FIRST EDITION

SCHROEDER'S ANTIQUES PRICE GUIDE

Edited by Sharon & Bob Huxford

COLLECTOR BOOKS
P.O. Box 3009
Paducah, KY 42001

The current values in this book should be used only as a guide. They are not intended to set prices, which vary from one section of the country to another. Auction prices as well as dealer prices vary greatly and are affected by condition as well as demand. Neither the Editor nor the Publisher assumes responsibility for any losses that might be incurred as a result of consulting this guide.

Additional copies of this book may be ordered from:

COLLECTOR BOOKS
P.O. Box 3009
Paducah, Kentucky 42001

@$9.95 Add $1.00 for postage and handling.

Copyright: Schroeder Publishing Co., Inc., 1983
ISBN: 0-89145-213-3

Just as any retail business judges its financial success or failure by the rise and fall of the economic barometer, so the business of buying and selling antiques and collectibles depends at least to some extent on general economic conditions. While some dealers report an overall decrease in the number of sales, the choice examples from every category continue to appreciate and to find a ready market. Quality goods are always the best buys. And whether involved in this business as a source of livelihood or enjoyment, the best insurance against poor investments is constant study of all available reference materials and observation of current market trends.

This book is intended only to inform you of these market trends; in the final evaluation, it is your good judgment that must prevail. Of the factors that contribute to that judgment, let this guide be only one of several. Never the only one.

The values in this price guide have been compiled from many sources. They have been gleaned from dealer's ads and lists from all over the country, from prices realized at some of America's finest auction houses, from shows and flea markets, and from nearly 200 dealers, authors and collectors who have contributed their specialized knowledge relating to specific areas. We have taken a full year to gather this information, during which time we have seen some items listed more than once---these prices were averaged. We did not include prices either at auction or from any other source that deviated extremely from the established norm. Obviously, such extremes occur from time to time, but to record them would only serve to misrepresent the market as a whole.

This book contains nearly 600 topics, listed alphabetically, either by manufacturer or by type of product. Consult the index if you have difficulty in locating your subject. Feel free to contact dealers listed in our directory. Many will be glad to ship you the merchandise you need. Several of the newer collector's clubs are also listed.

Every effort has been made to describe each item to the fullest extent possible in the space allotted by our format. Several standard abbreviations have been used throughout; they will be easy to read and understand if you will first take the time to quickly scan through them.

The Editors

Listing of Standard Abbreviations

The following is a list of abbreviations that have been used throughout this book in order to provide you with the most accurate descriptions possible in the limited space available. No periods are used after abbreviations, except for states. When two dimensions are given, height is noted first. If only one dimension is listed, height is indicated, except in the case of bowls, dishes, plates or platters, when it will indicate diameter.

Black . . . . blk
Cast iron ci
Composition. . . . . compo
Crossed . . . . x-d
Dark . . . . dk
Diameter . . . . dia
Embossed . . . . emb
Footed . . . . ftd
Green . . . . gr
Hand painted . . . . hp
Impressed . . . . imp
Individual. . . . . ind
Iridescent . . . . irid
Large . . . . lg
Light. . . . . lt
Lithograph . . . . litho
Mark . . . . mk
Mint in box . . . . MIB
Mother of pearl . . . . MOP
Numbered. . . . . #d
Opalescent. . . . . opal
Original . . . . orig
Patented . . . . pat
Piece. . . . . pc
Pint . . . . pt
Signed . . . . sgnd
Small . . . . sm
Square. . . . . sq
White . . . . wht
With . . . . w/

A B C Plates

Children's plates featuring the alphabet as part of the design were popular from as early as 1820 until after the turn of the century. The earliest English creamware plates were decorated with embossed letters and prim moralistic verses; later Staffordshire products were conducive to a more relaxed mealtime atmosphere and depicted playful animals with riddles, or scenes of pleasant leisure time activities. Braille plates for the blind were made, but are rather scarce, and therefore usually more valuable. You may also find an occasional bowl or mug...a matching set is rare.

Bowl, girl in field of poppies, gold relief alphabet, 7½″	**72.00**
Cup, Little Bo Peep, Staffordshire, 2″	**75.00**
Dish, children jumping rope, Germany, ceramic	**55.00**
Plate w/cup, animals playing in ABCs, Germany, 3 crown mark	**85.00**
Plate, ABCs, Adams, soft paste, ca 1840	**60.00**
ABCs, aluminum	**10.00**
ABCs, plain center, tin, 6″	**28.00**
Braille, numbers and ABCs, green and white ceramic	**55.00**
Bulldog in center, glass	**55.00**
Catch it Carlos, Staffordshire, polychrome, 5½″	**46.00**
Children & puppies, relief letters, ceramic 8½″	**38.00**
Children doing washing, Germany, ceramic, early 1900s	**65.00**
Children rolling hoops, tin, 3″	**50.00**
Children, parrot, dog, Germany, ceramic	**40.00**

Crusoe at work, BPCo, Tunstall, England, 7″	**50.00**
Franklin Farmer's scene & proverb, soft paste, polychrome	**75.00**
Gathering Cotton, Staffordshire, black transfer, 5½″	**45.00**
Girl on swing, polychromed tin, 3½″	**50.00**
Hey Diddle Diddle, ABCs in relief, metal	**45.00**
Independence Hall, Staffordshire, brown transfer, 7½″	**30.00**
Kittens, Ohio Art tin litho, 4″	**25.00**
Latest Thing Out, chicks in basket, ceramic	**32.00**
London Dog Seller, Powell & Bishop, Staffordshire	**42.00**
Lost, black transfer w/polychrome, 5½″	**30.00**
Man, spying on lovers, falls down hill, Staffordshire, 7½″	**75.00**
My Face is My Fortune, bulldog, England, blue & white,7½″	**36.00**
Paul & Virginia, ceramic	**25.00**
Pointed Hobnail, ABCs, glass	**12.00**
Rooster & hen, relief letters, grey border, 6½″	**40.00**
Rugby players, Staffordshire, 7½″	**75.00**
Sign language, ABCs in relief at rim, ceramic	**75.00**
Simple Simon, Oneida Tudor plate, 6″	**40.00**
Sioux Indian Chief, ceramic, 8½″	**58.00**
The Baker, ceramic, 5″	**40.00**
The Blind Girl, ceramic, 6″	**45.00**
The Gleaners, Staffordshire, polychrome, 6″	**45.00**

Tiger chasing boy, Powee, Bishop, Staffordshire, 6″	**55.00**
Tiger hunt, ceramic, 7½″	**24.00**
Two cows, chickens, verse, pink and green, Staffordshire, 7½″	**34.00**
Two men fishing, charging bull, ceramic, 7″	**68.00**

Who Killed Cock Robin, tin, 8″	**45.00**
Spoon & fork, Who Killed Cock Robin	**20.00**
Tray, ABCs, miniature oval, glass	**70.00**

Abingdon

From 1934 until 1950, the Abingdon Pottery Co. of Abingdon, Ill., made a line of art pottery with a white vitrified body, decorated with various glazes in an array of lovely colors--matt as well as glossy, crystalline and iridescent. Novelties, cookie jars, utility ware and lamps were made in addition to several lines of simple yet striking art ware. Fern Leaf, introduced in 1937 featured molded vertical feathering. La Fleur, in 1939, consisted of flower pots and flower arranger bowls with rows of vertical ribbing. Classic, 1939-40, was a line of vases, many with evidence of Chinese influence. Several marks were used, most of which employed the company name. In, 1950, the company reverted to the manufacture of sanitary ware that had been their mainstay before the Art Ware Division was formed.

101, vase, Classic, 10″	**9.00**
103, vase, Gamma	**32.00**
104, vase, Delta	**12.50**
107, vase, Gamma	**18.00**
110, vase, Classic, ivory gloss, original sticker	**14.00**
114, vase, Classic, rose	**16.00**
115, vase, Classic, green	**15.00**
117, vase, Classic, blue gloss, 10″	**15.00**
120, vase, Classic, chartreuse gloss	**14.00**
126, candleholder, Classic	**7.00**
132, vase, Classic, 8″	**12.00**
152S, flower pot w/saucer	**5.00**
156, vase, Classic, blue	**13.00**
176, vase, blue gloss	**14.00**
180, vase, Floral	**27.50**
305, bookends, Seagull	**42.00**
315, vase, Athenia Classic	**32.00**
320, vase, Tulip	**12.00**
335, vase, Chinese Scalloped, rectangular	**16.00**
350, vase, Fleur, oval	**15.00**
372, vase, Rhythm, 10″	**17.50**
377, wallpocket, Lily, yellow	**18.00**
389, vase, Geranium	**14.00**

411, vase, Volute, 11″ **35.00**
437, bowl, Han Pansy **15.00**
450, bowl, Asters **18.00**
462, bowl, Ribbon, pink **4.50**

463, vase, star, shrimp color **8.00**
474, cornucopia planter, blue **10.00**
479, candleholder, double, white **4.50**
482, double cornucopia, white gloss **14.00**
484, fan vase, blue gloss **10.50**
486, vase, yellow **13.50**
491, flowerholder vase, dark blue gloss **12.50**
494, vase w/ship, white gloss **13.00**
505, candleholders, double, Shell, pink, pr **15.00**
506, vase, Shell, pink, 5½x6″ **10.00**
507, vase, Shell, rose **10.00**
510, ash tray, donkey **27.50**
513, vase, white **14.00**
514, vase, Swirl, blue gloss **13.00**
514, vase, Swirl, pink, original sticker **14.00**
517, vase, Arden, pink matt w/white gloss interior **13.00**
522, vase, Barre, blue **8.50**
532, console bowl, Scroll, turquoise gloss **14.00**
533, bowl, Shell, blue **8.00**
545, bowl, streamliner medium, lt peach **6.00**
557, vase, Draped, ivory gloss **16.00**
564, bowl, scallop, green **13.00**
565D, cornucopia, pink & white **14.00**
569, cornucopia, rose **10.00**
575, candlestick, scallop, green, pr **20.00**
579, wall pocket, Daisy **22.50**
592, bowl, low, ivory gloss **6.50**
595, bookend, quill pen, white/black **15.00**
597, vase, pink w/ivory gloss **15.00**
599, vase, Quilted **23.50**
600, vase, Laurel, white gloss, 12″ **16.00**
616D, planter, Cactus **15.00**
626, vase, flared & scalloped, blue, 6½″ **8.50**
632, vase, anchor **18.00**
642, vase, Tulip **10.00**
652, puppy planter **15.00**
669, planter, donkey, double, blue, 7½″ **12.00**
708, vase, Square Leaf **12.00**
Console bowl w/handles, oval, pink, 13½″ **12.50**
Console set, Shell shape, rose, 11″ dia bowl **18.50**

Cookie jar, Baby **50.00**
   Hippo **38.50**
   Little Girl **35.00**
   Money Bag **40.00**
   Pig **30.00**
   Witch **42.00**
Desk accessory, advertising Abindgon, brown, 6½x4″ **65.00**

Adams See Also Spatter, Staffordshire

The firm of Wm. Adams & Sons was founded at Stoke-on-Trent in 1769, and still continues to operate. They made many types of earthenware, basalt, jasper and parian. From 1900-1965 they produced souvenir plates with transfer of American scenes, many of which were marketed in this country by Roth Importers of Peoria, Ill. In 1965, the company affiliated with Wedgwood. Although there were other Adams potteries in Staffordshire, their marks incorporate either the first name initial or a partners name, and so are easily distinguished from those of this company.

Adams Rose, creamer, rainbow spatter **275.00**
   Cup & saucer, rainbow spatter **210.00**
   Cup plate **45.00**
   Plate, 9½″ **135.00**
Coasters, Cries of London, corkback, set of 4, 4″ **35.00**
Cup & saucer, Cries of London, large, farmer's **65.00**
Cup & saucer, Seasons, Winter, pink, signed **40.00**
Cup & saucer, The Farmer's Arms, w/verse, large **45.00**
Hatpin holder, Jasper ware, blue/white w/classic figures, 4″ **55.00**
Plate, Andalusia, pink w/white border, 8″ **36.00**
Plate, Cries of London, hexagonal, 8½″ **22.00**
Plate, Dr Syntax Stopped by Highwaymen, signed, 10″ **38.00**
Plate, First Appearance of Samuel Weller, Tunstall, 10″ **35.00**
Plate, Shannondale Springs, Va, pink transfer, signed, 8″ **70.00**
Plate, The Bridal Veil Fall, Currier & Ives **35.00**
Plate, The Star of the Road, Currier & Ives **35.00**
Plate, Valentine series, colonial figures, No 7 . . . . **35.00**
Plate, View Near Conway, red/white, signed, 9″ **85.00**
Plate, Winter in the Country, Currier & Ives **35.00**
Platter, Leeds type, white w/blue embossing, 1830, 15x12″ **75.00**
Platter, Palestine, signed, 12x15″ **250.00**
Platter, Spanish Convent, pink transfer, 1820, 17x14″ **200.00**

Advertising

Early advertising items, with their colorful lithographed decorations portraying America's tastes and way of life from years gone by, have become a recognized art form; and judging from the amount of such items offered by dealers and auction houses, they are well received by many collectors. Our listings are alphabetized by company name, or in lieu of that information, by word content or other pertinent description.

A & P Great American Pepper, tin, cockatoo, tall, early **20.00**
ABC Brewing, sign, celluloid/cardboard, 1905, 6½x9″ **110.00**
AC Spark Plugs, clock **85.00**
Acme Ale, beer sign, tin, bulldog w/blanket, 1930, 17″ **120.00**
Acme, sign, tin, 1940s **50.00**
Aetna Insurance, hand mirror **28.00**
Aetna, sign, porcelain, 1920s, 12x18″ **75.00**
Air Float Talc, tin w/lady **18.00**
Akro Agates, cardboard stand-up, colorful, 15½x13″ **200.00**
Akron Brewing Co, tray, lady & tiger **135.00**
Alberly Coffee, tin, 1 lb **5.00**
Allen & Ginter Tobacco, tin **38.00**
Allis Chalmers, sign, porcelain, 1930s **35.00**

Ambassador Scotch, pitcher, white w/red & black, 5" dia **9.00**
American Brewing Co, sign, celluloid **135.00**
American Brewing Co, tray, w/Indian **130.00**
American Can, bank, Declaration of Independence **10.00**
American Express, sign, porcelain, double-faced, 1905 ...... **225.00**
American Express, sign, tin, Money Orders, 1920 .... **49.00**
American Line, pocket mirror, celluloid w/ship **20.00**
American Maid, tray **200.00**
American Navy Tobacco, tin tag **1.00**
Ampollina Dye cabinet, marquee, glass door, 24x15x7" **275.00**
Angelus Marshmallows, hand mirror, cupid w/horn **45.00**
Anheuser Busch Bevo, tray, probition era, non alcholic **125.00**
Anheuser Busch Ginger Ale, pocket mirror **50.00**
Anheuser Busch, paperboard, Custer's Fight, framed, 30" **95.00**
Anheuser Busch, paperboard, Custer's Fight, framed, 46" **350.00**
Anti-Plasma, sign, cures malaria--one week **175.00**
Apache Talc, tin **20.00**
Arm & Hammer, poster, boy laughing at hunter, 1910 .... **250.00**
Armour Peanut Butter, pail, Mother Goose, old **150.00**
Atlantic & Pacific Tea, die-cut, boys w/banjo, 1880, 7" **20.00**
Atlantic Coast Line, sign, tin, 1940s, 22" dia **75.00**
Atlas Prager Beer, tray **50.00**
Aunt Jemima's Pancake Flour, mask, 13x11½" **35.00**
Ayer's Catharatic Pills, die-cut, Doctor & children, 12" **45. 00**
B F Goodrich, ashtray, World's Fair 1939, diamond w/wreath .. **20.00**
B F Goodrich, ashtray, marblized agate, Safest Tire **20.00**
B F Goodrich, pen & holder, marblized agate tire **50.00**
Bab-O, bank **15.00**
Babbitt's Soap, poster, boy fishing, 1892, 27x14" **150.00**
Babcock's Corylopsis Talc, tin **22.00**
Bagley's Old Colony, pocket tin **50.00**
Babgipe Tobacco, soft pack **10.00**
Ballantines Beer, mirror, reverse painted **45.00**
Bank Note, tin w/paper label **20.00**
Bank Roll Cigars, tin, 6x5" **35.00**
Barbarosa Beer, sign, cardboard w/wood frame **35.00**
Bat Tobacco, tin tag **1.00**
Battleship Coffee, tin **30.00**
Bavarian, sign, tin, 1930s, 6x9" **18.00**
Beam, pitcher, 180th Anniversary, gold **75.00**
Beck's Hunting Tobacco, sign, tin yellow/black, 5x13" **13.00**
Beef, Wine & Iron Tonic, oiled paper, wood legs, w/bottle **135.00**
Beefeater Whiskey, pitcher **16.00**
Belbing Bros, thread cabinet, 13 drawers, 34" **28.00**
Bell Coffee, pocket mirror w/bell, celluloid, 2" **22.00**
Bell Public Telephone, sign, double sided, 18" **75.00**
Bell System, push plate, Underground Cable, porcelain **20.00**
Bell Telephone, Do Not Disturb, porcelain, 2½x7" **25.00**
Bells Scotch, pitcher **18.00**
Bergdoll Beer, goblet, 60th Anniversary **85.00**
Berghoff, bottle case, wooden **12.00**
Berghoff, mug **25.00**
Berghoff, picture of dog advertising **30.00**
Bergoff, sign, electric neon **300.00**
Berkshire Ale, tap knob, round **22.00**
Berry Bros Paints & Varnish, wagon wood/rubber wheels **395.00**
Betsy Ross, shoe polish box, 4 tins **45.00**
Beverwyck Beer, tray, wood grain **25.00**
Bevo Beer, tray, horses & wagon **65.00**
Big Kick Tobacco, soft pack **8.00**
Billy Baxter, tray, w/red bird, 1920s, 12" **40.00**
Birleys, thermometer **35.00**
Bissantz Ice Cream, tray w/lady **45.00**
Blackburn Hardware, tip tray w/girl, Bedford Pa., 1920 .... **85.00**

Blackman's Salt Block, rack & tin sign.................... **100.00**
Blatz Old Heidelberg, tray w/students, 1930s **80.00**
Bloodhound Tobacco,tin tag **1.00**
Blue Boar Tobacco, tin w/etched silverplated canister **225.00**
Blue Jacket Revolvers, poster, 1870, frame, 23x27" **160.00**
Blue Tiger Tobacco, lunch box **40.00**
Blue Valley Butter, pocket mirror, oval **18.00**
Boar's Head Tobacco, sign, porcelain, old, 24x7" **155.00**
Bobby Lou, sign, tin litho by Coffin, 1920s, 15x20" **50.00**
Bock Beer, poster, clothed goat w/Victorian woman, 27x21" .. **165.00**
Bohemian Club Beer, tap knob **17.00**
Bokar Coffee, bank **12.00**
Bombay Dry Gin, pitcher, Queen Victorian, 6" dia **20.00**
Bon Ami, tin, sample **8.00**
Boot Tobacco, tin tag **1.00**
Borden, flag to fly over factory, 5x8', 1975 .... **125.00**
Boye Needle case, tin w/wood base, round, store model **87.00**
Brand Paint, sign, tin w/wood trim, 48x96 .... **200.00**
Brasso Metal Polish, sign, porcelain enamel, 1920s, 16x24" **95.00**
Braumeister Beer, tray **25.00**
Breck's Brewing, tray, 1950s **17.50**
Briar Pipe Tobacco, poster, man smoking, 1910, 31x23" **195.00**
Bromo Seltzer, sheet music, Contains no cocaine or morphine . **12.00**
Brotherhood Tobacco, lunch box **120.00**
Brownie Baking Co, paperweight, 5" **25. 00**
Bruck's Beer, door-push, porcelain **75.00**
Bruck's Beer, tire cover, canvas, 28½" **60.00**
Buckeye Beer, sign, embossed tin, 1930s, 3x18" **20.00**
Buckeye Beer, sign, tin/cardboard, Captain & collie, 21x16" .. **100.00**
Buckingham Beer, tray, sample, pre-pro **85.00**
Buckingham Tobacco, pocket tin **30.00**
Buckshoe & Tiger Stripe Tobacco, poster, 1895, 28x14" **275.00**
Bud Fisher, cigar box, Mutt & Jeff **40.00**
Budweiser Levee, tray................................... **100.00**
Budweiser, hanging light w/revolving brewery wagon, old . **500.00**
Budweiser, paperboard, Bud Girl, frame, 1907, 36x21" **450.00**
Budweiser, sign, porcelain, 1920s, 11x21" **85.00**
Budweiser, tray, Colonial men before fireplace **75.00**
Budweiser, tray, Say When, man & woman making fondue, round **275.00**
Buffalo Peanut Butter, tin 1 lb **140.00**
Bull Durham Tobacco, sign, paper/glass, 5c, 21x17" **75.00**
Bull of the Woods Tobacco, tin tag...................... **1.00**
Bulldog Lager Beer, porcelain w/embossing, 15" **240.00**
Bunnies Salted Peanuts, can, 10 lb **200.00**
Burger Beer, sign, copper and wood **25.00**
Burger Beer, sign, tin, man w/canoe & case, 21x16" **60.00**
Burgon Blend, scoop, picture of elephant **22.00**
Burke & Barry, pitcher **12.00**
Burkes Ale, tray **70.00**
Burkhardt Beer, sign, cardboard, lady w/glass, 20x27" **35.00**
Busch Bavarian coach lamp, electric **20.00**
Busch Bavarian Beer, neon **55.00**
Busch Garden, dinner plates, set of 6 .... **60.00**
Busch Ginger Ale, sign, porcelain, 1920s. 11x21" **65.00**
Buster Brown & Tige, shoe lasts **50.00**
Buster Brown, tin, mustard **15.00**
California Wine House, calendar, 1908, 11½x23½" **125.00**
Calumet Baking Powder, can, Thank You Boy on lid **70.00**
Calumet Baking Powder, clock **695.00**
Camel Cigars, tin **55.00**
Campbell Kid, vinyl Scotsman **25.00**
Campbell Kids, tie clasp **15.00**
Campbells Coffee, tin w/camels **40.00**
Campfire Marshmallows, tin, campfire scene, 2x8" dia........ **40.00**

Canada Dry, sign, two sided steel, 1930s, 18x16″ **15.00**
Carter Inx, thermometer, porcelain **85.00**
Carter's Ink, print w/frame, Playfull Kittens, 11x13″ **35.00**
Centilivre Brewery, poster **450.00**
Central Union, canister **55.00**
Cresota Flour, pocket mirror **30.00**
Cetacolor, sign, oilcloth, Victorian woman, 1890, 36x25″ **75.00**
Champale, sign, electric, blinking **25.00**
Charles Denby cigars, framed ad, black porter, 17x12″ **48.00**
Checkers Confection, pocket mirror **55.00**
Chero Cola, calendar, 1917 w/wood frame, brunette, 36x20″ . . **350.00**
Chero Cola, poster, cardboard w/frame **65.00**
Cherry Blossoms, sign, embossed tin, 19x10″ **75.00**
Chesterfield, push plate, tin, 12x2½″ **15.00**
Chesterfield, sign, tin shelf strip **4.00**
Chi-Namel Varnish, metal die cut, Chinaman, 2 sided, 20″ **195.00**
Chicken Dinner, sign, embossed tin, 1940s, 12x28″ **40.00**
Chief Paints, sign, tin, 1940s, 12x28″ **20.00**
Chief of the West, Minneapolis Patent, flour sack **17.50**
Christian Feigewspan Breweries, tray, lady, 1910 . . . . **125.00**
Chrysler, sign, porcelain, 1930s, 24x36″ **95.00**
Clabber Girl, sign, tin, 1940s, 12x36″ **25.00**
Clark ONT, spool cabinet, 7 drawers **750.00**
Clark ONT, spool cabinet, walnut w/6 drawers **800.00**
Clark, spool cabinet, 3 long drawers over 6 halves **475.00**
Clarks Teaberry Gum, tray, glass, counter, amber **52.00**
Clicquot Club, sign, tin, 19½x8½″ **35.00**
Cloth of Gold Cigarettes, poster w/frame, blonde w/fan **295.00**
Clover Leaf, sign, embossed tin, 1915, 5x20″ **35.00**

Coca-Cola

The Coca-Cola Company was established in 1891, 5 years after John Pemberton, an Atlanta druggist served up the first batch of brew from an iron kettle in his backyard. After 1924, standard advertising designs were adopted and offered to bottlers around the country. Prior to that, outside of a few suggested guidelines, the individual bottler was free to choose his own. The unqualified success of the Coca-Cola Company is in itself evidence of the power of its extensive and continuing advertising campaign, and collectors of Coke memorabilia revel in a field of collecting that offers variety as well as challenge.

Bank, Linemar, battery operated **285.00**
Belt buckle, cigar cutter, Expo **250.00**
Blackboard, silouette of girl, 19x27″, 1940s, G **55.00**
Blotter, 1920s **20.00**
  1936, 50th Anniversary **28.00**
  1938 . . . . **7.00**
  1940, clown **48.00**
  1941 . . . . **5.00**
Booklet, 1907, "The Truth" **50.00**
Booklet, 1912, "The Truth" **37.50**
Booklet, in shape of case **7.50**
Bottle, Columbus Ohio, amber **60.00**
Bottle, miniatures in wood case **12.00**
Bottle, square, aqua, soda water No 49729 . . . . **24.00**
Bowl for ice, metal, 3 bottle legs **75.00**
Bowl for pretzels **70.00**
Calendar top, 1919, Knitting Girl, trimmed **165.00**
Calendar, 1943, March-April, 20x13″ **20.00**
Cards, Coke refreshes you best **35.00**
Cards, nature, 96 in orig box **25.00**
Carrier for 6 pack, 1923 . . . . **55.00**
Carrier for 6 pack, before 1929 . . . . **40.00**
Chair seat, embossed metal, 13½″ dia **23.00**
Clock, 1940 . . . . **265.00**
Cooler, 1939, salesman's sample, 10x12″ **695.00**

Cribbage set, no box, instructions **35.00**
Coupon w/frame, 1904, Lillian Russel **88.00**
Cut out, 1922, 3 girls w/umbrellas, 20x35″ **300.00**
Cut out, 1927, Toy Town, cardboard **39.00**
Cut out, 1932 Olympic, cardboard **39.00**
Cut out, 1932, circus, cardboard **39.00**
Die cut, Uncle Remus **25.00**
Dominoes w/box **65.00**
Glasses w/Santa, series 2, ea **4.00**
Holder for shopping cart, 1940 . . . . **20.00**
Ice pick & bottle opener, wood, old **18.00**
Ice pick, 1930s **17.50**
Magazine ad, 1905, Lillian Nordica w/coupon **75.00**
Magazine ad, 1919 Marion Doris, sepia **25.00**
Magazine cover w/ad, June 1910, Housewife **200.00**
Mechanical pencil w/mini bottle, sample **45.00**
Music box, cooler, 1940s **45.00**
Needle case, 1924, girl **45.00**
Note pad, 1945 . . . . **6.00**
Nut pick **50.00**
Pencil sharpener, 1933 . . . . **25.00**
Placard, WWII airplane **7.00**
Poster, w/Santa, 1952, 11x23″ **15.00**
Poster, 6 pack, 1951, 11x25″ **10.00**
Poster, Edgar Bergen w/friend, 1949, 11x24″ **35.00**
Print, 1906, Satisfied, no frame **325.00**
Radio, bottle shape **1,000.00**
Sidewalk sign, 1941, 20x28″ **40.00**
Sign, 1900, Hilda Clark, paper/wood, 15x20″ **750.00**
  1914, Betty, cardboard/wood, 22x32″ **410.00**
  1914, Betty, tin/self framed, 31x41″ **850.00**
  1917, Elaine, tin/self framed, 20x30″ **675.00**
  L. Russell, cardboard/tin, 8x11″ oval **425.00**
  Please Pay When Served, lighted **125.00**
  Drug store, porcelain, 28x16″ **95.00**
  Embossed tin w/bottle, 1923, 27x20″ **125.00**
Street marker, 1900s, brass **60.00**
Syrup bottle, block letters on enamel, 11½″ **165.00**
Syrup bottle, sm reverse glass label, 11½″ **270.00**
Syrup bottle, wreath around lettering, 11½″ **165.00**
Thermometer, 12″ dia **38.00**
  1900, wood **275.00**

Thermometer, 1942, 16″ **30.00**
  1958, gold, 7″ **20.00**

Bottle, 29″	58.00
Trade mark, Pat Dec, 1923, 5x16″	85.00
Tip tray, 1899, Hilda Clark, 5″	650.00
1900, Picture of bottle, 5″	575.00
1904, Hilda Clark w/glass, 9¾″ dia	350.00
1904, St Louis Fair, 4½x6″ oval	140.00
1909, Coca Cola Girl, 4x6″	140.00
1912, girl w/big hat	275.00
1914, Betty, 4x6″ oval	90.00
1917, Elaine	125.00
1920, Garden Girl, 4x6″ oval	80.00
Train set, 1974, Lionel, complete	130.00
Tray, 1898, Victorian lady, 9½″ dia	4,500.00
1904, St Louis Fair, 13x16″	325.00
1904, girl w/violets, 10¾x13″ oval	450.00
1905, Juanita, small oval	375.00
1906, Relieves Fatigue, 10¾x13″	275.00
1908, topless girl, 12½″ dia	425.00
1908, Western nude	1,900.00
1909	295.00
1912	300.00
1914, oval	230.00
1914, oval	275.00
1917, Elaine	140.00
1917, WWI Girl, 8x19″	85.00
1920, Garden Girl, 14x17″ oval	340.00
1921, Summer girl	220.00
1922, girl w/sailor hat, 10x14″	205.00
1923	65.00
1923, flapper girl	95.00
1923	125.00
1925, girl w/white fox fur, 10x14″	195.00
1926, Sports couple	300.00
1927, Curb Service	450.00
1927, soda jerk	135.00
1927, waiter w/glasses	125.00
1929, girl in swimsuit w/glass	235.00
1930, bathing beauty	135.00
1930, telephone girl	135.00
1931, boy w/dog	425.00
1932	250.00
1934, Weismuller	300.00
1935, Girl in white dress	185.00
1936, hostess	125.00
1937, running girl	85.00
1938	45.00
1939, springboard girl	62.00
1931, farm boy	400.00
1940, sailor girl fishing	60.00
1941, girl ice skater	65.00
1942, two girls w/car	65.00
1943, girl w/wind in hair	38.00
1950	25.00
Thanksgiving,	25.00
Truck, Smith-Miller, 6 full cases, MIB	450.00
Wallet in box, pigskin	15.00
Colonial Club, sign, two sided steel, 1920s, 18x8″	45.00
Colonial Ice, sign, Porcelain, 1930s, 12x20″	40.00
Columbian Rope, oil cloth, Its Waterproof, sailor, 50x30″	450.00
Columbus Brewery, tip tray w/Columbus, 4″	80.00
Cooke's Beer, sign, tin, redhead in red dress, 29x22″	175.00
Cooper Armored Cord, ashtray, tire, red striped, 6½″	15.00
Coors, ashtray, Colo. State Fair, 1936	95.00

Coors, bottle, comic ghoulish face w/logo	250.00
Copenhagen Snuff, can, 1915, cardboard w/tin, small round	4.00
Corby's Canadian Whiskey, sign, man w/newspaper, 31x23″	250.00
Corticelli Thread cabinet, oak, doors, medallion w/head	1,100.00
Cottolene, tip tray	85.00
Cottoline, tip tray, black woman, cotton field, 4″	50.00
Cow Brand Baking Soda, sign, 1910, dog in field, 29x20″	250.00
Crisco, sign, cardboard, 1930s, 11x13″	15.00
Crosby Radio, sign, cardboard	50.00
Crown Ice Cream, sign, tin w/wood frame	85.00
Cub Tobacco, sign, tin shelf strip, l5x1″	15.00
Cunningham Ice Cream, tray, factory, oval, 1915, 18″	165.00
Cupples Cord, sign, tin, rhino in tire, 20x28″	250.00
Curtiss Candies, counter jar	25.00
DM Ferry Seeds, sign, two women in wagon	385.00
Dad's, sign, tin, 1950s, 12x31″	16.00
Dad's, tin, blue, red, yellow, 28x20″	59.00
Dallas Brewery, tray, White Rose, vase, 14x17″oval	270.00
Dari-Rich, sign, tin, 1930s, 10x24″	25.00
Dark Horse Tobacco, soft pack	10.00
Dawes Brewery, tray, white/green, horse, pre-pro, 12″	205.00
Delaval Cream Separator, sign, We Use, 1920, 12x16″	65.00
Deppen Brewing, reverse on glass, elk, framed, 13x24″	300.00
Detroit Brewing, tray, The Invitation, 1911, 13″ dia	145.00
Devilish Good Cigars, sign, tin, 1910	85.00
Dewer's White Label, sign, composition, distillery, 13x20″	10.00
Dial Tobacco, poster, 1940s, 14x18″	8.00
Diamond Dye, cabinet, Evolution of Women	565.00
Diamond Dye, cabinet, children with balloons decor	525.00
Diamond Match, tin, black family pictured on lid	85.00
Dick & Bros Quincy Beer, tray, brewery scene, 10x13″	165.00
Dick's Beer, tray	75.00
Diehl Brewery, tip tray, woman w/bottle, 3″	40.00
Diehl Brewing, tray, girl, mountains, 1933, 12″ round	155.00
Dill's Best Tobacco, canister	8.00
Dill's Best Tobacco, pocket tin	9.00
Dilworth Bros Cigars, paperboard, girl w/flowers, framed	170.00
Dixie Beer, tray, waitress, 1930's, 13″ square	145.00
Dixie Cup, circus, 24-pc., premium	45.00

Dixie Maid Syrup pail	75.00
Dobler Brewing, sign, tin, horses & wagons, 20x24″	150.00
Dodge Bros, sign, porcelain, 1930s, 15x45″	95.00
Dolly Madison, sign, embossed tin, 1910, 5x20″	20.00
Double Cola, thermometer	10.00
Dr Ballard's, spoon w/dog design	6.00

Dr Blumer's, sign, tin, 1915, 3x18" **25.00**
Dr Davis Anti Head Ache, sign, 25c, woman in night gown **85.00**
Dr Kellogg's Asthma Remedy, sign, tin, old man **38.00**
Dr Meyer's Foot Soap, sign, black/white litho, 1940, G **12.00**
Dr Pepper, clock, Good for Life, 5c, w/pendulum **125.00**
Dr Pepper, sign, porcelain, 10x26", small chips **115.00**
Dr Scholl's display cabinet, products under glass **165.00**
Dr Swett's Root Beer, sign, paper, old man, boy, 1910 . . . . **150.00**
Draught Tea, tin, horses pulling wagon, 13x13x13" **300.00**
Drewry's Beer, tap knob **17.00**
Drink 76, sign, tin, patriotic, 1940s, 12x24" **18.00**
Drum Tobacco, soft pack **10.00**
Dubois Brewing, tray **245.00**
Dubois Export Beer, tab knob **15.00**
Duesseldorer Beer, sign, tin, baby, beer bottle, 12"dia **250.00**
Duffy's Pure Malt, hand mirror **30.00**
Duke's Mixture, paperboard, Our Comrade, framed, 32x22" . . . **395.00**
Duke's Mixture, print, Duke's Twins, framed, 1910, 24x30" . . . **395.00**
Duluth Imperial Flour, sign, tin, black cook, 1910, 18" **750.00**
Dupont Gunpowder, poster, H Pyle artist, 1911, orig tube **275.00**
Dupont Gunpowder, tin, w/2 labels, pat Sept 19, 1910 . . . . **30.00**
Dupont Stamping Powder, sign, tin/wood, 1915, 30x18" **125.00**
Dupont, print, cavalry man, buffalo, framed, 1895, 14x30" **295.00**
Dupont, print, hunter in field, wood frame, 1900, 10x15" **160.00**
Dutch Boy Paint, pulp figure, Dutch boy, 1935 pat, 22" **65.00**
Dutch Boy Paint, sign, die-cut tin, boy in swing **1,000.00**
Dutch Cleanser, bank, small **30.00**
Dutch Masters Cigars, litho canvas, 1910, 12x18" **125.00**
EJ York, dust pan, Lumber, Coal & Grain **35.00**
Eagle Beer, tray, Gypsy Girl, Utica N.Y. **110.00**
Eagle Brewing, tray, white/blue, eagle **45.00**
Early Times Whiskey, sign, plaster, distillery, 23x29" **300.00**
Ebbert Wagons, sign, tin, Old Apple Tree, framed, 25x37" . . . **785.00**
Ebling Brewing, mug, pictures brewery **75.00**
Edelweiss Beer, tray, w/Edelweiss girl, pre-pro **125.00**
Edelweiss Cheeses, sign, porcelain, convex, 12x16" **85.00**
Edison Mazda, lamp ad, Ecstacy, Parrish, framed, 1930s **275.00**
Ehlermann Beer, sign, tin, founder's portrait, 26x18" **650.00**
Ehret's Hell Gate Brewery, tray, pre-pro, oval **225.00**
El Bart Gin, sign, tin, bulldog w/chain, 1910, 9x13" **180.00**
Elgin Watch, paperboard, Father Time, frame, 1910, 16x22" . **175.00**
Emmerling Brewing, tray, 1913, 10½x13¼" **220.00**
Enterprise Brewing, tray, girl on table, flowers, 13" dia **240.00**
Erie Brewing, tray, woman w/tiger rug, l3" dia **190.00**
Eve Tobacco, tin, pocket **50.00**
Eveready Batteries, poster, George Washington, 1932 . . . . **90.00**
Eveready Prestone, thermometer **40.00**
Evinrude Rowboat & Canoe Motors, change tray, woman, boat . **54.00**
Exlax, thermometer, porcelain, 36" **85.00**
Fairbank's, sign, embossed tin, 1930s, 10x28" **40.00**
Fairbank's Soap, counter display box w/label, 16x17" **150.00**
Fairmount Furniture, tray, oval, 13x16" **140.00**
Fairy Soap, change tray, girl sits on soap bar, 4" dia **45.00**
Falls City Beer, tray, girl on horse, 13" dia **275.00**
Falls City Beer, tray, waitress, 1915, 12" dia **150.00**
Falstaff Beer, sign, Barbeque on Range, 42x30" **45.00**
Fan-Tan Cigars, glass **48.00**
Fashion Cut Plug Tobacco, lunchbox **100.00**
Fatima Cigarettes, moving picture dance booklet, 1914, G **8.00**
Fatima Cigarettes, thermometer, porcelain, 1913 . . . . **150.00**
Favorite Cigarettes, sign, 2-sided metal, hunting dog **125.00**
Feen-A-Mint, sign, porcelain, gum & package, 7x29" **125.00**
Fehr's Beer, sign, tin, man dreams, dancing girl, 23x33" **350.00**
Fehr's Malt Tonic, sign, tin woman w/cherubs, oval, 29" **300.00**

Finzer Tobacco, tin tag **1.00**
Firestone, ashtray, Transteel Radial, Spirit of 76, 6½" **8.00**
First Cabinet Cigars, box label **5.00**
Fisk Tires, sign, paper, boy & skyscraper, 48x28", G **60.00**
Five Bros, tobacco cutter **65.00**
Fleckenstein, sign, tin, 3 workers eating, 1910, 20x30" **275.00**
Fleers Double Bubble, ashtray, chalk, w/man shaped gum **75.00**
Flyer Cigar, sign, paper, Lindbergh's plane, 1927, 19x8" **20.00**
Ford, sign, porcelain, Ford Parts, 1920s **95.00**
Ford, sign, masonite board, tractor, 1939, 11x22" **65.00**
Forest & Stream, pocket tin w/duck **30.00**
Fort Pitt Beer, tap knob **10.00**
Foss-Schneider Brewing, tray, Cincinnati, flags, 14x17" **165.00**
Foster Hose Supporter, sign, celluloid, lady, 1900, 9x17" **150.00**
Foster Piano, fan, Harrison Fisher illustration **30.00**
Four Roses Tobacco, tin **25.00**
Fram Filter, thermometer **39.00**
Frank Fehr Brewing Co, tray, copper, king & queen **130.00**
Franklin Life Insurance, tip tray **45.00**
Freedom Oil, sign, 2-sided metal, bulldog **85.00**
Fring's Cigars, sign, embossed tin, clown, 1915, 14x10" **135.00**
Frostie Root Beer, blackboard, tin, old **35.00**
GO Blake Whiskey, tray, man w/bottle **45.00**
Gambrinus Cincinnati Beer, reverse on glass **100.00**
Genesee Club Pure Rye, Wellsville N.Y., tray, girl **45.00**
Geobel Brewing Co, tip tray, round, man at table **80.00**
George Esslinger & Son Brewers, sign, woman & child **150.00**
George Ringler Co, tray, oval **145.00**
George Washington, lunch box **45.00**
George Washington Corn Flakes, box, unopened, portrait **65.00**
George Washington Tobacco, tin w/handle, 7x4x4" **50.00**
Gertz Beer, tray **60.00**
Gibson Girl Cigarettes, can **45.00**
Gin Seng, tray, lady in rickshaw **60.00**
Glendorra Coffee, sample tin **8.00**
Gloria Ice Cream, tray, Cox's Brownies **135.00**
Gold Dust Scouring Cleanser, full can **22.00**
Gold Dust Twins, booklet, Fairbank Co, 1902 . . . . **45.00**
Gold Dust Washing Powder, box w/pickaninnies **12.00**
Gold Flake Cut Plug, paper under glass, woman w/dog **225.00**
Gold Flake Peanut Butter, pail **45.00**
Gold Medal Beer, Indianapolis Brewery, tip tray, 5" **50.00**
Golden Cola, sign, embossed tin, 1940s, 12x28" **30.00**
Golden Slipper Tobacco, tin tag **1.00**
Goldrock, sign, embossed tin, 1930s, 11x22" **20.00**
Goldrock Birch Beer, sign, tin 1930s, 9x20" **16.00**
Good Times Tobacco, barrel label, plowing, 7x13" **15.00**
Good Year Motorcycle Tire, sign, porcelain, man on cycle **450.00**
Goodyear Custom Power Cushion Polyglass, ashtray, pink **15.00**
Grain Belt Beer, paper w/wood frame, hunter & dog, 31x21" . **110.00**
Granger Tobacco, sign, cardboard, Frank Kelly **30.00**
Grants, pitcher, triangular **9.50**
Grape Nuts, framed tin sign, girl w/dog, 20x31" **650.00**
Great Supreme Biscuit Animal Show, tin litho, 13½x5½" **35.00**
Green River Soda, sign w/mermaid **50.00**
Green River Whiskey, counter display, man & horse, 11x14" . . **155.00**
Green River Whiskey, tray, 12" **350.00**
Griffith Boyd Co, sign, aluminum, 23x15" **20.00**
Grinnell Bros, pocket mirror, celluloid, old cars **30.00**
Growler Tobacco, soft pack **12.00**
Guarantor's Liability, framed, horses & buggies, 22x31" **190.00**
Gunos Beer, sign, self framed tin **350.00**
Hazel Club, sign, tin, 8" **9.00**
Hazel Club, thermometer, tin, 1940s, 6" **25.00**

Health Club, sign, tin, 1940s, 11x21″ **40.00**
Hepburn House Coal, tip tray, eagle, 4″ **30.00**
Heckers Flour, doll, cloth **12.00**
Heinekin, sign, lite-up **25.00**
Heinekin, windmill, electric, 18x11″ **18.00**
Helmar, tin, flat, 1950s **25.00**
Helmar Cigarettes, sign, cardboard w/frame, 36x25″ **295.00**
Helmar Cigarettes, sign, paper, brunette, 1900, 33x43″ **275.00**
Hemrich Bros, sign, sm girl w/flowers, frame, 18x31″ **350.00**
Heptol Splits, sign, cowboy on bronco, Russell, 1904 . . . . **125.00**
Hi Power, sign, tin, 1920s, 8x10″ **25.00**
Hibbeler Cigar Co, bottle/box opener, hatchet **18.00**
High Admiral Cigarettes, button, kid w/dice, 1896, 1¼″ **35.00**
High Plain Tobacco tin **15.00**
Hinckel, tray **135.00**
Hires Root Beer, die cut cardboard, life size lady, 1910 . . . . . . **900.00**
Hires Root Beer, dispenser, china, hour glass **325.00**
Hires Root Beer, mug, stoneware, corset shaped **55.00**
Hires, chalkboard **15.00**
Hires, cutout, cardboard **15.00**
Hires, electric display sign, sm **22.00**
Hires, mug, old **35.00**
Hires, sign, Double-Cola, 32″ **12.00**
Hires, sign, Double-Cola, 54″ **15.00**
Hires, thermometer, bottle shape, 28″ **42.00**
Hoffman House Cigars, sign, paper, men in tux, 32x36″ **295.00**
Hohenade Beer, sign, tin, John L Sullivan **375.00**
Holiday Tobacco, pocket tin **10.00**
Holsum, sign, embossed tin, 1940s, 6x22″ **25.00**
Home Federal Savings, bank **7.00**
Honest Scrap, sign, paper w/frame, cat & dog, 30x22″ **450.00**
Honey Dip Tobacco, canister, beehive graphics **125.00**
Homeymoon Tobacco, sign **200.00**
Hood's Sarsaparilla, calander, 1892 . . . . **38.00**
Hood's Sarsaparilla, puzzle, 2-sided, 1891 . . . . **200.00**
Hoody's Peanut Butter, pail, children on see-saw **85.00**
Hoonan Tea, sign **285.00**
Hornet, gasoline globe, plastic body **80.00**
Horseshoe Tobacco, sign, porcelain, 8x16″ **200.00**
Hot Shot Tobacco, tin tag **1.00**
Howell's Root Beer, sign, tin, 27x8″ **49.00**
Hub Tobacco, tin tag **1.00**

Hudson, gasoline globe, plastic, truck & trailer **350.00**
Hudson & Essex, sign, porcelain enamel, 1920, 24x38″ **125.00**
Hudson & Essex, sign, porcelain, 1920s, 14x30″ **115.00**
Hudson Fulton, button, celebration **12.00**
Hump Hairpins, die cut, tin, camel, 1910, 16x14″ **150.00**
Huntley & Palmers Biscuits, suitcase, tin, figural **80.00**
Hutchinson Flour Mills Co, blotter, logo **2.50**
Hyroler Whiskey, tip tray, gentlemen, 1910, 4″ **22.00**
IW Harper Whiskey, sign, milk glass w/wood frame, 30x24″ . . **850.00**
Illinois Watch, sign, Lincoln, litho canvas, 10x7″ **95.00**
Imperial Ruby, tobacco barrel label, 1870s, 7x14″ **15.00**
Independent Beer, tray, knight w/stein, Seattle **175.00**
Independent Brewing Co, sign, Seattle, Wa., 1912, 12″ dia **95.00**
Index Brand Cocoa, tin, 1 lb **48.00**
Index Brand Cocoa, tin, 5 lb **65.00**
Indian Gas, thermometer **10.00**
Indian Gasoline, sign, glass, Zuni Sign, 12x14″ **10.00**
Indianapolis Brewing Co, sign, paper, Union Labor **330.00**
Indianapolis Brewing Co, tip tray **75.00**
International, tobacco barrel label, w/nude, 1870s, 7x14″ **15.00**
Invincible Junior Vacuum, pocket mirror, celluloid **30.00**
Irish Cream Ale, tap knobs, plastic **25.00**
Ivory Soap, book, drawing & painting, 1886, 6x9″ **20.00**
JT Tobacco, poster, farmer, gambler, dude, 1895, 28x21″ **375.00**
Jack Sprat Peanut Butter, tin, 25 lbs **425.00**
Jackson Cookies, counter jar, plastic, metal lid & base **30.00**
James Foxe, pitcher **18.00**
James Meeds Furniture, tip tray **60.00**
Jani-Cola, tray lady w/horse, oval **150.00**
Jersey Ice Cream, sign, embossed tin, 1940s, 16x34″ **35.00**
Jetter Beer, poster/self frame, bottle, elk, 23x32″ **650.00**
Jewett Ice Cream, sign, tin, It's Pure, That's Sure **65.00**
Joe Louis Hair Pomade, jar **90.00**
John Deere, tape measure, deer figure both sides, 1847-1902 . . **50.00**
Johnny Walker Whiskey, tray, copper, 13½″ dia **45.00**
Johnson & Johnson, bandage tin, round **10.00**
Johnson & Johnson, paper litho, picking cotton, 14x28″ **225.00**
Jolly Time, sign on canvas, 1930, 17x36″ **95.00**
Jonteel Talc, tin **15.00**
Jose Cuervo, pitcher, Mexican style, 8″ dia **16.00**
Just Suits, canister, small top **75.00**
Kanm & Schellinger Brewery, poster **500.00**
Kato Beer, sign, convex glass, eagle, 15″ dia **125.00**
Kauers Beer, tray **38.00**
Kauffmann Bros & Bondy, pocket mirror, celluloid, pipes **18.00**
Kayo Beverage, sign, tin, 1920s 10x22″ **35.00**
Kayo, sign, embossed tin, 1930s, 28x14″ **60.00**
Kelloggs, pep pin, Dick Tracy **5.00**
Kelloggs, pep pin, Sandy **5.00**
Kelloggs, pep pin, Smilin' Jack **7.00**
Kelloggs, pep pin, Superman **7.50**
Kentucky Twist Tobacco, tin tag **1.00**
Kerosene, sign, embossed tin, 13x9″ **25.00**
Kessler Brewery, sign, embossed tin, Helena, 24x13″ **325.00**
Keystone Ammonia Carbonate, tin 5 lbs **38.00**
Keystone Beverage, glass **35.00**
King's Herald, tin, store **625.00**
King's Pure Malt, tip tray, Pan Pacific Expo **40.00**
King's International Expo, tip tray **65.00**
Kingsbury Beer, sign, 14x8″ **10.00**
Kirin Beer, sign, metal, Japan, 12x5″ **20.00**
Kirk's Flake Soap, sign, framed cardboard, Soap Girl, 38″ **385.00**
Kiss Me Gum, jar, glass **27.00**
Knickerbocker Beer, tap knobs, plastic **16.00**

Hudepohl, tray, 17x14½″ **100.00**

Knickerbocker Beer, tray	11.00
Knox Hosiery, cut out, flapper girls in parlor, 16x16″	45.00
Knox Hosiery, die cut, ladies w/wicker, 1920s	50.00
L Hoster Brewery, sign, tin w/wood frame, horses 39x30″	550.00
La Fendrich Cigars, sign, tin, 10x30″	55.00
La Fendrich Cigars, thermometer, porcelain, 5c cigar, 10x26″	95.00
La Raphaelle, poster, 1908, 60x48″	250.00
La Turka Tobacco, package, 1910 tax stamp	5.00
La Esferia Cigars, poster, lady w/umbrella, 1895, 25x15″	275.00
Labette's, sign, electric lite-up, seahorse	30.00
Lakeside Disc Talking Machine Needles, tin	22.00
Laquer Wax, sign, tin, car & can, 1930s, 12x16″	75.00
Larkin Soap, die cut, Chautauqua desk	22.00
Lash's Bitters, litho on wood, woman on horse, 14x21″	425.00
Laturka Tobacco, soft pack	8.00
Laverty's, sign, embossed tin, 6x9″	30.00
Lawrence Barrett Cigars, corner sign, porcelain, 21x31	400.00
Lee Tires, key chain, $1 Reward for Return	35.00
Lehigh Cement, sign, porcelain, blue/white, 16x60″	75.00
Leisy Beer Co, tray, factory, wagons, eagle, 16½″ oval	425.00
Lewis 66 Whiskey, sign, gent eating lobster	55.00
Liberty Tobacco, soft pack	18.00
Liberty, Pittsburgh Brewery, mug, pottery, Gibson girl	80.00
Lime Crush, syrup dispenser	300.00
Lipton Tea, sign, porcelain flange, 2 sides, 11x16″	175.00
Liquor Cure, sign, boy in cart pulled by rooster	400.00
Lite Beer, sign, neon	55.00
Little Pinkies, button	7.00
Log Cabin Syrup, bank, clear glass	25.00
Log Cabin Syrup, spatula, litho of log cabin	18.00
Log Cabin Syrup, tin, 4x3½″	38.00
London Life Cigarettes, paper w/frame, man, girl, 34x18″	225.00
London Life Cigarettes, self frame tin, 10 for 10c, 28x39″	500.00
London Life, sign, die cut, 16x2″, 1910	225.00
Lone Star, glass, etched	75.00
Lord Casper Cigars, sign	20.00
Lowenbrau, sign, plastic, gold lion, 16x14″	18.00
Lucky Strike Plug Tobacco, tin	25.00
Lucky Strike Tobacco, clock, original	750.00
Lucky Strike Tobacco, stand-up sign, bathing beauties, 52x30″	52.00
Lucky Strike Tobacco, tin, flat	9.00
Lydia Pinkham, calendar, 1927	28.00
Lydia Pinkham, perfume flask, silver, 2½x1½″	65.00
Ma's Root Beer, sign, Call Again	550.00
Maas & Steffen Fur Co, sign, animals, 1930s	75.00
Maier Brewery, tray, pre-pro, lady, 12″	70.00
Mail Pouch, sign, porcelain, blue, yellow, white, G	65.00
Mail Pouch, thermometer, porcelain, 38″	42.00
Mallard Baltimore Rye Whiskey, sign, tin, nude, 26x18″	1,200.00
Mark Twain Flour, bag	8.00
Marlow Coaster Brakes, poster, boys on bikes, 1930s	95.00
Maryland Club Tobacco, pocket tin	15.00
Mayo's, canister, small top	75.00
Mayo's Plug Light & Dark, poster, linen rooster, 30x18″	55.00
Mayo's Rooster Tobacco, tin tag	1.00
McBane's Extracts, display cabinet, stenciled marquee	275.00
McCall's Patterns, sign, porcelain, blue, white w/small flange	95.00
McCormick, sign, embossed tin, 1940s, 14x22″	25.00
Mecca Cigarettes, sign, girl by Christy, framed, 2x3″	375.00
Melachrino Cigarettes, sign, cardboard under glass	65.00
Memphis Electric, sign, embossed tin, 1930s, 9x20″	20.00
Meredith's Diamond Club Rye, jug, K T & K China, 1880	70.00
Merita Bread, sign, Lone Ranger	150.00
Merry World Tobacco, soft pack	12.00
Michelob Beer, sign, electric, logo, chain hung, 20x5″	18.00
Michelob Beer, tap knob	20.00
Mikado Pencils, sign, paper, Our Gang, 20x10″	75.00
Millar's Mountain Brand Coffee, tin, 1900s, 7″	50.00
Miller High Life, tray, girl on moon, oval	80.00
Miller Lite, sign, lite-up	15.00
Milwaukee Jim Beam, pitcher	30.00
Min Lax, tin, 1920s, 14x20″	25.00
Miner's Beer Malt, tureen, porcelain, figural steer head	165.00
Mission Orange, porcelain dispenser w/orange top	48.00
Mission Orange, sign, tin, 1940s, 2x2′	20.00
Mission Orange, sign, 30x12″	35.00
Modern Drug Co, display cabinet w/marquee, oak	275.00
Monarch Tea, tin, 8 oz	20.00
Monitor Stoves, sign, porcelain, curved, 24x18″	235.00
Monogram Tea, sign, porcelain, blue/white, 12x36″	85.00
Montgomery Ward, button	15.00
Monticello Whiskey, tip tray	75.00
Moor Mans, sign, embossed tin, 1930s 5x27″	25.00
Morton's Salt, blotter, vegetables on sled	7.00
Mother Hubbard Wheat Cereal, box, litho of Mother	20.00
Mother's Oats, poster, framed, child in tiger skin, 28x22″	145.00
Mother's Oats, sign, paper under glass, boy, 27x20″	165.00
Mountain Whiskey, framed paper, girl waterfall, 24x20″	150.00
Moxie, cardboard stand-up, w/bottle, 1930s, 9x21″	20.00
Change purse, plastic	25.00
Cigarette lighter, nickel over brass, man, horse	125.00
Fountain glass, Moxie acid etched	30.00
Fountain mug, fluted, embossed	30.00
Handfan, Laura Walker	18.00
Opener, red slide	16.00
Sign, Ted Williams	100.00
Sign, cardboard, 5c, prize under cap	15.00
Sign, embossed tin, Drink Moxie	250.00
Sign, tin, Hall of Fame, 1933, 54x19″	350.00
Sign, tin, driverless car, horse & rider	500.00
Sugar & creamer, silverplate, etched Moxie	200.00
Thermometer, Frank Archer picture	135.00
Thermometers	95.00
Tip tray	110.00
Mr Pickwick, Ale That is Ale, papier mache figure, 13″	38.00
Mt Hood Brewing, sign, brass, mountain & lake, 18x25″	335.00
Munsing Wear, stand-up, little girl in undies playing, gold	65.00
Munsing Wear, framed ad, mother & children, 33x21″	250.00
Murad Cigarettes, framed, Arabs w/rifles, horses, 26x41″	300.00
Murad Flat 100s, sign	35.00
Murad, tin	20.00
National Beer, tray, San Francisco, cowboy	250.00
National Lager, glass w/raised stem	28.00
National Phonograph, paperboard, elderly couple, framed	375.00
National Stoves & Ranges, sign, harp shape corner flange	275.00
Natural Cigarettes, poster, Arab w/rifle, framed, 26x28″	275.00
Navy Tobacco, sign, paper, 35x26″	290.00
Neallo, sign, embossed tin, 1940s, 7x4″	15.00
Nebo, sign, tin, 1920s, 15x13″	125.00
Nehi, sign, embossed tin, 1940s, 12x30″	30.00
New Bachelor Cigars, tin	48.00
New York Beer, tray, w/pretty lady, Spokane, Washington	175.00
Nip of Havana, tray, w/dog, easel back	320.00
Norka Ginger Ale, sign, tin, 1950s, 12x26″	15.00
Nu-grape, tray, woman w/child at fountain, rectangular	75.00
OFC Bourbon, sign, tin, stags drinking, barrel, 24x36″	225.00
Oceanic Cut Plug, lunch box	125.00
Oceanic Cut Plug, tin, 4x6″	75.00

Oconto, sign, 3-D paperboard, football players, 22x29" 95.00
Oertel's Brewing, tip tray, lady, dove **75.00**
Okla Vinegar Co, glass **18.00**
Old Abe Cigar Package cover **12.00**
Old Bushmills, pitcher, pyramid shape, 6" **8.00**
Old Colony Beer, mug, ironstone **30.00**
Old English Tobacco, store bin **135.00**
Old English, framed paper, men w/dog by fireplace, 31x24" . . **225.00**
Old Jed Clayton Whiskey, paper under glass, Hunting Scene . . **175.00**
Old Overholt Whiskey, framed tin, hunter w/farmer, 37x27" . . **495.00**
Old Partner Tobacco, pail, w/handle **75.00**
Old Reeding Beer, tap knobs, plastic **10.00**
Old Style Beer, tap knob, round **20.00**
Old Toothbrush, sign, tin, framed, 1890s **225.00**
Olympia Beer, sign, electric, It's The Water, G **20.00**
Olympia, tray, pre pro, horseshoe & waterfall **220.00**
Olympia, tray, w/cavalier decor **85.00**
Oneida Brewing Sparkling Cream Ale, tray **45.00**
Oneida Brewing, tray, Roderic, dog, fair **45.00**
Orange Crush, clock **650.00**
Orange Julep, tray, 1920s bathing beauty w/umbrella **155.00**
Oreno Fishing Tackle, cardboard standup, boy, boat, 3x4" . . . **115.00**
Orcico Cigars, tin **145.00**
Ortliebs Beer, tray **50.00**
P&G Soap, sign, cardboard, 1930s, 13x13" **15.00**
Pabst, sign, tin, hands hold bottle, factory, 1910, 36x48" **350.00**
Pacific Beer, tray, wood grain, ca 1912 . . . . **115.00**
Paddy, pitcher **45.00**
Pale Ale Beer, glass, etched Standard Pale **17.00**
Pale Rock, sign, tin, 14x20" **69.00**
Passport Scotch, pitcher, square, 7½" **9.00**
Pastime Plug Cut, tin **115.00**
Paul's Barber Shop, letter opener, Art Deco, gold tone **14.00**
Paunxsutawney Groundhog Sausage, tin, 10 lb **25.00**
Pearl Beer, sign, neon **55.00**
Pedro Cut Plug Tobacco, lunchbox tin **75.00**
Peerless Ale, tray **120.00**
Peerless Beer, tap knob round **20.00**
Peerless Ginger Ale, glass **23.00**
Peerless Tobacco, soft pack **8.00**
Peerless, can, tomatoes, label w/ship, hand soldered **65.00**
Penn Vacuum Cup Tires, sign, tin, 1914, 12x35" **125.00**
Penny Post Tobacco, lunchbox tin **150.00**
Pepo, bottle, full **10.00**
Pepo, sign, embossed tin, 1920s, 6x9" **30.00**

Pepsi-Cola
   Change tray, Victorian lady, soda fountain **225.00**
   Crate, ca 1920s **20.00**
   Cutout poster, large **20.00**
   Glass, old **10.00**
   Portable cooler, blue **30.00**
   Sign, tin, bottle shape, 5c, 8x29" **97.00**
   Tray, children singing, 1950s, 10x14" **45.00**
   Watch fob, embossed eagle & 2 bottles **225.00**
Perfection Dyes, cabinet, oak, 1900, 5x17x24" **245.00**
Peter Schuyler Cigar, sign, porcelain, color, 36x12" **90.00**
Peter's Cartridge, button **20.00**
Peter's Weatherbird School Shoes, blotter, dressed up birds . . . **6.00**
Peter's Shoes, sign, porcelain, 1900s, 26x16" **100.00**
Pflueger Fishing Tackle, stand-up, hooked fish, 20x18" **75.00**
Phillip Morris, sign, embossed tin, Johnny, 27x15" **60.00**
Piccadilly Little Cigars, framed paper, British officer **325.00**
Pickwick Ale, tray **65.00**
Pickaninny Brand Jumbo Salted Peanuts, tin, 9x8½" dia **200.00**

Piedmont Cigarettes, sign, tin, Gen Washington, 27x20" **250.00**
Piedmont, sign, porcelain, 2 sided, blue **35.00**
Pierce Cycles, paper/canvas, lady & bull, 1898, 4x7" **225.00**
Pilsener Beer, sign, tin, Hoboken N.J. 1910, 21x17" **450.00**

Planters Peanuts
    Mr. Peanut, the dashing peanut man with the top hat, spats, monocle and cane, has represented the Planters Peanut Company from 1916 to 1961 when the company was purchased by Standard Brands. He promoted the company's product by appearing on premium give-aways, store displays, jars, scales and in special promotional events.

Ashtray, Mr Peanut Silver Anniversary, 1906-1956 . . . . **40.00**
Ashtray, ceramic **60.00**
Bank, Atlantic City decal, Mr Peanut **35.00**
Bank, Gold Anniversary, Mr Peanut **45.00**
Bank, Mr Peanut, plastic **10.00**
Barrel jar, w/original label **250.00**
Blotter, peanut-shaped **20.00**
Bookmark, die-cut, 1930s **7.00**
Button, Mr Peanut, pink back, 1930 . . . . **4.00**
Cardboard cut-out, World's Fair, 1940, 6½" **12.00**
Cardboard stand-up, Mr Peanut, 12" **4.00**
Charm Bracelet, Mr Peanut **18.00**
Clock, masonite, 13x17" **35.00**
Container, plastic hat **10.00**
Counter display bowl **25.00**
Doll, Mr Peanut, cloth **7.00**
Doll, Mr Peanut, wood jointed, 9" **120.00**
Folding knife, Mr Peanut, 1960 . . . . **12.00**
Jar, 5c embossed, nut finial, large **29.00**
Jar, 6-sided, yellow, Mr Peanut **90.00**
Jar, full blown, 4 corner nuts, 14x10" **225.00**
Jar, Leap Year 1940 w/original box **45.00**
Jar, square, Planters embossed **85.00**
Mirror, 14x17" **30.00**

Mr Peanut figural, ci, 8" **150.00**
Nodder, w/original box **20.00**
Nut Set, 5 pc, 1939 World's Fair **18.00**
Nut Spoon, Mr Peanut figural, gold **20.00**
Paperweight, rectangular, 1938 . . . . **20.00**
Pencil, Mr Peanut **12.00**
Salt & Pepper, 1939, World's Fair **6.00**
Salt & Pepper, Mr Peanut figural, plastic **7.00**
Sign, metal **22.00**
Sign, plaster/wood, Mr Peanut in relief **350.00**

Tin, 10 lb, 1909 . . . . **55.00**
Tin,, 10 lb, w/red pennant **35.00**
Umbrella **35.00**
Wind-up walker, Mr Peanut **130.00**

Poll Parrot Shoes, ink blotter, red & white w/parrot **2.50**
Pollack Wheeling Stogies, thermometer **75.00**
Poole Pianos, reverse on glass, framed, 1895, 20x36″ **900.00**
Poppy Cigars, paperboard, artist's proof, bear, 18x27″ **110.00**
Pratts Foods Indian Village, sign **400.00**
Presidential Insurance, tip tray, rock **12.00**
Presidents Choice, pitcher **11.00**
Prestolite, thermometer, 27x8″ **20.00**
Prestone Antifreeze, thermometer **30.00**
Prestone Gas, thermometers **10.00**
Pride of Winston Tobacco, tin tag **1.00**
Prince Albert Tobacco, jar, glass, dated 1910 . . . . **45.00**
Prince Albert Tobacco, tin, w/lid **9.00**
Prudential Insurance, tray, Rock of Gibralter, blue rim **14.00**
Purity Salt, blotter, lady pouring salt **7.00**
Puritan Tobacco, tin container **85.00**
Putman Fadeless Dyes, ink blotter, girl in canoe **2.50**
Quaker Ice Cream, framed embossed tin, w/kewpie, 28x23″ . . . **195.00**
Queen Nefertiti, pitcher **24.00**
Quick Meal Ranges, tip tray **60.00**
R&G Corsets, sign, oscillating lady, w/key, 24x36″ **800.00**

RCA Victor

    Nipper, the RCA Victor trademark was the creation of Francis Barraud, an English artist. His pet's intent fascination with the music of the phonograph seemed to him a worthy subject for his canvas. Although he failed to find a publishing house who would buy his work, the Gramaphone Co. saw its potential and adopted Nipper to advertise their product. The company eventually became the Victor Talking Machine Co, and was purchased by RCA in 1929. Nipper's image appeared on packaged accessories, in ads and brochures. If you are very lucky you may find a life size statue of him--but all are not old, they have been reproduced! Except for the years between 1971 and '81 Nipper has seen active duty, and with just a bit of sprucing up, the ageless symbol of RCA still listens intently to His Master's Voice.

RCA, Nipper, papier mache, 14″ **300.00**
  Nipper, papier mache, 17½″ **375.00**
  Nipper, plaster, 1920, 3½ ft **900.00**
  Nipper, plaster, 1920, 4″ **50.00**
  Crate end, Nipper, His Master's Voice, 15x20″ **95.00**
  Record duster w/Nipper **25.00**
  Sign, 3-D light up, Nipper w/phonograph, 1940s **175.00**
Rainer Beer, calendar sign, cowgirl on stallion, 1906 . . . . . . **550.00**
Ramon's Pills, sign, cardboard **15.00**
Recruit Tobacco, soft pack **12.00**
Red Belt Cigar, framed poster, girl tying shoe, 1895, 22″ **375.00**
Red Belt Tobacco, pail, paper label **20.00**
Red Cross Cotton, framed paperboard, blacks picking cotton . . **375.00**
Red Cross Stoves, sign, tin, Maltese Cross, 16x20″ **125.00**
Red Elk Tobacco, tin tag **1.00**
Red Four Roses Tobacco, pocket tin **25.00**
Red Goose Shoes, clicker, pointed bill **10.00**
Red Indian Tobacco, tin canister **130.00**
Red Jacket Tobacco, pocket tin, 1930s, 4½″ **18.00**
Red Meat Tobacco, tin tag **1.00**
Red Raven, tip tray **95.00**
Red Raven, tray, bird, bottle **75.00**
Red Rock Tobacco, sign, tin, 1940s, 3x20″ **13.00**
Red Seal Battery, thermometer, porcelain **100.00**
Red Tiger Tobacco, lunch box, lg, 10″ **70.00**

Redford's Celebrated Tobacco, lithograph, 1920s, 20x25″ **45.00**
Reliable Seeds, wooden box, chromolitho lid, 25x12″ **75.00**
Remember the Maine, glass, etched **28.00**
Remember the Maine, tray w/battleship, 12″ **140.00**
Remington Arms, framed poster, hunter/ducks, 16x20″ **195.00**
Resinol Soap & Ointment, tip tray **80.00**
Richardson's Liberty Flair, glass **22.00**
Richmond Club Tobacco, box, small **15.00**
Richmond Strait Cut, sign, celluloid on board, 20x30″ **950.00**
Rexall Drugs, calendar, 1925, 17x11″ **20.00**
Rheingold Lager Beer, tray, 12″ **8.00**
Robert Smith Musty Ale, mug **75.00**
Robert Burns, wall plaque, plaid, 10c cigar, man, 24″ **165.00**
Rockford Watches, tip tray **65.00**
Rogers Paint & Varnishes, sign, porcelain w/flange **55.00**
Roly Poly, Dixie Queen **350.00**
  Dutchman Tobacco tin **480.00**
  Dutchman **550.00**
  Mammy **485.00**
  Red Indian, storekeeper **425.00**
  Satisfied Customer **475.00**
  Storekeeper **435.00**
Rome Ale, tray, gladiator **75.00**
Ross Seeds, wood box, w/inside label **65.00**
Round Up Tobacco, soft pack **5.00**
Royal Brewing, mug **40.00**
Royal Crown Cola, scale, bottle shape, plastic, 43″ **1,050.00**
Ruhstaller Brewery, tray, lady w/dove, 12″ **100.00**
Ruppert's Beer, tip tray, Hans Flato cartoon, 4″ **45.00**
Ruskin Cigars, framed paper, cowboy w/tobacco pack, 20x28″ . **850.00**

Russian Cigarette Tobacco, 4x3″ **55.00**
Ryders Scotch, pitcher **12.50**
S & H Green Stamps, tip tray **55.00**
San Antonio Beer, paperboard, cowboys at Judge Bean store . . **150.00**
San Antonio Brewing Pilsner, glass **85.00**
San Felice Cigars, framed, woman hugging man, 13x24″ **215.00**
Sanitary Ice Cream, tray, two children **110.00**
Santa Fe Peanut Butter, Pail, l-lb, picture of Indian **75.00**
Saratoga Chips Tobacco tin **17.00**
Satin Skin Cream, sign, litho, 1903, 27x41″ **40.00**
Satisfaction Tobacco, lunchbox tin **65.00**
Sauers Flavoring, thermometers, wooden **150.00**
Schenley Pure Rye, sign, tin, elegant couple, 1910, 11x13″ . . **285.00**
Schepp's, can, tapered w/round cap **60.00**
Schepp's, pail, yellow **60.00**
Schlitz Beer, mug, stoneware, blue & grey **125.00**
Schlitz Beer, sign, tin, pictures cone top can, 11x15″ **100.00**

Schlitz Beer, stretched canvas, winged nude, 14x22"	275.00
Schlitz Beer, tray, Schliterland, 1957, 12" dia	9.00
Schmidts Beer, sign, neon	55.00
Schmidts Beer, framed chromolitho, hunters, 1890, 38x28" . . .	690.00
Schmidt Brewery, self-framed tin, hunters w/moose, 33x23" . . .	350.00
Schoeny Grocers, Vienna Art Plate, brunette, 1905	65.00
School Boy Peanut Butter, pail, child's face decor	90.00
Seagrams VO, pitcher, metal	7.00
Seagram's VO Canadian, ashtray, gold on cobalt porcelain	18.00
Seal of North Carolina, small top can	175.00
Sears Roebuck, tape measure	25.00
Seaway Coffee, squat tin	5.99
Seitz Beer, coaster, tin	55.00
Sen-Sen Gum, box, bookshape	22.00
Sensible Tobacco, lunchbox tin	25.00
Sexton Ajax Garbage, tin, self frame, dog, 10x12"	85.00
Sharples Cream Separator, button	18.00
Sharples Tublar Cream Separator, sign, tin w/chain, 27x19" . .	575.00
Shawn's Malt, self-framed tin, mother w/child, 24x18"	325.00
Sherwin Williams, sign, Uncle Sam & clerk	18.00
Short Lance, counter jar, metal lid	25.00
Sickle Plus Cut Tobacco, poster, linen, 1900s, 13x36"	45.00
Silver Pine Healing Oil, poster, smiling horse, 28x21"	110.00
Silver Spring Brewery, sign, stone litho, 1915, 20x20"	40.00
Simon Pure Beer, tray	65.00
Smirnoff Silver, pitcher, white w/black, 4½" dia.	8.00
Smith Piano & Organ, framed paper, singing trio, 31x23"	250.00
Smoke Beck's Hunting tobacco, sign, tin	20.00
Sohio Diesel, gasoline globe	95.00
Spark Plug Tobacco, sign, cardboard, shows package	22.00
Spidel Authorized Dealer, sign, electric	20.00
Springfield Breweries, calendar, Poster Girl, 1912, framed	195.00
Sprite, blotter, w/Sprite boy & bottle	8.00
Squirrel Brand, Pail, 1 lb, Peanut Butter, no lid	125.00
Squirrel Brand, Pail, 5 lb, Peanut butter, no lid	195.00
Squirrel Peanuts, counter jar, embossed	125.00
Squirt, thermometer, embossed bottle	30.00
Stag Tobacco, canister	75.00
Star Beer, tray, old man & boat, 1905, Vancouver, Wash.	125.00
Star Shoes, framed tin, w/shoe shiner, 1920s, 19x24"	175.00
Star Soap, sign, porcelain, curved, 26x20"	275.00
Star Spangled Banner, glass, etched	16.00
Stars & Bars Tobacco, tin tag	1.00
Stearns Talc Powder, tin	70.00
Stegmaier Brewing, change tray, w/hand & bottle	58.00
Sterling Beer, sign, tin, clowns & circus horse, 21x28"	225.00
Stewart Hair Clipping Machine, self-framed tin, 24x20"	250.00
Stud Tobacco, soft pack	12.00
Sunoco Motor Oil, sign, die cut, 2 sides, 1920s, 26x16"	110.00
Sunoco, blotter, Donald Duck, 1946	5.00
Sunoco, map rack	20.00
Surbrug Tobacco Purse, lunch box	210.00
Sweet Burley Light, tin, hinged lid, yellow & red, 26" dia	110.00
Sweet Cuba Tobacco, bin, 10x8x8"	135.00
Sweet Hart Flour, sign, porcelain, 1915	165.00
Sweet Mist, sign, tin	85.00
Tanquery Gin, pitcher, dark green, 6½" dia.	9.00
Teachers, pitcher, blue & white	7.00
Teachers, pitcher, gray	9.00
Tetley Tea, clock, tin	295.00
Texaco Motor Oil, sign, porcelain, "T" w/oil can, flange	95.00
Texas Brewing, glass, etched, G	50.00
Theresa Bava Brewing Co, Vienna art plate	55.00
Tiger Bright Chewing Tobacco, lunch pail, 6x9x7" illus.	40.00

Tiger Tobacco, cardboard pouch	75.00
Tivoli Brewing, tip tray	45.00
Todd's Tonic, glass	28.00
Tom Keene Tobacco, tin	16.00
Tom Moore Tobacco, lunchbox tin	22.00
Toppers Cigarettes, sign, tin, 1930s, 16x11"	60.00
Town Talk Bread, thermometer	28.00
Triple A Root Beer, sign, tin, 1930s, 7x14"	4.50
Trommers Malt Beer, tap knob, round	30.00
Trout Line, pocket tin	350.00
Tuck, calendar, Sweet Message, 1897	40.00
Turkish Trophies Cigarettes, framed, girl, city, 22x30"	350.00
Tuxedo Tobacco tin	12.50
Twin Oaks Tobacco, pocket tin w/curved top	32.00
Twin Oaks Tobacco, treasure chest, silver-plate	45.00
US Cartridges, sign, cardboard, 15x12"	125.00
US Marine Tobacco, lunchbox tin	22.00
Union Girl Tobacco, soft pack	18.00
Union Leader Cut Plug Eagle tin, milk can shape, 9½"	85.00
Union Leader Cut Plug Tobacco, lunch box	70.00
Union Leader Uncle Sam canister	3.00
Union Workman Tobacco, soft pack	8.00
United Fireman's Insurance, fire mark, iron	130.00
United States Fur Co, paper litho, 1920s, 21x15"	275.00
Upton's, pail, 1 lb, peanut butter	88.00
Utica Beer, tap knobs, plastic	18.00
Vacuum Cup Tires, sign, 35x12"	60.00
Valley Forge Special, tray, waitress w/tray	80.00
Valtines Wisteria Blossom Talc, tin	24.00
Van Houten Cocoa, sign, cardboard, lady pouring, 23x31"	350.00
Vani Kola, tray, girl w/horse, oval	165.00
Vat 69, pitcher, white w/black & gold, 5½" dia	13.00
Velvet Tobacco, sign, porcelain, 12x36", G	65.00
Velvet Tobacco, sign, porcelain, pocket tin, 48x12"	150.00
Victoria Tea, tin, 5 lbs	75.00
Vi-Jon Sweet Pea Talc, tin	10.00
Vigorton, sign, tin, 1940s, 18x14"	25.00
Violet Talc, sign, cardboard	55.00
Virginia Dare Cigarettes, semi-nude male, female, 36x46"	550.00
WC Fields, pitcher	15.00
Washington Coffee, sign, metal side mount, 10x17"	65.00
Walkover shoes, sign, cardboard, man, 1910, 6x20"	6.50
Waltham, sign, paper under glass, factory, 36½x21"	85.00
Warnicke & Brown, lunchbox tobacco tin	48.00
Waukesha Brewery, tray, fox head, 13"	175.00
Way Up, sign, cardboard, balloon, 1930s, 5x7"	155.00
Weatherbird Shoes, whistle, round	8.00
Weatherly Ice Cream, sign, girl w/fur hat, stole, 1915	155.00
Webster Tobacco, tin	12.00
Welcome Nugget, tobacco barrel label, miner, 1970s, 11x11" . .	25.00
Welsbach Lighting, sign, child w/toys, mother	55.00
Western, wood frame, quail hunter w/dogs, 1920s, 15x27"	265.00
Western Ammunition, tin sign, relief hunting scene, 13x21" . .	150.00
Western Surety Co, mirror	18.00
Western Union, sign, porcelain, blue & white, 1905, 21x30" . .	265.00
Westinghouse, sign, tin, woman at machine	95.00
Westside, sign, Viking holds goblet	150.00
Whistle Orange Soda, mirror, 9x13"	32.00
White Cat Union Suits, pocket mirror, celluloid	35.00
White Eagle, gas globe	600.00
White Horse, pitcher, large, black	8.00
White Label Cigars, sign, embossed tin, cigars, 10x14"	95.00
Whitmans, sign, porcelain, green & white, 1918, 13x49"	135.00
Wholesale Drugs & Spices, Etc, pamphlet, 1850, 5x8"	10.00

Wiedemann Brewing, mug, Rookwood **150.00**
Wild Turkey Bourbon, pitcher, 101 proof, England **55.00**
Winchester, sign, cardboard, boxer, 1920s, 7x12″ **60.00**
Willard Battery, sign, porcelain, 1930 . . . . **35.00**
Wilson Whiskey, tin w/wood frame, carriage, people, 40x28″ . . **550.00**
Winchester, poster, 3 young hunters, 1900s **175.00**
Winchester Tires, sign, tin, 1940s, 18x48″ **35.00**
Winner Cut Plug Tobacco, lunchbox tin **85.00**
Winnie Winkle Cigars, box **20.00**
Wiss Tinner Snips, sign, tin, 13½x6″ **55.00**
Wm Crawford Biscuits, tin, figural globe **90.00**
Woochong, poster, Japanese ladies w/monkey **15.00**
Wooden Shoe Lager, tray, Dutch girls w/beer **85.00**
Woods Areca Nut Tooth Paste, box, porcelain, 2¾″ dia **90.00**
Woodward's Candy, tip tray, Jean Bregants, midgets **50.00**
Wright & Taylor Whiskey, Victorian girls, factory, 1900 . . . . . . **155.00**
Wrigley Chewing Gum, sign, w/4 old packs & gum man **110.00**
Wrigley's, trolleycard, 1923 . . . . **26.00**
Wrigley's Gum, sign, tin, 1920, 13x6″ **100.00**
Wrigley's Gum, counter display, half circle base w/elf **265.00**
Wyborowa Vodka, pitcher **7.00**
Yankee Girl Tobacco, tin tag **1.00**
Yusay Pilsner Beer, tray **30.00**
Zanzibar Sausage, tin, 50 lb, colorful pictures **195.00**
Zetts Bavarian Beer, framed litho, On Furlough **225.00**

Advertising Cards

From the mid l800s until the turn of the century, advertising trade cards were used by merchants to familarize the public with their products.

Adams Pepsin Gum, child w/dog, 5½x4½″ **7.50**
Albany Dry Goods, girl w/toboggan, 3½x5½″ **1.00**
Andes Stove Co, lady w/hat, 3x5″ **1.25**
Arbuckle Bros Coffee, Egyptian map, Sphinx, 1889, 3x5″ **2.25**
Arbuckle Bros Coffee, Hawaiian natives & alligators, 1893 . . . . **2.25**
Arbuckle Bros Coffee, Persian map, divers, weavers, 1899 . . . . **2.25**
Arbuckle Bros Coffee, soldiers & priests, 1881, 3x7″ **1.85**
Arm & Hammer, birds, lot of 49 . . . . **20.00**
Atlantic Tea Co, Autumn Boy, 1879, 4x6″ **2.50**
Berkshire Life Insurance, set of 8 . . . . **16.00**
Beverwyck Brewing Co, race horse & jockey, 1914 . . . . **3.00**
Bolding Bros & Co, Cupid in cart w/spool wheels, 3x5″ **1.75**
Chase & Sandborn, 1905, 3½x4½″ **8.50**
Cherry Smash, Mt Vernon & people in Colonial dress **2.25**
Church & Dwight Soda, set of 15, w/original envelope **8.00**
Clark's Thread Co, girl sewing boy's coat, color, 3x4½″ **1.10**
Comic, I'm A Farder, Victorian **4.00**
Currier & Ives, Bare Chance, 1879 . . . . **58.00**
Dan Patch, flip card, 1909, "World's Record Mile," Savage **55.00**
Deering Twine Binder **2.50**
Demorest's Family Magazine, w/1890 calendar, 5x7″ **2.50**
Doe-Wah-Jack, stove ads, Indian month series **11.00**
Dr JC Ayer & Co, Sarsaparilla, Sunny Hours **1.50**
Duplex corset, metamorphic, card opens, Mrs Brown **8.00**
Dupont, Gunpowder, dog, unused **26.00**
Fisk, Clark & Flagg's Gloves, Victorian gentlemen, 3x5″ **2.00**
Fleer, Three Stooges, black & white or color **2.50**
Fleming Bros, Mikado Perfume, red-head girl w/muff, 3x5″ **2.00**
French La Confiance Insurance, 1880 . . . . **10.00**
GE Marsh & Co, girl washing clothes **1.00**
Germania House Hotel, Cincinnati, Ohio, 1870 . . . . **3.50**
Gold Dust Twins, A Word to the Wife is Sufficient **21.00**
Gowers & Stover Co, Oak Leaf Soap w/muff, 3x5″ **1.10**

Great Atlantic & Pacific Tea Co, Grandma w/bonnet **2.00**
Heinz Co, airplane **2.00**
Hibbards Rheumatic Syrup Co, harem girl w/harp, 3x5″ **2.00**
Higgins Soap, day of the week, set of 7 . . . . **32.00**
Hill Brothers, The Climax, lady w/flowered hat, 1886 fashions . . **2.00**
Hires Root Beer, boy in electric car, 1900, 5x7″ **30.00**
Home Insurance, 1880 . . . . **8.00**
Indian Queen Perfume, ... **4.50**
Ivory Soap, Maud Humphrey illus, girl w/washtub **35.00**
J&P Coats Thread Co, boy w/girl in swing, 1881 . . . . **1.20**
J&P Coats Thread Co, lion bound w/thread, 3x4″ **1.50**
JC Mendenhall Co, Chill & Corn Cure, children w/butterfly **2.00**
JD Larkin & Son, girl w/rabbits, 1882, 3x5¼″ **1.50**
JD Larkin Co, boy w/butterfly, 1882, 3x5½″ **1.50**
Jello Co, Hawaiian girl, folding w/recipes . . . . **.85**
John Hancock Insurance **5.00**
Lautz Bros, Acme soap, girl w/pink bonnet, old **1.19**
Lord and Taylor, Mama Frog, ca 1880, 3x5″ **8.00**
Lydia Pinkham Co, bee & flowers, 2½x4″ **1.00**
McLaughlin's Coffee, President Cleveland, 1983, 5½x7″ **4.00**
Metro Life Insurance, 3 different cards **26.00**
Moxie, roadster, man on horse **26.00**
Niagara Starch, girl studying book, 1887, 3x5″ **1.10**
Official Photogapher, 4½x3″ **5.00**
Park & Tilford chocolates, elegant man and woman, Clapsaddle **46.00**
Parker Shot Gun **45.00**
Piedmont Cigarettes, Victorian ladies, 1902, 6x8″ **10.00**
Poole Pianos, beautiful ladies **2.50**
Putnam Nail, trotter & sulky, 1881, ... **9.00**
Singer Mfg Co, New Singer Building, N.Y. **2.50**
Singer Sewing Machine Co, Columbian Exposition set of 9 . . . . **4,00**
Singer Sewing Machine Co, birds, set of 16, large **8.00**
Singer Sewing Machine Co, birds, set of 16 . . . . **10.00**
Singer Sewing Machine Co, lady w/machine, Philippine Islands . . **2.85**
Singer Sewing Machine Co, Meadow lark & egg, JL Ridgeway, 1899 **1.50**
Tippecanoe Bitters, large **20.00**
Tobacco, steamship companies, lot of 7 . . . . **30.00**
Victorian, blacks w/musical instruments **45.00**
Walter Wood Enclosed Gear Mower, 4x6″ **5.50**
Waterbury Clock Co, three maids, 3x6″ **1.75**
White Sewing Machine Co, 18th century man & woman, color . . **1.20**
White Sewing Machine Co, snow scene w/bluebird, 4x5½″ **1.25**
White Sewing Machine Co, The Little Turk, 3½x5″ **1.50**
Willimatic Thread Co, boy w/ballon, 1881, 3x5″ **1.20**
Wings Cigarettes, lot of 59 . . . . **25.00**
Woolson Spice Co, 6¾x4½″ **6.00**

Advertising Dolls

Often the secret to finding advertising doll bargains hinges on being able to spot one. Many are unmarked. As you walk past merchandise at a flea market, can you spot trademark figures? What may look like a baby's squeeze toy may be the illusive Chiquita banana doll!

Common trademark figures used today are easy to identify: Mr. Peanut, the Jolly Green Giant and Pillsbuy's Doughboy; but what about Coco Wheat's Gretchen, or Peter Pan Ice Cream's doll--they are not marked, and haven't been used for several years.

Browse through old magazines...the old ads are a good source of information. Some companies and products no longer exist, and trademark figures change through the years.

When buying dolls, condition is very important. Check cloth dolls to make sure the fabric is not torn or rotted. Remember, it is almost impossible to clean a cloth doll that has been soiled for many years. And if it is faded, nothing can restore the color. Rubber items often disintegrate; check

unpainted areas to make sure they are solid. Plastics, though they may look hopeless, usually come out looking good as new with a little soap and water.

Never pay full price for a damaged advertising doll, unless it is very rare. At least you'll have one in your collection while you watch for a better example.

Collectors often build their collections by trading. Watch for dolls offered in your area and buy several. Watch for bargains, and exchange them for one you need.

New dolls and other toys are offered each month. Watch the grocery shelves, read the doll literature, and talk with fellow collectors. Many items sell for only a few months before the offer is withdrawn. Save the information relating to the advertising doll; clip ads, get extra coupons, and keep them in a scrapbook--in time, advertising literature will add greatly to the history of your doll collection.

A P W Paper Co, litho cloth trademark figure, 1925, 12″ **50.00**
Adam's Black Jack Gum, cloth rabbit, No 9 Chiclet Zoo, 11″ .. **55.00**
Alaska Yukon Pacific Expo, souvenir, The New Mail Baby, 5″.. **65.00**
Alka Seltzer, vinyl bank, Speedy, 5½″ **10.00**
American Airlines, plastic stewardess, blond, 1967, 11″ **10.00**
American Rice Food Mfg Co, Cloth Miss Flaked Rice, 1899, 21″ **65.00**
Arbuckle Bros, cloth Mary & Her Little Lamb, 14½″ **55.00**
Aunt Jemima Mills Co, litho cloth Aunt Jemima, 1910, 15″ ... **65.00**
Aunt Jemima Mills Co, litho cloth Wade, 1910, 12″ **50.00**
Aunt Jemima Mills Co, litho cloth Aunt Jemima, 1924, 15″ ... **40.00**
Babbitt Cleanser, cloth trademark boy w/can, 1916, 15″..... **200.00**
Baby Magic, litho cloth Snuggly Sammy, 1975, 2′ **12.00**
Baby Ruth, bean bag type baby w/plastic face & hands, 1973... **10.00**
Baker's Chocolate, china pincushion La Belle Chocolatiere, 7″ **300.00**
Beta Fiberglass Co, sad-faced Bad Doll, removable dress, 10½″.. **9.00**
Big Boy Restaurant, plastic w/cloth pants & shirt, 1974, 8½″ ... **8.00**
Blatz Beer, cast iron baseball player w/barrel body, 10½″ **55.00**
Blue Ribbon Malt Extract, litho cloth Lena, green dress, 1930, 14″. **200.00**
Borden Company, plush fabric w/vinyl head, Beauregard, 1950s. **15.00**
Bradlee Stores, gold plush bear Bruff, 14″................... **9.00**
Brer Rabbit Molasses, plush Easter rabbit, 1964, 27″ **15.00**
Brunswick Corp, cloth "iitywybts", 1967, 16″............... **12.00**
Buster Brown Shoes, cloth trademark dolls, 13″ **75.00**
C & H Sugar Twins, boy in sarong, girl in grass skirt, ea **8.00**
Campbell Kid, Horsman, compo head, stuffed muslin body, 1910 **90.00**
Campbell Cheer Leader, Ideal Toy, red skirt, sweater, 9½″ **20.00**
Cap'n Crunch doll, wool-like fabric, felt features, 15½″........ **8.00**
Caravelle Candy Bar doll, candy bar replica w/wire limbs........ **7.00**
Ceresota/Heckers Flour Boy, stuffed fabric cut out, 1972, 15″ ... **7.00**
Clark Candy Bar doll, soft vinyl, 7″ **15.00**
Club Aluminum Cook Ware, Cooky, plastic, vinyl w/rooted wig . **12.00**
Cox Gelatine, printed fabric w/instructions, Scottish dress **65.00**
Cream of Wheat Chef doll, stuffed cloth 1 pc legs............ **65.00**
Dairy Queen, Thor, stuffed cloth, 14″..................... **8.00**
Dodge Automobiles, Little Profit, nodder, 1960s, 6″ **10.00**
Domino Sugar, plush bear, 1975, 15″..................... **7.00**
Eastman Kodak Champion Retriever, 1971 .... **20.00**
Fab, American Doll, pink shoes, hat, 1957, 7¾″............. **15.00**
Faultless Starch, Lizabeth Ann, printed fabric to stuff, 19½″ ... **65.00**
Flintsones Vitamins, Fred Flintstone w/removable clothes **7.00**
Frostie Root Beer, prestuffed cloth litho w/beard, 16″ **10.00**
Gerber Baby doll, boy or girl, stuffed cloth, 8″ .... **Rare**
Gold Medal Flour, printed on flour sack, w/apron, 7½″ **40.00**
Gorton's Codfish vinyl fisherman doll, 7″ **10.00**
Hamm's Beer bear, celluloid black & white, display doll, 8″.... **12.00**
Hardee's Restaurant Gilbert Giddyup, 1971 .... **10.00**
Henderson Glove Indian doll, printed fabric, 11″............ **30.00**
Hoover Housewife w/vaccum, nodder doll, 8″................ **20.00**
Ideal Flour, Simple Sam, printed on flour sack, 14″ **15.00**

Jack's Restaurant, cloth 16″ **12.00**
Jello Girl, compositon w/cloth torso, 1905-20, 9″............. **85.00**
Keebler Elf, molded, painted vinyl, 1974................... **8.00**
Kellogg's Crinkle the Cat, printed fabric to stuff, 12″ **30.00**
Kellogg's Bingo, Banana Split doll, 10″ **60.00**
Kellogg's Tony the Tiger, molded vinyl, 1974, 8″ **9.00**
Kentucky Fried Chicken, Colonel Sanders bank, 12½″........ **10.00**
Kentucky Tavern Whiskey Snowman, 13″ **10.00**
Libby doll, litho cloth, talks by pulling cord **15.00**
Long John Silver Seafood girl, cloth litho................. **7.00**
Ma Brown Pickles, Ma Brown, all vinyl 15″ **20.00**
Maxwell House Coffee plush bear **10.00**
McDonald Corp, Ronald, cloth litho 1971.................. **8.00**
McDonald Corp, Big Mac in police uniform, 1975 .... **5.00**
Miller Beer, gold painted display figure.................. **20.00**
Mountain Dew Hillbilly doll, 18″........................ **25.00**
National Biscuit, Uneeda Kid, compo head, pat 1914, 16″.... **185.00**
Nestle Baby food, printed stuffed muslin, 1916 .... **45.00**
Old Crow Whiskey, felt figure in formal attire, 28″ **25.00**
Oxol, printed fabric to stuff, 17″ **40.00**
Peters Weather Bird shoes, all bisque doll, 2½″ **25.00**
Philip Morris Inc, Johnny, compo head, open close mouth 15″ **100.00**
Pillsbury Doughboy doll, cloth w/blue features, 1971, 16″...... **8.00**
Pillsbury Poppin' Fresh, pops out of can **8.00**
Pine Sol Bear, sitting, 15x15″.......................... **15.00**
Plymouth Chrysler Corp, Roadrunner, inflatable, 7½″......... **2.00**
Popeye Puffed Wheat, Popeye doll, stuffed cloth 15″ **7.00**
Procter & Gamble Mary Makeup, 11½″ **12.00**
Puritan Flour, Puritan cloth doll, 1920, 15½″ **65.00**
Revlon Inc, Little Miss Revlon, Ideal Toy, 1950, 10½″........ **25.00**
Royal Gelatin, King Royal vinyl bank, 9½″ **8.00**
Sambo's Restaurants, Sambo, rubber, 1972, 5″ **6.50**
Sea Island Sugar, cloth litho to stuff **20.00**
Sergeant's Sentry IV Flea Collar Dirty Dog, plush, 20″....... **8.00**
Seven Up, Fresh Up Freddie, cloth w/rubber head, 24″ **30.00**
Skookum Packers Assoc, compo head & hands, cloth body, 16″ **90.00**
Sunbeam Bread, Miss Sunbeam, plastic w/vinyl head, arms, 17″. **30.00**
Tastee-Freez International, Frenchy Fry, plush, 10″ **5.00**
Texas Dairy Queen, Cheerleader, cloth 1979 .... **4.00**
Travelodge International, Sleepy Bear, plush, 12″ **7.00**
United Hosiery Mills Corp, Dixie doll, ribbed knit, 13″....... **20.00**
Vlasic Stork, inflatable display figure, 4'3″ **4.00**
Westinghouse, Cozy Glo Kid, composition, 12½″ **200.00**

African Art

These artifacts of the African nation are a unique form of folk art, of interest not only in relation to the craftsmanship evident in their making but because of the culture they represent.

Bookends, Congolese tribal chief head **40.00**
Ebony carving, tribal woman, 9″ **25.00**
Fertility figure, carved wood, 25″ **55.00**
Mask cop Guro, pottery **36.00**
Mask, 36″ **30.00**
  Bauli **53.00**
  Carved, 21″ **25.00**
Shield & spear, colorful, large **85.00**
Voo Doo drum, authentic **135.00**
War axe, Zulu **25.00**

Agata

Agata glass is a very rare and expensive type of art glass that was made

at the New England Glass Co. in 1887. John Locke developed the method for achieving the characteristic mottled effect which was usually used on their lovely peach blow glass, although occasionally it was applied to opaque green. The procedure involved spraying an alcohol mixture on the surfaced of the glass while it was still very hot. The results produced a marbelized appearance not unlike the agate stone. Caution--be sure to use only gentle cleaning methods!

Fingerbowl, ruffled, raspberry to cream pink, 2½x5″	**1,000.00**
Punch cup, peach blow, mottled, 2½″	**685.00**
Toothpick, green opaque, New England Glass Co	**550.00**
Tumbler, creamy pink to deep rose, 3¾″	**800.00**
Vase, deep red to rose red, 10″	**1,585.00**

Akro Agate

The Akro Agate Company founded in 1914 in Clarksburg, West Va., was primarily a marble factory. Not until 1932, did they start to manufacture their popular lines of children's dishes, novelty items, etc. Although not always marked, much of their ware was made in a distinctive marbled or opaque glass that is easily recognized. Some of the children's wares were also made of clear colors. In the list that follows, colors not termed opaque or marble are clear. Pieces that are marked bear the circle seal with AKRO and a flying eagle carrying marbles in his talons. The company closed in 1951.

Box w/cover, green, Art Nouveau w/nudes in relief	**120.00**

Chiquita

Creamer, baked on cobalt	**9.25**
Creamer, opaque green	**4.50**
Creamer & sugar, baked on cobalt	**18.75**
Cup, baked on red	**5.75**
Cup & saucer, cobalt	**6.00**
Cup & saucer, opaque green	**4.75**
Plate, baked on green	**3.00**
Plate, dinner, opaque green	**5.00**
Service for 6, green, in box	**65.00**

Saucer, opaque green	**1.50**
Sugar, cobalt	**7.00**
Sugar, opaque green	**4.00**
Sugar, opaque turquoise	**25.00**
Teapot, opaque blue	**8.75**
Teapot, w/cover, baked on cobalt	**14.50**
Teapot, w/cover, cobalt	**12.00**
Teapot, w/cover, opaque aqua	**29.50**
Teapot, w/cover, opaque green	**3.75**
Plate, dinner, opaque green	**5.00**
Colonial Lady, lime green	**90.00**
Colonial Lady, powder jar, white	**35.00**

Concentric Rib

Creamer, opaque medium blue, small	**5.00**
Creamer, opaque white, small	**4.00**
Cup, opaque green, small	**3.75**
Cup, opaque orange, small	**8.75**
Cup, opaque white, small	**10.00**
Plate, opaque aqua, small	**2.00**
Plate, opaque green, small	**1.00**
Plate, opaque lavender, small	**7.00**
Plate, opaque light blue, small	**1.75**
Plate, opaque medium blue, small	**1.75**
Saucer, opaque white, small	**3.00**
Saucer, opaque yellow, small	**3.00**
Service for 2, opaque, small	**25.00**
Service for 4, opaque, 16-pc, small	**47.00**
Sugar & creamer, opaque green, small	**9.75**
Sugar & creamer, opaque light blue, small	**9.00**
Sugar & creamer, opaque white, small	**8.75**
Teapot, opaque blue, w/blue lid, small	**8.75**
Teapot, opaque green, w/beige lid, small	**9.25**
Teapot, opaque light blue, small	**3.00**
Teapot, opaque medium blue, small	**3.25**
Teapot, opaque white, w/green lid, small	**8.75**
Teapot, opaque yellow, w/green lid, small	**12.00**

Concentric Ring

Bowl, cobalt, large	**50.00**
Bowl, opaque cobalt, large	**18.00**
Creamer, blue, 1¼″	**75.00**
Creamer, cobalt, large	**32.75**
Creamer, opaque cobalt, large	**25.00**
Creamer, opaque green	**6.50**
Creamer, opaque medium blue, small	**8.75**
Creamer & Sugar, opaque light blue, small	**17.50**
Cup, blue	**6.50**
Cup, green	**3.00**
Cup, opaque green, 2″ dia	**5.00**
Cup, opaque orange, large	**18.00**
Cup & Saucer, cobalt, large	**65.00**
Plate, cobalt, large	**50.00**
Plate, green, small	**1.50**
Plate, opaque green, 3¼″	**5.00**
Plate, opaque green, large	**7.75**
Plate, opaque green, small	**4.50**
Saucer, opaque blue, small	**5.00**
Saucer, opaque green, 3½″	**4.50**
Saucer, opaque white, small	**1.50**
Saucer, opaque yellow, large	**6.00**
Saucer, opaque yellow, small	**3.00**
Service for 4, opaque, 16-pc, small	**60.00**
Service for 4, opaque, 21-pc, large	**190.00**
Sugar, blue, 1¼″	**7.50**
Sugar, cobalt, large	**24.75**
Sugar, opaque cobalt, w/lid, large	**24.75**
Sugar, opaque medium blue, small	**8.50**
Sugar, opaque cobalt, w/lid, large	**24.75**
Teapot, cobalt, w/lid, large	**55.00**
Teapot, opaque cobalt, large	**10.00**
Teapot, opaque green, w/white lid	**11.00**
Teapot, opaque light blue, small	**4.75**
Teapot, opaque medium blue, w/lid, small	**9.00**
Cornucopia, pink 3¼″No 765	**5.50**
Flowerpot, marble blue, 2¼″	**5.00**
Flowerpot, marble green, 2½″	**4.50**
Flowerpot, marble white, 2¼″	**4.00**

Flowerpot, orange, 1¾″	3.00
Flowerpot, white, 1¾″	3.00

Interior Panel

Bowl, green, large	12.00
Bowl, marble green/wht, large	18.75
Bowl, marble red/wht, large	25.00
Bowl, opaque blue, large	22.50
Bowl, opaque green, large	12.00
Creamer, green, large	15.00
Creamer, opaque blue, large	25.00
Creamer, opaque pink, small	20.00
Creamer, topaz, large	18.00
Cup, green, large	6.00
Cup, opaque blue, large	27.50
Cup, opaque pumpkin, large	20.00
Cup, opaque pumpkin, small	18.00
Cup, opaque yellow, small	30.00
Cup & saucer, amber, large	14.75
Cup & saucer, marble blue/wht. small	35.00
Cup & saucer, marble green/wht, small	25.00
Cup & saucer, opaque green, large	14.75
Cup & saucer, opaque green, small	12.00
Cup & saucer, opaque pink, small	28.00
Cup & saucer, opaque yellow, large	40.00
Plate, amber, large	2.50
Plate, green, large	4.00
Plate, green, small	2.75
Plate, marble blue/wht, large	10.00
Plate, marble green/wht, large	7.00
Plate, marble green/wht, small	5.00
Plate, marble red/wht, large	8.00
Plate, opaque blue, large	6.50
Plate, opaque green, large	4.00
Plate, opaque green, small	2.75
Plate, opaque pink, small	4.00
Plate, opaque yellow, large	7.00
Plate, opaque yellow, small	4.00
Plate, topaz, large	6.00
Saucer, marble green/wht, large	3.75
Saucer, marble red/wht, large	6.00
Saucer, opaque blue	4.50
Saucer, opaque cream, large	4.75
Saucer, opaque green, large	2.75
Saucer, opaque green, small	2.00
Saucer, opaque yellow	5.00
Saucer, topaz, large	4.50
Service for 2, marble red, open teapot	100.00
Service for 4, amber, 17-pc, large	125.00
Sugar, marble blue/wht, small	32.50
Sugar, opaque blue, small	26.00
Sugar, opaque blue, w/cover, large	35.00
Sugar, opaque cobalt, small	25.00
Sugar, opaque green, w/cover, large	26.50
Sugar, opaque yellow, large	27.50
Sugar, opaque yellow, small	25.00
Teapot, amber, w/cover, small	12.00
Teapot, green, large	10.00
Teapot, green, w/cover, small	11.00
Teapot, marble blue/wht, w/cover, small	30.00
Teapot, opaque blue, w/cover, small	20.00
Teapot, opaque cobalt, w/cream lid, large	25.00
Teapot, opaque green, w/cover, large	55.00
Teapot, opaque pink, w/cover, small	15.00
Teapot, opaque yellow, large	12.00

Teapot, opaque yellow, w/cover, large	57.50
Teapot, opaque yellow, w/cover, small	35.00
Teapot, topaz, open, small	10.00
Tumbler, green	5.75
Lamp, ivory w/clear beaded wafers, floral, 10½″	35.00
Lamp, ivory, 6½″	30.00
Lamp, octagonal base, stacked, rust, gold, grey marble, 7″	32.00
Mexicali, cigarette jar w/hat ash tray lid, orange/wht	40.00
Miss America, cup, white	20.00
Mortar & pestle, jar & lid, lt blue, pink/wht floral enamel	12.00

Octagonal

Ashtray, oxblood, 2 rests	8.00
Bowl, white, large	6.00
Creamer, blue, OH, large	8.75
Creamer, oxblood & lemonade, large	55.00
Cup, blue, CH, large	9.75
Cup, green, CH, large	4.00
Cup, light green, CH, large	12.50
Cup, orange, OH, small	12.75
Cup, pumpkin, CH, small	24.50
Cup, yellow, OH, small	15.00
Cup & saucer, oxblood & lemonade, large	35.00
Plate, aqua, large	5.00
Plate, blue, large	3.50
Plate, blue, small	6.50
Plate, green, large	2.25
Plate, green, small	2.75
Plate, lime green, small	4.00
Plate, opaque blue, small	4.00
Plate, opaque green, 4¼″	2.00
Saucer, opaque white, 3½″	2.25
Saucer, white, large	3.50
Saucer, white, small	4.50
Saucer, yellow, large	3.50
Saucer, yellow, small	6.75
Service for 4, 21-pc, OH, large	135.00
Sugar, blue, w/wht cover, large	9.00
Sugar & creamer, yellow, CH, large	12.75
Teapot, blue, w/wht cover	12.00
Teapot, blue, w/wht cover, OH, small	12.75
Tumbler, green	9.00
Tumbler, light green, small	6.00
Tumbler, medium green, small	6.00
Tumbler, opaque cream	10.00
Tumbler, opaque white	8.00
Tumbler, white, small	4.00
Tumbler, yellow, OH, small	7.00
Water set, 7-pc	47.50

Optic

Cup & saucer, jade	2.50
Cup & saucer, topaz, small	6.50
Plate, jade	3.75
Plate, topaz, 3¼″	3.00
Teapot, jade, w/lid	10.00

Panelled Plain Jane

Cup & saucer, cobalt	8.00
Plate, cobalt	5.00

Plain Jane

Bowl, baked on red	6.50
Creamer, green	45.00
Creamer & sugar, baked on	18.50
Cup, baked on red	2.75
Plate, baked on green	2.50
Saucer, baked on yellow	2.75

Service for 6, baked on, w/open teapot **60.00**
Teapot, baked on blue **4.75**
Teapot, green **25.00**
Planter, green/wht, 6x3½" **8.00**
Powder jar & lid, black base w/opaque yellow lid **25.00**
Powder jar & lid, pink amber, ribbed **35.00**

Raised Daisy
Cup, green **19.50**
Saucer, blue **8.00**
Teapot, blue **27.75**
Tumbler, yellow **24.50**

Stacked Disc & Interior Panel
Cup & saucer, marble blue/wht **6.00**
Teapot, marble blue/wht, lid **16.00**

Stacked Disc & Panel
Bowl, cobalt, large **19.75**
Bowl, opaque green, large **18.00**
Creamer, opaque aqua, large **20.00**
Creamer, opaque aqua, small **15.00**
Creamer, opaque cobalt, large **15.00**
Creamer, opaque cobalt, small **24.00**
Creamer, opaque white **3.00**
Creamer, opaque yellow **10.00**
Creamer & sugar, green, small **44.50**
Cup, cobalt, small **18.00**
Cup, marble blue/wht, small **37.50**
Cup, opaque green, small **4.25**
Cup, opaque medium blue, small **5.00**
Cup, opaque orange, large **22.50**
Cup, opaque pumpkin, small **17.50**
Cup, pumpkin, large **15.00**
Cup & saucer, azure blue, small **24.00**
Pitcher, green, 2 bands **9.75**
Pitcher, opaque green, small **8.00**
Pitcher, opaque medium blue, small **9.75**
Pitcher, water, opaque blue, small **35.00**
Pitcher, green, small **12.00**
Plate, azure blue, small **12.00**
Plate, blue, large **10.00**
Plate, cobalt, small **8.50**
Plate, opaque light blue **4.00**
Plate, opaque yellow, large **4.50**
Plate, opaque yellow, small **9.00**
Saucer, cobalt, large **3.00**
Saucer, opaque green, large **9.50**
Saucer, opaque green, small **8.00**
Saucer, opaque white, large **2.50**
Service for 4, opaque 21-pc, large **250.00**
Sugar, opaque cobalt, w/cover, large **25.00**
Teapot, azure blue, w/cover, small **30.00**
Teapot, blue, w/wht cover **12.00**
Teapot, cobalt, large **20.00**
Teapot, cobalt, w/wht lid, small **22.00**
Teapot, green, w/lid, small **17.75**
Teapot, opaque cobalt/wht, w/lid, small **39.75**
Teapot, cobalt, small **7.00**
Tumbler, azure blue **12.00**
Tumbler, clambroth **3.00**
Tumbler, green, small **12.75**
Tumbler, green-2 bands **6.75**
Tumbler, opaque beige, small **3.50**
Tumbler, opaque medium blue, small **9.75**
Tumbler, opaque pink **5.00**
Tumbler, opaque white, small **3.00**

Water set, 7-pc **45.00**
Water set, opaque, 5-pc **36.00**

Stippled Disc
Creamer, opaque yellow **10.00**
Cup, opaque green, small **4.25**
Cup, opaque medium blue, small **5.00**
Pitcher, opaque green, small **8.00**
Pitcher, opaque medium blue, small **9.25**
Plate, opaque light blue **4.00**
Tumbler, clambroth **3.00**
Tumbler, opaque medium blue, small **9.75**
Tumbler, opaque pink **7.00**
Tumbler, opaque white, small **3.00**
Water set, 7 pc **45.00**
Water set, opaque, 5 pc **35.00**

Stippled Band
Cup & saucer, dark amber, small **6.75**
Cup & saucer, green, small **7.00**
Cup & saucer, light amber, small **8.75**
Plate, dark amber, small **2.25**
Plate, green, large **3.00**
Plate, green, small **2.00**
Plate, light amber, small **3.25**
Saucer, dark amber, small **1.75**
Saucer, green, large **2.00**
Saucer, green, small **1.50**
Saucer, light amber, small **2.00**
Service for 4, green, 21-pc, small **110.00**
Set, blue 17-pc, w/original box **250.00**
Sugar, green, w/lid, large **17.75**
Teapot, dark amber, w/lid, small **12.00**
Teapot, green, w/lid, small **9.75**
Teapot, light amber, w/lid, small **12.00**
Tumbler, dark amber, small **8.00**
Tumbler, light amber, small **6.50**
Water set, green, 5-pc, small **8.75**
Treasure Trunk, wht/rust **75.00**
Vase, orange/wht, 3 footed, acanthus **6.50**
Vase, orange/wht, oval, floral, 4¼" **8.00**
Vase, orange/wht, square feet, bead rim, 3¼" **6.00**

Alexandrite

Alexandrite is a type of art glass introduced around the turn of the century by Thomas Webb and Sons, of England. It is recognized by its characteristic shading--pale yellow to rose and blue. It was also produced by other companies.

Creamer, honeycomb, citron handle, unusual shape, 5x2¾". **1,200.00**
Finger bowl & underplate **1,200.00**
Rose bowl, honeycomb, 2½" **725.00**
Tazza, w/ped, fluted, honeycomb, blued edge, 2x5½" **850.00**
Vase, wide scalloped top, faceted honeycomb, Moser, 8" **250.00**

Almanacs

Before the days of weather forecasters and mass communication, farmers and home gardeners alike had no alternative but to rely on the predictions of the almanac. It suggested the proper phase of the moon for planting and harvesting, offered household hints and "receipts", and often supplied a little humor on the side.

Ayer Almanac, 1864 . . . . **4.00**
Ayer Almanac, 1880 . . . . **4.00**
Boston Almanac & Register, 1852, hard back, 200 pgs **14.00**

Boston Almanac & Register, Father Time, hour glass, 1841 .... **14.00**
Clark's ABC Almanac, 1877 .... **4.00**
Comic Almanac, Philadelphia, Pennsylvania, 1891 .... **12.00**
Dr. Jayne's Medical Almanac, 1884 .... **4.00**
Dr. Jayne's Medical Almanac, 1885 .... **4.00**
Dr. McLean's Almanac, 1879 .... **4.00**
Farmer's Almanac, 1882 .... **4.00**
Farmer's Almanac, 1910 .... **6.00**
Flying Horse Almanac, 1938 .... **10.00**
Franklin Almanac for the Year, 1883, Phila on cover **10.00**
Frear's Almanac, 1855, Troy, N.Y. **7.00**
Goodrich Almanac, 1939 .... **17.50**
Hostetter's Almanac, 1891 .... **4.00**
Kate Greenaway, 1884 .... **150.00**

Peoples, 1856, Louden & Co **7.00**
Poor Richard's Almanac, 1898 .... **6.00**
Poor Will's Almanac, 1835, by Wm Collum, Philadelphia **25.00**
Rawleigh's Almanac & Cookbook, 1922 .... **7.50**
Steele's Almanac, 1843, Albany, N.Y. **8.00**
Swamp Root Almanac, 1939 .... **7.00**
Uncle Sam's Almanac, 1890 .... **12.00**
Vermont Register & Farmer's Almanac, 1828 .... **20.00**
Webster's Almanac, 1837, Albany, N.Y. **8.00**
Webster's Almanac, 1853, Albany, N.Y. **7.00**

Almaric Walter

Almaric Walter was employed from 1904 through 1914, at Verreries Artistiques des Freres Daum in Nancy, France. After 1919, he opened his own business where he continued to make the same type of quality objects d'art in pate-de-verre glass as he had earlier. His pieces are signed A. Walter, Nancy H. Berge' Sc.

Ashtray, frog figure, green **850.00**
Bowl, pate-de-verre, berries & leafage, H Berge, 5¾" **550.00**
Paperweight, pate-de-verre crab figural, 1720, 2¾" **715.00**

Aluminum

Aluminum, though being the most abundant metal in the earth's crust, always occurs in combination with other elements. Before a practical method for its refinement was developed in the late 19th century, articles made of aluminum were very expensive. After the process for commercial smelting was perfected in 1916, it became profitable to adapt the ductile, non-

tarnishing material to many uses.

By the late 30s, novelties, trays, pitchers, and many other tableware items were being produced. They were often hand crafted with elaborate decoration. Russell Wright designed a line of lovely pieces, such as lamps, vases and desk accessories, that are becoming very collectible. Many that crafted the ware marked it with their company logo, and these signed pieces are attracting the most interest.

Ashtray, autumn bouquet, Canterbury Arts, 5" dia............ **3.50**
Bowl, bouquet w/bow, 13½" **9.00**
Bowl, grapes in relief, Hammerkraft, 11½" **7.00**
Bowl, leaf scroll, ruffled, Admiration, 14" **7.00**
Bread tray, roses in relief, Barber Shlevin, 12" **8.00**
Candy dish w/cover, 3 part, Rodney Kent, No 457, 6" dia **6.00**
Candy dish w/cover, footed, blossom w/bow, Rodney Kent **8.00**
Coasters, ducks in relief, set of 12 .... **12.00**
Cocktail shaker, chrysanthemum design, No 530, Continental **7.00**

Eyeglass case, pat Feb 9/09 .... **12.00**
Ice bucket w/lid, handles, roses in relief, Everlast **12.00**
Lazy Susan, 8 petal flower, Buenilum, 17½" **12.00**
Leaf dish, Buenilum, 11" **7.00**
Plate, iris design, Chadwell, 13½" **8.00**
Plate, raspberry design, Farberware, 14" **9.00**
Samovar w/lucite handle, chrysanthemum, Continental **30.00**
Server, 2 tier, acorn design, No 525, Continental, 17½" **18.00**
Silent butler, pine cone & needles, Everlast **8.00**
Tea pot, coronation of Elizabeth, 1953 .... **9.00**
Tray, flying ducks, Designed Aluminum, 13½x9" **8.00**
Tray, handles, chrysanthemum design, Continental, 16x20" **12.00**
Tray, handles, crimped rim, Cromwell, 10x12" **9.00**
Tray, handles, hammered w/tulip design, Rodney Kent, 14" **27.50**
Tray, handles, pine trees, mountains, Arthur Amor, 11½x9" ... **10.00**

Amberina

Amberina glass was developed in 1883 by the New Enland Glass Co. Its characteristic amber to red or fuschia shading was due to a chemical reaction on the trace of gold in the formula during a reheating process. The same type of glass ware, called Rose Amber, was made by Mt. Washington. Today, both are refered to as Amberina. Pressed glassware was made in West Va., and later in Europe; the most rare type is plated Amberina, made briefly by New England.

Bowl, 3 ftd, signed Libbey **500.00**
Bowl, 6" dia **130.00**
Bowl, Diamond Optic, 4" **50.00**
Bowl, Hobnail, 5" **245.00**
Bowl, Honeycomb, 10" **100.00**
Bowl, oval, ruffled, birds & florals in gold, ftd 6½x8" **325.00**
Bud vase, 5" **100.00**
Bulb vase, Swirl, 8" **200.00**
Candy dish, signed Libbey, 7" **335.00**
Celery, 7" **235.00**
Celery, plated **2,250.00**

Champagne glass, hollow stem, red bowl **275.00**
Fingerbowl, New England, 2½x5" **185.00**
Goblet, 4½" **300.00**
Hanging lamp, plated, swirled, shade 14" **4,750.00**
Lemonade glass, swirled **185.00**
Lemonade, plated **2,500.00**

Mug, floral enameling, 3½" **150.00**
Pitcher, blown w/applied handle & spout, rough pontil, 8" **185.00**
   Cased, clear w/wht loops, clear handle, pontil **200.00**
   Clear twist handle, small **105.00**
   Gold & pink floral decor, 11½" **275.00**
   Herringbone, 8" **340.00**
   Honeycomb, good color, old **260.00**
   Inverted Diamond Thumbprint, reversed, 5" **365.00**
   Inverted Thumbprint, 3 corner top **300.00**
   Melon ribbed, applied handle, New England **150.00**
   Plated, bulbous, 7½" **3,750.00**
   Plated, 9" **6,000.00**
Plate, 7" **140.00**
Rose bowl, quilted, satin, large **285.00**
Sauce dish, Daisy & Button, square, Wheeling **145.00**
Shakers, Baby Thumbprint, decorated, orig tops, pr **180.00**
Spittoon, Swirl, gold ruffled top, hourglass shape, 9x5" **435.00**
Spoon holder, square top, much red, New England **200.00**
Toothpick, Diamond Quilted, 2 blown out bands, Sandwich . . . **135.00**
   Frosted, ribbed & fluted, blown **50.00**
   Ribbed, plated, kiln crack **2,200**
Tumbler, Diamond Optic, New England, deep color **120.00**
Tumbler, Inverted Baby Thumbprint, 4" **60.00**
Tumbler, Inverted Diamond Thumbprint, ground pontil **150.00**
Tumbler, Inverted Thumbprint **65.00**
Tumbler, plated **2,100.00**
Tumbler, ribbed **75.00**
Tumbler, Swirl, 4" **60.00**
Vase, Diamond Quilt Reverse, 8" **300.00**
Vase, Drape Pattern, baluster shape, 1800s, 9½" **235.00**
Vase, Expanded Diamond, square scallop rim, 7" **235.00**
Vase, floral enameling, 8" **350.00**
Vase, fluted, blue, white, pink flowers, 9½x4" **165.00**
Vase, gourd top, ornate handles, gold decor, beading 11" **285.00**
Vase, Inverted Thumbprint, ruffled, ftd, 6x6½" **250.00**
Vase, lily, New England Glass Co **210.00**
Vase, lovebirds, panel w/butterfly, florals, ruffled, 8" **300.00**
Vase, serpentine applied trim, large daisy, footed, 12" **225.00**
Vase, slightly concave sides, 6½x3½" **90.00**

Vase, Swirl, ftd, ruffled, gold floral decor, 11x5" **240.00**
Vase, wishbone ft, pointed top, rigaree, gold decor, 7½" **200.00**
Water pitcher, plated, 8¾" **5,750.00**
Wine glass, ftd, amber stem, 4½" **150.00**

American Encaustic Tiling Co

   AE Tile was organized in 1879 in Zanesville, Ohio. Until its closing in 1935, they produced beautiful ornamental and architectural tile equal to the best European imports. They also made vases, figurines and novelty items with exceptionally fine modeling and glazes.

Ashtray, brown glaze, 5x5" **10.00**
Ashtray, rectangular, light blue **12.00**
Box, w/cover, doghouse, ivory w/brown dog on roof **90.00**
Cuspidor, Art Nouveau female, gold **175.00**
Incense burner, Buddha, white glaze, 8½" **45.00**
Paperweight, figural scarab, blue-green mottled glaze **20.00**
Paperweight, ram, 3¾x5½" **45.00**
Plaque, ivory w/2 hunting dogs, 7" **50.00**
Plaque, lady's head, figural, brown, 6" **45.00**
Tile, floor, geometric multicolor, 3-layer encaustic, 6" **30.00**
Tile, floral, 6x6" **40.00**

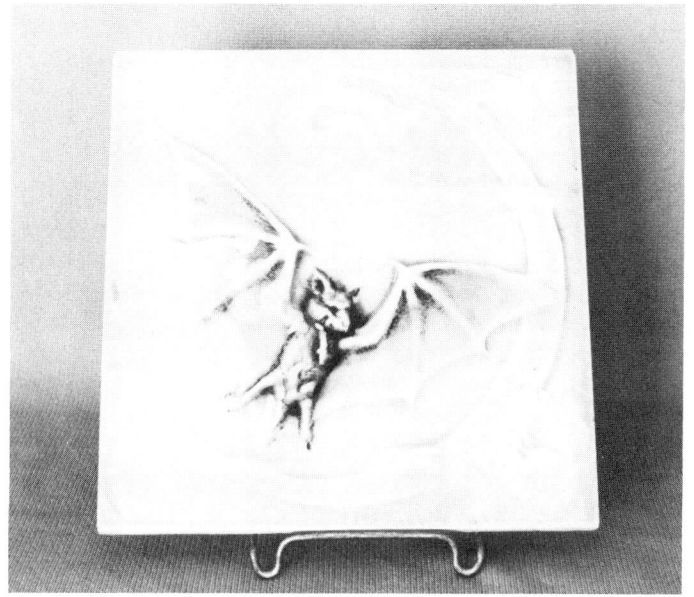

Tile, flying bat, moon, rare **135.00**
Tile, German girl w/stein, Mueller, panel w/four 6" tile **250.00**
Tile, hp ship, set of three, 4x4" **175.00**
Tile, hunting dog, Mueller design, brown, 1890, 6x18" **200.00**
Tile, maid & suitor, plum glaze, 1890, 6x18", pair **500.00**
Tile, male/female, 2 panels of 4 tiles, 1890, each 6x6" **600.00**
Tile, man w/tam, woman w/bonnet, brown, 1890, 6x6", pair . . **200.00**
Tile, owl & crescent moon, light green, 1890, 6x6" **75.00**
Tile, owl head w/winking eye, blue, 1890, 6x6" **85.00**
Tile, pot w/flowers, blue, 1890, panel of 6, 6" tile **300.00**
Tile, pseudo-renaissance male/female, 1890, 6x18", pair **400.00**
Tile, raised flowers **25.00**
Tile, reclining youth drinking wine, brown, 1890, 6x18" **200.00**
Tile, river mill scene by Frenzel, intaglio, 1890, 6x6" **100.00**
Tile, Roman soldier/Roman lady, rose colored, 6x6", pair **175.00**
Tile, squeeze bag peacock, Bergman, unmarked, 8x8" **150.00**
Tile, Victorian male/female, high relief, 8x8", pair **400.00**
Tile, women with flute & cymbals, 1890, 6x18", pair **400.00**
Tray, monks in relief, blue/white, 6½x5" **65.00**

Vase, bulbous, tubular neck, rose glaze, w/base, 11" **35.00**
Vase, rose in relief, brown, 6" **30.00**

American Indian Art

That time when the American Indian was free to practice the crafts and culture that was his heritage has always held a fascination for many. They were a people that appreciated beautiful and colorful decoration in their furnishings and clothing; and because instruction in these arts was a routine part of their rearing, they were well accomplished. Several tribes developed areas in which they excelled--the Navajo were weavers and silversmiths, the Zuni lapidaries. Examples of their craftsmanship are very valuable. Today, even the work of contemporary Indian artists--weavers, silversmiths, carvers and others--is highly collectible.

Arrowheads, Points and Chipped Blades

Arrow point, deer antler, 2" **4.00**
Arrow, Hupa, pre 1900 .... **45.00**
Arrow, Navajo w/metal point **45.00**
Arrow, Woodland, pre 1900, pair **100.00**
Arrowhead, Oregon, petrified wood, 1" **12.00**
Blade, Tn., beveled, 6½x2½" **120.00**
Blade, round base, 5" **25.00**
Cache blade, Hopewell, rounded base, 3¾" **20.00**
Point, Clovis type, 3" **35.00**
Point, Hohokam, deep serration, 1½" **35.00**
Point, Hopewellian, fine notched **12.00**
Point, Wash., translucent red/orange, 1" **15.00**
Point, corner notch, barbed, 3¾" **15.00**
Point, obsidian, 2¾" **30.00**
Skinning blade, Tenn., 5" **25.00**
Skinning celt, Mo., 7" **60.00**
Spear, Ill., large side notches, eared, 6" **150.00**
Spear, Ohio E-notch, 2¾" **35.00**
Spear, dark grey flint, ceremonial, 9x1¾" **30.00**
Tomahawk, flint **20.00**
Tomahawk, gray granite **22.00**

Apparel

Belt, Sioux, beaded hide, geometrics, ties, 2x28" **35.00**
Bodice, satin lined, fully beaded **45.00**
Boy's vest, stylized beading **450.00**
Breastplate, Plains, 100-5"pipes **1,250.00**
Bride dress, Sioux, fringed, beaded, 48" **375.00**
Child's vest, Sioux, pull over, velvet w/beads & elk teeth **150.00**
Gauntlets, Northern Plains, beaded leather **200.00**
Hat, Mic-Mac, geometric beadwork, pre 1870 .... **85.00**
Jacket, Woodlands, leather w/beaded cuffs, designs, fringed ... **200.00**
Leggings, Plains, buckskin fringe, beadwork **650.00**
Leggings, Northern Plains, wool w/beading, fur tassles **300.00**
Man's hat, Iroquoise, full beaded, feather and floral **185.00**
Mocassins, Arrapho, fully beaded, 1880, 10½" **200.00**
Mocassins, Cheyenne, near full bead, 1890 .... **60.00**
Mocassins, Cree, faceted metallic beads, florals, 10" .. **65.00**
Moccasins, Shoshone, beaded over top, toe & side strips, 9" ... **35.00**
Moccasins, Sioux, bands of beads, top, toes & sides, 8" **45.00**
Moccasins, Sioux, miniature, beaded w/cross, bands, 3½" **55.00**
Purse, Ojibwa, beadwork, butterfly design, 1915, 9x6" **95.00**
Vest, hide w/hp portrait on back, cloth leg pcs **225.00**
Awl case, Cheyenne, fully beaded, horsehair dangles, 8" **135.00**
Awl, bone, 5" **24.00**
Awl, copper, sharp both ends, 8" **50.00**
Bag, Apache, buckskin w/beaded fringe, geometric decor **85.00**
Bag, Iroquoise, velvet w/cloth binding, beaded both sides **100.00**
Bag, Yakima, trade cloth, beaded, elk, floral design, 1900 .... **175.00**

Baskets

Apache, burden w/buckskin & tin cone decor, 11x18" **300.00**
Apache, polychrome, terraced diamond & star, 3x12" **250.00**
Apache, terraced/arrowhead design, 1900, 3x11" **400.00**
Arrapaho Shoshoni, berry, pre 1900 .... **45.00**
Chippewa, birchbark, applique leaf decor, 10x12" **40.00**
Hopi, coiled polychrome, dog design, 6x9" **300.00**
Hopi, coiled polychrome, kachina mask design, 5x8" **175.00**
Hopi, plaque, coiled polychrome w/wedding design, 10" **95.00**
Hopi, plaque, coiled polychrome, eagle, 8" dia **75.00**
Hopi, plaque, polychrome, eagle design, 13½" **150.00**
Klamath, twined polychrome, butterfly & star, 6x10" **450.00**
Macah, lidded oval, 1895 .... **120.00**
Mach, oval, 1893 .... **110.00**
Makah, cedar checker base, striped, 2x4" **28.00**
Navajo, polychrome wedding design, 13" dia **60.00**
Ottawa, lidded, handle, grass, 12x4x3" **40.00**
Paiute, lidded, full decorated w/beads, 4x4" **205.00**
Paiute, water jug, one handle, 1900, 8x8" **200.00**
Papago, basket bowl, four lizard decor, 20" **200.00**
Papago, black 5 petal squash blossom, 4x17" **250.00**
Papago, fineweave, lizards, 4½" dia **35.00**
Papago, handles, fret design, 3½x7½" **55.00**
Papago, large fret design, 4x12" **225.00**
Papago, Man in the Maze, yellow & natural, 3x13" **75.00**
Papago, negative 5 part star/flower, 9½" dia **175.00**
Papago, plaque, Man in the Maze, 10½" **55.00**
Papago, plychrome star design, 4x17" **180.00**
Papago, stairstep design, 9x4" **235.00**
Papago, tray good decor, 12" **35.00**
Piaiute, oval single rod split stitch, 1900, 3x8" **85.00**
Pima, fancy designs, 5x13" **300.00**
Pima, grain basket, 11" **125.00**
Pima, multiple terrace design, 2x3" **80.00**

Pima/Papago, plaque, modified squash blossom, 12" **200.00**
Pima, plaque, squash blossom decor, 12" **200.00**
Pima, squash blossom decor in black, 1900, 4x14" **200.00**
Pomo, coiled, feathered **1,400.00**
Pomo, miniature, feathers on bottom & rim, 2½" dia **200.00**
Southwest, straight sides, brown geometric, 5x8" **85.00**
Tsimshian, lid, twined in Greek Key Hook, 1900, 4x7" **275.00**
Wahso, lidded, single rod split stitch, 1900, 2x3" **35.00**
Wahso, black geometric design, 1900, 3x5" **225.00**
Wahso, miniature, single rod, split stitch, 1900, 1¼x5" **18.00**
Washo, single rod split stitch, pedestal, 5x6" **115.00**
Water bottle, sealed w/pitch, 8½" **165.00**
Yokut, lidded, geometric, 1900, 4½x4½" **90.00**
Book, Scriptures for Indians, 1747 .... **200.00**
Bowl, wood, for food, frog design w/shell inlay, 4x11" **65.00**
Box, beadwork w/ribbons for hanging, dated, 1910 .... **50.00**

Cougar skin rug w/head 600.00
Cradle cover, leather, heavy beadwork 1,500.00
Deer skin rug, white tail 135.00
Dipper, gourd, Anasazi 25.00

Dolls

Composition face, wooden legs, has hair, 1920, 7″ 25.00
Hopi, kachina, Mudhead w/drum, 14½″ 205.00
Indian male, 1910, 16″ 50.00
Kachina, Hopi, Eagle Dancer, Lucas, 14½″ 675.00
Kachina, Hopi, Hemis Maiden, Tsosie, 15½″ 175.00
Kachina, Hopi, Wuyak-Kuita, Lucas, 20″ 275.00
Kachina, Tewa Clown, sitting, eating watermelon, Silas 145.00
Leather, cloth face & arms, bead trim, Sioux, 9½″ 120.00
Male w/human hair, beaded, 1900, 9″ 190.00
Pottery w/horsehair, bead necklace, cloth skirt 950.00
Squaw w/cloth body, 1920, Navajo, 12″ 140.00
Squaw in Indian dress, colorful beads, Plains, 9½″ 110.00
Eye glass case, Mohawk, floral beadwork, 1900 . . . . 300.00
Fish hook, copper, 1¼″ 10.00
Hot stone holder, bent wood, pre 1900 . . . . 30.00

Jewelry

Beads, Chevrons, 20″ 40.00
Bracelet, 10 large turq cluster, large center cab 350.00
Hairpin, bone, Ky., etched, 6″ 85.00
Mississippi, burial necklace, framed shell, barrel beads 60.00
Navajo, bracelet, 3 turq cabs w/bead & wire decor, 1940 . . . . . 95.00
Navajo, bracelet, silver w/5 large turq cabs 125.00
Navajo, buckle, free form chip inlay, sterling, old 200.00
Navajo, concho belt, 14 & buckle, pawn tag 400.00
Navajo, hat band, concho style, hand stamped w/one cab 115.00
Navajo, man's ring, stamped w/large turq cab, pawn 75.00
Navajo, necklace, one strand red clay beads, polished 35.00
Navajo, pin, stamped silver owl w/turq cab eyes, 1930 . . . . . . 30.00
Navajo, ring, sterling w/1x1½″ turq cab, 1930s 30.00
Navajo, shell w/coral inlay, turtle design, 2x3″ 25.00
Navajo, squash blossom, 10 w/large cab, sand cast Naja 275.00
Plains, quilled watch bracelet, beaded edges, hide, ¾″ 35.00
Pueblo, necklace w/jacklas, 3 strand, nuggets & heshe 350.00
Peblo, nuggets w/shell heshe, 2 strands, pr jacklas 250.00
Sioux, hair ties, spoke wheel quilling w/feathers, pr 25.00
Supai, collar, beaded by Keith Mahone, openwork, large 65.00
Trade beads, 5 elk teeth, 26″ 18.00
Trade beads, 1 strand, Hubbell glass 200.00
Ute, child's necklace, beadwork, wood & glass thunderbird 25.00
Yalalac, trade beads w/silver coins, old 300.00
Zuni, bracelet, 2 rows of tiny turq on stamped silver 80.00
Zuni, bracelet, large cluster, silver, turq, 1940 . . . . 110.00
Zuni, earrings, sterling horseshoe w/turq cluster 35.00
Zuni, pin, petit point, signed, 2¾x3″ 150.00

Knives

Blade, Tn., beveled, 6½x2½″ 120.00
Blade, round base, 5″ 25.00
Buffalo skinning knife, forged iron, 1700s 75.00
Cache blade, Hopewell, rounded base, 3¾″ 20.00
Celt, copper, flared, 4x3″ 50.00
Knife w/antler handle, Navajo 15.00
Knife w/beaded sheath, American flag, florals 175.00
Knife, Plains, for trade, pre 1900s 25.00
Knife, Bowie w/carved ebony/wood handle, leather sheath 60.00
Skinning blade, Tenn., 5″ 25.00
Skinning celt, Mo., 7″ 60.00
Trade knife, Sioux, pre 1900 . . . . 25.00
Trade knife, heavy copper, 1700s 250.00

Lariat, rolled rawhide, old 50.00
Medicine pouch, Plateau, beaded target design 30.00
Medicine pouch, Navajo, beadwork, linework, fringed 50.00
Medicine pouch, Navajo, beadwork 16.00
Medicine pouch, Sioux, calf shape w/cloth & glass features 65.00
Mortar & Pestle, lava stone 10.00
Needle case, Iroquoise, fully beaded, florals, 1890 . . . . 45.00
Needle, bone, 4″ 60.00
Needle, bone, 5″ 75.00
Needle, copper, 5″ 60.00
Needlecase, Mic-Mac, full beaded, 1875, 4½x3″ 60.00
Paint pallet, wood, 1880s, 6″ 50.00
Pestle, stone 18.00
Picture, Chipewa, birch bark w/buffalo, pre 1900 . . . . 15.00
Pincushion, 5 point star shape, beaded velvet, 1880, 7″ 70.00

Pipes and Ceremonial Items

Anasazi, pipe, pottery, T shape, slanted bowl 85.00
Anasazi, pipe, stone tube 85.00
Arapahoe, catlinite/pipestone, banded & cross decor, 1869 . . . . 375.00
Cheyene, pipe bag, beadwork w/fringe, 20x8″ 450.00
Chippewa, black stone w/inlay, 28″ puzzle stem, 1900 . . . . . . 425.00
Drum, hollow log w/rawhide, painted designs, 12x10″ 85.00

Fetish, Crow, umbilical form, beaded, 1800s, 6″ 190.00
Fetish, Sioux, turtle, beaded, 7″ 275.00
Hopewellian, pipe, bird figural w/prey in beak 325.00
Hopewellian, pipe, frog figural 275.00
Hopi, rattle, lizard, tadpole & ceremonial designs, 6″ 45.00
Hopi, rattle, painted gourd, swastica 35.00
Hopi, rattle, painted gourd, w/cross 25.00
Hopi, sash, fringed, embroidered woven yarn, fancy, 45″ 225.00
Kiowa, drum, both sides bird & geometric design, 12″ dia 75.00
Kiowa, fan, feathers, hide trim, trade beads, 16″ 200.00
Midwest, pipe, sandstone, barrel type, 2″ 35.00
Northwest coast, guessing rods, wood in leather pouch 700.00
Pipe bag, beadwork, fringe/brass thimble 1,200.00
Pipe, diegueno, soapstone tube, drilled, 5″ 200.00
Pipe, effigy, granite, bird figure, 3½″ 185.00
Pipe, steatite, elbow type, 2½x1½″ 100.00
Pipe-tomahawk, beaded shaft, horse tail decor, forged 600.00
Plains, pipe, bone cloud blower, many etched designs, 9″ 25.00
Rattle, wood handle, gut wrapped, contains beads 80.00
Sioux, pipe, catlinite, corkscrew stem, snake design 250.00
Sioux, pipe, effigy, lead & catlinite inlay 300.00
Winnebago, dance apron, beadwork, trade cloth, 1890 . . . . . . 90.00
Woodland, drum beater, pre 1900, fancy 25.00
Porcupine quill box, birch bark, rabbit on lid, 4½″ 55.00

Pottery

Acoma, bowl D Lewis, blk on wht, turkey design, 2x2¾″ 30.00
Acoma, bowl, Lucy Lewis, birds, flowers, 5″ 125.00
Acoma, bowl, Victorino, blk on wht w/orange, incised, 5x9″ . . 250.00

Acoma, canteen, polychrome, 1920, 4½x4″ **40.00**
Acoma, canteen, w/parrot, much detail **75.00**
Acoma, cooking pot, decorated rim, 1900, 7x8″ **35.00**
Acoma, effigy **10.00**
Acoma, jar, polychrome geometric, floral, 1930, 8x8½″ **215.00**
Acoma, jar, polychrome, 8x9″ **90.00**
Acoma, jar, polychrome, 9½x8½″ **130.00**
Acoma, jar, red ware, 7½″ **40.00**
Acoma, pot, Pena, blk on blk, relief sea serpent, old **150.00**
Acoma, pot, polychrome w/geometrics, 5x9″ **55.00**
Acoma, storage pot, red painted, rim decoration, 7x8″ **35.00**
Acoma, wedding vase, blk on wht, 8x6″ **55.00**
Avanyu, pot, Madeline, black, carved, 5x6″ **325.00**
Avanyu, vase, Rose, red, carved, 4½x6″ **275.00**
Casas Grande, jar, T Ortiz, polychrome checkerboard, 1¼x1¾″ **45.00**
Chaco, pitcher, blk on wht, lines, 1100 A D, sm repair, 8″ . . . **200.00**
Cherokee, bowl, Amanda Swimmer, 2 owls, 7″ **35.00**
Cherokee, bowl, Indian Chief head on either side, 4″ **32.00**
Cherokee, wedding jar, Louise Bigmeat Maney, blk, 7″ **35.00**
Cibecue, bowl, corrugated polychrome, 1200 A D, restored . **65.00**
Effigy, eagle, large, well made **30.00**
Gila, bowl, polychrome, geometric, 1300 A D, repair, 4x9″ . . **135.00**
Gila, bowl, polychrome, geometric, 1300 A D, 5x10″ **200.00**
Gila, bowl, polychrome, lines, circles, 1300 A D, 3½x7″ **95.00**
Gila, jar, 1300 AD, 5½x5″ **310.00**
Gila, jar, polychrome, lines, 1300 A D, mint, 5½x5″ **310.00**
Hohocom, bowl, bird effigy **85.00**
Hohokam, vessel, saguaro shoe, 1000 A D, sm repair, 7x9x7″. **150.00**
Hopi, bowl, R Silas, polychrome geometric, 2¾x4″ **55.00**
Hopi, bowl, geometrics inside, 1920s, 2½x9″ **100.00**
Hopi, bowl, orange, polychrome, 1900, 3x4½″ **30.00**
Hopi, jar, Joy Navasie, polychrome, geometric, 5½x7½″ **350.00**
Hopi, jar, R Silas, polychrome, geometrics, 4½x6″ **125.00**
Hopi, jar, orange w/blk, red, geometric, 1930, 3½x5″ **80.00**
Hopi, plate, Marcia Rickey, polychrome, geometrics, 5″ **45.00**
Hopi, tile, polychrome, geometric, 5½x8″ **20.00**
Hopi, wall plaque, R C Talashie, line, swirls, 6x4″ **20.00**
Isleta, plate, brown & red on wht, florals, 1930, 5½″ **18.00**
Jeddito, bowl, blk on orange, 1200 A D, 3½x9″ **150.00**
Maricopa, bowl, blk on red **35.00**
Mogollon, bowl, corrugated, 1000 A D, 1 repair, 3x6½″ **60.00**
Mogollon, jar, corrugated, 1000 A D, 3x4″ **40.00**
Mogollon, jar, corrugated, 1000 A D, repaired 4½x5″ **30.00**
Mogollon, olla, corrugated, lava flow, 900 A D, repair **75.00**
Navajo, bowl, pitch covered **28.00**
Navajo, water jar, pitch covered, pre 1900, 9x6½″ **55.00**
Pureco, bowl, blk on red, geometrics, 950-1150, 4x9″ **100.00**
Roosevelt, jar, 1200 AD, 5x5″ *illus* **300.00**
Roosevelt, jar, blk on wht, 1200 A D, 5x5″ **300.00**
Santa Clara, jar, red ware **25.00**
Santa Clara, pitcher, black, miniature **15.00**
Santa Clara, water bottle, red, polished **25.00**
Santa Clara, wedding vase, blackware, 1920s, 8x6″ **65.00**
Santa Domingo, jar, blk w/brown & wht decor, 6½x11″ **305.00**
Santa Domingo, jar, w/large flowers, 5″ **95.00**
Santa Dimingo, marriage pitcher, 8″ **125.00**
Santa Dimingo, pot, sienna/black w/floral, 1900, 6½x5″ **145.00**
Snowflake, bowl, blk on wht, ca 975-1200, swirls, 4x7″ **115.00**
Southwestern, jar, red w/blk & white decor, very large **3,200.00**
Tonto, jar, 1400AD, 6″ *illus* **250.00**
Tusayan, bowl, blk on wht, lines, 1200 A D, 3 repairs, 4x7″ . . **95.00**
Zia, canteen, Seferina Bell, large detailed bird **125.00**
Zia, jar, J Medina, polychrome, Indian figures, 12x10″ **275.00**
Zia, tile, wht w/brown, tan, rust, geometric, 4½″ sq **20.00**

Zuni, jar, J Laate, polychrome, lines, florals, 6x6″ **80.00**
Zuni, jar, Myraeriacho, polychrome, deer, floral, bird, 8x10″ . . **375.00**

Pouch, Iroquoise, full floral beaded design, 1890 . . . . **95.00**
Pouch, Mohawk, fine floral beadwork, allover design, cloth . . . **40.00**
Pouch, Ojibwa, both sides full beaded, 1915, 8x7″ **35.00**
Pouch, Ojibwa, full bead swastika w/cross, 10x4″ **75.00**
Pouch, Woodlands, multicolor beads, floral design, 2¾x3″ **65.00**
Powder horn, Plains, decorated w/tacks, dated 1889, 12″ **85.00**
Quirt, Hogan, pre 1900 . . . . **25.00**
Quiver, Hopi, w/5 arrows, pre 1900 . . . . **80.00**
Riding crop, Sioux, decorated end tab, braided hide strap **65.00**
Saddle, Crow, rawhide, 1890, 16x12″ **750.00**
Saddle, Navajo, rawhide, pre 1900 . . . . **125.00**
Sheath, hide w/beaded decor, hide handle knife **200.00**
Shield, Cheyenne, hide over metal w/bird decor, bone handle . **375.00**
Spoon, Navajo, made of horn, 7½″ **20.00**
Spoon, horn, quill work handle, 11″ **40.00**
Spoon, wood, 1850 . . . . **28.00**

Tools

Ax head, prehistoric, double groved & shaped, 2¾x3½″ **45.00**
Axe, Tenn., notched, 9″ **35.00**
Axe, child's 2x1¾″ **35.00**
Axe, stone, full grooved **30.00**
Fleshing tool, Hogan, wood & metal **26.00**
Pick, stone 14½″ **180.00**
Trade Ax, metal, 1700, 8x3½″ **80.00**

Wool comb, Navajo, rug tool **15.00**
Treaty Map, 1842 . . . . **85.00**
Wallet, Flathead, full bead, 1920 . . . . **25.00**
Washo, blk geometric design, 1900, 3x6″ **225.00**
Water container, hide, cloth handle, 1890, 8x5½″ **70.00**

Weapons

Arapaho, war ax, hide wrap, beading, 1860, 24″ **400.00**
Bow, Northwest coast, orig string, paint traces, 46″ **75.00**
Club, Sioux, 5½″ hide covered stone, 21″ handle, fringe **200.00**
Club, Sioux, hide covered rock, painted, horsehair tail **90.00**
Lance head, forged iron, pre 1870, 12″ **140.00**
Rabbit club, Pueblo, wood, carved and painted **18.00**
War ax, Arapaho, 24″ hide wrap handle, beaded, 7″ wedge . . **400.00**

War club, 6″ stone, beaded gut wrapped 30″ handle **250.00**
War club, 8″ stone, gut wrapped 24″ handle **250.00**
War club, hide wrapped grey quartz head, 36″ **250.00**
War club, Plains, shaft w/beads, fringe, buffalo tail **200.00**
War club, stone head, 9″ beaded handle w/red fluff **100.00**
War club, Tenn., both ends pointed, full groovrd **45.00**

Weaving

Navajo, red, grn, blk, tan, wht, Lena Toledo, 26x50″ **70.00**
Rug, by J B Moore, 1910, 7x4′ **1,500.00**
Rug, Grenada Red Arrows, 1910, 6x4′ **600.00**

Rug, Navajo, 1 winged Yei, 6 colors, 19x22" **90.00**
Rug, Navajo, 2 grey hills, traditional, 38x66" **900.00**

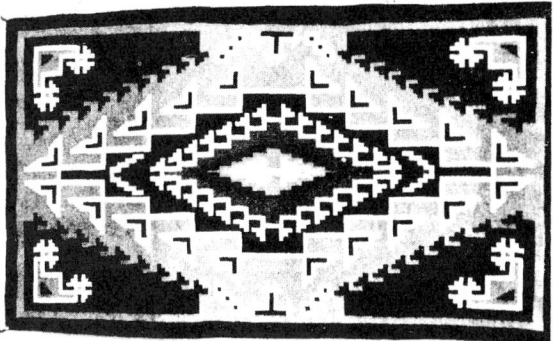

Rug, Navajo, 7 colors, vegetal dye, yei, F Tom, 24x32" **90.00**
Rug, Navajo, bands of diamonds, F Jones, 29x40" **250.00**
Rug, Navajo, brown, ivory, Greek key type design, 25x32" **70.00**
Rug, Navajo, Chief's, 52x57" **1,100.00**
Rug, Navajo, coal mine mesa/raised outline, 37x56" **375.00**
Rug, Navajo, diamond & sawtooth border, 14x22" **45.00**
Rug, Navajo, five color traditional, 32x50" **400.00**
Rug, Navajo, four in one, 1900, 5x6' **2,000.00**
Rug, Navajo, Ganado w/red, blk, wht, grey, Begay, 31x34" . . . **105.00**
Rug, Navajo, Greek key hook, T design, 1915, 40x70" **545.00**
Rug, Navajo, kachina figures, 17x21" **75.00**
Rug, Navajo, red, blk, grn, tan, wht, L Toledo, 26x50" **70.00**
Rug, Navajo, serrated & reg diamonds, cross, 44x60" **450.00**
Rug, Navajo, three colors, diamonds, crosses, 44x65" **375.00**
Rug, Navajo, transitional, 1890, 5x5' **1,900.00**
Rug, Navajo, Two Gray Hills, by Gladys Warren, 38x36" **900.00**
Rug, Navajo, vegetal, 5 colors, band & diamond, 31x42" **525.00**
Rug, Navajo, vegetal dye, wool, Storm design, 32x48" **375.00**
Rug, Navajo, water bug, Greek key, T decor, 44x84" **550.00**
Rug, Navajo, wide ruins, Habahie, vegetal, 23x37" **175.00**
Rug, by J B Moore, 1910, 7x4' **1,500.00**
Tapestry, Navajo, 2 grey hills traditional, Yazzie, 22x30" **650.00**
Teepee mat, Chehallis, pre 1900 . . . . **40.00**
Whistle, bone, from Tenn., incised design, 3" **35.00**

Amethyst Glass

Amethyst simply describes the rich purple color of this glassware, made by many companies both here and abroad since the 19th century.

Bud vase, enameled flowers on base & shoulder, 10" **95.00**
Cookie jar, floral w/gold decor, metal top & handle, 8½" **240.00**
Cracker jar, silver top & handle **70.00**
Creamer, wooden pail styling **135.00**
Pitcher, blown, fluted top, enamel flowers **235.00**
    Old South Jersey, Clevenger, 6" **38.00**
Rosebowl, enameled man drinking, gold house & scene, 4x4½" **110.00**
Tumbler, Sandwich Flute, flint **135.00**
Vase, Chicago Fair, 1933 . . . . **50.00**
    Ruffled top, gold flowers & leaves **90.00**
    With vaseline handles, applied opal flower, 14½" **300.00**
Vases, ground pontil, heavy, 12", pr **120.00**
    Ground pontil, vertical optic rib, 12", pr **125.00**
Water set, crimp top pitcher, gold, Lily of the Valley, 9½" . . . **335.00**

Amphora

The Amphora Porcelain Works of Teplitz, Austria, produced Art

Nouveau styled vases and figurines during the latter part of the 19th century. They marked their wares with various stamps, some incorporating the name and location of the pottery with a crown or a shield.

Basket, fully formed flowers & vines, 2-handled, 5x11" **210.00**
Basket, porcelain w/woven effect, angels/rosettes, 11x15" **595.00**
Bowl, applied duck on top **98.00**
Bowl, applied tropical birds **125.00**
Bowl, top w/raised apples & vines, footed, beige, 8" dia **150.00**
Bowl, w/lady figural at side, 12" dia **325.00**
Castle Tower, w/Arthur, Guinevere, Lancelot, turret top **125.00**
Compote, flaring base, Deco leaves, orig label, 7x10" **155.00**
Compote, floral, 4 vertical base-to-bowl handles, 9x9" **180.00**
Dish, covered, Nautilus-shaped, Czech, 5x5x8" **95.00**
Dish, square, w/Kate Greenaway figural child, pastel **165.00**
Figurine, Arab leading camel to water, 18x18" **975.00**
Figurine, Arab w/lyre sitting on camel, 9x12" **675.00**
Figurine, bird **225.00**
Pitcher, comical cat, 10½x4¾" **145.00**
Vase, 2 figural children playing in front, 13" **375.00**
Vase, allover silver, baluster, molded lobster, 14½" **745.00**
Vase, Art Nouveau, flowers & bird, 4 handles, 11" **130.00**
Vase, Art Nouveau, pink flowers & limbs, 11½" **150.00**
Vase, Art Nouveau, purple iridescence, cobalt flower **235.00**
Vase, bird in flight, flowers, 12" **145.00**

Vase, blue w/gold eagles either side, scrolled center panel, 13" **150.00**
Vase, blue w/gold embossed trees, 7½" **135.00**
Vase, bulbous w/owl, 5" **75.00**
Vase, bulbous w/parrots, 6½" **75.00**
Vase, bulbous, bunches of grapes in high relief, 8x8" **250.00**
Vase, cobalt/green, Greenaway girls, birds, 4 handles, 7" **180.00**
Vase, Deco large enamel birds, double handles **150.00**
Vase, gourd shape, lion on base, triple signed, 11" **300.00**
Vase, gourd, yellow roses, gold enamel, 4 handles, 9" **185.00**
Vase marbleized jewels, tan, Czech, 7" **60.00**
Vase, molded plums & leaves, iridescent grey **145.00**
Vase, molded squirrel & acorns, multi-color, 8" **225.00**
Vase, mosaic design owl w/flowers, 8½" **36.00**
Vase, multi-colored florals, solid rim band, 12" **130.00**
Vase, raised poppies, 4 handles, matte, 8½" **110.00**
Vase, reticulated, jewelled, 3 handles, Imperial mark, 7" **290.00**

Animal Dishes with Covers

Covered animal dishes have been made for nearly two centuries and

are as varied as their manufacturers. They were made in many types of glass--slag, colored, clear, and milk glass--as well as china and pottery. On bases of nests and baskets you'll find animals and birds of every sort. The most common was the hen.

Beaver, on scroll base, milk glass, sm chip rim **85.00**
Boar's head, red glass eyes, pat 1888, ribbed base, 9½″ **850.00**
Cat, lacy base, dated, Atterbury **100.00**
Cat, white, on ribbed base, milk glass **28.00**
Chick, in egg on sleigh, milk glass, old **50.00**
Chicks, on round basket, milk glass **35.00**
Dog, blue setter, signed Vallerysthal **125.00**
Dog, chow, on ribbed base, milk glass **40.00**
Dog, hunting dog top, wheat & quail bottom, Flaccus **70.00**
Dog, recumbent, woolly, milk glass **50.00**
Dove, McKee, signed **250.00**
Dove, w/hand, dated **125.00**
Duck, on basket, milk glass **30.00**
Duck, swimming, milk glass **35.00**
Eagle, sheltering eggs, American Hen, milk glass, 1898 . . . . . . **65.00**
Fish, entwined, milk glass, Atterbury **145.00**
Fish, on boat, milk glass **22.00**
Fox, on ribbed base, milk glass, dated **75.00**
Hen, basket base, milk glass, old, 7″ **20.00**
Hen, blue marble **150.00**
Hen, blue w/white head, milk glass **30.00**
Hen, large, marked Kemple **45.00**
Hen, milk glass, Hazel Atlas, 3″ **14.00**
Hen, on nest w/12 eggs, green/white, 11½x13″ **165.00**
Hen, on nest, milk glass, Vallerystahl, 2½″ **35.00**
Hen, Staffordshire, 11″ **150.00**
Hen, w/chick base, milk glass, Flaccus **145.00**
Hen, w/chicks, McKee **200.00**
Hen, white w/blue head, lacy base **150.00**
Hen, white w/blue head, milk glass, 5½″ **28.00**
Lamb, on lid, w/fluted box, 5½x3¾″ **22.00**
Lion, majestic, basket base **45.00**
Lion, ribbed, on lacy dish, dated **100.00**

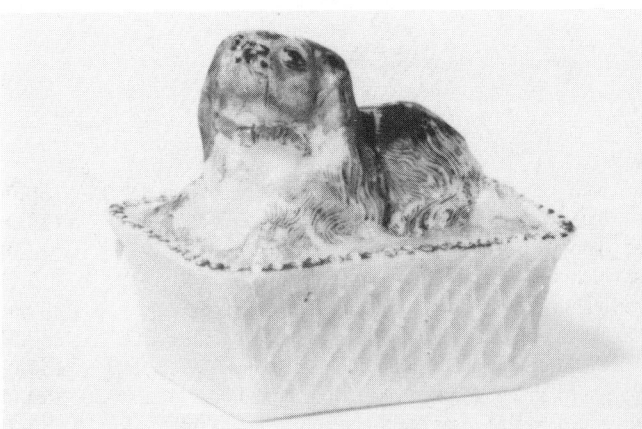

Pekingese, on rectangular basket, painted, 5″ **250.00**
Rabbit **165.00**
Robin, sitting on nest, opalescent blue **85.00**
Rooster, lacy edge basket, caramel slag, old Imperial mk **60.00**
Rooster, white w/ribbed base, milk glass **30.00**
Squirrel finial, dog handles, clear **110.00**
Stag, on fallen tree, milk glass, Flaccus **145.00**
Swan, McKee **175.00**
Swan, w/closed neck, milk glass **110.00**
Turkey, McKee **175.00**

Turtle, w/snail, white milk glass, Vallerystahl **80.00**

Apothecary Collectibles

Apothecary items--those articles dealing with the trade of drug preparation--are becoming recognized collectibles by not only people involved in the field today, but by collectors of "Americana" as well. In contrast to the advanced techniques of modern medicine, many of the implements used by the 19th century druggist have changed very little.

Book, Pharmaceutical Directory, Rudolphy, Riddle & Sons, 1872 **80.00**
Book, The Druggist's Handbook of Private Formulas, 1882 . . . . **80.00**
Bottle, apple green, pressed, reverse painted glass label, 10″ . . . **75.00**
Bottle, blown cobalt w/stopper, paper label, 9″ **40.00**
Bottle, blown, olive amber, w/label & tin cap, 14″ **325.00**
Bottle, cobalt, 18″ **20.00**
Case, contains bottles, etc, type used on ships, 1800s **340.00**
Case, mahogany w/brasses, fitted w/bottles, etc, 10x9x8″ **300.00**
Case, mahogany, ivory escutcheon, w/instruments, 6x7x9″ **310.00**
Chromolitho, pharmacist w/mortar & pestle, oak frame, 18x27″. **70.00**
Jar, blown in mould, blue, reverse glass label, tin lid, 10″ **180.00**
Jar, blown w/flared lip, pressed ground stopper, label, 9″ **125.00**
Jar, blown, cobalt blue, floral enameling w/gilt, 6″ **105.00**
Jar, cobalt pressed glass, ground lid, 7″ **60.00**
Jar, ironstone, green & white w/paper label, 10″ **160.00**
Jar, porcelain, gilt trim, French label Piper Cubeb, 10¼″ **90.00**
Jar, porcelain, gilt trim, polychrome label w/snake, 9″ **115.00**
Jar, pressed ribs, green w/reverse painted label, 9″ **35.00**

Jar, shelf type, either **15.00**
Mortar, cast bronze, leaf scroll handles, crest, 7x8½″ dia **725.00**
Mortar, cast bronze, w/handles, floral decor, 3x4½″ **125.00**
Mortar, early cast bronze w/decorative balusters, 3x5″ dia **125.00**
Mortar, early cast bronze, 4 faces of crowned monarch, 4¼″ . . . **75.00**
Mortar, soapstone, variegated green, 3½″ **45.00**
Mortar/Pestle, early cast bronze, griffins & dolphins, 5½″ **925.00**
Mortar/Pestle, white bisque, 4¾″ **30.00**
Mortar/Pestle, white stoneware, 1870 . . . . **45.00**
Mortar/Pestle, cast bronze w/bust in relief, 5x6½″ dia **180.00**
Scales, nickel on brass, mahogany, beveled glass, 10x9x19″ . . . **150.00**
Scales, nickel plate, mahogany/glass, hinged lid, Foremner **135.00**
Vapo lamp, complete, 6¼″ **40.00**

Appliances

As quaint as these old appliances may seem today, imagine how welcome each new innovation must have been when first introduced! The ice box

was invented in the very early 1800s by Thomas Moore, who built a box within a box, separated by insulation to keep the block of ice from melting. By the turn of the century, fancy oak boxes were offered at prices ranging from $5 to $50. Today, sans the drip pan, these lovely old boxes are refinished and used as cabinets to store everything from records to liquor.

Bulb, w/socket, Edison, double curl filament, 1903 . . . . **70.00**
Cornpopper, Stir & Pop, red & ivory, electric, 1920, working . . **24.00**
Fan, Emerson, oscillating **75.00**
Fan, GE, oscillating w/brass blade, 1916, 15″ **50.00**
Fan, Koldair, electric, 7″ blade, 1920 . . . . **20.00**
Fan, Table, battery, open armature, oak base, 19th century . . . **425.00**
Icebox, oak, brass hardware, 8 door, 7′11″x6′ **975.00**
Icebox, oak, small **325.00**
Icebox, oak, 6 door **350.00**
Icebox, oak, 4 doors, brass hinges, 7′x5′6″ **475.00**
Icebox, pressed oak, 3′x5′ **75.00**
Icebox, tiger oak, brass hardware **265.00**
Ice box, Mace Empire **275.00**
TV, Philco Predicta table model **300.00**
Vacuum cleaner, American Brush, non-electric **45.00**

Arequipa

The Arequipa Pottery operated from 1911 until 1918 at a sanitorium near Fairfax, California. Its purpose was two-fold--therapy for the patients, and financial support for the institution. Frederick H. Rhead was the originator and director. The ware was often hand thrown using local clays, simply styled and decorated. The marks were varied, but always incorporated the name of the pottery and the state. A circular arrangement encompassing a negative image of a vase beside a tree is most common.

Bowl, high gloss green, speckled, No 626, 2½x6½″ **60.00**
Bowl, thick plum glase w/grey drip, 1912, marked, 7″ dia **60.00**
Vase, blue over grey, 5½x6″ **300.00**
Vase, blue over grey, some crystalline, 5½x6″ dia **295.00**
Vase, deep blue w/slip decor at rim, marked 1912, 6″ **550.00**
Vase, grey/plum, square rolled rim, vert ribs, 4x4 3/8″ **100.00**
Vase, incised stylized butterflies, matt grey-blue, 6x5″ **550.00**

Vase, ribbed, square rim, blue **245.00**
Vase, thick blue glaze, narrow ribbing, No 102, marked, 6″ . . . **250.00**
Vase, w/carved butterfly, artist signed, 6″ **550.00**

Art Deco

The Art Deco movement began to emerge in the mid-20s after being

introduced at the Paris International Expo of 1925. Its sharp symetrical, often geometric, lines were a welcome respite to designers ready for a change from the heavy Victorian affectations that had been the fashion for many years. Chrome, glass and plastics were used in home accessories; lush fabrics, leather and rich colors offset any chance of starkness. Art Deco styling affected every phase of industry and design through the 30s and well into the 40s.

Ashtray, bronze terrier on green marble base, Germany **75.00**
Ashtray, combination cigarette/matchbox holder, metal nude . . . **30.00**
Ashtray holder, cartoon character Jigs, hp wood, 33″ **70.00**
Ashtray holder, wooden cat, glass eyes, 25x11x9″ **55.00**
Ashtray, woman on amethyst base, worn gilt tone **45.00**
Bathroom set, yellow overlay glass geometric, 6-pc . . **250.00**
Bedroom set, vanity, nightstand, chest, 2 beds, Johnson **1,100.00**
Bookends, bronze over copper, girl kneeling, pair **125.00**
Bookends, free-form male nude, plants on base, copper wash . . . **30.00**
Bookends, iron w/brass wash, The Thinker, 4x4″ **22.00**
Bookends, penguin, silver-plated, pair, 8x4″ **20.00**
Box, chrome, wood lined, lid w/flapper portraits, 8x4″ **38.00**
Candlesticks, scrolled copper tubing, pewter, 8½x4″ dia **35.00**
Cigarette box, phesant embossed on cover **12.00**
Cigarette dispenser, mechanical, ornate Flapper, 6x7″ **95.00**
Cocktail shaker, chrommetal w/red finial, 4 wines, Chase **20.00**
Coffee pot, electric, chrome, inset handles, faucet knob **25.00**
Coffee set, globular pot, sugar/creamer, tray, Chase **200.00**
Compact, chrome, rectangular, Houbigant **12.00**
Fairy lamp, round cottage, orange roof, green base, 2-pc **65.00**
Figurine, brass, Delilah At The Well **35.00**
Figurine, bronze and ivory, dancing figure, signed, 16″ **2,000.00**
Figurine, kneeling woman w/mirror, gilt metal, Chiparus **600.00**
Figurine, plane, mini D-C 2, cobalt milk glass/chrome **795.00**
Fireplace screen, wire w/brass archer & 2 hounds **350.00**
Incense burner, kneeling girl w/bowl, LN Aronson, 1923 . . . . . **115.00**
Ink stand, bronze w/head masks, 5″ square base **50.00**
Keith Murray for Wedgewood, pottery
  Bowl, footed, tapered sides, green, 7″ **350.00**
  Cigarette box, tubular pattern base to top, 8″ long **175.00**
  Jar, w/cover, ovoid, ring band at base, moonstone, 6″ photo **450.00**

  Pitcher, white, tight turnings on base & rim, 5″ **95.00**
  Vase, flat top w/sm lip, horizontal grooves, indent ft, 7″ photo **400.00**
  Vase, narrow base & lip, 8″ shoulder, moonstone, 12″ **550.00**
Lamp, Betty Beck, nude, cast metal, frosted glass diffuser **75.00**
Lamp, boudoir, panther figural w/pink camphor shade **45.00**
Lamp, bronzed, snake charmer, multicolor globe, Czech **150.00**
Lamp, camphor shade w/saturn, stars, moons, stepped base . . . **125.00**
Lamp, frosted shade & base, ladies on crescent moons **85.00**
Lamp, lighthouse w/chrome sailboat, stepped base **150.00**
Lamp, mushroom, brass w/prisms, 20″ **750.00**
Lamp, nude dances on plateaued amber glass base, 19½″ **150.00**
Lamp, nude metal figural, chartreuse glass background **95.00**
Lamp, nude w/deer, copper wash, red globe **40.00**

Lamp, plane, D-C 10 w/chrome wings & base, cobalt, 1930s .. **250.00**
Lamp, seated nude, frosted green/white, 1929, Lenox **850.00**
Lamp, semi-nude on globe, bronzed & brass, red shade, 24″ ... **80.00**
Lamp, woman archer & dog figural, frosted geometric shade .. **140.00**
Perfume bottle, china, yellow/green original stopper **19.00**
Perfume lamp, Egyptian Princess, German **175.00**
Powder box, octagonal, blue, frolicking nude in relief **30.00**
Set, pitcher w/nude stopper, 10 cups, Bottoms Up, pottery ... **195.00**
Tea set, platinum florals on white, 3-pc, Bavaria **85.00**
Vase, Kent, 12″ **75.00**
Vase, all-over 4-color pattern, Boch, 14″ **1,345.00**
Vase, brass w/tan lucite base, line banding, 6x6″ **24.00**
Vase, bulbous, French Deco, 1900s Rambers Miller, 7″ **95.00**
Vase, deco flowers & bands, ormolu top & base, Boch, 7″ **95.00**
Vase, tapered, all-over olive pattern, 3-color, Boch, 12″ **300.00**
Wine, set of 6, pyramid chrome base, Chase **60.00**

Art Glass Baskets

A popular novelty and gift item during the Victorian era, these one of a kind works of art were produced in just about any type of art glass in use at that time.

Cased, clear/yellow, swirl rib & rosette mold, ruffled, 7x5″ **150.00**
Cased, white/spatter, clear sq thorn handle, ruffled, 6″ **110.00**
Cut glass, 8 panels, intaglio sunflower, Heisey, 15½″ **275.00**

End of the Day, cased w/white, thorn handle, 7½″ **175.00**
Hand blown, frosted iridescent, heavy applied handle, 12x8″ .. **200.00**
Iridescent purple/rainbow luster bowl, 8 crimps, brass base.... **245.00**
Opaque white, red cherry applique, amber handle, 5x4″ **165.00**
Overshot, slender, clear w/applied flower & leaf at handle **180.00**
Peachblow, ruffled, swirled, camphor handle, 5½″ **850.00**
Pink slag cased w/clear, basket weave, rectangular, 7x5x4″ ... **160.00**
Satin Hobnail, white w/yellow casing, camphor handle, sm **75.00**
Satin, Tiffin, 10½″ **45.00**
Spangle w/clear overlay, swirl w/ruffled rim, 11″............. **55.00**
Spatter, blue w/white, crimped top, thorn handle, 6x5″ **240.00**
Spatter, melon ribbed, scalloped rim, thorn handle, 7x4″..... **125.00**
Square, vaseline/tan overshot on wht w/mica, 6 flower ft, crimped rim **365.00**
Vasa Murrhina, blue, 10″............................. **125.00**
Vaseline, stripe swirl, amber thorn handle **160.00**
Verre De Soie, raspberry prunts on handle, Steuben, 4x4½″ ... **90.00**
White cased w/lime & lavendar, ferns at rim, 10x9x12″ **375.00**

Aurene

Aurene, developed in 1904 by Frederick Carder of the Steuben Glass Works, is a metallic iridescent glassware similar to some of Tiffany's. Usually a rich lustrous gold, blue is also found, and occasionally red or green. It was used alone and in combination with calcite, a cream colored glass with a calcium base, also developed by Carder. It is usually marked Aurene or Steuben, sometimes with the factory number added, etched into the glass by hand. Paper labels were also used.

Atomizer, blue, 7½″ **350.00**
Basket, w/calcite, gold w/blue highlighted handle 11½x11″ ... **675.00**
Bon bon, clover shape, footed, ruffled rim, 3¾″ **175.00**
Bowl vase, calcite w/gold, ruffled rim, 2¼x5″............. **135.00**
Bowl, signed & numbered, 4½x7½″...................... **175.00**
Box, pagoda shape cover, gold, signed & numbered, 4x6″.... **750.00**
Candlestick, hi-light colors, signed & numbered, 8″ **185.00**
Candlestick, w/twist stem, blue, signed & numbered, 8″ **345.00**
Candlesticks, twist stems, blue, 10″ **850.00**
Centerpiece bowl, calcite & gold, flared & rolled top **170.00**
Cigarette holder-ash tray, gold, 2½x6″ **365.00**
Compote, calcite w/blue, 7x6½″ **550.00**
Compote, signed & numbered, 6¾″ **250.00**
Darner, gold **425.00**
Dessert bowl w/underplate, stretched & ruffled, gold **275.00**
Finger bowl, gold, signed **275.00**
Fruit bowl, w/bulbous base, w/calcite, 12″ dia............. **365.00**
Lamp, helmet shape, gold cut to calcite, F Carder, 14″....... **950.00**
Nut dish, gold, tri-lobe top, platinum iridescent, 2″ **150.00**
Perfume, acorn stopper, signed, 4″ **385.00**
Perfume, on ped, long dabber, blue, signed, 8″ **850.00**
Perfume, w/atomizer, blue hi-lights, 9″ **225.00**
Plate, stretched edge, signed Steuben, 7½″ **130.00**
Punch cup, w/ped, gold, signed & numbered **195.00**
Sherbet w/underplate, calcite stem, signed **345.00**
Sherbet w/underplate, gold, signed & numbered **235.00**
Stick vase, blue, Steuben numbered, 10″.................. **400.00**
Stick vase, mirror finish 10″ **285.00**
Vase, bulbous bottom, flaring top, ribbed, signed **280.00**
Vase, gold w/millefiori florets, green leaves & vines **2,250.00**
Vase, hollow ped foot, slender stem, floral flare, 8½″........ **425.00**
Vase, pinched bottom, waisted, long neck, 5″ **375.00**
Vase, stretched tri-corner ruffled top, signed, 4″ **175.00**

Wine, gold w/blue high lights, twist stem, 7¼″ **200.00**

Austrian Ware

At the turn of the century, Carlsbad, Austria, was the center of a thriving ceramic industry that produced fine quality china and pottery primarily for the American market. There were many potteries in and around the area, several are represented in the listings below.

Berry dishes, set of 6, florals, gold tracery, 5″, MZ Austria..... **32.00**
Boot, w/cupids, Victoria, 4½″ **35.00**

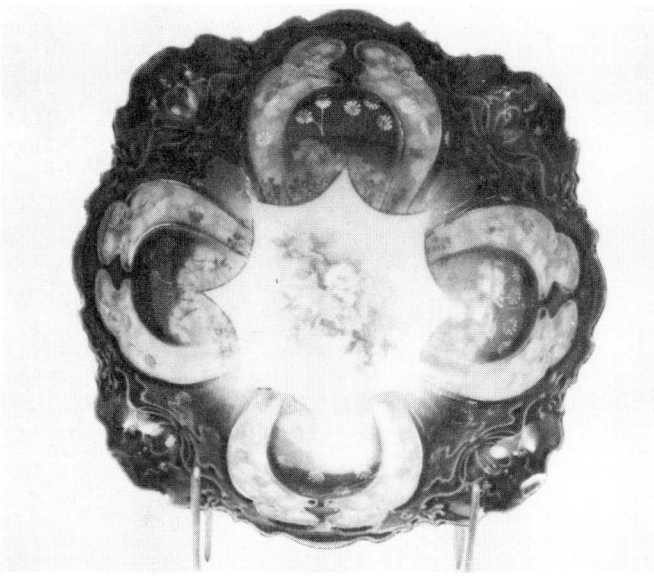

Bowl, blues w/wht cntr reserve, pk florals, Wheelock, Vienna, 10″ **200.00**
Bowl, centerpiece, Nouveau, 7x14″ long, crown mark........ **265.00**
Bowl, pearlized w/pink roses, scalloped, 10″, MZ Austria **110.00**
Bowl, scalloped edge, 3-color roses, 11″ dia, MZ Austria **95.00**
Bowl, scenic by Kauffman, pink & gold, Carlsbad, 9½″ **90.00**
Bowl/vase, irid, 4 gold ribbon handles, Carlsbad, 6x3″ **135.00**
Bowl/vase, peacock-feather irid, 4 handles, Carlsbad, 6x3″ **135.00**
Candleholders, white w/gold grapes & trim, 3 feet, 2″......... **18.00**
Chocolate pot, Falstaff & woman, much gold **125.00**
Chocolate pot, white w/florals, Carlsbad **30.00**
Dresser tray, scene with 7 pigs, large, MZ Austria **55.00**
Ewer, gold handle, floral reserve, baroque, Crown M, 15½″.... **95.00**

Ewer, lady w/rose on turquoise ground, gold handle, 11½″ ... **200.00**

Ewer, portrait on turquoise, ornate gold handle, 12″ **225.00**
Fish set, gravy boat, 20″ platter, 8-8″ plates, Carlsbad **350.00**
Humidor, pine cone decor, artist signed, Vienna **100.00**
Nut set, brown w/acorn decor, 7-pc, Royal Austria........... **50.00**
Pin tray, scene of 7 pigs in action, MZ Austria **48.00**
Plaque, hanging, roses & lilacs, Rococo border, 13″, LS&S **65.00**
Plate, apple blossom sprays, embossed leaves, 9½″, Carlsbad... **15.00**
Plate, blown-out azaleas, gold sprays, pointed edge, MZ, 10″... **45.00**
Plate, cream w/mulberry stems & ½″ border, Imperial, 8½″ ... **58.00**
Plate, Cupid, lt blue w/heart pierced border, Victoria, 8″ **25.00**
Plate, hp pink roses, blue & gold border, Imperial, 10″ **20.00**
Plate, hp raspberries, gold, Princess Louise, 8½″ **15.00**
Plate, portrait, dark-haired lady, MZ Austria **110.00**
Plate, portrait, dark-haired lady, signed Constance........... **95.00**
Plate, scalloped rim, autumn leaves, gold decor, 9″.......... **20.00**
Plates, portrait, maiden w/cherubs, set of 6, 8½″ **250.00**
Saucer, w/radish decor, 6½″, MZ Austria **20.00**
Vase, portrait of woman in yellow dress, Victoria........... **220.00**

Autographs

Philography, the hobby of collecting autographs, holds the interest of many people today, and judging from the prices observed in the market, they are a sound investment.

Several things must be considered in evaluating an autograph. The first is rarity, a factor which often takes thoughtful consideration to determine. Letters and papers are evaluated by the significance of their content. Condition is important, ink is prefered over pencil, and an autograph on an item other than conventional material--a baseball, a menu or a program--is more interesting and therefore more valuable, especially so if it pertains to their career.

Besides historical figures, world leaders, sports stars and novelists, autographs of movie stars and entertainers are widely collected. May West's often go for $50 or more, Carol Lumbard's well into the hundreds.

Abraham Lincoln,...................................... **950.00**
Abraham Lincoln, signed document, 1863 .... **2000.00**
Adlai Stevenson, typed letter, signed **12.00**
Adolph Hitler, document, 1937 .... **700.00**
Al Jolson, signed card, 1928 .... **45.00**
Alexander G Bell, typed letter, 1921 .... **125.00**
Alfred Hitchcock, signed magazine cover **80.00**
Andrew Johnson, document, 1864....................... **235.00**
Andrew Jackson, land grant, 1831 .... **160.00**
Andy Devine, signed photo **15.00**
Anne Blyth **10.00**
Audie Murphy **35.00**
Babe Ruth, 8x10″ photo **500.00**
Babe Ruth, signed baseball **500.00**
Barbra Streisand, signed photo, rare **20.00**
Bess Truman **15.00**
Carl Hubbell, signed baseball **25.00**
Carl Sandburg, presentation copy, signed, dated **85.00**
Carl Yastrzemski, baseball, picture postcard, 1969 .... **110.00**
Charles A Lindbergh, book, signed dated................. **350.00**
Charles De Gaule, ... **100.00**
Charles Dickens, bank check........................... **260.00**
Charles Huggins, 1966 Nobel Prize in medicine, photo....... **20.00**
Charlie Chaplin, photo **110.00**
Clarence Darrow, signed photo from magazine.............. **50.00**
Clark Gable, bank check **295.00**
Corretta Scott King, signed photo........................ **25.00**
David Brinkley **7.00**

Drew Pearson 15.00
Duke of Wellington, letter 32.00
Dwight Eisenhower, signed letter, White House letterhead 170.00
Edmond Randolph, sheepskin land grant, 1787 . . . . 400.00
Edna Ferber, letter 38.00
Eleanor Roosevelt 25.00
Elliot Maddox, baseball, on cardboard 12.00
Fay Wray, photo from King Kong 45.00
Fill Freehan, baseball, postcard w/picture 12.00
Fran Tarkenton, 5x7″ photo 35.00
George Bernard Shaw 40.00
George Bush, large color photo, signed, dated 45.00
George Washington, document, signed & dated, 1774 . . . . . 1,300.00
Gerald Ford, 8x10″ color photo, dated 1981 . . . . 85.00
Gerald Ford, inauguration program 100.00
Graig Nettles, baseball, on 4x6″ paper 25.00
Gypsy Rose Lee, 8x10″ photo 45.00
Hanging Judge Parker, Marshall's Oath, signed 235.00
Harriet Beecher Stowe, signed quote 150.00
Harry James 10.00
Harry Truman, photo at White house desk, framed, signed . . . 100.00
Helen Keller, pencil signature from letter 15.00
Helen Keller, presentation copy, book signed, dated 125.00
Henry Ford, rare 250.00
Henry Clay, document, 1831 . . . . 50.00
Henry Kissinger, Sec of State, signed photo 15.00
Herbert Hoover, signed booklet 35.00
Hoagy Carmichael, large black & white photo 30.00
Horace Greeley, signed letter, 1860 . . . . 75.00
Howard Pyle, handwritten letter, 1905 . . . . 100.00
Humphrey Bogart, pen and ink sig on paper 35.00
J Edgar Hoover 15.00
Jack Dempsey, large black & white photo 20.00
Jack Ruby, document 150.00
Jack Webb 15.00
Jackie Cooper 25.00
James F Walker, signed engraving, 1926 . . . . 125.00
James Fenimore Cooper, signed letter 100.00
James G Blain, statesman, letter, 1881 . . . . 35.00
James Garfield, Congressional envelope 68.00
James Whitcomb Riley, framed note, 1899 . . . . 60.00
Jane Mansfield, Christmas card 65.00
Jean Harlow, pencil inscription 235.00
Jerry Lucas, on 3″ sq paper bag, rare 80.00
Jimmy Stewart 10.00
Joan Crawford 25.00
Joe Louis & Carmen Basilo, program cover 38.00
John Coolidge, signed letter, 1973 . . . . 20.00
John Drew, actor of 1880s, handwritten letter signed 14.00
John F Kennedy, 1 pg contract 1,200.00
John F Kennedy, Jack, handwritten message 400.00
John Philip Sousa 45.00
John Quincy Adams, land grant 1826 . . . . 160.00
John Quincy Adams, note as senator, 1805 . . . . 95.00
John Quincy Adams, w/portrait 100.00
John Wayne, letter 45.00
John Wayne, on Australian Pound note 35.00
Johnny Case, signed record 10.00
Jonny Ray 10.00
Katherine Lee Bates, author, typed letter, signed 18.00
King George III, portion of document 50.00
Lauel & Hardy, both signatures on photograph w/note 425.00
Louis Armstrong, souvenir booklet, sig of his group 135.00
Lou Gehrig 150.00

Mamie Eisenhower, signed photo 35.00
Marilyn Monroe, autographed 5x7″ photo in orig envelope, 1952 250.00
Mary Baker Eddy, cut sig from letter 350.00
Maxfield Parrish, typed letter, signed, 1911 . . . . 250.00
Norman Rockwell, illustrated card, sig 45.00
Norman Rockwell, thank you note 80.00
Oliver Wendell Holmes, framed photo & verse, 1882 . . . . 140.00
Orville Wright, signed check 275.00
Paul Newman, 8x10″ photo 28.00
Paul Pender, boxing champion 15.00
Pearl Buck, page from book 14.00
Peggy Lee, signed letter 20.00
Pete Gogalak, football, 4x7″ snapshot 12.00
Queen Elizabeth II, traffic violation pardon, seal 375.00
Richard E Byrd, photograph dated 1928 . . . . 35.00
Richard Nixon, booklet of acceptance speech 125.00

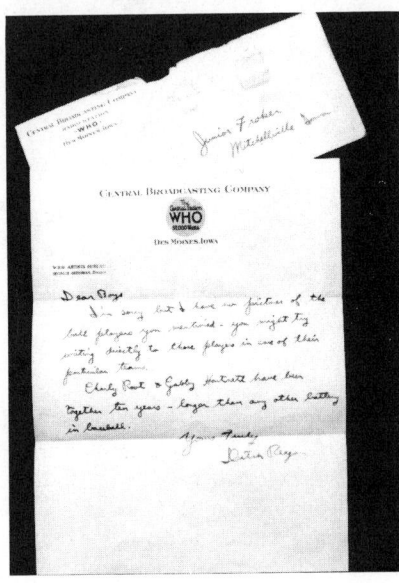

Ronald Regan, hand-written letter, re: baseball, Dutch, 1936 . . 675.00
Ronald Regan, letter concerning issue, 1972 . . . . 250.00
Rutherford Hayes, sm card 45.00
Salvador Dali, signed photo of painting 350.00
Samuel Adams, signed letter 300.00
Sean Connery, photo 15.00
Smiley Burnett, handwritten letter 20.00
Sparky Lyle, baseball on cardboard 12.00
Stephen A Douglas, letter 100.00
Steve Kline, baseball, on cardboard 12.00
Stewart Granger 15.00
Susan B Anthony, signed quote 210.00
Theodore Roosevelt, letter 95.00
Thomas A Edison, pen and ink on photo 45.00
Thomas Jefferson, military document, 1780 . . . . 865.00
WB Yeats, signed letter, 1913 . . . . 270.00
WL Garrison, founder Anti Slavery Soc sig on card 30.00
Wallace Beery, Jr. 15.00
Washington Irving, typed letter, signed 80.00
Will Rogers, bank check 175.00
William T Sherman, letter, dated 1878 . . . . 135.00
William Clark, document 365.00
William Howard Taft, signed letter 125.00
William IV, part of document 28.00
William T Sherman, letter, 1877 . . . . 136.00
William T Sherman, letter to Jefferson Davis 300.00
William Taft, letter 45.00
Willie Brandt, post card 15.00

Automobilia

While some automobilia buffs are primarily concerned with restoring vintage cars, others concentrate on only one area of collecting. For instance, hood ornaments were often quite spectacular. Made of chrome or nickel plate on brass or bronze, they were designed to represent the "winged maiden" Victory, flying bats, sleek greyhounds, soaring eagles and a host of other creatures. Today they bring prices in the $75 to $200 range. R. Lalique glass ornaments go much higher!

Horns, radios, clocks, gear shift knobs and key chains with company emblems are other areas of interest. Generally, items pertaining to the classics of the 30s are most in demand. Paper advertising material, manuals and catalogues in excellent condition are also collectible.

License plate collectors search for the early porcelain on cast iron examples. First year plates--e.g., Massachusetts, 1903; Wisconsin, 1905; Indiana, 1913--are especially valuable.

Accessory horn button, APCO, for Model T	10.00
Ampheres Shire Detroit, 2¾"	9.00
Ampheres Westinghouse, 2½"	9.00
Battery tester, pat date 1923 w/guage	30.00
Book, AAA Northeastern U S, 1936, 600 pgs	10.00
Book, Cadillac in WWI, 75 pgs, 1919	24.00
Book, Duryea, 1906, 142 pgs w/ads	10.00
Book, Dykes Encyclopedia, hard back, 1918, 916 pgs	16.50
Book, instructions for 1913 Hudson-37, 23 pgs	22.50
Book, instructions how to drive a Maxwell 25-4, 15 pgs	25.00
Book, reference, Brahnam, 1921, 320 pgs w/pictures	20.00
Booklet, Maxwell Motor Cars, 1912, 40 pgs	40.00
Box, tin, Edison Mazda Lamps for your car w/bulb, sm wrench	25.00
Catalog, The Cross Country Rambler, 1914	35.00
Catalog, No 20, Mitchell, 1909, 34 pgs	50.00
Chrome trim ring for wheels, 15"	2.00
Chrome trim ring for wheels, 16"	3.00
Clock, Studebaker, 1928 G C	35.00
Coil, Model T	9.00
Dash light cover, jeweled	4.00
Dash, complete w/instruments, Model A	35.00
Dashboard clock, Westclox, 1932 Ford, luminous, works, 2½"	25.00
Dome light, original make	10.00
Emergency kit, blue tin, Model T	24.00
Fender guide, illuminated	8.00
Fender guid, non-illuminated	5.00
Fire extinguisher, brass, pyrene, old	40.00
Flower vases, glass, pr	20.00
Fog light, cone shaped, 6 volt	10.00
Franklin lamps, brass, pr	150.00
Gas cap, w/brass eagle, Model A	20.00
Gas pump nozzle, brass	65.00
Gas pump w/glass cylinder	120.00
Gear shift knob, brown/white dog, glass, finger grooves	36.00
Gear shift knob, marble	8.00
Gear shift knob, swirled, 1920	25.00
Grille guards for 1930s model	10.00
Handbook/Manual, 1955 Thunderbird	20.00
Head light lens, flat	5.00
Headlight lens, 1937 Ford, pair	10.00
Headlight visors for cars of 1920s and 30s, pr	8.00
Headlight, Buick, 1920	14.00
Headlight, Model T, brass	75.00
Headlight, Packard, 1930	60.00
Headlight, brass, made for Cadillac, Gray & Davis	80.00
Headlights, Essex, 1928, pr	75.00
Heater, red w/silver top, Bunsen, Ind., Model T	40.00

Hood ornament, Lincoln	15.00
Hood ornament, Longchamps, R Lalique France	2,500.00
Hood ornament, Mercedes	20.00
Hood ornament, Pontiac, 1950s	30.00

Hood ornament, R. Lalique frosted, 1925, 5½"	650.00
Hood ornament, Ram's head	15.00
Hood ornament, lady w/flowing hair, not signed	100.00
Horn, a-oogah, hand operated, Steward Warner, 1920s	50.00
Horn, motor driven, 6 volts	15.00
Hub cap, Art Deco, chrome, mermaid	24.00
Hub cap, Model T	8.00
Hub cap, screw on type	5.00
Hubcap, Chevrolet, 1957	5.00
Hubcap, Dodge, 1922	3.00
Hubcap, Model T	4.00
Hubcap, threaded brass, nickel plate, Pierce Arrow	25.00
Interior clock mirrors w/auto script	15.00
Interior clock mirrors w/out auto script	10.00
Jack, 1934	18.00
Jack, cast iron w/cog wheel, early	18.00
Lamp, Dietz Eureka, 1914	55.00
License plate for 2 horse wagon, Mo., 1913, 3" dia	70.00

License plates, porcelain, 1911, 14x5", pr	275.00
Magazine, Motor, June 19, 1934	10.00
Magazine, The Horseless Age, Oct 6, 1912	22.00
Manual, Cadillac Owner, 1955	10.00
Manual, Edsel Service, 1958, 359 pgs	32.00
Monkey wrench, Ford in script	10.00
New Process Vulcanizer w/instructions, orig box, 1910	50.00
Oil can w/flexable spout, qt, pat 1861, Hoffman	25.00
Oil can, brass, Ford	10.00
Overland ignition box, K & W	45.00
Photo, Pierce Arrow Touring Car w/redwood tree, 7x5"	5.00
Photo, advertising Franklin Touring Car, Type C, 1906	20.00
Pin back button, Studebaker	18.00
Pin tray, brass, Graham Motor Cars emblem	40.00
Pin tray, copper General Motors emblem	40.00
Radiator cap, fish, Lalique	235.00
Radiator cap, Model T	3.00
Radiator cap, Motometer, no name	10.00
Radiator cap, Pontiac, 1924	15.00
Radiator cap, goddess, for 1928-31 Cadillacs	75.00

Radiator cap, heron, for 1928-31 Cadillacs	80.00
Radiator emblem, 1911 through 1920	20.00
Radiator emblem, 1921 through 1939	14.00
Radiator emblem, 1940 through 1950	5.00
Radiator gauge, Boyce Motor Meter for '30s Ford	34.00
Radiator ornament, eagle head molded & etched, R Lalique, 4"	725.00
Running board spot light	100.00
Showroom display, cardboard, Studebaker, 1950, 18x24"	40.00
Side lamp, Pierce Arrow truck Model 1923, engraved	235.00
Side light, Model T	15.00
Side light, oil, brass trim, Edmund & Sons, A14 Model 8	50.00
Side mount mirror	15.00
Speedometer, Standard, Model T	45.00
Spot light, chrome, 6 volt	15.00
Tail light lens, double	10.00
Tail light lens, single	50.00
Tail light lens, triple	15.00
Tire covers, metal, 17-19"	15.00
Tire gauge, Schrader, 1909	6.00
Tire gauge, orig pouch, Packard	85.00
Tire gauge, dial type, Buick, 28-20, 28-475, case & box	17.00
Tire gauge, tublar type, pocket size, for balloons, '24 Buick	12.00
Tire jack, cast iron w/cog wheel	20.00
Tire pressure gauge, Schrader, pat 1923	6.00
Tire pump, turned wood handle, cast iron base, 1920s	9.00
Tire remover, cast iron, JJ Miller, 19"	20.00
Tool envelope, fibercloth, w/tools, Model A	40.00
Traffic light finders	6.00
Trippe light, junior	20.00
Trippe light, senior	30.00
Trumpet horns, electric 6 volt, pr	30.00
Turn signals, tin men pointing fingers, swing out, 1915	195.00
Vaccum tank, Stewart Warner	15.00
Value grinder, Model T	12.00
Vulcanizer, cast iron, Adamson Mfg Co, pat 1912	20.00
Wheels, wire, for 1933 Plymouth, 5 for	150.00
Wind wings w/brackets, pr	25.00

Autumn Leaf

In 1933 the Hall China Company designed a line of dinnerware exclusively for the Jewell Tea Company, who offered it to their customers as premiums. Although you may hear the ware referred to as Jewell Tea, it was officially named Autumn Leaf in the 1940s. Other companies have been known to make a similar line, but these were never made in quantity, and values listed here are for the Hall product only.

Baking dish, swirl	12.50
Bean pot w/handles	42.00
Bowl, 5"	3.00
Bowl, 6"	4.00
Bowl, 7"	8.00
Bowl, Sunshine No 3	7.00
Bowl, Sunshine No 5	15.00
Butter dish w/cover, ¼ lb	80.00
Butter dish w/cover, 1 lb, MIB	125.00
Cake knife	22.50
Cake plate	12.00
Cake plate on ped	45.00
Cake safe, metal	20.00
Candle warmer base, round	92.00
Canister, round w/plastic lid	12.00
Casserole & lid	25.00
Casserole warmer, oval	16.00

Coasters, set of 6, metal	45.00
Coffee server w/cover, 8½"	36.00
Cookie jar, big ears	60.00
Cookie jar, beanbaker	60.00
Cream soup, 4½"	8.00
Creamer, new style	6.00
Creamer, 4¼"	7.00
Cup & saucer	6.00
Cup & saucer, St Dennis	16.00
Cup, St Dennis	13.50
Custard	3.75
Custard, swirl	4.75
Dinner plate, 10"	8.00
Divided vegetable	45.00
Drip jar w/lid	16.00
Dripolator, 8 cup, metal insert	32.00
Gravy boat w/underplate	20.00
Gravy boat	12.00
Irish mug	60.00
Jim Beam Jewell Tea Wagon	140.00
Marmalade w/underplate	45.00
Mixing bowl set, 3 pc	30.00
Mug, 10 oz	49.00
Mustard, 3 pc	45.00
Percolator, electric	160.00
Pickle dish	10.00
Pie baker	14.00
Pitcher, 2½ pt	15.00
Plate, 5½"	2.50
Plate, 6½"	3.00
Plate, 9"	7.00
Platter, 11"	11.00
Platter, 13"	12.50
Refrigerator stack set	55.00
Rolling pin, glass	10.00
Salad bowl, 9"	11.00
Salad plate, 7½"	6.00
Salt & pepper, casper, pr	12.00
Saucer	2.00
Shakers, range, pr	14.50
Soup, coupe shape	8.50
Sugar & creamer, 1934	28.00
Sugar & lid, new style	12.00
Sugar & lid, old style	15.00
Teapot, long spout, 1933	50.00

Teapot, Aladdin w/infuser	32.00

Tid bit, 3 tier	15.00
Tray, glass w/wood handles, 20″	20.00
Tumbler, frosted, 12 oz	13.50
Tumbler, frosted, 14 oz	14.50
Utility jug, 5 pint	16.00
Vase	110.00
Vegetable bowl w/cover	25.00
Wastebasket	145.00

Aviation

Aviation buffs are interested in items and material dealing with any phase of flying--magazines with information and photos of early airplanes, insignia and equipment from WWII, and ad cards and postcards depicting vintage war planes from various countries are popular collectibles.

Ad card, Runkel's Cocoa & Chocolates, aviation heroes	30.00
Altimeter, marked U S w/anchor, Kollsman Co	35.00
Bombardier wings, WWII, pin back, sterling	20.00
Book, Historic Airships, R S Holland, 343 pgs, 1928	15.00
Cigarette cards, Wings, all series, all cards	1.00
Goggles, 1 pc, nickle plate, rubber mask, WWII	100.00
Helmet, WWII aviator's, pile lined leather	45.00
Jacket, sheepskin w/large collar, WWII	250.00
Life vest, Mae West, grey, WWII	20.00
Magazine, Air Combat, Eagle Publishing Co, 1939-45	
Special, B17-G	10.00
Special, B24-D	12.00
Vol 1, all issues	15.00
Vol 2, all issues	10.00
Vol 3, all issues	8.00
Magazine, Air Classic, 1963 to present	
Vol. 1, No 1	35.00
Specials	7.00
Vol 1, No 2	20.00
Vol 1, No 3	25.00
Vol 2, all issues	10.00
Vol 3, all issues	9.00
Vol 4, all issues	9.00
Vol 5 or 6, all issues	8.00
Vol 7 through 9, all issues	6.00
Vol 10 through 14, all issues	5.00
Magazine, US Naval Aviation, Jan, 1942	25.00
Magazine, Wings and Airpower	
Vol 1, No 1, 1971	10.00
Vol 1, No 2, 1971	9.00
Vol 1, No 3, 1971	8.00
Matchsafe w/compass, WWII	6.00
Needle book, Trans-Atlantic Aeroplane, Czech	8.00
Photo, ME-163, German WWII Rocket Interceptor, 8x10″, framed	25.00
Photograph, P-39 in flight over Conn., official photo 17x21″	15.00
Pilot wings, WWII, pin back, sterling, pr	35.00
Propeller, hardwood w/brass trim on leading edge, 7′	350.00
Visor cap, khaki, leather bill & strap, brass eagle	35.00

Avon

The California Perfume Company, the parent of the Avon Co. was founded in 1886. Although an "Avon" line was introduced by the company in the mid-20s, not until 1939 did it become known as Avon Products, Inc. CPC products and award incentives are very collectible.

Albee, 1978	95.00

Alpine decanter, original, no box	35.00
American Eagle, 1976, full in box	18.00

Apple Blossom cologne, 6 oz, bubble sides, 1941-53	45.00
Baby powder & scent in box, CPC 1915	200.00
Bay Rum Keg, mint	7.50
Bleu Blazer, full in box	25.00
Bottle, 1906 CPC Avon Lady, 1977 issue	35.00
Bottle, 1926 Avon Lady, 1979	30.00
Bottle, lst Avon Lady, 1972	250.00
Bottle, Dale Robinson	24.00
Bottle, Family Scene	75.00
Bottle, McConnels, 1973	90.00
Bowl & pitcher, Victorian, marbelled, full, in box	25.00
Cake server, 1978	10.00
Calculator	22.00
Candle holder, Martha Washington	10.00
Casey Jones soap set	48.00
Chair	25.00
Charlie Brown, baseball suit & cap	25.00
Christmas Mouse, 5th Precious Moments	50.00
Christmas plate, 1975, MIB	16.00
Christmas plate, 1974	40.00
Christmas plates, set of 8	275.00
Circus Wagon soap	50.00
Courting lamp, 1970	11.00
Daisy Bouquet set	28.00
Daphine talcum, CPC, tin	26.00
Defender Cannon	8.00
Dollars 'N Scents, MIB	35.00
Dueling Pistol No 1	7.00
Dusting powder can, Jasmine, 1946	15.00
Electric Tray, CPC	25.00
Elizabeth figurine, pink	15.00
Fashion figurine, 1971	9.00
Fruit Flavors, CPC	10.00
Gavel, mint	4.50
Happy Father's Day set	15.00
Hunter stein	15.00
Kitten, milk white glass	6.00
Ladies' Awards, 1962	150.00
Lamp, cologne, base holds talc, full, carnival top	20.00
Lavender Powder Sachet, 1961	8.00
Lil Tom Turtle soap	25.00
Mexico Spanish Senorita, MIB	8.00
Parlor lamp, 1971	10.00
Perfection Coloring Set, CPC, tin box & bottles, signed	28.00
Pin cushion doll, Bicentennial Betsy Ross	25.00
Plates, Liberty Bell & Independence Hall, set	35.00
Poncho	12.00

Pool Paddlers	30.00
Scentiments, full, in box	12.50
Scottie dog, milk glass, full, in box	10.00
Sheriff's Badge soap	25.00
Smile Music Box	14.00
Speedy the Snail	18.00
Spoon, CPC, Panama Pacific Expo	75.00
Stanley Steamer	4.00
Stock Car Racer	4.00
Super Cycle, black glass, 1971	10.00
Talc for Men, WWII, cardboard container, Victory Package	28.50
Teddy Bear Pen Award, 1979	17.00
Teddy Bear cookie jar, 1979, team leader award	20.00
Tiffany Bangle Bracelet	60.00
Tiffany Sterling Acorn Necklace	80.00
Tooth Tablet, CPC, milk glass w/metal top, 1934	225.00
Trading Post	42.00
Umbrella, mint	25.00
Viking Horn, mint	7.50
Watering Can	10.00
Weatherwise thermometer & barometer, amber	8.00
Whitey the Whale	10.00

Baccarat

The Baccarat Glass company was founded in 1765 near Luneville, France, and continues to this day to produce quality crystal tableware, vases, perfume bottles and figurines. The firm became famous for the high quality millefiori and caned paperweights produced there from 1845 until about 1860. Examples of these range from $300 to as much as several thousand. Since 1953, they have resumed production on a limited edition basis. These are listed later in the Paperweight section.

Bobeche, amberina, swirled, Baccarat Depose, 4" dia	15.00
Box, pink crystal, Art Deco, 4"	135.00
Centerpiece, crystal winged female, w/silver holder	1,200.00
Cologne, pinwheel amberina, 6x2½"	65.00
Decanter, 8 panels, cut, w/stopper, tapered shape, 9½"	135.00
Dish, half circle, swirl, amberina, signed, 2x7½"	40.00
Oil lamp, amberina swirl, chimney shade, 10½"	100.00
Perfume w/atomizer, amberina swirl, 7"	45.00
Perfume w/atomizer, pressed amberina, 7"	45.00
Perfume w/stopper, bell shape, ribbed pattern	42.00
Perfume, crystal, Art Deco	55.00
Toothpick, cherubs holding barrel, frosted	150.00
Toothpick, signed	36.00
Tumblers, paneled w/green overlay, 4½", set of 6	345.00
Vase, bulbous base, slender neck, gilded florals, 12"	80.00
Vase, frosted, molded Deco nudes, etched mark, 7"	115.00

Badges

The breast badge became popular in this country before the Civil War. They were made from common metals--nickel, brass, occasionally silver, and rarely, even gold. Those issued during the 19th century, and particularly those from the "wild West" are much in demand.

Modern day badges dealing with areas of popular interest, those with a unique design, and all law enforcement badges are desirable.

Cab drivers, shield type, brass	35.00
Chauffeur, brass, 1942	10.00
Chauffeur, Ill., 1913	12.00
Chauffeur, Mo., 1929	14.00

Constable, New Mexico, eagle top	60.00
Constable, early oval	45.00
Deputy Bailiff, 5 point full ball star, Chicago, hallmark	62.50
Deputy Coroner, Mo.	45.00
Deputy Investigator, Mo., in old leatherette case	65.00
Deputy Marshall, star shape	45.00
Deputy Sheriff, Wyandotte Co, shield shape, eagle top, in case	65.00
Deputy Sheriff, ballpoint star, Texas Star in center	60.00
Detective Police, Pa. Electric R R, 3 color enamel	28.00
Dupont, Gopher Ordinance Works, Patrolman	48.00
Fire Department, Ca.	30.00
Fire Dept, ladder, pike & hydrant, early 1900s	24.00
Fire Inspector w/fireman's hat, horn	25.00
Fire Warden, heavy metal, N. Y.	20.00
Fireman's, N. Y., 1903	23.00
Game Patrol, bear in relief on gold metal shield	28.00
Guard, Berghoff	48.00
Guard, Jamestown Exp, 1607-1907	40.00
Investigator, Fidelity Casualty, brass & copper	68.00
Investigator, Hawaii, gold shield w/center logo, eagle	24.00
Licensed Chauffeur, NYC, 1927	55.00
Northwest Pacific RR, gold star w/3 color logo	28.00
Officer, AT & SF Ry, star shaped w/ball ends, hallmarked	65.00
Officer, Hospital Board, seal center, cut out Mo., Ks. City	65.00
Patrolman, eagle w/Ga. state seal, nickle finish	35.00
Police Captain, shield shape gold finish, Ind. seal	50.00
Police Chief, St Paul	50.00
Police Investigator, tutone shield	35.00
Police Patrolman	40.00
Police Petty Officer, nickled, ornamental top & bottom	38.00
Police, Sergeant, Gallup, New Mexico, original	95.00
Police Sergeant, gold metal w/enameling, Ca. logo	30.00
Police, Auxiliary, horses pulling covered wagon, pocket badge	48.00
Police, Chicago, 6 pointed nickled star, copper letters, heavy	85.00
Police, La. state seal, crouching eagle w/baton, nickled	40.00
Police, Minneapolis, early	30.00
Police, Mo., w/state seal	60.00
Police, Patrolman, Birmingham, Ala., hallmarked	50.00
Police, San Francisco, Chinatown, tong, silver metal, eagle	14.00
Police, Sergeant, Gallup, New Mexico, original	95.00
Police, gilt, round w/crouching eagle, Idaho state seal	65.00
Police, gold metal shield, center logo	20.00
Police, hat badge, brass & copper w/emblems	12.00
Police, shield shape, eagle top, Orlando, hallmark	65.00
Police, star in circle, silver metal, 1930	20.00
Posse Star, early, Omaha	75.00
Post Office, old	23.00
Protective Order Police, Fire, shield shape, eagle top	40.00
Railway Express Agency employee badge, porcelain, plated	38.00
Reporter, round w/Ky. state seal, eagle, maker proof, 1920	50.00
Republican State convention, Iowa, 1910	22.00
SFFD, scalloped, silver, 1930, 1½"	15.00
Sheriff, 6 point star, Calif., original	95.00
Special Police, Ks. City, circle type cut out star, 1919	70.00
Special Police, Oh., shield shape cut out star center	50.00
Special Police, sunburst w/crouching eagle w/banner, 1910	60.00
Special Detective, Atlantic City, N. J., custom die	40.00
Telephone Co employee badge, Ca., blue w/silver letter	20.00
Telephone Inspector	35.00
Texas Rangers, cut out star, marked 14K	175.00
Trooper, La., sunburst, eagle, outline of state, large	75.00
US Census, 1900	15.00
USNAF, nickled, ornamental top & bottom, crouching eagle	40.00
Union Pacific RR, brass, logo shape Spike Days 1929	28.00

Banks

Made from the late 1860s until modern times, mechanical banks, or those with parts that move when a coin is deposited, have been produced in thousands of varieties. Their amusing actions rewarded thrifty children who might otherwise have been sorely tempted to spend their money. They were made of cast iron, wood, tin, glass and pottery, and were a leading product of American toy manufacturers for many years following the Civil War.

Still banks, usually made of cast iron or tin, though lacking the entertainment quality, nevertheless offered an inducement toward saving money through appealing character themes, animal figures and fields of special interests.

Registering banks are those made to indicate the total amount of deposited money which changes as each coin is added through the proper slot.

Advertising banks have a two fold interest, both bank collectors and those who like antique advertising find them appealing.

Because many old banks are so valuable, reproductions are common. Some of these restrikes were themselves made over 40 years ago, so some study is required to be able to recognize the originals.

Condition is judged by the remaining percentage of original paint, and whether all parts are present, original and in working order. Rarity is a factor in evaluating worth, but those with an especially popular design may bring the higher prices. Some of the banks listed here are identified by Wh for Whiting and Cr for Cranmer, standard references used by many collectors. Ci indicates cast iron; np, nickelplated.

Advertising
Atlantic Stove Co, stove, pot metal, 5¼" **40.00**
Billiken Shoes, Cr-50, Bring Luck, ci, 4" **95.00**
Bokar Coffee, tin **10.00**
Browning King & Co Chicago, state bank, ci, 5½x4" **130.00**
Burdick, Cash Register, electroplated ci & steel, 5x5" **50.00**
Calumet Baking Powder, Calument Kid, tin, mechanical **280.00**
Calumet Baking Powder, litho tin can, cardboard baby, 5" **50.00**
Campbell Soup, Campbell Kids, WH-45, cast iron, 3x4" **185.00**

Clock, 1st National Bank & Trust, Pekin, 5" **22.00**
Coca-Cola bottle vendor **95.00**
Crescent Cash Register, combination lock door, nickled iron, 6" **500.00**
Crosley, radio No 70, Wh-141, tin & ci, no trap, 4½" **75.00**
Daisy Safe, Wh-319 . . . . **50.00**
Darche Electric Clock Co, Chicago, clock **100.00**
Economy Foundry & Machine, pig, Cr-276, ci, 3½x7½" **50.00**
Eight O'Clock, tin **10.00**

Exxon, World's Fair, 1939 . . . . **28.00**
F & M Bank, S Dakota, 4½x5½", girl w/balloon, tin **25.00**
Ford Enrollment Plan, metal w/leather cover **35.00**
General Electric, refrigerator, WH-237, ci, 3¾" **20.00**
General Electric, refrigerator, WH-237, ci, 4¼" **45.00**
Goodyear, zeppelin hanger, Cr-538, Dura Aluminum, no trap . . **35.00**
Green Cab Co, Buick Flat Top, ci, repainted wheels, 8" long . **675.00**
International Harvester Savings Bank, 4" **55.00**
JP Seeburg, piano, nickled iron, 6¾" wide **210.00**
Kelvinator Refrigerator, ci & tin, orig Arcade label, 4" **50.00**
Knox Hats, Santa w/top hat, plastic, 6" **45.00**
Lincoln Mutual, book w/leatherette cover, 1923 . . . . **20.00**
Log Cabin, 1st National Bank, 4x4" **40.00**
Magic Chef, stove, pot metal, 3½x3" **40.00**
People's Savings & Loan, beehive & base, nickled iron, 7" . . . **165.00**
Pepsi Cola bottle vendor **75.00**
Pittsburgh Paints, house, glass **24.00**
Red Goose School Shoes, Wh-212, 4½" **135.00**
Red Goose School Shoes, goose, Wh-215, 3¾" **100.00**
Red Goose Shoes, goose on pedestal, ci, not old, 5½" **65.00**
Red Goose Shoes, goose on stand, ci & brass, 5¾" **130.00**
Red Top Cab, cab, cast iron, 4¼x8" **375.00**
Rex Hot Water Heater, litho tin & painted steel, 7½" **30.00**
Rival Dog Food Can w/picture of dog **15.00**
Roper, gas stove, Wh-139, tin & ci, 3¼" **85.00**
Servel Electrolux, refrigerator, pot metal, 4" **10.00**
Tabernacle Savings, Wh-228, tabernacle, ci, 2¼" **750.00**
Templetone, radio, tin & ci, repainted, 4¼" **70.00**
Time Safe, Wh-397, nickel plated ci, 7¼" **210.00**
Union Bank, safe, iron **25.00**
Westoreland Mustard, log cabin, milk glass **100.00**
Yellow Cab, cab, Wh-158, cast iron, rubber tires, 4¼" **550.00**
York, Parlor stove, Wh-133, electroplated ci, 4" **140.00**

Mechanical
Acrobats, old recast **300.00**
Artillery **325.00**
Bad Accident, VG paint, good condition **975.00**
Book of Knowledge, Dentist, MIB, early, 1950s **60.00**
Book of Knowledge, Indian & Bear, MIB, early 1950s **60.00**
Book of Knowledge, Magician, MIB, early 1950s **55.00**
Bowling Alley **360.00**
Cabin **365.00**
Charlie McCarthy, on trunk, mouth opens, 1930s **145.00**
Chimpanzee, old recast **300.00**
Clown on Globe, in orig wood box **700.00**
Creedmore, 1877, all original **395.00**
Dapper Dan, dances on box, 1910 . . . . **750.00**
Eagle & Eaglets **425.00**
Elephant, man pops out of howdah **225.00**
Frog & Old Man, old recast **300.00**
Goat, old recast of rare bank **30.00**
Halls Excelsior **150.00**
Halls Lilliput, type III, No. 113 . . . . **225.00**
House w/dog on turn table, cast iron **225.00**
I Always Did 'Spise a Mule, Jockey **365.00**
Jolly Nigger, Starkey's pat **220.00**
Jolly Nigger, w/Beacon Product, 5½" **45.00**
Juke Box , plays music, plastic, 1920s style **140.00**
Kings Mfg Co., 4 coin **85.00**
Lion & 2 monkeys **375.00**
Little Joe, aluminum, 5" G **30.00**
Marx Buddy, tin mechanical boy, glass candy container **295.00**
Monkey, tips hat, tin litho, Chein **30.00**
Monkey **365.00**

Mule Entering Barn	495.00
Multiplying	195.00
Mystery bank, hand appears to grab coin, tin	45.00
Nodding Scotsman, poor paint	185.00
Novelty, No. 30	225.00
Organ bank, boy & girl	225.00
Organ bank, monkey	225.00
Owl, glass eyes, turns head, old, mint	295.00
Paddy & the Pig	475.00
Peg-leg Beggar	775.00
Penny Pineapple, bright yellow, hand feeds coins to mouth	350.00
Punch and Judy, tin, 1930s	150.00
Rocket Ship	20.00
Santa Claus, drops coin in chimney, 1889, all orig	650.00
Signal Cabin	475.00
Speaking Dog, dated 1885, excellent	275.00

Tammany Hall, 1920 restrike, 5½x3½″	50.00
Tammany, marked	190.00
Tammany, unmarked	280.00
Teddy Roosevelt & The Bear, ci	490.00
The Magician, original	550.00
The Thing, from the Adams Family	30.00
Trick Pony, No. 272	425.00
Trick dog, blue base, VG	325.00
Uncle Sam, cast iron, 10″long	325.00
Uncle Wiggly, tin, Chein	110.00
Watch Dog Safe	235.00
Woodpecker, tin litho, Germany	20.00

Registering

Bee Hive, 1888	165.00
Buddy L Savings and Recording, 6″	80.00
Burdick Corbin Pat 1902, copper	48.00
Kingsbury Mfg Co. clock, metal	40.00
Milk Pail, registers pennies, iron	85.00
Trunk, cent & dime, nickel plated ci	55.00
Uncle Sam's 3 coin, Durable Toy/Novelty Co, metal, 6″	50.00
Uncle Sam's Register Bank, 6x4½″	50.00

Still

Abe Lincoln, glass bottle	8.00
Airplane, Cr-293, nickel plated steel, 8″ long	65.00
Airplane, Cr-506 similar, die cast & pressed tin, 7″long	275.00

Andy Gump on Stump, ci, telling fish story, 4½″	750.00
Andy Gump savings, lead	300.00
Angel in relief on top, boy & dog on side, 4x2½x2½″	28.00
Animal Bank, tin, Cr-397	60.00
Apple, Wh-299, cast iron, 5½x3½″	575.00
Arabian Safe, Wh-346	55.00
Aunt Jemima, cast iron	65.00
Auto w/people, Wh-159	480.00
Ball on base, iron	250.00
Bank building, bank over door, cast iron	55.00
Bank building, tin, 3¼x3¼x2½″	15.00
Bank building w/cupola, Wh-306	35.00
Bank building w/dome roof, small, Wh-424	20.00
Barrel, Wh-285, cast iron	75.00
Baseball Player, Wh-10, cast iron, 5¾″	95.00
Baseball on Three Bats, Wh-220, nickel plated ci, 5½″	400.00
Battleship Maine, Wh-142, ci, jappaned, 4½x4½″	200.00
Battleship Massachusetts, Wh-143, replaced parts, 6x10″	400.00
Battleship Oregon, Wh-144, cast iron, 4x5″	300.00
Battleship Oregon, Wh-146, replaced twist pin, ci, 5x6″	210.00
Beaky Buzzard & Tree Trunk, pot metal, 4¼″	50.00
Bear, glass bottle, 4½x2″	8.00
Bear, Honey Bear, Wh-257, ci, 2½″	675.00
Bear, standing, 5¾″, cast iron	85.00
Bear, standing, Wh-328, cast iron, 7″	400.00
Bear stealing pig, Wh-246	985.00
Beauty, Horse, Wh-82	50.00
Beehive, Wh-169, English, ci, 7x4¼″	110.00
Beehive, w/pointed finial, redware w/black slip, 6x4″	175.00
Billiken, Good Luck, cast iron	60.00
Bird on Stump, Wh-209, cast iron, 5″	210.00
Black Kewpie, chalkware	48.00
Black Sharecropper, cast iron	55.00
Bonzo, papier mache, nodder, 8½″	180.00
Boston Bull, seated	90.00
Boy Scout, Wh-14	75.00
Brown face boy in blue turban, majolica	60.00
Buffalo, Wh-208, iron w/good paint	85.00
Bugs Bunny & barrell, pot metal, 5½″	80.00
Bugs Bunny, cast metal	90.00
Building, ornate w/4 dormers, 1881, Wh-381	125.00
Building, Wh-421 iron w/good paint	30.00
Building w/4 towers, Wh-376	150.00
Bulldog, seated, Wh-105	35.00
Buster Brown & Tige, iron horseshoe	150.00
Camel, "Kabba", lying down position, brass, 4½″ long	90.00
Camel, large, Wh-201	225.00
Camel, Wh-202, iron w/good paint	80.00
Camel w/pack, Wh-256, ci, 2¾″	475.00
Captain Kidd, Wh-38, ci, 5¾″	230.00
Carpetbag, Cr-352, bronze, 5¾″ long	60.00
Carpenter, Harper, nickelplated, ci, 4½″	1,350.00
Cash Register, Wh-241, wire mesh & ci, 3¾″	70.00
Cat, chalkware, blue & white, mid 1800s, 9¾″	300.00
Cat, Feed the Kitty, nickeled pot metal, 5¼″	30.00
Cat, seated, cast iron w/old black & gold paint, 1900s, 5x4″	50.00
Cat, standing, Wh-245, ci, bronze finish, 6¾″ long	900.00
Cat Tub, Wh-53, good paint	80.00
Cat with Bow Tie, Wh-244, ci, 4½″	5.00
Charlie Chaplin by barrel, Wh-393	125.00
Charlie McCarthy, open mouth, pot metal	125.00
Christ Child w/Lamb, metal, orig yellow paint	45.00
Church, ci, tin base, pot metal steeple, 7½x7½″	100.00
Church, Wh-354, ci, English, 3x2¾″	200.00

Cinder box w/litho cover, tin, early 1900s	20.00
Circus Elephant, on hind legs, trunk to side	75.00
Clock, Wh-221, ci, molded face, 5″	220.00
Clock w/Pendulum, Wh-217	325.00
Clown, Wh-29, cast iron, 6¼″	85.00
Columbia Bank, Wh-430, electroplated ci, 6x4½″	250.00
Confederate Saddled Horse, Wh-79, ci, repainted, 4½″	120.00
Coronation Souvenir 1953, crown, nickel plated ci, 3″	20.00
Cottage, cast iron, 5¼x3¾″	120.00
Cow, Skinny, Wh-188, cast iron, 2½x4½″	75.00
Cow, Wh-200, cast iron, 3½″	55.00
Daffy Duck & Barrel, pot metal, 4½″	50.00
Deer, Wh-195, iron w/good paint	55.00
Dick Whittington, tin w/key	32.00
Doc Yak, Cr-84, cast iron, 4¾″	400.00
Dog, Boston Bull Standing, ci, 5¼″	35.00
Dog, Cr-197, aluminum	40.00
Dog, English Bulldog seated, cast iron, 4″	65.00
Dog on Tub, Wh-54, ci, 4″	65.00
Dog, Retriever, Wh-104, cast iron, 4½″	160.00
Dog, Scottie, Cr-199, ci, 3″	225.00
Dog, Spaniel, Wh-109, cast iron, 3¾x6″	95.00
Dog, Spitz, Wh-103, cast iron, 4¼″	150.00
Dog w/Pack, cast iron, 3¾″	65.00
Dog w/Pack, Wh-82, cast iron, 5½″	20.00
Dog w/Pack, Wh-106, cast iron, 2¾″	30.00
Donald Duck, compo, 1930	130.00
Donkey, large, Wh-197	120.00
Donkey w/saddle, Wh-198	40.00
Dopey dime bank	100.00
Duck on Tub, Wh-323, cast iron, 5½x3¼″	62.00
Duck, Wh-324, cast iron, repainted, 5″	70.00
Duck, Wh-325, cast iron, 4″	200.00
Dutch Girl, Wh-24, cast iron, 6½″	425.00
Dutch Girl, Wh-35, cast iron	85.00
Eagle, Wh-255, cast iron, 4″	75.00
Egg Man, cast iron, 4¼″	2,600.00
Elephant, GOP Kansas City 1928, ci, 6½″ long	100.00
Elephant, GOP, Wh-73, ci, 4″	120.00
Elephant on Bench on Tub, Wh-55, ci, 4″	65.00
Elephant on Tub, Wh-60, ci, 5¼″	60.00
Elephant, seated on base, Wh-66, ci, 4½″	350.00
Elephant, swivel trunk, ci, 3½″ long	130.00
Elephant, small, Wh-69, cast iron, 2½″	50.00
Elephant, Wh-67, good paint	25.00
Elephant, Wh-73, no letters, ci, 4″	60.00
Elephant w/howdah, Wh-64, cast iron, 3¾″	60.00
Elephant w/howdah, Wh-68, cast iron, 3″	35.00
Every Copper Helps, English Bobby, ci, 4¾″	750.00
Fireman, Wh-9, cast iron, 5½″	340.00
Fish, IFC, cast iron, 7″ long	850.00
Flatiron Building, Wh-410, cast iron, 8¼″	160.00
Football Player, Wh-12	230.00
Foxy Grandpa, Wh-23, cast iron, 5½″	375.00
Frog, Professor Pug, Wh-230, cast iron, 3¼″	240.00
Gas Pump, Cr-467, cast iron, 5¾″	200.00
General Butler, Wh-294, cast iron, 6¾″	1,600.00
General Pershing, Wh-312, cast iron	100.00
George Washington	20.00
German Shepherd, iron w/orig paint, 9″	75.00
Globe, on base, pressed steel, 8″	25.00
Globe on Stand, embossed cast iron, 4½″	120.00
Globe w/Eagle, Wh-510, cast iron	150.00
Goats, 2 w/heads together, Wh-262, ci, 4½″	900.00

Graf Zeppelin, Wh-171, cast iron, 1¾x6¾″	60.00
Grandpa's Hat, top hat, 2″	60.00
Hanging Mail Box, Wh-382	50.00
Home Budget Bank Tudor, heavy tin	45.00
Home Savings Bank, Wh-375, cast iron, 5¾″	50.00
Horse, My Pet, Wh-85, ci, 4x5″	45.00
Horse on Tub, no saddle, Cr-139, fine	150.00
Horse w/Fly Net, Wh-80, cast iron, 4″	400.00
Horse, w/saddle, Wh-86, cast iron, 2¾″	65.00
House w/chimney, cast iron, some wear on paint, 3″	35.00
House, Wh-307, cast iron	35.00
House, w/porch, Wh-377, cast iron	95.00
House, wood, 1915, 7x5x5″	45.00

Humpty Dumpty	38.00
Indian Chief, Cr-104, pot metal, 3¼″	50.00
Indian Family, Harper, electroplated cast iron, 4″	750.00
Indian, Wh-39, standing w/hand shading eyes, ci, 6″	240.00
Jackie Robinson dime bank	100.00
Junior Cash Register, nickel plated ci, 4¼x3″	45.00
Kitten w/Bow	35.00
Liberty Bell 1876, Cr-376 variation, ci w/paper label	45.00
Liberty Bell, 1919	38.00
Liberty Bell, 1938 Iowa Womens Relief Corps, ci, 3½″	40.00
Liberty Bell, 1968 Wallace, cast iron, 3½″	10.00
Liberty Bell, Wh-279	25.00
Liberty Bell, Harper, electroplated ci, 4″	245.00
Lincoln High Hat, Wh-259	70.00
Lion, head slot, iron	40.00
Lion on Tub, cord in mouth, Wh-57, cast iron, 5½″	100.00
Lion, slot in forehead, applied features, sewer tile, 8″	170.00
Lion, Wh-91, cast iron, 3½″	15.00
Lion, Wh-93, tail on left leg, ci, 4x5½″	50.00
Lion, Wh-94, cast iron, 2½″	65.00
Lost Dog, cast iron, 5½″	600.00
Lucky Joe, glass	12.00
Lucky Jumbo, glass bottle	10.00
Mail Box, hole for hanging, 5x2½″	52.00
Mail Box w/eagle, small, cast iron	20.00
Mammy, hands on hips, Wh-20, cast iron, 5¼″	200.00
Mammy w/Clothes Basket, Cr-67, pot metal, 5¼″	160.00
Mammy, w/Spoon, black ci, 8″, G	95.00
Mammy w/Spoon, Wh-17, cast iron, 6″	40.00
Mascott-Boy on Baseball, partial repaint, ci, 5¾″	1,000.00
Mermaid, Wh-5, cast iron, 4½x4″	500.00

Mickey Mouse leatherette treasure chest **175.00**
Mickey Mouse Phone, 1930 . . . . **150.00**
Monkey, Thank You, tin **35.00**
Monkeys, three, Wh-236, cast iron, 3¼" **130.00**
Mother Goose, cast iron **165.00**
Mule, Wh-198, iron w/good paint **60.00**
Mulligan the Cop, Wh-8, cast iron, 5¾" **80.00**
Mutt & Jeff, Wh-13, ci, 5¼" **160.00**
Negro w/two faces, 3¼" **85.00**
Negro, Wh-42 . . . . **125.00**
Ohio Buckeye, cast iron **20.00**
Oriental Boy Baby on Pillow, cast iron, 5¼" **85.00**
Oriental Girl w/Mandolin, Wh-342, cast iron, 7" **140.00**
Owl on Stump, Wh-204, cast iron, 5" **135.00**
Owl, Wh-203, cast iron, 4¼" **90.00**
Panda Bear, Wh-229, cast iron **35.00**
Parlor Stove, Wh-138, cast iron, 7" **120.00**
Parrot on Tree Stump, cast iron, 6½" **525.00**
Peaceful Bill, Smiling Jim, Harper, electroplated ci, 4" **1,000.00**
Peters Weatherbird, Cr-15, ci, 4¼" **1,000.00**
Pig, Decker's, iron **75.00**
Pig, Rockingham brown, rust and cream, 4x6" **75.00**
Pig, Wh-184, cast iron, 4" wide **50.00**
Pig, Wh-179, iron w/good paint **30.00**
Pinochio, by barrel, metal **125.00**
Polar Bear Standing, cast iron, repainted, 6" **25.00**
Porky Pig & Barrell, pot metal, 4½" **80.00**
Porky Pig, Wh-27, cast iron, 5¾" **130.00**
Possum, on base, Wh-206, cast iron, 4¾" **2,300.00**
Possum, Wh-205 . . . . **400.00**
Prancing Horse, Wh-77 . . . . **25.00**
Prancing Pony, iron, 4¼" **40.00**
Puppy Dog, Cr-202, cast iron, 5x4" **40.00**
Rabbit on Base, Wh-97, ci, no paint, 2¼x2¾" **450.00**
Radio, Cr-446, pressed steel & nickeled ci, 3¼" **55.00**
Radio, upright console, combination lock, 4½" **60.00**
Radio, Wh-140, cast iron, 4" **55.00**
Refrigerator, cast iron, 3½" **60.00**
Republican Pig, cast iron, repainted 7" **45.00**
Rhino, Wh-252, cast iron repainted, 2¾" **120.00**
Rocking Chair, Wh-277, ci, 7" **775.00**
Rocking Horse, Still Bank Collectors Club, ci **300.00**
Roller Safe, iron **60.00**
Rooster, Polish, Wh-186, cast iron, 5½" **1,300.00**
Rooster, Wh-198, iron w/good paint **70.00**
Rudolph Reindeer, w/nose that lights, white metal . . . **15.00**
Sack of Chicken Feed, cast iron **50.00**
Safe, J & E Stevens Co, cast iron **55.00**
Sailor, Cr-55, small, cast iron, 5¼" **110.00**
Sailor, Wh-16, large, cast iron, 5¾" **145.00**
Santa, asleep in chair, painted plaster, 7" **35.00**
Santa, at chimney, painted lead, 4¼" **55.00**
Santa, sitting, hands on knees, painted plaster, 12" . . **45.00**
Santa, w/tree, cast iron, 5¾" **350.00**
Scotsman's Head, red hair w/green tam, Staffordshire, 3¾" . . . **125.00**
Scotty Dog, Wh-108, cast iron, 3¼" **80.00**
Scotty Dog, seated, Wh-110, cast iron, 5" **70.00**
Seal, Wh-199, cast iron, 3½x4¼" **190.00**
Sharecropper, Wh-18, cast iron, 5½" **50.00**
Shell, Wh-293, Shell Out, ci, with trap, 2½" **225.00**
Ship, Wh-249, When My Fortune Ship Comes In, ci, 5½" long . **15.00**
Sniffles & Barrell, pot metal, 5¼" **90.00**
Soldier, Wh-7, with gun, cast iron, 5½" **400.00**
Spaniel, Staffordshire, 4¼" **45.00**

Sparkle Plenty, boy w/arms extended **12.00**
Squirrel, w/nut, Wh-250 . . . . **525.00**
State Bank, Wh-442, cast iron, 3x2" **140.00**
State Bank, Wh-443, cast iron, 4¼x3" **40.00**
Statue of Liberty, Wh-268, cast iron, 9½" **160.00**
Statue of Liberty, Wh-269, cast iron **60.00**
Stop Light, Wh-233, nickel plated ci, 5¾" **130.00**
Stop Light, Wh-234, cast iron, 4½" **160.00**
Street Clock, Wh-219, cast iron, 6" **325.00**
Streetcar, cast iron, 2¾" **400.00**
Streetcar, Main St, Wh-164, w/people, ci, 6¾" **400.00**
Streetcar, Wh-166, cast iron, 6¾" **190.00**
Tally-Ho, Wh-168, ci, English, 4¾x4½" **100.00**
Tank, Wh-162, cast iron **75.00**
Teddy Roosevelt, bust, Wh-309 . . . . **235.00**
Terrier, seated, ci, 4¾" **85.00**
Thrifty Pig, Wh-175, cast iron, 6¾" **35.00**
Time Around The World, Wh-172, paper & ci, 3¾x2½" . . . **75.00**
Tiny Horse, Wh-86 . . . . **225.00**
Trolley Car, Wh-265, cast iron, 4½" **140.00**
Trunk, on handtruck, nickeled iron, w/combination, 5" long . . **110.00**
Turkey, Wh-139, cast iron, 2½" long **260.00**
US Mail, cast iron, 4x3½x1½" **20.00**
Uncle Wiggly, tin, Cr-280 . . . . **58.00**
Victorian House, 2 chimneys, cole slaw decor, Staffordshire . . **75.00**
Washington Monument, Wh-364, cast iron, 7½" **225.00**
Westwood Memorial, Cr-556, ci, 5¼" wide **50.00**
White City Puzzle Bank No 2, Cr-415, nickled iron, 3¼" . . **70.00**
White City Puzzle Barrel No 1, Wh-285, nickled iron, 3½" . . **60.00**
Woolworth Building, Wh-386, cast iron, 8" **80.00**
Woolworth Building, Wh-387, small, cast iron **40.00**
WWI Big Bertha Bomb, iron cross w/1914, 6¾" **165.00**
WWI Cannon Shell, Wh-385 . . . . **32.00**
WWI Hat, Wh-167, pressed steel, 3¾" wide **60.00**
WWI Helmet, U S Bank, brass eagle, pressed steel, 1¾" . . **50.00**
WWI Soldier, Wh-40 . . . . **350.00**
WWI Tank, Wh-169 . . . . **175.00**
WWII German Munsingen Helmet, pressed steel, 2¼" . . **400.00**
Young Nigger, Wh-42, cast iron, 4½" **90.00**
Zeppelin, Wh-171, good paint **130.00**

Barber Shop Collectibles

From as long ago as the 12th century, the barber has been a part of recorded history. The red and white colors of the barber pole traditionally represent the period when the barber was also the blood-letter, and ancient treatment for nearly any disease. Not until late in the 19th century was the patriotic blue added. Today's collectors are searching for these old poles, fancy chairs, barber bottles and shaving mugs from the past. Mugs and razors will be listed in separate sections.

Backbar, oak, beveled mirrors, wall mount, 5½x13' **1,200.00**
Backbar, oak, marble top, 15' **2,000.00**
Belt razor strap, leather, copper, wood handle, 1800s, w/box . . **35.00**
Bottles
Azure satin glass, silver overlay Nouveau flowers **195.00**
Bay Rum label, ribbed clambroth, bell-flower variant **295.00**
Blown cut glass, ruby, 10" **125.00**
Blue, white & clear spatter, 8" **32.00**
Blue Fern opalescent glass **95.00**
Colbalt blue, enamelled decor, wht milk glass stopper . . **60.00**
Cobalt blue, heavy enamelled daisies, gold leaves **100.00**
Cranberry, w/opalescent hobs, polished pontil **145.00**
Cranberry Swirl opalescent glass **110.00**

Heart & Thumbprint.................................. **60.00**
Hobbs, Brockunier, blue.............................. **80.00**
Intaglio cut, reticulated silver encasement & stopper **80.00**
Porcelain, hand painted roses decor, Bay Rum **65.00**

Bottle, quilted, blue w/enameling, 10½"................. **100.00**
Ruby frosted **32.00**

Chair, cherrywood, western era, restored................ **2,000.00**
Chair, Koken, wooden, good restorable condition **495.00**
Chair, oak, brass, leather seat & back.................. **1,500.00**
Chair, Paidar..................................... **250.00**
Chair, walnut, red velvet back insert & head rest **300.00**
Chair, wht marble w/red leather, iron filigree foot rest **400.00**
Chair, wooden, Pride of the West casting on base **2,000.00**
Hand clippers, metal, 1920s......................... **20.00**
Mustache/hair curler, w/alcohol heater, folding............. **50.00**
Photo, tin type, barber in shop, late 1800s **35.00**
Pole, 19th century hanging type, 32"................... **200.00**
Pole, floor model, porcelain, 8'x16" dia................. **395.00**
Pole, glass over revolving stripes, metal top/bottom, 26" **170.00**
Pole, key wound, restored **395.00**
Pole, Kochs..................................... **80.00**
Pole, Koken, ci, world's largest--9', no globe, needs paint ... **1,250.00**
Pole, leaded glass, mint restored, 34"................. **1,195.00**
Pole, leaded glass, porcelain top & bottom, 1920s, 34" **1,150.00**
Pole, window display, 19" **135.00**
Pole, wooden w/acorn finials, good folk art **325.00**
Razor strap, leather, Double Duck **12.00**
Razor strap, old **9.00**
Shaving mug rack, oak w/pigeonholes, carved top **300.00**
Shaving stand, oak, with mirror, 1900 .... **350.00**
Shoeshine chair, oak on wood base, iron footrest **500.00**
Shoeshine stand, wood base, wrought iron chair & footrest ... **300.00**
Sign, porcelain, square, curving, Barber Shop **50.00**
Sign, Wildroot w/embossed pole **60.00**
Sterilizer jar, clambroth, w/cover, star **37.00**
Stropper, Twinplex, w/display carton, metal case, directions **20.00**

Baskets

Unlike furniture, pottery, folk art, and glassware, there were relatively
few collectors of baskets in the decades prior to the 1970s. A study of antiques related magazines from the 1920s through the 1960s seldom turns
up advertisements or articles about country baskets.

A series of magazine articles in the early 1970s that displayed collectors' homes with handcrafted baskets hanging from pine beams probably
created a demand that had not previously existed.

From the mid 1970s until early 1980 basket prices probably increased
by ¼ to ½ each year. A cheese or curd basket that sold for $125 in 1975
was difficult to find for $350-$450 in 1982. In recent years the demand for
baskets has not grown as rapidly and the prices asked for baskets in shops
and at shows have tended to level off slightly.

When a basket approaches the price of a piece of country furniture,
most collectors would rather purchase the table, trunk, or small cupboard
than the comparably priced basket.

The most valuable baskets are those designed for a specific purpose
rather than the more commonly found utility baskets that had multiple uses.
The most costly forms include cheese baskets used to separate curds from
whey, fruit drying baskets, "lighthouse" baskets from Nantucket,
Massachusetts, herb gathering baskets, and finely woven Shaker miniature
baskets.

Most of the handcrafted baskets that collectors are still finding were
made in the period between the 1860s and the early 1900s. The invention
of the veneering machine in the late 1800s made splint quickly and inex-
pensively available to large basket factories that put the slower crafts people out of business. Factory made baskets with thick, wide splint cut by the
machine still have little value. Most can be found in the $10-$15 range in
most antique shops.

Amana Colony, oval unstripped willow, oak handle, 19x15x15" . **87.00**
Amana Colony, oval willow, pegged on oak handle, 16x12" **75.00**
Apple picker, oak splint, kicked in back, N. Y. **300.00**
Bobbin, green paint, wall hanging **125.00**
Buttocks, egg, double thick splint handle, 7½x9½" **125.00**
Buttocks, miniature, wide split handle, 4¼x3¼" **225.00**
Buttocks, ribbed, oak splint, w/handle **185.00**
Buttocks, ribbed, well made, 11" dia **175.00**
Buttocks, turned loop handle w/X at bottom, 10½x10" **140.00**
Buttocks, white oak, split handle, 7x12"................. **75.00**
Buttocks, X at handle, 6x7" **170.00**
Charcoal, open weave oak splint, carved, notched handle **150.00**
Cheese, good color, symmetry, 24"..................... **325.00**
Cheese, hexagon weave, 26" **465.00**
Cheese, large, 19th century, mint **595.00**
Cheese, open hexagon weave, New England, 26" **385.00**
Cheese, Shaker, hexagon weave, oak splint, 14" dia **500.00**
Cheese, splint, 10" dia............................. **140.00**
Cheese, splint, 18" dia............................. **235.00**
Cheese, splint, 20" dia............................. **230.00**
Cheese, splint, 26" dia............................. **265.00**
Cheese, splint, miniature, 1½" dia **65.00**
Cradle, pine floor, oak rim, stained, early 1800s, 16x41"..... **700.00**
Drying, footed, mortise & tendon constructed frame, 30x14x12" **400.00**
Egg, buttocks form, ribbed oak splint..................... **185.00**
Egg, flat back, twig handle, crude **100.00**
Egg, miniature, willow & splint, 6x5½x5" **125.00**
Egg, open weave splint, ash rim, splint wrapped handle, 1800s **270.00**
Egg, splint, wrapped handle, 11½"..................... **285.00**
Farm, painted, carved hickory handle, New England, 15"..... **200.00**
Feather, green paint, Shaker, slide cover **250.00**
Feather, w/swinging lid, carved handle, blue decor, 9x7½".... **140.00**
Feather, woven on mold, slide cover, ash splint............ **165.00**
Field, 16x32" **350.00**
Field, oak splint, carved bow handles, 14x18x9" **85.00**
Field, open plaited, Ill., 28" dia **385.00**
Field, oval w/carved handle, plaited weave, 22" long **225.00**

Field, ribbed, checkered, carved oak handles **200.00**
Field, woven splint, hand carved handles, 12½" **150.00**
Fruit drying, pine frame, ash splint, mortised ribs **350.00**
Garden, braided handle, ribbed oak splint, 13x18x32" **300.00**
Garden, plaited, wide splint, oak handle **85.00**

Half buttocks, 9x6" **150.00**
Herb tray, X-bound rim wrap, oak splint **125.00**
Horse feeding, splint **250.00**
Indian, splint, covered, painted and potato stamped **110.00**
Indian, splint, open, 2-handled, rectangular, potato stamped **90.00**
Indian, sq bottom, round top, floral decor, w/handle, 8x6½" . . **175.00**
Kidney, oak splint, handled, early 1900s, 14x14x14" **80.00**
Knife & fork, divided, green paint, bow handle, 5x11x6½" . . . **145.00**
Long Island eel pot **250.00**
Market, oak splint, checker, w/handle **130.00**
Market, ribbed oak splint w/twist handles **185.00**
Market, ribbed, oak splint, twist handle, large **260.00**
Market, ribbed, oak splint, twist handle, large **260.00**
Melon, mini, ribbed ash splint w/hickory handle, 5" dia **115.00**
Melon, miniature, 5¼x5" dia **125.00**
Miniature, carved handle, painted decorations, double rim **350.00**
Nantucket Lightship, nest of five, signed & dated **3,200.00**
Nantucket Lightship, ribbed, turned pine bottom, early 1900s . **350.00**
Nantucket, miniature, splint, circular, swing handle **435.00**
Pie carrier, holds 2, ash w/copper rivets, 2 handles **225.00**
Rectangular, oak handle, 16x15" **60.00**
Rice, straw, Pennsylvania German flower pattern **275.00**
Sewing, ribbed, demi-john bottom, double wrap rim **125.00**
Splint, berry-dyed decor, fixed loop handle, 11x5½x11" **175.00**
Splint, blue & red plaid, fixed handle, wrapped rim, 11x11" . . **175.00**
Storage, checkerwork, painted, hickory splint wrapped rim **95.00**
Storage, ribbed, oak splint w/hickory twist handle, 16x25" . . . **350.00**
Storage, tightly woven on mold, carved bows, ribbed, 13" . . . **1,400.00**
Storage, twig handle, pine feet, crude **110.00**
Swing handle, blue paint, wide steeples, mid 1800s **375.00**
Swing handle, green paint, carved ears, raised base, 15x16" . . **270.00**
Swing handle, splint, cylindrical, inverted bottom, 16" **235.00**
Swing handle, woven over mold, ribbed, New England **275.00**
Table, rectangular base, oval top, shallow, painted **110.00**
Tray, square, oak splint, handle **145.00**
Utility, drop handle, square bottom, round top, ribbed **250.00**

Utility, oak splint, hickory handle, 15" dia **220.00**
Utility, rye straw coil construction, 1 handle, 14" **150.00**
Wall basket **125.00**
Wicker, cloth liner, old, 14" **20.00**
Winnowing, openweave oak splint, wide loop handles **375.00**

Batchelder

Bowl, wide ribs, cast, stippled blue, 3x6" **65.00**
Tile, glazed geometric, marked "Los Angeles", 6x6" **35.00**
Tile, Mayan, engobe, marked "Pasadena", 6x6" **75.00**
Vase, plain, cast, pale purple, 9½" **125.00**

Battersea

Battersea is a term that refers to enameling on copper or other metal. Though originally produced at Battesea, England in the mid-18th century, the craft was later practiced throughout the Staffordshire district. Boxes are the most common examples, some are figurals and many bear an inscription.

Box, Accept this Trifle, w/female **425.00**
Box, bird figural, hinged, florals 2x2" **650.00**
Box, courting vignette, florals, hinged, 1x3½x2" **525.00**
Box, gherkin shape, hinged, blue/green, 2½" **550.00**
Box, hinged, Britannia, cupids, interior portrait, 1¾x2½x3½" . . **600.00**
Box, hinged, harbor scene & florals, 3x2½" **325.00**
Box, hinged, Moses in the bullrushes, 1x2½x2" **550.00**
Box, hinged, oval, scenic & floral decor, 1x2½x2" **400.00**
Box, May You Be Happy, small **145.00**
Box, Nelson's Victory, anchor, oval **225.00**
Box, Pump Room Bath, oval **160.00**
Box, rabbit figural, w/inscription, repaired, 1¼x1¾" **800.00**
Box, walnut figural, brown, 1¾x2¼" **400.00**

Box, yellow & white w/florals, 2x4" **300.00**
Case, cylinder, holds cut glass perfume, tape measure **775.00**
Patch box, A Token of Regard, inside mirror **135.00**
Patch box, dog's head **325.00**
Salt, cartouche decor w/gilt, 1 3/8" **85.00**
Snuff, lady & child in garden, 1x2x1½" **300.00**

Bauer

The J. A. Bauer Pottery operated in Los Angeles, Ca., from 1909 until 1962. Their initial products were redware pots, utilitarian stoneware and garden pottery. In 1916, they won a bronze medal at the Pacific Interna-

tional Exposition for a line of molded artware. The colorful tableware for which they are best known was introduced in 1932. Their first line, Ring, was made originally in 8 colors including black, which is highly prized by today's collectors. Other popular patterns were Moderne, 1935; Smooth, 1936; Speckware, 1946; and Monterey Moderne, 1948.

Bowl, ribbed, cobalt, #36, 5¾″	5.00
Ring, cereal, 5″	7.00
Ring, cobalt, #12	25.00
Ribbed, yellow, #24, 7½″	7.00
Soup, Ring, green, 7½″	10.00
Butter dish, Ring, round w/cover, green	35.00
Cake plate w/pedestal base, Monterey, turquoise	50.00
Candleholders, 3 lite, pink, 8″	25.00
Carafe w/lid, Ring, orange	50.00
Chop plate, Ring, yellow, 13″	15.00
Creamer & sugar w/lid, Ring	18.00
Cup & saucer, Ring, green	20.00
Juice tumbler, Ring, red	10.00
Yellow	9.00
Mixing bowl, Ring, #12, green	20.00
Orange, #9	40.00
Pitcher, Ring 3 qt, orange	50.00
Planter, swan, pink, 10″	20.00
Plate, Ring, 6″, yellow	4.50
Green, 8″	7.00
Green, 9″	10.00
Sandwich plate, Ring, 17″	20.00
Shakers, large, pr	10.00
Teapot, Aladdin, wide ribs, 8 cup, yellow	30.00
Tumbler, Ring, green, 4½″	15.00
Vase, Ring, cylindrical, black, 8″	50.00

Bavaria

Bavaria, Germany, was long the center of that country's pottery industry; in the 1800s, many firms operated in and around the area. China ware vases, novelties and table accessories were decorated by hand by artists who sometimes signed their work. The examples here are marked with 'Bavaria', and the logos of some of the various companies who were located there.

Ashtray, Disney, Minnie Mouse decor, 1932, 3½x3½″	25.00
Basket, blue w/floral decor, gilt handle & trim, Thomas Bavaria, 7x7″	65.00
Bowl, autumn leaves & purple berries decor, gold border	30.00
Covered, w/pink pansies decor, 4½″ dia	27.00
Cream soup, cream w/dk florals, gold rim, w/underplate	9.00
Fruit decor, pierced edge, oval, 12½″	45.00
Cake plate, decorated w/6 large pink & yellow roses, 11″ dia	16.00
Cake set, 7 pc, different color & floral decor for each plate	280.00
Celery tray, pink & wht rose decor, gold trim, 12″ long	32.00
Poppies & leaves decor, gold trim, 10x4½″	15.00
Chocolate pot, beige w/leaves & berries decor, gold trim	65.00
White w/roses decor, gold trim	35.00
Chocolate set, pearlized w/lavender bands, 13 pc	100.00
Coffee set, wht w/grey geometrics, pot, creamer & covered sugar	25.00
Cookie jar, Roman Key border, 2 handles, covered, large	37.00
Cracker jar	95.00
Cup & saucer, demitasse, overall floral decor on burdundy	20.00
Disney, Mickey & Minnie decor, gold trim, 1932	45.00
Gravy w/attached underplate, multicolor florals, scrolls, gold	12.00
Hair receiver, lavendar & yellow w/hp florals	15.00
Jardiniere, footed, scenic w/deer	48.00
Mug, 'Favorite', hp grapes on rust background	58.00
Pickle dish, rose decor, handled	18.00

Pitcher, raspberries decor	80.00
Plate, cobalt, gold roses, 10¾″	48.00
Disney, Mickey & Minnie decor, gold rim, 1932, 6¼″	45.00
Disney, Mickey & Minnie decor, gold rim, 1932, 7½″	55.00
Gold, green, brown w/acorns, signed Cranley, 7″	20.00
Portrait, bust of lady w/1890s hair style, gold trim, Mignon	36.50
Portrait, Indian, 10½″ dia	60.00
Portrait, Josephine	48.00
Portrait, Martha Washington, gold bands, Thomas, 9¾″	60.00
Portrait, Napolean	48.00
Red Riding Hood & Wolf decor, early, 7″	35.00
Powder jar, daisy decor, gold trim & finial	16.00
Salt dip, roses decor, pearlized inside, 3 feet	6.00
Sugar, covered, Disney, Mickey & Minnie decor, 1932, 4½x6½″	125.00
Tea set, child's blue w/silver overlay design, 15 pc	190.00
Toothpick holder, pink roses decor, barrel shape	23.00
Tray, parrots & floral decor, reticulated edge, oval, 13x7½″	60.00
Vase, bulbous, roses & acron decor, 10½″	75.00
Pink, yellow & red roses decor, gold looped handles, 11½″	85.00

Beehive

The beehive mark was originally used in 1720 on Royal Vienna, a highly decorated porcelain made in Vienna by Claude Innocentius de Paquier. Since then, both the ware and the mark have been widely copied. In the examples listed below, R V indicates Royal Vienna.

Bowl, A Kauffmann, 11x8″	235.00
Bowl, aqua & white w/relief & hp florals, gold, R V, 10″	100.00
Bowl, shallow, R V, 7″	105.00
Box, round w/classic scene, 2¾″	55.00
Celery tray, scalloped, portrait, florals, gold, 14″	75.00
Clock set, 3 pc, figural decorations, clock 9½″	1,200.00
Cup, saucer, cake plate, 7½″, A Kauffmann, heavy gold	90.00
Dresser box, portrait, gold beads & scrolls, covered, signed	125.00
Game plate, deep red w/gold trim, R V, 9″	100.00
Hanging bowl, A Kauffmann, Royal Vienna, 10″	125.00
Jar w/cover, Grecian lady, gold pine cones, ivy, R V, 7½″	230.00
Plate, brunette w/rose in hair, gold decor, signed, 8½″	95.00
Plate, Madonna portrait	85.00
Plate, monk drinking from mug, maroon & gold, R V, 12″	185.00
Plate, portrait of Constance, Austrian, 8″	295.00
Plate, portrait by Kauffmann, relief gold, 10″	110.00
Plate, portrait by Roberto, heavy gold, R V	650.00
Plate, portrait of Venus, signed Wagner, R V	675.00
Plate, portrait of young lady w/lilacs, R V, 10″	150.00
Plate, Queen Louise, signed Donath, R V, 9″	290.00

Tea set, service for 2, 2 sizes of cups, 2 urns, R V	1,500.00

Urn w/cap & underplate, scenic w/people, gold, R V, 19" . . . **2,200.00**
Urn, w/cap, gold snake handles, Venus, round base, R V, 18". **500.00**
Urn w/cap, scenic w/people, gold decor, R V, 14" **400.00**
Urn w/lid, colorful, much gold, 11" **165.00**
Urn, maroon w/gold beading, Remer, Geheimniss, 7" **75.00**
Vase, w/handles, A Kauffmann, women & child, gold, 9½" **80.00**
Vase w/handles, classical scene, R V, 6x6" **150.00**
Vase, w/handles, scenic decor, gold trim, 6½" **75.00**
Vase, girl w/harp, brown lustre, w/gold trim, Wagner, 14" . . . **525.00**
Vase, maidens & cupids, magenta w/gold **125.00**
Vase, owl, gold branches, pine needles, satin finish, R V, 6" . . . **95.00**
Vase, portrait by Wagner, 2 handles, R V, 9" **450.00**
Vase, w/handles, scenic w/gold trim, 10½" **140.00**
Vase, worship of Cora, R V, 8" **185.00**

Beer Cans

When the flat top can was first introduced in 1934 it came with printed instructions on how to use the triangle punch opener. Cone top, which are rare today, were patented in 1935 by the Continental Can Company. By the 1960s aluminum cans with pull tabs had made both types obsolete.

The hobby of collecting beer cans has been rapidly gaining momentum over the past ten years. Series types such as South African Brewery, Lion, and the Cities Series by Schmit and Tucker are especially popular.

Condition is an important consideration when evaluating market price. Grade 1 must be in like new condition, with no rust. However, the triangular punch hole is acceptable. Cans in less than excellent condition devaluate sharply.

Adler Brau, straight side steel **10.00**
Alpen Brau, Potosi, straight side steel **4.00**
Alpine, crimped steel **5.00**
Alpine, flat top **6.00**
Alpine, straight side steel **7.00**
Alt Heidelberg, flat top **80.00**
Amber Brau, straight side steel **8.00**
Arrow, Globe **4.00**
Ballantine Bock, flat top **22.50**
Becker's, flat top **8.00**
Berghoff Draft, straight side steel **12.00**
Billy Beer, bottom opened, 6 cans **12.00**
Black Horse Ale, pull top **1.00**
Black Label, black can, straight side steel **9.00**
Black Label, silver can, straight side steel **7.00**
Bohack Draft, aluminum **9.00**
Bohack Premium, aluminum **9.00**
Bonanza, pull top **14.00**
Brau Haus, straight side steel **8.00**
Brown Derby, Los Angeles, flat top **38.00**
Brown Derby, Maier, straight side steel **6.00**
Bull Frog, flat top **22.50**
Burgie!, Burgermeister, straight side steel **5.00**
Canadian Ace Bock, straight side steel **22.00**
Chief Oshgosh, straight side steel **8.00**
Circle Beer, flat top **7.50**
Circle, straight side steel **10.00**
Coburger, Old Dutch, straight side steel **10.00**
Corona, flat top **52.50**
Crystal Colorado, straight side steel **6.00**
Denver, flat top **24.00**
Drewery's Draft, crimped steel **3.00**

Du Bois, pull top **12.50**
Duke, straight side steel **8.50**
Einbock, straight side steel **7.50**
Excell, flat top **115.00**
F & G Drewerys **45.00**
Fabacher Bray, pull top **15.00**
Fisher B, Lucky, straight side steel **7.00**
Frankenmuth Light, straight side steel **9.00**
Gambrinus, pull top **2.50**
Garten Brau, straight side steel **6.50**
Gilley's No 2 . . . . **3.00**
Gipps Amerlin, flat top **28.00**
Grand Lager, pull top **5.00**
Great Lakes, straight side steel **16.00**
Hanley Pisner, flat top **6.50**
Hoffman House, straight side steel **9.00**
Holiday Bock, straight side steel **10.00**
Holland Brand, flat top **48.00**
Hynne, flat top **8.50**
Iriquois Draft Ale, pop top **30.00**
Iron City Beer Drinker's **2.50**
J R Beer **2.50**
Jamaica Sun, straight side steel **25.00**
King's, flat top **12.00**
King's Prem, Chicago **20.00**
Leisy's Dortmunder, flat top **50.00**
Lubeck, flat top **42.50**
Lucky Lager No 1672 . . . . **7.00**
Metz, green can, flat top **28.00**
Mickey's Malt Liquor, flat top **45.00**
Miller High Life, black **17.00**
Mountain Brew, Pull top **20.00**
Mustang Malt Liquor, 16 oz **20.00**
National Bohemian, flat top **20.00**
National Bohemian Bock, straight side steel **19.00**
Northern, yellow can, flat top **7.50**
Ohio Flag **2.00**
Old St Louis, flat top **50.00**
Old Style, Heilemn, crimped steel **3.00**
Old Tavern, old type **16.00**
Old Tavern, straight side steel **16.00**
Old Topper, cone top **70.00**
Orbit, flat top **22.50**
Original $1000, Gettlemen **15.00**
Paul Bunyan, flat top **110.00**
Pikes Pike Malt Liquor **32.50**
Queen's Brau, straight side steel **13.00**
R & H, flat top **145.00**
Rainier ale, cone top **65.00**
Razorback **2.00**
Renner, straight side steel **6.00**
Rolling Rock, flat top **10.00**
Rolling Rock, pull top **6.00**
Schlitz, old style, No. 2566 . . . . **9.00**
Schmidt's Ale, flat top **35.00**
Stite Malt Liquor, flat top **6.00**
Sunshine, rays, straight side steel **24.00**
Tex, Jackson, straight side steel **25.00**
Tiger Ale, cone top, 32 oz **28.00**
Van Dyke Export, pull top **20.00**
Velvet Glove Malt Liquor, pull top, 16 oz **25.00**
Walter's Bock B, straight side steel **25.00**
Wielands, miniature **25.00**
Wilco B, straight side steel **18.00**

Beleek, See Specific Manufacturers

Belleek is a very thin translucent porcelain that takes its name from the district in Ireland where it originated in 1857. The glaze is a creamy ivory color with a pearl like luster. Tablewares, baskets, figurines and such have been produced; Shamrock, Tridacna, Echinus and Lotus are but a few of the many patterns.

It is possible to date an example to within 20 to 30 years of manufacture by the mark. Pieces with an early stamp often bring prices nearly double that of a similar but later piece. With some variation, the marks have always incorporated the wolfhound, castle, harp and shamrock. Three of these were in black, used from 1863 until 1946, and three were in green, used from '46 until the present.

Aberdeen, cup & saucer, 2nd blk mk, white	250.00
Jug, 3rd blk mk, pearl, 6″	225.00
Vase, 2nd blk mk, 6″	225.00
Vase, 3rd blk mk, 6″	190.00
Vase, 3rd grn mk, 6″	68.00
Artichoke, cup & saucer, lst blk mk	200.00

Basket, applied roses, thistles, shamrocks, 1900, 12″ long	400.00
Basket, heart shape, 4 strand, braided corners 2x4″	190.00
Basket, heart shape, bud border, 4 strand	285.00
Basket w/cover, 3 strand, bird finial, very early	3,000.00
Basket w/cover, oval, 3 strand, 11½″	2,850.00
Blarney, creamer, 2nd blk mk, 4″	200.00
Teapot, 2nd blk mk, pink & gold trim, 7″	465.00
Bow & Ribbon, creamer, grn mk	20.00
Bowl, lattice w/shamrocks, roses, 1920, 5½″	295.00
Bowl, oval, reticulated, 3rd blk mk, 4x6½″	245.00
Bust of Clytie, 3rd blk mk	850.00
Cake server, 4 strand, large	285.00
Celtic, bread plate, 3rd grn mk, taffy trim	62.00
Sugar & cream, 3rd blk mk, taffy glaze	130.00
Vase, 2nd blk mk, blue decorated	495.00
Churn, miniature, 3rd grn mk, 2¼″	22.00
Cleary, spill, 4¾″	40.00
Conch shell, 2nd black mark, 4x6″	495.00
Condiment, 3 shells w/coral handle, 1st blk mk, 8″ dia	500.00
Cone teapot, 2nd blk mk, pink, gold trim	400.00
Corn vase, 1st blk mk, pearl, 6½″	345.00
Cornucopia, 2nd blk mk, pink trim, 3½″	110.00
Dolphin, comport, 1st blk mk	735.00
Dolphin, spill, 3rd grn mk, 6¼″	45.00
Double Shell, sugar & creamer, 3rd blk mk	120.00
Echinus, cup & saucer, 1st blk mk, white	200.00
Teapot, cream & sugar, 1st blk mk	800.00
Tray, 1st blk mk, pink trim, 18″	800.00
Egg cup, 1st blk mk	125.00
Egg server, 1st blk mk, pink trim, 7″ dia	1,250.00
Egg stand, 1st blk mk, w/4 egg cups	295.00

Envelope basket, 2nd blk mk, 4¼″	250.00
Erin, leaf plate, 3rd grn mk	30.00
Figurine, dog on pillow, contemporary grn mk, 4x5″	40.00
Erin, 1st blk mk	5,500.00
Girl w/basket, 1st blk mk, pearl, 9″	950.00
Greyhound, 1st blk mk, 6½″	700.00
Leprechaun, 2nd blk mk, 5½″	475.00
Pig, contemporary grn mk, 4″	25.00
Swan, 2nd blk mk, small	85.00
Finner, shell plate, 2nd blk mk, green trim	120.00
Flower pot w/applied roses, 2nd blk mk, 3½″	150.00
Grasses, honey pot, 2nd blk mk	490.00
Plate, 1st blk mk, No. 1, pale colors, 7¼″	65.00
Plate, 2nd blk mk, 6″	50.00
Tea set, 3 pc w/2 cups & saucers, 1st blk mk	1,450.00
Water kettle, 2nd blk mk, 8″	750.00
Green Ribbon, creamer, 2nd blk mk, 3¼″	75.00
Harp & Shamrock, cup & saucer, 3rd grn mk	75.00
Spill, 3rd grn mk, 7″	65.00
Harp handle, jug, 1st blk mk, pearl, 5½″	285.00
Harp, 3rd blk mk, painted shamrocks, 8½″	200.00
Hawthorn, plate, 1st blk mk	300.00
Tray, 1st blk mk, spider web	1,250.00
Henshall, basket, 4 strand, 1955, small	450.00
Hexagon, bread plate, 2nd blk mk, green & gold trim	38.00
Cup & saucer, 2nd blk mk, orange trim	200.00
Cup & saucer, 2nd blk mk, white	55.00
Plate, 2nd blk mk, 7½″	170.00
Horseshoe & Fan, cup & saucer, 1st blk mk, pearl	125.00
Institute, cup & saucer, 1st blk mk	125.00
Irish Pot, creamer, 2nd blk mk	60.00
Ivy, jug, 1st blk mk, 5″	130.00
Sugar & creamer, 1st grn mk, taffy trim	80.00
Lace, cup & saucer, 1st blk mk, footed	225.00
Leaf, plate, 2nd blk mk, 5″	75.00
Lily, basket, 3 strand, large, 10½″	1,200.00
Teapot, 2nd blk mk, plain	340.00
Sugar & creamer, 3rd blk mk, green trim	145.00
Limpet, bread plate, 3rd blk mk	100.00
Breakfast set, 20 pcs, 3rd blk mk	750.00
Cup, 3rd blk mk	100.00
Cup & saucer, 2nd blk mk, footed	190.00
Cup & saucer, 3rd blk mk, pink trim	180.00
Demi cup, 3rd blk mk	100.00
Plate, 1st grn mk, taffy trim, 8″	85.00
Plate, 3rd blk mk, pink trim, 7″	80.00
Sugar, 2nd blk mk, footed, pink trim	100.00
Tea set, 3 pc w/8 cups & saucers, 11″ plate, blk mk	700.00
Teapot, 3rd blk mk	215.00
Lotus, sugar, 3rd blk mk, taffy glaze, 3″	42.00
Sugar, 3rd blk mk	35.00
Marmalade, Beehive w/cloverleaf current green mark, 6″	165.00
Mask, plate, 3rd grn mk, 6″	62.00
Powder bowl w/cover, blk mk, large	175.00
Sugar & cream, 3rd blk mk	110.00
Menu holder, 2nd blk mk, pearl, 3″ wide	215.00
Nautilus, cup & saucer, contemporary grn mk	24.00
Jug w/coral handle, 1st blk mk	425.00
Neptune, cake plate, 2nd blk mk, pink trim	140.00
Cup & saucer, 2nd blk mk, pink	65.00
Cup & saucer, 2nd blk mk, taffy	190.00
Footed cup & saucer, 2nd blk mk, 2″	55.00
Hot water kettle, 2nd blk mk, pink trim	425.00
Teapot, 1st blk mk, taffy trim	425.00

Teapot, 2nd blk mk	250.00
New Shell, bread plate, 2nd grn mk, taffy trim	45.00
Cup & saucer, 3rd blk mk, pink trim	55.00
Nile, vase, 1st, blk mk, 10″, pink leaves	495.00
Vase, 3rd blk mk, yellow pearl	365.00
Plate, turquoise border, 1st blk mk	275.00
Prince Arthur, vase, 2nd blk mk, pink trim	300.00
Vase, 3rd blk mk, heavy decor, 11″	800.00
Prince of Wales, vase, 1869, 8½″	1,400.00
Queen's Institute, cup & saucer, 1st blk mk	200.00
Cup & saucer, 3rd grn mk	75.00
Rathmore, pitcher, 2nd grn mk	37.50
Vase, 3rd blk mk	130.00
Ribbon, bowl, 3rd grn mk	32.00
Sugar & creamer, 3rd blk mk, taffy trim	68.00
Vase, 2nd blk mk, 8″	295.00
Seahorse flower holder, 2nd blk mk	175.00
Serving basket, oval, large, early, 11½″	2,850.00
Shaker, 1st blk mk, multi-color, 3″	200.00
Shamrock & Basketweave, creamer, 3rd blk mk	35.00
Cup & saucer, 3rd blk mk	55.00
Demi cup, 2nd blk mk, 2″	40.00
Demi cup & saucer, contemporary grn mk	23.00
Plate, 3rd blk mk, 6½″	38.00
Plate, 3rd blk mk, 7″	42.00
Sugar, 3rd blk mk	35.00
Sugar & creamer, 1st grn mk	85.00
Teapot, 3rd blk mk	145.00
Shamrock, AC basket w/rod edge, 3 strand, 5¼″ dia	385.00
Basket, 3 strand, small	385.00
Bowl, 3rd blk mk, 2x3½″	60.00
Creamer, child's, 2nd blk mk	48.00
Cup & saucer, 2nd blk mk	150.00
Cup & saucer, 2nd grn mk	80.00
Cup & saucer, 3rd blk mk	55.00
Egg cup, 2nd blk mk	135.00
Honey pot w/lid, 2nd blk mk, 6¼″	400.00
Milk jug, 3rd blk mk	75.00
Mug, 1st grn mk, 3¾″	42.00
Mug, 3rd blk mk, 2½″	50.00
Plate, 2nd blk mk, 7″	62.00
Plate, 3rd blk mk, 6½″	58.00
Plate, contemporary grn mk, 9″	20.00
Salt, 2nd blk mk	65.00
Salt, 3rd blk mk, 2x3″	28.00
Sugar, child's, 2nd blk mk	42.00
Sugar & creamer, 2nd blk mk	95.00
Sugar & creamer, child's, 2nd grn mk	60.00
Teapot, 2nd blk mk	150.00
Teapot, 3rd blk mk	140.00
Tree trunk vase, 3rd blk mk, 6¼″	100.00
Shaving mug, sterling overlay	65.00
Shell & Seaweed, cup & saucer, 2nd blk mk	45.00
Shell bowl, low foot, 1st blk mk, 2½x5x4″	130.00
Shell w/rock base, 2nd blk mk, pink trim, 5½″	240.00
Shell, butter tub w/lid, blk mk	140.00
Compote, 2nd blk mk, 2½″	225.00
Coral foot, spiral, 2nd blk mk, pearl, 8½″	375.00
Creamer, child's, 2nd grn mk	32.00
Rock base, 1st blk mk, pink trim, 5½″	245.00
Snail jub, 1st blk mk, large, pearl	300.00
Snail shell, plate, 2nd blk mk, 7¼″	165.00
Swirl, plate, 2nd blk mk, 7″	175.00
Thistle, saucer, 1st blk mk, 5″	20.00

Vase, 2nd blk mk, pearl, 8½″	585.00
Tridacna, bread plate, 2nd blk mk, grn trim 7¾″	40.00
Creamer, 1st blk mk, pink trim, gold rim	100.00
Cup & saucer, 1st blk mk	200.00
Cup & saucer, 2nd blk mk, pink & gold trim	65.00
Cup & saucer, 2nd grn mk	45.00
Cup & saucer, 3rd blk mk, pink trim	185.00
Open salt, blk mk	32.00
Plate, 3rd grn mk, 5½″	38.00
Saucer, 1st blk mk, grn trim, gold rim	30.00
Sugar w/cover, 1st blk mk, pink & gold trim	100.00
Tea kettle, 1st blk mk, over handle	300.00
Tea pot, cream & sugar, 1st blk mk	645.00
Tea pot, 2nd blk mk, mid size, yellow trim	190.00
Tea set, 21 pcs, 3rd blk mk	1,200.00
Tulip, vase, 1st blk mk 9″	1,100.00
Tumbler, 1st blk mk, 4½″	195.00
Typha, jug, 2nd grn mk, 7″	20.00
Undine, milkmaid pitcher, 2nd grn mk, 4½″	20.00

Bells

Bells have been used throughout history to signify an alarm or a warning, a victory or a celebration, to call the people together for worship or for dinner. The earliest form was the crotal, or closed mouth bell, such as is commonly seen today in the sleighbell. Gongs, used in the Orient, have no clapper, and must be struck to sound. Bells have been made of metal, glass, and porcelain, in figurals as well as standard shapes.

Advertising, hand bell, Old Curiosity Shoppe	18.00
Art Deco, nude w/bell & mallet, brass	45.00
Art Nouveau, bronze, elaborate floral design	98.00
Boat bell, burnished brass, 8″	30.00
Brass, Baldwin Locomotive Works, 1921, orig yoke, 18″	850.00

Brass, embossed, Belgium	22.00
Brass, lady w/hoop skirt, mk China	38.00
Brass, set of 4 w/matched leaf engraving, 2″	13.00
Brass, w/wood 18″ stand, old, Made In China, 8″	100.00
Bronze, animals & people in relief, Albertano-Fondeurs, 8x9″	130.00
Bronze, in wrought iron tri-pod stand, lion decor, overall height 57″	175.00
Bronze, w/brass eagle handle, 5″	20.00
Cast bell metal, floral bands, early, inscription, 12″	300.00
Cast bell metal, inscription, 1634, 5½″	65.00
Colonial style, w/cross clapper, 1909	25.00
Cow, bronze, cast tassel clapper, 5″	12.50

Cow, hand made, 7½″ **12.00**
Cow, hand made, crudely seam-riveted, folded iron clapper, 7″ . **23.00**
Cow, set of 4, iron, handmade, riveted, 1½″, 2¼″, 2¾″, 4″ ... **23.00**
Desk, brass, on square marble base, dated 1887, 6″ **35.00**
Dinner, all bell brass including brass handle, miniature **25.00**

Dinner, farm-type, cast iron #1 .... **90.00**
Dinner, German porcelain, white, polychrome fruits, gold trim, 5″ **125.00**
Dinner, glass, 1893 Expo **145.00**
Dinner, International, 3″ **26.00**
Dinner, sterling silver, Wallace, small, .95 oz **25.00**
Dinner, sterling, Lebolt, hand made, 3″ **175.00**
Figural, Belgium country woman **65.00**
Figural, cat, celluloid, depress tongue to ring **50.00**
Figural, Clara Barton **58.00**
Figural Elizabethan woman w/clapper feet, brass, 3½″ **25.00**
Figural, lady w/ruffled skirt & bonnet, brass, 4½″ **30.00**
Figural, Mammy w/spoon, porcelain, 1940s, Japan, 3¼″ **20.00**
Figural, Napoleon, w/scenes of Waterloo, brass **175.00**
Glass, blue Finecut & Button w/threaded handle, old, 5¼″ **85.00**
Heisey, Victorian Belle, frosted **125.00**
Hemony, young warrior **200.00**
Maderin Hat Button **150.00**
Milk glass, blue rim **38.00**
Pairpoint, amethyst glass **125.00**
Plantation, bronze, w/cast iron stand & rocker arm, overall 24x22″ **375.00**
Railroad Crossing, 1909, 12″ dia. **95.00**
Schoolhouse, 6½″ **55.00**
Silver, green enameled, Chinese, very ornate **58.00**
Silver, sterling heavy American, 4½x2″ **55.00**
Sleigh, 7 open end horse bells w/clip ends, belly strap **185.00**
Sleigh, brass, set of 19 on original leather **165.00**
Sleigh, brass, set of 24 graduated, buckled strap, old **295.00**
Sleigh, set of 35 uniform size, unpolished brass crotal, strap .. **150.00**
Spode, Hammersley, 1971, in box **25.00**
Steam locomotive's, bronze, Kansas City Southern, 1937 ..... **400.00**
Steam locomotive's, bronze w/yoke & cradle, 16″ **975.00**

Bennington, See Also Stoneware

Although the term has become a generic one for the mottled brown ware produced there, Bennington is not a type of pottery, but rather a town in Vermont where two important potteries were located. The Norton company, founded in 1793, produced mainly redware and stoneware; only during a brief partnership with Fenton (1845-47) was any Rockingham attempted. Fenton organized his own pottery in 1847, manufacturing in addition to redware and stoneware many other types such as graniteware, scroddled ware, flint enamel, a fine parian and vast amounts of their famous Rockingham.

It is estimated that only one in five pieces were marked, and although it has become a common practice to link any fine piece of Rockingham to this area, careful study is vital to distinguish Bennington's from that of many other American and Staffordshire potteries who produced a similar product.

Among the more sought after examples are the bird and animal figures, novelty pitchers, figural bottles, and the more finely modeled items.

Book flask, brown & yellow mottled, 4½x6¼″ **350.00**
   Flint enamel, Departed Spirits, 5½″ **500.00**
   Flint enamel, For the Ladies **400.00**
Candlestick, flint enamel, blue, olive, ochre, 9½″ **325.00**
   Rockingham, 9½″ **275.00**
Croup kettle w/cover, Rockingham, 6½″ **350.00**
Curtain tie backs, 10 pointed stars, 4½″, pr **300.00**
Cuspidor, Rockingham, Lyman & Fenton, sm nicks, 4x9½″ ... **175.00**
Doorknobs, flint enamel, pr **125.00**
Mantle ornament, recumbent cow w/spill holder **900.00**
Mug, Rockingham, panels, one chip, 1849 mk, 3½″ **400.00**
Paperweight, spaniel top, Rockingham, 1849 mk, sm nick **375.00**
Picture frames, oval, Rockingham, 8x7¾″, pr **500.00**
Pitcher, flint enamel, Alternate Rib, age cracks, 1894, 11″ ... **425.00**
   Mask Lip, Rockingham, 1849 mk, 4½″ **775.00**
   Parian, Pond Lily, polychrome, age crack, mkd, 10″ **275.00**
   Parian, Wild Rose, 9¾″ **365.00**
   Parian, blue decor, 4½″ **50.00**
   Rockingham, Diamond pattern, 11″ **250.00**
Spill, parian, Wheat **55.00**
Stove tile, flint enamel, 1849 mk **525.00**
Tobacco jar w/lid, Alternate Rib **500.00**
Toby bottle, Rockingham, top hat, coat, holds bottle, mkd, 10″ **450.00**
Toby creamer, mottled brown, 1849 mk, seated **400.00**
Toby pitcher, seated, Rockingham, 1849 mk, 6½″ **375.00**
Toby snuff jar, flint enamel, 4¼″ **225.00**
   Rockingham, 1894 mk, 4¼″ **400.00**
Tulip vase, flint enamel, 10″ **450.00**
Wash bowl, flint enamel, Scalloped Rib, age cracks, 15¼″ **175.00**
Wash bowl, Rockingham, 1849 mk **375.00**

Beswick

Beswick & Co., of Longston, England, have produced figurines and other articles of fine bone china for about 40 years, which although still being produced are nevertheless hard to find. The discontinued figurines are being collected.

Angus Bull, 4x8″ **35.00**
Blue Jay, #2188, 4½x5″. **15.00**
Bullfinch **16.00**
Champion dog, Cuttail Cupie, 5x4½″ **25.00**
Chimpmunk, 4″ **22.00**
Dachshund, 11½″ **85.00**
Donkey, 7x5½″ **30.00**
Elephant, trunk up, 5½x7½″ **75.00**
Finch, #2973 .... **25.00**
Horse w/lady in riding habit, 8x8″ **110.00**
Lion, 5½x9″ **35.00**
Macawber, Toby pitcher, qt **175.00**

Parrot, #930 . . . . **55.00**
Pheasant, #1226 . . . . **95.00**

Pitcher, Robert Burns, #1045-2, Beswick, England, 8" **125.00**
Robin **16.00**
Sairey Gamp, figural Toby head pitcher, qt **60.00**
Sitting Fox **12.50**
Stonechat **16.00**
White Throat **16.00**

Big Little Books

Big Little Books--those cartoon illustrated hand-size sagas of adventure with such familiar heroes as Tarzan, Tom Mix, Flash Gorden and the 'G' Men--were popular with kids from the 1930s to the '50s. Created by the Whitman Co., others such as Goldsmith, Saalfield and World Syndicate soon followed suit. They originally sold for a dime, but eventually the price went to 20ᶜ; and though specifically made for the dime-store trade, some were premiums given away by the Coco Malt Co. These are highly prized by collectors today; so are Disney stories and super heroes.

Ace Drummond **10.00**
Admiral Bird **8.50**
Adventures Of Tiny Tim **16.00**
Air Fighters Of America **13.00**
Alice In Wonderland **22.50**
Alley Oop & Dinny In The Invasion Of Moo **22.00**
Andy Panda All Picture Comics **18.00**
Andy Panda And The Presto Pup **14.00**
Andy Panda And Tiny Tom **12.50**
Andy Panda In The City Of Ice **16.00**
Apple Mary & Dennie Foil The Swindlers **9.00**
Bambi **25.00**
Barney Baxter **12.00**
Betty Boop In Miss Gulliver's Travels **25.00**
Betty Boop In Snow White **22.00**
Big Little Mother Goose **19.00**
Blackie Bear **14.00**
Blondie & Dagwood, Everybody's Happy **9.00**
Blondie & Dagwood In Hot water **10.00**
Blondie & Dagwood Some Fun **10.00**
Blondie, Count Cookie In Too **14.00**
Blondie & Baby Dumpling **14.00**
Brenda Starr **10.00**

Brer Rabbit **18.00**
Bringing Up Father **24.00**
Buck Jones & The Killers Of Crooked Butte **25.00**
Buck Jones At Rock Creek In Ride E'm Cowboy **18.00**
Buck Jones At Rock Creek In The Fighting Code **18.00**
Buck Jones At Rock Creek In The Fighting Rangers . . . **20.00**
Buck Jones At Rock Creek In The Night Riders **24.00**
Buck Jones At Rock Creek and The Rough Riders **18.00**
Buck Rogers & The Depth Men of Jupiter, 1933 . . . . . **38.00**
Buck Rogers & The Doom Comet **35.00**
Buck Rogers & The Overturned World **35.00**

Buck Rogers & The Planetoid Plot, 1936 . . . . **40.00**
Buck Rogers In The City Below The Sea, 1934 . . . . . . **48.00**
Buck Rogers In The City Of Globes **50.00**
Buck Rogers 25th Century AD Doom Comet, 1935 . . . . **42.00**
Buck Rogers, War With The Planet Venus **42.00**
Bugs Bunny And His Pals **14.00**
Bugs Bunny And The Giant Brothers **12.00**
Bugs Bunny And The Klondike Gold **12.00**
Bugs Bunny In Risky Business **15.00**
Bugs Bunny The Masked Marvel **12.00**
Calling W-L-X-Y-Z, Jimmy Kean Behind Enemy Lines . . **12.00**
Calling W-L-X-Y-Z, Jimmy Kean Soldier Of Fortune . . . **12.00**
Captian Easy, Soldier Of Fortune **14.00**
Captian Midnight Verses The Terror of The Orient **20.00**
Captian Midnight And Sheik Jomak Khan **20.00**
Captian Midnight And The Secret Squadron **20.00**
Captian Midnight And The Moon Woman **22.00**
Charlie Chan **15.00**
Charlie Chan, Villainy On The High Seas **15.00**
Charlie McCarthy And His Pals **17.50**
Chester Gump At Silver Creek Ranch **14.00**
Chester Gump In The City Of Gold **15.00**
Cinderella & Magic Wand **22.50**
Clyde Beatty, Daredevil Lion Tamer **25.00**
Dan Dunn & The Zeppelin Of Doom **10.00**
Dan Dunn & The Underworld Gorillas **14.00**
Dan Dunn & The Boarder Smuggler **12.00**
Dan Dunn On Trail Counterfeiters **15.00**
David Copperfield **18.00**
Desert Eagle Rides Again **10.00**
Dick Tracy, premium giveaway issue **35.00**
Dick Tracy & Yogee Yama, 1946 . . . . **25.00**
Dick Tracy And Dick Tracy Junior **12.00**
Dick Tracy And His G-Men **12.00**
Dick Tracy And The Bicycle Gang **15.00**
Dick Tracy And The Frozen Bullet **18.00**
Dick Tracy And The Man With No Face **16.50**
Dick Tracy And The Racketeer Gang **15.00**
Dick Tracy And The Spider Gang **35.00**
Dick Tracy Mystery Of The Purple T **42.00**
Dick Tracy On Voodoo Island **15.00**
Dick Tracy Returns, 1939 . . . . **30.00**

Dick Tracy, Adventurers Of	60.00
Dick Tracy, Detective & Federal Agent	18.00
Don O'Dare Finds War	7.00
Don Winslow Secret Enemy Base	8.00
Donald Duck	14.00
Donald Duck And His Misadventures	22.00
Donald Duck And The Ducklings	32.50
Donald Duck And The Green Serpent	30.00
Donald Duck And Others	15.00
Donald Duck Forgets To Duck	25.00
Donald Duck Gets Fed Up	30.00
Donald Duck Hunting For Trouble	29.00
Donald Duck Lays Down The Law	20.00
Donald Duck Off The Beam	25.00
Donald Duck See's Stars	27.50
Donald Duck Up In The Air	25.00
Dumbo	27.50
Ella Cinders Mysterious House *illus*	15.00
Ellery Queen Forest Kingdom Of Mongo	35.00
Ellery Queen In Last Man Club	15.00
Ellery Queen Water World of Mongo	40.00
Ellery Queen Witch Queen of Mongo	42.00
Felix The Cat	32.00
Flash Gordon & The Tournaments Of Mongo, 1935	50.00
Flash Gordon & The Ape Men	35.00
Flash Gordon In The Forest Kingdom Of Mongo, 1937	50.00
Flash Gordon, Perils Of Mongo	42.00
Flash Gordon, Red Sword Invadors	38.00
Flash Gordon, Water World Of Mongo, 1937	40.00
Flash Gordon, Witch Queen Of Mongo, 1936	75.00
Frank Buck Presents	16.50
G-Man & The Gun Runners	15.00
G-Man & The Radio Bank Robbers	20.00
G-Man On The Crime Trail	14.00
Gang Busters In Action	15.00
Gene Autry & The Land Grab Mystery	18.00
Gene Autry & The Range War	14.00
Gene Autry In Gun Smoke	15.00
Gene Autry In Special Ranger Rule	20.00
Gene Autry Public Cowboy No 1	15.00
George Obrien & The Ghost Avenger	12.00
George Obrien & The In Gun Law	8.00
Green Hornet Cracks Down	25.00
Green Hornet Strikes	25.00
Houdini's Book Of Magic	30.00
Invisible Scarlet O'Neil Verses King Of The Slums	8.00
Jack Armstrong, Mystery Of The Iron Key	12.00
Jackie Cooper, Star Of Skippy & Sooky	15.00
Jackie Cooper In Peck's Bad Boy	12.00
Joe Louis, Brown Bomber	35.00
Joe Palooka	15.00
Jungle Jim And The Vampire Woman	35.00
Junior G-Men	8.00
Katzenjammer Kids	22.00
Kayo & Moon Mullins And The One Man Gang	9.00
Kazan, King Of The Pack	10.00
Ken Maynark In Western Justice	12.00
King Of The Royal Mounted	24.00
King Of The Royal Mounted Get's His Man	15.00
King Of The Royal Mounted In The Far North	15.00
King Of The Royal Mounted And The Northern Treasure	15.00
King Of The Royal Mounted Long Arm Of The Law	17.50
Laurel & Hardy	14.00
Life Among The Bumsteads	10.00
Little Abner Among The Millionaires	15.00
Little Annie Roonie And The Orphan House	12.00
Little Lulu, Alvin, Tubby	14.00
Little Orphan Annie In Rags To Riches	22.00
Little Orphan Annie, Underground Hide Out	25.00
Little Orphan Annie & Chizzler, 1933	35.00
Little Orphan Annie & Junior Commandos	20.00
Little Orphan Annie, Big Train Robbery	30.00
Little Orphan Annie, The $1,000,000 Formula	28.00
Little Orphan Annie With The Circus	25.00
Lone Ranger & His Horse Silver	25.00
Lone Ranger & The Dead Men's Mine	18.00
Lone Ranger & The Vanishing Herd	15.00
Lone Ranger & The Silver Bullets	14.00
Lone Ranger, Secret Of The Comber Canyon	15.00
Mac Of The Marines In Africa	14.00
Mandrake The Magician & The Flame Pearls	20.00
Mandrake The Magician, Mighty Solver Of Mystery	22.00
Maximo, Amazing Superman And The Crystals Of Doom	12.00
Mickey Mouse & The Pirate Submarine	38.00
Mickey Mouse & Nuggett Gulch	30.00
Mickey Mouse & Pluto	36.00
Mickey Mouse & The Bat Bandit	40.00
Mickey Mouse & The Magic Lamp	38.00
Mickey Mouse & The Seven Ghosts	35.00
Mickey Mouse, Bell Boy Detective	36.00
Mickey Mouse, Cave Man Island	35.00
Mickey Mouse, Haunted Island	36.00
Mickey Mouse In The Foreign Legion	35.00
Mickey Mouse In The Treasure Hunt	32.00
Mickey Mouse Presents A Walt Disney Silly Symphony, 1932	40.00
Mickey Mouse, Sail For Treasure Island, 1933	40.00
Mickey Mouse, The Miracle Maker	25.00
Mickey Mouse's Misfortune	20.00
Mickey Rooney, The Midnight Monster	15.00
Moon Mullins & Kayo The Plushbutton Twins	15.00
Moon Mullins & Kayo Cocomalt	18.00
Mutt & Jeff	28.50
Orphan Annie, 1934	15.00
Our Gang Adventures On The March	15.00
Peggy Brown & Jewel, Fire	8.00
Peggy Brown & The Mystery Basket	7.00
Peggy Brown In The Haunted House	7.00
Phantom And Desert Justice	38.00
Phantom, Girl Of Mystery	37.00
Phantom, Sign Of The Skull	37.00
Phantom, The, 1936	36.00
Pinnocchio & Jiminy Cricket	36.00
Pluto The Pup	18.00
Popeye, A Sock For Susan's Sake	20.00
Popeye & The Jeep, 1937	25.00
Popeye, Castor Oyl, Detective	22.00
Popeye, Quest For The Rainbird	20.00
Popeye The Spinach Eater	18.00
Porky Pig & His Gang	20.00
Radio Patrol Trailing The Safe Blowers	10.00
Red Barry, Undercover Man	10.00
Red Ryder & Squaw Tooth Rustlers	19.00
Red Ryder & Little Beaver	15.00
Red Ryder & The Rimrock Killer	15.00
Red Ryder & Western Boarder Guns	15.00
Red Ryder, Hoofs Of Thunder	18.00
Red Ryder, Outlaw Of The Painted Valley	14.00
Roy Rogers, King Of The Cowboys	15.00

Roy Rogers, Mystery Of The Lazy M **15.00**
Roy Rogers, Robin Hood Of The Range **14.00**
Secret Agent X9 . . . . **30.00**
Secret Agent X9 & The Mad Assassin **28.00**
Shadow & the Ghost Maker **28.00**
Shadow & The Living Death **28.00**
Skeezix, Military Academy **15.00**
Skeezix, On His Own In The City **15.00**
Smilin' Jack & The Boarder Bandits **20.00**
Smilin' Jack Escape From Death Rock **20.00**
Smilin' Jack In Wings Over The Pacific **20.00**
Smilin' Jack, Speed Pilot, 1941 . . . . **32.00**
Snow White And The Seven Dwarfs **25.00**
Story Of Johnny Weissmuller, The Tarzan of the Screen, 1943 . **25.00**
Sybil Jason In Little Big Shot **10.00**
Tailspin Tommy, Air Racer **15.00**
Tailspin Tommy And The Hooded Flyer **15.00**
Tailspin Tommy And The Sky Bandits **15.00**
Tailspin Tommy In Flying Aces **15.00**
Tailspin Tommy, Mountains Of Human Sacrifice **20.00**
Tarzan & The Ant Men **30.00**
Tarzan & The Jewels Of Opar **30.00**
Tarzan & The Lost Empire **28.00**
Tarzan In Land Of Giant Apes **28.00**
Tarzan The Avenger **28.00**
Tarzan Twins **28.00**
Tarzan, Son Of **30.00**
Terry & The Pirates And The Mystery Ship **15.00**
Terry & the Pirates In Mountain Stronghold **15.00**
Texas Ranger **10.00**
Thumper & Seven Dwarfs **35.00**
Tim McMoy Beyond The Law **15.00**
Tim McMoy In the Westerner **12.00**
Tim Tyler's Adventurers In The Ivory Patrol **22.00**
Tiny Tim & Mechanical Men **20.00**
Tom Beatty Ace Of The Service **12.00**
Tom Beatty Scores Again **15.00**
Tom Mix **20.00**
Tom Mix Avenges, Range King **15.00**
Tom Mix In The Range War **16.00**
Tom Mix, The Fighting Cowboy **15.00**
Tom Swift & His Giant Telescope **45.00**
Uncle Don's Strange Adventures **8.00**
Wash Tubbs In Pandemonia **15.00**
Wimpy, Hamburger Eater **30.00**
Wings Of The USA **15.00**
Zip Saunders **8.00**

Bing and Grondahl, See Also Collector Plates

Bing and Grondahl was founded in 1853 in Copenhagen, and still produce the fine figurines, dinnerware and Christmas plates that have made
them famous.

Figurine, Baby Goldfinch, 4¼" **100.00**
Baby Monkey, sitting, 3" **130.00**
Collie, 11x6" **275.00**
Girl kneeling, white cat in wicker basket, 4x4½" **145.00**
Girl w/doll, 1900, 7½" **245.00**
Little boy, sitting, drinking from cup, 5½" **65.00**
Madonna, standing w/infant, 9" **40.00**
Mother w/child on lap, 5x4½" **115.00**
Polar Bear, head raised, 5½x7½" **175.00**
Siamese Cat, #308, 5½" **85.00**

The Kissers **225.00**
Young girl w/pigtails, puppy in fold of skirt, 7" **100.00**
Young girl, reading book, 7½" **125.00**

Bisque

Bisque is a term referring to unglazed earthenware or porcelain that
has been fired only once. During the Victorian era, bisque figurines became
very popular. Most were highly decorated in pastels and gilt, and
demonstrated a fine degree of workmanship in the quality of the modeling.
Few were marked. Other bisque figurines are listed in sections on Piano
Babies and Heubach.

Bust, maid in blue hood, sq neckline w/bow, Lemaire, 19x12". **750.00**
Candelabra, 2 sockets, Colonial boy & tree trunk, gold **225.00**
Figurine, bathing beauty, flesh color, Germany, 3¼" **65.00**
Bathing beauty, polychrome, numbered **70.00**
Black boy in boat w/attacking alligator, 5x3½" **75.00**
Black boy on bench, watermelon & knife, 4" **45.00**
Black girl on chamber w/watermelon & slice, 4½" **100.00**
Black girl w/yellow dress, white hat, pink shoes, 2½" **135.00**
Boxer, early 1930s, numbered, 2¼" **18.00**
Boy & girl in parent's clothes, Schutz mk, pr, 12½" **225.00**
Boy & girl, musicians, gold bases, signed, 9½", pr **125.00**
Boy w/dog, blue beret, knee pants, gold, 17½" **200.00**
Boy w/pants rolled to knee, pail & basket on back, 10" **95.00**
Boy w/tray of fruit, knee pants, frock coat, 13" **125.00**
Bride & groom, early 1930s, 3½" **20.00**
Caricature of dachshund, green, German, 6½x4" **75.00**
Child w/baskets, rocks, pastels, Japan, 10½x9" **95.00**
Fishing boy forgets books, girl scolds him, 7½", pr **100.00**
Gardening boy & girl, papier mache bowers, #3772, pr **265.00**
Girl in bonnet by cart w/large wheels, 8½x9" **60.00**
Googlie girl w/crown, star & crown mk, 4½x3½" **90.00**
Igloo w/Eskimos, penguin on top, 2½" **18.00**
Lady w/flowing hair standing in boat 3¾x6" **110.00**
Maid w/book, patterned dress & apron, tall hat, French, 17" **275.00**
Man w/lute in 15th century dress, 10½" **150.00**

Figurine, potty boy, blue, gold trim, 4½" **50.00**
Ship's Captain, Germany, 2¼" **15.00**
Teddy & the Bear, Jamestown, N. Y. **35.00**
Three black boys, 2 w/hats, sitting on wall, 1890 . . . . **650.00**
Walnut shell w/black baby inside **37.50**
Whippet mother & pups, natural colors, 8x9" **145.00**
Night light, bull, glass eyes shine, German **195.00**
Cat, glass eyes, German **175.00**

Dog, glass eyes, German............................ **175.00**
Vase, boy on conch shell boat, 8x7x4″.................. **125.00**

Black Americana

Items representing the history of the Black race, particularly those legitimate historical artifacts dealing with slavery, should and do have value, for no matter how unfortunate the period from which they come, it is a part of our country's past.

The articles listed here with a derogatory connotation were from the early years of this century, and represent attitudes which thankfully are also a part of the past.

Alligator, metal, w/boy by seat of pants, 4″ **40.00**
Ashtray, chalk, Amos & Andy, I's Regusted, red, white, black .. **40.00**
   Figural baby on bed pan, For Butts & Ashes, porcelain **35.00**
   Figural boy & goose, Early Bird Catches the Worm......... **35.00**
Ashtray stand, wood, bellboy w/tray, 39″ **280.00**
Automaton, man smokes cigarette, turns head, musical **6,250.00**
Beer tray, Harvard Export Green Label, waiter, 12″ dia **35.00**
Book, Negro Recitations and Endman's Gags, 1946, 140 pgs **6.00**
   Poems of Cabin and Field, 1900 .... **50.00**
   Pore Lil Mose Entertains, Outcault color illustrations, 1901 .. **28.00**
   Rowena Teena Tot and the Blackberries, 1934 .... **25.00**
   Ten Little Niggers, RJ Williams, cloth, Dean's Rag Co....... **90.00**
Card game, In Dixieland, dated 1897, 50 different pictures ... **200.00**
Carte De Visite, female minstrel w/banjo in blackface production **70.00**
Cereal bowl, Cream of Wheat, Spirit of St Louis, with man's face, 6½″ **40.00**
Change tray, The Source of Cottolene, woman & child, 4¼″ dia **25.00**
Cheese knife, sterling, alligator w/boy's head in mouth, 5″ **55.00**
Cigar box, wooden log cabin, chromolitho of family, 8x5x5″ ... **90.00**
Comic strip, Misto' Sambo, Jan 23, 1910, Wood, museum mount **17.00**
Cookie jar, Mammy's head, wicker handle, 6″ **55.00**
Cream pitcher, boy w/high wheeler, Battery Park Hotel, blk/wht, 4″ **35.00**
   Girl's head, shirt collar base, red lips, china............. **100.00**
   Uncle Moe **28.00**
Die-cut, valet w/message & flowers, dog, 1880s, color, 10½″ ... **20.00**
Doll, cloth, girl w/kitten, Diana Aunt Jemima's.....,12″ **75.00**
   Cloth, w/embroidered eyes, nose, mouth, 1890s,.......... **40.00**
   Primitive Mammy, bald Pappy, 1800s, 9″, pr **275.00**
Drawing, boy singing w/broom, early 1920s, pastel, 17x14″ ... **140.00**
Egg, bisque, face on one side bare backside on other, hp **35.00**
Figurine, boy on potty w/watermelon, bisque, early 1900s, 4″ .. **50.00**
   Man & Mammy cottonpickers, souvenir New Orleans, 4″..... **50.00**
   Suffragette, Votes for Women, bisque, 6″ **140.00**
Frame, wood, plaster decor, 3 panels, children, 22½x9″....... **90.00**
Game, The Gold Dust Twins, 2 figures w/box top **60.00**
Humidor, basket w/boy & tobacco, lustre, 1885............. **145.00**

Humidor, boy on stump, 12″.......................... **150.00**

Ceramic, girl in tobacco pouch, 1890s, 8″ **250.00**
Illustration, Harper's Weekly, 1865, Gethering Corn **12.00**
   Harper's Weekly, 1877, First of May **20.00**
   Harper's Weekly, 1885, Possums & Persimmons **15.00**
   Harper's Weekly, 1897, Sunday Morning...Pines **25.00**
Incense holder, boy squatting holding vase, porcelain, 5″ **25.00**
Medal, copper, Martin Luther King, 1929-1968, I Have...Dream . **22.00**
Memo pad, Aunt Jemima **38.00**
Microphone dancer, Slapping Sam replica, orig box **200.00**
Movie poster, Ebony Parade, Mills Bros, Count Basie, 1-sheet . **150.00**
   Keep Punching, Henry Armstrong photo, 1-sheet.......... **200.00**
   Night Club Girl, Manton Moreland, 1-sheet............... **45.00**
Nodder, girl w/panties down, Lenwile China, Ardalt, 6″ **40.00**
   Man w/hands in air, Lenwile China, Ardalt, 6″........... **40.00**
   Papier mache, smiling gent w/top hat, early 1900s......... **100.00**
Pencil holder, alligator eats pencil with man's head, metal .. **22.00**
Photo, man in cook's uniform w/young white girl, 1900, framed. **35.00**
Plate, cartoon, CA Lewis, I'll Be Down...In A Taxi Honey **37.00**
   Who Is On The Line Honey, bright colors, 7″ **95.00**
Poster, Hercules Powder Co, I'se Lost De Lunch, 20x15″ **65.00**
   Little Eva's Temptation, Uncle Tom & Eva, 28x20″ **55.00**
   Pansy Blossom Octette, 1895, cardboard, b/w, 13x21″ **50.00**
   Vogel's Minstrels, Sam Harris, linen mounted, 42x28″...... **155.00**
Print, Our Colored Heroes, EG Renesch, 1918, framed, 16x20″ **65.00**
Puzzle, Amos/Andy & others, OK Hotel, Pepsodent Co, 8x10″ . **55.00**
   Woozy-Jig, 200 interlocking pieces, Brundage Inc **22.00**
Salt/pepper shakers, boy w/watermelon, china, 2-pc, 3¼″ **20.00**
   Mammy's salt/pepper, china, 3″, Japan **25.00**
   Man/woman, both cooks, ceramic, 1948 .... **35.00**
   Piggyback babies in canoe, 3½″ **25.00**
Shaving mug, man sitting on moon w/banjo, Amsbury in gold .. **80.00**
Sheet music, Brother Noah Gave Out Checks, baseball, 1907... **22.00**
   Coon Coon Coon, small photo of Johnson & Dean **40.00**
   Cinders, old bearded man w/hat & glasses, 1905 .... **25.00**
Sign, Jim Crow, Colored Seated in Rear, Aug 1, 1929, 4x11″ .. **50.00**
Sign, Mil-Kay, waiter w/tray, cardboard, 17x28″ **30.00**
Spoon, sterling, boy w/watermelon, Jacksonville souvenir....... **35.00**
String holder, porcelain, woman w/apron & red scarf, Japan, 7″ **30.00**
String holder, porter's head, Fredericksburg Pottery **65.00**
Syrup pitcher, woman w/plate of waffles, china, 5″, Japan...... **50.00**
Toothpick holder, dancing girl, glazed painted bisque, 1890s ... **40.00**

Toothpick holder, milk glass w/black face, 3½″............. **150.00**
Toy, Tapping Sam The Minstrel Man, 1920s, MIB **110.00**
   Tin wind-up, dancing Darky, litho, Lehmann, 6½″.......... **60.00**
   Tin wind-up, Jazzbo Jim, Unique Art Mfg, G **60.00**
   Tin wind-up, man playing banjo, head, arm moves, 8″ **180.00**
   Tin wind-up, man pushing cart, 6½x4″.................. **60.00**
Vase, sewer tile, fired-on cartoon, 1890s, 6″ **225.00**
Wall bracket, chalk, woman w/broom, Miller Studios, #2954, 9″ **30.00**
Wall brackets, chalk, pr, boy & girl w/watermelon, 1949, 6″ ... **40.00**
Wall hanging, cross-stitch, man/woman, We's Free, 1870, 4x5″ **100.00**
Wall plate, ML King, 1964 Nobel Peace Prize, tin, 8½″ **10.00**

Black Cats

Black cats are a line of figural kitchenware and novelties, from the early 1950s.

Ashtray, full body, 4″ **4.50**
Ashtray, green eyes, head. **10.00**
Ashtray, head, red bow, open mouth is ashtray **7.50**
Bookends. **15.00**
Bottle, yellow eyes, with 3 1¾″ shots **25.00**
Cinnamon shaker **10.00**
Condiment set, double head, spoons attached under lids. **18.50**
Cookie jar, head, w/lid, 5″. **45.00**
Creamer, 5½″ **9.50**
Cruets, oil & vinegar, sitting, red bows, 7½″, pair. **15.00**
Decanter, recumbant, w/6 shots hanging from back, 8″. **18.50**
Decanter, sitting, w/6 shots, all have red polka dots **14.00**
Egg cup, green eyes, single egg size **18.00**
Envelope holder, yellow eyes, w/sponge. **25.00**
Figurine, 3¼″ **4.00**
Letter holder, coil spring back. **24.00**
Marmalade, green eyes, double **40.00**
Measuring cups, set of 4 . . . . **25.00**
Pepper shaker, 3″ square. **4.50**
Relish, 2 heads **15.00**
Salt/pepper, green eyes, original label & tag, pair **12.00**
Salt/pepper, kittens in shoes, red bow tie, 3x2½″ **5.00**
Shakers, yellow eyes, 10½″ long, pair **12.00**
Spice set, green eyes, 8 compartments, wood triangular holder . **65.00**
Sugar & creamer, green eyes, red bow, tail is handle, pair **24.00**
Sugar, green eyes, original label **12.00**
Syrup **15.00**
Tea kettle, footed, cat's head on front, metal handle. **12.00**

Teapot, 2-cup, 4¾″ **15.00**
Teapot, 2-cup **15.00**
Teapot, 4-cup **20.00**
Teapot, 6-cup **25.00**
Utensil set, green eyes **45.00**
Wall pocket, green eyes **50.00**

Black Glass

Black Glass, sometimes called Black Milk Glass, is a term used to describe a type of colored glass. When held to a strong light, color can be seen through most items. Each glass house had it's own formula, so colors may vary, but the most common hue is a deep purple.

Occasionally it was decorated with silver, gold, enamel or coraline. It was sometimes etched or given a satin finish either by the glass house or by firms which specialized in decorating. Often, more than one of these devices was used. Crystal, jade, colored or milk glass was combined with the black as an accent.

Black glass has been made by many companies since the 17th century. Contemporary glass houses used black glass during the Depression, but many pieces are unmarked. It is still being made today.

Basket, tall handle, carnival mold, 6¼″ **25.00**
 Two handles, carnival mold, Imperial. **30.00**
Bath tub, souvenir, gold rim **12.00**
Boot, w/spur **40.00**
Bud vase, Mary Gregory girl, 7½″ **70.00**
Bushel basket, carnival mold, N in circle **50.00**

Cambridge

Bridge Dog, holds paper in mouth **12.00**
Candlestick, kneeling child holding flared pot, 1191 . . . . **55.00**
Candlestick, stem w/applied twist, Rebel, 8½″ **22.00**
Candlesticks, Calla Lilly, P-499, pr **35.00**
Candlesticks, Tracy, 7″, pr. **28.00**
Candy dish, domed lid, 3 feet, gold roses & decor, 6″ **50.00**
Cocktail, black nude steam, crystal bowl & foot, 3 oz, #3011. . . **42.00**
Console bowl, hp orange & purple roses, white edge, 15″ **90.00**
Ivy ball, crystal keyhold stem, 8″. **35.00**
Swan, 3¾″ **50.00**
Swan, 7½″ **75.00**
Swan, 9¼″ **100.00**
Swan, open 9¼″. **100.00**
Vase, floral & peacock etching #736, 8″. **45.00**
Vase, gold floral etching #748, Lorna #3400/17, 12″ **65.00**
Candlesticks, Licorice Life Saver, 5¾″, pr **25.00**
Reversible, Flower Cup, pr. **17.00**
Stepped bases, Deco, Triad, pr **16.00**
Central Glass Works, candlestick, Zaricar, florals, 9″. **16.00**
Co-op Flint Glass, elephant w/ashtray lid **75.00**
Elephant, w/lid **70.00**
Czechoslovakia, bathroom set, 14 pcs, castle scene **130.00**

Duncan Miller

Candlesticks, silver deposit Avalon, 57, pr 6¼″ **45.00**
Console bowl, silver deposit Avalon, 12″ **80.00**
Salt dip, three leaf, three toed **10.00**
Dish w/lid, Versailles, raised roses, green leaves, gold **45.00**
England, compote, Percy, 1877, 3¾″. **35.00**
England, match holder, Rippled Wave, 3¼″ **45.00**
England, match holder, Staggered Block, 3½″ **45.00**

Fenton

Bell, Craftsman, experimental. **48.00**
Bon-bon, dolphin handles, ruffled edge, 6½″. **30.00**
Bon-bon, Pond Lily & Leaf **35.00**
Bowl, basketweave w/blackberry **45.00**
Bowl, footed, dolphin handles, double pouring spout, 10½″. . . **85.00**
Bowl, footed, snake handles, double pouring spout, 10½″ **85.00**
Bowl, three toed, lattice, crimped, #1093 . . . . **25.00**
Bowl, tri-toed base, Chrysanthemum & Windmill **100.00**
Bowl, swans, necks loop to form handles, 11½″ **75.00**
Candle bowl, ped, notched rim, Fenton in oval **15.00**
Candleholders, 3 toed, lattice w/flat edge, #1093, pr **25.00**
Candlesticks, gold rings, wide disk base, #2324, 4″, pr. **18.00**
Candlesticks, swans, necks loop for handles, 6½″, pr. **55.00**
Candy jar, half pound, #835, tall finial, panels **40.00**
Candy dish, footed, dolphin handles, tall finial **75.00**
Elephant flower bowl, figural **225.00**
Figurines, praying boy & girl, pr **30.00**
Plate, gold rings & edge, Mayfair. **6.00**

Salt & pepper, pointed hobnail #3806, pr **15.00**
Salt dip, Three Leaf pattern............................. **15.00**
Swan, 1930s **25.00**
Vase, fish figural, white eyes & tail **55.00**
Vase, Empress Verly's mold **30.00**
Vase, Mandarin Verly's mold #8251 .... **30.00**
Wise Owl Decision Maker............................... **17.00**

Fostoria
Candlesticks, disk base & Deco handles, #2395, pr **18.00**
Candlesticks, scrolled disk handles, Deco styling, 5", pr ... **18.00**
Combination, bowl w/attached candleholders, Fern, #2415 ... **35.00**
Console bowl, scrolled disk handles, Deco, #2395, 10" ... **20.00**
Fan vase, silver deposit florals, #2385, 8½" **65.00**
Lusters, blk stem & ped, crystal top & prisms, 9", pr ... **40.00**
Nappy cupped "B", #2320, low foot, open work sides, 11".... **35.00**
Figural bulldog, satin finish, brown collar, red/white eyes ... **20.00**
Figural cat w/matte finish, gold ribbon, rhinestone eyes ... **20.00**
Frying pan, two pouring spouts, 5¼" **12.00**

Greensburg Glass
Candlestick, tri foot on disk base, Dilly................. **6.00**
Candlesticks, Yorkie, 3" pr **16.00**
Dog ash tray, 6" wide................................. **15.00**
Dog cigarette box & cover **15.00**
Elephant ash tray, 4" wide............................. **15.00**

Hobbs
Sugar shaker, Windermere's Fan, 1890s................. **125.00**
Sugar w/cover, Windermere's Fan, tall w/molded pattern ... **70.00**

Imperial
Creamer, Pillar Flute................................... **4.00**
Jelly dish, handle, Diamond Block...................... **4.00**
Lilly bowl, Diamond Block, #3305, 5" **4.00**
Sugar, Pillar Flute **4.00**

LE Smith
Bean pot, Daisy, floral design in silver, covered **35.00**
Bookends, rearing horse, 8" **25.00**
Candlestick, Mt Pleasant................................ **8.00**
Cup & saucer, Mt Pleasant, points & scallops **12.00**
Dresser set, hobnail, 7 pcs, crystal bottoms **25.00**
Elephant figural....................................... **16.00**
Fruit bowl, two handles, footed, disk handles........... **10.00**
Goose figural **16.00**
Nut tray, Mt Pleasant, center handle................... **10.00**
Plate, Mt Pleasant, points & scallops, 8" **8.00**
Plate, Mt Pleasant, tri-footed **15.00**
Reclining cat figural **16.00**
Scottish Terrier, 2½" **12.00**
Scottish Terrier, 3x3¾" **15.00**
Scottish Terrier, 5x6"................................. **25.00**
Swan, silver trim **45.00**
Tray, Mt Pleasant, for sugar, cream, salt & pepper **12.00**
Window box, Pan w/dancing nymphs, 8" long **15.00**
Ladies shoe, bow at front w/cube heel **60.00**
Lamp, Bullseye, Fleur-de-lis & Heart crystal font **110.00**
Lamp, bust of lady, Triple Peg & Loop crystal font...... **125.00**
Lamp, Crown, black foot w/crystal font, 1897, 10" **90.00**
Lamp, metal lined base, 2 pcs, 13¼" **550.00**
Lamp, Scottie decor on frosted cream shade, LE Smith ... **50.00**
Lamp, Sheldon Swirl, crystal swirled font, leaf base **100.00**
Lamp, Three Feather chimney, floral enameled, 9½" **110.00**
Luster, seven cut glass prisms, enameled floral on gold decor ... **75.00**

McKee
Candlesticks, Autumn, 4", pr **20.00**
Console bowl, Autumn, 7"............................. **18.00**
Tom & Jerry set, bowl & 10 mugs **75.00**

Mug, profile in relief, Laurel leaves, late 1800s **40.00**
Mug, toy, Feathered Friend, barber pole handle **35.00**

New Martinsville
Bowl, oval w/crystal swan handle, #679/1S, 12½" **40.00**
Candlestick, crystal swan handle........................ **27.00**
Flower bowl, open sphere w/tri-foot, crystal frog **20.00**
Perfume bottle, Queen Anne, long inside stopper **18.00**

Paden City
Candlestick, Echo, 7"................................. **15.00**
Candlestick, Garrett, bubble in well, 8½", pr **28.00**
Vase, bulbous base, flared body, Peacock & Rose, 10"..... **50.00**
Pin dish, gold painted relief design, 25 inside lid........ **15.00**
Pipe, rests on three legs, gold trim, 5¾" **10.00**
Plate, w/Club & Shell border, 9¼" **25.00**
   Gothis border........................... **15.00**
   Heart border **30.00**
   Keyhold border **15.00**
   Leaf and Scroll square edge border **30.00**
   Pinwheel border, 8¼"................... **25.00**
   Ring and Dot border.................... **15.00**
   Square S border, 9¼" **25.00**
   Stanchion border, Challinor, Taylor & Co ... **30.00**
   Triangle S border **30.00**
   Variant of Backward C square border **30.00**
   Wicket border, 9¼" **25.00**
Powder box, clown head, gold trim on base & lid **47.00**
Coraline parrot & flowers on lid **15.00**
Pattern Ruth on lid & under base...................... **15.00**
Silver deposit Face Powder on lid **15.00**
Sandwich glass, pomade bear, muzzle on face, 4" **110.00**
Toilet set, in plated holder, 2 bottles, jar, enameled ... **130.00**
Toothpick, Half Scroll, beads at rim, 1¾" **18.00**
Bee's on a Basket **65.00**
Pot Belly, blue enameled flowers & silver trim **27.00**
Tasseled Fan, Button & Daisy w/tassels on base **30.00**

United States Glass
Bath tub, souvenir, gold rim, ... **12.00**
Bud vase, disk foot, hp pink & gold florals, 10" **18.00**
Bud vase, disk foot, tapered body, petal rim, 16270, 7½" ... **9.00**
Bulb box, Elysium, classic relief, satin, 8127, 9½" long ... **40.00**
Cake plate, Shaggy Daisy **18.00**
Candlestick, satin, floral border, Garth, 3½", pr **20.00**
Canoe, souvenir, gold rim, 6" **12.00**
Chessie Cat, satin, 11"................................ **100.00**
Coal bucket, wire handle **10.00**
Frying Pan, two pouring spouts, gold rim 5¼" **12.00**
Oaken bucket, wire handle............................. **10.00**
Pipe, rests on three legs, 5¾" **10.00**
Top hat, English hobnail **10.00**
Vase, Asters in relief, 16273, 5" **15.00**
Vase, Iris in relief, 16254, 6" **15.00**
Vase, red & green poppies in relief, satin, 16255, 8" ... **30.00**
Vase, satin finish, Cattail design, disk foot **20.00**
Vase, satin finish, round flower arranger top, tapers, 8" ... **20.00**
Witches pot, three feet **10.00**
Vase, fluted, footed, enameled florals, pontil, 6¼" **22.00**
Fluted, footged, enameled florals, pontil, 9¾" **45.00**
Footed, enameled florals, butterfly, 11¼" **55.00**
Square, enameled stork on front, florals on 3 sides, 8" ... **35.00**
Viking Glass, Dish w/crystal swan handle, 5" **20.00**

Westmoreland
Ash tray, turtle figural **8.00**
Candlestick, Wrap Around, 6½" **18.00**
Cigarette box , turtle w/cover......................... **38.00**

Covered swan dish, lattice edge base **110.00**
Hen on nest, diamond weave base, 4½″ long **110.00**
Pistol **10.00**
Plate, For-Get-Me-Not border, enameled deer **30.00**
Plate, For-Get-Me-Not border, enameled fisherboy **30.00**
Plate, For-Get-Me-Not border, enameled girl, swinging **30.00**
Plate, three owls **30.00**
Robin on next, twig foot **110.00**
Salt dip, lotus **10.00**
Shell compote, dolphin stem, 1049, 6″ **50.00**
Standing rooster, 2 pc, 8½″ **80.00**
Sherbet, chicken head & tail in satin finish **18.00**

Blown Glass

Blown glass is rather difficult to date--18th and 19th century examples vary little as to technique or style. It ranges from primitive to the sophisticated. The metallic content of very early glass caused tiny imperfections that are obvious upon examination

In America, Stiegel introduced the English technique of using a patterned part size mold, a practice which was generally followed by many glasshouses after the Revolution. From 1820 to about 1850, glass was blown into full size 3 part molds.

Bottle, olive green, 18½x17½″ **350.00**
Bowl, footed, blue, 16 ribs, rolled rim, bubbled, 3x8″ **50.00**
Candlestick, clear w/spiral threading, Pittsburg, 10″ **575.00**
Creamer, cobalt, triangle rim, bulbous, 3¾″ **355.00**
Decanter w/pewter jigger top, Pillar mold, Pittsburg, 10″ **135.00**
Decanter, acorn stopper, 3 rigaree rings, Keene, qt size **225.00**
Decanter, sunburst, 12 diamond base, diamond quilt stopper, 10″ **195.00**
Decanter, three mold, sunburst pattern, acorn stopper, 11″ ... **130.00**
Fish bowl, waisted shape, 18x11″ **185.00**
Fishbowl, cone shape based, turned down rim, 1800s, 12″ **65.00**
Flask, blown in 20 diamond mold, amethyst, 6″ **380.00**
Flask, historical, double eagle, aqua, Pittsburg **65.00**
Hat w/folded rim, amber, 13″ **65.00**
Hat w/folded rim, three mold, 2″ **70.00**
Hyacinth vase, funnel base, folded rim, sapphire, 8″ **145.00**
Inkwell, olive, three mold, cylinder, 2¼″ dia **95.00**
Mug, opalescent blue, floral decor, applied handle, 2¾″ **110.00**
Paperweight, apple whimsey w/applied green leaves **110.00**
Pitcher, light emerald, 24 swirled ribs, Zanesville, 6″ **1,650.00**
Pitcher, pillar molded, 12 rib, 9″ **235.00**
Pitcher, wide rim, ovoid body, ribbed diamond, 6″ **240.00**

Rolling pin, amethyst, double handle, 15½″ **90.00**
Twine holder, applied blue rim, floral engraved, 5″ **265.00**
Vase, Pillar mold, applied foot & stem, Pittsburg, 9¾″ **95.00**
Vinegar bottle, double neck ring, cobalt **170.00**
Wig stand, footed, 1700s **600.00**
Wine glass, applied foot & stem w/wafer, 4½″ **40.00**
Whiskey taster, golden amber, 16 ribs broken swirl, 2½″ **215.00**

Blue and White Stoneware

Blue and white stoneware-- much of which was decorated with in-mold designs ranging from grazing cows to Dutch children--was made by practically every American pottery from the turn of the century until into the 1930s. Crocks, pitchers, washsets, rolling pins and canisters are only a few of the many items of the "country" pottery that has become one of today's popular collectibles.

Roseville, Brush-McCoy, U.H.L. Co. and Burley Winter were among those who produced it, but very few pieces were ever signed.

Baked bean pot, Boston Baked Beans, one handle, 10″ **20.00**
Baker w/lid, Chain Link, 7½x7″ **85.00**
Batter jar, Wildflower stencil w/lid, 8″ **150.00**
Batter pail, Basketweave & Flower, 7″ **135.00**
Bedpan, diffused blue, 12″ **100.00**
Beer cooler, Elves in shoulder band, brass spigot, 18x14″ **500.00**
Berry bowl, Cosmos, 2½x4¾″ **65.00**
Berry bowl, diffused blues, 2½x4½″ **55.00**
Bowl, Flying Bird, 6½″ **195.00**
Bowl, Wedding Ring, full set of 6 graduated sizes **375.00**
Brandy jug, hunting scene in relief, 8″ **375.00**
Butter crock w/lid, Draped Windows, flower finial, 8x9″ **200.00**
  Diffused blues, 1 lb, open **85.00**
  Victorian medallion w/stenciled Butter, 5x5″ **125.00**
  Advertising, 6x6″ **75.00**
  Apricots w/Honeycomb, clay lid, bail **175.00**
  Butterfly, 5 lb, no lid **95.00**
  Cows & Columns, open **175.00**
  Cows & Fence, clay lid, bail **300.00**
  Daisy & Trellis, clay lid, bail **125.00**
  Diffused blues, printed word, lid **110.00**
  Dragonfly & Flower, clay lid **175.00**
  Farm scene, wood lid **110.00**
  Grapes & leaves in relief band, 3x6½″ **100.00**
  Printed cows, no lid or bail **85.00**
  Swastika, clay lid, bail **85.00**
  Eagle, clay lid, bail, scroll bands, punching **300.00**
Canisters, Basketweave w/stenciled lettering, clay lid, ea **50.00**
  Diffused blue, stenciled lettering, open, ea **95.00**
  Snowflake stencil, open, 6½″, ea..................... **100.00**
Chamber, Beaded Rose Cluster & Spear Point **125.00**
  Blueband w/Earthworms **325.00**
  Bowknot, married lid **135.00**
  Fleur de Lis & Scroll, 13″ **225.00**
  Open Rose & Spear Point Panel **115.00**
  Wildflower stencil **100.00**
Cider cooler, Good to the Core, wood spigot, 15x13″ **250.00**
Cider crock, Brushed Leaves, stippled background, ears,18x16″ **150.00**
Coffee pot w/lid, diffused blues **225.00**
Coffee pot w/lid, Swirl, diagonal blue streaks, 11½x6″ **450.00**
Cookie jar, Flying Bird, 9″ **325.00**
  Grooved Blue w/lid **125.00**
  Put Your Fist In, Basketweave **150.00**
Creamer, Arc & Leaf Paneled, 4½″ **65.00**
Crock, Barrel Staves, pail style **175.00**

Crock, Three Apricots, w/Honeycomb, 10″ **100.00**
Cup, Bowtie w/blue bird transfer, 3″ **75.00**
   Paneled Fir Tree, 3½″ **75.00**
   Wildflower w/Embossed Ribbon & Bow, 4½″ **75.00**
Custard, Fishscale, 5″ **75.00**
Double roaster, Chain Link, 9x11″ **125.00**

Figural, Kewpie Thinker, attributed to Ungemach, 5½″ **335.00**
Footwarmer, diffused blue bands, A Warm Friend **175.00**
Footwarmer, Stone Pig for Cold Feet **250.00**
Grease jar, Flying Bird **250.00**
Hot water pitcher, Beaded Panels w/Open Rose **200.00**
Ice Tea cooler, Blue Banded, #3, pushbutton spigot, 13x11″ . . **275.00**
Ice crock, Barrel Staves, rope bands, ice tongs, 4½x6″ **150.00**
Ice water jug, Polar Bear, disk type, 10x9¾″ **375.00**
Johnston Cold Fudge Crock, 13x12″ **200.00**
Measuring cup, Spearpoint & Flower Panels, 6″ **115.00**
Milk crock, Daisy & Lattice, good color, 4x8″ **110.00**
   Lovebird, bail & grip, 9″ **125.00**
   Three Apricots w/Honeycomb, bail & grip, 10″ **110.00**
Mixing bowl, Currants & Diamonds, 5x9½″ **100.00**
   Diamond Point, sunburst base, 5½x10½″ **135.00**
   Feathers, 5½x10½″ **125.00**
   Flying Bird, 5x7½″ **100.00**
Mug, advertising, banded, 4½″ **45.00**
   Basketweave & Flower, roped sq top handle, 5″ **75.00**
   Diffused blue, 5½″ **100.00**
   Fannie Flagg, Robinson Clay Pottery, 5½″ **150.00**
   Flemish, golfer **65.00**
   Flying Bird, 5″ **150.00**
   Monk in reserve, 4½″ **85.00**
Mustard pot, Strawberry, Robinson Clay Pottery, 4x3″ **75.00**
Pickle crock w/lid, bail & grip, blue banded, 12x9″ **115.00**
Pickle crock, Heinze Co, advertising, 8x8″ **200.00**
Pie plate, Blue Walled Brick-Edge base, star mk, 10½″ **100.00**
Pitcher, American Beauty Rose, 10″ **225.00**
   Apricot in chain medallion, 8″ **150.00**
   Avenue of Trees, good color, 9″ **175.00**
   Bands & Rivets, 5½″ **115.00**
   Barrel Staves, 7″ **125.00**
   Basketweave & Flower, Morning Glory, 9″ **175.00**
   Bluebirds, blue bands top & bottom, 9″ **200.00**
   Butterfly in rope reserve, stippled background, 9″ **175.00**

Cattails, 10″ **145.00**
Cherries & Leaves in top & base band, 9½″ **250.00**
Cherry Cluster & Basketweave, 10″ **150.00**
Cherry Cluster, fine mesh background w/dots, 7½″ **175.00**
Columns & Arches, 9″ **275.00**
Cows in rope & bead reserve, 8½″ **175.00**
Daisy Cluster, bulbous **175.00**
Doe & Fawn, 8½″ **175.00**
Dutch Children & Windmill, 9″ **150.00**
Dutch Landscape, stencil **150.00**
Edelweiss, stippled background, metal rest, 9″ **200.00**
Flemish figures, 9½″ **500.00**
Flying Bird, 9″ **275.00**
Grape & Leaf Band, 9″ **125.00**
Grape Cluster in Shield, 8″ **175.00**
Grape Cluster on Trellis, 7x7″ **125.00**
Grape w/Rickrack on Waffle background, 8″ **100.00**
Indian Boy & Girl, sq branch handle, 6¼″ **225.00**
Indian in War Bonnet, 9″ **200.00**
Iris, quilted diamond band, 9″ **150.00**
Leaping Deer, 8½″ **150.00**
Lincoln Head, Uhl, 10″ **400.00**
Lovebird in beaded reserve, 8½″ **200.00**
Monastery & Fishscale, 9″ **175.00**
Paul Revere scene, 7″ **425.00**
Peacock w/palms & berries, 7¾″ **300.00**
Pine Cone, 9½″ **175.00**
Poinsettia, caned background, bulbous **175.00**
Printed Acorns, stencil, 8″ **135.00**
Printed Dutch Farm, stencil, 9″ **175.00**
Rose on Trellis, bulbous base **125.00**
Scroll & Leaf, 8″ **195.00**
Stag & Pine Trees in relief, 9″ **200.00**
Swan in reserve, deep blue shading, 8½″ **175.00**
Swastika, Indian Good Luck Sign, 9″ **185.00**
Wild Rose w/flower band at top, 9″ **150.00**
Wild Rose, spongewear bands, 9″ **225.00**
Wildflower stencil, blue bands **175.00**
Windmill & Bush, 9″ **200.00**
Pitcher & bowl, Basketweave & Flower **250.00**
   Feather & Swirl **300.00**
   Wild Rose **250.00**
Refrigerator jar, diffused blue w/lid, bail & grip, 6″ **125.00**
Roaster, diffused blues, lidded, 8½x12″ **125.00**
   Roaster, Heart & Drapery, open, 5x12″ **150.00**
   Wildflower stencil, lidded, 8½x12″ **125.00**
Rolling pin, advertising, Blue Bands **175.00**
   Advertising, Wildflower & Blue Band **200.00**
   Swirl, 13x13″ **225.00**

   Wildflower & Blue Band, no advertising **165.00**
Salt crock, Apricots in Medallions **150.00**
   Blackberry, wood lid **125.00**
   Blue Band, clay lid **95.00**
   Butterfly, wood lid **125.00**
   Daisy on Snowflakes, clay lid **175.00**
   Eagle w/arrow in its claws, clay lid **275.00**

Flying Bird, clay lid 300.00
Flying Bird 250.00
Grapevine on Fence, clay lid 175.00
Peacock, clay lid 175.00
Sand jar, polar bear & seals in relief, 13½" . . . 250.00
Scuttle mug, diffused blues, 6" 400.00
Soap dish, Cat's Head 150.00
Flower Cluster w/Fishscale 125.00
Indian In War Bonnet 150.00
Lion's Head 150.00
Spice jar, Cinnamon, clay lid 125.00
Spittoon, Lilies & Plumes 125.00
Peacock, 9x10" 250.00
Poinsettia & Basketweave, 9x9¾" 75.00
Sunflowers 135.00
Stein, Monk w/stein & mug, 11" 350.00
Syrup dispenser, Pep-So, 12x9" 275.00
Teapot w/lid, bail & grip, Swirl, 9x6½" 450.00
Tobacco jar, Basketweave, clay lid 150.00
Tobacco jar, Duke of Monmouth, blue, lidded . . 200.00
Toothbrush holder, Blue Band 45.00
Toothpick, Swan, 3¼x4" 65.00
Tumbler, diffused blues, 6" 65.00
Water cooler, Apple Blossom, brass spigot w/fishtail, 17x15" . . 525.00
Cupid in reserve, brass turn spigot, 15x12" . . . 525.00
Polar Bear, seals, Aurora Borealis, 17x15" . . . 525.00
Wesson oil jar, 5x5" 65.00

Blue Bird China

Made from 1910-1934, Blue Bird china is lovely ware decorated with flying blue birds among pink flowering branches. It was inexpensive dinnerware and reached the height of its popularity in the second decade of this century. Several potteries produced it; shapes differ from one manufacturer to another, but with only minor variations, the decal remains the same.

Among the backstamps, you'll find W. S. George, Cleveland, Carrollton, Homer Laughlin & Limoges China of Sebring, Ohio...and there are others.

Bowl, berry, Limoges China Co, USA, gold rim, 6" 5.00
Master berry, 8½x3" 14.00
Butter pat, relief molded edge w/gold rim, 3" 6.00
Butter w/cover, tab handles 60.00
Casserole w/lid, oval w/handles, 11½x4½" 45.00
Creamer, Homer Laughlin, squat, bulbous base, 4" . . . 12.50
Tall, waisted, 4½", *illus* 12.50
Cup & saucer, Carrollton China 12.00
Deep bowl, Madison, WS George, 5x3" 10.00

Demi cup, footed, 3½" 15.00
Mug, 3" 13.50
Plate, blue rim, 9" 7.50
Derwood, WS George, plain rim, 9½" 7.50

Platter, Homer Laughlin, Empress, oval, 15½x10" 18.00
Soup bowl, flat, paneled edge, 8½" 10.00
Sugar w/lid, Homer Laughlin, 3½" 14.00

Blue Ridge

Blue Ridge dinnerware was produced by Southern Potteries of Erwin, Tenn., from the late 1930s until 1956, in 8 basic styles and over 400 different patterns, all of which were hand decorated under the glaze. Vivid colors lit up floral arrangements of seemingly endless variation, fruit of every sort from simple clusters to lush assortments, barnyard fowl, peasant figures, and unpretentious texture patterns.

Although it is these dinnerware lines for which they are best known, collectors prize the artist signed plates from the 40s, and the limited line of character jugs made during the 50s most highly.

Antique Leaf, ashtray 10.00
Batter jug 15.00
Custard 2.75
Plate, 10" 3.50
Platter 6.75
Sugar w/lid & creamer 8.50
Autumn Apple, platter, 12" 6.00
Bowl, 5¼" 2.50
Bowl, 6¼" 3.25
Bowl, 9½" 4.75
Bowl, oval, 9" 4.00
Cup & saucer 4.00
Plate, 6¼" 1.25
Plate, 9" 2.75
Sugar w/lid & creamer 8.00
Blossom Top, shakers, 6", pr 15.00
Blue Heaven, platter, 11½" 6.50
Plate, 6" 2.00
Plate, 10" 4.50
Salt & peppers, tall, pr 12.00
Bountiful, platter, 11½" 5.50
Cherry Cobbler, plate, 7" 1.50
Chickory, plate, 10" 2.00
Chintz, leaf relish 14.00
Clover, platter, 11½" 6.00
Crab Apple, bowl, 5¼" 2.00
Creamer 2.50
Cup & saucer 4.50
Plate, 10" 4.00
Platter, big apple 8.50
Platter, small 6.00
Dutch Bouquet, vegetable bowl, 9" 7.00
Fantasia, bowl, 5¼" 2.50
Cereal, 6" 3.00
Cup 3.00
Plate, 6" 2.00
Plate, 7½" 3.00
Plate, 9½" 4.00
Plate, 10" 4.00
Platter, 11" 7.00
Platter, 13" 8.50
Saucer 2.00
Sugar w/cover & creamer 10.00
Teapot w/cover 16.00
Vegetable bowl, oval 8.00
Fruit Fantasy, coffee pot w/cover 24.00
Plate, 9½" 3.50
Salt & pepper, mushroom shape 4.50

Sugar & creamer **5.00**
Fruit Punch, shell relish **15.00**
Garden Lane, plate, 6″ **1.50**
Greenbriar, plate, 9½″ **3.50**
  Platter, 11½″ **6.00**
June Bouquet, plate, 9½″ **2.50**
Mayflower, bowl, 5¼″ **2.00**
  Plate, 9½″ **3.50**
Mountain Bells, cup & saucer **2.00**
  Plate, 6″ **1.00**
  Plate, 9″ **1.50**
Mountain Nosegay B, bowl, 5¼″ **3.00**
  Cup & saucer **6.50**
  Plate, 6″ **2.00**
  Plate, 7″ **3.50**
  Plate, 9½″ **4.50**
  Plate, 10″ **5.50**
  Sugar w/cover, large **6.50**
Pauline, platter, 11½″ **6.00**
Pinkie, cup, regular **3.50**
  Plate, 9½″ **3.50**
  Saucer, regular **2.00**
  Relish **5.50**
Posey, platter, 11½″ **6.00**
Quilted Fruit, cup & saucer **5.50**
  Plate, 6″ **1.50**
  Plate, 10″ **5.00**
  Sugar w/lid & creamer **17.50**
Red Apple, ashtray, green edge **6.00**
Roses, bowl, 5¼″ **2.00**
  Plate, 6″ **1.50**
  Plate, 8½″ **3.00**
  Plate, 10″ **4.00**
  Platter, 14″ **5.00**
  Relish, 3 part **16.00**
  Soup w/handles **3.00**
Ridge Daisy, cigarette box **6.00**
  Leaf relish w/handle **6.00**
  Plate, 8″ **1.50**
  Plate, 9½″ **2.50**
  Plate, 10″ **2.00**
  Platter, 14″ **5.00**
  Sugar w/cover **3.50**
  Tumbler, 12 oz **3.00**
Rooster, dinner plate **6.50**
  Plate, 10″ **6.50**
  Platter **12.50**
Rondelay, platter, 11½″ **6.50**
Rustic Plaid, plate, 9″ **3.00**
Sculptured Fruits, pitcher, 7″ **20.00**
Spray, relish green edge **15.00**
Sundrop, bowl, 5½″ **1.50**
  Cup & saucer **3.00**
  Plate, 6″ .... **.75**
  Plate, 9″ **1.75**
  Plate, 10″ **1.50**
Sunny, cup & saucer **4.50**
Sunny, plate, 10″ **3.00**
Wild Cherry, bowl, 5½″ **4.50**
  Bowl, 6¼″ **2.00**
  Cup & saucer **3.50**
  Plate, 9½″ **2.50**
  Plate, 10½″ **6.50**
  Sauce dish **1.00**

Soup, 8″ **2.00**
  Soup, flat **6.50**
Wild Strawberry, bowl, 5½″ **2.00**
  Bowl, 6″ **3.00**
  Creamer, large **4.00**
  Plate, 9½″ **3.50**
  Platter, 11¾″ **5.50**
  Platter, oval, 11″ **5.00**
  Salad fork **5.75**
  Salad spoon **5.75**
  Saucer, regular **2.00**
  Sugar & cover, large **5.00**
Yellow Mums, bowl w/handle, 6″ **3.50**
  Plate, 8″ **2.50**
  Plate, 9″ **3.50**
  Plate, 10″ **4.50**

Boehm

Boehm sculptures were the creation of Edward Marshall Boehm, a ceramic artist who coupled his love of the art with his love of nature to produce figurines of birds and animals in lovely background settings accurate to the smallest detail.

His first pieces were made in the very early 1950s, in Trenton, New Jersey, under the name of Ozzo Ceramics. Today, known as Edward Marshall Boehm, Inc., the private, family-held corporation produces not only the porcelain sculptures listed below, but collectors plates as well.

Ashtray, Acorn **50.00**
Figurine, Alba Madonna **950.00**
  American Cocker **350.00**
  Arabian Stallion **950.00**
  Baby Blue Bird, 4¾″ **250.00**
  Baby Blue Jay, 4½″ **175.00**
  Baby Buntings in Nest, 3½″, *illus* **180.00**
  Baby Cedar Waxwing, 3″ **145.00**
  Baby Chick **225.00**

Baby Crested Flycatcher, 5¼″, *illus* **200.00**
Baby Goldfinch, 4¼″ **190.00**
Baby Koala **725.00**
Baby Ocelot **600.00**
Baby Robin, 3½″ **250.00**
Baby Wood Thrush, 4¼″ **225.00**
Barn Owl, 5″, pr **250.00**
Blue Grosbeck **1,050.00**
Bobolink, issued 1964, 15″ **850.00**
Boreal Owl, 5″, pr **325.00**
Canada Geese **640.00**
Cardinals II **4,000.00**
Cedar Waxwing **175.00**
Charging Rhino **9,500.00**

Chick	225.00
Chipmunk, issued, 1961, #1513	300.00
Choir Boy	260.00
Cocker, brown & white	395.00
Colt, old, RPC 308-02	600.00
Common Tern, issued, 1968, 14″	4,500.00
Crested Flycatcher	2,700.00
Elephant	540.00
Female rabbit, old	150.00
Fledgling Blackburian Warbler, 4″	225.00
Fledgling Blue Jay	200.00
Fledgling Canada Warbler, issued 1967, 8½″	775.00
Fledgling Kingfisher	225.00
Fledgling Magpie, 6″	180.00
Fledgling Red Poll, 4″	160.00
Fledgling Western Bluebirds, 5¾″, illus	285.00
Giant Panda	5,200.00
Goldfinch	175.00
Great Horned Owl, 5½″, pr	320.00
Green Jayes	600.00
Hummingbird on Cactus	1,100.00
Kestrels, pr	2,400.00
King Tut Cheetah Head	350.00
King Tut Falcon Head	400.00
King Tut God Anubis	425.00
King Tut, 1977	70.00
Long Haired Angel	285.00
Mallards, 10½″, pr	1,900.00
Mergansers, pr	2,300.00
Mother Elephant & Calf	1,200.00
Mouse, 3½″	195.00
Mute Swans, female 10″, male 17½″, pr	5,500.00
Nuthatch	850.00
Nyala	5,700.00
Orangutan	450.00
Peace Rose	200.00
Penguin	250.00
Pied Wagtail	550.00
Poodle, 3x5″	195.00
Puffin	200.00
Queen of the Night Cactus	650.00
Reclining Panda	500.00
Reclining Poodle, old	240.00
Rhododendron w/Butterflies	1,000.00
Saw Whet, 5″, pr	300.00
Screech Owl, pr	320.00
Song Thrush	3,000.00
Standing Cygnet	200.00
Swan Lake Camellia w/Bumble Bee	825.00
Towhee, issued 1963, 8″	1,100.00
Tree Sparrow	700.00
Trumpeter Swans, taller, 17¾″, pr	5,000.00
Tufted Titmice	1,400.00
Woodthrushes, pr	6,000.00
Young & Spirited	1,500.00
Young American Bald Eagles, 9¾″, pr	1,500.00

Bohemian Glass

Bohemian glass has come to refer to a type developed in Bohemia in the late 6th century at the Imperial Court of Rudolf II, the Hapsburg Emperor. The popular artistic pursuit of the day was stonecarving, and it naturally followed to transfer familiar procedures to the glass making industry.

In the next century a formula was discovered that produced a glass with a fine crystal appearance that lent itself well to deep intricate engraving, and the art was further advanced.

Although many other types of art glass were made there, collectors today use the term Bohemian glass to indicate clear glass overlaid with color, through which a design is cut or etched. Red on crystral was used most often, but other colors may also be found.

Biscuit jar w/cover, deer & castle, ruby	150.00
Candlestick w/brass base & socket, ruby stem, 8″	40.00
Cologne bottle, red w/frosted scene	42.00
Decanter, cranberry, enameled design	125.00
With stopper, ruby, engraved deer & house, 8″	75.00
Finger bowl, Vintage decor, cobalt	32.00
Finger lamp, grape vine design, 1886 pat	165.00
Goblet, cranberry w/gold & enameled overlay, Holzner, 7½″	135.00
Lusters, white & pink, cut, enamel floral on prisms, pr 13″	250.00
Salt dip set, 6 dips & spoons, in orig box, Czech	30.00
Stein, red decor on clear, 3½″	75.00
Sweetmeat, ruby, fancy etching, 12″	80.00
Tumbler, burgandy overlay, bull's eye cutting, 5¼″	95.00
Vase, amber cut glass, 8½″	70.00
Cut ruby glass, 7″	60.00
Deer head & wreath, pedestal base, 10½″	50.00
Ruby, 4½″	30.00
Ruby, etched & panel cut, 13″	50.00

Ruby w/Vintage design on acid band, 10½″	50.00
Triple overlay white, clear, ruby, hp florals, 7″	300.00
White cut to green, florals, gold decor, 5x3½″	150.00
Whiskey tumbler, ruby glass, engraved & cut	12.00
Wine, knob stem w/frosted grape leaves	28.00

Bootjacks and Bootscrapers

Bootjacks were made from metal or wood--some were fancy figural shapes, others strictly business! Their purpose was to facilitate the otherwise awkward process of removing one's boots. Bootscrapers were handy gadgets that provided an effective way to clean the soles of mud and such.

Bootjack, cricket, ci, gilt paint, hole for hanging	33.00
Hand forged iron, 2 hearts	29.00
Pa. pine, Dutch carved tulips, 14″ long	85.00
Sycamore, early roughcut, 16″ long	25.00
Try Me, ci, 12″	35.00
Wooden, monkey in suit, primitive, early 1900s	40.00
Bootscraper, 18th century, hand forged iron, scrolled top, 6x8½″	60.00

Black Scottie dog, iron, 10x14″ **40.00**
Dachshund, sm **50.00**
Hand forged iron **15.00**
Mudder's Little Helper, ci **80.00**
Naughty Nellie, ci, detailed, late 1800s, 11x4x2″ **75.00**
Witch, hand forged iron **75.00**

Bottles and Flasks

As far back as 1 B.C., the Romans preferred blown glass containers for their pills and potions. Though you're not apt to find many of those, there are bottles of every size, shape and color to intrigue today's collectors.

American business firms preferred glass bottles in which to package their commercial products, and used them extensively from the late 18th century on. Bitters bottles contained "medicine", actually herb flavored alcohol, and judging from the number of these found today, their contents found favor with many! Scores of brands were sold; among the most popular were Dr. H.S. Flint & Co. Quaker Bitters, Dr. Kaufman's Anti-Cholera Bitters, and Dr. J. Hosetter's Stomach Bitters.

Perfume or scent bottles were produced abroad by companies all over Europe from the late 16th century on. Perfume making became such a prolific trade that as a result beautifully decorated bottles were fashionable. In America, they were produced in great quantities by Stiegel in 1770, and Boston and Sandwich in the early 19th century. Cologne bottles were made first in about 1830, and toilet water bottles in the 1880s.

Spirit flasks from the 19th century were blown in specially designed molds that produced various motifs including political subjects, railroad trains, and symbolic devices.

From the 20th century, early pop and beer bottles are very collectible, as are nearly every extinct commercial container.

Ceramic whiskey decanters were brought into prominence in 1955 by the James Beam Distilling Company. Few other companies besides Beam produced these decanters during the next 10 years or so; however other companies did follow suit, so that today there are at least 20 prominent companies and several on a lesser scale that produce these decanters.

Decanters very in size from miniatures (approximately 2 oz) to gallon sizes. Values vary from a few dollars to more than $3,000.00 per decanter. A mint condition decanter is one with no chips or cracks and all labels intact. Whether a decanter is full or not has no bearing on the value. A missing federal tax stamp does not lessen the value of the decanter. It is advisable to empty the contents of a ceramic decanter for many reasons--the thin glaze inside the decanter could crack, allowing the contents to seep through the porus china thus ruining the decanter.

B O & C Wilson Botanical Druggists **55.00**
Baby, 1860s **20.00**
  Acme **30.00**
  Baby Bear, picture of bear, Rutter Bros **15.00**
  Brighton nurser **22.50**
  Clear turtle, Bimal, Ralph's Nurser **25.00**
  Little Man Drink to Your Heart's Content, flat **18.00**
Beer, Bebe & Co, black glass, 3 part mold, 8″ **5.00**
  Bosch Lake, Linden, Mich. **6.00**
  Burgis & Calbourne, Leamington, dk green, 8″ **5.00**
  Calumet Brewing Co, Calumet, Mich. **7.00**
  Champagne Velvet, giant, amber glass, 30x8″ dia **135.00**
  Coors, embossed **2.00**
  Elks, embossed elk, aqua **7.00**
  Grulsch **5.00**
  Independent Brewing Assn Chicago **6.00**
  Schlitz, ruby red, qt **20.00**
Bitters, African Stomach, round, amber, 9½″ **35.00**
  American Life, rectangular, amber, 9″ **155.00**

Angostura, in castor **45.00**
Augauer, Chicago **28.00**
Bartlett's Excelsior, 8-sided **150.00**
Big Bill's Best **55.00**
Bininger, pressed amber, figural cannon barrel, 12½″ **180.00**
Bischoff's Stomach, Charleston, S.C., amber, 6½″ **295.00**
Brown's Celebrated Indian Herb, amber, rolled mouth, 12¼″ . **65.00**
Brown's Indian Herb, figural, yellow, lt green **1,100.00**
Cascara, square, amber, 9½″ **23.00**
Celebrated Crown, amber **70.00**
Colleton, plain base **50.00**
Dr Boyce's Tonic **39.00**
Dr J Hostetteer's Stomach, amber, sq, 8¾″ **15.00**
Dr Petzolds German Bitters, amber, crude **80.00**
Dr Soule Hop, very crude, blob top **26.00**
Dr Von Hopfs Curacoa, Chamberlain **28.00**
Electric Band, square, amber, 9¾″ **18.00**
Fish, WH Ware, pat 1866 . . . . **115.00**
Greeley's Bourbon/Bitters, barrel, red amber, 9¼″ **55.00**
HP Herb Wild Cherry Bitters, amber, fine **140.00**
Hop & Malt, square, amber, 9½″ **75.00**
Hopkins Stomach, honey amber, ABM **17.00**
Ladies Leg, amber, 12″ **25.00**
National, pat 1867, ear of corn, lt brown **775.00**
Old Carolina **250.00**
Peruvian, amber, square, monogram in panel on reverse **40.00**
Prickley Ash Bitters Co, amber **20.00**

Pineapple, amber, 9″ **250.00**
Rex Kidney & Liver, Best Laxative & Blood Purifier **12.00**
Sarracenia **75.00**
Suffolk, Life Preserver, pig figural, 9″ **80.00**
Blown, aqua blue, 25 rib, swirl **275.00**
Bride's, clear glass, enamel flowers, pewter collar, cordial, 4¾″ **200.00**
  Clear glass, woman w/shoulder yoke & water, florals, 5″ . . **275.00**
  Clear w/flower decor all sides, orig pewter screw top, 6¼″ . . **350.00**
  Fox w/birds in backpack, German script, 6″ **375.00**
  Opaque blue glass, British officer/wht horse, Stiegel, 6¼″ . . **650.00**
Calabash, Jenny Lind, Glass House, deep green, pontil, 10½″ . **460.00**
  Jenny Lind, aqua qt, 9¾″ **95.00**
  Kossuth, tree, lt green, 10″ **125.00**
Chattanooga, Tenn. emblem bottom **20.00**
Coca-Cola, Chattanooga, Tenn. emblem bottom **20.00**
  Chattanooga, Tenn. emblem both shoulders **22.00**

Chattanooga, Tenn. emblem shoulders, arrow bottom slug plate **28.00**
Green, straight 6 oz, Bottling Co, Tracy City, Tenn., block letters **22.00**
Hobble skirt, 6 oz, pat Nov 16th, 1915 emblem **6.50**
Hobble skirt, 6 oz, pat Dec 25th, 1923 emblem **6.50**
Huntsville, Ala, emblem center, script dk amber **20.00**
Knoxville, Tenn. emblem both sides w/straight arrows **27.00**
Nashville, Tenn. emblem bottom **20.00**
Script, Columbus, Ohio, straight sides, amber **10.00**
Cologne, blown Thumbprint, 6 sides, 7½" **70.00**
Blue opalescent, glass, gold decor, 7" **180.00**
Cranberry, w/clear stopper, multi floral w/gold, 7" **245.00**
Evening in Paris, original label, 4" **10.00**
French opaline, melon ribbing, gold decor, 5½" **100.00**
Moser, malachite, 6½" **225.00**
Ruby glass, enameled floral w/gold, opal jewels, 7" **140.00**
Wht cut to translucent blue, gold decor, 6½" **175.00**
Decanter, blown 3 mold, clear flint glass, Arch & Fern, Gin, 9½" **110.00**
Blown 3 mold, clear, melon stopper, Shell & Ribbing body, 10¾" **110.00**
Demijohn, blown in mold, honey amber, 1850s, Stoddard, 17" . **75.00**
Moulded kidney shape, lt green, sheared mouth w/ring, 16½" **25.00**
Ovoid freeblown, olive amber, sheared mouth w/ring, 11¾" . . **30.00**
Donut shape, stoneware, 9" **135.00**
Double Gemel, clear blown, applied foot, rigaree necks, 6½" . . . **15.00**

Ezra Brooks

American Legion, Hawaii, 1973 . . . . **10.00**
American Legion, Houston, Texas, 1971 . . . . **58.00**
Auburn-1932, Boat Tail, 1978 . . . . **28.00**
Badger #2, Football, 1974 . . . . **22.00**
Bulldog, Georgia, 1971 . . . . **18.00**
Chicago Legionaire, 1972 . . . . **75.00**
Christmas Tree, 1979 . . . . **35.00**
Clown Bust #1, Smiley, 1979 . . . . **40.00**
Clown Bust #3, Pagliacci, 1979 . . . . **35.00**
Corvette, Mako Shark, 1979 . . . . **38.00**
Deer, White-Tail, 1974 . . . . **22.00**
Dog, Setter w/Bird, 1970 . . . . **9.00**
Dog, Setter, 1974 . . . . **19.00**
Duck, Canadian Loon, 1979 . . . . **40.00**
Dueling Pistol, 1968 . . . . **8.00**
Dueling Pistol, Japanese, 1968 . . . . **30.00**
Elephant, Big Bertha, 1970 . . . . **12.00**
Ez Jug #1, 1977, Kentucky Whiskey **20.00**
Ford Mustang, Indy Pace Car, 1979 . . . . **42.00**
Fox, Redtail, 1979 . . . . **45.00**
Fresno Grape, 1970 . . . . **8.00**
Fresno Grape, 1970, w/no gold, rare **58.00**
Glass Series, Christmas 1965 . . . . **13.00**
Go Big Red #1, 1970 . . . . **28.00**
Greensboro Open, 1972 . . . . **28.00**
Greensboro Open, map, 1974 . . . . **44.00**
Groucho Marx, 1977 . . . . **26.00**
Hereford, 1971 . . . . **14.00**
Historical Flasks, Glass Series, 1970, each **5.00**
Iowa Farmer, 1977 . . . . **77.00**
Kachina #1, Morning Singer, 1971 . . . . **165.00**
#2, Hummingbird, 1973 . . . . **75.00**
#8, Drummer-Hopata, 1979 . . . . **45.00**
Leopard, Snow, 1980 . . . . **49.00**
Maine Lighthouse, 1971 . . . . **24.00**
Minnesota & Michigan Jug, 1974 . . . . **24.00**
Nugget Classic, 1970 . . . . **10.00**
Nugget Rooster, 1969 . . . . **40.00**
Owl, Eagle #2, 1978 . . . . **80.00**
Owl, Snowy #3, 1979 . . . . **45.00**

Panda, 1972 . . . . **20.00**
Phoenix Bird, 1971 . . . . **35.00**
Queen of Hearts, 1969 . . . . **7.00**
Raccoon, 1978 . . . . **45.00**
Saddle, Silver, 1972 . . . . **28.00**
South Dakota National Guard, 1976 . . . . **30.00**
Stagecoach, Dakota Express, 1977 . . . . **24.00**
Tiger, Bengal, 1979 . . . . **42.00**
Totem Pole, 1973, Heritage China Series **13.00**

Trout & Fly, 1970 . . . . **12.00**
Walgreen's, 1973 . . . . **25.00**

Figural, Coachman, Van Dunks, puce or black **75.00**
Hessian soldier, clear, 7" **28.00**
Honeymoon, emerald green **30.00**
Horn of Plenty **25.00**
Moses, green screwcap **50.00**
Poland Water, amber, few light stains **250.00**
Flask, AG Booze, 1840, amethyst **450.00**
All Seeing Eye, lt amber pt **60.00**
Amber blown chestnut, 24 vertical body ribs, 6½" **550.00**
Anchor, Log Cabin, Spring Garden, aqua pint, 7½" **65.00**
Anchor on side, aqua pt, 7¾" **8.00**
Clasped Hands, cannon, aqua, applied mouth w/ring, ½ pt . . **60.00**
Corn for the World, aqua qt **145.00**
Cornucopia & basket, lt amber half pt **50.00**
Double eagle, deep golden amber, half pint **45.00**
Double eagle, olive amber pint **85.00**
Double eagle, Pittsburgh in oval, olive amber pt **55.00**
Double eagle w/ovals, aqua half pt **20.00**
Eagle & Cornucopia, green, crude, 7" **100.00**
Eagle w/shield, For Our Country, olive amber pint **1,100.00**
Figural powder horn **25.00**
For Pikes Peak, aqua half pint **20.00**
For Pikes Peak, Eagle w/Pittsburg, aqua pint **35.00**
Freeblown amber, straight neck, ovoid body, 12" **70.00**
G Geo Washington, Eagle FL, lt green pt, flared lip, 7" . . **1,150.00**
Gen Taylor, Fell's Paint, green pt, 7½" **1,300.00**
Good Game, willow and stag, aqua pint, pontil, 7" **100.00**
Jenny Lind, double, w/lyre, aqua qt **850.00**
Jenny Lind, w/lyre, aqua pint, 7" **675.00**
Lady's, clear w/diagonal lines, silver top, Universal, 1927 . . . . **50.00**
Lancaster Glass Works, Cornucopia, urn, lt blue pt **295.00**
Louisville Ky Glassworks, iron pontil, pint **55.00**
Masonic, Eagle, TWD, clear pt, yellow/green tint **75.00**

Masonic, Eagle & oval, olive amber pt, pontiled, 7".........**75.00**
Masonic, Franklin, Free Trade, lt emerald pt, 6½".........**375.00**
Monument, corn, aquamarine qt.........**50.00**
Murdock & Cassel, Zanesville, lt green pt, 6¾".........**1,000.00**
New England Pitkin, blown half-post, olive green, ribbed, 4¾" **350.00**
PW, Keen, sunburst, 7½".........**200.00**
Pikes Peak, aqua.........**125.00**
Ravenna Glass Co, Traveler's Companion, amber pint.....**275.00**
Scroll, dark olive pint, 6¾".........**335.00**
Scroll, emerald green pint, 6½".........**295.00**
Scroll, sapphire blue, 7".........**825.00**
Scroll, yellow green half pint.........**610.00**
Stoddard, Granite Glass, amber pt.........**100.00**
Success To The Railroad, aqua pint.........**200.00**
Success To The Railroad, double, olive amber pt.........**95.00**
Success To The Railroad, olive amber, Mt Vernon Glass, pt..**70.00**
Summer-Winter, aqua, 7½".........**35.00**
Sunburst, light emerald, pontiled, 7".........**250.00**
Sunburst, olive amber, half pint, 6½".........**190.00**
Sunburst, olive pint, 7½".........**265.00**
Taylor & Washington, Father Of Our Country, pontil.....**150.00**
Travelers Companion, wheat, amber qt.........**45.00**
Tree & sheaf of wheat.........**60.00**
Trees, golden amber qt, 8¼".........**250.00**

Union, clasped hands, aqua pint, 7¾".........**80.00**
Union, clasped hands, double, aqua qt, 8¾".........**40.00**
Union, eagle & banner, aqua half pint, 6".........**20.00**
Union, Wm Frank & Sons, Cannon, amber qt, 8¾".......**310.00**
Urn & Cornucopia, olive green half pint, 5½".........**45.00**
Washington & Taylor, aqua, w/pontil, 7".........**45.00**
Washington & Taylor, lt blue qt, 8".........**510.00**
Washington & Taylor, med amber qt, 8¾".........**450.00**
Washington & Taylor, sapphire blue pint, 6¾".........**750.00**
Washington & Taylor, smoky grey, 8".........**900.00**
Westford Glass Co, sheaf of wheat pictorial, olive amber pt...**55.00**
Zanesville, 24 ribs, neck swirl, amber grandfathers.........**950.00**
Zanesville, 24 swirled ribs, dark amber, 8½".........**350.00**
Gallatin, aqua blown 2 part, applied joined lips, 5½".......**175.00**
Garwood's Salts.........**35.00**
Grain & Tree, collared mouth, aquamarine qt.........**35.00**
H Homer's Cooking Extract, sparkler.........**32.00**
H Lakes Indian Specific, crude.........**325.00**
Hand Cooler, peacock blue, 3".........**40.00**

Ink, Carter, cobalt cathedral, qt.........**55.00**
  Clear glass, w/slender glass-threaded neck, primitive, 2".......**8.00**
  Cone, olive green, Bertinquoit.........**225.00**
  Glass threaded neck, w/cork cap, 2".........**8.00**
  Umbrella, amber, Stoddard, open pontil.........**110.00**
  Umbrella, aqua, open pontil.........**22.00**
  Umbrella, med green, open pontil.........**45.00**
Jewell Tea Co, rectangular, clear, 6½".........**20.00**

Jim Beam

Agnew Elephant, 1970.........**1,900.00**
Aida, 1978.........**344.00**
Antique Globe, 1980.........**25.00**
Ashtray Donkey, 1956, political.........**16.00**
Bing's 32nd, 1972.........**30.00**
Bing's 34th, 1974.........**90.00**
Bob Hope 14th, 1973.........**15.00**
Bob Hope 15th, 1974.........**10.00**
Cardinal, Male, 1968, Trophy Series.........**50.00**
Carmen, 1978.........**380.00**
Cat, 1967, Tabby, Siamese, or Burmese.........**13.00**
Centennial, Chicago Fire, 1971.........**15.00**
  St Louis Arch, 1964.........**25.00**
  St Louis Arch, 1967-68.........**17.00**
Charlie McCarthy, 1976.........**40.00**
Convention, #1, Denver, 1971.........**13.00**
  #2, Anaheim, June 18-25.........**68.00**
  #2, Anaheim, June 20-23.........**100.00**
  #4, Lancaster, 1974.........**108.00**
Dancing Scot, 1963, short.........**113.00**
Dancing Scot, 1964, tall.........**14.00**
Doe, 1963, Trophy Series.........**30.00**
Dog, 1979, St Bernard.........**64.00**

Duck's Unlimited, #2, 1975.........**23.00**

Duck, 1957, Trophy Series	35.00
Executive, 1955, Royal Porcelain	450.00
1956, Royal Gold Round	125.00
1958, Gray Cherub	385.00
1959, Tavern Scene	67.00
1960, Blue Cherub	125.00
1966, Majestic	30.00
1978, Texas Rose	26.00
Figaro, 1977	325.00
Fox, 1965, green coat	37.00
Golden Gate, 1969	56.00
Harold's Club, Covered Wagon	23.00
Harold's Club, Man in Barrel, #2, 1958	230.00
Harrah's grey	826.00
Hawaii, 1959	50.00
Horse, Appaloosa, 1974	12.00
Horse, Black or Brown, 1967	20.00
Idaho, 1962	58.00
Jewel Tea Wagon	95.00
John Henry, 1972	60.00
Kentucky Derby 95th, 1969	5.00
Kentucky Derby 96th, 1970, w/double roses stopper	20.00
King Kong, 1976	18.00
London Bridge, 1971	5.00
London Bridge, 1971, w/Medallion	190.00
Madame Butterfly, 1976	695.00
Miami Beach Elephant, 1972 Republican Convention w/plate	920.00
Milwaukee Stein, 1972	78.00
Mortimer Snerd, 1976	40.00
New Hampshire Golden Eagle, 1971, Regal China Series	43.00
New Jersey, 1963, blue	63.00
Nutcracker, 1978	280.00
Pearl Harbor, 1972	24.00
Pennsylvania Dutch Club, 1974	19.00
Rockwell Series, 1975, each	5.00
Sailfish, 1957, Trophy Series	35.00
Short Timer, 1975, Regal China Series	29.00
Stutz Bearcat	39.00
Submarine Club, 1977	64.00
Telephone #1, 1975	75.00
Twin Bridges Club, 1971	53.00
Two Handles Jug, 1965 Zimmerman	97.00
Washington DC Elephant, Republican Dinner, 1972	745.00

Lionstone

Annie Christmas	20.00
Annie Oakley	24.00
Backpacker	45.00
Bar Scene w/Nude, frame	500.00
Barber	45.00
Bartender	30.00
Basket Weaver Oriental	30.00
Basketball	10.00
Basketball Player	25.00
Belly Robber	18.00
Blacksmith	26.00
Blue Bird Western	25.00
Bluejay	23.00
Boxer	20.00
Buccaneer	30.00
Buffalo Hunter	35.00
Calamity Jane	27.00
Camp Cook	25.00
Camp Follower	21.00
Canada Goose	80.00

Cannonade	40.00
Cardinal	35.00
Cardinal, fancy bird series	45.00
Cavalry Scout	11.00
Chinese Laundryman	20.00
Circus Clown-Lampy, m	30.00
Clown #1, m	20.00
Country Doctor	15.00
Cowboy	12.00
Cowgirl	32.00
Dancehall Girl	55.00
Engineer, RR	14.00
European, Horseshoer	23.00
European, Silversmith	23.00
Falcon	23.00
Fireman #1	125.00
Fireman #2	125.00
Fireman #3	65.00

Fireman #7, Red Hat	125.00
Fisherman	42.00
Football Players	21.00
Frontiersman	17.00
Gambler	13.00
Gardener	34.00
George Washington	25.00
God of Love & War	25.00
God of War	20.00
Goddess of War	20.00
Gold Panner	44.00
Highway Robber	20.00
Hockey Players	22.00
Indian Proud	14.00
Indian Squawman	26.00
Indian Weaver	27.00
Indian, Casual	12.00
Jessee James	16.00
Johnny Lightening #2	45.00
Judge Circuit	14.00
Judge Roy Bean	27.00
Lonely Luke	70.00
Lucky Buck	15.00
Madame	42.00
Mailman	20.00
Meadowlark	22.00

Mecklenburg	26.00
Molly Brown	26.00
Molly Pitcher	19.00
Monkey Business	30.00
Mountain Man	19.00
Owls	35.00
Paul Revere	20.00
Pheasant, m	15.00
Photographer	27.00
Pie in Face, m	28.00
Police Assoc Convention	26.00
Railroad Engineer	14.00
Rainmaker, m	13.00
Renegade Trader	22.00
Riverboat Captain	13.00
Road Runner	30.00
Robber, Highway	13.00
Rose Parade	25.00
STP Car	20.00
Safari Giraffe	13.00
Safari Series, Buffalo, m	12.00
Safari Series, Elephant, m	12.00
Salty Tails, m	24.00
Saturday Nite Bath	45.00
Say It w/Music, m	24.00
Screech Owl	45.00
Sheepherder	53.00
Sheriff	10.00
Shootout at OK Corral	350.00
Sodbuster	14.00
Stage Driver	20.00
Swallows, Silver Bell	55.00
Tea Vender	34.00
Telegrapher	20.00
Tinker	29.00
Trader	23.00
Trapper	30.00
Tribal Chief	36.00
Valley Forge	25.00
Vigilante	10.00
Wells Fargo Man	14.00
Woodhawk	28.00
Woodpeckers	28.00

McCormick

Alexander G Bell	25.00
Bat Masterson	22.00
Blue Bird	16.50
Caio Baby	27.00
Centurion	20.00
Charolais	35.00
Chas Lindbergh	27.00
Dune Buggy	30.00
Eleanor Roosevelt	26.00
Elvis #1	85.00
Elvis #2	55.00
Elvis #3	55.00
Elvis Bust	32.00
Elvis Gold	265.00
Elvis Silver	225.00
French Telephone	32.00
George Washington Carver	27.50
Keg	32.00
Kit Carson	24.00
Mark Twain	30.00

Mississippi Rebels	12.00
Muhammid Ali	46.00
Napoleon	20.00
Ozark Ike	42.00
Paul Revere	38.00
Pirate #10	22.00
Purdue Boilermaker	14.00
Renault Racer	40.00
Robert E Lee	26.00
Sam Houston	24.00
Sir Lancelot	35.00
Tennessee Volunteers	24.00
Texas Longhorn	32.00
Train, 4 pc series	225.00
U S Marshal	40.00
Wild Bill Hickock	22.00
Woman Feeding Chickens	42.00

Medicine Bottles

Bull Extract of Sarsaparilla, rectangular, aqua, 7″	18.00
Dr Dieter's Zokoro, cork top, 10″	20.00
Dr Kennedy's Medical Discovery, green	24.00
Dr McMunn's Opium, open pontil	18.00
Dr Porter's N.Y., open pontil	13.50
Dr SS Fitch, open pontil, flat lip	30.00
EA Buckhout Dutch Liniment, embossed Dutchman, aqua, 4¾″	290.00
ER Durkee, open pontil, flat lip	16.00
Fletcher's Castoria Laxative, clear, 7″	2.50
Graham's Dyspepsia Cure, rectangular, clear, 8¼″	12.00
Log Cabin Sarsaparilla, amber, 9″	98.00

McKesson's, Cod Liver Oil, 9″	28.00
Miles Nervine, rectangular, aqua, 8¼″	5.00
Milk of Magnesia, pat 1906, blue	10.00
Mrs Winslow's Soothing Syrup, open pontil	13.00
Preston, Boston, open pontil, flat lip	10.00
Rohrer's Expectoral Wild Cherry Tonic, amber, iron pontil, 10½″	75.00
Rubifoam for the Teeth, cork insert, metal screw cap, 4½″	9.00
St Joseph's, Assures Purity, w/cork top	8.50
Tricopherous for Skin & Hair, open pontil	15.00
University Free Medicine, Philadelphia, aqua	70.00
Warner's Safe Kidney & Liver Cure, amber, cork top	25.00
Winona, Ye Old Indian Herb Tonic, 8″	25.00

Mid-Western, globular aqua miniature, 4" **40.00**
Milk, Anchorage Dairy, Buttermilk, w/logo & milkmaid, round, pt **50.00**
    Bentley & Sons, Baby Face, qt **7.00**
    Buzby Dairy Fairbanks, round, pt **55.00**
    Matanuska Maid Anchorage, Seeing is Believing, round, qt . . . **50.00**
    Seward Dairy Alaska, round, pt **55.00**
Mineral Water, Buffalo Lithia, aqua, embossed girl w/pitcher, ½ gal **25.00**
Mineral Water, Old Blue Seltzer, Newport Mineral Water Co, Ky. **15.00**
Mineral Water, Poland, amber, figural **250.00**

Old Commonwealth

Alabama National Champs **25.00**
Coal Miner #1, m, ... **50.00**
Coal Miner #1 . . . . **175.00**
Coal Miner #2, w/pick **60.00**
Coal Miner w/shovel **60.00**
Coal Miner, Lunch Time **60.00**
Leprechaun **42.50**
Lumberjack **42.50**

Perfume, advertising Seeley, w/glass stopper **15.50**
    Amber glass, applied grapes, gold, insect on bottle, 4¼x1¾" **325.00**
    Amethyst, glass, French, fluted sides, brass cover, 1850s **48.00**
    Amethyst, w/white loops, pewter top, 2¼" **100.00**
    Atomizer, Art Deco, glass, triangular metal top, 4" **18.00**
    Atomizer, clear glass w/chrome, 1920, 4" **18.00**
    Atomizer, cut crystal, signed Marcel Franck, 3" **85.00**
    Atomizer, paneled, clear glass, 1940s, 3" **10.00**
    Atomizer, red cut to clear glass, Japan, 3" **35.00**
    Black glass w/polychrome florals, 1½" **38.00**
    Blue/white opaque glass, wht opaque ball stopper, 4¾" **85.00**
    Blue jade, bulbous, alabaster neck & stopper, 4¾" **95.00**
    Clear glass w/fancy cut stopper, Lubin, France, 4" **15.00**
    Clear w/mahogany & wht swirls, blown, 5" **50.00**
    Cobalt, melon bottom section, gold decor, 4x2½" **100.00**
    Cranberry, w/ornate silver overlay **139.00**
    Cranberry, glass, lavendar/gold stylized flowers, 4x2" dia . . . **165.00**
    Cranberry glass, pink & blue flowers, much gold, 4¾x1½" . . **110.00**
    Cranberry opalescent swirl, clear pressed swirl stopper, 6¼" **125.00**
    Enamel on copper, Art Deco, Germany, 4½" **15.00**
    Green glass w/lacy gold decor, gold decor stopper, 7¼" **65.00**
    Green w/enameled lilies of the valley, pewter cap **40.00**
    Heart shape, cut glass w/sterling top **125.00**
    Laydown, latticino, figure-8 shape, pink striping 1860 . . . . . **85.00**
    Pincushion doll, pink skirt, grey hair, 4" **35.00**
    Pink cased, crystal crest & stopper, Fenton, 5" **18.00**
    Porcelain, German figural, 3½" **30.00**
    Porcelain, German floral, 4¾" **30.00**
    Queen Anne, blue **20.00**
    Victorian red & gold decor, scalloped rim **130.00**
    With silver overlay **30.00**
    Wheel cut crystal, blue enamel over sterling stopper, 4½" . . . **38.00**
    White rigaree, looping, 3¼" **75.00**
    Yellow w/clear acid cut stopper, 2 heads in relief **35.00**
Pickle, Gothic arch, aqua, 9" **100.00**
Pickle jar, aqua, Q **55.00**
Poison, aqua, Poisonous, Not To Be Taken, applied top, 6¾". . **25.00**
    Aqua, ribbed, applied top, 10" **38.00**
    Aqua, ribbed, applied top, 7" **20.00**
    Cobalt Owl, triangular, large size **15.00**
    Figural skull, poison embossed above eyes, cobalt blue, 4¼" **155.00**
    Not To Be Taken, 6-sided, cobalt **6.75**
    Triloid's, cobalt, 100% labels **15.00**
Sarsaparilla, Warner's Log Cabin **55.00**
Shaker, Anodyne, embossed Shaker, 4" **22.00**

Cherry Pectoral Syrup, Canterbury, pontil, aqua **110.00**
Extract Valerian, aqua, Bimal embossed **40.00**
Hair Restorer, amber, embossed Shaker, 7½" **25.00**
Syrup #1, Canterbury, HH, Bimal embossed **70.00**
Syrup #1, embossed Shaker, 7½" **25.00**

Ski Country

Antelope **50.00**
Baltimore Oriole **44.00**
Bassett **45.00**
Birth of Freedom, m, ... **49.99**
Blackbird **44.00**
Bob Cratchet **50.00**
Bob Cratchit/Tiny Tim, m, ... **29.00**
Cardinal **63.00**
Chukar Partridge **46.00**
Cowboy Joe **70.00**
Coyote Family **39.00**
Deer Dancer **78.00**
Duck, Pintail, ½ gal **250.00**
    Pintail, m, ... **28.00**
    Wood **210.00**
    Wood, m, ... **150.00**
Eagle, Harpy **130.00**
    Hawk, ornate, m **45.00**
    Majestic **375.00**
    Majestic, gal **1,800.00**
    Majestic, m **150.00**
Falcon, Peregrine, G **475.00**
Falcon, White **60.00**
Flycatcher **58.00**
Fox Family, m, ... **18.00**
Fox on Log **115.00**
Game Cocks, Fighting **200.00**
Giraffe in Cage **30.00**
Hawk Eagle **125.00**
Holstein Cow **45.00**
Jenny Lind, yellow **165.00**
Labrador Dog w/pheasant **65.00**
Labrador Dog w/pheasant, m **19.00**
Lion on Drum **38.00**
Merganser **70.00**
Mrs Cratchit, m **22.00**
Owl, Horned, G **1,045.00**
Owl, Screech Family, G **425.00**
Phoenix Bird **85.00**
Ringmaster **25.00**
Saw Whet **54.00**
Scrooge **45.00**
Snow Leopard **50.00**
Wyoming Bronco **54.00**

Soda Bottles

    Albert Von Harten, Savannah, Georgia, teal green **22.00**
    Ashland Bottling Works, Wisc., blob top, amber **20.00**
    Belfast Ginger Ale, aqua, round bottom, blob top, no stopper, 9" **12.00**
    Canada Dry Ginger Ale, carnival **12.00**
    City Bottling Works, Cleveland, Ohio, dk aqua **30.00**
    Donald Duck Beverage, blue silk screen of Donald **4.00**
    Henry Kuck, 1878, Savannah, Georgia, teal green, blob top . . **30.00**
    Hires, embossing, clear, 1910-20, 9½" **6.00**
    Hutchinson, Bennington Vermont, aqua **30.00**
    Jacob's Bottling Works, Cairo N.Y., clear w/swirls, 7" **5.00**
    John Graf, Milwaukee, blob top, amber, 8 embossed panels . . **18.50**
    John's English Brew Ginger Beer, crock, blob top, pt **22.00**
    Pepsi, amber, embossed **16.50**

Star Brand Super Strong, embossed star, cobalt marble, lt green	**10.00**
WHH Chicago, blob top, pontil, cobalt, dug	**30.00**
Spaulding's glue, open pontil	**11.00**
Star Harden's Hand Grenade Fire Extinguisher, electric blue	**36.00**
Udophowolfe's Schnapps, olive green, iron pontil	**65.00**
Whiskey, Avan Hoboken & Co olive green, 11¼"	**22.00**
Bellows & Co round w/blob seal, clear, 11"	**15.00**
Bininger, AM & Co, round, green, 8"	**75.00**
Crown Distilleries, sample, amethyst, 3½"	**25.00**
Evaion *H* Evaia, flint, rectangle, 10½"	**20.00**
Golden Wedding, bell in relief, carnival glass, 6½"	**15.00**
Jo Jo, lt amethyst, 7½"	**20.00**
Little Brown Jug, brown pottery, 2¾"	**30.00**
Obermannm, JB, amber, 12"	**30.00**
Pumpkin seed, embossed owl	**15.00**
Remington Commercial, Distilled Right, 12"	**11.00**
Stampede, Sears, amber, 6"	**12.00**
Van Dunk's Genever Trade Mark, amber corker, 9"	**50.00**
Zimmerman, red amber, takes cork	**20.00**

Wild Turkey

#1 Female	**295.00**
#3 On the Wing	**90.00**
#4 With Poult	**110.00**
#5 With Flags	**38.00**
#6 Striding	**19.00**
#7 Taking Off	**21.00**
#8 Strutting	**45.00**
Baccarat Crystal	**225.00**
Mack Bulldog	**15.00**
NC Liggett Meyers	**325.00**
South Carolina, 1974	**60.00**
Turkey Lore #1	**45.00**
Turkey Lore #2	**35.00**

Zanesville, amber, 9"	**600.00**
Zanesville, blue, 8"	**400.00**
Zanesville, club shape, aqua, blown, 24 swirl ribs, 6"	**195.00**
Zanesville, globular, amber, 24 swirled ribs, 7½"	**340.00**

Boxes

Boxes have been used by civilized man since ancient Egypt and Rome. Down through the centuries specifically designed containers have been made from every conceivable material. Precious metal, papier mache, battersea, oriental lacquer and wood have held riches from the treasuries of kings, snuff for the fashionable set of the last century, China tea, and countless other commodities.

Ballot, metal, Fenton Metallic Mfg, N.Y., 14x16x18"	**60.00**
Band, floral, signed Levi Weaver, Maryland, 1830s, 14x9½"	**55.00**
Brass, gilt, mosaic lid, 4 side medallions, 4½"	**6.50**
Brass, w/enameling, florals, small	**25.00**
Bride's, bent wood, grey w/multicolor florals, people, 16" long	**700.00**
Pine, birch laced, Norwegian	**135.00**
Pine, laced seams, polychrome florals w/angel, 10" long	**535.00**
Burl veneer, w/cross banded veneer & brass edging, 2¾x5½"	**20.00**
Candle, chip carved, geometric & floral, slide top, 1800s, 4x10"	**850.00**
Pine, old paint, slide cover table model, 1820s, 6x7x11"	**95.00**
Walnut, w/sliding lid, 5x14½x8"	**210.00**
Collar, decorated w/young lady in outdoor scene	**30.00**
Document, black/red leather, brass, wallpaper lining, 1800s, 5x10"	**65.00**
Tin, black w/red band, shell decor, loops/swags, 8x4½"	**225.00**
Tinware, red/gold trim, 1890s, w/key, 12x8x5¼"	**27.00**
Wooden, grain paint, 1800s, 6x16x10½"	**85.00**
Domed lid, beech w/polychrome birds, florals, 9x9x14"	**565.00**
Bent wood, stamped designs, 3x7x4"	**135.00**
Grain paint, bail handles, lock, 12x30x15"	**300.00**
Pine, dovetailed, coil wire hinges, 1890s, 8½x9x16"	**185.00**
Glass, clear w/enameled roses, gold leaf, brass trim, 2½x4"	**65.00**
Cobalt w/gold hinged lid, yellow enamel, 4" dia	**125.00**
Cranberry w/overall enamel decor, hinged lid, ormolu ft, 4" dia	**165.00**
Cranberry, decorated, w/hinged lid, 3" dia	**135.00**
Vaseline, partially opaque, gold decor, enameling 4" dia	**110.00**
Glove, simulated ruby decor, Flemish art, satin lined	**55.00**
Hat, metal, tole decor, ceramic insert, brass latch	**40.00**
Horn, oval, tin/wood lid & bottom, tooled, 2¾" long	**30.00**
Lacquer, black & gold, butterfly top, for cigars	**190.00**
Black w/gold birds & flowers, small, old	**55.00**
Black w/mother-of-pearl inlay, birds, branches, 2x6x4½"	**25.00**
Costume box, black w/brass trim, large, old	**175.00**
Oblong, contoured, russet/gold/black flowers & bamboo	**115.00**
Red over gold, w/cranes, large	**90.00**
Sewing box, black/gold birds & flowers, ivory trim	**1,400.00**
Leather covered, brass rivet trim, stencilled lining, 1800s, 6x12"	**95.00**
Tacked initial cover, 1800s, 8¾x18"	**80.00**

Metal, blue, lavendar "Tiffany" finish, signed, 5x6½"	**500.00**
Norwegian, painted tin, 1830s	**725.00**
Oval, bent wood, unfinished, 10½x15x22"	**35.00**
Pantry, wooden, original yellow paint, 8" dia	**75.00**
Patch, amber glass, florals, brass hinge, 2" dia	**85.00**
Amber glass, floral lid w/brass hinges, 1½x2" dia	**95.00**
Blue glass, pink flowers, gold leaves, brass hinges, 3x3½" dia	**85.00**
Cricket shape, brown/orange, removable lid, Fisher/Meig,, 5x2"	**75.00**

Green w/multicolor floral, red enamel at base, brass hinges . . .	**98.00**
Shell shape, French porcelain, scenic medallion, Sevres	**110.00**
Tortoise shell & silver, old	**75.00**
Pine, for shaving brush/soap, 1-pc, 1700s, handled, 6½" long .	**110.00**
Primitive, sliding lid, 3x5x13"	**25.00**
Red/black graining, yellow striping, 4x9x12"	**65.00**
Transfer w/girl reclining, dovetailed, A Wilson, 9½" long . . .	**140.00**
Porcelain, heart shape, Limoges, 4½"	**50.00**
Round, blue, w/red lid, polychrome decor, 1865, Pennsylvania.	**280.00**
Scandanavian, wood w/florals, 2" long	**45.00**
Sewing, oval, handled, Shaker	**125.00**
Slide top, w/window insert, rose pattern paper, signed, 3x3x8"	**115.00**
Spice, dark pine, 8 drawers, replacement porcelain knobs	**130.00**
Round, red/green stencil decor, 8 canisters, patent 1858. . . .	**260.00**
Stamp, brass, 2 compartments, decorative lid	**70.00**
Brass, sloping lid, 2-compartments	**44.00**
Ivory, inscribed Stamps, 3-compartments	**140.00**
Monogrammed, marked Udall & Ballow, 2" dia	**40.00**
Silverplated cast brass, 3 compartments	**36.00**
Sterling, round w/cover, slot, spindle, Lebolt	**130.00**
Wood w/hinged lid, 1850s, 1x4½x1"	**10.00**
Wood, figural doghouse, bulldog w/glass eyes, 2x2x3½"	**28.00**
Storage, metal, gold stencil JS & Co, 20x12x18"	**50.00**
Tea caddy, stemmed, 2 part, wood, red/yellow apple, 5½" . . .	**45.00**
Tortoise shell, w/mother-of-pearl border, gold decor, 1¼x5½".	**350.00**
Treen, polychrome foliage, scrolls on graining, 2½x4" dia . . .	**255.00**
With threaded lid, polychrome florals on brown, wear, 3x4" . .	**40.00**
Trinket, stencilled parchment, maroon/white, brass handle, 2x4½"	**75.00**
Tulip wood, grain paint, brass bale, wallpaper lining, 7x10x18"	**200.00**
Wood, cherry w/hinged lid, brass bale, dovetailed, w/till, 7x12"	**170.00**
Chip carved, removable top, signed, 1776, 2x6"	**275.00**

Boyd's Crystal Art Glass

In 1978, Bernard C. Boyd and his son bought the Degenhart factory in Cambridge, Ohio, acquiring 50 of her glass molds with the 'D in heart' trademark removed. Many are used by Boyd, who also produces the Louise doll; the pony, Joey; and the elephant, Zack. These are issued each month in a new and different color of crystal as well as slag or 'marble' glass.

Bell, Louise, 1979	**65.00**
Joey, Candy Swirl	**25.00**
Chocolate	**38.00**
Delphinium	**12.00**
Firefly	**12.00**
Flame	**15.00**
Furr Green	**15.00**
Impatient	**12.00**
Mardi Gras	**15.00**
Olde Ivory	**12.00**
Persimmon	**35.00**
Sandpiper	**12.00**
Willow Blue	**12.00**
Zack Boyd Slag	**12.00**
Louise, Candy Swirl	**15.00**
Chocolate	**20.00**
Delphinium	**12.00**
Firefly	**15.00**
Flame	**12.00**
Heather	**20.00**
Ice Blue	**45.00**
Ice Green	**45.00**
Impatient	**12.00**

Mardi Gras	**15.00**
Olde Ivory Slag	**15.00**
Persimmon	**16.00**
Purple Variant	**20.00**
Sandpiper	**12.00**
Set of 12 plus bell, 1979	**350.00**
Willow blue	**12.00**
Zack Boyd Slag	**18.00**
Toothpick holder, forget-me-not, Elizabeth Slag #1, 1979	**10.00**
Zack, Delphinium	**15.00**
Flame	**45.00**
Furr Green	**15.00**
Mardi Gras	**15.00**
Old Ivory	**15.00**
Sandpiper	**14.00**

Bradley and Hubbard

The Bradley and Hubbard Mfg. Co. was a firm who produced metal accessories for the home. They operated during the early part of this century and their products reflect both the Arts and Crafts and Art Nouveau influence.

Their logo was a device with a triangular arrangement of the company name containing a smaller triangle and an Aladdin lamp.

Andirons, brass, goose neck stem, urn shaped finial, pair	**150.00**
Ashtray, brass, pair	**26.50**
Bookends, brass, spanish Galleons, pr.	**45.00**
Bookends, Lincoln Memorial, silver metal, heavy, pair	**20.00**
Candlesticks, brass, 5" square bases, 11", pair	**75.00**
Candlesticks, brass, 8", pair	**125.00**
Cigarette set, painted ballerina decor, 3-pc in 2x2¼x3¼" box . .	**50.00**
Desk set, pen tray, blotter, letter opener & holder, inkwell	**60.00**
Doorstop, flower	**50.00**
Figurine, stag & hounds	**100.00**
Hanging shade, brass frame w/slag, 9x16" sq tapering to 4½".	**250.00**
Inkwell, oval, oxidized ribbed brass, ball feet & finial, 4x2" dia .	**60.00**
Lamp, banquet, brass ftd urn, chased & repousse design, no globe	**175.00**
Banquet, spelter & copper bases, green & rose shades	**375.00**

Black metal frame, green glass, 19½"	**275.00**
Bordered panels, slag glass w/torch pattern overlay, 24x16" .	**500.00**

Floor, brass base, adjustable, w/floral leaded glass shade . . **1,800.00**
Gone With the Wind, bronze base, red satin globe **500.00**
Gone With the Wind, ornate, base w/8 ball forms, 22″ **600.00**
Hanging, ci frame, ornate, complete **375.00**
Oil, brass, 10″ dia butterscotch cased glass shade **165.00**
Oil, w/green & floral ball shade, 16″ **195.00**
Sq open-dome shade, russet glass panels, ornate metal work **375.00**
Table, figural base, torch reservoir, curved slag shade, 29″ . . **485.00**
Table, lily pad base, allover floral shade, 24″ **1,850.00**
Table, open-work leaves, leaves in relief on base, 2l″ **600.00**
Table, ornate brass overlay, 24″ **375.00**
Smokestand, bronze, 3 dolphin base, tails hold ashtray, 23″ . . **375.00**

Brass

Brass is an alloy consisting essentially of copper and zinc in variable proportions. It is a medium that has been used for both utilitarian items and objects of artistic merit. Today, with the inflated price of copper and the popular use of plastics, almost anything made of brass is collectible.

Andirons, solid feet & finials, fluted column w/ball, 20½″ **165.00**
Bird cage, Hendryx, dome shaped **100.00**
   Holds wind-up singing bird, fancy, French, 11″ **325.00**
Blotter corners, set of 4, Marshall Fields, floral relief **165.00**
Bookends, Art Deco, 6″, pr **35.00**
   Indian in full headdress, 8x5″, pr **110.00**
   Relief of 3 horseheads over stone wall, CJO, 4x5″ **50.00**
Bucket, iron bail handle, 1850s **100.00**
Candelabra, three branch, Art Deco, 15″, pr **165.00**
Candlestick, petal base, before 1750, 6½″ **250.00**
   Ruffled octagonal base, faceted, French, 1710, 9½″ **350.00**
   Silver plate, Benedict Arnak, Egyptian relief, 9″ **85.00**
   Georgian, push-up style, pr **85.00**
   Octagonal 3¾″ base, push up, 9¾″, pr **75.00**
Cigarette dispenser, Art Deco globe shape **65.00**
Desk set, floral scrolls, 7 pc, Bradley & Hubbard **385.00**
Dish, engraved Chinese dragon, made in China, heavy **65.00**
Door knocker, lion, brass screws, 7½x4½″ **33.00**
Fender, three bands of pierced work, four feet, 50″ **175.00**
Footman, rectangular top, cabriole front legs, 10½″ **150.00**
Hook, hinged arm, star bracket, 9½″ **50.00**
Humidor, glass w/brass lid, Benedict Arnak, Scarab motif **75.00**
Hunting horn, John Church & Co, 10″ **175.00**
Jardiniere, 8½x10″ **185.00**
   Floral basket frieze, ring handles, 3 ft, 8½″ **50.00**
   Hammered texture, roses in relief, 9¾x11½″ **55.00**
Kettle, iron basket handle, for jelly, 5¾x15″ **65.00**
   Iron rim & handle, 13″ **85.00**
   Signed Waterbury, Dec 16, 1851, 8½″ dia **85.00**
   With spider, 10″ **165.00**
Lantern, whale oil, pierced top & bottom, 12½″ **85.00**
Letter holder, wall type, Art Nouveau hand holds letter **20.00**
Money till w/tray **60.00**
Pail, spun, E Miller & Co, pat 1870, 13x9″ **75.00**
Paper clip, hand w/ring and lace cuff, 1800s, 5½″ **50.00**
Picture frame, oval, ornate, 5x3½″ **35.00**
Pot, hand engraved all over design, 6½″ **200.00**
Silent butler, ornamental, China **50.00**
Skimmer, fancy cut out handle, 20″ **75.00**
Spittoon, 6½x4¾″ **30.00**
   English, 1890, 12″ **150.00**
Stencils, complete alphabet, set **45.00**
Teakettle & stand, alcohol burner **110.00**
Toaster, one slice, scissor action handle, English, 13″ **50.00**

Tongs, hanging ring, claw ends, 11″ **15.00**
Tray, Carence Crafters, florals, handcrafted, sq, 5¾″ **130.00**
   Made in USSR, 12″ dia **25.00**
   With handles, engraved peacocks, India, 29x8″ **34.00**
Trivet, horse shoe, Good Luck to All Who Use This Stand . . . **30.00**
Umbrella stand, embossed outdoor tavern scene, rose border . . . **75.00**
Vase, leaf motif, 1880, 13″ **35.00**
   With handles, squirrels on tree limb, 7″ **200.00**
Whale, figural, 5½″ **50.00**

Bread Plates

Bread trays have been produced not only in glass, but in metal and pottery as well; but those considered most collectible were made during the last quarter of the 19th century of pressed glass with well detailed embossed designs representing a particular theme. Presidential campaigns, commemorations, and religion were among the most popular. Though most were made in crystal, colored glass, milk glass and goofus glass may also found.

Barred Forget-Me-Not, canary **45.00**
Bates, Lieut Colonel John Coulter Bates, bust in center **95.00**
Bible **55.00**
Bread Is The Staff Of Life **45.00**
Bunker Hill Monument **65.00**
Centennial, lion **65.00**
Columbus Pilot, wheel border **60.00**
Continental, Give Us This Day, 9x13″ **67.00**
Cupid & Venus, 11″ **36.00**
Daisy & Button, amber, oval **25.00**
Deer & Pine Tree, amber **60.00**
Deer & Pine Tree **32.00**
Dew Drop in Points **35.00**
Dewdrop with Sheaf of Wheat **21.00**
Diagonal Band, with motto Eureka, 9x11½″ **32.50**
Dog Cart **55.00**
Double Vine, 10½″ dia **28.50**
Egyptian, Cleopatra **48.00**
Faith, Hope, and Charity **75.00**
Fine Cut, w/lion head handles, amber **45.00**
Frosted Lion **40.00**
Garden of Eden **40.00**
Garfield Memorial, 10″ **60.00**
George Washington **120.00**
Give Us This Day Our Daily Bread, 12″ **45.00**
Gladstone **35.00**
Golden Rule **55.00**
Good Luck **45.00**
Good Mother **55.00**
Independence Hall **105.00**
It Is Pleasant To Labor **55.00**
Jenny Lind, 7¼x2″ **62.00**
Knights of Labor **250.00**
Last Supper **40.00**
Liberty Bell, with signer's names, 100 years ago **80.00**
Little Bo Peep **55.00**
Little Red Riding Hood **55.00**
Lotus Pattern, Give Us This Day **40.00**
Maltese Cross in Circles **17.00**
Maple Leaf, canary **60.00**
McKinley, It Is God's Way **50.00**
Nelly Bly **165.00**
Niagra Falls, glass, late 1800s **60.00**
Old Statehouse, Philadelphia **75.00**
Pacific Fleet **390.00**

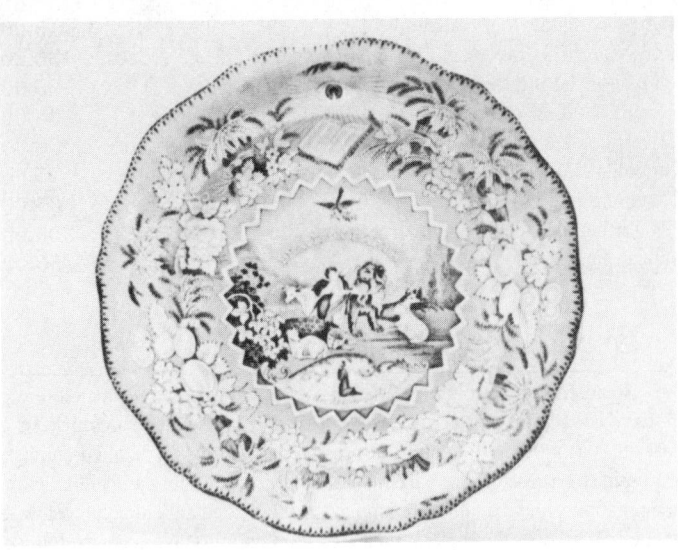

Peace on Earth, Millenium, brown transfer, Staffordshire **50.00**
Pleat & Panel **32.00**
Pope Leo XIII **20.00**
President Taylor, etched **345.00**
Queen Victoria **55.00**
Rock of Ages, milk glass center **150.00**
Roosevelt, w/dancing bear border **125.00**
Scroll with Flowers **10.00**
Sheaf of Wheat, Give Us This Day, Dewdrop Border, 11″ **45.00**
Single Horseshoe **32.00**
Swan & Flowers, clear w/handles, small **20.00**
Three Graces **65.00**
Three Presidents, clear **65.00**
Virginia Dare **65.00**
Warrior, frosted, signed Jacobus **165.00**
Waste Not, Want Not **45.00**
Wheat & Barley **24.00**

Bride's Baskets

Victorian brides were showered with gifts, as brides have always been; one of the most popular gift items was the bride's basket. Art glass inserts from both European and American glass houses, some in lovely clear color with dainty enameled florals, others of Peachblow, Vasa Murrhina, satin or cased glass, were cradled in complimentary silverplated holders. While many of these holders were simply engraved or delicately embossed, others such as those from Pairpoint and Wilcox were wonderfully ornate, often with figurals of cherubs or animals. The bride's basket was no longer in fashion after the turn of the century.

Apricot opalescent Hobnail, rectangle Meriden frame, 11x7″ . . **365.00**
Blue Spanish Lace, opalescent **135.00**
Blue cased w/wht, floral decor, Union Plate frame, 11x10½″ . . **295.00**
Blue finecut & oval panel, Derby Silver Co rectangle holder . . . **165.00**
Blue hobnail opalescent, Homan frame w/embossed florals **100.00**
Cased bristol, plated holder w/figural dolphin **165.00**
Cased, lime/wht to pink, Thomas Webb **750.00**
Cased, shaded pink, amber ruffle, Wilcox frame w/floral forms . **285.00**
Cased, wht w/salmon, satin, ruffled rim, plated ornate frame . . **150.00**
Cranberry, frilled, inverted thumprint, wht border **125.00**
Cranberry, iridescent w/enameling, 12″ **425.00**
Cranberry shades w/overlay, Honeycomb, plated holder **160.00**
Cranberry w/florals, footed plated holder w/3 figurals **215.00**
Heart shape, rose w/floral enamel, Forbes holder w/grapes **400.00**
Mauve cased w/white, ornate holder **125.00**

Mother of Pearl, enameled decor, signed Webb, plated holder . **450.00**
Opalescent, lacy orange enameling, crimped & fluted, 10x12″ . **180.00**
Opalescent Poinsetta, Rubin frame **195.00**
Overlay, pink, white, ruffled, ornate embossed plated holder . . **150.00**
Overlay, red to pink w/white outside, plated holder **350.00**
Overlay, red w/wht, scalloped, Simpson holder w/figurals **175.00**
Overlay, rose w/wht, ruffled, floral enamel, brass basket **200.00**
Overlay, ruffled w/floral decor, Union Plate holder **325.00**
Overlay, wht w/amber crimped rim, florals, fancy holder w/ped . **155.00**
Pink cut to wht w/cameos, Pairpoint frame w/figural angels . . . **945.00**
Pink ribbed w/lacy band, gold trim 5x10½x5″ **85.00**
Red to yellow bowl, Webster frame w/figural cherub stem, 11″ **285.00**
Red w/gold Prunus blossoms, plated ornate frame **450.00**
Rose to wht, amber rigaree rim, plated holder w/leaves **195.00**
Rubina, opalescent **195.00**
Ruby, enameled florals w/gold decor, 12″ **450.00**
Ruffled, exquisite enameled floral medallions, ornate holder . . . **525.00**
Satin glass, plated frame w/figural squirrels **200.00**
Verre de Soie, applied butterfly, ruffled **600.00**
Verre de Soie, pink w/crimped edge, enameled florals **275.00**
White overlay w/floral enamel, plated frame, 8x9″ **195.00**

Bristol Glass

Bristol is a type of semi-opaque opal glass which was made during the 18th and 19th century by glasshouses in England, France, Germany and Italy. It was popular during the Victorian era, and was produced in America by The New England Glass Co, and to a lesser extent by its contemporaries. It was often decorated with enamel work and cased with another color.

Bell, applied band, crimped rim **35.00**
Bottle, blue w/florals, matching stopper, 4″ **85.00**
Cracker jar, blue & white w/enameled lilacs, ornate **150.00**
Epergne, pedestal base, ruffled, single **65.00**
Ewer, butterfly & floral decor, ruffled, footed, 8″ **75.00**
Jar w/cover on pedestal base, brown w/floral decor, 8″ **25.00**
Jar w/cover, tall finial, lavendar w/florals, butterfly **35.00**
Plate, hp floral decor, 12″ dia **75.00**
Powder jar w/cover, tall semi-opaque w/florals, 6″ **50.00**
Sweetmeat w/plated lid, grey w/florals, gold decor, 5″ **85.00**
Sweetmeat w/plated lid, pink w/white liner, duck & florals, 5″ . **110.00**
Urn w/cover, pedestal, tan w/floral enameling, 24″ **245.00**
Vase, w/cover, forest scene w/deer, florals, 15″ **110.00**
Vase, bulbous, red throat, rose & gold decor, 10½″ **25.00**
Vase, butterflies, florals, 11″ **75.00**

Vase, cased cream/rose, florals & birds, enameled w/gold, 13½″ **125.00**

Vase, cased, white & pink, ruffled top, berries & florals, 6″ **38.00**
Vase, castle scene, Austria, 10″ **75.00**
Vase, cylinder, enamel scenery, chickens, 11x4½″ **45.00**
Vase, footed, ruffled rim, white on white, hp oranges, gold, 7″ . **50.00**
Vase, frosted w/autumn leaves, florals, gold trim, 9″ **25.00**
Vase, gold enamel, jewels on white satin, 12″ **200.00**
Vase, green, hand-blown, hp florals, 11½″ **175.00**
Vase, pale orchid shading to white w/windmills, 12″ **60.00**
Vase, pedestal, turquoise w/white florals, gold pontil, 8″ **35.00**
Vase, ruffled, blue w/beige casing, florals, pontil, 3x4″ **35.00**
Vase, ruffled, white cased w/pink, bird on branch, gold, 7″ **40.00**
Vase, white cased w/pink, triangular top, blue/white florals, 4″ .. **32.00**
Vase, white w/orange flowers & leaves, 1880, 9″ **80.00**
Vase, white, medallion w/winter scene, enameled florals, 9x5″ .. **40.00**

Broadsides

Webster defines the term as simply a large sheet of paper printed on one side. During the 1800s the broadside was the most practical means of mass communication. By the middle of the century they had become elaborate and lengthy with information, illustrations, portraits, and fancy border designs.

Fair, lists purses for livestock judging, 1883, 22x16″ **50.00**
Fire Insurance, City of Williamsburg, 17x21″ **375.00**
Joe Louis, black text on newsprint paper, pictures Lewis, 12x6″ **35.00**
July 4th Celebration, Vincennes, Ind., 1925, 8x12″ **16.50**
Magician, 3 wood engravings, extravagant text, pulp paper, 17x6″ **40.00**

Magician, woodcut illustration of performer, text, 1885, 27x10″. **75.00**
Second Annual Gala & Field Day of Maspeth, framed, 1891, 19x14″ **110.00**
Temperance, God's Wonderful Elixer of Life, Water, 1920 ..... **10.00**
Union Republican Ticket, Ward 2, ink write-in, 1886 .... **20.00**
Washington's Farwell Address, painted on silk, Phila., 1832, 17x21″ **650.00**

Bronze

Thomas Ball, George Bessell and Leonard Volk were some of the earliest American sculptors who produced figures in bronze for home decor, in about 1840. Pieces of historical significance were the most popular, but by the 1880s a more fanciful type of art work took hold. Some of the fine sculptors of the day were Daniel Chester French, Augustus St.-Gaudens and John Quincy Adams Ward.

Bronzes enjoyed the height of their popularity at the turn of the century. The American West was portrayed to its fullest by Remington, Russell, James Frazier, Hermon MacNeil and Solon Borglum. Animals of every specie were modeled by A. P. Proctor, Paul Bartlett and Albert Laessele, to name but a few.

Art Nouveau and Art Deco influenced the medium during the twenties, evidenced by the works of Allen Clark, Harriet Freshmuth, E. F. Sanford and Bessie P. Vonnoh.

Alexander wih Dagger & Lion, 1800s, Jacques Coichon, 12½″ **490.00**
Arab Stallion, 1850s, signed PJ Mene **2,400.00**
Archer & Doe, Daniel-Joseph Bacque, 17½″ **1,100,00**
Bird, red-tufted woodpecker, Vienna, 3x4″ **120.00**
Bison, reclining, signed, 8x16″ **1,050.00**
Bookends, anchor, pair **40.00**
    Figural Russian Wolf Hounds, Jennings, 6½″, pair **100.00**
    Figural heart & crouching cupid, Armour, pair **90.00**
    Greek busts of man & woman, plaster interior, dk green patina **70.00**
Bowl, medal of honor, raised woman warrior at base, 1867, 10″ **375.00**
Boy Snake Charmer, w/flute & cobras on carpet, polychrome, Vienna **300.00**
Boy on Camel, cross-legged reading book, boy leading camel, 3½″ **2,500.00**
Boy on Elephant, American Coin foundry mark **340.00**
Boy with Dolphin, 4″ **395.00**
Boy with Wheat, 1886, Franz Iffland **425.00**
Boys, pair, on black onyx bases, 4″ **60.00**
Buccaneer, Paul Herzal, Pompano Bros, 1928 .... **95.00**
Bull, brown patina, Rosa Bonheur, 1800s, 7½″ **850.00**
Bull on Mountain inscribed on marble base, PJ Mene, recast, 6½″ **295.00**
Bust, 5 children, wood base, Deco, Russian, signed, 15″ wide **1,290.00**
    Boy, on double tier marble base, Michetti, 10x4½″ **390.00**
    Charles Dickens, on square base w/plaque, 18″ **590.00**
    French woman, signed Chariclea, 15¾″ **275.00**
    Nubian Princess, French bronze & ormolu, 1800s **4,500.00**
Cake Walk, black girl w/hat, C Kauba, 6″ **525.00**
Candelabra, woman and deer, bird base, Hagenauer, Austria, 16x9″ **595.00**
Cannon, wood carriage coat of arms/MVS 1730, 18″ barrel . **1,100.00**
Cassack Warrior, w/two horses, Russian 3 pc group **4,000.00**
Cat, on chair, reading paper, Vienna, 1¾″ **85.00**
    Marble base inscribed Cat, Barye, recast, 4¼″ **115.00**
    Signed Barye, 4″ **350.00**
Chained Angel, Henri-Charles Levasseur, 22″ **700.00**
Chief Sitting Bull, 1884, relief, Edward Kemeys, 31x22 ..... **2,800.00**
Coffee Table Base, mottled dk brown patina, Giacometti, 15x54″ **3,500.00**
Cow, 4¾″wide bronze base, by Rosa Bonheur, 1800s, 3¼″ ... **400.00**
Cowboy & Bison, Isidore Bonheur, 1890s, brown patina, 16½″ **6,300.00**
Crayfish, Vienna, Geschutz **400.00**
Cupids with Basket, signed August Moreau **1,400.00**
Dancing Woman, bent backwards, hand touching ft, K Perl, 14″ **660.00**
Dante, full figure, Emile Blavier, 27″ **1,400.00**
David, w/head of Goliath, 1872, Antoine Mercie, 27½″ **900.00**
Dish, figural shell, nude in relief on wave w/fish, Ledru, 7½x6¾″ **375.00**
    Male & female figures, marble mounted, French, 1900, 19″ **1,100.00**
Dog and Mouse, marble base, recast, Barye, 4½″ **175.00**
Dog with Bird Nest, inscribed on marble base, PJ Mene, recast, 4¼″ **285.00**
Dog, Golden Retriever, reclining, attached head, 5¾″ **24.00**
    Marble base inscribed Sitting Dog, Barye, recast, 7″ **175.00**
    Setter, backing inscribed PJ Mene on marble base, 5x5½″ .. **215.00**
    Signed Barye, 6″ **475.00**
Dove Figure, perched on short planar support, marble base, 10½″ **1,100.00**
Dragon, on base, very heavy, 25″ **2,500.00**
Elephant, Austria, 7x5½″ **475.00**
    Trunk up, inscribed Sirio Tofanari, early l900s, 31″ long . **3,850.00**
Equestrian Figure, by Emmanuel Fremiet, 1800s, 14″ **400.00**
Figural Group, 2 dancing maidens w/center hoop, circular base **1,980.00**
Figures, pair, man w/fiddle, woman w/umbrella, Winkler, 9½″ . **470.00**
Fox, red-brown w/white crest & black hairs, seated, Vienna, 2″ . **85.00**
Girl, signed Moreau, 18″ **375.00**
Girl w/bow, draped gown, bust gold dore, 8½″ **360.00**
Girl w/tambourine, 1854, IJ Jacquet, 30¼″ **450.00**

Gladiator, signed Piccault **1,100.00**
Goddess Kali, 7 headed cobra, 17th century Indian, 13″ **150.00**
Greyhound, by Mene **1,500.00**
Harlequin, Art Deco, signed Nachtman, 14″ **450.00**
Horse, in full harness w/back legs entangled, TH Gechter, 15″ **1,050.00**
   Standing, on wooden base, 7½x10″ **75.00**
   With saddle, 3½″ **15.00**
Horse and Colt inscribed on marble base, PJ Mene, recast, 3½″ **245.00**
Hunting Dog, pointing, on marble base, Moigniez, 9x13″ **600.00**
   Signed Barye [Antoine Louis], 4¾x9½″ **1,500.00**
Huntsman & The Hounds, PJ Mene, 1869, green patina, 31x31″ **7,500.00**
Incense Burner, animal finial on lid **40.00**
Indian Chief, Shot-In-The-Eye, signed Kauba, Austrian foundry, 6½″ **375.00**
   With feathered headdress, brown patina, Humphriss, 10¾″ **2,200.00**
Inkstand,, nude w/foliage, Raoul Larche, gilt, 25″ wide **4,000.00**
Jaguar Reclining, gold patina, Eli Harvey, 1913, 24½″ **830.00**
Javelin Thrower, rectangular base, DH Chiparus, 1920s, 36″ . . **935.00**
King Charles Spaniel, 1840s, signed PJ Mene **300.00**
King Charles Spaniel & Greyhound, 1840s, signed PJ Mene . . . **600.00**
La Luxure, Rodin **7,500.00**
Lamp, figural dancing woman, G Van der Straeten, 17½″ . . **1,980.00**
   Figural, woman under ballooning tent on camel led by Arab, 14″ **3,575.00**
   Louis Potet, Nouveau girl, gilt, 1890 . . . . **1,350.00**
   Woman representing night w/star & owl at feet, marble base, 23″ **1,430.00**
Lamp base, armored man w/spear riding horse, signed Verona . **450.00**
Land Study, Rodin **3,200.00**

Le Gaucho, Rudolph Vanentino, wood base, 10½″ **750.00**
Lion, roaring stance, signed Oriental, 7½x13″ **950.00**
Lioness, reclining, brown patina, L Masson, 8¼″ **225.00**
Man on Horse, on rectangular base, signed W Wolff, 1862, 25″ **795.00**
Man with Hunting Dog, on leash, signed PJ Mene, dated 1879 **2,375.00**
Maternity, Paul Dubois, 27½″ **950.00**
Mechanical figure, seated dancer opens skirt, 1900, 5½″ **770.00**
Mozart, Paul Dubois, 25¼″ **1,600.00**
Nude Boy w/Arrows, marble base, old **350.00**
Nude Seated w/Flowers, bonnet rests on back, 1920s, Bouraine, 15″ **880.00**
Nude Woman w/Hoop, 1920s, inscribed L Alliot, 15¼″ **1,760.00**
Ophelia, gold patina, 1900, Maurice Bouval, 16¾″ **3,500.00**
Oriental Dancing Girl, 1900, 5½″ **100.00**
Oriental Leopard, 5½″ **86.00**
Parakeets, pair on tree trunk, signed G Gardet **1,300.00**
Pheasant & Chicks, 1870, Alphonse-Alaxendre Arson, 17″ . . . **695.00**
Phoenix Bird, marble base, Barye, 7x5½″ **285.00**

Planter, elephant decorated, footed, 4½x¾″ **65.00**
Queen Victoria, 1897, Sir EB MacKennal, 22½″ **900.00**
Romeo & Juliet, Miguel Berrocal, polished, 6¼x21x4¾″ **832.00**
Rough Rider Sargeant, Remington **5,000.00**
Rugby Players, 1800s, G Rovini, 13½″ **425.00**
Saint Sebastian, gold patina, Eduardo Paolozzi, 14″ **3,000.00**
Satanic Figure, cold-painted and composition, 1930s, onyx base, 10″ **770.00**
Shodo Flowing, 1960, Isamu Noguchi, 88″ **30,000.00**
Silent Thunder, Charles Russell, recast, 8″ **2,650.00**
Sleeping Cat, dk patina, William Zorach, 2½″ **1,500.00**
Soldier, leaving his wife, 1887, bas relief, 31¾x16″ **620.00**
St John, standing, late 1500s, Venice, 8¾″ **1,600.00**
Stallion, brown w/black mane & tail, Vienna, 5x6″ **225.00**
Temple Dancer, patina, 5″ **250.00**
Temple Musicians, set of 8, tall headdresses, 3½″ **330.00**
The Bathers, Guy Revol, 14¼″ **250.00**
The Blacksmith inscribed on marble base, Renoir, recast, 8½″ **1,285.00**
The Borghese Gladiator, late 1500s, dk patina, Italy, 16¾″ . **1,900.00**
The Bronco Buster, recast, Frederic Remington, 21½″ **2,650.00**
The Cheyenne, Frederic Remington, recast, signed, 21″ **2,650.00**
The Kiss, Jean Abel, 1900s, green, 47″ **1,000.00**
The Lovers, signed Lambeaux, 14x10x10½″ **3,500.00**
The Savage, Remington **6,000.00**
The Sunfisher, Richard Farrington Elwell, 1800s, #ed, 18″ . . **2,500.00**
The Vine, Frishmuth, 12″ **4,600.00**
The Washerwoman, inscribed Renoir, 12x10½″ **1,300.00**
Three Laughing Children, green-brown patina, J Clara, 13″ . . **675.00**
Tray, 12 zodiac symbols w/allover pattern, 23½″ dia **75.00**
Tray, handmade, Wendell August Forge, 11½x5¾″ **50.00**
Vase, clusters of dore grapes in relief, dark patina, 10″ **250.00**
   Dragon in relief on 2 sides, dog head handles, Chinese, 11″ **195.00**
   Goose standing, with long ivory tusk as vase, marble base, 13¾″ **880.00**
   Modified Amphora form, maiden in relief reaching for cherub, 8″ **440.00**
   Sterling overlay, gold dore finish, Aug 27, 1912, 5x5¼″ dia . . **90.00**
   With dard & dore patina, grapes in high relief, old, 9½x5″ . **325.00**
Venus A La Girafe, 1973, Salvador Dali, numbered, 22¼″ **950.00**
Venus After The Bath, Jean De Bologne, 1500s, dk patina, 17½″ **6,800.00**

Walking Tiger, after Barye, 1900, 17″ long **900.00**
Whippet, dore, signed Zach **265.00**
   Signed PJ Mene **575.00**
Wolf, by JE Masson, small shield medallion, Societe...Paris, 19½″ **700.00**
Wolves, worn silver finish, JE Masson, crest w/Societe...Paris, 19¼″ **850.00**
Woman & Recumbant Goat, Parcel-silvered, Morlon, wood base **1,350.00**
Woman & Standing Goat, parcel-silvered, Morlon, wood base **1,350.00**
Woman Playing Harp, neo-Egyptian costume, marble base, 27″ **935.00**
Woman in Flowing Robe, arms extended, octagonal onyx base **1,650.00**
Wounded Duck, black patina, 1913, Carl Ethan Akeley, 12″ **3,100.00**
Young Man Playing Violin, titled Inspiration, Moreau, 25″ . . . **275.00**

Brownies by Palmer Cox

Created by Palmer Cox in 1883, the Brownies charmed children through the pages of books and magazines, as dolls, on their dinnerware, advertising material and souvenirs. Each had his own personality--among them The Bellhop, The London Bobby, The Chairman and Uncle Sam--but the oversized trianular face with the startled expression, the protruding tummy and the spindle legs were characteristics of them all.

Book, Adventures of a Brownie, Mulock, 1893 . . . . **10.00**
  Brownies at Work **40.00**
Busy Brownies, Veal, Brownie illustrations by Cox, 1897 . . . . . . **20.00**
  Queer People, Cox Illustrations, 1888 . . . . **45.00**
  The Brownies, Their Book, lst edition, 144 pgs, 1887 . . . . **65.00**
  The Monkey's Trick, Veal, Cox illustration, 1897 . . . . **15.00**
Booklet, advertising, Orient Bicycles, w/Brownies **8.00**
Candlestick, Brownie Policeman, majolica, 7½" **145.00**
Candlestick, Brownie w/hands in pocket, majolica, 7½" **135.00**
Cereal bowl, china, w/Brownie decor, 5½" **45.00**
Character Brownie, acrobat, lithographed wood **50.00**
Character Brownie, cloth covered, 1891 . . . . **60.00**
Character Brownie, set of 10 wood litho **475.00**
Child's set, fork, spoon, knife, WB/B, Malabar, 5½" **75.00**
Frame, embossed border of Brownies, 8x10" **40.00**
Game, Brownie Horseshoe, tin & rubber horseshoe w/Brownies . **45.00**
Label, Palmer Cox Brownies Oranges, 10x12" **15.00**
Magazines, Queer People, 1894, set of 8 . . . . **75.00**
Mug, quadruple silver plate, Homan's, Brownies on seesaw **90.00**
Mug, white w/Brownies, gold trim, East Liverpool, 3" **40.00**
Mustache cup, Brownie decor **35.00**
Paperweight, w/Brownies **55.00**
Plate, Brownie decor, KTK & Co, 6" **20.00**
Plate, china, w/Brownie decor, 7" **45.00**
Sheet music w/Brownies **12.00**
Spoon, silverplate, Brownies on Ferris Wheel **15.00**

Stamping blocks in original box, 12 stamps **75.00**
Stickpin, Brownie Chinaman, rare **20.00**
Stickpin, Brownie Policeman **15.00**
Tray, tin, Brownie with ice cream, late 1800s **65.00**
Watch holder, bronze plated, 4 Brownies in relief, 6" **195.00**

Brush

George Brush began his career in the pottery industry in 1901, working for the J. B. Owens Pottery Co. in Zanesville, Ohio. He left the company in 1907 to go into business for himself, only to have fire completely destroy his pottery less than one year after it was founded.

Brush became associated with J. W. McCoy in 1909, and for many years served in capacities ranging from General Manager to President. (From 1911 until 1925, the firm was known as The Brush-McCoy Pottery Co., see that section for information.) After McCoy died, the family withdrew their interests, and in 1925 the name of the firm was changed to The Brush Pottery.

The era of hand decorated art pottery had passed for the most part, and would soon be completely replaced by the production of commerical lines. Of all the wares bearing the later Brush script mark, their figural cookie jars are the most collectible.

Basket, stylized leaf relief, yellow semi-mat #658 . . . . **12.00**
Bittersweet, flower pot, leaves & berries, 6½" **9.00**
  Pedestal planter, twig handles, 7" **10.00**
  Vase, narrow base, bulbous, 10" **10.00**
Bronze line, carafe, palette mk #928 . . . . **10.00**
  Flower arranger w/integral candlestick **9.00**
  Vase, palette mk #720, 8" **6.00**
Cookie jars, Antique Touring Car **24.00**
  Boy w/Balloons **17.00**
  Chick & Nest **24.00**
  Cinderella Pumpkin **30.00**
  Circus Horse **30.00**
  Clown w/yellow pants **28.00**
  Clown, Bust **18.00**
  Cookie House **24.00**
  Covered Wagon **24.00**

Cow w/Cat finial **24.00**
Davey Crocket **28.00**
Dog w/Basket **18.00**
Donkey & Cart **22.00**
Elephant in Baby Bonnet **30.00**
Elephant w/Monkey Finial **35.00**
Fish **15.00**
Formal Pig **30.00**
Granny **18.00**
Happy Bunny, white w/pastel **26.00**
Hill Billy Frog **65.00**
Hobby Horse **26.00**
Humpty Dumpty w/Beanie & Bow Tie **30.00**
Humpty Dumpty w/Peaked hat **22.00**
Laughing Hippo **28.00**
Little Boy Blue **22.00**
Little Girl **18.00**

Little Angel	22.00
Nite Owl, grey satin glaze	28.00
Old Clock	20.00
Old Shoe	15.00
Panda Bear	24.00
Peter Pan	22.00
Pumpkin Cookie Jar	24.00
Puppy Police	24.00
Raggedy Ann	22.00
Red Riding Hood	26.00
Sitting Hippo	24.00
Sitting Piggy	24.00
Smiling Bear	22.00
Squirrel in Top Hat	30.00
Squirrel on Log, grey, #W26	25.00
Stylized Owl	14.00
Stylized Siamese	18.00
Teddy Bear, feet apart	30.00
Teddy Bear, feet together	24.00
Treasure Chest	18.00
White Hen on Basket	20.00
Figurine, Fireside Cat, semi mat black Siamese 15½"	15.00
Fireside Cat, semi mat black Siamese, 12½"	12.00
Horace Falcon, black semi mat, 7"	14.00
Lawn ornament, Rooster, tan w/red comb	14.00
Planter, Basket Girl, small	12.00
Cactus figural w/double removable pots	10.00
Horse & carriage	12.00
Little Bo Peep	10.00
Mare w/foal	12.00
Rose jar, black gloss glaze, 11"	30.00
Stardust, flying saucer hanging pot	12.00
Hanging pot, plain, 4"	10.00
Vase, #601, 8"	6.00
Wall pocket, curled out point	10.00
Tankard, blue semi mat #609 Brush USA, 12½"	14.00
Vase, Southern Belle #218 USA	8.00
"V" for Victory, 8"	10.00
Wall pocket, Boxer,#542 USA	15.00
Bucking Horse	15.00
Doghouse	15.00
Horse, #545 USA	15.00

Brush McCoy

The Brush McCoy Pottery was formed in 1911 in Zanesville, Ohio, and alliance between George Brush and J. W. McCoy. Brush's original pottery had been destroyed by fire in 1907; McCoy had operated his own business there since 1899.

After the merger, the company expanded and produced not only their staple commerical wares, but also fine art ware. Lines such as Navarre, Venitian, Persian, Oriental and Sylvan were of a quality equal to that of their larger competitors. Because very little of the ware was marked, it is often mistaken for Weller, Roseville or Peters and Reed.

In the twenties, after a fire in Zanesville had destroyed the manufacturing portion of that plant, all production was contained in their Roseville (Ohio) Plant #2. A stoneware type of clay was used there, and the art ware lines of Jewell, Zuni-art, King Tut, Florastone and Panel-art are so distinctive that they are more easily recognized. Examples of these lines are unique and very beautiful--also quite rare and highly prized!

The Brush-McCoy Pottery operated under that name until after J. W. McCoy's death, when it became The Brush Pottery. The Brush-Barnett family retained their interest in the pottery until 1981, when it was purchased by The Dearborn Company.

Agean, umbrella stand, 21"	165.00
Basketware, jard & ped, Ivotint decor	300.00
Basketware, window box , Ivotint decor, 12x6"	115.00
Beauty Rose, umbrella stand, 21"	175.00
Blended, jardiniere & ped w/grapes in relief	150.00
Jardiniere, leaves & lilies in relief, 9½"	45.00
Umbrella stand, Liberty Bell, 21"	250.00
Umbrella stand, bow & swags in relief, 17"	85.00
Blue Banded Bristol chamber pot	95.00
Bug Door Stop, onyx, 9"	125.00
Bug Radio set	150.00
Bungalow Vase, Art Nouveau shoulder band w/grapes, 30"	250.00
Cleo, vase, stylized decoration, 11"	85.00
Corn, butter jar, w/natural colors & modeling, signed Cusick	75.00
Mug, 16 oz	35.00
Mug, 24 oz	45.00
Salt box	75.00
Spice jar	25.00
Stein	75.00
Tankard, 12¼"	125.00
Tobacco jar	45.00
Dandy-Line, butter w/cover, yellow ware w/wht band	45.00
Canister, sugar,	40.00
Pie baker,	10.00
Salt box w/cover	45.00
Duck, flower frog	20.00
Elephant book ends, pr	60.00
Floradora, blub log, 6"	10.00
Florastone, candlestick, stoneware w/stylized floral decor, tall	45.00
Jardinire, 11"	70.00
Vase, 8"	50.00
Vase, 10"	65.00
Frog, flower frog	20.00
Grape, butter jar w/cover, polychrome grape vines & lattice	50.00
Canister w/cover	40.00
Casserole w/cover, 9"	45.00
Cuspidor	50.00
Custard cup	10.00
Jug	45.00
Pitcher, brown w/white lining	50.00
Jetwood, bud vase, stoneware w/woodland enameling, 6"	80.00
Jardiniere, 10½"	150.00
Vase, bulbous, 8"	125.00
Vase, 12"	175.00
Jewel, bowl, stoneware w/enameled band decor, 5"	25.00
Candlestick, 4"	35.00
Jardiniere, 12"	75.00
Vase, 12½"	75.00
Vase, bulbous base, 9"	50.00
Jug Time clock, brown onyx	45.00
Kolorkraft, vase, Amaryllis relief, 9½"	20.00
Lotus, jard & ped, pointed panels	250.00
Loy Nel Art, cuspidor, brown glaze	55.00
Jardiniere & pedestal, hp leaves & berries	275.00
Jardiniere, footed, brown glaze, 10"	125.00
Jardiniere, hp tulips, 12" dia	135.00
Umbrella stand, hp leaves, 21"	200.00
Vase, handles, narrow neck, base, bulbous body, 12"	125.00
Vase, integral handles, brown glaze, 10"	75.00
Marble ware, jardiniere & ped, fluted column	200.00
Mat Green, jardiniere & pedestals, ring handles, Greek key	250.00
Mat Green, jardiniere, toed feet, Egyptian motif, 10½"	150.00
Mat Green, umbrella stand, Egyptian decor	175.00
Navarre, jardiniere & ped, Art Nouveau lady	850.00

Navarre, umbrella stand **650.00**
Navarre, vase, bulbous base, wide handles w/inner loops, 9″ . . **225.00**
Nurock, butter w/cover, Peacock at the Fountain **100.00**
Nurock, pitcher w/Peacock at the Fountain **125.00**
Nurock, pitcher, Hall Boy style **50.00**
Oak Leaf, jard & ped, tree stump base **325.00**
Old Ivory, jardiniere, Dutch children, 8″ **65.00**
Old Ivory, umbrella stand, deep fluting, 21″ **75.00**
Old Mill pitcher, blue & white **75.00**
Onyx, candlestick, 10½″ **20.00**
    Fruit bowl, 8″ **25.00**
    Vase, 6″ **20.00**
      12″ **35.00**
Oriental, floor vase, coral & ivory w/black scene, 23″ **350.00**
Ornament, turtle, 20″ **125.00**
Ornament, frogs w/tree **50.00**
Ornament, standing rabbit **100.00**
Our Lucile, combinet, bowknot w/floral decor **100.00**
Owl clock **100.00**
Panel-art, bowl, arched panels w/florals, stoneware, 5½″ **20.00**
Panel-art, candlesticks, 10½″, pr **100.00**
Panel-art, vase, 12″ **75.00**
Patriotic Bee lapel pin **35.00**
Roman decorated, jardiniere w/lions, printed, 7½″ **100.00**
Stonecraft, jardiniere, stoneware w/stylized florals, 9½″ **35.00**
Sweetheart Art Clock **45.00**
Sylvan, jard, 6½″ **35.00**
Tulip pitcher, bulbous, natural colors **35.00**
Venetian, candlestick, tan bands, floral pouncing, 6″, pr **90.00**
Venetian, jardiniere, 6″ **150.00**
Vestal, vase, cameo & swags, 8″ **30.00**
Vista, hanging basket, parading ducks, printed **75.00**
Vista, umbrella stand, ... **350.00**
Vista, vase, 12″ **150.00**

Vista, vase, hand decorated, 13″ **225.00**
Vogue, hanging basket, blk & wht fluted, 7″ **45.00**
    Jardiniere, 11″ **55.00**
    Umbrella stand, blk & wht fluted column **125.00**
    Vase, 9″ **20.00**
Wise Birds, bookends, pr **150.00**
    Bottle w/cork, majolica **125.00**
    Pitcher, pastel finish **115.00**
    Tumblers **25.00**
Woodland, cuspidor, caramel on ivory **100.00**
    Fern dish, caramel on ivory **45.00**

Jardiniere & pedestal, caramel on ivory **350.00**
    Umbrella stand, green glaze **150.00**
Zuni-art, candlesticks, swastika decor on stoneware 10″ **100.00**
    Jardiniere, 11″ **125.00**
    Vase, bulbous base, 6″ **100.00**
Vase, 12″ **150.00**

Buffalo Pottery

    The founding of the Buffalo Pottery, in Buffalo, N. Y. in l901, was a direct result of the success achieved by John Larkin through his innovative methods of marketing "Sweet Home Soap". Choosing to omit "middle-man" profits, Larkin preferred to deal directly with the consumer, and offered premiums as an enticement for sales. The pottery soon proved a success in its own right and began producing advertising and commemorative items for other companies, as well as commercial tableware.

    In 1905, they introduced their Blue Willow line, after extensive experimentation resulted in the developement of the first successful underglaze cobalt achieved by an American company.

    Between 1905 and 1909, a line of pitchers and jugs were hand decorated in historical, literary and outdoor themes. Twenty nine styles are known to have been made.

    Their most famous line, Deldare, from 1908 to 1911, was hand decorated after illustrations by Cecil Adams. Scenes of English life were portrayed in detail through unusual use of color against the natural olive green cast of the body. Emerald Deldare, made only in 1911, featured intricate allover Art Nouveau geometrics and florals. It is very rare.

Alaska Line, cup & saucer **18.00**
Bluebirds pitcher, 7″ **60.00**
Campbell Kids, ABC plate **40.00**
Deldare, bowl, Fallowfield Hunt, signed L Streissen, 9″ **165.00**
    Bowl, Village scenes, 9″ **425.00**
    Bowl, Ye Olden Days, 6½″ **65.00**
    Bowl, Ye Village Tavern, 9″ **345.00**
    Candlestick, 9½″, pr **610.00**
    Card tray, Fallowfield Hunt **235.00**
    Charger, An Evening at Ye Lion Inn, signed **425.00**
    Chop plate, The Start, signed Foster, 14″ **450.00**
    Chop plate, Ye Lions Inn, 12″ **475.00**
    Chop plate, Ye Lions Inns, 14″ **525.00**
    Cider set, Fallowfield Hunt, 6 pc, 1909 . . . . **1,700.00**
    Cup & saucer, Ye Olden Days **190.00**
    Dresser tray, Dancing Ye Minuet, signed Foster, 9x12″ **500.00**
    Fern bowl, Ye Village Street **400.00**
    Fruit bowl, Ye Village Tavern, 3x9″ **435.00**
    Hair receiver, Ye Village Street, Gerhardt, 1908 . . . . **325.00**
    Humidor, Ye Lion Inn, signed **765.00**
    Match holder, Ye Olden Days **375.00**
    Milk pitcher, To Demand My Annual Rent, signed, 1908, 8″ **450.00**
    Mug, Breakfast at Three Pigeons, signed Wade, 4¼″ **250.00**
    Mug, Fallowfield Hunt, 2½″ **265.00**
    Mug, Fallowfield Hunt, signed Hall, 1908, 4¼″ **275.00**
    Mug, Ye Lion Inn **235.00**
    Nut bowl, Ye Lion Inn **475.00**
    Pin tray, Ye Olden Days **180.00**
    Pitcher, octagonal, artist signed, 1908, 6½″ **350.00**
    Pitcher, This Amazed Me, 9″ **600.00**
    Pitcher, To Spare an Old Broken Soldier, 7″ **450.00**
    Plate, At Ye Lion Inn, 6½″ **110.00**
    Plate, Dr Syntax Disputing His Bill, 9¼″ **130.00**
    Plate, Fallowfield Hunt, Breaking Cover, 7″ **100.00**
    Plate, Fallowfield Hunt, Breaking Cover, signed, 10″ **195.00**
    Plate, Fallowfield Hunt, The Start, 9″ **170.00**

Plate, The Chase, 9″ **180.00**
Plate, The Death, 8½″ **195.00**
Plate, Ye Town Crier, signed Delaney, 8½″ **160.00**

Plate, Ye Village Gossips, sgnd Foster, 10″ **235.00**
Plate, Ye Village Street, 1908, 7″ **110.00**
Relish dish, Ye Olden Times **325.00**
Soup plate, Breaking Cover, 9″ **175.00**
Sugar & creamer, Ye Olden Days **365.00**
Sugar w/cover & creamer, Scenes of Village Life **400.00**
Tea tile, Dr Syntax **300.00**
Teapot w/cover, Scenes of Village Life **225.00**
Tray, Dancing Ye Minuet, signed, 9x12″ **495.00**
Tray, Fallowfield Hunt, signed Hall, 1908, 7″ **150.00**
Vase, Village scenes, 9″ **300.00**
Vase, Ye Village Parson, 8½″ **400.00**
Vegetable server, Ye Olden Times, 8½x6½″ **295.00**
Dusky Grouse, plate, 9″ **40.00**
Millefiori platter, 12x8½″ **18.00**
Mt Vernon plate, 1910, 7½″ **50.00**
Oriental scene, hand decorated plate,10″ **45.00**
Pilgrim pitcher, 1907, 9″ **475.00**
Quebec Tercentary, Wolfe & Montcalm, plate, 7½″ **55.00**

Robin Hood pitcher, 1907, 8¼″ **395.00**
Roosevelt Bears water pitcher, hand decor w//quote, 1907, 8″. **395.00**

Vienna, oval vegetable bowl **22.00**
Violets, child's tea service for 6 w/waste bowl............ **165.00**
Wild Ducks, 1907, 9¼″ **50.00**

Burmese

Burmese glass is opaque, in soft shades of yellow shading to pink. It was patented in 1885 by Frederick Shirley of the Mt. Washington Glass Co. The formula he developed contained gold which reacted with the fire to produce the delicate pink blush. It was made in both gloss and satin finish. Some pieces were decorated by hand or gilded.

Similar glass was later produced by Webb in England; it was reissued by Gunderson-Pairpoint, and again in 1978 by Bryden at the Sagamore Pairpoint factory.

Bottle vase, ivy decor, Webb, 7½″ **650.00**
Bowl, pansy decor, Diamond Quilted, Mt Washington, 2¼x4″. **210.00**
Bowl, ruffled, glossy finish, 2½″ **250.00**
Candlesticks, twist stem, Mt Washington, pr............. **800.00**
Condiment set, 4 pc, Pairpoint **995.00**
Creamer, yellow handle, acid finish **295.00**
Cruet, ribbed, acid finish, Mt Washington, 7″ **900.00**
Cup & saucer, shiny, very thin, Mt Washington **490.00**
Fairy lamp, acid, gold decor, clear Clarke base, 5¼″ **395.00**
   Clear Clarke base, 4½″ **175.00**
   Epergne on mirror base, 3 shades, 2 vases, 8½″ **1,650.00**
   Ivy decor, pressed insert, sq folded base, Webb, 5½x6″ .. **1,200.00**
Ginger jar, two handles, orig lid, Mt Washington **1,500.00**
Jack in the Pulpit vase, Mt Washington, 11″ **595.00**
Jack in the Pulpit vase, Mt Washington, 9″ **495.00**
Lamp, miniature Gone with the Wind shape **350.00**
Lemonade mug, lemon w/salmon blush................. **400.00**
Perfume, blue floral enameling, pink lined, silver top, 2″ **250.00**
Pitcher, Gunderson, applied reed handle, 10″ **350.00**
   Gunderson, fluted top, reed handle, 5½″ **250.00**
   Hobnail, 5½″ **350.00**
Plate, glossy, Mt Washington, 9¼″ **310.00**
Rose bowl, crimped rim, hp flowers, Webb, 4″ **395.00**
   Crimped top, white lined, English, 4x2½″ **265.00**
   Egg shape, crimp top, ruffled foot, 3½x2¼″ **275.00**
   Minature, Mt Washington **250.00**
   Satin, floral sprigs, Webb, 5″.................... **750.00**
   Scalloped, enameled leaves & berries, Webb, 3″ **325.00**
Shade, ruffled rim w/4¼″ fitter, 5x9″, Diamond Quilted **475.00**
Spooner, glossy, scalloped, Diamond Quilted, Mt Washington. **395.00**
Stick vase, Queen's design, 11¾″ **1,350.00**
Sugar on ped, open, glossy, Mt Washington, 2x3¼″........ **195.00**
Sugar shaker, acid w/fall leaves, berry jewels, Mt Washington.. **255.00**
Sweetmeat, butterfly, floral, gold band & bail, Queen's, Webb **395.00**
Sweetmeat, silver plated basket, glossy, applied shells, 5″..... **300.00**
Toothpick, acid, Diamond Quilted, sq top **300.00**
Top hat, basketweave, glossy, Bryden Pairpoint, 2¾x3½″ **45.00**
Tumbler, Diamond Quilted............................ **265.00**
Tumbler, miniature, Diamond Quilted, Mt Washington **250.00**
Urn, double handled, acid, round base, Mt Washington, 13½″ **675.00**
Vase, acid w/florals, Webb, 3½″ **365.00**
   Ball, w/flare & fluting, ivy w/ribbing, Webb, 3½″ **385.00**
   Bulbous, ribbed w/leaf decor, 4½x5″................. **575.00**
   Cased, pink shaded to ivory, 12″ **240.00**
   Four point ruffled top, acid finish, Mt Washington, 3½″.... **535.00**
   Glossy, crimped top, 4½″ **250.00**
   Glossy, folded star form rim, decorated, footed, Webb, 4″ .. **395.00**
   Lt rose to yellow, leaf decor, 4¼x3¼″ **365.00**
   Ruffled top, pinched in collar, 4″ **175.00**

Wide, tapers to ¾″ top, daisies, Mt Washington, 7½″ **400.00**
With ped, glossy, fluted top, Webb, 6x3½″ **395.00**
With ped, petal top, floral decor, Webb, 5¾x3¾″........ **650.00**
Yellow handles, floral decor, Queen's, Webb, 5x3″ **795.00**

Butter Molds & Stamps

The art of decorating butter begain in Europe during the reign of Charles II. This practice was continued in America by the farmer's wife who sold her homemade butter at the weekly market to earn extra money during hard times. A mold or stamp with a special design, hand carved either by her husband or a local craftsman, not only made her wares more attractive, but helped identify it as her product. The pattern then became the trademark of Mrs. Smith and all who saw it knew that this was her butter, "for butter or worse". It was usually the practice that no two farms used the same mold within a certain area, thus the many variations and patterns available to the collector today.

The most valuable of the collectible molds are those which have animals, birds, or odd shapes. The most sought after motifs are the eagle, cow, fish, and rooster.

These works of early folk art are quickly disappearing from the market.

Butter Molds

Box, w/flower & leaf, hoop type, machine made............. **30.00**
　　8 prints of fruit, 2 lb......................... **75.00**
　　With four simple designs, 1800s..................... **25.00**
Butterfly, miniature **45.00**

Cow, hand carved, 1 lb **175.00**
Double acorn w/rope edge, square, 2¾″.................... **40.00**
Double strawberry, 3½″.............................. **40.00**
Double star, rectangular **50.00**
Double wheat beside flower, rectangular **60.00**
Fern, machine made, 2½″ **30.00**
Flower, 6 sides, 3 parts, forms stick **45.00**
Flying duck, miniature **80.00**
Lamb, deep carving, 1800s, 3″ **300.00**
Pineapple, serrated edge, primitive, 3½″ **45.00**
Ram, stylized flowers, carved, 4½″ imprint **385.00**
Rose & bud, machine made, 3″ dia **30.00**
Sheaf of wheat, hand carved, primitive, 3½″ **45.00**
Six-leaf flower, hand carved, 1830s **40.00**
Star, round **50.00**

Sunflower w/leaves, 1800s **60.00**
Three pine twigs/machine made, 3½″ **30.00**
Two berries, two flowers, dovetailed w/brass clasp **40.00**
Wildflower & berries, machine made 3½″ **30.00**
Wildflower & pointed branches, beaded edge, 4½″ **35.00**
Wildflower w/rope edge, 3″ dia **25.00**

Butter Stamps

Cow w/gate, crimped edge **225.00**
Cow, hexagonal, pewter band, 4½″ surface **120.00**
Cow, stylized leaf, 4″ surface........................ **120.00**
Deer... **300.00**
Eagle **350.00**
Eagle w/branch in beak, 3½″ surface **225.00**
Eagle, knob handle, maple, 3½″....................... **250.00**
Eagle, star, 1800s, 2¾″ surface **115.00**
Fox, tree, 1800s, 2½″ surface........................ **165.00**
Geometric wheel, age crack, 1880s, 4″................. **60.00**
Grouse **300.00**
Heart, within wreath w/drying stand, 5″ dia, 4″ surface **230.00**
Lamb **275.00**
Leaf, double sided, 4″ **385.00**
Paddle, w/double stamp, cow & acorn **400.00**
Ram **350.00**
Rose, w/leaves, machine made **35.00**
Rosebuds, 1880s, 2½″ surface........................ **80.00**
Round, 4 pattern repeat **35.00**
Sheep, w/handle, fine cut **135.00**
Shell, 3 ring border, 1800s, 3½″ surface **115.00**
Thistle, hand carved **45.00**
Tree of Life, hand carved, reversible.................. **125.00**

Buttonhooks

Buttonhooks were made of bone, brass, iron or silver--simple utilitarian no-nonsense styles, fold up styles with jeweled gold handles, combination styles with built-in gadgets--all designed to ease the struggle of buttoning high top shoes, long kid gloves and stiffly starched collars.

Advertising, disc handle, 3″ **6.00**
　　Pat 1915, 3½″................................. **6.00**
　　Wire w/flat handle, 5″ **6.00**
Bone handle w/initials, 1910, 7″ **5.00**

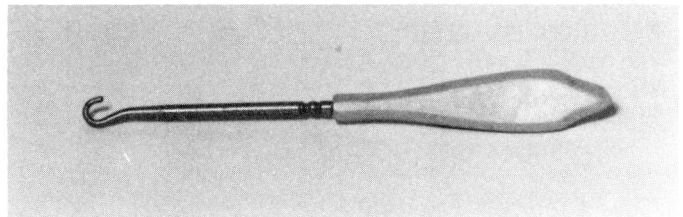

Celluloid handle, 5½″ **4.00**
French Ivory, tortoise shell handle.................... **4.50**
French Ivory **5.50**
Glass, w/red & wht swirls, attributed to Boston & Sandwich Glass, 6¾″ **70.00**
Sterling, Gorham repousse **38.00**
　　Art Nouveau, floral pattern, monogrammed.......... **16.00**
　　Art Nouveau, handle embossed woman's head, 7″ **22.00**
　　Heavy repousse handle, dated 1894, 10¼″ **24.00**
　　Repousse, faceted purple gemstone at top **35.00**
　　Wooden handle, for shoes, Keystone, 6½″ **15.00**
Victorian, shaped like gloved hand, finger is hook, nickeled brass, 11″ **45.00**
Wear-U-Well, metal **8.00**
Wire, flat handle w/scroll decor, 5″.................. **4.00**

C. D. Kenny

C. D. Kenny was determined to be a successful man, and he was. Between 1890 and 1934, he owned 75 groceries in 15 states. He accomplished this success in two ways: fair business dealings and premium give-aways. These ranged from trade cards and advertising mirrors to tin commemorative plates and kitchen items...there were banks and toys, clocks and tins. Today's collectors are finding hundereds of these items, all marked with Kenny's name.

Doll, bisque, wire jointed shoulders, marked, 4″	**55.00**
Figurine, porcelain poodle, Germany	**20.00**
Pitcher, miniature, blue	**20.00**
Plate, tin; Francis Scott Key, 1914	**40.00**
Girl w/muff, marked, 10″	**65.00**
Song book, patriotic, early, 6x3½″	**18.00**
Tin, little girls at table w/rabbit, self-framed, 8x12″	**60.00**
Tray, Democratic Convention	**85.00**
Girl praying, 4″ dia	**40.00**
Girl w/doll	**40.00**
Girl w/flowers, 4″ dia	**40.00**
Girl w/muff	**35.00**
Little girl in Thanksgiving scene	**35.00**
Raising the flag	**135.00**
Santa w/bag of toys, girl in bed, 9½″ dia	**45.00**
Soldier and sailor, 4″ dia	**40.00**
Three monkeys, 4″ dia	**35.00**
Victorian lady, sitting, 4″ dia	**45.00**

Calendar Plates

Calendar plates were popular advertising give-aways most popular from about 1906 until the late twenties. They were decorated with colorful underglaze decals of lovely ladies and handsome men, flowers, animals and birds--and, of course, the 12 months of the year of their issue.

During the late 30s they came into vogue again, but never to the extent they were originally.

Those with exceptional detailing, or those with scenes of a particular activity are most desirable--so are any from before 1906.

1906, flowers & berries decor	**25.00**
1907, bust of Colonial girl, 8″	**25.00**
1908, advertising, general merchandise, 9½″	**15.00**
New Year's Greetings, 7½″	**30.00**
Portrait of a lady, 9″	**40.00**
1909, advertising, Livermore Falls, Maine	**24.00**
Bust of Gibson type girl, 9½″	**25.00**
Flower & fruit decor	**15.00**
Fruit decor w/Illinois advertising, 7½″	**27.50**
Gibson Girl portrait, Morse & Bigelow Dept Stores, 9½″	**28.00**
Gibson Girl type, Westridge, Iowa	**18.00**
Man & woman in garden, initialed MK in gold, marked Sevres	**35.00**
Mountain scene in wreath of leaves & blue flowers	**18.00**
Multicolored poppies decor, 9½″	**15.00**
With pretty girl	**22.00**
1910, advertising, 8½″	**40.00**
1910, advertising, women's wear, 8″	**14.00**
Betsy Ross	**30.00**
Christy	**45.00**
Flowers decor, Dresden China	**30.00**
Gibson Girl w/rose border, signed A Gunn	**25.00**
Poppies w/Missouri advertising, 8½″	**25.00**
Portrait plate, signed	**35.00**
Washington House at Mt Vernon, 10″	**30.00**

With cherubs	**18.00**
Woman w/horse	**18.00**
1911, advertising, hunter & dog	**16.00**
Delft scene	**50.00**
Hunting scene, Markell Drug Co, 57 Park Street, Chelsea	**35.00**
Scenic w/flowers, advertising, Olpe, Kansas	**26.00**
Sunrise scene & advertising	**20.00**
1911-12, poppies w/California advertising, 8½″	**30.00**
1912, cherries & cherub decor, 8″	**25.00**
Martha Washington, 9″	**25.00**
Owl on book, Hayes, Dover, Deleware, 7½″	**25.00**
Wright Bros plane, 8½″	**31.00**
1913, boy under arch	**25.00**
Gibson Girl w/cherub border, artist signed	**25.00**
Holly & roses decor	**25.00**
Small boy, Bower, Shiremanstown, Pennsylvania, 7½″	**25.00**
1915, Panama Canal w/New York advertising, 7″	**25.00**
1916, man in canoe, advertising, 7½″	**25.00**
1918, US flag in center, bird & months border, 9″	**35.00**
1919, flag decor	**35.00**
1920, advertising, The Great World War, 7″	**27.50**
1921, blue birds & fruit decor, 9″	**25.00**
1928, Pickwick, Ridgway	**55.00**
1945, advertising, w/dog	**35.00**
1946, advertising, w/Indian	**35.00**

Calendars

Calendars are collected for their colorful prints, often attributed to a well recognized artist of the period. Advertising calendars from the turn of the century often have a double appeal when representing a company whose products are themselves collectible.

Advertising, 1911, furniture store, sepia photo, flip	**35.00**
1915, store, die cut w/4 girls	**65.00**
1923, die cut, embossed, fishing at the old mill	**65.00**
1924, grocery store, bath time, 8½x14″	**7.00**
Angler's Almanac, 1933, boy w/trout, large	**10.00**
Bakers, 1899	**45.00**
Bell-Cap-Sic, 1905, depicts dogs	**30.00**
Berlin Iron Bridge Co, 1897, depicts bridges	**45.00**
Boy Scouts, 1929, w/advertising, 15x7″	**15.00**
1931, Norman Rockwell	**100.00**
Brown & Bigelow, 1932, Boy Scout, Norman Rockwell	**365.00**
Brown & Bigelow, 1950, The 4 Seasons, Norman Rockwell	**85.00**
Buster Brown, 1920	**30.00**
Chero Cola, 1917, brunette w/bottle, 36x20″	**325.00**
Chesapeake & Ohio RR, 1943	**20.00**

Cleveland News, Carrier Greetings, 1911 .... **20.00**

Continental Insurance Co, 1897 . . . . **15.00**
Continental Insurance Co, 1932 . . . . **8.00**
De Laval Cream Separators, 1912, w/girl, 38x18″ **450.00**
De Laval, 1920 . . . . **60.00**
Dionne Quints, 1938, dairy calendar **25.00**
    1942 . . . . **35.00**
    1950, Sweet 16 . . . . **12.00**
    1951 . . . . **15.00**
Dodge, 1918, chafing dish, Maxfield Parrish **70.00**
    1924, Calendar of Friendship, Maxfield Parrish, in box **70.00**
    1925, Sunlit Road, Maxfield Parrish, orig box **70.00**
Dr Miles, 1905 . . . . **30.00**
Dr Pepper, 1948 . . . . **43.00**
Dr Pepper, 1949 . . . . **40.00**
Edison Mazda, 1925, Dreamlight, Parrish art, orig envelope . . . **225.00**
    1926, Enchantment, Parrish, orig frame **195.00**
    1927, Reveries, Parrish, orig frame **100.00**
    1928, Contentment, Parrish art, orig frame **110.00**
    1928, Norman Rockwell **70.00**
    1929, Golden Hours, Parrish, orig frame **350.00**
    1930, Ecstasy, Parrish art, 8x18″ **220.00**
    1931, Waterfall, Parrish, orig frame **175.00**
    1933, Parrish, complete **145.00**
Gibson Girl, 1905 . . . . **65.00**
Hamilton & Hunt Jewelers, 1882, Providence, R.I. **15.00**
Happy New Year, 1912, w/verse, framed, 20x24″ **65.00**
Hercules, 1919, hunting dogs, 14″ **150.00**
Hercules, 1938 . . . . **75.00**
Hood's Sarsaparilla, 1896 . . . . **30.00**
Hood's Sarsaparilla, 1894 . . . . **35.00**
Jackie Robinson, 1953, 12x15″ **60.00**
Jewel Tea, 1939 . . . . **30.00**
John Deer Centennial, 1837-1937 . . . . **175.00**
John Morrell, 1940 . . . . **25.00**
Kinter Milling Co, 1937, hunter w/dog, 38x18″ **130.00**
Listening In, 1944, J Erbit illustration **12.00**
Make It a Date, 1944, Rolf Armstrong **17.00**
Marilyn Monroe, 1955, Golden Dreams, w/date pad **30.00**
McCormick Reaper, 1931, Wyeth **50.00**
Metropolitan Life Insurance Co, 1908, Philip Boileau **170.00**
Mother's Joy, 1945, black mother & child **12.00**
National Life & Accident Insurance, 1939, 3 Little Pigs, 15x11″ **145.00**
Nestles Baby Food, Philip Boileau **190.00**
Nister, 1902, Young America, children in military uniform **40.00**
Ohio Farmers Insurance Co, 1904 . . . . **30.00**
Orange Crush, 1953 . . . . **40.00**
Peter's, 1925, mallards flying on marsh, 30x15″ **425.00**
Phoenix Insurance, 1901, 3 months, framed **18.00**
Prudential Insurance Co, 1898 . . . . **36.00**
Prudential Insurance Co, 1923, girl **12.00**
RR, Boston, 1930 . . . . **95.00**
Ruppert, 1950, w/envelope **20.00**
Sanford Ginger Ale, 1895, w/black men **40.00**
Savage & Stevens, 1922, deer on mountain, 14x28″ **295.00**
Savage & Stevens, 1927 . . . . **125.00**
Schlitz, 1910 . . . . **125.00**
Socony Gasoline, 1929, car, yacht, plane **125.00**
Spanish American, 1944, mother & child **12.00**
Squirt, 1949 . . . . **35.00**
The Author's Illustrated Quotation Kalendar, 1921, 65 pgs **8.00**
Travelers Insurance, 1936 . . . . **15.00**
Utica Beer, 1939, Franklin Roosevelt **75.00**
Winchester, 1920, man, boy unloading ducks at pier, 20x39″ . **525.00**
    1924, duck hunter in blind, 21x10″ **475.00**

Illustrated by Robert Robinson **280.00**
Wrigley's Chewing Gum, 1923 . . . . **12.00**
Youth's Companion, 1891 . . . . **18.00**
Youth's Companion, 1905, girl w/flowers, framed **80.00**
Zetts Beer, 1912 . . . . **200.00**

California Faience

    In 1916, Chauncey R. Thomas and William Victor Bragdon formed an association in Berkley, which by 1924 they called the California Faience Co. They produced simple art ware for the tourist trade, primarily from red clay with a monochromatic matt glaze, although occasionally a piece is found with a glossy finish. They also made decorative tile, hand pressed into molds designed to create an intaglio effect. The depressions were filled in with colors while the ridges between were left unglazed.

    Never a large company, two kilns were used and only a few workers were ever employed. Except for some tile made for the 1932 Chicago World's Fair, production stopped at the onset of the Depression.

    The artware was marked with the incised company name; the tiles with an ink stamp.

Bowl, matching frog, 2 values of blue, 10″ **225.00**
Bowl w/pr candlesticks, matt black w/maroon lining **325.00**
Flower frog, Chinese w/laundry bucket, Layes, mkd, 6x5″ **200.00**
Flower holder, figural, tan, blue, beige & rose matt, 6½x7″ . . . **250.00**
Jar w/cover, blue high glaze Persian shaded, #48, 5x3″ **135.00**
Planter, blue matt, shallow, 9″ dia **125.00**
Tile, architectural, 2 color, 3x3″ **40.00**
    Fleur de Lis, blue on white hi gloss **55.00**
    Fruit assortment, multicolor, 5″ **175.00**

Oriental face, 7x9″ **400.00**
Peacock in gold & blue, 5″ dia **140.00**
Shield, three color design, impressed mk, 12x9½″ **75.00**
Stylized face, 4 colors, 6x8″ **290.00**
Vase, blue, 4″ **125.00**
Vase, dark lavendar matt, script mark, 4x4½″ **160.00**

Calling Cards, Cases and Receivers

    The practice of announcing one's arrival with a calling card borne by the maid to the mistress of the house was a social grace of the Victorian era. Different messages were related by turning down one corner or another-condolences, a personal visit, or a goodbye. The custom was forgotten by WWI.

Fashionable ladies and gents carried their personally engraved cards in elaborate cases made of such material as embossed silver, mother of pearl with intricate inlay, or tortoise shell and ivory. Card receivers held cards left by visitors who called while the mistress was out or "not receiving".

Calling Card

Calling card, ea	3.00

Cases

Abalone & pearl, diamond design, 3x4″	30.00
Abalone & pearl, w/ivory edges, accordian center for cards, 4¼″	35.00
Art Deco, silver, basket of flowers w/stones on cover, Germany	60.00
Engraved pearl, w/ivory edges, reverse transfer on glass scene	22.50
Mother-of-pearl inlay	50.00
Pear shaped, carved center panel w/man & trees	35.00
Pear shaped, w/carved medallion w/dancing girls	40.00
Pearl, inlaid, w/carved central diamond, 2½x3½″	40.00
Pearl, w/carved classical woman's profile, floral engraving	30.00
Pearl, w/carved stag outlined in abalone, 2¾x3¾″	45.00
Reverse painted center, engraved pearl & ivory border	23.00
Sterling, cut bird design, chain handle, gold wash sections	135.00
Sterling, cut decor, chain handle, hinged compartment, marked	120.00
Sterling, engraved birds & flowers, chain handle	100.00
Tortoise shell, pearl, abalone parquetry, 2¾x4″	25.00
Tortoise, w/pearl & silver wire inlay, engraved silver plate	25.00

Receivers

Brass, hand shaped with wire spring	15.00

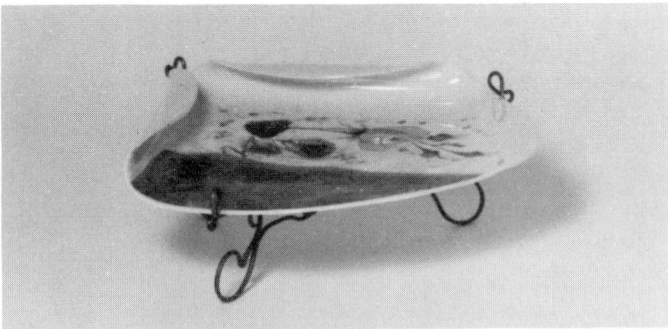

Bristol w/hp florals, wire holder	65.00
Ivory, carved inside & out, building w/people & trees, 4½x3″	196.00
Kate Greenaway style, boy & girl on fence in grape arbor	139.00
Milk glass, Indian	35.00
Silver plate, 6″ sq tray w/crimped edge, figural birds, Meridan	98.00
Victorian, 7″ tray, high relief angel w/2 infants, copper, bronze finish	80.00

Camark

The Camden Art and Tile Company, of Camden, Arkansas, was organized in 1926. John Lesell and his wife were associated with the company only briefly before he died that same year. After his death, his wife stayed on

and continued to decorate wares very similar to those he made for Weller. Le-Camark closely resembled Weller LaSa; Lessell was almost a duplication of Marengo. Perhaps the most outstanding was a mirror black line with luster decoration. Naturally, examples of these lines are very rare.

The company eventually became known as Camark, and began production of commercial ware of the type listed below.

Ashtray, turquoise, melon rib, #822, USA, 3¼″	3.00
Basket, cream w/pink & blue flowers, 4½x3¾″	8.00
Basket, double, blue, #138, 4½x5¾″	7.00
Bowl, centerpiece, turquoise, double flared shell, 12x5½″	13.00
Cream, scalloped rim, leaf handles, 12″	13.00
Green, scalloped, tab handles, 4½″	4.00
Turquoise, melon rib, scalloped, 9½x3″	8.00
Bowl & pitcher, apple green, fruit relief, 3¼x4½″	7.00
Cornucopia, cream, horizontal rib, 8x9″	13.00
Creamer, hi gloss black, decorated, 4½″	5.00
Double basket, cabbage leaf, maroon, 4½x5½″	7.00
Ewer, turquoise-plum w/yellow interior, melon rib, 10″	28.00
Flower holder, black & green, 4″	8.00
Cranes, maroon, 10x5″	13.00
Dancing nude figural, maroon, 9″	15.00
Ducks w/spread wings, black, 5¾x9″	13.00
Pitcher, Aladdin lamp style, maroon, #791, USA, 5½x8″	13.00
Bulbous, bead & scroll, maroon, 5″	7.00
Footed, scalloped, cream, 3¼″	4.00
White, black & white cat handle, orig label, 8″	26.00
Double swan	9.00
Double swans w/inter-twined necks, white, USA, #521	12.00
Elephant, trunk up, black gloss, 5½x6¼″	10.00
Green, 7x4½″	12.00
Heart shape, yellow, #099	20.00
Oval, fish, clam & water in relief, 10½″	13.00
Swan, blue w/label, 5″	15.00
Teapot, hanging strawberry, 8 cups, yellow, #609	8.00
Vase, bulbous, loop-top handles, green, brown, tan, 4x4½″	12.00
Fan, scalloped shell, yellow, 6x10″	13.00
Flared top, yellow, #288, 10x13″	11.00
Green w/yellow drip glaze, 8″	24.00
Grey & brown streaks, ring handles, 4½x4½″	11.00
Leaf shape, footed, flared split top, yellow 5″	6.00
Mirror black w/metallic hp rose, gold decor & mark, 9″	275.00
Wall plaque, horse head	20.00

Cambridge Glass

The Cambridge Glass Company began operations in 1901 in Cambridge, Ohio. They made primarily crystal dinnerware and well designed accessory pieces until the 1920s when they introduced the concept of color that was to become so popular on the American dinnerware market.

Always maintaining high standards of quality and elegance, they produced many lines that became best sellers; through the 20s and 30s they were recognized as the largest manufacturer of this type of glassware in the world.

Of the various marks the company used, the C in triangle is the most familiar. Production stopped in 1958.

Apple Blossom, amber; bowl, footed, low 11″	35.00
Comport, 7″	25.00
Apple Blossom, crystal; bowl, 2 handles, 10″	30.00
Butter w/lid in holder	75.00
Champagne	10.00
Cup & saucer #3400	17.50
Goblet	10.00

Ice bucket	50.00
Sandwich server, center handle	22.00
Sherbet	8.00
Water goblet	12.00
Fruit bowl, 5½"	5.00
Apple Blossom, green, tumbler, footed, 12 oz	25.00
Apple Blossom, topaz; console, footed, 12"	60.00
Plate, 8"	8.50
Water goblet, #3130	22.50
Wine	32.00
Blue Jay, candlefillers, pr	135.00
Cala Lily, candleholders, pr	25.00
Candlelight, Doulton jug, 76 oz	195.00
Caprice, blue; ashtray, 3 toed	9.00
Bon-bon, #33, 6"	40.00
Bon-bon, #147	22.50
Bowl, 2 handled, oval, #65, 11"	48.50
Bowl, 4 footed, 12"	40.00
Bowl, crimped, #61	50.00
Bowl, footed, 7"	25.00
Bowl, w/handles, 6"	22.50
Candleholders, #67, 2½", pr	22.50
Candleholders, triple, pr	75.00
Candy, w/lid, 3 footed	65.00
Champagne, 6 oz, thin	30.00
Cigarette box, #208	35.00
Cigarette box, Alpine, #208	45.00
Cocktail, 3 oz, thin	35.00
Cocktail, heavy	35.00
Comport, low, footed, #130	22.50
Comport, tall, #137, 7"	50.00
Creamer, medium	12.00
Cruet w/stopper	35.00
Cruets w/stopper, pr on tray	97.50
Cup & saucer	35.00
Dish, diamond, #171	15.00
Dish, heart, #169	15.00
Goblets, 10 oz, thin	30.00
Ice bucket w/tongs, 4 footed	145.00
Lemon tray, 2 handled, 4"	11.00
Mayonnaise & liner	30.00
Plate, 17"	75.00
Plate, 4 footed, Alpine, 15"	55.00
Plate, 7½"	16.00
Plate, 8½"	18.00
Plate, Alpine, 6½"	14.50
Plate, footed, low, 8"	25.00
Relish, 2 part	22.50
Relish, 3 part, #122	30.00
Shakers, pr	35.00
Shell, 3"	10.00
Sherbets, tall, heavy	27.00
Sugar & creamer, Alpine, med	40.00
Sugar & creamer, large	32.00
Tilt pitcher, 80 oz	150.00
Tumbler, 9 oz, #300	30.00
Tumbler, footed, 10 oz, #184	32.00
Tumbler, footed, 12 oz, #300	35.00
Vase, 4½"	35.00
Wine, 2½ oz, thin	40.00
Caprice, clear; Alpine bowl, 4 footed, 13"	12.00
Alpine plate, 15"	15.00
Alpine plate, rolled edge, 4 ft, 14"	14.00
Ashtray, 4½"	9.00
Bowl, 4 footed, oval, 11"	25.00
Bowl, Alpine, 4 footed, silver deposit, 11"	47.00
Bowl, crimped, silver deposit, 12½"	55.00
Bowl, footed, 13"	22.00
Bowl, oval, 11½"	17.00
Bowl, oval, scalloped, 4 footed, 12½x8½"	20.00
Bowl, ruffled, 11x5¼"	20.00
Bowl, scalloped, 4 footed, silver deposit, 10½"	48.00
Candy box & cover, #167	32.00
Plate, 8½"	10.00
Relish, 3 pt, 7½"	12.00
Rose bowl, Alpine, 4 footed, 8x5½"	16.00
Saucer	4.00
Sherbet, tall, #300	12.00
Sugar & creamer, 3"	13.00
Sugar & creamer, large	14.00
Sugar, 2½"	6.00
Tray, oval, #37	9.00
Tumbler, footed, 5 oz, #300	14.00
Tumbler, water, 9 oz, #300	12.00
Carmen, bowl, 10"	33.00
Bowl, crimped, 3 feet, 7"	30.00
Champagne	16.00
Comport	150.00
Sugar & creamer	45.00
Table goblet	125.00
Urn, 10½"	175.00
Cascade, crystal, ice tub	18.00
Dark green, sugar & creamer on tray	38.00
Chantilly, candleholders, 3 light w/prisms & bobeches	60.00
Champagne	15.00
Creamer, #3900, large	10.00
Creamer & sugar, #3900	30.00
Goblet	20.00
Juice, footed	14.00
Pitcher, #3900/115	100.00
Shakers, sterling top, pr	28.00
Sherbet, 4½"	14.00
Cleo, amber; cake tray, 10½"	18.00
Cup & saucer	17.50
Plate, 8¼"	7.50
Sugar & creamer, flat	29.50
Cleo, blue; candleholders, #27, pr	30.00
Champagne, 5½"	17.50
Console, #856 Decagon	35.00
Cup	8.00
Plate, 8½"	9.00
Sugar & creamer, #867, gold trim	40.00
Water goblet, 7"	22.00
Cleo, pink; cup & saucer	14.00
Salad set, 3 pc	45.00
Sugar & creamer	25.00
Cleo, topaz; creamer	15.00
Ice tea, footed, 6"	15.00
Water glass, footed, 5¼"	15.00
Water goblet, 7"	17.50
Crown Tuscan, ashtray, shell, hp roses, gold	8.00
Basket, 2 handles, Gadroon #3500/55, 6"	35.00
Bowl, 4 footed, square, #3400, 11¼"	65.00
Bowl, flying nude	200.00
Bowl, footed, gold, 12"	150.00
Candlesticks, dolphin stem #66, pr	110.00
Candy, 3 part w/lid, 8"	45.00
Cigarette box w/cover, gold, #35	35.00

Cocktail, nude stem, #3011 . . . . 105.00
Cornucopia vase, sea shell base, 10″ 85.00
Dish, 3 part, 8″ 32.00
Flower center, nautilis, footed, 6″ 90.00
Ivy ball, ring stem, 8″ 45.00
Lamp, urn shaped, 11″ 70.00
Nut, individual, footed 8.00
Seafood cocktail, shell shape, 4½ oz 50.00
Shell bowl, #18, 10″ 57.50
Shell compote, 6x4¼″ 38.00
Shell dish, nude stem, 6″ 85.00
Shell dish, nude stem, 7″ 100.00

Shell dish, w/nude stem, gold trim, 8″ 175.00
Shell dish, ped, 4x6″ 42.00
Shell dish, roses, gold, seaside scene, 7″ 90.00
Shell dish, w/lid, ped, 6¾x6″ 60.00
Vase, footed, 11″ 85.00
Decagon, amber; bowl w/handle, 6″ 6.00
Bowl, centerpiece, 12″ 16.50
Gravy 12.00
Sugar & creamer 16.00
Decagon, amethyst, ice bucket, bail 24.00
Decagon, black, sandwich server, center handle 18.50
Decagon, blue; bowl, 8″ 16.00
Cup 8.00
Sherbet 10.00
Decagon, cobalt; cup 9.50
Sugar & creamer, flat 22.00
Decagon, green; cup & saucer 6.50
Plate, 6″ 3.50
Plate, 8½″ 5.00
Shakers, #396, pr 20.00
Decagon, pink; cream soup, underplate 15.00
Ice tub w/handles 32.00
Waffle set, #816, 813 . . . . 80.00
Decagon, yellow, cocktail, 3 oz, #3120 . . . . 9.00
Diane, bon-bon, crystal, footed, 7¼″ 20.00
Candleholders, pink, key hole, pr 45.00
Cup & saucer, #3122 . . . . 25.00
Plate, #3122, 6″ 7.50
Relish, #3122, 5 part, 12″ 25.00
Water goblet 16.50

Water goblet, #3122 . . . . 17.50
Elaine, candy w/cover, 3 part, #3500/57 . . . . 35.00
Cocktail, crystal, 3 oz 25.00
Goblet, crystal 22.00
Oyster cocktail, 4¾″ 14.50
Relish, Gadroon, 4 part, flat, 14½″ 30.00
Sherbet, crystal, low 16.50
Tumbler, 2¼″ 20.00
Everglades, amber; bowl w/swans, 13″ 60.00
Bowl, dolphin foot, 12″ 45.00
Everglades, blue; double candleholder 35.00
Lunch plate 18.50
Sherbet 25.00
Everglades, crystal; candlesticks, double stem, pr 225.00
Covered candy 45.00
Goblet 14.50
Sherbet, footed & underplate 45.00
Farberware, amber; decanter, 38 oz 27.50
Relish tray, #397 floral cut 30.00
Sherbet, footed, 3¾″ 12.00
Farberware, amethyst; candy w/chrome lid 22.00
Condiment set on crystal handled tray 35.00
Stem, 4 oz 10.00
Farberware, cobalt; creamer 18.00
Stem, 4 oz 12.00
Cocktail shaker, 6 wines, tray 85.00
Nude compote, pierced floral 37.50
Nude w/amethyst bowl 50.00
Fighting Cocks, blue, champagne #3120 . . . . 22.00
Blue, water goblet #3120 . . . . 26.00
Pink, console, 3 pc #878, 977 . . . . 45.00
Yellow, tumblers, footed, 8 oz 15.00
Flower frog, Bashful Charlotte, crystal, 7″ 40.00
Draped Lady, #3 base, crystal, 8½″ 70.00
Draped Lady, crystal, 13″ 125.00
Draped Lady, green, 8½″ 100.00
Draped Lady, green, 13″ 165.00
Heron, 9″ 95.00
Gadroon, clear, plate, footed, Minerva etch, 12″ 22.00
Dark green, individual creamer 11.00
Gloria, amber, relish 2 part, 12″ 26.00
Pink, plate, 10″ 29.50
Yellow, shakers #3400, pr 75.00
Bon-bon, footed, 5½″ 13.50
Candy box w/cover, 7″ 50.00
Cup & saucer 20.00
Plate, 7½″ 10.00
Plate, 9½″ 20.00
Sherbet, tall, 6 oz 15.00
Sugar & creamer, footed, 6 oz 38.00
Tumbler, footed, 12 oz 13.50
Water goblet 18.00
Wine, 2½ oz 20.00
Heliotrope, bowl, 7½x2¼″ 38.00
Bowl, gold daisies, 12″ 60.00
Bowl, gold leaf band, 6x3″ 35.00
Bowl, gold leaf band, 8½x2½″ 60.00
Bowl, ram's head 175.00
Candlesticks, hexagonal, 7″, pr 75.00
Cheese/cracker, 2 pc set, 13½″ 95.00
Ice bucket w/bale, forest green 27.00
Ice bucket w/bale, ruby 35.00
Ivory, bowl, 1″ gold band, 3½x8″ 55.00
Ivory, plate, on ped, w/4 inserts, 12″ 65.00

Jade, bowl, 3x10″	48.00
Jug, milk glass, 32 oz	60.00
Milk glass, shell dish w/lid on ped, 6¾x6″	52.00
Mt Vernon, crystal; bowl, flared, 12″	27.00
Candlesticks, single, 4½″, pr	30.00
Goblet, 3 oz	15.00
Goblet, 10 oz	18.00
Nude, candlestick, crystal w/amber top	75.00
Cigarette box, covered, mandarin gold	165.00
Claret, crystal	75.00
Cocktail, crystal	75.00
Cocktail, ebony	85.00
Compote, blue cup	90.00
Ivy ball, amethyst, 9½″	145.00
Peacock, water set w/6 tumblers, clear	600.00
Portia, crystal; celery, #3500, 11½″	22.50
Sherbet, low, 7 oz	17.50
Sherbet, tall, 7 oz	17.50
Tumbler, footed, 10 oz	17.50
Vase, gold trim, 13″	105.00
Pressed Rosepoint, ice tea, royal blue, crystal foot	95.00
Oyster cocktail, carmen	125.00
Sherbet, amber w/crystal foot	70.00
Water goblet, carmen w/crystal foot	95.00
Rosepoint, ball jug, 80 oz, gold trim	95.00
Bon-bon plate, footed, #3500/55, 6″	20.00
Bon-bon plate, footed, #3900/1131, 8½″	20.00
Bon-bon w/handle, 6″	18.50
Bowl, footed, 11½″	32.00
#3900/54, 10″	35.00
Bud vase, #274, 10″	45.00
Cake plate, 2 handles, gold trim	28.00
Candelabrum, etched bobeche arm & vases	135.00
Candleholders, 3 light, #3900, pr	80.00
Candleholders, double, #495, pr	75.00
Candleholders, double, #647, pr	60.00
Candleholders, single, #646, pr	40.00
Candy 3 part, covered	65.00
Cheese & cracker #3900/135, 13½″	40.00
Cheese plate, 12″	28.00
Cigarette box, covered	150.00
Coaster set, 6 pc w/sterling base	200.00
Cocktail, #3121	32.00
Cocktail shaker, 13½″	95.00
Comport, blown, #3500, 5½″	45.00
Cordial, 1 oz, #3121	50.00
Cruet	75.00
Cup & saucer, #3900	35.00
Goblet, #3121, 8¼″	20.00
Goblet, #3500, 10 oz	23.00
Ice Bucket, Talley Ho	135.00
Ice tea, footed, 12 oz, #3121	25.00
Individual creamer, #3500/15	15.00
Lemon dish w/cover	150.00
Lunch plate	14.00
Mayonaise, #3900/19	26.00
Mustard w/cover & spoon, #515	135.00
Pickle dish, 3x9″	29.50
Plate, 6″	9.00
Relish, 2 part, #3400/90, 6″	35.00
Relish, 3 part, #3900/126, 12″	45.00
Relish, 3 part, round, 6½″	27.00
Relish, 4 part, gold trim	45.00
Salad dressing, double w/underplate & ladles #1491	70.00

Saucer	7.00
Shakers, flat, pr	40.00
Shakers, footed, #3400/73, pr	45.00
Sherbet, tall, #3121	25.00
Sugar & creamer, #3400/41	45.00
Tumbler, footed, 5 oz, #3121	24.00
Tumbler, ice tea, #3121	25.00
Tumbler, water, 9 oz	26.00
Vase, footed, #1238, 12″	60.00
Wine, 3 oz, #3121	60.00
Snowflake, cruet	45.00
Swan, Mandarin Gold, 8½″	95.00
Clear, 3½″	16.50
Clear, 5″	27.50
Peachblow, 3″, C in triangle	22.50
Yellow, 9¼″	110.00
Tally-Ho, amber, jug, #1402/49, 88 oz	45.00
Wildflower, bud vase #274, gold trim, 10″	25.00
Goblet	23.00
Sugar & creamer	22.50
Vase, 7½″	45.00

Cameo

Cameo glass was made in France from the late 19th century, and remained popular until about 1930. It consists of layers of colored glass banded together with the design, usually scenic or nature subjects, acid cut or hand carved to expose the underlying layer. From two to as many as five were used. Enamel or gilt was sometimes added to accent the motif. The finest work of this type was by Galle and Daum.

More cameo glass may be found listed under specific manufacturers. Only unmarked pieces are listed here.

Biscuit jar, iris decor, gold trim, plated top & rim; French	600.00
Bottle, white shell on olive, silver cap; English, 2½″	750.00
Bowl vase, 2 acid cuts, mountain scenic, 4¼x3½x7″	500.00
Perfume, acid cut red to frost, florals; St Louis, 2¼″	295.00
Perfume, blue w/leaves overall, silver top; English, 5¼″	795.00

Perfume flask, yellow iridescent ground, white Iris, 3x1½″	450.00
Powder dish w/cover, enameling, stork, mountains; Peynaud	250.00
Shade, red cut to frost, scenic	180.00
Vase, 2 acid cuts, sailboats, 3 colors; Michel, 8½″	850.00
3 colors, leaves & berries; French, 6″	325.00
Florals on citron, elaborate; English, 15″	1,450.00
Nude by R Krasna, 10x7″	1,950.00

Opaque cranberry, brass frame & rim, rippled, 8″ **345.00**
White cut to red, rose & butterfly, 7″ **3,800.00**
White florals cut to yellow; English, 5″ **875.00**
White florals on shaded pink body; English, 4¾″ **375.00**

Candleholders

Candleholders have evolved throughout the centuries in accordance with the time and manner of living of the period they represent. They may be primitive or elaborate, made from wood or precious metal.

Baker's, hand-forged, w/long handle & hooked end, early 1800s **450.00**
Bell metal, sq stepped molded bases, w/orig pushups, 1780s, 6″ **175.00**
Brass, 3 lions at base, 3 goats heads & grapes at top **125.00**
   9″, pair **80.00**
   English, 1820s, 11″, pair **95.00**
   King of Diamonds, w/push-ups, pair **495.00**
   Miniature, circular bases w/incised bead lines, 1780s pair . . . **125.00**
   Octagonal base w/circular stepping, push-ups, 1800s, 10″, pair **190.00**
   Octagonal raised bases & beehives, old, 12″ **90.00**
   Push-up wedding band, 1800s, 8½″ **255.00**
   Queen Anne, 8″ **195.00**
   Queen of Diamonds, w/push-ups, pair **395.00**
   Rectangular base w/incised rings & paw feet, early 1700s . . . **200.00**
   Square, 1920s, 13″, pair **49.00**
   The Diamond Princess, w/push-ups, pair **295.00**
   Turned shaping, square base, 7″ **135.00**
   With push-ups, 10″, pair **235.00**
Candelabra, French bronze, 1830s **250.00**
   Silvered brass, six branches, fine cut prisms, 1800s **80.00**
Chamberstick, brass, fingerhold, 1840s, 3″ **80.00**
Copper, early 1800s, 9″ **195.00**
Flat tin, finger roll handle, handmade **25.00**
French, silvered brass, w/crest & crown, 1700s, pair **375.00**
Glass, pressed pattern, New England Glass, 8½″, pair **125.00**
Hogscraper type, brass, 1700s, complete, 9″ **245.00**
   Iron, signed Shaw, 7″ **75.00**
   Pushup intact, mid to early 1800s, 7½″ **95.00**
Milk glass, crucifix, ornate, 10″ **45.00**
Minton, wht w/small floral transfer decor, 6″, pair **115.00**
Pairpoint, cobalt, 3¾″ base, bubble connector, 4″ **25.00**
Pewter, footed, ornate, 20″, pair **175.00**
'Pricket', wood base w/iron spike & drip cup, 1700s **250.00**
Spelter, Victorian man, woman w/torches, 15″, pair **300.00**
Spike, forged iron, to be driven into cabin walls, 1600s, large . **195.00**
   Forged iron, to be driven into cabin walls, 1600s, small **95.00**
   Hand-forged, 1700s **75.00**
Tin, push-up, 7″ dia drip plate, carrying handle, 1820s, 7″ **99.00**
Trammel, wrought iron, w/wick trimmers & snuffer **1,000.00**
Vaseline glass, hexegonal base, 7½″, pair **135.00**
Wood, crudely carved, mortised into rectangular base, 1800s . . . **80.00**
Wrought iron, combination candle & rushlight holder, 1850, 26½″ **235.00**

Candlewick

Candlewick was introduced by The Imperial Glass Corporation in 1936. It is recognized by the beads that decorate the bases and rims of most items. Others have beaded stems. During the time it has been produced, 741 different pieces have been made.

Ashtray **4.50**
Ashtrays, heart shape, set of 3 . . . . **18.00**
Basket, w/handle, 6½″ **14.00**
   #100/73/0 . . . . **36.00**

Bon-bon w/handle, 6″ **10.00**
Bon-bon w/handle, heart shape, 6″ **9.00**
Boudior set, 2 perfumes, mirror tray & puff jar **60.00**
Bowl, 10″ **17.00**
   #400/63B, 10½″ **24.00**
   Bell flared, 12″ **17.00**
   Bell shape w/red flashed beads **20.00**
   Centerpiece, mushroom **19.00**
   With handles, 8″ **12.00**
Bridge ashtray set, 4 pc **19.00**
Butter dish, ¼ lb **15.00**
Butter pat **12.00**
Cakestand, tall **40.00**
Candleholder, mushroom **8.00**
Candleholders, flower, pr **20.00**
   Rolled edge, pr **20.00**
   Silver floral design, pr **25.00**
   400/80, pr **15.00**
Candy, w/lid, 3 section **35.00**
Celery tray, 13½″ **15.00**
Champagne, 6 oz **10.00**
Cheese & cracker set, 400/88 . . . . **35.00**
Cheese compote, 400/88 . . . . **13.00**
Cigarette box & cover **16.00**
Claret, 5 oz **11.00**
Coaster, 4″ **5.50**
Cocktail, 4 oz **10.00**
Cologne bottle **12.00**
Compote, 8″ **16.00**
   Flat, 5½″ **8.00**
   Four bead stem, 5½″ **17.00**
   Low, no bead stem, 5½″ **18.00**
   Low, 2 bead stem, 5½″ **15.00**
Cup & saucer, large **10.00**
Fan vase, 8½″ **25.00**
Goblet, 9 oz **10.00**
Heart, 5″ **8.00**
Hurrican candleholder & shade, red flash **17.50**
Ice tub, cut monogram **35.00**
Ice tub, orig label **65.00**
Mayonnaise bowl, 5¼″ **9.00**
Mayonnaise set, 3 pc, Star Cut **25.00**
Mayonnaise spoon **7.00**
Mint tray, heart handle, 9″ **14.00**
Mustard w/cover **16.00**
Nappy, w/handles, 4¾″ **6.00**
Nut dish, 2¾″ **7.50**
Oil & vinegar w/tray **30.00**
Parfait glass **10.00**
Pickle, oval, 8½″ **7.00**
Pitcher, 400/24 . . . . **25.00**
Plate, 3 part, 12″ **12.00**
   6″ **4.00**
   8″ **6.00**
   10½″ **14.00**
   Crimped edge, 2 handles, 8½″ **15.00**
   Cupped, 17″ **32.50**
   With handle, 5½″ **6.00**
   With handle, 7½″ **12.00**
Punch cup **5.00**
Punch set, bowl, underplate, 12 cups **125.00**
Relish, 2 part **10.00**
Relish, 4 part, 4 handles **18.00**
Salad fork & spoon **15.00**

Salad set, bowl, fork, spoon, wood underplate **40.00**
Salt, pepper & tray **12.00**
Shakers, 400/96 . . . . **10.00**
    400/167, chrome top, pr **7.00**
    400/247 . . . . **6.00**
Sherbet, 5 oz **12.50**
Sugar, #400/30 . . . . **5.00**
Sugar, creamer & tray **15.00**
Tid bit, 3 pc set, heart shape **18.00**
Tray, handles, 12" **18.00**
    Oval, 9" **8.00**
    With heart handle **16.00**
Tumbler, 10 oz **8.50**
Vase, crimped, #400/287C, 6" **14.00**
    Crimped, beaded top & handles **25.00**
    Rolled, 7" **25.00**
Water tumbler, flat **8.00**

Wine goblet, 4 oz **12.50**
Wine, 3 oz **6.00**

Candy Containers

    Figural glass candy containers have been made in hundreds of designs from the early 1900s until the 40s. When full they held tiny sugar candy pellets of every color; when empty they became a toy or a bank. Some models were reissued with slight variations that can mean a subtantial difference in their value. Many had parts of wood or tin, and some had painted details. Values hinge on the condition of the paint, parts and whether or not the closure is original.

Airplane, patent 113053, clear, 4¾" long **28.00**
Airplane, Spirit of St Louis, lt pink glass, 4½" long **165.00**
Armored Tank **65.00**
Army Bomber **15.00**
Baby Chick Standing, excellent paint **110.00**
Baseball, Flying Red Horse, bank **20.00**
Battleship Maine, covered dish, milk glass, 7¼" **35.00**
Black Girl Sitting, papier mache, 5½" **70.00**
Bulldog, on round base, 4¼" **15.00**
Bureau, 3¾" **85.00**
Cane, glass, silver w/green stripes decor, 7¾" long **75.00**
Charlie Chaplin, Borgfeldt, 4" **80.00**
Chicken, on nest, covered dish, clear, 4¾" long **16.00**
Chicken, on sagging basket, traces of gold & red paint **40.00**
Christmas Boot, papier mache, red, 4" **8.00**

Clock, milk white, 3¼" **75.00**
Clock, octagon, 4", bank **75.00**
Coal Scuttle, blue, Victorian, wire bail **36.00**
Coupe, clear, 3½" long **32.00**
Dog, by barrel, bank, 3¼" **60.00**
Dog, w/bell, clear, 3¾" **28.00**
Doll Nurser, embossed with dog **12.50**
Dolly Milk Bottle, clear, 3" **20.00**
Drum Mug, clear, very good gilding, souvenir **22.00**
Duck, on rope top basket, green glass, 3" long **47.50**
Dutch Maid, bell **30.00**
Electric Runabout, clear, 3½" long **55.00**
Elephant, covered dish, pink glass, 7½" long **12.00**
Elephant, GOP, 2¾" **100.00**
Elephant, in swallow tail suit, clear, 3¾" **62.00**
Express Wagon, clear, 4" long **175.00**
Fire Engine, VG Co Little Boiler, 4¼" long **28.00**
Fish, papier mache, 5" long **65.00**
Frosty the Snowman, papier mache, 12" **16.00**
Gas Pump, clear, 4¼" **100.00**
Gun, w/candy, clear, 5¼" **15.00**
Hat, clear w/tin brim, 2" **24.00**
Hearse #2, clear, 4½" long **80.00**
Horn, Millstein 1948, plastic, green, red, blue, or yellow, 7", each **7.00**
Hound Pup, no closure **6.00**
Hurricane Lamp, clear glass **45.00**
Jack O' Lantern, pressed glass w/paint, 4" **75.00**
Kettle, w/three feet, 2" **12.00**
Kewpie, by barrel **90.00**
Kewpie, figural, signed **55.00**
Ku Klux Klan doll **325.00**
Lamp, floral paper shade, clear, 5½" **42.00**
Lamp, paper shade w/fairy tale motif, clear, 4¾" **58.00**
Lantern, ribbed base, w/candy **7.00**
Lantern, VG Co #1, 3¾" **8.00**
Lantern, Victory Glass Co, incorrect closure **4.00**
Lawn Swing, 6¾" wide overall **495.00**
Liberty Bell, amber glass, bank, orig closure **75.00**
Light Bulb, amber glass **45.00**
Lighthouse, clear, 3½" **10.00**
Limousine, w/rear trunk & tire, 4¾" **65.00**
Locomotive, double window 888, clear, red wheels, 5" long **25.00**
Locomotive, smokey clear glass, tin wheels, 5¼" long, Jent 888 **90.00**
Mailbox, clear, 3¼" **48.00**
Man on Motorcycle, w/sidecar, clear, 5" long **160.00**
Moon Mullins **35.00**
Mule Pulling 2 Wheel Barrel, w/driver, 4½" long **58.00**
Naked Child, clear, 6¾ **125.00**
Opera Glasses, swirl ribs, clear, 3¾" **46.00**
Peter Rabbit, orig painted cardboard, Millstein closure **20.00**
Phonograph, glass record, clear, 1¾" **195.00**
Piano, covered dish, clear, 7½" long **75.00**
Pierce Arrow, 1920, glass w/tin top **25.00**
Rabbit, covered dish, clear, 6¼" long **22.00**
Rabbit, covered dish, milk glass, 4½" long **15.00**
Rabbit, eating carrot **23.00**
Rabbit, emerging from egg **55.00**
Rabbit, running on log, 4¼" long **85.00**
Rabbit, standing, papier mache, 6¾" long **60.00**
Rabbit, w/wheelbarrow, 3¾" long **65.00**
Rabbit, with round nose, clear, 5¼" **50.00**
Radio, tune-in, clear, 4½" **25.00**
Radio, w/speaker **65.00**
Revolver, diamond in grip, light green glass, 7¼" long **10.00**

Revolver, Stough Whistling Jim, clear, 3½" long **15.00**
Revolver, West Bros Co, clear, 5½" long **8.00**
Rolling Pin, clear, 7" long **75.00**
Roly Poly, Santa Claus, papier mache, 4¾" **22.00**
Sad Iron, glass **15.00**
Safe, clear, 2¾" **30.00**
Sailboat, w/metal sail **10.00**
Santa Boot, metallic gold & red paint, no closure **15.00**
Santa Claus, leaving chimney, clear, 5" **55.00**
Santa Claus, plastic head **36.00**
Sedan, 6 vents, 4½" long **45.00**
Sedan, VG Co, 5" long **20.00**
Ship, no closure, silver paint overall **5.00**
Spark Plug, glass, dated 1922, King Features, orig paint . . **85.00**
Spark Plug, painted **65.00**
Spinning Top, clear, 2½" **16.00**
Spirit of Goodwill **100.00**
Station Wagon, no closure **11.00**
Stollwerck's, scenes from Hansel & Gretel, bank **85.00**
Straw Hat, glass, 3½" dia **32.00**
Street Lamp Post, 1892, clear, 6" **70.00**
Suitcase, clear, no closure **20.00**

Suitcase, milk glass w/bears **75.00**
Swan, with candy, 5" **30.00**
Tank, w/2 cannons, clear, 4¼" long, no closure **10.00**
Telephone, bell & crank, clear, 5½" **165.00**
Telephone, clear, #299 . . . . **75.00**
Telephone, desk type, clear, 1¾" **7.00**
Telephone, dial type, red, no closure, 5" **24.00**
Telephone, Lynn type **30.00**
Telephone, tall, VG Co, glass mouthpiece, clear, no closure . . . **90.00**
Telephone, w/glass receiver, painted green & gold, 4¾" **40.00**
Telephone, w/receiver **20.00**
Telephone, West Bros, 4¼" **28.00**
Telephone, wood mouthpiece, clear, 4¾" **42.00**
Tin litho, 2½ story house, 3x2x3" **14.00**
Tin litho, Engine Co, #23, horses & engine in door, 2¾x2½x3" **14.00**
Tin litho, Movie Theatre, 3x2½x2" **14.00**
Top Hat **35.00**
Touring Car, 4 door **75.00**
Traffic Sign, Don't Park Here, clear, 4½" **50.00**
Traffic Sign, stop & go, clear glass, mechanical, w/candy, 4¼" **200.00**
Turkey Gobbler, 3½" **80.00**
Ugly Duckling, papier mache, 9" **15.00**
Uncle Sam Hat, milk glass **45.00**
WWI Tank, 4½" long **65.00**
Watch, clear, 2" dia **150.00**
Wheelbarrow, clear, 6" long **35.00**

Willy's Jeep, no closure **15.00**
Wolf, w/book, 4¾" **58.00**

Canes

Fancy canes and walking sticks were once the mark of a gentleman. Handcarved examples are collected and admired as folk art from the past, and the glass canes that never could have been practical, as unique whimseys of the glass blowers profession.

Alligator handle, carved-in-the-round, 1890s, 35½" **68.00**
American flag & snake around bottom, early 1900s **155.00**
Arm & hand carved handle, dated 1846, folk art **185.00**
Carnival barker's, orange & black, lion head w/glass eyes **195.00**
Glass, amber w/wht threads, twist top & handle **70.00**
  Aqua, twisted, from Mason Jar factory, Belleville, Ill. **95.00**
  Blown, clear w/green core, ribbed, crooked handle, 41" **125.00**
  Blown, clear w/green interior, sq w/5" swirled corkscrew bottom **110.00**
  Blown, clear w/turquoise & amber swirls, 35" **110.00**
  Blown, crystal w/red threads, swirled, 36" **100.00**
  Clear w/double black interior spirals, 48" **85.00**
  Red & white, double 5 strand swirl encased in clear, 37" **75.00**
SS Great Eastern, inscribed on silver ferrule **265.00**
Walking stick, 4" lizard handle, gnarled, polished, carved acorn, 32" **120.00**
  Carved bamboo, Geisha girl heads **40.00**
  Carved, 6 snakes spiraled between bulbous dividers **205.00**
  Ebony w/round ivory handle **75.00**
  Handcarved doll-head handle, 1850s **165.00**
  Handcarved, figured, original blue **120.00**
  Lapis handled w/armadine garnet band in gold **275.00**
  Maple, mortised handle, chamfering, inlaid dots **85.00**
  Sterling, ferrule marked London 1898 . . . . **18.00**
Wood, 2 pc, w/brass eagle head handle **26.00**
Wood, carved man's head, primitive **80.00**

Canton

During the last part of the 18th century until late in the 1900s, china dinnerware was made in and around Canton, China, expressly for western export. The pattern whose name was borrowed from the city of its manufacture is decorated in blue on a white ground with a scene containing a bridge, willow trees, birds and a teahouse. The pattern is completed with various border designs, usually a solid band accompanied by scalloped lines.

Basket, w/undertray, reticulated, 9¾" **400.00**
Beakers, three, 2½" high **200.00**
Bowl, 5" **45.00**
  Deep, foliate shape, 9" dia **275.00**
  Mandarin decor inside & out, 3½x8½" **155.00**
  Salad, notched corners, 10½" **750.00**
  Scalloped, 1820, 9" **385.00**
  Stew, 9", 1820 . . . . **97.50**
Box, 7" long, covered **1,050.00**
  Barrel shape, mandarin scenes, covered, 5" high **170.00**
  Brush, covered, rectangular, 7" **750.00**
  Round, covered, 1½" high **110.00**
  Square, slightly domed lid, 7¼" high **957.00**
Butter dish, w/dome cover, separate strainer, 4½x7" dia **350.00**
Candlesticks, pr, 8¼" **1,300.00**
Celery dish, octagonal, 9¼" **200.00**
Charger, 11½" **175.00**
  18" dia **525.00**
Cider jug, breaks in handle **260.00**

Covered, foo dog finial, interlaced handle, 7¼" **500.00**
Creamer, ear shape handle, 4¼" high **100.00**
Creamer, helmet shape, 4" **160.00**
  Helmet shape, 5" high **300.00**
  Octagonal, 5½" high **225.00**
  Pear shape, 3½" high **160.00**
  Pear shape, 5" high **130.00**
  Snout nosed, 2¾" high **90.00**
  Snout nosed, 3¼" high **125.00**
  Snout nosed, 4" high **170.00**
Cup, w/saucer, 1870 . . . . **90.00**
Curry dish, footed, marquise shape, 10½" **325.00**
  Footed, square. **800.00**
Dish, 10" 1800s, blue. **40.00**
  Foliate shape, 9" dia **275.00**
  Kidney shape, 10¼ **225.00**
  Leaf shape, 10" **212.50**
  Leaf shape, scallop edge border, 7½" **175.00**
  Round, domed cover w/knob finial, wire bail handles, 7½" dia **425.00**
  Square, 8¾" **175.00**
Egg cup, 2¾" **100.00**
Ewer, drum shape body, tapered neck, 10½" **800.00**
Fish platter, w/mazzerine, 15" **900.00**
Ginger jar, covered, 7" **185.00**
  Mandarin landscape, electrified, 6½" **200.00**
  With orig cover, blue scenic decor, 7" **150.00**
Hot water plate, 1830, 9" **410.00**
  Octagonal, 10½" dia. **250.00**
Hot water platter, octagonal, 17" **700.00**
Meat platter, octagonal, 18" **325.00**
Mug, cylinder shape, interlaced handle, 4¾" **250.00**
Nut dish, quatrefoil shape, 4½" **90.00**
Pepper pot, 3¾" high **500.00**
Pitcher, 6" **250.00**
  With wash bowl, 15", dia bowl **650.00**
Plate, 7", 1840 . . . . **75.00**
  7", reticulated, ... **45.00**
  8¾", dia **35.00**
  9½", reticulated, ... **225.00**
  10", dia **77.50**
  10", 1820 . . . . **130.00**
  Mandarin design, early **31.50**
Platter, lemon peel glaze, sm rim flake, 17¼" **275.00**
  Octagonal, 11" **160.00**
  Oval, 12½" **150.00**
  Oval, 16" **250.00**
  Oval, well insert, minor edge flakes, 10x12¼" **170.00**
  With pierced liner, 17" **1,300.00**
Posset cup, twist handle, 1820 . . . . **120.00**
Pot de creme, interlaced handle, berry finial, 4" **75.00**
Punch bowl, mandarin scenes, slight rim repair, 13½" dia **550.00**
Sauce boat, scallop edge border, 7¾" **100.00**
Sauce tureen, 1880s, 3" dia. **35.00**
  With cover, 6¼" **175.00**
  With cover, oval, passion flower finial, repaired handle, 8½" **125.00**
  With cover, squash blossom finial, boar's head handles, 6". **225.00**
Saucer, 5", 1800. . . . . **55.00**
Serving dish, dome lid, octagonal body notch corners, lotus bud finial **275.00**
  Marquise shape, 10x5½", wide **275.00**
  Oblong, shallow, 9" **175.00**
  Oval, 13" **200.00**
Shrimp dish, 9¾" **400.00**
Soup tureen, stand & cover, blossom finial, boar's head handles, 14" **725.00**
Sugar, w/cover, 2 handle, 5" **175.00**

With cover, strawberry finial, 2 interlaced handles, 4½" **280.00**
  With twisted handles. **120.00**
Sweet meat set, 9 pc, fitted lacquer box, 10½" dia. **775.00**
Tazza, 6¾" dia **275.00**
  8¼" dia **325.00**
  10" dia. **600.00**
Teacup w/quatrefoil shape serving tray & cover **100.00**
  With undertray. **25.00**
  With undertray, wishbone handles **37.50**
Teapot, 5" high, 7¼" spout to handle **155.00**
  Censer shape, 4¾" **475.00**
  Dome top, 9¾" **450.00**
  Domed finial, swan's neck spout, 10" **300.00**
  Drum shape, 5½" **110.00**
  Drum shape, 1880, 6½" **425.00**
  Drum shape, berry finial interlaced handles, swan's neck spout **325.00**
  Lighthouse form, interlaced handle, berry finial 5½" **200.00**
  Lighthouse form, interlaced handle, domed lid, 8½" **375.00**
  Pear shape, swan's neck spout, 8" **140.00**
Terrapin, w/cover, oval, strawberry finial, 5½" **175.00**
Tile, chamfered, 5" dia **175.00**
  Octagonal, 4¾" dia **175.00**
  Round, 5" dia **135.00**
  Square, 6" dia **250.00**
Tray, oblong, galleried, notched corners, 8¼" **225.00**
Tureen, w/cover & original tray, boar's head handles. **1,450.00**
Umbrella stand, reeded w/mandarin scenes, 24" **775.00**
Urinal, covered w/foo dog finial **1,300.00**
Vase, bottle, mandarin scenes, 9" **125.00**
  Cylinder shape, 10¾" **275.00**
Vegetable dish, w/cover, 8" **200.00**
  9" **275.00**
  Marquise shape, lotus blossom finial, 9½" **175.00**
  Marquise shape, lotus blossom finial, 10¾" **325.00**
  Oblong, lotus blossom finial, notch corners, 9½" **200.00**
Vegetable dish, open, 9" **125.00**
Water bottle, acanthus leaves on neck, mandarin scene **750.00**
Platter, octagonal, 11" **160.00**

Carlton, See Art Deco

Carlton ware was the product of Wiltshaw and Robinson, who operated in the Staffordshire district of England from about 1890. During the 1920s they produced ornamental ware with enameled and gilded decorations such as flowers and birds, often on a black background. In 1958, the firm was re-named Carlton Ware Ltd. Their trademark was a crown over a circular stamp with W & R/Stoke on Trent surrounding a swallow. Carlton Ware was sometimes added by hand.

Bowl, Rouge Royal **30.00**
Pen holder, green w/deco type florals, 4" dia. **100.00**
Pitcher, classical figures in relief, florals, gilt, 6" **85.00**
  Cream w/blue florals, gilt, pewter lid, 1898, 6½" **85.00**
  Multiflorals, pewter lid, 6" **85.00**
  Presentation, Indian on spout, Mountie on horse, limited . **4,500.00**
Plate, white w/central fan decor, sm floral border, 8" **275.00**
Vase, black w/deco flying bird, jungle, 4" **125.00**
Vase, Deco, fan reverses to Oriental flower, 9" **350.00**
Vase, expanded ginger jar, fan reverses to Oriental flower, 9" . **350.00**
Vase, high flambe, Deco floral w/black centers, 11½" **425.00**
Vase, orange luster w/brown & gilt birds, signed, 8" **65.00**
Vase, trumpet shape, blue luster w/Persian design, signed, 10" . **85.00**

Carnival Glass

Carnival glass is pressed glass that has been coated with a sodium solution and fired to give it an exterior luster.

First made in America in 1905, it was produced until the late 1920s and had great popularity in the average American household; for unlike the costly art glass produced by Tiffany, Carnival glass could be mass produced at a small cost.

Besides being popular here, carnival glass gained great popularity in Europe and relatively large amounts were produced in England and Australia.

Colors most found are marigold, green, blue, and purple, but others exist in lesser quantities and include white, clear, red, aqua opalescent, peach opalescent, ice blue, ice green, amber, lavender, and smoke.

Companies mainly responsible for its production in America included the Fenton Art Glass Company, Williamstown, West Va.; the Northwood Glass Company, Wheeling, West Va.; the Imperial Glass Company, Bellaire, Ohio; the Millersburg Glass Company, Millersburg, Ohio; and the Dugan Glass Company (Diamond Glass), Indiana, Pennsylvania.

In addition to these major manufacturers, lesser producers included the U.S. Glass Company, the Cambridge Glass Company, the Westmoreland Glass Company, and the McKee Glass Company.

Carnival glass has been highly collectible since the 1950s and has been reproduced for the last twenty-five years. Several national and state collector's organizations exist, and many fine books are available on old Carnival glass including *The Standard Encyclopedia of Carnival Glass* by authority, Bill Edwards.

Acanthus, bowl, marigold, 8″	50.00
Acorn, Fenton, bowl, peach opal, 7″	98.00
Acorn Burrs, bowl, pastel, flat 10″	300.00
Bowl, dark, flat, 5″	45.00
Punch bowl & base, marigold	300.00
Punch cup, marigold	26.00
Covered butter, dark	225.00
Covered sugar, dark	125.00
Creamer or spooner, pastel	220.00
Water pitcher, dark	540.00
Tumbler, marigold	50.00
Age Herald, bowl, dark, 9¼″	850.00
Apple Tree, water pitcher, marigold	150.00
Tumbler, marigold	40.00
April Showers, vase, pastel	60.00
Autumn Acorns, bowl, marigold, 8¼″	28.00
Basket, either shape, aqua opal, footed	285.00
Basketweave, open edge hat shape, plain or blackberry interior, dark	45.00
Beaded Acantus, milk pitcher, smoke	140.00
Beaded Cable, rose bowl, pastel, footed	100.00
Candy bowl, marigold, footed	40.00
Beaded Shell, mug, marigold	150.00
Covered butter, dark	170.00
Covered sugar, marigold	75.00
Creamer or spooner, dark	90.00
Water pitcher, marigold	350.00
Tumbler, marigold	60.00
Beauty bud vase, regular size, dark	45.00
Bernheimer, bowl, dark, scarce, 8¾″	350.00
Big Fish, bowl, marigold, various shapes, rare	250.00
Birds & Cherries, bon bon, white	75.00
Compote, dark	60.00
Bird With Grapes, vase, marigold	52.00
Blackberry, open edge hat, red	165.00
Blackberry Block, water pitcher, dark	520.00
Tumbler, dark	60.00
Blackberry Wreath, bowl, vaseline, 7″	175.00

Blueberry, water pitcher, white, scarce	800.00
Tumbler, white, scarce	160.00
Bo-Peep, child's plate, marigold, rare	250.00
Child's mug, marigold, scarce	120.00
Bouquet, water pitcher, dark	375.00
Tumbler, dark	45.00
Brooklyn Bridge, bowl, marigold, rare	375.00
Butterflies, bon bon, dark	50.00
Butterfly, Northwood, bon bon, ice blue, plain or ribbed exterior	120.00
Butterfly & Berry, bowl, dark, footed, 10″	72.00
Bowl, marigold, footed, 5″	30.00
Water pitcher, dark	350.00
Tumbler, dark	60.00
Hatpin holder, marigold, rare	1,000.00
Butterfly & Fern, water pitcher, dark	450.00
Tumbler, dark	45.00
Butterfly & Tulip, large bowl, marigold, footed, scarce	300.00
Buzz Saw, cruet, small, dark, rare, 4″	375.00
Cruet, large, marigold, rare, 6″	350.00
Captive Rose, bowl, dark, 10¼″	48.00
Compote, smoke	75.00
Carnival Covered Hen, one size, dark, reproduced	140.00
Cathedral, chalice, marigold, 7″	75.00
Chatelaine, tumbler, purple, rare	400.00
Cherry, Millersburg, milk pitcher, marigold, rare	600.00
Covered butter, dark	150.00
Covered sugar, marigold	50.00
Creamer or spooner, dark	85.00
Water pitcher, marigold, scarce	700.00
Tumbler (2 variations), marigold	300.00
Cherry & Cable, water pitcher, marigold, rare	1,700.00
Tumbler, marigold, rare	210.00
Covered butter, marigold, rare	300.00
Sugar, creamer or spooner, marigold, rare, ea	155.00
Cherry Chain, bowl, marigold, 7½″	40.00
Bowl, white, 7½″	75.00
Plate, marigold, 9″	80.00
Plate, dark, 9″	100.00
Cherry & Cable Intaglio, bowl, marigold, 5″	36.00
Bowl, marigold, 10″	60.00
Cherry Circles, bon bon, marigold, 9″	36.00
Bon bon, dark, 9″	58.00
Cherry Smash, bowl, marigold, 8″	48.00
Covered butter, marigold	110.00
Tumbler, marigold	125.00
Christmas Compote, large, marigold, rare	2,700.00
Large, dark, rare	2,500.00
Chrysanthemum, bowl, marigold, flat, 10″	50.00
Bowl, pastel, flat, 10″	90.00
Bowl, red, flat, 10″	700.00
Bowl, marigold, footed, 10″	60.00
Bowl, dark, footed, 10″	85.00
Classic Arts, powder jar, marigold	145.00
Rose bowl, marigold	135.00
Vase, marigold, rare, 10″	175.00
Cleveland Memorial Tray, one shape, marigold, rare	2,200.00
Coin Dot, bowl, marigold, 6″	36.00
Bowl, dark, 10″	50.00
Pitcher, marigold, rare	295.00
Pitcher, dark, rare	410.00
Tumbler, marigold, rare	75.00
Tumbler, dark, rare	125.00
Coin Spot, compote, marigold	35.00
Compote, peach opal	60.00

Compote, aqua opal 210.00
Colonial, toothpick holder, marigold 50.00
   Toothpick holder, dark 85.00
   Open sugar or creamer, red 100.00
   Candlesticks, marigold, pr 185.00
Columbia, vase, marigold, 5″ 30.00
   Vase, dark, 5″ 46.00
   Compote, marigold 40.00
   Compote, dark 58.00
Concave Diamond, pitcher w/lid, ice blue 375.00
   Tumbler, vaseline 365.00
Concord, bowl, marigold, scarce, 9″ 65.00
   Bowl, amber, scarce, 9″ 100.00
   Plate, marigold, rare, 10″ 310.00
   Plate, dark, rare, 10″ 585.00
Constellation, compote, marigold 32.00
   Compote, peach opal 46.00
   Compote, vaseline 80.00
Coral, bowl, marigold, 9″ 42.00
   Bowl, white, 9″ 85.00
   Plate, dark, rare 500.00
Corinth, bowl, marigold, 9″ 35.00
   Bowl, peach opal, 9″ 70.00
   Banana dish, marigold 45.00
   Banana dish, dark 70.00
   Vase, smoke, 10″ 55.00
Corn Bottle, one shape, marigold 265.00
Corn Vase, regular mold, marigold 375.00
   Regular mold, peach opal 450.00
Cornucopia, vase, marigold, 5″ 60.00
   Candlesticks, white, 5″, pr 140.00
Cosmos and Cane, bowl, marigold, 10″ 55.00
   Bowl, white, 10″ 100.00
   Bowl, marigold, 5″ 32.00
   Bowl, white, 5″ 65.00
   Covered butter, marigold 150.00
   Covered sugar or creamer, white 230.00
   Spooner, marigold 85.00
   Spooner, white 195.00
   Pitcher, marigold, rare 900.00
   Pitcher, white, rare 1,300.00
   Tumbler, marigold, rare 165.00
   Tumbler, white, rare 180.00
Cosmos Vt, bowl, marigold, 9″ 30.00
   Bowl, pastel, 10″ 55.00
   Bowl, red, 9″ 165.00
   Plate, marigold, rare, 10″ 70.00
   Plate, dark, rare, 10″ 90.00
   Plate, peach opal, rare, 10″ 150.00
Country Kitchen, covered butter, marigold 290.00
   Covered butter, dark 350.00
   Sugar, creamer or spooner, marigold 165.00
   Sugar, creamer or spooner, dark 200.00
Courthouse, lettered, rare, dark 325.00
   Un-lettered, very rare, dark 485.00
Covered Little Hen, miniature, 3½″, clambroth, rare 100.00
Crackle, auto vase, marigold 25.00
   Candy jar, covered, dark 34.00
   Punch bowl and base, dark 55.00
   Punch cup, marigold 10.00
Cut Comos, tumbler, marigold, rare 275.00
Cut Flowers, vase, marigold, 10″ 60.00
Dahlia, bowl, footed, dark, 5″ 50.00
   Covered butter, footed, marigold 100.00

Covered sugar, footed, dark 100.00
Creamer, footed, dark 90.00
Pitcher, white, rare 650.00
Tumbler, dark, rare 110.00
Daisy, Fenton, bon bon, dark, scarce 55.00
Daisy and Drape, vase, marigold 110.00
Daisy Cut Bell, marigold, rare 395.00
Daisy Squares, rosebowl, dark green, rare 295.00
   Compote, amber, very rare 365.00
Dandelion, mug, marigold 345.00
   Pitcher, tankard, dark 595.00
   Tumbler, white 140.00
Dandelion, Paneled, pitcher, tankard, marigold 390.00
   Tumbler, dark 65.00
Diamonds, pitcher, marigold 125.00
   Tumbler, aqua 90.00
Diamond and Daisy Cut, vase, square, marigold, 10″ 70.00
   Pitcher, marigold, rare 310.00
   Tumbler, marigold, rare 45.00
Diamond Checkerboard, cracker jar, marigold 75.00
   Covered butter, marigold 70.00
   Tumbler, marigold 75.00
Diamond Lace, bowl, dark, 11″ 60.00
   Pitcher, dark 225.00
   Tumbler, dark 50.00
Diamond Ring, bowl, smoke, 5″ 20.00
   Fruit bowl, dark, 9½″ 50.00
Diving Dolphins, bowl, footed, marigold, 7″ 110.00
Dolphins, compote, dark green, rare 700.00
Double Dolphins, cake plate, center handle, pastel 55.00
   Compote, pastel 82.00
   Fan vase, pastel 54.00
Double Dutch, bowl, footed, dark, 9½″ 58.00
Double Scroll, candlesticks, pr, marigold, 9″ 45.00
   Punch cup, marigold 18.00
Double Star, pitcher, dark, scarce 350.00
   Tumbler, marigold, scarce 60.00
Double Stem Rose, bowl, dome, footed, white, 8½″ 64.00
Dragon and Lotus, bowl, flat, aqua opalescent, 9″ 225.00
   Bowl, footed, pastel, 9″ 110.00
   Plate, dark, rare, 9½″ 550.00
Dragon and Strawberry, bowl, flat, marigold, 9″, scarce 170.00
Drapery, rose bowl, pastel 95.00
   Candy dish, aqua opalescent 140.00
Duncan Cruet, one size, marigold 395.00
Dutch Plate, marigold, 8″ 35.00
Elegance, bowl, dark, 8¼″ 90.00
Elks, bowl, dark, rare 800.00
   Paperweight, dark, very rare, ... 995.00
Elks, Parkersburg plate, dark, rare 650.00
   Atlantic City plate, dark, rare 850.00
Embroidered Mums, bowl, aqua opalescent, 9″ 500.00
Engraved Grapes, covered candy jar, marigold 36.00
   Pitcher, squat, marigold 65.00
   Pitcher, tall, marigold 75.00
Estate, mug, pastel, rare 90.00
   Creamer or sugar, aqua opalescent 110.00
Fanciful, bowl, peach opalescent, 8½″ 60.00
Fan Tail, bowl, footed, marigold, 5″ 26.00
   Compote, dark 58.00
   Plate, footed, dark, very rare 1,000.00
Farmyard, bowl, various shapes, dark purple, 10″, rare 2,800
Fashion, fruit bowl and base, marigold 54.00
   Punch bowl and base, pastel 70.00

Punch cup, marigold **20.00**
Feather and Heart, pitcher, dark, scarce **500.00**
  Tumbler, marigold, scarce **80.00**
Feathered Serpent, bowl, marigold, 10″ **45.00**
  Bowl, dark, 5″ **38.00**
Fentonia, covered butter, dark **160.00**
  Creamer, marigold **60.00**
  Pitcher, dark **410.00**
  Tumbler, marigold **45.00**
Fentonia Fruit, tumbler, dark, rare **185.00**
  Pitcher, marigold, rare **375.00**
  Bowl, footed, dark, 10″ **150.00**
Field Flower, pitcher, pastel **375.00**
  Tumbler, dark **60.00**
  Milk pitcher, marigold, rare **155.00**
Field Thistle, plate, marigold, 9″, rare **265.00**
  Sugar, dark **60.00**
  Compote, marigold, large **75.00**
  Tumbler, marigold **36.00**
  Bowl, marigold, 10″ **40.00**
File, bowl, pastel, 10″ **45.00**
  Water, pitcher, dark, rare **420.00**
  Tumbler, marigold **145.00**
Fine Cut and Roses, rosebowl, footed, aqua opalescent **550.00**
  Candy dish, footed, pastel **165.00**
Fine Cut Rings, bowl, oval, marigold **35.00**
  Celery, marigold **40.00**
  Covered butter, marigold **65.00**
  Cake stand, stemmed, marigold **55.00**
  Jam jar w/lid, marigold **40.00**
Fine Rib, plate, peach opalescent, 9″ **90.00**
  Vase, pastel **50.00**
Fisherman's Mug, marigold **210.00**
Fishscale and Beads, plate, pastel, 7″ **80.00**
  Bride's Basket w/holder, peach opalescent **100.00**
Fleur De Lis, bowl, flat, pastel marigold, 8½″ **80.00**
  Bowl, dome footed, dark, 8½″ **125.00**
Floral and Grapes & VTS, pitcher, white **325.00**
  Tumbler, dark **36.00**
Floral and Optic, bowl, footed, red, 10″ **250.00**
Floral and Wheat, compote, marigold **30.00**
  Bon-bon, stemmed, peach opalescent **45.00**
Flowers and Spades, bowl, marigold, 10″ **40.00**
  Bowl, dark, 5″ **45.00**
Flute, Northwood salt dip footed, marigold **30.00**
  Pitcher, dark, rare **545.00**
  Tumbler, marigold, rare **45.00**
Flute, Millersburg, vase, dark, very rare **350.00**
  Punch cup, marigold **24.00**
  Berry bowl, w/base, marigold, rare, 10″ **115.00**
Flute #3, Imperial, sugar, creamer, or spooner, dark . . . **95.00**
  Punch bowl and base, marigold **260.00**
  Punch cup, marigold **24.00**
  Pitcher, green **495.00**
  Tumbler, dark **85.00**
Flute & Cane, milk pitcher, marigold **110.00**
Fluted Scroll, rosebowl, amethyst, footed, very rare . . . **950.00**
Footed Shell, large, marigold, 5″ **28.00**
  Small, marigold, 3″ **36.00**
Formal, hat pin holder, marigold, rare **175.00**
49'er, tumbler, marigold **70.00**
  Wine, marigold **48.00**
Four Flowers & Vts., bowl, marigold, 11″ **40.00**
  Bowl, peach opal, 11″ **65.00**

Plate, dark, 6″ **280.00**
Plate, peach opal, 10″ **400.00**
474, punch bowl and base, dark **475.00**
  Cup, marigold **26.00**
  Cup, dark **35.00**
  Milk pitcher, marigold, very scarce **120.00**
  Pitcher, dark, scarce **425.00**
  Tumbler, dark, scarce **85.00**
French Knots, hat shape, marigold **32.00**
Frolicking Bears, pitcher, dark, extremely rare **6,850.00**
Frosted Block, covered butter, marigold **65.00**
  Creamer, sugar, marigold, each **40.00**
  Milk pitcher, marigold, very rare **58.00**
Fruit & Flowers, bon bon, marigold, stemmed **36.00**
  Bon bon, aqua opal, stemmed **225.00**
Fruit Salad, punch bowl and base, dark **780.00**
  Cup, dark **36.00**
Garden Path & Vt., bowl, marigold, 10″ **40.00**
  Bowl, pastel, 10″ **85.00**
  Plate, marigold, rare, 6″ **225.00**
  Plate, peach opal, rare, 6″ **325.00**
Garland, rose bowl, dark, footed **65.00**
Gay 90s, pitcher, purple, very rare **6,000.00**
  Tumbler, dark, very rare **1,100.00**
God and Home, pitcher, dark, rare **1,850.00**
  Tumbler, dark, rare **195.00**
Golden Honeycomb, bowl, marigold, 5″ **25.00**
  Plate, marigold, 7″ **45.00**
  Creamer, sugar, marigold, each **35.00**
Golden Wedding, bottle, marigold, various sizes, from . . . **12.00**
Good Luck, bowl, marigold, 8¾″ **90.00**
  Bowl, aqua opal, 8¾″ **450.00**
  Bowl, ice green, 8¾″ **180.00**
  Plate, marigold, flat or ruffled, 9″ **195.00**
  Plate, dark, flat or ruffled, 9″ **275.00**
Grape, Heavy, Imperial, bowl, marigold, 9″ **38.00**
  Bowl, pastel, 9″ **70.00**
  Bowl, dark, 5″ **26.00**
Grape, Imperial, fruit bowl, marigold, 8¾″ **32.00**
  Fruit bowl, pastel, 8¾″ **70.00**
  Cup & saucer, marigold, complete **60.00**
  Sandwich tray center handle, marigold **35.00**
  Pitcher, dark **175.00**
  Tumbler, dark **35.00**
  Water bottle (vase), marigold, rare **120.00**
  Milk pitcher, dark, very rare **200.00**
  Decanter, with stopper, marigold **90.00**
  Decanter, with stopper, dark **170.00**
  Stemmed wine, marigold **28.00**
Grape, Fenton, orange bowl, marigold, footed **75.00**
  Bowl, dark, flat, 8½″ **50.00**
  Plate, red, footed, 9″ **485.00**
Grape, Northwood, banana boat, marigold, footed **185.00**
  Banana boat, pastel, footed **310.00**
  Candlesticks, dark, pr **260.00**
  Compote, marigold, large, covered **2,000.00**
  Compote, dark, large, open **500.00**
  Sweetmeat, marigold, covered **650.00**
  Cologne, marigold, w/stopper **250.00**
  Perfume, dark, w/stopper **585.00**
  Dresser tray, white **400.00**
  Pin tray, dark **135.00**
  Hatpin holder, marigold **210.00**
  Hatpin holder, aqua opal **3,000.00**

Powder jar, dark, w/lid **110.00**
Fernery, marigold, footed, rare **1,500.00**
Fernery, ice blue, footed, rare **3,000.00**
Plate, dark, handgrip **80.00**
Punch bowl & base (standard), pastel **1,000.00**
Punch cup, marigold **28.00**
Punch cup, pastel **70.00**
Covered butter, marigold **195.00**
Covered butter, pastel **300.00**
Covered sugar, marigold **85.00**
Creamer or spooner, dark **125.00**
Pitcher, standard, dark **300.00**
Tumbler, marigold **45.00**
Tumbler, dark **60.00**
Hatpin holder, dark, whimsey, very rare **1,000.00**
Grape & Gothic Arches, covered butter, dark **115.00**
Covered sugar, dark **75.00**
Creamer or spooner, dark **75.00**
Pitcher, marigold **200.00**
Tumbler, marigold **35.00**
Grape Arbor, bowl, marigold, footed, 11″ **125.00**
Pitcher, marigold **210.00**
Pitcher, ice green **3,100.00**
Tumbler, marigold **40.00**
Tumbler, ice blue **220.00**
Grape Leaves, bowl, marigold, 8¾″ **55.00**
Bowl, ice blue, 8¾″ **160.00**
Grape Wreath, bowl, dark, 9″ **65.00**
Grape Vine Lattice, pitcher, dark, rare **410.00**
Tumbler, dark, rare **75.00**
Greek Key, bowl, marigold, flat or dome footed, 8½″ **75.00**
Bowl, aqua opal, flat or dome footed, 7″ **220.00**
Pitcher, marigold, rare **550.00**
Tumbler, marigold, rare **75.00**
Hammered Bell Chandelier, complete, white, 5 shades **600.00**
Shade, white, each **90.00**
Harvest Flower, pitcher, marigold, very rare **700.00**
Tumbler, marigold, scarce **110.00**
Hattie, bowl, marigold, 9″ **30.00**
Bowl, pastel, 9″ **55.00**
Hearts & Flowers, bowl, marigold, 8½″ **36.00**
Bowl, pastel, 8½″ **75.00**
Compote, dark **55.00**
Compote, aqua opal **300.00**
Plate, marigold, rare, 9″ **160.00**
Heart & Vine, bowl, pastel, 8½″ **58.00**
Heavy Vine, atomizer, marigold **75.00**
Lamp, marigold **150.00**
Heron, mug, marigold, rare **700.00**
Mug, dark, rare **220.00**
Hobnail, Millersburg, pitcher, marigold, rare **3,200.00**
Tumbler, marigold, rare **470.00**
Rosebowl, dark, scarce **175.00**
Spittoon, dark, rare **275.00**
Covered butter, marigold, rare **295.00**
Sugar, creamer, spooner, marigold, rare, each **175.00**
Hobnail, miniature, tumbler, marigold, 2½″ tall **46.00**
Pitcher, marigold, very rare, 6″ tall **190.00**
Hobstar, Imperial, bowl, pastel, berry, 10″ **40.00**
Fruit bowl, dark, complete **75.00**
Cookie jar, w/lid, marigold **55.00**
Covered butter, dark **150.00**
Creamer, sugar, spooner, dark, each **85.00**
Hobstar & Arches, Imperial, fruit bowl, dark, 2 pc, complete . . . **70.00**

Hobstar & Feathers, punch bowl & base, marigold, rare **1,100.00**
Rosebowl, dark, giant, rare **950.00**
Punch cup, marigold, scarce **28.00**
Covered sugar, dark, very rare **800.00**
Compote, marigold, very rare **600.00**
Hobstar & Fruit, bowl, peach opal, 6″ **55.00**
Bowl, peach opal, 10″ **80.00**
Hobstar Reversed, English, spooner, marigold **42.00**
Covered butter, marigold **50.00**
Frog & holder, marigold **50.00**
Holly, bowl, dark, 8″ **32.00**
Plate, marigold, 10″ **75.00**
Holly Panelled, bon-bon, footed, dark **50.00**
Holly Swirl, (Sprig), nappy, tri cornered, dark **85.00**
Bon-bon, marigold **55.00**
Honeycomb & Clover, bon-bon, dark **50.00**
Compote, dark **55.00**
Horses Heads, bowl, footed, dark, 8″ **85.00**
Rosebowl, footed, dark **125.00**
Humpty-Dumpty, mustard jar, marigold **75.00**
Illusion, bon-bon, dark **60.00**
Bowl, marigold, 8½″ **50.00**
Indiana Statehouse, plate, dark, very rare **2,800.00**
Inverted Feather, cracker jar w/lid, green **185.00**
Pitcher, marigold, rare **1,400.00**
Tumbler, marigold, rare **460.00**
Compote, marigold, scarce **48.00**
Milk Pitcher, marigold, 7″, very rare **600.00**
Inverted Strawberry, bowl, dark, 9″ **85.00**
Candlesticks, marigold, rare, pr **250.00**
Compote, dark, large, rare **400.00**
Powder jar, complete, marigold, rare **400.00**
Ladies spittoon, dark, rare **625.00**
Milk pitcher, dark, very rare **2,000.00**
Pitcher, marigold, rare **1,000.00**
Tumbler, marigold, rare **350.00**
Iowa, miniature mug, marigold, rare **85.00**
Iris, Fenton, goblet, buttermilk, dark, scarce **65.00**
Iris, Heavy, Northwood-Dugan, pitcher, dark, scarce **1,050.00**
Tumbler, dark, scarce **120.00**
Isaac Benesch, bowl, advertising, dark, 6½″ **145.00**
Jewelled Heart, bowl, peach opal, 5″ **60.00**
Pitcher, marigold, rare **695.00**
Tumbler, marigold, rare **100.00**
Jewels, Imperial, bowl shape, red **165.00**
Hat shape, pastel **75.00**
Creamer, red **135.00**
Kittens, bowl, 2 sides up, scarce, marigold **120.00**
Cup & saucer, complete, scarce, dark **185.00**
Spooner, pastel, vaseline, rare, 2½″ **195.00**
Cereal bowl, marigold, scarce **140.00**
Kittens Bottle, pastel **47.00**
Knight Templar, mug, advertising, marigold, rare **495.00**
Lacy Dewdrop, banana bowl, pearl carnival, pastel **115.00**
Late Inverted Thistle, spittoon, dark, rare **2,350.00**
Pitcher, marigold, rare **2,200.00**
Tumbler, dark, rare **395.00**
Creamer, dark, rare **165.00**
Sugar, dark **165.00**
Lattice & Daisy, pitcher, pastel **210.00**
Tumbler, pastel **50.00**
Lattice & Grape, pitcher, peach opal **900.00**
Tumbler, marigold **32.00**
Lattice Heart, bowl, dark, 10″ **75.00**

Bowl, marigold, 5" **30.00**
Leaf & Beads, candy bowl, footed, dark **50.00**
   Rose bowl, footed, pastel, plain interior **140.00**
Leaf & Little Flowers, compote, miniature, dark amethyst **180.00**
Leaf Chain, bowl, red, 9" **325.00**
   Plate, marigold, 9¼" **55.00**
Leaf Column, vase, dark, 12" **32.00**
Leaf Tiers, covered butter, footed, marigold **165.00**
   Covered sugar, footed, marigold **85.00**
   Creamer or Spooner, footed, marigold **80.00**
   Pitcher, footed, dark, rare **620.00**
   Tumbler, footed, dark, rare **110.00**
Lily Of The Valley, pitcher, dark, blue, rare **2,900.00**
   Tumbler, marigold, rare **420.00**
Lion, bowl, dark, 7", scarce **120.00**
Little Barrel, pastel, amethyst **90.00**
Little Beads, compote, miniature, peach opal **45.00**
   Bowl, flat base, peach opal, 8" **40.00**
Little Fishes, bowl, flat or footed, pastel, white, 8½" **620.00**
   Bowl, flat or footed, dark, 5½" **65.00**
Little Flowers, bowl, red, 9¼" **800.00**
   Bowl, marigold, 5½" **28.00**
   Plate, marigold, rare, 10½" **600.00**
Little Stars, bowl, dark, 7" **70.00**
Loganberry, vase, old only, dark, scarce **195.00**
Long Thumbprint, vase, dark, green, 11" **30.00**
   Compote, marigold **30.00**
   Creamer, marigold **35.00**
Lotus & Grape, bowl, flat, dark, 7" **55.00**
Louisa, rose bowl, footed, amber **90.00**
Love Birds, bottle w/stopper, marigold **130.00**
Lustre & Clear, Imperial, creamer & sugar, pastel, pair **60.00**
   Compote, marigold, 5½" **40.00**
   Bowl, pastel, 10" **48.00**
   Vase, footed, dark, 8" **120.00**
   Rose bowl, pastel **85.00**
   Butter, covered, marigold **67.00**
Lustre Flute, bon-bon, dark **55.00**
   Creamer, marigold **32.00**
   Sherbet, dark **40.00**
   Nappy, marigold **30.00**
Lustre Rose, bowl, footed, red, 12" **825.00**
   Fernery, footed, marigold **37.00**
   Butter, covered, dark **72.00**
   Sugar, covered, pastel **70.00**
   Pitcher, marigold **70.00**
   Tumbler, dark **24.00**
   Milk pitcher, marigold **60.00**
Many Fruits, punch bowl and base, marigold **190.00**
   Cup, white **37.00**
Many Stars, bowl, ruffled, 9", scarce, dark **175.00**
Maple Leaf, bowl, stemmed, marigold, 9" **68.00**
   Bowl, stemmed, dark, 4½" **32.00**
   Pitcher, marigold **150.00**
   Tumbler, dark **46.00**
Marilyn, pitcher, dark purple, rare **1,000.00**
Mary Ann, vase, marigold, 7" **37.00**
Mayan, bowl, dark, 7½" **78.00**
Melon Rib, candy jar, w/lid, smoke **36.00**
   Powder jar, w/lid, marigold **30.00**
Memphis, punch bowl and base, ice blue **785.00**
   Cup, dark **35.00**
Mikado, compote, dark green, large **85.00**
Milady, pitcher, marigold **475.00**

Tumbler, dark **65.00**
Mirrored Lotus, bowl, dark, 8½" **58.00**
Moonprint, covered jar, w/lid, dark **80.00**
   Cheese keeper, marigold, rare **110.00**
   Banana bowl, marigold, rare **110.00**
   Covered butter, marigold **90.00**
Morning Glory, pitcher, dark, very rare **7,800.00**
   Tumbler, marigold, very rare **900.00**
Multi-Fruits and Flowers, punch bown and base, dark, rare . . **700.00**
   Cup, marigold, rare **40.00**
   Pitcher, dark, very rare **7,000.00**
   Tumbler, dark, very rare **1,000.00**
Nautilis, regular size, unlettered, peach opalescent, rare **220.00**
Near Cut souvenir mug, marigold, rare **165.00**
   Tumbler, marigold, rare **190.00**
Nesting Swan, bowl, clambroth, 10" **240.00**
New Orleans Shrine, champagne, clear **85.00**
Northern Star, card tray, marigold, 6" **32.00**
   Bowl, marigold, 6½" **28.00**
   Plate, marigold, rare, 6½" **65.00**
Northwood-Dugan Fan, gravy boat, footed, dark **65.00**
Northwood's Poppy, oval pickle bowl, pastel **75.00**
Nu-Art, plate, pastel, scarce **695.00**
Octagon, covered butter, marigold **80.00**
   Covered sugar, dark **72.00**
   Spooner, dark **60.00**
   Pitcher, pastel **175.00**
   Tumbler, marigold **28.00**
   Decanter, complete, dark **250.00**
   Wine, marigold **26.00**
   Milk pitcher, pastel, scarce **190.00**
Ohio Star, vase, aqua opalescent, rare **2,300.00**
Oklahoma, pitcher, marigold, very rare **460.00**
   Tumbler, marigold, rare **1,200.00**
Open Rose, bowl, footed, 12", pastel **80.00**
   Bowl, flat, dark, 9" **44.00**
Optic and Buttons, bowls, marigold, 8" **26.00**
   Bowl, handled, marigold, 12" **34.00**
Orange Tree, bowl, footed, white, 11" **110.00**
   Powder jar, w/lid, dark **85.00**
   Mug, pastel **70.00**
   Loving cup, aqua opalescent, scarce **2,000.00**
   Punch bowl and base, marigold **190.00**
   Cup, dark **28.00**
   Pitcher, footed, white **390.00**
   Tumbler, footed, marigold **35.00**
   Hatpin holder, white **250.00**
Orange Tree Orchard, pitcher, dark **400.00**
   Tumbler, white **70.00**
Oriental Poppy, tankard pitcher, dark **600.00**
   Tumbler, ice blue **140.00**
Oval and Round, plate, marigold, 10" **55.00**
   Bowl, flat, amber, 7" **40.00**
   Bowl, flat, dark, 9½" **45.00**
Palm Beach, bowl, white, 9" **75.00**
   Bowl, marigold, 5" **28.00**
   Pitcher, white, rare **500.00**
   Tumbler, marigold, rare **68.00**
Panelled Prism, jam jar w/lid, marigold **45.00**
Pansy, bowl, dark, 9½" **45.00**
   Dresser tray, flat, smoke **100.00**
   Nappy, one handle, marigold **18.00**
Panther, bowl, footed, dark, 10" **165.00**
   Bowl, footed, red, 5" **475.00**

Pastel Panels, pitcher, pastel	310.00
Tumbler, pastel	60.00
Peach, bowl, white, 9″	210.00
Pitcher, dark blue	575.00
Tumbler, white	90.00
Peach and Pear, bowl, large oval, dark	95.00
Peacock, Fluffy, pitcher, marigold	300.00
Tumbler, dark	60.00
Peacock, Millersburg, bowl, clambroth, 9″	360.00
Bowl, marigold, 5″	40.00
Plate, dark, rare, 6″	320.00
Spittoon whimsey, marigold, very rare	7,000.00
Bowl, ice cream, dark green, rare	395.00
Peacock and Grape, bowl, footed, vaseline, 7¼″	160.00
Peacock and Urn, Fenton, bowl, marigold, 8½″	50.00
Compote, red	595.00
Peacock and Urn, Northwood, bowl, ice cream, dark, 11″	250.00
Peacock At The Fountain, orange bowl, footed, pastel	1,400.00
Punch bowl and base, dark	370.00
Cup, aqua opalescent	300.00
Covered butter, pastel	210.00
Covered sugar, marigold	70.00
Creamer, dark	80.00
Pitcher, pastel	560.00
Tumbler, dark	50.00
Peacock Lamp, carnival base, red	485.00
Peacock Strutting, creamer, dark green	50.00
Peacock Tail, bon bon, marigold	28.00
Compote, dark	42.00
Hat shape with advertising, marigold	48.00
Peacocks, bowl, white, 9½″	200.00
People's Vase, straight top, dark, very rare	9,500.00
Perfection, pitcher, marigold, rare	3,800.00
Tumbler, dark amethyst, rare	595.00
Persian Garden, bowl, berry, pastel, 10″	185.00
Bowl, berry, dark, 5″	50.00
Plate, chop, pastel, rare, 13″	2,100.00
Plate, marigold, rare, 6½″	85.00
Persian Medallion, bon-bon, dark	45.00
Compote, marigold	38.00
Bowl, dark, 10″	60.00
Bowl, red, 5″	295.00
Plate, pastel, 9¼″	300.00
Hair receiver, collar base, dark	60.00
Peter Rabbit, bowl, marigold, rare, 9″	820.00
Plate, amber, rare, 10″	1,600.00
Pineapple, bowl, dome footed, dark, 7½″	65.00
Creamer, marigold	40.00
Compote, dark	90.00
Pine Cone, bowl, amber, 6″	45.00
Plate, dark, 6¼″	60.00
Pinwheel, bowl, marigold, 6″	36.00
Plate, marigold, 6¼″	50.00
Pipe Humidor, tobacco jar, w/lid, dark, very rare	3,000.00
Plaid, bowl, red, 8¼″	800.00
Poinsettia, Imperial, milk pitcher, smoke	120.00
Poinsettia, Northwood, bowl, flat, marigold, 8½″	110.00
Pony, bowl, dark, 8½″	120.00
Poppy, compote, large, dark green, scarce	250.00
Poppy Show, vase, amber, 12″	575.00
Bowl, dark, 8¼″	190.00
Premium, candlesticks, pr, clambroth, 8½″	80.00
Bowl, flat, smoke, 12″	95.00
Primrose, bowl, marigold, scarce, 8¼″	85.00

Prism and Daisy, vase, marigold	24.00
Bowl, marigold, 5″	18.00
Bowl, marigold, 8″	28.00
Propeller, compote, dark, small	37.00
Pulled Loop, vase, peach opalescent	45.00
Pump, Town, dark purple	550.00
Puzzle, bon bon, stemmed, pastel	55.00
Question Marks, bon bon, dark	45.00
Compote, peach opalescent	60.00
Quill, pitcher, marigold, rare	1,895.00
Tumbler, dark	450.00
Raindrops, bowl, dome base, dark, 9″	60.00
Ranger, creamer, marigold	35.00
Tumbler, marigold	250.00
Milk pitcher, marigold	150.00
Raspberry, bowl, dark, 9″	60.00
Bowl, marigold, 5″	28.00
Milk pitcher, ice green	1,500.00
Pitcher, ice blue	1,800.00
Tumbler, marigold	30.00
Rays and Ribbon, bowl, vaseline, 9½″	150.00
Ribbon Tie, bowl, red, 8¾″	1,200.00
Ripple, vase, marigold	22.00
Robin, mug, smoke	70.00
Pitcher, marigold	250.00
Tumbler, marigold	46.00
Roll, tumbler, cordial set, marigold	35.00
Rosalind, bowl, dark, scarce, 10″	120.00
Rose Column, vase, marigold, rare	1,050.00
Rose Garden, vase, dark, rare, 9″	300.00
Pitcher, communion, marigold, rare	1,200.00
Rose Show, bowl, pastel, 8¾″	250.00
Plate, aqua opalescent, 9″	575.00
Round-Up, bowl, white, 8¾″	90.00
Royalty, punch bowl and base, marigold	95.00
Cup, marigold	20.00
Rustic, vase, red	350.00
S-Repeat, punch bowl and base, dark	185.00
Cup, dark, rare	1,200.00
Sailboats, bowl, red, 6″	195.00
Wine, marigold	130.00
Scale Band, bowl, peach opalescent, 6″	37.00
Plate, flat, marigold, 6½″	37.00
Plate, dome base, red, 7″	295.00
Pitcher, dark	210.00
Scales, bowl, pastel, 10″	55.00
Scroll Embossed, bowl, dark, 8½″	42.00
Compote, marigold	40.00
Seacoast, pintray, dark, rare	225.00
Seaweed, bowl, marigold, rare, 9″	90.00
Bowl, ruffled, dark, scarce, 10½″	135.00
Shell, bowl, marigold, 9¼″	36.00
Shrine Toothpick, clambroth	175.00
Singing Birds, mug, pastel	450.00
Covered butter, dark	295.00
Covered sugar, marigold	100.00
Creamer, dark	100.00
Spooner, marigold	70.00
Pitcher, dark	245.00
Tumbler, marigold	42.00
Six-Sided Candlestick, smoke	145.00
Ski-Star, bowl, marigold, 10″	55.00
Bowl, dark, 5″	58.00
Bowl, dome base, peach opalescent, 10″	110.00

Banana boat, dome base, dark 110.00
Smooth Panels, tumbler, pastel 40.00
   Vase, pastel 55.00
Soda Gold, candlestick, marigold, 3½″ 22.00
   Bowl, pastel, rare, 9″ 50.00
   Pitcher, marigold 200.00
   Tumbler, pastel 75.00
Soldiers and Sailors, plate, Ill., dark, rare 695.00
   Plate, Indianapolis, dark, very rare 2,875.00
Split Diamond, creamer, small, marigold 30.00
   Sugar, marigold 40.00
Springtime, bowl, dark, 9¼″ 110.00
   Bowl, dark, 5″ 45.00
   Covered butter, marigold 160.00
   Creamer, dark 170.00
   Pitcher, pastel, rare 1,100.00
   Tumbler, dark 100.00
Stag and Holly, bowl, footed, red, 13″ 875.00
   Rose bowl, footed, dark, scarce 225.00
   Plate, footed, marigold, 13″ 260.00
Star and File, bowl, pastel, 9½″ 38.00
   Compote, large, marigold 42.00
   Pitcher, marigold 185.00
   Tumbler, marigold 58.00
   Rose bowl, dark 85.00
   Wine, marigold 40.00
Star Medallion, bowl, round, pastel, 9″ 35.00
   Compote, large, marigold 38.00
   Covered butter, marigold 80.00
   Milk pitcher, marigold 56.00
   Goblet, pastel 60.00
   Tumbler, dark green 45.00
   Celery tray, marigold 40.00
   Pickle dish, pastel 42.00
Star of David, bowl, pastel, scarce, 8¼″ 70.00
Star of David and Bows, bowl, dome base, dark, 8½″ 70.00
Stippled Rays, Fenton, bon-bon, red 310.00
   Bowl, dark, 9½″ 42.00
Stippled Rays, Northwood, bowls, marigold, 10″ 42.00
   Tulip style compote, dark 65.00
Stippled Strawberry, tumbler, marigold 72.00
   Spittoon whimsey, marigold, rare 220.00
   Syrup, marigold, rare 200.00
   Covered butter, marigold 75.00
Stork ABC, child's plate, marigold, 7½″ 65.00
Stork and Rushes, mug, dark blue 350.00
   Punch bowl and base, dark, rare 200.00
   Cup, marigold 16.00
   Pitcher, dark 275.00
   Tumbler, marigold 30.00
Strawberry, bowl, white, 10″ 150.00
   Plate, pastel, 9″ 170.00
   Plate, handgrip, dark, 7″ 90.00
Strawberry Scroll, pitcher, dark blue, rare 1,200.00
   Tumbler, marigold, rare 170.00
Studs, tray, large, marigold 56.00
   Juice tumbler, marigold 28.00
   Milk pitcher, marigold 65.00
Sunflower, Millersburg, pintray, dark, rare 225.00
Sunflower, Northwood, bowl, footed, pastel, 8½″ 70.00
Sunken Hollyhock, lamp, marigold, rare 2,500.00
Swan, Pastel, dark 95.00
Swirl Hobnail, rosebowl, marigold, rare 200.00
   Spittoon, dark amethyst, rare 500.00

Swirl Varient, bowl, pastel, 8″ 32.00
   Epergne, peach opalescent 147.00
   Plate, pastel, 8¾″ 45.00
   Pitcher, marigold, 7½″ 135.00
Ten Mums, bowl, white, 11″ 128.00
   Pitcher, dark, rare 865.00
   Tumbler, marigold 70.00
Thistle, bowl, dark, 10″ 42.00
Thistle, Fenton's, bowl, oval, footed, large, dark 185.00
Three Fruits, bowl, pastel, 9½″ 65.00
   Bon-bon, stemmed, dark 50.00
   Plate, aqua opalescent, 9″ 360.00
Three-In-One, bowl, dark, 8¾″ 36.00
   Bowl, marigold, 4½″ 15.00
   Plate, pastel, 6½″ 65.00
Three Row, vase, dark purple, 8″ 350.00
Tiger Lily, pitcher, marigold 125.00
   Tumbler, dark 37.00
Tornado, vase, ribbed, pastel 175.00
Tree Bark, pitcher, open top, marigold 60.00
   Tumbler, marigold 22.00
Tree Trunk, vase, dark, 22″ 40.00
Trout and Fly, bowl, marigold, scarce, 8¾″ 150.00
Tulip and Cane, claret goblet, 4 oz, marigold, very rare 54.00
   Goblet, 8 oz, marigold, very rare 60.00
Twins, bowl, marigold, 5″ 20.00
   Bride's basket, marigold 70.00
Two Flowers, bowl, footed, dark, 7″ 38.00
   Bowl, footed, white, 10″ 250.00
   Bowl, flat, dark, 8″ 48.00
   Rosebowl, marigold, rare 95.00
Venetian, vase, dark, very rare, 9¼″ 950.00
Victorian, bowl, dark, rare, 12″ 160.00
Vineyard, pitcher, peach opalescent 500.00
   Tumbler, white 150.00
Vining Twigs, bowl, marigold, 7½″ 26.00
   Hat shape, dark 40.00
Vintage, Fenton, epergne, one lily, dark 135.00
   Fernery, 3 feet, red 550.00
   Bowl, aqua opalescent, 8″ 650.00
   Punch bowl and base, wreath of roses exterior, dark blue . . . 330.00
   Cup, wreath of roses exterior, marigold 26.00
   Rose bowl, dark 60.00
   Compote, marigold 36.00
Vintage, Northwood-Dugan, Powder jar w/lid, marigold 50.00
   Oval dresser tray, marigold, 11″ 75.00
Vintage, Millersburg, bowl, hobnail, dk blue, very rare, 5½″ . . 400.00
   Bowl, hobnail exterior, marigold, very rare, 9½″ 325.00
Vintage Banded, mug, marigold 30.00
Waffle Block, basket, w/handle, smoke, 10″ 58.00
   Pitcher, clambroth 160.00
   Tumbler, marigold 200.00
   Punch bowl, no base, marigold 180.00
   Punch cup, marigold 18.00
   Shakers, pr, marigold 70.00
   Creamer, marigold 60.00
   Sugar, marigold 60.00
Waterlily and Cattails, Fenton, pitcher, marigold 285.00
   Tumbler, marigold 90.00
   Covered butter, marigold 125.00
   Sugar, marigold 85.00
   Spooner, marigold 75.00
Waterlily and Cattails, Northwood, pitcher, marigold 265.00
   Tumbler, dark 155.00

Weeping Cherry, bowl, dome base, peach opalescent......... **95.00**
  Bowl, flat base, marigold.............................. **40.00**
Whirling Leaves, bowls, clambroth, 10".................. **110.00**
Wide Panel, compote, marigold.......................... **28.00**
  Console set, 3 pcs, white **90.00**
  Goblet, red.. **125.00**
  Cup, marigold **18.00**
  Lemonade, handled, white **60.00**
  Miniature compote, marigold **30.00**
Wild Rose, Northwood, bowl, footed, open edge, ice blue, 6" . **295.00**
Wild Rose, Millersburg, lamp, medium, marigold, scarce..... **500.00**
Wild Strawberry, bowl, dark, 10½"...................... **120.00**
  Plate, dark, rare, 9"................................ **250.00**
Windflower, bowl, white, 8½"........................... **85.00**
Windmill, bowl, pastel, 9"............................. **42.00**
  Milk pitcher, dark **95.00**
  Pickel dish, marigold............................... **16.00**
  Pitcher, dark **158.00**
  Tumbler, marigold **20.00**
Wine and Roses, pitcher, cider, marigold, rare **195.00**
  Stemmed Wine, aqua **85.00**
Wishbone, bowl, flat, pastel, 10½".................... **185.00**
  Bowl, footed, dark, 9" **85.00**
  Epergne, center lily, marigold **165.00**
  Pitcher, dark, rare................................. **1,500.00**
  Tumbler, marigold, scarce........................... **70.00**
Wreath of Roses, rose bowl, dark **58.00**
  Bon-bon, stemmed, pastel............................ **60.00**
  Punch bowl and base, dark blue **350.00**
  Cup, marigold **24.00**
Wreathed Cherry, bowl, oval, white, 10½".............. **220.00**
  Bowl, oval, marigold, 5¾"........................... **28.00**
  Pitcher, dark **400.00**
  Tumbler, white...................................... **70.00**
Zipper Loop, hand lamp, smoke **295.00**
  Lamp, medium, marigold **175.00**
  Lamp, large, marigold............................... **225.00**
Zippered Heart, bowl, dark, 9"........................ **95.00**
  Bowl, marigold, 5" **32.00**
  Queen's vase, large, rare, dark..................... **900.00**

Carousel Figures

Who can forget the dazzle of the merry-go-round--lights blinking, animals prancing proudly by to the waltzes that bellowed from the band organ...

Gustav Dentzel, a German woodworker, created the first carousel in America in 1867. By the turn of the century his animals had evolved from horses with a military bearing to fanciful creatures in various postures with garlands of flowers, exotic saddles, and other adornments. Today these hand-carved creatures bring prices well into the thousands.

Although Dentzel is considered the master carver, Spillman and Parker animals are also very valuable.

Bear, carved wood, old............................... **4,000.00**
Camel, Philadelphia Toboggan Co, third row **7,000.00**
Chariot, Herchell Spillman, hand carved................ **500.00**
Giraffe, good original paint, 80" **18,000.00**
Goat, Philadelphia Toboggan Co, 1800s **5,600.00**
Horse, Allen Herchell, metal head, tail, legs, painted **800.00**
  Armitage Herchell, glass eyes, repainted, on rocking stand **2,000.00**
  Armitage Herchell, glass eyes, horse hair tail, restored ... **2,895.00**
  Carmel Borelli, stander, bevelled jewels, walnut, gold leaf . **7,895.00**
  Carved pine, laminated, old repaint, glass eyes, 56"........ **650.00**
  Cast iron, 1900, 32".................................. **2,800.00**

Cast metal, no paint **750.00**
Doll size, cast iron, cantering position................ **385.00**
Dentzel, standing, orig park paint **8,500.00**
Herschell Spillman, carved wood & aluminum **4,800.00**
Kiddie carousel, metal, 1930s, Pinto Bros Coney Island **250.00**
Orton & Spooner, 1900 .... **2,000.00**
Parker, wood, American flag, dog behind saddle, glass eyes **3,500.00**
Parker, wood, armoured, ear of corn behind saddle, glass eyes **3,500.00**
Wood, dapple grey, real mane & tail, full size **2,000.00**
Zebra, handcarved.................................... **1,295.00**
Zebra, Philadelphia Toboggan Co, third row **8,995.00**

Carpet Balls

Carpet balls are glazed china spheres decorated with intersecting lines or other simple designs that were used for indoor games in the British Isles during the early 1800s.

Black lines on white, 3"............................. **60.00**
Black, white rounds w/scalloped edge w/black inner circle, 4¼". **55.00**
Cobalt blue w/white star, blue center dot, 3¼" **50.00**
Charcoal grey, rows of white stars w/off-center grey circles, 3¼" **55.00**
Dark grey w/rows of white stars w/off-center dots, 3¼"........ **60.00**
Pink w/white scalloped round, pink inner circle, 4¼" **55.00**
White, 2½"... **52.50**

Cartoon Books

Cartoon books were the black and white forerunners of modern comics. They were popular from 1910 until late in the thirties.

Bringing Up Father, #21, 1932 .... **35.00**
  King Syndicate, 1930 .... **35.00**
  McManus, lst series, 1919........................... **45.00**
Mutt & Jeff, #6, 1919................................. **45.00**
  By Fisher, 1911.................................... **65.00**
Popeye, 1930s, 10x13"................................. **25.00**
Raemaker's Cartoons, Doubleday, 1916, 305 pgs **45.00**
The Adventures of Scrappy, 1935 .... **22.00**
Zipper, by Garr Williams, 1930s **25.00**

Cash Registers

Cash registers are being restored, rebuilt and used as they were originally intended, in business ranging from eating establishments to antique stores. Their brass and marble construction has made them almost imprevious to aging, and with just a bit of polish and shine they bring a bit of the grand Victorian era into modern times.

Barber Shop, oak, 1920s **195.00**
McCasky, golden oak, silent, 1900 .... **275.00**

Monitor, ci base & back, 2 orig wood trays w/tin money tickets **350.00**
  Small, oak, early **190.00**
  Wooden, w/orig marquee **425.00**
National, #2, w/ornate inlaid walnut, 1894 model case **1,250.00**
  #2 . . . . **700.00**
  #33, brass, pat 1891 . . . . **550.00**
  #50-7/4, candy store, brass, w/printer, unrestored **600.00**
  #52-¼, brass, w/wide base, unrestored **850.00**
  #54 . . . . **210.00**
  #92 . . . . **550.00**
  #129 . . . . **440.00**
  #130-B, brass, small size, good marble **650.00**
  #250, candy store, brass, unrestored **600.00**
  #312, candy store, ringing up to only .50 . . . . **995.00**
  #313, brass, restored **850.00**
  #332, brass **700.00**
  #336, ringing up to $3.00 . . . . **895.00**
  #356-G, brass **590.00**
  #357-2, w/tape, nickel plated over brass, 30 key, ornate **800.00**
  #455-A, brass **495.00**
  #532-3F, 6 drawer, oak cabinet **3,200.00**
  #542, brass w/time clock, punch in type **1,250.00**
  #1054X-C, brass **1,400.00**
  #1064-G **495.00**
  Brass w/Morocco finish **365.00**
  Brass, marble, oak base, 20½x9x16" **1,100.00**
  Floor model, 5 drawer **485.00**
  Saloon, brass, double drawer, w/pt & qt keys, restored . . . **1,000.00**

Cast Iron

In the mid 1800s the cast iron industry was raging in the United States. It was a medium recognized as extremely adaptable for uses ranging from ornamental architectural filigree to actual building construction. It could be cast into any conceivable design from a mold that could be reproduced over and over, at a relatively small cost. It could be painted to give an entirely versatile appearance. Furniture with openwork designs of grapevines and leaves and intricate lacy scrollwork was cast for gardens as well as inside use. Figural doorstops of every sort, bootjacks, trivets and a host of other useful and decorative items were made before the "ferromania" had run its course.

Bench, American Renaissance, Peter Timmes Son, 1895 . . . . . **800.00**
Bookends, Abe Lincoln profile, bronzed, pair, 4¾" **15.00**
  Art Nouveau, cut-out ends, expandable **38.00**
Gate weight, hand w/flowered cuff holding grape cluster, 1860s, 6½" **130.00**

Hitching posts, pair, black jockey w/ring in hand, orig paint, 12" **150.00**
Horse head, on marble base, signed Heidenrek, 10" **75.00**
Mermaid, 1800s, 5x4½" **40.00**
Pull toy, donkey w/cart, some tin, late 1800s, 7x3½x2¼" **100.00**
Shoelast, pat applied for St Louis **9.00**
Table bowl, 12¾" **58.00**
Target, shooting gallery duck, w/metal advertising base, 4" **42.00**
Turtle, step on head & shell opens up, some brass, 14" long . **185.00**
Wagon whip holder, 1850s, 7½" long **14.50**

Castor Sets

Castor sets became popular during the early years of the 18th century, and continued to be used through the late Victorian era. Their purpose was to hold various condiments for table use. The most common type was a circular arrangement with a center handle on a revolving pedestal base, and held at least shakers, a mustard pot, and oil and vinegar bottles. Some had extras; a few were equipped with a bell for calling the servant. Frames were made of silver, or plated, and some were of pewter. Though most bottles were of pressed glass, some of the designs were cut, and occasionally colored glass with enameled decorations was used.

Breakfast, footed, ornate bail, cruet, salt, mustard, 1860s **30.00**
Burmese, rare **375.00**
Button & Daisy, 4 inserts **235.00**
Cosmos **250.00**
Cranberry, w/enamel decor, floral frame **200.00**
Cut crystal, w/plated frame by Derby, 1879 . . . . **130.00**
Cut glass, Meriden frame w/cavalier head, medallions **275.00**
Etched floral, 5 bottle **75.00**
Gothic Arch, pewter frame, 5 bottle **95.00**
Jumbo, w/frosted figural elephant **585.00**
King's Crown, clear, 5-pc **95.00**
Mother-of-Pearl satin, green & gold **375.00**
Mt Washington Peach Blow, 3 barrel ribbed jars, Pairpoint holder **1,000.00**

Pewter, paneled bottles & shakers, 12½" **195.00**
Ruby Thumbprint **350.00**
Silver plate, egg cups, spoon slots, 6 bottles, ornate, 1800s . . . **250.00**
Thumbprint, frosted fern, frame w/chariot, unicorn, ostrich . . . **135.00**
Vaseline, etched leaf bottles, resilvered 4 hole castor **185.00**
Victorian, 5 bottles, etched Honeycomb, silver plated **120.00**
Wm Rogers, pedestal base, call bell, 5 bottles **235.00**
  Plated frame, flower handle, w/5 bottles, revolves **140.00**

Catalina Island

Founded on the eastern shore of Catalina Island in 1927 by William Wrigley, Jr, the primary product of the Catalina Pottery Co. was tiles, both architectural and decorative. After it was purchased by Gladding-McBean in 1937, vases and dinnerware were made, in seven beautiful colors and Obsidian, a high gloss black. The company marked their wares with the name Catalina Pottery, first as an impressed mark and later with an ink stamp.

Ash tray w/goat on side, Descanso Green on white clay **75.00**
Beverage pot w/6 tumblers, Toyon Red **75.00**
Bowl, low w/4 ears, Descanso Green on brown clay, 9" **65.00**
Coffee carafe, w/lid, Catalina Blue on white clay **30.00**
Cup & saucer, Descanso Green on brown clay **25.00**
Lamp base, bulbous, orig Avalon Ware label, 6½" **400.00**
Leaf dish, 14" **32.00**
Oil jar, brown clay w/heavy green matt, signed, 16" **300.00**
Plaque, Blue Marlin in relief, 14" **120.00**
Plate, Toyon Red on brown clay, 10" **30.00**
Plate, polychrome decorated w/undersea scene, 9" **200.00**
Vase, hi glaze red w/veining, 8½" **60.00**
Vase, matt green, 6½" **17.50**
Vase, red w/off-white lining, marked, 7" **75.00**
Vase, stepped, w/handles, Mandarin yellow on brown clay, 5" .. **75.00**

Catalogs

Catalogs are not only intriguing to collect on their own merit, but for the collector who is interested in a specific area, they are often the only remaining source of background information available and as such offer a wealth of otherwise unrecorded data.

The mail order industry can be traced as far back as the mid-1800s. Even before Aaron Montgomery Ward began his career in 1872, Loocke and Joys of Wisconsin and The Orvis Co. of Vermont, both dealers in sporting goods, had been well established for many years. The E C Allen Co. sold household necessities and novelties by mail on a broad scale in the 1870s. By the end of the Civil War, sewing machines, garden seed, musical instruments--even medicine--were available throughout the country through catalogue sales. In the 1800s, Macy's of New York issued a 127 page catalogue; Sears and Spiegel followed suit in about 1890.

A Cox Co Philadelphia, Stoves & Ranges, 1910, 113 pgs, 4x7". **30.00**
ACB Furniture Co, 1920, Wicker, etc **35.00**
Abbott-Detroit Cars, 1912, 32 pgs, 11x8" **55.00**
Acme Road Machinery Co, 1927, Rollers 14-A, steam rollers ... **23.00**
Albert Haman Watches & Watch Cases, 1919, 78 pgs **95.00**
Ames & Frost Co, Imperial Bicycles, 1893, 40 pgs **23.00**
Arlington Refrigeration Co, Vermont, 1918, ice boxes, 71 pgs .. **25.00**
Baker Shotguns, 1908, 6x3½" **20.00**
Barbie & Ken, 1961, shows all outfits & accessories **25.00**
Bathroom Fixtures, 1893, ornate faucets, toilets, etc, 465 pgs .. **55.00**
Beckan Jewelry, 1948, 445 pgs **45.00**
Benjamin & Allen Co, 1939, jewelry, 660 pgs **50.00**
Benjamin & Allen Co, 1929, jewelry, 870 pgs **60.00**
Benjamin Electric Mfg Co, 1906, lighting fixtures, 104 pgs **40.00**
Bibliotheca Aeronautica, Maggs Bros, 1920 .... **55.00**
Birdsall Advertiser, 1884, engines, threshers, 24 pgs **30.00**
Blue Book Jewelry, 1917, 1000 pgs **135.00**
Blue Book Jewelry, 1932, 550 pgs **60.00**
Brooks Boats, 1918, ... **20.00**
Brown & Sharpe, 1926, small tools **15.00**
Burhans & Black Hardware, 1922, hardcover, 979 pgs **75.00**
Burroughs Wellcome & Co, 1913, hardcover **20.00**
Butler Bros, 1887 Christmas, general merchandise **28.00**

Cadillac Illustrated Parts, 1955, 105 pgs **17.00**
Camera, 1913-14, includes stereopticons & enlarging lanterns .. **30.00**
Carriages & Harness Goods, 1901, salesman's leather bound, 146 pgs **50.00**
Cartercar, 1912, 36 pgs, 10x8" **45.00**
Central Cycle Co, 1895, Ben Hur Bicycles, 24 pgs **20.00**
Colt, 1916, guns, color cover w/horse logo, 5x4" **20.00**
Colt, 1921, guns & machine guns, 40 pgs **18.00**
Columbia Bicycles, 1898, Maxfield Parrish cover, 32 pgs, 7x9" . **30.00**
Columbus Carriage Co, 1904, vehicles, 144 pgs **30.00**
Continental Oil Well Supply, 1926, hardcover, 876 pgs **45.00**
Cooperative Supply Co, 1900, carriages, wagons, 32 pgs **18.00**
Dasco Tools & Cutlery **25.00**
DeLaval Cream Separators, Farm & Dairy Sizes, 36 pgs **35.00**
Donneleys National Jewelry, 1927, their first, 240 pgs **75.00**
Durro Brand Musical Instruments, 1926, 9x12" **22.00**
E Nason & Co, New York, 1884, wholesale watches, jewelry, etc **28.00**
Eagle Lock Co, Terryville, Conn., 1930, hardcover, 742 pgs ... **80.00**
Enderes, 1930, housewares **14.00**
Fairbanks Co Mill, Mine, Railway Supplies, 1920, 903 pgs **55.00**
Fostoria Glass, 1966, w/price list **25.00**
Geiser Mfg Co, 1907, portable engines & saw mills, 24 pgs **19.50**
Glove Machinery & Supply, 1930, contractor's, construction **8.50**
Grammes Inc, Allentown, Pa., 1929, metal advertising items.... **35.00**
Grand Union Tea Co, 1912, premium catalog **21.00**
Grolock Buggy, 1902, 113 pgs **25.00**
Hardware House of America, #8, early 1900s, carpenter tools ... **3.50**
Harley Davidson, 1921, 32 pgs **38.00**
Henry Disston & Sons, #92, 1932, saws, files **6.50**
Henry F Miller, Piano Fortes, 1882, 8 pgs **25.00**
Hercules Carriages, 1919, horse drawn vehicles, 9x10½" **65.00**
Horrock's Desks, Herkimer, NY, 1915, 63 pgs **45.00**
Indian Motorcycles, 1921, prices, 24 pgs **38.00**
Ithaca Guns, 1910 .... **30.00**
John Deere General Purpose Catalog, 1939, color **25.00**
Joseph Woodwell Toy Catalog, 1935 .... **40.00**
Keen Kutter Cutlery & Tools **25.00**
Keystone Jewelers Index, 1931, 584 pgs **60.00**
Kroeschell Bros Ice Machine Co, Chicago, 1913 .... **8.00**
LL Bean, Spring 1941 .... **15.00**
Lalance & Grosjean Tin Ware, 1922 .... **30.00**
Lehman Jewelry, from Denver, 1927, 416 pgs **100.00**
Lufkin Tools, #4, 1922 .... **12.50**
Marbles Outing Equipment, 1923 .... **26.00**
Marrston & Wells Fireworks, 1905, 84 pgs **14.00**
Marshall Field, Chicago, Holiday Goods, 1887, 95 pgs, 9½x12" **50.00**
Mayer Bros Jewelry, 1955, 350 pgs **20.00**
Mead Cycle Co, Crusader Bicycles, 1910, 12 pgs **11.00**
Meadows Mfg Co, 1919, Meadows Power Washers, wood tub machines **6.50**
Milwaukee Locomotive Co Parts, #162, Jan 1931, 19 pgs **6.50**
Montgomery Ward Fall & Winter, 1936 .... **18.00**
Montgomery Ward Spring, 1903 .... **20.00**
Montgomery Ward Spring & Summer, 1935 .... **18.00**
Montgomery Ward, 1921, 773 pgs **40.00**
Murray Co, Juvenile Steelcraft Vehicles, Mercury Bicycles, 1941 . **46.00**
Norris Allister Ball Jewelry, 1930, 700 pgs **75.00**
Otto Young & Co, 1929, jewelry, 1,191 pgs **135.00**
P Goldsmith's Sons, Spring & Summer Sports, baseball, 1913 .. **25.00**
Peck, Stow, & Wilcox Co, New York, 1911, tools **10.00**
Perin-Walsh Co, Truck Body & Equipment, 1920s, w/Coca-Cola **90.00**
Piedmont Wagon Co, 1911, wagons & drays, 48 pgs **35.00**
RR Howell Co, A-23, gas/steam engines, drills, pumps, 248 pgs . **17.00**
Rouse Hazard Co, 1893, bicycles & high wheelers, 50 pgs **30.00**
Schoenhut Circus, 1915, w/prices **15.00**
Schwab, 1929, jewelry, beaded bags, clocks, 640 pgs **30.00**

Sears 1944, big, girl w/ration stamps on corsage **22.00**
Sears Farm Implements, 1924, engines, buggies, 80 pgs **17.00**
Sears First Edition Harness, 1904 . . . . **28.00**
Sears Spring & Summer, 1931 . . . . **40.00**
Sears Wallpaper, 1921 . . . . **7.50**
St Louis Jewelry, Clock & Silver Co, 1934, 240 pgs **55.00**
Stanley Tools, 1927 . . . . **9.00**
Stanley Wrought Hardware, 1914, steel, brass & bronze, 260 pgs **35.00**
Starett Tools, 1927 . . . . **15.00**
Starrett Tools, 50th Anniv. #25, 1900 . . . . **20.00**
Stokes Mfg Co, 1893, Union Cycles, bicycles & accessories **15.00**
Stormer & Pennant Bicycles, 1898, 31 pgs, 6x8″ **14.00**
Swatchild, 1910, watch tools & parts, 760 pgs **145.00**
T Mills Co, nut machines, blanching, grinding & roasting, 15 pgs **20.00**
The American Railway, 1889, hardcover, 456 pgs **25.00**
Twitchell Co, Philadelphia, 1910, bottlers' supplies, 144 pgs . . . **35.00**
Unexcelled Fireworks, pre-1900, 80 pgs **45.00**
United Cigar Stores Premium Catalog, 1926 . . . . **25.00**
United Drug Co, 1914, drug store sundries, 163 pgs **40.00**
United Theater Co, 1918, motion picture equipment, 180 pgs . . **75.00**
WA Murray Co, 1905, carriages, farm wagons, 146 pgs **40.00**
Westervelt's Weather Vanes, 1889, 100 pgs **70.00**
Williamson, Chicago, 1920s, lighting fixtures **75.00**
Winchester Wholesale Retail, 1942 . . . . **32.00**

Celluloid

Celluloid was patented in 1869 by John W. Hyatt, who developed the formula by mixing pulp from the cotton plant with solvents and camphor. Although others claimed to have made the product earlier, it was ruled that Hyatt's celluloid was different enough to protect his patent rights. Today, celluloid is a generic term for all early plastics. WWII marked the end of its usefullness.

Earlier pieces have a creamy color with striations meant to imitate the texture of ivory or bone. Trademarks were not generally added until the 20th century when the color and weight became lighter, with little or no striations. During the 20s, tints were sometimes added; relief designs and gilding were popular decorative treatments.

Aunt Jemima set, syrup, salt & pepper, 6″ **27.00**
Baby rattle **8.00**
Bookmark, Libby Canned Meats, roses decor **7.00**
Collar box, Victorian woman, child & dog litho, beveled mirror . **88.00**
Comb, w/ornate metal holder **30.00**
Compact, w/embossed grapes **20.00**
Dresser box, Deco, 2 doors, 1 drawer, mirrors **85.00**
  Mirrored doors, 1 drawer, pretty ladies decor, 10½″ **110.00**
  Oval w/foot, brass finial, urn shape **12.00**
  Small, kittens illustration **33.00**
Dresser set, lemon w/tiny blue stones, 5 pc **30.00**
  Original case, 13 pc **100.00**
  Trimmed with amber decoration **30.00**
Frame, Imperial Brand Ivory Pyralin, easel back, 7x9½″ **35.00**
Glove box **45.00**
Hair receiver, amber, decagon, 4½″ **9.00**
Hen, figural, yellow, 2″ **9.00**
Jewelry box, small **10.00**
Manicure set, 3 pc **13.00**
Manicure set, green marbleized & topaz, 6¾″ holder, 4 tools . . **20.00**
Nodder, black poodle, marked Germany **10.00**
Powder jar, amber, decagon, 4½″ dia **9.00**
Rolly Polly, lady duck w/bonnet, American, 1920s, 3x2x2 . . . . . **30.00**
Rooster, metal legs, early 1900s, 4″ **23.00**
Set, scissors, buttonhook & manicure tool, 3 pc **18.00**

Tape measure, green bear **12.00**
Tape measure, Illinois Surgical Appliance Co, w/picture of truss . **10.00**
Tape measure, National Cleaners & Dyers, tinted picture of store **10.00**
Toiletry set, men's, leather case **27.00**

Chalkware

Chalkware is simply plaster of paris, made in a mold, and painted with water base paints. They were inexpensive substitutes for the more costly imported parian or glazed figurines from abroad. Some of the animal and bird figures that have survived from the early 19th century, are today selling for hundreds of dollars.

Carnival chalkware from this century is also collectible, especially the figures that are personality related.

Art Deco lady in hat w/2 dogs, New Art Ware, 13″ **85.00**
Art Deco nude w/deer **45.00**
Art Deco nude w/greyhound **32.00**
Ashtray, boy w/duck, The early bird catches the worm, 5″ **20.00**
Bird, on nest, orig paint, 4½″ **250.00**
Black woman w/broom, Paul Lighting Inc, 15½″ **15.00**
Boy at Fountain, w/2 colorful birds, 11″ wide base, numbered, 21″ **560.00**
Bulldog, seated w/collar, 7″ **65.00**
Cat, sitting, round base, 1850s, 13½″ **485.00**
Cat, sleeping, black & wht, early 1900s, 4x3x6″ **36.00**
Chinese boy w/lute, 5½″ **10.00**
Christ w/Mary, on base, Holy Water font, signed, 1928, 15″ . . . **50.00**
Clock, Art Nouveau female, dore, 1902, 24″ **435.00**
Deer, sitting, wht w/polychrome, 10″ **225.00**
Dog, carnival prize, Chicago's Riverview Park **35.00**
  Seated, orig wht paint, w/black spots & yellow collar, 8″ **165.00**
Frog, old paint, 3x3½x5″ **135.00**
Hen, setting, orig paint, early 1900s, 3¼x3″ **37.00**
Kewpie figural, Thinker **24.00**
Lad w/pipe, Com'a Papa, 14″ **265.00**

Lamp, Art Nouveau female, hands in hair, 28″ **130.00**
Lincoln, bust, Boston Sculpture Co, 1909, 13″ **90.00**
Rabbit, sitting, wht w/pink paws, ears, nose, 6″ **110.00**
Rooster, 1850s, 11″ **650.00**
Sailor girl, carnival prize, 14″ **45.00**
Spaniel, old brown, red & blue paint, mid 1880s, 8½″ **125.00**
Spaniel, standing on base, 7″ **160.00**

Victorian lady w/dog, color, Roman Art, Robia Ware, 11″ **42.00**

Champleve

Champleve, enameling on brass, differs from cloisonne in that the design is depressed or incised into the metal, rather than being built up, as cloisonne is, with fine wire dividers. The cells, or depressions, are filled in with color, and the piece is then fired.

Compote, 7¼x3¼″.. **140.00**
   Ribbed foot, 4 bands, 7¼x8¼″ dia................... **180.00**
Floor lamp, palace, 72″............................... **875.00**
Incense burner, w/cover, animal legs, foo lion finial, 18″.... **1,000.00**

Inkwell, tray & pen, 3x7″ **450.00**
Koro, w/cover, 1900, 9″............................... **170.00**
Lamp, 13¼″ dia base, 25″ **250.00**
Pin dish **15.00**
Tray, onyx center, 4 legs, French, 7x11″................. **350.00**
Urn, covered, w/elephant handles, 9x5¼″ dia **95.00**
Vase, 14x9½″... **200.00**
   4 bands of enamel, animal handles, 8½″ **125.00**
   Handled, 12″....................................... **135.00**
   Multicolor, gold, 12″............................... **165.00**
   Phoenix Bird decor, dragon handles, 14″ **195.00**

Chelsea

The Chelsea Porcelain Works operated in London from the middle of the 18th century, making porcelains of the finest quality. In 1770 it was purchased by the owner of the Derby Pottery and for about 20 years operated as a decorating shop. Production periods are indicated by trademarks: 1745-1750, incised triangle, sometimes with Chelsea and the year added; early 50s, raised anchor mark on oval pad; 1752-56, small painted red anchor, only rarely found in blue underlgaze; 1756-69, gold anchor; 1769-84, Chelsea Derby mark, the script D containing a horizontal anchor. Many reproductions have been made. Be suspicious of any anchor mark larger than ¼″.

Figurine, boy beside beehive, 7″........................ **250.00**
   Girl & man, both w/fruit baskets, gold anchor mk, 10″, pr .. **425.00**
   Girl w/basket of flowers, 6″ **95.00**
   Man w/basket of grapes, gold anchor mk, 5″........... **185.00**
   Monk reading book, 1750s **1,200.00**
   Shepherdess w/lamb, gold anchor mark................. **850.00**
Pitcher, blue anchor mark **275.00**
Teapot w/cover, white glaze, acanthus leaf in relief, early ... **2,000.00**
Vase, gilt swan w/handles, Royal Chelsea, 11″........... **225.00**

Chelsea Dinner Ware

Made during the 19th century in the Staffordshire district of England, this white porcelain ware is decorated with lustre embossings in the grape, thistle or sprig patterns. Because it was not produced in Chelsea as the name would suggest, dealers often prefer to call to it Grandmother's Ware.

Grape, berry dish **7.00**
   Cake plate, 10″.................................... **40.00**
   Creamer **50.00**
   Cup w/handle & saucer **35.00**
   Sugar, no top **50.00**
   Teapot, octagon **185.00**
Sprig, cup & saucer, lady's............................. **15.00**
   Cup & saucer, man's **30.00**
   Waste bowl **75.00**

Children's Books

Children's books, especially those from the Victorian era, are charming collectibles. Colorful lithographic illustrations that once delighted little boys in long curls and tiny girls in long stockings and lots of ribbons and laces have lost none of their appeal.

A Chance For Himself, Jack Hazard & His Treasure, 1872, 266 pgs **9.00**
A Jolly Circus, 1898 .... **8.00**
A Wonder Book For Girls & Boys, 1896/1902, 188 pgs **9.00**
Alice's Adventures in Wonderland, Rackham, illus............ **65.00**
Alice's Adventures in Wonderland, Lewis Carroll, 42 illus, 274 pgs **9.00**
Bible Characters, instructive & entertaining, numerous woodcuts, 1835 **6.00**
Book Of Magic, puzzles, tricks & stunts, Houdini, 1927, 295 pgs **8.00**
Brave & Bold, Alger **10.00**
Captain Bayley's Heir, Henty, 1920, 315 pgs **10.00**

Chatter Box, 1921, 10x7½″............................ **38.00**
Do And Dare, Horatio Alger, 1910 .... **8.00**
Poems From English & American Authors, Thomas Handford, 325 pgs **8.00**
Grimm's Fairy Tales, Scharl, 212 illus, 1944................. **7.00**
Happy Prince & Other Tales, Wilde, Shinn, 1940 .... **12.00**
The Little Jack Rabbit, Squirrel Brother, Cory, 1921........... **9.00**
Little Jack Rabbit's Adventures, Cory, 1921, 128 pgs **9.50**
Little Lord Fauntleroy, Burnett, Scribners, 1889, 209 pgs **10.00**
Nutcracker Of Nuremberg, Dumas, illus by Hosselriis, 1930, 154 pgs **6.00**
Only An Irish Boy, Horatio Alger Jr, 264 pgs **10.00**
Peter Newell's Pictures & Rhymes, illus, 1903 .... **5.50**
Rollo On The Thine, Abbott, illus, 1866, 218 pgs **8.00**
Rollo's Tour In Europe, Facob Abbott, Paris 1859, 226 pgs..... **9.00**
Songs Of Summer, James Whitcomb Riley, 1883/1908, 190 pgs. **10.00**
Story Of The World & Its People, For Little Juniors, Peabody, 389 pgs **12.00**
Summer Outing, WB Conkxey Co, 1901.................... **12.00**
Tarzan & The Jewels Of Opar, Edgar Rice Burroughs, 1918, 350 pgs **10.00**

The Backwoods Boy, H Alger, 1883, 1st ed **12.00**
The Fables Of Aesop, illus **9.00**
Three Good Friends, The Aunt Louisa's Big Picture Series, 1865 **8.00**
Tom Slade on Mystery Trail, Fitzhugh, 1921, 195 pgs **8.00**
Uncle Wiggily Indian Hunter, HR Garis, 1919/1924, 30 pgs **7.00**
Uncle Wiggily's Woodland, Games, HR Garis, 1922, 33 pgs **7.00**
What The Trees Taught The Little Girl, 1859, 36 pgs **7.50**

Children's Things

Nearly every item devised for adult furnishings has been reduced to child's size. Furniture, dishes, sporting goods--even some tools. All are very collectible. Toy glass dishes were made from the 1800s into the 1900s. They often fetch prices in the same range as grown up's!

Baby walker, pine, mortised & pinned, wood wheels, 16x23x38" **85.00**
   Wood w/horse head, 1880s **95.00**
Bed, drop sides, wht enameled iron, slightly chipped, 1890s . . **225.00**
   Foldaway, pine, 1880s **110.00**
   Rope, early handmade, mixed woods, lacing pegs intact **350.00**

Rosewood American Gothic, 1845, 38x38x53" **1,600.00**
   Walnut, Eastlake **380.00**
Bookcase, dropfront desk type, cherry, 1870s **375.00**
Carpet rocker, Victorian **85.00**
Chair, Mission, orig finish **55.00**
   Potty, oak, primitive **65.00**
   Pressed back, restored, set of 6 . . . . **450.00**
   Shaker youth, hickory, original woven seat **225.00**
   Straight, oak, primitive **75.00**
   Windsor arm type, walnut, wide carved splat, saddle seat . . . **250.00**

China

10 pc from set of 12, bright colored animals **78.00**
Berry set, pressed glass, Lacy Daisy, 6 pc **85.00**
Canister set, wht w/florals, 8 pc, German china **150.00**
Complete dinner set, wht w/brown floral, 1880s **175.00**
Cup & saucer, w/monkey pushing dog in wheelbarrow, Bavaria . **22.00**
Feeding dish, Ride A Cock Horse, DE McNicol, Liverpool **40.00**
Ironstone w/brown flowers print, set in tin warming dish **35.00**
Place setting, plate, cup, saucer, pink lustre w/girls & carriage . . **35.00**
Place setting, plate, fork & spoon, Little Miss Muffet, MIB **55.00**
Plate, House That Jack Built, 6" **18.00**
Plate, Maiden All Forlorn , 6" **18.00**
Service for 6 w/9 servers, brown calico on wht pottery, English **325.00**
Deco, orange flowers w/green designs, 6-sided pot, 21 pc **95.00**

Figural elephant pot, sugar & creamer, 13 pc **80.00**
Girls w/geese, pot, 4 cups & saucers, Germany **100.00**
Lustre w/cherry blossoms & birds, service for 4 . . . . **85.00**
Pink lustre, pot, cream, sugar, cups & saucers, 1860 . . . . **300.00**
Snow White, for 4 w/covered pot, in box **135.00**
Staffordshire, girl w/dog, 1887, 13 pc **200.00**
Tray w/5 bird-shaped pcs, Japan **35.00**
Tureen, toy decor, leaf handles, berry finial, 1860s, 4" dia **45.00**
Victorian China, portrait decor, 21 pc **85.00**

Cradle, field/slave, bentwood on wood stand, iron fasteners, 4 wheels **625.00**
   Hoodtop, walnut, handcut hood, edge, curves **350.00**
   Pennsylvania pine, orig mustard paint, iron rockers, early . . . **400.00**
Crib, poplar, turned splayed legs w/rockers, some wear, 23½x41" **150.00**
Desk, rolltop, w/orig swivel chair **275.00**

Dishes, nursery rhyme, litho on tin, Ohio Art & Co, 14 pcs . . . **100.00**
Dishes, tin, 12-pc table set, embossed animals **80.00**
Dresser-chest, walnut & maple, 4' **275.00**

Glass

Acanthus, mug, cobalt blue **24.00**
Acorn, creamer **80.00**
   Spooner **80.00**
Akro Agate Lustre, tea set, 7 pc, jade green **35.00**
American Rose, cake plate on tall pedestal, clear, 6" dia **32.00**
American Shield, castor set w/4 bottles **65.00**
Arrowhead in Ovals, table set, 4 pc **95.00**
Austrian, creamer, vaseline **50.00**
Banded Portland, water pitcher **32.00**
Bead & Scroll, butter w/cover **85.00**
Beaded Swirl Variation, butter w/cover, clear **30.00**
   Covered sugar **25.00**
   Creamer, clear **14.00**
Beads in Relief, mug, clear **18.00**
Button Panel, butter w/cover **65.00**
   Sugar w/cover **40.00**
Candlewick, cake plate **25.00**
Chimo, creamer **15.00**
   Punch cup **14.00**
   Spooner **20.00**
Clear & Diamond Panel, butter w/cover, blue **70.00**
   4 pc table set, blue **245.00**
   Creamer **25.00**
Colonial, covered sugar **15.00**

Pitcher	12.00
Spooner, Cambridge	10.00
Spooner, green, Cambridge	20.00
Table set, Cambridge	70.00
Water set, 7 pc	90.00
D & M, #30, honey jar,	38.00
#42, creamer, clear	45.00
#42, sugar w/cover	45.00
Deep Stars & Octagon, water pitcher	60.00
Tumbler	12.00
Diamond Band, mug	15.00
Diamond Sunburst, table set, butter, creamer, sugar	58.00
Dog & Cat, cup, blue	28.00
Doyle's 500, butter w/cover, amber	55.00
Tray, amber	20.00
Drape, castor set	70.00
Drum, butter dish	125.00
Spooner, clear	38.00
Table set, 4 pc, clear	325.00
Ellipse, goblet	16.00
Emerald Corn, pitcher	30.00
English Hobnail, cruet, tray & shaker	25.00
Fancy Cut, butter dish	25.00
Table set, 4-pc	90.00
Water pitcher, clear	32.00
Feather & Arches, punch bowl	22.00
Fernland, covered sugar	17.50
Creamer	12.50
Table set, 4 pc	85.00
Fine Cut, butter w/cover	30.00
Fine Cut, Star & Fan, butter w/cover	30.00
Spooner	19.00
Flat Diamond & Sunburst, table set, 4 pc	70.00
Flattened Diamond & Sunburst, butter w/cover	25.00
Punch set, 5 pc	55.00
Water tray, amber	45.00
Flute, berry bowl	5.00
Cream & sugar, Heisey	28.00
Galloway, water pitcher	20.00
Grape Vine in Ovals, creamer	55.00
Mug, 2″	13.00
Creamer, amber	20.00
Hawaiian Lei, table set, 4 pc	80.00
Heart Band, mug, enameled flowers, gilt trim, 2¾″	15.00
Mug, plain	10.00
Ruby flashed, no etching, 3½″	16.00
Heckman, condiment set	38.00
Hickman, condiment set, green	120.00
Hobnail, cream & sugar, wht opalescent	12.00
Tray, amber	40.00
Hobnail with opalescent, cream & sugar	15.00
Hobnail with Thumbprint, creamer, amber	20.00
Creamer, blue	28.00
Horizontal Threads, spooner	18.00
Horsehead Medallion, spooner, clear	36.00
Inverted Strawberry, berry bowl	22.00
Berry bowl, master	50.00
Lacy Daisy, berry bowl	7.00
Lamb, creamer	50.00
Liberty Bell, creamer	45.00
Milk, glass, mug	185.00
Lily of the Valley, water pitcher	85.00
Lion, covered sugar	85.00
Creamer	60.00

Table set, covered sugar, salt & pepper	200.00
Menagerie, spooner, amber	95.00
Michigan, water pitcher	22.00
Monk, stein, milk glass	25.00
Near Cut, pitcher, Cambridge	20.00
Water set, 4 pc, Cambridge	48.00
Nursery Rhymes, berry bowl	18.00
Creamer, clear	45.00
Pitcher w/4 tumblers	195.00
Pitcher	95.00
Plated, 6½″, Bo Peep w/ bears border	30.00
Punch bowl, milk glass	100.00
Punch cup	12.00
Punch set, 5 pc	180.00
Sugar w/cover, clear	55.00
Sugar	50.00
Table set, 4-pc	230.00
Water pitcher	110.00
Water set, 7 pc	260.00
Oaken Bucket, creamer, clear	28.00
Oval Star, covered sugar	12.00
Tumbler	10.00
Owl, creamer, blue milk glass	40.00
Clear, stippled base	45.00
Water set, 7 pc, pitcher w/amethyst petals	100.00
Pennsylvania, creamer	30.00
Salt & pepper	20.00
Pert, butter w/cover, clear	50.00
Spooner	45.00
Portland, pitcher, gold worn	18.00
Purtian, covered sugar	22.00
Creamer	20.00
Butter dish	25.00
Rexford, creamer	20.00
Creamer	80.00
Rooster, creamer	80.00
Spooner	85.00
Sawtooth Band, table set, 4 pc, Heisey	250.00
Star, candlesticks, pair	25.00
Stippled Arrow, mug	10.00
Stippled Leaf & Grape, cup, clear	17.50
Stippled Vine & Beads, covered sugar	65.00
Creamer	40.00
Spooner	40.00
Sultan, creamer, chocolate	75.00
Spooner, chocolate	65.00
Spooner, frosted	55.00
Swirl, butter w/cover, clear	22.00
Creamer, blue opal	55.00
Creamer, clear	18.00
Tappan, cream & sugar, green	30.00
Creamer	15.00
Sugar w/cover, green	16.00
Thousand Eye, jug, vaseline,	25.00
Tulip & Honeycomb, 4 pc table set	95.00
Butter dish	45.00
Punch set, 5 pc	60.00
Punchbowl	34.00
Table set, 4 pc	60.00
Twin Snowshoes, creamer	65.00
Twist, blue opal, creamer	65.00
Butter w/cover	30.00
Sugar w/cover	18.00
Two Band, creamer	30.00

Table set, 4 pc	**160.00**
Wabash, punch bowl	**15.00**
Punch set	**75.00**
Spooner	**10.00**
Table set	**115.00**
Wee Branches, covered sugar w/silver finial	**45.00**
Creamer	**45.00**
Cup & saucer	**60.00**
Open sugar	**25.00**
Plate	**45.00**
Wheat Sheaf, berry bowl, small, Cambridge	**8.50**
Creamer	**18.00**
Punch set, 5 pc Cambridge	**55.00**
Punch set w/4 cups	**45.00**
Whirligig, creamer	**15.00**
Punch set	**55.00**
Spooner	**16.50**
Sugar	**18.00**
Table set, 4 pc	**60.00**
Whirling Star, punch bowl	**22.50**
Wild Rose, butter w/cover, milk glass	**105.00**
Punch cup, milk glass	**18.00**
Punch set, 7 pc	**230.00**
Sugar, milk glass	**60.00**
Table set, 4 pc, milk glass w/stain	**260.00**
Butter dish, milk glass	**65.00**
Wooden Pail, creamer, clear	**28.00**
Hoosier cabinet, metal w/porcelain knobs & top, 39x22x15″	**145.00**
Ice skates, clamp on, Winchester	**38.00**
Racing model, brass inlay, 1850, Donahue	**75.00**
Wood w/iron runners, tie on, 8″ long	**70.00**
Wooden, 1900	**25.00**
Lamp shade, blue milk glass	**110.00**
Loveseat, Victorian w/velvet upholstery	**565.00**
Lunch box, tin, Educator Cakelets, mama & baby bears, 6x3½″	**15.00**
Pencil box, wood, hinged lid, orig paper label, 6″	**18.00**
Rocker, bentwood Adirondack style, 20x18x14″	**55.00**
Boston, orig black paint & stencils	**185.00**
Oak, pressed back w/spindles, turned arms & legs, refinished	**135.00**
Shaker style, tightly slatted back & seat, dated 1878	**150.00**
Wht wicker w/bluebird print cushions	**100.00**
Rocking horse, spotted, w/orig leather saddle, reins, stirrups	**385.00**
Sewing machine, Betsy Ross, metal, works, 5x7″	**75.00**
Skis, pair, late 1800s	**47.50**
Sled, 1 board top, orig paint, stenciled snowflakes & rose, 32″ long	**150.00**
Wood & iron, w/painting of lake,1860s 32x12x11″	**145.00**
Stove, Empire, l920s, repaint, rewire	**100.00**
Table, drop-leaf, pine	**48.00**
Table, rd, w/claw ft, w/4 chairs, oak table 23x26″, chair 31″	**1,650.00**
Wash set, blue & wht, 8-sided 1½″ bowl, 1¾″ pitcher, dragon handles	**95.00**
Wht w/pink & green flowers, 3 drawers, towel bar, 21x15″	**70.00**
Wheelbarrow, wood, old paint w/yellow stripes, Billy Spears, 34″	**125.00**

Christmas Collectibles

Christmas past...lovely momentos from long ago attest to the ostentatious Victorian celebrations of the season.

Some of the earliest examples of Christmas memorabilia are the pre-1870 ornaments from Dresden, Germany. These cardboard figures--angels, gondolas, umbrellas, dirigibles and countless others-- sparkled with gold and silver trim. Late in the 1870s, blown glass ornaments were imported from Germany. There were carrots and cucumbers, clown faces and angel heads, butterflies and stars--all painted inside with silvery colors. From 1890 through 1910, blown glass spheres were often decorated with beads, tassels and tinsel rope.

Later 20th century Christmas collectibles include figural electric lightbulbs, with character related examples the most popular. Non-working bulbs are indicated by the letters "nw".

Angel, stand-up, embossed litho paper, Germany, 14″	**15.00**
Bank, Santa, chalk-like, 1949	**9.00**
Bean bag board, Kriss Kringle, lithographed cardboard, w/box, 17″	**185.00**
Book, Christmas in Art & Song, 1880, illust by Gilbert, Birket, etc	**19.00**
Night Before Christmas, McLoughlin, 1896, linen, color	**45.00**
Box lid, Fairbank's Santa Claus Soap, paper label on wood, 14x9″	**55.00**
Bulb, Andy Gump, milk glass	**38.00**
Angel, early, arms crossed, clear glass, 3¼″, G	**50.00**
Angel, red sash w/gold trim, clear glass, nw, G	**30.00**
Apple, small, early European, clear glass, yellow/orange	**20.00**
Aviator, orange suit, milk glass, 2½″	**25.00**
Basket of fruit, milk glass, 2¾″ wide, nw	**20.00**
Bell, red, milk glass, 1¾″, nw	**4.00**
Betty Boop, *illus*	**45.00**
Bird cage, red & yellow, milk glass, 2″, nw	**14.00**
Bird, plastic, red	**2.00**
Blue w/embossed Santa, sleigh & reindeer	**7.00**
Boy In high boots, standing orange hair	**28.00**
Bulldog, on round ball, sitting up, clear glass, nw	**25.00**
Candy cane, peppermint stripes, large, milk glass, nw, G	**12.00**
Cat & banjo, clear glass, early, 2½″	**28.00**
Cat & banjo, w/red coat, milk glass, 3″	**14.00**
Cloverbuds, round balls, milk glass	**5.00**
Clown	**28.00**
Clown, hands in pockets, early German, clear glass	**40.00**
Coach light, red & wht w/snow on top, milk glass, 2″	**10.00**
Cross, blue, figural	**3.00**
Disney dwarf	**12.00**
Dog on basket, figural	**7.00**
Dog, figural	**15.00**
Doll head, two faces, milk glass, pink w/blue eyes, nw, G	**15.00**
Doll in stocking, milk glass	**22.00**
Donald Duck, milk glass, nw	**14.00**
Fish, red, base in nose, blunt tail, clear glass, early	**18.00**
Frog, base in nose, fine molding, milk glass, nw, G	**15.00**
Girl in bathing suit, red suit, green cap, milk glass, 2¾″	**25.00**
Girl, standing, w/red coat holding greenery, clear glass, nw	**25.00**
Grape cluster, milk glass, shaded green to yellow/orange leaves	**17.00**
Happy face, 2″ ball, painted face on milk glass, nw	**15.00**
Holly, on round ball, milk glass, 1¾″, nw	**6.00**
House, gothic windows, green, red, wht clear glass, 2″	**15.00**
House, red, orange, wht, 6 sided, milk glass, 2″	**10.00**
Humpty Dumpty, comic egg, milk glass, printing both sides	**45.00**
Jiminy Cricket, milk glass	**15.00**
Kewpie, milk glass, pink w/orange hair, long lashes, nw	**40.00**
Kristal Stars, set of 4	**10.00**
Lantern, green w/wht snow	**5.00**
Lantern, red, white, blue stars	**5.00**
Lemon, milk glass, nw	**12.00**
Little Jack Horner, egg shape, name printed both sides, large	**35.00**
Little Orphan Annie	**40.00**
Mickey Mouse	**50.00**
Minnie Mouse, nw	**35.00**
Moon Mullins, milk glass, nw	**30.00**
Oriental lantern	**5.00**
Oval, w/raised Santa heads, milk glass, nw	**20.00**
Parakeet, yellow, pink & green, milk glass, G	**9.00**
Parrot	**8.00**

Peacock **25.00**
Pear, shaded red to pale pink, large, milk glass, nw **15.00**
Pink star, w/moon face **4.00**
Pluto, Disney character, milk glass, nw **14.00**
Pocket watch, milk glass, nw **25.00**
Pouter pigeon, base in tail, early, clear glass, nw **12.00**
Queen of Hearts, milk glass, bright paint **28.00**
Red ball, w/white stars, milk glass, nw **7.00**
Rooster in knickers, striped socks, walking cane, milk glass, nw **30.00**
Rose **4.00**
Sandy, Orphan Annie's dog, "Arf", milk glass, nw **50.00**
Santa head, two faces, pointed beard, milk glass **10.00**
Santa, Japan, 7" **30.00**
Santa, milk glass, figural **12.00**
Santa, standing w/yellow pack, milk glass, nw **10.00**
Sing A Song of Sixpence, egg shape, words printed both sides **35.00**
Snowgirl, figural **12.00**
Snowman, holding carrot w/red mitten, early, clear glass **35.00**
Snowman, w/cocked head, yellow scarf, red hat, milk glass . . **12.00**
Square with scene, Santa w/reindeer & sleigh, nw, G **17.00**
Square with scene, hunters & horses, milk glass, nw **18.00**
Squash, orange to rose clear glass, early **12.00**
Star, green or red **3.50**
Three Little Pigs, milk glass, 3 pigs in set **45.00**
Tubular cross, clear glass, 2¾x2", nw **15.00**
Zeppelin, long green gondola, small flag, milk glass, nw **30.00**
Candle holder, tin, clip on tree, box of 19, early 1900s **35.00**
Candle shades, litho paper, revolve from heat, set of 4 . . . . . . **35.00**
Candy box, Santa, cardboard, National Candy Co, 11" **17.50**
   Snowman, cardboard, National Candy Co **12.50**
Candy container, Santa descending chimney, glass, 5" **65.00**
   Santa figural, painted glass, 5½" **15.00**
   Santa in stocking, papier mache & cloth, 6" **40.00**
   Santa on polar bear **45.00**
   Santa w/folded arms on round base, glass, 4½" **45.00**
   Santa, cloth, celluloid face, 3" **35.00**
   Santa, cloth, composition face & hands, 8" **100.00**
   Santa, glass, Stanley #892, 5¾" **55.00**
   Santa, papier mache, 7" **30.00**
   Santa's boot, red papier mache, 8" **12.00**
   Snowball w/snowman, papier mache, US Zone Germany **25.00**
Candy tin, Santa & children litho, Harvino Toffee, English, 4½" long **20.00**
Card, Christy color illustration, greeting inside, old **7.50**
   Double sided, w/children & fringe **5.00**
   Kate Greenaway signed, full length young boy, Marcus Ward . **40.00**
   Louis Frag, 1888, mother & child in snow w/holly, silk fringe . **18.00**
   Maxfield Parrish, Christmas Morn, Brown & Bigelow envelope . **6.50**
   Mechanical Santa feeding deer **8.00**
   Mickey Mouse, set of 4, England **15.00**
   Prange signed, fringed, 8x9" **100.00**
   Victorian boy, fringed edge, 1880, 3½x5" **12.00**
Chocolate set, child's, depicts Joseph & Mary on donkey, 14 pc **75.00**
Christmas light, amber glass, w/lady's head in relief on 4 sides . . **70.00**
   Blown, 15 diamond mold, folded rim **90.00**
   Cobalt quilted, drilled base w/metal fitting, 4½" **55.00**
   Diamond pattern, mold blown, clear or colored **18.00**
   Diamond pattern, mold blown, milk glass **28.00**
   Diamond Quilted, hung on tree w/candle, blue or green, 3¾" **13.50**
   Diamond Quilted, milk glass, 3¾" **20.00**
   Thousand Eye, dk blue **43.00**
   Thousand Eye, yellow **52.00**
Cigar box, Christmas Greetings, 1901 . . . . **95.00**
   Merry Christmas **35.00**
Cookie box, w/string handle, Merry Christmas, 1930s, 2x3½" . . . **6.50**

Cookie cutter, tin Santa, 5" **20.00**
Crate label, Santa from Santa Paula, Sunkist Lemons, matted, 16x20" **25.00**
Die-cut, Santa by chimney, 1930s, 10½" **25.00**
Egg cups, Mr & Mrs Santa, w/wool hats, orig box, 4", pr **20.00**
Fairy lamp, Santa, for oil, hp milk glass, brass holder, 9½" . . . **800.00**
Father Christmas figure, camphor glass, 1" **15.00**
   Cloth dressed, pot metal feet, wind-up, 8" **300.00**
   Papier mache, painted, 8½" **120.00**
Flashlight, Santa's face on lens, MIB **25.00**
Garlands, cellophane, 10" long, red or green, original wrapper, 1930s **4.00**
Icicles, old blown glass, each **2.00**
Lamp, Christmas tree miniature **130.00**
   Santa in milk glass, battery operated, Japan, 6½" **60.00**
   Santa standing figure is bulb, electric, 9" **55.00**
Light reflectors, tin, set of 10, old **18.00**
Mug, child's, Merry Christmas, Santa, pink lustre **28.00**
Nativity, cardboard w/chromolitho figures, 1880s, German, 15" . **45.00**
Nodder, Santa, composition w/wood base, old, 7" **25.00**

Ornaments

Airship, glass, silver & white, w/Father Christmas, 5" **125.00**
Anchor, Dresden, silver, 2½" **5.00**
Angel in snow, tinsel & paper, early 1900s, 5" **4.50**
   Litho w/tinsel, handmade, 5" **14.00**
Angel Head, glass, silvery green, on clip, 2¼" **165.00**
   Papier mache, 5" **6.00**
   With halo, Victorian **30.00**
Baby, diecut bust, blonde w/cotton batting dress, 16½" **35.00**
Ball, handmade, cotton w/tinsel, 5" **24.00**
Balloon, glass, scrap angel on stem, red/pink wire trim, 3" **25.00**
Banana, embossed Yes We Have No **95.00**
   Glass, old dull gold, 3¾" **55.00**
Bear, 3" **25.00**
Beetle **55.00**
Bell candy container, red silk, hp holly trim, 4" **15.00**
Bird, glass, on clip w/pendant berry in beak, old **75.00**
Black baby, diecut, wht hat & coat, on paper triangle, 5" **15.00**
Black girl, diecut, w/cotton batting dress & pearls, 9½" **50.00**
Boat, glass, gold/red/blue, wire wrapped, w/angel, 4x4½" **85.00**
Bottle, pressed cotton, long neck, gold decor cap, 3½" **25.00**
Boy, on cotton snowball, pressed cotton w/Heubach face **135.00**
Butterfly, composition w/spun glass wings, on clip, 3" **70.00**
   Candy container, Dresden, silver/gold, silk bag, 3" **175.00**
   Red glass, oval shaped, old **68.00**
   Silver, 1890s **9.00**
Camel, Dresden, 3-D, shaded brown w/curly tail, 2½x3¼" **45.00**
   Tan, Victorian, 2" **17.50**
Candelabra, 4 branch **22.00**
Carrot, orange, German **70.00**
   Pressed cotton, red-pink, sparkly, 3" **12.00**
Cat in shoe **45.00**
Cello, glass, brown **22.00**
Child's face w/glass eyes, w/box **150.00**
Clown, glass, "My Darling", pearly wht w/gold & silver suit **55.00**
   Glass, flat wht face, gold/blue hat, 3½" **90.00**
Clown head, glass, pearly wht w/gold collar, painted face, 3¼" **110.00**
Cluster of grapes, 2½" **39.00**
Coco-Cola bottle, 1923 Christmas special, 2" **100.00**
Coffee pot, glass, sparkly gold w/glass beaded rose, 4½" **30.00**
Cone candy container, green paper, gold lyre & tinsel, 5½" **10.00**
Crescent, Dresden, silver **7.50**
Crescent moon, diecut, w/stars & blonde child, 3¼" **8.00**
Cucumber, 4½" **85.00**
Curved horn, pressed cotton, yellow, red string hanger, 4" **25.00**
Dirigible, tinsel propeller, Victorian, 7" **45.00**

Dog in sack, My Darling.............................. **55.00**
Doll head w/applied eyes **60.00**
Doll head w/glass eyes **50.00**
Donkey, Dresden, gold w/red basket & flowers, 3x3¼"....... **20.00**
Duck, glass, pearly wht, blue eyes & wings, red bill, 3" **55.00**
Ear of corn, 4½" **45.00**
Elephant **95.00**
Elf's head, glass, red cap, gold hair, painted face, 2¼"....... **55.00**
Father Christmas, litho scrap in 5" tinsel rope ring.......... **15.00**
Father Christmas head, glass w/red hooded coat, 4½"........ **50.00**
Flounder, Dresden, silver & orange, 4" **145.00**
Flower, clip on **45.00**
Football candy container, Dresden, tan w/molded strings, 2½" . **45.00**
Four leaf clover, cotton batting, pink w/2 figural angels, 7" **20.00**
Frog, pink fantasy................................. **125.00**
  Pressed cotton, green/wht, Frog in Throat tag, 1½" **10.00**
Fruit basket, glass, old **8.00**
Girl, glass, blue dress w/wht frosted trim & purse, 3¼" **85.00**
Girl with dove, diecut, on pink net w/gold stars, 8"......... **12.00**
Girl's head, diecut, w/fancy hat & dress, 2½" **8.00**
  Glass, gold hair & hat, 2¼"....................... **50.00**
  Glass, w/glass eyes, red mouth & hat, 2½".......... **75.00**
Goldfish, Dresden, copper & orange, 3"................ **135.00**
Gondola w/tinsel, scrap Santa head, blown, Germany.......... **85.00**
Gun, glass, silver & green, 5" **55.00**
Heart, glass, old **8.00**
Hires Santa tradecard **9.00**
House candy container, sparkly cardboard, plaster Santa face... **28.00**
Hunting dog, Dresden, gold w/red collar & flowers, 3x5"...... **20.00**
Indian Chief, bust **125.00**
Lighthouse, glass, old **85.00**
Little Red Riding Hood, glass eyes, glass, old **110.00**
Lyre, Dresden, silver, flat w/red gel insert **9.50**
Man in the moon, tinsel, litho angel, early 1900s **32.00**
Occupied Japan, box of 12, small **5.00**
Owl, glass, silver & gold, gold & black eyes, 3¾" **45.00**
Parrot, Dresden, gold w/orange, red & tinsel trim, 7½"....... **25.00**
Peach, frosted glass **11.00**
  Pressed cotton, yellow w/orange & pink, 2" **14.00**
Peacock, spread tail **45.00**
Peanut candy container, Dresden, tan, Germany, 3" **30.00**
Pear, pressed cotton, yellow/orange/red, 2½" **15.00**
Pelican.. **125.00**
Pickle, glass, early, dull silver, 3" **55.00**
  Green, German **75.00**
  Glass, old, 4" **85.00**
Pinecone, old, glass **4.00**
Purse, glass, silver beads & wht rods, paper liner, 2½" **25.00**
Rabbit, glass, pearly wht w/black & pink, holding carrot **75.00**
Radio **55.00**
Rooster, Dresden, gold, on grass w/flowers, 2½x2¾" **10.00**
Rose, glass, w/diecut angel in center, on clip, 2¾" **55.00**
Sailboat, Dresden, detailed w/ropes & sails, gold patina, 7x5" . **45.00**
Santa, cotton litho paper, 8" **30.00**
  Cotton & paper, litho scrap face & tree, 6"........... **45.00**
  Cotton & tinsel, litho face, early 1900s **45.00**
  Embossed paper, spun glass, 10"................... **20.00**
  Glass, on chimney, old **75.00**
  Glass, pearly wht w/red & black, on clip, 3".......... **55.00**
  Glass, w/blue chenille legs, black compo boots, 5"...... **150.00**
  Glass, w/hands in pockets, old, 5" **95.00**
  Glass, w/shovel on stump, pearly gold, 2¾".......... **55.00**
  Mechanical, whiskers move, wood, old, 7" **90.00**
  On horse **150.00**

Plaster, set of 12, 3"............................... **30.00**
Santa head, Dresden, w/cap on star **40.00**
  Papier mache **30.00**
Slipper, Dresden, silver, ... **135.00**
Snake, glass, orange, old, 7" **85.00**
Snowflake, cotton batting, w/Father Christmas diecut & toys ... **25.00**
Snowman & broom, glass, green trim **35.00**
Squirrel, 3" **20.00**
Star, glass, alternating red, blue, silver points, 4" **22.00**
  Gold double sided, Victorian...................... **14.00**
Stocking, muslin, Father Christmas diecut, tinsel edged, 11" ... **45.00**
Strawberry, glass, old **3.00**
Tassel, Dresden, beaded **8.50**
Teapot, glass, red w/applied spout & handle............. **30.00**
Tiffany lamp, 3" **38.00**
Toadstool, clip on, w/box **55.00**
Trumpet, blown glass **12.00**
Umbrella, glass, red w/wht & blue, silver handle, 4½" **35.00**
  Tinsel wrapped................................. **22.00**
Vase, glass, sugared rose, clip on, Germany **60.00**
Violin, 5½"....................................... **45.00**
  Wine & wht satin covered, opens for candy **175.00**
Wax angel w/fiberglass wings **65.00**
Well, vine-covered, wood, clip on, 5" **30.00**

Outdoor display, Santa & reindeer, plastic, w/orig box, 20"... **20.00**
Paint book, The Night Before Christmas, 1939 .... **10.00**
Perfume bottle, Santa, clear glass, 7"................. **130.00**
Planter, Mr & Mrs Santa, Napco, 7".................... **8.00**
Puzzle, Aunt Louisa's Cube Puzzles, Santa Claus, McLoughlin 1884 **35.00**
Roly Poly, Santa candy container, painted papier mache, 8½". **120.00**
Salt & pepper shakers, Mr & Mrs Santa, w/orig box, 4", pair.... **6.00**
Santa & Sleigh, w/reindeer, ci, 17".................... **750.00**
Santa Band figurine, bisque, marked Japan **18.00**
Santa face, papier mache, large **48.00**
Santa head, painted plaster, 1913 Modern Tuscon Art Co, 17". **95.00**
Santa mask, painted paper w/beard **15.00**
Santa suit, J Halpern Co, Pittsburgh, w/orig box **35.00**
Santa in carriage, parasol, reindeer; straw, lace trim, tin wheels, 9" **335.00**
Santa in sleigh, mechanical, w/nodding cloth-covered deer, 42" long **425.00**
  Reindeer is candy box, leather trim, bentwood frame, 23" .. **800.00**
Santa on motorcycle, celluloid, 5".................... **55.00**
Santa on roller skates, battery operated, 12" **80.00**
Santa on sled, pulled by reindeer, celluloid, TR Win Co....... **25.00**
Santa with tree, cloth body, composition legs, early 1900s, 9". **65.00**
Santa, 3-D cardboard, w/bag & address book, on rockers, 10".. **15.00**
  Bisque, Germany, 1"............................. **30.00**
  Bisque, luminous, w/open-close blue eyes, S&H 1249, 24½" **765.00**
  Celluloid, Irwin, 9" **95.00**
  Celluloid, on wheels, 4" **13.00**
  Cloth doll, electric eyes that work, 25" **75.00**
  Cloth w/metal boots, 5" **35.00**
  Cloth, 3½".................................... **22.00**
  Cloth, for hanging, 18" **100.00**
  Enamel on lead, 3"............................. **17.00**
  Flocked, stand up easel back, 1930s, 13" **10.00**
  Flocked, w/toy bag & list, easel back, 1930s **20.00**
  Life-size, electric, cloth dressed, w/coke bottle **225.00**
  Mechanical toy, head rocks, eyes move **675.00**
  Oil cloth, 1920s, 13" **35.00**
  Papier mache, 1920s, 26x14x14" **265.00**
  Royalite Light-Up, w/tree, 8", MIB **20.00**
  Stand-up, embossed & flocked paper, basket & tree, Germany, 11" **55.00**
  Steiff, 12" **310.00**

Straw stuffed, mask face, long beard, light bulb eyes, 21"... **100.00**
Stuffed cloth w/papier mache face & hands, Japan, 5½".... **20.00**
Stuffed figure in silver suit, 1920s, 25".................. **115.00**
Wax & cotton, w/wood sled, early 1800s, German, 6x2".... **48.00**
Shade, Mickey Mouse & Pals decals, set of 8, 1930s......... **45.00**
Snowman, Royalite Light-Up, w/tree, 8", MIB.............. **15.00**
Still bank, Santa bust w/tophat, plastic, 6".............. **45.00**
   Santa figural, hooded cloak, painted cast iron, 6"........ **210.00**
Store display, large Santa head w/fireplace, clockwork, 20".. **400.00**
String of lights, candles, red, set of 7, Mazda............. **12.00**
   Disney characters, 7 plastic shades.................... **125.00**
   Disney characters, Silly Symphony, set w/orig box....... **335.00**
   Flames, realistic, old, set of 8...................... **16.00**
   Flash Gordon, set, 1934, MIB....................... **175.00**
   Mickey Mouse, 8 shades, w/orig box.................. **130.00**
   Noma Bubble-lites................................ **14.00**
   Stars, old, set of 8............................... **20.00**
Swizzle sticks, Christmas tree, green glass, set of 6.......... **9.00**
Tea set, child's, Santa in airship, 12 pc, German China...... **240.00**
   Santa in balloons, cars, etc, 21 pc, German china........ **350.00**
Tin Wind-up, Santa holds sign & rings bell............... **35.00**
   Santa on skis, Japan.............................. **18.00**
   Santa riding reindeer, litho tin, plastic & cloth, 5" long..... **25.00**
   Santa waving & ringing bell........................ **14.00**
   Santa, early Chein................................ **110.00**
   Santa riding tricycle.............................. **10.00**
   Santa Claus, in sleigh, 2 deers w/bells, Strauss, 11" long... **350.00**
Tree stand, ci, Merry Christmas........................ **28.00**
   Cast iron, 1890.................................. **45.00**
   Funnel shape w/Santa at chimnmey decals, Noma, 11"...... **35.00**
   Revolving music box , Germany...................... **65.00**
   With angels & stars............................... **137.50**
   With cherubs, painted ci, Germany, 7"................ **45.00**
   With Santa figure, painted ci, Germany, 8"............ **775.00**
Tree top ornament, angel, spun glass & paper............. **25.00**
   Cross, plush red velvet, 8 bulbs, w/orig box, 12".......... **17.00**
   Star, plush red velvet, 10 bulbs, w/orig box............ **20.00**
Wall clock, Santa, eyes move.......................... **60.00**
Wreath, composition Santa, w/light bulb, 13".............. **35.00**
   With pinecones, Santa head in center, plastic, electric, 26" dia **110.00**

Circus Collectibles

    The 1890s--the Golden Age of the circus. Barnum and Bailey's parades transformed mundane city streets into an exotic never-never land inhabited by trumpeting elephants with gold jeweled headgear, strutting by to the strains of the caliope that issued from a fine red and gilt painted wagon extravagantly decorated with wood carved animals of every description. It was an exciting experience--is it any wonder that collectors today treasure the momentos of that golden era?

    Posters that once wheted interest and stirred imaginations are today avidly sought, and though rarely signed by the artist, often carry the name of the printer or lighographer. Among them, many consider the work of the Strobridge Lithograph Co to be the finest. Other early printing companies were Gibson and Co. Litho, Erie Litho and Enquirer Job Printing Co.

Advertising Card, Cole's Circus, 1879, The Giants............ **19.00**
Banner, Hawaiian dancer w/2 musicians, canvas, 9x9"...... **295.00**
   Hindu man, on canvas, 1940s, 8x6"................... **345.00**
   Snakeology, canvas, 9x9".......................... **320.00**
   The Great Marlowe, Strong As A Lion, 8x10"........... **200.00**
   The Handcuffed Kings, 7x12"....................... **250.00**
   World's Smallest Man, on canvas, 1940s, 8x6".......... **395.00**
   Untitled, w/two clowns.......................... **2,200.00**

Billboard poster, Ringling Bros, w/clown & elephant, l940s, 6½x10" **85.00**
Book, Struggles & Triumphs of PT Barnum, 1869, autographed **30.00**
Litho, Biencke Circus Parade, 1855, 25x35"............... **300.00**
Magazine, The Billboard, 1911, carnival & circus supply....... **40.00**
Maul, hickory w/heavy iron end cups.................... **85.00**
Miniature circus, Delvan, 10 pc....................... **235.00**
Miniature circus, Schoenhut, barrel.................... **10.00**
   Chair... **12.00**
   Clown... **60.00**
   Donkey, painted eyes............................. **85.00**
   Elephant, glass eyes.............................. **200.00**
   Horse, painted eyes, w/saddle....................... **150.00**
   Horse, wht w/glass eyes & platform.................. **200.00**
   Ringmaster, wooden head.......................... **195.00**
Newspaper article, Robbins Bros, 1938, w/pictures of acts, 8 pgs **16.00**
Photograph, Schendel's Big 3-Ring Circus, 1901............ **11.00**
Poster, Clyde Beatty Cole Bros, Clyde w/lions & tigers, 28x21.. **14.00**
   Hagen Bros, 3-Ring, w/girl on horseback, 40x14"......... **18.00**

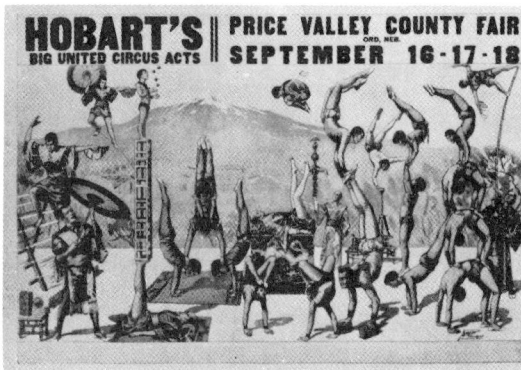

   Hobart's Big Circus Acts, 1906, 27x41"................. **275.00**
   Russell Bros 3-Ring, black man on mule, clowns, 28¼x20".. **80.00**
Print, Circus Kings of All Time, Barnum & Bailey, framed..... **70.00**
Program, Albee's New York Hippodrome, 1926............. **10.00**
   Cole Brothers, 1938.............................. **12.00**
   Ringling Bros & Bailey, 1924, clown cover.............. **11.00**
   Ringling Bros & Barnum & Bailey, 1924, w/program insert... **30.00**
Side show sign, nude mermaid, painted.................. **245.00**
Side show target, clown, papier mache, metal & fabric, early.. **150.00**
Window poster, two sided, Clyde Beatty, 1920s............. **25.00**
   King Bros...................................... **22.00**

Clambroth

    Clambroth is a term that refers to a type of glass popular during the Victorian period. It was semi-opaque and grey-white in color, said to resemble broth from the clam.

Barber bottle, cork & porcelain stopper.................. **38.00**
Candlestick, dolphin, petal socket...................... **550.00**
Egg cup, cable, flint................................ **500.00**
Jar w/nickle plated lid, "Cream", Hazel Atlas.............. **20.00**
Mug, souvenir, child's............................... **22.00**
Spill, rare scenic paneled............................ **325.00**
Tumbler, 5"...................................... **20.00**
Vase, corset shape, horizontal ribs, black band, 9".......... **35.00**
   Enameled florals, beading, 8½"..................... **70.00**
   Footed, enameled blue birds, 8x3", pr................. **135.00**
   Trumpet shape, black rim & disk ft, Steuben, 11"........ **180.00**

Clarice Cliff

    Clarice Cliff, born 1900, was trained in the art of ceramics at Burslem

School of Art. During her apprenticeship she decorated and designed ware for A. J. Wilkinson, Ltd; and until 1939 served as art director at Wilkinson's's Royal Staffordshire Pottery and its subsidiary, New Port Pottery. In the 30s she carried out designs for tableware styled by contemporary artists, that was exhibited by Harrod's of London. Many of her best works were decorated in vivid colors in the Art Deco style. Among these lines were My Garden, Bizarre, Fantasque and Biarritz. Some of her ware was marked with a gold transfer signature.

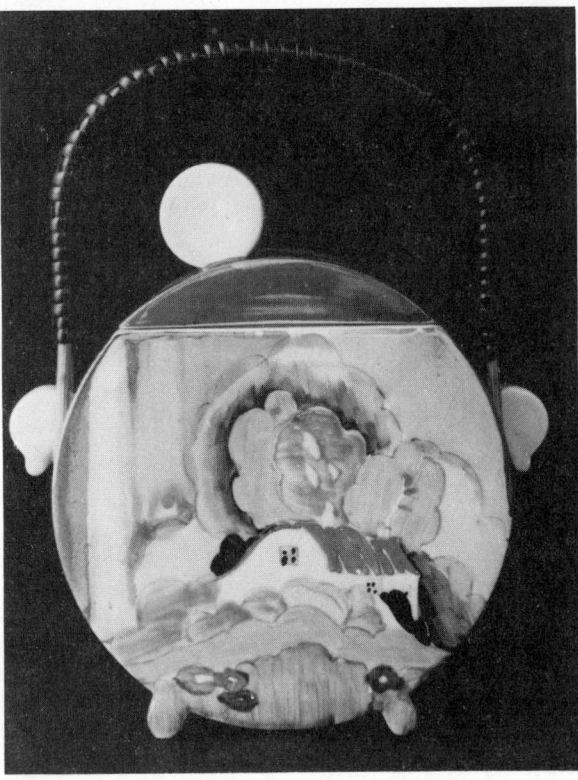

Bizzare, biscuit safe, house w/derby hat on top, forest scene, signed **325.00**
　Cake plate, cream w/blue trees, green grass, 7½x9″ **45.00**
　Covered jar, geometric, 3½″ **120.00**
　Creamer & sugar, fantasy trees, landscape **195.00**
　Cups & saucers, set of 6, Crocus pattern, signed **350.00**
　Jug vase, large, floral pattern, geometrics, signed **500.00**
　Sugar & creamer, cream, blue trees, green grass, signed **75.00**
　Sugar shaker, cone shape tree, spade shape bush, signed ... **125.00**
　Tea plate, cream, blue trees, green grass **28.00**
　Wall plate, house & forest scene, signed, 12″ **450.00**
Cigarette box w/lid, fish handle **75.00**
Coronation plate, '53, 6½″ **25.00**
Dinner set, Harvest, 88 pcs **300.00**
Fantasque, coffee set, 16 pcs **375.00**
Gayday, biscuit barrel **175.00**
Jug vase, large, floral pattern, geometrics, signed **500.00**
Plate, Confederation Series, Canada, Toronto, 11″ **50.00**
Plate, red turkey center, 10″ **10.00**
Set of 3 pitchers, Ravel pattern, 4″ to 10″ **400.00**
Tray, Tonquin, pink & white, Royal Staffordshire, 3½x6½″ **15.00**
Water Lily centerpiece, 1930, 9″ **150.00**

Clewell

Charles Walter Clewell was a metal worker who perfected the technique of plating an entire ceramic vessel with a thin layer of copper or bronze treated with an oxidizing agent to produce a natural deterioration of the surface. Through trial and error, he was able to control the degree of patina achieved. In the early stages, the metal darkened, and if allowed to develope

further, formed a natural turquoise blue or green corrosion. He worked alone in his small Akron, Ohio studio from about 1906, buying undecorated pottery from several Ohio firms, among them Weller, Owens, and Cambridge.

His work is usually marked. Clewell died in 1965, having never revealed his secret process to others.

Bud vase, excellent patina, #344-6, 7½″ **145.00**
Bulb bowl, 3 footed, w/patina, #421, 2½x5″ **125.00**
Mug, Art Nouveau shape, no mark, no patina, 6½x5″ **195.00**
　Copper clad w/brass plaque w/"w", circular mark, 4″....... **135.00**

Pitcher, 10″, priced with 6 matching mugs **750.00**
Powder box w/cover, squat, Clewell, Canton, O., 4″ **265.00**
Urn, all over green patina, 5½″ **150.00**
Vase, all over copper w/incised Indian type decor **300.00**
　Blue/green patina, 7x4″ **165.00**
　Bulbous base, narrow top neck, 5½″ **175.00**
　Bulbous bottom, Weller shape, #458, w/patina, 6x5½″ **200.00**
　Copper-turquoise, 6″ **150.00**
　Corroded patina finish, 8x4½″ **190.00**
　Cylinder, copper w/metallic patina, #328-2-6 .... **190.00**
　Early, no mark, Arc-en-Ciel blank, 1906, 8x4″ **190.00**
　Metallic copper patina, #344-215, 5x3 .... **95.00**
　No deterioration of patina, 5½″ **135.00**
　Ornate Egyptain motif, black shadows, no patina, 9½″..... **200.00**

Pottery, rare, green glaze, signed **150.00**
Red to green patina, 8½″ **160.00**

Clifton

Clifton Art Pottery, of Clifton, N.J., was organized in 1905, and until 1911 when they turned to the production of wall and floor tile, made art ware of several varieties.

The founders were Fred Tschirner and William A. Long. Long had developed the method for underglaze slip painting that had been used at the Lonhuda Pottery in Steubenville, Ohio, in the 1890s.

Crystal Patina, the first art ware made by the small company, utilized a fine white body and flowing, blended colors, the earliest a green crystalline. Indian Ware, copied from the pottery of the American Indians was decorated in black geometric designs on red clay. Robin's Egg Blue, pale blue on the white body, and Tirrube, a slip decorated matt ware were also produced.

Bank, monkey figural, slot on stomach, red bisque, 6″ **110.00**
Bowl, grey/green crystal patina, 2½″ mouth, 6x2″ **40.00**
  Tan/green gloss w/matt tan handles, #133, 1906, 3½x2x6″ . **170.00**
Pitcher w/lid, Crystal Patina, 5½″ **75.00**

Indian Ware, geometrics, glazed interior, #274, 4″ **50.00**
Teapot, covered, Crystal Patina, 5¾″ **70.00**
  Covered, Indian Ware, numbered **40.00**
  Tan Crystal Patina, modern, ink stamp #271-20, 3½x9″ **175.00**
  Teepee shape, Indian Ware, 4x9″ **125.00**
Vase, Crystal Patina, 1907 cipher #169 11¼″ **400.00**
  Green Crystal Patina w/caramel drip #160, 1906, 4½x8″ . . . **185.00**
  Indian Ware, Little Colorado, geometrics, #226, 5x7½″ **185.00**
  Red and black, Indian motif, 3x4″ **40.00**
  Red bisque w/slip jonquils by SB; 8x4″ **195.00**
  Red clay w/roses in white/grey by AH; Tirrube, 9x5″ **225.00**
  Red clay w/slip jonquils by SB; 8x4″ **195.00**
  Red clay w/stork by A Haubrick; Tirrube, #257, 12x7″ **500.00**
  Squat, "Arizona" Indian, 8″ **80.00**

Clocks

In the early days of our country's history, clockmakers were influenced by styles imported from Europe and Germany. They copied their cabinets and re-constructed their movements. But needed materials were in short supply--modifications had to be made. Of necessity was born mainspring motive power, and spring clocks. Wooden movements were made on a mass production basis as early as 1808; before the middle of the century, metal movements had been developed.

Aaron Willard, banjo, striker **3,500.00**
Abel Stowell, banjo, lyre, carved mahogany **4,500.00**
Advertising, Regulator, Sauer's Flavoring Extracts, walnut **725.00**
Alarm, WWII nostalgia piece, War Alarm, works **14.00**
Angelus, w/barometer, birdcage frame, pierced dome, 7″ **120.00**
Animated, alarm, 2 men hitting bell, brass plated, Forestville Co **48.00**

Betty Boop **400.00**
Big Bad Wolf, alarm **250.00**
Black minstrel w/blinking eyes, ci, 16″ **395.00**
Black Sambo, pendulette, 8¾x4½″ **220.00**
Blue bird, metal, Lux, 7x4″ **29.00**
Bulldog, Lux **225.00**
Bulldog, w/kittens, Keebler, 4¾x4″ **80.00**
Cat w/moving eyes & tail, Lux **90.00**
Cat, pink, California Clock Co, San Juan, Capistrano **20.00**
Charlie McCarthy **350.00**
Clown & seals, pendulette, Lux, 7x5¾″ **210.00**
Early Bird, w/farm sunrise scene, alarm **165.00**
Emile Zola figural, hand rings bell, brass plated, ornate **400.00**
German, figural clock w/mouse, eyes move, brass works **25.00**
Happy Days beer drinkers, dresser, 1930, Lux **175.00**
Holland scene w/windmill, electric, porcelain, 9¾″ **55.00**
Hula dancer, alarm, ivory celluloid, Florn Co, Germany **20.00**
Man at anvil **40.00**
Mickey Mouse, alarm, Ingersoll **175.00**
Racing car scene, alarm, 1930s, Jazz Clock **75.00**
Reindeer, Lux, 7x4″ **25.00**
Roy Rogers, alarm **115.00**
Shoe shine boy, dresser clock, Lux **162.00**
Showboat, paddle wheel revolves, alarm, Lux **185.00**
Spinning wheel, alarm, Lux **45.00**
Woody Woodpecker, plastic pendulette, Columbia, 7″ **240.00**
Woody Woodpecker, alarm w/box **175.00**
Ansonia, cabinet, Huntress Swing, figural, 1886, 25″ **800.00**
  Double figure, Don Juan & Don Caesar **1,200.00**
  Girl on swing, silveroid case **525.00**
  Gloria figural, swinging pendulum, 8-day **2,950.00**
  King model, 8-day, striker, spool pendulum, 24″ **300.00**
  Kitchen, 8-day, walnut w/bears **240.00**
  Mantel figural, Art & Commerce, 20½″ **750.00**
  Mantel figural, Florentine #3, greyhound on top, 13½″ **150.00**
  Mantel figural, Music, lady w/harp, 21¾″ **430.00**
  Mantel figural, Pizarro & Cortez, 1886, 10½″ **750.00**
  Mantel figural, Tasso, seated, 10½″ **350.00**
  Mantel, Antique #1, gilt dome, 5″ dial, 1886 . . . . **500.00**
  Mantel, Atlas, foliate decor on glass, 21″ **170.00**
  Mantel, Kentucky, 1886 . . . . **200.00**
  Mantel, Nile w/urn atop, ornate, 1886, 18″ **210.00**
  Mantel, Pompeii, ornate figural stork heads, wings **250.00**
  Novelty, Beauty, ormolu scrolls, leaves, round base **70.00**
  Novelty, Butterfly ink w/two wells, thermometer, 1886 . . . . . **120.00**
  Queen Mary, 8-day, time & strike, oak **875.00**
  Shelf, chimes, brass, glass case, jeweled face, 15″ **450.00**
  Tall case Regulator #8, weight, ornate pediment, 1886 . . . **5,000.00**
  Wall, Queen Elizabeth model, walnut **850.00**
Ansonia #11, Jeweler's Regulator, oak case **5,700.00**
Ansonia King, shelf spool pendulum, 24″ **280.00**
Arc De Triomphe, musical, gilt dial, columns, 17″ **775.00**
Art Deco, glass, acid Greek columns, girls head, wood base, 8″ **285.00**
  Green marble w/parrot, 8½″ **1,000.00**
  Sterling, 8-day, 5″ **465.00**
  Two nudes, brass, #205 USA, 8½″ **85.00**
Art Nouveau, digital, Plato-type, woman on top, celluloid **120.00**
Austrian, annular, vase form, onyx base, floral enamels, 7″ . . **1,750.00**
Banjo, alarm, scenic panel, 31″ **1,750.00**
  Decorated throat glass, eagle finial, 32″ **900.00**
  Mahogany w/tiger maple panel, brass weights, 28″ **550.00**
  Painted center panel w/deer & hounds **1,000.00**
  Rosewood, weight driven, nickeled brass face **880.00**
  Wall clock, mahogany, brass sidearms, Federal, 29″ **3,000.00**

Bartholomew, Federal, brass urn finials, half columns, 29".... **550.00**
Batman, talking figural **18.00**
Chelsea, #5, quarter sawed oak, 1 weight **3,250.00**
  Banjo, centennial weight **1,250.00**
Continental, mantel, ormolu & glass, enamel shepherdess, 10½" **675.00**
Cordey, porcelain w/pink rose sprigs, 10x7"............. **165.00**
Cuckoo, Black Forest walnut, pine cone weights, 46"........ **900.00**
  Hand carved figural mill w/water wheel, weight driven **75.00**
Currier, banjo, mahogany, reverse painted hunting scene ... **1,200.00**
DK Schoonman, tall case, ormolu, full calendar, 98"....... **4,600.00**
Dell & Co, 8-day, English oak, gothic, 39" **350.00**
EF Caldwell, desk, calendar, eight day movement, early 1900s **1,750.00**
E Howard & Co, Boston, Jeweler's Regulator, 26x72"...... **7,700.00**
EL Hausberg, carriage, French Rococo, alarm, scroll feet, 9" **3,850.00**
EN Welch, calendar, perpetual double dial, American........ **850.00**
Elgin #126, chronometer, mahogany case **2,650.00**
  Car's clock, leather case **40.00**
Eli Terry, pillar & scroll, mahogany, 1820s.............. **1,550.00**
  Shelf clock, reverse painting, pendulum, 31" **1,100.00**
English, bracket, ebonized case, lions, cupids, 13"......... **275.00**
  Bracket, oak Gothic, 8-day fusee movement, 1890s, 39".... **350.00**
  Gallery, fusee movement, restored **450.00**
  Grandfather, brass dial w/rocking ship **2,900.00**
  Mantel w/chimes, carved wood, 10½" **45.00**
Federal, cherry w/inlay, 1780s, 85".................... **3,500.00**
Forestville, wall, shaped case, reverse painting, 28"....... **1,200.00**
French, bracket, bronze, cloisonne w/porcelain insets **3,850.00**

Bracket, Louix XV, ormolu mounts, fig surmount, 28" ... **1,800.00**
Carriage, brass case, 7½"............................ **1,300.00**
Carriage, hour & ½ hour repeater, grand & petite sonniere, 5" **1,125.00**
Carriage, hour repeating, fluted columns, 7½" **1,100.00**
Carriage, repeater, gold dial, 8-day, Corniche case **625.00**
Carriage, triple face, square case, gilt, 1890s........... **3,750.00**
Drum, sunburst pendulum bob, marble columns, ½ hr strike, 1860 **600.00**
Mantel, barometer, figural angel, bronze, late 1800s **3,500.00**
Mantel, empire, gilt metal, 9" **475.00**
Mantel, ormolu, strikes, Wedgwood plaque, 14½"........ **825.00**
Mantel, perpetual calendar, columns, key wind, 1860s **3,300.00**
Picture frame, black lacquer w/abalone shell............. **425.00**
Shelf, china case, gilt decoration, signed Petit **425.00**
Wall clock, ebonized w/MPO & wood inlay, 24½"........ **145.00**

German, 6 hp nursery rhyme scenes, porcelain face, 8 day, 1910 **100.00**
  Bracket, Westminster chimes **730.00**
  Dresden, mantel **600.00**
  Grandfather, 2 weight, cherry case, brass dial **1,200.00**
  Grandfather, oak, 2 weight **1,050.00**
  Wall clock, carved walnut, enameled numerals, 48x30"..... **600.00**
  Wall, 2 weight **700.00**
  Wall, 3 panel bevelled glass door, oak **375.00**
  Wall, carved walnut w/enameled numerals, 48x30"...... **600.00**
Gibralter, Roosevelt figural, Wheel For New Deal, electric, 13½" **35.00**
Gilbert,12, wall, Jeweler's Regulator, oak **5,300.00**
  8-day, pillars & scrolls, gilt, 10"................... **40.00**
  Crystal regulator, cranberry glass w/ormolu **2,100.00**
  Grandfather, weight driven, brass face, 1912........... **950.00**
  Mantel, Arena, cherub w/mirror finial, 5½" dial **160.00**
  Mantel, Bishop, form suggests cathedral, 6" dial **160.00**
  Mantel, Eros, pendulum within drapery effect, 1880 ..... **175.00**
  Mantel, Laurell, oak w/ornate pressed leaves, 1900 ..... **200.00**
  Mantel, Melody, bell surmount, 5½" dial **145.00**
  Mantel, Palisade, 5½" dial, 4 columns, scroll feet **90.00**
  School clock, English, circular w/inlay, 26½"......... **75.00**
  Shelf clock, walnut, alarm......................... **300.00**
  Wall, light oak, 25x15½"........................ **155.00**
Gustav Becker, engraved dial, pendulum & 3 weights **1,700.00**
  Vienna Regulator, 3 weight, embossed case **1,850.00**
  Wall clock, w/calendar hand, walnut **275.00**
  Wall, spring wind regulator, time & strike **600.00**
Henri Jacot, carriage, hour repeating, serpentine case, 6"... **1,200.00**
Herschedes, grandfather, 9 tubular, mercury pendulum ... **12,500.00**
  Grandfather, walnut w/fluted posts, claw feet, chimes ... **7,250.00**
Howard 5#, banjo **2,200.00**
  #21, 8-day, weight, 24" marble dial **1,600.00**
  Wall Regulator #36, 1880......................... **5,000.00**
  Wall Regulator #60, 14" dial, ornate, 1880........... **6,000.00**
Ingraham, arch column **300.00**
  Banjo, 8-day, strike, pendulum, Treasure Isle, 39"........ **500.00**
  Banjo, Norse, eagle finial, reverse painted, 26" **275.00**
  Mantel, Belmont, wood w/round top, 5" dial, 1918 .... **50.00**
  Mantel, Majestic, ornate scroll feet, gilt columns......... **95.00**
  Mantel, Pekin, 1918 .... **65.00**
  Mosaic double dial calendar **1,275.00**
  Oak gingerbread w/alarm **175.00**
International Time Recording Co, time clock, oak case...... **350.00**
Ithaca, #8, shelf clock, walnut case **820.00**
  Calendar, #4 Hanging Office, 28", 1880 .... **1,200.00**
  Calendar, #6 Hanging Library, 1880, 32"............. **950.00**
  Calendar, parlour model, 8-day, time & strike.......... **3,700.00**
  Serpentine double dial, calendar **850.00**
  Wall, calendar, #0 Bank, fancy pediment, pendulum, 61" . **4,000.00**
  Wall, long case, spring driven, time & strike........... **1,050.00**
Ivory, carved, Victorian, rectangle case, turned legs, 8"... **440.00**
JE Caldwell, mantel, round face on scroll base, 22½" long ... **225.00**
James McCabe, mantel, 8-day, 19th century, 12x14"........ **775.00**
Jas Rankin, wall, English Victorian, mahogany **525.00**
Jerome & Darrow, 8-day, brass weights, wooden dial........ **385.00**
Jerome, shelf, 8-day weight driven, 1850s............... **450.00**
Jewelers Regulator, floor model, oak **3,500.00**
John Kline, tall case, mahogany w/moon dial **3,200.00**
John Walker, bracket, ormolu, chimes bail handles, 29".... **1,800.00**
Keebler, boy scout, pendulette, 6½" **85.00**
  Martha & George Washington, w/animated kissing birds **99.00**
  Tiny house figural, pendulette, 6¼x3½" **80.00**
Kienzle, carriage, music box alarm, 1890s, 6" **145.00**
Kroeber, walnut, 8-day, cut glass pendulum **300.00**

Le Coultre, desk, bronze, swinging, signed.............. **130.00**
Le Roy A Paris, lady at desk, 8-day, silk suspension, 11½″ . **1,800.00**
Lux, ballerina scene, dresser, brass works, 1920s **185.00**
    Clown w/seals, pendulette, w/orig box **225.00**
    Cuckoo, miniature, pendulette **60.00**
    Cuckoo, wall, green w/animated bird **30.00**
    Liberty Bell, pendulette............................. **225.00**
    Lindburg Plane figural............................... **60.00**
    Petunia, pendulette **250.00**
    Shmoo, wht, pendulette **85.00**
Mantel, brass, floral enamel, mercury pendulum dial, 11″..... **325.00**

Mantle, champleve & bronze, French, late 1800s, 14″ **1,100.00**
    Egyptian revival, black, red marble, sphinx, 4½″......... **225.00**
    Ormolu case, w/shepherdess, porcelain face, 10½″ **680.00**
Metzell, tall case, japanned w/polychrome & gilt, ornate **1,750.00**
Military Aircraft, 24 hour **85.00**
Morbier, concave enamel dial, brass repousse case, pendulum . **380.00**
    Lyre pendulum, Verge escapement, 1850s............... **725.00**
    Mystery, Jefferson Golden Hour, all glass face, gold plated numbers **55.00**
New Haven, banjo, 8-day, ship on pendulum, 33″........... **200.00**
    Banjo, miniature, striking, 17″...................... **325.00**
    Banjo, striking, Westminister **325.00**
    French carriage w/case **250.00**
    Iron case outside escapement, silver decor, 11″......... **130.00**
    Kitchen clock, walnut, 8-day time & strike, ornate **100.00**
    Mantel, Quincy, round dial, low scroll sides, oak **50.00**
    Mantel, fancy pressed oak case, pendulum, 1918 .... **160.00**
    Novelty, Eberle, figural cupid w/lute, bird **50.00**
    Novelty, Haines, fluted column support, 1918 .... **60.00**
    Oak, store Regulator............................... **295.00**
    Style B Merchants, 1918, 6″ dial **170.00**
    Travel, all brass w/red leatherette, folds................ **35.00**
    Wall, Mission, hanging, sq 12″ dial, pendulum **150.00**
    Waring, banjo, large **325.00**
    Westminster chime, tambour **140.00**
    Whitney, banjo **175.00**
Nixon Novelty, dressed in superman suit, wall, plastic, Lendan **70.00**
Occupied Japan, birdcage novelty **170.00**
Pillar & Scroll, mahogany w/paw feet, pineapples, 30″ **500.00**
Powder box, metal, musical w/animated heart beat, WWI **92.00**

Rimbault, bracket, mahogany w/brass handles, ogee feet, 20″ **1,500.00**
Robert Johns, castle figural, bronze plating, 1885, 13x10″.... **140.00**
    Frogs & banjo figural, iron w/copper wash, 1850s, 12x10½″ **155.00**
Robert Fletcher, tall case, oak, upper door, base panel, columns **650.00**
Samuel Terry, pillar & scroll, reverse painting **1,250.00**
Schatz, ship's clock, Royal Marine, brass **275.00**
Sempire, gallery, #3, 14″ dia **240.00**
    Wall, school model #9, 12″ dial **485.00**
Serves, bracket clock, scenics & figurals, 21″............ **1,400.00**
Sessions, alarm, 8-day, table model, 1930, 4½″........... **25.00**
    B-hive Puritan mantel, 8-day strike, porcelain dial **75.00**
    Banjo, 8-day, strike, pendulum, inlay neck, ship, 27″ **180.00**
    Banjo, Narragansett, sailboat scene, 1930 .... **125.00**
    Banjo, Salem, eagle finial, 8″ dial, sailboat **275.00**
    Banjo, standard size, 8-day movement **250.00**
    Keywind, steeple, w/sailing ship on front glass **165.00**
    Mantel, Westminster B, 6″ dial, 1930 .... **80.00**
    Oak, Mission **125.00**
    Regulator, 2-weight, 8-day **725.00**
    Tall case, #9003, broken pediment, columns, weights 78″. **3,000.00**
Seth Thomas #2, Regulator, w/factory stand, walnut **2,600.00**
    Regulator, weight driven **900.00**
Seth Thomas, Office #2, 1880s **200.00**
    Regulator #18, weight, 1885........................ **12.50**
    Art Nouveau novelty, Cis, 1910, 8″ **40.00**
    Art Nouveau novelty, Nan, 1910, 7″ **40.00**
    Banjo **235.00**
    Bank clock, round wht marble, 30-day **600.00**
    Bow front crystal Regulator, ornate dial **425.00**
    Calendar, walnut, brass works, pat 1875, 24″.......... **1,100.00**
    Crystal Regulator, fancy dial....................... **425.00**
    Dresser, Night Clock "A", 7″, 1910................... **40.00**
    Drop Octagon w/calendar, spring type, 1885, 23″ **260.00**
    Fashion, pat 1875, double dial **1,300.00**
    Lever, Lodge, house w/chimney, 3″ dial, 1885 .... **100.00**
    Mantel, Bosnia, black w/gilt trim, 5″ dial **100.00**
    Mantel, New York, 6″ dial, 1910 .... **130.00**
    Mantel, Toulon, gilt columns, 1905 .... **85.00**
    Mantel, Adamantine, w/detached horse **150.00**
    Mantel, Elba, scroll panels, feet, 1905 .... **85.00**
    Mantel, Orchid #6, oval glass, 1905 .... **365.00**
    Mantel, open pillars.............................. **600.00**
    Novelty, Syria, 1905, 16″ **200.00**
    Pendulum, Octagon Top, 1885, 9″ **150.00**
    Pillar & scroll, off-center wind **3,150.00**
    Plymouth Hollow, 30-hour **400.00**
    Regulator, octagonal long drop, 8-day **825.00**
    Serpentine double dial, calendar **950.00**
    Shelf, 2-weights pendulum, Rosewood, 1860 .... **375.00**
    Ship's clock w/bell, chrome case **320.00**
    Spring, Sharp Gothic, 1885, 21″ **145.00**
    Tambour, 8-day, striker, pendulum, 7½″............... **75.00**
    Turned columns, floral reserve, weight, 1885, 25″ **120.00**
    Wall Regulator #2, weight, scroll pediment **200.00**
    Wall Regulator #3, square dial, pendulum.............. **800.00**
    Wall, 8-day time, strike & alarm, rosewood case, reverse painted **425.00**
    Weight, tall case, Fine Regulator #15 .... **4,000.00**
    Weight, Office Calendar #11, 68″ **4,500.00**
    Westminster chime, tambour case, walnut.............. **330.00**
Sevres, bracket, Louis XV, porcelain, bronze mounted, scenic **1,400.00**
Ship's wheel style, brass, wooden spokes, 13″............. **175.00**
Shreve & Co, travel, w/case, brass, enamel face, 4″ **275.00**
Simon Hoadley, grandfather, mahogany tall case **1,850.00**
Sitzendorf, shelf, porcelain w/gilt, 4 figurines **495.00**

Spelter, floor standing, w/figure of Atlas, 5' **3,250.00**
Stannes, banjo clock, bird's eye maple case, 34½" **1,550.00**
Store, regulator, 8-day, cherry case **475.00**
Swiss, grandfather, carved fox & grapes, owl surmount, Trauffer **4,250.00**
Tall case, cherry w/inlay, moon phase, American, 95" **2,000.00**
   Cherry, enamel dial, 30 hr movement, 1800, 97" **1,650.00**
   Queen Anne, japanned, birds, florals, 72" **1,200.00**
   Walnut Chippendale, moon dial, second hand **1,100.00**
   Walnut inlay, swan neck pediment, wood face **1,200.00**
Terry, mahogany, pillar & scroll, reverse painting on glass . . **1,100.00**
Thermometer & barometer, 8 day time & strike, iron, English . **130.00**
Thos Botley, tall case, 8 day, 1820, 89" **1,750.00**
Thwaites Reed, temple style, rolling ball, 16" **1,700.00**
Tiffany & Co, tall case, intricate inlay, turn of the century . . **3,500.00**
Tiffany, ship's clock, Chelsea movement w/bells **425.00**
Time, master clock, standard electric, oak w/tape **690.00**
Train station clock, ci & brass Chelsea, w/place for train arrivals **400.00**
Treasure Isle, 8-day time striker, pendulum **500.00**
   Turtle figural, w/clock under shell, brass plated, Bentley **47.50**
Ungans, carriage, brass handle & ormolu, alarm, 7½" **240.00**
Unghans, bracket, w/chimes, German, 14½" **100.00**
Vermont, Art Nouveau, ci w/gilt wash, platform escapement . . . **600.00**
Vienna Regulator, wall clock, black, 2 weights, 1870, 40½" . . **450.00**
   Wall clock, single weight, transitional stained case, 1870s . . . **450.00**
   Wall clock, walnut, 2 weight, 39½" **400.00**
Wag on Wall, red roses on dial, ci weights **450.00**
Waterbury, Andes, wall model, 1918 . . . . **235.00**
   Drop Octagon, wall model, 1918 . . . . **235.00**
   Banjo, oak, 32" **300.00**
   Carriage, miniature **350.00**
   Crystal Regulator, front escapement **400.00**
   Hall, #74, simple lines, 12" dial, 1918 . . . . **1,000.00**
   Kitchen #9090, ornate oak, 6" dial, 1920 . . . . **150.00**
   Kitchen model #9093, 1930s **165.00**
   Mantel, Belfast, arched pediment, sq base w/scrolls **125.00**
   Mantel, Conductor, square brass & glass case, handle **100.00**
   Mantel, Dwyer, black w/4 gilt columns, scroll feet **90.00**
   Mantel, Florence, 1880 . . . . **125.00**
   Musical, plays on the hour **650.00**
   Octagonal drop, golden oak, 10" dial **250.00**
   Pinwheel Regulator, ornate golden oak, 75" **4,200.00**
   Shelf, mahogany, eagle, 17" **165.00**
   Study #4, 8-day, time & strike, oak **850.00**
   Wall Regulator #18, pendulum, scalloped pediment **600.00**
   Wall Regulator, Berlin, pendulum, Egyptian ornament **900.00**
   Wall Regulator, Ontario, arched pediment, pendulum **550.00**
   Wall, Arion, carved trim, 12" dial, 1918 . . . . **210.00**
   Wall, Fostoria, 1918 . . . . **435.00**
   Westminser chime, #503, mahogany, 24k scrolls, 16¼x13" . **335.00**
Welch, cabinet, #62, 5" dial **110.00**
   Mantel, Andree, scroll feet, gilt columns **100.00**
   Mantel, Dewey, flags, ships, 1900, 6" dial **250.00**
   Mantel, Ulmar, early 1900s, 5" dial **95.00**
   Mantel, Zella, 5" dial **100.00**
Westminster, mantle, mahogany w/reeded pilasters, chimes . . . **385.00**
Whiting, tall case, scrolled crest, grain paint, 89" **1,600.00**
Willard, tall case, mahogany, Federal, 97" **5,000.00**
Wurttenberg, bracket, Westminster chimes ¼ hr, brass works . **325.00**
Yale Co, miniature carriage, nickeled brass, 1881, 3" **80.00**

Cloisonne

Cloisonne is a method of decorating metal with enameling. Fine metal wires are soldered onto the metal body following the lines of a predetermin-ed design. The resulting channels are filled in with enamels of various colors, and the item is fired. The final step is a smoothing process that assures even exposure of the wire pattern.

Ashtray, turquoise & black, w/red, pink & wht flowers **26.00**
Bowl, green band w/multicolor design, 8½" **160.00**
   Green w/multicolor flowers, marked China, 4" **37.50**
   Plique-a-jour, green w/florals, 4¼" **654.00**
   With 5 claw dragons, large seal on bottom, 8" **250.00**
Box, egg shaped, dk green, 4" dia **495.00**
   Figural bird, blue w/black feathers & scrolls, miniature **58.00**
   Foil butterflies, scroll cloisons in blk, lid has foil medallions, 3" dia **155.00**
   Green floral **85.00**
   Oblong, dk red w/wht flowers, 4 compartments, 6x4½" **200.00**
   Quatrefoil, blue w/deer decor, fish scales **90.00**
   Quatrefoil, yellow w/phoenix decor, fish scales **95.00**
   Red w/wht florals, 3 compartments, 1½x3x7" **135.00**
   Round, black & floral, 4¾" dia **85.00**
   Terra cotta w/yellow design, brass foo dog finial, China, 5" dia **95.00**
Candlesticks, ball shape on bell pedestal, 1800s, 6", pair **450.00**
Charger, adventurine, w/dragons, 4 season floral, 12" **450.00**
   Circular center panel w/3 birds, 3" floral border, 12" **295.00**
   Herons, lily pond, blue & red bands, 14½" **350.00**
   Turquoise w/florals & fruit, multicolor border, Japan, 12" . . . **395.00**
   Turquoise w/phoenix, rim band of snakes & florals, 24" . . **2,200.00**
Chocolate pot, miniature, blk w/pink & wht foil goldfish, 3½" . **295.00**
Cockeral figure, rosewood pedestal, 1700s, 11" **750.00**
Cranes, standing, brown w/multicolor feathers & scrolls 7½" pr **665.00**
Foo dogs, w/dragons & birds, removeable heads, 8x9", pr . . **4,000.00**
Ginger jar, black w/pink & red flowers, 4" **85.00**
   Lotus & scroll decor, unmarked, 3x7 dia **225.00**
   Wisteria, blue ground w/lid 8" **950.00**
Horses, prancing, blue w/scroll work & gilding, 5x6" pr **990.00**
Incense burner, bronze, overall turtle design, foo dog finial, 4¼" dia **135.00**
   Gilt lion's heads, 3 legs, 1700s, 8" **450.00**
   Green goldstone, 4" **275.00**
Jar, covered, black w/multicolor flowers, 5½" **135.00**

Kylins, recumbent, 12, pr **1,200.00**
Lamp, Chinese, 37" **1,250.00**
   Hexagonal base, open work, wick, 2½" **165.00**
Opium pipe, multicolor, Chinese, 8" **210.00**
Opium water pipe, w/fixtures, 11x3" **225.00**
Pitcher, urn shape, black w/gold flecks, 4" **140.00**
Planter, swan, 1900, 5x5" **1,000.00**
Plate, blue w/florals, birds, & dragons in reserves, 11¾" **400.00**
Rose jar, w/cover, white w/red & blue florals, 5" **120.00**
Salt set, shaker & open dish, blossoms & foliage, autumn tones **70.00**
Smoke set, floral & animal decor, 3 pc **275.00**
   Floral decor, 4 pc **600.00**
   Match box holder & hinged, covered 3¾" long box **125.00**
Tea set, blue w/butterflies, teapot, creamer & sugar **700.00**
Teapot, goldstone w/phoenix birds & foliage, diaper pattern, 3½x5" **485.00**

Miniature, black w/pink & wht foil goldfish both sides **215.00**
Miniature, goldstone w/butterflies, birds & flowers **210.00**
Multicolor floral, scale decor spout, w/insert, 5″. **500.00**
Red goldstone, 3″. **325.00**
Toothpick holder, yellow w/red & blue flowers, 1½″. **45.00**
Tray, blue w/multicolor florals, 4″ dia. **20.00**
  Blue w/multicolored flowers, fans, 7½″. **100.00**
  Multicolor border, birds & butterflies on black, 8x10″. **275.00**
Vase, aventurine, dragon, flames, florals, 10″. **500.00**
  Beige w/florals, baluster shape, 15″. **675.00**
  Black & florals, 2″ border top & bottom, 11″. **200.00**
  Black & floral, 8¾″. **150.00**
  Black w/flowers & leaves, 5″. **75.00**
  Covered, dragons, flames & florals decor, 7½″. **425.00**
  Emerald green fish scales, wht & red stemmed roses, 7½″. . **290.00**
  Fish scale, sunset & trees, bird & border, 5″. **275.00**
  Florals, lily, flying birds, 1800s, 10″. **600.00**
  Foil panels, w/butterflies & flowers, 6″. **120.00**
  Gourd shape, powder blue w/allover design, 1800s, 11″. . . . **550.00**
  Green, blue florals, China impressed, 6″. **60.00**
  Grey & wht w/birds, trees & berries, 1900, 14″. **600.00**
  Mei ping, blue ground, wide shoulder, narrow base, 1800s, 11½″ **300.00**
  Ornate, 10″. **495.00**
  Ovoid, flaring rim, iris, lily, mum, bird, 12″. **400.00**
  Pigeon blood, ball shape, silver rims, bamboo motif base, 3½″ **85.00**
  Pink w/flowers, blue & wht bird, butterflies, 12x5½″ dia. . **1,000.00**
  Plique-a-jour, green foil w/florals & leaves, 1900, 10″. . . . **325.00**
  Plique-a-jour, shaded green w/multicolor blooming floral, 5″. **800.00**
  Russet w/white lotus scrolls, 6½″. **135.00**
  Shield shaped panels, florals, 1800s, 12″. **425.00**
  Yellow w/turquoise border, brass neck & foot, flowers, China, 5½″ **100.00**

Clothing and Accessories

"Second-hand" or "Vintage"? It's all a matter of opinion. But these days it's considered good taste--downright fashionable--to wear clothing from Victorian to WWII vintage. Jackets with padded shoulders from the 30s are "trendy". Art Deco jewelry from the Art Deco era is just as beautiful and often less expensive than current copies. Victorian blouses on models with Gibson Girl hair styles are pictured in leading fashion magazines--but why settle for new, when the genuine article can be bought for the same price with exquisite lace no reproduction can rival.

Apron, long, crochet & tatted hem & tie ends **40.00**
  Long, wht w/crocheted hem & insert, Victorian **17.00**
  White checked w/black feather stitching **18.00**
  White w/eyelet trim **18.00**
Bathing suit, grey wool, 1920s, buttons at shoulders, orig label . **15.00**
Bed jacket, cotton, wht w/rose print, peter pan collar, 2 tie closures **10.00**
  Sheer silk chiffon, turquoise, lace under yokes **25.00**
Bloomers **8.00**
Blouse, batiste w/middy collar, white embroidered **25.00**
  Black lace, button front, 1940s. **6.00**
  Sheer wht nylon, tucked & button front, collar, long sleeves, 1940 **14.00**
  Victorian, wht w/stripe pattern print, peplum, ¾ sleeve . . . **18.00**
Bodice, Silk, fiddleback, tucked bib, gingham lined, lapels, 1870 **45.00**
  Wool, high collar, inset silk yoke, bow at waist, 1895 . . . . . . **450.00**
Bonnet, baby's, crocheted roses w/petals, 1910 . . . . **8.00**
  Baby's handmade, blue satin, w/ribbons & rosettes. **30.00**
  Black velvet, aqua silk-lined brim w/flowers, back ribbons, 1910 **35.00**
  Infant's, fine lace **10.00**
  Riding, black velvet w/satin ties, 1920s **16.50**
  Victorian, navy velvet w/velvet flowers, bow, ribbon ties, 1880s **40.00**
  Victorian, straw, black w/purple ribbon, braid trim **35.00**

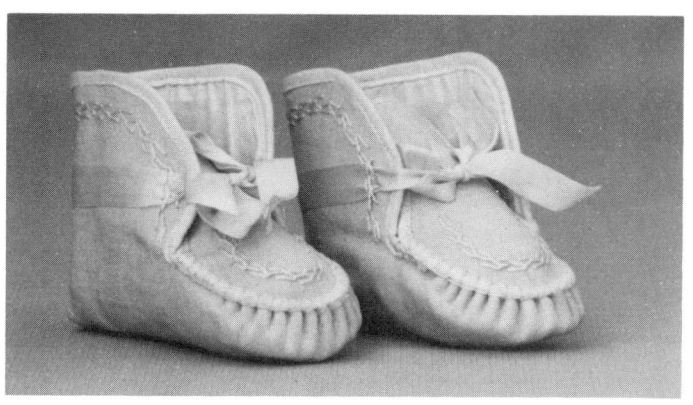

Booties, twill w/embroidery, lined, 1920s **15.00**
Buggy robe, baby's, fur-like w/quilted lining, ruffles, 35x22″. . . . **85.00**
Bunting, baby's, pink satin, seperate hood, 1930s **28.00**
Caftan, old Moroccan velvet, silver/gold ornate embroidery. . . . **450.00**
Camisole, batiste, embroidered flowers, button front, tucked. . . **35.00**
  Cotton w/crochet green top, elastic waist. **15.00**
  Cotton w/pink crochet trim, ribbon strap, button front **15.00**
Cap, black lace & net, lace ties **18.00**
Cape, black plush short 1895 . . . . **30.00**
  Black plush, looks like seal, 1920s **75.00**
  Floor length, purple wool, rolled velvet, bound border. **85.00**
  Hip length, blue, 1870s, Doucet, Paris **150.00**
  Lined broadcloth, ruffled collar, waist length **20.00**
  Peach satin brocade, small sleeves, silk fringe, Paris label. . . **125.00**
  Short, Victorian, black w/ribbon & jet bead trim **22.00**
  Shoulder, black velvet ribbon & taffeta panels, velvet trim. . . **25.00**
  Velvet, rust w/Deco closings, long, 1930s **75.00**
  Victorian, black long beaded & fringed **75.00**
Chemise, embroidered white, 1900s. **18.00**
  Filet crochet top **20.00**
  Irish lace, handmade, 1910. . . . . **10.00**
  Lace trim & insertions, pink embroidery, Wolfhead label. . . . **20.00**
  Pink silk w/lace trim **22.00**
Christening gown, baby's tucked w/lace collar & long sleeves . . . **12.00**
  Elaborate, much lace & tucking, w/petticoat **85.00**
  Much gathering & machine lace, very long, w/slip **50.00**
  Tucked & lace bodice, double ruffled hem **18.00**
Christening set, 3-pc, silk, 1890s **90.00**
Cloak, flapper style, silk velvet, Dolman sleeves, Marabou. . . . **200.00**
Coat, black Karacol, bell sleeves, 1940s **125.00**
  Black grosgrain, cut velvet flowers, black fox cuffs. **100.00**
  Black satin, fur Peter Pan collar, side-button, Hess Bros. . . . **125.00**
  Black velvet, collar forms scarf. **100.00**
  Childs, ecru w/braided frog closures, very old, 17″. **35.00**
  Evening, silk brocade, tone on tone trees, padded shoulders **125.00**
  Fox fur, full length, 1940 . . . . **165.00**
  Fur, street length, 1940s. **65.00**
  Grey Karacol, 1940s **65.00**
  Imitation leopard, suede backing **35.00**
  Man's, raccoon, large **110.00**
  Muskrat fur, ¾ length **750.00**
  Opera, black velvet w/wht fur collar, puffed sleeves **50.00**
  Opera, velvet w/rabbit collar, full length **85.00**
  Velvet, black, beaded, pearl trim at sleeve **90.00**
Collar, beaver fur **22.00**
  Black satin, velvet cord, wht couched embroidery, fringed, 54″ **35.00**
  Machine lace, comes to point in front, 10″ deep front. **22.50**
  Mink dyed marmot **20.00**
  Mink, 1930 . . . . **30.00**
  Red fox **15.00**

Wool w/fur tassels **12.00**
Collar set, mouton lamb, 1930s, 54″ collar, w/matching cuffs & muff **50.00**
Corset cover, pink knit, w/orig label **7.00**
Corset, wht **30.00**
Dress, 2-pc, blk wool, rhinestone studded lapels, Gloria Swanson label **45.00**
3-pc, tiered skirt w/crochet trimmed underskirt, matching bolero **75.00**
Afternoon suit, brown crepe & satin, 1930s **25.00**
Baby's, handmade calico print, lined bodice, 21″ **46.50**
Baby's, handmade, wht w/eyelet inserts, lace, 32″ **50.00**
Baby's, pink ruffles, lace inserts, sleeveless, cap collar, 1920s . **35.00**
Bare back, black crepe & satin, 1940s **20.00**
Batiste, 2 pc shadow stripe, lace at neck, long sleeves, 1905 . **70.00**
Black lace over silk, leg-o-mutton sleeve, fitted jacket, 1895 . **125.00**
Black net lace, 1920s, fancy **40.00**
Brown chiffon, elbow sleeves, apron panel, embroidery, 1900 . **75.00**
Chiffon, orange, slinky Harlow-style w/slip **35.00**
Child's, silk, 1910 . . . . **45.00**
Child's, Victorian, apron panels, ruffled front, much lace **45.00**
Child's, Victorian, beige, Paris Louvre **55.00**
Cocktail, black lace & velvet, 1940s **28.00**
Cocktail, sheer beaded w/wht underslip, fancy, signed Fanny's **110.00**
Embroidered wht, 1900s, double skirt, 1-pc **95.00**
Evening ensemble, jersey w/matching maribou trimmed coat . . **40.00**
Evening, crepe w/gold braid & red silk trim **45.00**
Evening, olive satin, 1940s **25.00**
Evening, taffeta, w/tiers of edged ruffles, velvet sash, 1920s . . . **40.00**
Flapper, all over beading on georgette, low pleats **85.00**
Flapper, beige beaded w/beige & pink satin sash **35.00**
Flapper, black lace tiered, scalloped **65.00**
Flapper, ivory georgette, beaded, silver sequins, Paris label . . . **85.00**
Flapper, navy georgette **20.00**
Flapper, satin w/all over fringe, straps **60.00**
Flapper, scalloped black lace, feather corsage **55.00**
Flapper, sheer, velvet paneled, rhinestone brass buckle **50.00**
Girl's, batiste, embroidered wht **25.00**
Girl's, cotton, crochet covered buttoned back, much lace, 1880s **75.00**
Girl's, organdy, embroidered ½ moons all over, net insert, 1919 **125.00**
Handkerchief silk, floral print, black velvet trim, 1905-10 . . . . **75.00**
Lawn, cream w/lace inserts, 1910 . . . . **22.00**
Long w/ruffle at hem, long sleeves, lined, 1890s **28.00**
Off-shoulder style, wht, mid-1800s **50.00**
Rose lace over taffeta, dubonnet velvet trim, Norman Original **35.00**
Satin, purple, w/slip, pre-WWI **40.00**
Sheer black & gold print, black underslip **25.00**
Velvet, black, w/puffed sleeves, bronze stripes on skirt **45.00**
Velvet, blue, belted, w/padded shoulders & puffy sleeves **27.50**
Victorian, cream silk, tiny florals, lace yoke, & cummerbund **110.00**
Victorian, handmade wht linen w/Irish lace, embroidery **240.00**
With jacket, wht pique w/heavily beaded trim **45.00**
With tucks & whitework embroider **10.00**
Wht lace pointed panels over net, encrusted pearl, Betty Parry **35.00**
Wht w/black polka dots, short sleeves, embroidery **95.00**
Wool, tweed w/lace trim **25.00**
Dress & coat ensemble, red, Gloria Swanson **55.00**
Dressing gown, wht cotton, embroidered lace ruffled yoke & cuffs **70.00**
Duster, auto, child's w/removeable Bertha collar **55.00**
Auto, lady's, cape style **35.00**
Auto, linen 2-pc, w/skirt, fancy, 1900s **45.00**
Auto, man's **25.00**
Auto, silk, 1900s **35.00**
Gloves, elbow length, wht kid **9.00**
Gloves, leather w/rhinestones, Germany **28.00**
Gown, evening, 2-pc grey taffeta, fringed bodice, peplum jacket, 1860s **75.00**
Evening, 2-pc brown satin brocade, velvet trim, 1870s **55.00**

Evening, black w/sequins, plunging neckline, 1930s, N.Y. Dress Co **45.00**
Evening, brown velvet, bias cut, low neck, brass buckled sash, 1920 **65.00**
Evening, coral velvet & net, w/snap on stole, 1950s **20.00**
Evening, taffeta, flecked design, 1939 . . . . **20.00**
Evening, velvet w/beaded trim, short sleeves, 1940s **55.00**
Evening, Victorian, black lace over ivory satin, short train, 1890s **75.00**
Evening, yellow sheer over taffeta, puff sleeves, ruffles, 1920s . **35.00**
Silk 2-pc, rust color, pre-Civil War **110.00**
Gymn suit, cotton sateen, 1-pc, bloomer type, early 1900s **8.00**
Hat & muff, brown Alaskan seal, pillbox hat, matching muff **40.00**
Hat, beret-type, black velvet w/velvet ties, 1920s **12.50**
Black velvet, full crown, swoop picture brim, feather trim, 1918 **35.00**
Bushel basket, 1905-10, black straw, large bow, flowers **30.00**
Felt, 1920s **48.00**
Imitation leopard, suede backing **10.00**
Navy velvet w/veil, Sally Victor **8.50**
Straw, turned-up brim, velvet trim, raffia flowers, net, 1915 . . . **35.00**
Velvet, 2-10″ ostrich plumes, handstitching, black bead hatpin **12.00**
Jacket, Asian mink, waist length, 1920 . . . . **1,700.00**
Baby seal fur, brown, flared back **250.00**
Bengaline, ¾-length black w/cardinal sleeves **65.00**
Bolaro, silk crepe, puckered **35.00**
Boxy, grey caracul fur, 1940s **50.00**
Cape-style, black Persian fur, collared **50.00**
Fox fur **350.00**
Lace over taffeta, early **15.00**
Maribou, grey, short, 1930s **75.00**
Waist, black crepe, Victorian **20.00**
Waist, black silk, tucked bodice & sleeves **25.00**
Kimono, pink rayon w/gold dragons **45.00**
Pure silk, much gilt, old **85.00**
Silk, floral decor, 1920s **90.00**
Silk, red w/birds & floral embroidery **265.00**
Mittens, baby's, cashmere, pr **16.00**
Muff, alpaca, square, flat **25.00**
Fur, 1920s **19.50**
Mink, lining in excellent condition, large, 1930 . . . . **35.00**
Ocelot **50.00**
Nightgown, long, wht w/tucked yoke, button front, long sleeves . **50.00**
Silk w/lace trim, 1940 . . . . **19.00**
Silk, aqua w/matching bed jacket **40.00**
Silk, coral w/wide lace straps & waist insert, 1930s **22.00**
Wht cotton, crochet yoke & pocket, tucking **18.00**
Pajamas, rayon w/lace trim, never worn, 1940s **26.00**
Pantaloons, wht cotton, eyelet trim **14.00**
Parasol, black chiffon, ruffled, 1890s **50.00**
Parasol, child's, pink paper & cloth **15.00**
Petticoat, long, black sateen w/flannel lining **18.00**
Long, fancy embroidered wht **35.00**
Long, wht w/pocket & ruffle at bottom **25.00**
Short, wht **6.00**
Wht cotton w/eyelet trim, tucking & embroidery **14.00**
Wht cotton w/eyelet trim **7.50**
Wht, Victorian, bustle back, w/lace & tucking **65.00**
Wht w/embroidery, open work lace, scalloped hem **22.00**
Robe, chenille, w/peacock on back, eyes along bottom **75.00**
Chinese embossed silk, 43″ **75.00**
Satin w/fur collar, Harlow-style **65.00**
Scarf, brown fox **30.00**
Fox, silver tip **58.00**
Mink, 2 skin **40.00**
Mink, 4 skin **45.00**
Russian squirrel, 2 skin **35.00**
Shawl, embroidered w/extra long fringe, heavy, large **85.00**

Silk, black w/ivory roses & long fringe, large **75.00**
Silk, cream w/long fringes, 42″ square................... **25.00**
Silk, peacocks & flowers decor....................... **50.00**
Wool paisley, mid-1800s **145.00**
Shirt, Hawaiian, blue w/green & wht sailboats, shell buttons **25.00**
Shoes, child's 5 button **12.00**
   Child's, leather w/brass toe trim, dated 1857. .... **55.00**
   High top silk, salesman's sample, dated 1860 .... **58.00**
   Lady's, black leather, 1890s **45.00**
   Lady's, high-top button, black velvet bottom, cloth uppers.... **45.00**
   Men's, leather hightop button, late 1800s **38.00**
Skirt, batiste, w/lace trim & tucks, wht embroidered **30.00**
   Blue early calico **60.00**
   Hoop, wire on linen, w/shoulder straps **25.00**
   Pink felt w/black poodles, 1950s **25.00**
   Thin, ribbon trim, Victorian **40.00**
   Tiered, embroidered wht............................ **50.00**
   Victorian, wht w/extensive floral cutwork, white work trim.... **65.00**
   Wht cotton gabardine, 32″ length w/pockets, 1915 .... **8.00**
   Wool, brown w/velvet & embroidered trim, Victorian **50.00**
   Wool, Victorian **25.00**
Slip, blue & wht check **45.00**
   Tucked w/lace insert, wht embroidered **30.00**
   Wht w/whitework embroidery **8.00**
Stockings, child's, handknit, early, tan & white stripe, buttons .. **24.00**
Stole, black seal, 5′ **40.00**
Stole, squirrel **21.00**
Suit, lady's, padded shoulders, tweed, 1940s............... **25.00**

Suit, velvet, satin & lace w/bead and embroidered trim **185.00**
Suit, man's, pongee w/2 pr pants, early 1930s **45.00**
Sunbonnet, brown calico, ruffled edge, long over shoulders, 1840s **55.00**
Tap pants, silk, peach, flower embroidery, scalloped legs, 1930s **15.00**
Teagown, printed linen, velvet yoke..................... **75.00**
Teddy, satin, blue, horizontal rows of lace, wide lace at bodice, 1930s **20.00**
Teddy, silk, peach, cutout sides, bra type back, lace trim, 1930s **25.00**
Top hat, black w/bow **60.00**
Trousseau ensemble, long robe w/train, short gown, bloomers, 1885 **150.00**
Trousers, gabardine w/pleats, 1930s **20.00**
Vest, man's, floral velvet, 1850s...................... **45.00**
Vest, man's, herringbone wool, 1930s **20.00**
Waist, purple taffeta, 1890s **17.00**
Waist, Victorian, lined w/velvet trim **40.00**
Wedding gown, full skirt, 1920 embroidered on net **43.00**
   Satin w/lace insert sleeves, bias cut, 1930 .... **54.00**
   Satin, floor length, 4′ train, seed pearls, 1920s **125.00**

Silk, 2 pc, skirt has train, 1900 .... **60.00**

Cluthra

Frederick Carder developed Cluthra glass while at the Steuben Glass Works. It is found in both solid color and shaded ware, and is characterized by a spotty appearance resulting from small air pockets traped between its two layers.

Torchere shade, white shading to rose, 11x7½″............ **215.00**
Urn vase, blue, Steuben **395.00**
Vase, Art Nouveau, female form, light blue **195.00**
   Bottle shape, royal blue & clear, pontil **60.00**
   Bulbous, 4 colors, wide rim, Kimball, 6½x6½″........... **795.00**
   Bulbous, blue, Kimble, 10″ **275.00**
   Bulbous, flaring, yellow, wht, lt orange, Kimble, 6½″ **495.00**
   Classic shape, pink/red, Steuben, 8½″ **800.00**
   Classic shape, tangerine, Kimball, dated, 7″ **175.00**
   Cylinder w/gourd base, white, Kimble, 7¾″ **155.00**
   Lavender, Steuben, 12x11″.......................... **800.00**
   Orange & grey mottled, Kimble, 9″ **350.00**
   Pink, Steuben, 5″ **275.00**
   Strawberry, signed Steuben fleu-de-lis, 11x9″.......... **950.00**
   Strawberry, #2683, Steuben, 8″ **650.00**

Coalport

John Rose purchased the Caughley factory from Thomas Turned in 1799 adding that holding to his own pottery he had built two years before in Coalport. The porcelain produced there before 1814 was unmarked, with very few exceptions. After 1820, some examples were marked with a number 2 with an oversize top loop. The term Coalbrookdale refers to a fine type of porcelain decorated in floral bas relief, similar to the work of Dresden.

After 1835, highly decorated ware with rich ground colors imitated the work of Serves and Chelsea, even going so far as to copy their marks.

From about 1895 until about 1920, the mark in use was Coalport over a crown, with England, A D 1750, indicating the date claimed as the founding, not the date of manufacture.

During the 1920s until 1945, Made in England over a crown, and Coalport below was used. Later Coalport again got top billing, over a smaller crown, with Made in England in a curve below.

Bouillon, Adelock #763/F, green & gold w/floral trim **28.00**
Cup & saucer, Tree of Life, large **35.00**
Figurine, silversmith, matt glaze, 8x8″ **595.00**
Flower pot, frog cover, florals in reserve, 1800s **850.00**
Jardiniere, w/separate footed stand, florals & fluting **200.00**
Mug, white w/leaf decor, 4½″ **85.00**
Plate, center w/hp bird in forest by JH Plant, 9½″ **275.00**
Plate, Tree of Life, scalloped, 6″..................... **60.00**
Plate, Tree of Life **35.00**
Sauce boat & underplate, Revelry, w/cupids **35.00**
Teacup, Tree of Life, small **20.00**
Urn, portrait, 6″ **130.00**
Vase, baluster w/lid, hp & encrusted florals, 1830, 16½″ **250.00**
   Scrolled feet, w/handles, hp & encrusted florals, 10½″ **350.00**

Coffee Grinders

In Grandma's day the task of choosing the brand of coffee she prefered was simple. She bought the whole beans in bulk from a wooden barrel, had them ground to order, or ground them at home to suit herself. There were patented grinders of every description to make the task a simple one.

Crown, #1, black enamel finish, brass cover **20.00**

Crystal, wall mount, glass jar **40.00**
Elgin National **365.00**
Elma, tin w/bottom drawer **50.00**
Enterprise, #1 . . . . **150.00**
   #9, eagle finial **345.00**
   #12, ci, large w/double wheel **400.00**
   #78, floor model **650.00**
   Orig red paint & labels, 2 iron wheels, handle **295.00**
   Store model, 2 wheels, eagle on hopper **400.00**
Ever Ready, #2, original & complete **420.00**
Everett, hand held, 1890 . . . . **24.00**
Grand Union, tin, wall hanging, picture of George Washington **195.00**
Grand Union Tea Co, red **85.00**
Lap, ci, brass plate signed Kenrick, porcelain-lined cup, iron drawer **69.00**
Lap, oak, ci top, Imperial **70.00**
My-T-Good Luck, 1906 . . . . **40.00**
Parker, #50 wall hanging, black ci & tin w/embossed eagle **40.00**
Star, #14, large double wheel, ci **525.00**
Star, iron, red paint w/black trim, 2 large wheels, handle 1 side **375.00**
Store Model, Fairbanks Morse **390.00**
Tabletop, w/glass bean bin **30.00**
Tin, blue paint, old **45.00**
Universal, #110, tin w/red decal **65.00**
Wall hanging, Golden Rule Coffee **40.00**
Wood, Delmew Coffee Mills, Simons Hardware, St Louis **60.00**
   Dovetailed 4 corners, fancy iron turnhandle, 1890s, pull drawer **85.00**

Coin Operated Machines

   Slot machines may be the fastest appreciating collectible on the market today. Legal in about half of the states, many are bought, restored and used for home entertainment. The rate of appreciation has been estimated at 20% per year to 5% monthly. Older machines from the turn of the century, and those with especially elaborate decoration and innovative accessories are most desirable, often bringing prices in excess of $5,000.00.

   Vending machines sold a product or a service. They were already in common usage by 1900, selling gum, cigars, matches and a host of other commodities.

   For one penny, arcade machines would entertain you with flip cards, test your strength or tell your fortune!

   The coin operated phonograph of the early 1900s paved the way for the jukeboxes of the 20s. Seeburg was first on the market with an automatic 8-tune phonograph. By the 1930s, Wurlitzer was the top name in the industry, with dealerships all over the country. As a result of the growing ranks of competitors, the 40s produced the most beautiful machines made. Wurlitzers from this era are probably the most popularly sought after models on the market today. The 1015 of 1946 is considered the all time classic, and often brings prices in excess of $4,500.00.

Advance Peanut machine **100.00**
Ajax Triple Hot Nut Vendor, restored **175.00**
American Eagle 1¢ gum dispenser **300.00**
Andes Sweet Chocolate 1¢ vendor **95.00**
Ansco Hot Nut Vendor, unrestored **75.00**
Apple Vendor, 5¢ **225.00**
Asco Hot Nut 1¢ vendor, all orig, 20″ **135.00**
Atlas Platter Gumball vendor **90.00**
Ball Spotlite, in line or bingo game, 1950s **500.00**
Bally Coin Pay out gaming device **1,750.00**
Barbell Strength Test machine, floor model, 1¢ **900.00**
Best Hand **295.00**
Bluebird Penny Drop **235.00**
Boop-a-Doop 1¢ Whirlball, restored **300.00**
Buffalo 1¢ Shooting Game w/gum dispenser **145.00**

Call-o-Scope, card viewer, refinished **975.00**
Catch Kicker, 1¢ counter top game **285.00**
Challenger **145.00**
Chicago Coins Band Box, attachment for jukebox **2,300.00**
Cigar vendor, Peter's Mfg Co, oak, 1903 . . . . **750.00**
Climax 10 Peanut Machine, mint **1,100.00**
Columbus "A" Peanut, restored **195.00**
Columbus Vendor Model 21, hex globe **250.00**
Derby Lite, counter top horse race **135.00**
Dice game, Exhibit Supply, counter model **130.00**
Dice machine, 1¢, ci, mint **495.00**
Double Nugget Peanut, restored **125.00**
Duck Shoot gum machine **110.00**
EZ Derby gumball machine **500.00**
EZ Gumball, Zodiac model, mint **500.00**
Evans Races, Long Shot Model 5¢, restored **5,000.00**
Exhibit 1¢ coin changer, ci & brass, restored **235.00**
Filling Station for Pocket Lighters, 1¢ **225.00**
Ford vendor, orig green paint, slug rejector **85.00**
Game-o-Skill, Mills 5¢ **450.00**
Gator Grandfather Clock Strength Test, mint **1,750.00**
Globe Ball Grip machine, mint restored **2,295.00**
Golden Arm Strength Tester **160.00**
Grip Tester 1¢, Kennedy, Wright City, Mo. **135.00**
Hawk Eye, book match dispenser, orig **80.00**
Hershey's Chocolate 1¢ vendor **85.00**
Ironclaw digger restored, early **1,250.00**
Jaw Breaker gum ball 1¢, WWII **35.00**
Jennings The Target Penny Drop, restored **500.00**

Juke Box
AMI Model C, restored **495.00**
Capehart w/radio combination, wood case, 5¢ **1,500.00**
Phono Junior **1,000.00**
Rock-Ola, 3 . . . . **525.00**
   160 Rhapsody **495.00**
   1422 . . . . **1,750.00**
   1426 . . . . **1,250.00**
   1428 . . . . **1,350.00**
   1934 . . . . **550.00**
   1939 . . . . **995.00**
Sabels **2,700.00**
Seeburg 147A **350.00**
   1947 . . . . **2,500.00**
   Selectaphone 5¢ back if you guess the record **700.00**
   Stereo Showcase **495.00**
Sonata 1050, excellent orig condition **3,800.00**
Speaker, counter, chrome Art Deco, 1930s **375.00**
Wurlitzer, P10 . . . . **535.00**
   51 . . . . **1,950.00**
   61 countertop **1,350.00**
   61 w/base **1,500.00**
   81 . . . . **2,400.00**
   750 . . . . **2,100.00**
   780L **3,800.00**
   789 . . . . **950.00**
   800 . . . . **1,000.00**
   850 . . . . **6,500.00**
   950 . . . . **3,600.00**
   1015 . . . . **4,750.00**
   1080 . . . . **3,650.00**

Kandy King Tab Gum vendor, good orig **45.00**
Kicker-Catcher **145.00**
Love Meter **125.00**

Lucky Strike 1ᶜ for 1 cigarette dispenser 400.00
Magna gumball 1ᶜ vendor 200.00
Match dispenser, Albert Pick 125.00
Match vendor, 4 column 425.00
   Ci, 3-column, pat 1904 Kelley Mfg Co 650.00
Mercury Grip Tester 95.00
Mercury athletic scale grip machine, 1ᶜ 150.00
Mills 1ᶜ Punching Bag 1,000.00
   Counter Upright Owl, complete 4,600.00
   Electricity Is Life, orig, restored 5,850.00
   Special, ci gambling machine, 1905 . . . . 2,500.00
Mint vendor, 5 slots, 1923 . . . . 145.00
Moderne Gum Ball Machine, aluminum, good orig 375.00
Monkey Lift Test 995.00
Mutoscope, Magic Pen Digger type 1,400.00
   Punching bag, oak & ci, 1ᶜ, ex 1,685.00
   Tin 175.00
NW Booze Barometer 5ᶜ 150.00
National Vendors mint, restored 245.00
National gum machine, 1925 . . . . 125.00
Nickelodeon, Seeburg L Model, restored 6,500.00
Northwestern 1ᶜ match vendor, restored 65.00
   33 Gumball, restored 140.00
   33 Jr vendor, blue porcelain, ex restored 450.00
   Porcelain gum machine, #31 . . . . 135.00
Ohio 1ᶜ match dispenser, orig decals 75.00
Parker Pencil vendor, 5ᶜ 200.00
Penny Arcade photo card viewer w/cards 475.00
Penny Flipper, 5 jacks, solid oak case, ornate, w/key 750.00
Pinball, 5 Star Final, 1ᶜ 150.00
   Baffle Ball, 1ᶜ, 1930 . . . . 380.00
   Bally Fireball 1,700.00
   Big Broadcast 650.00
   Bingo 5ᶜ, orig 375.00
   Gottlieb Bank a Ball 300.00
   Gottlieb & Co, 2 player Thoroughbred in play 265.00
   Gottlieb Hurdy Gurdy 400.00
   Juggle Ball, 1ᶜ 750.00
   Lucky Seven, 5ᶜ, 1930, oak 385.00
   Mat-cha-skor 200.00
   Negroes shooting dice, 1920 . . . . 400.00
   Play-Boy, w/stand 495.00
   Racehorse, cash payout, 1941 . . . . 750.00
   Williams Jalopy w/Auto Race, 1950s 500.00
Playball Baseball 1ᶜ game 190.00
Pollard Football 1,350.00
Professor, Dr Kings Peppermint Gum vendor, animated 1,750.00
Pulver Chocolate Cocoa Gum machine, pat 1889 . . . . 675.00
Pulver Gum 1ᶜ dispenser, 36" 125.00
Rock-Ola scales, Low Boy 130.00
Rocket ship gum ball, 6 for 1ᶜ, plastic 30.00
Roovers Floor Shocker 1,950.00
Rowe Art Deco cigarette vendor 180.00
Scoopy Baker Boy 1ᶜ gum vendor 1,100.00
Shooting Gallery, Challenge, 1940s 165.00
Silver King vendor, ci w/orig paint & decal 150.00
Silver King, gum ball machine, restored 65.00
Simmons Peanut vendor, orig globe, ci base 200.00
Slot
20th Century 25ᶜ 9,750.00
Buckley Pointmakers, electric 495.00
Buckley 25ᶜ 1,200.00
Caille, 5ᶜ Cadet 800.00
   5ᶜ Commander 800.00

5ᶜ Sphinx, restored 1,400.00
10ᶜ Doughboy, rebuilt 845.00
10ᶜ Superior Jackpot, mint 1,150.00
25ᶜ Victory Center Pull, nude front, restored 6,750.00
Centaur, ex orig 13,250.00
Dewey, 5ᶜ floor model, orig condition 6,900.00
Dutchess 5ᶜ window mint vendor 1,250.00
Gabels 5ᶜ Chicago 12,850.00
Groetchen 10ᶜ Columbia 1,100.00
Jennings, 1ᶜ Little Duke w/side vendor, restored 2,250.00
   5ᶜ 4-Star Chief 1,150.00
   5ᶜ Bronze Chief, good 850.00
   5ᶜ Club Special, ex orig 1,900.00
   5ᶜ Dixie Belle, restored 1,800.00
   5ᶜ Duchess vendor front, restored 1,050.00
   5ᶜ Dutch Boy, restored 1,650.00
   5ᶜ Operators Bell, ci w/side vendor 2,600.00
   5ᶜ Sun Chief 1,150.00
   5ᶜ Vest Pocket, restored 550.00
   5ᶜ Victoria #7 w/Deco front 1,450.00
   5ᶜ Victory Chief 1,150.00
   5ᶜ Witch, restored 5,000.00
   10ᶜ Silvermoon Club 1,050.00
   25ᶜ Monte Carlo 3,250.00
   25ᶜ Standard Chief 1,200.00
   25ᶜ Sun Chiefs Tic Tac Toe, restored 1,500.00
   5ᶜ/25ᶜ Challenger 1,650.00
   $1 Silver Chief 2,150.00
   $1 Standard Chief 2,500.00
   Jack Pot Dutch Boy, 1929 . . . . 3,000.00
   Little Duck 1,750.00

Operators Bell, wood front 2,200.00
Rockaway, 5 jacks, restored 1,200.00
Keeney 5ᶜ Bonus Super Bell 795.00
Liberty 5ᶜ counter top, 3 reels, w/keys 495.00
Mills 1ᶜ Firebird QT, orig 1,600.00
   1ᶜ OK Goose Neck 1,250.00
   1ᶜ Skyscrapper Gooseneck, orig 1,400.00
   5ᶜ Black Cherry 1,100.00
   5ᶜ Bursting Cherry, restored 1,400.00
   5ᶜ Castle Front 1,100.00
   5ᶜ Club Extraordinary, ex 1,400.00
   5ᶜ Firebird QT, restored 1,200.00
   5ᶜ Futurity 2,495.00
   5ᶜ Hi-Top 777, ex orig 1,350.00
   5ᶜ Hi-top 21, guaranteed jackpot, ex 1,200.00
   5ᶜ Hightop, restored 1,100.00
   5ᶜ Illusion, curved glass ci front & top, restored 2,100.00

5ᶜ Lion's Head, restored	1,500.00
5ᶜ Poinsettia, original	1,500.00
5ᶜ Roberts Goose	1,200.00
5ᶜ Rock-ola Triple Jackpot	1,450.00
5ᶜ Roman Head, gold award, restored	2,700.00
5ᶜ Silent FOK vendor front, restored	1,550.00
5ᶜ Skyscraper	1,050.00
5ᶜ Vest Pocket	225.00
5ᶜ War Eagle, original	1,800.00
5ᶜ War Eagle, restored	2,100.00
10ᶜ Brown Front, Bursting Cherry iron case, ex	2,000.00
10ᶜ Cherry Front	1,075.00
10ᶜ Club Extraordinary, ex	1,400.00
10ᶜ Diamond Front	875.00
10ᶜ War Eagle	1,750.00
25ᶜ Black Cherry front	1,150.00
25ᶜ Bursting Cherry, orig parts, restored	1,375.00
25ᶜ Golden Falls, restored	1,750.00
25ᶜ War Eagle, restored	1,750.00
50ᶜ Poinsettia, restored	1,900.00
50ᶜ Roman Head	2,500.00
Check Boy	4,000.00
Mystery Castle Front	2,000.00
Pace 1ᶜ Bantam, excellent	1,350.00
5ᶜ Bantam, good orig condition	1,600.00
5ᶜ Comet w/mint vendor, fortune strips	1,350.00
10ᶜ Butterfly conversion skill stops	1,185.00
10ᶜ Comet, restored	1,350.00
25ᶜ 1929, restored	1,750.00
25ᶜ Royal Comet, floor model	3,250.00
Skelly Bell Jr 25ᶜ, 1928	1,850.00
Stolks Flying Heels	1,250.00
Watling, 5ᶜ Bird of Paradise, good orig	3,500.00
5ᶜ Blue Seal, orig cond	1,200.00

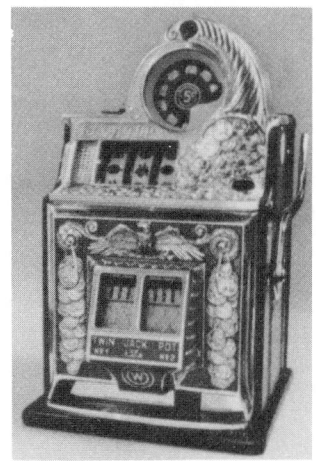

5ᶜ Coin Front Roll-A-Top Bell	3,300.00
5ᶜ Bird of Paradise, good orig	3,500.00
5ᶜ Treasury, restored	3,500.00
10ᶜ Torch Front	1,450.00
Brownie Jackpot, good orig	4,350.00
Checkerboard, restored	3,000.00
Chicago, excellent	13,000.00
Fancy Front twin jackpot	1,200.00
Roll-A-Top, coin front, restored	3,500.00
Roll-A-Top, twin jackpot, Skil Stops, Fortune Reels	3,665.00

Superior Confection gumball, brass body & top	250.00
Talking Scale, 3 jacks, 1ᶜ	650.00

5ᶜ, 1902, ex	4,500.00
Target Penny Drop, Jennings, mint restored	495.00
Test Your Grip, Bottlieb	125.00
Topper 1ᶜ gum vendor	85.00
Trade Stimulator, 5ᶜ I O U	75.00
Ad-Lee 25ᶜ Beat It	250.00
American Eagle 1ᶜ, ex	295.00
American Eagle 5ᶜ, restored	395.00
Bakers 1ᶜ Pick a Pack	425.00
Buckley Puritan	300.00
Chicago Club House	350.00
Daval 1ᶜ Cub, restored	295.00
Daval Free Play	200.00
Daval Reel 21	200.00
Garden City Gem	175.00
Gem Cigarettes, gum vendor	400.00
Gold Rush	125.00
Groetchen High Stakes	400.00
Groetchen Klix	200.00
Groetchen Mercury	175.00
Groetchen Pok-O-Reel	300.00
Groetchen Sparks	350.00
Hi Fly Baseball 5ᶜ flip	265.00
Jennings Ciga-Rola 5ᶜ, buy or win	1,450.00
Kalamazoo Kazoo	200.00
Lark 3-reel, gum dispenser, 9″	250.00
Mills Bell Boy	1,750.00
New Deal w/jackpot	325.00
Pok-O-Reel, Poker game, 1ᶜ or 10ᶜ	550.00
Roulette, restored	450.00
The Bicycle 1893	3,500.00
Wood Deuces Wild	225.00
UG Grandbois 1ᶜ gum	95.00
United ABC, 3 card Bingo, 1950s	500.00
Victor V vendor, restored	95.00
Watling 1ᶜ Fortune Teller, Weighing Machine, 1918	900.00
Watling 1ᶜ scales	395.00
Zena Fortune Teller, English	235.00
Zeno gum machine, wood	475.00

Coin Spot

Coin spot is similar to Inverted Thumbprint, except the despressions are opal glass. It was made by many manufacturers.

Bowl, cranberry, 9½″	80.00
Honeysuckle, 7x3½″	40.00
Creamer, blue w/clear handle, 4″	40.00
Blue w/reed handle, 4″	36.00
Cranberry w/clear handles, 4″	38.00
Cruet, blue cased, 7¾″	65.00
Blue opal	75.00
Blue, 8″	75.00
Vaseline, Baby Coinspot, 7″	40.00
Hat, cranberry, old & thin, 3½x3¾″	50.00
Hurricane lamp, cranberry, 8½″	85.00
Pitcher, blue w/ruffled top, large	75.00
Green opal, crimped & ruffled, applied handle, 9½″	90.00
White opal w/clear handle, 9½x6″	75.00
Shade, white opal, ruffled, 6½″	45.00
Sugar shaker, blue, orig top	95.00
Syrup, clear to opal	60.00
Cranberry opal	90.00
Tumbler, blue opal	25.00

Cranberry opal **35.00**
Green opal, 5x3″ **15.00**
Vase, Baby Coin spot, cranberry w/crimped ruffled top, 8″ **50.00**
Cranberry, ruffled & crimped, 8x8″ **75.00**
Cranberry, ruffled rim, 4x5″ **30.00**
Cranberry w/opal, ruffle edge, 10″ **150.00**
Green & lime opal, 11″ **65.00**
White opal, ruffled rim, 3½x4¼″ **22.00**
White opal, ruffled rim, 6x61½″ **35.00**

Collector Plates

After a period of reduced activity in the market of limited edition plates, a renewed enthusiasm, brought on perhaps by full-scale publicity effected through direct mailing, magazines and national television has established what many collectors optimistically regard as a solid secondary market. As a result, values of choice issues are steadily appreciating--first editions usually prove the best investment. In the listings that follow, they are indicated by the letters FE.

Two of the earliest manufacturers of Christmas plates were Bing and Grondahl who issued their first plate in 1895, and the Royal Copenhagen Porcelain Manufactory following with their series in 1908. In this country, Frankoma Pottery began producing limited edition plates in 1965. Today they have been joined by well over 100 manufacturers and marketing organizations, world-wide.

There are several specific publications and many other sources of information available to keep today's collector aware of current market trends. Only a few are listed here to represent some of the more familiar companies.

Anna Perenna
1978, Firebird **90.00**
1978, June Dream **60.00**
1979, Oliver's Birthday **140.00**
1979, Romeo and Juliet **100.00**
1980, Jerusalem Triptych **315.00**
1981, Clowns and Unicorns **85.00**
Anri
1971, St Jakob in Groden **110.00**
1972, Alpine Mother & Children **45.00**
1972, Boy **135.00**
1972, Children Play House **125.00**
1972, Christ in the Manger **150.00**
1972, Finishing Cradle, FE **210.00**
1972, Pipers at Alberobello **115.00**
1973, Alpine Horn **315.00**
1973, Wedding Scene **80.00**
1974, Alpine Father & Children **75.00**
1974, Young Man and Girl **90.00**
1975, Christmas in Ireland **90.00**
1975, Flight into Egypt **105.00**
1975, Mother & Dove **100.00**
1976, Knitting **60.00**
1976, Mother & Child **90.00**
1976, Sailing **95.00**
1977, Cliff Gazing **80.00**
1978, Klockler Singers **100.00**
1978, Leading the Way **85.00**
1979, All Hearts **105.00**
1979, The Drummer **105.00**
1980, Rejoice **155.00**
1980, Wintry Churchgoing **155.00**
Bing & Grondahl
1895, Frozen Window **3,420.00**
1896, New Moon **1,900.00**

1897, Sparrow **1,170.00**
1898, Roses and Star **720.00**
1899, Crows **1,800.00**
1900, Church Bells **720.00**
1901, Three Wise Men **360.00**
1902, Gothic Church Interior **350.00**
1903, Expectant Children **260.00**
1905, Christmas Night **145.00**
1907, Little Match Girl **120.00**
1909, Yule Tree **95.00**
1910, Easter Plaque **115.00**
1910, The Old Organist **95.00**
1911, Angels & Shepherds **85.00**
1911, Easter Plaque **80.00**
1913, Bringing Home the Tree **90.00**
1915, Dog Outside **125.00**
1917, Christmas Boat **90.00**
1918, Easter Plaque **60.00**
1919, Outside Lighted Window **85.00**
1920, Church Bells **105.00**
1920, Easter Plaque **70.00**
1922, Star of Bethlehem **70.00**
1925, Child's Christmas **75.00**
1925, Dog Outside Window **190.00**
1928, Eskimos **70.00**
1929, Easter Plaque **140.00**
1930, The Old Organist **225.00**
1930, Town Hall **105.00**
1931, Easter Plaque **180.00**
1932, Lifeboat **90.00**
1934, Easter Plaque **515.00**
1935, Easter Plaque **675.00**
1935, Lillebelt Bridge **80.00**
1935, Little Match Girl **900.00**
1938, Lighting Candles **125.00**
1940, Three Wise Men **1,800.00**
1941, Horses **295.00**
1944, Sorgenfri Castle **110.00**
1945, Amalienborg Castle **295.00**
1947, Dybbol Mill **90.00**
1950, Eskimos **245.00**
1950, Kronborg Castle **140.00**
1953, Royal Boat **80.00**
1955, Kalundborg Church **110.00**
1956, Christmas in Copenhagen **125.00**
1959, Christmas Eve **125.00**
1960, Kronborg Castle **190.00**
1962, Winter Night **75.00**
1965, Bringing Home the Tree **55.00**
1965, Churchgoers **115.00**
1968, Christmas in Church **45.00**
1969, Dog & Puppies **440.00**

1970, Pheasants in Snow **25.00**

1971, Cat & Kitten 15.00
1971, Christmas at Home 20.00
1974, Christmas in Village 17.00
1975, Doe & Fawn 25.00
1980, Christmas in Woods 40.00
1981, Hare & Young 35.00

Goebel
1971, Heavenly Angel 800.00
1972, Hear Ye 70.00
1973, Globe Trotter 170.00
1974, Goose Girl 90.00
1974, Robin 55.00
1975, Rabbits 30.00
1975, Ride into Christmas 80.00
1976, Apple Tree Girl 70.00
1976, Barn Owl 45.00
1977, Apple Tree Boy 100.00
1977, Pandas 40.00
1978, 12 Tribes of Israel 110.00
1978, Happy Pastime 90.00
1979, 10 Commandments 155.00
1979, Owls 60.00
1979, Singing Lesson 65.00
1980, Schoolgirl 80.00
1980, Traditions 200.00
1981, Umbrella Boy 80.00

Gorham
1971, Boy & Dog, Rockwell, set of 4 . . . . 445.00
1971, Quiet Waters, FE 20.00
1971, Rembrandt, FE 25.00
1972, Little Boatyard 130.00
1972, Young Love, Rockwell, set of 4 . . . . 180.00
1973, Ages of Love, Rockwell, set of 4 . . . . 305.00
1973, Christmas March, FE 35.00
1973, Mother's Day, FE 30.00
1973, New Year on the Cimarron 35.00
1974, Grandpa & Me, Rockwell, set of 4 . . . . . . 155.00
1974, Tiny Tim 75.00
1975, Me and My Pal, Rockwell, set of 4 . . . . . . 170.00
1975, Mother's Day 15.00
1975, Old Ramond 35.00
1975, Our Heritage 55.00
1976, 200 Years With Old Glory 55.00
1976, A Scout Is Loyal 50.00
1976, Cavalry Officer 40.00
1976, Christmas Tree 15.00
1976, Christmas Trio 55.00
1976, Grand Pals, Rockwell, set of 4 . . . . 190.00
1976, Kennedy 50.00
1976, Moppet Couple 13.00
1977, A Good Sign 35.00
1977, Christmas Visit 29.00
1977, Going on Sixteen, Rockwell, set of 4 . . . . 180.00
1977, The Scoutmaster 55.00
1977, Yuletide Reckoning 35.00
1978, Mother's Day 10.00
1978, The Tender Years, Rockwell, set of 4 . . . . 105.00
1979, A Helping Hand, Rockwell, set of 4 . . . . . 90.00
1980, Beyond the Easel 40.00
1980, Dad's Boy, Rockwell, set of 4 . . . . 120.00
1980, Letter to Santa 28.00
1980, Summer Respite 40.00
1981, Moppets Christmas 12.00
1981, Old Timers, Rockwell, set of 4 . . . . 90.00

Lenox
1970, Wood Thrush 270.00
1971, Goldfinch 80.00
1972, Bird of Peace 270.00
1972, Mountain Bluebird 60.00
Lincoln 25.00
1973, Raccoons 80.00
1974, Red Fox 45.00
1974, Rufous Hummingbird 60.00
1976, Cardinals 50.00
1976, Chipmunks 55.00
1978, Mockingbirds 55.00
1978, White-tailed Deer 55.00
1980, Black-Throated Blue Warbler 70.00
1980, Bobcats 85.00

Pickard
1970, Woodcock & Grouse, pr 290.00
1973, Pheasant & Wild Turkey, pr 175.00
1974, American Bald Eagle 550.00
1976, Alba Madonna 215.00
1976, American Buffalo 170.00
1977, Nativity 125.00
1978, Girl with Watering Can 205.00
1978, Rest on the Flight into Egypt 90.00
1979, At the Piano 105.00
1979, Red Foxes 105.00
1980, Madonna and Child 70.00
1980, Miracle 180.00

River Shore
1976, Lincoln 360.00
1977, Bronco Buster 45.00
1977, Triple Self-Portrait 110.00
1979, Adoration 450.00
1979, Akiku 60.00
1979, Spring Flowers 80.00
1980, Cheyenne 55.00
1980, Looking Out to Sea 90.00
1980, Virgin & Child 400.00

Rockwell Museum
1978, Baby's First Step 70.00
1978, First Haircut 30.00
1978, Happy Birthday Dear Mother 40.00
1979, Birthday Party 29.00
1979, Bride and Groom 29.00
1979, Day After Christmas 70.00
1980, New Arrival 30.00
1981, Courageous Hero 33.00
1981, Good Food, Good Friends 33.00
1981, Little Shaver 33.00
1981, Space Pioneers 32.00

Rockwell Society
1974, Scotty Gets His Tree 135.00
1975, Angel With Black Eye 85.00
1976, A Mother's Love 100.00
1977, Toy Maker 245.00
1977, Toy Shop Window 45.00
1978, Bedtime 85.00
1978, The Cobbler 145.00
1979, Somebody's Up There 25.00
1980, A Mother's Pride 25.00
1981, Music Maker 20.00
1981, Wrapped up in Christmas 25.00

Royal Copenhagen
1908, Madonna & Child 1,450.00

1909, Danish Landscape	135.00
1910, The Magi	120.00
1911, Danish Landscape	140.00
1912, Christmas Tree	140.00
1913, Frederik Church Spire	135.00
1914, Holy Spirit Church	110.00
1915, Danish Landscape	125.00
1916, Shepherd & Angel	85.00
1917, Our Saviour's Church	85.00
1918, Shepherds in Field	85.00
1919, The Park	85.00
1920, Mary & Jesus	95.00
1921, Aabenraa Marketplace	75.00
1922, Three Singing Angels	75.00
1923, Danish Landscape	80.00
1924, Star over the Sea	95.00
1925, Christianshavn	90.00
1926, Christianshavn Canal	80.00
1927, Ship's Boy at the Tiller	170.00
1928, Vicar's Family	80.00
1929, Grundtvig Church	75.00
1930, Fishing Boats	90.00
1931, Mother & Child	95.00
1932, Frederiksberg Gardens	95.00
1933, Ferry & The Great Belt	110.00
1934, Hermitage Castle	115.00
1935, Kronborg Castle	130.00
1936, Roskilde Cathedral	125.00
1937, Scene in Main Street	125.00
1938, Round Church in Osteriars	250.00
1939, Greenland Pack-Ice	235.00
1940, The Good Shepherd	325.00
1941, Danish Village Church	340.00
1942, Old Church Bell Tower	380.00
1943, Flight into Egypt	445.00
1944, Typical Winter Scene	185.00
1945, A Peaceful Motif	335.00
1946, Zealand Village Church	150.00
1947, The Good Shepherd	195.00
1948, Nodebo Church	190.00
1949, Church of Our Lady	200.00
1950, Boeslunde Church	235.00
1951, Christmas Angel	375.00
1952, Christmas in the Forest	125.00
1953, Frederiksborg Castle	105.00
1954, Amalienborg Palace	135.00
1955, Fano Girl	195.00
1956, Rosenborg Castle	225.00
1957, The Good Shepherd	110.00
1958, Sunshine Over Greenland	140.00
1959, Christmas Night	175.00
1960, The Stag	215.00
1961, Training Ship Denmark	200.00
1962, The Little Mermaid	180.00
1963, Hojsager Mill	95.00
1964, Fetching the Tree	75.00
1965, Little Skaters	70.00
1967, The Royal Oak	45.00
1967, Virgin Islands	25.00
1969, Danish Flag	25.00
1969, The Old Farmyard	30.00
1971, American Mother	20.00
1971, Hare in Snow	25.00
1972, Munich Olympiad	20.00

1972, Oriental Mother	12.00
1973, Danish Mother	16.00
1975, Queen's Palace	25.00
1977, Twins	24.00
1978, Yellowstone	75.00
1981, The Everglades	75.00
Royal Delft	
1910, Halley's Comet	699.00
1915, Christmas Bells, 10″	5,995.00
1916, Cradle with Child, 10″	335.00
1916, Star Floral Design, 10″	675.00
1917, Christmas Star, 10″	245.00
1917, Shepherd, 10″	400.00
1918, Christmas Star, 10″	235.00
1918, Shepherd, 10″	335.00
1919, Church, 10″	365.00
1920, Church Tower, 10″	344.00
1920, Holly Wreath, 10″	240.00
1921, Canal Boatman, 10″	395.00
1921, Christmas Star, 10″	285.00
1922, Christmas Wreath, 10″	250.00
1922, Landscape, 10″	390.00
1923, Christmas Star, 10″	270.00
1923, Shepherd, 10″	395.00
1924, Christmas Star, 10″	250.00
1924, Shepherd, 10″	380.00
1925, Christmas Star, 10″	240.00
1925, Towngate in Delft, 10″	415.00
1926, Bell Tower, 7″	195.00
1926, Christmas Star, 10″	260.00
1926, Windmill Landscape, 10″	420.00
1927, Christmas Star, 10″	270.00
1927, Sailboat, 10″	435.00
1928, Christmas Poinsettia, 10″	285.00
1928, Lighthouse, 10″	335.00
1928, Mill, 7″	290.00
1929, Christmas Bell, 10″	340.00
1929, Small Dutch Town, 10″	340.00
1930, Christmas Rose, 10″	295.00
1930, Church Entrance, Delft, 10″	320.00
1930, Sailing Boat, 7″	196.00
1931, Christmas Star, 10″	270.00
1931, Snow Landscape, 10″	335.00
1932, Bell Tower, 7″	265.00
1932, Christmas Star, 10″	340.00
1933, Interior Scene, 10″	415.00
1934, Interior Scene, 10″	425.00
1935, Interior Scene, 10″	425.00
1936, Interior Scene, 10″	400.00
1937, Interior Scene, 10″	400.00
1938, Interior Scene, 10″	395.00
1939, Interior Scene, 10″	395.00
1940, Christmas Tree, 10″	400.00
1941, Interior Scene, 10″	395.00
1955, Christmas Star, 9″	150.00
1955, Church Tower, 10″	290.00
1956, Landscape, 10″	290.00
1956, Flower Design, 9″	115.00
1957, Christmas Star, 9″	115.00
1957, First Earth Satellite	85.00
1958, Christmas Star, 9″	115.00
1959, Landscape, 10″	320.00
1959, Landscape with Mill, 7″	115.00
1960, Landscape, 7″	140.00

1960, Street in Delft, 10″	**320.00**
1961, Village Scene, 10″	**310.00**
1962, Tower in Leeuwarden, 10″	**310.00**
1963, Mill in Zeddam, 7″	**135.00**
1963, Tower in Enkhuisen, 10″	**310.00**
1964, Tower in Hoorn, 10″	**310.00**
1965, Corn Mill in Rhoon, 10″	**310.00**
1966, Snuff Mill in Rotterdam, 10″	**300.00**
1966, Towngate in Medemblik, 7″	**135.00**
1967, Tower in Amsterdam, 10″	**335.00**
1968, Tower in Amsterdam, 10″	**315.00**
1969, Church in Utrecht, 10″	**315.00**
1969, Mill near Gorkum, 7″	**115.00**
1970, Cathedral in Veere, 10″	**315.00**
1971, Dom Tower in Utrecht, 10″	**310.00**
1971, Mother & Daughter, Volendam	**75.00**
1971, Towngate at Zierikzee, 7″	**110.00**
1972, Church in Edam, 10″	**300.00**
1973, De Waag in Alkmaar, 10″	**370.00**
1973, Father & Son, Hindeloopen	**70.00**
1973, Valentine, Enduring Beauty	**140.00**
1974, Dutch Easter Palm	**130.00**
1974, Kitchen in Hindeloopen, 10″	**335.00**
1974, Watergate at Sneek, 7″	**145.00**
1975, Apollo Soyuz	**115.00**
1975, Farmer in Laren, 10″	**335.00**
1975, Father & Son, Zuid-Beveland	**105.00**
1976, Dutch Easter Palm	**200.00**
1976, Farm in Staphorst, 10″	**325.00**
1976, George Washington, 9″	**315.00**
1976, Mother & Daughter, Scheveningen	**125.00**
1977, Dromedaris Tower, 7″	**130.00**
1977, Farm in Spakenburg, 10″	**315.00**
1978, Winter Skating Scene, 10″	**240.00**
1979, Christmas in Rhenen, 10″	**225.00**

Royal Doulton

1972, Christmas in England	**45.00**
1973, Christmas in Mexico	**35.00**
1973, Colette & Child	**460.00**
1974, Christmas in Bulgaria	**45.00**
1974, Harlequin	**90.00**
1974, Sayuri & Child	**142.00**
1975, Christmas in Norway	**48.00**
1975, Kristina & Child	**125.00**
1975, San Francisco	**90.00**
1975, Spring Harmony	**80.00**
1976, Christmas in Holland	**40.00**
1976, Dreaming Lotus	**90.00**
1976, Garden of Tranquility	**90.00**
1976, Marilyn & Child	**110.00**
1976, Pierrot	**90.00**
1976, Sailing with the Tide	**115.00**
1976, Victorian Boy & Girl	**65.00**
1977, Christmas in Poland	**60.00**
1977, Columbine	**80.00**
1977, Pennsylvania Pastorale	**90.00**
1977, Running Free	**110.00**
1977, Venice	**65.00**
1977, Winter Fun	**55.00**
1977, A Brighter Day, Lisette De Winne	**78.00**
1978, Christmas Day	**25.00**
1978, Christmas in America	**55.00**
1978, Country Bouquet	**75.00**
1978, Lovejoy Bridge	**80.00**

1978, Kathleen & Child	**85.00**
1978, Punchinello	**75.00**
1978, Sleigh Bells	**70.00**
1979, Christmas	**30.00**
1979, Four Corners	**75.00**
1979, My Valentine	**35.00**
1980, Panchito	**180.00**
1980, Village Children, Lisette De Winne	**65.00**
1981, Adrien	**105.00**

Wedgwood

1969, Windsor Castle	**240.00**
1970, Trafalgar Square	**35.00**
1971, Sportive Love	**30.00**
1971, Zodiac	**30.00**
1972, Boston Tea Party	**40.00**
1972, Sewing Lesson	**30.00**
1973, Butterfly	**145.00**
1973, Paul Revere's Ride	**105.00**
1973, Tower of London	**55.00**
1974, Camelot	**155.00**
1975, Children's Games	**60.00**
1975, Across the Delaware	**100.00**
1975, Mother & Child	**35.00**
1975, Tower Bridge	**45.00**
1976, Declaration Signed	**40.00**
1976, Robin	**25.00**
1977, Innocence	**100.00**
1977, Leisure Time	**30.00**
1977, Westminster Abbey	**45.00**
1979, Sacred Scarab	**35.00**
1980, Oliver Twist & Fagin	**60.00**
1981, Micawber Denouncing Uriah Heep	**60.00**

Compasses

Boy Scout, canvas case, 1920s	**24.00**
Bronze, Cohassett, 23″	**80.00**
Enterprise, two wheel, iron drawer, 8½″	**275.00**
Nautical, brass, w/walnut box & orig instructions	**325.00**
Ship's, old, box 5¼x7½″ wide, Wilcos, Crittendon & Co	**125.00**
Ship's, WWI destroyer, w/orig box	**295.00**
Wood case, polaris, MC Co, 4″ card	**50.00**

Cookbooks

Among the most valuable of the old cookbooks that are becoming popular with collectors today are those issued as advertising premiums. Especially desirable are the figurals that were shaped like a jar, a slice of bread, or some other form pertinent to the product. Others with unique features such as illustrations by well known artists or references to famous people or places are priced in accordance.

Aceola Cookbook, 2nd ed, 1900, 235 pgs	**8.00**
Arm & Hammer Valuable Recipes, 1922, 31 pgs	**4.00**
Boston Cooking School Cookbook, Fannie Farmer, 1945	**12.50**
Calumet Baking Powder Master Cake Baker, 1927	**8.00**
Century of Progress	**12.00**
Coca-Cola, When You Entertain, hardcover, 1932, 124 pgs	**25.00**
Common Sence In The Household, 1887	**20.00**
Cottolene Shortening, 52 Sunday Dinners, 1915, 192 pgs	**4.00**
Denver Post, Prize Recipes, 1932	**5.00**
Dr Morse's Indian Root Pills Cookbook, 1896, 32 pgs	**6.50**
Dr Pierce's Good Cooking, 1900s, 32 pgs	**4.00**
Electric Refrigerator Recipes, Alice Bradley, Gen Elect, 1929, 144 pgs	**3.00**

Everyday Cookbook, 1892 . . . . **20.00**
Favorite Cookbook, 1896 . . . . **45.00**
Favorite Dishes, Columbian Souvenir, 1893 . . . . **22.00**
Fleischmann Yeast Recipe Booklet, 1902, 14 pgs **3.00**
Foods & Household Management, Kinne & Cooley, 1917 . . . . . . **15.00**

Goldmedal Cookbook, 1904 . . . . **8.50**
Gone With The Wind Cookbook, Pebeco Toothpaste, No Date, 48 pgs **7.50**
Granite Ironware Cookbook, 1885, 61 pgs **5.00**
Horsford Almanac & Cookbook, 1886, 36 pgs **5.00**
Jack & Mary's, Gen Foods, cartoon of Benny & Livingston, 1937 **10.00**
Jell-O Cookbook, Rockwell cover, 1923 . . . . **10.00**
Kate Smith's Favorite Recipes, 1940 . . . . **7.00**
Larkin Houswives Cookbook, 1916 . . . . **6.00**
Libby's Evaporated Milk Recipes, can-shaped booklet **3.00**
Lowney's Cookbook, 1912 . . . . **18.00**
Majestic Cookbook, early 1900s, 96 pgs **24.00**
Mickey Mouse Recipe Card, 1930s **6.00**
Mrs Lincoln's Boston, What To Do & What Not To Do, 1886 . . **65.00**
Mrs Rohrer's New Cookbook, 1902 . . . . **10.00**
Pepsi-Cola Recipe Book, 1940 . . . . **9.00**
Pet Milk recipes, 1931 . . . . **3.00**
Ralston Mother Goose Recipe Book, CM Burd, illus, 1919, 15 pgs **5.50**
Ralston Recipes, Burk, illus of Mother Goose, 1922, 25 pgs **3.00**
Royal Baking Powder Co, Baker & Pastry Book, 1911 . . . . **3.00**
Rumford Complete Revised, 1836 . . . . **15.00**

Sleepy Eye Milling Co, figural bread slice **250.00**
Small Sunkist Recipe Book, 1924 . . . . **5.00**
Snow Drift Secrets, gingham cover, 1913, 46 pgs **2.00**
The Enterprising Housekeeper Recipe Book, 1902, 90 pgs **15.00**
The Table How To Buy, Cook & Serve Food, Filippini, 1891, 182 pgs **8.00**

Wesson Oil Let's Enjoy Eating, 1932, 48 pgs **8.00**
WFBL Cookbood Of The Stars, w/photos of radio stars, 1941 . . . **4.00**
White House Cookbook, 1902 . . . . **80.00**
   Ziemann & Gillette, 1905, 590 pgs **25.00**
   1911 . . . . **60.00**
Woman's Exchange Cookbook, 1894 . . . . **40.00**
   Superbly illus, 1902, 510 pgs **15.00**

Cookie Jars

The appeal of the cookie jar is universal; folks of all ages, both male and female, love to collect 'em! The early '30s heavy stoneware jars of a rather nondescript nature, quickly gave way to figurals of every type imaginable. Those from the mid to late '30s were often decorated over the glaze with "cold paint", but by the early '40s underglaze decorating resulted in cheerful, bright, permanent colors and cookie jars that still have a new look 40 years later.

The jars listed here were made by companies other than those represented by other sections.

Alice in Wonderland **25.00**
Aunt Jemima's, plastic, red & white, opens at waist, 10½" **25.00**
Bald Monk, Shalt Not Steal, marked USA **25.00**
Butter Churn with Flowers, USA **18.00**
Cat in Basket, USA **16.00**
Cat on Beehive, American Bisque **16.00**
Cat, sitting, yellow, pink, blk, wht **17.00**
Chick on Chicken, USA Fabco **18.00**
Chick, blue jacket and tan, American Bisque **12.50**
Churn, brown w/red flowers, American Bisque **13.00**
Coffee Pot, wht w/embossed cookies & cup, American Bisque . . **13.00**
Cookie Garage, Cardinal **15.00**
Cookie Truck, mostly yellow, bird finial, old **13.00**
"Cookies", w/animals in relief, round, American Bisque **18.00**
Cornline, Stanford **25.00**
Dog in Basket, USA **10.00**
Donald Duck w/nephews, Disney **30.00**
Dutch Boy, American Bisque **13.00**
Dutch Girl, w/tulips on skirt, American Bisque **18.00**
Dutch Windmill, Fapco **15.00**
Elephant, w/crossed feet, upraised trunk, USA **20.00**
Elf's Head **22.00**
Fat Man **15.00**
Fluffy Cat **22.00**
Gingerbread Man, candy cane handle **30.00**

Globe with Astronauts, no mark **24.00**

Goldilocks, marked USA................................. **60.00**
Hound Dog, green, marked USA........................... **25.00**
Incised ship on front, gold w/brown speckles, Holiday Designs, 1965 **12.50**
Kittens, w/green ball of yarn, American Bisque Co **17.00**
Locke & Co, Warwick, Eng, green repousse leaves, gold buds, 5″ dia **245.00**
Locomotive, w/smiling face, Sierra Vista **22.00**
Magic Bunny, in top hat, American Bisque Co.............. **15.00**
Milk Can, After School Snacks, American Bisque **16.50**
Milk Wagon, pulled by horse, black cat finial, old **17.50**
Momma Pig, flowers in hair, apron **8.00**
Overall Bear, marked USA............................... **25.00**
Owl Reading Book, USA **32.00**
Pig **15.00**
Pigeon, Fapco **15.00**
Pinochio, Metlox **20.00**
Poppytrail Elsie Cow, marked USA **22.00**
Pot Belly Stove, pipe to side, USA **16.00**
Rabbit in Basket **15.00**
Rabbit in Hat, marked USA.............................. **25.00**
Red Riding Hood, marked USA........................... **50.00**
Ring For Cookie Bell, USA **22.00**
Schoolhouse, After School Cookies, American Bisque **18.00**
Sitting Bear, w/pink bib, American Bisque Co **15.00**
Squirrel, Metlox **30.00**
Thumper, Walt Disney character **48.00**
Turnabout, bears...................................... **38.00**
  Donald Duck, Joe **40.00**
  Mickey Mouse, Minnie Mouse **50.00**
  Pluto, Dumbo **55.00**

Copper

    Handcrafted copper was made in America from early in the 18th century until about 1850, with the center of its production in Pennsylvania. Examples have been found signed by such notable coppersmiths as Kidd, Buchanan, Babb, Bently and Harbeson.

    Of the many utilitarian items made, tea kettles are the most desirable. Early examples from the 18th century were made with a dovetailed joint which was hammered and smoothed to a uniform thickness. Pots from the 19th century were seamed.

    Coffee pots were made in many shapes and sizes, and along with mugs, kettles, warming pans and measures are easiest to find; stills, ranging in sizes up to 50 gallon, are popular with collectors today.

Ashtray, hammered, w/removable lid, 2x4½″, Apollo Studios, N.Y. **20.00**
Basket, cherubs in relief, Art Nouveau, 14″ **85.00**
Bath tub **125.00**
Bathtub, enclosed in pine **450.00**
Bedwarmer, pierced heart decor, turned handle, 42″ **165.00**
  Turned wooden handle, engraved bird decor, late 1800s, 44″ **125.00**
  Turned wooden handle, simple engraving on lid, 42½″..... **145.00**
Bowl, hand hammered, silver lined, Novick, 3x8″ **165.00**
  Heavy, w/wrought iron rim handles, 8x17½″ dia **105.00**
Bucket, brass spout, handles & decor, 14″................. **95.00**
  Iron bail, 13″ dia **65.00**
Candle snuffer, cone shape w/handle, eagle & shield mark **68.00**
Candlestick, short, craftsman **20.00**
Candy kettle, 1850s, 19″ dia............................ **195.00**
  Set of 6, iron handles, dovetailed, polished.............. **700.00**
Chafing dish, wood handles, w/tray, orig & complete........ **50.00**
Chestnut roaster, pierced cover, twisted wrought shaft **135.00**
Coal bucket... **110.00**
Coffee pot, brass finial, 8½″ **15.00**
  Wood handle, brass trim **35.00**

Coffee set, china cup inserts, 12 pc, w/warmer............. **220.00**
Cream skimmer, oval, 1 pc, hammered, 4½″ **35.00**
Cup, flared sides, 5″................................... **35.00**
Desk set, early 1900s, pierced decor, 5 pc **155.00**
Dipper, burnished **59.00**
Engraving, hand colored, framed, Paris, 1796, 13½x16½″, pr. **180.00**
Evaporating pan, dovetailed, rolled rim, iron handle & rings ... **80.00**
Funnel, for wine decanters, offset curved tube, mesh screen insert, 7″ **30.00**
Hot water bottle, 11″.................................. **35.00**
Kettle, dovetailed seams, iron bail & under rolled edge, w/iron cradle **450.00**
  Dovetailed, flat rim, 1800s, 15½″ **80.00**
  For apple butter, tongue & groove iron handle, 24x18″ **265.00**
  In iron tripod stand, 16″ dia **395.00**
  Plantation, 1830s, 25″ dia **275.00**
Measure, set of 4, brass trim, ½ pt to 2 qt **160.00**
  Wide spout, applied handle, tapered sides, late 1800s, 10¼″ . **50.00**
Measuring jugs, set of 7, haystack, dovetailed & marked **1,400.00**
Milk bucket, iron handle, 1880s **95.00**
Milk jug, strap handle, dovetailed **75.00**
Mold, bundt, old, 9″................................... **90.00**
Mug, lead lined, double handled, early 1800s, 6″ **145.00**
Pan, dovetailed bottom................................ **135.00**
  Iron handle, hanging eye **145.00**
  Unpolished, tubular copper handles, mkd A&N-G&L, 5x17″ dia **145.00**
  Wrought iron handle stamped Boudes, applied rim, 12¼″ dia **65.00**
Pitcher, dovetailed, ½ gal **35.00**
Pot, hand made, w/handles, copper rivets, early 1800s, 12″ **80.00**
Samover, w/stand, tinned inside,"Jos. Henricks...8 patent," 12″ . **55.00**
Saucer pan, tin lined, wrought copper handle initialed TR, 7″ dia **40.00**
Skillet, wrought copper handle, 8½″ dia **30.00**
Soup pot, w/cover, both have iron handles, 13″ **110.00**
  Wrought iron handle, signed **170.00**
Spatula, wrought iron handle, signed **170.00**
Spittoon, tall, w/Bull Dog & Cat Plug emblem **30.00**
Still, complete & orig, works **95.00**
Tasting spoon, tapered tubular handle, 1830s, 8½″ **65.00**
Tea pot, brass handle, marked Majestic in large letters....... **185.00**
Teakettle, 1850s, Savannah, Georgia..................... **65.00**
  Brass trim, footed, 8″ dia, on brass stand w/burner, English. **165.00**
  Chuckwagon style, 2 gal, nickel plated **55.00**

Teakettle, hand made, 7″ **125.00**
  Oval w/goose neck, 8½″................................ **135.00**

Wood handle, 1 gal, 1930s, Portugal 12.50
Tray, rectangular, hammered, brass handles, 16x12″ 40.00
Sandwich, w/foot, hand hammered, silverlined, Gebelein, 11″ wide 100.00
Umbrella stand, reticulated decor, brass trim, 1890s 125.00
Vase, French pleated w/brass lining & gold bows, 4″ 45.00
Warming pan, pierced decor, turned handle 70.00
Wash basin, round, 11½″ dia 60.00
Wash boiler, w/lid, all copper 75.00
Water jug, hinged lid, strap handle 60.00
Weathervane, horse, running, 1800s, 32″ 375.00

Copper Lustre

Copper luster is a term referring to a type of pottery made in Staffordshire from around the turn of the 19th century. It is finished in a metallic rusty brown glaze resembling true copper. Pitchers are found in abundance, ranging from simple styles with dull bands of color, to those with ornately fashioned handles and bands of embossed polychromed flowers. Bowls are common; goblets, mugs, teapots and sugar bowls much less so. It's easy to find, but not in good condition.

Bowl, blue band w/gold decor, 3x6″ 50.00
    Cobalt trim, footed, 3½x6½″ 75.00
    Yellow floral band, 2½″ 55.00
Compote, blue band w/embossed polychrome florals 4″ 85.00
Creamer, blue & cream stripes, 4½″ 35.00
    Blue band w/embossed florals, 3½″ 38.00
Cup, handleless, yellow floral band, 2¾″ 55.00
Goblet, white band, hp floral enameling, 4½″ 95.00
Mug, blue band w/embossed polychrome cherubs, 3½″ 45.00
    Florals, hp decor, 4″ 75.00
    Purple lustre resist floral band, 3½″ 60.00
    Yellow band w/pink lustre decor, 4″ 40.00
Pitcher, 3 black transfers on wht band, Jackson, 1804, 5″ 850.00

Pitcher, bird head handle, blue bands & polychrome florals, 7½″
    Blue & gold bands, 3½″ 60.00
    Blue band, 5½″ 70.00
    Blue band w/girl & cat, 3½″ 75.00
    Blue bands, floral enameling, birds head handle, 7½″ 85.00
    Cobalt & gold decor, fancy handle, 5″ 68.00
    Four feet, floral decor, 3″ 42.00

No decor, 3½″ 35.00
Sanded band, 4″ 18.00
Sanded band, 6″ 25.00
Wide cream band w/black scenic, 7″ 100.00
Yellow band w/2 raised red roses, beading 42.00
Yellow band w/transfers, 6″ 126.00
Rice bowl, white cherubs in relief, 6″ 65.00
Shaving mug, blue band w/embossed polychrome florals, 3½″ . . 65.00
Tea set, square, enameled leaves & flowers 200.00
Teapot, pink, yellow & green enameled decor, 7½x10½″ 300.00

Coralene

Coralene is a unique type of art glass easily recognized by the tiny grains of glass that form its decorations. Lacy allover patterns of seaweed, geometrics and florals were used, and well as solid forms such as fish, plants and single blossoms. It was made by several glass houses, both here and abroad.

Bride's basket bowl, blue satin cased, diamond quilted 280.00
Pitcher, diamond quilted, blue satin, frosted ribbed handle 275.00
Vase, cased satin, diamond quilted, allover geometric, 6½″ . . . 245.00
    Cased satin, seaweed pattern, 6″ 385.00
    Cranberry inverted thumbprint, floral decor, 5¼″ 390.00
    Cranberry w/enamel florals, coralene outlined, footed, 10x5″ dia 335.00
    Fleur de Lis decor on blue MOP satin, diamond quilted, 7″ . 575.00
    Overall decor on shaded blue satin, 6″ 432.00
    Pair, 3 color lady slipper decor on clear blue, footed, 10″ . . 900.00
    Epergne shape, MOP bugs, butterfly floral, 7¼″ 660.00
    Pink satin w/gold washed pedestal 500.00
    Pink to blue, Flemish window panes, Mt Washington, 7″ . 1,250.00

Rose amber, water lily, fish on obverse, footed 250.00
Rose overlay satin, wht lining, yellow decor, 7x5″ dia 550.00
Seaweed decor on rubina crystal, 7¾″ 200.00
Shaded blue w/yellow & red beading, pat pending 1908, 9″ . 335.00
Yellow seaweed on blue satin, wht lining, 8½″ 550.00
Yellow seaweed on pink shaded satin, diamond quilted 295.00

Cordey

The Cordey China Company was founded in Trenton, N.J., in 1942, by Boleslaw Cybis. They produced figurines, vases, lamps and similar wares

much of which was marketed through gift shops. They closed in 1950, when Cybis Porcelains began operations.

Box, covered, w/4 feet, florals, #6038, 4½x4″ **70.00**
Bust, Jr Miss #5026 w/scarf, 7″ **95.00**
   Lady w/gold tiara #5014, 6½″ **65.00**
   Lady w/hat, roses & leaves, gold decor, 6″ **80.00**
   Lady w/ruffled lace cap, bare shoulders w/roses **65.00**
   Male, #5038 . . . . **45.00**
   Man w/ruffled jabot, coiffure w/bow at back **70.00**
   Napoleon, Raleigh #5038, 7½″ **85.00**
   Pink hat, collar w/blue bow, Chantillion #3003, 6″ **75.00**
   Shawl over head & shoulders, Chantillion #5025, 6″ **78.00**
Console set, bowl, candlesticks w/cherubs **150.00**
Figure, lady w/parasol, bonnet, puffed sleeves, ruffles **90.00**
Figurine, boy w/basket of flowers on shoulder, #5048, 10½″ . . **140.00**
   Girl carrying urn w/berrys, #5047, 10½″ **140.00**
   Girl w/basket gathering fruit #30, 16″ **225.00**
   Lady #303, 16″ **95.00**
   Lady in riding habit, pink & maroon, 16″ **145.00**
   Lady w/lace shawl, basket of flowers, bonnet, 10″ **100.00**
   Lady w/parasol, bonnet, puffed sleeves, ruffles 3-quarter figure **90.00**
   Man #302, 16″ **95.00**
   Man w/top hat, vest & gloves 3-quarter figure **90.00**
   Oriental, 12″ **95.00**
Lamps, 18th century man, lady figurals, pr **300.00**
Leaf dish, reticulated, rose decor, 5½″ **35.00**
Perfume bottle **35.00**
Sugar & creamer on tray **100.00**
Tray, #7007 . . . . **32.00**
Wall plaque, cream, pastel florals in relief, gold, #7002, 12″ . . **85.00**
Wall shelves, w/roses, pr **75.00**

Coronation Collectibles

British souvenir items have been made to commemorate coronations as well as other notable occasions involving the royal families for many years. Bells, thimbles, postcards, mugs, plates and spoons are the most common.

Ashtray, Edward VIII, 1937, Royal Doulton **15.00**
   Queen Elizabeth II, shield, glass, 3½″ **15.00**
Baby's feeding dish, coronation, 1911, mkd Shelly, England **75.00**
Beaker, Edward VII, 1902, Royal Doulton **65.00**
   Edward VIII, 1937 . . . . **30.00**
   Queen Elizabeth II, portrait, crown, flowers, Spode, 4½″ . . . **50.00**
Bowl, Edward VIII, profile, oak leaves, Shell Ware Eng, 6½″ . . **45.00**
   Elizabeth II, 1953, 7″ **10.00**
   George V, 1911, 10″ **15.00**
   Victoria, 1897, stoneware **45.00**
Brandy snifter, King Edward VIII **35.00**
Cup & saucer, George VI & Elizabeth, 1937 . . . . **22.50**
   George VI, Portrait **17.00**
Cup, Edward VII **36.00**
Cup & saucer, Queen Elizabeth II, sepia portrait, Royal Albert China **40.00**
Dish, Victoria & Albert, names & profile busts, pressed glass, 5″ **175.00**
Jar, Queen Elizabeth II coronation, Lancaster & Sandland Ltd, 5x4″ **55.00**
Medal, George V, 1911 . . . . **21.00**
   George VI **15.00**
Mug, Queen Victoria, Diamond Jubilee 1837-1897, portrait & decor **55.00**
   Coronation, Edward VIII, May 1937, 2½″ **20.00**
   Coronation, George VI, 1937, tin **18.00**
Pitcher, Edward VIII, color portrait in wreath, Nelson Ware, MIE **60.00**
   Elizabeth II, 1953, Worcester **50.00**
Plate, Edward VIII, coronation, portrait, crown, Spode Copeland **100.00**

George VI, portrait **15.00**
Mayor & Mayoress of Worcester, Royal Worcester, 1896 . . . . . **75.00**
Queen Victoria, 1887 Jubilee, bust, parian, 7½″ **150.00**
Queen Victoria, 50th Anniversary, painted on porcelain, oval 6¾x5″ **87.50**
Queen Victoria, Jubilee, 1837-1887, mkd Hobson, 9½″ **15.00**

Post cards, King Edward VII, Queen Alexandra, ea **25.00**
Teapot, Elizabeth II, 1953, portrait & crest **42.00**
Tin, Elizabeth II, 1959, portrait **9.00**
Toby mug, George V & Queen Mary, 1910 . . . . **50.00**
Tray, Queen Elizabeth II, 1953 . . . . **24.00**
Tumbler, George VII, portrait, crown flag, 3¼″ **25.00**

Cosmos

Cosmos, sometimes called Stemless Daisy, is a patterned milk glass tableware produced from 1894 through 1915 by Consolidated Lamp & Glass Company. Relief molded flowers on a fine cross-cut background were painted in soft colors of pink, blue and yellow. In addition to the tableware, lamps were also made.

Butter dish, pink band **175.00**
Condiment set, 3 pc w/tops, orig holder **325.00**
Creamer, white w/pastels **125.00**
Lamp, large, orig shade **250.00**
   Miniature, clear glass, complete **50.00**
   Miniature, pink band, complete **285.00**
Shakers, pink band, 3½″, pr **95.00**
Spooner **90.00**
Sugar & creamer **250.00**
Sugar w/cover **155.00**
Syrup **145.00**
Tumbler **65.00**
Water pitcher **215.00**

Coverlets

The Jacquard loom, made in the early 1800s in France, made possible the production of intricately woven coverlets in various designs. They were made of wool, dyed and natural, from patterns punched into paper cards that indicated the colors of woof and warp necessary to develop the motif. Many were dated and had the name of the owner woven into a corner

Andrew Kump Damask Coverlet Mfg, Pennsylvania 1849, 4 colors **700.00**
Beiderwand weave, N.Y., corners w/company name & 1844, 72x88″ **395.00**
Child's, large leaf reserve, w/geometric star, 1850 . . . . **200.00**
Crib, wool, 3 colors **135.00**

Dekalb County Indiana, 1859, handwoven **150.00**
Double Weave, blue & wht, pine trees & snowflake, 2 pc, 68x82″ **195.00**
   Indigo & natural, pine tree border, 1840s 82x76″ **325.00**
   Pine tree border, geometric center, blue & wht w/red, 2 pc . **300.00**
Eagles, blue & wht, signed, 1888 . . . . **765.00**
Goose Eye Twill, navy, lt blue & red plaid, early, 80x84″ **175.00**
Independence Hall, eagles, 1829, some wear **400.00**

Jacquard, 4 colors, 2 pc, signed dated 1844, 74x84″ **350.00**
Jacquard, bird & courthouse border, 1860s, 80x84″ **325.00**
   Blue & wht, 2 pc, building border, eagle corners, 64x80″ . . . **275.00**
   Blue & wht, florals, scrolls, 1850s, 96x85″ **200.00**
   Blue & wht, star flower designs, 2 pc, 76x86″ **175.00**
   Blue, red & wht, bird border, 1848, signed corners, 75″ . . . **155.00**
   Blue, red & wht, w/vine border, eagle corners, center floral . **100.00**
   Double weave, 3 colors, pine tree & snowflake, 1840, 74x80″ **410.00**
   Double weave, 3 colors, urns w/florals, peacocks, 79x83″ . . . **425.00**
   Double weave, blue & wht w/floral medallions, 2 pc **165.00**
   Double weave, blue, wht & red, dated 1850 corners, 2 pc, 72x81″ **450.00**
   Double weave, red, blue & wht intricate, 2 pc, signed, 74x100″ **250.00**
   Double weave, red, wht & blue star medallions, 2 pc, 72x82″ **130.00**
   Double weave, signed, 1850 . . . . **750.00**
   Eagle & vintage border, dated 1853 & signed corners, 72x81″ **200.00**
   Eagle corners, 2 colors, 2 pc, minor wear, 78x86″ **300.00**
   Four colors, 1852 . . . . **550.00**
   Navy & wht, dated 1840 corners, 2 pc, 74x92″ **350.00**
   Oakland Co on 4 sides, 4 roses, repeat border, 1850, 70x90″ **575.00**
   Rose & flower pot border, star medallions, floral center, 1862 **400.00**
   Single star, red, gold & wht, 79x88″ **145.00**
   Star center, eagle corners, foliage & letters borders, 78″ . . . **225.00**
   Signed E Showerman, 1833, stylized trees, double weave, 88x78″ **380.00**
   Signed HG Wilkin, 1842, double weave, 84x90 . . . . **395.00**
Overshot weave, brown, green & natural, w/fringe, 1840s, 78x96″ **250.00**
   Green, gold, red, some wear, 1840s, 76x72″ **175.00**
   Indigo & wht, fringe on 3 sides, wht warped, 64x90″ **350.00**
   Navy & natural, w/fringe, 1850s, 80x87″ **250.00**
   Two shades of blue & wht, 90x108″ **250.00**
Rose medallion, blue/wht urns border, signed & dated corners, 1855 **325.00**
Strawberry medallion, signed, dated corners, vintage & bird borders **275.00**
Summer-Winter, blue & wht eagles, signed, 1887 . . . . **750.00**
   Navy & natural, True Lover's Knot, 74x79″ **260.00**
   Pre Civil War, center seam, 74x80 . . . . **145.00**
Sunburst & Lily, w/bird border, red, blue, green & beige **850.00**

Cowan Pottery

   Guy Cowan opened a small pottery near Cleveland, Ohio, about 1912, where he made tile and artware on a small scale, from the natural red clay available there. He developed distinctive glazes--necessary, he felt, to cover

the dark red body. After the war and a temporary halt in production, Cowan moved his pottery to Rocky River, where he made a commercial line of art-ware utilizing a highly fired white porcelain. Although he acquiesced to the necessity of mass production, every effort was made to insure a product of highest quality. Fine artists, among them Waylande Gregory, Thelma Frazier Winter and Viktor Schreckengost, molded figurines often produced in limited editions, some of which sell today for upwards of $1,000.00. Most of the ware was marked Cowan or Lakewood, not to be confused with the name of the 1927 mass produced line called Lakeware. Falling under the crunch of the Great Depression, the pottery closed in 1931.

Ashtray, Pierrot figurine, green, 3″ **40.00**
   Duck figural, Daffodil Yellow, 2½″ **19.00**
   Sea shell decor, #927F, Apple Blossom Pink, 3½″ **10.00**
Bookend, Art Deco, geometric, 10″ **500.00**
Bookends, Boy & Girl figurals, #519, by Wilcox, Ivory, 6½″ . . **275.00**
   Boy & Girl, #519, Ivory glaze, 6½″, unsigned **125.00**
   Elephants, #E-2, Oriental red, impressed mk, 7″ **150.00**
   Scottie Dogs, Shadow White, E6, 8″ **250.00**
   Sunbonnet Girls, #E521, Verde Green glaze, 7″ **135.00**
   Thinker, #522, Pine Green matt, 7″ **145.00**
Bowl, blue lustre, 7″ **25.00**
   Female figural frog, high glaze 8″ **110.00**
   Footed, cream w/pink interior, impressed, 4x12″ **35.00**
   Footed, tu-tone high glaze, 5″ **45.00**
   Ftd, w/frog-candleholder, vine form, Mayflower, 9x12½″ **55.00**
   Pterodactyl heads, Apple Blossom, 7x7½x10″ **75.00**
   With frog, orange lustre **18.00**
Candleholders, diamond base, grapes, Oriental Red, 4″ **35.00**
   Square w/florals, base relief leaf form stem, 6″ **45.00**
Candlestick lamp base, blue luster, ink stamp, 11″ **60.00**
Candlesticks, #501C, early pink luster, ink stamp, 14″ **175.00**
   Byzantine angels, #764, crackled, impressed, 9″ **250.00**
   Bulbous w/leaf form holder, Ivory, 4″, pr **22.00**
   Diamond base w/vine decor, S782, caramel, 3″, pr **22.00**
   Matt mustard, impressed, 3½x4″, pr **25.00**
Cigarette box, w/lid, sea horse finial, copper luster, 6x4″ **55.00**
Cigarette jar, w/lid, goat finial, Oriental Red, 7½″ **95.00**
Compote, seahorse stem, ivory w/orchid liner, impressed, 6½″ . . **25.00**
Console set, bowl w/reticulated base, B6, candles, Etruscan, Red **100.00**
   Bowl, B741, candles S751, vines, Amalfi **75.00**
   Fan vase, 8″ candles, sea horses, Apple Blossom **55.00**
   Female figural, 6 pcs, Waylande Gregory **2,400.00**
   Spanish dancers, D793, Special Ivory, 9½″ **275.00**
Decanters, King & Queen, standing, X12-13, red, hp, 1931, 11″ **500.00**
Figurine, Adam, ltd edition, RG Cowan, repaired **1,800.00**
   Flamingo, D-20, black impressed mk, 11½″ **325.00**
   Horse, DL-82, terra cotta crackle, 8¾″ **375.00**
Flower frog, dancing nymph, #686, ivory, impressed mk, 6½″ . **135.00**
   Dancing nymph, #686, Sea Green, impressed mk, 7″ **250.00**
   Dancing nymph, #687, ivory, impressed mk, 12″ **275.00**
   Dancing nymph, #698, caramel, impressed mk, 6½″ **225.00**
   Dancing nymph, #698, ivory, impressed mk, 6½″ **125.00**
   Dancing nymph, #709, ivory, impressed mk, 6″ **125.00**
   Dancing twins, #685, ivory, impressed mk, 7½″ **225.00**
   Female in Deco pose, high glaze, 5″ **95.00**
   Flamingo, D-2-F, ivory, impressed mk, 11½″ **175.00**
   Mushroom figural, F9X, Special Ivory, 4¾″ **27.00**
   Scarf dancer, #686, ivory, 1925 1st Prize winner **75.00**
Lamp, green crystalline, molded perpendicular decor, 11½″ . . **145.00**
   Lustre, 7″ **75.00**
Match holder, sea horse base **25.00**
Paperweight, elephant figural by Postgate, D3, ivory, 4½″ **75.00**
   Elephant, D-3, Arabian Night blue, impressed mk **150.00**

Elephant figural by Postgate, D3, ivory, 4½" **75.00**
Plate, blue on blue fish design, 11½" **295.00**
Punchbowl, Jazz design, Schreckengost, 1931, 18" **2,200.00**
Set, bowl #859B w/dolphin candles #755, mkd, green/orange . . **250.00**
Soapdish, seahorse stand, blue, ink stamp, 4" **50.00**
Strawberry jar, SJ-2, April Green, straight sides, 11" **85.00**
Tea set, 7 pc, ftd tea tile, pot 3x4", melon ribs, yellow **110.00**
Vase, 6 sides, V9, orange lustre, Marigold, 7" **30.00**
   Artichoke, green, 12½" **125.00**
   Birds, squirrels in relief, Gregory, V19, green, 9" **125.00**
   Black jet gloss, #548, ink stamp COWAN, 5½" **50.00**
   Blue & aqua, 12" **165.00**
   Blue luster, #619C, ink stamp COWAN, 12" **125.00**
   Blue luster, #691A, ink stamp COWAN, 7½" **45.00**
   Bulbous w/cylinder top, Rasberry lustre, 6" **35.00**
   Chinese bird, #V747, Oriental Red, imp COWAN, 11½" **275.00**
   Copper luster, V554B, long tapered top, 12" **65.00**
   Exotic foliage, Waylande Gregory, 1930, marked, 10" **600.00**

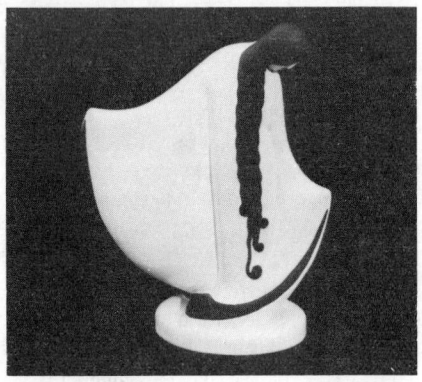

Female figure, white cape, long hair, mkd, 9½" **1,100.00**
Fish & seaweed, Dry Point, V91, dark green, 6½" **295.00**
Floral handle, V649B, Logan Award 1924, Larkspur, 8½x7" . **55.00**
   Green, 6½" **30.00**
Larkspur Blue luster, decorated handles, #649B, 8" **60.00**
Marigold luster, #564, 6 sides, ink stamp COWAN, 6" **45.00**
Mirror Blue, #598, bulbous, 3x5" **25.00**
Orange lustre, 9x7" **65.00**
Peacock Blue, hand thrown effect, 9", 38" circumference **75.00**
Relief animals, Waylande Gregory, V19, blue/wht, 9" **95.00**
Round, tab handles on collar, blue crackle, V99, 6" **75.00**
Square base w/flare top, V1, Cowan Black, Princess, 6" . . . **325.00**
Wall pocket, blue luster, #653, ink stamp, 9x3½" **125.00**

Cracker Jacks

Kids began buying Cracker Jacks in 1908. Before the first kernel was "krunched" the free prize had been retrieved from the depth of the box--actually no easy task, considering the care one had to take to keep the contents so swiftly displaced by eager fingers from spilling over the side! Tho a little older perhaps, many of those same kids still are looking--just as eagerly--for the Cracker Jack prizes.

Cast Metal
Air corps wings, silver or blk, CJ, 3" **35.00**
Angelus horse & wagon, 3-D, silver or gold, CJ, 2½" **85.00**
Angelus thimble, aluminum w/red paint fill, CJ **42.00**
Animals w/shoes, tools, pipe, etc, no mk, about 1" **2.50**
Cars, trolleys, trains, bikes, etc, no mk, about 1" **3.75**
Dollhouse items: lantern, tray, mug, candle, etc, no mk **12.00**
Presidential coin set, 31 pc, aluminum, CJ **10.00**
Stand up flats w/base, colored, not game piece, no mk, ... **17.50**

Stud button, crossed bats & ball, "Pitcher" **48.00**
Tootsie toy series, boats, cars, animals, 1-3", CJ **8.25**
Paper
Baseball cards, 1906 & 1907 series CJ **32.00**
   Score counter, CJ **95.00**
Bear post cards, 1907, series of 16, CJ, ea **14.00**
Book marker, bulldog, CJ **9.25**
CJ Animals to Color, book **48.00**
   Birds to Color, book **48.00**
   Riddles Book: Boy & Dog, RWB **28.00**
   Riddles Book: Jester, RYBK **30.00**
Comic books ads **10.00**
Drawing book, CJ **40.00**
Halloween masks, CJ, 10" or 12" **37.50**
Hats, overseas vendor cap, RWB, CJ **68.00**
Jackie's Friends, mini books, CJ, ea **38.00**
Jumping frog, toy, CJ **10.00**
Letter heads & envelopes, 1900-1920, CJ **60.00**
Movies, pull tab for 2nd picture, CJ, about 3" **48.00**
Old packages, bid as per date & condition . . . . **Valuable**
Puzzles: envelope w/metal puzzle, CJ, series of 15, ea **22.00**
Riddle cards, CJ, series of 20 . . . . **12.00**
Saturday Evening Post ads, 1918-1920 . . . . **22.00**
Spinner w/string, 1½" round, CJ **22.00**
     Rectangle, CJ **22.00**
Stories of the Presidents, CJ, series of 6 mini books **38.00**
Uncle Sam's Famous National Songs, book, CJ **38.00**
Plastic
Baseball players & spacemen, 3-D, plastic, CJ **8.50**
Fobs, alphabet letter, plastic, CJ **5.00**
Nosco, rocking base, animals & people, plastic, CJ **4.50**
   Stand up semi-flat animals & people, plastic, CJ **1.75**
Railroad train engine & cars, plastic, 3-D, CJ, about 2" **9.50**
Tin
Angelus truck, ad on each side, 1½", CJ **28.00**
Bank, book shape, Vol 1, green, 2" tall, CJ **48.00**
Boy & dog, die cut, CJ, with bend over tabs in place **48.00**
Boy & dog, die cut, RBW, 2" **22.00**
CJ shows, circus animals in cage, 1¾", RBY **34.00**
CJ band, gold or silver, 1¾" round, Hummer, CJ **34.00**
Clicker, Noisy Cracker Jack, tearshape, CJ, 2" **17.50**
Comic characters, oval stand ups, 2", CJ **47.50**
Doll dish, silver/gold, CJ, 1¾ **25.00**
   Plate, silver, CJ, 2" **25.00**
Horse & wagon **15.00**
Lunch box **14.00**
Model T Ford, N.Y. 1916 #999, B & W, CJ, 2" **58.00**
Our Boy Sailor Knife, 2¾" **90.00**
Pocket watch, silver/gold, CJ, 1½" **32.00**
Sulky, 2 wheels, 5" w/stick, CJ **10.00**
Top, Fortune Teller, CJ **45.00**
Two toppers, CJ **45.00**
Tops, variety of types **22.00**
Toy tray w/picture of pkg, large, CJ **60.00**
Train engine & tender #512, CJ, 2", RBW **35.00**
Whistle, "life saver", 1¼" dia, CJ **42.00**
   Close end w/fingers, ID etched, CJ **37.50**
   Close end w/fingers, ID in relief, CJ **22.00**
   Enameled twin tune, CJ, 2½" **37.50**

Cranberry

Cranberry glass is named for its resemblence to the color of cranberry juice; it was made by many companies, both here and abroad.

Bottle, gilt & enamel decor, 5″ **85.00**
Bowl, 3 scroll feet, applied petal decor, 4½x5″ **240.00**
  Amber handles, draped rigaree middle & rim, 4x5½″ **230.00**
  Applied crystal feet & loopings, 6″ **70.00**
  Clear applied ruffled edge, 6″ **100.00**
  Craquelle, 3″ **25.00**
  Crystal garlands & berry prunts, scroll feet, 5″ **375.00**
  Gold enameling **35.00**
  Hobnail, white opal, Victorian, 8½″ **145.00**
  Inverted Thumbprint, 5″ **38.00**
  Three tiered crystal petals, 3 scroll feet, 4¾″ **225.00**
Box, w/cover, gilt & enamel decor, 2¾″ **65.00**
Celery, handled, 8″ **40.00**
Cologne, gold florals, 7″ **95.00**
Comport, oval, clear bubble stem, 5″ **75.00**
  Footed, bubble ball stem & base, 5x4″ **65.00**
  Threaded Diamond, clear rigaree rim, ft, 3½x8″ **115.00**
Creamer, clear foot, reeded handle, 2¾″ **60.00**
Cruet, clear ball stopper, polished pontil, 6″ **70.00**
  Clear handle, bubble stopper w/berry brunt, lilies, 8″ **150.00**
  Dasies, scrolls, gold trim, 7″ **150.00**
  Enamel lilies, clear handle & stopper **100.00**
Decanter, clear bubble stopper, wht lilies, gold trim, 8″ **145.00**
  Faceted stopper, scroll & foilage engraved, ped, 12″ **135.00**
  Orchid decor, clear steeple stopper, 11″ **125.00**
Epergne, single lily, ruffled, plated ped, 10½″ **150.00**
Ewer, clear handles & edge, gold spangling, 9¾″ **195.00**
  Gold scrolls, pink & blue florals, 15″ **496.00**
Finger bowl, overshot, flint **30.00**
Jam jar, Baby Thumbprint, clear rigaree at middle, gold wash . **225.00**
  Plated filigree holder & lid **110.00**
  Rigaree top, footed ornate hallmarked frame, 6x6 ...... **135.00**
Lampshade, 4¾″ fitter flares to 5¾″, 9¾x10″ **175.00**
  Cylindrical, swirl, 5″ fitter, 7¾″ **160.00**
  Hobnail, 4″ fitter, 7″ **160.00**
  Hobnail, 5″ fitter, 6½″ **175.00**
  Ribbed, 4″ fitter, 7¾″ **160.00**
  Swirl, both openings, 4x7x7½″ **160.00**

Mug, floral enameled, clear handle, Austria, 4½″ **45.00**
Open salt, clear glass applied center & base, 2½″ **45.00**
Patch box, lacy gold decor **65.00**
Pickle castor, plated holder w/tongs, Inverted Thumbprint **140.00**
Pitcher, clear twist handle wraps around neck, Sandwich, 8½″ **175.00**
  Cut dragonfly, leaves in gold, 6½″ **160.00**
  Fluted rim, med size **155.00**
  Fluted rim, white enamel deer, small **175.00**
  Fluted top, lacy white dot decor, 6½″ **115.00**
  Inverted Thumbprint, clear handle, enamel florals, 7½″ **165.00**
  Inverted Thumbprint, 4 sided mouth, 7½″ **165.00**

Ribbed effect, clear handled, ruffled, 7½″ **125.00**
Ruffled top, enamel decor, ribbed, Victorian, 8″ **140.00**
Squat, Inverted Thumbprint, clear handle **190.00**
Swirl, clear reeded lion foot handle, 1890 .... **195.00**
Threaded, slim neck, w/ruffled, 5″ **40.00**
Threaded, slim neck, 5″ **35.00**
Plate, 7″ **45.00**
Rose bowl, footed, daisies, foilage, gold trim, 6½x4½x8″ **160.00**
  Plain, 5″ **65.00**
Rosebowl, arboresque, crimp, wht craquelle, Stevens & Williams, 3″ **125.00**
  Enamelled white lace **145.00**
Scent bottle, white lace enamel decor, 5″ **120.00**
Shakers, bulbous **45.00**
Sugar & creamer, wht threading, rigaree, petal feet **350.00**
Sugar shaker, opal dots, 4½″ **35.00**
  Silverplate top, cut panels, 5½″ **60.00**
Sweetmeat, plated holder, 5½″ dia **65.00**
Tray, 12x5½″ **135.00**
Tumble-up, Inverted Thumbprint **48.00**
Tumbler, Inverted Thumbprint **25.00**
Urn, covered, crystal handles & thorny finial, gold decor, 11″ . **275.00**
Vase, blown, floral enameling, upward taper, 10¾″ **225.00**
  Bulbous, fluted, baby Thumbprint, 7″ **55.00**
  Clear applied leaves, florals, three corner top, 5x4″ **195.00**
  Clear rigaree & ped foot, 12″ **95.00**
  Clear rigaree rim, applied feet, 13″ **325.00**
  Crystal handles & feet, silver crackle, 12″ **195.00**
  Crystal leaves at top & base, 8¾x4″ **120.00**
  Crystal reeded handles, florals, 22″ **295.00**
  Floral branches, sanded gold leaves, 8¾x5″ **115.00**
  Gold & white all over enameling, footed, 8″ **110.00**
  Gold flecks, blown, 4″ **30.00**
  Gold floral, scrolls, 12″ **150.00**
  Heavy gold decor, 5″ **80.00**
  Melon section, crystal feet & leaves, 7″ **95.00**
  Swirl w/white rim, 11½x6½″ **135.00**
  Trumpet shape, ruffled top, clear foot, 11½″ **75.00**
  With multicolor enamel, 6″ **75.00**
  White florals w/pink centers, gold leaves, ribbed, 13″ **150.00**
Vases, forget-me-nots, gold trim, 11″, pr **285.00**
  White daisies, green leaves, gold trimmed, 4¾″, pr **145.00**

Crown Devon

Crown Devon was the trade name of S. Fielding and Co. Ltd., an English firm founded about 1879. They produced majolica, earthenware, pottery mugs, vases and kitchenware. In the 1930s they manufactured an exceptional line of Art Deco vases that have recently been much in demand.

Charger, Deco floral pattern, marked, 12″ **500.00**
Charger, couple, trees, 3 unbrellas, Charlotte Rhead, 1925 .. **1,100.00**
Humidor, crimson w/enameled galleons, D Cole, 1930 .... **125.00**
Plate, Deco forest scene, marked, 6″ **125.00**
Plate, lusterine, fish decor in gold, 9″ **65.00**

Crown Milano

Crown Milano was introduced in 1884 by the Mt. Washington Glass Co. When the company merged with Pairpoint in 1894, it continued to be one of their best sellers. It is an opaque, highly decorated ware, with gold or colored enamels in intricate designs on pale backgrounds, nearly always in a satin finish. Many pieces are marked CM with a crown.

Biscuit jar, blown out pebbles, starfish & jewels **1,200.00**

Burmese shading, wht interior, gold decor	**1,050.00**
Coral & yellow shading, gold florals, beads, ruffled, 8″	**1,250.00**
Cream w/mottling, heavy gold threads, melon ribs	**1,150.00**
Delicate floral branch w/plated lid	**685.00**
Floral enameling, marked MW	**275.00**
Peach & yellow shading, gold, ruffled bail top, 8″	**850.00**
Squat, Fuji mums, plated lid, signed	**650.00**
Box, hinged cover, florals, gold, brass collar, signed	**600.00**
Bride's bowl, in Pairpoint plated frame	**1,100.00**
Cockle shell salt, white w/florals, shaker top, 2¾″	**495.00**
Compote, pairpoint silver plated stand, signed	**1,100.00**
Cruet	**795.00**
Marmalade, pastel pansies, silver plated lid w/butterfly	**895.00**
Muffineer, lt green w/floral bouquet, ribbed melon, 4½″	**585.00**
Mustard, florals, plated lid & handle	**650.00**
Pickle castor	**750.00**
Pitcher, rope handle, tan w/enamel thistles, leaves, gold	**1,850.00**
Sugar & creamer, gold decor	**900.00**

Sugar shaker, melon rib, floral enameled, 2½x3½″	**400.00**
Sweetmeat, decorated w/silver plated cover, signed	**1,250.00**
Diamond pattern, green leaves, red berries, 4″	**500.00**
Tray, floral decor, triangle, signed & #d	**400.00**
White w/pastel columbines, 2 rolled sides, signed	**395.00**
Tumbler, florals & gold	**385.00**
Vase, 7″	**625.00**
Allover floral nosegays, 8¾x6½″	**1,250.00**
Autumn leaves, jeweled, snake at neck, 10½″	**1,650.00**
Blue w/geese, moon & stars, 14″	**1,900.00**
Cream w/gold foliage & edge decor, signed & #ed, 12½″	**1,400.00**
Cream w/pink & grey mottling, gold florals, 6″	**1,300.00**
Ferns, heavy gold, 8″	**750.00**
Gold florals, on cream, paper label, 6″	**1,600.00**
Ovoid w/narrow neck, green & brown thistles, mkd, 9″	**690.00**
Peony decor on white w/blue shadow leaves, 7″	**175.00**
Pink & grey mottled w/cream & gold florals	**1,300.00**
Shiny w/gold chrysanthemums, 9″	**295.00**
Shiny, bulbous, 3 handles, scenic w/Arab & camel	**3,500.00**
White shading to pink satin w/florals	**6,750.00**

Cruets

Cruets, containers made to hold oil or vinegar, are usually bulbous with tall narrow throats and a stopper. During the 19th century and for several years after, they were produced in abundance, in virtually every type of glass ware available.

Amber, blue rope handle & stopper, cut star base, 9″	**146.00**
Cathedral	**75.00**
Frosted, w/millefiori canes, orig stopper	**98.00**
Amberina, orig stopper	**265.00**
Cased glass, fuschia & blue, applied handle & floral decor, 10″	**165.00**
Cobalt, w/tiny wht enamel florals, 1830s	**155.00**
Cranberry, ground pontil, blown stopper, 9¼x5″ wide	**135.00**
Diamond Quilted, blue satin, frosted thorn handle & stopper, 5″	**650.00**
Esther, green w/gold, orig stopper	**145.00**
Forget-me-not, wht, orig stopper	**80.00**
Olive amber, enamel flowers & foliage, amber ped foot, 9x3″ dia	**85.00**
Opalescent, blue Seaweed	**115.00**
Oval Star Variant, miniature, w/stopper, 3¾″	**35.00**
Pewter embossed neck & handle, w/pewter open-work stopper, 11″	**60.00**
Ruby, cut, engraved to clear vintage pattern, w/stopper	**65.00**
Shoshone, emerald green, w/orig stopper	**69.00**

Spangle, cranberry w/gold flecks, amber twist handle, 10″	**145.00**
Swirl, deep blue, 8 distinct swirls, orig stopper, 8″	**135.00**
Green w/Lily of the Valley decor, gold foliage stopper	**270.00**
Tokyo, green w/opal, orig stopper	**145.00**
Webb, blue w/clear amber base & stopper, berry prunt handle, 10½″	**325.00**

Cup Plates Staffordshire, See Staffordshire

In the early 1800s, it was the fashion to pour hot beverages from the cup into a deep saucer to cool before drinking. The cup plate was used as a coaster for the cup. While many companies made them, Sandwich was probably the largest manufacturer of the type called 'lacy'. Those made by Midwestern firms are identified by techniques, characteristics and peculiarities of design attributed to that area.

In these listings, numbers refer to *American Cup Glass Plates* by Ruth Webb Lee and James A. Rose. Staffordshire and Pairpoint cup plates are listed later in other sections

Hard cider, log house & flag	**60.00**
LR-90, opalescent	**75.00**
LR-103, clear w/slight bluish tint	**70.00**
LR-132, Midwestern, lacy	**150.00**
LR-133, Midwestern, lacy, thistle center	**90.00**
LR-159, clear, Midwestern, lyre center	**130.00**
LR-167A, clear, Midwestern	**120.00**
LR-243, opalescent	**75.00**

LR-246, opalescent	275.00
LR-262, dk blue lacy	130.00
LR-269A, peacock blue lacy	290.00
LR-321C, amethyst	150.00
LR-332B, yellow	175.00
LR-334A, clear	18.50
LR-334A, opalescent	65.00
LR-440, clear	38.00
Electric blue	125.00
Peacock blue lacy heart	140.00
LR-440B, blue	225.00
Clear	15.00
LR-459D, green lacy heart, rare	300.00
Peacock blue lacy heart	110.00
LR-465J, opalescent	60.00
LR-465L, violet-blue lacy heart	260.00
LR-561, Washington, Midwestern, clear	300.00
LR-565B, Henry Clay, blue	115.00
LR-576, Victoria, clear	85.00
LR-610, light blue	175.00
LR-610A, blue	110.00
LR-610A, clear	27.00
LR-619, Benjamin Franklin, clear	70.00
LR-640, Bunker Hill, clear	65.00
LR-651A, eagle, fiery opalescent	450.00
LR-665, eagle, clear	85.00
LR-668, eagle	200.00
LR-670A, eagle, clear	85.00
LR-676B, dk blue, lacy, eagle, Ft Pitt Glass Works	600.00
LR-680E, eagle, clear	120.00
LR-686, blue, Midwestern, lacy harp, rare	325.00
LR-807, eagle, blue	340.00

Custard

As early as the 1880s, custard glass was produced in England. Migrating glassmakers brought the formula for the creamy ivory ware to America. One of them was Harry Northwood who in 1898 founded his company in Indiana, Pa., and introduced the glassware to the American market. Soon other companies were producing custard, among them Heisey, Tarentum, Fenton and McKee. Not only dinnerware patterns, but souvenir items were made. Today, custard is the most expenive of the colored pressed glassware patterns. The formula for producing the luminous glass contains uranium salts which imparts the cream color to the batch and causes it to glow when it is examined under a black light. Although not true custard in the strictest sense, the blue opaque version of Northwood's Chrysanthemum Sprig is listed here also.

Argonaut Shell, berry, master	125.00
Covered butter	225.00

Pitcher, 8″	400.00

Salt & pepper shakers, orig tops	280.00
Spooner	125.00
Sugar, covered	140.00
Beaded Circle, creamer	115.00
Master berry	245.00
Pitcher, Northwood	420.00
Spooner, Northwood	115.00
Beaded Swag, goblet, Heisey	45.00
Sauce, souvenir Avoca, Wisconsin	48.00
Biscuit jar, w/brass lid, English	200.00
Bulging Teardrop, condiment set	150.00
Cane Insert, spooner, w/gold, Tatentum	79.00
Sugar, covered, w/gold, Tarentum	110.00
Cherry & Scale, bowl, 6-sided, stalking lion, Fenton	92.00
Berry set, 7 pc, mint nutmeg, Fentonia	350.00
Covered butter, brown trim	210.00
Sugar, covered, nutmeg stain	145.00
Tumbler, nutmeg trim	55.00
Chrysanthemum Sprig, bowl, oval, 10½″	180.00
Compote, jelly, tall	95.00
Covered butter, good gold & decor	245.00
Master berry, gold trim	180.00
Salt & pepper, pair	100.00
Shaker, gold decor	80.00
Spooner, Northwood, signed	95.00
Sugar, covered	145.00
Toothpick, Northwood	230.00
Tray, small	49.00
Tumbler, w/gold & enamel decor	60.00
Water set, 7 pc	650.00
Chrysanthemum Sprig, blue; celery vase, w/gold, Northwood	935.00
Compote, jelly	390.00
Covered butter, mint gold	625.00
Creamer	325.00
Cruet tray	1,750.00
Cruet, orig stopper	785.00
Master berry	495.00

Pitcher, 8″	950.00
Salt & pepper	395.00
Sauce	120.00
Spooner	270.00
Sugar, covered, mint gold	425.00
Table set, 4 pc	1,695.00
Toothpick, Northwood	400.00
Tumbler, water	195.00
Corn, salt & pepper, orig lids	90.00
Delaware, pin tray, blue	45.00

Sauce, boat shape, green decor 75.00
Tumbler 45.00
Diamond Maple Leaf, creamer, silver decor 100.00
Spooner, gold decor 105.00
Table set, 4 pc, very good 575.00
Diamond with Peg, covered butter, rose decor 200.00
Salt & pepper, w/red rose, souvenir 80.00
Shot glass, souvenir 45.00
Toothpick 52.00
Duthridge Princess Swirl, condiment set 190.00
Salt shaker, enameled flowers 38.50
Double Fan Band, syrup 195.00
Dugan Fan, table set, 4 pc, excellent gold, signed 450.00
Everglades, creamer, Northwood 120.00
Salt & pepper, Northwood 240.00
Sauce 65.00
Spooner 110.00
Tumbler, Northwood 85.00
Fan, Spooner, gold decor 90.00
Sugar, covered, gold decor 140.00
Table set, 4 pc, mint gold 600.00
Tumbler 65.00
Finecut & Roses, rose bowl 60.00
Fluted Scrolls, master, berry, footed, gold decor 100.00
Puff jar, covered, blue opalescent, mint gold 55.00
Fruit & Flowers, bowl, fluted w/spiked edges, nutmeg stain, 7¼" 100.00
Geneva, banana boat 155.00
Compote, jelly, red & green decor 78.00
Covered butter 180.00
Creamer, red & green decor 75.00
Cruet, red & green decor, orig stopper 275.00
Master berry, round 125.00
Spooner, w/red & green decor 75.00
Toothpick 85.00
Tumbler, red & green decor 50.00
Georgia Gem, berry set, 7 pc, enameled flower decor 175.00
Covered, butter, enamelled floral decor 170.00
Covered, butter, gold trim 160.00
Creamer, breakfast, floral decor, Tarentum 45.00
Cruet, floral decor, Tarentum 210.00
Gold trim 175.00
Master berry, gold decor 95.00
Sugar, open, enamelled floral decor 40.00
Table set, 4 pc, excellent gold 395.00
Toothpick holder, gold decor 60.00
Grape, banana boat, fruit bowl, pink stain, ruffled edge, footed 360.00
Plate, nutmeg stain, Northwood 45.00
Punch cup, blue decor 80.00
Pedestal, Northwood 45.00
Grape Arbor, pitcher, pink satin, Northwood 545.00
Tumbler, pink satin, Northwood 88.00
Vase, nutmeg stain, Northwood 55.00
Grape & Cable, berry, Pedestal, thumbprint & nutmeg stain, small 45.00
Grape & Gothic Arches, covered butter, carnival finish, w/gold 185.00
Goblet, no stain 40.00
Goblet, nutmeg trim 45.00
Spooner, carnival finish w/nutmeg stain 75.00
Sugar, covered, gold trim 95.00
Vase, stemmed, from goblet mold 80.00
Heart With Thumbprint, finger lamp, floral decor, Tatentum .. 140.00
Wine, Tarentum 94.00
Honeycomb, cordial, tiny 45.00
Intaglio, compote, fruit, gold & green decor, large 195.00
Compote, jelly, blue & gold decor 95.00

Covered butter, green & gold decor 200.00
Cruet, green/gold clear stopper 200.00
Master berry, pedestal, blue & gold decor 185.00
Sauce, pedestal, blue & gold decor 50.00
Spooner, green trim 100.00
Table set, 4 pc, decorated 600.00
Tumbler, blue decor 55.00
Inverted Fan & Feather, berry set, 7 pc 650.00
Compote, jelly 250.00
Covered butter 245.00
Master berry, pink & good gold 105.00
Punch cup 250.00
Salt & pepper, pink & gold 400.00
Sauce footed, Northwood, 2½x4½" dia 70.00
Spooner 110.00
Table set, pink & gold decor, 4 pc 695.00
Toothpick 495.00
Tumbler, water, gold & pink trim 75.00
Iris, creamer, excellent gold & decoration 110.00
Jackson, spooner 30.00
Water set, pitcher & 4 tumblers, good trim 375.00
Jefferson Optic, sauce 34.00
Spooner 80.00
Tumbler, red rose 38.00
Louis XV, covered butter 200.00
Creamer 85.00
Master berry 135.00
Pitcher 240.00
Salt & pepper 165.00
Sauce 50.00
Spooner 80.00
Tumbler 60.00
Maple Leaf, covered butter 240.00
Creamer 95.00
Pitcher, Northwood 250.00
Salt & pepper 550.00
Sauce, Northwood 85.00
Spooner 105.00
Sugar, open 45.00
Table set, 4 pc, Northwood 495.00
Tumbler, Northwood 82.00
Water set, 5 pc 600.00
Panelled Poppies, lampshade, hanging, nutmeg on satin finish . 675.00
Peacock & Urn, ice cream dish, large, nutmeg decor 220.00
Ice cream dish, small, nutmeg decor 65.00
Pitcher, milk, souvenir Toronto, Canada, 4¼" 90.00
Poppy, pin tray, Northwood 78.00
Ribbed Drape, compote, jelly 165.00
Creamer, Jefferson 92.00
Tumbler, Jefferson 69.00
Ribbed Thumbprint, mug, rose decor 45.00
Tumbler, rose decor 50.00
Ring Band, berry set, gold band decor, Heisey 350.00
Pitcher, water, State Fair 1906, Heisey 295.00
Salt & pepper, rose decor 145.00
Spooner, w/rose decor 85.00
Sugar, covered, w/rose decor 125.00
Syrup, rose decor 265.00
Table set, gold chrysanthemum w/persimmon dot, 4 pc 395.00
Toothpick holder, decorated 80.00
Tray 175.00
Tumbler, red rose decor, Heisy 45.00
Water set, rose decor, 7 pc 750.00
Ring box, hinged w/Cupid, French 225.00

Rose bowl, blown, painted Victorian lady **90.00**
Salt & pepper, souvenir, hp florals **40.00**
Sawtooth Band, cup, Heisey, signed **40.00**
Shell, mug, Northwood **60.00**
Sweetmeat container, handled, birds & flowers decor **125.00**
Three Fruits, plate, 7½″ **75.00**
Tiny Thumbprint, creamer, Crysanthemum decor **95.00**
   Salt & pepper, Crysanthemum decor, pair **100.00**
   Spooner, Chrysanthemum decor, Tarentum **80.00**
   Table set, Chrysanthemum decor, 4 pc **585.00**
Trailing Vine, covered butter **150.00**
Vermont, card tray, small **83.00**
   Covered butter **150.00**
   Creamer **84.00**
   Pickle tray **55.00**
   Tumbler, floral decor **60.00**
   Vase, US Glass **85.00**
Victoria berry set, 6 pc **575.00**
   Master berry **185.00**
   Pitcher, water, green **350.00**
   Sauce **55.00**
   Spooner **80.00**
Wild Bouquet, creamer **105.00**
   Sauce, Northwood **70.00**
   Spooner **120.00**
   Sugar, arched cover, no finial **220.00**
   Sugar, finial cover, Northwood **180.00**
   Tumbler **100.00**
Winged Scroll, berry set, 7 pc, gold decor **525.00**
   Bon-bon, Heisey **55.00**
   Card dish w/turned over sides, Heisey **85.00**
   Dresser tray, mint decor **200.00**
   Master berry **120.00**
   Match holder, Heisey **177.00**
   Sauce **35.00**
   Toothpick holder, rose decor, Heisey **130.00**
   Vase, no gold, Heisey **85.00**
   Water set, tankard w/6 tumblers, Heisey **495.00**

Cut Glass, See Also Specific Manufacturer

   The brilliant period of cut glass covered a span from about 1880 until 1915. Because of the pressure neccessary to achieve the deeply cut patterns, only glass containing a high grade of metal could withstand the process. For this reason, and the amount of hand work involved, cut glass has always been expensive.

   Key:

straw.....strawberry   x-.............cross
dia..........diamond   pt.............point

Ashtray, hobstars, mitre cuts, pineapples, x-hatching **20.00**
Banana boat, Harvard w/floral pattern **200.00**
Banana bowl, scalloped, Russian, oval medallions, 11x7″ **95.00**
   Scalloped, hobstars w/band of same, cane **85.00**
Basket, 6″ **65.00**
   8 panels, intaglio engraved sunflowers, Heisey **185.00**
   Double twisted handle, hobstars w/x-hatching, 5½″ **225.00**
   Engraved fruit pattern **375.00**
   Florence hobstar & cane w/hobstar base, 16″ **1,650.00**
   Hobstars & thistles, step cut ends, star base, 7″ **145.00**
   Pinwheel, hobstar & zipper, 6″ dia **175.00**
   Twist handle, hobstars, fan, buzz, 6½″ dia **130.00**
Bishop's hat, Sunflower, allover cut, 11½″ **350.00**
Bon-bon, Alhambra, sterling rim, 5″ **485.00**

Bowl, allover dia, buttons & ferns, 3 footed, 8″ **125.00**
   Banana, hobstars in bottom, allover cut, Hunt, 8x11½″ **475.00**
   Blue cut to amber to clear, Vintage, 2½x5″ **525.00**
   Comet, 7″ dia **170.00**
   Expanding star pattern, 9″ dia, 4″ deep **150.00**
   Football shape, 4 fancy deep cuts, 1920 . . . . **250.00**
   Footed, 6x5″ **159.00**
   Footed, pinwheel w/x-hatching & fans, heavy cut, pressed . . . **45.00**
   French cut, swirl design filigree silver mounts, 10″ **225.00**
   Fruit, hobstars & cane, scalloped edge, 9x9″ **450.00**
   Garland, heavy blank, excellent polish, 4x9″ **325.00**
   Hobstars & cane shields separated by fans, 8″ dia **160.00**
   Hobstars, x-hatch, dia pt & notched panels, heavy, 8¼″ **175.00**
   Hobstars, dia pt, x-hatching, notch panels, 8″ dia **160.00**
   Marquis, 8″ **235.00**
   Oblong, 3 fruit gravic cutting **100.00**
   Prisms & flutes, 8″ **200.00**
   Rolled rim, straw dia in x-cut w/hobstars, 9½″ **195.00**
   Round, hobstars, x-hatching, fan cutting, 8″ **275.00**
   Russian cutting, 10x10″ square **1,025.00**
   Sawtooth edge, straw, fans, pinwheels, 7″ **85.00**
   Signed Clark, floral & straw quilt pattern, 8¼″ **110.00**
   Snowflake & Shield, heavy, 8″ dia **150.00**
   Straw fans, pinwheels, 7″ **120.00**
   Three feet, 7½″ **75.00**
   Venetian, w/silver floral rim, 4x9″ **850.00**
Box, collar & cuff, round, large **525.00**
   Dresser, covered, Harvard pattern, 24 pt base, 6″ dia **135.00**
   Gold wash sterling lid, straw dia & x-cut dia, 5x7″ **575.00**
   Heart-shape w/plated fittings, flowers & leaves, 32 pt base, 5x6″ **215.00**
   With cover, Creswick, Hoare **340.00**
   With cover, hinged, intaglio, 7½″ **250.00**
   With cover, hinged, Viscaria, Pairpoint, 6″ dia **190.00**
Bread tray, Harvard, Florence, hobstar center, shaped, 4x6x10″ **175.00**
   Hobs, vesicas, very heavy **275.00**
   Turned in sides, hobstars **315.00**
Bud vase, dia & fan, 9½″ **100.00**
Butter dish, profuse hobstars **325.00**
Butter pats, 4 . . . . **75.00**
   Carolyn, x-cut ovals & hobstars, J Hoare, 4 . . . . **225.00**
   Set of 8 . . . . **195.00**
Butter, w/cover, hobnail **150.00**
Butter tub, 2 eared, brilliant cut, 4½x7″ **185.00**
   Tab handles, scalloped rim, florals, fans & hobnail **125.00**
   With underplate, Arcadia pattern **350.00**
Candelabra, plated stem & 4 arms, hobs, straw dia & beads, 15½″ **450.00**
Candle holders, tall fluted teardrop, 6 prism bobeches, Libbey, pr **500.00**
Candlestick, teardrop stem, hobstars, straw, dia cane **295.00**
Candlesticks, scalloped hobstar base, 11″, pr **800.00**
Candy dish, w/handles, hobstars, dia & fan, 3x6½″ **60.00**
Candy jar, covered, x-cut dia, faceted knob **295.00**
   Lid w/high finial, fine x-hatching, 4 ft, 6″ **45.00**
   W/lid, triangular, spike finial, some cutting on pressed blank . **15.00**
Carafe, Broadway, octagonal neck, 7½″ **115.00**
   Chrysanthemum, hobstar base, by Hawkes, 7″ **595.00**
   Hobs & fans, 24 pt base, for water, 7½″ **95.00**
   Strawberry fan, 24 pt base, 9x6″ **60.00**
Celery, fish scale background, signed Libbey, 11½x4½x2″ **225.00**
   Hobstars, vexicas, fans, caning, x-hatch & hobnail, 12″ **125.00**
Champagne, ruby cut to clear **65.00**
Cheese & cracker, sterling rims, hobstars, straw dia fans **395.00**
Cheese dish, oversize, hobstar, buzz, dia, cane & fan **285.00**
   Covered, flashed pinwheel, fan, x-hatch & hobnail **550.00**
   Covered, scallop tooth rim, hobs, straw dia in sq **450.00**

Clock, boudoir, flowers, leaves & cane, 5½" tall **225.00**
   Boudoir, Harvard & Cosmos, working 5½x4" **220.00**
Cologne, Brazilian, cut stopper **250.00**
   Star & Clear buttons, 24 pt base, 5½" **220.00**
Comport, hobstars, dia fan w/scalloped hobstar base, 7" **245.00**
Compote, 1 pc, daisy & fan, scalloped rolled top, 12" **650.00**
   2 handle, heavy cut, 10" **400.00**
   2 handle, Harvard, 6½x9" **150.00**
   2 pc, scalloped bowl, Harvard & floral, 24 pt ft, 8x8" **450.00**
   8" stem, hobstars **160.00**
   Dia & fan, 11x9½" **275.00**
   Dia cut petticoat base, scallop tooth rim, hobs, hobnail, beading **600.00**
   Fan & cane cutting, 12" **390.00**
   Hobs, cane & straw dia notched stem w/blown teardrop **150.00**
   Hobs, x-hatch vesicas, scalloped hob base, 9½x6" **225.00**
   Hobstar base, teardrop stem, flashed hobstars, fans, 9½x6" . **285.00**
   Hobstars, cane, mitre cuts, heavy, sq, 7½x10" **125.00**
   Hobstars, dia & cane, knobbed stem, 8x7" **175.00**
   Hobstars, dia & cane, scalloped base, 11" **265.00**
   Hobstars, straw dia, honeycomb stem, 24 pt base, 8x8" **35.00**
   Hobstars, vesicas, zippered stem, rayed base **195.00**
   Hobstars & Harvard, hobstar pedestal, 8x11½" **275.00**
   Notched prism, hob base, 9½x6" **200.00**
   Paperweight base, allover cutting, 6½x7" **330.00**
   Paperweight base, hobnail & fan, 11x9½" **265.00**
   Pedestal, handles, Harvard, 9x6½" **200.00**
   Pedestal, hobstars, x-hatching & fans, 6¼x4" **65.00**
   Redmond, 10x9" **600.00**
   Russian cut lace & dia pattern, 10x7" **385.00**
   Teardrop in stem, 32 pt hobstar base, 9x9" **525.00**
   With teardrop, toothed rim, hobstars, straw dia, 8" **275.00**
Cookie jar, with cover, allover pinwheel, fan & hobnail, 9x6" . **575.00**
Creamer & sugar, Acme pattern, Hoare **155.00**
   Corinthian **175.00**
   Footed, hobstar, cane & straw dia, 5" **500.00**
   Miniature, sharply cut hobstars, heavy **195.00**
   Pedestal base, w/hobstars & cane, 4½" **400.00**
   Pinwheel, fan, straw **125.00**
   Straw dia & fan **90.00**
   Notched handles, sawtooth edge, Fry **200.00**
   Thumbprint handle, pinwheels, mitred, notch rim **85.00**
Cruet, dia & fan **32.50**
   Flashed fan, flairs, modified hobstars, w/stopper **115.00**
   Hobs, dia oval punties, 24 pt base, 6¾" **65.00**
   Stars & vesicas, rayed bottom, 9" **95.00**
   X-hatching & fan cutting, 6" **90.00**
Decanter, 9" **110.00**
   Allover buzz saw, hobs, fans, faceted stopper, 10½" **135.00**
   Diagonal block w/band of x-cutting, stopper **150.00**
   Flat, fluted mushroom stopper, panel cut, 10" **75.00**
   Gold cut to clear, with stopper, 12" **85.00**
   Hobstar, pinwheel & fan, 9" **135.00**
   Marlboro, hobstar base, handle, silver stopper **685.00**
   Music box, orig hollow stopper, Modern America series **185.00**
   Pinwheel, 6 cordials **200.00**
   Ring-handled, fern feather & flashed star w/stems, 11" **145.00**
   Ruby cut to clear, 12" **135.00**
   St Louis, zipper, thumbprint, w/handle **130.00**
   Thumbprint, matching stopper, 11" **140.00**
   Whiskey, hobstar pattern **285.00**
   With 6 cordials, pinwheel **170.00**
   Zipper pattern, w/handle, 9" **125.00**
Dinner bell, geometric allover cut, hobstars & canes, 5" **235.00**
Dish, 3 section, 3 handles, fern **190.00**

Crescent shape, Russian cut **225.00**
   Imperial pattern, diamond cut, 6" **65.00**
   Russian, Persian buttons, 6" **110.00**
Dresser box, allover Harvard, 24 pt base, 3½x6" **160.00**
Dresser tray, apple green cut to clear, hobstar center, oval ... **265.00**
Ewer, 1 qt, plated spout, ornate handle, leaf overlay, 12½" ... **125.00**
Flask, w/sterling cap, hobstar 1 side, rayed obverse, 4¼x3¾" . **225.00**
Fruit bowl, 14" dia **150.00**
   Plymouth, Empire, 3½x8" **250.00**
Glasses, juice, set of 6, straw dia fan **110.00**
Globe, Russian, 22 pt center, ball shape, 6" **200.00**
Goblet, hobstars, notched stems, 25 pt star base **25.00**
Goblets, Vintage, set of 12, hobstar & fan cranberry overlay, 8" **595.00**
   Water, stemmed, sharp buzz star, heavy, 6 .... **595.00**
Humidor, covered, pinwheels, 32 pt rayed base, 9x6" **500.00**
   Marlboro w/single star bottom, 10" **1,000.00**
     11" **1,200.00**
Ice cream tray, Harvard pattern, 8x14" **350.00**
   Harvard pattern, 12" **380.00**
   Scalloped, notched rim, hobnails, straw **285.00**
Ink well, cane, sterling top **285.00**
Jar w/cover, pinwheel & zipper, 5" **90.00**
Jewelry box, hinged cover, primrose & hobstars **750.00**
   Thumbprint at top & base edge, florals, 6" dia **365.00**
Juice glass, buzz pattern **20.00**
Juice glasses, 8 pt florence star, stars & checks, 3½x6" **150.00**
Knife rest, master, notched prism cut ball ends & bar, 5½" ... **90.00**
Lamp, 2 light, 10" dia shade, hobstars & fan **2,150.00**
   Dome 8½" dia, w/alternating 5" & 4" prisms, 24" **1,400.00**
   With prisms **1,050.00**
Lamps, hurricane w/prisms, pr **400.00**
Lemonade, Kalana Poppy, Dorflinger **95.00**
Liquor bottle, sterling collar "Scotch", Harvard **110.00**
Loving cup, 3 handles, buzz star & cane, 5½" **395.00**
Mayonnaise bowl w/underplate, hobstars & bars, single stars .. **150.00**
   Hobstars, notched prism, 7" plate, 4" cup **575.00**
Muffineer, silver top, hobstars fan, x-cut, rayed bottom, 4" ... **85.00**
Mustard, w/lid & underplate, vertical notch prism **135.00**
Napkin ring, hobstars **60.00**
   Russian cut **125.00**
Nappy, allover fine cutting, signed Libbey, 5" **75.00**
   Cranberry to clear, dia, x-cut & straw, 6½" **450.00**
   Floral, 6" **25.00**
   Hobstars, handles, signed Hawkes **35.00**
   Wild Rose, hobstar border, w/handle, 6" **75.00**
   Wild Rose, x-hatching, fan cutting, 4" **90.00**
Nut cup, w/underplate, allover dia, bottom ribs, octagon **72.00**
Paperweight book, Harvard, large **275.00**
Perfume, cranberry cut to clear, cane **295.00**
   Laydown, heart-shape, allover cut, sterling collar **65.00**
   Overall cane, sterling screw-on top, 3" dia **18.00**
   Panel flute, sterling top **140.00**
   Silver hinged top, single star & x-cut dia, 2½" **125.00**
Pickle dish, canoe, Harvard pattern **85.00**
Pitcher, Brunswich cutting, 11" **435.00**
   Bulbous, circles, ovals, cylinder ice insert, plated handle, sm.. **45.00**
   Bulbous, circles, ovals, vertical lines, 12 pt star base, sm..... **34.00**
   Cider, cathedral vesicas w/hobstars, Hoare **595.00**
   Cider, tankard-style, hobstars, straw, dia, fans, 6" **350.00**
   Hobstars, fans & straw dia, daisies, 10" **175.00**
   Lotus, Egginton, 7" **245.00**
   Martini w/sterling ice lip & spoon, Iris, Hawkes, 6" **185.00**
   Milk, Harvard cutting, 8" **390.00**
   Scallop rim, notch handle, hobs, block dia, 4¾" **160.00**

Navarre, barrel shape, signed Hawkes, 8" **475.00**
Pedestal, hobstars & notched prism, handle, 10" **995.00**
Tankard-shaped, heavy, 10¼" **150.00**
Triple notch handle, hobstars, dia, J Hoare, 1853, 8½x7" . . **450.00**
Water, bull's eyes & prisms, 8" **275.00**
Plate, Ellsmere, signed Libbey, sabre mark, 6¾" **95.00**
Harvard button cut in straw dia, J Hoare, 7" **300.00**
Standard foot, 24 pt flashed hobstar, 10" **275.00**
Straw dia band, sterling border, 9" **55.00**
Powder box, hinged, star flower w/variants, 5½" **190.00**
Punch cup, cobalt medallion, 22K crest **145.00**

Punch bowl, 2 pc, amethyst cut to clear, 16" **2,800.00**
Punch bowl, 2 pc, pinwheel, hobstars & straw dia, 10" **700.00**
2 pc, Meriden cut #136, 1900, 12" dia **1,200.00**
2 pc, pinwheel cutting, 15" **1,400.00**
Pedestal, 12" **800.00**
Tulip shape, buzz star, cane, hobstars, 2 pt, 13" **950.00**
With lid, pineapple & fan, 1890 . . . . **550.00**
Punch cups, Colonna pattern, signed Libbey, 5 . . . . **280.00**
Punch ladle **375.00**
Punch set, bowl on pedestal w/10 cups **1,500.00**
Relish, canoe shape, 7" **50.00**
Canoe shape, Clark, 12x4" **215.00**
Ring tree, Florence pattern **115.00**
Rose bowl, deep cut w/gold & enamel decor, 7" dia **190.00**
Dia, sq ft, scallop top, fan cuttings **175.00**
Gold and enamel decor, 1800s, 7" **225.00**
Miniature, Middlesex, hobs base, 2¾x3½" **85.00**
Miniature, tiny rayed pedestal **95.00**
Straw & dia, 5x4" **180.00**
Straw & dia, 32 pt star bottom 6½x7" **210.00**
Rose jar, signed Clark **525.00**
Rosebowl, hobstars w/notched columns, star base, 3" **35.00**
Salt, crosscut, straw dia, fans, 24 pt star base **16.00**
Salt & peppers, Celtic, Dorflinger **28.00**
Spooner, all over cut, Harvard, hobstar bottom, heavy 4¾" . . . **170.00**
With handles, starburst, dia fan **100.00**
Tankard, applied handle, floral, lead cutting, 11" **30.00**
Heavy, 10¼" **150.00**
Large & small hobstars, dia chains, 8½" **145.00**
Notched prism, cupids heads, heavy, 15" **550.00**
Sterling rim, hobstars, straw dia, 11" **350.00**
With hobstars, 12" **380.00**

Tatting holder, prism, Gorham top, 3¼x3¼" **250.00**
Toothpick, star, fan, notched ribs, barrel shape **16.00**
Tray, cake, scallop tooth rim, hobs, hobnail w/ovals **400.00**
Celery, 4 elipses join in center w/flowers , leaves, 12" **120.00**
Gold cut to clear intaglio fruits, oblong, 13" **80.00**
Gravic Iris, oval, 10x7" **295.00**
Kidney shape, hobstars & diamond, 8x3½" **75.00**
Marlboro, very heavy, 12" dia **865.00**
Russian, 15x8" **750.00**
With handles, hobstars, dia & star, 8x4" **100.00**
Tumbler, hobstars, fan **18.00**
Russian pattern **65.00**
Set of 4, intricate cuttings, 24 pt base, Hoare **300.00**
Vase, Athens, single star base, 10x4½" **285.00**
Chalice trumpet, blown, hobstar base, Hoare, 12" **375.00**
Cobalt to clear, 10x8" **225.00**
Genoa pattern by Clark, 6x6" **550.00**
Green cut to clear, floral & mitre, England, 8" **75.00**
Hobs, prisms, bull's eyes & dia points, 14" **225.00**
Hobstars & thumbprint, notched prisms, scalloped, Maple City, 8" **235.00**
Hobstars, hobnails & x-hatching, hobstar base **695.00**
Kohinoor & dia, flaring, Hawkes, 10" **275.00**
Monarch, w/handles, 12" **1,000.00**
Pinwheel, heavy blank, 5x6½" **85.00**
Russian & Pillars, trumpet shape, footed, 12" **1,250.00**
Sawtooth rim, rayed base, zippered stem, 10" **125.00**
Scalloped w/hobstars, prism & panels, ft, 15" **195.00**
Trumpet, graduated bull's eyes & prism, 20" **650.00**
Trumpet, hobstars & notched prism, some wear, 15" **295.00**
Trumpet, hobstars, fan & x-hatching, 10" **95.00**
Trumpet, Tuthill, intaglio grape, notched panels, scallops, 12" **195.00**
Trumpet, waffle pattern & thumprint rim, Hawkes, 9" **165.00**
Waisted, cone/x-hatch band at top, floral, leaf cut, 6" **45.00**
Wild Rose w/butterflies, ped base, Clark **200.00**
With notched stem, 24 pt ray star bottom, 12x5" **350.00**
With ped, flashed fans, step cut scallop top 14" **650.00**
Car, no holders, 4x7", pr **350.00**
Vinaigrette, sterling embossed top, ring notched ribs, 3" **26.00**
Whiskey bottle, w/faceted collar, hobstars, x-cut dia fans . . . **300.00**
Whiskey glass, hobstar base **90.00**
Pinwheel **15.00**
Wine glass, knobbed teardrop stem, Russian, green **350.00**
Louis XIV, knob stem, 4" **65.00**
Wine tureen, w/6 sm glasses **300.00**

Cybis

Boleslaw Cybis was a graduate of the Academy of Fine Arts in Warsaw, Poland, and was well recognized as a fine artist by the time he was commissioned by his government to paint murals in the Polish Pavillion's Hall of Honor at the 1939 World's Fair. With the outbreak of WWII, the Cybises found themselves stranded in the United States, and founded an artists' studio, first in Astoria, N. Y. and later in Trenton, N. J., where they made fine figurines and plaques with exacting artistry and craftsmanship entailling extensive handwork. The studio still operates today producing exquisite porcelains on a limited edition basis.

Abigail Adams **750.00**
Alexander w/pink saddle **245.00**
Alice **250.00**
Allegra **225.00**
Apple Blossoms **350.00**
Baby Chicks, Downey & Lemon **180.00**
Baby Owl **75.00**

Beatrice	1,150.00
Betty Blue	250.00
Bonbonnier	75.00
Boys Playing Leap Frog	300.00
Boys Playing Marbles, Rusty & Johnny	300.00
Bunny Pat-A-Cake	75.00
Bunny, Mr Snowball	40.00
Bunny, Muffet	85.00
Burro, Fitzgerald	85.00
Calla Lily	900.00
Cinderella	365.00
Circus Rider Equestrienne Extraordinarie	2,000.00
Columbine	1,500.00
Daisies Don't Tell	75.00
Deermouse in clover	125.00
Desiree, The White Deer	600.00
Dormouse, Maximillian	150.00
Doves of Peace, 1957	4,500.00
Duckling, Baby Brother	100.00
Edith	275.00
Edward	250.00
Elephant	250.00
Elizabeth Ann	250.00
Enamoured Prince	700.00
Eros	200.00
Eskimo Boy	265.00
Felicity	335.00
First Flight	110.00
Frollo the Juggler	465.00
Golden Winged Warbler	765.00
Goldilocks	210.00
Good Queen Anne	775.00
Great Horned Owl	1,200.00
Great White Heron	1,500.00
Guinevere	1,000.00
Harlequin	1,200.00
Heidi	225.00
Holiday Child	200.00
Jeannie w/the Light Hair	300.00
Jogger, Lance	250.00
Kara, Girl on the Beach	275.00
Kazmar Golden Eagle, signed	175.00
Lady MacBeth	860.00
Lily #189, wood base, 5″	275.00
Little Blue Hero	850.00
Little Boy Blue	325.00
Little Eagle	350.00
Little Miss Muffet	225.00
Little Owl	65.00
Little Red Riding Hood	150.00
Madonna w/Bird, decorated	325.00
Madonna w/lace veil, 4½″	110.00
Madonna, Queen of Peace, decorated	190.00
Mary, Mary	450.00
Melissa w/blue bow	485.00
Monkey Bosun	275.00
Mushroom Jack O'Lantern	250.00
Nancy & Ned Sledding	320.00
Noah	1,600.00
Oriental Boy	280.00
Oriental Girl	280.00
Oriental Head	300.00
Pandora	175.00
Pegasas, Free Spirit	500.00

Pinto Colt	150.00
Pip, the Elfin Player	450.00
Pollyanna	250.00
Poppy Performing Pony	600.00
Prairie Dog, Poke	160.00
Psyche	200.00
Queen Esther	900.00
Raffles the Raccoon	240.00
Red Riding Hood	115.00
Rose Jar Pastel	150.00
Rose, Pink Parfait	140.00
Rumples, the Clown	425.00
Running Deer & Little Eagle, pr	975.00

Snail	235.00
St Joseph, colored glaze, early 11″	300.00
Suzanne, Girl w/Kitten	250.00
Thoroughbred	600.00
Tiffin	200.00
Victoria	250.00
Wendy w/Flowers, special edition	185.00
Wendy w/Flowers	175.00
Windflower	165.00
Yankee Doodle Dandy	275.00

Czechoslovakian Collectibles

Czechoslovakia, located in the heart of Europe was a land with the natural resources necessary to support a glass making industry that dates back to the mid-14th century. To this day it remains an important industry. Pottery and china has also been made there; many pieces are ink stamped Czechoslavakia.

Ashtray, deer, ceramic, Art Deco, mk, 6″	8.50
Basket, clear w/scalloped rim, frosted relief roses	40.00
Candlesticks, saucer & handle, blue Delft type, pr	18.00
Canister & spice set, ceramic, blue on white, 15 pcs	65.00
Creamer, moose head figural, ceramic, marked	28.00
Figurine, lady in evening gown, seated, w/cigar, ceramic	40.00
Seated hunter w/gun, dog, porcelain, 8″	125.00
Inkwell, double, 24k gold decor	125.00
Jam jar, ceramic, ivory/tan basketweave, berries, Coronet	10.00
Lamp, mushroom figural, camphor glass, 7″	75.00
Marionette, King, compo head, hands, feet, painted, 8″	22.00
Nut dishes, 4 pc, spade, heart, club, diamond	5.00

Perfume, camphor glass, fan stopper, florals, scrolls, 6″ **35.00**
   Clear cut, round stopper, small **15.00**
   Purse flask, ruby to clear, 3″ **45.00**
Pin tray, jeweled, w/cut glass insert **40.00**
Pitcher, bird figural, ceramic hp red, yellow, blk, mkd, 9″ **30.00**
Planter, bird on log, ceramic, 4″ **5.50**
Salts, ceramic, set of 4 in box **20.00**
Sugar & creamer, hexagon, blk w/hp florals, gold handles **45.00**
Teapot, w/tray, orange & black, Art Deco **30.00**
Vase, art glass, fluted top, 8″ **35.00**
   Art glass, spatter to clear, metal collar w/geese, 12″ **195.00**
   Black ameythst, applied flowers, 14″ **30.00**
   Cased glass, red, wht w/lt red handles, mkd, 7x7″ **38.00**
   Cased, red & grey spatter, black snake, ruffled, 8″ **80.00**
   Painted glass, green sides, amber base, ruffled, 6″ **20.00**
   Pearl luster w/blue handles, scalloped, 5½″ **6.50**

Vase, Peloton-type, clear glass, w/red, white, 7½″ **25.00**
   Satin & clear glass alternate in panels, 7½″ **15.00**
   Yellow & green luster, black handles, ceramic, 5½″ **6.00**
Wall pocket, bird on branch, 3 openings, orange/yellow, #32 .... **8.00**
   Bisque owl on castle wall **12.00**

D'Argental

   D'Argental cameo glass was produced in France from the 1870s until about 1920, in the Art Nouveau style. Browns and caramels were often used to compliment florals and scenic designs developed through acid cuttings.

Bowl, flowering vines, leafage, mustard & green, 9¼″ **825.00**
Box, florals & leaves, yellow on brown, 3¾″ **550.00**
Vase, florals & leaves in detail, bulbous w/slim neck, 2 colors, 4″ **400.00**
Vase, florals, blue on maroon, 13½″ **900.00**
Vase, jonquils, maroon, salmon, frosted maize, 4 cuttings, 12x6″ **875.00**
Vase, lake scene, 4 cuttings, wide base, slim tapered neck, 14″ **975.00**
Vase, landscape, maroon on gold frost, 6¼″ **585.00**
Vase, leaves, berries, shaded ground w/acid & gloss decor, 5″ . **475.00**
Vase, lily pond scene, yellow & red w/red flora, 4x4″ **550.00**
Vase, pine cones & branches, red on green, 13″ **800.00**

Daum Nancy

   Daum was an important producer of French cameo glass, operating from the late 1800s until after the turn of the century. They used various techniques—acid cutting, wheel engraving and hand work—to create beautiful scenic designs and nature subjects in the Art Nouveau manner. Today, marked examples are much in demand and command very high prices.

Bottle, green Deco florals on frosted stippled ground, 7″ **165.00**
Bowl, lime & salmon w/winter landscape, rolled, scalloped, 6″ . **605.00**
   Red & purple poppies, green leaves, 2 handles, 8″ **1,100.00**
   Winter scene, square, 2¼x6″ **550.00**
   Yellow/orange ground w/brown leaves, cherries, 5½″ **595.00**
Box, acid stippled ground w/red apples & vines, 4″ dia **80.00**
   Covered, autumn leaves, nuts, 4″ sq **400.00**
   Covered, disk foot, domed cover, rose branches, 5¾″ **550.00**
   Covered, winter scene, 3″ sq **600.00**
Bud vase, bulbous w/tall thin neck, lakeside forest, 16″ **1,100.00**
   Gray w/carmel pine boughs, 7″ **400.00**
   Gray w/purple wildflowers, leaves, 6¾″ **375.00**
Candle lamp, blue w/Venetian boat scene 12¾″ **375.00**
Compote, blue/brown w/leafage, 8″ **475.00**
Cup & saucer, Clair de Lune scenic, man, sailboats **700.00**
Ewer, bellflowers on mottled gold & clear ground, 11½″ **250.00**
   Clear serpentine handle trails body **420.00**
   Silver top & handle, enameled flowers, signed, dated **250.00**
Flagon, waisted w/applied handle, marine & landscape motif, 3″ **715.00**
Goblet, butterscotch cameo, signed **250.00**
Juice tumbler, green w/pods & berries **115.00**
Master salt, four feet, shamrock pattern **350.00**
Perfume, w/atomizer, florals **775.00**
   Mottled w/yellow iris, green leafage, 5½″ **600.00**
Pitcher, miniature, violets, frosted **695.00**
Rosebowl, clover cut top, all over cameo **500.00**
   Winter scenic, oblong, gold mottled frost ground, 4½x6″ ... **695.00**
Salt, green w/gold enamel **300.00**
   Turquoise thistles, frosted ground, 2″ **545.00**
   Windmills, ships, 1¾″ **385.00**
Shot glass, winter scenic, orange ground, signed, 1¾″ **350.00**
Toothpick, oval scenic w/swan, signed **450.00**
Tumbler, blue w/gold pods & berries, signed **150.00**
   Pink w/gold pods & berries **145.00**
   Summer scene, blue frost w/enameled detail, 4¾″ **540.00**
Vase, frosted w/sunflowers in ivory, gilt, 13″ **1,210.00**
   Baluster, gray mottled w/blue clematis, 12½″ **1,045.00**
   Black raspberry, 2 cuttings, polished, 8″ **575.00**
   Black Duck, deep carving on wings & tail, 17″ **100.00**
   Blue w/winter scene in gray & wht, 1910, 9½″ **770.00**
   Bulbous w/squared rim, dandelions, 3″ **500.00**
   Citron & gray w/raspberries in natural colors, 21″ **1,100.00**
   Cylinder neck, cushion foot, wisteria pods, leaves, 13½″ **770.00**
   Cylinder, gray w/purple, fuschia cuttings, 8½″ **375.00**
   Cylinder, wine iridescent, enamel roses, 8¾″ **525.00**
   Flattened ovoid, mottled blue w/spring meadow, 4¾″ **770.00**
   Floriform, gold to brown, insects, webs, fern base, 8″ **1,200.00**
   Fox & Raven w/enameling, ice-like to emerald, 8″ **1,275.00**
   Frosted ground w/leaves & berries, gold, 4¾″ **500.00**
   Frosted w/sunflowers in ivory, gilt, 13″ **1,210.00**
   Gondola, sailboat, Venice in background, 5x3″ **1,450.00**
   Gray w/lime streaks, ivory pods & leafage, 14″ **715.00**
   Gray w/red & yellow mottling, branches, grasses, 13″ **770.00**
   Mottled ground w/cut & enameled bleeding hearts, 4¾″ **360.00**
   Multicolor mottling w/seven black junks, 14″ **1,210.00**
   Ovoid, on foot, mottled yellow, gray, enamel florals, 3½″ ... **350.00**
   Ovoid, yellow w/enamel poppies, gilt foot, 4″ **450.00**
   Purple violets, green leaves, 4½″ **565.00**
   Purple w/roses in relief, gold, 9″ **575.00**
   Satin cobalt to gray, streaks of blue & rust, 4″ **875.00**

Squared, green thistle w/gold enamel, 4½"............. **335.00**
Summer scenic, green frost w/enameled detail, flattened, 5". **850.00**
Sunset scenic, black pedestal, pulled up corners, 4½x7".... **925.00**
Sunset w/sailboats, pedestal base, 9½"................. **995.00**
Tapered cylinder on pedestal, apricot w/leafy branch, 16"... **770.00**
Winter scenic, 2"..................................... **935.00**
Winter scene, flattened oval, brown trees on orange, 3¼".. **425.00**
Winter scenic w/church & windmills................... **895.00**
Wooded landscape, mottled lime ground, 14"........... **935.00**
Yellow & apricot ground, winter scene, 11¾"........... **1,210.00**
Yellow & gray w/violet, autumn landscape, 6¾".......... **990.00**
Yellow, orange, green, w/blk grapevines, pedestal, 15"..... **770.00**

Davenport

W. Davenport & Co. were Staffordshire potters operating in that area from 1793-1887 producing earthenwares, creamwares, porcelains and ironstone. Many different stamps, all with 'Davenport', were used to mark the various types of ware.

Bowl, landscape, blue & wht, early 1800s, mkd......... **60.00**
Cup & saucer, Imari, early 1800s...................... **65.00**
Panels w/scrolls, gold decor, 1850s................... **78.00**
Pitcher, octagonal, Winchester Cathedral, purple luster, mkd, 8" **295.00**
Plate, castle w/mountains, hand painted, 9"........... **60.00**
Multifloral decor, scrolled & reticulated border, 9"....... **50.00**
Plates, black & white w/Yarmouth scenes, set of 6, 7"...... **120.00**
Platter, oriental decor, reticulated border, blue & wht, 11"... **100.00**
Tea set, Persian Bird, 3 pc w/3 handleless cups & saucers.... **450.00**
Urn, portrait in reserve, low handles, ped, mkd........... **250.00**

De Vez

De Vez was a type of acid cut French cameo glass produced by Cristallerie de Pantin in Paris around the turn of the century.

Bowl, diamond shape, bears in forest, 3 acid cuttings, 3½x5½" dia **1,100.00**
Cologne, footed, heart shape body, floral on yellow, 5"...... **250.00**
Vase, fisherman & boats, 3 acid cuts, rose & leaf frame, 7½" **2,000.00**
Frosted aqua, boat, vines frame, 3 acid cuts, 4x2½"....... **525.00**
Frosted green, sailboats, 3 acid cuts, branches frame scene, 10" **995.00**
Gold w/3 cuttings, Venice scenic, top w/pulled points, 6"... **850.00**
Green to rose, Venetian scene w/gondola, 3 acid cuts, 6"... **895.00**
Green w/peach Roman Temple, sailboats, 8".......... **1,200.00**
L'Meteor Village, gold frost w/rose, navy, 3 cuts, 8½".... **1,000.00**
Lemon w/pink blush, navy foliage, 3 flamingos, 7¾"....... **695.00**
Pink, navy, yellow, sailboats, mountains, trees, 10"........ **750.00**
Sailboat, house, trees & mountain, 3 cuttings, 8"......... **795.00**
Scenic, 3 acid cuttings, blues & greens................ **650.00**

Decoys

For some years decoys have been recognized as folk art, but even more recently an increasingly competitive market has attracted the serious attention of collectors. Distinguishing between factory decoys and those of individual artists is not always an easy task, since some factory-made decoys involved individual workmanship. Inexperienced collectors should beware of repainted or otherwise altered models.

Key:
RR--repaint   OP--original paint
WOP--worn original paint   OWP--original working paint
ORP--old repaint   WRP--working repaint

American Merganser, Herter's, glass eyes, OP, 1893, 19"..... **55.00**

Open beak, cocked head, glass eyes, OP, 14"........... **65.00**
Bird, glass eyes, bristle comb, by Schifferl, 21x16"......... **630.00**
Tin, pat 1874.. **60.00**

Black Duck, deep carving on wings & tail, 17"............. **100.00**
Glass eyes, OP w/scratch detail, splits, 1910, 15".......... **80.00**
Hollow Premiere, early mason, black repaint............. **120.00**
Turned head, glass eyes, OP, 14"...................... **105.00**
Blue Goose, flat wood field stick-up, tack eyes, OP, 1930, 24".. **90.00**
Blue Wing Teal drake, turned head, tack eyes, WOP, 11"..... **80.00**
Primitive, tack eyes, OP, 1920, 12".................... **75.00**
Bluebill, carved, New Jersey, 9"...................... **45.00**
Bluebill drake, glass eyes, OP, 1920, 12½".............. **45.00**
Glass eyes, WOP, by Ackerman, 12".................... **95.00**
Glass eyes, WRP, Baumgardner, 1930, 12"............. **60.00**
Mason's Premier, 1900............................... **575.00**
Primitive, glass eyes, repainted bill, 13½".............. **48.00**
Primitive sleeper, glass eyes, OP, 1920, 12"............. **55.00**
Updike, WOP... **150.00**
Bluebill duck, tin stick-up, ornate painting, 1920, 9x14"...... **50.00**
Bluebill hen, hollow, glass eyes, WRP, 1900, 13½"......... **50.00**
Low head position, tack eyes, carved feathers, OP......... **80.00**
Primitive, balsa, glass eyes, WOP, 1930s, 14"........... **30.00**
Primitive, WOP, 1920s, 14½"......................... **45.00**
Tack eyes, turned head, incised feathers, OP............ **125.00**
Bufflehead drake, carved, Eastern shore, Va., OP, 11½"..... **30.00**
Hollow, by Croft, Mi., tack eyes, OP, 10"............... **65.00**
Primitive, by Croft, glass eyes, 10"................... **60.00**
Canadian Goose, primitive, glass eyes, Ackerman, WOP, 17".. **100.00**
Carved wings, OP, w/slight wear...................... **230.00**
Early 1900s, OP, 23x12x9".......................... **220.00**
From Easton, Md.................................... **195.00**
Swimmer by Gibson, OP, 30"........................ **165.00**
Swimmer, tack eyes, OP, 22"........................ **75.00**
Swivel head, textured, OP, old....................... **175.00**
Tack eyes, carved bill, old paint, Lincoln............. **600.00**
Wood & canvas on wire, OP, 19"..................... **30.00**
Canvasback drake, glass eyes, OP w/touch up, Nelo, 1930, 14". **60.00**
Hollow, premiere grade, OP.......................... **425.00**
OP, Walter Evans, 1920s............................ **170.00**
Coot, glass eyes, OP, 1910, 13"...................... **135.00**
Primitive, glass eyes, OP, 1900, 11½"................. **70.00**
Primitive, tack eyes, OP, 1900, 9½"................... **115.00**
Crow, glass eyes, OP, by Seidel, Delaware River, 16"...... **130.00**
Curlew, Virginia, WOP............................... **235.00**
Duck, cork w/wood head & base....................... **20.00**
Hand carved, 1900, 13"............................. **47.50**
Ill. Red Head, OP, early 1900s....................... **170.00**
Mason's challenge grade, RP......................... **100.00**
Mason's premier grade, OP.......................... **275.00**
Shoveler, Mason cedar body, hand carved............... **90.00**

Stained, glass eyes, 1920, 17″ **65.00**
Eider, primitive WOP, 15″ **75.00**
Goldeneye drake, glass eyes, OP, wing carving, 1930, 14″ **75.00**
    Glass eyes, WRP, 1930, 15″ **55.00**
    Turned head, by Jobes, OP, 14″ **60.00**
Goldeneye sleeper, wing & tail carved, glass eyes, OP, 11″ **55.00**
Goose, hissing, Maine, OWP, 1920s **245.00**
    Preening position, Brandt, never painted, 20″ **140.00**
    Tin stick-up, OP, 1900, 22x29″ **55.00**
Great Black Backed Gull, cedar w/details, glass eyes, 27″ . . . **270.00**
Green Wing teal drake, cedar, glass eyes, OP, 10″ **80.00**
    Glass eyes, OP, from Knotts Island, 9½″ **105.00**
Hooded Merganser, Primitive, tack eyes, OP, 10″ **60.00**
Loon, primitive, Nova Scotia, carved back, OP, 1900, 18″ **65.00**
Mallard drake, carved hollow body by P Wilcox, 1920s **200.00**
    Miniature on driftwood, contemporary, Long Island **25.00**
    Miniature, W R Case, 1971, Long Island **35.00**
    Perdew, WOP, no weight **480.00**
    Pratt, OP **60.00**
    Primitive, feeder, Saginaw Bay, Mi., 1920, 18″ **75.00**
    Schmidt Bros, 1930s, ex OP **375.00**
    Sleeper, Op, 14″ **55.00**
    Swimmer, by Smith, Mi., glass eyes, OP, 21″ **125.00**
Mallard hen, glass eyes, carved, stamped detail, OP, Monamee . . **55.00**
    Hollowbody, Ill. River, signed, 1930s **220.00**
    Tin stick-up, fancy paint, 1920, 9x14″ **50.00**
Mallard, Mason's challenge grade **90.00**
Merganser drake, Mason's premier grade, hollow, OP, repair **1,700.00**
Merganser, glass eyes, signed Archer, OP, 16½″ **180.00**
Pigeon, English, 15″ **150.00**
    Primitive style folk carving, OP, 14½″ **165.00**
Pintail drake, Castle Haven, glass eyes, WRP, 16″ **75.00**
    Cedar, glass eyes, OP, 21″ **150.00**
    Cloth covered, 13″ **25.00**
    Field stick-up, metal wings, OP, 17½x24″ **150.00**
    High head, elongated tail, by Gibson, OP, 18″ **85.00**
Pintail hen, head to left, OP, by Ward Bros, some damage . **3,100.00**
    Standard, tack eyes, WOP **185.00**
Red Breasted Merganser drake, hollow, Hendrickson, OP, 16″ **130.00**
Red Breasted Merganser hen, hollow, McNair, horsehair comb **345.00**
    Relief carved, tack eye, OP, 15″ **85.00**
Red Breasted Merganser, cocked head, open beak, glass eyes, OP, 14″ **65.00**
Redhead drake, Jess Urie, OP **135.00**
    Turned head, wing carving, WOP, 13″ **60.00**
Redhead hen, glass eyes, old RP, Dodge Factory, 1800, 14½″ **155.00**
    Sellers, OP **80.00**
Ruddy duck, carved details, inletted head, cocky, OP, 7″ **150.00**
Sea duck, Tollers, Eiders, from Hulls Harbor 1940, pr **175.00**
Sea gull, minniature on driftwood, contemporary, Long Island . . **60.00**
Sea gull, tack eye, primitive, OP, early 1900s **140.00**
Shore bird, Black Bellied Plover, OP, by Bieder, East coast **80.00**
    Sandpiper, by Bieder, OP, East coast **70.00**
    Snowy Egret, stretching neck, carved bill **95.00**
    Wood, yellow-legs, square nail beak, 1890 . . . . **95.00**
    Yellowlegs, by Bieder, OP, East coast **85.00**
Swan, decorative, by Paul, 7½″ **215.00**
    Miniature w/snake at neck, Vern, 8″ **95.00**
    Tack eyes worn WRP, base added, 26x29″ **550.00**
Trumpeter Swan, hollow carved, OWP, repair **3,250.00**
Turkey, wood & compo w/glass eyes, OP restored, repair, 27½″ **800.00**
Whistler Drake, Coombs, OP **380.00**
White Winged Scoter, inlet head, OP **140.00**
    Mason's standard, glass eye, OP **400.00**
Widgeon drake, miniature, by Crowell, ... **300.00**

Wood duck, primitive hand carved, flat head, old paint **20.00**
Yellowlegs, spike bill, WOP **170.00**

Dedham Pottery

Originally founded in Morrisville, Pennsylvania as the Chelsea Pottery, the name was changed to Dedham Pottery in 1895, after the firm relocated in Dedham, near Boston, Massachusetts. The move was effected to make use of the native clay deemed more suitable for the production of the popular dinnerware designed by its founder, Hugh Robinson. The ware utilized a grey stoneware body with a crackle glaze and simple cobalt border designs of flowers, birds and animals. Decorations were brushed on by hand using an ancient Chinese method which suspended the cobalt within the overall glaze. There were thirteen standard patterns, among them Magnolia, Iris, Butterfly, Duck, Polar Bear and the Rabbit, which was chosen to represent the company on their logo. On the very early pieces the rabbits face left; decoraters found the reverse position easier to paint, and the rabbits were turned to the right.

In addition to the standard patterns, other designs were produced for special orders. These and artist signed pieces are very popular with collectors.

The firm was operated by succeeding generations of the Robertson family until it closed in 1943.

Ashtray, Polar Bear, sm chip, 4″ **135.00**
Bowl, Azalea, slight age crack, 8½″ **175.00**
    Covered, Rabbit, 9″ **90.00**
    Double Ear Rabbit, marked, 4″, illus **75.00**
    Magnolia, scalloped rim, 9″ **300.00**
    Oval, Magnolia, age crack, 10″ **120.00**
Child's plate, Rabbit, 4½″ **195.00**
Child's punch bowl, Rabbit, 3½″ **150.00**
Chop plate, Iris, 12″ **345.00**
Creamer, Azalea, tankard shape, 3″ **170.00**
    Elephant, tankard shape, special order, 5″ **500.00**
Pitcher, Rabbits, 5″ **240.00**
    Azalea, 3½″ **165.00**
Plate, Azalea, 8½″ **95.00**
    Dolphins, upside down, experimental, 8¾″ **550.00**
    Double Ear Rabbit, marked, 6″, illus **85.00**

Double Ear Rabbit, marked, 8½″ **90.00**

Duck, 8″	80.00	Dk Amber	95.00
Duck, Maude O Davenport, 8½″	275.00	Dk Slag	95.00
Grape, 2 mks: ink & impressed rabbit, 8½″	140.00	Opaque Blue	95.00
Grape, 7½″	125.00	Pink Crystal	12.50
Grape, 8½″	95.00	Elephant, Vaseline	15.00
Horsechestnut, 8½″	95.00	Gypsy Kettle, Milk White Opal	12.50
Iris, signed Humphrey, 9″	100.00	Hand, Amethyst	12.50
Lobster, 2 marks: ink & impressed rabbit, 9″	550.00	Tuscan	15.00
Magnolia, 8″	60.00	Hat, Daisy & Button, Sapphire	15.00
Magnolia, 10″	85.00	Hen, 2″, Bloody Mary	25.00
Moth, 6″	175.00	5″, Amber	45.00
Mushroom, 6″	195.00	5″, Bloody Mary	85.00
Polar Bear, 6″	185.00	8″, Charcoal Opaque	30.00
Polar Bear, artist signed, 2 mks: ink & immpressed, 10″	360.00	8″, Crown Tuscan	25.00
Pond lily, 8½″	95.00	8″, Green	20.00
Rabbit, 6¼″	60.00	8″, Vaseline	20.00
Rabbit, 8″	85.00	Jewel box, heart, Amber, signed	45.00
Rabbit, 8½″	95.00	Heart, Sapphire	25.00
Turkey, 6½″	120.00	Heart, Yellow Opaque Custard	50.00
Turkey, 7½″	145.00	Lamb, 5″, Amberina	45.00
Turkey, 8½″	165.00	5″, Blue	45.00
Saucer, Swan	175.00	5″, Sapphire	35.00
Shaker, Bunnies	110.00	Mini Pitcher, Amberina	23.00
Vase, caramel drip glaze, 8″	250.00	Crystal	10.00
Green & blue glaze, signed HCR, hairline, 5½″	450.00	Sapphire	12.50
Volcanic dark olive high glaze, DP69A, HCR, 8½x7″	265.00	Vaseline	10.00

Degenhart

The Crystal Art Glass factory in Cambridge, Ohio, opened in 1947 under the private ownerhsip of John and Elizabeth Degenhart. John had previously worked for the Cambridge Glass Company, and was well known for his superior paperweights. After his death in 1964, Elizabeth took over management of the factory, hiring several workers from the defunct Cambridge Co, including Zack Boyd. Boyd was responsible for many unique colors, some of which were named after him. From 1964 to 1974, more than 27 different molds were created, most of them resulting from Elizabeth Degenharts work and creativity, and over 145 official colors had been developed. In 1978, Elizabeth died, and the molds were sold to Island Mold Co, and the familiar 'D' in heart trademarks removed. The factory was eventually bought by Zack's son, Bernard Boyd.

Mini slipper, Amethyst	20.00
Milk Blue	20.00
Sapphire	15.00
Mug, stork, Cobalt	12.00
Owl, Amber	27.00
Angel Blue	25.00
Blue, Green & Wht slag	90.00
Charcoal Slag	55.00
Chartreuse	39.00
Chocolate	45.00
Crown Tuscan	22.00
Crystal	20.00
Dickie Bird	90.00
Dk Blue	32.00
Dk Green	95.00
Indigo	21.00
Jade	45.00
Lavender Blue	65.00
Lemonade	32.50
Limeade	33.00
Lt Yellow	120.00
Midnight Sun	45.00
Milk Blue	35.00
Moonglo	38.50
Peachblo	16.50
Pearl Grey	50.00
Pigeon Blood, Carnival	162.00
Pigeon Blood	95.00
Red Carnival	145.00
Rose Marie	21.00
Sapphire	25.00
Shell	37.50
Sunset	33.00
Tiger Ivory	48.50
Willow Blue	19.50
Paperweight, Bicentennial	300.00
Colored Crystal, controlled bubbles	200.00
First Lady of Glass	225.00

Bell, Charcoal	25.00
Crystal	10.00
Milk Blue	15.00
Sapphire	10.00
Tuscan	15.00
Chick, 2″, Cobalt	15.00
2″, Milk Blue	15.00
Coaster, Pearl Grey	15.00
Covered candy, Milk Blue	25.00
Cream & sugar, Daisy & Button, Cobalt	50.00
Daisy & Button, Golden Amber	50.00
Daisy & Button, Sapphire	50.00
Texas, John D. Ruby	75.00
Texas, Cobalt	85.00
Texas, Dk Amber	70.00
Cup Plate, Cobalt	12.50
Heart & Lyre, Crown Tuscan	50.00
Heart & Lyre, Custard	50.00
Heart & Lyre, Opalescent Blue	50.00
Dog, Bittersweet Slag	65.00
Cobalt	18.50
Creamy Pink	35.00

Rose, Yellow	300.00
Portrait plate, Amberina	55.00
Pottie, Bluebell	10.00
Priscilla, Amethyst	75.00
April Green	80.00
Ebony	100.00
Ivory	80.00
Jade	90.00
January Blizzard	75.00
Periwinkle	80.00
Willow Blue	75.00
Salt, bird, Crystal	10.00
Milk Blue	15.00
Sapphire	12.50
Salt, Daisy & Button; Bittersweet	20.00
Milk Blue	20.00
Milk White Opal	15.00
Vaseline	7.00
Salt, Star & Dewdrop; Milk Blue	15.00
Vaseline	12.50
Salt, Star; Cobalt	10.00
Slipper, bow, Crown Tuscan	25.00
Milk Blue	25.00
Slipper, cat, Tiger	35.00
Tuscan	25.00
Vaseline	17.50
Sugar, Daisy & Button; Milk Blue	25.00
Milk White	25.00
Toothpick holder, Beaded Oval, Amethyst	12.50
Beaded Oval, Milk Blue	15.00
Beaded Oval, Tuscan	15.00
Bird, Amethyst	18.00
Daisy & Button, Bittersweet	18.50
Daisy & Button, Blue Milk	15.00
Daisy & Button, Vaseline	10.00
Forget-Me-Not, Blue Slag	18.00
Forget-Me-Not, Bluebell	12.00
Forget-Me-Not, Cobalt	10.00
Forget-Me-Not, Ebony	20.00
Forget-Me-Not, Lime Ice	12.00
Gypsy Kettle, Blue Jay Slag	16.00
Heart, Cobalt	12.00
Heart, Milk White	12.50
Heart, Opaque Jade	15.00
Heart, Vaseline	12.00
Turkey, 5"; Amber	45.00
Bittersweet	75.00
Lt Pink	35.00
Pink	35.00
Sapphire	35.00
Wine, Buzzsaw, Amberina	27.50
Buzzsaw, Amethyst	20.00
Buzzsaw, Cobalt	20.00
Buzzsaw, Milk Blue	25.00
Daisy & Button, Cobalt	35.00

DeLatte

DeLatte was a manufacturer of French cameo glass. Founded in 1921, their style reflected the influence of the Art Deco era, with strong color contrasts and bold design.

Atomizer, mottled, deco motif, 5½"	185.00
Bottle, blue mottled w/Deco enamel florals	525.00

Chandelier, mottled orange shade, rose garland support, 18"	715.00
Vase, delphiniums, color florals, 10"	995.00
Lime frost w/bird, tree branch, handles, 2 cuts, 6½"	895.00
Pink w/yellow-orange florals, green leaves	475.00
Salmon frost w/mauve scene, 2 cuttings, 7½"	675.00
With handles, scenic w/river, trees, 14"	350.00

Delft

Old Delft ware, made as early as the 16th century, was originally a low-fired earthenware coated with a thin opaque tin glaze with painted-on polychrome designs. It was not until the last half of the 18th century, however, that the ware became commonly referred to as Delft, acquiring the name from the Dutch village that had become the major center of its production.

English potters also produced Delft, though with noticeable differences, both in shape and decorative theme.

In the early part of the 18th century, the German potter, Bottger, developed a formula for porcelain; in England, Wedgwood began producing creamwares--both of which were much more durable. Unable to compete, one by one the Delft potteries failed. Soon, only one remained. In 1876, De Porcelyne Fles reintroduced Delft ware on a hard white body with blue and white decorative themes reflecting the Dutch countryside, windmills by the sea, and Dutch children. This type continues to be produced and can be found today in nearly any giftship.

Ashtray, chrome top, late, 4½"	20.00

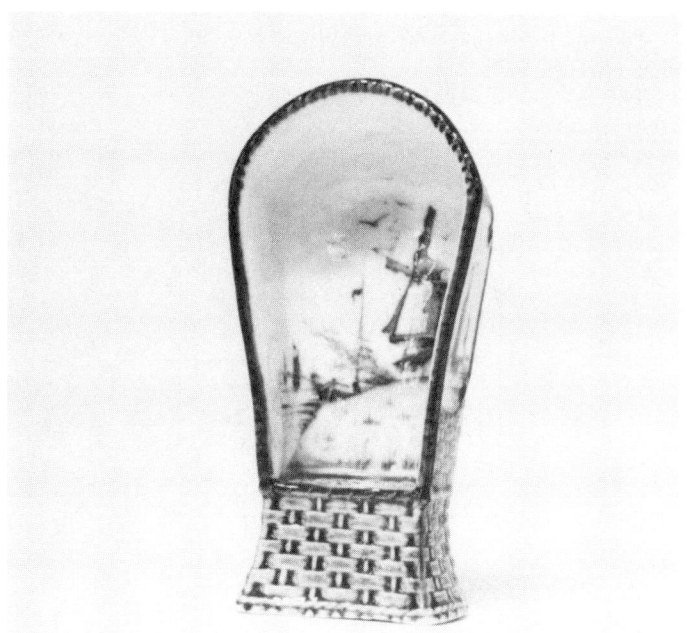

Beach chair novelty, basketweave effect, w/windmill, 6"	85.00
Bowl, floral reserves & lattice effect, 1700s, 10½"	375.00
Candlestick, polychrome florals, saucer base, 6½"	100.00
Charger, blue, white florals, very early, 13½"	1,600.00
Signed BFK, 14"	50.00
Urn w/flowers in center, repetitive border design, 14"	450.00
Cow creamer, 3"	65.00
Crown mark, 5"	65.00
Cup & saucer w/windmill	25.00
Dish, peacock decor, 1700s	345.00
Figurine, cat on cushion, 8"	465.00
Inkwell, sleigh shape w/well in seat, 5x7"	150.00
Jar, dog finial, reserve w/ship, blue & wht, mk JT & L, 16x7"	160.00
Florals w/gold decor, early, 12"	180.00
Jars, peacocks, 18th century, pr	750.00

Plaque, oval w/river, trees, boat, signed, 1800s, 15″ **1,230.00**
Plate, blue & white w/inscription, 9″ **180.00**
   Blue & wht florals, yellow rim, late 1800s, 12″ **375.00**
   Polychrome, Lambeth 1730s, 9″ **325.00**
   Scalloped rim, canal scene in winter, 15″ **85.00**
Rolling pin, windmill, etc, early **165.00**
Tiles, 20 pc, farm scene, blue & wht, 1700s, 20½x25½″ **55.00**
Tobacco jar, blue & white, brass cover, 1700s **500.00**
Vase, buildings, trees, water, windmills, 5″ **50.00**
   Octagon shape, picture panel, mkd, dk blue, 11½x7½″ **165.00**
   Paneled w/landscape, river & man, 6½″ **165.00**

Depression Glass

Other than coins and stamps, colored glassware produced during the depression era is probably the most sought after collectible in our field today. There are literally thousands of collectors in the United States and Canada buying, selling and trading "Depression Glass" on today's market.

Depression Glass is defined by Gene Florence, author of several best selling books on the subject, as "the inexpensive glassware made primarily during the Depression era in the colors of amber, green, pink, blue, red, yellow, white and crystal." This glass was mass produced and sold through five and dime stores and mail order catalogs and given away as premiums with gas and food products.

The listings in this book are far from being complete. If you want a more thorough presentation of this fascinating glassware, we recommend THE COLLECTOR'S ENCYCLOPEDIA OF DEPRESSION GLASS by Gene Florence. This beautiful full color volume contains thousands of descriptions and prices. It is available at your favorite bookstore or public library.

Adam, Jeannette Glass Company 1932-1934

Ash Tray, 4½″, Pink **18.50**
Bowl, 7¾″, Pink **12.50**
Butter Dish & Cover, Green **217.50**
Candy Jar & Cover, 2½″, Green **57.50**
Cup, Pink **4.00**
Plate, 6″ Sherbet, Green **10.50**
Plate, 9″ Grill, Pink **72.50**
Salt & Pepper, 4″, Green **9.00**
Sugar, Pink **32.50**
Tumbler, 5½″ Iced Tea, Pink **32.50**
Vase, 7½″, Green **32.50**

American Pioneer, Liberty Works 1931-1934

Bowl, 5″ handled, Pink **8.00**
Bowl, console 10-3/8″, Green **45.00**
Candy Jar and Cover, 1½ lb., Pink **55.00**

Coaster, 3½″, Pink **12.50**
Cup, Green **6.50**
Goblet, Wine, 4″, 3 oz., Pink **17.50**
Lamp, 8½″ tall, Pink **55.00**
Plate, 8″, Pink **5.00**
Sherbet, Green **12.00**
Sugar, 3½″, Pink **12.50**
Tumbler, 5″, 12 oz., Pink **16.50**
Vase, 7″, three styles, rolled, or crimped edge, straight, Pink **55.00**

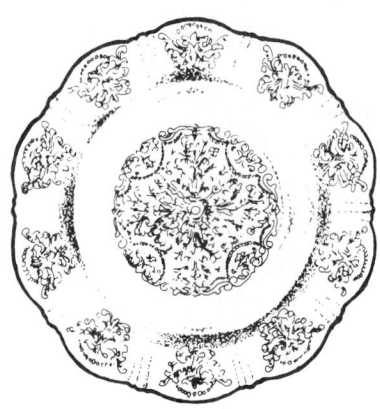

American Sweetheart, Macbeth Evans Glass Company 1930-1936

Bowl, 3¾″ Flat, Berry, Pink **21.50**
Bowl, 9″ Round, Berry, Monax **35.00**
Creamer, Footed, Pink **7.00**
Plate, 8″ Salad, Pink **5.50**
Plate, 12″ Salver, Monax **12.00**
Pitcher, 8″, 80 oz., Pink **300.00**
Sherbet, Footed, 4″, Pink **10.50**
Sugar Cover, Monax **152.50**
Tumbler, 4½″, 10 oz., Pink **35.00**

Anniversary, Jeannette Glass Company 1947-1949

Bowl, 4-7/8″ Berry, Crystal **1.50**
Butter Dish and Cover, Pink **42.50**
Cake Plate, 12½″, Crystal **5.50**
Cup, Pink **4.00**
Plate, 9″ Dinner, Crystal **3.50**
Relish Dish, 8″, Pink **6.50**
Sugar, Crystal **2.00**
Vase, Wall Pin-up, Crystal **10.00**
Wine Glass, 2½ oz., Pink **8.50**

Aunt Polly, U.S. Glass Company Late 1920's

Bowl, 4-3/8″ Berry, Green **4.00**

Bowl, 7-7/8″ Large Berry, Blue **16.50**
Candy, Cover, Two Handled, Green **25.00**
Plate, 6″ Sherbet, Green **3.00**
Sherbet, Green **7.50**
Tumbler, 3-5/8″, 8 oz., Blue **12.50**

Avocado, (Sweet Pear), No. 601, Indiana Glass
Company 1923-1933

Bowl, 5¼″, Two-Handled, Pink **20.00**
Bowl, 7½″ Salad, Green **37.50**
Bowl, 9½″, 3¼″ Deep, Pink **55.00**
Pitcher, 64 ozs., Green **450.00**
Plate, 10¼″ Two Handled Cake, Pink **22.50**
Sugar, Footed, Green **27.50**

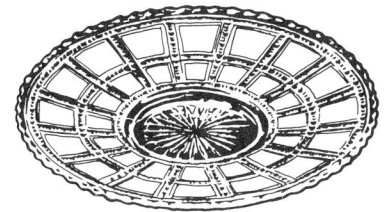

Beaded Block, Imperial Glass Company 1927-1930's

Bowl, 4½″, 2 handled jelly, Pink **5.50**
Bowl, 5½″, 1 handle, Pink **6.50**
Bowl, 6½', round, Opalescent **12.50**
Bowl, 7¼″, round, flared, Pink **8.00**
Bowl, 8¼' celery, Opalescent **13.50**
Plate, 7¾″ Sq., Pink **5.00**
Stemmed Jelly, 4½″, flared top, Opalescent **15.50**
Vase, 6″, bouquet, Pink **8.00**

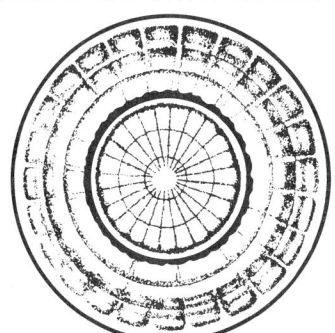

Block Optic, (Block), Hocking Glass Company
1929-1933

Bowl, 4¼″Berry, Pink **4.00**
Bowl, 8½″ Large Berry, Pink **9.00**
Candlesticks, 1¾″, Pr., Pink **24.50**

Candy Jar Cover, 6¼″, Green **30.00**
Cup, Four Styles, Green **5.00**
Goblet, 5¾″, 9 oz., Green **12.50**
Mug, Flat Creamer, No Spout, Green **27.50**
Plate, 6″ Sherbet, Pink **2.00**
Salt and Pepper, Footed, Pink **40.00**
Saucer, Pink **4.50**
Sherbet, 4¾″, 6 oz., Pink **8.50**
Tumbler, 3½″, 5 oz. Flat, Pink **11.50**
Tumbler, 9 oz. Footed, Green **12.50**
Tumble-up Night Set: 3″ Tumbler Bottle and Tumbler, 6″ High . . . **42.50**

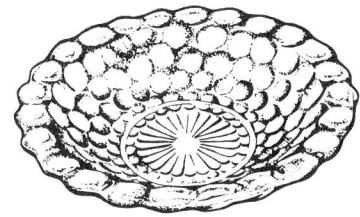

"Bubble", "Fire King", Hocking Glass Company
Company 1934-1965

Bowl, 4″ Berry, Crystal **3.00**
Bowl, 7¾″, Flat Soup, Blue **8.00**
Cup, Blue **3.50**
Plate, 6¾″ Bread & Butter, Crystal **1.00**
Platter, 12″, Oval, Blue **8.50**
Tumbler, 6 oz., Juice, Red **6.00**
Tumbler, 16 oz., Lemonade, Red **15.00**

Cameo, (Ballerina or Dancing Girl), Hocking
Glass Company 1930-1934

Bowl, 4¾ Cream Soup, Green **42.50**
Bowl, 8¼″ Large Berry, Green **22.50**
Bowl, 11″ 3 Leg Console, Green **40.00**
Candlesticks, 4″ Pr., Green **67.50**
Cocktail Shaker (Metal Lid) Appears in Crystal Only, Yellow **175.00**
Creamer, 3¼″, Green **16.00**
Decanter, 10″, W/Stopper, Green **77.50**
Domino Tray, 7″ With 3″ Identation, Green **65.00**
Goblet, 6″, Water, Green **35.00**
Pitcher, 5¾″, Syrup or Milk, 20 oz., Yellow **287.50**
Pitcher, 8½″, Water, 56 oz., Green **35.00**
Plate, 8½″ Square, Yellow **55.00**
Plate, 10½″, Grill, Yellow **6.00**
Platter, 12″, Closed Handles, Yellow **20.00**
Salt & Pepper, Footed, Pr., Green **47.50**
Saucer 6″ (Sherbet Plate), Yellow **2.00**
Sugar, 3¼″, Yellow **10.00**
Tumbler, 4″, 9 oz. Water, Green **18.00**
Tumbler, 5¼″, 15 oz., Green **35.00**

Tumbler, 5¾", 11 oz. Footed, Green **30.00**
Water Bottle (Dark Green) Whitehouse Vinegar, Green **17.50**

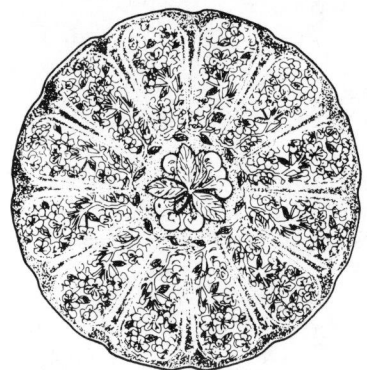

Cherry Blossom, Jeannette Glass Company 1930-1939

Bowl, 4¾" Berry, Green **11.50**
Bowl, 8½" Round Berry, Pink **15.50**
Bowl, 10½", 3 Leg Fruit, Green **36.50**
Coaster, Pink **11.50**
Mug, 7 oz., Green **127.50**
Pitcher, 8" PAT, 42 oz. Flat, Green **45.00**
Plate, 9" Dinner, Pink **12.00**
Platter, 11" Oval, Green **22.50**
Saucer, Pink **4.50**
Sugar Cover, Green **12.50**
Tumbler, 4½", 9 oz. Round Foot AOP, Green **27.50**
Tumbler, 4¼", 9 oz. Flat PAT, Green **16.50**

Cherry Blossom — Child's Junior Dinner Set

Creamer, Pink **22.50**
Sugar, Pink **22.50**
Original Box, Pink **10.00**
Plate, 6", Pink **7.50**
Cup, Pink **17.50**
Saucer, Pink **5.00**
14 Piece Set, Pink **175.00**

Chinex Classic, Macbeth-Evans Division of Corning Glass Works, Late 1930 - Early 1940's

Bowl, 5¾" Cereal, Decorated **4.50**
Butter Dish, Ivory **52.50**
Plate, 6¼" Sherbet, Decorated **3.00**
Saucer, Ivory **2.00**

Circle, Hocking Glass Company 1930's

Bowl, 4½", Green **3.00**
Cup, Pink **2.00**
Goblet, 8 oz. water, Pink **6.50**

Plate, 9½" Dinner, Green **5.00**
Sherbet, 4¾", Green **4.75**
Tumbler, 8 oz. Water, Pink **4.00**

Cloverleaf, Hazel Atlas Glass Company 1930-1936

Ash Tray 4", Match Holder in Center, Black **52.50**
Bowl, 5" Cereal, Yellow **20.00**
Candy Dish and Cover, Green **37.50**
Plate, 6" Sherbet, Yellow **5.00**
Salt and Pepper, Pair, Yellow **85.00**
Sugar, Footed, 3-5/8", Green **7.00**
Tumbler, 5¾", 10 oz. Footed, Green **15.00**

Colonial, (Knife and Fork), Hocking Glass Co. 1934-1938

Bowl, 3¾", Pink **22.50**
Bowl, 4½" Cream Soup, Green **35.00**
Bowl, 10" Oval Vegetable, Pink **13.00**
Cup, Green **8.50**
Goblet, 4½", 2½ oz. Wine, Green **18.50**
Mug, 4½", 12 oz., Pink **125.00**
Plate, 6" Sherbet, Green **3.50**
Plate, 10" Grill, Green **17.50**
Saucer (Same as sherbet plate), Pink **3.00**
Sugar, 5", Green **11.00**
Tumbler, 4", 9 oz. Water, Pink **8.50**
Tumbler, 15 oz. Lemonade, Pink **25.00**
Tumbler, 5¼", 10 oz. Ftd., Green **20.00**

Colonial Fluted, (Rope), Federal Glass Company 1928-1933

Bowl, 4" Berry, Green **3.50**
Bowl, 7½' Large Berry, Green **8.50**

Plate, 6″ Sherbet, Green **1.50**
Saucer, Green **1.50**
Sugar Cover, Green **7.50**

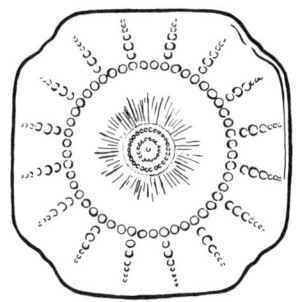

Columbia, Federal Glass Company 1938-1942

Bowl, 5 Cereal, Crystal **6.50**
Bowl, 10½″ Ruffled Edge, Crystal **12.50**
Cup, Pink **7.00**
Plate, 11¾″ Chop, Crystal **5.50**
Snack Plate, Crystal **12.50**

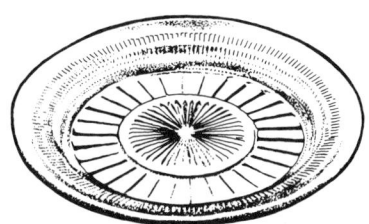

Coronation, (Banded Fine Rib), (Saxon),
Hocking Glass Company 1936-1940

Bowl, 4¼ Berry, Pink **3.00**
Cup, Red **4.50**
Saucer, Pink **1.50**
Tumbler, 5, 10 oz. Footed, Pink **7.50**

Cremax, Macbeth-Evans Division of Corning Glass Works,
Late 1930's - Early 1940's

Bowl, 5¾″ Cereal, Ivory **3.00**
Cup, Ivory Decorated **3.50**
Plate, 9¾ Dinner, Ivory **4.00**
Saucer, Ivory Decorated **2.50**
Sugar, Open, Ivory Decorated **5.50**

Cube, (Cubist), Jeannette Glass Company 1929-1933

Bowl, 4½″ Dessert, Pink **4.00**

Butter Dish and Cover, Green **47.50**
Creamer, 2″, Pink **2.00**
Pitcher, 8¾″, 45 oz., Green **137.50**
Powder Jar and Cover, 3 Legs, Pink **11.50**
Sherbet, Footed, Green **6.00**
Sugar/Candy Cover, Green **8.50**

Cupid, Paden City Glass Co., 1930's

Bowl, 8½″, Oval, ftd., Pink **30.00**
Bowl, 11″, Console, Green **32.50**
Creamer, 4½″, ftd., Pink **25.00**
Mayonnaise, 6″ Diameter (fits 8″ plate), Pink **37.50**
Sugar, 4¼″, ftd., Green **25.00**
Tray, 10-7/8″, Oval, ftd., Green **35.00**

"Daisy", Number 620, Indiana Glass Company

Bowl, 4½″, Berry, Crystal **2.50**
Bowl, 7-3/8″ Deep Berry, Amber **9.50**
Creamer, Footed, Crystal **4.50**
Plate, 7-3/8″ Salad, Amber **6.00**
Plate, 10-3/8″ Grill, Crystal **4.00**
Plate, 11½″ Cake or Sandwich, Amber **9.00**
Saucer, Crystal **1.00**
Tumbler, 9 oz. Footed, Crystal **5.00**

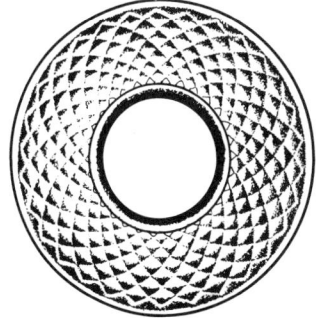

Diamond Quilted, (Flat Diamond),
Imperial Glass Company Late 1920's - Early 1930's

Bowl, 4¾″ Cream Soup, Green **6.50**
Bowl, 7 Crimped Edge, Blue **10.00**
Candlesticks (2 Styles) Pr., Green **8.50**
Creamer, Blue **9.50**
Goblet, 2 oz. Wine, Green **5.00**
Ice Bucket, Blue **55.00**
Plate, 6″ Sherbet, Green **2.00**
Plate, 14″ Sandwich, Green **8.50**

Sherbet, Blue **8.00**
Tumbler, 12 oz. Iced Tea, Green. **7.00**
Tumbler, 12 oz. Footed, Green. **12.50**

Diana, Federal Glass Company 1937-1941

Ash Tray, 3½", Pink **3.00**
Bowl, 9" Salad, Amber **5.50**
Candy Jar & Cover, Round, Pink **17.50**
Cup, Amber. **4.00**
Plate, 6" Bread & Butter, Pink **1.50**
Platter, 12" Oval, Pink **6.50**
Sherbet, Amber **5.00**

Dogwood, (Apple Blossom), (Wild Rose), MacBeth-Evans Glass Company 1929-1932

Bowl, 5½" Cereal, Pink **13.50**
Cake Plate, 11" Heavy Solid Foot, Pink **152.50**
Creamer, 3¼" Thick, Pink **13.50**
Pitcher, 8", 80 oz. (American Sweetheart Style), Pink **457.50**
Plate, 9¼" Dinner, Pink **16.50**
Platter, 12" Oval (Rare), Pink. **237.50**
Sugar, 2½" Thin, Green **35.00**
Tumbler, 4" 10 oz. Decorated, Green. **52.50**

Doric, Jeannette Glass Company 1935-1938

Bowl, 4½" Berry, Pink **5.00**
Bowl, 8¼" Large Berry, Green **12.50**

Butter Dish and Cover, Pink **57.50**
Candy Dish, Three Part, Green **5.50**
Cup, Green **6.50**
Plate, 6" Sherbet, Green **3.00**
Plate, 9" Grill, Pink **7.00**
Relish Tray, 4" x 8", Pink **6.50**
Sherbet, Footed, Green **8.50**
Tray, 10" Handled, Pink **7.50**
Tumbler, 4", 11 oz. Ftd., Green **28.50**

Doric and Pansy, Jeannette Glass Company 1937-1938

Bowl, 4½" Berry, Pink **6.50**
Butter Dish and Cover, Ultramarine **657.50**
Plate, 6" Sherbet, Pink **6.50**
Salt and Pepper, Pr., Ultramarine **387.50**
Tray, 10" Handled, Ultramarine **17.50**

Doric and Pansy, "Pretty Polly Party Dishes"

Cup, Pink **15.00**
Creamer, Ultramarine **30.00**
Sugar, Pink **22.50**
14 Piece Set, Ultramarine **205.00**

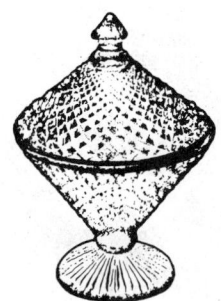

English Hobnail, Westmoreland Glass Company 1920's-1970's

Ash Tray, Several Shapes, Pink **18.50**
Bowls, 6", Several Styles, Green **9.50**
Bowls, 11" and 12" Nappies, Pink **35.00**
Candlesticks, 3½", Pair, Pink **30.00**
Candy Dish and Cover, Three Feet, Green **55.00**
Cigarette Box, Pink. **22.50**
Cup, Pink **12.00**
Egg Cup, Green **32.50**
Goblet, 3 oz. Cocktail, Green **12.50**
Grapefruit, 6½", Flange Rim, Green **12.50**
Marmalade and Cover, Pink **30.00**
Pitcher, 60 oz., Pink **127.50**
Plate, 7¼", Pie, Green **3.50**

Salt and Pepper, Pr., Round or Square Bases, Pink **57.50**
Sherbet, Green **11.50**
Tumbler, 4″, 10 oz. Iced Tea, Green **13.50**
Tumbler, 9 oz., Footed, Pink **13.50**

Fire-King Dinnerware, Anchor Hocking Glass
Company 1937-1938

Bowl, 5½″ Cereal, Blue **25.00**
Candy Jar, 4″ Low, with Cover, Pink **140.00**
Cup, Pink **75.00**
Pitcher, 8½″, 54 oz., Green **500.00**
Plate, 10″ Heavy Sandwich, Pink **27.50**
Plate, 11-5/8″ Salver, Green **30.00**
Sugar, 3¼″ Ftd., Crystal **60.00**
Tumbler, 5¼″ Ftd., 10 oz., Pink **37.50**

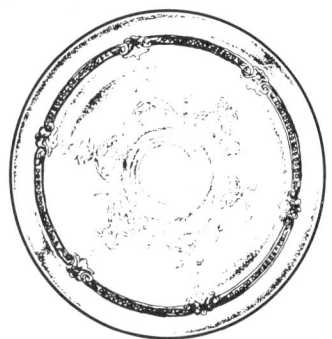

Fire-King Oven Glass, Anchor Hocking Glass
Company

Baker, 1 pt., rd. or sq., Blue **3.00**
Baker, 2 qt., Blue **8.00**
Casserole, 1 qt., Knob Handle Cover, Blue **8.00**
Casserole, 1 qt., Pie Plate Cover, Blue **10.00**
Casserole, 10 oz., Tab Handle Cover, Blue **8.00**
Custard Cup, 5 oz., Blue **2.50**
Nurser, 4 oz., Blue **15.00**
Pie Plate, 5-3/8″ Deep Dish, Blue **5.00**
Pie Plate, 9-5/8″, Blue. **8.00**
Refrigerator Jar & Cover, 4½″x5″, Blue **6.00**
Utility Pan, 10½″, Rectangular, Blue **8.00**

Floragold, (Louisa), Jeannette Glass Company 1950's

Bowl, 4½″ Square, Iridescent **4.00**
Bowl, 5½″ Ruffled Fruit, Iridescent **4.00**
Bowl, 9½″ Salad, Deep, Iridescent **25.00**
Butter Dish and Cover, Round, Iridescent **35.00**
Candy, 5¼″ Long, 4 Feet, Iridescent **4.50**
Cup, Iridescent **4.50**
Plate, 8½ Dinner, Iridescent. **15.50**
Salt and Pepper, Plastic Tops, Iridescent **32.50**

Sugar, Iridescent **4.50**
Tumbler, 11 oz., Footed, Iridescent **12.50**

Floral (Poinsetta), Jeannette Glass Company
1931-1935

Bowl, 4″ Berry, Pink **8.00**
Bowl, 8″ Covered Vegetable, Green **27.50**
Candlesticks, 4″ Pr., Pink **42.50**
Coaster, 3¼″, Green **7.50**
Ice Tub, Oval, 3½″ High, Pink **327.50**
Pitcher, 8″, 32 oz. Footed Cone, Green **25.00**
Plate, 8″ Salad, Pink **6.00**
Platter 10¾″ Oval, Green **12.50**
Salt and Pepper, Pr., 4″ Footed, Pink **30.00**
Sherbet, Green **9.50**
Tray, 6″ Square, Closed Handles, Green **10.00**
Tumbler, 5¼″, 9 oz. Footed Lemonade, Pink **22.50**
Vase, 6¼″ Tall (8 Sided), Green **377.50**

Floral and Diamond Band, U.S. Glass Company
1927-1931

Bowl, 4½″ Berry, Pink **5.00**
Butter Dish and Cover, Pink **77.50**
Creamer, 4¾″, Green **10.00**
Sherbet, Pink **4.50**
Sugar Lid, Green. **25.00**

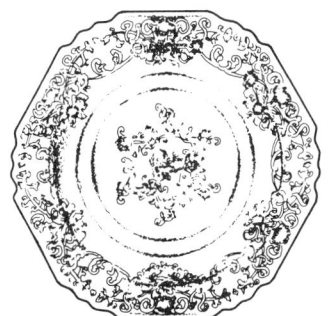

Florentine No. 1, (Poppy No. 1), Hazel Atlas
Glass Company 1934-1936

Ash Tray, 5½″, Green **16.50**

Bowl, 8½" Large Berry, Yellow **18.50**
Coaster/Ash Tray, 3¾", Green **12.50**
Cup, Yellow **6.50**
Plate, 6" Sherbet, Green **3.00**
Plate, 10" Grill, Yellow **10.00**
Saucer, Green **2.00**
Sugar Cover, Green **11.50**
Tumbler, 4¾", 10 oz. Footed Water, Yellow **15.00**

Florentine No. 2, (Poppy No. 2), Hazel Atlas
Glass Company 1932-1935

Bowl, 4½" Berry, Green **7.00**
Bowl, 6" Cereal, Yellow **20.00**
Butter Dish and Cover, Green **77.50**
Coaster, 3¼", Yellow **15.00**
Compote, 3½" Ruffled, Green **12.50**
Custard Cup or Jello, Yellow **57.50**
Pitcher, 7½" 54 oz., Green **39.50**
Plate, 6¼" with Indent for Custard, Yellow **22.50**
Plate, 10¼" Grill, Green **6.50**
Relish Dish, 10", 3 Part or Plain, Green **12.00**
Sherbet, Footed, Yellow **8.50**
Tumbler, 3½", 5 oz. Juice, Green **7.00**
Tumbler, 3¼" 5 oz. Footed, Green **8.50**
Tumbler, 5", 12 oz. Footed, Yellow **25.00**

Flower Garden (With Butterflies,
Butterflies and Roses), U.S. Glass Co. Late 1920's

Ash Tray, Match-Pack Holders, Black **137.50**
Candlesticks, 8", Pr., Green **75.00**
Cheese and Cracker Set (4" Compote, 10" Plate), Pink **57.50**
Creamer, Green **67.50**
Powder Jar, Footed, All Colors **37.50**
Saucer, Green **35.00**
Tray, Rectangular, 11¾"x7¾", All Colors **42.50**

Forest Green, Anchor Hocking 1950's-1967

Ash Tray, Dark Green **2.50**
Bowl, 7-3/8" Salad, Dark Green **6.00**
Plate, 6-5/8" Salad, Dark Green **1.50**
Pitcher, 3 qt., Rnd., Dark Green **17.50**
Sugar, Flat, Dark Green **4.00**
Vase, 4" Ivy, Dark Green **3.00**

"Fortune", Hocking Glass Company 1937-1938

Bowl, 4" Berry, Pink **2.50**
Bowl, 5¼ Rolled Edge, Pink **4.00**
Cup, Pink **3.00**
Saucer, Pink **2.00**
Tumbler, 4", 9 oz. Water, Pink **4.00**

"Fruits", Hazel Atlas and other glass companies 1931-1953

Bowl, 5" Cereal, Pink **12.50**
Pitcher, 7" Flat Bottom, Green **37.50**
Sherbet, Green **6.00**
Tumbler, 4" (Combination of Fruits), Pink **8.50**

Georgian (Lovebirds), Federal Glass Company
1931-1936

Bowl, 4½" Berry, Green **5.00**
Bowl, 6½" Deep, Green **42.50**
Bowl, 9" Oval Vegetable, Green **45.00**
Cold Cuts Server, 18½" wood w/seven 5" openings for 5"coasters **477.50**
Cup, Green **7.00**
Plate, 8" Luncheon, Crystal **6.00**
Platter, 11½" Closed Handled, Green **42.50**
Sugar, 3" Footed, Green **8.00**
Sugar Cover, 4", Green **30.00**

Harp, Jeannette Glass Company 1954-1957

Ash Tray/Coaster, Crystal **3.00**
Cake Stand, 9", Crystal **15.00**
Saucer, Crystal **1.50**

Vase, 6", Crystal **8.50**

Heritage, Federal Glass Company Late 1930's-1960's

Bowl, 5" Berry, Pink **4.50**
Cup, Crystal **3.50**
Plate, 8" Luncheon, Green **5.00**
Plate, 9¼" Dinner, Crystal **6.00**
Saucer, Crystal **2.50**

Hex Optic, (Honeycomb), Jeannette Glass Company
1928-1932

Bowl, 4¼" Berry, Ruffled, Pink **2.50**
Creamer, 2 Style Handles, Green **3.50**
Pitcher, 5", 32 oz. Sunflower Motif in Bottom, Pink **10.00**
Plate, 8" Luncheon, Green **4.50**
Salt and Pepper, Pr., Any Color **17.50**
Sherbet, 5 oz. Footed, Green **3.50**
Tumbler, 7" Footed, Pink **5.50**

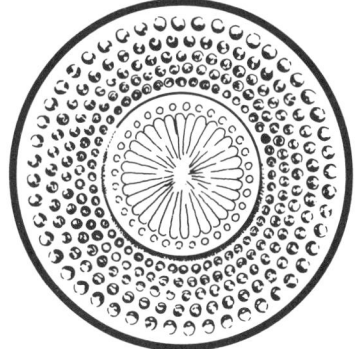

Hobnail, Hocking Glass Company 1934-1936

Bowl, 5½" Cereal, Crystal **2.50**
Decanter and Stopper, 32 oz., Crystal **12.50**
Pitcher, 18 oz. Milk, Pink **12.50**
Saucer, Crystal **1.00**
Tumbler, 5 oz. Juice, Pink **3.00**
Tumbler, 3 oz. Footed Wine, Crystal **5.00**

Holiday, (Button and Bows), Jeannette Glass
Company 1947-1949

Bowl, 5-1/8" Berry, Pink **6.50**
Bowl, 9½" Oval Vegetable, Pink **11.50**
Cake Plate, 10½", 3 Legged, Pink **52.50**

Cup, Two Sizes, Pink **5.00**
Plate, 6" Sherbet, Pink **3.00**
Platter, 11-3/8" Oval, Pink **9.50**
Sherbet, Pink **5.00**
Tumbler, 4", 10 oz. Flat, Pink **13.50**

Homespun, (Fine Rib), Jeannette Glass Company
1939-1940

Bowl, 4½", Closed Handles, Pink **4.50**
Butter Dish and Cover, Crystal **39.50**
Cup, Crystal **4.00**
Platter, 13" Closed Handles, Pink **8.50**
Sugar, Footed, Pink **6.50**
Tumbler, 4", 5 oz. Footed, Pink **7.00**

Homespuns's Child's Tea Set

Cup **20.00**
Saucer **6.00**
Plate **8.00**
Tea Pot **20.00**
Tea Pot Cover **30.00**
Set 14 Pieces **185.00**

Indiana Custard (Flower and Leaf Band),
Indiana Glass Company

Bowl, 4-7/8" Berry, Ivory **5.50**
Bowl, 8¾" Large Berry, Ivory **19.50**
Cup, White **29.00**
Plate, 7½" Salad, White **8.50**
Platter, 11½" Oval, Ivory **22.50**
Sugar, Ivory **8.50**
Sugar Cover **13.50**

Iris (Iris and Herringbone), Jeannette Glass
Company 1928-1932, 1950, 1970

Bowl, 4½" Berry, Beaded, Crystal **27.50**
Bowl, 7½" Soup, Iridescent **19.50**
Bowl, 11" Fruit, Ruffled, Crystal **8.50**
Candlesticks, Pr., Iridescent **22.50**

Creamer, Footed, Crystal **6.00**
Demitasse Saucer, Iridescent **47.50**
Goblet, 5¾", 4 oz., Crystal **12.00**
Plate, 5½'Sherbet, Crystal **5.00**
Plate, 11¾" Sandwich, Crystal **9.50**
Sherbet, 4" Footed, Crystal. **9.50**
Tumbler, 4"Flat, Crystal **37.50**
Vase, 9", Crystal **13.50**

Jubilee, Lancaster Glass Co., Early 1930's

Bowl, 9'''", Fruit, Handled, Topaz **30.00**
Creamer, Topaz **15.00**
Goblet, 6-1/8", 12½ oz., Topaz **22.50**
Plate, 8¾", Luncheon, Topaz **7.50**
Sugar, Topaz. **15.00**

Lace Edge (Open Lace), Hocking Glass Company
1935-1938

Bowl, 6-3/8" Cereal, Pink **10.50**
Bowl, 10½" 3 Legs, Pink **117.50**
Candy Jar and Cover, Ribbed, Pink **32.50**
Cookie Jar and Cover, Pink. **35.00**
Fish Bowl, 1 gal. 8 oz. (Crystal Only), Pink **14.50**
Plate, 8¾" Luncheon, Pink **11.00**
Plate, 13" 3 Part Solid Lace, Pink **17.50**
Relish Dish, 7½" Deep, 3 Part, Pink **35.00**
Sugar, Pink **13.50**
Vase, 7", Pink. **192.50**

Lake Como, Anchor Hocking Glass Company 1934-1937

Bowl, Berry, Blue & White **4.50**
Bowl, Vegetable, 9¾", Blue & White **10.00**
Cup, Blue & White **5.50**
Plate, Dinner, 9¼", Blue & White **7.00**
Salt & Pepper, pr., Bue & White **22.50**
Sugar, Footed., Blue & White **7.50**

Laurel, McKee Glass Company 1930's

Bowl, 5" Berry, Ivory. **4.00**
Bowl, 9", Large Berry, Green **8.00**
Bowl, 11", Ivory **20.00**
Creamer, Short, Green **7.00**
Plate, 6" Sherbet, Ivory **2.50**
Plate, 9-1/8" Grill, Green **5.00**
Saucer, Green **2.00**
Sugar, Tall, Ivory **8.00**

Children's Laurel Tea Set

Creamer, Green **17.50**
Cup, Green **12.50**
Plate, Green **7.50**
Saucer, Green **5.50**
Sugar, Green **17.50**
14 Piece Set, Green **135.00**

Lincoln Inn, Fenton Glass Company Late 1920's

Ash Tray, Blue **10.00**
Bowl, 5", Fruit, Pink **4.50**
Bowl, Handled, Olive, Red **8.50**
Bowl, 10½", Ftd., Red **13.50**
Creamer, Blue **16.50**
Goblet, Wine, Red **12.50**
Plate, 8", Blue **6.00**
Salt, Pepper, Pr., Pink **77.50**
Sugar, Red **15.00**
Tumbler, 7 oz., Ftd., Pink **8.00**
Vase, 12", Ftd., Green **37.50**

Lorain (Basket), "No. 615", Indiana Glass Company
Company 1929-1932

Bowl, 6" Cereal, Yellow **37.50**
Bowl, 9¾'Oval Vegetable, Green **25.00**

Plate, 5½″ Sherbet, Yellow 5.00
Plate, 10¼″ Dinner, Green 27.50
Saucer, Green 3.50
Tumbler, 4¾″, 9 oz. Footed, Yellow 18.50

Madrid, Federal Glass Company 1932-1939

Ash Tray, 6″ Square, Amber 122.50
Bowl, 7″ Soup, Green 9.50
Bowl, 9½″, Deep Salad, Amber 18.50
Butter Dish and Cover, Green 67.50
Creamer, Footed, Amber 6.00
Hot Dish Coaster, Green 27.50
Jello Mold, 2-1/8″ High, Amber 8.00
Pitcher, 8½″, 80 oz., Green 177.50
Plate, 7½″ Salad, Amber 7.50
Plate, 10½″ Grill, Green 15.00
Platter, 11½″ Oval, Amber 9.50
Saucer, Amber 2.50
Sugar Cover, Green 25.00
Tumbler, 5½″, 12 oz., 2 Styles, Green 23.50
Wooden Lazy Susan, 7 Hot Dish Coasters, Amber 500.00

Manhattan, (Horizontal Ribbed), Anchor
Hocking Glass Company 1939-1941

Ashtray, 4″, Crystal 4.50
Bowl, 7½″ Large Berry, Pink 6.50
Bowl, 9½″ Fruit, Crystal 15.00
Candy Dish & Lid, Crystal 17.50
Creamer, Oval, Pink 6.00
Relish Tray, 14″, 5 Part, Crystal 8.50
Plate, 6″ Sherbet (Same as 6″ Plate), Crystal 2.50
Plate, 14″ Sandwich, Crystal 8.50
Sherbet, Pink 5.50
Vase, 8″, Crystal 7.50

Mayfair Federal, Federal Glass Company 1934

Bowl, 5″ Sauce, Amber 4.50
Bowl, 5″ Cream Soup, Green 13.50
Bowl, 6″ Cereal, Green 13.50
Bowl, 10″ Oval Vegetable, Green 14.50
Creamer, Footed, Amber 9.00
Cup, Green 7.00
Plate, 6¾″ Salad, Amber 4.50

Plate, 9½″ Dinner, Green 9.50
Plate, 9½″ Grill, Green 8.50
Platter, 12″ Oval, Amber 13.50
Saucer, Green 2.50
Sugar, Footed, Amber 9.00
Tumbler, 4½″9 oz., Green 14.50

Mayfair, (Open Rose), Hocking Glass Company
1931-1937

Bowl, 5″ Cream Soup, Pink 28.50
Bowl, 9″, 3-1/8″ High, 3 Leg Console, Pink 1,750.00
Bowl, 10″ Covered, Blue 72.50
Butter Dish and Cover or 7″ Covered Vegetable, Pink 42.50
Celery Dish 10″ or 10″ Divided, Pink 17.50
Cup, Blue 32.50
Goblet, 4½″ Wine, 3 oz., Pink 47.50
Pitcher, 6″, 37 oz., Blue 77.50
Plate, 6″ (Often Substituted as Saucer), Pink 7.50
Plate, 8½″ Luncheon, Blue 22.00
Plate, 12″ Cake W/Handles, Pink 25.00
Salt and Pepper, Pr., Flat,Blue 167.50
Saucer (Cup Ring), Pink 18.00
Sherbet, 3″ Footed, Pink 12.50
Sugar Lid, Pink 625.00
Tumbler, 4¾″, 11 oz. Water, Blue 82.50
Tumbler, 5¼″, 10 oz. Footed, Pink 23.50
Whiskey, 2¼″, 1½ oz., Pink 57.50

Miss America, Hocking Glass Company 1933-1937

Bowl, 6¼″ Berry, Crystal 6.00
Bowl, 10″ Oval Vegetable, Pink 15.00
Candy Jar and Cover, 11½″, Crystal 47.50
Compote, 5″, Pink 15.00
Goblet, 3¾″, 3 oz. Wine, Crystal 14.00
Pitcher, 8″ 65 oz. w/Ice Lip, Pink 87.50
Plate, 8½″ Salad, Pink 12.50
Platter, 12″ Oval, Crystal 10.00
Salt and Pepper, Pr., Crystal 22.50
Sugar, Pink 11.00
Tumbler, 6¾″, 14 oz. Iced Tea, Pink 45.00

Moderntone, (Wedding Band), Hazel Atlas Glass
Company 1934-1942

Ash Tray, 7¾″ Match Holder in Center, Cobalt 87.50
Bowl, 5″ Cream Soup Ruffled, Amethyst 11.50
Bowl, 8¾″ Large Berry, Cobalt 20.00
Creamer, Amethyst 6.00
Plate, 5¾″ Sherbet, Cobalt 3.00

Plate, 8-7/8″ Dinner, Amethyst **6.50**
Platter, 12″ Oval, Cobalt **20.00**
Sherbet, Cobalt **6.50**
Tumbler, 9 oz., Cobalt **12.50**

Moondrops, New Martinsville 1932-1940's

Ash Tray, Red **25.00**
Bowl, 7½″, Pickle, Pink **9.50**
Bowl, 9½″ Three Legged, Ruffled, Blue **17.50**
Bowl, 9¾″ Two Handled, Oval, Green **25.00**
Bowl, 13″, Console with "wings", Red **57.00**
Candles, 4½″, Sherbet Style, Pr., Green **15.00**
Candlesticks, 8½″ Metal Stem, Pr., Black **20.00**
Compote, 4″, Red **12.50**
Creamer, 3¾″, Regular, Blue **12.00**
Decanter, Medium, 8½″, Pink **32.50**
Goblet, 2-7/8″ ¾ oz. Liquor, Green **12.50**
Goblet, 4¾″, 5 oz., Red **12.50**
Goblet, 6¼″, Water, 9 oz., Green **13.50**
Pitcher, Small, 6-7/8″, 22 oz., Red **125.00**
Pitcher, Large, No Lip, 8-1/8″, 53 oz., Red **145.00**
Plate, 6″ Round, Off-Center Indent for Sherbet, Green **4.00**
Plate, 9½″ Dinner, Red **12.50**
Platter, 12″ Oval, Green **12.50**
Sherbet, 4½″, Blue **15.00**
Tumbler, 2¾″, Shot, 2 oz., Green **6.50**
Tumbler, 3-5/8″, 5 oz., Red **10.00**
Tumbler, 4-7/8″, Handled, 9 oz., Green **9.50**

Moonstone, Anchor Hocking Glass Company 1941-1946

Bowl, 5½″ Berry, Opalescent **6.50**
Bowl, 7¾″ Flat, Opalescent **8.00**
Bowl, Cloverleaf, Opalescent **8.50**
Cigarette Jar and Cover, Opalescent **14.50**
Goblet, 10 oz., Opalescent **13.50**
Plate, 8″ Luncheon, Opalescent **7.50**
Saucer (Same as Sherbet Plate), Opalescent **2.50**
Vase, 5½″ Bud, Opalescent **8.50**

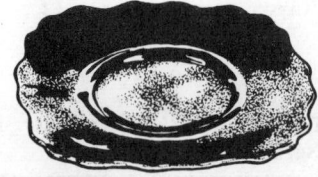

Mt. Pleasant, (Double Shield), L.E. Smith
Company 1920's-1934

Bon Bon, Rolled Up Handles, Black **8.50**
Bowl, 8″ Two Handled Square, Cobalt **15.00**

Creamer (Waffle-like Crystal) **4.00**
Cup, Black **6.00**
Plate, 10½″ Cake with Solid Handles, Cobalt **13.50**
Sherbet, Scalloped Edges, Cobalt **10.00**

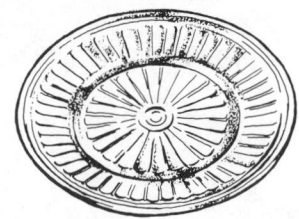

New Century, and incorrectly, Lydia Ray,
Hazel Atlas Glass Company 1930-1935

Ash Tray/Coaster, 5-3/8″, Green **25.00**
Bowl, 8″ Large Berry, Green **9.50**
Cup, Green **4.50**
Goblet, 2½ oz. Wine, Green **11.50**
Pitcher, 8″, 80 oz., with or without Ice Lip, Green **27.50**
Plate, 8½″ Salad, Green **5.50**
Platter, 11″ Oval, Green **10.00**
Saucer, Green **2.00**
Sugar Cover, Green **8.50**
Tumbler, 5″, 10 oz., Green **9.50**
Tumbler, 4-7/8″, 9 oz. Footed, Green **10.50**

Newport, (Hairpin), Hazel Atlas Glass Company
1936-1940

Bowl, 4¼″ Berry, Amethyst **7.50**
Bowl, 8¼″ Large Berry, Cobalt **20.00**
Plate, 6″ Sherbet, Amethyst **3.50**
Platter, 11¾″ Oval, Cobalt **20.00**
Sherbet, Cobalt **7.50**

Normandie, (Bouquet and Lattice), Federal
Glass Company 1933-1940

Bowl, 5″ Berry, Amber **4.00**
Bowl, 10″ Oval Veg., Pink **18.50**
Pitcher, 8″, 80 oz., Amber **45.00**
Plate, 9¼″ Luncheon, Pink **6.50**
Platter, 11¾″, Amber **9.50**
Sherbet, Pink **7.50**
Tumbler, 4″, 5 oz. Juice, Amber **11.50**
Tumbler, 5″, 12 oz. Iced Tea, Pink **29.50**

No. 610, (Pyramid), Indiana Glass Company
1928-1932

Bowl, 4¾" Berry, Pink	11.50
Bowl, 9½" Pickle, Yellow	42.50
Ice Tub and Lid, Yellow	377.50
Sugar, Pink	16.50
Tumbler, 11 oz., Footed, Yellow	49.50

No. 612 (Horseshoe), Indiana Glass Company
1930-1933

Bowl, 4½" Berry, Yellow	13.00
Bowl, 8½" Vegetable, Green	15.50
Butter Dish and Cover, Green	477.50
Cup, Yellow	7.50
Plate, 8-3/8" Salad, Green	5.00
Plate, 10-3/8" Grill, Green	16.50
Relish, 3 Part, Footed, Green	12.00
Sugar, Open, Yellow	10.50
Tumbler, 9 oz., Footed, Yellow	13.50

No. 618, (Pineapple & Floral), Indiana Glass Company 1932-1937

Ash Tray, 4½", Crystal	13.00
Bowl, 7" Salad, Amber	8.50
Creamer Diamond Shaped, Crystal	6.50
Plate, 6" Sherbet, Amber	4.00
Plate, 11½" Sandwich, Crystal	12.50
Saucer, Amber	3.00
Tumbler, 4¼", 8 oz., Crystal	22.50

Old Cafe, Hocking Glass Company 1936-1938; 1940

Bowl, 3¾" Berry, Pink	2.00
Bowl, 9", Closed Handles, Pink	7.50
Lamp, Red	15.00
Plate, 10" Dinner, Pink	12.50
Tumbler, 3"Juice, Red	5.00
Vase, 7¼", Pink	8.50

Old English, (Threading), Indiana Glass Company
Late 1920's

Bowl, 4" Berry, Green	9.50
Candlesticks, 4", Pr., Pink	20.00
Compote, 3½" Tall, 7" Across, Amber	12.50
Goblet, 5¾", 8 oz., Green	16.50
Plate, Indent for Compote, Green	16.50
Sherbet, Green	13.50
Tumbler, 4½" Footed, Green	10.00
Vase, 13", Pink	27.50

Ovide, incorrectly dubbed "New Century", Hazel Atlas Glass Company 1930-1935

Bowl, 4¾" Berry, Black	7.00
Candy Dish and Cover, Green	12.50
Cup, Green	1.50
Salt and Pepper, Pr., Black	19.50
Sugar, Open, Green	2.50

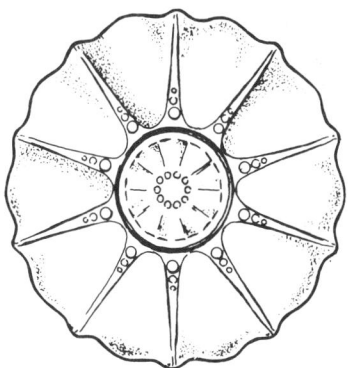

Oyster and Pearl, Anchor Hocking Glass 1938-1940

Bowl, 5¼" Round or Handled, Pink	5.00
Bowl, 6½" Deep, Handled, Red	11.50
Candleholder, 3½", Pr., Pink	15.00
Relish Dish, 10¼" Oblong, Pink	5.50

"Parrot", Sylvan, Federal Glass Company 1931-1932

Bowl, 5" Berry, Amber	9.50
Bowl, 8" Large Berry, Green	45.00
Butter Dish and Cover, Amber	557.50
Cup, Green	20.00

Jam Dish, 7", Green 22.50
Plate, 5¾" Sherbet, Amber 9.50
Plate, 9" Dinner, Amber 19.50
Plate, 10½" Grill, Square, Amber 15.50
Platter, 11¼" Oblong, Green 25.00
Salt and Pepper, Pr., Green 175.00
Sherbet, 4¼" High, Green 117.50
Tumbler, 4¼", 10 oz., Green 60.00

Patrician, (Spoke), Federal Glass Company 1933-1937

Bowl, 4¾", Cream Soup, Green 15.50
Bowl, 8½" Large Berry, Green 25.00
Butter Dish and Cover, Green 89.50
Cup, Amber 7.50
Plate, 6" Sherbet, Green 4.50
Plate, 10½" Dinner, Amber 5.00
Salt and Pepper, Pr., Green 45.00
Sugar, Amber 6.00
Tumbler, 4½", 9 oz., Green 25.00

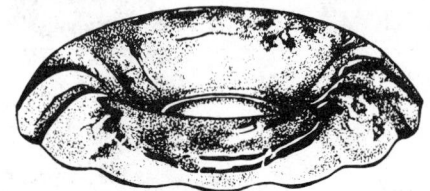

"Peacock & Wild Rose", Line #300, Paden City Glass Co., 1930's

Bowl, 8½", Flat, Pink 22.50
Bowl, 8¾", Ftd., Pink 25.00
Bowl, 10½", Fruit, Green 32.50
Bowl, 11", Console, Green 30.00
Candlesticks, 5", Green Base, Pr., Pink 37.50
Comport, 6¼", Pink 20.00
Ice Bucket, 6", Green 45.00
Plate, 8", Pink 15.00
Saucer, Green 15.00
Vase, 10", Green 57.50

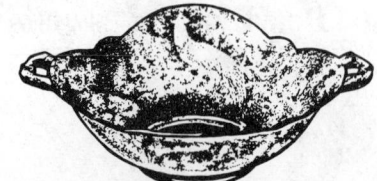

"Peacock Reverse", Line #412, Paden City Glass Co., 1930's

Bowl, 4-7/8", Square, Red 20.00
Candlesticks, 5¾" Sq. Base, Pr.,Blue 67.50
Cup, Red 25.00

Sherbet, 4-5/8" h; 3-3/8" base, Red 30.00
Sugar, 2¾", Flat,Blue 45.00
Tumbler, 4", 10 oz. Flat, Blue 40.00

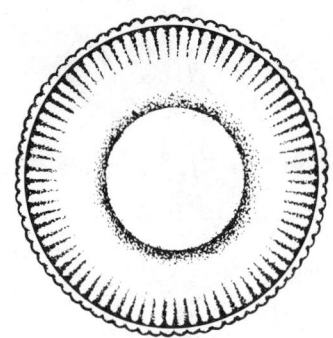

Petalware, MacBeth Evans Glass Company 1930-1940

Bowl, 4½" Cream Soup, Monax 7.50
Cup, Pink 2.50
Mustard with Metal Cover in Cobalt Blue Only 6.00
Plate, 9" Dinner, Pink 3.50
Saucer, Monax 2.00

Princess, Hocking Glass Company 1931-1935

Ash Tray, 4½", Pink 57.50
Bowl, 9" Salad Octagonal, Green 20.00
Butter Dish and Cover, Pink 65.00
Candy Dish and Cover, Green 32.50
Creamer, Oval, Green 8.00
Pitcher, 7-3/8", 24 oz. Footed, Pink 400.00
Plate, 8" Salad, Green 8.50
Plate, 11½", Grill, Closed Handles, Pink 5.00
Relish, 7½", Divided, Green 17.50
Saucer (Same as Sherbet Plate), Pink 3.00
Sugar Cover, Green 11.50
Tumbler, 5¼", 12 oz. Iced Tea, Pink 16.00
Tumbler, 6½", Footed, 12½ oz., Green 42.50

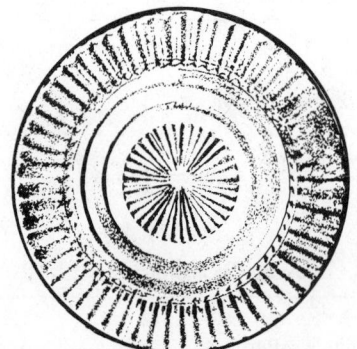

Queen Mary, (Vertical Ribbed), Hocking Glass Company 1936-1940

Ash Tray, Oval, 2"x3¾", Pink 2.00

Bowl, 5″ Berry, 6″ Cereal, Crystal 3.50
Butter Dish or Preserve and Cover, Pink 80.00
Candlesticks, Ruby Red Pr., Crystal 27.50
Cigarette Jar, Oval 2″x3″, Pink 4.50
Compote ,5¾″,Crystal 5.00
Plate, 6″ and 6-5/8″, Pink 2.00
Plate, 12″ Sandwich, Crystal 6.00
Relish Tray, 14″, 4 Part, Pink 8.00
Sherbet, Footed, Crystal 4.00
Tumbler, 4″, 9 oz. Water, Pink 4.00

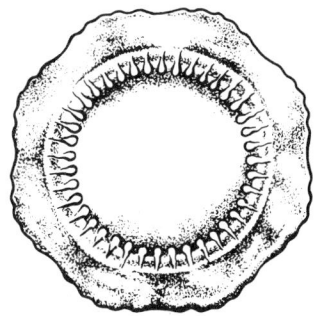

Radiance, New Martinsville 1936-1939

Bon Bon, 6″, Crystal 6.00
Bowl, 5″, 2 Handled, Nut, Red 10.00
Bowl, 8″, 3 Part Relish, Amber 9.00
Bowl, 10″ Flared, Red 20.00
Butter Dish, Blue 147.50
Cheese and Cracker, 11 Plate Set,Red 27.50
Condiment Set, 4 pc. On Tray, Crystal 87.50
Cup, Red 8.50
Lamp, 12″,Crystal 37.50
Plate, 8″ Luncheon, Red 6.50
Punch Bowl, Crystal 37.50
Salt & Pepper, Pr., Red 32.50
Tray, Oval, Blue 15.00
Vase, 12″, Crimped, Red 47.50

Raindrops, (Optic Design), Federal Glass Company
1929-1933

Bowl, 4½″ Fruit, Green 2.50
Creamer, Green 5.00
Salt and Pepper, Pr., Green 45.00
Sherbet, Green 4.00
Sugar Cover, Green 22.50
Whiskey, 1-7/8″, Green 4.00

Ribbon, Hazel Atlas Glass Company 1930-1932

Bowl, 4″ Berry, Green 3.00
Creamer, Footed, Black 11.50

Plate, 8″ Luncheon, Green 3.00
Saucer, Green 1.50
Sugar, Footed, Black 19.00
Tumbler, 6½″, 13 oz., Green 13.50

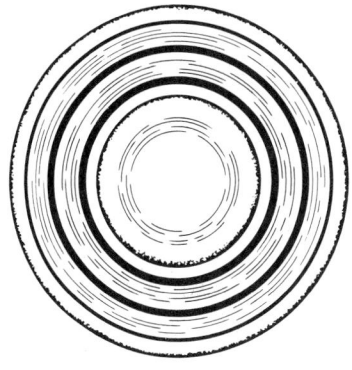

Ring, (Banded Rings), Hocking Glass Company
1927-1932

Bowl, 5″ Berry, Decorated 3.00
Butter Tub or Ice Bucket, Crystal 8.50
Creamer, Footed, Crystal 4.50
Ice Tub, Crystal 8.00
Plate, 6¼″ Sherbet, Decorated 1.00
Salt and Pepper, Pr., 3″, Crystal 12.00
Saucer, Decorated 2.00
Sherbet, 4¾″, Footed, Crystal 4.00
Tumbler, 4¼″, 9 oz., Decorated 4.00
Tumbler, 5½″, Footed Water, Crystal 3.50
Whiskey, 2″, 1½ oz., Decorated 5.00

Rock Crystal, (Early American Rock Crystal), McKee Glass Company 1920's and 1930's

Bon Bon, 7½″, S.E., Crystal 6.50
Bowl, 5 Finger Bowl with 7″ Plate, P.E., Pink 15.00
Bowl, 9, 10½″ Salad, S.E., Crystal 10.00
Bowl, 12½″ Footed Center Bowl, Pink 52.50
Candelabra, Two Lite, Crystal 27.50
Candlesticks, 8½″ Tall, Pr., Pink 62.50
Compote, 7″, Crystal 12.50
Cup, 7 oz., Pink 12.50
Jelly, 5″ Footed, S.E., Crystal 10.00
Pitcher, ½ Gal., 7½″ High, Pink 117.50
Plate, 7½″, 8½″ Salad, P.E. & S.E., Crystal 3.50
Salt and Pepper 2 styles, Pink 67.50
Saucer, Crystal 3.50
Stemware, 1 oz., Footed Cordial, Pink 17.50
Stemware, 6 oz., Footed Champagne, Crystal 10.00
Sugar, 10 oz. Open, Pink 15.00
Sugar, 10 oz., Covered, Crystal 27.50
Tumbler, 5 oz., Old Fashioned, Pink 15.00
Tumbler, 12 oz., Concave or Straight, Pink 17.50

Rosemary, (Dutch Rose), Federal Glass Company
1935-1937

Bowl, 5" Berry, Amber	3.50
Bowl, 6" Cereal, Green	11.50
Creamer, Footed, Amber	6.00
Plate, 6¾" Salad, Green	5.50
Plate, Grill, Amber	4.50
Saucer, Green	2.50
Tumbler, 4¼, 9 oz., Amber	9.00

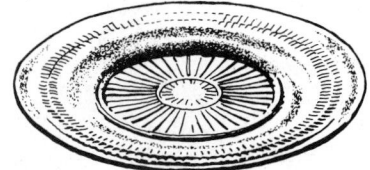

Roulette, (Many Windows), Hocking Glass
Company 1935-1939

Bowl, 9" Fruit, Pink	7.00
Pitcher, 8", 64 oz., Green	22.50
Plate, 8½" Luncheon, Pink	3.50
Saucer, Green	2.00
Tumbler, 3¼", 5 oz. Juice, Pink	4.00
Tumbler, 4-1/8", 9 oz. Water, Pink	6.00
Tumbler, 5½", 10 oz. Footed, Green	9.50

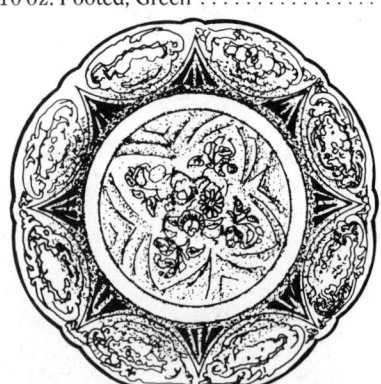

Royal Lace, Hazel Atlas Glass Company 1934-1941

Bowl, 4¾" Cream Soup, Pink	11.00
Bowl, 10", 3 Leg, Straight Edge, Blue	40.00
Bowl, 11" Oval Vegetable, Pink	15.00
Candlesticks, Pr., Rolled Edge, Blue	92.50
Creamer, Footed, Pink	9.00
Pitcher, 8", 68 oz., Blue	100.00
Plate, 6" Sherbet, Pink	3.50
Plate, 9-7/8" Grill, Blue	19.50
Saucer, Pink	3.50
Sugar, Blue	20.00
Tumbler, 4-1/8", 9 oz., Pink	9.50

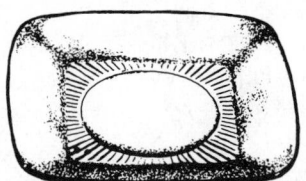

Royal Ruby, Anchor Hocking Glass Company 1939-1960's

Ash Tray, 4½" Square	2.50
Bowl, 8" Oval Vegetable	11.50
Creamer, Footed	6.50
Lamp	17.50
Pitcher, 3 qt., Tilted or Upright	27.50
Plate, 7¾" Luncheon	4.00
Punch Cup	2.50
Sugar, Flat	6.00
Tumbler, 5 oz., Juice, 2 Styles	4.50
Tumbler, 13 oz. Iced Tea	7.00
Vase, 4" Ball Shaped	4.50
Vases, Several Styles (Large)	10.00

"S" Pattern, (Stippled Rose Band), MacBeth
Evans Glass Company 1930-1933

Bowl, 5½" Cereal, Amber	3.50
Cup, Thick or Thin, Crystal	2.50
Plate, 8" Luncheon, Amber	2.50
Plate, Grill, Crystal	2.50
Saucer, Amber	2.00
Tumbler, 3½", 5 oz., Crystal	2.50
Tumbler, 4¼", 10 oz., Amber	6.00

Sandwich, Hocking Glass Company 1939-1964

Bowl, 4-7/8" Berry, Crystal	2.50
Bowl, 7" Salad, Green	27.50
Bowl, 8¼" Oval, Crystal	4.50
Creamer, Green	13.50
Custard Cup Liner, Crystal	6.50
Plate, 7" Dessert, Green	1.00
Plate, 9" Indent For Punch Cup, Crystal	3.00
Sherbet, Footed, Crystal	5.00
Tumbler, 9 oz. Water, Green	3.00

Sandwich, Indiana Glass Company 1920-1970's

Ash Tray Set (Club, Spade, Heart, Diamond Shapes) each, Crystal . . . **2.00**
Bowl, 6″, 6 Sides, Pink **3.50**
Bowl, 9″ Console, Crystal **10.00**
Candlesticks, 3½″, Pr., Pink **13.00**
Cruet, 6½ oz. and Stopper, Crystal **37.50**
Decanter and Stopper, Pink **65.00**
Plate, 6″ Sherbet, Crystal **1.25**
Plate, 8-3/8″ Luncheon, Pink **4.00**
Sandwich Server, Center Handle, Crystal **17.50**
Tumbler, 3 oz. Footed Cocktail, Crystal **15.00**
Tumbler, 12 oz. Footed Iced Tea, Crystal **12.00**

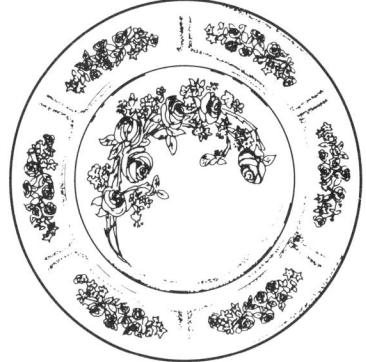

Sharon, (Cabbage Rose), Federal Glass Company
1935-1939

Bowl, 5″ Berry, Pink **6.50**
Bowl, 7½″, Flat Soup Two Inches Deep, Amber **22.50**
Bowl, 10½″ Fruit, Pink **22.50**
Candy Jar and Cover, Amber **32.50**
Cup, Pink **9.00**
Plate, 6″ Bread and Butter, Amber **2.50**
Platter, 12½″ Oval, Pink **13.50**
Sherbet, Footed, Amber **8.50**
Tumbler, 4-1/8″, 9 oz. Thick or Thin, Pink **19.50**

Sierra, (Pinwheel), Jeannette Glass Company
1931-1933

Bowl, 5½″ Cereal, Pink **6.00**
Butter Dish and Cover, Green **45.00**
Pitcher, 6½″, 32 oz., Pink **35.00**
Salt and Pepper, Pr., Green **27.50**
Sugar, Pink **6.00**

Spiral, Hocking Glass Company 1928-1930

Bowl, 4¾″ Berry, Green **4.00**
Creamer, Flat or Footed, Green **4.00**

Ice or Butter Tub, Green **12.50**
Plate, 6″ Sherbet, Green **1.00**
Salt and Pepper, Pr., Green **16.00**
Saucer, Green **1.00**
Sugar, Flat or Footed, Green **4.00**

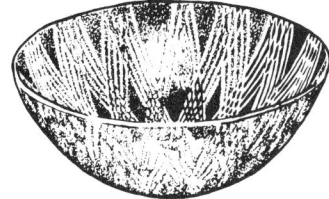

Starlight, Hazel Atlas Glass Company 1938-1940

Bowl, 5½″ Cereal, Pink **3.50**
Plate, 6″ Bread and Butter, Crystal **2.00**
Plate, 8½″ Luncheon, Pink **3.50**
Relish Dish, Crystal **2.50**
Sugar, Oval, Crystal **3.00**

Strawberry, U. S. Glass Company 1928-1931

Bowl, 4″ Berry, Pink **6.50**
Butter Dish and Cover, Pink **122.50**
Creamer, Large, 4-5/8″, Pink **10.00**
Pickle Dish, Green **9.00**
Plate, 7½″ Salad, Green **8.50**
Sugar Large, Pink **12.00**

Swirl, (Petal Swirl), Jeannette Glass Company
1937-1938

Bowl, 5¼″ Cereal, Ultramarine **7.50**
Bowl, 10½″ Console, Footed, Pink **12.50**
Candy Dish, Open, 3 Legs, Pink **7.50**
Creamer, Footed, Pink **6.50**
Plate, 6½″ Sherbet, Ultramarine **3.50**
Plate, 9¼″ Dinner, Pink **6.50**
Saucer, Pink **3.00**
Sugar, Footed, Pink **6.50**
Tumbler, 9 oz., Footed, Ultramarine **16.50**

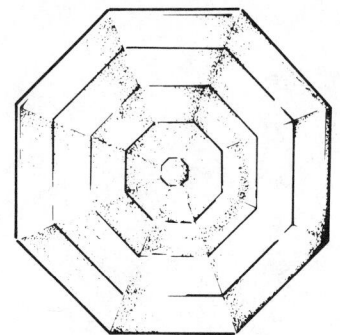

Tea Room, Indiana Glass Company 1926-1931

Bowl, 7½″ Banana Split, Green **42.50**
Bowl, 9½″ Oval Vegetable, Pink **32.50**
Creamer and Sugar on Tray, 3½″, Green **42.50**
Ice Bucket, Pink **32.50**
Parfait, Green **37.50**
Plate, 8¼″ Luncheon, Green **19.50**
Relish, Divided, Green **15.50**
Sherbet, Three Styles, Pink **12.50**
Sundae, Footed, Ruffled, Green **27.50**
Tumbler, 9 oz., Footed, Pink **16.00**
Vase, 9″, Green **27.50**

Twisted Optic, Imperial Glass Company 1927-1930

Bowl, 4¾″ Cream Soup, Pink **5.50**
Candlesticks, 3″, Pr., Green **9.50**
Cup, Pink **2.50**
Plate, 7″ Salad, Pink **2.00**
Sandwich Server, Center Handle, Green **12.50**
Saucer, Green **1.00**
Tumbler, 4½″, 9 oz., Pink **4.50**

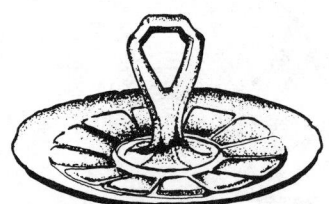

Victory, Diamond Glass-ware Company 1929-1932

Bowl, 6½″ Cereal, Green **5.50**
Candlesticks, 3″, Pr., Pink **14.00**
Creamer, Green **7.50**
Gravy Boat and Platter, Green **95.00**
Plate, 6″ Bread and Butter, Green **2.50**
Plate, 9″ Dinner, Pink **9.00**
Saucer, Pink **2.00**

Vitrock (Flower Rim), Anchor Hocking Glass
Company 1934-late 1930's

Bowl, Cream Soup, 5½″, White **3.50**
Bowl, Cereal, 7½″, White **2.50**

Creamer, Oval White **3.00**
Plate, Salad, 7¼″, White **1.50**
Plate, Soup, 9″, White **3.00**
Platter, 11½″, White **4.50**

Waterford, (Waffle), Hocking Glass Company
1938-1944

Ash Tray, 4″, Pink **5.50**
Bowl, 8¼″ Large Berry, Crystal **6.00**
Creamer, Oval, Pink **7.50**
Plate, 9-5/8″ Dinner, Crystal **5.00**
Plate, 13¾″ Sandwich, Crystal **5.00**
Sherbet, Footed, Pink **6.50**
Sugar Cover, Oval, Pink **8.50**
Tumbler, 4-7/8″, 10 oz. Footed, Crystal **6.50**

Windsor, (Windsor Diamond), Jeannette Glass
Company 1932-1946

Ash Tray, 5¾″, Crystal **11.50**
Bowl, 5-1/8″, 5-3/8″ Cereals, Pink **9.50**
Bowl, 9½″ Oval Vegetable, Crystal **5.00**
Butter Dish, Pink **35.00**
Candy Jar and Cover, Crystal **8.00**
Compote,, Pink **7.50**
Pitcher, 4½″, 16 oz., Crystal **17.50**
Plate, 7″ Salad, Pink **8.50**
Plate, 13-5/8″ Chop, Crystal **7.00**
Salt and Pepper, Pr., Pink **25.00**
Sugar and Cover, Crystal **4.50**
Tray, 8½″x9¾″, Pink **18.50**
Tumbler, 5″, 12 oz., Crystal **5.50**

Derby

   William Duesbury operated in Derby, England from about 1755, purchasing a second establishment, The Chelsea Works, in 1769. During this period fine porcelains were produced which so impressed the King that he issued the company the Crown Derby patent. In 1810, several years after Dunesbury's death, the factory was bought by Robert Bloor. The quality of the ware suffered under the new management, but in 1876 a newly con-

structed pottery and new owners revived the company's former high standards of excellence. The Queen bestowed the firm the title Royal Crown Derby in 1890; it still operates under that name today.

Bough pot w/liner, apricot w/scenic, x-baton & D mk, 8½", pr **1,900.00**
Butter tub, oriental scene, cable border, blue & wht, 1810.... **250.00**
Cache pot, yellow w/scenic reserve, 2 tab handles, 1790 .... **1,200.00**
Creamer, multiflorals, twig handle, 1760s **200.00**
Cup & saucer, Near Cromford, Derbyshire, hp, early 1800s ... **125.00**
    Cobalt w/church, gilt border, Bloor Derby, 1820 .... **135.00**
Figurine, lady w/scarf & plumes, playing triangle, 10" **675.00**
    Man w/keg, by tree stump, 1765, 8" **300.00**
Platter, Japan tree, rust, cobalt, gold, 1780-1800, 17" **400.00**
Sauceboat, shell form, blue & white, 1770 .... **400.00**
Vase, florals, hp, standard mark, 1800-1825, 12½", pr **1,600.00**

De Vilbiss

Atomizer, black w/goldstone, signed, 7" **160.00**
    Black, w/silver metal top, sgnd, 6½" **90.00**
    Colbalt blue cut glass, 3½" **60.00**
    Etched amber, signed, 7" **60.00**
    Green w/cut leaf design, signed **60.00**
    White opal, 6" **38.00**
Cologne, gold top, mauve opaque, signed, 6" **40.00**
Perfume lamp, Ivorene w/gold loop, gilt base, Steuben, 7½" .. **625.00**
    Torchiere, Deco black birds on pink, blue **130.00**
    Art Deco, orange, black, gold.......................... **60.00**
    Bulbous base, encrusted gold, gold & black stopper, 4" **38.00**
    Clear w/heavy gold engraved decor **20.00**
    Gold w/3 etched panels & foot, signed, 5" **75.00**
    Green opal coinspot, 3" **35.00**
    Green satin glass, signed............................. **55.00**
    Pink geometric, signed, 2¾" **35.00**

Devon Ware

Devon ware is a unique type of art pottery made in the South Devon area of England from the 1870s. At the height of productivity, at least a dozen companies flourished there, producing simple folk pottery from the area's natural red clay. The ware was both wheel turned and molded, and decorated under the glaze with heavy slip resulting in low relief nature subjects or simple scroll work.

Three of the best known of these potteries were: Watcombe (1870-1900); Aller Vale (in operation from the mid-1800s producing domestic ware and architectural products); and Longpark (1890 until 1957). Watcombe and Aller Vale merged in 1901 and operated until 1962 under the name of Royal Aller Vale & Watcombe Art Pottery.

Perhaps the best known type of ware potted in this area was Motto Ware, so called because of the verses, proverbs, and quotations that decorated it. This decor was achieved by the sgraffito technique, that is scratching the letters through the slip to expose the red clay underneath. The most popular accompaniment to these mottos was a stylized crocus design in slip work. Occassionally, the interior of a piece was glazed in a cream color, but often only a clear glaze was used to enrich the red of the clay. Other popular decorative devices were cottages, stylized daisies, and a scroll work pattern called Sandringham.

Aller Vale ware may sometimes be found marked H.H. & Co, a firm who assumed ownership from 1897 to 1901. Watcombe Torquay was an impressed mark used from 1884 to 1895.

Bowl, blue & green w/flower in center, 2x4" **38.00**
Candlestick, blue kingfisher, Longpark Torquay, 3½"........ **35.00**
Motto Ware, candle holder, w/finger grip, MIE............... **45.00**
    Ashtray, Cottage, Royal Watcombe **15.00**
    Ashtray, square, Cottage, Royal Watcombe **15.00**
    Butter tub, Cottage, Watcombe **30.00**
    Candy dish on ped base, mauve florals **30.00**
    Cauldron, footed & scalloped, 4¾" **35.00**
    Cereal bowl, Cottage, Watcombe **35.00**
    Cheese dish, Pixie, Watcombe **45.00**
    Coffee pot, Scandy, Longpark, 7" **60.00**
    Creamer, Cottage, MIE **20.00**
    Cup & saucer, Cottage, Dartmouth Devon................ **30.00**
    Hatpin holder, Scandy, Longpark **38.00**
    Hot water pot, Cottage, Royal Watcombe, 8½" **65.00**
    Hot water pot, pear shape, Cottage, MIE **35.00**
    Ink pot, Scandy, brown & green, Exeter **35.00**
    Ink pot, Scandy, matching stopper..................... **40.00**
    Ink pot, Shearer, Glasgow............................ **35.00**
    Inkwell, Scandy, Torquay **32.00**
    Jam dish, handled, Scandy, 5¼" **28.00**
    Jug, Cottage, MIE, 4¾" **30.00**
    Jug, pinched spout, cream/brown, Aller Vale............ **30.00**
    Milk jug, Thistle, Longpark Torquay **35.00**
    Pitcher, Daisy, Aller Vale **32.00**
    Pitcher, Scandy, Exeter.............................. **29.00**
    Pitcher, Shamrock, Longpark **25.00**
    Pitcher, barrel shape, 3x3"........................... **30.00**
    Pitcher, sailboat, 3 handles, 4½" **40.00**
    Salt w/ped base, Scandy, Exeter **18.00**
    Sugar & creamer, Cottage, MIE, pr **35.00**
    Sugar bowl, Cottage, Dartmouth....................... **15.00**
    Sugar bowl, ped base **30.00**
    Sugar, Cottage, large, MIE **30.00**
    Sugar, Scandy, Watcombe............................ **18.00**
    Teapot tile, round, Scandy, Longpark **40.00**
    Teapot, Cottage, Dartmouth Devon, 5" **35.00**
    Teapot, Cottage, MIE, 4½" **38.00**
    Vase, Cottage, Longpark, 6½"......................... **45.00**
    Vase, green drum design............................. **24.00**
Mug, blue, large **24.00**
Plaque, terra cotta, Watcombe.......................... **55.00**
Trivet, terra cotta, Longpark **45.00**
Vase, Kingfisher, Longpark **30.00**

Documents

Documents are collected for their historical significance. Those of a military nature are especially valued.

American Express, 1860	**10.00**
Bearer Demand Note, Ky., 1819, pink w/vignette farmer & river scene	**45.00**
R.I., 1855, vignette steamboat	**25.00**
S.C., 1800, vignette/sailing ships	**18.00**
Bill of Lading, horses Conn. to Barbados, sloop 'Gule', 1765	**35.00**
British passport, coat of arms & revenue stamp	**24.00**
Certificate, apprentice Pharmacist, Ill., 1899, 8½x10″	**12.00**
Business College, 1864	**12.00**
Pension, Civil War	**14.00**
Voters, 1866	**8.00**
Civil War, Confederate No 22, use wagons, teams, drivers, 1865	**20.00**
Confederate orders, authorize collection supplies, N.C.	**30.00**
Confederate Texas muster roll, 1863	**95.00**
Connecticut line note, to soldiers, treasurer signed, 1782	**60.00**
Discharge certificate, part printed	**5.00**
Draft notice, Mass., 1863	**15.00**
Enlistment papers, S.C., 1864	**27.50**
Field order, Ala., 1865, muster out, hand-written	**12.00**
Gen Orders No 153, New Orleans, 1864, 'courtesies military life'	**8.50**
Record court martial proceedings, Va., dessertion	**16.00**
Requisition for Forage, Fla., 9/22/1863	**4.00**
Special Orders No 38, Tenn., 1865, dismiss special board	**6.00**
Constitution, Fredericksburg Society, 5/23/1829, intemperance	**105.00**
Deed, Fire Ins, Lancashire Ins Co. w/company crest, 1898	**12.00**
Underwriters Agency, blue Liberty, 1905	**12.00**
Deed, Land, Mo., Wright Co, 1869	**6.00**
Land, Texas, Harris Co, filed 1884	**6.00**
Phila, vellum, 1868, 18x24″	**15.00**
Deposition, Cost & Labor Slave Jeff, died in service to S.C.	**65.00**
Discharge paper, Civil War, 1864, 8x11″	**25.00**
Estate settlement, Franklin's seal, 1766, 7½x12½″	**85.00**
Knights Ku Klux Klan, Grand Dragon, 1927-28, 7 documents	**70.00**
Land grant, England, parchment w/seals & signatures, 3/31/1797	**40.00**
Ill., vellum document, signed Filmore, 1852, 10x16″	**28.00**
Ill., vellum, signed Pierce, 1854, 10x16″	**28.00**
Parchment, signed for Franklin Pierce, 1854	**22.50**
Parchment, signed for James Polk, 1848	**15.00**
St Cloud, Minn., signed by Grant's secretary, 1876	**35.00**
Land lease, signed Baine, Hunter	**52.00**
List of Men, Company C, 45th	**14.00**
Manifest, Schooner Hiram, Portland, 1801	**35.00**
Nat'l Guard Certificate, Honorable Service, 1864, sgnd Lincoln	**100.00**
Note to pay loan, printed, 1780, 7x5″	**35.00**
Ohio Gov Appointing Post, 1815	**24.00**
Revenue stamps, Maryland, sheet of 4, 30 cents	**100.00**
Summons, Alabama, 1866, 7x12″	**9.00**
Indiana, 1860s, 3½x8″	**4.50**

Dolls

Collecting dolls of any sort is one of the most rewarding hobbies in the United States. The rewards are in the fun, the search and the finds, plus there is a built in factor of investment. No hobby, be it dolls, glass or anything else, should be based completely on the investment, but any collector should ask; 'Can I get my money back out of this item if I should ever have to sell it?' Many times we buy on impulse, rather than with logic, which is understandable; but by asking ouselves this question we can save ourselves a lot of 'Buyer's Remorse', which we have all experienced at one time or another.

Since we want to train ourselves to invest our money wisely while we are having fun, we must learn what things devaluate a doll. If bisque, watch for eye chips, hairline cracks and chips or breaks on any part of the head. Compositon should be clean, not crazed or cracked. Vinyl and plastic should be clean, with no pen or crayon marks. Though a quality replacement wig is acceptable for bisque dolls, composition and hard plastics should have their originals, in uncut condition. Original clothing is a must, except in bisque dolls, since it is unusual to find one wearing its original costume. However, they should be well dressed and ready for your collection.

A price guide is only a guide. It suggests to the collector the range of value for each doll. Bargains can be found for less than suggested values; and 'unplayed-with' dolls in their original boxes may cost more. Dealers must become aware of condition so that they do not overpay and overprice their dolls---which seems to be a common practice across the country. Quantity does not replace quality, as most find out in time. A faster turnover of sales with a smaller margin of profit is far better than being stuck with an item that does not sell because it is over-priced. It is important to remember that prices are based on condition and rarity.

Barbie dolls are priced mint in box.

Key:

bsk	bisque	ptd	painted
c/m	closed mouth	ShHd	shoulder head
hh	human hair	ShPl	shoulder plate
jtd	jointed	SkHd	socket head
MIG	Made In Germamy	str	straight
o/c	open closed	Trn	turned
o/m	open mouth		

Alexandre, Henri, Phenix Bebe, c/m, ball jtd compo, str wrists, 22″	**2,800.00**
Alice in Wonderland, cloth, yarn hair, Childhood Classics, 16″	**55.00**
Amberg, compo w/molded hair, ptd eyes, c/m smile, 14″	**125.00**
Newborn, compo head/cloth/celluloid, claps hands, #45520, 12″	**175.00**
American Character, Ben Cartwright, 8″	**85.00**
Ricky, Jr, 21″	**100.00**
Amosandra, Sun Rubber, 13″	**45.00**

Aranbee Dolls

Angel Face, cloth/vinyl, o/c eyes/lashes, 1954, 23″	**38.00**
Army, compo limbs & head, excelsior body fill, 15½″	**95.00**
Baby Marie, plastic/vinyl limbs, head; o/c eyes/lashes, 8″	**10.00**
Baby Nancy, compo, ¾ compo limbs, o/c eyes, o/m 4 teeth, 26″	**45.00**
Boy, from Nancy Lee mold, compo, mohair wig, 14″	**75.00**
Bride, hard plastic, o/c eyes/lashes, 1953-54, 14″	**55.00**
Carolyn Lee, ptd molded hair, c/m, R&B Doll Co, 8½″	**45.00**
Carolyn the Show Queen, compo, mohair wig, o/c eyes/lashes, 20″	**95.00**
Dream Baby, oil cloth body, o/c eyes/lashes, saran wig, 19″	**65.00**
Happy Time, hard plastic w/wig, tin o/c eyes, R&B 250, 15″	**65.00**
Juliana Coronation doll, hard plastic, o/c eyes/lashes, 17″	**75.00**
Miss International, compo, o/c eyes, o/c 4 teeth, 16½″	**65.00**

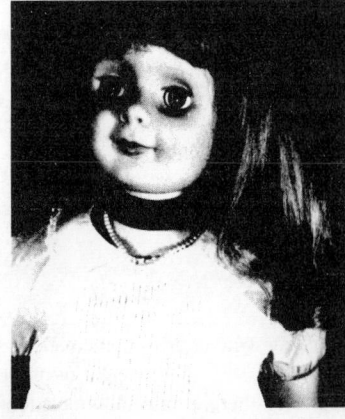

My Angel, plastic/vinyl, walker, rooted hair, 36″	**85.00**

Nancy Jean, compo, jtd, hh wig, o/c eyes, 21″ **95.00**
Nancy Lee, compo, o/c eyes w/eyeshadow, hh wig, 14″ **75.00**
  Hard plastic, saran ponytail, 1951, 17″ **55.00**
  Heavy vinyl, o/c eyes/lashes, 1954, 14″ **95.00**
Nancy, all comp, jtd limbs, ptd hair & eyes, 1930s, 12″ **45.00**
  Cloth w/compo ShHd, tin o/c eyes, o/m 2 teeth, 23″ **95.00**
Original Bottletot, compo/cloth/celluloid hands, o/m, 18″ **75.00**
Princess Betty Rose, compo, o/c eyes, c/m, hh wig, 1938, 18″ . . **95.00**
Rosie, swivel head, cloth/compo body, 1935, 19″ **50.00**
Scarlet, compo, o/c eyes/lashes, 15″ **75.00**
Sonja Henie, compo, mohair wig, o/c eyes/lashes, c/m, 21″ **95.00**
Teen, o/c eyes, hard plastic, plaid formal, 14″ **100.00**
WW II Nurse, compo/cloth, o/c eyes, c/m, wig, 11″ **65.00**

Armand Marseille
3/H/41 K/AM, SkHd baby, 16″ **235.00**
5/6/3/2K, closed dome baby, o/m, 16″ **235.00**
248/Fany/A 2/0 M, SkHd, mkd DRGM, 9″ **435.00**
  16″ **1,500.00**
  20″ **2,000.00**
  24″ **2,600.00**
341, flange or SkHd, My Dream Baby, c/m, 9″ **165.00**
  9″, black **235.00**
  13″ **285.00**
  13″, black **385.00**
  21″ **425.00**
  21″, black **425.00**
351/AM OK/Germany, SkHd, My Dream Baby, o/m, 7″ **150.00**
  14″ **150.00**
  18″ **265.00**
  25″ **385.00**
352/Germany, SkHd, 1914, mkd AM, 12″ **220.00**
  18″ **325.00**
  23″ **425.00**
353 12/OK, SkHd, oriental, mkd Am/Germany, 9″ **450.00**
  12″ **550.00**
  16″ **675.00**
370, ShPl, o/m, kid body, 15″ **150.00**
  17″ **170.00**
  21″ **200.00**
  24″ **225.00**
370/AM, 2-1/2 DEP/MIG, ShPl, brown tones, 22″ **295.00**
390, SkHd, o/m, 12″ **120.00**
  18″ **175.00**

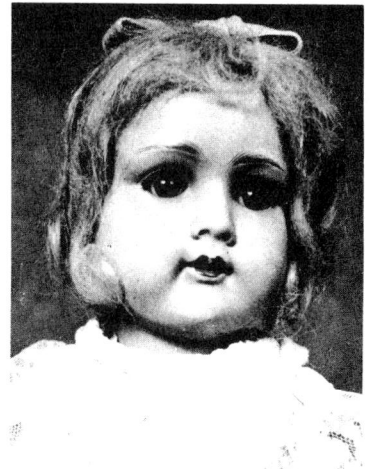

  23″ **225.00**
  30″ **400.00**
  40″ **900.00**
390/A 2 M, talker, (mama), SkHd, 17″ **225.00**

390/A 8/O, 16, SkHd, My Dream Baby, 1910, Armand Marseille, 10″ **110.00**
  23″ **215.00**
390/DRGM 246 1/A 3-1/2 M, SkHd, MIG/AM, 24″ **225.00**
390N, SkHd, o/m, 11″ **165.00**
  22″ **265.00**
560/DRGM 232, SkHd, toddler, 1924, Armand Marseille, 9″ . . **185.00**
  15″ **350.00**
  20″ **485.00**
640/A 3 M/Germany, ShPl, 1909, ptd eyes, 22″ **385.00**
975 M/Germany, SkHd, baby, Armand Marseille, 9″ **150.00**
  14″ **245.00**
  20″ **325.00**
  25″ **500.00**
1894 AM/0 DEP/MIG, SkHd, black, 15″ **265.00**
1894 AM/2/0/DEP, SkHd, black, 12″ **185.00**
1894 AM/8/0 DEP/MIG, ShPl, 1901, 12″ **150.00**
  17″ **210.00**
  22″ **265.00**
  26″ **300.00**
3200/AM 10/0x DEP, musical jestor, 1900, 10″ **350.00**
A 1 M, SkHd, closed dome, 11″ **195.00**
A 3 M, SkHd, 1915, c/m, intaglio eyes, mkd MIG, 18″ **650.00**
A 7/0 M/MIG, ShPl, boy, 14″ **145.00**
A 8/0 M, SkHd, side glance eyes, 13″ **325.00**
A 11M, walker, SkHd turns, mkd Armand Marseille/Germany, 26″ **345.00**
A 980 M 16/Germany, mechanical, eyes & tongues move, 26″. **850.00**
AM, SkHd, black, 12″ **365.00**
AM 2 DEP, SkHd, 16″ **225.00**
AM DEP/Germany/9, ShPl, 12″ **125.00**
  26″ **325.00**
AM Germany, SkHd, oriental, voice box, 10″ **365.00**
AM Germany/12, flange neck, 1907, 16″ **350.00**
Alma/10/0/Germany, ShPl, 12″ **110.00**
  18″ **175.00**
  26″ **250.00**
Armand Marseille, SkHd, 18½″ **175.00**
Baby Gloria/Germany 3, ShPl, 16″ **300.00**
Baby Phyllis, cloth body, 1915, 4/240/MIG, 12″ **225.00**
  23″ **375.00**
Baby/O/Betty/DRGM, 1912, ShPl & SkHd, MIG, 12″ **135.00**
  17″ **200.00**
  26″ **325.00**
Beauty/MIG, ShPl, 1898, mkd AM, 12″ **95.00**
  20″ **250.00**
  26″ **350.00**
Bonnie Babe, 1926, bisque, Corp/Georgene Averill/Germany/11, 8″ **550.00**
CM Bergmann, A 12M, SkHd, mkd MIG, 27″ **385.00**
Columbia/MIG, ShPl, 1904, 24″ **325.00**
Duchess, 1914, Germany/A 6 M, 14″ **125.00**
  20″ **250.00**
  26″ **375.00**
Floradora/A 2/0x M/MIG, SkHd, closed dome, 19½″ **245.00**
  A 3/0 M, SkHd, mkd MIG/Armand Marseille, 18″ **225.00**
    SkHd, mkd MIG/Armand Marseille, 22½″ **275.00**
    26″ **345.00**
    14″ **165.00**
  A 4/0 M/MIG, ShPl, turned, 16½″ **175.00**
  A 6M/DRGM 3748 30, ShPl, hair eyebrows, mkd 1374, 26″. **345.00**
    20″ **245.00**
  A 8/0 M/MIG, ShPl, 13″ **135.00**
    16″ **200.00**
    21″ **265.00**
    24″ **285.00**
    28″ **325.00**

Germany, ShPl, mkd 16/0 Germany/body, 6″ **125.00**
GB/AM 3-04, SkHd, closed dome, c/m, 18″ **425.00**
Googly, 253 M, Nobbikid, SkHd, c/m, 1915, US Pat Germany, 7½″ **425.00**
   10″ **795.00**
   A11/0/M/Germany/DRGM, SkHd, painted eyes, 7½″ **425.00**
   Mkd AM, 9″ **550.00**
   Just Me, SkHd, c/m, Registered/Germany A 3l0 3/0, 9″..... **700.00**
     12″ **1,100.00**
   Painted bisque, Just Me, SkHd, c/m, Registered/A 310 3/0 M, 9″ **385.00**
     12″ **495.00**
Indian, AM/7/0, mkd Germany, SkHd, 9½″ **295.00**
   Mkd AM 8/0, 12″ **325.00**
   Mkd AM/xGermany 4/0, SkHd, 11″ **325.00**
Kiddiejoy/1/0, closed dome baby, mkd Germany, 9″ **165.00**
   18″ **400.00**
   372/A 1 M, ShPl, closed dome, 1926, Germany, 9″ **165.00**
   AM 375/6, 1918, o/m, Germany, 9″ **165.00**
     18″ **400.00**
Lilly/3/0/Germany, ShPl, 12″ **125.00**
   16″ **165.00**
   20″ **250.00**
   26″ **345.00**
Mabel 5 Germany/Armand Marseille, ShPl, turned, SkHd, 20″. **250.00**
Mabel/0, ShPl, mkd Germany, 12″ **135.00**
   18″ **225.00**
   22″ **275.00**
   26″ **345.00**
My Companion, 1911, mkd AM Germany, 18″ **265.00**
My Playmate, 1903, c/m, stocknet body, mkd AM Germany, 18″ **325.00**
   Closed dome & mouth, 18″ **325.00**
New Born Baby, mkd LA&S 1914/G45520 4/Germany, 12″ .. **250.00**
   18″ **400.00**
Otto Gans/A 11 M, SkHd, baby, 26″ **550.00**
Puppet baby in a blanket, mkd AM, 8″ **185.00**
Queen Louise/7/Germany, SkHd, 1910, 12″ **145.00**
   16″ **175.00**
   22″ **275.00**
   30″ **450.00**
Rosebud/A 3/0 M, ShPl, 1902, 18″ **200.00**
   26″ **350.00**
Rosland/A 0 M, 1910, 18″ **225.00**
Special/Germany, SkHd, 1904, 12″ **125.00**
   16″ **165.00**
   20″ **250.00**
   26″ **345.00**
The Dollar Princess/Germany/A 3 1/2 M, SkHd, 26″ **375.00**

Bannister Baby, Sun Rubber, 13″ **45.00**
Barbie & Friends
Allen, 1963 .... **45.00**
   1964, bendable leg **100.00**
Barbie, 1959, #1 .... **700.00**
   #2, blonde **400.00**
   Brunette **450.00**
   1960, #3 .... **100.00**
   #4 .... **75.00**
   1961, first hollow body, 3 different hair colorings, each...... **60.00**
   1962, bubble cut hair style, 3 different hair colors, each **50.00**
   1963, Fashion Queen, w/3 interchangeable wigs **75.00**
   1964, Miss Barbie, w/sleep-eyes & wigs **300.00**
     Without box, w/suit, cap & wigs **150.00**
     Swirl ponytail, 3 different hair colors, each **55.00**
   1965, bendable leg, American Girl hair, blonde or redhead, each **50.00**
     Black hair **55.00**

Side-part hairstyle **150.00**
   1966, Twist 'N Turn **45.00**
   1967, standard **35.00**
     Twist 'N Turn **45.00**
   1968, talking **50.00**
     Twist 'N Turn **45.00**
   1969, Dramatic New Living **45.00**
     Living **45.00**
     Talking **50.00**
     Twist **45.00**
   1970, standard **35.00**
   1971, Hair Happenin's, Sears Limited edition **200.00**
     Live Action Barbie **45.00**
     Live Action Barbie on Stage **60.00**
     Malibu Barbie **20.00**
     Talking **50.00**
     Twist **45.00**
     With Growin' Pretty Hair **50.00**
   1972, Busy Barbie with Holdin' Hands **65.00**
     Talking Busy Barbie with Holdin' Hands **65.00**
     Walk Lively **60.00**
     Ward's Anniversary Barbie Doll **100.00**
     With Growin' Pretty Hair **60.00**
   1973, Malibu Barbie **10.00**
     Quick Curl **30.00**
     Quick Curl w/extra outfit, store promotion issue **50.00**
   1974, Gold Medal Barbie **20.00**
     Gold Medal Skier **25.00**
     Newport Barbie **45.00**
     Sun Valley **35.00**
     Sweet Sixteen **25.00**
     Sweet Sixteen, promotional, w/extra outfit **30.00**
   1975, Free Moving Barbie **30.00**
   1976, Ballerina, first issue, hair pulled to back **20.00**
     Ballerina On Tour, dept store special **35.00**
     Beautiful Bride, first issue, dept store special **35.00**
     Deluxe Quick Curl **20.00**
   1978, Ballerina On Tour, reissue, selected stores only, 3 styles, each **25.00**
     Ballerina, second issue, heavier make-up, side curl **15.00**
   Living Barbie Action Accents Gift Set, Sears Exclusive **150.00**
   Sparkling Pink Gift Set **200.00**
   Twinkle Town Gift Set, Sears Exclusive **125.00**
   Twist 'N Turn, limited edition w/extra outfit **75.00**
Barbie & Stacey Fashion Boutique, case w/4 dolls, orig outfits. **250.00**
Brad, 1970, New Talking **45.00**
   1971, Bendable Leg **40.00**
Buffy & Mrs Beasley, 1968 .... **45.00**
Cara, 1973, Quick Curl **25.00**
   1975, Free Moving **30.00**
   1976, Ballerina, in pink tutu **25.00**
     Deluxe Quick Curl **20.00**
Casey, 1967, blonde or brunette, each **60.00**
   1975, Baggie Casey, last market issue **15.00**
Chris, 1967 .... **45.00**
Christie, 1969, New Talking **35.00**
   1969, Twist **35.00**
   1970, Talking **35.00**
   1971, Live Action **50.00**
   1973, Malibu Christie **10.00**
Curtis, 1975, Free Moving **30.00**
Fluff, 1971 .... **45.00**
Francie, 1966, bendable leg **35.00**
   1966, straight leg **40.00**
   1967, Black Francie, dk brown eyes & hair **150.00**

Black Francie, lt brown eyes, red oxidized hair......... **160.00**
   Twist 'N Turn.................................. **45.00**
1969, Twist 'N Turn **45.00**
1970, Hair Happenin's **60.00**
   Twist 'N Turn.................................. **45.00**
   With Growin' Pretty Hair....................... **50.00**
1971, Malibu Francie **10.00**
   Twist 'N Turn, referred to as 'No Bangs Francie' **75.00**
1972, Busy Francie with Holdin' Hands................ **70.00**
1973, Quick Curl **30.00**
1975, Baggie Francie, last market issue.............. **15.00**
   Quick Curl, limited edition w/special costume offer..... **45.00**
   Rise 'N Shine Gift Set, Sears Exclusive **125.00**
Ginger, 1976, Growing Up **20.00**
Jamie, 1970, Walking **60.00**
   Walking, Strollin' In Style Gift Set, Sears Exclusive **150.00**
Julia, 1969, Talking **35.00**
   Twist 'N Turn, wearing 2-pc uniform **50.00**
1970, Twist, wearing 1-pc uniform **45.00**
Kelley, 1973, Quick Curl **35.00**
1974, Yellowstone Kelley **55.00**
Ken, 1961, first issue, flocked-hair **65.00**
   Second issue, flocked hair **65.00**
1962, painted hair **45.00**
1964, bendable leg **100.00**
1969, Talking **45.00**
1970, bendable leg **40.00**
1971, Live Action **40.00**
   Live Action On Stage **50.00**
   Malibu Ken **15.00**
1972, Busy Ken **45.00**
   Talking Busy Ken **45.00**
   Walk Lively..................................... **60.00**
1973, Mod Hair Ken **20.00**
1974, Sun Valley **30.00**
1975, Free Moving **20.00**
   Gold Medal Skier **25.00**
1976, Now Look Ken, shoulder-length or chin-length hair, each **20.00**
   Malibu Surf's Up Gift Set, Sears Exclusive **100.00**
Midge, 1963, bendable leg **75.00**
   Blonde w/lt blue & dk blue swimsuit **45.00**
   Brunette, w/pink & red swimsuit **45.00**
   Red hair, w/green & orange swimsuit **45.00**
   With teeth **100.00**
Miss America, 1972, Walk Lively, Kellogg Co promotional **30.00**
1973, Quick Curl, blonde **15.00**
   Quick Curl, brunette, longer hair, twist waist............ **75.00**
PJ, 1969, New 'N Groovy Talking **50.00**
1969, Twist 'N Turn **45.00**
1971, Live Action PJ.............................. **45.00**
   Live Action PJ On Stage **60.00**
1972, Malibu PJ **20.00**
1974, Malibu PJ **10.00**
1975, Free Moving **30.00**
1976, Deluxe Quick Curl **20.00**
Pretty Pairs, 1970, Angie 'N Tangie **75.00**
1970, Lori 'N Rori **75.00**
   Nan 'N Fran **75.00**
Ricky, 1965..................................... **45.00**
Skipper, 1964 .... **40.00**
1965, bendable leg **45.00**
1967, bendable leg, re-issued **65.00**
1968, Twist 'N Turn **35.00**
1969, New Twist 'N Turn **35.00**

1970, New Living................................. **35.00**
   Twist **35.00**
1971, Malibu Skipper **15.00**
1973, Pose 'N Play, Baggie **15.00**
   Quick Curl **20.00**
1975, Growing Up **11.00**
   Party Time Gift Set **125.00**
Skooter, 1965 .... **40.00**
1966, bendable leg **45.00**
Stacey, 1968, Talking **40.00**
1968, Twist 'N Turn **35.00**
1969, New Twist 'N Turn **40.00**
Steffie, 1972, Busy Steffie with Holdin' Hands **70.00**
1972, Talking Busy Steffie with Holdin' Hands **70.00**
   Walk Lively **60.00**
Tiff, 1972 .... **75.00**
Todd, 1966 .... **45.00**
Truly Scrumptious, 1969, Standard.................... **200.00**
1969, Talking **200.00**
Tutti, 1966, blonde or brunette, each **40.00**
1966, Me and My Dog play set **125.00**
   Melody In Pink play set, pale pink or hot pink, each **75.00**
   Night Night Sleep Tight play set **65.00**
   Walkin' My Dolly play set **65.00**
1967 .... **30.00**
   Cookin' Goodies play set **75.00**
   Swing-A-Ling play set............................ **75.00**
1969 .... **30.00**
1975, Night Night Sleep Tight play set, re-issued in Europe .. **35.00**
   Swing-A-Long play set, re-issued **35.00**
   Walkin' My Dolly play set, re-issued in Europe **35.00**
Tuttie & Tod, 1966, Sundae Treat play set **125.00**
Twiggy, 1967.................................... **60.00**

Barbie & Friends Accessories

Barbie & Francie Color Magic Fashion Designer Set........ **100.00**
Barbie Baby Sits Layette **125.00**
   First issue..................................... **100.00**
Barbie Diary **15.00**
Barbie Fan Club Magazine, early **4.00**
   Later.. **3.00**
Barbie Good Grooming Manicure Set.................. **25.00**
Barbie Hair Fair Set **20.00**
Barbie Hot Rod **60.00**
Barbie Music Box GE-TAR **20.00**
Barbie Photo Album **15.00**
Barbie Record Set, 'Barbie Sings' **20.00**
Barbie Sportscar **50.00**
Barbie Stand, #1................................. **50.00**
   #2 .... **40.00**
   #3 .... **30.00**
Barbie's Horse, Dancer **45.00**
Barbie's Wig Wardrobe, 1964, 3 wigs on card **45.00**
Boat, Sears Exclusive **35.00**
Clothes, 1959, Easter Parade, MIB **100.00**
1959, Gay Parisienne, MIB......................... **100.00**
   Roman Holiday, MIB **100.00**
1963-64, Masquerade, #794, MIB................... **35.00**
1964-65, Little Theatre Costume, 'Arabian Nights', #0774, MIB **50.00**
   Little Theatre Costume, 'King Arthur', #0773, MIB **75.00**
   'The Prince', #0772, MIB.......................... **75.00**
1965, Mr Astronaut, #1415, MIB.................... **125.00**
Dog 'N Duds Set **100.00**
   Dog only **20.00**
Midge's Wig Wardrobe, 1964, 3 wigs on card **75.00**

Belton

Concave head, 2 or 3 hole, fine bisque & body, o/m or c/m w/wig, 12″ **750.00**

   15″ **900.00**

   18″ **1,250.00**
   20″ **1,500.00**
   23″ **1,700.00**
   26″ **2,400.00**

Betty Boop, compo/wood, extra jtd, molded hair, by Fleiscker, 12″ **450.00**

Bisque

Baby, molded bottle, jtd shoulders & hips, painted diaper, 5″ . . **50.00**
Bunny, jtd shoulder, egg basket on back, Heubach, 4½″ **115.00**
Campbell Kid, jtd shoulders, molded clothes, German, 4½″ . . . **115.00**
Character child, shoulder jtd, molded hair, ptd features, 7″ . . . **175.00**

Dutch boy, molded clothing, hands in pockets, Japan, 6½″ **25.00**
Fully jtd, glass eyes, o/m, good wig, German, dressed, 4″ **175.00**
   7″ **275.00**
Jtd shoulders & hips, painted shoes, Occupied Japan, 5½″ **20.00**
Molded hair, wht w/ptd eyes, cloth w/wht bsk arms & legs, 12″ . **80.00**
Molded hair & bow, shoes, 1 pc, mk: 22797-G, 3¼″ **45.00**
Molded on bonnet & bow, cloth w/wht bsk limbs, 14″ **295.00**
Nodder boy, molded clothes, bobbing neck, Japan, 6″ **45.00**
Oversize head, ptd jeatures, jtd arms, fused legs, Germany, 4½″ **50.00**
Set eyes, c/m, 1 pc head & body, ptd shoes, mk: 620/0, 4½″ . **165.00**
Stone bsk, bonnet & bow, shoulder decor, cloth w/leather, 13″ **225.00**

Stone bsk, bonnet & bow molded on, cloth w/wht bsk arms, 16″ **360.00**
Tommy Peterkin, molded longjohns, 1915, Horsman, Germany, 4″ **150.00**

Bru

Closed mouth, all kid body, bisque lower arms; Bru, 16″ . . . **6,500.00**
   18″ **7,400.00**
   21″ **8,300.00**
   26″ **9,500.00**
Closed mouth, kid/wood body, bisque lower arms; Bru Jne, 12″ **5,000.00**
   14″ **6,600.00**
   16″ **8,500.00**

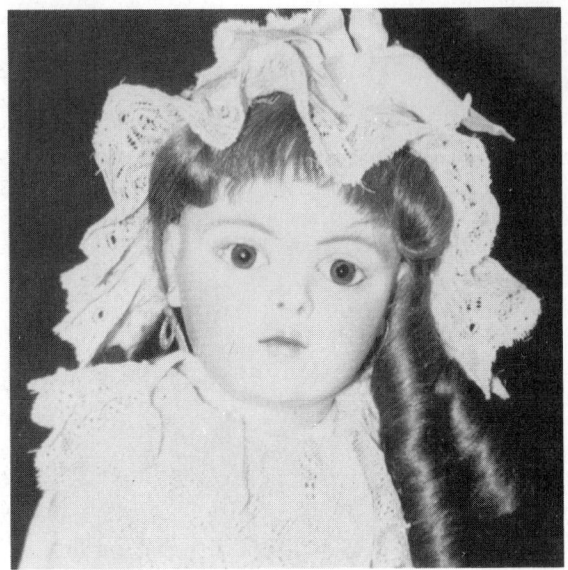

   20″ **9,600.00**
   25″ **12,500.00**
   28″ **14,500.00**
   32″ **17,500.00**
   36″ **20,000.00**
Closed mouth, mkd Bru, circle dot, 16″ **7,400.00**
   19″ **11,500.00**
   23″ **14,500.00**
   26″ **16,000.00**
   28″ **17,300.00**
Closed mouth, socket head on composition body; Bru, R, 14″ **3,400.00**
   17″ **4,000.00**
   22″ **4,800.00**
   25″ **5,600.00**
   28″ **6,200.00**
Open mouth, comp walker's body, throws kisses, 18″ **2,400.00**
   22″ **3,000.00**
   26″ **4,200.00**
Open mouth, nursing Bru (Bebe), early & excellent bisque, 12″ **3,400.00**
   15″ **6,500.00**
   18″ **7,200.00**
Open mouth, nursing (Bebe), high color, late SFBJ, 12″ **1,200.00**
   15″ **2,200.00**
   18″ **2,800.00**
Open mouth, socket head on comp body; Bru, R, 14″ **2,200.00**
   17″ **2,900.00**
   22″ **3,400.00**
   25″ **4,000.00**
   28″ **4,800.00**
   32″ **5,700.00**

China

Adelaine Patti style, wht center part, double chin, 14″ **300.00**
Baby, Common style molded hair, exposed ears, 15½″ head, 26″ **650.00**
Biedermier, blk area on solid dome head, hh wig, china limbs, 8″ **225.00**

Boy, blonde Common style molded curly hair, exposed ears, 22″ **575.00**
Boy, brush stroke hair, exposed ears, cloth body, china limbs, 14″ **500.00**
Boy, side part molded hair, 2 curls on forehead, kid body, 10″ **425.00**
Boy, side part molded hair, deep swirls & comb mks, 18″ **395.00**
Boy, side part molded hair, molded shirt & tie, 20″ **1,600.00**
Common, molded on corset, red eye liner, molded hair, 34″ .. **400.00**
Common, molded blonde hair, o/m w/teeth, cloth body, 10½″ .. **50.00**
Common, printed pictures on cloth body, molded hair, 10½″ .. **70.00**
Countess Dagmar, glazed head, pierced ears, molded hair, 16″ **675.00**
Covered Wagon, glass eyes, ears exposed, molded hair, 19″ .. **950.00**
Covered Wagon, wht center part, pink luster, 22″........... **550.00**

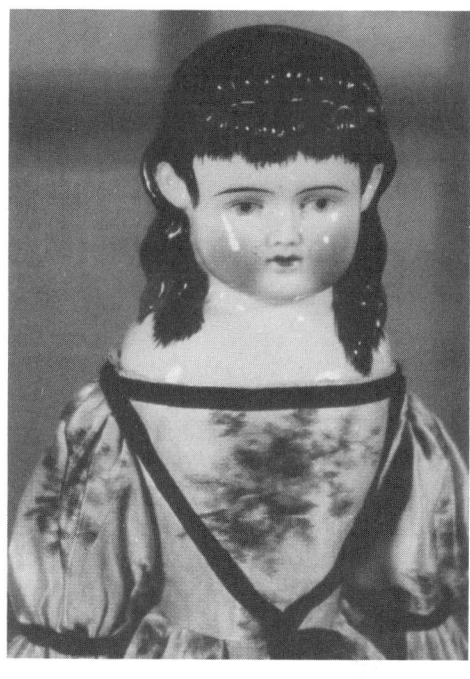

Currier & Ives, black molded hair, exposed ears, cloth body, 18″ **650.00**
Dolly Madison, red liner over blue eyes, pink luster, molded hair, 21″ **425.00**
Highland Mary, pink luster, black molded hair, 25″ **475.00**
Highland Mary, red liner over blue eyes, blonde molded hair, 20″ **375.00**
Japanese, pierced ears, 2 sew holes, adult features, 1920s, 12¼″ **75.00**
Scarf & grapes, molded on, center part molded hair, kid body, 13″ **750.00**
Spill Curls, molded hair w/long curls down back, kid body, 25″ **825.00**
Wig, blk thread w/shell earrings attached, orig clothes, 10″ **50.00**
Wig, w/long shoulder length curls, glass eyes lined w/blue, 14″ **1,200.00**

Cloth, ptd features on buckram, mohair wig, separate fingers, 20″ **65.00**
Danel & Cie, compo jtd body, c/m, Paris Bebe, Tete Dep/9, 21″ **2,700.00**
    25″ **3,100.00**
Daniel Boone, cloth, pressed plastic face, UAW-CIO, 1956, 20″ **28.00**
Denamur, compo jtd body, o/m, E 6 D/Depose, 17″ **895.00**
    C/m nurser, E 2 D/Depose, 16″ **1,650.00**
    20″ **2,300.00**
Disney, Mickey Mouse, bendable vinyl, Benda-A-Twist, 18″..... **85.00**
    Pinocchio, compo, jtd, molded hair, ptd eyes, 11½″ **125.00**
    Tinkerbell, vinyll w/rooted hair, set eyes, 12″ **35.00**

Effanbee
Amish, 1939, 7″ **85.00**
Amosandra, 1936, 9-10″ **145.00**
Anne of Green Gables, 1935, 22″....................... **100.00**
Antique Bride, 1979-80, ea **55.00**
Autumn, 1976-80, ea **65.00**
Baby Beauties, 1973, ea............................... **45.00**
Baby Bright Eyes, 1916, 11″ **85.00**
Baby Buds, 1919-20, 7″ **85.00**
Baby Cuddle, 1967-68 .... **45.00**

Baby Dainty, 1912-25, 24″ **175.00**
Baby Huggins, 1913-25, 9″ **50.00**
Baby Snowball, 1915, 12″ **145.00**
Baby-kin, 1940-49, 9″ **95.00**
Baroness, 1976-77 .... **75.00**
Beautee-Skin Baby, 1944, 19″.......................... **85.00**
Betty Ann, 1938, 15″.................................. **185.00**
Bicentennial Boy and Girl, 1976, ea **125.00**
Blue Bayou, 1979 .... **75.00**
Bobby, 1913, 11″ **75.00**
Bobby Bounce, 1913, 11″ **75.00**
Boudoir Doll, 1958, 28″ **125.00**
Brother, 1918, 14″ **175.00**
Bubbles, 1958-60, 23″ **45.00**
Bubbles, Betty, 1924, 22″ **195.00**
Bubbles, Walking, 1926, 26″........................... **300.00**
Button Nose, 1968-81, 16″ **45.00**
Candy Ann, 1954, 24″ **95.00**
Candy Land Collection, 1973, ea........................ **55.00**
Carousel Collection, 1974, ea **55.00**
Central Park, 1978 .... **65.00**
Charleston Harbor, 1978-81 .... **65.00**
Charming Cheeks, 1974, ea **55.00**
Christening Baby, 1918, 29″ **165.00**
Cleopatra, 1978....................................... **75.00**
Coco, 1980 .... **75.00**
Cookie, 1968-69, 16″.................................. **45.00**
Cotton Candy Collection, 1980, ea **45.00**
Country Look, 1973, ea **55.00**
Crowning Glory, Limited Edition, 1978................... **250.00**
Currier & Ives Collection, 1978-80, ea **65.00**
Denise, 1981 .... **65.00**
Dolly Dumpling, 1918, 18″ **195.00**
Dutch, 1937, 9″ **100.00**
DyDee Baby, 1930s, 20″ **100.00**
DyDee Baby, New, 1967, 16″ **55.00**
DyDee Jane, 1940, 20″ **100.00**
DyDee Lou, 1955, 20″ **100.00**
Elizabeth, 1938, 29″ **125.00**
Enchanted Garden Collection, 1973-74, ea **65.00**
Flapper, 1978-79...................................... **65.00**
Fluffy, Tiny, 1957, 8″ **35.00**
Frontier Series, 1968-71, ea **55.00**
Genevieve, Baby, 1981 .... **55.00**
Girl with Watering Can, 1981 .... **150.00**
Grandma, 1934, 10″................................... **175.00**
Grumpy, Baby, Jr, 1915, 12″........................... **125.00**

Gumdrop, 1962-77, 15½″ **45.00**

Half Pint Collection, 1976-77, ea......................... 55.00
Harmonica Joe, 1924, 15"............................... 225.00
Heartbeat Baby, 1942, 17".............................. 150.00
Her Royal Highness, 1976-78 .... 75.00
Honey, 1948, 18"....................................... 100.00
Honey Bun, 1967, 18".................................... 50.00
Honeybunch, 1923, 16".................................. 100.00
Hyde Park, 1980.. 75.00
Ice Queen, 1938, 15"................................... 395.00
Jambo, 1940, 14"....................................... 125.00
Joan Carol, 1929, 20".................................. 175.00
John Wayne, Cowboy, 1981............................... 65.00
Junior Miss, 1958, 15"................................. 125.00
Katie (Katy), 1954-57, 8".............................. 55.00
Lady Ashley, 1977 .... 75.00
Lady Diane, Limited Edition, 1982 .... 200.00
Lenox, 1919, 20"....................................... 365.00
Lil' Darlin', 1959, 16"................................ 35.00
Little Boy Blue, 1912, 12"............................. 75.00

Little Lady, 1939-46, 21"............................. 400.00
Little Luv, 1970-77, 14".............................. 35.00
Lovey Mary, 1926, 14"................................. 95.00
Lovums, 1928, 28".................................... 200.00
Luv, 1970, 18"....................................... 65.00
Madeleine, 1980 .... 45.00
Mam'selle, 1976-77, ea............................... 75.00
Marilee, 1924, 24"................................... 200.00
Mary Jane, 1917-23, 20".............................. 135.00
Mary Jane Toddler, 1963, 13"......................... 45.00
Mary Sue, 1927, 18" 95.00
Memories, 1978, ea 55.00
Mickey Baby, 1950-69, 20"............................ 65.00
Mint Julip, 1976 .... 75.00
Miss Black America, 1977-79.......................... 65.00
Miss Chips, 1965-80, 18"............................. 75.00
Miss Glamour Girl, 1942, 21"......................... 150.00
Miss Holland in trunk, 1977 .... 100.00
Miss Israel, 1980-81 .... 65.00
Miss Russia, 1978-81 .... 65.00
Mommy's Baby, 1949-52, 28"........................... 95.00
My Baby, 1963-65, 14" 35.00
My Fair Baby, 1958-69, 22"........................... 85.00
My Precious Baby, Limited Edition, 1975.............. 450.00
Nancy Ann, 1923, 23"................................. 225.00
Nap Time Gal, 1959, 22".............................. 65.00

New Born Baby, 1925, 12"............................. 125.00
Night on the Hudson, 1978 .... 65.00
Opal, 1981 .... 75.00
Pajama Baby, 1913, 14"............................... 50.00
Passing Parade, 1977-80, ea.......................... 65.00
Patricia Walker, 1954, 21"........................... 125.00
Patsy, 1946, 13½"................................... 145.00
Patsy Ann, Music Box, 1939, 18"...................... 250.00
Patsy Baby-kin, 1932, 9"............................. 135.00
Patsy, Jr, 1930, 11"................................. 145.00
Patsyette, 1931, 9".................................. 135.00
Peaches & Cream, 1976, ea............................ 75.00
Pennsylvania Dutch, 1936, 1939, 9"................... 100.00
Pimbo, 1950, 14".................................... 75.00
Plymouth Landing, 1978-80 .... 65.00
Popeye, 1933, 16".................................. 165.00
Precious Baby, Limited Edition, 1975................ 450.00
Prince Charming, 1952, 18".......................... 150.00
Queen Mother, 1977-78 .... 75.00
Red Cross Nurse, 1918, 12".......................... 95.00
Regal Heirloom Collection, 1976-78, ea 75.00
Riverboat Gambler, 1981, 9"......................... 100.00
Rootie Kazootie, 1954, 12".......................... 85.00
Rosemary, 1925, 28"................................. 225.00
Salvation Army Lass, 1921, 16"...................... 95.00
School Girl, 1913, 11".............................. 85.00
Shauna, 1981 .... 65.00

Skippy, 1928-43, 14"................................ 200.00
Sleeping Beauty, Disney, 1977-78.................... 100.00
Snow White, Disney, 1977-78......................... 100.00
Soldier, 1918, 16".................................. 100.00
Sonja on Skates, 1938, 16".......................... 125.00
Spirit of '76 boy & girl, 1976, ea.................. 125.00
Sugar Baby, 1936-40, 20"............................ 95.00
Sugar Plum, 1963-80, 20"............................ 65.00
Sunny, 1969-73, 16"................................. 45.00
Suzette, 1959, 15".................................. 35.00
Sweet Nostalgia, 1973, ea........................... 45.00
Sweetie Pie, 1938-48, 24"........................... 175.00
Teddy Bear, 1919, 12"............................... 100.00
Tinkerbelle, 1978 .... 75.00
Tiny Tad, 1912, 1916-18, 11"........................ 125.00
Toddle Tot, 1958-70, 22"............................ 65.00
Touch of Velvet Collection, 1977-78, ea 55.00
Touslehead, Black, 1943, 15"........................ 175.00
Twinkie, 1952-80, 15"............................... 45.00
Uncle Mose, 1915, 14"............................... 150.00

Vanilla Fudge Collection, 1977, ea **45.00**
Violette, 1977 .... **75.00**
W C Fields, 1929, 22" **400.00**
   1980 .... **65.00**
Winkie, 1963, 16" **35.00**
Wonder Doll, DyDee's Cousin, 1940, 20" **95.00**
Yesterday's Collection, 1977, ea **45.00**

Dorothy Collins, Star Doll Co, hard plastic, o/c eyes, 14" **65.00**
Ferte, deep crown slice, c/m, 1875, marked BF, 15" **1,800.00**
   C/m, 1875, marked BF, 22" **2,600.00**

Frozen Charlotte
China finish; molded blk hair, Common style, unmkd, 4" **50.00**
   8" **75.00**
   Molded hair, Black doll, 1" **25.00**
      3" **50.00**
      5" **65.00**
      7" **95.00**
   Molded hair, blonde, 4" **60.00**
      8" **85.00**
   Molded hair, boy, 15½" **350.00**
   Wigged, 7" **175.00**
Parian, luster lavender boots, pin jtd shoulders, molded hair, 5½" **250.00**

Fulper, bsk on compo, o/m set glass eyes, marked vertically, 17" **375.00**
Gaultier, compo, str wrists, mk F 7 G, 17" **2,200.00**
   Compo, str wrists, mk F 7 G, 20" **2,700.00**
   On marked Gesland body, c/m, FG in scroll, 20" **2,900.00**

Germany
Black, jtd body, o/m 4 teeth, Caracul wig, 10½" **250.00**
Brown bsk, jtd, stick legs, o/c eyes, o/m; S/PB/H/1909/10/0, 11" **245.00**
Brown bsk, o/m w/teeth, set eyes, MIG, 16" **365.00**
Compo, 1880s molded hair style, cloth/leather arms, 20" **325.00**
Jester clown, bsk head, molded on scarf, ptd teeth, o/c mouth, 10" **375.00**
Mache squeeze box clown, tips hat, walks, 12" **165.00**
Negro, o/c mouth pierced ears, jtd compo, 10" **150.00**

Gobel, My Daisy, bsk ShHd, kid body, compo limbs, o/m, 21" **435.00**

Half Dolls
Bisque, fancy hairdo, free hands, #3905, 4" **175.00**
Blonde, pink tie & rose, bed lamp, 4" **65.00**
China legs, hands away, fancy hair, shoes, #10044, 9" **115.00**
Colonial lady, hands free, feathers in hair, dressed, 5½" **225.00**
D&K, hands away, dutch bonnet, good features, 3¼" **185.00**
Fancy hairdo, gray curls, both hands free, #14753, 4¾" **150.00**
Flapper, arms extended, hat, 3" **150.00**
   Holding mirror, 4" **240.00**
Germany, arms away, good details, #1124, 3½" **85.00**
   Arms not open, lacy shawl & rose, #16924, 3½" **45.00**
   Elaborate hair w/band, #8030, 3¾" **55.00**
   Hands away, bobbed hair, china legs w/shoes, 4" **50.00**
   High hairdo w/good feathers, open arms, dressed, 4" **85.00**
   One hand away, curls, clothing, feathered hat, 5½" **250.00**
   Open arms, 1 raised to hair, 1 to waist, 4" **60.00**
   Open arms, feathers in hair, well dressed, 5" **55.00**
   Open arms, sitting, skirt flared, #1459, 3" **85.00**
   Orig wig, dressed, w/fan, #6181, 3¼" **85.00**
Googly w/glass eyes, wig, moveable arms, 3" **350.00**
Holding dog, arms not open, #8900, 5" **45.00**
Mimi, wrapped wire body & limbs, cloth clothes, 9" overall ... **125.00**
Open arms, hands to hair, dressed, bows in hair, #15466, 4" .. **85.00**
   Holds rose, nude, #12756, 5" **150.00**
Open arms, strapless top, hairband, 3" **35.00**
Orig mohair wig, hands away from body, nude, #6186 .... **125.00**

Spanish dancer, open arms, comb in hair, orig wrap, 4" **27.00**
Upsweep w/throat band, hands away from body, #14990, 2¾" .. **95.00**
Wearing hat, clothed, open arms w/rose in hand, #19177, 4" .. **80.00**
Wearing riding habit, putting on gloves, 4" **225.00**

Hallmark, Ben Franklin, cloth litho for Bi-Centennial, 7" **32.00**
   Betsy Ross, cloth litho, for Bi-Centennial, 7" **65.00**
   George Washington, cloth litho for Bi-Centennial, 7" **32.00**
Handwerck, bsk on jtd compo, o/c eyes/lashes, X on forehead, 24" **475.00**
   Bsk ShHd, papier mache/wood, jtd, 109/DEP-15, 30" **695.00**
Hasbro, flying nun, all vinyl, rooted hair, ptd features, 5" **28.00**
Hendren, Doret Doll, cloth/compo, ptd eyes, 15" **115.00**
   Scout, cloth/compo, molded hair, ptd eyes, 15" **125.00**

Heubach
5 pc bent leg baby, intaglio eyes, o/m, ptd hair, #3/77/59, 11" **595.00**
   Pouty c/m, o/c eyes, #72/48/4, 13" **925.00**
Dolly Dimples, SkHd, jtd compo, o/m, o/c eyes, #717/DEP/7½, 19" **170.00**
Negro ShPl, cloth/bsk, intaglio eyes, ptd hair, 2/0, 11" **1,200.00**
SkHd, 5 pc body, ptd shoes, o/c eyes/lashes; 8-192, 11" **300.00**

Heubach-Koppelsdorf
5 pc compo/mache, o/c eyes, pierced ears, #399/13/0, 9" **350.00**

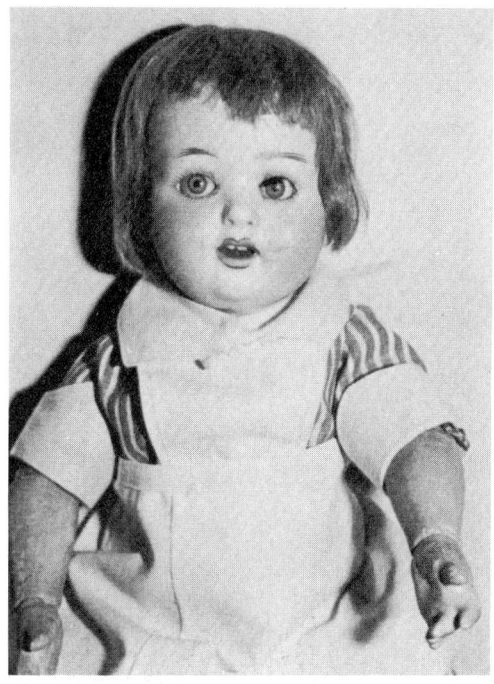

Bent leg baby, o/c eyes, o/m 2 teeth, 300/8/0, 25" **450.00**
SkHd, jtd compo, o/c eyes, o/m, #250 6 1/2, 14" **195.00**

Horsman
Baby Dimples, compo/cloth, o/m, o/c tin eyes, 22" **95.00**
Betty Jo, compo, mohair wig, 15" **75.00**
Campbell kid, compo head, limbs, cloth body, 1912, 15" **95.00**
Chubby Toddler, compo, tin o/c eyes, mohair braids, 22" **55.00**
Cindy Ruth, c/m smile, o/c eyes/lashes, rooted hair, 18" **65.00**
Cindy Strutter, hp walker, 27" **85.00**
Compo head, celluloid eyes, mohair wig, jtd compo/wood, 15½" **495.00**
Mama w/cryer, cloth/compo, o/m, o/c eyes, 26" **45.00**
Peterkin, cloth w/compo, ptd eyes, c/m, 13½" **125.00**
Petite Sally, compo, tin o/c eyes, mohair wig, 19½" **100.00**
Ruth's Sister, plastic, vinyl head & arms, 26" **45.00**
Sweet Marie, compo on cloth, sausage curls, 1915, 10" **85.00**

Hoyer, hard plastic, o/c eyes, glued on wig, 14" **85.00**
Hulss, SkHd, 5 pc baby, voice box, o/c eyes, 1916, 19" **365.00**
Hummel, boy, basket w/pig, 18-2, 1800 on back, 1966, 8" **95.00**

Girl, 1803, 1800 on back & feet, 8″ **95.00**
Ice Capades, American girl, 1970s, Kaysam 1961, 24″ **325.00**
   Parisian Percision, 1958-59, 18″ **325.00**
   Sentimental Journey, 1974, Kaysam 1961, 21″ **325.00**

Ideal
Baby Betsy Wetsy, vinyl, rooted hair, o/c eyes, 12″ **22.00**
   23″ **46.00**
Baby Coo's, latex 1 pc body & legs, 30″ **85.00**
Baby Jo Anne, early vinyl jtd, separate fingers, 16″ **28.00**
Bye Bye, vinyl & plastic, o/c eyes, o/m nurser, 25″ **165.00**
Carole Brent, ptd eyes, all vinyl; M-15-1, 15½″ **35.00**
Daddy's Girl, plastic & vinyl, jtd waist & ankles, 42″ **800.00**
Deanne Durbin, compo, o/c eyes, o/m, hh wig, 15″ **250.00**

Fannie Brice, compo/wood, ptd eyes, o/c mouth, 1938, 12″ . . . **225.00**
Flossie Flirt, cloth body, compo head & legs, 1934, 19″ **95.00**
Honey Baby, cloth w/compo, molded hair, o/c eyes, 1943, 15″ . **65.00**
Judy Garland, Wizard of Oz costume, 15″ **750.00**
Kissy, plastic, rooted hair, o/c eyes/lashes, 22″ **42.00**
Miss Ideal, plastic & vinyl, o/c eyes, rooted hair, 29″ **85.00**
Patti Playpal, plastic & vinyl, 1961, 36″ **95.00**
Posie, hp vinyl head, rooted hair, 23″ **50.00**
Tammy, in skier outfit, 1962″ **20.00**
Thumbelina, rooted hair o/c mouth cloth body, 1967, 20″ **28.00**
Toni, hp o/c eyes, nylon wig, 1949, 14″ **65.00**

Japan, celluloid boy w/molded baby bottle, jtd neck, 3½″ **9.00**
   Celluloid on velvet body, luxury liner souvenir, 12″ **12.00**

Jumeau
211/Jumeu, swivel head, o/m, inset eyes, The Screamer, 17″ **10,000.00**
Closed mouth, mkd EJ (incised) Jumeau, 10″ **2,650.00**
   14″ **2,850.00**
   16″ **3,600.00**
   19″ **4,700.00**
   21″ **5,200.00**
Closed mouth, mkd Tete Jumeau, 10″ **1,650.00**
   14″ **2,200.00**
   16″ **2,600.00**
   19″ **2,800.00**
   21″ **3,000.00**
   23″ **3,200.00**
   25″ **3,600.00**
   28″ **4,200.00**
   30″ **4,600.00**
Depose/Tete Jumeau, swivel head, pierced ears, long curls, 18″ **2,700.00**

28″ **4,200.00**
E 6 J/Jumeau, swivel head, inset eyes, kid body, 16″ **3,600.00**
   20″ **4,850.00**
EJ/Depose Brevete, swivel head, inset eyes, 'mama/papa' 16″ **2,600.00**
Jumeau 1907, SkHd, applied ears, o/m, 18″circumference, 32″ **2,800.00**
   Swivel head, o/m, o/c eyes pierced ears, 18″ **1,200.00**
   23″ **1,700.00**

Jumeau 1909, swivel head, o/m,inset eyes, pierced ears, 21″ **1,400.00**
Long face, closed mouth, 21″ **8,700.00**
   25″ **10,500.00**
   30″ **12,700.00**
Open mouth, mkd 1907 Jumeau, 14″ **750.00**
   17″ **1,100.00**

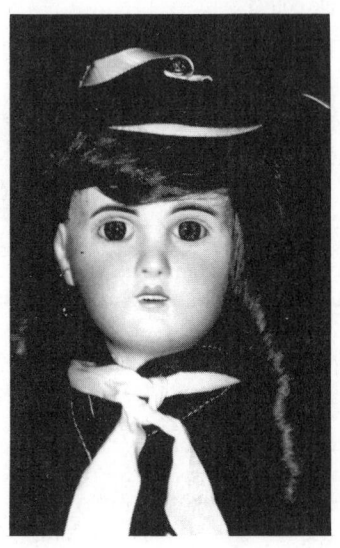

20″ **1,300.00**
   25″ **2,100.00**
   28″ **2,400.00**
   32″ **2,800.00**
Open mouth, mkd Tete Jumeau, 10″ **450.00**
   14″ **900.00**
   16″ **1,000.00**
   19″ **1,500.00**
   21″ **1,600.00**
   23″ **1,900.00**
   25″ **2,200.00**
   28″ **2,550.00**
   30″ **2,800.00**
Phonograph in body, o/m, 20″ **2,400.00**
   25″ **2,850.00**
Portrait Jumeau, closed mouth, 16″ **3,500.00**
   20″ **4,600.00**

Kammer & Reinhardt
#101, boy or girl w/glass eyes, 9″ **1,300.00**
   12″ **1,700.00**
   16″ **1,950.00**
   20″ **2,500.00**
#101, boy or girl w/painted eyes, 9″ **1,000.00**
   12″ **1,400.00**
   16″ **1,650.00**
   20″ **2,200.00**
#109, rare, 15″ **3,600.00**
   18″ **4,200.00**
#109, rare, w/glass eyes, 15″ **3,900.00**
   18″ **4,500.00**
#112, rare, 15″ **3,600.00**

18″ **4,200.00**	20″ **450.00**
#112, rare w/glass eyes, 15″ **3,900.00**	150.1, bsk, Kestner seal on body, 8″ **375.00**
18″ **4,500.00**	152, SkHd, made for Wolf, 1916, o/m; LW & CO 12, 20″ . . . **395.00**
#114, rare, 15″ **3,600.00**	154, SkHd & ShHd, kid w/bsk ½ arms, o/m set teeth, DEP, 14″ **300.00**
18″ **4,200.00**	17″ **375.00**
#114, rare, w/glass eyes, 15″ **3,900.00**	20″ **395.00**
18″ **4,500.00**	26″ **495.00**
#115, closed mouth, 15″ **2,000.00**	
18″ **2,650.00**	
22″ **3,200.00**	
#115, open mouth, 15″ **1,400.00**	
18″ **2,000.00**	
22″ **2,500.00**	
#115a, closed mouth, 15″ **1,650.00**	
18″ **2,200.00**	
22″ **2,800.00**	
#115a, open mouth, 15″ **600.00**	
18″ **900.00**	
22″ **1,200.00**	
#116, closed mouth, 15″ **1,650.00**	
18″ **2,200.00**	
22″ **2,800.00**	
#116, open mouth, 15″ **600.00**	
18″ **900.00**	
22″ **1,200.00**	
#116a, closed mouth, 15″ **1,650.00**	
18″ **2,200.00**	
22″ **2,800.00**	
#116a, open mouth, 15″ **600.00**	
18″ **900.00**	
22″ **1,200.00**	
#117, closed mouth, 18″ **1,900.00**	
24″ **3,000.00**	
30″ **4,200.00**	
#117a, closed mouth, 18″ **1,900.00**	
24″ **3,000.00**	
30″ **4,200.00**	

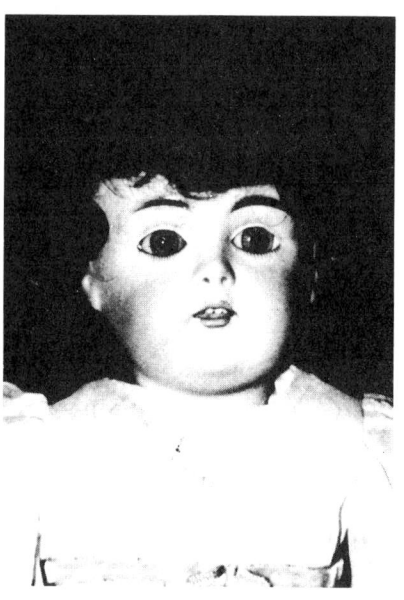

Dolly face, open mouth, mold #400-403-109, etc, 16″ **325.00**	167, SkHd, jtd compo, o/m, pierced ears; F 1/2/MI6 1/2/G, 16″ **325.00**
20″ **395.00**	20″ **395.00**
24″ **475.00**	168, SkHd, o/m; MID/G7, 26″ **495.00**
28″ **595.00**	169, SkHd, jtd compo, c/m o/c eyes; B 1/2/BI6 1/2G, 16″ **800.00**
38″ **1,100.00**	18″ **1,200.00**
40″ **1,400.00**	171, ShHd, o/m; INCIDEIN F 1/2, G/10 1/2, 20″ **395.00**
Kestner	26″ **465.00**
7 1/2/B, ShHd, kid w/bsk ½ arms, o/c eyes, o/m w/teeth, 19″. **395.00**	171, SkHd, jtd compo, o/m o/c eyes, 'Daisy'; F/MI10, 15″ **300.00**
10, SkHd, bsk shoulder plate, c/m, 21″ **1,350.00**	18″ **375.00**
10, SkHd, o/c mouth 2 teeth; JDK/MIG, 12″ **325.00**	22″ **395.00**
10/G, SkHd, c/m, 1912; JDK, 12″ **550.00**	172, ShHd, ball, kid fashion w/bsk arms, c/m, pierced ears, 14″ **1,300.00**
11, SkHd, o/c mouth ptd eyes to side; JDK/MIG, 11″ **425.00**	180 12/Ox/Crown seal, SkHd, o/m, 16″ **365.00**
12, SkHd, 5 pc baby, o/c eyes, o/m 2 teeth, JKD/MIG, 15″ . . . **400.00**	201, ShHd, celluloid on kid, set eyes/lashes, o/m, JDK, 19″ . . . **300.00**
13, SkHd, o/m; JDK/MIG, 18″ **400.00**	211, SkHd, 5 pc baby, o/c mouth, o/c eyes, MI10/G/JDK, 12″. **325.00**
16, SkHd, o/m; JDK/MIG, 21″ **400.00**	15″ **400.00**
16/GES#1, ShHd, o/c mouth, ptd eyes, molded boy's hair, 16″ **1,000.00**	215, SkHd, jtd compo, fur eyebrows, o/m; MI9/GJDK, 21″ **400.00**
26, K & Co/JDK/MIG/81, 16″ **350.00**	217A/Kestner, bsk, c/m smile, googly ptd eyes, 12″ **995.00**
143, ShHd, kid w/bsk ½ arms, o/m, 17″ **375.00**	221/GES/GESCH, SkHd, c/m smile, googly eyes; G/JDK, 21″.. **400.00**
145, ShHd, kid w/bsk ½ arms, o/c mouth, 15″ **750.00**	236, SkHd, 5 pc baby, o/m modeled tongue, set eyes, JDK, 18″ **495.00**
145, SkHd, c/m; 143/4/0/JDK, 11″ **500.00**	245, SkHd, 5 pc baby, o/m, G/MIG/11/JDK Jr/1914 Hilda, 14″ **2,395.00**
145, SkHd, c/m; MI/O/G/18, 14″ **700.00**	17″ **2,750.00**
146, SkHd, swivel, on shoulder plate, o/m; JDK, 18″ **395.00**	257, SkHd, 5 pc baby, o/m, G/JDK, 10″ **275.00**
147, TrnShHd, o/m; JDK, 25″ **495.00**	16″ **450.00**
148, ShHd, kid w/bsk ½ arms, o/m, 7 1/2, 18″ **385.00**	20″ **550.00**
21″ **425.00**	24″ **750.00**
151, SkHd, 5 pc baby, intaglio eyes, o/m 2 teeth, MIG/5, 12″ . **300.00**	270, SkHd, o/m, made for Carl Trautman; CP/39, 38″ **1,500.00**
16″ **375.00**	639, TrnShHd, closed dome, c/m; G/6, 18″ **995.00**
	1070, SkHd, o/m; G11/237 15/JDK Jr 1914 HILDA/GES, 16″ **2,550.00**
	A, ShHd, o/m, MIG/Kestner, 19″ **385.00**
	A/5, ShHd, o/c mouth, 23″ **1,150.00**
	B, SkHd, o/m, 1896; MIG/Excelsior; DRP #70686/G, 22″ **425.00**
	B/6, ShHd, kid w/bsk ½ arms, o/c eyes, o/m w/teeth, 19″ **395.00**
	B/6, SkHd, jtd compo, o/m 2 teeth, set eyes, 22″ **425.00**
	Bergmann, SkHd, made for CM Bergmann, o/m; JDK/CM, 14″ **300.00**
	17″ **375.00**
	20″ **395.00**

Century Doll Co, flanged closed dome, c/m, 15″ **600.00**
D/8, SkHd & ShHd, kid w/bsk ½ arms, c/m, 15″ **750.00**
E/9, ShHd, o/m, MIG, 26″ **495.00**
    SkHd, o/m, 1892, 26″ **495.00**
G/8, TrnShHd, o/m; MI/JDK, 19″ **395.00**
G/11, SkHd, brown, o/m, 16″ **500.00**
Grace Putnam, bsk, 1 pc body & head, 1923, 1/copy, 6″ **365.00**
    Bsk, 1 pc, ptd eyes; 20/10/COPR, 6″ **325.00**
    Bye-lo baby, 1927, 6-12/Copr, 16″ **525.00**
H 1/2, ShHd, o/m, 23″ **395.00**
H/12, SkHd, o/c mouth, 1892, 23″ **1,500.00**
Handwerck, SkHd, made for Handwerck, o/m; JDK/H/12, 23″ . **395.00**
    27″ **475.00**
I/13, SkHd, o/m, 1892, JDK, 16″ **350.00**
    26″ **495.00**
J/13, SkHd, o/m, 1896, 27″ **500.00**
JDK, bsk head on celluloid, R Gummi Co, turtlemark, 18″ . . . **695.00**
K/12, ShHd, made for Century, o/c mouth, molded hair, 21″ **1,350.00**
KK/14 1/2d, o/m, 1896, 26″ **495.00**
Kewpie, bsk, 1913, Rose O'Neill/10 945G, 8″ **250.00**
L 1/2/15 1/2, SkHd, c/m, 14″ **700.00**
L/15, SkHd, c/m, 21″ **1,400.00**
    SkHd, swivel, shoulder plate, c/m, 21″ **1,400.00**
L/3, ShHd, o/c mouth molded teeth, 23″ **1,150.00**
N/17, SkHd, o/m, 1892, 17″ **375.00**
    SkHd, oriental, o/m; JDK/Kestner, 14″ **750.00**
    Ptd eyes, JDK/3 4/0, 8″ **265.00**
TrnShHd, 18½″, Kidoline w/bsk ½ arms, o/c eyes, G/MIG, 16″ **325.00**

Lenci, felt orig, pre World War II, 11″ **265.00**
Lori, Swaine & Co, o/m/tongue/2 teeth, bent leg, jtd arms, 19″ **1,000.00**

Madame Alexander
African, hp, 1966-71, 8″ **245.00**
Alexander-kins, Wendy Ann, bend knee, walker, 1956-64, 8″ . **100.00**
    Wendy Ann, bend knee, non-walker, 1965-72, 8″ **100.00**
    Wendy Ann, straight legs, non-walker, 1973-75, 8″ **45.00**
Alice In Wonderland, Margaret, Compo, 14½-18″ **225.00-250.00**
    Margaret, hp, 1948, 14½″ **250.00**
    Maggie & Margaret, hp, 1950, 23″ **350.00**
    Wendy Ann, hp, 1955-56, 8″ **250.00**
    Lissy, 1963, 12″, from **850.00**
    Disneyland-World, Disney Crest Colors, 1972-76, 8″ **175.00**
Amish, boy, Wendy Ann, hp, 1966-69, 8″ **395.00**
    Girl, Wendy Ann, hp, 1966-69, 8″ **395.00**
Argentine Boy, Wendy Ann, hp, l965-66, 8″ **325.00**
Argentine Girl, Wendy Ann, hp, bend knees, l965-72, 8″ **95.00**
Baby Brother, Mary Mine, cloth/vinyl, 1977, 20″ **80.00**
Baby Clown, Wendy Ann, hp face, 1955, 8″, from **650.00**
Baby Genius, all cloth, 1930s, 11″ **125.00**
    Vinyl, hp, 1956, 8″ **85.00**
Ballerina, Wendy Ann, hp, 1953-56, 8″ **145.00**
    Elise, hp, 1957-57 & 62, hp, 16½″ **125.00**
    Cissette, hp, 1957-59, 10-11″ **165.00**
Bill/Billy, Wendy Ann, boy's clothes & hair, hp, 1953, 8″ . . . **110.00**
    Wendy Ann, groom, hp, 1953-57″ **175.00**
Binnie Ballerina, Cissy, hp, 1956, 14″ **150.00**
    1954, 15-18″ **180,00**
Blue Boy, cloth, 16″ **300.00**
    Wendy Ann, hp, 1956, 8″ **300.00**
Brenda Starr, hp, 1964, 12″ **125.00**
Bride, Tiny Betty, compo, 1935-39, 7″ **150.00**
    Margaret, hp, in pink, 1950, 17″ **145.00**
    Elise, hp, 1957-58 & 64, 16½″ **135.00**
    Cissy, hp, 1956, 20″ **225.00**

Cissette, street dresses, hp, 1957-63, 10-11″ **125.00**
    Ballgowns **280.00**
    Queen/trunk/trousseau, 1954, from **500.00**
Cissy, street dresses, hp, 1955-59, 20-21″ **165.00**
    Ballgowns **375.00**
Coco, plastic/vinyl, various clothes, 1966, 21″, from **1,700.00**
Cowboy, Wendy Ann, hp, 1967-69, 8″ **325.00**
Cowgirl, Wendy Ann, hp, 1967-79, 8″ **325.00**
Davy Crockett Boy, Wendy Ann, hp, 1955, 8″ **250.00**
Davy Crockett Girl, Wendy Ann, hp, 1955, 8″ **300.00**
Denmark, Cissette, hp, 1962, 11″, from **475.00**
Dionne Quints, babies, molded hair & painted eyes, 7½-8″, each **100.00**
    Set **950.00**
    Toddlers, compo, 20″, each, ... **250.00**
    Set **1,500.00**
    Toddlers, molded hair & sleep eyes, compo, 11″, each **185.00**
    Set **1,100.00**
    Toddlers, molded hair & painted eyes, compo, 8″, each . . . **125.00**
    Set **950.00**
    Toddlers, wigs & painted eyes, compo, 8″, each **125.00**
    Set **950.00**
    Toddlers, wigs & sleep eyes, compo, 11″, ea **185.00**
    Set **950.00**
Dr Dafoe, compo, 1937, 14″ **450.00**
Easter Doll, Wendy Ann, hp, 1968, 8″, from **975.00**
Ecuador, Wendy Ann, hp, 1963-66, 8″ **300.00**
Elise, vinyl arms, street clothes, hp, 1957-60, 16½″, from **185.00**
    Ballgowns, from **200.00**
English Guard, Wendy Ann, hp, 1966-68, 8″ **425.00**
Eskimo, Wendy Ann, hp, 1967-69, 8″ **400.00**
Fisher Quints, Little Genuis, hp/vinyl, 1964, 7″, set **325.00**
Flora McFlimsey or McFlimsy, Prin Elizabeth, compo, 22″ . . . **275.00**
    14″ **185.00**
    15-16″ **200.00**
Funny, cloth, 1963, 18″ **55.00**
Gibson Girl, Cissette, hp, 1962, 10″, from **650.00**
Gold Rush, Cissette, hp, 1963, 11″, from **850.00**
Grandma Jane, Mary Ann, plastic/vinyl, 1970, 14″ **175.00**
Greek Boy, Wendy Ann, hp, 1965-68, 8″ **275.00**

Hawaiian, Wendy Ann, hp, 1966-69, 8″ 400.00
Hiawatha, Wendy Ann, hp, 1967-69, 8″ 350.00
Jacqueline, hp/vinyl arms, 1961-62, 21″ 525.00
   Cissette, hp, 1962, 10″ 375.00
Jane Withers, c/m, compo, 1937, 12-13½″ 350.00
   15-17″ 350.00
Klondike Kate, Cissette, hp, 1963, 11″, from 850.00
Laurie Little Men, Wendy Ann, hp, bend knees, 1966-72, 8″ . 125.00
   Straight legs, mks: Alex, 1973-75 .... 55.00
   Lissy, hp, 1967, 12″ 450.00
Leslie, Black Polly, vinyl, 1965-71, 17″ 175.00
   Bride 175.00
   In formal 185.00
   Ballerina... 165.00

Lissy, hp, 1956-58, 11½-12″ 135.00
   Coco, 21″, from 1,500.00
Little Shaver, cloth, 1940, 10″ 245.00
Little Women, Meg/Jo/Amy/Beth, cloth, 1933, 16″ 200.00
   Margaret/Maggie, (Marme 1947-56), hp, 14-15″ 185.00
   Amy w/loop curls, 14-15″ 225.00
   Wendy Ann, bend knees, hp, 1956-59, 8″, each 125.00
      Set 700.00
   Bend knees, 1960-72, 8″, each 100.00
      Set 575.00
Madame Doll, Coco, hp/vinyl arms, 1966, 21″, from 1,500.00
   Mary Ann, plastic/vinyl, 1967-74, 14″ 300.00
Maggie, hp, 1948, 15″ 145.00
   17-18″ 165.00
Maggie Mixup, Elise body, hp/vinyl, 1960, 16½″......... 200.00
   Hp, 1960, 8″ 275.00
   Hp Angel, 1961, 8″ 500.00
   Plastic/vinyl, 1961, 17″ 175.00
Margaret O'Brien, compo, 14½″......................... 300.00
   17″... 350.00
   18″... 400.00
   19″... 450.00
Mary-bel, doll that gets well, rigid vinyl, 1959-65, 16″........ 125.00
   In case 175.00
Mary Martin, Margaret, hp, 1949, 14-17″ 425.00

McGuffey Ana, cloth, 16″............................. 300.00
   Hp, 17-18″ 200.00
   Lissy, hp, 1963, 12″, from 900.00
   Prin Eliz, compo, 1937, 14-16″ 200.00
Miss USA, Wendy Ann, hp, 1966-68, 8″ 225.00
Morocco, Wendy Ann, hp, 1968-70, 8″ 295.00
Nancy Drew, plastic/vinyl, 1967, 12″.................. 300.00
Nurse, Tiny Betty, compo, 7″ 150.00
   Wendy Ann, hp, 1956, 8″, from 300.00
Parlour Maid, Wendy Ann, hp, 1956, 8″, from 650.00
Peruvian Boy, Wendy Ann, hp, 1965-66, 8″ 350.00
Peter Pan, Margaret, hp, 1953, 15″ 350.00
   Mary Ann, plastic/vinyl, 1969, 14″ 250.00
   Wendy Ann, hp, 1953, 8″ 275.00
   Complete set of 4 dolls, 1969 .... 1,250.00
Pocahontas, Wendy Ann, hp, 1967-70, 8″ 325.00
Poor Cinderella, Margaret, hp, 1950, 14″ 275.00
President's Ladies, 1st set 1,400.00
      Singles 165.00
   2nd set... 600.00
      Singles 100.00
Princess Elizabeth, Tiny Betty, compo, 7″ 175.00
   Compo, 15″ 200.00
   24″ 275.00
Queen, Margaret, hp, 1953, 18″ 350.00
   Cissette, hp, 1957, 10″ 325.00
      1972-73-74, 11″ 300.00
   Cissy, hp/vinyl arms, 1957-58, white gown, 20″ 475.00
      1961-63, gold gown 475.00
   Elise 275.00
   Wendy Ann, hp, 1954-55, 8″ 300.00
Scarlett O'Hara, Tiny Betty, compo, pre-movie, 1936-38, 7″ .. 175.00
Cissette, hp, 1968-73, 11″ 375.00
   Lissy, hp, 1963, 12″, from 900.00
   Wendy Ann, 14″.................................... 275.00
      16″ 290.00
      17″ 300.00
      Compo, 18-21″ 375.00
      Hp, 1955-57, 7½-8″ 250.00
Shari Lewis, 1959, 14″ 185.00
   21″ 300.00
Sleeping Beauty, Little Betty, compo, 1941, 9″ 175.00
   Cissette, hp, 1960, 10″ 300.00
   Hp, 1959, 16½″ 350.00
   1959, 21″ 400.00
Snow White, Prin Eliz, compo, ptd eyes, 1937, 13″ 185.00
   Compo, 16″ 250.00
   Disney Crest Colors, #1455, 1967, 14″ 275.00
   Margaret, hp, 21″ 400.00
   Margaret, hp, 1952, 15″ 325.00
   Mary Ann, plastic/vinyl, Disney colors, 14″ 250.00
Sonja Henie, compo, 1939, 13-15″..................... 175.00
   Compo, 17-18″ 250.00
   Compo, jtd waist, 13-14″ 200.00
   Hp/vinyl, 1951, 15-18″ 200.00
Sound of Music, Louisa, large, 14″ 225.00
Sound of Music, Maria, small, 12″ 150.00
Sweet Tears, vinyl, 1965-74, 9″ 85.00
   With layette in box 145.00
Vietnam, Wendy Ann, hp, 1968-69, 8″.................. 350.00
   With Maggie Mixup face 375.00
Wendy Angel, Wendy Ann, hp, 1954, 8″, from 600.00

Mammy doll, compo head, o/c mouth, ptd teeth, Tony Sarg, 18″ 425.00

Melba, bsk on jtd mache, o/c eyes, o/m sculptured teeth, 14″ . **375.00**
Metropolitan, compo, ShHd, molded hair w/ribbon loop, 21½″ **100.00**
Miss America, Sayco, vinyl jtd waist, o/c eyes, 10½″ **30.00**
Morimura, SkHd, o/c eyes, o/m 2 teeth, 5 pc baby, #10, 13″.. **175.00**
  18″ **225.00**
Nancy Ann, Mary Had a Little Lamb, #152, 5″ **65.00**
  Monday's Child, #180, 5″ **65.00**
  Muffie, hp, o/c eyes, mohair wig, 8″ **75.00**
  Sunday's Child #186, 5″ **65.00**
Nippon, bsk head, 5 pc bent leg baby, o/m, o/c eyes, 18″ .. **250.00**
  SkHd, 5 pc bent leg baby, h/h wig, inset eyes, o/m, 12″ .. **165.00**
  SkHd, 5 pc bent leg baby, o/c eyes, o/m 2 teeth; B/9, 20″ .. **285.00**

Papier mache
Cloth body w/wood arms, long fingers, glass eyes, 1840s, 19″ . **795.00**
Fashion type, French, ptd eyes & hair, 18″ **850.00**
In orig French Morrocco, 1890s, 7″ **300.00**
Inset glass eyes, ptd hair, bamboo teeth, 1825, 30″ **200.00**
Kid body, ptd eyes & hair, 1830s, 8″ **395.00**
Leather body, wooden limbs, 1830s, 11½″ **625.00**
Negro, o/c mouth, glass inset eyes, 1880, 11″ **285.00**
Rare hairdo, crude peg jtd wood body, 1820s, 4½″ **325.00**
Set eyes, o/m 6 teeth, excelsior filled, German, 20″ **265.00**
ShHd, hh wig, glass eyes, cloth body, 14½″ **145.00**

Parian
1860 hairstyle, cloth w/china arms, 10″ **350.00**
Blonde ringlets, cloth w/leather arms, mk: 1056 #7, 18″ **425.00**
Blonde w/glass eyes, ShHd, cloth w/parian limbs, 20″ **995.00**
Boy, cloth w/bisque arms, 10″ **225.00**
Countess Dagmar, paperweight eyes, cloth w/parian limbs, 20″ **995.00**
Dresden wreath, ribbon, tassel; cloth w/parian limbs, 19″ ... **1,200.00**
Empress Eugenia, cloth body w/leather arms, wears snood, 16″ **995.00**
Molded bow & collar trim, cloth w/stone bisque limbs, 12″ ... **325.00**
Molded on blk hair, snood, clothes, cloth w/parian limbs, 21″. **995.00**
Molded on blk long curls, Dresden flowers & necklace, 15″. **1,200.00**
Molded on br hair, clothes; ears show, ptd features, 18″ **950.00**
Swivel neck, molded hair, cloth w/parian arms, mk: 2 1/2, 12″ **225.00**

Perle, bsk head, o/m sculptured teeth, printed features, 24″ .. **695.00**
Princess/1/Germany, SkHd, jtd compo, o/c eyes, o/m, 25½″... **425.00**
Putnam, Grace, bsk head Bye-Lo, o/c eyes, celluloid hands, 10½″ **300.00**
Rabery & Delphieu, SkHd, o/m, R ID, 20″............... **1,000.00**
  SkHd, c/m, R OD, 17″ **1,950.00**

SFBJ
11, compo w/bsk swivel head, c/m, inset eyes, 16″ **500.00**
20, molded ptd shoes & eyes, 5 pc body, Paris/12, 10″ **200.00**
60, French WWI nurse, 5 pc body, SFBJ/13/0, 8½″........ **200.00**
60, SkHd, compo w/straight legs, o/m, curved arms, 15″ **500.00**
60, SkHd, mache/compo 1 pc body, plunger cryer, o/m, 11″ .. **400.00**
203, 1900 bsk head on compo, o/c mouth, inset eyes, 20″.. **1,500.00**
215, bsk swivel on compo, c/m, inset eyes, 15″ **1,500.00**
223, bsk, closed dome, o/m 8 teeth, molded hair, 17″ **1,500.00**
227, brown swivel closed dome head, animal skin wig, 15″.. **1,600.00**
  18″ **1,750.00**
227, closed dome, o/m, inset eyes, ptd hair, 15″ **1,500.00**
227, French boy, jewel eyes, o/c mouth, eyes, hair lashes, 18″ **1,600.00**
228, toddler, c/m, inset eyes, mache body, 16″ **1,600.00**
229, swivel head, o/c mouth, inset eyes, compo, 18″...... **1,750.00**
229, wood walker, o/c mouth, inset eyes, 18″ **1,850.00**
230, pierced ears, compo walker, o/m, inset eyes, 16″ **950.00**
230, SkHd, pierced ears, o/m, o/c eyes, 23″............. **1,400.00**
235, closed dome, molded hair, o/c mouth & eyes, 8″ **750.00**
  16″ **1,650.00**
236, laughing Jumeau, o/m, o/c eyes, double chin, 12″...... **800.00**
  20″ **1,300.00**

238, swivel head, o/m, inset eyes, compo body, Paris 6, 15″ **3,500.00**
239, Poulbot, c/m, street urchin, red wig, 14″ **3,700.00**
  17″ **4,300.00**
245, boy, large glass eyes, googly, ptd shoes, o/c mouth, 8″. **3,800.00**
  12″ **4,500.00**
247, toddler, o/c mouth/2 inset teeth, 16″ **2,000.00**
  20″ **2,800.00**
  24″ **3,200.00**
247, twirp, o/c eyes & mouth/2 teeth, SkHd, 21″ **2,800.00**
251, 1099 character baby, o/c mouth, eyes, hair lashes, 16″. **1,300.00**
  18″ **1,600.00**
252, character, pouty, c/m, inset eyes, mache body, 18″ **3,000.00**
  22″ **5,500.00**
257, 1900 toddler, o/c mouth, inset eyes, 16″ **1,600.00**
266, bsk head, closed dome, o/c mouth, character, 20″ **1,500.00**
301, bsk SkHd on compo, o/m, inset eyes, 16″........... **500.00**
  22″ **800.00**
  30″ **1,200.00**
Bebe Parisiana, 1902, bsk head, c/m, inset eyes, 16″ **1,700.00**
Celestine, bsk SkHd on mache, o/m, inset eyes, 18″....... **900.00**
Tete Jumeau, pierced ears, o/c eyes/lashes, o/m, 18″...... **1,000.00**
SkHd, fully jtd mache/wood body, o/m, o/c eyes, 30″ **1,000.00**

Schmitt&fils, 1879 bsk swivel head, c/m, inset eyes, 16″.... **4,200.00**
  18″ **4,800.00**
  24″ **5,800.00**
Schnitz, PH, Bebe Moderne, c/m, inset eyes, 18″ **1,300.00**

Schoenhut

All wood, o/c mouth/ptd teeth, orig wig, 17″............... **350.00**
Baby w/bent limbs & ptd features, 15″ **400.00**
Bareback rider, circus figure, girl **250.00**
Boy w/molded hair, orig clothes, 14½″ **950.00**
Boy, ptd features, w/wig, 15″............................ **300.00**
Clown, 8″ **185.00**
Common, dolly faced, wigged, 16″ **300.00**
Dolly faced, sleep eye, 19″ **625.00**
Girl, character, molded hair, ribbon, comb marks, 14″....... **900.00**
Girl, decal eyes, spring jtd, ptd features, 16″ **300.00**
Milkman, ptd eyes, hair, moustache, jtd, 7½″ **375.00**
Pouty, o/c mouth, ptd teeth, 16″ **400.00**
  19″ **450.00**
Toddler, pouty, c/m, 11″ **300.00**

Schornau & Hoffmeister, 1906, SkHd, o/c eyes/lashes, o/m; H, 22″ **350.00**
  28″ **485.00**
  Clown, SkHd, jtd compo & wood, o/m, o/c eyes, 27″ **695.00**
Schuetzmeister & Quendt, 'Belton', c/m, jtd limbs, wardrobe, 9″ **695.00**
  Baby, SkHd, 5 pc, o/c eyes, o/m/teeth, 17″ **325.00**

Shindana, Flip Wilson/Geraldine, pull string talker, cloth, 16″ . . **12.00**
    Marla Gibbs, plastic w/vinyl, 15½″ **30.00**
Shirley Temple
Arranbee, compo, 'Nancy', 19″ **150.00**
Bisque, fully jointed, painted on shoes, mkd Germany, 4″ **65.00**
Bisque, jtd shoulders & hips, painted on shoes/socks, Japan, 6½″ **50.00**
Bisque, made from the compo molding, recent, 16″ **50.00**
Bisque, recent, 13″ **50.00**
Goldberger Co, compo, mkd EG, Miss Charming, o/m, o/c eyes, 18″ **125.00**
Horsman, compo, tin o/c eyes, o/m, mohair wig, Bright Star, 14½″ **95.00**
Ideal, baby, compo head, cloth body, o/c eyes, o/m, molded hair, 16″ **600.00**
    Compo head & limbs, w/cloth, o/c eyes, o/m, 22″ **350.00**
    Compo, mkd, cowgirl, 11″ **625.00**
    Compo,13″ **425.00**
      15″ **425.00**
      16″ **425.00**
      17″ **475.00**
      18″ **475.00**
      20″ **475.00**
      22″ **565.00**
      25″ **650.00**
      27″ **785.00**
    Compo, mkd, brown o/c eyes, w/orig trunk, 13″ **525.00**
    Compo, mkd, w/trunk & clothes, 1936, 17″ **625.00**
    Compo, mkd, w/orig taffeta Little Colonel dress, 18″ **525.00**
    Compo, mkd, Littlest Rebel, 20″ **575.00**
    Mechanical, compo, mkd, motor in stand, 27″ **2,500.00**
    Vinyl, 12″ **125.00**
      15″ **150.00**
      16-17″ **175.00**
      19″ **175.00**
      35″ **1,400.00**
    Vinyl, Captain January, 12″ **125.00**
    Vinyl, flirty eyes, 17″ **175.00**
      19″ **225.00**
    Vinyl, w/store display, 16″ **60.00**

Simmone, F, bsk swivel head, Rue Derivoli 188, fashion, 18″ **3,600.00**
Simon & Halbig
10, SkHd, o/m; G/Halbig/S&H, 16″ **325.00**
    19″ **400.00**

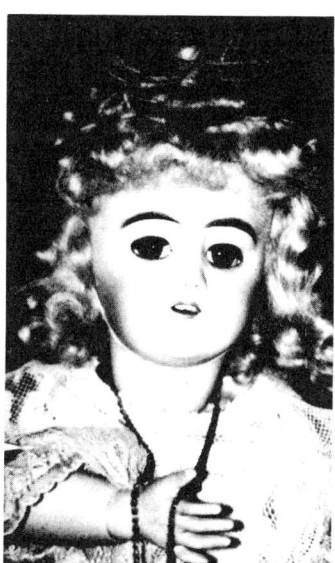

    22″ **450.00**
10 1/2, SkHd, o/m, flirty o/c eyes; S&H, 18″ **950.00**
30, SkHd, w/3 extra heads, 1920; L/Simon & Halbig/K*R, 12″ **3,000.00**

48m SkHd, o/m, 1905; Simon & Halbig/K*R, 27″ **550.00**
50, SkHd, c/m; Simon & Halbig, 16″ **650.00**
50, SkHd, o/m, 1900; K*R/Simon & Halbig, 14″ **300.00**
53, SkHd, c/m, brown bsk; Simon & Halbig/K*R, 16″ **850.00**
70, SkHd, o/m, 1896, Halbig/K*R, 26″ **550.00**
99, SkHd, o/m, 1899, 11 1/2 Handwerck/Halbig, 16″ **325.00**
100, SkHd, o/m; Simon & Halbig/S&C/G, 15″ **300.00**
    22″ **425.00**
101, SkHd, c/m; Simon & Halbig/K*R, 16″ **1,650.00**
109, SkHd, o/m, 1895; Handwerck/G/Halbig, 23″ **425.00**
114, SkHd, c/m; Simon & Halbig K*R/L, 9″ **1,000.00**
    14″ **2,100.00**
    20″ **3,400.00**
115, SkHd, c/m, 1912; K*R, Simon & Halbig, 16″ **2,000.00**
115a, SkHd, c/m pouty; K*R/Simon & Halbig, 15″ **2,000.00**
116a, SkHd, c/m; K*R/Simon Halbig, 17″ **1,700.00**
117, SkHd, c/m, 1919; Simon & Halbig/K*R, 16″ **1,900.00**
    20″ **2,600.00**
117a, SkHd, c/m; K*R/Simon & Halbig, 16″ **1,900.00**
    20″ **2,600.00**
117n, SkHd, c/m; Simon & Halbig/K*R, 20″ **1,000.00**
118, SkHd; K*R/Simon & Halbig, 14″ **1,000.00**
119, SkHd, o/m, 13/Handwerck 5/Halbig, 16″ **275.00**
120, SkHd, o/m; SH, 28″ **625.00**
121, SkHd, o/c mouth 2 teeth, flirty o/c eyes, 1920; K*R, 16″ **525.00**
121, SkHd, o/c toddler, 16″ **650.00**
121, SkHd, o/m, 1920; K*R/Simon & Halbig, 14″ **400.00**
    19″ **525.00**
122, SkHd, 1920; K*R/Simon & Halbig, 14″ **450.00**
126, SkHd, o/c mouth; SH, 23″ **675.00**
126, SkHd, o/m; Simon & Halbig/K*R, 14″ **425.00**
    19″ **575.00**
127, SkHd, o/m; K*R, Simon & Halbig, 18″ **425.00**
128, SkHd, o/m; K*R/Simon & Halbig, 14″ **400.00**
    19″ **535.00**
151, SkHd, o/c mouth, ptd eyes; S&H/1, 16″ **2,900.00**
156, SkHd, 1925, S&H, 18″ **350.00**
    22″ **500.00**
159, SkHd, o/m; Simon & Halbig, 16″ **325.00**
191, SkHd, o/m; Bergmann/CB, 18″ **350.00**
246, ShKd, o/m, 1900, K*R/Simon & Halbig, 18″ **300.00**
282, SkHd, o/m; S H, 14″ **275.00**
    18″ **375.00**
    22″ **425.00**
383, SkHd, flapper body; S H, 14″ **700.00**
402, SkHd, o/m; K*R SH, 16″ **325.00**
403, SkHd, o/c mouth; K*R, Simon & Halbig, 20″ **750.00**
403, SkHd, o/m, walker; K*R SH, 21″ **675.00**
409, SkHd, o/m; S&H, 24″ **475.00**
    26″ **525.00**
    30″ **650.00**
530, SkHd, o/m; G/Simon & Halbig, 21″ **495.00**
540, SkHd, o/m; G/Halbig/S&H, 30″ **850.00**
540, SkHd, swivel on bsk shoulder plate, o/m; S&H, G, 16″ . . **325.00**
550, SkHd, o/m, for Gimbel Bros; G/G/Simon & Halbig/S&H, 21″ **375.00**
550, SkHd, o/m; Simon & Halbig/S&H, 16″ **325.00**
570, SkHd, o/m, walking, head turns; G/Halbig S&H, 18″ **625.00**
570, SkHd, o/m; Halbig S&H/G, 18″ **475.00**
576, SkHd, o/m; Simon & Halbig, 16″ **325.00**
612, SkHd, o/m; MIG/ S&H/CM Bergmann, 16″ **375.00**
616, flanged compo head, 1920, o/m; Simon & Halbig/MIG, 12″ **185.00**
670, SkHd, o/m; Simon & Halbig, 16″ **325.00**
719, SkHd, c/m; S&H DEP, 16″ **1,500.00**
719, SkHd, o/m; Simon & Halbig S11H DEP, 20″ **600.00**

719, SkHd, swivel, shoulder plate, c/m; S&H, DEP, 20″ **1,500.00**
739, SkHd, c/m, brown; S 5 H DEP, 14″ **750.00**
  18″ **950.00**
759, SkHd, o/m, brown; S 10 H DEP, 20″ **600.00**
769, SkHd, S&H DEP, 17″ **1,600.00**
905, SkHd, swivel on shoulder plate, c/m; S H, 21″ **1,500.00**
908, SkHd, swivel on shoulder plate, c/m; S H, 16″ **1,300.00**
929, SkHd, c/m; S&H, DEP, 20″ **1,600.00**
  25″ **2,300.00**
939, SkHd, c/m; S 11H DEP, 17″ **1,600.00**
  23″ **2,000.00**
940, SkHd, closed dome, o/c mouth; S 2 H, 26″ **1,700.00**
940, SkHd, swivel on shoulder plate, o/c mouth; S 2 H, 14″ .. **895.00**
945, SkHd, c/m; S 2 H DEP, 16″ **850.00**
1019, SkHd, c/m, swimming doll for Martin; Halbig/S&H/G2, 12″ **850.00**
1059, SkHd, swivel on ShPl, wood w/kid fashion, o/m; 19″ . **1,400.00**
1159, SkHd, adult body, 1905; G/Simon & Halbig/S&H7, 14″. **725.00**
  18″ **1,000.00**
  24″ **1,500.00**
1279, SkHd, o/m, musical & mechanical; S&H DEP/G/7 1/2, 18″ **750.00**
1296, SkHd, 1911; FS&Co/Simon & Halbig, 14″ **350.00**
1329, SkHd, o/m, olive; G/Simon & Halbig/SH, 14″ **850.00**
1848, SkHd, o/m; Jutta Simon & Halbig, 16″ **450.00**
1923, SkHd, o/m; SH Sp 53/4/G, 14″ **300.00**
  21″ **400.00**
  26″ **550.00**
AW, SkHd, o/m; SH/13, 21″ **425.00**
Baby Blanche, SkHd, o/m baby; S&H, 16″ **300.00**
  21″ **450.00**
Baby Compolite, SkHd, o/m, for Handwerck 1895; S&H, 530/G, 16″ **325.00**
CM Bergmann, SkHd, o/m, 1895; Halbig/S&H5, 30″ **850.00**
CM Bergmann, SkHd, o/m, 1897, S&H6, 12″ **145.00**
CM Bergmann, SkHd o/m; Simon & Halbig, 3 1/2, 18″ ... **375.00**
Elenore, SkHd, o/m; CMB/Simon & Halbig, 18″ **450.00**
G68, SkHd, flirty eyes, 1908; S&H/K*R, 16″ **500.00**
Handwerck, SkHd, o/m, 1893, 16″ **250.00**
Handwerck, SkHd, o/m, 1895; G/S&H/1, 16″ **250.00**
Handwerck, SkHd, o/m; G/Halbig, 4, 26″ **550.00**
S&H3, all bisque, c/m, inset eyes, molded on shoes, 6″ .. **150.00**
Santa, SkHd, o/m, for Hamburger 1900; incised 'angel' H Co, 14″ **400.00**
SkHd, 2 teeth, tongue; K*R/Simon & Halbig, 116a-38, 17″ ... **600.00**

Smith, P D, o/m/2 teeth, flirty glass eyes, jtd body, 1918, 20″ **1,000.00**
So Wee, Sun Rubber, Ruth Newton, 10½″ **40.00**
Steiner
A 7, brown bsk head, c/m, inset eyes, compo, 16″ **2,500.00**
  20″ **3,200.00**
A 13, bsk head, c/m, inset eyes, F1 AF, 18″ **2,600.00**
  22″ **3,200.00**
  26″ **3,800.00**
C 1, swivel head, o/m, o/c eyes, compo body, STE, 18″ ... **2,800.00**
C 5, swivel head, pierced ears, voice, c/m, STE, 25″ **3,600.00**
Bebe Liege, 1899 bsk head, c/m, inset eyes, 18″ **1,800.00**
Bebe Modele, 1901 bsk head, c/m, inset eyes, 18″ **1,600.00**
Bourgion, mache/copo, c/m, 21″ **4,200.00**
Keywind, kit, compo & cartouche, o/m 2 rows teeth, 20″ ... **1,475.00**
Majestic, Edmund, SkHd, c/m, jtd compo/wood, 32″ **995.00**
Mechanical, wax over mache, o/c eyes, ptd hair & wig, 22″ . **1,250.00**
Wire-eye, fully jtd compo/wood body, o/c eyes, 18″ **2,800.00**

Superman, felt & plush w/vinyl head, Commonwealth Toys, 1966 ″ **65.00**
Superior, cloth body, leather arms, blonde sausage curls, 14½″ **325.00**
Thuillier, mache, jtd, big hands, pierced ears, A12T, 25″, from **12,000.00**
Unis, 5 pc body, ptd eyes, ptd on shoes, Unis in oval/60, 12″. **325.00**

Bsk on mache, paperweight eyes, ptd on shoes, France, 7″ . **185.00**
Vogue
Ginny, bent knee orig, 8″ **50.00**

Ginny, hh, ptd eyes, all orig, 8″ **95.00**
Ginny, straight leg walker, orig, 8″ **75.00**
Musical Baby Dear, cloth/vinyl, 1960, 12″ **42.00**
My Angeline, all vinyl, o/c eyes/lashes, 15″ **35.00**
Toodles, compo, ptd eyes to side, 7″ **95.00**
Toodles Baby, original clothes **95.00**

Wax, creche woman, inset glass eyes, c/m, wax arms, 17½″ .. **425.00**
Wax, glass eyes, cloth body, leather arms, English, 26″ **350.00**
Wax, peg jtd wood body & limbs, inset glass eyes, 11″ **1,695.00**
Wax on mache, cloth, moldled hi-top boots, 1800s, 20″ **185.00**
Wax on mache, cloth body, compo limbs, glass eyes, German, 25″ **300.00**
Wax on mache, pumpkin head, inset eyess, cloth body, 1880, 9″ **110.00**
Webber, singing mechanism, set eyes, c/m, 1800, 26″ **895.00**
Welsch, SkHd, mache/wood jtd body, made for Arnold, 19″ .. **375.00**
Welsh, SkHd, ptd on shoes, o/c eyes, o/m, 9″ **175.00**
Zorro, Sun Rubber **65.00**

Doll Furniture

Little girls have always loved their dolls, and loving parents have bought them steamer trunks, cupboards, bureaus, and beds--everthing a child needed to make her doll comfortable. Some were lovingly hand crafted and rather primitive, while other pieces were commercially made. All make charming collectibles.

Armchair, Mission oak, 9½x7½x5″ **25.00**
Bathroom set, stool, lavatory, tub, German porcelain **95.00**
Bed, brass, early, 18x12″ **130.00**
  Brass **75.00**
  Iron, folding **35.00**
  Iron, hp scene & prayer, old **550.00**
  Rope, Empire style, rolled top headboard, 10x15½″ **78.00**
  Spindle sides, applied sawtooth star, old paint w/gold ... **30.00**
  Spool turned ash, late 1800s, 24x15x13″ **55.00**
  Walnut, Victorian, intricate carving, high headboard **600.00**
  Walnut, high poster rope style, early 1800s, 17x18x13″ ... **180.00**
  Wicker, satin lining & pillows, 1936, Germany, 10½″ long .. **30.00**
  Wood, handmade, red paint, lengthwise slats **115.00**
  Wood, wht paint, 15½″ long **35.00**
Blanket chest, hinged top, bottom drawer, oilcloth cover, 7x7″. **60.00**
  Poplar, turned feet w/till, 7x10x5½″ **175.00**
Bureau, mahogany, elephant trunk scrolls, 2 drawers on 4, 16″ **275.00**

Carriage, wicker, 30″	90.00
Chair, twisted wire, rolled tops, scrolls, ornate, 28½″	75.00
Windsor bowback, saddle seat, yellow paint, 16″	235.00
Wood w/slats, 1930s, 10″	40.00
Chest of drawers, bracket base, scrolls, pat 1878, 8x11″	125.00
Mahogany, 4 half drawers over 2, 7x11x5″	165.00
Chest, 2 drawers w/mirror, 1930s, 12x6x9″	35.00
Two drawers, brass pulls, shaped base, 6x6½x3½″	60.00
Three drawer, scroll backboard w/tree shape center, 1878	85.00
Cradle, box type, wht paint	45.00
Hooded, 1800s	100.00
Hooded, orig dk blue paint, handmade mattress	75.00
Hooded, poplar, orig red paint, 16″ long	80.00
Wicker, swinging removeable basket, 16x27″	130.00
Cupboard, 2 open shelves over 2 doors, painted, brass knobs	35.00
Glass doors, 2 shelves, brass knobs, 15x13″	40.00
Desk/bureau, slant-top, pine, 5 drawers	85.00
Dresser, Victorian, w/stenciled mirror frame, 20″	50.00
Walnut, carved Eastlake lines, 1870s	185.00

With mirror, 3 drawers, oak, 16x10″	80.00
Wood, 2 drawers, 1890s	12.00
Fainting couch, upholstered, 21″ long	35.00
Hamper, wicker, 12″ long	35.00
Highchair, Firehouse Windsor, maple, eyecaned seat, 30″	285.00
Folds to chair height, maple, orig eyecaned seat	150.00
Oak, pressed back, tray, 1890s, 38½x15″	150.00
Ice box, tin, 2 doors, Mary Lu	85.00
Laundry set, tub, washboard, round clothesline w/pins, MIB	25.00
Living room set, Victorian, tufted velvet/cardboard, sofa & chair	22.00
Wicker, 2 chairs, round table & settee	65.00
Wicker, table, chair & 11½″ long settee	60.00
Rocking chair, maple w/rush seat, 9x5½″	25.00
Maple, slat-back w/splint seat	35.00
Sideboard, mahogany w/inlay, 3 drawers, turned legs, 1800s	140.00
Stroller, wicker, green	75.00
Table, bentwood, w/4 chairs	45.00
Table set, painted, rectangular 20″ table, 25″ chairs, 1920s	100.00
Pine, 2 drawers, china knobs, double stretchers, 11x9″	190.00
Trunk, camel back	65.00
Steamer, paper covered wood frame, 2 drawers	55.00
Steamer, tin	25.00
Wood, floral lined, drawers & hangers, 9½x10½x20″	100.00
Wash tub, octagonal, w/brass banded scrub board	80.00

Dollhouses and Furnishings

Dollhouses were introduced commercially in this country late in the 1700s by Dutch craftsmen who settled in the East. They were meticuously designed and executed to the most minute detail. Of the examples left available to collectors today, those by Bliss and Schoenhut are most desirable.

Furnishings by Biedermeier feature stenciled decorations and Victorian styling, and often sell for several hundred dollars each. Other early pieces made of papier mache, pewter and porcelain are also quite valuable.

Arm chair, Empire, Biedermeier	45.00
Rolled arms, upholstered, 4x2″	20.00
Rolled arms, velvet, Germany, 1920, 3½″	35.00
Upholstered, turned legs, 4x2″	10.00
Wood frame, padded seat & back, Germany, 1930s 4″	14.00
Armoir, German, wood, opens	14.00
Bathroom, cabinet	30.00
Portable heater, Strombecker	4.00
Scale, Tootsie Toy, lavender & wht	17.00
Set, 6 pc, Strombecker, orig box	18.00
Set, brass, cup holder, towel rack, running water, 1920	280.00
Set, Tootsie Toys, 4 pc	30.00
Set, wood, all stationary, tub flush to floor	14.00
Set, wood, toilet & sink, brass faucets, 1915	70.00
Sink & mirror	30.00
Sink, Renwal	50.00
Sink, Tootsie Toy, lavender & white	14.00
Sink, wooden, white	4.00
Toilet, Petite Princess	65.00
Toilet, Plasco, aqua & white	3.00
Toilet, porcelain, blue wooden lid	9.00
Toilet, Strombecker, white	6.00
Toilet, Tootsie Toy, lavender & white	12.00
Tub, Plasco, aqua & white	3.00
Tub, plastic, lt blue w/white fixtures	3.00
Tub, Strombecker, green	6.00
Tub, Strombecker, white	6.50
Tub, Tootsie Toy, lavender & white	14.00
Tub, wooden, white	5.00
Bathtub & wash stand, Tootsie Toy	20.00
Bean pot w/cover, pewter, ¾x1¼″ dia	12.00
Bed, brass, 3x7x6″	20.00
Brown wood	7.00
Oak, simple	10.00
Tin, wire bottom, Germany	15.00
Twin, Strombecker, wood	5.00
Twin, Tootsie Toys, 1¼x3¼″	7.00
Bed warmer, Colonial	12.00
Bedroom set, 6 pc, Strombecker, orig box	18.00
Oak, marble top washstand, 8″ bed, bureau	345.00
Bird cage, ormolu, wire sides, top, 2″	110.00
Bookcase, wood, top shelf behind 2 doors, 2 open at bottom, 5x3″	30.00
Books, row of 10	6.00
Bucket, plastic, ca. 1940s, yellow	00.75
Buffet, mahogany w/3 pull out drawers, turned legs, 3x5x2″	38.00
Plastic, 1940s, center drawer opens, brown	5.00
Royal, Petite Princess	30.00
Tootsie Toy, removeable drawers	17.00
Bureau, 2 drawers, attached mirror, oak	10.00
Aenwal, brown	4.00
Strombecker, white, partially finished	5.00
With mirror, marble top, turned columns, 3 drawers, 7″	130.00
Cabinet, Treasure Trove, Petite Princess	30.00
Candelabra, Fantasia, Petite Princess	8.00

Canned goods, lot **2.00**
Carpet sweeper, metal w/moveable wheel, 6″ **22.00**
    Wood & wire, 4½″ **18.00**
    Wood, metal dust pan **7.00**
Chair, bathroom, Tootsie Toy, lavender & white **9.00**
    Cast metal, France, 1920, 2¾″ **22.00**
    Curved legs, otherwise simple, 1900, 4x1½″ **5.00**
    Occasional, Petite Princess, aqua velveteen **7.00**
    Old ornate brass, velvet seat **15.00**
    Straight, German, wood, fabric seat, black w/flowers **9.00**
    Tin & pewter, 3″ **14.00**
    Wing, Petite Princess, orange brocade **12.00**
    Wing, salon, Petite Princess, red brocade, orig box **12.00**
    Wood w/rush seat, fancy back, 4″ **9.00**
Chandelier, silverplate, 12 candleholders, 7x5″ **125.00**
Chest of drawers, Biedermeier, needs mirror, 14″ **220.00**
Chest, cedar, lift top w/loop handles, 1½x4″ **17.50**
    Wood, w/3 drawers, flush to floor, 3½x4x2″ **14.00**
China cabinet w/curved front, isinglass door opens, 1 shelf, 4″.. **25.00**
Clock, alarm, wood, Strombecker **5.00**
    Mantel type, pillars, pendulum gilded tin, Germany 2½″ **14.00**
    Oak, wall type w/pendulum, bonnet top, 4½″ **50.00**
    Ormolu base, copper figural horse & rider, 2″ **50.00**
    Stamped metal, tin base, 1885, 2″ **35.00**
    Strombecker, green w/numbers in gold **3.00**
    With brass pendulum, fancy, 1900, 7¼″ **18.00**
Closet, oak, Victorian, w/mirrored door, pewter feet, 5″ **35.00**
Coal bucket, metal **4.00**
    Scuttle **60.00**
Coffee grinder **6.00**
Commode w/drawer, 2 doors, oak **12.00**
Corner cupboard, plastic, 1940s, 2 open shelves **4.00**
Cradle, pewter filigree, 1¾x2¼″ **22.00**
    Swinging, pewter filigree, mid 1800s **90.00**
    Wood, blue w/flower decal **9.00**

Dollhouse
    American, 1930, wood, red roof, wht w/green, 26x29x28½″. **150.00**
    American, 1900, wood, red roof, glass windows, 25x18x27″. **200.00**
    American, 1920, wood, 6 rooms, glass windows, 23x20x23″. **100.00**
    Bungalow w/porch, bay window, 1 room, 1920s, 22x20x13″.. **55.00**
    Bungalow, 1930s, 1 room **65.00**
    Colonial, wood, 1930, 8 rooms, electrified, 15x27x22″ **100.00**
    Dutch Colonial, American, 1940, 7 rooms electrified, 32x57x27″ **175.00**
    Dutch Colonial, wood, 1925, 5 rooms, furnishings, 20x26x15″ **450.00**
    German, 1900, red roof, 18½x11x20″ **485.00**
    German, wood w/litho paper, FAO Schwarz label on base . **2,000.00**
    Paper litho-on-wood, 2 rooms, 1900 .... **225.00**
    Petite Princess, 5 rooms w/furniture, no roof, display model . **400.00**
    Schoenhut, 2 rooms w/furniture **185.00**
    Uncle Wiggily Stump House, w/figures, rare **225.00**
    Victorian, Bliss, 2 story, open front, 13x9″ **600.00**
    Victorian, litho, paper over wood, 2 story, porch **300.00**
    Victorian, wood, farmhouse, 1880s, back opens, 28x20x20″. **125.00**
    Wood, stencilled inside and out, removable windows, 11½″ .. **45.00**
    Wood, 2 story, 4 rooms furniture w/dolls, 1930's **450.00**
    Wood, w/litho, 7½″ **45.00**
    Wood, w/litho, 2 story, 10″ **160.00**
Desk, w/bentwood chair, Biedermeier stenciled, marble top ... **135.00**
Dining room hutch, Germany, wood, open shelves, doors open . **17.00**
    Set, 6 pc, Strombecker **35.00**
    Set, 10 pc, Strombecker, walnut **35.00**
    Set, Bestmaid **30.00**
    Set, Donna Lee **20.00**
    Table, wood, brown **8.50**

Dust pan **3.00**
Fainting couch, Petite Princes **15.00**
Fence, Victorian, cast iron **195.00**
Fireplace w/logs, Petite Princess **12.00**
    Attached mirror, brown wood **6.00**
    Tin w/pewter decor, simulated fire, 2¾x3½″ **38.00**
    With brass and irons **15.00**
    With mirror, ormolu, w/metal fire, 6x3″ **230.00**
    White House Toys, 3½x5″ **15.00**
Firewood basket **3.00**
Flower pot, Austrian bronze w/irises **25.00**
    With flowers **6.00**
Grandfather clock **15.00**
    Cast metal w/weights & moving pendulum, 5″........... **75.00**
Hall stand, mirror, oak, pressed, Art Nouveau, 9½″ **24.00**
Hamper, bathroom, Tootsie Toy, lavender & white **14.00**
Hutch, Petite Princess **50.00**
    Renwal, brown **4.00**
Iron pot **3.00**
Ironing board, Renwal, legs fold, pink **4.00**
Kitchen, Tootsie Toys, cabinet w/doors, 2 chairs, table, stove... **30.00**

Sink **12.00**
Brass lamp **25.00**
Clock **4.00**
Copper teakettle **10.00**
Dipper **7.00**
Goblet **5.00**
Iron **5.00**
Metal table service **15.00**
Pitcher **5.00**
Rolling pin **2.00**
Skillet **3.00**
Washboard **4.00**
Kitchenette, range, dishwasher, frig, sink, Cragstan, 6″........ **17.50**
Ladder, metal, gray **12.00**
Lamp, oil, brass.. **9.00**
    Petite Princess **3.00**
Lawn furniture, 5 pc, metal **35.00**
Living room, chair, Renwal, blue **5.00**
    Set, 6 pc, Donna Lee, Deluxe, wood Deco **45.00**
    Set, 6 pc, Strombecker, orig box **18.00**
Metronome, Petite Princess **2.00**
Music room furniture, Tootsie Toy, in orig box **85.00**
Paint roller **2.00**
Palace chest, Petite Princess **18.00**
Pans, copper, 5 pc **9.00**

Parlor set, 6 pc, golden oak, 4 chairs, sofa, table **300.00**
Piano, grand, gold metal, Durham, Ind. **6.00**
   Petite Princess, bench & metronome, orig box **23.00**
   Petite Princess, grand, in box **38.00**
   Upright, wood w/paper keys, 4x4" **16.00**
   With stool, pressed oak, moveable keys, 5x4x2½" **115.00**
Picnic table, wood, natural, attached benches **9.00**
Potty chair w/tray, Marx **5.00**
Radio, console w/lower cabinet, door opens, 3½x2¼" **45.00**
   Console, top & door opens, turned legs, wood, 3x3" **20.00**
   Console, walnut **8.00**
   Renwal, floor model **5.00**
   Strombecker, brown, nice detail **12.00**
Rug, braided, round, mostly green, 6" dia **12.00**
   Braided, silk, 10" dia **27.50**
   Woven Indian design, green, orange, fringe, 7¾x6½" **14.00**
   Woven floral design, maroon, 8½x10¾" **29.00**
Scoop, plastic, 1940s, yellow, 1" **00.50**
Settee, curved back, ornate, iron, 1¾x4½" **25.00**
Sewing machine, metal, 2" **6.00**
   Pewter filigree, movable treadle, 3" **120.00**
   Tin w/moveable wheel, needle **42.00**
Sewing table, oak, pull out drawer, 3" **95.00**
Side chair, oak, turned posts & legs, velvet upholstery, 4½" . . . **28.00**
Sideboard, Biedermeier, stencilled, mirror, 2 doors, 4½" **115.00**
   Wood, 2 doors open, turned legs, fancy, 3¾x4" **24.00**
Sink, Strombecker, white **5.00**
Sofa, Biedermeier, stenciled, cotton upholstery, 2½x4½" **130.00**
   Petite Princess, gold brocade **17.00**
   Plasco, green **3.00**
   Rolled arms, round back w/curved legs, ci, Arcade, 4x7" . . . **25.00**
   Tootsie Toy **10.00**
Stool, round, Strombecker, unfinished **3.00**
Stove, coal, pewter, 4" **75.00**
   Gas, ci, double oven w/4 burners, Geneva, Champion **30.00**
   Gas, ci, silver, Royal, 2 burners, hood, 4" **25.00**
   Pot bellied, lead, 4" **145.00**
   Pot belly, 2¾" **2.00**
   Royal, iron, 2½x2x2½" **22.00**
   Tin, 5x3x3" **25.00**
Straight chair, wood, rung back w/velvet seat, 4½" **7.50**
Table, ci w/simulated marble top, late 1800s, 3x4" **38.00**
   End, oval, brown wood, turned legs **4.00**
   German, wood, top 2½x4" **12.00**
   Lyre, Petite Princess **4.00**
   Magazine, Strombecker, walnut, marked **12.00**
   Oval, ci, green, scalloped aprons, red legs **24.00**
   Parlor, both ends curved turned legs, dark wood, 3x4½" . . . **18.00**
   Renwal, white **5.50**
   Round, telephone, Petite Princess, clear **4.00**
   Round, Petite Princess, dark marble top **5.00**
   Round, Petite Princess, green swivel top **6.00**
   Tier, Petite Princess **7.00**
   Tier, set **12.00**
   Trestle, Sturbridge, stained pine, 2¼x5" **9.00**
   With 4 chairs, sterling, 1850, ornate repousse **490.00**
   With 5 chairs, metal tubes, floral gray/pink, Japan **45.00**
   With marble top, pewter base, 2x2½" **125.00**
Table lamp, w/shade, round base, 1¾" **2.50**
Tea set, Germany, blue wood, 11 pc **17.00**
Tea cart, Tootsie Toy **14.00**
Tea wagon, drop sides, lower shelf, wheels turn, wood **30.00**
Telephone, old upright **20.00**
   Tootsie Toy **10.00**

Wall type, wood and metal, 2" **12.00**
Tray, pewter filigree, floral decor, 2½x1½" **15.00**
Trunk, Victorian, humpback, metal w/wood trim **60.00**
Vase, pewter, ornate, 2½" **22.00**
Wardrobe, wood, 2 doors open w/handles, 5x4" **30.00**
Washboard, Durham, metal **3.00**
Washstand, oak w/marble top, turned columns, 4x3½" **120.00**
   Pewter filigree w/candleholders, 5½" **100.00**
Waste basket, Strombecker **2.00**
Wheelbarrow, Tootsie Toy **10.00**
Wringer washer, Renwal **10.00**

Doorknobs

Decorative doorknobs are found in Bennington type pottery, fancy Victorian brass, glass and hand painted porcelain....just about any interesting old knob is collectible.

Bennington, w/shaft, excellent mottling, pr **45.00**
Brass, egg shape **10.00**
   Key plates & lock w/key set, fancy **20.00**
   No shaft **15.00**
   With shaft **20.00**
Cut glass, amethyst, pr **60.00**
Mercury glass, pr **20.00**
Porcelain, black **8.00**
   Hp dancing couple, brass hanks **20.00**
   Hp florals, brass hanks **20.00**
Iron basket w/flowers, inside **20.00**
Iron minute man **18.00**

Doorknockers

Doorknockers, those charming precursors of the door bell, come in an intriguing array of shapes and styles---the very rare ones come from England.

Brass, eagle, ca 1926, 6" **28.00**
   Lion, brass screws, 7½x4½" **33.00**
   Man's head, 8½" **80.00**
   Old horse **35.00**
Bronze, hand holding 'pearl', ruffled cuff, w/woman's head **85.00**
   Lion's head, 1½x4¼" **20.00**

Cast iron, lady's hand holding apple, no paint **25.00**
   Lady's head pattern, 1860, 8x4½" **75.00**
   Nickel plated, lady's hand w/cuffed sleeve, 4" **57.00**
   Parrot on perch, painted **17.50**

Doorstops

Although introduced in England in the mid-1800s, cast iron door stops were not made to any great extent in this country until after the Civil War. Once called 'door porters', their function was to keep doors open to provid better ventilation. They have been produced in many shapes and sizes, and in the past few years have become a popular yet affordable collectible. While cast iron examples are the most common, brass, wood, and chalkware were also used. Average prices are in the, $40-50 range, though some are valued at more than one hundred dollars. Doorstops retained their usefullness and appeal well into the '30s.

Advertising, Bear Bros Paint, 2 figural bears **20.00**
Aunt Jemima, not full bodied, 13¼" **140.00**
Aunt Jemima, wood **23.00**
Basket of flowers, 9" **38.00**
Basket of flowers, blue & pink, 6" **35.00**
Berry basket, small **45.00**
Black man, metal, on iron cotton bale **170.00**
Black man with colorful livery, 8½" **55.00**
Campbell's Kid, w/teddy bear **185.00**
Cat, black, heavy, 9½" **82.00**
Cat, Deco, mkd Hubley **75.00**
Cat, sitting, orig paint, green eyes, yellow whiskers, 7" **95.00**
Cat, sitting **25.00**
Cavalrymen, mounted, English, brass, pair **95.00**
Chalet & trees **65.00**
Clipper ship **34.00**
Clown, large **32.00**
Coach, w/horse & drivers **70.00**
Colonial lady, 11½" **35.00**
Cottage, w/flowers **35.00**
Covered wagon, old orig paint **35.00**
Covered wagon, with oxen team, orig paint, 12" **68.00**
Dog, Airedale, standing, 10x11" **75.00**
   Boston Bull, brown & tan, 9" **90.00**
   Boston Terrier, brown & wht **50.00**
   Boxer, orig brown paint, 7½" **38.00**
   Fox Terrier **50.00**
   French Bull **48.00**
   Pug, blk & wht, 10" **80.00**
   Russian Wolfe Hound, orig wht paint, 10x15½" **130.00**
   Scottie, wht, large, heavy **65.00**
   Setter, orig blk/wht paint, 15" **55.00**
   St Bernard, orig gold paint, early 1900s, 12x9" **75.00**
   Terrier, after Staffordshire **110.00**
Dutch boy & girl, Hubley **85.00**
Dutch girl, w/2 water pails **14.00**
Elephant, raised trunk **24.00**
Falcon, old paint, 7¼" **60.00**
Fox, sleeping, early 1900s, 7" long **65.00**
Frog, heavy, old **40.00**
   Orig green & yellow paint, 6x6x3" **60.00**
Grape cluster **25.00**
Horse, prancing, solid brass, much detail, 1860s, 10x9x2½" . . **110.00**
Horse, work, large **35.00**
Lady, early Victorian figural, 4½" **60.00**
Lady's shoe, blk w/wht buttons **55.00**
Lighthouse **35.00**

Lincoln's cabin, 6" long green base, heavy, 5" **55.00**
Lion, old gold paint, late 1800s, 9x6x4" **90.00**
Lion, recumbant, oval base, late 1800s, 7x5" **73.00**
Lion, with serpent on his back **25.00**
Marie Antoinette, orig paint **40.00**
Mayflower, orig paint, copyright 1913/Creation 403, 11½" **40.00**
Milk maid, blue dress & bonnet, wht apron **52.00**
Parrot, on a ball, orig paint, 12x6" **85.00**
Parrot, on perch, orig paint, early 1900s, 8" **50.00**
Penguin **55.00**
Peter rabbit, orig paint, 11¾" **65.00**
Pirate ship, orig paint, 10¼" **65.00**
Popeye, wooden cut-out, 1930s, orig paint, 15" **50.00**
Pot of tulips, 8" **85.00**
Rabbit, wht, from Alice in Wonderland, old paint, 10" **85.00**
Rabbit **55.00**
Ram, "Julia" in relief across back, 7x10" **150.00**
Robert E Lee, figural, orig paint, 7" **95.00**
Rooster, w/wood handle **140.00**
Ship, 3-masted, bronze patina **35.00**
Ship, full sail, on rough sea, orig paint, 9½" **35.00**
Ship, orig gold, black, brown paint, 1930s, 12" **70.00**

Squirrel, 11½" **65.00**
Stagecoach, 20" **185.00**
Tambourine, w/Mickey Mouse decor, 7" dia **22.50**
Tropical bird, colorful **30.00**
Windmill, bronzed iron, 7x7" **23.00**

Doulton and Royal Doulton

The range of wares produced by the Doulton Company since its inception in 1815 has been vast and varied. Their earliest wares produced in the tiny pottery in Lambeth, London, were salt glaze pitchers, plain and fancy figural bottles---all utility-type stoneware geared to the practical need of everyday living.

The original partners, John Doulton & John Watts, saw the potential for success in the manufacture of drain and sewage pipes, and during the 1840s concentrated on this highly lucrative type of commercial ware. Watts retired from the company in 1854, and Doulton began experimenting with a more decorative style of product. As time went by, many glazes and decorative effects were developed, among them Faience, Impasto, Silicon, Carrara, Marqueterie, Chine and Rouge Flambe. Tiles and architectural terra

cotta were an important part of their manufacture. Late in the 19th century, at the original Lambeth location, fine art ware was decorated by such notable artists as Hannah and Arthur Barlow, George Tinworth and J.H. McLennan. Stoneware vases with incised animal drawings, gracefully shaped urns with painted and cleverly modeled figurines rivaled the best of any competitor.

In 1882, a second factory was built in Burslem, which continues even yet to produce the famous figurines, character jugs, series ware and table services so popular with collectors today. Their Kingsware line, made from 1899 to 1946 featured flasks and flagons with drinking scenes usually on a brown glazed ground, some of which were limited editions, while others were commemorative and advertising items. After 1902, these wares were marked with a lion, with or without a crown, over a circular 'Royal Doulton'.

Animals

Airdale, 1023	60.00
Airdale Terrier, 1024	135.00
Alsatian, 1115	275.00
1117, small	100.00
American Foxhound, 2525, medium	175.00
Boxer, 2543, medium	50.00
British Bull Dog, large	425.00
Bulldog, Brindle, 1044	110.00
Bulldog, 1047, small	35.00
Cairn, 1035	35.00
K-11	25.00
Cairn puppy, 2589	20.00
Cat, Persian, 999	100.00
Rouge flambe, 9	60.00
Character dog, standing, 2509	95.00
Cocker & Pheasant, 1001	225.00
1020	75.00
1062	125.00
Cocker Spaniel, 1002	275.00
1021	100.00
1037	100.00
1078, black & white, small	75.00
1109, black & white, small	75.00
1188, golden, small	75.00
Collie, 1059, small	100.00
Dachshund, K-19	25.00
1029	110.00
1129	85.00
Dalmatian, 114, small	125.00
1113	60.00
Dragon, rough flambe, 2085	475.00
Drake, miniature, 807	45.00
Rouge flambe, 137	60.00
Duck, rouge flambe, 112	40.00
Rouge flambe, 112	40.00
Rouge flambe, 395	35.00
Elephant, rouge flambe, 489	80.00
Rouge flambe, 489A	125.00
English Setter, 1050	60.00
1051, small	110.00
Fox, rouge flambe, 14	55.00
Rouge flambe, 39	40.00
Foxhound, K-7	245.00
2525, medium	245.00
Guinea Hen, rouge flambe, Noke, 6x3½"	175.00
Hare, 2594	22.00
Rouge flambe, 1157	55.00
Irish Setter, 1056	90.00
Kingfisher	135.00

Kitten, setting, 2584	20.00
Llama, 2665	135.00
Lucky Cat, K-12	40.00
Mallard, 2152	55.00
Owl, rouge flambe, 2249	265.00
Pekinese, K-6	30.00
1012, small	35.00
Penguin, rouge flambe, 4	60.00
Pointer, 2624	150.00
Poodle, 2631	55.00
Rabbit, ear up, rouge flambe, 113	55.00
Rhino, rouge flambe, 19"	425.00
Scotch Terrier, 1015, black, medium	200.00
Sealyham, K-3	30.00
K-4	30.00
1032	140.00
Springer Spaniel, 2516, medium	150.00
2517	55.00
Terrier, 1014	35.00
1110	85.00
Tiger, rouge flambe, crouching, 20, 9"	385.00
Welsh Corgi, 2558, medium	175.00
2559	35.00
Ashtray, Auld Mac, A mk	125.00
Bateman character	25.00
Country scene, Noke, Flambe, 4½"	35.00
Gypsy Caravan, 4½"	22.00
The Major, yellow	45.00
Basket, Welsh Ladies, 3"	45.00
Biscuit barrel, plated lid, cows, H Barlow, Lambeth, 1800, 8"	550.00
Bottle, Dewars, Here's Health Unto His Majesty, full	700.00
Silver overlay in floral & leaf, w/stopper, 7½"	695.00
Zorro, black, 4"	35.00
Bowl, FC Pope, 8½"	90.00
Coaching Days, silverplate rim, 8"	85.00
Gnomes, 8"	70.00
Robert Burns inside, scenes outside, 7½"	135.00
Robin Hood, King of Archers, octagonal, 6½"	50.00
Willow, flow blue, 7"	65.00
Willow, flow blue, 8"	75.00
Bunnykins, mug, Barbara Vernon	28.00
Baby set, dish & silver bunny spoon	16.00
Bank, soldier	30.00
Child's 3 pc set, mug plate & bowl, in box	30.00
Egg cup, bison	22.50
Egg cup, dog	25.00
Egg cup, otters	25.00
Egg cup, owl	22.50
Egg cup, rabbits	22.50
Plate, Barbara Vernon, 6"	15.00
Plate, Barbara Vernon, 9"	28.00
Santa plate, Barbara Vernon	40.00
Candleholder, Dutch scene, 6x2"	125.00
Centerpiece, Neptune & Barnacle, 1885	150.00
Cookie jar, cows, Hannah Barlow, Lambeth, 6¼"	595.00
Creamer, black cat figural, Depoier	60.00
Cup & saucer, Coaching Days	40.00
Decanter, Zorro, A mk, black, 10½"	50.00
Demi cup & saucer, hp florals	55.00
Ewer, applied decoration, florals, Bowditch, 1890	200.00
Flow blue w/gold, florals, 11"	165.00
Pink roses in relief, Mary Burton, 12½"	85.00
Plant forms, mk V, Marshall, 1880, 13"	225.00

Figure, Oriental man, wireless speaker holder, for Artandia ... **595.00**
   Crinoline, salt glaze, matt wht/blue **500.00**
   Dutch girl, salt glaze, matt blue, 4½″ **200.00**
Flask, Jim Crow, Doulton-Watts, 8½″ **225.00**
Fruit bowl, brown w/forest in silhouette, 4x9″ **125.00**
Humidor, Dickens figures in relief, browns, 6″ **120.00**
   Natural foliage ware, artist signed, Lambeth, 6x4″ **95.00**
Jam jar, plated holder, blue & white, Burslem **115.00**
Jardiniere, cobalt rim, base, 4″ tapestry band, mums, 9″ **150.00**
   Cobalt, wht, farm & country scene, 8½x10″ **200.00**
   Cows, Hannah Barlow, 1887, 7x9″ **650.00**
   Reticulated rim, florals on brown, Lambeth, 6x9″ **185.00**
Jug, Art Nouveau, Burrough Distillers, 7½″ **100.00**
   Brown leather look, motto, 8x6″ **145.00**
   Cavaliers toasting, cream w/blue, purple, orange, 8½″ **95.00**
   Concord, Bayeux Tapestry, 6″ **95.00**
   Figures in relief, 1869, 5¾″ **85.00**
   For whiskey, grey ship, Lambeth **80.00**
   Girls dancing, flow blue w/green, Morrisian, 6″ **165.00**
   Leatherware, Landlord Invitation, silver rim, 1896 .... **150.00**
   Men in chariot w/horses, flow blue, 7½″ **150.00**
   Monks, cream w/brown, Refectory Bell, D3608, 6½″ **115.00**
   Morrisian, dancing girls & garlands, flow blue, 6½x5″ **165.00**
   Old Curiosity Shop, Nell & Grandfather, 5½″ **100.00**
   Profile of Queen Victoria, Jubilee, motto, 7½″ **175.00**
   Shakespeare, scene w/quote, Henry 4th **75.00**
   Stoneware, motto w/silver rim, 8″ **160.00**
   Tan & blue w/beading, stoneware, Simmance, 1876, 6″ **195.00**
   Teniers paintings, Village Fete **50.00**
Loving cup, silver rim, running antelopes, H Barlow, Lambeth . **675.00**
Matchholder, Mr Squeers **95.00**
Pitcher, Aldin's Dogs **75.00**
   Blue & white florals, Burslem **60.00**
   Brown & tan bulbous, wht relief figures, 5½″ **85.00**
   Camel, incised & applied decor, signed, 1894, 6″ **125.00**
   Chaucer, Famous Authors, Ye Tabard Southwark, 7½″ **110.00**
   Cobalt, brown bands, horizontal ribs, florals, 7″ **100.00**
   Flow blue w/girls dancing, Gloriana, Burslem **250.00**
   Fox Hunt, signed, 7½″ **200.00**
   Gaffers, 5″ **85.00**
   Inn series, Author, Raleigh **90.00**
   Longfellow Mansion on brown glaze, 4½″ **55.00**
   Moorish gate, 4½″ **85.00**
   Old Bob Ye Guard, 8½″ **95.00**
   Old Lady & Cat, 4½″″ **85.00**
   Pewter lid, Slater's Pat, 7½″ **65.00**
   Pewter mount, Florie Jones, 8″ **60.00**
   Santa in sleigh, quote on back **100.00**
   Tapestry band, incised lilies, Slater's Pat, Burslem **165.00**
   World's Fair, 1904, Dutch scene, 2½″ **46.00**
   Ye Canterbury Pilgrims **115.00**
Place setting, 5 pc, Angelic **45.00**
Plaque, Terra Cotta, Tinworth **300.00**
Plate, A Thing of Beauty Is A Joy Forever, Old English Saying . **70.00**
   Ainsdale, dinner................................. **17.50**
     Salad **12.50**
   Angelic, bread & butter............................ **8.50**
   Boats, wht borders, gold lace, signed, JH, 10½″ **225.00**
   Columbine **50.00**
   Dickens character, Capt Cuttle **58.00**
     Dickens portrait w/character border **85.00**
     Tony Weller, brown mk **70.00**
   Eglington Tournament, Knights in Sword Combat **65.00**
   English Cottage, 10″.............................. **60.00**

English Countryside.................................. **65.00**
Exotic bird, 8″ **25.00**
Gen Washington Marching on Trenton, Christmas, 1776..... **68.00**
Gibson Girl, A Message From the Outside World **65.00**
   A Quiet Dinner With Dr Bottles **78.00**

Day After Arriving at Her Journey's End **95.00**
Miss Babbles the Authoress Calls & Reads Aloud **65.00**
Mrs Diggs is Alarmed For the Safety of Her Child **65.00**
She Becomes a Trained Nurse **85.00**
She Contemplates The Cloister **85.00**
She Decides To Die in Spite of Dr Bottles **115.00**
She Finds Some Consolation In Her Mirror............. **85.00**
She Finds That Exercise **85.00**
She Goes to the Fancy Dress Ball **65.00**
She Longs for Seclusion **85.00**
She Looks for Relief Among the Old Ones **85.00**
She is Disturbed by a Vision **80.00**
Some Think She Has Remained in Retirement Too Long .. **65.00**
They All Go Fishing **110.00**
We Leave Her **75.00**
Historical Britain, Tower of London **35.00**
Hurtsmonceaux Castle, 10″ **60.00**
Jackdaw of Rheims, Off That Terrible Curse He Took **65.00**
Muckrose Abbey, 10½″ **35.00**
Nursery Rhyme, Old Mother Hubbard **40.00**
   To Market to Buy a Fat Pig **45.00**
Oriental figures among ruins, 10″ **60.00**
Pan in forset setting, 10″ **60.00**
Pierrot **40.00**
Ploughing, 10″ **60.00**
Robin Hood, Under the Greenwood Tree, square **68.00**
   Scalloped, 10½″ **70.00**
Sampler, 1916, D3749, 7½″ **25.00**
Shakespeare character, Wolsey........................ **68.00**
   Orlando.. **68.00**
Sherwood, salad **12.50**
The Falconer **65.00**
The Hunting Man **45.00**
The Jester, 10½″ **50.00**
Titanian ware, grey w/blue, brown, yellow, bird, 8½″........ **55.00**
Set of 10, florals w/red rims, E Percy, 10½″ **600.00**

Vienna Gondola, 10″ **75.00**
Slop bucket, flow blue, complete, old **195.00**
Soap dish, rose & beading, 4¾″ dia **68.00**
Soup bowl, Coaching Days, 7½″ **20.00**
Tankard mug, watchmen, cream w/blue & blk, 5½″ **65.00**
  Cobalt w/gilt scrolls, roses, E Wood, 9″ **475.00**
  Tan & brown stoneware w/motto, Lambeth, 5″ **85.00**
Tea tile, Coaching Days **20.00**
Teapot, blue birds, Florence Barlow **750.00**
  Brown w/witch, cat & cauldron, Kingsware **250.00**
  Oval, windmill finial, Dutch harbor scene, 9½x6″ **350.00**
  Tapestry ground w/florals, gold, D & Slaters, 5″ **195.00**
Tobacco jar, florals, hp, brass handle, Alfred Dunhill, NY **135.00**
  Monks, 5½″ **230.00**
Toothpick, Dr Johnson & Fleet St **35.00**
Tray, Robin Hood, Under the Greenwood Tree, 5x10½″ **85.00**
Tumbler, horses grazing, Hannah Barlow, 1876, 4¼″ **335.00**
  Tan, cobalt scroll, brass rim, mk: GT, Lambeth, 1881 ..... **170.00**
Vase, Art Nouveau leaves, scrolls, rust, cobalt, Lambeth, 9″ **90.00**
  Babes In Woods, flow blue, girls under tree, 7½″ **245.00**
  Blue/grey w/brown relief leaves, Roberts, 1885, 10x5″ **195.00**
  Brown & blue w/cows & geometrics, 1885, 12x5″ **695.00**
  Buff w/red & green floral decor, 4″ **75.00**
  Caramel, ladies in black, Morrisian, Burslem, 7x3¾″ **125.00**
  Celedon shoulder, neck, tapestry body, florals, 9x5″ **300.00**
  Coaching Days, 3½″ **55.00**
  Cobalt top, bottom, 3″ tapestry band, florals, 6″ **60.00**
  Cobalt w/olive, rust, Nouveau stems, E Simmance, 8″ **275.00**
  Deer, Hannah Barlow, 9½″ **595.00**
  Flambe, veined, 11½″ **150.00**
  Flambe, veined, Sung decor, ovoid, #1616, 10″ **235.00**
  Flared rim, colorful mosaic on brown, gold, Lambeth, 8″ **100.00**
  Floral over band of gold leaves, Burslem, 9½″ **250.00**
  Friar Tuck Joins Robin Hood, 9″ **125.00**
  Ftd, cobalt floral base band, tapestry body w/mums, 12″ **300.00**
  Green & gold w/etched horse, H Barlow, 1886, 11x7″ **795.00**
  Green ovoid w/wht relief florals, 8½″ **185.00**
  Jackdaw of Rheims, Cardinal Lord Archbishop, 5″ **85.00**
  Notched foot, low handles, 2 children, 7″ **325.00**
  Ovoid w/ped, flared, cows, sheep, Barlow, 1880, 7½″ **560.00**
  Rouge Flame, scenic w/florals, #1032, 5″ **88.00**
  Scenic w/cows, Rouge Flambe, 8½″ **235.00**

Sheep, Hannah Barlow, 9″ **485.00**
Stoneware, blue/gold w/brown natural foliage, sq, 5″ **75.00**
Stoneware, blue/grey, brown leaves, E Simmance, 6″ **195.00**
Stoneware, relief leaves, Florence Roberts, 1885, 10″ **225.00**

Figurines
A La Mode, 2544 .... **190.00**
A 'Courting, 2004 .... **450.00**
Abdullah, 2104 .... **525.00**
Adrienne, 2152, purple **138.00**
  2304, blue **95.00**
Affection **55.00**
Afternoon Tea, 1747 .... **195.00**
Alchemist, 1259 .... **700.00**
Alexandra, 2398 .... **142.00**
Alice **78.00**
Allison, 2336 .... **93.00**
Anna, 2802 .... **60.00**
Annabella, 1872 .... **440.00**
Annette, 1550 .... **225.00**
Antoinette, 1850-1, ... **550.00**
  2326 .... **130.00**
Ascot **110.00**
Apple Maid **285.00**
At Ease, 2473 .... **165.00**
Autumn, 2087 .... **275.00**
Autumn Breezes, 1911, pink **185.00**
  1913, green **170.00**
  1934, red **100.00**
  2147 .... **200.00**
Awakening **500.00**
Baba **325.00**
Babie, 1679 .... **48.00**
Baby, 12 .... **700.00**
Baby Bunting, 2108 .... **100.00**
Bachelor, 2319 .... **190.00**
Ballad Seller, 2266 .... **175.00**
Ballerina **230.00**
Balloon Man **100.00**
Balloon Seller, 583 .... **325.00**
Barbara, 1421 .... **350.00**
  1461, potted **475.00**
Basket Weaver, 684 .... **750.00**
  2245 .... **425.00**
Beachcomber, 2487 .... **170.00**
Beat You To It **190.00**
Bedtime Story, 2059 .... **130.00**
Beggar, 2175 .... **490.00**
Belle, 754 .... **450.00**
  776 .... **450.00**
  2340 .... **40.00**
Belle O' The Ball, 1997 .... **175.00**
Bernice, 2071 .... **600.00**
Bess, 2002 .... **215.00**
Beth **62.50**
Betsy, 2111 .... **250.00**
Betty, 402-3 .... **550.00**
  435-8 .... **550.00**
  477-8 .... **550.00**
  1404-5 .... **225.00**
  1435-6 .... **225.00**
Biddy, 1513 .... **175.00**
  Potted **200.00**
Biddy Penny Farthing, 1843 .... **105.00**
Blacksmith Of Williamsburg, 2240 .... **120.00**

Blighty **300.00**

Blithe Morning, 2021, pink **175.00**
   2065, red **175.00**
Blossom **500.00**
Bluebeard, 75 . . . . **800.00**
   410 . . . . **800.00**
   1528 . . . . **400.00**
Boy on Crocodile **700.00**
Boy on Pig **400.00**
Boy With Turban **275.00**
Bride, 1588, ... **250.00**
   1600 . . . . **250.00**
   1762 . . . . **250.00**
   1841 . . . . **250.00**
   2166 . . . . **125.00**
   2873 . . . . **100.00**
Bridesmaid, M12 . . . . **245.00**
   1433-4 . . . . **100.00**
   1530 . . . . **100.00**
   2148 . . . . **100.00**
   2196 . . . . **100.00**
   2874 . . . . **60.00**
Bridget **260.00**
Broken Lance **425.00**
Bunny, 2214 . . . . **90.00**
Buttercup, 2309 . . . . **95.00**
Called Love, A Little Boy, 1545 . . . . **150.00**
Calumet, 2068 . . . . **550.00**
Camellia, 2222 . . . . **240.00**
Camille, 1648 . . . . **325.00**
Captain, 778 . . . . **500.00**
Captain, 2260 . . . . **145.00**
Captain Cook **220.00**
Captain MacHeath, 464 . . . . **750.00**
Carmen, 1267 . . . . **400.00**
   1300 . . . . **400.00**
   2545 . . . . **180.00**
Carnival **850.00**
Carolyn, 2112 . . . . **185.00**
Carpet Seller, 1464 . . . . **230.00**
Carpet Vendor **600.00**
Carrie, 2800 . . . . **65.00**
Catherine Parr **50.00**
Cavalier, 369 . . . . **500.00**
   2716 . . . . **120.00**
Celeste, 2237 . . . . **190.00**
Celia **500.00**
Cellist, 2226 . . . . **410.00**

Cerise **145.00**
Charley's Aunt, 35 . . . . **420.00**
   Potted, 35 . . . . **495.00**
Charlotte, 2421 . . . . **110.00**
Charmian **550.00**
Check Point **825.00**
Chelsea Female **525.00**
Chelsea Male **525.00**
Chelsea Pr, 577 & 579 . . . . **1,100.00**
Cherie, 2341 . . . . **60.00**
Chief, 2892 . . . . **120.00**
Child of Williamsburg, 2154 . . . . **70.00**
Child on Crab **425.00**
Child's Grace **700.00**
Chinese, Dancers of the World **595.00**
Chitarrone, 2700 . . . . **750.00**
Chloe, 1765 . . . . **250.00**
   1767 . . . . **275.00**
   M-9 . . . . **325.00**
Choice **500.00**
Choir Boy, 2141 . . . . **90.00**
Chorus Girl **525.00**
Christine, 1839-40 . . . . **500.00**
   2792 . . . . **155.00**
Christmas Morn, 1992 . . . . **100.00**
Christmas Parcels, 2851 . . . . **120.00**
Christmas Time, 2210 . . . . **375.00**
Cicely **450.00**
Cissie, 1809 . . . . **85.00**
Clare **150.00**
Claribel, 1951 . . . . **175.00**
Clarinda, 2724 . . . . **160.00**
Clarissa, 1525 . . . . **375.00**
   1678 . . . . **375.00**
   2345 . . . . **100.00**
Clemency, 1633 . . . . **445.00**
Cleopatra And Slave, 2868 . . . . **875.00**
Clockmaker, 2279 . . . . **215.00**
Clothilde, 1598 . . . . **505.00**
Clown, 2890 . . . . **180.00**
Coachman, 2282 . . . . **375.00**
Cobbler, 1705, 8½″ **375.00**
   1706 . . . . **220.00**
Collinette, 1999 . . . . **325.00**
Columbine, 1285 . . . . **95.00**
   1297 . . . . **250.00**
   1439 . . . . **250.00**
Coming of Spring **850.00**
Constance **450.00**
Contentment **450.00**
Convent Garden **550.00**
Cookie, 2218 . . . . **105.00**
Coppelia, 2113 . . . . **525.00**
   2115 . . . . **735.00**
Coquette **650.00**
Coralie, 2307 . . . . **90.00**
Corinthian **575.00**
Country Lass, 1991 . . . . **87.50**
Court Shoemaker **550.00**
Courtier **550.00**
Cradle Song, 2246 . . . . **375.00**
Craftsman **300.00**
Crinoline Lady **325.00**
Crouching Nude **350.00**

Cup Of Tea, 2322	92.00
Curly Knob	250.00
Curly Locks	220.00
Curtsey, 66A	700.00
Cymbals, 2699	750.00
Cynthia, 1685	350.00
Daffy-Down-Dilly, 1712	215.00
Dainty May, 1639	225.00
Daisy, 1575	115.00
Damaris	600.00
Dancing Eyes, 1543	225.00
Dancing Years	250.00
Dandy	450.00
Daphne, 2268	100.00
Darby, 1427	230.00
Darling, 1	550.00
1319	80.00
1985	35.00
71-2	65.00
Dawn, 1858	325.00
Daydreams, 1731	925.00
1944	225.00
2380	100.00
Debbie, 2385	60.00
Debutante, 2210	250.00
Deidre, 2020	290.00
Delicia	425.00
Delight, 1772	155.00
Delphine, 2136	225.00
Denise, 2273	225.00
Derrick	600.00
Detective, 2359	100.00
Diana, 1986	100.00
Digger	275.00
Diligent Scholar	650.00
Dimity	225.00
Dinky Do, 1678	46.00
Do You Wonder, 1544	150.00
Doctor, 2858	115.00
Dolly Varden	475.00
Dorcas, 1558	300.00
Doreen	425.00
Doris Keene as Cavallini	1,200.00
Double Jester	700.00
Dreamland	700.00
Dreamweaver, 2283	190.00
Matte	175.00
Drummer Boy, 2679	215.00
Duke of Edinburgh	555.00
Dulcie	115.00
Dulcinea	700.00
Dunce	650.00
Easter Day, 2039	250.00
Elaine	110.00
Eleanor, 1754	500.00
Eleanor of Provence	500.00
Elegance, 2264	892.50
Elfreda	450.00
Eliza, 2543	195.00
Elizabeth Fry	1,250.00
Ellen Terry	700.00
Elsie Maynard, 639	500.00
Elyse, 2429	95.00
Embroidering	125.00
Emir	450.00
Emma, 2834	60.00
Enchantment, 2178	95.00
Ermine Coat, 1981	220.00
Esmeralda, 2168	275.00
Estelle	550.00
Eugene	375.00
Europa and Bull	1,500.00
Evelyn	375.00
Eventide, 2814	85.00
Fair Lady, green, 2193	95.00
Pink, 2835	92.50
Red, 2832	92.50
Fair Maiden, 2211	60.00
Family Album, 2321	210.00
Family, White, 2720	72.00
Faraway, 2133	170.00
Farmer's Boy	500.00
Farmer's Wife	350.00
Fat Boy, 1893	450.00
2096	220.00
Favorite, 2249	90.00
Fiddler	500.00
Fiona, 1924-5	325.00
1933	325.00
2694	110.00
First Dance, 2803	102.50
First Steps	250.00
First Waltz, 2862	145.00
Fisher Woman	750.00
Fleur, 2368	110.00
Fleurette	250.00
Flora, 2349	135.00
Flounced Skirt	650.00
Flower Seller's Children, 1206	400.00
525	400.00
551	400.00
1342	255.00
Foaming Quart, 2162	95.00
Folly	700.00
Forget-Me-Not	300.00
Fortune Teller, 2159	385.00
Forty Theives, 667	195.00
Forty Winks, 1974	165.00
Four O' Clock	350.00
Fragrance, 2334	102.50
Francine, 2422	62.50
Frangoon	400.00
French Peasant, 2075	400.00
Friar Tuck	275.00
Fruit Gathering	850.00
Gaffer	250.00
Gainsborough Hat, 705	600.00
Gay Morning, 2135	295.00
Geisha	600.00
Genevieve, 1952	200.00
1962	175.00
Gentle Woman	325.00
Gentleman From Williamsburg, 2227	120.00
Georgiana, 2093	265.00
Geraldine, 2348	140.00
Gillian	325.00
Girl in Yellow Frock, 588	1,100.00
Girl with Sunshade	650.00

Giselle, 2140	370.00
Gladys	375.00
Gloria	500.00
Gnome	450.00
Golden Days	90.00
Gollywog	185.00
Good Catch, 2258	105.00
Good King Wenceslas	175.00
Good Morning, 2671	135.00
Goody Two Shoes, 2037	65.00
Goose Girl, 425	600.00
Gossips, 1429	250.00
2025	325.00
Grace, 2318	110.00
Grand Manner, 2723	147.50
Grandma, 2052	240.00
Granny	500.00
Granny's Heritage	250.00
Granny's Shawl, 1647	225.00
Greta	195.00
Gretchen, 1397	525.00
Griselda, 1993	375.00
Grizel	400.00
Grossmith's Perfume	515.00
Grossmith's Tsany Ihang	400.00
Guy Fawkes	550.00
Gwendaline	350.00
Gwynneth, 1980	275.00
Gypsy Dance, 2157	250.00
2230	185.00
Happy Joy Baby Boy	150.00
Harlequin	95.00
Harlequinade Masked	500.00
Harmony, 2824	105.00
Hazel, 1797	195.00
He Loves Me, 2046	105.00
Heart to Heart	250.00
Helen, 1508	550.00
Helmsman, 2499	122.50
Henrietta Maria, 2005	515.00
Henry Irving	1,000.00
Henry Lytton as Jack Point	475.00
Henry VIII	600.00
Her Ladyship, 1977	240.00
Here A Little Child	150.00
Hermione	500.00
Highwayman, 527	450.00
Hilary, 2335	112.50
Hinged Parasol, 1578	400.00
Home Again, 2167	75.00
Honey, 1910	425.00
Hornpipe, 2161	625.00
Hostess of Williamsburg, 2209	120.00
Houndsman	120.00
Hunt's Lady	450.00
Hunting Squire	550.00
Huntsman, 1226	450.00
1815	450.00
2492	160.00
Ibrahim	400.00
In Grandma's Days	500.00
In the Stocks, 1474-5	700.00
2163	400.00
Indian Brave, 2376	2,400.00
Innocence, 2842	92.50
Invitation, 2170	100.00
Iona	600.00
Irene, 1621	250.00
Irish Colleen	500.00
Irishman	550.00
Ivy, 1768	58.50
Jack	85.00
Jack Point, 85	1,200.00
91	1,200.00
99	1,200.00
Jacqueline	225.00
Jane	400.00
Janet, 1538	150.00
1575	75.00
1737	150.00
1916, 5"	150.00
Janine, 2461	110.00
Japanese Fan	600.00
Jasmine	375.00
Jean, 2032	250.00
Jennifer	200.00
Jersey Milk Maid, 2057	165.00
Jester, 2016	120.00
458	450.00
Jill, 2061	90.00
Joan, 1422	235.00
Jolly Sailor, 2172	500.00
Jon Peel	600.00
Jovial Monk, 2144	175.00
Judge, 2443	105.00
Matt	200.00
Judge & Jury	900.00
Judith, 2089	225.00
Julia, 2705	110.00
June, 1691	290.00
Karen, 1994	300.00
Kate, 2789	92.50
Kate Hardcastle, 1719	475.00
Katherine, 314	550.00
Kathleen, 1252	500.00
Kathy	65.00
Katrina, 2327	265.00
King Charles, 2084	975.00
404	895.00
Kirsty, 2381	108.50
Kitty	450.00
Ko Ko, 1266	400.00
1286	400.00
Kurdish, Dancers of the World	650.00
La Sylphide, 2138	310.00
Lady April, 1958	285.00
Lady Betty, 1967	230.00
Lady Bird	375.00
Lady Charmain, 1947	200.00
1948, blue	210.00
1949	225.00
Lady Clare, 1465	410.00
Lady Clown	500.00
Lady Ermine, 54	550.00
Lady Fayre, 1265	390.00
Lady Jester	450.00
Lady Pamela, 2718	135.00
Lady & Blackammor	600.00

Lady from Williamsburg, 2228	120.00
Lady of Georgian Period	900.00
Lady of Time of Henry VI	700.00
Lady of Elizabethan Period	900.00
Lady with Fan	600.00
Lady with Rose	600.00
Lady with Shawl	700.00
Laird, 2361	105.00
Lambeth Walk, 1881	1,000.00
Lambing Time, 1890	130.00
Land of Nod	600.00
Last Waltz, 2315	107.50
Laurianne, 2719	135.00
Lavinia, 1955	70.00
Leading Lady, 2269	140.00
Leisure Hour	300.00
2055	375.00
Lido Lady	450.00
Lights Out, 2262	185.00
Lilac Shawl	500.00
Lilac Time	185.00
Lily	110.00
Linda, 2106	110.00
Lisa, 2310	105.00
Lisette	400.00
Little Boy Blue	110.00
Little Bridesmaid, 1433	185.00
Little Child So Rare	150.00
Little Jack Horner	150.00
Little Lady Make Believe, 1870	290.00
Little Land	750.00
Little Mistress, 1449	240.00
Little Mother	550.00
Lizana, 1756	375.00
Lobster Man, 2317	105.00
London City	425.00
Long John Silver, 2204	500.00
Loretta, 2337	100.00
Lori	60.00
Lorna, 2311	75.00
Love Letter, 2149	275.00
Lovers, black, 2763	72.00
Lucy Ann, 1502	175.00
Lucy Lockett, 524	595.00
Lunchtime, 2485	140.00
Lydia, 1908	75.00
Lynne, 2329	100.00
M' Lady's Maid	450.00
Madonna of the Square	400.00
Maisie, 1619	290.00
Make Believe, 2225	60.00
Mam'selle, 724	550.00
Man in Tudor costume	600.00
Mandarin	1,200.00
Mantilla, 2712	215.00
Margaret	185.00
Margaret of Anjou, 2012	525.00
Margery	285.00
Marguerite, 1928	285.00
Marie, 1370	50.00
Marjorie, 2728	110.00
Market Day, 1991	225.00
Mary Had a Little Lamb, 2048	60.00
Mary Jane, 1900	385.00
Mary Mary, 2044	125.00
Mask Seller, 2103	117.00
Masque, 2554	105.00
Masquerade, 600	350.00
Master, 2325	102.50
Matilda, 2011	610.00
Maureen, 1770	265.00
1771, blue	750.00
Mayor, 2280	435.00
Meditation, 2330	130.00
Melanie, 2271	100.00
Melissa	110.00
Melody	250.00
Memories, 2030	350.00
Mendicant, 1365	250.00
Mephistopheles & Marguerite	700.00
Meriel	375.00
Mermaid, 97	412.50
Meryll	500.00
Mexican, Dancers of the World	650.00
Michelle, 2234	95.00
Midinette, 1289	350.00
1306	350.00
2090	265.00
Midsummer Noon, 1899	450.00
Milady	425.00
Milking Time	750.00
Milkmaid, 2057	85.00
Millicent	425.00
Minuet, 2019	250.00
2066	395.00
Mirabel	425.00
Miranda	450.00
Mirror	450.00
Miss 1926	650.00
Miss Demure, 1402	145.00
Potted	210.00
Miss Fortune	275.00
Miss Muffet	110.00
Miss Winsome	275.00
Modena	425.00
Modern Piper, 756	1,050.00
Moira	600.00
Molly Malone	600.00
Monica, 1467	65.00
Moorish Minstrel	800.00
Moorish Piper Minstrel	800.00
Mother's Help	100.00
Motherhood	600.00
Mr Micawber, 2097	250.00
Mr Pickwick, 2099	255.00
Mrs Fitzherbert	550.00
My Love, 2339	110.00
My Pet, 2238	85.00
My Pretty Maid	115.00
My Teddy, 2177	235.00
Nana	95.00
Negligee	450.00
Nell Gwynne, 1887	440.00
New Bonnet	250.00
Newhaven Fishwife	500.00
Newsboy, 2244	350.00
Nicola, 2839	145.00
Nina, 2347	140.00

Ninette, 2379	110.00
Noelle, 2179	375.00
Old Balloon Seller, 1315	105.00
Old King, 2134	365.00
Old King Cole, 2217	695.00
Old Lavender Seller, 1492	600.00
Old Meg, 2492	250.00
2494	200.00
Old Mother Hubbard, 2314	190.00
Olga, 2463	175.00
Olivia	235.00
Omar Khayyam, 2247	105.00
Omar Khayyam & Beloved	900.00
Once Upon a Time	110.00
One That Got Away	150.00

Orange Lady, pink, 1759	175.00
Green, 1953	185.00
Orange Seller	325.00
Orange Vendor	450.00
Organ Grinder	425.00
Out For a Walk	550.00
Owd Willum, 2042	230.00
Paisley Shawl, 1914	200.00
1987, 9"	225.00
1988, 6"	160.00
Palio	2,500.00
Pamela, 1469	475.00
Pan on Rock	425.00
Pantalettes, 1362	280.00
Parisian	145.00
Parson's Daughter, 564	280.00
Past Glory, 2428	160.00
Patch Work Quilt, 1984	275.00
Patricia, 1567	350.00
1414	500.00
Paula	110.00
Pauline	185.00
Pavolona	625.00
Peace, black, 2433	40.00
Pearly Boy, 2035	180.00
Pearly Girl, 1483	180.00
Pecksniff, 2098	300.00
Peggy, 2038	70.00
Penelope, 1901	285.00
Penny, 2338	40.00
Pensive Moments, 2704	105.00
Phillippine, Dancers of the World	650.00
Phyllis, 1486	575.00

Picnic, 2308	60.00
Pied Piper, 2102	185.00
Pierrette, 643	900.00
Pillow Fight, 2270	175.00
Pirouette	200.00
Poacher, 2043	295.00
Poke Bonnet, 612	950.00
Polka, 2156	245.00
Polly Peachum, 549	400.00
620	350.00
Potter, 1493	245.00
Premiere, 2343	137.50
Priscilla, 1340	350.00
Primrose, 1617	650.00
Professor	160.00
2281	125.00
Prue	225.00
Puff & Powder	650.00
Punch & Judy Man	195.00
Puppet Maker	375.00
Pussy	600.00
Pyjams	150.00
Quality Street	500.00
Rachel	120.00
Rag Doll, 2142	45.00
Rebecca	195.00
Reflections	800.00
Regal Lady, 2709	100.00
Regency	450.00
Regency Beau	600.00
Rendezvous	195.00
Repose, 2272	210.00
Rest Awhile	135.00
Return of Persephone	1,500.00
Reverie, 2306	150.00
Rhapsody	125.00
Rhoda	250.00
Rhythm	450.00
Rita	275.00
River Boy	75.00
Robert Burns	850.00
Rocking Horse	1,600.00
Romance, 2430	135.00
Romany Sue	500.00
Rosabelle	475.00
Rosalind, 2393	185.00
Rosamund, 1320	500.00
Rose, 1368	40.00
Roseanna, 1926	300.00
Rosebud	350.00
Rosemary, 2991	300.00
Rosina, 1364	325.00
Rowena, 2077	700.00
Royal Governors Cook, Williamsburg	120.00
Ruby	185.00
Ruth, 2799	60.00
Sabbath Morn, 1982	210.00
Sailor's Holiday, 2442	155.00
Sairey Gamp, 7"	200.00
Sandra, 2275	85.00
Sara	145.00
Saucy Nymph	150.00
Schoolmarm, 2223	125.00
2239	130.00

2430	115.00
Scotch Girl	400.00
Scotties, 1349	325.00
Scottish, Dancers of the World	650.00
Scribe, 305	600.00
Sea Harvest, 2257	145.00
Sea Sprite, 1261	150.00
2191	85.00
Seafarer, 2455	145.00
Seashore	135.00
Secret Thoughts, 2382	125.00
Sentimental Pierrot	500.00
Sentinel	500.00
Serena	700.00
She Loves Me Not	90.00
Shepherd, 81	700.00
627	700.00
632	700.00
75l,	500.00
1975	150.00
Shepherdess	500.00
Shore Leave, 2254	165.00
Shy Anne, 65	800.00
Shylock	700.00
Sibell, 1668	360.00
Siesta, 1305	950.00
Silks & Ribbons, 2017	95.00
Silversmith of Williamsburg, 2208	120.00
Simone, 2378	100.00
Sir Thomas Lovell	425.00
Sir Walter Raleigh, 2015	590.00
Skater, 2117	310.00
Sketch Girl	750.00
Sleep	500.00
Sleepy Head	500.00
Sleepy Scholar	650.00
Smiling Buddha	650.00
Snake Charmer	550.00
Soiree, 2312	100.00
Solitude, 2810	125.00
Sonia	500.00
Sonny	325.00
Sophie, 2833	65.00
Southern Belle, 2229	100.00
Spanish Lady, 1262	375.00
Spanish Lady, 1294	800.00
Spook	700.00
Spring, 2085	260.00
Spring Flowers, 1807	300.00
Spring Morning, green, 1922	235.00
Pink, 1923	210.00
Springtime	250.00
Squire	450.00
St George, 385-6	1,800.00
1800	1,800.00
2067	1,800.00
St George & Dragon	275.00
Standing Beefeater	550.00
Stayed at Home	90.00
Stephanie, 2807	100.00
Stitch in Time, 2352	130.00
Stop Press, 2683	135.00
Suitor	225.00
Summer, 2086	325.00

Summer's Day	225.00
Sunday Best, 2206	182.50
Sunday Morning	185.00
Sunshine Girl	500.00
Susan, 2056	325.00
Susanna	500.00
Suzette, 2026	260.00
Sweet & Fair	450.00
Sweet & Twenty, 1298	175.00
Sweet Anne, 1330	170.00
1496	175.00
Sweet April	275.00
Sweet Dreams, 2380	90.00
Sweet Lavender	225.00
Sweet Maid	325.00
Sweet Seventeen, 2734	100.00
Sweet Sixteen	100.00
Sweet Suzy	275.00
Sweeting, 1935	125.00
Swimmer	600.00
Sylvia	350.00
Symphony, 2287	335.00
Tailor	400.00
Taking Things Easy, 2677	140.00
Tall Story, 2248	170.00
Tea Time, 2255	100.00
Teenager, 2203	240.00
Teresa	500.00
Tess, 2865	65.00
Tete A Tete, 798	1,000.00
Tete A Tete, 798, potted	1,150.00
Thanks Doc, 2731	115.00
Thanksgiving, 2446	170.00
This Little Pig, 1793	50.00
Tinkle Bell, 1677	50.00
Tinsmith	300.00
To Bed, 1805	120.00
Toinette	500.00
Tom	65.00
Tony Weller, 346	700.00
Tony Weller, 684	825.00
Tootles, 1680	95.00
Tootles, 1688	85.00
Top O The Hill, 1833	150.00

1834	102.50
1849	165.00
Town Crier, 2119	215.00
Toymaker, 2250	340.00

Toys	700.00
Tranquility, black, 2426	55.00
White, 2469	55.00
Treasure Island, 2243	110.00
Tulips	550.00
Tuppence A Bag, 2320	110.00
Twilight, 2256	145.00
Two-a-Penny	450.00
Uncle Ned	235.00
Under the Gooseberry Bush	500.00
Upon Her Cheeks She Wept	700.00
Uriah Heep, 2101	290.00
554	275.00
Valerie, 2107	65.00
Vanessa	350.00
Vanity, 2475	65.00
Veneta, 2722	108.50
Veneta, 2772	125.00
Vera	350.00
Verena	350.00
Veronica, 1517	230.00
Victoria, 2471	130.00
Victorian Lady, M2	245.00
1529	350.00
Viking, 2375	205.00
Vivienne, 2073	220.00
Votes for Women, 2816	130.00
Wandering Minstrel	500.00
Wardrobe Mistress, 2145	475.00
Wayfarer, 2362	135.00
Wedding Morn	750.00
Wee Willie Winkle	145.00
Welsh Girl	50.00
Wendy, 2109	45.00
Wigmaker of Williamsburg, 2239	115.00
Willy Won't He	185.00
Windflower, 2029	325.00
Windmill Lady	600.00
Winner	500.00
Winsome, 2220	90.00
Winter, 2088	290.00
Wistful, 2396	200.00
Wizard, 2877	130.00
Woman Holding Child	500.00
Wood Nymph	85.00
Yardley's Old English Lavender	350.00
Yeoman of the Guard	400.00
Young Knight	600.00
Young Love, 2735	440.00
Young Master	195.00
Young Miss Nightingale	475.00
Young Widow	650.00
Yum Yum, 1286	490.00

Jugs

Anne Boleyn, large, D6644	48.00
Miniature	20.00
Apothecary, large, D6567	48.00
Miniature, D6581	20.00
Small, D6574	30.00
Aramis, Miniature, D6508	20.00
Small, D6454	30.00
'Ard of 'Earing, large, D6588	700.00
Miniature, D6594	1,195.00
Small	675.00

'Arriet, large	150.00
Miniature	55.00
Tiny	200.00
'Arry, large	160.00
Miniature, D6249	55.00
Small, A mk, D6235	85.00
Tiny, D6255	195.00
Athos, large, D6439	48.00
Miniature, D6509	20.00
Small, D6452	30.00
Auld Mac, large, A mk	65.00
Large, D5823	58.00
Miniature, A mk, D6253	55.00
Miniature, D6253	20.00
Small, D5824	30.00
Bacchus, miniature, D6521	20.00
Small, D6505	30.00
Beefeater, large	48.00
Miniature, D6251	20.00
Small, D6233	42.50
Blacksmith, large, D6571	48.00
Miniature, D6585	20.00
Bootmaker, large, D6572	48.00
Miniature, D6586	20.00
Small	30.00
Cap'n Cuttle, small, A mk	95.00
D5842	95.00
Captain Ahab, large, D6500	48.00
Miniature, D6522	20.00
Small, D6506	30.00
Captain Henry Morgan, large, D6467	48.00
Miniature, D6510	20.00
Small, D6469	30.00
Captain Hook, large, D6497	325.00
Small, D6601	280.00
Cardinal, large, D5614	135.00

Miniature, A mk, D6129	55.00
Miniature, D6129	60.00
Small, A mk	75.00
Tiny, D6258	245.00
Catherine of Aragon, large, D6643	48.00
Miniature	20.00
Small	30.00
Cavalier, large, A mk, D6114	125.00
Clown, White Hair, large, D6322	1,000.00
Dick Turpin, large, Horse Handle, Masked, D6528	55.00
Large, Unmasked	120.00
Miniature, Gun, Mask Up, D6128	45.00

Small, A mk, Gun, Mask, D5618	70.00
Small, Gun Handle, Mask Up, D5618	60.00
Small, Horse Handle, Masked, D6535	30.00
Dick Whittington, large, D6375	325.00
Don Quixote, large	50.00
Miniature, D6511	20.00
Small, D6460	35.00
Drake, large, A mk, D6115	120.00
Small, A mk, D6174	70.00
Small, D6174	70.00
Falconer, large, D6533	48.00
Miniature, D6547	20.00
Small, D6540	30.00
Falstaff, large, D6287	48.00
Miniature, D6519	30.00
Small, D6385	30.00
Farmer John, large, A mk, D5788	140.00
Small, A mk, D5789	75.00
Fat Boy, miniature, D6139	65.00
Small, D5840	80.00
Tiny, D6142	105.00
Field Marshal Smuts, large, D6198	1,900.00
Fortune Teller, large, D6497	385.00
Miniature, D6523	385.00
Friar Tuck, large, D6321	400.00
Gaoler, large, D6570	48.00
Miniature, D6584	20.00
Small, D6577	30.00
Gardener, large, D6630	75.00
Miniature, D6638	25.00
Small, D6634	35.00
Gladiator, large, D6550	500.00
Miniature, D6556	375.00
Small, D6553	325.00
Golfer, large, D6623	48.00
Gondolier, large	500.00
Gone Away, large, D6531	48.00
Miniature, D6545	20.00
Small, D6538	30.00
Granny, large, A mk, D5521	60.00
Large, D5521	48.00
Miniature, D6520	20.00
Small, D6384	30.00
Guardsman, large, D6568	48.00
Miniature, D6582	20.00
Small, D6575	30.00
Gulliver, large, D6560	500.00
Miniature, D6566	395.00
Small, D6563	385.00
Gunsmith, large, D6573	48.00
Miniature, D6587	20.00
Small, D6580	30.00
Henry VIII, miniature	20.00
Small, D6647	30.00
Isaac Walton, large, D6404	48.00
Jane Seymour, large, D6646	48.00
Jarge, large, D6288	295.00
Small, D6295	165.00
Jester, small, A mk	100.00
D5556	90.00
Jockey, large, D6625	175.00
John Barleycorn, large, A mk, D5327	135.00
Large D5327	130.00
Miniature, A mk, D6041	65.00
Small, A mk	75.00
Small, D5735	70.00
John Peel, large, D5612	120.00
Miniature, A mk	55.00
Miniature, D6130	50.00
Small, A mk, D5731	60.00
Small, D5731	58.00
Tiny	230.00
Johnny Appleseed, large, D6372	260.00
Lawyer, large, D6498	48.00
Miniature, D6524	20.00
Small, D6504	30.00
Lobster Man, large, D6617	48.00
Miniature	20.00
Small, D6620	30.00
Long John Silver, large, D6335	65.00
Miniature, D6512	20.00
Small, D6386	30.00
Lord Nelson, large, D6336	250.00
Lumberjack, large, D6610	42.50
Large, special Canadian, centennial edition	125.00
Small, D6613	33.00
Mad Hatter, large, D6598	48.00
Miniature, D6606	20.00
Small, D6602	30.00
Mark Twain	48.00
Mephistopheles, large	2,200.00
Merlin, large, D6529	48.00
Small, D6536	30.00
Mikado, large, D6501	355.00
Miniature	300.00
Small, D6507	275.00
Mine Host, large, D6468	48.00
Miniature, D6513	20.00
Small, D6470	30.00
Monty, large, A mk	75.00
Mr Micawber, miniature, A mk, D65138	50.00
Miniature, D6138	70.00
Small, A mk	70.00
Small, D5843	100.00
Tiny	110.00
Mr Pickwick, large, A mk, D6060	155.00
Miniature, D65254	55.00
Tiny	200.00
Neptune, large, D6548	48.00
Miniature, D6555	20.00
Small, D6552	30.00
Night Watchman, Large, D6569	48.00
Miniature, D6583	20.00
Small, D6576	30.00
North American Indian, large, D6611	48.00
Miniature	20.00
Small, D6614	30.00
Old Charley, large, A mk	150.00
Large, D5420	48.00
Large, seated Toby	140.00
Miniature, A mk, D6046	35.00
Miniature, D6046	20.00
Small, A mk	39.50
Small, D5527	30.00
Tiny, D6144	10.50
Toby, small	135.00
Old King Cole, small, D6037	90.00
Old Salt, large, D6551	48.00

Small, D6554 . . . . **30.00**
Paddy, large A mk, D5753 . . . . **125.00**
  Large **125.00**
  Miniature, A mk, D6042 . . . . **45.00**
  Miniature, D6042 . . . . **50.00**
  Small, A mk **59.00**
  Small, D5768 . . . . **50.00**
  Small, dated 1942 . . . . **55.00**
  Tiny, D6145 . . . . **105.00**
Parson Brown, large, A mk **100.00**
  Large **130.00**
  Small, A mk, D5529 . . . . **60.00**
  Small, D5529 . . . . **70.00**
Pearly Boy, large, brown **850.00**
Pied Piper, large, D6403 . . . . **57.50**
  Miniature **30.00**
  Small, D6462 . . . . **35.00**
Poacher, large, D6429 . . . . **48.00**
  Miniature, D6515 . . . . **20.00**
  Small, D6464 . . . . **30.00**
Porthos, large, D6440 . . . . **48.00**
  Miniature, D6516 . . . . **20.00**
  Small, D6453 . . . . **30.00**
Punch & Judy Man, D6593 . . . . **380.00**
Regency Beau, small, D6562 . . . . **400.00**
Regency Coach, ltd edition **500.00**
Rip Van Winkle, miniature, D6517 . . . . **20.00**
  Small, D6462 . . . . **30.00**
Robin Hood, large **48.00**
  Miniature, A mk, D6252 . . . . **55.00**
  Small **65.00**
Robinson Crusoe, large, D6532 . . . . **48.00**
  Miniature, D6546 . . . . **20.00**
  Small, D6539 . . . . **30.00**
Sairey Gamp, large, A mk, D5451 . . . . **85.00**
  Large, D5451 . . . . **48.00**
  Miniature, A mk **35.00**
  Miniature, D6045 . . . . **20.00**
  Miniature, dated 1942 . . . . **30.00**
  Small, A mk **40.00**
  Small, D5528 . . . . **30.00**
  Small, dated 1942 . . . . **39.00**
  Tiny, A mk, D6146 . . . . **110.00**
  Tiny **100.00**
Sam Johnson, large, D6289 . . . . **250.00**
  Small, D6296 . . . . **175.00**
Sam Weller, large, A mk, D6064 . . . . **120.00**
  Miniature, A mk, D6140 . . . . **50.00**
  Miniature, D6140 . . . . **55.00**
  Small, A mk **75.00**
  Small, D5841 . . . . **110.00**
  Tiny, D6147 . . . . **110.00**
Sancho Panzo, large, D6456 . . . . **48.00**
  Miniature, D6518 . . . . **20.00**
  Small, D6461 . . . . **30.00**
Scaramouche, large **500.00**
  Miniature, D6564 . . . . **390.00**
Sergeant Buz Fuz, small, A mk **80.00**
Simon The Cellarer, large, A mk, D5504 . . . . **135.00**
  Large **130.00**
  Small, A mk **70.00**
  Small, D5616 . . . . **60.00**
Simple Simon, large, D6374 . . . . **475.00**
Sleuth, large, D6631 . . . . **48.00**

Miniature, D6639 . . . . **20.00**
Small, D6635 . . . . **30.00**
Smuggler, large **65.00**
  Small, D6619 . . . . **35.00**
St George, large, D6618 . . . . **105.00**
  Small, D6621 . . . . **68.00**
Tam O'Shanter, large, D6632 . . . . **60.00**
  Large **60.00**
  Miniature, A mk **30.00**
  Miniature, D6640 . . . . **28.00**
  Small, D6636 . . . . **35.00**
Toby Philpots, large, A mk **140.00**
  Large, D5736 . . . . **120.00**
  Miniature, A mk, D6043 . . . . **45.00**
  Miniature, D6043 . . . . **50.00**
  Miniature **45.00**
  Small, A mk, D5737 . . . . **55.00**
  Small **55.00**
Tony Weller, large, A mk, D5531 . . . . **108.00**
  Miniature, D6044 . . . . **45.00**
  Small, A mk **59.00**
  Small, D5530 . . . . **65.00**
Touchstone, large, A mk, D5613 . . . . **220.00**
  Large, D5613 . . . . **215.00**
Tower Of London, ltd edition **600.00**
Town Crier, large, D6530 . . . . **140.00**
  Miniature, D6544 . . . . **125.00**
  Small, D6537 . . . . **210.00**
Trapper, large **48.00**
  Small, D6612 . . . . **30.00**
Ugly Duchess, large **325.00**
  Miniature, D6607 . . . . **270.00**
  Miniature **300.00**
  Small, D6603 . . . . **248.00**
Uncle Tom Cobbleigh, large, D6337 . . . . **415.00**
Veteran Motorist, large, D6633 . . . . **48.00**
  Miniature, D6641 . . . . **20.00**
  Small, D6637 . . . . **30.00**
Vicar Of Bray, large, A mk, D5615 . . . . **180.00**
  Large, D5615 . . . . **200.00**
Viking, large, D6496 . . . . **95.00**
  Miniature, D6526 . . . . **120.00**
  Miniature **120.00**
  Small, D6502 . . . . **65.00**
Walrus And Carpenter, large, D6600 . . . . **85.00**
  Miniature, D6608 . . . . **27.50**
  Small, D6604 . . . . **42.50**
Yachtsman, Large, D6622 . . . . **85.00**

Dresden, See Also Meisen

Today, the term Dresden is used to indicate the porcelains that were produced in Meissen and Dresden, Germany, from the very early 18th century, well into the next. John Bottger, a young alchemist discovered the formula for the first true porcelain in 1708, while being held a virtual prisoner at the palace in Dresden because of the King's determination to produce a superior ware. Two years later, a factory was erected in nearby Meissen, with Bottger as director. There, fine tablewares elaborate centerpieces and exquisite figurines with applied details were produced. In 1731, to distinguish their product from wares of such potters as Serves, Worcester, Chelsea and Derby, Meissen adopted their famous crossed swords trademark. During the next century, several potteries were producing porcelain in the 'Meissen style' in Dresden itself. Their wares were marked with their own logo and the Dresden indication. Those listed here are from that era. See the Meisen

section for examples with the crossed swords marking.

Biscuit jar, white w/relief flowers, vines, Crown mk, 6½″ **40.00**
Box, covered, oval, hp scenic, floral relief, 3½x4″.......... **120.00**
   Woven, ribbed, Oriental scene, twig handle, 3½x4″........ **85.00**
Bust, colonial man & lady, lt green, pink, 9½″, pr **150.00**
Candelabra, couple, applied fruits & flowers, gold, 8″, pr **300.00**
Candle lamp, double, ballerina, mirror, flowers, brass, marble . **175.00**
Candlesticks, relief florals, foilage, swirls, 6½″, pr **240.00**
   Swirls, w/colorful florals in relief, 6½″, pr **250.00**
Centerpiece, angel figurals, florals in relief, 12x6″.......... **450.00**
Clock, mantel, 8 day, 3 figures, scrolls, ornate **1,200.00**
Compote, white, figurals, early, 12″ **165.00**
Cracker jar, hp roses, gold decor, Dresden............ **90.00**
Creamer, Shelby Touraine **70.00**
Cup & saucer, Shelby Touraine **50.00**
Demitasse cup & saucer, portrait in yellow............. **185.00**
Dresser tray, palatte shape, wht w/pink roses, gold, 11x8″ **3.50**
Ewer, fluted ped base, ornate handle, florals, 1800s **235.00**
Figurine, ballerina, Made in Germany,4″................. **80.00**
   Ballerina, Popplesdork mk, 7″............... **150.00**
   Ballerina, delicate lace, pink & white........... **185.00**
   Ballerina, old mark, 4″.......................... **80.00**
   Colonial couple on settee, 10″................. **475.00**
   Girl, 17th century costume, 5″................ **115.00**
   Girl, bonnet w/flowers, feather, 5″............. **175.00**
   God of Wine on goat, s through X-swords mk, 8½″ **395.00**
   Hunter w/dogs, 13½″ **650.00**
   Lady on couch, lace, Fritze, 8x6″ **400.00**
   Monika, 5½″................................. **150.00**
   Nude, Wallingford, 11″...................... **135.00**
   Parrots, blue/green, yellow/green, on stump, 6½″, pr **345.00**
   Peasant child, 11″............................ **235.00**
   Ring Around the Rosy, 7x7″ **300.00**
   The Musical Vagabond, signed Stahl, 7″......... **145.00**
   Woman on tree stump **280.00**
Group, Fall, boy w/rust coat, girl, pastels, blue crown N mk... **275.00**
   Winter, boy & girl, pastels & cobalt **275.00**
   Boy & girl in warm clothes play on icy rocks **275.00**
Perfume w/stopper, green, florals, by Thieme, Saxony, 3″...... **70.00**
Plaque, oval, w/portrait, late 1800s **565.00**
Plate, florals, w/gold rococo border, open handles, 10½″ **60.00**
Platter, Del Monte pattern **82.00**
Pot, woman w/basket of flowers, 7½″.................. **125.00**
Teapot, duck figural in teak stand, signed **300.00**
Vanity mirror, cupid figurals, roses & scrolls, blue mk, 18″ ... **525.00**
Vase, bulbous w/cylinder neck, hp scenic, late 1800s....... **1,200.00**

Dresser Accessories

Box, cut glass, ornate sterling top **75.00**
Manicure set, silver plated, w/lady's head & flowing hair, 4 pc .. **75.00**
Mirror, brass scrollwork frame w/roses, free standing.......... **65.00**
Set, aluminum, mirror & brush, w/hp porcelain bouquet **14.00**
   Art Deco, 4 pc, sterling **175.00**
   Art Deco, 13 pc, repousse sterling & cut crystal **300.00**
   Art Deco, comb & brush w/orig gold case........ **65.00**
   Celluloid, 9 pc, amber & gold **80.00**
   Cut glass, powder box & hair receiver, sterling tops **155.00**
   Ebony w/sterling initials, mirror & 3 brushes **23.00**
   French Ivory, 13 pc............................ **99.00**
   German, 4 pc white w/4 color flowers **65.00**
   Gold filigree & stones, 4 pc, w/domed jewelry box **125.00**

Half-dolls, 3 pc, porcelain ladies w/pompadour hair **98.00**
Porcelain, 3 pc, blue, hp daisies, footed, Limoges **55.00**
Schumann Bavaria, 5 pc, on 16″ tray, hp floral decor...... **175.00**
Sterling, 3 pc, rose & feather design, ornate, Gorham...... **285.00**
Sterling, 3 pc, w/ornate roses decor, monogram, Kirk & Son **225.00**
Sterling, 4 pc, 'Love's Dream', Unger Bros............... **575.00**
Sterling, 4 pc, Webester **285.00**
Sterling, 5 pc, cut & etched glass, 1800s, Simpson Hall Miller **450.00**
Sterling, 6 pc, Art Nouveau, Gorham **500.00**
Sterling & cut glass, 3 pc, embossed florals, Watson **125.00**
Sterling & cut glass, 6 pc, engraved 'Irene', Gorham **150.00**
Sterling & cut glass, 8 pc & case, stepped border, Wallace.. **250.00**
Sterling & cut glass, 13 pc, engraved foliage, International .. **225.00**

Sterling, brush & mirror, red velvet insert................. **50.00**
Talcum dispenser, working top, Ivory Pyralin, 3½″ **7.00**
Tray, French Ivory, 10x6½″......................... **9.00**
   Mirrored, Art Deco, blue w/ivorene & steel, 14x19″........ **35.00**
   Mirrored, spiral glass rods, gold leaf corners, 16x9″ **17.00**

Duncan and Miller Glass

   The Duncan and Miller Glass Company was built in 1894 in Washington, Pa. Their earliest products were pressed glass tablewares and vases. In the 20s, colored glassware was introduced, and new patterns were developed, the most notable their recreation of Sandwich's #41. During the 40s, simple lines of high quality glass were made in opalescent colors of pink blue, yellow and chartreuse. The company was sold in 1955 to US Glass.

#21 Plaza, bowl, 4½″............................... **3.00**
   Juice, flat **3.00**
   Plate, 6″.................................. **1.25**
#22 Astaire, bon-bon, footed, 6″, clear.................. **10.00**
   Puff box, amber **25.00**
#24, butter pat **8.50**
   Champagne, saucer type **29.00**
   Creamer **21.00**
   Finger bowl **21.00**
   Open sugar **15.00**
   Sugar shaker **29.00**
   Wine **29.00**
#28, bowl, flat, 5″................................. **14.00**
   Champagne, saucer type **36.00**
   Cordial **36.00**
   Jelly compote **24.00**
   Punch cup **7.00**
   Shakers, plastic tops, pr **14.50**
   Syrup, 3¾″ **40.00**
   Toothpick................................. **19.50**
#29, champagne **35.00**
#30 Pall Mall, bowl, flat, 8¼″ **17.00**
   Butter pat................................. **10.00**

Champagne	30.00
Creamer, 3¼"	14.50
Creamer, 5"	20.00
Cruet, orig stopper	32.50
Punch cup	8.00
Sauce dish, flat w/gilt trim, 4"	8.00
Sugar w/cover, bar type, 5¾"	24.00
Sugar w/cover, bar type, 5"	18.00
Toothpick	26.00
Trumpet vase, 6½"	16.00
Tumbler, gilt trim	26.00
Vase, 10"	18.50
Water pitcher, applied handle	45.00
Wine w/gilt trim	23.00
Wine	26.00
#40 Spiral Flute, carafe	29.00
Egg cup	18.50
Nappy, green	6.50
Parfait, green, 5½"	10.00
Punch cup	6.00
Soup, handled, green	8.50
Tumbler, ruby stained	42.00
#41 Sandwich, basket, w/handle, 6½"	20.00
Bowl, 12"	25.00
Bowl, oblong, 12"	24.00
Candelabrum w/cut prisms#1-41	40.00
Candles, 4" pr	20.00
Candlestick, blue, 4"	55.00
Candy w/cover, 8½"	27.50
Champagne	7.50
Coaster, crystal, 5"	7.50
Cocktail, 3 oz	8.50
Cologne & stopper, clear	12.00
Cologne bottle, pink opal, 7"	55.00
Comport, crimped, low, 5½"	12.00
Creamer	7.50
Cup	9.00
Cup & saucer	12.00
Finger bowl, green	15.00
Fruit bowl, 12"	30.00
Goblet, 9 oz	8.50
Goblet, blue, 6"	35.00
Grapefruit, green	16.50
Ice cream, 4¼"	6.50
Juice tumbler	6.50
Plate, 6¼"	3.00
Plate, green, 8"	17.50
Sherbet, 4¼"	4.50
Vase, crimped, clear, 8"	14.00
Wine	9.00
#42 Mardi Gras, bud vase, 6¼"	10.00
Butter pat	9.50
Carafe	40.00
Cordial	38.00
Creamer, oval, 2½x3¾"	8.00
Creamer, large	17.00
Cruet	35.00
Plate, 5"	10.00
Punch bowl, flared, 2 pc, 15"	100.00
Punch cup	7.50
Rose bowl, 4"	32.50
Sherry, 2 oz	26.00
Swan, pink opal, Sylvan	40.00
Tankard pitcher, 9½"	45.00

Toothpick w/gilt trim	26.00
Toothpick w/scalloped top	30.00
Wine	26.00
#44, tumbler, gilt trim	23.00
Wine, gilt trim	24.00
#45, cakestand, 10"	65.00
Plate, 6"	17.00
Punch cup	6.00
Relish, 7½x3½"	12.00
Sauce w/ruby stain, 4¾"	24.00
#48 Amberette, creamer, 5"	65.00
Bowl, flat, 8"	14.50
Champagne	30.00
Champagne, saucer type	29.00
Claret	32.00
Egg cup, handled	20.00
Gas shade	14.00
Goblet	32.00
Jam jar	27.00
Plate, 8"	16.00
Punch bowl, 15"	60.00
Wine, gilt trim, 4½"	21.00
#71, plate, star shape, 14"	38.00
Vase, flared, 8"	30.00
#78 American Way, candleholder, pink opal, pr	55.00
Candlesticks, 2", pr	7.00
#101 Ripple, plate, amber, 6"	3.00
Sherbet, amber	5.00
Sugar w/cover, amber	10.00
#112 Caribbean, bowl, clear, 4½"	4.25
Bowl, blue, deep, 9½"	25.00
Bowl, w/handles, blue, 6"	10.00
Candles w/brass trim, prisms, 7½", pr	45.00
Candy w/cover, blue	30.00
Console set, 3 pc, blue	145.00
Cruet w/stopper, crystal	24.50
Goblet, water, blue	30.00
Mayonnaise, divided, 6½"	18.00
Mint tray, stemmed, clear	12.00
Plate, blue, 8½"	9.00
Plate, clear, 8½"	6.50
Plate, handles, 6"	8.00
Plate, handles, blue, 10½"	12.00
Relish, 4 pt, blue, 11½"	27.00
Sherbet, blue, 4"	15.00
Sherbet, crystal, 4½"	8.00
Vase w/2 handles, blue, 6½"	32.50
#114, bon-bon w/handle, blue opal	17.00
#115 Canterbury, ashtray, 3"	4.00
Bowl, crimped, crystal, 9"	16.00
Candy dish, 3 part, vaseline	10.00
Candy w/cover, 3 part, blue opal	45.00
Console bowl	4.00
Cup & saucer	14.00
Goblet, chartreuse, 6½"	18.00
Goblet, water	4.00
Hat vase, crimped, 5½"	12.50
Pickle dish, clear, 8½"	8.50
Rose bowl	25.00
Sugar, large	4.00
Tumbler, 8 oz, blue opal	26.00
Vase, pink opal, 5x5"	30.00
Wine, lead crystal, 3½"	8.50
#117 Three Feathers, cornucopia vase, blue opal	50.00

#118 Hobnail, cream & sugar **10.00**
    Goblet, water **8.00**
    Ice tea, 13 oz, amber **24.00**
    Water jug, green **35.00**
#122 Sylvan, butter w/cover **33.00**
    Sandwich plate, 14″ **40.00**
#127 Murano, bowl, crimped, vaseline, 10″ **40.00**
    Console set, blue opal, 3 pc **110.00**
    Vase, flared, 7″ **20.00**
#150, butter w/cover, footed, clear **22.00**
    Goblet, etched **17.00**
    Sugar w/cover **18.50**
#301 Teardrop, bowl, handled, sq, 6″ **9.50**
    Butter w/silver plate cover, oblong **10.00**
    Celery tray, 10¾″ **7.50**
    Cheese comport **6.00**
    Condiment set, 5 pc **40.00**
    Cream & sugar **12.00**
    Creamer and sugar on tray **18.00**
    Cruet **12.50**
    Cup & saucer **8.50**
    Dish, heart shape, divided **9.50**
    Goblet, water **10.00**
    Mayonnaise set, 3 pc, clear **40.00**
    Nut dish, 2 pt, clear, 3″ **6.00**
    Pickle, 2 pt, 6″ **3.50**
    Pitcher, ice lip, ½ gal **60.00**
    Plate, 7½″ **4.00**
    Plate, 10½″ **10.00**
    Plate, w/handles, 11″ **8.00**
    Relish, 5 pt, 10″ **18.00**
    Shaker **5.00**
    Torte plate, 16″ **22.50**
    Tumbler, 9 oz, 4¼″ **12.00**
    Tumbler, 10 oz, 5¼″ **15.00**
    Tumbler, 12 oz, 5¾″ **15.00**
    Tumbler, flat, 4½″ **7.50**
    Tumbler, flat, 9 oz **7.00**
    Tumbler, flat, 12 oz **9.00**
    Tumbler, flat, 14 oz **10.00**
    Water goblet, crystal **7.00**
    Water set, floral cut, 7 pc **60.00**
#Flower Scroll, syrup w/amber decor **195.00**
Arlis, tumbler, ruby **25.00**
Ashtray, duck **24.50**
Bowl, floating garden, pink, 13x14″ **125.00**
Cigarette box, duck **35.00**
Donkey **325.00**
Fat goose **425.00**
First Love, champagne **13.50**
    Cordial **14.50**
    Cream & sugar on tray, miniature **75.00**
    Creamer, large **20.00**
    Decanter & stopper, 16 oz **70.00**
    Ice cream, 4″ **12.50**
    Juice, 5¼″ **15.00**
    Oyster cocktail **24.00**
    Plate, 8½″ **9.50**
    Vase, 3 feathers **95.00**
    Water goblet **13.50**
    Wine **13.50**
Heron **100.00**
Language of Flowers, bowl, w/handles, crystal, 6½″ . . . **12.00**
Perfume bottle, Swan on ball, 4″ **50.00**

Swan, Sanibel, pink opal, 8¼″ **65.00**
    Chartreuse, 8½″ **35.00**
    Crystal, 5″ **25.00**
    Crystal, short body, 12″ wing span **50.00**
    Open red, 6″ **32.00**
    Open, 3½″ **14.00**
    Solid, 3″ **20.00**
    Solid, 4½″ **43.00**
Swordfish **175.00**
Viking boat **385.00**
Willow, cheese & cracker, handled **40.00**
    Creamer **14.00**
    Plate, 7½″ **15.00**
    Sugar **14.00**
    Water goblet, crystal, cut, 6½″ **25.00**

Durand

Durand Art Glass was a division of Vineland Glass Works in Vineland, N.J. Created in 1924, it was geared specifically toward the manufacture of fine hand-crafted art ware. Iridescent, opalescent and cased glass was used to create such patterns as King Tut, reminiscent of Tiffany and Steuben. Production halted in 1931, after the death of Victor Durand.

Bowl, blue, 7″ dia **775.00**
    Gold, footed, King Tut decor, 5″ **375.00**
Candy dish, gold irid, flaring, scalloped rim, 6″ dia . . . **245.00**
Centerpiece bowl, flashed ruby w/wht feathers & pink bands, 12″ **445.00**
Compote, blue & silver irid w/vines & leaves, gold foot, 3″ . . . **575.00**
    Blue w/lily pad decor, 2¾x4½″ **400.00**
Cup & saucer, red w/wht feathering″ **350.00**
Dish, blue irid, signed, 1½x6½″ **175.00**
Goblet, blue w/amber hollow stem, wht edged ruffle top **325.00**
Lamp, blue King Tut, gold shaft, mask finial, 24″ **280.00**
    Candle, terra cotta w/cut crystal, clear & amber, pr **1,300.00**
    Floor, red King Tut, flared, brass base, 12″ **550.00**
    Gold irid w/threading, 13″, pr **1,450.00**
Plate, lustre glass w/opal & red peacock feather, 8″ **115.00**
    Ruby, pulled feather, Bridgeton Rose engraved **300.00**
Rose bowl, clear bubbles, signed, 4″ **225.00**
Shade, King Tut flared top for brass floor lamp, 12″ **375.00**
    White, green, grey swirl block, for hanging lamp, 11½″ . . . **425.00**
Sherbet, green paneled w/wht rim, hollow amber stem, pr . . . **270.00**
    Red w/amber stems, 1 w/orig paper label, pr **300.00**
    With wht feathering, red stem & base **200.00**
Sweetmeat, w/cover, King Tut, 7″ **700.00**
Vase, amethyst, pedestal base, ribbed body, signed, 16″, pr . . . **500.00**
    Amethyst, sharp ribbing, signed, 12″ **350.00**
    Blue & wht over gold, craquelle glass, 11½″ **1,600.00**
    Blue King Tut decor, 4¼″ **650.00**
    Blue irid, modern shape, signed, 7″ **325.00**
    Blue on lustre crystal, Moorish crackle, 13″ **365.00**
    Blue w/wht lily pads & vines, pedestal, 8″ **550.00**
    Blue water lily pads w/green leaves & vines, 7″ **435.00**
    Butterscotch w/green lily pads & vines, 7″ **425.00**
    Clear blue top, feathered, signed, 12½″ **650.00**
    Cobalt blue irid w/orange irid in neck, 11½″ **400.00**
    Gold, green irid w/pink & blue, ruffled, King Tut, 6¾″ . . . **875.00**
    Gold irid, 9½″ **425.00**
    Gold irid King Tut decor w/pink & lavender, 12½″, pr . . . **1,500.00**
    Gold irid w/blue lily pads & vines, 10″ **425.00**
    Gold irid w/blue lily pads & green vines, 7¼″ **400.00**
    Gold irid w/blue lily pads & vines, 10″ **500.00**
    Gold irid w/threading & lion head jewels, feathered, 10″ . . . **425.00**

Gold irid w/threading, peacock plume, 7¾" **625.00**
Gold irid, signed 1812-8, 8" **350.00**
Gold lustre w/green King Tut decor, 6½" **450.00**
Green craquelle w/satin swirled design, blue liner, 8" **700.00**
Green King Tut, brass pedestal base, 10½" **400.00**
Green w/pink, lavender, gold King Tut decor, 12½" **750.00**
Intaglio cut, signed, #20161-8 .... **1,350.00**
Lavender, ribbed, 6" **150.00**
Orange & gold irid, 8½" **150.00**
Orange irid, bulbous w/narrow neck, flared, 6½" **275.00**
Orange lustre, 6" **175.00**
Orange w/blue vines & leaves, pedestal, signed, 12" **650.00**
Peacock blue, signed, #1710-4 .... **300.00**
Pink King Tut, chartreuse liner, blemishes, signed, 19" **800.00**
Purple ribbed crystal, squat, w/flare, 5½" **150.00**
Red, ribbed, gold liner, 10½" dia, 7½" high **450.00**
Salmon w/green leaves, 8½" **300.00**
Silver & gold decor, 10" **375.00**
Trumpet, red w/brown interior, calcite verre de soie ft, 8" .. **350.00**
Various colors, 9¼" **650.00**
White, w/red & blue liner, overlay, signed, pr **500.00**
Wine, clear red w/feathering, footed **300.00**
Cobalt blue w/wht loopings & cut band, vaseline stem, ft ... **225.00**
Red cup & base w/amber stem **300.00**
Red w/clear stem & light green base, pr **380.00**
Ruby bowl w/ribbed Spanish yellow stem, 7" **225.00**
With matching ribbed goblet, amethyst **190.00**

Durant

The Durant Pottery Co. operated in Bedford Village, N. Y., in the early 1900s.

Cake plate, and server, floral relief border, floral sprays **15.00**
Cheese dish w/cover, stylized florals, panels, gold trim, 5½x7".. **12.00**
Compote, turquoise glaze, 1921, 3x6" **225.00**
Salt box w/wood lid, scenic w/couple, fence and trees, ivory **18.00**
Vase, magenta phlox, gold background, 4 handles, 8x4" **25.00**
Wall pocket, bird decor, matt blue, brown, yellow, 7" **12.00**

E S Prussia

E.S. Prussia was a mark used by the Erdman Schlegelmilch porcelain manufactory established in 1861, in the Prussian province in Saxony, Germany. Most examples seen today date from the early 1900s until the factory closed in the 1920s.

Bowl, autumn leaves, fruit, wht w/nature colors, 6" **35.00**
Open handle, robin on picket fence, 7" **50.00**
Oriental lady, embossed heads, reticulated, 11" **275.00**
Scroll border, 6 side recesses, satin, florals, 10½" **275.00**
Vegetable, hp robbins, oblong **125.00**
Cake plate, open handles, lady w/doves, wht, red, gold, 10"... **550.00**
Open scrolled handles, roses on wht **135.00**
Cake set, bird w/floral branch, 7 pcs, hp **285.00**
Cheese & cracker dish w/poppies **50.00**
Cookie server, center handle, bird w/floral branch, 8½" **60.00**
Cup & saucer, burgandy & gold, Kauffmann, RS **65.00**
Cup, footed w/saucer, pastel flowers on white **45.00**
Ped base, portrait of children reserve on red, gold, 5" **285.00**
Dish, 3 compartments, portraits, handle, 10" **200.00**
Divided, autumn leaves, horse chestnuts **65.00**
Tall center handle, yellow roses **75.00**

Ewer, girl w/birds, pearlized, gold handle, 8" **65.00**
Hair receiver, pink roses **30.00**
Lobster dish, gold figural handle, divider, reticulated **120.00**
Pin tray, Queen Louise, pearlized **35.00**
Plaque, portrait of woman in period dress, pink & gold, 10" ... **60.00**
Portrait, 10" **70.00**
Plate, Gibson girl portrait, 8½" **450.00**
Pierced border, gold luster, green, pink roses, 10" **125.00**
Red & gold beaded border, portrait w/floral center, 8" **325.00**
Reticulated rim, fruit decor, 10" **95.00**
Semi-nudes at water's edge, red & gold border, 8" **75.00**
White w/wht & pink roses, 8½" **50.00**
Windmill & water scene, 8½" **125.00**
Relish dish, portrait, gold border, 8½" **30.00**
Toothbrush holder, wht w/gold scroll edges, dainty florals ... **165.00**
Tray, 3 ladies & cherubs, green border, handles, 12x8½" **95.00**
Blackcap Chickadee, hp, 13" **125.00**
Dresser, classic scene, 11" **45.00**
Open handles, portrait, 10x6" **125.00**
Reticulated edge, fruit decor **100.00**
Vase, Art Nouveau, lady w/peacock, wht w/heavy gold, 11½" .. **900.00**
Art Nouveau, portrait, ornate handles, beaded, 11" **300.00**
Bust portrait, maroon, lime, clovers, gold, ... **145.00**
Girl w/leaf crown, lilac lustre, gold etched, 2 handles **125.00**
Lady w/peacock, gold, ornate handles, tapestry, 10" **1,000.00**
Lady w/peacock, shaded, fluted top, 9" **165.00**
Maroon luster w/turquoise neck, scenic panel, handles, 8" .. **275.00**
Portrait of lovely lady, 11½" **265.00**
Portrait, red lustre w/gold, cobalt, 7½" **160.00**
Portrait, yellow, 2 gold handles, 6½" **55.00**
Rococo, portrait reserve, blue body, 3 loop handles, 11" ... **500.00**

Elephants

Elephants have always had a special significance to many people; collectors are no exception. In fact, if you're interested, in the directory you'll find the address of a newly organized elephant collectors club and newsletter.

Bank, gold color ci, 2 pc w/screw bolt, 3x4" **45.00**
Mechanical, twirling elephant on drum, 1930s **65.00**
Bookmark, ivory, carved top is 2 elephants **6.00**
Brass, tusk shaped vesica box, 2¾" **45.00**
Bronze, bull attacked by tigers, 1800s, 24x41" **3,250.00**
Charging w/upraised trunk, large, 1900 .... **225.00**
Bud vase, Staffordshire, cole slaw decoration, 1850 .... **300.00**
Cast iron, figural w/old silver paint, 7" long **30.00**
In wheeled cart, bell on trunk, 1910 .... **1,200.00**
Ceramic, GOP w/Senator Bridges, blue, 1½x2½" **10.00**
Christmas light bulb, celluloid, pink w/red **10.00**
Cigarette dispenser, ci, turn tail to dispense **55.00**
Cigarette package holder, 2 pc, yellow/green, Germany **35.00**
Coconut shell, carved elephant on cover, 3 on base, 7" **25.00**
Cookie jar, elephant w/split trunk, McCoy Pottery Co **50.00**
Doorstop, full figure, ci **38.00**
Ebony, hand carved, ivory tusks, 3" **35.00**
Felt, stuffed, standing, sitting, lace collar, 1900, pr **25.00**
Incense burner, figural w/howdah, gold metal, France, 4x4" **20.00**
Ivory, 4½x1¾" **40.00**
Five graduated elephants, detailed, largest 5" **300.00**
Holds baboon aloft in trunk, China 4x1¾" **17.00**
Kenton, man in Egyptian cart, 1910 circus series **190.00**
Lamp, black cast metal figural, gold trim howdah **40.00**
Milk glass, kneeling figural w/saddle, 1890, 5" **200.00**
White metal figurals, amber crackle glass shade **60.00**

Match holder, elephant head, amber glass, hanging **58.00**
   Elephant w/howdah, frosted glass, 3½″ **47.00**
   Yellow w/green trim, RT 923D, 1½x2¾″ **15.00**
Necklace, ivory, graduated elephants w/elephant pendant **20.00**
Netsuke, elephant w/3 men **85.00**
Peanut butter jar, Jumbo, embossed head, glass, 1 lb **15.00**
Pipe holder, teakwood figural **18.00**
Pitcher, McCoy Pottery Co, 1940s **40.00**
Planter, china, figural, child on trunk, Japan **20.00**
   Wicker, metal container, black button eyes, 12x7″ **20.00**
Porcelain, head w/trunk & tusks raised, wht, English, 14x8″ . . **150.00**
   Trunk up, ivory tusks, brown & wht blend, 4½x6″ **18.00**
Poster, Elephant Walk, Elizabeth Taylor, Peter Finch **65.00**
Powder dish, clear cover w/2 elephants, green bottom **15.00**
Print, Battle of the Bridge, hand colored, 1800s **30.00**
Program, Hullo Elephant, Italian film starring Sabu **10.00**
Salt & peppers, Shawnee Pottery, wht/red, 3″ **10.00**
Schoenhut, glass eyes, multi-jointed, 4x7″ **150.00**
Silverplate, advertising figural, Freed Co, 3x6″ **25.00**
Steiff, from circus, on wheels, blanket, 1930s, 17″ **300.00**
Sterling, charging w/trunk raised, ivory tusks, 3¾x7½″ **600.00**
Stuffed, pink, button eyes, 4 bells, embroidery, 1900s **140.00**
Toothpick, elephant head, clear glass **15.00**
Toy, early American tin bell, Fallows, w/clockwork monkey . . **1,500.00**
   Elephant Ride #252, Britain Ltd, howdah & children **380.00**
   Windup w/key, felt covered metal, animated **35.00**
Wood carving, humorous, trunk raised, red, Thai, 18x40″ **200.00**
   Ivory tusks, on base, 2½x3″ **13.00**
   Sitting, trunk raised, black/yellow, 28″ **300.00**

Epergnes

   A popular item during the Victorian era, epergnes were fancy centerpieces often consisting of several tiers of vases, called lilies, candleholders or dishes, or a combination of components. They were made in all types of art glass, and some were set in ornate plated frames.

Applied green base, pink petal edge, single stem, 10″ **200.00**
Blue shading to clear, 3 lilies, 20x12″ **185.00**
Bronze Roman figure base, clear to opal, green ruffle, Webb . . **450.00**
Cased, 4 lilies, each with rigaree decor **385.00**
Cased Vasa Murrhina, plated holder, single lily, 12″ **165.00**
Cranberry, 5 lilies, clear rigaree, opal bowl, 20″ **350.00**
   Gold flecked filigree, 3 trumpet vases **185.00**
   Pull-up technique, NE Glass Co, 13½″ **250.00**
Cranberry opal, metal base, w/figural girl, 22″ **240.00**
Diamond Quilted MOP, pink, stem w/3 arms, mirror plateau . . **550.00**
Fenton, Hobnail, milkglass, 4 pc, 10½″ bowl **30.00**
Green opal, 4 ruffled lilies & bowl, 20″ **325.00**
Hobnail in Square, aqua opal **190.00**
Hobnail, opal, 3 tier, fluted bottom bowl **125.00**
Milk glass, Hobnail, 3 lilies, 9x10″ **30.00**
Opal vaseline, 3 ruffled Jack in Pulpits on base, 21″ **385.00**
Overlay, enameled decor, ormolu holder w/figural man, leaves . **800.00**
Pink milk glass, 3 lilies **45.00**
Satin, frost shaded to rose, flat flower forms, Spelter base **350.00**
Silver, Martin Hall & Co, 23¼″ **3,000.00**

Eskimo Artifacts

   While ivory carvings made from walrus tusks or whale teeth have been the most emphasized aricles of the Eskimo art, basketry and woodworking are other areas in which these Alaskan Indians excell. Their designs are effected through the appliciaton of simple yet dramatic lines and almost stark decorative devices. Though not pursued to the extent of American Indian art, the unique work of this northern people is beginning to attract the serious attention of today's collectors.

Adz, wood handle, ivory head **185.00**
Adz-blade, walrus tusk, early, 8¼″ **100.00**
Awl, ivory, engraved **50.00**
Basket, 5x10x12½″ **25.00**
   Aleut, braided grass, braided strap, 11″ dia **200.00**
   Baleen, w/ivory bear & seal **150.00**
   Swirling stairstep design, w/lid, 12x11″ dia **165.00**
   With lid, early 1900s, 9x13″ dia **135.00**
Boat, painted, 14x5″ **65.00**
Boots, sealskin, man's, thigh-length, waterproofed seams **300.00**
Bowl oil lamp, soapstone, oblong, 13″ long **135.00**
Box, walrus ivory, scrimshaw **60.00**
Bracelet, fossilized ivory, polar bears carved in relief **120.00**
   Fossilized ivory **45.00**
Carving, bone, sled & dogs **80.00**
   Ivory, man w/gun hunting walrus, polychrome, 1890s **335.00**
   Walrus ivory, snowy owl **40.00**
Chisel, ivory, w/whale tooth set in bone handle **170.00**
Comb, bone, very old, 2¾″ long **35.00**
Cribbage board, walrus ivory, 1930s **100.00**
Cup, made from a walrus jaw bone **65.00**
Dish, drift wood, 10x14″ **60.00**
Doll, carved wood, w/skin parka, early 1900s, 5″ **75.00**
   Dressed in 5-pelt parka, felt/lace trim, w/carved knife, 11″ . . **65.00**
Fetish, bear, ivory, 1½″ **65.00**
   Fish, wood **45.00**
   Walrus, ivory, 1¼″ **45.00**
Fire-making set, curved fire-bow, drill stick & base **45.00**
Harpoon tip, ivory, double barbs each side, 3¼″ **85.00**
Lure, figural fish w/drilled eyes, iron hook, carved bone, 4″ . . . **50.00**
Mask, seal skin w/applied fur trim, 9″ **85.00**
   Whalebone, ivory teeth & eyes, baleen pupils, jade labrets . . **105.00**
   Whalebone, very old, 8¾″ **375.00**
Meat hook, bone w/ivory inset holding barb, 14½″ **185.00**
Mittens, leather, 14½″ **75.00**
Mukluks, baby's, leather, 5¼″ **18.00**
   Caribou w/fur, 34″ **325.00**
   Sealskin w/walrus hide, early 1900s, 15″ **20.00**
Napkin ring, bone, handcarved fish & bird, 2″ wide **45.00**
Netting tool, bone, notched on both ends, 4″ **15.00**
Parka, duck feather lined, full length, 1880s **800.00**
Seal retreiver, w/rope **90.00**
Sled bag, walrus, 1880s, 18″ **240.00**
Snow goggles, carved ivory, prehistoric, 1½x4½″ **350.00**
Snow knife, walrus ivory, scrimshaw ship & whale scene, 18″ . **750.00**
   Wood, 22″ **55.00**
Snow shovel, bone blade, 1900, 48″ **140.00**
Stool, 3 legs, 1890s, 5x12″ **100.00**
Storyboard, w/carved figures attached **800.00**
Tobacco container, ornate beadwork, early 1900s **98.00**
   Prehistoric, St Lawrence Island, edge chips, 6¼″ **95.00**
Umiak, miniature, gut-covered wood frame, w/4 paddles, 17″ . **200.00**
Wristguard, ivory, to protect against bowstring, 4½″ **100.00**

Fans

   The Japanese are said to have invented the fan. From there it went to China, and Portuguese traders took the idea to Europe. Though usually

considered milady's accessory, even the gentlemen in 17th century England carried fans! More fashionable than practical, some were of feathers and lovely handpainted silks with carved ivory or tortoise sticks---some French fans had peepholes. There are mourning fans, calendar fans, and those with advertising. All are collectible!

Advertising, Baker's Chocolate, folding **35.00**
   Coolerator girl, cardboard w/wood handle **15.00**
   DeCoursey Ice Cream, w/boy & girl twins picture **13.00**
   Generale Transat Lantique Steamship, 1915, signed **40.00**
   Moxie, celluloid **40.00**
   Putnam Dyes, cardboard, butterfly & Art Nouveau figures **24.00**
   Singer Sewing Machines, paper, blue w/roses **12.00**
Bone sticks, wht w/hp designs, lace trim, w/orig box **25.00**
Calendar, 1914, lacy foldout **22.00**
Celluloid, 1900 . . . . **12.00**
Cockade, red cloth, guard sticks, leather, 13x9" **24.00**
Elks, paper, 1909 . . . . **14.00**
Embroidered, Chinese dragon on silk, ivory sticks, 1830s **75.00**
   Red & blue designs on blk satin, framed, 24x14" **125.00**
   Silk, ivory sticks, butterfly mount, w/orig box **60.00**

Feathers, hp florals, tin butterfly & beads decor, 14½x9½" **25.00**
French, blk lace & silk, hp butterflies, old **110.00**
   Blk 24" ostrich plumes, MOP sticks, 1860 . . . . **185.00**
   Lacquered, w/hp ladies **145.00**
   MOP sticks, peach hp silk & lace, 1850 . . . . **135.00**
   Minuet, silk & lace, tortoise sticks, 1840 . . . . **130.00**
   Silk, 'peep' style, horn & ivory sticks, 1830 . . . . **145.00**
Ivory, carved both sides, Chinese, 18th century Brise, ornate . . **375.00**
Ivory sticks, carved, w/hp silk, old, signed **165.00**
   Hp silk, large, w/orig box **30.00**
   Hp silk, old, signed **65.00**
   Silver studded, w/hp silk, 1850 . . . . **110.00**
   With silver decor, wht silk & lace, brass hook **15.00**
   White, lace on silk, w/sequins, old, 18" wide **40.00**
Lace, wht w/embroided florals, MOP silk tassel, w/orig box **85.00**
Lacquered sticks, blk, lace & sequins, gold trim, w/matching box **125.00**
Lacquered sticks, blk, silk w/gold Oriental figures, old **110.00**
Lithographed, signed, 1909 . . . . **28.00**
Mourning, satin, ebony sticks w/carved tulips, 1870, Pa. Dutch **115.00**
Occupied Japan, bamboo & MOP, hp silk, orig silk tassel **22.00**
Organdy, black w/silver sequins, carved sticks, 8½" **35.00**
Ostrich feathers, black, tortoise sticks, dated 1850 . . . . **110.00**

Black, tortoise sticks **35.00**
Blue, framed for hanging, marroon velvet case **75.00**
Orange, tortoise sticks, old **90.00**
Pink, plastic handle, 11", w/orig box **35.00**
Simulated tortoise sticks, 9x12" **12.00**
Sky blue, tortoise sticks, 16" **50.00**
Paper, blk w/silver bird & flowering branch, 11x24" **20.00**
   Japanese motif, wood sticks, 17x9" **10.00**
   Painted floral design, bamboo sticks, 24" dia **10.00**
Peacock feathers, 10" **24.00**
   Carved teakwood, beaded tassel, 21" wide **85.00**
   Filigreed teakwood, birds & flowers, 12x20" **85.00**
Satin, ivory w/florals, feather tufts, ivory sticks, 12" **75.00**
   Painted wedding in forest scene, MOP sticks, 10" **45.00**
   Red, hp leaves & flowers, 13" **85.00**
Silk, Chinese motif, silver & gold on maroon sticks, 13½" **35.00**

Herons, embroidered, carved ivory sticks, 13" **16.00**
   Hp roses decor, wooden sticks, 14" **45.00**
   Pink & silver w/sequins, hp florals, 9x17" **30.00**
Silk & lace, large oval, black **40.00**
Silver, w/evening compact **175.00**
Victorian, silk & lace, hp child & woman **95.00**
   Hp portraits **89.00**
Wood, handcarved, folding, 1850s **30.00**

Farm Collectibles

Country living in the 19th century entailed plowing, planting, harvesting —gathering eggs and milking—making soap from rendered lard on butchering day—and numerous other tasks performed with primitive tools of which we in the 20th century have had little firsthand knowledge.

Barn decoration, iron star hex sign, orig paint, Penn., 12" . . . **115.00**
Barn peg board, hickory, Indiana Amish, 72" long, 8" pins . . . **175.00**
Bean sorter, pedal run, Saginaw, 1803 . . . . **225.00**
Beehive box, pine, dovetailed 4 corners, layered, lift lid **100.00**
Blinder, leather & iron, fits over head, Mean Mule **35.00**
Breast chains, for work horse team, pair **20.00**
Brick snugger, 1 pc wood, iron bottom, 54" long **26.00**
Bridle harness, square leather blinders, 1800s **29.00**
Buggywheels, pair, iron wheel rims & fittings, 40" dia **55.00**
Buggywhip holder, maple, iron band fastener to vehicle **25.00**
Calf muzzle, handcarved, open tube for breathing, 1870s **22.00**
Carriage step, ornate iron, slant bolted at each side **18.00**
Chicken feeder, wood, 36" long, low tray 6" wide, 3½" high . . . **32.00**
Chicken snatcher, iron rod w/hook end, wood handle, 47" overall **45.00**
Collar, leather, wood & iron singletree, for small animal **65.00**
Cornsheller, 2 14" planks w/wood peg, easel-type holder, 1700s **350.00**
Cotton bale sampler, iron hook, brass ferrule, hickory grip, 1840s **45.00**

Cutter, binder twine, homemade, wood handle, iron blade, 40" . **12.00**
    Broom corn, 10" long, 8" curved blade **65.00**
Drag hook & handforged chains, set **40.00**
Dryer, seedcorn, ci, late 1800s, 20" long **10.00**
    Seedcorn, iron, hanging eyes **18.00**
Egg carrier, folding, wire **15.00**
    Star, holds 1 dozen, 1906 . . . . **32.00**
    Wood slats & dividers, wire handle, holds 12 dozen **25.00**
Equipment seat, iron, Stoddard **47.00**
Fence stretcher, iron **19.00**
Fodder stripper, hickory, 7 carved scallops one side near top . . . **23.00**
Grain gleaner, hickory, 1 pc, curved handle, grip eye, iron teeth **85.00**
Grain measure, wooden, 2 qt, Royalston, Mass. **17.50**
Grain seed sorter stand, wood, orig red stain, tinned roller, 4 legs **150.00**
Grinding wheel, stone, 14" dia, 4" thick **45.00**
    19" dia, 2½" thick **25.00**
Grist mill pulley, wood, center stored wedges, Tennessee **98.00**
Hammer, wagon, iron **18.00**
Harness stitcher, hickory legs, hard pine seat **175.00**
Hayfork, wood, 3 prongs, handcarved, 58" **90.00**
    Wood, 6 19" prongs, hand fashioned, 62" **145.00**
Hogstretcher, hickory, handmade, Amish, 20" **28.00**
Honey press, handmade, early 1700s **500.00**
Horse collar, leather, solidly packed, late 1800s **45.00**
Horse collar hames, pair, wood, brass tips, iron fittings **80.00**
Horse collar hook **27.50**
Horse comb, bronze teeth, wood handle **28.00**
Horse scraper, wood, carved hearts, 1800s, 17" **45.00**
Horseshoe, iron, ice caulks **17.50**
Lamp, brooder, center galvanized iron, red painted side lamps . . **45.00**
Lard paddle, hickory, long handle, worn **30.00**
Lard press, Enterprise Mfg Co, Phila, USA 2092, works **85.00**
    Hickory, iron hinged serrated inside paddles, large **125.00**
    Sensible Press, MR Steere & Co **37.50**
    Small round paddles, 1890s **25.00**
Lard skimmer, handwrought iron **48.00**
Milk can, 1 gal, heavy gauge tin, wire bail **25.00**
Milk container, tinned copper, lidlock & bail, mkd deLaval . . . **300.00**
Milk strainer, tin, cheesecloth over base w/loose collar, 10" dia . **28.00**
Milking stool, hickory legs, pine seat **65.00**
    Hickory slab **55.00**
    Maple, deep saddle seat, outside grooved **95.00**
    Maple, wood pulled into handle for carrying **85.00**
    Oak, short legged, Michigan **45.00**
    Poplar, 2 boards thick, Indiana **40.00**
    Tiger maple **95.00**
Mill palette paddle, handcut wood, thumb & finger holds **25.00**
Millstone, granite, 16" dia, 5" thick, Georgia **110.00**
Mule collar, iron, early **70.00**
Planter, bulb, hand, factory made, iron & wood **25.00**
    Cabbage, hand, iron & wood, factory made **25.00**
    Potato, wood handle, 1885 . . . . **90.00**
    Seedcorn, wood/iron/tin, orig label, Champion Hand **80.00**
Saddle bags, leather **200.00**
Saltbox, calves', rosetop nails to spare rim from tongues **22.00**
Sap spigot, New England pine **23.00**
Sausage press, tin, maple stomper, 1840s, 18" long **80.00**
Seed grain separator, wood, iron jaws, crude homemade **15.00**
Seed sorter, early 1900s **125.00**
Sickle, iron, wood handle **55.00**
Silage fork, handforged tines, 34" wood handle, 1700s **185.00**
Silage knife, iron blade, adjustable hickory handles **35.00**
Snowplow, hardwood, horsedrawn, handfashioned, New England **200.00**
Snowshovel, wood, tin patch, homemade **150.00**

Stirrup, lady's, blacksmith crafted 18th century iron, heart shape **40.00**
Sugar kettle, ci, shallow, 1800s, Kelly, Kentucky, 50" dia **225.00**
Wagon, goat, hickory wood slats, iron axles & fasteners, 1880s **495.00**
    Grease bucket, oak staves, iron bands, bail, 1800s **40.00**
    Pine, carved from 1 pc wood, w/lid, rope handle, early 1800s **145.00**
    Hickory, removable stake sides, iron axles, ironbound wheels **115.00**
    Pony, old wagon green w/yellow stripes, Indiana homemade . **400.00**
    Wheels, pair, wood, 2" wide iron wheel rims, 42" dia **65.00**
Water keg, field, iron banded & handled oak staves, w/spigot . . **95.00**
Well grappling hook, iron, 1800s **35.00**
Well plug, wood, w/traces of moss, ironbound, 1800s **55.00**
Yoke, calf, bentwood over the neck, handle was the poke **40.00**
    Harness, hickory, brass studded leather ring at center **45.00**
    Oxen, orig red stain, double, complete, 1830s **275.00**
    Poplar, handcarved, for human shoulders to carry pails, 1830 . **55.00**
    Trainer, oxen, hickory, single, iron fittings, orig red stain . . . **250.00**

Fenton, See Also Carnival

    Frank and John Fenton were brothers who founded the Fenton Art Glass Co in 1906 in Martin's Ferry, Ohio. The venture was first only a decorating shop using blanks purchased from other companies. This operation soon proved unsatisfactory, and by 1907 they had constructed their own glass factory in Williamstown, West Virginia. John left the company in 1909, and organized his own firm in Millersburg.

    The Fenton Company produced over 150 patterns of carnival glass. They also made custard, chocolate, opalescent and stretch glass; and during the 20s, manufactured the colored glassware so popular during that era. Free hand, or off hand pieces introduced in 1925 were made without molds, and because the process proved to be unprofitable, the line was discontinued by '27. Even their newer glassware made in the past 25 years is already regarded as collectible. Various paper labels have been used since the 1920s; only since 1967 has the logo been stamped into the glass.

Aqua Crest, bowl, 10" **38.00**
    Bowl, triangle, crimped, #1522, 4½x9½" **24.00**
    Comport, crimped, 7" **30.00**
    Fan vase, 4" **18.50**
    Nappy, 5" **15.00**
    Nappy, double crimp, 6" **18.00**
    Plate, 8" **22.00**
    Plate, 11¼" **35.00**
    Sherbet **18.50**
    Tulip vase, 6½" **30.00**
    Tulip vase, rib bottom, 4" **27.50**
    Vase, 7" **35.00**
    Vase, 11½" **48.00**
    Vase, plain top, 9¾" **55.00**
Basket, #6437, aventurine green & blue, 1964-76, 11" **145.00**
Beaded Melon, bowl, ruffled, green overlay, 7" **35.00**
    Salt & peppers, white opal **35.00**
Bell, crimped, blue **20.00**
    Crimped, Velva Rose **20.00**
Bicentennial, bell, Patriot, Chocolate **40.00**
    Paperweight, Eagle, Chocolate **12.00**
    Planter, Patriot's, Chocolate **12.00**
    Plate, Eagle, Chocolate **18.00**
    Plate, Lafayette, Chocolate **18.00**
Block & Star, bowl w/pr candles, #5673, turquoise opaque **50.00**
Bon-bon w/dolphin handles, Jade, crimped, 6½" sq **25.00**
Bowl, #601, shallow, cupped, Pekin Blue, 1928, 11" **125.00**
    #847, Mongolian Green, flared, 7½" **45.00**
Bubble Optic, vase, #1359, Wild Rose, 1961, 11½" **180.00**
Cake plate, #3513, footed, rose pastel **45.00**

Candle bowl, #3872, black, mkd pat pending **12.50**
Candleholders, cornucopia #950, Silvertone, ruffled, 6″, pr **40.00**
Candy box, #6080, Coral, 1961 . . . . **160.00**
Candy, covered #7390WD, wht daisies on blk, 1973-74 . . . . **35.00**
Carolina Dogwood, bowl #942, Rosalene **35.00**
    Bowl, ruby irid **20.00**
Cat slipper, Daisy & Button, hair on cat, #1900, 1937 . . . . **45.00**
Chicken server, #5188, milk glass w/blk, 1953-54 . . . . **100.00**
Chou Ting ceremonial light, Rosalene **25.00**
    Ruby irid **25.00**
Chrysanthemum, bowl, marigold irid, 3 toed, 1914, 11″ **72.00**
Closed petal tulip bowl, lilac, #552, no ped **75.00**
Coin Dot, chandelier, 3 globes, French opal, brass **125.00**
    Hat, #1922, French opal, 6x8″ **50.00**
    Hat, white, 3½″ **24.00**
    Perfume, #92, blue **35.00**

Pitcher, 8½″ **80.00**
Vase, #189, blue, 10″ **65.00**
Vase, #1450, white, 5″ **22.00**
Vase, #1925, white, 8″ **45.00**
Vase, bottle shape, white, 6″ **22.00**
Console set, #950, cornucopia, royal blue, 1934 . . . . **120.00**
Curtain, bowl, Rosalene **28.00**
Daisy & Button, fan vase, #1900, Emerald Green, 10″ **45.00**
    Fan vase, blue, 8″ **38.00**
    Fan vase, pastel green, 8″ **38.00**
Dancing Lady, comport, crystal, 8½″ **45.00**
Diamond & Rib, swing vase, carnival, 11½″ **22.00**
Diamond Lace, bowl, ruffled, opal blue, 10½″ **40.00**
    Cake stand, blue opal, 13″ **35.00**
    Console bowl & candles, white **45.00**
Diamond Optic, bowl, low dolphin foot, pink, 9″ **35.00**
    Comport, green pastel, 6¾″ **25.00**
    Goblet, #1502, royal blue, 1928, 7″ **25.00**
    Salt shaker, ruby **35.00**
    Server w/dolphin center handle, pink **48.00**
    Vase, #1720, blue, 7½″ **48.00**
Dolphin bowl, #1502, flared, aquamarine Diamond Optic, 1927 . **42.00**
    #1608, Jade, 10½″ **65.00**
    Chinese Yellow, low, 1931, 11½″ **115.00**
    Footed, Jade **77.00**
    Persian Blue w/tooling in mold, 1933 . . . . **250.00**
Dolphin candlesticks, #1623, Wisteria, 1930, pr **38.00**
Dot Optic, bottle vase, yellow, 7″ **30.00**

Bowl, triangle, blue, 7″ **35.00**
Hurricane shade, turquoise opal, wht swirl candle base **75.00**
Pitcher, French opal w/blue handle, 1929 . . . . **100.00**
Elephant, #618, Jade Green, 1929 . . . . **225.00**
Emerald Crest, bowl, 7½″ **22.50**
    Comport, 7″ **30.00**
    Fan vase, 4″ **18.50**
    Plate, 8″ **18.50**
    Plate, 12″ **45.00**
    Plate, 1951, 10½″ **35.00**
    Vase, low, squat, 4″ **24.00**
Empress, vase, Pekin Blue **75.00**
Epergne, 4 pc, Hobnail, white milk glass, 6½x8″ **30.00**
    Plum opal Hobnail, 3 lilies, sm, 1960 . . . . **150.00**
    Rose pastel Hobnail, 3 lilies, sm, 1954-56 . . . . **75.00**
    Hobnail, Lime Sherbert **12.50**
Fentons, basket candleholders, royal blue, 1933 . . . . **55.00**
Fish vase, #5156, blk w/milk eyes, 1953, 6½″ **150.00**
Five Petal Dogwood, basketweave vase #9324, blue **40.00**
    Comport, #7429, blue **45.00**
Georgian, candlesticks, ruby, 1931, pr **72.00**
    Cocktail, amber, 3½″ **12.00**
    Decanter w/stopper, 6 glasses, #1611, 1931 . . . . **200.00**
    Goblet, pink, 5½″ **17.00**
    Plate, ruby, 6″ **3.00**
    Shaker, cobalt **24.00**
    Sherbet, low, cobalt **10.00**
    Sherbet, tall, red **12.50**
Gold Crest, bowl, 10½″ **32.50**
    Bowl, 14″ **45.00**
    Cake plate, 12″ **20.00**
    Candles, 5½″, pr **38.50**
    Cornucopia candles, 6″, pr **38.50**
    Epergne, petal, 5½″ **15.00**
    Vase, 6″ **30.00**
    Vase, #36, 4″ **25.00**
    Vase, sq, 5″ **20.00**
Hanging Heart, basket, blue & black, illus **135.00**
    Footed bowl, #3026, turquoise, 1928 . . . . **300.00**

Vase, pinched sides, ruffled **90.00**
Happiness Bird, Rosalene **20.00**

Hat vase, #1922, Peachblow, 1940-41, 19″ **100.00**
Hobnail, 3 part relish, crystal **5.00**
  Basket, turquoise pastel, 7″ **35.00**
  Bon-bon, #3937, white opal, 7″ **12.50**
  Bon-bon, blue opal, 3½″ **10.00**
  Bowl, crimped, sq, blue opal, 4½″ **9.50**
  Bowl, deep, yellow opal, 6½″ **22.00**
  Bowl, footed, yellow opal, 8″ **30.00**
  Bowl, green pastel, 10″ **40.00**
  Bowl, lime opal, 5½″ **28.50**
  Bowl, triangle, blue opal, 6″ **10.00**
  Bowl, white opal, 11″ **22.00**
  Candleholders, #3870, cranberry **32.50**
  Candles, amber, 3½″ pr **20.00**
  Candy w/lid, footed, turquoise **80.00**
  Compote, blue opal, 6″ **40.00**
  Cornucopia candles, white opal, 3½″, pr **16.00**
  Cornucopia vase, blue opal, 6″ **35.00**
  Cruet w/stopper, blue opal **28.00**
  Cruet w/stopper, white opal **22.00**
  Fan vase, blue opal, 8″ **45.00**
  Fan vase, white opal, 6″ **22.00**
  Flip vase, blue opal, 8½″ **45.00**
  Goblet, blue opal, 5″ **18.00**
  Individual cream, blue opal, 3¼″ **12.50**
  Individual creamer, milk glass **6.00**
  Individual sugar, blue opal, 3¼″ **12.50**
  Lamp, bottle, blue opal, 6½″ **20.00**
  Mustard w/lid & spoon, blue opal **18.00**
  Mustard w/lid, milk glass **8.00**
  Mustard w/lid, white opal **15.00**
  Nappy, Peachblow, 6″ **18.00**
  Nappy, blue opal, 5″ **15.00**
  Pitcher, w/4 juices, milk glass, 5″ **15.00**
  Plate, round, blue opal, 8″ **18.50**
  Plate, square, blue opal, 5½″ **12.00**
  Plate, sq, blue opal, 8½″ **25.00**
  Pot, green pastel, 4″ **15.00**
  Salt & pepper, blue opal **28.00**
  Salt & pepper, cranberry, pr **38.50**
  Shakers, red, pr **45.00**
  Sherbet, blue, 4″ **15.00**
  Slipper, yellow optic, 6″ **28.00**
  Sugar #3, blue opal **18.00**
  Sugar, ruffled, white opal, 3″ **12.50**
  Tumbler, #3947, 12 oz, cranberry **22.00**
  Tumbler, flat, white opal, 4″ **15.00**
  Tumbler, flat, white opal, 6″ **16.00**
  Tumbler, footed, blue opal, 6″ **15.00**
  Tumbler, footed, white opal, 6″ **13.00**
  Underplate, blue opal, 5¾″ **9.50**
  Underplate, yellow opal, 5¾″ **7.00**
  Vase, #389, lime opal, 6″ **35.00**
  Vase, #3850, blue opal, 4½″ **25.00**
  Vase, Peachblow, 6¾″ **35.00**
  Vase, blue opal, 3½″ **18.00**
  Vase, clear cranberry, 5½″ **35.00**
  Vase, clear green, 6″ **18.00**
  Vase, footed, dusty rose, 4″ **23.00**
  Vase, lime opal, 5½″ **35.00**
  Vase, triangle top, yellow opal **24.00**
  Vase, yellow opal, 5½″ **30.00**
  Wine, blue opal, 4″ **15.00**
Honeycomb, vase, cased satin butterscotch, 8½″ **85.00**

Vase, cased satin, blue, 8½″ **85.00**
Hurricane shade, Peachblow, 9¾″ **45.00**
Independence, comport, Jefferson, blue **65.00**
  Paperweight, Eagle, blue **12.00**
  Plate, Eagle, blue **12.00**
Ivory Crest, vase, #201, square, 5″ **45.00**
Jacqueline, salt & pepper, #160, powder blue, 1961 . . . . **35.00**
Lamp base, sq marble base, round font, 10x7″ **60.00**
Lavabo, #3867, turquoise pastel **175.00**
Lincoln Inn, champagne, pink **9.50**
  Juice, footed, red **15.00**
  Water goblet, pink, 6″ **15.00**
Lovebird vase, #8258, custard satin, 1975-76 . . . . **15.00**
Macaroon jar, #1681 Big Cookies, Ebony **125.00**
Mandarin & Empress vases, Jade, pr **40.00**
Ming, candles, #349, crystal, pr **30.00**
  Candles, #1800 Sheffield, crystal, pr **35.00**
Nativity scene fairy light, Antique Blue, 1980 . . . . **25.00**
Nut bowl, orange tree, 3 ftd, Rosalene **35.00**
Overlay, basket, pink, 11x10½″ **75.00**
  Bowl, #711, white over gold, 1949, 7″ **28.00**
  Bowl, blue, 7″ **25.00**
  Bowl, pink, 10″ **35.00**
  Bowl, rose, 7″ **25.00**
  Jug, #192, blue, 5″ **42.50**
  Tulip vase, #711, beaded melon, gold, 1949, 6″ **35.00**
  Vase, #192, blue, 5″ **25.00**
  Vase, #192, blue, 6″ **24.00**
  Vase, #376, ruby, 6″ **35.00**
  Vase, globe #192, blue, 5x6″ **29.00**
  Vase, rose, 5½″ **35.00**
Owl fairy light, lavender satin **12.50**
Peach Crest, bowl, 10½″ **45.00**
  Candy jar, open, #1522, 1940-41 . . . . **100.00**
  Cornucopia vase, #1523, 1941 . . . . **100.00**
  Jug, #192, 8½″ **55.00**
  Tulip vase, 8½″ **45.00**
  Tulip vase, like #320 . . . . **36.00**
  Vase, #192, 6½″ **35.00**
  Vase, #7254, 4½″ **35.00**
  Vase, Beaded Melon, 6″ **25.00**
  Vase, cornucopia, #1523, 1941 . . . . **100.00**
Persian Medallion, basket, ruby irid **30.00**
  Bon-bon, w/handle, aqua w/gold irid, 1912 . . . . . . **100.00**
Petticon Crest, comport, covered, silver, 6″ **35.00**
  Cornucopia candles, silver, pr **25.00**
  Creamer & sugar, aqua **50.00**
  Fan vase, aqua, 6½″ **15.00**
  Heart shape relish, wht/red **25.00**
  Nut dish, footed, silver, 4″ **7.50**
Pineapple, goblet, pink **22.00**
Pink Blossom, candy, footed, w/cover **24.00**
Plymouth, basket, ruby w/metal handle, 1933-34 . . . . . . **125.00**
  Sherbet, amber **8.00**
  Sherbet, red, 4″ **12.50**
  Water goblet, red, 5½″ **15.00**
  Wine goblet, red, 4″ **18.00**
Polka Dot, tulip vase, #2250, cranberry opal, 1955, 8″ . . **65.00**
Praying Boy & Girl, Jade Green, pr **17.50**
Priscilla, bowl, flared, blue, 11″ **25.00**
  Sherbet, blue **15.00**
Prism Band, tankard, Florentine Green, 1924 . . . . **350.00**
  Tumbler, no pattern, painted **52.00**
Rib Optic, bottle w/stopper, #667, cranberry, 13½″ **70.00**

Rose Crest, bowl, 7" **18.50**
  Nappy, 6" **12.00**
  Vase, 7" **25.00**
  Vase, 11½" **48.50**
  Vase, #36 . . . . **25.00**
September Morn Nymph, w/frog, ruby, 1933-36 . . . . **150.00**
  Frog, Rose Crest, milk glass bowl **175.00**
  Hobnail bowl, pink **95.00**
  Jade, frog, candles, closed petal tulip bowl **200.00**
Sheffield, vase, #1800, amber, 1936, 6¼" **30.00**
Silver Crest, basket, 4¾" **18.50**
  Bowl, 6" **8.50**
  Candles, 5¾", pr **22.00**
  Comport, 8" **18.50**
  Heart shape bowl w/1 handle, 6¾" **22.00**
  Triangle hat, 3¾" **15.00**
  Vase, 6½" **15.00**
Silver Turquoise Crest, cake plate, footed, 13" **38.50**
  Comport, 6¾" **24.00**
  Plate, 8½" **18.50**
Slipper, rose pastel, Hobnail, 1954-55 . . . . **20.00**
Snow Crest, hurricane lamp, iron base, #170, cranberry **65.00**
  Planter, #401, Emerald Green, 1951-55 . . . . **75.00**
  Vase, #1925, amber, 8¾" **55.00**
  Vase, #3004, cranberry, 1949 . . . . **65.00**
  Vase, #3005, amber, 7½" **45.00**
  Vase, ruby overlay, 1951, 7½" **35.00**
  Vase, spiral optic, #1925, crimped, azure, 4x9" **35.00**
Spiral Optic, vase, cranberry opal, 12" **120.00**
Spiral, rose bowl, #201, blue opal **55.00**
  Vase, Blue Ridge, tall w/bulbous base, 7½" **65.00**
Stretch, candlesticks, #8, braid, Jade, pr **75.00**
  Candlesticks, pink, 4" pr **27.00**
  Fan vase, blue, 8" **32.50**
  Fan vase, etched ship, blue **95.00**
  Lemon dish w/center handle, yellow **37.50**
  Server w/center handle, vaseline **32.00**
Sung Ko, bowl, #152, 1934-35 . . . . **250.00**
Swan, open, Rosalene **20.00**
Tumbler, #1933, cobalt, 4" **12.50**
Vase, #184, Wisteria etching, 1938, 11½" **45.00**
  #379, crimped, French opal, 6x6¾" **29.00**
  #621, Mongolian green, flared, 8" **45.00**
  #6459, rose w/aventurine gr, Vasa Murrhina, 1960s, 14" **150.00**
  Dolphin handles, Jade, 6" **35.00**
Vintage, bowl, #466, blue opal, 8¾" **50.00**
  Fern dish, Chocolate, 1910 . . . . **195.00**
Water Lily bowl, 3 ftd, Rosalene **45.00**
Water pitcher, #465, blue mist, Vasa Murrhina, 1964 . . . . **175.00**
Waterlily & Cattails, bowl, amethyst opal, 1908 . . . . . . **60.00**
Wine decanter, 6 wine glasses, ribbed, cranberry opal **300.00**
Wriskey bottle, orig stopper, cranberry opal **75.00**

Ferrandiz Figurines

Artist Juan Ferrandiz designes the figurines, bells, ornaments, music boxes and bells that are sculped by carvers at the world's most renowned woodcarving workshop, Anri, in St. Ulrich, Italy. Discontinued or retired editions often bring many times their original price on the secondary market.

Cowboy, 3" **70.00**
Cowboy & Harvest Girl, set, ltd, 6" **1,000.00**
Drummer Boy, 3" **95.00**
Drummer Boy, 6" **150.00**

First Blossom, 6" **90.00**
Freedom Bound, 6" **225.00**
Friends, 6" **200.00**
Friendship, 3" **50.00**
Girl in Egg, 6" **200.00**
Girl w/Rooster, 3" **75.00**
Going Home, 3" **80.00**
Going Home, 6" **110.00**
Good Shepherd, 6" **110.00**
Greetings, 6" **399.00**
Happy Strummer, 6" **100.00**
Happy Wanderer, 6" **125.00**
Harvest Girl, 3" **50.00**
He's My Brother, 3" **60.00**
High Riding, 10" **279.00**
Jolly Piper, 1981, 6" **130.00**
Leading the Way, 6" **300.00**
Love Gift, 3" **46.00**
Love Gift, 6" **175.00**
Melody for Two, 1981, ltd, 6" **135.00**
Merry Melody, 1981, 6" **130.00**
Musical Basket, 3" **65.00**
Nature Girl, 6" **180.00**
Night, Night, 6" **100.00**
Peace Pipe, 3" **65.00**
Reverence, old mark, 6" **130.00**
Rock-a-Bye, 6" **200.00**
Romeo, 3" **115.00**
Spreading the Word, 6" **165.00**
Spring Arrival, ltd, 20" **1,250.00**
Spring Arrival, 10" **435.00**
Spring Arrivals, 6" **125.00**
Spring Dance, 24" **2,900.00**
Stepping Out, 3" **45.00**
Stepping Out, 6" **100.00**
Stitch in Time, 6" **100.00**
Stolen Kiss **215.00**
Sugar Heart (Baker), 6" **400.00**
Sweet Arrival Pink, 6" **170.00**
Sweet Arrival Blue, 3" **150.00**
Talking to the Animals, 20" **1,740.00**
Talking to the Animals, 3" **40.00**
Talking to the Animals, 6" **125.00**
Tender Moments, 6" **345.00**
The Adoration, 6" **220.00**
The Bouquet, 3" **85.00**
The Chorale, 6" **120.00**
The Helper, 6½" **175.00**
The Poor Boy, 3" **50.00**
The Quintet, 6" **125.00**
The Stray, 6" **125.00**
Threadbare, 3" **60.00**
Tiny Sounds, 1981, 6" **120.00**
Trumpeter, 6" **125.00**
Umpapa, 4" **125.00**
Wonderlust, 6" **125.00**
Rock-a-Bye, 3" **67.00**

Fiesta

Fiesta is a line of dinnerware produced by the Homer Laughlin China Co., of Newell, West Virginia, from 1936 until l973. It was made in 11 different solid colors, with over fifty pieces in the assortment. The pattern was developed by Frederic Rhead, an English Stoke-on-Trent potter who was

an important contributor to the art pottery movement in this country during the early part of the century. The design was carried out through the use of a simple band of rings device near the rim. Fiesta Red, a strong red-orange glaze color, was made with depleted uranium oxide. It was more expensive to produce than the other colors, and sold at higher prices. Today's collectors still pay premium prices for Fiesta Red pieces.

During the '50s the color assortment was grey, rose, chartreuse and medium green. These colors are relatively harder to find, and along with Fiesta Red will usually command prices at least 25% higher than those listed below.

Fiesta Kitchen Kraft was introduced in 1939; it consisted of 17 pieces of kitchenware such as pie plates, refrigerator sets, mixing bowls and covered jars, in four popular Fiesta colors.

As a final attempt to adapt production to modern day techniques and methods, Fiesta was restyled in 1969. Of the original colors, only Fiesta Red remained. This line, called Fiesta Ironstone, was discontinued in 1973.

Two types of marks were used, an inkstamp on machine jiggered pieces, and an indented mark molded into the holloware pieces.

Ashtray 15.00
    Advertising 30.00
    Ironstone 5.00
Bread and butter, 7" 3.00
Bud vase 23.00
Cake plate, 10" 55.00
Calendar plate, 1954, 10" 18.00
    1955, 10" 24.00
Candleholder, bulb, pr 24.00
    Tripod, pr 75.00
Carafe, 3 pt 45.00
Casserole, Ironstone, w/cover 12.00
    Med green or 50s colors 38.00
    With cover 30.00
Chop plate, 12" 12.00
    15" 15.00
    Decal decor, 15" 33.50
    Turkey decal, 13" 50.00
    With metal handle, 13" 32.00
Coffee mug, Ironstone 4.50

Coffee pot, regular 33.00
Coffee server, Ironstone 14.00
Compartment plate, 10½" 10.00

11½" 12.00
Comport, 12" 32.00
Cream soup cup, med green 17.00
Creamer, individual, red 32.00
    Individual, turquoise 60.00
    Ironstone 3.00
    Regular 6.00
    Stick handle 8.50
Deep plate, 8" 12.00
Demitasse cup & saucer 20.00
    50s colors 40.00
    Red 24.00
Demitasse pot 65.00
Dessert bowl, 6" 9.00
    Med green, 6" 22.00
Dessert plate, 6" 2.50
Dinner plate, 10" 8.00
Egg cup 18.00
    Lazarus 25.00
Fiestawood, bowl 40.00
    Hors d'oeuvre tray 45.00
    Lazy Suzan, 20" 42.00
    Tray, 16½" 35.00
French casserole, yellow 78.00
Fruit bowl, 4¾" 6.50
    11¾" 55.00
    Ironstone, sm 3.50
    Med green, 4¾" 22.00
Gravy boat 13.00
Ice pitcher, 2 qt 22.50
Individual salad bowl, 7¾ 22.00
Jug, 2 pt 17.00

Kitchen Kraft
Cake plate 22.00
Casserole, 7½" 40.00
    7½" 40.00
    8½" 40.00
    Individual 45.00

Covered jug, either size 75.00
Covered refrigerator jars, mix colors 55.00
Fork 32.00
Jar, covered, large 78.00
    Covered, med 75.00
    Covered, small 76.00
Metal holder for: casserole 16.50
Metal holder for: pie plate, 10" 13.00
Metal holder for: platter 16.50
Mixing bowl, 10" 35.00
    6" 18.00
    8" 32.00
Pie plate, 10" 25.00

9"	27.00
Platter, oval, 13"	40.00
Salt & pepper, pr	37.00
Server	35.00
Spoon	30.00
Lamp base, fabricated body, any type	75.00
Luncheon, 9"	5.00
Marmalade, Ironstone	22.00
Metal holder for cream soup, jam set	25.00
Jug & tumblers	30.00
Juice set	17.00
Marmalade	25.00
Mustard & marmalade	40.00
Nappy, 9½"	8.00
Salt, pepper & mustard	30.00
Mug, advertising	18.00
Mustard	45.00
Nappy, 9½"	12.00
8½	10.00
Nappy, Ironstone, large	6.00
Nested bowl, #1, 5"	18.50
#2, 6"	13.00
#3, 7"	18.00
#4, 8"	21.00
#5, 9"	25.00
#6, 10"	28.00
#7, 11"	38.00
Nested bowl lid, any size	36.00
Onion soup bowl	78.00
Turquoise or red, illus	108.00
Pitcher, dish, 2 qt	22.00
Disk, Ironstone	10.00
Juice, 30 oz, yellow	9.00
Juice, 30 oz red or gray	40.00
Plate, 10", Causal	9.00
7", Casual	7.00
Ironstone, 7"	2.00
Dinner, Ironstone, 10"	3.50
Platter, oval, 12"	13.00
Oval, Casual	20.00
Oval, Ironstone, 13"	6.00
Relish tray	60.00
Decal floral decoration	45.00
Salad bowl, Ironstone	9.00
Any color but yellow, 9½"	60.00
Footed	68.00
Yellow, 9½"	28.00
Salt & pepper, pr	9.00
Sauceboat, Ironstone	5.50
Sauceboat, Ironstone, other colors	12.00
Sauceboat, Ironstone, red	35.00
Saucer	2.00
Casual	6.00
Ironstone	1.00
Shakers, Ironstone, pr	5.00
Sit 'n Sip sets	26.00
Sta-Brite stainless steel flatware, 3 pc place setting	6.50
Sugar, cover	9.00
Cover, Ironstone	4.00
Sugar, creamer and tray, individual, yellow, navy blue	50.00
Sweets comport	16.00
Syrup pitcher	67.00
Tablecloth and napkins	30.00

Tea cup	12.00
Ironstone	4.00
Teapot, large, illus	30.00
Med	27.00
Ironstone	11.00
With metal dripolator insert	45.00
Tidbit tray, 3 tier	38.00
Tom & Jerry mug	20.00
In red	40.00
Tumbler, 10 oz	20.00
Juice, 5 oz, 6 orig colors & rose	12.00
Juice, 5 oz, other colors	27.00
Utility tray	12.00
Vase, 8"	83.00
10"	120.00
12"	140.00

Findlay Onyx

Findlay, Ohio, was the location of the Dalzell, Gilmore and Leighton Glass Company. Their most famous ware, Onyx, is very rare. It was produced in 1889, in several colors---cream, rose, raspberry and amber among them---developed by layering two or three compatible shades together. Lustre trapped between the layers accented the dainty pattern. Heavy losses were incurred in the manufacturing process, and it was made for only a short time.

Bowl, 2¾x8"	750.00
Butter w/cover, 6x5"	850.00
Celery, 6"	485.00
Creamer & covered sugar, excellent color	850.00
Pitcher, silver onyx, cream, 8"	900.00
Salt shaker, cream	245.00
Spooner, raspberry	435.00
Sugar shaker, original top, platinum worn	475.00
Silver decor, no top	260.00
Sugar w/cover	650.00
Syrup, metal pourer, 7"	700.00
Toothpick, cream	150.00
Tumbler, barrel shape, platinum lustre florals, 3"	295.00

Fire-fighting Collectibles

Fire-fighting collectibles from the early 19th century reflect the feeling of pride the men felt for their brigades and for their roll as volunteer fire fighters. Dress uniforms and fancy helmets recall the charisma of the unit on parade; the leather buckets, blown glass, liquid-filled fire extinguishers and brass hatchets serve as reminders of their heroism and dedication to their calling.

In the 1860's, volunteer units were replaced by municipal fire departments. Equipment evolved from horse drawn wagons and bucket brigades to fire engines with sirens and water wagons with hoses. Today, many collectors find a fascination with these fire-fighting relics of the past.

Alarm, "Fire Alarm Station No 432", w/internal alarm	80.00
Round, 8½" dia	18.00
With watch box, ci, pat'd March 31, 1908, oval	28.00
Alarm box, iron, Gamewell, 17"	95.00
Alarm information card, paste board w/metal borders, colorful	30.00
Alarm system, Gamewell box, tape system, bell, 2 keys	315.00
Ax, early parade model	125.00
Hooked handle	129.00
Axes, pair, painted, "Ladder 1"	65.00
Badge, Boston type, "Quincy FD", city seal, chrome plated	30.00
Metropolitan FD type, die struck, "Greenbush", gold plated, 1860s	75.00

NYFD, 1860s **50.00**
With 3″ Maltese Cross, 2 wire loops on back, 1880s **24.00**
Bell, alarm, brass w/iron back, 11″ dia **95.00**
American La France **300.00**
With transformer, "Edwards 1872", D.C., 10″ **15.00**
Belt, "Columbia-We Yield To None", black leather **60.00**
"Progress-2", white leather, 42″ **40.00**
"Protection", black leather, red & wht trim, 40″ **115.00**
"Rescue-3", black leather, spanner wrench **80.00**
Book, Our Firemen, Costello **100.00**
Bucket, "Ezra Wheeler, 1806-No 2 Providence", decorated ... **250.00**
Leather, 1875 .... **195.00**
Leather, painted black, 14″ w/handle **95.00**
Leather, with decorations, missing handle **170.00**
Leather, with Italian designs, 1700s **350.00**
Pair, "Varrell, 1812", green & gold, 13″ w/handle **1800.00**
"Phoenix" painted scene, some deterioration **645.00**
Plain w/name **125.00**
With fire scene **500.00**
Catalogue, LaFrance Equipment, 1910 .... **35.00**
LaFrance Fire Engine Equipment, 1919 .... **16.00**
Steam fire engines **75.00**
Certificate, NYFD, framed, 1830 .... **200.00**
Coloring book, Fire Department, 1910 .... **50.00**
Engine light, 6 sided engraved glass **1,000.00**
Extinguisher, "Badgers", 2½ gal, copper & brass, 24″ **28.00**
"Badgers Pony", copper & brass, 1¼ gal **80.00**
Chemical, "Pat Aug 12, 1873", extra nozzles **130.00**
Dry Chemical **32.00**

Glass, light bulb shape, hangs from ceiling, early **20.00**
Kent, grass, 21″ gauge **24.00**
Red Comet, salesman's sample **80.00**
"Rex", 2½ gal, copper & brass, 24″ **28.00**
Sireen, cardboard **14.00**
Fire bag, "M Parry Jones, FFS 1789", 43x39″ **525.00**
Fire mark, carved wood, 1 pc oval, black on white, 8½x11¼″ **450.00**
Cast iron, F.A. **125.00**
Cast iron, Greentree **400.00**
Fire marks, lot of 4, cast, all different **60.00**
Fire torch, nickel plated brass, 1800s **775.00**
Fireman's gear, slicker & boots **10.00**
Frock coat, blue wool, 1850s, 12 F.D. buttons **100.00**
Game, Fighting the Flames, old **100.00**
Gong, oak case w/brass bell, "Pat June 7, 1881", Gamewell ... **470.00**
Grenade, brown glass, "Hasletons", handle intact, ½ gal **105.00**
Clear glass, diamond design, pint, Hayward **89.00**
Glass, "Hardens Hand Grenades", w/star, Pint, 6½″ **125.00**

Red Comet, clear, w/wall bracket **15.00**
Hat, leather, eagle on top **85.00**
Parade, leather, Palmer Hose #1, 1845, Kinderhook **250.00**
Parade, painted scene **1,750.00**
Hatchets, lot of 3, all different **60.00**
Helmet, Austrian **195.00**
English, brass **178.00**
"Firemans Active Philadelphia", high eagle, red leather **385.00**
French dress, brass **270.00**
French, brass **165.00**
German, black **177.00**
Leather, 1880s, eagle finial **155.00**
Leather, black, high eagle, missing hat plate **100.00**
Leather, firemen shield holder, Washington/Hartford **315.00**
Leather, high eagle holder, "Chief AFD" **145.00**
Leather w/animal finial **175.00**
Leather w/eagle finial **135.00**
Leather w/fireman finial **150.00**
Leather, with presentation plate **200.00**
Helmet parade torch, nickel plated on wire yoke gimble, 1870s **100.00**
Helmet patch, old **40.00**
Holder, for play pipe nozzle, brass/iron, w/leather strap **50.00**
Hose rack, ci, red & green paint, 19x10″, w/hose **155.00**
Hose reel, aluminum, 14″ dia **15.00**
Indicator, Gamewell, w/15″ gong **1,500.00**
Journal, NYFD, 1875 .... **30.00**
Lantern, brass & copper, nickel plated, 19″ **360.00**
Brass, #39 Fire Dept. **250.00**
Engraved globe **350.00**
Nickel plated brass, 1899 .... **65.00**
Painted silver, Dietz Fire King **115.00**
Wagon style, brass font, Dietz **165.00**
Lantern carrying pole, wood w/wrought iron hook, 1800s **125.00**
Life net, all rope **105.00**
Log book, Boston Fire Dept, Jan 7-April 14, 1904 .... **40.00**
Nozzle, brass, 1′ **15.00**
Brass, 3′ **75.00**
Brass, AJ Morse & Son, Boston, 15¼″ **45.00**
Pair, copper & brass, 20″ **125.00**
Pair, play pipe, copper & brass, 27″ **145.00**
With adaptor, US Rubber Co, 10″ **35.00**
Wooster Brass, 10″ **30.00**
Parade pennant, 1800s **117.00**
Parade shirt, wool, flap front, covered buttons, 1860s **125.00**
Patches, lot of 80, different fire companies **65.00**
Photograph, firemen on parade, 1870s, 8½x5″ **40.00**
"North & South Watch...Liverpool Fire Dept", 6x8″ **50.00**
Pair, Portland, Maine company w/Casco Steamer #5 ...... **160.00**
Steamer, hose cart & firemen, walnut frame **135.00**
Powder flask, made w/fire hose, wooden ends **40.00**
Print, Currier & Ives, Always Ready **250.00**
Puzzle, sectional steamer **50.00**
Rattle, wood, 11″ long **80.00**
Repeater, brass mechanism, glass case, marble base, 33x13″ **1,050.00**
Sheet music, Midnight Fire Alarm **20.00**
Sheet music, Zepher Quick Step, 1850s **60.00**
Spot light, for truck, nickeled brass, 12½″ dia, Gray & Davis . **160.00**
Sprinkler head, 1911 .... **7.50**
Steam Engine, Cole Bros, Southbridge No 1 .... **25,000.00**
Steam Gauge, Stutz Fire Engine, chrome, 5″ dia **60.00**
Tape Alarm System, arrow punch, key **50.00**
Tape Alarm System, ticker tape, round punch, key **105.00**
Truck markers, lot of 6 .... **30.00**
Trumpet, brass, copper trim, 16″ **435.00**

Plain brass, 18″	350.00
Presentation, brass, rough but orig, 16½″	560.00
Silver plated, engraved, 23″	750.00
Speaking, collapsible, brass, 13″	850.00
Speaking, silver plated, 21″, 1857	2,600.00
Turnout coat, heavy rubber, corduroy lined, NYFD, 1930s	65.00
Uniform, dress, Niagara Fire Co	315.00
Weather vane, wrought iron, fireman w/bucket & torch	470.00

Fire Marks

During the early 18th century, insurance companies used fire marks, or signs of insurance to indicate to the volunteer fire fighters which homes were covered by their company. Handsome rewards were promised to the brigade that successfully extinguished the blaze, so competition was fierce between rivals, and sometimes resulted in an altercation at the scene to settle the matter of which brigade would be the one to fight the fire!

Fire marks were originally made of cast iron or lead; later examples were sometimes tin or zinc. They were used abroad as well as in this country, and those from England tended to be much more elaborate.

When municipal fire departments were organized in 1865-70, the volunteer departments and fire marks became obsolete.

English, Royal, copper	40.00
Royal Exchange, lead	75.00
Sun, copper	35.00
Lead	60.00
United States, Aetna, tin	125.00
Continental, tin	75.00
Eagle, Cincinnati, ci	600.00

Fire Association, ci	115.00
Hartford, tin	110.00
Hope Mutual, zinc	180.00
Lumbermans, ci	135.00
Phoenix, tin	90.00
Protector, copper, 1825	175.00
St Louis Mutual, zinc	160.00
United Firemen, ci	125.00

Fireplace Implements

In the colonial days of our country, fireplaces provided heat in the winter, and were used year round to cook food in the kitchen. The implements that were a necessary part of these functions are varied and are treasured collectibles today, many put to new use in modern homes as decorative accessories. Gypsy pots may hold magazines; copper and brass kettles, newly polished and gleaming, contain dried flowers or green plants. Firebacks, highly ornamental iron panels that once reflected heat and protected masonry walls, are now sometimes used as well decorations.

By Victorian times, the cookstove had replaced the kitchen fireplace, and many of these early utensils were already obsolete. But as a source of heat and comfort the fireplace continued to be used for several more decades.

Andirons, blacksmith, drawn open ring finials, early 1800s, pair	195.00
Brass, 14″	85.00
Brass, 15½″	95.00

Brass, 30″	275.00
Brass, ball top, 15½″	185.00
Brass, ball top w/bulbous ring turned shaft, arched legs	220.00
Brass, vase shaped baluster, hollow ball finial, 1800s	125.00
Brass, w/ball top & feet, 17″	165.00
Bronze, urn w/flame, 12″	10.00
Christmas tree figural, ci w/brass balls, 13″	65.00
Cast iron, caricature of black colonial couple, 16½″	585.00
George Washington figural, ci, 20″	195.00
Hessian soldier figural, ci, early 1800s, 19¾″	900.00
Iron rams heads, 12″ log space, 1700s, pair	325.00
Steeple top, paw feet, 22″	125.00
Bellows, oak, hp, 20″	32.00
Ornate, French, cast brass nozzle	24.00
Turtle top, painted, stencilled decor, 1850s, 19″	135.00
Bucket, brass, swinging bail handle, mid-1800s	90.00
Cinder box, oak w/tin liner	85.00
Fire back, ci, basket of flowers & scrollwork decor, 18x28″	115.00
Fire dogs, brass, Victorian, pair	65.00
Fire fender, brass, 10x14x42″	185.00
Brass, molded base w/lion head corners, 1880s	200.00
Fireback, full length gentleman, castle background, ci	55.00
Scene of hunting dogs, cattails, ducks, ci, 27x21″	190.00
Fireplace, wht marble, 1800, 50x72″	500.00
Frame, mythological creatures in relief, ci, w/door, small	135.00
Ornate, ci, w/door	125.00
Kettle shelf, wrought iron, openwork shelf w/good details	75.00
Mantel, carved floral side columns, oak, VG	200.00
Pine w/old paint, Federal, 61x62½″	70.00
Oven peel, iron, ram's horn shaped handle	85.00
Wrought iron, handle w/button terminus, 45″	45.00
Oven, tinned sheeted iron, bonnet shape, iron frame legs	75.00
Pan, handled, round bottom, 3 legs, ci, early 1800s, 8″ dia	95.00
Pan, round bottom, 3 legs, ci, 15x8x3″	80.00

Pastry iron, Norwegian, long-handled, ornate, 1800s **100.00**
Screen, copper, 31″ **100.00**
Spatula, wrought iron, round & flattened shaft, late 1700s, 14″. **48.00**
Toaster, iron worked in artistic shapes **255.00**
   Iron, plain **125.00**
Toasting fork, 3-tine, diamond-tapered shaft, late 1700s **65.00**
Tongs, hand forged **30.00**
   Primitive, ci, 10″ **6.50**
Tool Set, brass, steeple tops, poker, tongs & stand **145.00**
Trammel, chain, w/kettle & meat holders, handforged, 1700s .. **350.00**
   Chain, wrought iron, 3 links varying from 5-18″, 77″ **65.00**
   Iron, sawtooth cooking extention, handforged, 1700s **285.00**
Trivet, iron, heart shape w/3 feet **125.00**
   wrought iron, triangular, 18″ sides, 7″ high **45.00**

Fischer

Fine porcelain has been produced in the Herend area of Hungary since the late 18th century. In 1839, Moritz Fischer founded a pottery that continues today to produce hard paste porcelain dinnerware, vases and figurines similar to those of Serves and Meissen.

Charger, allover enameling, Budapest **300.00**
Ewer, blue/beige, gold beads, medallions in relief, 9½″ **215.00**
Jug, blue butterflies, deer, allover florals **380.00**
   Enameling & gold, Budapest **250.00**
Urn, enameled birds, gold decor, 24x16″ **1,500.00**
Vase, 4 leaf lip, handles, bulbous, all reticulated, 12″ **185.00**
   All over floral reticulation, 4 cobalt ring handles, 11″ **180.00**
   Bulbous, flared rim, handles, filigree decor, 6½″ **145.00**

Fishing Collectibles

Fishing as a sport was unheard of in America before 1800. During the 19th century one patent after another was issued for various reels, rods and artificial plugs. Today's collector may choose to specialize in one area only...some search for wooden plugs, while others are interested in the products of one specific manuafacturer. The hobby is only newly established, so market values are variable. Older plugs are most valuable; condition is very important, and original cartons add to net worth.

Decoy, bullhead, Reno, glass eyes, rubber whiskers, orig paint, 14½″ **90.00**
   Glass eyes, copper fins, tail, 1920, 14½″ **65.00**
   Glass eyes, tin fins, sponge brushed, 11½″ **65.00**
   Perch, tack eyes, metal fins, orig paint, 14½″ **90.00**
   Wood, tin fins, carved tails, lot of 8, 4″-7″ **75.00**
Fish spear, 3 tine, wooden handle **15.00**
   Hand wrought, 12″ **30.00**
Fishermans Companion, box w/slide cover & line winder, 3″ ... **90.00**
Guide-Catalogue, Helin Fishing Tackle, 1948 .... **5.00**
Lure, codfish, lead, 2 iron hooks, 8″ **18.00**
   Fishmaster Minnow, 1940s **5.00**
WAB, Fenner Weedless Bait Co, 1926 .... **10.00**
Minnow bucket, tin w/gold stencil, "Wade In..", 1900, 8″ **50.00**
Plug, Bite-Em Water Mole, 1920 .... **10.00**
   Charmer Minnow, 1911 .... **10.00**
   Decker, underwater, w/propellers, 3′ **20.00**
   Dowagiac Muskollonge Minnow 700-3 Treble **25.00**
   Luny Frog #3500, 4½″ **15.00**
Reel, Bronson Mercuury #2550, engraved, jewelled **10.00**
   Chicago Fishing Equip Co Champion #805 .... **20.00**
   Edwards #30, aluminum fly **4.50**
   Meisselback Triton **75.00**
Ocean Big Pflueger, brass pat 1908, Douglass **14.00**

Ocean City #1591 .... **5.50**
Pflueger Skilkast 1953, need cleaning **8.00**
Pflueger Summit 1993L **10.00**
Pflueger Summit **12.00**
Shakespeare 1837 Tru-Art Automatic Trout Reel, box **18.00**
Shakespeare, Direct Drive Model EH **10.00**
UCO, 3½″ old **25.00**
Union Hdwr Co Samson **15.00**
Wondereel Deluxe Model GE **16.00**
Winchester **70.00**
Seine ball, cobalt, 5″ **20.00**
   Orange, 2″ **15.00**
Spinner, Archer, Milwards, Redditch, England, mint **10.00**
Spoon, Skinners #5, feathered treble, fluted spoon, 1930s **7.00**

Flags

Of most interest to serious collectors of American flags are those with 38 stars or less, and those which are hand stitched. Design, size, construction, scarcity and condition are factors to be considered in arriving at a fair market price. Reproductions or commemorative flags have little or no value.

Larger American Flags of All Sewn Construction
    (5 ft fly and up; ordinary star patterns)
49-48 star **10.00-25.00**
46-44 star **25.00-55.00**
43 star, rare .... **Negotiable**
42-38 star **55.00-100.00**
37-34 star **100.00-200.00**
33 stars or less .... **200.00 up**

Larger All Printed American Flags
    (Silk most preferred)
50-75% of above listing

Smaller All Printed American Flags
    (Silk most preferred)
20-50% of above listing

American Flags of Unusual or Special Design

Flatirons

Irons come in all shapes and sizes; there are sadirons, fluting irons, tailors irons and ruffling irons, to name but the most common. Hooded sadirons, patented about 1870, supposedly shielded the ironer's hand from the heat. Box irons from the late 1800s had hinged rear doors to accomodate heated slugs. Charcoal irons worked on the same principal, but removing the ashes was a nuisance! Even the gas irons of the early 20th century had drawbacks. Pressure on the tank controlled the flame. Too little meant no heat, too much could result in an accident! Denatured alcohol and boiling water were also used as heat sources. Electric irons, though invented around the turn of the century, were not used to any great extent until electricity became a commonplace commodity several decades later.

Almond shaped, w/removeable wooden handle, AC Williams Co, 6¾″ **20.00**
Brass, rear hinged plate opens, w/lock **20.00**
Cast and wrought iron, polished surface, ingot, wood handle, 8″ **28.00**
   Sliding door, ingot, turned wood handle, 6¾″ **35.00**
Cast iron w/hinged wrought handle, spring fastener, PW Weidat, 1870 **40.00**
Cast iron w/twisted wrought handle, Dale Co #14, 10¼″ **10.00**
   Monito's, St Louis, 11″ **12.00**
Charcoal, bird perched on front to open & close **85.00**
   Cast iron w/ wooden handle, Pagoel **30.00**

Hand forged, 1700s, has door for coals **85.00**
Nickeled steel, w/chimney & wood handle, 7½″ long **22.00**
Ornamental ci lift off lid, side doors, wood handle **35.00**
Ornate lift off lid **36.00**
Chattanooga, #8 . . . . **15.00**
Child's, swan, Cathedral pattern, old red paint, w/trivet **75.00**
Commercial pleater, electric, ci base, brass rollers **77.00**
Compartment for iron slug insert, w/door, 1860 . . . . **46.50**
   1865 . . . . **50.00**
Crimping, brass rollers, orig paint, 1875, complete **75.00**
Enamelware body, tank & handle **20.00**
Polisher, linen covered beeswax ball, w/wood handle **15.00**
Fluting, 1 piece, iron rocker & slug signed The Best **40.00**
   American, straight **45.00**
   Cast iron, crank handle, 2 brass rollers, missing slugs **48.00**
   Footed, Syracuse **40.00**

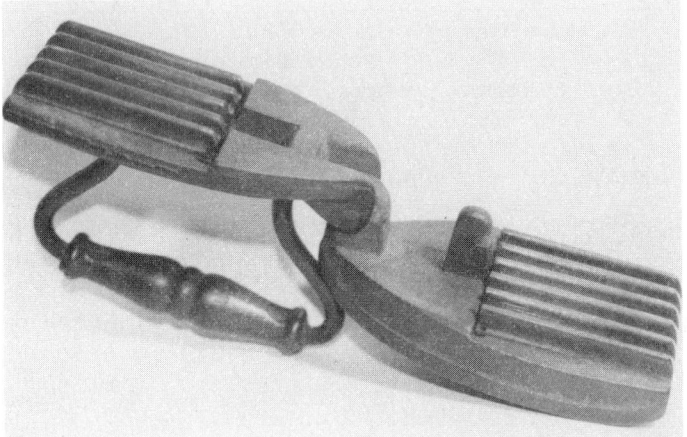

Geneva, Ill., hand fluter **75.00**
Goffering iron, hand wrought handle, w/holding stand **50.00**
Iron, w/iron handle, #4, 1860s, 4½″ long **18.00**
   With strap-type handle, hand forged, 4 lbs, 1860s, 4½″ **17.00**
Lion's head finial, charcoal, old **60.00**
McCoy, unusual shape, cut out middle, 4¾″ **35.00**
Miniature, asbestos, Dover Mfg Co, May 22, 1900 . . . . **20.00**
   Ober, Chagrin Falls, Ohio, 4″ long **25.00**
Polishing, Dover, Boston **50.00**
Primitive, ci w/wrought handle, 10½″ long **25.00**
Sensible, #2, 1887, detachable handle, w/trivet **50.00**
Tailor's **38.00**

Flow Blue

Flow Blue ware was produced by many Staffordshire potters, among the most familiar were Meigh, Podmore and Walker, Samuel Alcock, Ridgway, Wedgwood and Davenport. It was popular from about 1825 through 1860, and again from 1880 until the turn of the century. The name describes the blurred or flowing effect of the cobalt decoration, achieved through the introduction of a chemical vapor into the kiln. The body of the ware is ironstone, and Oriental motifs were favored. Later issues were on a lighter body, and often decorated with gilt.

Acantha, plate, 8″ dia **14.00**
   Plate, 9″dia **18.00**
   Plate, 10″ dia **20.00**
Agra, plate, 1891, F Winkle, 6¾″ dia **25.00**
Alaska, vegetable dish, covered **100.00**
Aliwal, plate, (lily pattern), 1850s, 10½″ dia **60.00**
Alvin, wash bowl, handled, 18″ dia **98.00**
Amoy, bean bowl, Davenport, 11½″ **250.00**

Cream & sugar, straight sides, Davenport **415.00**
Cup & saucer, handleless, Davenport **105.00**
Cup plate **39.00**
Master butter, covered, Davenport **345.00**
Pitcher, milk, 2 qt, Davenport **325.00**
Plate, Davenport, 8¼″ **65.00**
Plate, Davenport, 10½″ **85.00**
Rim soup, Davenport, 10½″ **90.00**
Sauce, Davenport **48.00**
Tea Set, pot, creamer & sugar, Davenport **715.00**
Teapot, Davenport **415.00**
Vegetable dish, rectangular, open, 9¼x7¾″ **215.00**
Ancient Ruins, soup bowl **28.00**
Arabesque, sauce dish **35.00**
Arcadia, soup plate w/rim, A Wilkinson, 1907, 9″ dia **18.00**
   Vegetable bowl, open, oval **45.00**
Argyle, butter w/cover, Grindley **145.00**
   Gravy w/tray, Grindley **165.00**
   Plate, Grindley, 10″ **58.00**
   Platter, Grindley, 10″ **75.00**
   Platter, Grindley, 15x10½″ **155.00**
   Platter, Grindley, 16″ **215.00**
   Rim soup, Grindley, 9″ **55.00**
   Soup tureen, Grindley **410.00**
   Vegetable dish, covered, oval **210.00**
   Vegetable dish, covered, square **210.00**
   Vegetable dish, open, oval, 10″ **95.00**
Ashburton, soup plate, 1891, Grindley, 7¾″ dia **25.00**
Astoria, platter, Johnson, 14″ **65.00**
   Vegetable dish, covered, 10″ **85.00**
Baltic, bone dish, Grindley **40.00**
   Gravy boat, 7½″ **60.00**
   Plate, 10″, Grindley **45.00**
   Serving bowl, round, 10″ dia **45.00**
   Vegetable, covered, oval, Grindley **165.00**
   Vegetable, covered, round, Grindley **185.00**
Beaufort, bone dish, Grindley **40.00**
   Pitcher, milk, 2 qt, Grindley **155.00**
   Plate, 10″ **34.00**
   Platter, 15¼x10½″, Grindley **110.00**
   Vegetable dish, open, oval, 8¼″ **65.00**
   Waste bowl, pedestal, Grindley **65.00**
Beauties of China, vegetable bowl, 11x8″ **140.00**
Bejapore, sauce tureen, covered, w/matching ladle **250.00**
Brush stroke, mug **50.00**
   Sugar bowl **80.00**
California, soap box w/drainer & lid, PW & Co, 1849 . . . . **110.00**
   Soup plate w/rim, PW & Co, 1849, 9½″ dia **45.00**
Cambridge, soup plate w/rim, New Wharf, 1891, 9″ dia **45.00**
Canton, cup & saucer, handleless, 1845 . . . . **65.00**
Carlton, creamer, S Alcock, 1850, 6″ **85.00**
Carnation, platter, Furnival, 11x9″ **125.00**
Castle, cup plate, J Tams, 1875 . . . . **35.00**
Chapoo, coupe plate **75.00**
   Cream & sugar set, Wedgwood **425.00**
   Cup & saucer, demitasse **100.00**
   Cup & saucer, handleless, Wedgwood **85.00**
   Plate, J Wedgwood, 8¼″ **50.00**
   Plate, J Wedgwood, 9¼″ **70.00**
   Plate, Wedgwood, 10½″ **90.00**
   Plate, Wedgwood, 11″ **85.00**
   Sauce dish, Wedgwood **48.00**
   Vegetable dish, rectangular, open, Wedgwood, 7½″ **195.00**
Chusan, plate, F Morley, 1850, 9″ dia **50.00**

Soup tureen, very large, pedestal base, open, Morley **460.00**

Teapot, J Clementson, 10″ **225.00**
Ciesha, soup tureen, upper Handley **250.00**
Circassia, soup, 10½″ **65.00**
Clarence, butter pat, Grindley **16.00**
Cluny, sauce dish, Furnivals, 1910, 5″ dia **10.00**
Clytie, plate, 8″ **39.00**
   Platter, Wedgwood Imperial Porcelain, 17x14″ **225.00**
Coburg, teapot, J Edwards, 1860 . . . . **270.00**
Colonial, butter pat **20.00**
   Plate, Meakin, 1891, 8″ dia **20.00**
   Saucer, Meakin, 1891 . . . . **6.00**
Colonial, tea cup & saucer, Meakin **40.00**
Conway, vegetable dish, round, open, 8″ **40.00**
Corinthia, vegetable dish cover, Wedgwood **20.00**
Countess, plate, 6¾″ **12.00**
Cup & saucer, farmer's, scenes inside, flared cup, 8″ saucer **38.00**
Dahlia, sugar bowl, Challinor **120.00**
   Waste bowl, 1840 . . . . **85.00**
Davenport, soup plate w/rim, Wood & Sons, 1907, 9″ dia **25.00**
Del Monte, set, 42 pc, Johnson Bros **1,250.00**
Delaware, plate, J Ridgway, 1847, 10½″ dia **35.00**
Derby, creamer, Grindley, 1891, 5″ **75.00**
Dresden, cup & saucer, Johnson Bros **52.50**
   Soup plate w/rim, S Hancock, 1900, 9″ dia **25.00**
Duchess, soup tureen, w/lid, platter & ladle, Grindley **375.00**
   Sugar bowl cover, Grindley, 1891, 5″ dia **15.00**
Dundee, 8 place dinner service & 10 serving pcs, Ridgway . . **1,750.00**
   Pie plate, Ridgway, 1910, 6″ dia **15.00**

Ebor, cream & sugar, Ridgway **80.00**

Cup & saucer, Ridgway **64.50**
Elgar, plate, 8″ **12.00**
   Platter, Upper Handley, 10½″ **15.00**
   Sugar bowl **50.00**
Excelsior, serving platter, 1900 . . . . **115.00**
Fairy Villas, bowl, Adams, 2x10″ **35.00**
   Bowl, soup, 9″ **25.00**
   Butter pat **20.00**
   Cup & saucer, Adams **60.00**
   Plate, 7″ **18.00**
   Platter, Adams, 17½″ **150.00**
   Relish dish, Adams **85.00**
   Rim soup, Adams, 9″ **45.00**
   Sauce dish, Adams **24.00**
   Serving bowl, open, 10″ dia **110.00**
   Vegetable dish, covered, Adams, 12x9½″ **220.00**
Fern, teapot, grape cluster finial **450.00**
Ferrara, plate, soup, mkd Wedgwood, 1½x9½″ dia **40.00**
Floral Design, jardiniere, 1891, gold decor **150.00**
Florida, cream & sugar, Grindley **195.00**
   Plate, Grindley, 6¾″ **28.00**
   Platter, 16½″, Johnson Bros **150.00**
   Platter, Grindley, 14x10″ **115.00**
   Waste bowl, Grindley **48.00**
Gem, cup & saucer, set of 6, Maddock **270.00**
Gironde, cup & saucer, Grindley **28.00**
   Platter, 15″ **60.00**
   Sauce, Grindley, 5¼″ **10.00**
   Tureen, covered **78.00**
   Vegetable bowl, Grindley, 9½″ **38.00**
Grace, turkey platter, 21″, Grindley **150.00**
Granada, sugar bowl, finial reset **48.00**
Haddon, cup & saucer, Grindley **55.00**
Hamilton, cup & saucer, J Maddock, 1896, 2 flakes **15.00**
   Plate, J Maddock, 1896, 8″ dia **20.00**
      9″ dia **25.00**
   Platter, J Maddock, 1896, 17x12″ **75.00**
   Sauce dishes, J Maddock, 1896 . . . . **15.00**
   Soup plate, w/rim, Maddock, 8″ **26.00**
Hindustan, platter, Maddock, 10x13½″ **95.00**
Hofburg, cup & saucer, Grindley **30.00**
Holland, gravy boat, w/rim chip **22.00**
Hong Kong, dinner plate **65.00**
   Honey dish **38.00**
   Soup plate w/rim, 1850, hairline **15.00**
   Vegetable, 1845, C Meigh, 12″ dia **140.00**
Hudson, butter pat **26.00**
   Gravy boat & tray **42.50**
Indian Stone, plate, E Walley, 1850, 9¾″ dia **60.00**
Irene, butter dish, 3 pc, round, Wedgwood **150.00**
Iris, bowl, sauce, 5½″ **15.00**
   Cup & saucer, w/age line, Grindley **20.00**
   Plate, Grindley, 6″ **12.50**
      8″ dia **14.00**
      9″ dia **20.00**
      10″ dia **25.00**
   Platter, Grindley, 10x7½″ **20.00**
      12x8½″ **30.00**
   Soup plate, Grindley, 1910 . . . . **20.00**
   Vegetable tureen, open, Grindley, 1910 . . . . **35.00**
   Waste bowl, Grindley, 1910 . . . . **35.00**
Italia, cup & saucer, scenic **77.00**
Janette, platter, 15″ **85.00**
Japan, creamer, Fell **195.00**

Plate, Fell, 6½" 40.00
Jeddo, cup & saucer, handleless, Adams & Son, 1845 . . . . 55.00
Jewel, butter dish, w/cover, Johnson Bros 130.00
Kaolin, sugar bowl, PW & Co 120.00
Kyber, butter pat, Adams 30.00
  Compote, fruit, open 210.00
  Cup & saucer, Adams 65.00
    Demitasse, Adams 58.00
  Handleless cup & deep saucer, 1850s, Meir 86.00
  Plate, 6" 35.00
    10", W Adams & Son 45.00
  Platter, Adams, 10x7¼" 115.00
    12x9½" 125.00
  Saucer, Adams 22.00
  Soup, 8", Adams 45.00
  Vegetable dish, covered, Adams 380.00
    Open, 7½x5½" 115.00
    Rectangular, open, 10¼x7¾" 165.00
LaBelle, dish, serving, scalloped w/ribbing, Wheeling 75.00
  Plate, 9" 44.50
  Sandwich plate, indented for cup, signed, 8" dia 95.00
  Sandwich tray, small back chip 85.00
  Saucer 20.00
  Syrup jug, w/orig lid, signed 165.00
Lahore, creamer, Phillips 195.00
Lancaster, cup & saucer, New Wharf 50.00
  Plate, New Wharf Pottery, 1900, 10" dia 35.00
Lewis & Clark, saucer 35.00

Lincoln, plate, Wedgwood Royal, ca 1885, 10" 70.00
Linda, butter pat, Maddock 16.00
  Creamer, J Maddock, 1896, 4" 65.00
  Cup & saucer, Maddock 24.00
  Dinner plate, Maddock 20.00
  Plate, 9" 18.00
  Platter, Maddock, 9x12" 55.00
  Relish dish, Maddock, 4x8½" 28.00
  Soup tureen, cover w/slot, Maddock, 9½" 130.00
  Teapot, large, 1896, Maddock 145.00
Lobelia, cup plate, G Phillips, 1845 . . . . 40.00
Lonsdale, platter, Ford & Son, 13½x11" 55.00
Lorne, butter pat 16.00

Creamer, Grindley 95.00
Plate, Grindley, 6" dia 20.00
  8" dia 25.00
  10" dia 35.00
Platter, Grindley, 14x10" 115.00
  16x11½" 125.00
Saucer, Grindley, 1900, 6" dia 6.00
Soup plate w/rim, Grindley, 1900, 9" dia, edge roughage 20.00
Lotus, pitcher, 2½ qt, Grindley 110.00
  Soup ladle, 12", Grindley 100.00
  Soup plate w/rim, Grindley, 1910 . . . . 20.00
Louise, cup & saucer, New Wharf 35.00
  Sugar, New Wharf 52.00
Lucania, soup plate w/rim, E Clarke, 1885, 9" dia 26.00
Luzerne, sauce dish, Mercer 16.00
Lynton, bowl & pitcher, Ceramic Art Co 395.00
Madras, cereal bowl, Doulton, 1900 . . . . 22.00
  Egg cup, Royal Doulton 53.50
  Plate, 9½", Doulton 35.00
    10½" 50.00
  Platter, Doulton, 11" 48.00
Manhattan, butter pat 15.00
Manilla, cup & saucer, handleless, PW & Co, 1845 . . . . 85.00
  Cup plate, Walker 68.00
  Cup, posset, Walker 78.00
  Gravy, Walker 235.00
  Pitcher, milk, straight sides, 3 cup 245.00
  Plate, 7¾", Walker 60.00
    8½", Walker 68.00
    9¾", Walker 72.00
    10½" 75.00
  Platter, Walker, 12½x9¼" 235.00
  Relish, Walker 175.00
  Sugar bowl 225.00
  Teapot 290.00
  Vegetable, covered, Walker 450.00
Marechal Niel, butter pat, Grindley 22.00
  Butter, covered, w/insert, Grindley 155.00
  Creamer, Grindley, 1895, 4" 75.00
  Gravy, Grindley 95.00
  Gravy & tray, Grindley 145.00
  Plate, Grindley, 1895, 10" dia 35.00
  Platter, 8½" 75.00
    12½" 110.00
    14½" 125.00
    16" 145.00
  Rim soup, 9", Grindley 40.00
  Sauce dish, Grindley 24.00
  Soup, 7½" 40.00
  Sugar w/cover, Grindley 115.00
  Vegetable, covered, Grindley 155.00
    Oval, 9x6" 85.00
Marguerite, compote, 4¾x9" dia, Grindley, rare 165.00
  Gravy boat & tray, Grindley, 1891 . . . . 75.00
Marie, cup & saucer, Grindley 30.00
  Pitcher, 8" 125.00
Marlboro, bowl, soup, Grindley, 8¾" 25.00
Martha Washington, cup, Woods & Sons, 1900 . . . . 20.00
Melbourne, butter pat, Grindley, 1900 . . . . 20.00
  Creamer, Grindley, 1900, hairline 20.00
  Gravy, Grindley 95.00
  Plate, Grindley, 8" 20.00
    9" 25.00
    10" dia 40.00

Platter, 14x10" 80.00
  Soup plate w/rim, Grindley, 1900, 9" dia 30.00
  Soup tureen, Grindley 375.00
  Vegetable dish, covered, round 175.00
Mersey, bone dish, Grindley, 1900, slate blue 12.00
Mongolia, plate, 1860, 9¼" dia 38.00
Nantucket Harbor, plate, 9", Wedgwood 50.00
Napolean, plate, portrait, open ends, Old Paris 150.00
Ning Po, waste bowl 95.00
Non Pareil, creamer, Burgess & Leigh 115.00
  Gravy, Burgess & Leigh 110.00
  Plate, 6", Burgess & Leigh 28.00
    6¾" 32.00
    7¾", Burgess & Leigh 35.00
    8¾", Burgess & Leigh 38.00
    10", Burgess & Leigh 50.00
  Platter, Burgess & Leigh, 13½x11" 140.00
  Sauce dish, Burgess & Leigh 25.00
  Spoon rest, Burgess & Leigh 65.00
  Vegetable dish, covered, Burgess & Leigh 255.00
  Vegetable dish, oval, 9¾" dia 90.00
Old Curiosity Shop, bowl, Ridgway, 1910, 8½" dia 45.00
  Plate, Ridgway, 9" dia 25.00
    8" dia 20.00
Olympic, bone dish, Grindley 47.50
Oregon, creamer, straight sides, Mayer 200.00
  Cup & saucer, handleless, Mayer 95.00
  Plate, Mayer, 7½" 48.00
    8½", Mayer 50.00
    9½", Mayer 55.00
    10¼", Mayer 75.00
  Platter, Mayer, 13½x10½" 200.00
  Potato bowl, round, Mayer, 12" 245.00
  Rimmed soup, Mayer, 9" 60.00
  Sauce dish, Mayer 55.00
  Sauce tureen, rectangular, Mayer 285.00
    With ladle & tray, Mayer 550.00
    With rosebud finial, Mayer 290.00
  Tea set, pot, creamer & covered sugar, Mayer 725.00
  Teapot, Mayer 380.00
Oriental, bone dish, Ridgway 52.00
  Cup & saucer, Ridgway 58.00
  Cup, New Wharf 30.00
  Plate, J Edwards, 1850, 10" dia 50.00
    Ridgway, 1891, 9" dia 38.00
  Rimmed soup, Ridgway 30.00
  Serving bowl, oval, 8" 127.50
  Vegetable dish, open, Ridgway, 9½" 130.00
  Vegetable, covered, Ridgway 265.00
  Waste bowl, Ridgway 85.00
Ormonde, bone dish, Meakin 35.00
Osborne, creamer, Ridgway, 1891, 4" 65.00
  Egg cup, Ridgway 95.00
  Plate, Ridgway, 7¾" 28.00
    9¾" 47.00
  Serving bowl, oval, 9¾" 52.50
  Vegetable bowl, clover shape, Ridgway 80.00
Paisley, platter, Mercer, 15½" 75.00
  Sugar, covered, Mercer 65.00
  Vegetable dish w/cover, Mercer, 12" 80.00
Paris, vegetable dish, covered, oval, New Wharf, 1891 ... 125.00
Peach Blow, vase, raised gold flowers, branch handles, Jones .. 225.00
Pekin, cup, 12 panel, Dimmock 38.00
  Cup & saucer, handleless, 1845 .... 75.00

Plate, 7½" 55.00
  7¾", Wilkinson 32.00
  9", Wilkinson 45.00
Pelew, cup & saucer, paneled, handleless, Challinor 80.00
  Plate, Challinor, 8½" 50.00
Persian Moss, butter dish, covered 75.00
Pitcher, mkd Masons Patent Ironstone China, 6½" 120.00
Platter, allover blue flowers, Crown & Banner, 9x12" 59.00
  Blue birds, 2 handles, 11½" 68.00
Plymouth, plate 25.00
  Sugar & creamer, New Wharf 190.00
Poet, plate 50.00
Princess, sauce tureen, covered 140.00
Regent, sugar bowl, Meakin 97.50
Regina, rimmed soup 29.50
Renown, sauce boat & tray 90.00
Rhone, plate, T Dimmock, 1844, 10½" dia 50.00
  Plate, T Furnival, 1845, 10½" dia 45.00
Richmond, bread tray, Meakin 80.00
  Plate, Johnson, 7" 15.00
    Meakin, 10" 50.00
Rock, dinner plate 55.00
Rose, plate, Grindley, 7½" 24.50
  Plate, Grindley, 9" 27.50
  Sauce boat, Grindley 59.50
Roseville, rimmed soup, Maddock 28.00
Royston, bone dish, Johnson Bros, 1900 .... 20.00
Savoy, cup & saucer, Johnson Bros 67.50
  Platter, Johnson Bros, 9½x12¾" 98.50
  Serving bowl, round, Johnson Bros, 9" 78.00
Saxony, sauce boat 67.50
Scinde, creamer, Alcock 250.00
  Cup & saucer 80.00
    Handleless, Alcock 105.00
  Fruit compote, Alcock 600.00
  Gravy boat, Alcock 220.00
  Plate, Alcock, 8" 60.00
    Alcock, 10½" 95.00
    T Walker, 9½" 70.00
  Relish, Alcock 135.00
  Sauce dish, Alcock 60.00
  Sugar, covered, Alcock 225.00
  Teapot, Alcock 410.00
  Vegetable dish, open, rectangular, Alcock, 8¾x6¾" 200.00
  Vegetable, covered, square finial, 10x13" 425.00
Sefton, vegetable dish, covered, Ridgway 125.00
Seville, platter, New Wharf, 12½x9" 125.00
  Vegetable dish, covered, New Wharf 220.00
Sevres, vegetable, covered, Wood & Sons, 1900, 12" long ... 120.00
Shanghai, butter w/cover, drainer, Grindley 110.00
  Cup & saucer, Grindley 46.00
  Plate, Corn, 8½" 18.00
  Platter, J Furnival, 1860, 15½x12" 150.00
  Serving bowl, oval, 8¾" 60.00
Shantong, rimmed soup, Dimmock & Smith, 1845, 10¾" 75.00
Shell, platter, E Challinor, 1860, 18x14" 275.00
Shusan, plate, F & R Pratt, 1855, 8¼" 40.00
Simla, plate, Elsmore & Forester, 8½" 43.50
Sloe Blossom, pitcher, Wm Ridgway & Co, 1820, 8½" 115.00
Snowflake, creamer, 3½" 60.00
  Cup & saucer, early ironstone 80.00
  Cup, early ironstone 65.00
  Plate, heavy ironstone, 8½" 52.00
Sobraon, plate, Alcock, 8¼" 48.00

Plate, Alcock, 9½" **55.00**
Platter, Alcock, 13x10½" **190.00**
Potato bowl, round, Alcock, 10½" **99.00**
Vegetable dish, covered, Alcock **325.00**
Sugar bowl, covered, 1850 .... **120.00**
Spinach, creamer **87.50**
  Cup & saucer **57.50**
Splendid, cup & saucer, Maastricht **55.00**
St Louis, casserole w/cover **87.00**
  Dinner plate **36.00**
  Gravy bowl **45.00**
  Luncheon plate **30.00**
  Platter, large **65.00**
Steak platter, cattle scene, Wedgwood **225.00**
Sterling, serving bowl, oval, New Wharf, 10" **52.00**
Sydney, creamer, Wood & Son **60.00**
  Plate, New Wharf, 9" **21.00**
Temple, chamber pot, 6x8" dia, no lid **225.00**
  Plate, PW & Co, 8" **55.00**
    8¾" **60.00**
    9" **75.00**
    9½" **85.00**
    10", Walker **90.00**
  Platter, J Wedgwood, 13¼" **165.00**
    PW & Co, 13¼" **150.00**
The Olympic, cup & saucer **50.00**
Togo, plate, 7" **25.00**
  Soup plate, rimmed, F Winkle, 1900, 8¾" dia ... **25.00**
  Soup tureen, Winkle **125.00**
Tonquin, cup plate, Heath **50.00**
  Plate, W Adams & Son, 1845, 10¼" dia **75.00**
Touraine, butter pat **32.50**
  Creamer, Alcock & Stanley **150.00**
  Cup & saucer, Alcock & Stanley **65.00**
  Egg cup **165.00**
  Gravy boat **85.00**
  Pitcher, milk **185.00**
    Water **245.00**
  Plate, 6" **22.00**
    Alcock, 6½" **30.00**
    Alcock, 8" dia **30.00**
    Shelby, 8½" **30.00**
    Stanley, 6¼" **25.00**
    Stanley, 8½" **32.00**
  Platter, Stanley, 15" **85.00**
  Relish **65.00**
  Sauce dish, Stanley, 1898, 5¼" **20.00**
  Saucer, Stanley **16.00**
  Soup plate, rimmed, Alcock, 1898, 10" dia **40.00**
  Sugar, Alcock & Stanley **135.00**
Tulip, vegetable dish, covered, Johnson Bros **98.00**
Vase, 8 scenic panels, double handle, 12" **260.00**
Vermont, cup & saucer, demitasse, Burslem **47.50**
Versailles, relish tray, Furnival **48.50**
  Sauce dish, Furnival **35.00**
  Cup & saucer, Furnival **45.00**
Victoria, serving bowl, round, Wood & Son, 10" ... **47.50**
  Vegetable bowl, round, Wood, 10" **35.00**
Vienna, wash set, 6 pc, Johnson Bros **595.00**
Virginia, platter, John Maddock, 12" long **72.50**
Wagon Wheel, shaving mug **27.50**
  Waste bowl from child's set **70.00**
Waldorf, creamer, New Wharf **72.00**
  Cup & saucer, New Wharf **80.00**

Plate, New Wharf, 6" **20.00**
  6½" **30.00**
  6¾" **33.00**
  9" **35.00**
  9½" **45.00**
  10" **50.00**
  Gold trim, New Wharf, 7¾" **35.00**
  Gold trim, New Wharf, 9" **40.00**
Platter, New Wharf, 10½x8" **50.00**
  16x11½" **150.00**
  Small **40.00**
Rimmed soup, gold trim, New Wharf, 9" **37.00**
Sauce dish, New Wharf **24.00**
  With gold trim, New Wharf **29.00**
Serving bowl, round, New Wharf, 9" **87.50**
Soup plate, rimmed, New Wharf, 1892 .... **35.00**
Vegetable dish, covered, New Wharf **235.00**
  Open, gold trim, New Wharf, 9¼x6½" **72.00**
Waste bowl, gold trim, New Wharf **46.00**
Washington, coffee pot, Walker, 1848 .... **195.00**
  Plate, T Walker, 8½" **55.00**
Watteau, tureen, pedestal, covered, round, Doulton **275.00**
Wentworth, butter pat, Hanley **16.00**
Willow, compote, low, footed, Doulton **127.50**
York, serving tray, fluted & scalloped, Corn, 9½x11¾" ... **40.00**

Flue Covers

When spring housecleaning started and the heating stove was taken down for the warm weather season, the unsightly hole where the stove pipe joined the chimney was hidden with an attractive flue cover. They were made with a colorful litho print behind a round glass piece with a chain for hanging. The most popular motifs were florals, children and lovely ladies.

Boy, w/red cap, finger in mouth **21.00**
Children, Victorian dress, 9½" **40.00**
Fishing scene **18.00**
Girl, gold border, chain for hanging **15.00**

Lady & roses, 9¾" **55.00**
Little boy & girl **30.00**
Little girl, w/bonnet of flowers **35.00**
Sailboat, silverplate, floral engraved border, James Tufts ... **38.00**

Fostoria

The Fostoria Glass Company was built in 1887 at Fostoria, Ohio; by 1891 it had moved to Moundsville, West Virginia. During the next two decades they produced many lines of pressed patterned tableware and lamps. Their most famous pattern, American, was introduced in 1915, and has been produced continuously since that time, in well over 200 different pieces. From 1920 to 1925, top artists designed tablewares in colored glass---canary, (vaseline), amber, blue, orchid, green and ebony---in pressed patterns as well as etched designs. By the late '30s Fostoria was recognized as the largest producer of handmade glassware in the world. The company continues in operation today, making the same quality glassware for which it is famous.

American

Almond dish, small	11.00
Ashtray, 3″ sq	8.00
Individual, 2½″ sq	4.00
Oval, 3″	12.00
Basket, w/handle	55.00
Bitters bottle, w/stopper	35.00
Boat, 2 handles	13.50
8½″	9.00
Divided, 12″	16.50
Bon-bon, 3 legs	7.00
Bowl, 2 handles, 8″	22.50
2 handles, 9″	17.50
2 handles, oval, 7″	14.00
3 corner, 4½″	15.00
3 corner, toed, 7″	18.00
3 legs, 11″	22.00
5″	8.00
7½″	14.00
8″	18.00
11½″	18.00
Deep, 7½″	18.00
Deep, 10½	20.00
Flared, 3½x18″	22.00
Fruit, 3 toed, 12″	35.00
Handled, tri corner, 4½″	20.00
Handled, 4½″ sq	7.00
Handled, 5″	7.00
Loving cup, flat, 8¾″	40.00
Low, 12″	30.00
Oval, 6″	12.50
Oval, 9″	14.00
Oval, 10″	16.00
Oval, 11¾″	18.00
Oval, divided	30.00
Salad, 4½x10″	20.00
Salad, 8″, #188	18.00
Shallow, 13″	25.00
Shallow, footed, 13″	32.50
With cover, 5½″	24.00
Box w/cover, cigarette	15.00
Puff, 3″	50.00
Cake stand, footed, sq	40.00
Candlesticks, 3″, pr	17.50
6¼″, pr	20.00
Twin, pr	27.50
Candy dish, 3 part w/cover	40.00
Covered, #505, 5″	14.00
Footed, 6¾″	15.00
Footed, covered, tall	18.00
Celery boat, 10″	7.00

6″	14.00
Coaster, 3″ dia	5.00
Cocktail icer, juicer insert	20.00
Cocktail, footed, 3 oz	14.00
Cologne bottle, stopper, 6″	35.00
Cracker & cheese	55.00
Cruet, orig stopper, 5 oz	27.50
Cup, footed	5.00
Cup & saucer	10.00
Custard, handled, flared,	6.50
Handleless	6.50
Reg	4.00
Decanter, regular, qt	55.00
Rye, qt	80.00
Scotch, qt	80.00
Finger bowl	12.50
Blue	25.00
Goblet, 6″	10.00
7″	12.00
Hex foot	12.00
Ice bucket, hotel	28.00
Ice cream, handled	5.00
Ice tub, large	50.00
Small	40.00
With 9″ liner	55.00
Individual salt & pepper w/tray, set	30.00
Sugar	5.00
Jelly, flared, 4½″	6.50
Jelly dish w/cover, footed	27.50
Jug, milk, pt	25.00
No ice lip, ½ gal	50.00
No ice lip, 3 pt	32.00
Straight side w/ice lip, ½ gal	35.00
Lamp, rose bowl, 5″	40.00
Vanity	35.00
Mayonnaise, liner & ladle	30.00
Mustard w/cover	20.00
Nappy, flared, 6″	10.00
One handle, 4½″	5.50
One handle, shallow, 5″	10.00
Oil cruet & ground stopper	35.00
With stopper, 5 oz	29.50
Olive, oval, 6″	16.00
Oyster cocktail, #33	9.00
Pickle dish, 8″	8.00
Plate, 6″	4.50
8″	6.00
8½″	6.50
Dinner, 9″	12.50
Dinner, 9½″	14.50
Rolled edge, 14″	18.50
Sandwich, 2 handles	8.00
Torte, 13½″	16.00
Punch cup, flat, #615	6.50
Relish, oval, 10″	8.00
3 part, oval, 9½″	15.00
3 part, oval, 10½″	17.50
4 part, #624	20.00
Rose bowl, 5″	24.00
Sm	12.50
Salt & pepper, cone, pr	8.00
Square, 2½″, pr	10.00
Straight, pr	12.00
Salt dip	6.00

Sauce boat w/underliner, oval, rare 60.00
Server w/center handle, orig label 42.00
Sherbet, 7 oz. 4.00
   Hex foot, 4¼″ 6.00
   High, flared 6.00
   Low, flared 5.00
   Round foot, 4¼″ 6.00
   Round foot, low, 3½″ 5.50
Spooner 28.00
Sugar & creamer, individual 12.00
Sugar w/cover & creamer, large 25.00
Sugar, creamer, bulbous, round handles 15.00
   Pointed handles, on tray, 3 pc 20.00
Sundae, footed 4.00
Syrup, chrome lid, 4¾″ 52.00
   Dripcut 20.00
Tid-bit, tier, Shepherd's Crook 30.00
   2 tier, Shepherd's Crook 35.00
   3 toed, 8″ 6.00
Tom & Jerry mug, #708 . . . . 12.50
Toothpick 8.00
Top hat, 2¼″ 22.00
   3″ 22.00
   4¼″ 30.00
Tray, 7″ 12.00
   9x6½″ 35.00
   Comb & brush, oval, 10½″ 42.50
Tumbler, 8 oz, #76 . . . . 10.00
   9 oz 8.50
   Flat, 4¼″ 7.50
   Flat, 4¾″, 5 oz 8.50
   Flat, 5¼″ 7.50
   Flat, flared, 8 oz 12.00
   2½″ 10.00
   Ice tea, 6″ 12.00
   Juice, footed, 5 oz 8.00
   Low, ball, 3½″ 10.00
Vase, 6″ 15.00
   8″ 18.00
   8¼″ 12.50
   10″ 22.00
   Bud, 6″ 12.50
   Bud, flared, 6″ 9.00
   Flared, round, 8″dia, 9½″ rare 70.00
   Flared, square bottom, 9½″ 20.00
   Flat, flared, 5″ 15.00
   Straight sided, flared, 9½″ 45.00
   Straight, #785, 8″ 20.00
   Swung, 10″ 15.00
Water bottle 60.00
Whiskey, footed, 2 oz 10.00
   Tumbler 8.00
Wine, hex foot, 2½ oz 10.00
   Hex foot 10.00

Baroque
Blue, bowl, 11½″ 32.00
   Candlestick, #2496, 5½″, pr 30.00
   Candy w/cover, 7½″ 35.00
   Creamer, 3″ 8.00
   Goblet, 6¾″ 22.00
   Individual sugar 12.00
   Juice, footed, 3″ 16.50
   Nappy, triangle, one handle 15.00
   Plate, 7″ 12.00

   9¼″ 20.00
   Relish, 2 part 10.00
   Sherbet, cone 14.50
   Sugar, 3″ 8.00
   Sugar & creamer 26.00
   Tray, 9″ 8.00
   Vase, 8″ 32.50
Crystal, bowl, vegetable 19.00
   Candle, trindle 17.00
   Candlelabra, double, bobeches/prisms 70.00
   Cup & saucer 15.00
   Pickle dish, oval 10.00
   Plate, dinner 10.00
   Sherbet, cone 9.50
   Sugar, creamer & tray, individual 22.00
   Vase, 7″ 22.00
Topaz, bon-bon, 3 toed 16.00
   Bowl, 11″ 25.00
   Candle, low 12.50
   Candy, 3 part w/cover 45.00
   Cocktail, 2¾″ 14.50
   Cup & saucer, footed 17.50
   Goblet, 6¾″ 17.50
   Individual sugar 9.50
   Mayonnaise underliner 8.50
   Mustard, lid & spoon 32.50
   Pickle dish, 8″ 15.00
   Plate, 6″ 5.00
     Torte, 14″ 20.00
   Relish, 3 part 25.00
   Rose bowl, 4″ 22.00
   Sherbet, cone 14.50
   Sweetmeat, square, 6″ 14.00
   Tid-bit, 3 toed 15.00

Beverly
Amber, candleholders, 3″ 25.00
   Creamer 20.00
   Cup & saucer, footed 10.00
   Goblet, water, 7″ 17.50
   Ice tea, 6″ 18.00
   Server, center handle 25.00
Crystal, ice bucket 18.00
Green, creamer 12.00
   Plate, 7½″ 4.00
     8½″ 5.00
   Tumbler, footed, 6″ 22.00

Chintz
Bowl, handled, 8½″ 22.00
Candlestick, single, pr 28.00
Cheese & cracker, footed 30.00
Comport, mint 25.00
Console, handled, 10½″ 30.00
Creamer, large 17.50
Goblet, 7½″ 22.00
Individual creamer & sugar on tray 30.00
Mayonnaise, 3 pc 30.00
Nappy, round, 1 handle, 5″ 10.00
Plate, 8½″ 15.00
   9½″ 20.00
   Handled, 10″ 22.00
   Torte, 14″ 27.00
Relish, 3 part, 10″ 28.50
Server, center handle 28.00
Sherbet, low, 4½″ 18.00

Sugar, 3″ **10.00**
   Large **17.50**

Colony

Bon-bon, 3 leg **9.00**
Bowl, flared, 11″ **10.00**
   Float, 11″ **12.00**
   Footed, 8½″ **25.00**
   Oval, 9¼″ **18.00**
Butter w/cover, ¼ lb **16.00**
Candlesticks, 3″, pr **12.00**
   2 socket, 6½″ **30.00**
Champagne, Empire green top **10.00**
Cheese stand **9.50**
Cocktail goblet, Empire green top **12.00**
Comport, 4″ **9.50**
Cruet **30.00**
Cup & saucer **8.50**
Goblet, 5½″ **8.00**
   9 oz **10.00**
   Water **12.00**
Juice, flat, 5 oz **7.00**
Mayonnaise **8.50**
Mayonnaise set, 3 pc **19.00**
Olive, 7″ **10.00**
Oyster cocktail **8.00**
Plate, 6″ **5.00**
   7″ **5.00**
   8″ **6.00**
   9″ **7.50**
   Handled, 6″ **6.50**
   Handled, 10″ **14.00**
   Turned up, 6″ **8.00**
Relish, 2 part, 9″ **10.00**
   3 part, oval, handles **12.50**
Salt & pepper, chrome lids, pr **15.00**
Sandwich tray, center handle **12.50**
Sherbet **4.00**
Sugar & creamer **15.00**
   Small **8.00**
Tray for sugar & creamer **6.00**
Tricorne, 3 toed, 7″ **7.00**
Tumbler, flat, 9 oz **6.50**
   Flat, 12 oz **8.00**
   Footed, 5″ **9.50**
   Footed, 12 oz **12.50**
Vase, bud, flared, 6″ **8.50**
   Cornucopia **30.00**
   Flared, 6½″ **11.00**
Water goblet, Empire green top **15.00**
Wine goblet, Empire green top **15.00**
Wine, 3½ oz **9.00**

Fairfax

Amber, bowl, cereal, 6″ **10.00**
   Bowl, fruit, 5″ **8.50**
     Whip cream **13.50**
   Butter dish, w/cover **60.00**
   Candlesticks, #2375, 4″, pr **25.00**
   Celery, 11½″ **15.00**
   Champagne, #5299 .... **12.00**
   Cream soup w/underplate **18.00**
   Cream soup **10.00**
   Creamer **7.50**
   Cup & saucer, footed **7.50**
   Demitasse cup & saucer **18.00**

Finger bowl, blown **12.00**
Goblet, #5099, 8″ **22.00**
   Water, #5299 .... **15.00**
Juice icer, no insert **6.00**
Mayonnaise **10.00**
Plate, 2 handled, 7″ **9.00**
   2 handled, 10″ **12.00**
   6″ **4.00**
   7¼″ **5.00**
   8½″ **8.00**
   9½″ **10.00**
   10½″ **13.50**
Relish, 3 part, oval, 11½″ **12.00**
   Divided, 8½″ **10.00**
Server, center handle **15.00**
Sugar & creamer, footed **16.00**
Tray, #2429, service **25.00**
Tumbler, footed, 8 oz **10.00**
   10 oz **11.00**
Azure, baker, 9″ **25.00**
   Bon-bon **9.50**
   Bowl, berry, 5″ **9.50**
     Cereal, 6″ **14.50**
     Handled, 6″ **9.50**
   Butter w/cover **125.00**
   Coaster **4.50**
   Cup & saucer **9.75**
   Cup **8.00**
   Demitasse cup & saucer, footed **24.00**
   Finger bowl **9.00**
     With underliner **12.00**
   Goblet, water, 8″ **22.50**
   Individual nut bowl, footed **9.00**
   Pickle dish, 8½″ **12.00**
   Plate, 6″ **4.00**
     7″ **6.00**
     8½″ **8.00**
   Relish, 2 part, 8½″ **12.00**
   Sugar & creamer, footed **26.00**
   Tankard, #5000 .... **155.00**
Ebony, individual creamer & sugar **29.50**
   Plate, canape, 6″ **3.00**
   Tumbler, 13 oz, crystal & black **15.00**
Green, bon-bon, 2 handles **9.00**
   Bowl, 3 legs, 6½″ **15.00**
     5″ **8.00**
     6″ **10.00**
     8″ **24.00**
     Footed, 12″ **22.50**
   Celery, oval, 11½″ **13.00**
   Coaster **3.00**
   Confection, oval, footed w/cover **30.00**
   Covered butter **65.00**
   Cream soup w/underliner **12.00**
   Cup & saucer, footed **8.00**
     Flat **8.00**
   Demitasse cup & saucer **18.00**
   Finger bowl **9.50**
   Grapefruit, w/insert **22.00**
   Ice bowl **6.00**
   Ice bucket, #2350 .... **25.00**
   Individual sugar **5.00**
   Master nut dish, 6½″ **13.00**
   Plate, 6″ **4.00**

7½″	5.00
8½″	7.50
9½″	12.00
10″	15.00
Canape	4.00
Platter, oval, 12″	22.00
Relish, 2 part, 8½″	11.00
3 part, 11″	15.00
Sauce boat w/underliner	12.00
Sugar and lid	25.00
Sweet meat	10.00
Tankard, #5000	135.00
Orchid, ashtray	12.50
Bowl, fruit, 5″	12.00
Coaster	4.00
Cream soup, footed	13.00
Cup & saucer	5.00
Footed	12.00
Ice bucket	32.00
Plate, 8½″	8.00
10″	22.00
Relish, 2 part, 8½″	11.00
Tray	12.50
Vase, optic, 8″	22.00
Pink, ashtray	9.50
Baker, oval, 9½″	22.50
Bowl, 5″	6.00
12″	20.00
Dessert, 2 handles	26.00
Whip cream	12.50
Candy w/cover, 3 foot	35.00
Coaster	3.00
Cream soup	10.00
Creamer, footed, large	5.00
Cup & saucer	9.00
Footed	10.00
Demitasse cup & saucer	20.00
Individual cream & sugar	12.00
Nut dish, 3 legs	15.00
Plate, 6″	3.00
7½″	5.00
8½″	7.00
10″	20.00
Platter, oval, 12″	20.00
Sherbet, low	8.50
Sugar, footed, large	5.00
Tumbler, water, footed, #2000	10.00
Water, footed, #5298	15.00
Topaz, bowl, 5″	8.00
Bowl, cereal	10.00
Dessert, 2 handles, 8½″	20.00
Oval, 10″	25.00
Whip cream	10.00
Candlesticks, low, pr	25.00
Scroll, pr	50.00
Cocktail	20.00
Cream soup	8.00
Cruet w/faceted stopper	50.00
Cup & saucer, footed	7.00
Demitasse cup & saucer	15.00
Finger bowl	10.00
Goblet, water	15.00
Ice tea, footed	18.00
Individual sugar & creamer	12.00

Mayonnaise w/underplate	25.00
Nut dish, footed	15.00
Oyster cocktail	15.00
Plate, 6″	5.00
7″	7.50
8″	9.00
9½″	12.00
10¼″	20.00
13″	15.00
Platter, oval, 12″	20.00
Oval, 15½″	25.00
Relish tray, 5 inserts, 13″	65.00
Salt & pepper, glass top, pr	75.00
Salt, open	8.00
Sauce boat w/liner	95.00
Sherbet, #6206	10.00
Low	6.00
Sugar w/cover, creamer, large, lid rare	150.00
Tumbler, juice, footed	8.00
Water, footed	9.00
Wine	20.00

Heather

Crystal, cocktail, 5″	20.00
Goblet, 6½″	22.50
Mustard w/lid	22.50
Pickle, oval, 8½″	12.00
Relish, 3 part, 11″	25.00
Sherbet, 5″	18.00
Wine, 6″	22.50

Hermitage

Azure, cup	6.50
Ice tub	60.00
Crystal, celery, oval, 11″	8.50
Coaster	3.50
Goblet, 5″	10.00
Ice dish	6.50
Icer w/fruit liner	11.00
Plate, 8½″	7.00
Tumbler, 3½″	5.00
5¾″	6.00
Footed, 3 oz	4.00
Topaz, cup & saucer	8.50
Plate, 7″	4.00
Sherbet	5.00
Vase	25.00

June

Azure blue, candlestick, low, pr	50.00
Candlesticks, 4″, pr	40.00
Candy w/cover, 3 part	125.00
Celery, 11″	40.00
Champagne, 6″	25.00
Claret	35.00
Comport, footed	75.00
Cup & saucer	42.50
Demitasse saucer	25.00
Goblet, water	35.00
Ice dish	45.00
Ice tea, 6″	25.00
Oyster cocktail	30.00
Pitcher	550.00
Plate, 7½″	12.50
8¾″	15.00
9½″	22.50
10¼″	60.00

For cream soup	15.00
Salt & pepper	140.00
Server, center handle	48.00
Sugar	27.50
Tray, 6 sides, rare	270.00
Tumbler, 5″	24.00
Whipped cream pail	125.00
Crystal, goblet	20.00
Plate, 13″	26.00
Relish, divided, 8½″	15.00
Sugar	15.00
Pink, bon-bon	17.50
Bowl, cereal, 6″	28.00
Fruit, 5″	22.00
Candlesticks, #2395½, 5″, pr	45.00
Cocktail, 3 oz	42.00
Creamer	20.00
Demitasse cup & saucer	50.00
Goblet, 8″	25.00
Grapefruit dish, footed	36.00
Ice tea, 6″	24.00
Plate, 6″	7.00
7½″	9.00
8½″	13.50
For finger bowl, 6″	9.00
Salt & pepper	90.00
Sugar	20.00
Whiskey, 3″	32.50
Topaz, bowl, footed, 12″	32.50
Bowl, handled, 6″	12.50
Handled, 7½″	10.00
Scroll, 10″	45.00
Toed, 12″	32.50
Candle, block, 4″	15.00
Candlesticks, 2″, pr	24.00
Champagne, 6″	18.00
6½″	21.00
Claret	30.00
Cocktail	35.00
Creamer, footed	22.00
Cup & saucer	25.00
Cup, footed	20.00
Finger bowl liner	9.00
Goblet, #5298, 8″	27.00
Water, 8″	25.00
Oyster cocktail	18.00
Pitcher	335.00
Plate, 6″	6.00
7½″	9.00
8¾″	12.00
10½″	25.00
Relish, divided, 8¾″	22.50
Salt & pepper	95.00
Sherbet, 4¼″	12.00
Sherbet, low	22.50
Sweet meat	18.50
Tumbler, footed, 9 oz	16.50
Footed, 12 oz.	18.00
Water, 5″	18.00
Wine	40.00

Lafayette

Burgandy, sugar & creamer	22.00
Cobalt, cup & saucer	19.00
Crystal, relish 3 part	8.00

Dark green, creamer, footed	13.00
Lemon dish	9.00
Sweetmeat	9.00
Green, pickle, 8½″	12.00
Sugar & creamer, footed	22.00
Topaz, sweetmeat	7.00

Mayfair

Amber, relish, 2 part	8.50
Black, plate, 7″	5.00
Crystal, relish, 4 part	12.00
Green, cup, footed	5.00
Relish, 4 part	14.00
Sugar, individual	7.00
Sugar, large	6.00
Pink, bowl, oval, 10½″	18.50
Demitasse cup & saucer	17.50
Topaz, comport, footed	20.00
Cup & saucer	7.50
Demitasse cup & saucer	20.00
Plate, 6″	3.00
Plate, 7″	5.00
Plate, 8″	5.00
Platter	18.00
Sugar, footed	8.00

Meadowrose

Crystal, bowl, 2 handles, 4 legs	22.00
Bowl, 2 handles, 8¾″	35.00
With handles, 12″	20.00
Champagne	16.00
Cocktail, 5″	18.00
Goblet, 7½″	22.00
Plate, 6″	3.50
Relish, 3 part, 10″	18.00
Sherbet	12.50
Tumbler, footed, 4½″	12.00

Navarre

Crystal, bowl, handled, 8½″	22.50
Candleholders, double flame, pr	60.00
Candlesticks, double, #2496, pr	32.00
Champagne, 5½ oz	18.00
Cocktail, 3½ oz	16.00
Comport, 5½″	28.00
Cordial, 1 oz	22.00
Creamer & sugar	27.50
Goblet, 7½″	24.00
Goblet, water, 9 oz	18.00
Ice tea, footed, 13 oz	18.00
Juice, footed, 5 oz	12.00
Nappy, tri corner, 1 handle	12.00
Plate, 6″	6.00
7½″	9.00
Relish, 3 part	17.50
Salt & pepper shakers, pr	30.00
Sherbet, 5½″	20.00
Tumbler, 5″	15.50
Footed, 6″	18.50
Wine, 3 oz	20.00

New Garland

Yellow, cream soup	12.50
Cup & saucer	25.00
Plate, 6″	6.00
Plate, 8″	10.00
Plate, 9″	15.00
Sugar	12.50

Oak Leaf

Crystal, candlestick **15.00**
   Cheese & cracker, 2 pc **25.00**
   Confection & cover **40.00**
Green, confection & cover **70.00**
   Plate, 8½″ **18.00**
Pink, console, oval, 13″ **40.00**

Romance

Crystal, bowl, flared, 12″ **18.50**
   Candleholder, double **15.00**
     5½″ **18.50**
   Champagne, 5½″ **17.50**
   Cocktail, 5″ **18.00**
   Cream & sugar **24.00**
   Cup & saucer **15.00**
   Goblet, #6017 . . . . **14.00**
   Ice tea, 12 oz **14.00**
   Plate, 7½″ **7.00**
     9½″ **16.50**
   Relish, 2 part, 6½″ **14.50**
   Sherbet **10.00**
   Tumbler, footed, 4¾″ **16.00**
   Wine, #6017 . . . . **18.50**

Royal

Amber, celery, 11″ **22.50**
   Champagne, 5″ **15.00**
   Comport, 5″ **25.00**
   Cup & saucer, flat **2.00**
   Demitasse cup & saucer **35.00**
   Goblet, water, 7″ **25.00**
   Grapefruit dish, footed **22.50**
   Ice tea, 6″ **17.50**
   Pickle, 8″ **15.00**
   Plate, 7½″ **5.00**
     8¼″ **7.50**
     10½″ **15.00**
   Salt & pepper, #5000, pr **35.00**
   Sherbet, tall **14.00**
   Soup, 7½″ **22.50**
Green, bouillon w/liner **22.50**
   Bowl, berry, 5½″ **2.50**
     Cereal, 6½″ **17.50**
     Footed, 10½″ **32.00**
   Candlestick, 3½″ **12.00**
   Candy w/cover, footed **50.00**
   Cup & saucer, flat **22.50**
     Footed **25.00**
   Grapefruit, footed **25.00**
   Plate, 6″ **5.00**
     7½″ **6.50**
     8½″ **7.50**
   Server, center handle **23.00**
   Vase, flared, 7″ **40.00**
   Wine **7.00**

Seville

Amber, bouillon **10.00**
   Cream soup w/liner **15.00**
   Cup & saucer, footed **12.50**
   Goblet, water, 7″ **20.00**
   Plate, 6″ **2.25**
     7½″ **4.00**
     9½″ **9.00**
     10½″ **12.00**
   Sherbet, 4″ **10.00**

Soup, 7¾″ **15.00**
Wine **20.00**
Green, champagne, sherbet **10.00**
   Comport, 7″ **22.50**
   Demitasse cup & saucer **30.00**
   Goblet, tall **20.00**
   Oyster cocktail **8.00**
   Vase, footed, 7″ **22.50**

Sunray

Crystal, ashtray **4.50**
   Bowl, berry **6.00**
     Fruit, 12″ **25.00**
     Salad, 8″ **25.00**
   Butter w/cover, ½ lb **45.00**
   Candy & cover, footed **50.00**
   Cheese & cracker **25.00**
   Coaster **4.50**
   Cocktail shaker **30.00**
   Compote, footed **10.00**
   Condiment set, 2 oils, 2 mustards w/lids & spoons, tray **100.00**
   Console, ped, 12″ **24.00**
   Cruet w/stopper **22.50**
   Cup & saucer **10.00**
   Ice bucket **24.00**
   Jug, 2 pt, 8½″ **50.00**
   Onion soup, covered **35.00**
   Plate, 6″ **3.00**
     7½″ **4.00**
     8″ **4.75**
     9½″ **7.00**
     13″ **20.00**
   Torte, 14″ **25.00**
   Punch cup **5.00**
   Relish, 4 part **17.50**
     Divided, w/handle, 10½″ **14.50**
   Rose bowl, small **15.00**
   Rye decanter w/stopper **35.00**
   Sherbet, footed **6.00**
   Sugar & creamer on tray **18.00**
   Sugar, 2¾″ **6.00**
   Tray, ice cream **12.50**
     Oblong, 10½″ **15.00**
   Vase, 10″ **25.00**

Trojan

Pink, ice bucket **95.00**
   Individual cream & sugar **65.00**
   Vase, 8″ **75.00**
Topaz, bowl, berry, 5″ **12.50**
   Champagne, 6″ **17.50**
   Cocktail **22.00**
   Console, footed, 12″ **25.00**
   Creamer, footed **17.50**
   Cup & saucer **17.50**
   Demitasse cup & saucer **35.00**
   Goblet, water, 8″ **22.00**
   Juice, footed, ... **14.00**
   Lemon dish **14.50**
   Mayonnaise, footed **20.00**
   Mint comport **27.00**
   Plate, 6″ **5.50**
     7¼″ **6.50**
     8¾″ **9.50**
     10½″ **14.50**
   Torte, 14″ **35.00**

Sherbet, tall	**14.50**
Sugar	**17.50**
Metal handle	**75.00**
Tumbler, 9 oz, 5¼″	**16.00**
Water pitcher	**295.00**
Whip cream pail, metal handle	**75.00**

Vernon

Amber, candle, #2375, 4″	**14.00**
Cream & sugar	**27.50**
Cup & saucer	**15.00**
Finger bowl	**12.50**
Ice tea, 6″	**12.50**
Parfait	**16.00**
Plate, 7½″	**6.00**
8¾″	**6.00**
10½″	**25.00**
Server, center handle	**22.00**
Tumbler, footed, 9 oz	**16.50**
Azure, console, oval, 13″	**55.00**
Demitasse cup & saucer	**35.00**
Finger bowl	**18.00**
Orchid, ice bucket	**75.00**
Plate, 10″	**25.00**
Tumbler, footed, 2½ oz	**14.50**
Wine, #877	**45.00**

Versailles

Azure blue, boullion, w/liner	**29.50**
Bowl, w/handles, 9″	**35.00**
Candlesticks, #375, 4″, pr	**45.00**
Candy, w/cover	**165.00**
Cocktail	**40.00**
Console, #2394, 3 legs	**40.00**
Cordial, rare	**65.00**
Cream soup w/liner	**40.00**
Creamer	**27.50**
Cruet, w/stopper	**250.00**
Cup & saucer	**30.00**
Demitasse cup & saucer	**60.00**
Finger bowl, blown	**27.00**
Goblet, water, 8″	**27.50**
Ice bucket	**120.00**
Ice tea, footed	**25.00**
Parfait	**40.00**
Plate, 6″	**7.00**
7″	**10.00**
8¾″	**15.00**
10″	**45.00**
Salt	**35.00**
Saucer	**9.50**
Shaker	**60.00**
Tumbler, footed, 5 oz	**22.00**
Footed, 12 oz	**28.00**
Water pitcher	**450.00**
Whip cream bowl	**35.00**
Wine	**50.00**
Green, Champagne, #5298	**25.00**
Claret/parfait, 6½oz	**28.00**
Fingerbowl, w/underliner	**17.50**
Goblet, 8″	**25.00**
Ice tea	**20.00**
Juice, footed	**15.00**
Plate, 6″	**5.00**
Pink, bon-bon, 2 loop handle	**16.50**
Bowl, whip cream	**17.50**

Candlesticks, #2375½, pr	**35.00**
#2394, pr	**22.00**
2″, pr	**22.00**
Candy, w/cover, flat	**50.00**
Champagne, 6″	**20.00**
Comport, 7″	**22.00**
Console set, footed, #2375 candles	**55.00**
Console, mushroom, 12″	**35.00**
Creamer	**20.00**
Creamer & sugar	**42.50**
Cup & saucer	**18.50**
Goblet, 8″	**25.00**
Ice bucket	**45.00**
Liner, 6″	**6.50**
Plate, 6″	**5.00**
7½″	**7.50**
8¾″	**8.50**
9″	**15.00**
Torte, 14″	**20.00**
Salt & pepper, pr	**85.00**
Server, center handle	**30.00**
Sherbet, high	**20.00**
Low	**14.00**
Sugar	**20.00**
Tumbler, footed, 9 oz	**20.00**
Water pitcher	**275.00**
Topaz, ashtray, sm	**32.00**
Bon-bon, handled, 7″	**10.00**
Bowl, cereal, 6″	**9.00**
Fruit, 5″	**7.50**
Salad, 2 handles	**50.00**
With handles, 9″	**28.00**
Candleholders, 5″, pr	**32.00**
Champagne	**20.00**
Cheese & cracker	**60.00**
Claret	**32.50**
Console bowl, 3 legs	**40.00**
Handled	**25.00**
Cordial, gold trim	**35.00**
Creamer	**15.00**
Cruet w/stopper, rare	**350.00**
Cup & saucer	**22.50**
Demitasse cup & saucer	**45.00**
Finger bowl	**15.00**
Goblet, water, 8″	**22.00**
Ice bucket	**70.00**
Ice tea, footed	**22.00**
Juice, footed, rare	**40.00**
Liner	**6.50**
Oyster cocktail	**20.00**
Plate, 6″	**6.50**
7″	**7.50**
8¾″	**8.50**
10½″	**12.00**
Handled, 7″	**10.00**
Platter, 12″	**30.00**
Relish, 3 feet	**20.00**
Sherbet, low	**14.00**
Soup, 7″	**27.50**
Sugar	**20.00**
Tumbler, footed, 9 oz	**18.00**
Water pitcher	**275.00**

Vesper

Amber, boullion cup	**15.00**

Bowl, berry, 5" **12.50**
Candleholder, 3", pr **30.00**
Celery, 11" **9.50**
Cocktail, 5" **22.00**
Cream soup **17.50**
Cup & saucer, footed **22.00**
Demitasse cup & saucer **35.00**
Finger bowl **14.00**
Goblet **24.00**
Pickle, 8" **15.00**
Plate, 6" **2.50**
  7½" **5.75**
  8¾" **8.00**
  10½" **20.00**
Server, center handle **32.00**
Green, boullion **14.50**
Bowl, cereal, 6½" **14.50**
Candlesticks, 3½", pr **25.00**
Cream soup **17.50**
Creamer, flat **17.50**
Cup & saucer, flat **22.50**
  Footed **22.50**
Finger bowl, blown **20.00**
Goblet, water, 7¼" **25.00**
Grapefruit/mayonnaise, ... **30.00**
Ice bucket, complete **65.00**
Ice tea **18.00**
Plate, 6" **4.50**
  7" **6.50**
  10" **20.00**
  Torte, 14" **40.00**
Server, center handle **35.00**
Sugar & creamer, footed **35.00**
Sugar, flat **17.50**
Tumbler, 10 oz, 6" **18.00**
Willowmere
Crystal, bowl, w/underplate, flared, 12½" **70.00**
Candlesticks, 6", pr **70.00**
Claret **35.00**
Cocktail **12.00**
Cream & sugar, footed **35.00**
Goblet, water **15.00**
Ice tea **15.00**
Oyster cocktail **12.00**
Plate, 8" **10.00**
Relish, 2 part **16.00**
  3 part **20.00**
Tumbler, footed, 5 oz **12.00**
  Footed, 9 oz **16.00**
Wine **17.50**

Fraktur

   Fraktur is a German style of black letter text type. To collectors, the fraktur is a type of hand lettered document used by the people of German decent who settled in the area of Pennsylvania and New Jersey. These documents recorded births, baptisms and marriages, were used as bookplates, and as certificates of honor. They were elaborately decorated with colorful folk art borders of hearts, birds, angels and flowers. Examples by recognized artists, and those with unusual decorative motifs, bring prices well into the thousands of dollars. Not all were done completely by hand however; in the last quarter of the 19th century, lithograph companies sold prepared forms on which the text was hand lettered, and the decorations often enhanced.

Baptismal certificate, printed,Stark & Lange, Hanover **220.00**
Birth and Baptismal certificate
2 ladies, flowers, Oley Twp, PA artist **1,625.00**
2 standing men, rooster, 1802 .... **5,300.00**
Peters, PA **17.50**
Ritter, Reading, angels, birds **85.00**
Strenge, floral, heart, bird, 1793 .... **600.00**
Birth and Baptismal record
Flying Angel, branches, parrot, swan, 1809, 23x15½" **1,430.00**
Pennsylvania births, 1851 & 1863, English, Scheffer, 14x17" .. **40.00**
Young, PA, woman, flowers, parrots, 1819, 10x8¼" **6,875.00**
Birth record
Birds & trees in red, blue, & yellow, 1820, 12¼x7¼" **3,850.00**
Ohio, Peters, PA, red, yellow block, 15½x18¼" **65.00**
Printed w/hand colored eagle, angels, 1865, 16x19" **55.00**
S Peters, 1820, framed, 14x18" **70.00**
Trewitz, PA, heart, tulips & birds **1,650.00**

Bookplate, red, blue, yellow tints, pen & ink, flowers, framed, 6x7¾" **385.00**
Name plate, Franica Brand, bright colors, bird on tree, 10¼x8" **2,970.00**
Vorschrift, colored floral vines & hearts, PA, 1786, 11¾x16½" **600.00**

Frames

   Styles in picture frames have changed with the fashion of the day, but those that especially interest today's collectors are the deep shadow boxes made of fine woods such as walnut or cherry, those with Art Nouveau influence, and the oak frames decorated with molded gesso and gilt from the Victorian era.

Acorns carved on 12" ovals, pair **35.00**
Brass plated & painted iron, easel type, w/Art Nouveau lady.... **25.00**
Brass, US Airman, embossed service wings, star in corners, 1940 **18.00**
  Ball feet, embossed Drape & Tassel design, oval, 7" **12.00**
  Open grape & leaf pattern, beaded inside, no glass, 6¾" **10.00**
  Ornate scrolling, grapevines, Bacchus in relief, 14¾" **68.00**
  Rectangular, embossed, beaded border, dated 1900, 4½x6" .. **12.00**
  Table top, ball feet, recticulated, 1800s **32.00**
  Table top, ribbon cut-out, ball feet, 1800s **30.00**
  Victorian, w/mosaic florals, 2x1¾" **48.00**
Celluloid, pearlized gold, metal corners, 9x7½" **9.00**
Embossed allover pattern on gesso, 14x17" **18.00**
Frame holder, ci, Victorian, black girl w/bow & arrow **80.00**
Iron, gilded ornate scrolls, easel back, oval 5½x3¾" opening .. **30.00**
Limestone, carved flowers & vines, dated 1880, w/tin types, 10x7" **130.00**
Octagonal, w/relief carved flowers, curved glass, 12x18" **25.00**
Pine, blk paint, relief gilded gesso flowers, pair **85.00**
Rosewood, carved, easel back, 8x10", 4¼x6¼" opening **40.00**
Seashells set in plaster, wood base, Victorian, oval, 14" **50.00**
Shadow box, walnut, black & gold, 17x15" **70.00**
  Wood w/gilt liner, 9½x8"opening **35.00**

Silver finish w/gold trim, ornate, 16x20" **110.00**

Walnut, 13x10″ . . . 12.00
Black line trim, 9x11″ . . . 20.00
Deep, inner gilt liner, 23½x27″ . . . 37.50
Gilt liner, 13″ square . . . 22.00
Gold liner, semi-deep, 18½x22″ . . . 25.00
Oval, semi-deep, 8½x10″ . . . 20.00
Wooden with red marbelized inner frame, 12x14″ . . . 30.00
With gilt relief, 15x18″ . . . 40.00
With gilt relief, 6¾x8¾″ . . . 28.00
Wood, ornate, curved glass, oval, 18″ dia . . . 40.00

Franciscan

Franciscan ware was developed by Gladding McBean and Company at their site in Glendale, California. First introduced in 1934, it has been made in many lovely patterns that are today attracting the attention of collectors interested in modern American dinnerware. Perhaps the best known of their early lines is Swirl, or Coronado, as it was officially named. It was made in more than sixty shapes and fifteen colors. The first mark, used in the late 30s was a large F within a double walled square. In the 40s, a 2 line Franciscan mark was adopted. It was replaced in 1947 by a circular device, Franciscan Ware centered by Made In California USA.

Apple
Bowl, 5¼″ . . . 5.00
6″ . . . 6.00
8″ . . . 16.00
Butter w/cover, ¼ lb . . . 14.00
Chop plate, 14″ . . . 16.00
Cookie jar . . . 40.00
Creamer . . . 8.50
Cup & saucer . . . 7.00
Large . . . 18.00
Gravy boat . . . 15.00
Gravy w/attached underplate . . . 15.00
Jug, open . . . 8.00
Mug, 10 oz . . . 8.00
Pitcher w/ice lip, 8½″ . . . 35.00
Plate, bread & butter . . . 2.75
Dinner . . . 7.50
Salad . . . 5.00
Platter, 12″ . . . 12.50
Rim soup, 8½″ . . . 8.50
Salt & pepper, pr . . . 10.00
Service for 4, 25 pc, w/6 extras . . . 125.00
Soup . . . 4.50
Sugar w/cover . . . 12.00
Sugar, open . . . 5.00
Teapot . . . 35.00
Vegetable bowl, 8½″ . . . 8.50
Coronado
Bowl, 6½″, satin rose . . . 3.50
9″, gloss rose . . . 9.00
Creamer, satin ivory . . . 9.00
Cup, gloss maroon . . . 4.00
Gloss yellow . . . 4.00
Satin rose . . . 4.00
Satin yellow . . . 4.00
Pitcher, illus. . . . 15.00
Plate, 6½″, gloss maroon . . . 2.50
6½″, gloss turquoise . . . 2.50
6½″, gloss yellow . . . 2.50
6½″, satin rose . . . 2.50
6½″, satin turquoise . . . 2.50
8″, gloss maroon . . . 3.50
8″, satin yellow . . . 5.00
9½″, gloss maroon . . . 4.00
9½″, gloss yellow . . . 4.00
9½″, satin blue . . . 4.00
9½″, satin rose . . . 4.00
10½″, satin yellow . . . 8.00
12″, chop, gloss rose . . . 10.00
14″, chop, satin ivory . . . 15.00
Sauce dish, satin rose, 6″ . . . 2.50
Saucer, satin rose . . . 1.00
Gloss yellow . . . 1.00
Sugar, covered, satin ivory . . . 10.00
Teapot, gloss maroon, w/lid . . . 14.00

Teapot without pedestal base, turquoise gloss . . . 15.00
Desert Rose
Bowl, 5″ . . . 5.00
6″ . . . 6.00
9″ . . . 18.00
Divided vegetable . . . 12.00
Candleholders, pr . . . 16.00
Creamer . . . 8.50
Cup & saucer . . . 8.50
Demitasse . . . 10.00
Pitcher, pt . . . 18.00
2½ qt, w/6 14 oz tumblers . . . 60.00
Plate, dinner . . . 7.50
Luncheon . . . 6.00
Salad . . . 4.00
Platter, oval, 14½″ . . . 24.00
Relish, 3 part, oval . . . 12.00
Rim soup . . . 8.50
Salt & pepper, pr . . . 10.00
Saucer . . . 1.50
Sugar w/cover . . . 12.00
El Patio
Bowl, 8½″ . . . 6.00
Fruit, 9″, turquoise . . . 8.00
Oval vegetable . . . 7.50
Carafe w/wood handle, lid . . . 17.50
Chop plate . . . 12.00
Creamer . . . 6.00
Cup, brown . . . 5.00
Maroon . . . 5.00
Pitcher . . . 14.00
Plate, 6″, cobalt . . . 4.00
6″, turquoise . . . 2.00
8″, cobalt . . . 5.00
8″, pumpkin . . . 5.00

8″, turquoise	4.00
8″, yellow	5.00
9½″, turquoise	6.00
10½″, turquoise	7.50
Platter, oval, 13″	12.50
Salt & pepper, pr	8.00
Saucer, turquoise	4.00
Yellow	2.00
Soup	6.50
Sugar w/cover	7.50
Tumbler w/handle	8.00

Ivy

Bowl, 8″ dia	15.00
Casserole, covered, double handled, 8″ dia	25.00
Plate, chop, 11¾″	14.00
Plate, chop, 14″	22.50

Square

Cup, yellow	4.00
Plate, 6″, chartreuse	2.00
9″, yellow	4.00
Toaster set, jam jars w/yellow tray, set	8.00

Swirl

Baker, oval, w/flange	9.00
Casserole w/lid	12.50
Cream soup w/underplate	12.00
Creamer & sugar	18.00
Cup & saucer	10.00
Pitcher	15.00
Plate, 6½″	4.00
7½″	6.50
8½″	6.50
9½″	7.00
Platter, 15½″	18.00
Oval, 10½″	10.00
Salt & pepper, pr	10.00
Sherbet	7.50
Teapot	15.00

Francisware

Francisware, produced by Hobbs, Brokunier & Co. of Wheeling, West Virginia in the 1880s, is a clear or frosted tableware with amber stained rim bands. The most often found pattern is hobnail, but a swirl design was also made.

Clear: butter w/cover	90.00
Creamer	45.00
Pitcher, 8½″	135.00
Pitcher, 11″	195.00
Salt & pepper	50.00
Sauce dish, square	28.00
Spooner	45.00
Table set: sugar w/cover, covered butter, cream, spooner	225.00
Toothpick, hobnail	40.00
Tumbler	38.00
Frosted: berry set, ruffled rims, 7 pc	180.00
Bowl w/underplate, square	80.00
Bowl, square, 9″	58.00
Butter & cover	120.00
Fingerbowl	38.00
Fingerbowl, swirl	50.00
Ice cream set, 5 pc	130.00
Pitcher, rare, 7″	265.00
Pitcher, 8½″	165.00

Pitcher, bulbous w/applied handle, 11″	245.00
Salt & pepper	65.00
Set: pitcher, 2 tumblers, finger bowl, cloverleaf tray	395.00
Spooner	60.00

Sugar	75.00
Syrup, swirl	95.00
Table set, 4 pc	300.00
Toothpick	55.00
Toothpick, swirl	95.00
Tray, cloverleaf	100.00
Tray, oval, 12x7″	40.00
Tumbler	50.00
Waste bowl	65.00

Frankart

During the 1920s, Frankart Inc. of New York, N.Y., produced a line of metal accessories such as lamps, bookends and ashtrays in a green patina finish. Animals and bird figurals were used, but their nudes were the most popular. Many pieces were marked Frankart, with the patent number and date of manufacture.

Bookends, nudes, knee up, chin on shoulder, w/frog, 1922, pr	215.00
Springer Spaniels, bronzed finish, pair	45.00
Bust, woman	69.00
Figurine, head turned, knee up, w/frog, good paint, 1922, 10″	135.00
Nude, 10″	110. 00
Nude ash tray, No T301	105.00
Smokers stand, No T333, nude supports 8″ glass ash tray, 27″	600.00
Statue, horse, signed, 6″	50.00
Table lamp, 2 nudes form 'A' shape, custard glass globe, 19″	450.00
Wall plaques, No 242, silver finish, pr	395.00
No W903, decorative masks, Art Deco style, pr	475.00

Frankoma

The Frank Pottery, founded in 1933 by John Frank, became known as Frankoma in1935. The company produced decorative figurals, vases and such, marking their ware from 1936-38 with the Leopard & Pot, Frankoma mark. These pieces are highly sought. The entire operation was destoryed by fire in 1938 and new molds were cast---some from surviving pieces---and a similar line of production was pursued.

The body of the ware was changed in 1956 from a light cream to a red burning clay and this, along with the color of the glazes (over 35 have been used), helps determine the period of production.

A desert theme has always been favored in design as well as in color selection. In 1965 they began to produce a limited edition series of Christmas plates, followed in 1969 by a bottle series. Considered very collectible are their political mugs, bi-centennial plates, Teenagers of the Bible plates and their Wildfire series. Their ceramic Christmas cards, especially those sent after 1969, are very popular items with today's collectors.

The pottery is still operating, and continues to produce lovely dinner-ware lines, kitchen accessories, flower pots and figurines.

Ash tray, elephant	45.00
Windproof	15.00
Bean pot, w/cover, beige & brown	22.50
Bottle vase, V1, 1969, 1st issue, John Frank, 15″	110.00
V1	60.00
V3	30.00
V4, 1972, signed John Frank, 12″	75.00
V4	45.00
V5	30.00
V8, 1976, stars & stripes, Joneice Frank	40.00
With cat mark, square, #30	40.00
Bowl, bronze, 1 handle, 3¾x2¼″	6.00
Candleholder, Christ the Light of the World, Desert Gold	20.00
Chop plate, Mayan-Aztec, Woodland Moss, 15″	25.00
Christmas card, 1950 Frankoma	70.00
1960 Gracetone	65.00
1962 Frankoma	50.00
1966	30.00
1975 Grace Lee & Milton Smith	80.00
1972	15.00
Cornucopia, #58, 7″	25.00
Cream & sugar w/lid, Plainsman, Onyx Black	12.00
Dog food spoon	25.00
Donkey mug, 1976, red/white	30.00
1977, Carter-Mondale, pink/white	25.00
Elephant mug, 1969, Nixon, Agnew, red & white	85.00
1970	30.00
1971	30.00
1972	20.00
1973, Nixon-Agnew	50.00
1974	20.00
1975, yellow/white	30.00
1976	20.00
1977	15.00
1978, moss/white	15.00
1979	8.00
Flask, Aztec decor, leather thong, ceramic loops, green, brown	17.00
Flowerabrum, #58	30.00
Jewelry, bolo	15.00
Ear clip	8.00
On Silla Gem card	14.00
Jug, tan, 7″	9.00
Lamp base, barrel	25.00
Leaf dish, #226, green/bronze, 12″	8.00
Liquor jug w/cork, green/bronze, decorated, 5x5½x3½″	17.00
Miniature, bull	35.00
Elephant	35.00
Fish vase	75.00
Hobby horse vase	75.00
Horse	25.00
Terrier	45.00
Thunderbird vase, #506	20.00
Uncle Slug jug	15.00
Vase, #500	12.00
Mint bowl, small, #34	25.00

Pitcher, w/6 mugs, barrel, Dessert Gold	30.00
Mayan-Aztec, Woodland Moss, 2 qt	12.00
With ice lip, green/bronze, 8x6½″	15.00
Plaque, Will Rogers, no border	35.00
Will Rogers, w/border	25.00
Plate, Battles for Independence, 1974, White Sand, 8½″	85.00
Birth of Eternal Life, 1977, signed Joneice Frank	15.00
Bob White Quail, 1972, 1st issue, Prairie Green, 7″	100.00
Christmas 1968	35.00
Christmas 1979	30.00
Conestoga Wagon, 1971, 8½″	245.00
Good Will..., 1965, 1st issue, signed John Frank	225.00
Grace Madonna, 1977, Rubbed Bisque, 8½″	15.00
Gray Squirrel, 1977, Prairie Green, 7″	50.00
Jesus the Carpenter, 1971, 1st issue, signed John Frank	45.00
Jonathan the Archer, 1975 signed Joneice Frank, 7″	20.00
King of Kings, 1970, Della Robbia, signed John Frank	35.00
Lazy Bones, Peach Glow, 10″	7.00
Madonna of Love, 1978, Rubbed Bisque, 8½″	15.00
Peter the Fisherman, 1977, signed Joneice Frank, 7″	15.00
Provocations, 1972, 1st issue trial run, gold	260.00
Provocations, 1972, 1st issue trial run, green	260.00
Provocations, 1972, 1st issue, White Sand, 8½″	150.00
Symbols of Freedom, 1976, White Sand, 8½″	32.00
The Annunication, 1973, signed John Frank	25.00
Salt & pepper, Dutch shoes	25.00
Bull	50.00
Monogrammed	15.00
Sculpture, buffalo	175.00
Charger Horse bookend	40.00
Circus Horse	25.00
Dreamer Girl bookend	55.00
Fandancer, light clay	100.00
Flower Girl	75.00
Gardener Boy w/shirt & pants	90.00
Gardener Boy w/overalls	85.00
Gardener Girl	80.00
Indian Bowl Maker, light clay	65.00
Indian Madonna, Bronze Green, 13½″	25.00
Irish Setter bookend	50.00
Medicine Man	50.00
Pacing Leopard, 15″	65.00
Prancing Colt, 8″	85.00
Reclining Puma, light clay	45.00
Seahorse bookend	175.00
Seated Puma, light clay	40.00
Tragedy Mask, Rubbed Bisque, 9″	20.00
Trojan Horses bookend	40.00
Western Bronco, bookends, patina	35.00
Sugar, Mayan-Aztec, bronze, 1 handle, #7U	7.00
Teapot, Wagon Wheel, 6 cup, Red Bud	18.00
Toby mug, Cowboy, Flame, 4½″	15.00
Uncle Sam, blue, 4½″	20.00
Trivet, Wagon Wheel, Clay Blue	18.00
Cattle brand symbols	20.00
Tumbler, green/bronze, 2¾″	4.00
Tureen, West Wind, Woodland Moss, 2½ qt	12.00
Vase, A Fireside Pitcher, #77A	25.00
Black Foot, #55	10.00
Cactus Bloom	35.00
Fireside Vase, #77	25.00
Flying Goose, #60B	12.00
Phoebe, white sand	42.50
Shell	20.00

Stovepipe, #72 . . . . **25.00**
Swirl, #73 . . . . **25.00**
Tall Ram's Head, w/cat mark/#74 . . . . **45.00**
Wagonwheel **15.00**
Wheat **25.00**
With Cat mark/#76 . . . . **40.00**
Shell, Peach Glow, 6″ **30.00**
Wall Pocket, 196, Prairie Green, 12″ **20.00**
Acorn, light clay **12.00**
Boot **15.00**
Phoebe, light clay **35.00**
Ram's Head **40.00**

Paperweight, temple **15.00**
Pitcher, Royal Dulton Flow Blue, 1906 centennial, 8½″ **165.00**
Plate, Los Angeles, roses, emblem, 1906, 6″ **55.00**
Stick pin, 10k, trowel **18.00**
Sword, silverplate & steel, plate & chrome scabbard **250.00**
Watch fob & strap w/emblem, 1912 . . . . **16.00**
Watch fob, 32nd, 14k **185.00**
Moose, tankard w/4 mugs, Howdy Pap, Acme Art Co **80.00**
Velvet robe for officer, old **125.00**
Shrine, chalice, cranberry glass, 1908 . . . . **65.00**
Champagne, swords & tobacco leaf base, 1909 . . . . **75.00**
Plate, shriner w/fez, camel caravan, 10½″ **65.00**

Fraternal Organizations

Fraternal memoribilia is a vast and varied field. Emblems representing the various organizations have been used to decorate cups, shaving mugs, plates and glassware. Medals, swords, documents and other ceremonial paraphernalia from the 1800s are especially prized.

Eagles, shaving mug, Limoges, 4″ **75.00**
Elks, badge, convention 1936 . . . . 9.00
Cigarette case, brass w/emblem **15.00**
Demitasse spoon, figural, BPOE Carnival, 1902 . . . . **18.00**
Mug, advertising, Minn. Brewery, BPOE, 4½″ **130.00**
Mug, BPOE, 5″ **65.00**
Pen knife, BPOE **85.00**
Plate, BPOE, Buffalo Pottery **55.00**
Tin litho, 2 elk, Mt Hood, 1912 . . . . **38.00**
Tin litho, BPOE, Philadelphia, 1907 . . . . **40.00**
Tin litho, w/elk, 1907, 9½″ **38.00**
Stamp box, w/figural head, 14k w/amethyst **325.00**
Masons, book, The Master Mason, 1925-27 . . . . **10.00**
Bookends, metal, heavy, w/emblem, pr **15.00**
Bookmark, copper **5.00**
Chalice, w/emblem, 1908 . . . . **90.00**
Champagne, man w/camera **90.00**
Champagne, New Orleans, 1910, Neptune, alligator **75.00**
Glass, frosted, Grand Consistory Ky., 1917, 3″ **30.00**
Glass, Osiris 1920 w/emblems, 3½″ **40.00**
Goblet, Louisville, 1909, horseshoe, emblem **75.00**
Grand Masonic Hall Lottery ticket, Mo., 1842 . . . . **100.00**
Medal, Mass. Consistory, SPRS, MIB, 3x2¼″ **30.00**
Mug, Atlantic City w/sailboat, lady, sword, 1900 . . . . **75.00**
Niagara Falls, emblem w/bridge, 1905 . . . . . . **65.00**
River, bridge, emblem, 3 sword handles, 1905 . . . . . . **68.00**
Sword handle, 1903 . . . . **70.00**
Nappy, chocolate glass w/insignia **145.00**

Fruit Jars

As early as 1829, canning jars were being manufactured for use in the home preservation of foodstuffs. For the past 15 years, they have been sought as popular collectibles. At the last estimate, over 4,000 fruit jars and variations were known to exist----some are very rare, perhaps one of a kind examples known to have survived to the present day. Among the most valuable are the black glass jars, the amber Van Vliet and the cobalt Milville. These often bring prices in excess of $500 when they can be found. Aside from condition, values are based on age, rarity, and special features.

ABC, aqua, qt **350.00**
ARS, in fancy script, aqua, qt **65.00**
Acme, on shield, w/stars & stripes, ½ gal **8.00**
Atlas E-Z Seal, amber qt **31.00**
4 leaf clover Good Luck, clear, ½ gal **12.00**
Aqua, ½ gal **3.00**
Aqua, ½ pt **6.00**
Whole fruit jar, clear, ½ gal **3.00**
BB Wilcox, pat'd March 26, 1867, aqua, qt **55.00**
Ball, blue, ½ pt **30.00**
Blue, ½ gal, dated **6.00**
Blue, ½ pt, dated **35.00**
Clear, ½ gal, dated **3.00**
Clear, ½ pt, dated **3.00**
Deluxe Jar, clear, quart **4.00**
Sanitary Sure Seal, clear, ½ pt **8.00**
Sure Seal, blue, ½ gal **6.00**
Sure Seal, blue, ½ pt **35.00**
Beaver, embossed beaver w/log over word, amber, qt **450.00**
Embossed beaver w/log over word, aqua, qt **30.00**
Bee Hive Trademark, with bees & hive, aqua, qt **135.00**

Blown, aqua, cork pealer, ½ gal **300.00**

Champion Syrup & Refining Co, Indianapolis, aqua, qt........ **30.00**
Clark Peerless, ground lip, aqua, pt or qt................... **8.00**
Clyde, in circle, clear, ½ gal........................... **8.00**
   In script, clear, ½ gal................................ **8.00**
Cohansey, aqua qt..................................... **15.00**
Commonwealth, Fruit Jar, clear, ½ gal.................. **95.00**
Crown Emblem, clear, midget........................... **9.00**
Double Safety, clear, ½ pint........................... **4.00**
Electric Trademark, in circle, aqua, pt.................. **8.00**
Empire, in stippled cross w/in frame, clear, ½ pint or ½ gal ... **15.00**
Eureka, pat'd Dec 27, 1864, aqua, qt.................... **75.00**
Gem, base, ground lip, glass insert, screw band, aqua, midget .. **25.00**
   Improved, Made in Canada, amber, qt............... **60.00**
Globe, amber, pt...................................... **85.00**
Hamilton, original clamp, qt............................ **60.00**
Hazel HA Perserve jar, clear, qt........................ **4.00**
Hero, above cross, aqua, qt............................ **30.00**
Jewell Jar, Made In Canada, ½ turn clamp, clear, qt.......... **50.00**
King, on banner below king's head, clear, pt or qt.......... **14.00**
Lightning, Trademark, amber, pt........................ **75.00**
   Trademark, aqua, salesman sample, aqua, ½ pt.......... **95.00**
Lockport Mason, zinc lid, aqua, pint or quart.............. **4.00**
Mason's, CFJ Improved, reverse Clyde NY, aqua, pt or qt....... **3.00**
CFJ Improved, zinc band, glass insert, aqua, midget.......... **9.00**
   Keystone within circle, zinc lid, aqua, midget.......... **22.00**
Myers Test Jar, w/orig clamp, aqua, quart............... **115.00**
P Lorillard Co, ground lip, glass lid wire clamp, amber........ **18.00**
Protector, vertically, w/rare orig lid, ½ gal.............. **65.00**
Red, superimposed over a key, Mason, aqua, qt............. **9.00**
Root Mason, olive green, qt............................ **50.00**
Royal, crown emblem, AG Smalley & Co, April 7, 1896, ½ gal .. **8.00**
   In crown, Trademark Full Measure Registered, amber, qt.... **65.00**
Sealfast, base Foster, smoke colored, ½ pt................ **3.00**
Smalley, Full Measure Quart, amber..................... **58.00**
Star, emblem, encircled by fruit, aqua, qt............... **110.00**
Sun, aqua, qt.. **55.00**
Superior RG Co, w/in circle, aqua, pint................. **18.00**
The American Nagco, porcelain, ground lip, aqua, ½ gal..... **30.00**
The Burlington, BG Co, 1876, clear, ½ gal................ **55.00**
The Daisy, FE Ward & Co, aqua, pint.................... **12.00**
The Marion Jar Mason's, zinc lid, aqua, qt............... **15.00**
The Rose, clear, ½ gal................................ **50.00**
The Whitney Mason, pat'd 1858, aqua, quart.............. **6.00**
The Wide Mouth Famous Jar, glass lid, wire bail, aqua, pt..... **14.00**
Veteran, clear, ½ pt.................................. **25.00**

½ pint... **25.00**
1 gal.. **22.00**
Whitney Mason, 3 dots under Mason, smooth lip, zinc top, aqua, pt **6.00**
Wide Mouth Telephone, aqua, ½ gal.................... **15.00**
   Pint or quart..................................... **6.00**

Fry

Henry Fry established his glassworks in Rochester, Pennsylvania, in 1901, and until 1933 when it was sold to the Libbey Co., produced many types of fine glassware which gained for him a reputation of quality. In the early years they produced beautiful cut glass, and when it began to wane in popularity, Fry turned to the manufacture of occasional pieces and oven glassware. He is perhaps most famous for the opalescent pearl glass called Foval. It was made in combinations with crystal or colored trim, and because it was in production for only a short time in 1926-27, it is hard to find.

Collectors of depression era glassware look for the opalescent reamers and opaque green kitchenware made during the early 30s.

Bowl, Hobstar & Fan cutting, 1900, signed, 9"............ **185.00**
Candlesticks, opal & clear, 9", pr...................... **60.00**
   Twist stems, Delft Foval trim, 11", pr.............. **275.00**
Coffee pot, Delft Foval trim........................... **185.00**
Cup & saucer, Delft Foval handle....................... **60.00**
   Jade handle....................................... **65.00**
Decanter, footed, opalescent w/cobalt handle, 9".......... **160.00**
Ewer, clambroth w/blue handle, 8"...................... **120.00**
Fruit bowl, Delft Foval, 14".......................... **325.00**
Glasses, crystal & black, 14 oz, set of 8................ **60.00**
Goblet, Optic, pink & green........................... **15.00**
Grill plate, opal..................................... **25.00**
Lemonade glass, Foval w/Jade ped & handle.............. **65.00**
Lemonade pitcher, crackle body w/green handle, 8"........ **85.00**
   Opal stripes, cobalt handle & lid.................... **145.00**
Pie plate, opalescent, 1916, 10"....................... **15.00**
Pitcher, crackle w/blue thorn handle, 13"............... **125.00**
   Diamond Optic, ground pontil, green, 9¾"............ **60.00**
   Foval blue w/cobalt handle........................ **85.00**
   Squat, green handle, 6"............................ **70.00**
   With cover, blue handle & finial.................... **140.00**
Plate, Brighton cutting, 7", sq........................ **180.00**
Plates, Diamond Optic, octagon, golden glow, set of 6, 7½" ... **45.00**
Set, teapot, sugar, creamer, 4 cups, saucers, Foreign Pagoda... **35.00**
Soup bowl, Foval, 6½"................................ **35.00**
Syrup pitcher, clambroth opal, 6"...................... **75.00**
Teapot, Foval, lg..................................... **145.00**
Toothpick, blue handle, Foval......................... **50.00**
Tray, Duquesne cutting, signed, 14".................. **1,250.00**
Tumbler, Foval blue w/cobalt handle.................... **17.00**
Vase, crackle glass, blue leaves, 7¼".................. **65.00**
   Foval blue base & trim, signed, 6".................. **100.00**
Water tumbler, footed, Optic.......................... **15.00**
Wine, Optic, pink & green............................. **15.00**

Fulper

The Fulper Pottery was founded in 1899 after nearly a century of producing utilitarian stoneware under various titles and managements. Not until 1909 did Fulper venture into the art pottery field. Vasekraft, their first art line, utilized the same heavy clay body used for their utility ware. Shapes were severe, unadorned and rather ungraceful. But the glazes they developed were used with such flair and imagination, alone and in unexpected combined harmony, that each piece was truly a work of art. In contrast to the

Wier, stoneware jar & lid, wire & metal clamp, 1 pt........ **18.00**

Vasekraft line, graceful Oriental shapes were produced to compliment the important 'famille rose' glaze developed by W. H. Fulper, Jr. Other designs were developed with an Art Deco influence.

During WWI, doll's heads and Kewpies were made as a substitute for imports. Figural perfume lamps and powder boxes were made both in bisque and glazed ware. Although the plant was in operation until 1935, the most prized examples pre-date 1930. Much of the ware was marked with a vertical FULPER in line reserve, although a horizontal mark as well as a Vasekraft paper label was also used.

Bowl, #61, green & yellow crystalline **130.00**
  Aqua, 4 feet, ink mk, 7½″ dia **40.00**
  Blue & ivory, scalloped edges, incised signature, 9½″ long . . . **50.00**
  Blue crystalline, vertical ink mk, 7″ dia **115.00**
  Blue matt w/multicolor flambe, roll edge, 13″ dia **235.00**
  Blue wisteria, Chinese blue & wht flambe, 4 feet, 10″ dia **60.00**
  Boat shape, blue crystals, silver tag, impressed mk **200.00**
  Boat shape, green matt **50.00**
  Brown w/blue drips **40.00**
  Copper oxide green, footed, 3 leaf flower frog, 7¾″ dia **75.00**
  Dk blue drip over rose, 11″ dia **90.00**
  Flared lip, shades of blue over rose matt, mkd, 9″ **130.00**
  Green w/brown overglaze mirror finish, incised signature **33.00**
  Metallic matt green & tan, 10½x3½″ **48.00**
  Mottled green & blk, crystals, 3 footed, 8x2¼″ **75.00**
  Mottled green, rolled edge, 9x2½″ **95.00**
  Purple & rose w/froth & speckles, 8¾x4½″ **74.00**
  Tan flambe over brown mustard, decagon, 9″ dia **85.00**
  Tan w/brown streaks, mirror glaze, 4 feet, ink mk **30.00**
Bud vase, heavy wht drip over brown, 8¼″ **110.00**
  Med blue, handled, 4½″ **45.00**
  Rose flambe w/blue, square, footed, mkd, 8″ **50.00**
Bulb dish, dk green, 8x2″ **25.00**
Candlestick, green crystal, 8″ oval **40.00**
  Green crystalline, 2 handles, 4x5″ **36.00**
  Green into rose, w/handles, 3x5″ **40.00**
  Pair, green crystalline, vertical ink mk, 7x4″ base **140.00**
  Pair, mirror black, vertical mk, 11½″ **350.00**
  Pair, olive over green crystal, 3 Deco handles, 6″ dia **80.00**
  Pair, oval, blue & mustard **65.00**
  Pair twist shape, hi-gloss green/copper flecks, 8″ **85.00**
  Tan & blue underglaze, brown trim, 2″, ink mk **30.00**
Candy dish, lt green w/gold scalloped edges, oval, ink mk **18.00**
Compote, crystalline, flambe exterior, 4 legged base, 6x11½″ . . **85.00**
Console bowl, matt rose, scalloped, 13″ dia **85.00**
  Olive over green crystal, scalloped edge, 16″ **115.00**
Curtain tie-backs, pair, tri-level, rose tones, ink mk **46.00**
Dish, oval, mottled blue, beige streaks, scalloped, 10″ long **24.00**
  Oval, scalloped, aqua w/green edge, mirror glaze, incised mk **25.00**
Doll, open/close eyes, ball-jointed wood body, incised Stangel, 26″ **345.00**
Flower frog, 3-leaf, dk green, no mark, 2″ **10.00**
  Figural pelican, brown, green, 7″ **135.00**
  Lady sitting on rock, mulitcolor flecks, 5½″ **15.00**
  Metallic green over tan, no mk, 4½″ dia **39.00**
  Swan figural, cream on brown lustre, 6x4½″ **170.00**
Jar, cafe au lait semi matt, handled, ink mk, 4¼x6″ **35.00**
  Matt blue, blue & green flambe, #452, handled, 6″ wide **60.00**
  Yellow, verte antique overglaze at top, ink mk, 6″ **55.00**
Jardiniere, dk green matt, 3 feet, ink mk **30.00**
  Varigated lt green matt, reticulated, 6½x10¾″ **160.00**
  Violet matt, semi-mirror, 3 handles, incised mk, 8″ dia **55.00**
Jug, silver overlay w/ship, music box, 7½″ **1,500.00**
Jug, whiskey, musical, dk browns & yellow, much copper dust . . **60.00**
Lamp, green matt over rose, musical decanter blank, 10″ **80.00**

Perfume, ballerina, pink, signed **225.00**
  Perfume, blonde lady w/wht & blue dress, incised signature . **150.00**
Powder box, Egyptian lady decor, 8″ **225.00**
  Girl finial, 6½″ **150.00**
Sugar & creamer, plain yellow glaze, octagonal, faience **60.00**
Urn, two tone green crystalline glaze, shoulder handles, 12″ . . **350.00**
Vase, #26, dk blue flambe, 6″ **60.00**
  #436, verte antique, crystalline, green flambe **140.00**
  #585, matt antique verte, handled, 10½″ **90.00**
  Aqua & green, mirror glaze, incised signature, 8″ **30.00**
  Beehive, black lustre, shoudler handles, 6½x5¼″ **120.00**
  Blue crystalline, handled, horizontal mk, 4½x6″ **140.00**
  Blue lustre, handled, vertical hand incised mk, 8″ **185.00**
  Blue streaks into purple, raised vertical mk, 6¾x4½″ **95.00**
  Blue w/blue wisteria, 11″ **225.00**
  Bowl, 3 handles, rose w/green, turquoise flambe, 6½x8″ . . . **230.00**
  Cream w/green, brown, vertical mk, 5½x7″ **200.00**
  Bowl, handled, brown over green crystalline, 6x8″ **230.00**
  Brown crystalline, 2 handles, signed, 11″ **200.00**
  Brown gloss over green, vertical mk, 12″ **200.00**
  Brown over green gloss, handled, ink mk, 6″ **130.00**
  Brown shades w/cream gloss, ovoid, ring handles, 13″ **450.00**
  Brown, black flambe, handled, vertical ink mk, 7½″ **160.00**
  Chocolate, copper, cream flambe, 7¼″ **115.00**
  Cream volcanic w/black & blue, Panama Pacific tag, 10″ . . . **720.00**
  Deco handles, 3½x7″ dia **70.00**
  Dk blue bottom, lt blue top, cruet shape, vertical ink mk, 5″ . **55.00**
  Dk blue matt, square, 8″, vertical ink mk **35.00**
  Drip, green glaze, signed, 6x4″ **35.00**
  Famille rose, bulbous w/flared neck, 7½″ **70.00**
  German Art Glaze, maroon, drip, 3 handles, 8½″ **65.00**
  Gold w/black flambe streaking, square, vertical ink mk **125.00**
  Green & rose, bulbous, 7½″ **74.00**
  Green & tan crystalline, handled, 7¼″ **135.00**
  Green crystalline, impressed leaves, 5½″ **50.00**
  Green drip glaze, 6x4″ **40.00**
  Green flambe, brown mirror glaze, handled, 3½x7″ dia **65.00**
  Green flambe, globular, 7″ **80.00**
  Green matt over rose, fan shape, 125 Anniversary seal **65.00**
  Green over rose, small crystals, trumpet shape, 9″ **60.00**
  Green, black flambe, vertical ink mk, 4½″ **50.00**
  Green, rose, trumpet shape **60.00**
  Green/blue lustre, gourd shape, 4½x5″ **130.00**
  Heavily reticulated foliage & star, high glaze, 7½″ **1,800.00**
  Leopard skin glaze, shaded green, crystalline, 8″ **50.00**
  Lt & dk blue, high glaze, bowl shape, unmarked, 5x6″ **75.00**
  Matt green w/applied leaves & flowers, 4x7″ dia **55.00**
  Mottled blue volcanic, #642, handled, glazed over mk **65.00**
  Mottled blue, bulbous, 10½″ **90.00**

Reticulated floral rim, aqua, #4061, 10″ **150.00**

Rose & purple, bowl shape, handled, 4½x4½"............ **66.00**
Rose over green, heavy drip glaze, handled, 6x7"......... **110.00**
Shaded blue bottom, green top, matt, ink mk, 3¾x3¼" dia .. **24.00**
Shaded green matt, 12"................................ **70.00**
Streaked blue glaze, handled, 8x5"..................... **95.00**
Tan, green flambe, crystalline, ribbed octagonal, 8x7"..... **300.00**
Trumpet, famille rose matt, green volcanic drip, 9"........ **140.00**
Varigated greens, classical Chinese shape, handled, 8½".... **60.00**
Wall pocket, rose w/cream ridges, mixed blue & aqua, ink mk.. **22.00**

Furniture

From the cabinet maker's shop of the early 1800s, with apprentices and journeymen who learned every phase of the craft at the side of the master carpenter, the trade had evolved by the mid-century to one with steam powered saws and turning lathes and workers who specialized in only one operation.

By 1870 the industrial revolution had been accomplished and large factories in the East and Midwest turned out increasingly elaborate styles, ornately machine carved and heavily inlaid. Rococo, Egyptian and Renaissance Revival furniture lent themselves well to factory production. Eastlake offered a welcome respite from Victorian frumpery, and a return to quality hand crafting. All of these styles remained popular until the turn of the century.

As early as 1880, factories began using oak; early mail order catalogues offered oak furniture simply styled and lighter in weight, since long distance shipping was often a factor.

Mission, or Craftsman, a style introduced around 1890, was simple to the extreem. Stickley and Hubbard were two of the leading designers.

Other popular Victorian styles were Colonial Revival, Cottage, Bentwood and Windsor. Prices are as variable as the styles.

Key:

Am----American	Hplwht----Hepplewhite
Chpndl----Chippendale	mahog----mahogany
dbl----double	N.E.----New England
do----door	ped----pediment
drwr----drawer	prim----primitive
Fr----French	rnd----round
ft----feet	str----straight
ftbd----footboard	trn----turning
grad---graduated	Vict----Victorian
hdbd----headboard	wal----walnut
hdw----hardware	

Armoire, Country French Louis XV, carved pine, 1700s, 86" **4,500.00**
Satinwood, single door w/beveled glass **575.00**
Bedroom set, Eastlake, walnut, 3 pc **1,600.00**
Renaissance Revival walnut, 3 pc, marble top **1,900.00**
Vict oak, intricately carved, bed 80", 3 pc **3,600.00**
Beds
Black Forest walnut, flower basket crest, elaborate **600.00**
Brass, and porcelain, 8' posts w/brass canopy, elaborate **5,000.00**
Chinese, canopy w/3 sides, ornate, 1890 .... **5,250.00**
Twin size, square tubing............................ **340.00**
Wide daisy decor, wide hdbd, w/rails, polished **1,200.00**
Cannonball, 4 trn maple posts, pine hdbd & ftbd, stain **300.00**
Canopy, Sheraton, arch hdbd, ring/urn trn posts, stencil **700.00**
Mahogany, 1800s.................................. **600.00**
Day, country pine & poplar w/orig red paint, 68x23" **160.00**
Eastlake, rope twist design, ¾ size **400.00**
Empire, painted oval decor on shaped ftbd & 54" hdbd...... **650.00**
Four thick trn posts, maple, double w/trundle, lacing pins .. **1,250.00**
Gustav Stickley, no mk, same as #923, 42", 4 slat **600.00**
Half tester, Eng Vict, curtain rings, barley twist trn ftbd...... **800.00**

Infirmary, Shaker, pine & basswood, curtain rod, trn legs..... **300.00**
Iron & brass, double, 1890 all orig...................... **650.00**
Ornate, dbl, 1850 .... **875.00**
Low post, maple, hdbd w/turn toprail, arch ftbd, trn posts **110.00**
Mahog, Empire, tall posts w/pineapple finials, carvings, 62".... **725.00**
Maple, Federal, 4 turned posts, canopy, 68x54"........... **1,400.00**
Oversize cannonballs, cherry, double **1,050.00**
Poster, 1800s, 85" **2,750.00**
Mahogany, Empire w/pineapple finials, 64x76"........... **750.00**
Tiger maple, panel hdbd w/rolled top, trn post........... **600.00**
Queen Anne, low post, Va. origin, 1720s, painted **2,400.00**
Rope, 4 low turned posts, hdbd/ftbd w/6 spindles, 1829 .... **1,200.00**
Cannonball, rock maple **450.00**
Maple trnd posts, matching crests, refinished **195.00**
Maple tulip top posts, coverlet roller **360.00**
Poplar w/acorn finials **295.00**
Poplar w/some orig red stain, carved hdbd, 1850s **1,100.00**
Sleigh, curly maple, scroll panel hdbd/ftbds, legs w/ball ft..... **150.00**
Tester, Sheraton, cherry, 79x78"...................... **3,500.00**
Country Federal, pointed arch hd & ftbd, painted, 1790 .... **550.00**
Mahog Federal, pointed arch canopy, spiral trn post **550.00**
Spiral post, 1820, 65" **900.00**
Walnut, lion head on high hdbd, silver & pearl inlay....... **1,000.00**

Bench, bucket, pine **225.00**
Water, pine, splash board, 2 drawers, 2 doors, 47x42"..... **600.00**
Bookcase
Chpndl, 2 pc, 2 glazed do on 2 drw, ogee ft **350.00**
Mahog Regency, 2 do over drop desk, 2 drw & cupboard... **4,000.00**
Stickley, #523, paper label, 44x39"..................... **1,500.00**
Craftsman, oak w/double doors, 44x39" **1,600.00**
Oak, 56x54" **1,650.00**
Walnut, 2 doors w/glass, beaded molding, 68x45".......... **435.00**
Bookcase-secretary, drop front, oak, bevel mirror, 2 drw **950.00**
Oak, drop front, beveled mirror **425.00**
Walnut, barrel front **795.00**

Buffet, oak, carved, orig brass hdw **275.00**
Bureau
Birch, Federal bowfront, 4 drw in bird's eye veneer **850.00**
Cherry, 4 drw, ogee bracket ft, Federal, 36x40" **1,800.00**
Federal, 2 half drw over 3, 1790, 41x40".............. **900.00**
Hplwht bow front, 4 drw, eagle & banner decor **1,000.00**
Overhang top, 4 grad drw w/beading, 1800 .... **1,000.00**
With inlay, Federal, 4 drw, 34x35x17" **1,500.00**
Chpndl/Hplwht swell front w/4 drw, fan inlay corners...... **2,500.00**
Curly birch & maple, 4 drw, 36" wide.................. **2,200.00**
Curly birch, Sheraton, 4 drws & fluted corner posts **350.00**
Hepplewhite, 4 drw, cockbeaded, brass hdw, bracket base **525.00**
Inlaid mahogny, 4 drw, fluted columns & skirt, orig hdw... **1,100.00**
Inlaid mahog Chpndl, serpentine front, 4 drw, ogee base ... **3,250.00**
Inlaid mahogany, Chpndl w/serpentine front **8,000.00**
Inlaid maple, Federal bowfront, 4 drw, 35x39".......... **1,200.00**
Mahogany, Empire, 46x42"......................... **350.00**
Mahog, Empire, 6 long drw, carved panels & columns, paw ft . **150.00**
Geo III, writing fall front, fitted interior, 41"........... **1,800.00**
Mahogany, Hepplewhite, 4 drw, 45" long **950.00**
Swell front, 4 drw, trn columns, 40x42"............... **400.00**
Pine, 4 drawers, cottage quality, 36"................... **85.00**
Victorian Cottage, repainted **85.00**
Cabinet
Bow front, carved & gilded, Louis XVI **3,000.00**
Carved oak, 3 glass do over base w/2 drw & do, 84x72" ... **1,200.00**
China, oak w/curved glass & mirror dolphins & claw ft..... **700.00**

Oak w/curved glass, lion head carving **310.00**
Oak w/mirror back, 1910 . . . . **695.00**
Corner, pine, open face, 1 base door, 72x32″ **1,700.00**
Curio, French, gold leaf, curved glass, 38x18½″ **2,000.00**
   Louis XVI, bronze mounted, inlaid **2,100.00**
   Mahog w/inlay, cloth on shelves & back, traditional **335.00**
Eastlake, 2 pc, cupboard w/mirror over 2 do, 3 drw **950.00**
File, 30 drawers, walnut, 1890s **400.00**
Hoosier, oak w/flour bin, roll top **340.00**
Kitchen, oak, porcelain top, flour bin, 6½x4½′ **365.00**
   Oak, roll front w/flour bin, very good cond **300.00**
   Oak, Nappanee, zinc top, flour sifter **550.00**
Rosewood, Renaissance, birds eye interior, 1830, 4x4x2′ . . . **1,175.00**
Spool, walnut, 5 drawer **600.00**

Candlestand

Birch, Federal, turned post, tripod base, 1800s **385.00**
Cherry & curly maple, 3 snake ft, refinished **265.00**
Cherry, Queen Anne, oval top, vase trn post, snake ft **525.00**
   Chippendale, trn post, tripod, pad ft, 27″ **400.00**
Grain paint, sq top & post, snake ft, 1780 . . . . **375.00**
Hplwht, 1 drw, orig red, 1790s **825.00**
   Oval chamfered edge tip top, trn shaft **425.00**
Mahog, Queen Anne, 3 snake ft, octagon top **425.00**
   Chippendale turned post, 27″ **650.00**
Maple, Hplwht, needs refinishing **100.00**
   Short tri-pod, snake feet, 1800s **550.00**
   Tri-pod base, late, 1800s **135.00**
N.J. origin, original paint, 1790s **1,150.00**
Octagon tip top, mahogany w/inlay, 28½″ **600.00**
Oval tip top, cherry, vase trn post, 3 legs, 27″ **400.00**
Queen Anne, rectangle top w/cut corners, turned, 27″ **175.00**
Unique finialled drop at base, 1 board top, 1750 . . . . **250.00**
Walnut, trn stem, tri-pod base **250.00**

Chair Set

1 arm, 3 side, shield back mahog, cloth seats, 1790 . . . . . . **1,100.00**
3 Belter, Rosalie pattern **8,000.00**
4 arrow back, painted decor, 1820 . . . . **385.00**
4 clothespin Windsor, old mustard paint, 1820s **2,200.00**
4 country Chpndl ladder-backs, 1789 . . . . **3,300.00**
4 fancy pressed back, ash **215.00**
4 ladderback w/rush seats **160.00**
4 press back w/cane seat **400.00**
4 side, w/curved crests, turned tiles & legs, caned 1810 . . . . **225.00**
4 str tiger maple, straight crestrail & splat, 1800 . . . . **325.00**
4 Windsor bentwood kitchen, mix wood, 1860 . . . . **300.00**
4 Windsor style, orig paint, stenciled **450.00**
5 side w/1 arm, maple Hitchcock, rush seats **900.00**
6 Fed mahog, Duncan Phyfe, 1816, concave crestrail **2,800.00**
6 hand carved Georgian **2,100.00**
6 Hitchcock, grained, stenciled, rush seats, ball feet **375.00**
6 oak, 4 spindle back, solid seat, 1850s **1,250.00**
6 Vict laminated rosewood, Belter type **1,750.00**

Chair

Arm, Windsor, carved crest, 6 spindles, saddle seat, 48″ . . . **3,900.00**
   Carved lions heads, claw legs, mahogany **1,100.00**
   Chinese Chpndl carved rosewood, pierced backsplat **325.00**
   Chinese, 1800s, dragon arms w/inset ivory eyes **850.00**
   Geo III, leaf carved knees, claw & ball feet, upholstered . . **1,650.00**
   Gothic Revival, leather seat & back **465.00**
   Ladder-back, donkey ear top stiles, woven seat **150.00**
   Ladder-back, maple w/woven seat, 1800s **175.00**
   Queen Anne, cabriole legs, Dutch ft & backsplat **95.00**
   Rococo Revival, medallion back, carved legs, 40″ **190.00**
   Sheraton, rush seat, early 1800s **150.00**

Slatback, rush seat trn legs & stretchers, 1700s **375.00**

Victorian, walnut, original upholstery, 41½″ **225.00**
   Windsor bow back bulbous trn legs, 1 board seat **475.00**
   Windsor country comb back, refinished, 1800s **150.00**
   Windsor step down crest, triple arrowback splats **130.00**
   Windsor, fan back **650.00**
Banister back, concave crest rail, rush seat, 41″ **235.00**
   Turned finials, stiles, arm supports, 45″ **685.00**
   With scroll arms, rush seat, orig paint **1,100.00**
Bowback Windsor, shaped arms, saddle seat, painted, 35″ . . . **550.00**
   Vase turnings, saddle seat, 41″ **850.00**
Cage back, Windsor **345.00**
Chpndl, curved top rail, shaped splat, sq chamferred legs . . . **250.00**
   Str back w/mahog arms, sq legs & stretchers **100.00**
Comback Windsor, refinished, no repairs, 1810 . . . . **1,650.00**
Corner, block turned legs, rush sat, refinished, 1700s **350.00**
   Maple w/rush seat, turned legs **340.00**
   Queen Anne, shaped handholds, trn posts & legs **550.00**
   Scrolled arms, vase splat, burled seat, trn legs **375.00**
Country Chpndl, earred crest, simple, orig paint, 1750 . . . . . **175.00**
Horn, Victorian **300.00**
Hplwht w/shield back, pierced, carved backsplat, 1780 . . . . . **210.00**
Ladder-back, 4 slats, acorn finials, bulb ft, splint seat **160.00**
   Child's, rush seat, old paint, 29″ **335.00**
   Maple & ash, 4 slats, rush seat, 44″ **275.00**
   Tiger maple, 4 slats, rush seat, 41″ **700.00**
   With arms, mix woods, spool trn stretchers **1,500.00**
   With arms, trn finials, stiles, stretchers, 4″ **650.00**
   With rolled arms, mushroom finials, 4 splat **200.00**
Lady's oak spindle, leather cushion, attrib Stickley **2,300.00**
Lolling, Chpndl, serpentine crestrail, upholstered, 1780 . . . . . **675.00**
Mahog, arched crest w/feather carvings, late 1700s **500.00**
   Scroll arm w/trn legs, stretchers, upholstered **60.00**
Morris w/writing stand, carved oak frame, upholstered **450.00**
Office swivel, press back, slat seat & back **230.00**
Side, Am Sheraton, trn fluted legs, rnd rush seat, decor **55.00**
   Banister-back, rush seat **225.00**
   Cane back & seat, fruitwood **200.00**
   Carved crest, Chippendale **825.00**
   Cherry Queen Anne, vase backsplat, rush seat, detailed **700.00**

Chinese Chippendale **385.00**
Chpndl, shaped crestail, pierced splat, 1789 . . . . **125.00**
Curved crest rail, rush seat, Spanish ft, 42″ **475.00**
Gustav Stickley #350 . . . . **140.00**
Ladder-back, 1800s **60.00**
Mahog Chpndl ribbon back, 4 pierced slats **950.00**
Maple, Queen Anne, trn legs, Spanish ft **740.00**
New Eng Queen Anne, paint over maple, round crestrail . . . **170.00**
Turned finials, stiles, legs, 4 slat, rush seat, 45″ **365.00**
Walnut Chpndl, shell carved crest & knees, cloth seat **3,000.00**
Steerhorn & hide, elaborate, excellent condition **2,000.00**
Straight, Orkney Isles, Am usage, hand roping, curved back . . **225.00**
Homemade w/solid seat, primitive, 1840 . . . . **150.00**
Vict gentleman's, carved crest, re-upholstered **130.00**
Finger carved, good velvet **325.00**
Windsor, 7 spindle back, refinished **265.00**
Bow back, 7 spindle, bamboo turnings **450.00**
8 spindle, saddle seat, 35″ **400.00**
9 spindles, turned legs, 37″ **275.00**
Incised back, turned legs, saddle seat **150.00**
Saddle seat, refinished **350.00**
Comb back, 9 spindles, knuckle arms **850.00**
Continuous arm, comb, knuckle carving **3,100.00**
Hoop back, turned legs, saddle seat **150.00**
Spindle & splat back, refinished, 1820 . . . . **650.00**
Step down crest w/cut out, bamboo trn, refinished **225.00**
Triple comb back w/arms, refinished, 1800s **1,650.00**
With orig paint & striping **260.00**
With writing arm, orig decor **2,300.00**

Chest

4 drawer, Hplwht, well decorated, 41x41″ **1,850.00**
Orig red paint, replaced brasses, 1825 . . . . **1,025.00**
Sliding top, stepped box, grain paint **240.00**
Apothecary, maple, glass knobs, 20 drw, bracket ft **1,100.00**
Bachelors, mahog, Georgian, pull out side, 3 drw, brasses . . . **250.00**
Birch, 4 drw, bracket base, 1765, 42x40″ **675.00**
Am Sheraton, 4 drw, trn corner post, 1800s, 44″ **285.00**
Bird's eye & tiger maple, Heplwht **2,300.00**
Blanket, cherry & poplar, sponge decor, 1800s **175.00**
European, 1854 . . . . **625.00**
Floral & fruit decor, boot jack ends **100.00**
Grain paint w/eagle plaque, till w/2 drw **270.00**
Grain paint, black & red, lift top, base drw, 35″ **385.00**
Maple, Queen Anne, 5 simulated drws over 2 . . . . **1,500.00**
Pine, Chpndl, dovetailed case w/till, red paint **225.00**
Pine, Federal, lift top, 1 drw, 32x42x19″ **225.00**
Pine, Queen Anne, 3 drw, 36x50x18″ **1,200.00**
Pine, Queen Anne, red, 1 drw, 1740, 29x39″ **250.00**
Pine, base drawer, 42″ wide **325.00**
Pine, grain paint, 1 drw, brasses, 27x44″ **190.00**
Pine, grain paint, 1800s **1,000.00**
Pine, lift top, 1 drw, cut out sides, 33x44x19″ **345.00**
Pine, sm inner shelf box, dovetailed corners, 1840 . . . . **400.00**
Poplar, l board top, concealed hinges, 23x35x18″ **190.00**
Queen Anne, base w/center arch, bootjack ends, 2 drw, 1750 **700.00**
Queen Anne, boot jack ends, 3 simulated drw **200.00**
Walnut, 1 board top, dovetailed corners, 24x44″ **230.00**
Champhorwood, China trade origin, brass corners, lifts, 35″ . . **420.00**
Cherry, Chpndl, 4 drw, 41x38″ **1,500.00**
Cherry, Country Sheraton, trn legs, 7 drw, 68″ **775.00**
Cherry, Hplwht, inlaid top & 4 drw fronts, 35½″ **1,600.00**
Cherry, Hplwht, bow front w/French ft, 1790 . . . . **1,500.00**
Cherry, maple inlay, Hplwht bow front **2,700.00**
Cherry & tiger maple, Sheraton, 4 drw, scroll apron, trn legs . **880.00**

Chpndl, molded cornice, 5 drw w/maple front, brasses, 1760 . . **700.00**
Cove crown, 3 over 2 over 4 drw, brasses, ¼ fluted columns **3,000.00**
Curly maple, Chpndl, 4 drw, willow brasses **550.00**
Chpndl, 6 graduated drws, 57x36″ **2,000.00**
Flame grain, 3 drw base, lift lid, 40x40″ **400.00**
Mahog, Sheraton, bowfront, 4 drw, trn ft, 1810, 41″ **475.00**

Gilt, bronze mounted, walnut marquetry, 1860, 39x29″ **1,200.00**
Grain paint, Hplwht, 4 drw **1,700.00**
Highboy, oak, 6 drw w/mirror **225.00**
Highboy, walnut, raised side panels, Pa., 9 drw **8,800.00**
Hplwht, bow front, 4 drw, inlaid & veneered **2,100.00**
Mahogany, 4 drw, pull out slide, 35x33″ **850.00**
Mahog, Chpndl, blocked front & 4 drw, cockbead edge **450.00**
Inlay top, 4 drw, shaped skirt, brasses **575.00**
Mahog, Federal, swell front, 4 drw, 41x43″ **950.00**
Mahog, Georgian Chpndl, 2 over 3 drw w/wood pulls, 1790 . . **375.00**
Mahog, Sheraton, bow front, inlay top w/cookie corners **375.00**
Inlay top, cookie corners, fluted columns **375.00**
Maple, Chpndl, 6 drw, bracket base **5,500.00**
Molded cornice, 5 drw, brass hdw, 1780 . . . . **1,100.00**
Oak, 3 drw, refinished **165.00**
Pine & mahog, Hplwht, 4 dr w/brasses, flared French ft, sm . . **600.00**
Quilt, maple, 1 board top, 22½x43″ **175.00**
Sea, pine, 1 board top, handforged hinges & lock, rope handle **325.00**
Pine, dovetailed corners, 1 board top, iron lock, 38″ long . . **275.00**
Sugar, walnut, wide board, 2 inner compartments, 1 drw . . . **1,250.00**
Tiger maple, 2 half drw over 5, old brass & finish, 48″ **1,900.00**
Chpndl, 6 drw, molded cornice, 56x36″ **2,400.00**
Walnut, 4 drw & 2 handkerchief drw on top, 1880s, refinished **395.00**
Walnut, Hplwht, 4 drw w/beaded trim **750.00**
Hplwht, inlay top, 4 graduated drw, corner columns **900.00**
Yellow & brown grain paint, 4 drw, N.H. **450.00**

Chifforobe, oak, 4 drw, beveled mirror, sm size **300.00**
Oak, 1 lg, 7 sm drw, beveled mirror, 1800 . . . . **1,000.00**
China cabinet, mahog, 2 do, carved pillars, cornice **650.00**
Oak, curved glass, 3 shelves, refinished **985.00**
China closet, oak, L & JG Stickley, leaded glass panels, 67″ **1,000.00**
Coat rack, Mission, 6 hooks, 37″ **70.00**
Commode, ash, 3 drw, 1890 . . . . **225.00**
Flame mahog, ring & ball ft, simulated drw, 1800 . . . . **160.00**
Pine, Vict, lift top w/door **85.00**

Tier maple, 3 simulated drw, cut out base, 19″ **425.00**
Couch, fainting, tufted velvet, wood trim castors **425.00**
   Mahog, Empire, arm scrolls w/dolphins, paw ft w/cornucopia **700.00**
   Walnut, trn arm supports & ft, simple board back, 75″ long **700.00**

Cupboard
2 drw over 2 do on molded base, early 1800s **270.00**
Cherry, Pa. Dutch, 4 do, 3 spice drw **2,300.00**
Corner, cherry & pine, arched top w/shelf, fluted columns . . **1,300.00**
   Cherry & pine, country, refinished, 72″ **750.00**

Cherry & poplar, rope turnings, 64x42″ **1,800.00**
Cherry & walnut, open shelves, 2 do, 83x41″........... **1,200.00**
Cherry, 2 pc, broken arch pediment, 11 pane do over 2 in base **900.00**
Cherry, do chamfered inside, 1820, 81″ **3,200.00**
Cherry, pediment, 2 glaze do over 2 in base, 1800s **700.00**
Cherry, scalloped & scribed crown board w/do, 1789 ..... **2,600.00**
Curly maple, 12 pane top, base trim, trn ft **3,400.00**
Hanging, country Chpndl, ogee crown, 2 do, 50″ **200.00**
H-hinges, sq nails, wood pegs, 1750s **3,200.00**
Pine & basswood, 9 pane do, Chpndl **1,500.00**
Pine, 1860, 72″.................................... **895.00**
Pine, bow front 2-8 pane do over 2, 87″ **1,750.00**
Rupp decor, Pa., 80x58″ **500.00**
Shennandoah Valley, molded crown over 2 dbl do **750.00**
Walnut, 2 part, 1 panel do over 2, 1800, 76″ **450.00**
Walnut, fine arhcitectural construction, 1750 .... **5,000.00**
Country type w/open front, orig paint, early 1800s........ **1,750.00**
Dough, 1 board top, 1 lg & 1 sm panel do w/screen inset **275.00**
Hanging, bow front, original mustard finish, 1830 .... **750.00**
   Pine, 9 drw, towel bar, 1860, 4′ **285.00**
   Walnut, cornice mold, raised panel, 26x22″ **450.00**
Jelly, country Hplwht, Ohio, Shaker blue, 1820 .... **1,500.00**
   Grain paint, wide pine boards, 1880, 60″ **675.00**
   Midwest origin, orig blue, 1800s **490.00**
Kitchen, maple, 2 glass do, 5 spice drw, refinished **625.00**
Oak, spice drws................................... **1,200.00**
Pine, open face, 2 shelves, step back, 2 do, 73″ **1,400.00**
   Step back, open top, base door, restored, 1760s **500.00**
Primitive Welsh w/bonnet top, 1750s **1,250.00**
Secretary combination, mahogany, writing desk, 2 do, 3 drw . . **750.00**
Walnut, 2 pc, refinished, 1860....................... **1,195.00**
   Dutch, cornice top, 2-8 pane do over 2 do & 2 drws..... **3,000.00**

Desk
Black walnut, Wells Fargo type, 1872, 54x33x64″......... **1,100.00**

Burl veneer, Biedermier, fall front, ebonized interior **1,100.00**
Burled walnut, davenport, slant lid, 33x22½x22″.......... **2,750.00**
Cherry, 2 carved dogs.............................. **2,500.00**
   Chpndl, slant front elaborate inlay, 43x36x19″ **3,600.00**
   Federal, 4 drw, slant front, 42x39x19″ **2,600.00**
   Hplwht, fall front, fitted, tiger maple drw facings **3,000.00**
   Plantation, 2 pc, slant front, table base, 30x33″........ **295.00**
   Sheraton, plantation, fitted interior **700.00**
   Slant front w/maple interior, 3 drw, 43x42″ **1,900.00**

Davenport, walnut & burl walnut, 1845, 36x21″ **900.00**
Dressing table combination, walnut, fancy carving, cabriole legs **300.00**
French lady's secretary, marble top, inlaid, 3 drw **800.00**
Mahogany davenport, leather slant top, trn columns, 4 drw ... **600.00**
Mahog, Empire, curved legs............................ **325.00**
   Federal, inlaid tambour **7,200.00**
   Hplwht, slant front, graduated drw.................. **1,600.00**
Mahog & pine, Geo III, batchelor's, graduated drw **2,500.00**
Maple Chpndl, slant lid, 3 drws **1,200.00**
Maple & birch, Chpndl, slant drop front, 3 drw, 43″...... **2,000.00**
Maple & mahog, Sheraton, lady's, fitted interior, reeded legs **3,800.00**
Mustard graining, lift top **700.00**
Oak, Country English, 8 drw, 1690.................... **3,750.00**
   Dropfront, side drawers & doors, Victorian............ **950.00**
   Larkin, mirror & gingerbread top, candle shelves.......... **145.00**
   Library, mission, 1 drw, shelf stretcher **300.00**
   Slant front w/pigeon holes, brass bound **295.00**
   Stickley, fall front, minor restoration, 1905 .... **600.00**
   Telephone, w/glass inkwell, Burnhardt, 1909............. **80.00**
Oriental, carved, 1800s, 57x44x27″.................... **1,650.00**
Pine, Sheraton, master's, drop front, fitted.............. **450.00**
Queen Anne, slant front, fitted, leather surface, 30x25″ **2,200.00**
Roll-top, burl walnut veneer, Eastlake cylinder, gallery **1,275.00**
   Mahog, 2-curve, paneled sides, 42 drw & holes, 60″ **1,800.00**
   Oak, 84″ long................................. **1,850.00**
   Oak, S-curve, raised panel, 54″ **2,450.00**
   Oak, S-roll, 1894, refinished **1,995.00**
   S-roll w/5 drw & filing surface, Dearborn Co **975.00**
Rosewood, 2 base drw, fitted, drop front, china trade **955.00**
School master's, lift top, pigeon holes, refinished, 33x34″ **150.00**
Secretary, Hplwht, fall front, fitted, inlay on legs **1,500.00**
Slant front, 4 drw, fitted interior, late 1700s **1,650.00**
Walnut, butler's secretary, open below **1,000.00**
   Cylinder, carved **1,100.00**

Drop front w/applied fruit carvings	850.00
Gallery, slant front, 1 drw, trumpet legs	1,400.00
Hplwht, drop front, fitted interior, 4 drw	2,800.00
Lady's partner, leather insert, brasses, 1850	695.00
Wooten, black walnut w/maple finish, elephant ft, back glass	9,000.00
Cabinet-secretary, Standard Grade	7,700.00
Standard, small	8,300.00
Walnut & burl w/bird's eye maple interior, standard	8,500.00

Dinning set, Duncan Phyfe, table, buffet, 6 chairs, 1940s	950.00
L & JG Stickley, #722 table w/2 leaves, 6 chairs	650.00
Dresser, burl & carved front, marble top, candle posts, 1870	375.00
Cherry & mahog, orig mirror, 1835	375.00
Mahogany, Empire, 4 drw, stepped top	450.00
Walnut, Eastlake, marble top, glove	575.00
Dry sink, old paint, lower wood box compartment	445.00
Pine, 2 do, 1 drw, 38x60″	500.00
Pine, 2 do, 5″ well, sm drw top right, splashboard	695.00
Pine, lift top, sq nails, primitive	275.00
Pine & poplar, revamped w/drawers, 42″ long	275.00

Etagere

Corner, mahog, fretwork galleried shelves, small	425.00
Walnut, 12 carved fretwork brackets, w/4 shelves, 62″	2,350.00
Renaissance Revival, cupboard base, 74″	550.00
Rococo, marble top, 2 drw base, mirror	2,350.00
Victorian w/oval mirror, 5x4′	450.00
Vict, glass enclosed shelves, 3 beveled mirrors, 6 sm shelves	700.00

Footstool, iron, lacy design, plush cover	50.00
Louis XVI, incised, Grecian Cross legs, hoof ft	250.00
Walnut, Rococo, serpentine legs, velvet over coil springs	175.00

Hall Piece

Chair, walnut & burl, Renaissance, drw in seat, 50″	450.00
Foyer mirror, butternut, Greek scroll top, fluted columns	3,000.00
Pier glass, walnut & burl, Renaissance, marble shelf, crest	800.00
Rack, oak pillars, lift seat, beveled mirror	635.00
Stand, oak, large and ornate, extra wide seat	650.00
Oak, lift seat, applied crest decor, hooks, 7½′	700.00
Oak, ornate hooks, beveled mirror, lift seat	600.00
Walnut & burl, marble shelf, Renaissance Revival	1,500.00
Tree, cast iron, Rococo, leaf & vine decor, umbrella holds	400.00
Iron, Art Nouveau	800.00
Oak, Victorian, mirrored, lift seat, 84″	125.00

Highboy

Birch, Connecticut 1740s	7,500.00
Cherry, Chpndl, bonnet top, fan carving, 82″	4,000.00
Queen Anne, 2 over 3 drw, base w/mid-drw w/side-drws	3,000.00
Curly maple, Queen Anne, 62x39″	2,600.00
Maple & walnut, 2 section, 8 drw, double arches, 69″	4,500.00
Maple, Queen Anne, 5 drw over base w/1 over 3 drw, 1740s	2,000.00
Walnut, Queen Anne, 3 over 2 over 3 drw, base w/drw, ¼ columns	3,400.00
Queen Anne, bonnet top w/broken arch, 80″	6,000.00

Hutch, pine, flat cornice w/2 shelves, base w/2 do, cutout, 74″	500.00
Linen press, cherry, Empire, trn ft, pilasters, 43″	1,000.00
Mahog, inlay shields in upper section	4,200.00
Oak, 2 do over 6 drw, English, 1700s	3,500.00
Pine, walnut knobs, 2 do, base drw	700.00
Love seat & chair, carved cupids, carved legs & arms, velvet	5,000.00
Lowboy, burl walnut, inlay, Stair & Co, 1800s, 28x30″	1,750.00
Jocobean, 1 drw, triple arch apron w/2 finial drops	450.00
Maple & walnut, 3 drw, 1800s, 32″ wide	4,000.00
Sheraton, overhanging top, 1 drw over 2 divided drw	450.00
Meridienne, rosewood, Belter	4,500.00

Night table, tiger maple, 1 drw, trn legs, 20x18½″	275.00
Walnut, marble top, 1 drw, 1 panel do	375.00
Ottoman, mahog, Empire, needlepoint over coil spring	175.00
Parlour set, Eastlake, 5 pc	1,800.00
Rosewood, Sleepy Hollow, 1880, 3 pc	865.00
Settee, armchair & 3 sm chairs, velvet	1,200.00
Pew, walnut, Renaissance, applied carvings, burl insets, arms	300.00

Pie Safe

2 drws, pierced tin do, cut out base, 53″	365.00
Painted, tin sides	125.00
Pine, mesh inserts, 2 do, solid sides, top drw	225.00
Orig heavy tin pierced do & sides	295.00
Punched tin do, bottom drw	300.00
Tulip punched tin inserts	880.00

Rack

Bedding, walnut, cut out sides, 3 do & 2 lower bars	225.00
Linen, black walnut, cameo bust pediment	175.00
Black walnut, handcarved bird on branch	225.00
Inset tiles, needlework, carved wings & finials	200.00
Walnut, double bar, Rococo cherub & carvings	175.00
Pie cooling, tilt shelves	125.00
Plate, oak, molded protector, top shelf	150.00

Rocker

Bentwood, cane seat & back, excellent	700.00
Painted, caned seat	135.00
Boston, hard maple, carved headpiece, 1830s	225.00
Cage back, 4 spindle comb	550.00
Cherry, needs refinishing	95.00
Curly maple, Rococo carved oval top, demi arms	350.00
Floral press back w/cane seat	145.00

Folding, ca 1890, 33″	200.00
Ladder-back w/turn arm support, ring trn finials, splint seat	190.00
Maple & ash, 4 slat, 1790s, 44″	190.00
Sausage trn w/4 stiles, ball trn finials	190.00
Lincoln, black walnut, Rococo velvet seat & back	400.00
Maple, curved arms, eye caning, bentwood scrolls	350.00
Mission, L&JG Stickley, no arms	125.00
W/arms, L&JG Stickley	175.00
Mix wood, homecrafted, seat rewoven, Miss.	175.00
Nursing, maple, incised, baluster & spindle trn	250.00
Oak, 4 spindle each side under rolled arms, 41″	295.00

Press back, 7 trn spindles, country **150.00**

Vict., applied leaf carvings 8 trn back, 5 ea side spindles **225.00**

Platform, cherry, spring seat, 1870 . . . . **250.00**

Incised, carved, walnut w/leather **300.00**

Signed Hunzinger **750.00**

Poplar, wht paint, restored pressed paper seat, Ky. **125.00**

Sewing, cane seat & back **75.00**

Oak w/spindle back **60.00**

Victorian, cane back & seat **250.00**

Walnut, Belter style, cabriole legs, scroll arms **2,000.00**

Carved frame, Sleepy Hollow **475.00**

Windsor, rolled arms, stepdown crestrail, bamboo trn **425.00**

Arrow-back **125.00**

Spindle back, needs refinishing **110.00**

Screen, cherry frame, 3 panels, hp silk **550.00**

French, hp 3 panels canvas, floral & lattice **150.00**

Walnut w/silk insets, 1 tall & 2 shorter spindled panels **450.00**

Walnut, adjustable frame, tapestried, 1 wide panel **195.00**

Secretary

Black walnut, cylinder, roll barrel, 2 glaze do, 3 drw **2,500.00**

Flame mahog, Eng Regency, drop front, brass grills & trim . **3,500.00**

Grain paint, cornice, 2 do, fold out desk, 57x33" **1,100.00**

Hplwht, glass do over drw in base **3,600.00**

Oak, side by side w /bookcase **665.00**

Walnut & burl, cylinder, incised decor, bookcase top, 8½' . **2,600.00**

Walnut & burl veneer, bulter's, glaze do, 5 drw base, 91" . . **1,100.00**

Walnut, Chpndl, arch pediment, rosettes, shell carved **1,350.00**

Eastlake, cylinder, side do in base w/2 drw **2,400.00**

Server, rosewood & burl, Empire, marble top **750.00**

Walnut & burl veneers, marble top, brass pulls, Eastlake . . . **750.00**

Walnut & matched veneer, 2 end columns on ball ft, 60". **1,600.00**

Settee

Lacquered, caned panels w/hp scenes, trn legs, slip seat, 1800 **375.00**

Mahog, Sheraton, arch crestrail, trn fluted legs **450.00**

Mahog, arched crest, trn, reeded arms, legs, 74" **4,000.00**

Straight crest, acanthus carved arms, 1830, 88" **500.00**

Walnut & velvet, Eastlake, carved mirror, incisings **475.00**

Walnut, carved, serpentine back, upholstered, 1900 . . . . **550.00**

Eastlake, upholstered sides, back w/wood panel **300.00**

Walnut, reupholstered, 34x38" **210.00**

Wing-back, Queen Anne, 65" **675.00**

Settle, Penn Dutch, hp w/rush seat **2,500.00**

Shaving Stand

Black walnut w/bevel mirror, 1870 . . . . **550.00**

Curly maple, bow front, drw, 18" **95.00**

Ornate inlay of Admiral Dewy, US Shield, sidecabinets, 1 drw base **425.00**

Mahog, brass steeple trn finials, 1 drw, 20" **130.00**

Mahog & brass, marble top, spindle column, 1 drw **600.00**

Mahog veneer w/inlay, bowfront drw, 16" **85.00**

Mirror, w/towel bar, razor baskets **40.00**

Shelf, clock, grain paint, Penn. **75.00**

Corner, ebony, handcarved dog head, on fancy pendant **200.00**

Pine, 3 shelves, red stain, shaped sides, 24x21" **135.00**

Walnut, clock, incised **125.00**

Sideboard

Cherry, double reeded pillasters, trn legs **345.00**

Crotched mahog, Sheraton, trn fluted legs, arch panel **375.00**

Mahog, Empire, carved columns, claw ft, 48x52" **400.00**

Hplwht, 'D' top, inlay, 1 drw over 2 drw, 1 bottle drw **500.00**

Hplwht, inlaid top w/mid-draw over 2 do, 2 drw, 42x69" . . **2,600.00**

Hplwht, inlay, serpentine front **4,000.00**

Hplwht, serpentine do, compartments in top, sm **650.00**

Inlaid, bow front, 3 drws & doors, 36x45" **1,000.00**

Regency, 2 drw, round & trn legs, box stretcher **275.00**

Misson, Gustav Stickley **1,100.00**

Oak, medallion frame mirror, Ionic columns, lions ft **975.00**

Bowed drw, lion ft, 1900 . . . . **895.00**

Victorian, 3 mirrors, 2 galleries, florals, 90x72" **2,200.00**

Walnut w/burl veneers, Renaissance, marbel top w/shelves . **1,900.00**

Walnut, blk & wht marble, mirror w/sides shelves, 94x40" . **2,900.00**

Carvings frame oval door centers, mirror, side shelves **1,600.00**

Sofa

Chpndl, camel back, roll arms, 3 cushion, H stretcher **475.00**

Scroll arms, shaped back, stretcher legs, slip seat **500.00**

Duncan Phyfe type, carved panels, 80" **2,000.00**

Empire, horsehair upholstery, eagle carvings, cornucopia arms **2,400.00**

Mahog, Empire Revival, 6 lion paw ft, leaves, fruit **1,450.00**

Rococo frame w/tufted velvet, 72" long **750.00**

Rosewood frame, legs & arms, damask seat, back **1,250.00**

Rosewood & tufted velvet, serpentine pierced trim **2,800.00**

Vict, 3 crests, carved, orig upholstry, 92" **1,000.00**

Walnut & tufted velvet, full upholstered back, carved apron . . . **700.00**

Walnut frame, Victorian, triple crest, velvet **1,100.00**

Stand

Four sq chamfered spay legs, curved scalloped apron, 15" **80.00**

Birch, 1 drw, early 1800s **450.00**

Cherry, 1 drw, trn legs **450.00**

Sheraton, 1 drw w/wood knob, 1840, 29x22½x20" **275.00**

Mahog, fluted column w/pineapple, domed base **225.00**

Heavy post w/twist carving, bronze ft **450.00**

Sewing, mahog, drop leaves w/inlay, 2 drw **300.00**

Sheraton, 1 drw, 1 board top, trn legs, 28" **160.00**

Teakwood, Chinese, prunus blossom carvings, 32" **550.00**

Round w/marble insert, intricate, 36x11" **250.00**

Walnut, 3 drw, inlay, drop leaves **3,750.00**

MOP inlay, 4 spindle legs **350.00**

Carved stag head figural **175.00**

Eastlake scalloped apron, finial pendants, 30" **250.00**

Heavy spiral post, brass animal ft, sq top **375.00**

Stool

Jacobean, block & trn supports w/trestle base **70.00**

Kneeling, simple quartered oak **100.00**

Walnut, handcarved biblical theme **795.00**

Organ, Eastlake w/velvet upholstery **200.00**

Empire, iron grips raise & lower height 375.00
High back 300.00
Maple w/tufted velvet, ornate scroll ft 275.00
Maple, Eastlake 175.00
With back, refinished 235.00
Piano, maple w/trn legs, adjusts 125.00
Wooden w/high back, glass ball & claw ft 95.00
Slipper, black walnut, pierced sides, carved crests 350.00
Table
Banquet, 2 part, Sheraton, flute ring trn legs, molded frieze . 2,000.00
Flame mahog, 3 trn ped, fluted legs, brass paw ft 1,750.00
Mahog, 2 part, Hplwht, 30x46x87" 550.00
Mahog, Federal by Henredon, 2 peds, 2 leaves, ... 700.00
Birdcage, mahog, Georgian, ped w/leaf carving, tripod base ... 350.00
Mahog, Chpndl, scroll top, trn shaft, arch legs 575.00
Mahog, tilt top, vase trn ped, 3 cabriole legs, ball & claw ... 600.00
Breakfast, cherry, drop leaf w/end drw, N.E., 1810 .... 450.00
Card, brass inlay, intricate carving, 1810 .... 1,500.00
Chpndl, fly leaf, scalloped apron, serpentine top 650.00
Crotched mahog veneer frieze w/canted corner 375.00
Hplwht demi-lune, inlaid frieze, sq legs, w/cuff inlay 1,400.00
Mahog w/inlay, Federal, 1700, 28x35x16" 1,650.00
Hplwht demi-lune, 29x36½" 700.00
Sheraton, Wm Hook, serpentine 2,800.00
Bow front, Federal, 29x36x18" 1,200.00
Mahog, Sheraton, serpentine top, shaped corners w/inlay ... 325.00
Hplwht, serpentine top & skirt w/inlay 325.00
Mahogany, Sheraton, hinged top, reed legs, 30x36" 425.00
Serpentine, swivel top w/coin pockets 290.00
Sheraton, demi lune, ball ft, sliding back leg, 1 drw 475.00
Cherry & pine, 26x30x21" 265.00
Drw 1 end, side apron lifts, trn legs 375.00
Half round w/drop leaf 400.00
Pembroke, cut corners, 1810 .... 735.00
Sq legs, 1 drw, 3 board top, 29x34" 625.00
Coffee, walnut turtleback, scrolled, marble top 600.00
Console, mahog w/inlay, early 1800s 850.00
Dining, birch, drop leaves, 28x36x34" 225.00
Cherry, drop leaf, 33x75" 785.00
Flame mahog, Sheraton, drw in ea end, brasses 300.00
Mahog, Federal, 1 board top, drop leaves 500.00
Gate leg, drop leaves, sq taper legs, 28x42" 400.00
Lions ft, 7' w/3 leaves 1,000.00
Sheraton, 2 pedestals 2,100.00
Dressing, butternut, 4 drw, 1700s, 29x33" 225.00
Mirror, 1 drw, vase trn legs, serpentine stretcher 200.00
Drop leaf, birch, Federal, red stain, 29x42" 475.00
Cherry w/inlay, Federal, 27x35" 500.00
Country Queen Anne, 1 board top, 27x42" 1,035.00
Trn legs, wide boards, 29" 270.00
Mahog, Chpndl, 28½x42" 435.00
Hplwht, gate leg, 1 board top, sq legs 325.00
Oval w/inlay, late 1700s 1,100.00
Maple, Queen Anne, oval top, pad ft, 28x45" 1,500.00
Oval, carved cabriole legs, restored 1,750.00
Queen Anne, base w/scalloped apron, cabriole legs 750.00
Sheraton, black walnut & cherry, 1850 .... 250.00
Tiger maple w/inlay, rectangular, 29x36" 600.00
Tiger maple, 28x42x40", open 225.00
Trestle ft, Stickley, 32" 2,500.00
Walnut, Sheraton, 1 board top, trn legs, 30x48" 280.00
Cherry, 27½x34" 475.00
Mahog, Gerogian, 1 drw, oval top 550.00
Pine, Hplwht, 1 drw 700.00

Drum, Jacobean, ring & bulbous trn legs, X stretcher w/finial, 34" 325.00
Mahogany, Duncan Phyfe, hexagonal, leather inset 375.00
Empire, carved eagle heads, sm, round 2,000.00
Entry, walnut, demi lune w/carved urn, florals, leaf 450.00
Extension, walnut, Vict, extends to 10' 300.00

Foyer, marble top, ca 1890s, England, 32x26" 325.00
Game, cherry, French, drop leaf, 1890 .... 375.00
Mahog w/inlay 1,200.00
Gate leg, oak, English, oval, late 1800s 750.00
Hall, carved bird pediments, long & narrow 900.00
Harvest, pine, 3 board top, tonque & groove, 10' 1,900.00
Hplwht, Pembroke, serpetine top, gate leg support 450.00
Hunt, Sheraton, 6 trn fluted legs, deep drop molded leaves ... 850.00
Hutch, pine, old paint, 1780s 50" dia 1,350.00
Pine, painted, top dia, 50" 1,400.00
Kitchen, pine, chestnut legs, w/drawer, N.C. 365.00
Kneading, pine, pegged top, sq legs, 1 drw, 31x30x30" 465.00
Lamp, brass & oak, Vict, ornate pierced apron 350.00
Chinese, 1800s, 42" dia 750.00
Vict, marble, turtle top, 25½" 225.00
Library, claw ft, North Wind head, carved panels 875.00
French style, serpentine ends, scroll apron, 1 drw 290.00
Gustave Stickley in red stamp, 26# 525.00
Oak, Stickley, 29x48" 335.00
Heavy trn legs 100.00
Mahog, oval top, trn post, tripod base, 1790s 700.00
Mahogany w/inlay, Federal, serpentine front, 29x36x39" 2,800.00
Mahogany, Pembroke, drop leaf, sq legs, X stretcher, 1 drw .. 925.00
Maple & curly maple, Pembroke, 2 drop leaves, 1 drw end ... 450.00
Hplwht, taper legs, drw 130.00
Marble top, grape carving, turtle top 625.00
Mahogany, ogee carved base, 39" dia 550.00
Occasional, Hplwht, 2 drws, 1 board top 350.00
Oriental carved rosewood, 1880, 30" 550.00
Parlor, rosewood, Vict, ornate carvings, marble top, 30x46" . 1,100.00
Walnut, Eastlake w/inlaid top 600.00
Pine & poplar, country, 2 board wide top, 23x23" 195.00
Pine, 1 board top, side drw, spoon trn legs, 1840 .... 1,200.00
Plank top, cherry spool legs, 28" dia 265.00
Round 2 board top, 5½" deep apron, 28" 190.00
Sawbuck, 25x25" 185.00
Turn table top, 52", 1800's 550.00
Round, oak, hexagon ped, claw ft, 52" wide 885.00
Pedestal w/claw ft, 48" 600.00
Serving, tiger maple, 2 drw, rectangle, 29x42x18" 390.00

Sewing, 2 drw, sponge grain, orig striping **285.00**
  Cherry, 1 drw, trn legs **290.00**
  Hplwht, shaped top w/inlay **3,400.00**
  Mahog, Sheraton, w/orig sewing bag, 27″ **500.00**
    Rope trn legs, Sheraton **230.00**
Sheraton Pembroke, 1 drw, ring & spiral trn legs **250.00**
Side, sq w/serpentine gallery, shelf, inlay, X stretcher **575.00**
Square oak w/5 press back chairs, eagle claw **1,500.00**
Tavern, 2 drw, Penn Dutch **1,000.00**
  Cherry, drawer, trn legs, box stretcher **1,100.00**
  Curly maple, oval top, 25x32″ **1,100.00**
  Maple & pine, oval top, trn legs, 1720s, 24x34″ **450.00**
  Oval top, trn spayed legs, sq stretchers, 23″ **2,655.00**
  Pine, 1 drw, maple base, 30x40″ **185.00**
    Refinished, 26″ **350.00**
  Pine & maple, Chpndl, old paint, 25″ **1,000.00**
  Queen Anne, 1 drw, 1 board top shaped corners **625.00**
  Vase, ring & block trn, 1 drw, 1 board top, breadboard ends **500.00**
Tea, Chpndl, cabriole legs, spade ft **2,900.00**
  Federal, tip top, trn ped set on 3 arched legs **110.00**
  George II, tilt top, carved ped on tri pod base, 23″ dia **500.00**
  Mahog, Queen Anne, dish top, pull out candle slides **200.00**
    Square tip top, Chpndl, 30x41″ **1,350.00**
    Tilt top, octagonal, 1800s **700.00**
  Queen Anne, tip top, trn ped, arch legs, snake ft, 30″ **185.00**
  Tip top, mahog, trn post, 3 legs, 1770, 19″ **550.00**
  Mahogany, vase & ring trn post, tripod base **200.00**
  With 4 chairs, Duncan Phyfe **500.00**
  Walnut, Queen Anne, tilt top, 27″ dia **550.00**
  Regency, dolphin legs **1,200.00**
  Vict, deep apron, legs carved at top, 1862 . . . . **675.00**
Work, birch, Federal, 2 drw, trn legs, 29x20″ **390.00**
  Cherry, Sheraton, 1 drw, beaded lip, 1 board top **230.00**
  Federal, 2 drw, scroll legs, rosettes, brass paw ft **525.00**
  Sheraton, 2 drw drop leaf, trn legs, 29x19½″ **235.00**
  Tiger maple & cherry, 3 drw, star inlay, trn legs **1,250.00**
Writing, lady's Hplwht, pin w/pewter pulls, 1790 . . . . **650.00**

Taboret, oriental, carved top w/marble inset, pierced skirt, 29″ **300.00**
Tea cart w/lid, walnut **100.00**
  Walnut w/glass tray, spoke wheels, 1885 . . . . **100.00**
Vitrine, mahog, 4 curved glass panels, oval top, 28″ **190.00**
Wall unit, Oriental lacquer, 3 pc, MOP inlay, carving **2,000.00**
Wardrobe, chestnut, 2 recess panel do, 2 base drw, 84″ **1,300.00**
  Oak, double do, fancy carved top, 1910 . . . . **650.00**
    Vict, carved & fancy **500.00**
    Vict, ornate carved top, sectional **600.00**
  Pine, orig paint, cornice, inner shelf, 1800s, 72x50″ **450.00**

Washstand
Butternut, burl panels, marble, teardrop pulls **575.00**
Corner, mahog w/inlay, Hplwht, galleried back, X stretcher . . . **350.00**
Federal, scrolled stepped gallery back, bow front **220.00**
Hplwht, sq legs, 1 drw, scalloped frieze, backsplash **190.00**
Oak, Eastlake, incisings, 1 do, 1 long & 2 short drw **300.00**
  Hotel model, Eastlake, towel bar, 2 drw, 2 do **350.00**
  Mirror & towel rack **175.00**
  Pressed back board **250.00**
Pine, sponge decor, 1 drw shelf, 30x15x15″ **485.00**
  Vict, orig paint & stencil decor **300.00**
Regency, scroll backsplash, 2 drw, trn legs **210.00**
Walnut & burl, 1 do, 1 long & 2 short drw, marble top **350.00**
  Dovetailed drw, cutout for bowl, backsplash **375.00**
  Marble top, backsplash & candlerests **485.00**
Walnut, applied burl panels, round front corners **325.00**

Backsplash w/candleshelves, bracket ft **350.00**

G. Argy-Rousseau

  Gabriel Argy-Rousseau produced both fine art glass and commercial quality ware in 1918 in Paris, France. He favored Art Nouveau as well as Art Deco, and in the 20s produced a line of vases in the Eyptain manner, made popular by the discovery of King Tut's tomb. One of the most important types of glass he made was pate de verre. Most of his work is signed.

Bowl, black, raspberry, pineapples & leafage, 1925, 4½″ **825.00**
  Translucent tan, berries on rim, 2x4½″ **645.00**
Box, w/red mask lid, amber, orange, charcoal, 1925, 6″ dia . **1,760.00**
Lamp, frosted blue & green, hammered metal base, 7½″ . . . **2,900.00**
Lamp base, w/orig harp, finial & brass base, signed **1,495.00**
Pin tray **950.00**
Tray, red & purple, w/Egyptian head, lattice bottom, 6x3½″ **1,300.00**

Galle

  Emile Galle was one of the most important producers of French cameo glass. His firm, founded in 1874, in Nancy, France, produced beautiful wares in the Art Nouveau style during the 1890s, using various techniques. He also made enameled wares, as well as some pottery.

Cameo Glass
Bowl, shaded w/polished green & brown leaves, 4x8½″ **1,500.00**
Box, w/cover, purple leaves & berries **1,150.00**
Bud vase, frosted w/yellow, green, apricot foliage, 3½″ **350.00**
Egg, light green w/dark green ferns **1,400.00**
Lamp, red butterflies, wrought iron on marble base, 5½″ . . . **1,600.00**
Night light, gold w/red polished bleeding hearts **1,350.00**
Perfume lamp, red acorns on gold, polished, bronze base . . . **1,400.00**
Pitcher, pink w/purple bleeding hearts, 2 cuttings, 2x3″ **850.00**
Rose bowl, yellow w/polished red flowers & leaves **375.00**
Vase, 3 color allover florals, bulbous, 9½″ **1,850.00**
  Acid ground w/florals, 7″ **725.00**
  Amber w/pink & green wisteria, partial polish, 23″ **4,400.00**
  Apricot/rose w/red berries, silver leaf collar, 10″ **450.00**
  Aqua w/amber iris, scalloped rim, 15″ **1,800.00**
  Beige w/cranberry berries, polished, 5″ **650.00**
  Blown out leaves and pods, yellow w/amethyst, 9½″ **5,450.00**
  Blue w/purple hydrangeas, green leaves, polished, 13″ . . . **1,750.00**
  Blue/gray w/pink & lime florals, polished, 9½″ **1,750.00**

Carnelian w/floral decoration, 14½".................. **2,000.00**
Frost w/3 color pine cones & needles, 9"............... **815.00**
Frost w/coral splashes, brown leaves, 6½" **800.00**
Frosted & pink, w/green florals, 17" **1,950.00**
Frosted w/green & brown pine stems, blossoms, 7"....... **650.00**
Frosted, mauve to clear floral, cameo signature, 4"....... **350.00**
Gold frost w/flowers & leaves, 6"...................... **550.00**
Gold w/lavender flowers & leaves, 5¾" **510.00**
Gold w/lavender flowers, signed, 5".................... **400.00**
Gray w/greens, wisteria, cylinder, cushion ft, 13½"...... **770.00**
Gray w/pink splash, lavendar & green wisteria, 12½"..... **1,210.00**
Gray w/plum branches, bulbous w/cylinder neck, 5¾"...... **465.00**
Green stick form, 3 cuttings, 3¾" **450.00**
Green w/red landscape, ped, tapered, 9"............... **1,100.00**
Green, frost, & peach, w/acorns, flask shape, 5¾"....... **1,100.00**
Grey to amber, amber & russet primrose & foliage, 14"... **2,310.00**
Landscape in great detail, 3 colors, 6" **975.00**
Lavendar overlaid clematis, partial polish, 9" **770.00**
Light blue w/purple flora, green leaves, 13½x5½" **1,400.00**
Milky w/lavender & green hydrangea, bulbous to slender, 12" **715.00**
Milky w/purple sweet peas, cylinder w/disk base, 23", illus. **1,210.00**
Milky w/red lotus, bulbous, small neck, 4" **770.00**
Milky w/rust ivy, polished, bulbous w/thin neck, 12"...... **1,540.00**
Ochre w/allover red & maroon clematis, bulbous, 9½" ... **4,675.00**
Orange & white w/acid etched florals, 24".............. **1,700.00**
Pink to frost w/purple wisteria, green leaves, 11½" **800.00**

Pink w/green blossoms, cylinder into disk base, 17"...... **1,045.00**
Pink/white w/amber landscape, disk base, tapers, 18", illus **1,980.00**
Rose w/plum florals, bulbous w/cylinder neck, 6¾" **880.00**
Scenic w/man in boat, trees, 3 colors, 4½x7".......... **1,750.00**
Scenic w/mountain & forest, 3 colors, cylinder, 18½" **3,500.00**
Tan w/blue floral, green, brown leaves, 5½"........... **600.00**
Tan, frost w/3 shades of brown leaves, slender, 4½"....... **950.00**
Wheel cut scenic, mountain & lake, ped, 6½" **1,100.00**
White to light blue w/royal florals, 7".................. **925.00**
White w/purple iris, 16" **1,600.00**
White, w/lavender florals, polished, bulbous, 8" **850.00**
Yellow w/red flowers, 2½" **375.00**
Yellow w/lavender florals, bulbous base, 8"............. **565.00**
Yellow w/lavender flowers, signed, 4" **495.00**

Yellow w/mold blown blue & brown fruit, leaves, 11"..... **6,000.00**
Yellow w/red chrysanthemums, low foot, bulbous, 6¾" ... **2,200.00**
Pottery
Ewer, beetle & lotus decor, 8" **650.00**
Plaque, fleur-de-lis form w/portrait, 8½x7"............ **375.00**
Teapot, swirled & ribbed, bird spout, floral, mica, 11"....... **950.00**

Gambling

Books
Card Manipulations, Hugard, 163 pg, 1930 .... **12.00**
Card Mastery, MacDougall, 202 pg, 1944 .... **15.00**
Chance And Luck, Proctor, 263 pg, 1889 .... **35.00**
Cheated At Dice, King, 16 pg, 1951 .... **25.00**
Diamond Jim, Morell, 278 pg, 1934 .... **18.00**
Doctrine Of Chances, Rouse, 349 pg **100.00**
Encyclopedia Of Indoor Games, Foster, 625 pg, 1903........ **27.00**
Ethics of Gambling, MacKenzie, 90 pg, 1899 .... **22.00**
Expert At The Card Table, Erdnase, 178 pg, 1902 .... **35.00**
Fools Of Fortune, Quinn, 638 pg, 1891 .... **150.00**
Forty Years A Gambler On The Mississippi, Devol, 288 pg, 1926 **42.00**
Foster's Practical Poker, Foster, 253 pg, 1905............. **23.00**
Frauds Exposed, Comstock, 576 pg, 1880 .... **150.00**
Gamblers Don't Gamble, MacDougall, 167 pg, 1940 .... **28.00**
Gambling, Romain, 230 pg, 1891 .... **75.00**
Gambling World, Rouge et Noir, 373 pg, 1898 .... **45.00**
Gin Rummy, Jacoby, 241 pg, 1947 .... **6.00**
Hand Book Of Games, Bohn, 617 pg, 1850.............. **55.00**
History of Gambling, Ashton, 285 pg, 1898 .... **55.00**
How To Control Fair Dice, 16 pg **35.00**
How To Figure The Odds, Jacoby, 215 pg, 1947............. **8.00**
Hoyle's Games, 519 pg, 1897 .... **22.00**
If You Must Gamble, Lenihan, 127 pg, 1946 .... **20.00**
Jackpots, Stories Of The Great American Game, Edwards, 1900 **25.00**
Jo-Jotte, Culbertson, 160 pg, 1937 .... **8.00**
Monaco And Monte Carlo, Smith, 466 pg, 1912 .... **49.00**
Monte Carlo Casino, Polovisoff, 283 pg **20.00**
Paddle Wheels And Pistols, Anthony, 329 pg, 1930 .... **15.00**
Play The Devil, Chafetz, 459 pg, 1960 .... **19.00**
Pole On Whist, Pole, 218 pg, 1883 .... **20.00**
Policy Pete's Dream Book, 99 pg, 1934 .... **39.00**
Protection, The Sealed Book, Meyer, 123 pg, 1911 .... **125.00**
Round The Green Cloth, Chester, 254 pg, 1928 .... **20.00**
Scarne On Dice, Scarne, 379 pg, 1945................... **17.00**
Sealed Book Of Roulette, 262 pg, 1924 .... **45.00**
Sharps And Flats, Maskelyne, 335 pg, 1894................ **125.00**
Such Was Saratoga, 365 pg, 1940 .... **45.00**
Suckers Progress, Asbury, 469 pg, 1938................. **49.00**
The Arts & Miseries Of Gambling, Green, 1845............. **120.00**
The Open Book, Johnson, 155 pg **125.00**
Traps For The Young, Comstock, 246 pg, 1883 .... **65.00**
Treasury Of Gambling Stories, 382 pg, 1946 .... **65.00**
Webster's Poker Book, 126 pg, 1925 .... **30.00**
What's The Odds, Ullman, 155 pg, 1903 .... **20.00**
Why You Can't Win, Scarne, 44 pg **75.00**

Card case, 2 deck, paper covered wood **22.00**
Card corner rounder, rosewood top, steel & brass, 5x3¼".. **1,200.00**
Card press, rosewood base, ivory mounted, 10½x5x9" **345.00**
Card trimmer, ivory handle, nickel silver base, 6x5½"...... **1,800.00**
   Shear style, brass base, G Henry & Co **1,500.00**
Chip rack, Faro, wood trim, 25x12½" **95.00**
Crap layout, unmounted, full size **125.00**
Dealing box, German silver, side squeeze, gaffed, Ball Bros ... **595.00**

Dice, bone, crude, ½″ 35.00
 Celluloid, transparent, ¼″........................ 6.00
 Poker, advertising, Seagram's VO, imitation ivory 25.00
  Ivory, Elk Brand, w/orig box, ½″ 28.00
 Porcelain, black w/gold pips, ¼″ 7.00
 Put & take, imitation ivory, ½″ 16.00
 Solid Steel, unusual, ½″ 10.00
Dice boat, all wood, lined interior, 3x6″............. 28.00
Dice cup, turned ivory, carved ribs, 4½x1½″ 125.00
Faro casekeeper, closed box style, hearts & ivory beads, G Williams 400.00
Faro dealing box, gaffed, inside lock & release, unmkd 625.00
Faro layout, oil cloth w/applied cards in clubs, Will & Finck .. 765.00
 Suit is spades, wood trim, Wm Ellis Mfg................ 625.00
Horse race game, 12 hp lead horses, complete w/wood case... 325.00
Keno hopper, carved wood/brass hardware, early style, 21½x12″ 565.00
 Walnut, furniture style, acorn finial, German silver hardware, ftd 750.00
Lotto, boxed set w/all cards, markers & buttons 24.00
Money belt, for gold coins, leather, 8 pockets, brass buckles ... 99.00
Playing cards, *see Playing Cards*
Poker chip, brass, embossed w/Recreation both sides 2.00
 Ivory, 25 scrimshawed on sides 25.00
  Plain 7.00
  Red border, letter D in script 18.00
Poker chip rack, holds 100 chips, 24 laminated layers, blonde wood 22.95
 Holds 250 chips, all wood, metal handle 20.00
Roulette cloth, unmounted, hp numbers, 54x37″........... 100.00
Roulette layout, folds, hp, William Ellis, 54x31″ 900.00
Roulette table & wheel, veneered legs, BC Wills 3,000.00
Roulette wheel, full size, early, Albert Pic & Co, complete .. 1,695.00
 Traveling, press plunger, tin case, 4¾x1½″ 35.00
 Turned wood w/wood & metal center, 9″ dia 79.00
 Wood, cast aluminum center, 19½″ dia 349.00
 Wood, cast center, 3 wood ft, 11½″ dia............. 195.00
Slot machines, *see Coin-Operated Machines*
Table, blackjack, Queen Anne legs, cloth top, set-in chip rack, 3½x6′ 895.00
 Chuck-a-Luck, heavy wood, Queen Anne legs, 3x5′ 795.00
 Crap, wood legs, high sides, wood chip rack, 12x5′ 1,700.00
 Faro, sit-down, Queen Anne legs, carved cross bar....... 1,695.00
 Wheel of fortune, ci feet, eagle at top, carved pole, 48″.... 1,795.00
 Horse race wheel, odds maker on top, HC Evans, 60″ ... 3,695.00

Games & Puzzles

 Among the most popular 19th century games attracting collectors today are the board games and their components which are hand-carved and painted, often with great attention to detail. Near the last decade of the century, commercially marketed games were introduced, some by companies who are still working. As is true today, many Victorian games were instructional & educational as well as entertaining. Colorfully-lithographed boxes and game parts add to their appeal, and subject matter often exhibits customs and attitudes of a bygone era.

 Puzzles were invented in 1760 by an English mapmaker whose intention it was to facilitate the teaching of Geography. By the mid 1850s, both America and Europe were producing children's puzzles. The earliest examples were made of wood, and were hand cut. Die cut cardboard puzzles were first manufactured in the 1890s, and 'adult' puzzles came into vogue. Although wood continued to be used, plywood replaced solid wood during the '20s and '30s and interlocking pieces made them easier to construct.

 Hand colored, hand cut or special interest 19th century puzzles are favorites of todays collectors; character related and quality wooden puzzles are also very desirable.

Alley Oop, 1937 .... 12.00
Anagrams, 1934, excellent & w/instructions 28.00

Authors, McLaughlin, 1902 .... 15.00
Bezique, French card game, 4 decks w/score pads, early....... 64.00
Bob Feller Big League Baseball.................... 22.00
Buster Brown, cloth litho, pin tie on Buster, w/tie cut outs 55.00
Camelot, Parker Bros, 1931.................... 18.00
Checkerboard, 2 pc, round, used on cracker barrel, 1890 .... 275.00
 Intricate hand-carving, orig paint, 1800s, 10x13″........ 225.00
 Pine, w/blue & wht squares, 24x10½″ 145.00
 Reverse painted glass, oak frame 110.00
Chiromagica, McLaughlin Bros, rare 100.00
Cinderella, card game w/color litho cards, 1895 .... 27.00
Dominoes, wood, Wharton Bros., in box, 1890s 45.00
Game board, checkerboard reverses, primitive, carved, 17x17″.. 75.00
 Handcarved, old paint, signed & dated 1906 .... 290.00
Gee-Wiz Horse Racing, 1920s, 29″ 88.00
Movie Sticks, Parker Bros, colored sticks, 1937........ 18.00
Parcheesi set, 1918............................ 10.00
Pit, Parker Bros, 1904 .... 8.00
Pretty Village, boathouse set, McLaughlin Bros 40.00
Puzzle, Battleship, Parker Bros.................... 145.00
 Snow White & Red Rose, reversible, McLaughlin, set of 6 .. 400.00
Puzzle Peg, owl on front, 1923.................... 15.00
Puzzle, 5 Victorian child's scenes, wood, orig wood box..... 165.00
 Down on the Farm, 300 combinations, in box, 11x8½″ 65.00
 Map of USA.................................. 15.00
 Parker Bros, orig wooden box, 1917.................. 27.00
 RR & Country Map of N.Y., hand tint, 1887, 13x17″ 95.00
Radio Questionnaire, orig box, pat 1928 .... 15.00
Telegraph Boy, McLaughlin Bros.................... 35.00
Touring, Parker Bros, 1937, MIB 20.00
Uncle Wiggly, paper litho hat game, excellent 40.00

Gas Globes and Panels

 Gas globes and panels, once a common sight, have vanished from the country side, but are being sought by collectors as a unique form of advertising memorabilia. They were often reverse painted and displayed the name of the gas company as well as their logo.

American, gas globe inserts, pair...................... 200.00
Flying A, curved gas pump sign.................... 50.00
Gulf, gas globe inserts, pair 100.00
Imperial No Lead, gas globe inserts, pair 75.00
Indian, glass panel, 10x4″ 10.00
Sinclair Power X, gas globe lenses, pair 75.00
Sky Chief, glass panel, 10x4″ 10.00
Sunoco Dynafuel, gas globe lenses, pair 175.00
Texaco Diesel Chief, gas globe inserts, pair 75.00
White Eagle, gas globe, excellent detail, 22″.............. 600.00

Gaudy Dutch

 Gaudy Dutch, made in England from 1780-1820, was a hand decorated ware on a soft paste body with rich underglaze blues, accented in orange, red, pink, green and yellow. It differs from Gaudy Welsh in that there is no luster. There are sixteen patterns, most of which were inspired by the Japanese Imari wares. Some of the most commonly found designs are War Bonnet, Grape, Dahlia, Oyster, Urn, Butterfly, Carnation and Single Rose.

Butterfly, cup & saucer, mint.......................... 700.00
 Milk jug, 4″ 1,100.00
 Plate, vines & dotted decor at blue banded rim, 9¾″ 1,320.00
 Plate, wavy line & vine decor at rim, 6½″ dia 660.00
 Teabowl & saucer, 3¾″ & 5½″ dia, pair 650.00

Teapot, covered, squat baluster form, 5″ **2,090.00**
Carnation, plate, 7½″ **430.00**
    8¼″ dia **575.00**
Double Rose, cup & saucer **550.00**
    Plate, 7¼″ dia **450.00**
    Tea set, 3 pc, w/red fenced garden & blue plateaux decor . **2,860.00**
Grape, plate, 7″ dia **425.00**
Oyster, cup & saucer **425.00**
    Plate, 8″ **325.00**
    Plate, 9¾″ dia **450.00**
Primrose, toddy plate, 4¾″ dia **355.00**
Single Rose, coffee pot, double gourd form, covered, 10¾″ ... **880.00**
    Creamer, wide mouth **280.00**
    Cup & saucer **300.00**
    Plate, impressed Riley, 8¼″ dia **325.00**
Sunflower, 8″ dia **300.00**
    Plate, russet line & yellow wavy line on blue border, 6½″ .. **500.00**
    Toddy plate **120.00**
Urn, cup & saucer **350.00**
Urn, plate, 8¼″ dia **375.00**
War Bonnet, cup & saucer **500.00**

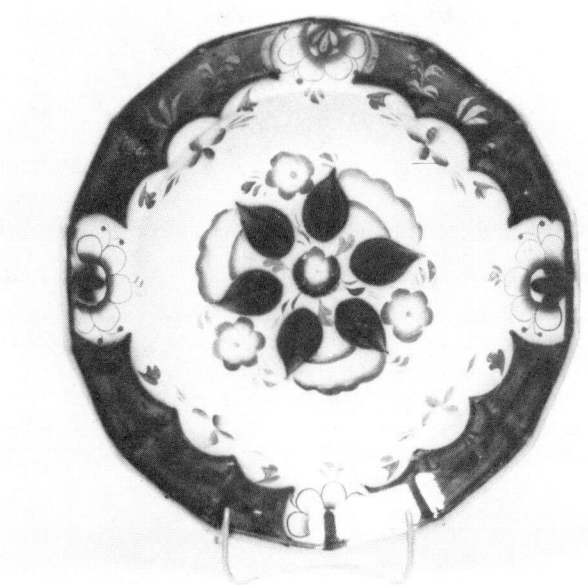

Plate, 8″ dia **450.00**

Gaudy Ironstone

Gaudy Ironstone was produced in the mid 1800s in Staffordshire, England. Some of the ware was decorated in much the same colors and designs as Gaudy Welsh, while other pieces were painted in pink, orange and red, with black and light blue accents. Lustre was used on some designs, omitted on others. The heavy ironstone body is its most distinguishing feature.

Bowl, Amherst Japan pattern, footed, 7½″ dia **110.00**
Cigarette caddy, Mandarin, gold trim, Mason's 2½″ **15.00**
Compote, Amherst Japan pattern, green & orange, 7″ dia **115.00**
Creamer, Imari-pattern, lion handle, Ironstone China, 5″ **45.00**
    Imari-pattern, snake handle, Mason's, 4″ **30.00**
Cup, handleless, cobalt, lustre **45.00**
Egg-nog bowl, hummingbirds, overpainted, peach lustre, 1870 . **140.00**
Mug, child's, pinched handle, Mason's **25.00**
Pitcher, floral & figures, snake handle, 1845, Mason's, 6″ **110.00**
    Milk, Metz **60.00**
    Rust peonies & green foliage, decorated spout & handle, 7″ .. **65.00**
    Snake handle, multicolor & gold lustre, 1845, Mason's, 7″ ... **98.00**

Plate, Imari pattern, Mason's Patent, 9½″ **25.00**
    Red, green & blue decor, copper lustre trim, E Walley **55.00**
Platter, blue leaves & orange florals, Ironstone China Warranted **110.00**
    Oriental design, Mason's, 16¾″ **100.00**
Serving dish, Carlton pattern, 2 handled, orange & yellow, 9½″ **57.50**
Soup, flanged, early Imari-decor, Mason's, 1825 .... **95.00**

Soup plate, 10″ **85.00**
Teapot, Mason's (Ashworth), vivid coloring, w/stand **195.00**
Teapot & underplate **275.00**
Tureen, Imari decor, cover w/flower finial, underplate, Mason's **195.00**

Gaudy Welsh

Gaudy Welsh was an inexpensive hand decorated ware made in both England and Wales from 1820 until 1860. It is characterized by its colors---principally underglaze blue, orange-rust, and copper luster---and by its bold uninhibited patterns. Accent colors may be yellow and green; and pink luster may be present, since luster applied to the white areas develops pink rather than the copper affected over dark colors. The body of the ware may be heavy ironstone, creamware, earthenware or porcelain; even style and shapes vary considerably. Patterns, while usually floral, are also sometimes geometric, and may have trees and birds.

Bowl, Grape VI pattern, pink lustre bands, 1825, 6½″ dia **195.00**
Bowl, Imari colors, 6¾″ dia **75.00**
    Oyster **148.00**
    Wagon wheel, 7½″ dia **38.00**
Creamer, 5″ **45.00**
    Oyster **60.00**
Cup & deep saucer, tulip early **47.00**
    Wagon wheel **45.00**
Cup & saucer, Carousel **30.00**
    Columbine, 1840s **50.00**
    Demitasse, Oyster, copper lustre trim **40.00**
    Floral, typical colors **35.00**
    Grape **30.00**
    Marigold **45.00**
    Oyster **30.00**
    Rhonda **135.00**
    Tulip, blue, green, rust, yellow & brown **55.00**
    Wagon Wheel **50.00**

Ginger jar, cobalt blue, iron-red & copper lustre, covered, 7¼". **75.00**
   Covered, 7x4½" **110.00**
Hot water jug, Imari-decor **55.00**
Jug, oyster pattern, 1830s, 5¾" **210.00**
Mug, miniature **35.00**
   Orange tree pattern, 3½" **55.00**
   Tulip, 2½" **45.00**
Pitcher, Bethesda, tiger handle, orange, blue & green, 5½"... **125.00**
   Forget-Me-Not, 6" **125.00**
   Milk, Wagon Wheel, 8½" **140.00**
   Oyster, 4x4" dia **55.00**
   Oyster, squatty, 3¼" **150.00**
Plate, cobalt blue, gold lustre, Imari motif, 9" **150.00**
   Decagonal, flowers & leaves decor, lustre, 9½" **75.00**
   Morning Glories, 9" dia **65.00**
   Oyster, 5½" **35.00**
   Oyster, copper & purple lustre, 6" dia **45.00**
   Tulip, 6¼" **22.00**
   Tulip, 8½" dia **65.00**
   Urn, 8½" **65.00**
   Wagon Wheel, 5½" **34.00**
   Wagon Wheel, 8¼" **50.00**

Child's teapot **100.00**
Child's teacup & saucer **50.00**
Tea set, child's Oyster pattern, copper & purple lustre, 3-pc .. **125.00**
   Feather, 8-pc **350.00**
   Tulip III, w/stylized florals, pink lustre, 28-pc **770.00**
   Tulip, 16-pc **350.00**
Tureen, Urn, covered, footed, 9½" wide **150.00**

Geisha Girl

Geisha girl porcelains have only recently attracted a following in the collectible market. They were made primarily for export, in dinnerware, tea sets and vases, in several patterns featuring Geisha girls in various daily pursuits. Some were entirely handpainted, others were hand decorated over decals or with stencils. Pieces were bordered in one of many bright colors---red, yellow, blue, green or brown---and collectors generally prefer to match border colors when reassembling a matching set.

Berry set, 7 pc, Geishas feeding herons **77.00**
Bowl, 5½" **5.00**
   Blue trim, 3 feet, scalloped, 3" **8.00**
   Red, scalloped rim, 7½" **18.00**
Chocolate pot, reserve panels, umbrellas, butterflies **75.00**
   Blue trim **26.00**
Chocolate set, pot w/6 cups & saucers **225.00**

Red, pot w/8 cups & saucers **110.00**
Cracker jar, Kutani **55.00**
Creamer, olive rim **9.00**
Cup & saucer, cobalt, chocolate **10.00**
   Demitasse **10.00**
   Tea **12.00**
Cup & saucer, geometric border, building & cherry blossoms, gold **16.00**
   Orange border **12.00**
Dish, red, heart shaped **7.50**
Egg cup, rust trim, footed, 2¼x1½" dia **6.00**
Hair receiver, red trim **20.00**
Luncheon set, lake scene, 22 pcs, floral finials, much gold, mkd **140.00**
Match holder, blue **25.00**
Mustard jar, red **10.00**
Nut bowl, footed, Japan, 5¼" **9.00**
   Footed, red **3.00**
Nut set, master bowl w/4 individuals, scalloped **40.00**
   Orange trim, 3 footed bowl & individual bowls **49.00**
   Red trim, 7 pc **35.00**
Perfume **15.00**
Pin tray, red, kidney shaped **8.00**
Plate, 8", Nippon **15.00**
   Geometric border, buildings & cherry blossoms, gold, 8½" ... **20.00**
   Orange trim, scene w/6 Geishas, Made In Japan, 6½" dia **7.00**
Powder jar, blue trim, 2 Geishas, Japanese mk, w/lid, 4" dia ... **28.00**
Rice bowl, cobalt, flared, Imari **12.00**
Salt, round, red **5.00**
Saucer, orange trim, 5½" dia **4.00**
Shaker, orange trim, 3½" **8.00**
Tea set, gold, pot w/4 cups **150.00**
   Lake scene, much gold, pot w/wicker handle, 13 pcs, mkd .. **115.00**
   Orange border, pot, cream & sugar **75.00**
   Red w/gold trim, pot w/4 cups & saucers **149.00**
Teapot w/matching sugar, mkd Nippon **22.00**
Teapot, vivid colors, raffia bail handle, gold trim, Kutani mk, 6 cup **45.00**
Toothpick holder **8.00**
Vase, scalloped, flared, 7" **35.00**
   Stick **25.00**
   Trumpet, 2 handles, scenic, orange trim, Nippon, 10" **85.00**

German Porcelain

The porcelain listed in this section is marked simply Germany. Products of other German manufacturers are listed under specific name. The pink pigs series refered to in the listing are very collectible, though produced by an anonymous maker.

Bowl, fruit, hp **55.00**
Box, w/cover, pincushion doll type, holding parrot, 6" **50.00**
   With lid, for playing cards, dog finial **16.00**
Canister set, saltbox w/wood lid, vinegar & oil cruets, 25 pc .. **175.00**
Celery tray, w/6 salts **85.00**
Chocolate pot, w/cover, floral, scallop top & base, 10½x6" **75.00**
Chocolate set, pot w/6 cups & saucers, pink w/roses **165.00**
   Pot w/cover & 4 cups, mkd crest & 1828, hp flower **130.00**
Container, 2 pt, figural lady dancing, green crackle, 8¼" **90.00**
Demitasse set, hp roses, Altwasser, 9 pc **98.00**
   Medallions w/floral baskets, pearl, 13 pc **100.00**
Dish, double shell, applied flowers, 11" **38.00**
   With handles, reticulated rim, florals, gold, 12" dia **20.00**
Figurine, boy and girl, 9", pr **85.00**
   Blonde bathing beauty on stomach, lustre, 1½x3½" **80.00**
   Depicting arts & sculpture, 19th century **175.00**
   Lady, parts at waist, 3" **45.00**

Little girl, Winifred Jones, Mezzotint **185.00**
Napoleon standing in full uniform, 9″ **165.00**
St Bernard puppy, 19th century, 8½x5¼″ **145.00**
Wolfhounds, brown w/wht base, sealed back opening, 10¾x8¾″ **135.00**
Fish set, 21″ platter & six 8½″plates, trout & floral **195.00**
Mustache cup & saucer, lavender & blue pansies, folded trim . . . **35.00**
Painting, Dolores, gold frame, signed Wagner, 11½x10″ . . . **1,000.00**
Lotus Blume, signed Grunez, oval, 7x5½″ **900.00**
Melon Eater, 3½″ **50.00**
Perfume bottle, figural w/china flapper, 3″ **30.00**
Pink pig, 2 by pump **56.50**
2 in purse **64.50**
2 in roadster **120.00**
2, 1 looking in outhouse at other, 4½″ long **98.00**
Bathing at pump, 5″ **98.00**
By purse **65.50**
In auto w/policeman holding up traffic, 6″ long **135.00**
In cup **64.50**
Matchholder, by jar beans, Scratch My Back **78.00**
On binoculars **112.00**
On purse bank **66.50**
Pitcher, green w/wht cat handle, 3½x2½″ **30.00**
Plaque, rural scene w/wht figures in relief, framed 7x10″ **175.00**
Winged cherubs peering over clouds, heavy frame, 4x6″ . . . **315.00**
Plate, chop; maroon, lady's bust, scalloped, gold trim, 12″ . . . **85.00**
Hp w/apples & wht flowers, gold border, 8½″ **20.00**
Hp w/apples, florals, gold border, 8½″ **20.00**
Hp w/tulips & cherries in relief, aqua basketweave, 11″ **40.00**
With handles, scrolls, scalloped, lustre rim, rose, 9½″ **25.00**
Wildflower & leaf, 8½″ **50.00**
Punch bowl, w/8 cups, signed Elizabeth Shelly, many colors . . **395.00**
Tea set, 24 pc **195.00**
Vase, floral, many colors, cobalt rim, signed **50.00**
Vases, figural boy & girl, Sitzendorf, pair, 7″ **175.00**

Vase, "Pomona", hp brown w/fruit, 7″ **100.00**
Wall pocket, 2, figural lady, pr **65.00**
Girl holding seashell **10.00**

Goebel

F.W. Goebel founded the Hummelwork porcelain manufactory in 1871, located in Rodental, West Germany. They produced porcelain figurines, plates and novelties, the most famous of which are the Hummel figurines;

those are listed in a separate section. There were many other series produced by Goebel---Disney characters, birds, animals, and the Friar Tuck Monks that are especially popular.

Ashtray, Friar Tuck **18.00**
Ashtray, figural Disney Thumper, Full Bee with V **75.00**
Bank, Friar Tuck, Stylized Bee, SD29, 4½″ **40.00**
Bird, Bluejay, large, bisque **110.00**
Canary, yellow, 1973, 5″ **45.00**
Great Spotted Woodpecker, black & wht, 7″ **65.00**
Kingfisher, blue, green & rust, 1972 . . . . **65.00**
Nightingale, brown, 1973, 5″ **55.00**
Parakeet, blue & wht, 1973, 7″ **65.00**
Waxwing, brown, 1967, 6½″ **55.00**
Box, Santa Claus decor, lift off lid, Full Bee, 4¾x2¾″ **28.00**
Tall, bright green & orange, 5½″ tall **185.00**
Cookie jar, Friar Tuck **80.00**
Creamer, cow, Full Bee **40.00**
Figural, baby face, monk garb in orange, 4″ **24.00**
Kewpie face, clown body, 7½″ **175.00**
Friar Tuck, 2½″ **39.00**
Decanter, Friar Tuck, 1956, 11″ **90.00**
Friar Tuck, skinny, KL95, blk feet, Stylized Bee **48.00**
Friar Tuck, fat, KL92, Stylized Bee, pink feet **78.00**
Dog, Pekingese, 5″ Full Bee **50.00**
Red w/metal fly on nose, 2″ **35.00**
Egg timer, Friar Tuck, double, Full Bee, E96 . . . . **40.00**
Friar Tuck, single, blue lettering, V above E **25.00**
Font, angel holding font, impressed crown mark, Full Bee, 5½″ long **75.00**
Jigger, Friar Tuck, KL94, Stylized Bee, Friar Tuck sticker **12.00**
Liquor bottle, clown, 1923 mk, Art Deco **75.00**
Match holder, Friar Tuck, brown, RX111 . . . . **135.00**
Red dog, w/black match striker, S642 . . . . **65.00**
Mug, Friar Tuck, brown, T74/0, Stylized Bee, 4″ **35.00**
Friar Tuck, handled, 5″ **49.00**
Mustard bowl, Friar Tuck, brown, Stylized B, S183 . . . . **25.00**
Nativity scene, 16 figures & stable, 26-A-S **1,700.00**
Parrot, large, bright colors **110.00**
Pepper shaker, Friar Tuck, brown w/red book, Stylized Bee **25.00**
Friar Tuck, brown, P153/1, 3″ Stylized Bee **15.00**
Pitcher, figural red elephant, S487/0½ **45.00**
Friar Tuck, brown, S141 2/0, Full Bee, 2½″ **15.00**
Friar Tuck, brown, S141/0, Stylized Bee, 4″ **20.00**
Friar Tuck, brown, S141/1, Full Bee, 5¾″ **30.00**
Parrot, 6¼″ **125.00**
Salt & pepper shakers, Monk, all bisque, pair **20.00**
Friar Tuck, red w/blk feet, Stylized Bee, 2½″ **85.00**
Sugar bowl, Friar Tuck, brown, Z37, Stylized Bee circ led, 4½″ **20.00**
Table set, Friar Tuck, salt, pepper & covered mustard, w/handled tray **85.00**
Friar Tuck, covered sugar & creamer w/tray, Stylized Bee **85.00**

Goldscheider

Goldscheider Pottery Ltd. of Staffordshire, England, produced earthenwares and bone china figurines from 1946 until 1959.

Ashtray, Dutch girl decor **30.00**
Box, w/head of German Shepard on lid **65.00**
Figurine, Chinese Guitarist, 9¾″ **50.00**
Chinese Poet, 9¾″ **50.00**
Duchess of Devonshire, signed Peggy Porcher **48.00**
Juliet with Doves **85.00**
Madam Pompadour, signed Peggy Porcher **48.00**
Prince of Wales, signed Peggy Porcher **50.00**

Reclining bull dog	30.00
Russian Wolfhound, USA, 10x10″	250.00
Siamese cat	75.00
Squirrel dancer, signed Claire Weiss, 16″	300.00
Vienna, lions, 22x10″	400.00
Yankee Doodle Dandy, signed Peggy Porcher	48.00

Gonder

Lawton Gonder grew up a ceramist. By the time he opened his own pottery in December, 1941, he had a solid background in both production and management. Gonder Ceramic Arts, Inc., purchased the old Peters and Reed-Zane Pottery in South Zanesville, Ohio. There they turned out quality commerical ware with graceful shapes in both Oriental and contemporary designs. Their greatest achievements were the development of their superior glazes: flambe; 24k gold crackle; and Chinese crackle glazes in celadon, ming yellow and blue. Most of the ware is marked with Gonder impressed in script, and a mold number.

Creamer and sugar w/lid, brown drip & spatter	20.00
Ewer, gold crackle	25.00
Grey w/pink interior, B-60, 6″	15.00
Maroon mottled, bulbous w/lid,#944, 7½″	25.00
Turquoise, 7½″	25.00
Fern dish, gondola shape, green w/grey interior	7.50
Figurine, Coolie w/water buckets, magenta, mkd, 14½″	30.00

Panther, tan & light gold mottled, #210, 19″	50.00
Planter, bowl, ribbed sides, yellow, 6½″ dia	6.50
Grey & pink mottled, #518, 7″	12.00
Kneeling Coolie, blue & grey gloss	12.00
Madonna, pink & grey mottled	10.00
Standing Coolie, blue, 7½″	12.00
Swan, turquoise to pink gloss, E-44	12.00
Teapot, brown w/yellow drip glaze	12.00
Vase, beaded petal & scroll, 8″	9.00
Bird's nest base, leaf handles, H-602, 6¾″	12.00
Cornucopia, blue & pink, 8½″	12.00
Cornucopia, brown & grey, 7¼″	10.50
Cornucopia, grey w/pink interior, 6″	9.00
Cornucopia, pink, 9″	15.00
Dogwood, brown & yellow, E-3, 8″	9.00
Double cornucopia, mottled pink & grey, H-82, 5″	9.00
Draped w/tieback, glossy blue	15.00
Fan shape, green mottled, 10″	11.00
Fan shape, handles, grey mottled, pink inside, 9″	13.00
Figural leaves & flowers, blue lustre, 11″	25.00
Flower & leaf forms, blue gloss, 12″	20.00
Flower shape, mottled tan & brown, 7½″	10.00
Molded florals, yellow w/blue & pink, H-79, 8″	12.00
Twist, mottled grey, 6″	8.00
Two swans at base, scalloped, 8″	23.00

Goofus Glass

Goofus was an inexpensive type of lustre painted pressed glassware made by many companies during the first two decades of the 20th century. Bowls and trays are most common, and red and gold combinations are found more often than blues and greens.

Bowl, gold & red roses	25.00
Red & silver, 7½″	17.50

Bread tray, Last Supper	50.00
Compote, flint w/Goofus border, 7″	27.50
Oil lamp, embossed grapes and leaves	60.00
Pickle jar, Goofus on milk glass, 15½″	100.00
Roses, gold, 7½″	25.00
Plate, gold & red apple	15.00
Poppies, 8″	25.00
Powder jar, lady on lid	12.50
With lid, allover rose in relief, 5″	28.00
Rose bowl, clear w/silver rose, 3½x4″	15.00

Goss

The Goss Pottery was established in 1858 at Stoke-On-Trent in England. Their earliest products were quality porcelains, parian and earthenware. Later, they also produced 'farings'---small souvenir items decorated with decals that were sometimes overpainted by hand. The decals represented English landmarks, coats of arms, or scenes of historical significance. Early wares were marked WHG, or W H Goss. After 1862, a falcon mark was used. The company was purchased in 1934 by Cauldon Potteries, Ltd.

Bowl, model of Lincoln	14.00
Bust, Shakespear, 4½″	69.00
Shakespear, 9″	150.00
Cup & saucer, Jack Newberry Arms, medium size	35.00
Jug, model of Lincoln	14.00
Model of Shakespeare, 3¼″	25.00
Ornament, Anne Hathaway's cottage	100.00
Lady Betty	150.00
Pitcher, wht, woman & pillars on red shield, Falcon mk, 2½″	38.00
Vase, model of Lincoln	14.00

Gouda

Since the 18th century the main center of the pottery industry in Holland was in Gouda. One of its earliest industries, the manufacture of clay pipes, continues to the present day. The art ware so easily recognized by collectors today was first produced about 1885. It was decorated in the Art Nouveau manner. Stylized florals, birds and geometrics were favored motifs; only rarely

is the design naturalistic. The Nouveau influence was strong until about 1915. Art Deco was attempted, but with less success. Most of the workshops failed during the depression. Watch for the Gouda mark, which is usually a part of the backstamps of the various manufacturers.

Ash tray, advertising **70.00**
Basket, square, black w/yellow, green & wht **220.00**
Bowl on ped, w/flower frog, bird form, Melsa **175.00**
Candleholders, mkd, 8½", pr **165.00**
Candlestick, saucer base, multicolor w/black, Beaca, 6¼x6½" . . **80.00**
   Henley, 7½" **40.00**
   Roba, 14" **70.00**
Chamberstick, 5½" **45.00**
   Beek, saucer base, 4" **45.00**
Compote, Casino, 7½x5¼" **70.00**
   Multi floral, 10" **65.00**
Creamer & sugar, w/cover, mini, Areo **35.00**
Dish, Madeleine, 3¾" dia **20.00**
Ewer, hi-glaze, multicolor, Art Nouveau, 9" **95.00**
Humidor, w/cover, Mero, 8" **135.00**
   With lid, Verona, 5" high **60.00**

Liquor bottles, boy & girl figural, multicolor, glossy, pr **100.00**
Matchholder, w/striker, mkd **38.00**
Pipe, w/figural bowl, early clay, paper label **70.00**
Pitcher, 1900, 11" **150.00**
   Art Nouveau, floral painting, artist signed, 4½" **125.00**

Irene, 6½" **50.00**
Planter, oblong, Yssel, 12x7x4" **60.00**
Plaque, Unica, 12" dia **70.00**
Teapot, Aladdin, matt floral, signed, Holland, 9½" **175.00**
Tobacco jar, Art Deco, 7" **150.00**
Vase, Art Deco, black, gray & green, 6½" **65.00**
   Art Nouveau, multicolor, mkd & numbered, 4" **35.00**
   Beek, 6¾" **50.00**
   Bergen, 3" **30.00**
   Bird decor, bulbous, 2 handles, 8½x8½" **165.00**
   Black bands, wide gold & blue center band, 5½" **70.00**
   Black & tan w/orange & yellow flowers, w/large handles, 9½" **120.00**
   Candia, w/handle, 8¼" **70.00**
   Damascus, 11¼" **80.00**
   Eskaf, w/handles, 12" **170.00**
   Hi-glaze, Nouveau flowers, 6 colors, 6" **115.00**
   Hollandia, 10" **70.00**
   Lattice top, ivory w/flowers, Zenith, 7½" **48.00**

Graniteware

Graniteware, thin iron ware with an enamel coating, derives its name from its appearance. The speckled or mottled effect of the vari-colored enamels may look like granite---but there the resemblance stops! It wasn't especially durable! Expect at least minor chipping if you plan to collect.

Graniteware was featured in 1876 at Phily's Expo. It was massproduced in quantity, and enough of it has survived to make at least the common items easily affordable. Color is an important consideration in evaluating an item; purple, brown or green swirl is unusual, and so are more expensive. Pieces with wire bales and wooden handles are premium---so are decorated pieces.

Bed pan, grey **15.00**
Bowl, blue, 6½" **10.00**
   Dk blue w/wht speckles, shallow, 7" **10.00**
   Mixing, child's, 2 cup, blue & wht marbleized **8.00**
   Mixing, grey mottled, 7" dia **4.50**
Bread box, wht w/blue lines, round, hinged **45.00**
Bucket, blue & wht marbleized, straight sides, bail handle, wood grip **29.00**
   Grey, bail handle, 3" **35.00**
Butter dish, grey mottled w/pewter trim & finial, dome lid **275.00**
Candleholder, blue **16.00**
Casserole, grey, w/cover **20.00**
Chamber pot, blue & wht swirl, w/lid **25.00**
   Child's, grey **10.00**
   Cobalt, 13" dia **19.50**
   Grey, w/lid **15.00**
   Wht w/blk trim, w/lid, 13" dia **12.00**
Chamberstick, cobalt **19.50**
   Wht w/fluted bottom **30.00**
Cheese grater, rotary, wht **32.00**
Child's cook set, mottled turquoise & wht, 8 pc **110.00**
Coffee boiler, blue & wht marbleized, enamel lid, 8 qt **38.00**
   Green & wht marbleized, enamel lid, 6 qt **55.00**
Coffee pot, blk & wht, 12 qt **20.00**
   Blk & wht, small **8.50**
   Blue, Agate, 9" **20.00**
   Blue, Imperial, w/label **30.00**
   Blue & wht, gooseneck **30.00**
   Brown & wht swirls, 10" **45.00**
   Brown enamel w/pewter top, 1899 . . . . **75.00**
   Grey, 10" **24.00**
   Grey, gooseneck, iron handle, wood finial, 8" **37.50**
   Grey, w/pewter top, 13" **150.00**

Grey, pewter spout, lid & fittings, 1876, 11″ **130.00**
Grey mottled, gooseneck, pewter lid, wood finial **45.00**
Teal & wht swirl, gooseneck, 7″ **32.50**
Wht w/pink bird, egg shaped, pewter lid & handle, 10″ **100.00**
With orig Nash's Coffee decal............................ **30.00**
Colander, blue w/wht marbleized swirls, footed, w/handles, 10″ dia **19.00**
Grey mottled, footed, w/handles, 10″ dia **13.00**
Cream can, dk grey, w/lid & bail handle, 1 qt **28.00**
Cup, blk & wht **3.00**
Blue & wht marbleized **12.00**
Grey, large **9.00**
Red & wht **8.00**
Cup & saucer, grey **14.00**
Cuspidor, brown, 2 pc **23.50**
Grey **15.00**
Lady's, grey mottled **25.00**
Dipper, blue & wht marbleized w/blk handle, 5″ dia **17.00**
Blue & wht splash, 5″ dia **18.00**
Blue & wht splash, wht interior **12.00**
Brown & wht swirl.................................... **20.00**
Grey, mottled **7.50**
Wht w/red trim **7.50**
Dishpan, blue & wht marbleized, w/handles, 20″ dia **19.50**
Shaded green, hole for hanging, 20″ dia **17.00**
Double boiler, blue marbleized, w/lid **27.50**
Grey, w/lid **18.00**
Wht... **9.00**
Fish poacher, grey, complete w/insert **55.00**
Flask, grey **52.00**
Foot tub, blue & wht **42.00**
Funnel, blue, handled.................................... **14.00**
Dk blue w/marbleized swirls **15.00**
Grey mottled, blue trim, side handle, 3″ **10.00**
Grey mottled, handled, 5½″ dia **8.50**
Grey mottled, handled, for canning, 4″ **7.50**
Grocery scoop, grey **54.00**
Heater, kerosene, sky blue, bail handle, 22″ **45.00**
Irrigator, flat back, wht w/blue trim, Austria **15.00**
Lunch bucket, blue & wht marbleized, bail handle, tin lid **40.00**
Grey mottled, miner's type, oblong w/thermos top **48.00**
Sky blue, bail handle, tin lid.......................... **22.00**
Milk can, wht, 1 gal **29.00**
Wht w/enamel lid, 1 qt **16.50**
Mold, food, grey, 7″ **24.00**
Pudding, blue & wht swirl............................ **35.00**
Muffin tin, blue & grey mottled **28.00**
Grey mottled, 8 cup **22.00**
Turquoise marbleized **50.00**
Mug, blue & wht marbleized **19.00**
Grey **10.00**
Royal blue, wht band, gold trim **14.00**
Napkin Holder, wht **28.00**
Pail, berry, blue spatter, w/cover, 6″ **40.00**
Blue-grey, 6″ **20.00**
Blue marbleized, wire bail, w/cover, 6x6″ dia **40.00**
Brown & wht, Majestic **22.00**
Grey, 4½″ **20.00**
Grey, w/cover, 4″.................................... **32.00**
Grey mottled, miniature **17.50**
Milk, grey mottled, bail handle, w/lid, 1½ qt........... **22.00**
Pan, baking, grey **9.00**
Blue & wht, 8½x18″.................................. **30.00**
Bread, grey.. **6.00**
Bundt, grey mottled.................................. **24.00**

Cake, angel food, grey mottled........................... **15.00**
Cake, square, blue & wht **10.00**
Cobalt & wht swirl, 10″ **23.00**
Cream w/green trim, w/lid **6.00**
Jelly roll, blue & wht splash, 10″ dia **12.00**
Loaf, grey **8.00**
Milk, blue & wht marbleized, colored inside, 10″ dia **18.00**
Percolator, blue & wht marbleized, 6 cup................. **22.00**
Yellow, gooseneck **15.00**
Pie pan, child's, grey mottled **7.75**
Dk blue & wht outside, wht inside, 9″................. **7.00**
Grey, 9″ **5.00**
Grey, 10″ **7.00**
Grey mottled, 9½″ **6.00**
Turquoise **9.00**
Pitcher, grey mottled, 1 pt **23.00**
Grey mottled, 4 cup, bulbous, 7″ **24.00**
Pitcher & bowl, wht w/blk trim **25.00**
Plate, cobalt & wht marbleized, 9″ **12.00**
Green, 9″ **3.50**
Grey mottled, set of 5, 8″ **35.00**
Red & wht **14.00**
Sky blue, Elite, 8″ **7.50**
Potty, child's, side handle, blue & wht marbleized, wht interior . **35.00**
Covered, blue, minor chips **25.00**
Potty chair pot, blue **8.00**
Preserving kettle, brown **30.00**
Grey **10.00**
Roaster, oval, grey **10.00**
Salt box, blue & wht splash, Seife lettered on front.......... **42.00**
Saucepan, blue & wht marbleized, 1 qt................... **25.00**
Grey **16.50**
Saucer, cobalt & wht marbleized, 6″ dia................. **12.00**
Scoop, mottled grey, 5″ handle, overall 10″.............. **12.00**
Serving dish, turquoise & wht, 1 qt...................... **14.50**
Sieve, round, grey **10.00**
Skillet, large, cobalt blue & wht swirl **47.50**
Large, grey **29.00**
Small, grey **18.00**
Soap dish, grey, wall type, w/strainer **15.00**
Wht, 2 pc **18.00**
Soup kettle, grey w/tin lid **28.00**
Spittle cup, grey mottled **12.50**
Spittoon, blue & wht **35.00**
Lady's, grey **25.00**
Rust colored, 2 pc **20.00**
Spoon, blue & wht **10.00**
Grey mottled, 11″ **7.50**
Mixing, turquoise & wht, old **9.00**
Wht w/blue handle, 16″ **5.50**
Steamer insert, grey, 10½″ **50.00**
Stew pot, blue & wht marbleized, bail handle, wood grip, w/lid . **30.00**
Sky blue, pour spout, bail handle, 8″ dia **21.50**
Sugar bowl, grey mottled, pewter trim, covered........... **175.00**
Tea cup, grey mottled, 3¾″ dia.......................... **8.50**
Tea kettle, blue over ci, Wrought Iron Range Co **90.00**
Cream & green **8.00**
Grey mottled, 6 qt, covered **30.00**
Sky blue, gooseneck, heavy **20.00**
Teapot, blue, Fry Foval top, 8½″ **75.00**
Tea set, child's, wht w/blk rim, painted flowers, 11 pc **85.00**
Tea strainer, grey **17.50**
Wht, for cup, tab ring handle **15.00**
Teapot, blue w/pewter & copper lid, glass knob............ **139.00**

Child's, rust colored, 1 cup size **15.00**
Grey, gooseneck, tin cover **25.00**
Turquoise & wht, gooseneck, w/cover **30.00**
Thunder mug, grey **15.00**
Toothbrush holder, wht **19.50**
Tumbler, grey, rough **10.00**
Water, rust colored w/wht interior, 3¼" **6.00**
Utensil rack, wht w/blue lines, 14x20" **65.00**
Wash basin, blue marbleized, 6¾" **12.00**
Green & wht **32.00**
Grey, 22" **19.00**
Washboard, blue **30.00**
Cobalt scrub surface **35.00**

Green & Ivory

Green and ivory are the colors of a type of country pottery decorated with in-mold designs very similar to those of the more familiar blue and white wares. It is unmarked and was produced from about 1910 to 1935 by many manufacturers as part of their staple line of kitchenwares.

Bank, Waffle & Grape, inscribed Penny's Pennies, 3½" **150.00**
Bowl, 12" dia **45.00**
Apricots, 9½" dia **48.00**
Butter crock w/cover, daisy **60.00**
Waffle & Daisy, 6" **75.00**
Chamber pot, Rose & Fishscale, 5½" **75.00**
Mug, Admiral Dewey, Burley-Winters, Crooksville 0, 4" **40.00**
Grape, 4" **40.00**
Swirl decor, 6" **50.00**
Pitcher, cow in relief, 6" **60.00**
8" **85.00**
Grapes, 8" **65.00**
Indian head, 8" **150.00**
Rose & Fishscale, 11" **85.00**
Spittoon, grapes, 5½" **55.00**
Waffle & Grape, salesman's sample, 2" **65.00**
Umbrella stand, irises, 20" **200.00**
Vase, pebbly texture, 8½" **65.00**

Greentown Glass

Greentown glass refers to the product of the Indiana Tumbler & Goblet Co. of Greentown, Ind., ca. 1894 to 1903. Their earlier pressed glass patterns were #1, a pseudo-cut glass design, #137, Pleat Band, and #200, Austrian. Another line, Dewey, was designed in 1898. Many lovely colors were produced, in addition to crystal. Jacob Rosenthal, who was later affiliated with Fenton, developed his famous Chocolate glass in 1900. The rich shaded opaque brown glass was an overnight success. Two new patterns, Leaf Bracket and Cactus were designed to display the glass to its best advantage, but previously existing moulds were also used. In only three years, Rosenthal developed yet another important color formula, Golden Agate. The Holly Amber pattern was designed especially for its production. The figural Dolphin dish and cover with fish finial is perhaps the most famous and easily recognized piece ever produced. Other animal dishes were also made; all are highly collectible. There have been many repros---not all are marked!

#11, compote, clear, 6½x6½" **40.00**
Master berry bowl, clear **22.00**
Rose bowl, clear **22.00**
Austrian, creamer, canary, 5¾" **65.00**
Creamer, child's, canary **95.00**

Creamer, table size, clear **35.00**
Goblet, canary **55.00**
Goblet, clear **45.00**
Ind creamer, clear **25.00**
Ind sugar, clear **25.00**
Punch cup, clear w/gold **22.00**
Salt shaker, clear **35.00**
Tumbler, clear w/gold **30.00**
Vase, clear, 8" **60.00**
Wine, vaseline **120.00**
Beehive, goblet, clear **75.00**
Cactus, berry set, 7 pc chocolate **350.00**
Bowl, 3¾x7" **105.00**
Butter w/cover, chocolate **185.00**
Compote, scalloped rim, chocolate, 5½" **120.00**
Compote, small, chocolate **135.00**
Compote, chocolate 6¼" dia **145.00**
Cracker jar w/cover, chocolate **195.00**

Cruet, chocolate **165.00**
Mug, chocolate **70.00**
Plate, chocolate, 7½" **80.00**
Salt & pepper, w/orig lids, chocolate **80.00**
Spooner, chocolate **80.00**
Syrup pitcher, chocolate **95.00**
Toothpick, chocolate **68.00**
Tumbler, chocolate **65.00**
Cat on Hamper, tall chocolate **285.00**
Cord Drapery, bowl, w/hand fluting, small, green **135.00**
Pickle dish, clear **30.00**
Punch cup, clear **16.00**
Relish, 9x5½" **20.00**
Sweetmeat dish, covered, amber, 5¼" **165.00**
Dewey, butter w/cover, ¼ lb, amber **65.00**
Chocolate **165.00**
Vaseline **90.00**
Creamer, large, amber **25.00**
Small, chocolate **45.00**
Vaseline **50.00**
Cruet w/stopper, amber **125.00**
Emerald Green **135.00**
Nile green **750.00**
Vaseline **125.00**
Ind sugar w/cover, amber **32.00**
Mug, green **45.00**
Pitcher, vaseline **185.00**
Relish, vaseline **50.00**
Serpentine relish, small, amber **45.00**

Sugar, open, vaseline 60.00
Tumbler, green 55.00
Dog's Head, toothpick nile green 55.00
Dolphin, w/lid, beaded top, chocolate 265.00
    Golden agate 350.00
    Sawtooth top, chocolate 200.00
Dust pan, vaseline 135.00
Elves, mug, opaque blue 45.00
Geneva, fruit bowl, oval, chocolate, 6x9½" 175.00
    Master berry, oval, 5x8½" 185.00
Hen covered dish, chocolate 250.00
    On nest, amber w/milk glass head 115.00
Heron, pitcher, water, clear 195.00
Herringbone Buttress, cake stand, clear 150.00
    Mug, chocolate 85.00
    Sugar w/cover, clear 75.00
Holly, relish, clear 68.00
    Toothpick holder, clear 37.50
Holly Amber, berry, individual, 4¼" 185.00
    Berry bowl, 8½" 600.00
    Berry set, 5 pc 1,400.00
    Bowl, oval, 7" 275.00
    Butter dish 1,400.00
    Jelly compote 850.00

Mug, 4½" 500.00
Tumbler 750.00
Honeycomb, dish, rectangular, chocolate 350.00
Leaf Bracket, 4 pc table set, chocolate 285.00
    Berry set, 7 pc, chocolate 295.00
    Celery tray, chocolate 110.00
    Cruet w/stopper, chocolate 130.00
    Dish, oblong w/scallops, chocolate 1½x7x5" 75.00
    Triangle nappy, red agate 65.00
    Tumbler, chocolate 48.00
Masonic, nappy, chocolate 120.00
Mug, castle drinking scene, flared top, Nile green 125.00
Rabbit, domed, covered dish, chocolate 225.00
Ruffled eye, water pitcher, canary 195.00
    Water pitcher, green 50.00
Shuttle, bowl, clear, 8" 50.00
    Cup, chocolate 50.00
    Mug, clear 20.00
    Punch cup, chocolate 50.00

Punch cup, clear 15.00
Spooner, chocolate 265.00
Syrup pitcher, chocolate 125.00
Tankard creamer, chocolate 65.00
Tumbler, chocolate 55.00
Wine, clear 12.00
Six Flutes, bowl, chocolate 165.00
Stag Alert, pitcher, clear 145.00
Stein, indoor drinking scene, chocolate 125.00
    Indoor drinking scenr, pour spout, chocolate 150.00
    Outdoor drinking, pour spout, chocolate 175.00
Teardrop & tassel, butter dish, blue 150.00
    Creamer, blue 100.00
    Spooner, cobalt 65.00
    Tumbler, blue 45.00
    Tumbler, clear 30.00
Uneeda Biscuit, tumbler, chocolate, tall 115.00
Witch head, toothpick, blue satin 55.00

Grueby

    William Henry Grueby joined the firm of the Low Art Tile Works at the age of 15, and in 1894, after several years of experience in the production of architectural tiles, founded his own plant, the Grueby Faience Co., in Boston, Mass. Grueby began experimenting with the idea of producing art pottery, and had soon perfected a fine glaze---soft and without gloss---in shades of blue, grey, yellow, brown and his most successful, cucumber green. In 1900 his exhibit at the Paris Exposition Universelle won him three gold medals.

    Grueby pottery was hand thrown and hand decorated in the Arts and Crafts style. Vertically-thrust stylized leaves and flowers in relief were the most common decorative devices. Tiles continued to be an important product--unique, due to the matt glaze decoration, as well as durable. Grueby tiles were often a full inch thick. Obviously incompatible with the Art Nouveau style, the artware was discontinued soon after 1910.

    The ware is always marked in one of several ways: Grueby Pottery, Boston USA; Grueby, Boston, Mass.; or Grueby Faience. The artware is often artist signed.

Bowl vase, matt blue, thick glaze, 5x6½" 355.00
Paperweight, blue w/wht winged scarab, 2½" 225.00
    Scarab, 4" 135.00
Tile, architectural design, 4 colors, 4x6" 60.00
    Flower, 4x4" 100.00
    Hexagonal, matt tan, green leaves, 3" 100.00
    Houses, trees, water, 4 colors, 4" 175.00
    Knight, 6x6" 225.00
    Mermaid, 6x6" 225.00
    Multicolor landscape, hills, 6x6" 700.00
    Sailing ship, sgnd, AS, 6x6" 600.00

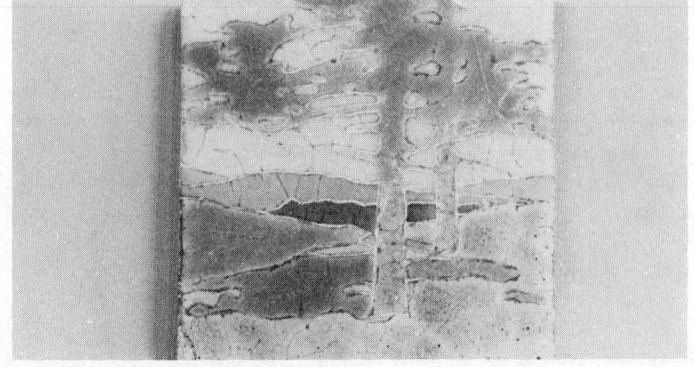

Scenic w/trees, 6x6x1" 450.00

Stylized leaf, 6x6″ **250.00**
Stylized trees, 4x4″ **175.00**
Trees, river, in blue, green, ivory w/blk outline, 4″ **185.00**
Windmill, 4 color **185.00**
Vase, blue matt, 5x3″ **100.00**
  Blue pebble grained, 6½″ **350.00**
  Bulbous, narrow neck, matt green, petal decor, 7½″ **425.00**
  Incised band oblong panels, shaded greens, Newman, 7½″ .. **450.00**
  Leaf design, green matt, 10x4″ **500.00**
  Leaf design, green matt, 9x4″ **375.00**
  Leaves in relief, green matt, bulbous, sgnd JE, 12″ **2,000.00**
  Leaves in relief, textured green Faience, 13″ **1,450.00**
  Matt green, 8x3″ **100.00**

Matt green, bowl **275.00**
Matt green, lotus mark, #250, 10″ **200.00**
Matt green, lotus mark, 4½″ **150.00**
Molded leaves, flower buds, matt green, sgnd Pierce, 11″ ... **700.00**
Mustard, leaves at base, Faience, artist sgnd, 19″ **4,700.00**
Pumpkin shape, ribbed, yellow, paper label, 3x4″ **150.00**
Wide base, w/molded leaves, sgnd Erickson, #32, 13″ **335.00**
White matt, 6x3″ **100.00**

Gutta-Percha

Gutta-percha is the plastic substance from the latex of several types of Malaysian trees. It resembles rubber but contains more resin. A patent for the use of this material in manufacturing an early type of plastic was issued in the 1850s, and it was used extensively for daguerreotype cases and picture frames.

Collar box, collars & cuffs on lid in relief, brass band **25.00**
  Soldiers monument scene **32.00**
Compact, Art Deco w/gazelle, 3½″ dia **25.00**
Daguerreotype case, 'Angel with Horn', 4x3¼″ **65.00**
  Birds & ornate birdbath, dated 1854, 3¾x3¼″ **25.00**
  Cupid decor **65.00**
  Embossed farm related items, 2½x3″ **55.00**
  Embossed flowers, flower basket medallions, 3x3″ **23.00**
  Embossed Victorian lady & child w/cat, 4-photo **150.00**
  Heavy, 5¼x6¾″ **75.00**
  Ninth plate, 'The Genius of Poetry With Her Celestial Pen' .. **75.00**
  Octagonal, man & woman playing chess, 3x2½″ **40.00**
  Ornate scrolls, ambrotype, 2½x3″ **40.00**
  Oval w/miniature roses, tintype, 2½x2½″ **36.00**
  'The Huntress', woman w/Victorian type dress, 3½x4″ **75.00**
  'The Tryst', 5x4″ **85.00**
  Three children playing, double tintypes, 2¼x3½″ **80.00**
  Wounded stag **65.00**
Frame, embossed jewels & florals, gold mat, 5½x6½″ **60.00**
  Florals in relief, pat July 21, 1868, 6x8¾″ **50.00**
Matchsafe, coronation of Edward VII **45.00**
  Glucks, Minn. **65.00**
Mirror, dresser, deer head embossed on back **38.00**

Hand, Egyptian figures decor, 1866 .... **38.00**
Shaving box, US Navy, 'Don't Give Up The Ship', w/mirror, 1850s **75.00**
Tape measure, ornate, pat 1870 .... **36.00**

Haeger

In 1871 David Henry Haeger, a young son of German immigrants, purchased a brick factory at Dundee, Illinois, and began an association with the ceramic industry that his decendents have pursued to the present time. Soon their production was expanded to include drainage tile. By 1914 they had ventured into the field of commercial art ware. Vases, figurines, lamp bases and gift items in a pastel matt glaze carried the logo of the company: a block H in diamond or rectangle with the last five letters of the company name written over the bar of the H. From 1929-33, a dinnerware line of assorted solid colors—blue, rose, green and yellow—was made, and marketed through Marshall Fields. Royal Haeger, their premium line designed in 1938 by Royal Hickman, and the Flower Ware line, 1945-50 marked RG for Royal Garden, are especially desirable with collectors today. Ware produced before the mid-30s sometimes is found with a paper label; these are also of special interest. A stylized script mark, Royal Haeger, was used during the 40s; later a paper label in the shape of a crown was used.

The Macomb, Ill., plant, built in 1939, primarily made ware for the florist trade. A second plant, built there in 1969, produces lamp bases.

Basket, horizontal ribs, blue matt, 8x8¾″ **15.00**
Bowl, green/turquoise, ribbed w/pedestal base, mkd, 6″ **5.00**
  Stylized sunfish, orange & green, 1½x8x9½″ **10.00**
Bud vase, eggshell, #68, silver sticker, 7″ **8.00**
Candleholder, green leaf shape, 75th anniversary sticker, 6x5″ ... **4.00**
  Calla Lily, green & blue, 5″, pr **15.00**
Centerpiece, leaf w/fruit cluster, green w/blk exterior, 20″ **25.00**
  Mermaid, prone, w/console bowl, #505, 22″ dia **45.00**
Console set, ftd bowl, pr 10″ candles, grapes, purple **55.00**
Cornucopia, basketweave, ftd, pink & blue marble, 12″ **12.00**
  Basketweave, gloss green, 14″ **12.00**
  Pink & blue marble, #R1705 .... **10.00**
  Footed shell, hi gloss, grey, 5x8″ **9.00**
Dish, leaf form, reticulated philodendron, blue & green, 14x11″ **18.00**
Planter lamp, leaping gazelle, dk green gloss **25.00**
Planter, figural fish, blue & green, #R752, 9x7½″ **15.00**
  Girl w/basin in lap, green, yellow, ivory, 10x11″ **30.00**
  Girl, basket, pool, ivory, 10x6½x12½″ **30.00**
  Stork w/glasses, basket w/bow, pink, 9″ **20.00**
Vase, Colonial Girl, aqua, 7″ **8.50**
  Figural ballerina by disk, orig label, 8″ **8.00**
  Figural gazelle, yellow/green, orig sticker, 9″ **15.00**
  Modernistic deer, cream, 7″ **11.00**
  Running deer, ftd, 9″ **17.00**
  Sculptured leaves, mottled mustard over green, 11″ **12.00**
Wall pocket, fish, green, 13½″ **15.00**
Windowbox, mottled green, 4½x13x6″ **12.00**

Hall

The Hall China Company of East Liverpool, Ohio, was established in 1903. Their earliest product was whiteware toilet sets, mugs, jugs, etc. By 1920, their restaurant type dinnerware and cookingware had become so successful that Hall was assured of a solid future. They continue today to be one of the country's largest manufacturers of this type of product. Many of these lines produced from the 30s through the 50s are popular with collectors today.

Hall introduced the first of their famous teapots in 1920; new shapes and colors were added each year until about 1948, making them the largest teapot manufacturer in the world.

Advertising, jug, Teacher 12.00
   Keen's Chop House Bowl, wht w/gold, florals 10.00
   Palmer House, ashtray w/match holder, rectangle 16.00
   Palmer house, ashtray w/match holder, round 15.00
   Palmer House, candle stick 15.00
Blue Boquet, casserole, no handles, large 29.00
   Coffee pot, banded 40.00
   Cookie jar, pretzel handle 55.00
   Cup 6.00
   Jug, ball shape 24.00
   Left-over, w/cover, Mary Lou, square 30.00
   Left-over, w/cover, Mary Lou, rectangle 20.00
   Pitcher, Colonial 15.00
   Plate, 6″ 6.00
   Refrigerator dish, oblong 22.00
   Refrigerator dish, square 30.00
   Salad bowl 16.00
   Saucer 4.00
   Soup 11.00
   Soup tureen, w/lid 45.00
   Sugar, w/cover 9.00
Batter bowl, pouring spout & handle, red, large 15.00
Beanpot, Vegie 58.00
Beverage set, 2 mugs, 2-cup pot, Sanka, red & wht 47.00
Bowl set, 5 pc, Morning Glory, wht w/decals, blue exterior 60.00
Bowl, #3, Morning Glory 12.00
   #5, Morning Glory 20.00
   Emerald green, 6″ 5.00
   Red outside/wht inside, 2½x5¼″ 6.00
Chinese Red, bean pot 30.00
   Jug, Sandigrid, sm 17.00
   Pitcher, Sanidgrid, 5″ 17.00
   Teapot, Sandigrid 17.00
Crocus, baker, French, large 15.00
   Bean pot 48.00
   Bowl, Sunshine #5 . . . . 15.00
   Cake plate 15.00
   Casserole, Sunshine 30.00
   Cereal bowl 4.00
   Coffee pot, Colonial 25.00
   Coffee pot, Crest style, rare 35.00
   Cookie jar, w/pretzel handles, large 55.00
   Cup 4.00
   Gravy boat 18.00
   Jug, ball shape, large 26.00
   Pitcher, sunshine, 6″ 18.50
   Plate, 6″ 4.00
   Plate, 8″ 5.00
   Plate, 9″ 5.50
   Platter, oval, 11″ 15.00
   Salad bowl 20.00
   Salt & pepper, loop handle, pr 20.00
   Sauce, large 4.50
   Soup 12.50
   Vegetable bowl, round, large 15.00
Cameo Rose fruit, 5″ 1.50
   Plate, 9″ 2.00
   Plate, 10″ 4.00
   Plate, bread & butter 1.50
   Platter, large 9.00
Candlestick, black 5.00
Casserole, 488 pattern, no handles, large 28.00
   Blue Garden 45.00
   Cadet Star, blue & gold 24.00

Pink w/copper holder, big lip, made for Forman 24.00
Rust w/pearl lustre lid, made for Forman 20.00
With handles, Poppy & Wheat, 1 qt 35.00
With handles, round, Fantasy, Sunshine 20.00
Cereal jar, Sunshine, flour, red 28.00
   Sunshine, tea, red 28.00
Coffee maker, Big Boy, mint 60.00
Coffee pot, Arch 32.00
   Banded, 9-cup 25.00
   Blaine, Cadet 35.00
   Colonial, 4 pcs, all ceramic 95.00
   Crest, w/jonquils 25.00
   Crest, w/yellow roses 30.00
   Flower Spray, aluminum dripolator 25.00
   Green Duse 26.00
   Ivory w/gold dots, aluminum dripolator 25.00
   Jonquil 20.00
   Poppy Golden key 23.00
   Red Sash 25.00
   Springtime 20.00
   Sweep 25.00
Cookie jar, Banded, red 25.00
   Cadet Star, w/tab handle, blue & gold 20.00
   Safe handle, red 40.00
Creamer, New York style, Delph & gold 10.00
   Philadelphia style, black & gold 10.00
Creamer & sugar, w/cover, Canary Lipton 11.00
   With cover, Colonial, pink mums 20.00
   With cover, light green, 4″ 8.00
Cup, Arlington 3.00
Drip bowl, pink mums 18.00
   With cover, Black Gold 11.00
Flare Ware, bowl set, 3 pc 20.00
   Coffee pot 25.00
   Cookie jar 20.00
Gold Dot Ware, bowl set, 3 pc, big lip 30.00
   Casserole 20.00
   Cookie jar 20.00
   Teapot, Boston 27.50
   Teapot, Windshield 20.00
Gravy, Mary Lou, pink Morning Glory 18.00
Heather Rose, coffee pot, stepdown, metal drip 35.00
   Creamer & sugar w/cover 10.00
   Cup 4.00
   Jug, Sunshine, 1 qt 8.00
   Pitcher, Sunshine 12.00
   Plate, 6″ 3.00
   Plate, 9″ 4.00
   Salad bowl 12.00
   Sauce 3.00
   Sugar w/cover 15.00
Humidor, mottled green glaze, inside cover 110.00
Individual casserole, w/handle, red 5.00
Individual teapot, w/lid, octagonal, hi-gloss yellow, 3¾″ 7.00
Irish coffee, green 5.00
Jug, ball shape 24.00
   Chinese Red Banded, 1½ pt 8.00
   Doughnut, Delphinum, sm 15.00
   Doughnut, red & wht 18.00
   Loop Handle, red w/wht interior 17.00
   Princeton, blue turquoise 17.50
   Royal Rose, ball shape 20.00
   Springtime, ball shape 23.00
   Tilt ball, ice lip, powder blue 11.00

With lid, Chinese red, Sunshine	**50.00**
With lid, Sunshine, red	**40.00**
Mount Vernon, cereal	**3.00**
Creamer	**5.00**
Gravy boat, 2 pc	**8.00**
Plate, 6″	**2.50**
Plate, 7″	**3.00**
Plate, 9″	**4.00**
Platter, large	**8.00**
Platter, small	**7.00**
Sugar w/cover	**5.00**
Orange Poppy, baker	**4.50**
Bean pot	**45.00**
Cake plate	**12.00**
Casserole, oval	**24.00**
Casserole, round	**20.00**
Cereal	**6.00**
Coffee pot, S-lid	**30.00**
Coffee pot, S-lid w/metal drip	**35.00**
Cookie jar, pretzel handle	**50.00**
Cup	**5.00**
Drip w/cover	**15.00**
Jug, Sunshine	**14.00**
Left-over w/loop handle	**24.00**
Platter, 9″	**8.00**
Platter, 11″	**10.00**
Salad bowl	**12.00**
Salt & pepper	**18.00**
Soup	**12.00**
Teapot, Melody	**60.00**
Vegetable bowl	**22.00**
Pitcher, Banded, forest green	**9.00**
Empire, blue, 8 oz.	**5.00**
Hollywood, black & gold	**10.00**
Marine & gold, ball shape	**24.00**
Mottled yellow/green/blue, coiled form, 5x6″	**38.00**
New York, light blue & gold	**10.00**
Philadelphia, black & gold	**12.00**
With cover, blue, decorated, 8″	**15.00**
Punch bowl, w/8 cups, Tom & Jerry, ivory	**65.00**
With 8 mugs, Tom & Jerry, black	**80.00**
Punch cup, black, 5 oz.	**5.00**
Punch mug, ivory & gold, 7 oz	**7.00**
Ramkins, fluted white	**2.00**
Range shakers, salt & pepper, 5″	**6.00**
Red Poppy, bowl #3	**10.00**
Bowl, #4	**12.00**
Bowl set, 4 pc, Sunshine	**45.00**
Cake cover, metal, snap handle	**28.00**
Cake plate	**12.00**
Canister, 6″	**7.00**
Casserole, Sunshine	**20.00**
Cereal	**9.00**
Coffee pot, Stepdown	**22.00**
Creamer, Rickson	**8.00**
Cup & saucer	**8.00**
Drip, covered	**18.00**
Jug, Sunshine, large	**18.00**
Pitcher, Mary Lou	**9.00**
Plate, 6″	**4.50**
Plate, 7″	**5.00**
Dinner	**9.50**
Platter, oval, 11″	**18.00**
Oval, 13″	**20.00**

Range shakers, pr	**6.50**
Rubbish pail, metal, 14½″	**30.00**
Salad	**14.00**
Salt & pepper, egg-drop	**12.00**
Salt & pepper, loop handle	**18.00**
Sauce	**3.50**
Soup	**11.00**
Sugar w/cover	**8.00**
Teapot, Aladdin, oval infuser	**60.00**
Teapot, New York	**25.00**
Teapot, oval lid	**45.00**
Vegetable bowl, 9″	**18.00**
Rose Parade, bean pot	**20.00**
Bowl set, #3, #4, #5, straight sides	**45.00**
Casserole, large	**20.00**
Creamer & sugar w/cover	**15.00**
Custard	**4.50**
Jug, Sanigrid, large	**18.00**
Jug, Sanigrid, med	**14.00**
Jug, Sanigrid, small	**11.00**
Salt & pepper	**12.00**
Teapot, 3 cup	**12.00**
Teapot, 6 cup	**15.00**
Rose White, bowl #3	**10.00**
Casserole, tab handles	**20.00**
Creamer & sugar w/cover	**14.00**
Jug, Sanigrid, large	**20.00**
Jug, Sanigrid, medium	**16.00**
Jug, Sanigrid, small	**14.00**
Teapot, 3 cup	**15.00**
Teapot, 6 cup	**18.00**
Salad bowl, black & gold	**10.00**
Salt & pepper, Eureka, loop handle	**18.00**
Red Sash	**10.00**
With handles, Royal Rose	**11.00**
Soup, Arlington	**8.00**
Eureka	**9.00**
Syrup, red, Safe Handle	**26.00**
Taverns, baker, French Swirl, large	**12.00**
Bobby nappy, small	**7.00**
Bowl set, 3 pc, Colonial	**35.00**
Casserole, Colonial	**20.00**
Coffee pot, Colonial w/chrome drip	**45.00**
Coffee pot, Colonial	**30.00**
Coffee pot, Banded	**25.00**
Cookie jar, pretzel handle	**55.00**
Creamer & sugar w/cover, Colonial	**20.00**
Dinner plate	**7.00**
Jug, Classic	**50.00**
Leftover w/lid, oblong	**20.00**
Leftover w/lid, square	**30.00**
Mixing bowl set, 3 pc	**48.00**
Salad bowl	**15.00**
Salt & pepper, Colonial, large	**22.00**
Salt & pepper, ball type, Banded	**10.00**
Tankard mug	**30.00**
Teapot, New York, 6 cup	**30.00**
Vegetable dish, 8″	**24.00**
Tea cup, Philadelphia, maroon, 1 cup	**7.50**
Tea set, Boston, ivory, 8 cup pot, 3 pc	**47.00**
Hollywood, white, 3 pc	**40.00**
New York, marine blue, 8 cup pot, 3 pc	**47.00**
Tea tile, light green, 6″	**40.00**
Teapot, Addison French, cobalt w/gold flowers, 6 cup	**13.00**

Airflow, Canary 20.00
Airflow, cobalt 40.00
Airflow, Marine 45.00
Airflow, red 35.00
Aladdin, Canary 18.00
Aladdin, Red Poppy 40.00
Albany, brown/gold w/infuser 35.00
Albert, Celadon 25.00
Auto, cobalt w/silver trim 150.00
Baltimore, Lettuce 45.00
Basket, emerald 85.00
Basketball 150.00
Bellevue, emerald green, 1 cup 7.00
Birdcage, maroon 130.00
Boston, ivory, 1 cup 6.00
Boston, sunken lid, metal spout, blue, 2 cup 7.00
Buffet, grey, 2 cup 6.00
Buffet, modified white, 2 cup 7.00
Cadet Star, blue & gold 37.00
Cleveland, lavender-rose 45.00
Coffee Queen, Celadon 7.00
Cube, orange, British copyright 20.00
Disraelia 20.00
Doughnut jug, brown, 64 oz 60.00
Doughnut jug, marine 45.00
French, blue turquoise, 2 cup 10.00
French, Cadet blue w/gold 24.00
French, cobalt w/gold, 8 cup 35.00
French, lustre black, 6 cup 18.00
French, maroon w/wht lid, 1 cup 7.00
French, matt black, 6 cup 20.00
French, warm orange w/gold flowers, 6 cup 18.00
Gladstone 20.00
Globe 75.00
Hollywood, Lettuce 25.00
Hollywood, maroon 25.00
Hook Cover, Cadet 20.00
Illinois 75.00
Inverted Spout 40.00
Ionic, blue & white 9.00
Ionic, grey, 2 cup 9.00
Ionic, matt black 8.00
Lipton 20.00
Los Angeles, Cadet 37.50
Los Angeles, light green & gold 22.00
Los Angeles, cobalt 40.00
Manhattan, brown 25.00
McCormick turquoise 25.00
Melody, light buff, oval, 2 cup 30.00
Miss Terry 22.00
Moderne, Cadet blue & gold 20.00
Moderne, yellow & gold 15.00
Nautilus 60.00
National, black lustre, 2 cup 8.00
New York, light blue & gld, 2 cup 15.00
New York, marine blue, 2 cup 7.00
New York, maroon & gold 20.00
New York, yellow w/gold, 2 cup 16.00
Parade Canary 20.00
Parade, blue & gold 23.00
Philadelphia, ivory w/gold 25.00
Philadelphia, turquoise 25.00
Red, squat, 6 cup 17.00
Safe Handle, cobalt, 6 cup 35.00

Safe Handle, yellow w/gold trim 30.00
Streamline, Canary 20.00
Streamline, Chinese red 50.00
Streamline, yellow w/silver trim 24.00
Surfside 60.00
Teataster 50.00
T-Bail, round 35.00
Thorley type, blue turquoise, rhinestones, gold 45.00
Twin Spout 25.00
Warm orange, Tricolator Pour Right 35.00
Windshield, Camellia 20.00
World's Fair 100.00
Tulip, bowl, big lip #4 .... 15.00
    Bowl, big lip #5 .... 20.00
    Coffee pot, all ceramic, Colonial, 4 pc 30.00
    Cup & saucer 8.00
    Fruit, 5″ 30.00
    Gravy boat 12.50
    Plate, 9″ 8.00
    Salad bowl 15.00
    Soup 4.00
    Teapot, Dodeca 20.00
Water jug, Bingo, dark blue, large 45.00
Water server, #628, turquoise green 20.00
Wildfire, baker, French 10.00
    Bowl set, 4 pc, big lip 45.00
    Casserole, sunken handle 20.00
    Casserole, tab handled, large 30.00
    Coffee pot, S-lid 25.00
    Cup 6.00
    Custard 4.00
    Drip, tab handle 12.00
    Drip w/lid, knot handles 15.00
    Gravy 9.00
    Jug, Sanigrid, large 38.00
    Jug, Sunshine, large 25.00
    Plate 7″ 3.00
    Plate 9″ 5.00
    Plate 10″ 8.00
    Platter, large 15.00
    Salad bowl 12.00
    Salt & pepper, Sanigrid 12.00
    Salt & pepper, egg drop 10.00
    Salt & pepper, loop handle 20.00
    Sauce 3.50
    Saucer 2.00
    Saucer server, 3 tier 30.00
    Soup 11.50
    Teapot, Aladdin w/infuser 45.00
    Teapot, Boston 30.00
    Vegetable bowl, oval, 9″ 15.00
Wild Rose, bowls, set of three, Sunshine 20.00
    Coffee pot, Colonial 3.50
    Custard 4.00
    Soup plate 8.00
    Teapot, Crest lid 25.00
Zeisel Holiday, ashtray 3.00
    Creamer & sugar 11.00
    Cup & saucer 5.00
    Dinner plate 5.00
    Demitasse cup & saucer 7.00
    Gravy boat 12.00
    Salad bowl, large 12.00
    Salad bowl, medium 8.00

Teapot 12.00
Vinegar & oil set 15.00

Hampshire Pottery

The Hampshire Pottery Co. was established in 1871 in Keene, New Hampshire, by James Scollay Taft. Their earliest products were redware and stoneware utility items such as jugs, churns, crocks and flower pots. In 1878 they produced majolica ware which met with such success that they began to experiment with the idea of manufacturing art pottery. By 1883, they had developed a Royal Worcester type of finish which they applied to vases, tea sets, powder boxes and cookie jars. It was also utilized for souvenir items that were decorated with transfer designs prepared from photographic plates.

Cadmon Robertson, brother-in-law of Taft, joined the company in 1904, and was responsible for developing their famous Matt glazes. Colors included shades of green and brown, red and blue. Early examples were earthenware, but eventually the body changed to semi-porcelain. Some of his designs were marked with an M in a circle as a tribute to his wife, Emoretta.

Robertson died in 1914, leaving a void impossible to fill. Taft sold the business in 1916 to George Morton, who continued to use the matt glazes that Robertson had developed earlier. After a temporary halt in production during WWI, Morton returned to Keene and re-equipped the factory with the needed machinery to manufacture hotel china and floor tile. Because of the expense involved in transporting coal to fire the kilns, Morton found he could not compete with the potteries of Ohio and New Jersey who were able to utilize locally available natural gas. He was forced to close the plant in 1923.

Bowl, florals in relief, Robertson, 6″ 60.00
    Green w/molded decor, 2½x5½″ 40.00
Bud vase, sea serpent shape, green, 6¼″ 50.00
Chamberstick, matt green, concave sides, 3x7″ 50.00
Clock, matt blue, #2002 . . . . 200.00
Lamp base, applied rings, green matt, 11″ 325.00
Mug, girl, handmade, 7″ 85.00
    Indian portrait, gold decor, 7″ 130.00
    Leaf relief rim, Worcester green & brown glaze, 5½″ 75.00
Pitcher, creamer w/transfer Saranac Lake, gilt, 6½″ 50.00
    Matt green, impressed mark, 8″ 60.00
    Melon shape, Worcester finish, sgnd, large 65.00
    Roman Key, 6″ 35.00
Stein, green, 8″ 60.00
    Worcester finish, clipper ship decor, mkd, 5½″ 65.00
Vase, grape design, green, #125, 4″ 35.00
    Leaves & buds in relief, Robertson, 7½″ 80.00
    Leaves decor, green matt, 3½″ 125.00
    Matt green, 8″ 100.00
    Matt green, #54, 3½″ 30.00
    Matt green, #146, 3½″ 35.00
    Matt green, signed MO, 3″ 35.00

Handel Lamps

Philip Handel was best known for his production of art glass lamps at the turn of the century. His work is similar to the Tiffany lamps of the same era. Handel made gas and electric lamps, with both leaded glass and reverse painted shades.

Banquet, ornate brass, w/decorated globe, 31″ 650.00
Chipped ice, red scenic shade, 18″ 2,500.00
    With scenic border shade, 6½x4½″ 185.00
Desk, bronze base, leaded 6½″ dia shade 1,900.00
Brown Mosserine shade, bronze base 635.00

Goose neck, sgnd shade 195.00
Reverse painted oak & berry shade, sgnd 2,850.00
Floor, bronze gooseneck, leaded shade, 5′ 1,500.00
Floral overlay, 15″ dia, early 2,250.00
Gridwork over green hexagon panels, 21″ 375.00
Leaded shade, allover floral pattern, 14x9″ 500.00
    Dogwood band, 16″; copper color base 1,650.00
    Florals, hanging, 22″ 1,800.00
    Flowers & birds border, 18″ dia 2,250.00
    Full floral, 18½″ dia, brass base, 25½″ 3,850.00
    Geometric Deco, brass cabbage design base, 20″ 1,600.00
    Grapevines, cylindrical base, #d 1,800.00
    Green & pink florals, 21x18″ 2,750.00
    Hibiscus, baluster base, w/3 legs, #d 2,400.00
    Lillies & buds w/lily pad bronze base, 16x22″ 2,000.00
    Poinsettia border, honeycomb top, tree base, 26x20″ 1,650.00
    Scalloped, geometrics, 18″ dia 1,700.00
    Spoke design, scalloped, sgnd, 21x18″ 1,600.00
    Top & bottom floral ring, metal base, 24x18″ 880.00
Mica shade, sgnd base & shade 880.00
Mushroom shape Etruscan shade, brass base, sgnd 685.00
Night light, craquelle, birds & trees, wht metal base 275.00
Reverse painted, autumn scene, conical; metal base, 24x18″ . . 1,320.00
    Birds & branches overall, gilt base, 23x18″ 5,775.00
    Pastel country scene 5,200.00

Trees & sunset, metal base, 23x18″ 1,430.00
Student lamp, double, green shades, Mosserine 1,800.00
Wall lites, frosted glass w/bronze holder 350.00

Harker

The Harker Pottery was established in East Liverpool, Ohio, in 1840. Their earliest product was yellowware and Rockingham produced from local clay. After 1800, whiteware was made from imported materials. The plant eventually grew to be a large manufacturer of dinnerware and kitchenware, employing as many as 300 people. It closed in 1972, after it was purchased by the Jeanette Glass Co.

Perhaps their best known line was their Cameo ware, decorated with a white silhouette or cameo effect on a contrasting solid color. Floral silhouet-

tes are standard, but other designs were also used. Blue and pink are the most often found background hues; a few pieces are found in yellow.

Bowl, Pate sur Pate, grey, 9″	**5.00**
Cake plate, Tulip	**7.00**
With handles, blue Cameo	**8.00**
Casserole, 1 qt w/lid, underplate, pink Cameo	**12.00**
Child's set, mug, bowl, plate, blue Cameo	**2.50**
Creamer, Pate sur Pate, grey	**3.00**
Cup & saucer, Pate sur Pate, grey	**3.00**
Custard cup, Petipoint	**3.00**
Mixing bowl, Tulip, 10″	**8.50**
Pickle dish, Pate sur Pate, grey, 8¾″	**5.00**
Pitcher, blue w/red trim, Mexican scene, 5½″	**12.50**
Yellow Cameo, 10″	**15.00**
Plate, dinner, Tulip, 9½″	**5.00**
Pate sur Pate, grey, 10½″	**3.50**
6″	**1.00**
Platter, Pate sur Pate, grey, oval, 12″	**4.00**
Pate sur Pate, grey, oval, 13½″	**5.00**
Rolling pin, blue	**50.00**
Salt & peppers, blue Cameo, pr	**8.00**
Salt shaker, Liberty Bell, 1776-1876 Centennial	**10.00**
Stack set, 2 bowls, lids, Cameo, 2x6½″	**10.00**
Sugar w/lid, Pate sur Pate, grey	**5.00**

Harlequin

Harlequin dinnerware produced by the Homer Laughlin China Co., of Newell, West Virginia, was introduced in 1938. It was a lightweight ware, made in maroon, mauve blue, and spruce green, as well as all the Fiesta colors, except ivory. It was marketed exclusively by the Woolworth Stores, who considered it to be their all-time best seller. For this reason, they contracted with Homer Laughlin to reissue Harlequin to commemorate their 100th anniversary in 1979. Although three of the original glazes were used in the reissue, the few serving pieces that were made have been restyled, and the new line offers no threat to the investment of collectors of old Harlequin.

The Harlequin animals, including a fish, lamb, cat, penguin, duck and donkey, were made during the early 1940s, also for the dime store trade. Today these are highly regarded by collectors of Homer Laughlin China.

Animals, each	**40.00**
Ashtray, basketweave	**22.00**
Regular	**18.00**
Baker, oval, 9″	**6.00**
Bowl, '36s	**5.00**
Butter w/cover	**32.00**
Candleholders, pr	**32.00**
Casserole w/lid	**20.00**
Coffee cup, after dinner	**10.00**
In '50s colors	**15.00**
Cream soup	**5.50**
Creamer, regular	**4.00**
With high lip	**18.00**
Deep plate	**5.00**
Egg cup, double	**6.00**
Individual	**12.00**
Fruit, 5½″	**3.00**
Jug, 22 oz	**11.00**
Marmalade	**37.50**
Nappy, 9″	**5.00**
Novelty creamer	**6.00**
Nut dish, 3″	**5.50**

Oatmeal, '36s, 6½″	**4.00**
Perfume bottle	**25.00**
Plate, 6″	**1.00**
7″	**2.00**
9″	**3.00**
10″	**4.00**
Platter, 13″	**6.50**
Relish tray, 5 pc	**35.00**
Salt & peppers, pr	**7.00**
Sauceboat	**6.00**
Saucer	**.75**
After dinner	**4.50**
'50s colors	**7.00**
Saucer/ashtray	**20.00**
Spoon rest, '50s colors & red	**125.00**
Advertising	**65.00**
Harlequin colors	**80.00**
Sugar w/cover	**5.00**
Syrup	**55.00**
Tankard cup	**30.00**
Tea cup	**4.00**
Teapot	**15.00**
Tumbler w/car decal	**16.00**
Water jug	**14.00**
Water tumbler	**12.00**

Hatpins

A hatpin was used to securely fasten a hat to the hair and head of the wearer. Hatpins, measuring from 4″ to 12″ in length, were worn from approximately 1850 to 1920. During the Art Deco period, hatpins became ornaments rather than the decorative functional jewels that they had been. The hatpin period reached its zenith in 1913 just prior to World War I, which brought about a radical change in women's headdress and fashion. About that time, women began to scorn the bonnet and adopt 'the hat' as a symbol of their equality.

The hatpin was made of every natural and manufactured element, in a myriad of designs that challenges the imagination. They were contrived to serve every fashion need and compliment the milliner's art. Collectors often concentrate on a specific type: hand painted porcelains, sterling silver, commemoratives, sporting activities, carnival glass, Art Nouveau and/or Art Deco designs, Victorian gothics with mounted stones, exquisite rhinestones, escutcheon engraved and brass mounted heads, gold and gems, or simply primitive types made in the Victorian parlor. Some collectors prefer the long pin-shanks while others select only those on tremblants or nodder type pin-shanks.

Abalone, claw mounted, 6″ steel pin	**8.00**
Amber, 1¼″ head, socket mounted, 7½″ pin	**45.00**
Amythest, imitation glass, 1¼″ head, claw mounted, 10″ pin	**30.00**
Art Deco, enameled, fan shaped 1″ head, on 8½″ pin	**25.00**
Art Deco, painted celluloid, 2½″ head, 4″ pins, pr	**20.00**
Art Nouveau, 1¼″ glass head, decorated; 5¾″ pin	**30.00**
Art Nouveau, coral cabochon, 1″ on 9¾″ pin, Sterling	**75.00**
Art Nouveau, coral-color plastic rose, 1″, on 9″ pin, 1900	**45.00**
Art Nouveau, sterling thistle motif, hallmarked: CH, Charles Horner	**35.00**
Art Nouveau, sterling, enameled floral motifs	**45.00**
Art Nouveau, sterling figural or portrait, hallmarked	**45.00**
Art Nouveau, sterling Unger Bros, florals & portraits	**55.00**
Bead, polished wood, ¾″ head on 7½″ steel pin	**8.00**
Beaded, 2½″ 2-color beads, on 4½″ pins, pr	**12.00**
Bird, figural, 4½″ sterling head w/stone eyes, 8″ pin	**95.00**
Blown glass, 1¼″ Bohemian, hand painted, on 4½″	**25.00**

Carnival glass, 1½″ grape mold, purple, 8″ pin **22.00**
Commemorative, 2″ enameled sterling, 'Georgetown Univ' **22.00**
Commemorative, 1½″ chased & engraved, silver plate **15.00**
Damascene, 1¾″ head, floral motif on 11″ pin **45.00**
Escutcheon, 1″ baroque head, engraved escutcheon, 7″ pin **20.00**
French ivory, 2½″ pierced molded head on 6″ pin **12.00**
Gift boxed hatpins, 1¼″ enameled, hallmarked, pr **150.00**
Goldstone, ½″ cube, socket mounted on 9½″ steel pin **15.00**
Glass, peacock eye, bezel set, sterling hallmarked **85.00**
Golf club figurals, sterling, 8¼″ overall **22.00**
Indian figurals, sterling, Hiawatha & Laughing Water, pr **175.00**
Ivory, 8½″ carved floral on 7″ pin **45.00**
Jet, imitation glass, cut and polished on 8″ steel pin **15.00**
Jet, w/japanned frame & pin, hand set, rivited stones **95.00**
Kewpie figural, 1″, marked 'Kewpie' & copyright, sterling **95.00**
Mosaic, 1″ oval, filigree frame, 6″ brass pin **35.00**
Mosaic, 1¼″ button type, metal sleeve mounting, 8″ pin **55.00**
Nodder, figural butterfly mounted, 7″ gilt pin **35.00**
Porcelain, hand painted, portrait type **65.00**
Porcelain, hand painted, scenic type **55.00**
Porcelain, ceramic transfer, hand painted highlights **45.00**
Rhinestone, variety of infinite shapes, mountings, sizes, from **25.00**
Satsuma-type, brass sleeve mounted, floral or scenic, from **75.00**
Satsuma-type, pear shape, socket mounted, floral or scenic, from **85.00**
Satsuma-type, pear or octagon shaped, figure or portrait, from . . **95.00**
Scarab, carnival glass figural, 1½″ head on 11½″ brass pin **95.00**
Scarab motif, metallic or glass molded, from **25.00**
Shell, 2″, wire mounted on 7½″ pin **12.00**
Silver ornamental, hallmarked sterling variety, from **35.00**
Sporting activity, variety in sterling silver, from **25.00**
Swastika motif, enameled or sterling variety **15.00**
Tortoise, pique work, 1½″ head on 11″ pin **75.00**
Tortoise shell, imitation, 3″ head on 4″ pin, rhinestones **12.00**
Tooth (not tusk), trophy mounted, 1″ tooth, gold socket, 6″ pin **95.00**
Vanity heads, compact, rouge rag, straight pin holder **95.00**
Venetian glass beads as pin heads, 5″ steel pins **10.00**
Wood, lacquered & hand painted, 1½″ head on 7″ pin **12.00**

Hatpin Holders

Most hatpin holders were made from 1860 to 1920 to coincide with the period during which hatpins were popularly in vogue. The taller types were required to house the long hatpins necessary to secure the large bonnets that were in style from 1890-1914. They were usually porcelain, either decorated by hand or by transfer with florals or scenics, although some were clever figurals. Glass examples are rare, and those of slag or carnival glass are especially valuable.

In the listing below, RM refers to Red Mark Prussia.

Bavaria, bulbous w/attached saucer, pearl w/gold decor, 5″ **50.00**
Carnival glass, amythest, Grape & Cable **145.00**
  Blue, Butterfly & Berry **500.00**
  Cobalt, Orange Tree, Fenton **200.00**
  Green, Orange Tree, Fenton **250.00**
  Ice blue, Grape & Cable, Northwood **775.00**
  Ice green, Grape & Cable, Northwood **800.00**
  Marigold, Butterfly & Berry, Fenton **850.00**
  Marigold, Grape & Cable, Northwood **210.00**
  Purple, Grape & Cable, Northwood **200.00**
ES Prussia, base & rim flare, ivory w/roses, 13 holes, 7″ **80.00**
Geisha Girl, flared bottom, 4″ **30.00**
Jasperware, hp lady w/crown, German **70.00**
  Pink w/Kewpie decor **250.00**
Nippon, attached dish, gold w/florals, 4½″ **120.00**

Hp florals **40.00**
  Mountain scenic in reserve, moriage beading, 5″ **45.00**
  Three feet, gold scroll medallion w/roses, 4½″ **80.00**
PK Silesia, florals **40.00**
Pickard, w/saucer, florals, signed **150.00**
Pink slag, Grape & Cable, Northwood **775.00**
Porcelain, cylinder w/saucer, hp pears, foliage, 4½″ **45.00**
  Multi-florals, gold decor, Germany, 4½″ **30.00**
RS Germany, hp lily, 4½″ **65.00**
  Multi-color florals **75.00**
  Shaded green w/Calla Lily decor **50.00**
  Yellow to brown w/white roses, 6 sides, 4½″ **45.00**
RS Prussia, 3 handled, w/ring tray, unmarked **120.00**
  Brown w/mill scene, large **350.00**

Floral, wht w/turq & gold, RM, 4½″ **120.00**
Hp multi-color roses, RM, 5″ **115.00**
Roses, daisies, pond, RM **120.00**
Three handled, florals, RM **200.00**
Rosenthal, pale green w/pink roses, gold **38.00**
Royal Bayreuth, figural Dachshund, blue mk **400.00**
  Rose Tapestry, 3-color roses **350.00**
  Sunbonnet Babies, blue mk **400.00**
Silverplate, Egyptian decor, 3 ball feet, Karnak Brass, 4½″ **48.00**
  With cushion **45.00**
Sterling, w/cushion, hallmark **75.00**
Willets, belleek, allover silver scroll work **58.00**

Haviland

The Haviland China Co. was organized in 1840 by David Haviland, a New York china importer. His search for a pure white, non-porous porcelain led him to Limoges, France, where natural deposits of suitable clay had already attracted numerous china manufacturers. The fine hand painted china he produced there was translucent and meticulously decorated, with each piece fired in an individual sagger.

It has been estimated that as many as 60,000 chinaware patterns were designed, each piece marked with one of several company backstamps. H & Co was used until 1890, when a law was enacted making it necessary to include the country of origin. Various marks were used since that time including Haviland, France; Haviland & Co Limoges; and Decorated by Haviland & Co.

Various associations with family members over the years have resulted in changes in management as well as company name. In 1892, Theodore

Haviland left the firm to start his own business. Some of his ware was marked Mont Mery. Later logos included a horseshoe, a shield, and various uses of his initials and name. In 1941, this branch moved to the United States. Wares produced here are marked Theodore Haviland, N.Y., or Made In America.

Bouillon cup & saucer, allover flowers trimmed in gold **17.00**
   Covered, Ranson, white" **27.00**
   Fleur-de-lis, handled, Limoges **30.00**
Bowl, berry, wht & gold, Ranson, 5" **8.00**
   Cereal, pink & wht florals, #520, Limoges **6.00**
   Covered, Apple Blossom, gold handles, Limoges, 10½" **60.00**
   Princeton **40.00**
   Silver pattern, 9" dia **65.00**
   Soup, red edge, gold trim, center medallion, Limoges, 7½" . . **12.00**
   Soup, Rosalinde, Theo Haviland, America **24.00**
   Soup, wht & gold, Ranson **15.00**
   White Drop Rose, 9" **110.00**
Butter pat, Marseille **8.00**
   Pink Shasta Daisy design **8.00**
Cake plate, 3 branches w/4-color hp roses, pierced handles, 11" **40.00**
   Baltimore Rose **70.00**
   Napkin fold blank, floral decor, Limoges, 10¼" **150.00**
Cake set, Castiglione, 12" platter, 12 plates, Limoges **150.00**
   Olive border w/leaves & gold, 13-pc, Limoges **175.00**
Chamberstick, wht & pink florals, H & Co, Limoges **65.00**
Chocolate pot, delicate floral decor, ribbon handle **139.00**
   Floral sprays, gold scalloped base, 10" **179.00**
   Pink & blue floral bands, Limoges **125.00**
   Ranson blank, pink floral decor, 10" **140.00**
   Ribbon handle & finial **169.00**
Chocolate set, orange florals on pearlized ground, 9-pc **175.00**
Coffee pot, moss rose, CFH, Limoges **70.00**
   Pink roses on embossed blank, gold trim, CFH **90.00**
Compote, basketweave, white, 1870s **78.00**
Cream & sugar, Bretagne **60.00**
   Moss Rose, Limoges **60.00**
   Pink roses, lavender violets, #87D **65.00**
Cup, wht & gold, Ranson **15.00**
Cup & saucer, #19 . . . . **32.00**
   Autumn Leaf, Haviland & Co **25.00**
   Baltimore Roses, very large **45.00**
   Delaware **25.00**
   Demitasse, Delaware **20.00**
   Demitasse, Marie **25.00**
   Emily **20.00**
   Gotham **20.00**
   Montabello **28.00**
   Pasadena **22.50**
   Pink & wht flowers #520, Limoges **14.00**
   Princeton **22.50**
   Rosalind, Theo Haviland, America **33.00**
   Varelene **17.50**
   Wht & gold, Ranson **30.00**
Dessert set, 19-pc, 9" pot, #575 . . . . **235.00**
Dresser tray, star blank #5, lg floral sprays, 11" dia **48.00**
Egg cup, #500A **20.00**
   Pink floral garlands, gold trim, Theo Haviland, Limoges **22.00**
Game plate, green background, lion, much gold, H & Co, 13" **115.00**
Game plate set, birds, yellow border, gold trim, signed, 5 pc . . **340.00**
   Folded corners, hp & dated 1885 . . . . **125.00**
Gravy boat, 2-pc, blue florals, gold trim **30.00**
   With attached underplate, Gotham **45.00**
   With attached underplate, Silver Anniversary **66.00**

With attached underplate, Stewart **35.00**
Liquor decanter, Chantilly **95.00**
Oyster plate, 5 wells, floral decor, scalloped edge **55.00**
   6 wells, starfish center, hp, 8½" **95.00**
Pitcher, milk, blank 12 w/beaucoup gold **48.00**
   Milk, Drop Rose, 8" **185.00**
   Milk, seascape w/flying swallows, gold trim, 6½" **70.00**
Plate, Autumn Leaf, Haviland & Co, 6" dia **12.00**
   Blue & gold scroll decor **32.00**
   Blue w/hp floral decor, gold border, 8½" **75.00**
   Bread & butter, coupe, #19 . . . . **14.00**
   Bread & butter, Gotham, 6½" **12.00**
   Bread & butter, Ranson #1 . . . . **14.00**
   Bread & butter, Silver Anniversary **14.00**
   Brown, w/hp monk, 12½" Haviland & Co, Limoges **260.00**
   Cobalt blue w/silver & gold overlay, H & Co **65.00**
   Dessert, wht & gold, Ranson, 7½" **13.50**
   Dinner, Gotham, 10½" **18.00**
   Dinner, Kate Greenaway figures & verse, #12 . . . . **45.00**
   Dinner, pink & wht flowers, #520, Limoges **12.00**
   Dinner, Princeton **16.00**
   Fish, gold seaweed decor, cobalt rim, signed, 1899, 9" **55.00**
   Hp red poppies, 12" dia **75.00**
   Luncheon, Delaware **20.00**

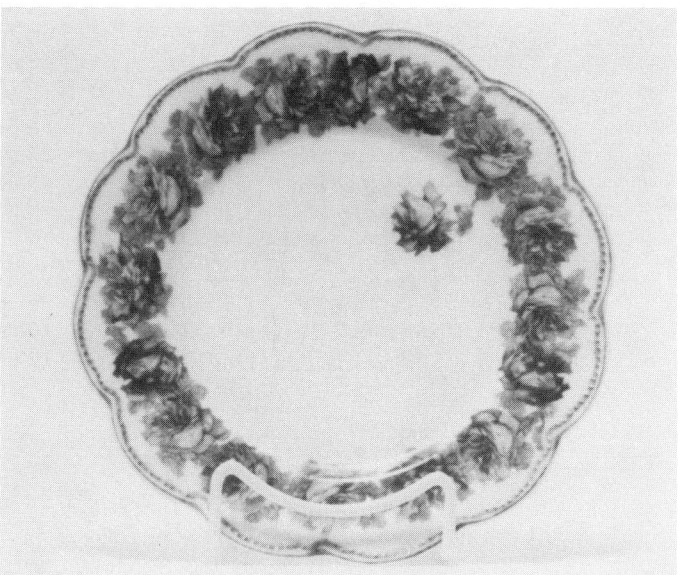

Luncheon, Dropped Rose, 8½" **75.00**
Luncheon, Montabello **12.00**
Luncheon, pink & wht flowers, #520, Limoges **10.00**
Luncheon, Ranson #1 . . . . **16.00**
Luncheon, rimmed, #19 . . . . **18.00**
Marie, 7½" **11.00**
Pink & wht flowers, #52Q, Limoges, 7½" **8.00**
Portrait, lady w/red roses, pink border, signed **110.00**
Princess, 8½" **20.00**
Ranson, #1, white, 9½" dia **20.00**
Ranson, 8½" **16.00**
Ranson, Haviland & Co, 6" **9.00**
Salad, coupe, #19 . . . . **16.00**
Salad, Gotham, 9" **15.00**
Salad, wht & gold, Ranson, 7¼" **13.50**
Soup, rimmed, Princess **15.00**
The Ardennes, Theo Haviland, Limoges, 8½" **8.00**
Varelene, 7½" **10.00**
Varelene, 10½" **13.00**

Platter, Apple Blossom, Theo Haviland, Limoges, 14″ long **40.00**
  Arcadia, Theo Haviland, Limoges, 13″ oval **99.00**
  Fish, Charonne, 23″ long............................ **190.00**
  Gotham, 14″ **65.00**
  Pink & wht flowers, #52Q, oval, Limoges, 12″ **15.00**
  Pink carnations, 18x12½″ **65.00**
  Pink flowers, gold trim Haviland & Co, Limoges, 11½″ oval.. **50.00**
  Princess, 12″ long............................... **29.00**
  Princeton **48.00**
  Rosalind, Theo Haviland, America, 14″ long **80.00**
  Wht & gold, Ranson, oval, 9x13½″..................... **30.00**
Pudding set, bowl w/liner on large charger, Ranson w/gold.... **175.00**
Punch bowl, hp rose decor inside & outside, Limoges, 14″ dia **400.00**
Relish dish, #72 .... **39.00**
  Princess **25.00**
Sauce dish, #19.................................... **14.00**
  Ranson #1 .... **14.00**
Sauceboat w/attached underplate, fluted basket, sea scenic **60.00**
Saucer, Delaware.................................... **4.00**
  Pink & wht flowers, #52Q, Limoges **4.00**
  Princeton **8.00**
Service for 8, White Diana, 48-pc including serving pieces **375.00**
Serving dish, Baltimore Rose **70.00**
  Irregular edge **30.00**
Snack tray & cup, Marseille blank, factory decorated florals, gold **45.00**
Tea set, maroon on wht, gold trim, ribbon handle, 9-pc **350.00**
  Ranson, 6″ tankard, w/creamer & covered sugar **115.00**
  Scalloped base, gold hp florals, 3-pc, Theo Haviland **230.00**
Teapot, cream w/3-color hp decor, gilt trim, 7″ **70.00**
  Deco design, heavy gold trim on border, large **45.00**
  Mellon shape, Woodbine.......................... **65.00**
  Pink roses, green leaf swags, #547A **47.00**
Tureen, covered, Princeton **48.00**

Vase, barbotine decor, sgnd Richard, 1878, 8½″ **450.00**
Vegetable dish, cloverleaf, covered, Limoges, 10″ oval **80.00**
  Covered, pink & wht flowers, #52Q, Limoges **17.00**
  Covered, Ranson #1, oval **65.00**
  Pink & wht flowers, #52Q, oval Limoges................ **14.00**
  Pink florals, gold trim, open, Limoges, 10″ oval........... **40.00**
  Rosalind, oval, Theo Haviland, America **60.00**
  Round, Ranson #1 .... **60.00**

Hawkes

Thomas Hawkes established his factory in Corning, New York, in 1880. He developed many beautiful patterns of cut glass, two of which were awarded the Grand Prize at the Paris Exposition in 1889. By the end of the century, his company was renowned for the finest in cut glass production. The company logo was a trefoil form enclosing a hawk in each of the two bottom lobes, with a fleur-de-lis in the center.

Ashtray, intaglio vintage **30.00**
  Yellow w/gilt sterling overlay & center rest, 3½″ **125.00**
Boat dish, blown out, scalloped, hobstars & geometrics, 7x4″ . **485.00**
Boat tray, hobstars, sm stars in points, fans, blazed fans, 12″ . **350.00**
Bon-bon, blown out, scalloped, hobstar on ea of 6 panels, 6″ . **395.00**
Bottle, etched & decorated, stopper, 8″ **80.00**
Bowl, 6 cut 5-petal flowers, fine ribbed section, 6″ **90.00**
  Etched, silver stem handle, 10½″ **80.00**
  Garcia, 6″ **140.00**
  Gravic florals, 3 feet, 4½x9″ **250.00**
  Gravic Iris, 3x6″ **250.00**
  Gravic, Strawberry, 8½″ **365.00**
  Gravic, Wild Roses & leaves........................ **265.00**
  Hobstars alternate w/flowers, draped leaves, 48 pt base, 8″.. **130.00**
  Hobstars, bulls eye, 6″ **85.00**
  Hobstars, flowers, draped leaves, 2½x8″................ **145.00**
  Holland, 7″ **230.00**
  Sheraton, star base, 8″ **385.00**
  Stylized floral cutting, 8″ **175.00**
  Triumph, 9″ **300.00**
Box, fans, hobstars in dia, hobstar in lid & base, barrel shape. **495.00**
Candlesticks, Gravic flower & vine, 10½″ **365.00**
  Round base & top, blown, 4x6½″, pr **340.00**
Candy jar, floral cutting, footed, 9″.................... **70.00**
Carafe, Brazilian, single star base, 7½″ **525.00**
  Chrysanthemum, hobstar base, 7½″ **525.00**
Cheese bowl, covered, 9¾″ **300.00**
Compote, emerald green stem & base, wheel decor.......... **120.00**
Console bowl, Wedgwood, blue w/gold band & white decor ... **175.00**
Cordial, verre de soie, engraved flowers **70.00**
Cruet, silver overlay stopper.......................... **100.00**
  Sterling stopper, 7½″ **135.00**
  Strawberry diamond, hobstar & fan, double notch handle, stopper **65.00**
  With stopper, signed both pcs, 7″ **50.00**
Decanter, signed stopper & base **300.00**
Decanter & 6 goblets, Sierra **375.00**
Finger bowl, Venetian............................... **90.00**
Fruit bowl, hobstar & x-hatching, Corning, N.Y., 3¾x12″ **450.00**
Humidor, notched prisms, repousse lid, 7″................ **435.00**
Ice bucket, cut glass, 5½″ **850.00**
  Green, engraved w/silver handle **120.00**
Ice tub, Queens, hobstar base, 4½x6″ **580.00**
Martini pitcher w/metal stirrer, Rock Crystal, 16″ **250.00**
  Iris, sterling lip & spoon, 6″ **185.00**
Napkin ring, floral engraving **80.00**
Nappy, flashed stars, w/handles **70.00**
  Wreath & Flower, 5½″............................ **78.00**
Perfume tray, Gravic Iris, oval, 10x7″ **300.00**
Pitcher, Navarre, barrel shape, 8″...................... **475.00**
Plate, engraved border, green crystal, 7½″................ **15.00**
Relish, leaf form, Holland **120.00**
  Lexington, 2 part, silver handle **65.00**
Salt, open, cut glass w/trefoil mk...................... **22.50**
Tray, celery, Classic, 10x4½″ **210.00**
  Celery, Queens, 11x5″ **485.00**

Centauri, 12" **955.00**
Deep panel cutting, 10" **875.00**
Gravic Iris, gallery rim, oval, 10x7" **295.00**
Panel cuttings, 10" **925.00**
Tumbler, Navarre **34.00**
  Queen's **155.00**
  York **45.00**
Vase, Brunswich cutting, 9" **250.00**
  Chinese temples, bridges, black to clear, engraved, 8½" **145.00**
  Cylindrical cut, engraved, 14" **200.00**
  Floral engraved, blue over clear, silver deposit bands **115.00**
  Grape leaves engraved, green, fan shape, 7" **95.00**
  Gravic cut, 8" **140.00**
  Gravic florals, 14" **160.00**
  Gravic Iris, sterling base, chalice shape **465.00**
  Heavily cut decor, 12½x5" **275.00**
  Hobstar & scalloped top, bullseye, undercut ped, 12" **350.00**
  Kohinoor & diamond, flared top, 10" **275.00**
  Scalloped hobstar base, trumpet, 14" **325.00**
  Verre de soie, 10½" **295.00**
  Waterford, amethyst cut glass, 7¾x6", pr **800.00**
  Wheel engraved, applied cobalt rim, urn shape, 4" **75.00**
Whiskey glass, Brunswick, 2¾" **75.00**
Wine glass, Louis XIV, knob stem, 4" **65.00**

Heisey

A.H. Heisey was associated for a time with the firm of Geo. A. Duncan and Sons, but in 1895 began producing glass in his own factory located in Newark, Ohio. The plant closed in 1956, and a few years later the Imperial Glass Corporation acquired the molds and patents. Although Imperial used some of the molds to reproduce some of the original pieces, the H in diamond trademark was first removed.

During their highly successful period of production, Heisey made fine handcrafted tableware with simple yet graceful designs. In the 20s and 30s colored glassware lines were often marked with a paper label only. Today Heisey glass is highly collectible.

Animals and Figurines

Airedale **550.00**
Ashtray, horsehead **50.00**
Asiatic Pheasant **275.00**
Bookend, fish **95.00**
  Horsehead **140.00**
Candle, fish **150.00**
Chick, head down **125.00**
Clydesdale **400.00**
Colt, kicking **175.00**
  Standing, amber **475.00**
Cygent, marked **150.00**
Donkey **200.00**
Duck flower frog, Flamingo **285.00**
  In green **250.00**
Elephant, large **240.00**
  Medium **195.00**
  Small **175.00**
Elephants, set of 3 .... **650.00**
Fighting Roosters, pr **235.00**
Gazelle **1,350.00**
Geese, set of 3 .... **450.00**
  Wings up, pr **140.00**
Giraffe, head back **175.00**
  Head forward, 11" **150.00**
  Head turned **195.00**

Giraffes, pr **250.00**
Goose, wings down **325.00**
  Wings half up **70.00**
  Wings up **100.00**
Kingfisher, pink **250.00**
Madonna, paper label, 9" **225.00**
Mallard, wings, half up **100.00**
  Wings up **75.00**
Mallards, set of 3 .... **575.00**
Piglets **65.00**
Plug horse, Oscar **95.00**
Ponies, set of 3 .... **365.00**
Pouter pigeon **500.00**
Ringneck Pheasant **120.00**
Rooster **485.00**
  Vase **80.00**
Scottie **90.00**
Sparkie **95.00**
Sparrow **75.00**
Swan **850.00**
  Individual nut dish **15.00**
  Master nut dish **20.00**
Tropical fish **1,500.00**
Victorian Belle **125.00**

Acorn, Flamingo, plate, 10½" **35.00**
Banded Flute, cruet, 4 oz **22.50**
Bead & Daisy, console bowl, silver rim decor, rayed base, 10" .. **70.00**
Beaded Panel & Sunburst, punch cup **12.00**
Beaded Swag, mug, souvenir, 1901 .... **65.00**
  Punch cup **9.00**
  Toothpick, opaque white **65.00**
Beehive, Flamingo, plate, 5" **15.00**
Carasonne, Lafayette, sherbet **10.00**
  Old Colony Etch, champagne **15.00**
  Old Colony Etch, goblet, short stem, 11 oz **20.00**
  Old Colony Etch, goblet, tall stem, 11 oz **25.00**
  Sahara, goblet, short stem **20.00**
  Sahara, sherbet, low **15.00**
  Old Colony Etch, champagne **15.00**
Colonial, cocktail **13.00**
  Compote, #353, 5¾x3" **17.00**
  Cordial, ¾ oz **20.00**
  Creme de mint, 2½ oz **12.00**
  Goblet, 9 oz **25.00**
  Marmalade w/cover **28.00**
  Orchid vase, puntied neck, cut bottom, scalloped, 5" **25.00**
  Punch bowl, 2 pc w/12 cups **275.00**
  Sherbet, high stem, 4 oz **15.00**
  Tumbler, star bottom, 7 oz **9.00**
  Vase, flared, 5x4" **15.00**
  Vase, sweet pea, flared, 6x5½" **18.00**
  Vase, trumpet, 15" **125.00**
  Wine, 2½ oz **8.50**
Colonial Panel, nappy, scalloped, 4½" **6.00**
  Olive, 9" **10.00**
  Punch cup, 4½ oz **10.00**
Continental, compote, 5½" **40.00**
Crinoline, cup **16.50**
Crystolite, ashtray, 3" **5.00**
  Black, candlesticks, pr **30.00**
  Box, gold floral & filigree metal, covered, 4½" dia **17.50**
  Candleblocks **22.00**
  Candles, low pr **16.50**

Candles, single lite, pr	12.50
Candy dish w/brass cover, glass flower handle	28.00
Cigarette box, 4 ashtrays, set	40.00
Coupe soup, 7½″	12.00
Hurricane lamp, cut glass shade	200.00
Individual nut dish, 1 handle	6.50
Master nut dish, 1 handle	14.00
Relish, 3 part, 5x13″	19.00
Relish, 4 part leaf, 9″	18.00
Sugar, creamer, tray, ind	35.00
Sugar, large	13.00
Diamond Optic, green, lemon dish, tub handles	15.00
Green plate, 6″	3.00
Moongleam, sauce boat	35.00
Moongleam, sherbet	9.50
Sahara, wine	25.00
Topaz platter, 12″	25.00
Diamond Quilt, creamer, flat, #7019	15.00
Donna, soda, 12 oz	50.00
Empress, vase, grape etch, 9″	85.00
Empress, Sahara: almond, 3″	20.00
Bowl, 6½″ sq, w/underliners	30.00
Coffee cup	10.00
Console set, bowl, 11″, toed candlesticks	225.00
Goblet, 8″	35.00
Mayonnaise & ladel	36.00
Plate, 7″	9.00
Plate, 8″	15.00
Plate, sq, 6″	6.00
Plate, sq, 8″	15.00
Relish, 3 part, 7½″	18.00
Shakers, pr	60.00
Fancy Loop, goblet	75.00
Plate, 8″	25.00
Punch cup	15.00
Fandango, jug, squat	450.00
Flat Panel, cheese & crackers plate	45.00
Deep plate, 9″	20.00
Fruit jar w/cover, 2 qt, 1908	95.00
Tray, floral cut, 5 pt, 10½″	40.00
Grandeur, Sabrino, goblet	15.00
Greek Key, cream & sugar, hotel	60.00
Goblet, 7 oz	180.00
Punch bowl & ped, 15″	235.00
Sherbet	9.50
Tankard, 3 pt	225.00
Water pitcher	110.00
Hawthorne, candles, #114, pr	50.00
Creamer	15.00
Heisey Rose, candles, 2 lite	65.00
Goblet	28.00
Ice tea	32.00
Sherbet	25.00
Ipswich, champagne	20.00
Goblet	15.00
Plate, 8″	16.00
Soda, footed, 5 oz	10.00
Water goblet	25.00
Killarney, cocktail, Spanish stem	50.00
Lariat, bowl, intaglio roses, 12½″	50.00
Candleholders, 2″, pr	18.00
Candleholders, 2 lite, pr	32.00
Candlestick, 3 lite, 7″	26.00
Candy dish, divided, floral etch, 6″	20.00
Cocktail shaker	150.00
Comport, low footed, 6½″	42.50
Creamer & sugar	35.00
Cruet, fancy	175.00
Cruet, original stopper	30.00
Decanter	160.00
Fan vase	55.00
Floral bowl, 12″	45.00
Jelly, footed, handled, 6″	45.00
Moonglow, champagne, 5″	90.00
Relish, 3 part, 13″	25.00
Vegetable, oval, floral etch	25.00
Minuet, plate, 8″	10.00
Symphone stem, champagne, 6 oz	25.00
Symphone stem, claret	12.50
Symphone stem, goblet	35.00
Symphone stem, soda, 12 oz	18.00
Toujours, marmalade w/cover	150.00
Monte Cristo, Olympiad, goblet	15.00
Narrow Flute, celery, 9″	20.00
Finger bowl, w/underplate	14.00
Individual almond, silver overlay	95.00
Pitcher, 1 pt	50.00
Oceanic, bowl, 2x12″	17.00
Orchid Etch, bowl 3x7″	30.00
Bowl, dolphin leg, 5½″	25.00
Butter dish	125.00
Candles, 2 lite, #134	58.00
Candlesticks, 1 lite, 3″, pr	65.00
Celery, 12″	37.50
Champagne	25.00
Cream, sugar, tray, individual	75.00
Cup & saucer	38.00
Dinner plate	85.00
Goblet, short stem	26.50
Goblet	32.50
Honey dish, 7″	40.00
Oyster cocktail	35.00
Plate, luncheon	17.00
Plate, salad	13.50
Relish, 3 part, 11½″	38.00
Sherbet	26.50
Soda, footed, 12 oz	28.00
Torte, 14″	35.00
Tumbler, flat tea	32.50
Tumbler, footed, 6″	30.00
Peacock Etch, goblet, 11 oz	20.00
Peerless, sherbet, footed, 4½ oz	35.00
Sherbet, low, shallow, 5 oz	12.00
Pinwheel & Fan, water pitcher	120.00
Plantation, goblet, footed, 6½″	17.00
Jelly	38.00
Mayonnaise, liner & spoon	50.00
Punch cup	12.00
Sherbet, 4½″	13.00
Plantation Ivy, champagne	16.00
Cocktail	20.00
Water goblet	20.00
Pleat & Panel, Flamingo, boullion	20.00
Candy, tall, cut w/sterling	42.50
Compote w/lid, footed, 8″	50.00
Cruet w/stopper	35.00
Ice tea, 12 oz	20.00
Jelly, 2 handles	20.00

Plate, 7″	**8.00**
Plate, 8″	**10.00**
Plate, 10¾″	**15.00**
Sherbet, low footed, 3½″	**15.00**
Sugar, w/cover & creamer, ftd	**35.00**
Tray, 5 part, 10″	**30.00**
Tumbler, 8 oz	**22.00**
Prince of Wales, water set, 7 pc	**275.00**
Priscilla, champagne, saucer type	**12.00**
Compote, 11½″	**110.00**
Custard, handled, 5 oz	**7.50**
Prison Stripe, punchbowl, ped & 8 cups	**395.00**
Puritan, bowl, footed, 8x8½″	**30.00**
Bowl, shallow, 8½″ dia	**24.00**
French dressing bottle	**14.00**
Goblet, 6 oz	**13.00**
Oil & vinegar bottle w/stopper	**16.00**
Pitcher, ½ gal	**75.00**
Punch cup, shallow, 4½ oz	**10.00**
Queen Ann, cup & saucer	**30.00**
Dressing bowl, divided, 7″	**35.00**
Floral bowl, footed, rose etch	**65.00**
Ice bucket, grape & vine overlay	**110.00**
Jelly, 2 handled	**15.00**
Relish, 3 part, round	**50.00**
Old Colony, celery, 13″	**30.00**
Orchid Etch, party plate, 16″	**75.00**
Orchid Etch, torte plate	**55.00**
Sahara, plate, sq, 8″	**14.00**
Ramshorn, Flamingo, champagne	**15.00**
Flamingo, goblet	**20.00**
Rib & Panel, basket, Flamingo	**90.00**
Bon-bon, 2 handles, turned up sides	**12.00**
Green, bon-bon, 2 handles, turned up	**12.00**
Parfait	**12.00**
Ridgeleigh, celery, 12x4″	**16.00**
Cigarette cylinder, 3x2½″	**20.00**
Plate, elaborate silver plate, sq, 8″	**18.00**
Plate, sandwich, 13½″	**16.00**
Punch cup	**8.00**
Relish, star	**35.00**
Wine	**15.00**
Rosalie, dressing bowl, 2 part	**35.00**
Mayonnaise set, 3 pc	**32.00**
Relish, 13″	**25.00**
Shawl Dancer, champagne	**16.50**
Goblet	**18.00**
Plate, 7½″	**12.00**
Tankard, ½ gal	**150.00**
Stanhope, cocktail	**87.50**
Creamer, sugar, plastic plugs in handle	**35.00**
Cup & saucer, etched	**10.00**
With plugs	**12.00**
Plate, ruffled edge, 7½″	**7.00**
Sugar	**12.50**
Sunburst, ice cream set, 7 pc	**120.00**
Nappy, scalloped, 10″	**30.00**
Swingtime, creamer	**17.00**
Trojan, soda, #445 etch, 5″	**22.00**
Tryolean, cocktail, 4 oz	**37.50**
Champagne	**25.00**
Goblet, 10 oz	**30.00**
Juice	**375.00**
Twist, Moongleam bowl, 4″	**15.00**

Moongleam oil w/stopper	**65.00**
Moongleam plate, 6″	**12.50**
Moongleam, soda	**14.00**
Twist, bon-bon, 2 handles,	**15.00**
Unid, bowl, underplate, rolled edge, sculptured band, 9″; 10½″	**45.00**
Sugar, gold trim, hp flowers, fluted base, 2 ring handles	**10.00**
Sugar, scalloped rim, hex ft, floral & butterlfy engraved	**30.00**
Victorian, goblet	**14.50**
Tumbler, 4″	**9.50**
Wabash, Fontenac, goblet	**12.00**
Warlick, bowl, 10¾″	**50.00**
Candlestick, 2 light, #1428	**25.00**
Cornuopia	**30.00**
Waverly, candy jar, seahorse handled	**115.00**
Cream & sugar, individual	**50.00**
Epergnette, 6½″	**8.50**
Plate, 8″	**17.50**
Sherbet	**5.00**
Torte plate, 14″	**45.00**
Violet vase, footed, 4″	**72.50**
Waverly, Enchantress, comport, footed, 6½″	**30.00**
Waverly, Orchid Etch, bowl, crimped, 3x9″	**32.00**
Orchid Etch, bowl, sea horse ft	**70.00**
Orchid Etch, comport, low ftd, 6″	**45.00**
Orchid Etch, relish, 3 part, 11″	**35.00**
Whirlpool, candleholders, block, pr	**35.00**
Celery, 13″	**25.00**
Champagne, saucer, 5 oz	**8.50**
Coaster	**7.00**
Cream & sugar, footed	**22.00**
Creamer, large	**15.00**
Goblet, water	**12.50**
Juice, footed, 4″	**8.00**
Oyster cocktail	**14.00**
Sherbet, 3¾″	**8.00**
Torte plate	**35.00**
Winged Scroll, emerald green, cigarette holder	**135.00**
Emerald green, tumbler	**45.00**
Yeoman, Moongleam, bar glass, flared	**15.00**
Bowl, rose engraved, 2 handles	**10.00**
Cake salver w/floral cutting	**50.00**
Cream & sugar w/Daisy cutting	**35.00**
Creamer, oval hotel	**10.00**
Sugar, roses, silver deposit	**12.00**
Zodiac, ice tea, 12 oz	**18.00**
Ice tea, 12 oz	**15.00**

Miscellaneous

Beer mug, Sportsman	**175.00**
Club drinking scene	**175.00**
Bitters bottle, Tally Ho	**110.00**
Buffet platter, Nimrod & Diana etch, 16″	**85.00**
Skier, fern etch, 14″	**185.00**
Candelabrum, Sahara, 2 arms, 3 lites, 20½x14″	**850.00**
Candelabrums, Marigold, #300, 1 lite w/prisms, etched, 11½″	**300.00**
Cornucopia	**35.00**
Card case	**85.00**
Cocktail shaker, Legionaire, 3 pc	**100.00**
Orchid etch	**130.00**
Rooster	**85.00**
Tally Ho, 2 qt, 3 pc	**165.00**
Cocktail, rooster head	**55.00**
Rooster stem	**55.00**
Skier footed	**90.00**
Compote, Dolphin, Flamingo	**140.00**

Console set, Asiatic Pheasants & bowl **550.00**
Creamer & sugar, individual, dolphin foot **45.00**
Goblet, Duquesne stem, Tangerine **175.00**
    Spanish stem, cobalt blue **105.00**
Hair receiver, silver deposit on crystal **100.00**
Ice bucket, dolphin foot **100.00**
    Green swirl, aluminum bail **65.00**
Lamp, #201, glass shade w/A shaped prisms **800.00**
    Glass font, mushroom shade, 'C' cut prisms **800.00**
Muddler, #10 . . . . **8.00**
Old Fashioned, equestrian **50.00**
Plate, Mah Jongg, 12″ **125.00**
Powder box, silverplate Art Nouveau lid **40.00**
Soda, 12 oz, fisherman **70.00**
    Club drinking scene **40.00**
    Tally Ho **35.00**
Soda glass, sailboat **35.00**

Heubach

    Gebruder Heubach is a German porclain company that has been in operation since the 1800s producing quality figurines and novelty items. They are perhaps most famous for their doll heads and piano babies, most of which are marked with the circular rising sun device containing an H superimposed over a C.

Boy, sitting, arms up, leg out to side, intaglio googly eyes **95.00**
Children, in nighties w/songbooks, 10″, pr **395.00**
Chinese boy, open parasol, red/gold hat & suit, sgnd, 6″ **185.00**
Clown w/urn, mkd, 10″ **85.00**
Colonial gentleman w/outstretched arm, hi-glaze, 8″ **95.00**
    Blue costume w/gilded trimmings, mkd, 8″ **110.00**
Dickens figure, Fat Boy, grey coat w/yellow trim, 4½″ **65.00**
Dog, 3½x8″ long **75.00**
Dove, white, mkd **265.00**
Dutch boy, sitting, blue & wht, 4½x3¾″ dia **88.00**
    Sitting, grey-blue & wht, mkd, 7″ **75.00**
Dutch children, 5″, pr **225.00**
    One couple back-to-back, 1 couple kissing, 4½″, pr **225.00**
    Seated, red/green clothes, 3¼″, pr **125.00**
Dutch girl, seated, red skirt, hands on knees, 4½″ **60.00**
    Sitting, blue & wht, mkd, 4½″ **88.00**
Ewers, miniature, scenic decor, green, pr **110.00**

Girl, blue bonnet, coy pose, mkd, 6″ **150.00**
    Bubble blower, oily bisque, mkd, 13″ **425.00**
    Dancing pose, rose trellis base, 7¾″ **125.00**

Reading book, sitting on bale of wheat, 11″ **145.00**
    With bonnet & hay fork, pastel colors, 10″ **165.00**
Great Dane, lying on stomach, head erect, paws crossed, 4x8″ **110.00**
Hound dog, sitting, grey & wht, 3½x3½″ **90.00**
Mouse, sitting on haunches, eating grain, white, 2x3½″ **105.00**
Nude baby, Googly, 3½″ **110.00**
    Grumpy, 5″ **150.00**
    Sitting, throwing kisses, wearing cap & shoes, 5″ **200.00**
Piano baby, blond curls, 1 hand up, 1 w/rattle, green dress . . . **175.00**
    Blonde, w/2 front teeth showing, blue bow, 6½″ **280.00**
    Crawler, mkd, 4″ **140.00**
    Crawler, aqua bow, incised sunburst, 12x7¾″ **395.00**
    Crawler, largest size, oily bisque, 12″ **450.00**
    Crawler, wht nightie w/blue trim, 5x7¾″ long **195.00**
    Crawler, wht nightie w/blue trim, impressed mk, 4″ **135.00**
    Lying on back playing w/toes, 6x9″ **340.00**
    Lying, mkd, 8½″ **375.00**
    Playing w/feet, nightgown, sunburst, 7½″ **185.00**
    Sitting, mkd, 6½″ **275.00**
    Sitting, playing w/toes, wht gown w/green trim, 8″ **265.00**
    Sitting, touching toes, good detail, 8¼″ **295.00**
    Squatting nude, excellent detail, 9″ **375.00**
    With attached vase, aqua trim, incised sunburst, 9x6½″ **425.00**
Piano child, sitting, 9″ **295.00**
Pirate boy, bandana w/red, w/shovel in hand, signed, 8½″ **225.00**
Planter, basket w/raised lid, children peeking out, 3x3½″ **130.00**
Rabbit, grey w/wht & pink tones, tall & realistic **150.00**
Shaggy dog, white, sitting up, 9″ **225.00**
Spaniel, scratching himself, sad eyes, 6x6″ **100.00**
Sunbonnet girl, blonde, blue ruffled hat, wht pleated dress **125.00**
    Seated, aqua & wht dress, blue hat, 6″ **150.00**
Tray, sea gull form, 9″ **85.00**
Vase, brown w/hp fruit decor, 7″ **130.00**
    Pate-sur-pate, Art Nouveau lady w/scarf, gold interior **175.00**
Vases, rich gold & bisque, signed, pair **350.00**
Woodpecker, perched on stump, mkd, 6½x8″ **145.00**

Homer Laughlin China

    The Homer Laughlin China Co. of Newell, W. Va., was founded in 1871. The superior dinnerware they displayed at the Centennial Exposition in Philadelphia in 1876 won the highest award of excellence. From that time to the present, they have continued to produce quality dinnerware and kitchenware, many lines of which are becoming very popular collectibles. Their most famous pattern, Fiesta, is included in another chapter.

    Most of the dinnerware is marked with the name of the pattern, and occasionally with the shape name as well. The HLC trademark is usually followed by a number series which indicates the year of its manufacture by the first two digits.

American Potter, cake set **23.00**
    HLC World Fair plate **35.00**
    Marmalade & cover **22.00**
    Small vase, any size **20.00**
    Zodiac cup & saucer **37.50**
American Beauty, cup & saucer **2.50**
    Plate, dinner **2.50**
    Platter **8.50**
    Vegetable bowl **8.50**
Bone dishes, 6 pcs, King Charles **45.00**
Conchita, cream & sugar w/cover **10.00**
    Cup & saucer **8.00**
    Dessert, 5″ **4.00**
    Plate, 9″ **4.00**

Platter, 11½″ 6.50
Platter, 13½″ 8.00
Conchita, Kitchen Kraft, cake plate, 10½″ 18.00
Covered jar, large 55.00
Covered jar, medium 55.00
Covered jug 75.00
Underplate, 9″ 15.00
Dogwood, bowl, 5½″ 2.00
Cream & sugar 6.00
Cup & saucer 4.00
Gravy boat 5.00
Plate, 6″ 2.00
Plate, dinner 3.00
Platter, 12″ 5.00
Georgian, casserole w/cover 15.00
Cream & sugar 10.00
Cup & saucer 6.00
Demitasse cup & saucer, gold on red 8.50
Gravy boat 6.00
Plate, bread & butter 2.00
Plate, dinner 3.00
Platter, 12″ 6.00
Platter, 17″ 7.00
Soup, bowl 2.00
Hacienda, casserole, Nautilus, 8″ 30.00
Cream & sugar w/cover 9.50
Cup & saucer 8.00
Deep plate, 8″ 5.00
Fruit, 5″ 4.00
Plate, 6″ 2.00
Plate, 9″ 3.50
Plate, 10″ 5.00
Platter, w/sq well, 11″ 8.00
Teapot w/lid 22.00
Vegetable, 8″ 7.00
Historical America, plate, mulberry & wht, Betsy Ross, flag 10.00
Jubilee, cream & sugar 13.00
Cup & saucer 10.00
Plate, 7″ 4.00
Plate, 8½″ 6.00
Sandwich plate w/handles 18.00
Tumbler, footed 25.00

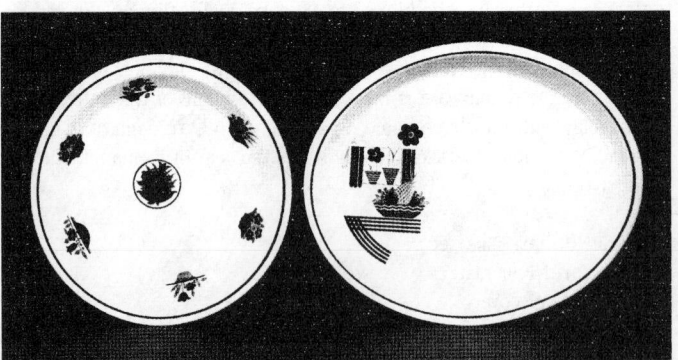

Kitchen Bouquet, pie plate 10.00
Kitchen Bouquet, platter 12.00
Laughlin Art china, BPOE mug, old eagle mark 25.00
Mexicana, '36s oatmeal, 6″ 5.50
Cream & sugar w/cover 10.00
Deep plate 5.50
Fruit, 5½″ 4.50
Glass tumbler 10.00
Plate, 9″ 4.00

Plate, 10″ 5.50
Platter, 13″ 8.00
Sauceboat 8.00
Teacup 6.50
Mexicana, Kitchen Kraft, casserole, 8½″ 30.00
Fork 20.00
Mixing bowl, 10″ 20.00
Pie plate, 10″ 18.00
Pie server 20.00
Salt & pepper, pr 24.00
Spoon 20.00
Priscilla, ball jug w/ice lip 17.50
Cake plate, 10″ 8.00
Casserole, w/cover, 9″ 12.00
Creamer 4.50
Cup & saucer 5.00
Fruit, 5½″ 2.50
Gravy boat 7.00
Milk pitcher 15.00
Mixing bowl, 6″ 6.00
Mixing bowl, 10″ 10.00
Pie plate, 9½″ 8.00
Plate, dinner 5.00
Platter, 14″ 6.00
Soup, flat 4.00
Sugar 5.50
Underliner 3.00
Rhythm, cup & saucer, illus 5.00
Dessert plate, 6″, illus 2.50
Fruit, 5½″, illus 2.50

Plate, 9″, illus 4.00
Rhythm Rose, cake plate, 10½″ 7.00
Cake server 8.00
Cream & sugar w/cover 10.00
Cup & saucer, A D 8.00
Deep plate, 8″ 4.00
Nested bowl, large 12.00
Nested bowl, med 10.00
Nested bowl, small 8.00
Plate, 6″ 1.50
Plate, dinner, 9″ 3.00
Sauceboat 6.00
Teapot 20.00
Rhythm Rose, Kitchen Kraft, casserole, 8½″ 14.00
Coffee pot 20.00

Jug pitcher	10.00
Pie plate	10.00
Underplate, 9″	10.00
Serenade, chop plate, 13″	6.50
Cup & saucer	5.00
Fruit, 6″	3.50
Plate, 7″	2.50
Plate, 9″	4.00
Salt & pepper, pr	7.00
Vegetable bowl, 9″	5.00
Serenade, Kitchen Kraft, casserole w/lid	15.00
Swing, cream soup, yellow	3.00
Plate, flowers w/yellow border, 10″	3.00
Tango, cup & saucer	5.00
Deep soup	3.50
Dessert plate, 6″	2.00
Egg cup	5.00
Salt & pepper, pr	4.50
Virginia Rose, bowl, 9½″	9.00
Butter dish w/cover, ½ lb	25.00
Casserole w/cover, 10½″	18.00
Cookie jar	32.50
Creamer	4.00
Cup & saucer	4.50
Deep bowl	4.00
Deep plate	4.00
Double egg cup	6.00
Fruit, 5″	2.50
Milk pitcher, 5″	9.00
Mug	10.00
Nested bowl, large	12.00
Nested bowl, medium	10.00
Nested bowl, small	8.00
Oatmeal, 6″	3.00
Pie plate, 9½″	10.00
Plate, 6″	1.50
Plate, 7″	2.50
Plate, 9″	3.00
Plate, 10½″	4.00
Platter, 9½″	4.00
Platter, 10½″	3.00
Platter, 11½″	5.00
Platter, 15½″	6.00
Salt & pepper, pr	6.00
Sauceboat	6.00
Sugar w/cover	5.00
Vegetable bowl, 7½″	4.00
Vegetable bowl, 8½″	3.50
Vegetable bowl, 9″	4.00
Vegetable bowl, oval, 8″	3.50
Vegetable bowl, oval, 9″	6.00
Virginia Rose, Kitchen Kraft, casserole	15.00

Hobbs & Brockunier

Hobbs & Brockunier's South Wheeling Glass Works was in operation during the last quarter of the 19th century. They are most famous for their peachblow, amberina and Daisy and Button pattern glass. The mainstay of the operation, however, was druggist items and plain glassware---bowls, mugs and simple footed pitchers with shell handles

Berry bowl, pale lemon w/applied cranberry ruffle, 10″ dia	165.00
Cheese dish, quilted lime cased w/wht, swirl finial	130.00
Lemonade set, vertical row relief colored daisies, 5 pc	225.00

Syrup, crystal w/in-mold lip, pewter top, 8″	**75.00**

Hull

The A.E. Hull Pottery was formed in 1905 in Zanesville, Ohio, and in the early years produced stoneware specialties. They expanded in 1907, adding a second plant, and employing over two hundred workers. By 1920 they were manufacturing a full line of stoneware, art pottery with both air-brushed and blended glazes, florist pots and garden ware. They also produced toilet ware and kitchen items with a white semi porcelain body. Although these continued to be staple products, after the stock market crash of 1929, emphasis was shifted to tile production. By the mid 30s, interest in art pottery production was growing, however, and over the next fifteen years, several lines of matt pastel floral decorated patterns were designed, consisting of vases, planters, baskets, ewers and bowls in various sizes.

The Red Riding Hood cookie jar, patented in 1943, proved so successful that a whole line of figural kitchenware and novelty items were added. They continuted to be produced well into the 50s.

Through the 40s, their floral artware lines flooded the market, due to the constriction of foreign imports. Although best known for their pastel matt glazed ware, some of the lines were high gloss. Rosella, glossy coral on a pink clay body, was produced for a short time only, and Magnolia, although offered in a matt glaze, was produced in gloss as well.

The plant was destroyed in 1950 by a flood which resulted in a devestating fire when the floodwater caused the kilns to explode. The company rebuilt and equipped their new factory with the most modern machinery. It was soon apparent that the matt glaze could not be duplicated through the more modern processes, however, and soon attention was concentrated on high gloss art ware lines such as Parchment and Pine, and Ebb Tide. Figural planters and novelties, piggy banks and dinnerware were produced in abundance in the late 50s and 60s. By the mid 70s, dinnerware and florist ware was the mainstay of their business. The firm continues to operate.

Ashtray planter, metal stand, hi gloss, black & pink, 26″	**30.00**
Athena, wallpocket, hi gloss lilac, 8½″	**18.00**
Bak-Serve, bean pot, ivory w/black bands, covered, 7″	**32.00**
Jug, ivory w/red bands, pint	**25.00**
Blossomflite, basket, T-2, C in circle, 55, 6″	**12.00**
Basket, square, T-9, 10x5½″	**20.00**
Candleholders, w/handles, T-11, pr	**14.00**
Cornucopia, T-6, 10½″	**16.00**
Blue Bird cereal set, 15 pc, square	**325.00**
Bow Knot, basket, 12, pink & blue, 10½″	**50.00**
Basket, B-29, 12″	**90.00**
Candleholder, B-17, 4″	**15.00**
Console bowl, B-16, blue & green, 13½″	**32.00**
Console set, 3 pc	**65.00**
Cornucopia, B-5, pink & turquoise, 7½″	**20.00**
Jardiniere, B-18, blue & pink, 5¾″	**30.00**
Vase, B-3, blue & green, 6½″	**20.00**
Vase, B-8, pink & blue, 8½″	**30.00**
Vase, B-10, 10½″	**40.00**
Vase, B-11, 10½″	**45.00**
Vase, B-14, 12½″	**55.00**
Wall plaque, 10″	**75.00**
Wall pocket, cup & saucer	**30.00**
Wall pocket, whisk broom, 8″	**30.00**
Butterfly, pitcher, B-11, 9″	**28.00**
Planter, scalloped, gold rim & decor, B-8	**12.00**
Vase, 3 footed, triangular, B-14	**20.00**
Calla Lily, vase, blue, USA 360-32, 13″	**60.00**
Capri, urn, lion in relief	**18.00**
Cinderella Blossom, shaker set, floral w/handles, 3½″, pr	**16.00**
Conventional, vase, hi gloss, evergreen, 8½″	**12.00**

Conventional Tile, salt box, square w/wood lid **64.00**
Crescent, shaker set, maroon hi gloss, 3½", pr **12.00**
Cuspidor, maroon banded **50.00**
Debonair, cookie jar, high gloss, band decor, 8¾" **25.00**
Delft, salt box, round w/wood lid, blue & white **65.00**
Dogwood, basket, 501, 7½" **35.00**
   Bowl, 521, 7" **24.00**
   Ewer, 519, 13½" **60.00**
   Vase, 502, 6½" **25.00**
   Vase, 510, 10½" **40.00**
Ebb Tide, ash tray, mermaid on shell, hi gloss **35.00**
   Basket, pink & turquoise, E-11, 16" **30.00**
Figural, dachshund, hi gloss black, 6x14" **35.00**
Grecian, cruet set, pottery stoppers, gold border, sq **60.00**
House & Garden, creamer & sugar w/cover, brown **9.00**
   Milk pitcher, brown, 7" **8.00**
   Pitcher, brown, 9½" **12.00**
Iris, basket, 408, 7" **40.00**
   Ewer, 401, 13½" **55.00**
   Vase, 406, 8½" **24.00**
   Vase, 414, 10½" **40.00**
Jardiniere, semi-porcelain, orange tree decor, 7" **30.00**
Lavabo, 2 pc set, orig metal hanger, 16" **65.00**
Magnolia, centerpiece, H-23, glossy pink, footed, 13" **22.00**
   Cornucopia, double matt, 12" **40.00**
   Double cornucopia, 6-12, yellow matt **35.00**
   Ewer, 14, yellow matt, 4¾" **15.00**
   Ewer, high gloss matt, 13½" **65.00**
   Fan vase, 12, cream & tan matt, 6½" **14.00**
   Fan vase, glossy pink, H-8, 8½" **18.00**
   Pitcher vase, cream & tan matt, 7¼" **18.00**
   Teapot w/lid, glossy pink, H-20, 6½" **27.00**
   Vase, 1, pink & blue matt, 8½" **25.00**
   Vase, 3, yellow & rose, handled matt, 8½" **24.00**
   Vase, 4, w/handles matt, 6¼" **15.00**
   Vase, 7, yellow matt, 8½" **25.00**
   Vase, 8, footed, handles matt, 10½" **25.00**
   Vase, 11, yellow matt, 6¼" **18.00**
   Vase, 12, yellow matt, 6¼" **18.00**
   Vase, 13, pink & blue matt, 4¾" **15.00**
   Vase, matt, 15" **90.00**
   Vase, 15, pink & blue matt, 6½" **18.00**
Mayfair, vase, hi gloss spring green, 7¾" **12.00**
Open Rose, basket, 140, 10½" **45.00**
   Ewer, 105, 13¼" **60.00**
   Planter, 104, 10½" **55.00**
   Vase, 108, 8½" **30.00**
   Vase, 123, 6½" **20.00**
   Vase, 126, 8½" **34.00**
   Vase, 4¾" **15.00**
Orchid, bookends, 7", pr **80.00**
   Vase, 304, pink & blue, handles, 10¾" **45.00**
Parchment & Pine, teapot w/lid, small, S-15 . . . . **28.00**
   Vase, footed, S-4, 10½" **22.00**
Pitcher, utility, brown banded stoneware, 4¾" **22.50**
Planter, goose, green, maroon, yellow, 11" **15.00**
   Kitten, ivory, USA 61, 7¾x7" **11.00**
   Poodle, high gloss maroon & green, 8" **16.00**
   Siamese cat & kitten, 12" long **17.50**
   Swan, hi gloss greens, 8½" **18.00**
   Telephone, grey **15.00**
Plaque, AE Hull Co Pottery, matt, 5x11" **250.00**
Poppy, basket, 12" **95.00**
   Ewer, 610, 13½" **55.00**

Vase, 606, 10½" **45.00**
Wallpocket, 609, 9" **45.00**
Red Riding Hood, bank, wall or hanging **195.00**
   Bank **150.00**
   Butter **85.00**
   Canister, large **190.00**
   Canister, spice **95.00**
   Cookie jar, large **50.00**
   Cookie jar, small **95.00**
   Creamer & open sugar **60.00**
   Creamer, pouring from head **65.00**
   Creamer, pouring from sash **65.00**
   Jar w/cover, small, blue bowl **95.00**
   Match safe, holder **125.00**
   Milk or syrup pitcher, leaning on side **85.00**
   Milk pitcher, reg **75.00**
   Mustard w/spoon **115.00**
   Shakers, large, pr **30.00**
   Shakers, small, pr **15.00**
   String holder **195.00**
   Sugar, open, feet out front **50.00**
   Teapot **85.00**

Wall pocket **145.00**
Rosella, lamp base, 11" **110.00**
   Vase/ewer, R11, pink, 7" **25.00**
Salt box, round, green stoneware, wood lid, 6" **40.00**
Serenade, ashtray, S-23, blue, 14" **20.00**
   Basket, S-5, yellow, 6x7" **20.00**
   Candy w/cover, S-3, turquoise **24.00**
   Fruit bowl, ped base, scalloped top, 7" **35.00**
   Hat vase, S-4, yellow **12.00**
   Pitcher, S-7 #621, blue, 10½ **22.00**
   Vase, S-1, footed, yellow, 6½" **15.00**
Stein, stoneware, American Legion logo, 6½" **25.00**
Sueno Tulip, basket, 102-33, 6" **40.00**
   Ewer, 109-33 . . . . **60.00**
   Flower pot & saucer, 116-33 . . . . **25.00**
   Vase, 107-33 . . . . **16.50**
   Ewer, 13" **55.00**
   Vase, 10½" **30.00**
   Vase, pine cone, pink, 6½" **25.00**
Swing Band set, 5 pc, ivory w/gold **60.00**
Tankard, stoneware, Alpine decor, 9½" **75.00**
Thistle & Pinecone, vase, 52, 6½" **18.00**
   Vase, 55, 6½" **10.00**
   Vase, 405, 10½" **35.00**

Vase, 414, 16″ **70.00**
Tile, decorated border, 3x6″ **12.00**
Tokay, comport w/cover, pink, 7″ **16.00**
  Cornucopia, pink & green, 10¾″ **15.00**
  Urn, pink & green gloss, 5½″ **15.00**

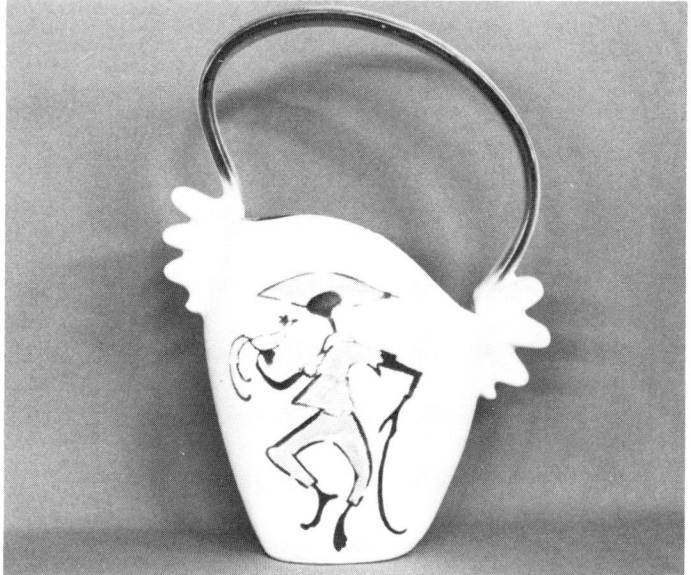

Tropicana, basket, figures on white hi gloss, 12¾″ **95.00**
  Ewer, 12½″ **25.00**
  Vase w/dancing figure, 12½″ **75.00**
  Vase, 8½″ **10.00**
  Vase, 14½″ **20.00**
Tuscany, candy dish, covered, pink & grey, 7x8½″ **22.00**
Vase, flamingo, footed, pink, yellow, & green hi gloss, 85, 9″ . . **15.00**
  Leaf shape, hi gloss, green, 9″ **12.00**
Wall pocket flying goose, hi gloss, 6½″ **18.00**
Water Lily, basket, 10½″ **55.00**
  Console bowl, L-21, pink & green, 13½″ **38.00**
  Jardiniere, L-23, pink & green, 5½″ **30.00**
  Vase, l-9, yellow, 8½″ **12.00**
  Vase, L-1, pink & green, 5½″ **15.00**
  Vase, peach & rose, footed, tab handles, 1-12, 10½″ **30.00**
Wildflower, ewer, 11, yellow, 8½″ **40.00**
  Teaset, 3 pc **110.00**
  Vase, 4, pink & blue, 6½″ **18.00**
  Vase, 6, pink & blue, 7½″ **20.00**
Woodland, cornucopia, yellow & green matt, W-10, 11″ **22.00**
  Hanging basket, 3 legs, scalloped, 7½″ **75.00**
  Tea set, hi gloss 2 tone **50.00**
  Vase, W-8, gloss chartreuse & pink, 7½″ **18.00**
  Vase, double handles, 12½″ **85.00**
  Vase, peach & pink gloss, W-8, 7½″ **18.00**
  Wallpocket, glossy pink & green **14.00**
  Window box, glossy blue & green, rectangular, W-14, 10″ . . . **15.00**

Hummel

Hummel figurines were created through the artistry of Berta Hummel, a Franciscan nun called Sister M. Innocentia. The first figures were made about 1935 by Franz Gobel of Gobel Art Inc., Rodental, West Germany. Plates, plaques and candy dishes are also produced, and the older, discontinued editions are highly sought collectibles.

Generally speaking, an issue can be dated by the trademark. The first Hummels, from 1934-1950, were either incised or stamped with the Crown WG mark. The full bee mark was employed with minor variations until 1959.

At that time the bee was stylized and represented by a solid circle with symetrical angled wings completely contained within the confines of the V. The three line mark, 1964-1972, utilized the stylized bee, and included a three line arrangement '© by W. Goebel, W. Germany'. Another change in 1970 saw the stylized bee in V suspended between the vertical bars of the b and l of a printed 'Goebel, West Germany'. Collectors refer to this mark as the last bee mark, since the current mark, in use since 1979, omits the bee in V.

  Key:

Stylized bee---Sty Bee   Last bee------------LB
Full bee------------FB   Current mark--------CM

A Stitch in Time, #255, Sty Bee, 6¾″ **155.00**
Accordian Boy, #185, Sty Bee, 5¼″ **125.00**
  #185, LB **70.00**
Adoration, #23/I, LB, 6¼″ **140.00**
Angel Serenade, #83, LB, 5″ **120.00**
Angel With Birds, font, #22/I, 3-line mark, 3¾x4″ . . **50.00**
Angelic Song, #144, Sty Bee, 4¼″ **110.00**
Apple Tree Boy, #142/3/0, 3-line, 4″ **90.00**
  #142/3/0, Sty Bee **95.00**
  #142/I, LB, 6″ **115.00**
Apple Tree Girl, #141/3/0, 3-line, 4″ **90.00**
  #141/I, LB, 6″ **115.00**
Ashtray, Boy with Bird, #166, LB, 3¼x6¼″ **85.00**
  Happy Pastime, #62, Sty Bee, 3½x6¼″ **135.00**
  Joyful, #33, Sty Bee, 3½x6″ **100.00**
  Let's Sing, #114, Sty Bee, 3½x6¾″ **100.00**
  Singing Lesson, #34, LB, 3½x6¼″ **75.00**
Auf Wiedersenhen, #153/0, LB, 5¼″ **110.00**
Baker, #128, 3-line mark, 4¾″ **80.00**
Band Leader, #129, FB, 5¼″ **240.00**
Barnyard Hero, #195/I, LB, 5¾″ **115.00**
Be Patient, #197/2/0, LB **70.00**
  #197/I, Sty Bee, 6¼″ **190.00**
Bell, 1978 Annual, #700, LB, 6″ **275.00**
  1979 Annual, #701 . . . . **85.00**
  1980 Annual, #702 . . . . **90.00**
Birthday Serenade, #218/0, LB, 5¼″ **120.00**
Blessed Event, #333, LB, 5½″ **240.00**
Bookends, Farm Boy & Goose Girl, #60/A&B, LB, 6″, pair . . . **200.00**
  Good Friends & She Loves Me, #251/A&B, LB pair **150.00**
  Little Goat Herder & Feeding Time, #250/A&B, LB, pair . . . **150.00**
  Playmates & Chick Girl, #61/A&B, LB, 6″ pair **210.00**
Boots, #143/I, FB, 6¾″ **290.00**
Boy With Toothache, #217, LB, 5½″ **75.00**
Brother, #95, Sty Bee, 5½″ **110.00**
Candleholder, Angel Duet, #193, LB, 5″ **80.00**
  Angelic Sleep, #25/I, Sty Bee, 3½x5″ **140.00**
  Candlelight, #192, LB, 6¾″ **60.00**
  Herald Angels, #37, 3- line mark, 2¼x4″ **120.00**
  Little Band, #388/M, w/music box, LB **195.00**
  Lullaby, #24/I, LB, 3¼x5″ **70.00**
  Silent Night, #54, Sty Bee, 4¾x5½″ **170.00**
Candy box, Chick Girl, #III/57, 3-line mark, 5¼″ . . . **125.00**
  Joyful, #III/53, LB, 6¼″ **90.00**
  Let's Sing, #III/110, 3-line mark, 6″ **120.00**
  Playmates, #III/58, Sty Bee, 5¼″ **160.00**
  Happy Pastime, #III/69, 3-line mark, 6″ **130.00**
  Singing Lesson, III/63, LB, 5¼″ **90.00**
Chick Girl, #57/0, Sty Bee **125.00**
  #57/I, FB, 4¼″ **310.00**
Chimney Sweep, #12/2/0, 3-line, 4″ **60.00**
  #12/2/0, Sty Bee **70.00**

Cinderella, #337, LB , 5½"	120.00
Close Harmony, #336, LB, 5½"	120.00
Coquettes, #179, Sty Bee, 5¼"	200.00
Culprits, #56/A, Sty Bee, 6¼"	210.00
Doctor, #127, Sty Bee, 4¾"	100.00
Doll Bath, #319, 3-line mark, 5¼"	140.00
#319, LB	95.00
Doll Mother, #67, Sty Bee, 4¾"	195.00
Drummer, #240, 3-line mark	85.00
#240, LB	60.00
Duet, #130, LB, 5¼"	100.00
Easter Playmates, #384, LB, 4"	120.00
Eventide, #99, FB, 4¾"	350.00
Farewell, #65, LB, 4¾"	145.00
Farm Boy, #66, 3-line mark, 5¼"	145.00
#66, FB	188.00
Feathered Friends, #344, Sty Bee, 4¾"	240.00
Feeding Time, #199/I, Sty Bee, 5¾"	175.00
Follow the Leader, #369, LB, 7"	475.00
Font, Angel At Prayer, #91/A&B, LB, 2x4¾", pair	45.00
Angel Cloud, #206, 3-line mark, 2¼x4¾"	275.00
Angel Duet, #146, CM, 2x4¾"	135.00
Angel With Birds, #22/I, Sty Bee, 3¼x4"	70.00
Angel With Flowers, #36/I FB, 3½x4½"	115.00
Child Jesus, #26/0, Sty Bee, 1½x5"	40.00
Good Shepherd, #35/0, LB, 2¼x4¾"	25.00
Heavenly Angel, #207, FB, 2x4¾"	85.00
Holy Family, #246, 3-line mark, 3x4"	50.00
Seated Angel, w/bird, #167, 3-line mark, 3¼x4¼"	50.00
Worship, #164, FB, 2¾x4"	135.00
For Father, #87, Sty Bee, 5½"	160.00
For Mother, #257, 3-line mark, 5¼"	110.00
Friends, #136/I, 3-line mark, 5"	140.00
Gay Adventure, #356, LB	90.00
Globe Trotter, #79, Sty Bee, 5"	150.00
Going to Grandma's, #52/I, LB, 6"	260.00
Good Friends, #182, 3-line mark, 4"	110.00
Good Shepherd, #42, FB, 6¼"	195.00
Goose Girl, #47/0, LB	90.00
#47/0, Sty Bee, 4"	140.00
#47/II, LB, 7½"	220.00
Happiness, #86, FB, 4¾"	155.00
Happy Birthday, #176/I, LB, 6"	135.00
Happy Days, #150/0, LB, 5¼"	130.00
#150/2/0, FB, 4¼"	240.00
Happy Traveler, #109/0, FB, 5"	200.00
#109/0, Sty Bee	90.00
Hear Ye, Hear Ye, #15/0, Sty Bee	125.00
Heavenly Angel, #21/I, Sty Bee	160.00
Heavenly Protection, #88/II, LB, 9¼"	250.00
Hello, #124/0, green pants, Sty Bee	120.00
#124/0, grey pants, Sty Bee	140.00
#124/I, LB, 7"	135.00
High Tenor, #135, 3-line mark, 4½"	70.00
Home From Market, #198/I, Sty Bee, 5¾"	170.00
Joseph, #214B, white, nativity piece, FB	135.00
Joyful, #53, 3½", Sty Bee	115.00
#53, FB, 4"	165.00
Just Resting, #112/1, 3-line mark	105.00
#112/3/0, Sty Bee, 3¾"	110.00
Kiss Me, #311, 3-line mark, 6"	165.00
Latest News, #184, Sty Bee, 5¼"	200.00
Let's Sing, #110/0, 3-line mark	115.00
#110/I, LB, 3¾"	85.00

Little Cellist, #89/I, Sty Bee, 6"	160.00
Little Fiddler, #4, 3-line mark, 5"	115.00
Little Gabriel, #32/0, Sty Bee, 5"	105.00
Little Gardener, #74, FB, 4¼"	170.00
Little Goat Herder, #200/I, LB, 5¼"	100.00
Little Helper, #73 LB, 4¼"	65.00
Little Hiker, #16/2/0, Sty Bee	85.00
Little Hunter, #16/2/0, LB	50.00
Little Pharmacist, #322, 3-line mark, "	150.00
Little Scholar, #80, 3-line mark, 5½"	80.00
Little Shopper, #96, FB, 4¾"	165.00
Little Sweeper, #171, Sty Bee, 4½"	95.00
Little Thrifty, #118, CM, 5"	300.00
Lost Sheep, #68/0, Sty Bee, 5½"	160.00
Madonna Praying, #46/I, 3-line mark, 11¼"	65.00
Madonna With Halo, #45/0, CM, 10½"	175.00
March Winds, #43, Sty Bee, 5"	105.00
Max & Moritz, #123, 3-line mark	95.00
Meditation, #13/0, LB, 5"	90.00
Merry Wanderer, #11/2/0, Sty Bee	80.00
#7/I, 3-line mark, 7"	235.00
Mischief Maker, #342, 3-line mark	150.00
Mother's Darling, #175, 3-line mark, 5½"	100.00
#175, LB	80.00
Mother's Helper, #133, Sty Bee, 5"	150.00
Mountaineer, #315, LB, 5¼"	100.00
Music Box, Little Band, #392/M, LB	225.00
Nativity Set, #214/D, Sty Bee, 3"	70.00
Angel Serenade, Sty Bee, 3"	70.00
Infant Jesus, #214/A, LB, 1½x3¾"	35.00
Madonna, #214/A, LB, 6½"	110.00
Shepherd Boy Kneeling, #214/G, LB, 3¾"	70.00
Out of Danger, #56/B, 3-line mark, 6¼"	175.00
Plaque, Ba-Bee Rings, #30/IA&B, 3-line mark, 5" dia	65.00
Child-in-Bed, #137, LB, 2¾x¾", round	35.00
Flitting Butterfly, #139, Sty Bee, 2½x2½"	110.00
Little Fiddler, #93, LB, 4¾x5¼"	70.00
Madonna, #222, Sty Bee, 4x5"	950.00
Madonna, #48/0, Sty Bee, 3x4"	100.00
Mail Coach, #140, LB, 4½x6¼"	130.00
Merry Wanderer, #92, Sty Bee, 4¾x5¼"	140.00
Quartet, #134, LB, 6x6"	150.00
Retreat To Safety, #126, 3-line mark, 4¾x5"	150.00
Swaying Lullaby, #165, Sty Bee, 4½x5¼"	140.00
Vacation Time, #125, LB, 4x4¼"	100.00
Playmates, #53/0, 3-line, 4"	105.00
Postman, #119, Sty Bee, 5¼"	145.00
Prayer Before Battle, #20, Sty Bee	135.00
Puppy Love, #1, Sty Bee, 5"	135.00
Retreat To Safety, #201/I, 3-line mark, 5½"	180.00
School Boy, #82/0, 3-line mark, 5½"	90.00
#82/2/0, Sty Bee	95.00
School Girl, #81/0, 3-line mark, 5¼"	100.00
#81/2/0, Sty Bee, 4¼"	110.00
Sensitive Hunter, #6/0, 3-line mark, 4¾"	95.00
#6/1, LB	80.00
#6/I, Sty Bee, 5½"	140.00
Serenade, #85/0, 3-line mark, 4¾"	70.00
She Loves Me, #174, LB, 4¼"	65.00
Shepherd, #214G, kneeling, nativity scene, LB	70.00
Shepherd Boy, #64, FB, 5½"	250.00
Singing Lesson, #63, FB	180.00
#63, LB, 2¼"	65.00
Sister, #98/0, LB, 5¾"	65.00

#98/0, Sty Bee **90.00**

Skier, #59, FB, 5¼" **250.00**
Spring Cheer, #72, Sty Bee, 5" **90.00**
St George, #55, LB, 6¾" **185.00**
Store Display Plaque, #187, 3-line, 4x5½" **220.00**
Stormy Weather, #71, Sty Bee, 6¼" **400.00**
Strolling Along, #5, CM, 4¾" **290.00**
Surprise, #94/3/0, LB, 4¼" **60.00**
Sweet Music, #186, 3-line mark, 5¼" **110.00**
Table lamp, Culprits, #44/A, LB, 9½" **200.00**
  Out Of Danger, #44/B, 3-line mark, 9½" **245.00**
  To Market, #223, LB, 9½" **200.00**
  Wayside Harmony, #224, LB, 9½" **185.00**
To Market, #49/3/0, 3-line mark, 4" **105.00**
  #49/3/0, LB **85.00**
Trumpet Boy, #97, Sty Bee, 4¾" **95.00**
Umbrella Boy, #152/A/0, Sty Bee, 5" **600.00**
Umbrella Girl, #152/B/II, 8" **430.00**
  #152/B/0, LB, 4¼" **350.00**
Village Boy, #51/2/0, 3-line mark, 5" **60.00**
  #51/I, LB, 7¼" **150.00**
Volunteers, #50/2/0, LB, 5" **115.00**
Waiter, #154/0, Sty Bee, 6" **130.00**
Watchful Angel, #194, 3-line mark, 6½" **200.00**
Wayside Harmony, #111/3/0, 3-line mark, 3¾" **75.00**
Weary Wanderer, #204, LB, 6" **80.00**
  #204, Sty Bee **145.00**
Worship, #84/0, Sty Bee, 5" **130.00**

Hunter Glass

Vi Hunter of Akron, Ohio, is an artist who designed the Jenny doll, first pressed in 1979 by Mosser Glass of Cambridge, Ohio. The first issues were made in crystal, cornflower blue and cobalt. When these are found today, they often bring prices of about $200 each. They are issued monthly, each in a new color. Hunter's Josh doll, a companion to Jenny, was introduced in 1981. An annual bell is produced each Christmas from the Jenny mold. Each piece is marked with a combination HC device and dated in the glass.

Bell, Jenny, Pearl **25.00**

Aztec Flame **35.00**
Azure Blue **20.00**
Black Pearl **9.50**
Cameo Bronze **20.00**
Cameo Custard **15.00**
Golden Opaline **15.00**
Irish Mist **18.00**
Jasmine **15.00**
Kashmir Green **30.00**
Mandarin Slag **10.00**
Morning Glory Slag **50.00**
Mystery Red **55.00**
Sea Breeze **15.00**
Set of 12 plus bell, 1979 .... **875.00**
Set of 12 plus bell, 1980 .... **285.00**
Starlight Blue **20.00**
Topaz **18.00**
Turquoise **20.00**
Twilight Pink **30.00**
Wind Frost **25.00**

Hutschenreuther

Established in 1845 in Hohenberg, Bavaria, the Hutschenreuther porcelain manufactory continues to produce fine china figurines and limited edition plates of interest to collectors today.

Cake plate, green & floral, heavy engraved gold, 2 handled **68.00**
Figurine, bantam rooster, white glaze, 6x4" **235.00**
  Bear cubs, natural brown glaze, 3½x5" **285.00**
  Bird, red, green & tan finch, 3½x3½", Granget **45.00**
  Bluebird on trunk, #2664, 5½" **125.00**
  Butterfly **55.00**
  Canary, insect in beak, wings outstretched, 5½x4¼" **160.00**
  Cardinal, signed Granget **135.00**
  Cat, Selb, 6¾", by Fritz Brown **125.00**
  Colonial soldier leapfrogs over gold ball, Tutter, 5½" **165.00**
  Elephant **48.00**
  Girl dancing, matt & hi-glaze, signed Achtziger, 8½x6" ... **350.00**
  Girl w/arms outstretched, w/matching bowl **148.00**
  Hummingbird w/flower, 4½" **90.00**
  Ice skater, sit-spin position, blue costume, 6x6½" **285.00**
  Maiden in long gown, crying cupid at feet, white glaze, Selb, 9½" **140.00**
  Monkey, Archtziger **105.00**
  Nude dancer w/outstretched arms, matt finish, 9¼x7" **170.00**
  Nude girl, kneeling w/head back, hands on head, lion mk, Tutter **210.00**
  Peking duck, wht w/orange beak, glazed, 5¾x5" **175.00**
  Pekingese dog, standing, 3x4½" **78.00**
  Rabbit, brown & wht, sitting, 5½" **68.00**
  Rhino, 2x4" **75.00**
  Robins on branch, signed Tutter **125.00**
  Twin donkeys, grey, matt finish **290.00**
Plate, dinner, Bavaria Dresden pattern, 10" **35.00**
  Hp roses, 8½" **60.00**
Tray, lt blue w/wht & pink flowers, gold, handled, 12x5½" **35.00**

Imari

Imari is a generic term which covers a broad family of wares. It was made in more than a dozen Japanese villages, but the name is that of the port from whence it was shipped to Europe. There are several types of Imari. The most common features a design with panels of birds, florals or people, surrounding a central basket of flowers. The colors used in this type are underglaze blue, with overglaze red, gold and green enamels. The Chinese

also made Imari wares, which differ from the Japanese type in several ways-- the absence of spur marks, a thinner type body, and a more consistent control of the blue. Imari type wares were copied on the continent by Meissen; and by English potters, among them Worcester, Derby and Bow.

Bowl, blue & white w/children, 10″	150.00
Meifi, chop marks, 2½x5″	140.00
Repaired, 22″	650.00
Scalloped & fluted, floral reserves, panels, 10″	135.00
Scalloped rim, ribbing, 11″	170.00
With cover, 2½x5″	135.00
Charger, blue & white 1900, 18″	175.00
Blue & white, 1830, 18″	1,000.00
Cobalt decor, 15″	165.00
Floral rim w/fans, 13″	95.00
Pierced for hanging, 4 reserves, early 1900s, 14″	125.00
Red w/blue, oriental figures, gilt, 18½″	235.00
Scalloped edge, ribbed, birds, mums, tree, 22″	265.00
Scalloped rim, urn w/flowers, gilt trim	600.00
Sky, mountains, fish; red, wht, blue, gold trim, 13″	65.00
Dish, w/cover, handles, 11″	250.00
Figural, elegant lady in kimono, 1800s, 12″	450.00
Fish basin, Island of Immortals, 1700s, 5x27″	9,000.00

Garden seats, 19″, pr	1,000.00
Jardiniere, raised floral panels w/Peacocks, gilt, 12″	275.00
Red w/birds, flowers, 1850, 20″	1450.00
Plate, red, blue & white, 8½″	50.00
Scalloped edge, florals, 12″	165.00
Three panels, 10″	80.00
Plates, scalloped; orange, blue, red, green, panels, dragon, pr	90.00
Platter, fish shape, 14″	425.00
Punch bowl, ribs, scallops, fish border, garden, hairline, 16″	225.00
Scalloped rim, ribbed, floral, 12″ dia	650.00
Sake bottles, white, red & blue decor, 5″, pr	185.00
Temple vase, flaring, red w/cobalt, birds, florals, 24″	675.00
Umbrella stand, cylinder w/blue & wht decor, 1850, 24″	350.00
Vase, flared, orange w/florals, applied dragon, 14″	340.00
Flared, ornate handles, scenes, 16″	340.00
Iris, foilage, butterfly bands, 15″	775.00

Imperial

Although the Imperial Glass Co. was organized in 1901, it was not until three years later that they began to manufacture glassware. Their early products were jelly glasses, hotel tumblers, etc, but by 1910 they were making a name for themselves by pressing quantities of Carnival Glass, the iridescent colored glassware that was popular during that time. From 1916 to 1920, they used the lustre process to make a line they called Imperial Jewels, now referred to as stretch glass. Opalescent glassware was introduced in the 30s, and was made in Sea Foam, Harding Blue, Moss Green and Burnt Almond. In contrast to these colored lines, Candlewick was a simple pattern in crystal glass, yet one for which the company is best known. All of

these types are listed in specific sections.

Freehand Ware, art glass made entirely by hand using no molds was made for a short time only, from about 1923 to 1928. Nu-Cut was made to imitate cut glass; it was produced in crystal as well as color and was introduced in 1914.

The company closed in 1931, but soon reorganized and reopened as the Imperial Glass Corporation. In 1940, they bought the molds and assets of the Central Glass Works of Wheeling, W. Va.; and in 1958 they purchased molds from Cambridge and Heisey. Although Imperial later used these molds to reproduce the older pieces, they marked the reissues with the I superimposed over a G trademark used since 1951. The company sold out to Lenox in 1973, but continues today to make hand pressed giftware items.

Ashtray, Top Dawg, caramel slag	8.00
Basket, w/wht handles, purple slag, shiny	28.00
Bell, Dresden lady, caramel slag, Cambridge	13.00
Purple slag, dull	28.00
Bookend, scottie, caramel slag, Cambrigde	13.00
Bowl, daisy cut w/sawtooth edge, footed, caramel slag	28.00
Daisy cut w/sawtooth edge, footed, purple slag, dull	28.00
Fluted, open rose, caramel, shiny	28.00
Fluted, open rose, footed, caramel slag, dull	28.00
Fluted, open rose, footed, purple slag, dull	28.00
Fluted, open rose, purple slag, dull	28.00
Fluted, open rose, red slag, dull	28.00
Purple slag, large open swan, dull	45.00
Purple slag, large open swan, shiny	45.00
Purple slag, small open swan, shiny	20.00
Bunny, caramel slag, Heisey	5.00
Butter dish, w/cover, red slag, dull	37.00
Candleholders, purple slag, shiny, pr	28.00
Candy dish, footed, grape, crimped, caramel slag	28.00
With cover, Herringbone, purple slag, sm	20.00
With cover, dog, caramel slag	16.00
With cover, footed, Louis IX, purple slag, dull	28.00
With cover, large owl, purple slag, shiny	35.00
Comport, w/cover, caramel slag, 9½″	20.00
Creamer & sugar, sm owl, purple slag, shiny, pr	35.00
Cruet, w/stopper, purple slag, shiny	35.00
Cygnet, caramel slag, Heisey	10.00
Dish, w/cover, eagle, purple slag, dull	50.00
Donkey, slag	28.00
Elephant, #3 caramel slag, Heisey	28.00
Honey jar, w/cover, beehive w/bees, caramel slag, 3¾x5″	16.00
Lamp, electric, purple slag, no shade	50.00
Lion on Nest, slag	45.00
Mallards, slag	28.00
Milk pitcher, windmill, purple slag, dull	35.00
Minuet girl, caramel slag, Heisey	8.50
Mug, singing birds, purple slag, shiny	20.00
Pie wagon, w/cover, caramel slag	30.00
Pitcher, miniature, purple slag, dull	16.00
Miniature, purple slag, shiny	16.00
Rooster on Nest, slag	45.00
Scolding bird, caramel slag	13.00
Tiger, caramel slag, Heisey	10.00
Toothpick holder, cornucopia, purple slag, dull, 3″	16.00
Miniature, footed, flared, purple slag	16.00
Vase, cobalt w/light blue looping, 10½″	190.00
Freehand, blue w/marigold inner throat, 10″	225.00
Freehand, gold w/wht loopings, 10″	162.00
Freehand, orig sticker, 10″	148.00
Freehand, pearl lustre w/green leafage, 9″	285.00
Loganberry, 10½″	17.50

Mosaic threaded, 6″ **147.00**
Wht iris w/green leafage, veined orange collar, 9¼″ **285.00**
Yellow w/wht looping, orange lustre interior, 11″ **190.00**

Imperial Porcelain

The Blue Ridge Mountain Boys were created by cartoonist Paul Webb and translated into three dimension by The Imperial Porcelain Corporation of Zanesville, Ohio, in 1947. These figurines decorated ashtrays, vases, mugs, bowls, pitchers, planters and other items. The Mountain Boys series were numbered 92 through 108, each with a different and amusing portrayal of mountain life. Imperial also produced American Folklore miniatures---23 tiny animals one inch or less in size--- and the Al Capp Dogpatch series. Because of financial difficulties, the company closed in 1960.

Ashtray, Buffy, #95, 8″, combo **40.00**
  Luke, #103 .... **40.00**
  Willie, #101A **40.00**
Beer mug set, 24 oz, set of 6 w/relief decor, #99 .... **300.00**
Cigarette box, #98 .... **25.00**
Cigarette holder, Pa, #102A **40.00**
Dealer sign, large **100.00**
  Small **50.00**
Dogpatch characteristics, each **45.00**
Figurine, bull **20.00**
  Burro **20.00**
  Calf **20.00**
  Colt **20.00**
  Cow **20.00**
  Duck **15.00**
  Flat piggy **35.00**
  Fox **20.00**
  Frog **15.00**
  Horses **20.00**
  Hound dogs **20.00**
  Kitten, large **20.00**
  Kitten, small **15.00**
  Lamb **20.00**
  Mule **20.00**
  Philpot Baby **15.00**
  Rabbit **20.00**
  Sheep **20.00**
  Skunk, large **20.00**
  Skunk, small **15.00**
  Sow **20.00**
  Turtle **20.00**
Liquor container, w/stopper, #100B **45.00**
  Willie, #101B **40.00**

Mug, 4″ **45.00**

Jake, Ma, Pa, #94 1502 .... **35.00**
  Riding High, signed Paul Webb, 6″ **29.00**
Pitcher, 1½ qt, #93, rabbit hunting **75.00**
Planter, Buffy, #100 .... **45.00**
  Ma, #104 .... **40.00**
  Pa, #102 .... **40.00**
Popcorn bowl, #96 .... **75.00**
Salt & pepper shakers, Grandma & Old Doc, #97 .... **25.00**
Vase, barrel, #106 .... **40.00**
  Willie, #101 .... **40.00**

Indian Tree

Indian Tree was a popular dinnerware pattern produced by various potteries since the early 1800's to contemporary times. Although backgrounds and borders vary, the Oriental theme is carried out with the gnarled brown branch of a pink blossomed tree. Among the manufacturers marks, you may find represented such notable firms as Coalport, S. Hancock & Sons, Soho Pottery and John Maddock & Sons.

Bouillon cup & underplate, Coalport **30.00**
Bowl, cereal, Johnson Bros **7.00**
  Soup, green rim, 7¾″, John Maddock 1896 .... **16.00**
  Soup, Johnson Bros **10.00**
Cream & sugar, covered, crown & wreath, Staffordshire **22.00**
Cream pitcher, Coalport **30.00**
Creamer, Johnson Bros **18.00**
Cup, green rim, John Maddock, 1896 .... **18.00**
Cup & saucer, Coalport **30.00**
  Demitasse, Minton impressed **35.00**
  Johnson Bros **18.00**
  Medina shape, Meakin, 1935 .... **40.00**
  Mkd Indina Tree in circle, Myott 1959 .... **20.00**
  Red shield mk, Myott 1930 .... **30.00**
Gravy boat, green rim, 1896, John Maddock **32.00**
Pitcher, bulbous, gold trim, 8″, Davison, England **27.50**
Plate, 6″, crown mk, Myott 1930 .... **15.00**
  6″, mkd Indian Tree in circle, Myott 1959 .... **15.00**
  6½″, red shield mk, Myott 1930 .... **7.50**
  6¾″, green rim, John Maddock 1896 .... **12.00**
  6¾″, scalloped, Coalport **20.00**
  7¾″, red shield mk, Myott 1930 .... **8.50**
  8″, crown mk, Myott 1936 .... **12.00**
  8″, Maddock **9.00**
  9″, Coalport **10.00**
  9″, green rim, John Maddock 1896 .... **17.50**
  9½″, brown rim, earthenware, John Maddock **17.50**
  10″, Maddock **15.00**
  Dinner, Johnson Bros **18.00**
  Grill, Booth **10.00**
  Salad, Johnson Bros **7.00**
Platter, 11½″, S Hancock & Sons **35.00**
  14″, crown mk, Johnson Bros **22.00**
  16″, Maddock **50.00**
Sauce dish, Johnson Bros **5.00**
Saucer, gold rim, John Maddock **4.00**
  Green rim, John Maddock, 1896 .... **2.50**
Server, handled, 8½″ sq, Coalport **55.00**
Sugar, covered, Coalport **35.00**
Teapot, Coalport **45.00**
Vegetable bowl, oval, 9″, Staffordshire **18.50**
  Oval, 10″, Davison **30.00**
  Oval, 10″, Maddock **35.00**
  Oval, gold rim, 7x9″, John Maddock **26.00**

Oval, Johnson Bros **18.00**

Inkwells

Ink, the fluid form as we know it today, was not developed until 1836. The inkwell was a natural follow-up. They were made in many materials, glass the most common since it was non-porus and stain resistant. Pewter, silver, brass and even gold was used, depending on the station and financial status of the owner. During the Victorian era, inkwells became more elaborate---some had two wells, others trays and penholders, and a few had a well or shaker for fine sand or steel powder to sift onto wet ink to blot up the excess. Cut glass inserts and ornate brass frames were popular.

With the development of the fountain pen, the inkwell's usefullness began to decline.

Advertising, Carter's Fountain Pen Liquid, embossed glass **60.00**
    Globe Insurance, 1923, brass **20.00**
Art Nouveau, brass holder w/glass insert **17.50**
    Brown enamel, centered in tray, bud shaped lid **35.00**
    Copper cube w/sterling design, hinged compositon insert **40.00**
    Copper on pewter, deer decor **50.00**
    Lady's head, crystal & silverplated **45.00**
    Pyramid, brass w/clear insert, Germany **40.00**

Silver on pewter, domed floral base w/molded swirl base band, 3" **90.00**
    Silverplated figural dog stand w/inkwell tree trunk **95.00**
    Sterling on copper, covered, monogrammed, composition insert **40.00**
Bear figural, sitting, ci, hinged head, complete w/insert **42.00**
    Sitting, removable head, interior inkwell **45.00**
Bisque, 2 pc, man & woman on sofa, Germany, 1880s **475.00**
Brass, embossed stand w/double dome lid **120.00**
    Footed base, ornate, w/cut glass square well, 3½x7½" **165.00**
    Pyramid shape w/clear glass insert **35.00**
    Ship's, signed Mellenship & Harris **125.00**
    With framed calendar set, hinged lid, glass well, K & Co, 1908 **55.00**
Bronze, double, 3 figures of Dutch children **450.00**
    Woven wire creel w/hinged cover, applied bronze shellfish . . **250.00**
Camel figural, resting, enameled metal **45.00**
Cast iron, Eastlake **40.00**
    Horseshoe on back, horse head pen holder, glass well **65.00**
    With 2 milk glass figural snails, footed, 6" square **125.00**
Cat, procelain, w/pen holder, yellow w/green eyes, Germany **55.00**
Champleve, inkwell & pen, 3x7" **450.00**
Clock, works, brass, 1890s, English, 8" **345.00**
Cloisonne, cobalt blue & red, footed, covered, 3½x2½" square **125.00**
Combination, brass wells, pen tray & stamp drawer, Victorian . . **58.00**
    Silver, 2 inkwells & pen tray, 1915 . . . . **35.00**
Copper pyramid, hinged cover, glass liner, MF & Co, Artmetal **130.00**
Copper stand & lid, glass insert, dog finial, McClelland Barclay, 1932 **75.00**
Crab figural, metal, coppery decor, orig clear insert, 7x6½" **68.00**
Crystal, 4 sided, sterling silver top **95.00**
    Brass hinged cut glass top, 3¼x2½" sq **55.00**
    Hinged sterling top, cut blocks bottom, 2x2¼" **45.00**

Cupid & horse figural, Rockingham type **70.00**
Cut glass, clear w/sterling silver cap, Unger Bros **125.00**
    Cranberry w/panel cutting, brass base & lid, 4" **135.00**
    Leaded, silver top, w/pen **140.00**
    Nailhead diamonds, w/silverplated, hinged top & tray **125.00**
    Sapphire blue w/prism cutting, sterling hinged lid, 2½" **135.00**
Deer hoof mounted on velvet stand, ornate silverplated pen holder **42.00**
Dog figural wearing red dunce cap, lidded fruit basket **125.00**
    With baby bottle & 4 dolphins, glass insert, 1900 . . . . **100.00**
Dog head figural, metal, hinged, 3½" **50.00**
Dresden, yellow & white, gold decor & finial, w/underplate, mkd **85.00**
French, pump style, wht porcelain, brass chain & caps, 1893 . . **250.00**
German helmet figural, silverplate w/glass insert, 3½x2¾x3¾" . . **45.00**
Giraffe figural w/palm tree, silverplated, J Deakin & Sons, 10½" **375.00**
Glass, aqua, 1882, 2½", Carter's Raven Black, orig labels **10.00**
    Beveled black stand, 3 velvet lined indentations **130.00**
    Black w/wht painted flowers, 12 sided, hinged, 2¼x1½" sq . . **140.00**
    Blown three mold, diamond diapering above ribbing, olive . . . **82.50**
    Blown, cylinder form, olive, 2" **100.00**
    Blue opaque, metal hinged lid, mushroom shape **110.00**
    Blue, 12 sided, hinged, 2¼x1½"sq, w/wht painted flowers . . **150.00**
    Blue, hinged top, beveled, 2x2½" **200.00**
    Boat shape, milk glass **150.00**
    Clear w/blue peaked lid, octagonal **150.00**
    Coal scuttle ribbed shape, metal lik, PN Mfg Co, 1884 . . . . . **75.00**
    Cobalt cut to wht cut to clear, heavy, sterling band & hinge . **225.00**
    Flint, early round dome, 2¼x4", w/ci hinged top **35.00**
    Hobnail pattern, amber, w/lid, 2" sq **110.00**
    Olive amber, embossed diamonds & ribbing at base, Keene, N.H. **145.00**
    Olive green, pontil, 8 sided, Stoddard, N.H., whittle mkd **95.00**
    Pale green, ribbed, cork stopper w/brass top, 1¼x1¼" **140.00**
    Sapphire blue, 3 part, 4x4½" **140.00**
    Thousand Eye, amber, w/cover **125.00**
    Thousand Eye, blue, w/matching cover **185.00**
    Thousand Eye, vaseline, covered **180.00**
    Vaseline, double, covered sander & vaseline wells, old, 7¾" long **375.00**
    Vaseline, w/wht painted flowers, 12 sided, hinged, 2¼x1½" sq **175.00**
    Wht flint opaque, pyramid shape w/hinged mushroom lid . . . **135.00**
Golf ball, metal w/green glass insert **30.00**
Iron stand w/horsehead & horseshoe, footed, 1877, w/crystal well **75.00**
Japanese green glass & silver overlay **27.00**
Joseph Scammell, stand, 3 wells w/glass inserts, 1794, 4x9" . **1,550.00**
Kate Greenaway boy standing behind hinged nest w/eggs, metal **65.00**
Kittens on ottoman w/mother cat, compo material, 3" **75.00**
Leprechaun figural, seated, hinged hat, ci, signed **115.00**
Letter scale figural, brass, Victorian, English, 9½x4½" **350.00**
Lobster figural, black, 7" **95.00**
Loetz, green insert, brass lid, pewter lily pad frame, 3x2½" . . . **180.00**
    With hinged brass lid **125.00**
Ma & Pa figurals, Carter Inx, German mk, pat date, pair **150.00**
Majolica, on tray **105.00**
Monument shaped, Reynolds Revolving Inkwell, Louisville, Ky . . **85.00**
Nippon, matt finish, jewelled cover, much gold, green wreath mark **175.00**
Owl head, yellow glass eyes, lift-off lid, German bisque, china insert **195.00**
Partner's, large wood, brass, cut glass, 1850s **250.00**
Pewter, cylinder w/hinged lid, marked SO & crown, 3¼" dia . . **120.00**
Plymouth Rock glass paperweight, 1876 Centennial, Providence Co **52.00**
Porcelain, figural Geni, 2 pc, Germany **45.00**
    Ribbed, russet & blue decor, underplate w/fan-molded corners **65.00**
    With underplate, 'A Present From Cork', English, 2½" **30.00**
Pottery, relief lions, figural dog, sander insert, Swopes Pottery, 1851 **875.00**
School type, glass w/Bakelite top **8.00**
Sangbusch, self-closing, glass & Bakelite top, 1903-14 . . . . **7.50**
Ship figural w/pewter top **85.00**

Silver overlay on emerald glass w/clear domes, double well, signed **345.00**
Silver overlay, green glass, double, General Supply Co, pat #879470 **395.00**
Silver patterned, quad plate; cut, frosted glass, Simpson, Hall, Miller **150.00**
Silver, tennis racket base, ball inkwell, "1st Prize 1895"...... **135.00**
    With glass covered compartment on each side, 1900 ...... **660.00**
Snail figural, cobalt, w/ornate stand, brass fittings, pat 1878... **175.00**
    Double, w/ornate iron stand **85.00**
    Milk glass, in iron frame **50.00**
Soccer ball figural, silverplated, green glass insert **38.00**
Staffordshire deer & doe, salmon color w/wht base, pair **250.00**
Staffordshire, figural boy feeding birds, gold & wht **125.00**
Sterling inlaid copper, monogrammed, compo insert **40.00**
Stevens & Williams, hinged, w/applied cherry, 3" **225.00**
Stoneware, figural face w/Liberty cap, 2 pen holes, 2x2½x3½" **100.00**
    Grey, 3 quill holes, 3¾" dia..................... **60.00**
    Grey, round, single hole, 2¼" dia **50.00**
Tin, enamel w/decoupage, milk glass insert, English, 3" **50.00**
Traveling, egg shape w/hinged cover, silver, hallmarked, 1868 . **605.00**
Turtle figural, aqua glass, octagon base, J & IEM **14.00**
Walnut curve handled stand, 2 swirled hinged wells, English .. **100.00**
Waterman's Ideal, wood w/screw top, bottle inside, litho-labels, 1900s **43.00**
Wood stand w/candleholders, 1860s **120.00**

Insulators

    The telegraph was invented in 1844. The devices developed to hold the electrical transmission wires to the poles were called insulators. The telephone, invented in 1876, intensified their usefullness and by the turn of the century thousands of varieties were being produced in glass of various colors and sizes, pottery and wood. Of the more than 3,000 types known to exist, today's collectors evaluate their worth by age and rarity of color. Aqua and green are the most common colors in glass, dark brown in ceramic. Threadless insulators, made between 1850 and 1870, bring prices well into the hundreds.

AT&T, aqua **11.00**
    Frosty lavender **12.00**
    Jade milk glass......................... **11.00**
    Purple................................. **14.00**
    Turquoise **10.00**
Armstrong DPI, olive **11.00**
    Smoke **5.00**
B&O (on crown) pat Jan 25, 1870, light blue **9.00**
'B' aqua, 2 pc transposition **11.00**
    Aqua.................................. **5.00**
    Blue **10.00**
    Dark purple **11.00**
    Emerald green **8.00**
Beehive, porcelain, carmel & yellow two tone....... **12.00**
Brookfield #9, aqua....................... **7.00**
    #36, blue **8.00**
    #41, aqua **9.00**
    Aqua, dome embossed **4.00**
    Green, w/amber streaks **7.00**
    Threadless, dark amber, illus **400.00**
CCG, purple **35.00**
CEW, blue, (The Tallone) **65.00**
CGI Co, green **8.00**
    Lt purple **10.00**
    Rose **11.00**
CNR Standard, lt aqua **7.00**
Cable #3, aqua **7.00**
    #3, green **20.00**
Cable Top, porcelain, blue **10.00**

Porcelain, brown **4.00**
    Porcelain, white **8.00**
California, aqua **145.00**
    Blue **11.00**
    Clear... **20.00**
    Sage green **10.00**
    Smoke & strawberry **11.00**
    Yellow-strawberry **40.00**
Canada, ice-blue, milky swirls..................... **10.00**
Canadian Pacific Ry Co, lt lavender **14.00**
    Purple.. **16.00**
Columbia #2, aqua **50.00**
    #2, green **50.00**
Dominion #42, peach **8.00**
EDR, lt aqua **8.00**
Foster Bros, base emblem **500.00**
GTP Tel Co, lt aqua **9.00**
GTR, emerald green **9.00**
Gayner #44, aqua **7.00**
    #90, lt blue **10.00**
HBR, lt aqua **17.00**
HG Co, dark aqua **4.00**
    Jade, milk glass **11.00**
Hawley, PA. USA, lt blue......................... **10.00**
    Aqua... **10.00**
Hemingray #2 Transposition, blue-green **19.00**
    #5, dark aqua **9.00**
    #9, jade milk glass............................. **12.00**
    #10, dark aqua **6.00**
    #21, blue **6.00**
    #38, aqua **13.00**
    #60, ice blue **17.00**
    #62, turquoise-blue **9.00**
    Clear, (Big Mouth) **40.00**
    Cobalt blue **60.00**
Jumbo, lime green, base emb Oakman MFG **175.00**
Kimble #820, smokey-clear....................... **7.00**
Locke #14, dark aqua **13.00**
    #20, Victor, N.Y., dark aqua **10.00**
    #20, yellow-green **14.00**
Lynchburg #10, green **7.00**
    #36, yellow-green **11.00**
    #44, yellow-green **9.00**
    #530, aqua-green **14.00**
Manhattan, aqua **30.00**
Maydwell #9, lt purple **13.00**
    #9, smoke.................................... **6.00**
    #19, lime-yellow **12.00**
McKee, threadless, blue **400.00**
McLaughlin #9, lt yellow **11.00**
    #10, lt green **6.00**
    #16, black-glass **11.00**
    #20, delft-blue **8.00**
    #40, aqua **45.00**
    #42, delft-blue **10.00**
NEGM, emerald green, straight sides............... **65.00**
NEGM Co, lt green **8.00**
New England T&T, aqua **7.00**
    Green **6.00**
    Ice blue **5.00**
OVG Co, dark aqua **14.00**
    Lt aqua....................................... **16.00**
    Lt green...................................... **8.00**
PSSA #9, clear **11.00**

Yellow-green **9.00**
Yellow **28.00**
Pony porcelain, double groove, brown **6.00**
   Single groove, brown **4.00**
Postal, aqua **7.00**
   Green **7.00**
   Purple **14.00**
Pyrex #661, strawberry **7.00**
   Deep orange carnival **13.00**
Roman Helmet, procelain, white **12.00**
S MCKee, aqua **150.00**
SF, aqua **5.00**
   Green **7.00**
Santa-Anna, blue **13.00**
Signal, porcelain, lt blue **9.00**
   Porcelain, two-tone brown **5.00**
Spool, porcelain, cobalt blue **9.00**
Standard, purple **17.00**
Star, olive green **4.00**
Sterling, aqua **11.00**
TCR, lt aqua **7.00**
Tillotson, aqua **200.00**
WFG Co, clear **17.00**
   Lt blue, Denver, Co **9.00**
   Purple **17.00**
   Purple **23.00**
Whitall Tatum #1, dark smokey plum **17.00**
   #1, extra dark purple **9.00**
   #1 peach **8.00**
   #2 olive-yellow **11.00**
   #3, clear **5.00**
   #9, purple **13.00**
   #13, clear **9.00**

Ironstone

During the last quarter of the 18th century, English potters began experimenting with a new type of body that contained calcinated flint and a higher china clay content to produce a fine durable white ware---heavy, yet with a texture that resembled porcelain. To remove the last trace of yellow, a minute amount of cobalt was added, often resulting in a bluish white tone. Wm. and John Turner of Caughley, and Josiah Spode II were the first to manufacture the ware successfully. Others, such as Davenport, Hicks and Meigh, and Ralph and Josiah Wedgwood, followed with their own versions. The latter coined the name 'Pearl' to refer to his product and incorporated the term with his trademark.

In 1813 a 14 year patent was issued to Charles James Mason, who called his ware Patented Ironstone. Francis Morley, G.L. Asworth, T.J. Mayer and other Staffordshire potters continued to produce ironstone until the end of the century. While some of these patterns are simple to the extreme, many are decorated with in-mold designs of fruit, grains and foliage on ribbed or scalloped shapes. In the 1830s, transfer printed designs in blue, mulberry, pink, green and black became popular, and polychrome versions of Oriental wares were manufactured to compete with the Chinese trade.

Bouillon cups & underplates, pink, Mason's, set of 8 . . . . **85.00**
Bowl, covered, white w/brown spray, EM&CF, 2x6x9" **26.00**
   Fruit, white, square, Meakin **25.00**
   Oval, Wedgwood, 2½x10x12" **22.00**
   Oval, white, Meakin, 8x10" **32.00**
   Soup, deep, Johnson Bros, 8½" **8.00**
   Soup, white, Meakin **10.00**
   White, 1850, 7½" dia **10.00**
   White, Edwards, 3½x9½" **26.00**

White, footed, Adams, 8x10" **75.00**
White, footed, handled, 8¼" **25.00**
Butter dish, covered, flower finial, white **30.00**
Butter pat, J&G Meakin, 2½x2½" **8.00**
Coffee pot, corn & oats, corn finial, large, mkd Davenport **125.00**

White, A Meakin, 10½" **68.00**
Compote, small, T&R Boote **25.00**
   Vista pattern, blue transfer, Mason's **70.00**
Cream & sugar, raised leaf design, Red Cliff **30.00**
Cup, handleless, white, very early, heavy, 3½x3½" **15.00**
Cup & saucer, handleless, black transfer, Corean **20.00**
   Handleless, molded panels & berries, blk & gold, mkd XP . . **65.00**
   Vista pattern, blue transfer, Mason's **25.00**
Cuspidor, miniature, masked spout, handle, white, 3x4" **40.00**
Dish, covered, fluted, white, Pankhurst **65.00**
Ginger jar, covered, Oriental form, 7" **95.00**
Gravy boat, covered, w/ladle, 7" **40.00**
   Royal, Clemenston **25.00**
   White, Royal, oak leaf handle, A Meakin **25.00**
Honey pot, covered, w/ladle, 7" **45.00**
Nappie, oval, Meakin, 5x6½" **9.00**
Pickle dish, oblong, scalloped edge, JW Parkhurst, Hanley **22.00**
Pitcher & bowl, Mason's **395.00**
Pitcher, 8-sided, decorated, Masons's, 4¼" **58.00**
   8-sided decorated, Masons's, 5¼" **68.00**
   Flowers, leaves & tendrils, high relief, Adams, 9½" **50.00**
   Hot water, white, late 1800s **35.00**
   Leaves & berries, gold trim, Boote, Waterloo, 10½" **80.00**
   Milk, Eugenia, green transfer, J&C Meakin **38.00**
   Octagonal, serpent handle, Blue Willow, Mason's, 5¼" . . . **85.00**
   Violet decor, green leaves, 12" **50.00**
   Water, large, Dogwood pattern **35.00**
   Water, small, Dogwood pattern **30.00**
Plate, 8", white, Wheat pattern, Staffordshire **20.00**
   9", white, Royal, A Meakin **7.00**
   10", Maddock & Co, England **10.00**
   10", fern, Wilkinson **10.00**
   10", white, Royal, A Meakin **8.75**
   Birds decor, floral border, blue transfer, Mason's **38.00**
   Imari style, open cake handle sides, A Broyden, 8" **45.00**
Platter, blue & wht, landscape, 19½" **165.00**

Corn pattern, scalloped, W&E Corn, Burslem, 19″ **55.00**
Floral designs, 8¼x12½″ **12.00**

Lozere, mk E Challinor, 15½x12″ **145.00**
White w/floral border, 13″ **30.00**
White, 16½x11″, Meakin, England **25.00**
White, Burgess & Leigh, 10½x12½″ **14.00**
White, Meakin, 8x11″ **15.00**
White, Meakin, 12″ **12.00**
White, Meakin, 14x19″ **45.00**
White, lion & unicorn mk, Hanley, #20, 14″ **15.00**
White, oval, Elsmore & Forster, 14x18″ **75.00**
White, Royal, A Meakin, 13½″ **10.00**
White, Royal, A Meakin, 19″ **30.00**
Serving dish, round, wht raised flower border, 12¾″ **15.00**
Shaving mug, white, Shaw **55.00**
Soap dish, Cable pattern, white **9.00**
Spit cup, ladies, handled, 1840s, flared top, 4x4″ **40.00**
Sugar bowl, Cable & Knot pattern, white, 6″, H Burgess **50.00**
Sugar, covered, Pacific shape, 1871 . . . . **50.00**
Teapot, Bow & Tassel pattern, white, Burgess & Goddard, 1878 **30.00**
Octagon shape, slender, Rice pattern, mkd, 6½″ **30.00**
Ribbed body, crimped rim, nut finial, J Edwards, 10″ **90.00**
Tulip pattern, bud finial, painted decor, Elsmore & Forster . . **95.00**
White, Burges & Leigh, 3½″ **27.00**
Tray, wht w/fig pattern, 1880s **40.00**
Tureen, octagonal, impressed April 30/02, w/ladle **90.00**
Soup, covered, blue transfer, 1830s, 10¾″ **385.00**
Urn, octagonal, blue/wht transfer, Corinth pattern, 1845, Phillips **25.00**
Vegetable bowl, covered, Wheat pattern, brown transfer, Boote . **20.00**
White, 8x10x3½″ **40.00**
Wash basin, Corella pattern, mulberry transfer, 12″ dia **125.00**
Water dispenser, barrel type, 5½x14″ dia **125.00**

Ispanky

Ispanky figurines, designed by Lazlo Ispanky, have been produced at his Pennington, New Jersey workshop since 1966.

Annabel Lee **1,350.00**
Antony **750.00**
Awakening **195.00**
Claudia **195.00**
Cleopatra **1,950.00**
Coppelia **325.00**
Dianne **495.00**
Feathered Friends **165.00**
Holy Family, 1974, white **900.00**

King Solomon **2,400.00**
Lorelei, 1973 . . . . **525.00**
Lydia **475.00**
Melinda **125.00**
Melody **135.00**
Pegasus, 1968, decorated **550.00**
Poppy, 1977 . . . . **395.00**
Romance **650.00**
Sophistication **500.00**
Spirit of the Sea **1,150.00**
Sugar Plum Fairy **175.00**
Ten Commandments, 1980 . . . . **85.00**
Tubby **185.00**
Twelve Tribes, 1979 . . . . **75.00**

Ivory

Technically, true ivory is the substance composing the tusk of the elephant; the finest type comes from those of Africa. However, tusks and teeth of other animals---the walrus, for instance, the hippopotamus, and the sperm whale---are similar in composition and appearance and have also been used for carving. The Chinese have used this substance for centuries, preferring it over bone because of the natural oil contained in its pores, which not only renders it easier to carve, but also imparts a soft sheen to the finished product. Aged ivory usually takes on a soft caramel patina, but unscrupulous dealers sometimes treat new ivory to a tea bath to 'antique' it!

A bill passed in 1978 reinforced a ban on the importation of whale and walrus ivory.

Backscratcher, ornately carved lady's fingers, 7½″ **32.00**
Beads, 8mm, strand **25.00**
Box, flowers & butterflies in MOP, agate, 1800s, 2½″ dia **450.00**
Round, braid decor, hinged Sheffield lid & base, 3½x5x4½″ **165.00**
Bracelet, handcarved, old **145.00**
Cane handle, drummer boy, 5¾″ **150.00**
Chess set, carved, in wooden box **695.00**
English, kings & queen are crowns, w/incised grisaille board **550.00**
French, pawns are farmers w/cloth hats, late 1700s, Dieppe . **750.00**
Japanese style pieces, fitted playing board case **475.00**
Oriental pieces, board w/blk & gold lacquer decor, ped stand **250.00**
Chopsticks, 7″ **195.00**
Cigar holder, carved floral decor **22.00**
Cigarette holder, carved **50.00**
Cribbage board, carved roses decor, w/pins **48.00**
Doctor's doll, black hair, w/stand, 8½″ **225.00**
Carved female figure, w/moveable bracelet, 3″ **55.00**
Carved nude female reclining on wooden table, 7″ **175.00**
Full female figural w/moveable bracelet, 6″ **140.00**
With stand, 12½″ **675.00**
Figurine, angel w/flower, 9″ **260.00**
Angel, standing, 11″ **270.00**
Apple w/carved front, multi-colored scene inside, wood base . **165.00**
Apple w/ladybug, opens to reveal erotic scenes **110.00**
Beauty w/bird, 11″ **320.00**
Boy sitting on stump holding outstretched frog **150.00**
Chinese woman w/basket, carved ivory stand, 5½″ **185.00**
Cupid kneeling, 2½″ **150.00**
Deity in kimono w/fan, happy/sad face, 3″ **200.00**
Eagle, 7″ **325.00**
Elephant being attacked by 3 lions, 2½x8″ **325.00**
Elephant bridge on stand, 18″ long **650.00**
Elephant w/passengers, 3½″, Indian **150.00**
Fisherman, 8″ **150.00**
Fisherman, Qianlong, 15″ **600.00**

Gardener in kimono, standing, w/rake & fruit, 4¼" **220.00**
Geisha playing samisen, kneeling, 3" **180.00**
Group of 4 figures representing different sages, 2" **160.00**
Japanese girl in kimono, 16" **650.00**
Kuan Yin, 12" **285.00**
Longevity w/boy, 11" **220.00**
Man w/dragon, 14" **300.00**
Old man, 8" **150.00**
Old man w/boy, 10½" **250.00**
Oriental warriors w/horsemen & flag bearer, carved stand ... **275.00**
Pair, king & queen, 11" **430.00**
Pair, man fishing, woman w/poles & gear, 6" **335.00**
Reclining man reading book w/pointer, 7x8x2" **75.00**
Rhinocerus, old, African, 5" **135.00**
Seated man in robe, knife, carp, signed, 2¼" **135.00**
St George on horse killing dragon, grouping on rosewood stand **300.00**
Flower pot, 17" **1,200.00**
Glove stretcher, 9½" **45.00**
Jewel box, reticulated, ornate, Chinese **600.00**
Letter opener, w/paper folder, 10½x1½" **30.00**
Mask, emperor & empress, wood stand, carved, 5" pr **150.00**
Mask, emperor & empress, 5" plus 1" stand, ornately jeweled, pair **275.00**
Match box, etched scenes of Red Riding Hood, Vesta **95.00**
Mystery ball, 6 layers, 4" dia, held up by 3 elephants, ped base . **75.00**
  7 layers, 3½" dia, ped base w/3 'standing' elephants **85.00**
  Many layers, 17" **800.00**
Needle case, carved Oriental figures **50.00**
Painting on ivory, beautiful woman, miniature **95.00**
  Court lady, brass frame 4x5" **140.00**
  Lady in lavender dress, signed Hardy, miniature **130.00**
  Praying woman w/halo, celluloid/brass frame, miniature **50.00**
  Woman & girl, tortoise frame, 2½x3½" **75.00**
  Woman w/horse, signed Andre **175.00**
Pill box, 3 stacking interlocking compartments on cord **50.00**
  Carved oriental zodiac animals, 4 compartments, beaded cord **160.00**
  Mountain paradise scene, 4 rows Japanese characters **90.00**
Ruler, folding center, brass fittings, 6" **35.00**
Sealer, foo dog, monkeys, imprints Japanese characters **240.00**
Snuff bottle, dragon & Phoenix bird, ring handles, 2½" **60.00**
Snuff bottle, pair, figural oriental w/cane, wife w/book, 4½" ... **235.00**
Tusk, 38" **1,725.00**
  45" **2,875.00**
  70" **6,000.00**
  Carved dragon decor, ornate, 21" **250.00**
  Carved warriors, women, children climb wooded mountain, 18½" **945.00**
  Head of Buddah, w/crown, 14" **1,000.00**
Umbrella handle, lizard under mushroom, detailed **85.00**

Jack in the Pulpit Vases

Popular novelties at the turn of the century, Jack in the Pulpit vases were made in every type of art glass produced. Some were simple; others elaborately appliqued and enameled. They were shaped to resemble the lily for which they were named.

Art Deco, amber on crystal base, 15" **85.00**
Art glass, amber to green swirls, cranberry crimped edge, 11". **135.00**
  Clear to deep purple, 11" **35.00**
Cranberry glass, tulip form, 12" **75.00**
MOP, raindrop satin, bulbous, ruffle top, blue, 7" **265.00**
Opalescent, oxblood, deep ruffled, pleated rim, 8x7" **85.00**
  Purple to green, enamel scrolls & daisies, 5½" **95.00**
  Wht w/red & black shaded lip, 7" **125.00**
Rubina Verde, applied swirled rigaree, pr, 13x5" **395.00**

With applied regaree, Stevens & Williams, pr, 13x5" **495.00**
Satin glass, blue bowl, decor & jewels, 7" dia **179.00**
Stourbridge, fuchsia, fluted, wht applied flowers, vaseline ft, 6" **195.00**
Vasa Murrhina, clear w/green, pink, rose, mica, 10½x6" **130.00**

Jackfield

Jackfield has come to be a generic term used to refer to wares with a red clay body and a high gloss black glaze. It originated at Jackfield, in Stropshire, England; however, it was also produced in the Staffordshire district as well. While some pieces are decorated with relief motifs or painted on florals and gilting, many are unadorned. Teapots produced in the 18th century were known locally as 'black decanters'. These pots, and figural dogs and roosters are the items most often found.

Cheese dish, enameled decor, finial, 12" dia **235.00**
Coffee pot, decorated w/vines, footed, 9¾" **200.00**
Creamer, cow, w/orig gilt decor & lid, 1800s **50.00**
Pitcher, wht floral design, 6" **95.00**
Spaniels, pair, 1700s, England **400.00**
Syrup pitcher, pewter top, 7½" **70.00**
Teapot, 3-color decor, gold trim **80.00**

Jewelry

Jewelry as objects of adornment have always been regarded with special affection. Whether it be a trinket or a costly ornament of gold, silver, or enameled work, jewelry has personal significance to the wearer.

The art of the jeweler is valued as is any art object, and the names of Lalique or Faberge on collectible pieces bring prices demanded by the signed works of Picasso.

Once the province of kings and noblemen, jewelry now is a legacy of all strata of society. The creativity reflected in the jewelers' art has resulted in a myriad of decorative adornments for men and women, and the modern usage of 'lesser' gems and base metals has elevated the values and increased the demand for artistic merit on a par with intrinsic values. Luxuriously appointed pieces of Victorian splendor and Edwardian grandeur, now compete with the unique, imaginative renditions of jewelry produced in the exciting Art Nouveau period, as well as the adventurous translation of jewelry executed in man-made materials versus natural elements.

Today, prices for gems and gemstones crafted into antique and collectible jewelry, are based on artistic merit, personal appeal, pure sentimentality, and intrinsic values.

Barrette, jet glass, French, 1890 .... **25.00**
Belt, Chatelaine, silver w/imitation jasperware cameo, 1895..... **60.00**
Bouquet holder, bridal, bronze & silver, Art Nouveau, 1895 .. **250.00**
  Bridal, silver baroque, w/handkerchief ring, 1850 .... **225.00**
Bracelet, 3-matched bangles, carved plastic, 1930 .... **30.00**
  3-strand cultured pearls w/marcasites, 1950 .... **150.00**
  14k & 6 hollow gold charms, 1900 .... **345.00**
  14k & enamel links, Art Deco, 1920 .... **250.00**
  14k, w/genuine gems & pearls, 1930 .... **350.00**
  16, 10-14k slides w/genuine stones, 1925 .... **500.00**
  Art Deco, copper & oxidized silver, simulated carnelian...... **85.00**
  Art Deco, 14k w/diamonds & emerald **1,000.00**
  Art Deco, link design, sterling w/marcasites, 1925 .... **75.00**
  Art Deco, silver set w/Egyptian motifs **25.00**
  Art Deco, sterling w/green & black enameling **45.00**
  Art Moderne, chrome & sterling mesh, 1940 .... **35.00**
  Art Nouveau, 14k w/diamonds & sapphires, w/slides **1,850.00**
  Art Nouveau, gold over sterling, blue molded glass **650.00**
  Bangle, brass w/gold wash, handmade, 1935, set **25.00**
  Bangles, silver setting for turquoise, 1950 .... **85.00**

Bangle-type, sterling w/imitation stones, 1900 . . . . **35.00**
Cabochon & rose cut, low karat metal, 1900 . . . . **300.00**
Cinnabar & filigree sterling silver, 1920 . . . . **75.00**
Coral beads, finely braided, 1910 . . . . **100.00**
Cuff-style, carved plastic, 1930 . . . . **20.00**
Cuff-type, pink gold, heavily engraved, 1890 . . . . **75.00**
Gilt links w/3 monkeys & elephant charms, 1900 . . . . **45.00**
Gold bangle set w/paste stones, 1910 . . . . **50.00**
Gold base metal, imitation stones, 1925 . . . . **75.00**
Gold links set w/stones, 1 of pair, 1890 . . . . **250.00**
Gold wash bangle, 1900 . . . . **20.00**
Gold washed silver, set w/amythests, 1940 . . . . **150.00**
Gold-coil bangle, set w/garnets, 1925 . . . . **150.00**
Gold-filled bangle w/pink paste stones, 1910 . . . . **45.00**
Green turquoise in silver mounting, 1940 . . . . **95.00**
Hollow gold tube, garnet & half pearls, 1885 . . . . **450.00**
Inlaid turquoise, 1950 . . . . **135.00**
Lava cameos, bezel-set, sterling, 1890 . . . . **175.00**
Mesh gilt w/mother-of-pearl in buckle, 1910 . . . . **45.00**
Pave' set garnets in 14k links, 1910 . . . . **225.00**
Peking glass bangle, dark green, 1930 . . . . **8.00**
Red glass set in mounting, gold wash, 1880 . . . . **85.00**
Rhodium, *Pave'* mounted rhinestones, 1950 . . . . **75.00**
Shell cameo, gold wash over silver, 1900 . . . . **85.00**
Sterling & enamel w/genuine stones, 1890 . . . . **275.00**
Sterling & jet bangle, 1900 . . . . **25.00**
Sterling w/green onyx stones & marcasites, 1925 . . . . **75.00**
Sterling w/gold wash, cut amythest, 1920 . . . . **50.00**
Sterling w/synthetic sapphires, 1910 . . . . **65.00**
Thunderbird design w/turquoise, Gallup, 1940 . . . . **135.00**
Victorian, gold link chain w/lock, 1900 . . . . **250.00**
Victorian, gold wash, 6 amythests, 1890 . . . . **75.00**
Zuni needlepoint in silver, hand-wrought, 1945 . . . . **150.00**
Bracelet & earrings set, Bakelite & chrome, Art Moderne, 1930 **28.00**
Bracelet & pin, gold finish w/simulated topaz & quartz, 1950 . **125.00**
Brooch, Art Deco, brass insect, w/glass stones, 1920 . . . . **15.00**
   Art Deco, green glass stones, brilliant white alloy **20.00**
   Art Deco, set w/chrysoprase, 1920 . . . . **18.00**
   Art Deco, silver w/enamel badge, 1915 . . . . **20.00**
   Art Deco, sterling free form, George Jensen **65.00**
   Art Deco, white alloy, set w/rhinestones **15.00**

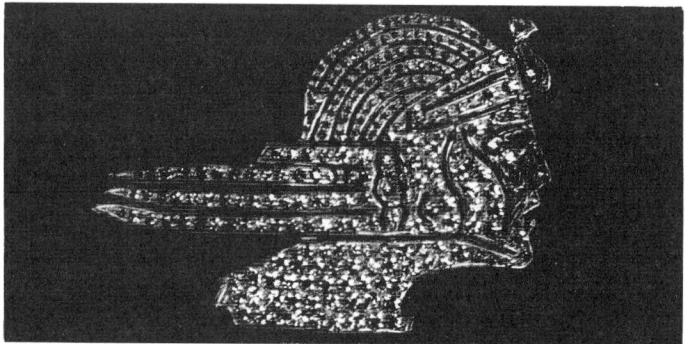

   Art Deco, white alloy, winged & helmeted Hermes **45.00**
   Art Moderne, gold plated, dog & lady w/chain, mkd Coro, 1940 **25.00**
   Art Nouveau, bumble bee in flight, carved horn **95.00**
   Art Nouveau, Charles Horner, enamel on sterling **125.00**
   Art Nouveau, copper & silver, 1910 . . . . **45.00**
   Art Nouveau, dragonfly, base metal, colored glass stone, 1910 **25.00**
   Art Nouveau, dragonfly, carved horn **150.00**
   Art Nouveau, embossing & repousse work, sterling **300.00**
   Art Nouveau, gilt over brass w/simulated topaz **35.00**
   Art Nouveau, gilt on brass, peacock-eye glass accent **75.00**

Art Nouveau, gold & enamel w/opal, 1910 . . . . **125.00**
Art Nouveau, gold wash on brass, set topaz, 1910 . . . . **35.00**
Art Nouveau, gold wash over brass amythest, 1900 . . . . **45.00**
Art Nouveau, gold, 4 mine-cut diamonds, Flore **425.00**
Art Nouveau, horn butterfly w/mock turquoise accent **350.00**
Art Nouveau, marked sterling, enameling **85.00**
Art Nouveau, marked sterling, George Jensen **95.00**
Art Nouveau, plique-a-jour enamel, marked sterling **850.00**
Art Nouveau, round w/Diane, sterling mk Unger Bros **185.00**
Art Nouveau, silver w/enamel, 1910 . . . . **20.00**
Art Nouveau, silver, intricate open work, sterling **450.00**
Art Nouveau, mother-of-pearl inlay, 1910 . . . . **50.00**
Art Nouveau, silver, 4x2½″, floral motif **60.00**
Art Nouveau, sterling & cloisonne, 1910 . . . . **35.00**
Art Nouveau, sterling dragonfly, plique-a-jour **450.00**
Art Nouveau, sterling portrait, 1910 . . . . **45.00**
Art Nouveau, sterling set w/hematite stone, 1910 . . . . **50.00**
Art Nouveau, sterling, gold wash, ½ moon & bat, Whiting & Co **225.00**
Art Nouveau, sterling w/gold wash, Unger Bros **350.00**
Art Nouveau, sterling w/gold wash, ½ shell w/pearl **400.00**
Art Nouveau, sterling w/lady's head, La Pierre Mfg Co **375.00**
Art Nouveau, sterling, w/female head, Unger Bros, Newark, N.J. **275.00**
Art Nouveau, thistle motif, Celtic, sterling **45.00**
Art Nouveau, w/simulated stones, gold wash, 1915 . . . . **45.00**
Art Nouveau, 900 silver w/lapis stone insect, 1910 . . . . **30.00**
Bohemian garnets set in 14k gold, 1900 . . . . **195.00**
Bohemian glass, flower form, mkd Coro, 1940 . . . . **20.00**
Cameo in copper & gold sculptured frame, 1860 . . . . **200.00**
Carved Bakelite, diamond shape, 1930 . . . . **5.00**
Cinnabar oval, engraved gold washed sterling, 1910 . . . . **50.00**
Coral branch in 14k gold wire mount, 1910 . . . . **25.00**
Decal on Limoges porcelain, brass frame, 1935 . . . . **25.00**
Enameled Dutch girls, child's, 1890 . . . . **15.00**
German silver floral mount cabochon-cut rose quartz, 1900 . . **20.00**
German silver, hand painted portrait, 1890 . . . . **20.00**
Gilt on brass, blue glass cluster, 1950 . . . . **25.00**
Gold frame, hand painted jet glass, sq, 1890 . . . . **95.00**
Gold frame, oval porcelain w/portrait, 1880 . . . . **85.00**
Gold memorial piece marble mosaic, contains lock of hair, 1890 **250.00**
Gold w/branch coral, 1910 . . . . **35.00**
Gold washed brass, ornate mount w/citrine TOC, 1900 . . . . . **30.00**
Gold washed silver, wht leaf open circle, 2 Trifari, 1940 . . . . **35.00**
Gold washed sterling bird on branch, paste turq & lapis, 1950 **35.00**
Half pearls in gold set w/rose-cut diamond in 'C', 1900 . . . . . **95.00**
Hand carved & painted, Scottie dog, 1930 . . . . **5.00**
Hand carved wood spread wing eagle, 1950 . . . . **5.00**
Hand painted porcelain, gold bead frame, 1875 . . . . **125.00**
Heavy gold frame, hp on porcelain, 1890 . . . . **125.00**
Jasperware, 14k yellow gold frame, Wedgwood, 1860 . . . . . . **165.00**
Jet, clasped hands w/mourning wreath, 1890 . . . . **50.00**
Jet, cut & faceted pair hearts in gold, 1890 . . . . **40.00**
Jet, large oval portrait, 1890 . . . . **95.00**
Jet, mourning, beads on wire, cluster, 1890 . . . . **25.00**
Jet, mourning, oval set w/marcasites, 1890 . . . . **75.00**
Marcasites & carnelian set in sterling, 1920 . . . . **65.00**
Moss agate set into engraved silver frame, 1930 . . . . **20.00**
Onyx cameo, 4 old mine cut diamonds, 1900 . . . . **500.00**
Polished wood & clear plastic, spread wing bird, 1935 . . . . **5.00**
Portrait in heavy Baroque gilt frame, 1900 . . . . **45.00**
Red & white onyx cameo, 1875 . . . . **700.00**
Rhinestone cluster, wax bead pearl drops, 1930 . . . . **25.00**
Rhodium & enamel free form leaves, buds, mkd MB, 1940 . . . **25.00**
Rhodium, rhinestones w/simulated pearls, 1950 . . . . **25.00**
Rubies & diamonds plique-a-jour butterfly, ivory face, Feuillatre **15,000.00**

Shell cameo, 14k gold, gypsy setting, 1920 . . . . **45.00**
Silver & gold, openwork rose cut diamonds, drop pearl, 1865 **275.00**
Silver w/gold wash, genuine amythest floral form, 1910 . . . **450.00**
Sterling, bar set, w/3 large chrysoprase & marcasites, 1925 . . . **75.00**
Sterling, bird on branch, engraved, repousse, 1930 . . . . **20.00**
Sterling, circle, open, side, w/coral & turq drops, 1920 . . . . . **40.00**
Sterling, 'Danecraft', flying bird, 4½", 1940 . . . . **75.00**
Sterling, George Jenson, Art Deco, 1925 . . . . **75.00**
Sterling w/amythest-cut stones, leaves, bug & buds, 1940 . . . . **35.00**
Sterling w/French paste stone cluster, 1950 . . . . **10.00**
Sterling & marcasite leaves, 1920 . . . . **75.00**
Sterling & marcasite scarab, 1900 . . . . **45.00**
Sterling & marcasite, Art Deco bow, 1920 . . . . **110.00**
Stylized Art Deco butterfly, enamel, 1920 . . . . **18.00**
Tortoise shell, pique work, set w/paste stones, 1925 . . . . **75.00**
Wedgwood w/gold chain & frame set w/seed pearls, 1875 . . . **200.00**
Wedgwood Jasperware, sterling frame, The Singer, 1880 . . . . . **95.00**
Wedgwood Jasperware, oval silver mounting, cupids at play, 1890 **125.00**
Wooden, hand-cut from Americus wood, cameo, 1935 . . . . **25.00**
Buckle, belt; Art Deco, gold wash, open oval, 1920 . . . . **55.00**
Art Deco, peacock motif, painted plastic, brilliants **65.00**
Art Deco, white alloy frame, triangle ends, set rhinestones . . . **15.00**
Art Nouveau, 2 pc, Japanese cloisonne w/florals **165.00**
Art Nouveau, 6 peacock-eye glass sets **75.00**
Art Nouveau, engraved sterling, coiled snakes, w/garnet, 1910 **65.00**
Art Nouveau, large, female head, coiled snake, gilt over brass **425.00**
Art Nouveau, large, swirling irises in marked sterling **95.00**
Steel beads, French, 1900 . . . . **35.00**
Buckle, hat; sterling filigree w/French jet center, 1900 . . . . **35.00**
Buckle, sash; Art Nouveau, gold washed, silver female head, 1900 **55.00**
Art Nouveau, gold washed, silver leaf frame w/paste amethyst . **85.00**
Sterling silver, ornate open square, 1920 . . . . **25.00**
Buckles, shoe; Art Nouveau, hand cut steel beads, Deco pattern **55.00**
Buttons, stud; man's 10k gold, engraved, 1900 . . . . **25.00**
Woman's, 10k gold w/chain, 1890 . . . . **75.00**
Cameo, shell, 14k gold frame, Moon Goddesses, Phoenix bird, 1950 **375.00**
Shell, claw-set, gold w/pendant loop, 1910 . . . . **75.00**
Shell, simple gold cage, 1910 . . . . **100.00**
Chain, double-strand, 10k solid gold, 1900 . . . . **450.00**
Watch or knife, 10k Roman gold, 1920 . . . . **15.00**
Chain, vest; low karat gold heavy links, 1870 . . . . **200.00**
Chain, w/slide; 14k gold flat link chain w/tab, 1910 . . . . **450.00**
14k gold, slide w/pearls & rubies, 1890 . . . . **250.00**
14k gold, w/garnets, opal & pearls, 1900 . . . . **250.00**
Chain, watch; 14k gold, ornamental flat link chain, 1900 . . . . . **110.00**
Art Nouveau, gilt over brass, vermeil **65.00**
Chain, watch w/slide, Art Nouveau, rolled & plated gold **250.00**
Charm, 14k engraved w/inscription, period couple, 1911 . . . . . . **45.00**
Charms, set of 7, sterling hunter, African animals, 1930 . . . . . **75.00**
Charms, four, sterling and enamel, Christian symbols, 1890 . . . . **85.00**
Chatelaine, spectacle case, sterling, 1905 . . . . **185.00**
Clip, hat or fur, gold wash, large, paste aquamarine, 1940 . . . **20.00**
Clip, dress; Art Deco, gold wash, feather motif, metalic head, 1925 **15.00**
Art Moderne, Bakelite & metal, 1925 . . . . **7.00**
Art Moderne, chrome, leaves and red berries, 1935 . . . . **10.00**
Bakelite, 3 diagonal bars, 1935 . . . . **5.00**
Cinnabar, mkd made in China, 1920 . . . . **35.00**
Gold wash, Etruscan work w/simulated stones, 1930 . . . . **10.00**
Sculptured brass florals w/filigree backing, 1930 . . . . **15.00**
Set w/blue glass leaf, rhinestone trim, 1930 . . . . **10.00**
With simulated diamonds & sapphire Art Deco, 1930 . . . . **10.00**
Clip, fur; enamel w/rhinestones, 1930 . . . . **25.00**
Coin carrier, engraved sterling, w/chain, small, 1910 . . . . **55.00**
Coin carrier & compact, sterling, w/carrying chain, 1900 . . . . . **85.00**

Comb, celluloid, English, Art Deco fan shape, 1925 . . . . **45.00**
Celluloid, French, Art Nouveau, small, 1900 . . . . **20.00**
Decorative, celluloid, Art Nouveau, 2 prong, 1900 . . . . **45.00**

Faux tortoise, w/gilt brass & turq glass, pr **75.00**
Ivory, intricate bird carving, oriental, Victorian, 1860 . . . . . . **135.00**
Rodium and rhinestones, small, 1940 . . . . **10.00**
Sterling, fan shape, French Victorian, 1860 . . . . **225.00**
Tortoise, English w/pique work, Victorian, 1890 . . . . **60.00**
Comb, back; celluloid, French paste, notched ½ circle, 1890 . . . **55.00**
French ivory w/paste stones ornate, Art Nouveau, 1910 . . . . . **55.00**
Jet black glass, lacy fan sections, Victorian, 1910 . . . . **20.00**
Large tortoise, scrolls & brilliants, Spanish, 1870 . . . . **110.00**
Pierced design w/zig-zag decor, Art Deco, 1920 . . . . **45.00**
Tortoise w/jade butterfly form, French, Art Nouveau, 1910 . . . **95.00**
Tortoise, English lattice w/floral, 1890 . . . . **135.00**
Comb, side; celluloid, Art Deco, blue brilliants, open work, 1925 **20.00**
Celluloid, Victorian, blue brilliants & scrolls, sm, 1890 . . . . . . **15.00**
Cross, bog oak, hand carved, 1880 . . . . **75.00**
Gold w/simulated cabochon-cut sapphire, 1900 . . . . **175.00**
Gold wash, w/topaz-color glass stones, 1930 . . . . **35.00**
Gold, engraved w/ivy motif, 1920 . . . . **65.00**
Hollow gold, Etruscan type, applied-design work, 1890 . . . . . **250.00**
Silver florals, w/turquoise centers, 1930 . . . . **45.00**
Sterling & jet w/glass bezel-set enclosure, 1860 . . . . **85.00**
Cross & chain, old gold filled, w/amythests, 1895 . . . . **150.00**
Gold thread chain, Gothic cross, 1930 . . . . **75.00**
Cuff links, gold, engraved, snail shell in sterling, burnished **35.00**
Rare collector's piece w/photo, 1910 . . . . **15.00**
Earrings, Art Deco Bakelite, beads, elongated triangles, 1930 . . **10.00**
Art Deco, drops, gilt over brass frames, molded Czech glass . . **25.00**
Art Deco, transition to moderne, enamel & chrome, 1930 . . . . **25.00**
Art Nouveau hoops w/female head 14k w/bezel-set opals, 1x1" **425.00**
Black & wht onyx cameo, gold w/gold wire, 1885 . . . . **150.00**
Brass, w/imitation jade, Phoenix bird motif, 1920 . . . . **15.00**
French jet glass tear-drop w/gold wire, 1880 . . . . **75.00**
Garnet clusters, small drops, w/stud wires, 1920 . . . . **85.00**
Gold w/black enamel w/gold wire, 1850 . . . . **100.00**
Gold wash, scroll-leaf both ends of ear wire, made by Cartier, 1930 **35.00**
Jet glass triangles & rhinestones, screw-type, sm, 1930 . . . . . . **5.00**
Jet w/wire for pierced ears, teardrop style, 1900 . . . . **35.00**
Marcasite in sterling, 1920 . . . . **25.00**
Marcasites in sterling w/bead drops, 1920 . . . . **40.00**
Millefiori beads set in Florentine silver drops, 1910 . . . . **10.00**
Silver mesh drops, screw backs, 1940 . . . . **25.00**
Sterling w/emerald-color Bohemian glass w/marcasites, drops, 1920 **75.00**
Victorian, gold w/plunger stud wires, drops, 1860 . . . . **95.00**
Victorian, 14k gold, coral beads, Etruscan work, drops **165.00**
Victorian, 14k gold filigree w/seed pearl drops, 1885 . . . . **135.00**
With clips, Art Deco, inverted 'V's w/large bottom stone **125.00**
With posts, Art Deco, sterling w/marcasites, long tiered drops **125.00**

Earrings & bar pin set, gold w/half pearls, 1860 . . . . **150.00**
Earrings, bracelet, brooch; gold washed silver, gr enamel leaves, 1950 **65.00**
Fob, Art Nouveau, gold wash, female head, 1898 . . . . **50.00**
 Gold, scalloped and bezel-set, glass photo insert, 1920 . . . . . . **50.00**
 Man's, grosgrain, pendant w/rubies, gold engraved, frame, 1920 **25.00**
 Man's, grosgrain, narrow w/tiny gold buckle, low karat gold, 1910 **20.00**
Glasses, lorgnette; w/good frame & chain, 1925 . . . . **85.00**
Glove holder, gold mesh, clasp & tassel & finger ring, 1890 . . . . **65.00**
Hatband or sash ornament, rhinestone & gilt wire sunburst, 1915 **20.00**
Holder, pendant-type for fan, lorgnette, Nouveau, 14k, female form **850.00**
Lavaliere, 14k gold, 3 rings & chain w/half pearls, 1925 . . . . . . **100.00**
 14k gold, triangle w/coral cameo, pearl drop gold chain **150.00**
 Art Deco, sterling set w/sq sodalite gemstones, marcasites . . . **115.00**
 Art Nouveau, 14k, 1¼" scroll center, ½" jade drop w/2 pearls **385.00**
 Art Nouveau, gold, sm amythest cluster & seed pearls, 1900 **135.00**
 Art Nouveau, lg turquoise cab, chains, gilt over brass, F&B . **275.00**
 Art Nouveau, elongated triangle, gold w/opal & half pearls, chain **150.00**
 Art Nouveau, Jablonec rivited cut blk glass on wire frame . . . **350.00**
 Art Nouveau, mosaic floral in gilded hand wrought silver **85.00**
 Art Nouveau, 14k, set w/peridots, pearls & ruby **525.00**
 Art Nouveau, sterling, bottle shape, enamel disks, pearl drop . **75.00**
 White gold filigree, camphor glass w/diamond, 1890 . . . . **95.00**
Locket, 3 color gold wash, vine w/wax bead pearls, 1900 . . . . . . **35.00**
 Gold wash set w/Persian turquoise, 1850 . . . . **35.00**
 Gold wash w/chain of gold nuggets, 1910 . . . . **250.00**
 Gold-filled, w/smoke-color rhinestones, 1915 . . . . **25.00**
 Sterling engraved, w/sterling chain, 1896 . . . . **75.00**
Locket & chain, imitation tortoise-shell w/loop chain, 1920 . . . . **30.00**
Lorgnette, Art Nouveau, gold wash over brass, 1895 . . . . **75.00**
Necklaces, 3-strand branch coral bits, 1920 . . . . **125.00**
 Amber color Bohemian glass beads, single strand, 1920 . . . . . **25.00**
 Amythest color beads w/glass ring inset, 1920 . . . . **65.00**
 Art Deco, Bohemian cut & faceted glass **45.00**
 Art Deco, Bohemian glass beads w/larger 2 color squares **35.00**
 Art Deco, brass w/Bakelite beads & large pendant, 1925 . . . . . **50.00**
 Art Deco, Czech pink foiled glass w/enamel & filigree drops . **75.00**
 Art Deco, enameled vermeil, silver over copper **150.00**
 Art Deco, gilt over brass, Egyptian, triangles w/glass beads . . **450.00**

Art Deco, silver on copper w/enameling, 3 'V' sections **225.00**
Art Deco, silver tube beads w/mock lapis beads & bar, drop . **165.00**
Art Moderne, Bakelite & celluloid, 1925 . . . . **60.00**
Art Moderne, Bakelite & chrome, 1930 . . . . **85.00**
Art Nouveau, amber & pink waxbase pearls w/drop, 1915 . . . . **25.00**
Art Nouveau, blue enamel on silver w/blister pearls, free form **350.00**
Art Nouveau, damescene butterfly center w/drop, 1910 . . . . . . **65.00**
Art Nouveau, enamel on sterling squares w/connecting chains **2,800.00**
Art Nouveau, green Czech glass w/enameled leaves **55.00**
Art Nouveau, sterling-14k, moonstones & amythest **850.00**
Blood coral, 2 rows round beads between long faceted, 1935 **285.00**
Bohemian garnets, center section on gold chain, 1895 . . . . . **250.00**
Carnelian & marcasite in sterling, 1925 . . . . **125.00**

Festoon type, gold w/Persian turquoise cabs & pearls, 1895 . **950.00**
Festoon type, silver & gold, rose cut diamond, snake chain . **300.00**
Gilt, lapis-color glass w/enamel Czech, 1920 . . . . **85.00**
Gold washed, synthetic coral, Victorian style, 1930 . . . . **75.00**
Green enameling & faux jade in silver Mayan style mounts . . **35.00**
Paste stones in rhodium, large tiered center cluster **35.00**
Pendant w/coral bead, gold beaded links, 1850 . . . . **500.00**
Tortoise shell w/locket, 1890 . . . . **125.00**
Victorian, w/amythest teardrop stones, 1900 . . . . **285.00**
Necklace & bracelet set, w/Peking glass & French paste, 1925 **100.00**
Necklace & earrings set, Art Moderne, rhodium , fine wire fringe **35.00**
 Bohemian glass, multi strand, faceted beads, tiny-med, Weisse, 1950 **50.00**
 Gold washed silver, heavy drop w/turq & coral inlay, 1950 . **175.00**
 Rhinestone & imitation emeralds, 1950 . . . . **100.00**
 Squash Blossom, Zuni cluster turquoise, 1940 . . . . **650.00**
Necklace & ring set, kachina, hand-inlaid in silver, 1940 . . . . **950.00**
Necklace, beads; 10" strand of matched size garnets, 1920 . . . . **40.00**
 12" strand, graduated garnets, 1920 . . . . **70.00**
 Amber, Baltic, 1920 . . . . **275.00**
 Amythest color seed beads, 1920 . . . . **55.00**
 Amythest quartz beads w/silk tassels, 1920 . . . . **85.00**
 Art glass type beads w/gold flecks, 1930 . . . . **100.00**
 Bohemian citrine color, gilt findings, 1930 . . . . **35.00**
 Bohemian garnets, 3-stranded, 1910 . . . . **225.00**
 Bohemian-cut & polished jet rope, 1895 . . . . **100.00**
 Camelian, hand-carved, single-strand, 1920 . . . . **125.00**
 Ceylon jade, 1900 . . . . **125.00**
 Ceylon jade, w/gold wash over silver, 1915 . . . . **85.00**
 Cherry amber, hand-cut, 1890 . . . . **250.00**
 Crochet w/glass ring & bead weights, 1920 . . . . **65.00**
 Crochet, Bohemian beads, long rope, 1930 . . . . **45.00**
 Cut & faceted amber, 1920 . . . . **150.00**
 Cut crystals, rondell-type, quartz, 1925 . . . . **150.00**
 Ebony wood beads, 1925 . . . . **15.00**
 Faceted French jet, Bohemian **35.00**
 Fresh water pearls & oriental jade, 1930 . . . . **3,800.00**
 Mikimoto cultured pearls, 1950 . . . . **100.00**
 Milkglass w/clear glass bead weights, 1920 . . . . **65.00**
 Peking glass, Venetian, 1930 . . . . **35.00**
 Venetian iridescent beads, 1925 . . . . **100.00**
 With Cabochon clasp set in sterling, 1920 . . . . **75.00**
 With gilt pierced links & rhinestones, 1930 . . . . **30.00**
Ornament, hat, coral plastic w/simulated stones, 1935 . . . . **10.00**
 Floral design w/imitation stones, 3½", 1935 . . . . **15.00**
 Jeweled sword, Florenga, 1950 . . . . **25.00**
 Pearl & Peking glass beads, rhinestone accent, 1925 . . . . **8.00**
 Rhinestones & simulated pearls, 4¾", 1925 . . . . **10.00**
Ornament, sash; Art Nouveau, w/simulated jade & hasp, 1910 . . **15.00**
 Gilt, Art Nouveau w/simulated ruby, 1910 . . . . **20.00**
 Paste stones set in cups w/gilt wire, 1915 . . . . **25.00**
Pendant, Art Deco, gilt on brass basket w/glass moonstone floral, 1930 **15.00**
 Art Deco, sterling; summer, youth; obverse: winter, old age . **175.00**
 Art Deco, vermeil, silver over copper, enamel abstract **55.00**
 Art Nouveau, 14k, champleve tulip, 5 diamonds **895.00**
 Art Nouveau, 14k, extended lily & female w/diamond & emerald **685.00**
 Art Nouveau, 14k, mermaid, enamel w/diamond **585.00**
 Art Nouveau, 14k, w/blister pearls **485.00**
 Art Nouveau, floral enamel, sterling w/drop, English **300.00**
 Art Nouveau, lady on lily pad, 14k enamel w/diamond **685.00**
 Art Nouveau, plique-a-jour daffodil w/diamond & pearl drop . **385.00**
 Art Nouveau, plique-a-jour gold washed silver, 2 pc w/mirror **2,000.00**
 Brass & Bakelite w/grosgrain, King Tut motif, 1925 . . . . **55.00**
 Cameo w/fresh-water pearls, w/chain, 1895 . . . . **125.00**
 Enamel & silver w/gold wash, good luck symbol, 1897 . . . . . . **65.00**

Gilt over brass frame, hp miniature porcelain, 1890 . . . . **75.00**
Gold wash, w/simulated moonstones & garnets, 1920 . . . . **40.00**
Jade & coral w/fine link chain, 1900 . . . . **75.00**
Molded plastic cameo & link chain, 1920 . . . . **30.00**
Oriental jade angel fish w/14k gold chain, 1925 . . . . **75.00**
Pendant w/chain, 14k gold framed, carved shell cameo, lg triangle **250.00**
14k plique-a-jour wings, female form, pearl drop **585.00**
14k plique-a-jour wings, female head, pearl drop, diamond **1,250.00**
14k wht gold, diamonds & sapphire, sm, 1925 . . . . **185.00**
Art Deco, platinum w/diamonds **1,750.00**
Art Deco, sterling w/chysoprase cab & marcasites **95.00**
Art Nouveau, 14k, 2 profiles joined w/opal **485.00**
Art Nouveau, 14k gold w/seed pearls & drop, Arts & Crafts . **750.00**

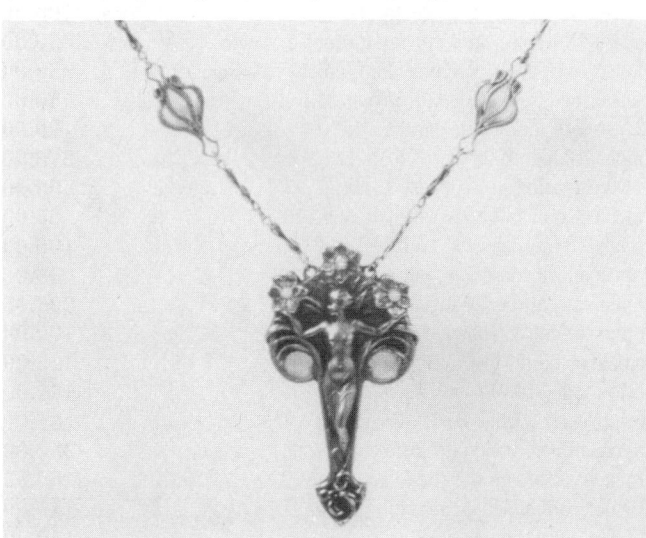

Art Nouveau, 14k, plique-a-jour, female, diamonds, opals . . **1,250.00**
Art Nouveau, 14k set w/emeralds, Butterfly Lady **785.00**
Art Nouveau, carved horn dragonfly w/claw-set moonstone . . **600.00**
Art Nouveau, enamel on sterling, insect, Charles Horner **235.00**
Art Nouveau, floating blue enamel on silver, Charles Horner **250.00**
Art Nouveau, plique-a-jour on silver, drop ring, Fahrner . . **2,500.00**
Art Nouveau, sterling female head, scrolls **375.00**
Pin, Art Nouveau, collar pin, blue enamel, Horner **35.00**
Twisted wire, 14k gold, 1900 . . . . **200.00**
Pin, Bar; Art Deco, plastic, 1925 . . . . **10.00**
Art Deco, platinum, diamonds & amythests **1,500.00**
Black onyx, gold floral, half pearls, 1895 . . . . **125.00**
Cut & faceted garnets, 1900 . . . . **65.00**
Jet w/pearls, 1890 . . . . **150.00**
Plastic, scarab center, 1925 . . . . **10.00**
Sterling & marcasite, geometric design, 1920 . . . . **65.00**
White gold w/platinum top, w/diamond, 1900 . . . . **95.00**
Pin, breast; 14k gold, set w/ruby & pearls, 1910 . . . . **75.00**
Low karat gold w/Bohemian garnets, sm, 1920 . . . . **85.00**
Pin, hair; 10k gold w/chain and loop, 1920 . . . . **25.00**
Art Deco, Bakelite, ornate, 1925 . . . . **15.00**
Celluloid w/French paste, Art Moderne, 1930 . . . . **10.00**
Fleur-de-lis, tortoise, Art Nouveau, 1910 . . . . **20.00**
Tortoise w/14k heavy gold piercework, 1870 . . . . **110.00**
Pin, scarf; gold plate, synthetic stone, 1920 . . . . **10.00**
Gold wire circular design, 1920 . . . . **45.00**
Goldstone, 1910 . . . . **15.00**
Rhodium tassels, mid-Victorian piece, 1950 . . . . **25.00**
Pin, tie; German silver w/synthetic stones, 1920 . . . . **10.00**
Gold cross, 14k, 1910 . . . . **35.00**
Gold plate, half pearls, 1920 . . . . **35.00**
Locket-type w/photos, 10k gold, 1910 . . . . **65.00**

Pin, watch; half pearls & diamond center, 1895 . . . . **175.00**
Heavy gold, sculptured & engraved, 1900 . . . . **75.00**
Woman's, gold set w/diamonds, 1900 . . . . **375.00**
Pin w/watch hook, Art Nouveau, female head, sterling w/gold wash **375.00**
Ring, 18k engraved gold set w/emerald & pearl, 1860 . . . . . . **100.00**
Art Deco, enamel & gold, 1925 . . . . **125.00**
Art Nouveau, 14k, full female face w/1 diamond & 2 rubies . **435.00**
Art Nouveau, 14k, head w/4 diamonds in hair **385.00**
Art Nouveau, female head, 14k, diamond & rubies in hair . . **385.00**
Baroque engraving set w/opal & *pave'* diamonds, 1900 . . . . . **200.00**
'Dragon's Breath' in sterling, 1930 . . . . **45.00**
Gold w/cabochon-cut garnet, 1910 . . . . **85.00**
Gold w/claw-set ruby doublet, 1900 . . . . **75.00**
Gold w/genuine emeralds & pearls, 1890 . . . . **150.00**
Gold w/Persian turquoise & half pearls, 1890 . . . . **85.00**
Marcasite & onyx in sterling, 1920 . . . . **50.00**
 Marcasite & sterling, 1930 . . . . **50.00**
Marcasite & jade in sterling, 1920 . . . . **45.00**
Scarf holder, Art Nouveau, silver w/gilt slide w/stickpin back . . . **35.00**
Slide, gold, for fan chain, set w/jet & agate, rare, 1880 . . . . . . **75.00**
Stickpin, Art Nouveau, all gold carat **135.00**
Studs, woman's, porcelain blouse studs, 1890 . . . . **35.00**
Vanity case, Art deco, nickel w/gold wash, for coins, lipstick, 1925 **125.00**
Sterling, engraved w/floral enamel, for rouge, 1925 . . . . **35.00**

Jewelry Boxes

Jewelry boxes of a long rectangular form, usually on legs and designed in the Art Nouveau style, are called jewelry caskets. Today, these have become popular collectibles.

Art Nouveau, gilded w/pink satin lining, 3x4½" **28.00**
Brass, gilded w/Limoges portrait inserts, 5" **950.00**
Hinged lid, Art Nouveau style, jeweled w/hp portrait, 6x5" . . . **50.00**
Bronze, gilded, ornate embossed decor, maidens scene in relief . **60.00**
Gilded, ornately embossed, classical maidens in relief **60.00**
Casket, Art Nouveau, copper metal, 2½x3x2½" **20.00**
Brass, octagonal top, scroll handle on lid **60.00**
Casket, cobalt, lion head ormolu legs, enamelled florals, gold **175.00**
Dore bronze, floral inlaid medallions, satin lined, 1885 . . . **1,625.00**

Gold metal, Art Nouveau styling, 3½x5½" **45.00**
Plated, scrolls in relief, 2½x4", illus **30.00**
Silver plated, Victorian figural cherubs, bail **100.00**
Chinese, teakwood & MOP inlay, floral decor, 1800s, 11x16x29" **250.00**
Glass, foiled blue w/enamelled beading & silver embossed ormolu **435.00**
Ruby w/wht enamelled florals, ormolu feet, brass trim **250.00**
Ivory, braided decor, hinged Sheffield lid, round, 3½" **165.00**

Silver plated, ornate, footed, orig blue satin lining, signed Tuffts **35.00**
 Ornate bird & cherub on top, round ormolu feet **195.00**
Sterling, allover floral engraving, monogram, velvet lining **250.00**
Victorian, papier-mache & MOP inlay, floral motifs, 1860, 4x11x8″ **170.00**

John Rogers

 John Rogers was a machinist from Manchester, New Jersey, who turned his hobby of sculpting into a financially successful venture. From the originals he meticulously fashioned from red clay, he made molds and cast plaster copies which he painted in dull grey to suggest a metal composition. He specialized in large detailed groupings that portrayed scenes of everyday life as he saw it during the mid 1850s.

Charity Patient **350.00**
Chess **700.00**
Council of War, 24″ **700.00**

Favored Scholar **550.00**
Fetching the Doctor **700.00**
Going for the Cows **350.00**
One More Shot **300.00**
Playing Doctor **650.00**
Returned Volunteer **500.00**
Rip Van Winkle at Home **400.00**
Rip Van Winkle on the Mountain **500.00**
Taking the Oath **600.00**
The Checker Players **650.00**
The Elder's Daughter, late 1800s **600.00**
The Fugitive's Story, 22″ **500.00**
Uncle Ned's School **375.00**

Jugtown

 The Jugtown Pottery was started about 1920 by Juliana and Jacques Busbee, in Moore Co., N.C. Ben Owen, a young descendant of a Staffordshire potter, was hired in 1923. He was the master potter, while the Busbees experimented with perfecting glazes and supervising design and modeling. Preferred shapes were those reminiscent of traditional country wares, and classic Oriental forms. Glazes were various: natural clay oranges, buffs, 'tobacco spit' brown, mirror black, white, frogskin green, a lovely turquoise called Chinese blue, and the traditional cobalt decorated salt glaze. The pot-

tery gained national recognition and as a result of their success several other local potteries were established. Jugtown closed in 1959.

Baking dish, fluted, brown, 1970s, 3x11½″ **35.00**
Bowl, fluted edge, wht, Chinese translation, 4x7¾″ **75.00**
 Salt glaze w/Chinese blue interior, 3x7½″ **75.00**
 Salt glaze w/blue gloss interior, floral stencil, 3x5″ **35.00**
 White, Oriental, crimped edge, 2x6″ **55.00**
Bowl vase, Chinese translation, gray stone w/wht drip, 3½″ **70.00**
Candlesticks, mirror black, 1970s, pr, 12″ **45.00**
Cup, no handles, salt glaze, 3x3½″ **12.00**
Jug, frogskin, 4″ **28.00**
Pie plate, fluted, brown, 1970s, 9½″ dia **20.00**
Pitcher, salt glaze, blue decor on gray, mkd, 4½x5″ **40.00**
Salt shaker, chicken figural, hand made, orange, 1930s, 5″ . . . **120.00**
Teapot, w/sugar & creamer, orange glaze, 1970s, 7½ & 5″ **50.00**
Vase, blue & black gloss drip over red clay, mkd, 5x4″ **75.00**
 Chinese blue, 3½x1½″ **45.00**
 Chinese blue, blue/green glaze, 7½x4½″ **200.00**
 Chinese blue, impressed mark, 4x2″ **65.00**
 Chinese translation, plum w/wht drip, 4½x6″ **150.00**
 Chinese translation, wht glossy drip over brown, ovoid, 5½″ . . **80.00**
 Chinese white, 6x5″ **110.00**
 Gourd, frogskin, 6½″ **65.00**
 Green frogskin glaze, oriental blank, 5x3″ **35.00**
 Green, impressed circular mark, 4x3″ **38.00**
 Thick wht glaze, dimpled, 6″ **35.00**

KPM Porcelain

 Under the tutelage of Frederick the Great, King of Prussia, porcelain manufacture was instituted in Berlin in 1751 by William K. Wegeley. In jealous competition with Meissen, hard paste porcelain was produced---dinnerware, figurines, vases, etc---some of which was undecorated while other pieces were hand painted in Watteau scenes, landscapes or florals. Never able to seriously compete, the King withdrew his support and the factory failed in 1757.
 In 1761, Johann Ernst Gotzkowsky bought the rights and attempted a similar operation which soon failed due to financial difficulties. Still determined to gain the same recognition enjoyed by Meissen, the King bought the plant in 1763, and ruled the operation with an iron hand, often assuring his success by taking advantage of his position. The King died in 1786, but production has continued and quality tableware and decorative porcelains are still being made on a commercial basis.
 Earliest marks were simply G or W, followed by the sceptre mark. After 1830, KPM with an orb or eagle was adopted.

Bowl, covered, portrait, turquoise w/gold handles **225.00**
 Trefoil server, allover floral, gold trim, 10x12½″ **180.00**
 White, melon ribs, twig handles, oval, 9x7½″ **45.00**
Cake set, pastel blue & yellow floral, Silesia, 8 pc **150.00**
Candleholder, finger ring, wht w/pink & cream roses, gold, mkd, 3x5″ **60.00**
Chamberstick, highly decorated, 1883 . . . . **230.00**
Cup & saucer, demitasse, Royal Ivory, The Claridge **27.50**
Dessert set, wht w/pink flowers, gold rim, 27 pc **325.00**
Figurine, 2 dancers, incised Conte, sgnd, 7x12″ **70.00**
 Classical youth, mkd, 1830-1840 . . . . **650.00**
 Cleopatra **2,000.00**
 Geisha w/removable parasol, 9½″ **110.00**
 Madonna & Child **700.00**
 Shepherd boy carrying lamb, wht, 4¼″ **70.00**
 Tiger, applied flowers, leaf base, 4½″ **100.00**
 White w/blk & gold decor, Empire dress, mkd, 8½x3½″ pr . **495.00**
Freedom bell, ltd ed, 1950 . . . . **60.00**

Plaque, Judith w/head of Holofernes, 13x11″ **2,900.00**
    Marie Antoinette w/children, sgnd Knoeller, 9½x6″ **1,900.00**
    'Psyche', sgnd Wagner **2,700.00**

Young soldier, late 19th century, 11″ **1,500.00**
Plate, open handled, #626, wht w/pink & green floral, 10½″ ... **45.00**
Platter, lady & man scenic, open handles, 12½x17¾″ **495.00**
Portrait, girl, oval, frame, 6¼x9½″ **950.00**
Powder box, round, gold & floral painting, 3″ dia **55.00**
Soup bowl, heavy gold, pink roses, sgnd, 7¾″ **15.00**
Sugar & creamer, blue w/gold design, mkd, sgnd Kuykendall ... **75.00**
Sweet meat dish, painted floral on pink, gold, 11″ **90.00**
Vase, w/serpent handles, flower & leaf, 18½″ **1,200.00**

Kate Greenaway

Kate Greenaway was an English artist who lived from 1846 to 1901. She gained world wide fame as an illustrator of children's books, drawing children clothed in the styles worn by proper English and American boys and girls of the very early 1800s. Her book, *Under the Willow Tree*, published in 1878, was the first of many. Her sketches appeared in leading magazines, and her greeting cards were in great demand. Manufacturers of china, pottery and metal products copied her characters to decorate children's dishes, tiles, salt and pepper shakers, as well as many other items.

Almanac, 1885 .... **110.00**
    1887, Geo Routledge **65.00**
    1924, hard cover **35.00**
Birthday Book **35.00**
Book, alphabet, ca 1880, mint **65.00**
    Little Ann & other poems, Frederick Warne & Co **50.00**
    Mother Goose, mkd 'Author's Edition', fair **75.00**

Child's set, 3 pc, Germany **125.00**

Chocolate set, in orig basket, rare **225.00**
Inkwell, figural boy behind hinged nest w/eggs, metal, 3″ **65.00**
Print, 'The Little Jumping Girls', signed, 2½x5½″ **20.00**
Print, 'The Pied Piper of Hamlin' **60.00**
Statue, Grandpa, gold leathering at base, 6″ **65.00**
Toothpick holder, Meriden #43 .... **85.00**
Top hat, bisque w/3 girls sitting on brim, w/flowers **95.00**

Keen Kutter

Keen Kutter was a brand name of E.C. Simmons Hardware, used from about 1870 until the mid 1930s. In 1923, Winchester merged with Simmons, but continued to produce Keen Kutter marked knives and tools. The merger dissolved and in 1940 the Simmons Company was purchased by Shapligh Hardware. Older items are very collectible.

Advertisement, paper; 2 sided, lawn mowers & tools, 15x20″ ... **24.00**
    2 sided, pocket knives, & hand tools, 15x20″ **28.00**
    Tools-Cutlery-Mowers, 15x43″ **20.00**
Ax, double bit, head shows no use, never ground **45.00**
Box opener **15.00**
Brace & bit **35.00**
Brace, corner, #K300 .... **195.00**
Brace **35.00**
Breast drill **30.00**
Can opener, cast still, single blade, pre-1918 .... **38.00**
Carpenter's pencil **12.00**
Carving set, knife & fork, stag handle **45.00**
Catalog, 1935, EC Simmons, hard bound; 2,118 pgs **380.00**
Chisel, wood, ¼″ **28.00**
    ½″, plastic handle **25.00**
Cork screw **18.00**
File, flat **10.00**
Food chopper, hand held, 2 blade **28.00**
Hammer, claw, small **15.00**
    Curved claw, octagon head, 16 oz **32.00**
    Sawset **13.00**
    Straight claw, 16 oz **30.00**
Hatchet, broad head **30.00**
Key, KK emblem, punched for key ring **20.00**
Knife, boning, 6″ blade **20.00**
    Hunting, leather laminated handle, leather sheath, Schrade ... **55.00**
    Pocket, Grand Dad's Barlow, blk plastic, brass lined, Schrade **25.00**
    Pocket, Old Timer, 3 blade, stag handle, Schrade **35.00**
    Set, Kountry Kitchen, 3-pc, 3″, 6″, 8″ blade **45.00**
    Steel **15.00**
Level, w/brass ends **35.00**
Meat cleaver **40.00**
Nail clippers **25.00**
Nail set, 1/16″ point, #1217 .... **9.00**
Padlock, KK emblem shape, bronze cast **94.00**
    Brass **55.00**
    Bronze cast w/word Simmons **48.00**
Plane, block, 6″ **25.00**
Pliers, slip joint **12.00**
Razor, safety, by Christy, w/orig box & instructions **12.00**
    Orig box **15.00**
    With velvet lined box, 1x2x4¼″ **18.00**
Razor hone, K-15, w/metal box, round corners **28.00**
Ruler, folding, brass ends, 2 ft **14.00**
Saw, hand **25.00**
Scissors, barber shears, 7½″ **22.50**
    Bent trimmer, 6″ **16.50**
    Bent trimmer, 9″ **20.00**

Scissors, button hole, 4½″ **22.00**
Mule shears, 10¼″ **28.00**
Straight trimmer, 6″ **11.50**
Straight trimmer, 7″ **19.00**
Screwdriver, cabinet, #3542, 8″ **21.00**
Phillips, #3548, 6″ blade **16.00**
Stubby, #3503 .... **12.00**
Scribe, wooden **20.00**
Sharpening steel, for carving knife **20.00**
Shears, 7½″ **5.00**
Used for boning chicken **25.00**
Sign, ci, raised letters, 4x4″ **25.00**
Silverware, service for 6, in orig dovetailed oak box **45.00**
Spade, tiling, 14x16″ blade **20.00**
Square, K3, 16x24″ **40.00**
Small **22.00**
Wood auger bit, #5 .... **12.00**
#16 .... **18.00**
Wood chisel **14.00**
Wrench, crescent, mkd Shapleighs, 10″ **13.00**
Monkey, black jack, 6″ **40.00**
Pipe, 18″ **50.00**
Yardstick, w/KK advertising **10.00**

Kelva

    Kelva was a trademark of the C.F. Monroe Co. of Meriden, Conn., used on an opaque mold blown glassware that was hand decorated with pastel florals and often set in ormolu holders. It was very similar to the company's other lines, Nakara and Wave Crest; only those pieces bearing the Kelva mark are listed here. All three types were in production from about 1900 until WWI.

Box, blue w/pink floral decor on hinged lid, 2x3½″ **250.00**
Enameled azaleas, brass frame w/North Wind decor, 5″ dia . **460.00**

Floral on pink, 2½″ **250.00**
Moss leaf decor w/pink & wht florals, 4″ dia **300.00**
Rose color w/orchid decor, repousse brass fittings, hinged .. **340.00**
Wht w/enameled florals, ormolu rims & ft, hinged lid, 4½″ sq **330.00**
Humidor, green w/enameled florals, gold trim & 'Cigars', hinged lid **465.00**
Jardiniere, green w/enameled azaleas, ornate brass rim, large .. **400.00**
Planter, mottled green w/enamel lilies, ormolu collar & ft, 8″ wide **475.00**
Vase, green-grey w/enameled florals, ormolu handles & ft, 14″. **535.00**
Mottled apricot w/enameled carnations, silver rim, 8″ **185.00**
Vases, florals on pink, 6″, pr, illus **675.00**

Kenton Hills

    Kenton Hills Porcelain was established in 1940 in Erlanger, Ky., by Harold Bopp, former Rookwood superintendent, and David Seyler, noted artist and sculptor. Native clay was used; glazes were very similar to those that were currently being used at Rookwood. The work was of high quality, but because of the restrictions imposed on needed material due to the onset of the war, the operation failed in 1942. Much of the ware is artist signed and marked with the Kenton Hill name and shape number.

Lamp base, Lotus, peach-beige ground, sgnd Hentschel, 12½x6″ **350.00**
Vase, #109, fish & bubbles, Stratton, 8″ **475.00**
#125, florals, Stratton, 6x4½″ **385.00**

Keramos

Bowl, w/poppies, swastika mk, 4x10″ **60.00**

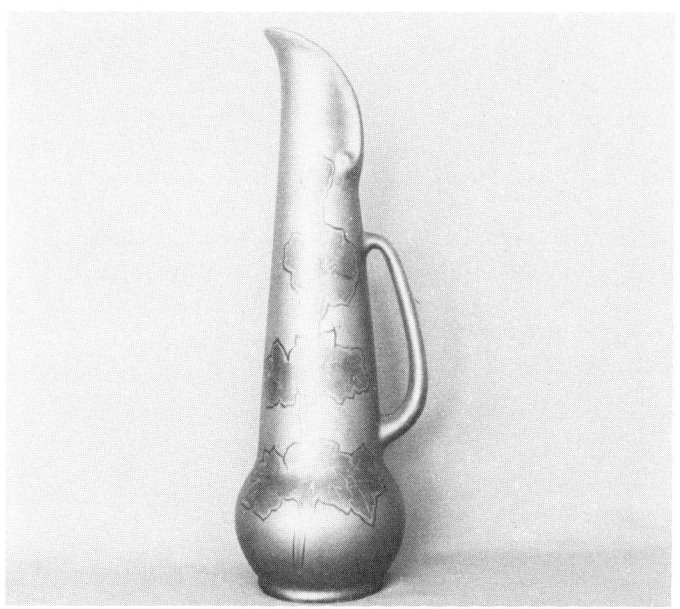

Ewer, swastika mk, gold lustre, 13″ **600.00**
Vase, decal of cavalier & lady, wht/pink, hi-gloss, 7½″ **115.00**
Decal, wht w/pink tint, 8″ **140.00**
Gold w/green leaves & gold veins, swastika mk, 10½″ **295.00**

Kew Blas

    Kew Blas was a trade name used by the Union Glass Co. of Somerville, Mass., for their iridescent art glass produced from 1890 until about 1920. The glass was made in imitation of Tiffany, and achieved notable success.

Bowl, irid green, 6½″ **495.00**
Compote, gold irid w/blue feathering, 4″ **450.00**
Tumbler, tapered w/round foot, inner ribs, gold irid, 3½″ **135.00**
Vase, bulbous w/narrow neck, gold w/blue pulled feather design, 2½″ **285.00**
Butterscotch w/blue & wht feathering, signed, 2¾″ **385.00**
Gold high luster, internal ribs, bulbous, tiny neck, 8″ **200.00**
Gold luster w/platinum irid, pulled feathers in blue outline, 9½″ **1,250.00**
Green irid fishscale pattern, blue irid loops, gold lined, 8″ .. **325.00**
Sweet pea, opal glass w/pulled green & gold lustre leaf decor, 10″ **950.00**

Keys and Locks

    The earliest type of lock in recorded history was the wooden cross bar used by ancient Egyptians and their contemporaries. The early Romans are

credited with making the first key operated mechanical lock. The ward lock was invented during the Middle Ages by the Etruscans of Northern Italy, the lever tumbler and combination locks followed at various stages of history with varying degrees of effectiveness. In the 18th century, the first precision lock was constructed---it was a device that utilized a lever tumbler mechanism.

Two of the best known of the early 19th century American lock manufacturers are Yale and Sargent. Today's collectors also value names such as Winchester and Keen Cutter. Other factors to consider are rarity, condition and construction. Brass and bronze locks are generally priced higher than those of steel or iron.

Keys

Clock, w/ornate bows	4.50
English, night latch lift keys	18.00
Sliding ring style, 1800s, 8″	30.00
Flat, US folding, 1900s, stamped w/mfg name	15.00
Folding, 19th century	25.00
French, night latch lift keys	30.00
German, casket, 1600s, spikes on bow, star-cut bit	85.00
Closed trefoil bow, 1600s	80.00
Folding, 17th century	90.00
Open cloverleaf bow, 1600s	75.00
Hotel, brass w/brass tags, 1900s	15.00
Roman bronze, various designs & sizes	135.00
Rope bed, 2 keys on one shaft, wooden	42.00
Safe, various styles, 1800s	27.50
Thieves pick, 18th-19th century	18.00
US Brass, 18th century	30.00
19th century	17.50
20th century	9.00

Locks

Bohannan, heart shaped, 1878	10.50
Boxlock, handwrought, 1700s, w/orig brass key	55.00
Brass, #999	40.00
1890 w/embossed crown	10.50
Good Luck horseshoe	45.00
Heart shaped	10.00
Climax, 6-lever pancake push key	20.00
Combination, Slaymaker	4.00
Corbin, 6-lever pancake push key, Excelsior	18.00
Eagle, 6-lever pancake push key	15.00
Brass cylindrical, w/key	19.00
Fraim Slaymaker, pin tumbler push key, Blue Grass #44	19.00
Illinois Lock Co, wafer type	5.00
Iron w/enamel, brass keyhole cover, 1865, 3x2½″	9.00
JMV & Co, ward lock, heart shape	27.00
Jail, wafer, Scandinavian type, JW Climax	20.00
Wafer, Scandinavian type, Star	35.00
Keen Kutter, Frisco	125.00
Laglade, brass 6-lever push key	30.00
Southern Pacific Railroad, brass	45.00
Steel Railway Express Agency, w/key	48.00
Ward, wrought iron, NH & Co	18.00
Western Union Telegraph Co, brass, heart shaped	50.00
Yale, badge shaped, w/brass key door	9.50
Incised, w/key	35.00

King's Rose

King's Rose is a soft paste ware made in Staffordshire, England, from about 1820 to 1830. It is closely related to Gaudy Dutch in the colors of the hand decoration as well as body type. The pattern consists of a large full blown orange-red rose with green, pink and yellow leaves and accents.

Creamer	350.00
Cup & saucer	375.00
Plate, rare size, 1810, 5¼″	195.00
Plate, broken border, 10″	185.00
Solid border, 8″	110.00
Soup plate, broken border, 10″	175.00
Teapot, oyster, 11″	500.00

Kitchen Collectibles

During the last half of the 1850's, mass-produced kitchen gadgets were patented at an astonishing rate. Most were ingeniously efficient. Apple peelers, egg beaters, cherry pitters, food choppers and such were only the most common of hundreds of kitchen tools well designed to perform only specific tasks. Today all are very collectible.

Apple corer, carved bone, early 1800s, 4″	40.00
Apple peeler, 3 gears, clamp on type, pat 1863, 12″	45.00
Cherry, mounted on 4 leg walnut table, 1700s	285.00
Ci, table mounted, hand crank, 1881	30.00
Iron, Goodell, pat 1884	30.00
Keyes, 1856	50.00
Monroe Fitchburg, Mass, 1856	50.00
Ornate, Reading Hdw Co, Penn., 1877	57.50
Rival #296, 3 gear, 1889, lg gear 11½″ dia	150.00
Wood, crank handle, 2 size belt driven gears	150.00
Asparagus buncher, burnished iron, mounted on walnut board	150.00
Berry press, A Burritt, Chicago Mfg Co	65.00
Bin, meal, pine, slanted worktop lid opens front or back	695.00
Biscuit board, walnut table, square, w/lift off lid, marble slab	890.00
Biscuit cutter, rotary, dated 1892	20.00
Biscuit roller, wood board w/grooved roller, side handturn, 1860s	110.00
Bowl, crock, yellow glaze inside, brown clay outside, 12x19″ dia	95.00
Bread peel, knob end handle, handcrafted, 1840s, 49″ long	80.00
Butcher knife, stag handle, 13½″	15.00
Cabbage cutter, pine, 3 iron blades, very large, late 1800s	175.00
Wood, 6½x17″	18.00
Iron center blades, 33″ long x 12″ wide	35.00
Walled sides, iron blades, 3″ high	45.00
Cake maker, tin, 3 gears, wood handle, Universal, 1905, 8″	50.00
Can opener, ci, heavily embossed Keen Kutter on handle	17.50
Canner, stovetop, tin w/copper base, 2-door, Conservo	25.00
Cheese curds knife, 4 flexible iron prongs, wood handle	125.00
Cheese cutter, thin steel wire knife, wood handle	65.00

Cheese press, iron "Starrett's" pat Apr 15, 1873 . . . . 175.00

Cherry pitter, Enterprise #2, ci **15.00**
    Enterprise, 1870, iron, 4 'spider' legs w/bolts **40.00**
    Goodell Co, USA, ci, double......................... **28.00**
    Logan Strobridge 'Electric' **22.00**
    New Standard, on legs **31.00**
    Reading Hdw Co, Reading Penn., 4 legs **29.00**
    Rollman #8, w/orig cardboard box **26.50**
Chopper, 6 blades, rosette form, 6½" **20.00**
    Burl handle, hand wrought steel, 6½" **150.00**
    Double tang, wood handle, iron blade, handmade **50.00**
    Manufactured single or double tang **35.00**
    Single tang, handwrought 1 pc iron, 1700s **80.00**
       Wood handle, iron blade, handmade **45.00**
    Universal #0, 1897 .... **12.00**
    Vegetable, hand forged, wood handle, mid 1800s, 12"...... **40.00**
Chopping knife, stainless blade, iron handle, Samson, 1910 .... **10.00**
Churn, Daisy, 1 qt **38.00**
    Stoneware, wood dasher, lid, Brothers, 10" **36.00**
    Tabletop, ci, works **37.50**
    Wood frame, windmill paddles, side turn handle, 16" **225.00**
    Wood staved, 3 iron hoops, w/dasher, 3 gal **175.00**
Clothes sprinkler, Chinese man, blue & wht, California Cleminsons **14.50**
    Chinese man, hp, Clemson **18.00**
    Clothespin w/cute face............................. **16.00**
    Elephant... **20.00**
    Flatiron figural **13.50**
    Lady w/long dress & mutton sleeves, Cal. Cleminsons **14.00**
Cookie cutter, bear, tin, 5" **15.00**
    Bird, tin, 4" **25.00**
    Bird in flight, perforated back **18.00**
    Butterfly, tin.................................... **18.00**
    Chick, perforated back **10.00**
    Donkey, tin **17.50**
    Full length man, tin, 5½" **20.00**
    Galvanized lady in skirt, 5 "........................ **14.00**
    Goose, tin, 3¾"................................... **35.00**
    Guitar, tin, 7" **20.00**
    Heart, tin, 3".................................... **15.00**
    Horse, old, tin **12.00**
    Leaping deer, tin **30.00**
    Peafowl, tin **35.00**
    Rabbit, old, tin **12.00**
    Set of 12 mini size, w/tin lidded box, 1900............ **50.00**
    Star, tin **25.00**
    Steer, perforated back............................. **16.50**
Corn stick pan, ci, Martin Stove & Range **24.00**
Dipper, applebutter, burnished iron, wood handle, 9" dia, 1700s **110.00**
    Iron & brass, hammered bowl, 17½"................... **55.00**
       Hammered bowl, 20½" **65.00**
Dishpan, iron, slant sides, heavy handles, late 1800s, 15" dia .. **48.00**
    Tin, strap handles, early **35.00**
Doughboard scraper, iron, Penn. Dutch, 1800s **35.00**
Doughbowl, fine ironstone, 10x14" dia **95.00**
Doughnut cutter, tin, 2 way scalloped edge is also cookie cutter **17.00**
Egg beater, Androck Turbine Lutz File Co, 13" **10.00**
    Cast iron, 1908, New Britain, Conn., 13"............... **17.00**
    Dover Pattern Improved, pat 1904, iron **24.00**
    Lyon, dated 1897, also cream whip **22.50**
    Rotary, iron & tin **15.00**
    Tin cylinder-shaped, 1910.......................... **23.00**
    Toplin Mfg Co, pat '03, 4 beaters **28.00**
    Turbine Beater, Washburn Co, pat 1920 .... **19.00**
    Wonder Cream Whip & Egg Beater, tin **16.00**
Egg poacher, tinware, wire handle, for single egg, old........ **15.50**

Flour sifter, Duplex, 5-cup, 1922, wood handle works sideways . **20.00**
    Tin, Bromwell **6.00**
    Wood frame & teeth, crank hdl, brass label O Bond, 1875... **85.00**

Food chopper, Starretts, 1865, ci, 13½x16" **275.00**
Food grinder, Universal #0, 1897 .... **10.00**
Fork, cooking, wrought iron, 2 prong, 1800s, 18" long **45.00**
    Testing, wrought iron, 2 prong, 1800s, 16" long **40.00**
Fruit auger, sugar devil, iron w/wood handle, pat **150.00**
Fruit jar sealer, nickle plate, dome shape w/3 legs.......... **10.00**
Fruit press, cherry, woodpinned, drainage spout, 1800s **225.00**
Fruit pulper, walnut, iron blades, w/stand, embossed label, 1890s **175.00**
Funnel, tin, for filling canning containers, early 1900s **20.00**
Grater, handled, handmade, 1800s, 12x8" **50.00**
    Punched tin semi-circle, on pine box w/drawer **40.00**
    Tin, arched & pierced, full length drawer, rolled edges **75.00**
       Punched holes, semi-circle, 1870s, 16x7" **38.00**
       Round, 1901.................................. **9.00**
    Wood top lifts, tin grater over 2 drawers, 9x9" **65.00**
Griddle, ci, 8x16" **14.00**
Ice pick, advertising, steel handle, 8" **14.00**
    Iron, 2 sided handle, Run Right to Reads.............. **35.00**
Ice shaver, Wrightsville Howe Co, Wrightsville, Penn......... **45.00**
Jar lid remover, ci, mechanical, Champion 1863, 4½" dia **85.00**
Kraut cutter, Indianapolis Kraut Cutter, 1905 .... **45.00**
Ladle, for skimming, tin, 14"........................... **15.00**
    Iron, handwrought, long handle drawn into hook, 1840s..... **45.00**
    Wood handle, pewter basin bowl, 1850s, 15" **65.00**
Lemon squeezer, ci, late 1800s **60.00**
    Iron, 2-pc, hanging eye **15.00**
Marshmallow toaster, wire, long handle **6.00**
Masher, hickory, 6x2" dia **28.00**
    Metal w/wood handle, 25" **12.00**
Measure, tin, qt, Dover **15.00**
Mortar & pestle, iron, signed Savery & Co, Philadelphia....... **95.00**
Muffin pan, 5 hearts, 8 ruffled, eye rings each end, iron...... **145.00**
    Cast fruit designs, 9 sections **110.00**
    Cast iron, 8x12½" **12.00**
       With 9 round sections, Erie **25.00**
       With fruit designs, 2 sections **110.00**
Muffin rings, ci, miniature size, hearts, spades, clubs, diamonds . **10.00**
Nutmeg grater, ci & tin, turned wood handles, pat, 4" **40.00**
    Cast iron, pat 1870, 4".............................. **45.00**
    Edgar, pat date Nov 10, 1896 .... **48.00**
    Tin & wood, pat 1898, 5" **45.00**
Paddle, food, 36" long, 1¼" top width to 3" base **35.00**
    Scrapple, 1-pc iron w/paddleturn, wood handle, 86" **48.00**

Stirring, iron one end, early **65.00**
Pancake turner, opener combo, advertising, pat 1914 . . . . **8.00**
Pastry board, tin, rolling pin cradle, hanging ring, 22x18½" . . **135.00**
    Tinned sheetiron, w/pin, can all be hung on wall **275.00**
Pastry jigger, forged iron, faceted ball end, 1700s, 5¾" **50.00**
Pea huller, ci **37.50**

Peanut grinder, #00, 6x3½" **80.00**
Pie crimper, wood handle, The Dandy, Gold Medal, April 28, 1925 **3.50**
Pie lifter, wire, old **25.00**
    Wire, wood handle **16.00**
Potato peeler, bright metal, Clipper, 6½" **3.00**
Potlid, revolving, rattail & ornate handle, 1600s **185.00**
Raisin seeder, table model, The Gem, 1895 . . . . **21.00**
    Wood & wire, The Everett, w/directions, 1890s, 3¼" **50.00**
Rolling pin, amethyst blown glass, 1800s, 15" **100.00**
    Glass w/maple handles, Cincinnati Galv Co **25.00**
    Glass w/wood handles & inner rod, 1879, 20½" **25.00**
    Heavy glass w/tin screw cap **25.00**
    Metal handle strips, 28" long, 3" dia, 5 lbs **35.00**
    Milk glass, hand blown, glass nob ends, 15" **40.00**
    Pressed glass, tin screw cap, grip ridged handles **25.00**
Scrapple pan, tinned iron, Penn. Dutch **656.00**
Set, tin, Deco, canisters, wastebasket, etc, 24-pc, Crummer Trans **295.00**
Skillet, ci, w/wrought handle, 10" dia **12.00**
Skimmer, iron, handcrafted, handle pulled into hooks, 1800s . . . **48.00**
    Tin, l900, 6" **5.00**
Soap saver, mesh w/iron loop handle **8.00**
Spatula, iron, handcrafted, ring end w/extra hanger, 1700s **95.00**
Steam cooker, tin, handled top, pat date 1879, 12½" dia **28.00**
Steamer, pudding, w/lid, Kreamer **25.00**
Sugar scoop, tin, small w/strap handle, kitchen container type . . **12.50**
Tea kettle, ci, 7x11" dia **40.00**
    Copper w/brass & wood handle, 1 gal, Portugal **14.00**
Teacake pan, ci, hanging eyes each end, 1800s **115.00**
Toaster, 4 sided, Pyramid Stove Top **5.00**
    Double wire maltese cross frame, wood handle, old, 18" **29.00**
    Fireplace, iron, rattail handle end, rotates, 2 legs, 1700s . . . **250.00**
Tomato slicer, pat George Edwards **18.00**
Universal Tool, Cleveland 1881, ci, 7-way, lid lifter, pleater, etc . **45.00**
Vegetable cutter, maple board, corrugated tin, 1880s **20.00**
Vegetable slicer, wood, dated 1890, 20" **30.00**
Waffle iron, ci on tall stand, Griswald American, 1908 . . . . **22.00**

Cast iron w/stand, Shapleigh #8 . . . . **28.00**
Cast iron w/stand, Wagner, 1892 . . . . **23.00**
Wrought iron, double handle, 1800s **40.00**
Wire w/spiral handle, brass ferrule, 8½" **19.00**
Wire w/tin handle, 18" **25.00**
Wire w/wood handle, 12" **7.50**
Whisk broom, fits in handle of 7" crumb tray, Fuller, early **35.00**

Knives

Knife collecting as a hobby began in earnest during the 1960s when government regulations required for the first time that knife companies mark their product with the country of origin. The few collectors and dealers cognizant of this change at once began stockpiling the older knives made before this law was enacted. Another impetus to the growing interest in this area came with the Gun Control Act of 1968, which severly restricted gun trading. Frustrated gun dealers transferred their attention to knives. Today there are collectors clubs in many of the states.

The ones to look for are old bone handled knives in mint, unsharpened condition, pearl handles, Case doctor's knives and large display models.

Adophus Bush, 3 blade w/corkscrew **140.00**
Adophus Bush, peep hole w/picture, 4 blade **115.00**
Advertising, Carl Miller Tractor Co, Des Moines, Caterpillar **37.50**
    Coke, Remington **80.00**
    Foot Fashion Fine Shoes, Remington in circle, 3" **85.00**
    Glover Packing Co, Colonial, gold w/pearl, 3" **18.00**
    Harms Oil Co, Colonial, Prov RI, 2½" **15.00**
    Nehi Beverages, figural boot, Remington **185.00**
    Payne's Strong Wear Shoes, Topeka, steel handle, 3" **25.00**
    Traveler's Insurance Co, embossed train, 3" **125.00**
    US Rubber Co, 2 blades w/corkscrew **10.00**
    Y-B Cigars, double blade **10.00**
BPOE, brass **75.00**
Bowie, boot, Joseph Allen & Sons, Sheffield, MOP handle **150.00**
    Boot, Manhattan Cutlery, Sheffield, bone handle **150.00**
    Coral sets in handle, stars & moon in blade **200.00**
Boy Scout, Remington, 4 blade, 3¾" **60.00**
    Spear, blade, chisel & scraper, stag handle, Cattaraugus **125.00**
Camper's horn handle, w/eating utensils & corkscrew, Germany . **35.00**
Chinese watch chain, all brass, embossed Chinese girl **40.00**
Clasp, bone handle, 1 blade, brass loop, J Rogers & Son, Scheffield **48.00**
Doctor's celluloid handle, very early, Curtin & Clark **23.00**
Figural lady's shoe, turquoise, on chain for belt, Germany **27.50**
    Lady's leg, ornate celluloid handle, Union Cut Co **150.00**
Founders, stag handle, w/display case **65.00**
Hunting, RH51, Remington **30.00**
Jack, green marbled w/shield, 2 blades, Valley Forge Cutlery . . . **25.00**
    MOP, 2 blades, Robeson Suredge USR **35.00**
    Wood handle, 1 blade, Watter Bro, Germany **10.00**
Lady's metal case w/embossing, 2 sterling blades **20.00**
    Metal embossed handles, engraved 'Lottie', 2 blades **18.50**
    Sterling, 'Mollie' engraved on blade **28.00**
Landers Frary & Clark, pearl handle, 2 blades, 2¾" **18.00**
Pruning, ebony handle, Southington **14.00**
Remington Acorn w/ground punch **16.00**
Robeson Shur-Edge, Safety First Pays, 2 blades, brass handle . . **45.00**
Sailor's Ford & Medley, Sheffield, 2 blades, w/spike **9.00**
Souvenir, Long Beach, California, The Pier, metal handle, 2 blade **70.00**
Souvenir, World's Fair, 1933 . . . . **33.00**
Texas Ranger 1973, w/wood case **100.00**
Union Cut Co, abalone pearl handle, 2" long rectangle, 2 blade **160.00**
United States Navy, old stag handle, Williams, Sheffield, England **225.00**
Wadsworth, horn handle, crown grape pattern, locks, early **150.00**

Pocket Knives

Advertising, Pearl handle, 4 blades, Germany, 3″ **35.00**
Ambassador USA, Pearl handle, 1956 Shriners, 2″ **18.00**
BPO Elks, Germany, metal handle, 3½″ **24.00**
Bone w/scrimshawed buffalo, Schrade SC500 . . . . **70.00**
Case, #5254, tested, stag handle, 4″. **218.00**
   #51215-½F, bone handle **300.00**
   #53131, tested, stag handle, 3½″ **500.00**
   #6100, green bone handle, 3¼″ **350.00**
   #6391, tested, green bone handle, 4½″. **1,015.00**
   #62042, stag handle **18.00**
   #M100XX, nickeled silver handle, 3″ **95.00**
Cattaraugus #206, shrine emblem, 2 blade, 3¼″ **45.00**
   #305, 10k gold, 3 blade, 2¾″ **50.00**
   #5003, 3 blades w/scissors & corkscrew, MOP **115.00**
   #12099L, stag handle, lock, 1 blade, 4½″ **135.00**
   #12819, stag handle, 1 blade, 5½″ **590.00**
   #12839, stag handle, 1 blade, 5½″ **650.00**
   #32653, MOP handle, 3 blades, 3½″ **210.00**
   #P1, knife, pencil & file combo **65.00**
Celluloid ivory handle, 2 blades, crown in circle mk **6.00**
Craftsman #9491 . . . . **18.00**
JP Lovell, Boston Army Co, American Bulldog, hunting scene . **135.00**
Kent, double blade **8.50**
Lady leg, 1900, 3″, illus **22.00**
Lady leg, United, 3″, illus **22.00**
New York Knife Co, timber scribe, very scarce. **44.00**
Peakhole w/girl smoking, pearl handle, Wadsworth & Son . . . **125.00**
Pearl handle, Key Work Clothes, Hammer, USA **15.00**

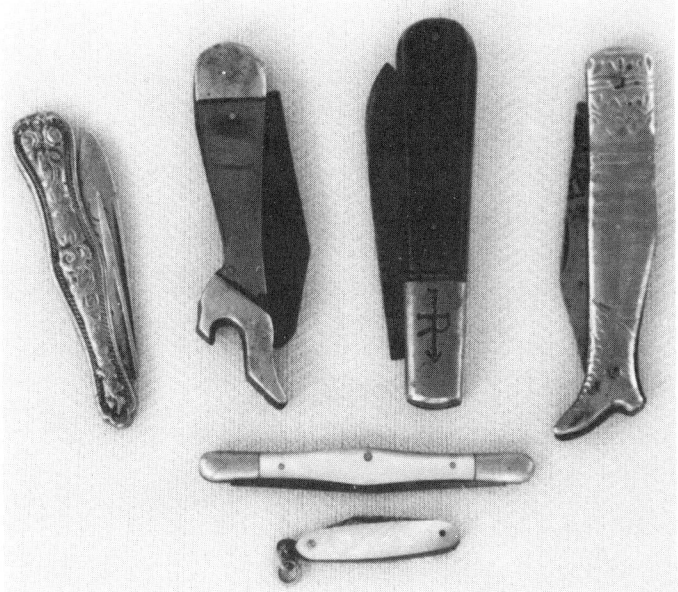

Pearl handle, 1½″ **12.00**
Pearl handle, 3″, illus. **14.00**
   Embossed, Munchen, Germany, 3″ **15.00**
   With bottle opener, 3″ **18.00**
Pictures Washington & Lincoln, other side has Klansman **110.00**
   Washington, Lincoln & Wilson, 2 blade **80.00**
Pipe smoker's, chrome, w/reamer, gouge, tamper, 3¼″ **10.00**
Queen Steel #22, double blade **9.00**
Quick Point, Remington **60.00**
Remington #R21, redwood handle, 2 blades, 3½″ **50.00**
   #R453, stag handle, 2 blades, 3½″ **60.00**
   #R684, pearl handle, 3″, 2 blade. **190.00**
   #R3453, 3 blades, acorn stag handle. **120.00**

#R4353, 2 blades, stag handle **600.00**
#R6032, black handle, 4 blades, 3″. **80.00**
#R6949, nickeled silver handle, 2 blades **50.00**
#R7500, buffalo horn handle, 3 blades **70.00**
Russell #226, cocobola handle, 2 blades, 3½″ **230.00**
   #6354, genuine stag handle, 3 blades, 3½″ **450.00**
   #44H13X, ebony handle, 1 blade, 4¼″. **125.00**
Russel, bone, 3″, illus **38.00**
Scene w/hunter, dog & deer, John R Lovell Arms Co **30.00**
Silver handle, ring in end, 3 blades, ornate **45.00**
Silver, lady's, Art Nouveau, 2¾″, illus. **55.00**
Souvenir Niagra Falls, Arrow Co Germany, 1½″ **25.00**
   Woolworth Bldg, World's Tallest **19.00**
Stag handle, Hawkbill Blade, Surrolk Works, Sheffield **65.00**
   US Navy, Cox & Sons, 4¾″ **95.00**
Sterling, w/inlay Indian design, 2 blade, Robeson Suredge **80.00**
   2 blade, colored Indian emblems, Robeson, 3½″ **130.00**
Winchester #1201, nickeled silver, 1 blade, 3½″ **160.00**
   #1920, stag handle, 1 blade, 5¼″ **650.00**
   #2070, celluloid, 2 blade, 3½″ **100.00**
   #2853, bone handle, 2 blade, 3½″ **165.00**
   #3962, buffalo horn, 3 blade, 4″ **210.00**
   #4341, pearl handle, 4 blade, ... **195.00**
Wire handle, Geo Schrade, 1926. . . . . **10.50**

Knowles, Taylor, Knowles

   Isaac Knowles and Isaac Harvey operated a pottery in East Liverpool, Ohio, in 1853, where they produced both yellowware and Rockingham. In 1870, Knowles bought Harvey's interests and took as partners John Taylor and Homer Knowles. Their principal product was Ironstone china. But Knowles was confident that American potters could produce as fine a ware as the Europeans, and to prove his point hired Joshua Poole, an artist from the Belleek Works in Ireland. Poole quickly perfected a Belleek type china, but fire destroyed this portion of the company and before it could function again, their hotel china business had grown to the point that their full attention was required to meet market demands. By 1891 they were able to try again. They developed a bone china, as fine and thin as before, which they called Lotus. Henry Schmidt from the Meissen factory in Germany decorated the ware, often with lacy filigree applications, or with hand formed leaves and flowers to which he added futher decoration with liquid slip applied with a squeeze bag. Due to high production costs, with so much of the fragile ware damaged in firing, and of course changes in taste and style of decoration, the Lotus Ware line was dropped in 1896. Some of the early ware was marked KTK China, later marks have a star and a crescent, with Lotus Ware added.

Chocolate set, wht embossed flowers, gold bands, gold drape. . **750.00**
Creamer. **110.00**
Lotus, cream & sugar, gold fishnet, panels w/hp violets, signed **610.00**
   Creamer, floral decor, gold, signed, 4″ **190.00**
   Ewer, ribbed, lacy, small beading on neck, handles **450.00**
   Jar, covered, apple blossom decor, openwork on lid **750.00**
   Pitcher, bulbous, fishnet overlay, rose & forget-me-not decor **325.00**
   Pitcher, squatty, fishnet design **225.00**
   Tea set, 3-pc, feather design **650.00**
   Teapot, fishnet decor, bamboo handle. **300.00**
   Vase, cylinder, morning glories decor, w/large gold insect, 8″ **675.00**
   Vase, floral decor, gold handle, signed, 7½″ **335.00**
   Vase, gold fishnet, gold ball feet, 4 triangular panels, 8″. . . **625.00**
   Vase, ivory colored w/hp flowers, ewer shape, 9″ **350.00**
   Vase, ornate gold handles, waisted, florals **400.00**
Mug, child's, Little Boy Blue scene both sides, 3¼″ **28.00**
Platter, fighting ducks, 14″ **42.00**

Punch bowl, 1870s **300.00**
Tea set, wht w/blue flowers, 19 pc & 6″ teapot **75.00**

Kutani

Kutani, named for the Japanese village where it originated, was first produced in the 17th century. The early ware, Ko Kutani, was produced for only about thirty years. Several types were produced before 1900, but these are rarely encountered. The later, more familiar type, has large areas of red with gold designs on a white ground decorated with warriors, birds, florals, etc., in controlled colors of red, gold, and black. In the 19th century, kilns located in several different villages began to copy the old Kutani wares.

Bowl, fish decor, white w/gold bands, 8″ **120.00**
   Footed, genre scenes, mums, red, blk, & gold, 4x4″ **390.00**
Cup & saucer, Thousand Faces, polychrome, red border **25.00**
Cups & saucers, demitasse, Bird of Paradise, set of 8 . . . . **240.00**
Dish, ped base, hexagonal, boys, trees, mountains, 1800s, 11″ **350.00**
Figurine, woman w/fan, 12″ **295.00**
Mustard, covered, w/spoon, marked **20.00**
Plates, set of 12, each w/different sea shore scene, 8½″ **665.00**
Punch bowl, 3 scenes--figural, floral, landscape--22″ dia **1,650.00**
Saki set, donut shape bottle, 4 cups w/erotic Geisha, round tray **165.00**
Tea set, butterflies decor, cups & saucers w/Geisha lithophane, 15-pc **160.00**
   Demitasse, Wisteria pattern, 19 pc **325.00**
Tray, scenic w/woman & children, red border, gilt, 13″ long . . **295.00**
Vase, bottle, flowering branches decor, red & gold, 6″ **70.00**
   Figures in carp masks, gilt, 11″ **375.00**
   Girls & scenery decor, 2 handles at top, 3″ widest part **75.00**
   Green dragons, 13″, pair **425.00**

Labels

Before the advent of the cardboard box, wooden crates were used for transporting products. Paper labels were attached to the crates to identify the contents and the packer. These labels often had colorful lithographed illustrations, covering a broad range of subjects. Eventually the cardboard box replaced the crate, and the artwork was imprinted directly onto the carton. Today, these labels are becoming collectible, not only for the artwork, but for their advertising appeal as well.

Apple crate, America's delight **2.00**
   Hula **4.00**
   Kentucky Cardinal **10.00**
Bumble Bee brand, Royal Anne cherries **3.50**
Butterfly brand, Refugee beans **3.50**
   Succotash **3.50**
   Sweet Pears **3.50**
   Wax beans **3.50**
Cigar box, Alcazar **3.00**
   Call again **3.00**
   Commander **2.50**
   Cuban, 4x4″ **2.00**
   Elsie **4.00**
   FDR **4.00**
   First Blush **5.00**
   Gettysburg Commanders, 4x4″ **6.50**
   Gettysburg Commanders **18.00**
   Greater Columbia **18.00**
   Iris **8.00**
   La Boda, 4x4″ **1.00**
   La Cantarina, 4x4″ **6.00**

Little African, 4x4″ **5.00**
Little African **19.00**
Medal of Honor **5.00**
Two Friends **6.50**
Cloth of Gold Bantam corn **3.50**
Delta brand sugar corn **3.50**
Kentucky Cardinal, 1918, 9½x11½″ **12.00**
Kentucky Mountain Pride Corn Meal flour sacks, water mill **1.00**
Lemon crate, Arab, San Dimas, 12x9″ **6.00**
   Collie, San Dimas, 12x9″ **18.00**
   Cutter, 1937, 12x9″ **4.00**
   Pansy, 12x9″ **7.00**
   Tom Cat, Orosi, 12x9″ **20.00**
   Woodlake Nymph, nude, Woodlake, 12x9″ **12.00**
Long Distance Tobacco **15.00**
Majestic brand, War Time colorful box, spark plugs **2.00**
Orange crate, Albion, Placentia **18.00**
   Annie Laurie **6.00**
   Annie Laurie, Strathmore, 10x11″ **3.00**
   Double A **4.00**
   Glider, Fillmore, 10x11″ **9.00**
   Golden Gate, Lemon Cove, 10x11″ **5.00**
   Golden Trout, Orange Cove, 10x11″ **11.00**
   Homer Brand, black bird, 10x10″ **12.00**
   Legal Tender, Fillmore **3.00**
   Pacoast, L A **1.00**
   Redskin, Rialto **7.00**
   Stalwart, Santa Paula, 10x11″ **6.00**
   Sunny Cove, Redlands, 10x11″ **2.00**
   Unicorn, E. Highlands, 10x11″ **9.00**
Palace Garden Pumpkin **3.50**
Pear crate, Big Game, 11x7″ **3.00**
   Places, 11x7″ **4.00**
Red bird, Blue Hill brand corn, mountain lake scene **3.50**
Red poppie brand Morrow squash **5.00**
Ted Williams Moxie **4.00**

Lace, Linens and Needlework

It has been recorded that lace was found in the tombs of ancient Egypt. Lace has always been a symbol of wealth and fashion. Italian laces are regarded as the finest ever produced, but the differences between them and the laces of France are nearly indistinguishable. In Munich a type of lace was woven, not by human fingers but by insects. Caterpillar lace was made by smearing a flat surface with an edible paste, over which the desired design was outlaid in oil. The catterpillars were repelled by the oiled areas, but ate the paste, all the while spinning their silken threads.

Needlework was revived during the middle of the 18th century, and became the favorite of feminine pastimes. Examples of many forms are readily available today--tatting, embroidery, needlepoint and crochet---and although fragile in appearance have withstood the ravages of time with remarkable durability.

Banquet cloth, linen, Damask, 4 hunting scenes, cutwork, 56″ dia **75.00**
Bedspread and sham, ½ moon shape, ruffled, silky rayon, 1930 **37.00**
   Crochet, beige, heirloom, 120x90″ **225.00**
   Crochet, popcorn stitch, handmade, 1915 . . . . **225.00**
   Crochet, popcorn stitch, stars, 95x80″ **235.00**
   Crochet, wht medallion, 90x106″ **65.00**
   Crochet, wht w/butterflies & stars, 82x112″ **120.00**
   Lace, ecru, single **135.00**
Blanket, homespun, red/blue plaid on natural, 2 pc, fringed, 74x87″ **175.00**
Bookmark, needlepoint, Victorian, black couple, Goodby Dixie, 2½″ **65.00**
Collar w/matching cuffs, tatted **85.00**

Cotton, printed, on orig bolt, Lindberg, 1927, 3 yd **100.00**
Crib canopy, crochet **32.00**
Doily, crochet, pink, 16″ dia **13.00**
    Crochet, wht w/ruffled edge, 14½″ **10.00**
    Linen, 1¾″ crochet edging, pair, 12″ oval & 5″ dia **9.00**
Dresser scarf, lace, beige, intricate, 31x13″ **15.00**
Firescreen, petitpoint, dutch room scene w/lady, walnut frame, 1900s **195.00**
Framed picture, girl skating, wools & silk, 1860, Russian, 7¼x9¼″ **225.00**
    Needle/petitpoint, Happy Days of Charles I, 1883, 54x46″ .. **800.00**
    Needlework, hp paper on silk, scenic, floral, 12x18″ **425.00**
Lace, hairpin, framed, 15x28″ **45.00**
Linen, ecru, 16 different embroidered scenes, 98x85″ **150.00**
Mantilla, black lace, Berlin, made by Franciscan Monks **100.00**
    Spanish black lace, open roses, scalloped edge, 42″ **185.00**
Motto, embroidery on cardboard, Home Sweet Home, framed, 5x11″ **45.00**
Mourning picture, Shakespear's tomb, painted features, 13x12″ **185.00**
Pillow, woolwork, 1850s **95.00**
Pillow case, calico patchwork, embroidery outline, ruffle, 1890 .. **70.00**
    Embroidered florals, crochet edging, pair **12.00**
Pillow cover, hand embroidered, linen, 1920s, 20x18″ **12.00**
Runner, crochet, wht, 41x14″ **18.00**
    Ecru, crochet, 6 point star design, 45x13″ **20.00**
    Linen w/embroidered teacups & strawberries, 26x17″ **12.00**
    Linen, 1½″ crochet edging, 37x11″ **14.00**
    Linen, ¾″ crochet edging, embroidered flowers, 37x11½″ ... **16.00**
Shawl, piano, Victorian, silk crepe, embroidery, fringe, 50″ **80.00**
    Red satin w/floral embroidery, fringe, 50x30″ **50.00**
    Spanish black lace, Victorian, floral design, 21x45″ **135.00**
Table cloth, all Battenburg w/18″ cloth center, 52″ **85.00**
    French, handmade, 72x111″ **50.00**
Table rug, hooked, Tree of Life, on burlap, 1850s, 14x20″ ... **165.00**
Tablecloth, 13½″ crocheted border, 4″ lace insert, 72″ dia ... **150.00**
    All Battenburg lace except 18″ center, 52″ **85.00**
    Battenburg, 60″ dia **95.00**
    Crochet, 6 point star medallion, 56x70″ **90.00**
    Crochet, ecru lacy medallion, handmade, 54x46″ **35.00**
    Crochet, filet, colonial man, woman in corner, 70x70″ **100.00**
    Crochet, heavy thread, round medallions, 85x63″ **85.00**
    Crochet, medallion w/8 point stars, 70x86″ **180.00**
    Crochet, Queen's Lace, ecru, 66x80″ **70.00**
    Cutouts, wide lace in points around edge, linen, 66″ dia **135.00**
    French, handmade, 72x111″ **50.00**
    Linen, handwoven, 2 pc, stripes, 1850, 60x120″ **40.00**
    Linen, many handmade lace inserts & wide border **135.00**
    Linen, woven in 2 pcs, 1792, 46x50″ **60.00**
    Wht Battenburg lace, grape pattern, 60″ dia **95.00**
    Wht cotton, lace insert & border, 90x78″ **45.00**
Wall hanging, hooked, deep pile, multicolor geometric, 8x14″ .. **35.00**
    Hooked, farm scene, detailed, 12x20″ **100.00**
    Hooked, geometric design, handmade, 1800s, 8x17″ **25.00**
    Hooked, geometric design, handmade, 8x17″ **30.00**
    Petitpoint on silk, framed **45.00**
Wedding cloth, linen, Damask, chrysanthemum pattern, 178x70″ **100.00**
    Linen, Damask, embroidered signature, 180x88″ **100.00**

Lalique

Beginning his lengthy career as a designer and maker of fine jewelry, Rene Lalique at first only daubled in glass, making small panels of pate-de-vere (paste on paste) and cire perdue (wax casting) to use in his jewelry. He also made small flacons of gold and silver with his glass inlays, which attracted the attention of M.F. Coty, who commissioned Lalique to design bottles for his perfume company. The success of this venture resulted in the opening of his own glasshouse at Combs-la-Ville in 1909. In 1921, a larger factory was established at Wingen-sur-Moder, in Alsace-Lorraine. By the 30s, Lalique was world reknown as the most important designer of his time.

Lalique glass is lead based, either mold blown or pressed. Favored motifs during the Art Nouveau period were dancing nymphs, fish, dragonflies and foliage. Characteristically the glass is crystal in combination with acid etched relief. Later, some items were made in as many as ten colors---red, amber and green among them---and were occasionally accented with enameling. These colored pieces, especially those in black, are rare and highly prized by advanced collectors.

During the 20s and 30s, Lalique designed several vases and bowls reminiscent of American Indian art. He also styled a line of Art Deco vases with stylized birds, florals and geometrics. In addition to vases, clocks, automobile mascots, stemware, bottles and many other useful objects were produced.

Items made before his death in 1945 were marked R. Lalique; later the R was deleted even though some of the original molds were still used. Numbers found on the bases of some pieces are catalogue numbers.

Ashtray, figural turkey **225.00**
    Naiade, intaglio nymph, 4″ **325.00**
Atomizer, 6 nudes **210.00**
Bowl, fish in opalescent water, bubbly center, 2x11¾″ **395.00**
    Frosted & clear, molded hounds, w/brown enamel **850.00**
    Nemours, mk Lalique **220.00**
    Opal & clear, angels facing, each side, 14½″ **3,500.00**
    Opalescent blownout mistletoe pattern, 9½″ dia **675.00**
    Starfish **250.00**
Box, covered, deeply embossed roses, 3½x5″ **950.00**
    D'Orsay, molded signature, 4¼x1½″ dia **190.00**
    Rose on cover, opal, 10″ dia **500.00**
Candy box, fish, opal amber cover, mk Lalique, 10¼″ ... **1,700.00**
    Round, birds **295.00**
Car mascot, Victoire, clear & frosted w/chrome & wood, 10″ **3,200.00**
Centerpiece bowl, frosted & molded waterlilies & pads, 11¼x4½″ **395.00**
    Pale blue irid, wheat stalks, 14½″ **475.00**
Champagne glass, blk enamel grapes on stem **85.00**
Chandelier, mottled orange & wrought-iron, garlands, 1925, 18½″ **715.00**

Clock, deux figurines, parcel-gilt illuminated metal socle, 15¼″ **4,400.00**
    Floral decor, mk Lalique **1,100.00**

Half circle, birds, 6″ **2,400.00**
Cordial, w/openwork stem, Deco design, 6½″ **65.00**
Decanter, w/blue stopper, Neptune & mermaid, 1934, 8¼ **715.00**
Dish, Martigues, relief swirls, opal, wood stand, 14½″ dia... **1,500.00**
  With cover, scalloped opal rim, floral, ... **500.00**
Figurine, bison, mk Lalique **150.00**
  Cat, mk Lalique..................... **370.00**
  Cat, reclining, mk Lalique, 9½″ **475.00**
  Chrysis, colorless frosted glass, 6″ **145.00**
  Elephant, mk Lalique **300.00**
  Owl, black onyx base, detailed, overall 3x8½″ **295.00**
  Perche, colorless frosted glass, 6″ **150.00**
  Salamander, green, mk Lalique **125.00**
  Seagull, Daphnis, mk Lalique **280.00**
  Sparrow, mk Lalique **280.00**
  Turtle, amber, mk Lalique **140.00**
Fruit bowl, Margeurite, frosted & clear, 15″ dia **500.00**
Liquor glass, frosted fish design................. **65.00**
Paperweight, Deux Aigles, R Lalique **875.00**
  Sirene, sea nymph, 4″.................... **2,000.00**
Pendant, Fioret..................... **325.00**
  Floret **135.00**
Perfume bottle, 6 nudes, leaves & flowers **200.00**
  Blue, flattened circle shape, w/stopper, 4¼″ **150.00**
  Encircled w/roses..................... **145.00**
  Moon & star w/stopper, mk Lalique, 3¼″........... **400.00**
  Tiara stopper w/nudes, D'Orsay, Lalique, 5″ **1,750.00**
  Worth, cobalt blue crystal, 3¼″.................. **120.00**
Perfume bottles, clear, frosted tops, pair **225.00**
Pin tray, swan, mk Lalique **100.00**
Plate, bubble-like design in center, opal, 11″ dia........ **190.00**
Powder box, 3 dancing nudes, 3¾x1½″ **200.00**
  Emiliane **275.00**
  Marguerite **245.00**
  Wheat pattern, 9½″ dia **190.00**
Scent bottle, allover floral moulded..................... **150.00**
Serving dish, peacock feathers w/opalescent eyes, 11″ dia **375.00**
Vase, 8 standing nudes, frosted brown-stained, 18″ **4,200.00**
  Amber, 1925, 6½″ **522.00**
  Amber, Milan, 11″..................... **4,800.00**
  Aras, frosted & clear, birds in berry branches.......... **1,800.00**
  Art Nouveau, frosted, 10¼″ **5,000.00**
  Avallon, birds w/cherries & leaves, olive green, 5¾″ **2,250.00**
  Baies, frosted & blk enamel, thorned & berried branches, 7¾″ **3,750.00**
  Brambles, frosted w/thorn branches on green ground, 9¼″ **1,050.00**
  Branches & berries, w/brown, frosted, 9½″............. **1,650.00**
  Carthage, molded gray glass, bowl shape, 7″ **700.00**
  Champagne, molded gray glass, cone shape projections, 6½″ **495.00**
  Chardons, frosted, 4 sides, w/thistle leaves, 7½″ **870.00**
  Cherries & leaves, frosted, 5½″..................... **210.00**
  Coqs et Plumes, frosted, 6¼″ **850.00**
  Deer feeding in foliage, brown patinated enamel, 6½″.... **1,050.00**
  Enameled blk, wht & turquoise, lime green, 1925, 6½″ **220.00**
  Escargot, spiral snail shell, frosted, mk Lalique, 8¼″ **600.00**
  Fish motif, seahorse handles **350.00**
  Formose, frosted, round, molded w/goldfish, 6¾″........ **1,250.00**
  Grey, 1925, 7″..................... **550.00**
  Gui, frosted, molded w/mistletoe plants, 6¾″ **670.00**
  Gun metal, Champagne pattern, 7″ **600.00**
  Horse motif, signed, 7″..................... **235.00**
  Lievres, frosted w/ferns & bands of rabbits, brown traces, 6¼″ **1,000.00**
  Mimosa, pyriform vessel w/mimosa leaves, frosted, 6½″.... **260.00**
  Molded bubbles in relief bubbles, inside frosted, 7½″ **675.00**
  Opalescent w/curling feathers, 1925.................. **380.00**

Panels of caryatids, 8″ **525.00**
Petrarque, colorless glass, large molded glass handles, 8¼″ **1,210.00**
Pierrefonds, gold-amber, Art Deco, handles, 14x6″ **3,100.00**
Poivre, frosted, flask form, w/pepper plant branches, 9½″ . **1,450.00**
Ronsard, cased & frosted, round w/nudes on handles, 8¼″ **1,200.00**
Sage green, 11″..................... **2,700.00**
Seaforms, frosted w/blk letters, mk Lalique, 10″ **415.00**
Thistle w/blue, frosted, 7½″..................... **925.00**
Thorns in relief, frosted w/green enamel, 9″ **1,100.00**
Toubillons, clear & blk enamel, intaglio whirlwinds, 7¾″ . **3,750.00**
Tournesol, frosted, sunflowers in relief, 4¾″ **610.00**
Water glass, 2 nudes on stem, 6½″ **85.00**
  Frosted fish design **85.00**
Wine glass, Duncan, 2 nudes on stem, 5½″............. **85.00**
  Blk enamel background w/molded cherries on stem, flaring... **95.00**
  Blk enamel grapes on stem **80.00**
  Frosted fish design .... **75.00** .
  Stem is figural male & female nudes, sgnd, 5¾″ **65.00**
  Stemmed w/open rectangle near top, 7″ **75.00**

Lamps, Lanterns & Lighting Devices

The earliest known lamp was the primitive grease lamp, a small alabaster dish holding openly burning grease. An improved version, the Betty lamp introduced in the 18th century, made use of a lid and cloth wick. The developement of the tubal wick by Swiss inventor Aime Argand in 1784 brought about a more sophisticated oil lamp, featuring a glass chimney. With the discovery of petroleum in 1859, new methods of producing artificial light were made possible. Bigger, heavier and more elaborate lamps came into vogue.

The most popular of the kerosene lamps were the Aladdins, introduced in 1908 by the Mantle Lamp Company of America. Aladdin lamps were made in over 18 models and more than 100 styles.

Banquet lamps were kerosene lighting devices with round glass globes, often with hand painted decorations. They were quite similar to the Gone With the Wind lamps of the 1870s.

Other types of early lamps were 'spark lamps', small night-lights with limited illumination; and 'student lamps', useful for late-night reading. Gas lamps were used, especially for outdoor lighting.

With the invention of the electric bulb in 1879, oil lamps slowly became obsolete. The light from the electric bulb was so bright, ornamental shades were necessary to reduce the glare. Glassmaker Louis C. Tiffany devoted most of his career in the latter 1800s to producing original and elaborate glass and bronze lamps for the electric bulb.

Aladdin
#1, brass mantle lamp **500.00**
#5, mantle..................... **110.00**
#8, mantle..................... **130.00**
#11, mantle lamp **50.00**
#12, mantle **50.00**
#12, mantle, red satin glass shade..................... **120.00**
Alacite, Cupid lamp, short base..................... **120.00**
  Candlestick w/shades, pr **40.00**
  Dancing Ladies urn, G-375 .... **395.00**
  Hanging lamp font, B burner **35.00**
  Hopalong Cassidy, gun in holster **125.00**
  Lincoln Drape, B-75 .... **70.00**
  Lincoln Drape, B-75 w/scallop foot, 10½″ **250.00**
  Lincoln Drape, short, B-60 .... **265.00**
  Lincoln Drape, tall, 701A shade..................... **120.00**
  Melon shape, 4 feet, orig shade & finial **65.00**
  Simplicity, B-27, gold luster **225.00**
  Simplicity, B-76A..................... **115.00**

Urn lamp, melon rib, w/lid, lamp finial, 11″ **95.00**
Beehive, B-80, clear **50.00**
  B-81, green **70.00**
  B-83, ruby **250.00**
Cathedral, #107 .... **60.00**
  #108, green **70.00**
  #109, amber crystal **70.00**
  B-111, green moonstone **115.00**
  B-112, rose moonstone **115.00**
Clarissa, #2 Ts85 .... **400.00**
Colonial, B-104, clear **60.00**
  B-105, green **75.00**
  B-106, amber **85.00**
Corinthian, B-104, clear font w/black foot **55.00**
  B-114, white moonstone **80.00**
  B-116, rose moonstone **80.00**
  B-124, wht moonstone font, blk ft **95.00**
  B-125, wht moonstone font, green ft **80.00**
  B-126, wht moonstone font, rose ft **100.00**
  Black amethyst **60.00**
  Pink **80.00**
Lincoln Drape, short, B-62, ruby **325.00**
  Tall, B-76, cobalt **375.00**
  Tall, B-77, ruby **310.00**
Little Jewel, S44 .... **100.00**
Majestic, green **95.00**
Orientale, B-131, green **80.00**
  Replated, new shade, B-134 .... **65.00**
Queen, white **95.00**
Quilt, B-65, white moonstone **100.00**
  B-86, green moonstone **100.00**
  B-90, wht moonstone font, blk fot **120.00**
  B-91, wht moonstone font, rose ft **85.00**
Simplicity, B-28, rose **80.00**
  B-29, green **85.00**
  White, B-30 .... **75.00**
Solitaire, B-70 .... **700.00**
Venetian #99 clear, B burner **110.00**
  #100 .... **70.00**
  #103, rose **80.00**
Vertique, B-87, rose moonstone **120.00**
  B-88, yellow moonstone **260.00**
  B-92, green moonstone **115.00**
  B-93, white moonstone **325.00**
Washington Drape, B-47, bell stem, 701A shade **115.00**
  B-48, bell stem, green **140.00**
  B-49, bell stem **140.00**
  B-51, green **65.00**
  B-52, amber **65.00**
  Plain, B-53 .... **35.00**
  Plain, B-54 .... **55.00**
  Plain, B-55 .... **80.00**
  Round base, B-39, clear **45.00**
  Round base, B-40, green **65.00**
Hanging lamp #1 .... **600.00**
  #2 .... **500.00**
  #4 .... **300.00**
  #5 font, brass **120.00**
  #6 .... **200.00**
  #7 w/retractor **475.00**
  #8 .... **400.00**
  #9 .... **200.00**
  #10 .... **325.00**
  #11, #3 extension, 516 shade **175.00**

#12 w/716 shade **190.00**
  #12 w/decorated shade **425.00**
  B, chain **150.00**
Hanging lamp B w/716 shade **150.00**
Hanging lamp w/parchment shade **150.00**
Hanging store lamp, #6, style 116, opal shade 215 ... **300.00**
Shade, 201 .... **120.00**
  203 .... **50.00**
  215 .... **100.00**
  301 .... **95.00**
  401 .... **100.00**
  501 .... **90.00**
  501 #9 deluxe **350.00**
  516 .... **100.00**
  550 .... **500.00**
  601 .... **85.00**
  601S, cabin **225.00**
  616S, gristmill **340.00**
  620S **340.00**
  701A **90.00**
  701B, hobnail **100.00**
  716 .... **130.00**

Applesauce, frosted leaf font, etched shade, dated, orig dome . **800.00**
Argand, bronze, orig oil, elecrified, frosted shades, pr **500.00**
Art Deco, boudoir, all glass frosted umbrella shade, 12″ **450.00**
  Bronze dancing girl holding sm bulb, onyx base, 12″ ... **350.00**
  Geometric, grey marble glass, 3″ **40.00**
  Roman chariot w/horses, green shade, 12x11″ **70.00**
Art Nouveau, bronze dancer, millefiori shade, Collection Francaise **295.00**
Astral, cut & etched globe, brass stem & base, 24″ **475.00**
  Cut glass shade, grapes & leaves, brass & marble base **495.00**
Bronze nude on threaded glass light **125.00**
  Flame shape globe on ped, 9½″ **40.00**
  Lavender slag glass dome shade & base, 20″ **275.00**
  Musical jesters, frosted globe **100.00**
  Nude on sea lion, spatter globe, 18½x12″ **150.00**
  Nude w/basket, wht metal, tortoise shade **140.00**
Baccarat, oil, Amberiina pinwheel swirl shade, 10½″ **110.00**
Banquet, brass & slate base, Sandwich shade, prisms, 27″ **340.00**
  Diamond & Fan, clear, ball shade **250.00**
  Miniature, Delft globe, openwork base, slip-in font, 14″ **295.00**
  Miniature, Florette, green, no shade, CGCO **195.00**
  Pineapple & Fan, clear **320.00**
  Pyramid brass base, vaseline stem & etched shade, 28″ **485.00**
Basket, woven brass base, multicolor glass flowers, 10½″ **220.00**
Bergman, bronze w/gold paint, Austrian, 30x12½″ **3,950.00**

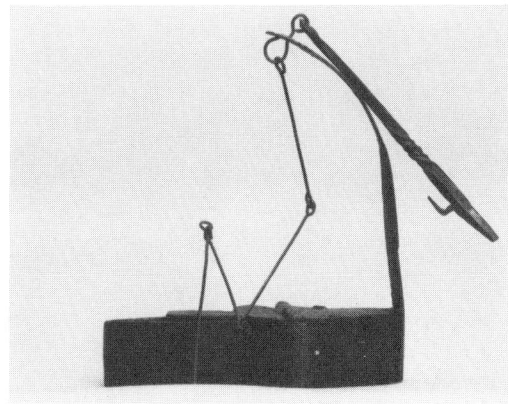

Betty lamp, wick-pick & hook, 4½″ **175.00**
Bicycle, carbide, Old Sol, Hawthorne, nickeled brass **55.00**

Carbide, Search Light, polished brass, 1900 . . . . **70.00**
Bigelow & Kennard, leaded shade, 12"; bronze base, 18" . . **3,750.00**
Blown molded, Blackberry, Owl & Shield, brass & marble base, 8" **75.00**
Boudoir, glass w/overlay of classic figures, florals, 11½" **175.00**
Bracket, Banded Rib, Owl & Moon chimney, mercury reflector, 1881 **120.00**
    MM & Co, clear, 3½" high, 4½" font **32.00**
    Oil, Fo Dewy & Sons, applied handle, 3½" **38.00**
Bradley & Hubbard, oriental filigree 6 panels, top & base lite . **750.00**
Camphene, wood w/pewter fittings, New England, 1830 . . . . . . **250.00**
Candle, double, tin shades, saucer base, scrolled arms, 18" . . . **565.00**
    Green satin w/frosted petal bases, 9¼", pr **350.00**
    With brass reflector **75.00**
Carriage, w/holders, modern, 17½", pr **185.00**
Ceiling, pitcher form w/spout & lid, lead on tin, Penn. 1800 . . **350.00**
    Pull down, cranberry w/prisms, 15" high dome, 1870 . . . . **1,200.00**
Chandelier, 4 arm, gas, ornate w/orig etched shades, 44" dia **1,500.00**
    Pull down, 3 milk glass globes, Jones, 1859, 28" dia **495.00**
    Pull down, prisms, signed scenic shade, brass, 1890 . . . . **635.00**
    Wood w/12 tole fixtures, fish decor, 42" dia **1,400.00**
    Wrought iron, holds 6 candles, 1850s **525.00**
Classique, bronze base, 8" shade **1,650.00**
Cut & pressed glass, 6" dome w/30 prisms, 12" **375.00**
    2 lights, 10" dia shade **2,150.00**
    32 prisms, 19" **2,500.00**
    Dahlia & cones, 22 prisms, 7-8"; 30" tall **3,650.00**
    Mushroom globe, 24 prisms, 14" **350.00**
DeCroismare, hanging, etched 14" dome, 3 side shades **2,250.00**
Desk lamp, cased green Verdelite shade, 2 adjustments **200.00**
    Verdelite, bronze w/double inks, 1912 . . . . **450.00**
Dining, side lamp, Fostoria candlesticks w/Cricklite shades, pr . **295.00**
Doll lamp, chalkware princess w/lace skirt, MIB, 17½" **30.00**
Dressmaker's brass, cranberry shade, kerosene, orig chimney . . **350.00**
Duffner & Kimberly, bronze Egyptains in base & leaded shaded **5,500.00**
    Leaded glass shade, 32" **2,350.00**

Lily blossoms, blue green ground, cattails & pads on base, 22" **2,200.00**
Duffner, filigree & caramel slag panels, bronze base **800.00**
Durand, King Tut art glass, table lamp **300.00**
Emeralite, desk lamp, 1916, orig **275.00**
    Desk lamp, brass filigree, slate base, Zebra shaded, 30" **795.00**
    Desk lamp, signed & dated **395.00**

Single knuckle lamp **225.00**
Student lamp, 2 shades, bell pulls **900.00**
Student lamp, 2 shades **400.00**
Fairy lamp, amber opal swirl pyramid, clear Clarke base, 3¾" . . **95.00**
    Blue Diamond Quilted MOP satin on Tunncliffe vase **295.00**
    Blue Hobnail pyramid, Davidson's **75.00**
    Blue shade w/Diamond Clarke base **60.00**
    Burmese, Clarke Cricklite base, 5" **345.00**
    Citron ribbed satin, Clarke base **85.00**
    Clarke Cricklite, crystal w/gilt fittings, 11" **225.00**
    Cranberry Verre Moire w/Clark's clear base, 5" **170.00**
    Cranberry w/fairies & foilage, clear base, 5" **165.00**
    Diamond Quilted MOP, rose w/clear Clarke base **145.00**
    Diamond Quilted MOP, w/holder, blue **150.00**
    Diamond Quilted ruby pyramid, clear Clarke base, 3½" **75.00**
    German Dog, 4" **170.00**
    Hanging, on mirror, red w/wht loop shade & bowl **850.00**
    Nailsea, rose w/candle cup, clear Cricklite base **285.00**
    Overshot, green pyramid, clear Clarke base, 4" **110.00**
    RS Germany **175.00**
    Ruby glass shade on Clarke base **65.00**
    Satin w/ribbed pink shade, clear holder, Cricklite **120.00**
    Sq folded base w/Burmese insert, ivy decor, large **1,250.00**
    Yellow satin glass pyramid, Clarke base, 3½" **110.00**
Figural, Admiral Dewey's copper & brass bullet, oil, 9" **400.00**
    Bisque lady, Schaffer & Vatter, 1890s **145.00**
    Cherub & lamb, Spelter base, Queen Anne #1 burner **125.00**
    Porcelain owl, pink overlay swirl shade, 13" **400.00**
    Santa Claus **1,500.00**
Findlay Dalzell, Oval Windows, green, 10" **150.00**
Finger lamp, amethyst w/reflector **300.00**
    Aquarius, amber **90.00**
    Aquarius, light blue, pedestal **130.00**
    Blue w/white opal swirls, handle **150.00**
    Bulls Eye, flat, green **120.00**
    Bulls Eye, green, pedestal **160.00**
    Coin Dot, blue opal **320.00**
    Coin Dot, clear & opal, pedestal **210.00**
    Coolidge Drape, cobalt **220.00**
    Corn, clear, 3" **115.00**
    Cranberry opal windows, clear handle **395.00**
    Diamond Band & Shield, cobalt **280.00**
    Dome shape, star bottom **20.00**
    Filley flat, clear, 1862 . . . . **60.00**
    Fishscale base, honeycomb font, ped, 2 handles, amber **145.00**
    Harp, Sandwich, whale oil **125.00**
    Heart pattern **70.00**
    Light green opal swirl, flat **180.00**
    Milk glass ball shaded, Bridgeport Brass Co **75.00**
    Peacock Feather, blue, w/ped **275.00**
    Pelotan, multicolor threads on wht **950.00**
    Pillows encircled, on standard blue **195.00**
    Primrose, opal-clear, flat **200.00**
    Prince Edward, green, tall ped **200.00**
    Riverside panel, green over clear, pedestal **120.00**
    Shrine, on pedestal **80.00**
    Sweetheart, green over clear, pedestal **400.00**
    Torpedo, pedestal base **78.00**
    Wedding Ring **95.00**
    Wheat, clear, pedestal **120.00**
Flat lamp, clear w/applied handle, 3½" tall w/4½" dia font . . . **38.00**
Fluid lamp, polychrome lithophane umbrella shade, 4 panels, 20" **575.00**
    Sandwich opaque wht pear-shape font, opal base, 11" **250.00**
Fulper, perfume lamp, Ballerina, 627 . . . . **185.00**

Going to Bed, brass, embossed lid, inside fitted for matches & tapers **80.00**
  Bronze squirrel, hinged head, 2″ **75.00**
  Ebony beehive w/brass & ivory detail, 3½″ **35.00**
  Englomise scenic, cylindrical, brass ft, 1862, 2½″ **30.00**
  Figural peacock, saucer base, top socket, 2″ **35.00**
  Papier mache w/lacquer & pewter ivy, 2½″ **30.00**
  Prince Albert Safety Box, brass, floral relief lid, 2¾″ **75.00**
  Reticulated brass, reverse scenic lid, 2½″ **20.00**
  Treen w/threaded lid, 2″ **18.00**
  Treen w/transfer scene, ivory socket, 2½″ **50.00**
Gone With the Wind, Bulls Eye, red satin, 1895, 25″ **800.00**
  Cherubs, green satin **1,600.00**
  Diamond Quilted, orange satin, 29″ **750.00**
  Font & globe w/4 lions heads, wht satin, Glo-Mar Artworks . **125.00**
  Green w/roses **400.00**
  Maple Leaf, red satin, half shade **675.00**
  Milk glass w/child's face, 25″ **550.00**
  Pillar & Chain, red satin **490.00**
  Pink & white w/florals, 23″ **325.00**
  Puffed out Maple Leaf, brass slip in font, 1897, 24″ **795.00**
  Red satin, Spelter base, brass burner & fittings, 24″ **675.00**
Galle, frosted glass w/pastel florals, top & base light, 14″ ... **5,500.00**
  Night light, gold w/bleeding hearts **1,400.00**
Gas light, w/mantle, orig box, 1912 Reflex **45.00**
Grease, wrought & cast iron, hook for hanging, heart shape, 7½″ **75.00**
HA Best, pryamid art glass shade, base w/entwined fish **325.00**
Hall lamp, Amberina, paneled swirl, ornate brass fittings ... **395.00**
Hand lamp, chartreuse overlay, beige scroll, panel base, complete **110.00**
  Cranberry glass cut panels, complete, 5″ **125.00**
  Feather Duster, amber, 3½″ **125.00**
  Opaque blue w/embossed water lilies, 5″ **110.00**
  Opaque green, embossed scrolls, square, complete, 5″ **95.00**
  Pink & chartreuse spatter overlay, 5″ **115.00**
Hanging, 8 panel carmel slag, orig glass beads **1,000.00**
  Brass, Victorian, all orig, rewired **450.00**
  Hall lamp, red satin **375.00**
  Pull down, hp shade, complete **200.00**
  Regal Iris, puffed out, butterscotch satin cased **595.00**
Hitchcock, mechanical, nickel on brass **350.00**
Hurricane, cranberry chimney, tin candle, w/hanging chain **85.00**
Jefferson, reverse painted 18″ floral shade, tapered base **1,800.00**
  Reverse painted scenic, sgnd & #d **975.00**
  Reverse poppy 16″ shade, bronze base **1,500.00**
  Scenic w/red sunset, fence, 16″ **1,000.00**
Kerosene, Apollo, amber, hobnail open top w/scallops, 15½″ . **150.00**
  Aquarius, med blue, 10″ **150.00**
  Aquarius, table lamp, amber, 9″ **135.00**
  Bull's Eye, green, 10″ **160.00**
  Bull's Eye Grape & Bead **95.00**
  Bull's Eye w/Diamond Point, applied handle, 5″ **85.00**
  Canadian Drape, 9½″ **100.00**
  Cathedral, blue font, clear base, 13″ **200.00**
  Chicago, amber, 10½″ **150.00**
  Cobalt w/scrolls, footed, 10″ **100.00**
  Columbian Coin, white, 9½″ **300.00**
  Copper base, floral ball shade, Miller **400.00**
  Copper feet & base, signed floral shade, 1890, 10″ **300.00**
  Dahzell Windows, green #2 burner, 10″ **175.00**
  Embossed daisies, clear, 1880 .... **85.00**
  Feather Duster, amber, 8¼″ **150.00**
  Feather Duster, iron base, 8″ **24.00**
  Findlay Sweetheart, clear #2, 11″ **165.00**
  LaBelle & Corn, clear, 7″ **110.00**
  Moon & Stars, med blue, 10½″ **120.00**

Mountain Laurel, clear, 8″ **85.00**
New York, amber, 9″ **160.00**
Open Rose, clear **30.00**
Peacock Feather, blue, 9″ **245.00**
Peacock Feather, blue, 11″ **265.00**
Primrose, clear opal, clear stem, 8″ **195.00**
Reverse swirl, amber opal **200.00**
Sheldon swirl, clear, blue, black, 8¾″ **150.00**
Sheldon swirl, opal & clear, 8″ **150.00**
Sheldon swirl, vaseline opal, 8″ **195.00**
Snowflake #2, cranberry, ... **325.00**
Snowflake, blue opal, 8″ **265.00**
St Louis, amber **175.00**
Stripe, blue opal on clear pattern, 8″ **250.00**
Sweetheart, green, 9¾″ **215.00**
Sweetheart, green, 10¼″ **225.00**
Swirl band, star base, ribbed medallion font **24.00**
Thick green glass, brass cup base, 1880s **150.00**
Wheat, table lamp, clear, 7″ **110.00**
Wildrose & Bowknot, caramel & clear **650.00**
Wildrose & Bowknot, clear **300.00**
Lantern, amber globe, Dietz Universal **30.00**
  Brass w/bevel glass, red lens & font, back bracket **125.00**
  Buckboard, Warren Sta-Lit **35.00**
  Buggy, 2 Bull's Eye, red & clear, Dietz Jr **65.00**
  Candle, tin, 3 glass sides, dome top, 11″ **55.00**
  D-Lite #2, frame & globe date 1912 .... **25.00**
  Dash, Buckeye, Dietz **68.00**
  Doctor's, slit & open faces, 1800s, 8″ **75.00**
  Farm, amber globe, Dietz **60.00**
  Folding, Miner's pat 1865, w/match compartment, 5x3″ **145.00**
  Hooded Blizzard #2, Dietz **35.00**
  Kerosene, decorative brass, bevel glass, handle, 10″ **70.00**
  Miner's brass Justrite Carbide **85.00**
  Punched tin, Paul Revere type, 13″ **80.00**
  Whale oil, punched tin, glass globe, 1830s **195.00**
Larkin, oil lamp, brass metal, urn, floral satin shade, Miller ... **225.00**
Leaded glass, spider web shade, split leaf brass base **700.00**

Wisteria, conical, irregular edge, 23½″, ht w/base 31″ ... **6,000.00**
Library, matching shade & font holder w/florals, prisms **695.00**

Pull down, hp shade, prisms..........................300.00
Millefiori, 17″......................................500.00
Miner's, tin, long spout, eagle, 1904, 2¾″..........65.00
  Tin, long spout, hinged top, signed, 2½″..........45.00
Miniature, beaded heart sweetheart, clear, 5″......110.00
  Bull's Eye, red eyes, base rim......................75.00
  Bull's Eye, clear USGC..............................60.00
  Christmas tree, painted............................185.00
  Coreopsis, pink & green, Consolidated..............250.00
  Cosmos, yellow band................................285.00
  Daisy, blue..120.00
  Daisy, clear, USGC..................................80.00
  Delft, milk glass w/blue ships.....................150.00
  Embossed sunbursts, w/stem, clear...................80.00
  Evening Star, clear, opal chimney..................100.00
  Iron & brass, swirled glass........................145.00
  Lincoln Drape w/red shade...........................70.00
  Little Favorite, bristol shade.....................110.00
  Maltese Cross, gold decor..........................245.00
  Milk glass, blue trim, red daisies.................365.00
  Milk glass, plumes in relief........................50.00
  Milk glass, Rib & Panel............................120.00
  Mission octagon, milk glass, USGC..................175.00
  Nellie Bly, blue & wht.............................120.00
  Nellie Bly, milk glass, clear Deco shade...........125.00
  Optic, clear, USGC..................................60.00
  Pairpoint, Delft w/boats & windmills...............400.00
  Raindrop, tall stem, orig burner, no shade..........40.00
  Raindrop w/amber stem...............................80.00
  Sandwich, opaque blue, hex font w/stars, plumes....350.00
  Spider web, milk glass, rose decor.................320.00
  Torquay, milk glass painted blue...................225.00
Mission, oak, 4 slag panels.........................400.00
  Oak, caramel glass panes, 20″......................650.00
  Oak, dark finish, green slag shade, kerosene.......275.00
Moe Bridges, miniature, reverse scenic..............450.00
  Night light, hp glass shade........................375.00
  Reverse scenic, linen texture, 18″...............1,500.00
  Triple water fall scenic, 18″ shade, 2 lite base.2,800.00
Night light, Bead & Panel, Fostoria, clear w/red....50.00
  Bisque bull's head, wht horns, amber eyes, German..185.00
  Bisque cat w/green eyes, German....................185.00
  Bisque dog's head, brown w/amber eyes, German......185.00
  Bridgeport Brass All Night Lamp, nickel plate.......85.00
  Cranberry thumbprint, Wright.......................130.00
  Fleur de Lis, Imperial..............................40.00
  Narrow swirl, clear................................250.00
Nutmeg, pressed glass, brass fittings, embossed.....140.00
Oil, Artichoke, red satin, 21″......................250.00
  Kinnears pat 1851...................................80.00
  Lutz type font, clear w/wht threading, 7½″.........225.00
  Peanut w/chimney....................................50.00
  Pewter, Capen & Molinweaux, double burner, 9″......125.00
  Pewter, double burners, 6½″.........................90.00
  Pewter, drip pan, font w/tin wick support, 1851, 11½″..500.00
  Rayo, white shade, 1894.............................90.00
  Ribbed Bellflower..................................150.00
  Sandwich, brass collar, 1820s, 10½″................185.00
  Snowflake, cranberry opal, stand lamp..............310.00
  Tin disk, tubular wick support, brass lever, 4½″ dia..55.00
  Tin w/brass fittings, clear pleated shade, small....48.00
  Tubular, 1876, pat date, 12″.......................150.00
  Zippered Loop, metal collar, marigold..............135.00
Overlay, double-cut, pear-shape font, overlay stem, 13″..750.00

Ruby cut to clear, grapes, marble base, 14″.........300.00
Parade torch, kerosene, tin, primitive...............22.00
Pittsburg, farm scene w/red house, lake & people, 16″..1,000.00
Post, CT Ham, 1897..................................250.00
Pump, French pewter.................................145.00
Reverse painted 5 panel scene w/sheep, Miller, 6″ dia..1,000.00
Reverse painted mountain lake shade, 16″, metal base, 22½″..880.00
  Ochre w/lower border, 16″, metal base, 22″.........440.00
  Tropical shade, 14″, Pittsburg, 18″..............1,500.00
  Woodland scene, 6 side base, 18″ shade.............550.00
Royal Bonn, oil, urn style china font, green & gold.165.00
Student lamp, 3 layered cased shade, Bradley & Hubbard, 10″..650.00
  Brass, 3 layered cased yellow shade, Miller, 10″...750.00
  Brass, 1879, CA Kleeman............................495.00
  Brass w/orig wht shade, Manhattan Brass Co, 1876...275.00
Table lamp, brass holder w/cherub handles, Handel shade, Miller..350.00
  Coin dot, clear & opal, 8½″........................240.00
  Curved panel, screw on shade, tree trunk base, 22″ dia..3,500.00
  Curved slag shade, 6 panels, brass base, 24″.......340.00
  Dore & slag glass, 10″ dia.........................425.00
  Embossed brass, glass prism, beaded fringe, pr.....700.00
  Porcelain & brass base w/colonial couple, 22x36″, pr..350.00
  Sandwich frosted globe & chimney, 21″..............185.00
  With caramel slag shade.............................60.00
Wall lamp, ci, kerosene w/10″ reflector..............80.00
  Double, tin w/glass globe, milk glass shades.......225.00
  Tin w/reflector, 1800s.............................155.00
Wedding lamp, blue base, clear font, match holder, Ripley..1,250.00
  Clambroth fonts & base, blue match holder, Ripley..750.00
Welsbach, carbide harp w/tank........................65.00
Whale oil, blown font, brass collar, pressed base w/claws, 12″..140.00
  Blown molded on brass & marble base, clear, 7″.....65.00
  Brass, saucer base w/handle, 6½″...................185.00

Cast iron, chicken finial, 8½″.......................150.00
Hand forged, hanging................................100.00
Hyde, 5″...85.00
Israel Trask sgnd, 9″, pr...........................500.00
Pewter, 6″..100.00
Pewter, Capen & Molineux, 1850, pr..................600.00
Pewter, hand or hanging, Gimbal, 4″, pr.............220.00
Pewter, single wick, conical, Smith & Co, 1850s, 5″..165.00

Pottery, heart shape w/handle, 4½″ **675.00**
Punty & Loop, glass stem, round base, 7″ **75.00**
Sandwich glass **175.00**
Saucer base, turned shaft & bulbous font, wick holder **60.00**
Saucer base, finger ring, witch-hat font, mica, 4″ **150.00**
Tin w/crimped saucer, conical w/handle, 5″ **30.00**
Wilkinson, floral leaded glass shade, 22″ dia, bronze base . . **4,950.00**
Jeweled leaded glass shade, 16″, bronze base **1,750.00**
Poppy leaded glass shade, 20″ dia, metal base, 27″ **3,300.00**

Lap Desks

Lap desks were popular during the last half of the 19th century and were often used by travelers who filled some of their lengthy travel time with correspondence. They provided a portable writing surface and were fitted with an inkwell and compartments for ink and other writing accouterments.

Chinese, teakwood w/scroll & ivory inlay, hinged cover **240.00**
Ebony, w/elephant **85.00**
Green paint, mustard & red diamond borders, dated 1781 . . . . **175.00**
Mahogany, brass bound, inner leather writing surface, mid-1800s **300.00**
Brass flower form inlay, fitted interior, late 1800s **95.00**
Brass inlay, gilted tooled leather writing surface **105.00**
Brass mounted, interior drawers & inkwell, 1800s **360.00**
With key plate, 9x12″ **150.00**
Oak, sloped lid, brass mounts, inner compartments, 1800s **125.00**
Papier mache, black lacquer, inlaid MOP, hp floral panels, carved top **100.00**
Pine, dovetailed construction, 8x11″ **55.00**
Printed floral decor, 8x12″ **40.00**
Rosewood & MOP, bird & floral motifs, hinged lid, 1800s **375.00**
Folding cover, side drawer, inscription plate, 1800s **412.00**
Walnut, hinged lid, fitted interior, 1800s, 14x9″ **49.00**
Inset MOP, velvet lined, interior glass wells, all orig **162.00**

Law Related Collectibles

Billy club, leather wrapped top, thong handle, pat dated 1874 . . **65.00**
Walnut, thong handle, 1880-1890, marks, 12½x1¾″ **55.00**
Broadside, C bunker etc., swindler, 1910, has nicks **75.00**
OC Klingman, embezzlement, photo, 1911, 11x8½″ **50.00**
Reward, Alexander Frederick Givens, photo, 1894, 9½x12″ . . **150.00**
Reward, Arthur Leroy Lowrie, robbery, photo & mug shots, 1916 **100.00**
Reward, subject absconds w/funds, mug shots, 1916, 13x11″ **200.00**
Chair, judge's, mahog w/tufted leather seat & back **2,600.00**
Club, walnut, thong handle, 1880-1890, marks, 12½x1¾″ **55.00**
Gavel, judge's, walnut, highly polished **85.00**
Handbill, wanted for murder & robbery, 1921, mug shot, 11x8½″ **75.00**
Handcuffs, iron, Green County 1876 . . . . **80.00**
Leg iron, Ten Slave, iron, ends pointed, 2x12″ **85.00**
Smithy fashioned, 1870, pr **65.00**
Mantrap, New Eng, iron, for game poachers **195.00**
Rockbreaker, prison, iron doughnut on wood handle **45.00**
Wrist restraint, chain, early 1800s **62.00**

Le Verre Francais

Le Verre Francais was produced during the 1920s by Schneider, at Epinay-sur-Seine in France. It was a commercial art glass in the cameo style, composed of layered glass with the designs engraved by acid. Favored motifs were styled leaves and flowers, or geometric patterns. It was marked with the name in script or with an inlaid filigrane.

Night light, cameo florals, metal leaf base, 15½″ circumference **695.00**
Vase, ball shape w/stem & base, floral cameo, signed, 8½″ . . . **425.00**
Burgandy w/cameo florals & leaves, bulbous base, 32x12″. **1,750.00**
Cameo, Art Deco & wheel engraved, 3 color, blown foot, 5½″ **385.00**
Cameo, Deco motif, 3 color, footed, 11½″ **480.00**
Cream w/cameo berries & leaves, urn shape, ped, 10x6″ **750.00**
Orange & yellow cameo, signed, 18″ **800.00**
Orange w/brown cameo design, wht flecks, 5½″ **395.00**

Leeds

The Leeds Pottery was established in 1758 in Yorkshire, and under various managements produced fine creamware, often highly reticulated or transfer printed; shiny black glazed Jackfield wares; and figurines similar to those made in the Staffordshire area. Little of the early wares were marked; after 1775, the impressed Leeds Pottery mark was used. From 1781 to 1820, the name Hartley Greens & Co. was added. The pottery closed in 1898.

Basket, bulbous, scalloped rim, openwork w/twig handles **165.00**
Bowl, floral etched, 10¾″ **28.00**
Coffee pot, pear-shape, multi floral, 10¼″ **325.00**
Cup & saucer, handleless, enameled 3 color floral, miniature . . **100.00**
Cup plate, blue feather edge, 4½″ dia **55.00**
Dish, deep, raised blue floral medallions, feather edged, 10″ . . . **90.00**
Jug, notched rim, man by river, 5¼″ **250.00**

Loving cup, 3 handles, w/maxim, 5″ **75.00**
Mug, child's, green & cream check, 3″ **30.00**
Child's, lustre decor scene, pin-striped borders **60.00**
Plate, octagonal, 5 color floral, blue feather edge, 6½″ **290.00**
Platter, 3 color floral, 5x4″ **275.00**
Soup plate, w/flange rim, blue feather edge, 10″ dia **40.00**
Stallion, pearlware, tan & black, oblong base, 16¾″ **385.00**
Sugar bowl, w/cover, Gaudy, blues, 7″ **95.00**

Legras

Legras and Cie was founded in St. Denis, France, in 1864. Production continued until about 1914. They made cameo art glass in pastel shades decorated with landscapes in Art Nouveau and Art Deco designs executed by acid cuttings through two to six layers of glass. Their work is signed Legras in relief.

Bowl, basket shape, cherries & leaves, enamel decor, 8″ **335.00**
Cameo country scene, oval, 4x4½″ **575.00**
Centerpiece, w/pair of vases, all w/scenic decor, 23″ **2,450.00**

Cracker jar, cameo, burgundy floral w/brass fittings, covered .. **795.00**
Decanter, cameo, frosted body w/yellow trim, signed, 7½ **395.00**
Rose bowl, cameo winter snow scene, signed, 3x3¼" **125.00**
Vase, acid cut, Art Deco type floral, 10½" **395.00**
   Acid cut, geometric, 5½" **345.00**
   Ball shape, cameo, shaded lavender berries, frosted ground, 6" **350.00**
   Cameo w/enamel, forest scene, 13" **450.00**
   Cameo, purple ivy on peach-to-frosted textured body, 11½". **550.00**
   Cameo, red w/birds decor, 9½x12" **700.00**
   Cameo, seaweed pattern, cream, tan & brown, 14" **1,375.00**
   Cylinder, flare neck & base, frosted orange w/vintage decor, 14" **350.00**
   Enamel winter scene w/woman walking, signed, 14½" **225.00**
   Spherical w/long neck, etched glass w/enameled trees, 23½" **1,000.00**
   Tapered cylinder, mottled oranged w/painted lake scene, 13¾" **350.00**
   Wht swans on lake, greens & browns, 13" **495.00**

Lenox

    Walter Scott Lenox, former art director at Ott and Brewer, and Jonathan Cox founded The Ceramic Art Company (CAC in the listing below) of Trenton, New Jersey, in 1889. By 1906, Lenox had formed his own company which he called Lenox, Inc. Originally he produced high quality ornamental art wares; but always striving for improvements, he imported two potters from the Belleek district of Ireland and became the first in America to produce the fine fragile chinaware known as Belleek. Because of this development, he began to concentrate on the superior dinnerware for which the company became famous. Since 1917, Lenox has been chosen the official White House china.

Angel, white, 4½" **95.00**
Ashtray, Atlantic Sail Fish, signed, gr mk, 8" dia **37.00**
   Lenox Rose **10.00**
   Statford, wht, gold trim, gr mk, emb sides, 7" dia **30.00**
Atomizer, Devilbiss, round emb flowers w/blue dots, gr mk..... **78.00**
   Atomizer, penguin **65.00**
Basket, basketweave pattern................................ **25.00**
Bird, green crested, 4"................................... **35.00**
   Green open body, rare, 6½"........................... **65.00**
   Pink crested....................................... **35.00**
   Pink open body, rectangular base, 6½" long **60.00**
   White, 3½" **15.00**
   White, green wreath mk, 7".......................... **32.00**
Bottle, w/figural stopper, Hattie Carnegie, wht **130.00**
Bouillon cup & saucer, Golden Gate **23.00**
   With underliner, Maryland **14.00**
Bowl, centerpiece, Lenox Rose, 3x10½" **110.00**
   Coral, ruffled rim, green wreath mk, 4x6¼"............. **85.00**
   Hexagon, silver overlay, palette mk, w/handles, 8" dia....... **75.00**
   Peacocks in relief, floral & scroll borders, 8½" dia **87.50**
   Salad/dessert, Blue Ridge **22.00**
Box, cigarette, w/2 ashtrays, green, Fleur de Lis, gr mk **47.00**
   Green/wht finial, gold trim, sides pinched, green wreath mk, 3x7" **125.00**
   With cover, Art Deco heart, twig finial, green wreath mk **48.00**
   With lid, florals, gold rim, 2x5x3½" **37.50**
   White, gold trim, feather handle, green mk, 8½x3½" **40.00**
Cake plate, ftd, Ming, 10¾" **75.00**
Candleholder, lyre-shape, green mk, 8" **40.00**
   Nantucket Chairback, decorated, gr mk, 5x7½"........... **45.00**
Chocolate cup, w/Mauser sterling holder & saucer, gr w/rose swags **120.00**
Chocolate pot, w/creamer, Belleek, CAC, pink roses, 7"...... **245.00**
Cider pitcher, Belleek, CAC, blackberries, 6½x8" **125.00**
Cider pitcher, pink roses, green handle, CAC, 6x9" **120.00**
   Shaded, pink roses, green studded handles, CAC, 6x9"..... **110.00**
Cigarette box, World's Fair, 1939 .... **75.00**

Coffee pot, Westchester, shape #1960, gold mk............. **165.00**
   Gold lily of the valley, green mk, 8½" **95.00**
Coffee set, silver overlay flowers, 3 pc.................... **350.00**
Compote, boat-shape, gold handles, grapes **125.00**
   Gold handles, pedestal, rim band; florals, 4½x10" **70.00**
   Yellow, lavender floral; gold handles, palette mk, 4¼x3¼" ... **75.00**
Condiment set, oranges, leaves, gold decor, Belleek, palette mk, 3 pc **75.00**
Cornucopia, fluted top, ftd, rope trim handle, leaves **85.00**
Cream soup, Aurora, w/stand **40.00**
   Belvedere, w/stand **23.00**
   Blue Ridge **35.00**
   Golden Gate, w/stand **34.00**
   Lenox Rose, w/stand **40.00**
   Orchard, w/stand **35.00**
   Windsor, gr mk, #1307, w/stand **45.00**
Creamer & sugar, w/cover, Belleek, CAC, Hawthorne, wht w/gold gilt **225.00**
Cruet, white, gold trim, gold stopper, gr mk, 8½"........... **34.00**
Cup & saucer, Antoinette **64.00**
   Aurora **40.00**
   Beltane Coral **40.00**
   Cambridge **56.00**
   Cobalt, CAC, hexagon **65.00**
   Cynthia **25.00**
   Engagement, Belleek, wht, green wreath mk............. **115.00**
   Essex Maroon **53.00**
   Golden Wreath **38.00**
   Imperial **35.00**
   Lowell.. **25.00**
   Ming **22.00**
   Peachtree **25.00**
   Renaissance **55.00**
   Rhodora **34.00**
   Rhodora Variation **42.00**
   Roslyn **20.00**
   Savoy Maroon **45.00**
   Sonata **40.00**
   Westbury **48.00**
   Weschester, green mk **62.00**
   Windsor, green mk, shape #1620....................... **45.00**
Cup, Imperial **24.00**
Demi cup & saucer, Belleek, cobalt w/silver overlay, gr wreath mk **95.00**
   Belleek, ivory w/silver geese overlay, octagonal **50.00**
   Dark gray, rare **30.00**
   Green, green wreath mk **25.00**
   Ribbed, black wreath mk **24.00**
   Sterling silver holder, Belleek **50.00**
   Washington-Wakefield pattern **35.00**
   White ribbed, blk wreath mk **20.00**
   White shell **20.00**
Demitasse pot, cream w/silver overlay **130.00**
Dish, pink w/wht handle, gold trim, green mk, 3½x6" **20.00**
   White shell, gold trim, green mk, 6x3½x2½" **30.00**
Dressing bowl, ftd, w/underplate **40.00**
Ewer, red roses, gold handle & ruffled spout, CAC, 8½" **155.00**
   Rose, wht embossed panels, feathery handles, 6" **80.00**
Figurine, Floradora, Belleek, hi-glaze wht.................. **250.00**
   Mistress Mary...................................... **475.00**
   Standing nude, wht bisque, 12" **235.00**
Fish plates, Morley, wide gold band, 12 .... **750.00**
Flower holder, circular rope, 2 apertures, handle............ **32.00**
   Rib base, 4 apertures, green mk **35.00**
Fruit dish, Ming **14.00**
Fruit saucer, Antoinette **34.00**
   Aurora **20.00**

Gravy, Aurora	**92.00**
Windsor, green mk, shape #1112½, w/stand #1118	**90.00**
Inkwell, hp florals, CAC, green wreath mk, 3 pc	**225.00**
Jug, deer, dragon handle, Belleek, 6″	**125.00**
Lamp, lady w/fan, wht bisque, sgnd	**275.00**
Lamp shade	**50.00**
Leaf dish, crushed gold rim, 8½″ long	**27.50**
Mug, barrel shape, blue & wht, football players, CAC gr wreath, 5″	**195.00**
Belleek, CAC, 3 handles, pink, blue & gold, purple palette mk	**65.00**
Belleek, CAC, gooseberries, sgnd	**95.00**
Elk head, gold dragon handle, fruit decor, Belleek, 6″	**95.00**
Monk, CAC	**65.00**
Pen holder, custom made for Shaeffer, wht w/gold trim, 6x6″	**50.00**
Pitcher, Bouquet, wht w/gold trim, gr mk, 5½″	**20.00**
Carolina, wht, gold trim w/embossed flowers, gr mk, 7x3x7½″	**35.00**
Colonial, pink w/wht handle, gr mk, 5x4x5½″	**35.00**
Belleek, CAC, Indian in headdress, 14″	**495.00**
Brown glaze w/sterling overlay, monogram, 4″	**45.00**
Plate, bread & butter; Antoinette	**22.50**
Aurora	**15.00**
Avon	**9.50**
Cambridge	**21.00**
Cynthia	**7.50**
Festival	**15.00**
Golden Wreath	**12.00**
Imperial	**10.00**
Lenox Rose	**15.00**
Renaissance	**18.00**
Rhodora	**12.00**
Royal Oak	**17.00**
Sheffield Plain	**10.00**
Starlight	**9.50**
Windsor, green mk, shape #5½, 6¼″	**15.00**
Plate, dinner; Antoinette	**42.50**
Aurora	**26.00**
Cambridge	**38.00**
Classic, w/pumpkin colored band on rim	**26.00**
Cynthia	**15.00**
Fountain	**24.00**
Imperial	**21.00**
Notre Dame Sheffield, w/blue band on rim	**17.00**
Peachtree	**25.00**
Renaissance	**36.00**
Rhodora	**21.00**
Romance	**43.00**
Rose	**27.50**
Royal Oak	**35.00**
Sheffield Plain	**18.00**
Starlight	**24.00**
Windsor, green mk, shape #10½	**30.00**
Plate, luncheon; Blue Ridge	**23.00**
Colonial	**26.00**
Lenox Rose	**22.00**
Renaissance	**26.00**
Starlight, 9″	**15.00**
Plate, salad; Alden	**24.00**
Antoinette	**31.00**
Aurora	**20.00**
Avon	**12.00**
Cambridge	**26.00**
Cynthia	**13.00**
Golden Wreath	**18.00**
Imperial	**18.00**
Lenox Rose	**20.00**
Renaissance	**26.00**
Rose	**16.00**
Starlight	**14.00**
Windsor, green mk, shape #6, 7½″	**20.00**
Platter, Aurora, 13¾″	**65.00**
Aurora, 17″	**95.00**
Avon, 10x13″	**47.50**
Rhodora, 16″	**70.00**
Maryland, round, 12½″	**100.00**
Windsor, green mk, shape #12, 13½″	**68.00**
Powder box, Hattie Carnegie, Art Deco head, 4x3½″	**80.00**
Rose, round, 8x3¾″	**110.00**
Relish jar, Rose	**35.00**
Salt & pepper, orange w/foliage, gold decor, Belleek	**42.00**
Salt, swan, green wreath, 2½″ long	**27.00**
Saucer, Aurora	**12.50**
Cynthia	**7.00**
Golden Wreath	**11.00**
Golden Wreath, fruit	**20.00**
Lenox Rose	**13.00**
Sheffield Plain	**9.00**
Trent	**13.50**
Windsor, fruit, green mk, shape #5	**21.00**
Server, Greenbriar, gold trim, green mk, no USA, 8½″ w	**50.00**
Shell dish, Rose, 6″	**35.00**
Sherbet, Belleek, ftd, CAC, fluted edge, gold paste, 3½″	**130.00**
Shoe, undecorated	**75.00**
White embossed pattern, rare	**125.00**
Soup, rim style; Colonial	**33.00**
Golden Wreath	**27.00**
Imperial	**25.00**
Pagoda, w/yellow rim	**28.00**
Souvenir bowl, Yale Stadium in relief, 1914, 7″ long	**150.00**
Sugar & creamer, Betty Ware, brown w/silver overlay	**200.00**
Washington's 200th birthday 1732-1932	**125.00**
Sugar, w/cover, Oak Leaf maroon	**15.00**
Swan, 12″	**140.00**
Closed back, 4½x5½″	**45.00**
Cream, gold mk, 4x4¾″	**24.00**
Pink, 4½x2½″	**34.00**
Green mk, pr, 3x4½″	**35.00**
White, gold trim, green mk, 5x3″	**32.00**
Tea set, Art Deco piano key design, blk & wht, gr wreath mk	**225.00**
Belleek, geese & trees, ivory, yellow, green, 3 pc	**275.00**
Hawthorne, ltd ed, 3 pc	**225.00**
Washington-Wakefield, green mk, 3 pc	**195.00**
Tea tile, Lenox Rose pattern	**60.00**
Teapot, w/lid, brown glaze w/silver overlay, mkd, 3½x3¾″	**145.00**
Toby jug, Wm Penn, Indian handle, green wreath mk	**175.00**
Wm Penn, undecorated	**125.00**
Vase, Belleek, CAC, red & wht roses, sgnd, 1903, 15″	**325.00**
Belleek, floral, sgnd W Marsh, 11½″	**375.00**
Belleek, ivory w/hp Japanese maidens, beaded gold, 10″	**265.00**
Belleek, pastel roses, sgnd W Marsh, 11½″	**345.00**
Bud, Lenox Rose, bulbous, gr mk, 8″	**32.00**
Colonial Lady, wht glaze	**155.00**
Coral w/floral & ribbing relief, green mk, 6″	**45.00**
Cylinder, floral design, green mk, 10x3″	**35.00**
Gothic, green & wht, fluted top, gold trim, green mk, 9″	**51.00**
Horn Plenty, fluted edge, 10″	**48.00**
Pedestal w/gold leaf design handles, CAC, 12½″	**85.00**
Reda and the Swan, glazed	**300.00**
Regal, blue & wht, platinum trim, green mk, 9″	**62.00**
Regal, green & wht, gold trim, green mk, 9″	**60.00**

Rose, Ardmore Rhodora, wht w/gold trim, 5½x9¼" **50.00**
Trumpet, blk bands & flowers, Belleek palette, 1919, 9" **35.00**
White w/gold handles in leaf form, CAC, 12" **75.00**
With dog, 8" **295.00**
Vegetable dish, Antoinette, oval, open **109.00**
Aurora, oval, large, open **69.00**
Avon, oval **37.50**
Southern Gardens, oval, large, open **95.00**
Windsor, green mk, covered, shape #1112½ **180.00**
Windsor, green mk, round w/2 handles, shape #1929 ...... **80.00**
Woman's head, #2138, glazed, 4½" **134.00**

Letter Openers

Advertising, Adkins Motor Co, Omaha Ford Cars, bronze plate handle **16.50**
Dupont Explosives, aluminum laminated handle **22.00**
Embalmers Supply Co, bronze, bottle handle **14.00**
Fort Pitt Casket Co, bronze, triple thick handle **14.00**
Frank Mossberg & Co, picture of factory.................. **18.00**
Gates Vulco V-Belt, bronze, v-belt cast in handle **11.00**
Hawley & Hoops, NY, 1875-1925, Quality Candy, nickeled steel **14.00**
Ice Cream Mfg, Silver Anniv, picture of ice cream sundae **28.00**
Illinois Life Insurance Co, 1913, porcelain handle **22.00**
Irwan Auger Bit Co, made from steel auger bit **6.00**
Knowled & Moudry Pharmacy **22.00**
Martin Metal Mfg Co, Wichita, Kansas, brass **8.00**
Northern Pacific Railroad, bronze **14.00**
Pittsburgh Steel Co, made from large steel nail **6.00**
Red Ball Transfer Co, brass blade, figural lady's leg **6.00**
Remington UMC, knife in handle **16.00**
Uneeda Boy **75.00**
Wagner Mfg Co, Cedar Falls, Iowa, celluloid **5.00**
Weber Implement & Auto Co, St Louis, brass **8.00**
Welsbach Co **40.00**
Wheeling Steel Corp, made from La Belle cut nail **6.00**
Art Deco, Egyptian brass dagger in sheath **12.00**
Bone, figural Indian, souvenir, 5½" **15.00**
Hand carved, 9" **15.00**
Brass, Art Nouveau figural handle **50.00**
Claw handle, Germany................................. **60.00**

Dragon handle, 8" **28.00**
Figural bare-chested Indian............................. **20.00**

Owl, 8½" **35.00**
Viking sword, dated 1895, Germany, 9" **18.00**
Celluloid, figural Indian w/pipe........................... **18.00**

Elephant, 7" **14.00**
Figural alligator **9.50**

Figural owl handle.................................... **13.50**
Geisha Girl, Germany **14.00**
Copper, figural Army rifle, advertising Army & Navy goods **11.00**
Dagger shape, bullet shell handle, 7" **15.00**
English broad sword, ornate handle **13.00**
Figural, alligator swallowing black man **23.00**
Chicken foot handle, cast bronze **27.50**
Rifle w/bayonet, 8" **15.00**
Rooster, sterling, Art Deco **23.00**
Seated Indian, arrowhead blade **20.00**
Goat's horn handle, 5", overall length 11" **22.00**
Ivory, carved elephants **17.00**
Carved rabbit, 7".................................... **16.00**
Carved windows handle, sterling blade, 5½" **22.50**
Handcarved, Victorian **75.00**
Scrimshawed floral design, old **25.00**
Jade, carved pug dog head, faceted ruby eyes & collar **1,100.00**
Pewter, figural gargoyle of Notre Dame, 9¼" **22.00**
Figural girl's head, Art Nouvea........................ **18.00**
Souvenir, Century of Progress, Chicago, 1933, bronze **11.00**
Empire State Building, NY, very early **18.00**
Mardi Gras, 1910, brass **80.00**
Washington DC, late 1800s, 7" **30.00**
Sterling, Aksarben, Omaha, 1902 .... **27.50**
Acorn pattern, stamped George Jensen, Denmark.......... **66.00**
Embossed wave motif & Greek Revival medallion, 1890 .... **880.00**
Repousse design, Shreve Crump & Low **32.00**
With MOP blade **19.00**
Sword in sheath **12.50**

Libbey

The New England Glass Co. was established in 1818 in Boston, Mass. In 1892, it became known as the Libbey Glass Company. At Chicago's Columbian Expo in 1893, Libbey set up a ten pot furnace and made glass souvenirs. The display brought them world wide fame. Between 1878 and 1918, Libbey made exquisite cut and faceted glass, considered today to be the best of the brilliant period glassware. The company is credited for several innovations---the Owens bottle machine that made mass production possible; and the Westlake machine which turned out both electric light bulbs and tumblers automatically. They also developed a machine to polish the rims of their tumblers in such a way that chipping was unlikely to occur. Their glassware carried the patented Safedge guarantee.

Libbey also made glassware in numerous colors-cobalt, ruby pink, green and amber. In 1935, it was bought by Owens-Illinois, and remains a divison of that company.

Bowl, covered, satin glass, floral trim, sgnd **350.00**
Cut glass, 8", sgnd **125.00**
Cut glass, Glenda pattern, 2x9" dia **325.00**
Cut glass, Stars & Ferns pattern, sgnd, 10" dia **275.00**
Cut glass, Wedgemere pattern, 3½x8" **795.00**
Box, trinket, cut glass, sgnd **350.00**
Bread tray, cut glass, hobstar, fan, strawberry, sgnd, 12x6" ... **285.00**
Bucket, champagne, cut glass, 32 point star on base, hobstars, 6" **480.00**
Candlestick, camel in stem **100.00**
Celery, cut glass, 8" **150.00**
Celery boat, cut glass, Colonna pattern, deep, sgnd........ **245.00**
Celery tray, cut glass, 8" long **135.00**
Champagne, squirrel stem, sgnd **115.00**
Twisted stem, ribbed w/narrow green lines, 6" **135.00**
Compote, cut glass, geometrics, knobbed stem w/teardrop, 10½" dia **625.00**
Decanter, cut glass, Harvard pattern, w/matching stopper, 13". **550.00**
Fruit bowl, cut glass, Gloria, sgnd, 9" **300.00**

Goblet, black panther stem, sgnd, 7" **145.00**
Ice cream dish, scalloped edge, hobs, strawberry & diamond, 8" dia **160.00**
Maize, bowl, opaque wht w/green husks, 9" dia............. **95.00**
   Syrup, opaque wht w/green husks **270.00**
   Tumbler, opaque w/blue husks, 4" **150.00**
   Vase, blue opal **65.00**
   Vase, wht opal **35.00**
Pitcher, champagne, cut, Harvard pattern, 11" **375.00**
   Cut glass, Middlesex, sgnd **700.00**
   Cut glass, sgnd, 9x5½" round **165.00**
   Water, cut glass, flute cut w/notching, hobstar, 8"........ **295.00**
Plate, Santa Maria, beige w/brown decor, sgnd, 7¾" **250.00**
Relish, oval, allover cut, sgnd **135.00**
Sweetmeat, melon ribbed, blue flowers, mkd **350.00**
Tray, cut glass, Colonna pattern, sgnd, 12" **650.00**
Tumbler, cut glass **32.00**
Vase, cut glass, swirl, incised leaves & flowers, sgnd, 14"..... **350.00**
   Cut glass, trumpet shape, engraved fruits & flowers, sgnd **90.00**
   Cut glass, trumpet shape, ped base, heavy, old, 8" **175.00**
Wine, opal, polar bear stem, sgnd..................... **125.00**

Limoges

From the mid 18th century, Limoges was the center of the porcelain industry of France, where at one time more than forty companies utilized the local kaolin deposits to make a superior quality china, much of which was exported to the United States. Various marks were used; some included the name of the American export company rather than the manufacturer, and 'Limoges'. After 1891 'France' was added.

Bouillon cup & saucer, roses on green vines **20.00**
   White w/gold border & handle, T&V **12.00**
Bowl, Elite, pink & lavender flowers, gold edge, 5¼" **10.00**
   Green w/hp pink roses, gold trim, ftd, T&V **30.00**
   Hp blackberries, mkd JPD **75.00**
   Scallop edge w/pink roses, Elite pattern, large **75.00**
   With cover, hp leaves & berries, ruffled borders, 4x7" **145.00**
Box, w/cover, boat scene, sgnd, T&V, rectangular **70.00**
Butter dish, scalloped edge, pink, lavender & wht flowers **55.00**
Charger, earthtone colors, sgnd, 12½"................... **135.00**
   Wht w/hp leaves & berries, scalloped gold edge, sgnd **125.00**

Chocolate pot, lime to wht satin, gold florals, 10"........... **250.00**
   Pink roses, leaves, gold handle & ring finial, 10"........... **80.00**

Chocolate set, 8-sided, brown & orange on beige, 6 pc **155.00**
   Green w/water lily, sgnd, 9 pc **220.00**
Cider set, crab apples & foliage, rust & green, Xmas 1907, 5 pc **285.00**
   Grape design, gold trim, ornate, sgnd, 7 pc **450.00**
   Grape design, lustre trim, 5 pc **175.00**
Coffee pot, wht ribbed, gold spout, handle & finial, 2 mks, 8½" **60.00**
Compote, courting couple, sgnd Fragonard, 4¼x9".......... **79.00**
   Openwork at corners, decorated, 8x7" **180.00**
Cream soup, w/underplate, blk & gold, hp Deco, handles, T&V . **12.00**
Creamer & sugar, w/cover, lilacs, gold rims, pearlized, sgnd **75.00**
Cup & saucer, Coronet, wht w/green & gold **15.00**
Dresser tray, diamond-shape, hp violets, Moltog, 8x10¼"..... **75.00**
   Kidney-shape, hp pink flowers, 13x9" **45.00**
   White w/gold floral, scalloped, fluted rim, 11x15" **55.00**
Ewer, green clover, AK France, 1903, 12¾" **140.00**
Fish set, green border, 14 pc **250.00**
   Hp, sgnd, 8 pc **400.00**
   Shell form, design varies ea pc, hp, 7 pc **185.00**
Game plate, 2 grouse, gold scroll edge, pierced for hanging, sgnd, 10" **75.00**
   Duck, trees & bird, gold rococo border, sgnd, 9¼"........ **45.00**
   Game birds, hp, muted natural colors, 11".............. **185.00**
   Game birds, sgnd Jean, 10", pr **375.00**
   Gold rope edge, sgnd, T&V, 9" **40.00**
   Grouse, gold scalloped, sgnd, 13" **235.00**
   Mallard & basket, T&V **75.00**
   Pheasants & daisies, gold rococo scalloped, embossed, 10¾" **135.00**
   Quail in woods, hp, gold border, sgnd Jean, T&V 1800, 12" **150.00**
   Quail, gold rococo border, sgnd, 9" **85.00**
Game set, deer & game birds, gold scalloped, D&C, hp, 12 pc **750.00**
   Game birds, sgnd Muville, 8 pc **900.00**
   Ornate border, sgnd, 7 pc **695.00**
Handkerchief box, square, purple violets................. **85.00**
Honey pot, w/lid, 2 handles, roses & scrollwork, 6" **70.00**
Ice bucket, w/plate, wht w/grapes & leaves, gold handles & edge, T&V **95.00**
Inkwell, melon-shape, lt blue & wht w/gold trim liner **38.00**
Jardiniere, green w/lavender flowers, fluted gold top, 6x7" **95.00**
Lemonade pitcher, hp apple design..................... **155.00**
Oyster plate, marine life, hp, scalloped rim, 8½"............ **45.00**
Pin tray, hp owls on pine bough, T&V, 1917, sgnd, 9¼x6¼" .. **85.00**
Pitcher, bulbous, hp lemons, T&V, sgnd, 6½" **165.00**
   Cream w/flowers, gold trim, T&V, mkd June 3, 1884........ **50.00**
   Green w/plums & leaves, gold trim, 5x7" **75.00**
   Hp apples & branches, border, mkd, 6" **150.00**
   Hp grapes & leaves, gilt handle, flaring to base, 13¾" **325.00**
Plaque, birds w/gold border, S&S, 13½" **275.00**
   Classical maiden, sgnd, 8¼x11" **450.00**

English Pointer, quail, scroll border, 12½" **185.00**
Mallard, scalloped, Coronet, gold border, 16" dia **235.00**

Medallion w/hp roses, scalloped, 10x14″ **125.00**
Pate-sur-pate, Art Deco **225.00**
Portrait, gold & silver on copper, enamel, 9¼x7″ **175.00**
Purple, wht & pink flowers, 13″ **95.00**
Plate, Art Deco, yellow & green, gold band, Porter 1910 ..... **85.00**
Blue w/roses, sgnd M Burkholder, H&C over L **45.00**
Cavalier, scalloped, embossed rim, 10″ **78.00**
Cherubs drinking wine w/grapes & roses, scalloped, S&S, 8¾″ **95.00**
Elite, pink & lavender florals, gold edge, 9¾″ **14.00**
Lady of the Night, sgnd LaValiere **40.00**
Lady on Bench, Coronet, 10″ **75.00**
Pine cones & gold decor, 2 handles, 10½″ **75.00**

Lithophanes

Lithophanes are porcelain panels with relief designs of varying degrees of thickness and density. Transmitted light brings out the pattern in graduated shadings, lighter where the porcelain is thin, and shaded in the heavy areas. They were cast from wax models prepared by artists, and depict genre views of life in the 1800s, religious themes, or scenes of historical significance. First made in Berlin about 1825, they were used as lamp shade panels, window plaques, or candleshields. Later, steins and mugs cups had lithophanes in their base. Japanese wares were sometimes made with dragons or Geisha lithophane bases.

Candle shield, boys in grass, castle background, Baroque holder **250.00**
Chamber stick, 4 scenic panels, double handle, 4 holes at top . **650.00**
Cup & saucer, cup has oriental house, trees & mountains **21.00**
Demitasse, turquoise & blk decor w/dragons, etc **16.00**
Demitasse set, dragons in relief, 10 pc **110.00**
Dish, shell figural, Dom zu Koelm, florals, Victorian, 7″ **58.00**
Lamp, 3 panels children, 2 scenic, candlestick electric base, PPM **850.00**
Oil, 6 panel scenic, brass base, 9½″ dia shade **1,350.00**
5 trapezoid panels, electrified oil lamp base, PPM **600.00**
Pair, 5 panels, all children, turned brass electrified bases . **1,800.00**
Match box, porcelain w/lithophane bottom, 3x2″ **100.00**
Mug, occupational, carpenter **195.00**
Peasants w/skirts blowing, gold handle & band **55.00**
Souvenir World's Fair, St Louis, Machinery Hall in base ... **160.00**
Panel, boat w/passengers paddled by standing man, 4¾x6¼″ . **175.00**
Boy & girl pushing swing, KPM, 3¾x3″ **160.00**
Courting mishap, in color, PPM, 4½x6″ **235.00**
Cupid setting trap for 2 girls, colors fired in, 4x5″ **225.00**
Large building w/open square, brass edge frame, KPM w/scepter **225.00**
Lovers in woods crossing stream, signed #1407, 4x4½″ **125.00**
Titled 'Beatrice', PPM, 4½x5¼″ **160.00**
Woman at window, suitor below, brass rim frame, 4x5″ **125.00**
Woman eating, impressed German word for breakfast, PPM, 4x6″ **125.00**
Woman w/spinning wheel, mkd PR & sickle sign, framed, 4x5″ **125.00**
Pin tray, fox hunt scene, scroll border, gold, 6x3″ **48.00**
Plaque, 2 girls at roadside chapel, 5x4½″ **265.00**
Ascension of Mary into the clouds, 5x4½″ **115.00**
Child on father's shoulders, mother making bed, 4x5″ **265.00**
Courting scene, boy & girl on bridge, blk & wht, 5x4½″ ... **225.00**
Girl w/dog, KPM, 5x7½″ **180.00**
Hunters bidding lady goodby, blk & wht, 6½x5½″ **395.00**
Ladies in living room w/baby & children, color, 4x5″ **265.00**
Little girl in bed w/nightcap, German inscription, brass frame **265.00**
Miniature, child holding puppet, 1½x1″ **125.00**
Saki set, 6 cups w/lady in each, hp pot w/florals & whistling bird **65.00**
Shade, 5 panels, KPM, 4¼x5¼″ **600.00**
Stein, 83rd Air Rescue Squad **110.00**
Fur Erinnerung, pewter top, ½ liter **140.00**
Zum Andenken, floral, man & women at table, ¼ liter **125.00**

Tea set, Kutani, matt blk w/geishas in cup, gold dragons, 13 pc **185.00**
Kutani, silver hp design, 21 pc **175.00**
Satsuma type **400.00**
Thousand Face, lithophane in cups, 15 pc **375.00**
Tea warmer, 1 pc cylindrical panel, holder w/cast metal legs ... **300.00**

1 pc flared insert, chrome over brass frame, 4½″ **250.00**
4 panels, brass holder w/orig burner, 4½x5″ **295.00**
4 panels, nickel plated **290.00**
Window ornament, girl in garden, stained glass border, 7x6½″ **295.00**
Man & wife in museum, stained glass border, 7x6½″ **235.00**

Liverpool

In the late 1700s, Liverpool potters produced a creamy ivory ware, sometimes called Queens ware, which they decorated by means of the newly perfected transfer print. Made specifically for the American export trade, patriotic inscriptions, political portraits or other States themes were applied in black with colors sometimes added by hand. (Obviously their loyalty to the crown didn't stand in the way of their business success!) Before it lost favor in about 1825, other English potters made a similar product; today Liverpool is a generic term used to refer to all ware of this type.

Bowl, American war ship transfer; 1 inside, 4 outside, 10″ ... **675.00**
Neptune & mermaids outside, war ship transfer inside, 9″ dia **525.00**
Polychromed w/transfer of British warship, 11″ **450.00**
Cup & saucer, Wellington & Lewis transfer, silver luster **115.00**
Jug, transfers of American ship & Masonic emblems, 11″ **400.00**
Mug, transfer of The Sailor's Return, lustre trim **150.00**
Pitcher, creamware w/black landscape, 1809, 8″ **350.00**
Creamware w/transfer, The Church Militant, 7″ **165.00**
Transfers of Peace & Plenty; w/eagle, 6½″ **350.00**
Tankard, polychromed w/transfer of Northumberland 74, 5¾″ . **295.00**

Lladro

Lladro porcelains are currently being produced in Labernes Blanques, Spain. Their limited edition figurines are popular collectibles

L-1010, Girl w/lamb **100.00**
L-1018, King Baltasar **1,200.00**
L-1030, Don Quixote w/stand **685.00**
L-1034, Girl w/basket **127.50**
L-1035, Girl w/geese **105.00**
L-1052, Girl w/Duck **120.00**
L-1081, Girl w/brush **100.00**
L-1082, Girl manicuring **100.00**
L-1083, Girl w/doll **100.00**

L-1084, Girl w/mother's shoe 100.00
L-1127, Puppy Love 162.50
L-1147, Girl w/bonnet 100.00
L-1148, Girl, shampooing.............................. 100.00
L-1151, Elephants, 10x12¼" 215.00
L-1181, Boy w/donkey 172.50
L-1230, Friendship 210.00
L-1249, The Race 1,060.00
L-1255, Seesaw 325.00
L-1270, Reminiscing 1,070.00
L-1277, Feeding Time 227.50
L-1278, Devotion 260.00
L-1279, The Wind 515.00
L-1280, Playtime 310.00
L-1288, Aggressive Duck 270.00
L-1306, On the Farm 192.50
L-1309, Girl w/cats 192.50
L-1311, Girl w/puppies in basket 210.00
L-1312, Little Bo Peep 195.00
L-1356, Phyllis 100.00
L-1360, Laura 100.00
L-1372, Anniversary Waltz 340.00
L-1374, Waiting in the Park 257.50
L-1380, Cathy & Her Doll, w/base 285.00
L-3506, Maiden 345.00
L-3507, Flower Seller 330.00
L-4510, Girl w/parasol & geese 145.00
L-4575, Mother & Child 172.50
L-4576, Pastoral 135.00
L-4584, Girl w/sheep 100.00
L-4602R, Doctor 105.00
L-4603R, Nurse 120.00
L-4608, Boy w/pig 112.50
L-4618, Clown 227.50
L-4621, Sea Captain 157.50
L-4655, Horses 422.50
L-4659, Shepherd 132.00
L-4676, Shepherd w/lamb 50.00
L-4678, Girl w/basket, 8¾" 50.00
L-4682, Girl w/milk pail 132.00
L-4684, Hebrew Student 145.00
L-4730, Bird Watcher 190.00
L-4750, Romeo & Juliet 620.00
L-4762R, Dentist 132.00
L-4779, Children, praying 110.00
L-4807, Geisha 290.00
L-4808, Wedding 112.50
L-4809, Going Fishing 100.00
L-4810, Young Sailor 100.00
L-4828, Cinderella 132.00
L-4838, Clean Up Time 105.00
L-4840, Oriental Girl 290.00
L-4844, Pharmacist 235.00
L-4854, Don Quixote 122.50
L-4856, Waltz Time 270.00
L-4860, Dutch Girl 115.00
L-4866, Girl w/swan & dog 115.00
L-4867, Seesaw, 7½x9" 205.00
L-4868, Girl w/candle 46.50
L-4874, Boy & Girl 80.00
L-4875, Girl w/jugs 132.00
L-4877, Boy w/flute 200.00
L-4882, Carnival Couple 177.50
L-4907, Admiration 345.00

L-4909, Dove on Lap 137.50
L-4915, Girl w/pigeons 170.00
L-4918, Girl at Pond 190.00
L-4922, Windblown Girl 235.00
L-4934, Dainty Lady 147.50
L-4935, Closing Scene 320.00
L-4938, Baby's Outing 417.50
L-4951, Missy 535.00
L-4969, Sheriff puppet 120.00
L-4970, Skier puppet 112.50
L-4981, Ironing Time 107.50
L-4988, Oriental Spring 192.50
L-4989, Sayonara 192.50
L-4991, Butterfly 192.50
L-5000, Reading 165.00
L-5003, Sunny Day 210.00
L-5007, Bashful 77.50
L-5009, Curious 77.50
L-5013, Daughters 550.00
L-5029, Flower Peddler, 10¼" 880.00
L-5039, Party Girl 185.00
L-5040, Pixie 192.50
L-5045, Belinda w/doll 125.00
L-5050, Dancer 110.00
L-5052, At the Circus 665.00
L-5053, Festival Time 250.00
L-5056, Boy Clown w/clock 290.00
L-5060, Girl Clown w/trumpet 290.00
L-5064, Gretel 255.00
L-5065, Ingrid 370.00
L-5067, Halloween 450.00
L-5074, My Hungry Brood 295.00
L-5079, Pottery Seller 300.00
L-5080, South of the Border 320.00
L-5081, Jugs for Sale 300.00
L-5083, Lullabye & Goodnight 485.00
L-5086, My Baby Brother 275.00

Locke Art

Bowl, lobster, fish, seahorse etching, sgnd, 2½x5" 245.00
Goblet, ivy decor, twisted stem, 6½" 50.00
Muffineer, acanthus leaf design, silver-plated top, 6" 75.00
Tumbler, poppy decor, sgnd, 4½" 55.00
   Sheaves of wheat etching, 2¾" 75.00
Vase, mum decor, flared, paper label, 5" 450.00
   Peonies decor, ruffled, 5" 445.00

Loetz

Loetz glass is an iridescent art glass produced by Johann Loetz Witwe in Klostermule, Austria. Previous to the purchase of his own glassworks in 1840, Loetz worked for LC Tiffany, and some of his glass bears a resemblance to Tiffany's style. Although the gold iridescent glass is the most readily recognized, he also made other types, including cameo. Loetz died in 1848, but the glassworks remained in operation until WWII.

Bowl, cobalt, irid mottling, dimples, 4x10"................ 475.00
   Irid gold rib w/purple hi-lites, 2½x6" 160.00
   Irid purple, blue, deep ruffle top, pinch base, 4x10" 650.00
   Low w/ruffled top, salmon w/blue oil spots, signed 475.00
   Magenta w/silver blue ribbon decor, 10" dia 1,430.00
Bulb planter, spider webb rib, brass collar w/grapes, 9½" dia . 350.00

Bulb vase, rubina verde **80.00**
Candy dish, bronze Nouveau holder w/3 tree form ft, 6x6″ ... **450.00**
Centerpiece, irid mottling on purple, dimpled, 4x10″ **600.00**
Compote, cranberry mottled, bronzed base, ruffled rim **165.00**
   Cut glass, 7½x4″ **125.00**
Inkwell, irid Phenomen glass, brass hinged lid **200.00**
Rose bowl, silver overlay w/gold iridescence, 4″ **450.00**
Vase, apricot w/violet, green, silver dots & striations, 8″ **750.00**
   Blue & green irid, pinched top, dimpled sides, 4″ **225.00**
   Blue irid w/tortoise shell interior, 14x7″ **250.00**
   Blue w/allover blue/green irid mottling, 7″ **375.00**
   Blue w/yellow threads, 4″ **225.00**
   Blue wave on irid green optic rib, pinched sides, 4″ **375.00**
   Cameo, 2 cuttings, ped foot, ruffle top, signed, 8″ **750.00**
   Cameo, ped ft, ruffle top, 2 colors, 7½″ **575.00**
   Cased, irid, ribs, silver overlay florals, vines, 5″ **100.00**
   Cobalt papillion, irid, rib handles, 6″ **300.00**
   Cone top on ovoid base, irid gold/green, 6″ **275.00**
   Corset shape, treebark body, blue irid, ground pontil, 5″ ... **125.00**
   Crackled, green & amethyst irid **125.00**
   Cranberry w/irid swirls, signed, small **295.00**
   Enameled florals on red irid, 2¾″ **125.00**
   Fish net decor, pale grn, bulbous base, 6¾″ **275.00**
   Floriform, aqua irid, marbleized **200.00**
   Footed gourd, pinched, rust trailing, mottled, 7″ **75.00**
   Formosa pattern, blue threads on green, 3½″ **175.00**
   Gold luster w/silver irid, ribs, applied fruits, 9″ **200.00**
   Grecian urn, amber & green irid, oil & gold trailing, 10″ ... **100.00**
   Green irid w/gold dust, pinched & swirled, 14x7″ **400.00**
   Green, irid, 5½″ **160.00**

   Green irid, dimpled base, 10″ **175.00**
   Irid w/clear applied decor, 4½″ **115.00**
   Iridescent green oilspots, 9½″ **325.00**
   Orange & silver, sq base, 8½″ **145.00**
   Overshot, brass collar w/grapes, owls, irid, 8½″ **600.00**
   Pearl w/threading & rigaree at flare top, 7″ **250.00**
   Pulled blue decor over amber irid, 6½″ **375.00**
   Purple pulled feather, 5″ **500.00**
   Red irid w/floral enamel, signed, 3″ **200.00**
   Red iridescent, swirled stripes, 12″ **450.00**
   Reds & greens, iridescent oil spots, 12″ **225.00**
   Ruffle top, amber irid, signed, 8″ **120.00**

Ruffle top, green crackle irid, signed, 3½x3″ **350.00**
Ruffled, green, signed, 4″ **245.00**
Shaded honey to purple irid, petal top, twist waist, 11″ **175.00**
Shellform, silver-blue & amber spots, clear irid ft, 7″ **770.00**
Silver floral overlay on lime w/oil spots, 8½″ **1,210.00**
Silver overlay, 10″.................................. **900.00**
Silver overlay, rainbow irid on amethyst, Nouveau, 4½″ ... **425.00**
Silver overlay on irid, Art Nouveau, 7½″ **600.00**
Silver overlay on irid, flare on bulbous body, 8½″ **700.00**
Silver overlay on wavy silver blue, 13″ **400.00**
Square rim, shaded, swirled irid, 12x6″................. **295.00**
Striated ribbons in amber on silver, 11″ **400.00**
Top lip turned in, marble marquetry insets, 12″ **650.00**
Tortoise w/irid blue pulled loops, gold & silver, 5½″ **120.00**
Waisted, sq bottom, vari-colors w/burgandy stripes **450.00**
Wide shoulder, amber irid w/silver blue feathering, 5½″ **385.00**

Longwy

   The Longwy workshops were founded in 1798, and continue today to produce pottery in the north of France near the Luxembourgh-Belgian border. The ware for which they are best known was produced during the Art Deco period, and decorated in bold color and geometric designs. Earlier wares made during the lst quarter of the 19th century reflected the popularity of Oriental art, cloisonne enamels in particular. The designs were executed by impressing the pattern into the moist clay, and filling in the depressions with enamels. Examples are marked Longwy, either impressed or painted under glaze.

Ashtray, narrow bulbous swirl base, gold ft, 5″ dia **55.00**
   Vivid florals & leaves on turquoise, 3½″ **35.00**
Charger, running deer, palm fronds, Primavera, 15″ **1,200.00**
Dish, pelicans, water, flowers, shallow form, mkd, 9″ **200.00**
Plate, wood scene w/hunting dogs, 9″..................... **45.00**
Powder box, allover florals, square, typical **90.00**
   Ram, mystic trees, 3½″ **325.00**
   Recling nude, Primavera, after Mattise, 3½″ **375.00**
   Vase & florals, after Magrette, 3½″.................... **250.00**
Tile, bird & flowers, 8x8″ **175.00**
Tray, scalloped, mkd, 6x4″ **45.00**
Trivet, woman w/exotic foliage, Primavera, after Mattise, 8″ ... **850.00**
Vase, 8 sided, bulbous, cobalt top & bottom, 6″ **95.00**
   Allover florals, typical, 3″ **75.00**
   Cylindrical, 3½″ **40.00**
   Deco florals, square, 5″ **135.00**
   Mattise nudes, exotic foliage, Primavera, 12x10″ **1,200.00**

Peacock, Deco balloon trees, geometric base design, 11″ ... **910.00**
Purple nudes, lush foilage, balloon trees, base design **1,500.00**

Lonhuda

William Long was a druggist by trade, who combined his knowledge of chemistry with his artistic ability, in an attempt to produce a type of brown glaze slip decorated artware similar to that made by the Rookwood Pottery. He achieved his goal in 1889, after years of long and dedicated study. Three years later, he founded his firm, the Lonhuda Pottery Company. The name was coined from the first few letters of the last name of each of his partners, W.H. Hunter and Alfred Day. Laura Fry, formerly of the Rookwood company, joined the firm in 1892, bringing with her a license for Long to use her patented air brush blending process. Other artists of note, Sarah McLaughlin, Helen Harper and Jessie Spaulding joined the firm and decorated the ware with nature studies, animals and portraits, often signing their wares with their initials. Three types of marks were used on the Stubenville Lonhuda ware. The first was a lineal composite of the letters LPCO with the name Lonhuda impressed above it. The second, adopted in 1893, was a die stamp representing the solid profile of an Indian, used on ware patterned after pottery made by the American Indians. This mark was later replaced with an impressed outline of the Indian head, with 'Lonhuda' arching above it. Although the ware was successful, the business floundered due to poor management; in 1895, Long became a partner of Sam Weller and moved to Zanesville where the manufacture of the Lonhuda line continued. Less than a year later, Long left the Weller Company.

Ewer, florals, sgnd JRS, shield mk 215, 7″ **350.00**
Florals, shield mk, 6″ **250.00**
Pillow vase, herd of cows, man, shield mk 275, 11½″ **4,000.00**

Vase, berries, wide base, flare rim, sgnd LM, ½ circle seal, 7″ **110.00**
Floral, artist sgnd, petal rim, 8″ **250.00**
Floral, loop handles, sgnd AH, shield mk 820, 4½″ **200.00**
Florals, sgnd Taylor, #248, 3½x4½″ **200.00**
Florals, sgnd S Reid McLaughlin, shield mk, 5½″ **150.00**

Lu Ray Pastels

Lu Ray Pastel dinnerware was introduced in the early 1940s by Taylor, Smith and Taylor, of East Liverpool,Ohio. It was offered in assorted colors---Persian Cream, Sharon Pink, Surf Green, Windsor Blue and Gray---in complete place settings as well as many service pieces. It was a successful line in its day and is once again finding favor with collectors of American dinnerware.

Bowl, 5¼″. **2.00**
9″ **6.00**
10″ **7.00**
Buttered, covered, ¼ lb **12.00**
Cream pitcher **4.00**
Creamer **4.00**
Cup, tea **5.25**
Cup & saucer **4.25**

Demitasse **9.00**
Egg cup **4.00**
Fruit, 5″ **3.75**
Gravy w/underliner **12.00**
Plate, 6″ **1.50**
7″ **2.50**
8″ **2.25**
9″ **3.00**
10″ **3.50**
Chop, 15″ **9.00**
Platter, 11″ **6.00**
12″ **7.00**
13″ oval **8.00**
Salt & pepper, pair **5.00**
Sauceboat **7.00**
Saucer **1.00**
Soup, coupe **5.50**
Soup, lug **5.00**
Sugar, covered **6.00**
Teapot **14.00**
Utility tray **6.00**

Lustre Art Glass Co.

The Lustre Art Glass Company operated in Long Island, New York from about 1920 until 1925, manufacturing iridescent lampshades similar to those of Durand and Quezal.

Candlestick, blue irid, graceful form, sgnd, 9″ **185.00**
Shade, blue double pulled feather, outlined in gold, on opal, 5¼″ **225.00**
Shades, gold ribbed, pear shaped, flared edge, set of 5, 5½″ . . **375.00**
Shades, green/gold leaves on opal, gold lining, set of 4, sgnd . **480.00**

Lutz

Nicholas Lutz worked for the Boston and Sandwich Glass Co. from 1869 to 1888, where he produced the threaded and striped art glass that was popular during that era. His works were not marked, and since many other glassmakers of the day made similar wares, the term Lutz has come to refer not only to his original works but to any of this type.

Bowl, pedestal, ruffled edge, 4¼″ dia **65.00**
With underplate, threaded, opal lustre, pink ruffled, 5″ dia . . **80.00**
Dish, threaded, flint, ruffled, 4¾″ **45.00**
Finger bowl w/underplate, crimped w/ 1″ threaded rim, 5½″ . . **130.00**
Nut dish, applied raised enamel flowers **35.00**
Tumbler, cranberry threading on clear glass, Sandwich **55.00**
Vase, clear, green & wht latticino, goldstone base & handles, 7″ **110.00**

Maastricht

Maastrich, Holland, was the site of the De Sphinx Pottery, founded in 1836 by Petrus Regout. They made earthenware decorated with transfer prints. Potteries are still working in this area today.

Bowl, end of day, 4″ dia **40.00**
Cup & saucer, flow blue, Oriental **35.00**
Plate, blue parakeets, P. Regout & Co, 8″ **25.00**
Commemorative, Eisenhower, 1944, 8″ **18.00**

Magazines

Magazines are collected primarily for their cover prints, and for the in-

formation pertaining to defunct companies and their products that can be gleaned from the old advertisements.

Amazing Stories, 1928, Aug, debut of Buck Rogers **145.00**
Boys' Life, 1937, Feb, Rockwell, 2 scouts & old seaman...... **25.00**
   1938, Feb, Rockwell, scout building birdhouse **25.00**
   1943, Feb, Rockwell, scout & family looking at map **15.00**
Century, 1904, Dec, I am Sick of being a Princess, Muchas **22.00**
   1905, Oct, Sandman, NC Wyeth **20.00**
   1911, Feb, Sing a Song of Sixpence, Parrish illus **30.00**
Cinema Arts, 1937, June **25.00**
Click, 1938, Feb **10.00**
Collier's, 1903, Jan, Jesie Wilcox Smith cover, Gibson centerfold **18.00**
   1903, Christmas, Leyendecker cover **22.50**
1904, Jan, Sherlock Holmes 5th Adventure, Steele cover **25.00**
   1905, July, Maxfield Parrish cover **25.00**
   1905, Sept, Maxfield Parrish cover................... **25.00**
   1906, Dec, Parrish print, Search for Singing Tree **50.00**
   1909, July 3, Parrish cover **38.00**
   1915, Nov, Leyendecker cover **15.00**
Collier's Photographic History of WWII, 1946 .... **27.50**
Coronet, 1936, Nov **20.00**
   1941, Sept **7.00**
Cosmopolitan, 1934, Apr, Harrison Fisher cover, Roosevelt sketches **15.00**
   Louisiana Purchase edition **10.00**
Delineator, 1895, June **12.00**
Focus, 1938, Apr **20.00**
Good Housekeeping, 1923, Apr **5.00**
Harpers Monthly, 1865, Dec **4.50**
   1888, Sept, Western Journalism **4.50**
   1896, Jan **5.00**
Hearst, 1922, Mar, color cover Mucha, good **65.00**
Holiday, 1946, Mar.................................. **25.00**
Incidents of Western Life, 1905, CM Russell, Stars of Broadway **17.50**
Ladies Home Journal, 1900, Aug, Howard Chandler Christy cover **18.00**
   1904, Sept, Air Castles cover **35.00**
   1904, Dec, JW Smith illus **10.00**
   1905, Mar, Parrish Circus Quilt design **14.00**
   1905, July, Justice cover **10.00**
   1911, bride cover, Sarah Bernhardt story **12.50**
   1927, Dec, Santa cover, Rockwell colored Xmas **25.00**
   1937, May **10.00**
Leslie's Illustrated Weekly, 1911, Dec 7, Xmas cover.......... **6.00**
Leslie's Monthly, 1886, Nov.......................... **18.00**
   1902, Feb, includes portrait of McKinley................ **4.50**
Liberty, 1924, May 10, Rockwell Fiske Tire ad **50.00**
Life, 1936, Nov 23, 1st issue **50.00**
   1936, Dec 23 .... **35.00**
   1941, Sept 1, cover story: The Great Ted Williams **80.00**
   1959, Apr, Marilyn Monroe cover **11.00**
Look, 1937, Feb, Vol 1, No 2 .... **40.00**
Music & Life, 1904, JW Smith & Harrison Fisher illus **20.00**
National Geographic, 1901, Oct, Discovery of the Pole **16.00**
   1904, Jan, very good, complete **85.00**
   1905, Jan, complete **135.00**
   1905, Feb, very good, complete **135.00**
   1905, Mar, complete **135.00**
   1911, July, Reptiles of All Lands **13.50**
   1912, Oct, China................................ **12.50**
   1913, Apr, Wonderland of Peru **24.00**
   1913, Sept, Ancient Egypt **11.50**
   1913, Nov, Phillippines **11.50**
   1914, Jan, Northern Africa **9.50**
   1914, May, Birds of Town & Country **9.50**

1914, Aug, Grand Canyon............................. **9.50**
1914, Nov, Young Russia **9.50**
1915, May, American Wild Flowers **7.00**
1915, Aug, American Game Birds **7.00**
1915, Nov, The Beauties of France **7.00**
1916, May, Land of the Incas......................... **7.00**
1916, June, Common American Wild Flowers **7.00**
1916, Nov, Larger North American Mammals **9.00**
1917, Oct, Our Flag Number **16.00**
1918, May, Smaller North American Mammals **9.00**
1919, Mar, Dogs **16.00**
1919, Dec, Military Insignias......................... **12.00**
1920, May, Common Mushrooms of US................. **7.00**
1920, Dec, Falconry **8.50**
1921, Mar, America in the Air **7.00**
1921, June, Familiar Grass & Their Flowers **7.00**
1922, July, Cathedrals (Old & New World) **9.00**
1923, May, Tomb of Tutankhamen **8.50**
1923, Oct, The Auto Industry......................... **7.00**
1923, Nov, The Story of the Horse **9.00**
Vol 1, No 1, very good, complete.................... **3,950.00**
Vol 1, No 2, very good, complete **900.00**
Vol 1, No 3, very good, complete.................... **1,200.00**
Vol 1, No 4, very good, complete **900.00**
Vol 2, No 1, very good, complete **350.00**
Vol 3, No 1, very good, complete **225.00**
Vol 4, No 1, very good, complete **300.00**
Vol 5, No 1, very good, complete **225.00**
Vol 6, No 1, very good, complete **200.00**
Vol 6, No 2-5, very good, complete, ea **300.00**
Peek, 1938, Jan **10.00**
Physical Culture, 1904, Sept, on Roosevelt............... **6.00**
Picture, 1938, Feb **10.00**
Pleasure, 1937, Winter............................... **20.00**
Psychology, 1927 .... **10.00**
Punch, 1916, July-Dec, war material **20.00**
Radio Age, 1924, lifeguard cover, 'Future Radio Movies'...... **10.00**
Saturday Evening Post, 1888-1899, any issue **40.00**
   1905, Aug 19, black maid on cover.................. **20.00**
   1906, Dec 1, Leyendecker cover, Xmas **10.00**
   1906, Dec 29, Leyendecker cover, New Years **10.00**
   1907, Feb 2, Harrison Fisher cover, lady **20.00**
   1908, Dec 26, Leyendecker cover, Children Xmas **16.00**
   1913 .... **14.00**
   1916, May 20, Rockwell cover **450.00**
   1917, June 16, Rockwell cover **75.00**
   1918, Sept 21, Rockwell cover **70.00**
   1919, Lyendecker Easter cover **20.00**
   1919, Mar 22 .... **42.00**
   1919, Aug 9, Rockwell cover **43.00**
   1919, December 2, Rockwell cover **50.00**
   1920, May 1, Rockwell cover **40.00**
   1920, Aug 28, Rockwell cover **40.00**
   1921, Mar 12, Rockwell cover **50.00**
   1921, Aug 13, Rockwell cover **35.00**
   1921, Dec 3, Rockwell cover **26.00**
   1922, April 29, Rockwell cover **35.00**
   1922, June 10, Rockwell cover **40.00**
   1923, June 23, Rockwell cover **40.00**
   1923, Dec 8, Rockwell cover, 3 Xmas carolers **80.00**
   1924, April 5, Rockwell cover, Cupid whispering in young mans ear **37.50**
   1924, May 3, Rockwell cover **60.00**
   1924, Aug 30, Rockwell cover **30.00**
   1924, Dec 6, Rockwell cover, Santa looming over house **75.00**

1925, April 18, Rockwell cover **32.00**
1925, Aug 29, Rockwell cover **35.00**
1925, Nov 21, Rockwell cover **65.00**
1926, May 29, Rockwell cover **50.00**
1926, June 26, Rockwell cover **24.00**
1926, Aug 14, Rockwell cover **50.00**
1926, Aug 28, Rockwell cover **24.00**
1927, Mar 12, Rockwell cover **50.00**
1927, April 16, Rockwell cover **50.00**
1927, Sept 24, Rockwell cover **37.00**
1927, Dec 3, Rockwell cover, Santa holding tiny boy **45.00**
1928, April 14, Rockwell cover **50.00**
1928, May 26, Rockwell cover **23.00**
1928, July 21, Rockwell cover **38.00**
1928, Aug 18, Rockwell cover, fisherman 'Contentment' **33.00**
1928, September 22, Rockwell cover **30.00**
1929, Mar 9, Rockwell cover, 'The Doctor and the Doll', classic **450.00**
1929, April 20, Rockwell cover, constable behind 'Welcome' sign **33.00**
1929, May 4, Rockwell cover **35.00**
1929, June 15, Rockwell cover **30.00**
1929, Dec 7, Rockwell cover **45.00**
1930, Mar 22, Rockwell cover **30.00**
1930, Sept 13, Rockwell cover **34.00**
1930, Dec 6, Rockwell cover **40.00**
1931, July 25, Rockwell cover **34.00**
1931, Nov 7, Rockwell cover **25.00**
1932, Oct 21, Rockwell cover **25.00**
1932, Dec 10, Rockwell cover **45.00**
1934, June 30, Rockwell cover **30.00**
1934, Dec 15, Rockwell cover **60.00**
1935, April 27, Rockwell cover **35.00**
1935, Sept 14, Rockwell cover **32.00**
1936, Mar 7, Rockwell cover **25.00**
1936, May 30, Rockwell cover **45.00**
1936, Sept 26, Rockwell cover **38.00**
1936, Oct 24, Rockwell cover **27.50**
1936, Dec 19, Rockwell cover **32.00**
1937, April, Rockwell cover **25.00**
1937, Oct 2, Rockwell cover **25.00**
1937, Dec 25, Rockwell cover **35.00**
1938, June 4, Rockwell cover **55.00**
1938, Dec 17, Rockwell cover **45.00**
1939, Feb 11, Rockwell cover **37.00**
1939, Mar 18, Rockwell cover **40.00**
1939, April 29, Rockwell cover **27.00**
1939, July 8, Rockwell cover **50.00**
1939, Dec 16, Rockwell cover, Santa on ladder by world map **70.00**
1939, Dec 23, Leyendecker cover, Xmas child **10.00**
1940, April 27, Rockwell cover **23.00**
1940, May 18, Rockwell, barbershop **32.00**
1940, July 13, Rockwell cover **24.00**
1941, Jan 4, Leyendecker cover, New Years Baby **10.00**
1941, Mar 3, Rockwell cover, complete **55.00**
1941, July 26, Rockwell cover **22.00**
1941, Oct 4, Rockwell cover **35.50**
1941, Nov 29, Rockwell cover **35.00**
1941, Dec 20, Rockwell cover **25.00**
1942, Feb 7, Rockwell cover **35.00**
1942, April 11, Rockwell cover **34.50**
1942, June 27, Rockwell cover, Willie Gillis **27.50**
1943, Mar 6, Rockwell cover **24.00**
1943, June 26, Rockwell cover **34.00**
1943, Sept 4, Rockwell cover **33.50**
1943, Nov 27, Rockwell cover **20.00**

1944, Jan 1, Rockwell cover **33.00**
1944, July 1, Rockwell cover **20.00**
1944, Sept 16, Rockwell, Gillis & GI ancestors **40.00**
1944, Nov 4, Rockwell cover **20.00**
1945, Sept 15, Rockwell, sailor & dog in hammock **20.00**
1945, Oct 13, Rockwell cover **60.00**
1945, Nov 24, Rockwell 'Thanksgiving' cover **18.00**
1945, Dec 15, Rockwell cover **20.00**
1946, April 6, Rockwell, 2 cleaning women in theater **40.00**
1946, Oct 5, Rockwell, Gillis as college student **35.00**
1946, Dec 7, Rockwell cover **20.00**
1947, Jan 11, Rockwell cover **18.50**
1947, Dec 27, Rockwell cover, complete **20.00**
1948, Jan 24, Rockwell, clowning skiiers **30.00**
1948, Mar 6, Rockwell cover **32.00**
1948, Oct 30, Rockwell cover **12.00**
1949, Mar 19, Rockwell cover, bobby-soxer w/evening gown . . **10.00**
1949, Sept 24, Rockwell cover **15.00**
1950, Oct 21, Rockwell cover **15.00**
1951, July 14, Rockwell cover **15.00**
1952, May 245, Rockwell cover **25.00**
1953, Jan 3, Rockwell cover **14.00**
1954, Jan 9, Rockwell cover, lion & zookeeper **18.00**
1954, Mar 6, Rockwell cover **70.00**
1955, April 16, Rockwell cover **15.00**
1955, June 11, Rockwell cover **60.00**
1956, Mar 17, Rockwell cover **25.00**
1956, Oct 13, Rockell cover **15.00**
1957, May 25, Rockwell cover **15.00**
1959, Feb 14, Rockwell cover **15.00**
1960, Aug 27, Rockwell cover **10.00**
1961, Sept 16, Rockwell cover **10.00**
1962, Nov 3, Rockwell cover **10.00**
Scribners, 1907, Aug, Old Romance, Fishers, Flaggs illus **30.00**
    1910, Aug, Errant Pan, NC Wyeth **22.00**
Sports Illustrated, 1954, Aug 16, baseball cards **100.00**
The Commentator, 1937, Feb **10.00**
The Curio Informant, 1899, Aug, 4 pgs **3.00**
The Golden Star, 1893, Nov, magazine for boys **3.50**
The Idler Monthly, 1893, Nov **3.50**
The New York Woman, 1936, Sept 9 . . . . **15.00**
The Shadow, 1940, Dec **25.00**
The Young Naturalist, 1886, Feb, Chicago, Ill. **4.50**
Variety, 1949, Jan, #5, slot machines **10.00**
    1956, Jan, 50th Anniversary **25.00**
Vogue, 1921 . . . . **12.00**
    1930s, ea **10.00**
    1940s, ea **8.00**

Majolica

Majolica is a type of heavy earthenware, design molded, and decorated in vivid colors with a lead or tin type of glaze. It was popular during the Victoria era. Nearly every potter of note, both here and abroad, produced large majolica jardinieres, umbrella stands, pitchers with animal themes, leaf shapes, vegetable forms and nearly any other theme or decorative device that came to mind. Few, however marked their ware. Among those who did were Wedgwood and George Jones in England; Griffin, Smith and Hill (Etruscan) in Phoenixville, Pa.; and Chesapeake Pottery (Avalon and Clifton) in Baltimore.

Ash tray, black boy **50.00**
    Frog peeking out of deep well **40.00**
Basket, applied flower decor, birds on branch handles, 18" . . . **400.00**

Basket, applied roses, twisted twig handle, #d, 14" 125.00
Berry dish, florals, leaves, scalloped, small 15.00
   Scalloped, ribbon edged 20.00
Biscuit barrel, florals, biscuits on finial, brass bale & cover . . . 115.00
Bowl, butterflies, gold Greek Key rim, 6 panels, Wedgwood, 4" 300.00
   Hummingbirds, blue w/orange interior, 2½x4" 275.00
   Turquoise Picket Fence, large 75.00
   Water Lily & Pad, ftd, 3½x9½" 45.00
Bread plate, Begonia, 10½" 50.00
Bread tray, Oak Leaf, Etruscan 45.00
   Water Lily, 13" 100.00
Bust, bisque face, delicate colors 800.00
Butter pat, leaf form, green 12.00
   Shell & Seaweed 18.00
   Tan w/leaf 20.00
Butter plate, Fern 22.00
Cake plate, Shell & Seaweed 65.00
   Basketweave, maroon w/yellow flower, 7 pc 85.00
   Tree trunk w/grape leaves, Smith, Griffin & Hill 125.00
Cake stand, Maple Leaf w/Basketweave border, ftd, Etruscan, 5x9" 75.00
   New England Astor 85.00
   Shell & Seawood 65.00
Candle holder, pastel, Griffin 62.00
Candy dish, lattice border, footed, 9" 140.00
Card holder, girl w/sheep 90.00
Cauliflower, covered 85.00
Cauliflower plate, Etruscan 40.00
Charger, swan, 13" 35.00
Coffee pot, Shell & Seaweed, Etruscan 215.00
Compote, Basketweave 145.00
   Cupid on lion, rose-beige, Etruscan, 4x8" 55.00
   Dolphin, Wedgwood 175.00
   Flowers & leaves, 2 branch handles, 3 colors, 9½" 60.00
   Leaf, Basketweave ground, green & yellow, Etruscan, 9" 75.00
   Leaves, pink & green, footed, Etruscan, 9½" 85.00
   Turquoise, ftd, shell 75.00
Condiment, Blackberry 220.00
Creamer, owl 60.00
Cream & sugar, Blackberry, Etruscan 65.00
   English Bamboo, Etruscan 65.00
   Shell & Seaweed, Etruscan 150.00
Creamer, Butterfly, Etruscan 55.00
Cup & saucer, Pineapple 35.00
   Seaweed pattern 90.00

Cuspidor, Bamboo & Fern 100.00
   Shell & Seaweed, Etruscan 90.00
Dish, leaf, large 20.00
   Strawberry, 10" 35.00
   Sunflower, oval, 14" 100.00
Ewer, five colors, 11" 55.00
   Lizard handle, mouth open, applied flowers, 13" 125.00
Figurine, turtle, 11½" 150.00
   Boy & girl, Borghese, pr, 9" 50.00
Humidor, Sunny Bank, Avalon 140.00
Jardiniere, pedestal, pink, brown & green, 35" 400.00
Jug, baseball & soccer players, cobalt, Etruscan 250.00
   Fern, Etruscan 30.00
   Rustic leaves, Etruscan 165.00
Leaf dish, dragonflies, scalloped w/handle, 7" 25.00
Match holder, Black boy, w/striker, large 120.00
   Castle, 5x7" 100.00
   Egyptan girl, w/striker, pastel 90.00
   Indian, w/striker, wht & pastels 125.00
   Peasant girl, w/striker, large 90.00
   Queen of Sheba w/striker, 5½" 115.00
Mug, Basketweave w/Oak Leaf, Etruscan, 3½" 500.00
Mustache cup, Shell & Seaweed 200.00
   Lily, footed, Etruscan 65.00
Oyster plate 45.00
   Seaweed 50.00
   Shell & Seaweed, Wedgwood, 9" 200.00
Paperweight, elf, 6" 85.00
Pitcher, Basketweave, yellow flowers, butterfly spout, Etruscan, 4½" 70.00
   Bird's nest, 9½" 100.00
   Blackberry 65.00
   Bow & Floral 27.00
   Cat, mouth is pouring spout, 11" 125.00

Cat, w/mandolin, 9½" 100.00
   Cobalt, sanded, large 45.00
   Corn, large, crazing inside 50.00
   Duck figural, cattails form handle, French, 12" 65.00
   Elephant scene, beige w/pink lining, twig handle 115.00
   Fish, 10" 75.00
   Florals, English 25.00
   Grape, 7½" 45.00

Majolica	
Hound handle, rabbit finial, w/lid, 11″	11.00
Lizard in robe, 13½″	135.00
Morning Glory	35.00
Mottled w/pink blossoms, 6½″	70.00
Shell & Seaweed, Etruscan, 6″	35.00
Sunflower, 7″	325.00
Sunflower, textured background, Etruscan, 6″	420.00
Swan figural	260.00
Water lilies, yellow w/lavender lining, bulbous, 7″	55.00
Water, American Rose	40.00
Plate, Albino, Etruscan	65.00
Apples, Etruscan	25.00
Bamboo, Etruscan	80.00
Basketweave border, Wedgwood	60.00
Basketweave, pink flowers	30.00
Cauliflower, Etruscan	60.00
Cream & green leaf on brown cane, Etruscan, 8″	35.00
Deer, green w/brown, 8″	30.00
Geranium, Etruscan	75.00
Grape Leaf, Wedgwood	70.00
Green leaves, Etruscan, 9″	45.00
House & forest, blownout, Zell	45.00
Kitten design, in wire basket holder	150.00
Leaf on Cane, Etruscan, 8″	38.00
Maple Leaf, Etruscan, 9″	70.00
Pedestal, pink w/green leaves, Etruscan, 5¼″	78.00
Rose, w/Lilies of Valley	20.00
Shaggy dog house, 10½″	55.00
Shell, Wedgwood, 8″	45.00
Turquoise w/birds & grape vines, 8″	15.00
Platter, Begonia Leaf, green & brown w/wht	41.00
Platter, Shell & Seaweed, Etruscan, 13½x9¼″	85.00
Sunflower	55.00
Relish, Astor	45.00
Salt, open, ftd, green & brown mottled w/pink lining, 2″	25.00
Serving dish, Maple Leaf w/fox handle, Stoke on Trent, 10″	500.00
Spooner, Bamboo, Etruscan	55.00
Stein, nudes & grapes	70.00
With pewter lid, brown, yellow & green, 12x4¾″	60.00
Sugar, Cauliflower/covered	85.00
Pear/covered	48.00
Pineapple/covered	85.00
Wild Rose, Etruscan	40.00
Sugar & creamer, florals, pr	32.00
Syrup, pewter top, Etruscan, 7″	35.00
Sunflower, Etruscan	150.00
Tea set, Water Lily, 3 pc	100.00
Teapot, Bird & Fan	70.00
Tobacco jar, Arab	70.00
Elephant	100.00
Man in hat, 7″	95.00
Monk, no cover	10.00
Pipe w/cows	48.00
Pipe w/flowers	50.00
Toby jug, lg	38.00
Small	28.00
Toothbrush holder	20.00
Tray, Oak Leaf, Etruscan	48.00
Tureen, green w/red crab	100.00
Umbrella stand, dragon in relief, 26″	165.00
Pink inside	125.00
Vase, cherries, blossoms, leaves, bulbous w/handles, 4″	20.00
Florals, brown glaze, green leaves, 1859, 13″, pr	190.00
Flowers, large handles, 13″	110.00

Majolica (cont.)	
Girl on bridge, figural, Etruscan, 9″	145.00
Girl w/sheep, card holder	70.00
Moor boy, figural, Etruscan, 9″	135.00
Multi-color fish, handle w/bamboo modeling, 8″	125.00
Vegetable bowl, Bird & Fan	75.00
Wall pocket	30.00

Maps & Atlases

Maps are highly collectible, not only for historical value, but also for their sometimes elaborate artwork, legendary information, or data that has since been proven erroneous. There are many types of maps, including geographical, military, celestial, road and railroad. The most valuable are those made before the mid-1800s.

American Publishing, Lawrence, Massachusetts, indexed, 1889	45.00
Appleton, General War Map, Railroads of US, 1861, 20″	30.00
Atlas, A New General Atlas, A Finley, Young & Delleker, 1824	400.00
Appleton's Railroad & Steamboat Companion, Williams, 1849	95.00
Johnson Family New Illustrated, 1864	110.00
Lake County, Ohio, Stranahan, 1898, 17½x15″	100.00
Morse's New Atlas of the US, 1823	135.00
New Official Map of Alaska, Boyce Co, 1897, 28 pgs	55.00
Plymouth County, Massachusetts, Walker & Co, 1879	295.00
United States on an Improved Plan, Se Morse, 1823	115.00
Authorized Map of 2nd Byrd Arctic Expedition, 1934, color, 18x24″	80.00
Bancroft, History of the US, French & Indian War areas, 9x5″	10.00
Blaeu, America Nova Tabula, 17th century, copper-plate engraving	2,500.00
Chatelain, World	300.00
Civil War, Battlefield of Bull Run, 7/21/1861, very detailed	45.00
Battlefield of Gettysburg, July 2-3, 1863, topographical, 10x10″	25.00
Boundaries of Union & CSA Geographical Div, 12/31/1861	40.00
Defenses of Washington Under McDowell, July 1861, 16x27″	37.00
Military Defenses of NE Virginia, 1/1/1862, 16x27″	37.00

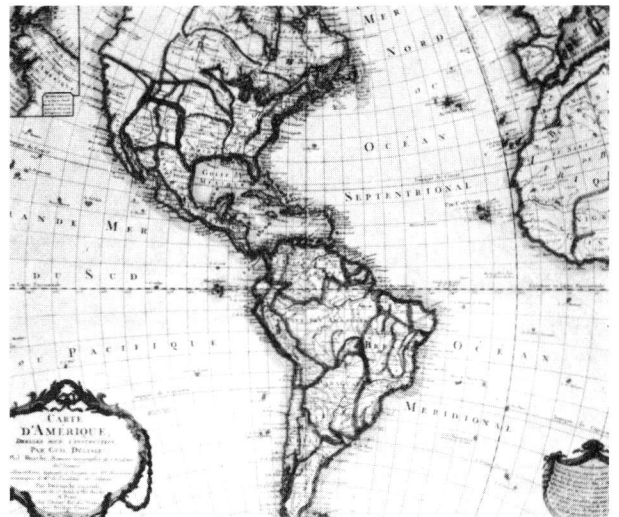

Delisle, North & South America, 1790, w/color, 19x24″	400.00
Ensign & Thayer, Pictorial Map of Great West, 1848, 23x31″	25.00
George, MA, Thirty Miles Around Boston, 1775, 10x10″	90.00
Johnson & Ward, Ireland & Scotland, 1836	75.00
Marshall, Battlefields of the Revolution, from *Life of Washington*	50.00
Munster, America, 1540, woodblock	1,650.00
Ortelius, Abraham, America, 1570	2,500.00
Peters, Indian Reservations, Washington, DC, 1885, 35x24″	50.00
Speed, John, America, early 17th century	2,500.00
Flintshire, early 17th century	750.00
State, Arkansas, TG Bradford, Boston, 1838	60.00

California, Gaskell, 1887, 18x24", color **20.00**
Connecticut, engraved, Doolittle for M Carey, Philadelphia, 1795 **150.00**
Georgia, Matthew Brady, Philadelphia, 1814 .... **120.00**
Illinois, 1822, cartographical, Carey & Lea **500.00**
Illinois, 1837 .... **225.00**
Indiana, Colton, 1889, 17x13", color.................... **25.00**
Maryland, by S Lewis for Matthew Carey, Philadelphia, 1800 **130.00**
Michigan & Wisconsin, Johnson's & Ward, 1836 .... **65.00**
Missouri, TG Bradford, Boston, 1838 .... **60.00**
Ohio, 1822, cartographical, Carey & Lea **175.00**
Oregon, Bien, N.Y., 1863 .... **30.00**
Townsend, Sperm Whaling Grounds of the 19th Century, 1900 . **20.00**
United States, New Map of Our Country, Doty, N.Y., 1857, 73x66" **300.00**
World on Mercator's Projection, Philadelphia, J Melish, 1817 . **150.00**

Marblehead

What began as therapy for patients in a sanitarium in Marblehead, Mass., has become recognized as an important part of the Arts and Crafts movement in America. Results of the early experiments under the guidance of Arthur E. Baggs in 1904 met with such success that by 1908 the pottery had been converted to a solely commercial venture. Baggs bought the company in 1915 and relocated. Simple vase shapes were often incised with stylized animal and floral motifs or sailing ships; others were decorated in low relief. Simple matt glazes in soft yellow, gray, wisteria, rose, tobacco brown, and their most popular, 'Marblehead Blue', were used alone, or in combinaton. The Marblehead logo is distinctive---a boat with full sail, and the letters M and P. The pottery closed in 1936.

Bowl vase, blue matt w/hi gloss interior, 3x5" **95.00**
  Matt green, brown hi gloss interior, 3½x5" **85.00**
Bowl, black luster, 6" dia................................. **78.00**
  Blue, 7½" **65.00**
  Dark green, 5" dia **45.00**
  Floral, three colors **200.00**
  Hi gloss olive w/brown interior on red clay, 4x5".......... **90.00**
Perfume, figural Egyptian mummy, paper label **250.00**
Planter, blue matt, 4½" **60.00**
Tile, ship decor, paper label, incised mk **135.00**
  Stylized florals, copper lustre & green, 4½" **120.00**
Vase, blue matt w/brown hi gloss interior, ship mark, 4" **55.00**
  Blue, 4½" **45.00**
  Blue, 4½x7¾x7".. **70.00**
  Blue, squatty, 4½" **60.00**
  Brown, 6x¾x3½" **55.00**
  Bulbous, matt blue, 7½" **50.00**
  Cylinder, blue matt, 8" **55.00**
  Florals, olive and dk blue on blue, 6½x5" **595.00**
  Green, 6"... **65.00**
Wall vase, beehive shape, rings, blue matt, mkd, 6" **65.00**

Marbles

Marbles have been popular with children since the mid-1800s. They've been made in many types from a variety of materials. Among some of the first glass items to be produced, the earliest marbles were made from a solid glass rod broken into sections of the proper length, which were placed in a tray of sand and charcoal, and returned to the fire. As they were reheated, the trays were constantly agitated until the marbles were completely round. Other marbles were made of china, pottery, steel and natural stones.

When size is not otherwise indicated, prices are listed for mint condition marbles of average size, ½" to 1".

Agates, stone marbles of many different colors, bands of color alternating

with white usually encircle the marble, most are tranlucent ... **12.50**
Akro Agates, among the earliest machine-made marbles, glass simulating the look of agate. Those in original boxes are rare **1.50**
Ballot Box, handmade (with pontils), opaque white or black, used in lodge elections **7.00**
Bloodstone, green chalcedony w/red spots, a type of quartz.... **40.00**
China, with or without glaze, in a variety of handpainted designs--parallel bands or bulls-eye designs most common **18.00**
Clambroth, opaque glass with outer evenly spaced swirl of one or alternating colors, ¾"..................................... **40.00**
  ½" **25.00**
Clay, one of the most common older types, some are painted, while others are not .... **.75**
Comic Strip, a series of machine-made marbles with faces of comic strip characters; Peltier Glass Factory, Ill., 12 characters.
    Andy Gump **40.00**
    Betty Boop **40.00**
    Emma **40.00**
    Ko Ko.. **40.00**
    Orpan Annie **45.00**
    Sandy **40.00**
    Smitty **40.00**
  Set of all 12 characters, mint...................... **495.00**
Crockery, sometimes referred to as Benningtons, most are either blue or brown, although some are speckled. The clay is shaped into a sphere, then coated with glaze and fired........................ **4.00**
End of the Day, single pontil glass marbles, the colored part often appears as a multicolored blob or mushroom cloud **60.00**
Indian Swirls, usually black glass, with a colored swirl appearing on the outside, next to the surface, usually irregular **20.00**
Latticinio Core Swirls, double pontil marble, with an inner area with net-like effects of swirls coming up around the center **25.00**

    1½", (left) **50.00**
    2½" **130.00**
Lutz, (goldstone), glass with colored or clear bands alternating with bands which contain copper flecks.
    3/4".. **45.00**
    5/8"... **25.00**
Micas, clear or colored glass with mica flecks which reflect as silver dots when marble is turned. Red is rare.
    Blue, 5/8"....................................... **10.00**
    Clear, 5/8" **8.00**
Onionskin, spiral type which are solidly colored instead of having individual ribbons or threads; multicolored..................... **25.00**
  Multicolored, 1 7/8", illus **90.00**
Peppermint Swirl, made of white opaque glass with alternating blue and red outer swirls **20.00**
  1" **60.00**
Ribbon Core Swirls, double pontil marble, center shaped like a ribbon with swirls that come up around the middle **22.50**
Rose Quartz, stone marble, usually pink in color, often with fractures in side and on outer surface **40.00**
Solid Core Swirls, double pontil marble, middle is solid with swirls coming

up around the core **22.50**

2″ **95.00**

Steelies, hollow steel spheres marked with a cross where the steel was bent together to form the ball. **12.00**

Sulphides, generally made of clear glass with white figures inside. Rarer types have colored figure or colored glass; from **40.00**

Bear, walking, 2″dia **85.00**

Cow, 1¾″ **70.00**

Dog, 2½″ **40.00**

Elephant, 1½″ **60.00**

Frog, 2¼″ **100.00**

Girl, 1¾″ **200.00**

Grazing sheep **60.00**

Horse, 1½″ **60.00**

Lamb, 1¼″ **45.00**

Lion, 1½″ **65.00**

Number, each, from 0 to 9, 1¾″ **250.00**

Pig, 1¾″. **70.00**

Poodle, 1¾″ **135.00**

Rabbit, 2″ **85.00**

Rearing horse, 2″ **125.00**

Squirrel, 1¾″ **80.00**

Wild boar, 1½″ **65.00**

Tiger Eye, stone marble of golden quartz with inclusions of asbestos, dark brown with gold highlights **40.00**

Vaseline, machine-made of yellowish-green glass with small bubbles **12.00**

Marine Collectibles

Apothecary set, bottles, scales, etc, w/case, 1800s **325.00**

Artifact, bronze hatch bolt from USS Constitution, 1797, 10″ . . **60.00**

Barometer, US Coast Guard, brass, Taylor Co, 5″ dia **110.00**

Basket, sailor's, stringwork, scalloped edges, intricate **75.00**

Single rope work, w/red, wht & blue coloring **15.00**

Belaying pin, wood w/octagonal handle, 7¾″ long **15.00**

Bell, bell metal w/ci hanger, 16x18″ **490.00**

Brass, 17x12″ dia **250.00**

Deborah, signed, 80 lbs **525.00**

Havkong, signed, 45 lbs **425.00**

Binnacle, brass & wood **975.00**

Brass, large **1,275.00**

Mahogany dome, compass, light, 1930, 11″ **145.00**

Book, Harpooner, 4 Year Voyage..., Ferguson, 1936 . . . . **50.00**

Chart bag, sail cloth, hand sewn, w/several charts **90.00**

Chart chest, grain painted, hinged cover, 14x46x9″ **40.00**

Compass, early dry card type, Gimbal rings, Robert Merril, NY . **35.00**

Course corrector, brass, 10″ dia **100.00**

Cutlass, double edge, brass knuckle guard, grip, Naval, 1841 . . **275.00**

Desk, captain's, mahogany, brass handles, slant top, 26x26x8½″ **225.00**

Door plate, Captain's Quarters, Officers Only, 2½x8½″ **20.00**

Flags, signal, wool, lot of 28 . . . . **50.00**

Flare gun, brass, rope lanyard, iron barrel, 13″ **75.00**

Handle for sailor's chest, rope & leather **95.00**

Harpoon, whaling, Lilly Iron, arrowhead tip, movable barbs, 36″ **340.00**

Whaling, for Eban Pierce gun, 37″ **240.00**

Helmet, diver's, brass, copper, glass, 17″ **450.00**

Diver's, glass, copper, US Navy, 20″ **800.00**

Journal log book, Capt Eldridge, 1863-1866, 179 pg, whaling **5,100.00**

Pacific Ocean whaling voyage, 1852-1856 . . . . **3,000.00**

Journal, Civil War, US Sloop of War Vandalia, G **350.00**

Knife, diver's, USS FDR, 13½″ **115.00**

Knot board, w/examples of knots, flag signals **140.00**

Lantern, blk body w/red lens **80.00**

Brass, 360 degree clear lens, burner, 11″ **90.00**

Brass, bail handle, round cage, 1880s, National, 9½″ **150.00**

Brass, handmade, wick light, 9″ **90.00**

Line of position computer, w/box & instruction manual, 15″ . . . **60.00**

Marlinspikes, steel, 14″, lot of 2 . . . . **20.00**

Needle case, wood, w/25 sail maker's needles, 5″ **25.00**

Octant, ebony, brass, ivory scales, Walker, 12″ **650.00**

Ebony, w/box, Gilbert, London **650.00**

Parallel rules, ebony & brass, 12″ long closed **25.00**

Photograph, bark under full sail w/sailors on deck, framed, 17x19″ **25.00**

Whaler 'Janet', at New Bedford, 1874, 20x16″, framed **70.00**

Portholes, brass, 7″, lot of 4 . . . . **100.00**

Portrait, oil on canvas, Governor Dingley ship, 1899, 22x36″ **1,900.00**

Quadrant, ebony, brass, ivory scales, Thos Jones, w/case, 16″ . **950.00**

Sailing card, Mary Goodell, 1860s, 3½x6½″ **165.00**

Sea chest, red paint, inside cover has painted ship, 24½″ long **700.00**

Seam rubber, mahogany, w/faceted knob-end, initialed, 4½″ . . **65.00**

Sextant, brass w/silver scales, cased w/some accessories **300.00**

Brass, silver scale, case **275.00**

US Coast Guard, w/case & accessories, Heath Co **325.00**

Shears, sail maker's, iron **25.00**

Telescope, brass w/wood barrel, 4-draw, w/round wood case, 39″ **400.00**

Day/night, 3-draw scope, brass w/blk enamel barrel, 1800s . . **225.00**

Single-draw, all brass, 36″ **150.00**

Trident, 5 prongs, 11″ **60.00**

Valentine, double hinge mahogany case, varnished shells, 9″ opened **700.00**

Octagonal case, bright colored shells, 9¾″ opened **400.00**

Wheel, ship's, complete w/standards & wood drum, 1800s, 60″ **600.00**

Window, stained glass, flying pennant w/fouled anchor, 27x29″ **300.00**

Martin Bros.

The Martin Bros. were studio potters who worked from 1873 until 1914, first at Fulham, and later at London and Southhall. There were four brothers, each who excelled in their peculiar area. Robert, known as Wallace, was an experienced stonecarver. He modeled a series of grotesque bird and animal figural caricatures. Walter was the potter, responsible for throwing the larger vases on the wheel, firing the kiln and mixing the clay. Edwin, an artist of stature, prefered more naturalistic forms of decoration. His work was often incised or with relief designs of seaweed, florals, fish and birds. The fourth brother, Charles, was their business manager. Their work was incised with their name, place of production, and letters and numbers indicating month and year.

Bottle vase, florals, 6″ **125.00**

Jug, fish, seeweed, incised decor, 2½″ **100.00**

Pitcher, flowering Lotus, 7½″ **200.00**

Squat shape, 5″ **75.00**

Shelf, flowers & leaves in relief, blue, grey, 6 sides, 5″ **500.00**

Vase, brown glaze, 4½″ **50.00**

Grotesque fish, 9″ **350.00**

Orchids, beige w/brown & cream, 9½″ **350.00**

Salamanders, tadpoles, 10″ **400.00**

Mary Gregory

Mary Gregory glass, for reasons that remain obscure, is the namesake of a Boston and Sandwich Glass Co employee who worked for the company for only two years in the mid 1800s. Although the company's museum says no evidence exists to indicate that glass of this type was even produced there, the fine colored or crystal ware decorated with figures of children in white enamel is commonly referred to as Mary Gregory. The glass, in fact, originated in Europe, and was imported into this country where it was copied by several

eastern glass houses. It was popular from the mid 1800s until the turn of the century.

Atomizer, cranberry, inverted thumbprint, girl w/puppet, 5″ ... **145.00**
Berry bowl, clear w/boy and girls, 9½″ dia **95.00**
Bottle w/stopper, amber, pastoral scene w/girl, 8″ **150.00**
Bowl, lime, ormolu feet, boy & girl in wht, 4x6″ **225.00**
Box, sapphire, 2 girls w/bird, 5x5″ dia **395.00**
Cologne, diamond form, beveled, cut stopper, girl, florals, 8″ . **225.00**
Cruet, cobalt, girl **300.00**
Cruet, lime w/green handle, stopper, boy w/colored clothes, 7″ **145.00**
Ewer, green, wht mountaineer **180.00**
Goblets, sapphire, 1 w/boy, 1 w/girl, 5″, pr **110.00**
Jewel casket, ormolu foot, brass rings, girls w/birds, 5x5″ **400.00**
Lady's stein, amber, girl w/kite, pewter & glass top, 3¾″ **195.00**
Liqueur cruet, sapphire, bubble stopper, girl in wht, 10″ **225.00**
Pitcher, cranberry, clear handle, girl w/birds, 11½″ **350.00**
  Cranberry, ribbed, boy w/boat **130.00**
  Emerald, applied handle, boy, 4″ **100.00**
  Pale beige w/wht boys playing football, 11½″ **265.00**
Salt & peppers, amber, orig tops & ratchet **225.00**
Stein, cobalt w/boy in wht, 4″ **200.00**
Tankard, cranberry, clear handle, girl w/birds, 9″ **335.00**
Tumbler, amber, boy in wht, 4″ **45.00**
  Clear, 1 w/boy, 1 w/girl, pr **180.00**
  Sapphire, boy in white, 3¾″ **45.00**
  Sapphire, sitting boy, 4½″ **65.00**
Vase, amber, gold trim, reed handles, boy in white, 10″ **195.00**
  Blue spatter, girl w/butterfly net, 6″ **160.00**
  Blue, cylinder, boy w/hat, 9½x3″ **75.00**
  Blue, pedestal, boy running w/flowers, 6½″ **125.00**
  Bristol pink overlay, girl w/bird, horn, 10″ **195.00**
  Cobalt w/brass handles & rim, girl, 6x2″ **110.00**
  Cranberry, 1 w/boy, 1 w/girl, 9″, pr **365.00**
  Cranberry, boy w/stick, 8½″ **165.00**
  Cranberry, boy w/whip, 5″ **100.00**
  Cranberry, girl & foliage in wht, 6½″ **145.00**
  Cranberry, girl blowing horn, bird on hand, 12″ **275.00**
  Cranberry, girl w/baloon in wht, 5″ **100.00**
  Cranberry, girl w/bubble pipe, gold trim, 7″ **150.00**
  Cranberry, girl w/horn, 12″ **300.00**
  Flat disk body w/notched rim, blk w/wht girl, 16″, pr **1,250.00**
  Green satin, girl w/hat & birds, wht dot trim, 6″ **150.00**
  Green, child w/florals, 12″ **175.00**
  Green, crystal trim, girl, 11″ **150.00**
  Green, straight sides, flared rim, pontil, girl **135.00**
  Lavender bristol, gold trim scalloped, girl w/basket, 12″ **195.00**
  Lime crackle, girl w/hat, 6″ **135.00**
  Lime, boy & bird in wht, beaded top band, 9″ **195.00**
  Lime, cylinder, girl w/tinted features, 13½″ **110.00**
  Lime, girl & foliage, 4x3½″ **95.00**
  Lime, girl w/hat & butterfly net, 7½″ **135.00**
  Opaque green w/girl at pump, man w/hat, 14″ **295.00**
  Pink opaque, girl on tree branch, 12″ **195.00**
  Sapphire w/gold bands at base, 18½″, pr **1,200.00**
  Sapphire, cylinder, boy w/hat in wht, 9½″ **80.00**
  Sapphire, ornate crystal handles, 1 w/boy, 1 w/girl, 9″, pr .. **395.00**
Wine bottle, green, girl, stopper, 9″ **135.00**

Massier

Clement Massier was a French artist-potter who established a workshop at Golfe Juan, France, in 1881, where he experimented with metallic lustre glazes. (One of his pupils was Jacques Sicardo, who brought the knowledge

he had gained through his association there to the Weller Pottery Company of Zanesville, Ohio). The lustre lines developed by Massier incorporated nature themes with allover decorations of foliage or flowers on shapes modeled in the Art Nouveau style. The ware was usually incised with the Massier name, his initials or the location of the pottery. Massier died in 1917.

Bowl, irid 3-color outside, lustrous 3-color inside, scrolling, 3x5″ **350.00**

Bowl, irid w/florals, handles, 7x7″ **450.00**
Charger, multicolor lustre, bees & lillies decor, 16¾″ **1,200.00**
Vase, deep gold w/applied locust, sgnd Sicard, 3″ **150.00**
  Thorny branches decor, irid, 9″ **700.00**
  Yellow w/flowers in field, gold hi-lighted, sgnd, 17½″ **400.00**

Match Holders

Before the invention of the safety match in 1855, matches were kept in matchboxes and carried in pocket sized matchsafes because they ignited so easily. John Walker, an English chemist, invented the match more than 100 years ago, quite by accident. Walker was working with a mixture of potash and antimony, hoping to make a combustible that could be used to fire guns. The mixture adhered to the end of the wooden stick he had used for stirring. As he tried to remove it by scraping the stick on the stone floor, it burst into flames. The invention of the match was only a step away!

Advertising, Adriance Farm Machinery, hanging type, colorful .. **70.00**
  De Laval Separator Co, hanging type **40.00**
  JS Kemp Mfg, cast iron w/crocodile paperweight, 8½″ **50.00**
  Judson Whiskey, wall type, cast iron **40.00**
Bisque, girl figural stands beside basket shaped holder, Germany **90.00**
Boar tusk, American, w/stag candle holder, lucite base, 1910 ... **50.00**
Brass, w/eagle & arch border, schooner on pocket, hanging type **30.00**

Deer, gun, game & double pouch, ci, 11″ **75.00**
Elephant, figural, amber glass **40.00**

Glass, Art Noveau woman in relief, wall type **40.00**
Mechanical, cast iron, Phoenix Bird picks up matches w/beak . . **95.00**
Wood, chip carved, hanging type, 1 pc, Kansas leaves decor . . . **40.00**

Matchsafes

Matchsafes, aptly named cases used to carry matches in the days before cigarette lighters, were used during the last half of the 19th century until about 1920. Some incorporated added features--hidden compartments, cigar cutters, etc.---some were figural, and others were used by retail companies as advertising give-aways. They were made from every type of material, but silver plated styles abound.

Advertising, Anheuser Busch, German Silver, 'A' w/eagle **50.00**
    Dr Shoop's **95.00**
    Fontiues Gents Fine Footwear, Denver, Pocket style **34.00**
    Gillette **22.00**
    Juicy Fruit Gum **145.00**
    Luden's Menthol Cough Drops 5ᶜ, under celluloid **55.00**
    Marshall's Merchant's Row, Boston, 1899, w/orig matches **33.00**
    Old Judson **135.00**
    Ridgewood Tobacco Co, nickeled brass, pocket size **90.00**
    Schlitz Milwaukee Beer, pocket size w/cigar cutter **35.00**
    Standard Clothing Co, Boston **19.00**
    US Machine & Supply, 1880 . . . . **10.00**
    Val Blatz Brewing Co **95.00**
Agate **125.00**
Art Nouveau, plated, floral embossing, 2½", illus **30.00**
Aluminum, brite-cut, 1907 . . . . **15.00**
Bloomers, nickeled brass, ruffled knees, opens top, striker bottom **195.00**
Brass, antique, horseshoe-shaped **60.00**
    Embossed owl in flight **60.00**
    Figural basket of flowers & fruit, striker bottom **175.00**
    Glove figural **150.00**
    Tooth-shaped w/boar finial **90.00**
Cloisonne, intricate, w/jade inserts **56.00**
Corset, brass, full figural, laces in back **285.00**

Devil, 2", illus **27.50**
Figural, Columbus **125.00**
    Hoof **75.00**
    Indian, sterling **125.00**
    Oriental warrior, sterling **65.00**
Gold, 14K, coat of arms, 'Justus Esto et Non Metus' **375.00**
Greenaway **45.00**
Hanging, 3 owls on horseshoe **32.00**
    Cast iron,, lacy, grape pattern, open pocket **23.00**
    Lacy, open double section pocket, 3 strike surfaces **47.00**
    Lacy, signed C Parker, 1868 . . . . **60.00**

Lacy, swing lid, Parker pat 1869 . . . . **65.00**
    Urn shape, dated 1867 . . . . **35.00**
Knights of Columbus, 1919 . . . . **120.00**
Nouveau lady's head & filagree on cover, push-button opener, 1904 **30.00**
Package, nickeled brass, tied in four sections w/cord **95.00**
Silver plate over brass, ornate, old **32.00**
    Art Nouveau, 2 fisherman, 2½" **50.00**
Silver plate w/etched hunting scene, 3", illus **27.00**
Souvenir, Union Station, St Louis, 1904, w/cigar cutter **38.00**
Sterling silver, Art Nouveau Cupid kissing lady, w/mono **55.00**
    Embossed scrolls & flowers, dated 1907 . . . . **55.00**
    Ornate Victorian design w/mono **55.00**
    Totally ribbed, front raised leaf, 1¾" **28.50**
    With Cupids **85.00**
    With hunt scene **85.00**
    Winged nude in bower of lilies, #1197 . . . . **95.00**
    Woman's head w/flowing hair in relief, both sides **65.00**
Tiffany & Co, overall engraving, 'Justice' w/scales & etc **110.00**
Tiger maple, turned ped, heavy uniform stripes, table model, 3½" **75.00**
Unger Bros, embossed florals & scrolls, 2 Cupids, unique shape **175.00**
    Sterling, nude lying in water, monogram **275.00**

Mayer

From as early as 1790 the Mayers operated potteries in Staffordshire, often marking their wares with the surname and first initials. The first, Elijah Mayer, 1790-1804, produced creamware, basalt, and Wedgwood-type wares. His son, Joseph, joined the firm in 1805, and in 1822 founded his own firm where he made earthenwares marked either with his full name or Mayer & Co. Thomas Mayer, 1826-35, produced blue transfer printed dinnerware for export to the United States, which he marked T. Mayer.

The Mayer Bros., Thomas, John and Joseph Mayer, operated the Furlong Works and Dale Hall Pottery at Burslem in Staffordshire, in 1843-55. They made quality products and were especially noted for their molded Parian wares. Their trademark was T.J. & J. Mayer, or Mayer Bros.

Although others by this name operated at various times, their marks did not include 'Mayer'. Currently in business in Stoke, the Elton Pottery, established in 1956 for the production of earthenwares, is under the direction of a Thomas Mayer. Their logo is a T over M device, or Elton Pottery, MIE.

Cup & saucer, handleless, 12 panels, blue X & dot decor, 1830 **65.00**
Cup, handleless, Abbey Ruins, blue, 1835 . . . . **35.00**
Pitcher, Canova, pink & green transfer, 1½ qt, mkd **80.00**
    Paul & Virginia, stippled w/hi-relief figures, mkd, 1851, 8" . . **225.00**
Place setting, Avonlea, 5 pc **70.00**
    Stanwood, 5 pc **70.00**
Plate, 7½", Canova, red & green **20.00**
    9", Canova, pink **37.50**

McCoy

The third generation McCoy potter in the Roseville, Ohio area was Nelson, who with the aid of his father J. W. established the Nelson McCoy Sanitary Stoneware Company in 1910. They manufactured churns, jars and jugs, poultry fountains and footwarmers. By 1925, they had expanded their wares to include majolica jardinieres and pedestals, umbrella stands and cuspidors, and an embossed line of vases and small jardiniers in a blended brown and green matt glaze. From the late '20s through the mid '40s a utilitarian stoneware was produced, some of which was glazed in the soft blue and white so popular with collectors today. They also used a dark brown mahogany color, and a medium to dark green---both high gloss. In 1933, the company became known as the Nelson McCoy Pottery Company, and they continue to use that title currently. They expanded their facilities in

1940, and began to make the novelty art wares, cookie jars, and dinnerware that today are synonomous with 'McCoy'. To date, more than 200 cookie jars of every theme and description have been produced. Some are very common. Mammy, the Clown, and the Bear, although very old are easy to find; while the Dalmations, Christmas Tree, and Kangaroo, for instance, though not so old are harder to locate. The Indian and the Teepee, both made in the '50s are two of the most popular and some of the most expensive!

More than a dozen different marks have been used by the company; nearly all incorporate the name McCoy, although some of the older items were marked NM USA.

Apollo decanter, len 30.00

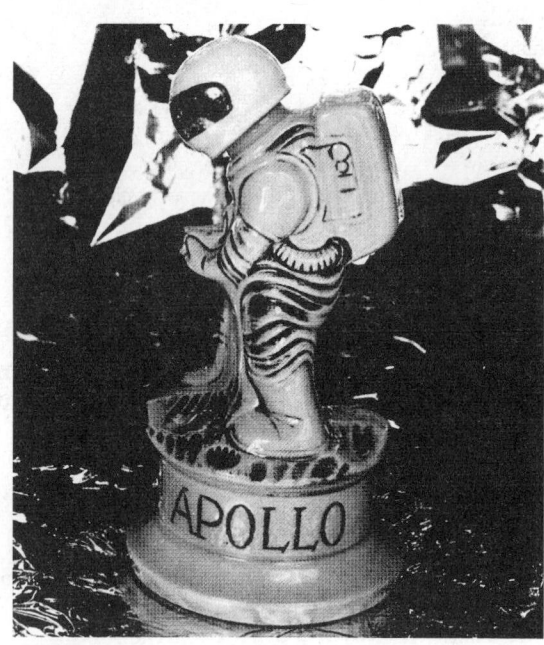

Astronaut decanter 30.00
Bank, 1st Money Chest 12.00
    Eagle, Immigrant Industrial Savings 12.00
    Liberty Bell 12.00
    Seaman's for Savings, figural sailor 12.00
    State Federal Savings of Puerto Rico 12.00
    Woodsey Owl 15.00
Basket; basketweave, double handles 15.00
    Leaves, braided handle 16.00
    Oak leaf & acorn, 1962 . . . . 15.00
    Pine cones, green & brown on white 15.00
Bean pot; bean pod decor, w/lid, brown 20.00
    Brown glaze, no decor 8.00
    Cream w/hp red apple, green leaf, Kathy Kale 12.00
    Stoneware, brown & white, #3 . . . . 12.00
    Suburbia, 2 qt w/cover 12.00
Beverage jug, Sunburst Gold 25.00
Beverage server; blue streaks, Eastman 8.00
    Purple & gold on wht 20.00
Birdbath; greystone finish, 27" 65.00
    Greystone, leaves & berries at base" 85.00
Bookends, hunting dog w/pheasants, pr 30.00
    Lilys w/leaves, pr 20.00
    Rearing horses, white glaze, pr 15.00
    Swallow, w/planter, pr 20.00
    Violin, w/planter, 1959, pr 15.00
Bud vase, zig zag Deco type 6.00
Butterpot, yellow w/white band, crockery lid 45.00
Cabbage grease jar 18.00

Cabbage salt & peppers 12.00
Cache pot, double lily w/bird 12.00
Canning jar, stoneware, brown, 1 qt 10.00
Casserole, blue & black mottled w/black lid 8.00
Cat feeder, yellow stoneware 10.00
Centerpiece; Antique Curio, wht w/blue berries 8.00
    Basket line, 1959 . . . . 15.00
Churn; salesman's sample, 3¾" 30.00
    Stoneware, #3 . . . . 85.00
Coffee pot, Grecian 30.00
Coffee server w/warmer, El Rancho Bar-B-Que 35.00
Comport, Garden Club 10.00
Cookie jar; Animal Cracker, round w/animal decor, finial, 1959-60 24.00
    Apple, 1950-64 . . . . 18.00
    Apple on Basketweave, 1957 . . . . 16.00
    Bananas, 1950-52 . . . . 25.00

Barnum's Animals, Nabisco Wagon, 1972-74 . . . . 30.00
Bear, w/bow-tie, 1942-45 . . . . 18.00
Bobby Baker, 1974-75 . . . . 10.00
Brown Milk Can, 1970-74 . . . . 8.00
Caboose, 'Cookie Special', 1961 . . . . 35.00
Chef, 1962-64 . . . . 28.00
Chipmunk, 1959-62 . . . . 40.00
Christmas Tree, 1959 . . . . 90.00
Circus Horse, 1962 . . . . 45.00
Clown Bust, 1943-49 . . . . 18.00
Clown in Barrel, 1953-56 . . . . 28.00
Coalby Cat, 1967 . . . . 15.00
Coffee Grinder, 1961-64 . . . . 12.00
Coffee Mug, USA, 1965 . . . . 15.00
Colonial Fireplace, 1967 . . . . 25.00
Cookie Barrel, 1958-67 . . . . 12.00
Cookie Boy, 1940-43 . . . . 45.00
Cookie Cabin, 1957-60 . . . . 25.00
Cookie Log, squirrel finial, 1967 . . . . 12.00
Cookie Safe, blk, mkd USA on leg, 1962-63 . . . . 18.00
Cookstove, rectangular wood stove, 1962-64 . . . . 12.00
Corn, 1959 . . . . 75.00
Country Stove, pot-bellied stove, 1967 . . . . 15.00
Covered Wagon, 1959-62 . . . . 28.00
Dog on Basketweave, 1956-57 . . . . 22.00
Dog, 'Mac', USA, 1967 . . . . 18.00
Drum, drum finial, 1959-60 . . . . 20.00

Duck on Basketweave, 1956	**25.00**
Dutch Boy, 1945	**18.00**
Dutch Girl, w/Dutch boy on reverse side, 1945	**40.00**
Dutch Treat Barn, 1970-73	**15.00**
Early American Chest, chiffonier, 1967	**35.00**
Elephant, 1943	**32.00**
Elephant, split trunk, 1943	**50.00**
Engine, 1963-64	**35.00**
Flower Pot, tulip decor, tulip finial, 1959	**28.00**
Flower Pot, w/plastic flower top, 1950s	**15.00**
Forbidden Fruit, rope-look basket w/apple finial, 1967	**18.00**
Fortune Cookie, Chinese lantern, 1967	**35.00**
Globe, hand decorated countries, 1959	**28.00**
Grandfather Clock, mkd USA, 1962-64	**22.00**
Granny, USA 1972-73	**15.00**
Have A happy Day, round w/smile face, 1971-75	**12.00**
Hen on Nest, USA, 1959	**25.00**
Hexagon Jar, floral decor, sq handles, 'W' finial, 1947	**15.00**
Hillbilly Bear, early 1940s, limited	**75.00**
Hobby Horse, 1950-51	**35.00**
Honey Bear, 1953-55	**22.00**
House, 'Cookie House', 1960	**42.00**
Indian Head, 1954-56	**95.00**

Kangaroo w/joey in pouch, rare	**125.00**
Kettle, blk w/immoveable bail, floral decor, 1962-64	**15.00**
Kettle, blk w/'Kookie Kettle' in gold, moveable bail	**12.00**
Kettle, jumbo size, moveable bail, 1963-64	**15.00**
Kitten on Basketweave, 1956-69	**18.00**
Kittens on Ball of Yarn, 1945-55	**22.00**
Lamb on Basketweave, 1956-57	**25.00**
Little Clown, full figural, 1945	**25.00**
Lollipop, w/lollipop finial, 1958-60	**22.00**
Love Birds, penguins kissing, 1945	**22.00**
Mammy, checked apron, 'Cookies...', 1948-57	**24.00**
Mammy with Cauliflowers, 1939, limited	**85.00**
Monk, 1970	**15.00**
Mother Goose, 1947-51	**40.00**
Mr & Mrs Owl, 1953-55	**22.00**
Oaken Bucket, USA, 1961-71	**10.00**
Old Churn, no mk, 1961	**12.00**
Old Fashioned Auto, touring car, 1962-64	**28.00**
Pears on Basketweave, 1957	**16.00**
Pelican, 1940-43	**45.00**

Picnic Basket, mkd USA, 1962-63	**25.00**
Pineapple, 1955-57	**20.00**
Pineapple, modern, 1970	**12.00**
Pirates Chest, 1970-71	**15.00**
Pumpkin Jack-O-Lantern, 1955	**30.00**
Puppy, 1961-62	**25.00**
Quaker Oats, USA, 1970	**12.00**

Reclining cow, Cookies & Milk, rare	**175.00**
Rocking Chair with Dalmations, 1962	**65.00**
Rooster, 1955-57	**28.00**
Round w/hp leaves, 1964	**15.00**
Snoopy, USA, 1970	**25.00**
Snow Bear, holding flower, 1965	**18.00**
Spaceship Friendship, 1962-63	**28.00**
Strawberry, 1955-57	**18.00**
Strawberry, new, 1972-75	**12.00**
Tea Pot, 1071	**12.00**
Teepee, 1957-59	**75.00**
Turkey, 1959-60	**45.00**
Uncle Sam's Hat, 1973	**12.00**
WC Fields, USA, 1972-74	**40.00**
Wedding Jar, wht w/gold trim, 1961	**25.00**
Windmill, 1961	**25.00**
Wishing Well, 1961-70	**12.00**
Woodsy Owl, USA, 1972-74	**28.00**
Wren House, 1959-60	**25.00**
Creamer; dog w/bow figural, aqua	**15.00**
Grecian	**5.00**
Crock, RV Cry Co, pr	**7.00**
Cucumber & mango, salt & pepper, pr	**12.00**
Cuspidor, grape	**25.00**
Dish, w/applied bird, 1950	**10.00**
Dog dish; bird dog w/pheasant, paneled	**18.00**
Hunting dog, green stoneware	**15.00**
Man's Best Friend	**15.00**
Dresser caddy; buffalo, for Swank	**15.00**
Dog w/brush tail, for Swank	**15.00**
Lion, for Swank	**15.00**
Dripolator, white, paneled 2 pc	**15.00**
Duck, figural, small, wht glaze	**5.00**
Fan vase, Wild Rose	**10.00**
Fern box, stylized band of butterflies, Deco sides	**5.00**
Fernery; butterfly, small	**7.00**
Hobnail, 1940	**6.00**

Flower pot; basketweave, small **2.50**
   Basketweave, large **7.00**
   Basketweave, med **4.50**
   Leaves & berries at base, wht matt, 1935 . . . . **7.00**
   Lotus motif, #4 . . . . **10.00**
   Shield mark #14 . . . . **10.00**
   Lattice w/roses, bisque, 1926 . . . . **10.00**
Foot warmer, stoneware, 1910 . . . . **25.00**
Hanging basket; Basketweave, late '30s, 7½" **15.00**
   Early American, blue trim on wht **9.00**
   Green & brown glaze w/leaves & berries, 1926 . . . . **15.00**
Hillbilly, novelty, small **5.00**

Ice tea server, barrel, El Rancho Bar-B-Que **45.00**
Ivy bowl or hanging basket, leaves, 1949 . . . . **15.00**
Jar; stoneware, #4 . . . . **22.00**
   Stoneware, #8 . . . . **22.00**
Jardiniere; Basketweave w/leaves, cherries at top, 10½" **22.00**
   Butterflies & panels, 1940 . . . . **12.00**
   Fern motif, brown glaze **18.00**
   Flying birds, 7½" **15.00**
   Flying birds, small, white matt **8.00**
   Green & brown blend, shield mark #16 . . . . **15.00**
   Holly motif, aqua, large **15.00**
   Leaves at base, med, 1940s **9.00**
   Leaves in relief, tassels on sides, large **10.00**
   Pine cones, green & brown matt, large **12.00**
   Roses around top in relief, pink **7.00**
   Springwood **8.00**
Jard & ped; matt white, berries & leaves, 21" **75.00**
   Matt white, butterflies, 21" **75.00**
   Tufted w/butterfly border, large **70.00**
   Turquoise w/cobalt drip, 1924, 41" **250.00**
Jug, stoneware, #3 . . . . **30.00**
Lamp base; boots, large **35.00**
   Boots, small **20.00**
   Horse, gold glaze **20.00**
   Pitcher & bowl **12.00**
Lamp, panther, black glaze, log base **12.00**
Lazy Susan, 7 sections on revolving base **15.00**
Mirth is King, decanter **25.00**
Mug; buccaneer, green stoneware, #6 . . . . **12.00**
   Grape motif, green stoneware **10.00**
   Robin Hood **7.00**
   Suburbia **4.00**
   Willow Ware, green glaze **10.00**
Oil jar; 2 handles, 1930-50, 16" **50.00**
   No handles, 12" **35.00**
Pencil holder, boot **6.00**
Pigeon, small **5.00**
Pitcher; angel fish motif **15.00**
   Antique Rose, 1959 . . . . **7.00**

Batan, 1940s **30.00**
Birds & cherries, matt **12.00**
Blended Scotch Whiskey for Seagrams **20.00**
Buttermilk, shield mark #21 . . . . **15.00**
Chicken figural, 1943 . . . . **15.00**
Deco panels & leaves, twig handle, sq spout, 1950s **20.00**
Disk w/leaves at base, aqua **20.00**
Duck head handle, relief decor, 1935 . . . . **30.00**
Embossed cloverleaf, 1948 . . . . **15.00**
Fish figural, aqua, 1949 . . . . **28.00**
Old Crow Distillery **20.00**

Parrot figural, 1952 . . . . **22.00**
Plain, green glaze, ½ gal, 1926 . . . . **15.00**
Water lily, #124 . . . . **10.00**
Water lily w/fish handle, #30, large **30.00**
Willow Ware, green glaze **30.00**
Planter; 2 fawn **8.00**
   2 kittens w/basket **7.00**
   2 quail & fleging, green & brown blend **18.00**
   2 rabbits by stump **9.00**
   3 fawn, log base, trees, large, natural colors **45.00**
   3 poppies, leaves, twig base **12.00**
   4 scotties in a row **10.00**
   Alligator **12.00**
   Antique Curio, white w/blue berries **6.00**
   Anvil w/chain & hammer, 1953 . . . . **10.00**
   Arcature, rectangle w/bird in center **15.00**
   Arcature, square w/bird in center **15.00**
   Baby crib **4.00**
   Banana boat, Calypso line **18.00**
   Barrel w/singer, Calypso line **18.00**
   Bird dog w/pheasant, fence, large **50.00**
   Bird of paradise **10.00**
   Bird & nest, 1957 . . . . **9.00**
   Bunny w/carrot **8.00**
   Butterfly figural **12.00**
   Carriage w/separate umbrella **35.00**
   Cobblers bench **8.00**
   Coffee, tea, sugar, salt **15.00**
   Cradle w/swag & flowers **7.00**
   Discus thrower **14.00**
   Doe & fawn, wht glaze **9.00**
   Dog & carriage, What About Me **10.00**
   Dog w/coat in mouth **9.00**
   Duck, 2 eggs **8.00**
   Duck carrying egg **10.00**
   Duck w/separate umbrella **35.00**
   Dutch shoe, applied flower **6.00**
   Elephant, trunk turned back, 1940s **8.00**

Fan w/bow, pink, 1956 .... **6.00**
Fish & fowl w/bucket **9.00**
Fish figural, large **15.00**
Flying ducks, leaves at base **18.00**
Frog & lotus **8.00**

Frog w/separate umbrella **35.00**
Goat, head down **8.00**
Gondola, black w/flowers **12.00**
Goose w/cart **9.00**
Hand, hole in palm **10.00**
Hand w/bowl **7.00**
Hand w/cornucopia **8.00**
Hat, rolled brim **5.00**
Heart & roses **8.00**
Hobby horse **10.00**
Humpty Dumpty **6.00**
Keats, hands hold book **8.00**
Kitten, recumbent **7.00**
Kitten w/basket, 1941 .... **7.00**
Lamb, white w/blue bow **10.00**
Liberty Bell **55.00**
Lion, recumbent **10.00**
Log w/chain **4.50**
Log w/wheel **10.00**
Mary Anne shoe **4.00**
Old mill, 1953 .... **8.00**
Orange, figural on leaf **7.00**
Parrot w/tub, leaves at base **12.00**
Pear figural on leaf base **7.00**
Pelican, 1941 .... **9.00**
Pheasant, woodland base, natural colors .. **12.00**
Piano **12.00**
Pig, 1947 .... **5.00**
Plow boy, 1955 .... **12.00**
Pony w/saddle **9.00**
Poodle **9.00**
Pussy at the well **12.00**
Robin Hood **9.00**
Rocking chair, 1954 .... **12.00**
Rodeo cowboy, 1950s, natural colors **15.00**
Rolling pin w/Blue Boy, 1952 .... **12.00**
Rooster, 1951 .... **10.00**
Santa & sled, North Pole **8.00**
Scoop w/mammy, 1954 .... **15.00**
Sheep, Baa, Baa, Black Sheep **5.00**
Singing angels, Noel **8.00**
Singing bird, 1943 .... **5.00**

Sitting dog w/cart **9.00**
Spinning wheel **8.00**
Spinning wheel w/cat **7.00**
Spotted puppy, 1959 .... **8.00**
Springwood, triple foot **11.00**
Squirrel w/nut **8.00**
Stork & basket **10.00**
Stork w/basket & baby **9.00**
Swan, large, leaves at base **10.00**
Triple lily on log base, natural colors **9.00**
Trivet w/pot **7.00**
Turtle, open back, large **15.00**
Twin shoes **7.00**
Twin swans, 1953 .... **7.00**
Uncle Sam w/eagle **18.00**
Village smithy **14.00**
Wishing well, 1950 .... **8.00**
Zebra & baby **10.00**
Planting dish; butterfly **10.00**
  Cross w/leaves **9.00**
  Pair of doves **7.00**
  With swan behind **10.00**
Plate, Suburbia, dinner **4.00**
Pot, lotus leaf, attached saucer **8.00**
Pretzel jar, green stoneware w/wood effect modeling **35.00**
Salt box; brown glaze w/butterfly motif, open **30.00**
  Green & ivory, crockery lid **40.00**
Sand jar, sphinx head motif, green & brown, 1940s **65.00**
Shoulder bowl; green stoneware, #11, 1926 ..... **10.00**
  USA, cream w/red & blue bands **8.00**
Sombrero centerpiece, El Rancho Bar-B-Que **45.00**
Spoon rest; butterfly, 1953 .... **18.00**
  Penguin figural **18.00**

Sport Phantom decanter **35.00**
Sprinkler, turtle **18.00**
Stein, beer advertising **15.00**
Strawberry pot, yellow w/leaves in relief, #2, 7" **15.00**
Strawberry jar w/bird, flowing tail, blended glaze **14.00**
Stretch dachshund **7.00**
Stretch doggy **7.00**
Stretch horse **5.00**
Stretch lion **5.00**
Sugar & creamer, sunburst gold **20.00**
Sugar, Grecian **6.00**
Tankard; Buccaneer, green stoneware **30.00**
  Banded barrel, green stoneware **25.00**
  Grape, green stoneware **30.00**
  Indian Peace Sign, brown glaze **30.00**
Tea set; daisy decor, brown & green on white, 3 pc **30.00**
  Pinecone, 3 pc **35.00**
  Two tone green leaves, twig handles, 3 pc **35.00**
Teapot; cat w/pink bow, tail is handle, paw spout **15.00**
Train decanter, Jupiter 60, 4 pc **200.00**
Tray, hands w/leaves & berries, 1941 ..... **7.00**

Urn, Deco, 2 rows of points, blended glaze	**20.00**
Vase; 5 fingers, Antique Curio	**9.00**
Birds & cherries, w/cherries on obverse	**8.00**
Blossomtime w/handles	**10.00**
Butterfly, cylinder, 6″	**8.00**
Butterfly, cylinder, 8″	**9.00**
Butterfly, tall, ped foot	**12.00**
Cornucopia, green, 1926	**10.00**
Deco, 2 rows of points, stepped shoulder, handles	**25.00**
Disk w/florals, wheel handles	**9.00**
Double bud, leaves & berries at base	**8.00**
Double tulips, natural colors	**9.00**

English ivy, green & brown on ivory	**12.00**
Fawns in curl of cornucopia	**12.00**
Grape cluster w/leaves at top	**12.00**
Green & brown blend, leaves & florals	**10.00**
Hobnail, 8″	**8.00**
Horseshoe decoration, 1950s	**12.00**
Hyacinth, 1950	**12.00**
Leaves & stylized berries, handles, aqua, 12″	**20.00**
Lizard handles, water lily motif, green matt	**18.00**
Magnolia blossoms, natural colors, 1953	**10.00**
Onyx, brown, pear shape w/handles, disk ft, 6″	**12.00**
Onyx, green, convex sides w/leaves in relief	**12.00**
Paneled sides, ric rac top, 12″	**15.00**
Pine cones down sides	**12.00**
Ram's head, 1950s	**22.00**
Sailboat, square base	**8.00**
Single lily w/leaves	**10.00**
Springwood, ball base w/sq throat	**7.00**
Sunflower w/basket base, 1954	**9.00**
Swan, 9″	**8.00**
Tulip in relief, green glaze	**8.00**
Uncle Sam, 1943	**14.00**
Wild Rose, 1942	**8.00**
Wall pocket, apple	**12.00**
Banana	**12.00**
Basketweave cornucopia	**10.00**
Bellows	**12.00**
Bird bath	**12.00**
Clock	**20.00**
Early American, blue trim on wht	**10.00**
Grapes	**12.00**
Iron on trivet	**12.00**
Lady in hat w/bow	**12.00**
Leaves	**10.00**
Leaves & berries	**12.00**
Lily	**10.00**
Love bird on trivet	**15.00**

Mail box	**10.00**
Mexican, blue matt	**15.00**
Orange on leaf	**12.00**
Owl on trivet	**15.00**
Pear	**12.00**

Sunburst Gold fan	**15.00**
Sunflower w/bird	**12.00**
Umbrella	**10.00**
Violin	**12.00**
Wall shelf, bird, wht glaze	**15.00**
Window box; butterfly	**8.00**
Rustic, pine cone feet	**6.00**
Window planter, Grecian	**12.00**

McCoy, J.W.

The J.W. McCoy Pottery Company was incorporated in 1899. It operated under that name in Roseville, Ohio, until 1911 when McCoy entered into a partnership with George Brush, forming the Brush-McCoy Company.

During the early years McCoy produced kitchen wares, majolica jardinieres and pedestals, umbrella stands and cuspidors. By 1903, they had begun to experiment in the field of art pottery, and though never involved to the extent of some of their contemporaries, nevertheless produced several art lines of merit.

Their first line was Mt. Pelee, examples of which are very rare today. Two types of glazes were used, matt green and an iridescent charcoal grey. Though the line was primarily mold formed, some pieces evidence the fact that while the clay remained wet and pliable, it was pulled and pinched with the fingers to form crests and peaks, in a style not unlike George Ohr.

The company rebuilt in 1904, after being destroyed by fire, and other art ware was designed. Loy Nel Art and Renaissance were standard brown lines, hand decorated under glaze with colored slip. Shapes and artwork were usually simple but effective. Olympia and Rosewood were relief molded brown glaze lines, decorated in natural colors with wreaths of leaves and berries or simple floral sprays. Although much of this ware was not marked, you may find examples with the die stamped Loy Nel Art, McCoy or an incised line identification.

Bowl, Loy Nel Art, florals, 2 handles, large	**80.00**
Console bowl, Mt Pelee, green, 3½x12″	**300.00**
Divided tray w/handle, Mt Pelee, black irid, 2x7″	**125.00**
Ewer, Mt Pelee, grey irid, large	**275.00**
Olympia, molded roses, 9½″	**180.00**
Rosewood, grapes & leaves in relief, 10″	**200.00**
Jardiniere, Loy Nel Art, Hayley's Comet, 1910, 4½″	**200.00**
Loy Nel Art, pansies, ball ft, 6″	**100.00**
Loy Nel Art, smoking cigars, 4″	**200.00**
Rosewood, ftd, large, 9″	**95.00**
Jardiniere & ped, Loy Nel Art, tulips, 28″	**350.00**
Jug vase, Olympia, floral, ftd, 1 handle	**120.00**
Jug, Olympia, molded ear of corn, 7½x3½″	**180.00**

Mug, Olympia, molded leaf band at top rim, 5x4½" **125.00**
Pretzel bowl, Olympia, leaves, on pedestal **250.00**
Punch bowl, Olympia, molded grapes & leaves, 10x17" **400.00**
Spittoon, Loy Nel Art, florals, 4½" **100.00**
Vase, Loy Nel Art, daffodil, integral handles, 11" **125.00**
   Loy Nel Art, floral, brown glaze, handles, 13½" **225.00**
   Loy Nel Art, pansies, w/handles, 8" **125.00**
   Olympia, Aladdin lamp form, leaves & berries in relief **145.00**
   Olympia, molded ear of corn, 4½" base, 2" top, 11" **190.00**
   Olympia, molded irises, 9x5" **150.00**
   Olympia, molded leaves, 10x3½" **175.00**
   Olympia, molded leaves, handles, 5" **110.00**
   Olympia, molded roses, handles, 6x6" **155.00**
   Olympia, molded tulips, Art Nouveau, handles, 12x6" **200.00**

Rosewood, grapes & leaves in relief, 7" **125.00**
Rosewood, molded florals, 5" **110.00**
Rosewood, orange streaks on brown, 3" **30.00**
Rosewood, orange streaks on brown, 6" **35.00**
Rosewood, orange streaks on brown, 9" **50.00**

McKee

McKee Glass was founded in 1853, in Pittsburg, Pa. Among their early products were tableware of both the flint and non-flint variety. In 1888, the company relocated to avail themselves of a source of natural gas, thereby founding the town of Jeanette, Pa.

One of their most famous colored dinnerware lines, Rock Crystal, was manufactured in the 1920s. During the '30s and '40s, colored opaque dinnerware, Sunkist reamers, and 'bottoms up' cocktail tumblers were popular, as well as a line of black glass vases, bowls and novelty items. All are popular items with today's collectors.

The company was purchased in 1916 by Jeanette Glass, under which name it continues to operate.

Bowl, blue cane, coach, 1886 .... **65.00**
   Light green, flower design, footed, 1917, mkd, 14" **95.00**
   Rock Crystal, clear, plain edge, 4½" **10.00**
Candy jar, Rock Crystal, clear, covered, 16 oz **55.00**
Champagne, Rock Crystal, clear, footed, 6 oz **17.00**
Clock, Tambour, blue **495.00**
Cocktail, Rock Crystal, clear, footed, 3½ oz **18.50**
Cordial, Rock Crystal, ½ oz **12.50**
Egg cup, custard, 4¼" **5.00**
Juice, Rock Crystal, 3½ oz **7.50**

Rock Crystal, 5 oz **16.00**
Mug, Tom & Jerry, wht & gold **2.50**
Nappy, custard, 4¼" **3.00**
Pitcher, Rock Crystal, pink, w/lid **155.00**
Punch bowl, Wiltec, clear, 14" **45.00**
Punch set, Tom & Jerry, wht w/red decals, bowl & 9 mugs **30.00**
Refrigerator dish, jadeite w/clear lid, 5x4" **5.00**
   Jadeite, 5x8½" **12.00**
Sandwich server, Rock Crystal, amber, center handle **45.00**
Sherbet, Rock Crystal, clear, 3½ oz **15.00**
Sugar shaker, jadeite, square, 4½" **10.00**
Sundae, Rock Crystal, clear, low, footed, 6 oz **14.00**
Tumbler, bottoms-up, carmel, w/crystal & gold coaster **65.00**
   Bottoms-up, carmel **55.00**
   Bottoms-up, crystal satin, w/black coaster **75.00**
   Bottoms-up, jade, w/coaster **75.00**
   Bottoms-up, jade, w/crystal & green coaster **65.00**
   Bottoms-up, jade coaster **75.00**
Tumbler, Sunbeam, green **25.00**
   Whiskey, Rock Crystal, clear, 2½ oz **21.50**
Vase, green milk glass, triangular shape, 3 nudes, 8½" **98.00**
   Rock Crystal, clear, bulbous, footed, 11" **57.50**
Wine, Rock Crystal, clear, footed, 3 oz **18.00**
   Sunbeam **24.00**

Medical Collectibles

The field of medical-related items encompasses a wide area, from the primitive bleeding bowl, to the X-ray machines of the early 1900s. Other closely-related collectibles include apothecary and dental items. Many tools that were originally intended for the pharmacist found their way to the doctor's office, and often dentists used surgical tools when no suitable dental instrument was available. A trend in the late 1700s toward self-medication brought a whole new wave of home care manuals and 'patent' medical machines for home use. Commonly referred to as 'quack' medical gimmicks, these machines were usually ineffective, and occasionally dangerous.

Advertising sign, Antiplasma Cures Malaria...cured by Sunday . **165.00**
Apothecary bottle, hand finished lip, eglomise label, amber, 7½" **65.00**
   Coblat blue, 7¼" **30.00**
   Ground stopper, eglomise label, clear 8¼" **15.00**
   Ground stoppers, eglomise labels, 5, 6 to 9" **28.00**
Apothecary jar, acron finial & embossed label, milk glass, 6½" . **85.00**
   Clear blown, paper label & replaced tin lid, 9" **20.00**
   With ground stoppers, amber, eglomise labels, 4½" **21.00**
Balance scales, 6 weights, Pelouze Mfg Co, Chicago, 9" **25.00**
   With brass pans, ci, brown w/gilded striping, 14½" **55.00**

Bellows, dental, chestnut, w/iron fixtures **75.00**
Bleeder, Will & Finck, brass & steel **325.00**

Bleeding bowl, London Delft, late 17th century, 6¾" dia **900.00**
  Silver, 1688, 7" dia **2,000.00**
  White porcelain, kidney-curved, rare **225.00**
  White porcelain w/blue hp, oval, 1870 . . . . **200.00**
Blood cell calculator, 1922 . . . . **32.50**
Bottle, ether, blown in mold, chamois stopper cover **50.00**
Cabinet, w/marble top shelf, glass knobs, refinished, 1870-80 . . **950.00**
Case, rosewood, leather interior, w/instruments, 3x6x16" **425.00**
Chair, doctor's carved oak, iron base, makes bed, 1800s **700.00**
Chest, wooden, 'Quaker Family Medicine Chest', 12x6" **65.00**
Corkpress, Art Nouveau handle, 2 hinged sections joined **75.00**
Corn Cure, paper label **10.00**
Cot, folding, walnut frame, eyecaned top **225.00**
Dental case, folding Civil War era, 5 instruments **235.00**
Dental chair, Ritter 103, 1921 . . . . **500.00**
  Chrome sides, tray, lamp, 1920 . . . . **285.00**
Dental drill, electric, 1907 . . . . **100.00**
Dental kit for gold crowns, oak dovetailed box **200.00**
Dilator, nasal, brass, bivalve, ivory lined, 1875 . . . . **95.00**
Doctor's bag, leather, bottles in compartments, 1865 . . . . **100.00**
  Leatherette covered wood, 1900, 11x5x5" **18.50**
Ether mask, brass, 1900 . . . . **50.00**
Examining table, oak w/door & 4 drawers, wheels **1,100.00**
Eyecup, clear **10.00**
  Colbalt **20.00**
  Frosted **15.00**
  Green glass, John Bull on base **49.50**
Fleam, 3, 3" blades, folding, in narrow brass case **150.00**
  Three steel blades, horn cover, 1840 . . . . **90.00**
Forceps, bullet, scissors type w/2 needle prongs, 1900s **125.00**
  Horn handles, nickel plated, 11" **130.00**
Guillotine, tonsil, steel & brass, ebony handle, 1860 . . . . **80.00**
Heating pan, porcelain on iron, slip-on iron handles, 3x12" **45.00**
Lancet, ivory handled, in case, 1700s, set of 6 . . . . **275.00**
  Tortoise covered, 1840 . . . . **50.00**
Lens set, velvet-lined box w/12 pr lenses **22.00**
Medicine case, folding, Civil War era **18.00**
Microscope, Bausch & Lomb, cased, mint cond, 1915 . . . . **175.00**
  Bausch & Lomb, lg, pat 1915, 5x & 10x, case **280.00**
  Brass w/iron base, accessories mint cond, cased, 8" **90.00**
  Brass, mkd, Henry Crouch, London, wooden box **165.00**
  Cylinder **65.00**
Mortor & pestle, stoneware, wood handle on stoneware pestle . . **70.00**
Mortors, 3 white bisque w/2 wood handled pestles **50.00**
Needle holder, steel casing, for surgery, 1880 . . . . **20.00**
Opthalmic tester, brass arm w/sliding frame, late 1800s **225.00**
Otoscope, silverplated, 3 ear pieces, 1860 . . . . **150.00**
Plow plane **45.00**
Pocket scales, in box, 1885 . . . . **45.00**
Post mortem set, w/saw, scalpels, hooks, mahog case **249.75**
Quack machine, Bleadon-Dunn Co, ultraviolet, glass tubes, in box **35.00**
  Oak cabinet, Auto Kure w/instruction **52.50**
  Oxygenator, Wisconsin, plus orig book **22.00**
  Radiation outfit for home, early 1900s **30.00**
  Super Marvel w/attachments **100.00**
  The Electreat, called Mechanical heart, w/instructions, orig box **55.00**
  Ultra violet, 5 electrodes, w/instructions, MIB **20.00**
Saddle bags, leather w/medications both sides **150.00**
Saw, bone, etched ebony handle, hinged, 1820 . . . . **140.00**
  Skull, etched ebony handle, 1820 . . . . **65.00**
Scarificator, brass body, 12 blades, 1830 . . . . **175.00**
Speculum, ear, 3 pc silver, cased in horn, 1860 . . . . **85.00**
  Nasal, steel, needlenose w/etched handles, 1890 . . . . **20.00**
Stereoscopic Atlas of Anatomy, 1900, 9x7" mounts, excel **375.00**

Sterlizer, Renwal Electric #5, porcelain tank, 5x3" **12.50**
Stethoscope, monaural, turned wood, ivory earpiece, 1830 . . . . **150.00**
Surgeon's saw, French made, American usage **325.00**
Surgical scissors, 9" **8.50**
  With amber celluloid handles, 5" **4.25**
  With ornate celluloid handles, 5" **7.00**

Tins, cure-all ointments **12.00**
Tongue depressor, black Bakelite, double hinged, 1890 . . . . **30.00**
  Silver, 1896 . . . . **75.00**
Tooth extractor, rosewood handle, w/pearl inlay, 1846 . . . . . . **105.00**
  Turned ebony handle, 6¾" **75.00**
Wooden block, drilled for 11 brass scale weights, 3¾x8" **30.00**
X-Ray machine, 1900, museum quality **1,500.00**

Meissen, See Also Blue Onion, Dresden

The Royal Saxon Porcelain Works was established in Meissen, Saxony, in 1710. Under the direction of Johann Freidrick Bottger, who in 1708 had developed the formula for the first true porcelain body, fine ceramic figurines with exquisite detail, and tableware of the highest quality were produced. Although every effort was made to insure the secrecy of Bottger's discovery, others soon began to copy his ware, and in 1731 Meissen adopted the famous crossed sword trademark to identify his own work. The term Dresden ware is often used to refer to the Meissen porcelain, since Bottger's discovery and first potting efforts were in nearby Dresden.

Basket, applied florals, interior decor, Marcolini mk, 11x7x7" . **500.00**
Bowl, antique gold w/florals **180.00**
  Deep pink w/heavy gold decor, X-swords, 12" **325.00**
  Florals in relief, cobalt border, blue X-swords **300.00**
  Gold trim florals, X-swords, 12" **175.00**
  Relief gold decor, scalloped, butterflies, 1800 . . . . **150.00**
  With wood handle, 4" **110.00**
  White w/gold, fan trim on base, X-swords, 4½" **60.00**
Bust, distraught maid w/bird, pastels, X-sword, 11½" **675.00**
  Wild Mustang, sgnd Oeline 1949, wht X-swords, 7x7½" **400.00**
Butter pat, yellow & red dragon, X-swords **18.00**
Cake plate, white w/gold trim, X-swords **150.00**
Centerpiece, female musicians sit under tree, hold compote, 8" **650.00**
Charger, white w/gold trim, X-swords, 11" **300.00**
Chocolate pot, florals on white, ornate handle, X-swords **95.00**
Coffee cup & saucer, gold relief, leaf edge, 19th century **150.00**
Coffee pot, florals, rose finial, X-sword, 9" **275.00**
Compote, 3 winged cherubs, florals, 18" **800.00**
  Cherubs, Greek scroll border, old mark #447 . . . . **200.00**
  Floral decor, X-swords, 9x8" **400.00**
  Foliage decor, pink & green, Rococo border, 6x10" **285.00**
  Gold traced on floral reticulation, top & base, 7x9" **210.00**
  Leaf pattern, gold & wht, 5x9½" **375.00**
Cream & sugar, wht w/gold trim, X-swords **90.00**
Cup & saucer, florals, gold band, late 1700s **75.00**
  Kakiemon style, Red Dragon pattern, 1900 . . . . **75.00**
Demi cup & saucer, floral & insects, scalloped gold rim, X-mk . . **90.00**
Figurine, 18th century couple, Saxe au Point, pr **700.00**
  Bacchus, group, from 1774-1813 period **2,500.00**

Boy & girl cherubs, cooking, w/aprons, X-swords, 6″, pr.... **750.00**
Boy on stick horse, girl on stick, X-swords, 5″, pr......... **525.00**
Cherub, X-swords, 9″ **350.00**
Colonist w/sword & cane, X-sword, 6½″ **550.00**
Cupid sharpening arrows, X-swords, 1850, oval base, 6x4″.. **500.00**
Cupid standing near alter, applied florals, X-swords, 5¾″ ... **475.00**
Griffon dog, 6x5″ **785.00**
King & Queen, pr, 8″............................. **300.00**
Kingfisher, X-swords, 6x7″ **395.00**
Lady w/flowers, X-swords, 9″ **425.00**
Lady w/watering can, X-sword, 4″ **285.00**
Monkey w/lute, X-swords............................ **190.00**

Nymphs w/net, group, 12½″ **900.00**
Philomele, X-swords, early 19th century, 17″ **1,000.00**
Rooster, X-sword mk........................... **275.00**
Shepherd & girl under tree, lamb, X-swords, 10x9x8″...... **850.00**
Spring, X-swords, 5½″ **400.00**
Strolling musician, 19th century reissue, X-swords **650.00**
The Chase & the Putti, group **2,200.00**
The Children's Orchestra, group, 18th century **900.00**
The Oboeist, 18th century **700.00**
The Vanquished Romance, group **1,200.00**
Turkey, X-sword **275.00**
Inkwell, florals, turquoise w/gold, X-swords............. **100.00**
     Single, X-swords, Deutche Blummen, 1800s **100.00**
Keg on stand, 19th century **3,250.00**
Leaf plate, cobalt, ivory & gold, enameling, X-sword, 9″ dia .. **170.00**
Master double salt, lady sitting in center, 5x5½″........... **425.00**
Plate, florals, gold raised & fluted decor, X-swords **160.00**
     Multi-floral center on wht, scalloped, gold, X-mk, 11″...... **185.00**
     Portrait, cobalt & gold **135.00**
     Scalloped & ribbed, gold & floral hp, 9½″............. **150.00**
Platter, 22″................................. **325.00**
     Scenic, floral border, marquee shape, 1775, 13″ **600.00**
Salt, florals in relief, bugs; ped, tri-cornered, X-swords **150.00**
Sugar bowl, cobalt, 4½″ **110.00**
Tea caddy, wht w/roses, X-swords, 5″ **100.00**
Tea set, florals on white, 3 pc w/10″ pot **600.00**
Urns w/lids, applied florals, maidens, 29″, pr **775.00**
Vase, applied florals, scenic, pedestal, X-swords **285.00**
     Cobalt w/hp florals, X-sword, 9½″................. **195.00**
     Pate sur pate, cobalt, w/Cupid, 6″ **295.00**
     Red Dragon, baluster w/silvered mounts, 14″ **600.00**
     White w/green leaves, X-swords, 9″ **175.00**

Mercury Glass

Mercury glass was popular during the 1850s, and enjoyed a short revival at the turn of the century. It was made with two thin layers, either blown with a double wall or joined in sections, with the space between the walls of the vessel filled with a mixture of tin, lead, bismuth and mercury. The opening was sealed to prevent air from dulling the bright silver color.

Bud vase **10.00**
Candlesticks, pr............................. **15.00**
Dish, w/lid, 7″ **85.00**
Goblet, ivy & grapes engraved, seal 'P' on bottom, 7½x3¾″ .. **135.00**
Mug, clear handle, For a Good Boy **37.50**
Pitcher, w/clear handle, 8″ **100.00**
Spooner, Vintage **65.00**
Sugar & creamer, ftd, applied & crimped clear glass handle, 1855 **175.00**
Tiebacks, embossed floral, pewter shanks, pr, 3½″ dia **30.00**
Toothpick holder **15.00**
Vase, 10¼″................................. **12.00**

Floral decor, 11″............................... **25.00**
Enamel, inside gold wash w/lead seal, 10″ **160.00**
Wig stands................................... **50.00**

Metlox

The Metlox Manufacturing Company was founded in 1927 in Manhattan Beach, Ca., but it was not until the '40s that they began producing the dinnerware for which they have become famous.

Poppytrail, figurine, Dancing Lady, decorated, by Romanelli, 9¼″ **75.00**
     Planter tray, ivory exterior, limegreen interior, 15″ **8.50**
     Platter, turquoise, 12½″ dia **9.00**
     Tumbler, ring band, w/detachable metal & wood handles, 8 oz . **6.50**
     Vegetable bowl, deep gloss blue, 2½x9″ dia **6.00**
     Vegetable bowl, soft matt powder blue, 2½x9″ dia.......... **9.00**
     Vase, swordfish, satin green, by Romanelli, 9″ **35.00**
Poppytrail California Ivy, creamer **4.50**
     Bread & butter............................. **3.00**
     Cup & saucer **5.00**
     Planter, square, small **4.50**
     Saucer................................. **1.00**
Poppytrail California Provincial, bowl, double pour lip, stick handle **8.50**
     Cup, coffee, 2½″............................. **4.00**
     Plate, 6¼″ **3.50**
     Plate, 7¼″ **5.00**
     Plate, 10″................................. **7.00**

Salt & pepper, pair 10.00
Sauce dish, 6″ 4.00
Saucer 2.00
Sugar & creamer, pair 15.00
Poppytrail Cape Cod, platter, 14½″ 12.00
Poppytrail Provincial Fruit, bowl, 7″ 3.50
Bowl, 8½″ 4.50
Bowl, vegetable, 10″ 8.00
Covered sugar 6.00
Creamer 5.00
Cup & saucer 5.00
Fruit dish, 6½″ 2.50
Plate, bread & butter 3.00
Plate, dinner, 10½″ 4.00
Plate, salad″ 3.00
Platter, 13½″ 11.00

Mettlach

In 1836, Nicholas Villeroy and Eugene Frances Boch, both of whom were already involved in the potting industry, formed a partnership and established a stoneware factory in an old restored abbey in Mettlach, Germany. Decorative stoneware with in-mold relief was their specialty, steins in particular. Through constant experimentation, they developed innovative methods of decoration. One process, called chromolith, involved inlaying colorful mosaic designs into the body of the ware. Later underglaze printing from copper plates was used. Their stoneware was high quality, and their steins won many medals at the St. Louis Expo and early world's fairs. Most examples are marked with an incised castle and the name Mettlach. The numbering system indicates size, date, stock number and decorator. Production was halted by a fire in 1921---the factory was not rebuilt.

Beaker, #2327, elderly violinist 60.00
#2327, Tyrolean longhorn player 65.00
#2968, sgraffito, ¼ liter 50.00
Grape decor, silver lustre 40.00
Beer set, pitcher #2332/1031, 3 liter, 6 mugs #2333/1032, dwarfs 500.00
Bowl & underplate, raised leaves, green & brown on wht 120.00
Cheese dish, #3321, etched, covered 95.00
Coaster, #1032, dwarf w/radish & beer, another taps keg 115.00
#1692, portrait of Salem witch, Salem Mass., 4¾″ dia 95.00
Creamer, #3321, etched 75.00
Jug, #1577, banquet scene, pewter lid, 21″ 1,500.00
Mug, barrel shape, Drink Hires Root Beer, w/Hires boy 120.00
Pitcher, #1169, portraits in relief, pewter lid 265.00
#2107, etched, King Gambremus, 1895, castle mk, 2 liter . . . 800.00
#2210, round, figures in relief, turnips & pipe on inlay lid, 3 liter 950.00
#2947, elaborate tree decor, 7½″ 110.00
Figures in relief, scrolls, grapes, insects, 14½″ 250.00
Parian, grapes & vines in relief, vine handle, 7¾x7½″ 225.00
Plaque, #305, seascape scene, mercury mk 109.00
#1003, girl w/cockatoo, F Feils, 8½″ 165.00
#1044, doe & fawn, 12″ dia 150.00
#1044/5176, blue castle scene 275.00
#1048, etched, coronation scene, border, 15¾″ dia 425.00
#1387, etched, bust of man w/beard, border, 11″ 350.00
#1652, barefoot maiden w/flower basket, sgnd Warth, castle mk 510.00
#1678, castle scene, 13¼″ 400.00
#1694, etched, floral motif, border, 8½″ 200.00
#2041, etched, equestrian scene, 15″ dia 700.00
#2102, pastoral scene, blue & wht, 15″ 350.00
#2143, Gen Von Moltke, gold etched, 15½″ 900.00
#2196, castle, 17″ 1,200.00
#2305, boat scene, matt glaze, 10″ 120.00
#2542, Art Nouveau, girl in profile, castle mk, 15½″ 900.00
#2544, etched, lady's portrait, leaf border 650.00
#2626, etched, 1903, castle mk, 7¾″ 300.00
#2860, etched, village in valley & on mountainside, 17½″ dia 700.00
#2805, deer, 16″ 600.00
#3041, stag, blue & wht, 11½″ 200.00
#3042, doe & stag, blue & wht, 11½″ 200.00
#3225, Dresden coat-of-arms, mercury mk, 10½x13″ 110.00
#5042, man's portrait, 12″ dia 235.00
#5176, blue & wht castle scene, 12″ dia 225.00
#5177, blue & wht castle scene, 12″ dia 225.00
#7041, scene w/castle, 12″ 225.00
#7071, blue, sgnd, 7¾x5¾″ 375.00
#7072, cameo, 8x8″ 875.00
Scene w/horses & pony on river bank, mercury mk, 12″ 125.00
Scenic, man & horses, mercury mk, sgnd, 11½″ 125.00
Plate, #2712, young girl's portrait 250.00
Punch bowl, #2087, relief dancing figures, covered, w/underplate 750.00
Stein, #6, cameo relief serving, 3 liter 550.00

#228, bear thumbrest, ½ liter, 8″ 500.00
#0171, mercury mk, ½ liter 250.00
#0675, barrel, ½ liter 160.00
#1028, relief, ½ liter 325.00
#1050, etched, pink, slipper on lid, castle mk, ½ liter 500.00
#1077, sgnd HS, ½ liter 250.00
#1146, etched, ½ liter 450.00
#1196, painted 250.00
#1370, cameo relief, ½ liter 295.00
#1395, etched, ½ liter 425.00
#1467, ½ liter 200.00
#1476, dwarfs, ½ liter 465.00
#1508, tavern scene, Gorif, inlaid lid, ½ liter 565.00
#1646, panel w/man at table drinking, ½ liter 150.00
#1724, etched, standing fireman, inlaid lid, fireman finial, ½ liter 1,000.00
#1786, etched, St Florian, mercury mk, ½ liter 800.00
#1789, mosaic, ½ liter 345.00
#1863, Stuttgart, ½ liter 475.00
#1909, comic tavern scene, pewter lid, Munich Child, ½ liter 335.00
#1909/1179, man playing mandolin, pewter lid, ¼ liter 125.00
#1914, 4-F Stein, ½ liter 635.00
#1951, etched, Four Seasons, figured pewter lid, castle mk, 2 liter 995.00

#1997, etched picture of George Ehret, inlaid lid, ½ liter ... **175.00**
#2001-A, shelf-of-books decor, lawyer, insert inlay lid, ½ liter **550.00**
#2001-B, shelf-of-books decor, doctor, insert inlay lid, ½ liter **450.00**
#2017, polychrome king on keg, sgnd H Schlitt, 12″ **625.00**
#2024, 'Berlin', ½ liter **600.00**
#2044, ½ liter **475.00**
#2054, man raising beer mug, ½ liter **550.00**
#2057, relief, ½ liter **275.00**
#2077, mercury mk, .3 liter **265.00**
#2082, etched William Tell scene, bust inlaid on lid, ½ liter **650.00**
#2086, brick red w/11 figures in relief, inlaid lid, ¼ liter..... **70.00**
#2090, ½ liter **475.00**
#2134, etched, ½ liter **575.00**
#2181/957, lady w/stein decor, pewter lid, ¼ liter **150.00**
#2182, bowling, castle mk, ½ liter **245.00**
#2184, elves, ½ liter **275.00**
#2230, cavalier w/maiden, fox scene on lid, ½ liter **585.00**
#2231, ½ liter **550.00**
#2246, panels w/dancing couples in relief **255.00**
#2248, .3 liter **300.00**
#2373, scenes of St Augustine, alligator handle, ½ liter **575.00**
#2394, Siegfried, ½ liter..................................... **580.00**
#2441, castle mk, ½ liter **695.00**
#2455, etched, 6 liters **2,750.00**
#2526, etched **385.00**
#2557, blue w/wht figures in relief, ½ liter **450.00**
#2719, polychrome coat-of-arms, lions, 7¾″............ **700.00**
#2784/6129, pewter lid, Bard, 3 liter **500.00**
#2796, Heidelburg scene, 3 liter...................... **1,500.00**
#2829, castle top, houses, polychrome, 11″ **345.00**
#2921, hunters, 3 liter **1,200.00**
#2936, etched elk's head, Elk's motto, 9½″............ **395.00**
#2958, 3 liter **985.00**
#3070, raised design of man w/monkey on barrel, ½ liter ... **250.00**
#3136, etched geometric, 1 liter **600.00**
#3253, etched, ½ liter **360.00**
Printed flowers **225.00**
Sugar, #3321, etched, covered............................ **85.00**
Tile, Rosy Finch on bittersweet branch, brass footed.......... **45.00**
Tumbler, #2327, water, Stadt Munceten, ¼ liter **45.00**
Urn, #7017, mythological figures in relief, cameo line, Stahl, 10″ **345.00**
Vase, #1289, stylized leaf snowflake design, footed, castle mk, 10½″ **400.00**
#1462, sgnd Warth, 14½″ **500.00**
#1591, etched, enamel decor, ped base, bulbous, 12″...... **475.00**
#1749, etched, girls, 1912, castle mk, 12¾″ **600.00**
#1804, etched, beaded, applied florettes, footed, 7″....... **250.00**
#1829, etched, enamel decor, beads, 8½″ **300.00**
#1874, cobalt w/etched design, castle mk, 8″ **450.00**
#2416, Art Nouveau, sgnd H, 17″...................... **550.00**
#2857, flared top, blue & brown w/decor, castle mk, 8¼″ .. **225.00**
#2859, turquoise w/fleur-de-lis, bulbous, castle mk **100.00**
#2909, Art Nouveau, 16″ **350.00**
Cameo dancing figures, silver lustre, 9″ **225.00**
Elephant trunk, 14″ **800.00**
Etched berries, birds & flowers, gold trim, 12¼″.......... **600.00**

Militaria

Because of the wide and varied scope of items available to collectors of militaria, most tend to concentrate mainly on the area or areas that interest them most, or that they can afford to buy. Some items represent a major investment, and because of their value have been reproduced. Buy with caution.

While uniforms, daggers, rings, toys and medals represent the high end

of investment potential, there are many areas of interest that are less expensive. Paper items, such as books, discharge papers, diaries, manuals and posters can be interesting and enjoyable to collect, yet on today's market, most are priced within easy reach.

Accoutrements, orig, leather pouch, brass, emblems, bayonet.. **300.00**
Action cover, British Lee Enfield **3.00**
Ammunition pouch, German, 1870 .... **15.00**
  German, WWII, 3 section **10.00**
  Soviet, 2 pocket, leather & canvas **8.00**
Anvil iron, Civil War, hand forged, 4x14″ **48.00**
Arm band, Army Air Force observer, WWII **1.50**
  Red & blk, straight wing eagles, Deutscher Volksturm Wehrmacht **20.00**
  Standard issue, red, blk swastika on wht circle **12.00**
  Wht & blk, 'Hilfs Krankentrager' **18.00**
  Wht & blk, straight wing eagle, swastika **18.00**
  Yellow & blk, 'Deutsche Wehrmacht' **20.00**
Artillery cannon primer hole cleanout pick, Civil War, brass halfcap **38.00**
Ashtray, Shanghai Volunteer Corps, w/badge, silver **50.00**
Backpack, German, WWII, fur............................... **45.00**

Badge, GAR w/ribbon, Ft. Wayne, Ind....................... **25.00**
  GAR w/ribbob, Maine on top bar, fob drop, Gettysburg **14.00**
  Glider Army **5.60**
Baker patch, WWI, loaf of bread, on disk, wool............... **4.00**
Banner, Boxer Rebellion, painted dragon **200.00**
  Nazi, red guard w/blk swastika on wht, 9x3″ **175.00**
Battleship signal lamp, US Navy, WWII, sgnd, 1933, 110 volts, pr **500.00**
Bayonet, British, WWII, MK4 prong, w/carrier **4.00**
  Civil War, ESA officer's, iron **95.00**
  Confederate **20.00**
  For 1812 Springfield, US **25.00**
  French saber, w/scabbard, 1877 model **30.00**
  German sawback **60.00**
  Japanese **25.00**
  Revolutionary War, American, 12″....................... **30.00**
  WWI, Swiss, Waffenfalrik, w/scabbard **20.00**
Bazooka manual, German, WWII **45.00**
Belt & buckle, Civil War, leather is 45″ long **35.00**
  Spanish American War, naval officer's sword hangers **15.00**
  US Navy, 1898.. **28.00**
  With cartridge holder **65.00**
Belt buckle, 7th Cavalry, Hartley & Co N.Y., Anson Mills...... **15.00**
  Asiatic fleet, silver, Bantamweight Champ 1930 .... **250.00**

Civil War, brass **120.00**
Civil War, puppy paw, 'US' **75.00**
Indian war period, late 1800s **40.00**
Lakehurst Naval Station 'US', Anson Mills, 1925 . . . . **15.00**
Regulation, US Indian war, Anson Mills, 1881 issue **15.00**
Shanghai Volunteer Corps, foliated **150.00**
WWI, US Expeditionary Forces, Balloon Corps, Anson Mills . **15.00**
Belt knife, handmade, small, no sheath **25.00**
Beret badge, Shanghai Volunteer Corps, Armoured Car Unit . . **100.00**
Binoculars, Civil War period, brass, lg **39.00**
Book, Civil War, The Rifled Musket, Fuller **12.00**
History of the War w/Spain parts l-12, pictorial, Harper's **50.00**
Hitler Youth Handbook, German text, over 300 pages **20.00**
Hitler's Propaganda, number on spine, 1933 . . . . **500.00**
Breast badge, Russian, St Stanislaus, gold & enamel, 3rd class **485.00**
Breast plate, armor, pre 1750 . . . . **1,600.00**
Civil War, round heavy brass, eagle center **125.00**
Bridle rosettes, Civil War, Cavalry, CSA brass, small, pr **65.00**
Civil War, Cavalry, US brass, pr **45.00**
Civil War, leather, twisted iron bit, Kennesaw, Georgia **39.00**
Bucket, Civil War, for artillery grease, chain handle, blk sheet iron **350.00**
Buckle, Nazi, eagle w/swastika, iron, 2½x1¾" **9.00**
Bugle, Cavalry, brass **140.00**
French Foreign Legion, w/banner, current **200.00**
US regulation, brass **40.00**
With 7th Cavalry cross sabers affixed **40.00**
Bullet, brass, 1942, 7" **10.00**
Bullet mold, brass **45.00**
Civil War, battlefield brass pistol **30.00**
Civil War, iron, 2 hinged sections, for lead bullets **29.00**
Cannon shell, 37mm, 1940 . . . . **23.00**
Cannonball tongs, Civil War, lg, Federal Pennsylvania Foundry . **78.00**
Battle of Lake Erie, bronze, 1813 . . . . **150.00**
Canteen, Civil War, bull's eye, w/cover **95.00**
Civil War, CSA burnished iron **135.00**
Civil War, wood, 9 dia **35.00**
German, copper **55.00**
Spanish American War, pewter neck **25.00**
Cap, French, General's visor **150.00**
Cap badge, British Colonial, Hong Kong Vol Machine Gun Co . **75.00**
British, 25th Fusiliers/Legion Frontiersmen, WWI **75.00**
Ceylon, planters rifles **25.00**
Falkland Islands Defence Force **25.00**
Gold Coast Rifle Volunteers **50.00**
Imperial Camel Corps **50.00**
Malacca Volunteer Rifles **50.00**
Palestine Volunteer Force **50.00**
Shanghai Volunteer Corps, general service **50.00**
Shanghai Volunteer Corps, medical unit **75.00**
Singapore Volunteer Corps **50.00**
Somaliland Camel Corps **50.00**
Tonga, Defence Force **25.00**
Transjordan Defence Force **50.00**
Cartridge pouch, Civil War, US impressed, blk leather **85.00**
Certificate, FFL Good Conduct, Indochina & Algerian **75.00**
Cigarette box, Union **10.00**
Coat button, Indian War **2.00**
Collar badge, Shanghai Volunteer Corps **50.00**
Colour, Shanghai Volunteer Corps, miniature, 6x9" **200.00**
Commission case, Civil War, officer's, maps, dispatches, 19" . . **125.00**
Cross, German, ring, inscriptions on both sides, iron **32.00**
WWI medal, German, iron w/orig ribbon **45.00**
Cross belt w/badge, British Indian Army, whistle, pouch, Geo V **200.00**
Cup, Civil War, pewter, folds, in tin container **22.00**

Civil War, tin **30.00**
Tin, from Indian War, 4x5" **15.00**
Dagger, AEF Siberia, hand crafted, w/scabbard, 1919 . . . . . . **125.00**
Army, officer's **110.00**
Nazi officer's, w/potopee **210.00**
Nazi, WWII **200.00**
With sheath, Nazi, 'SA', 1940 . . . . **100.00**
Dauerausweis Paris, lg swastika stamp **20.00**
Diary, Civil War, Union Captain's, Chaplain, w/letters to wife . . **200.00**
Discharge, Ohio, Charles D Rothburn, March 4, 1863 . . . . . . **100.00**
Dog tag, WWI US Army **5.00**
Dress, Red Cross, yellow, 1940s **12.00**
Dress epaulettes, French Foreign Legion, NEO, current **50.00**
Dress tunic, Shanghai Volunteer Corps, SVC in gold bullion . . **200.00**
Drill jacket, Women's Land Army, khaki canvas, 1940s **16.00**
Drum majors baldric, British Indian Army, George V **300.00**
Envelope, postmkd, 1861-65 . . . . **8.00**
Epaulets, Civil War, officer's, gilt metal fishscales, pr **135.00**
Civil War, Bran **30.00**
Epaulets box, Civil War, blk tole finish w/gilt stripes, hinged lid **85.00**
Farewell address, by Horatio B Reed, printed, 1865, 5x8" **22.00**
Field flask, Nazi German, oval, w/orig cover & strap **10.00**
Field glasses, civil war, w/case, French made **85.00**
Flag, Imperial German battle, swallow tail w/tassels **38.00**
Nazi, circle symbol on flag, 4x6' **65.00**
Nazi, w/IC in corner, lg **75.00**
Nazi, WWII **175.00**
Office, 30x55" **85.00**
Fob, shield shape w/howitzers, mountain scene **9.00**
French, unit Guidon, Voltigeurs L'euphrate Levant, 1920 . . . . . **250.00**
Fuse cutter, Civil War **15.00**
Garrison cap, US, WWII, small . . . . **.50**
Gas mask, German, WWII **35.00**
Gun oiler, British Lee Enfield, brass **1.50**
Gunners gimlet, Civil War **8.00**
Gunners pick **8.00**
Hat, Red Cross, blue, 1940s **12.00**
Sailor's, USS Chattanooga, mkd, 1900s **20.00**
Hat cord, Artillery **6.00**
Helmet, blk leather fur-lined flight deck **20.00**
Flying, Army Air Force, WWII, tan cloth version **18.00**
French, WWII, w/liner **7.00**
German, Kaiser regime, leather **100.00**
German, WWI, camouflage **50.00**
Italian, WWII, w/liner **7.50**
Nazi Army, steel w/leather liner **44.00**
Nazi felt spike, 'Koenig FR' **225.00**
Nazi, SS, steel **125.00**
Nazi, WWII **22.00**
Pith, African Corps, eagle & swastika, blk & silver metal **85.00**
Pith, Nazi, Africa corp **85.00**
Police, leather, Mettendorf **200.00**
Prussian, spiked, metal, refinished, blk & silver, 1915 . . . . **80.00**
Swedish **25.00**
US as used in Pearl Harbor **7.50**
WWI, doughboys **15.00**
Helmet net, Canadian Army **1.50**
Holster, Read Gun Co, 1885 . . . . **30.00**
Horse bridle bit, US Cavalry, mkd #2 . . . . **15.00**
Horse brush, Civil War, Cavalry **25.00**
Horse curry brush, Civil War, leather, US & Herbert Mfg, pr . . . **35.00**
Horsebit, Civil War, Cavalry, lg mouth, smithy made **48.00**
Identification bar, Civil War **15.00**
Instrument case, Civil War, tin, ironmonger's brass label, 7x1" dia **55.00**

Iron balls, anti-cavalry solidshot, Civil War **25.00**
Iron cross, Nazi, on 1 side 1813; obverse: 1939 w/swastika **65.00**
Jacket, WWII, EM, CBI & Aircorps patches, w/wool shirt **23.00**
Jetton, bronze, 100th Anniversary War 1812 . . . . **10.00**
Kepi insignia, Civil War, field artillery, crossed cannon, 2″ **18.00**
Knapsack, Union **20.00**
   WWI, canvas & leather **16.00**
Knife, Japanese, WWII, Paratroopers, combat **65.00**
   WWI, American combat, w/scabbard **25.00**
Kukri, British Indian army, etched blade, silver scabbard **200.00**
Letter, Civil War **8.00**
Letters, 10, eyewitness destruction of Merrimac **250.00**
Machete, Spanish, brass guard & tipped handle, w/scabbard, 1900s **50.00**
   WWII, Camillus, folding **20.00**
   WWII, Jungle, w/canvas case **3.00**
Magazine, Civil War, Century **9.00**
   Civil War, Harper's **7.00**
Manual, WWI, featuring equipment, 31 pages, 6x9″ **22.00**
   WWI, handbook of the Browning machine gun, 125 pages . . **14.00**
Map case, Civil War, crudely tinner made, 30″ long **32.00**
   Civil War, lt wood, screw top, 14″ long **50.00**
Medal, Austrian, WWI, for bravery, Franze Joseph Kaiser **15.00**
   Austrian, WWI, Franz Joseph Order **25.00**
   British Legation Guard, Adis Ababa, May 2-6, silver, 1936 . . **200.00**
   Centennial, Commemoration American Indian, 1776- 1876, in case **15.00**
   Crimean war, bronze w/ribbon **45.00**
   Dutch, for bravery, bronze, late 1860s **15.00**
   Japanese China Campaign **70.00**
   Marine Corps Service, WWII, 3 stars, sterling & blue, 1″ . . . **10.00**
   Nazi German Mothers, 1936 . . . . **60.00**
   Nazi, Winter Front **12.00**
   Purple Heart in Presentation box w/2 bars **25.00**
   Shooting, 2 pc bronze 1904 on top bar, shield drop **6.50**
   Shooting, German, WWI **15.00**
   Shooting, Tientsin, Sergeant, 14th Infantry, set of 6, 1930s . **200.00**
   Silver Star **26.00**
   US Army Legion of Merit, WWII, Oak Leaf **48.00**
   Victory, WWI, one bar France, campaign bar **14.00**
   WWI, bronze, Rainbow Divison **35.00**
   WWI, Federal, single bar, France, for service **10.00**
   WWI, French Croix De Guerre w/palm leaf **20.00**
   WWI French Verdun, bronze **8.00**
   WWI, good conduct **23.00**
Mess plate, British, WWII, tin **1.00**
Mess tray, officer's, porcelain, w/serving dish **45.00**
Military paper, Civil War, muster rolls, sick & prisoner lists **23.00**
Mirror, Civil War, Spotsylvania, 5th Infantry Star, pocket **45.00**
Mug, Shanghai Volunteer Corps, Company A/SVC, pewter **100.00**
Musket, Civil War, contract 58 caliber rifle **400.00**
Musket lockplate, Civil War, found at battle of Richmond site . **100.00**
Musket nipple, Civil War, Enfield **5.00**
Naval boarding Pike head, Civil War, iron **125.00**
Naval dividers tool, Civil War, brass, 18″ long **110.00**
Naval utensils, Civil War, knife, fork & spoon **100.00**
Neck badge, Russian, St Anne, 2nd class, no swords, Edouards **650.00**
Newspaper, Civil War, common, no big battle described **4.50**
   Civil War, famous battle described **22.00**
   Harper's Weekly Pictorial History, 2 volumes, 1894 . . . . . . **195.00**
Nipple protector, Civil War, Enfield, w/chain **8.00**
Nipple wrench **5.00**
Oil painting, Civil War, of Lincoln, framed, 9x12″ **110.00**
Overcoat, Nazi Party officials **150.00**
Pants, WWII, Cavalry riding, lg **25.00**
Pass, Civil War, railroad **15.00**

Civil War, soldier's **18.00**
Patch, 504th Parachute Regiment **7.00**
   B-29 shield **5.25**
Pay voucher, Civil War **24.00**
Periscope, WWII, American tank **10.00**
Phial, doctor's, flip open pewter lid, cobalt blue, name **95.00**
Picture, Kaiser Wilhelm II w/family, military dress, 14x18″ **375.00**
   Metal, Union & Confederate soldiers **2.00**
Pike head, Civil War, iron, Georgia origin **95.00**
Pin, Spanish American War, battleship & flag, celluloid, 1¼″ . . . **4.00**
Pincushion, chalk figure of Hitler **85.00**
Pipe banner, British Indian Army, 5th BN, 1st Prince, Ed 7 . . **200.00**
Plate, cartridge box, Civil War, US, brass, Stone River, Tenn . **155.00**
Plumbob, Civil War, engineers', iron **48.00**
Powder flask, Civil War, pewter, plain, brass lid-measure **68.00**
Raincoat, USAF, size 36 . . . . **40.00**
Regimental records, 2nd Brigade, Conn., leather, 1850s **120.00**
Ribbon badge, Civil War Naval Veteran, round drop w/eagle . . . **14.00**
   WE lst Defenders, bar w/drop, 1861 . . . . **20.00**
Rifle pin, Spanish American war, w/16 star flag, 'Off to Spain' . . **25.00**
Rifle sling, British Lee Enfield **3.00**
Ring, WWI souvenir w/Cross of Lorrain **12.00**
Saber, 3 branch brass, eagle, stars, mkd, 41¼″ long **450.00**
   Cavalry, 3 branch brass guard, 1864, 43″ long **468.00**
   Cavalry, w/scabbard **375.00**
   Civil War, cavalry, 1840 . . . . **86.50**
Service book, French Foreign Legion, Indochina & Algerian . . . **75.00**
Shell loader, Civil War, iron, wood handles **15.00**
Shoulder straps, Civil war, Captain's **75.00**
Shoulder title, Shanghai Volunteer Corps, metal, SVC **35.00**
Snaphook, Cavalry carbine **15.00**
Soap dish, British, WWII **1.00**
Spurs, Civil War, CSA officer's, iron, pr **150.00**
   Civil War **75.00**
   Indian War, grass, US **40.00**
Stretcher, Navy, oak & canvas, 1917 . . . . **95.00**
Sword, Civil War, Ames M & Co, Chicopue, left handed **160.00**
   Civil War, US Calvary, w/scabbard, curved steel blade, 35″ . **250.00**
   German, WWI **225.00**
   Japanese Marine Samurai, WWII **250.00**
   Japanese Military Police **125.00**
   Nazi, lions on handle, ruby eyes **125.00**
   Nazi, officer's **225.00**
   Nazi, youth leaders **124.00**
   New Hampshire State Militia, mkd, 1870, 37″ **155.00**
   Shanghai Municipal Police, w/scabbard **200.00**
   US Army officer, etched blade, metal scabbard, 1900s, 30″ . **100.00**
   With scabbard, Civil War, wrist breaker **175.00**
Telegram, Civil War, civilian **6.00**
   Civil War, military **20.00**
   Nazi, heavy stock paper, depicts Hitler **35.00**
Timetable, Civil War, railroad **50.00**
Token, Civil War, wreath w/Liberty, Union on reverse, 1863 . . . . **4.00**
Trace chain, artillery, pr **15.00**
Trumpet banner, Free French, Commandos d'Afrique **250.00**
   US Marines, 4th... Shanghai, Fessenden Fifesi **350.00**
Tumbler punch, Civil War **5.00**
Uniform, Civil War, Ohio Volunteer Infantry, orig brass, 1862 . **150.00**
   French Foreign Legion, Saharan, w/capes, bandolier **500.00**
   Marine, pre WWI **42.00**
   US, WWI complete, hat, leggings, coat, pants, helmet **55.00**
   US, WWII, complete 5 pc, w/mess kit **70.00**
Unit guidon, French Foreign Legion, Indochina & Algerian . . . **500.00**
Veterans banner, French Foreign Legion, current **300.00**

Visor cap, French Foreign Legion, officer's, current **100.00**
Volunteer enlistment form, US Army, 1863, 8x10″ **14.00**
Voucher, Ohio & Mississippi, for troop movement, 1862....... **10.00**
Wall banner, British Legation Guard, Peking 1908-09......... **75.00**
　　Chinese Maritime Customs Service, Ninpo 1901 .... **150.00**
　　SHS 1912-14 .... **250.00**
Warrant, NY National Guard, appointment to rank, 1865, 9x13″ **32.50**
　　State of NY, Whedon appointed to Sergeant Major, 1865 .... **32.50**
Water keg, Civil War, wood w/brass bands, 3 gallons **40.00**
Window sticker, WWII...a man from this family in Navy **5.00**
Wings, RAF, crown over flag **25.00**
　　US Army, sterling silver, Master Air Crew **20.00**
　　USAF, sterling silver, 1½″ **7.50**
　　USAF, sterling silver, Flight Surgeon, 3″ **30.00**
　　USAF, sterling silver, Master Air Crew **35.00**
　　USAF, sterling silver, Master Navigator **35.00**
　　USAF, sterling silver, Senior Air Crew, 3″ **30.00**
　　USAF, sterling silver, Senior Navigator, 3″ **30.00**
　　USAF, sterling silver, Senior Pilot, 3″ **30.00**
Worm, for ramrod...................................... **4.50**

Milk Glass

　　Milk glass, so named because of its milky white color, has been produced since the 18th century. The early glass, made with cryolite, looks
very much like true porcelain, and rings with a clear bell tone when tapped.
It was made both here and in England. Though not technically correct, collectors sometimes refer to colored opaque glassware as milk glass.

Ashtray, Helping Hand, McKee **8.00**
Bottle, slipper **8.00**
　　World's Fair 1939 .... **18.00**
Bowl, Daisy & Tree of Life, Challinor, 8″................. **55.00**
　　Scroll, green **85.00**
　　Scroll, round **65.00**
Box, heart shape, gold scroll, 3½″ **22.00**
　　With cover, lily, some paint **35.00**
　　With cover, scrolls, 4″ **16.00**
Candlestick, blue, embossed leaf & swirl **88.00**
Card tray, double hands & grapes, 7½x5¾″ **20.00**
　　Embossed hearts, diamonds, etc.................... **14.00**
Cheese jar, w/cover, metal handled holder **45.00**
Compote, Atlas, open edge, green..................... **250.00**
　　Atlas, open edge **125.00**
　　Atterbury lattice edge, basketweave stem, wht, 6½x9″ **30.00**
Compote, Ball & Chain **20.00**
　　Jenny Lind, wht................................. **105.00**
　　Lacy edge, open tripod base, bell-tone, 7x9″ **65.00**
　　Lattice edge, large.............................. **38.00**
　　Opaque scroll................................... **55.00**
　　Scalloped lacy edge **25.00**
　　Scroll **100.00**
　　Scroll, green **175.00**
　　Thousand Eye **70.00**
　　Tri-leg, fruit & leaves underside, French **30.00**
　　With cover, sawtooth, flint, 6½x8¾″ **100.00**
Condiment, w/cover, basketweave, blue **23.00**
Couch, covered dish, w/orig colors **150.00**
Creamer, little boy, no eyes **160.00**
　　Owl miniature, Challinor, blue, 3½x2″ **55.00**
　　Owl miniature, Challinor, wht, 3½x2″ **35.00**
Cruet, w/clear faceted stopper, wht guttate, gold decor **90.00**
Deer, on fallen tree base, fiery opalescent edges, rare, 6¾″... **135.00**
Dish, chicks & eggs cover, lacy edge base, 1880s, Atterbury **120.00**

Cow, embossed, with cover **35.00**
Hand & dove, w/cover.............................. **75.00**
Moses in the Bullrushes, with cover.................. **130.00**
Wooly lamb, with cover **130.00**
Double salt, facing chickens **12.50**
Dresser tray, 9½″ **9.00**
Duck, blue, Atterbury, dated **500.00**
　　Wht, Atterbury, gold-brown eyes, dated............... **120.00**

Egg cup, hatching yellow chick **20.00**
　　Rooster... **18.00**
Fish covered dish, supported on fins, glass eyes, 1880s **150.00**
Fish set, 9 pc fish-shaped, dated pat 1872 .... **295.00**
Fruit bowl, on standard, lattice, hp flowers, 9″ **65.00**
Hen, black w/wht head, basketweave base, rare **135.00**
Ivy ball, hobnail **13.50**
Jam jar, blackberry, orig ladle **47.50**
Lion covered dish, lacy base, Atterbury dated **100.00**
　　Rib base, Atterbury, dated **120.00**
Mug, Greentown Troubadour **18.00**
Mustard jar, Old Abe **90.00**
Nugget bottle, w/original metal cap, mk Klondike **135.00**
Paperweight, Washington Monument **110.00**
Perfume bottle, boot, no stopper **18.00**
　　Figural w/painted pewter head, oriental............... **220.00**
Pickle dish, figural fish, dated 1872 .... **30.00**
Pin tray, heavy scroll **12.00**
Pitcher, dolphin **65.00**
Plate, Easter, 3 rabbits in cabbage patch **38.00**
　　Arch border, smooth center **12.00**
　　Backward-C edge, 8½″ **12.00**
　　Battleship Maine, 7¼″ **14.00**
　　Block border, blue............................... **25.00**
　　Blue, angel head **50.00**
　　Bryan **60.00**
　　Chrysanthemums, double fleur de lis, chalky wht **50.00**
　　Club & Shell, 9½″ **10.00**
　　Cupids heads on lacy border, 9″ **35.00**
　　Eagle, flag & star border, slightly muddy, 7″ **15.00**
　　Easter bunny & egg, 7¼″........................... **65.00**
　　Easter ducks, grayish............................. **30.00**
　　Easter rabbits, gilt **25.00**
　　Easter rabbits, 'Easter', 7¼″ **30.00**
　　Flag w/eagle border, stars, 1903 .... **42.00**
　　Floral center, criss-cross border, 10″ **22.00**
　　Girl with flower **29.50**
　　Heart shape, reticulated heart border, 8″ **18.00**
　　Keyhold border, black............................. **16.00**

Keyhole variant, uncommon **18.00**
Open edge, pink floral, Atterbury, 10½″ **50.00**
Owl lovers, 7″ **30.00**
Rooster w/hen & chicks, No Easter Without Us **38.00**
Taft **55.00**
Three Bears, 7″ **35.00**
Triangular, Leaf & Chain **22.50**
Washington, 13 star border, 8¼″ **45.00**
Wicket, 7½″, Atterbury **19.00**
Woof-Woof, 5½″ **30.00**
Yacht & Anchor **20.00**
Platter, Retriever **125.00**
   Rock of Ages, clear rim **140.00**
Portrait, pewter frame, sgnd **200.00**
Powder jar, w/cover, octagonal, palmette pattern, 3x3½″ **35.00**
Quail, covered dish, base w/oval & scallops, 6½x4½″ **25.00**
Rabbit, covered, large glass eyes, dated **100.00**
Robin on nest dish, flowered base, unpainted **75.00**
Rolling pin, advertising Columbus Flour Co, Detroit **285.00**
   With painted ship **38.00**
   With sailors farewell **48.00**
Rose jar, colored floral decor **35.00**
Salt & pepper, Centennial Boot, pewter tops **35.00**
Salt, Strawberry, ft, flint **35.00**
   Swan, open **50.00**
   Swan **10.50**
   With top, Billiken **75.00**
Saltcrock, w/new wood hinged lid, embossed 'Salt', 6½x6″ **200.00**
Santa on sleigh **90.00**
Sleigh, w/bird cover **25.00**
Spooner, Blackberry **35.00**
   Little girl, no eyes **130.00**
   Sandwich Loop **75.00**
   Sunflower **25.00**

Spooner sugar bowl, Wheat, spoon slots at rim **65.00**
Stein set, monk, red trim, 7 pc **155.00**
Sugar, w/cover, Swan, gold trim **50.00**
Sugar & creamer, w/cover, crown top **22.00**
   With cover, hp cherries & grapes, Westmoreland **25.00**
Swan, knobbed basketweave, 6¼x7″ **135.00**
Syrup pitcher, fishnet background w/poppy decor, pewter top, 7″ **90.00**
   Pewter top, applied handle, dated 1872 . . . . **50.00**

Tankard, Scroll, green **125.00**
   Scroll **85.00**
Toothpick, Swan & Cattail **25.00**
Tray, buffalo heads, 11″ **20.00**
   Figural fish, Atterbury pat 1872 . . . . **55.00**
   Rose Garland, 7x10″ **10.00**
Tumbler, Beaded Swag, Heisey, souvenir **20.00**
   Scroll **25.00**
   Scroll, blue **35.00**
Vase, blue, panels w/oriental figures, sgnd, sq, 4½″ **45.00**
   Bulbous, molded floral, painted, 12″ **38.00**
Water pitcher, wht guttage, gold rim & handle **100.00**
Water set, w/4 tumblers, Wild Iris, yellow, pink & green **345.00**

Millefiori, See Also Paperweights

   Millefiori glass was a type of art ware produced during the late 1800s. Literally, the term means thousand flowers, an accurate description of its appearance. Canes, fused bundles of multicolored glass threads such as often used in paperweights, were cut into small cross sections, arranged in the desired pattern, refired and shaped into articles such as cruets, lamps and novelty items.

Cruet, w/stopper, frosted, applied handle, 8″ **95.00**
Lamp, 11″ **425.00**
Paperweight vase, sgnd, 9″ **850.00**
Plaque, Frederick Carder, 10¼″ **1,100.00**

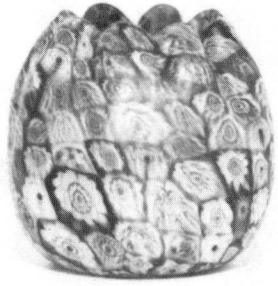

Rosebowl, 3″ **100.00**
Tumbler **65.00**

Miniatures

   There is some confusion as to what should be included in a listing of miniature collectibles. Some feel the only true miniature is the salesman's sample. Common during the latter part of the 19th century, these were small-scale copies of a particular product. Other collectors consider certain small-scale children's toys to be appropriately referred to as miniatures, while yet others believe a miniature to be any small-scale item used to display the craftsmanship of its creator. All of the above have been included in this listing.

Baking pan, graniteware, scalloped edge, 3″ dia **20.00**
Bowl & pitcher, white china, pink flowers, 1870s, 2″ **32.00**
Butter mold, 3½″, illus **35.00**
Candelabra, sterling, 5 light, 1½″ **85.00**
Candlesticks, brass, 1¾″, pr **17.00**
   Star, pr **28.00**
Canister set, Germany, 6 pieces **55.00**
Castor set, 4 pcs in stand, 6½″ **100.00**
Chambersticks, swirl, blue milk glass, pr **48.00**
China wash set, 6 pcs, pitcher 5″, blue & wht, pink florals . . . **150.00**
Clothes wringer, Horseshoe brand, rubber rolls, 5x6″ **55.00**
Coffee grinder, 3½″ **75.00**

Wht w/blue trim, granite, brass funnel, 2″ **75.00**
Coffee pot, brass, slant sides & spout, 1850s, 2¼x3″ **40.00**
Coffee pot with lid, brass, red finial, Japan, 2½″ **3.50**
Couch, fainting, tufted velvet, w/fringe, 21x6½x7½″ **125.00**
Cream pitcher, blue & wht, graniteware, 2¼x2″ **16.00**
Curling iron, wood handles, 3″ **18.00**
Desk, sterling, fall front w/pierced drawer decor, ftd, 1½x2x1″ **185.00**
   Walnut, slant front, 1 drawer supports lid 7½x8½x4″ **250.00**
Dresser, oak, 2 drawer, beveled mirror, 15x7x23″ **150.00**
General Store scale, ci, works, 1900, 5x3x3″ **20.00**
Goblet, sterling, English, 1″ **10.00**
Ice tongs, 2″ **7.50**
Iron kettle, footed **20.00**
Jug, stoneware, brown glaze, Centennial July 4, 1876, 3″ **75.00**
Ladle, graniteware, 4″ **18.00**
Meat grinder, 3″ **12.00**
Mortar & pestle, brass, 1½x1″ dia, 3″ pestle **30.00**
   Heavy cast brass, 1½″ **20.00**
Mug, Humpty Dumpty, pressed glass, 1890s **28.00**
Oven, Houlis Master Bake, detailed, works, 27x21″ **1,500.00**
Pail, brass, Mayan applied medallion, Columbia, 1¾″ **5.00**
Pan, w/handle & pouring spout, graniteware, grey & wht, 2½″ . **22.00**
Pestle, brass, 1¼″ **4.00**
Pie plate, graniteware, grey & wht, 2″ **22.00**
Platter, blue & wht, graniteware, 5″ **16.00**
Player piano, Hobart Cable, w/stool **800.00**
Pot w/handle **10.00**
Rolling pin, wood, 4″ **5.00**
Sadiron, curved-up front, clip-on wood handle, 3¾″ **30.00**

W/trivet, ci, 4½″ long **20.00**
Salesman's sample, corn cultivator **95.00**
   Cream Separator **80.00**
   Furnace, wood or coal burning, water tank on back **150.00**
   Hat **35.00**
   Kitchen meat press, working parts, 3″ **45.00**
   Ox yoke **85.00**
   Stock gate, wood, 3 bars, old paint, 6x12½″ **140.00**
   Stove, kitchen, ci, Royal **250.00**
   Stove, wood or coal burning, Lilly **225.00**
   Washing machine, wood **60.00**
   Wheelbarrow **160.00**
Skillet, granite, grey, 2″ dia **42.00**
Spinning wheel, working, 16x16″ **65.00**
Stepladder, ci, hinged, old ivory paint, 3″ **20.00**
Stove, Crescent, ci, sample-size **125.00**
   Eagle, ci, complete w/lifter, fry pan & pot, 5¼x6″ **58.00**
   Star, ci, hinged oven door **25.00**
Strainer, granitware, 4″ **18.00**
Tea kettle, cast brass w/hinged lid, 2″ **35.00**
Teapot, brass, w/lid, red finial, Japan, 2½″ **3.50**
   Grey graniteware **24.00**

Urn, heavy cast brass, 2¼″ **14.00**
Waffle iron, ci, 1800s, 4″ dia, illus **70.00**

Minton

    Thomas Minton established his firm in 1793 at Stoke on Trent, and within a few years began producing earthenware with blue printed patterns similar to the ware he had learned to decorate while employed by the Caughley Porcelain Factory. The Willow pattern was one of his most popular. Neither this nor the porcelain made from 1798 to 1805 was marked, (except for an occasional number series), making identification often impossible.

    After 1805 until about 1816, fine tea services, beehive shaped honey pots, trays, etc., were hand decorated with florals, landscapes, Imari-type designs and neo-classic devices. These were often marked with crossed 'Ls'.

    From 1816 until 1823, no porcelain was made. Through the '20s and '30s the ornamental wares with colorful decoration of applied fruits and florals and figurines in both bisque and enamel were usually left unmarked. As a result, they have been erroneously attributed to other potters. Some of the ware that was marked bears a deliberate imitation of Meissen's crossed swords.

    From the late '20s through the '40s, Minton made a molded stoneware line---mugs, jugs, teapots, etc.---with florals or figures in high relief. These were marked with an embossed scroll with an M in the bottom curve. Fine parian ware was made in the late 1840s, and in the '50s Minton perfected and produced a line of quality majolica which gained them widespread recognition.

    During the Victorian era, M.L. Solon decorated and signed pieces in the pate-sur-pate style; these examples are considered to be the finest of their type. After 1862, all wares were marked Minton, or Mintons, with an impressed year cypher.

Cabinet plate, cherub center, swags of roses, magenta & gold . . **60.00**
Cache-pot, blue w/floral reserves, gilt jewelled ground, 5″ **225.00**
   Pink w/raised floral & fruit decor **325.00**
Candlesticks, white w/floral transfer, 6″, pair **130.00**
Center bowl, majolica, daisy border, basketweave, vine base, 12¼″ **85.00**
Cup & saucer, 1889, impressed 'S' **45.00**
Flask, moon, gilt stencilled decor on plum ground, printed mk, 8¼″ **100.00**

Game dish w/cover & liner, majolica, 13x7″ **200.00**
Medallion, pate sur pate, blue ground w/wht, sgnd A Birks, 2″ **145.00**
Mug, miniature, florals, gold trim, 3 handles, 1½″ **40.00**
Oyster plate, Shell & Seaweed, majolica **75.00**
Oyster plate, varigated, raised shells, dated 1873 . . . . **150.00**
Pitcher, raised acorns, salt glaze, 5″ **17.50**
Plaque, pate sur pate, red, sgnd Birks, 6x8½″, framed **1,100.00**
Plate, tiger kittens, one has rat in mouth, 7″ **35.00**
Service for 4, bone china, white w/real gold border, 36 pc, 1900 **1,100.00**
Tankard, red & gold leaf design, tall, pewter top, 1842 . . . . . . **85.00**

Tazza, blue & coral, cupid base, early **165.00**

Tile, child's head in relief, 6x6″ **70.00**
   Cream ground w/scene of cow & calf, W Wise 1879 . . . . **70.00**
   Cream gound w/scene of horses in farmyard, W Wise 1879 . . . **70.00**
   European canal scene, 7x12″, oak frame **150.00**
Vase, earthenware, Art Nouveau, burgundy w/gr & cream design, 9¾″ **80.00**
   Mahogany; daisies, gold leaves & insects, rams head handles, 7½″ **110.00**
   Trophy shape, pink w/center hp floral medallion, 10″ **565.00**
Vases, blue w/floral & fruit panels, gilt, covered, bird finial, 13″, pr **3,750.00**

Mirrors

    Englomise (reverse glass painted) mirrors were made in this country from the late 1700s, and remained popular through the next century. The simple hand painted panel was separated from the lower mirrored section by a simple narrow slat, and the frame was either the dark finished Federal style or the more elegant, often gilded Sheraton.

    Mirrors changed with the style of other furnishings, but whatever type you purchase, as long as the glass sections remain solid, even broken or flaking mirrors are more valued than replaced glass. Careful resilvering is acceptable if excessive deterioraton has taken place.

Architectural, mahog 2-part, overhanging crown w/15 balls, 17x39″ **150.00**
Art Deco, sterling vanity, full-bodied woman & floral design **50.00**
Art Nouveau, cast bronze lady holding beveled mirror, 10x12″ **180.00**
   Copper over tin, hanging, 3 ornate brass hooks, 18x18″ **68.00**
Black turning w/gold on frame, englomise scene, old glass, 11x19″ **160.00**
Carved wood w/eagle, early 1880s, 42″ **400.00**
Cherry, top & bottom shaped crest, 9½″ **265.00**
Chinese, bronze, w/stand **200.00**
Chippendale; crest w/eagle, 26x14″ **275.00**
   Crest w/eagle, foliate sides & floral base, old glass, 34″ **250.00**
   Cutout pine tree border, line inlaid inner edge, old glass, 32x19″ **140.00**
   Fret work w/carved gilt innerliner, 1700s, small **130.00**
   Gilt, scrolled crest, carved base w/glass insert, 45″ **90.00**
   Mahogany; arched pediment eagle & lions head, gilt **825.00**
     Carved & gilded Phoenix, inner molding, orig back boards **275.00**
     Scrolled crest & base, gilt raised decor, 42″ **130.00**
   Mahogany & pine, scrolled frame, 17″ **185.00**
   Mahogany scroll; old glass, 12½x21″ **585.00**
     Orig glass, 1809, 11x19″ **425.00**

Oval, gilt frame & floral pediment **450.00**
   Scrolled base, ears & crest, applied gilt eagle, 23x13½″ **150.00**
   Scrolled crest, gilt liner, 27″ **365.00**
   Scrolled crest, base & ears, inside edge band inlay, old glass, 25″ **150.00**
     Molded inner edge, 1780s, 18x11½″ **160.00**
   Scrolled fretwork crest, skirt & ears; all orig **210.00**
Clothier's, cast iron **330.00**
Dressing, mahogany, 3-drawer, 1800s **160.00**
Empire; englomise fishermen scene, 32″ **135.00**
   Englomise panel, 25″ **100.00**
   Grain painted, englomise picture, 21x11″ **95.00**
Englomise; split spindles, ring turnings, brown paint, 30x11″ . . **125.00**
   Split balusters, rosette corners, orig glass, 1800s, 20x11″ . . . **210.00**
Federal; englomise eagle, 31″ **475.00**
   Englomise; gold leaf, new glass, 24″ **165.00**
     Split balusters, brass corner rosettes, orig glass, 44x21″ . . **225.00**
   Gilt, leaf corners, turned, carved & fluted split balusters, 46x26″ **90.00**
   Mahogany; 2-pt, molded cornice, 15 acorn drops, baluster columns **110.00**
     2-pc, englomise harbor scene, reeded molding, orig glass . . . **95.00**
     On stand w/block & turned supports, shaped ft **140.00**
   Split balusters, rosette corners, raised panel w/cornucopia, 44x21″ **160.00**
Folding, 3 beveled 9x11″ mirrors, oak frame, brass trim, oak peg ft **95.00**
Hall, walnut carved frame **190.00**
Hand, Art Nouveau, silver plate **25.00**
   Brass w/allover floral decor, 9″ **24.00**
   Bronze, beveled, 1x1″ painting on ivory on reverse side, 10″ **200.00**
   Celluloid; hp Grecian lady, diamond shape frame, beveled, 14″ **28.00**
     Ivorene w/hp cameo of Grecian young man & florals, beveled, 14″ **26.00**
     Pearlized gr w/inserted colored stones, beveled, 14″ **25.00**
     Pearlized green & black, 13″ **17.00**
   Lady's ornate brass, 1900s **25.00**
Mahogany, gothic frame, mid-1800s **100.00**
   Half columns, englomise scene, 5½x10″ **325.00**
   Shaped crest w/phoenix, gilt lined, 30″ **375.00**
Pier, gold leaf, w/carving, 7′x30½″ **375.00**
Plateau, beveled edge, brass frame, 12″ dia **45.00**
   Lion head & claw ft, scroll & floral sides, double beveled, 15″ **120.00**
   Miniature, ornate ft & sides, elevated rim, full metal underside, 7¼″ **45.00**
   Ornate silver sides, floral ft, beveled glass, 14″ **85.00**
   Silver plate, florals & scrolls, double bevel, 12″ **155.00**
   Wide scrolls, floral ft, tin underside, 12″ **90.00**
Queen Anne, mahog & pine, crest over molded frame, beveled, sm **300.00**

Rococo, giltwood, beveled plate, 20th century, 56x36″ **1,200.00**

Shaving, 3 section beveled, free standing case, mythological decor **145.00**
   Eastlake style frame **125.00**
   Sheraton, bow front, drawer, brass escutcheon, old glass, 17½" **140.00**
   Triangular frame, red lacquer design, wood & brass-fitted abacus **45.00**
Triple, silver, Victorian, dated 1887 . . . . **2,200.00**
Vanity, bronze, Art Nouveau, oval **85.00**

Mocha

Mocha was made in England from as early as 1780, in Scotland, Wales, and even America, until well after the turn of the 20th century. The term refers to the distinctive effect achieved by the slip decoration. Among the most common designs are worm, seaweed, cats-eye and marbling. These patterns resulted from colored slip being allowed to flow or drip onto the ware's surface as it was turned on a lathe. While the finished product partially reflected the skill of the turner, a second factor involved the reaction of the slip when sprinkled with drops of a chemical fluid. Although very little of this ware was ever marked, researchers believe that at least some mocha was made in America by J. Vodrey, George S. Harker, Edwin Bennett and John Bell.

Beaker, marbleized sienna & wht, green incised top band, 4" . **245.00**
Bowl, brown & mustard bands w/seaweed, blue incised top band, 5" **190.00**
   Whiteware w/earthworm in wide band, 4¾" dia **140.00**
   Yellow, brown & wht bands, seaweed decor, 5½" dia **300.00**
   Yellowware w/undulating seaweed decor, 1" brown band, 5" dia **200.00**
Cream jug, marbleized; wht spout, finial, foot & handle, 6" . . . **300.00**
   Vellum, w/cover **450.00**
Cup & saucer, demitasse, marbleized swirl **400.00**
   Demitasse, yellowware w/3 color speckles, ribbed band **210.00**
   Handleless, speckled, blk & wht checkered band **250.00**
   Marbleized, swirl decor **350.00**
Humidor, blk & wht check, chocolate/blue/wht bands, acorn finial **1,300.00**
Jar, yellowware clay body w/earthworm decor, 4" w/lid **200.00**

Yellowware w/earthworm decor, 6½" **250.00**
Jug, black bands enclosing blue band w/worm, green top band, 5" **400.00**
   Blue w/marbleized leaf, wht foot, spout & handle, 6½" **485.00**
   Grey w/standing seaweed, geometric & green ribbed top band, 7" **475.00**
   Marbleized, blue over-sponging, top bands, wht spout & handle, 8" **650.00**
Mug, black & blue bands w/seaweed decor, handled, 4¾" **150.00**
   Blue band w/cat's eye, blue & wht bands, wht stepped base, 3½" **175.00**
   Cat's eye, worm decor **575.00**

Cream w/2 narrow cream & grey bands **90.00**
Cream w/broad wht & 2 narrow brown bands, handled, 4x4" . **85.00**
Cream w/brown seaweed decor, black bands, handled, 5" . . . **185.00**
Marbleized, green incised band at top, wht handle, 4x4½" dia **200.00**
Mustard pot, speckled, blk & wht checkered band, flower finial **245.00**
Pitcher, blue band, looped worm, 5" **450.00**
   Blue seaweed decor, footed, 7½" **175.00**
   Earthworm decor **345.00**
   Marbleized, blue sponge effect, 8" **685.00**
   Seaweed pattern, mkd VR 93 . . . . **98.00**
Posset cup, mustard band, looped worm between brown & wht bands **300.00**
Potty, seaweed decor **120.00**
Punch pot, wht w/bands overall, wht spout, handle & ball finial, 12" **625.00**
Saucer, black, blue, wht & sienna bands, 6" dia **175.00**
Shaker, cat's eye on blue ground, brown/mustard stripes, 4½" **150.00**
Spill, cream, brown & tan bands, incised green bands, 3½" . . **200.00**
Sugar bowl, marbleized leaf, flaring rim, covered **500.00**
Tea caddy, marbleized, wht top & bottom bands, 5½x2½" dia **325.00**
Teapot, marbleized, gr incised band, wht spout & handle, 3½" **325.00**
Teapot, miniature, mustard w/seaweed decor, blue bands, w/lid **700.00**

Molds

Food molds have become a popular collectible; not only for their value as antiques, but because they also revive childhood memories of elaborate ice cream Santas with candy trim, or barley sugar figurals adorning a Christmas tree. Ice cream molds were made of pewter and came in a wide variety of shapes and styles. Chocolate molds were made in fewer shapes, but were more detailed. They were usually made of tin, copper, and occasionally of pewter. Hard candy molds were usually metal, although the primitive maple sugar molds of hearts, rabbits and other animals were carved from wood. Cake molds were made of cast iron or cast aluminum, and were most common in the shape of a lamb, a rabbit or Santa Claus.

Barley sugar, basket, fluted, 3 pc, 1¾x2¾" **35.00**
   Rabbit, sitting, ears up, #6-L, 4½x6", heavy **45.00**
   Two rabbits, facing, ears down, 1x4" **25.00**
   Three chickens on nest, fine design, 2x7" **20.00**
   Three roosters, bumps fit dents to unite metal **15.00**
Cake, lamb marked Baker's Coconut, cast aluminum, 2 pc, 8x12" **75.00**
   Rabbit w/directions & recipes, aluminum, 8x10" **7.00**
   Rabbit, 2 pc, Griswald Mfg Co, cast iron, 9x11" **95.00**
   Rabbit, 2 pc, left & right, cast iron **35.00**
   Santa with pack of toys, Hello Kiddies, cast aluminum, 12" . . **80.00**
   Sitting rabbit, 2 pc, cast iron **40.00**
Cheese, stave construction, iron bands **55.00**
Chocolate molds, basket, clamped, 1½x4" **35.00**
   Basket, clamped, 3x9" **55.00**
   Basket, hinged, latched, 4 pcs **75.00**
   Baskets, one inverted on the other, hinged & clamped, 6½x9" **75.00**

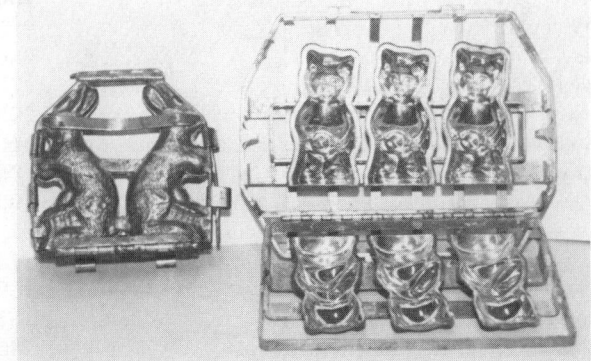

Bears, makes 3, banded **75.00**

Bird, 1 pc, tin w/copper, 1¼x4¼"	**25.00**
Boy, Gesetzl Geschutizi, Swedish, 2 pc, 5½"	**40.00**
Cat, 8230, USA, Eppelsheimer, 8"	**85.00**
Chick, 3 pc, hinged, banded, clamped, 3½x4"	**20.00**
Chicks, roosters, rabbits, makes 16 assorted, 6x8"	**75.00**
Christmas stocking, w/toys, 59+4271, Larrosh, Schw Gmund, 8"	**125.00**
Christmas scene, tree, 3 children, 1 pc, flat, 4½x8"	**35.00**
Christmas trees, makes 3, pat pend, Janion Reiche, 8x11"	**75.00**
Clown w/concertina, 15262, 2 pc, 9"	**75.00**
Dog head, France, 2 pc, 4"	**15.00**
Donkey, on base, large ears, 15919, Holland, 7"	**35.00**
Easter egg, rabbit scene, tin washed copper, 6x5x9"	**50.00**
Easter egg, rabbit w/flag, 2 pc, 4½"	**15.00**
Easter egg w/rabbit in swing ea side, pewter, 3x5x7"	**85.00**
Elephant, 1 pc, 2½x4"	**15.00**
Girl standing w/rabbit, 273, 7"	**55.00**
Heart, 8006, USA, Eppelsheimer, 9x9"	**65.00**
Hearts, 2, To My Valentine, 2 pc	**65.00**
Hershey bar, flat mold	**20.00**
Indian, full regalia, Germany, 1 pc, 7½"	**35.00**
Jack O Lantern, heavy wire clamp, 2 pc	**35.00**
Pencils, pair, 8½"	**30.00**
Plate mold, assorted chicks & rabbits, 2215S, 11x17"	**95.00**
Plate mold, coin-type candies, Eppelsheimer, 6x15"	**20.00**
Rabbit & cart scenic, 5x7½"	**30.00**
Rabbit houses, makes 4, 2 pc, 2½x6½x9½"	**65.00**
Rabbit lollipops, flat, makes 8, 8x10"	**55.00**
Rabbit riding rooster, 8350, 2 pc, 5½x6"	**40.00**
Rabbit w/cane & backpack, 6170, 237, Eppelsheimer, 6"	**25.00**
Rabbit w/lock dents, 324 USA, 4050, Eppelsheimer, 2 pc	**15.00**
Rabbit, 1749, lying ears down	**25.00**
Rabbit, 8074, USA, Eppelsheimer, copper, hinged, 4"	**35.00**
Rabbit, artist wearing glasses, 3 pc, hinged & banded, 8"	**75.00**
Rabbit, boxing, 11748-1, Germany, Janion Reich Dresden, 6"	**55.00**
Rabbit, defined fur detail, lock dents, 3½x4"	**20.00**
Rabbit, on hind legs, head turned, 2 pc, 13"	**75.00**
Rabbit, plastic, Tomric, 1173	**5.00**
Rabbit, pulling cart, 2 pc, 4x8"	**25.00**
Rabbit, round base, backpack, 15"	**125.00**
Rabbit, running, tin washed copper, 3x5"	**25.00**
Rabbit, sitting, 437-TC Weygandt, 3 pc, 6½x8"	**45.00**
Rabbit, sitting, ears erect, 12"	**50.00**
Rabbit, sitting, ears up, makes three, 1 upside down, 7x11"	**50.00**
Rabbit, sitting, ears up, makes two, 7x8½", illus	**55.00**
Rabbit, sitting, makes three, 16523-7DRGM Germany, 3½x7"	**40.00**
Rabbit, smooth, little detail, Germany, 2 pc, 5x5"	**25.00**
Rabbit, standing, basket on back, Eppelsheimer, 948146, 4x9"	**50.00**
Rabbit, Uncle Wiggley, 3 pc, 4½"	**45.00**
Rabbit, w/lock dents, 6626-1-13, 4¼"	**20.00**
Rabbits, in cars, 2 sections, tin on copper, 4x8"	**60.00**
Rabbits, 2, either side of basket, 265, 6x8½"	**40.00**
Rabbits, 2, either side of basket, 4682, Eppelsheimer, 7x7½"	**55.00**
Rabbits, 2, either side of egg, lock dents, 9"	**60.00**
Rabbits, 3, dressed, Eppelsheimer, pat'd 1939, 6x9"	**65.00**
Rabbits, 4, 307 Germany, 6x11½"	**50.00**
Rabbits, 4, w/violins & bows, 4½x7"	**65.00**
Rabbits, riding rooster, makes two, banded, clamped, 6x11"	**50.00**
Rabbits, standing, makes 8 identical, 2 pc, 11" sq	**50.00**
Rooster, 312, 2 pc, 9"	**40.00**
Santa, Janion Reich Dresden, German 21335S, 3'	**1,500.00**
Santa, makes 3 identical, 8x11"	**75.00**
Santa, one hand to beard, one to belt, flat 1 pc, 4½"	**20.00**
Santa, tall cone shape hat, elongated form, 4"	**20.00**
Santa's head, flat 1 pc	**20.00**

Scarecrows, 3, in battered top hats, 6"	**85.00**
Sedan, 4 door, w/trunk, 3x5"	**10.00**
Snowman in top hat, 2 pc, 4"	**50.00**
Strip, for individual candies, Schrafts Co, 15"	**5.00**
Teddy Bear, 2644+11	**150.00**
Turkey, 3 pc, hinged & clamped, Germany	**45.00**
Witch, riding broom, 3 pc, 6"	**75.00**
Ice cream mold, 4-leaf clover, E335	**32.00**
Ace of Diamonds	**28.00**
Ace of Hearts	**30.00**
Ace of Spades	**28.00**
American Legion Emblem	**32.00**
American Flag	**35.00**
American Shield	**32.00**
Apple, E240	**29.00**
Aster, #236, hinged	**45.00**
Automobile, S & Co 5162	**50.00**
Baby, in long dress, S & Co, 286	**55.00**
Baby cradle, 3 pc, #344	**32.00**
Ball, 4 per qt	**22.00**
Banana	**35.00**
Banjo	**67.00**
Baseball Bat	**45.00**
Basket, 3 part mold	**60.00**
Basket, Brevete, SGDG Remarque Fabrique CC, banquet size	**250.00**
Battleship, large size, 1½-2 qt	**300.00**
Bear, sitting, E614	**32.00**
Boat, hinged at both ends	**35.00**
Boat, with cover E935, 934 on boat	**32.00**
Box, wild rose decor, #455, individual	**50.00**
Bride, large, detailed	**39.00**
Bride, small	**38.00**
Bride, w/veil	**50.00**
Bride & groom, E & Co, M1201	**40.00**
Brownie, Eppelsheimer #1031, double row of buttons	**65.00**
Bunch of asparagus, no mark, miniature	**45.00**
Bunch of carrots	**70.00**
Bunch of violets	**55.00**
Calla lily, S & Co, 210, 3 pc, double hinge, early	**50.00**
Cannon, #273	**35.00**
Carnation w/stem, #554, 5 part leaf	**32.00**
Carnation w/stem, E361, 6 part leaf	**33.00**
Cat, E644	**35.00**
Cherries, 4 in mold, #108	**30.00**
Chick in egg, #599	**32.00**
Chicken, E & Co, 652, early	**45.00**
Christmas bell, #404	**65.00**
Christmas fireplace, E & Co, M1202, individual	**75.00**
Christmas stocking, 596, rare	**85.00**
Christmas tree, decorated in detail, 641-K, tin over copper	**45.00**
Chrysanthemum, #313	**55.00**
Cow, E659	**35.00**
Cradle	**50.00**
Cross, Knights Templar, E1005	**30.00**
Crown, no mark, 2½"	**45.00**
Cucumber, E & Co, large	**22.00**
Cup, open top, E976	**30.00**
Cupid, #492	**55.00**
Cupid, seated	**50.00**
Cupid in rose, E959	**35.00**
Daisies, bunch of 3, #365	**34.00**
Daisy #363	**32.00**
Daisy, E & Co #317, detailed	**45.00**
Diploma	**54.00**

Dove of Peace, in flight, E & Co 667, rare **85.00**
Dove of Peace, seated w/flowers, #342 . . . . **55.00**
Doves, cooing **35.00**
Drum, 3 pc, double hinge, Krauss #511A **75.00**
Duck, CC on ea half, flared French hinge **50.00**
Duck, Krauss #44 banquet size **350.00**
Duck, S & Co, #15 . . . . **36.00**
Dutch clog **40.00**
Ear of corn, S & Co, 270, detailed, individual **50.00**
Egg, #907 . . . . **30.00**
Elephant, #169 . . . . **36.00**
Elk's head medallion, E1101 . . . . **32.00**
Engagement ring, E & Co 1141 K, tin washed copper **25.00**
Engine & coal car, 377, 47B, ea **75.00**
Fish, E604 . . . . **34.00**
Fleur de Lis, E997 . . . . **32.00**
Flying stork w/baby **65.00**
Football, E381, 3 pc **32.00**
Four leaf clover **53.00**
Foxy Grandpa **50.00**
Geo Washington #460, D & Co on hinge **65.00**
Geo Washington bust **50.00**
Girl on bicycle, wearing hat **65.00**
Gladiolus, E349 . . . . **30.00**
Golfer, female, #464 . . . . **35.00**
Golfer, male, #1042 . . . . **35.00**
Gondola, 3 prt mold **60.00**
Good Luck Horseshoe **42.00**
Grapes, #159, no leaves **45.00**
Groom, E1149, large **39.00**
Groom, E1149, small **35.00**
Harp, #361 . . . . **38.00**
Hat, lady's, E1006 . . . . **30.00**
Heart, #475 . . . . **32.50**
Heart a flame, Love, 300 . . . . **50.00**
Heart w/cupid, E1102 . . . . **35.00**
Hobby horse, E & Co, early, rare **65.00**
Horn of plenty, 287, tin washed copper, individual **25.00**
Horn of plenty, E & Co, 1004, pewter **75.00**
Hyacinth, E356 . . . . **32.00**
Indian, #458 Des Cop'd 1896, hand shading eyes **75.00**
Jack of Diamonds, E928 . . . . **35.00**
King of Diamonds, E923 . . . . **35.00**
Kiwanis club emblem, E111 . . . . **32.00**
Lemon, E308 . . . . **27.50**
Lily, 3 pc, double hinged, early **35.00**
Lime, CC 814 Brevete SGDG, early **35.00**
Lion, E618 . . . . **35.00**
Log, E & Co #987, individual **55.00**
Log, banquet size, 10″ **250.00**
Masonic compass **35.00**
Masonic emblem, Shrine, E1081 . . . . **32.00**
Melon slice **53.00**
Morning Glory, E297 . . . . **32.00**
Old Mother Hubbard, E & Co 981 Des Cop'rd 1890 . . . . **70.00**
Orange, E307 . . . . **27.50**
Orange, S357 . . . . **27.50**
Orange blossoms, E360 . . . . **32.00**
Orchid, 319, Des, cop'd 1892 . . . . **65.00**
Pansy w/stem, 269 . . . . **45.00**
Parrot **60.00**
Peach, E234 . . . . **28.00**
Peach half w/stone **28.00**
Pear, E248 . . . . **28.50**

Petunia, E298 . . . . **27.50**
Pineapple, #156 . . . . **32.00**
Pipe, smoking, #374 . . . . **32.00**
Pond lily, E318 . . . . **28.50**
Poppy, #495 . . . . **28.50**
Potato, S154 . . . . **30.00**
Pumpkin, 600 . . . . **35.00**
Pumpkin, no mark, unusual latch **35.00**
Queen of Clubs, E925 . . . . **35.00**
Queen of Diamonds **55.00**
Queen of Hearts, E927 . . . . **35.00**
Queen of Spades, E924 . . . . **35.00**
Rabbit crouching, E & Co #658 . . . . **65.00**
Rabbit, half standing, Krauss 189 . . . . **50.00**
Rabbit, half standing, Krauss 297 . . . . **45.00**
Rabbit, recumbent, head to right, 190, hinge at rear **45.00**
Race car & driver, E1218 . . . . **45.00**
Rooster, banquet size, 11½″ **400.00**
Rose bouquet, #194 . . . . **32.00**
Rose, #582, full blown **50.00**
Rose, CC, flared French hinge, small, 1½″ **35.00**
Rose with leaves & bud, S & Co, good detail **55.00**
Rosebud, CC on ea half, natural size, French flare hinge 2½″ **35.00**
Roses, three in cluster, #391, individual **45.00**
Rowboat, individual **60.00**
Santa, E & Co, banquet size, #194 . . . . **400.00**
Santa, from Stohlman's, individual, pewter **45.00**
Santa, hands in muff, hinged, individual **45.00**

Santa, 'Hello Kiddies', 13″ **100.00**
Santa, in sleigh, pulled by reindeer, individual **65.00**
Santa, letting his pack down chimney, E & Co, N.Y., 1171 . . . **75.00**
Santa, pack on back, 1 leg in chimney, no mark, individual . . **45.00**
Santa, S & Co #427, hood, long beard, hand in bag, individual **45.00**
Santa face in holly wreath, flat, individual **45.00**
Shamrock, E1039 . . . . **32.00**
Sheaf of wheat **70.00**
Shell, S & Co 311 . . . . **75.00**
Shoe, hinged in front **50.00**
Skull & crossbones, #506 . . . . **37.50**
Slipper, 2 pc, E899 . . . . **32.00**
Slipper, 3 pc, #570 . . . . **34.00**
Spade, S211 . . . . **27.50**
St Bernard dog, E654 . . . . **57.50**

Strawberries, makes 3, natural size, S & Co **55.00**
Strawberry, #503, individual **65.00**
Swan, E630 . . . . **34.00**
Teddy Bear, E & Co 1103 . . . . **65.00**
Tomato, S153 . . . . **30.00**
Train, passenger car #479, 3 pc **300.00**
Tulip, E352 . . . . **32.00**
Turkey, E & Co, 650, individual **45.00**
Turkey, roasted, #364, D & Co on hinge **40.00**
US flag in breeze **62.00**
Washington's head on hatchet, E & Co **35.00**
Watermelon slice, S & Co 557, early **65.00**
Wedding bell, #285 . . . . **45.00**
Wedding bell w/cupid, E1019 . . . . **34.00**
Wedding ring, E1142 . . . . **32.00**
Witch on broomstick, #1153 . . . . **75.00**
Witch's cat, E & Co 1175 . . . . **75.00**
Wreath, E & Co, 1146, 5½″ **95.00**
Maple sugar; for chunks, moveable sections, wood **170.00**
Heart, wood **61.00**
Large house, wood **147.00**
Rabbit, 2 piece with 2 pegs, wood **35.00**
Two part rooster, 8½x11″, wood **197.00**
Three deep heart sections, wood **227.00**
Three lb, blocks, 19x2½″, wood **87.00**
Muffin, heart & star design, small, cast iron **10.00**
Pudding, melon shapped, 2 pc, tin **14.00**
Sheep, 7x13″ ci **120.00**
Various fruits, 8½x5x6″ **70.00**

Monmouth

The Monmouth Pottery Co. was established in 1892, in Monmouth, Ill. Their primary products were stoneware crocks, churns and jugs, in salt glaze, Bristol, spongeware and brown glaze. In 1906, they were absorbed by a conglomerate called the Western Stoneware Co. Monmouth became their #1 plant, and until 1930, continued to produce stoneware marked with their maple leaf logo. Items marked Monmouth Pottery Co. were made before 1906; after the merger, 'Co' was dropped, and 'Ill' was substituted.

Bowl, daffodils in relief, hi-gloss green inside, 7½ ″ dia **10.00**
Cookie jug, w/cork **18.00**
Pitcher, tan, horizontal ribs, 5½″ **8.00**
Poultry fountain, blue print on wht, 2-pc, 'Splash Proof', 10x6″ **115.00**
Vase, matt green, 8″ **6.00**
Stylized leaves, handled, brown & orange, 7½x5½″ **10.00**

Mont Joye

Mont Joye was a type of acid cut French cameo glass produced by Cristallerie de Pantin in Paris around the turn of the century.

Rose bowl, violets decor, gold rim, sgnd, 4½x5″ dia **250.00**
Vase, acid etched, purple irises w/gold leaves, sgnd, 13½″ . . . **300.00**
Cameo acid cut back, amethyst w/carved flowers, textured, 12″ **350.00**
Cranberry floral cameo, brass base & rim, rippled, 8″ **345.00**
Frosted w/heavy enamel & cut, mkd **265.00**
Green acid cut, 1½″ top flared to 3″ bottom, sgnd, 7″ **250.00**
Green frosted w/gold enamel leaves & silver acorns **295.00**
Green w/brown flowers & gold trim, sgnd **260.00**
Green w/gold flowers in cameo, enamel, gold trim, sgnd **395.00**
Rubina, melon ribbed, floral enamel, 12″ **335.00**

Moorcroft

William Moorcroft was an English potter who established a workshop in Burslem, England, in 1913. He produced tablewares and a line of fine Art Nouveau vases, bowls, etc., which until 1919 were marked with the printed or impressed block lettered 'Moorcroft', Burslem. After that, the patented W. Moorcroft signature mark was used. Wm. Moorcroft died in 1945, and the work was continued by his son. Modern wares are marked 'Moorcroft', and Made In England.

Ashtray, green w/pink poppies **35.00**
Bowl, blue & green background, large flower inside, 4¼″ dia . . **40.00**
Cobalt w/wisteria inside & out, sgnd, 3¼x11″ **165.00**
Flower & leaves, 7″ dia **90.00**
Low, cobalt w/pansy, 3″ **40.00**
Low with 3-color leaves & purple berries, 4½″ **55.00**
Yellow & green, w/purple & red orchids, 3½″ **68.00**
Bowl vase, cobalt w/iris & multi-color florals, squeeze bag, MIE, 3½″ **50.00**
Box, floral decor, w/lid, 6″ dia **175.00**
Compote, green & pink lustre, 1910, 9½″ dia **75.00**
Covered dish, poppies on cobalt, 6¾″ **135.00**
Cup, demitasse, Florian, blue & wht **300.00**
Cup & saucer, cobalt w/wisteria floral, orig paper label, sgnd . . **145.00**
Demitasse, blue w/colorful fruit **70.00**
Cup w/ped, saucer, heavy ware, lt to dk green, orchids **55.00**
Fruit bowl, flambe glazed, iris florals, painted monogram, 9″ . . **195.00**
Ginger jar, irid orange lustre, w/cover, 8¾″ **125.00**
Pink magnolia, 4″ **50.00**
Jardiniere, Florian, blue w/3-color florals, McIntyre, 12″ **450.00**
Pitcher, cobalt w/floral, 3″ **38.00**
Sugar & creamer, mushroom decorated, 1914 . . . . **260.00**
Teapot, pale blue w/pink & yellow hibiscus, dk blue trim **250.00**
Trivet, mushrooms, green signature, 5½″ dia **175.00**
Urn, miniature, seaweed in the Breeze pattern, w/wood base, 3x4″ **295.00**
Vase, blackberry, 6″ **220.00**
Cobalt blue & green, pomegranates & grapes, sgnd **175.00**
Cobalt blue w/floral, mkd Potter to HM the Queen, 3¼″ . . . **80.00**
Cobalt w/pansies, script signature, 7″ **185.00**
Cobalt w/poppies & green stems, sgnd, 6¼″ **145.00**
Cobalt w/red fruit & yellow leaves, Potter to the Queen, sgnd, 7¼″ **145.00**
Cobalt w/yellow & red freesia, 5″ **95.00**
Dark green w/beige & rust florals, sgnd, 6″ **450.00**
Flambe, bulbous, orig paper label, 2¾″ **75.00**

Florals, red and gold, 8″ **125.00**
Florian, blue & green floral, wide base, narrow neck, McIntyre **600.00**
Flower & leaves decor, 6½″ **85.00**
Mushroom design, 3½″ **175.00**
Orange lustre, 1913, 9″ **120.00**
Orchid decor, 4″ **50.00**
Pink magnolia, 6″ **50.00**

Pomegranate, 3½x4″ wide **95.00**
Red & blue pansies, impressed mk Burslem, 3½″ **135.00**
Rose panel, 2 handled, 1915, 10½″ **175.00**
Rust floral decor, 12″ **465.00**
Sang de Boeuf, 9½x7″ dia **395.00**
Tree design w/pewter **250.00**
Vases, cobalt w/orchids, Royal mk, 3½″, pr **145.00**

Moravian Pottery & Tile Works

Dr. Henry Chapman Mercer was an author, anthropologist, historian, collector and artist. One of his diversified interests was pottery. In 1898, he established the Moravian Pottery and Tile Works in Doylestown, Pa., the name inspired by his study and collection of decorative stone plates made by the early Moravians. Because the red clay he used there proved unfit for tableware, he turned to the production of handmade tile which he himself designed. Though never allowing it to become more than a studio operation, the tile works was nevertheless responsible for some important commercial installations, one of which was in the capitol building at Harrisburg.

Mercer died in 1930. Business continued in the established vein under the supervision of Mercer's assistant, Frank Swain, until his death in 1954. Since 1968, the studio has been operated by The Bucks County Commision and tiles are still fashioned in the handmade tradition. They are marked 'Mercer', and are dated.

ndleholder, sconce, Viking ship decor **125.00**
e, grapes & leaves on blue, square, Mercer, 2¾″ **11.00**
Knight in armour on horse **45.00**
Moravian ship decor **65.00**
Sculptured fawn, buff & dk green, Mercer, 4½″ **30.00**
Shield, grey-blue, County-Duty-Honor, Mercer, 4″ **23.00**
Zodiac sign decor **56.00**

Morton Pottery

Morton Pottery Works-Morton Earthenware Company (1877-1914)
Bowl, mixing, yellow glaze, lattice w/wht top bands, 15¼″ dia . . **36.00**
Milk boiler, brown Rockingham glaze, 4½x4″ dia **40.00**
Mug, coffee, brown Rockingham glaze, 3½″ **35.00**
Pitcher, water, blue glaze, 3 pint, 6¼″ **25.00**
Stein, brown Rockingham glaze, German motto at top & bottom, 6″ **55.00**
Teapot, Rebecca at the Well, brown Rockingham glaze, 8½″ . . **65.00**
Cliftwood Art Potteries, Inc. (1920-1939)
Beer set, barrel shaped pitcher w/6 mugs, gr glaze **40.00**
Bookends, elephant figurals, blue mulberry drip glaze, 4½x6″ . . **25.00**
Bowl, batter, orchid & pink drip glaze over wht, handled, 4½x9″ dia **25.00**
Candlesticks, blk semi-lustre glaze, 7″, pair **35.00**
Figurine, police dog, chocolate drip glaze, 11x18″ **65.00**
Vase, snake w/fish figural handles, chocolate drip glaze, 18¼″ . . **40.00**
Midwest Pottery, Inc. (1939-1944)
Creamer, cow figural, brown drip glaze, yellow handle, 5″ **12.00**
Figurine, female nude, September Morn, wht glaze, 12″ **20.00**
  Mother duck w/2 ducklings following, wht glaze, yellow trim, 3x6½″ **4.50**
  Two kissing rabbits, wht glaze, gold trim, 2¼″ **6.50**
  Two yellow canaries perched on gold stump, 4¼″ **15.00**
Pitcher, duck figural, cattail handle, brown & grey spray glaze, 9¾″ **18.00**
Morton Pottery Company (1922-1976)
Bowl, brown glaze, A&J Double Action Egg Beater, 5½x4½″ dia **30.00**
Bowls, mixing, 3 nested, gr/yellow/brown spatter glaze, 7, 8 & 9″ dia **55.00**
Cookie jar, figural hen, chick finial, wht glaze w/brushed blk trim, 7½″ **35.00**
Pie bird, yellow, green & red brushed decor on wht glaze, 5″ . . **18.00**
Stein, beer, embossed parrot on lattice ground, brown glaze, 5″ **25.00**
Sugar & creamer, hen & rooster, wht glaze w/brushed blk trim, 4″ **12.00**

American Arts Pottery (1947-1961)
Doll head, hand decorated, blk hair, 3″ dia, w/arms & legs, set . **25.00**
Figurine, Hampshire Hog, blk glaze w/wht ribbon, gr base, 5½x7½″ **10.00**
Lamp/planter, titmice on limb, pink & grey spray glaze over wht, 11″ **9.00**
Planter, figural swan, blue & pink spray glaze on wht, 11″ **3.50**
Planter, teddy bear w/wht glaze sits on hp building blocks, 6x9″ . **5.00**
Vase, ewer, pink glaze, 14″ **5.00**

Mosaic Tile Co.

The Mosaic Tile Co. was organized in Zanesville, Ohio, in 1894 by Herman Mueller and Karl Langenbeck, both of whom had backgrounds in the indusry. They developed a faster, less costly method of potting decorative tile, utilizing paper patterns rather than copper molds. By 1901, the company had grown and expanded, with offices in many major cities. Faience tile was introduced in 1918, greatly increasing their volume of sales. They also made novelty ashtrays, figural boxes, bookends, etc., though not to any large extent. Until they closed during the 1960s, Mosaic used various marks. Many include the company name, another their initials---MT superimposed over Co in a circle.

Bookends, figural, child w/book, sitting on books, 7½″ **80.00**
Dish, trefoil shape, grey-green gloss, 3x7x9″ **8.00**

Figurine, bear, black, 10½x5¾″ **135.00**
  German Shepherd, tan, lying down, 6x10½″ **105.00**
Tile, A Lincoln, blue & wht, hexagonal, 3½″ **55.00**
  Black w/pot of multicolor flowers, red clay, 1920, 6x6″ **100.00**
  Black w/silver, Art Deco, red clay, 1930, 4½x4½″ **50.00**
  Deer, 10x6″ **120.00**
  Duck in flight, faience type, 6x6″ **85.00**
  Gen Pershing **35.00**
  Mollie Pitcher, 6x10″ **90.00**
  Oxen & covered wagon, 6x6″ **80.00**
  Story book, blk line process, multicolor, 4½″ **50.00**
Trivet, cast iron & tile, 3-color floral decor **13.00**

Moser

Ludwig Moser founded the Moser Glassworks in Czechoslovakia in 1857. He produced Art Nouveau style glass---cameo, intaglio cut, iridescent and enameled ware. Most valued by collectors are items made between 1860 and 1920. The firm is still in operation.

Ashtray, cobalt blue, women, triangular **175.00**
  Horses form feet, Malachite **125.00**
Bowl vase, ftd, sapphire blue, enamel bird, scrolls, 9x8½ **695.00**
Bowl, amber, sgnd, 8″ dia **100.00**
  Cranberry, paneled w/gold floral, sgnd, 4x6″ **290.00**

Lt blue, w/flowers & leaves, 2¾x4½" **165.00**
Bud vase, clear to lt green, enamel, sgnd, 15" **200.00**
Bud vases, lavender to clear w/flowers, yellow x-hatched pr, 4½" **145.00**
Compote, blue w/enamel acorns & ferns, 3 corner 5½x7¼" . . **385.00**
   Cranberry, gold decor, clear stem, 12" **200.00**
   Green, gold decor, clear stem, 12" **200.00**
Cruet, w/stopper, 5 color enamel, 8¼" **295.00**
Decanter, ruby w/applied gold bees, 10½" **475.00**
Demi cup & saucer, amber w/gold dots, leaves and grapes **75.00**
Ewer, w/brass cover, handle, green w/clear foot, 6" **120.00**
Juice glasses, clear swirl w/gold & red band, sgnd, 6" **150.00**
Pitcher, amber, clear reed handle, flowers & leaves, gold trim, 7½" **225.00**
   Cranberry, crackle, fish handle, enamel **345.00**
   Ftd, snake handle, amethyst to cranberry w/enamel, 10¼" . **950.00**
   Lizard decor, ruffled, top **295.00**
Tumbler, amber w/gold bands, panels 3" **60.00**
   Green, multi-color acorns & buds **235.00**
   Lt blue, w/flowers & leaves, sgnd **60.00**
Vase, amethyst, ducks, marquise-form, 7¾" **700.00**
   Blue, ruffle top, amethyst ped gold trim w/jewels, 15½" . . . **250.00**
   Cameo, jungle scene, red/amber w/gold, sgnd, 13½" **1,500.00**
   Cobalt, gold elephant scene, sgnd, 8" **1,200.00**
   Ftd, frieze, w/figures, purple/gold, Carlsbad, 20" **400.00**
   Ftd, multi colors, beads, gold trim, 4½" **295.00**
   Intaglio, corset-shape green to clear, cut flower, 6x2½" . . . **200.00**
   Lavender to clear, x-hatch enamel & gold, 4½" **75.00**
   Purple, paneled, 5x4" **75.00**
   Twist stem, scalloped base, pink/opal, jeweled w/gold, 14" . . **400.00**
Vases, amber, crackle, w/colored seaweed, pr, 11" **450.00**
   Cranberry, applied bees, gold decor, 11x4½", pr **725.00**

Vase, topaz w/enameling, applied teardrops, 8" **165.00**
Water pitcher, w/2 tumblers, blue w/clear applied handle, bird . **350.00**
Wines, intaglio cut, sgnd, pr **175.00**

Moss Rose

Moss Rose patterned dinnerware was a favorite of many Staffordshire and American potters from the mid 1800s. The Wheeling Pottery in West Virginia introduced their version in the '80s, and it became one of their best sellers, remaining popular well into the '90s.

Coffee pot, Haviland, Limoges **60.00**

Coffee set, 10" pot, 6" creamer, 7½" sugar bowl **100.00**

Cup & saucer, Bridgwood, 1840s **30.00**
   Bone china, Royal Albert **15.00**
Fruit saucer, Bridgwood, 5" **10.00**
Gravy boat **30.00**
Mustard pot, beaded sterling foot & lid, sterling ladle, Rosenthal **50.00**
Plate, Bridgwood, 7" **8.00**
   Bridgwood, 9" **30.00**
   Meakin, 8" **15.00**
Platter, Haviland, 7½x11" **20.00**
   Haviland, 9x13" **25.00**
Sauce dish, Bridgwood, 5" **9.00**
Shaving mug **45.00**
   George Scott Stone China **85.00**
Teapot, large **49.00**
Tea set, service for 10, 53-pc, Haviland **275.00**
Tureen, Empire Pottery Ironstone **48.00**

Mosser Glass Co.

Tom Mosser founded the Mosser Glass Co. in Cambrige, Ohio, during the late 1960s. Among the most popular of its art glass wares is the Clown series. Near-monthly issues are produced, each in a newly developed color or type of glass, with each clown given a different name.

Bear, Chablis **35.00**
   Chocolate **10.00**
   Cloud 9 . . . . **9.50**
   Cloud 9 Frosted **10.50**
   Coral Mist **8.00**
   Coral Mist Frosted **9.50**
   Crystal **8.00**
   Crystal Frosted **9.50**
   Fiesta **50.00**
   Fiesta Cinnamon **55.00**
   Honey **10.00**
   Honey Frosted **12.00**
   Milk White **45.00**
   Misty Rose **8.00**
   Sunflower **9.00**
   Tawny **12.00**
   Turquoise **12.00**
   Violet D'or **30.00**
Clown, Arty **125.00**
   Bags **35.00**
   Cleo **35.00**
   Daisy **45.00**
   Eros **18.00**
   Flip **9.00**

Gabby **9.00**
Hoagy **15.00**
Iffy **9.00**
Jaggs **9.00**
Koko **12.00**
Lyle **9.00**
Maxi **9.00**
Lion, Gold Krystal **8.00**
   Green Irid **8.50**
   Tawny **9.00**
Paperweight, Hunting Dog, Crystal Satin **9.00**
Rabbit, Sapphire, large **10.25**
Robin, Aztec Flame, 5″ **40.00**

Mother of Pearl

Mother of Pearl glass was a type of mold blown satin art glass popular during the last half of the 19th century. A patent for its manufacture was issued in 1886 to Frederick S. Shirley, and one of the companies which produced it was the Mt. Washington Glass Co. of New Bedford, Mass. Another was the English firm of Stevens and Williams.

Its delicate patterns were developed by blowing the gather into a mold with inside projections that left an intaglio design on the surface of the glass, then sealing the first layer with a second, trapping air in the recesses. Most common are the Diamond Quilted, Raindrop and Herringbone patterns. It was made in several soft colors, the most rare and valuable is rainbow shaded. Some pieces are decorated with coralene, enameling or gilt.

Biscuit jar, Dia Quilt, pink & wht stripes, plated top, 6½″ **750.00**
   Ribbon, silver plate top, handle, blue, 5¾″ **495.00**
Bowl, Dia Quilt, applied ft, flower prunt, apple green, 4″ **700.00**
   Dia Quilt, tri-corne, ftd, blue, 5½x5″ **750.00**
Creamer, Herringbone, blue w/rose lining, ruffled **345.00**
Cruet, Dia Quilt, cut stopper **300.00**
Ewer, Dia Quilt, rainbow, 12½″ **900.00**
   Herringbone, cranberry, white, 6½″ **200.00**
   Herringbone, glossy, thorn handle, 14″ **160.00**
   Herringbone, ruffled 3 petal top, thorn handle, 7″ **285.00**
Fairy lamp, Dia Quilt, blue shade on pottery base **300.00**
   Dia Quilt, clear Clarke base, yellow **165.00**
   Dia Quilt, rigaree & petal base, rainbow, miniature **1,950.00**
Fingerbowl, Dia Quilt, rainbow, mkd patent, crimped, 2½x5″ . **850.00**
Pitcher, Dia Quilt, coralene & enameling, camphor handle **500.00**
   Dia Quilt, raspberry to pink **425.00**
   Herringbone, pink to rose, sq top, 8″ **400.00**
   Herringbone, square mouth, raspberry to pink **425.00**

   Raindrop, butterfly & florals, gilt trim, blues, 8″ **400.00**
   Spiral, apricot, 6″ **165.00**
Plate, Drape, wht to raspberry, mk pat, 7″ **190.00**

Rosebowl, Coin Dot, blue to wht, wht lining, 3″ **145.00**
   Dia Quilt, box pleated, Stevens & Williams, blue, 4″ **235.00**
   Dia Quilt, dimpled sides, blue, 8 crimps, 3½x4″ **200.00**
   Dia Quilt, rainbow, clear appendages, crimped **1,000.00**
   Dia Quilt, rainbow, mkd Pat, 4½″ dia **850.00**
   Dia Quilt, rose, egg shape, crimped, mkd Pat, 3¾″ **300.00**
   Dia Quilt, yellow, crimped, 3″ **200.00**
   Herringbone, 4 crimp, blue, 3½″ **195.00**
   Herringbone, 8 crimp, rose, 3½x3½″ **200.00**
   Herringbone, 8 crimp, blue shades, 4″ dia **125.00**
   Herringbone, 8 crimp, blue to white, wht lining, 3¾″ **165.00**
   Herringbone, 8 crimp, rose, 3½x3½″ **225.00**
   Ribbon, rose w/wht lining, crimped, 3″ **300.00**
   Striped, crimped top, wht, 2¾″ **120.00**
   Striped, pinched top, mocha, 3″ **135.00**
Salt & pepper, Dia Quilt, pewter 2-part top, blue, pr **300.00**
Salt shaker, Raindrop, apricot **115.00**
Sweetmeat, Dia Quilt, plated top, handle, rose, 5½″ **300.00**
   Rib Dia Quilted, rose, silver top, handle, 3x5″ **435.00**
   White w/gold blossoms, silver lid **600.00**
Tumbler, Herringbone, blue, 3¾″ **110.00**
   Raindrop, butterfly & florals, gilt trim, blues, 3½″, illus **110.00**
Vase, Concentric Diamond, camphor applique, gilt, beads, 10½″ **500.00**
   Dia Quilt, bulbous, slim neck, apricot, 10″ **260.00**
   Dia Quilt, camphor petal feet, pink, 6″ **95.00**
   Dia Quilt, ormolu flowers & feet, frilled, lime, 10x4″ **525.00**
   Dia Quilt, peach to caramel, 10″ **185.00**
   Dia Quilt, rainbow, 6″ **975.00**
   Dia Quilt, rainbow, ball body, slim neck, 6″ **550.00**
   Dia Quilt, rainbow, fluted, waisted, 7″ **500.00**
   Dia Quilt, rainbow, shoulder rings, rim skirt, 6″ **950.00**
   Dia Quilt, rose to pink, 6″ **130.00**
   Dia Quilt, rose w/wht casing, 11x5″ **265.00**
   Dia Quilt, ruffled, mocha, 6½″, pr **335.00**

   Dia Quilt, waisted, rolled & pinched rim, apricot, 7½″ **175.00**
   Flower & Acorn, pinched bottom, tri-corne top, lime, 4″ . . . **435.00**
   Herringbone, ruffled, peach, 5½x3½″ **165.00**
   Hobnail, blue **185.00**
   Raindrop, hand w/cornucopia, ruffled, blue, 10½″ **600.00**
   Ribbon, blue w/wht casing, pinched neck, 4½x6″ **495.00**
   Ribbon, gold w/wht casing, frosted disk ft, gold prunus, 4″ . **345.00**
   Ribbon, lime, frosted disk ft, 2¾″ **195.00**
   Ribbon, rose, frosted disk ft, gold prunus & top edge, 3″ . . **400.00**
   Spiral, keyhole rim, blue w/gold pattern, 5″ **235.00**

Striped, gold w/wht lining, 4″ **120.00**
Swirl, rose to gray w/gold decor, 8½″ **150.00**

Movie Memorabilia

Movie memorabilia covers a broad range of collectibles, from books and magazines dealing with the industry in general, to the various promotional materials which were distributed to arouse interst in a particular film. Many collectors specialize in a specific area---posters, press books, stills, lobby cards or souvenir programs (also referred to as premier booklets).

Arcade card, Tim Mix **9.00**
Book, Actor Guide to the Talkies, 2 vols, 1967 .... **15.00**
Book, souvenir, Marilyn Miller in Sunny, 22 pgs, photos **25.00**
Books from the movies; Abie's Irish Rose, 1929, 324 pp **6.50**
  And Then There Were None, 1945 .... **7.50**
  Auction of Souls, 1919, lst ed, 254 pg **25.00**
  Case of Sgt Grischa, The; 1930, 449 pg **10.00**
  Clothes Make the Pirate, 1926, Photoplay ed **10.00**
  Dawn Patrol, 1930 .... **10.00**
  Diamond From the Sky, The; 1916, 440 pg **40.00**
  Duel in the Sun, 1946, 246 pg **7.50**
  Gone With The Wind, lst ed, 1st printing, 1939, 391 pg **20.00**
  Hunchback of Notre Dame, The; 1923, 144 pg **25.00**
  Last Days of Pompeii, 1935, 254 pg **12.50**
  Love Parade, The; 1929 .... **7.50**
  Man Who Laughs, The; 1928, 530 pg **12.50**
  Misfits, The; 1961, 1st paperback ed 223 pg **7.50**
  Sky Hawk, The; 1929 .... **12.00**
  Tarzan and the Golden Lion, 1927, 33 pg **12.50**
  Temple, Shirley, Little Colonel, 1935 .... **26.50**
  Ten Commandments, Richard Dix **10.00**
  Twenty Thousand Leagues Under The Sea, 1916, 386 pg **25.00**
  When Knighthood Was in Flower, Marian Davies **8.00**
Brochure, Columbia Picture, 7 group of shorts, 1930-31 ..... **195.00**
Celluloid drawing, Alice in Wonderland, Walt Disney Studio .. **150.00**
Chandelier, from movie theatre, gaudy w/nudes, 2 for **295.00**
Coloring book, Gone with the Wind **40.00**
Costume sketch, Lady L Sophia Loren, 1965 by Ora Kelley **50.00**
Handbill; Knock on Any Door, Humphrey Bogart, 10x8″ **16.50**
  Tex Ritter **5.00**
Lobby card; Acquitted, Houghs, Livingston, Columbia, title+7 .. **80.00**
  Bat, Vincent Price, 1959 .... **15.00**
  Blood of the Vampire, 1958 .... **10.00**
  Boom!, Burton & Taylor, special, 1968 .... **40.00**
  Bronze Venus, Lena Horne, Toddy Pictures, 11x14″ **45.00**
  Casablanca, rare, orig **1,250.00**
  Dance Hall, Lake & Borden, title card+7 .... **95.00**
  Delightful Rogue, LaRoque, LaRoy, Radio pict, title+7 ..... **95.00**
  Drake Case, Brockwell, Stanley, Universal, title+7 .... **80.00**
  Drums, Sabu & Massey, 1938, set of 6 .... **90.00**
  Gold Rush, Chaplin, 1942, lot of 3 .... **85.00**
  Grapes of Wrath, shows cast & book, 1940 .... **50.00**
  Great Dictator, Chaplin & Godard, 1940, title card **50.00**
  Hearts Up, Harry Carey, Universal, title card, B/W **12.00**
  House Rent Party, Pigmeat Alamo Markham **20.00**
  It Happened One Night, Colbert & Gable, 1934 .... **90.00**
  Jazz Heaven, O'Neil, Johny Mack Brown, title+7 .... **95.00**
  Jealousy, Jeanne Eagles, Paramount, 6 in set **135.00**
  Kibitzer, Green & Brian, Paramount **10.00**
  Klondike Annie, Mae West, 1936, 14x18″ **200.00**
  Man's Plaything, Grace Davison, B/W, 4 in set **45.00**
  Marianne, Davies & Grey, MGM, title card+7 .... **110.00**
  Marriage Pit, Frank Mayo, title card **12.00**

Midlanders, Bessie Love, Federated, title+4, B/W **60.00**
Midnight Shadow, George Randol Production, 11x14″ **10.00**
Mr Wu Stoll Film Mystery, Matheson Lang, title card+7 ..... **95.00**
Nat'l Velvet, Liz Taylor, Rooney, set of 6 .... **100.00**
Night Club Girl, Mantan Moreland, 11x14″ **10.00**
Paragan, Ramon Navarro, Metro, set of 7 .... **85.00**
Rebel Without a Cause, Dean, Wood & Mineo **100.00**
Shanghai Lady, Nolan & Murray, Universal, title+7 .... **100.00**
Song of Love, Baker & Graves, Columbia, title+7 .... **85.00**
Sundown Slim, Harry Carey, Universal, title+5, B/W **95.00**
Tiger True, Frank Mayo, Universal, title+7 .... **85.00**
Tom Mix **35.00**
Under Crimson Skies, Elmo Lincoln, title card+7 .... **95.00**
Wagon Master, Ken Maynard, set of 6 .... **90.00**
Welcome Danger, Harold Lloyd, title+6 .... **125.00**
Woman Trap, Brent & Morris, Paramount, title+7 .... **100.00**
Magazine, Film Fun, May 1932 .... **7.00**
  Modern Screen, Aug, 1944, Lana Turner **8.00**
  Movie Magazine, Mary Pickford cover, 1918 .... **20.00**
  Movie Mirror, Vol 1 .... **45.00**
  Photoplay, June, 1945, Bacall **8.00**
  Picture Play, July 1929, Lily Damita by Stein cover **5.00**
  Screen Album, Rogers & Astaire on cover **20.00**
  Screenland, March 1930, Evelyn Brent by Armstrong cover .. **15.00**
Photo, Brian Aherne, w/auto, 8x10″ **15.00**
  Carmen Miranda, framed **60.00**
  Clark Gable, Adventure in China, 1936, 8x10″, framed **12.50**
  Clark Gable, Dixie Cup Premium, 9x11″ **35.00**
  Esther Williams, 5x3½″ **15.00**
  Gary Cooper, Dixie Cup Premium, 9x11″ **25.00**
  Gene Tunney, w/auto **40.00**
  Jackie Cooper, Dixie Cup Premium, 9x11″ **15.00**
  Jeffery Hunter, inscribed, 8x10″ **25.00**
  Marilyn Monroe, inscribed, 8x10″ **125.00**
  Orig publicity shot, Other Men's Shoes, B/W **35.00**
  Orig publicity shot, West is West, Harry Carey, 8-8x10″ **15.00**
  Red Ryder, 5x7″ **20.00**

Photo cards, 1916, ea **8.00**
Photo Postcard, Crawford, w/auto **25.00**
  Tremayne, w/auto **10.00**
Portraits, Academy Award Winners, 1961, boxed set **15.00**
Poster, A Texas Ranger, 1900, 28x41″ **200.00**
  All The Fine Young Cannibals, Natalie Wood, 1 sheet, 1960 . **10.00**
  Anna Karenina, Vivian Leigh, 1948, 1 sheet **100.00**
  Baby the Rain Must Fall, Steve McQueen, 3 sheet, 1965 ..... **15.00**
  Barbarella, Fonda, 1968, 27x41″ **55.00**
  Beware, Louis Jordan, Astor Pictures, 1 sheet **65.00**
  Big Sleep, 1 sheet, 1946 .... **150.00**
  Black Cat, Karloff & Bellalugosi **35.00**

Blazing Saddles, 27x41" **15.00**
Blondie's Hero, 1 sheet, 1950 . . . . **20.00**
Bronze Venus, Lena Horne, Toddy Pictures **150.00**
Call It Murder, Bogart, 41x27" **125.00**
Circus World, John Wayne, 1965, 27x41" **35.00**
City That Stopped Hitler, propaganda, 1 sheet **50.00**
Courage of Black Beauty, 1957 . . . . **8.00**
Coming Attractions, 1930s, 22x14" **15.00**
Dick Tracy vs. Cueball, 1 sheet, 1946 . . . . **55.00**
Dillinger, Warren Oates, 1973, 27x41" **20.00**
Double Trouble, Elvis **45.00**
Fight Never Ends, Joe Louis, Toddy Pictures **140.00**
Fly My Kite, Little Rascals, 28x42" **18.00**
Girl of the Golden West, 1905, 21x28" **25.00**
Golden Rush, Chaplin, 1941, 1st talkie, 27x41½" . . . **180.00**
Greatest, Muhammad Ali, 27x41" **18.00**
Heidi, 1968 . . . . **8.00**
Here Comes the Marines, Gorcey & Bowery Boys, 1943 . . . . . **14.00**
I Was a Teenage Werewolf, 1 sheet **45.00**
King Kong, Jeff Bridges, 1976, 27x41" **18.00**
King's Row, orig linen back **800.00**
Limelight, Chaplin, 1952, 22x28" **150.00**
Little Rascals, Our Gang **75.00**
Mister Roberts, 27x41" **75.00**
Niagra, Monroe, 1953, 14x22" **50.00**
One Million BC, Victor Mature, Landess & Chaney, 1 sheet . **150.00**
One Round Jones, Eddie Green, Helen Lewis, 1946 . . . **130.00**
Pat & Mike, Hepburn & Tracy, 1952, 1 sheet, 27x41" . . **60.00**
Perils of the Jungle, C Beatty, 1953, 27x41" **25.00**
Place in the Sun, Taylor & Cliff **100.00**
Pursued, Ames & Jory, 1934, 14x18" **8.00**
Rebel Without a Cause, 1 sheet, 1957 . . . . **65.00**
Road to Rio, Lamour, Andrew Sisters, Hope & Crosby, 1947 **170.00**
Sands of Iwo Jima, 27x41" **75.00**
Sinbad the Sailor, 1 sheet, 1947 . . . . **100.00**
Spartacus, 1 sheet **10.00**
Stormy Weather, Lena Horne, Bill Robinson, 1 sheet, 1950 . . **35.00**
Swanee Showboat, Nina McKinney & Pigmeat **35.00**
Swiss Miss, Laurel & Hardy, Get Gay, Get Goofy, 1947 . . **80.00**
Tarzan & Leopard Woman, Weissmuller, 20x28" . . . **36.00**
Tarzan Triumphs, 3 sheet, 1943 . . . . **100.00**
The Robe, Burton, 1963, 27x41" **20.00**
Under the Red Robe, 1937, 11x18" **45.00**
Urban Cowboy, 27x41" **15.00**
Vanishing Pioneer, Holt, Powell & Kohler, 11x14" . . . **40.00**
War Gods of the Deep, V Price, 1965, color, 27x41" . . **27.00**
Pressbook, Angels in Disguise, Bowery Boys, 1949 . . **9.00**
Barefoot in the Park, Redford, Fonda **9.00**
Drowning Pool, Paul Newman **9.00**
Exorcist, Ellen Burstyn **12.00**
Gidget Goes to Rome, James Darren **15.00**
Girl Happy, Elvis **22.00**
Let's Make Love, Marilyn Monroe **20.00**
Love & Death, Woody Allen **9.00**
Misfits, Monroe, Gable, Cliff **28.00**
Monte Carlo Story, Marlene Dietrich **9.00**
Mystery of the Hooded Horsemen, Tex Ritter, 1937 . . **45.00**
Outlaw Deputy, Tim McCoy, 1937 . . . . **65.00**
Outlaw Trail, Hoot Gibson, Bob Stelle, 1943 . . . . . **30.00**
PT-109, Cliff Robertson **14.00**
Playgirls After Dark, Jane Mansfield, 6 pgs **45.00**
Red Line, 7000, James Caan **14.00**
Rollin' Plains, Tex Ritter, 1937 . . . . **45.00**
Shadow-Missing Lady, 1946 . . . . **50.00**

Smokey & the Bandit, Reynolds **14.00**
Spy Who Came in From the Cold, Richard Burton . . . **14.00**
Star Wars, Mark Hamill **23.00**
Tammy & the Doctor, Peter Fonda, Sandra Dee . . . **14.00**
Tarzan & the Great River, Mike Henry **9.00**
That's My Boy, British, Martin & Lewis, 12 pg **40.00**
Whirlwind Horseman, Ken Maynard, 1937 . . . . **65.00**
Zorro Rides Again, John Carroll, Renaldo, 1958 . . . **20.00**
Program, Big Fisherman **15.00**
Birth of a Nation, souvenir **35.00**
Cort Theatre, NY, Alice Brady, 1928 . . . . **4.00**
Dr Zhivago **10.00**
Ethel Barrymore Theatre, NYC, Irwin Shaw, 1936 . . **5.00**
Four Horsemen of the Apocalypse, Valentino, souvenir . . **30.00**
Gone With the Wind, souvenir, orig 18 pg **30.00**
How the West Was Won **25.00**
King of Kings **25.00**
Lyceum Theatre, NY, Basil Sydney, 1929 . . . . **3.50**
Porgy & Bess **35.00**
Scaramouche, Ramon Navarro, souvenir **22.00**
Scarlett Letter, Lillian Gish, souvenir **22.00**
Taming of the Shrew **15.00**
Stills, set of 41, Day the World Stood Still, 1951 . . **135.00**
Toby mug, Frank Morgan, hp by Warren, USA, 5½" . . **95.00**
William Bendix, hp by Warren, USA, 5½" **95.00**

Mt. Washington

The Mt. Washington Glass Works was founded in 1837 in South Boston Mass, but moved to New Bedford in 1869, after purchasing the facilities of the New Bedford Glass Co. Frederick S. Shirley became associated with the firm in 1874. Two years later the company reorganized and became known as the Mt. Washington Glass Co. In 1894, it merged with the Pairpoint Manufacturing Company, a small Brittania works nearby, but continued to conduct business under its own title until after the turn of the century. The combined plants were equipped with the most modern and varied machinery available, and boasted a working force with experience and expertise rival to none in blowing and cutting glass.

In addition to their fine cut glass, they are recognized as the first American company to make cameo glass; theirs developed by acid cutting. In 1885, Shirley was issued a patent to make Burmese, the yellow glassware tinged with a delicate pink blush. Another patent issued in 1886 allowed them the rights to produce Rose Amber, or amberina, a transparent ware shading from ruby to amber. Pearl Satin Ware and Peachblow, so named for its resemblence to a rosy peach skin, were patented the same year. One of their most famous lines, Crown Milano, was introduced in 1893. It was an opal glass, either free blown or pattern molded, tinted a delicate color and decorated with enameling and gilt. Royal Flemish was patented in 1894, and is considered the most rare of the Mt. Washington art glass lines. It was decorated with raised gold enameled lines dividing the surface of the ware in much the same way as lead lines divide a stained glass window. The sections were filled in with one or several transparent colors, and further decorated in gold enamel with florals, foliage, beading and medallions.

Biscuit jar, Albertine, swirled ribs, spider mums, silver lid **875.00**
Yellow to orange, w/florals, plated Pairpoint lid **400.00**
Box, Cupid, scrolls & flowers, hinged lid, 2¾", dia **85.00**
Bud vase, ruby overshot, bronze crane & dragonfly, 13½" **385.00**
Cracker jar, swirled satin, enameled & jeweled, 5" **175.00**
Jar, leaves & acorns, shaded ground, plated top, 6" **100.00**
Plate, white w/painted birds & nest **45.00**
Rose bowl, Shell & Seaweed, satin **175.00**
Salt & pepper, burmese, ribbed, in plated Tufts holder **285.00**
Salt & pepper castor, opal shakers w/florals, plated frame . . . **125.00**

Salt shaker, 5 lobed, pansies on yellow **42.00**
   Egg shape, Columbian 1893 Exhibit **85.00**

Egg shape, opaque w/brown & orange fuschia **60.00**
Egg shape, pink & blue florals **45.00**
Egg shape, pink top, enameled **60.00**
Fig, yellow & peach w/pink flowers **95.00**
White to blue, florals, mellon ribbed, orig top **35.00**
Yellow w/blue flowers **60.00**
Sugar shaker, blue w/floral enameling **300.00**
   Cut glass, egg w/lid **175.00**
   Egg shape, pewter top, enameled florals on blue **175.00**
   Egg shape, yellow enameling, orig top, 4½" **150.00**
   Tomato, acid cut w/enamel florals **180.00**
   Tankard, Butterfly & Flowers, St Louis diamond handle, 9½" **225.00**
Toothpick, burmese, tri-foil top, Diamond Quilt, 2" **320.00**
Tumbler, butterfly & flowers **25.00**
Urn, satin glass, disk ft, 13½" **650.00**
   Vase, burmese, Egyptian style handles **850.00**
   Burmese, yellow edge, 6" **375.00**
   Lava, 2 handles, 5½x6" **425.00**
   Red w/blooming branches, birds, landscape, 12", pr **300.00**
   White, bulbous w/slender neck, oval mouth, 7x3" **55.00**

Mulberry China

Mulberry china was made by many of the Staffordshire area potters from about 1830 until about the 1850s. It is a transfer printed earthenware or ironstone named for the color of its decoration, a purplish brown resembling the juice of the mulberry. Shades vary; some pieces look almost gray, with only a hint of the purple visible. Some of the patterns, Corean, Jeddo, Pelew and Formosa for instance, were also produced in Flow Blue ware. Others seem to have been used exclusively with the mulberry color.

Athens, plate, Adams, 9" **25.00**
   Plate, Adams, 10" **40.00**
Bachara, plate, Edwards, 1847, 9" **22.00**
   Plate, 10½" **32.00**
   Saucer dish **20.00**
   Sugar w/cover **100.00**
Cabul, plate, 10½" **45.00**
Canova, plate, Phillips, 7½" **16.00**
   Vegetable dish w/cover, Mayer, 1830, 10x12½" **85.00**
Castles, Pembroke, milk pitcher, Woods **27.50**
Castle Scenery, plate, Furnival, 10½" **32.00**
Corean, bowl, 14½" **125.00**
   Cake plate, 10" **40.00**
   Cup plate **40.00**
   Handleless cup & saucer, Walker, 1830 . . . . **100.00**

Pitcher, 12½" **165.00**
Plate, PW & Co, 6¾" **20.00**
Plate, 7½" **28.00**
Plate, Clementson, 9" **35.00**
Plate, PW & Co, 9¾" **35.00**
Plate, Clementson, 10½" **50.00**
Platter, PW & Co, 13½x10½" **95.00**
Cottage girl, cup & saucer, 1840 . . . . **65.00**
Cyprus, plate, 6¼" **25.00**
   Plate, 9" **40.00**
Dora, deep plate, Challinor, 10½" **25.00**
Gingham Flower, platter, 14x10½" **85.00**
Hong, plate, 10" **40.00**
   Platter, 13" **75.00**
   Vegetable w/lid, octagonal, footed, 1850 . . . . **75.00**
Jeddo, plate, Adams, 1840, 7½" **16.00**
   Plate, Adams & Son, 9¼" **30.00**
   Vegetable w/cover, Adams **100.00**
   Wash pitcher, Adams, 12" **65.00**
Kan-Su, creamer **75.00**
Kyber, milk pitcher, 1½ pt **120.00**
   Waste bowl **65.00**
Leipzig, platter, Clementson, 14" **75.00**
Neva, creamer **80.00**
Ning-Po, vegetable w/cover, baroque style **195.00**
Octagonal pitcher, 9x5½" **100.00**
Pekin, handleless cup, Wood, 1835 . . . . **20.00**
Pelew, coffee pot **175.00**
   Creamer, 5½" **85.00**
   Gravy boat **95.00**
   Handleless cup & saucer **45.00**
   Milk pitcher, rope handle, 8" **125.00**
   Posset cup **30.00**
   Sauce dish **32.00**
   Shaving mug **145.00**
   Soup plate, Challinor, 9" **25.00**
   Sugar **85.00**
   Waste bowl, slight rim wear, 3½x5" **65.00**
Peru, gravy tureen & stand **125.00**
   Soup plate, w/rim, Holdcroft, 1850s, 10¾" **35.00**
Rhone Scenery, plate, 7½" **20.00**
   Plate, 8½" **25.00**
   Service for 8, 40 pcs **1,400.00**
Rose, plate, Walker, 9¾" **24.00**
   Vegetable bowl, 8x6" **48.00**
Shapoo, handleless cup & saucer **45.00**
Swiss Scenery, plate, 10½" **40.00**
Tavoy, cup plate **30.00**
   Plate, 6¾" **25.00**
Temple, plate, PW & Co, 7" **20.00**
   Plate, PW & Co, 9¾" **30.00**
   Wash basin, 14" dia **135.00**
Tillenberg, vegetable, open **45.00**
Tivoli, handleless cup & saucer **32.00**
   Plate, Meigh, 1840, 7" **16.00**
   Plate, Meigh, 1840, 9" **20.00**
Tonquin, plate, 6" **40.00**
   Platter, Heath & Co, retangular, 12½x9½" **125.00**
Venture, vegetable dish w/cover, 1840, 8x9½" **85.00**
Vincennes, platter, 10½" **48.00**
   Platter, 15½x12½" **95.00**
   Vegetable bowl, 9¾x7½" **60.00**
Washington Vase, creamer, 5½" **75.00**
   Handleless cup & saucer **48.00**

Plate, 7″	**15.00**
Plate, 8¾″	**35.00**
Plate, PW & Co, ironstone, 9¾	**45.00**
Platter, 16″	**100.00**
Vegetable, w/cover	**145.00**

Muller Freres

Henri Muller established a factory in 1900 at Croismare, France. He produced fine cameo art glass decorated with florals, birds and insects in the Art Nouveau style. The work was accomplished by acid engraving and hand finishing. Usual marks were Muller, Muller Croismare, or Croismare, Nancy.

In 1910, Henri and his brother Deseri formed a glass works at Luneville. The cameo art glass made there was nearly all produced by acid cuttings of up to four layers, with motifs similar to those favored at Croismare. A good range of colors were used, and some pieces were gold flecked. Handles and details were sometimes applied. To commerate Lindberg's first flight, they designed a series of vases with cameo scenes featuring the monoplane. Their glass was signed Muller Freres, or Luneville.

Chandelier, grapevine brass, 1 lg w/3 sm shades, blue & wht	**695.00**
Lamp, Art Deco w/signed shade	**650.00**
Cameo wisteria shade, 19″ dia, 27″	**3,500.00**
Shades, ivory w/multi color mottling, set of 5, 6″	**275.00**
Vase, fisherman & woman, on wht, cameo, 6″	**1,400.00**
Floral on yellow, cameo, 8″	**2,000.00**
Florals, 3 acid cuttings, green, clear w/pink, 6″	**1,195.00**
Hyacinth decor on blue, cameo, Lunville, 14″	**600.00**
Lillies in ivory on green translucent, Croismare, 13¼″	**1,045.00**
Mountain scenic w/deer, multi cut & color, 11x14″	**6,000.00**
Red orchid, cameo, 3 cuttings, 8″	**825.00**

Muncie

The Muncie Clay Products Co. was founded in 1922 in Muncie, Indiana, by Charles Benham. By 1939, it had closed--- a casualty of the Great Depression. Little is known about the ware they manufactured; only an occasional piece was marked with the name of the company., Others bear only an A, 1A, 2A, or 3A. The body of the ware is heavier than that of most of their contemporaries; the style of their vases is sturdy and simple. Glazes are varied; you will find subdued matt solids, mottled effects, and a drip glaze similar to Roseville's Carnelian.

Bud vase, pink & green, 8½″	**15.00**
Pitcher, green drip over pink matt, 5½″	**25.00**
Vase, blue, incised H, 5x3″	**10.00**
Green & rose, handles, 9x5″	**35.00**
Green drip over rust, handles, 10x5″	**43.00**
Green to tan gloss, 2 handles, 6½″	**22.00**
Terra cotta w/green drip, large	**25.00**

Musical Instruments

The field of automatic musical instruments covers many different categories ranging from tiny dolls and trinkets concealing musical movements to huge organs and orchestrions which weigh many tons. Music boxes, first made in the late 18th century by Swiss watchmakers, were produced in both disc and cylinder models. The latter type employs a cylinder studded with tiny projections. As the cylinder turns, these projections lift the tuned teeth in the 'music comb' and cause a melody to play. The value of the instrument depends upon the length of the cylinder and the quality of workmanship, as well as other factors. Those in ornate cabinets or with extra features such as bells, mechanical birds, etc., often sell for much more. Units built into matching tables sell for about twice as much. While small and medium size units are still being made today, most of the larger ones date from the 19th century.

Disc type music boxes utilize interchangeable steel discs with projecting studs, which by means of a intervening 'star wheel' cause a music comb to play. There are many different variations and mechanisms. Most were made in Germany, but some were produced in the United States. Among the most popular makes are Polyphon, Symphonion, and Regina. The latter was made in Rahway, New Jersey, from about 1894 through 1917.

Player pianos were made in a wide variety of styles. Early varieties consisted of a mechanism which pushed up to a piano and played on the keyboard by means of felt-tipped fingers. These use 65 note rolls. Later models have the playing mechanisms built in. At first these also used 65 note rolls, but those produced from about 1908 until 1940 use 88 note rolls.

Coin-operated electric pianos were made in many different sizes, shapes and formats. Important makers included Link, Seebury, Hupfeld, Weber, Wurlitzer, Coinola, Cremona and others.

Reproducing pianos are deluxe versions of player pianos which incorporate expression mechanisms so that by using special rolls made for the instruments the pianos will play back the hand-recorded rolls by famous pianists. Popular makes incude Ampico, Duo-Art and Welte.

Roll operated organs were made in many different forms, ranging from table-top models to large foot pumped versions. Of the latter, the Aeolian Orchestrelle is one of the most popular.

Unless noted, prices given are for instruments in fine condition, playing properly, with cabinets or cases in excellent condition. In all instances, unrestored instruments sell for much less, as do pieces with broken parts, damaged cases, and the like. On the other hand, particularly superb examples in especially ornate case designs, and pieces which have been particularly well restored often will command more.

Accordian, rosewood, brass & MOP, 1880	**150.00**
Automaton, magician, musical movement, 20″	**3,800.00**
Band organ, Wurlitzer Style 125 w/brass trumpets	**22,000.00**
Banjo, 4 string, Gibson Mastertone, nickle or chrome plate	**700.00**
4 string, Paramount, Style A, 4 string	**550.00**
4 string, Paramount, F tenor, 19 frets w/resonator	**1,200.00**
4 string, Trujo, 1930s, carved, engraved, fancy	**600.00**
4 string, Vega Professional tenor, w/resonator, 1920s	**350.00**
4 string, Weymann, 1920s, w/resonator, fancy	**300.00**
5 string, Fairbanks Electric, engraved pearl	**500.00**
5 string, Gibson Mastertone, 1930	**2,500.00**
5 string, Orpheum, #1, 1915, fancy, pearl	**450.00**
5 string, SS Stewart #2, The Amateur, 1890s	**240.00**
5 string, SS Stewart Presentation, 1900, fancy	**1,500.00**
5 string, SS Stewart Thoroughbred Special, 1890s	**500.00**
5 string, Vega Tubaphone #9, 1919, carved, engraved	**1,200.00**
5 string, Vega Whyte Laydie #7, 1919, fancy	**1,250.00**
Tenor, Bacon & Day, Special Ed #2, 1930, w/case	**250.00**
Box, Celesta, 15½″ discs	**2,200.00**
Clarola, hand crank, QRS	**75.00**
Criterion, 10½″ discs	**1,200.00**
Cylinder w/mandolin, inlaid lid 8x23″	**900.00**
Euphonia, 12″	**800.00**
French, cylinder coin-op, hand carved case & table	**4,000.00**
German toy, litho scenes, wind-up	**75.00**
Imperial Symphonion, coin-op, 2 comb, 18¼″ discs	**1,950.00**
Italian organ grinder w/monkey, 2 children, large	**220.00**
Kalliope, 10 bells, 11″ discs	**2,500.00**
Kalliope, 6 saucer bells, 9″ discs	**1,100.00**
Keywind, inlaid case, 10½″ cylinder, 8 tune	**1,100.00**
Mermod Freres, interchangeable cylinder, handles, fancy	**3,495.00**
Mermod Freres, 12″ silver cylinder, 27x10x9″	**1,850.00**

Mermod Freres, 12 tune, 13½″ cylinder	1,300.00
Mira, console model, 15¾″ discs, restored	3,900.00
Mira, uses 6¾″ discs	900.00
Nicole, stone inlay key wind, 11″ cylinder, restored	2,150.00
Olympia, carved case, restored, 15½″ discs	2,900.00
Paillard, 2 cylinders, carved case restored	3,750.00
Polyphon, coin-op w/storage bin, restored, 24½″ discs	6,500.00
Polyphon, upright, 16 bells, 22¼″ discs	7,800.00
Polyphone upright, 19½″ disc, storage cabinet	6,900.00
Regina, 2 comb, oak cabinet, coin-op, 15½″ disks, 5′8″	2,750.00
Regina, 2 comb, serpentine case, Style 11A	3,200.00
Regina, 15½″ discs in mahogany case, restored	2,250.00
Regina, automatic changer, tall cabinet, 10¾″ discs	15,000.00
Regina, coin-op, double comb, 15½″ disc	3,100.00
Regina, oak bow front changer, 20¾″ discs	10,800.00
Regina, portable, 1897, #26391, 12½x9½x7″	1,250.00
Regina, Style 11, 15½″	2,150.00
Regina, table model, 2 comb, 15½″ discs	2,795.00
Regina, table model, 8¼″ disc	1,300.00
Regina, table model, 11″ disc	1,800.00
Regina, table, 20¾″ disc	4,500.00
Regina, upright w/12 15½″ discs & automatic changer	12,000.00
Regina, wall model w/dancing girls, 15½″ disc	2,000.00
Regina, w/changer in tall cabinet, 27″ discs	14,000.00
Regina Bell, 15½″ discs	5,495.00
Regina Hexaphone, mahogany case	5,000.00
Regina Sublima Corona #39, iron legs, coin-op	12,500.00
Regina Sublima Corona, round front parlor model	14,500.00
Stella, 168, mahogany, 17½″ discs	2,500.00
Stella, 1897 w/40 metal discs	3,000.00

Swiss, MOP & line inlay on burl, 16″ cylinder	1,200.00
Swiss L'Pee, rosewood, marquetry case, cylinder	1,395.00
Symphonion, 5¾″ discs	235.00
Symphonion, Germany, 5x7x7½″	500.00
Calliope, National, 53 note	15,000.00
Trangley, 43 note, manual or roll played	7,650.00
Trangley, 48 whistle	12,000.00
Cello, Prescott, tiger maple, 49″	435.00
Conductor's baton, ebony, in papier mache case, 16″	18.00
Dulcimer, 2 heart shape cutouts, 4 legs, 33″	145.00
Guitar, Martin D 18, 1940	900.00
Martin D 28, 1940	1,600.00
National Metal Body, 1930s, round neck	400.00
Harmonica, Brass Band, 1910	20.00
Chardomonica I, leather pouch	50.00
Mandolin, Gibson, A, 1920	300.00

Gibson, A-2, 1920	400.00
Gibson, A-2, 1925 w/case	600.00
Gibson, A-4, 1920	500.00
Gibson, F-2, 1920	700.00
Lyon & Healy, Artist model, 1920	800.00
Marxophone, orig box w/sheet music, 1912	55.00
Melodeon, Mac Nutt, Phila, carved folding legs, restored	700.00
Treat & Linsley, rosewood, Victorian	625.00
Nickelodeon, Coinola Build Up	5,000.00
Cremona Upright	3,200.00
Johnson A, stained glass	4,850.00
Peerless cabinet style 10 tune rolls	5,500.00
Seeburg, oak cabinet, art glass, rotary pump	4,400.00
Seeburg E	6,000.00
Seeburg L, oak & stained glass cabinet model	5,750.00
Seeburg-Selesta	3,000.00
Style A, oak cabinet, art glass rotary pump	4,400.00
Welte Grand	1,200.00
Wurlitzer IX	2,750.00
Orchestrion, coin-op, 9 instruments, stained glass front	6,500.00
Happy Jazz Band, Popper, Germany, 1925	7,600.00
Hupfeld Atlantic, silvered English oak case, 9′x4′x2′	6,000.00
Hupfeld Helios Class I	55,000.00
Margot barrel coin-op, stained glass, 7′	3,800.00
Philip Pianella Carona PC w/ferris wheel changer	3,800.00
Seeburg, piano, mandolin, xylophone, castanets	15,000.00
Seeburg G, piano, mandolin, 2 ranks of pipes, drums	40,000.00
Seeburg H, 4 instruments, 2 ranks pipes, ornate case	70,000.00
Organ, Aeolian Orchestrelle, 58 note, foot pump, small size	4,000.00
Aeolian Orchestrelle, 58 note, foot pump, upright, 7′	12,000.00
Aeolian Orchestrelle, Model V, oak, orig condition	5,500.00
Aeolian Orchestrelle, Style F, player, mahogany	22,000.00
Aeolian Orchestrelle, vaccum-op, self player	5,000.00
Aeolian Solo, for 2 types rolls, ornate	17,000.00
Aeolian Style F Solo, delux, self-player	15,000.00
Barrel portable, Gavioli-flute, 9 selections, 26″ wide	1,100.00
Barrel street, Poirot, 35 key, 65 flute pipes	4,750.00
Estey Vox Humana Tremolo, 1869, pump, ornate cherry wood	1,200.00
Fairground, Gavioli, 89 key	100,000.00
Gem Roller, table model, uses wooden cobs	800.00
Mason & Hamlin reed, walnut, restored	1,000.00
Merry-go-round, Wurlitzer Style 153	50,000.00
Merry-go-round, Wurlitzer Style 165	85,000.00
Molinary, street, brass, brass pipes	6,000.00
Monkey, hand-cranked, used wooden cylinder	6,000
Orguinatte table model, mechanical for paper rolls	1,100.00
Pump, early Beckwith, carved walnut, 17 stops, 86x50″	1,400.00
Pump, Gulbransesn, 1930s	1,000.00
Reed type barrel monkey	2,500.00
Ruth, 96 key, in ornate case	175,000.00
Seeburg Celesta Piano-98 pipe	7,800.00
Street, on cart	3,500.00
Vox Humana Tremold spinet w/horse hair stool, 1865	2,000.00
Piano, Aeolian Duo-Art, George Steck grand, 6 legs	3,800.00
Ampico Mason & Hamlin Model B, reproducing	40,000.00
Ampico symphonique B grand, restored	9,800.00
Ampico upright, reproducing	5,000.00
Apolo grand, fancy case, w/bench, refinished	4,250.00
Bechstein Welte-Migon grand, reproducing	8,000.00
Chickering Ampico, grand, lt walnut, restored w/rolls	8,500.00
Chickering Ampico B, William & Mary art case	19,500.00
Chickering Ampico B, mahogany, square legs, 5′4″	8,500.00
Chickering, grand, walnut, restored	9,800.00
Coinola, keyboard w/mandolin, bells, drums, coin-op	25,000.00

Fisher Ampico A, reproducing **3,500.00**
Franklin, reproducing, 5'8" **6,000.00**
G&B Barmore rosewood veneer sq back, 1851 . . . . **2,100.00**
Haynes baby grand, reproducing **6,000.00**
Kimball Recordo, grand, player, 5' **6,000.00**
Knabe Ampico A, walnut, art case, Louis XVI legs, 5'8" . . **9,000.00**
Knabe Ampico B, walnut, art case, Louis XVI legs, 5'4" . . **9,000.00**
Link, mandolin & xylophone, coin-op, ... **14,000.00**
Marshall & Wendell Ampico A, mahogany, 5'4" **9,500.00**
Mazzoletti street **1,400.00**
Melville Clark Apollo player, 1905 . . . . **4,000.00**
Ronish upright, reproducing, w/50 rolls **4,650.00**
Schiller Welte, carved burl walnut art case, player **10,000.00**
Schumann Welte, Louis XVI art case, gold leaf, player . . **13,500.00**
Seeburg, keyboard w/mandolin rail, coin-op, 10 tunes **6,000.00**
Seeburg, w/mandolin, xylophane, pipes, coin-op **12,000.00**
Steck, Duo-Art, upright, reproducing **6,000.00**
Steinway, Duo Art, grand, AR **15,000.00**
Steinway, Duo Art, grand, OR **4,500.00**
Steinway, Duo Art, grand, XR **9,800.00**
Steinway, grand, restored, 1903, 7' **12,000.00**
Steinway, square, rosewood, 1856 . . . . **15,000.00**
Stroud Duo-Art, grand, walnut, restored, 5'2" **8,500.00**
Wurlitzer, baby grand, player **6,000.00**
Wurlitzer IX, art glass front, coin-op, restored **8,500.00**
Piano roll, Aeolina 633497, Pryor, Mister Black man, 2 Step, box **6.00**
Aeolian 71479, Sloanne, Gingerbread Man, 11", in box **5.00**
Aeolian, 72945, Herbert, Whistle It, 11", in box **5.00**
Aeolian, 8628, B Jerome, Bunch of Rags, 11", w/box **5.00**
Chase & Barker, 34BC, Nevin, Day in Venice, in box **4.50**
Regal D444, Lamp, Dreamy Eyes March, 11" **5.00**
Virtuoso 5515, Wade, Hindoo Honey, 11", w/box **5.00**
Piccolo, wood, early 1900s **35.00**
Saxaphone, mechanical, plays rolls, 14" **360.00**

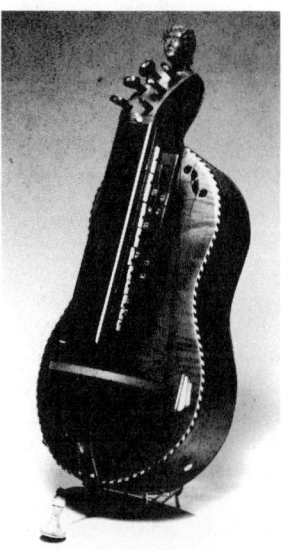

Vielle, hickory w/ivory & bone inlay **475.00**
Violin, curly maple, silver & pearl inlaid bow, wood case **350.00**
Mills Automatic **9,500.00**
Zither, German, ebony w/inlay, 1800 . . . . **150.00**

Mustache Cups

Mustache cups were popular items during the late Victorian period, designed specifically for the man with the mustache! They were made in silver plate as well as china and ironstone. Decorations ranged from simple transfers to elaborately applied and gilted florals. To properly position the 'mustache bar', special cups were desiged for the 'lefties'; these are the rare ones!

Cup w/saucer; blue w/floral spray, cherub handle **45.00**
Cobalt w/embossed florals, 'Think of Me' in gold, large **85.00**
Floral w/gold accent **95.00**
German china w/'Papa' in gold letters, 3" cup **40.00**
Pink, gold lattice, red branches, ftd" **75.00**
Salmon pink w/blue & purple florals, gold trim **42.00**
Silver plate w/floral engraving **75.00**
Violet motif on one side **30.00**
White & pink cup, wht saucer, gold rim **35.00**
Cup only; bouquets on shaded ground, gilt garlands at rim **35.00**

Floral on wht w/gold trim & lining, cobalt leaves, 3" **40.00**
Florals, relief scrolls, gold decor, ornate handle **35.00**
Souvenir, Boston, Mass., flowers around bottom, 3" **65.00**
Mug, advertising Yankee Girl Chewing Tobacco, brown pottery **145.00**

Nailsea

Nailsea is a term referring to clear or colored glass decorated in contrasting spatters, swirls or loops. These are usually white, but may also be pink or blue. It was first produced in Nailsea, England, during the late 1700's, but was made in other parts of Britain and Scotland as well. Originally used for decorative novelties only, by 1845 pitchers, tumblers and other practical items were produced in Nailsea glass.

Candlesticks, 12", pr **70.00**
Flask, clear, w/wht loops, cobalt lip, leather holder **185.00**

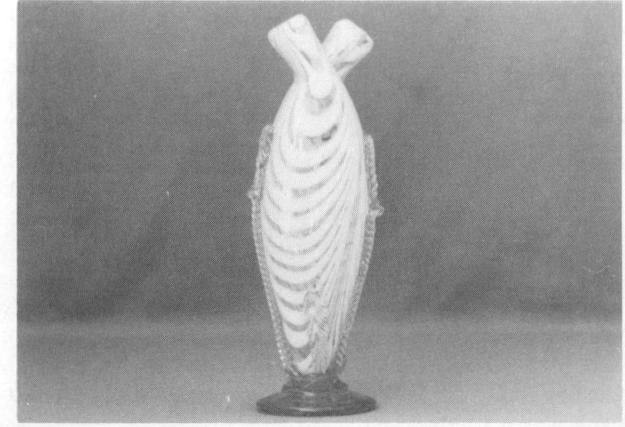

Double clear, w/white opal, 11" **110.00**

Red, white, & blue swirls, 1820s, blown 150.00
Wht loops, blue applied lip, flint, 4x7½″ 75.00
Pitcher, water, white looping 110.00
Powder horn, early 1800s 275.00
Rolling pin, blue loops 125.00
Lavender & white loops 120.00
Pink loops 120.00
Sugar shaker, pear shape, peacock w/diagonal loops 95.00
Toothpick holder 50.00
Vase, blue, 10½″ 80.00
Blue looping, 12½″ 120.00
Blue w/clear handle, 11″ 85.00
Clear handles & footed bases, 11″, pr. 145.00
Peacock blue w/wht loops, 5x4½″ 40.00
Pink satin w/loops, 8¾″ 185.00

Nakara

Nakara was an opaque glass ware made soon after the turn of the century by the C.F. Monroe Co. Though shapes were plainer and colors deeper, it was very similar to their famous Wave Crest line. Boxes of all sizes, pin trays, and dresser items of every sort were decorated with delicate hand painted florals, and 'squeeze bag' lace reserves with detailed transfer printed portraits of classical figures, birds or Victorian garbed ladies. Ormolu handles, bases and collars, and scented satin box linings added opulence to the already elegant ware.

The C.F. Monroe company closed in 1916.

Box, beige w/blue Irises, octagonal, 6½″ 550.00
Bishop's Hat, brass ormolu frame, 6½″ dia 675.00
Bishop's Hat, footed, orange w/blue florals, orig lining 675.00
Bishop's Hat, ormolu ftd base, orig lining, hp florals, 4″ 400.00
Blue floral enamel, 4x8″ 650.00
Blue florals, orig lining, 3½x4″ 495.00
Blue w/enameled florals, mirror inside, signed, 4″ sq 385.00
Blue w/floral enamel, 3½″ 365.00
Green shading to purple w/florals 350.00
Green w/lavendar base, floral lid, 3¾″ 475.00
Light green w/florals in relief, 9½x4x4″ 900.00
Pink & wht florals on blue, 3½″ 245.00
Portrait on cover, rose ground, orig lining 525.00
Rose decor, inside mirror, 5½″ 500.00
Rust w/purple florals, ormolu frame, 5½″ 650.00
Cigar box, green & pink florals 675.00
Powder jar, stand up swivel mirror & orig puff 295.00
Smoke set, ormolu holder & feet, cigarette box & match holder 650.00
Tobacco jar, Indian in full headress, signed 1,250.00
Tray, green w/pink & wht florals, scrolls, ormolu rim, 6″ dia . . 225.00
Ormolu rim & handles, Bishop's Hat, 5½″ dia. 250.00
Vase, green w/florals, 16″ 785.00

Napkin Rings

Napkin rings became popular during the late 1800s, and were made from various materials. Among the most popular were the silverplated figural types, many of which are listed below. For other types, see specific materials.

Baseball player w/bat, ready to swing, plated 180.00
Bear figural, Victorian 145.00
Bird in flight, by ring on plateaued base, Queen City 95.00
Bird on nest w/eggs, on ring, twig feet, Meriden 65.00
Bird w/long tail on stem of base leaf, engraved ring, Meriden . 100.00
Book w/clasp 80.00
Bow shape, silver plate 20.00

Boxer dog, silver plate 65.00
Boy pulling off sock, shoes along side, Derby plate 135.00
Boy riding dog by ring 215.00
Boy riding turtle w/ring on back 185.00
Bulldog guarding doghouse, silver plate 275.00
Cat pushing hoop ring, ornate 125.00
Cat w/glass eyes, plated 85.00
Chick figural by ornate ring on oval base, Rogers Smith 125.00
Chick figural, silver plate 45.00
Chinaman, hand on hip, beside basketweave ring, plated . . . 280.00
Cow grazing, sheaf of wheat ring, Wilcox 250.00
Cow w/horns beside ring, silver plate 165.00
Crane stands beside ring, oval base, sterling 250.00
Crossed rifles, ornate filigree ring, silver plate 225.00
Dachshund w/ring on back 185.00
Dog sitting beside barrel ring, silver plate 150.00
Dog sitting w/tassel, embossed oval base, Schnadig 115.00
Dog w/front paws on ring, barks at cat atop ring, silver plate . . 235.00
Dog, sitting, Simpson, Hall & Miller 65.00
Eagles carrying ring, Rogers Bros triple plate 80.00
Eagles, wings spread each side of ring, Meriden 60.00
Fans each side of ring, butterfly below, sq base, 4 ball ft 125.00
Fawn 145.00
Footed barrel, Comin Thru the Rye 35.00
French maid, hands behind back, base w/4 feet, Rogers 175.00
Frog on lily pad, silver plate 130.00
Girl playing w/dog 195.00
Girl w/big hat pushing ring, footed base 215.00
Goat pulling ring, wheels turn 150.00
Griffin on top of ring, ornate base, silver plate 195.00
Horse pulling cart, moveable wheels, Rogers & Bros 275.00
Horse, prancing, w/ring on back 185.00
Hound dog supports ring, engraved base & ring, Simpson, Hall 100.00
Kalo sterling, 4¼x5″ 35.00
Kangaroo & ostrich by ring w/boomerang 110.00
Kate Greenaway boy by ring w/grapes & leaves in relief 170.00
Kate Greenaway girl before bow tie, rectangle base, plated . . . 250.00
Kate Greenaway girl by fawn, R Strickland & Co 175.00
Kate Greenaway girl by ring on wheeled base pulled by Cupid . 225.00
Kate Greenaway girl holding dog's reins, on fancy seat 185.00
Kate Greenaway girl w/rifle in front of ring, footed base 185.00
Lady, barefoot, watering flower, silver plate 280.00
Lady in Victorian gown & large hat, pierced ring, Rogers . . . 175.00
Leaf base, coiled stem handle, Good Luck, horseshoe, Bridgeport 50.00
Lily leaf w/bud, curling stem, plated 85.00
Lily pad & flower, ring center, Rogers & Bros 55.00
Lily pad base w/branch of cherries & leaves, Toronto plate . . . 95.00
Monkey in clothes, w/dog 215.00
Oriental man w/cymbals, 6″ 85.00

Palm leaf w/flower, sterling 25.00
Peasant girl w/hands on hips, barefoot, 3½″ 150.00

Porcupine figure, silver plate, Wilcox **50.00**
Ring on butterpat, 2 pcs, floral cuttings **40.00**
Rooster figural, Pairpoint Mfg Co **65.00**
Sailor w/anchor **215.00**
Silverplate ring w/ribbed edges **15.00**
Soldiers in tunics w/horns in hands each side of ring, plated . . **165.00**
Souvenir, old Detroit scenic, gilt metal **15.00**
Squirrel eating nuts, branches of acorns, James Tufts **55.00**
Squirrel pushing ring w/squirrel on top **195.00**
Stag, ring on back, rectangle base, Meriden **165.00**
Turtle crawling w/ring on back, silver plate **125.00**
Violin leaning against elevated base, Good Times **65.00**

Nash

A. Douglas Nash founded the Corona Art Glass Co. in 1929, in Long Island, N.Y. He produced tableware, vases, flasks, etc., using delicate artistic shades and forms. After 1933, he worked for the Libbey Glass Co.

Candleholder, vertical green & blue stripe design, sgnd & #d, 3½x4″ **75.00**
Vase, flower form, gold lustre w/floral relief on stem, 5½″ **400.00**
  Gold irid, free-form allover design in relief, sgnd & #d, 7½″ **290.00**
  Gold irid, notched top rim, molded rib pattern, sgnd, 4½″ . . **145.00**
  Red opaque lustre w/irid, blue chintz pattern, sgnd, 10¼″ . . **650.00**

Netsukes

Netsukes are miniature Japanese carvings made with holes, either channeled or within the carved design that allow it to be threaded onto a waist cord and worn with the kimono. Although most are of ivory, others were made of wood, metal, porcelain or semi-precious stones. Some were inlayed or lacquered. They are found in many forms, but figurals are the most common and desirable. They range in size from 1″ to 2″, with a few up to 5″. Prime considerations are condition, workmanship, subject matter, and material.

Basket, upside down, 2 mice on top **40.00**
Buddha, standing, holding bag & scythe, 2½″ **140.00**
Cat on turtle, 2″ **36.00**
Daruma, pop out eyes, gold lettered base **175.00**
Devil head, pop eyes, 2½″ **140.00**
Devil with hammer, 2½″ **145.00**
Dog, recumbent, 2½″ **110.00**
Dogs, pair, realistic type, 2½″ **140.00**
Dragon **95.00**
Dragon, coiled tail, golden color, 2½″ **100.00**
Father Time w/pitchfork & incense burner, polychrome, 2″ . . . **50.00**
Frog w/frog on back, 2″ **40.00**
Hand, holding devil, 2½″ **135.00**
Head, large, w/hands crossed in front of beard **140.00**
Horse, recumbent, 2″ **40.00**
Horse, recumbent, carved wood **160.00**
Horse w/ring, 2½″ **140.00**
Man, bearded, arm around water buffalo, 1½″ **110.00**
Man clipping toenails, 2½″ **300.00**
Man, frog on back, 2½″ **145.00**
Man holding lantern, 2″ **40.00**
Man holding rabbit by the ears, sack in other hand, 2″ **50.00**
Man in robe w/pipe, sitting on log, monkey along side, color . . **100.00**
Man, led by donkey, 2½″ **140.00**
Man loading basket on water buffalo, 2″ **40.00**
Man looking at horse's hoof, 2″ **40.00**
Man mounting horse, 2″ **40.00**

Man on rope coil w/hammer & sack, polychrome **295.00**
Man riding bull, 2½″ **140.00**
Man sawing huge log in half, 2″ **40.00**
Man sitting, arms enfolding snarling tiger **125.00**
Man sitting, beating durms w/drumsticks **40.00**
Man sitting on crab, wearing kimono, hands over face **110.00**
Man standing, wearing robes, w/pipe to ear **110.00**
Man stooping, faces on back, 2½″ **335.00**
Man stooping, with two snakes, 2½″ **140.00**
Man, swivel head, 2½″ **145.00**
Man with fan, polychrome, 2½″ **295.00**
Man with kneeling boy, fish & basket, polychrome, 2½″ **85.00**
Man with snake & pipe, pop eyes, 2½″ **150.00**
Man wrestling huge dragon **125.00**
Mice, playing in rice bale, 1800s, ex **200.00**
Monkey, riding turtle, 2″ **40.00**
Monkey, sitting, holding sm monkey w/outstretched arm **35.00**
Mythical animal w/hooves, 2½″ **140.00**
Mythical creature, half dragon, half horse, recumbent **50.00**
Mythical creature, w/elephant trunk, lion mane & tail, 2″ **60.00**
Mythical dog, 2½″ **140.00**
Mythical dog & rabbit, 2½″ **130.00**
Mythical dogs, two, 2½″ **135.00**
Mythical lion/dog, 2½″ **145.00**
Mythical lion/dog w/elephant trunk nose, 2½″ **135.00**
Octopus w/3 turtles & rat, 2½″ **300.00**
Old man w/hammer, small horse, 2½″ **150.00**
Old man w/turtle shell on back, 2½″ **170.00**
Old woman w/fangs, 2″ **80.00**
Rabbits, two, one coming out of basket, 2½″ **120.00**
Rat catcher, 2½″ **160.00**
Rat on rope barrel, 2nd nose pops out side **140.00**
Rats, three, on log, 2½″ **140.00**
Rats, two, one entwined in rope, 2½″ **110.00**
Samo wrestler, polychrome,, 2½″ **110.00**
Samurai, carrying large bell, sgnd **375.00**
Snuff bottle, intricate carving, round, 2½″ **220.00**
  King & boy in bas-relief, etched birds **120.00**
  Nut tree branch figural, 2½″ **150.00**
Tasmanian Devil, 2½″ **95.00**
Toad, small toad on back **35.00**
Turtle, 2½″ **130.00**
Twelve faces, 2½″ **300.00**
Warrior, standing w/sword & brimmed hat, hand to hat **65.00**
Wild boar, 2″ **50.00**
Woman & boy, walking, minimal color, 2″ **120.00**
Woman & child carrying huge vase up stairs **50.00**
Woman, feeding Kiwi, standing on wicker basket, 2″ **40.00**
Woman, semi-nude, washing hair, boy & dog **135.00**
Woman, w/closed fan, polychrome, 2½″ **295.00**
Wrestlers, two, standing side by side, 2″ **40.00**

New Martinsville

The New Martinsville Glass Co. took its name from the town in West Virginia where it began operations in 1901. In the beginning years, pressed tablewares were made in crystal as well as colored opal glass. Considered an innovator, the company was known for their imaginative applications of the medium in creating lamps made entirely of glass, vanity sets, figural decanters and novelty figurines. The company was purchased by Viking Glass in 1944. It is still in production; current wares are marked Viking or Rainbow Art.

Baby bear **45.00**

Baby bear & cart	**75.00**
Basket, Janice, lt blue, 13x10″	**60.00**
Bookends, cornucopia, pair	**25.00**
Elephant, pair	**120.00**
Harp, pair	**45.00**
Squirrel, pair	**55.00**
Bride's bowl, peachblow, ribbed, fluted edge	**95.00**
Candleholder, double, fan shape, amber, pair	**35.00**
Candlesticks, Radiance, azure blue, pair	**95.00**
Chicks	**42.50**
Cruet, Janice	**18.00**
Cup & saucer, Radiance, blue	**10.00**
Duck, amberina, 5″	**38.00**
Hen	**50.00**
Mama bear	**125.00**
Mustard, Janice, w/cover & spoon	**25.00**
Nautilus shell	**24.50**
Pig, large	**500.00**
Pitcher, Radiance, red	**160.00**
Police dog	**45.00**
Powder jar, coach, covered	**35.00**
Rabbit, lt blue, 6½″	**40.00**
Rooster, Epic, red, 9½″	**65.00**

Salt shaker, Many Petals, opaque, 1905	**25.00**
Swan, emerald, 7½″	**20.00**
Swan, Janice, 11″	**28.00**
Janice, cobalt head & neck, 12″	**52.00**
Tumbler, Radiance, red	**12.00**
Vase, cornucopia, crystal, 6″	**38.00**
Wolfhound	**75.00**

Newcomb

The Newcomb College of New Orleans, La., established a pottery in 1895 to provide the students with first hand experience in the fields of art and ceramics. Using locally dug clays---red and buff in the early years; white burning by the turn of the century---potters were employed to throw the ware which the ladies of the college decorated.

Until about 1910, a glossy glaze was used on ware decorated by slip painting or incising. After that, a matt glaze was favored. Soft greens and blues were used almost exclusively, and the decorative themes were chosen to reflect the beauty of the South. 1930 marked the end of the matt glaze period, and the art pottery era.

Various marks used by the pottery include an N within a C, sometimes with HB added to indicate a 'hand-built' piece. The potter often incised his initials into the ware, and the artists were encouraged to sign their work. Among the most well known artists were Sadie Irvine, Henrietta Bailey, and Fannie Simpson.

Bud vase, geometric floral, 6½″	**335.00**
Paperweight, green, 3½″	**400.00**
Pitcher, blue gloss w/incised blue & wht flowers, Ryan, 6″	**950.00**
Blue w/green bands, SI, 3½″	**300.00**
Plaque, matt gray w/blue morning glories, Bailey, framed, 9x12″	**1,450.00**
Tile, blue morning glories, artist sgnd S, 6x10″	**1,300.00**
Vase, black glaze, experimental, 1910, 5″	**150.00**
Blue matt w/floral, Simpson, 9x5″	**450.00**
Blue w/dark blue banding at rim, florals, Irvine, 5″	**375.00**
Blue w/pink & green incised floral, Bailey, 5½x6″	**335.00**
Blue w/pink floral, 8½″	**600.00**
Blue w/wht berries, 5½″	**475.00**
Blue w/wht floral, 5½″	**475.00**
Blue w/wht flowers, green leaves, Simpson, 5x5½″	**450.00**
Blue w/yellow iris, Irvine, bowl shape, 8x4″	**300.00**
Decorated bulbous base, stems trail to top, Irvine, 8½″	**695.00**
Dimpled, blended gr, lavendar & rose, 4x2¾″	**230.00**
Floral, blue, 3″	**225.00**
Floral, handles, Bailey, 5x4½″	**275.00**
Geometric decor, 6½″	**380.00**
Geometric hi-gloss, JM, 6x2″	**450.00**
Green hi-gloss, no decor, gourd shape, 4x2″	**50.00**
Incised trees & bars, Leona Nicholson, 1903, 10½″	**2,100.00**
Matt green drip over blue, JM, #237, 5x3″	**120.00**
Moss & moon, Irvine, 4½x5½″	**500.00**
Relief snowdrops w/gr stems on blue, paper label, FES, 6¾″	**650.00**

Stylized floral, sgnd GLE, 4″	**350.00**
Three color blue w/scenic, Bailey, 8x4″	**550.00**
Three color blue, Irvine, 5x3″	**400.00**
Tree w/moss & moon, Irvine, 6″	**600.00**

New Hall

The New Hall Company was established in the early 1780s in the Shelton district of England. During its productive years the number of partners who were attached to the firm often varied from the original eleven. In the early years, they produced hard paste dinnerware typically decorated with simple floral sprays, often assigning a number rather than a name to their patterns. By 1812, a bone china body was favored and styles revised to suit the fashion. Decorations became more elaborate. Much of the ware was unmarked and is often attributed to Worcester. Occasionally a piece was marked New Hall within a double circle. Production ceased by 1835.

Box w/lid, cream, fireplace scene, Mr Pecksniff	**30.00**
Cup & saucer, early 1800s	**50.00**
Dish, black & gray florals, #241, 8½″ dia	**120.00**
Sugar w/cover, gilt decor, 1790, 4″ dia	**220.00**
Tea bowl & saucer, 1770	**135.00**
Typical decor, 1790	**82.50**
Teapot, silver form mkd, 1770s	**575.00**
Waste bowl, 1800s, 8″	**175.00**

Newspapers

Newspapers are primarily collected for their news content. Those reporting important political or military events in the history of our country are usually of greater value.

Bangor Jeffersonian, April 18, 1865, 1st report Lincoln assassination **66.00**
  July 14, 1863, Battle of Gettysburg **34.00**
Boston Chronicle, Aug 29, 1768, rebellion in Philadelphia **50.00**
  May 23-26, 1768, articles on vegetation, hogs **39.00**
  July 4, 1768, Franklin & electricity **75.00**
  Oct 31, 1768, Vol 1, #47 . . . . **25.00**
Boston Daily Journal, Feb 2, 1849, gold discovered in California **17.00**
Boston Weekly Globe, Aug 11, 1885, burial President Grant **4.00**
Buffalo Commercial Advertiser, April 27, 1865, Lincoln assassination **38.00**
Charleston Daily Courier, 1862, Confederate States of America . **44.00**
Chicago Daily Times, April 30, 1945, Mussolini's death **7.50**
Chicago Daily Tribune, Nov 3, 1948, Dewey Defeats Truman . . **200.00**
Columbian Register, Connecticut, June 5, 1819, Seminole War, 4 pg **9.00**
Connecticut Gazette, April 26, 1782, anti-taxation **75.00**
  June 28, 1792, Paine's Rights of Maine, 4 pg **25.00**
Connecticut Journal, Sept 18, 1793, New French Constitution, 4 pg **30.00**
Daily Alta Californian, May 22, 1851, Democratic state convention **48.00**
Daily Index, Nevada, Aug 19, 1881, Garfield's condition, 4 pgs . **22.00**
Daily Puget Sound Courier, Washington Territory, May 20, 1874 **30.00**
Democrat Union, Dec 12, 1848 . . . . **5.00**
Detroit Free Press, June 5, 1864, General Custer **12.00**
  March 3, 1864, war news **8.50**
  March 29, 1864, Paducah captured by rebels **8.00**
Edinburgh Evening Courant, 1728, decorative woodcut title pg . **28.00**
Freeman's Journal, Philadelphia, Nov 14, 1781, letter, Silas Deane **89.00**
Harper's Weekly, Feb 21, 1863, Tom Thumb Gets Married **43.00**
  Oct 12, 1878 . . . . **10.00**
Illustrated London News, 1899 . . . . **4.00**
Illustrated Police News, Oct 13, 1888, Billy the Kid, Jack the Ripper **32.00**
Independent Chronicle, Boston, Oct 16, 1777 . . . . **225.00**
  Boston, Sept 28, 1780 . . . . **135.00**
Kenosha Telegraph, Wisconsin, 1865, Lincoln assassination, 4 pg **34.00**
London Gazette, Aug 17-20, 1668, French garrisons in Germany **17.00**
  Jan 14, 1666, Turks march on Persian front, 1 pg **20.00**
  May 7-11, 1668, Don Juan expected in Bruges **17.00**
  Nov 21-25, 1667, Spanish Armada, 1 pg **19.00**
London News, 1937, Coronation, illustrated, color plates **15.00**
Louisiana Advertiser, New Orleans, August 16, 1823 . . . . **26.00**
Loyal Protestant & True Domestic Intelligencer, 1682 . . . . **48.00**
Massachusetts Spy, August 23, 1781, famous paper by Isaiah Thomas **45.00**
  Dec 23, 1773, masthead by Revere, Boston Tea Party **350.00**
  May 26, 1861, Col. Ellsworth's funeral, 8 pg **13.50**
  June 30, 1861, map of war in Virginia, 8 pg **9.00**
  Feb 25, 1863, Sherman's march unopposed, 8 pg **11.00**
  May 29, 1864, Gen. Cook raids southwest Virginia **11.00**
  Feb 18, 1865, Sherman's capture of Branchville, 8 pg **11.00**
  April 15, 1865, Lincoln Assassination, front page **800.00**
  April 26, 1865, Lincoln Assassination, blk border **42.00**
New York Independent, Jan 8, 1863, Emancipation Proclamation **35.00**
New York Mercantile Advertiser, 1816, Jefferson & Adams death **34.00**
New York Mirror Weekly Journal, Nov 10, 1838, literature, fine arts **9.00**
New York Times, July 1969, Men Walk On The Moon, ... **15.00**
  Sept 1, 1864, Ft Morgan Surrender, 8 pgs **11.00**
New York Tribune, Dec 22, 1862, Battle of Prairie Grove, Arkansas **11.00**
  July 30, 1862, Missouri Union Victory, 8 pg **9.00**
  Nov 28, 1863, Great Chattanooga Victory, 8 pg **9.50**
Newark Daily Advertiser, April 18, 1865, Lincoln Assassination, 4 pg **65.00**
Pennsylvania Chronicle & Advertiser, June 22-29, 1776 . . . . . . **66.00**

1769, fine masthead **48.00**
Pennsylvania Gazette, Oct 6, 1784, state legislature news, ads . . **20.00**
Philadelphia Inquirer, Nov 7, 1861, civil war **5.00**
Portsmouth Oracle, Jan 21, 1809, the Enforcement Act **28.00**
Press Telegram, Long Beach, Cal., Nov 22, 1963, Kennedy Slain **800.00**
Providence Gazette, 1772, fine masthead w/royal coat of arms . . **24.00**
Richmond Examiner, Dec 31, 1862, Jefferson Davis Proclamation **30.00**
Richmond Whig, Jan 31, 1865, end of slavery, 4 pgs **25.00**
The Allentown Democrat, 1867 . . . . **5.00**
The Evening Fire-Side or Weekly Intelligence, April 20, 1805 . . **11.00**
The Guardian, 1713, Sir Richard Steele **17.00**
The Rambler, 1751, Dr. Samual Johnson **12.00**
The Sentinel of Freedom, Jan 18, 1862, death of John Tyler, 4 pg **17.00**
The Village Herald, June 2, 1830, political articles **12.50**
The War, NY, May 4, 1813, news of War of 1812 . . . . **30.00**
The World, 1755, Moore, Walpole & Chesterfield **3.50**
  London, 1756 . . . . **10.00**
Utica Telegraph, NY, April 7, 1865, early report end of war . . . **59.00**
Washington Democrat, Dec 17, 1864, President's message **49.00**

Niloak

Benton, Arkansas, was an area rich with natural clay, high in quality and easily accessible. During the last half of the 1800s, a dozen potteries flourished there, but by 1898, the only one remaining was owned by Charles Dean Hyten. In 1909 he began to experiment, trying to preserve in his finished ware the many colors of the native clay. By 1912, he had perfected a method that produced the desired effect. He obtained a U.S. Patent for his handcrafted Niloak Mission pottery, characterized by swirling layers of browns, blues, red and buff clays. Only a few early pieces were glazed both inside and out; these are extremely rare. After the process was perfected, only the interior was glazed. The ware was marked Niloak, the backward spelling of Kaolin, a type of fine porcelain clay. No sooner had production began than the pottery burned. But Hyten rebuilt, and added a stoneware line called Eagle Pottery. Hywood, an inexpensive novelty ware, was introduced in 1929---an attempt to boost sales during the onset of the depression years. Until 1934, when the management changed hands, the line was marked Hywood-Niloak. After that, Hywood no longer appeared on the ware.

Hyten left the pottery in 1941; in 1946 the operation closed.

Ashtray, Mission Ware, swirl **60.00**
Bowl; Mission Ware, swirl, 3x10″ **55.00**
  Mission Ware, swirl, red, cream, blue, green, 5x2¾″ **25.00**
  With turtle flower frog **39.00**
Candleholder; Mission Ware, swirl, 2″ **15.00**
  Mission Ware, swirl, pr, 7″ **115.00**
  Mission Ware, swirl, 8½″, pr **225.00**
  Mission Ware, swirl, 12″ **60.00**
Ewer; hi-gloss brown, relief mk, 6½″ **18.00**
  Winged eagle on side, rose & green, semi-glaze, Hywood, 10″ **30.00**
Figural; canoe, white matt, 7½″ **30.00**
  Elephant, white, sgnd **25.00**

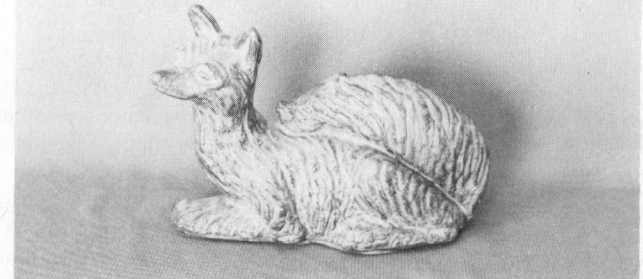

Fox, rare glaze, tan **60.00**

Frog **15.00**
Lady, in long gown, 10″ **75.00**
Polar bear, w/basket, matt, 3½x5½x5″ **33.00**

Jug, maroon **65.00**
Juice set, square pitcher & 6 cups **60.00**
Lamp, Mission Ware, swirl, w/paper shade **200.00**
Paperweight, rabbit, paper label, 2½″ **25.00**
Pitcher; square, blue, stylized relief flowers, hi-gloss, 7″ **20.00**
With eagle, 10″ **20.00**
Planter; bear, 3″ **25.00**
Bird, spread wings, rose/green **20.00**
Bull dog, lying **25.00**
Camel, white & brown, 3½″ **25.00**
Camel, white & red, 3½″ **25.00**
Camel, 2-hump, reclining, tan **14.00**
Deer, pink/gray, 9″ **38.00**
Deer, rose/green, 9″ **39.00**
Elephant, hi-gloss pink, 12″ **42.00**
Elephant, matt pink, 6½″ **30.00**
Fox **11.00**
Parrot, 6″ **25.00**
Rabbit, rose matt **25.00**

Rabbits, pink & green **35.00**
Seal, brown matt, 5″ **25.00**
Seal, white matt, 5″ **25.00**
Squirrel, cobalt blue, 6″ **34.00**
Squirrel, white & green, 6″ **32.00**

Stork, matt, 8″ **25.00**
Swan, cobalt blue, 7″ **28.00**
Swan, pink hi-gloss, 7″ **18.00**
Wooden shoe, pink & green, 5″ **8.00**
Punch bowl & cups, Mission Ware, swirl **1,500.00**
Sugar & creamer, rose w/green shade **32.00**
Vase; blue, wing side handle, melon rib, bulbous base, 6x5″ . . . **11.00**
Green, scalloped, bulbous, melon rib bottom, handle, 6½″ . . . **11.00**
Hywood, hand thrown, applied handles, 6″ **30.00**
Jug, Mission Ware, imp mk, 2½x5½″ **57.00**

Mission Ware, swirl, 4½″ **35.00**
Mission Ware, swirl, 8¼″ **80.00**
Mission Ware, swirl, 9½″ **100.00**
Mission Ware, swirl, 4x6″ **38.00**
Mission Ware, swirl, 5x4″ **45.00**
Mission Ware, swirl, bud, 6″ **52.00**
Mission Ware, swirl, bud, 9½″ **60.00**
Mission Ware, swirl, brown, blue & cream, 6″ **50.00**
Mission Ware, swirl, brown, tan, green & blue, 3x4″ **31.00**
Mission Ware, swirl, bulbous bottom, long flaring neck, 9¼″ . **95.00**
Mission Ware, swirl, floor vase, 18x8″ dia **250.00**
Mission Ware, swirl, incised block letters, 5″ **35.00**
Mission Ware, swirl, marbleized brown w/blue, 6¾″ **55.00**
Mission Ware, swirl, rare 'red' & brown swirl, 10x4½″ **90.00**
Mission Ware, swirl, wide flare, 10″ **85.00**
Mission Ware, swirl, wide cupped rim, 9″ **75.00**
Winged handles, tan to green matt, mkd, sticker, 7″ **28.00**

Nippon

Nippon generally refers to Japanese wares made during the period from 1891 to 1921, although it was also used to a much lesser extent on later wares. Nippon, meaning Japan, identified the country of origin to comply with American importation restrictions. After 1921, 'Japan' was an acceptable alternative. The term does not imply a specific type of product, and may be found on items other than porcelains. In the listings that follow, the numbers refer to these specific marks:

1. China E-OH   5. Rising Sun
2. M in wreath   6. Royal Kinran
3. Cherry blossom   7. Maple leaf
4. Double T Diamond in circle

Ash tray, scenic w/swans, crown mk **75.00**
Allover color, ships & trees, orange & lavender, 5″ dia, green #2 **75.00**
Hand painted hoo bird, enamel beading, #2 . . . . **85.00**
Pine cone decor, 4″ wide, #2 . . . . **85.00**
With match box, hp Fatima cigarettes on each side, #2 . . . . **140.00**
Yellow w/horses, riders & dog, 3 rests, 4¾″ dia, #2 . . . . . . **125.00**
Basket, butterfly w/gold decor **30.00**

Chestnuts, wavy edge & raised beading, #2 . . . . **80.00**
Pink & blue morning glories, gold thistles & handle, #2 . . . . . **55.00**
Pink rose design w/gold, cobalt trim **78.00**
Sailboat scene, enameled decor, handled, 9″ long **125.00**
Berry set, cobalt trim, pink & red roses decor, 6 pc **150.00**
Dark shaded ground, wht swans decor, 7 pc **395.00**
Octagonal, swan scene w/raised border, 6 pc, Torii Nippon . . . **75.00**
Scenic, beading, gold, sgnd, 5 pc **110.00**
White w/gold outlined leaves & flowers, 7 pc, #2 . . . . **220.00**
White w/heavy raised gold band, 7 pc **135.00**
Bouillon cup & saucer, wht w/violet interior decor, #2 . . . . **30.00**
Bowl, 5-sided, pears & flowers decor, footed, 8″, #2 . . . . **110.00**
6 panels w/house & meadow scene, scallops, gold trim, 10″ dia, #2 **215.00**
Allover roses, heavy gold, 10″ **110.00**
Basketweave, molded acorns, 7¼″ dia, #2 . . . . **110.00**
Bisque finish peanut shell, peanut & leaves inside, 8″, #2 . . . **140.00**
Bisque windmill scene, 3 jeweled handles, #2 . . . . **115.00**
Bisque, scene w/house, trees & water, 2 handles, 8″ dia, #2 . **135.00**
Blue Wedgwood decor, wht w/pink roses interior, #2 . . . . . . **280.00**
Blue w/roses, gold trim, 10″ wide, #2 . . . . **170.00**
Brazil nut relief molded decor, beaded handles, 9½″ **160.00**
Cherry blossom decor, pedestal **115.00**
Doll face pattern, 5¾″ dia, blue #5 . . . . **90.00**
Gold grapes & leaves decor, 4x7″ dia, #2 . . . . **85.00**
Gold roses & scrolls, handled, 2x9″ dia, #2 . . . . **125.00**
Gold w/blk rim & hp roses, 6½″ dia, #2 . . . . **85.00**
Gold w/red roses, scalloped, 14″ **175.00**
Grape decor in center, gold trim & beading, 8½″ dia, #2 . . . **115.00**
Hand painted floral interior, 10″ dia, Wedgwood, #2 . . . . . . **319.00**
Hunting scene border, 9″ dia **195.00**
Moriage trees, relief gold leaf border, on pedestal **225.00**
Orchid floral decor, gold border w/raised beading, 9″ dia, blue #7 **160.00**
Peanuts molded in relief, slipwork on ft, 7½″ dia, #2 . . . . . . **160.00**
Red w/orange flowers, handled, gold trim, 9″ dia, #2 . . . . . . **120.00**
Red/wht/cream, heavy gold, ruffled rim, 3′, 6½″ dia, blue #7 . **90.00**
Scenic w/trees & water, gold handles, 12″ dia, #2 . . . . **185.00**
White w/pink roses, 11¼″ dia, #2 . . . . **165.00**
Windmill scene, 3 beaded handles, 6″, #2 . . . . **55.00**
Yellow w/scenic decor, handled, 10″ **75.00**
Box, casket shape, bisque scene of small house, covered, 5″, #2 **150.00**
Heart shape, gold & turquoise beading, heart medallion, green #7 **85.00**
Heart shape, rose decor, covered, sgnd **40.00**
Large poppy decor, gold beaded rim, covered, ftd, 6″ dia, blue #7 **95.00**
Butter dish, geisha scene, red & gold, #2 . . . . **70.00**
Red roses w/gold beading, plate is 7½″ wide, #2 . . . . **135.00**
Cake plate, scenic, 2 handled, 12″ **65.00**
Shrines & bridge scene, gold w/red border, 10¼″ dia, #2 . . **135.00**
Cake set, floral decor, 7-pc, sgnd **50.00**
Scene of house by lake, 7-pc, #2 . . . . **120.00**
Turquoise w/flying egrets, gold & jeweled border, 7-pc **225.00**
White w/bluebird decor, 7-pc, #2 . . . . **220.00**
Calling card tray, turned-in sides, 2 rose medallions, 7½″, blue #7 **200.00**
Candlestick, blue w/gold beading, pelicans, 6¼″, S&K in diamond **60.00**
Geometric pattern, 8″, #2 . . . . **140.00**
Moriaga, handled, 7½″ **160.00**
Red & blue enamel decor, 9″ **165.00**
Red floral trim, gold design & beading, 9½″ #2 . . . . **95.00**
Scenic w/boat & trees, 6½″, #2 . . . . **110.00**
Candlesticks, blue w/floral medallions, gold trim, 8″, #2 pair . **290.00**
Candlesticks, blue w/wht Wedgwood decor, 8″, #2 pair **235.00**
Overall sunset scene, brown rim, 5″, blue #7 pair **250.00**
Celery dish, boat shape, blue Wedgewood decor, 7½″, #2 . . **280.00**
Scenic w/trees & sailboats, rolled ends, 9″, #2 . . . . **80.00**
Celery set, blue flowers & butterflies, 7-pc, #2 . . . . **50.00**

Open handle dish, pink roses w/gold decor, 7-pc **75.00**
Wht w/heavy gold band, 13″ tray, sq ends, 7-pc **95.00**
Wht w/pink flowers, gold trim, 13″ long dish, 6 salts, #2 . . . **135.00**
Cheese & cracker plate, miniature, hp morning glories, gold border **65.00**
Cheese & cracker set, pink roses, gold outlined **60.00**
Chocolate pot, all over scenic, cobalt & gold **110.00**
Bulbous bottom, allover roses, gold, 10½″ **155.00**
Butterfly decor w/gold trim **75.00**
Green ground w/red & pink roses, moriage **250.00**
Green w/large floral center medallions, 11″, blue #7 . . . . . . **240.00**
Purple wisteria decor, 10″, #2 . . . . **225.00**
Red/yellow/purple flowers, cobalt & gold trim, 8½″, #2 . . . . **235.00**
Wht w/pink florals, gold trim, 9½″, blue #5 . . . . **150.00**
Wild rose decor, gold trim **185.00**
Chocolate set, cobalt, geisha girl, 9-pc, Torii Nippon mk **295.00**
Cream w/raised gold & floral, 9-pc, 10″ pot, #2 . . . . **280.00**
Geisha girl decor, much gold, Royal Kaga mk **250.00**
Green w/pink florals, relief molding, 10-pc **165.00**
Mottled green w/large purple orchids, 9-pc, #2 . . . . **395.00**
Orange w/wht poppies, 7 pc **300.00**
Purple & red fruit decor, heavy gold trim, 9-pc, #2 . . . . **350.00**
Scene w/oriental people in field, orange trim, 13-pc, pagoda mk **285.00**
Wht w/band of pastel flowers, gold trim, 11-pc, blue #5 . . . . **325.00**
Wht w/blk scenic, gold trim, 9-pc, #2 . . . . **260.00**
Wht w/bluebirds in flight decor, 11-pc, #2 . . . . **275.00**
Wht w/floral borders, gold trim, 10-pc **130.00**
Wht w/florals, gold traced, 13 pc **115.00**
Wht w/ivy bands, raised gold, 30-pc **405.00**
Wht w/pink poppies, hexagon 11″ pot, 13-pc, Imperial Nippon mk **350.00**

Child's set, Googly Eye, 3 pc **200.00**
Cider set, 5-pc, grape design **165.00**
Cigarette holder, tumbler shape, blue bisque w/owl in flight, 3½″, #2 **160.00**
Coaster, scene of sailboat on water, 3¾″ dia, #2 . . . . **25.00**
Coffee pot, individual, cream w/scene of man on camel, pyramids, #2 **125.00**
Coffee server, individual, Arabian scene, blue #7 . . . . **115.00**
Coffee set, lt blue, wht bands w/lacy blk decor, 13-pc **185.00**
Compote, butterflies decor, floral panels, flower frog cover, 10″ . **75.00**
Grapes & gold decor, 6″ dia including handles, #2 . . . . **75.00**
Moriage **250.00**
Wht w/hp roses, 6½x8½″ dia, #2 . . . . **120.00**
Condensed milk container, wht w/blue forget-me-nots, 6″, #2 . **140.00**
Condiment set, florals, gold decor, 4-pc, spoke mk **40.00**
Scene w/blue sky & wht egrets, 4-pc, #2 . . . . **145.00**
Cookie jar, gold w/red roses, cobalt trim, 7½″, #2 . . . . **325.00**
Roses & buds decor, cobalt & gold trim, ftd, magenta #7 . . . **280.00**
Scenic, melon ribbing, cobalt & gold, 3 ft **300.00**
Wide cobalt trim, scenic w/swans, jeweled **275.00**

Covered dish, 3-color pagoda decor, w/base & ladle, #2 .... **70.00**
Cracker jar, all over decor red roses, heavy gold, handles..... **145.00**
   Cobalt trim, pink & lilac flowers **175.00**
   Pink wild rose decor **75.00**
   Red/yellow/pink roses, double handle, 9″ wide, #2 .... **165.00**
   Wht w/violets, gold trim, handled, #5 .... **65.00**
Cream & sugar, moriaga dragon decor, mk of Kugawa **50.00**
   Oriental village scene, gold overlay florals **90.00**
   Windmill, trees, lake, gold decor **30.00**
Cucumber dish & underplate **65.00**
Cup & saucer, pedestal cup, blk & gold w/flowers, #7 .... **25.00**
   Wedgwood landscape, green ground **225.00**
Demitasse set, flower basket decor, blue/gold trim, 9-pc, blue #5 **290.00**
Desk set, pastel scene w/floral overlay, 4-pc, #2 .... **185.00**
   Scenic w/floral medallions, 10-pc, #2 .... **550.00**
Dish, pine cone decor, footed & handled **65.00**
   With center well, on ped, poppies, gold, 2x10 .... **45.00**
Doll, boy baby, 4½″ long, incised Nippon **130.00**
   Kewpie-style, moveable arms, painted suit, 3½″, incised Nippon **175.00**
Dresser set, pink roses decor w/gold outline, 5-pc, green #7 .. **175.00**
Dresser tray, pink & red rose decor **125.00**
Dutch shoe figural, green w/scattered flowers, 3¼″ long, #2 .. **160.00**
Egg cup, blown out doll face, signed...................... **85.00**
   Copper & violet lustre, 3½″, #2 .... **60.00**
   Delft blue, Royal Somitake mk......................... **28.00**
Egg warmer, pink roses, orange & purple flowers, w/gold, 4-egg, #2 **140.00**
   Scenic w/brown enamel trim, 4-egg, w/cap, #2 .... **150.00**
Ewer, gold medallions w/roses, ribbed, gold beading, 7½″, blue #2 **275.00**
   Green w/portrait, gold beading, reverse has rose medallion, 12″,#2 **550.00**
   Green w/yellow & purple orchids, moriage trim, 12″, #2 .... **340.00**
   Red & pink rose decor, cobalt blue & gold trim, 9½″, #2 .. **250.00**
   Red w/roses decor, much gold, 9″..................... **225.00**
   Roses in center, moriage green & cream trim, 8″, Royal Moriye mk **290.00**
   Roses, cobalt w/gold handle, spout & ped, 9″ **200.00**
   Tapestry ground w/4-color roses, bulbous, 7¼″, green #7 ... **595.00**
Ferner, Egyptian motifs w/3 molded Egyptian heads, #2 ...... **340.00**
   Hexagonal, floral decor w/gold trim, 7¾″ wide, #2 .... **195.00**
   Hexagonal, panels w/lake scene, 7″ wide, blue #7 .... **175.00**
   Square, lake scene, matt finish, ftd, 7″ wide, #2 .... **190.00**
   Triangular, green w/scene of horse & plow, 8″ wide, #2 .... **200.00**
Figurine, bird, rare, green #2 .... **120.00**
Ginger jar, pink w/round medallion decor, wht beading, 9″, #2 **315.00**
Gravy boat & underliner, allover blue & gold scrolls & beads... **95.00**
Hair receiver, red w/overlaid gold & roses, ftd, 4½″ wide, #2... **90.00**
   Wht w/many pink & yellow roses, 5″ wide, #2 .... **75.00**
   Wht w/rose decor, gold trim, ftd **22.00**
Hair receiver & powder bowl, palm trees decor **55.00**
Hairpin holder, pink w/gold beading & flowers, 3″, #2 .... **120.00**
Hatpin holder, pink flowers, gold beading, 5″, #2 .... **27.00**
   Airplane decor.................................... **110.00**
   Hanging heart shape, gold/turquoise beads, medallion, green #7 **125.00**
   Multicolored, RC mk................................ **37.00**
   Pink wild rose decor **45.00**
   Wht w/pastel blue flowers, open top, #2 .... **65.00**
Humidor, Collie dog molded in relief, 6¼″, #2 .... **895.00**
   Four seascapes, Deco trim, 5″, #2..................... **250.00**
   Hexagonal, green w/floral decor around top & lid, #2 ...... **350.00**
   Hexagonal, pipe & cigar decor, bisque finish, #2 .... **500.00**
   Lamplighter scene molded in relief, 7¼″, #2 .... **999.00**
   Landscape, windmill **150.00**
   Lion & lioness scene molded in relief, 7¼″, #2 .... **925.00**
   Moriage playing cards decor, 3-handled, #2 .... **435.00**
   Orchid decor, gold rim & beading, matt finish, 6¼″, blue #7 **380.00**
   Playing cards & poker chips decor, large **275.00**

Small scenic medallions, raised beaded border **175.00**
Stag & doe scene, moriage trim, ball ft, 5½″, #2 .... **450.00**
Stag on hillside, enameled trees, jeweled knob, 5″, TN mk.. **325.00**
Inkwell, bisque water scene w/boat, complete w/liner, 2½″, #2. **155.00**
   With pen rest, wht w/floral decor, lavender & floral border.. **175.00**

Jug, 2 scenic panels, sq, 7½″ **135.00**
Knife rest, pink floral decor, gold trim, 3½″ long, blue #5 ... **125.00**
Lamp, pink w/cascading vines & wht flowers, 11″, #2........ **245.00**
Lazy susan, scenic decor, 5-pc in blk lacquered box, blue #5.. **125.00**
   Scenic sailboats & palm trees, in papier mache box........ **120.00**
Lemonade set, geese in flight, pitcher & 6 mugs, TS Nippon mk **265.00**
   Wht w/cascading purple wisteria, 7-pc, #1................ **265.00**
Mayonnaise bowl, wht/peach, footed, w/underplate & ladle, #2. **105.00**
   Wht w/butterfly decor, w/underplate..................... **95.00**
Milk pitcher, red & pink roses, 7″ **50.00**
Mug, grey w/moriage dragon, beading as trim, 5½″, #2 ...... **225.00**
Mustache cup & saucer, cream w/multi floral, beaded, blue #7. **150.00**
   Deep rose w/gold overlay, pink, rosebuds, blue #7 .... **185.00**
   Floral & geometric decor **60.00**
Mustard jar, w/underplate, bisque w/yellow flowers, gold trim, #2 **50.00**
   With underplate, rose decor, blue & gold trim, #2 .... **55.00**
Napkin ring, blue, green, gold flowers, green #2 .... **49.00**
   Triangular, ornate **40.00**
   Yellow bisque w/sailboat decor, 2″ long................. **65.00**
Nappy, cobalt & gold scalloped rim, heavy gold, 7½″ dia, #2 .. **90.00**
   Heart shape, nut decor **45.00**
   Yellow floral decor, signed W Rose, #2.................. **40.00**
Nut bowl, gold w/red roses, footed, 6½″, blue #7 .... **80.00**
   Oak branch w/acorn, bisque finish, jeweled, 7″, #2 .... **75.00**
   Peanut decor, bisque & enamel trim, 3 ball ft, #2 .... **42.00**
Nut cup, scalloped edge, hp interior, 2x3″................. **30.00**
Nut set, aqua w/swans, gold relief florals, beads, 5 pc **125.00**
   Cherry decor on green/tan ground, 7-pc, blue #7.......... **195.00**
   House scene in greens & oranges, pierced handles, 7-pc, #1.. **65.00**
   Orange floral decor, 7-pc, crown mk **45.00**
   Shepherd & sheep, gold beading & jewels, 7-pc, #2 .... **220.00**
Pancake dish, brown & beige geometric design **50.00**
Pancake server, gold cameos w/pink roses, turq beading, blue #7 **150.00**
   White w/orchids & leaves, #2......................... **135.00**
Pancake warmer, raised gold floral & leaves on cream, #2 ..... **45.00**
Pitcher, scenic w/autumn design, moriage trees **85.00**
   Windmill scene, cobalt w/heavy gold, bulbous, 7″, #2 ...... **200.00**
Plaque, American Indian on horseback in relief, 10½″ dia, #2 **900.00**

American Indian w/turkey scene, 10″ dia, #2 . . . . **925.00**
Birds in flight over lake, heavy gold leaves, 10¼″ dia **195.00**
Bisque scene of path winding to house, 10½″ dia, #2 . . . . . . **270.00**
Buffalo scene in relief, 10½″ dia, #2 . . . . **875.00**
Country scene w/cottage, 10¼″ dia **175.00**
Ducks in front of cottage, 9″ dia **165.00**
Landscape scene, pink & blue jeweled border, 9″ dia, blue #7 **260.00**
Newfoundland dog portrait, self-framed, 10½x8″, #2 . . . . **450.00**
Owl in sunset, 10″, #2 . . . . **125.00**
Pagoda temple & Mt Fuji, 10″ dia, #2 . . . . **285.00**

Parrot on branch scene, 10″ dia, #2 . . . . **275.00**
Pastel sailboat scene, colorful border, gold trim, 10½x8″, #2 **375.00**
Purple flowers, gold beads & jeweling, 9″ dia, #2 . . . . **200.00**
Red lobster, sea shells, 12″, mkd **195.00**
Sailboat & palm tree scene, 14″ dia, #2 . . . . **200.00**
Scene of ducks walking in road, 9″ dia, #2 . . . . **325.00**
Scene of man standing in boat, 9″ dia, #2 . . . . **265.00**
Scene of woodland stream in Autumn, 10″ dia, #2 . . . . **220.00**
Scene w/cottage in Spring, 10″ dia, #2 . . . . **250.00**
Scenic floral, 10½″ dia **125.00**
Scenic w/palm trees & pineapple plants, 9″ **90.00**
Scenic w/raised blossoms on tree, 7½″, #2 . . . . **50.00**
Scenic w/gold decor border, beads & jeweled flowers, 10″, blue #7 **185.00**
Spring scene, 11″ **200.00**
Squirrel molded in relief, 10½″ dia, #2 . . . . **900.00**
Still life of pheasant & milk jug on table, 12¼″ **375.00**
Sunbonnet baby playing w/dog, 7½″, #2 . . . . **275.00**
Sunset Arabian desert scene, 10¼″ **155.00**
WWI airplane, 7¾″ dia **145.00**
Plate, butterfly decor, blk/gold fan border, 10½″ dia, #1 . . . . **110.00**
Chestnuts, Jonroth Studios, 8½″ **45.00**
Dogwood roses, raised gold trim, open handles, 11″, IC Nippon **75.00**
Green bisque w/large orchid decor, 7½″ dia, #2 . . . . **90.00**
Landscape w/cow, matt, 10″ dia **145.00**
Moriage bird decor, 8″, mkd **98.00**
Parrots, floral, 8½″, mkd **35.00**
Pink & yellow rose decor, 6½″ dia, #2 . . . . **60.00**
Scene of Nile & pyramids, gold border, 10″ dia, #2 . . . . **115.00**
Snow-goose, beaded, 4 birds, much gold, sgnd, 9″ **45.00**
Underwater scene w/2 fish, gold design rim, 8½″ dia, #2 . . . **100.00**
Powder box & hair receiver, ribbed, floral decor, gold & wht beads, #2 **48.00**
Powder jar, coralene, yellow w/pink flowers **90.00**
Punch bowl, cobalt w/gold swans, 2-pc, claw ft, #2 . . . . **400.00**
Fruit decor, gold handles, w/gold ftd base, sgnd, #2 . . . . . **245.00**
Punch set, grape decor w/gold trim, handled bowl, 6 cups, tray, #2 **700.00**
Landscape scene, pedestal bowl, 4 cups, blue pagoda mk . . . **495.00**

Red rose decor, 2-pc bowl, 5 pedestal shape cups, #2 . . . . . . **950.00**
Relish dish, American Indian head handles, 8½″ long, #2 . . . . **125.00**
Desert scene, 2 sections, handle, 7½″ long, blue #7 . . . . **95.00**
Green aqua & navy stylized decor, Spoke mk **19.00**
Relish, medallions w/roses, ornate gold, oval, open-handled, green #2 **38.00**
Raised gold dragon decor, 9″, Shofu mk **40.00**
Relish set, windmill decor, 7-pc in 10″ papier mache box **145.00**
Ring tree, boat scene, raised hand, gold trim, #2 . . . . **45.00**
Hand w/attached underplate, rose decor, 3″, blue #7 . . . . . . **60.00**
Rose bowl, brown w/moriage cherry blossom decor, 5¾″ dia, blue #7 **165.00**
Ivory w/red berries, leaves, miniature **75.00**
Salt, individual, wht w/yellow flowers, gr leaves, #2 . . . . **18.00**
Salt & pepper, portrait, footed, green w/heavy beading **125.00**
Sardine set, wht w/geometric design, box, lid & underplate, #2 **200.00**
Smoke set, Hoo bird design, 3-pc on 7″ tray, #2 . . . . **200.00**
Yellow matt w/scenic decor, humidor & cigarette box, mkd . . **400.00**
Stein, portrait of monk, grape & leaves border, 7″, #2 . . . . . **450.00**
Winter scene, 7″, #2 . . . . **375.00**
Stickpin holder, blue w/lt blue flowers, attached tray, #2 . . . . **140.00**
Sugar & creamer, allover gold etching, RE Nippon **90.00**
Gold w/beaded drape **37.50**
Gold w/grape & leaf pattern, #2 . . . . **135.00**
Meadow scene, Art Nouveau decor, gold trim, #2 . . . . **130.00**
On pedestals, large pink roses outlined in gold **160.00**
Windmill scene, #2 . . . . **65.00**
Sugar shaker, allover color **85.00**
Bulbous, floral decor, sgnd **30.00**
Ivory w/rose decor, 4″, blue #7 . . . . **125.00**
Roses w/gold swirls decor, #2 . . . . **85.00**
Syrup, w/underplate, cobalt w/floral decor, blue #7 . . . . **125.00**
With underplate, gold on wht, turq beading, blue #7 . . . . . . **110.00**
With underplate, gold rim, handle finial, 6″ **60.00**
With underplate, wht w/violet decor, #2 . . . . **85.00**
Tankard, cobalt blue w/red & pink floral decor, gold beading, 12″ **275.00**
Purple w/large blue waterlilies, gold trim, 12″, Royal Nishiki mk **395.00**
Tankard set, fisherman scene molded in relief, w/4 mugs, #2 **4,500.00**
Scenic, raised enamel florals, moriaga & jeweled rim, 7-pc . . **495.00**
Stag scene molded in relief, w/6 mugs, #2 . . . . **3,700.00**
Tazza, lavender, Wedgwood decor, 5½x7″ dia **350.00**
Tea set, panels w/lake scene or grapes; 13-pc Pickard etched mk **225.00**
Blue upper portion, birds on off-wht base, gold trim, 9-pc, #4 **135.00**
Blue w/allover pink & yellow roses, gold trim, sgnd, 13-pc . . **325.00**
Blue-gray, much gold, 3-pc **135.00**
Country scene, blk & gold bands, 11-pc, #2 . . . . **195.00**
Cream w/encircling stylized blue florals, gold trim, 11-pc . . . **195.00**
Garden scene, ladies, pagoda, Mt Fuji, 3-pc, Nippon Torii mk **190.00**
Large rose decor, gold trim, footed, 15-pc, blue #7 . . . . **425.00**
Moriage dragon decor, 3-pc, raised 5-pt star, Japan **85.00**
Mother & child, cherry trees, pagodas, 17-pc, Royal Kinran mk **300.00**
Multi florals, 21 pc **195.00**
Pale green w/floral decor, 11-pc, very old, #3 . . . . **195.00**
Pink & green florals, cobalt & gold border, 15-pc **175.00**
Red & pink rose decor, cobalt trim, 3-pc, #2 . . . . **200.00**
Scenic in bright blues & oranges, 3-pc **85.00**
Turquoise w/flying egrets, gold & jeweled border, 7-pc **350.00**
Wht w/house scene, 15-pc, #2 . . . . **250.00**
Wht w/pink flowers outlined in gold, 3-pc, #2 . . . . **160.00**
Tea strainer, pastel hp roses & geometric designs, 2-pc, #2 . . . **135.00**
Pink & blue floral, #2 . . . . **33.00**
With bowl, roses decor **65.00**
With undercup, pink roses w/gold decor, large **50.00**
Wht w/purple violets, gold beading, blue #7 . . . . **125.00**
Yellow & brown, roses decor, gold trim, 2-pc, Royal Kinran mk **120.00**
Tea tile **52.00**

Toothpick, brown w/American Indian portrait, 3 handles, #2 .. **120.00**
  Corset shape, pink floral decor, 3 handles, #2 .... **90.00**
  Floral decor, 3 feet, 3 handles, #2 .... **40.00**
  Sailboat & windmill scene, 3 handles, 2½", #2 .... **85.00**
  Scenic, souvenir Newport, Rhode Island, #2 .... **35.00**
Tray, blue Wedgwood decor, handles, 10x6" **325.00**
  Maple leaves, 7x10" **40.00**
  Woodland scene, 10" dia **200.00**
Trivet, lake scene, 6" dia, #2 .... **55.00**
Urn, cameo portrait of woman, pedestal base, ornate, 12", blue #7 **465.00**
  Cobalt w/gold trim, medallions w/swans, covered, 12", blue #7 **450.00**
  Gold, medallions w/mums, covered, 14", #2 .... **600.00**
  Scenic band of Roman ruins, gold & enamel trim, covered, 15" **475.00**
Vase, basket shape, windmill scene silhouetted in blk, 6", gr #2 **160.00**
  Beige w/sunflower decor, 11", green #2 .... **240.00**
  Beige w/swan scene, 10", green #2 .... **220.00**
  Blue w/grape clusters, bulbous, ring neck, 12", green #7 ... **110.00**
  Boat scene w/palm trees, 10¼", green #2 .... **225.00**
  Bottle shape, floral decor, gold trim, 7½", poppy mk **85.00**
  Brown w/iris pattern, 11½", green #7 .... **240.00**
  Brown w/wht & lavender flowers, ribbed, handled, 11", blue #7 **250.00**
  Castle & forest scene, bisque, 3-claw ft, 12", blue #7 ...... **250.00**
  Cobalt & heavy gold, fluted beaded rim, oval w/figures, 8½" **225.00**
  Cobalt w/floral decor, gold trim, bulbous, handled, 5½", blue #7 **150.00**
  Cobalt w/floral panels, gold trim, 4 handles, 12¼", blue #7 . **435.00**
  Cobalt w/lake & mountain scene both sides, gold trim, #7 .. **125.00**
  Cobalt w/large orchid decor, gold trim, 9½" **525.00**
  Cobalt w/rose decor, gold trim, ftd, 5x8" dia **345.00**
  Cobalt w/scenic decor, gold border, 6", blue #7 .... **135.00**
  Coralene cherry blossom decor, gold beading, 5" **225.00**
  Cottage, lake, birch trees overall; bulbous w/tiny neck, 6" .. **160.00**
  Cream w/boat scene, green #2 .... **275.00**
  Dk blue w/floral decor, gold border, 7", green #2 .... **160.00**
  Dk blue w/iris design, gold handles, 12¼", Royal Nippon mk . **75.00**
  Dragon decor, ftd, loop handles, 3¼", green #2 .... **70.00**
  Dragon motif in slipwork, ruffled neck, bulbous, 7½", blue #7 **180.00**
  Duck scene, cobalt w/heavy gold trim, 8¾", T Nippon mk .. **250.00**
  Farmer & 2 oxen scene, gold decor & handles, 8½" **245.00**

  Floral, handles, gold trim, 8", gr #2 .... **120.00**
  Floral medallions w/gold borders & beading, 8½", blue #7 .. **200.00**
  Gold traced florals & leaves, gold handles, 16" **70.00**
  Gold w/red iris, ped base, cobalt top & bottom, 9", green #2 **200.00**

Grape, flowers & leaves, outlined in gold, silver beading, 8", #2 **155.00**
Green w/allover acorn motif molded in relief, 7", green #2 .. **450.00**
Green w/large flowers, melon ribbed, gold trim, 10", blue #7 **220.00**
Green w/large pink roses, gold trim, 10", green #7 .... **220.00**
Grey w/moriage dragon decor, turquoise enameled eyes, 13" **250.00**
Hour-glass shape, scenic, handled, 11", blue #7 .... **390.00**
House on country road scene, handled, 9", green #2 ...... **195.00**
Iris decor, bisque, 8¾", Royal Kinran mk **190.00**
Jug, boat scene, much beadwork, 4", green #2 .... **55.00**
Lake & boat scene, early, 16x9" at widest point **450.00**
Lake scene, cobalt & gold trim, 6" **85.00**
Lakeside scene, large orange flowers, gold trim, 10¼", green #2 **225.00**
Large 3-color flowers w/wht enameling, handled, 9½", blue #7 **200.00**
Large red poppies, cobalt & gold trim, Royal Kinran, 16" .. **450.00**
Lavender to wht w/red & yellow flowers, handled, 6", #3 ... **145.00**
Lavender w/house & lake scene, 5½", green #2 .... **125.00**
Lilies on matt finish, handled, 10", blue #7 .... **165.00**
Lime green w/pink rose decor, gold beading, 10", green #2 . **220.00**
Lizard around top, brown, ribbed, 3x3" **245.00**
Lt blue w/lily-of-valley, dk blue top & bottom, 10¾", green #2 **225.00**
Man & camel scene, bisque, 3 ped ft, 11¾", green #7 .... **380.00**
Man on camel scene, blue & tan ground, ftd, 8", green #2 . **250.00**
Man on camel scene, melon shape, cobalt trim, 8½", green #2 **250.00**
Moriage butterfly front decor, hp butterfly back, 9", blue #7 **295.00**
Mottled green on lime green, orchid decor on front, 6", blue #7 **145.00**
Mum decor, gold handles, beading, 9x6½", green #2 ...... **195.00**
Mum slip decor, gold overall beads, handled, ftd **275.00**
Orange w/egrets standing in water, 4½", green #2 .... **80.00**
Owl on tree branch decor, pillow shape, handled, 8", green #7 **225.00**
Phoenix bird & butterfly decor, mkd **265.00**
Pink floral center, cobalt blue top & bottom, 7", blue #7 ... **145.00**
Portrait, full length, jeweled, 12", blue #7 .... **460.00**
Portrait of lady on front, rose medallion on back, gold decor, 7½" **225.00**
Portrait of lady w/flowers, heavy cobalt trim, 6¾", blue #7 .. **225.00**
Portrait of Princess Potocka, heavy gold decor **385.00**
Rose decor w/leaves outlined in gold, blue trim, handled, 7", gr #2 **135.00**
Rose decor, moriage trim, handled, 8", blue #7 .... **210.00**
Rose & gold decor, large ring handles, 11½x9" dia **525.00**
Ruffled top, 3-color ground w/floral decor, gold trim, 7½", gr #2 **160.00**
Rust & green floral decor, gold trim & handles, 8½", Spoke mk **95.00**
Scenic, gold handles & legs, 13" **300.00**
Scenic w/lavender & orange tones, 12½", green #2 .... **135.00**
Scenic w/thatched roof cottage near lake, bulbous, 6¼", green #2 **150.00**
Seascape w/moriage birds, 5½" **85.00**
Seascape, 8", green #2 .... **275.00**
Shaded pink & gr, brown band w/gold tracings, 13x5½", gr #2 **145.00**
Swans, cobalt w/heavy gold, 10½" **485.00**
Tapestry w/flowers, gold beaded swags, handled, 8", blue #7 **550.00**
Tapestry w/grape decor, heavy gold trim, 5¼x6½", blue #7 . **150.00**
Turquoise w/red roses decor, encrusted in gold, ovoid, 13" . **425.00**
WWI airplane decor, handled, brown trim w/enameling, 3", gr #2 **165.00**
Water scene, pinks & greens, beadwork, handled, 4¼", green #2 **45.00**
Wedgwood blue & wht decor, ornate ring handles, 8½", green #2 **535.00**
Wht w/pink flowers, gr leaves, gold trim, 6¾", green #2 .... **110.00**
Wild rose decor, flared neck w/geometric trim, 5" **90.00**
Wisteria decor, geometric & floral bands, 4 handles, 12", green #2 **285.00**
Yellow & brown floral decor, gold ring handles, 9½x8½", gr #2 **200.00**
Yellow & wht, 3-color rose decor, gold trim, 12½", Niskiki mk **125.00**
Whiskey jug, clusters of grapes & leaves **235.00**
  Landscape scene, beaded trim, 6½", #2 .... **375.00**
Wine jug, bulbous, wisteria decor, 11" **395.00**
  Eagle decor, w/stopper, 11", #2 .... **595.00**
  Ear of corn & husks, fall colors, mkd **245.00**
  Egyptian scene w/moriage decor, w/stopper, 11", blue #7 ... **600.00**

Nodders

So called because of the nodding action of their head and hands, nodders originated in China where they were used in temple rituals to represent deity. Early in the 18th century, the idea was adapted by Meissen and by French manufacturers who produced not only china nodders but bisque as well. Most nodders are individual--couples are unusual. The idea remained popular until the end of the 19th century, and was used during the Victorian era by toy manufacturers.

Alligator, jaws move, Germany	55.00
Andy Gump, comic strip character, 1930s, German bisque	125.00
Black girl, w/slate, sitting in chair, bisque, 8"	135.00
Bobs Bailey, Germany	75.00
Cat playing violin, candy container, Germany	170.00
China Chow, Germany	75.00
Clown, porcelain, Germany, 7½"	65.00
Sitting, both head & legs nod	145.00
Denny Dimwit, 1930s, 11"	115.00
Donkey, celluloid	35.00
Fat man w/top hat, both body & head nod	145.00
Flapper, German bisque, 4"	24.00
Girl, Victorian style dress & hat, bisque, 4"	185.00
Herby, Germany	27.50
Indian w/fruit	125.00
Kayo, comic strip character, 1930s, German bisque	95.00
Lady, seated, pink tiara, fan, gold beads & decor, German bisque, 4"	155.00
Man w/cigar & glass eye, papier mache, 6"	47.50
Monk, scowling, one arm raised, hiding wine jug, German bisque	125.00
Moon Mullins, comic strip character, 1930s, German bisque	95.00
Oriental figure, triple, German porcelain, 5"	450.00
Oriental man, sitting, holds pearlized fan behind hand, Germany, 7"	295.00
Oriental man, sitting, holds knife & sheath, skull hat, bisque, 6"	165.00
Pair; bisque bowls w/Oriental woman & man in relief, nodding fan	340.00
Man & woman, china & bisque, 6"	500.00
Man & woman, papier mache, Germany	70.00
Oriental figures, floral decorated porcelain	225.00
Standing couple, she w/cup, he w/umbrella, Heubach, 6"	175.00
Rachel, comic strip character, china, 3½"	65.00
Salt & pepper; kangaroo mother & baby	45.00
Monkey mother & baby	45.00
Skeezix, comic strip character, 1930s, German bisque	95.00
Tilda, comic strip character, 1930s German bisque	125.00
Uncle Bim, comic strip character, 1930s, German bisque	125.00
Uncle Walt, comic strip character, 1930s, German bisque	95.00
Woman, wearing dress & cape, w/field glasses, Germany, 6½"	150.00
Zero, comic strip character, King features	18.00

Noritake

The Noritake Company was first registered in 1904 as Nippon Gomei Kaisha. In 1917, the name became Nippon Toki Kabushiki Toki. The M in wreath mark is that of the Morimura Brothers, distributors with offices in New York. It was used until 1941. The tree crest mark is the crest of the Morimura family.

The Noritake Company has produced fine porcelain dinnerware sets and occasional pieces decorated in the delicate manner for which the Japanese are noted. Their Azalea pattern was produced exclusively for the Larkin Company, who gave the lovely ware away as premiums to club members and their home agents.

From 1916 through the 30s, Larkin distributed the fine china decorated in pink Azaleas on white with gold tracing along edges and handles. Early in the 30s, six pieces of crystal glassware with the handpainted pattern was offered: candleholders, comport, tray with handles, scalloped fruit bowl, cheese and cracker set, and cake plate. All in all, 70 different pieces were offered. Some, such as the 15 pc child's set, bulbous vase, china ashtray and the pancake jug, are quite rare. Marks varied over the years; the earliest was the blue rising sun Nippon mark, followed by Noritake M in wreath with variations. Later, the ware was marked Noritake, Azalea, handpainted, Japan.

Azalea, basket, #193	115.00
Bon-bon dish, #184	35.00
Bouillon cup & saucer, #124	15.00
Bowl, #55	88.00
Bowl, #172	23.00
Bowl, deep, #310	43.00
Bowl, divided, #439	175.00
Bowl, round, 10", #12	28.00
Butter tub w/insert, #54	25.00
Candy dish, #313	450.00
Casserole, #372	295.00
Casserole, covered, #16	55.00
Celery, #444	160.00
Celery, 12½", #99	30.00
Cheese, covered, #314	70.00
Coffee pot, #182	295.00
Compote, #170	80.00
Condiment set, 5 pc, #14	35.00
Creamer, #122	50.00
Cruet w/stopper, #190	130.00
Cup & saucer, #2	13.50
Egg cup, #120	29.00
Grapefruit dish, #185	85.00
Gravy boat, #40	25.00
Jam jar set, #125	98.00
Lemon dish, #121	15.00
Mayonnaise set, 3 pc, #3	25.00
Mustard jar, handled, #191	35.00
Nappy, handled	25.00
Pitcher, milk, #100	120.00
Plate, 6¼", #8	7.00
Plate, 7½", #4	6.00
Plate, breakfast, 8½", #98	15.00
Plate, cake, #10	30.00
Plate, dinner, #13	14.00
Plate, grill, #338	55.00
Plate, square, #315	35.00
Platter, 10¼", #311	110.00
Platter, 12", #56	35.00
Platter, 16", #186	295.00
Relish, 4 section, #119	99.00
Relish, oval, #18	12.00
Relish, oval, handled, 7¼", #194	35.00
Relish, twin, #171	35.00
Relish, twin-loop, #450	275.00
Salt & pepper, #11, pair	10.00
Salt & pepper, #89, pair	11.00
Salt & pepper, #126, pair	10.00
Sauce dish, 5¼", #9	7.50
Shell dish, #188	210.00
Snack set, #39	30.00
Soup, flat, #19	15.00
Spoon holder, #189	60.00
Sugar, gold finial, #401	55.00
Sugar, open, #123	35.00
Sugar & creamer, #123	55.00
Sugar & creamer, #7	28.00

Sugar & creamer, gold finial, #401, pair **110.00**
Sugar shaker & creamer, #122 . . . . **98.00**
Syrup pitcher w/underplate, #97 . . . . **70.00**
Tea set, pot, sugar & creamer **110.00**
Tea tile, #169 . . . . **30.00**
Teapot, #15 . . . . **70.00**
Teapot, gold finial, #400 . . . . **300.00**
Vase, fan, #187 . . . . **100.00**
Vegetable, oval, 9½″, #172 . . . . **25.00**
Vegetable, oval, 10½″, #101 . . . . **28.00**
Basket, blue w/relief decor of nuts **40.00**
Berry set, green w/hp orchids, gold edge, 7 pc **60.00**
Biscuit jar, scenic Arab astride camel by tent, metal top & handle **125.00**
Bon-bon, raised gold pattern **10.00**
Bowl, gold & wht, scalloped edge, 10″ **42.00**
  Low, center bouquet decor, open handled **14.00**
  Scene w/house & trees, brown rim & beading, M in wreath, 8¾″ **23.00**
Box, lady's portrait on lid, Greek Key border **60.00**
Butter tub, scenic decor **22.00**
Cake plate, lusterware, scenic center, gr & blk border, 9¾″ **25.00**
Cake set, floral decor w/encrusted gold, 7 pc **100.00**
Cake set, ivory band, blk & gold trim, blue urns, 7 pc, red M mark **45.00**
Candleholders, double gold handles, blue luster, 4″, pair **15.00**
Candy dish, cover w/apple finial, sgnd **32.00**
Celery dish, gondola scene, gr to blue ground, 11½″ **32.00**
Cheese server, scenic, silver & blue, side handle **8.00**
Chocolate pot, all over scenic **42.00**
Chocolate set, blue w/red roses, pre-war, 11 pc on 12″ tray . . . **210.00**
Chocolate set, parrot w/flowers decor, 11 pc **175.00**
Cigarette box, flapper girl & parrot decor **20.00**
Coffee pot w/trivet, orange & blue luster **58.00**
Compote, cottage scene, scrolled peach & gold border, handled, 5″ **70.00**
Compote, fruit decor, 2 pc, gold handles, claw feet **230.00**
Condiment set, gr w/florals, 9 pc, 'pot of flowers' mustard **38.00**
Condiment set, wht w/red floral decor, shakers & mustard w/lid . **29.00**
Creamer, child's, nursery rhyme decor **45.00**
Demitasse set, pot, 6 cups & saucers, raised gold pattern **300.00**
Demitasse set, scene w/tree, lake & windmill, 5 pc on 12″ tray **150.00**
Fruit dish, lg yellow roses decor, matt finish, 9½″ sq **42.00**
Hair receiver, floral decor on lid, 3 gold feet, 4x4″ **22.00**
Humidor, blue w/geometric & floral decor, sq top, round body . . **85.00**
Humidor, lg scale all over scenic **130.00**
Jam jar, blown-out oranges & leaves, luster ground, w/ladle . . . **28.00**
Jam jar, blue w/red apple finial **38.00**
Jam jar, melon figural w/ladle, leaf like underplate **48.00**

Marmalade, w/spoon & undertray **30.00**
Match holder, figural flapper's head, Art Deco **10.00**
Mayonnaise set, 3 color decor, 4″ bowl w/matching ladle **38.00**
Mustard w/cover, attached liner, floral medallions, blue & gold . **26.00**

Napkin ring, finger ring shape, gr w/flowers & leaves setting . . . **55.00**
Navarre, gravy w/attached tray, bird w/flowers **25.00**
  Plate, bread & butter, crested bird w/flowers **3.50**
  Plate, dinner, crested bird w/flowers **6.00**
  Plate, salad, crested bird w/flowers **4.00**
  Sauce dish, crested bird w/flowers **3.00**
  Vegetable, covered, round, bird w/flowers **35.00**
  Vegetable, open, oval, handled, bird w/flowers **25.00**
Nut dish, lusterware, blue, wht interior w/floral decor, 5½″ **15.00**
Nut dish, swan on lake scene, handled, 5½″ sq **12.50**
Nut set, wht w/gold geometric design, ftd, 6 pc, blue M in wreath **50.00**
Planter, continual sunset scene, gr mk, 3x6x5″ **70.00**
Platter, ivory band, gold encrusted & beaded floral, 16″ **20.00**
Platter, sedan pattern, wht w/pastel flowers on rim, 14″ **18.50**
Powder, box, lustre, cover has red-haired lady finial, w/10″ tray . **85.00**
Relish tray, floral rim & base decor, ruffled, gold bead trim, 7″ . **12.50**
Salt & pepper, w/handled holder, yellow w/dainty florals **7.50**
Sheridan, butter tub w/insert **20.00**
  Casserole, covered **40.00**
  Cup & saucer **10.00**
  Egg cup **20.00**
  Gravy boat **25.00**
  Lemon dish **10.00**
  Plate, dinner **9.00**
  Relish, oval, handled, 7½″ **25.00**
  Sauce dish **5.00**
  Sugar & creamer **20.00**
  Vegetable, oval, 10½″ **25.00**
  Vegetable, round, 10″ **22.00**
Spoon holder, scenic decor **32.00**
Spooner, lay-down, handled, hp flowers w/gold luster, 8″ long . . **18.50**
Sugar & creamer, luster, Japanese lantern scene, gold & blk handles **15.00**
Sugar & creamer, sunset lake scenic, satin finish, gold handles . **35.00**
Sugar shaker & creamer, beige w/gold trees, pagoda & birds . . **45.00**
Sugar shaker & creamer, raised gold pattern **40.00**
Sweetmeat dish, lustre, cover w/apple finial, handled, 6½x8″ dia **65.00**
Syrup pitcher, wht w/luster brown bands & floral, w/top **15.00**
Syrup w/underplate, florals & gold decor **34.00**
Tea set, child's, nursery rhyme decor, 21-pc, w/orig box **295.00**
  Child's, scene w/house & stream, 7-pc, sgnd **85.00**
  Gold encrusted basket w/scrolls, ivory bands, 15-pc **95.00**
  White w/butterflies & floral decor, lacy gold, 3-pc **175.00**
Tea tile, water scenic, brown rim, square, green M mk **7.50**
Tree In Meadow, basket **85.00**
  Bowl, 5¼″ **5.00**
  Bowl, 5¾″ **8.00**
  Bowl, oatmeal **10.00**
  Bowl, open handled, 10″ **20.00**
  Bowl, oval, 7″ **15.00**
  Bowl, 9″ **20.00**
  Bowl, shell-shape **165.00**
  Butter tub w/pierced insert **28.00**
  Cake set, 7-pc **65.00**
  Coffee pot, demitasse **65.00**
  Compote **60.00**
  Condiment set, 3-pc on tray **30.00**
  Cruet **85.00**
  Cup **9.00**
  Cup & saucer **12.00**
  Gravy boat, w/attached underplate & ladle **38.00**
  Jam jar set, w/underplate, ladle, figural cherries on lid **58.00**
  Lemon dish, handled, 5½″ **15.00**
  Mayonnaise, w/underplate & spoon, footed **20.00**
  Plate, 6½″ **3.00**

Plate, 8½″ **12.00**
Plate, cake **28.00**
Plate, salad **7.50**
Platter, oval, 11½″ **25.00**
Salt & pepper, bulbous, 3″ **14.00**
Saucer **3.00**
Sugar, covered **10.00**
Sugar, open **10.00**
Sugar shaker **25.00**
Sugar shaker & creamer **40.00**
Tea pot **65.00**
Tea set, pot, sugar, creamer, 4 cups & saucers **115.00**
Vase, fan **85.00**
Vegetable, oval, 9¼″ **30.00**
Vegetable, oval, 10½″ **35.00**
Urn, hexagon, blue w/scenic medallion, leaf handles, 13″ **160.00**
Vase, all over scenic, gold trim, 8½″ **45.00**
Fan w/fruit & vines decor, green & blue base w/ruffled top, 7″ **18.50**
Hexagonal, sunset lake scene, gold rim, red M mk **45.00**
Imari style hp decor, attached ped base, handled, 1930s, 11¼″ **55.00**
Pink & wht mum decor, blue band at neck, gold trim, 8½″ . . **45.00**
Ruffled top, orange, grey & wht geometric design, 4½x5″ **20.00**
Scene of city park, cobalt top/bottom, gold handles, 9½″ . . . **120.00**
Vegetable bowl, pink & orange floral, mustard edges, handled, 8¼″ **15.00**
Wall pocket, scene w/swan on lake **22.00**

Norman Rockwell

Norman Rockwell began his career in 1911 at the age of 17 doing illustrations for a children's book entitled *Tell Me Why Stories*. A few short years later in 1916, he did the *Saturday Evening Post* cover that made him one of America's most beloved artists. Though not well accepted by the professional critics of his day, who did not consider his work to be art but 'merely' commercial illustration, Rockwell's popularity grew to the extent that today there is an overwhelming abundance of examples of his work, or those related to the theme of one of his illustrations. The Gorham Company was among the first to attempt to place examples of Rockwell's work in the hands of collectors. In 1971, the Four Seasons porcelain plate set was issued; today the set is worth more than 10 times its original $60 retail price. For additional Rockwell listings, see Collector Plates.

Bell, Chilling Chore, wooden handle, 8½″ **45.00**
Chilly Reception, 1980, wooden handle, 8½″ **30.00**
Grandpa Sowman, porcelain, 7″ **55.00**
Puppy Love, porcelain, 7″ **55.00**
Sweet Song So Young, wooden handle, 9″ **82.00**
Bottle, Ben Franklin, Sat Eve Post cover 2½x6½x26″ **15.00**
Game Called Because Of Rain, Sat Eve Post 4/23/49 . . . . **15.00**
Bowl, Ben Franklin, 5½x8½″ dia **115.00**
Figurines, At The Doctors, 1978, 5½″ **112.00**
Barbershop Quartet, 1975, 7″ **1,000.00**
Bedtime **50.00**
Buttercup Test, Hummel, 5″ **275.00**
Caroler, 1973, 5½″ **30.00**
Discovery, 1979, 6″ **160.00**
Doctor & Doll, miniature, 1979, 3½″ **40.00**
Doctor & Doll, 1974, 10″ **300.00**
Dreams Of Long Ago, 1979, 6″ **100.00**
Family Collection, 4″ **90.00**
Four Ages Of Love, Fall, Fondly Do We Remember **290.00**
Four Ages Of Love, Spring, Sweet Song So Young **290.00**
Four Ages Of Love, Summer Flowers In Tender Bloom **290.00**
Four Ages Of Love, Winter, Gaily Sharing Vintage Times . . . **290.00**
Friends In Need, 1974, 5¼″ **86.00**

Huckleberry Finn Secret, 5¼″ **110.00**
Lazybones, 1973, 3¼″ **300.00**
Leapfrog, 1973, 6¼″ **600.00**
Lighthouse Keeper's Daughter **50.00**
Little Leaguer, The; 1979, 8″ **175.00**
Love Letter, miniature, 1979, 3″ **26.00**
Marble Player, miniature, 1979, 3″ **36.00**
Mother's Helper, Hummel, 5½″ **275.00**

No Swimming, miniature, 1979, 3½″ **22.00**
No Swimming, 1975, 9″ **300.00**
Puppy Love, 4¾″ **65.00**
Redhead, miniature, 1979, 3½″ **18.00**
Springtime Of '27, musical, Talk To The Animals **150.00**
Take Your Medicine, miniature, 1980, 4½″ **36.00**
Teachers Pet, 1979, 5¾″ **70.00**
The Cobbler **50.00**
The Four Seasons, Fall, Pride Of Parenthood **380.00**
The Four Seasons, Spring, Adventurers Between Adventures **380.00**
The Four Seasons, Summer the Mysterious Malady **380.00**
The Four Seasons, Winter, A Boy Meets His Dog **380.00**
The Home Cure, Hummel, 6″ **275.00**
The Toy Maker **50.00**
Wrapping Christmas Presents, 4″ **90.00**
Ingots, Charles Dickens, silver, 1977 . . . . **45.00**
Christmas Trio, silver, 1974 . . . . **30.00**
Santa Planning a Visit, silver, 1978 . . . . **40.00**
Magazine, American Boy, December, 1916 . . . . **21.00**
Look, July 4, 1916 . . . . **4.50**
McCall's December, 1964 . . . . **9.50**
Newsweek, December 28, 1970 . . . . **3.50**
Recreation, January, 1915 . . . . **8.50**
Saturday Evening Post, *see magazines*
Medal, Sat Eve Post 250th Anniversary **50.00**
Ornament, Drum For Tommy, Sat Eve Post, cover date 1921 . . **30.00**
Tiny Tim, porcelain, 3″ **15.00**
Paperweight, leaded crystal, Christmas Trip **125.00**
Prints; At The Barber, 22x30″ **3,000.00**
County Agricultural Agent, 24x35″ **2,700.00**
Expected And Unexpected, The; 17x20″ **2,200.00**
Four Seasons, Autumn, 20x21″ **1,500.00**
Four Seasons, Spring, 20x21″ **1,500.00**
Four Season, Summer, 20x21″ **1,500.00**
Four Seasons, Winter, 20x21″ **1,500.00**

Freedom Of Speech, 29x35″ **4,700.00**
Holiday In Karachi, 30x24″, 1980 .... **125.00**
Ichabod Crane, 20x26″............................. **5,000.00**
Moving Day, 24x30″ **2,000.00**
No Swimming, signed, 19x25″ **500.00**
On The Ice, 1979, 20x27″ **100.00**
Pals, 1978, 20x27″ **125.00**
Prescription, 24x30″ **3,900.00**
Roadblock, signed, 19x25″ **500.00**
Runaway, 28x32″.................................... **4,600.00**
School Days, Baseball, 20x26″ **1,850.00**
School Days, Cheering, 20x26″ **1,850.00**
School Days, Golf, 20x26″ **1,850.00**
School Days, Studying, 20x26″...................... **1,850.00**
Settling In, 20x26″ **1,400.00**
Spelling Bee, 14x30″................................ **5,500.00**
Texan, The; 24x30″ **2,300.00**
Tired But Happy, signed, 19x25″ **500.00**
Walking To Church, signed, 19x25″ **500.00**
Welcome, 20x26″ **1,600.00**
Spoon, Caroler, pewter, 6¾″........................ **35.00**
  Circus, pewter, 6¾″ **35.00**
  Lovers, pewter, 6¾″ **35.00**
Stamp, Commemorative, Boy Scouts Of America, 4 cent, issued 1960 .**28**
  Tom Sawyer, 8 cents, issued 1972 .... **.28**
Stamps, Foreign & Cachets, A Good Scout, 1925 .... **7.00**
  Beyond The Easel, 1969 .... **7.00**
  On My Honor, 1953 .... **7.00**
Toby mugs, Jester, 1939 Sat Eve Post cover date **35.00**
Tray, Coca-Cola Company, 10½x13″ **175.00**
  Green Giant Niblets Corn, 17½x12¾″ **45.00**

Norse

The Norse Pottery was established in 1903 in Edgerton, Wisconsin, by Thorwald Sampson and Louis Ipson. A year later it was purchased by A.W. Wheelock and moved to Rockford, Ill. The ware they produced was inspired by ancient bronze vessels of the Norsemen. Designs were often incised into the red clay body, dragon handles and feet were favored decorative devices, and they achieved a semblance of patina through the application of metallic glazes. The ware was marked with a stylized N containing a vertical arrangement of the remaining letters of the name. Production ceased after 1913.

Bowl, owls in relief, circular foot, bronze, 4x5½″ **265.00**
Dish, dragon handles, oval, 2½″ **75.00**

Pot, covered blk glaze, 3½″ **325.00**
Vase, footed, #55, 2½x4½″............................ **70.00**
  Head-shaped feet, 5¼x8x4½″ **55.00**

North Dakota School of Mines

The School of Mines of the University of North Dakota was established in 1890, but due to a lack of funding, it was not until 1898 that Earle J. Babcock was appointed as Director and efforts were made to produce ware from the native clay he had discovered several years earlier. The first pieces were made by firms in the east from the clay Babcock sent them. Some of the ware was decorated by the manufacturer, some was shipped back to North Dakota to be decorated by native artists. By 1909 students at the University of North Dakota were producing utilitarian items--tile, brick, shingles, etc.--in conjunction with a ceramic course offered through the Chemistry Department. By 1910 a Ceramic Department had been established, supervised by Margaret Kelly Cable. Under her leadership, fine art ware was produced. Native flowers, grains, buffalo, cowboys and other subjects indigenous to the state were incorporated into the decorations. Some pieces have an Art Nouveau-Art Deco style easily attributed to her association with Fredrick H. Rhead, with whom she studied in 1911. During the 20s the pottery was marketed on a limited scale through gift and jewelry stores in the state. From 1927 until 1949, when Miss Cable announced her retirement, a more widespread distribution was maintained, with sales branching out into other states. The ware was marked in cobalt with the official seal: Made at School of Mines, N.D. Clay, University of North Dakota, Grand Forks, N.D., in a circle. Very early ware was sometimes marked U.N.D. in cobalt by hand.

Bowl, 9″, McBride **75.00**
  Blue, sgnd Chuck Gowran, 5″ **42.00**
  Green semi-matt, incised squirrel, S Mattson, 2¼x6½″ **175.00**
  Low, turquoise **25.00**
  Signed Pincombe, 9″ **75.00**
  Squirrel sgraffito, brown, Cable, 3x6½″ **180.00**
  Tan w/hp multicolor florals, M Cable, 6″ dia **60.00**
Candlestick, crude.................................... **20.00**
Coyote, figural, matt tan............................. **95.00**
Dish, 3″... **25.00**
  Grey, 2x7½″ **40.00**
Experimental, Hebron clay sample test pc, 2″ **46.00**
Paperweight, aqua, 3½″ dia........................... **75.00**
Pitcher, floral sgraffito, maroon, 8½x6½″ **140.00**
Plate, Persian design, birds, unicorn, 1932, M Cable, 10″ **90.00**
Pot, Cable, 2¾″ **55.00**
  Tapered, Cable, 4¼″ **125.00**
Tea set, stylized crocus decor, 3-pc, 1922, MKC, 7½″, 3½″ .. **165.00**
Vase, aqua, sgraffito rings at neck, Cable, 7½″ **100.00**
  Blue w/stylized trees, cylinder w/rolled edge, 8″, FLH **95.00**
  Blue, bowl shape, 3x4″.......................... **35.00**
  Brown w/covered wagon, oxen at shoulder, M Cable, 6″ **95.00**
  Dutch girls sgraffito, brown/green, Cable, 4x4½″ **155.00**
  Green w/incised daffodils, Mattson, 5½″ **200.00**
  Green w/tulip sgraffito, Huck, 4x3½″ **125.00**
  High glaze mottled terra cotta & cream w/incised leaf, 7½″ .. **95.00**

Incised wheat, 5″ **125.00**

Oak leaf sgraffito, green & brown, Cable, 6½x7″ **200.00**
Sgraffito, fish decorated band at shoulder, Huckfield, 8″ **95.00**
Tan w/stylized purple flowers, 1925, JM, 6″ **55.00**
White w/blue slip painted floral spray, 5″ **75.00**
Yellow, 3″ **35.00**

Northwood, See Also Carnival, Custard, Goofus & Pressed Glass

The Northwood Company was founded in 1896 in Indiana, Pennsylvania, by Harry Northwood, whose father, John, was the art director for Stevens & Williams, an English glassworks. Harry Northwood joined the National Glass Company in 1899, but in 1901 again became an independent contractor, and formed the Harry Northwood Glass Company of Wheeling, West Va. He marketed his first Carnival glass in 1908, and it became his most popular product. His company was also famous for its custard, goofus, and pressed glass. Northwood died in 1923, and the company closed.

Nut Crackers

The nutcracker, though a strictly functional tool, is a good example of one to which man has applied ingenuity, imagination and engineering skills. Though all designed to accomplish the same end, hundreds of types exist in almost every material sturdy enough to withstand sufficient pressure to crack the nut. Figurals are popular collectibles, as are those with unusual design and construction.

Alligator, figural, ci, early 1900s, 14x3½x2″ **70.00**
Dazey, St Louis, Mo., ratchet type **22.50**
Dog, figural, brass, 6″ **40.00**
Dog, figural, ci on metal base **65.00**
Elephant, figural, iron **45.00**
Female, figural, wooden **20.00**
Gnomes head, figural, handcarved wood, 7½″ **45.00**
Home, iron, takes 3 sizes of pecans, table clamp **12.00**
Iron, wood handle **13.50**
Japan, ci on wood base **35.00**
Lady's legs, brass, 4½″ **35.00**
Lady's legs, solid brass, primitive, 1900, 5½″ **19.50**
Man thumbing nose, ci, screws to counter **25.00**

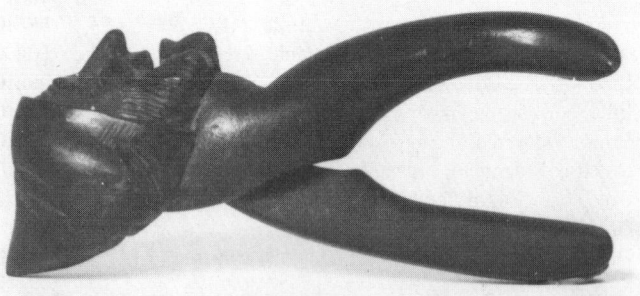

Man w/beard, pointed hat, wood **50.00**
Parrot, figural, ci, orig gr & orange paint, 1880s, 10″ **65.00**
Parrot, figual, ci **25.00**
Pecan, iron, 1915 . . . . **14.00**
Perfection, Waco, Tex., 1914 . . . . **15.00**
Punch & Judy, brass **14.00**
Rooster, figural, brass **20.00**
Shakespeare portrait, Hathaway cottage, brass **30.00**
Squirrel, figural, Tyler, Tex., 1913 . . . . **17.50**
Squirrel, figural, brass **36.00**
Squirrel, figural, ci **40.00**

Squirrel, figural, ratchet type, 1925 . . . . **22.50**
Squirrel on branch, figural, bronze **55.00**
St Bernard, figural, ci w/old gold paint, 1900s, 11x6½″ **60.00**
The Hamilton, ci, table model **11.00**
Vienna bronze, Geschuzt Nutcracker, w/walnut, 3½x2¾″ **125.00**

Occupied Japan

Items marked Occupied Japan have become popular collectibles in the last few years. They were produced during the period from the end of World War II until April 18, 1952, when the occupation ended. By no means was all of the ware exported during that time marked Occupied Japan---some was marked Japan, or Made In Japan. It is thought that because of the natural resentment felt by the Japanese toward the occupation, only a fraction of these wares were marked Occupied Japan. Even though you may find identical 'Japan' marked items, because of the limited use of the Occupied mark only these are being collected to any great extent.

Angel child, w/accordian, 2¼″ **2.75**
   With book, 2¼″ **2.75**
Ashtray, metal, w/bucking horse design impressed **4.50**
   Orange ceramic, little girl figure perched on edge, 4x2¾″ . . . **12.50**
Atomizer, perfume, glass w/rubber bulb, 3½″ **23.00**
Bandit, Mexican, carries shotgun, bisque, 6¼″ **25.00**
Baseball player, celluloid **25.00**
Bicycle, 2 wheel fold-up, standard size **220.00**
Bird, perched on books, 2″ **6.00**
Boat, bisque, 9″ long, 8″ boy stands in front **150.00**
Bowl, steam cover, lacquerware, flowers, 18k gold trim, 6″ **35.00**
Box, heart shape, sailboat on lid, gold trim, 2¾″ **9.00**
Boy, holding staff, w/dog, 3½″ **10.00**
   Pink trousers, lt blue coat, holding rose, bisque, 7½″ **18.00**
   Playing banjo, w/dog, Hummel type, 4½″ **17.50**
   Playing flute, w/duck, Hummel type, 3″ **10.50**
   With bag over shoulder, 3½″ **10.00**
   With dog, standing by fence, Hummel type, 3½″ **17.50**
   With fiddle, Hummel type, 4½″ **12.00**
Bud vase, bottle shaped, w/recumbant nude figural cherub **14.00**
   With bisque girl figural, 7½″ **18.50**
Camera, Minolta, adustable, folding leather case also mkd **125.00**
Candelabra, bisque, double holder, lotus, 6″ **30.00**
Candelstick, Colonial lady, 3½x3½″ **15.00**
Celluloid, dancing couple w/box & key, 4x1¾″ **30.00**
Cherub, plays banjo, 2″ **8.00**
Cigarette box, inlaid wood, bird picks up cigarettes, orig box . . . **18.00**
Cigarette set, silver plate, 3 pc **45.00**
Clock, animated elephant, T&Z Co **55.00**
   Bird cage w/stand, musical bird **165.00**
   Oak, wall type, key & strike **450.00**
   Wall, 8 day, chimes hour & ½ hour **200.00**
   Wood cuckoo, weights, MIOJ on gear plate & face plate **135.00**
Coal scuttle, maroon, floral medallion, gold trim, 4″ **8.00**
Coaster set, lacquerware, red container, 6 coasters, w/different designs **45.00**
Colonial boy & girl, arm in arm, 1 pc, 2½x3½″ **9.50**
Colonial couple, 1 pc, 5″ **8.50**
   Standing, 1 pc, 2½x3½″ **15.00**
Colonial lady, holding bouquet, bisque, 4″ **17.50**
   Holding skirt, 4″ **8.50**
   Porcelain, fancy dress, 7″ **17.00**
   Porcelain, perfume bottle inside, 8″ **80.00**
Colonial man, playing fiddle, 4¼″ **7.50**
   Playing mandolin, 6″ **14.50**
   Standing, blue open coat, 2½″ **7.50**
   With powdered wig, 3½″ **6.50**

Couple, 18th century dress, 8½", pr **30.00**
Couple, lady w/basket, man w/red coat, 1 pc, 6" **40.00**
Creamer, cow, brown & orange, 3½x5½" **20.00**
Cup & saucer, demitasse, dragon, translucent porcelain **35.00**
   Demitasse, hp rose, raised gold trim, Chubu **16.00**
   Demitasse, lovers in landscape, SGK **14.00**
   Demitasse, multicolor flowers, gold trim **7.00**
   Hand painted large iris, gold trim, Merit **10.00**
   Lusterware, hp house & trees scene **12.75**
Demi-pot, w/lid, multicolor florals, gold trim, 7¾" **18.00**
Dinner set, 52 pc, no logo, plain pattern **250.00**
Dinner set, 98 pc, logo & pattern name, ornate **620.00**
Dog, Dalmation, recumbent, 3x2" **12.00**
   German Shepard, standing, black, brown, & wht, 3x2½" **12.00**
   Seated, bone in mouth **13.00**
   Sitting up, gr bow at neck, 2½" **8.00**
   Wire Hair Terrier, porcelain **11.50**
   Spaniels, porcelain, 1 pc **15.50**
Doll, baby, 'Betty Boop', celluloid, nude, 3" **9.00**
   Baby, rubber, squeaks when squeezed, finger in mouth **20.00**
   Boy, celluloid, moveable arms/legs, 5" **12.00**
Dollhouse figure, colonial man seated in chair, porcelain, 2½" . . . **8.50**
Dollhouse furniture, chair w/wht floral decor, porcelain, 2" **9.50**
Dwarf, base player, bisque, 3½" **12.00**
Elf, pink, riding on snail, 2¼x4" **16.00**
Girl, playing mandolin, 3½" **5.00**
   Sitting on fence, Hummel type, 4¼" **20.00**
   Sitting, Hummel type, 6" **22.00**
   With roses, 3½" **5.50**
Incense burner, man, seated, 3½" **16.00**
Italian man, playing accordian, 4" **15.00**
Jewelry box, grand piano, enamel top, 5x3x2" **23.00**
Lady, w/basket of fruit, 5" **7.50**
Lamp, Colonial couple, 10½" **45.00**
   Lacquerware, flowers, square pedestal w/shade **65.00**
Lamps, single colonial lady & man, w/orig shades, pair **65.00**
Lighter, Aladdin lamp, 4x2¾", on tray, 7x5" **25.00**
   Baseball, chrome **18.00**
   Camera on tripod, chrome **30.00**
   Camera w/stand, 4" **13.00**
   Car, Buick, chromed brass, hood pops up for lighter **60.00**
   Desk telephone, chrome **30.00**

   Electric fan, chrome **25.00**
   Gun, chrome **10.00**
   Jet plane, chrome **8.00**
   Lamp-shape, metal **30.00**
   Metal, w/tray, Horn of Plenty **25.00**
   Piano, baby grand, chrome **30.00**
   Pipe, brass color, chrome **18.00**
   Typewriter, chrome **30.00**
   Western boot **18.00**
Man, w/harpsichord, 2 pc **18.00**
Match holder, double basket figural, wall type **98.00**
Mug, beer, German style, tavern scene on cobalt, 6¾" **40.00**
   Beer, tavern scene & hops on cobalt, 5" **13.00**
   Brown, purple grapes, 4" **10.00**
   Douglas McArthur, 4" **35.00**
   Figural man w/beard, 5" **35.00**
   Figural man w/glasses, 5" **35.00**
   Moonshiner **22.00**
   Nude lady handle **45.00**
Musician lady, 4¾" **5.50**
Musician man, 4¾" **5.50**
Newsboy, elephant mark, 'City of Life', 5½" **8.00**
Nut set, lacquerware, 5" bowl, 6 dishes, ladle, 18k gold trim . . . **55.00**
Opera glasses, ornate **55.00**
Oriental boy, brown coolie hat, 4½" **14.00**
Oriental girl, w/flowers, 4" **8.00**
Oriental lady, w/basket & fan, finely detailed, 7¼" **25.00**
Oriental man, playing horn, 4¾" **4.00**
Oriental warrior, bisque, 4¾" **17.00**
Pair, colonial boy & girl, 5" **25.00**
Perfume bottles, three 3" on round glass tray, quilted **28.00**
Pipe rest, cobalt, gold, floral, 2 pc **32.00**
Pitcher, windmill, 4" **17.00**
Planter, baby boot, lt blue, pierced for hanging, 2¼" **5.50**
   Camel, recumbent, 4x7½" **16.50**
   Cherub w/bucket of grapes, 2½x2½" **12.00**
   Doe & fawn, 8" **27.50**
   Donkey & sleeping Mexican, 4x6" **14.00**
   Free standing birds, 6x2½" **15.00**
   Girl & boy beside well, 2¾" **12.00**
   Kitten & basket, 3½" **9.00**
   Motor launch & driver, 8" long **17.00**
   With figural dog; green, wht, brown & blue, 4¼x3" **10.50**
   With figural rabbit; Belleek type porcelain, 3½x3" **11.50**
Plaques, pair, oval, pastel lady & gent under tree, Chase **39.00**
Plate, hp lakeside scene, glazed back, sgnd T Hiyake **45.00**
Rabbits, set of 4, each playing different instrument **24.00**
Rice bowl, porcelain, embossed dragon, 6" **23.00**
Rickshaw, w/two figures, 5" long **6.50**
Salt & pepper, 10 gal hat **18.00**
   Beehive set on stand **14.00**
   Boy & girl seated on single holder **17.00**
   Colonial children w/big bonnets, 3" **15.00**
   Ducks, hp, multicolored, orig box **10.00**
   Dutch boy & girl, seated, 2½" **10.00**
   Rooster, & hen, sitting, orange & yellow, 2¼x3½" **15.00**
   Senore & Senorita, 3¼" **14.00**
   Steins w/undertray, wht w/floral decor **20.00**
   Tomatoes, 4" **18.00**
   Tomatoes w/leaf ped, 2½" **12.0**
Salt shaker, Raggedy Ann, 4½" **7.00**
Schooner, bamboo sails & rigging, 2 masted, 4x4" **23.00**
Sewing machine, portable, foot control, Admiral Emporer **110.00**
Shelf sitter, boy fishing, painted details, 6x2½" **35.00**

Girl playing banjo, 4½" **12.00**
Girl w/basket of flowers, 3½" **12.50**
Shepherd, holds silver horn, dog, bisque, 6¼" **23.00**
Slide rule, w/leather case & instruction book **75.00**
Sugar & creamer, Dutch windmill figural **7.00**
    Tomatoes **25.00**
Tea set, pot w/lid, cream, sugar, 6 cups/saucers, Bone China ... **75.00**
    Raised moriage-type dragon decor, grey/coral/blue/gold, 24 pc **185.00**
Teapot, w/lid, windmill, 5" **23.00**
Tin windup, jockey on horse, in box **20.00**
Toby, double face, each seated John Bull holding mug **23.00**
    English gentleman, ceramic, 3x2¼" **17.00**
    Indian chief, 2½" **35.00**
    Jailer, ring of keys, wooden club, 7½" **25.00**
    Man w/beard, squirrel handle, 5" **28.00**
    Man w/can & medallion, 5" **22.00**
    Miniature, colonial lady **13.50**
    Miniature, lady's face **15.00**
    Muskateer, green hat, yellow feather, 4½" **23.00**
    Pirate, blk mask, 3¼" **18.00**
Toothpick holder, boy & girl holding cornucopia, 2¼" **9.00**
    Gentleman horn player **5.50**
Toy, wind-up, remote control car, MIB **26.00**
Toys, 6 wind-up cars, 3 Chevy, 3 Studebakers, w/boxes, set ... **135.00**
Vase, bisque, w/cherubs, hp, 2 handles, 4¾x4¼" **17.50**
    Souvenir Lake Okaboji, Iowa, hp bird & florals, 2½" **10.00**
    Waggles **10.00**
Wall pocket, circular w/ballerina, net skirt, 5" **22.00**
    Cup & saucer, hp flowers, scalloped rim, 3¼" **8.00**
    Lady leans out window, 3¾x2¾" **13.00**
    Mallard duck diving into water, hp, 4¾" **13.00**
    Plate, molded and hp apples **9.50**
Wind chimes, square glass blades hung from racks **55.00**

Ohr, George

George Ohr established his pottery around 1893 in Biloxi, Miss. The unusual style of the ware he produced, and his flamboyant personality earned him the dubious title of the 'mad potter of Biloxi'. Though acclaimed by some of the critics of his day to be perhaps the most accomplished thrower in the history of the industry, others overlooked the egg shell thin walls of his vessels, each a different shape and contortion, and saw only that their 'tortured' appearance contradicted their own sedate preferences.

Ohr worked by himself with only minimal help from his son. His work was typically pinched and pulled, pleated, crumpled, dented and folded. Lizards and worms were often applied to the ware, each with detailed, expressive features. He was well recognized, however, for his glazes, especially those with a metallic patina.

The ware was marked with his name, alone or with Biloxi added. Ohr died in 1918.

Baby jug, unglazed, marbleized, 6½" **325.00**

Bowl, blue & brown bisque, 4x5" **85.00**
    Crimped, grey w/olive & grey interior, 2½x5" **165.00**
    Crimped, mottled grey & brown, w/yellow interior, 2x4" ... **140.00**
    Mottled tan & green, minutely crimped rim, 2½x3" **165.00**
    Olive glaze w/gunmetal highlights, folded, pinched, 3x5" ... **200.00**
    Speckled gr & brown, 5½x2¾" **200.00**
    White, brown & blue, unglazed, crazed bottom, 4½x5¼" **95.00**
Candlestick, block letters, 5" **225.00**
Creamer, brown speckled glaze, pinched, 3" **360.00**
Mug, gr & purple glaze, 2 handles, 3½" **350.00**
    Puzzle, mottled blk & brown glaze, rabbit handle, 3½" **250.00**
Pitcher, mottled blue & gr, pinched, 4½" **450.00**
    Red speckled glaze, pinched neck, 6½" **500.00**
Vase, brown w/mustard specks, pleated rim, 5x4" **245.00**
    Brown speckled, ornate double handles, twist, pleat waist, 7½" **700.00**
    Cup shape, green w/orange & gr specks, 2 handle, red clay . **230.00**
    Cup shape, mottled, gritty blk/red, 3 horizontal ribs, 3x3" .. **200.00**
    Dark brown, pleated & pinched, 3¼x5¼" **200.00**
    Green glaze w/orange blush, crimps & twist, 5" ornate handles, 7" **725.00**
    Gunmetal, 4½x4½" **160.00**
    Hi gloss, pleated, pinched-in belly, 3¼x5¼" **245.00**
    Metallic, script signature, 4½" **150.00**
    Olive high glaze, cylinder body, narrowing neck, 6" **165.00**
    Raspberry w/flecks, brown interior, pinched rim, 3¼x3½" .. **230.00**
    Red on grey, blk inside, wide horizontal ribs, 3x3" **230.00**
    Speckled gr, single & double handles **200.00**

Old Ivory

Berry set, #16, 7-pc **195.00**
    #76, 7-pc **200.00**
Bone dish, #200 .... **95.00**
Bowl, soup, #28 .... **85.00**
    Vegetable, #16 .... **45.00**
    #84, 6¼" **20.00**
Cake plate, #16, open handle, 10" dia **60.00**
    #28 .... **50.00**
    #75, open handle, 10¼" **55.00**
    #84, Ohme mk, 10" **68.00**
    #200 .... **50.00**
Cake set, #16, open handled platter & 6 small cake plates.... **125.00**
    #84, 7-pc **195.00**
Candy dish, #11, ring handle, 1½x6¼" dia **50.00**
Celery dish, #69 .... **50.00**
Celery tray, #16, Silesia, 11½" **50.00**
Charger, #82, 13" dia **130.00**
Chocolate pot, #11 .... **255.00**
    #200, w/cups, #27 .... **425.00**
Chocolate set, pot & 5 cups/saucers, rose design **325.00**
Cracker jar, #16, w/handles, 6x8½" **190.00**
Creamer, #75 .... **46.00**
Cup & saucer, #10, Clarion **45.00**
    #200 .... **50.00**
    Tea, #VII **35.00**
Cups & saucers, chocolate, #66, set of 5 .... **150.00**
Hair receiver, #16, 2-pc **200.00**
Nappy, #12, Clarion, inside handle, 6½" **45.00**
Pickle dish, #84, 8¼" **35.00**
Plate, #16, 6¼" **18.00**
    #16, 7½" **25.00**
    #16, 8½" **35.00**
    #73, 8½" **37.50**
    #84, dinner **100.00**

#200, dessert, 7½" **25.00**
Relish dish, #16, oval **30.00**
Salt & pepper, #75, roses **85.00**
#84 .... **95.00**
Sugar, covered, #16, Silesia **55.00**
Sugar & creamer, #31 .... **95.00**
#84 .... **110.00**
#VII **175.00**
Tea tile, #16, sgnd **125.00**
Waste bowl, #84, scalloped rim, 5½" dia **80.00**

Old Paris

Old Paris porcelains were made from the late 18th century until about 1900. Seldom marked, the term refers to the area of manufacture rather than a specific company. In general, the ware was of high quality, and characterized by classic shapes, colorful elegant decoration and gold application.

Bowl, open basketweave, paw feet, gold florals............. **195.00**
Cache pots, gr w/gilding, floral & figural scenes, 9½" **1,450.00**
Compote, gold & purple florals, deep open work, ftd, 8x8¾"... **75.00**
Inkstand, reclining man cover, w/3 inserts, 15x11x11" **450.00**
Tea set, child's, blue floral decor, red dots, gold tracing, 26-pc **395.00**
Toilet set, brass hinged jar, 2 bottles, children & cupid decor . **400.00**
Tureen, floral panels, much gold, ornate handles........... **150.00**
Vase, cobalt & blue floral painting, much gold, 2 handles, 12" **165.00**

Courting couple in reserve, black & aqua, gilt trim, 16½" .. **275.00**
Flair, vignette, gold & blue, 14x8" **149.00**
Pillow shape, birds & foliage, 4 gold feet, 11x8½" **320.00**
Portrait, maroon, gold & green, 13x8" **149.00**
Side-by-side, applied foot & floral decor, 3½" **45.00**

Old Sleepy Eye

Old Sleepy Eye was a Sioux Indian Chief who was born in Minnesota in 1780. His name was used for the name of a town, as well as a flour mill. The Sleepy Eye Milling Co., of Sleepy Eye, Minnesota, contracted The Weir Pottery Co. of Monmouth, Illinois, to make steins, vases, salt crocks and butter tubs which the flour company gave away to their customers in each bag of their flour. A bust profile of the old Indian and his name decorated each piece of the blue and gray stoneware. In addition to these four items,

the Minnesota Stoneware Co. of Red Wing made a mug with a verse which is very scarce today.

In 1906, Weir Pottery merged with six others to form the Western Stoneware Co. in Monmouth. They produced a line of blue and white ware using a lighter body, but these pieces were never given as flour premiums. This line consisted of pitchers, (5 sizes), steins, mugs, sugar bowls, vases, trivets, and mustache cups. These pieces turn up only rarely in other colors and are highly sought by advanced collectors.

Advertising items, such as trade cards, pillow tops, thermometers, paperweights, letter openers, post cards, tradecards, cookbooks and thimbles are considered very valuable.

The original ware was made sporadicaly until 1937. Brown steins and mugs were produced in 1952.

Breadboard scraper **495.00**
Butter carton, old **15.00**
Calendar, 1906, Sleepy Eye Milling Co **135.00**
Crock, butter, blue & grey stoneware **500.00**
Crock, salt, stoneware **575.00**
Fan, Indian head **100.00**
Label, barrel **135.00**
Egg crate, colorful, old **15.00**
Letter opener **400.00**

Match holder, chalkware, painted, right................ **1,500.00**
Mug, blue & wht, sgnd Monmouth, 4¾" **185.00**
Mug, brown, 1952 issue **300.00**
Convention item, 1976 .... **195.00**
Convention item, 1977 .... **145.00**
Convention item, 1978 .... **95.00**
Convention item, 1979 .... **50.00**
Convention item, 1980 .... **45.00**
Mug, poem, Minnesota Stoneware Co **1,250.00**
Paperweight, bronze, illus **495.00**
Pillow cover....................................... **600.00**
Pitcher, cobalt on white, #1......................... **180.00**
#2 .... **200.00**
#3 .... **215.00**
#4 .... **225.00**
#5 .... **235.00**
Pitcher, Flemish, blue & grey, #1 .... **190.00**
#2 .... **245.00**
#3 .... **260.00**
#4 .... **275.00**

#5	300.00
Pitcher w/Standing Indian	1,500.00
Post card	65.00
Salt crock, stoneware	575.00
Sign, tin, 19x13¼″	700.00
Spoon, Indian head on handle	95.00
Stein, all blue	660.00
All brown	1,000.00
Blue & grey stoneware	490.00
Brown, Western Pottery, 40 oz, 1952	550.00
Brown & wht	700.00
Brown & yellow	720.00
Cobalt blue & wht	490.00
Sugar, open, cobalt blue & wht	500.00
Thimble, aluminum, various colors	170.00
Trivet	1,150.00
Vase, blue & wht pottery, dragonflies decor	400.00
Brown & yellow, cattail decor	700.00
Flemish blue & grey, w/cattails & dragonfly	200.00
Green, cattail decor	520.00

Onion Pattern

The familiar pattern known to collectors as Onion acquired its name through a case of mistaken identity. Designed in the early 1700s by Johann Haroldt of the Meissen factory in Germany, the pattern was a mixture from earlier Oriental designs. One of its components was a stylized peach, which was mistakenly percieved to be an onion, causing the pattern to become known by that name. Usually found in blue, an occasional piece is also found in pink. The pattern is commonly associated with Meissen, but it has been reproduced by many others including Villeroy and Boch and Royal Copenhagen.

Bone dish, Meissen, crossed swords	55.00
Bowl, Meissen, china, 9¾″	35.00

Box, crossed swords mark, 3½x1¼″	85.00
Butter dish, Meissen, 2 pc	110.00
Canister, Japan, 4 pc, paper label	65.00
Nudelin & Reis, 8½″	100.00
Charger, Meissen, 14″	300.00
Meissen, 16″	350.00
Cheese board, 11″	150.00
Meissen, pink, wood handles, 6x11″	235.00
Chop plate, Meissen, crossed sword, round deep center	255.00
Coffee pot, crossed swords, rosebud finial	275.00
Colander, crossed swords	28.00
Creamer, Meissen, 3½″	65.00

Meissen, crossed sword mkd, floral decor, 1925, 4″	27.50
Crimper, Meissen	135.00
Cutting board, 7″	100.00
Darner, wood handle, unmkd	75.00
Demitasse cup & saucer, Meissen	30.00
Dish, Meissen, deep pinched sides & corners	110.00
Meissen, rectangular dome cover	350.00
Meissen, square, 8″	150.00
Meissen, 10½″	175.00
Feeding cup, impressed Germany, 7″	43.00
Five point mixer, Meissen	135.00
Food warmer, Grimwade, Staffordshire, 11″	85.00
Funnel strainer, Meissen, wood handles	235.00
Gravy boat, Meissen, attached underplate, handled	125.00
Hanging cheese dish, Meissen, mkd, 10x6″	320.00
Hanging salt box, Meissen, orig wood lid	385.00
Hot plate, 7″	75.00
Masher, Meissen, blue	135.00
Pink	185.00
Measuring set, crossed swords, 4 small pitchers	30.00
Meat tenderizer	85.00
Meissen mk	145.00
Mixing spoon, Meissen	135.00
Mortar & pestle, Meissen, pink	350.00
Ocarina, Meissen, unusual	150.00
Pepper	55.00
Pitcher, 3″	50.00
Plate, Meissen, 6″	250.00
Meissen, 9½″	35.00
Meissen, crossed swords, round feather design	335.00
Platter, Cauldon, 16x12″	78.00
Meissen, crossed swords, 11½″	165.00
Meissen, crossed swords, 13½″	185.00
Meissen, crossed swords, 16″	195.00
Meissen, crossed swords, pierced insert, 22″	325.00
Villeroy & Boch, oval, 17″	100.00
Rolling pin, Meissen, blue	185.00
Meissen, pink	235.00
Sauce boat, Meissen, double handle, double lip, 9¾″	250.00
Villeroy & Boch, large	22.50
Scoop, Meissen, 3″ deep	195.00
Spoon, Meissen, blue, decorated bowl, wood handle, 8½″	145.00
Meissen, pink, 4¼″	235.00
Strainer, Meissen, blue, round, 3″	135.00
Meissen, pink, wood handle, 6x3″	185.00
Sugar w/cover, Meissen, crossed swords, melon shaped	95.00
Tea tile, Meissen, ball ftd, sq, 5″	125.00
Tea pot, crossed swords, rosebud finial	175.00

Opalescent Glass

First made in England in 1870, opalescent glass became popular in America around the turn of the century. Its name comes from the milky white opalescent trim that defines the lines of the pattern. It was produced in table sets, novelties, toothpick holders, vases and lamps.

Banana boat, Alaska, vaseline opal	225.00
Barber bottle, Daisy & Fern, vaseline opal	75.00
Basket, Caroline, wht opal, large	35.00
Old Man Winter, large, green opal	55.00
Old Man Winter, vaseline opal	75.00
Ringhandled, wht opal	45.00
Western Daisy, large, wht opal	35.00
Berry, bowl, Alaska, blue opal, footed, 8½x8½″	138.00

Beatty Swirl, wht opal, master **35.00**
Chrysanthemum Base Swirl, cranberry opal, master **85.00**
Double Greek Key, blue opal, 8″ **35.00**
Drape, blue opal w/enamel, small **30.00**
Everglade, blue opal, master **145.00**
Everglade, blue opal, small **45.00**
Fluted Scroll, vaseline opal, master **95.00**
Fluted Scroll, vaseline opal, small **32.00**
Inverted Fan & Feather, blue opal, gold decor, small **38.00**
Iris, small, wht opal **12.00**
Iris & Meander, blue opal, small **20.00**
Jackson, blue opal, small **12.00**
Jefferson, wht opal, small **5.00**
Jeweled Heart, blue opal, small **22.00**
Ribbed Spiral, vaseline opal, sm **8.00**
Vesta Hobnail in Square, wht opal **8.00**
Wild Bouquet, blue opal, master **90.00**
Wild Bouquet, wht opal, master **65.00**
Berry set, Flora, vaseline opal, 7 pc **265.00**
   Flower & Jewel, vaseline opal, gold decor, 7 pc **345.00**
   Jeweled Heart, blue opal, 7 pc **135.00**
   Jeweled Heart, green opal, 7 pc **145.00**
   Scroll w/Acanthus, 7 pc, wht opal **55.00**
   Wild Bouquet, 7 pc, wht opal **125.00**
   Wreath & Shell, wht opal, 7 pc **225.00**
Biscuit jar, on plate, sanded gold decor, blue opal, 8″ **225.00**
Blackberry Hat w/paint, wht opal **12.50**
Bon bon, Beaded Fan, blue opal **35.00**
   Blossom & Palms, wht opal **29.00**
Bowl, Abalone, green opal **14.00**
   Argonaut Shell, blue opal, footed, 6½x8″ **27.00**
   Barbell, ruffled, blue opal, 6½″ **30.00**
   Basketweave, green opal **25.00**
   Beaded Drapes, footed, vaseline opal **32.00**
   Beaded Stars, blue opal **20.00**
   Blossom & Palm, green opal **25.00**
   Blossom & Web, blue opal **60.00**
   Cashews, green opal, 8″ **25.00**
   Cherry, ruffled, gold & red trim, wht opal, 10″ **25.00**
   Consolidated Crisscross, cranberry opal, 8″ **135.00**
   Daisy & Plume, blue opal, 3 feet, ribbon candy edge **65.00**
   Daisy & Plume, footed, green opal, 7″ **45.00**
   Daisy & Plume, 3 feet, wht opal **35.00**
   Daisy Dear, green opal **35.00**
   Desert Garden, green opal **30.00**
   Fancy Fantails, footed, vaseline opal, red rim, 7½″ **35.00**
   Fancy Fantails, footed, wht opal, red trim, 8″ **25.00**
   Fluted Scrolls, cranberry opal, ftd, 6½″ **37.50**
   Fluted Scrolls, footed, blue opal, 7″ **28.00**
   Greek Key & Rib, footed, wht opal **30.00**
   Hobnail, vaseline opal, Hobbs, 5x3″ **100.00**
   Honeycomb & Clover, green, 9″ **38.00**
   Jackson, blue opal, 3 feet **35.00**
   Jefferson Shield, blue opal **75.00**
   Jewel & Fan, blue opal **28.00**
   Jewel & Fan, wht opal, 5x8½″ **22.00**
   Jewels & Drapes, blue opal **28.00**
   Jolly Bear, wht opal **125.00**
   Lattice Medallion, blue opal **30.00**
   Leaf & Beads, footed, blue opal **28.00**
   Leaf & Beads, footed, green opal, 7″ **25.00**
   Leaf & Leaflets, w/gold & red trim, wht opal **26.00**
   Lined Heart, green opal, 8″ **18.00**
   Loop, wht opal **100.00**

Many Loops, blue opal **22.00**
Meander, blue opal, footed **65.00**
Meander, green opal, 9″ **30.00**
Meander, wht opal, 3 feet **30.00**
Milkyway, large **25.00**
Peacock on the Fence, blue opal **90.00**
Pearl Flowers, green opal **25.00**
Rays & Lines, blue opal **22.00**
Reverse Drapery, ruffled, green opal **22.00**
Rose Show, blue opal **175.00**
Ruffles & Rings, wht opal, 3 legs, 9″ **30.00**
Scroll w/Acanthus, wht opal, 5½″ **15.00**
Shell & Wild Rose, footed, green opal **26.00**
Spanish Lace, oval, large **18.00**
Spokes & Wheels, wht opal **22.50**
Swag w/Bracket, flared edge, cranberry opal, 6″ **35.00**
Swirl, ruffled, large, green opal **28.00**
Three Fruits, Meander, blue opal **45.00**
Tokyo, blue opal, 8″ **27.00**
Tokyo, fluted, footed, wht opal, 8″ **26.00**
Tokyo, shallow, wht opal, 9″ **17.00**
Western Daisy, blue opal **45.00**
Wheel & Block, wht opal **18.00**
Windflower, wht opal **22.00**
Winter Cabbage, footed, blue opal **35.00**
Bud vase, Tiny Twig, wht opal, 4¾″ **16.00**
Butter, Diamond Spearpoint, vaseline opal **250.00**
   Double Greek Key, wht opal **95.00**
   Drapery, blue opal **130.00**
   Everglades, blue opal **325.00**
   Fluted Scrolls, blue opal **250.00**
   Fluted Scrolls, vaseline opal **195.00**
   Fluted Scrolls, wht opal **125.00**
   Hobnail, footed, blue opal **115.00**
   Jackson, ¼ lb, wht opal **45.00**
   Jewel & Flower, vaseline opal **250.00**
   Panelled Holly, blue opal **280.00**
   Regal, green opal **175.00**
   Seaweed, blue opal **225.00**
   Tokyo, blue opal **200.00**
   Tokyo, green opal **135.00**
   Wreath & Shell, blue opal **150.00**
   Wreath & Shell, vaseline opal **200.00**
Candy dish, Wishbone, blue opal **45.00**
Carafe, water, Reverse Swirl, blue opal **45.00**
Card tray, Argonaut Shell, wht opal **29.00**
   Nautilus, vaseline opal **45.00**
Celery, Alaska, blue opal **150.00**
   Alaska, blue opal w/enamel **235.00**
   Alaska, vaseline opal **145.00**
   Beatty Swirl, blue opal **55.00**
Chalice, Maple Leaf, wht opal **35.00**
Chop plate, Northern Star, blue opal **45.00**
Compote, Berry Patch, green opal **14.00**
   Dolphin handles, blue opal **45.00**
   Fluted Bars & Beads, wht opal **25.00**
   Hearts & Flowers, blue opal **25.00**
   Intaglio, small **25.00**
   Maple Leaf, green opal **35.00**
   Maple Leaf, vaseline opal **35.00**
   Ocean Shell, wht opal **28.00**
   Popsicle Sticks, blue opal, large **28.00**
   Popsicle Sticks, wht opal, large **18.00**
   Spool & Threads, blue opal **25.00**

Thistle Patch, wht opal, small............................ **14.00**
Compote, jelly, Argonaut Shell, blue opal, tall **58.00**
  Everglade, vaseline opal **125.00**
  Intaglio, blue opal **39.00**
  Iris w/Meander, vaseline opal **45.00**
  Maple Leaf, green opal **45.00**
  Regal, blue opal **85.00**
  Ribbed Spiral, blue opal **45.00**
  Swag w/Brackets, blue opal **30.00**
Cracker jar, Beatty Ribbed, blue opal **355.00**
Creamer, Circled Scroll, green opal **85.00**
  Alaska, blue opal **75.00**
  Alaska, vaseline opal **65.00**
  Beatty Honeycomb, wht opal **20.00**
  Beatty Waffle, wht opal, 3″ **20.00**
  Circled Scroll, blue opal **85.00**
  Circled Scroll, green opal **85.00**
  Drapery, blue opal **50.00**
  Everglades, blue opal **48.00**
  Fan, footed, green opal **28.00**
  Feather, green opal **65.00**
  Fluted Scroll, blue opal **50.00**
  Fluted Scroll, cranberry opal **65.00**
  Fluted Scroll, vaseline **40.00**
  Fluted Scroll, wht opal **50.00**
  Intaglio, wht opal **45.00**
  Iris, green opal **80.00**
  Jewel & Flower, wht opal **40.00**
  Panelled Holly blue opal **100.00**
  Regal, green opal **35.00**
  Reverse Swirl, blue opal **60.00**
  Scroll w/Acanthus, vaseline opal **50.00**
  Shell, blue opal **65.00**
  Shell, wht opal **30.00**
  Tokyo, green opal **45.00**
  Waterlily & Cattails, blue opal **40.00**
  Wild Bouquet, wht opal **35.00**
Cruet, Alaska, blue opal **300.00**
  Alaska, wht opal **68.00**
  Argonaut Shell, blue opal **225.00**
  Argonaut Shell, wht opal **90.00**
  Daisy & Fern, wht opal **75.00**
  Everglades, blue opal **395.00**
  Fluted Scroll, blue opal, clear stopper **120.00**
  Fluted Scroll, w/enamel, vaseline **145.00**
  Herringbone, cranberry opal, cut stopper **155.00**
  Intaglio, blue opal **90.00**
  Intaglio, wht opal **80.00**
  Jackson, blue opal **75.00**
  Regal, wht opal **70.00**
  Reverse Swirl, vaseline, clear stopper **75.00**
  Ribbed Lattice, blue opal, clear stopper **135.00**
  Seaweed, blue opal **155.00**
  Seaweed, wht opal **90.00**
  Tokyo, green opal **95.00**
  Tokyo, wht opal **70.00**
  Wild Bouquet, wht opal **95.00**
Cup, Ribbed Spiral, vaseline opal **35.00**
Dish, Open O's, wht opal **25.00**
  Squirrel & Acorn, green opal **85.00**
Epergne, Vesta, 3 lily, wht opal **55.00**
Ewer, applied florals, vaseline handle, leaf, wht opal, 8½″ **125.00**
  Wht w/blue stripes, pink flowers, vaseline handle **135.00**
Finger bowl, Windows Swirl, cranberry opal **30.00**

Hobnail, *see Pattern glass*
Log Trough, blue opal **28.00**
  Wht opal **20.00**
Maize, *see Libbey*
Match holder, Waterlily & Cattails **20.00**
May Basket, green opal **35.00**
Mug, Diamond & Spearhead, vaseline opal **35.00**
  Stork in Rushes, blue opal **38.00**
Mustard w/lid, Reverse Swirl, vaseline opal **38.00**
Nappy, Blooms & Blossoms, handled, wht opal **16.00**
Perfume, Plumes, blue opal **25.00**
Pitcher, Alaska, blue opal **375.00**
  Alaska, vaseline opal **350.00**
  Arabian Nights, cranberry opal **450.00**
  Beatty Rib Swirl, blue opal **200.00**
  Beatty Swirl, wht opal **95.00**
  Buttons & Bows, blue opal **165.00**
  Clover & Honeycomb, wht opal **125.00**
  Coronation, blue opal, tankard **125.00**
  Daisy & Fern, wht opal, 8½″ **115.00**
  Drape, cranberry opal, tankard **275.00**
  Drapery, blue opal **200.00**
  Drapery, green opal **155.00**
  Drapery, wht opal **95.00**
  Flora, wht opal **95.00**
  Fluted Scroll, blue opal **200.00**
  Fluted Scroll, wht opal **80.00**
  Hobnail w/Thumbprint, blue opal **90.00**
  Intaglio, blue opal **225.00**
  Intaglio, wht opal **75.00**
  Open Windows, wht w/clear handle, ruffled, 7½″ **80.00**
  Poinsettia, blue opal, tankard **100.00**
  Reverse Swirl, cranberry opal **295.00**
  Reverse Swirl, gold rib, 9¾″ **130.00**
  Reverse Swirl, tankard, wht opal **85.00**
  Reverse Swirl, vaseline opal, Burlington mk **170.00**
  Spanish Lace, blue opal, ruffled top **165.00**
  Spanish Lace, cranberry opal **325.00**
  Swag w/Brackets, wht opal **135.00**
  Wild Bouquet, wht opal **65.00**
  Windows, blue opal, Burlington **175.00**
Plate, Beaded Stars, footed, green opal **24.00**
  Iris & Meander, wht opal, 7½″ **20.00**
  Palm Beach, blue opal **48.00**
  Spokes & Wheels, blue opal, 8½″ **30.00**
  Tokyo, green opal, 8½″ **28.00**
  Vintage, dome ft, flat top, green opal **25.00**
  Waterlily & Cattails, turned up edge, amethyst opal, 10″ **45.00**
Punch cup, Swirl, blue opal, clear handle **25.00**
Relish, Jewel & Fan, wht opal, 8½x4¼″ **18.00**
Rose bowl, applied flowers, striped vaseline opal branch, 4″ .. **100.00**
  Beaded Drape, blue opal **32.00**
  Beaded Fan, blue opal **48.00**
  Button Panels, blue opal **32.00**
  Button Panels, vaseline opal **32.00**
  Daisy & Fern, blown, wht opal **32.00**
  Fancy Fantails, blue opal **35.00**
  Fluted Bars & Beads, blue opal **28.00**
  Opal Open, flared & scalloped, blue opal **35.00**
  Opal Open, stemmed, wht opal **25.00**
  Open Stemmed, blue opal **28.00**
  Pearls & Scales, blue opal **25.00**
  Pearls & Scales, footed, green opal **45.00**
  Piasa Bird, blue opal **40.00**

Piasa Bird, wht opal **65.00**
Swirl satin blue opal, Stevens & Williams, 3½" **195.00**
Wreath & Shell, footed vaseline **65.00**
Salt & pepper, Alaska, blue opal **150.00**
Salt shaker, Jewel & Flower, wht opal **65.00**
Vertical Ribbon, canary opal **26.50**
Sauce, Acorn & Burr, blue opal **45.00**
Alaska, vaseline opal **25.00**
Beatty Swirl, blue opal **15.00**
Inverted Fan & Feather, blue opal w/gold, footed **38.00**
Jewel & Flower, wht w/gold **40.00**
Palm Beach, vaseline opal **60.00**
Plume, acorn base, wht opal **115.00**
Roman Rosette, wht opal **95.00**
Scroll w/Acanthus, wht opal **18.00**
Swag Bracket, footed, blue opal **24.00**
Wild Bouquet, wht opal **20.00**
Sherbet, Intaglio, wht opal **28.00**

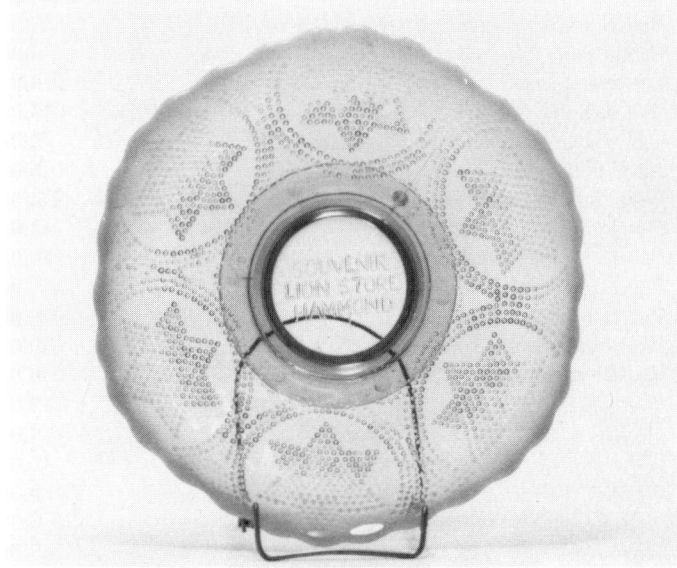

Souvenir, plate w/stars, blue opal, 9" **65.00**
Spooner, Alaska, blue opal **65.00**
Double Beetle Band, blue opal **50.00**
Drapery, wht opal **35.00**
Feather, green opal **75.00**
Fluted Scroll, blue opal **50.00**
Fluted Scroll, wht opal **42.00**
Fluted Scroll, vaseline opal **45.00**
Intaglio, blue opal **75.00**
Iris, green opal **85.00**
Iris & Meander, blue opal **55.00**
Jewell & Flower, yellow opal **80.00**
Palm Beach, blue opal **60.00**
Regal, blue opal **65.00**
Reverse Swirl, blue opal **50.00**
Ribbed Lattice, cranberry opal **95.00**
Scroll Acanthus, vaseline opal **45.00**
Seaweed, cranberry opal satin **90.00**
Spanish Lace, cranberry **75.00**
Tokyo, green opal **40.00**
Waterlily & Cattails, blue opal **40.00**
Waterlily & Cattails, green opal **40.00**
Wild Bouquet, wht opal **30.00**
Wreath & Shell, yellow opal **80.00**
Stump Mug, blue opal **35.00**

Sugar, Bubble Lattice, covered, cranberry opal **115.00**
Diamond Spearhead, w/cover, vaseline opal **90.00**
Double Greek Key, covered, wht opal **95.00**
Fluted Scroll, covered, wht opal **75.00**
Fluted Scroll, open, vaseline opal **25.00**
Fluted Scroll, open, vaseline opal w/enamel **30.00**
Jewel & Flower, wht opal, covered **40.00**
Regal, blue opal **75.00**
Reverse Swirl, covered, blue opal **115.00**
Seaweed, covered, cranberry opal satin **110.00**
Sunburst on Shield, wht opal **20.00**
Water Lily & Cattails, open, green opal **28.00**
Wild Bouquet, open, wht opal **25.00**
Sugar shaker, Reverse Swirl, blue opal **110.00**
Spanish Lace, blue opal **68.00**
Syrup, Bubble Lattice, blue opal **195.00**
Coin Spot & Swirl, blue opal **80.00**
Daisy & Crisscross, blue opal **175.00**
Fern, blue opal **65.00**
Gonderman Swirl, blue opal **175.00**
Lattice, bulbous, blue opal **145.00**
Windows Swirled, blue opal **180.00**
Table set, Alaska, vaseline opal **500.00**
Drapery, 4 pc, blue opal, gold decor **370.00**
Fluted Scroll, 4 pc, vaseline opal **450.00**
Fluted Scroll, 4 pc, wht opal **125.00**
Swag & Bracket, 4 pc, green opal **350.00**
Tokyo, 4 pc, blue opal **500.00**
Toothpick, Chrysanthemum Base Swirl, cranberry opal **115.00**
Overall Hobnail, blue opal **40.00**
Tumbler, Buttons & Braid, blue opal **40.00**
Chrysanthemum Base Swirl, blue opal **40.00**
Circled Scroll, blue opal **90.00**
Coin Spot, blue opal **40.00**
Daffodil, blue opal **50.00**
Drape, blue opal **28.00**
Florette, pink opal **60.00**
Honeycomb, rainbow opal **250.00**
Iris Meander, vaseline opal **48.00**
Jackson, wht opal **22.00**
Palm Beach, blue opal **90.00**
Palm Beach, vaseline opal **45.00**
Panelled Holly, blue opal w/gold trim **30.00**
Poinsettia, blue opal **48.00**
Poinsettia, wht opal **42.00**
Polka Dot, blue opal **60.00**
S-Repeat, blue opal **40.00**
Spanish Lace, blue opal **45.00**
Swag w/Brackets, wht opal **35.00**
Swirl, blue opal **30.00**
Vesta, wht opal **38.00**
Waterlily & Cattails, blue opal **30.00**
Vase, Basketweave, open edge, footed, green opal **15.00**
Beads & Bark, blue opal **50.00**
Boggy Bayou, amethyst opal **32.50**
Boggy Bayou, wht opal, large **15.00**
Calyx, blue opal **35.00**
Corn, vaseline opal **75.00**
Diamond Optic, cranberry opal, 7½" **60.00**
Diamond Point & Oval Thumbprint, wht opal **15.00**
Diamond Stem, wht opal **12.50**
Fluted Bars & Beads, green w/pink lip **35.00**
Iris & Meander, blue opal, large **28.00**
Jack in Pulpit, red glass edge, blue opal **25.00**

Jack in Pulpit, wht opal, 7″	20.00
Jefferson Spool, novelty, green opal	15.00
Leaf pattern, wht opal, large	16.00
Lined Heart, blue opal	50.00
Lorna, vaseline opal	16.00
Lorna, wht opal	12.00
Many Ribs, blue opal	22.00
Open Windows, bulbous, ruffled, wht opal, 7½″	70.00
Pulled Loop, wht opal	15.00
Thin Rib, blue opal, 8″	20.00
Tree Bark, blue opal	25.00
Tree Bark, green opal, large	20.00
Tree Bark, wht opal, 12″	15.00
Twig, vaseline opal, large	35.00
Zipper & Loops, green opal	40.00
Pink opal to vaseline, footed, 3¼″	50.00
Water bottle, Reverse Swirl, blue opal	110.00
Water set, Buttons & Braid, blue opal, 5 pc	275.00
Coin Spot, cranberry opal, Burlington mk, 7 pc	325.00
Daisy & Fern, cranberry opal, 7 pc	365.00
Drapery, blue opal w/gold decor, 7 pc	485.00
Fern, blue opal, 7 pc	350.00
Poinsetia, blue opal, 7 pc	375.00
Regal, blue opal, 7 pc	685.00
Spanish Lace, bulbous, cranberry opal, 7 pc	645.00
Windows, blue opal, Burlington mk, 5 pc	315.00

Openers

Around the turn of the century, manufacturers began to seal bottles with a metal cap that required a new type of bottle opener. Now the screw cap and the flip top are making bottle openers nearly obsolete.

There are many variations, some in combination with other tools. There are those in silver or brass; some are figural, many are advertising--all are collectible.

Corkscrews

Advertising, Anheiser Busch, bottle shape w/shaft inside	20.00
Davis, pat 1891, McMannammy Bar Supplies	25.00
GG liquor, w/cap puller	8.00
Hamm's Brewery	20.00
Old Snifter, chrome, w/opener	49.00

Old Snifter, figural standing man 45.00

Schlitz Beer, wood handle	7.50
Wacker & Birk Brewing, wood handle	9.00
Williamson's New Century, bottle tap, chrome	34.00
Ah-so, prong type, German	5.00
Bar, wine corkscrew, wood/metal	35.00
Bar Bum, figural of a drunk w/opener	35.00
Boar tusk handle	40.00
Brass; 2-lever, one on each side	15.00
Bullet, Williamson, dated 1897	17.00
Dog, Hootch Hound, 4″	35.00
Key, corkscrew in shaft	15.00
With bell, old, 5½″	19.00
With lever action	55.00
Chrome, parrot, w/opener	11.00
With shot measure & opener	15.00
Double lever, Heeley & Sons, English	50.00
English, Magic Lever cork puller	35.00
Figural; antler handle, large	15.00
Bird, Art Deco, ci, w/lifter, 1920s	10.00
Butler, wood, unscrews at waist, old, 8″	75.00
Cannon, wood barrel, w/opener	14.00
Cat, brass, small, corkscrew tail	10.00
Golf bag and club, heavy	80.00
Grape vine, vine handle	5.00
Harp, folds	5.00
Key, brass, w/corkscrew in shaft	15.00
Mermaid, folds, English	15.00
Parrot, standing, corkscrew in tail	10.00
Pig, brass, corkscrew tail	5.00
Pig, standing, corkscrew tail	15.00
Pig's hind quarters, metal	26.00
Red devil, standing	10.00

Waiter, standing, Syroco wood, 8½″	40.00
German, tubular w/more tools in case	10.00
Iron, w/interior screw, turned wood handle	8.00
Silver look, relief grapes, Italy, w/opener	55.00
Sterling, folds, double hinged, 3″	30.00
Wood handle, w/metal cork lifter	10.00
Zig Zag, accordian type, France	10.00

Bottle Openers

Advertising, Ballantine Beer, can piercer & lifter, plastic	12.00
Ballantine Beer, wood baseball bat, 12″	25.00
Ballantine, lifter w/open 3 ring symbol	10.00
Budweiser, bow-tie, steel, red & white, 5″	10.00

Budweiser, fishing lure, lifter & piercer **6.00**
Buffalo Brewery, figural boot **25.00**
Columbia Brewing Co, w/ice pick, wood handle **12.00**
Esslinger's Beer, tin figural **30.00**
Esslinger's Beer-Ale, w/spoon **12.00**
Gay-Ola, figural leg & shoe **5.50**
Giffon's Beer, lifter & bell combination **23.00**
Girl Beer, woman serving beer, Germany, old **22.00**
Gold Top Beer, baseball player, flat metal **18.00**
Iroquois Beer, figural Indian, brass, early **30.00**
Joachim Cigar Co, hacket type **17.00**
Kingsbaker Cigar Co, nickel plate, hacket end **35.00**
Lone Star Beer, Sheriff's Badge, steel **6.00**
Michelob, mini-bottle, wood/metal, 1960s **10.00**
Over the top lifter, bottle shape, lithograph **15.00**
Pabst, Tapster **250.00**
Sheridan Export Beer, steel w/brass case **70.00**
Silverman's Strand Theatre, leg & foot, chrome **7.00**
Sprenger Brewing Co, man w/beer mug, brass **160.00**
West End Brewing Co, leg, ivory, w/2 blades **55.00**
White Rock, figural girl, early **15.00**
White Rock, figural nymph on rock **20.00**
Bottle, with opener formed in glass bottom, 5¾" **14.00**
Brass, figural nude lady, 1913 Braum & Co **22.00**
    King with crown, robe, and crossed sword, old, ornate **55.00**
    Lady's leg **25.00**
Bronze, man **60.00**
Cap lifter w/ornate cast iron handle, pat Feb 6, '94 . . . . **25.00**
Cap lifter w/wire breaker, cigar cutter, tamper, ci, 4¾" **22.00**
Chrome, gold club **9.00**
Combination, lifter & pencil **25.00**
    Lifter, lid pry, jar top opener, 5½" **25.00**
    Lifter & slotted ladle, pat 1915, 10½" **30.00**
    Opener & bell, brass, Bells of Barna, India **15.00**
Easi-Ope can & bottle opener, Ranson, 4¾" **6.00**
Figural; auto jack, 1920s style, cast iron **10.00**
    Barber shop quartet **19.50**
    Baseball cap, cast iron **13.00**
    Bird, Toucan, white w/orange beak, cast iron **30.00**
    Black Egyptian woman, cast iron **15.00**
    Black face w/bow tie, mouth is opener, painted cast iron **32.00**
    Black man holding beer, iron **16.50**
    Bulldog, cast iron **15.00**
    Bulldog, solid brass **25.00**
    Car, Model-T **15.00**
    Donkey, cast iron, old paint, 3½" **80.00**
    Donkey head, cast iron **30.00**
    Drunk w/lamp post, iron, old, 4" **7.50**
    Eagle head on bottle shape, pat 4-30-12, 2¾" **10.00**
    Elephant, sitting, cast iron **25.00**
    Elephant, trunk is opener, cast iron **11.00**
    False teeth, cast iron, old paint, 3½" wide **70.00**
    Fat waiter carring beer mugs, papier mache, 1920s **35.00**
    Fish, brass, w/corkscrew **15.00**
    Fish, spinner, spin to see who pays, Dow Co, 3¼" **25.00**
    Horse's hind quarters, cast iron **11.00**
    Horsehead **30.00**
    Lady's shoe **15.00**
    Lobster, cast iron **15.00**
    Mini-bottle, wooden, w/metal cap & cap lifter, 3½" **20.00**
    Nude female, Deco **18.00**
    Nude pouring from bottle, 3" **10.00**
    Nude, Sept Morn, high relief brass, 1913, 3¼" **30.00**
    Parrot on perch, cast iron, old paint, 5" **55.00**

Pelican, cast iron **16.00**
Pretzel, cast iron **20.00**
Rooster, opener in tail, cast iron **11.00**
Rooster, standing, cast iron **30.00**
Seagull, cast iron, painted, 3½" **18.00**
Shark, cast aluminum **23.00**
Walrus, cast iron, original paint **85.00**
Wolf head, chrome, crescent shaped handle **29.00**
Woman with 4 eyes, cast iron **20.00**
Key shape, combo lifter, screw driver, cutter, ED Mfg, 3" **25.00**
Silver, sterling, hollow handle, swirled ribs, scrolls, 6" **22.00**
Souvenir, Cypress Gardens, anchor, w/corkscrew, brass, old **12.00**
Tap Knob, Anheuser-Busch **15.00**
Wall, 4 eyes, cast iron **35.00**
    Black face, cast iron **65.00**
    Bulldog, cast iron **45.00**
    Clown, cast iron, 4x4¼" **50.00**
    Coal miner w/pick & mug, cast iron, Laier Brewing **200.00**
    Brewmaster w/mug, brass, Sprenger Brewing **100.00**
    Man w/mustache & 4 eyes, cast iron **30.00**
    Parrot, standing, cast iron **25.00**
    Woman, painted, marked Wilton **18.00**

Opera Glasses

Chevalier, Paris, silver & brass, w/MOP handles, case **25.00**
Dubois, Paris, red enamel, white MOP eye pieces, gold fleur-de-lys **450.00**
Laymayre, Paris, MOP, w/case **40.00**
LeMaire, brass, pink MOP, in case, Paris **38.50**

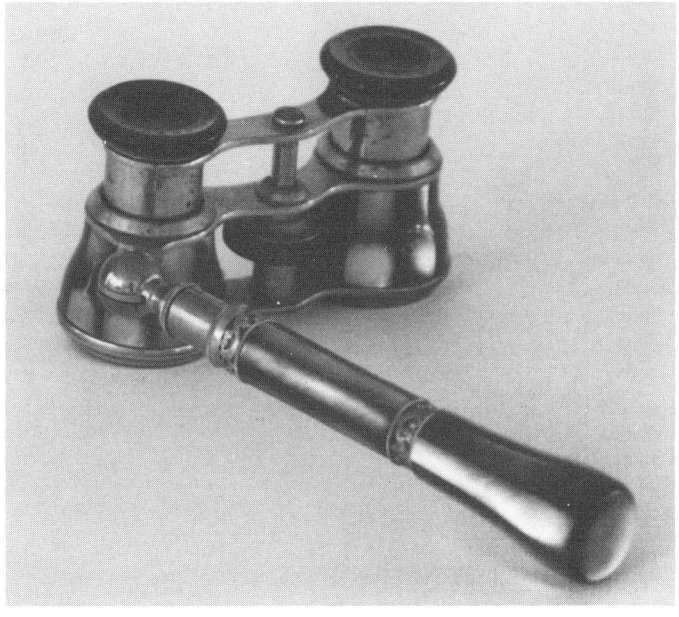

MOP & brass **50.00**
MOP & brass, orig leather case **35.00**
Officer, military souvenir kit, mkd DRGM, cloth snap bag **15.00**
Sportier, Paris, tan w/plated brass **24.00**

Optical Items

    Collectors of Americana are beginning to appreciate the charm of antique optical items, and those involved in the related trade find them particularly fascinating. Anyone, however, can appreciate the evolution of technology apparent when viewing a collection of old eyewear, and at the same time admire the primitive ingenuity involved in their construction.

Binocular, Chevalier, Paris, Day & Night Glass Co **40.00**
   Brass, sgnd Lanier, Paris **15.00**
Lorgnette, 14k gold filigree, 1800s **275.00**
   Sterling w/niello enameling, 1920 . . . . **185.00**
   Tortoise shell, carved open scroll work handle **55.00**
   Tortoise shell, silver frame, France **150.00**
Spectacle case, 14k gold, mkd w/initials, Tiffany & Co **1,500.00**
   Lacquered black w/gold, scroll design, cloth lining **18.00**
   Silver gilt & cloisonne enamel, V Rassadin, Moscow **2,100.00**
   Sterling, mkd, scroll design, velvet lining **55.00**
Spectacles, Ben Franklin style, sun w/case **9.00**
   Ben Franklin style, sun glasses, orange lenses **25.00**

Folding frames, paperboard case **15.00**
Gold chain & hairpin, Omaha, Doctors Bryant & Bushman . . . **45.00**
Octagonal lenses, 10k gold **40.00**
Old sunglasses, dark green lenses **20.00**
Old sunglasses, gray lenses **20.00**
Oval lenses, temple slides, Silveroid **20.00**
Rimless, gold fittings, leather case, Pincenez **12.00**
Rimmed, gold nose clip, chain & hairpin, w/case **17.00**
Silver, 1820s, Georgian **175.00**
Silver, adjustable sides, mkd **85.00**
Tin, w/case, 1874 . . . . **20.00**
White base metal **25.00**
Women's, 12k gold framed, 1940 . . . . **35.00**
Yellow base metal **25.00**

Orientalia

   The art of the Orient is an area of collecting that has recently enjoyed a surge of interest, not only in those examples that are truly 'antique', but in the 20th century items as well. Auction prices seem to well exceed their estimates with a regularity not apparent in many other collectible fields.

   Because of the many aspects involved in a study of Orientalia, we can only try through brief comments to acquaint the reader with some of the more readily available examples and suggest specialized reference sources for detailed information.

   Celadon, introduced during the Chin Dynasty, is a green glazed ware developed in an attempt to imitate the color of jade. Designs are often incised or painted on over glaze in heavy enamel applications.

   Chinese export ware was designed to appeal to Western tastes, and was often made to order. During the 18th century, vast amounts were shipped to Europe and on westward. Many of these dinnerwares were given specific pattern names---Rose Mandrin, Fitzhugh, Rose Medallion, Canton and Armorial are but a few of the more familiar.

   Cinnabar is carved laquer work, often involving hundreds of layers built one at a time on a metal or wooden base. Later pieces are red; older examples tend to darken.

   Moriage is a 20th century innovation characterized by heavy applications of enamel in relief designs of scrollwork, florals or beaded lace.

   See also sections on cloisonne, ivory, snuff bottles, Rose Medallion, Satsuma, Geisha Girl China, Kutani, Imari, Netsuke, Nippon, Noritake, Canton, Champleve and Peking glass.

Banko, teapot, basketweave lid, bird on branch, bows **120.00**

Teapot, brown clay w/enameled cranes, florals, 3″ **75.00**
Teapot, elephant **115.00**
Teapot, gray w/birds, & flowers, 2½″ **45.00**
Teapot, gray w/movable finial, painted birds, foliage, 4½″ **65.00**
Teapot, marbleized w/glaze modeled 5 masks **425.00**
Teapot, white w/blue/yellow ground, cranes, foliage, 3″ **45.00**
Tumbler, articulated figures, 3½″ **90.00**
Vase, black w/mottled colors, boys w/bucket, artist seal, 12″. **235.00**
Vase, sgraffito trees, brown glaze, 1½″ **50.00**
Vase, slip & sgraffito decor, on ped, w/handles, bisque, 3½″ . **80.00**
Basket, w/carved wood handle, brass lock, footed, 12x12x7″ . . **240.00**
Bell, w/dragon in wooden stand, 2 figures w/flowers, inlaid wire **700.00**
Blue & white, aquarium, immortals on mythical animals, 18x20″ **1,200.00**
   Box, w/lid, crane & foliage, 4″ dia **110.00**
   Cache pots, hexagonal, w/undertrays, 15″ dia, pr **1,250.00**
   Charger, florals, Ming, 11″ dia **150.00**
   Charger, landscapes & man, scalloped, 17″ **350.00**
   Charger, phoenix in flight, Ming, export, 11½″ **150.00**
   Crocus vase, squared ovoid, dragons, ftd, loose ring handles, 10″ **350.00**
   Deep dish, florals, Annamese, 1600s, 17½″ **300.00**
   Garden seats, barrel shaped, 19½″, pr **1,200.00**
   Ginger jar w/cover, florals allover, 1850 . . . . **130.00**
   Incense burner, hp, 3 men hold up world & foo dog **1,500.00**
   Jar, genere, children at play, Kang Hsi, 10″ **295.00**
   Jar, sages walk through pines, covered, late 1800s **300.00**
   Teacup, Ming Wanli, 1573-1620 . . . . **70.00**
   Teapot, scenes w/men, both sides, flattened shape, export, 10x9″ **400.00**
   Temple urn, 1850, 17″ **325.00**
   Vase, allover dragon, dragon straps, Ming, pr **4,800.00**
   Vases, 4 Accomplishments, covered, 22″ **1,850.00**
Bodhisattva on lotus throne, Cire Perdue bronze, 6½″ **125.00**
Bookend, Bonheur horses **50.00**
Bowl, coat of arms, export **165.00**
   Floral swags, & sprays, export porcelain, 10½″ **300.00**
   Immortals, in scene w/deer & bats, blue, wht & red, 15″ . . . **325.00**
   Orientals in landscape, dog, export, 1775, 7½″ **345.00**
   Porcelain, chipped ice pattern, signed, 1820, 10½″ **325.00**
   Provincial Ming blue & white, 6″ dia **250.00**
   Ship decor, export, repaired, 11″ **285.00**
Box, brass, hand engraved, wood lined **40.00**
   Brass, w/enameled cranes, 4x6″ **70.00**
   Condiment, porcelain export, 3 section **125.00**
   Japanese Damascene, black enamel over brass, gold decor, 3x4½″ **90.00**
   Japanese Damascene, black w/18k butterfly, florals, w/mirror **125.00**
   Peach shape, export, 5½″ dia **130.00**
   Silver w/engraved garden scene, for incense, 3″ **365.00**
   Wedding, Korean, red & black, 24x11″ **100.00**
   Wedding, w/lid, 4 part, china, birds, florals, carp, 10″ **450.00**
   Wood carved, domed lid, reticulated mums, scrolls, 5″ **40.00**
   Wood carved, w/carved jade insert, 1900, 3x5″ **120.00**
   Wood, Hotei's bag devoured by rats **3,250.00**
Brush box, cobalt, w/gilt florals, divided, export, 2½x7″ **290.00**
Brush pot, 3 color ware, yellow, w/relief design, Ming style . . . **100.00**
Buddha, bronze, attached base, 1700s, 6½″ **200.00**
   Bronze, lotus position, 1800s, 5″ **200.00**
   Sitting, polychrome, 1900, 9″ **140.00**
   Porcelain, enameled robe, w/prayer beads, 5″ **75.00**
   Porcelain, floral enamel robes, holds prayer beads, 10x9″ . . . **185.00**
Butterfly & Cabbage, bowl, 9″ **195.00**
   Plate, 8½″ **30.00**
   Plate, 9½″ **40.00**
   Tea set, 11 pc **265.00**
Candlestick, brass, 1800s, 20″, pr **235.00**
   Brass, figural storks, fish, 1900, 19″, pr **245.00**

Bronze, figural flying dragons, pr **150.00**
Bronze, phoenix, cloisonne sockets, 11½″ **700.00**
Cane, teakwood elephant, hand carved **85.00**
Canton, *see Canton*
Celadon, bowl, interior decor of dragons, locust **265.00**
   Bowl, late 1800s, 8½″ **85.00**
   Bowl, underglaze decor, Ming type, 13″ **275.00**
   Duck figurals, pr **75.00**
   Planter, blue design & rice pattern **30.00**
   Planter, prunus blooms in blue & white, 1½x5x7″ **55.00**
   Planter, scroll ft, blue lozenges, wht scroll, 7x10x7″ **135.00**

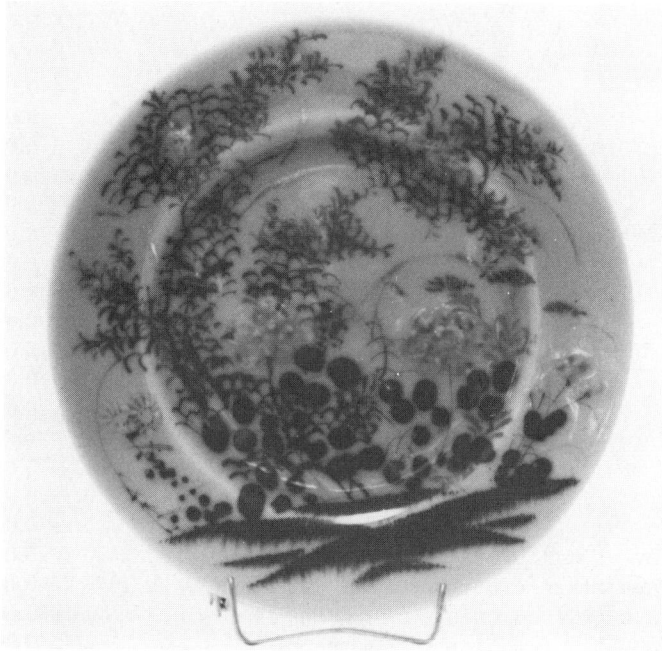

Plate, heavy floral enameling, 8½″ **125.00**
Umbrella stand, 3 carp, flora, scroll work, blue & wht, 24″ **1,300.00**
Urn, green w/swans & clouds in relief, 1850s, 9″ **245.00**
Urn, open work, on wooden stand, 3x2½″ **48.00**
Vase, animal handles, cobalt decor, 9″ **140.00**
Vase, birds & iris, underglaze blue & wht, 14″ **550.00**
Vase, cylinder, footed, geometrics, 8½″ **750.00**
Vase, quilted ground, florals, birds, branches in gold, 15″ . . **160.00**
Champleve, *see Champleve*
Charger, coat of arms, export, porcelain, 1700s, 13″ **650.00**
   Millifleur, black decorated & signed, 1850, 16″ dia **495.00**
   Porcelain, floral & bird center panel, vivid color, 11″ **40.00**
Chocolate cup, Faux Armorial, twist handle, export, 1780 . . . . **55.00**
Cigarette holder, w/rose carving, 4½″ **25.00**
Cinnabar, box, red w/black scene w/4 figures, 6x8½″ **150.00**
   Box w/domed cover, allover floral & figure carving, 7x4″ . . . **110.00**
   Bracelet, silver over copper, China **55.00**
   Bracelet w/5 stones, Made In China **40.00**
   Tray, dragons, reign mark, 2x7x11½″ **135.00**
Cloisonne, *see Cloisonne*
Coffee can, bittersweet decor, export, 1760 . . . . **80.00**
Coralene, tankard, w/purple 1909 pat mk, 4½″ **215.00**
   Vase, multi color, 7″ **175.00**
   Vase, yellow florals, green leaves, blue handles, pat mk, 5″ . **200.00**
Creamer, helmet, florals, export, 1760, 4″ **220.00**
   Helmet, iron red hand, famille rose decor, export, 4″ **125.00**
   Helmet, polychrome florals, export, 5½″ **85.00**
   Helmet, w/florals, export porcelain, 4½″ **60.00**
Dish, blue decor w/long life symbol, bats, rice pattern, 1½″ . . **22.00**
Embroideries, silk w/birds, & flowers, framed, 14x15″, pr **40.00**

Famille Jaune, ginger jars, child & lady on horse, 1800s, 8″ . . **400.00**
   Snuff bottle w/stopper, foliage decor **50.00**
   Temple lion, seated, 1800s, 17″ **350.00**
Famille Rose, bottle, twig handles, children w/kites, 11″ **230.00**
   Bowl, religious scene, florals, 6x16″ **600.00**
   Bowl, trees & calligraphy, bats, 1800s, 7″ **100.00**
   Bridal lamp, children playing, 15″ **160.00**
   Candleholder, elephant figural, 4″ **1,000.00**
   Charger, 18″ **295.00**
   Charger, flowering ming tree, rose & bird, 12″ **100.00**
   Chop plate, on celadon, late 1800s, 12″ **145.00**
   Cider jug, strap handle, figures in garden, 1820, 8½″ **400.00**
   Fish bowl, indoor scene w/people, fish, 7″ **300.00**
   Food pot, 8x8″ **185.00**
   Plate, 4 Mandarin figures, butterfly border, 7½″ **250.00**
   Plate, dragon & peony border, peafowl, butterfly, etc, 10″ . . **200.00**
   Plate, ladies, calligraphy, floral corder, Canton, 10″ **175.00**
   Spoon, allover dragon decor, 1870s **22.00**
   Sweetmeat dish, ladies in courtyard, export, 1800, 10″ **300.00**
   Teapot, w/lid & 4 c/s, court scenes, 1800s, 4″ pot **485.00**
   Urn w/lid, children & ladies, blossom finial, 16″ **500.00**
   Vase, birds & trees in heart shape reserve, 10″ **850.00**
   Vase, foo dog handles, florals, birds, 1800s, 6″ **60.00**
Famille Verte, charger, couple in pavillion, plant, repeat border, 11″ **450.00**
   Dish, lotus, birds, & blossoms, K' and Hsi, 8½″ **285.00**
   Fish bowl, indoor scene, playing children, 20½″ **1,650.00**
   Jar w/cover, cabbage & butterflies, 11¾″ **300.00**
   Plaque, seascape w/boats, verse, 1800s, 12″ dia **345.00**
   Server, ormolu mount, 1800, 16″ **1,200.00**
   Urn w/cover, Emperor & attendants, 15″ **765.00**
Fan, painting of flowers & calligraphy, framed & matted, 1800s **220.00**
Fertility figure, silver repousse **125.00**

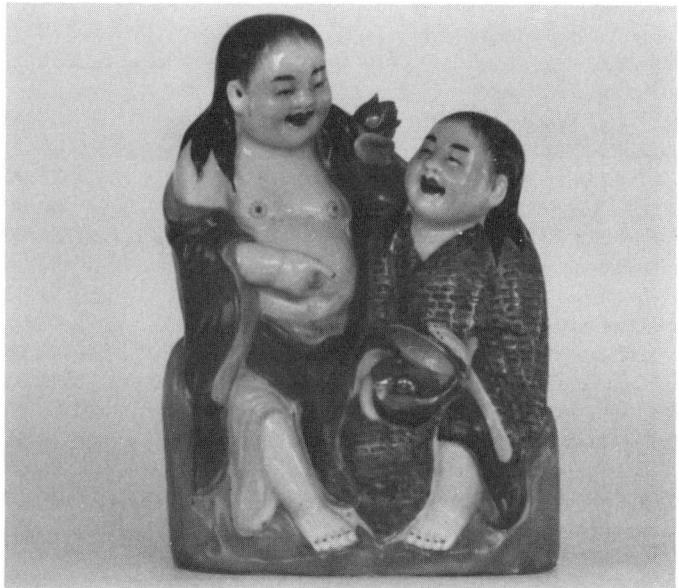

Figurine, 2 men in kimono w/bat in box, 10x7½″ **135.00**
   Court lady, Tank Dynasty, 13½″ **4,000.00**
   Duck w/spread wings, attached base, bronze, 16x19″ **375.00**
   Monkey, loose head, tongue rolls forward, 1800s, 4½″ **285.00**
   Porcelain female, cloud base, reign mark 9½″ **150.00**
   Porcelain, Geisha in dance posture, 1800s, 11½″ **450.00**
   Porcelain, lady in kimono, 1800s, 15″ **300.00**
Fingernail guard, enameled **110.00**
   Tortoise shell **110.00**
Fitzhugh, cup & saucer, green **125.00**
   Hot water dish, 1810, 9¾″ **450.00**

Mug, barrel shape, 5″ **275.00**
Plate, green, 9½″ **225.00**
Platter, oval, 1810, 11½″ **175.00**
Flag, Japanese Rising Sun, allover writing **50.00**
Foo dogs, carved white marble, on stands, 6″, pr **50.00**
   Bronze, crouched, encrusted w/inlaid stones, 34″, pr **900.00**
   Porcelain, brown base, yellow & green, 12″, pr **190.00**
Garden seat, pottery, hexagon body, floral designs, 20″ **525.00**
Ginger jar, 2 scenes, polychrome, rose color **235.00**
   Yellow w/scrolls & flowers, covered, 8½x7″ **150.00**
Ginger jars, applied birds, water lilies, 6″, pr **125.00**
Handwarmer, hand engraved copper stand **225.00**
Hard stone carving; coral, Buddha, 1½″ **50.00**
   Jade, bangle bracelet, pale green Burmese **440.00**
   Jade, cap vase, squared ovoid **6,500.00**
   Jade, elephant, on rosewood stand, 2x3¼″ **245.00**
   Jade, fan-tail goldfish, mottled green, 3x2¾″ **135.00**
   Jade, figure of bearded Oriental, 7″ **120.00**
   Jade, foo dog pendant, bright green **95.00**
   Jade, plaque, oval, w/figures & scenic, white, w/stand, 6″ . . **575.00**
   Jade, pop-eye gold fish, 1½x3½″ **120.00**
   Jade, tree, white metal, green jade, 3½″ **165.00**
   Jade, winged beast, recumbent, green, 4½x10″ **350.00**
   Jade, zodiac figure chicken, 1x2½″ **65.00**
   Malachite, group of Immortals, 4½″ **260.00**
   Rose quartz, Buddha, lotus position, celestial veils on shoulders **275.00**
   Rose quartz, Hotei, 5″ **850.00**
   Serpentine, quail, pr **225.00**
Hotei, porcelain, sitting, floral decor pink & yellow robes, 5½″ . **55.00**
Horn, carved female figural, 1910 . . . . **70.00**
Incense burner, brass, reticulated base, lion head & foo dog, 12″ **140.00**
   Bronze w/dark patina, 1800s **45.00**
   Bronze w/ring handles, fish scale, enamel, 5½″ **165.00**
   Foo dog, brownware, 7½″ **275.00**
Inro, 2 case gold lacquer, takamai-e, aogi & pewter inlay . . . **2,250.00**
Ivory, *see Ivory*
Knife, silver blade, ivory handle, MOP & amber decor, 8″ . . . **135.00**
Kutani, *see Kutani*
Lacquer, box, cover w/hp gold birds **25.00**
   Box, MOP, octagon shape, removable compartments **90.00**
   Figure of Jizo, large **2,750.00**
   Handle on pickle fork, gold, 6½″ **50.00**
   Hat box **250.00**
   Letter holder, 2 section, black ground, gold figures **45.00**
   Miniature alter table, w/gold, silver & MOP inlay, 3″ . . . **1,400.00**
   Plaque, scene w/children, inlaid rocks, gold, 10x30″ **400.00**
   Screen, 4 panel, MOP pagoda & lady, 72x72″ **300.00**
   Tea chest, hexagonal, 6x7″ **110.00**
   Vase, allover florals leaves, fine work, 6½″ **50.00**
Lamp, bronze base, slag glass dome, 29x29″ **400.00**
Lowestoft-type, cup & saucer, flowers in bowl **95.00**
   Handleless cup & saucer, strawberry motif **200.00**
   Pitcher, lavender banding & enamel decor on base, 5″ **85.00**
Marriage lamp, 2 pc, porcelain, reticulated, 11″ **345.00**
Money pouch, attached carved ivory snuff bottle & bead . . . **120.00**
Moriage, basket tray w/handle, 8½″ **125.00**
   Basket vase, hp roses, allover lacy slipwork, 9″ **350.00**
   Chocolate pot, green w/allover wht slipwork, hp roses **275.00**
   Chocolate pot, ornate handle, ftd base, animal finial, florals . **190.00**
   Chocolate set, 13 pc, cobalt w/pastel enamel birds **550.00**
   Condiment set, mustard w/lid & spoon, salt & pepper, on tray **55.00**
   Creamer & covered sugar, slip trail dragon **22.00**
   Cruet w/stopper, slip trail dragon **25.00**
   Cup & saucer, gold ground w/leaf decor **125.00**

Cup & saucer, scalloped **75.00**
Demi cup & saucer, slip trail dragon **10.00**
Ewer, green w/pink & lavender flowers, 7″ **275.00**
Jar w/cover, blue w/allover decor, 6½x6½″ **145.00**
Match holder, crown shape, maroon, & white, ornate **175.00**
Mustard w/cover, slip trail dragon **20.00**
Plate w/floral medallions, 10″ **45.00**
Tea caddy, mosaic work, beaded, 4½″ **135.00**
Tea set, 3 pc, floral hp panels **300.00**
Tea set, dragon decor, serves 6 + pot, sugar & creamer . . **195.00**
Tea set, 14 pc, blue w/slipwork parrot, prunus, leaves **225.00**

Tray, 12½x9″ **175.00**
Vase, allover beads, ornate handles, floral reserves, ftd, 10″ . **240.00**
Vase, birds on limb, prunus, heavy slip, 9″ **195.00**
Vase, bottle shape, irises, w/beading, 9¾″ **155.00**
Vase, floral reserves, ornate handles, bulbous base, 8″ . . . **110.00**
Vase, roses in center medallion, on green ground, 9″ **225.00**
Vase, turquoise, gold medallion w/bird, slip trailing 14″ . . . **125.00**
Mud figure, 2 elders, sitting, playing game, polychrome **80.00**
   Elder, carrying staff, 6″ **75.00**
   Elder, sittting, w/fish, blue & brown, 5″ **65.00**
   Sitting female deity w/prayer beads, 5″ **45.00**
Mug, coat of arms, bell shape, export, 1755, 5″ **385.00**
   Coat of arms, export **275.00**
   Strap handle, polychrome florals, export porcelain, 6″ . . . **250.00**
Nanking, cream pot, w/cover, 1800 . . . . **265.00**
   Leaf shape dish, 1800s, 6″ **125.00**
   Tea bowl & saucer, 1800 . . . . **135.00**
Netsuke, *see Netsuke*
Nippon, *see Nippon*
Nortitake, *see Nortitake*
Opium pipe, silver w/hand carved & ebony case, Ming **4,500.00**
Oxblood, vase, unglazed lip, very dark base, 1800s, 11″ **700.00**
Painting, reverse on glass, 2 fishermen, carved pierced frame, 19x14″ **25.00**
   Thanka, Nepal, Lives of Buddha, 16x19″ **350.00**
Palace Ware, bowl, dignitaries & attendants by pavilion & river, 9½″ **750.00**
   Dinner plate, 2 ladies, 3 attendants by river, 1790, 9¾″ . **1,100.00**
   Dinner plate, seated dignitary & scholar, 9¾″ **1,000.00**
   Soup plate, 3 figures by riverside, pine trees, 9¾″ **1,000.00**
Panels, mounted Samurai, bamboo, MOP & ivory, 65″ **500.00**
Peking glass, *see Peking glass*
Plate, vine border, deer heads in reserve, armorial, export, 9″ . **375.00**
Platter, figures in court scene, butterfly border, export, 10″ . . **385.00**
Punch bowl, cobalt decor, 1790s, 18″ **1,300.00**
   Masonic emblems, export, 1795, 10″ **1,000.00**

Rice basket, 3 tier, large **280.00**
Rice set, 6 pc, china, leaf shape, blue hp flowers, mkd **155.00**
Rose Canton, cache pot, butterfly decor **525.00**
Rose Mandarin, bowl, figures on terrace, 1780, 11″ **500.00**
    Bowl, sacred carp & scroll border, 1800 . . . . **325.00**
    Candlesticks, 7½″, pr **500.00**
    Cup & cup plate, 1800 . . . . **65.00**
    Cup & saucer, sacred carp & scroll border **75.00**
    Deep plate, sacred carp & scroll border **90.00**
    Lotus bowl, butterfly, rose & peony border, 10″ **475.00**
    Plate, carp & scroll border, court scene, 1800, 8″ **75.00**
    Platter, sacred carp & scroll border, garden scene, 1800 . . . . **475.00**
    Punch bowl, figures & landscapes, 1770, 10″ **750.00**
    Sauce boat, scalloped rim w/handle, 7½″ **400.00**
Rose Medallion, *see Rose Medallion*
Samurai, Miyao figural, metal on wood base, w/inlay, 6½″ **700.00**
Samurai General on horse, sculpture, bronze, 1800s, 13″ **700.00**
Sang de boeuf, bottle vase w/stand, early 1900s, 17″ **365.00**
    Stick neck w/bulbous base, large **375.00**
Satsuma, *see Satsuma*
Sauceboat stand, Faux Amorial, cobalt, gilt, export, 1780 . . . . **550.00**
Screen, 4 panel, hp landscape w/people, 14½x39″ **120.00**
    Four panels, ea 19x6″, in rosewood frame, elaborate **500.00**
Soapstone, *see Soapstone*
Soup plates, Faux Armorial, cobalt, gilt, restored, 6 for **880.00**
Sumida Gawa, ashtray, in form of a man **195.00**
    Pitcher, applied elephants, 11¾″ **175.00**
    Sugar bowl w/cover, relief scene of children playing **125.00**
    Tankard w/2 figures, 1 pouring water on 2nd, 9½″ **225.00**
    Toby jug **175.00**
Tea bowl, gold floral tracings, w/blue, export, 1700s, 4″ **75.00**
    With saucer, blues, export, 1760-80 . . . . **190.00**
Tea caddy, roses & butterflies, export, porcelain, 4½″ **60.00**
Tea table, octagon shape **100.00**
Teapot, bronze, dragon spout, 1850 . . . . **375.00**
    Floral sprays, export, porcelain, 5″ **150.00**
    Foo dog, tail is handle, dog leans over pot, 1900, 6½″ **110.00**
    With lid, sepia eagle w/gilt trim, export, 1795 . . . . **650.00**
Temple Dancer, figural w/cymbals, red sandstone, 1600s, 18″ . **800.00**
Temple jar, cobalt & wht cherry blossoms, w/lid, 10″ **240.00**
Temple jars w/lids, figural & floral decor, noire field, 17″, pr . . **350.00**

Temple lions, late 1800s, 9½″ **90.00**

Temple toy, bronze, Shiva & Parvati on Divine horse Dadhikra **160.00**
    Bronze, elephant, early 1800s **145.00**
    Bronze, ram, early 1800s **195.00**
Temple vase, porcelain, cobalt florals, foo dog handles, 24″ . . . **675.00**
    Porcelain, cobalt flowers & vines, shoulder bands, 24″ **550.00**
Terra cotta, pitcher, dragon handle, multicolors, 11″ **375.00**
    Teapot, w/twig spout, enameled handle & finial, 4x7″ **50.00**
Thousand Faces, creamer & sugar **150.00**
    Creamer, red trim **85.00**
    Cup & saucer **115.00**
    Demitasse cup & saucer, lithophane **12.00**
    Demitasse pot, lithophane, 7″ **55.00**
    Plate **28.00**
    Sugar & creamer, lithophane **37.00**
Tobacco Leaf, cream pitcher, 1775, 6″ **1,000.00**
    Dish, scalloped rim, leaf form, 1700, 11″ **650.00**
    Platter, scalloped rim, oval, 1770, 15″ **1,400.00**
    Soup plate, octagonal rim, 1775, 8½″ **350.00**
Tray, brass, floral etched, 1900s, 3″ dia **8.00**
    Turned wood handles, black w/red scenic decor, 10½x7″ **60.00**
Tureen, cover w/boar head handles floral sprays, gilt, 1700s . **1,250.00**
Vase, bronze, dragon, phoenix, tree, bat, 1700s, 11½″ **700.00**
    Bronze, eagle & parrot relief, Meiji, 13″ **1,200.00**
    Crackle, bottle form, animal & foliate relief, 1800s **100.00**
    Egg shell, jade green w/allover white florals, 1915, 5″ **70.00**
    Egg shell, scenic, verte **55.00**
    Export, cylinder, oriental figures, red seal mk, 11″ **90.00**
    Floral reserves, pierced handles, bulbous base, 8″ **115.00**
    Florals, & foo dog, export, slender flared neck, ftd, 19″ **50.00**
    Flowering trees & birds, export, 22″ **495.00**
    Kinkozan, dk blue w/dragons, gold filigree, scenic panels, 9″ **700.00**
    Oatmeal crackel, 1850 . . . . **200.00**
    Ochre w/allover blue decor, w/stand, Kang Hsi, 13″ **485.00**
    Panels w/flower vases & butterflies, export, 10″ **275.00**
    Shoulder vase, porcelain, peacocks, florals, geometrics, 24″ . **335.00**
    Turquoise crackle glaze, w/stand, 1900, 14″ **170.00**
Vases, applied foo dog & dragon decor, figural panels, 31″, pr **1,150.00**
    Florals & peafowl, polychrome on brick, applied decor, 19″, pr **350.00**
    Orientals in landscape, reticulated, export, 4¼″, pr **285.00**
Waste bowl, florals, diaper pattern, export porcelain, 5½″ **100.00**
Watercolor, ducks, lotus blossoms, Japan, 8x13″ **45.00**
    Japanese, yellow mums tied to stake, 10x15″, 1800s **95.00**
    Woodblock, tiger & mountains, Japan, 10x15″ **100.00**
Wedding teacup set, in cushioned box, w/stands, 1800s **300.00**
Wig stand, dogs & calligraphy, 10″ **175.00**
Woodcarving, bust of man w/beard, on platform, 10″ **185.00**
    Deity holds up fruit, w/gilt, 19½″ **360.00**
    Dragon, polychrome, 1700, 9x26″ **775.00**
    Elderly Oriental man & child, gilt & polychrome, 60″ **325.00**
    Elephant, teakwood, on wood base, 15½x16½″ **200.00**
    Guardian dogs, polychrome, 7½″, pr **135.00**
    Hermit in cave, from ginger root, 1600s, 7″ **500.00**
    Oriental figure w/staff, gilt & polychrome, 61″ **325.00**
    Oriental man on foo dog, ivory eyes & teeth, 12″ **100.00**
    Temple lion w/paw on pup, inlaid ivory teeth, 1800s **350.00**

Orrefors

    Orrefors glassworks was founded in the early 1900s in the Swedish province of Smaaland. Utilizing the expertise of designers such as Lindquist and Gate, it produced quality art glass. Various techniques were used in achieving the decoration; some were wheel engraved, and others blown through a unique process that formed controlled bubbles or air pockets resulting in unusual patterns and shapes.

Bowl, blue, heavy, sgnd, 5¼" dia **40.00**
   Green w/maroon swirls, sgnd E Olmstorm, 4¼" dia **30.00**
   Half moon cut out designs, 5" dia **50.00**

Decanter, Neptune w/mermaid, clear w/blue stopper, sgnd KR, 8" **715.00**

Ott & Brewer

The partnership of Ott & Brewer began in 1865 in Trenton, New Jersey. By 1876 they were making decorated graniteware, parian and 'ivory porcelain'---similar to Irish belleek, though not as fine and of different composition. In 1883, however, experiments toward that end had reached a successful conclusion and a true belleek body was introduced. It came to be regarded as the finest china ever produced by an American firm. The ware was decorated by various means---hand painting, transfer printing, gilding, and luster glazing. The company closed in 1893, one of many that failed during that depression.

Cracker jar, blue & gold on wht, 6" **80.00**
Creamer, pansy nosegays decor, 3½" **135.00**
Cup & saucer, Tridacna, lavender tint, gilt trim, crown & sword mk **110.00**
   Belleek, Cactus pattern **90.00**
   Demitasse, belleek, glossy wht w/cream interiors, sgnd **165.00**
   Fluted w/twig handle **250.00**
Ewer, unusual shape, gold decor, 6¾" **500.00**
Fruit bowl, triangular, factory decor, gold paste Thistle, 9" dia **775.00**
Pitcher, belleek, raised gold floral decor, 3 colors, 6" **675.00**
Plate, hp w/gold trim, #d, 9¾" **120.00**
Rose bowl, gold Thistles, 4" **325.00**
Saucers, blue & pastel, #d, 6 for **120.00**
Sugar, belleek, Tridacna pattern, faint pink trim, gold accents . **175.00**
Teapot, belleek, Tridacna pattern, faint pink trim gold accents **200.00**

Overbeck

The Overbeck Studio was established in 1911 in Cambridge City, Ind., by four Overbeck sisters. It survived until the last sister died in 1955. Early wares were often decorated with carved designs of stylized animals, birds or florals with the designs colored to contrast with the background. Others had tooled designs filled in with various colors for a mosaic effect. After 1937, Mary Frances, the last remaining sister, favored hand made figurines with somewhat bizarre features in fanciful combinations of color. Overbeck ware is signed OBK.

Figurine, bluejay, blue & grey, 2x1" **85.00**
   Cat, wht, tan glaze, 2x1" **75.00**
   Crow, black glaze, 2x1" **85.00**
   Dog, brown, tan & wht glaze, 2x1½" **75.00**
   Gentleman in suit w/top hat, multi color glaze, 4x1½" **100.00**
   Lady in wht dress, multi colored glaze, 4x1½" **100.00**
   Skunk, black & wht glaze, 2x1¼" **75.00**
Flower form, pink, blue & green, 3" **175.00**
Vase, 3 carved Art Nouveau panels, sgnd E & F, 6x20" **600.00**
   Geometric design, green & brown, 4x2" **250.00**
   White w/blue flowers, 3x2" **200.00**

Overshot

Overshot glass is characterized by the beaded or craggy appearance of the surface. Earlier ware was irregularly textured, while 20th century examples tend to be more uniform.

Fairy lamp, cranberry overshot on clear, mkd Clarke, 3¾x3" dia **115.00**
Finger bowl, flint **30.00**
Mug, 3" **17.00**
Pitcher, bulbous, blown, applied amber ribbed-shell handle, 7" **190.00**
   Milk, 6¾" **69.00**
   Rubina to ¾ way down, 7¾" **165.00**
   Water, 7¾" **85.00**
   Water, blue w/pink applied handle, 7¾x6" dia **165.00**
Plate, 6½" **15.00**
Sauce, 5½" **17.00**
Vase, blue overshot, amber reeded handle, Sandwich **65.00**
   Bulbous base twisted into tall round shaft, purple w/silver, 6½" **35.00**
   With snake band, 8½" **59.00**

Owens Pottery

J.B. Owens founded his company in Zanesville, Ohio, in 1891, and until 1907, when the company decided to exert most of its energies in the area of tile production, made several quality lines of art pottery. His first line, Utopian, was a standard brown ware with underglaze slip decoration of nature studies, animals and portraits. A similar line, Lotus, utilized lighter background colors. Henri Deux, introduced in 1900 featured incised Art Nouveau forms with colors inlaid within the design. Other important lines were Opalesce, Rustic, Feroza, Cyrano and Mission, examples of which are rare today.

The factory burned in 1928, and the company closed shortly thereafter.

Bowl, Utopian, autumn leaves, 4½x6" **110.00**
Bud vase, Alpine, slip leaves on bisque, #1127, 8" **230.00**
Dish, w/cover, Opalesce, cigars & matches, green, 5½" **700.00**
Ewer, Utopian, florals, artist Steel, 6" **175.00**
Honey jug, Utopian, raspberries, artist sgnd, 5x6" **250.00**
Jardiniere & ped, Utopian, matt, wht & brown tulips, 24" **375.00**
   Embossed griffins, pink w/gold fleck trim, 7½x8½" **65.00**
   Henri Deux, 8x10" **185.00**
   Lotus, butterflies, 7½x10½" **225.00**
Jug, Utopian, large florals, imp Owensart Torch #820 . . . . **150.00**
Lamp, Soudanese, floral shoulder band, tapering, wide base, 14" **195.00**
   Utopian, floral/leaf decor, artist DH, 11½" base **185.00**
   Utopian, orange florals, artist F, 10" **165.00**
Mug, Utopian, cherry decor, artist sgnd, 5" **190.00**
Pillow vase, 4 ftd, flying ducks, 8x9" **600.00**
   Lightweight, 4 ftd, violets decor, #846, 4x4¾" **175.00**
   Utopian, 4 ftd, 3 flying geese, moon by Leffler, 8x9" **600.00**
   Utopian, 4 ftd, cherries, #821, 5½x4½" **90.00**
   Utopian, 4" **40.00**

Utopian, chick in reeds, artist FF, 4x5″ **500.00**
Tankard, Utopian, matt, berries, leaves on lt brown, 12″ **175.00**
Tankard mug, Utopian, w/leaves & cherries, sgnd **100.00**
Vase, Aborigine, 6″ **65.00**
    Brushmodel Lotus, brown w/orange florals, mkd, 7″ **275.00**
    Green, Owensart, 7″ **65.00**

Henri Deux, narrow neck expanding to wider base, w/head, 7″ **350.00**
Lightweight, Lady Slippers, artist sgnd, imp Owens, 7″ **145.00**
Lotus, ovoid w/purple carnations, Owensart, 10¾″ **370.00**
Lotus, water lilies, mkd, 7″ **350.00**
Matt green w/overglaze cacti, 11½″ **125.00**
Opalesce, red/gold metallic, florals, black leaves, 10″ **165.00**
Parchment Lotus, pink florals on gray, Haubrich, 11″ **245.00**

Soudanese, leaves & florals, #1258, 8″ **700.00**
Utopian, 3 feet, floral, artist sgnd, 7″ **150.00**
Utopian, autumn leaves, imp Owens, artist sgnd, 7½″ **145.00**
Utopian, berries, 8″ **150.00**
Utopian, bottle shape, autumn leaves, 10″ **125.00**
Utopian, cherries decor, 10″ **115.00**
Utopian, cylindrical neck, brown w/orange florals, 14″ **150.00**
Utopian, florals, 4″ **60.00**
Utopian, grey leaves & florals, 9½″ **125.00**
Utopian, matt, golden cherries, green leaves, #1114 . . . . **500.00**
Utopian, matt, trumpet shape, floral, artist HL, 12″ **245.00**
Utopian, orange & green leaves, #105, 3¾″ **125.00**

Utopian, orange roses/green leaves, 12½″ **150.00**
Utopian, ovoid w/wild rose, 2/Owens/1060, 3½″ **280.00**
Utopian, swirled, nasturtiums, 14″ **135.00**
Venetian, 10″ **165.00**
Wall pocket, Aqua Verdi, large acorn **85.00**

Pacific Clay Products

Pacific Clay Products Co., founded in 1881, had several locations in southern California that were involved in the production of yellowware and red clay products such as brick and tile. By 1936, however, they had developed a full line of products, including a low-fired pastel glazed dinnerware called 'Coralitos'. About the same time, they designed a dinnerware in the more vivid hues to compete with the highly successful Fiesta, by Homer Laughlin, and Ring, made by the Bauer Co. With the onset of WWII, the company began to manufacture insulators for radio equipment, and the dinnerware lines were discontinued.

Cake plate, yellow, 16″ **45.00**
Cereal bowl, cobalt, 5½″ **5.00**
Coffee pot/chocolate pot, orange **75.00**
Grill plate, green, 11½″ **15.00**
Mixing bowl, cobalt, 11½″ **30.00**
Salad bowl, ftd, green, 11″ **35.00**
Sandwich tray, chrome center handle, cobalt, 11½″ **15.00**
Tea pot, low, 2-cup, green **30.00**
Tumbler, dark blue, 4″ **10.00**
Vegetable bowl, yellow, 7½″ **10.00**

Paden City

The Paden City Glass Company began operations in 1916, in Paden City, West Virginia. The company's early lines consisted largely of the usual pressed tablewares, but by the 1920s their product had developed to include color, in crystal as well as opaque glass, in a variety of patterns and styles. The company maintained its high standards of handmade perfection until 1949, when under new management, much of the work formerly done by hand was replace by automation.

The Paden City Glass Co. closed in 1951, and its earlier wares, the colored tableware in particular, is becoming very collectible.

Bowl, Cupid etching, pink, 10″ **30.00**
    Delilah Bird, amber, 9½″ **25.00**
    Lucy, 2-handled, ruby, 9¼″ **24.00**
Candy dish, Gadroon/Wotta variation, round, 3-pt, covered, ruby, 6¾″ **45.00**
Cream soup, Crows Foot, ruby **12.00**
Creamer, Cupid etching, pink **12.50**
Cup, Gadroon/Wotta line variation, cobalt **6.50**
Mayonnaise, Gadroon/Wotta line variation, 3-pc, ruby **20.00**
Owl, Gazebo, crystal w/gold, 9½″ **15.00**
Pheasant, lt blue **95.00**
Plate, Chavelier, cobalt, 6″ **2.50**
    Gadroon/Wotta line variation, ruby, 6¼″ **5.50**
    Gazebo, crystal w/gold, double handled, depressed center, 11½″ **25.00**
    Nora Bird, green, 8½″ **7.00**
Platter, Gadroon/Wotta line variation, ruby, 10″ **15.00**
Pony, standing tall **74.50**
Sandwich server, Gadroon/Wotta, center handle, floral & scroll etch **60.00**
Wine, Chavelier, yellow **4.00**

Pairpoint

The Pairpoint Manufacturing Company was built in 1880 in New Bedford, Mass. It was primarily a metalworks, whose chief product was coffin

fittings. Next door, the Mt. Washington Glass Works made quality glasswares of many varieties. By 1894 it became apparent to both companies that a merger would be to their best interest. (See Mt. Washington for more information concerning their art ware lines).

From the late 1890s until the 1930s, lamps and lamp accessories were an important part of Pairpoint's production. There were three main types of shades, all of which were blown: puffy---blown out reverse painted shades, usually floral designs; ribbed---also reverse painted; and scenic---reverse painted with scenes of land or seascapes, usually on a smooth surface, although ribbed shades were also scenic decorated. Cut glass lamps and those with metal overlaid panels were also made. Scenic shades were sometimes artist signed, and although many are unmarked, some are stamped Pairpoint Corp. Blown out shades may be marked Pat July 9, 1907. Bases were made from bronze, copper, brass, silver or wood, and are always signed.

Because they produced only fancy hand made artware, their sales lagged seriously during the depression, and as time and tastes changed, their style of artware was less in demand. As a result, they never fully recovered and consequently part of the buildings and equipment were sold in 1938. They reorganized in 1939 under the direction of Robert Gunderson, and again specialized in quality hand blown glassware. Isaac Babbit regained possession of the silver departments, and together they established Gunderson Glass Works, Inc. After WWII, having incurred considerable loss of sales, it again became necessary to reorganize. The Gunderson-Pairpoint Glass Works was formed, and the old line of cut, engraved artware was reintroduced.

The company moved to East Wareham, Mass. in 1957, but closed only one year later. However, in 1970 new facilities were constructed in Sagamore under the direction of Robert Bryden, who had been sales manager since the 1950s.

Since 1974, the company has been producing lead glass cup plates which were made on commission as fund raisings for various churches and organizations. These are signed with a P in diamond, and are becoming quite collectible.

Baby mug, quadruple plate, 1887, engraved **25.00**
Basket, quadruple, ornate swing handle, raised apples, ftd **40.00**
    Silver plate, engraved florals, floral cut-out bails, 4" **70.00**
Biscuit jar, hp flowers, ftd removable base, quadruple plate, sgnd **325.00**
    Oval, hp flowers, sgnd & #d, w/lid & ftd brass stand **375.00**
Bowl, amber rim & ft, engraved Wagon Wheel pattern, clear stem, 6" **75.00**
    Heavy cut crystal, pinwheel pattern, 9" dia **150.00**
Box, decorated Mt Washington glass inset top, quadruple plate, 2x6" **350.00**
    White w/gold decor, hinged, pewter collar & ring, sgnd, 6" dia **275.00**
Butter dish, covered, silver plated, engraved flowers, knife rest, mkd **100.00**
Candelabras, silver 3-light, cobalt blue base, 12½", pr **375.00**
Candlestick, silver plate, repousse, 7½" **110.00**
    Sunburst pattern, cranberry cut to clear, teardrop stem, 10½" **275.00**
Candlesticks, amber w/controlled bubble connector, 12", pr . . . **125.00**
    Blue, bubble base, 6", pr **149.00**
    Green w/8 hanging prisms, w/bubble ball, 9", pr **150.00**
    Topaz w/bubble, 4½", pr **85.00**
Candy dish, clear cut Viscera pattern, w/cover **135.00**
Canister, brass, rooster finial, 40th Anniv Rooster Guard 1870-1910 **75.00**
Centerpiece, Rosario Expanded Diamond, w/bubble paperweight **150.00**
Compote, canaria, Vintage design, bubble ball stem, 14" **250.00**
    Colias pattern, cut notched rim & stem, 6½x6½" dia **85.00**
    Cut crystal on 5" silver plated cherub, marble base, 8" **125.00**
    Green, prisms at rim, bubble ball base, grape pattern, 7" dia **150.00**
    Green w/bubble connector, Gunderson, 12" **175.00**
Console set, green w/bubble ball, 9" candlesticks, 6½" compote **170.00**
Cracker jar, sq body w/gold floral motif, silver plated cover, 10" **300.00**
Cup plate, Aptuxcet Windmill, ice blue **10.00**
    Barbershop Chords, green **25.00**
    Call to Freedom, green opal **15.00**

Cape Cinema, teal **50.00**
Cape Playhouse, amethyst **95.00**
Christ Episcopal Church 1976, green **95.00**
George Washington, amethyst **12.00**
Harwich Jr Theatre, amber **35.00**
Heisey Horse & Rider, crystal **12.50**
Mrs Peter Rabbit **10.00**
NBGM 1979 (Whaleman) **50.00**
NBGM Christmas 1980, Snowflake, crystal **10.00**
NBIS 1865-Auroria **35.00**
Ntl Heisey Association, crystal **25.00**
Ocean Spray, cranberry stain **50.00**
Peter Rabbit **10.00**
Quota Club, amethyst **10.00**
Sandwich Press, amber **35.00**
Spotty the Turtle, amethyst **10.00**
Surratt House, amber, 60 scallops **12.00**
The Study Gallery, apple green **25.00**
Thistle, green opal **25.00**
Worcester Art Museum, dk amethyst **14.00**
Fairy lamp, blue w/coraline flowers **350.00**
Goblets, yellow w/etched vintage pattern, set of 12 . . . . **350.00**
Jewel box, Murrilo pattern, intaglio flowers, 2 rows thumbprint, 5" **195.00**
    Viscaria pattern, multi-rayed base, hinged, 6½" dia **269.00**
Juice bowl, amber intaglio grape pattern, on pedestal, 9x9¼" dia **245.00**
Ladle, cut glass, Hobstars & Fan, sgnd **300.00**
Lamp, Bedford Harbor scene, 16" **2,200.00**
    Berkley, forest & deer scene, sgnd W Macy, 18" **1,950.00**
    Blown out roses, sgnd & dated 1907, 10" **1,800.00**
    Boudoir, Bedford Harbor scene on 8½" shade, 14" overall **1,185.00**
    Boudoir, puffy shade w/flowers, butterflies & gingham, sgnd . **950.00**
    Boudoir, reverse painted floral mottled shade, 13½" **475.00**
    Boudoir, reverse painted; nickel plated figural child base . . . **850.00**
    Carlisle, parrots & foliage decor, sgnd, 18" **3,100.00**
    Carlisle, Provincetown Sand Dunes, 18" **2,150.00**
    Copley, Dutch windmill scene & seascape, 16" **1,250.00**
    Copley, seagull scene, w/glass seagull base, 20" **4,500.00**
    Directorie shade w/flowers, onyx base, 14" **995.00**
    Four panel shade, bronze finish base, mkd, 12" **350.00**
    Hexagonal reverse painted shade, silver plated base, 15" . . **1,950.00**
    Hexagonal shade w/ship scene & nautical designs, onyx base **2,450.00**
    Lansdowne, ships & harbor scene, 20" **2,950.00**
    Painted scenic shade, patinated metal base, sgnd & #d, 26" **1,320.00**
    Puffy, pink roses & green leaves, sgnd, 15" **2,300.00**
    Puffy, white & tan poppies, red poppies, 14" **4,250.00**
    Reverse painted floral, sgnd shade & base, 21" **1,500.00**
    Table, harvest scenes, artist sgnd, 20" **2,900.00**
    Table, puffy lacy shade w/birds & roses decor, sgnd, 14" . . **3,500.00**
    Table, Venetian harbor shade, pedestal base, 20" **2,750.00**
Master salt, silver plate, reticulated, ftd, cobalt dish **27.50**
Mirror, plateau, silvered cut-out sides, petal border, 12" **65.00**
Mustache cup & saucer, silver plated, repousse floral band **95.00**
Nut bowl, cabbage figural, squirrel on rim, ftd, 10¾x7½" **115.00**
Paperweight & clip holder, clear, pin bubbles **150.00**
Perfume, clear ribbed pear shape, long ribbed stopper, w/label, 7" **125.00**
Salt & pepper, quadruple plate, dragonflies & spider web design, sgnd **95.00**
Toothpick holder, twig type handles, sgnd **60.00**
Tray, purple, intaglio grape, 14" dia **150.00**
Urn, purple, grapes decor, w/lid, 10" **120.00**
Vase, bell-tone cut, controlled bubble knob stem, 13½x6½" . . **165.00**
    Blue w/etched grapes, clear bubble ball, 13" **145.00**
    Clarrissa engraved, 12" **160.00**
    Delft, harbor village & castle scene, 12" **400.00**
    Green, Colias pattern, 9¾" **200.00**

Heavy cut crystal, floral w/scalloped rim, cylindrical, 14″.... **200.00**
Orange florals, dragonflies, gilt, #d 1225, 18″.......... **1,000.00**
Ruby Gundersen Teardrop **225.00**
Ruby standing cornucopia on clear controlled bubble base .. **110.00**
Trumpet, ruby applied overlay twist, ruffled, 10″ **125.00**
Trumpet, ruby, clear ball stem w/bubbles, ruby base, 13″ ... **175.00**
Trumpet, wheel engraved grapes, bell-shape base, amber, 12″ **125.00**
Water set, blue base & handle, inverted ribs, engraved star, 5-pc **375.00**
Wine, Flambeau, red w/blk stems, 5¼″ **32.00**

Paper Dolls

No one knows quite how or when paper dolls originated. One belief is that they began in Europe as 'pantins' (jumping jacks) and were frequently worn as part of the costume. By the late 1790s, they were being mass-produced.

During the 19th century, most paper dolls portrayed famous dancers and opera stars such as Fanny Elssler and Jenny Lind. In the late 1800s, the Raphael Tuck Publishers of England produced many series of beautiful paper dolls. Also about this time, retail companies used them as advertisements to further the sale of their products. Around the turn of the century many popular women's magazines began featuring a page of paper dolls.

Most familiar to today's collectors are the books with dolls on the cardboard covers, and clothes on the inside pages. These made their appearance in the late 1920s and early 1930s. The most collectible of these, and the most valuable, are those representing celebrities, movie stars and comic strip characters of the 30s and 40s.

Paper doll books in their original, uncut condition will, of course, demand higher prices than those with missing, bent or torn parts.

Air Hostess, Saalfield, 1947 .... **15.00**
Airline Stewardess, Samuel Lowe, 1957...................... **6.00**
Airliner, Merrill, 1941.................................... **18.00**
Alice Fay, Merrill, 1941 .... **90.00**
Amy Jo, Saalfield, 1972 .... **4.00**
Angel Baby, Merrill, 1943 .... **18.00**
Animal, Saalfield, 1950................................... **15.00**
Ann Blyth, Merrill, 1943 .... **42.00**
Ann Southern, Saalfield, 1943 .... **48.00**
Annette, Merrill.. **48.00**
Annie Laurie, Samuel Lowe, 1941.......................... **17.00**
Around The Clock With Sue & Dot, Merrill, 1952............. **6.00**

Artist Models, Saalfield, 1945............................ **12.00**
B Is For Betsy, Merrill, 1954 .... **6.00**
Babs, Saalfield, 1949..................................... **7.00**
Babs & Her Doll Furniture, Samuel Lowe, 1943 .... **6.00**
Baby Anne Smiles & Crys, Samuel Lowe, 1964 .... **5.00**

Baby Brother, Saalfield, 1959.............................. **7.00**
Baby Dear, Saalfield, 1964................................ **30.00**
Baby Doll, Samuel Lowe, 1957............................. **5.00**
Baby Dolls, 12, Merrill, 1939............................. **30.00**
Baby Dolls, Saalfield, 1941............................... **9.00**
Baby Mine, Merrill, 1944................................. **18.00**
Baby Sandy, Merrill, 1941................................ **48.00**
Baby Show, Samuel Lowe, 1940............................ **22.00**
Baby Sisters, Merrill, 1938............................... **24.00**
Baby Sitter, Saalfield, 1956.............................. **9.00**
Badgett Quadruplets, Saalfield, 1941....................... **55.00**
Barbara Britton, Saalfield, 1954........................... **29.00**
Bette Davis, Merrill, 1942 .... **60.00**
Bettina & Her Playmate Rosalie, Saalfield, 1931 .... **30.00**
Betty Blue & Patty Ping, Merrill, 1949 .... **10.00**
Betty Bo-Peep, Samuel Lowe, 1942......................... **22.00**
Betty Field, Saalfield, 1943 .... **30.00**
Betty Grable, Merrill, 1953............................... **42.00**
Big Doll Betty, Samuel Lowe, 1960 .... **3.00**
Big 'N' Easy, Merrill, 1949 .... **8.00**
Big 'N' Little Sister, Merrill, 1951 .... **6.00**
Billy Boy, Samuel Lowe **2.00**
Boarding School, Merrill, 1942 .... **18.00**
Bob and Betty, Saalfield, 1945 .... **20.00**
Bobbsey Twins, Samuel Lowe, 1952 .... **12.00**
Bonnets and Bows, Saalfield, 1963 .... **6.00**
Bonnie, Samuel Lowe, 1963............................... **5.00**
Boy & Girl Cut-Out Doll Book, Saalfield, 1937 .... **30.00**
Brand New Baby, Saalfield, 1951.......................... **8.00**

Brenda Starr, Saalfield, 1964............................. **17.00**
Bridal Party, Saalfield, 1956............................. **9.00**
Bride and Groom, Merrill, 6 pg, 1949...................... **6.00**
Bride and Groom, Merrill, 8 pg, 1949...................... **7.00**
Bye Baby Bunting, Samuel Lowe, 1953...................... **3.00**
Candy Stripers, Saalfield, 1973........................... **4.00**
Captain Big Bill, Samuel Lowe, 1956 .... **2.00**
Career Girls, Samuel Lowe, 1942 .... **16.00**
Career Girls, Samuel Lowe, 1950 .... **12.00**
Cathy Goes To Camp, Merrill, 1954 .... **6.00**
Cecelia My Kissin' Cousin, Samuel Lowe, 1960 .... **18.00**
Children In The Shoe, Merrill, 1949 .... **12.00**
Children 'Round The World, Merrill, 1955 .... **9.00**
Cinderella, Saalfield, 1950............................... **18.00**
Cinderella Steps Out, Samuel Lowe, 1948 .... **12.00**
Cindy, Samuel Lowe, 1964................................ **4.00**

Circus Time, Samuel Lowe, 1952 . . . . **2.00**
Clothes Make A Lady, Samuel Lowe, 1942 . . . . **17.00**
College Style, Merrill, 1941 . . . . **18.00**
Colonial America, Saalfield, 1974 . . . . **5.00**
Corinne, Saalfield, 1954 . . . . **6.00**
Cowboy and Cowgirl, Merrill, 1950 . . . . **6.00**
Cowboys and Cowgirls, Samuel Lowe, 1950 . . . . **6.00**
Cradle Tots, Merrill, 1945 . . . . **14.00**
Curiosity Shop, Saalfield, 1971 . . . . **3.00**
Daddy's Girl, Saalfield, 1974 . . . . **4.00**
Dancing School, Merrill, 1938 . . . . **36.00**
Day With Diane, Saalfield, 1957 . . . . **7.00**
Deanna Durbin, Merrill, 1941 . . . . **72.00**
Diana Lynn, Saalfield, 1953 . . . . **25.00**
Dick The Sailor, Samuel Lowe, 1941 . . . . **10.00**
Dolls We Love, Merrill, 1936 . . . . **36.00**
Dolly and Me, Saalfield, 1969 . . . . **3.00**
Donna Reed, Saalfield, 1959 . . . . **17.00**
Double Date, Saalfield, 1957 . . . . **7.00**
Double Wedding, Merrill, 1939 . . . . **30.00**
Down On The Farm, Samuel Lowe **12.00**
Dr Kildare Play Book, Samuel Lowe **4.00**
Dream Girl, Merrill, 1947 . . . . **14.00**
Dude Ranch, Samuel Lowe, 1943 . . . . **12.00**
Dutch Treat, Saalfield, 1961 . . . . **6.00**
Elizabeth, Samuel Lowe, 1963 . . . . **5.00**
Emilie, Merrill **48.00**
Esther Williams, Merrill, 1950 . . . . **42.00**
Eve Arden, Saalfield, 1953 . . . . **30.00**
Farmer Fred, Samuel Lowe, 1943 . . . . **6.00**
Fashion Previews, Samuel Lowe, 1949 . . . . **12.00**
First Date, Merrill, 1944 . . . . **18.00**
Five Little Peppers, Samuel Lowe, 1941 . . . . **17.00**
Flying Nun, Saalfield, 1968 . . . . **7.00**
Gabby Hayes, Samuel Lowe, 1954 . . . . **6.00**
Gigi Perreau, Saalfield, 1951 . . . . **18.00**
Gina Gillespie, Saalfield, 1962 . . . . **13.00**
Girls In The War, Samuel Lowe, 1943 . . . . **17.00**
Girls In Uniform, Samuel Lowe, 1942 . . . . **16.00**
Gisele MacKenzie, Saalfield, 1957 . . . . **17.00**
Gloria Jean, Saalfield, 1941 . . . . **37.00**
Golden Girl, Merrill, 1953 . . . . **12.00**
Goldilocks & The 3 Bears, Saalfield, 1939 . . . . **37.00**
Gone With The Wind, Merrill, 1940 . . . . **90.00**
Good Little Dolls, Saalfield, 1941 . . . . **18.00**
Good Neighbor, Saalfield, 1944 . . . . **12.00**
Greer Garson, Merrill, 1944 . . . . **72.00**
Grown-Up, Merrill, 1936 . . . . **22.00**
Gulliver's Travel, Saalfield, 1939 . . . . **50.00**
Happiest Millionaire, Saalfield, 1967 . . . . **7.00**
Happy Birthday, Merrill, 1939 . . . . **30.00**
Happy Family, Samuel Lowe, 1973 . . . . **2.00**
Hedy Lamarr, Merrill, 1942 . . . . **72.00**
Hedy Lamarr, Saalfield, 1951 . . . . **30.00**
Heidi and Peter, Saalfield, 1957 . . . . **8.00**
Henry & Henrietta, Saalfield, 1938 . . . . **25.00**
Here Comes The Bride, Saalfield, 1967 . . . . **7.00**
Here Comes The Bride, Samuel Lowe, 1955 . . . . **6.00**
High School, Merrill, 1940 . . . . **24.00**
High School Dolls, Merrill, 1948 . . . . **12.00**
Honeymooners, Samuel Lowe, 1956 . . . . **30.00**
Ice Festival, Saalfield, 1957 . . . . **8.00**
In Our Backyard, Samuel Lowe, 1941 . . . . **17.00**
Jack, Samuel Lowe, 1963 . . . . **18.00**

Jane Arden, Saalfield, 1942 . . . . **36.00**
Janet Leigh, Merrill, 1953 . . . . **42.00**
Janet Leigh, Samuel Lowe, 1957 . . . . **30.00**
Jeannie and Gene, Samuel Lowe, 1975 . . . . **2.00**
Jill, Samuel Lowe, 1963 . . . . **18.00**
Judy, Merrill, 1951 . . . . **6.00**
Julia, Saalfield, 1968 . . . . **9.00**
Julie Andrews, Saalfield, 1958 . . . . **17.00**
Jungletown Jamboree, Samuel Lowe **2.00**
Junior Misses, Samuel Lowe, 1958 . . . . **7.00**
Junior Prom, Samuel Lowe, 1942 . . . . **14.00**
Karen Goes to College, Merrill, 1955 . . . . **6.00**
Keepsake Folio-Mini Doll, Samuel Lowe, 1964 . . . . **6.00**
Keepsake Folio-Trudy Doll, Samuel Lowe, 1964 . . . . . . **17.00**
Kewpie Dolls, Saalfield, 1964 . . . . **17.00**
Kewpie Kin, Saalfield, 1967 . . . . **9.00**
Kewpies, Saalfield, 1963 . . . . **19.00**
Kiddie Circus, Saalfield **5.00**
Kim Novak, Saalfield, 1958 . . . . **29.00**
Kissy, Saalfield, 1963 . . . . **5.00**
Kitchen Play, Saalfield, 1938 . . . . **13.00**
Kitty Goes to Kindergarten, Merrill, 1956 . . . . **6.00**
Lace and Dress Kitty, Samuel Lowe, 1975 . . . . **3.00**
Lace and Dress Puppy, Samuel Lowe, 1975 . . . . **3.00**
Laugh-In Party, Saalfield, 1969 . . . . **12.00**
Let's Play Store, Saalfield, 1933 . . . . **25.00**
Let's Play With the Baby, Merrill, 1948 . . . . **7.00**
Liberty Belles, Merrill, 1943 . . . . **17.00**
Lilac Time, Saalfield, 1959 . . . . **7.00**
Linda Darnell, Saalfield, 1953 . . . . **25.00**
Lindy-Lou 'N' Cindy-Sue, Merrill, 1954 . . . . **9.00**
Little Ballerina, Merrill, 1953 . . . . **6.00**
Little Cousins, Samuel Lowe, 1940 . . . . **6.00**
Little Dolls, Samuel Lowe, 1972 . . . . **2.00**
Little Fairy, Merrill, 1951 . . . . **6.00**
Little Girls, Samuel Lowe, 1969 . . . . **2.00**
Little Kitten To Dress, Samuel Lowe, 1942 . . . . **12.00**
Little Miss America, Saalfield, 1941 . . . . **20.00**
Little Princess, Merrill, 1936 . . . . **36.00**
Little Toddlers, Saalfield, 1954 . . . . **10.00**
Little Women, Saalfield, 1960 . . . . **12.00**
Little Women, Samuel Lowe, 1941 . . . . **17.00**
Lollipop Kids, Samuel Lowe, 1961 . . . . **3.00**
Lost Horizon, Saalfield, 1973 . . . . **5.00**
Lucille Ball, Saalfield, 1944 . . . . **48.00**
Many Things To Do, Saalfield, 1932 . . . . **7.00**
Mardi Gras, Saalfield, 1956 . . . . **9.00**
Marie Osmond, Saalfield, 1973 . . . . **7.00**
Marilyn Monroe, Saalfield, 1953 . . . . **57.00**
Mary Martin, Saalfield, 1942 . . . . **56.00**
Masquerade Party, Samuel Lowe, 1955 . . . . **2.00**
Mimi From Paree, Samuel Lowe, 1960 . . . . **3.00**
Mini Mods, Saalfield, 1969 . . . . **3.00**
Molly Dolly, Samuel Lowe, 1962 . . . . **3.00**
Mommy & Me, Saalfield, 1943 . . . . **20.00**
Mopsy and Popsy, Samuel Lowe, 1971 . . . . **2.00**
My Bonnie Lassie, Saalfield, 1957 . . . . **7.00**
My Little Margie, Saalfield, 1954 . . . . **25.00**
Nanny and the Professor, Saalfield, 1970 . . . . **7.00**
Navy Girls and Marines, Merrill, 1943 . . . . **18.00**
Navy Scouts, Merrill, 1942 . . . . **18.00**
New Baby, Merrill, 1943 . . . . **14.00**
New Quintuplet Dolls, Merrill, 1936 . . . . **58.00**
Nurse and Doctor, Saalfield, 1952 . . . . **12.00**

Once Upon A Wedding Day, Saalfield **5.00**
Our New Baby, Merrill, 1937 . . . . **20.00**
Ozzie and Harriett, Saalfield, 1954 . . . . **22.00**
Paper Doll Ballet, Saalfield, 1957 . . . . **12.00**
Paper Doll Family, Saalfield, 1935 . . . . **30.00**
Paper Doll Playmates, Saalfield, 1955 . . . . **7.00**
Paper Doll Wedding, Merrill, 1943 . . . . **18.00**
Paper Dolls On Parade, Saalfield, 1940 . . . . **15.00**
Papoosie, Saalfield, 1949 . . . . **9.00**
Partridge Family, Saalfield, 1971 . . . . **5.00**
Patchwork, Saalfield, 1971 . . . . **4.00**
Patchy Annie, Saalfield, 1962 . . . . **5.00**
Patience & Prudence, Samuel Lowe, 1957 . . . . **8.00**
Patti Doll Book, Samuel Lowe, 1961 . . . . **3.00**
Patti Page, Samuel Lowe, 1957 . . . . **30.00**
Peggy and Peter, Samuel Lowe, 1962 . . . . **20.00**
Penny, Saalfield, 1964 . . . . **6.00**
Penny's Party, Samuel Lowe, 1952 . . . . **3.00**
Pert and Pretty, Merrill, 1948 . . . . **12.00**
Peter Pumpkin's House, Merrill, 1955 . . . . **6.00**
Petunia & Patches, Saalfield, 1937 . . . . **37.00**
Picnic, Saalfield, 1952 . . . . **12.00**
Pig-Tails, Merrill, 1949 . . . . **7.00**
Pink Prom Twins, Merrill, 1956 . . . . **6.00**
Pink Wedding, Merrill, 1952 . . . . **9.00**
Piper Laurie, Merrill, 1953 . . . . **42.00**
Playmates, Samuel Lowe, 1961 . . . . **3.00**
Playtime Pals, Samuel Lowe, 1946 . . . . **6.00**
Polly and Her Playmates, Merrill, 1951 . . . . **6.00**
Polly Bergen, Saalfield, 1958 . . . . **22.00**
Polly Pal, Samuel Lowe, 1976 . . . . **2.00**
Preschool, Saalfield, 1958 . . . . **6.00**
Pretty As A Rose, Saalfield, 1963 . . . . **8.00**
Prince and Princess, Saalfield, 1949 . . . . **12.00**
Prom Home Permanent, Samuel Lowe, 1952 . . . . **12.00**
Quiz Kids, Saalfield, 1942 . . . . **30.00**
Ranch Family, Merrill, 1957 . . . . **6.00**
Ride A Pony-Judy & Jill, Merrill, 1944 . . . . **18.00**
Rita Hayworth, Merrill, 1942 . . . . **72.00**
Rock-A-Bye Baby, Saalfield, 1945 . . . . **9.00**
Roller Rhythm, Merrill, 1944 . . . . **18.00**
Rosemary Clooney, Samuel Lowe, 1956 . . . . **42.00**
Sally Ann, Samuel Lowe, 1960 . . . . **2.00**
Sally Lou, Saalfield, 1931 . . . . **30.00**
Sally, Sue and Sherry, Samuel Lowe, 1969 . . . . **2.00**
Santa's Band, Samuel Lowe, 1962 . . . . **3.00**
School Girl, Saalfield, 1942 . . . . **20.00**
Schoolmates, Saalfield, 1947 . . . . **10.00**
Shari Lewis, Saalfield, 1958 . . . . **17.00**
Shari Lewis & Her Puppets, Saalfield, 1960 . . . . **6.00**
Sherlock Bones, Samuel Lowe, 1955 . . . . **2.00**
Shirley Temple, Saalfield, 1958 . . . . **22.00**
Shirley Temple Play Kit, Saalfield, 1958 . . . . **22.00**
Shirley Temple Playhouse, Saalfield, 1935 . . . . **60.00**
Shirley Temple Standing Doll, Saalfield, 1935 . . . . **60.00**
Six and Sweet 16, Merrill, 1955 . . . . **7.00**
Sleepy Doll, Saalfield, 1971 . . . . **5.00**
Slumber Party, Merrill, 1943 . . . . **18.00**
Sonja Henie, Merrill, 1939 . . . . **60.00**
Southern Belles, Saalfield, 1953 . . . . **8.00**
Square Dance, Saalfield, 1950 . . . . **12.00**
Star Babies, Merrill, 1945 . . . . **15.00**
Sub-Deb, Merrill, 1941 . . . . **36.00**
Sugar and Spice, Saalfield, 1966 . . . . **3.00**

Sugar Plum Pals, Saalfield, 1966 . . . . **6.00**
Sunbeam, Saalfield, 1972 . . . . **3.00**
Susan Dey, Saalfield **7.00**
Suzy, Samuel Lowe, 1961 . . . . **3.00**
Sweet 16, Merrill, 1944 . . . . **18.00**
Sweetheart Dolls, Saalfield, 1954 . . . . **12.00**
Teen Boutique, Saalfield, 1973 . . . . **2.00**
Teen Shop, Saalfield, 1948 . . . . **8.00**
Texas Rose, Saalfield, 1959 . . . . **12.00**
Three Darling Dolls, Saalfield, 1964 . . . . **8.00**
Timmy, Samuel Lowe, 1956 . . . . **2.00**
Tina and Tony, Samuel Lowe, 1940 . . . . **17.00**
Tom & His Toys, Samuel Lowe, 1943 . . . . **6.00**
Tom & The Aviator, Samuel Lowe, 1941 . . . . **10.00**
Toni Hair-Do Cut-Out Dolls, Samuel Lowe, 1950 . . . . **17.00**
Town and Country, Saalfield, 1954 . . . . **12.00**
Trinket, Samuel Lowe, 1953 . . . . **2.00**
Trudy In Her Teens, Merrill, 1943 . . . . **14.00**
Tuesday Weld, Saalfield, 1960 . . . . **17.00**
Turnabout Dolls, Samuel Lowe, 1943 . . . . **16.00**
Twin Babies, Merrill, 1942 . . . . **18.00**
Two Marys, Merrill, 1950 . . . . **6.00**
Umbrella Girls, Merrill, 1956 . . . . **10.00**
Uncle Sam's Little Helpers, Saalfield, 1943 . . . . **30.00**
Victory Volunteers, Merrill, 1942 . . . . **20.00**
Watch Me Grow, Merrill, 1944 . . . . **18.00**
Wedding Party, Saalfield, 1951 . . . . **12.00**
Wee Wee Baby Doll Book, Samuel Lowe, 1945 . . . . **17.00**
When We Grow Up, Samuel Lowe, 1971 . . . . **2.00**
White House Paper Dolls, Saalfield, 1969 . . . . **6.00**
Wiggie The Mod Model, Saalfield, 1967 . . . . **5.00**
You Are A Doll, Saalfield **12.00**
Yvonne, Merrill **48.00**
Ziegfeld Girl, Merrill, 1941 . . . . **88.00**
Zoo Revue, The New, Saalfield, 1974 . . . . **4.00**

Paperweights

The term 'paperweight' technically refers to any small, heavy object used to hold down loose papers. They have been made from a broad range of materials; many have been sold as souvenirs or given away by retail companies as advertising premiums. But today, those attracting the most interest are the glass collector weights.

During the mid-1800s, the interest in these paperweights reached a high point, during which three major French factories were in close competition. The St. Louis, Baccarat and Clichy companies were among the first to produce paperweights as a commercial venture, and their products are among the most valued. In the late 1860s, an unexplained decrease in their popularity caused the market for paperweights to diminish, and all three major companies eventually discontinued production.

The manufacture of paperweights in the United States which began in the 1850s did not experience this decline, and they have continued in production to the present time. The most valued antique American weights are from the New England, Sandwich and Milleville companies. In 1954, a renewed surge of interest resulted in the organization of collectors clubs and an exciting new era of paperweight production. Because of this, the manufacture of weights by St. Louis and Baccarat was resumed, and contemporary artists such as Kaziun, Stankard and Ysart are bringing their own ingenuity to this rediscovered art form.

Advertising, Badger Insurance, badger figural **27.00**
    Battery figural **21.00**
    Hill's Bros Coffee **15.00**
    Imperial Varnish Co, Akron, O., 3" **45.00**

Oil can figural **19.00**
Planters, Mr Peanut, 1938 .... **30.00**
White Cat Cigar.. **12.00**
Art glass, cranberry, clear overlay w/controlled bubbles, early ... **45.00**

Ayotte, Rick
Baltimore Oriole on acorn branch, clear................ **300.00**
Blackburnian Warbler, male & female compound **425.00**
Black-Capped Chickadee, in clear, compound single **350.00**
Herring Gull **250.00**
Mallard Duck, 1980 .... **300.00**
Mute Swan, dk blue ground, single **300.00**
Wester Meadowlark, single, compound w/rainbow **450.00**

Baccarat, Antique
Blue spiraling, qauze cable canes, B-1848 cane, 2¼" dia **850.00**
Close pack mf, no silhouette canes, magnum **900.00**
Close pack mf mushroom, blue & wht spiral torsade **1,050.00**
Close pack mf w/B-1848 cane, 5 silhouette canes.......... **1,500.00**
Concentric, 4 rings, central red/wht cane, miniature **250.00**
Pansy w/bud, central red bull's eye cane................... **400.00**
Red & wht Primrose, star center cane, star cut base........ **925.00**
Spaced mf on muslin, B-1848 cane, 9 silhouette canes **1,550.00**
Spaced mf, complex center cane & garland have arrow heads, 2" **390.00**

Baccarat, Modern
Lampwork, basket of fruit, 1976 .... **295.00**
Blue & wht concentric, 1972 .... **160.00**
Coiled yellow snake, speckled rock ground **425.00**
Grapes, 1975 .... **315.00**
Mushroom o/l, blue & wht, 1973 .... **275.00**
Mushroom o/l, red & wht double, 1978.................. **425.00**
Seahorse, underwater scene, 1975 .... **315.00**
Snake of the Orient, brown, 1979 .... **375.00**
Strawberries, 1974.. **395.00**
White double Clematis w/bud, 1974 .... **215.00**
Sulphide, Franklin, o/l, red round, 1955 .... **700.00**
Gridel series, butterfly.................................. **325.00**
Gridel series, stag **200.00**
Kennedy 1963, ltd ed **200.00**
Kennedy Memorial, ltd ed **250.00**
Lincoln, o/l, purple ground, 1954 .... **500.00**
Martin Luther King, gilded cameo **140.00**
Mount Rushmore, o/l **400.00**
Will Rogers, o/l **200.00**
Will Rogers, regular **90.00**
Zodiac, Capricorn dk blue ground, faceted **115.00**
Kennedy, red & wht dbl o/l **500.00**

Bandford, Bob
Bicentennial, red/wht/blue flower, 5 & 1 faceting, 1976....... **300.00**
Five flower bouquet, 3 buds, star cut base, 3"............. **500.00**
Pink Clematis & bud w/dragonfly, turquoise ground, faceted .. **500.00**
Purple flower & buds, yellow double o/l, radiant cut **500.00**
Snake & upright blue flower, yellow ground................. **400.00**

Banford, Ray
Lilies of the valley on cranberry, 6 & 1 faceting **500.00**
Pears against parallel wht lacy cane **425.00**
Single rise w/2 buds, star cut base **400.00**
Triple iris & red rose bouquet, diamond cut base **595.00**

Bohemian, antique, concentric mf, stars, bull's eye, 1¾" **95.00**
Brass, army hat figural **20.00**
Bronze, eagle fiural w/6" wingspan, 5".................... **75.00**
Embossed building sitting on coal, Capital Fuel Co, 3" dia ... **30.00**
Brown floral, '1875', 3" dia.............................. **45.00**
Bubble weight, high dome, crimped splatter, American, 3".... **75.00**
Burl wood, book figural w/inlay, 2½x3½"................. **35.00**

Cast iron, Irish Setter figural **35.00**
Kewpie in relief, Purdue Foundry, 1½x3" dia............. **70.00**
Mammy.. **40.00**
Parking stanchion mkd Don't Park Here, 4" **15.00**
Chinese, close concentric, crimped canes, 2" **25.00**
End of day; red, blue, pink, green & yellow, 3" **50.00**
Floral w/center cane, stem w/leaves, 2¾" **45.00**
Millifiori blown glass, mkd China **65.00**
Civil War soldier in clear glass **120.00**

Clichy, Antique
Blue & wht swirl, gr & wht center cane **1,035.00**
Central pink cane, 5 mf circlets, green ground **1,050.00**
Close pack mf w/5 wht roses & 2 pink, wht stave basket, 1¾" **995.00**
Looped garland motif on opaque wht ground................ **800.00**
Scattered mf on lace, pastry mold canes, central pink roses ... **995.00**
Star canes & 2 concentric rows, stave basket.............. **500.00**

Cut glass, cobalt blue, 30-sided, 3½" dia **50.00**
Pineapple & Fan, recessed center **75.00**

D'Albret
Albert Schweitzer, regular **55.00**
Lindberg, o/l **165.00**
Paul Revere, regular **60.00**
Prince Charles, o/l **165.00**
Regular **55.00**

End of day, blown glass, 3½" dia **80.00**
Fairbanks Glass, Roosevelt **150.00**
General J Pershing, glass, 1917 embossed on reverse **35.00**
Gillinder, Victoria silhouette cane, faceted **425.00**
Home Sweet Home, 1910.................................. **35.00**

J Glass
Blue bouquet, upset muslin ground, flash o/l, faceted **300.00**
Center butterfly, mf entwining garlands, purple ground, faceted **325.00**
Pink & blue interlaces mf garlands, muslin ground **150.00**
Three pastel flowers, wht latt ground, 1980 .... **150.00**

Kaziun, Charles
Morning glory on trellis **1,100.00**
Pedestal w/lavendar rose, miniature **1,200.00**
Pedestal w/spider lily, gold flecked ground, miniature **400.00**
Tilted pedestal, bee on rose, 3 mf canes, cobalt ground **600.00**

Kiwanis, blue & yellow **20.00**
Lalique, conical shape w/berries, clear & acid, R Lalique **245.00**
Libbey, Wisconsin State Building, made at Columbian Expo.... **85.00**
Lundbert Studios, fish & stylized jellyfish, blue ground **135.00**

Manson, William
Blue shark, underwater scene **350.00**
Butterfly, amber, pulled canes form basket................. **325.00**
Butterfly, garland w/complex gr canes **140.00**
Elizabeth of Glamis Rose, mf garland, faceted **350.00**
Lilac blossom, rich & complicated, deep purple ground **295.00**
Three candles surrounded by circle of wht canes........... **200.00**
Two swans, deep blue ground, mf garlands, faceted **250.00**

Manson/Scotia
Dragonfly, mf canes for garland, dk ground **145.00**
Purple fish on blue & wht jasper ground, 8 mf canes **75.00**
Snowman, yellow scarf & cap **100.00**
Spaced mf, 5 circlets spaced w/6 complex canes **135.00**
Thistle on lavender ground, mf garland **150.00**

Maryland Glass Co, Christmas 1926, cobalt w/plated coin **24.00**
Midwestern, 5 petal lily, crimped ground, fragments, high dome, 3" **40.00**
Mushroom shape, mf, ruby double o/l w/6 windows **80.00**

New England Glass, clear obelisk w/red, wht & blue twist, 1860s, 13″ **245.00**
    Red/wht Poinsettias w/fruit, latt, magnum **200.00**
Orient & Flume, pastel mabrie, bird silhouette center cane . . . **135.00**
Palmer Cox Brownie **30.00**
Perthshire
Blue & wht Primrose, triple o/l **400.00**
Christmas Mistletoe, brilliant red ground, 1972 . . . . **100.00**
Christmas, colored angel silhouette, garland, 1979 . . . . **200.00**
Colored rooster silhouette cane, red ground, garlands, 1977 . . **320.00**
Crown, red/blue twist ribbon, wht latt, 1969 . . . . **225.00**
Dragonfly, blue w/wht latt wings, garland, 1979 . . . . **225.00**
Flat bouquet, yellow bow, dragonfly, faceted **465.00**
Millifiori garland w/colored flower silhouette, orange ground, 1974 **135.00**
Seal, ruby o/l, 1979 . . . . **320.00**
Sprig of Scottish Heather, 1978 . . . . **175.00**
Tropical fish, faceted, 1980 . . . . **395.00**

Plymouth Rock figural, 1620-1876, w/legend, glass **110.00**
Roger Brown, sulphide, Norman Rockwell, French crystal, 1979 **100.00**
Sandwich Glass Co, concave, mf design, 2¾″ dia **150.00**
Souvenir, Alaska Yukon-Pacific Expo, 1909 . . . . **22.00**
    Chicago, Milwaukee & St Paul Railway, bear figural **65.00**
    Empire State Building, sailboat figural, Jenning Bros, 6x4″ . . . **26.00**
    Pan American Expo **15.00**
    Statute of Liberty, eagle on rock figural, K & Co, 3½″ **38.00**
    World's Fair 1893, acid etching **95.00**
    World's Fair 1893, ferris wheel **20.00**
    World's Fair 1893, view of fair **38.00**
St Louis, Antique
Blue double Clematis, wht latt threads, faceted **1,100.00**
Center cane on blue & wht jasper, 5 complex canes **495.00**
Complex gr & wht center cane, red & wht jasper ground **250.00**
End of day, canes & lacy twists **275.00**
Fruit in latt basket **1,350.00**
Fuchsia blossom & berry, wht latt **2,500.00**
Nosegay w/4 florets, amber diamond cut ground **575.00**
Purple Dahlia, 5 leaves, in clear crystal **2,250.00**
St Louis, Modern
Cherries on wht latt, 1975 . . . . **350.00**
Gold foil Washington on horse, cobalt ground, 13 stars **250.00**
King Tut 24k gold medallion, orange ground, mf garland **350.00**
Miniature fruit on wht latt **260.00**
Overlay mushroom, Pistachio, 1970 . . . . **300.00**
Pair of wax seals, 1974 . . . . **95.00**
Red Dahlia on royal blue ground, 1980 . . . . **270.00**
Sulphide, 1953 Coronation, amber base, mf garland **300.00**
Stankard, Paul
First Bouquet, 1977 . . . . **1,500.00**
Spider Orchid, 1978 . . . . **850.00**
St Anthony's Fire, compound, 1975 . . . . **775.00**
Triple Wild Rose, 1975 . . . . **775.00**

Steuben, Zodiac, Taurus the Bull, 4½x3½x1½″ **135.00**
Tarsitano, Debbie
Colorful blooms fill clear ground **1,250.00**
Pink zinnia w/bumblebee, star cut, faceted **450.00**
Purple flowers, clear crystal, window cut **395.00**
Red flowers & bud, clear ground, early **275.00**
Yellow flowers & buds, basket cut base, clear ground **300.00**
Tarsitano, Delmo
Cherries on branch, ornate faceting **375.00**
Green snake, sand ground **350.00**
Pears on branches, earth ground **250.00**
Peppers & blossoms, clear crystal **300.00**

Strawberries & blossoms **475.00**
Trabucco, Victor
Dendrobium **350.00**
Green fish, faceted **250.00**
Nature in Ice series, strawberry w/blossom **350.00**

Train figural, NY Central lines **65.00**
Turtle figural, blown green glass, 6x4″ **135.00**

Papier Mache

    The art of papier mache was mainly European. It originated in Paris around the middle of the 18th century, and became popular in America during Victorian times. Small items, such as boxes, trays, inkwells, frames, etc., as well as extensive ceiling moldings and larger articles of furniture were made. The process involved building layer upon layer of paper soaked in glue, coaxed into shape over a wood or wire form. When dry, it was painted or decorated with gilt or inlays. Inexpensive 20th century 'notions' were machine processed and mold pressed.

Animal mask, German, lot of 9 . . . . **295.00**
Box, Czar's head, Russian, 1882, hp peasant scene, 4x6x2″ . . **350.00**
Bulldog **250.00**
Collar box, orig latches, satin lining, bottom drawer **30.00**
Cow, wind-up **725.00**
Crow, glass eyes **28.00**
Duck, US Zone Germany, 3″ **20.00**
French bucket, iron handle, old, large **85.00**
Funnel, orig red stain **35.00**
Horse, on wheeled stand, orig paint, 1880s **90.00**
Lamb, wood & cotton trim, early 1900s, 5x5x2″ **40.00**
Santa in sleigh, Hubley **800.00**
Spectacle case, MOP inlay, w/spectacles **25.00**
Spectacle case, oval w/end hinged cover, w/spectacles, gold decor **25.00**
Tea caddy, Victorian, MOP inset **65.00**
Tent, Schoenhut **450.00**
Tobacco jar, Mandarin, figural **60.00**
Toy bear, twist & turn, 4x6″ **65.00**
Tray, Chippendale, polychrome floral, gilt, 23x31″ **125.00**

Parian Ware

    Parian is hard paste unglazed porcelain made to resemble marble. First made in the mid 1800s by Staffordshire potters it was soon after produced in the United States by U.S. Pottery at Bennington, Vermont. Busts and statuary were favored, but plaques, vases, mugs and pitchers were also made.

Basket, Copeland, 5x10x2½″ **45.00**
Bust, Burns, sgnd Copeland **60.00**
    Chopin, 2¾″ **22.00**
    Psyche, mk J&TR, 6½″ **50.00**
    Sir Walter Scott, mkd, J&TB, imp Scott, #307, 10x7″ **85.00**
Candy dish, hand holding basket, diamond mk, 1870, 8″ long . **175.00**
Child's set, holly decor, 2 c/s, cream, sugar w/lid, tray, 10x8″ . **145.00**
Figurine; boar, recumbent, sgnd Valton, 1906, 10″ **145.00**
    Boy w/jug, wheat sheaf on shoulder, larger 1 behind him, 10″ **60.00**
    Classic maid, finger to chin, 1 hand on hip, anchor mk, 12″ **135.00**
    Eggshell, open w/2 mice inside, 2¼″ **25.00**
    Girl w/harp, 8″ **80.00**
    Grouping, warrior, horses, 7½″ **75.00**
    Man w/basket of grapes, mk Robinson & Leadbeater, 8½″ . . **145.00**
    Semi-nude in drape holds mask in hand, 14″ **135.00**
    Simply to Thy Cross I Cling, group, Bennington, 13½″ **150.00**
    Victorian girl, w/mandolin, 6½″ **45.00**

Victorian girl, w/mandolin, 8½″ **70.00**
Victorian girl, w/sheaf of wheat vase on back, 7″ **55.00**
Woman, classic hairdo & gown, imp anchor, 12″ **145.00**
Woman, mkd Robinson & Leadbeater, 9½″ **145.00**
Jug, gleaners, pewter cover & thumb rest, Reg mk 1858, 7″ . . **110.00**
Soldiers & Arabs, lavender w/wht, 5¾x3½″ **145.00**
Pitcher, drinking scene, dancers, boy on base ledge, Reg 1852, 9″ **150.00**
Grandmother & girl from Grimms, relief scene, 8½″ **200.00**
Leaf & flower pattern, blue & white, 9″ **260.00**
Tulip design, 8″ **125.00**
Twig handle, Bachinal scene, grapes & leaves in color, 8″ . . . **85.00**

Plaque, advertising, N C Smoking Tobacco, 9½″ **185.00**
Garden scene w/couple, pastels, gilded frame, 12x15″ **45.00**
Ring holder, hand holding ear of corn, w/ring & bracelet in relief, 7½″ **85.00**
Hand w/fancy cuff, 4″ **60.00**
Trinket box, shell shaped, white **35.00**
Vase, 2 cupids in relief, 9″ **65.00**
Grape clusters, 1860, 6½″ **60.00**
Portraits, vintage decor, wht w/blue, 1890, 8½″ **185.00**
Vases, 1 w/colonial girl figural, 1 w/boy, tree trunks, 6x4″, pr . . . **80.00**

Pattern Glass

The process for making mold pressed glass ware was perfected in the 1820s. Many early glass houses produced tableware in hundreds of patterns and variations. In the early years, flint glass was used. This type of glass contained lead, which gave the ware resonance and clarity of color. Through the remaining years of the century until about 1915 when glass ware of this type lost favor, soda lime was used to replace the lead. Glass of this type is referred to as non-flint.

Though in the past, collectors have tended to ignore all but the early flint glass, today there are many who appreciate the later glass as well, and prices within the last few years reflect this attitude. There are several important non-flint patterns. The rare portrait goblet and the American Coin pattern are both non-flint, as are the States series, made by U.S. Glass Company which are enjoying a newfound popularity.

In the listing that follows, if color is not noted, the glass is clear.

Aberdeen, butter w/cover **35.00**
Compote, open **35.00**
Compote w/cover **50.00**
Creamer **25.00**

Goblet. **20.00**
Sauce, flat **8.00**
Sugar, open **15.00**
Sugar w/cover **35.00**
Acorn, butter w/cover **32.00**
Celery **35.00**
Compote, open **35.00**
Compote w/cover **45.00**
Creamer **35.00**
Egg cup **20.00**
Goblet **25.00**
Salt, footed **15.00**
Sauce, 4″ **9.50**
Sauce, footed **15.00**
Spooner **20.00**
Sugar, open **17.50**
Sugar w/cover **35.00**
Water pitcher **50.00**
Acorn Band, champagne, flint **45.00**
Acorn Band w/Loops, goblets **18.00**
Acorn w/Wreath, goblet **35.00**
Actress, bread tray, Miss Neilson **50.00**
Bread tray, scene for Pinafore **50.00**
Butter w/cover **75.00**
Cakestand, large **125.00**
Cakestand, small **95.00**
Celery **95.00**
Cheese dish **150.00**
Compote, 3¼x6″ **35.00**
Compote w/cover, 6″ **85.00**
Compote w/cover, 10″ **110.00**
Creamer **50.00**
Dresser bottle, milk glass **30.00**
Goblet **65.00**
Master salt **68.00**
Milk pitcher **95.00**
Pickle, flat, 'Love's Request is Pickles' **35.00**
Relish **30.00**
Sauce, flat **9.00**
Sauce, footed, 4½″ **17.50**
Spooner **45.00**
Sugar w/cover **65.00**
Tumbler, clear **75.00**
Water pitcher **125.00**
Admiral Dewey, *See Dewey*
Alabama, toothpick **27.00**
Alba, syrup, decorated milk glass **60.00**
Albany Peerless, spooner, green w/gilt trim **25.00**
Alligator, goblet, clear **100.00**
Toothpick **55.00**
Alligator Scales, goblet, clear **24.00**
Alligator Scales w/Spearpoint, goblet, clear **12.00**
Water tumbler, amber **17.00**
Almond Thumbprint, bowl, flint **17.50**
Bowl, non-flint **8.75**
Celery vase **20.00**
Compote, open, flint, 4¾x8½″ **40.00**
Creamer, flint **37.50**
Creamer, non-flint **18.50**
Egg cup, flint **25.00**
Egg cup, non-flint **12.50**
Goblet **16.50**
Goblet, flint **30.00**
Goblet, non-flint **15.00**

Spooner, non-flint	8.50
Sugar w/cover, non-flint	25.00
Tumbler, flint	35.00
Tumbler, non-flint	17.50
Water pitcher, flint	50.00
Water pitcher, non-flint	25.00
Wine, flint	25.00
Wine, non-flint	14.50
Amazon, bowl	25.00
Butter w/cover	45.00
Cakestand, large	40.00
Cakestand, medium	35.00
Cakestand, small	30.00
Celery, tall	30.00
Champagne	35.00
Claret	35.00
Compote, open, 7¼x8¾"	35.00
Compote w/cover	45.00
Creamer	35.00
Dish, oval, w/cover	23.00
Dish, oval, w/lion handle	35.00
Goblet	28.00
Olive dish w/handle	12.00
Relish, flat	12.00
Salt dip	8.00
Salt shaker	12.00
Sauce, flat	8.00
Sauce, footed	10.00
Spooner	25.00
Sugar, open	22.00
Sugar w/cover	35.00
Syrup	45.00
Tumbler	20.00
Vase	22.00
Water pitcher	45.00
Water tumbler	20.00
Wine	30.00
American Shield, butter w/cover	155.00
Butter, horizontal, no final, round top	125.00
Castor set, 4 bottles w/stand, child's	95.00
Creamer	95.00
Spooner	95.00
Sugar w/cover	155.00
Andes, *See Beaded Tulip*	
Angora, butter w/cover	40.00
Creamer	25.00
Goblet	35.00
Sugar w/cover	36.00
Anthemion, berry bowl	35.00
Butter w/cover	70.00
Plate, curled edge, 10"	35.00
Sauce, large, square, flat	16.00
Spooner	25.00
Sugar w/cover	35.00
Tumbler	32.00
Water pitcher	42.00
Apollo, bowl	15.00
Butter w/cover	32.50
Cakestand	32.50
Celery	28.00
Compote, open	30.00
Compote w/cover	40.00
Creamer	32.50
Goblet	32.00

Pickle dish	20.00
Sauce, 3½"	10.00
Saucer, etched, footed, 4"	14.00
Spooner	25.00
Sugar, open	28.00
Sugar w/cover	38.00
Syrup, etched, metal handle	45.00
Tray, for water set	28.00
Tray, wine	28.00
Arabesque, butter w/cover	40.00
Celery	30.00
Compote w/cover, 6"	37.50
Creamer	37.50
Goblet	25.00
Sauce, flat	6.50
Spooner	18.50
Sugar, open	25.00
Sugar w/cover	37.50

Archfoot & Daisy, bowl, 9x4"	45.00
Arched Fans, goblet	25.00
Arched Fleur-de-lys, cruet & stopper	30.00
Arched Grape, butter w/cover	65.00
Celery	30.00
Creamer	40.00
Goblet	22.00
Sauce, flat	15.00
Spooner	35.00
Sugar, open	35.00
Sugar w/cover	45.00
Water pitcher	65.00
Arched leaf, goblet, flint	75.00
Goblet, non flint	20.00
Plate, large, flint	30.00
Plate, large, non-flint	20.00
Salt, footed, flint	30.00
Arched Ovals, goblet	22.00
Goblet, red flashing	30.00
Tumbler, etched, ruby stained	30.00
Wine, red flashing	24.00
Argus, champagne	38.00
Compote, open flint, 5½x5"	56.00
Tumbler, short	50.00

Wine, flint	27.50
Art, banana dish	75.00
Butter w/cover	50.00
Cakestand, 9″	65.00
Celery	40.00
Compote, open, 7½″	40.00
Compote, open, 8¾x10″	50.00
Compote w/cover	60.00
Creamer	30.00
Cruet	35.00
Goblet	35.00
Milk pitcher, rare, ruby stained	150.00
Relish	25.00
Sauce, flat	10.00
Sauce, footed	15.00
Spooner	30.00
Sugar, open	30.00
Sugar w/cover	40.00
Wine	28.00
Artic, goblet	80.00
Ice bowl	75.00
Waste bowl	75.00
Water pitcher	145.00
Water tray, oval	125.00
Water tray, round	125.00
Ashburton, ale glass, flint, 6½″	60.00
Bar bottle, flint, qt	85.00
Bar bottle, flint, pt	65.00
Bar tumbler, flint	60.00
Bitters bottle, flint	65.00
Celery vase w/scalloped top	135.00
Celery, plain top, flint, footed	75.00
Celery, flint, scalloped	125.00
Champagne, flint	60.00
Claret, w/low stem, flint	45.00
Cordial, flint	60.00
Creamer, flint, scarce	185.00
Egg cup, flint, double	35.00
Egg cup, flint	20.00
Goblet, flint, flared	45.00
Goblet, flint, gilt	100.00
Sugar, open, flint	75.00
Water tumbler, flint	50.00
Whiskey tumbler, flint, handled	78.50
Wine, flint	32.00
Wine, flint, gilt	90.00
Ashland Snowdrop, goblet	27.50
Ice cream tray	40.00
Leaf dishes	17.50
Plate, large	40.00
Ashman, bowl	15.00
Butter w/cover	45.00
Cakestand	20.00
Celery	30.00
Compote w/cover, 6″	40.00
Compote w/cover, 12″	50.00
Creamer	32.50
Goblet	32.50
Pitcher, water, etched	75.00
Relish dish	12.50
Sauce dish	9.00
Spooner	32.50
Sugar, open	32.50
Sugar w/cover	42.50

Water tray, large	35.00
Wine	15.00
Aster & Leaf, salt shaker, blue	42.00
Aster Band, goblet	18.50
Atlas, bowl, red flashing	28.00
Bowl	12.00
Butter	35.00
Butter, red flashing	75.00
Cakestand, 8″	25.00
Cakestand, red flashing 10″	75.00
Champagne	28.00
Creamer, red flashing	42.50
Creamer, flat, etched	22.50
Goblet	22.00
Goblet, red flashing	52.00
Jelly compote	26.50
Milk pitcher, 10″	34.00
Sauce, footed	12.50
Sauce, footed, red flashing	25.00
Spooner	20.00
Spooner, red flashing	40.00
Sugar, open, amber	25.00
Sugar w/cover	30.00
Sugar w/cover, red flashing	55.00
Toothpick	14.00
Tumbler, gr	30.00
Water pitcher, 11″	45.00
Water pitcher, red flashing	75.00
Wine	22.50
Wine, red flashing	75.00
Aurora, wine, etched	20.00
Wine, ruby stain	38.00
Wine tray, ruby stain, 10″	50.00
Aztec, bon bon, footed, 4½x7″	25.00
Tumbler	14.00
Bakewell Block, celery	74.00
Spill w/straight top	40.00
Bagware, spooner, amber	25.00
Butter w/cover, amber	60.00
Balder, bowl, gold, 8½″	25.00
Butter w/cover	50.00
Carafe	36.00
Creamer	23.00
Creamer, individual, gold	14.00
Decanter w/orig stopper	85.00
Goblet	18.00
Juice glass	9.50
Master berry	28.00
Plate, 7½″	12.00
Plate, 8″	14.00
Punch cup	12.00
Rose bowl	15.00
Sauce, flat, 4½″	5.00
Sauce, flat, 5″	9.00
Shot glass	9.50
Spooner	18.50
Sugar, open	18.50
Syrup, 5″	40.00
Toothpick	24.00
Toothpick, gr	85.00
Tumbler	19.50
Whiskey, gr	35.00
Wine	16.00
Ball & Swirl, creamer	22.50

Goblet, etched	20.00
Sauce, footed	6.50
Balloon, goblet	15.00
Wine	12.00
Bamboo Edge, butter w/cover	36.00
Compote, open	24.00
Compote w/cover, 7″	40.00
Relish, retangle, large	20.00
Relish, rectangle, small	16.00
Salt & pepper, pair	36.00
Sauce, footed	10.00
Spooner	20.00
Sugar w/cover	34.00
Banded Buckle, egg cup	24.00
Syrup, hollow handle	110.00
Banded Cube, butter w/cover, etched	30.00
Goblet	14.00
Sauce, flat, etched, 4″	8.00
Banded Knife & Fork, egg cup	11.00
Banded Portland, butter w/cover, Maiden Blush	175.00
Creamer, 4″	14.00
Creamer, individual, w/gold	16.00
Relish, 8½″	12.00
Relish, oval, w/gold	22.00
Shaker, w/gold	16.00
Syrup, w/gold	60.00
Toothpick, w/gold	25.00
Tumbler, w/gold	25.00
Vase, 6″	14.00
Wine, w/gold	35.00
Barberry, compote w/cover	30.00
Egg cup	20.00
Plate, 6″	14.00
Water pitcher, w/applied handle	75.00
Wine	30.00
Barley, goblet	22.00
Pitcher	28.00
Plate, 11½x9½″	35.00
Sauce, footed, 4″	8.50
Barred Hobnail, mug	13.50
Shaker	14.00
Spoonholder	20.00
Barred Ovals, celery w/flat base	18.00
Creamer	15.00
Pitcher	45.00
Barrel Argus, champagne	38.00
Goblet	35.00
Bartlett Pear, creamer	25.00
Goblet	22.50
Sauce, flat	6.00
Spooner	18.00
Sugar, open	18.00
Sugar w/cover	30.00
Basketweave, cup & saucer, yellow	32.00
Egg cup, dated	24.50
Goblet, amber	29.00
Vaseline	38.00
Yellow	27.00
Pitcher, vaseline	65.00
Spooner, amber	35.00
Tray, rural scene, blue, 12″	50.00
Tray, rural scene, yellow, 12″	50.00
Bead & Scroll, goblet	17.00
Mug	14.50

Spooner, cobalt	65.00
Wine, engraved	16.00
Beaded Acorn Medallion, goblet	28.00
Pitcher	50.00
Sugar	20.00
Beaded Band, butter w/cover	38.00
Spooner	20.00
Syrup	45.00
Beaded Circle, butter w/cover	85.00
Celery	48.00
Compote, open	65.00
Compote w/cover	95.00
Creamer	50.00
Egg cup	35.00
Goblet, flint	75.00
Mug w/handle	45.00
Spooner	40.00
Sugar, open	50.00
Sugar w/cover	75.00
Beaded Dewdrop, dish, 6x4″	20.00
Individual sugar & creamer	30.00
Mug w/handle, large	38.00
Syrup, 6½″	50.00
Beaded Grape, bowl, sq, green, 5½″	26.00
Butter w/cover, green w/gold	110.00
Celery, clear	35.00
Cruet, green	100.00
Platter, clear, 10x7″	20.00
Toothpick, green	55.00
Water pitcher, green	85.00
Wine, green w/gold	38.00
Beaded Grape Medallion, bowl, flat, 10x7″	27.00
Creamer	58.00
Egg cup	22.00
Goblet	30.00
Relish dish, 8½x4½″	16.00
Sugar w/cover	45.00
Beaded Loop, berry bowl	15.00
Cakestand, 6″	30.00
Cakestand, 8″	45.00
Cakestand, 9½″	55.00
Celery	25.00
Compote, open	28.00
Compote w/cover, large	45.00
Creamer	23.00
Cruet	25.00
Goblet	35.00
Honey dish, 3½″	9.50
Mug w/handle	22.50
Pitcher, milk	40.00
Platter, 11x8″	26.50
Relish, 7½x4″	20.00
Salt shaker	22.00
Sauce, flat	6.00
Sauce, footed, 3½″	9.50
Spooner, footed	20.00
Sugar w/cover, flat	28.00
Sugar w/cover, footed	35.00
Syrup pitcher	40.00
Toothpick	25.00
Vase toothpick	30.00
Water pitcher	45.00
Whiskey carafe	40.00

Beaded Mirror, castor set, 5 bottle	85.00
Goblet	35.00
Plate, large	45.00
Sugar, open	40.00
Beaded Ovals, creamer	16.50
Butter w/cover	42.50
Celery	28.00
Cream	30.00
Goblet	25.00
Spooner	25.00
Sugar w/cover	38.00
Beaded Swirl, berry set, green w/gold, 7 pc	145.00
Butter	40.00
Creamer	25.00
Egg cup	24.00
Finger bowl	20.00
Goblet	25.00
Punch cup, green w/gold	22.00
Relish, flat	20.00
Sauce, flat, 4½"	5.00
Sauce, green, 4"	25.50
Spooner	20.00
Sugar, open	20.00
Sugar w/cover	35.00
Tumbler	25.00

Beaded Tulip, pitcher, qt, rare size	70.00
Wine tray, 9"	32.00
Bear Climber, goblet	100.00
Bearded Man, butter w/cover	50.00
Beautiful Lady, salt shaker	14.00
Beaver Band, goblet	300.00
Beehive, goblet	38.00
Wine	36.00
Bellflower, bar tumbler	80.00
Bowl, coarse rib, ftd, 8"	68.00
Champagne, fine rib	125.00
Compote, low, scalloped, 5x8"	60.00
Egg cup	28.00
Goblet, barrel, flint	50.00
Goblet, fine rib	40.00
Goblet, w/loops	125.00
Master salt	40.00

Pitcher, double vine, 7¼"	400.00
Salt, footed, flint, 2¾"	35.00
Spooner, double vine, flint	60.00
Sugar, open	24.00
Sugar w/cover	65.00
Syrup, applied handle	350.00
Tumbler	65.00
Wine	85.00
Belmont Royal, bread platter, amber	110.00
Bread platter, crying child in center, clear	60.00
Butter w/cover, 6-sided skirted base	140.00
Celery, ball feet	80.00
Creamer, 6-sided skirted base	60.00
Master salt, ftd, 6-sided skirted base	20.00
Sugar w/cover, ball feet	90.00
Belt Buckle, creamer	26.00
Mug	25.00
Punch cup	18.00
Relish	12.00
Tumbler	25.00
Wine	28.00
Belted Worchester, tumbler, footed	33.50
Bethlehem Star, compote w/cover, 4½"	50.00
Creamer	35.00
Sauce, 4½"	10.00
Sugar w/cover	42.00
Beveled Diamond & Star, sauce, 4"	11.00
Tumbler, ruby stained	42.00
Bigler, bar bottle, qt	60.00
Celery, footed	95.00
Goblet	33.00
Lamp, 7"	75.00
Birch Leaf, egg cup, flint	24.00
Goblet	25.00
Spooner, flint	24.00
Tumbler, footed	16.00
Wine	25.00
Bird & Strawberry, bowl, footed, 9x5½"	42.00
Bowl, oval 4 legs, 9½"	62.00
Butter dish	78.00
Cakestand, 9"	50.00
Celery vase	65.00
Creamer	50.00
Punch cup	22.00
Spooner	40.00
Sugar w/cover	65.00
Tumbler	40.00
Water pitcher	165.00
Wine	58.00
Birds & Roses, goblet	25.00
Birds at Fountain, compote w/cover, 8"	60.00
Goblet	38.00
Blackberry, bowl, oval, 8x5½"	40.00
Butter w/cover	65.00
Goblet	48.00
Sauce, flat, 4"	17.50
Spooner	52.00
Blackberry Band, creamer	45.00
Sugar w/cover	55.00
Blaze, creamer, molded handle	55.00
Oil bottle w/orig stopper, 6"	49.00
Sugar w/cover	65.00
Bleeding Heart, bowl, flat, oval, 9¼x6½"	26.00
Butter w/cover	60.00

Compote, open	36.00
Creamer	45.00
Goblet, plain	35.00
Goblet, knob stem	35.00
Mug	45.00
Sauce, flat, 4″	14.00
Spooner	35.00
Block, rose bowl, ruby stained, late	65.00
Syrup, ruby stain	145.00
Tumbler, ruby stained, late	31.00
Tumbler, amber	25.00
Block & Bar, creamer	45.00
Water pitcher	95.00
Block & Circle, goblet	23.00
Wine	18.00
Block & Double Bar, pitcher, ruby stained, 11″	150.00
Block & Fan, bowl, collared base, 8″	23.00
Carafe	45.00

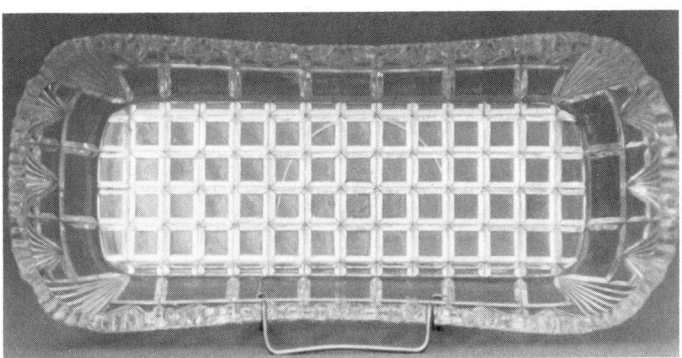

Celery, 12x5″	25.00
Celery vase	25.00
Cruet, medium	29.50
Ice bowl	41.00
Plate, 6″	19.50
Plate, large	19.50
Rose bowl, 4″	28.00
Sauce dish, footed	10.00
Sugar shaker	37.00
Syrup	67.00
Wine	32.50
Block & Honeycomb, goblet	20.00
Pitcher	60.00
Block & Iris, goblet	8.00
Block & Lattice, celery, ruby stained	75.00
Cruet, ruby stained	105.00
Block & Rosette, tumbler	34.00
Blocked Arches, bowl, frosted, 9¼″	22.00
Bone Stem, goblet	35.00
Bow Tie, bowl, flat, 6¾″	16.00
Goblet	36.00
Jam jar	45.00
Water pitcher	75.00
Bradford Blackberry, bar tumbler	95.00
Champagne	68.00
Goblet	60.00
Sugar w/cover	85.00
Broken Column, berry bowl, ruby stained, 2x6″	48.00
Bowl, flat, 2½x7¼″	25.00
Cakestand, 9″	65.00
Carafe	65.00
Celery	33.00
Cruet w/orig stopper, red flashing	150.00

Dish, oval, 11x5″	28.00
Relish dish, 7¾x5″	25.00
Relish dish, 8x4″	26.00
Brooklyn, goblet	44.00
Buckle, compote, open, 8″	49.50
Creamer, flint	52.00
Egg cup, flint	35.00
Goblet, flint	35.00
Master salt, flint	34.00
Sauce, flat	9.00
Spooner	26.00
Sugar w/cover	45.00
Sugar w/cover, flint	65.00
Buckle w/Diamond Band, water pitcher	75.00
Buckle w/Star, butter w/cover	42.00
Creamer	28.00
Wine	24.00
Budded Ivy, creamer	45.00
Goblet	26.00
Bulging Loops, toothpick, pink cased	45.00
Bull's Eye, decanter w/orig stopper, pt	85.00
Goblet	67.00
Spooner	40.00
Water bottle	47.00
Wine	60.00
Bull's Eye & Bar, goblet, flint	175.00
Bull's Eye & Broken Column, goblet	69.00
Tumbler, footed	40.00
Bull's Eye & Button, creamer	75.00
Pitcher, Illinois	180.00
Shot, Pennsylvania	35.00
Sugar, Vermont	65.00
Tumbler	30.00
Wine, finecut, tiny	22.00

Bull's Eye & Daisy, champagne, gilt trim	16.00
Tumbler, purple eyes	16.00
Bull's Eye & Diamond Point, goblet	100.00
Honey dish, 3½″	28.00
Sauce, flat, 4¼″	17.00
Tumble-up	150.00
Water tumbler	90.00
Bull'e Eye & Fan, bowl, flat, blue w/gilt trim, 8½″	31.00
Goblet	16.50
Milk pitcher, blue w/gold	95.00
Punch cup	11.00

Sauce, flat, 4″	5.00
Sauce, flat, 5¼″	6.00
Spooner	13.00
Toothpick, green	125.00
Tumbler	13.00
Tumbler w/gilt trim	13.00
Wine	16.50
Wine, saucer type, 3¾″	16.50
Bull's Eye & Rosette, whiskey tumbler, 3¾″	43.00
Bull's Eye & Wishbone, goblet	100.00
Button Arches, individual sugar, ruby stained	25.00
Punch cup, ruby stained	15.50
Tumbler, ruby stained w/frosted band	25.00
Tumbler, ruby stained, vintage etched	28.00
Water set, ruby stained w/frosted band, 7-pc	300.00
Wine, clambroth	30.00
Cabbage Rose, bar tumbler	40.00
Bowl, oval, flat, 7½x5″	25.00
Master	30.00
Tumbler	40.00
Cable, decanter w/cable stopper, qt	225.00
Goblet, flint	65.00
Honey dish, 3½″	13.00
Spooner, flint	35.00
Water tumbler	45.00
Whale oil lamp, 8¼″	155.00
Camel Caravan, goblet	65.00
Cane, boat relish, amber, 7½x3½″	26.00
Celery	20.00
Goblet	20.00
Goblet, amber	28.00
Goblet, green	25.00
Kettle, blue	18.00
Plate, blue, 4½″	14.00
Plate, green, 4½″	14.00
Tumbler, blue	28.00
Waste bowl, amber	35.00
Water pitcher, amber	49.00
Water tray, amber, 11½″	50.00
Cape Cod, goblet	35.00
Capitol Building, champagne	36.00
Goblet	36.00
Cardinal Bird, butter w/cover	65.00
Creamer	40.00
Goblet	36.00
Carnation, bud vase, flat, scalloped, plated holder	42.00
Cathedral, berry bowl, amber	35.00
Cruet, vaseline	48.00
Relish, blue, fish-shaped	35.00
Water pitcher	125.00
Wine, amber	52.00
Wine, blue	52.00
Cattails & Fern, goblet	25.00
Celtic Cross, celery vase, etched	13.50
Spooner	13.50
Ceres, spooner	26.00
Chain, butter w/cover	40.00
Compote w/cover, 12″	55.00
Goblet	20.00
Plate, 7″	16.50
Wine	20.00
Chain & Shield, creamer	19.00
Pitcher	28.00
Spooner	16.00

Goblet	18.00
Chain w/Star, creamer	22.00
Goblet	25.00
Plate, 7″	12.00
Plate w/handle	27.00
Spooner	17.00
Chandelier, celery, flat-base	24.00
Celery, tall	35.00
Creamer	31.00
Goblet	69.00
Master salt	24.00
Checkerboard, butter	55.00
Creamer, 4″	20.00
Goblet	22.00
Punch cup	9.00
Wine	14.00
Cherry, butter w/cover	40.00
Goblet	25.00
Spooner	24.00
Spooner, milk glass	43.00
Sugar, open	25.00
Cherry & Cable, berry, clear w/gold, small	10.00
Berry, clear w/pink, small	10.00
Cherry & Fig, milk pitcher	30.00
Sauce	8.00
Cherry Lattice, butter w/cover, gilt trim w/color	65.00
Sauce w/color, 4½″	16.00
Water, clear w/good gold & pink, 6-pc	195.00
Chrysanthemum Leaf, butter w/cover, clear	55.00
Butter w/cover, gold trim	55.00
Creamer, gold trim	35.00
Classic, bowl, log feet, 8¼″	120.00
Butter w/cover, log feet	295.00
Celery, collared base	185.00
Compote w/cover, lg, log feet	325.00
Compote w/cover, small, log feet	295.00
Creamer, log feet	175.00
Milk pitcher, log feet	295.00
Plate, warrior, signed	155.00
Sauce, log feet, 4¼″	55.00
Spooner, log feet	75.00
Sugar w/cover	150.00
Sugar w/cover, log feet	250.00
Sweetmeat w/cover	250.00
Clear & Diamond Panels, goblet, jelly-type	12.00
Sugar, open	14.00
Clear Circle, compote, open	36.00
Creamer	30.00
Cruet, frosted	38.00
Goblet	28.00
Plate, 5″	7.00
Punch cup	16.50
Cleat, milk pitcher	135.00
Clematis, goblet	12.00
Sugar w/cover	25.00
Colonial, champagne	60.00
Creamer	70.00
Goblet, knob stem	60.00
Master salt	20.00
Sugar w/cover	78.00
Colonial w/Diamond Band, wine	14.50
Colonial w/Garland, wine	13.50
Colorado, bowl, ftd, gr, 7½″	30.00
Bowl, ftd, gr, 9½″	35.00

Butter w/cover, gr w/excellent gold 135.00
Celery vase, etched 30.00
Compote, 3 corners, green 135.00
Creamer, gr w/excellent gold 48.00
Dish, ftd, blue w/gilt trim, 6½″ 24.00
Nappy, clear 12.00
Sauce, ftd, gr, 4¾″ 18.00
Sugar, open, enamelled cross, crown & angels, 1898 . . . . 45.00
Toothpick, gr w/gold, souvenir 35.00
Tumbler, gold 30.00
Violet bowl, blue w/gilt trim 42.00
Water pitcher, gr w/gold 250.00
Columbian Coin, celery, frosted 80.00
   Creamer, frosted 85.00
   Milk pitcher 190.00
   Syrup 145.00
   Tray 115.00
Comet, bar tumbler 110.00
   Goblet 85.00
   Water tumbler 135.00
   Whiskey tumbler 95.00
Connecticut Flute, goblet, 5½″ 17.00
Cord & Tassle, goblet 34.00
   Spooner 23.00
   Wine 29.00
Cord Drapery, bowl, flat, 7¼″ 14.50
   Compote w/cover, small 40.00
   Punch cup 10.00
   Relish, oval, 9½″ 20.00
   Tumbler, gr 55.00
Cordova, creamer, gr, 3½″ 20.00
   Toothpick, gr 36.00
Cornucopia, wine 15.00
Cottage, creamer 25.00

Pitcher, 5″ 25.00
Plate, 6″ 12.00
Plate, 8″ 14.50
Saucer, ruby stained, 5″ 14.00
Creased Bale, salt shaker, milk glass 14.50
Crescent & Fan, champagne 19.50
Croesus, berry, large 155.00
   Berry, purple w/excellent gold, small 40.00

Butter w/cover, amethyst w/gold 245.00
Butter w/cover, clear 95.00
Butter w/cover, gr w/excellent gold 245.00
Celery vase, amethyst w/excellent gold 225.00
Cruet, gr, gold decor, large 245.00
Individual creamer, green 100.00
Sugar 145.00
Tumbler, purple 75.00
Water set, 6 pc, gr & gold 325.00
Crossed Disks, butter w/cover, etched 24.00
   Creamer, etched 14.00
   Egg cup, double-handled 15.00
   Sauce, ftd 7.00
   Sugar w/cover, etched 20.00
Crowfoot, sauce, flat, 5½″ 7.50
   Sugar w/cover 35.00
   Tumbler 20.00
Crystal Wedding, plate, etched, sq, 8″ 55.00
   Tumbler 55.00
Crystal, celery, ftd 16.50
   Egg cup 17.00
   Goblet 17.00
Cube & Square Stem, butter w/cover, etched 30.00
   Creamer, etched 25.00
   Goblet, etched 17.00
   Sugar w/cover 25.00
Cube w/Fan, sauce, flat, 4″ 5.50
Cupid & Venus, bread plate 38.00
   Creamer 35.00
   Goblet 47.00
   Jam jar w/cover 45.00
   Milk pitcher 58.00
   Mug, 2″ 30.00
   Mug, 3½″ 36.00
   Plate, 10 . . . . 27.50
   Plate, 10½″ 29.00
   Sauce, ftd, 3¾″ 8.00
   Sauce, ftd, 4½″ 10.00
   Sauce, ftd, small 8.00
   Sugar, open 20.00
   Water pitcher 52.00
Cupid's Hunt, compote w/cover, 9x8″ dia 65.00
   Sauce, ftd, 4″ 10.00
Currant, butter w/cover 39.00
   Goblet 26.00
   Spooner 21.00
Currier & Ives, goblet 20.00

Keresene lamp, 9½" 85.00
Milk pitcher 33.00
Curtain Tieback, goblet 18.00
Cut Log, butter w/cover 75.00
Cakestand, 9" 45.00
Celery 40.00
Compote, jelly, high standard, 6" 65.00
Compote, low standard, scalloped, 9" 60.00
Compote, open, high standard, scalloped, 9" 70.00
Compote, w/cover, high standard, 8" dia 90.00
Creamer 50.00
Cruet w/orig stopper, small 50.00
Goblet 50.00
Honey dish w/cover, sq, large 160.00
Individual creamer & sugar w/cover 55.00
Mug 15.00
Nappy, 2x5" dia 20.00
Pitcher, tall tankard 80.00
Salt & pepper, pr 60.00
Sauce, ftd, plain edge 35.00
Sauce, ftd, scalloped 35.00
Spooner 35.00
Sugar w/cover 60.00
Tumbler 25.00
Vase, 16" 45.00
Vase, 17" 65.00
Water pitcher, regular 85.00
Wine 28.00
Dahlia, creamer, 4½" 21.00
Cakestand, 9½" 32.00
Cakestand, amber, 9" 70.00
Creamer 22.00
Goblet 32.00
Mug, amber 40.00
Pitcher" 35.00
Plate, 7 " 15.00
Plate w/handle, amber, 8¾" 38.00
Relish dish 15.00
Water pitcher 40.00
Daisy & Button, boat, amberina, 8" 210.00
Hat spooner, vaseline 30.00
Plate, ruby stain, 7" 20.00
Rose bowl 18.50
Shoe, amber, 5¾" 20.00
Shoe, blue, 5¾" 25.00
Spooner, sq 42.00
Sugar shaker, cranberry 90.00
Tumbler, vaseline 27.50
Daisy & Button in Oval Panels, berry bowl, ftd, amber 35.00
Creamer 19.00
Goblet, gold trim 22.00
Tumbler 12.00
Daisy & Button w/Amber Panel, *see Amberette*
Daisy & Button w/Cross Bar, bowl, flat, 9x6" 10.00
Bowl, flat, amber, 8x5½" 22.00
Bowl, flat, blue, 9x6" 23.00
Compote, 7" 12.50
Compote, 8½" 15.00
Cruet, amber 110.00
Goblet, amber 38.00
Goblet, yellow 47.00
Milk pitcher, blue 48.00
Platter, 10¾x8" 15.00
Sauce, flat, amber, 4" 15.00

Sugar w/cover, amber 47.00
Waste bowl, yellow 27.00
Water pitcher, yellow 65.00
Wine, amber 39.00
Daisy & Button w/Red Dots, berry, sq, 4½" 20.00
Pitcher, round 210.00
Daisy & Button w/V Ornament, toothpick 18.00
Tumbler 11.00
Dakota, ale 145.00
Butter w/cover, etched 65.00
Cakestand, etched, 9½" 65.00
Celery, flat base, etched 30.00
Celery, ftd 20.00
Celery, ftd, etched 39.00
Champagne 155.00
Compote, 5x5" dia 50.00
Compote w/cover, etched, 5x8" 65.00
Condiment stand 110.00
Goblet 30.00
Goblet, etched 35.00
Goblet, etched, ruby stained 52.00
Sauce, ftd, etched, 4" 20.00
Spooner 26.00
Spooner, etched 39.00
Sugar w/cover 55.00
Sugar w/cover, etched 67.50
Tankard water pitcher 75.00
Tumbler, ruby stain 35.00
Wine 30.00
Wine, ruby stained 50.00
Darling Grape, tumbler 14.00
Deer & Dog, celery vase 65.00
Goblet, U-shaped, etched 85.00
Water pitcher 150.00
Deer & Pine Tree, butter w/cover 75.00
Butter, open 45.00
Compote w/cover, on standard 75.00
Creamer 57.50
Goblet 35.00
Mug, gr 95.00
Plate, cake, pedestaled 85.00
Punch cup 25.00
Sauce, oval 25.00
Spooner 53.50
Water pitcher 80.00
Delaware, boat sauce, pink w/gilt trim 5x3¼" 42.00
Bowl, octagonal, gilt trim, 9" 30.00
Butter, gr w/gold 145.00
Cruet w/orig stopper 100.00
Master berry, round, gr w/excellent gold 40.00
Pin tray, 7x3½" 17.00
Pin tray, 9x4¾" 21.00
Sauce, flat, gr w/gilt trim, 3½" 21.00
Spooner, gr w/gold 45.00
Sugar w/cover 60.00
Toothpick, gr w/gold trim 90.00
Toothpick, Maiden's Blush w/gold 75.00
Tumbler, clear w/gold 18.00
Tumbler, gr w/gilt trim 40.00
Water pitcher 50.00
Water set, gr w/gold trim, pitcher 9½" 200.00
Derby, *see Pleat & Panel*
Dew & Raindrop, cordial 23.00
Creamer 32.00

Sherbet cup **20.00**
Dewberry, tumbler, gilt trim **15.00**
Dewdrop, butter w/cover **20.00**
   Cakestand, 8½" **24.00**
   Goblet, vaseline **25.00**
   Goblet w/band **12.00**
Dewdrop & Flowers, creamer **28.00**
Dewdrop in Points, plate, 8¾" **17.00**
   Spooner **28.00**
Dewdrop w/Star, berry bowl **20.00**
   Master salt **7.00**
   Sugar w/cover **45.00**
Dewey, pitcher **55.00**
   Plate, 6" **18.00**
   Relish, serpentine shape, amber, 8¼" **40.00**
   Sauce, ftd, amber, 4¾" **18.00**
   Serpentine tray, amber, 10" **45.00**
Diagonal Band, creamer **18.00**
   Goblet **21.00**
   Relish, 7x4½" **8.50**
Diagonal Band w/Fan, goblet **23.00**
   Plate, 6" **13.00**
   Sauce, ftd **7.00**
   Spooner **18.50**
   Wine **19.00**
Diagonal Sawtooth Band, wine **34.00**
Diamond & Sunburst, cakestand **30.00**
   Celery vase **28.00**
   Goblet **20.00**
   Syrup, applied handle **55.00**
   Tumbler **18.00**
Diamond & Sunburst Variation, punch cup, ruby stained **21.00**
   Tumbler **18.00**
   Tumbler, ruby stained **29.00**
Diamond Band, goblet **24.00**
   Mini mug **15.00**
Diamond Block, *see Art*
Diamond Block w/Fans, creamer **28.00**
   Pitcher **45.00**
   Sugar w/cover **40.00**
Diamond Cut w/Leaf, creamer **26.00**
   Goblet **24.00**
   Plate, 7¼" **14.50**
   Sugar w/cover, rare amber **85.00**
Diamond Horseshoe, *see Aurora*
Diamond Medallion, cakestand, 8¾" **22.00**
   Celery, ftd **16.00**
   Compote, open, 6¼x6¼" dia **24.00**
   Goblet **24.00**
   Sauce, flat, 4½" **6.00**
   Sugar w/cover **23.00**
   Water pitcher, 9½" **38.00**
Diamond Point, bar tumbler **65.00**
   Bowl, 6¼" dia **20.00**
   Celery, flared top **62.00**
   Celery, ftd **75.00**
   Champagne, 5½" **75.00**
   Claret **70.00**
   Compote, flared top, 10½x8½" **70.00**
   Compote, open, 7¼x7¼" dia **50.00**
   Creamer **85.00**
   Decanter w/orig stopper, qt **100.00**
   Egg cup **25.00**
   Egg cup, clambroth **110.00**

Goblet **55.00**
   Sauce, flat, 5½" **14.00**
   Spooner **35.00**
   Spooner, clear w/gold **45.00**
   Spooner, flint **45.00**
   Sugar w/cover, flint **75.00**
   Water tumbler **75.00**
   Whiskey w/handle, flint **75.00**
   Wine, flint **50.00**
Diamond Quilted, bowl, flat, yellow, 4¼x9" dia **26.00**
   Celery, amberina, 6½" **265.00**
   Celery, ftd, yellow **49.00**
   Creamer, amethyst **45.00**
   Creamer, ftd, blue **88.00**
   Goblet, blue **35.00**
   Goblet, yellow **24.00**
   Mug w/handle, blue **40.00**
   Sauce, flat, blue, 4" **11.00**
   Sauce, ftd, amethyst, 4" **15.00**
   Sauce, ftd, blue, 4½" **15.00**
   Sauce, ftd, yellow, 4½" **13.00**
   Spooner, light amber **20.00**
   Tumbler, amberina **90.00**
   Tumbler, amethyst **40.00**
   Tumbler, blue **40.00**
   Wine, clear **12.00**
   Wine, vaseline **30.00**
Diamond Ridge, toothpick **25.00**
Diamond Splendor, goblet, gold **20.00**
Diamond Thumbprint, carafe, open, large **115.00**
   Celery vase, scalloped rim, 9½" **200.00**
   Champagne **250.00**
   Compote, open, 7x4¾" **43.00**
   Goblet **275.00**
   Honey dish, individual **14.00**
   Sauce **15.00**
   Spooner, flint **65.00**
   Water tumbler **95.00**
   Whiskey **100.00**
Diamonds in Diamonds, goblet **16.00**
   Spooner, ftd, scalloped **22.00**
   Water pitcher, applied handle, bulbous **67.00**
Dickinson, goblet **34.00**
   Sauce, 4" **18.00**
   Spooner **45.00**
Diedre, goblet **25.00**
Dinner Bell, *see Cottage*
Dirigo Pear, sauce, flat, 4x5" **7.00**
Divided Diamonds, egg cup **65.00**
Divided Hearts, celery ftd **65.00**
   Compote, open, 8" **60.00**
   Goblet **70.00**
   Sugar, open **36.00**
Divided Squares, sauce, flat, triangle, frosted amber, 4¼" . . . **16.00**
Dogwood, sauce, color w/gilt trim, 3¾" **25.00**
Dolly Madison, water set, 7 pc, blue w/gold **285.00**
Dominio, shakers, pair, milk glass **55.00**
Doric, *see Feather*
Double Beetle Band, goblet **21.00**
   Goblet, amber **35.00**
Double Block, wine set, 5 pc, orig stopper, 'H 1892' . . . **210.00**
Double Dahlia & Lens, toothpick, clear w/stain, mint color . . . **58.00**
Double Diamond Panels, sugar, open **26.00**
Double Fan, toothpick **15.00**

Double Leaf & Dart, goblet **25.00**
Double Loop, *see Ribbon Candy*
Double Petal Tulip, goblet **20.00**
Double Red Block, tumbler **42.00**
Double Ribbon, compote w/cover, 12½x8″ dia **70.00**
  Lamp, dated, 9¼″ **88.00**
Double Rosette, celery **25.00**
Double Snail, rose bowl, large **40.00**
  Squat milk pitcher, 6½″ **78.00**
Double Spear, goblet **13.00**
Douglass, banana stand **38.00**
Draped Fan, creamer **19.00**
Draped Red Block, goblet **59.00**
  Sugar w/cover **29.00**
  Tumbler **34.00**
Draped Window, goblet **95.00**
Drapery, creamer **29.00**
  Goblet **25.00**
  Plate, 6″ **16.00**
  Spooner, blue opalescent w/gold **55.00**
Drapery Variant, *see Tidy*
Duchess Loop, wine **29.00**
Duke, goblet **22.00**
Duncan #27, *see Block Band*
Duncan Block, berry bowl, etched, amber flash **35.00**
  Spooner, amber flash **30.00**
  Water pitcher, etched, ruby stained **145.00**
Duquesne, goblet **12.00**
Early Thumbprint, bitters bottle **135.00**
  Celery **100.00**
  Celery, pattern in base **125.00**
  Goblet **55.00**
  Goblet, baluster stem **68.00**
  Honey dish, 3¼″ **7.00**
  Paperweight **350.00**
  Sauce, flat, 4¼″ **8.50**
  Sauce, flat, 5¼″ **10.00**
  Spooner **58.00**
  Tumble-up **450.00**
  Tumbler, ftd **32.00**
  Wine **55.00**
Egg & Dart, individual creamer **12.50**
Egg in Sand, goblet **27.00**
  Spooner, amber **55.00**
  Water tray **50.00**
Egyptian, butter w/cover **75.00**
  Celery vase **55.00**
  Compote w/cover, high standard, sphinx at base, 8″ **145.00**
  Creamer **32.50**
  Goblet **40.00**
  Pickle dish **30.00**
  Spooner **35.00**
  Sugar, open **30.00**
  Sugar w/cover **55.00**
Elegant, bitters bottle **26.00**
  Goblet, flint **85.00**
Elmino, goblet, etched **15.00**
Empire Colonial, goblet, flint **85.00**
Empress, butter w/cover, gr w/gold decor **145.00**
  Creamer **120.00**
  Master salt **65.00**
  Punch cup, emerald gr w/excellent gold **110.00**
  Sugar **145.00**
  Table set, 4 pc **400.00**

Toothpick, gr **120.00**
English Hobnail Cross, *see Klondike*
  Creamer **15.00**
Esther, berry, large **55.00**
  Celery **120.00**
  Creamer **125.00**
  Cruet **145.00**
  Salt **55.00**
  Spooner, gr w/gold trim **50.00**
  Toothpick **110.00**

Tumbler, green & gold, 4″ **40.00**
Etched Band, *see Colonial w/Diamond Band*
Etched Dakota, *see Dakota*
Etched Morning Glory, *see Morning Glory*
Etched Pavonia, *see Pavonia*
Etched Zinnia, *see Zinnia*
Euclid, toothpick **24.00**
Eureka, egg cup **25.00**
  Goblet **26.00**
Excelsior, bar bottle, pt **39.00**
  Cordial, flint **30.00**
  Goblet **38.00**
  Master salt, ftd **18.00**
  Tumbler, vaseline, 4″ **100.00**
  Water pitcher **225.00**
Eyewinker, compote w/cover, 11x6½″ **45.00**
  Fruit stand, 8½x7½″ **58.00**
  Salt & pepper, pr **45.00**
  Syrup **85.00**
Fairfax Strawberry, *see Strawberry*
Falling Leaves, water pitcher **35.00**
Fancy Diamonds, tumbler **14.00**
  Wine **12.00**
Fancy Loop, goblet, some gilt **38.00**
  Toothpick **60.00**
Fans w/Diamond, bowl, oval, 6x8″ **13.00**
  Goblet **24.00**
  Sauce **18.00**
  Spooner **18.00**
  Wine **20.00**
  Feather, bowl, flat, 8½″ **16.00**
Feather Duster, spooner, gr **29.00**
  Butter w/cover **35.00**
  Cakestand, 8″ dia **24.00**
  Creamer **27.00**
  Goblet **45.00**
  Honey dish, 3½″ **18.00**

Milk pitcher **50.00**
Sauce, flat, sq, 4″ **17.00**
Spooner **18.00**
Spooner, gr **75.00**
Sugar w/cover **32.00**
Sugar w/cover, gr **80.00**
Water pitcher **35.00**
Wine **36.00**
Fedora Loop, goblet **32.00**
Feeding Swan, goblet **62.00**
  Water pitcher, 7¾″ **75.00**
Ferguson Inverted Thumbprint, goblet, amber **16.00**
  Goblet **9.00**
Fern Whirl, wine **12.00**
Ferris Wheel, goblet **17.00**
Festoon, bowl, flat, 7″ **16.00**
  Cakestand, 9″ **34.00**
  Creamer **26.00**
  Sauce, flat, 4½″ **6.50**
  Tumbler **24.00**
  Water tray, 10″ **24.00**
Fickle Block, water pitcher, sq **125.00**
  Wine, gilt trim **7.00**
Figure 8, *see Ribbon Candy*
Fine Cut, boat celery, 11x3½″ **18.50**
  Bowl, flat, 8¼x5″ **13.50**

Brides basket, 11x10″ **85.00**
Creamer **28.00**
Cruet, vaseline **65.00**
Dish, rectangle, 9x6″ **13.50**
Goblet **19.50**
Mustard w/cover & under plate **26.50**
Plate, 6¼″ **11.00**
Plate, 7¾″ **12.50**
Plate, 10½″ **16.00**
Plate, amber, 7¼″ **14.50**
Plate, amber, 10½″ **19.50**
Plate, blue, 6¼″ **16.00**
Spooner **30.00**
Toothpick, canary **28.00**
Tumbler **19.00**
Tumbler, vaseline **30.00**

Water pitcher, blue **95.00**
Water pitcher, vaseline **55.00**
Fine Cut & Block, berry bowl, ftd, blue, small **14.00**
  Creamer, amber blocks **82.00**
  Creamer, clear **65.00**
  Egg cup **19.50**
  Goblet, pink blocks **67.00**
  Goblet, yellow blocks **67.00**
  Plate, 5¾″ **14.00**
  Sauce, ftd, 5¾″ **7.50**
  Sauce w/handle, blue **16.50**
  Sauce w/handle, yellow blocks **19.50**
  Tumbler **19.50**
  Tumbler, amber **42.00**
  Tumbler, blue blocks **60.00**
  Tumbler, yellow blocks **60.00**
  Water pitcher, blue blocks **115.00**
  Water pitcher, clear **95.00**
Fine Cut & Diamond, *see Diamond Medallion*
Fine Cut & Feather, *see Feather*
Fine Cut & Panel, goblet **25.00**
  Platter, 13x9″ **25.00**
  Platter, blue, 13x9″ **34.00**
  Relish dish, 7x3½″ **7.00**
  Sauce, ftd, yellow, 3¾″ **15.00**
  Wine, amber **37.00**
  Wine, blue **37.00**
Fine Cut Band, *see Cottage*
Fine Cut Diamond Point, champagne **29.00**
  Cup plate **9.50**
  Goblet **24.00**
Fine Prism, champagne **33.00**
  Wine **26.00**
Fine Rib, butter w/cover **75.00**
  Claret **75.00**
  Compote, open, low standard **40.00**
  Goblet, flint **50.00**
  Goblet, non-flint **50.00**
  Master salt **26.00**
  Milk pitcher, bulbous, applied handle **75.00**
  Sauce, flat, 4¼″ **9.50**
  Spooner **55.00**
  Sugar w/cover **75.00**
  Wine **45.00**
  Wine, plain band **29.00**
Fine Rib to Top, *see Fine Rib*
Fingerprint, *see Thumbprint*
Fishbone, goblet **14.50**
Fishscale, berry dish, sq, 4″ **8.00**
  Berry set, 7 pc, 8½″ **39.00**
  Bowl, 7″ **14.00**
  Bread plate, sq, 9″ **23.00**
  Cakestand, 8½″ **19.50**
  Cakestand, 9″ **22.00**
  Compote, 6½x8½″ **22.00**
  Compote, jelly **12.50**
  Goblet **33.00**
  Milk pitcher **21.00**
  Pickle w/handle **12.00**
  Pitcher, water **26.00**
  Plate, 7″ dia **20.00**
  Plate, 8″ **25.00**
  Plate, sq, 9″ **27.50**
  Relish, 8½x4″ **14.00**

Flaming Pleat & Panel, cruet............................ **65.00**
Flamingo Habitat, compote, open, high standard, 8″ dia **25.00**
    Creamer **42.00**
    Goblet... **31.00**
    Sherbet, 4¼x3¾″ dia **22.00**
    Sugar w/cover **49.00**
Flat Diamond, cordial, 3½″ **24.00**
    Goblet... **17.00**
    Sugar w/cover **30.00**
    Wine **18.00**
Flat Diamonds & Panels, *see Lattice & Oval Panels*
Flat Panel, *see Pleating*
Flattened Diamond & Sunburst, cup, gr **14.00**
    Cup.. **10.00**
    Punch bowl **22.00**
    Toothpick.. **30.00**
Flattened Hobnail, water pitcher **38.00**
Fleur-de-Lys, cakestand, late, 9½″ **24.00**
    Goblet... **30.00**
    Mug, late, 3¼″ **15.00**
    Plate, gr, 8″ **37.00**
    Plate, late, sq, 7″ **15.50**
    Tumbler, late, ruby stained **26.00**
    Water pitcher, gr **68.00**
Fleur-de-Lys & Drape, *see Fleur-de-Lys & Tassel*
Fleur-de-Lys & Tassel, celery, flat, 10¼x4½″............. **17.00**
    Compote, jelly, green, 5″ **28.00**
    Compote, Maine **125.00**
    Creamer **19.50**
    Dish, rectangle, gr, 8x5¼″ **17.00**
    Kerosene lamp, 8″ **45.00**
    Pitcher, green **95.00**
    Sauce, flat, 4″ **8.50**
    Sugar w/cover **25.00**
    Syrup, Maine **195.00**
    Table set, Medallion Sprig **350.00**
    Tumbler **25.00**
    Water set, 5 pc, green **250.00**
    Water tray, 11½″ **19.50**
Flora, butter, white opalescent........................... **85.00**
    Tumbler, gr w/gold **25.00**
    Water pitcher, gr, w/gold **85.00**
Florette, toothpick, gr milk glass **30.00**
Florida Palm, creamer **17.00**
    Goblet... **19.50**
Flower & Honeycomb, spooner **18.00**
    Sugar w/cover **28.00**
Flower & Scroll, wine, amber............................. **40.00**
Flower Band, goblet **48.00**
Flower Flang, *see Dewey*
Flower Medallion, relish dish, gilt & color **12.50**
    Tumbler, clear w/gold & pink........................... **20.00**
Flower Pot, creamer **30.00**
    Sauce w/handle, ftd **9.00**
Flower w/Cane, sauce dish **12.00**
    Tumbler **25.00**
Flowered Pan, celery **20.00**
Flowered Tulip, goblet, small **26.00**
Flute, bar bottle, pt **25.00**
    Bar bottle, qt... **34.00**
    Bar tumbler, large **24.00**
    Claret **24.00**
    Egg cup, double **27.00**
    Egg cup, single **18.50**

Goblet... **22.00**
    Whiskey taster, blue **37.00**
    Whiskey taster, clear **10.00**
    Whiskey tumbler w/handle **24.00**
    Wine **17.00**
Flute & Cane, decanter, qt.............................. **28.00**
Flute w/Bull's Eye, champagne........................... **48.00**
    Wine **29.00**
Fluted Icicle, goblet **32.00**
Fluted Ribbon, sugar w/cover, frosted **32.50**
Fluted Scroll, salt shaker, blue opalescent **35.00**
    Salt shaker, blue w/enamel decor & gold............... **45.00**
Fluted Scrolls, creamer **21.00**
Flying Robin, *see Hummingbird*
Forest Ware, *see Ivy in Snow*
Forget-Me-Not, spooner, barred **22.00**
Four Petal Flower, *see Delaware*
Frazier, tumbler, cranberry w/enamel decor **28.00**
Fringed Drape, cruet, clear w/gold **18.00**
Frosted Apollo, butter w/cover.......................... **45.00**
Frosted Artichoke, spooner w/handle **65.00**
Frosted Banded Portland w/Purple, *see Barred Ovals*
Frosted Circle, cruet w/orig stopper..................... **30.00**
    Sauce, flat **10.50**
    Tankard pitcher, 12″ **55.00**
Frosted Diagonal Band, goblet........................... **25.00**
Frosted Dolphin, compote, jelly **38.00**
Frosted Eagle, sugar w/cover, etched **230.00**
Frosted Flower Band, sauce, ftd, 3½″ **14.50**
Frosted Leaf, egg cup, flint **95.00**
    Goblet, ladies **85.00**
    Sauce, flat, 4¼″ **25.00**
Frosted Lion, bread tray................................. **60.00**
    Celery, etched **145.00**
    Compote w/cover, 11½″ **115.00**
    Compote w/cover, lion rampant, 4x7″ **85.00**
    Creamer **65.00**
    Egg cup **60.00**
    Goblet... **50.00**
    Marmalade jar w/cover................................. **55.00**
    Relish, lion handles **48.00**
    Sauce, 4″ **18.50**
    Sauce, ftd **22.00**
Frosted Ribbon, celery **42.00**
Frosted Ribbon w/Double Bars, celery, ftd **24.00**
    Water pitcher, bulbous **75.00**
Frosted Roman Key, celery, ftd **78.00**
    Egg cup **40.00**
    Goblet... **60.00**
    Tumbler, ftd.. **75.00**
    Wine **65.00**
Frosted Victoria, creamer **45.00**
    Celery vase **45.00**
Frosted Waffle, *see Hidalgo*
Fushia, spooner... **20.00**
Gaelic, water goblet **25.00**
Galloway, bowl, oval, 8½x4½″ **14.50**
    Bowl, oval, 8½x6½″................................... **16.00**
    Cakestand, 9½″ **52.00**
    Celery, flat-base **17.00**
    Creamer **17.00**
    Cruet, panelled stopper **28.00**
    Goblet, gilt trim **35.00**
    Individual creamer **11.50**

Milk pitcher	45.00
Punch cup	7.50
Sauce, flared, flat, 4½″	7.00
Sauce, flat, 3½″	6.50
Sauce, ftd	11.50
Spooner	16.00
Sugar w/cover	29.00
Tumbler	27.00
Tumbler, gilt trim	27.00
Vase, 13½″	16.00
Vase, flared, 7″	21.00
Water pitcher, miniature	27.00
Wine	30.00
Garden Fruits, goblet	16.50
Sugar w/cover	17.00
Water pitcher, bulbous, 10″	55.00
Garden of Eden, platter	24.00
Garfield Drape, creamer	36.00
Milk pitcher, 8½″	67.00
Plate, 11″	17.00
Sauce, flat, 4″	8.50
Spooner	22.00
Water pitcher	80.00
Gargoyle, goblet	175.00
Gathered Knot, celery	32.00
Gem, *see Nailhead*	
Geneva, bowl, oval, gr, 9½″	35.00
Pitcher, gr, w/excellent gold	100.00
Georgia Gem, breakfast sugar, custard	49.00
Butter w/cover, gr w/gold	75.00
Salt shaker, gr	20.00
Sauce, flat, custard, 4″	36.00
Toothpick	18.00
Tumbler, gr w/gold	30.00
Georgia, *see Peacock Feather*	
Giant Baby Thumbprint, *see Early Thumbprint*	
Giant Block & Lattice, tankard pitcher, ruby stained	140.00
Giant Bull's Eye, goblet	70.00
Giant Prism, champagne	155.00
Ale	145.00
Giant Prism w/Thumprint Band, ale glass	27.50
Giant Sawtooth, goblet	80.00
Water tumbler	75.00
Gibson Girl, tumbler	25.00
Goat's Head, sugar w/cover	100.00
Gonterman Swirl, tumbler, amber top w/frosted base	65.00
Good Luck, *see Horseshoe*	
Gooseberry, bar tumbler	40.00
Creamer	20.00
Goblet	30.00
Spooner	15.00
Gothic, celery, ftd	95.00
Egg cup	42.00
Goblet, flint	65.00
Sauce	14.50
Sugar w/cover, flint	42.00
Water tumbler	75.00
Grand, *see Diamond Medallion*	
Grant Memorial, plate, yellow, 10″	95.00
Grape & Festoon, creamer, gr	40.00
Goblet	18.00
Goblet, small American shield	90.00
Plate, 6″	7.00
Relish, scoop-shaped	19.00

Spoon holder	23.00
Grape & Festoon w/Shield, goblet	24.00
Mug, 1¾″	17.00
Sauce, ftd	6.00
Grape & Festoon w/Stippled Leaf, goblet	25.00
Grape & Gothic arches, bowl, shallow, custard, 7½″	42.00
Creamer	40.00
Goblet, custard w/trim	67.00
Sugar w/cover	55.00
Table set, 4 pc, gr w/mint, gold	335.00
Tumbler, gr w/gold, sgnd w/circle	28.00
Water set, 7 pc, gr w/excellent, gold	225.00
Grape Band, bar tumbler	29.00
Goblet	22.00
Grape Bunch, bread tray w/motto, 10″	19.50
Egg cup	10.00
Grasshopper, butter dish, no insect	33.00
Creamer, no insect	30.00
Sauce, ftd, etched, 4″	9.00
Greek Cross Band, water pitcher, blue	46.00
Greek Key, banana split dish	24.00
Butter	165.00
Ice tea, flat bottom	75.00
Plate, 5″	12.00
Plate, 9¼″	45.00
Relish, oval, 9″	38.00
Relish, oval, 12″	48.00
Sherbet	17.00
Spooner	85.00
Water goblet	85.00
Grenade, toothpick	17.50
Gridley, pitcher	105.00
Grogan, goblet	16.00
Tumbler	14.00
Grooved Bigler, master salt, flint	20.00
Tumbler, ftd	45.00
Guardian Angel, *see Cupid & Venus*	
Hairpin, bowl, flat, 7¼″	17.00
Bowl, oval, 8x5″	19.50
Celery, ftd	41.00
Champagne	36.00
Decanter w/orig stopper, qt	85.00
Egg cup	19.00
Egg cup, opaque white	70.00
Goblet	22.00
Sauce, flat, 4″	8.00
Spooner	22.00
Sugar, open	19.00
Hairpin w/Thumbprint, goblet	43.00
Haley's Comet, tumbler	16.00
Wine, etched band	30.00
Hamilton, butter w/cover	65.00
Compote, open, 5x7¾″ dia	43.00
Egg cup	35.00
Honey dish, 3½″	15.50
Sauce, flat, 4″	8.00
Spooner	26.00
Sugar, open	25.00
Water tumbler, flint	75.00
Hamilton w/Leaf, bar tumbler	75.00
Goblet	55.00
Sugar, open	30.00
Hand, compote, open, 5x9″ dia	25.00
Goblet	50.00

Sauce, flat, 4¼″ **7.00**
Hanover, celery **34.00**
 Goblet **25.00**
Harp, spill **50.00**
 Whale oil lamp **250.00**
Hartley, dish, flat, blue, 9x6″ **17.00**
 Goblet, amber **42.00**
 Milk pitcher, amber, 7″ **55.00**
 Sauce, ftd, amber, 4″ **14.00**
 Water pitcher, yellow **85.00**
Harvard, plate, gr, 7¾″ **14.00**
Hawaiian Lei, berry bowl **15.00**
 Salt shaker, pair **15.00**
 Wine **16.00**
Hawaiian Pineapple, goblet **115.00**
Heart & Spades, *see Medallion*
Heart Band, creamer, ruby flashed **30.00**
 Toothpick, ruby stain **22.00**
Heart Stem, celery, ftd, amber **45.00**
 Creamer **30.00**

 Spooner **25.00**
Heart w/Thumbprint, bowl, 9¼″ **35.00**
 Bowl, flat, 8″ **29.00**
 Bowl, fluted edge, gilt trim, 8″ **29.00**
 Bowl, gold trim, 4¾″ **15.00**
 Card tray, 8x4¼″ **22.00**
 Celery, flat base **29.00**
 Comport, 7½″ **55.00**
 Goblet **55.00**
 Individual creamer **20.00**
 Jar, powder, silver top **30.00**
 Punch cup **18.50**
 Rose bowl **17.00**
 Sauce, flat, gilt trim, 5″ **16.50**
 Sauce, flat, sq, 4″ **14.00**
 Sugar, open **32.00**
 Tray, 9x4¼″ **26.00**
 Vase, 10″ **20.00**
 Vase, gr, 6″ **50.00**
 Wine **55.00**
Heavy Drape, egg cup **12.00**
Hercules Pillar, ale glass **12.00**
 Syrup w/orig lid, amber **50.00**
 Syrup w/orig lid, blue **65.00**
Hero, spooner, ruby stain **32.00**

Heron, water pitcher **125.00**
Herringbone, berry, large, clear **35.00**
 Creamer **17.50**
 Cruet w/orig stopper, emerald gr **95.00**
 Goblet, emerald gr **35.00**
 Goblet, clear **20.00**

 Pitcher, 9″ **55.00**
 Sugar w/cover, clear **23.00**
 Tumbler, green **25.00**
 Water set, 7 pc, emerald **200.00**
 Wine, emerald gr **55.00**
Herringbone Band, goblet **15.00**
Hexagon Block, celery, ruby stained **55.00**
 Compote, open, ruby stained, 7x7¼″ dia **35.00**
 Dish, crimped, 10½x5″ **21.00**
 Spooner, etched, amber stained **36.00**
 Syrup, ruby stained **135.00**
 Tumbler, etched, amber stained **39.00**
 Tumbler, ruby stained **39.00**
 Water pitcher, etched, amber stained, 12½″ **85.00**
Hexagon Star, toothpick, clear w/gold **26.00**
Hickman, bowl, flat, 5″ **11.00**
 Creamer **24.50**
 Jack in Pulpit dish, 6x8″ **13.00**
 Punch cup **6.50**
 Sugar, open, oval, ruby stained **19.50**
 Tray, 12¾x8″ **55.00**
 Wine, gilt trim **18.50**
Hidalgo, celery vase, frosted **45.00**
 Celery, flat base, amber stained **37.00**
 Celery, flat base, etched **26.00**
 Creamer, etched **29.00**
 Cruet, enamelled rosebud **24.00**
 Goblet, etched **15.00**
 Goblet, frosted **17.00**
 Sauce w/handle, flat, 4½″ **11.00**
 Sugar shaker w/orig lid, frosted **60.00**
Hinoto, *see Diamond Point w/Panels*
Historical, bank w/orig tin base, amber **67.00**
 Inkwell base, Memorial Hall **30.00**
 Match holder, Bible **40.00**
 Plate, Columbus Pilot Wheel **48.00**
 Plate, Garfield Star **20.00**
 Plate, McKinley, 7½″ **35.00**

Plate, Pope Leo, 10″	40.00
Tumbler, Cleveland in wreath	30.00
Tumbler, Garfield in wreath	30.00
Tumbler, Grant, 'Let Us Have Peace'	50.00
Tumbler, McKinley, 'Protection & Plenty'	30.00
Tumbler, McKinley large face in base	50.00
Whiskey tumbler, Bumper to Flag	38.00
Hobnail, creamer, blue opalescent, 3½″	12.00
Pitcher, 7″	40.00
Pitcher, reeded handle, 8″	48.00
Rose bowl w/stem, ftd, vaseline w/opalescence, 6½″	26.00
Toothpick, canary opalescent	55.00
Clear w/white opalescent	24.00
Toothpick, opalescent	27.00
Hobnail-Ruffled Top, bowl, oval, amber, 8x5½″	40.00
Dish, cranberry, 3½x6″	35.00
Finger bowl, blue opalescent	35.00
Goblet, cranberry, 5½″	90.00
Hobnail w/Fan Top, bowl, 10x7½″	14.50
Goblet	24.00
Hobnail w/Thumbprint, butter w/cover, blue	65.00
Waste bowl, amber	29.00
Holbrook, see Pineapple & Fan	
Holly, compote w/cover, 9x8¾″ dia	159.00
Goblet	115.00
Tray, 9″	100.00
Holly Band, master salt	65.00
Holly Leaves, goblet	24.00
Holly w/Cord & Tassel, creamer	55.00
Sugar, open	24.00
Honeycomb, celery, flint	25.00
Goblet	15.00
Tumbler, ftd	45.00
Honeycomb & Clover, tumbler, water, sapphire blue, gold trim	35.00
Water pitcher, blue w/gold trim	65.00
Honeycomb w/Diamond, egg cup	20.00
Goblet	28.00
Honeycomb w/Flower Rim, creamer, amber	30.00
Honeycomb w/Ovals, champagne	34.00
Goblet	21.00
Hops & Barley, see Wheat & Barley	
Hops Band, goblet	20.00
Sugar, open	18.00
Wine	27.00
Horn of Plenty, bar tumbler	70.00
Champagne	150.00
Creamer	170.00
Egg cup	43.00
Goblet	65.00
Honey dish, flint, 3¼″	18.50
Plate, 6″	40.00
Sauce, 5″	25.00
Sauce, flat, 4½″	14.50
Sauce bottle, clear w/orig pewter top	125.00
Spillholder	40.00
Sugar w/cover	50.00
Water tumbler	75.00
Wine	125.00
Horsehead's Medallion, celery, ftd	40.00
Horsemint, sauce, gold trim, 4″	8.00
Horseshoe, bread tray	33.00
Creamer	25.00
Goblet	30.00
Goblet, knob stem	40.00
Pitcher	115.00
Plate, 10″	40.00
Platter, 9x13″	30.00
Relish dish, 9x5″	20.00
Sauce, ftd, 4″	8.00
Spoon holder	20.00
Sugar shaker, amber, small	35.00
Hotel Thumbprint, goblet	14.00
Huber, ale glass, 5½″	24.00
Celery, ftd, etched	24.00
Champagne	26.00
Cordial	29.00
Egg cup	17.00
Goblet	26.00
Master salt	15.50
Mug, 3″	26.00
Whiskey tumbler, 3″	20.00
Whiskey w/handle	47.50
Wine	21.00
Huckle, see Feather Duster	
Hummingbird, bar tumbler, amber	55.00
Celery	24.00
Compote, 7″	55.00
Waste bowl	38.00
Water pitcher, amber	130.00
Water set, 7 pc, blue, 1870's	365.00
Iceburg, see Arctic	
Icicle w/Chain Band, goblet, flint	45.00
Icicle w/Loops, goblet	35.00
Inconoclast, goblet	43.00
Idyll, cruet, gr w/gold	120.00
Toothpick, apple gr	50.00
Illinois, master berry, clear, sq, 8″	35.00
Plate, sq, 7″	35.00
Toothpick, clear w/gold	30.00
Indiana, see Cord Drapery	
Indian Swirl, see Feather	
Interlocking Hearts, creamer, gr	27.00
Sugar w/cover, clear	19.50
Syrup	52.00
Wine	14.00
Inverted Baby Thumbprint, toothpick, pigeon blood	90.00
Inverted Fan & Feather, berry, gr w/gold, small	25.00
Table set, 4 pc, gr w/gold	275.00
Tumbler, gr	38.00
Inverted Fern, butter w/cover	57.00
Egg cup, flint	25.00
Goblet, rayed base	37.00
Goblet	30.00
Honey dish	12.50
Punch cup, signed	25.00
Sauce, flat, 4″	8.50
Sugar, open	25.00
Water tumbler	80.00
Inverted Honeycomb, tumbler, amber w/D&B base	20.00
Inverted Strawberry, compote, jelly, 4½″	18.00
Tumbler	24.00
Inverted Thistle, berry set, 6 pc, gr w/excellent gold	105.00
Butter w/cover, gr w/excellent gold	135.00
Creamer	25.00
Sugar w/cover	85.00
Inverted Thumbprint, box w/cover, amberina, 7″	295.00
Cruet, amberina	230.00
Cruet, ruby	80.00

Syrup w/applied handle, amber	**60.00**
Wine, amber	**30.00**
Wine, blue, claret size	**40.00**
Wine, tapered bowl, teardrop stem, blue	**40.00**
Inverted Thumbprint w/Star, goblet, amber	**29.00**
Ionia, goblet	**16.50**
Iowa, cruet	**38.50**
Tumbler, excellent gold	**12.00**
Iowa City, bowl, clear stork, 6½"	**65.00**
Irish Column, *see Broken Column*	
Isis, spooner, ruby stained	**45.00**
Ivy Scroll, compote, jelly, gr	**28.00**
Pitcher	**75.00**
Tumbler	**18.00**
Ivy in Snow, bowl, flat, 8x5½"	**11.00**
Cakestand	**24.00**
Celery vase	**20.00**
Plate, 10"	**20.00**
Sauce, flat, gold leaves, 4¼"	**7.00**
Sugar, open	**8.50**
Water pitcher	**24.00**
Jackson, salt shaker, blue opalescent w/goofus decor	**42.00**
Salt shaker, clear opalescent	**25.00**
Jacob's Coat, butter w/cover, blue	**48.00**
Creamer, blue	**38.00**
Jacob's Ladder, butter w/cover	**48.00**
Celery, 9"	**30.00**
Compote, 5¾x8½"	**30.00**
Compote, 7x7½"	**28.00**
Compote, 8x8½"	**32.00**
Creamer & sugar	**60.00**
Dish, oval, 7¾x5½"	**20.00**
Dish, oval, 8¾x6"	**22.00**
Goblet, 6½"	**55.00**
Honey dish, 3½"	**12.00**
Pitcher, water, large	**140.00**
Plate, 6"	**25.00**
Relish, 7¾x5½"	**12.00**
Relish, Maltese Cross handles, 9¾x5½"	**25.00**
Salt, ftd, 2¾"	**20.00**
Sauce, flat, 4"	**9.00**
Sauce, flat, 4½"	**12.00**
Spooner, 5¾"	**30.00**
Sugar	**24.00**
Syrup jug w/spring lid	**110.00**
Water pitcher, bulbous	**185.00**
Wine, 4"	**32.00**
Jasper, *see Belt Buckle*	
Jefferson Optic, table set, 4 pc, clear w/salmon & enamel decor	**195.00**
Toothpick	**20.00**
Jenny Lind, compote, amber, large	**195.00**
Compote, flint	**100.00**
Jersey Swirl, plate, 6"	**10.00**
Plate, 10"	**12.00**
Plate, amber, 8"	**19.50**
Tumbler, etched	**12.00**
Wine	**14.50**
Jewel & Dewdrop, bread plate, oval, 'Our Daily Bread'	**50.00**
Cakestand, 9"	**55.00**
Compote, clear, 6"	**40.00**
Mug, 3½"	**22.00**
Relish plate, clear	**35.00**
Tumbler	**55.00**
Jewel Band, creamer	**24.00**

Wine	**18.00**
Jewelled Heart, creamer, blue	**40.00**
Creamer, gold	**17.50**
Jewelled Moon & Star, bowl, flat, clear, 7½"	**18.50**
Cakestand, clear, 8½"	**35.00**
Compote, open, 7¾x9"	**29.00**
Compote w/cover, 6¾x8"	**60.00**
Goblet, gilt trim	**45.00**
Wine, clear	**21.00**
Job's Tears, *see Art*	
Jubilee, goblet	**32.00**
Jumbo, compote	**450.00**
Spoon rack	**550.00**
Kaleidoscope, water pitcher	**75.00**
Kallbach, goblet	**13.00**
Spooner	**15.50**
Kansas, *see Jewel & Dewdrop*	
Kayak, water tray, 10"	**22.00**
Kentucky, cakestand, 9½"	**45.00**
Sauce, ftd, 3¼"	**6.50**
Tumbler, gr	**25.00**
Keystone Grape, goblet	**24.00**
King's Breast Plate, goblet, gilt trim	**9.50**
King's Crown, goblet w/purple thumbprints	**23.00**
Goblet, amethyst eyes, gilt trim	**16.50**
Goblet, green eyes, gold trim	**14.00**
Goblet, trace of gilt	**22.00**
Sugar, open	**13.00**
Wine, gr eyes	**18.00**
Klondike, butter w/cover	**400.00**
Cruet w/orig stopper	**600.00**
Goblet	**350.00**

Salt & pepper, pair, amber trim	**250.00**
Sugar & creamer, pair	**400.00**
Sugar w/cover, frosted & gold	**290.00**
Knights of Labor, goblet	**18.00**
Mug	**30.00**
Knives & Forks, goblet, flint	**16.00**
Knobby Bull's Eye, goblet, amethyst eyes	**21.00**
Tumbler	**11.00**
Water set, 7-pc, amethyst eyes	**95.00**
Wine, gilt trim, 4½"	**22.00**
Kokomo, celery, flat base	**19.50**
Compote, open, 4½x8½" dia	**16.00**
Compote, open, 5¾x7½" dia	**20.00**
Condiment holder	**20.00**
Creamer, 5"	**36.00**
Cruet, 8½"	**36.00**
Goblet	**25.00**
Salt shaker	**11.00**
Sauce, flat, 4¼"	**8.00**

Sauce, footed, 4″ 6.50
Sauce, footed, 5″ 8.00
Syrup 55.00
Tankard water pitcher 47.00
Lace, goblet 30.00
Lace Checkerboard, goblet 25.00
Lacy Dewdrop, goblet 28.00
Lacy Medallion, *see Princess Feather*
Lacy Valance, salt shaker, blue 19.00
Ladder w/Diamond, carafe 25.00
    Goblet, ice water, 4¼″ 24.00
    Punch bowl, base 19.50
    Punch set, 8 cups, bowl 8″ 77.00
    Salt & pepper, pair 24.00
    Sugar, open, 3″ 11.00
    Tumbler, gilt trim 14.50
    Water tray, 12½″ 15.00
    Toothpick 25.00
Ladders, wine, clear w/gold 15.00
Laminated Petals, wine 42.00
Late Block, water set, 7-pc 365.00
Late Buckle, *see Belt Buckle*
Late Moon & Star, *see Priscilla*
Late Thistle, tumbler, gr w/gilt trim 20.00
Later Sawtooth, goblet 19.50
    Wine 13.00
Lattice & Oval Panels, claret 77.00
    Goblet 110.00
Lattice, cakestand, 10½″ 45.00
    Plate, 6½″ 12.00
Lattice Bar, *see Diamond Bar*
Lawrence, *see Bull's Eye*
Le Clede, *see Hickman*
Leaf & Dart, goblet 24.00
    Water pitcher, bulbous 79.00
    Wine 36.00
Leaf & Flower, butter w/cover, frosted w/amber stain 120.00
    Table set, 4-pc, clear & amber stained 230.00
Leaf & Star, creamer & sugar w/cover, pr, good gold & color .. 70.00
Leaf Band, spooner 23.00
Leaf Medallion, berry set, 7-pc, amethyst w/gold 300.00
    Creamer, gr w/gold regent 60.00
    Tumbler, amethyst w/excellent gold 35.00
Leaf Mold, berry, cranberry spatter, mica, small 32.00
    Pickle insert, 2″ opening 135.00
    Spooner 135.00
    Tumbler 65.00
Leaf Umbrella, syrup, mauve 330.00
Lens & Star, *see Star & Oval*
Liberty, *see Cornucopia*
Liberty Bell, butter w/cover 75.00
    Goblet 45.00
    Master berry bowl, ftd 65.00
    Pitcher, water 550.00
    Plate, 7″ 60.00
    Salt shaker, pewter lid, "1776 Liberty 1876" 80.00
    Sauce, ftd, 4½″ 25.00
    Sugar, open 50.00
    Sugar w/cover 110.00
Lily of the Valley, butter w/cover 50.00
    Creamer, 3 legs 45.00
    Goblet 33.00
    Milk pitcher w/applied handle 75.00
    Relish dish 9.50

Tumbler, etched, flint 22.00
Water pitcher 9.50
Lincoln Drape, egg cup 39.00
    Goblet, flint 60.00
    Spooner, flint 50.00
Lincoln Drape w/Tassel, goblet, flint 95.00
Lined Smocking, goblet, flint 55.00
Lion, butter w/cover, 2 face lion finial 90.00
    Goblet, etched 65.00
    Spooner 53.00
Lion's Head, bowl, 5x8″ 45.00
    Butter w/cover 60.00
    Cake plate, ftd 95.00
    Compote 6″ 135.00
    Compote, w/cover, 5″ 85.00
    Cream pitcher 40.00
    Goblet 45.00
    Jelly dish, ftd 38.00
    Relish dish, oval 45.00
    Sauce 30.00
    Toothpick 35.00
    Water pitcher 110.00
Lion's Leg, *see Alaska*
Lippman, *see Flat Diamond*
Locust, *see Grasshopper*
Log & Star, cruet, blue 45.00
Log Cabin, creamer 135.00
    Pitcher 295.00
    Relish dish, large 85.00
    Sauce dish 40.00
    Spooner 85.00
Loganberry & Grape, milk pitcher 30.00
    Sauce, ftd 7.00
Long Spear, *see Grasshopper*
Loop, *see Seneca Loop*
Loop & Argus, goblet 14.50
    Wine 14.00
Loop & Block, goblet, ruby stained 38.00
    Tumbler, ruby stained 27.50
Loop & Dart, celery 34.00
Loop & Dart w/Diamond Ornaments, egg cup 19.50
    Goblet 18.00
    Sauce, flat, 4″ 5.00
Loop & Dart w/Round Ornaments, bowl, flat, 8x5″ 18.00
    Goblet 23.00
    Sauce, flat, 3¾″ 7.00
    Spooner 32.00
    Tumbler, ftd 27.00
Loop & Dewdrops, goblets 23.00
Loop & Fan, cakestand, 9½″ 34.00
    Compote, jelly, 4x5″ dia 16.50
    Goblet 33.00
    Plate, 7″ 14.50
    Sauce, 3¾″ 7.00
    Sauce, flat, gr 18.00
    Wine 19.50
Loop & Honeycomb, goblet 19.50
Loop & Moose Eye, bar bottle, qt 40.00
    Bar tumbler 55.00
    Champagne 59.00
    Compote, open, 3½x7″ dia 40.00
    Egg cup 36.00
    Goblet 45.00
    Spooner 29.00

Sugar, open	29.00	Goblet	24.00
Sugar w/cover	65.00	Spooner	23.00
Loop & Pillar, *see Michigan*		Martha's Tears, goblet	15.00
Loop w/Dewdrops, creamer	15.00	Goblet, amber	22.00
Goblet	24.00	Maryland, compote, jelly	15.00
Sauce, flat, 4¼″	5.00	Mascotte, celery, ftd	16.00
Sugar w/cover	22.50	Celery vase, etched	35.00
Tumbler	22.00	Creamer	19.50
Loop w/Fish Eye, goblet	19.00	Creamer, etched	35.00
Loop w/Frosted Band, goblet	12.00	Goblet, etched	40.00
Loop w/Stippled Panels, *see Texas*		Individual salt	5.50
Lotus, goblet	45.00	Jar w/cover, milk glass	65.00
Relish, 9½x5¼″	13.00	Sauce, ftd, 3¾″	7.00
Sauce w/handle, flat, large	14.00	Sauce, ftd, 4″	9.50
Sauce, flat, small	9.00	Spooner, etched	28.00
Sauce, ftd	8.00	Sugar etched	45.00
Lotus & Serpent, mug	45.00	Sugar, w/cover	26.00
Louis XV, berry, large	75.00	Wine	24.00
Creamer, gr & gold decor	45.00	Massachusetts, carafe	42.00
Sauce, oval, gr w/gilt trim	25.00	Creamer, gravy-boat type	26.00
Louisiana, compote, scalloped edge, 5¼″	20.00	Tumbler	35.00
Milk pitcher	40.00	Vase, 6½″	14.50
Magnet & Grape w/Clear Leaf, sauce, 4″	5.50	Vase, green, 10″	40.00
Magnet & Grape w/Frosted Leaf, celery, flint	175.00	Master Argus, goblet, flint	45.00
Champagne	145.00	Master Honeycomb, goblet, flint	85.00
Egg cup	90.00	Medallion, cakestand, 9¼″	26.00
Goblet, knob stem, flint	52.00	Goblet, amber	35.00
Goblet, low stem, flint	85.00	Goblet, yellow	39.00
Sauce, flat, 4″	22.00	Sauce, flat, amber, 4¼x3¾″	8.00
Sugar w/cover	125.00	Spooner, amber	30.00
Water tumbler	100.00	Spooner green	45.00
Magnet & Grape w/Frosted Leaf & Shield, goblet	285.00	Sugar w/cover, vaseline	55.00
Magnet & Grape w/Stippled Leaf, goblet	19.50	Water pitcher, yellow	80.00
Maine, butter w/cover	50.00	Medallion Sunburst, plate, sq, 7″	13.00
Cakestand, gr	50.00	Mellor, creamer, flint	30.00
Compote, 8″	50.00	Melon Leaf w/Net, creamer, blue	55.00
Compote, w/cover, jelly	40.00	Melrose, celery	28.00
Master berry	30.00	Goblet	21.00
Sauce, flat, 4″	14.50	Spooner	28.00
Wine	45.00	Tankard pitcher, 10″	47.00
Majestic, cruet w/pattern stopper	20.00	Wine	13.00
Cruet, ruby stained	120.00	Memphis, berry set, 7-pc, gr	125.00
Sauce, flat, ruby stained, sq, 4″	14.50	Creamer, gr w/gold	50.00
Toothpick	18.00	Water set, 7-pc, gr w/gold	255.00
Maltese, *see Jacob's Ladder*		Michigan, berry, open, flared, 3½x10″ dia	30.00
Manhattan, plate, 6″	10.00	Berry w/cover, spoon groove, 4½x8″ dia	60.00
Plate, scalloped, turned-up sides, 5″	10.00	Bowl, gold rim, 2½x3¼″ dia	9.00
Sauce, amber, 4½″	8.50	Bowl, gold rim, 2½x4½″ dia	11.00
Sauce, cranberry eyes, oval, 3½x5″	18.50	Celery vase, pink flashed, gold trim	110.00
Toothpick, clear w/mint gold	35.00	Custard cup, flared	10.00
Manting, bar tumbler	55.00	Dish, flat, gold, 1½x7½x5¼″ dia	15.00
Champagne	54.00	Finger bowl, 2¾x4¾″ dia	12.50
Goblet	40.00	Goblet, gilt trim	32.00
Wine	40.00	Goblet, green flashed rim, blue enameled circlets	35.00
Maple Leaf Band, goblet	16.00	Goblet, rose decal, gold to jewels	25.00
Creamer	12.00	Honey cup	8.00
Goblet, twig stem, vaseline	85.00	Jelly w/cover, 2½x3″ dia	7.50
Plate, yellow, 10½″	30.00	Pickle dish	12.50
Platter, 13¼x9½″	30.00	Pickel dish, 7¾x4¼″ dia, cranberry edge	15.00
Sugar w/cover, gr w/excellent gold	65.00	Pickle dish, gold edge	12.00
Tumbler	28.00	Punch cup	10.50
Mario, tankard water pitcher	135.00	Salt & pepper, pr	32.00
Marquisette, butter w/cover	47.00	Sauce, 4½″ dia	9.50
Celery, ftd	26.00	Sauce, flared, blue edge w/ivory enameled circlets	12.50

Sauce, flared, cranberry edge & jewels	**15.00**
Sauce, flared, gold jewels	**10.00**
Sauce, flared, green edge w/blue enameled circlets	**12.50**
Spooner, yellow	**40.00**
Table set, pink flashed w/gold grooves	**325.00**
Tumbler	**21.00**
Tumbler, gold to jewels	**25.00**
Tumbler, green flashed, blue enameled circlets	**30.00**
Tumbler, green flashed, gold grooves	**30.00**
Tumbler, top gold band	**22.00**
Water carafe	**28.50**
Water pitcher, blush stain w/gilt trim	**75.00**
Water pitcher, clear w/cranberry edge	**75.00**
Millard, spooner, ruby stained	**44.00**
Minerva, butter	**60.00**
Creamer	**42.00**
Goblet	**85.00**
Goblet, sun tint	**70.00**
Plate, w/warrior, handles, 9½"	**67.00**
Relish, clear	**30.00**
Sauce, ftd, 4"	**13.00**
Minnesota, creamer, 3¼"	**26.00**
Cruet w/orig stopper	**38.00**
Goblet	**20.00**
Goblet, gold trim	**22.00**
Mug	**14.00**
Relish dish	**10.00**
Sugar w/cover	**35.00**
Toothpick, 3 handled	**20.00**
Tumbler, gilt trim	**15.50**
Minor Block, *see Mascotte*	
Mioton, champagne	**14.50**
Goblet	**8.50**
Goblet, ruby stained	**25.00**
Mirror, goblet	**34.00**
Sugar, open	**21.00**
Wine	**30.00**
Mirror & Fan, wine decanter, excellent red	**95.00**
Mirror w/Loop, goblet, flint	**40.00**
Missouri, berry, small	**15.00**
Wine	**85.00**
Mitered Diamond, bowl, flat, amber, sq, 7½"	**26.00**
Tumbler, amber	**26.50**
Tumbler, blue	**26.00**
Tumbler, vaseline	**25.00**
Wine, amber	**45.00**
Mitered Diamond Point, celery vase	**20.00**
Moesser, *see Overall Lattice*	
Monkey, sugar, open	**65.00**
Moon & Star, berry bowl	**15.00**
Compote, hi standard, 8"	**38.00**
Compote, open, 6½"	**28.00**
Compote, w/cover, 9¼x6¼" dia	**46.00**
Creamer, frosted ovals	**32.00**
Relish, 8x4¾"	**11.00**
Sauce, flat, 4"	**5.00**
Sauce, flat, 4½"	**7.00**
Sauce, footed, 4"	**11.00**
Sauce, footed, 4½"	**13.00**
Moon & Star w/Waffle Stem, *see Jewelled Moon & Star*	
Moongleam Pleat & Panel, cruet	**120.00**
Morning Glory, egg cup	**125.00**
Goblet	**14.50**
Sauce, ftd	**7.00**

Wine	**175.00**
Nail, bowl, etched, ruby stained, 2¾x6" dia	**55.00**
Cakestand, 9"	**55.00**
Creamer	**35.00**
Sauce, ftd, 3½"	**11.00**
Sugar, open	**30.00**
Syrup, etched	**75.00**
Water pitcher	**60.00**
Nailhead, bowl, flat, 6"	**18.00**
Cakestand, 9"	**25.00**
Compote, open, 6¼x6¼" dia	**20.00**
Compote, w/cover, 9½x6¼" dia	**46.00**
Goblet	**20.00**
Plate, round, 9"	**16.00**
Plate, square, 7"	**19.50**
Relish dish, 8¾x5¼"	**12.00**
Sugar, open	**14.00**
Water pitcher, 1870	**48.50**
Wine	**20.00**
Naturalistic Blackberry, *see Blackberry Variant*	
Nellie Blye, tray	**185.00**
Neptune, *see Bearded Man*	
Nestor, berry set, complete, gr	**250.00**
Butter w/cover, amethyst decor	**145.00**
Compote, jelly, blue	**26.00**
Creamer, blue w/gold	**35.00**
Creamer, green	**40.00**
Master berry bowl, gr	**60.00**
Spooner, gr	**40.00**
Sugar w/cover, gr	**65.00**
Water pitcher, amethyst	**125.00**
Wine, gr w/gold & enamel	**35.00**
Netted Oak, sugar shaker, milk glass	**62.00**
Nevada, biscuit jar	**38.00**
New England Pineapple, butter w/cover, 5½"	**165.00**
Castor bottle, mustard	**40.00**
Egg cup	**42.00**
Goblet	**65.00**
Master salt	**40.00**
Spooner, flint	**40.00**
Sugar, open	**31.00**
Tumbler, bar, flint	**100.00**
Water tumbler	**85.00**
Wine	**145.00**
New Hampshire, cruet	**24.00**
Goblet	**22.00**
Mug, Maiden's Blush, large	**45.00**
Sugar	**18.00**
Toothpick	**15.00**
New Jersey, goblet, gold	**33.00**
Plate, 8¾"	**15.00**
Plate, 11½"	**18.50**
Plate, deep, 10½"	**19.50**
Sauce, flat, 4¼"	**9.50**
Water pitcher, gold	**58.00**
Wine, flared, gilt trim	**35.00**
Noah's Ark, butter w/cover	**475.00**
North Pole, *see Arctic*	
Notched Rib, *see Broken Column*	
O'Hara Diamond, plate, gr, 10"	**18.00**
Oak Leaf Band, buttermilk	**25.00**
Celery vase	**30.00**
Goblet	**27.50**
Spooner	**23.00**

Oak Leaves, goblet 22.00
Oaken Bucket, bucket amber, 2¾" 12.00
   Sugar, open 25.00
   Sugar w/cover 35.00
   Sugar w/cover, blue 50.00
   Sugar w/cover, vaseline 85.00
   Tumbler 16.50
Oats & Barley, *see Wheat & Barley*
Old Abe, *see Frosted Eagle*
Old Man, *see Bearded Man*
Old Man of Woods, *see Bearded Man*
Old Man of the Mountain, *see Bearded Man*
One-O-One, celery, ftd 39.00
   Creamer 37.00
   Goblet 29.00
   Plate, 7" 18.50
   Plate, 8" 20.00
   Sauce, flat, 4" 8.50
Open Rose, creamer w/applied handle 45.00
   Egg cup 20.00
   Goblet 19.50
   Sauce, flat, milk glass, 4" 26.00
   Spooner 26.00
   Tumbler 18.00
   Water pitcher 80.00
Opposing Pyramid, goblet 18.00
   Wine 11.00
Optic, spooner, amethyst 25.00
   Sugar w/cover 35.00
Oregon, *see Beaded Loop*
Oriental, celery 38.00
Orion, *see Cathedral*
Ornate Star, wine tray 14.50
Oval & Fine Pleat, goblet 20.00
Oval Mitre, compote, open, 5¾x6¾" dia 43.00
   Goblet 31.00
   Sugar, open 19.50
Oval Panels, goblet, amber 26.00
Overall Lattice, goblet 12.00
Overlapping Grape, goblet 33.00
Ovoid Panels, goblet 20.00
Owl & Possum, goblet 45.00
Owl & Pussy Cat, cheese dish, rare 195.00
Owl in Fan, *see Parrot*
Paling, goblet 12.00
Palm Stub, goblet 20.00
Palmette, celery 30.00
   Dish, oval, 7x4¾" 12.00
   Goblet 31.00
   Master salt 26.00
   Plate, amber, 9" 24.00
   Sauce, flat, 4" 8.00
   Sauce, flat, 5" 14.50
   Tumbler, bar 45.00
Pampas Flower, sauce, ftd, 3½" 5.50
Panama, wine 11.00
Panelled Acorn Band, egg cup 33.00
   Goblet 32.00
   Spooner 33.00
Panelled Apple Blossom, goblet 19.50
Panelled Cane, goblet 16.00
   Water tray, gr, 10¼" 19.50
Panelled Daisy, bowl, flat, 8½" 13.00
   Plate, sq, 9" 24.00

   Sauce, sq, 4" 6.00
   Spooner 25.00
   Water tray, 11" 36.00
Panelled Daisy & Button, *see Queen*
Panelled Dewdrop, berry bowl, oval 20.00
   Celery vase 35.00
   Goblet 30.00
   Mug w/applied handle 40.00
   Sauce, ftd, 4½" 8.50
   Sugar, open 20.00
   Wine 21.00
Panelled Diamond Cut & Fan, *see Hartley*
Panelled Diamonds & Flowers, goblet 24.00
Panelled Dogwood, *see Dogwood*
Panelled Fern, spooner 33.00
   Spooner, opaque white 28.00
   Sugar w/cover 52.00
Panelled Fine Cut, salt shaker, blue 19.50
Panelled Finetooth, goblet, flint 33.00
   Wine 36.00
Panelled Forget-Me-Not, butter w/cover 42.00
   Compote w/cover, 8½x6" dia 57.00
   Creamer 34.00
   Goblet 38.00
   Honey dish, 3½" 11.00
   Relish dish 12.00
Panelled Forty-Four, goblet 27.00
Panelled Heather, butter dish 48.00
   Cruet w/orig stopper 28.00
   Goblet 24.00
   Plate, 12" 17.00
   Sugar w/cover 35.00
Panelled Herringbone, bowl, oval, gr, 8½x5½" 19.50
   Goblet, gr 43.00

   Pitcher, emerald, footed, 10" 90.00
   Sauce, flat, gr, 4½" 8.00
Panelled Hobnail w/Ropes, punch cups, amber 15.50
Panelled Holly, water set, 7 pc, gr w/gold 350.00
Panelled Iris, punch cup 7.00
Panelled Jewel, goblet 16.00

Goblet, amber	35.00
Panelled Long Jewels, goblet	25.00
Panelled Nightshade, goblet	25.00
Wine	20.00
Panelled Oak, water pitcher	55.00
Panelled Ovals, champagne	60.00
Egg cup	40.00
Panelled Palm, wine	15.00
Panelled Sprig, see Sprig	
Panelled Star & Button, creamer	20.00
Panelled Stippled Bowl, see Stippled Band	
Panelled Stippled Scroll, creamer	7.50
Panelled Strawberry w/Roman Key, tumbler, gilt & color	15.50
Water set, 7 pc, gilt & color	145.00
Panelled Thistle, cakestand, signed, 9¼″	38.00
Dish w/cover, sq, 5½″	20.00
Goblet, Bee mark	30.00
Milk pitcher, 7¼″	30.00
Plated, 10¼″	19.50
Relish, oval, 8¼x4¼″	12.00
Salt & pepper, pair	40.00
Sugar w/cover	30.00
Panelled Wheat, creamer	17.00
Sugar w/cover	45.00
Panelled Zipper, sauce, flat, 4½″	7.50
Goblet, gold rim	25.00
Pangyric, see Prism & Crescent	
Pansy, toothpick, pink opaque	55.00
Parrot, goblet	35.00
Wine	35.00
Patee Cross, cruet	20.00
Pathfinder, goblet	13.00
Tumbler	12.00
Wine	12.00
Pavonia, butter w/cover, ped, maple leaf etching	65.00
Celery, ftd	19.50
Creamer, etched	50.00
Goblet	25.00
Sauce, ftd, 4″	8.50
Spooner, etched	40.00
Sugar w/cover, etched	55.00
Tumbler, etched, ruby stained	34.00
Water pitcher, etched	55.00
Water set, 7 pc, ruby stained	285.00
Peacock Feather, butter w/cover	44.00
Compote, open, 3¼x6½″ dia	15.50
Creamer	24.00
Cruet, 7½″	35.00
Dish, footed, 7x2½″	25.00
Sauce	11.00
Tumbler	22.50
Pear, see Bartlett Pear	
Pecorah, goblet	14.50
Wine, 4½″	14.00
Peerless, egg cup	19.50
Goblet	19.50
Spooner	17.00
Sugar, open	11.00
Water pitcher, bulbous	75.00
Pennsylvania, see Balder	
Pentagon, wine	17.00
Pequot, goblet	33.00
Periwinkle, salt shaker, blue	20.00
Petticoat, creamer	30.00

Philadelphia Centennial, goblet	36.00
Picket, butter w/cover	45.00
Goblet	32.00
Picket Band, spooner	22.00
Pigs in Corn, goblet	250.00
Pillar, claret, 6″	65.00
Goblet	47.00
Wine	39.00
Pillar & Bull's Eye, goblet	55.00
Wine	59.00
Pillar Molded, celery, ftd	75.00
Pillar Encircled, berry set, 4 pc, ruby stained	125.00
Celery, flat base	14.50
Celery, frosted, enameled forget-me-nots	75.00
Pitcher, etched, 13″	43.00
Spooner, etched, ruby stained	35.00
Tray, gr, 9½x5½″	24.00
Tumbler, etched	16.50
Tumbler, etched, ruby stained	29.00
Pineapple, goblet, flint	45.00
Toothpick, gr	37.00
Pineapple & Fan, cruet	65.00
Pineapple & Sunburst, sugar w/cover	28.00
Pineapple & Stem, see Pavonia	
Pioneer, see Westward Ho	
Pioneer's Victoria, sauce, flat, ruby stained, 4″	14.00
Tankard style pitcher, ruby stained, 12″	65.00
Tumbler, ruby stained	40.00
Wine, ruby stained	46.00
Wine tray	45.00
Pitcairn, goblet	13.00
Pittsburgh, tumbler, saphire blue, 3½″	55.00
Whiskey, 6 panels, deep amethyst, 2¼″	70.00
Pittsburg Centennial, goblet	75.00
Pittsburg Daisy, wine	11.00
Pittsburg Flute, goblet, flint	2.00
Plain Scalloped Panel, toothpick, gr	20.00
Pleat & Panel, cakestand	50.00
Celery	40.00
Creamer	28.00
Milk pitcher	40.00
Sauce, handled, 4″	8.50
Sugar, open	25.00
Pleating, pitcher, ruby stained, large	80.00
Spooner, ruby stained	24.00
Toothpick, ruby stained	42.00
Plume, bowl, flat, scalloped, 7″	15.50
Cake plate, 5¾x9¼″	42.00
Celery, flat base, vertical plume	23.00
Creamer	35.00
Goblet	34.00
Sauce, flat, flint, 4″	8.00
Sauce, flat, sq, 4¾″	11.00
Tumbler, etched, ruby stained	50.00
Water pitcher, ruby stained	155.00
Plume & Block, celery	20.00
Pogo Stick, plate, 7″	9.00
Pointed Jewel, compote, jelly	15.00
Creamer	25.00
Goblet	23.00
Pitcher	40.00
Punch cup	9.00
Sugar w/cover	33.00
Pointed Panel Daisy & Button, see Queen	

Pointed Thumbprint, *see Almond Thumbprint*
Polar Bear, *see Arctic*
Popcorn, creamer w/ears 29.00
   Goblet, w/lined ears 34.00
   Milk pitcher 75.00
   Spooner 22.00
   Spooner, w/ears 24.00
   Sugar w/cover 45.00
Portland, celery, flat base 19.00
   Compote, open, 5½x7½" dia 24.00
   Individual creamer 14.50
   Sauce, flat, 4½" 8.00
   Sugar w/cover 30.00
   Toothpick 14.50
   Tumbler 20.00
Portland w/Diamond Point Band, *see Banded Portland*
Post, goblet, etched 47.00
Powder & Shot, creamer, w/applied handle 110.00
   Egg cup 40.00
   Goblet 55.00
   Sauce, flat, 4" 16.50
   Sugar, open 29.00
Prayer Rug, *see Horseshoe*
Pressed Diamond, *see Zephyr*
Pressed Leaf, egg cup 20.00
   Goblet 25.00
   Master salt 18.00
Sauce, flat, 4" 11.00
   Sugar, open 28.00
   Water pitcher w/applied handle 65.00
Primrose, creamer, amber 29.00
   Plate, amber, 4½" 14.00
   Plate w/handle, 9" 14.50
   Platter, amber, 12x8" 27.00
   Relish, 8x5¼" 13.50
   Relish, amber, 9¼x5" 20.00
   Sauce, flat, blue, 9" 9.00
   Toddy plate, 4½" 12.00
   Toddy plate, blue 22.00
   Wine, amber 43.00
Prince Albert, goblet 16.50
Princess Feather, butter w/cover, 5½" 70.00
   Celery vase 45.00
   Egg cup 35.00
   Goblet 30.00
   Plate, 7" 29.00
   Plate, 9" 36.00
   Spooner 24.00
Printed Hobnail, tumbler 13.00
Priscilla, berry bowl, small 10.00
   Butter w/cover, gr w/gold 75.00
   Cakestand, 10" 40.00
   Cakestand, 11x6½" 65.00
   Compote, open, slightly flared side, 4¾x5" 35.00
   Compote, open, slightly flared side, 8¾x9¾" 60.00
   Compote w/cover, 9x6" 65.00
   Compote w/cover, jelly 50.00
   Deep dish, 2x9½" 45.00
   Deep dish, 10½x2½" 50.00
   Donut stand, 5¾x4¼" 45.00
   Donut stand, 9x5¾" 60.00
   Double relish, 5x7¼" 20.00
   Master berry bowl, slightly flared side, 8x3½" 60.00
   Mini mug 20.00

Mustard, no lid 25.00
Nappy w/handle 10.00
Shallow bowl, 10½" 24.00
Tankard 75.00
Prism, double egg cup 29.00
   Egg cup 25.00
   Goblet 24.00
   Spooner 18.00
Prism & Block Band, butter w/cover, etched 31.00
   Mug, etched, 3" 14.50
Prism & Bull's Eye, goblet 14.00
Prism & Clear Panels, goblet 18.00
   Wine 14.00
Prism & Crescent, goblet 65.00
   Wine 55.00
Prism & Daisy Bar, goblet, amber 20.00
Prism & Diamond Band, wine, flint 30.00
Prism & Sawtooth, bar bottle, qt 43.00
   Goblet 29.00
Prism Arc, goblet 24.00
   Water pitcher 28.00
   Wine 18.00
Prism w/Diamond Point, bar tumbler, flint 50.00
   Creamer w/applied handle, flint 60.00
   Egg cup, flint 25.00
   Master salt 15.50
Prophet, *see Bearded Man*
Proxy, Ashburton, goblet 49.00
Psyche & Cupid, celery vase 45.00
   Creamer 50.00
   Goblet 38.00
   Sauce, ftd, 2¼x3¾" dia 12.00
   Spoon holder 50.00
   Sugar, open 40.00
Puffed Bands, goblet 16.00
Punty Band, toothpick, ruby flash 35.00
Purple Block Portland, *see Barred Ovals*
Pygmy, *see Torpedo*
Pyramid, *see Mitered Diamond*
Quaker Lady, goblet 22.00
Queen, butter w/cover, amber 55.00
   Compote, open, high standard, amber, 8" 27.50
   Goblet 20.00
   Goblet, amber 39.00
   Spooner 15.50
   Spooner, amber 20.00
   Wine, sun-tint 24.00
Queen Anne, creamer 35.00
Quihote, goblet 24.00
   Plate, 10½" 11.00
   Salt & pepper, pair 19.50
   Sauce, collared, 4¼" 7.00
Quilted Diamond, tumbler, amethyst 40.00
R & H Swirl, *see Kokomo*
Rabbit Tracks, goblet 19.50
Radiant, goblet 10.00
   Water pitcher 40.00
Radiant Daisy & Button, *see Isis*
Rail Fence Band, goblet 15.50
Raindrop, creamer, amber, 4½" 24.00
   Creamer, sapphire blue 33.00
   Sauce, ftd, blue, 4¼" 13.00
   Water pitcher, amber 54.00
   Water tray, amber, 11" 24.00

Ramsey Grape, berry bowl **30.00**
Rayed Flower, tumbler, gilt w/cover **14.50**
Reardon, goblet, etched **14.00**
Recessed Ovals, champagne **20.00**
Recessed Pillar w/Red Top, *see Nail*
Recessed Pillar w/Thumbprint Band, *see Nail*
Red Block, bowl, flat, ruby stained, 8″ **60.00**
    Butter w/cover, ruby stained **75.00**
    Creamer, ruby stained **54.00**
    Goblet, ruby stained **46.00**
    Spooner, ruby stained **35.00**
    Sugar w/cover, ruby stained **60.00**
    Table set, 4 pc **235.00**
    Tankard water pitcher **120.00**
    Tumbler, amber blocks **42.00**
    Tumbler, ruby stained **40.00**
    Wine, ruby stained **43.00**
Red Top, *see Button Arches*
Regal Block, wine; gilt trim **9.00**
    Wine tray, 9¼″ **18.00**
Reticulated Cord, creamer **26.00**
    Sauce, flat **7.00**
Reverse 44, creamer, silver trim **18.50**
    Cruet **68.00**
    Dish w/handle, signed, 5½x4¼″ **18.00**
    Goblet, amethyst stain **19.50**
    Pickle relish, 5x8″ **25.00**
    Tumbler, trace of amethyst **15.50**
Reverse Swirl, sugar shaker, old lid, blue **110.00**
    Tankard water pitcher **110.00**
Reverse Torpedo, creamer **75.00**
    Spooner **55.00**
    Sugar w/cover **85.00**
Rib & Bead, toothpick, ruby stained **25.00**
Ribbed Acorn, sauce, 4″ **14.50**
Ribbed Band, *see Ripple*
Ribbed Grape, goblet **43.00**
    Plate, 6″ **43.00**
    Spooner, flint **48.00**
Ribbed Ivy, bar tumbler **85.00**
    Butter w/cover **100.00**
    Egg Cup **30.00**
    Goblet **39.00**
    Water tumbler **80.00**
    Wine **95.00**
Ribbed Lattice, sugar shaker, old lid **70.00**
Ribbed Leaves, mug **12.00**
Ribbed Opal, celery vase **35.00**
Ribbed Oval, creamer, large **25.00**
Ribbed Palm, egg cup **30.00**
    Goblet **34.00**
    Master salt **29.00**
    Water tumbler **70.00**
    Wine **50.00**
Ribbed Pillar, salt shaker, pink spatter shiny **22.00**
    Syrup, cranberry spatter **165.00**
Ribbon, berry bowl, round, 7″ **17.00**
    Berry dish, 4″ dia **8.00**
    Berry dish, round, ftd, 3x4″ **13.00**
    Bowl, serving, 2½x11″ dia **18.00**
    Bowl, sq, 3x8x8″ **17.00**
    Bread tray, 7x11″ **20.00**
    Butter dish w/cover, 7″ dia **32.00**
    Cakestand, 6½x8¼″ dia **25.00**

    Cakestand, 7½x9″ dia **25.00**
    Cakestand, 8x10″ dia **30.00**
    Celery, etched, 9″ **26.00**
    Compote, open, 6x5″ dia **25.00**
    Compote, open, etched, 8x7″ dia **25.00**
    Compote w/cover, 6x5″ dia **30.00**
    Compote w/cover, 8x7″ dia **32.00**
    Compote w/cover, etched, 7x7″ dia **40.00**
    Cream pitcher, 6½″ **15.00**
    Goblet, etched **25.00**
    Master salt, not pure Ribbon **8.00**
    Plate, shallow serving, 10″ dia **16.00**
    Relish dish, 7″ **18.00**
    Salt w/small spoon, 2″ **9.00**
    Sauce w/handle, flat, sq, 3¾″ **13.50**
    Sugar w/cover, 6½″ **15.00**
    Tray, etched, 12x16″ **44.00**
    Water pitcher, large **48.00**
Ribbon Candy, bowl, 8¼″ **25.00**
    Cakestand, 8½″ **26.00**
    Creamer **19.00**
    Plate, 8″ **14.50**
    Relish dish **10.00**
Richmond, water pitcher, etched **25.00**
Ring Neck, syrup, spatter **165.00**
Ringed Beehive, cruet w/orig stopper, amber **45.00**
Ripple, creamer w/applied handle **37.00**
    Egg cup **19.50**
    Goblet **16.50**
    Plate, 5″ **8.50**
    Spooner **18.00**
    Sugar, open **17.00**
Rising Sun, celery, flat base, gilt trim **29.00**
    Compote, jelly, amethyst eyes, 5″ **16.50**
    Goblet, gr **20.00**
    Tumbler, gilt trim **15.50**
Riverside, tumbler, vaseline, gold trim **25.00**
Roanoke, bowl, flat, ruby stained edge **30.00**
    Cakestand, 10½″ **17.00**
    Creamer, gr, 3½″ **24.00**
    Pitcher, water, ruby stained **95.00**
    Sauce, flat, 4½″ **6.50**
    Sauce, flat, ruby stained edge 4½″ **12.00**
    Tumbler, ruby stained **30.00**
    Waste bowl, etched, ruby stained **38.00**
Roanoke Star, goblet **14.00**
Rochelle, *see Princess Feather*
Rock Crystal, tumbler **10.00**
Roman Cross, goblet **14.00**
Roman Key, bar tumbler **32.00**
    Goblet **32.00**
    Sugar, open **30.00**
    Sugar w/cover **45.00**
Roman Rosette, bread tray **27.00**
    Compote, jelly **45.00**
    Compote w/cover, 10x6½″ dia **45.00**
    Creamer **35.00**
    Mug, 3½″ **12.50**
Romeo, *see Block & Fan*
Rope & Rib, butter w/cover, blue **72.50**
Rope & Thumbprint, butter w/cover, blue **68.00**
    Creamer **35.00**
    Spooner **35.00**
    Sugar w/cover, vaseline, small **45.00**

Rope Bands, *see Clear Panels w/Cord Bands*
Rope Panels, salt shaker, milk glass 13.00
Rose Point Band, creamer 14.00
   Tumbler 11.00
Rose Sprig, boat dish, amber, 7¾x3½" 24.00
   Bowl, collared, blue, 8x7" 37.00
   Celery 30.00
   Compote, oval, amber, 8x7½x6" 24.00
   Goblet 27.00
   Mug w/applied handle 62.00
   Plate, sq, 6½" 18.00
   Tumbler 30.00
Rose in Snow, bar tumbler 43.00
   Butter w/cover, round 45.00
   Butter w/cover, sq 45.00
   Cologne bottle, orig stopper 110.00
   Compote, open, yellow, 5¾" dia 65.00
   Creamer, round 35.00
   Creamer, sq 65.00
   Creamer, vaseline 70.00
   Double pickle 75.00
   Goblet, amber 35.00
   Mug, 'In Fond Remembrance' 20.00
     Yellow 55.00
   Perfume bottle w/orig top 50.00
   Plate, 9¼" 20.00
   Plate w/handle, 9½" 30.00
   Powder jar w/cover 21.00
   Spooner 18.00
   Sugar, open 15.00
Rosepoint Band, bowl, 10" 15.00
Rosette, compote, jelly 8.00
   Goblet 24.00
   Pitcher 26.00
   Plate w/handle, 9" 17.50
   Spoon holder 14.00
Rosette & Palm, celery, flat base 20.00
   Compote, open, 5½x9" dia 20.00
   Goblet 20.00
   Plate, 10" 13.00
   Spooner 18.50
Rosette Medallion, *see Feather Duster*
Rosette w/Pinwheels, wine 16.50
Round Thumbprints, goblet 30.00
Royal Crystal, bowl, ruby stained, 7" 45.00
   Sauce, flat, ruby stained, 4" 18.50
   Sugar w/cover 25.00
   Syrup, 7½" 29.00
   Tumbler, ruby stained 45.00
   Wine 16.00
Royal Ivy, rose bowl, frosted deep cranberry 125.00
   Salt & pepper, pair 70.00
   Salt & pepper, rubina clear, pr 120.00
   Salt shaker, frosted 40.00
   Sauce, cranberry to clear, frosted 40.00
   Syrup, frosted & clear 130.00
   Toothpick 58.00
   Tumbler, clear rainbow crackle 80.00
   Tumbler, frosted 60.00
Royal Lady, butter w/cover 35.00
Royal Oak, pitcher, cranberry to clear, large 310.00
   Sugar shaker, milk glass 47.00
   Water pitcher, clear 200.00
Royal Thumbprint, celery vase 55.00

   Champagne 35.00
Ruby Rosette, *see Pillow Encircled*
Ruby Thumbprint, celery vase 65.00
   Compote, high standard, 6" 75.00
   Compote, jelly 45.00
   Creamer, individual 28.00
   Goblet 34.00
   Individual sugar 28.00
   Pitcher 95.00
   Sauce, scalloped 20.00
   Spooner 42.00
   Tankard milk pitcher 100.00
   Toothpick 28.00
   Tumbler 45.00
   Wine 32.00
S-Repeat, cruet w/clear stopper, amethyst 75.00
Sampson, pitcher 90.00
Sandwich Holly, spooner w/Cord & Tassel base 125.00
Sandwich Loop, *see Hairpin*
Sandwich Star, bar bottle, qt 170.00
   Decanter w/orig stopper & ovals, pt 75.00
   Spill 60.00
   Spill, canary 300.00
   Spill, flint, clambroth 375.00
   Spill, flint, electric blue 675.00
Santa Claus, *see Bearded Man*
Sawtooth, butter w/cover 90.00
   Carafe 55.00
   Celery 32.00
   Celery, ftd 65.00
   Celery, scalloped, non-flint 25.00
   Champagne, knob stem 65.00
   Champagne, non-flint 137.00
   Compote, deep, non-flint, 5½x7½" 38.00
   Compote, shallow, non-flint, 6¾x10" 50.00
   Creamer, applied handle, bulbous flint, 6½" 75.00
   Creamer, applied handle, rayed bottom, flint 5½" 75.00
   Creamer, molded handle, non-flint, 6" 25.00
   Dish, ftd, oval, non-flint, 7x4¾" 25.00
   Goblet, flint, 5½" 48.00
   Goblet, non-flint, 6½" 22.00
   Master salt 16.50
   Spooner, flint 55.00
   Spooner, milk glass 60.00
   Spooner, non-flint 35.00
   Sugar, open, non-flint 28.00
   Sugar w/cover, non-flint 45.00
   Wine, 'GEH 1906', ruby stained 25.00
Sawtoothed Honeycomb, toothpick 16.00
   Tumbler, ruby stained 33.00
Scalloped Band, *see Scalloped Lines*
Scalloped Daisy, *see Button Arches*
Scalloped Daisy & Fern, goblet, emerald gr 45.00
Scalloped Diamond Point, plate, 5" 8.50
   Plate, 8" 13.50
Scalloped Lines, egg cup 15.00
   Spooner 22.00
Scalloped Loop, *see Yolked Loop*
Scalloped Swirl, toothpick, ruby stained 38.00
Scalloped Tape, *see Jewelled Band*
Scroll, egg cup 19.50
   Goblet 18.00
   Shaker, ftd, gr, milk glass 18.50
   Spoon holder 18.00

Tumbler, blue, milk glass **39.00**
Scroll w/Cane Band, cruet w/matching stopper, clear w/gold **25.00**
   Toothpick, ruby stained **90.00**
   Tumbler, clear w/excellent gold trim **20.00**
Scroll w/Flower, goblet **19.00**
   Egg cup, handled **14.00**
   Relish **15.00**
   Spooner **34.00**
   Table set, 4 pc **115.00**
Sedan, *see Panelled Star & Button*
Seed Pod, celery vase, gr w/gold **45.00**
   Master berry bowl, blue w/gold **60.00**
   Table set, 4 pc **400.00**
   Vase **145.00**
Selby, goblet **14.00**
Semi-Loops, goblet **20.00**
Seneca Loop, champagne **45.00**
   Egg cup **20.00**
   Goblet **16.50**
   Water Pitcher **47.00**
   Wine **17.00**
Sequoia, bar tumbler **19.50**
   Bowl, 3½x9¾x4¾" **19.50**
   Champagne **25.00**
   Creamer, 6" **15.50**
   Salt shaker **11.00**
   Tumbler **14.00**
Serrated Block & Loop, *see Sawtoothed Honeycomb*
Sheaf & Diamond, *see Fickle Block*
Sheaf of Wheat, goblet **32.00**
Shell & Jewel, butter w/cover, 4¾" **14.50**
   Pitcher **30.00**
   Pitcher & 4 tumblers, set **95.00**
   Tumbler **14.50**
   Tumbler, amber **42.00**
   Tumbler, blue **30.00**
Shell & Spike, *see Shell & Tassel*
Shell & Tassel, berry, ftd, sq, 4" **16.00**
   Bowl, 6½x12" **55.00**
   Bowl, oval, ftd, 12" **75.00**
   Butter pat, shell-shaped **11.00**
   Butter w/cover, dog finial **95.00**
   Cakestand, sq, 9" **30.00**
   Celery, ftd, sq **57.00**
   Compote, jelly, sq, 5x4¾" dia **35.00**
   Compote, open 5¾x5¾" dia **36.00**
   Platter, 9x13" **60.00**
   Sauce w/handle, sq, 4" **13.00**

Water pitcher **75.00**

Celery, vase, 8" **20.00**
Compote, 6¾x5" **20.0**
Compote w/lid, 8" dia **35.00**
Creamer **18.00**
Creamer, amber **25.00**
Flower pot **34.00**
Pitcher, milk **20.00**
Pitcher, water, 9" **28.00**
Platter, 8x10" **12.00**
Relish, octagonal, amber, 8¾x4" **18.00**
Sauce, ftd **12.00**
Spooner **16.00**
Spooner, amber **34.00**
Sugar w/cover, amber **45.00**
Wine **12.00**
Sherwood, goblet **12.00**
Shields, *see Tape measure*
Shimmering Star, tumbler **17.00**
Short Tidy, goblet **15.00**
Shoshone, banana stand **26.00**
   Cakestand, 8½" **16.00**
   Compote, open, 9" **23.00**
   Cruet **24.00**
   Cruet, gr **77.50**
   Wine **18.00**
Shovel, goblet **15.50**
Shrine, mug, 3¼" **42.00**
   Pickle dish **32.50**
Shuttle, wine **6.50**
Side Wheeler, salt shaker, old, blue **22.00**
Single Rise, creamer **23.00**
   Spooner **18.50**
   Sugar w/cover **26.00**
   Tumbler **19.00**
   Tumbler, gr **27.00**
Skilton, *see Beaded Loop*
Slashed Swirl, goblet, border etched **21.00**
   Sauce, ftd, 3½" **6.00**
Smocking, champagne, knob stem **99.00**
   Spill **42.00**
   Sugar, open **30.00**
Smocking Band, *see Double Beetle Band*
Snail, berry bowl, flat **45.00**
   Celery **48.00**
   Spooner **30.00**
   Tumbler, etched **44.00**
Snakeskin w/Dot, plate, milk glass, 7" **17.00**
   Toddy plate, amber, 4½" **11.00**
Snowband, *see Puffed Bands*
Snowdrop, *see Ashland*
Souvenir w/Red Panels, *see Millard*
Spades, *see Medallion*
Spearhead, butter w/cover **28.00**
   Compote, open, 6x6½" dia **19.50**
   Sugar, open **14.50**
   Sugar w/cover **24.00**
Spearpoint, compote, jelly **14.00**
   Punch cup **9.50**
Spearpoint Band, sauce, ruby stained, 4" **17.00**
   Spooner, ruby stained **50.00**
   Tumbler **10.00**
Spirea Band, bowl, amber, 7x4½" **12.00**
   Bowl amber, 9x5¼" **14.50**
   Compote, open, amber, 5x7" dia **21.00**

Creamer, amber	35.00
Creamer, blue	38.00
Goblet	16.00
Goblet, amber	29.00
Platter, amber, 10¾x8½"	18.50
Platter, blue, 10¾x8½"	21.00
Sauce, flat, amber	7.00
Wine, amber	19.50
Sprig, berry bowl	20.00
Butter w/cover	45.00
Cakestand, 10"	50.00
Celery vase	45.00
Compote, flared, 7x8" dia	24.00
Compote, open, 5½x6¾" dia	19.50
Goblet	25.00
Sauce, flat	10.50
Sauce, ftd	10.00
Spooner	23.00
Sugar, open	20.00
Sugar w/cover	25.00
Water pitcher	50.00
Square Panes, see Post	
Stamen, see Tidy	
Stanley Inverted Thumbprint, wine, amber	13.00
Star & Oval, tumbler, frosted band	11.00
Star & Palm, goblet	16.00
Star & Pillar, creamer	38.00
Star Band, see Bosworth	
Star Flower Band, see Stippled Star Flower	
Star in Bull's Eye, relish, gr	12.00
Toothpick	20.00
Wine	27.00
Star Medallion, punch cup	6.00
Spooner	13.00
Star of Bethlehem, water pitcher, ruby stained	175.00
Star Rosetted, sauce, flat, 4¼"	5.50
Sauce, ftd, 4¼"	5.50
Water pitcher, bulbous	69.00
Star Whorl, wine, gilt trim	11.00
Stars & Bars, cruet, blue	95.00
Cruet, w/stopper, amber	75.00
Goblet	14.00
Salt & pepper, pair	10.00
Stars & Stripes, cordial	7.00
Creamer	20.00
Water pitcher	45.00
Wine	11.00
States, creamer, gold	23.00
Goblet	25.00
Pickle dish	18.00
Punch cup	10.50
Salt & pepper, pair	30.00
Toothpick	25.00
Stedman, butter w/cover	30.00
Champagne	35.00
Egg cup	23.00
Sugar, open	25.00
Steele, see Priscilla	
Stepped Flute, champagne	43.00
Stippled Band, goblet	19.50
Spoon holder	14.00
Stippled Bowl, master salt	23.00
Stippled Chain, goblet, flint	20.00
Sauce, flat, 4½"	5.50

Spooner	22.00
Stippled Cherry, bowl, 8"	19.00
Creamer	26.00
Stippled Dahlia, syrup, milk glass	65.00
Stippled Daisy, compote, open, 8"	28.00
Tumbler	20.00
Water tray, 10"	19.50
Stippled Diamond Band, goblet	18.00
Stippled Forget-Me-Not, pitcher, 8"	42.00
Stippled Fuschia, goblet	23.00
Stippled Grape & Festoon, celery	38.00
Compote w/cover, 8x8"	49.00
Creamer, clear leaf	35.00
Goblet	23.00
Spooner	20.00
Spooner, ftd, scalloped	33.00
Sugar, open	35.00
Stippled Ivy, goblet	24.00
Sugar, open	20.00
Stippled Medallion, egg cup	34.00
Goblet	34.00
Stippled Panelled Flower, see Maine	
Stippled Roman Key, goblet	23.00
Stippled Scroll, see Scroll	
Stippled Star Flower, goblet	16.50
Straight Huber, wine	12.00
Strawberry, goblet	39.00
Goblet, water	25.00
Relish, milk glass, 8½x4¾"	30.00
Sauce, flat, milk glass, 4"	13.00
Strawberry & Currant, goblet	24.00
Syrup w/applied handle	80.00
Strigil, bowl, 8" dia	23.00
Bowl, sq, 7"	23.00
Cakestand	30.00
Creamer	18.00
Pitcher, milk	40.00
Wine, gilt trim	16.00
Sunbeam, toothpick, gr	30.00
Sunburst, plate, 7"	11.00
Plate, 8"	12.00
Relish w/cover, flower finial	23.00
Sauce, ftd, 4¼"	7.00
Sauce w/handles, flat, 3½"	6.50
Sauce w/handles, flat, 5"	7.50
Sunburst Medallion, goblet	25.00
Sunk Daisy, cracker jar w/cover	50.00
Goblet	23.00
Goblet, gr	45.00
Plate, turned up edge, 7½"	14.50
Spooner	16.00
Toothpick	23.00
Sunk Honeycomb, creamer, ruby stained, 4½"	29.00
Cruet w/orig stopper, etched, ruby stained	125.00
Individual salt	6.50
Punch cup	7.50
Rose bowl, 6"	16.50
Salt shaker	7.50
Salt shaker, ruby stained	23.00
Tumbler	30.00
Wine, etched	17.00
Sunken Buttons, see Mitered Diamond	
Sunken Primrose, compote, high standard, 9¾"	26.00
Sauce, ruby w/clear & amber	15.00

Sunken Teardrops, creamer	**19.00**
Swan, creamer	**39.00**
Sauce, ftd, 4″	**12.00**
Spooner	**33.00**
Swirl Band, goblet, etched	**16.00**
Tackle Block, goblet, rounded	**38.00**
Tacoma, spooner, ruby stained	**45.00**
Tailored Band, goblet	**12.00**
Tape Measure, goblet	**16.00**
Sauce, flat, 4″	**7.00**
Sugar, open	**17.00**
Teardrop & Tassel, pitcher	**90.00**
Sauce, 4″	**9.50**
Texas, sauce, flat, 4½″	**9.50**
Toothpick	**18.00**
Texas Bull's Eye, goblet	**23.00**
Texas Star, sugar, open	**45.00**
Thayer, goblet	**19.50**
Thistle Shield, goblet	**32.00**
Thousand Eye, butter w/cover, knob finial	**40.00**
Celery, amber	**48.00**
Compote, blue, 5½″	**40.00**
Compote, blue, 8½″	**65.00**
Compote, open, amber, 3½x8¼″ dia	**35.00**
Compote, open, amber, 5¾x8¼″ dia	**40.00**
Compote, open, gr, 3½x8″ dia	**44.00**
Compote, open gr, 6½x10″ dia	**55.00**
Compote, open, gr, 6x8¼″ dia	**45.00**
Goblet, amber	**33.00**
Goblet, blue	**36.00**
Goblet, gr	**36.00**
Mug, gr, 2½″	**19.50**
Mug, yellow, 2″	**21.00**
Plate, amber, sq, 7¾″	**20.00**
Plate, gr, 5¾″	**20.00**
Plate, sq, 6″	**9.00**
Platter, blue, 11x8″	**42.00**
Sauce, flat, blue, 4″	**13.00**
Sauce, ftd, 3½″	**7.50**
Sauce, ftd, opalescent, 3½″	**13.50**
Sleigh salt, hobnail, amber	**54.00**
Spooner, knob stem	**19.50**
String-holder	**36.00**
Toothpick, blue	**35.00**
Tumbler	**15.50**
Tumbler, blue	**38.00**
Water tray, yellow, 11½″	**46.00**
Wine, amber	**45.00**
Thousand Eye Band, wine, etched	**13.00**
Three Face, celery vase	**75.00**
Compote w/cover, large	**225.00**
Creamer w/medallion under spout	**110.00**
Goblet	**9.00**
Salt & pepper w/orig top	**85.00**
Sauce, ftd	**20.00**
Sugar w/cover	**135.00**
Three Panel, berry bowl, ftd, blue	**45.00**
Berry, sm, amber	**15.00**
Berry, sm, clear	**10.00**
Berry, sm, vaseline	**15.00**
Creamer, blue	**45.00**
Creamer, clear	**25.00**
Creamer, vaseline	**40.00**
Fruit bowl, amber, 11x4″	**50.00**
Fruit bowl, blue, 10¾x4″	**65.00**
Fruit bowl, vaseline, 10x3¾″	**55.00**
Goblet, amber	**37.50**
Master berry bowl, blue	**35.00**
Master berry bowl, clear, small	**28.00**
Pitcher, milk, clear, 7″	**45.00**
Sauce, ftd, amber, 3¾″	**12.00**
Spooner, amber	**35.00**
Spooner, clear	**22.00**
Sugar, open	**20.00**
Sugar w/cover, clear	**33.00**
Sugar w/cover, vaseline	**65.00**
Thumbprint, berry set, 5 pc, boat shaped, ruby stained	**165.00**
Berry set, 6 pc, boat shape, ruby stained	**195.00**
Celery vase	**45.00**
Claret, ruby stained	**45.00**
Compote, clear flint, 9½x8½″	**90.00**
Compote, hexagonal foot, 7x10″	**120.00**
Compote, jelly	**45.00**
Creamer	**55.00**
Decanter, cork top, clear flint, 11″	**95.00**
Goblet	**40.00**
Sauce	**14.50**
Tankard, mid size, ruby stain	**90.00**
Toothpick, ruby stain	**45.00**
Tumbler, clear, 3¾″	**37.00**
Wine, clear flint, 5½″	**55.00**
Wine, ruby stained	**40.00**
Thumbprint & Diamond, goblet	**11.00**
Tidy, sugar w/cover	**25.00**
Water pitcher, bulbous	**60.00**
Tiny Fine Cut, decanter w/orig stopper, green	**34.00**
Wine	**12.00**
Tiny Optic, spooner, amethyst	**25.00**
Sugar w/cover, amethyst	**35.00**
Tokyo, berry, opalescent, large	**75.00**
Butter	**70.00**
Tong, egg cup, flint	**16.00**
Tumbler, ftd	**17.00**
Torpedo, berry bowl, 3½″	**12.00**
Bowl, flat, 8″	**25.00**
Bowl, master berry, ruby stained	**55.00**
Celery vase	**30.00**
Compote, open, 6x7″	**34.00**
Compote, jelly	**32.00**
Finger lamp	**75.00**
Goblet	**45.00**
Syrup, ruby stained	**165.00**
Triangular Prism, bar tumbler, non-flint	**14.00**
Covered butter	**40.00**
Goblet, lady's, non-flint	**17.00**
Triple Bar, goblet, etched	**17.00**
Triple Bar w/Cable, butter w/cover	**45.00**
Sugar w/cover	**40.00**
Triple Triange, celery, flint	**33.00**
Goblet, ruby stain	**45.00**
Spooner, ruby stain	**27.00**
Table set, 4 pc, ruby stain	**235.00**
Tumbler, ruby stain	**35.00**
Water set, 7 pc, ruby stain	**265.00**
Wine, ruby stain	**45.00**
Truncated Cube, creamer, ruby stain, 3″	**28.00**
Cruet, ruby stain	**95.00**
Goblet, ruby stain	**30.00**

Wine, ruby stain **35.00**
Tulip, sugar, open **27.00**
   Syrup **65.00**
   Whiskey tumbler, handled, 3″ **38.00**
Tulip & Honeycomb, table set, 4 pc **95.00**
Tulip w/Ribs, egg cup **30.00**
   Goblet **40.00**
Tulip w/Sawtooth, bar bottle, pt **70.00**
   Bar tumbler, non-flint **35.00**
   Celery, footed, non-flint **27.00**
   Champagne, non-flint **38.00**
   Decanter, orig stopper, pt **50.00**
   Decanter, orig stopper, qt **110.00**
   Goblet, flint **60.00**
   Goblet, non-flint **33.00**
   Master salt, non-flint **16.50**
   Spooner, flint **35.00**
   Wine, flint **50.00**
   Wine, non-flint **26.00**
Two Panel, berry bowl, amber **20.00**
   Berry bowl, vaseline **35.00**
   Compote, amber, 6½x8x7″ **45.00**
   Compote, yellow, 9x7½x4″ **49.00**
   Goblet, amber **27.50**
   Goblet, blue **45.00**
   Goblet, green **35.00**
   Goblet, vaseline **25.00**
   Salt dip, blue **18.00**
   Salt dip, green **10.00**
   Sauce, flat, oval, amber **11.00**
   Sauce, flat, oval, blue **13.00**
   Tray, blue **40.00**
   Tumbler, blue **33.00**
   Water set, 7 pc, blue **265.00**
   Water tray, amber, 10x15″ **57.00**
   Water tray, vaseline **44.00**
   Wine, blue **40.00**
   Wine, clear **19.50**
   Wine, green **38.00**
Unid, bowl, prescut, 8½x4½″ **15.00**
   Compote, beaded, scalloped rim, 3½x7½″ **20.00**
   Punch bowl, panelled, 16″ **40.00**
US Coin, butter w/cover, dollar, half dollar, sq, 6½″ **500.00**
   Cakestand, dollar & quarter **460.00**
   Celery tray, frosted, 7½x4″ **200.00**
   Celery vase, quarter **340.00**
   Compote, open, quarter, 8½x6½″ . . . **375.00**
   Spooner, quarter, 5¾″ **230.00**

Sugar, quarters & half dollars, Liberty Head finial **450.00**
Tumbler, dollar, 3½″ **225.00**

US Rib, toothpick, green w/gilt trim **45.00**
US Thumbprint, goblet **18.00**
Utah, spooner **17.00**
   Water pitcher **48.00**
Valencia Waffle, butter /cover **36.00**
   Compote w/cover, 1880, blue, 8x7″ . . **55.00**
   Compote, open, blue **36.00**
   Goblet, amber **40.00**
   Goblet, blue **45.00**
   Salt & pepper, orig top, apple green, sq, pr **45.00**
   Sauce, ftd, amber, sq, 4″ **15.00**
   Water pitcher, amber **75.00**
Valentine, goblet **155.00**
Vermont, basket, custard, 4x5½″ **55.00**
   Berry set, 6 pc, green **50.00**
   Butter w/cover, green, 5″ **19.50**
   Candlestick, custard w/decor **65.00**
   Celery, flat, 11½x5½″ **16.00**
   Creamer, clear **18.00**
   Creamer, green, 4″ **46.00**
   Spooner, clear **16.00**
   Toothpick, green w/mint gold **45.00**
   Toothpick, milk glass **30.00**
   Tumbler, green w/gold **40.00**
Vertical Strip, salt shaker, vaseline opal . **38.00**
Victor, *see Shell & Jewel*
Viking, *see Bearded Man*
Virginia, *see Galloway*
Virgo, toothpick **20.00**
Waffle, celery, ftd **45.00**
   Claret **75.00**
   Compote, open, 5¼x7″ dia **38.00**
   Compote, open, 8x9½″ dia **50.00**
   Egg cup **33.00**

Pitcher, 5½″ **30.00**
Sugar w/cover, large **70.00**
Waste bowl, ruffled top, 5½x4″ **85.00**
Wine **75.00**
Waffle & Thumbprint, claret, flint **100.00**
   Compote, 6″ **85.00**
   Egg cup **35.00**
   Goblet **65.00**
   Whale oil lamp, double-burner, 10″ . . . **150.00**

Wine **50.00**
Waffle w/Fan Top, goblet **16.00**
Waffle w/Spearpoint, goblet **14.50**
Wahoo, goblet **16.50**
Washboard, *see Adonis*
Washington, bowl, flat, 6x9¼" **13.00**
  Claret, flint **155.00**
  Egg cup, flint **75.00**
  Goblet, etched panels, flint **87.00**
  Master salt, flint, ftd **55.00**
  Shaker, decor **18.00**
  Water tumbler **110.00**
Washington Centennial, ale glass **16.00**
  Bowl, berry, clear, small **12.00**
  Cakestand, clear, 8¼" **50.00**
  Celery vase, clear **45.00**
  Compote, open 7" dia **40.00**
  Compote, open, 8¼x7½" **50.00**
  Compote w/cover, clear, 7x10½" **70.00**
  Compote w/cover, clear 8¼x12" **105.00**
  Creamer, clear **85.00**
  Dish, oval, 9x6" **24.00**
  Egg cup **50.00**
  Goblet, clear **45.00**
  Master salt, oval **33.00**
  Milk pitcher **90.00**
  Pitcher, 1976 . . . . **135.00**
  Platter, George Washington, frosted **110.00**
  Platter, Independence Hall, clear **105.00**
  Relish w/paw handles, dated, clear **32.50**
  Sauce, flat **11.00**
  Spooner, clear **45.00**
  Sugar, open, clear **25.00**
Waterford, cut saucer champagnes, flint **40.00**
Waterlily, *see Rosepoint Band*
Waterlily & Cattails, tumbler, opalescent, blue **25.00**
Way's Currant, goblet **22.00**
Wedding Bells, celery, blush, 9¾x3½" **33.00**
  Goblet **55.00**
  Sauce, 4" **9.50**
  Sauce, gilt & rose **7.00**
Westmoreland, celery **18.00**
Westward Ho, butter mold, figural glass cow, round wooden handle **65.00**
  Butter w/cover **150.00**
  Carafe, 8½" **110.00**
  Compote, open, 6" dia **45.00**
  Compote w/cover, 5" **165.00**
  Compote w/cover, hi ped, Indian finial, 8" dia **250.00**
  Creamer **85.00**
  Goblet, deer, lion, trees, log cabin **75.00**
  Marmalade **225.00**
  Milk pitcher **195.00**
  Sauce, ftd **25.00**
  Spooner **90.00**
  Sugar w/cover **145.00**
Wheat & Barley, butter w/cover **30.00**
  Compote, jelly **19.50**
  Creamer **20.00**
  Goblet **30.00**
  Goblet, amber **45.00**
  Goblet, blue **45.00**
  Mug, amber, 3¾" **35.00**
  Plate, 7" **17.00**
  Sauce, ftd, 4" **12.00**

Sauce, ftd, amber, 4" **16.50**
Sauce w/handles, flat, amber, 4" **12.00**
Spoon holder **15.00**
Sugar, open, amber **15.00**
Sugar, w/cover **25.00**
Tumbler, amber **38.00**
Wheeling Block, rose bowl **14.50**
Whirligig, spooner, 2 handled, 6" **35.00**
Whitton, goblet **18.50**
Wild Fruits, pitcher **50.00**
Wildflower, bowl, flat, gr, sq, 7½" **27.00**
  Bowl, ftd **20.00**
  Bread platter, apple gr **25.00**
  Cake basket, pedestal, gr **110.00**
  Celery vase **55.00**
  Compote, open, amber, 7" **40.00**
  Creamer, amber **35.00**
  Creamer, clear **21.00**
  Goblet, amber **37.00**
  Goblet, clear **29.00**
  Goblet, gr **45.00**
  Relish dish, amber, 9x4" **18.00**
  Relish dish, blue, 9x4" **20.00**
  Relish dish, clear **16.00**
  Relish dish, gr, 9x4" **20.00**
  Salt & pepper, gr, pr **60.00**
  Sauce, flat, amber, sq, 4" **12.00**
  Sauce, flat, clear **7.00**
  Sauce, flat, gr, 4" **13.00**
  Spooner, blue **30.00**
  Tumbler, amber **30.00**
  Tumbler, clear **23.00**
  Tumbler, yellow **34.00**
  Water tray, amber, oval, 11x13" **52.00**
  Water tray, clear **48.00**
  Water tray, gr, oval **60.00**
Willow Oak, cakestand, 10" dia **28.00**
  Cakestand, amber, 8¾" **49.00**
  Creamer **20.00**
  Goblet **20.00**
  Plate, amber, 7" **35.00**
  Sauce w/handles, flat, amber, 4" **11.00**
  Spooner **19.00**
  Sugar, open **20.00**
  Water tray, 10½" **21.00**
Windflower, goblet **30.00**
  Sugar, open **19.50**
  Tumbler **42.00**
Winged Scroll, powder jar w/cover **45.00**
  Sauce, ftd, opalescent, 4" **19.50**
  Toothpick, custard **95.00**
  Toothpick, gr w/gold **145.00**
Wisconsin, *see Beaded Dewdrop*
Wishbone, creamer **25.00**
  Wine **12.00**
Wooden Pail, creamer **35.00**
  Spooner, amber **30.00**
  Spooner, vaseline **45.00**
  Sugar w/cover, vaseline **65.00**
Wreath & Bars, goblet **30.00**
Wyoming, wine **45.00**
X-Logs, *see Prism Arc*
X-Ray, butter **65.00**
  Butter **65.00**

Pitcher	**65.00**
Sugar w/cover, gr w/gold	**55.00**
Toothpick, gr	**55.00**
Tumbler	**28.00**
Water set, 7 pc, gr w/mint gold	**195.00**

Yale, *see Crowfoot*

Yoked Loop, goblet	**28.00**
Sugar, open	**23.00**
Water tumbler	**45.00**
Whiskey w/handles	**35.00**
York Herringbone, butter w/cover	**95.00**
Yuma Loop, goblet	**14.00**
Tumbler, ftd	**15.00**
Zephyr, individual salt, yellow	**8.50**
Salt shaker, amber	**12.00**
Zipper, celery vase	**20.00**
Cheese dish	**40.00**
Goblet	**19.00**
Spooner	**15.00**
Zipper Slash, berry bowl, etched, frost w/amber flash	**55.00**
Master salt	**8.50**
Toothpick	**23.00**
Wine, souvenir, ruby stained	**25.00**
Zippered Block, nappy, 5½"	**11.00**
Salt & pepper shakers, ruby stained	**42.00**

Paul Revere Pottery

The Saturday Evening Girls were a social group of young Boston, Mass., ladies who met to pursue various activities, among them pottery making. Their first kiln was bought in 1906, and within a few years it became necessary to move to another location. Because their new quarters were near the historical Old North Church, they chose the name Paul Revere Pottery. With very little training, the girls produced only simple ware. Until 1915, the pottery operated at a deficit. Then a new building with four kilns was constructed on Nottingham Road. Vases, miniature jugs, children's tea sets, tiles, dinnerware and lamps were produced, usually in soft matt glazes with simple stylized nature decorations often incised on the ware. Occasional examples in a dark high gloss may also be found.

Several marks were used, P.R.P., S.E.G., or the circular Boston, Paul Revere Pottery with the horse and rider.

The pottery continued to operate, and even though their product sold well, the high production costs of the handmade ware caused the pottery to fail in 1946.

Bookends, blue-green house & trees, sgnd E Brown, 1923, SEG	**175.00**
Bowl, boat decor, sgnd SG, 1920, SEG, 11"	**225.00**
Boat design in bottom, 3 colors, sgnd, dated, SEG, 4" high	**295.00**
Geese decor, sgnd EG, 1922, SEG, 5½"	**170.00**
Greek Key decor, sgnd SG, 1917, SEG, 8"	**170.00**
Lotus decor, sgnd FL, 1910, SEG, 6" dia	**120.00**
Roosters decor, sgnd FL, 1917, SEG, 11"	**250.00**
Trees at rim, 4 colors, sgnd, dated, SEG, 7" dia	**375.00**
Yellow, lotus decor, sgnd FL, 1915, SEG, 5½" dia	**170.00**
Box, covered, blue & wht, lotus decor, sgnd JMD, 1919, SEG, 3x5"	**275.00**
Covered, yellow, sgnd SM, 1921, SEG, 2¼x3"	**60.00**
Bread & milk set, tortoise & hair decor, 3-pc, sgnd AM, 1913, SEG	**650.00**
Butter dish, blue w/wht band, sgnd SG, 1919, SEG	**90.00**
Calendar holder, blue-green w/trees decor, sgnd AM, 1920, SEG	**170.00**
Candlestick, saucer w/ring handle, blue w/tree border, 1914, SEG	**225.00**
Charger, boats decor, sgnd AM, 1914, SEG, 12" dia	**900.00**
Cookie jar, grey, SEG, 7"	**170.00**
Creamer, blue & grey, lotus decor, sgnd JG, 1914, SEG, 3½"	**90.00**
Yellow & wht, ducks decor, SEG, 3½"	**90.00**

Cup, geometric design, sgnd SG, 1912, SEG, 5"	**115.00**
Cup & saucer, gr w/wht band, sgnd SG, 1913, SEG	**60.00**
Greek Key design, sgnd SG, 1913, SEG	**170.00**
Trees decor, 1917, SEG	**90.00**
Cups & saucers, tea, 2-color w/blk stripe, set of 6, SEG	**475.00**
Jam jar & plate, rabbits decor, sgnd SG, 1914, SEG	**285.00**
Rabbits decor, unsgnd, 5"	**70.00**
Jar, covered, bulbous, boats decor, sgnd SG, 1914, SEG, 5"	**290.00**
Hexagonal, gr & wht, sgnd SG, 1916, SEG, 5"	**115.00**
Turquoise glaze, handled, w/cover, SEG	**25.00**
Lamp base, floral decor, SEG, 12"	**440.00**
Mug, anniversary, MIT, 1911, SEG	**195.00**
Paperweight, swan, SEG	**90.00**
Tree, SEG	**90.00**
Pen tray, trees decor, sgnd EG, 1917, SEG	**115.00**
Pitcher, floral 3-color decor at rim, sgnd, SEG, 9"	**450.00**
Planter, Greek Key design, 4 handles, sgnd SG, 1914, SEG, 7x9"	**1,100.00**
Plate, border design w/little chickens, sgnd, SEG	**65.00**
Dark blue w/lt blue band, sgnd FG, 1926, SEG	**40.00**
Floral 4-color border, SEG, 8"	**325.00**
Geometric 4-color decor, sgnd, dated, SEG, 9" dia	**400.00**
Greek Key decor, sgnd IG, 1909, SEG, 7¾"	**115.00**
Greek Key decor, sgnd IG, 1911, SEG, 10"	**170.00**
Grey w/blk-rimmed blue border, 1920, SEG, 7"	**45.00**
Rabbits decor, sgnd SG, 1912, SEG, 6¾"	**90.00**
Trees decor, sgnd EG, SEG, 8¼"	**120.00**
Sponge pot, blue-green w/trees decor, sgnd EG, 1914, SEG	**170.00**
Tea pot, green, SEG	**90.00**
Yellow, SEG	**90.00**
Tile, geometric, ftd, 1922, SEG, 5½x5½"	**115.00**
Goose decor, unmkd, 5x5"	**140.00**
Hart House, sgnd LS, 1910, SEG, 4x4"	**145.00**
Wolf decor, unmkd, 5x5"	**140.00**
Tray, blue, sgnd EG, 1921, SEG, 14x9½"	**90.00**
Tumbler, two colors, no pattern, sgnd, dated, SEG, 7"	**70.00**
Vase, 1919, SEG, 11"	**85.00**

Blue glaze, signed, 4"	**110.00**
Blue & gr, trees decor, sgnd SG, 1917, SEG, 8¼x7" dia	**475.00**
Blue & wht, lotus decor, sgnd SG, 1917, SEG, 10"	**475.00**
Blue, sgnd EG, 1922, SEG, 14"	**115.00**
Brown, SEG, 10"	**105.00**
Cylindrical, trees decor, sgnd FL, 1917, SEG, 8"	**335.00**
Drip glaze, sgnd RB, 1917, SEG, 21"	**335.00**
Drip glaze, sgnd AM, 1920, SEG, 11"	**225.00**
Floral green, sgnd SG, 1914, SEG, 8½"	**335.00**

Miniature, two flowers, sgnd, SEG, 1" **50.00**
Overall floral 4-color decor, sgnd, dated, SEG, 7" **750.00**
Scenic 4-color design overall, sgnd, dated, SEG, 11" **1,200.00**
Trees decor, sgnd AM, 1916, SEG, 4½" **170.00**
Yellow trees, sgnd FL, 1914, SEG, 8" **335.00**
Yellow, buttercup decor, SEG, 5" **40.00**
Wall pocket, blue-green, lotus decor, sgnd E Brown, 1922, SEG **115.00**

Pauline Pottery

Pauline Pottery was made from 1883 to 1888 in Chicago, Ill., from clay imported from the Ohio area. Its founder was Mrs. Pauline Jacobus, who had learned the trade at the Rookwood Pottery. Mrs. Jacobus moved to Edgerton, Wisconsin, to be near a source of suitable clay, thus eliminating shipping expenses. Until 1905, she produced high quality wares, able to imitate with ease designs and styles of such masters as Wedgwood and Meissen. Her products were sold through leading department stores, and the names of some of these firms may appear on the ware. Not all were marked, and unless signed by a noted local artist, positive identificaton is often impossible. Marked examples carried a variety of stamps and signatures: Trade Mark with a crown, Pauline Pottery, and Egerton Art Pottery are but a few.

Bowl, hp roses w/gold trim, 3½x9½" **775.00**

Peachblow

Peachblow, made to imitate the colors of the Chinese Peachbloom porcelain, was made by several glass houses in the late 1800s. Among them were New England Glass, Mt. Washington, Webb, and Hobbs Brockunier and Company. Its pink shading was achieved through action of the heat on the gold content of the glass. While New England Peachblow shades from pink to cool white, Mt. Washington's tends toward an ivory shade. Although usually glossy, a stain finish was also produced, and many pieces were enameled and gilded.

Bowl, enamel scene on inside **350.00**
Webb, gold prunus decor, acid finish, cream lining, 4" dia . . **395.00**
Condiment set, Wheeling, salt, pepper & mustard, plated holder **1,850.00**
Creamer, Libbey, ribbed **195.00**
Webb, decorated **275.00**
Wheeling, 3¾" **750.00**
Yellow to peach, 4½" **250.00**
Cruet, Wheeling **850.00**
Darner, New England, shiny finish, 6x2½" dia **180.00**
Dish, deep red/cream, ruffled, sawtooth edge, 7" **175.00**
Ewer, Webb, wht lining, 12" **400.00**
Finger bowl, Mt Washington, acid finish **900.00**
Finger lamp, Webb, kerosene, enameled decor **425.00**
Jar, covered, Webb, acid, gold prunus decor, cream lining, 4½" **650.00**
Mug, monkey, peachblow, shiny **135.00**
Pear, New England, stem intact **295.00**

Perfume, Webb, lay-down, gold prunus, hallmkd silver cap, 5" **295.00**
Pitcher, hobnail, ribbed camphor handle, 6½" **500.00**
Mt Washington, acid finish, 6" **1,900.00**
Wheeling, acid finish, sq top & frosted amber handle, 8" . **1,400.00**
Wheeling, shiny w/amber handle, 5" **325.00**
Punch cup, New England, reeded opaque wht handle, 2½x2½" dia **385.00**
Wheeling, amber handle, red shaded to yellow, wht lining . . **325.00**
Salt & pepper, Gutta pattern, 4" **125.00**
Wheeling, shiny finish **225.00**
Sugar & creamer, New England, ribbed satin, gold World's Fair 1893 **400.00**
Sugar bowl, Mt Washington, 3¾" **500.00**
Wheeling **500.00**
Sweetmeat jar, Webb, gold prunus, shiny, silver plated top & handle **495.00**
Toothpick holder, New England, square **375.00**
New England, triangle top **325.00**
Tumbler, New England, satin finish, 3½" **325.00**
Webb, enameled decor **165.00**
Wheeling, shiny finish, 3¾x3" dia **350.00**
Vase, applied amber florals, ruffled, 13" **575.00**
Applied glass plums, leaves & vines on amber applied ft, 14¼" **550.00**
Cased blue interior, 6" **110.00**
Flower form, wht shading to pink, acid finish, 6" **295.00**
New England, acid finish, ovoid w/slightly flaring rim, 14½". **675.00**
Lily, shiny finish, 8" **375.00**
Lily, shiny finish, 17½" **425.00**
Shiny, 4 dimples at widest part, 10½" **850.00**
Trumpet, undulating rim, circular base, label, 8" **825.00**
Satin glass w/Lace De Boheme Cameo, 1880s, 9" **275.00**
Webb, bulbous w/narrow neck, coralene coral decor, 12" . . **250.00**
Decorated w/glass birds, propeller mk **375.00**
Double gourd, flare top, acid w/gold florals, 8" **850.00**
Fishscale, soft gold decor around middle, 8" **200.00**
Gold bee & flowers, shiny, propellor mk, 5x2½" dia **250.00**
Gold bird & flowers, shiny, off-wht lining, 8x4" dia **295.00**
Gold dragonflies & flowers, shiny, frosted handles, 7" . . . **395.00**
Shiny, crystal applique: rigaree, flowers, loop ft, 5¾" . . . **550.00**
Yellow coralene decor, frosted clear handles, ribbon rigaree, 6" **445.00**
Wheeling, gourd shape, shiny finish, 7" **800.00**
Mahogany cased, 8¼" **495.00**
Shiny, applied amber foot, 1890s, 8¾" **275.00**
Stick shape, acid finish, 8¼" **375.00**
Vases, enamel cherries, gold trim, 10½", pair **800.00**

Peking Glass

The first glass house to be established in Peking in 1680 produced glassware made in imitation of porcelain, a more desirable medium to the Chinese. By 1725, multi-layered carving with a cameo effect resulted in a wider range of shapes and colors. The factory was closed from 1736 to 1795, but glass made in Po-shan and shipped to Peking for finishing continued to be called Peking glass.

Twentieth century ware is usually decorated in soft frosted colors on relief molded designs.

Bowl, cameo, turquoise frogs on lily pads, beautifully cut **350.00**
Pair, floral & bird decor, gr cameo on wht ground, 8" **530.00**
Demitasse cup & saucer, blue, in brass holder w/handle **50.00**
Jar, covered, cranberry flowers cut to wht, 3" **135.00**
Snuff bottle, red overlay, carved sides, lt gr jade top, 1700s . . . **235.00**
Reverse painted, scenes of women in teahouse, 4½" **265.00**
Tea caddy, Chinese fan shape, turquoise w/enameling, 4½x6" . . **55.00**
Vase, cameo cut, blue to wht, 8¾" **350.00**
Cameo, wht w/gr bird & floral design, 8" **370.00**
Imperial yellow on wht, relief butterfly & florals, 1865 . . . . . **295.00**
Waisted, gr on wht **400.00**

Peloton

Peloton glass was first made by Wilhelm Kralik in Bohemia in 1880. This unusual art glass was produced by rolling colored threads onto the transparent or opaque glass gather as it was removed from the furnace. Usually, more than one color of threading was used, and some items were further decorated with enameling. It was made with both shiny and acid finishes.

Cruet, clear applied handle & faceted stopper **375.00**
Finger bowl, multi-colored threads on crystal **145.00**
Pitcher, water, blue w/enameled yellow flowers & long leaves . . **345.00**
Sugar, w/cover, melon ribbed, clear w/wht threads, 4½" **135.00**
Vase, clear lined w/pink, ruffled fan top **500.00**
  Filaments of deep pink, blue & yellow decor, pink lining . . . **445.00**
  Rainbow, swirled frosted rigaree decor, 13¼" **175.00**
  Red, blue, wht on cased light gr, pr **1,100.00**

Pens and Pencils

The first metallic writing pen was patented in 1809 and soon machine produced pens with steel nibs gradually began replacing the quill. The first fountain pen was invented in 1830, but due to the fact that a suitable metal for the tips had not been developed, they were not manufactured commercially until the 1980s. The first commercial producers were Waterman in 1884, and Parker with the Lucky Curve in 1888.

The self-filling pen, in 1890, featured the soft interior sack which filled with ink as the metal bar on the outside of the pen was raised and lowered. Variations of the pumping mechanism were tried until 1932 when Parker introduced the Vacumatic, a sackless pen with an internal pump.

Fountain Pens
Aiken Lambert Mercantile, red hard rubber, gold plated tip, 1925 **35.00**
Carter Inx, green jade marble, gold plated tip, 1932 . . . . **20.00**
Carter 10117 Inx, coral marble, gold plated tip, 1928 . . . . **185.00**
Conklin, lady's ribbon, self-filler, orange **20.00**
  Self-filling, marbleized brown & red, orig box, 1909 . . . . **85.00**
Dreadnaught, 1920, Dunn, Pennsylvania **18.00**
Esterbrook, green, orig box **6.00**
Eversharp, green pearl lustre, gold filigree band, 1930s **12.00**
  Doric, gold lined marble, gold plated tip, 1940 . . . . **45.00**
  Gold Seal Doric, marble, 1931 . . . . **240.00**
  Skyline, gold filled cap, 1940s **8.50**
  Skyline, maroon, gold plated tip, 1944 . . . . **15.00**
JC Rider, red & black, 1903 . . . . **20.00**
Japanese Jumbo, black, gold plated tip **24.00**
John Holland, blue marble, gold plated tip, 1931 . . . . **30.00**
Laughlin New Departure, red & black marble, gold plated tip, 1901 **30.00**
Lefoeuf, gold plated tip, 1932 . . . . **40.00**
Moore, emerald pearl marble, gold plated tip, 1934 . . . . **10.00**
Parker, '5l' demi size, grey, copper plated tip, 1954 . . . . **15.00**
  '51' Demonstrator, w/stainless cap, copper plated tip, 1927 . . **68.00**
  '51' gold filled cap **10.00**
  '51' grey gold filled cap, gold plated tip, 1951 . . . . **10.00**
  Black hard rubber, pat 1894 . . . . **55.00**
  Big Red Duo-Fold **50.00**
  Challenger, burgandy pearl marble, gold plated tip, 1937 . . . **12.00**
  Duofold Deluxe, black & pearl, 3 rings, 4½" **35.00**
  Duofold Jr Lucky curve pen **25.00**
  Duofold, burgandy pearl, gold plated tip, 1933 . . . . **25.00**
  Duofold, green, 1927 . . . . **20.00**
  Duofold, mottled ivory & blk cap, russet & blk body **25.00**
  Gold filled metal, gold plated tip, 1957 . . . . **35.00**
  Lady Duofold, black rubber, gold plated tip, 1924 . . . . **15.00**
  Lucky Curve, gold filled metal, gold plated tip, 1918 . . . . **65.00**

Maxima Blue Diamond Vacumatic, gold pearl w/black, 1941 . **175.00**
Sheaffer Lifetime, mottled green, 1914 . . . . **29.00**
  '33', dark green, 14k tip **35.00**
  '33', gold w/black stripe, gold plated tip, 1936 . . . . **7.50**
  '34' Self Filling, hard rubber, nickel plated tip, 1915 . . . . **25.00**
  '46 Special', orange **100.00**
  Feathertouch, black, gold plated tip **6.00**
  Snorkel, black, copper plated tip, 1958 . . . . **42.00**
  White Dot Snorkel, grey, gold plated tip, 1953 . . . . **18.00**
  White Dot, black, gold plated tip, 1926 . . . . **30.00**
  White Dot, blue, gold plated tip, 1949 . . . . **14.00**
  White Dot, jade marble, gold plated tip, 1923 . . . . **32.50**
Stratford, black, 1930s **4.00**
Swan Eternal '46', black lined pearl marble, gold plated tip, 1929 **100.00**
  Green jade marble, gold plated tip, 1926 . . . . **55.00**
Travelers, brown w/blk stripe, see through center, 14k tip **12.00**
Wahl Eversharp, Gold Seal Doric, blue, 1927 . . . . **28.00**
  14k gold point, revolving ball clip, 1928 . . . . **19.00**
  Red & blk marble, gold pointed tip, 1927 . . . . **85.00**
Waterman '52', black hard rubber, 1922 . . . . **22.00**
  '52', hard rubber, nickel plated tip, snake clip, 1923 . . . . **55.00**
  '55', red ripple hard rubber, gold plated tip, 1924 . . . . **67.50**
  '56', black hard rubber, nickel plated tip, 1921 . . . . **85.00**
  '56', black hard rubber, nickel plated tip, 1922 . . . . **100.00**
  '92', pearl green & red marble, gold plated tip **20.00**
  100 Year Super Size, black, gold plated tip, 1940 . . . . **225.00**
  Black, 1903 . . . . **25.00**
  Citation Taperite, grey, 1946 . . . . **18.00**
  Commando, blue, gold plated tip, 1943 . . . . **35.00**
  Duofold, green w/center gold band, Sept 26, 1905 . . . . **65.00**
  Duofold, sterling **45.00**
  Ideal, 14k gold point, brown lustre body **20.00**
  Ideal, 14k gold, engraved foliage, monogram reserve **285.00**
  Patrician, onyx, gold plated tip, 1933 . . . . **300.00**
Webster Four Star, black hard rubber, gold plated tip, 1923 . . . **78.00**
Mechanical Pencils
Amethyst colored stone at top, 14k gold shell, engraved, old . . **150.00**
Eversharp Lady's, gold filled, 1920s, 4¼" long **30.00**
  Red hard rubber, 1926 . . . . **20.00**
German, 3 color, brass, 1908 . . . . **35.00**
Parker Duofold Big Brother, red hard rubber, gold plated tip . . **80.00**
  Mottled jade, gold filled cap, tip & clip **10.00**
Sheaffer Lifetime, green mottled, wide gold filled cap **15.00**
Stan Musial baseball pencil **12.00**
Sets
Eversharp Ventura, maroon, gold filled caps, 1956 . . . . **18.00**
Parker Parkette Deluxe, pearl green, 1935 . . . . **28.00**
  Vaccumatic, 1930s **65.00**
Conklin Endura, gold & brown marble, gold plated tip, 1926 . . **95.00**
Schaefer White Dot, 1938 . . . . **38.00**
WS Hicks, 14K **45.00**
Wahl, sterling silver **49.00**

Personalities, Fact & Fiction

One of the largest and most popular areas of collecting today, if tradepaper ads and articles be any indication, are character related collectibles. Everyone has a favorite or favorites, whether they be comic strip personalities or true life heroes. The earliest comic strip dealt with the adventures of the Yellow Kid, the smiling, bald headed Oriental boy always in a nightshirt. He was introduced in 1895, a product of the imagination of Richard Fenton Outcault. Today, though very hard to come by, items relating to the Yellow Kid bring premium prices. In 1902, Buster Brown and Tige, his dog and constant companion, another of Outcault's progenies, made

it big in the comics as well as in the world of advertising. Shoe stores appealed to the younger set through merchandising displays that featured them both; today, the items from their earlier years are very collectible.

Other early comic figures were Moon Mullins, created in 1923 by Frank Willard; Little Orphan Annie, by Harold Gray in 1923; Buck Rogers by Philip Nowlan in 1928; and Betty Boop, the round-faced, innocent-eyed, chubby-cheeked Boop-Boop-a-Doop girl of the early 1930s. Bimbo was her dog, and KoKo her clown friend.

Tarzan, created around 1930 by Edgar Rice Burroughs; and Captain Midnight, by Robert Burtt and Willfred G. Moore are popular heroes with today's collectors. During the days of radio, Sky King of the Flying Crown Ranch, also created by Burtt and Moore, thrilled boys and girls of the mid 1940s. Hoppalong Cassidy, Red Rider, Tom Mix and The Lone Ranger were only a few of the other 'good guys' always on the side of law and order.

But of all the fictional heroes and comic characters collected today, probably the best loved and well known is Mickey Mouse. Created in the late 1920s by Walt Disney, he became an instant success with his first film, Steamboat Willie. His popularity was parlayed through wind-up toys, watches, figurines, cookie jars, puppets, clothing, and numerous other saleables. Today, collectors find a market plagued by wildly fluctuating prices---due to speculation in this area, many have not yet stablized. It is important to be aware of which are the older items, since Mickey Mouse remains a popular commodity.

Not all personalities being collected today are fictional, however. Dan Patch, for instance, was a champion trotter who set a world record in 1906. His owner, M.W. Savage, used him to represent his many business enterprises, among them the Dan Patch Music Company, M.W. Savage Co., and Northland Biscuit Works. Dan Patch Tobacco tins were released through the Scotten Dillon Co. of Detroit, Mich.

Shirley Temple 12 oz. pitchers were a premium offered in the early 1930s by the General Mills Co. They were free inside boxes of their cereal. All in all, over 10,000 were produced by the U.S. Glass Co. of Pittsburg. Four more items were added later, an 8 oz. mug, 6 and 6½″ bowls, and a 4″ nappy; these are more difficult to find. Look for a well preserved decal!

Al Jolson, salt & pepper shakers, figural, pr	15.00
Alice in Wonderland, clock, w/oscillating Mad Hater	175.00
Game, early Parker Bros	95.00
Playing cards, MIB	65.00
Sewing card, Walt Disney	45.00
Tea set, Walt Disney	45.00
Watch	45.00
Amos, tin wind-up, 1930	145.00
Amos 'n Andy, book, Amos 'n Andy & Their Creators	55.00
Fresh Air Taxi, Marx	525.00
Map of Weber City w/letter, orig envelope	35.00
Andy Gump, bisque figure, 1½″	10.00
Doll, wood w/tin legs, 9″	45.00
Nodding bisque figure, molded clothes, 4½″	45.00
Aunt Jemima, family dolls, set of 4	52.00
Note pad	25.00
Spice set	65.00
Sugar & creamer, pr	35.00
Syrup	25.00
Babe Ruth, pocket watch, w/fob, rare	250.00
Watch	150.00
Bambi, figurine w/label, American Pottery, 8″	125.00
Planter	16.00
Bambi & Thumper, bookmark, Prevent Forest Fires, WDP	5.00
Barney Google, game	12.00
Barney Google & Sparkplug, sheet music, 1923, King Features	20.00
Bashful, puppet, orig clothes, Madame Alexander	40.00
Batman, clock, talking alarm, 1975	40.00
Coloring book, 'Adventures of Batman', 1976, Whitman	3.50
Figurine, hard plastic, 4″	9.00
Record, 'Batman Vs the Riddler', 1975	5.00
Utility belt, 1941	75.00
Beatles, figures, 4 w/instruments & microphones	50.00
Inflatable dolls, set of 4	130.00
Nodders, boxed, 8″	400.00
Official pillow, 4 pictures	45.00
Bebe Daniels, ashtray, 1930s, 4½″	12.00
Bert & Ernie, hand puppets, pr	16.95
Betty Boop, bisque figurines, set of 3, playing instruments	275.00
Chalk figure, 14½″	12.00
Doll quilt	98.00
Pin, Roxy Theatre, N.Y.	4.00
Bing Crosby, figural record cleaner	22.50
Blondie, ring toss target game	45.00
Blondie & Dagwood, game, orig box, 1941	18.00
Bobby Bensen, bowl	10.00
Bonzo, bisque figures, sgnd, 4 playing different instruments	185.00
Buck Jones, horseshoe pin	25.00
Buck Rogers, binoculars, super sonic glasses, 1953	35.00
Book, 'Adventure of Buck Rogers on Planetoid Eros'	55.00
Book, Pop-Up, 'A Dangerous Mission', 1934	95.00
Figurine, painted metal, 1934, Rappaport	25.00
Flashlight, Lite Buster	24.00
Glow in the dark ring, Ring of Saturn	100.00
Gun, sonic w/signal ray	55.00
Helmet, metal & leather	35.00
Liquid helium pistol, tin litho	300.00
Pocket watch, 1930s	300.00
Press book, 'Planet Outlaws', 1939	25.00
Record, orig broadcast, 25th century, 1973	30.00
Roller skates	18.00
Smoke ring ray gun, w/ammo	37.00
Space ship, orig box	585.00
Strato blazer flashlight	50.00
Zoopa Pop Pistol, lithograph	35.00
Bugs Bunny, clock, 1970, Seth Thomas	10.00
Doll, 1941, Warner Bros	95.00
Figural camera, orig box	45.00
Watch w/carrot hands	45.00
Buster Brown, 2 for 5 cent cigar tin	45.00
Blocks, alphabet, puzzle & picture combination	105.00
Camera, 1910, Outcult	350.00
Cardboard store display, 1940	45.00
Child's cup & saucer, Buster Brown & Tige	25.00
Child's plate, 6¼″	25.00
Mug	85.00
Playing cards, orig box, 1906	85.00
Trolley book, 'Boston to the Bronx'	24.00
Campbell Kids, feeding dish, Grace Drayton	65.00
Captain Kangaroo, game, MIB, 1956	6.00
Captain Marvel, club buttons	20.00
Junior ski jump	15.00
Picture puzzle	22.00
School bag	55.00
Captain Midnight, airplane, Aerial Torpedo, 1941	52.00
Detecto-Scope, MIB	47.00
Ring, Mistic Eye Detector, 1942	55.00
Secret Squadron manual	55.00
Shake-Up Mug, orig papers inside	65.00
Captain Video, child's 2 pc suit & hat	70.00
Figure, orig box w/8 rockets	29.00
Charles Lindbergh, 30 pcs sheet music, 1898-1935	27.00
Carved cane, massive	25.00

Glider toy, celluloid tail, 9″ **12.00**
Jewelry box, marbleized metal, 1927 .... **48.00**
Lucky Lindy perfume w/plane logo, 1927............... **6.00**
Metal bracelet, w/plane & flag buildings............. **12.00**
Pocket watch w/fob, New York to Paris **600.00**
Tapestry, 1927 .... **125.00**
Tin pencil box, plane & Lindy, has pencil & ruler **35.00**
Tin print, 7x12½″................................... **85.00**
Token, gilt, pictures Lindy & Spirit St Louis........... **7.00**
Charlie Chaplin, chalkware statue, twisted wire cane, 1925 ..... **49.50**
Plaster of Paris figure, mkd, 11″ **20.00**
Poster, hand done on cardboard, early **600.00**
Rag doll w/porcelain face, hands & feet, 21″ **38.00**
Tin button puppet, English, 4″...................... **80.00**
Walking toy, Waterbury Clock Co, 1920, 12″.......... **1,000.00**
Charlie Chaplin & Jackie Cooper, tin pencil box, 1930s, pr ... **73.00**
Charlie McCarthy, cardboard puppet, 20″............. **12.00**
Crazy Car wind-up.................................. **325.00**
Figural glass perfume bottle **20.00**
Game of Topper, 1938 .... **30.00**
Cinderella, planter................................... **20.00**
Watch **35.00**
Cisco Kid, neckerchief, nickel sombrero slide.......... **22.00**
Daddy Warbucks, stamp, comic, rubber, 1930 .... **9.50**
Dagwood, tin wind-up airplane....................... **475.00**
Daisy Mae & Lil Abner, paper dolls, 1942, Saalfield **60.00**
Dale Evans, watch, leather band, The Ingraham Co, Bristol **55.00**
Dan Patch, coaster wagon, 'Dan Patch 1:55' **600.00**
Plate, 'Dan Patch 1:55', 7½″........................ **300.00**
Stop watch, 'Dan Patch 1:55'........................ **550.00**
Tin, 1920s, 4x4x6″................................. **30.00**
Davey Crockett, belt & buckle **25.00**
Game, MIB, 1955 .... **12.00**
Indian craft **27.50**
Pocket knife....................................... **18.00**
Deputy Dawg, tin wind-up **75.00**
Dick Tracy, badge, crime stoppers.................... **15.00**
Book, 'Ace Detective', 1943, Chester Gould **15.00**
Button, pin back **8.00**
Cards, 1935, Caramels **25.00**
Cookie set, 1937, Pillsbury......................... **35.00**
Detective fingerprint set, 1933 .... **100.00**
Figure, painted **15.00**
Official electronic 2-way wrist radio, orig box **80.00**
Pop pistol, MIB.................................... **50.00**
Pop-up book **85.00**
Record, orig radio broadcast, 1972 .... **30.00**
Ring, secret compartment **75.00**
Second Year Star badge **15.00**
Secret Service Patrol Sergeant badge................. **20.00**
Siren pistol, decal, red **45.00**
Stamp, comic strip, rubber, 1932.................... **12.00**
Target game, Marx................................. **30.00**
Walking nursemaid toy, orig box, 1951 .... **28.00**
Wallpaper, late 1930s, 50 ft, large roll **25.00**
Dionne Quintuplets, book, 'Going on Three' **13.00**
Book, 'The Story of Dionne Quintuplets'.............. **25.00**
Book, 'We Were Five', paperback, Brough **12.00**
Cereal bowl, metal................................. **25.00**
Paper doll book, 'All Aboard Shut Eye Town' **95.00**
Plate.. **55.00**
Scrapbook, 100 pg **20.00**
Disney, television playhouse tin & plastic figure, MIB, Marx, 1940 **450.00**
Disney characters, rug, super color, 5½x8½′............ **1,650.00**

Disneyland, tin tea set, for 4, Chein **85.00**

Donald Duck, bank, Walt Disney, 6½″.................... **18.00**
Bisque figure, long billed, 1930s, 3½″ **30.00**
Bisque twin toothbrush holder **265.00**
Board game, 1938, Walt Disney Enterprises **25.00**
Book, 'Donald Duck & His Friends', Heath, 1939 .... **95.00**
'Donald Duck & His Nephews', Heath, 1939 .... **95.00**
First published, 1935, Whitman **325.00**
Camera, 1947, Herbert George Co.................... **40.00**
Candy bucket, 1949 .... **50.00**
Celluloid pencil sharpener **145.00**
Celluloid figure, early, 3½″ **175.00**
Clock, animated, Bayard **110.00**
Delivery Tricycle, plastic, Marx, 5″.................. **30.00**
Drawing board, lithographed tin, big Donald figural **20.00**
Figural soap....................................... **110.00**
Figure, 1939, Brayton Laguna Pottery, 6½″............. **225.00**
Sun Rubber, 6½″ **35.00**
Drum Major, Knicker-Bocker, 14″ **550.00**
Party game, 1938, Walt Disney Enterprises............. **25.00**
Planter, Donald in cowboy outfit **18.00**
Plaster doll, 20″................................... **25.00**
Plastic feet **25.00**
Playboard, 1946, 9″................................ **17.50**
Pull toy, Fisher Price, 10″.......................... **85.00**
Roly poly **8.00**
Shakers, ceramic, WDP, pr......................... **40.00**
Tea set, china luster, 13 pc, long billed Donald **55.00**
Tin wind-up on skis, Linemar....................... **285.00**
Wallpaper trim, 10′................................ **70.00**
Watch **75.00**
Dopey, doll **100.00**
Wind-up, rolling eyes, 1930s **250.00**
Dumbo, cream pitcher **20.00**
Figure, pointed hat, ear to ground, American Pottery, 4″ **40.00**
Turnabout cookie jar, no paint **35.00**
Vinyl figure, movable legs, WDP Hong Kong, VS, 4″ **10.00**
Edward G Robinson, tobacco package w/picture, 1930 .... **12.00**
Elvis, belt, picture of Elvis, 1956..................... **25.00**
Movie script, MGM **30.00**
Paramount **30.00**
Watch **35.00**
Felix the Cat, baby plate, 1925, large.................. **125.00**
Board game, 1960.................................. **14.00**

Celluloid figure	85.00
Figure, 16″	175.00
Figure, wood jointed, Schoenhut, 4″	150.00
Platform toy, Nifty	150.00
Toy, Schoenhut, 9″	250.00
Ferdinand Bull, bisque figure	35.00
Fibber McGee, glossy picture, entire radio cast, 8x10″	2.00
Flash Gordon, cards, set of 8, picture	10.00
Insignia wings, pin-back, metal	6.00
Kite, paper, 1930s	35.00
Medal, pin-back, color	4.00
Movie poster, color, Italian, 22x28″	39.00
Pop-up book, 1935, Pleasure Books	185.00
Press book, 'Mars Attacks the World', 1930	22.00
Puzzle, comic strip, 1942, 14x9″	25.00
Fred Flintstone, hand puppet	12.00
Toy, battery operated, on Dino, Marx, 22″	250.00
Gene Autry, book, Whitman, 1950	6.00
Cast iron cap gun, 1940s, 8″	36.00
Coloring book	18.00
Display sign, 9x12″	100.00
Galoshes, orig box	35.00
Guitar, MIB, Emenee	50.00
Record, orig sleeves, 78 rpm	5.00
Watch, moving 6 gun	95.00
Gomer Pyle, tin lunchbox, raised figures	20.00
Green Hornet, wallet, 1966	12.00
Happy Hooligan, figure, 12″	95.00
Roly poly, papier mache, 1920s, 9″	200.00
Henry, bisque figure, 3½″	60.00
Hopalong Cassidy, 8mm film, 'Heart of the West'	17.50
Alarm clock, black metal case, Hopalong picture	60.00
Autograph book w/zipper	65.00
Bedspread	95.00
Bicycle, complete w/holsters, orig paint, 1948	175.00
Binocular, 1950	25.00
Birthday card, w/balloon	25.00
Birthday card, with rope	18.00
Brass star	8.00
Bronze color plastic bank	9.00
Camera	60.00
Cap pistol w/black grips	25.00
Child's knife	15.00
Colorful tin badge	9.00
Comic, 1950s	8.00
Good Luck Bar 20 ring, 1949, Post cereal	25.00
Kerchief	17.00
Lucky piece	10.00
Magazine, Life, 1950s	12.00
Milk bottle, glass, ½ gallon	25.00
Mirror, sgnd, 4x6″	9.00
Newspaper comic strip, 1950s	5.00
Night light, 'Gun in Holster', Aladdin	135.00
Picture, black & white	12.00
Plate, WS George, 10″	22.00
Pocket knife, Hoppy on a white horse	40.00
Publicity manual	20.00
Radio, Hoppy & Topper, 1946, Arvin	110.00
Record, 2, w/story & photo, 'Singing Bandit'	10.00
'Square Dance Holdup', w/pictures	34.00
Revolver w/holster, Ex, 9½″	85.00
Rocking horse cowboy, Marx	70.00
Tin dart board	18.00
Tin wind-up	18.00

Token	13.00
Toy viewer & 5 films w/Gabby Hayes, orig box	35.00
Tumbler, milk glass	14.00
Watch, orig band	40.00
Writing paper set	35.00
Howdy Doody, apple bag	8.00
Doll, plastic, mouth moves	17.00
Marionette	40.00
Orange bag	8.00
Play desk	50.00
Ring, Face Flashlight, 1950	60.00
TV game	35.00
Jack Armstrong, Egyptian whistle ring	22.50
Flashlight	17.50
Game, Big 10 Football	65.00
Pedometer	18.75
Propeller gun, 2 propellers	75.00
Telescope	20.00
Jackie Coogan, pencil box, metal	27.50
Jackie Robinson, watch	500.00
Jiggs, wood figure	10.00
Jiminy Cricket, wood w/top hat & umbrella	125.00
Jimmy Carter, doll, sgnd, 22″	150.00
Joe Palooka, colored comics, 1942	145.00
Palooka, lunch pail	65.00
Watch	235.00
Kathlyn Williams, plate, 1918, Star Players Photo Co, 9″	15.00
Katzenjammer Kids, figurines, Captain, Hans & Fritz, mkd, 1944	85.00
Hockey game	22.00
Kayo, bisque figure, orig box	275.00
Wood plaque, 12″	25.00
Killer Kane, figurine, painted metal, 1934, Rappaport	25.00
Lamb Chop & Charlie Horse, hand puppets, pr	19.00
Laurel & Hardy, in model T, boxed, Politoy	50.00
Wind-up toy, picture of Harmon	26.00
Lawrence Welk, champagne bubble machine	8.50
Lil Abner, animated wrist watch, American Flag	180.00
Candy vending machine, 1940	450.00
Little Orphan Annie, 3 way whistle, orig mailer & instructions	37.50
Ashtray, Sandy standing, 1930	125.00
Bisque figurine, 3″	35.00
Book, 'Gila Monster Gang', 1944	10.00
Circus, in mailer, premium	45.00
Dime bank	135.00
Face ring	20.00
Game, Pursuit, Selchow & Righter, 1938	13.00

Mug	40.00
Necklace, enamel figure, 1936	35.00
Pastry set, Transogram	35.00
Pop-up book	85.00
Purse, small, red	35.00

Radio w/Sandy & Daddy Warbucks **275.00**
Radio, Secret Society, orig envelope, 1934 . . . . **50.00**
Record, orig radio broadcast, 1974 . . . . **30.00**
Secret Society pin **12.50**
Stamp, comic, rubber, 1930 . . . . **15.00**
Tin 4 burner stove, Annie & Sandy on front **45.00**
Wrist watch, 1934 . . . . **95.00**
Little Red Riding Hood, plate, w/picture & verse, pr, 6" **45.00**
Lone Ranger, 6 shooter ring **26.00**
17th Anniversary lucky piece **28.00**
Adventure set, Blizzard, 1973, Gabriel **18.00**
Carson City Bank Robbery **25.00**
Hidden Rattler, 1973, Hubley **19.50**
Hidden Silver Mine, 1973 . . . . **25.00**
Hopi Medicine Man, Hubley **24.00**
Landslide, 1973, Hubley **17.00**
Red River Floodwaters, 1973 . . . . **30.00**
Tribal Pow-wow, 1973, Hubley **24.00**
Arcade card, sgnd, 3½x5½" **4.00**
Book, 'Gold Robbery', hardcover, 1939 . . . . **5.00**
'The Lone Ranger', 1936, F Striker **13.00**
Bullet **12.00**
Button, yellow & black w/silver **18.00**
Buttons, silver **15.00**
Cards, set of 16, 1950 . . . . **40.00**
Clicker pistol, decal, gray, jewel **35.00**
Clothes brush, 1939 . . . . **22.00**
Color book **28.00**
Comic books, 4, 1955-1956 . . . . **10.00**
Deputy star badge **20.00**
Figure, Lone Ranger on Silver, 1938, 4½" **22.00**
Game, 1938, Parker Bros **50.00**
Harmonica, orig display **22.00**
Knife, red handled **28.00**
Lunch box, early version, w/Tonto coin **40.00**
Movie poster, 'Lone Ranger & Lost City of Gold' **99.00**
Pedometer, 1943 . . . . **20.00**
Play watch **10.00**
Printing set, 8 rubber stamps, 1939 . . . . **30.00**
Puzzle **10.00**
Record player, all wood case **100.00**
Ring, Atom Bomb **28.00**
Scrapbook **15.00**
Silver bullet pen, orig card **25.00**
Silver bullet, secret compartment compass **35.00**
Tin wind-up, Marx, 1938, MIB **225.00**
TV bank **60.00**
Wallet, 1948 . . . . **23.00**
Mandrake the Magician, pin, 1934, King Features **35.00**
Marilyn Monroe, change tray **285.00**
Mickey Mouse, 50th birthday music box, Schmid **50.00**
50th birthday plate, Schmid **65.00**
50th birthday plate, Viletta **75.00**
Alarm clock, Ingersoll, 1947 . . . . **300.00**
Alarm clock, eyes move, Phinney Walker, West Germany **50.00**
Band **250.00**
Bean bag game, MIB **200.00**
Belt buckle, brass, 1937, Tiffany **45.00**
Book, 'Mickey Mouse & His Friends', Heath, 1939 . . . . . . **95.00**
'Mickey Mouse & His Horse Tanglefoot', McCay **45.00**
'Mickey Mouse Stories', 1934 . . . . **60.00**
'Mickey Mouse Story Book', McCay, 1931 . . . . **75.00**
'Mickey Mouse in Pigmy Land', soft cover **95.00**
'Mickey Never Fails', Heath, 1939 . . . . **95.00**

'Mickey Sees the USA' **95.00**
'Mickey Mouse Waddle Book' **450.00**
Bowl, Beetleware **15.00**
Bucket, 1930s, made in England, 6x7" dia **45.00**
Camera, ear is shutter, 1969 . . . . **145.00**
Camera, figure of head, Child Guidance **24.95**
Canasta junior w/tray, MIB, 1950 . . . . **25.00**
Candy mold, 1930s, 7" & 5", pair **95.00**
Candy tin, 1980, Christmas **10.00**
Card game, Old Maid, orig box, 1935 . . . . **45.00**
Clock, weight driven, Japan, 5x2½" **68.00**
Club button, pin-back, 1928, Disney, 1¼" **45.00**
Club cap, felt **10.00**
Club picture puzzle, Walt Disney **11.00**
Color print, 8¼x9¾" **35.00**
Cookie jar, ceramic, birthday **55.00**
Cufflinks, Hockok **18.00**
Doll, felt, Steiff 12" **850.00**
Doll, Gund **45.00**
Doll, pull string talks, 13" **48.00**
Drum, tin litho, Ohio Art, 6" **75.00**
Drummer, battery operated, Linemar **375.00**
Early china set, service for 4 w/servers **400.00**
Ferris wheel, Chein **175.00**
Figure, w/drum **35.00**
Figure, w/sax **35.00**
Figure, wooden, jointed, 1933, 8" **650.00**
Figures, playing horn & mandolin, pair **70.00**
Glass enclosed BB Puzzle, 'The Farmer' **135.00**
Globe map **85.00**
Hairbrush set, orig box, 1935 . . . . **75.00**
Inkograph fountain pen, 1930s **38.00**
Iron on appliques, orig package, 1946 . . . . **12.00**
Kaleidoscope, Mickey design **30.00**
Little books, 6 in half holder, 1934 . . . . **100.00**
Lunch box, tin school bus **10.00**
Magazine, Volume 1, 1935 . . . . **60.00**
Melody player & 6 rolls **75.00**
Mouseketeer girls costume, MIB **37.50**
Movie Jector, 2 rolls of film, 1935 . . . . **265.00**
Movie poster, Touchdown Mickey, black & white, 27x41" **16.00**
Movie stories, 1931, McKay Publisher **475.00**
Mug, bowl & plate set, w/pluto & Minnie **75.00**
Patrol car w/siren **35.00**
Pencil holder, 1930, Dixon, 6" **235.00**
Phonograph, MIB, 1950s **38.50**
Pillow, 1932, Vogue Needlecraft **285.00**
Playing cards, boxed, Walt Disney Enterprises **40.00**
Pocket watch, bicentennial, boxed **50.00**
Radio, 1950s, Mickey face in knob, 14" long **35.00**
Rocker, decal on seat **250.00**
Sand strainer & shovel, Ohio Art **45.00**
School clock, electric, arms clock hands, 10x15½" **90.00**
Soap statue, boxed, 1930, Castile Soap **40.00**
Soldier set, pop gun, soldiers, large **295.00**
Sparkler, tin **135.00**
Stuffed toy, early 1930s, 14" **250.00**
Suitcase w/wood blocks, Walt Disney, West Germany **18.00**
Tea set, blue w/white & excellent images **195.00**
Tin bank safe w/candy **15.00**
Tin jack-in-box, 1940 . . . . **37.00**
Top, tin **18.00**
Train, Mickey driving, 56x45" **100.00**
Typewriter, MIB **65.00**

Valentine, 1936	25.00
Watch, Bradley	50.00
Watch, oblong Ingersoll	200.00
Watch, rectangular Ingersoll, MIB, 1938	500.00
Watch, round Ingersoll	300.00
Water sprinkler bucket, 1930s, small	45.00
Wind-up, Mickey climbing ladder, MIB	24.50
Wind-up, Plastic, tail twirls, Marx	65.00
Wood train, 5 pc, 30″ long	110.00
Yoyo	22.00
Mickey Mouse & Donald Duck, china tea set, 23 pc, Marx	295.00
Fire engine, rubber, 4x6½″	175.00

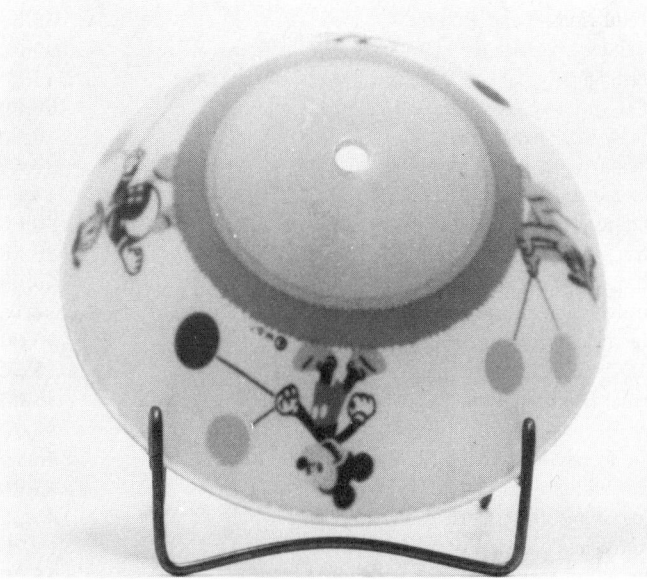

Shade, reverse painted, 8″	35.00
Mickey & Minnie Mouse, child's rug	120.00
Handcar, Lionel 1100	400.00
Noisemakers, cone shaped, heavy board	165.00
Salt & pepper, ceramic, Leed's China, 1940s	12.00
Mickey & Minnie & Pluto & Donald, soap, 4 bars w/decals	255.00
Bisque figure, Christman, Grolier	195.00
Milton Berle, car, MIBS	125.00
Minnie Mouse, Minnie knitting in rocking chair, Linemar	175.00
Bavarian cup & saucer, 1932, Walter E Disney	45.00
Book, 'The Pop-Up Minnie Mouse', Blue Ribbon, 1933	335.00
Cloth doll, WDP, VG, 6″	12.00
Cowgirl, 1936, Knicker-Bocker, 18″	450.00
Doll, clothed, 1930, 12″	130.00
Figure w/broom, early 1940s, Evan Shaw, 4½″	95.00
Figurine w/accordion	35.00
Figurine w/mandolin	35.00
Hand puppet, 11″	20.00
Plate, Minnie in rocker w/mice, 7½″	35.00
Tin wind-up in rocking chair, Linemar	195.00
Monkees, lunch box, thermos, VG	140.00
Moon Mullins, bisque figure, orig box	275.00
Mortimer, cardboard figure	15.00
Mutt & Jeff, brass stickpin, pair, 1930s	45.00
Figures, pair, 1911	175.00
Peanuts, lunch box, G	10.00
Peter Pan, china set, 23 pc, Marx	285.00
Pinky Lee, tin tray	25.00
Pinocchio, book, 'Adventures of Pinochio'	15.00
Book bank	48.00
Paint book	11.00

Puppet show	245.00
Record, 2 albums, 78 rpm	17.50
Pluto, clock, animated, Bayard	110.00
Figure, howling sitting position, 1939, Brayton Laguna	65.00
Hand puppet, 11″	15.00
Planter	16.00
Toy, Roll Me Over, MIB	150.00
Wood pop-up, Fisher Price	75.00
Popeye, animal cookies, orig box, 1930s	45.00
Ashtray, 12″	175.00
Bif Bat Paddle toy, 1929	48.00
Book, 'Popeye at the Holiday Parade', 1976	12.00
Card game, 1972, Milton Bradley	18.00
Cards, picture, set of 50, 3rd series, 1962	15.00
Costume, 5 pc, 1935, MIB	185.00
Figure, 1930, 3½″	55.00
Figure, rubber, color, 1972, B Cooper Inc, 6″	8.00
Juggler pocket game, 1929, King Features	40.00
Lamp w/orig shade, 1935, King Features	225.00
Lamp, rubber	45.00
Lantern, MIB	125.00
Pen & pencil, 1930s	75.00
Pencil & crayon box, Eagle Pencil Co	30.00
Pipe, ivory Meerschaum replica, MIB	45.00
Pipe Toss Game, MIB	25.00
Pirate Pistol, MIB, 1936	125.00
Puppet, early 1930s	125.00
Ring, flasher, color	3.50
Soap Suds, MIB	35.00
Tie clip, enameled character	40.00
Tin wind-up in the barrel	275.00
Tin wind-up on a house, 1930s	140.00
Viewmaster reel, 'Football Fans', 1959	12.00
Watch, 7 jewels, Swiss	175.00
Popeye & Sweet Pea, coloring book, 1970, Whitman	4.00
Popeye & Olive Oyl, salt & pepper shakers	45.00
Porky Pig, bisque figural bank	45.00
Red Ryder, target game, 1939	35.00
Richard Nixon, doll, signed	75.00
Watch, 'I'm No Crook', 1973, Honest Time	50.00
Robert Edward Perry, mug, 5″	85.00
Roy Rogers, alarm clock, animated, Ingraham	125.00
Badge, tin	7.00
Bandana, yellow, red	50.00
Big Little Book	8.00
Buttons	4.50
Camera	18.00
Cap gun, miniature	5.00
Cap gun, orig box, 7″	14.00
Flashlight, pocket size	15.00
Flashlight w/siren signal	25.00
Guitar w/case, all orig	125.00
Harmonica	15.00
Lantern, Ohio Art	10.00
Lucky horseshoe, hard rubber	12.00
Mug, figural	14.50
Pinback	5.00
Rodeo Ranch, Marx	75.00
Rodeo Sticker Fun	18.00
Tell-a-Tell book	5.00
Watch, Roy & Trigger on band, The Ingraham Co, Bristol	55.00
Watch, Roy & Trigger on face, 1950s, Ingraham	62.50
Sergeant Preston, police whistle	12.00
Seven Dwarfs, compo dolls, w/orig clothes, beards, hats, names	1,150.00

Perfume bottles, set of 7 .... **275.00**
Rubber figures, set of 7 .... **40.00**
Shirley Temple, birthday card **20.00**
Book of paper dolls, Saalfield **100.00**
Book, 'Little Colonel', 1935 .... **22.00**
Book, 'Little Star' **30.00**
Book, 'My Crayon Book' **28.00**
Book, 'Now I Am Eight', 1937, Sallfield, **26.00**
Book, 'Shirley Temple's Favorite Poems', Saalfield ... **12.00**
Book, 'Sing w/Shirley Temple', 1935 ..... **50.00**
Cereal bowl **40.00**
Creamer, cobalt, w/picture **35.00**
Figurine, saltstone, w/dog, 4½" **17.50**
Mug, cobalt w/picture **50.00**
Picture frame **7.50**
Pocket watch **150.00**
Postcard **12.00**
Teaset, plastic, white cameos of Shirley . **40.00**
Trading card **12.00**
Writing tablet **25.00**
Skippy, Beetleware bowl **8.00**
Sky King, Detecto Writer **45.00**
Smilin' Jack, puzzle, comic strip, 1943 .. **25.00**
Smitty, bisque figure, 3" **35.00**
Watch **125.00**
Sneezy, plaster figure, 6" **14.00**
Snow White, clock, house shape, dwarf head moves, W Germany **22.50**
Bisque figurine, fully marked **30.00**
Book, 1st, 1937 .... **225.00**
Dime bank **45.00**
Figurine, Goebel **125.00**
Soap figurine, some color, boxed **225.00**
Tin refrigerator, 15" **30.00**
Watch **25.00**
Snow White & Seven Dwarfs, candy tin ... **20.00**
Figurines, Goebel, Full Bee **2,450.00**
Glitter ornaments, orig box, German **275.00**
Miniature playing cards **95.00**
Musical top, Chein, 6½" **30.00**
Tea service for 4 .... **85.00**
Bisque figures, 1938, Japan **275.00**
Sparkle Plenty, figurine, miniature, painted **12.00**
Spiro Agnew, watch, orig band in metal container, Dirty Time Co **200.00**
Stan Musial, baseball glove in display box ... **75.00**
Superman, book, 'Last Son of Krypton', paperback, 1978 ... **5.00**
Cards, set of 50, color, 1968 .... **26.00**
Coloring book, 'Luther's Lost Island', 1975 ... **3.50**
Doll, wood ball joint & compo w/caps, 13½" **395.00**
Figure, hard plastic, Clark Kent, 4" ... **12.00**
Figure, pliable rubber, Mego, 5" **9.00**
Premium Club set, certificate, button, decoder **100.00**
Pressbook, 'Superman Campaign Book', 1943 ... **185.00**
Ring, Crusader **65.00**
Rollover Tank, 1940, Marx **165.00**
Tarzan, book, 'Tarzan of the Apes', Story Digest, Burroughs **13.00**
Book, 'The Return of Tarzan', 1915, Burroughs ... **26.00**
Cards, set of 50, 1966, Barratt Ltd **17.00**
Pressbook, 'Tarzan & Great River', Mike Henry ... **9.00**
Cards, set of 66, puzzle back, 1966 .... **27.00**
Texas Ranger, knife in case, 1973 ...... **95.00**
Three Little Pigs, book, 1933 .... **60.00**
Tea set, 10 pc **40.00**
Three Stooges, color cards, set **85.00**
Thumper, figure, 1940, American Pottery, Evan Shaw, Disney, Ca **30.00**

Planter **16.00**
Tiger Man, figurine, painted metal, 1934, Rappaport ... **18.00**
Tim Tyler, pop-up book **85.00**
Tom Corbet, atomic rifle, MIB **45.00**
Punch out book **18.00**
Space pistol, MIB **90.00**
Space rifle, MIB **95.00**
Sub machine gun, MIB **45.00**
Tom Mix, 2 in 1 compass, radio premium . **27.50**
Badge w/siren, Sheriff of Dobie County, 1930s ... **40.00**
Badge, Ranch Boss **60.00**
Big Little Book, 'Hoard of Montezuma' .. **14.00**
Bracelet w/charms, steer head, gun **35.00**
Brand ring, Secret Photo **28.50**
Decoder pins, set in orig mailer **95.00**
Flashlight, signal **45.00**
Film, MIB **60.00**
Lucky wrist band, 1936 .... **70.00**
Magnifying glass, radio premium **27.50**
Manual, Life of Tom Mix **45.00**
Sliding whistle ring **20.00**
Straight Shooter, Ralston **28.50**
Straight Shooter's Decoder & Life Story Book, Ralston ... **40.00**
Straight Shooter's Make-up Tin **7.75**
Watch fob, gold ore **30.00**
Tonto, arcade card, full figure **4.50**
Tweedle Dum, figurine **40.00**
Uncle Remus--Br'er Rabbit, pin ball game, marble shooter type . **35.00**
Uncle Wiggly, car **350.00**
Uncle Willie, bisque figure, orig box . **275.00**
Walter Johnson, baseball game **135.00**
Waltons, lunch box, VG **10.00**
Whimpy, rubber figure, 10" **65.00**
Squeaker **30.00**
Wilma, figurine, painted metal, 1934, Rappaport ... **25.00**
Winnie the Pooh, baby dish, 1946, Germany ... **65.00**
Game, MIB, 1933 .... **12.00**
Wizard of Oz, board game **25.00**
Wizard of Oz--Scarecrow, music box **24.50**
Woody Woodpecker, alarm clock, 'Woody's Cafe', animated ... **205.00**
Wyatt Earp, record **22.50**
Yellow Kid, die cut stick pin **50.00**
Zoro, hand puppet **20.00**
Pressbook, 'Zoro Rides Again', 1958 serial ... **20.00**
Watch **35.00**

Peters and Reed

John Peters and Adam Reed founded their pottery in Zanesville, Ohio, just before the turn of the century, using the local red clay to produce a variety of wares.

Moss Aztec, introduced about 1912, has an unglazed exterior with designs molded in high relief, and the recesses highlighted with a green wash. Only the interior is glazed to hold water. Pereco, named for Peters, Reed & Co., is glazed in semi-matt blue, maroon, or cream. Orange was also used very early, but such examples are rare. Shapes are simple with in-mold decoration, sometimes borrowed from the Moss Aztec line.

Wilse Blue is a line of high gloss medium blue with dark specks on simple shapes. Landsun, characterized by its soft matt multi-colors or blue and grey combinations, is decorated either by dripping or by hand brushing, in an effect sometimes called Flame or Herringbone. Chromal, in much the same colors as Landsun, may be decorated with a realistic scenic, or the swirling application of colors may merely suggest one.

Shadow ware is a glossy, multicolor drip over a harmonious base color.

When the base is black, the effect is often iridescent.

Perhaps the most desirable line is the brown high glaze art with the 'sprigged' type designs. Although research has uncoverd no positive proof, it generally accepted as having been made by Peters and Reed. It is interesting to note that many of the artistic shapes in this line are recognizable as those made by Weller, Roseville and other Zanesville area companies.

Other lines include Mirror Black, Persian and an unidentified line which collectors call Mottled Colors. In this high gloss line, the red clay body often shows through the splashed-on multicolors.

In 1922, the company became known as the Zane Pottery. Peters and Reed retired, and Harry McClelland became president. Charles Chilcote designed new lines, and production of many of the old lines continued. The body of the ware after 1922 was light in color.

Marks include the impressed logo or ink stamp Zaneware in a rectangle.

Chromal
Jardiniere, scenic, meadow & house on hill, #12, 6x7" **225.00**
  Lamp/vase, rainstorm over stylized hills, #2, 5½x4½" **150.00**
  Vase, impressionistic scene, predominately blue, 9x5" **135.00**
    Indistinct mountains & lake, good color, #5, 9x3½" **175.00**
    Scenic, field w/trees & fence, #6, 8x4" **145.00**
    Scenic, moon sinking into ocean, gulls, 8½x5½" **200.00**

    Scenic, trees, house, 8" **150.00**
    Scenic w/house, trees & fence, #5, 10x4" **195.00**
    Scenic w/islands & palm trees, #1, 5x4" **90.00**

High Glaze Brown Ware
Chalice, leaf band at top, 2 handles, 6x9" **85.00**
  Hair receiver, loop handle, front opening, garland **125.00**
  Jardiniere, grapes, leaves at top rim, 9x11" **225.00**
  Jug, decorated handle, lion's head, grape clusters, 6x5" **105.00**
    Man w/pipe, man drinking, 3x6" **35.00**
    Pinched waist, grapes, lion head, 5x4½" **96.00**
    Snail shape, cavaliers, flower under spout, 6x6x4" **120.00**
    Trapezoidal, 4 different scenes, 5x5½x4" **110.00**
  Mug, grapes & leaves decor, 5½x5" **65.00**
  Pitcher, 2 cavaliers, long leaf under spout, goldstone effect, 7" **125.00**
    3 ft, wreath decor, 5" **80.00**
  Tankard, swirl, Weller shape, grapes, leaves, 12" **165.00**
  Tea pot, nonfunctional, 3 ft, pumpkin shape, garlands, 6x5½" **85.00**
  Vase, 3 handles, 3 ft, cavaliers heads decor, 5" **100.00**
    Art Nouveau shape, fluted, Medusa heads, 6x4" **80.00**
    Double loop handles, florals, cherubs, 16x6" **185.00**
    Garland, w/handles, 14" **90.00**

    Garlands & lion's heads, 10½x6½" **125.00**
    Handled, 4 ft, George Washington, leaves, 8½x8" **225.00**
    Narrow neck, flared rim, garlands, lion's heads, 14" **225.00**
    Pinched cylinder, large flower, 12" **90.00**
    Squarish narrow base, 4 lions, 6x3½" **75.00**
    Wide base, narrow neck, flared rim, floral garlands, 12" .. **145.00**

Landsun
Bowl, blue, #24, 2½x8" **20.00**
Lamp base, bulbous bottom, chimney neck, grey-blue, 6½x7" .. **85.00**
Rose jar w/cover, Herringbone, #1, 4x3½" **35.00**
Vase, bulbous bottom, flared, tan/blue/green, 5x4¾" **35.00**
  Dripped on, #25, 11½x5" **90.00**
  Flaring shape, #43, 6x3½" **30.00**
  Herringbone, #40B, 7½x3" **35.00**
  Herringbone, #40C, 10x3½" **45.00**
  Multi-color drip over ivory, #24, 11½x5" **90.00**

Moss Aztec
Bowl, green, #602, 2½x5" **15.00**
Compote, classic design w/band of roses, 6½x7½" **85.00**
Hanging planter, stylized roses, #107, 4½x6" **40.00**
  Woven basket, #105, 5x5½" **55.00**
Jardiniere, dancing nymphs, 6x7½" **75.00**
Molded pine cones, branches, #404, 4x7½" **45.00**
Jardiniere & ped, grapes, leaves & vines, Ferrell, #232, 36"... **325.00**
Spittoon, stylized tulips, #320, 5½x7" **50.00**
Umbrella stand, band of grapes, vines, fluted bottom, 21x11" . **225.00**
Vase, blackberries, #172, 8x5" **45.00**
  Irises, #105, 15x5" **90.00**
  Nasturtiums decor, #160, 10x4" **40.00**
Wall plaque, Grecian women picking grapes, 8x5" **150.00**
Wall pocket, grapes, #160, 8x4" **60.00**
  Roses & branches, 8x5" **55.00**
  Roses & vines, gr wash, red clay, Zane **40.00**

Mottled colors
Bowl, yellow, black, blue, #625, 2½x7½" **25.00**
Vase, blk over green, matt, no red clay shows, #178, 9x4" **65.00**
  Flared top, yellows, black, #37, 8x5½" **55.00**
  Handled, blue, blk, yellow, red clay, fluted, 13½x9" **75.00**
  Multicolor splashes w/much clay showing, #650, 10" **85.00**
  Narrow neck, wide base, greens & yellow over lt blue, 10" ... **55.00**
  Octagon base, trefoil ft, blk & yellow on royal blue, 6x4" **65.00**
Wall pocket, cylinder front, loop handle, front opening, 7x3½". **50.00**

Pereco
Bookends, half columns w/laurel branches, tan w/green, #2, pr . **80.00**
Bookends, stylized floral in circle on sq panel, #1, pr **65.00**
Bowl, dk blue w/berries & leaves, 8½x3¼" **60.00**
  Flared sides, molded butterflies, 2x7" **22.00**
  Laurel branches, leaves & berries, #9, green, 3x8½" **65.00**
  Rare maroon glaze, #9, 3x8½" **85.00**
Jardiniere, classic form, cream w/green shadows, 3x4" **22.00**
Vase, corset shape, ivy in relief, matt green, 8x5½" **35.00**
  Moss Aztec blank, roses, dk blue, #175, 14x6" **125.00**
  Moss Aztec blank, ivy, white, 11x5" **85.00**
Wall pocket, Egyptian blank, stylized lotus leaves, #81 .... **50.00**

Shadow Ware
Lamp base, bright green over irid blk, #753, 8x6½" **85.00**
Pot, high glaze green w/blue drip, 5x5" **35.00**
Vase, blk & gr over bright med blue, 9x4" **50.00**
  Blue, carmel over tan, #772, 4x3½" **55.00**
  Blue, tan, green, over tan, #753, 7½x6" **65.00**
  Blue, yellows over tan, #754, Zane mk, 9½x5½" **65.00**
  Blues over tan, #774, 8x3½" **65.00**
  Bright gr dripping over irid blk, #768, 13x7" **140.00**
  Ivory, blk, yellow over bright blue, 9x5" **65.00**

Wilse Blue

Bowl, #656, Zane stamp, 4x6½" **30.00**
    Molded dragonflies, Zane stamp, 2x5" **24.00**
Bowl vase, #604, Zane stamp, 4x4½" **18.00**
Bud vase, 8x4" **25.00**
Candlesticks, twisted shaft, #630, Zane stamp, 10x5", pr **60.00**
Lamp base, factory made, #705, 11½x5" **85.00**
Vase, #605, 7x3" **22.00**
    #612, 9" **55.00**
    #650, Zane mk, 10" **60.00**
    Cylinder shape, Zane stamp, 4x3½" **18.00**
Wall pocket, faint molded floral decor near rim, 8x4"........ **40.00**

Pewabic

The Pewabic Pottery was formally established in Detroit, Michigan, in 1907, by Mary Chase Perry Stratton and Horace James Caulkins. The two had worked together since 1903, firing their ware in a small kiln Caulkins had designed especially for use by the dental trade. Always a small operation who relied upon basic equipment and the skill of the workers, they took pride in being commissioned for several important architectural tile installations.

Some of the early art ware was glazed a simple matt green; occasionally other colors were added, sometimes in combination, one over the other in a drip effect. Later, Stratton developed a lustrous crystalline glaze.

The body of the ware was highly fired and extreemly hard. Shapes were basic, and decorative modeling, if used at all, was in low relief. Mary Stratton kept the pottery open until her death in 1961. In 1968, it was purchased and reopened by the Michigan State University.

Several marks were used over the years: a triangle with Revelation Pottery (for a short time only); Pewabic with 5 maple leaves; and the impressed circle mark.

Ashtray, metallic glaze, ¾x4x5" **35.00**
Bowl, deep blue irid w/gold, Detroit, 4" **300.00**
Figurine, Madonna, red irid, 7" **90.00**

Planter, w/hand incised maccaws, 4½" **250.00**
Pot, green w/red, grey & green irid dripping, circle mk, 7x7" . **190.00**
Tile, Holy Ghost bird, gold luster, unmarked **50.00**
    Indian Maiden **135.00**
Vase, blue & silver metallic, 6x3" **150.00**
    Blue flambe, circular mk.......................... **450.00**
    Blue irid, 4x3" **175.00**
    Blue matt, 3x2".................................. **100.00**
    Blue metallic, 8x4" **300.00**
    Brown-red irid to brown glaze ground, circle mk, 3½x4" ... **250.00**
    Dk matt green, ribbed, mk: maple leaves, 14½x10" ... **575.00**
    Gold, green & ruby irid, mkd, 3" **275.00**

Heavy silver luster, bulbous w/cylinder neck section, 9½" ... **950.00**
Orange matt, 12x6" **350.00**
Red & silver metallic, 6x4" **175.00**

Pewter

Pewter is a metal alloy of tin combined with small amounts of lead, copper or brass. It has been used since the days of Ancient Rome, and was imported to this country from England by the American Colonists. Much of the Colonial pewter was melted during the American Revolution to make bullets, which accounts to some extent for the scarcity of examples from this period. Production of pewter in the United States reached its peak after the Revolution.

Basin, by Josiah Danforth, Middletown, Conn., 8" dia **155.00**
    Communion bowl, engraving, Richard Yates, London 1773, 9" **195.00**
    Samuel Hamlin, Hartford & Providence, 1767-1801, 7½" ... **250.00**
    Unmarked, polished, 7½" **150.00**
    Unmarked, polished, 10" **210.00**
    Unmarked, polished, interior is pitted, 6" dia............ **100.00**
Beaker, flared, set of 6, 2 tooled grooves at top & 3 at bottom . **65.00**
    With handle, Ashbill Griswold, 1830 .... **80.00**
Bottle holder, holds 4, Israel Trask...................... **75.00**
Bowl, ftd, engraved rim, 1709, 3x5" **70.00**
    Footed, outfolded rim, early 19th century, 2½x5¼" dia **165.00**
    With 2 handles, mk Abrahan, English, 6½".............. **125.00**
Box, w/cast feet, handles & lid, finial matches handle, 10" long **125.00**
Bucket, sgnd **49.00**
Candle garniture, 3 pc, 2-2 arm sticks & 1-3 arm candelabra, 1900 **715.00**
Candle sconces, pair, backpiece w/lion heads, scrolls, 11"... **1,010.00**
Candelabra, pair, branch-type, sgnd, 12" **49.00**
Candlestick, early, rare size, 5"......................... **185.00**
    Engraved, by Henry Hopper, New York City, 1842-47 ...... **400.00**
    Lady holding 2 candles, Art Nouveau, Berlin, 13" **395.00**
Push-up, pair, 8" **100.00**
    Push-up, pair, Meriden Brittania Co, 1867 .... **175.00**
Chalice, mk: FF, Rogers, Smith & Co, Hartford, Conn., 6¾ .. **105.00**
Chamberstick, heavy, sgnd, 7".......................... **35.00**
Charger, Austin, early 1800s **365.00**
    By Hamlin, Providence & Hartford, 1700s, 13½" **425.00**
    Engraved hunting scene, Cooke, 16½ **330.00**
    Marked, 12"....................................... **75.00**
Coffee pot, bulbous w/gooseneck, spout, by Thomas Smith, 1835 **60.00**
    Lighthouse, Hiram & Charles Yale..................... **400.00**
    Lighthouse, beaded & floral chased, Israel Trask, 13"...... **225.00**

On stand, w/leaf feet, leaf & grape finial, 18"............. **450.00**
Pear shaped, short spout, Roswell Gleason, 10"............ **190.00**
Pear shaped, lid w/grape decor, mid 1800s, 10"............ **70.00**

Pigeon-breasted, 4 ftd base, Roswell Bleason, 1822-1871 . . . **375.00**
Pouter pigeon shape, mk: Leonard, Reed & Barton, 10″ . . . **175.00**
Round, cone shaped top, mkd **70.00**
Tapered sides, goose neck, Dunham, 10½″ **230.00**
Dish, deep, by B & J Harbeson, Philadelphia & Lancaster, 11″ **650.00**
Deep, mk: Joseph Danforth, 1780, 13¼″ **600.00**
Eggleston, 13″ **750.00**
T & C, 8″ **135.00**
Feeding spoon, FH, 1800, 5″ long **50.00**
Flagon, Graves, Middletown, Conn., 1850 . . . . **500.00**
Molded base, cyma-scrolled handle, domed lid, American . . . **225.00**
Reed & Barton, 11½″ **175.00**
Sheldon & Feltman, Albany, N.Y., 1847 . . . . **425.00**
With Guernsey cover, inverted neck, applied handle, 1790 . . **200.00**
Funnel, w/ring, 5½″ **50.00**
Invalid feeder, pap boat, unmarked, 5″ long **65.00**
Ladle, 13″ **25.00**
Lamp, orig fluid burner w/brass spouts, Capen & Molineux, 8¾″ **185.00**
Leaf dish, handled, hand hammered, Nebrassoff, 17½x7½″ **45.00**
Measure, 1 litre, French **75.00**
Tankard, ½ pint, City Bristol, 4″ **30.00**
Tankard, ½ pt, w/lid, Imperial **235.00**
With handle, mk: GILL, English, 3″ **95.00**
With lid, Boulanget, 6″ **85.00**
Moneyclip, Art Nouveau **20.00**
Mug, child's, incised birds, handle w/man's head in relief, 3″ . . . **55.00**
Pint size, English **65.00**
With ear handle, unmarked, 4¼″ **70.00**
Yates, English, ½ pt **55.00**
Nut Dish, center sculptured bird handle, oval, 9½x7″ **35.00**
Pitcher, covered, 1 gallon, Daniel Curtiss, Albany, N.Y., 1822-1840 **750.00**
Embossed grapes & leaves, Art Nouveau lines, 10½x7″ dia . **125.00**
Gooseneck handle, sgnd, 7″ **42.00**
With lid, 11″ **90.00**
With lid, Stimpson, 1800s, 11½″ **285.00**
With side spout, engraved D, stamped Quart, BJ Grimes, 6½″ **80.00**
Plate, 9½″ **35.00**
American, Gleason, 10″ **110.00**
Bassett, late 1700s **475.00**
Boardman, 1800s, 11″ **365.00**
Bush, London, 1785, 8″ **90.00**
Calder, 1800s, 10½″ **380.00**
Danforth, early 1800s, 8″ **420.00**
Eagle, mk: Blakeslee Barns, Phila, American, 1812, 8″ **140.00**
Edgar Curtis, London, 1785, 8″ **100.00**
Engraved rim initials, pair, German, 8″ **95.00**
Engraved w/dove w/an olive branch, mk: SG, 9″ **115.00**
German, 9½″ **50.00**
Gershom Jones, Providence, 1774, #175, 8¼″ **375.00**
Hot water, Yates, 8½″ **80.00**
J Harbeson, Philadelphia, 1765-1800, 8″ **300.00**
Lacquered, Thomas D Boardman, Hartford, Conn., 1805-1850, 9″ **250.00**
Make: by Richard Danforth, Connecticut, 1700s, 8″ **100.00**
Nathaniel Austin, Charleston, Ma., 1763-1800, #4, 8½″ . . . **425.00**
Rolled lip, hammered booge, mk: Ashbil Hinchum **140.00**
Rolled rim, 3 series of marks, by Samuel Ellis, 1700s **150.00**
Rolled rim, hammered booge, mk: Robert Bush & Richard Perkins **85.00**
Roswell Bleason, Dorchester, Massachusetts, 9″ dia **155.00**
Scalloped rim, beaded edge, 10″ **55.00**
Shaped rim, mk: LB Smith, Boston, 14″ dia **95.00**
Smith & Feltman, Albany, 1847-48, 19½″ **185.00**
Smooth brim, mk: Townsen & Giffen, London, 1777, 8¾″ . . . **95.00**
Thomas Boardman, 9½″ **300.00**
Thomas S Derby, Middletown, Conn., 1812-1852, 8¾″ . . . **1,000.00**

Mark: B Barns Phila, 8″ **145.00**
Mark: Compton, Thomas & Townsend, Made in London, 7¾″ **70.00**
Mark: Townsend & Compton, London, 10¾″ **95.00**
Townsend, 9″ **70.00**
Wallace, 10″ **55.00**
Porringer, TD & SB, 5″ **360.00**
Crown handle, TD & SB, 5″ **435.00**
Crown handle, unmarked, 5″ **220.00**
Heavy, 2 handles, 6″ **70.00**
Turned rim, applied crown handle, mkd, I Green **22.00**
With cast handle, 2½″ dia **180.00**
Pot, tall, mk: G Richardson, polished, handle painted blk, 10½″ **270.00**
Pudding mold, cylinder, 1 qt, dated 1868 . . . . **140.00**
Salt & pepper, w/handles, pair, mk: RAY, 3″ **20.00**
Salt shaker, traces of engraving, Continental, 2½″ **15.00**
Shaker, ftd, 5″ **85.00**
Spoon, cast figural handle, 4½″ **12.00**
Curved handle, Wolstenholm, 1830, 11½″ **60.00**
Spoon mould, bronze die w/wood handles, w/spoon, 9″ **160.00**
Stein, sgnd **22.95**
Syrup, angel torchmark, tall **95.00**
Tankard, ale; circular base, bulbous, applied strap handle, 1800 **70.00**
Pint, w/English mk CB, 5″ **50.00**
With lid, 6″ **75.00**
Tea caddy, lacquer container, fine engraving, large **225.00**
Teapot, bulbous, Dixon & Smith, 6x12″ **225.00**
Bulbous, gooseneck spout, cyma handle, mkd, 8″ **70.00**
Bulbous, scrolled spout, finial hinged cover, 6½″ **150.00**
By Boardman & Hart w/x-quality mark **125.00**
By Israel Trask **200.00**
Copper bottom, TD & SB **100.00**
Cornish, by Dixon & Sons, 1842 . . . . **85.00**
Danforth, early 1800s **260.00**
Gleason, 1800s **185.00**
Griffin spout, sgnd **49.00**
High dome cover, molded spout, Porter, 1840s, 7″ **120.00**
Lighthouse, top & bottom bands, I Trask, 1807-1856, 11″ . . **695.00**
Low ftd base, wishbone handle, Bailey & Putnam, 1830s . . . **245.00**
Mark: G Richardson No C, polished, handle painted blk, 9¼″ **225.00**
Mark: Morey & Ober, Boston, polished handle painted black, 7¾″ **175.00**
Mark: R Gleason, Dorchester Massachusetts, polished, 7¼″ . **225.00**
Mark: Smith & Co **150.00**
Mark: w/bee on bottom, Austrian, 1800, 7″ **75.00**
Queen Anne, 6″ **130.00**
Short rectangularly chased body, hinged lid, by Dixon **50.00**
Tankard shape, G Richardson, 10″ **500.00**
Tea service, Reed & Barton, 6 pc **350.00**
Tobacco humidor, tulip shape, mk: Rose & Crown, 7½x5″ dia . **40.00**
Tray, oval, shaped edge, mkd, English, 8½x6½″ **125.00**
Trencher salts, crown mark, 1709, pr **190.00**
Urn, fish decoration, 2 handles, Kayserzinn **135.00**
Vase, sgnd, Orvit, 3 cut-out handles, overall gilding, 7″ **85.00**

Pfaltzgraff

The Pfaltzgraff family were making utilitarian stoneware early in the 1800s in York Co., Pa. Over the years, the products have evolved to keep pace with changing times. The early blue decorated salt glazed storage crocks and jugs eventually gave way to animal and poultry feeders, red clay flower pots and baking pans. During the 40s and 50s, mixing bowls, planters, ashtrays and cookie jars decorated in colorful glazes became popular variety store wares. Today, the company is best known for their dinnerware lines, produced since the early 40s. They have adopted the Pfaltzgraff family castle which still stands in Rhineland, Germany, as their trademark.

Bowl, fluted rim, matt blue, 5½x6″ **20.00**
Coffee server, w/lid, hi-gloss brown, beige froth at top **17.00**
Pitcher, creamy to hi-gloss brown, ice guard, 7½″ **13.00**
Vase, matt pumpkin to brown, shoulder handles, 8¼x7″ **40.00**
    Rose w/gr, 5¼″ **13.00**

Phoenix

The Phoenix Glass Company of Beaver County, Penn., began production in 1880. In the early years its main product was commercial glassware. It is best known today for the sculptured, cameo-like molded wares produced there from the 1930s to the 50s.

Bowl, lemons & foliage **75.00**
    Nasturtiums, green, 10″ **75.00**
    Nude maid, grey-blue w/frosted nude, 4x6x14″ **245.00**
    Nudes swimming, green to clear, 14″ **155.00**
    With underplate, nudes dancing, frosted lt green **65.00**
Dresser box, kidney shape, w/cover, fruit, peach color **50.00**
Lamp, berries, wht w/blue & green **90.00**
    Berries & foliage, orange & green, 10″ base, 21½″ **145.00**
    Larkspurs, 12″ base **250.00**
    Praying mantis, amber **240.00**
Planter, fruit & vines, 3 colors **70.00**
Puff box, florals, w/leaf finial, 4½x6¾″ **80.00**
Rosebowl, pink, 7″ **65.00**
Vase, acorns, orange & cream, 7″ **65.00**
    Birds, cream & gold, 10½x4″ **75.00**
    Birds, flowers, leaves & branches, 3 colors, 6″ **70.00**
    Birds, orange, green & white, 7″ **85.00**
    Birds, pillow shape, mint green w/wht irid, 10x12″ **145.00**
    Birds of paradise, gold & wht flowers, 7″ **100.00**
    Birds on cherry tree branch, cream w/gr, 10x9″ **180.00**
    Bluebell, pink w/wht irid florals, 7″ **70.00**
    Bluebell, white w/green & blue, 10½″ **95.00**
    Bluebell, yellow w/wht, 7″ **80.00**
    Catalonian, aqua, 12″ **40.00**
    Cattails & dragonflies, wht w/turquoise, 6″ **60.00**
    Cosmos flowers, wht on blue ground, 7½″ **85.00**
    Dogwood, purple w/white, 7″ **85.00**
    Dogwood, red, blue & brown decor, 11x8″ **190.00**

Dogwood, white, pink, 11″ **165.00**

Fern, frosted, 6″ **40.00**
Ferns, blue & clear, 7½″ **40.00**
Ferns, opal & ivory, 7½″ **60.00**
Florals, green, 7″ **120.00**
Florals, tan & wht, 7½x6½″ **80.00**
Florals, tapered body, multi colors, 12½″ **110.00**
Florals, waisted shape, frost on aqua, 7½″ **120.00**
Florals, yellow w/wht, 11″ **140.00**
Florals & birds, squared curving shape, 6½″ **100.00**
Florals & birds, white w/purple, pink & blue, 6½″ **130.00**
Flowers, rare ice finish, blue & clear, 11″ **100.00**
Foxglove, wht w/pink, green, 10½x5″ **260.00**
Geese, brown, ovoid, 9″ **145.00**
Geese, dark blue w/wht, sgnd, 9″ **145.00**
Geese, oval, white & frosted, 9½″ **95.00**
Geese, ovoid, red, 9¼″ **165.00**
Geese, pillow shape, 12x9½″ **145.00**
Goldfish, milk glass **100.00**
Grasshopper, white w/gold **135.00**
Hummingbird, green, 6″ **40.00**
Hummingbird, turquoise & cream, 6″ **60.00**
Leaves frame small florals, custard, 7″ **165.00**

Love Birds, 10″ **100.00**
Madonna head in relief, w/orig label, blue, 10″ **230.00**
Nudes, frolicking, brown w/tan & wht nudes, 11½″ **375.00**
Nudes, frolicking, pink w/frosted **175.00**
Pan w/frolicking nudes, pink & blue on wht, 11½″ **265.00**
Philodendron, blue ground, 11″ circumference **160.00**
Profile bust of lady, wht on 2 shades of blue **225.00**
Roses, leaves, wht w/purple & blue, 12″ **100.00**
Seagulls, aqua on cream, 10½x10″ **225.00**
Starflower, pink **95.00**
Trumpet vine, custard w/blue, 10½″ **100.00**
Wild rose, lt blue **115.00**

Phoenix Bird

Blue and white Phoenix Bird china has been produced by various Japanese potteries from the early 1900s. With slight variations the design features the Japanese bird of paradise and scroll-like vines of Kara-Kusa, or Chinese grass. Although some of the earlier ware is unmarked, the majority is marked in some fashion. More than 40 different stamps have been reported, with 'Made in Japan' the one most often found. Newer items, if

marked at all, carry a paper label. Compared to the older ware, the coloring of the new is whiter and the blue more harsh; the design is sparse, with more ground area showing. Although collectors buy even 'new' pieces, the older is of course more highly prized and valued.

Bowl, 2¼x4½"	12.50
Ftd, w/cover, blown-out mold	35.00
Rice	15.00
Round, large, 7½"	30.00
With handles, oval, 7"	28.00
Butter, tub w/liner	55.00
Butter pats	10.00
Creamer & sugar, w/lid, M in gr wreath	42.00
Cup & saucer, demitasse, Nippon Rising Sun	15.00

Japan, reg	12.00
Dish, fruit; blue flowers & leaves decor, mkd wreath & M, 6¼".	15.00
Egg cup	12.00
Large, 3½"	18.00
Ginger jar, 5½"	32.50
Covered, 7"	50.00
Hot plate	45.00
Nut set, melon shaped ftd master bowl, 5 matching nut bowls	45.00
Pitcher, 3"	10.00
Milk, 6¼"	30.00
Plate, 6"	7.00
Leaf shaped, 7¼"	20.00
Leaf shaped, 10" dia	35.00
Shaker, small, round	10.00
Soup, flat, 7"	12.00
Teapot, squatty shape, holds 6 cups, covered	50.00
Tumbler	20.00
Tumbler, mkd Old Blue Flower, Japan	10.00
Tureen, w/cover, 7½"	48.00

Phonographs

The phonograph, invented by Thomas Edison in 1877, was later manufactured by various companies who incorporated their own variations with the original Edison model. Those with the large morning glory horns are especially desirable.

Amberola 75	425.00
Beam, AC motor, acoustical sound	80.00

Billard Echophone	500.00
Burns Pollack, combination lamp & phonograph	1,250.00
Busy Bee, cylinder	325.00
Disc machine	425.00
Calois Cylinder Machine, Gem	775.00
Cameraphone	150.00
Columbia A	350.00
AG, concert, 5"	1,200.00
AH, front mount, black horn w/brass bell	650.00
AN	375.00
B, Eagle	325.00
BD, w/mahogany wood horn	950.00
BD, w/nickel horn	650.00
BG, w/nickel horn	600.00
BGT, back mount	1,250.00
BH, disc phono w/wood horn	800.00
BK	350.00
BKT, back mount	525.00
BV	375.00
Grafanola	6,000.00
Grafanola Deluxe, table model, mahogany case	4,000.00
Grafanola Regent, desk style	600.00
Gramaphone, table model, plays cylinders, 1900	1,500.00
Home Grand, 5"cylinders	2,200.00
Crown Cylinder Machine	400.00
Edison, #30	250.00
#70	250.00
Amberola, large table model, oak	450.00
Amberola 30	300.00
Amberola DX	350.00
BC	350.00
Concert, G, 5", w/drawer, brass horn w/20" bell & stand	2,500.00
Concert, Suitcase, 5" cylinder	1,800.00
D, Model K reproducer, 2 pc horn, cylinder phono	700.00
Gem, key wind	400.00
Home, 2 minute	350.00
Home, Cylinder	450.00
Home, Cylinder, floor stand, brass horn	450.00
Home, with H reproducer, black horn w/brass bell	350.00
Home, wood signet horn	1,100.00
Home A	425.00
Home B	375.00
Long play flat disc, low boy case, 2 reproducers	600.00
Opera, cylinder phono, w/mahogany horn, 1912	4,000.00
Standard, 19" horn	350.00
Standard, 30" brass horn	450.00
Standard, cylinder player, morning glory horn	435.00
Standard w/Cygnet	565.00
Standard X	325.00
Suitcase Home	600.00
Talking wax doll, crank operated	4,800.00
Triumph	550.00
Triumph, recorder w/gooseneck horn, plays cylinder	800.00
Triumph A	750.00
Class M, electric, #4782 w/NA Phonograph Co plaque	1,800.00
Geib, portable wind-up	85.00
Gramaphone, American Berliner, all orig	2,200.00
Graphophone BC	875.00
Hexaphone, Union I	4,500.00
Union II	4,250.00
Ideal, cylinder & disc	6,500.00
Lambertphone, model Q	385.00
Lioret Cylinder Machine	6,000.00
Maroon Gem	750.00

Mignonphone **150.00**
Mikkiphone **175.00**
Multiphone, coin op, cylinder player, plain tall case **10,000.00**
Panola, portable wind-up **135.00**
Pathe Aiglon, cylinder **375.00**
Pathe Black Diamond, cylinder **375.00**
Pathe Coin-op **800.00**
Pathe Concert, disc **1,200.00**
Pathe duplex cylinder machine **2,000.00**
Phonix I **400.00**
RCA Victor, 45 rpm, model 45EY2 . . . . **60.00**
Rosenfield, coin operated **3,700.00**
Small Talk O Phone, disc phono **350.00**
Standard Talking Machine Co, Model A, outside horn, mint decal **325.00**
Victor I **500.00**
Victor II, w/large black horn, orig **625.00**
Victor II, w/large wood horn **850.00**
Victor III, Monarch case **550.00**
Victor III, w/large black horn, orig **625.00**
Victor III, w/large wood horn **1,300.00**
Victor IV **625.00**
Victor V, brass bell horn **750.00**
Victor V, large black horn w/dog decal **900.00**
Victor V, large oak horn **1,800.00**
Victor VI, fibroid horn **2,000.00**
Victor VI, mahogany horn, ex orig **2,200.00**
Victor VV-VI, internal horn, oak case **200.00**
Victor D, restored **1,200.00**
Victor E, front mount **650.00**
Victor E, rear mount **525.00**
Victor Electrola Coin-op **650.00**
Victrola, 78 rpm, windup in dovetailed mahogany case, 11" sq . **50.00**
Victrola Orthophonic, #1050, ornate walnut case **1,250.00**
Victrola XVI, mahogany cabinet w/album storage, 1915, 24x24x50" **750.00**

Photographica

Photographic collectibles include not only the cameras and equipment used to 'freeze' special moments in time, but also the photographic images produced by a great variety of processes that have evolved since the Daguerrean era of the mid-1800s.

Among the earliest cameras was the box-like view camera with a sliding lens. The lens slid in and out of a protective wooden 'drawer' which was replaced on later models with leather bellows. These were the fore-runners of the multi-lens cameras developed in the late 1870s, which were capable of recording many small portraits on a single plate. Double lens cameras produced stereo images which, when veiwed through a device called a stereoscope, achieved a 3-dimensional effect. In 1888, George Eastman introduced his box camera, the first to utilize roll film. This greatly simplified the process, making it possible for the amateur to enjoy photography as a hobby. Detective cameras, those disguised as books, handbags, etc., are among the most sought after by todays collectors.

Many processes have been used to produce photographic images: daguerrotypes---the most valued examples are the full plate which measures 6½x8½"; ambrotypes, produced by an early wet-plate process whereby a faint negative image on glass is seen as positive when held against a dark background; and tintypes, contemporaries to ambrotypes, but produced on japaned iron, and not as easily damaged.

Other collectible images include cartes de visites, known as CDVs, which are portraits printed on paper, and produced in quantity. The CDV fad of the 1800s enticed the famous and the unknown alike to pose for these cards, which were circulated among the public to the exent that they became known as 'publics'. When the popularity of CDVs began to wane, a new fascination developed for the cabinet photo, a larger version measuring about 4½x6½".

Stereo cards, photos viewed through a device called a stereoscope, are another popular collectible. The glass stereo plates of the mid-1800s and photo prints produced in the darkroom are among the most valued.

Album; celluloid front cover, w/Teddy Roosevelt **95.00**
   Gold clasp, gr velvet, floral design on page corners **35.00**
   Holds 4 small tintypes per page, 24 pgs, full **25.00**
   Maroon velvet **35.00**
   Musical, w/drawer **200.00**
   Ornate leather, 26 cartes de visite, double brass clasps, old . . **40.00**

Portrait, scenic, velvet back, 1890, 13x10" **80.00**
Silver plated **85.00**
Upright on stand, 30 photo openings, Victorian lady portrait . **80.00**
With music box, leather **105.00**
With music box, litho girl w/harp **185.00**
With stand, velvet plush w/beveled mirror, 1890s **95.00**
Album photo; armed batallion band, Boston, orig mount, 8x10" **100.00**
   Blackface minstrels, sgnd Chas A & Ceree L Buzzell, 1880 . **100.00**

German Lancers, w/orig card mount, 11x14½" **150.00**
Military band, 1885, wood frame, 9x6" **30.00**
Ambrotype; ½ plate, Niagara Falls, taken from Babbitt's Point . **70.00**
   ½ plate, young dandy **30.00**
   ¼ plate, boy w/black doll, half case **70.00**
   6th plate, gentlemen holding adze, dressed in suspenders **50.00**
     Girl w/cat, tinted **90.00**
     Man w/dog, tinted, full case **60.00**
     Men, well dressed on horse-drawn carriage, 1855 . . . . **40.00**
     Woman in fancy dress w/lace collar, 1854 . . . . **70.00**
   9th plate, child w/drum & dog, tinted, brass matt, preserver . . **38.00**

House, 2-story w/white wood fence, 1857 . . . . **30.00**
Man wearing glasses **22.00**
Matt reads: Union Now & Forever, gutta percha case **50.00**
Middle-aged man, 1860 . . . . **15.00**
Full plate, Niagara Falls w/people & buildings, gilt frame . . **1,250.00**
Book, Around the World With a Camera, WWI Rockwell illus . . **35.00**
Cabinet photo; 2 Salvation Army women in uniform **12.00**
Amelia Earhart w/Mayor Burke, airplane **125.00**
Baseball player **18.00**
Boy w/rocking horse **7.50**
Cape Cod beach houses & children playing, by Nickerson, 1880s **12.00**
Carnival photographer, ferris wheel, 1800 . . . . **50.00**
Chauncey Moorlano & wife, each weighs over 525 lbs, by Wendt **10.00**
Child in sled **16.00**
Circus scene, outdoors, monkey on handcart, by Drum **25.00**
Clergyman **7.50**
DW Griffith, moviemaker, 2½x4″ **85.00**
Denver, Colorado, taken from Union Depot, by WH Jackson . **20.00**
Execution, Trenton, Mo., 1893 . . . . **35.00**
Fannie Johnson w/high boots & whip, by Newsboy **17.50**
Fatal drop, 4½x6½″ **35.00**
General Grant & family, 1885 . . . . **20.00**
General Kilpatrick **20.00**
General Logan w/civilian clothes **15.00**
General Rush **20.00**
General Sheridan **13.00**
Girl on horse led by silk hatted man, by Rushworth **6.00**
Horses, buggies & riders **7.50**
Indian woman wrapped in blanket, EP Butler, Nevada Art Gallery **35.00**
John L Sullivan, waist up, 1890 . . . . **15.00**
Last Prayer **35.00**
Lillian Russell, back view **9.00**
Man, camera, cigar **40.00**
Man w/rifle, sitting w/dog at feet **8.00**
Men in front of clothing store **19.50**
Musical McGibeny family, 2 poses, both **21.00**
Negro magician w/top hat & wand **15.00**
Negro in full evening dress w/wife & child **15.00**
Negro w/mandolin, 1900 . . . . **15.00**
Photo buff, Camp Quiet **40.00**
Policeman w/badge, belt buckle, billy club & hat **9.00**
Prince & Princess Henry of Prussia **8.00**
Red Cross worker **10.00**
Rhode Island Militia soldier, lst Sergeant, 1880-90 . . . . **8.50**
Small child w/big horn & violin **15.00**
Soldier in kepi, uniform, knapsack, rifle, 1880 . . . . **10.00**
Tatooed man, 2 poses, both **46.50**
Three midgets **18.00**
Trick shot **7.00**
Two giants **11.00**
William Gladstone **10.00**
Camera; 8mm Revere model 85 w/case **150.00**
8mm Revere model K66 w/case **285.00**
Agfansco Folding, 1913, 2½x4¼″ pictures **14.95**
Ansco Memo Wooden Model, wood tropical model, 1920 . . . **330.00**
Ansco Vest Pocket #2, 8 exposure, #120, 1916 . . . . **35.00**
Antique Oak Detective, brass fittings, 1890 . . . . **800.00**
Argoflex, Argus, TLR of 7 different models, 1950s, #620 . . . . **16.50**
Argus C3, Brick body, 35 mm, Cinar f3.5 anastigmat rangefinder **45.00**
Autographic Folding Kodak, #2-A, #A-116 film, 1917 . . . . . . **14.95**
#A-116 film, 1921 . . . . **14.95**
Autographic Kodak, Jr, 1921 . . . . **80.00**
Bessamatic, SLR, Voightlander, 35mm, w/various lenses, 1960s **80.00**
Blair Century Hawk-Eye, black wooden bed, 7x9″ folder, 1900 **300.00**

Brilliant, TLR, Voightlander, #120, 1933 . . . . **40.00**
Brownie #2, in orig box showing orig Brownie, 1901 . . . . **85.00**
Bullard, folding plate, wood interior, red bellows, 4x5″ plates . **65.00**
Buster Brown, in orig box, Anthony & Scovill Co **225.00**
Cherry wood, red bellows, orig case, 5x7″ photo, 1907 . . . . . **120.00**
Circo 35, Graflex 35mm, split image rangefinder, 1955 . . . . **25.00**
Conley, cherry wood, 5x7″ photos, red bellows, 1907 pat . . . **120.00**
Conley, mahogany, red bellows, tripod, case, film holders, 4x5″ **145.00**
Contax, Zeiss, Model D, German, 1932 . . . . **110.00**
Contax, Zeiss, Model I, German **565.00**
Contax, Zeiss, Model II, German, 1932 . . . . **185.00**
Contax, Zeiss, Model III, German, 1932 . . . . **235.00**
Contax, Zeiss, Model S, German, 1932 . . . . **140.00**
Contessa Nettel Tropical, tripod & extra plate pack, 1920 . . **725.00**
Dejur, TLR, Dejur-Amsco, #120, Models 10, 20 or 400, 1952 **35.00**
Detrolia 400, Wollensak lens, 35mm rangefinder, 1939 . . . . . **275.00**
Edixa Stereo, Wirgin, 35mm, 1950 . . . . **90.00**
Edixa Stereo, Wirgin, Model II, 35mm, 1954 . . . . **110.00**
Edixa Stereo, Wirgin, Model III, 35mm, 1955 . . . . **110.00**
Ensignette by Houghtons, London, brass case, folds, 1907 . . . **45.00**
Exakta, Ihagee trapezoidal, 35mm, Model VX **92.00**
Exakta, Ihagee, Kine, trapezoidal shape, 35mm, 1936 . . . . . **140.00**
Exakta, Thagee, Model 66, trapezoidal, 35mm **225.00**
Exakta, Thagee, Model H, trapezoidal, 35mm **125.00**
Exakta, Thagee, Model B, trapezoidal, 35mm **130.00**
Exakta, Thagee, Model C, trapezoidal, 35mm **110.00**
Exakta, Thagee, Model I, trapezoidal, 35mm **72.00**
Exakta, Thagee, Model II, trapezoidal, 35mm **58.00**
Exakta, Thagee, Model V, trapezoidal, 35mm **60.00**
Expo Watch Camera, orig carton w/cassette, 1905 . . . . **180.00**
Foth Derby, German, 16 exposure, #127, 1930s, Model I . . . **52.00**
Foth Derby, German, 16 exposure, #127, 1930s, Model II . . . **72.00**
Fotron, Triad, 'pictures in dark w/out flashbulbs', 1966 . . . . . **55.00**
Goldeck, Germany, 16mm film, 30 exposure, 10x14mm negatives **140.00**
Graflex, Series D, w/bag magazine **145.00**
Graphic 35 Electric, German, for Graflex, 35mm, 1959 . . . . . **170.00**
Isolette, Agfa, #120, Model II or I **38.00**
Isolette, Agfa, #120, Model III **32.00**
Kewpie, Conley, box #120, Model #2 . . . . **30.00**
Kewpie, Conley, box #120, Model #2A **19.00**
Kewpie, Conley, box #120, Model #3 . . . . **32.00**
Kewpie, Conley, box#120, Model #3A **38.00**
Keystone 8mm K32 w/case **55.00**
Kodak #1-A, #616 film, 1920, 2½x4¼ photos **15.00**
Kodak #2 string set w/case **450.00**
Kodak #3-A, folding, postcard size pictures, 1913 . . . . **14.95**
Kodak Bulls-Eye, #1, leather box, wood interior, 1896 . . . . . . **50.00**
Kodak Bulls-Eye #2, #103 film, 1896-1913 . . . . **5.00**
Kodak Bulls-Eye #3, #124 film, 1908-1913 . . . . **58.00**
Kodak Bulls-Eye #4, #103 film, 1896-1904 . . . . **72.00**
Kodak Duraflex, LV w/case & flash **35.00**
Kodak Panoram #1, swinging lens, #105 film, 1900-14 . . . . . **210.00**
Kodak Panoram #3A, swinging lens, #122 film, 1926-28 . . . . **220.00**
Kodak Panoram #4, swinging lens **345.00**
Kodak Panoram #4D, 1900-07 . . . . **165.00**
Kodak Screen Focus, swinging back, 1905 . . . . **245.00**
Kodak Stereo, 35mm, 1954-59 . . . . **95.00**
Kodak Tourist II, #628, Kodet lens, 1951-58 . . . . **30.00**
Kodak Tourist II, #620, Anaston lens, 1951-58 . . . . **55.00**
Kolibri, Zeiss, #127, half frame setup, pullout lensboard, 1930 **215.00**
Le Physiographe Stereo Binocular Camera, 1896 . . . . **4,000.00**
Linex, Lionel, 16mm, plastic body, early 1950s **165.00**
Linex stereo w/flash **85.00**
Mandelette, Chicago Ferrotype, 2¼x3½″ on direct positive paper **160.00**

Mentor, Goltz & Greutmann, folding reflex, 1915-30	**210.00**
Pathex Motion Picture w/orig leather case & instructions	**57.00**
Perfex 44, 35mm rangefinder, 1950s	**98.00**
Primo B Rochester optical, 4x5″ red bellows	**110.00**
RD Gray, forerunner of Stirn Concealed Vest Camera, 1885	**2,000.00**
Ralls, Chicago, 1937, orig box, sold thru Krogers	**7.50**
Rexoette, Burke & James, box type, 6x9cm negative, roll film, 1910	**20.00**
Rouch Eureka Detective, mahogany & leather, English, 1888	**1,000.00**
Rover Detective, mahogany, Lancaster, England, 1892	**875.00**
Scovill Detective Waterbury, black wood box, 5x7″ plate, 1888	**635.00**
Scovill Stereo, mahogany & brass, accordian septum	**600.00**
Seneca, pocket #29, in case w/wood slides, 1905	**75.00**
Soroco, Dry Plate w/darkroom outfit, 1901	**115.00**
Tom Thumb Camera Radio, Automatic Radio Mfg Co, 1948	**120.00**
Vest Pocket Folding Kodak, #127 film, 1913	**9.95**
Vitessa, Voightlander, 35mm, coupled rangefinder, 1950	**98.00**
Vitessa, Voightlander, Model N, 35mm, changeable lenses, 1954	**110.00**
Vitessa, Voightlander, Model T, 33mm, fs.8 lens	**110.00**
Wollensack, w/tripods, glass slides, orig case, 1908, 5x7″	**175.00**
Wollensak portrait, dated 1908, 5x7″, w/tripods & case	**325.00**
Zeiss-Ikon Ikoflex, orig leather case	**43.00**
Carte De Visite; Abraham Lincoln, Anthony print, Brady negative	**38.00**
Alexander Dumas	**15.00**
Anna Swan, Nova Scotia Giant Girl, Bailey & Silver	**9.50**
Bear's den, zoo	**32.00**
Black woman in costume, Charles Eisenmann	**10.00**
Civil War soldier	**5.00**
Fat lady, Barnum exhibit, 1863 tax stamp on back, E & HT Anthony	**9.50**
Fat lady from sideshow, Case & Getchell, 1870	**10.00**
Gen Daniel Butterfield, Brady 1800s	**50.00**
Gen Franz Sigel, 1800s	**55.00**
Gen George B McClellan, Fredricks, 1800s	**90.00**
Gen Gilmore	**30.00**
Gen Grant, full length, seated, 1865	**10.00**
Gen Kilpatrick	**15.00**
Gen Rosecrans	**15.00**
Gen Scott	**15.00**
Gen Sherman, signed	**100.00**
Giant, wearing a CW uniform & helmet, holding a sword	**12.00**
Girls holding doll, 2	**7.50**
James Lowell	**10.00**
James Murphy, giant boy, 1863, E & HT Anthony	**9.50**
Lincoln, w/signature	**10.00**
Lincoln in relief oval, w/eagle & flags	**10.00**
Louis Napoleon w/son & wife picture, 1860	**7.50**
Mary Todd Lincoln, by Brady	**80.00**
Nathaniel P Banks, by Brady, 1800s	**60.00**
Pauline Cushman	**7.00**
Sailboat Atlantis, North, 1879	**50.00**
Schyler Colfax	**14.50**
Surveyor w/transit, tripod, target, European	**15.00**
Tom Thumb, wife & child	**8.50**
Union Generals, Phil Sheridan, by Brady, autographed	**150.00**
William Cullen Bryant	**10.00**
Daguerreotype; ½ plate, 2 young men Upton, gutta percha frame	**1,000.00**
½ plate, children, posed in front of school w/teacher	**350.00**
Gentleman, by Augustus Washington, stamped	**400.00**
Young dandy in top hat	**85.00**
¼ plate, boy w/white hat, blue ribbon	**90.00**
Meeting house	**390.00**
Woman in shawl, by Fredricks, tinted	**155.00**
6th plate, 2 girls, colorful plaid dresses, in case	**150.00**
2 men, matt sgnd Anson	**32.00**
Boy, 12 years old seated at table, 1850	**30.00**

Boy with dog	**175.00**
Boy with riding crop & hat	**80.00**
Child with doll, tinted	**165.00**
Engraving, cherubs, flowers	**80.00**
Girl, 1851, star burst vignette	**275.00**
Man in tux, velvet collar, tinted, ½ case	**70.00**
Musician holding clarinet & rolled sheet of paper	**165.00**
New England factory, 1850	**750.00**
Old woman in blk dress & wht lace bonnet	**25.00**
Woman with dog	**165.00**
9th plate, Young woman, red plaid skirt, by Weston, ½ case	**60.00**
Brooch, open face, gent	**145.00**
Children, fourth plate, MH Root, Philadelphia	**90.00**
Edgar Allen Poe, 1848	**35,000.00**
Man, hair bracelet	**145.00**
Oversize half plate, man, wife, fancy wood frame	**300.00**

With case, 3x2″	**35.00**
Edward Curtis, photogravure; Corn Mountain, Zuni, 6x8½″	**60.00**
Indian: Star Morning, 6x8½″	**75.00**
The Monastery & Church at Zuni, 6x8½″	**60.00**
The Pima Woman	**500.00**
The Vanishing Race	**3,000.00**
The Yuma	**600.00**
Edward Weston; Cypress Point	**3,800.00**
Point Lobos	**4,000.00**
Silver print, Onion Halved	**5,500.00**
Folder w/12 photos Yellowstone, Haynes Studio, color	**100.00**
Glass slide; Capitol at Richmond w/Union Flag	**8.00**
Skagway Alaska, 1900, 3¼x4″	**4.00**
Take Me Up in an Airship, girl, boy & plane in color	**5.00**
Magic lantern; brass & tin, w/burner, wood base	**75.00**
Brass w/wood base, ornate lens bracket	**90.00**
Delineascope/Spencer Model D36053	**100.00**
Keystone, Radioptocin	**60.00**
Laterna Magica, duplex brass burner, Gloria EP w/slides	**250.00**
Tin, deer decoration, 8″	**20.00**
Tin w/copper clawfeet, burner w/double wick, MIB	**150.00**
Magic lantern slides, 12, orig wooden box, sgnd EP, Germany	**75.00**
48, American History, 16 color, w/box	**50.00**
70, Social Studies, American History	**70.00**
79, b&w, box, Egypt, Palestine, Africa	**80.00**
87, b&w, Orient, w/box, 1920	**100.00**
Movie set, The Hollywood, by Montgomery Ward, w/reel WWI action	**65.00**
Neck brace, cast iron daguerrean, ornate, rare	**350.00**
Photo; booklet, San Francisco fire, 10 pgs, 1906, 6x7″	**5.00**
Buffalo Bill, sgnd	**25.00**
Circus	**4.00**
FDR, addressing 74th Congress, matted & framed, 14x25″	**35.00**

Firemen, 9, wearing firemen outfits, WFD initials on hat **9.50**
In Memorian, Lincoln, Garfield & McKinley, 1901, 16x20" . . . **70.00**
Jefferson, dated Oct 10, 1896 . . . . **20.00**
Long haired woman **10.00**
Negro family, 4¼x6½" **20.00**
Tattooed woman **12.00**
The Burning City, San Francisco, 10 AM, April 18, 1906, 52x9" **35.00**
Weight lifter, 500 lbs in hands, Jos Barton, 4½x6" **15.00**
WWI troopship, USS Maui, framed, 12x18" **45.00**
Projector; 8mm Ampro #A8 w/case **400.00**
Delineascope, Model D, Spencer Lens Co, 10½x20x5¾" case **100.00**
Kodascope, Model #125, 8mm, 1928, EX **30.00**
Radiopticon Postcard, w/orig Mazda bulbs **50.00**
Slide, Bausch & Laumb, w/wood slide holder, 1911 . . . . . . **165.00**
Stereopticon, Keystone, w/light & cards **100.00**
Western Electric, theater, 1928 . . . . **750.00**
Pyrographhic Heart, Flemish Art Co, tintype insert, 3" **75.00**
Ring, gold filled, w/tintype of lady **275.00**
Sepia print, 100 Sioux Indians dressed in tribal costumes, 7x43" **47.50**
Stereo book; contains metal viewer, 36 views of Germany **70.00**
Le Stereo Bijou, souvenir, w/views **95.00**
Tintype; ½ plate, outdoor scene w/large group of people **18.00**
¼ plate, boxers, in dueling stance **16.50**
   Boy w/milk pail, tinted **20.00**
   Civil War officer in kepi **55.00**
   Couple in car, open car **16.50**
   Grinning dog, humorous, color **32.00**
   Lady Biker, paper matt **22.00**
   Man on donkey **15.00**
   Man, matt sgnd AM Allen **28.00**
¾ plate, peddler w/dog on wagon, 'GS Rollins' on wagon **75.00**
6th plate, 4 men w/bicycles, 1870-75 . . . . **9.50**
   Bikers, 2 men **28.00**
   Bisque head doll **60.00**
   Black women, bust shot **16.50**
   Candian soldier, full length, full dress, 1870 . . . . **15.00**
   Cat, brass matt & preserver **38.00**
   Civil War soldier **20.00**
   Girl in comic costume **16.50**
   Man w/bicycle, 1890 . . . . **40.00**
   Militia bandsman, 4 men, full length, wearing kepis . . . **15.00**
   Occupational: printers in aprons & hats, 1870 . . . . **5.00**
   Parrot, woman, child, bird, brass matt & preserved **30.00**
   Soldier in kepi, tinted **45.00**
   Soldier, blue uniform, shako w/feather plum **22.00**
   Uniformed soldier w/wife, tinted **45.00**
   Vase of flowers, color **65.00**
9th plate, black boy, in case **18.00**
Boy on horseback, 5x7" **38.00**
Boy w/wagon, 2½x3½" **14.00**
Little boy on stool wearing kepi hat **15.00**
Little girl standing by lg wooden wheeled tricycle **20.00**
Peddler wagon, dog w/peddler, GS Rollins & peddled item list **75.00**
Sleeping dogs, 5 hunting dogs, 5x7" **68.00**
Whole plate, Negro baby in crib **130.00**
View card; 3 black gentlemen, hand tinted, 1850 . . . . **28.00**
135 Pa. Avenue, taken from White House, street scene, 1866 **15.00**
A Visit to Central Park, set of 13, E & HT Anthony, 1863 . . . **50.00**
Abraham Lincoln Floral Wreath **16.50**
Barnum Circus Parade, 2 views, elephants & camels, 1880 . . . **60.00**
Barnum Parade, Washington DC **22.00**
Bird's View, Paris Expo, Kilburn **6.00**
Broadway, New York City, Keystone, Trolleys, 1901 . . . . . . **3.50**
Centennial, Pa., 1876, 4x7" **8.00**

Crocodile, Frith #335 . . . . **12.00**
Crystal Palace, TR Williams, African w/camel **28.00**
Delaware Water Gap, revenue stamps, 1865 . . . . **3.00**
Denver, 15th St, 1880 . . . . **30.00**
Eclipse of the sun, Mar 6, 1867, Alfred Bros **165.00**
GAR Review downtown Pittsburgh, 1885 . . . . **5.00**
Ghost in the Stereoscope, Yeates & Son, 1856 . . . . **20.00**
Grand Avenue Inn, Milwaukee, 1885 . . . . **5.00**
Grand Union Hotel parlor, New York **3.00**
Humorous, children, barbers, ladies, 60 . . . . **50.00**
Hunting & fishing **1.50**
Hutching's Hotel, Anthony #109, Glories of Yosemite **20.00**
Indians **3.50**
Lake Superior scenery, 4 views, Brubaker **18.00**
Main Street, St Louis, 1885 . . . . **5.00**
Marine views, lot of 28 . . . . **60.00**
Milford, Ct., Anthony #3771 . . . . **5.00**
Montana, Boulder Divide #210, Savage, Ottinger **6.00**
New Britain, Ct., Wallingford Tornado **7.50**
Oakland Wharf in San Francisco, 1885 . . . . **5.00**
Palace Hotel in San Francisco, 1885 . . . . **5.00**
Playing leap frog, 1850 . . . . **18.00**
Razzle Dazzle, Coney Island, Campbell, 1896 . . . . **6.00**
Risque ladies, group of 25 . . . . **40.00**
Robins & nest, Bennett #38, Wayside Gems **18.00**
Roosevelt Inauguration Parade, 24 . . . . **45.00**
Salt Lake City, CW Carter, horses, carts, people **35.00**
San Julien Ranch, Hayward & Mussall #205 . . . . **17.50**
Shakespeare's house, hand tinted, London Stereo, 1860 . . . . **14.00**
Snake, Anthony #125, Glories of Yosemite **9.00**
Spanish American War, Rough Riders, 1899 . . . . **7.00**
St Petersburg, Florida, 1885 . . . . **5.00**
Steamship views, lot of 5 . . . . **15.00**
Street scenes, 15 . . . . **17.00**
Switch-Back RR, Mauch Chunk, Pa., 1896 . . . . **6.00**
Teddy bear playing piano for raccoon **15.00**
Wicked Eyes, hand tinted **10.00**
Viewbook, NYC 1904, 160 Underhill views: subways, buildings, etc **25.00**
Savannah, Ga, 1900 . . . . **10.00**
Viewer; Brewster, burl wood, brass, ornate, for glass or paper . **500.00**
Brewster, mahogany, curved sides, for paper or glass slides . **225.00**
Keystone, Tour of the World, 6 books, 12 volumes, 600 cards **295.00**
Keystone, WWI, w/95 cards **250.00**
Keystone, w/Bausch & Laumb lens, carrying case, 50 slides . **315.00**
Perfectoscope, 1895, brushed engraved aluminum & wood . . . **35.00**
Symetroscope, tin w/gold litho, 1899, 6" **230.00**
Underwood, aluminum embossing, 1901 . . . . **35.00**
Zeiss Aerotopograph, metal w/leatherette case, 6 cards **75.00**

Piano Babies

A familiar sight in Victorian parlors, piano babies languished atop shawl covered pianos in a variety of poses: crawling, sitting, on their tummies, or on their backs playing with their toes. Some babies were nude and some wore gowns. Sizes ranged from about 3" up to 12". The most famous manufacturer of these bisque darlings was the Heubach Brothers of Germany who nearly always marked their product; see Heubach for more listings. Watch for reproductions.

Boy in socks w/dog, 8½x5" **75.00**
Crawling baby, white nightdress, blue trim, 4" **140.00**
Girl, bonnet & dress w/green trim, 7" **185.00**
Girl, Negro, lying down, in bonnet, 6x3½" **85.00**
Lying, w/thumb at mouth, bisque, pink & white gown, 2½x5¾" **48.00**

Sitting baby holding apple, bisque, gown trimmed w/lime, 4½". **65.00**
Sitting baby, German, wht gown, hand up, holding flowers, 6½" **195.00**
Sitting boy, hands over head, white nightdress, pink trim, 3½" **170.00**

Pickard

Founded in 1897 in Chicago, Ill., the Pickard China Co. was originally a decorating studio, importing china blanks from European manufacturers. Some of these early pieces bear the name of those companies as well as Pickard's. Trained artists decorated the wares with hand painted studies of fruit, florals, birds and scenics, and often signed their work. In 1915, Pickard introduced a line of 23k gold over a dainty floral etched ground design.

In the 1930s, they began to experiment with the idea of making their own ware, and by 1938 had succeeded in developing a formula for fine translucent china. Since 1976 they have issued an annual limited edition Christmas plate. They are now located in Antioch, Ill.

The company has used various marks: Pickard w/double circles; the crown mark; Pickard on a gold maple leaf; and the current mark, the lion and shield.

Bon-bon, red poppies, gold scalloped rim, open handled, LOH . **55.00**
Bowl, berries decor, open handles, 8" dia **125.00**
  Ears of corn decor, gold scalloped rim, 1898-1904 mk, 9" . . **265.00**
  Entirely gilded, Art Nouveau interior, Osborne, 10" **125.00**
  Low ped, shamrocks & gold harp decor, handled, MGS, 9" . **155.00**
  Orange poppies in ring of gold poppies, gr band, 1895 mk, 9¾" **175.00**
  Strawberry & gold decor, 6" **60.00**
Cake platter, floral decor, maple leaf mk, 9½" **35.00**
Candlesticks, Aura Argenta Linear, sgnd OP, early circle mk, 5", pr **165.00**
  Gold/silver luster, berry decor, circle mk, 5", pr **135.00**
Charger, raspberries, scalloped gold border, 1894-04 mk, 12½" **185.00**
Cheese & cracker dish, Dutch girl decor, artist sgnd, 9" dia . . . **60.00**
Chocolate pot, fruit decor, much gold, sgnd, 1912, 8½" **135.00**
  Pink sweet clover, sgnd Reuvy **325.00**
Coffee pot, allover florals, heavy gold, Wagner, 1905, 8½" . . . **160.00**
Coffee set, Aura Argenta Linear, 3-pc, gold/silver, sgnd, circle mk **325.00**
Compote, fishscale ground w/pink florals, gold band, 9" **135.00**
  Gold ped, gold floral bowl, center rose medallion, 9" **135.00**
Creamer, blue/orange scrolls on blk/orange luster, Hessler, circle mk **48.00**
Cup & saucer, grapes decor, gold luster, sgnd, 1898-04 mk **75.00**
Dresser set, pink/blue floral, heavy gold trim, 3-pc on oval tray **175.00**
Jug, Corn Likker, sgnd Gifford, 1898, 6¼" **245.00**
Mug, tulips, wide decorated band, Bek, 1910-12 mk, 5¼" **135.00**
Mustard, allover gold etching, w/spoon, 1920 mk **45.00**
Nappy, currants decor, 8" **95.00**
  Scene w/castle, handled, sgnd, 7½" dia **85.00**
Nut set, ftd master, 6 nut decor individuals, sgnd Vokral **295.00**
Perfume, cream w/pink flowers outlined in gold, gold stopper . **100.00**
Pitcher, Aura Argenta Linear, Podlaha, 8" **200.00**
  Aura Argenta, silver rim, gold handle, sgnd OP, 6" **235.00**
  Hexagonal, continuous forest scene, Limoges, Yeschek **260.00**
    Scenic superimposed w/fruits, Yeschek, 9¼" **285.00**
  Peaches, florals, gold handle, sgnd Mott, 5" **130.00**
  Trees, lilies, water decor, 1910 gold mk, France, gr mk **160.00**
Plate, 6 flowers, 2" gold center, scalloped, sgnd, Limoges, 9" . . **85.00**
  Art Deco, w/gold decor, 10½" **80.00**
  Autumn scene, sgnd Marker, circle mk, 8½" **125.00**
  Floral decor, gold trim, artist sgnd, 1905, 7½" **65.00**
  Frosted seascape, sgnd Challinor, 8½" **140.00**
  Handled, Oriental bird, wht w/florals, gold border, 10" **85.00**
  Iris decor, gold leaves & border, artist sgnd, 8½" **65.00**
  Pink/wht morning glories, scalloped gold edge, 1905-10 mk, 8½" **85.00**
  Poppies & daisies decor, gold, Schoner, 1900, 8½" **130.00**

Purple floral decor, artist sgnd, 1905, 6½" **32.00**
Violets decor, sgnd Ray, circle mk, 8½" **55.00**
Wht/blk/gold bell florals, fuschia irid, red bands, 8¾" **100.00**
Woodland scene, matt, handled, Challinor, maple leaf mk, 11" dia **300.00**

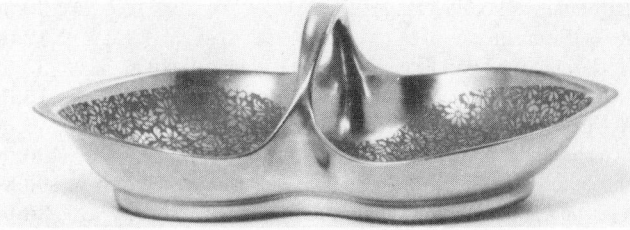

Relish, 2-part, 8¼" **35.00**
  Borders of hp fruit, gold center, open handled, sgnd, 12½" . . **89.00**
Salt & pepper, currants decor, pr **40.00**
  Dutch girl decor, artist sgnd, pr **50.00**
  Individual, allover gold decor, pr **18.00**
Salts, pedestal, gold floral, unsgnd, pr **15.00**
Serving dish, 2-part, etched gold w/petite floral, handled **55.00**
Sugar bowl, covered, large size, all gold, 1919 . . . . **40.00**
Sugar & creamer, blue & gr bellflower design, heavy gold **50.00**
  Currant pattern, sgnd O Goess **195.00**
  Gold floral, square shape, sgnd **45.00**
Tankard, Dutch girl decor, artist sgnd, 8½" **130.00**
Tea set, Dutch girl decor, 3-pc, artist sgnd **225.00**
  Floral decor, gold handles, 3-pc, James, 1912-19 mk **125.00**
  Pink floral, gr leaves, much gold, 15-pc, mkd **280.00**
Tray, oval, colorful, 11½" **135.00**

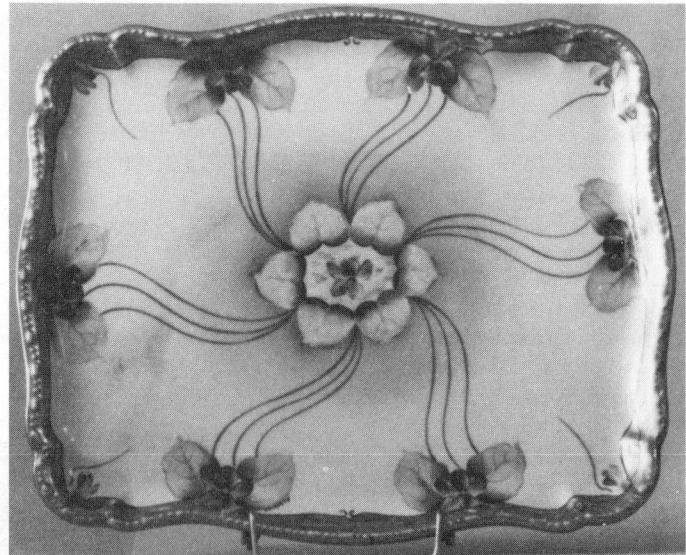

Violets, gold trim, artist sgnd, 10½x8½" **80.00**
Vase, allover gold etched floral, gr interior, 5" **55.00**
  Allover gold etched flowers, hp basket, medallion, 9¾" **225.00**
  Allover violets decor, gold, Brauer, 1910-12 mk, 6¼" **85.00**
  Amphora shape, 2 handles, gold/blk, peacock, sgnd, 8" **425.00**
  Chinese enamel peony & plum blossoms, sgnd, 1912-19 mk, 9" **299.00**
  Garden & fence w/flowers, matt, E Challinor, 7" **350.00**
  Gold w/2" band of water lilies on blue, artist sgnd, 7" **155.00**
  Green & gold w/cherry & blossom luster decor, Lindner, 8" . **135.00**
  Red flowers & ground, leaves & vines, gold neck/handles, 6" **145.00**
  River scene w/palm trees, matt, Challinor, 1912 . . . . **395.00**
  Scenic, Wildwood pattern in pastels, James, 8¼" **395.00**
  Stylized purple florals, gold trim, 1898, 7" **125.00**
  Sunset lake scene w/palm trees, 2 handles, 7" **180.00**
  Violets w/grn & gold leaves, gold neck, 1905-10 mk, 6½" . . . **78.00**
Vase/lamp, scene w/3 pointing Setters, F Cirnacty, 1919-22 mk **495.00**

Pickle Castors

The pickle castor is a novel table item made popular during the Victorian period. It consisted of a glass insert, usually a type of colored art glass, contained in a decorative metal frame. A pickle fork or tongs were usually attached to the frame.

Amberina, enameled	235.00
Thumbprint, enamel floral & fruit, Rogers frame	375.00
Berlin block insert; Meriden frame, w/panel of dove & nest w/eggs	85.00
Blown, hand cut, Pairpoint frame w/tongs	95.00
Blue, enameled florals, plated frame, large	295.00
Blue cane, tongs, highly ornate frame	150.00
Blue glass insert w/tongs, Meridan plated frame	175.00
Burmese, w/enamel decor, rare	375.00
Cased, yellow, plated frame	250.00
Clear, panelled	95.00
Clear insert w/ornate resilvered frame, lid	70.00
Clear to blue w/enameling	350.00

Cobalt, enameled scrolls & florals, 11½"	600.00
Cranberry, Cone pattern, complete	250.00
Enamel decor, floral frame	200.00
Inverted Thumbprint w/enamel; Simpson plated, ftd frame	280.00
Inverted Thumbprint; lid, frame plated, scroll finial	90.00
Inverted Thumbprint, Roger & Bros frame w/tongs	275.00
Maiden Hair & Fern enameled; Queen City, ornaments & tongs	295.00
Optic, horizontal ribbing, ftd Meriden frame	165.00
Pairpoint frame w/applied flowers & leaves	200.00
Thumbprint jar, VanBergh frame w/tongs	175.00
Windows, opal	235.00
Crystal, Cane; bird's head holds tongs, Britannia finish	45.00
Crystal w/vertical cuttings, Meriden plated frame	145.00
Cupid & Venus, tongs & ornate ftd frame by Wilcox, 1880	175.00
Cut crystal w/plated frame, by Derby, 1879	130.00
Daisy & Button, blue, silverplate frame w/tongs	115.00
Daisy & Fern, blue opalescent	295.00
Diamond Cut, blue, embossed frame w/tongs, ornate bail	165.00
Diamond Quilted, clear/blue w/enameling; ornate high ftd frame	425.00
Cranberry, enameled, plated frame w/birds on lid	350.00
Double, brilliant blue; spread eagle on top, w/fork	175.00
Fine Cut; ftd resilvered Wilcox frame, floral cut-outs	210.00
Insert, vaseline; orig frame, mk: Beacon Silver Co, 10½"	135.00
Panel insert; Pairpoint, trimmed frame, w/tongs	95.00

Fireglow enameled; ftd frame w/high standard	425.00
Frosted, birds & butterflies on jar & frame, mk: Reed & Barton	125.00
Herringbone, MOP, 12"	600.00
Hobbs, clear w/wht loops, cranberry threading, orig holder	325.00
Hobnail, blue, w/ornate frame	250.00
Inverted Thumbprint, blue w/hp flowers, frame w/2 birds	130.00
MOP, apricot satin Herringbone, plated frame w/tongs	300.00
Satin, gr/gold	375.00
Mary Gregory, ruby, all orig	495.00
Nailsea, clear w/loopings & cranberry threading, Simpson Hall frame	335.00
Paneled, clear; silverplate lid, Meriden frame	80.00
Paneled Sprig, cranberry; silver plate frame, ftd	185.00
Peachblow, swirled; Homan silver plated frame w/tongs	200.00
With Acme Silver Co plated frame	220.00
Pressed glass; Meridan frame, w/seminude & floral ornaments	70.00
Pressed glass, crystal; resilvered frame, 11x3½"	135.00
Reverse Swirl, coffee opal, ped base, trimmed Homan frame, tongs	165.00
Royal Ivy, clear; w/bow knot frame	150.00
Rubina, enameled decor	350.00
Rubina Inverted Thumbprint, floral enameling, ftd, frame	385.00
Rubina w/coralene; dog finial on frame, 11"	600.00
Ruby, gold enamel, 12", illus	600.00
Stork & Rushes, plated frame, tongs	135.00

Pie Birds

Pie birds or vents were used until about 1930 to prevent pies from boiling over in the oven. When the juices began to bubble and expand, they were contained within the hollow forms; as the pie cooled, the juices drained back into the pie.

Baby Bird, US made, long necked	12.00
Benny Baker Novelty, US made	14.00
Bird, US made, multicolor	12.00
Pink w/yellow beak	15.00

Black Bird, 1940s, 4"	14.00
W/wht base, 2 pc, Royal Worcester, England	25.00
Black Chef, US made	15.00
Chicken, wht, w/pink & gr	12.00
Donald Duck, US made	30.00
Duck, rose	12.50

Yellow w/brown **14.00**
Duckling, US made **17.00**
Dutch Girl, US made **23.00**
Mammy, US made **23.00**
Negro **20.00**
Patrick Rooster, US made **12.00**
Peasants, wooden hand carved, Soviet Union, pair **15.00**
Rooster, Blue Willow **12.50**
   Red, large **8.00**
   US made, long necked **14.00**
   Wht w/gr on brown trim **15.00**

Pigeon Blood

Pigeon blood glass, produced in the late 1800s, may be distinguished from other dark red glass by its distinctive orange tint.

Bowl, master berry, open heart arches, enamel decor, frosted . **165.00**
Compote, ftd, etched, 7″ wide, 3½″ high **22.50**
Cracker jar, florette, silver plated top **150.00**
   Melon shaped, silver plated top, handle **190.00**
   Torquay, orig silver plated bale & lid **245.00**
Perfume, w/stopper, wht enamel decor & jewel, 9″ **70.00**
Salt, Banded Flower **40.00**
Salt & pepper, Bulging Loops, pair **100.00**
   Pewter tops, pair **100.00**
Sweetmeat, Torquay **175.00**
Table set, Venicia w/wild rose decor, 4 pc **600.00**
Tumbler, blown, old, set of 6 . . . . **275.00**
   Thumbprint, 4½″ **35.00**
Vinegar cruet, blown-out bulbous panels **95.00**

Pink Lustreware

Pink lustre was produced by nearly every potter in the Staffordshire district in the 18th and 19th centuries. The application of gold lustre on white or light colored backgrounds produced pinks, while the same over dark colors developed copper. The wares ranged from hand painted plaques to transfer printed dinnerware.

Boot, red & gold trim, 4¼x1¼x3¾″ **40.00**
Creamer, hunter & hounds, old **38.00**
Cup & saucer, feather design w/gr **42.00**
   Footed, panels w/branch, florals, early 1800s **45.00**
   Handleless, girl w/dog & lamb, 1840 . . . . **70.00**
   House **50.00**
   Pink & gr feather pattern, wht background **25.00**
   Portrait of woman & child **25.00**
   Red bud & gold leaves, early 1800s **50.00**
   Strawberry **150.00**
   Sunflower **45.00**
   Transfer on cup Faith & Hope, on saucer Charity **55.00**
   With foot, Faith, Hope & Charity theme, 1840 . . . . **95.00**
   Wishbone handles, gr w/floral decor, deep saucer **42.00**
Jug, hunters in relief, Staffordshire, 6½″ **150.00**
Pitcher, 3½″ **42.00**
   Softpaste, gadrooned border, raised vine decor, dog scene, 5″ **200.00**
Plaque, iris, open handles, 11″ **65.00**
   Moralistic verse, copper lustre decor, 1830s, 9x10″ **65.00**
Plate, deep, 'Shepherd Boy', 1820, 7¼″ **48.00**
   Dickens scene, 5¼″ **50.00**
   Relief scrolls, shades of pink w/enameling, 9½″ sq **42.50**
   Wide band w/leaf & floral decor, set of 4 . . . . **100.00**

Pisgah Forest

The Pisgah Forest Pottery was established near Mount Pisgah in Arden, North Carolina, in 1914 by Walter B. Stephen. Stephen is best known for his cameo ware which he decorated by hand in the pate-sur-pate style with scenes portraying covered wagons and other subjects related to the pioneer days. He sometimes signed these pieces 'Stephen' within the paste decoration. He also produced a turquoise crackled ware, and developed a fine crystalline glaze, examples of which are highly prized by today's collectors. The ware was marked Pisgah Forest, often with a potter at the wheel. Stephen died in 1961, but the work was continued by his associates.

Ashtray, turquoise, 1939, 5″ dia **19.00**
Plate, glazed turquoise, mkd & dated, Stephen **25.00**
Pot, ivory, blue crystals, Stephen, 3½″ **100.00**

Sugar & creamer, Cameoware, Stephen **250.00**
Vase, blue/silver crystals on cream, sgnd Stephen, 6″ **250.00**
   Bulbous, w/heavy crystals, 6″ dia **275.00**
   Crystalline, 4″ **125.00**
   Full crystals on coffee-colored ground, 1940, 6″ **175.00**
   High-glaze grape color, 1946, Stephen, 10″ **50.00**
   Ivory, blue crystals, 6″ **135.00**
   Ivory, Stephen, 5½″ **200.00**
   Maroon drip on blue, sgnd, 4½″ **52.00**
   Matt lavender w/matt wht interior, potter at wheel mk, early . **150.00**
   Pastel gr crystals on beige, classic shape, dated & sgnd, 9¼″ **262.00**
   Turquoise & maroon, 1929, 9″ **40.00**
   Wht, green w/crystalline highlights, 1953, 7½x5″ **220.00**

Pittsburg

As early as 1797, utility window glass and hollowware were being produced in the Pittsburgh area. Coal had been found in abundance, and it was there that it was first used instead of wood to fuel the glass furnaces. Because of this, as many as 150 glass companies operated there at one time. However, most failed due to the economically disasterous effects of the War of 1812. By the mid-1850s those that remained were producing a wide range of flint glass items including pattern-molded and free-blown glass, cut and engraved wares, and pressed tableware patterns.

Candlestick, clear w/3 colored spiral threads, 10″ **575.00**
Cruet, expanded 24 rib, folded rim, blown stopper, 9″ **185.00**
Decanter, pillar mold, pewter jigger top, 10″ **135.00**
Vase, pillar mold, applied foot & stem, 9¾″ **95.00**
Whiskey, flute, emerald green **95.00**

Playing Cards

Playing cards can be an enjoyable way to trace the course of history. The art, literature and politics of any era can be gleaned from a study of its playing cards. When royalty lost favor with the people, Kings and Queens were replaced by common people. During the periods of war, Generals, of-

ficers and soldiers were favored. In the United States, early examples had portraits of Washington and Adams as opposed to Kings, Indian Chiefs instead of Jacks, and goddesses for Queens.

Tarot cards were used in Europe during the 1300s as a game of chance, but by the 15th century they were used to predict the future, and were regarded with great reverence.

The backs of cards were of no particular consequence until the 1800s. The marble design used by the French during the late 1800s, and the colored wood-cut patterns of the Italians in the 19th century, are among the first attempts at decoration. Later, the English used cards printed with portraits of royalty. Eventually cards were decorated with a broad range of subjects from reproductions of fine art to advertising.

Advertising, Air Canada, Estrie Graphics, gold maple leaf, MIB . **18.00**
  Bohemian Ale, w/box **10.00**
  Coca-Cola, Coke Refreshes You Best, girl w/coke, orig box . . . **35.00**
    Enjoy Coca-Cola, Be Really Refreshed **35.00**
    Airplane spotter, WWII **40.00**
    Girl w/Coke & score pad **25.00**
  Dr Pepper, sweater girl, revenue stamp cut but all there, 1940s **65.00**
  Edison Mazda, Night Is Fled, 1918, single card **6.00**
  Gerber, w/picture of Gerber baby **8.00**
  Green River Whiskey, MIB **53.00**
    Pinochle, w/orig box **33.00**
  Jack Daniels #7, double deck in tin box **35.00**
  Page Dairy, shows milkmaid & cow **17.00**
  Standard Oil Co, Des Moines District **15.00**
Beatles, 1964, MIB **7.00**
Bee #92, w/box **13.00**
Betty Boop, 1926, w/orig box mkd Fleishman Studios **35.00**
  1932 . . . . **30.00**
Buster Brown, w/box, 2½" **45.00**
C&O Railroad, kittens, double deck w/box **25.00**
CM & St P Railroad, 53 different scenes, many trains **34.00**
Civil War/Union, 1862, shows officers, Lady Liberty, w/box . . . **275.00**
De La Rue, sq corners, no indices, 2-way courts, floral backs, 1880s **135.00**
Everywhere West, Burlington Route, 1940, in case, used **14.00**
Fact & Fancy, 1961, designed by Dick Martin for CPCC, MIB . . **25.00**
Faro, complete deck, hand painted **95.00**
  Russell & Morgan, complete deck, Consolidated Card Co **90.00**
Flinch, Flinch Card Co, lithographed, in old carton **9.00**
French, pink backs, 2-way courts, no indices, small, Gratteaux, 1850s **55.00**
German made, 2-way courts, no indices, red & beaded backs, 1870s **90.00**
Hardy & Sons, sq corners, no indices, 1-way courts, hand colored **140.00**
Hunt & Sons, plain backs, Fizzle Ace, complete, 1820s **120.00**
Little Lord Fauntleroy, w/ivory celluloid covered case, 1¾x2½". **18.00**
Man from UNCLE **8.00**
Maxfield Parrish, Ecstasy, 1930, single card **5.00**
  Enchantment **35.00**
    1926, single card **5.00**
  Limited edition, unopened decks **15.00**
  Reveries, MIB **40.00**
  The Lampseller of Bagdad, 1923, single card **6.00**
  The Venetian Lamplighter, 1924, single card **5.50**
Movie Stars, Ronald Colman, Ken Maynard, Monte Blue, etc . . . **28.00**
Movie souvenier, 52 cards **35.00**
Norman Rockwell, set of 4 seasons **12.00**
Nude Bernice, copyright 1900, complete deck, no box **90.00**
Penn Railroad, w/orig box **20.00**
Pin-ups, sgnd Mac Thorson, double deck, w/orig 1945 box **9.00**
Politicards, full deck, all different, Nixon, Reagan, etc, issued 1971 **10.00**
Reynolds & Sons, floral backs, 1-way courts, hand colored, 1850s **130.00**
  Plaid backs, hand colored, round corners, 1830s **115.00**
Shirley Temple **50.00**

Southern Railway System, double deck, sealed & mint in orig box **18.00**
Souvenir, British Columbia, Clarke & Stuart, 1890s, w/box **45.00**
  Century of Progress, Chicago, 1934, globe, orig box **18.00**
  Paris Exposition, 1900, by Tom Jones **70.00**
  Pittsburg, WJ Gilmore Co, 1901 . . . . **40.00**
  St Louis, 53 views, 1903 . . . . **22.00**
  Texas Centennial, 1936, w/box **5.00**
  World's Fair, 1933, 53 views of fair **15.00**
Spirit of Night, 1919, single card **6.50**
Steamboats, '999', complete deck **45.00**

Political Entourage

The most valuable political items are those from the 19th century and those from any period which relate to a political figure whose term was especially significant or marked by an important event, or one whose personality was particularly colorful. Pinback buttons from the 40s through the 70s, posters, ribbons, badges and photographs are but a few examples of the items popular with collectors of political memorabilia.

Address Book, JFK, 1960 . . . . **15.50**
Bandanna, Alfred E Smith picture, 14x18¾" **65.00**
  Cleveland-Stevenson, red & wht, 1892, eagle & crest each corner **95.00**
  Cleveland-Thurman picture, rooster & broomstick, 1888 . . . . **105.00**
  Eisenhower bust in center, red & wht & blue, 1952 . . . . **45.00**
  Harrison-Morton photo, red & wht & blue **95.00**
  Harrision-Reid, flag in center, 1892 . . . . **120.00**
  Parker-Davis, 1904 . . . . **45.00**
  Protection to American Industries, silk, 1888 . . . . **50.00**
  Roosevelt, 1912 . . . . **70.00**
Banner, McKinley bust w/cane **125.00**
  Teddy Roosevelt-Charles Fairbanks, cloth, 22x23" **120.00**
Book, Cleveland & Thurman for Pres & Vice, 588 pgs, 1888 . . . **10.00**
Booklet, Anti-Woman Suffrage, Massachusetts, 48 pgs, 1915 . . . **25.50**
  Cleveland-Harrison Presidential, 1888, Waterbury Watch Co . . **10.00**
  Hoover photo, 1928 . . . . **9.00**
  James M Cox Presidential Campaign, w/portrait **22.00**
  Lincoln Campaign Songster, 1959, reprint **5.00**
Bubble gum, Story of President Kennedy **10.00**
Bubble gum cigars, Humphrey, orig box, Win w/HHH **20.00**
Bullet pencil, Theodore Roosevelt photo **30.00**
Button, 1952 Primary, litho metal **30.00**
  Anderson for President, litho metal **7.00**

Ashbrook, Re-elect to Congress **5.00**
Bush for President, picture, celluloid **18.00**
Carter, Re-Elect Carter-Mondale, litho metal **6.00**
Carter-Mondale, celluloid, 3¼x2¼" **12.00**
Carter-Mondale Polish America, celluloid **18.00**

Dewey, litho metal **12.00**
Dewey-Bricker picture **22.00**
Eisenhower, I Like Ike, litho metal **18.00**
Eisenhower, 'Ike' in gold script **5.00**
Eisenhower, litho metal **18.00**
Eisenhower, Welcome Home Ike, w/ribbon, from WWII **45.00**
Eisenhower-Nixon, litho metal **18.00**
FDR, litho metal **25.00**
Ford, Our 38th, picture, celluloid **12.00**
Goldwater in 64, litho metal **8.00**
Goldwater-Miller, litho metal **8.00**
Goldwater-Miller picture, celluloid **12.00**
Harding picture, celluloid, 1920 . . . . **40.00**
Hoover-Curts GOP, litho metal **35.00**
Humphrey In '68, picture, celluloid **12.00**
Humphrey-Muskie, litho metal **8.00**
JFK, New Frontier, litho metal **12.00**
JFK, Our 35th, picture, celluloid **23.00**
Johnson, LBJ All The Way, picture, celluloid **12.00**
Kennedy in 1980, celluloid **12.00**
Kennedy-Illinois Citizens, celluloid **12.00**
Landon-Knox, litho metal, felt daisy **40.00**
Landon-Knox, picture **50.00**
Landon-Knox, yellow felt backing **15.00**
McGovern, litho metal **8.00**
McGovern-Eagleton, celluloid **23.00**
McGovern-Shriver, litho metal **8.00**
McKinley, In McKinley We Trust, In Bryan We Bust **15.00**
Nixon, lithographed, metal **7.00**
Nixon for President, picture, celluloid **12.00**
Nixon Now, litho metal **7.00**
Nixon's The One, litho metal, illus **8.00**
Nixon-Agnew, litho metal **9.00**
Nixon-Lodge, I'm for Nixon & Lodge, litho metal **12.00**
Reagan, In 76, picture, celluloid **23.00**
Reagan, Our President Reagan, '80, celluloid **7.00**
Reagan, The Time Is Now---Reagan-Bush, litho metal **5.00**
Stevenson-Liberal Party, litho metal **23.00**
Taft, celluloid **110.00**
Taft-Sherman, sepia brown, 1″ **30.00**
Truman, litho metal **50.00**
Udall, Udall for President, celluloid **10.00**
Wallace, litho metal **8.00**
Wallace-Lemay, litho metal, illus **9.00**
Wilkie-McNary, litho metal **18.00**
Wilson, Woodrow Wilson Safety First, celluloid **40.00**
WIN, litho metal **12.00**
Calendar, Wilkie-McNary picture **20.00**
Candy box, McKinley-Roosevelt, WT Cardy & Sons, Mass. **61.00**
Card, Hoover, It Won't Be Long Now, color, 5x4″ **4.00**
  Smith, I'm Going to Vote for Al Smith, 3½x3½″ **6.00**
  Truman-Dewey magic change card, 1948, 4x7¼″ **32.00**
Cartoon book, Roosevelt-Hoover, Erbie & 'is Playmates **22.50**
Certificate of donation, $10.00, Republican Nat'l Committee, 1892″ **19.00**
Clock, Roosevelt, Spirit of USA **75.00**
Comic book, Stevenson **6.00**
Composition book, Teddy Roosevelt, red & wht & blue **16.00**
Convention report, Republican National, 1924, 256 pgs **15.00**
Convention ticket, Democratic National, 1892, Cleveland **7.00**
  Democratic National, 1920, Roosevelt-Cox, stub **11.50**
  People's Party National, 1896 . . . . **7.50**
  Republican National, 1888, Harrison **15.00**
Dartboard, Nixon **20.00**
  Spiro Agnew **7.00**

Elephant, Hoover, for buttonhole **30.00**
  Brass, red saddle, GOP, ¾x1¼″ **8.00**
Excursion ticket, Republican, to Gay Head on Steamer Frances, 1886 **5.00**
  Salt River Anti-Democratic, 3¼x5″ **6.00**
Fan, Thomas Dewey, presidential candidate, blue & wht cardboard **17.50**
Folder, Smith-Hoover, red & gr cellophane, ad on back **7.00**
Glass, William McKinley, handled, tin, small **200.00**
Guest ticket, Republican National Convention, 1900 . . . . . . **15.00**
Handkerchief, Cleveland-Thurman busts, pink, gray & blue border **75.00**
Inaugural invitation, Eisenhower-Nixon, 1953 . . . . **7.00**
  Hoover-Curtis, 1929, orig envelope **26.00**
  Roosevelt-Garner, 1937 . . . . **30.00**
  Reagan, in envelope, 8½x11½″ **14.00**
Inauguration program, Washington, 1889 . . . . **24.00**
Jug, Harrison-Morton, miniature, brown **14.00**
Lantern, Garfield-Arthur picture, campaign 1880 . . . . **200.00**
  Grant-Wilson, folding type **192.50**
  Harrison-Morton, 24x56″ circumference **250.00**
Liberty Bell, Teddy Roosevelt, bronze bear on bell, 5″ base . . . **37.50**
License plate, Eisenhower, attachment, Republican Congress, 1954 **10.00**
  Johnson, inauguration flags picture, 1965 . . . . **35.00**
  Nixon, inauguration, White house & flag picture, 1969 . . . . **35.00**
Luncheon reception program, Democratic women w/Truman, 1948 **47.50**
Magazine cover, Puck, Sept 18, 1912, Teddy Roosevelt **45.00**
Mechanical button, Cleveland picture, 1888 . . . . **150.00**
Medal, Roosevelt, Country & Humanity in Memorium, bronze, 3″ dia **30.00**
Mug, FDR, figural barrel, The New Deal shield, 4″ **32.50**
  Howard Taft, 5″ **85.00**
Mug, William J Bryan, glass, The Peoples Money **75.00**
Necktie, Truman **18.00**
Newspaper, The National Intelligencer, political, slavery, 1844 . . . **5.00**
Paper cup, Eisenhower **7.50**
Paperweight, General Pershing, WWI era **37.50**
Pennant, Hoover picture **15.00**
  Roosevelt picture **15.00**
Photo, Dewey, w/back stand, full face in color, 1944, 17x24″ . . **14.00**
Pin, Coolidge portrait, Keep Coolidge **10.00**
  Dewey-Bricker picture **22.00**
  FDR, raised profile, red & wht & blue porcelain **40.00**
  Herbert Hoover portrait **10.00**
  McKinley-Roosevelt portrait, 1″ **20.00**
  Taft portrait, 1″ **15.00**
  Teddy Roosevelt portrait, 1″ **10.00**
  Wilson portrait, 1¼″ **15.00**
Pinback button, McKinley-Roosevelt portrait, jugate **20.00**
  Roosevelt-Wallace, jugate **10.00**
  Truman **20.00**
  Wilson, color **15.00**
  Kennedy, Hake **50.00**
  MacArthur for American Hopeful **13.00**
Plaque, FDR, Wedgwood cameo, MIB, 2½″ dia **44.00**
  J F K, Royal Copenhagen, 3″ **50.00**
  Parker-Davis, cardboard, 1904, 7½x3½″ **30.00**
Plate, Garfield for President, portrait, porcelain, 8″ **40.00**
  Grover Cleveland Picture, ironstone, 8″ **30.00**
Pocket mirror, William J Bryan for President, sepia pic, 2¼″ . . **38.00**
Poster, Roosevelt-Truman, 11x15″ **20.00**
Presidential Forecast folding card, 1912, 6x6½″ **20.00**
Press pass, Democratic National Convention, 1924 . . . . **12.50**
Program, Roosevelt-Wallace, 1941 inaugural, 64 pgs **15.00**
Progressive Party Charter membership certificate **22.50**
Progressive Party Founder's Certificate, 1912 . . . . **27.50**
Propaganda, Communist Party, USA, Keep America Out, 1940 . **12.00**
Puzzle, Spiro Agnew dressed in superman suit, 16x20″ **5.00**

Ribbon, Cleveland-Hendricks, silk 1884 . . . . **25.00**
   McKinley-Roosevelt, w/words **8.00**
Ribbon w/brass token, Truman, inauguration 1949 . . . . **42.50**
Senate pass, for impeachment of Andrew Johnson, May 2, 1868 **50.00**
Senate chamber ticket, Robert Kennedy, 1966, unissued **9.00**
Snuff box, Woodrow Wilson, Wilson's head on top in brass, 2". **28.00**
Sticker, Coolidge-Dawes, window, 5x12" **9.00**
   Democrats for Wilkie **6.50**
   Forward w/Roosevelt, 1936, 6" **8.00**
   Kennedy, lot of 36, red & wht & blue **10.00**
   Landon-Knox, sunflower **13.00**
   Roosevelt, 1936-40, 8" **8.00**
Straw hat, Wallace, Wallace for President **25.00**
Tradecard, William McKinley, 4x6½" **6.00**
Tray, Roosevelt & McKinley, 1900, 12" **75.00**
Tumbler, Roosevelt-McKinley pictured w/eagle **58.00**
   William McKinley portrait **27.50**
Voting box, wooden, 18 china marbles, wht & black **65.00**
Watch fob, James Cox picture, 1920 presidential campaign . . . **125.00**
   Roosevelt picture, 1920 presidential campaign **125.00**
   Roosevelt-Fairbanks, brass, leather strap, 1904 . . . . **47.00**
Whig circular, Massachusetts, 1851, to get out the vote, 5¼x5½" **19.00**

Pomona

Pomona glass was patented in 1885 by the New England Glass works. Its characteristics are an etched background of crystal lead glass dcecorated with simple designs painted on with metallic stains of amber or blue. The etching was first achieved by hand cutting through an acid resist. This method, called first grind, resulted in an uneven feather-like frost effect. Later, to cut production costs, the hand cut process was discontinued in favor of an acid bath, which effected an even frosting. This method is called second grind.

Bowl, 1st grind, crimped amber edge, 2½x5" **175.00**
   1st grind, deep crimping, cornflowers, 5" **140.00**
   2nd grind, 2½x4½" **60.00**
   2nd grind, cornflowers, 4x3" **175.00**
   2nd grind, cornflower, crimped rim, 3½x8" **300.00**
   2nd grind, ruffled, clear reserves w/engraving, 2½x5" **150.00**
Candlesticks, rolled tops, center prunts, waffle pontils, 4", pr . **125.00**
Finger bowl, 1st grind, ruffled amber rim **120.00**
   2nd grind, amber crimped rim, 4½" **60.00**
Pitcher, 1st grind, amber stained sq trim, cornflowers, 6½" . . . **350.00**
   2nd grind, Diamond Optic, gold stain top, trefoil handle, 8" **350.00**
Punch cup, 1st grind, acanthus leaves **95.00**
   1st grind, blue cornflowers **95.00**
Sugar bowl, 2nd grind, Inverted T'print, fluted, amber stain . . . **65.00**
Toothpick, 1st grind **150.00**
   Tri-cornered **140.00**
Tumbler, 1st grind, lt amber trim **110.00**
   1st grind, blue cornflowers, amber stain **140.00**
   2nd grind, Acorn Band Inverted Thumbprint **125.00**
   2nd grind, cornflower decor, 3½" **60.00**
   2nd grind, Diamond Optic, lt amber top **110.00**
   2nd grind, Diamond Quilted, amber top band **95.00**
Vase, 2nd grind, crimped amber edge, 6½x4" **225.00**

Popcorn and Peanut Machines

The popcorn and peanut machines that were a popular sight a century ago were often elaborately decorated. Some were designed with special attention-getting features, such as a small clown to turn the peanut roaster, or a fascinating steam engine placed where curious onlookers could watch

it power the rotating corn popper. The vendor hoped that should the enticing aroma of his wares go unnoticed, the appeal of his machine would capture the attention of those passing by!

Peanut machine, Climax 10, orig paint **750.00**
   Royal, good orig **1,250.00**
   Victor Model Bartholomew, pre 1900 . . . . **5,500.00**
Peanut & popcorn machine, RO Stutzman, burns wht gas, 1900 **5,500.00**
Popcorn machine, Holcomb & Hoke, oak **2,500.00**

Post Cards

A German by the name of Von Stephan is credited for inventing the post card, first printed in Austria in 1869. They were eagerly accepted by the continentals and the English alike, who saw them as a more economical way to send written messages. Three years later post cards were introduced in America.

The first to be printed in the United States were plain U.S. postal cards. Photo cards, first sold here in the 1880s, were made in Germany by order of the Leighton Company of Portland, Maine. But the Columbian Exposition in 1892-93 was the spark that ignited the post card phenomenon. Souvenir cards by the millions were sent to folks back home---Expo scenes, transportation themes, animals, birds and advertising messages became popular. There were patriotic themes, black themes, and cards for every occasion.

In 1907, the Payne-Aldrich Bill placed such a high tariff on imported cards that dealers began to turn to American printers and lithographers. Some of the earliest post card publishers were Raphael Tuck, Gibson Art, and Nister and Gabriel. Early 20th century illustrators such as Winsch, Brundage, Rose O'Neill and Clapsaddle designed cards that are especially valued today.

Though the post card rage waned at the onset of WWI, they rank today among the most sought after paper collectibles!

Advertising, 5A Horse Blankets, Stratton Duck Stable Blanket . . **12.00**
   Bell Telephone, The Social Call by Telephone, R-6 . . . . **22.00**
   Campbell's Kids, chubby girl at table, 1913 issue **80.00**
   Campbell's Kids, slide down rail, 1910 issue **60.00**
   Cracker Jack Bears, #6, dancing w/vendor in N.Y., Moreland . **19.00**
   Cracker Jack Bears, #7, w/Teddy Roosevelt at White House . . **20.00**
   Dupont, Dupont dog, Count Gladstone **70.00**
   French music store, cut out & assemble violin & parts **55.00**
   Gold Dust Twins, There's A Washout On The Line **25.00**
   Swifts Premium Oleomargarine, Ireland, copyright 1912 . . . . **12.00**
   Teddy Bear Bread, '...Anything In It?', bear w/basket **14.00**
   Texaco, shows products: pump, oil, etc, 1937 . . . . **10.00**
   Tobler Chocolate, Disney, Pinochio, French, 1930s **15.00**
Alligator border, Ramble & Cove, Palm Beach, Fla., #8520, Langsdorf **24.00**
   The Smile That Won't Come Off, blk man w/melon, Langsdorf **26.00**
Automobile, Everitt six-cylinder car, yellow & blk advertising . . . **65.00**
   Great Chadwick Six, red/blk advertising w/specifications **55.00**
   Oldsmobile, hold-to-light, tiller-type auto, 1905 . . . . **150.00**
   Studebaker Electric, blue-tinted, 'Shopping in a ...' **60.00**
Bathing Beauties, On The Beach, embossed, 1909, Taggert Co, #25 **8.00**
Bouileau, Philip---Published by Reinthal & Newman unless noted
A Gift of Love, valentine, National Art Co **20.00**
At Home, Connoisseur Series, very rare **150.00**
Autumn, issue #19 by National Art Co **20.00**
Baby Mine, mother & baby **17.00**
Chic, Water Color Series, last image done before his death **40.00**
Here Comes Daddy (Babyhood), Water Color Series **50.00**
June, Blessed June, image of Emily Boileau, Series 108 . . . . . . **40.00**
My Big Brother, older girl hugging younger boy **17.00**
Poppies, Boileau Head Series, Taylor Platt & Co **75.00**

Ready for Mischief, Series 108, semi-nude **45.00**
School Days, three young girls **18.00**
The Fruit of the Vine, scarce **45.00**
The Parting of the Ways, (Maidenhood), Water Color Series . . **45.00**
The Secret of Flowers, Series 108, semi-nude **35.00**

Boy Scouts, Guarding Sleeping Baby, sgnd Fred Spurgin, #445, color **12.00**
Brundage---Published by Gabriel unless noted
Christmas, mother & girls at fireplace, #200-10, sgnd **10.00**
Evangeline, calendar series #284, sgnd **20.00**
Halloween, 3 girls, apples in tub of water, red border, sgnd, ... **9.50**
Little Hollanders, series 6910, sgnd Tuck **23.00**
The Christening, Colored Folks Series 2723, sgnd, Tuck **20.00**

Button Face, dog w/wagging tail, sgnd JG, 'Every little movement...' **21.00**
     Little girl holding cat, 'Alice Rawling Went A Calling' **17.00**
Caldecott, Randolph, Nursery Rhymes, complete set of 48, 1930s **75.00**
Chief Sitting Bull, #3420, nicely embossed, sgnd Peterson, Tammen **8.00**
Clapsaddle---Published by Inter Art Co unless stated otherwise
Birthday, #6, baby in cariage w/balloon & toys, sgnd **10.00**
Christmas, blk girl/bench, cat peeks out, 'Wishing You..Cheer', sgnd **10.00**
Christmas, boy w/turkey on platter, 'Hearty...Greeting', sgnd, Wolf **9.00**
Cradle roll, #4, boy in yellow suit w/can & shovel, sgnd **13.00**
Cupid w/mechanical kaleidoscope heart, scarce, sgnd **30.00**
Easter, boy in blue w/egg basket, 'Best Easter Wishes', sgnd, Wolf **9.50**
Easter, silver cross in flowers, 'Risen for thee...', sgnd **7.00**
Halloween, blk boy in wht robe, w/moveable arm, sgnd **30.00**
St Patrick's, boy in wht w/shamrock corsage, sgnd **9.50**
Valentine, boy w/cane, girl w/blue bonnet, '...Pain is love!', sgnd . **9.00**

Disney, 1 Round of Fun, #1744, Mickey & Goofy on carousel, 1930s **18.00**
     The Fishing is Swell, #4045, Mickey, Minnie & Donald, 1930s **20.00**
Dwarf, sitting on grass, songbird on branch, sgnd Mather **8.00**
Firefighters, A Fire Scene, N.Y. City, steamer in action **20.00**
     Langsdorf, Sounding The Alarm **30.00**
     Oswego, N.Y., Chemical & Engine Co w/horse drawn pumper, 1908 **15.00**
Fisher, Harrison---Publisher is Reinthal & Newman unless noted
All's Well, #381 Water Color Series, woman in sailor suit **18.00**
American Girl in England, American Girl Abroad Series **22.00**
Beauties, girl w/hat holds dog **20.00**
Beauties, girl holds tiger cat **15.00**
Compensation, #844, nurse reads to patient, Cosmopolitan Print Dept **16.00**
Day Dreams, blonde rests head on pillow **20.00**
Good Morning Mama **20.00**
I'm Ready, girl in uniform **30.00**
Mary, girl w/hat, scarce **22.00**
Paddling Their Own Canoe, #611, 2 women in canoe **13.00**
Sense of Sight, The First Meeting, The Senses series **20.00**
The Honeymoon, Greatest Moments of a Girl's Life series **20.00**
The Kiss, ½ view **14.00**
     Full-length view **30.00**
Welcome Home, #387 Water Color Series, woman & man on ship **18.00**

French, L'Equitation, woman on horse is nude when seen w/red film **25.00**
Golliwog, 2 playing cards w/2 stick dolls, silver ground, BB London **25.00**
     Mr Golliwog Good Night, child w/candle, sgnd A Richardson . **15.00**
Hold-to-light, cut-out, Bathing at Coney Island, #61llL, Koehler . **26.00**
     Child angel praying, DRGM **27.00**
     Cupid's Message, cupid in rowboat **35.00**
     New York & Brooklyn Bridge, #1500, Koehler **29.00**
     Rabbit w/umbrella puts eggs in basket **30.00**
Installment set, Huld's Puzzle Series 1, alligator, 4 cards **40.00**
     Je Suis L'Immaculee Conception, set of 10, Fauvelle #190 . . **125.00**
     Pope Leo XIII, set of 8, used, VG **250.00**

Kewpies, 1 holding Santa mask, 'Kewpies Playing Santa', sgnd O'Neill **28.00**
     Happy New Year, one holds attractive gift, sgnd O'Neill **35.00**
     Votes for Women, 3 fife & drum poses, sgnd O'Neill, Campbell Art **19.00**
Kirchner, Raphael, man kisses girl on back of neck **30.00**
     Raphael, set of 6 redheaded girl on bicycle, different poses . **700.00**
Langsdorf State Girl, Maryland, silk midshipman outfit **50.00**
     Oregon, embossed outfit, holding staff **35.00**
Mucha, Alphonse, Job Cigarette Papers, advertisement image . . **175.00**
     Lilies, from the set of Four Flowers **150.00**
     Moet & Chandon Champagne **400.00**
     Winter, from the set of Four Seasons **170.00**
Niagara Falls Summer, set of 12 copyrighted 1897, unused . . . **140.00**
PFB, Children #6727-6, boy in straw hat w/hen in basket **10.00**
     Children #9025-3, girl in fur coat holds puppy & holly **14.00**
     Comics #8808-5, The Morning After The Night Our **12.00**
Parrish, Maxfield, The Broadmoor, poster painting of hotel, sgnd **28.00**
Puzzle card, What is nicer than a pretty girl, Dederick Bros, 1906 **8.00**
Real hair, blonde, on cupid inserting key into heart, photo card **25.00**
     Woman w/dk purple silk cloche, yellow ribbon **22.00**
Roosevelt bear, #31,... At Hunter, shooting at hunters, Stern . . . **25.00**
     #31,...At Washington, meeting Teddy Roosevelt, Stern **30.00**
Santa, 2 girls at window, Santa in gonolda, Winsch 1913 . . . . . . **15.00**
     Advertising Hyler's Bonbons, watching children write letters . . **20.00**
     Blue silk robe, shows toys in sack to children, series 606 . . . **35.00**
     European, red robed w/tree & basket of toys in snowstorm . . **14.00**
     Hold-to-light, cut-out, w/purple robe, in roadster **85.00**
     Leather card, red coat, holding up sock, HS Heal **10.00**
     Transparency, boy & girl by tree, Santa, 'appears' **20.00**
     Tuck oilette, #C1059, full size, red robe, w/golliwog **20.00**
Shirley Temple, glossy sepia photo, Hawaiian outfit, w/Buddy Epsen **14.00**
Sonja Henie & Tyron Power, glossy photo, Second Fiddle, #FS 196 **10.00**
St Louis Exposition, 1904, set of 10, illuminate, silver ground . . **80.00**
Suffragettes, Suffrage First, EH Chamberlin, National Suff Publ Co **25.00**
Sunbonnet Babies, Days of the Week, Ulman series #72, set of 7 **140.00**
Toy Model Series, #5, locomotive, cut out & assemble, Henderson **45.00**
     Our Pretty Pets, donkey, #3173, cut out & assemble **50.00**
Transparency, man w/wine turns to drunk on ground, Hagelburg **23.00**
     Paris #14, LePantheon et la Rue Soufflot, day-to-night **18.00**
Tuck, Characters from Dickens, Mr Pickwick, #540, sgnd KYD . **15.00**
     Homes of US Presidents, A Lincoln, Springfield, Ill. **9.00**
     Homes of US Presidents, John Adams, Quincy, Mass. **7.00**
     Juliet w/skull cap, sgnd A Asti **7.00**
     Little Men & Women, Waiting for Orders, boy w/basket **10.00**
     Madam Butterfly, complete set of 6, #2635, oilette **250.00**
     Memorial Day Confederate, Gen Robert E Lee, on bronze medal **15.00**
     Model Cottage, Series II #3388, cut out & assemble **55.00**
     Nursery Rhymes Doll, Series III #3383, Betty Blue, oilette . . . **80.00**
     Our Boy Scouts, The Eagle, oilette **100.00**
     Poster Girl, w/tennis racket **50.00**
     Wild West USA, Cowboy Fun, oilette, sgnd Harry Payne #9531 **12.00**
Main, Louis, cat 'couple' going to theatre, sgnd, Davidson Bros . **25.00**
Weiner Werkstatte, Flora, woman w/flowers, sgnd Loffler #913 **225.00**
     Hop In Weissenkirchen, sgnd K Schwetz #719 . . . . **150.00**

Posters

Advertising posters by such French artists as Monet and Toulouse-Lautrec were used as early as the mid 1800s. Color lithography spurred their popularity. Circuses, movies, and patriotic causes are popular categories with poster collectors today. Works of noted artists such as Fox, Parrish and Herrick bring high prices. Other considerations are good color, interesting subject matter, and, of course, condition.

Advertising, Baldwin's Nervous Pills, 1905, 26x20" **40.00**

Bock Beer, clothed goat, Victorian woman, 1893, 27" **165.00**
Centlivre Brewery, 1900 .... **550.00**
Chero Cola, pretty girl drinking, 1930s, 12x18" **75.00**
Collie Malt Whiskey, copyright 1910 .... **47.50**
Cunard, 1920s **125.00**
Eveready Battery, art by Robert Robinson **95.00**
Hercules Powder, Don't Fool Me, Dog, 1920, 20x15" **65.00**

Italian, mounted on linen, artist's mark, 55x38" **200.00**
Kimball Cigarettes, show-girls, 1890s, 13x27" **275.00**
Moore's Ice Cream, giant cone, 1940s, 15x21" **85.00**
Red Man Chewing Tobacco, 1930s, 20x22" **65.00**
Silver Pine Healing Oil, bleeding horse, 1900, 28" **110.00**
United States Fur Co, St Louis, blk man & skunk, 20x16"... **32.00**
Boxing, Ali-Frazier Fight, Philippines 1975, by Leroy Neiman, 14x22" **25.00**
 Mace's Challenge to Heenan & Sayers, London, April 13, 1862 **200.00**
Minstrel, Al G Fields, Harry Skunk-That Minstrel Man, 41x26". **60.00**
 Apollo Club, 1889, 13x38" **100.00**
 Bryant's Opera House, Nov 9, 1896, NYC, 9x22" **110.00**
 Famous Troubadours Colored Comedy Company, 1922, 9x12" **35.00**
 Kola Touring, French, 3 blk men's heads, linen back, 50x37" **120.00**
 Lew Dockstater's, Al Jolson in black face **95.00**
 Sprague's Original Georgia, pictures Layton & Warwick, 19x25" **100.00**
Political, Harding & Coolidge, 1920, blk & wht oval pictures, 16x14" **35.00**
 Herbert Hoover, window type, This Home is for Hoover, 8x12" **20.00**
 Landon & Knox For US Deeds... Not Deficits, 14x21" **20.00**
 Roosevelt & Johnson, 1912, w/Kipling poem, 19x25" **55.00**
Red Cross, American, Junior, Walter Beach Humphrey, 21x15". **10.00**
 Christmas Roll Call, Dec 16-23, color litho, 28" **15.00**
 Fisher, 1918 .... **120.00**
 'Join' on US map, color, 1930, 12x18" **9.00**
Theatrical, Miss Billie Burke in The Runaway **40.00**
 Pianos Daude, Art Deco overhead view of pianist, 1930s, 64x46" **450.00**
 Prof Adams' Monster Specialty Company, 1880s, 9x24" **45.00**
 Take It From Me, artist: F Crepaux, Miner Litho NYC, 80x40" **110.00**
 The Great Dayton Show, 1910 stone litho, 42x26" **125.00**
 Thurston the Magician, Do The Spirits Come Back?, 1920s .. **75.00**
Travel, Bermuda, A Treidler illus, Art Deco, couple dancing, 42x28" **125.00**
 Come To Ulster, hikers w/backpacks, SC Allen & Co, 39x24" **100.00**
 Denmark, Bendix illus, cyclists in country, 39x25" **85.00**
 International Leipzig Trade Fair, silver letters on blue globe.. **75.00**
 Orient Calls, stylized figures, ship background, Toppan, 39x25" **135.00**
WWI, 1st Aerial Express, War Weapons Into Peacetime Tools.. **14.00**

American Library Assoc, Hey Fellows, 30x20" **20.00**
And They Thought We Couldn't Fight, Forsythe **48.00**
Clear the Way, Christy illus, Forbes Lithographic Co, 20x30" **350.00**
Emprunt Defense Nationale, A Bersnard, Maquet, Paris, 44x32" **200.00**
Fight or Buy War Bonds, Christy illus, Forbes Lithographic, 1917 **350.00**
For Home & Country, soldier w/wife & child, color **14.00**
Goodby Dad...Government Bonds, Harris, 30x20" **30.00**
Help Crush the Menace of the Seas, 27x18" **20.00**
I Want You for the Navy, Christy illus, 1917, 27x41" **250.00**
Journee l'Armee d'Afrique...Troupes Coloniales, Lucien Jonas . **70.00**
Keep Him Free, War Bonds, CL Bull **70.00**
Keep Them Smiling, color **14.00**
Lest We Perish, Greek girl w/arms outstretched, color **14.00**
Liberty Loan, Boy Scouts of America, Lyendecker **75.00**
Remember Belgium, Ellsworth Young, 30x20" **40.00**
Remember Your First Thrill of American Liberty, 30x20".... **30.00**
Shall We Be More Tender With Our Dollars..., 1917........ **30.00**
Spirit of 1917, US Marines, 4 soldiers, 2 w/flags, 40x30" **50.00**
Sure We'll Finish the Job, Gerrit Beneker, 40x26" **30.00**
The Army Builds Men, Army trade sign, hp colors & gold leaf **245.00**
The First Three Boys Killed in WWI, Kidder, 20x30" **75.00**
The Spirit of America, Christy illus, 1919, 20x30"........ **300.00**
War Camp Community Service, w/sailors & dough boys, 30x20" **20.00**
Woman's Liberty Loan Committee, Columbia w/torch, 14x21" **18.00**
YMCA War Campaign, 20x27" **125.00**
YMCA, His Home Over There, Albert Herter illustration **12.00**
YMCA, United Work Campaign Nov 11-18, 1918, w/Gen Pershing **12.00**
WWII, A Careless Word, A Needless Sinking, 1942, Fischer, 37x28" **25.00**
Attack, Attack, Attack, War Bonds, B Warren, US Printing Office **50.00**
Fire Away, Buy Bonds, sub sailor w/field glasses, 1944 ...... **10.00**
Food Is A Weapon, place setting w/bones, color............. **9.00**
I Want My Daddy Back, Daugherty **26.00**
Save Food & Equipment, Revolutionary soldier w/cook fire **9.00**
The Marines Have Landed, Flagg illus, US Printing Office, 28x40" **125.00**
Till We Meet Again, Buy War Bonds, soldier on transport ... **10.00**
Together We Win, Flagg illus, Powers Co, 28x40" **125.00**
We've Made A Monkey Out Of You, Hitler monkey, 1943, 20x15" **20.00**
World's Fair, New York 1939; New Yorkers are Friendly, 13x20" **40.00**
 Penn Railroad, 24x40" **200.00**
 Sgnd Culin, 28x40" **400.00**

Pot Lids

Pot lids were pottery covers for containers that were used for hair dressing, potted meats, etc. The most desirable were decorated with colorful transfer prints under the glaze in a variety of themes, animal and scenic. The first and probably the largest company to manufacture these lids was F.& R. Pratt, of Fenton, Staffordshire, established in the early 1800s. The name or initials of Jesse Austin, their designer, may sometimes by found on exceptional designs. Although few pot lids were made after the 1880s, the firm continued into the 20th century.

'A Pair' **75.00**
Bear picture, Pratt-Fenton, 1851, 3" **85.00**
Dr Johnson **100.00**
Garibaldi **75.00**
Man & his dog, upright holding a dish, framed, Pratt **75.00**
Peace, sgnd Austin **55.00**
Residence of Anne Hathaway, Pratt, 4" **115.00**
Rustic lovers scene, quotation around edge **75.00**
Scene w/dog & table, Shakespear bust, book & inkwell, framed, 6" **100.00**
The Shrimpers, 4" **98.00**
Uncle Toby **115.00**
View of Strasbourg, framed, 5" dia **50.00**

Village Wedding **95.00**
Walmer Castle, w/pot **105.00**
Winter scene of woman & boy, 3″ **78.00**

Powder Horns and Flasks

Flask, brass shot, embossed eagle on both sides, 4″ **75.00**
  Brass shot, emb scrolls & medallion w/3 horse heads, mkd, 8″ **135.00**
  Brass shot, embossed stag & foliage, gilded top, 8½″ **100.00**
  Brass shot, shell embossing, 8¾″ **105.00**
  Copper shot, brass top, 6½″ **40.00**
Powder horn, American, engraved animals, fish, inscribed, 1804, 10″ **145.00**
  American, engraved Masonic emblems, Peace Pipe, war club, 9½″ **105.00**

Carved, snake, dog, 16″ **400.00**
Carved end, inserted wood base, American Revolution, mkd, 15½″ **55.00**
European, engraved scrolls, inscription, 1748, 6″ **60.00**
European, engraved w/primitive animals, birds, flowers, 9¼″ **220.00**
European, floral engraving, 6¼″ **175.00**
European, primitive engraving, no plug, 6″ **30.00**
European, relief carving, animals, men on horseback, 6″ . . . **135.00**
Map, medallions, portrait, eagle w/shield & flag, 13″ **750.00**

Pratt

    Prattware is a type of relief molded earthenware with polychrome decoration. Scenic motifs with figures were popular; sometimes captions were added. Jugs are most common, but teapots, tableware, even figurines were made. 'Pratt' refers to Wm. Pratt of Lane Delph, who is credited with making the first of this type, though similar wares were made later by other Staffordshire potters.

Bowl, scene of The Blind Fiddler, oval on ped, leaf handle, 12x9″ **350.00**
Compote, rare mark, Godden **375.00**
Creamer, heart frames 2 young girls, doll & dog, 5″ **195.00**
Cup & saucer, 2 scenes on 5¼″ cup, 1 on 6½″ dia saucer . . . **135.00**
  Blue-green, geometric border, 3 transfers, large **155.00**
Figurine, lady, 3″ **80.00**
Jar, blue, hunting scene **20.00**
Jug, The Wine Makers, embossed design, soft paste, 1820s . . . **135.00**
Pitcher, blue w/scenes from 1856 hunting print, 6″ **85.00**
  Family scene in relief, 5″ **120.00**
  Pink luster w/Roman scenes, 7″ **120.00**
  Sportive Innocence & Mischievous Sport, 1815 . . . . **195.00**
Plate, classic figure border, transfer center, 9″ **125.00**
  Garibaldi, 6″ dia **115.00**
  Linlithgow Palace, blue transfer w/colors added, 1830, 9½″ . . **95.00**
  Persuasion **55.00**
  Preparing for the Ride, pink border **75.00**
  Scene of Statford on Avon, Fenton, 7″ **75.00**
  Scene w/Roman ruins **50.00**
  T Webster, 1834 litho, 9½″ dia **195.00**
  The Skewbald Horse, apple green border **80.00**
  Village Wedding, dated 1861, 7″ **36.00**
Tea set, Old Greek, 3-pc, Fenton **200.00**

Pre-Columbian Artifacts

    The term 'pre-Columbian' loosely refers to some time prior to 1492, when Columbus arrived in America. In particular, it indicates pre-1492 artifacts of Central and South America, some of which can be dated as early as 4000 B.C. Artifacts representing the cultures of the Inca, Maya, and Aztec Indians are avidly sought by the collector. These may be made of precious metals and hardstones, or of pottery. Some were used in rituals and religious rites, while some such as bowls and other utensils, though strictly utilitarian, nevertheless convey through form and decoration the craftsmanship of these early tribes.

Bowl, polychrome, highly decorated, cream slip, Mayan, 6″ dia **350.00**
Figure, queen, seated, winged headress, terra cotta, 4″ **150.00**
  Seated god, 3″ **45.00**
Jar, terra cotta, dark slip; flat & round; narrow, short neck **30.00**
Plate, rimmed, 3 long legs, terra cotta, red slip **110.00**
Sacrificial head, terra cotta, large headress, slant eyes, 3″ **50.00**
Skull, jade, pierced, 1½″ **125.00**
Snake, coiled, pale green Beryl, handcarved, 1¼″ **100.00**
Stirrup bottle, Peruvian, reddish-brown decor w/man's figure . . **350.00**
Whistle, queen figural, terra cotta, Mayan **100.00**

Primitives

    Like the mouse that ate the grindstone, so has collectible interest in primitives increased, a little bit at a time, until demand is taking bites instead of nibbles into their availabiltiy. Long generally restricted to survival essentials somehow contrived by our American settlers, the term 'primitives' has been expanded to include objects needed or desired by succeeding generations, those from cabin-'n-cornpatch existence to those from larger farms and towns. And through popular usage, it also respectfully covers what are actually 'country collectibles'.

    From the 1600s into the latter 1800s, factories employed carvers, blacksmiths and other artisans, whose handwork contributed to turning out quality items. In buying, exciting discoveries are 'touchmarks', a company's name and/or location, and maker's or owner's initials.

    Primitives are uniquely individual. Following identical forms, results more often than not show typically personal ideas of handcrafters---minimal or extensive. A price guide as this one combined with circumstances of age, condition, desire to own, etc., can only be used as directional arrow to arrive at individual pricing. For items not listed, consult comparable examples.

    In business for profit, dealers cannot reach buying levels of emotional evaluations a seller of inherited artifacts might expect, nor can they pay retail prices, but may instead be able to offer only 50% of retail due to their considerable expenses. To continue reading and visiting exhibits is to better approach knowledgeable purchasing.

Bathtub, tinned iron, 1830 . . . . **550.00**
Bedwarmer, ash handle, brass, 1850 . . . . **175.00**
  Brass, engraved, pierced lid **275.00**
  Burnished iron, brass screw tops w/rings, German, pr **95.00**
  Turned wood handle, copper pan, w/engraved bird, 44″ **135.00**
Bee smoker, metal can w/handle, bellows, wood base, New England **22.00**
Bee Smoker, tin, leather bellows **35.00**
Bench, barbershop, 6 braced legs oak slats, 1880-90, 17x9x28″ **185.00**
  Bucket, tin top, walnut, serpentine legs, 19x24x17″ **135.00**
  Crock, pine, stop shelf, deep lower shelf, base bar, 27x37x12″ **300.00**
  Mammy's rocking, N.E. pine, removable guard-gate, 1800 . **1,350.00**
  Pine, 4 leg supports through seat w/wood pins, 16½x48″ . . . **125.00**
  Pine, bracket ft mortised into seat, 17x13x82″ **195.00**
  Pine, carved hearts ea bracket ftd side, 17½x14x70″ **250.00**
  Pine, deep side aprons, center carrying cutout, 16x9x18″ . . . **125.00**
Washtub, oak slats, deep stain, 22x13x51″ **65.00**

Waterbucket, cypress, 2 top drawers, 2 base doors, 66x40″ . **350.00**
Bin, grain, slant lid, 1-board wide, 22″, 42″ high, 1870s **295.00**
    Meal, pine, 2 drawers, shelf back, 40″ wide **375.00**
    Meal, pine, roll front lid, 2 low doors, 3 top drawer, 72″ ... **700.00**
Bucket, galvanized iron, bail, for well **29.00**

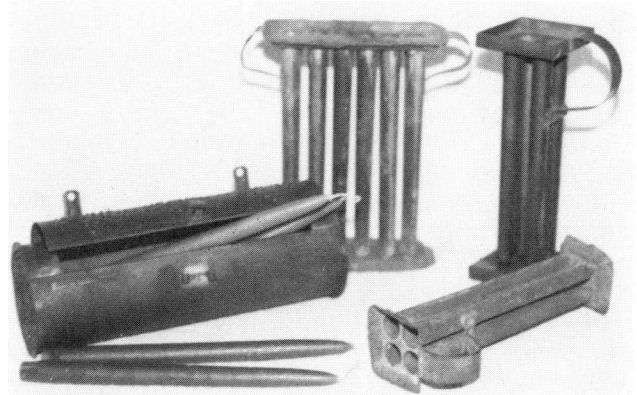

Candle box, tinner made, hanging, hinged cover, 1840, illus .. **210.00**
Candle lantern, pierced tin top, walnut frame, 15″ **265.00**
Candlemold, 6 sections, early **45.00**
    Tin, 4 tube, 10″ **30.00**
    Tin, 12 hole, 1800s **80.00**
    Tube, single handle, 1800s, illus **210.00**
    Two tube w/handle, tin, 1800s, 10½″ **75.00**
    With drip cup & handle, tin, Cathedral, 17¾″ **120.00**
Carpet beater, looped wire pattern **20.00**
    Wire, 3 center heart designs, wood handle **35.00**
Carriage jack, oak w/heavy iron, 1850 .... **130.00**
Cider press & grinder, oak **125.00**
Clothes plunger, made by MB Little, Chicago **45.00**
Coals carrier, sheetiron, sq w/flared top handle, lid, Arizona .. **130.00**
Comb, lady's, wrought iron, flat wood crown, New England **90.00**
Cranberry picker, tinned iron, handle, 45 teeth, 4½x14½x10″ . **75.00**
Cranberry scoop, metal tines, 10″ **75.00**
    Wood tines, 20″ **130.00**
    Wood tines, 22″ **140.00**
Crane, handwrought, iron, hooks for kettles, 1830s **55.00**
Doughbox, pine, splay leg base, fitted 2 board cover **165.00**
Drawing, Spenserian eagle, sgnd, 1861 .... **130.00**
Feather fluffer, 7-2″ loops, 18x2x5″ **65.00**
Flax breaker, Massachusetts, dated 1844 .... **175.00**
Flue cleaners, iron, 36″ **25.00**
Footwarmer, charcoal tray, old carpet covered **25.00**
    Buggy, oval, tin, charcoal w/handle, Taplex **22.00**
    Double, pierced tin, side door, tin coal pan, 7x16″ **125.00**
    Double, sloped top, brass handle, tin body, 8x19″ **225.00**
    Pierced tin, maple **140.00**
    Pierced, tin, soapstone insert, orig whale oil burner **120.00**
    The Clark, buggy, tin, charcoal, carpeted **19.00**
    Wood & tin, bail handle, New York, 19th century, 9x6½″ ... **95.00**
Grasshopper, wooden pull toy, old paint, early 1900s **75.00**
Harness holder, wooden, 2 wooden uprights **22.00**
Heat vent cover, ornamental ci, impressed Adams Co, 1897 .... **35.00**
Hitching block, ci, 1850-1860 .... **45.00**
Ice card **7.50**
Ice pick, Dayton, Ohio **15.00**
Ice tongs, 24″ **28.00**
    Factory made, iron, heavy handle, 1800s to early 1900s **45.00**
Jug, pressed glass in tin frame for filling kerosene lamps **39.00**
    Vinegar, brown clay top saltglazed, wht stoneware base **40.00**
Kettle, gypsy, 3 legged, w/iron bail **22.00**

Marionette, carved wood, leather joints, 28″ **300.00**
Mop wringer, orig labels, refinished wood, Pa., dated 1924 .... **69.00**
Noise maker, rachet-style, wooden **30.00**
Pan, iron, handle, hanging eye, 1800s, 40″ **115.00**
    Rolled sheet iron, Soapmaker, 10x26″ dia **50.00**
Pleating board, pine, 2 rows wire loops, 10 brass slats, 11x31″ . **25.00**
Pot, cast iron, encircled by iron band, 7″ dia **21.50**
    Ftd, bail handle, Barstow Stove Co **35.00**
    Heavy wire bail, 6x10″ **28.00**
    Iron band, bail, 3 legs, 7″ dia **22.00**
Pump plunger, 1 pc wood, illus **19.00**
Shoe last, cast iron, hand held to use, child & adult **9.50**
Soap cutter, blade w/turned wood handle, 1890s **25.00**
Steam boiler, iron & mesh, factory made, 1800s **80.00**
Stove shaker, cast iron **10.00**
String holder, hanging pine shaped splat **14.00**
Sugar nipper, spring handle, wide mouth, half-moon cutters, 1840s **115.00**
Tool carrier, orig blue & gr paint, eagle decor **245.00**
Town pump, long wooden handle 32½″, Kansas City Pump Co #1 **500.00**
Toy, carved wood man on wire, glass eyes, late 1800s **165.00**
Warming pan, brass & copper, floral design, 42″ **165.00**
Washboard, blue porcelain, cobalt, soap saver, dated 1918 ... **125.00**
    Brass & wood, Made-Rite, large **22.00**
    Brass, The Brass King, National **10.00**
    Glass ridges, drip slots in wood, soap ledge, Glass King **22.00**
    Roller, Mother Hubbard's Mendota **85.00**

Washer, copper, to dash clothes up and down in tub **75.00**
Watercolor, multiplication table, sgnd, reframed, 1838 .... **105.00**
Whiskey funnel, copper, strap handle, point gone, early **60.00**
Wind baffle, candle-powered, 1800s, 36″ **1,300.00**
Yoke, wooden, red, handwrought iron re-inforcements **35.00**

Prints

The term 'print' may be defined today as almost any image printed on paper by any available method. Examples of collectible old 'prints' are Norman Rockwell covers and Maxfield Parrish posters and calendars. 'Original print' refers to one achieved through the efforts of the artist, or under his direct supervision. A 'reproduction' is a print produced by an accomplished print maker, who reproduces another artist's print or original work.

Thorough study is required on the part of the collector to recognize

and appreciate the many variable factors to be considered in evaluating a print. Prices vary from one area of the country to another, and are dependent upon new findings regarding the scarcity or abundance of prints as such information may arise. Although each collector of old prints may have their own varying criteria by which to judge condition, for those who deal only rarely in this area, or newer collectors, a few guidelines may prove helpful. Staining, though unquestionably detrimental, is nearly always present in some degree, and should be weighed against the rarity of the print. Professional cleaning should improve its appearance and at the same time help to preserve it. Avoid tears that affect the image; minor margin tears are another matter, especially if the print is a rare one. Moderate 'foxing', brown spots caused by mold or the fermentation of the rag content of old paper, and light stains from the old frames are not serious unless present in excess. Margin trimming was a common practice, but look for at least ¾" to 1½" margins, depending on print size.

Audubon: Viviparous Quadrupeds of North America, Imperial Folio

Audubon is the best known of American & European wild life artists. This is one of his less familiar series, assembled in corroborate with John Bachman from 1839 until 1851. The prints are 28x22" each.

11 Northern Hare, Summer		850.00
14 Fremont's Squirrel		850.00
21 Grey Fox		1,000.00
31 Collard Peccary		900.00
47 American Badger		850.00
56 American Bison or Buffalo		1,000.00
61 Raccoon		1,000.00
66 Virginia Opossum		1,000.00
72 White American Wolf		850.00
73 Rocky Mountain Sheep		825.00
77 Prong-horned Antelope		850.00
90 Common Mouse		1,000.00
106 Columbian Black-tailed Deer		1,000.00
116 American Black or Silver Fox		950.00
118 Long-tailed Deer		875.00
136 Common or Virginia Deer		1,000.00
143 Rocky Mountain Flying Squirrel		775.00

Audubon: The Bien Edition

Audubon's first series of prints, 'Birds of America', was produced by Robert Havell of London. They were printed on Whitman watermarked paper, bearing dates of 1826 to 1838. The Octavo Edition of the same series were printed in three editions, the 1st by J.T. Bowers under Audubon's direction. There were 7 volumes of prints, each 11x7", the first 5 bearing the J.J. Audubon and J.B.Chevalier mark, the last 2, J.J. Audubon. They were produced from 1840 through 1871. The Bein Edition were full size reprints made under the direction of Audubon's son and daughter in the late 1850s. Due to the onset of the Civil War, only 105 plates were finished. These are considered to be the most valuable of the reprints of The Birds of America.

In the 1950s New York Graphics reproduced the full color prints through photolithography; and in 1971 the complete set was reprinted by Johnson Reprint Corp. of N.Y. and Theaturm Orbis Terrarum of Amsterdam. Examples of the latter bear the watermark G. Schut and Zonen.

7 Red-tailed Hawk		1,250.00
14 White-headed Eagle		2,250.00
19 Iceland Falcon		2,250.00
34 Barn Owl		1,850.00
48 Republican or Cliff Swallow		300.00
63 Wood Pewee		300.00
74 Kentucky Warbler		350.00
114 Black and White Creeper		350.00
119 Pine Grosbeak		350.00
200 Common Crossbill		1,250.00
205 Rose-breasted Grosbeak		1,500.00

217 Baltimore Oriole		2,250.00
220 Boat-tailed Brackle		1,500.00
225 American Crow		1,850.00
253 Ruby-throated Humming Bird		1,800.00
255 Belted Kingfisher		1,250.00
257 Pileated Woodpecker		1,250.00
273 Gold Winged Woodpecker		1,250.00
275 Yellow Billed Cuckoo		1,500.00
278 Carolina Parrot		2,500.00
280 White-headed Pigeon		1,500.00
287 Turkey Cock		6,000.00
296 Pinnated Grouse		1,400.00
332 Red-backed Sandpiper		300.00
358 Glossy Ibis		1,500.00
367 Green Heron		1,250.00
368 Great White Heron		2,250.00
371 Reddish Egret		2,250.00
372 Blue Crane		2,250.00
385 Mallard Duck		2,500.00
386 Dusky Duck		1,850.00
391 Summer Duck or Wood Duck		2,500.00
414 Smew or White Nun		1,250.00
423 Brown Pelican		2,500.00
465 Great Auk		1,500.00

Audubon: Birds of America, Original Edition, Havell and Son

6 Hen Turkey (Great American Hen)		12,000.00
17 Carolina Turle Dove		4,000.00
26 Carolina Parrot		4,500.00
27 Red-headed Woodpecker		2,500.00
31 White-headed Eagel		4,000.00
41 Ruffed Grouse		4,500.00
62 Passenger Pigeon		4,000.00
76 Virginia Partridge		4,500.00
81 Fish Hawk		3,700.00
86 Black Warrior		2,700.00
90 Black and White Creeper		850.00
95 Blue-eyed Yellow Warbler		850.00
101 Raven		3,700.00
111 Pileated Woodpecker		4,500.00
121 Snowy Owl		4,000.00
126 White-headed Eagle (young)		3,200.00
131 American Robin		4,000.00
136 Meadow Lark		4,000.00
156 American Crow		3,250.00
176 Spotted Grouse		4,000.00
181 Golden Eagle		4,000.00
199 Little Owl		1,300.00
211 Great Blue Heron		4,500.00
217 Louisiana Heron		4,000.00
222 White Ibis		2,700.00
231 Long-billed Curlew		4,500.00
242 Snowy Heron		4,500.00
251 Brown Pelican		4,500.00
261 Whooping Crane		4,000.00
272 Richardson's Jager		775.00
281 Great White Heron		4,500.00
301 Canvasback Duck		4,500.00
321 Roseate Spoonbill		4,000.00
331 American Merganser		3,000.00
340 Least Stormy Petrel		775.00
351 Great Cinereous Owl		3,300.00
361 Long-tailed Grouse		3,000.00
366 Iceland Falcon		4,000.00
376 Trumpeter Swan		4,000.00

386 White Heron **4,000.00**
400 Arkansas Siskin **1,250.00**
406 Trumpeter Swan **4,000.00**
411 Common American Swan **4,000.00**
421 Brown Pelican **4,000.00**
430 Slender-billed Guillemot **775.00**

Boileau

    Philip Boileau (1864-1917) was well known for his illustrations of women, particularly those painted during the early 20th century. He did three dozen covers for *The Saturday Evening Post*, dozens of postcard subjects, and many other illustrations.
Madonna & Jewels, framed, 1916, 10x17″ **75.00**
   Magazine cover, any 1900-17, detached **9.00**
   Magazine cover, any 1900-17, intact **18.00**

Christy, Howard Chandler

Couple, 1909 . . . . **135.00**
Looking Backward, 1903, 13x16″ **35.00**
   Spring Scene, sgnd, orig frame, 23x19½″ **75.00**
   Winter Scene, sgnd, orig frame, 23x19½″ **75.00**

Currier & Ives

    Nathaniel Currier was in business by himself until the late 1850s when he formed a partnership with James Merrit Ives. Currier is given credit for being the first to use the medium to portray newsworthy subjects; and the Currier and Ives views of 19th century American culture are familiar to us all.
A Black Squall, 1879 . . . . **175.00**
A Broadway Belle, girl **40.00**
A Clearing on the American Frontier, small folio **250.00**
A Crack Trotter--Coming Around, Thomas Worth on stone **55.00**
A Fast Team--Out on the Loose **215.00**
A Halt by the Wayside **175.00**
A Home in the Wilderness, small folio, 1870 . . . . **475.00**
A Home on the Mississippi, small folio, 1871 . . . . **395.00**
A Line Shot--The Aim, small folio, 1881 . . . . **175.00**
A Lovely Calm, small folio, 1879 . . . . **175.00**
A Mountain Ramble **125.00**
A Mule Train on a Down Grade, small folio, 1881 . . . . . . **150.00**
A Mule Train on an Up Grade, small folio, 1881 . . . . **150.00**
A New England Home, small folio **165.00**
A New England Home, med folio, orig frame **220.00**
A New England Homestead, the Franklin Pierce home, NC, 1852 **185.00**

A Staunch Pointer, small folio **185.00**
A Stopping Place on the Road--The Horse Shed, lg folio . . . **2,250.00**
A Virginia Home in the Olden Time, 1872 . . . . **195.00**
A Year After Marriage, 1847, NC, sm **80.00**
Abraham Lincoln--The Nation's Martyr, small folio **70.00**
Abraham Lincoln/The Nation's Martyr, medium folio, blk & wht **145.00**
Alnwick Castle, small folio **110.00**
American Brook Trout, small folio, 1872 . . . . **275.00**
American Express Train, lg folio, 1864 . . . . **7,500.00**
American Field Sports--On a Point, lg folio, 1857 . . . . . . **345.00**
American Game, lg folio **795.00**
American Homestead--Autumn, small folio, 1869 . . . . . . **225.00**
American Homestead--Spring, small folio, 1869 . . . . **225.00**
American Homestead--Summer, small folio, 1868 . . . . . . **215.00**
American Homestead--Winter, small folio, 1868 . . . . **595.00**

American Hunting Scenes, A Good Chance, 1863, lg **1,200.00**
American Speckled Brook Trout, lg folio, 1864 . . . . **950.00**
American Winter Sports--Deer Shooting on the Shatagee, lg, 1855 **800.00**
American Country Life--Pleasures of Winter, lg folio, NC, 1855 **1,250.00**
Among the Pines--A 1st settlement family **275.00**
An Easter Offering, 1871 . . . . **45.00**
Andrew Jackson--Seventh President of the US, NC **75.00**
Art Gallery--Grand United States Centennial **145.00**
Autumn, small folio, 1871 . . . . **60.00**
Autumn Fruits, medium folio, 1861 . . . . **190.00**
Autumn on Lake George, small folio **170.00**
Ballston Springs, 1838 . . . . **20.00**
Battle at Cedar Mountain, Aug 9, 1862 . . . . **165.00**
Battle of Cerro Gordo, April 18, 1847, NC **125.00**
Battle of Gettysburg, July 3, 1863 . . . . **150.00**
Battle of the Kings, large folio **375.00**
Bear Hunting--Close Quarters, small folio **650.00**
Bombardment & Capture of Fort Henry, Tenn., small folio . . . **95.00**
Bothwell Bridge--On the Clyde, medium folio **150.00**
Bouquet of the Vase, 1870 . . . . **80.00**
Bridal Veil--Yosemite Valley, California **265.00**
Brook Trout--Just Caught, medium folio **345.00**
Burial of the Bird, small folio, blk & wht **85.00**
Burning of the Steamship Austria, Sept 13, 1859 . . . . **200.00**
Byron in the Highlands, small folio **65.00**
California Scenery, small folio **150.00**
Capture of Andre, 1780, NC **160.00**
Capture of Atlanta, Sept 2, 1864 . . . . **145.00**
Catterskill Falls **165.00**
Celebrated Trotting Stallion Patron **160.00**
Central Park--The Bridge, small folio **350.00**
Chappaqua Farm--Westchester City, NY, 1872 . . . . **150.00**

Children in the Wood.................................... 50.00
City Hall, New York, NC 225.00
City of New York, from Jersey City, 1849, NC 475.00
Clipper Ship Lightening, NC, lg folio................ 3,000.00
Clipper Ship Ocean Express, lg folio, 1865 .... 750.00
Colonel Elmer E Ellsworth............................. 85.00
Cornelia... 45.00
Cutter Yacht Thistle, small folio 325.00
Darktown Fire Brigade, 1889 .... 160.00
Day Before Marriage--The Bride's Jewels............... 75.00
De Boss Rooster, negro comic 125.00
Death of Major Ringgold, NC.......................... 45.00
Death of Washington, Dec 14, 1799, small folio, NC 100.00
Deer in the Woods.................................... 225.00
Deer Shooting on the Shattagee, 1859, 18x27" 900.00
Delicious Fruit, medium folio, 1865 .... 245.00
Dorothy, NC 40.00
Dwight L Moody--The American Evangelist, blk & wht 30.00
Easter Flowers, 1869 .... 48.00
Ethan Allen & Mate & Dexter, lg folio, 1867........... 1,100.00
Evening Star 42.00
Eventide--The Curfew, small folio..................... 45.00
Fall of Richmond on the Night of April 2, 1865 .... 170.00
Falls of Niagara, From Clifton House, NC 145.00
Fanny, NC... 45.00

Farmers Home--Summer, 1864, lg...................... 600.00
Father & Child, NC, 1849 .... 56.00
Feeding the Swans, small folio......................... 85.00
Fire Department Certificate, medium folio, 1877 .... 300.00
First Pants, medium folio.............................. 110.00
Flight of the Mexican Army, small folio, 1847 .... 60.00
Floral Tribute, small folio 110.00
Flushing a Woodcock.................................. 145.00
Fording the River, medium folio, NC 325.00
Fort Pickens, Pensacola Harbor, Fla................... 165.00
Fort Sumter, Charleston Harbor, S.C.................. 245.00
Fox Chase--Gone Away, small folio, NC, 1846 .... 225.00
Fox Chase--Throwing Off, small folio, 1846 .... 135.00
Fox Hunting--The Death, medium folio................. 85.00
Fox Hunting--The Meet, medium folio 800.00
Frozen, small folio 575.00
Fruit, apples, plums, grapes & butterflies 65.00
Fruit & Flowers, 1870 .... 85.00
Fruit Vase, 1870 .... 95.00
Fruits of the Golden Land, small folio 35.00
Fruits of the Seasons, 1872 .... 75.00

Fruits of the Tropics, 1871 .... 80.00
General Andrew Jackson--At New Orleans, Jan 8, 1815, NC 80.00
General Grant & Family, med folio 85.00
General Grant & Family, small folio 75.00
General Israel Putnam--The Iron Son of 76, NC 150.00
General James A Garfield, small folio, blk & wht 85.00
General Taylor--Rough & Ready, NC, 1847 .... 75.00
General Tom Thumb & Wife, Col Nutt & Minnie Warren 175.00
General Z Taylor--Hero of the Rio Grande, NC, 1846 .... 95.00
George M Patchen--Brown Dick & Miller's Damsel, lg folio, 1859 650.00
George Washington, bust portrait 100.00
George Washington--First President of the US, NC, small folio.. 55.00
Getting a Hoist, A Bad Case of the Heaves, Thomas Worth on stone 150.00
Glencariff Inn 85.00
God Bless Our Home, small folio 75.00
Good Little Sisters, small folio, blk & wht 60.00
Good Times on the Old Plantation, small folio 350.00
Grand Horse St Julien--The King of Trotters 195.00
Grand National American Banner, NC, 1856 .... 195.00
Grand National Democratic Banner, 1864 .... 168.00
Grand National Democratic Banner--Press Onward, NC, 1844 . 150.00
Grand National Temperance Banner, small folio, NC, 1851 ... 135.00
Grand National Whig Banner--Onward, NC 100.00
Grand United Order of Odd-Fellows Chart, Medium folio, 1881 . 75.00
Great Salt Lake, Utah, small folio 150.00
Grottos of the Sea, 1869 .... 50.00
Harry Bassett & Longfellow, small folio, 1874 .... 300.00
Harvest, oxen pulling hay wagon over bridge 110.00
Haying Time, The Last Load, large 1,500.00
He is Saved, small folio, blk & wht 50.00
Hiawatha's Wedding, medium folio 250.00
Hiawatha's Wooing, medium folio, 1860............... 475.00
High Water in the Mississippi, lg folio, 1868 .... 1,450.00
Home Sweet Home, med folio, orig frame 220.00
Home Sweet Home, small folio 115.00
Home of Washington, Mount Vernon, Va., medium folio 195.00
Homeward Bound, small folio 495.00
Honorable Abraham Lincoln, medium folio, blk & wht, 1860 ... 95.00
Household Pets, mother holding young girl, NC, 1845 .... 60.00
Household Treasures, small folio 48.00
Household Treasures, baby, little girl, dog & puppy 45.00
Hudson River--Crow Nest, small folio 245.00
Hues of Autumn--Racquet River, small folio 200.00

Husking, 1861, lg 1,800.00
Hunting on the Plains, small folio..................... 425.00

In the Harbor, hand colored, 12½x16″ **200.00**
In the Mountains **225.00**
In the Woods **145.00**
Indian Buffalo Hunt, orig frame, med folio **150.00**
Initiation Ceremonies of the Darktown Lodge--Part First, sm, 1887 **175.00**
Initiation Ceremonies of the Darktown Lodge--Part Second, sm, 1887 **95.00**
Innocence, young girl, NC **55.00**
Into Mischief, orig 21x16¼″ frame **95.00**
Iroquois, small folio, 1881 .... **275.00**
James Madison--Fourth President of the US, NC **125.00**
James Monroe--Fifth President of the US, NC **150.00**
John Quincy Adams--Sixth President of the US, NC **90.00**
John R Gentry, small folio **175.00**
Josephine, small folio **50.00**
Just Married **38.00**
Kate, small folio **35.00**
Kenilworth Castle, lg folio **160.00**
Kilkenny Castle, small folio **70.00**
King of the Forest, small folio **170.00**
Lafayette at the Tomb of Washington--Mt. Vernon, NC, sm folio **85.00**
Lake George, Black Mountain **125.00**
Lake Memphremagog, Owls Head **145.00**
Lakeside Home, medium folio **250.00**
Landing of the Pilgrims at Plymouth 11th Dec 1620, small folio **125.00**
Landscape, Fruit & Flowers, large folio, 1862 .... **1,750.00**
Life on the Prairie/The Trapper's Defense/Fire Fight Fire, lg, 1862 **4,500.00**
Lily Lake, framed **65.00**
Little Annie & Her Kittie, small folio, 1868 .... **55.00**
Little Daisy Girl...................................... **50.00**
Little Fairy, little girl **45.00**
Little Johnny--Quite Tired, small folio **50.00**
Little Manly **34.00**
Little Minnie, Taking Tea, small folio, blk & wht........... **45.00**
Little Nelly... **45.00**
Little Red Riding Hood **100.00**
Little Rosebud, small folio, 1870 .... **30.00**
Little Teacher, blk & wht.............................. **26.00**
Londonderry, on the River Foyle, Ireland, small folio **65.00**
Longfellow, by Lexington, J Cameron on stone **150.00**
Longfellow, small folio, 1871 .... **225.00**
Loss of the USM Steamship Artic, small folio, NC, 1854 ..... **235.00**
Love is the Lightest **45.00**
Ma Ma's Pets, small folio, NC, 1847 .... **35.00**
Major General George B McClellan, small folio, blk & wht **85.00**
Major General John C Fremont **45.00**
Major General Philip H Sheridan........................ **45.00**
Marcus Morton--Govenor of Massachusetts, framed, NC........ **45.00**
Martha Washington, medium folio....................... **100.00**
Martha Washington, small folio **70.00**
Martin Van Buren--Eighth President of the US, NC........... **55.00**
Mary Ann, NC... **18.00**
Mayflower Saluted by the Fleet, lg folio, 1886 .... **495.00**
Melrose Abbey, small folio **45.00**
Mischief & Music, small folio, blk & wht.................. **55.00**
Mother's Blessing, med folio **60.00**
Moonlight Promenade................................... **45.00**
Moonlight in the Tropics, small folio **135.00**
Moosehead Lake, small folio **175.00**
Mountaineer's Home, small folio **150.00**
Mr Wm H Vanderbilt's Celebrated Road Team/Sm Hopes/Lady Mac **160.00**
My Favorite Pony **48.00**
My Highland Girl **35.00**
My Little Playfellow, small folio, NC **75.00**
My Little White Kittens--Playing Ball, small folio **60.00**

My Little White Kittens--Playing Dominoes **60.00**
Naval Bombardment of Vera Cruz, NC, 1847............... **165.00**
New York Bay--From Bay Bridge........................ **400.00**
New York Bay--From Bay Bridge, medium folio **450.00**
New York Clipper Ship 'Challenge', NC **325.00**
New York Ferry Boat **375.00**
Niagara Falls--From Goat Island, medium folio............. **200.00**
Night After the Battle, small folio **70.00**
Night by the Campfire, medium folio, 1861 .... **295.00**
Noah's Ark, small folio **85.00**
Noontide a Shady Spot, small folio **165.00**
O! There's a Mousie! **75.00**
O'Sullivan's Cascade, small folio **125.00**
Old Blandford Church--Petersburg, Virginia **110.00**
Old Oaken Bucket, small folio.......................... **120.00**
Old Saw, LI, small folio, NC **275.00**
On the Coast of California **150.00**
On the St Lawrence, Indian encampment **225.00**
Our Pets--Fast Asleep **60.00**
Our Pets--Wide Awake **60.00**
Phebe, NC **45.00**
Placid Lake, Adirondacks............................... **175.00**
Prairie Hens, small folio **325.00**
President Lincoln at Home, small folio, 1865 .... **70.00**
Profit & Loss, small folio, 1880........................ **225.00**
Quail Shooting **350.00**
Republican Banner for 1860, Lincoln & Hannibal **195.00**
Roadside Cottage, medium folio **135.00**
Robinson Crusoe & His Man Friday, small folio **195.00**
Robinson Crusoe & His Pets, small folio **165.00**
Roses of May, 1870 .... **95.00**
Saratoga Lake, small folio **185.00**
Saratoga Springs, small folio **175.00**
Scenery of the Cattskills, mountain & house in distance **195.00**
Scenery of the Wissahickon, near Philadelphia **185.00**
Scholars Rewards, small folio, 1874 .... **200.00**
Search the Scriptures, NC **20.00**
Seige of Charleston **345.00**
Shantying on the Lake Shore, lg folio, 1867 .... **1,800.00**
Skating Scene--Moonlight.............................. **650.00**
Sleepy Hollow Bridge **245.00**
Sleepy Hollow Church--Near Tarrytown, NY, medium folio **595.00**
Sons of Temperance, Love, Purity & Fidelity, NC **60.00**
Spirit of the Union, 1860 .... **125.00**
Spring, 1870, framed **110.00**
Spring, Girl **45.00**
Squirrel Shooting **375.00**
Star Pointer, small folio **175.00**
Strawberries, small folio, 1870 .... **95.00**
Striped Bass, 1872 .... **145.00**
Summer, small folio, 1871 .... **65.00**
Summer Fruits, medium folio, 1861 .... **180.00**
Summer in the Country **110.00**
Summer Morning **225.00**
Sunnyside--On the Hudson, small folio **155.00**
Sweet Spring Time, medium folio **150.00**
Sylvan Lake **90.00**
Take Care **32.00**
Terrific Combat Between the Monitor, small folio **475.00**
The American Beauty................................... **40.00**
The Assassination of President Lincoln, small folio, blk & wht, 1865 **60.00**
The Battle at Five Forks, Va., April 1, 1865, small folio....... **35.00**
The Battle of Bunker's Hill, small folio, blk & wht **60.00**
The Battle of Cedar Creek, Va., Oct 19, 1864............... **125.00**

The Battle of Fair Oaks, Va., May 31, 1862, small folio **175.00**
The Best Likeness, medium folio, 1858 .... **135.00**
The Bewildered Hunter, small folio, 1872 .... **135.00**
The Black Eyed Beauty **45.00**
The Bouquet of Roses **55.00**
The Brave Wife, General McClellan.................... **85.00**
The Burning of Chicago, small folio, 1871 .... **300.00**
The Celebrated Clipper Ship Dreadnought **395.00**
The Celebrated Trotting Stallion Ethan Allen, small folio, 1872 **175.00**
The Children's Picnic **45.00**
The Clipper Yacht America of New York, small folio, NC..... **600.00**
The Cottage Door--Yard, Evening, medium folio, blk & wht ... **135.00**
The Cottage by the Cliff.............................. **148.00**
The Cove of Cork, small folio **70.00**
The Darktown Hook & Ladder Corps, small folio, 1884 ...... **195.00**
The Death Bed of the Martyr President Lincoln, medium folio **185.00**
The Declaration of Independence, 4/4/76, NC **145.00**
The Eastern Beauty **40.00**
The Fairest of the Fair, small folio **40.00**
The Farmer's Friends **165.00**
The Favorite Horse, small folio **165.00**
The Ferry Boat, medium folio, NC **195.00**
The First Ride, small folio **45.00**
The First Step--Come to Mamma, L Maurer on stone, med folio **85.00**
The Flower Vase, small folio, 1848 .... **70.00**
The Fruit Girl, NC **45.00**
The Fruits of Intemperance, small folio, 1870 .... **235.00**
The Girl I Love, small folio **60.00**
The Golden Morning, small folio **175.00**
The Great East River Bridge, small folio, 1872 .... **385.00**
The Great East River Bridge, Connecting New York and Brooklyn **200.00**
The Great Fight Between the Merrimac & Monitor, March 9, 1862 **350.00**
The Great Fire at Boston, small folio, 1872................ **200.00**
The Great Mississippi Steamboat Race, small folio.......... **550.00**
The Great West **550.00**
The Happy Home, small folio, NC...................... **95.00**
The Hudson From West Point, medium folio, 1862 .... **675.00**
The Hudson Highlands, Near Newburg, NY **75.00**
The Hudson Near Coldspring, Chapel of Our Lady, small folio.. **85.00**
The Ingleside Winter **400.00**
The Jockey's Dream **50.00**
The Lake of the Dismal Swamp **100.00**
The Lakes of Killarney, small folio **95.00**
The Lexington of 1861--The Massachusetts Volunteers **100.00**
The Life & Age of Woman **85.00**

The Life of a Fireman--The Metro System, 1886, lg **850.00**
The Life of a Fireman--The Ruins, lg folio, NC, 1854 ..... **1,200.00**
The Life of a Hunter--Catching a Tartar, lg folio, 1861 ..... **5,000.00**

The Life of a Sportsman--Camping in the Woods **325.00**
The Life of a Sportsman--Coming Into Camp, small folio, 1872 **325.00**
The Life of a Sportsman--Going Out, small folio, 1872 .... **450.00**
The Lincoln Family, 1867 .... **125.00**
The Little Beauty, 1872 .... **28.00**
The Little Favorite, NC **35.00**
The Little Volunteer, small folio, 1861 .... **20.00**
The Lovers Quarrel, small folio, NC, 1846 .... **85.00**
The Lovers Reconciliation, small folio, NC, 1846.............. **85.00**
The Man of Words, The Man of Deeds, med folio, blk & wht . **175.00**
The Marriage, small folio, NC, 1847 .... **95.00**
The Merry, Merry Maiden & the Tar **150.00**
The Morning, small folio **55.00**
The Mother's Dream................................. **40.00**
The Narrown, New York Bay, From Staten Island, sm folio ... **225.00**
The New Fashioned Girl................................. **65.00**
The Notch House, White Mountains, New Hampshire **125.00**
The Old Farm House, small folio, 1872 .... **625.00**
The Old Manse, view of the Vander Hayden Palace **150.00**
The Pasture--Noontide, medium folio **130.00**
The Peaceful River, small folio **125.00**
The Presidents of the US, small folio, 1844 .... **60.00**
The Puzzled Fox, small folio, 1872 .... **225.00**
The River Side, couple on bank viewing rowboat **125.00**
The Roadside Mill, small folio, 1870 .... **165.00**
The Sailor, Far-Far at Sea, NC **90.00**
The Sale of the Pet Lamb, small folio **165.00**
The Sleigh Race, small folio.......................... **1,500.00**
The Soldier's Record, 16th Regiment, Vermont Volunteers, 1862 **70.00**
The Soldiers Dream of Home, small folio **45.00**
The Soldiers Home--The Vision, small folio, 1862 .... **110.00**
The Source of the Hudson, In the Indian Pass **265.00**
The Tomb of Washington, Mt Vernon, medium folio, blk & wht **60.00**
The Trapper's Last Shot, medium folio **800.00**
The Union Clad Monitor Montauk, small folio............ **375.00**
The Vase of Flowers, 1847 .... **195.00**
The Washington Family, blk & wht....................... **65.00**
The Washington Family, small folio, blk & wht, 1867 .... **125.00**
The Wedding Day, NC, 1846 .... **65.00**
The Wedding Day, small folio, NC **85.00**
The Wonderful Mare Maud S, Scott Leighton on stone **115.00**
The Yacht Countess of Dufferin, small folio **290.00**
The Young Continental--The Spirit of '76, small folio **245.00**
The Young Mother, NC **45.00**
Through to the Pacific, 1870.......................... **675.00**
Thy Kingdom Come, small folio, 1872 .... **110.00**
To the Memory of...., NC............................. **25.00**
To the Rescue, blk & wht **35.00**
Tobogganing on Darktown Hill--An Untimely Move, sm folio .. **175.00**
Tobogganing on Darktown Hill--Getting a Hist, sm folio, 1890 . **175.00**
Toll-gate, Jamaica Plant Road, sm folio, NC................ **195.00**
Tree of Death--The Sinner, NC **32.00**
Tree of Intemperence, saloon on left, NC **75.00**
Tree of Life--The Christian, sm folio **85.00**
Trotting Cracks at Home--A Model Stable, lg folio, 1868 ... **3,200.00**
Trotting Mare Nancy Hanks, sm folio **175.00**
Trout Fishing on Chateaugay Lake, N Currier, 20x27"....... **950.00**
Two Little 'Fraid Cats................................. **58.00**
US Post Office, NY.................................. **275.00**
Under Cliff--On the Hudson **275.00**
Under Cliff--On the Hudson, sm folio **60.00**
United American, Patriotism, Charity, Harmony, NC **95.00**
Valley Falls, Virginia, small folio **170.00**
View From Fort Putnam, West Point, Hudson River, NY **245.00**

View on the Rondout, med folio 195.00
Washington as a Mason, sm folio, 1868 . . . . 130.00
Washington at Princeton, January 3, 1777, NC 500.00
Washington's Reception by the Ladies, NC 75.00
Washington's Reception by the Ladies, sm folio, 1845 . . . . 160.00
Watkins Glen, New York Hotel & Bridge 235.00
Wild Turkey Shooting, small folio 400.00
William Henry Harrison--Ninth President of the US, NC 65.00
Winning Hands Down with a Good Second, lg folio, 1887 . . . . 355.00
Winter Morning in the Country, small folio, 1873 . . . . 750.00
Winter Morning, medium folio, 1861 . . . . 125.00
Wm Penn's Treaty w/the Indians 1661, small folio 125.00
Woodcock Shooting, small folio 450.00
Wound Up, small folio 175.00
Yacht Meteor of NY--293 Tons 295.00
Yosemite Falls, California, sm folio 275.00

Fisher, Harrison

Harrison Fisher (1875-1934) was America's most highly paid illustrator circa 1910 when he earned $50,000 a year. He did nearly 100 covers for *The Saturday Evening Post*, over 200 covers for *Cosmopolitan*, as well covers for many other magazines. He also did postcards, prints and other illustrations, among them several large books including *The Harrison Fisher Book, A Dream of Fair Women, Maidens Fair, American Belles*, and *A Girl's Life and Other Pictures*. Many of the 'prints' seen today are pages removed from these magazines. These have value, but not as much as individual prints issued as such.

Any large size, usually 15-16″ 75.00
Any small size, usually 9x7″, or similar 23.00
Bonnet Girl, sgnd, framed, 6x9″ 50.00
Magazine cover, any Cosmopolitan, detached 4.00
Magazine cover, any Cosmopolitan, intact 11.50
Magazine cover, any Ladies Home Journal, detached 11.00
Magazine cover, any Ladies Home Journal, intact 18.00
Magazine cover, any Saturday Evening Post, detached 9.00
Magazine cover, any Saturday Evening Post, intact 14.00
Out For Spin, 1907, 11x16″ 38.00
So Nice to Have Money, 11x16″ 38.00
The Honeymoon, 12x16″ 70.00
The King of Hearts, 10x14″ 68.00
Times in a Girl's Life, set of 4, gold frame, 6½x4½″ 75.00
Times in a Girl's Life, set of 4, orig gold leaf frame, 8½x6½″ . 100.00

Gutmann, Bessie Pease

A Little Bit of Heaven, orig frame 35.00
Awakening, orig gold frame, 19½x15″ 60.00
Chums 150.00
Dreamland's Border, orig frame 45.00
Mischief, old octagon frame 75.00
Our Alarm Clock, 9x12″ 25.00
Sunbeam, old octagon frame 75.00
The 1st Dancing Lesson, framed, 17½x12½″ 78.00
The Butterfly, framed 65.00
The Message of the Roses 90.00
The New Love, 1907, 9x12″ 30.00

Humphrey, Maud

Four girls w/baby chick, framed, 1890 . . . . 125.00
Girl w/pink dress holding a mirror, sgnd, 8x10½″ 75.00
Two girls in field picking flowers, sgnd, 11x8″ 35.00
Two girls playing w/fire crackers, sgnd, 8x10½″ 75.00
Young lady w/flowered hat, matted, 15½x11″ 120.00

Icart

Louis Icart was a French artist who immortalized the French woman through his etchings, which were widely produced during the 1920s. Most of his post-1920 etchings carry a U.S. copyright notice in the margin, as well as Icart's personal intaglio seal.

Apple Girl, 1929 . . . . 95.00
Arrival & Departure, framed, pair 1,150.00
Autumn, etching & drypoint colors, sgnd, 1928 . . . . 650.00
Bathers, 3 women in a pond, framed 875.00
Belle Rose 1,200.00
Bird Seller, framed 895.00
Blue Buddha 1,100.00
Broken Jug, framed 595.00
Casanova 895.00
Charm of Montmarte 825.00
Coach, 2 women, umbrella, framed 750.00
Cocktail Martini 2,095.00
Conchita, framed 995.00

Coursing II 2,000.00
D'Artagnan, framed 1,000.00
Don Juan 950.00
Eager to Play 1,395.00
Eve, etching, framed, oval sepia 1,350.00
Fair Model, framed 1,450.00
Farewell--Au Revoir, mended 1,200.00
Faust 900.00
Feeding Time, framed 575.00
Forbidden Fruit, etching, unframed 1,200.00
Inquest 1,600.00
Japanese Garden, 12x16½″ 250.00
Joan of Arc, framed 750.00
Joy of Life, framed 1,995.00
Kittens, sgnd, oval frame, 1925 . . . . 575.00
La Cigarette, etching & drypoint in color, 1925 . . . . 1,400.00
La Lettre, orig print, 1928, 22x18″ 65.00
Lady of the Camelias, orig frame & mat, 1927, 21x17″ 1,250.00
Laziness 995.00
Lilies, etching & drypoint in colors, sgnd, 1934, 28½x20″ . . 1,350.00
Lovers 800.00
Madame Butterfly, etching & drypoint in colors, sgnd, 1927 . . . 850.00
Maid with Greyhounds, 16x26″ 765.00
Musetta, etching & drypoint in colors, sgnd, 1927 . . . . 850.00
Orange Blossom, etching, 1935 . . . . 850.00
Parisian Lady, sgnd, 1912, 5x7″ 450.00
Picking Apples 895.00
Playful Pup Terrier, pulling woman's dress at hem 700.00
Rainbow, framed 1,995.00
Salome, etching & drypoint, color, 21x14″ 575.00
Sea Nymph, no frame 1,250.00
Seated Woman with Parasol 1,870.00
Secrets--Ecoute 1,980.00
Sleeping Beauty 900.00
Smoke, orig frame, sgnd & sealed, 19½x14½″ 1,200.00
Springtime Promenade, framed 595.00

Symphony in Blue, etching & drypoint in colors, sgnd, 1936 **1,000.00**

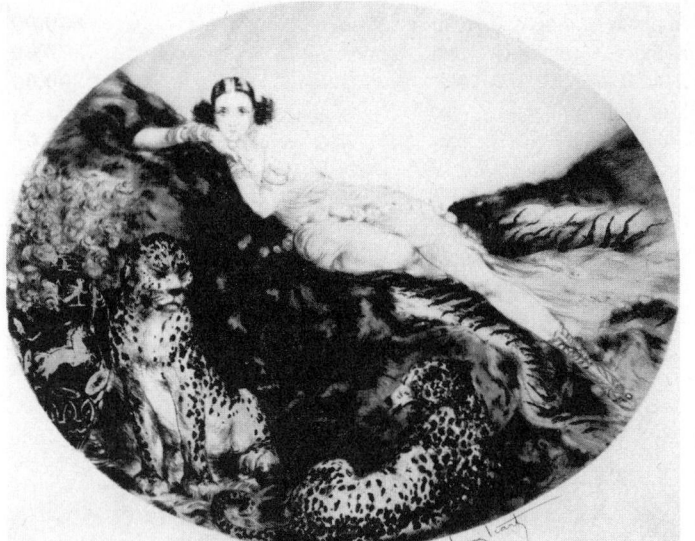

Thais **1,950.00**
The Angry Steed **1,600.00**
The Blue Chair **1,795.00**
The Blue Dairy, etching, oval sepia, unframed **1,550.00**
The Four Dears **1,300.00**
The Nurse **800.00**
The Pink Slip **1,600.00**
The Pool **2,200.00**
Tosca **1,000.00**
Venus **1,400.00**
Waltz Echoes, 1″ margins, framed **1,475.00**
Werther, framed **1,075.00**
White Handkerchief, framed, rare **950.00**
White Underwear **950.00**
Wisteria **1,395.00**
Wistfulness, framed................................. **575.00**
Young Lady & Dog, 20x28″ **245.00**
Young Woman in Vineyard, sgnd, oval, color, 23½x28″ **500.00**
Zest **1,400.00**

Japanese
Hiroshige I, Great Wave at Satta, 1858, Tsutaya, 15x10″ ... **2,150.00**
Hiroshige I, Moonlight at Fuchu, 1855, Tsutaya, 15x10″ **355.00**
Hiroshige II, Bikuni Bridge in Snow, 1858, Uoei, 15x10″... **1,750.00**
Kunisada, 10x14″.................................... **125.00**
Kunisada, Poetess Sagami, #65, 1845, Sanoki, 15x10″...... **325.00**
Kuniyoshi, Underwater Battle, 1856, Iseyoshi, 15x10″........ **725.00**
Kura in Tomonoura, 1930, 10x15″..................... **495.00**
Parrot in a palm tree, framed, matted, 12½x21½″ **25.00**
Shinsai, The Purple Shell, 1809, 5½x7½″................. **360.00**
Toyokuni, 10x14″.................................... **125.00**
Tse Ching Shien, Dogwood, paper cutout, hand colored, 1978 **100.00**
Yeisen, 10x14″...................................... **125.00**
Yoshitoshi, Hotei Pointing at Moon, 1888, A Buemon, 15x10″ **260.00**
Yoshitsuya, Kintaro Riding Carp, 1849, E Rinnosuke, 15x10″. **535.00**

Kurz & Allison
　Louis Kurz founded the Chicago Lithograph Co. in 1833. Among his
most notable works were a series of 36 Civil War scenes and 100 illustrations of Chicago architecture. His company was destroyed in the Great Fire
of 1871, and in 1880 Kurz formed a partnership with Alexander Allison,
an engraver. Until both retired in 1903, they produced hundreds of
lithographs, in color as well as black and white.
Ben Franklin Opening Masonic Lodge, 1896 .... **110.00**
Desoto's Discovery of the Mississippi, color, 22x28″ **55.00**

Die Hermann's, color, 38x25″.......................... **60.00**
Garfield & Family, 1882, 22x28″....................... **28.00**
Lakes of Killarney, 22x28″............................ **35.00**
Mammoth Hot Springs, 22x28″......................... **95.00**
Rubio Canyon Falls, 22x28″........................... **95.00**
St Patrick, 22x28″ **40.00**
The Lincoln Family, no date, 22x28″.................... **85.00**

Mucha, A
Champagne Ruinart, gold leaf mat, orig frame, 21x43″..... **4,000.00**
Four Seasons, hand cut mat, gold & silver frame, small size. **3,000.00**
Gismonda, velvet & gold leaf antique frame, 14x19″........ **900.00**
La Samaritene, excellent framing, 14x24″ **850.00**
Nestle's Food for Infants, Art Nouveau frame, 20x32″..... **3,500.00**
Paris 1900 Ostereich, large poster, linen back, no frame.... **4,500.00**
Slavnostni, poster, Art Nouveau frame, 11½x22″.......... **2,600.00**

Nutting, Wallace
Accommodating Curves, framed......................... **60.00**
An Afternoon Tea, sgnd, 1909, 17x14″ **55.00**
Beyond the Daisies, framed **60.00**
Candlestand, large frame **65.00**
Corner Decoration, A; sgnd, framed, 18x14″ **88.00**
Decked as a Bride, scene of a road & apple blossoms, 22½x19″ **55.00**
Drying Apples, large frame............................ **110.00**
Elm Drapery, framed, sgnd **50.00**
Guardian Mother, framed, orig WN label, 17½″......... **135.00**
Larkspur, orig frame, sgnd, 9¼x7¼″ **30.00**
Laughing Water, framed, 1921, 7½x9½″................. **38.00**
Mary's Little Lamb, framed, sgnd, 17x14″ **53.00**
Mother's Day Greeting, verse, sgnd, florals **68.00**
Pine Pool, framed, sgnd, 7¾x9½″ **47.50**
Scenic, w/cows, stone walls, tree, framed, 11½″........... **48.00**
Sea Ledges, seascape, framed, 11x16½″.................. **57.00**
Sip of Tea, A; framed, sgnd, 11¼″ **55.00**
Stitch in Time, framed **50.00**
Swimming Pool, sgnd, framed, 12x18″ **35.00**
The Canopied Road, sgnd **65.00**
The Coming Out of Rosa, framed, 4½x6½″............... **30.00**
The Cup That Cheers, framed, sgnd, 13x11″.............. **60.00**
The Heart of Maine, framed............................ **38.00**
The Valley Orchard, framed, sgnd, 1907, 17x14″ **34.00**
Three Women, interior of a bedroom, framed, sgnd, 8½x7¼″.. **45.00**
Warm Spring Day, framed, sgnd, 23x19″ **70.00**
Water Gambols, 7½x9½″ **30.00**
Where Grandma Was Wed, framed, sgnd, 17x15″.......... **48.00**

Parrish, Maxfield
　Maxfield Parrish was a painter and illustrator who began his career in
the last decade of the 19th century. His work remained prominent until
the early 1940s. His most famous painting, *Daybreak*, was published in print
form and sold nearly 2,000 copies between 1910 and 1930. Prices are for
unsigned prints, unframed unless noted.
Air Castles, framed, new mat, 1906.................... **90.00**
Aladdin **55.00**
Aladdin Cave of 40 Thieves, 13x17″.................... **75.00**
　18½x22″ **95.00**
Ancient Tree, orig print, large........................ **145.00**
Arabian Nights, portfolio **275.00**
Aucassin Seeks Nicolette, 8x11″ **27.50**
Birches, unframed.................................... **35.00**
Candy box w/illustrated Cleopatra, geso over wood, 14x10½″. **500.00**
Canyons, new frame, 6x8″............................ **85.00**
Cassim, orig print **70.00**
Centaur **75.00**
Codadad, orig print.................................. **70.00**
Daybreak, 6x10″..................................... **45.00**

Daybreak, orig print, 10x18″ **48.00**
Daybreak, orig frame, 18x30″ **200.00**
Dinkey Bird, sgnd, orig frame, 16x12″ **100.00**
Dream Garden, garden, waterfall, L Tiffany mural, orig frame . . . **75.00**
Early Autumn, calendar print, sgnd, dated, orig border **80.00**
Enter King Pompdebile, comical king w/attendants, orig frame . . **50.00**
Evening, sgnd, framed, 16½x12½″ **85.00**
Father Knickerbocker, sgnd, 1898, 8x10¾″ **30.00**
Fisherman & Geni **50.00**
Garden of Allah, 9x18″, orig frame **30.00**
Garden of Allah, 15x30″ **165.00**
Garden of Allah, 32x17½″, color, sealed, framed **200.00**
Glen Mill, orig print, large **150.00**
Golden Hours--Mazda print **80.00**
Harvest, 5x7″ **25.00**
Hilltop, 13½x21½″ **400.00**
    23x32½″ **450.00**
Interlude **185.00**
King of Black Isles **60.00**
Knave of Hearts, small **25.00**
Knave on Wall **125.00**
Lady Violetta, maiden w/golden hair in kitchen, orig frame **69.00**
Lamp Seller of Bagdad, 10x10″ **150.00**
Land of Enchantment, 8¼x11″ **35.00**
Land of Make Believe, 27x33″ **200.00**
Lute Players, 10x18″ **85.00**
Lute Players, 18x30″ **425.00**
Magazine cover, Colliers; 1/5/1907, New Year, orig frame **50.00**
    3/11/1911, Comical Soldier, orig frame **40.00**
    11/16/1912, Marching Soldiers, orig frame **40.00**
    5/17/1913, The Comic Cop, orig frame **40.00**
Manager, comical gent holding curtain, orig frame **40.00**
Mare & Colt, gold frame **22.00**
Morning Light, framed, matted, sgnd, print size 8½x7″ **70.00**
Old King Cole, seated w/jesters, knaves, fiddlers, orig frame . . . **320.00**
Old Romance, 6x8″ **25.00**
Peaceful Valley, orig print, large **110.00**
Phoenix Throne, boulder, caricatures a face, orig frame & matt . **76.00**
Perrot, clown, 1912 sample, 12x15″ **65.00**
Prince Codadad, 13x16″ **65.00**
Prosperina & Sea Nymphs, orig print **70.00**
Quiet Solitude, 14x18″ **17.50**
Romance, knave, maiden in foreground, castle, orig frame **345.00**
Rubiyat, orig frame, 7½x29″ **350.00**
Sheltering Oaks, 14x18″ **20.00**
    19½x22½″ **90.00**
Sing A Song of 6-Pence, king & blackbird pie, orig frame & matt **39.00**
Solitude, w/calendar pad, 1932, 8x18″ **125.00**
Stars, 24x29″ **450.00**
The End, comical gent w/long red cape, orig frame **52.00**
The Knave, knave sitting in flowers, waterfall, orig frame **98.00**
The Page, knave sitting on wall, orig frame, 12½x15½″ **98.00**
The Prince **95.00**
Thy Templed Hills, landscape, unframed **75.00**
Twilight, 1937 . . . . **85.00**
Under Summer Skies, 14x17″ **17.50**
Venetian Lamplighter, calendar print, 8x10″ **85.00**
Violetta & Knave, knave & maiden in kitchen, orig frame, 12x14″ **54.00**
Waterfall, new frame, 19x8″ **80.00**
White Birch, farmer, plow, horse, near birch, orig frame, 10x12″ **44.00**
Wild Geese, orig print **90.00**

Prang, Louis
A Midday Rest, matted, 1895, 14½x22″ **52.00**
Battle of Antietam, 17x23½″ **50.00**

Battle of Kenesaw Mountain, 17x23½″ **50.00**
Children Playing in Snow, sgnd, 1904, 28x11″ **58.00**
Cupid Awake, oval frame, 9x7″ **20.00**
Fall Fruits, cherry frame **175.00**
Monument 2nd Battle of Bull Run, framed **50.00**
Murandia, 1885, 7½x11″ **12.00**
Snowballs, 1886, 7½x10½″ **15.00**
Spring Fruits, cherry frame **175.00**
Sunlight in Winter, guilded frame, 30x30″ **148.00**

Remington, Frederic
A Cavalry Officer, blk frame, sgnd, 14¾x11¾″ **45.00**
Busting Broncos, pair, framed, sgnd, 13¾x17¾″ **125.00**
Dead Men, 12x16½″ **25.00**
E Pluribus Unum **35.00**
Erin Go Bragh, 15x19″ **35.00**
Evening on a Canadian Lake, color, 1906, 18¾x12¾″ **50.00**
Highland Fling **35.00**
Indians in Canoe, wht man standing, 14x19½″ **25.00**
Man in Canoe Aiming at Moose, blk frame, sgnd, 1905, 25x19½″ **65.00**
Man in Canoe Aiming at Moose, sgnd, 1908, 15½x10¾″ **40.00**
Men in Canoe on Rough Waters, 14x19½″ **35.00**
Men in Canoe w/Dog, 11x15½″ **25.00**
Pool in Desert, 12x17″ **25.00**
Queen's Own **35.00**
Snow Trail, 12x16½″ **25.00**
Stagecoach Attack by Indians, 14x19½″ **25.00**
The Parley, 14x19½″ **25.00**
Warriors Last Ride, 11½x16½″ **25.00**
With Eye of Mind, 12x16½″ **25.00**

Robinson, Robert
    Robert Robinson (1886-1952) painted in the style of Norman Rockwell with human interest themes. From about 1907 until his death in 1952 he did hundreds of magazine covers, post cards and posters. Most show school boys escaping their teacher's watchful eye, policemen in predicaments, and other such interesting subjects.
Magazine cover, any American Druggist, 1926-33, detached **4.50**
Magazine cover, any American Druggist, 1926-33, intact **9.00**
Magazine cover, any Motor, 1926-52, detached **4.50**
Magazine cover, any Motor, 1926-52, intact **9.00**
Magazine cover, any Saturday Evening Post, 1907-25, detached . . **9.00**
Magazine cover, any Saturday Evening Post, 1907-25, intact . . . **18.00**

Wyeth, Andrew
April Wind, 18x15″ **10.00**
Canvasbacks, unframed, 17x13″ **15.00**
Christina's World, 18x27″ **10.00**
Christina's World, 24x18″ **35.00**
Mrs Kuerner, 12x17″ **10.00**
Shed Lantern, 16x25″ **15.00**
Shed Lantern, framed, 17x20″ **32.00**
Storing Up, unframed, 17x13″ **15.00**
Study for April Wind, sgnd, 28x22″ **75.00**

Contemporary Artists
Abbett, Robert; English Setter Family, 28x18″ **200.00**
    First Season, 30x22½″ **250.00**
    Split Rail Bobs, 27x18″ **185.00**
Adamson, Harry C; Conclave-Desert Bighorns, 16½x25″ **70.00**
    The Loafing Bar-Mallards, 16x25″ **300.00**
Akers, Gary; Winter's Grays, 16x28″ **125.00**
Armstrong, David; Drifted Snow, 29x23″ **125.00**
Balke, Don; Gray Fox, 28x32″ **175.00**
    Gray Squirrel Family, 21x17″ **85.00**
    Red Fox, 35x24″ **275.00**
Bama, James; Rookie Bronc Rider, 22x17½″ **135.00**
Bateman, Robert; Coyote in Winter Sage, 35x20″ **245.00**

Bierly, Edward J; Ready Fox, 27x21″ **90.00**
  Snow Leopard, 25x35″ **270.00**
Birdsall, Byron; McKinley Meringue, 21x27″ **75.00**
Blish, Carolyn; Last Leaves, 32x21¾″ **75.00**
  Wonderment, 28x22″ **250.00**
Booth, Herb; Home Place, 27x20″ **150.00**
Boren, James; Wintertime in Stephenville, 28x21″ **100.00**
Boutwell, George; Texas Classic, 24x12″ **150.00**
  Tribute to Two Trees, 22x17″ **150.00**
Brehm, Marv; Lilli, 14x24″ **200.00**
Brod, Stan; Cat and Rainbow, 16x16″ **45.00**
Brown, Paul; Grissomn's Pond, 25x19½″ **30.00**
Brown, William H; Tarpon Reef, 36x24″ **80.00**
Brubaker, Lee; Sioux War Party, 27x18″ **65.00**
Burger, E Howard; Yesterday, 20x16″ **55.00**
Calle, Paul; The Trail Boss, 30x24″ **100.00**
Campbell, John Reed; Misty Mountain, 32x22″ **100.00**
Carlson, Ken; Bald Eagle, 22x17½″ **60.00**
Carter, John L; Ruffs on the Edge, 26x13″ **80.00**
Ching, Raymond; Treasure Chest, 25x18½″ **100.00**
Christie, Robert A; Gus and Blue **95.00**
Clark, Robert; August Still Life, 16x23″ **50.00**
Clymer, John; Whiskey Whiskey **150.00**
Coheleach, Guy; Baby Bubo, 12x21″ **250.00**
  Bald Eagle, 32x40″ **725.00**
  Fox Den, 26x35″ **350.00**
  Jaguar Head, 16x20″ **155.00**
  Leopard Head, 16x20″ **285.00**
  Raccoons, 20x26″ **175.00**
  Siberian Chase, 15x26″ **300.00**
  Siberian Tiger, 21x21″ **300.00**
Cook, Arthur M; The Traveler Rests--Artic Tern, 21x15″..... **100.00**
Cooke, Roger; Gathering for the Huckleberry Feast **75.00**
Cowan, John P; Boat Blind, 27x19″ **125.00**
  Sunkin Blind, 27x19″ **125.00**
Cox, Tim; Fall Along the Animals, 20x13″ **75.00**
Crandall, Jerry; Smoke Up Ahead, 30x20″ **65.00**

  Pursued, 28x22″ **65.00**
Cross, Penni Anne; Bia-Wa-Ja-Ches, Woman Chief **100.00**
Crowley, Donald V; Hudson's Bay Blanket, 20½x17″ **100.00**
Cybis, Boleslaw; Hopi, Old Woman, 17x23″ **65.00**
Dance, Robert B; Gemein House, 28x22″ **300.00**
Daniel, Kevin; Getting Familiar--Black Lab, 24x18″ **60.00**

Darro, Peter; The Sentinel, 19x24″ **160.00**
Davenport, Ray; By Gone Summer, 26½x21″ **40.00**
Davies, Ken; Ripe Fruit, 22x29″ **80.00**
  Transparencies, 34x16″ **85.00**
Davis, Lowell; Plum Tuckered Out, 19x22″ **75.00**
Deer, Gary White; Peyote Eagle Song **1,000.00**
Deloney, Jack C; Granny's Little Helper, 26½x17½″ **50.00**
Denault, Charles H; Antler, 20x16″ **50.00**
Depaolis, Lou; Willoughby's Pride, 17½x20″ **60.00**
Dodson, Larry; April Morning, 22x16″ **90.00**
  Winter Reflection, 18x23″ **100.00**
Dowden, Anne Ophelia; Crab Apple/Apricot, 10x13″ **65.00**
Duran, Gilbert; Bob White Quail, 37½x24½″ **100.00**
Eckelberry, Don; Fulvous Tree Duck, 26x23½″ **75.00**
  White Gyrfalcon, 23x30½″ **125.00**
Enes, Mary; Scent of September, 29x22″ **60.00**
Evers, Carl; Battle of the Monitor and Merrimac **175.00**
Ewell, Ned; Mid-Mourning Mallards, 22x16″ **40.00**
Farm, Gerald; Queen of Hearts, 28x22″ **100.00**
Farnsworth, Imogene; Lion, 19x21″ **55.00**
Fellows, Fred; The Welcome Committee, 33x24″ **100.00**
Fisher, James P; American Goldeneye, 16x20″ **60.00**
Flattmann, Alan; Silk Flowers, 20x27″ **50.00**
Floeck, Wayne; Resting, 18x22″ **30.00**
Forbis, Stephen D; Sundown Council, 16x20″ **15.00**
Forrest, Don; Spruce Grouse, 14x18″ **30.00**
Frace, Charles; Giant Panda, 21x24½″ **175.00**
  The Lions, 30½x23½″ **185.00**

Frisino, Louis; Black Lab With Mallard, 11x14″ **100.00**
  Yellow Lab With Canvasback, 11x14″ **100.00**
Fritz, Charles J; Robins Wake Trillium, 19¼x14¼″ **60.00**
Garrison, Webb; Redwinged Blackbird/Cat Tails, 20x23″ **40.00**
Gee, Frank; Snowbound Cottontails, 21½x26½″ **75.00**
Gilbert, Albert Earl; Amazon Jungle Jaguar & Cub, 40x32″... **150.00**
Golden, Francis; Canada and Young, 25x18″ **65.00**
Gray, Jim; Field Daisies, 19x24″ **1,200.00**
Gromme, Owen J; Barn Owl, 17¾x22″ **100.00**
  Frosty Morning--Whistling Swans **100.00**
  Misty Morning--Woodcock, 20x17″ **1,200.00**
  Misty Morning--Quail, 20x17″ **700.00**
  Misty Morning--Ruffed Grouse, 20x17″ **1,100.00**
  Sharptails on the Rise, 17¾x23½″ **100.00**
  Wintering Quail, 17x22½″ **1,300.00**
Hagerbaumer, David; Thru the Pines--Mourning Doves **400.00**
  Woodlot Covey--Bobwhite Quail, 18x27″ **950.00**
Hampton, Ben; Monument to an Era, 19x26″ **1,000.00**
Haney, Enoch; American Bald Eagle **600.00**

Hardy, Carole Pigott; Sunrise Mallards, 30x20″ **50.00**
Harm, Ray; American Eagle, 24x32″ **400.00**
   Bald Eagle Family, 23x29″ **650.00**
   Eagle and Osprey, 39¼x26½″ **2,000.00**
   Pelicans, 32x24″ **150.00**
   Whitetail Deer, 22x28″ **125.00**
   Wood Duck, 19¼x23″ **225.00**
Harper, Brett; Mellow Yellow, 13½x19½″ **100.00**
Harper, Charles; Bobwhite Family, 24¾x9½″ **125.00**
   Cardinal, on corn, 20½x15¼″ **275.00**
Harper, Edie; Dan's Den, 20x8½″ **150.00**
   Noaz Ark, 15¾x16¼″ **210.00**
Harrison, Jim; Brush & Bucket, 26¼x18¼″ **300.00**
   Philip Morris, 26x17″ **185.00**
Harvey, G; Drifting Cowhand, 29½x24¾″ **120.00**
   The Silent Hunter, 17½x22″ **75.00**
   Times Remembered, 22x13½″ **100.00**
Hennbessey, Tom; Sentinels at Sun-Up, 22x15″ **60.00**
Hibel, Edna; Beggar, Plate #44, 27¾x38¼″ **800.00**
   Cheryll & Wendy, Plate #300 . . . . **3,900.00**
   Chinese Mother & Baby, Plate #119, 24x36″ **750.00**
   Colette & Child, Plate #206, 14½x20″ **750.00**
   David the Shepherd, Plate #260, 41x30″ **1,700.00**

   Doris & Children, 19x24″ **550.00**
   Elsa & Baby, Plate #138, 16½x24″ **1,200.00**
   Girl w/Kerchief, Plate #100, 12¼x18″ **700.00**
   Japanese Doll, Plate #157, 17½x11¼″ **1,000.00**
   Krista & Child, Plate #276, 13x10½″ **950.00**
   Lenore & Child, Plate #234, 7½x9½″ **950.00**
   Mayan Man, Plate #190, 28½x41¼″ **1,000.00**
   Ruth-Ann, Mother & 3 Children, Plate #132 . . . . **700.00**
   Sami Thinking, Plate #27, 10¼x12¾″ **1,100.00**
   Sampan, on Silk, Plate #174, 9x12″ **500.00**
   Torah, Plate #13, 11x14¼″ **750.00**
   Vases of Flowers, Plate #76, 22x31″ **600.00**
   Wedding of David and Bathsheba, Plate #218 . . . . **1,000.00**
Hood, Rance; War on the Plains, 24x28″ **470.00**
Howd, Van; Bib Tom, 30x20″ **150.00**
   Mt Kilimanjaro, 30x22″ **140.00**
Hughes, Allen; The Challenge, 19x23″ **175.00**
Johnson, Russell; Morning, 24x18″ **75.00**

Jones, Herb; Dare County, landscape, 14x20″ **165.00**
   Lowery Road, landscape, 14x20″ **125.00**
   Road to Nowhere, landscape, 22x28″ **435.00**
   Winters Past, landscape, 14x20″ **175.00**
Joyce, Marshall Woodside; Sea Moss Gatherer, 28x20″ **95.00**
Kapp, Gary; Navajo Sky, 18x12″ **60.00**
Keel, Barbara; White Siberian Tiger Cub, 20x24″ **40.00**
Kerr, Vernon; Venture to the Sea, 30x20″ **60.00**
Kester, Mel; Barn Bee, 25x22″ **60.00**
   Road Home, 20x16″ **75.00**
Killen, James H; Wilderness Retreat, 24x16″ **90.00**
Knaack, Terrill; Morning Stillness--Loon, 16½x25″ **300.00**
Koelpin, William J; The Poacher **60.00**
Krumrey, Dietmar; Otters, Series III, 8x10″ **60.00**
   Ruffed Grouse, Series II, 9x12″ **200.00**
Kuhn, Bob; Soft Touch, 30x24″ **80.00**
Kunstler, Mort; Apache Raiding Party, 30x23″ **150.00**
   War Cry **70.00**
Lansdowne, J Fenwick; Pintail Ducks, 24x18″ **155.00**
   Wood Ducks, 18x24″ **140.00**
Leblanc, Lee; A Cache River Memory, 24x16″ **125.00**
   Obion River Memory, 24x16″ **150.00**
Lockhart, David G; Autumn Calm--Black Ducks, 25x17″ **70.00**
Lougheed, Robert; Navajo Tapestry **115.00**
Lucy, Gary R; Merriam's Wild Turkeys, 17x13″ **45.00**
Maass, David A; Abandoned Orchard--Ruffed Grouse, 25x17″ . **125.00**
   Early Wintermorning--Bobwhite, 18x21″ **150.00**
   Monarchs of the Hardwoods--Wild Turkeys **1,000.00**
   Two Away--Woodcock, 15x18″ **85.00**
MacDonald, Grant; Hill Country Pastoral, 26x20″ **50.00**
Magee, Alderson Sandy; Trout, 10x8″ **200.00**
Malone, Betty; Curiosity, 20x16″ **30.00**
Martin, Bernard; Eastern Bluebird, 16x18½″ **100.00**
   Wood Duck, 16x18½″ **100.00**
Martin, Larry K; Winter Whitetails, 20x27″ **55.00**
Matsumoto, Ikki; Butterfly Tree, 22x22″ **250.00**
McCalla, Irish; Mail Order Bride, 18x24″ **85.00**
McCarthy, Frank C; Retreat to Higher Ground, 32x22″ **200.00**
   Smoke Was Their Ally, 26x18¾″ **250.00**
McCoy, John T; The Wright Brothers at Fort Myer, 29x22″ . . **160.00**
McDonald, Ralph J; Carolina Wren **25.00**
   Chairman of the Board Mallards **90.00**
   Little Diamond and Toto **105.00**
   Sentinel **200.00**
   Tennessee Waterfowl Stamp **150.00**
   Uncle Johnny's Covey **150.00**
McGaughy, Clay; Bachelor, 24x27″ **150.00**
   Rival, artist proof, 31x25″ **80.00**
McGehee, Paul; Chesapeake Bay Harbor, 35x24″ **100.00**
   Memories, 32x18″ **75.00**
   Winter in Heidelberg, 25x19″ **100.00**
McPhail, Roger; First Light--Wood Ducks, 17x25″ **80.00**
Middleton, Sallie; Cardinals, 26x22″ **95.00**
   Robin, 17x26″ **290.00**
   Yellow-shafted Flicker, 20x29″ **440.00**
Miller, Kathryn; Land of the Trembling Earth, 28x22″ **50.00**
Miller, Vel; Plenty Trouble, 20x15″ **60.00**
Moore, Burton E Jr; Harry Shourdes Redhead **85.00**
Moore, Tara; Lab Pups and Water Bug, 20x17″ **250.00**
Moriarty, Harvey; Tiger, 18x20″ **45.00**
Moss, Gary W; Canadas on the Coast, 24x18″ **75.00**
Moss, P Buckley; Hail the Day, Solace, 22x22″ **75.00**
   Quilting Bee, 16x17″ **55.00**
Murphy, Charles; Wood Ducks, 28x22″ **55.00**

Nass, Lori Pearson; Mountain Reveille--Elk, 22½x16" **300.00**
Neel, Jerry; Carr's Island, 25x17" **100.00**
Neelson, Susan; Autumn Shadows, Whitetail Deer, 23x17".... **50.00**
    Pretty Teddy, 11x14" **30.00**
Neiman, Leroy; Al Capone, 40x30".................. **675.00**
    Florida Racing, 45x31"................. **1,500.00**
    High Altitude Skiers, 24x36" **2,000.00**
    Jockey, 22x26" **1,100.00**
    Lion Pride, 36x48" **4,100.00**
    Love Story, 28x42" **1,900.00**
    Roulette, 50x60" **3,800.00**
    Rushing Back, 32x45" **2,200.00**
    Surfing, 31x23" **1,600.00**
Niblett, Gary; Confirming the Count, 22x16" **100.00**
Nipp, Robert; Blue Wings Over Yucatan, 24x19" **40.00**
    The Wood Duck, 21½x17¾" **100.00**
Owen, Bill; Since Sunup, 30x32" **100.00**
Parnall, Peter; River Otter, 29x17" **120.00**
Pearson, Charles E; Autumn Arrivals--Canadian Geese **35.00**
    Breakout--North Link Honkers, Canadian **100.00**
Perkinson; Yellow Hills, 22½x19¼" **80.00**
Peterson, Roger Tory; Bald Eagle, 23x31".......... **450.00**
    Great Horned Owl, 23x31"................. **900.00**
Pfeiffer, Jacob; Out of Winter's Silence, 24x30"......... **75.00**
Phelps, C E; Cheetah, 19½x13" **65.00**
Phillips, Gordon; Rendezvous, 31x23" **100.00**
Pitcher, John C; Horned Puffin, 15x22" **50.00**
Pleissner, Ogden M; Crossing, 22x18" **900.00**
Polseno, Jo; Canada Geese, 24x18" **40.00**
Preuss, Roger; American Goldeneyes, 9¼x6¾" **2,400.00**
    Canada Geese--Feeding Time **100.00**
    OOlinka--American Forest Indian Girl **550.00**
    Rutting Time--Misty Morning Whitetails **80.00**
Pummill, Robert; Back to Texas, 22x13" **85.00**
    Wet Weather Wanderers, 22x15" **85.00**
Putman, Donald ' Putt'; His Favorite Spot, 22x17" **85.00**
Reece, Maynard; Afternoon Shadows--Bobwhites, 28x20" **350.00**
    Edge of the Hedgerow--Bobwhites, 30x25" **670.00**
    Flooded Oaks--Mallards, 32x23" **350.00**
    Thunderhead--Canada Geese, 17x21" **350.00**
    Wood Ducks, 32x26" **325.00**
Reneson, Chet; The Bay Gunners, 29x21" **100.00**
    Winter Marsh, 26x26" **80.00**
Reynolds, James; The Good Life, 32x23".......... **150.00**
Rice, Hal; Deer Among Aspen, 28x20".......... **65.00**
Rippel, Morris; Fall Pajoaque Valley, 22x14".......... **70.00**
Ripper, Chuck; Mid-Winter Bobwhites, 16x22¾".......... **40.00**
Robinson, John E; Big Sur Coast, 22x28".......... **40.00**
    Full Moon, 28x22" **60.00**
Robinson, Rex W; Natural Friends, 19x16".......... **25.00**
Rodrigue, George; Alone With the Oak, 24x18".......... **150.00**
Rogers, Charles D; Passing Leaves, 24x14".......... **60.00**
Ruthven, John A; Bald Eagle, 24x18".......... **800.00**
    Cinnamon Teal, 12x15" **100.00**
    Eastern Wild Turkey, 30x22".................. **350.00**
    Gray Fox, 25x33" **1,200.00**
    Passenger Pigeon, 27x42" **1,200.00**
    Red Fox, In the Snow, 33x26" **300.00**
Saito, Manabu; Mai **125.00**
Sander, Tom; Black Labrador and Mallard.......... **125.00**
Sandoval, Secundo; Mysterious Shadow, 23x18" **70.00**
Savitt, Sam; Going Home, 25x20" **75.00**
Sawyier, Paul; An Old Kentucky Home **65.00**
    Fish Trap **135.00**

Lover's Leap **195.00**
    Rainy Day in Frankfort **635.00**
    River Cliffs **150.00**
    Shakertown Ferry **340.00**
Schatz, Manfred; Mallards, 19x25" **200.00**
Schexnayder, A J; Flaring the Edge **50.00**
Schoenherr, John; Sahib, 30x20" **150.00**
Shanika; Max Creek Road, 19x12¾" **20.00**
Shields, Bonnie; The Odd Couple **40.00**
Simmons, Roger; Falcon and Grey Hawk, 11x14" **30.00**
Singer, Arthur; Baltimore Oriole, 20x26".......... **90.00**
    Peregrine Falcon, 18x38".................. **115.00**
Sloan, Michael; Spring House, 26x22" **100.00**
Sloan, Richard; Ambush--Bobcat and Wild Turkey, 27x22" ... **100.00**
    American Goldfinch.................. **125.00**
    Lark Bunting **50.00**
    The Orchard, 22x19" **100.00**
Sloane, Eric; Sky Cathedral, 22x19".......... **100.00**
Smith, Charles Roy; Cabin in the Sky, 28x20".......... **100.00**
Smith, E Darrell; Barred Owl, 21x27".......... **150.00**
Smith, Tucker; Hay Sled, 24x20".......... **185.00**
    Malamute, 17x20½".................. **115.00**
Snidow, George; American Paint, 33x24".......... **100.00**
Snidow, Gordon; Buckaroos, 28x22".......... **100.00**
Solberg, Morten E; At Water's Edge, 20¾x17".......... **75.00**
    Kodiak Bears, 29x22".................. **205.00**
    Polar Bear, 23¼x11¼".................. **275.00**
Soldwedel, Kipp; Operation Sail--Boston, 28x21".......... **50.00**
Sorrels, Gary; Winter Rendezvous--Whitetail Deer **225.00**
Soule, Evan R Jr; Steamboats, Mabel Comeaux, 15x12"...... **40.00**
Spradley, Wayne; Early Morning Mist, 25x18".............. **35.00**

Huckleberry Pond, 21½x19" **35.00**
Steinke, Bettina; Santa Clara Dancer, 19x25" **70.00**
Stone, William F Jr; New England Barn, 21½x17¾" **35.00**
Stone, Lester Jay; Bluenose on the Grand Banks **75.00**
Stonington, N Taylor; Crow Creek Mercantile, Girewood, Alaska **50.00**
    Old Salmon Cannery, Hoonah, Alaska.................. **40.00**
    Whidbey Island, Washington, 24x18" **50.00**
Swanson, Gary R; Storm Over Laredo, 24x18" **150.00**
Teague, Donald; Ambush, 32x22".......... **65.00**
Thomas, Sharkey J; Cheetah and Cubs.................. **100.00**
Thompson, Richard; Autumn Day, 24x18".......... **100.00**
    Downwind, 29x24" **150.00**

Lovely Day, 18x24″	**100.00**
Tiger, Jerome; Intermission, 13x23″	**175.00**
Trail of Tears, 28x21″	**350.00**
Tiger, Johnny; Dancer's Desire, 9x11″	**75.00**
Timberlake, Bob; Afternoon at the Petrea's, 24x17″	**310.00**
Another World, 24x18″	**900.00**
Baldhead Lighthouse	**525.00**
Mr Garrison's Slab Pile	**1,400.00**
Study of His Coat, 11x14″	**1,300.00**
Timm, Richard; Badger	**75.00**
Prairie Dog	**50.00**
Tollas, Harry; Scenting the Wind--German Shorthair	**55.00**
Topah, Paul Pahse; Buffalo Hunt, 22x21″	**170.00**
Toschik, Larry; Ahead of the Storm--Mallards, 19x25″	**140.00**
Sundown Ballet--Mallards, 26x16″	**75.00**
The Present Tenants--Wild Turkeys, 29x21″	**45.00**
Towar, Bruce; Alice, 24x16″	**17.00**
Tyner, William; Decoy--Carver's Bench, 23x16″	**75.00**
Velazquez, Joseph E; Mountain Man, 17x21″	**150.00**
Vidal, Hahn; Flower Market--Paris, 20x29″	**125.00**
Voorhees, Donald; Yellows of Spring, 25x18″	**150.00**
First Light, 23x17″	**100.00**
Wagoner, Robert; Approaching Storm, 20x11″	**60.00**
Wampler, Maryrose; Magnolia	**50.00**
Ward, Wellington; At Water's Edge	**100.00**
Still Waters	**100.00**
Wells, Ronnie; Rural Setting, 30x18½″	**80.00**
Wesling, Bill; American Eagle, 23x29″	**75.00**
West, Gordon E; All the Way Home, 33x25″	**40.00**
Whitlatch, Don; American Woodcock, 18x20″	**125.00**
Barred Owl, 18x22″	**100.00**
Long-eared Owl, 18x23″	**150.00**
Snowy Owl, 13x18″	**250.00**
Wilson, Nick; Elephants and Baboob Tree, 18x23″	**100.00**
Jaguar, 24x17″	**140.00**
Windberg, Dalhart; Renewal of Season	**280.00**
The Flourish of Nature's Hues, 24x18″	**45.00**
Timeworn Shelters	**165.00**
Wysocki, Charles; Butternut Farms, 30x26″	**125.00**
Yee, Steve; Goldfish, 18x14″	**100.00**
Younger, Richard Evan; Bobcat, '72, 26x17″	**150.00**
Cheetah, 40x20″	**125.00**
Eastern Timber Wolf, 33x20″	**65.00**
October Morning, 20x24″	**150.00**
Zamora, Frank; The Hunt--Indian, 24x18″	**45.00**
Zimmerman, William; Folio	**300.00**
Open Water, 30x24″	**175.00**
Silent Wings, 21x30″	**75.00**
Wood Duck, 20x24″	**75.00**

Purses

A popular new collectible, one that seems to have captured the attention of many, is metal mesh and beaded bags. They are found in floral beaded velvets that represent the tastes of the turn of the century, or in styles recalling the flapper era. Deco styling is also represented, and these are usually made from metal mesh in a gold or silver finish. Some of the mesh bags are enameled with florals or birds, and some are fitted inside with mirrors and compacts. All are very collectible, and prices reflect their popularity.

Art Deco, fitted, silver, on chain, cloisonne	**275.00**
Beaded; birds, illus, 6x4″	**50.00**
Blk w/silver, Deco, strap, snap close	**20.00**
Blue crystal on mustard crochet square, filigree frame, 1910	**95.00**

Blue stylized florals, swan chain holders, silver frame, fringe	**60.00**
Cloth lining & cord, 9″	**30.00**
Clutch bag, blue florals, gr leaves, 11x6″	**45.00**
Cobalt carnival, looped beads at top & bottom, handled	**47.00**
Copper carnival design on red weaving, metal expandable top	**68.00**
Copper carnival draped beaded design, 5½x7″	**49.00**
Cut steel in paisley design, w/coin purse, gilt frame, 1900	**150.00**
Dk blue carnival, metal frame, 7x7″	**25.00**
Dk carnival w/silver & copper, floral motif, fringe, silver frame	**59.00**
Fine crystal w/red beaded rose motif, gilt carnelian clasp, 1910	**200.00**
Floral on shaded brown, brass frame w/glass stones, lined	**65.00**
Florals on clear ground, silver geometrics, brass frame, fringe	**55.00**
Jet, Nouveau cherubs, trees, florals, w/sterling handle	**125.00**
Lg roses & violets, ornate silver hallmkd frame, lined	**125.00**
Marquisite vertical rows on gray knit, metal frame, lined	**32.00**
Multifloral on blk pouch, 1922	**48.00**
Navy/marcasite envelope, 7½x4½″	**28.00**
Over deerskin, 1910	**36.00**
Victorian, blue & silver	**275.00**
Celluloid, cloth handles, lined, 'Maxim'	**20.00**
Czechoslovakian, drawstring, beaded, lt blue & gray, tassels, orig label	**15.00**
Drawstring; beaded, lg roses against foliage, opal beaded ground	**25.00**
Beaded, multi-color bands w/rose design, oblong, metal chain	**40.00**
Beaded, purple, oblong w/2 rows fringe, long beaded tassel	**30.00**
Beaded, silver alternating w/pale gr weaving	**20.00**
Blk crochet, jet glass lg cut beads, beaded fringe drops, 1900	**50.00**
Crochet, silver metal bead fringe	**24.00**
Crochet, yellow beading, fringe, large	**40.00**
Purple & marcasite allover beads, loop fringe	**20.00**
Silvertone ends, beaded overall floral lattice, silk lined	**38.00**
Embroidery; on beige silk, ornate frame & chain	**30.00**
On blk taffeta, ornate frame, 'Jeweled' clasp, Deco, 1910	**100.00**
Envelope style, Deco, pears & bugle beads	**25.00**
Faille, blk, fitted for lipstick, comb, compact, button snap	**10.00**
French; beaded pink satin, enameled clasp/frame, 1930s, MIB	**250.00**
Brass frame, Deco beaded geometrics, webbed fringe, lined	**60.00**
Scalloped brass frame, beaded stylized florals & fringe	**70.00**
German silver, Art Nouveau frame engraved AGN, w/chain, 6x7″	**40.00**
Goldtone; basket weave, fitted for lipstick, powder, rouge, cigarettes	**20.00**
Flowers & leaves design, Art Moderne, fitted, mink handle	**45.00**
Hallmarked silver cherubs, 1904	**325.00**
Mesh; all silver, silver ornate frame	**65.00**
Blue & gr enamel, Mandalian Co	**48.00**
German silver, Art Nouveau, w/belt clip	**78.00**
German silver, etched frame, finial shaped tassels, small	**30.00**
German silver, heavy floral design frame, ball tassels	**40.00**

Gold, lead stripes, 6½x5″	**40.00**
Goldplated, metal frame w/florals, blue stone clasp, braided handle	**35.00**
Lead, multicolor, orig box, 5x6½″	**140.00**
Lead, multicolor, w/chain, 4x6½″	**80.00**

Nickel silver, star shaped links, hanging tassel	**65.00**
Silver metal, plated frame, shoulder bag	**45.00**
Silverplate w/hp florals, marcasite stones, scalloped fringe	**60.00**
Sterling silver, floral etched frame, mesh tassel	**50.00**
Sterling silver, narrow floral engraved frame, mesh handle	**40.00**
Whiting-Davis silver, Deco, floral frame, small	**32.00**
Whiting-Davis silver, enameled, frame w/flower basket motif, 1910	**150.00**
Whiting-Davis silver, enameled geometrics, cabochons, 1910	**200.00**
Needlepoint, florals on cream, faille trim, brass frame, clasp insert	**23.00**
Petitpoint; 2 different scenes, floral border, brass tooled frame	**40.00**
Birds & Deco designs, original lining	**125.00**
Nickeled brass top, Angel Kissing the Dead motif, dated 1890	**29.00**
Ornate brass frame dated 1928	**45.00**
Ornate frame & chain	**30.00**
Pink roses on navy, marcasite closure	**45.00**
Plastic, vanity purse; blk w/geometric design, rhinestones, 1925	**50.00**
Rectangular, imitation jewels, blk tassel, 1925	**55.00**
Rectangular, ivory w/imitation jet, Deco, 1925	**40.00**
Satin, blk w/jet glass beads, floral motif, sterling frame, 1890	**75.00**
Silk; blk moire, butterflies & Phoenix bird decor	**30.00**
Blk, w/rhinestones, seed pearls, yellow beads	**25.00**
Floral bouquet in vase applique, gold braid handle	**30.00**
Silver; floral engraving, on chain, small	**175.00**
Gorham, 10 putti, floral repousse, w/2nd interior frame, 1890s	**125.00**
Slipper figural, coin purse, allover silver & gold beading	**12.00**
Sterling; coin purse, Victorian, cupid motif w/cut steel beads, 1898	**50.00**
Engraved scenic pattern, 3x2¼″	**30.00**
Hinged, engraved, card section, mirrored powder	**90.00**
Purse/compact, coin compartments, bills, powder & rouge	**45.00**
Suede, reverses to beading, round floral embossed frame, loop fringe	**35.00**
Tortoise frame, blk w/allover beading, floral design, fringe	**35.00**
Velvet; cut steel beads, 9-ball fringe, self-loop handle, 1895	**75.00**
Pearls/gold color beads, gold embossed frame, griffin loops, 1910	**125.00**

Quezal

The Quezal Art Glass and Decorating Company of Brooklyn, N.Y., was founded in 1901 by Martin Bach. A former Tiffany employee, Bach's glass closely resembled that of his former employer. Most pieces were signed Quezal, a name taken from a Central American bird. After Bach's death in 1920, his son-in-law, Conrad Vohlsing, continued to produce a Quezal-type glass in Elmhurst, N.Y., which he marked Luster Art Glass.

Bowl, flared stretched rim, gold irid, sgnd, 6x9½″	**475.00**
Gold King Tut, sgnd, 9¾″	**700.00**
Compote, orange, sgnd, 5x5″	**375.00**
Top: gold/opal; ft: scales; wht, silver feather, 6″	**1,750.00**
Jack-in-the-Pulpit vase, blue w/blue & gold interior, 11″	**1,100.00**
Lamp, glass shade & base, blue-green w/silver, 26″	**1,100.00**
Nut dish, fluted rim, irid gold, 1½x3″	**175.00**
Rose bowl, opal w/top half gold feathered, gr edge, 3¾″	**460.00**
Salt, gold irid w/blue hi-lites, 2½″	**125.00**
Shade, bell form, ivory w/gold interior w/amber feathers, 6″	**125.00**
Blue hearts & vines	**135.00**
Blue irid, feather w/gold tracing & lining, sgnd, 4 for	**1,100.00**
Calcite w/gold pulled feather & lining, 6x4½″, pr	**325.00**
Floriform, amber, sgnd	**85.00**
Gold feather on opal, pr	**275.00**
Gold webbing, leaves & lining, notched rim	**145.00**
Minaret shape, lavender, sgnd, pr	**440.00**
Notched gr rim; opal w/gr & gold leaves & webbs, pr	**300.00**
White w/blue feathers, gold lined, 5¾″	**225.00**
White w/gr pulled feathers, pr	**330.00**
Shade/wall sconce, Otpic Rib, gold/wht, pulled feather	**190.00**

Vase, 3 loop feet, gold w/blue King Tut, good irid, 8½″	**2,200.00**
Blue w/silver King Tut, sgnd, 9″	**750.00**
Blue/gold w/floral silver overlay, sgnd, 7″	**1,400.00**
Bulbous to slim, gr w/silver feathers, ribs twists, 5″	**1,750.00**
Fluted, stretch top, opal w/gold interior, gr feathers, 8″	**1,175.00**
Gold leaves & green thatching, 7″	**650.00**
Gold/silver feathers on shaded gr; wht top w/gold, 8″	**2,250.00**
Green w/lt stripes, platinum feathers, wht neck w/gold, 6″	**1,550.00**
Green w/gold decor, paper label, 5″	**1,250.00**
Lily form, gold irid, 8½″	**475.00**
Opal, gold lined, blue hi-lites, King Tut, ped base, 16″	**550.00**
Opal w/gold King Tut design, signed, 12½″	**1,200.00**
Ovoid, shaded gr w/wht top, lily pad decor, sgnd, 4¾″	**1,000.00**
Platinum ribbing, 8x8″	**450.00**
Pulled gr lattice w/gold feathering & interior, 6½″	**1,000.00**
Square base w/4 indents, narrow neck, sgnd, 5¾″	**250.00**
Stick, irid blue, gr & purple w/silver overlay, sgnd, 10″	**1,050.00**
Sweet pea, opal w/pulled gr threads, gold inside, ped, 6″	**1,500.00**
Trumpet, opal w/gold interior & rim, gr feathers, 5½″	**1,250.00**
Tulip form, wht w/gr, gold decor & interior, sgnd, 8½″	**1,250.00**

Quilts

Quilts, while made out of necessity, nevertheless represent an art form which expresses the character and the personality of the designer. During the 17th and 18th century, quilts were considered a necessary part of a bride's hope chest---the traditional number required to be properly endowed for marriage was a 'bakers dozen'! Quilts were used not only for bed coverings, but for curtains, extra insulation, and matresses as well. The early quilts were made from pieces salvaged from cloth items that had outlived their original usefulness, and from bits left over from sewing projects. Regardless of shape, these scraps were fitted together following no organized lines; these were called crazy quilts.

In 1793, Eli Whitney developed the cotton gin, and as a result, textile production in America became industrialized. Soon inexpensive fabrics were readily available, and ladies were able to choose from colorful prints and solids to add contrast to their work. Both pieced and appliqued work became popular----pieced quilts were considered utilitarian, while appliqued work was shown with pride of accomplishment at the fair. Today many collectors prize the pieced quilt and their intricate geometric patterns above all other types. Many of these designs were given names: Daisy and Oak Leaf, Grandmother's Flower Garden, Log Cabin, and Ocean Wave are only a few. Appliqued quilts involved stitching one piece, carefully cut into a specific form such as a leaf, a flower, or a stylized shape, onto either a large one piece ground fabric or an individual block. Often the background fabric was quilted in a decorative pattern.

Amish women scorned printed calicos as 'worldly', and instead used colorful blocks set with black ground fabrics to produce a stunning pieced effect.

During the Victorian era, the crazy quilt was revived, but the ladies of the 1870s used plush velvets, brocades, silks and linen patches and embroidered along the seams with feather or chain stitches.

Another type of quilting, highly prized and rare today is trapunto. These quilts were made by first stitching the outline of the design onto a solid sheet of fabric which was backed with a second with a much looser weave. White was often favored, but color was sometimes used for accent. The design (grapes, flowers, leaves, etc.) was padded through openings made by separating the loose weave of the underneath fabric; a backing was added and the three layers quilted as one.

Besides condition, value is judged on intricacy of pattern, color effect and craftsmanship.

Amish

Bars, green, purple, maroon, Lancaster, Pa., 1930s, 73x80″	**2,500.00**

Basket, blue, blk, purple, 4 flower quilt, Ohio, sgnd, 1900, 74x84″ **275.00**
Child's, all wool, blue on blk, fine quilting **800.00**
Crosses & Losses, pieced cotton, 1850 . . . . **1,000.00**
Midwest, crib, vibrant colors on cotton, 1930s **630.00**
    All wool, red, gr, mauve, 1900s **1,900.00**
Nine Patch, cotton w/vegetable dyes, some fading **440.00**
Ohio, blk double pink border, Ocean Wave & Diamond, 1920, sgnd **300.00**
    Daisy & Oak leaf, 5 color woolens, 1920, 68x83″ **450.00**
Pieced, 20 golden star design on blue & gr, homespun back, 70x88″ **135.00**

Appliqued
Alphabet, w/trailing vines, 1894, 76x72″ **950.00**
Baskets, yellow on wht, early, full **450.00**
Ben-Hur's Chariot Wheels, 1850s, double **750.00**
Butterfly, embroidery detail, 82x70″ **145.00**
Christmas cacti in vase w/trailing vine border, 1841, 8′ **1,100.00**
Compass on wht field, oak leaf & acorn border, 90″ sq **200.00**
Double Heart variation, red on wht, 4 lg sq w/red border **400.00**
Floral design, pink & gr calico, pieced, 82x84″ **215.00**
Floral medallions, lg, cut whole, 1850s, double **400.00**
Flowers on squares w/multicolor borders, 1800s, 81x92″ **465.00**
Friendship Daisy, 1915 . . . . **115.00**
Grandmother's Flower Garden, full size **345.00**
Graphic, exceptional quilting but edge wear **185.00**
Hawaiian, red on wht, swag w/tassle border, early, 84x65″ **475.00**
Nine fleur-de-lis type quatrefoils, scalloped border, 78″ **65.00**
Red oak leaves on cream for 4 poster, 1855 . . . . **190.00**
Red rose on wht scalloped border, 1870, 81x78″ **350.00**
Stylized flowers, floral & leaf trailing border, 80x101″ **600.00**
Stylized oak leaves on homespun back, 80″ **90.00**

Stylized tulips, meandering border, feather quilting, 84x102″ . . **525.00**
Swags & Pinwheel, red, ecru & goldenrod, feather quilting, 84″ sq **385.00**
Tree of Life, dark yellow on wht, 90½x88″ **750.00**
Whig's Rose, red, gr, wht border, 1880s **650.00**

Embroidered
Forty-eight states & state flowers, blue & wht, 1912 . . . . **325.00**
Friendship, 499 names, 1913, 84″ sq **240.00**
    Floral, sgnd, sq, 1932 . . . . **100.00**
Silk; silver, gold, maroon, blk bands, 66x60″ **375.00**
Sunbonnet Girl, 72x75″ **185.00**

Mennonite, Grandmother's Flower Garden, wool, 1880s **345.00**
    Patchwork, magenta, red & gr, Lancaster, Pa., 1930, 68x76″ **295.00**

Pieced
Around the World, calico prints, Pennsylvania, 1880s **360.00**
Bear Paw, early calicos, blues, reds **295.00**
Block, mixed colors, cotton **75.00**
Boston Commons, 2½″ squares, percale on wht, 1940s, EX . . **150.00**
Bow Tie, blues, reds, earth tones on ivory, 1910, 84x80″ **250.00**
    Mixed colors, 1930s **75.00**
Broken Star, sawtooth border, indigo calico print, 1840, 79x63″ **525.00**
Butterfly, wht sq, 1950s **58.00**
Calico Nine Patch & Star, late 19th century **225.00**
Calico red gr & blue, brown & wht print backing, 86x88″ **450.00**
Calico red, brown & blue, brown calico backing, 90″ sq **375.00**
    Yellow & gr, wht homespun backing, 80″ sq **370.00**
Calico, blue & wht, 1½″ squares, 1910 . . . . **115.00**
    Burgundy brown & beige, 1870s, 83x78″ **255.00**
Catch-Me-If-You-Can, red w/calico, Pennsylvania, 1870s **330.00**
Checkerboard, top, only 70x85″ **40.00**
Chevron, calico prints, allover pattern, double, late 1800s **250.00**
Chintz, w/overall diagonal quilting & star border, 88x99″ **400.00**
Clay's Choice, calicos on wht **98.00**
Courthouse Square, 1850s, 69x89″ **100.00**
Crazy comfort, tacked, calico pieces w/briar stitch **75.00**
Crazy quilt, floral print backing, 1900, 74x80″ **135.00**
Crazy quilt, percale & feed sacks, 88x70″ **100.00**
Crazy quilt, silk, 20 squares, small components, early **950.00**
Cross in Sawtooth square, red & wht, wear, 1880, 74″ **120.00**
Crown & Thomas, reds, blues & greys, 75x72″ **90.00**
Diamond, reversible, 1920, 83x70″ **95.00**
Diamond Patches, sunburst effect, cotton, early 1900s **165.00**
Double Irish Chain, calico prints, 85x96″ **120.00**
    Red & wht **175.00**
Double Wedding Ring, 1920s, 90x77″ **110.00**
    74x90″ **115.00**
    Calicos on wht, scalloped **120.00**
    Pastels, double border, sm pieces on wht, 1930, 77x91″ . . . **225.00**
    Scalloped edge, multicolor w/grey, 82x65″ **90.00**
Dresden Plate, allover pattern, excellent quilting, 1930s **200.00**
    Variant, unused, Ephrata area Pa., 1880 . . . . **2,000.00**
Drunkard's Path, percale on muslin, good used 1930 . . . . **145.00**
    Pink & wht, 1920s **180.00**
Eight Point Star, calicos & ginghams, 72x70″ **280.00**
    Top only, blue & wht cotton **55.00**
Fan, allover pattern, 1940s, 82x86″ **185.00**
    Made from old suit materials, early 1900s, 74x60″ **145.00**
    Percales w/solid strips, diagonal quilting **195.00**
Flower Basket, 1930, 71x77″ **50.00**
Four Feather, quilted wreaths divided by bands, 80″ **330.00**
Friendship, 30 pinwheels on blk, Ind., 1911, 78x90″ **65.00**
    Each sq sgnd, 1934, 80x68″ **100.00**
Friendship Ring, 1932 . . . . **100.00**
Geese Toward the Moon, double **375.00**
Geometric design, red & wht, applique initials, 82″ sq **55.00**
Grandmother's Fan **70.00**
    Top only, 68x75″ **50.00**
Grandmother's Flower Garden, gr, unused, early 1900s **175.00**
Grandmother's Flower Garden, scalloped border, 1930s **235.00**
Improved Nine Patch, 1930, 68x78″ **150.00**
Indiana Puzzle, blue & wht calico, 1920, 71x80″ **150.00**
Irish chain, red w/blk on wht, 4 central hearts, 1900, 86x72″ . **125.00**
Jackson Star, multicolored calicos & ginghams, 84x68″ **160.00**
Jacob's Coat, 2 pointed edges, double, 1940s **175.00**
Lady of the Lakes, modified, sgnd, 1871 . . . . **650.00**
Large Star, rayed from center, floral chintz background, 82″ sq **400.00**
Lavender organdy w/lace trim, pillow sham, child's, 1930 . . . . . . **18.00**

Log Cabin, 1900, 82″ sq	175.00
Barn Raising, silks, velvets, 1800s	175.00
Court House Steps pattern, cotton, early 1900s	185.00
Graphic Barn Raising, browns, pre 1880s, 86x86″	250.00
Log Cabin, 3 homespun colors, homespun back, 72x88″	105.00
Straight Furrow, 1950s″	70.00
Lone Star, exquisite quilting, 1880s	600.00
Multi-print on blue, super quilting	235.00
Mexican Star, large blocks, mixed colors, cotton, early 1900s	185.00
Mosaic, various colors, calicos & ginghams on a wht field, 80x68″	100.00
Nine Patch, 1930, 68x78″	165.00
Blue & wht sq, red strips, yellow back, 1882	125.00
Nine piece square on diagonal within block, print back	175.00
Ocean Wave, cotton, print back, double, 1895	95.00
Ozark Cobblestone, percale & feed sack, 1930s, 88x70″	85.00
Pinwheel, calico prints on red calico field, 1880s	265.00
Princess Feather, Providence, 1860s	800.00
Red Baskets, w/Sawtooth Handles, wht w/blk block print, 1880s	285.00
Robbing Peter to Pay Paul, gr & rose calico, 78x74″	440.00
Seven Star, red & orange stars, wht background, 1890s	275.00
Shoo Fly, 6″ sq, 1930s, 70x80″	275.00
Pieced w/calico strips, 1920s, 74x88″	125.00
Single Star radiating to edges in diamond patch, Pa., 84″ sq	325.00
Sisters Choice, various prints, machine stitched binding	165.00
Six Point Star, hexagon center, used, double, 1940s	175.00
Small Hexagon Star, prints w/quilted wht center, double	185.00
Star, Victorian shirt fabrics, Lancaster, Pa., 1900	**1,850.00**
Yellow & blue on a red field, 19th century, 82x80″	775.00
Star Design, multicolor, Montgomery, Pa., 80″ sq	575.00
Star of the East, squares w/in-between wreath pattern, 1840	375.00
Stars & Squares, twin size	275.00
Sunbonnet Babies, 41 squares, w/pillow sham, 1900, 83x80″	270.00
Texas Star, percale, all over pattern, 1940s, 92x70″, EX	160.00
Trip Around World, 5 colors of flowers, 90x83″	230.00
Victorian, blk silk patches & colored feather stitching	285.00
Wedding Ring, 84x66″	115.00
Whirlwind, diagonal wht stripes between squares, 81x91″, VG	200.00
Pink w/gr, 1920s, 71x71″	175.00
Wild Goose Chase, linsey-woolsey	220.00

Trapunto

Block type pattern, floral embroidery, yellow on wht	150.00
Center Wreath, 4 baskets of flowers, wht homespun, 88x90″	**1,700.00**
Mamie Rowe, red & wht, floral, Texas, 1850s, 80x82″	400.00

Sawtooth Border red & gr, red & gr stars, pieced, 76x86″	250.00
Tulip, cream, lavender, gr, 70x85″	210.00

Quimper

Quimper is a type of pottery produced in Quimper, France. A tin enamel glazed earthenware pottery with hand painted decoration, it was first produced in the 1600s by the Bousquet and Caussy factories. Little of this early ware was marked.

By the late 1700s, several factories were operating in the area, manufacturing the same type of pottery. The Grande Maison de HB, a company formed because of a marriage joining the Hubaudiere and Bousquet families, was a major producer of Quimper pottery. They marked their wares with various forms of the HB logo, but of the pottery they produced, collectors value examples marked with the HB within a triangle most highly.

Francois Eloury established another pottery in Quimper in the late 1700s. Under the direction of Charles Porquier, the ware was marked simply 'P'. Adolph Porquier replaced Charles in the 1850s, marking the ware produced during that period with an 'AP' logo. Of all the Quimper products, this is considered to be the most rare and valuable.

Jule Henriot began operations in 1886, using molds he had purchased from Porquier. His mark was 'HR', and until the 20th century he was in competition with The Grande Masion de HB. In 1926, he began to mark his wares 'Henriot Quimper'.

In 1968, the two factories merged. They are still in operation under the name Les Faenceries de Quimper.

Basket dish, yellow w/florals, peasant man, NS & S H3	150.00
Bell, figural bagpipe	85.00
Peasant lady, skirt is bell, sgnd HC	75.00
Pinecone decor, HD, 5x4	60.00
Bottle, peasant lady knitting, HB, 14″	375.00
Bowl, crimped edge, cream w/florals, peasant lady, 6″ dia	60.00
Oval w/handles, 4 sm ft, peasant, Henriot, 3x6x4″	50.00
Scalloped & fluted, peasant man & foliage, HB, 6″	55.00
Box, covered, brown brushstrokes, spongeware finial, HB, 4x5″	65.00
Busts, boy in hat, girl in bonet, 1840, pr	465.00
Butter dish w/cover, attached plate, octagonal, man w/bagpipe	165.00
Butter pat, bird & floral, 3″	36.00
Casket, 5″ long	210.00
Creamer, pink daisies, HB, Quimper, HM, 3¼″	70.00
Cup & saucer, fluted, lady & foliage, large, Henriot	80.00
Wishbone handle, grey w/blue floral	50.00
Yellow, 6 sides, mk: Henriot	30.00
Cup plate, scalloped, lady w/foliage, 4″	30.00
Demitasse cup & saucer, hexagon w/panels of florals	30.00
Dish, 3 wells, dancing couple, wht w/cobalt & yellow, 11″	340.00
Fish shape, blue trim, Henriot, France	90.00
Portrait of man, Henriot, 6½″	65.00
Egg cup, basket of flowers on yellow ground	45.00
Double, man w/staff & florals, HB	25.00
Swan, Henriot	48.00
Ewer, man in blue jacket w/pipe, Breton hat spout, Henriot, 5½″	90.00
Figurine, mother w/child, sgnd R Micheau-Vernez, Henriot, 15″	565.00
St Ives, HR, 6½″	130.00
St Vierge, Henriot, 3½″	85.00
Goblet, figural stem of man w/bowl on back, artist sgnd	195.00
Inkwell, hat shape, 5x6″	165.00
Jar w/cover, allover decor, HB, 16″	400.00
Jug, 2 sided, 7½″	140.00
Male figure, pale green, Henriot, 6″	75.00
Peasant lady, Henriot, France, 8″	165.00
Jug pitcher, w/handle on side & 1 on top, figure, florals	175.00
Knife rests, triangle form, yellow trim, florals, set of 4	100.00
Oil-vinegar cruets, criss-crossed, florals, HB	85.00
Pig, flower arranger, old mark	150.00
Pipe rest, duck figural, sgnd Quimper, France	125.00

Pitcher, lady w/flowers, foliage, Henriot, 8″ **145.00**
 Ovoid, sepia w/blue trim, 4 panels w/lady, HB, 8½″ **350.00**
 Peasant man w/basket, florals, 9½″ **350.00**
 Pinch lip, peasant woman, Henriot, France, 5″ **75.00**
 Stylized floral branch, base & rim band, large **160.00**
 Woman's head figural, hat forms spout, 6½″ **125.00**
Planter, scalloped, man, prine, blowing horn **700.00**
Plate, male figure, HB, 7″ **30.00**
 Scalloped rim, male figure, 9½″ **130.00**
Porringer, blue & rust decor, HB, 5″ **45.00**
 Blue sponge w/peasants, Nellie, HB, 5″ **55.00**
Puzzle jug, reticulated, w/motto, 5″ **85.00**

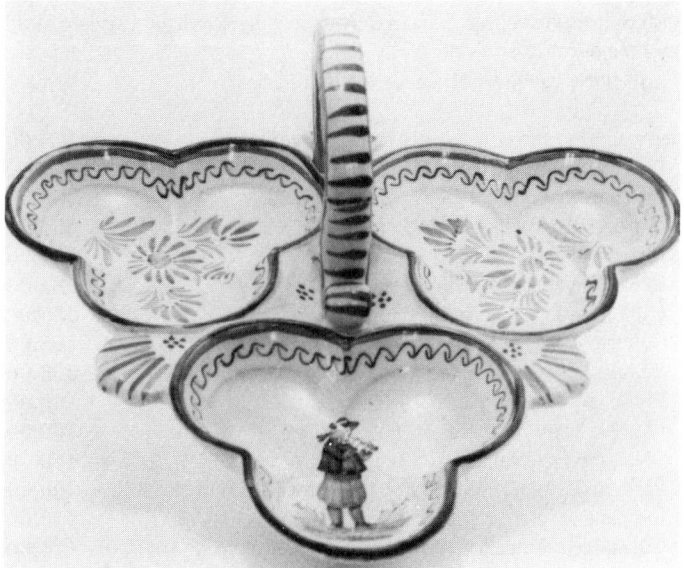

Relish, 3 part, peasant musician & florals, 11½x11½″ **85.00**
Salt, 4 handles, blue decor, HB, 2″ dia **24.00**
 Bagpipe **35.00**
 Double swan **24.00**
 Double, cat figural, mk: HB **235.00**
 Double, heart shaped, 1930 . . . . **48.00**
Shakers, peasant man & woman, HB, 3½″, pr **110.00**
Tea set, yellow w/peasant figures, octagonal, 3 pc **250.00**
Teapot, Breton figures **100.00**
Tray, scalloped, oblong, w/handles, man & lady, 10x6″ **200.00**
Vase, 5 finger; peasant lady, mk: HB, 7½″ **100.00**
 Brown & white vines, metal top & base, 9″ **150.00**
 Crescent, dolphins on base, man & lady, 7½″ **225.00**
 Mosaic decor, reserve w/table, 2 men, barmaid, 12x12″ . . . **1,200.00**
 Narrow neck, wide base, lady, mk on front HB, 7″ **150.00**
 Peasant lady w/shuttle of wool, 2 handled, 9″ **185.00**
 Peasant lady, HB, 5½″ **75.00**
 Peasant lady, various designs, tricorn, Henriot, 7″ **135.00**
 Portrait, w/handles, Henriot, 10½″ **190.00**
Wall plate, scalloped border, Henriot, 8″ **135.00**
 Hanging bagpipe, peasant man, 8x6″ **285.00**
 Peasant man, sgnd Pontivy, Henriot, 8″ **90.00**
 Woman holding basket, front mk: HR Quimper, 10½″ **150.00**
Water jug, man w/basket, cobalt trim, heavy faience, PB, 9½″ **400.00**

RS Germany

In 1869, Reinhold Schlegelmilch began to manufacture porcelain in Tillowitz, in upper Silesia. He had formerly worked with his brother, Erdmann, in his factory in Suhl, in the German province of Thuringia. Both areas were rich in resources necessary for the production of hard paste porcelain. Wares marked with the name Tillowitz, and the accompanying 'RS Germany' phrase, are attributed to Reinhold. The most common mark is a wreath and star in a solid color, usually under the glaze. Items marked RS Germany are decorated somewhat more simply than RS Prussia. Some reflect the Art Deco trend of the 1920s. Certain hand painted floral decorations, and hand painted themes such as 'Sheepherder', 'Man with Horses' and 'Cottage' are especially valued by collectors; those in a high gloss finish or on Art Deco shapes in particular.

Not all hand painted items were painted at the factory. Those with an artist's signature, but no 'Hand painted' mark, indicate that the blank was decorated outside the factory.

 Key:

 BM--------blue mark   GM-------green mark

Berry set, lilac clusters, hp, artist sgnd Wallet, 9 pc, GM **325.00**
 Yellow w/allover floral decor, gold trim, fluted, 7 pc **265.00**
Bone dish, teardrop shape, wht w/wide gold banded rim, BM, 5x3½″ **24.00**
Bowl, allover gold, 4 pierced sides, game bird medallion, BM, 7½″ **225.00**
 Art Deco mold, sheepherder scene, gold rim, GM, 9″ square **300.00**
 Berry, poppies & lilacs decor, plume molded edge, gold, 10½″ **135.00**
 Center mill scene, pierced sides, pearlized lustre, BM, 7½x6″ **200.00**
 Deep, ftd, pierced, wht poppies, gold trim & band, BM, 2½x6″ dia **55.00**
 Fruit, nasturtiums decor, large **38.00**
 Game birds scene, pierced handles, BM, 7x5½″ **175.00**
 Oblong w/buldging sides, pierced, stylized florals, pearl lustre . **90.00**
 Pastel roses, leaves, gold border, GM, 8½″ dia **30.00**
 Pearlized beige, center multicolor florals, BM, 9¼″ **27.00**

Roses, hp, 5 in-mold flowers at rim, gold & green, 10″ **125.00**
 Scalloped edge, lt gr poppy, pearl lustre, GM, 5″ dia **30.00**
 Scalloped, blue w/tiger lilies, florals, gold decor, 10″ **75.00**
 Scalloped, wide gold border w/roses, florals, 9″ **90.00**
 Snowball florals, brown leaves, gr band & gold rim, BM, 10″ dia **115.00**
 Tulips, hp, gold leafy border, BM, 9½″ dia **105.00**
Bread tray, floral decor, gold trim, BM, 11x7″ **115.00**
Bun tray, basket of roses decor, GM, 14″ long **200.00**
Celery, blue & wht floral decor, hp, GM, 12½″ long **125.00**
 Green w/wht flowers, gold trim, handled, GM, 14″ **75.00**
Cheese & cracker dish, tiered, stylized poppies, orange luster . . **48.00**
Chocolate pot, Art Deco mold, allover cottage scene, silver trim, GM **450.00**
 Art Deco mold, wht w/gold trim, GM **195.00**
Chocolate set, floral decor, gold, 10½″ pot, 4 c/s, sgnd **265.00**
 Floral on gr gound, 11 pc, BM **365.00**

White w/grapes, gold, 7 pc, BM, red script **565.00**
Compote, tulips, hp, gold leafy border, BM, 3x7″ dia **110.00**
Cracker jar, floral on ivory, gold bands, handles, BM **145.00**
    Roses decor, GM **75.00**
Creamer, wht w/delicate leaf band between pink roses, gold trim, 4″ **45.00**
Cup & saucer, demitasse, pink roses, scalloped ft & rim, gold trim, GM **50.00**
    Tea, roses decor **28.00**
Demitasse set, tulip decor, BM **495.00**
Dish, floral decor, oval, handled, 4″ **20.00**
Dresser set, tray w/3 other pcs, beige & gr w/lilies decor **145.00**
Egg cup, cotton plant decor, inside liner, handled, BM, 3½″ . . . **70.00**
Game plate, w/pheasants, 10″ **200.00**
Gravy boat, w/underplate, pink lilacs decor, BM **55.00**
Hatpin holder, dk blue bottom shades to wht top, floral, GM, 4½″ **135.00**
Inkwell, wht w/4 floral panels, floral decor on lid, BM, 3x3″ dia **145.00**
Inkwell & pen holder, red roses decor, GM **75.00**
Muffineer, wht w/wide gold band at bottom, BM, 4½″ **100.00**
Mustard jar, steeple mk **48.00**
Nail buffer set, 3 pc, wht roses & gold, sgnd **75.00**
Perfume bottle, roses decor **48.00**
Pin box, round, wht w/peach poppy on dome lid, 2″, GM **40.00**
Pitcher, milk, orange shaded glaze, peonies decor, sgnd **50.00**
Plate, calla lilies decor, gold rim, BM, 9″ dia **85.00**
    Floral decor, hp, dark border, artist sgnd Pavec, GM, 8″ dia **115.00**
    Gardenias decor, gold trim, 8″, rare mk **33.00**
    Green & gold, w/handles, 9½″ **30.00**
    Large peach poppy, gold rim, GM, 6″ dia **25.00**
    Man with Horses scene, pierced sides, gold rim, BM, 10″ . . **340.00**
    Multicolor florals, gold rim, integral handles, 10½″ **55.00**
    Poppies decor, gold trim, w/handles, 10″ **40.00**
    Scalloped rim, open handles, hp violets, 10″ **25.00**
    Shaded brown, green w/wht florals, gold, BM, 10″ **36.00**
    Stylized tulip bouquet, hp, gold mk, 8″ dia **125.00**
    Tulips decor, fleur-de-lis band, BM, 7″ dia **85.00**
    Tulips, gold leafy border trim, hp, matt, BM, 8″ **99.00**
    Yellow daffodils, wht ground, gold rim, BM, 8½″ dia **40.00**
Powder box, floral sides, scenic top, gold hinges & rim, orange mk **97.00**
Powder jar, pink roses decor, hinged lid **35.00**
    White water lily decor **40.00**
Relish, boat form, scalloped, gold florals & geometrics, GM, 7¾″ **22.00**
    Poppies decor, handled **35.00**
    Tiered, satin, green w/lilies & gold design **48.00**
Relish tray, Art Nouveau decor, matt, BM, 8½″ long **110.00**
    Large wht & peach fowers, silver rim, GM, 8¼x4″ **70.00**
    Pastel roses, scroll handles, BM, 7½x4″ **70.00**
Salt & pepper, daffodils decor, BM **60.00**
Sauce, wht w/hp florals, wide gold rim band, handled, BM, 6″ long **25.00**
Shell dish, pearl lustre finish, arch of pink roses, BM **250.00**
Spoon tray, slotted, w/large wht poppies **58.00**
Sugar, covered, pink roses decor, ornate gold trim, 3x6″ dia . . **65.00**
Sugar & creamer, cottage scene **65.00**
    Garlands of cascading sprays, gold, ftd, sgnd **75.00**
    Violet mums on yellow ground, GM **45.00**
    Water lily decor, pearl lustre, BM **250.00**
Sugar shaker, handles, BM **90.00**
Syrup, bluebells on sides & lid, gold trim, BM, 3½″ **78.00**
    With underliner, wht lilies on green ground, GM **68.00**
    With underplate, florals, gold decor **52.00**
Talcum shaker, ribbed, pearl w/gold enamel, scalloped ft, BM, 4″ **170.00**
    White w/pink & white floral clusters, gold trim, BM, 4½″ . . . **200.00**
Tankard, wht Art Nouveau, blown out florals, gold, 9″ **200.00**
Teapot, irises & florals, 8″ **60.00**
Toothpick holder, pink roses, 3 large gold handles, BM **70.00**
Tray, cherubs decor **240.00**

Wht florals w/yellow centers, gold designs, oval, handled, GM, 5½″ **115.00**
Vase, orange glaze, roses in wicker basket on back & front, 5½″ **47.00**
    Scene by Rembrandt, double handles, gold, GM, 5½″ **325.00**
    Scenic w/pheasants, handled, 3½″ **240.00**
    Winter scenic, artist sgnd, BM, 5″ **80.00**
Wall pocket molded parrot & floral: undecorated blank, GM, 9″ **150.00**

R.S. Prussia

    Art porcelain bearing the mark R.S. Prussia was manufactured by Erd-mann and Reinhold Schlegelmilch from the late 1870s to the early 1900s in a Germanic area known until the end of WWI as Prussia. The vast array of mold shapes in combination with a wide variety of decoration is the basis for R.S. Prussia's appeal. Themes can be categorized as figural (usually based on a famous aritist's work), birds, florals, portraits, scenics, and animals.

    In these listings, RM stands for Red Mark.

Berry set; blown out aqua iris mold, w/pink poppies, 6-pc **475.00**
    Petal mold, florals, gold, 7-pc, RM **425.00**
Biscuit jar, green, gold allover rose decor **200.00**
Bowl; berry, iris edge mold; pink, wht & yellow roses **58.00**
    Blown out melon edge, poppies decor, RM **200.00**
    Blown out tulips, floral center, pearl, RM, 10″ **185.00**
    California poppy, satin, 4 handles, 4x11″ **235.00**
    Cottage scene, ornate gold, green, yellow, 10″ **265.00**
    Embossed leaves, cherries, gold border, satin, 10½″ **265.00**
    Ftd, chain of pink roses & wreaths, gold rim band, 3x6″ . . . **50.00**
    Ftd, irid ivory, pink florals, fluted, RM **300.00**
    Gold ribbon scalloped rose bouquets, garlands, RM, 10″ . . . **170.00**
    Icicle mold, blown out floral border, roses, RM, 10½″ **200.00**
    Iris mold, winter scenic, RM, 8½″ **950.00**
    Iris molded & beaded rim, center roses, scalloped, 10¼″ dia **175.00**
    Ivory satin w/roses, gold decor, ftd, 5½″ **150.00**
    Jewels, roses & snowball florals, 11″ **175.00**
    Lavender border, Christmas holly, satin, 10½″ **165.00**
    Lebrun portrait, w/medallions **725.00**
    Lt gr to cream, mums, blown out mold **85.00**
    Magnolia blossoms, w/gold, wht, gr & tan, RM, 10½″ dia . . . **285.00**
    Melon Boys, RM, 10½″ **1,600.00**

Melon Eaters, 10½″ **875.00**
Nut mold, floral decor, 10″ **300.00**

Pedestal, wht satin, ivy decor, RM 200.00
Pink carnations decor, RM, 10″ 125.00
Scalloped lustre border w/gold, lavender/pink florals, RM, 10½″ 165.00
Sunflower mold w/roses. 150.00
The Courtship, 1 of the Serenade patterns, RM, 9½″ 600.00
Wht/pink lilies in water, scalloped rim, 10½″ dia 175.00
Winter, satin, iris mold, 10½″ 1,050.00
Bun tray, mill scene, 12″ 880.00
Butter pat, gr & yellow flowers, satin, gold border, RM 59.00
Cake plate; Dice Players 675.00
Embossed iris w/roses 125.00
Flower basket decor, pearlized, open handle, RM, 11″ 235.00
Hp roses, handled, 9½″ 140.00
Newport Belle, 21½″ dia 75.00
Purple w/pink roses, handled, 11″ 270.00
Swan decor 260.00
Cake set, satin, scalloped w/red roses, 7-pc 365.00
Card tray, lustre finish, ftd 90.00
Celery; blue & red floral design, handled, RM, 9½″ 125.00
Gr w/wht flowers 145.00
Wild roses decor, open handles 145.00
Chocolate pot; blown mold, hp roses, RM 245.00
Carnation mold, satin, florals 395.00
Castle scene, RM, 8″. 1,050.00
Floral on satin, beaded rim & base, RM 230.00
Summer, satin, carnation. 2,300.00
Chocolate set; demitasse, floral decor, 13-pc 1,750.00
Floral decor, 13-pc 1,025.00
Gray to orange, gardenias, relief stems, 7-pc 485.00
Swan & urn on portico, 7-pc 875.00
Compote, hanging floral basket decor in center 625.00
Cracker jar; floral decor, matt 245.00
Floral decor, satin finish, w/lid, 5″. 380.00
Floral on gr, RM, 8½″ 325.00
Iris mold, red/pink large poppies, iris finial, satin, RM 355.00
Ivy trim, matt. 200.00
Lily pattern, pearlized, RM 190.00
Melon Eaters 1,500.00
Cup, chocolate, satin swans decor, RM 45.00
Cup & saucer; coffee, gr w/pink roses, ivory beaded rim, gold, RM 105.00
Embossed stars in saucer & base of cup, roses 130.00
Entirely blown, dainty florals, gr blown base, RM. 110.00
Fruit decor, RM. 75.00
Ped, roses decor, gold traced, RM 78.00
Demitasse pot, blue, cream w/pink roses, pink ribbon 285.00
Dish, notched rim, pink & yellow roses, handled, gold, 3½x8″ . 45.00
Dresser set, pink roses, wht flowers, gold, 5-pc on 12½″ tray, RM 800.00
Dresser tray; cobalt, wht florals, RM, 12″ 400.00
Icicle mold, barnyard scene 925.00
Lt gr w/roses, 7x11″ 150.00
Rectangular, scalloped w/snowball florals, 12x8″. 120.00
Shepherds decor, RM 725.00
Ewer; Summer, 9″ 1,500.00
Wht satin, w/Bird of Paradise, RM 985.00
Hair receiver, dogwood decor, scalloped, ftd, much gold, RM . . 149.00
Hatpin holder; floral, 5″. 200.00
Floral decor, 3 handles, 5″ 330.00
Hexagonal, floral decor, RM. 140.00
Leaf-form dish, lily-of-the-valley decor 90.00
Loving cup, Melon Boys 1,400.00
Mustard; melon blossom mold, lavender & gr, gold trim, w/ladle 58.00
Ped, floral decor, w/cover, RM 225.00
Swans decor, w/lid, 3″ 250.00
Nut dish, oval, sunflower edge, florals, handles, RM, 5x4″ . . . 80.00

Plate; cobalt band, 5 women's portraits, florals, gold, RM, 6″ . 475.00
Cobalt border, w/5 portraits, 8″. 475.00
Fleur-de-lis border mold, alternating floral panels, handled, 11″ 185.00
Four Seasons, 8″, ea. 1,700.00

Four Seasons, Autumn, keyhole portrait, RM, 9″ dia 950.00
Icicle mold, swans, w/open handles, RM, 11″ 425.00
Ivory & gr w/large pink & wht roses, gold, scalloped, 10″ dia 165.00
Lavender shaded ground, wht jonquils, gold tracing, 11″ dia 160.00
Lily decor, lustre finish, 10″. 150.00
Lt gr shades to cream, florals, RM, 8″ 140.00
Scalloped, beaded gold stars & florals border, embossed florals, 8″ 70.00
Scalloped gold rim, satin w/florals, 6″ 40.00
Tigers, open handle, 10½″. 3,200.00
Wht/pink lilies in blue water, scalloped, handled, 10″ dia . . . 160.00
Yellow/brown ground, pink/wht open poppies, gold, 11″ dia . 160.00
Relish; floral decor, carnation mod, 11″. 295.00
Oval, scalloped blown rim, gold, lilies, 9½″ 125.00
Swans decor, 7″ 465.00
Swan scene, beaded rim, RM, 10″. 225.00
Salt & pepper, wht satin w/violets, RM 150.00
Shaving mug, hanging floral basket decor, RM 145.00
Sugar & creamer; blown mold, dogwood, scalloped rim & base, RM 195.00
Egg mold on ped, pink roses, RM. 200.00
Gr feather mold w/pink poppies, RM 250.00
Mill scene, RM 500.00
Petite gold, gr w/pink roses, pearl, ftd. 195.00
Swan & urn on portico 525.00
Syrup & underplate, blown blossoms, w/scene, steeple finial . . 350.00
Tankard; acorn mold, roses decor, 10″ 675.00
Dice Players, jeweled 4,000.00
Floral, w/blown out mold, 12″ 700.00
Four Seasons, Summer, blown out poppy mold w/portrait . 4,500.00
Mill scene, acorn mold, brown 1,800.00
Ped, 6 panels, raised gold scrollwork, RM, 11½″. 575.00
Roses decor, 4 ft, RM, 10½″. 385.00
Ship, rare mold, unmkd, 11″ 1,800.00
Tea set, child's, cottage scene, 17-pc 350.00
Tray; iris mold, florals & cattails, satin, open handle, 12x6″ . . 225.00

Mill scene, oval, RM, 12x6″ **550.00**
Mill scene, rectangular, RM, 11x7″ **595.00**
Pink & yellow rose clusters, shaded gr ground, satin, RM, 12x9″ **185.00**
Portrait, Allegory series, unique oval shape, 7¾x4½″ **425.00**
Sunflower mold w/roses decor **140.00**
Vase; bulbous, hummingbirds decor, 8″ **975.00**
Dice Players, 28 jewels, handled, 10″ **1,400.00**
Farmyard scene, pheasant on back, RM, 10″ **725.00**
Melon Boys, jeweled, handled, 9″ **650.00**
Miniature, pheasants decor, 3½″ **380.00**
Miniature, turkeys decor, 3½″ **925.00**
Swan scenic, ftd, double handles, scalloped neck, gold, RM, 10″ **700.00**

Radford Jasper

The Jasperware listed below was made in Zanesville, Ohio, at the A. Radford Pottery Co. incorporated there in 1903. It was first designed and produced in 1896 when Albert Radford worked in Tiffin, Ohio. The Zanesville Jasper, in contrast to the original line, was decorated with Wedgwood type cameos in relief that were not applied, but were formed within the general mold. The only mark found on the ware is a two digit shape number. The Tiffin Jasper, though not always marked, is sometimes impressed 'Radford Jasper'.

After only a few months Radford sold the plant to Arc-En-Ciel and moved his works to West Virginia.

Letter holder, lady w/bow & target scene, bark trim, #61 . . . . . **500.00**
Mug, grapes decor, #25, 5″ **150.00**
Pitcher, grapes, Old Man Winter on handle, #17, 9″ **600.00**
Vase, boy w/lion, #50, 2″ **110.00**
Bust of Lincoln; reverse: eagle; bark trim, #12, 7″ **300.00**
Bust of Washington; reverse: eagle; bark trim, #20, 7″ **300.00**
Cone shape, Grecian lady & man, bark trim, #21, 9″ **600.00**
Flat twisted, running girl, deep blue, #53, 3½″ **100.00**
Flat, lady w/flowers, grapes reverse, #59, 4″ **150.00**
Grecian man w/spear, #52, 6″ **150.00**
Kneeling lady, arms up, bird in hand, bark trim, #24, 9″ . . . **600.00**
Lady under grape arch, #58, 5½″ **150.00**
Lady w/dog; reverse: Roman, man kneeling; bark trim, #18, 7″ **300.00**
Lady w/fire beside her, grapes reverse, #55, 3½″ **100.00**

Lady, arm raised, flowing robe, #19, 9″ **600.00**

Sitting lady, trees & dog, bark trim, #22, 9″ **600.00**
Three horses in clouds pulling chariot, bark trim, #16, 7″ . . **300.00**
Twisted, man's head both sides, 3″ **100.00**
Two children w/lion; reverse: same; bark trim, #15, 7″ **300.00**
Two cupids w/flower garland; reverse: 1 cupid; #57, 5½″ . . . **150.00**
Two cupids w/instruments, column on 1 side, bark trim, #14, 7″ **300.00**

Radios

Antenna, loop **20.00**
Atwater Kent; #10 . . . . **150.00**
#10C, breadboard **350.00**
#20, compact w/tubes **200.00**
#20, large w/tubes **200.00**
#30, battery, Bakelite front **70.00**
#33, w/tubes **165.00**
#35 . . . . **15.00**
#55 . . . . **15.00**
#82 . . . . **400.00**
Breadboard #4700 w/tubes **800.00**
Model E, radio speaker **110.00**
Model H, horn **235.00**
Baseball shaped, 1930s **250.00**
Clarion, 5 tube, battery, table model **75.00**
Clasp Eastman Regenerative, 1 tube, HR **225.00**
Coil Tuner **24.00**
Crosley; #51 . . . . **55.00**
Ace-3b **150.00**
Table top, 6 tube, iron cased, battery **53.00**
Crystal set; homemade **5.00**
Manufactured **25.00**
Dayton, #25 . . . . **27.00**
Deforest, F-5 . . . . **35.00**
Dicto Grand honr, blk **200.00**
Drum Speaker **12.00**
Echophone **40.00**
Fada; #185 A **200.00**
Neutrola **85.00**
Federal **150.00**
Freshman Masterpiece, table model, wooden cased **62.00**
Grebe CR9, brass base tubes, 3 tube set **750.00**
Grebe Syncrophase **50.00**
Grundig, #59 . . . . **95.00**
Hallicrafter **60.00**
Kennedy, Colin P, table model, battery, w/5 tubes, wood . . . **90.00**
Kennedy V **70.00**
Michigan Radio Corp, 1 tube **300.00**
Nazi **85.00**
Peerless Cathedral **115.00**
Pepsi-Cola, bottle, large **150.00**
Philco; 20 . . . . **150.00**
#84 . . . . **185.00**
Jr, #80 . . . . **300.00**
Jr Cathedral **35.00**
RCA Victor; #100A, loud speaker **38.00**
#224 . . . . **350.00**
Electric, 5 tube, Bakelite case w/Chinese figures, 75x17″ . . **80.00**
End table model **65.00**
Radio Sadder, horn w/phones, 1922 . . . . **260.00**
Radiola; #16 . . . . **12.00**
III & amp **165.00**
IIIA **25.00**
AR 812, MN **200.00**
Horn #1320 . . . . **200.00**

Horn #1325	**185.00**
Sparton, blue mirror, 'Bluebird'	**1,200.00**
Steinert, crystal set	**100.00**
Stewart Warner, #305	**22.00**
Stromberg Carlsen, #1105, wooden table model	**50.00**
Tubetester, 1925	**10.00**
WD 11, radio tube	**22.00**
Zenith; #15, w/antenna	**1,200.00**
#10S-130, table model, 23x16½"	**85.00**
#R216, wood	**110.00**
Trans-Oceanic Wave, magnet, #5H40	**120.00**
Wavemaster, #6G60, electric, 9½x15x6½"	**20.00**

Railroadiana

As evidenced by the growing number of ads in the trade papers today, collecting railroad related memorabilia is fast becoming one of America's most popular hobbies. The range of collectible items available is almost endless, considering the fact that there are more than 175 different railroad lines represented.

Some collectors prefer to specialize in one railroad in particular, while others attempt to collect at least one item from every railway line that is known to have existed. For the advanced collector, there is the challenge of locating rarities from short-lived railroads; for the novice there are abundant keys, buttons, passes and playing cards. Among the most popular specializations are dining car collectibles--flatware, glassware, dinnerware, etc.---in a wide variety of patterns and styles.

Ashtray, B&O glass, Capitol dome logo, 4½" sq	**7.50**
Chessie, C&C, top mkd	**80.00**
George Washington, silhouette, C&O, top mkd	**70.00**
GN, china, Syracuse, round, mountain goat, 4"	**65.00**
L&N, glass, hexagon, red logo, 5"	**8.00**
M&StL, ceramic, round, wht & blue, 5½"	**45.00**
NP, glass, octagon, Monad logo, 5x5"	**12.00**
SOO Line, metal, blk finish, round, 6"	**15.00**
T&P, china, Hall, oval, gold logo, 4x6"	**55.00**
Badge, breast; C&NW RY police, 6 pointed star, embossed	**185.00**
M&StL Special Police, 6 star, nkl plated, 2½"	**55.00**
NP RY Deputy Sheriff, 6 pointed, nkl plated, 2½"	**65.00**
NP RY Watchman, 6 pointed, nkl plated, 2½"	**55.00**
Special Officer, shield, star center, 2¾"	**125.00**
ST PUD 318 Baggage & Mailman, 2"	**45.00**
Badge, convention; ORC, ticket punch pinclasp bar, St Paul, 1901	**30.00**
Badge, lodge; B of LF&E, Taylor 175, Newark, Ohio, 9x2¾"	**30.00**
Baggage check, brass; B&O RR LO 39590, 1½x2¼"	**30.00**
C&NW 633, 1½x1¾"	**10.00**
Claim baggage at UN PAC RY Depot	**60.00**
GNRY 86, key tag, 1¼"	**8.00**
M&StL RY 307, 1½x1¾" strap	**35.00**
P&R RY from Chaddsford, 1½x2¼"	**30.00**
Baggage rack, ornate brass, 13x63"	**250.00**
Bell, steam loco, cast bronze, iron yoke & stand	**650.00**
Berth ladder, wood, 4 steps, sleeping car	**75.00**
Blanket, rose, w/Pullman Co logo & blk #4	**38.00**
Blotter, CSTPM&O, fireman shoveling coal, 1895	**10.00**
GN, Chief Two Guns White Calf, 1932	**2.50**
NYC, 20th Century Ltd, and railroad stations, 1930s	**3.50**
Wabash, lady seated in coach, logo, 1920s	**5.00**
Bond, South Mountain Railroad Co, $500 gold bond, 1837	**12.50**
Book, Appleton's, Northern & Eastern Traveler's Guide, 1853	**65.00**
AT&SF Rules and Regulations, 1959	**3.50**
Car Builder's Encyclopedia, 13th Ed, 1931	**100.00**
GN Book of Rules, 1908	**3.50**

History of the Baldwin Locomotive Works, 1831-1923	**25.00**
History of the N PAC RR, Eugene V Smalley, 1883	**65.00**
Locomotive Encyclopedia, 10th Ed, 1938, 1232 pages	**125.00**
Moody's Steam RR Manual, 1941	**30.00**
Official, Northern Pacific RR Guide, 1893	**55.00**
Poor's Manual of RRs, 1901	**85.00**
SP, The Overland Trail, 1923, string-tied	**12.50**
Story of the B&O RR, 1827-1927, E Hungerford, 2 vols	**25.00**
The Official Guide of the Railways, Sept, 1935	**45.00**
The Official Guide of the Railways, Oct, 1962	**10.00**
Wonders and Curiosities of the Railway, Kennedy, 1884	**15.00**
Bottle opener, Canadian National Steel, flat type, 3¾"	**5.00**
Bottle, milk; Missouri Pacific, ½ pt	**7.50**
Brochure, Central Iowa RY, The Great Northwest, 1887	**30.00**
CMS & P&P, The Trail of the Olympian, 1930	**6.50**
FEC, East Coast of Florida, 1900	**12.00**
NP, Along the Scenic Highway, 1914	**12.50**
Santa Fe, Along Your Way, 1949	**3.00**
Brush, coach seats, NYC&HR RR, early 1900s	**17.00**
Paint, pure bristle, PRR, Rubico, 2"	**8.00**
Bucket, fire; cone shaped, 19x13½"	**45.00**
Button/pin, lapel; 8, RR brakemen, gold brakewheel & letters	**10.00**
B of RR clerks, green & red pen & pencil	**8.00**
B of RR ticket agents validator, blue enameled	**15.00**
B of RR trainmen, 25th Anniv, 1883-1908	**15.00**
B of RT 15 years, gold wreath	**10.00**
BLF&E, 20 yrs, enameled white logo, 10K	**20.00**
B of LE of NYCS, March 20, 1900	**27.50**
O of RC, caboose, 1" dia	**3.50**
Button, uniform; agent, large, gold dome	**4.50**
Alton, large, gold, flat	**2.50**
Alton, small, gold, flat	**2.00**
American Exp Co, shield, large, gold dome	**8.50**
B&A, large, gold, flat	**1.75**
B&A, small, gold, flat	**1.00**
B&MRR, Maltese Cross, large, silver dome	**4.50**
B&MRR, Maltese Cross, small, silver dome	**3.50**
Baggage master, large, silver dome	**4.00**
Brakeman, star, large, silver dome	**2.00**
C&IW, large, silver dome	**4.00**
C&NW, large, silver dome	**2.50**
C&NW, small, silver dome	**1.50**
Conductor, star, large, gold dome	**2.00**
DM&V, monogram, large, gold dome	**6.00**
Frisco, large, gold, flat	**2.50**
Grand trunk, large, gold dome	**1.75**
IC, large, silver, flat	**2.50**
IC, small, silver, flat	**1.50**
MRR, large, silver dome	**3.00**
NC&STL, large, gold, flat	**2.50**
NYC&H RRR, large, gold dome	**4.00**
NP, monogram, pat'd catch, large, gold dome	**1.75**
NP, monogram, pat'd catch, small, gold dome	**1.00**
Penn., large, silver dome	**2.50**
Peoria Railway Co, large, gold, flat	**3.50**
Porter, star, large, silver dome	**2.00**
Portland Railroad, large, gold, flat	**4.00**
Pullman, across, large, gold, flat	**1.75**
Reading lines, R in diamond, large, gold dome	**2.50**
Rutland, large, silver dome	**2.00**
Southern, large, gold dome	**1.50**
Southern, small, silver dome	**1.00**
Toronto Railway Co, beaver, large, gold dome	**4.00**
Vandalia Line, VL monogram, large, gold dome	**6.00**

Wabash, pat'd catch, large, silver dome **2.00**
Wagner Palace Car Co, large, gold dome **18.00**
York St RY Co, large, gold, flat **2.50**
Cabinet, stationery, wood, marked Great Mountain Exress **350.00**
Cabinet, ticket; oak, slanted roll front, Pool Bros, Mfgrs **275.00**
Oak, vertical roll front, National Ticket Case Co **200.00**
Calendar, AT&SF, 1954 Navajo Shepherdess, 13¼x24¼". **7.50**
B&O, 1827-1927, Centennial, 20¾x28½" **35.00**
C&O, 1948, Here Comes Your Train, 14x24" **12.50**
CRI&P, 1888, man w/umbrella, 14x22" **95.00**
GN, May, 1928, Chief Two Guns, 10¼x22" **30.00**
HP, perpetual tin wall, The Eagle, 12½x19" **95.00**
NYC, 1926, 20th Century Ltd, Walter L Green **45.00**
PRR, 1947, Working Partners, Grif Teller, 29x28½". **40.00**
Can, water, galvanized; Burlington Rt, logo on front, 9½" **20.00**
NPRY, wood spool bail, 14" **16.00**
Candy container, glass w/litho tin depicting cab interior **25.00**
Cap badge, cap complete; AT&SF RR brakeman, nickle finish. . **22.50**
Boston & Maine Baggage Master, nickle **35.00**
C&NWRY Freight Conductor, nickle finish **22.50**
GNRR US Mail, nickel finish, pointed top **45.00**
LIRR Brakeman, nickle finish. **20.00**
LIRR Conductor, nickel finish **22.00**
Milwaukee Road Trainman, black rectangle. **20.00**
Minnesota & Int'l Agent, red & gold **75.00**
PRR Usher, red Keystone logo, ornate top **30.00**
Pullman Conductor, pebbled gold **20.00**
Pullman Porter, pebbled silver **20.00**
Southern RY Flagman, nickel finish. **30.00**
UP RR Electrician, silver finish **30.00**
UP Station Baggage, pebbled gold **35.00**
Wabash RR Conductor, nickel finish **30.00**
Cap complete, non-RR marked; Conductor, gold finish, rectangle **10.00**
Engineer, nickel finish, rectangle **20.00**
Fireman, nickel finish, rectangle **20.00**
Cap complete, trainman; CMSTP&P RR Police Officer, nickle finish **85.00**
GN RY Porter, nickel finish, printed top **35.00**
Pullman Conductor, blk letters on gold **30.00**
Card, playing; ACL, diesel locomotive, 525 & palm trees **3.00**
C&A, red cowboy girl, original, 1903. . . . . **55.00**
CMSTP&P, Hiawatha figure, 1965 . . . . **10.00**
D&RG, train in Royal Gorge, 1922 . . . . **38.50**
GN, double deck, original slipcase box, 1951 . . . . **20.00**
IC, Floridan Ltd, orig case, 1935. . . . . **42.50**
NP, double, Yellowstone Park Line, orig case. **27.50**
NYC, 20th Century Ltd, original box, 1926 . . . . **45.00**
PRR Locomotive, 1846-1946 on backs, orig case **18.00**
PRR, double deck, Keystone logo **15.00**
SP, Mt Shasta on backs, orig 2-piece slipcase, 1915 . . . . . **47.50**
UP, 1869-1969, Driving Golden Spike **8.00**
Cart, depot, hand, 2-wheel, wood & cast iron, old. **125.00**
Carton, Wonder Orange drink, ½ pt, B & O RR. **6.00**
Chime, dining car, Deagan **45.00**
Cigarette lighter, Frisco, logo, gold on red, Vulcan **12.50**
GN, logo, red/black on silver **10.00**
Clock, depot, Seth Thomas, wall, SOO Line, eight-day **225.00**
Club, Brakeman's, wood, marked M&StL RY Co, 28". **20.00**
Coat hanger, wood, The Property Of The Pullman Co **8.00**
Corkscrew, folding metal, Take The Soo For Fishing And Hunting **15.00**
Currency, Erie & Kalamazoo RR Bank, $1.00, ships in center. . **15.00**
South Carolina RR Co, $2.00, 1880s. **3.00**
Cuspidors, UP, white porcelain, steel, black, Union Pacific **47.00**
Date nail, GN RR, steel, round head, '25' raised . . . . **.50**
IC, steel, square head, '24' raised. **4.00**

Dinnerware

Bouillon cup & saucer, Yellowstone, Northern Pacific **38.00**
Bouillon cup, Winged Streamline, Union Pacific, top mk **6.00**
Bowl, Banner, Wabash, top marked, 5" **55.00**
Banner, Wabash, soup, top mk, 7". **80.00**
Bluebells, Fla. East Coast, bottom stamp, 5" **80.00**
Calumet, Pullman, top mark, sauce **22.00**
Capitol dome, B&O, top marked, cereal **32.50**
Carolina, Fla. East coast, bottom stamp, soup **28.00**
Cavalier, Norfolk & Western, top mkd, 5" **28.00**
CMStP&P, oval, green rim stripe, bottom stamp, sauce . . . **45.00**
Desert Flower, Union Pacific, bottom stamp, cereal **28.00**
Eagle, Mo. & Pacific, 6". **450.00**
Flora of South, Atlantic Coast, 5" **65.00**
GN, Rock, mountain goat logo, NBM, SYR, cereal **150.00**
Keystone, Pa. System, top mkd **38.00**
Princeton RI monogram, top marked, cereal **110.00**
Prospector, Rio Grande, top marked, 5" **32.50**
Prospector, Rio Grande, top marked 7" **55.00**
Traveler, Milwaukee Rd, bottom stamp, soup **22.00**
Union Pacific, Desert Flower, soup, bottom stamp **28.00**
Violets & Daisies, CB&O, bottom stamp, soup **45.00**
Butter pat, AT&SF, Mimbreno, flying bird, BM, SYR **25.00**
Denver & Rio Grande, top mkd **55.00**
Celery, floral design, Erie, Susquehana, 9¾x5" **75.00**
Keystone, P RR, top marked **45.00**
Compote, Flora of the South, Atlantic Coast, bottom stamp . . . **220.00**
Cream pitcher, Blue Line, Centennial, B&O, bottom stamp **82.50**
Creamer, Indian Tree, Pullman, side mk **38.00**
Keystone, P RR, side mk **32.50**
Sunset, Southern Pacific, side mark, individual **55.00**
Cup, B&O, bottom stamp, 2¾x3½" **6.00**
Caroline, Atlantic Coast Line, 1952. . . . . **35.00**
De Witt Clinton, NYC, bottom stamp **38.00**
Erie, side mk **33.00**
Feather River, Western Pacific, top mk **38.00**
Mountain Wildflower, Southern Pacific, bottom stamp **38.00**
Sunset logo, green floral border **85.00**
Cup & saucer, B&O, Lamberton Scammell, 1927 . . . . **85.00**
Blue Line, B&O, bottom stamp **80.00**
Centennial, B&O, bottom stamp **55.00**
Mimbrena, ATSF, bottom stamp **80.00**
Olympian on saucer, CMStP&P **125.00**
Olympian, Milwaukee Road, top mark **110.00**
Prospector, Rio Grande, top mark **80.00**
Public Service N.J. Railway, side mark **110.00**
Violets & Daisies, CB&O, bottom stamp **82.50**
Demitasse cup, Desert Flower, Union Pacific, bottom stamp . . . **28.00**
Heraldic, Florida, East Coast, bottom stamp **80.00**
Mountain Wildflower, Southern Pacific, no mk **28.00**
Demitasse cup & saucer, Baltimore & Ohio, 1927 . . . . **75.00**
Blue Line, Centennial, B&O, bottom stamp **80.00**
Flying geese, CMStP&P **38.00**
Logan, SOO Line, bottom stamp **55.00**
Winged Streamliner Union Pacific **27.50**
Winged Streamliner Union Pacific, bottom stamp **33.00**
Demitasse set, Allegheny P RR, bottom mark **275.00**
C&O, Silhouette, bottom mark. **220.00**
Central of N.J. & Reading, green & gold **335.00**
Dish, Atlanta & West Point Rt, sauce, top mark **330.00**
Harriman Blue, Union Pacific, bottom stamp **16.50**
Indian Tree, NY, NH&H RR, celery, bottom stamp **55.00**
Monad, Northern Pacific, top marked, 4" **29.00**
Penn. Keystone, brown pinstripes, oval, 4½x9" **35.00**

Egg cup, double, Desert Flower, Union Pacific, bottom stamp . . **28.00**
 Monogram, ICRR side mk **65.00**
 Winged Streamline, Union Pacific, no bottom stamp **11.00**
Gravy boat, Blue Band & seahorse, Fla., E Coast, stamp **110.00**
 Harriman blue, southern Pacific Ogden & Shasta, top mk . . . **110.00**
 New Haven, Platinum blue, nude figure **55.00**
 Purple Laurel, P RR, bottom stamp **45.00**
Oatmeal, Rio Grande, Prospector, top mk, 6" **45.00**
 Southern, Peach Blossom, bottom stamp **28.00**
 Union Pacific, Zion, no bottom stamp **38.00**
Pitcher, Bleeding Blue, ATSF, top mark **330.00**
Plate, ARSF, Adobe, bottom stamp, 9½" **110.00**
 ATSF, Mimbreno, dinner, bottom stamp **65.00**
 Alaska RR, McKinley, top mark, 6" **110.00**
 Atlanta & West Point Rt, top mark, 6" **550.00**
 Atlantic Coast, Flora of the South, 5½" **65.00**
 Atlantic Coast, Flora of the South, 9" **220.00**
 B&O, Centennial, bottom stamp, 8" **55.00**
 B&O, Centennial, bottom stamp, 9" **70.00**
 B&O, Centennial, Shenango, 10" **32.50**
 Baltimore & Ohio, Harpers ferry, 1927, 9" **125.00**
 C&O, Chessie, dinner, top mark **110.00**
 C&O, George Washington, service, 10½" **700.00**
 D&H, state seal, bread, top mark **22.00**
 Florida E Coast, Heraldic, bread, no stamp **27.00**
 GN monogram, top mark, 9" **80.00**
 GN, Glory of the West, bottom stamp, 6" **38.00**
 IC RR, monogram in center, top mk, 10" **270.00**
 IC RR, Pirate, no bottom stamp, 10" **110.00**
 Kansas City, Southern Flying Crow, 10" **435.00**
 Lehigh Valley, top mk in flag, luncheon **300.00**
 Lehigh Valley Tractin, Liberty Bell, 8" **300.00**
 Lord Baltimore, 9" **75.00**
 MD&T RR, Old Abbey, blue rim, Buffalo China **275.00**
 Milwaukee Rd, Galatea, no stamp, 10" **55.00**
 Mo. Pacific, Diesel, top marked, 10½" **200.00**
 Mopac State Capitols, Diesel Streamliner, service, 10½" **300.00**
 Mowhawk, NY Central, syracuse, dinner **90.00**
 NYC, Country Gardens, birds, no stamp, 10½" **45.00**
 NYC, DeWitt Clinton, bottom stamp, 9" **55.00**
 NYC, double mkd, ornate border, top mark, 7" **220.00**
 NYC Central, Pacemaker, green on ivory, dinner **80.00**
 Northern Pacific, Villand, top mark, 10" **80.00**
 P RR, Broadway, top mark, 9" **55.00**
 P RR, Mountain Laurel, dinner, bottom stamp **45.00**
 P RR, Purple Laurel, dinner, bottom stamp **38.00**
 Panama Ltd IC RR, service, bottom stamp **500.00**
 Southern, Peach Basket border, bottom stamp, 10" **80.00**
 Southern, Peach Blossom, bottom stamp, 5" **28.00**
 Southern, Peach Blossom, bottom stamp, 10½" **65.00**
 Southern, Piedmont, bottom stamp, 9" **27.50**
 Southern Pacific, Mountain Wildflower, bread, bottom mk . . . **28.00**
 Southern Pacific, Sunset, dinner, top mark **80.00**
 Southern Pacific, Syracuse, Prairie Mountain Wildflower, 10" . **90.00**
 Southern RY System, Peach Blossom, 7½" **55.00**
 Southern RY System, Peach Blossom, dinner **100.00**
 StLSW, Greek Key, top mark, 10" **550.00**
 Texas & Pacific, flower border, top mark, 11" **800.00**
 Texas Midland, wht & gr pinstripe, top mkd, 10" **330.00**
 Union Pacific, Challenger, top mark 9" **70.00**
 Union Pacific, Challenger, top mark, salad **55.00**
 Western Pacific, Feather River, top mark, 7" **28.00**
Plate, divided; D&H, Canterbury, top mark, 11" **110.00**
Plate, oval; ATSF, Black Chain, bottom stamp, 6" **55.00**

C&O, Charlottesville, top mk, 8" **165.00**
GN monogram, top mk, 10" **110.00**
Missouri Pacific, Syracuse, eagle, 10" **85.00**
NY Central, DeWitt Clinton, dinner, Buffalo **75.00**
NY, NH&H RR, Indian Tree, bottom stamp, 9" **45.00**
NY, NH&H RR, Platinum Blue, bottom stamp, 9" **45.00**
Pullman, Indian Tree, top mk, 8" **55.00**
Rio Grande, Prospector, top mk, 8" **55.00**
Rio Grande, Prospector, top mk, 12" **110.00**
SOO Line, Logan, bottom stamp, 5" **32.50**
Southern Pacific, Prairie Mountain Wildflower, 6½x9½" **55.00**
Stotesbury, Reading, 9" **38.00**
Stotesbury, Reading, bottom stamp, 9" **75.00**
Texas & Pacific, geometric, top mk, 12" **550.00**
Vicksburg Rt, top mk, 9" **165.00**
Washington Terminal, Gray Lattice, 8" **55.00**
Washington Terminal, green pin stripe, 7" **45.00**

Platter, Cumberland Narrow, Shenango, B&O, 11½x8" **45.00**
 Erie, Gould, rectangular, 8¾x6" **57.00**
 MO Pacific, Eagle, top mk, 11" **68.00**
 NYC, DeWitt Clinton, bottom stamp, 8" **48.00**
 NYC, Hundson, Limoges **135.00**
 NYC, Syracuse, DeWitt Clinton, 8x12" **120.00**
 Pullman, Calumet, top mk, 8" **55.00**
 Pullman, Indian Tree, 8¼x5¾" **75.00**
 Southern, Pelican, top mk, 14" **165.00**
 Union Pacific, Harriman Blue, bottom stamp, 11" **33.00**
 Union Pacific, Harriman Blue, bottom stamp, 13" **55.00**
Saucer, Southern Pacific, Mountain Wildflower, bottom stamp . . **16.50**
Soup plate, B&O, Derby, bottom stamp **32.50**
 CP, Maple Leaf brown, 9¼" **32.00**
Tea plate, ATSF, California Poppy, bottom stamp **38.00**
 ATSF, Griffin, top mk, 8" **110.00**
 Atlantic Coast Line, Caroline, 7½" **200.00**
 Southern Pacific, Mountain Wildflower, bottom stamp **22.00**
 Union Pacific, Harriman Blue, bottom stamp, 7" **16.50**

Dipper, water; StLSF RWY Co, embossed on bottom, 8" handle **20.00**
Door handle set, coach 2 pc, cast brass, 1900s **45.00**
Door plate, depot, brass, SOO Line logo, 3½x16½" **35.00**
Drumhead, electric lighted, 28¼x20½" **300.00**
Fan, Japanese folding; NP, ship & train, 1890s **35.00**
Fire extinguisher, glass tube, chemical type, embossed C&NWRY **65.00**
Flare, 9" **14.00**
Flare, cone shape, B&O, 10" **20.00**
Flashlight, Bakelite, 2 cells, AT&SF RY Co, 7" **12.50**

Funnel, GN RY, embossed, 6x4¼″ dia **10.00**

Glassware

Cordial, NYC System, stemmed, NYC Logo 4¼″ **10.00**

High ball, PRR, large, w/red Keystone & Diesel **6.00**

Sherbet, cut glass stem, Canadian National RY **35.00**

Shot, UP, clear, etched Union Pacific Shield Logo **5.50**

Wine, stemmed, clear, frosted IC Diamond Logo **15.00**

Head rest, Look Ahead/Look South, gr on pink, 15x19″ **7.50**

   Milwaukee Rd, red Logo, brown on tan, 13x18″ **6.00**

Headlight, steam locomotive, electric, Pyle Natl, 1920s **185.00**

Heralds, tin, set of 28, cereal premiums, 1950s **50.00**

Holder, toothpick; CSTPM&O RY, 3¼″ **75.00**

Insignia, lapel; Rock Island, Logo, blue letters on gold, set **16.00**

   The Milwaukee Rd, red canted box, logo, set **20.00**

Insulator, B&O, white porcelain, B&O indented on base **13.00**

   CPR, light blue glass, raised letters on base **15.00**

   PRR, aqua gr glass, raised initials on dome **10.00**

Jug, pullman thermos, Stanley Super Vac, nickel plated **95.00**

   Stoneware, Rock Island Lines, blue on white **75.00**

Key, Misc; ACL, Adlake, long solid barrel, caboose, brass **10.00**

   CNR, Mitchell, long hollow barrel, coach, brass **15.00**

   GN, short solid barrel, brass **9.50**

   M&SL RR, switch key type, hollow barrel, brass **35.00**

   NP RY, US mail car, key, hollow barrel, brass **30.00**

   PRR, short hollow barrel, iron key, brass **6.00**

   Unmarked, Adlake, long solid barrel, caboose, brass **5.00**

Key, switch; AT&SF RY, S, 13679, Adlake, brass **16.00**

   B&M RR, Bohannan, brass **16.00**

   CStPaul M&O Ry, S, Slaymaker, brass **22.50**

   CM & PS RR, Loeffelhotz, brass **35.00**

   CM & ST Paul Ry, B, steel key **20.00**

   CRI & P RR, S, 37860, A&W Co, brass **12.50**

   D&H Co, S, 1533, huge letters, brass **16.00**

   D&I R RR, S, 356, steel, oiler key **35.00**

   ERR, slaight, small key, brass **25.00**

   GB & W RR, W 110, brass **40.00**

   KCS Ry, 10284, huge fancy marking, brass **17.50**

   L&N RR, D, 39976, Dayton, thick short barrel, brass **16.00**

   M&StL RR, S, 0152, Bohannan, brass **28.50**

   MK&T Ry, Fraim, in banner, thick short barrel, brass **20.00**

   Omaha, Adlake, brass **22.50**

   PRR, F-Shdwe, knobs around hilt, brass **22.00**

   RF&P, climas, brass **22.50**

   SP Co, CS-4-S, Adlake, brass **11.50**

   SP Ry, huge letters, long barrel, brass **16.00**

   St P M&M RR, S, brass **50.00**

   WC Ry, Loeffelholtz, brass **28.00**

   W&St P RR, S, Wilson, Bohannan, brass **65.00**

Knife, pocket; C&NW, Stainless Steel, Zippo **10.00**

Lamp, CM & St P Ry, flat top, electric, two lens, no maker's mrk **100.00**

   CM & St P Ry, Star Lantern Co, pat'd 1910, car inspector . **100.00**

   E J&E Ry, Dressel, dome top, oil, two clear lens **150.00**

   GN Ry, Pyle National, 1924, electric, two clear lens **125.00**

   Unmarked, Oxweld, 1926, car inspector, carbide **75.00**

   UPRR, CT, Ham, pat'd 1909, track-walker, kerosene **115.00**

Lamp, marker; C&NW, Dressel, dome top, oil four prongs **95.00**

   CRI&P RR, Handlan, dome top, oil, passenger car **115.00**

   DM & I R, Adlake, square top, oil, bell bottom **125.00**

   NP, Adlake, square top, oil, caboose **100.00**

   500 Line, Armspear, dome top, brass, 4 prongs **135.00**

Lamp, Semaphore; GNRR, Adlake, oik, fuel pot intake **95.00**

   NP, Adlake, electric, single bulls-eye lens **65.00**

Lamp, wall; Adams & Westlake, coach, brass bracket arm **150.00**

Aladdin, caboose, brass fuel pot, glass chimney **50.00**

   Safety Co NY, caboose, brass candle lamp **45.00**

Lantern, A&StL RR, embossed on globe, whale oil type, 1850 **500.00**

   Adams & Westlake Co, conductor, nickel plated **700.00**

   Adams & Westlake Co, nickel plated, pullman on base **300.00**

   B&ORR Loco, Adlake Reliable, 1913, clear globe **185.00**

   C&NW Ry, Adlake Reliable, 1913, clear globe **62.00**

   CCC&StL Ry, Dietz Vesta, 1929, clear globe **45.00**

   CM&StP Ry, brass top, Adams & Westlake Co **135.00**

   CNR, Hiram L, Piper, 1955, etched CNR **36.00**

   D&IR RR, Adlake Reliable, 1913, etched D&I RR **145.00**

   Erie RR, CT Ham 39 railroad, 1893, clear globe **75.00**

   GNRY, Armspear, 1925, clear globe **50.00**

   K&IT RR, Dressel, red 3¼″ globed, unmarked **45.00**

   LVRR, RR Signal L&L Co, 1889, clear globe **125.00**

   M&StL RR, Keystone, Cassey, 1903, clear globe **145.00**

   NPRY, Adams & Westlake Co, 1938, green globe **45.00**

   NYCRR, Adlake Reliable, 1913, clear 5½″ globe **55.00**

   OSI, The Adams, 1909, clear 5½″ globe **175.00**

   Peter Gray, Boston, nickel plated, clear globe **250.00**

   SOO line, Dressel, amber 3¼″ globe, unmarked **40.00**

   SPCO, Adlake 250 Kero, 1923, clear 3¼″ globe **34.00**

ST Louis, Handlan, pat 1928, blue globe, 14½″ **55.00**

Linens

Napkins; Burlington Rt, white on white, 18½x21″ **8.00**

   Frisco Lines, white on white, 22x20½″ **8.00**

   Milwaukee Rd, magenta on tan, 10¾x16½″ **8.00**

   S Pacific Lines, white on white, 21x21″ **15.00**

Tablecloth, Baltimore & Ohio, white on white, 34x34″ **15.00**

   RI, white on white, 34x33″, floral design **12.00**

   Union Pacific, rose pink, 50x42″ **10.00**

Towel, hand; AT&SF, red center stripe, 13x17″ **10.00**

   GN on 1 of 2 red stripes, 18x24″ **15.00**

   Pullman, 1928, blue stripes, white, 17x25″ **10.50**

Link & pin coupling set, 2 pc, UP RR, 1880s **65.00**

Lock, C&A, signal, small heart shape, Miller on drop, brass . . . **17.50**

   M&StL RR, Road Dept, small heart shape, Fraim, brass **60.00**

   Ry Ex Agy, steel, pat'd 11-21-05, no maker's mark **30.00**

   SOO Line, signal, small heart shape, 1930s, brass **35.00**

   Southern Ry, signal, large heart shape, A&W CO, brass **45.00**

   Union Pacific with CS-21 Roadway & Bridge, brass **40.00**

Wabash, Signal Dept, incised, Yale, brass **25.00**
Lock, switch; Burlington, incised on shackle, steel, brass rivets . **10.00**
   CM&StP RR, heart shape, Hansl Mfg, 1956, brass **25.00**
   CM&StP RR, heart shape, Loeffelholz, brass **55.00**
   CPR, raised on key drop, steel, Mitchell **17.50**
   CStPM&O RY, heart shape, Slaymaker, 1900s, brass **135.00**
   M&StL RY, steel, 'F S HDW' on drop, 1938, chain **25.00**
   N&W RY, heart shape, 1952, no maker's mark, brass **38.00**
   NPR, heart shape, Fraim, 1911, brass **55.00**
   UP RR, heart shape, 1951, no maker's mark, brass **50.00**
Magazine, Locomotive Engineer's Journal, Sept, 1920 . . . . **3.50**
   Northwestern Railway, C&NW RR, Oct, 1923 . . . . **4.00**
   Pluck & Luck, True As Steel, July 11, 1906 . . . . **10.00**
   Railroad Man's Magazine, Mar, 1939 . . . . **2.50**
   Railroad Trainmen's Journal, May, 1903 . . . . **5.00**
   Trains Magazine, small, Feb, 1944 . . . . **2.00**
Map, MO-PAC, World, classroom type, 1950, 38x51" **25.00**
   NP, wall mount, Line & Connections, 1893, 23x35" **35.00**
   UP, tourist folding, U.S. & System, 1922, 18x32" **8.50**
Match case, Burlington, stainless steel, Zephyrus Emblem, 1934 **22.50**
Match, book; ACL, logo silver printing on purple . . . . **.75**
   C&NW, logo & streamliner, 400 Fleet **1.00**
   GN, logo & Indian, Route of the Empire Builder **1.25**
   IC, diamond logo & blk steam locomotive, gr & gold **2.50**
   N&W, steam train, Pocahontas & Cavalier **2.00**
   Rock Island, black logo on red . . . . **.35**
Matchbox, ci hinged, shape of old Katy logo **65.00**
Medal, IC, 1851-1951, bronze, diamond logo & map, 3" dia . . . **35.00**
Menu, AT&SF, The Chief Dinner, 1939, red monogram on cover **5.50**
   Burlington Rt, Zephyr Luncheon, 1943 . . . . **5.50**
   C&NW, 400 Dinner, Dec, 1954 . . . . **6.50**
   GN, Empire Builder, breakfast, 1936, Indian on cover **22.50**
   IC, Panama Ltd, breakfast, 1963, transition of locomotive **2.00**
   Lehigh Valley, Black Diamond Express Dinner, 1927 . . . . **25.00**
   NP, baked potato shape, 4 pages, dinner, 1914 . . . . **20.00**
   Union Pacific, Domeliner City of L.A., breakfast, 1971 . . . . . . **1.50**
Menu stand, UP RR, w/2 pencil holders, Int'l **37.50**
Mirror, pocket; Frisco System, train & advertisement **37.50**
Mug, shaving, occupational, locomotive, 1875 . . . . **125.00**
Number plate, Baldwin locomotive, brass, 16½" **250.00**
Oil can, kerosene/signal; AT&SF RY, 10½x7" dia **22.50**
   GN RY, 8½x5¼" **15.00**
   NPR, 6x7" **25.00**
Oiler, Engineer's long spout; CRI&P RY, 31½" **35.00**
   PRR, no lever, 26" **25.00**
Oiler, short spout; GN R, 9" spout, 1912 . . . . **20.00**
Paperweight, CM&StP, grizzly bear, bronze finish **85.00**
   NYC, britannia metal, silver finish, 1940s **75.00**
   Rock Island, octagon, 1880s, glass **85.00**
Pass, Atlantic, Mississippi & Ohio RR, 1873, ornate engraving . . **18.50**
   Burlington & Lamoille RR, 1884 . . . . **10.00**
   Chesapeake & Ohio RR, 1930 . . . . **3.00**
   Chicago & Alton RR, 1895, full length passenger train **12.00**
   Chicago & Northwestern RY, employee, 1884, trip **10.00**
   Dayton & Union RR, 1868, ornate **20.00**
   Erie Railway, 1874, picturesque **16.00**
   Flint & Pere Marquette RY, 1873, train on bridge **16.50**
   Great Northern RY, employee, 1901, time **6.50**
   Illinois Central RR, 1865, picturesque depot scene **25.00**
   Iowa Central RY, 1898, farming & industry scene **10.00**
   Lake Erie & Western RY, 1882, editor's pass **30.00**
   Manitoba & Northwestern RY of Canada, 1895, locomotive . . **11.00**
   Missouri Pacific RR, 1920 . . . . **4.00**
   Mobile & Birmingham RR, 1897, passenger train **10.00**

National Mail Company, misc, 1895, stagecoach **12.00**
   Northern Pacific RR, employee, 1904, exchange trip **6.00**
   NY, Penn. & Ohio RR, 1883, clergyman's certificate **12.00**
   Parmelee Co Chicago Omnibus Line, misc, 1903 . . . . **6.50**
   Pere Marquette RR, 1902 . . . . **5.00**
   Rock Island & Peoria RY, 1895, train **15.00**
   Seneca Lake Steam Navigation Co, misc, 1895, train **15.00**
   Southern Pacific, 1946-1948 . . . . **1.50**
   Southern Railway, employee, 1914, annual **4.00**
   St Paul & Duluth RR, 1892, engraved scenes **10.50**
   StPM&M RY, 1881, Jas J Hill **35.00**
   Utah, Central RR, 1876 . . . . **15.00**
   Wisconsin Central Lines, 1889, train on bridge **12.50**
Pen, BN, gr logo on wht, Tucker, USA **1.00**
   MO-PAC, red logo, blk train, Quick Point, St Louis **6.00**
Pencil, BCR&N RY, gold on maroon, round, no eraser **12.50**
   CGW, gold printing on green, hexagon, eraser **3.50**
   KCS, silver printing on tan, round, no eraser **1.25**
   MO-PAC, white on maroon, hexagon, eraser . . . . **.35**
   SOO Line, gold letters on tan, round, no eraser **2.00**
   Wabash, flag logo, blue letters on white, round, eraser **5.00**
Pencil, mechanical; Frisco, gold logo & printing on black, gold . . **7.50**
   M&StL, diesel freight on white, black ends **15.00**
   Rock Island, rocker streamliner, red logo **10.00**
Pillow case, Burlington Rt, logo stenciled in black **3.00**
   Pullman, white, standard size **4.00**
Pin, lapel; Atlantic Coast Line, white on green **12.00**
   Burlington Rt, Safety First, around center logo **15.00**
   Cotton Belt Rt, logo, silver & blue **13.00**
   GN, goat logo, pre-1935 . . . . **17.00**
   N Pacific, Monad logo, 10K, diamond gemstone **60.00**
   NYC Lines, gold on black, oval **12.00**
   Union Pacific, shield logo, The Overland Rt **18.00**
Pinback, Amtrak, Tracks Are Back, blk letters on white **3.00**
   BCR&N RY, red diamond logo on white, 1" dia **20.00**
   Burlington Rt, silver zephyr on dark blue, 1¼" **5.00**
   C&O RY, Chessie kitten on white background, 1½" **12.00**
   CM&StP RY, red logo on white & yellow, 1½" **20.00**
   GN RY, The Red River, orange, green & white, 1¼" **15.00**
   LV RR, red flag logo with wreath, 1" **12.50**
   Northwestern Line, logo at center, 1¼" **10.00**
Plaque, coach, brass, raised letters, 4x12" **35.00**
Postcard, AT&SF, view of shops, Topeka, Kansas, unused **3.00**
   BCR&N, train wreck, May 28, 1899, JP King **22.00**
   CGW, view of standard sleeping car, unused **2.50**
   GN, view of Lake McDonald, Montana, postmarked 1910 . . . . **2.00**
   MC, view of Niagara Falls from Mich. Central Train **7.50**
   NP, scenes of western route to Spokane, Wash. **8.00**
   NYNH&H RR, passenger depot, Springfield, Mass. **12.50**
   UP, view of Santa Barbara Mission, California **1.00**
Poster, BCR&N, promoting harvest excursions, 1900 . . . . **50.00**
   SP, Klondikers should take the Shasta Rt to Alaska, 1898 . . **100.00**
   UP, WWII, 'In the Service of Supply' **15.00**
Postmark, Bangor & Bos-RPO, April 11, 1898 . . . . **8.00**
   Heron Lake & Pipestone-RPO, East, Sept 30, 1931 . . . . **5.00**
   MIC, Central RR, 1853 . . . . **75.00**
Pot, tallow; C&NW RY, teapot style, 7x5x7¼", oval base **15.00**
   RI Lines, coffee pot style, 7x5" **18.50**
Press, Waybill, ci, wheel style handle **135.00**
Rug, parlor car, wool, GN RY goat logo in center **100.00**
Ruler, C&NW, 15", wood, logos front, diesel trains back, 1940s **10.00**
   GM&O, 12", plastic, logos, diesel freight **3.00**
   KCS, 15", wood, Port Arthur Route, front **35.00**
Scale, counter; Railway Express Agency, double face dial **125.00**

Sheet music, 'Casey Jones, The Brave Engineer', Seibert & Newton **15.00**
  'In the Baggage Coach Ahead', Gussie L David **20.00**
  'Song of the Great Big Baked Potato', 1912 .... **22.50**
  'The Pennsylvania Special', F N Innes, 1905 .... **18.00**
Sheet, cloth; GN RY, white, 81x64″ **12.00**
Shop cloth, C&NW, blue on orange, 14x17″ **4.00**
Sign, Burlington Rt, white, black, red, CB&O RR, 21x27″.... **150.00**
  Railway Express Agency, Packages Received Here, steel **75.00**
  UP System, Tickets for Children, white on blue steel...... **100.00**
  Watch Your Step, steel, white letters on black **25.00**
  Western Union Telegraph & Cable Office, white on blue..... **35.00**
Silver, flatware
    Numbers refer to Dominy & Morgenfruh guide
ATSF, fork, D-M 36 .... **10.00**
  Fork, D-M 37 .... **8.00**
  Knife, D-M 36 .... **10.00**
  Oyster fork, D-M 37 .... **10.00**
  Tablespoon, D-M 36 .... **12.00**
  Teaspoon, D-M 36 .... **15.00**
Atlantic Coast Line, knife, short, D-M 3 .... **15.00**
  Teaspoon, D-M 3 .... **10.00**
  Teaspoon, D-M 4 .... **15.00**
B&O, ladle, D-M 39 .... **40.00**
C&A, knife, D-M 40 .... **40.00**
  Ladle, D-M 40 .... **50.00**
  Salad fork, D-M 15 .... **10.00**
C&NW, knife **5.00**
  Serving spoon, script **25.00**
Canadian National, fork, D-M 26 .... **5.00**
  Knife, D-M 26 .... **5.00**
  Tablespoon, D-M 26 .... **5.00**
  Teaspoon, D-M 26 .... **5.00**
Canadian Pacific R, dessert spoon, D-M 26 .... **10.00**
  Knife, D-M 50 .... **10.00**
  Ladle, D-M 11A **20.00**
  Mustard spoon, D-M 26 .... **15.00**
  Sugar tongs, plain **15.00**
  Teaspoon, D-M 38 .... **5.00**
  Teaspoon, D-M 26 .... **5.00**
DL&W RR, serving fork, D-M 9 .... **18.00**
Denver & Rio Grande RR, teaspoon, D-M 35............. **15.00**
Erie, teaspoon, D-M 6 .... **15.00**
Florida East Coast, demi spoon D-M 4 .... **20.00**
Fred Harvey, dinner knife, D-M 121 .... **8.00**
  Tablespoon, D-M 4 .... **5.00**
  Tablespoon, D-M 45 .... **8.00**
  Teaspoon, D-M 4 .... **8.00**
Frisco, knife, D-M 83 .... **5.00**
Great Northern, bouillon spoon, D-M 35 .... **10.00**
  Fork, D-M 35...................................... **10.00**
  Knife, D-M 35 .... **10.00**
  Teaspoon, D-M 35.................................. **10.00**
Ill Central, fork, D-M 25 .... **14.00**
  Ice teaspoon, D-M 99 .... **15.00**
  Oyster fork, D-M 10 .... **10.00**
  Teaspoon, D-M 10 .... **15.00**
Mo Pac, teaspoon, D-M 1............................. **12.00**
  Teaspoon, D-M 14 .... **15.00**
N&W, teaspoon, D-M 4 .... **10.00**
New Haven, fork, D-M 4 .... **10.00**
New York Central, fork, D-M 1 .... **8.50**
  Fruit spoon, D-M 1 .... **10.00**
  Oyster fork, D-M 1 .... **8.00**
  Tablespoon, D-M 1 .... **8.00**

Northern Pacific, bouillon spoon, D-M 37............... **14.00**
  Dinner fork, D-M 43 .... **15.00**
  Dinner knife, D-M 43 .... **13.00**
  Ice teaspoon, D-M 43 .... **20.00**
  Oyster fork, D-M 67 .... **10.00**
  Sugar tongs, D-M 118.............................. **20.00**
  Teaspoon, D-M 37................................. **17.00**
  Teaspoon, D-M 67 .... **8.00**
PRR, fork, D-M 2 .... **10.00**
  Knife, D-M 2 .... **12.00**
  Teaspoon, D-M 2 .... **12.50**
Pullman, sugar tongs, plain pattern **15.00**
  Tablespoon, D-M 21 .... **8.00**
  Teaspoon, D-M 21 .... **8.00**
Rio Grande, dinner knife, D-M 7 .... **15.00**
  Fork, D-M 6 .... **15.00**
Rock Island, tablespoon, D-M 110..................... **13.00**
  Teaspoon, D-M 4 .... **10.00**
SP&S, dinner fork, D-M 118 .... **20.00**
  Fork, D-M 37 .... **15.00**
  Table knife, D-M 118 .... **20.00**
  Tablespoon, D-M 118 .... **20.00**
Salt Lake Route, grapefruit spoon, D-M 50 .... **35.00**
  Teaspoon, D-M 50 .... **25.00**
Seaboard, bouillon spoon, D-M 63 .... **10.00**
Seaboard, fruit knife, D-M 4 .... **20.00**
Seaboard, teaspoon, D-M 1 .... **10.00**
Southern Pacific, bouillon spoon, D-M 6............... **8.00**
  Dinner fork, D-M 55 .... **15.00**
  Mustard spoon, D-M 6 .... **18.00**
  Table knife, D-M 108 .... **15.00**
  Tablespoon, D-M 31 .... **15.00**
  Teaspoon, D-M 2 .... **10.00**
  Teaspoon, D-M 6 .... **18.00**
  Teaspoon, D-M 10 .... **10.00**
Southern, fruit knife, D-M 1.......................... **10.00**
  Knife, D-M 8 .... **10.00**
  Sugar tongs, D-M 8 .... **15.00**
Union Pacific, dinner fork, D-M 13 .... **5.00**
  Dinner knife, D-M 8 .... **5.00**
  Ice teaspoon, D-M 3 .... **15.00**
  Teaspoon, D-M 3 .... **6.00**
  Teaspoon, D-M 10 .... **10.00**
  Teaspoon, D-M 13 .... **5.00**
Wabash, ice teaspoon, D-M 18 .... **15.00**
Western Pacific, demitasse spoon, D-M 35 .... **15.00**
  Dinner knife, D-M 35 .... **15.00**
  Fork, D-M 35 .... **15.00**
Silver, hollowware
Bowl, ice, PRR, Int'l................................. **65.00**
Butter pat, UPPR, Int'l............................... **25.00**
Coffee pot, GN, Int'l, 14 oz **55.00**
Crumb scraper, NP RY, Rogers Bros, 1847, 12″ **125.00**
Pitcher, GM&C, 4 pint, hinged cover, Int'l............. **120.00**
Salt & pepper, S Pacific, small winged logo, Int'l....... **75.00**
Sauce boat, L&N, Int'l **45.00**
Sugar & creamer, NPR, pagoda style, R&G, pr **150.00**
Sugar, covered, ACL, MER BR, 8 oz **75.00**
Syrup, w/attached drip tray, GN, Int'l **65.00**
Tray, Boston & Albany, top mk **110.00**

Stationery, D&RGW, scratch pad, diesel freight in Rocky Mountains **1.50**
    GN, sheet of paper, 8½x11″........................... **.25**
    LV, envelope, business size, 4x9½″ .... **.35**

Rock Island, paper, envelope, Route of the Rockets	**2.00**
Step box, pullman, metal, made by Utica	**125.00**
Sticker, Burlington Rt, round foil, blue w/silver zephyr	**5.00**
Milwaukee, Olympian, 3 colors, round	**8.00**
Santa Fe, square, blue & silver, logo, Super Chief	**3.50**
Stir stick, AMTRAK, plastic, blue, arrow top	**1.00**
GN, plastic, Empire Builder, goat at top	**3.00**
Hiawatha, Nothing Finer on Rails, glass, spoon tip	**15.00**
UP, plastic, red, gold shield logo top	**1.50**
Stock, CB&O, 100 shares capital, brown border, 1895	**3.50**
CW&B, 10 shares common, loco in center, 1880s	**10.00**
GM&N, 100 shares common, brown border, 1929	**5.00**
MK&T, 100 shares common, green border, 1907	**4.50**
Telegraph, key, Vibroplex, ci base, brass plate	**75.00**
Key, yellow brass, Chas Cory & Sons, N.Y.	**65.00**
Relay, ci base, 150 OHMS, rectangular	**55.00**
Resonator, adjustable ci arms, triangle box	**130.00**
Resonator, stationary, no maker's name, 9″	**25.00**
Sounder, yellow brass, rectangle mounted on wood base	**45.00**
Telephone, bell box, oak, 6½x9″, type 295A	**45.00**
Desk phone, candlestick type, pat'd Jan 14, 1913	**110.00**
Scissors phone, desk mount style, pat'd 1915	**155.00**
Wall phone, long box type, push to talk button	**185.00**
Thermometer, wall, metal, GN RY, black numerals on brass	**50.00**
Ticket dater dies, NO PAC RY, Ritzville, Wash.	**45.00**
Ticket dater, COSMO Model No 2, complete w/die & ribbon	**55.00**
Hill's Model A, Centennial, complete w/die	**85.00**
Ticket envelope, C&O, Chessie kitten frontside, green/wht	**2.00**
Milwaukee Road, views of Superdome Hiawathas	**1.00**
Rock Island, logo/rocket frontside, red	**1.25**
Ticket punch, B&M, Fleur-de-lis mark, pat'd July 18, 1882	**20.00**
CNW, ½″ punch mark	**12.50**
PRR, L punch mark, pat'd Dec 23, 1884	**18.00**
Unmarked, clover punch mark	**6.00**
Ticket, B&M Commutation, 5 rides, card type, 1892	**3.00**
CGW, 1,000 mile ticket booklet, 1903	**5.00**
GN, one first class passage, local, 1922	**1.25**
Monon, carbonized booklet, paper stock, 1960s	**2.00**
NYNH&H, one passage ½ fare, local, 1890	**2.25**
PRR, coach ticket, local, card stock, 1926	**1.50**
SOO Line, 6 month round trip coach ticket, 1951	**1.50**
Ticket, rubber stamp; one way coach, black, rubber die cast	**2.50**
Roomette, one piece finger-molded die	**1.00**
Timetable, AT&SF, 1882, Dec 21, pictorial fold-out	**30.00**
B&O, 1936, April 26	**5.00**
C&NW, employee, Wisconsin Div, No 441	**4.00**
Colorado, Midland, 1909, July	**22.50**
CStP&KC, 1889, July 28, maple leaf emblem	**25.00**
GN, employee, Willmar Div, No 124	**3.50**
GN, 1916, May 14, local	**7.50**
Harlem Extension RR, 1871, May 29, single sheet	**65.00**
IC, 1899, April 20, Southern Fast Mail emblem	**15.00**
KCS, 1947, June 22, Southern Belle streamliner	**3.00**
LS&MS, 1857, Mar 31, card type	**50.00**
MKT, 1901, Jan, figure of Katy	**15.00**
New Haven Railroad, 1967, April 30	**1.00**
NP, employee, Dakota Div, No 20, July 6, 1902	**12.50**
PC, 1971, March 3	**.75**
Rock Island, 1924, June 22	**6.00**
SP, 1912, Dec, Sunset Ogden & Shasta Route logo	**10.00**
UP, 1953, March 1, steam & diesel trains	**2.50**
W&LE, 1894, Feb 15, pictorial fold-out	**12.75**
W&StP, employee, No 113, Nov 25, 1883	**25.00**
Timetable, holder; metal, wall mounted	**75.00**

Token, aluminum; UP, 1934 Century of Progress lucky piece	**4.50**
Token, wood; engine No 136, ½ cord, brass	**75.00**
Tongs, sugar; Southern, Sierra, R&B	**15.00**
Tool, C&NW, double headed open ended curved wrench	**10.00**
CB&O, track shovel, Husky	**15.00**
CM&StP RY, monkey wrench, all metal, 12″	**12.50**
DSS&A RY, spiking maul, Slug Devil	**25.00**
GN RY, ball pein hammer, True Temper	**6.50**
IC, track Adz, Aldusht, Chgo, 12″ long	**15.00**
M&StL, hatchet, depot type, claw nail puller head	**40.00**
NPRR, hand saw, EC Atkins, wood handle	**18.00**
NYC RR, cold steel chisel, 9″	**6.00**

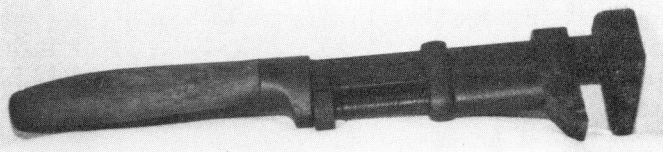

NYC RR, monkey wrench	**40.00**
RI Lines, tie tongs, Aldusht Co Chgo	**26.00**
Torch, CM&StP, teapot type, grip handle, 6″	**20.00**
GN RY, candle type, all brass, 13″	**25.00**
Teapot style, 4¾x9″	**25.00**
UP RR, ci torch, wick, 10″	**35.00**
Toy train, ci, set, #999 loco, marked MCRR, 1890	**250.00**
Electric, Lionel, #1666 engine, O gauge set	**150.00**
Train order hoop, bentwood type, w/metal clip, 43″ long	**37.50**
Wall lamp, pullman berth, electric brass, w/shade	**45.00**
Watch, Ball, Hamilton, 21 jewels, yellow gold filled case	**325.00**
Elgin, BW Raymond, 19 jewels, yellow gold case	**750.00**
Hampden, Special Railway, 2l jewels, yellow gold	**225.00**
Howard, Railroad Chronometer Series, 21 jewels	**275.00**
Illinois, Bunn Special. 60 hour, 21 jewels, yellow gold	**275.00**
South Bend, Studebaker, 21 jewels, white gold filled	**185.00**
Waltham, Vanguard, 23 jewels, yellow gold filled	**275.00**
Watch charm, B of RR Trainmen, Maltese cross type, gold/black	**35.00**
Davenport locomotive, works, oval, silver plated copper	**85.00**
NP, Monad logo, enamel on gold, black ribbon type	**85..00**
Wax seal, Adams Express Co, 5186, Burlington, Iowa	**85.00**
American Railway Express Co, 2154, Messenger	**25.00**
AT&SF RY, agent, Gage, Okla., tall iron handle	**95.00**
B&MR RR, in Neb., Nelson, brass toadstool	**150.00**
CGW RR, 142, New Hampton, Ia., hollow brass handle	**150.00**
CM&StP RY, Mitchell Station, wood handle	**75.00**
Kansas City Southern RY, freight station, Joplin	**95.00**
KCM&B RR, Sullicent, Al., iron bulb handle	**115.00**
M&StP RY, Algona, wood toadstool handle	**175.00**
Nor Pac Exp, NPRR Co, Clear Lake, Minn., brass	**250.00**
Ry Ex Agy Inc, Public, Hastings, Minn.	**27.50**
W&StP RR, Redwood Falls Station, hollow brass	**150.00**
Wabash RR, dining car dept, nickel handle	**125.00**
WC RR, Ore Docks, Ashland, Wis., fancy wood handle	**135.00**
Wells Fargo & Co Express, 442, iron handle	**100.00**
Whistle, police; brass, B&O RR incised on top	**25.00**
Steam locomotive, brass, Powell's, 15″	**125.00**

Razors

The razor has gone through several substantial changes since the first primitive, hand-hammered steel variety. Those models made before 1800, though very collectible because of their antique value, were very plain, with little etching or engraving. During the 1800s, the competition between English and German manufactures brought about many innovations. Prior

to 1820, most blades were marked 'Cast Steel'. M. Farraday discovered the process of adding silver to cast steel in 1820, and blades cast by this method were marked 'Silver Steel.' During this same period, it became a common practice to stamp the blade with the initials of the current sovereign along with the cutlers marks, which is sometimes helpful when determining age and origin.

The hollow ground blade was another important development of the 19th century, along with a much more detailed tang. By the mid-1800s, etched blades and fancy handles were becoming popular. The elaborate syles of this period are most treasured by the collector.

Abrams & Son, GD; Wayland, NY, super wedge shop work **10.00**
Adam, Chas; Rochester, NY, Tonsorial gem **10.00**
Arnold Fountain, Safety, 1906, looks like fountain pen **48.00**
Baker & Co, Sheffield, Phoenix razor **10.00**
Barber, LD English **20.00**
Barber, John; Masonic Square **16.00**
Benitz, Leo C; Philadelphia, Sensation **10.00**
Boker & Co, Germany, black plastic tang **16.00**
    Hand Forged **30.00**
    Silver King **24.00**
    The King **20.00**
    Tree Brand **24.00**
Case, made in USA, Ace **20.00**
    Corn Husker **30.00**
    Gold Nugget, Double X **30.00**
    Red Imp **16.00**
    Temperite **20.00**
Damascara Fremont, Ohio, The Razor of Quality **10.00**
Denison, BS Co; Texas, Blue Steel **10.00**
Dolle, Fred; Chicago, Ill., Special **10.00**
Droescher, SR; Solingen Germany, Deluxe **12.00**
Durham Domino, Made in USA, pat May 28, 1907 . . . . **10.00**
Eagle Razor, The Improved, magnet steel **16.00**
Electric Cutlery, New York, Arlington **10.00**
Empire Razor, Winsted, Conn, Empire Razor silver steel **16.00**
Enders, brass, in original case **6.00**
Engles, FW; Solingen, Germany, FWE Special **12.00**
Ern, Freidrick C, Wald, Germany, Rattler **12.00**
Fox Cutlery Co, The Celebrated for #44 . . . . **16.00**
    Solingen, Germany, The Old Platina **16.00**
    Solingen, Germany, Trade Mark Fox **16.00**
Friedmann & Lauterjung, US Hollow Ground **12.00**
    Celebrated Razor **10.00**
Garland Cutlery Co, Germany, 1856 coins **50.00**
Genco Geneva, NY, USA, Henry's X **10.00**
Genco Razors Geneva, NY, Vanadium **10.00**
Gevoso, Solingen, Germany, Fromm Bros **16.00**
Greaves & Sons Sheaf Works, Cast Steel Warranted **12.00**
Hall, JM Cutler; Wigan, very old **12.00**
Hamburg, hollow ground, WB Speed **14.00**
Hessen-Bruch & Co, HT Cushwa & Bro **14.00**
Howell Gano & Co, Germany, Magnetic Boss **12.00**
Hustler, Made In Germany, AW NY **10.00**
Imperial Razor, 20507, Germany, Imperial Safety **30.00**
    Army & Navy **32.00**
Jermania Cutlery Works, Germany, Oxford razor **10.00**
Johnson, James; Silver Steel **8.00**
Jordan, AJ Sheffield, England, Old Faithful **10.00**
Kaiser, Gustav; Germany, Diamond Steel **10.00**
Kama, Solingen; Kama **16.00**
Keen Kutter, #44 . . . . **18.00**
    #741, in original box **25.00**
    Safety, in original box **12.00**

Simmons, brass, in original case **11.00**
Kennedy & Co, John A Boston, Black Diamond **24.00**
Kinfolks Incorporated, Real Red Point **12.00**
    The Ace **10.00**
    Wedge **10.00**
Kion, Made & Ground in Sheffield, England **14.00**
Koch & Schafer, Kama **10.00**
Kochs, Theodore A; Chicago, Diamond Steel **10.00**
Koken, St Louis, USA, Army & Navy **20.00**
Krusius Brothers, Germany, barber's model **12.00**
LG & Co Germany, Pathfinder **10.00**
LE Champion, Switzerland, Qualite Garantie, Ad Abrenz **16.00**
Le Grelot, France, P Hospital & CIE **16.00**
Louper, Solingen, Flame, 214 Louper **14.00**
M S Co, Philadelphia, Warranted **10.00**
Marples & Co, Golden Bee Hive **10.00**
Marples & Co, Bee Hive, Fine Surgical Steel **10.00**
Morley & Sons, W H Germany, Admiral **12.00**
Mount & Co, Warranted **12.00**
N.Y. Razor Co, Boston, Swift **10.00**
Oxford Razor Co, Germany, Germania Cutlery Works **12.00**
    The Improved Eagle Razor **14.00**
Pabst & Kohler, Columbus, Oh., Tramp **12.00**
Pearl Duck, Solingen, Germany, Dubl Duck Swarf **16.00**
Ph-hahn, N.Y.; hollow ground **12.00**
Pritzlaff, Hardware Co, John, Brilliant **12.00**
Pritzlaff Hardware Co, John, Victor **12.00**
Progress 665, Germany, Extra Hollow Ground **12.00**
Pumacker, G H New York, Black Diamond Wedge **10.00**
Radiumite Co, Dayton, Ohio, Radiumite **10.00**
Rankins-Snyder Hardware, Silver King **10.00**
Rector & Wilhelmy Co, XX Clean Clipper **12.00**
Reider Co, Minneapolis, Minn., Sat Suma **12.00**
Reppenhagen, M E; Germany, Diamond #7 . . . . **12.00**
Reynolds, Fredrick; Sheffield, The Champion **18.00**
    The Prince's Own **18.00**
SPEC Co, Derby, Conn., The Herbrand Razor **10.00**
Sample, W H; Commander **10.00**
Savage & Sons, Geo; Tempered **16.00**
Schoolhouse, Cast Steel, very old **16.00**
Sears & Son, Henry; 1865, Premier **20.00**
    Magnetic 3060 . . . . **20.00**
    Queen ¾ **18.00**
Shaw's John; Celebrated Razor **10.00**
Sheaf Works, Cast Steel Warranted, very old & crude **14.00**
Shumate Razor Co, St, Louis, Shumate Barbers Antiseptic **10.00**
Simmons Hardware Co, English Standard Hollow Ground **12.00**
    Hollow Ground Keen Kutter **30.00**
    Hornet **12.00**
    Keen Kutter **30.00**
    Royal **12.00**
    Royal Keen Kutter **30.00**
Simmons Hardware Co, USA, Keen Kutter-Blue Steel **24.00**
Smith, Joseph, Sheffield, Silver Steel Razor **16.00**
Standart Bros, Detroit, The Boss Razor **10.00**
Sterling Razor Works, Rattler **10.00**
Stevens & Son, J, England, Fine Surgical Steel **12.00**
Superior Razor, Warranted Well Known **10.00**
Tadross, Antoni, Made In Germany, Antoni Tadross **12.00**
Taylor, Sheffield, Clean Shaver **10.00**
    The 1000 . . . . **10.00**
Taylor, W; England, corporate mark-X Q SI TE **14.00**
Tiki, bone handle **16.00**
Tonsorial, Sheffield Steel **10.00**

Tuckmar, Silver Steel, Solingen, black & white **14.00**
Tuckmar, Solingen, Siber-Stahl **18.00**

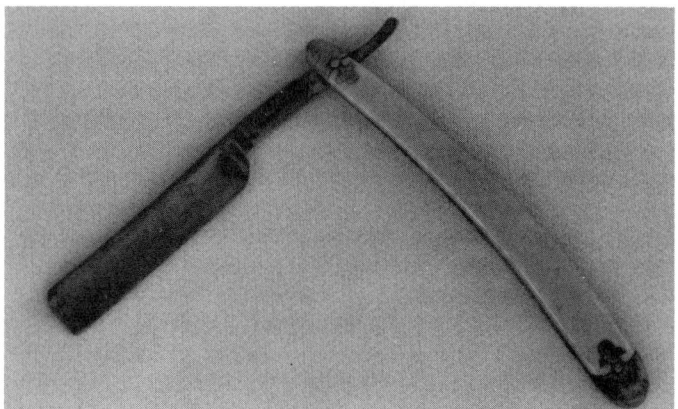

Turner, Thomas & Co, Sheffield, Full Concave **10.00**
Turners Encore **10.00**
Underland, A L, Omaha, Neb., Black Diamond **10.00**
Union Cutlery Co, Olean, N.Y., Spike **10.00**
United Drug Co, Tidioute, Permedge **10.00**
Valentine & Yule, Chicago, 311 . . . . **12.00**
Vom Cleff & Co, New York, Diamondine **10.00**
Voos, Emil; Solingen, Germany, Black King **10.00**
Wade & Butcher, Barbers Use **16.00**
Elars **15.00**
Straight type **6.00**
Wade & Butcher, Celebrated, Patent Temper **16.00**
Wade & Butcher, Sheffield, By All the World Approved **20.00**
Diamond Edge **16.00**
Hollow Ground **18.00**
Made for W H Carter **20.00**
Wayne Cutlery Co, Trade Mark-Rochester **10.00**
Weck & Son, E N.Y., USA, pat July 27 '09 . . . . **10.00**
Wester Bros, New York, Yankee Wedge **12.00**
Winchester, #8425, bone handles, leather case **35.00**
Trade Mark **50.00**
Witte, A, Germany, Gold Bug **10.00**
Worchester Razor Co, Red Tobacco **12.00**
Wragg & Son, John, Sheffield, The Empire **16.00**
Wright & Wilhelmy Co, Clean Clipper **10.00**
Wyeth's, Germany, Warranted Cutlery **10.00**
Yankee Cutlery Co, Germany, Lion Brand **10.00**
Without Equal **10.00**

Reamers

Reamers have been made in hundreds of styles and colors, and by as many manufacturers. Their purpose is to extract the juices from lemons, oranges and grapefruits. Some are footed; others flat bottomed.

The largest producer of glass reamers was McKee who pressed their products from many types of glass---custard; delphite and Chalaine blue; opaque white; Skokie green; black; caramel and white opalescents; Seville yellow; and transparent pink, green and clear. Among these, the black and the caramel opal are the most valuable.

The Fry Glass Co. also made reamers that are today very collectible. Their vaseline glass juicers, both the straight sided and ruffled top models, are valued at well over $100. So is the Hazel Atlas Crisscross orange reamer in pink or deep blue. Hocking Glass produced a light blue orange reamer and, in the same soft blue, a 2-pc reamer and measuring cup combination. Both are considered rare and very valuable, with $200 and up for the 1-pc and $150 and up for the 2-pc currently quoted estimations.

In addition to the colors mentioned, red glass examples---transparent

or slag---are rare and costly. Regarded as one of the most valuable reamers ever made, the Cambridge bottom beaded 'Pat Jan. 6, 1909', in cobalt blue is worth in excess of $300.

Amber, shaker type, complete, Paden City **50.00**
Tab handle, plain side, Federal **115.00**
Tab handle, seed dam, ruffled, Federal **9.00**
Antique White, blocked-in embossing **45.00**
Black, pitcher & top **225.00**
Pointed, Saunders **325.00**
Black Amethyst, 'Orange Juice Extractor' **160.00**
Blue, Cambridge, Jan 6, 1909 . . . . **350.00**
Fruit juice, 1 qt, Hocking **160.00**
Quart pitcher & reamer, Hazel Atlas **135.00**
Opalescent **115.00**
Caramel opalescent, McKee **375.00**
Caramel swirl, McKee **125.00**
Ceramic, 2-pc toby, Japan **85.00**
2-pc, Royal Rudolstadt **95.00**
Double handle, child's, chicks, 2-pc, 4″ **30.00**
Figural clown, 5½″ **30.00**
Figural dog, 2-pc **65.00**
Figural duck, 2-pc, 2¾″ **35.00**
Figural swan, rose flowers, 2-pc, 4¼″ **38.00**
Lemon shape, 3-pc **25.00**
Orange shape, 2-pc, Goebel Germany **40.00**
Chalaine blue, grapefruit, McKee **225.00**
Sunkist **75.00**
Clambroth, tab handle, Hazel Atlas **55.00**
Cobalt, 2-pc **135.00**
Crisscross pattern, 1-pc **95.00**
Crystal, Cambridge **15.00**
Common ribbed **4.00**
Czechoslavakia **45.00**
Embossed Sunkist in bottom, Federal **160.00**
Hand reamer, 'Little Handy Lemon Squeezer' **55.00**
Jennyware, Jeannette **50.00**
No spout, 2-pc **20.00**
Platinum trim **30.00**
'Radnt' **55.00**
Thumbprint type reamer, 'Easley pat pend' **45.00**
Two handled **12.00**
Custard, ftd, embossed 'McK', small **20.00**
Delphite blue, ftd, embossed 'McK', small **160.00**
Emerald green, ruffled top, Fry **125.00**
Floral, ceramic, 2-pc, pitcher/reamer, w/tumblers, 7¾″ **45.00**
Ceramic, pitcher w/reamer top, 5½″ **25.00**
Ceramic, saucer shape, 1-pc **20.00**
Forest green, McKee **200.00**
Frosted, w/chicks, 2-handle **55.00**
Fry Glass, tab handle, 3″ **15.00**
Green, Servmor, slick handle type, US Glass **50.00**
Bucket reamer, 'Hex Optic', Jeannette **17.50**
Dark, Tufglas **80.00**
Flattened loop handle, Westmoreland **80.00**
Lemon/orange, Westmoreland **115.00**
Mechanical w/attachment feature **125.00**
Orange Juice Extractor **40.00**
Tab handle, plain side, Federal **4.00**
Tab handle, short, Jenkins Glass Co **50.00**
US Glass **20.00**
Jadite, dark, Jeannette **22.00**
Dark, pitcher w/reamer, Jeannette **35.00**
Kwicky Juicer, pat #141788 . . . . **15.00**

Milk glass, blk, oval, top only **110.00**
  Black, Saunders Reamer Pat Applied For **400.00**
  Slick handle **50.00**
  Sunkist **10.00**
  'Valencia' embossed **60.00**
  White, embossed Sunkist **9.00**
New Standard Green, metal, w/2-pc glass attachment **100.00**
Pink, complete, two handle, 2-pc **70.00**
  Etched **25.00**
  Grapefruit, McKee **375.00**
  Jeanette **90.00**
  Jennyware **80.00**
  Loop handle, orange reamer, 'Crisscross' **135.00**
  Ribbed, loop handle, Federal **15.00**
  Shaker type w/metal insert, Paden City **35.00**
  Sunkist **15.00**
  Tab handle, seed dam, ribbed, Federal **70.00**
  Tab handle, small, Jeannette **40.00**
Pottery, matching pitcher, panels & florals, Japanese ... **18.00**
Puddinhead **120.00**
Red slag, 'Fleur-de-Lis' **225.00**
Seville yellow **35.00**
Skokie green, ftd, unembossed, McKee, large **20.00**
USA Jiffy, 1-pc **38.00**
Vaseline, straight side, embossed, Fry **125.00**
  Straight side, unembossed, Fry **35.00**
Vitrock, embossed, loop handle, orange reamer, Hocking .. **12.50**
White, gr tinge, ftd, embossed 'McK', large **18.00**
  Sunkist **10.00**
  Two handle w/rabbit **70.00**
  US Glass **60.00**
White top, lemon shaped bottom, leaf spout & handle, Germany **30.00**
Yellow clown **45.00**

Records

Records that were made in limited quantities, early works of a performer who later became famous, and those issued in special series or aimed at a limited market are being sought by collectors at prices well in excess of their original cost. The most widely collected categories are Jazz, Dance Bands, Celebrity, Blues, Rhythm and Blues, Country and Western, Hillbilly, Rockabilly, and Rock and Roll.

Aladdins, The; I Had A Dream Last Night, Aladdin, 3275 ..... **30.00**
Alexander, Texas; Frisco Train Blues, Okeh, 8658 .... **60.00**
  Tell Me Woman Blues, Okeh, 8673 .... **60.00**
Alix, May; Experience Blues, Harmograph, 873 .... **50.00**
Allen Brothers, Glorious Night Blues, Victor, 23707 ...... **70.00**
  New Salty Dog, Victor, 23514 .... **50.00**
Allen, Henry & His Orchestra; Dancing Dave, 38121 .... **40.00**
  Sugar Hill Function, 38140 .... **40.00**
Anderson, Andy; Gimme A Lock-A Yo' Hair, Century, 601 .... **20.00**
Anderson, Jelly Roll; Free Women Blues, Herwon, 92020 .... **75.00**
Anka, Paul; Diana, ABC Paramount, 420 .... **15.00**
Armstrong, Louis; Basin Street Blues, 8690 .... **40.00**
  Heebie Jeebies, 8300 .... **50.00**
  Sweet Little Papa, 8379 .... **50.00**
Arnold, Eddy; Country Classics, RCA Victor, 3027 .... **30.00**
  When It's Round-Up Time In Heaven, 3249 .... **20.00**
Arnold, Kokomo; Milk Cow Blues, Decca, 7026 .... **20.00**
Arthur, Emry; I Tickled Her Under The Chin, 3301 .... **20.00**
  The Bluefield Murder, Paramount, 3222 .... **20.00**
Atkins, Chet; At Home, RCA Victor, 1544 .... **16.00**
Autry, Gene; Cowboy Yodel, Gennett, 7243 .... **80.00**

Living In The Mountains, QRS, 1044 .... **100.00**
The Girl I Left Behind, Superior, 2561 .... **130.00**
Western Classics, Columbia, 9001 .... **12.00**
Avalon, Frankie; Young Frankie Avalon, Chancellor, 5002 .. **15.00**
Avalons, The; Chains Around My Heart, Groove, 0141 .... **35.00**
Baldwin, Luke; Travelin' Blues, Champion, 16343 .... **25.00**
Barbecue Bob, It Just Won't Quit, Columbia, 14614 .... **35.00**
  Telling It To, Columbia, 14546 .... **35.00**
Basie, Count, & His Orchestra; Honeysucke Rose, 1141 .... **10.00**
  One O'Clock Jump, 1363 .... **10.00**
Beach Boys, The; Spirit of America, Capitol **50.00**
  Surfin', Candix, 331 .... **35.00**
Beale Street Sheiks; Hunting Blues, Paramount, 12774 .... **110.00**
Beatles, The; Ain't She Sweet, Atco, 169 .... **25.00**
  Meet The Beatles, Capitol, 2047 .... **40.00**
  Penny Lane, Capitol, 5810 .... **30.00**
  Please Please Me, Vee Jay, 498 .... **100.00**
Berry, Chuck; Chuck Berry Is On Top, Chess, 1435 .... **15.00**
Bird's, Elmer, Happy Four; Muscle Shoals Blues, Gennett, 7182 **70.00**
Blind Blake; Depressions's Gone From Me Blues, 13137 ..... **90.00**
  Dissatisfied Blues, Paramount, 13115 .... **90.00**
  Night And Day Blues, Paramount, 13123 .... **90.00**
  Rope Stretchin' Blues, Paramount, 13103 .... **90.00**
Blind Lemon Jefferson; Empty House Blues, Paramount, 12946. **50.00**
  Long Distance Moan, Paramount, 12852 .... **50.00**
  Mosquito Moan, Paramount, 12899 .... **50.00**
Blythe's Blue Boys; Oriental Man, 15676 .... **80.00**
  There'll Come A Day, 15344 .... **100.00**
Bodine; Wabash Cannon Ball, Superior, 2608 .... **30.00**
Bond, Eddie; Slip Slip Slippin' In, Mercury, 70882 ...... **30.00**
Boone, Pat; Pat, Dot, 3050 .... **12.00**
Bradley, Tommie; When You're Down And Out, 16308 .... **50.00**
Brown, Charles; Mood Music, Aladdin, 702 .... **80.00**
  Seven Long Days, Aladdin, 3092 .... **20.00**
Brown, Hi Henry; Hospital Blues, Vocalion, 1715 .... **120.00**
  Titanic Blues, Vocalion, 1728 .... **120.00**
Brown, Roy; Hip Shakin' Baby, Imperial, 5510 .... **15.00**
  Roy Brown And Wynonie Harris, King, 607 .... **60.00**
Brown, Willie; M and O Blues, Paramount, 13090 .... **120.00**
Bumble Bee Slim; Chain Gang Bound, Paramount, 13109 ..... **75.00**
  Yo Yo String Blues, Paramount, 13102 .... **75.00**
Bunn, Teddy & Williams; Spencer, Goose And Gander, 38602.. **50.00**
Burnett, Johnny; Tear It Up, Coral, 61651 .... **25.00**
Burse, Charlie; Tappin' That Thing, Champion, 16654 ..... **90.00**
Burston, Clara; Good And Hot, Champion, 16756 .... **50.00**
Burton, John; Pal Of My Sunny Days, Superior, 2810 ...... **75.00**
Butcher, Dwight; By A Little Bayou, Victor, 23794 .... **30.00**
Butler, Mary; Mad Dog Blues, Brunswick, 7049 .... **50.00**
Butterbeans & Susie; Kiss Me Sweet, Okeh, 8182 .... **40.00**
Cadillacs, The; Down The Road, Josie, 778 .... **15.00**
  The Crazy Cadillacs, Jubilee, 1089 .... **60.00**
Cakkiway, Blanche; Casey Jones Blues, Victor, 22640 ..... **20.00**
Calicott, Joe; Fare Thee Well Blues, Brunswick, 7166 .... **100.00**
California Ramblers; Tip-Toe Through The Tulips With Me, 52629 **15.00**
Campbell, Gene; Wedding Day Blues, Brunswick, 7197 ...... **50.00**
Campbell, Glen; Turned Out Blues, Brunswick, 7226 .... **50.00**
Candullo, Joe & His Orchestra; Spanish Mama, Buddy, 8052 .. **20.00**
Cannon, Freddy; Freddy Cannon Steps Out, Swan, 511 ...... **40.00**
Cannon's Jug Stompers; Money Never Runs Out, Victor, 23262 **100.00**
  Wolf River Blues, Victor, 23272 .... **100.00**
Cardinals, The; She Rocks, Atlantic, 972 .... **20.00**
Carlisle, Cliff; Box Car Blues, Champion, 16212 .... **30.00**
  Nobody Wants Me, Champion, 16329 .... **30.00**
Carr, Leroy; I Know That I'll Be Blue, Brunswick, 1519 ... **30.00**

Let's Disagree, Brunswick, 1624 . . . . **30.00**
Naptown Blues, Vocalion, 1400 . . . . **30.00**
Carrol, Johnny; Hot Rock, Decca, 30013 . . . . **30.00**
Carson, Fiddlin' John; I Intend To Make Heaven My Home, 45555 **40.00**
John Henry Blues, Okeh, 7004 . . . . **60.00**
Sugar In The Gourd, Okeh, 4994 . . . . **60.00**
The Baggage Coach Ahead, Okeh, 7006 . . . . **60.00**
The Lightning Express, Okeh, 7008 . . . . **60.00**
Carter Family; Gold Watch And Chain, Victor, 23821 . . . . **50.00**
I Loved You Better Than I Know, 23835 . . . . **50.00**
I Wouldn't Mind Dying, Victor, 23807 . . . . **50.00**
Carter, Bo; I Want You To Know, Okeh, 8935 . . . . **50.00**
I'm An Old Bumble Bee, Okeh, 8852 . . . . **50.00**
Casa Loma Orchestra; Dixie Lee, Brunswick, 6726 . . . . **10.00**
White Jazz, Brunswick, 6092 . . . . **10.00**
Cash, Johnny; All Aboard The Blue Train, Sun, 1270 . . . . **20.00**
Folsom Prison Blues, Sun, 232 . . . . **5.00**
Cawley's Ridge Runners; The Vine-Covered Cottage, 23570 . . . . **30.00**
Chantels, The; I Love You So, End, 1020 . . . . **15.00**
Maybe, End, 1005 . . . . **20.00**
Chapman, Charlie; Moanin' The Blues, Broadway, 5079 . . . . . . **75.00**
Charles, Ray; Rockhouse, Atlantic, 2006 . . . . **15.00**
The Sun's Gonna Shine Again, Atlantic, 984 . . . . **12.00**
What'd I Say, Atlantic, 2031 . . . . **25.00**
Charms, The; Heaven Only Knows, DeLuxe, 6000 . . . . **50.00**
My Baby Dearest Darling, DeLuxe, 6056 . . . . **20.00**
Checker, Chubby; The Class, Parkway, 804 . . . . **60.00**
Flame In My Heart, King, 4558 . . . . **50.00**
Night Curtains, King, 4581 . . . . **50.00**
Childers, WC; I'll Smoke My Long Stemmed Pipe, 7113 . . . . . . **50.00**
Two Little Girls In Blue, Gennett, 7223 . . . . **30.00**
Clifton, Kaiser; Cash Money Blues, Victor, 23278 . . . . **80.00**
Cline, Patsy; Patsy Cline, Decca, 8611 . . . . **15.00**
Clovers, The; Crawlin', Atlantic, 989 . . . . **15.00**
Don't You Know I Love You, Atlantic, 934 . . . . **50.00**
The Clover's Dance Party, Atlantic, 8034 . . . . **20.00**
Coasters, The; One By One, ATCO, 123 . . . . **30.00**
The Coasters, ATCO, 101 . . . . **40.00**
Cochran Brothers, The; Fool's Paradise, Ekko, 3001 . . . . **75.00**
Cochran, Eddie; Never To Be Forgotten, Liberty, 3220 . . . . . . **60.00**
Singin' To My Baby, Liberty, 3061 . . . . **80.00**
Collins Kids, The; Hop, Skip And Jump, Columbia, 40921 . . . . **12.00**
Rock Boppin' Baby, Columbia, 41225 . . . . **12.00**
Collins, Sam; The Jail House Blues, Black Patti, 8025 . . . . **120.00**
Yellow Dog Blues, Black Patti, 8026 . . . . **120.00**
Concords, The; Monticello, Harlem, 2328 . . . . **100.00**
Connie's Inn Orchestra; You Rascal, You, Crown, 3194 . . . . . . **25.00**
Coronets, The; It Would Be Heavenly, Chess, 1553 . . . . **40.00**
Cox, Bill & Hobbs, Cliff; Alabama Blues, Gennett, 7080 . . . . . . **50.00**
California Blues, Gennett, 6928 . . . . **50.00**
Cox, Ida; Coffin Blues, Paramount, 12318 . . . . **80.00**
Jail House Blues, Paramount, 12965 . . . . **80.00**
Crayton, Pee Wee; Pappy's Blues, Imperial, 408 . . . . **20.00**
Crests, The; Fabulous Hits, Coed, 904 . . . . **30.00**
The Crests Sing All Biggies, Coed, 901 . . . . **40.00**
Crickets, The; Not Fade Away, Brunswick, 55035 . . . . **25.00**
That'll Be The Day, Brunswick, 55009 . . . . **25.00**
Crosby, Bing; Can't We Be Friends, Columbia, 2001 . . . . **12.00**
St Louis Blues, Brunswick, 20105 . . . . **15.00**
Sweet Georgia Brown, Brunswick, 6320 . . . . **10.00**
Cruse, Manny & The Sounds; Any Time Any Place, Dart, 127 . . **50.00**
Have Faith In Me, 6037 . . . . **50.00**
Daddy Stovepipe; Depression, Bluebird, 6023 . . . . **50.00**
Darby, Tom & Jimmie Tarlton; Going Back To My Texas Home **60.00**

The Black Sheep, 15674-D **50.00**
Darren, James; Sings For All Sizes, Colpix, 424 . . . . **20.00**
Davenport, Charles; Atlanta Rag, Broadway, 6869 . . . . **60.00**
Chimes Blues, Broadway, 5046 . . . . **60.00**
Davis, Dale & The Tomcats; Why'd You Leave Me Blues, l04/l05 **25.00**
Davis, Jimmie; Cowboy's Home Sweet Home, Victor, 23718 . . . . **50.00**
Lonely Hobo, Victor, 23648 . . . . **50.00**
The Gambler's Return, Victor, 23778 . . . . **50.00**
Davis, Link; Don't Big Shot Me, Starday, 255 . . . . **15.00**
Grasshopper Rock, Nucraft, 2026 . . . . **10.00**
Davis, Walter; Howling Wind Blues, Victor, 23308 . . . . **80.00**
Lonesome Hill Blues, Victor, 23325 . . . . **80.00**
Night Creepin', Victor, 23414 . . . . **50.00**
Railroad Man Blues, Victor, 23291 . . . . **80.00**
Dee, Jimmy; You're Late Miss Kate, Dot, 15721 . . . . **15.00**
Deep River Boys, The; Midnight Magic, Que, 104 . . . . **30.00**
Spiritual And Jubilees, Waldorf, 108 . . . . **15.00**
Del Vikings, The; Come Go With The Del Vikings, 1000 . . . . . **50.00**
Swinging Singing Record Session, 20353 . . . . **50.00**
The Del Vikings & The Sonnets, Crown, 5368 . . . . **15.00**
Whispering Bells, Fee Bee, 211 . . . . **15.00**
Dells, The; Tell The World, Vee Jay, 134 . . . . **300.00**
Delmore Brothers; I Got The Kansas City Blues, 6002 . . . . **10.00**
Smoky Mountain Bill, Bluebird, 5589 . . . . **12.00**
The Frozen Girl, Bluebird, 5338 . . . . **15.00**
Diamonds, The; The Diamonds Meet Pete Rugold, 20368 . . . . . **30.00**
The Diamonds, Mercury, 20309 . . . . **30.00**
Diddley, Bo; Bo Diddley, Chess, 1431 . . . . **30.00**
Dixieland Jug Blowers; Banjoreno, Victor, 21472 . . . . **40.00**
Southern Shout, Victor, 20954 . . . . **40.00**
Dixon, Floyd; Change Your Mind, Kent, 311 . . . . **10.00**
Come Back Baby, Aladdin, 3151 . . . . **15.00**
Wine Wine Wine, Aladdin, 3135 . . . . **16.00**
Domino, Fats; Cheatin', Imperial, 5220 . . . . **35.00**
Going To The River, Imperial, 5231 . . . . **16.00**
How Long, Imperial, 5209 . . . . **20.00**
Rock And Rollin', Imperial, 9000 . . . . **40.00**
Rockin' And Rollin' With Fats Domino, 9004 . . . . **40.00**
Dominoes, The; Love Love Love, Federal, 12072 . . . . **40.00**
Weeping Willow Blues, Federal, 12039 . . . . **60.00**
Dorsey Brothers, The; Singing In The Rain, Okeh, 41272 . . . . . **12.00**
Dorsey, Tom; Tiger Rag, Okeh, 41178 . . . . **12.00**
Duke Of Earl; Duke Of Earl, Vee Jay, 1040 . . . . **15.00**
Dupree, Jack; Cabbage Greens, Okeh, 12103 . . . . **30.00**
Champion Of The Blues, Atlantic, 8056 . . . . **16.00**
Natural & Soulful Blues, Atlantic, 8045 . . . . **16.00**
Duprees, The; You Belong To Me, Coed, 905 . . . . **30.00**
Dylan, Bob; Blowin' In The Wind, Columbia, 42856 . . . . **50.00**
Corrina Corrina, Columbia, 42656 . . . . **50.00**
Edwards, Bernice; Hard Hustlin' Blues, Paramount, 12766 . . . . **40.00**
Long Tall Mama, Paramount, 12633 . . . . **40.00**
El Dorados, The; Rock 'N' Roll's For Me, Vee Jay, 180 . . . . . . **12.00**
Tears On My Pillow, Vee Jay, 250 . . . . **15.00**
At My Front Door, Vee Jay, 147 . . . . **10.00**
Ellington, Duke; Immigration Blues, Vocalion, 1077 . . . . **70.00**
New Orleans Low-Down, Vocalion, 1086 . . . . **70.00**
Red Hot Band, Vocalion, 1153 . . . . **70.00**
Enchanters, The; Bottle It Up And Go, Coral, 61916 . . . . **15.00**
Oh Rosemarie, JJ & M, 1562 . . . . **15.00**
Spellbound By The Moon, Stardust, 102 . . . . **100.00**
Esquerita; Esquerita, Capitol, 1186 . . . . **100.00**
Estes, John; Expressman Blues, Victor, 23318 . . . . **100.00**
Poor John Blues, Victor, 38628 . . . . **100.00**
Stop That Thing, Champion, 50001 . . . . **25.00**

T-Bone Steak Blues, Victor, 38595	**100.00**
Everly Brothers, The; Everly Brothers, Cadence, 3003	**30.00**
Keep A-Loving Me, Columbia, 21496	**30.00**
Fabian; Hold That Tiger, Chancellor, 5003	**20.00**
Rockin' Hot, Chancellor, 5019	**24.00**
Falcons, The; Now That It's Over, Falcom, 1006	**20.00**
Fascinations, The; Come To Paradise, Capitol, 4137	**15.00**
Feathers, Charlie; Tongue-Tied Jill, Meteor, 5032	**100.00**
Why Don't You, Kay, 1001	**15.00**
Feathers, The; Johnny Darling, Show Time, 1104	**30.00**
Fender, Freddy; Little Mama, Duncan, 1004	**10.00**
Mean Woman, Duncan, 1000	**20.00**
Five Crowns, The; A Star, Rainbow, 179	**90.00**
Alone Again, Rainbow, 206	**100.00**
God Bless You, Gee, 1001	**15.00**
Five Discs; Roses, Dwain, 803	**30.00**
Five Dollars; You Fool, Fortune, 833	**12.00**
Five Keys, The; I Hadn't Any One Till You, Aladdin, 3136	**125.00**
Tear Drops In Your Eyes, Aladdin, 3204	**100.00**
The Glory Of Love, Aladdin, 3099	**100.00**
Five Satins; In The Still Of The Night, Standord, 1005	**75.00**
To The Aisle, Ember, 1019	**15.00**
Five Willows, White Cliffs Of Dover, Allen, 1003	**120.00**
Flamingos; Golden Teardrops, Chance, 1145	**100.00**
In A Letter, Chance, 1162	**100.00**
Would I Be Crying, Checker, 853	**10.00**
Fleming & Townsend; Blowin' The Blues, Victor, 23635	**35.00**
Blues Have Gone, Victor, 23758	**50.00**
Gambler's Advice, Victor, 23829	**50.00**
Foley, Red; Beyond The Sunset, Decca, 8296	**15.00**
Ford, Tennessee Ernie; Sixteen Tons, Capitol, 3262	**8.00**
Foster, Jim; Do That Thing, Silverstone, 5131	**100.00**
The Jail House Blues, Champion, 15320	**100.00**
Foster, Little Willie; Crying The Blues, Cobra, 5011	**15.00**
Four Buddies; Heart And Soul, Savoy, 817	**40.00**
What's The Matter With Me, Savoy, 866	**30.00**
Four Lovers; Never Never, RCA, 6648	**10.00**
The Girl In My Dreams, RCA, 6518	**9.00**
Four Tunes; The Lonesome Road, RCA Victor, 50-0042	**30.00**
They Don't Understand, RCA Victor, 4828	**8.00**
Fulsom, Lowell; Best Wishes, Swing Time, 289	**30.00**
Black Widow Spider, Swing Time, 308	**30.00**
Good Party Shuffle, Swing Time, 320	**20.00**
Georgia Melodians; Charleston Ball, Edison, 51678	**15.00**
Rhythm Of The Day, Edison, 51730	**15.00**
Gibbs, Hugh; Chicken Feel, Paramount, 3003	**25.00**
Gibson, Clifford; Stop Your Rambling, Paramount, 12923	**100.00**
Whiskey Moan Blues, QRS, 7087	**100.00**
Gilley, Mickey; Drive In Move, Princess, 4004	**12.00**
Now That I Have You, Supreme, 101	**8.00**
What Have I Done, Daryl, 101	**8.00**
Your Selfish Pride, Lynn, 503	**8.00**
Glover, Mae; Gas Man Blues, Gennett, 7040	**50.00**
Grass Hopper Papa, Champion, 16351	**40.00**
Golden Gate Orchestra; Button Up Your Overcoat, Edison, 52513	**20.00**
The Pay Off, Edison, 52181	**20.00**
Third Roll, Edison, 52206	**20.00**
Goodman, Bennie; A Jazz Holiday, Vocalion, 15656	**50.00**
Love Or Leave Me, Columbia, 2871	**25.00**
That's A Plenty, Vocalion, 15705	**50.00**
Grant And Wilson, Scoop It, Paramount, 12379	**30.00**
You Dirty Mistreater, Paramount, 12324	**50.00**
Graves, Roosevelt & Brother; Bustin' The Jug, Paramount, 12859	**60.00**
When I Lay My Burdens Down, 12974	**60.00**
Gray, Owen; Be Home Early Tonight, My Dear, 5301	**20.00**
Midnight Special, Vocalion, 5337	**20.00**
Green, Lee; Dud-Low Joe, Vocalion, 1467	**50.00**
Gambling Man Blues, Vocalion, 1533	**50.00**
Greer, John; Cheatin', RCA Victor, 50-0096	**10.00**
Drinkin' Wine, Spo-Dee-O-Dee, 50-0007	**15.00**
Gross, Helen; Last Journey Blues, Ajax, 17090	**40.00**
Rockin' Chair Blues, Ajax, 17046	**40.00**
Haley, Bill; Jukebox Cannonball, Holiday, 113	**90.00**
Rock 'N' Roll, Decca, 2209	**12.00**
Rock Around The Clock, Decca, 8225	**20.00**
Rocket 88, Holiday, 105	**100.00**
Rockin' Around The World, Decca, 2564	**8.00**
Hamilton, George; Atlanta Rag, Champion, 15726	**60.00**
Handy's Memphis Blues Band; Beale St Blues, Lyratone, 4211	**30.00**
Yellow Dog Blues, Lyratone, 4212	**30.00**
Harlem Footwarmers, The; Old Man Blues, Okeh, 8869	**35.00**
Sweet Chariot, Columbia, 14670	**35.00**
Harptones; My Memories Of You, Bruce, 102	**12.00**
Since I Fell For You, Bruce, 113	**10.00**
Harris, William; Kansas City Blues, Gennett, 6707	**130.00**
Harris, Wynonie; Blood Shot Eyes, King, 4461	**12.00**
Night Train, King, 4555	**15.00**
Quiet Whiskey, King, 4685	**12.00**
Harvey, Roy; Dark Eyes, Columbia, 15714	**30.00**
Railroad Blues, Champion, 16255	**30.00**
We Will Outshine The Sun, Gennett, 6350	**30.00**
You're Bound To Look Like A Monkey, 16331	**30.00**
Heartbeats; A Thousand Miles Away, Hull, 720	**20.00**
Henderson, Fletcher & His Orchestra; Dinah, 15204	**40.00**
Hay Foot, Straw Foot, 15174	**40.00**
Memphis Bound, 15030	**40.00**
Henderson, Katherine; If You Like Me, QRS, 7041	**100.00**
Higgins, Chuck; Pachuko Hop, Combo, 300	**60.00**
Highlanders; Richmond Square, Paramount, 3184	**50.00**
Hill, Bertha; Panama Limited Blues, Okeh, 8367	**35.00**
Hines, Earl & His Orchestra; A Monday Date, QRS, 7037	**120.00**
Chimes In Blues, QRS, 7038	**120.00**
Off Time Blues, QRS, 7036	**120.00**
Panther Rag, QRS, 7039	**120.00**
Hokum Boys, The; Hip Shakin' Strut, Champion, 1623	**60.00**
Holly, Buddy; Buddy Holly, Coral, 577210	**40.00**
Love Me, Decca, 30543	**15.00**
Reminiscing, Cora, 57426	**30.00**
That'll Be The Day, Decca, 30434	**30.00**
Wishing, Coral, 62369	**12.00**
Hooker, John Lee; House Of The Blues, Chess, 1438	**30.00**
I'm John Lee Hooker, Vee Jay, 1007	**30.00**
Plays And Sings The Blues, Chess, 1454	**30.00**
Horton, Johnny; Lover's Rock, Columbia, 41043	**10.00**
Houchins, Kenneth; My Little Ozark Mountain Home, 16775	**30.00**
Tennessee Blues, Champion, 16501	**30.00**
The Old Missouri Moon, Champion, 16637	**30.00**
Hutchison, Frank; Johnny And Jane, Okeh, 45361	**20.00**
Worried Blues, Okeh, 45114	**20.00**
Jackson, Charlie; I'll Be Gone Babe, Paramount, 12905	**30.00**
Self Experience, Paramount, 12956	**40.00**
James, Skip; Devil Got My Woman, Paramount, 13088	**150.00**
Drunken Spree, Paramount, 13111	**250.00**
Jeffries, Speed, & His Night Owls; Kentucky Blues, 2670	**90.00**
Tiger Moan, 2755	**90.00**
Johnson, Big Bill; Mr Conductor Man, 16426	**60.00**
Saturday Night Rub, Champion, 16081	**60.00**
Johnson, Edith; Honey Dripper Blues, Paramount, 12823	**60.00**

Johnson, Lonnie; Home Wreckers Blues, Columbia, 14667..... **30.00**
    Unselfish Love, Columbia, 14676 .... **30.00**
Johnson, Mary; Muddy Creek Blues, Brunswick, 7093 .... **60.00**
    Western Union Blues, Brunswick, 7081.................. **60.00**
Johnson, Tommy; Canned Heat Blues, Victor, 38535 .... **120.00**
Jordan, Charlie; Cherry Wine Woman, Vocalion, 1707 .... **50.00**
    Working Man Blues, Victor, 23304 .... **80.00**
Jordan, Luke; If I Call You Mama, Victor, 23400 .... **70.00**
Kansas Joe; Pickin' The Blues, Vocalion, 1660 .... **50.00**
Keese, Howard; Memphis Special Blues, Gennett, 7166....... **50.00**
    The Longest Train I Ever Saw, 16374 .... **35.00**
Kelly, Willie; Hard Luck Man Blues, Victor, 23320 .... **60.00**
Kincaid, Bradley; After The Ball, Gennett, 7081 .... **25.00**
    Let The Mule Go Aunk, Aunk, 6944 .... **25.00**
Lee, Ruth; Maybe Someday, Nordskog, 3008 .... **150.00**
Leecan, Bobbie Needmore Band; Midnight Susie, Victor, 20251 **35.00**
Lenoir, JB; I Want My Baby, JOB, 1016 .... **60.00**
Lewis, Furry; Cannon Ball Blues, Victor, 23345........... **80.00**
    Creeper's Blues, Vocalion, 1547.................... **75.00**
Lewis, Smiley; Caldonia's Party, Imperial, 5241 .... **30.00**
    Too Many Drivers, Imperial, 5316 .... **15.00**
Lightnin'; In New York, Candid, 8010 .... **20.00**
    Lightnin' Hopkins, Herald, 1012 .... **40.00**
    Lightnin's Jump, TNT, 8002..................... **20.00**
Little Hat Jones; Little Hat Blues, Okeh, 8794......... **70.00**
Little Richard; Long Tall Sally, Specialty, 572 .... **7.00**
    The Fabulous Little Richard, Specialty, 2104 .... **20.00**
Little Son Jackson; Lonely Blues, Imperial, 5229 .... **30.00**
    Piggly Wiggly, Imperial, 5276.................... **25.00**
    Sugar Mama, Imperial, 5339.................... **12.00**
    Upstairs Boogie, Imperial, 5165 .... **40.00**
Lymom, Frankie; I'm Not A Juvenile Delinquent, 1026 .... **7.00**
Ma Rainey; Jelly Bean Blues, Paramount, 12238 .... **100.00**
    See See Rider Blues, Paramount, 12252................. **100.00**
Macon, Uncle Dave; Carve That Possum, Vocalion, 5151 ...... **40.00**
    Farm Relief, Vocalion, 5341.................... **40.00**
    I'm The Child To Fight, 292 .... **30.00**
    Put Me In My Little Bed, 5397 .... **40.00**
    When The Train Comes Along, 16805 .... **100.00**
Mainer, JE; When I Reach My Home Eternal, 6385 .... **10.00**
    Won't Be Worried Long, Bluebird, 6738................ **10.00**
Martin & Roberts; Gwine Down To Town, Gennett, 7050 ...... **25.00**
    Put On Your Old Gray Bonnet, 7242 .... **25.00**
Martin, Blind George; Southern Rag, Broadway, 5053........ **40.00**
Martin, Janis; Let's Elope Baby, RCA Victor, 6744 .... **10.00**
Martin, Sara; Death Sting Me Blues, QRS, 7042 .... **100.00**
    Kitchen Man Blues, QRS, 7043 .... **100.00**
McCoy, Charles; Glad Hand Blues, Brunswick, 7165 ...... **40.00**
    Too Long, Vocalion, 1712 .... **40.00**
McCracklin, Jimmy; She's Gone, Peacock, 1605.......... **10.00**
McFadden, Ruth & The Supremes; Cherry Red, 312 .... **30.00**
McGee, Samm; Kickin' Mule, Gennett, 7022 .... **40.00**
    Only A Step To The Grave, Gennett, 6778 .... **40.00**
McMichen, Clayton; Corn Licker Still, Part 11/12, 15618-D **20.00**
    Wild Cat Rag, Columbia, 15775-D **50.00**
Mello-Kings; Tonite, Tonite, Herald, 502 .... **7.00**
Memphis Jug Band; Fourth Street Mess Around, Victor, 23251 **100.00**
    Meningitis Blues, Victor, 23421 .... **100.00**
    Taking Your Place, Victor, 23347 .... **100.00**
Memphis Minnie & Kansas Joe; Fishin' Blues, 1711 .... **40.00**
    Garage Fire Blues, 1601 .... **50.00**
Midnighters; Midnighters Sing Their Greatest Hits, 333........ **40.00**
Miles, Lizzie; I Hate a Man Like You, Victor, 38571.......... **60.00**
Miller, Al; Saturday Night Hymn, Black Patti, 8049.......... **60.00**

Mississippi John Hurt, Avalon Blues, Okeh, 8759 .... **100.00**
    Stack O'Lee Blues, Okeh, 8560 .... **100.00**
Mississippi Sheiks, Shooting High Dice, Paramount, 13142 ... **100.00**
    Tell Me To Do Right, Paramount, 13156 .... **100.00**
Missourians, The; Two Hundred Squabble, Victor, 38145 ..... **40.00**
Mitchell, Bobby; One Friday Morning, Imperial, 5250 .... **50.00**
    Wedding Bells are Ringing, Imperial, 5295 .... **60.00**
Moonglows; I Was Wrong, Chance, 1156 .... **100.00**
    Secret Love, Chance, 1152.................... **100.00**
    Train, 1161 .... **120.00**
Moore & Poteet; John Henry, Paramount, 3023 .... **40.00**
    Land Where We'll Never Grow Old, 3296.......... **40.00**
    Lazy Tennessee, Paramount, 3063.................. **40.00**
Moore, Alice; Lonesome Dream Blues, Paramount, 13107 ..... **90.00**
    Serving Time Blues, Paramount, 12947 .... **90.00**
Moore, Byrd; Back Water Blues, Gennett, 6686.......... **60.00**
    Mama Toot Your Whistle, Gennett, 6586.......... **60.00**
Morton, Fred; Fish Tail Blues, Autograph, 606 .... **300.00**
    London Blues, Okeh, 8105 .... **100.00**
    Weary Blues, Autograph, 607.......... **300.00**
    Wolverine Blues, Autograph, 623.......... **300.00**
Muddy Waters; Screamin' and Cryin', Aristocrat, 406 ...... **100.00**
Mullican, Moon; Good Deal, Lucille, King, 1337 .... **10.00**
    Oogle, Oogle, Olglie, King, 1164 .... **10.00**
Narmour & Smith; Limber Neck Blues, Okeh, 45548 .... **30.00**
    Texas Breakdown, Okeh, 45492.................... **25.00**
Nelson, Ricky; Lonesome Town, Imperial, 5545 .... **18.00**
    Teen Time, Verve, 2083 .... **35.00**
Newbern, Hambone Willie; She Could Toddle-oo, Okeh, 8740. **100.00**
Nichols, Red & His Orchestra; Keep a Song in Your Soul, 6068 **15.00**
Nicholson's Players; Let Me Call You Sweetheart, Gennett, 7241 **18.00**
Nix, Willie; All By Myself, Sabre, 570 .... **40.00**
    Baker Shop Boogie, Sun, 179 .... **120.00**
Noble Sissle & His Orchestra; Basement Blues, Brunswick, 6129 **25.00**
    Roll on, Mississippi, Roll On, 6111 .... **25.00**
Noland, Terry; Terry Noland, Brunswick, 54041 .... **75.00**
Noone Jimmie, Orchestra; A Monday Date, 1229 .... **50.00**
    I Know That You Know, 1584 .... **50.00**
North Carolina Ramblers; Bill Mason, Paramount, 3079 .... **30.00**
    Blue Eyes, Paramount, 3072 .... **30.00**
Note Makers; It Hurts To Wonder, Sotoplay, 007 .... **40.00**
Nutones; Believe, Hollywood Star, 798 .... **120.00**
Oliver, Joe King, Jazz Band; Canal Street Blues, Gennett, 5132 **200.00**
    King Porter, Autograph, 617 .... **600.00**
    Krooked Blues, Gennett, 5274 .... **300.00**
Original Dixieland Jazz Band; Oriental Jazz, Vocalion, 12097 .. **30.00**
    Ostrich Walk, Vocalion, 1206.................... **30.00**
Orioles; At Night, Jubilee, 5025 .... **110.00**
    Forgive and Forget, Jubilee, 5016 .... **120.00**
    I'd Rather Have You Under the Moon, 5031 .... **120.00**
Orlando, Tony & The Milds; Ding Dong, Milo, 101 .... **15.00**
Patton, Charley; Joe Kirby, Paramount, 13133 .... **140.00**
    Magnolia Blues, Paramount, 12943 .... **110.00**
    Some Summer Day, Paramount, 13080.................. **140.00**
Patton, Jimmy; Teen-Age Heart, Sims, 104 .... **8.00**
Penguins; Cool Cool Penguins, Dooto, 242 .... **25.00**
Perkins, Carl; Whole Lotta Shakin', Columbia, 1234 .... **50.00**
Piano Red; Decatur Street Blues, Groove, 0023 .... **8.00**
    Piano Red in Concert, Groove, 6 .... **15.00**
    Rockin' With Red, RCA Victor, 587 .... **15.00**
Platters; Roses of Picardy, Federal, 12181 .... **40.00**
    Take Me Back, Federal, 12204 .... **20.00**
    The Platter, Federal, 549 .... **120.00**
Presley, Elvis; All Shook Up, Victor, 6870 .... **25.00**

Blue Moon, Victor, 6640 .... **30.00**
Elvis Sails, Victor, 5157 .... **30.00**
I Beg of You, Victor, 7150 .... **30.00**
I Got Stung, Victor, 7410 .... **70.00**
King Creole, RCA Victor, 5122 .... **30.00**
Milkcow Blues Boogie, Victor, 6382 .... **25.00**
Price, Lloyd; Just Because, Paramount, 9792 .... **15.00**
The Exciting Lloyd Price, Paramount, 277 .... **25.00**
Puckett, Holand; Little Bessie, Gennett, 6720 ..... **20.00**
Puckett, Riley; Somewhere In Old Wyoming, Columbia, 15631 . **30.00**
The Cat Came Back, Columbia, 15656 .... **30.00**
Waitin' For The Evenin' Mail, Columbia, 15605 .... **30.00**
Rainwater, Marvin; Hot And Cold, MGM, 12240 ..... **30.00**
Ravens; Count Every Star, National, 9111 .... **150.00**
You Don't Have To Drop A Heart, 39112 .... **60.00**
Red Onion Jazz Babies, Santa Claus Blues, 4032 .... **150.00**
Reed, Jimmy; Boogie In The Dark, Vee Jay, 119 ..... **20.00**
Now Appearing, Vee Jay, 1035 .... **20.00**
Reneau, George; C&W Wreck, Vocalion, 14897 ..... **12.00**
On Top of Old Smoky, Vocalion, 15366 .... **20.00**
Wild Bill Jones, Vocalion, 14998 .... **12.00**
Robbins, Marty; Rock' n' Roll and Robbins, Columbia, 2601 .. **100.00**
Roberts, Fiddlin' Doc; Farewell Waltz, Gennett, 6717 .. **20.00**
Jack's Creek Waltz, Gennett, 7017 .... **20.00**
Rye Straw, Gennett, 7221 .... **20.00**
Robins; How Would You Know, Victor, 5434 .... **80.00**
I Made A Vow, Crown, 106 .... **50.00**
Robinson, Elzadie; Elzadie's Policy Blues, Paramount, 12635 .. **75.00**
Rodgers, Jimmie; Blue Yodel No. 9, Victor, 23580 .... **60.00**
Mississippi Delta Blues, Victor, 23816 .... **60.00**
Mother, The Queen of My Heart, 23721 .... **40.00**
My Time Ain't Long, Victor, 23669 .... **35.00**
The Southern Cannon Ball, Victor, 23811 ...... **60.00**
The Yodeling Ranger, Victor, 23830 .... **60.00**
Sloppy Drunk, Chess, 1574 .... **20.00**
Royals; Are You Forgetting, Federal, 12113 .... **100.00**
Sammy Stewart & His Orchestra; Copenhagen, Paramount, 20359 **40.00**
Sanders, Bessie; Shake a Little Bit, Champion, 15471 .... **40.00**
Scott, Jack; What Am I Living For, Carlton, 122 .... **50.00**
What In The World's Come Over You, 326, 626 .... **40.00**
Scottsdale String Band, Goin' Crazy Blues, Okeh, 45201 ...... **12.00**
Scruggs, Irene; Back to the Wall, Paramount, 13046 .... **100.00**
Good Meat Grinder, Paramount, 13023 .... **100.00**
Self, Ronnie; Ain't I'm A Dog, Columbia, 2149 .... **60.00**
Shirley & Lee; I'm Gone, Aladdin, 3153 .... **20.00**
Smith, Bessie; Safety Mama, Columbia, 14634 .... **35.00**
Smith, Clara; Clara Blues, Black Patti, 8035 .... **75.00**
Sand Raisin' Blue, Black Patti, 8034 .... **75.00**
Smith, Iva; Doin' That Thing, Gennett, 7040 .... **50.00**
Smith, Trixie; Mining Camp Blues, Paramount, 12256 .... **75.00**
Railroad Blues, Paramount, 12262 .... **75.00**
Snow, Hank; Hank Snow, RCA Victor, 3026 .... **30.00**
Old Doc Brown, RCA Victor,1156 .... **20.00**
Solataires, The; Lonely, Old Town, 1008 .... **50.00**
Sons of the Pioneers; How Great Thou Art, RCA Victor, 1431 . **15.00**
Spand, Charlie; Hard Times Blues, Paramount, 13112 .... **100.00**
She's Got Good Stuff, Paramount, 13005 .... **100.00**
Thirsty Woman Blues, Paramount, 13047 .... **100.00**
Spaniels; Baby It's You, Vee Jay, 101 .... **150.00**
Goodnite Sweetheart, Goodnite, Vee Jay, 107 .... **50.00**
Spiders; I Didn't Want To Do It, Imperial, 9140 .... **60.00**
Squires; Sindy, Mambo, 105 .... **20.00**
State Street Ramblers; Careless Love, Champion, 16464 ...... **75.00**
Tiger Moon, Champion, 16147 .... **75.00**

Stidham, Arbee; Barbecue Lounge, Victor, 50-0037 .... **15.00**
Stokes, Frank; Frank Stokes' Dream, Victor, 23411 .... **100.00**
I'm Going Away Blues, Victor, 23341 .... **100.00**
Stoneman, Ernest V; John Hardy, Okeh, 7011 .... **30.00**
Silver Bells, Challenge, 153 .... **10.00**
The Fatal Wedding, Domino, 3984 .... **10.00**
When The Redeemed Are Gathered In, 52290 .... **20.00**
Swallows; Dearest, King, 4458 .... **150.00**
I Only Have Eyes For You, King 4533 .... **100.00**
Since You've Been Gone Away, King, 4466 .... **200.00**
Tampa Red; That's Her Own Business, Victor, 50-0041 .... **18.00**
Tampa Red The Guitar Wizard; Down In The Valley, 1254 ... **40.00**
The Duck Yas-Yas-Yas, 1277 .... **50.00**
Through Train Blues, Paramount, 12685 .... **50.00**
Tanner, Gid & His Georgia Boys; Bully of the Town No. 2, 15640 **20.00**
Devilish Mary, 15589 .... **20.00**
Four Cent Cotton, 15746 .... **40.00**
Miss McLeod's Reel, 15730 .... **40.00**
Taylor, Eva; Candy Lips, Okeh, 40715 .... **30.00**
I've Found a New Baby, Okeh, 8286 .... **35.00**
Teardrops; The Stars Are Out Tonight, Josie, 766 .... **40.00**
Terry, Sonny; And His Mouth Harp, Riverside, 12-644 ..... **30.00**
Sonny Terry, Everest, 206 .... **30.00**
Thomas, Henry; Run, Mollie, Run, Vocalion, 1141 .... **50.00**
Thomas, Hociel; Deep Water Blues, Okeh, 8297 .... **35.00**
Listen To Ma, Okeh, 8346 .... **35.00**
Tiny Parham & His Forty Five; Golden Lily, Victor, 23426 ... **80.00**
My Dreams, Victor, 23432 .... **80.00**
Tom, Georgia; Pig Meat Blues, Supertone, 9507 .... **50.00**
Rolin' Mill Stomp, Supertone, 9512 .... **50.00**
Six Shooter Blues, Gennett, 7130 .... **50.00**
Trammell, Bobby Lee; Arkansas Twist, Atlanta, 1503 ...... **40.00**
Traumbauer, Frankie; Baby, Won't You Please Come Home, 41286 **30.00**
Blue River, Okeh, 40879 .... **30.00**
Turner, Joe; Boss of the Blues, Atlantic, 1234 .... **30.00**
Joe Turner Sings Kansas City Jazz, 1243 .... **30.00**
Twilighters; Please Tell Me You're Mine, Marshall 702 ...... **120.00**
Valentines; Christmas Prayer, Rama, 186 .... **30.00**
Velvets, The; The Tried, Red Robin, 120 .... **35.00**
Venuti, Joe; Beale Street Blues, Vocalion, 15864 .... **30.00**
Farewell Blues, Vocalion, 15858 .... **30.00**
Vincent, Gene & The Blue Caps; Bluejean Bob, Capitol, 764 ... **75.00**
Walker, T-Bone; T-Bone Walker, Capitol, 370 .... **35.00**
Wallace, Sippie; Dead Drunk Blues, Okeh, 8499 .... **50.00**
Jack O'Diamonds Blues, Okeh, 8328 .... **50.00**
Waller, Thomas; I'm Crazy 'Bout My Baby, Columbia, 14593 ... **35.00**
Ward, Billy & His Dominoes; Federal 548 .... **80.00**
Washboard Sam; Ocean Blues, Bluebird, 5983 .... **18.00**
Want To Woogie Some More, Bluebird, 7440 .... **15.00**
Washington, Lizzie; Lord Have Mercy Blues, 92039 .... **50.00**
Mexico Blues, Black Patti, 8054 .... **60.00**
Waters, Ethel; Craving Blues, Paramount, 12312 .... **75.00**
Tell 'Em 'Bout Me, Paramount, 12189 .... **30.00**
Welling & McGhee; Almost Persuaded, Paramount, 3310 ..... **20.00**
Too Many Parties and Too Many Pals, 3157 .... **20.00**
Wheatstraw, Peetie; Can't See Blues, Vocalion, 1727 .... **30.00**
School Days, Vocalion, 1569 .... **30.00**
White, Georgia; Your Worries Ain't Like Mine No. 2, 7143 .... **10.00**
Whitman, Slim; Slim Whitman Sings & Yodels, Victor, 3217 ... **50.00**
Slim Whitman Favorites, Imperial, 9003 .... **20.00**
Whitter Old Jimmy Sutton, Gennett, 6436 .... **20.00**
Sally Goodin, Gennett, 6733 .... **30.00**
Snow Storm, Herwin, 75537 .... **25.00**
Wilkins, Robert; Get Away Blues, Brunswick, 7158 .... **100.00**

Police Sergeant Blues, Brunswick, 7168	**100.00**
Williams, Clarence; New Orleans Hop Scop Blues, 4975	**100.00**
Pane In The Glass, Paramount, 12870	**125.00**
Speakeasy, Paramount, 12884	**125.00**
Squeeze Me, Paramount, 12885	**125.00**
Williams, Fess & His Royal Flush; Wimmin Aah, 3259	**100.00**
Williams, Hank; Hank Williams as Luke The Drifter, MGM, 3267	**15.00**
Honky Tonkin, MGM, 242	**50.00**
Williamson, Sonny Boy; Frigidaire Blues, Bluebird, 7404	**20.00**
Good For Nothing Blues, Bluebird, 8237	**15.00**
Suzanna Blues, Bluebird, 7352	**20.00**
Wolverine Orchestra; Riverboard Shuffle, Gennett, 5454	**75.00**
Wrens; Betty Jean, Rama, 175	**75.00**
Yas Yas Girl, The; About My Time To Check, Vocalion, 04150	**12.00**
Love Shows Weakness, Vocalion, 04094	**12.00**
Young Creole Jass Band; Dearborn Street Blues, 12088	**80.00**

Red Wing

The Red Wing Stoneware Company, founded in 1878, took its name from its location in Red Wing, Minnesota. In the 1920s, the name was changed to the Red Wing Union Stoneware Company after a merger with several of the other local potteries. For the most part, they produced utilitarian wares such as flowerpots, crocks and jugs. In about 1930, their catalogues offered a line of art pottery vases in colored glazes, some of which featured handles modeled after swan's necks, snakes or female nudes. Other examples were quite simple, often with classic styling. After the addition of their dinnerware lines in the early '30s, 'Stoneware' was dropped from the name, and the company became known as Red Wing Potteries, Inc. They closed in 1967.

Blossom Time, bowl, 5½"	**2.50**
Bowl, 8½"	**6.00**
Cup & saucer	**6.00**
Plate, 6"	**3.00**
Plate, dinner	**6.50**
Platter, 13"	**8.00**
Bob White, bowl, salad, 12"	**50.00**
Bowl, soup	**10.00**
Bowl, vegetable	**22.50**
Bread tray, 23"	**50.00**
Casserole, covered, 2-qt	**25.00**
Cookie jar, w/lid	**40.00**
Cup & saucer	**6.50**
Gravy, covered	**24.00**
Hors d'oeuvres, bird figural in center	**60.00**

Pitcher, 11½"	**30.00**
Plate, 8"	**3.00**

Plate, 11"	**7.50**
Plate, dinner	**9.00**
Platter, 13"	**15.00**
Salt & pepper, tall, pair	**15.00**
Sauce dish	**8.00**
Server, 2-tier	**22.50**
Sugar, covered	**16.00**
Sugar & creamer, tall	**25.00**
Teapot, large	**55.00**
Tray, cocktail	**25.00**
Brittany, saucer	**1.00**
Teapot	**20.00**
Commercial art ware, ashtray, 1965 World Series, Minnesota Twins	**35.00**
Ashtray, maroon	**25.00**
Bowl, 75th Anniversary, 1953, maple leaf, gold label, 15"	**35.00**
Bowl, floral design, 2¼x15½", w/matching deer figural	**45.00**
Bowl, pink, Deco relief, tab handles, 8½x3¼"	**9.00**
Bowl, white, leaves, berries & bows in relief, 6¾x3"	**10.00**
Casserole, wht w/turquoise interior, oval, #1055	**8.50**
Celery, ducks in flight decor	**6.00**
Cornucopia, antique wht, 8½x8½"	**11.00**
Cornucopia, green w/yellow interior, leaf base, 5½x7½	**10.00**
Cornucopia, magenta high-gloss w/grey interior, leaf base	**10.00**
Dish, freeform, 1950s, grey w/pink interior, 13x10½"	**13.00**
Dish, ivory ped, green top, 2 cherubs, 7x9"	**29.00**
Dish, maroon w/grey interior, freeform, 13x10x2"	**13.00**
Figurine, cowgirl, 11"	**70.00**
Ginger jar, covered, cream w/blown-out flowers, 12"	**24.00**
Piano, yellow	**35.00**
Pitcher, swirl, dusty rose color, ice lip, 7"	**18.00**
Planter, green w/brown specks, deer, lady & harp, 5x7x14"	**16.00**
Planter, hi-gloss beige combed ridges, dk gr interior, 3x14x9"	**10.00**
Planter, hi-gloss speckled gold, vertical flute, 2¾x12x4¼"	**13.00**
Planter, ivory, 16", w/deer flower frog	**28.00**
Planter, semi-gloss grey w/pink interior, leaf decor, B1402	**5.00**
Rose jar, raised dragons, blk pottery cover & stand	**30.00**
Salt & pepper, wht, large	**20.00**
Teapot, chicken, yellow	**20.00**
Vase, blue w/deer in relief, 8"	**20.00**
Vase, blue w/pink interior, shaped like 2 leaves, 9"	**13.00**
Vase, bud, cat w/mouth open, #878, blue glaze, 5"	**20.00**
Vase, bulbous, Amphora, elephant handles, tan, gr & blue, 8x9"	**150.00**
Vase, bulbous, green gloss, brown, #182, 7"	**18.00**
Vase, bulbous w/long narrow neck, green crackle glaze, mkd	**35.00**
Vase, cream w/lt green interior, 5-finger fan, 12"	**30.00**
Vase, cream w/pink interior, handled, curved relief, 7½x6½x5"	**13.00**
Vase, dark green w/yellow interior, 2-pt freeform, 8"	**13.00**
Vase, fan, blue w/pink interior, ftd, scrolled, 7½"	**13.00**
Vase, fan, cream w/green interior, shape of 2 leaves, 7½"	**23.00**
Vase, fan, green semi-matt w/cream interior, acanthus in relief, 9"	**30.00**
Vase, green w/wht interior, leaf decor, handled, #1115, 7"	**7.00**
Vase, Roman motif, #159, 15"	**125.00**
Cookie jar, French Chef Pierre, beige	**30.00**
Blue Monk	**30.00**
Hen on Nest	**24.00**
Mexican Dancers	**17.00**
Pig, in cookie jar	**30.00**
Rooster	**24.00**
Crazy Rhythm, bowl, 6"	**4.00**
Bowl, vegetable, divided	**9.00**
Relish, divided, 13"	**8.00**
Salt & pepper, small	**5.00**
Saucer	**1.50**
Lotus, bowl, fruit	**3.00**

Bowl, vegetable, 8½" **7.00**
Cup & saucer **6.00**
Gravy w/attached tray **6.00**
Plate, 10½" **5.00**
Platter, 11x13" **5.00**
Saucer **2.00**
Magnolia, bowl, fruit **4.00**
Bowl, sauce, 5" **4.00**
Coffee pot **14.00**
Creamer **6.00**
Cup **4.00**
Cup & saucer **7.00**
Plate, bread & butter, 6" **3.00**
Plate, dinner, 10½" **4.50**
Plate, salad, 7¼" **3.50**
Platter, oval, 11x13" **8.00**
Salt & pepper **7.00**
Normandie, bowl, fruit **6.00**
Bowl, vegetable, large round **12.50**
Casserole, covered **30.00**
Cup & saucer **8.00**
Flat soup **9.40**
Plate, 7" **4.50**
Plate, dinner **6.75**
Platter, round, 12" **10.00**
Saucer **3.50**
Stoneware, spongeware, bowl, 6" **65.00**
Spongeware, bowl, 9" **80.00**
Spongeware, bowl, mixing, blue & orange, 11" **75.00**
Spongeware, bowl, rust & blue on tan, mkd, 4¼x7" dia **70.00**
Bean jar, w/advertising **46.00**
Bean jar, w/bail & cover, brown top, 4½" **30.00**
Birdhouse, hanging, Brushware **95.00**
Bowl, beater; You Beat Eggs, We Beat Prices **55.00**
Bowl, Greek Key, 7" **70.00**
Bowl, Greek Key, 8" **75.00**
Bowl, Greek Key, 9" **80.00**
Butter crock, deep blue, 1-lb **20.00**
Canning jar, ½-gal. **110.00**
Canning jar, 1-gal, Union Stoneware **225.00**
Cherry Band, pitcher, large **120.00**
Pitcher, small **110.00**
Pitcher w/advertising, 2-qt **140.00**
Chick feeder, Ko-Rec, complete **50.00**
Cookie jar, barrel, Saffron **25.00**
Crock, 40-gal **175.00**
Crock, fish lure decor, 3-gal **150.00**
Fruit jar, Mason, Union Stoneware, pat Jan 24, 1899, 6½" . **135.00**
Fruit jar, Mason, blue letters, 1-gal **320.00**
Gray Line, butter jar, 3-lb **195.00**
Canning jar, dome top shield **650.00**
Casserole, w/blue advertising, 7" dia. **95.00**
Cookie jar **350.00**
Custard **90.00**
Pitcher, small size **145.00**
Salt, hanging **750.00**
Salt & pepper **450.00**
Sugar & creamer **125.00**
Jar, Bowey's Hot Chocolate, tan cattail design **125.00**
Jar, pantry, small **265.00**
Pencil holder, sewer pipe, brown glaze **20.00**
Pitcher, grape w/ric-rac, blue & wht, 9x6" **125.00**
Pitcher, saffron, w/advertising, 8" **75.00**
Vase, brown w/cattails, 7" **40.00**

Vase, Brushware w/stork **32.00**
Vase, green & wht w/incised warriors at top, 12" **45.00**
Water cooler, 3-gal, Red Wing Union Stoneware **210.00**
4-gal, blue/grey, Red Wing Stoneware **280.00**
5-gal **125.00**
Tampico, plate, 6½" **3.00**
Plate, 8½" **4.00**
Plate, 10" **5.00**
Saucer **2.00**
Town & Country, sugar, covered, sand **7.50**

Redware

The term redware refers to a type of simple earthenware produced by the Colonists as early as the 1600s. The red clay used in its production was abundant throughout the country, and during the 18th and 19th centuries redware was made in great quantities. Intended for utilitarian purposes such as every-day tableware, or use in the dairy, redware was simple in design and decoration. Glazes of various colors were used, and a liquid clay referred to as 'slip' was sometimes applied in patterns such as zigzag lines, daisies or stars. With such decorations it is referred to as 'slip ware'.

Bank, salmon-yellow glaze w/daisies, bulb shape, mushroom finial **65.00**
Bed pan, maganese splotching **75.00**
Bowl, 4 line yellow slip, coggled edge, 13½" **350.00**
Coggled edge, 3 line yellow slip, 13½" **185.00**
Light green exterior, interior same w/brown flecks, 3½x7¾" **125.00**
Mottled green & amber, br flecks, attributed to Gonic, 6¾" **75.00**
Ovoid, applied handles, tooling, green-clear w/brown, 3" . **160.00**
Rectangular, coggled edge, yellow slip decor, w/damage, 13x18" **150.00**
White inside, brown glaze outside, 5x3½" **20.00**
Candlestick, clear glaze w/brown splotches, sgnd, 1976, 4¾" **20.00**
Charger, coggled edge, 3 line yellow slip decor, 12" dia . **240.00**
Yellow slip decor, coggled edge **300.00**
Churn, allover cream slip w/green spotting, 17" **45.00**
Cradle, clear w/incised 'Baby', June 4, 4½" **215.00**
Crock, black glaze, 7" **35.00**
Cobalt bands, & '2', 17" **35.00**
Impressed DM Baker, Pa. **55.00**
Cuspidor, 1800s **17.50**
Dish, 3 triple zigzag bands, rectangle w/crimped edge, deep, 15½" **400.00**
7" **22.50**
Cobbled edge, crossing wavy lines & dots in yellow slip, 12" **300.00**
Coggled edge, yellow slip decor, 10x16" **575.00**
Finger crimping, amber & tan mottled, 3½" **30.00**
Green-amber mottled, 3½" **45.00**
Yellow slip daisy in center, rim band, 11½" **175.00**
Flower pot, saucer, finger crimped rims, tooled, brown sponge, 2" **250.00**
Jar, green & amber mottled w/running brown splotches, Gonic, 4" **90.00**
Green-brown mottled, 2" **210.00**
Impressed Necco Boston Baked Beans, 1½" **30.00**
Mustard w/brown spots & splotches, 8" **260.00**
Ovoid, greenish w/brown splotches, 9" **50.00**
Ovoid, impressed John Bell, Pa., brown specks, 5½" **65.00**
Ovoid w/cover, red-orange, black specks, 5½" **165.00**
With handle, imp Eberly, cream inside, brown pebbled outside, 9" **75.00**
Wax sealer, 7½x5" **35.00**
Jug, dk gr w/orange spots, some damage, 7½" **135.00**
Green-amber w/tan hi-lite & brown flecks, hairline, 5" ... **85.00**
Light green w/flecks of rust, minor damage, 6½" **185.00**
Strap handle, gr glaze w/orange spots, Gonic, N.H., 11" . **775.00**
Unglazed, 2½" **15.00**
Lighting stand, incised straight & wavy line, gr w/drips, 4" **340.00**
Loaf dish, 3 bands of wavy lines, lg **1,050.00**

Milk pan, brown-green glaze, 8x18½" **60.00**
Milk pan, yellow slip decor, 3x11½" **185.00**
Milk pitcher, sky blue glaze, 7x5½" **45.00**
Mold, depicts flight into Egypt, 5" dia **65.00**
  Swirl design w/center post, 11" **85.00**
  Turk's head, mottled green & amber w/brown, 3x7" **85.00**
Mug, strap handle, clear glaze, dk brown & blk runs, 5½" ... **165.00**
  Swirl & daisy decor, 4" **400.00**
Paperweight, book figural, marbelized yellow-tan, 3½" **110.00**
Pie plate, central 8 pointed star, 8½" **1,700.00**
  Coggled edge, 4 line yellow slip decor, 9¾" **295.00**
  Zigzag decor, 8" **110.00**
Pitcher, green-amber w/brown splotches, 3" **315.00**
  Green-amber, running brown flecks, 4" **155.00**
  Light green over all but ft, 5" **165.00**
  Light green w/amber spots, 5½" **135.00**
  Orange glaze w/brown spots, 2½" **275.00**
Plate, 2 color tulip, yellow, green, brown, 8" **850.00**
  Coggle edge, 2 line yellow slip crowsfoot, 8" **175.00**
  Coggled edge, 2 line yellow slip crowsfoot, 10" **215.00**
  Coggled edge, 3 line yellow slip decor, 9" **200.00**
  Coggled edge, 3 line yellow slip decor, 9¾" **300.00**
  Coggle edge, clear glaze w/brown flecks, 10½" **35.00**
  Coggle edge & crowsfoot, yellow slip, 8½" **145.00**
  Crows foot center, spatter edges, 10" **600.00**
  Double zigzag decor in yellow slip, coggled edge, 3½" **320.00**
  Marbleized pattern **250.00**

Parallel zigzag lines, slip decor, 9½" **100.00**
Porringer, green w/brown sponge, 3¾x4x5" **115.00**
Preserving jar, green w/orange spots, w/lid, 8" **100.00**
Spice jar, 1850s **25.00**
Sugar bowl, no handle, gr & amber w/brown runs, Gonic, 5¾" . **85.00**
  With lid, border decor **135.00**
Urn, double handle, small **45.00**
Vase, coggle wheel edge, 2 handles, green w/brown runs, 10½" **85.00**

Religious Items

Book, The Book of Common Prayer **75.00**
  Celluloid, full color cover, Jewish, 1926, 3½x2½" **8.00**

Figure, marble, carved, St Mary **130.00**
Mold, cast iron, fish form, 1840, 5½x3x21" long **65.00**
Rosary box, tortoise pique, sterling inlay, 3x1½" **135.00**
Triptych, hinged doors, guesso facings, hp figures, Russian, 30" **375.00**

Reverse Painting on Glass

   Verre eglomise is the technique of painting on the underside of glass. Dating back to the early 1700s, this art became popular in the 19th century when German immigrants chose historical figures and beautiful women as subjects for their reverse glass paintings. Advertising mirrors of this type came into vogue at the turn of the century.

Blarney Castle, extra fancy gold frame, Ireland **30.00**
Boxer, bare knuckle, fighting pose, orig frame, 1860, 20¼x14¼" **295.00**
Castle, in Belgium, fancy gold frame **65.00**
Game table, ornate w/door; 2 women, Chinese, 1800s, 14x13½" **165.00**
Lamp, house & snow scene **410.00**
Statute of Liberty, oval, plain frame, 25" **48.00**
Tinsel, multi floral on blk, framed, 13x18" **45.00**
US Capitol, oval, framed **65.00**
Varied Arts Building, orig frame, St Louis, 1904 .... **85.00**

Rhead

   Associated with many companies during his career---Weller, Vance Avon, Arequipa, A.E. Tile and finally Homer Laughlin China---Frederick Hurten Rhead organized his own pottery in Santa Barbara, Ca., in about 1913. Admittedly more of a designer than a potter, Rhead hired help to turn the pieces on the wheel, but did most of the decorating himself. The process he favored most involved sgraffito designs inlaid with enameling; Egyptian and Art Nouveau influences were evidenced in much of his work. The ware he produced there was often marked with a logo incorporating the potter at the wheel and 'Santa Barbara'.

Bowl, heavy green drip glaze, 7" dia **375.00**
  Sea green to rust, crazed, Oriental look, 2x6" **325.00**
Desk tray, advertising, green matt, sgnd, Rhead, 6" **350.00**
Vase, 3 handled, blue flambe hi glaze, 4½" **325.00**
  Gray matt w/incised geometrics, 8" **950.00**

Ovoid, green blistered glaze, 4½" **500.00**

Richard

   Richard, who at one time worked for Galle, made cameo art glass in France during the 1902s. His work was often multi-layered and acid cut with florals and scenics in lovely colors. The ware was marked with his name in relief.

Bowl, village scenic w/trees & mountains, brown & lime, 4½x7" **775.00**

Lamp, scenic, black & mauve, signed, 30″ **2,000.00**
Vase, Alpine village scene, 2 cuttings, rose to pink, 15″ **1,450.00**
   Chateau w/trees, 2 cuttings, orange, brown, 10½″ **900.00**
   Lake scene w/sail boats, maroon to pink frosted, 4″ **475.00**
   Scene w/florals, ped base, ovoid, flare rim, 2 cuts, 8x4″ **485.00**
   Scenic, 2 cuttings, orange satin w/brown, 10½″ **1,000.00**

Ridgway

   As early as 1792 Ridgway brothers, Job and George, produced fine quality earthenwares in Shelton, Staffordshire, marking their product Ridgway,
Smith & Ridgway, and later, Job & George Ridgway. About 1800, the brothers
split and each had his own firm, both in Shelton. They were joined in the
business by various members of the Ridgway family, and in fact their
descendents still operate there today.

   The two firms created by the split were the Bell Works and the Cauldon
Pottery. Bell produced stone china and earthenware decorated with blue
transfer printing. Their mark was J. & W. Ridgway or J. & W.R., until 1848
when William Ridgway was used.

   The Cauldon Pottery made earthenware, stone china and high quality
porcelains fine enough to win them the distinction of being appointed potters to the Queen. From 1830, their wares attest to this fact, bearing the
Royal Arms mark with J.R. within the crest. In 1840, '& Co.' was added.

   Most examples of their wares found today are transfer printed historical
scenes. See also Flow Blue and Staffordshire, Historical.

Bowl, Dickens, Very Good Girl, 9″ **35.00**
   Oblong, Coaching Days, Down the Hill on a Frosty Morn, 5x15″ **145.00**
Child's tea set, Maiden Hair Fern, 15 pcs, octagonal, 1888 . . . **195.00**
Cup & saucer, Coaching Days, 1850 . . . . **60.00**
   Dragons, oriental birds, soft paste, 1800s **75.00**
   Forget-me-not, 1830s **75.00**
Jug, Coaching Days, caramel w/black scenes, silver trim, 5″ **65.00**
Mug, 2 handles, Coaching Days, Walking up the Hill, 4½″ **95.00**
   Coaching Days, straight sides, blk on caramel, 4¾″ **40.00**
   Coaching Days, Breakdown on the Mails, 5″ **50.00**
Pitcher, Coaching Days, 5½x5″ **65.00**
   Coaching Days, 7″ **75.00**
   Coaching Days, Taking up the Mail, 9½″ **120.00**
   Coaching Days, caramel w/blk scenes, 3¼″ **35.00**
   Figural Dionysus handle, allover relief, 9″ **75.00**
   Gray w/gold rope bands top & lower part, twist handle, 12″ . . **90.00**
   Tournament theme, 1810 . . . . **195.00**
   Coaching Days, 7″ **30.00**
   Dickens, green scene on cream, hp edges **35.00**
   Marmora, blue decor, 1830s, 10½″ **40.00**
   Oriental, blue decor w/gold trim, 7″ **15.00**
   View from Ruggles House, black transfer . . . . **50..00**
Platter, Palestine, octagonal, 13x10½″ **45.00**
   Willow, red w/multi color, bowl & quiver mk, 2x9½″ **65.00**
Saucer, Oriental, blue decor w/gold trim, 1890s, 6″ **6.50**
Sugar w/lid, Oriental, blue decor w/gold trim **50.00**
Tankard, Coaching Days, 5″ **45.00**
   Taking Up the Mail, 9½″ **110.00**
Tankard pitcher & 6 ½ pt mugs, Coaching Days **265.00**
Teapot, Coaching Days, Racing the Mail, 5″ **95.00**
Tumbler, Coaching Days, black on caramel, 4″ **30.00**
Tureen w/lid, Oriental, blue decor w/gold trim, 8½x11″ **130.00**

Riviera

   Riviera was a line of dinnerware introduced by the Homer Laughlin
China Co. in 1938. It was sold exclusively by the Murphy Co. It was unmarked, light weight, and inexpensive. It was discontinued sometime prior

to 1950. Colors are mauve blue, red, yellow, light green and ivory. On rare
occasions dark blue pieces are found, but this was not a standard color.

Baker, oval, 9″ **5.00**
Batter set, complete **70.00**
Butter, covered, ½ pound **30.00**
Casserole, w/lid **23.00**

Creamer, regular **4.00**
Cup & saucer, demitasse **16.00**
Fruit, 5½″ **3.00**
Jug, covered **35.00**
   Juice, yellow **35.00**
Nappy, 8¼″ **5.50**
Plate, 6″ **1.50**
   7″ **2.50**
   9″ **4.00**
   10″ **6.50**
   Deep **5.00**
Platter, w/handles, 11¼″ **6.50**
   With handles, 12″ **9.00**
Salt & pepper, pr **5.00**
Sauceboat **6.00**
Saucer **2.00**
Sugar, covered, illus **5.00**
Syrup, covered **30.00**
Tea cup **5.00**
Teapot **22.00**
Tumbler, juice **20.00**
   With handles **20.00**

Robertson

   Fred H. Robertson, clay expert for the Los Angeles Brick Co. & son
of Alexander Robertson of the Roblin Pottery, experimented with crystalline
glazes as early as 1906. In 1934, Fred and his son George established their
own works in Los Angeles, but by 1943 they had moved operations to
Hollywood. Though most of their early wares were turned by hand, some
were also molded in low relief. Fine crackle glazes and crystallines were
developed. The ware was marked with Robertson, F.H.R. or R., with the
particular location of its manufacture noted. The small pottery closed in 1952.

Bowl, low, oblong, turquoise crackle, 6″ **55.00**
Vase, persian blue, cabinet size **40.00**
   Pink-beige crackle, mkd, 5½″ **65.00**
   Turquoise crackle, mkd, 3″ **55.00**

Robinson Clay Products

   In the early 1900s, Whitemore, Robinson & Company merged with the
E.H. Merrill Company to form Robinson Clay Products of Akron, Ohio. They
produced stoneware, fine glazed Rockingham and yellowware until 1915,
when the emphasis was shifted to bricks, tile, etc. In 1920, the company
merged with the Ransbottom Brothers Pottery Company of Roseville, and
was there after known as the Robinson-Ransbottom Company.

Mug, 4 golfers, blue/grey stoneware, 1890s, 5¾"........... **175.00**
Water cooler, wishing well, blue/wht **450.00**

Robinson Ransbottom

In 1900 the four Ransbottom brothers founded the Ransbottom Bros. Pottery Co. in Ironspot, Ohio, very close to Roseville. They produced utilitarian stoneware products until 1920, when they merged with the Robinson Clay Products Company of Akron. Production was broadened to include kitchen wares, and 'Early American' accessories. Cookie jars were an important line from the 1930s until recent times. The company is still in operation in Roseville, Ohio. Items made after the merger were marked 'RRPCO', (for Robinson-Ransbottom Pottery Co.), 'Roseville'. The green and brown streaky glazed flower pots, jardinieres and pedestals which they produce today are often mistaken for older products of the Roseville Pottery Company, which operated there until the 1950s.

Bowl, fishscale design, turquoise, 8½"..................... **9.00**
Cookie jar, Cookie Stories **35.00**
    Cow Jumped over the Moon **20.00**
    Hey Diddle Diddle **35.00**
    Hootie Owl........................ **18.00**
    Yellow w/3 color stripes, 2 tigers on lid........... **20.00**
Jardiniere, brown & green majolica, spike & disc, 7x8"....... **15.00**
Pitcher, cherry decal, old, 9½"..................... **35.00**
Planter, bug figural, yellow, #420........................ **8.00**

Roblin

In the late 1800s, Alexander W. Robertson and Linna Irelan established a pottery in San Francisco, combining parts of their respective names to coin the name Roblin. Robertson was responsible for potting and firing the ware, which often reflected his taste for classic styling. Mrs. Irelan did much of the decorating, utilizing almost every method, but favoring relief modeling. Mushrooms and lizards were her favorite subjects. Vases were a large part of their production, all of which was made from native California red, buff and white clays. The ware was well marked with the firm name or the outline of a bear. Roblin Pottery was destroyed in the earthquake of 1906.

Creamer, wht bisque, 2" **250.00**
Tile, floral, matt glaze, 6x6" **700.00**
Vase, 3½"................................. **300.00**

Rockingham

In the early part of the 19th century, American potters began to favor brown and buff burring clays over red because of their durabilty. The glaze favored by many was Rockingham, which varied from a dark brown mottling to a sponged-effect sometimes called tortoise shell. It consisted in part of manganese and various metallic salts, and was used by many potters until well after the 20th century.

Bank, book figural, 1840 .... **60.00**
Bed pan, bird figural **125.00**

Bottle, boot, early 1800s **120.00**
    Boot, imp Victoria, 6½x7" **60.00**
    Fish shape **300.00**
    Mermaid figural **125.00**
    Shoe w/slide laces, Victoria, 6½"......................... **30.00**
Bowl, 2x9" **25.00**
    4½x10" **50.00**
    9" **50.00**
    Covered, fluted, 4x6" **65.00**
Butter dish w/lid, Peacock, Brush Pottery **110.00**
Cake mold, 9½" **65.00**
    Fluted **75.00**
Coal skuttle **350.00**
Creamer, bulbous w/flared lip, floral spray at top, 5"....... **35.00**
    Bulbous w/flared lip, leaves in relief, 5" **40.00**
Cuspidor, mk Pruden 9" **95.00**
Decanter, fox handle, hunt scene in relief, Crown Devon **50.00**
Dish, oval, 5½x8"......................... **35.00**
Flask, embossed leaves & man smoking, woman, 7½" **145.00**
Milk pan, 2½x9"......................... **85.00**
    13½" **125.00**
Mold, turk's head, 9½" **75.00**
Mug, 2 handles, frogs inside, man smoking & woman, 6½"... **225.00**
    2 hound handles, hunters **60.00**
    6" **30.00**
    Frog inside, people, grapes & leaves in relief, 4" **95.00**
    Leaves in relief, 5" **40.00**
    Strap handle **62.00**
Pie plate, 8½" **85.00**
    9¾" **75.00**
    10" **85.00**
Pitcher, 7" **75.00**

    Arched panels, floral decor, 10" **500.00**
    Band w/scrolls, yellow streaks, 7" **85.00**
    Covered, hound handle w/embossed dog & deer, 9" **245.00**
    Embossed children & goat, 7½" **95.00**
    Embossed dancers, 6"......................... **60.00**
    Embossed tulips, 5½" **50.00**
    Embossed tulips, 9¾" **50.00**
    Hound handle, deer, rabbit, bird, 10"......................... **175.00**
    Hound handle, emb hunt scene, vintage rim, 11" **260.00**
    Hound handle, hunting scene, presentation piece.......... **175.00**
    Hunting scene 7" **95.00**
    Hunting scene, 10" **325.00**
    No decor, 5" **75.00**
    Tulip pattern, 5½" **50.00**
Platter, brown bear paw glaze, 14" **200.00**

Octagonal, 15" long **225.00**
Oval, 13" **65.00**
Preserving jar, 8½" **65.00**
Soap dish, 2¼x4½" **35.00**
Wreath edge, drain holes, 2½x7x5" **45.00**
Spittoon **35.00**
Panelled ferns & beaded bottom **60.00**
Syrup, w/hinged pewter lid **40.00**
Teapot, Rebecca at the Well, 6½" **75.00**
Rebecca at the Well, 10" **95.00**

Rookwood

The Rookwood Pottery Co. was established in 1879, in Cincinnati, Ohio. It's founder was Maria Longworth Nichols Storer, daughter of a wealthy family who provided the backing necessary to make such an enterprise possible. Mrs. Storer hired competent ceramic workers and through constant experimentation they developed many lines of superior art pottery. While in her employ, Laura Fry invented the air brush blending process for which she was issued a patent in 1884. From this, several lines were designed that utilized blended backgrounds.

One of their earlier lines, standard, was a brown ware decorated with underglaze slip painted nature studies, animals, portraits, etc. Iris and Sea Green were introduced in 1894, and Vellum, a transparent matt glaze line, in 1904. Other lines followed: Ombroso in 1910, and Soft Porcelain in 1915. Many of the early art ware lines were signed by the artist.

Soon after the turn of the 20th century, Rookwood manufactured 'production' pieces that relied mainly on molded designs and forms, rather than freehand decoration, for their esthetic appeal.

Only rarely will you find an unmarked piece. Though many marks were used, the most familiar is the reverse RP monogram. First used in 1886, a flame point was added above it for each suceeding year until 1900. After that, a Roman numeral added below indicated the year of manufacture. Impressed letters that related to the type of clay used for the body were also used---G for ginger, O for olive, R for red, S for sage green, W for white and Y for yellow.

Art ware must be judged on an individual basis. Quality of the artwork is the prime factor to consider. Portraits, animals and birds are worth more than florals; and pieces signed by a particularly reknowned artist are highly prized.

The Depression brought on financial difficulties from which the pottery never recovered. Though it continued to operate, the quality of the ware deteriorated, and the pottery was forced to close in 1967.

Ashtray: 1922, Viking ship, matt blue, fraternal, 5½" **50.00**
1940, nude, ivory matt, 4½" **75.00**
1949, advertising baseball equipment, Siegle **45.00**
With figural owl, 4" **90.00**
Beer stein, advertising, G Weiderman Brewing Co **175.00**
Bookends: birds, pink matt, pr **110.00**
Eagles, dark green, pr **175.00**
Elephant figural, 1944, pr **100.00**
Floral basket, 1927, 5 colors, pr **225.00**
Horseheads, white, McD, 1936, 6x5½" pr **275.00**
Lady reading book, #6037, pr **200.00**
Rooks, 1921, brown & buff speckled, large size, pr **225.00**
Rooks, 1946, matt blue, McD, 5½", pr **150.00**
Rooks, 1950, hi glaze, McD, pr **135.00**
Trees, 1930, rust, red-brown, MCD, 4", pr **110.00**
Water lilies, 1919, #2863, pr **125.00**
Bowl: 1884, floral & butterfly, clear glaze, Mary Taylor, #87, 6" **300.00**
1924, mirror black, #9578 .... **30.00**
1926, squeeze bag abstract, Hentschel, #2254E, 4¼" **300.00**
Mirror black, green speckled interior, #2875, 11" **95.00**

With cover, 1920, ram handles, tan w/turquoise inside, 5" ... **75.00**
With figural frog, girl w/basket, 1915 .... **155.00**
Bowl vase, 1919, Egyptian figurals, Arthur Comant, #2358.... **125.00**
Bowl & frog, 1921, matt yellow, #2529, 2¾x12" **85.00**
Cameo: bowl, dogwood, wht on peach/pink, Valentien, 1889, 11" **465.00**
Chocolate pot, pk floral on pink/peach, Valentien, 8" **410.00**
Demitasse cup & saucer, apple blossoms, Toohey, 1887 .... **150.00**
Candleholders, blossom design, yellow, 4x4", pr **65.00**
Candlesticks, 1921, modeled cherubs, McDonald, 24" **1,100.00**
Centerpiece, 1927, Art Nouveau female forms handles **500.00**
Console bowl, 1921, molded pattern, rose matt w/green, 12" ... **60.00**
Cream & sugar, 1940, blue matt, #547 .... **45.00**
With lid, 1919, green gloss w/blk bands, #2496 .... **140.00**
Creamer, 1885, sgraffito clovers, blue on red clay, AMB, #43 . **350.00**
Dish, covered, red glaze, 6½" **95.00**
Faience: plaque, Christ Child in swaddling clothes, 14x19" ... **785.00**
Tile, grapes & leaves in relief, 8x8" **240.00**
Tile, stylized flower, #3278, 3" **50.00**
Figurine, 1928, sitting nude, Abel, green hi-glaze, 4" **110.00**
Cocker Spaniel, tan glaze **85.00**
Flower frog, 1917, floral **18.00**
1919, water lily **22.00**
Incised Matt: jug, swirl decor, REM, 1901, #273CZ, 6¼" **175.00**
Jug, tan, Menzel, 1901, #273CZ, 7" **150.00**
Shades of blue, Rose Fecheimer, 1904, 3x6" **140.00**
Vase, abstract, green, 1904, #935E, 6" **90.00**
Vase, flowers, Todd, 1919, #271C, 9" **220.00**
Vase, matt green, artist sgnd, 1901, 6" **235.00**
Iris: mug, silver overlay handle, 1905, commemorative by Sax **1,800.00**
Vase, berries, Van Horne, 1908, #905E, 5½" **350.00**
Vase, bleeding hearts, green, Diers, 1903, 11" **945.00**
Vase, blue bells, Shirayamadani, 6½" **775.00**
Vase, dandelions, pedestal, shaded blue, DVH, 1907, 9" **765.00**
Vase, dogwood, gray & black, GVD, 1902, #926D, 7" **800.00**
Vase, floral, ACR, 4" **425.00**
Vase, floral, CA Baker, 1898, 10" **800.00**
Vase, floral, Steinle, 1906, #901D, 7" **575.00**
Vase, floral, yellow & green, Zettell, 1901, 6" **545.00**
Vase, florals, at base, Steinle, 1911, #1358E, #1358E, 7x4". **490.00**
Vase, florals, pink, CA Baker, 1901, 6" **545.00**
Vase, florals, yellow on tan to green, Zettel, 1904, 7½" **550.00**
Vase, iris, blue on lavener, F Rothenbusch, 1905, 8½" **675.00**
Vase, magnolia blossoms, artist sgnd, 1904, 8½x4" **575.00**

Vase, milkweed,1902, E.D., #905D, 8" **1,400.00**
Vase, palm fronds, cream, Ed Diers, 1907, bulbous, 9½" ... **750.00**

Vase, stylized peacock feather, MAD, 1900, #S1674 .... **400.00**
Vase, sweet peas, Irene Bishop, 1906, #935E, 6″ **450.00**
Vase, Venetian canal scene, Carl Schmidt, 1923, 7¼″ **4,000.00**
Jar, 1919, wht band w/flowering branch on blue body, LE, 3½x3″ **75.00**
Jug, 1882, incised clover, gray matt, sgnd S, 5″ **200.00**
   1882, incised, brown, HW, #61, 4½″ **400.00**
   1882, tri-color brushed decor, kiln mk, #61, 4½″ **650.00**
   1883, bird, black on brown w/gilt, sgnd R, 5″ **250.00**
   1883, florals, wht on tan, 4½x3″ **185.00**
   1883, unglazed red clay w/carved irises #101 .... **220.00**
   1886, birds in flight, bisque, MAD, #101A, 11″ **950.00**
Mug, 1894, mountaineer portrait, B Horsfall, 5″ **1,400.00**
Paperweight: Basset Hound **70.00**
   Cocker Spaniel........................ **80.00**
   Deco girl, 1931, Abel, #28668, 4″ **125.00**
   Duck figural, 1941, #6064, green gloss **60.00**
   Elephant, 1926, blue, McDonald, 3x4″ **95.00**
   Girl, 1929, ivory, L Abel, 4x4″ **125.00**
   Girl, 1943, turquoise gloss, Abel, 4x4″ **85.00**
   Rabbit, 1946, ivory, 3x3″ **65.00**
   Rook, lt brown, 1925, #1623, 3″ **125.00**
   Rook, navy, 1915, 3x4½″ **125.00**
   Rooster figural, 1946, multi colored gloss **135.00**
   Rooster, 1928, #6038 .... **100.00**
   Seated nude, 1932, white, Louis Abel, #2868 .... **125.00**
   Squid, sgnd P, #1053, 6″ **45.00**
   Squirrel, 1933, ivory, Sallie Toohey, 4x4″ **85.00**
Pitcher, 1882, bushes, birds, Wm McDonald, gold hi-lights, 5″ **850.00**
   1883, dragonflies, clear glaze, ARV, #116, 6½″ **1,250.00**
   1884, incised wisteria, clear green hi-glaze, 1884, 11″ **460.00**
Plaque, Christ Child, 21″ oval **480.00**
Plate, 1964, Valparaiso Univ, #7218, 7¾″ **35.00**
Sea Green, vase, floral, Sally Toohey, 1899, 8½″ **1,650.00**
Standard: bowl, foliage & butterfly, M Raylor, #87, 6½″ **250.00**
   Box w/cover, holly decor, 1893 .... **400.00**
   Bud vase, berries, Van Briggle, 1902, #780, 8½″ **850.00**
   Chocolate pot, clover & bees, Carl Schmidt, 1900, 8½″ .. **1,150.00**
   Coffee pot, bird on branch, M Nourse, 1894, 9″ **2,000.00**
   Creamer, butterflies, M Nourse, 1891, 2¾″ **310.00**
   Dish, daisies, Sprague, 1889, #521C, 7″ **195.00**
   Ewer, floral, #469C **465.00**
   Ewer, floral, Bookprinter/Valentien, #304, 9″ **425.00**

Ewer, floral, DD, 1897, #715, 6″ **425.00**
Ewer, holly berries, Steinle, 1899, #40, 6″ **320.00**
Ewer, oak leaves & acorn JG, 10½″ **485.00**
Ewer, wild roses, AMY, 1896, 10″........................ **500.00**

Humidor, pipes, cigars, Zettel, 1990, #3812, 6″ **400.00**
Jardiniere, floral, CFB, 3″ **325.00**
Jardiniere, silver overlay, BA, 1907 .... **1,500.00**
Jug, cherries, Hurley, 1903, 6″ **220.00**
Jug, wheat by O Geneva Reed, 1893, 6½″ **475.00**
Loving cup, 3 handles, Indian, Lenore Asbury, 1897, 7½″ **6,000.00**
Match holder, floral w/matches, Swing, #355, 2x3½″ **260.00**
Mug, corn, Ashbury, 1902 .... **215.00**
Mug, corn, Rothenbush, 1899 .... **475.00**
Pitcher, clover, butterfly handle, MR, 4″................. **300.00**
Pitcher, clover, flower form handle, MR, 4″ **245.00**
Pitcher, floral by Sadie Markland, 1893, 4″ **345.00**
Pitcher, grapes, A Van Briggle, 1889, #367, 8″ **935.00**
Sugar w/cover, holly **475.00**
Tankard, Harriet E Wilcox, 1891, 9½″.................. **1,000.00**
Tankard, pine cone, OG Reed, 1893, 9½″ **600.00**
Teapot, roses, cube knob, sgnd CS, 1908, #770 .... **400.00**
Urn, poppies, 3 handles, Sprague, #S1454, 1899, 10″...... **850.00**
Vase, Ed Diers, 1897, 4″ **295.00**
Vase, autumn leaves, Altman, 1904, 8″................. **565.00**
Vase, autumn leaves, Steinle, 1903, #913D, 7″ **330.00**
Vase, blackberries, Swing, 1904 #935E, 6″................. **385.00**
Vase, blueberry clusters & leaves, Anna Valentien, 1899, 11″ **595.00**
Vase, clover, artist sgnd, 1899, 4″ **500.00**
Vase, floral, handles, Coyne, 1896, 6″ **485.00**
Vase, floral, ruffled rim, 1886, #272C, 5½″ **425.00**
Vase, florals, 1886, imp, #272C, 5½″ **375.00**
Vase, florals, C Steinle, 1907, 6½″ **465.00**
Vase, holly, Toohey, 1898, 11″ **445.00**
Vase, lion portrait, Hurley, 1902 .... **4,100.00**
Vase, maple leaves, Carrie Steinle, 1904 .... **250.00**
Vase, pansies & poppies, ball shape w/3 ball ft, 1886 ...... **275.00**
Vase, poppies, Tom Lunt, 1896, 6″.................... **465.00**
Roses, Toohey, 1895, 8½″ **250.00**
Vase, silver overlay, pods & leaves, Swing, 1903, 5½″.... **1,500.00**
Vase, stylized poppies, Grace Hall, 1903, 5½″ **375.00**
Whiskey jug, corn by Lenore Asbury, 7½″ **1,000.00**
Tea caddy, 1905, lt green sweet clover, silver lid, CS **475.00**
Tiger Eye, ewer, florals, AMB, #101C, 9″ **945.00**
Vase, Albert Valentien, 1886, R270, 10½″ **1,600.00**
Vase, crabs & seaweed, MAD...................... **410.00**
Tile, 1900, rooks, celadon, 6″........................ **145.00**
   Parrot............................... **75.00**
Tray, 1946, bunch of grapes on leaf, lime green, 7x6″ **85.00**
   1950, rook on tray, #1139 .... **90.00**
Trivet, 1918, seagulls in flight, #2351 .... **105.00**
   1924, grapes, #1683, 6x6″ **80.00**
Urn, 1912, green matt w/handles, #339B, 12″ **235.00**
Vase: 1883, fired overglaze gold, AR Valentien, 9¼″ **1,000.00**
   1885, floral enamel on bisque, Fry, 5x7″ **875.00**
   1886, birds, MA Daly, 11″ **1,600.00**
   1897, florals, bisque w/gold rim, AMB, #304, 8½″ **945.00**
   1900, incised decor on brown matt, WHM, 5½″ **300.00**
   1902, green, 8½″ **60.00**
   1904, shaded blue w/wht & roses, S Coyne, #917E, 5½″ ... **600.00**
   1906, green matt, #819, 5″ **35.00**
   1907, grapes on ivory, Rothenbusch, #900C, 8″ **700.00**
   1911, amber, 9½″.......................... **45.00**
   1912, carved decor, Hentschel, 13″................. **575.00**
   1913, relief decor, matt glaze, #1068, 4″ **45.00**
   1914, shephard & sheep in relief, brown, 5½″ **75.00**
   1914, tulips, blue, #1711, 10″ **135.00**
   1915, lavender, 5¾″.......................... **35.00**
   1916, birds & berries in relief, dk green, 5½″ **65.00**

1917, floral porcelain, Van Horne, #162D, 5¼" **325.00**
1920, florals, porcelain, Epply, 1920, 6½" **360.00**
1920, rooks, blue, 7½" **95.00**
1921, abstract florals, matt, Louis Abel **160.00**
1921, sgraffito leaves, berries, L Able, 1921, #2066, 7½" ... **350.00**
1922, cattails, 5" **40.00**
1922, small floral relief decor, matt, 7½x5" **185.00**
1922, wht matt, 4" **25.00**
1923, burgundy, 3¾" **30.00**
1923, tulips in relief, lavendar matt, 10½" **95.00**
1923, tulips in relief, lavender matt, 10½" **95.00**
1924, brown, cream spatter, 8½" **45.00**
1924, butterfly, matt lavender, 5¾" **25.00**
1924, panels of daisies, turquoise w/wht hi-lites, 5½" ... **25.00**
1926, yellow, 6½" **30.00**
1928, blue matt, #2394, 9" **110.00**
1928, incised floral band, #2394, 9" **30.00**
1928, square, aqua matt on four feet, 7½" **50.00**
1929, florals, cream w/purple, H Wilcox, #357F, 6" **295.00**
1929, leaf in relief, blk on turquoise, Barret, 11" **295.00**
1930, abstract, spittoon shape, Shirayamadani **335.00**
1930, floral, matt glaze, Jensen, #2544, 8" **170.00**
1931, berries, turquoise, semi gloss, #6217, 5x6" **65.00**
1931, iris on ivory, HEW designer, #6171S, 13½" **250.00**
1932, experimental production, #6315, 6x5" **90.00**
1934, 5 sided, rooks, trees, green, #1795 .... **85.00**
1934, National Conference Catholic Charities, blue, 5x4½" . **120.00**
1940, leaves, blue semi gloss, #2282, 5" **35.00**
1943, gr to yellow hi glaze, w/blk florals, W Rehm, 5" ... **295.00**
1945, seagulls in relief, lt green, 9" **90.00**
1945, stylized florals, blue 1945, #6767, 6½" **60.00**
1946, 3 floral panels in relief, beige & blue, 5" **185.00**
1946, hi glaze turquoise, #6777, 12¼" **135.00**
1949, blue jays on crystalline, Ora King, 11½" **1,000.00**
1950, Mexican village scene in relief, 6" **85.00**
1955, shepherd & flock, turquoise hi glaze, 5½" **25.00**
1957, mushrooms, #7057 .... **21.00**
1962, tulips, matt turquoise, #1711, 10" **70.00**
199, florals in relief, hi gloss brown-grey, #6833........ **70.00**
Florals, incised, LNL, #16 .... **200.00**
Peacock feathers, brown matt over green, #1904, 6"...... **75.00**
Vellum: compote, roses, CS Todd, 1913, 6½x7½" **300.00**

Plaque, scenic, LA, 1921, 9x5" **1,300.00**
Plaque, scenic w/mountain & stream, Epply, 1919, 6x8" .. **1,000.00**
Plaque, The Poplars, L Epply, framed, 8x6" **1,350.00**
Plaque, trees & pond, C Schmidt, 1919, 4½x8½" **1,600.00**
Vase, 3 colored drip on blue-grey, LNL, 1921, 7½" **175.00**
Vase, abstract flowers at top, Todd, 1917, 7" **325.00**

Vase, birches by lake, all around decor, Diers, 1922, 10" . **1,500.00**
Vase, cherries on burgandy, Abel, 1919, #1096, 5" **150.00**
Vase, dogwood, Coyne, 1917, #2101, 7" **400.00**
Vase, floral, Diers, 1927, #551, 7" **385.00**
Vase, floral, E Hurley, 1928, 5x7" **445.00**
Vase, floral, Elizabeth Lincoln, 1906, 4¾" **285.00**
Vase, floral, F Rothenbush #942B, 9" **675.00**
Vase, floral, gourd shape, McD, 1914, 5½" **288.00**
Vase, floral, Lincoln, 1907, 6½" **280.00**
Vase, floral, McD, 1913, 8½" **375.00**
Vase, florals, on brown, Feichimer, 1905, 6½x3½" **300.00**
Vase, floral, PC, 1917, #1660E, 8" **425.00**
Vase, floral, Rothenbusch, 1916, #2033E, 8x4" **205.00**
Vase, florals, Todd, 1917, 7" **250.00**
Vase, forest scene w/geese, Shirayamadani, 1910, 8½x4½" . **950.00**
Vase, geometric design, CAD, 1909, #955, 4" **145.00**
Vase, river & trees, Rothenbusch, 1919, 14" **1,300.00**
Vase, sailboats, seascape, Sara Sax, 1911, 8" **2,000.00**
Vase, scenic, 1920, X'd, 8" **670.00**
Vase, scenic, E Hurley, 1931, 13½" **1,000.00**
Vase, scenic, E Hurley, 1940, 8" **2,000.00**
Vase, scenic, Ed Deirs, 1931, 9½" **900.00**
Vase, scenic, Ed Diers, 11" **1,000.00**
Vase, scenic, F Rothenbusch, 1910, 9" **750.00**
Vase, seascape w/boats, Coyne, 1914, #551, 6½" **1,200.00**
Vase, snow fall w/reindeer, ETJ, #839C, 9" **1,500.00**
Vase, sunrise scene all around, FR, 1911, #1655F, 6½" **775.00**
Vase, top band, w/Deco florals, Elizabeth Lincoln, 1908, 6½" **275.00**
Vase, trees & lake at sunset, Diers, 1919, #951B, 12" **1,800.00**
Vase, trees & sunset, Coyne, 1920, 8" **950.00**
Vase, trees, blue-yellow sky, Asbury, #901C, 10" **1,000.00**
Vase, trees, lake, Hurley, 1939, #614E, 8" **1,110.00**
Vase, tulips, red on aqua, CS Todd, 1920 .... **195.00**
Vase, winter scenic, Sally Coyne, 1918, 7¾" **1,600.00**
Wax Matt: vase, carved flowers, MH McDonald, 1926, 6"..... **275.00**
Bowl, autumn leaves, J Harris 1928, 9" **250.00**
Box w/cover, floral, VT, 1923, #622C, X'd **175.00**
Rose bowl, florals, E Barrett 1929, 5½"............... **300.00**
Vase, floral, HM Moose, 1924, 9" **385.00**
Vase. floral, K Jones, 1929, 7" **350.00**

Rosemeade

Rosemeade was the name chosen by Wahpeton Pottery Co., of Whapeton, N. D., to represent their product. The founders of the company were Laura Meade Taylor and R.J. Hughes, who organized the firm in 1940. It is most noted for small bird and animal figural designs, either in high gloss or a Van Briggle-like matt glaze. The ware was marked Rosemeade with an ink stamp, or carried a Prairie Rose sticker. The pottery closed in 1961.

Ashtray, w/turkey, Worthington, Mn. **25.00**
Centerpiece, tan & lt gr w/frog, mk, 9" **65.00**
Figural, blue elephant, sgnd, 5" **25.00**
   Pink swan **21.00**
Flower holder, bird on log, matt finish **10.00**
Pitcher, miniature **10.00**
Planter, double parakeet, sgnd **15.00**
   Kangaroo figural, blue w/lavander shaded matt, 6" **15.00**
Rose bowl, shiny pink, North Dakota **20.00**
Salt & pepper, cat figurals, rose hi glaze, pair **10.00**
   Elephant, pair **9.00**
   Leaping fawn, beige, 4", pair **8.00**
   Swordfish, blue, 4", pair **8.00**

Tid-bit server, pheasant, orig label, 4½″................ **15.00**

Tray, mouse in relief, maroon **15.00**
Vase, deer, matt, 8″ **35.00**
  High, gr exterior, cream interior, 4″ **8.00**

Rose Medallion

    Rose Medallion is one of the patterns of Chinese export porcelain produced from the early 1800s until the first part of the 20th century. It is decorated in rose colors with panels of florals, birds and butterflies that form reserves containing Chinese figures. Earlier examples were decorated with gold tracery; some were heavily reticulated.
    Key:
        MIC......Made In China

Bouillon bowl, double handle, MIC w/red block outline....... **125.00**
  Porcelain stand & lid, 1800s **100.00**
Bowl, 3½″, footed, 1890 .... **35.00**
  3½x8½x9¾″, reticulated sides **175.00**
  4½x11x10″, for fruit, oval, reticulated **365.00**
  5″ **50.00**
  5¼″, 1820 .... **75.00**
  7½″, deep **90.00**
  7½x6″, oval, scalloped **50.00**
  8½″, round, scalloped, shallow, gold trim............. **225.00**
  9″ **75.00**
  9″, square, 1875 .... **140.00**
  9½″, rectangular, serving **160.00**
  10″, shallow, lotus shape, 1875 .... **140.00**
  With cover, 8½x7″, nut finial **250.00**
    Vegetable **275.00**
Box, portrait on lift off lid & sides, 1½x1¼″ **55.00**
  With cover, 2″ **65.00**
Brush pot, 1800 .... **200.00**
Butter dish, 12 sided base, gold enamel **375.00**
  Covered, round **360.00**
  Pierced insert, gold enamel **440.00**
Butter pat, 2¾″, 6 for **145.00**
  3½″ **50.00**
Candlestick, 8¼″ **250.00**
Charger, 11½″, no mk **225.00**
  15″, 1850s **395.00**
Chocolate pot, 9½″ **275.00**
Chop plate, 14½″ **275.00**
  Paneled base, birds & butterfly, gilt decor, 1820 .... **110.00**

Creamer & sugar **125.00**
  Covered, bulbous, 5½″, pr **280.00**
Cup & saucer **75.00**
  Red China in circle **35.00**
Demitasse cup & saucer **60.00**
Demitasse saucer..................................... **15.00**
Dish, 3½″, scalloped & footed **30.00**
  4½″, scalloped edge **40.00**
  6½x5″, leaf shape **45.00**
  8″ across, 4 lobed **36.00**
  9″, oval, flat rim, serving **165.00**
  With cover, marquise shape, 1860, 10″ **275.00**
  With cover, marquise shape, shallow, 8¾″ **250.00**
  With cover, rectangular, 1860, 8¼″ **225.00**
Flower arranger, mushroom shape, 1830, 9″ **1,250.00**
Fruit basket, oval, reticulated, 11x10x4½″............. **275.00**
Jar w/cover, 1800s, 17″ **950.00**
Marriage lamp, reticulated shade, 11″ base **325.00**
Plate, 6″ **45.00**
  6½x4½″, oval **50.00**
  7″, cut corner sq **55.00**
  7¼″ **45.00**
  8½″ **55.00**

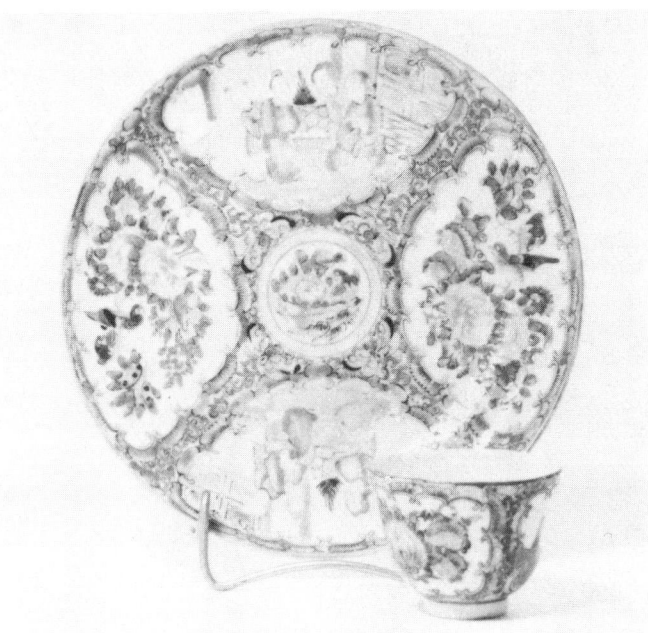

  8½″, lattice edge, 1910 .... **75.00**
  9½″ **60.00**
  10″, 1900.. **65.00**
  10″, birds & people, 1800s **135.00**
  11″, oval, footed **95.00**
  12″ **125.00**
Platter, 10½″, oval, floral & birds..................... **65.00**
  11x8½″, 1800 .... **650.00**
  13¾″, interior scenes w/birds, 1875 .... **200.00**
  16x13″, 1850s...................................... **365.00**
  18¼″ **400.00**
Punch bowl, 10″ **600.00**
  15″ **950.00**
Ramekin, w/underplate, 1800s **50.00**
Rice bowl w/cover, 4½″ **50.00**
Rice spoon, 1820 .... **50.00**
Salt & pepper, pr **40.00**
Sauce boat, double lip, 1860, 8″ **200.00**
Saucer **10.00**

4¼″	20.00
5½″, deep	28.50
Sugar, twist handles, 5″	250.00
Twist handles, covered, 1840, 3½″	440.00
Tea cup, 3″, handleless, illus	30.00
Tea set, pot & 2 cups in fitted wicker cozy, 1920	250.00
Teapot, cylinder, wht spout, wicker handle, 5½″	200.00
Domed lid, 1890, 9¾″	625.00
Pear shape	280.00
Pear shape, gold finial, 1900, 6″	115.00
Wrapped raffia handle, 1850s, 7¼″	250.00
Tray, 7″, oval	65.00
8¾″, oval	80.00
10″, reticulated, lemon peel glaze	185.00
11½″, clover leaf	235.00
Tureen, w/underplate, 14″ handle to handle, plate, 13½x10½″	1,850.00
Vase, 8½″	200.00
Applied salamanders, foo pup finials, scalloped, 14½″	300.00
Foo dogs & snakes, 1890, 12″	225.00

Rose O'Neill

Rose O'Neill's Kewpies first became popular in 1909, when they were used to conclude a story in the December issue of Ladies Home Journal. They were an immediate success, and soon Kewpie dolls were being produced world-wide. German manufacturers were among the earliest, and also used the Kewpie motif to decorate chinaware as well as other items. The Kewpie is still popular today, and can be found on products ranging from Christmas cards and cake ornaments to fabrics and wallpaper.

Bell, brass, figural, Kewpie	27.50
Book, 'Clever Betsy', Rose O'Neil illustrations	8.00
'Cordially Yours'	10.00
'I Wanna Be Loved by You'	10.00
'I'm Glad You Came Into My Life'	10.00
'The Master Mistress', poetry, drawings, 1922	37.50
Booklet, Jell-O	25.00
Box w/cover, gr Jasperware, 10 action Kewpies, high relief	190.00
Calendar, 1916, Campbell Art Co Kleverkard, Kewpie, sgnd	32.00
Kewpie, 1975	10.00
1976	10.00
Chamberstick, pink Jasper, 8 Kewpies, mkd Kandlelite	195.00
Chocolate mold, tin, Kewpie, 1930	10.00
Clock, jasper, sgnd, blue w/Kewpie	340.00
Creamer, German lustre w/Kewpie	80.00
Blue & white jasper, Kewpie, 2½″, Germany	165.00
Cup & saucer, w/Kewpie, sgnd, Royal Rudolstadt	95.00
Demi cup, lustre, Kewpie	40.00
Doll, Gingles, compo w/molded hair, jtd, 14″	195.00
Embroidery set, Kewpie, orig envelope	95.00
Flannel, Kewpie, 5x6″	15.00
Frame, metal w/figural Kewpie, sgnd	280.00
Ice cream tray, Kewpie	65.00
Kewpie, Anniversary, MIB, gold sticker	65.00
Bisque, arms raised, 2″	150.00
Bisque, box sgnd, MIB, Germany, 8″	350.00
Bisque, Cupid, moveable arms, marked, 4½″	95.00
Bisque, hugging Cupids, 3½″	110.00
Bisque, Italian soldier w/hat, standing by tree, 4½″	425.00
Bisque, jointed, 5¼″	595.00
Bisque, lapel doll w/paper label, 2″ long	145.00
Bisque, on stomach, 4″	340.00
Bisque, seated, hands propped under chin, eyes to right, 5″	225.00
Bisque, set of 6, 1950s, Lefton	27.00

Bisque, sgnd, 4½″	75.00
Bisque, sgnd, heart label, 5¼″	95.00
Bisque, sgnd on foot, moveable arms, blue wings, 5¼″	95.00
Bisque, shoulderhead, 2″	295.00
Bisque, snow baby, seated w/rabbit, 1¾″	110.00
Bisque, soldier, prone, firing rifle, 3″	395.00
Bisque, w/flower, sitting, 1¾″	240.00
Bisque face, JDK doll, glass googly eyes, jointed, 12″	4,250.00
Brass ho ho	15.00

Bride & groom, fully clothed, sgnd, 1913, 4½″	200.00
Bride & groom, wedding cake decoration	80.00
Cameo, Miss Peep's	39.00
Cameo, old w/strong body & very poseable, 27″	155.00
Cameo, yellow dotted sunbonnet outfit	65.00
Cardboard, fur hat, advertising, 1913, 12″	125.00
Carnival figurine	7.50
Carved wooden, colored	25.00
Celluloid, 2¼″	65.00
Celluloid, blue wings, mkd Pat 111-4, 1913, 2¼″	12.00
Chalkware, Thinker, sgnd, Germany	240.00
Cheerful cherub, compo/cloth, 25″	185.00
China, on stomach, 2¼″	95.00
Cloth, large	185.00
Compo, jointed arms, red heart sticker, eyes to right, 11″	175.00
Compo, jointed shoulders, blue wings, dressed, 12″	85.00
Compo, red heart on chest, 1913 label, 9″	78.00
Cuddle, by Kruger, blue	80.00
Folded paper cutout, dated 1928, 3x4″	10.00
Gal	50.00
German soldier w/helmet & tie tac	12.50
Hapifat, 4″	475.00
Hot 'n Tot, colored, marked	89.00
Huggers, heart sticker, 3″	145.00
Negro, painted compo, jointed arms, 11½″	375.00
Playing, signed	145.00
Red plush	22.50
Santa Claus, standup, signed, 1913, Royal Society	24.00
Scootles	150.00
With glasses, label in front & back, orig apron, 7″	395.00
Wax	7.50
Lamp, chalk, Kewpie w/movable arms, early pc	150.00
Letter opener, figural Kewpie, marked	50.00
Magazine, Ladies Home Journal Christmas, Kewpie, 1927	25.00
Perfume, Kewpie figural, German	65.00
Pitcher, blue jasper, white figures, signed, Germany	185.00

Gr w/pink jasper, 4 action Kewpies & butterfly, 4½"....... **225.00**
Place card holder, Kewpie, scholar w/bud vase, 2½"........ **355.00**
 Kewpie w/guitar.. **275.00**
Planter, heart-shaped, Kewpie playing mandolin, Old Lefton.... **25.00**
Plate, 6 Kewpies, sgnd, Royal Rudolstadt, 7"............ **95.00**
 8 Kewpies in action, Prussia Royal Rudolstadt, 7½"....... **100.00**
Postcard, Kewpie.. **35.00**
Print, Kewpie, sgnd, 1920s, 14x8"............................ **20.00**
Sand pail, Kewpie, Maud Humphrey, Muffet Xmas Party print, 1895 **75.00**
Soap, Kewpie, marked, 4¼"................................... **65.00**
Stamps, Kewpie.. **2.50**
Sugar, lusterware, 4 action Kewpies, sgnd, pink trim, 3½".... **125.00**
Talcum shaker, compo, Kewpie w/jointed arms, 1917........ **125.00**
Teapot, w/cover, German lustre w/Kewpie.................. **145.00**
Tin, Kewpie on swing, 2".. **27.00**
 Kewpie, 6".. **10.00**
Tray, tin, advertising, Kewpie, sgnd, 13x13"................ **165.00**
Vase, bisque, Kewpie w/guitar, blue, 5"................... **575.00**
Wall plaque, Jasperware, 'Start the Day', Happy Note, 7x5"... **58.00**

Rosenthal

In 1879, Phillip Rosenthal established the Rosenthal Porcelain Factory in Selb, Bavaria. Its earliest products were figurines and fine tablewares. The company has continued to operate to the present decade, manufacturing limited edition plates.

Bowl, strawberries & leaves, 1 handle, scalloped, gold trim, 10". **75.00**
Cake plate, Apollo, violet background, cameo, gold rim, 10"... **60.00**
Candelabra, figural couple, tree trunk, 9x6"............. **1,250.00**
Charger, Delft scenic, 15"................................... **240.00**
Chocolate, violets, 13 pc................................... **150.00**
Coffee pot, silver overlay, espresso, 7 pc on oval tray, Art Nouveau **395.00**
Cup & saucer, silver overlay, Maria......................... **55.00**
 White w/gold sprays, trim.................................... **16.00**
Demitasse set, ivory w/roses, sterling, 3 pc................ **140.00**
Dresser jar, silhouette on lid, Art Deco, Wiinblad, 5"........ **65.00**
Figurine, 3 figures, Selb Bavaria, A Caogmann, 8x10"....... **325.00**
 Bird, brown w/red head, sgnd Distelfink................. **110.00**
 Yellow, sgnd Karner....................................... **110.00**
 Bird of Paradise, 20".................................... **1,750.00**
 Bull & matador, pr... **495.00**
 Duck, sgnd, 2½"... **40.00**
 Dying Swan, ballerina..................................... **565.00**
 Eagle, brown shades, 15x16"............................ **1,500.00**
 French Bulldog, sgnd, 2½x3½"............................. **50.00**
 Horse, 3½"... **34.00**
 Horse, dapple grey, rearing, 12x17"................... **2,000.00**
 Nefertite, 11½x4".. **195.00**
 Penguin, 5¾".. **50.00**
 Pouter pigeon, chest puffed out, 6"...................... **145.00**
 Rabbit, wht w/pink accents, 2"............................ **45.00**
 White w/pink accents, 6¼"................................. **85.00**
 Robin on pedestal, artist sgnd, 5"........................ **80.00**
 Rooster, sgnd, 6"... **95.00**
 Rooster & hen, sgnd F Heidenreich, 4".................. **110.00**
 Russian Wolf Hound, lying down, blk & wht, 11"........ **140.00**
 Squirrel w/walnut, 7x7".................................... **160.00**
 Tiger, Karner, 18x8"...................................... **650.00**
 Turtle, 1x2½x1½".. **55.00**
 Wippet, wht, Karner, 5"................................... **125.00**
Fish set, gold trim, platter 15x11", 6 plates 10"........... **125.00**
Lunch set, Magic Flute, service for 6 w/accessories, Wiinblad.. **350.00**
Plate, floral, 9¼"... **10.00**

10"... **15.00**
Serving dish, strawberries & leaves, rococo gold trim, scalloped, 11" **75.00**
Teapot, silver overlay on lt blue, Art Nouveau.......... **125.00**
Vase, angel fish, fan shape, beige, pate-sur-pate, 5x6½"....... **80.00**
 Blue w/berries in wht relief, ovoid, flaring collar, 11"...... **180.00**

Roseville

The Roseville Pottery Company was established in 1892 by George F. Young in Roseville, Ohio. Finding their facilities inadequate, the company moved to Zanesville in 1898, erected a new building and installed the most modern equipment available. By 1900 Young felt ready to enter into the stiffly competitive art pottery market.

Roseville's first art line was called Rozane. Similar to Rookwood's Standard, Rozane featured dark blended backgrounds with slip painted underglaze art work of nature studies, portraits, birds and animals.

Azurean, developed in 1902, was a blue and white underglaze art line on a blue blended background. Egypto (1904) featured a matt glaze in a soft shade of old green and was modeled in low relief after examples of ancient Egyptian pottery. Mongol (1904) was a high gloss oxblood red line after the fashion of the Chinese Sang de Boeuf. Mara (1904), an iridescent luster line of magenta and rose with intricate patterns developed on the surface or in low relief, successfully duplicated Sicardo's work.

These early lines were followed by many others of highest quality: Fudjyama and Woodland (1905-06) reflected an Oriental theme; Chystalis (1906) was covered with beautiful frost like crystals.

Their most famous was Della Robbia, introduced in 1906, which was decorated with designs ranging from florals, animals and birds, to scenes of Viking warriors and Roman gladiators. These designs were accomplished by sgraffito with slip painted details.

Very limited but of great importance to collectors today, Rozane Olympic (1905) was a red ware decorated with scenes of Greek mythology.

Pauleo (1914) was the last of the art ware lines. It was varied---over 200 glazes were recorded---and some pieces were decorated by hand, unuslly with florals.

During the 2nd decade of the century until the plant closed 40 years later, new lines were added regularly, each reflecting the tastes of its time. Some of the more popular of the middle period lines were Donatello, 1915; Futura, 1928; Pine Cone, 1931; and Blackberry, 1933. Floral lines of the later years have become highly collectible. Pottery from every era of Roseville production---even its utility ware---attest to an unwavering dedication to quality and artistic merit.

Examples of the fine art pottery lines present the greatest challenge to evaluate. Scarcity is a prime consideration. The quality of art work varied from one artist to another---some pieces show fine detail and good color, and naturally this influences their value. Studies of animals and portraits bring higher prices than the floral designs. Artist's signatures often increase the value of any items, expecially if the artist is one who is well recognized.

Antique Matt Green
The Gate, double bud.. **25.00**
Wall pocket, cone w/relief florals, 10"...................... **125.00**
Apple Blossom
Basket, #310, 10"... **60.00**
 #311, 12"... **85.00**
Bowl, #326-6, 2½x6½".. **35.00**
Cornucopia, #381, 6".. **30.00**
Ewer, #316, 8".. **50.00**
Hanging basket.. **65.00**
Jardiniere, #342-6, 6".. **50.00**
Tea set, #371, 3 pc... **85.00**
Vase, #192-15, 15½"... **125.00**
 #382, 7".. **35.00**
 #388-10, 10".. **55.00**

#390-12, 12½″ **75.00**
Wallpocket, twig handle, blue, 8½″ **40.00**
Window box, #368-8, 2½x10½″ **35.00**

Artwood
Planter set, 3 pc, #1050 center, #1051-6 sides **40.00**
Planter, #1054, 8½″ **35.00**
#1055-9, 7x9½″ **35.00**
#1056-10, 6½x10½″ **35.00**
Vase, #1057-8, 8″ **35.00**

Autumn
Pitcher, 8½″ **650.00**
12½″ **900.00**
Shaving mag, 4″ **400.00**
Soap dish/liner, 5½″ **450.00**
Toothbrush holder, 5″ **400.00**
Wash bowl, 14½″ **500.00**

Aztec
Lamp base, lt blue, 11″ **275.00**
Pitcher, deep blue, 5″ **250.00**
Lt blue, 5½″ **250.00**
Vase, deep blue, 10″ **250.00**
Deep blue cylinder, 9½″ **250.00**
Deep blue cylinder w/widened shoulder, flare rim, 11½″ **300.00**
Pale gray-blue w/stylized florals, 11″ **300.00**
Tan, waisted w/flare rim, 11″ **300.00**

Azurean
Candlestick, florals by V Adams, no mark, 9″ **450.00**
Mug, leafage, RPCO #4 die stamp **450.00**
Vase, bulbous, scenic, 9″ **1,600.00**
Florals by B Myers, trumpet shape, #856, 18″ **1,000.00**
Florals by Leffler, #822/7, 15½″ **1,000.00**
Grapes by W Myers, futuristic shape, mkd, 14″ **1,000.00**
Slender neck, florals by Leffler, mkd, 7½″ **450.00**

Azurine
Orchid & Turquoise, 8″ **50.00**
Double bud vase, 5x8″ **50.00**
Vase w/handles, 10″ **85.00**

Baneda
Bowl, 3½x10″ **50.00**
Hexagon w/low handles, 3x11″ **60.00**
Candleholder, red, 4½″, pr **85.00**
Console, red, 13″ dia **100.00**
Jardiniere, red, 9½″ **175.00**
Vase, ball shape, shoulder handles, disc ft, 8″ **65.00**
Broad U Shape on disc, sm handles at narrow neck, 12″ . . . **100.00**
Flared w/disc ft, low handles, 12″ **85.00**
Green, loop handles at rim, disc base, 6″ **50.00**
Inverted cone w/sm neck handles, disk base, 4½″ **40.00**
Loop handles at base, red, 8″ **75.00**
Sm neck handles, disc base, 7″ **55.00**
Sm neck handles, red, 5½″ **60.00**
Wall pocket, 8″ **150.00**

Banks
Beehive, 2½″ **175.00**
3″ **200.00**
Buffalo, 3x6″ **150.00**
Cat head, 4″ **175.00**
Dog head, 4″ **150.00**
Eagle head, 2½″ **175.00**
Large pig, 4x5½″ **125.00**
Pig on 4 legs, 2½x5″ **100.00**
Pig, on base, 3x4″ **100.00**
Uncle Sam **125.00**

Bittersweet

Basket, #807-8, 8½″ **45.00**
#808, 6″ **35.00**
#809, 8″ **50.00**
#810, 10″ **60.00**
Cornucopia, #857-4, 4½″ **45.00**
#882, 8″ **45.00**

Double bud vase, #873, 6″ **40.00**
Ewer, #816, 8″ **50.00**
Planter, #868, 8″ **40.00**
Tea set, #871, 3 pc **95.00**
Urn, #842-7, 7″ **60.00**
Vase, #87 4-7, 7″ **45.00**
#883, 8″ **45.00**
#888-16, 15½″ **100.00**
#972, 5″ **35.00**
Wallpocket, #866-7, 7½″ **40.00**

Blackberry
Bowl, small rim handles, 8″ dia **110.00**
Candlestickes, 4½″, pr **125.00**
Console bowl, angle sides, sm rim handles, 13″ **150.00**
Jardiniere & ped **850.00**
Rim handles, 6″ **150.00**
Urn vase, bulbous, sm rim handles, 6″ **125.00**
Vase, ball shape, flare rim band, sm handles, 4″ **95.00**
Bulbous lower half, cylinder upper, shoulder handles, 5″ . . . **95.00**
Top flares, shoulder handles, 6″ **110.00**
Narrow shoulder curving to wider base, 5″ **95.00**
Ovoid w/short straight neck, rim to shoulder handles, 8″ . . . **150.00**
Short cylinder neck on wide curving body, rim handles, 12½″ **175.00**
Very bulbous w/short straight neck, angle shoulder handles, 4″ **110.00**
Waisted w/straight top & waist handles, 8″ **150.00**
Wide cylinder upper ½, lower tapers, rim handles, 6″ **110.00**
Wide waisted body, angle base section, long waist handles, 10″ **175.00**
Wall pocket, fan shape **175.00**

Bleeding Heart
Basket, #360, 10″ **60.00**
#360-10, 9½″ **60.00**
#361, 12″ **85.00**
Bowl, #377-4, 4″ **35.00**
Console bowl w/frog, #384-14, 17″ **75.00**
Ewer, #963, 6″ **40.00**
#972, 10″ **75.00**
Hanging basket, 8″ dia **75.00**
Pitcher, #1323 . . . . **65.00**
Plate, #381, 10½″ **50.00**

Pot, #651, 3½" **25.00**
Vase, #138, 4" **30.00**
  #964-6, 6½" **30.00**
  #968-9, 8½" **35.00**
  #969-8, 8" **40.00**
  #976-15, 15" **90.00**
Wall pocket **55.00**
  #1287, 8" **50.00**

Burmese
Candleholder/bookend, blk #70-B, or wht #80-B **100.00**
Candlestick, #75-B, pr **30.00**

Bushberry
Basket, #369, 6½" **45.00**
  #370, 8" **50.00**
  #372, 12" **95.00**
Bowl, #411, 4" **30.00**
  #657, 3" **30.00**
Cider pitcher, #1328 .... **85.00**
Console bowl, #385-10, 13" **50.00**
Cornucopia, #153, 6" **35.00**
  #154, 8" **35.00**
  #3 .... **45.00**
Double bud, #158-4 .... **40.00**
Double cornucopia, 6" **45.00**
Ewer, #1, 6" **45.00**
  #2, 10" **85.00**
Hanging basket, 7" **85.00**
Mug, 3½" **35.00**
Tea set, #2, 3-pc **125.00**
Vase, #29, 6" **35.00**
  #38-12, 12½" **75.00**
  #257-8, 8" **125.00**
Wall pocket, #1291, 8" **45.00**

Capri
Ashtray, #598-9, 9" **35.00**
  #599-3, 13" **50.00**
Basket, #510-10, 9" **75.00**
Bowl, #525-7, 7" **30.00**
  #529-9 .... **35.00**
Leaf, #531-14, 15" **45.00**
  #532-16, 16" **45.00**
Planter, #558, 7" **75.00**
  C1010-10, 5x10½" **50.00**
Shell, C1120, 9" **55.00**
Vase, #582-9, 9" **50.00**
Window box, #569-10, 3x10" **45.00**

Carnelian I
Bowl, plain, narrow disc base, rim handles, RV ink mk, 3x9" .. **30.00**
  With frog, 3x8½" **30.00**
Candleholder/frog, RV ink stamp, 3½" **30.00**
Console bowl, disc base w/wide flare rim, RV ink mk, 5x12½" . **55.00**
Ewer, 15" **100.00**
Flower frog, 4½" **30.00**
Urn, angle shoulder, extended shoulder to base handles, 8".... **60.00**
Vase, angle shoulder w/rim handles, 7" **45.00**
  Bottom half ball shape, 3 neck rings, ornate handles, 8" **45.00**
  Cylinder top half on ball w/disc ft, center handles, 10" **60.00**
  Fan shape, RV ink mk, 6" **30.00**
  Paneled fan top, cone base, low handles, RV ink mk, 8" **35.00**
  Wide shoulder narrows to base, angled rim handles, 10" **70.00**
    Rim to shoulder handles, 9½" **70.00**

Carnelian II
Bowl vase, angled sides, short flare neck band, w/handles, 5" .. **40.00**
Ewer, 12½" **45.00**

Ovoid on flare foot, cylinder neck section, 18½" **175.00**
Planter, on platform w/handles, 3x8" **30.00**
Urn, flat flare neck, short slope to bowl body, long handles, 6" . **60.00**
  High angle shoulder, disc ft, long shoulder-to-base handles, 8" **60.00**
  Sides w/low angle buldge, large ornate handles, 8" **60.00**
Vase, buldging base tapers to trumpet body, large low handles, 10" **45.00**
  Ovoid w/slight flare rim, 14" **95.00**
  Ovoid w/wide flare rim, straight handles rim to body, 12" ... **100.00**
  Ovoid, short flare rim, milkcan handles, 12" **100.00**
  Short cylinder neck, body w/angled buldge, lg handles, 7" ... **45.00**

Cherry Blossom
Bowl vase, narrow neck w/sm rim handles, 6" **95.00**
  Slight rim flare, sm shoulder handles, 5" **85.00**
Candleholders, 4", pr **125.00**
Hanging basket **200.00**
Jardiniere & pedestal, 25" **650.00**
  With handles, 10" **200.00**
Lamp base **250.00**
Vase, bulbous w/short cylinder neck, sm high handles, 8" **150.00**
  Bulbous w/sm rim handles, 5" **85.00**

Cylinder body w/slight rim curve, sm handles, 7½" **85.00**
High shoulders w/closed handles at wide rim, 7" **95.00**
Low buldge, convex sides, low handles, 8" **110.00**
Low, squat, narrow neck band w/sm handles, 4" **85.00**
Ovoid body, high handles, 10" **125.00**
Ovoid w/sm neck opening, sm handles, 7" **125.00**
Shoulder handles, 5" **85.00**
Wall pocket, 8" **200.00**

Chloron
Jug vase, relief leaves & buds, 1 shoulder handle, 9" **275.00**
Vase, Art Nouveau style, relief berries, scroll handles, 9" **325.00**
  Flat flare rim, tapered body, 3 large squared ft, 12" **250.00**
  Simple relief striated neck widens to buldge at base, 6½" .. **175.00**

Clemana
Bowl, #281-5, 4½" **65.00**
Flower frog, #23, 4" **35.00**
Vase, #112-7, 7½" **85.00**
  #208-6, 6½" **85.00**
  #749-6, 6½" **75.00**
  #750-6, 6½" **80.00**
  #752-7, 7½" **85.00**
  #754-14, 14" **175.00**
  #754-8, 8½" **125.00**
  #756-9, 9½" **125.00**
  #758-12, 12½ **125.00**

Clematis

Basket, #387, 7″	45.00
#388, 8″	40.00
#389, 10″	60.00
Bowl, #445, 4″	25.00
Bud vase, #187, 7″	30.00
Candleholder, #11, 4½″, pr	40.00
Cookie jar, #3, 10″	85.00
Cornucopia, #140, 6″	30.00
Double bud vase, #194, 5″	35.00
Ewer, #16, 6″	45.00
#17, 10″	60.00
#18, 15″	110.00
Tea set, #5, 3-pc	85.00
Vase, #108, 8″	35.00
#188, 6″	35.00
Wall pocket, #1295	40.00

Colonial

Combinet w/lid, 12″	275.00
Pitcher, 7½″	100.00
Pitcher & bowl	400.00
Toothbrush holder, 5″	85.00

Columbine

Basket, #365, 7″	45.00
#367, 10″	85.00
#368, 12″	80.00
Bookend/planter, 5″, ea	35.00
Bowl, #401, 6″	35.00
#655, 3″	30.00
Cornucopia, 5½″	30.00
Ewer, #18, 7″	50.00
Hanging basket, 8½″	65.00
Vase, #20, 8″	40.00

Corinthian

Ash tray, 2″	50.00
Candleholder, 8″	35.00
10″	40.00
Compote, 10″ dia	50.00
Double bud vase	35.00
Jardiniere & pedestal, 24″	325.00
Vase, bulbous, 10½″	50.00
Cylinder w/slightly flared rim, 8″	40.00
High shoulder, narrow base, 6″	35.00
Narrowed neck & disc foot, 8″	30.00
Wall pocket, 12″	65.00

Cornelian

Mush bowl & pitcher	80.00
Pitcher & bowl	350.00
Shaving mug, 4″	65.00
Soap dish, w/cover, 4″	85.00
Toothbrush holder, 5″	70.00

Cosmos

Basket, 12″	85.00
Bowl, #376, 6″	45.00
Candleholder, 2½″, pr	50.00
Console bowl, 15½″	75.00
Ewer, #951, 15″	95.00
Flower frog, 3½″	25.00
Hanging basket, 7″	70.00
Vase, 3″	25.00
#954	25.00
Disc ft, shoulder handles, 12½″	80.00

Creamware

Ashtray, Fatima, 3″	175.00
Advertising, 2″	40.00
Candlestick, Good Night, shield back, 7″	225.00
Mug, shrine emblem, 5″	100.00
Novelty stein, Try it on the Dog, 5″	225.00
Smoker combination w/Indian decal, 7½″	350.00
Batchelors Coat of Arms	275.00
Tobacco jar, 6″	250.00
Trivet w/cherries, 6″	100.00

Cremona

Candleholders, 4″, pr	40.00
Console bowl, squared, 9″	45.00
Flower frog	20.00
Vase, disc ft, trumpet shape, 8″	45.00
Elongated ovoid, 8″	45.00
Fan on disc ft, 5″	25.00
Ovoid w/narrow rim, angle handles, arrowhead leaves, 10″	70.00
Sharp side angle, 5″	40.00
Squared, on disc ft, 7″	50.00
Wide flare rim, high shoulders, tapering, 10½″	60.00
Wide flat rim, slender w/high shoulder, 3 rings on disc ft, 12″	60.00

Crocus

Vase, bulbous, short foot, ring neck, 7″	400.00
Bulbous top section, slender body, 9″	450.00
Buldging neck ring, tapering sides, 9½″	450.00
Flared sides, short narrow neck, 7″	350.00
Waisted shape, 9″	400.00

Crystallis

Candlestick, 9″	1,000.00
Pot, buldging ring at shoulder & base, 3 straight handles, 3″	2,000.00
Vase, cylinder w/wide base flare, l-pc 3-handle neck section, 14″	3,000.00
Narrow neck w/flare, broad shoulder, tapering, 11″	2,500.00
Ovoid body w/narrow neck ring, orange, 5½″	1,500.00
Simple shape, high shoulder, 13″	950.00
Slightly flaring, 3 futuristic 2-pt handles, sq ft, 12½″	1,350.00

Dahlrose

Bowl vase, low & squat, 4″	45.00
Bowl, angle handle, sm disc base, 10″	50.00
Bud vase, 8″	45.00
Candlestick, 3½″, pr	40.00
Double bud vase	30.00
Hanging basket	85.00
Jardiniere & ped, 30½″	550.00
Pillow vase, 5x7″	40.00
Triple bud vase, 6″	35.00
Vase, angled rim handles, 8″	75.00
Small shoulder handles, 6″	40.00
Squared, wide flare rim, 6″	35.00
Wide shoulder, sm rim handles, 6″	50.00
Wall pocket, 10″	70.00
Window box, buldging sides, 6x16″	125.00
Straight tapering sides, 6x12½″	75.00

Dawn

Bowl, #318-14, 16″	50.00
Ewer, #834-16, 16″	125.00
Vase, #826, 7″	40.00
#827, 6″	40.00
#833-12, 12″	65.00
#838, 8″	45.00

Della Robbia

Letter holder, caramel w/stylized iris decor, 3½″	650.00
Mug, band w/Dutch children, 4″	500.00
Teapot, tall flared shape, stylized flowers in panels, 5½″	1,100.00
Vase, blue lake w/swans, checkerboard neck band, 11½″	3,700.00
Broad ovoid w/reticulated top w/waterlily, 14″	2,700.00

Bulbous, tan w/br shoulder band w/wht florals, 8½" **1,400.00**
Narrow neck, bulbous, rings of daisies, leaves at base, 8" . **1,700.00**
Ovoid, rimless, stylized mum & leaf decor, 8½" **1,400.00**
Pale green w/cherries & leaves, reticulated neck, 13".... **2,000.00**
Reticulated rolled top w/repetitive daffodil decor, 12" **2,500.00**
Slender, white w/fan-like decor in gray Nouveau reserves, 9½" **1,100.00**

Dogwood I
Bowl, low................................. **45.00**
Hanging basket **95.00**
Vase, ovoid, 6"........................... **50.00**
   Ovoid, 7"............................. **70.00**
Wall pocket, 9½"......................... **60.00**

Dogwood II
Basket, 6"................................ **40.00**
   Bulbous, 8"........................... **40.00**
Bowl..................................... **25.00**
Bud vase, 9"............................. **35.00**
   With open twig handle, 8"............. **30.00**
Double bud, 8"........................... **45.00**
Double lily wall pocket **50.00**
Jardiniere, 8"............................ **70.00**
Planter, boat shape, 6"................... **45.00**
Tub, 4".................................. **50.00**
Vase, angle top, 9"....................... **35.00**
   Barrel shape, 8"...................... **40.00**
   Irregular top, 12".................... **65.00**
   Openwork top, 14½"................... **175.00**
Wall pocket, 9".......................... **70.00**
   15".................................. **125.00**

Donatello
Ash tray, flared top, 3".................. **75.00**
   Slightly flared, panels alternated w/columns............... **75.00**
Basket, 7½".............................. **150.00**
   Tall pointed handle, 15".............. **200.00**
Bowl, 6"................................. **45.00**
   Curved sides, 8"...................... **70.00**
   Sharply angled sides, 9½"............. **65.00**
   Straight sides, 8½"................... **75.00**
Candlestick, 1 base handle, 6½".......... **60.00**
Comport, tall standard, 9½".............. **125.00**
Compote, 5".............................. **60.00**
Cuspidor, 5½"............................ **70.00**
Double bud vase, center reserve w/cupid, handles, 7"....... **125.00**
Flower pot w/saucer **50.00**
Hanging basket........................... **125.00**
Incense burner, 3½"...................... **175.00**
Jardiniere, round body, flared fluted rim, 6" **85.00**
Jardiniere & ped, 24".................... **350.00**
   34".................................. **600.00**
Pitcher, 6½"............................. **175.00**
Plate, 8"................................ **175.00**
Powder jar, 2x5"......................... **175.00**
Vase, 3 ribbed neck rings, buldging base, long handles, 6" ... **100.00**
   Flare base, trumpet flare w/fluted rim, 10" **70.00**
   12".................................. **100.00**
   Gentle S curve sides, flared neck, 12".. **175.00**
   Unusual grey color, 8½"............... **175.00**
   Wide base, shoulder band, 8".......... **40.00**
Wall pocket, 9".......................... **60.00**

Dutch
Combinet, 10½"........................... **250.00**
Creamer, side pour, 3"................... **60.00**
Humidor, w/advertising, 6"............... **175.00**
Milk pitcher, 4½"........................ **150.00**

Mug, 4".................................. **75.00**
Pin tray, 4"............................. **35.00**
Pitcher, 7½"............................. **125.00**
Plate, rolled edge, 11".................. **90.00**
Soap dish, w/lid, 3"..................... **150.00**
Tankard, tall slender standard shape, 11½................. **110.00**
Teapot, 4½".............................. **100.00**
   Squared feet, scroll finial, J shape handle, 6½".......... **200.00**
   Squat flare w/angle finial, 4"........ **100.00**
   Tall flared panels, squeeze bag trim, 7".. **225.00**
Toothbrush holder, 4".................... **60.00**

Earlam
Bowl, squared, w/handles, 3x11½"......... **50.00**
Candlestick w/attached saucer, 4"........ **95.00**
Planter, 5½x10½"......................... **50.00**
Vase, U shape w/ear handles, 6".......... **55.00**
   Shoulder handles, 4".................. **40.00**
   Squared, rolled edge, 9".............. **75.00**
Wall pocket, 6½"......................... **120.00**

Early Pitchers
Boy, 7½"................................. **175.00**
Bridge, 6"............................... **40.00**
   Blended glaze, 6"..................... **50.00**
Cow, no horns, 6½"....................... **200.00**
   7½".................................. **100.00**
   With horns, 7½"....................... **150.00**
Goldenrod, 9½"........................... **85.00**
Grape, 6"................................ **75.00**
Landscape, 7½"........................... **40.00**
Mill, 8"................................. **175.00**
Poppy #11................................ **100.00**
   #141, 9".............................. **100.00**
Spearhead leaves in relief, mottled, 6½".. **60.00**
Tulip, 7½"............................... **40.00**
   Undecorated........................... **80.00**

Wild Rose, 9½"........................... **85.00**

Egypto
Bud vase, shoulder points, bulbous bottom w/slim neck, 5½". **175.00**
Circle jug, open center, 11"............. **500.00**
Compote, flowering tree shape, 9"........ **300.00**
Creamer, tricorn rim, 3½"................ **175.00**
Lamp base, 3 elephants w/riders, 10"..... **750.00**
Oil lamp, 5"............................. **275.00**
Pitcher, disk foot, no decor, 5"......... **225.00**

Vase, flared neck, relief shoulder bands, mkd, 11″ **275.00**
   Square, tapering w/Roman head medallions, 12½″ **275.00**

Elsie the Cow

Bowl, #B3 . . . . **60.00**
Mug, #B1 . . . . **60.00**
Plate, #B2, 7½″ **60.00**

Falline

Bowl, 11″ **150.00**
Bowl vase, w/handles, 6″ **175.00**
Candlestick, 4″ **100.00**
Lamp **175.00**
Vase, ball shape w/cylinder neck, ornate handles, 6″ **160.00**
   Corrugated bottom half, handles, 9″ **175.00**
   Disk foot, straight flared sides, handles, 8″ **150.00**
   Ovoid w/small neck handles, 7½″ **150.00**

Ovoid, large handles, 7″ **150.00**
Ovoid, w/handles, 6″ **150.00**
Straight sides, large handles, 6″ **150.00**
Tall cylinder on wider base, low handles, 12½″ **225.00**
Tapered ovoid, high shoulder handles, 8″ **150.00**

Ferella

Bowl, w/frog, deep, red, 5″ **175.00**
   Red, 12″ **175.00**
Candlestick, sherbet shape, brown, 4½″ **75.00**
Lamp base, blue, 10½″ **200.00**
Urn vase, buldging center w/tiny handles, brown, 6″ **150.00**
Vase, elongated ovoid w/close to body handles, 9″ **150.00**
   Ovoid, brown, 8″ **175.00**
   Shoulder buldge, w/handles, 4″ **95.00**
   Slender top w/low buldge & large handles, 6″ **110.00**
   Squat w/low buldge, pointed handles, slim neck, 4″ **100.00**

Florane

1920s, basket, 8½″ **80.00**
   Bowl, low, 8″ **30.00**
   Bud vase, 8″ **30.00**
   Urn vase, rimless ball shape, 3½″ **35.00**
   Vase, 12½″ **75.00**
   Shoulder handles, 6″ **35.00**

Florentine

Basket, 8″ **50.00**
Bowl, low, 9″ **35.00**
Compote, 5″ **35.00**
   10″ **45.00**
Double bud vase, 6″ **35.00**
Jardiniere & ped, 25″ **650.00**
Lamp **85.00**
Sand jar, light color **225.00**

Umbrella stand **350.00**
Vase, 8½″ **30.00**
   Ovoid, rimless, 6½″ **25.00**
Wall pocket, 7″ **30.00**
   9½″ **45.00**

Foxglove

Basket, #373, 8″ **55.00**
Candleholder, #1150, 4½″, pr **45.00**
Conch shell, #426, 6″ **35.00**
Cornucopia, #164, 8″ **35.00**
Double bud vase, #160, 4½″ **35.00**
Ewer, #4, 6½″ **50.00**
   #5, 10″ **60.00**
   #6, 15″ **80.00**
Jardiniere & pedestal, 30½″ **350.00**
Vase, #42, 4″ **25.00**
   #659, 3″ **25.00**
Wall pocket, 8″ **50.00**

Freesia

Basket, #391, 8″ **45.00**
   #392, 10″ **60.00**
Bookends, #15, pr **50.00**
Bud vase, #195, 7″ **30.00**
Candleholder, #1161, 4½″ **25.00**
Cookie jar, #4, 10″ **85.00**
Cornucopia, #198, 8″ **30.00**
Ewer, #19, 6″ **35.00**
   #31, 15″ **110.00**
Flower pot, #670, 5″ **40.00**
Jardiniere & ped **350.00**
Pitcher, #20, 10″ **60.00**
Teaset, #6 . . . . **85.00**
Urn, #196, 8″ **50.00**
Vase, #120, 7″ **40.00**
   #122, 8″ **45.00**
Wall pocket, 8½″ **35.00**

Fudji

Vase, buldging shoulder, narrowing body, 10½″ **1,350.00**
   Round base, tapering to throat, full top, 9″ **1,100.00**
   Square, twisted shape, 10″ **1,350.00**
   Twisted Rozane shape, squeeze bag decor, 9″ **1,100.00**
   Wide base tapers to throat, gourd top, 10″ **1,200.00**

Fuschia

Bowl, #346, 4″ **40.00**
Candleholder, #1132, 2″ **20.00**
Console bowl, #351, 3½x12½″ **50.00**
Ewer, #972, 10″ **75.00**
Pitcher, #1322, 8″ **65.00**
Vase, #645, 3″ **35.00**
   #879, 8″ **45.00**
   #891, 6″ **40.00**
   #893-6, 6″ **35.00**
   #895, 7″ **45.00**
   #896, 8½″ **45.00**
   #898, 8″ **50.00**
   #903, 12″ **75.00**

Futura

Bud vase, cone base, slender body, straight handles, leaf & bud **50.00**
Candleholders, sq elevated base, ivory w/gr leaf, 4″, pr **45.00**
Candlestick/bud vase, stacked cones w/disk ft, tan w/leaves, 10″ . **75.00**
Graduating buldging rings, disk ft, flare neck, 10″ **150.00**
Jardiniere, angled shoulder, sq rim handles, leaves, 6″ **75.00**
Pillow vase, sq sides, diagonals w/common point, blues, 5″ **45.00**
Planter, square base, flare sides, ivory w/leaf, 7″ across **50.00**

Pot, sq cone on sq base, 4 vertical posts, 4″ **50.00**
Shaded chrome blue to tan w/stylized seagulls, 10″ **85.00**
Vase, acorn shape body w/4 vertical stepped half panels, 7″ **75.00**
   Ball w/circle decor on elevated sq base, 4 posts, 8″ **95.00**
   Ball w/flat trapezoidal base, lt blues, greens, 7½″ **60.00**
   Cylinder w/stepped neck & square handles, 6″ **45.00**
   Deep wide flare top, Deco handles, tan w/peacock body, 8″ . . **60.00**
   Disk ft, bulbous bottom w/tapered stepped top, 12½″ **150.00**
   Ovoid on flared disk w/horizontal rings, relief decor, 6″ **60.00**
   Pink & gray gloss w/accordian folded sides, 8″ **50.00**
   Pink & gray gloss, stepped neck, rectangular, w/handles, 8″ . . **85.00**
   Stepped shoulder, tapered body, spear panels, 6″ **40.00**

   Tipped base, futuristic, rare shape, 11″ **500.00**
   Tan, steps from below neck to broad shoulder, tapers, 10″ . . . **85.00**
   Wide disk ft, cone body w/4 vertical stepped half panels, 8″ . . **55.00**
Wall pocket, 8″ **55.00**
Window box, 4 stepped vertical half columns, 5x15″ **150.00**

Gold Traced
Candleholder, More Light Goeth, 4″ **75.00**
Candlestick, little decor, 9″ **100.00**
Gold Traced & Decorated, candlestick, 9″ **125.00**

Holland
Mug, 4″ **40.00**
Pitcher, 6½″ **135.00**
   12″ **275.00**
Powder jar, 3″ **95.00**
Tankard, 9½″ **125.00**

Imperial I
Basket, #7, 9″ **65.00**
   Bowl base, 6″ **45.00**
   Cylinder, diagonal rim, 8″ **45.00**
   Tall arched handle, wide base, 13″ **60.00**
   Wide handle, 11″ **65.00**
Bud vase, 12″ **50.00**
Comport, 6½″ **80.00**
Planter, boat shape, 14x16″ **90.00**
Triple bud vase **45.00**
Vase, bulbous base w/cylinder neck, waist handles, 10″ **80.00**
   Bulbous w/handles, 8″ **70.00**
   Bulbous, rim handles, 10″ **80.00**
   Ovoid w/irregular rim, long handles, 10″ **60.00**
   Rimless ovoid w/bulging base, 12″ **90.00**

   With handles, 8″ **35.00**
Wall pocket, 8″ **45.00**

Imperial II
Bowl, corrugated bottom, relief decor top, 5x9″ **175.00**
   Disk ft, wide flare, corrugated base, 5x12″ **200.00**
Bowl vase, deep, round base, yellow/mauve dripping, 4½″ **150.00**
Bowl vase, side base, straight tapered sides, 4½″ **125.00**
Pot w/flared top, tan w/green 'moss', 6″ **175.00**
Vase, angled shoulder, cylinder neck w/wht relief, 7″ **175.00**
   Bulbous body, tapering neck w/incised rings, 7″ **150.00**
   Bulbous w/narrow rim, tight band of rings, 8″ **125.00**
   Elongated ovoid w/narrow rim, blue w/splotches, 11″ **200.00**
   Flaring tumbler shape, irregular incised lines, 8″ **175.00**
   Ovoid, relief decor rim band, blue mottled, 10″ **175.00**
   Sm high shoulder handles, tapers, rings, 8″ **175.00**
   Wide base, tapering, band of rings, aqua, 5½″ **100.00**
Wall pocket, pot w/irregular lines, 6½″ **175.00**
   Triple vase, tan w/moss, 6½″ **175.00**

Iris
Basket, #354, 8″ **65.00**
   #355-10, 9½″ **85.00**
Bowl, #2117, 4″ **35.00**
   #359, 5″ **45.00**
Candleholder, #1135, 4″, pr **45.00**
Console bowl, #361, 3x10″ **45.00**
Ewer, #926, 10″ **65.00**
Planter, #364, 14″ **60.00**
Vase, #914, 4″ **30.00**
   #917, 6½″ **30.00**
   #920, 7½″ **35.00**
   #922, 8½″ **45.00**
   #923, 8″ **50.00**
   #928, 12½″ **85.00**
Wall pocket, 8″ **55.00**
Wall shelf, 8″ **85.00**

Ivory II
Bowl, Matt Color shape, milkcan handles, #550, 6″ **30.00**
Dog figural, 6½″ **150.00**
Hanging basket, Matt Colors shape, 7″ **70.00**
Nude figural, 9″ **200.00**
Urn vase, Russco shape, #259, 6″ **40.00**
Vase, Carnelian shape, 10″ **50.00**
   Savona shape, 6″ **60.00**

Ixia
Basket, #346, 10″ **60.00**
Bowl, #326, 4″ **30.00**
   #387, 6″ **40.00**
Candleholder/bud vase, #1128, 3 sections, 5″ **40.00**
Candlestick, #1127, double **35.00**
Console bowl, #330, 3½x10½″ **60.00**
Vase, #835, 6″ **30.00**
   #857, 8½″ **40.00**
   #862, 10½″ **40.00**

Jonquil
Basket, cylinder w/pointed handle, 10″ **125.00**
   Pointed handle, 9″ **125.00**
Bowl, low buldge w/rim to buldge loop handles, 3″ **35.00**
Bowl vase, bulbous wf/rim handles, 4″ **60.00**
   Spherical w/pointed handles **40.00**
   With rim handles, 5½″ **60.00**
   With handles, 3½x9″ **50.00**
Bud vase, 7″ **45.00**
Crocus pot, w/saucer attached, 7″ **70.00**
Flower pot w/frog, 1 pc, 5½″ **60.00**

Jardiniere & ped, 29″ **850.00**
Vase, angled base buldge, rim handles, 4″ **50.00**
  Ovoid w/flared rim, handles, 12″ **150.00**
  Ovoid, close to body handles, 8″ **85.00**
  Short cylinder neck, bulbous bottom, handles, 4½″ **35.00**

Juvenile
Bear, bowl, 6″ **75.00**
  Creamer, 4″ **85.00**
  Mug, 3½″ **85.00**
Chicks, creamer, 3″ **40.00**
  Cup & saucer **60.00**
  Custard, 2½″ **50.00**
  Mush bowl **35.00**
Dog, cup & saucer **60.00**
  Mug w/2 handles, 3″ **50.00**
  Rolled edge plate, 8″ **60.00**
Duck, creamer, 4″ **50.00**
  Custard, 2½″ **65.00**
  Mug, 3½″ **50.00**
  Plate, 7″ **65.00**
Duck w/Hat, creamer, 3½″ **40.00**
  Cup & saucer **60.00**
  Mug, 3″ **40.00**
  Plate, 8″ **45.00**
Fancy Cat, divided plate, 8½″ **200.00**
  Mug, 3″ **125.00**
  Plate, 8″ **175.00**
  Rolled edge plate, 8″ **175.00**
Fat Puppy, creamer, 3½″ **70.00**
  Mug, 3½″ **50.00**
  Pitcher, 3½″ **50.00**
  Plate, 7″ **65.00**
Nursery Rhyme, sugar, 3″ **125.00**
Teapot, 6″ **225.00**
Pig, creamer, 4″ **125.00**
  Rolled edge plate, 8″ **175.00**
Rabbit, egg cup, 4″ **95.00**
  Mug, 3″ **50.00**
  Rolled edge plate, 8″ **45.00**
Santa Claus, creamer, 3½″ **95.00**
  Cup & saucer **150.00**
  Rolled edge plate, 8″ **45.00**
Sitting Rabbit, custard, 2½″ **50.00**
  Egg cup, 3″ **95.00**
  Pitcher, 3″ **40.00**
  Plate, 7″ **35.00**
  Plate, 8″ **40.00**
Sunbonnet Girl, creamer, 3½″ **40.00**
  Cup & saucer **60.00**
  Egg cup, 4″ **95.00**
  Mug w/2 handles **50.00**
  Plate, 8″ **40.00**

La Rose
Bowl, low, 6″ dia **50.00**
Candleholders, 4″, pr **45.00**
Console bowl, 9″ **50.00**
Double bud vase **35.00**
Jardiniere, 6½″ **60.00**
Vase, bulbous, scroll handles, 4″ **40.00**
  Elongated ovoid, 10″ **50.00**
Wall pocket, 9″ **50.00**

Landscape
Creamer, 3″ **45.00**
Planter, 4½″ **75.00**

Sugar w/cover, 3½″ **50.00**

Laurel
Bowl, rolled rim, narrow base, turquoise, 7″ dia **30.00**
Vase, bulbous bottom, top half bucket shape, closed handles, 9″ **75.00**
  Bulbous, short straight neck band w/closed handles, 8½″ **60.00**
  Ovoid w/closed handles, old gold, 6″ **50.00**
  Ovoid w/stepped top, closed handles, turquoise, 7″ **35.00**
  Stepped top, straight sides flare, angle handles, 8″ **45.00**
  Wide rim, tapers to narrow ft, low closed handles, 6½″ **35.00**

Lombardy
Jardiniere, footed, 6½″ **150.00**
Vase, 3 feet, 6″ **150.00**

Lotus
Bowl, #L6-9, 3x9″ **75.00**
Pillow vase, #L4-10, 10½″ **100.00**
Planter, #L9-4, 3½x4″ **85.00**

Luffa
Candlestick, 5″ **45.00**
Jardiniere, 5¼″ base size **115.00**
Lamp base, 8½″ **200.00**
Vase, broad shoulder, tapers to disk ft, rim handles, 8″ **60.00**
  Pedestal, tapering, shoulder handles, 15½″ **275.00**
  Slight flare, handles, 8½″ **45.00**

Lustre
Basket, flat bowl w/pointed handles, 6½″ **100.00**
  Pointed handle, 10″ **200.00**
  Pointed handle, slender, 6″ **175.00**
Bowl, 5″ **35.00**
Candlestick, 5½″ **35.00**
  10″ **45.00**
Vase, angular high shoulder, 12″ **55.00**
  'Broken' glaze effect, 12″ **100.00**

Magnolia
Basket, #384, 8″ **50.00**
  #385, 10″ **85.00**
Bowl, #665, 3″ **25.00**
Cider pitcher, #132, 7″ **75.00**
Cookie jar, #2, 10″ **85.00**
Double bud vase, #186 . . . . **30.00**
Ewer, #13, 6″ **40.00**
  #15 . . . . **125.00**
Mug, #3, 3″ **40.00**
Planter, #389, 8″ **30.00**
Tea set, #4 . . . . **85.00**
Vase, #86, 4″ **25.00**
Wall pocket, 8½″ **40.00**

Mara
Vase, low buldge, narrows to rim, relief decor, handles, 5½″ **3,000.00**
  Slender, 13″ **1,500.00**
  Slender, dominate scroll pattern, 13″ **1,500.00**
  Thick pear shape w/loop rim handles, #13, 5½″ **2,750.00**

Mayfair
Bowl, #1110, 4″ **25.00**
Cornucopia, #1013-6, 3″ **30.00**
Jardiniere, #1109-4 . . . . **25.00**
  #90-4, 7½″ **30.00**
Pitcher, #1101-5, 5″ **30.00**
  #1102-5, 5″ **30.00**
  #1105, 8″ **45.00**
Planter, #1113-8, 3½″ **30.00**
Tankard, #1107, 12″ **75.00**

Ming Tree
Basket, #508, 8″ **65.00**
  #509, 13″ **110.00**

#510, 14½″ 85.00
Bookend, #559, 5½″, pr 85.00
Candleholder, #551, pr 35.00
Conch shell, #563, 8½″ 40.00
Console bowl, #528, 10″ 65.00
Ewer, #516, 10″ 75.00
Floor vase, 15½″ 200.00
Vase, #581, 6″ 35.00
   #582, 8″ 50.00
   #583, 10½″ 65.00
   #584, 12½″ 85.00
   #585, 14½″ 200.00
Wall pocket, 8½″ 125.00

Mock Orange
Basket, #908, 6″ 45.00
   #909, 8″ 50.00
Bowl, #90, 4″ 25.00
Ewer, #916, 6″ 35.00
Pillow vase, #930, 7″ 45.00
Planter, #931, 3½″ 35.00
   #932, 4″ 40.00
Tall planter 45.00
Vase, #973, 8½″ 45.00
   #985, 13″ 85.00
Window box, #956, 8″ 35.00

Moderne
Comport, #295, 5″ 55.00
   #297, 6″ 60.00
Lamp, #799, 9″ 100.00
Triple candleholder, #112, 6″ 45.00
Urn, #299, 6½″ 45.00
Vase, #787, 6½″ 35.00
   #789, 6″ 45.00
   #794, 7″ 30.00
   #796, 8½″ 45.00

Mongol
Cylinder vase, 15″ 900.00
Mug, 3 handles, 6″ 700.00
Pitcher, high shoulder handle, 6½″ 700.00
Vase, beehive base, bar handles center buldge to flare lip, 10″ 1,500.00
   Egg shape body w/sm neck, short foot, 5″ 600.00
   Flat flare over angled shoulder, concave sides, 14″ 900.00
   Trumpet body, base w/wide flare, 16″ 900.00

Monticello
Basket, pointed handle, 6½″ 100.00
   Pointed handle, cylinder top half, bottom buldges, 6½″ 150.00
Vase, bulbous, ear handles, 6″ 45.00
   Elongated ovoid, small handles, 7″ 60.00
   Long U shape on short base section, low handles, 10½″ 80.00
   Low angled buldge, disk ft, handles, 4″ 45.00
   Wide midpoint, rim to center handles, 9″ 70.00

Monticello
Basket, ball shape, disk ft, 10½″ 250.00
Bowl vase, white, 4″ 125.00
Candlestick, 5″, ea 75.00
Console bowl, 4½x11½″ 150.00
Pot, disk ft, center handles, 5″ 125.00
Urn vase, white, 6″ 125.00
Vase, angle shoulder w/extended handles, blue, 12″ 200.00
   Bulbous base, neck handles, 10″ 175.00
   Concave sides, elevated disk ft, blue, 6″ 125.00
   Narrow fan on disk ft, low handles, wht, 7″ .. 125.00
   Ovoid, large angle handles at rim, white, 8″ .. 150.00
   Shoulder handles, 15″ 300.00

Wall pocket, 8½″ 200.00
Moss
Candleholder, #1107, 4″, pr 45.00
Candlestick, #1104, 2″ 20.00
Console bowl, 13″ 60.00
Pillow vase, #781, 8″ 45.00
Triple bud vase, #1108, 7″ 45.00
Urn, #290, 6″ 60.00
Vase, #774, 6″ 35.00
   #774, 8″ 50.00
Wall pocket, 10″ 100.00

Mostique
Bowl, high gloss 25.00
   Low w/handles, 9″ dia 55.00
Comport, 7″ 65.00
Hanging basket, 7″ 125.00
Jardiniere, closed handles, 10″ 90.00
Vase, cylinder w/rim buldge, 6″ 35.00
   Shoulder band, 10″ 55.00
   Wide base & rim, concave sides, 6″ 25.00
      8″ 30.00
      Handles, 12″ 100.00
Nursery, baby plate, rolled edge, 8″ 95.00

Olympic
Pitcher, Pandora Brought to Earth, bulbous, 7″ 2,250.00
   Ulysses at the Table of Circle, 7″ 2,500.00
Vase, 3 legs w/ball ft, Persia & Ionia Yoked to...Xesxes, 14½″ 4,500.00
   Slim neck w/handles, flare body, Juno commanding the sun, 20″ 4,500.00

Orian
Bowl vase, w/curving handles, 6″ 70.00
Comport, 4½″ 110.00
Vase, angle shoulder, wide narrows to raised base, handles, 7½″ 125.00
   Cylinder top, 2 mid flanges, squat base, handles, 7″ 65.00
   Slim top half to bulb on short ped, handles, 12″ 95.00
   Red, 12″ 150.00

Panel
Bowl vase, wide shoulder, disk ft, collar, 4″ 45.00
Candlestick, 8″, pr 85.00
Double bud vase 35.00
Fan vase w/nude, 6″ 150.00
   8″ 150.00
Jar w/cover, 10″ 300.00
Lamp base w/nude, 10″ 225.00
Vase, angle shoulder, trailing vines, no panels, 10″ 75.00
   Bulbous, no collar, disk ft, 8″ 60.00
   Slender, 6″ 40.00
Wall pocket, 8″ 85.00

Pasadena
Bowl, #L24, 3″ 35.00
Flowerpot, #L36, 4″ 35.00
Occasional piece, #526, 7″ 25.00

Pauleo
Vase, bulbous body, flare neck, trees, 19″ 800.00
   Cylinder w/low buldge & 3 tab ft, textured, 12″ 700.00
   Elongated ovoid, wine w/blue speckles, 19″ .. 1,200.00
   Ovoid, w/art work, leaves & berries, 16½″ ... 900.00
   Shoulder, ivory & lavendar w/iris, 19″ 1,200.00
   Stand up collar, ovoid, 'broken' glaze, 9″ ... 500.00
   Wide flare rim, low buldge, disk ft, mottled, 19″ 1,000.00

Peony
Basket, #376, 7″ 45.00
   #378, 10″ 60.00
Bowl, #427, 4″ 30.00
   #661, 4″ 35.00

Double cornucopia, #172 . . . . 40.00
Ewer, #7, 6″ 35.00
  #8, 10″ 75.00
Tea set, #3 . . . . 85.00
Vase, #57, 4″ 25.00
  #57, 4″ 25.00
Wall pocket, #1293, 8″ 40.00

Persian
Bowl, 3 rim handles 75.00
Candlestick, 8½″ 125.00
Hanging basket, 9″ 250.00
Jardiniere, large 150.00
Sugar & creamer 85.00

Pine Cone
Ashtray, #499, 4½″ 30.00
Basket, #353, 11″ 85.00
Boat dish, #427, 9″ 50.00
Bowl, #320, 4½″ 35.00
  #457, 4½″ 40.00
Candlestick, #112, 2½″ 25.00
Centerpiece/candleholder, #324, 6″ 75.00
Console bowl, 11″ 60.00
Jardiniere & ped 450.00
Mug, #960, 4″ 50.00
Pillow vase, #845, 8″ 60.00
Pitcher, #485, 10½″ 60.00
  #708, 9½″ 125.00
Planter, #124, 5″ 40.00

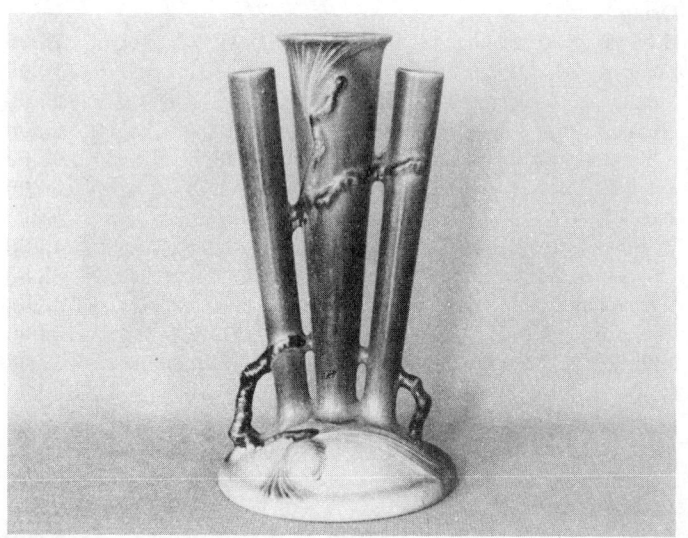

Triple bud vase, green, 8½″ 47.50
Tumbler, 5″ 45.00
Urn vase, #908, 8″ 70.00
Vase, #121, 7″ 45.00
  #747, 10½″ 60.00
  #850, 14½″ 150.00
  #907, 7″ 40.00
Wall pocket, 8½″ 65.00
Wall shelf 85.00
Window box, #431, 3½″ 60.00

Primrose
Bowl, 4″ 40.00
Vase, #761, 6½″ 40.00
  #765, 8″ 50.00
  #767, 8″ 50.00

Raymor
Bean pot, #194 . . . . 25.00

#195 . . . . 25.00
Casserole w/lid, 13½″ 35.00
Casserole, #185, 13½″ 25.00
Casserole, med, #183, 11″ 30.00
Covered butter, #181, 7½″ 30.00
Cruet, 5½″ 18.00
Cup & saucer, #151 . . . . 15.00
Dinner plate, #152 . . . . 10.00
Divided vegetable bowl, #165, 13″ 20.00
Gravy, #190, 9½″ 12.00
Hot plate & casserole, #84-#158 . . . . 50.00
Hot plate, #159 . . . . 15.00
Individual casserole, #199, 7½″ 18.00
Individual corn server, 12½″ 15.00
Individual covered ramekin, #156, 6½″ 15.00
Luncheon plate, #153 . . . . 7.00
Mustard, 3½″ 30.00
Salad bowl, #161, 11½″ 15.00
Salad plate, #154 . . . . 7.00
Salt & pepper, 3½″, pr 20.00
Shirred egg, 10″ 18.00
Swinging coffee pot, #176 . . . . 90.00
Tray, 8½″ 20.00
Vegetable, #160, 9″ 12.00
Water pitcher, #189 . . . . 60.00

Rosecraft
Bowl, w/flower frog 40.00
Bud vase, 8″ 50.00
Vase, slim w/neck handles, 6″ 35.00
Vase, sm rim handles, cylinder, 8″ 35.00

Rosecraft Black
Bowl, 3x8″ 75.00
Comport, 4x11″ 125.00
Ginger jar, 8″ 200.00
Vase, cylinder neck w/flare, bulbous bottom, ornate handles, 10″ 125.00
Vase, high shoulder, 13½″ 150.00

Rosecraft Hexagon
Bowl, 7½″ 75.00
Candlestick, 8″ 100.00
Double bud, 8″ 125.00
Vase, 6″ 100.00
Vase, blue hi-gloss, 5″ 125.00

Rosecraft Vintage
Bowl, 3″ 40.00
Jardiniere & ped, 30½″ 475.00
Vase, 12″ 125.00
Vase, angle shoulder w/handles, 8½″ 75.00
Vase, ball body w/sm neck handles, 4″ 45.00
Vase, ovoid, 6″ 60.00
Window box, 6x11½″ 125.00

Rozane
Bowl, #927, floral, 2½″ 125.00
Bud vase, #862, 4″ 125.00
Chocolate pot, #936, artist sgnd, 9½″ 400.00
Ewer, #828, floral 275.00
Ewer, #879-4, floral, 11″ 250.00
Ewer, 4″ 150.00
Ewer, brown glaze, undecorated, 8″ 175.00
Jug, #888, 4½″ 250.00
Jug, cherries by Josephine Inlay 7″ 275.00
Mug, florals by G Gerwick, 5″ 175.00
Paperweight, floral by Grace Neff 225.00
Pillow vase, #882, 2 dogs, hat w/plume, F Steele, 9″ 3,500.00
Pillow vase, bird w/pheasant, 8½″ 1,400.00

Pillow vase, ruffled w/handles, bulldog, 9" **2,000.00**
Pitcher, floral by Mae Timberlake, 5" **250.00**

Tankard, cherries, artist signed, 10½" **175.00**
   Ears of corn by V Adams, 15½" **450.00**
Tobacco jar, pipe decor by Walter Myers, 6" **600.00**
Vase, #821, floral, 9½" **175.00**
Vase, #923, commemorative, 5" **165.00**
Vase, bulbous base, long neck w/ruffle, berries, Mitchell, 14" . . **275.00**
Vase, horse by Leffler, 13" **4,000.00**
Vase, Indian in headdress, #891, 14" **3,000.00**
Vase, kitten, by HS, ovoid w/stand up collar, 9½" **2,000.00**
Vase, w/handles, florals, 4" **125.00**

Rozane, 1917

Basket, 11" **80.00**
Comport, 8" **65.00**
Jardiniere & ped 28½" **350.00**
Jardiniere & ped, 35" **450.00**
Vase, 8" **45.00**
Vase, 10" **60.00**

Rozane Light

Ewer, grapes by J Imlay, grey-green/ivory, 11½" **50.00**
Pillow vase, scalloped top & ft, cherries by W Myers, 10x10" . **300.00**
Pitcher, grey/ivory, floral & squeeze bag, Mary Pierce, 7" **600.00**
Tankard, pink/ivory/gray w/ear of corn, J Imlay, 10" **400.00**
Vase, angle shoulder, slight concave, teal/ivory floral, V Adams, 6½" **200.00**
Vase, ball shape body w/angle rim handles, 4" **175.00**
Vase, flat flange rim, 3 tab ft, pansies on grey/ivory, 9" **225.00**
Vase, gourd shape, florals on grey & white, Mae Timberlake, 8" **200.00**
Vase, pink grapes on shaded ground, bulbous, J Imlay, 14" . . . **500.00**
Vase, pink roses on teal/ivory, J Imlay, 16" **600.00**
Vase, twist panels, grey/ivory w/florals, Walter Myers, 10" **250.00**

Russco

Bowl vase, ball shape, stacked handles, crystals, 6½" **55.00**
Bowl vase, ball shape, stacked handles, matt, 6½" **50.00**
Double bud vase, matt, 8½" **35.00**
Triple corncupoia, 8x12½" **70.00**
Vase, body tapers to raised base, rim to base handles, crystals, 8" **95.00**
Vase, flare rim tapers to raised foot w/low handles, crystals, 8" . **60.00**
Vase, stacked shoulder handles, disk ft, matt, 14½" **10.00**

Savona

Candlesticks, 9½" pr **175.00**
Urn w/cover, 8" **150.00**
Vase, broad shoulder w/angle handles, short ped ft, 12" **300.00**

Silhouette

Ashtray, #799 . . . . **25.00**
Basket, #708, 6" **35.00**
Basket, #708, 8" **40.00**
Candleholder, #751, 3", pr **30.00**
Cigarette box **35.00**
Cornucopia, #721, 8" **30.00**
Ewer, #716, 6" **40.00**
Ewer, #717, 10" **50.00**
Fan Vase, #783, w/nude, 7" **90.00**
Planter, #731, 14" **50.00**
Planter, #756, 5" **30.00**
Urn, #763, w/nude, 8" **110.00**
Vase, #782, 7" **30.00**
Vase, #785, 9" **35.00**
Wall pocket, #766, 8" **35.00**

Snowberry

Ashtray **30.00**
Basket, #1BK, 7" **35.00**
Basket, #1BK, 8" **45.00**
Bowl, #1RB, 5" **35.00**
Bud vase, #1BV, 7" **30.00**
Candleholders, #1CS-1 . . . . **25.00**
Console bowl, #1BL1, 10" **40.00**
Cornucopia, #1CC, 6" **30.00**
Ewer, #1TK, 6" **35.00**
Ewer, #1TK, 10" **60.00**
Tea set **85.00**

Sunflower

Bowl, angled shoulder, 4" **55.00**
Jard & ped, 29" **850.00**
Jardiniere, 9" **100.00**
Umbrella stand **500.00**
Urn vase, wide shoulder, 5½" **50.00**
Vase, flared top half tapers to rounded bottom, 7" **60.00**
Vase, ovoid w/cylinder neck w/sm handles, 10" **85.00**
Vase, ovoid w/flare rim, neck handles, 8" **70.00**
Vase, straight sides w/angled rim handles, 6" **50.00**
Wall pocket, 7½" **125.00**
Window box, 3½x11" **85.00**

Teasel

Basket, #394, 10" **75.00**
Bowl, #342, 4" **30.00**
Bowl vase, w/cylinder neck & handles, 5" **30.00**
Ewer, #890, 18" **125.00**
Urn vase, #384, 6" **35.00**

Thornapple

Basket, #3342, 10" **65.00**
Candleholders, 2½", pr **35.00**
Candleholders, 5½", pr **70.00**
Cornucopia vase, 6" **30.00**
Planter, #262, 5" **45.00**
Vase, #308, 4" **35.00**
Vase, #812, 6" **35.00**
Wall pocket, 8" **60.00**

Topeco

Bowl, red glaze **100.00**
Urn vase, ball shape, short collar, 6" **85.00**
Vase, bulbous, 9" **85.00**
Vase, ovoid w/flare collar, 6½" **70.00**
Vase, red glaze, 9½" **150.00**

Tourist

Vase, 8" **450.00**
Vase, 12" **500.00**

Window box, 8½x19″ **1,000.00**

Tourmaline
Bowl, pink/grey speckles, 8″ **50.00**
Candlestick, flared ft, 5″, pr **40.00**
Cornucopia, 7″ **45.00**
Pillow vase, vertical lines, low handles, 6″ **50.00**
Squarish w/wide sq collar w/relief work, 7½″ **50.00**
Urn vase, sharp shoulder angle, relief decor at collar, 4½″ **50.00**
Vase, 6 panels taper, relief on alternating panels, 10″ **65.00**
Vase, ball body w/stand up collar & handles, 6″ **60.00**
Vase, ball w/wide lip, disk ft, 6″ **60.00**
Vase, twist panels, pink/grey/ivory 8″ **60.00**

Tuscany
Flower arranger w/handles, 5½″ **40.00**
Vase, comport shape, 4″ **35.00**
Vase, elongated ovoid, stand up collar, rim handles, 12″ **85.00**
Vase, ovoid w/high handles, ring lip, 6″ **35.00**
Vase, squarish body w/flange rim, disk ft, handles, 6″ **40.00**
Vase, straight neck, bulge below midpoint, handles, 9″ **60.00**
Wall pocket, 8″ **45.00**

Velmoss
Bowl, w/handles, 3x11″ **45.00**
Vase, broadens to width below midsection, high angle handles, 12½″ **95.00**
Vase, pointed handles at widened midsection, 9½″ **70.00**
Vase, sharp shoulder & angle handles, tapers, 8″ **55.00**
Vase, wide top tapers to raised ft, high angle handles, 14″ ... **115.00**
Wall pocket, 8½″ **150.00**

Velmoss Scroll
Bowl, flaring rim, 3″x7″ **40.00**
Ring lip, stand up collar, ovoid body, disk ft, 10″ **80.00**
Vase, elongated oval w/stand up collar, 8″ **60.00**
Vase, large ovoid, ring lip, 12″ **100.00**
Vase, ovoid w/stand up collar, 8″ **60.00**
Vase, slim curving shape on wide base, 10″ **70.00**
Vase, wide shoulder, 5″ **50.00**
Wall pocket, 11″ **95.00**

Victorian Art Pottery
Bowl vase, wide shoulder, ring neck, 4″ **85.00**
Jar w/cover, ovoid, flat lid, gloss, 8″ **225.00**
Vase, bulbous, ring neck, 8″ **125.00**
Vase, sm ring neck, wide angle shoulder, tapers to disk ft, 7″ .. **95.00**
Vase, wide shoulder, ring neck, 6″ **90.00**

Vista
Basket, 9½″ **75.00**
Basket, 12″ **85.00**
Jardiniere & ped, 28″ **500.00**
Vase, #134, 18″ **175.00**
Vase, #212, 15″ **125.00**
Vase, angle shoulder, slight taper to flaring bottom, 10″ **60.00**
Vase, flat band rim w/sm handles, full body w/disk ft, 18″ **175.00**
Wall pocket, 9½″ **85.00**

Volpato
Candlestick, 3½″ pr **120.00**
Candlestick, 10″ **100.00**
Console bowl, w/handles, footed, 4x10″ **150.00**
Pot w/saucer, 6″ **130.00**
Vase, rolled edge, ovoid, disk ft, 9″ **125.00**
Window box, 2½x9″ **85.00**

Water Lily
Basket, #381, 10″ **60.00**
Basket, #382, 12″ **80.00**
Bowl, #663, 3″ **25.00**
Cookie jar, #1, 10″ **95.00**
Cornucopia, #177, 6″ **35.00**

Cornucopia, #178, 8″ **40.00**
Ewer, #10, 6″ **35.00**
Ewer, #11, 10″ **60.00**
Ewer, #12, 15″ **110.00**
Vase, #72, 6″ **30.00**
Vase, #73, 6″ **30.00**
Vase, #75, 7″ **35.00**
Vase, #81, 10″ **50.00**
Vase, #81, 12″ **60.00**

White Rose
Basket, #363, 10″ **60.00**
Basket, #364, 12″ **75.00**
Bowl, #387, 4″ **30.00**
Bowl, #653, 4″ **30.00**
Bowl, #653, 3″ **25.00**
Cornucopia, #143, 6″ **25.00**
Cornucopia, #144, 8″ **35.00**
Double cornucopia, #145, 8″ **40.00**
Ewer, #981, 6″ **35.00**
Ewer, #990, 10″ **75.00**
Ewer, #993, 15″ **100.00**
Frog, #41 .... **25.00**
Pitcher, #1324 .... **60.00**
Tea set, #1 .... **85.00**
Urn vase, #147, 8″ **50.00**

Wincraft
Basket, #208, 8″ **40.00**
Basket, #209, 12″ **60.00**
Cornucopia, #222, 8″ **30.00**
Ewer, #216, 8″ **40.00**
Ewer, #217, 6″ **35.00**
Planter, #231, 10″ **45.00**
Tea set, #271, 3 pc **75.00**
Vase, #272, 6″ **30.00**
Vase, #282, 8″ **40.00**
Vase, #284, 10″ **50.00**
Vase, #285, 10″ **50.00**
Vase, #290, 10″ **150.00**

Windsor
Candlestick, w/handles, 4½″ pr **95.00**
Vase, w/fern, ball bottom, concave top w/handles, 9″ **200.00**
Vase, w/fern, large ear handles, 7″ **175.00**
Vase, w/handles, 5″ **60.00**

Wisteria
Bowl vase, w/handles, 4″ **65.00**
Console bowl, 12″ **85.00**
Jardiniere & ped, 24½″ **650.00**
Urn vase, ball shape w/sm shoulder handles, 7½″ **75.00**
Vase, broad top, funnel bottom w/long angled handles, 9″ ... **95.00**
Vase, bulbous w/angle rim handles, 7″ **75.00**
Vase, cylinder w/angle rim handles, 10″ **95.00**
Vase, flared sides, rim handles, 8″ **75.00**
  Narrow neck, handles, 8″ **80.00**
Vase, widens to below midpoint, handles, 6″ **65.00**
Wall pocket, 8″ **175.00**

Woodland
Vase, bulbous w/narrow flared neck, 15″ **900.00**
Vase, floral, 6″ **450.00**
Vase, large floral, 19″ **1,500.00**
Vase, slim neck, bulb bottom, floral, 7″ **450.00**
Vase, square top half, full bottom, petal ft, 11″ ..... **650 .00**
Vase, twist panels, floral, 10″ **600.00**
Vase, wide shoulder, floral, 6½″ **450.00**

Zephyr Lily

Ashtray	35.00
Basket, #393, 7"	45.00
Basket, #394, 8"	50.00
Basket, #395, 10"	65.00
Bowl, #474, 8"	40.00
Bowl, #671, 4"	30.00
Console boat, #475, 10"	45.00
Cookie jar, #5, 10"	95.00
Cornucopia, #203, 6"	35.00
Ewer, #23, 10"	75.00
Ewer, #24, 15 "	95.00
Jardiniere & ped	275.00
Tea set, #7	85.00
Vase, #137, 10"	50.00
Vase, #138, 10"	45.00
Wall pocket, 8"	35.00

Rowland & Marsellus

Though the impressive back stamp seems to insist otherwise, Rowland Marsellus & Co. were not Staffordshire potters, but American importers who commissioned various English companies to supply them with the blue printed historical ware, a popular import item since the early 1800s. Plates, cups and saucers, pitchers and platters with historical events, famous people or commemorative themes were sold as souvenirs from 1890 to 1920. The mark may be in full or R. & M. in a diamond.

Cup & saucer, scenic reserves	40.00
Cup, farmer's; Take Ye a Cup of Kindness	50.00
Pitcher, American Independence, 7"	225.00
American Pilgrims, 5½"	200.00
Discovery of America, 7½"	225.00
Historical scenes, 8"	150.00
Plate, 1620 Plymouth Rock	45.00
Bangor, Maine	45.00
Charles Dickens portrait, rolled edged, 10"	35.00
Charlotte, N.C.	45.00
Clara Burton Birthplace, fruit rim	35.00
Cleveland, Ohio, central vignette & border	40.00
Denver, rolled edge	35.00
Detroit	45.00
Famous Musicians & Composers	45.00
John & Priscilla Alden, 10"	20.00
Kalamazoo, Mich.	45.00
Landing of Hendrich Hudson	50.00
Mass. State House, 10"	20.00
Miles Standish, blue & white, 10"	50.00
Miles Standish, yellow, brown & green, 10"	95.00
New York City	50.00
Plymouth Rock, rolled rim, 7 vignettes, 10"	48.00
Views of Peoria, 10"	65.00
Washington at Prayer at Valley Forge, 10"	65.00

Royal Bayreuth

Founded in 1794 in Tettau, Bavaria, the Royal Bayreuth firm originally manufactured fine dinnerwares of superior quality. In more recent times, they have produced lines of dinnerware and accessory items such as humidors, vases, ashtrays and boxes in patterns called Rose Tapestry, Sunbonnet Babies, Beach Babies and Devil and Cards. These are highly sought by today's collectors. Figural creamers, sugar bowls and shakers in the shape of tomatoes, grapes, shells and animals were made in abundance.

In the listing that follows, BM indicates pieces that are stamped with the logo in blue ink, GM indicates a green mark.

Ashtray, accordion player, china, sgnd Honer	32.00
Clown, MOP, lg	135.00
Corinthian	30.00
Devil & Cards, BM	65.00
Devil's head, BM	170.00
Eagle	165.00
Elk	125.00
Goose, BM	375.00
Goose girl & farm, figural spade w/blue rim edge	55.00
Goose w/frog in beak	285.00
Heart, lady w/man playing lyre, castle, boat, 5"	55.00
Hunting scene, triangular, sgnd, gold trim	50.00
Turkey	295.00
Basket, florals, heavy gold, reticulated triple handle, 8"	140.00
Little Bo Peep, mini, ftd	225.00
Basket, Rose Tapestry, 3 color roses, 5x5x3"	375.00
Rose Tapestry, 3 color roses, 4¼" wide	350.00
Rose Tapestry, entwined handle, 4"	290.00
Rose Tapestry, lg pink roses, 6x6½x3¾"	475.00
Tapestry, dancing couple, gold banded, BM, 4¼"	239.00
Tapestry, w/portrait, ruffled top	425.00
Bell, Beach Babies, orig clapper	275.00
Little Bo Peep, china, unmkd	95.00
Sunbonnet Babies	275.00
Bon-bon, men in sailing ships scene, leaf shape, BM, 6½"	80.00
Sunbonnet Babies fishing, spade shape, 5¼"	190.00
Bowl, enameled ivory, ftd, open work	145.00
Grapes, purple & green, blown out, sgnd, 10½"	235.00
Jack & Jill, 3"	105.00
Jack Horner, 3"	105.00
Lettuce, 10x4"	240.00
Little Boy Blue, 4"	115.00
Poppy, red, deep, unmkd, 6½"	75.00
Rose Tapestry, master berry, 10½"	465.00
Rose, pink, yellow, small	245.00
Roses, blown out cornucopias, fluted rim	80.00
Sand Babies, cereal, 7½"	125.00
Seal on sea shore, 4¼"	50.00
Snow Babies, 2 girls w/sled, ftd, scalloped	85.00
Sunbonnet Babies, 2 children darning, baby's serving bowl	165.00
Sunbonnet Babies, large serving	105.00
Tomato, salad	75.00
Box, colonial scene tapestry, pin, oval	145.00
Colonial scene tapestry, powder, dome shaped, unmkd	155.00
Fisherman, w/cover, 2½x4"	60.00
Little Miss Muffet, pin, oval	75.00
Rose Tapestry, 3 color, 4x4¾" across, 1¾" tall	350.00
Rose Tapestry, 3 color, covered, lg	245.00
Rose Tapestry, 3 color, powder, round	215.00
Rose Tapestry, jewel, round, covered	225.00
Rose Tapestry, orange roses, powder, covered	235.00
Rose Tapestry, powder, covered, pink	145.00
Tapestry, powder, melon shaped, 3 gold feet, BM	195.00
Cake plate, Brittany Girls, open handled, 10½"	95.00
Little Bo Peep, open handled, 10½"	145.00
Little Jack Horner, open handled, lg	145.00
Rose Tapestry, 3 color roses, lg open handle	235.00
Cake set, Rose Tapestry, 7 pc	900.00
Candleholder, prospector, BM, 5½"	100.00
Girl w/dog, shieldback, gr background	245.00
Little Bo Peep, shieldback, BM	275.00
Little Miss Muffet, shieldback	275.00
Storks, blk w/wht enameling, pale gr color, BM, 4"	90.00
Sunbonnet Babies, shieldback, BM	295.00

Ship scene, blue, pair, 6″ 185.00
Celery, lobster, BM 125.00
Chocolate pot, Rose Tapestry, w/4 cups & saucers 1,500.00
   Rose Tapestry 1,000.00
   Snow Babies 225.00
   Sunbonnet Babies 225.00
Clock, daisy tapestry 375.00
   Rose Tapestry, 3 color roses, 4″ 375.00
Compote, poppy, pastel orange satin lustre, leaf stem, 3¾″ ... 265.00
   Poppy, pastel 250.00
   Sunbonnet Babies, 2¾x5¾″ 295.00
Cracker jar, tomato 285.00
Creamer, alligator, BM, 4½″ 145.00
   Apple, BM, 3¾″ 80.00
   Beetle, red, old Tettau mk 200.00
   Bellringer, BM 245.00
   Bird of paradise 185.00
   Bull, blk, red trim, BM, 'Plympkton, NS' 95.00
   Bull, brownish 145.00
   Bull, grey 125.00
   Butterfly, w/spread wings 150.00
   Cavaliers, BM, 3″ 67.50
   Cat, blk 135.00
   Cat, calico 295.00
   Cat, grey 78.00
   Chimpanzee, BM, 4″ 190.00
   Chrysanthemum Tapestry, BM, 3″ 180.00
   Clown, red, BM, 3¾″ 145.00
   Coachman, redcoat, BM, 4¼″ 150.00
   Conch, pearlized, gr leaves, sgnd, 5″ 65.00
   Conch shell & red lobster, low scuttle form 70.00
   Corinthian, blk, 4½x1½″ 65.00
   Corinthian, yellow w/rust lining, BM, 3¾″ 85.00
   Cow, figural, blk 135.00
   Cow, figural, brown, mottled 175.00
   Cow scenic, 2¾″ 50.00
   Cow scenic, tankard shape, BM, 3¾″ 65.00
   Crow, blk 100.00
   Devil, red 115.00
   Devil & Cards, GM 75.00
   Duck 120.00
   Eagle 135.00
   Elk, GM 82.50
   Fish head, BM 150.00
   Frog, gr 120.00
   Frog, red 135.00
   Girl w/basket, BM 325.00
   Girl w/candle 85.00
   Girl w/dog 75.00
   Jack & Beanstock 115.00
   Jack & Jill 65.00
   Jack Horner 115.00
   Kangaroo 350.00
   Lemon 75.00
   Little Bo Peep, BM 100.00
   Little Boy Blue 55.00
   Little Jack Horner 65.00
   Little Miss Muffett, tall 120.00
   Lobster, red 60.00
   Man in mountain, BM 110.00
   Man in mountain, unmkd, 4″ 70.00
   Mountain goat, BM, 3¾″ 145.00
   Oak leaf, BM 100.00
   Orange 85.00

Pansies, purple 115.00
Parakeet 175.00
Peach 165.00
Pelican 80.00
Penguins, blk, sq, yellow 95.00
Pig 295.00
Pink poppy, MOP, 3¾ 125.00
Platypus 350.00
Platypus, BM 550.00
Polar bear 375.00
Poodle, blk 120.00
Poodle, grey 135.00
Poppy, BM, 3½″ 80.00
Robin, sgnd 175.00
Rooster 165.00
Rose Tapestry, 3 color roses, squat shaped 125.00
Rose Tapestry, BM, 3½″ 195.00
Rose Tapestry, pinched nosed, pink, 3½″ 125.00
Rose Tapestry, waisted, pink 125.00
Sand Babies, BM 120.00
Seal, grey, BM, 4″ 185.00
Seal, grey, GM, 4″ 125.00
Seal on sea shore 70.00
Sheep in field, BM, 3½″ 67.50
Shell, BM, 3″ 80.00
Snow Babies 85.00
St Bernard head 165.00
Storks, gr background, blk w/wht, BM, 4¾″ 70.00
Strawberry 100.00
Strawberry, leaf front, gold entwined handle, 3¾″ .. 77.00
Sunbonnet Babies, squat 125.00
Tapestry, pinch snout, 'Cavaliers', sgnd Dixon 450.00
Tavern scene, tapestry 125.00
Tomato 50.00
Turtle, BM 250.00
Water buffalo, blk 115.00
Water buffalo, grey 110.00
Water buffalo, wht 115.00
Watermelon 135.00
Woman w/basket, seashore, BM, 3½″ 67.50
Cup & saucer, dice, BM 110.00
   Jack & Jill, full size 175.00
   Old Mill, waterfall, church, demitasse 35.00
   Poppy, red, demitasse 160.00
   Rose, pink 165.00
   Shell 65.00
   Sunbonnet Babies, demitasse 105.00
   Sunbonnet Babies, sweeping & mending, BM 195.00
Cup, grape, white pearlized, demitasse 40.00
   Sunbonnet Babies 105.00
Desk set, 4 pc, pink w/gold, gold mk 395.00
Dish, apple, w/cover 65.00
   Conch shell, candy 45.00
   Conch shell, w/handle 150.00
   Inn scene, Club-shaped, GM, 4½x4¾″ 35.00
   Leaf, iridescent, BM, 7x6″ 85.00
   Little Jack Horner, Club 65.00
   Lobster, covered, BM, 5″ 85.00
   Maple leaf, nut 150.00
   Pearlware, candy, leaf form 68.00
   Rose Tapestry, BM, 5¾″ 165.00
   Rose Tapestry, clover leaf shape, orange roses ... 175.00
   Rose Tapestry, clover leaf shape, pink 125.00
   Rose Tapestry, covered 200.00

Rose Tapestry, leaf, candy 175.00
Sunbonnet Babies, cleaning, pin, heart shape, BM 175.00
Dresser tray, Colonial scene tapestry 195.00
Goat scene tapestry 150.00
Rose Tapestry, 3 color roses, sgnd, BM 375.00
Rose Tapestry, pink, 19″ 195.00
Sand Babies 165.00
Tapestry, pin, roses w/courting scene in center, BM 450.00
Violet Tapestry 195.00
Frame, Rose Tapestry 425.00
Hair receiver, oyster & pearl, gold lid 185.00
Pansy, pink pearlized 185.00
Rose Tapestry, 3 gold feet 245.00
Rose Tapestry, gold foot, BM 140.00
Rose Tapestry, pink 135.00
Sheep, hp 70.00
Sunbonnet Babies 140.00
Hatpin holder, floral decor 38.00
Sunbonnet Babies, w/pin tray 150.00
Humidor, tobacco 280.00
Troubadours, sgnd Dixon, tall 295.00
Inkwell, elk, orig insert, w/cover, place for desk pcs & pen rests, BM 250.00
Sand Babies, no lid 125.00
Snow Babies 95.00
Jam jar & plate, green grape 185.00
Jar, farmer & turkeys, powder 98.00
Grape, cracker, pearlized, unmkd 350.00
Strawberry 195.00
Jug, Jack & Beanstalk, mini 75.00
Loving cup, Sunbonnet Babies, ironing, 3-handles, miniature . . 300.00
Match holder, clown, hanging 190.00
Devil & Cards, hanging 235.00
Rose Tapestry, 3 color roses, hanging 220.00
Mountain goat, hanging 250.00
Snow Babies, triangle shape, hanging 225.00
Mayonnaise, Goose Girl 105.00
Jack & Jill 115.00
Man fishing 105.00
Mug, Devil & Cards, beer, GM, 5″ 135.00
Jack & Beanstalk, child's 95.00
Snow Babies, 3″ 100.00
Sunbonnet Babies, BM 125.00
Mush set, Sunbonnet Babies, child's 220.00
Mustard, lobster, covered, w/spoon 45.00
Lobster, w/ladle & underplate 89.00
Poppy, red 75.00
Rose, BM 225.00
Shell 45.00
Tomato, w/spoon 40.00
Nappy, Jack & Jill, heart-shaped, verse border, 5½″ 65.00
Sunbonnet Babies 240.00
Pin tray, Rose Tapestry, GM, 5¼″ 175.00
Sand Babies, 3½x5″ 90.00
Pitcher, clown, milk 165.00
Clown, water 525.00
Coachman, milk 160.00
Coachman, water 285.00
Conch, 4″ 80.00
Corinthian, milk, red lining, BM 85.00
Crow, blk, milk 165.00
Dachshund 260.00
Dachshund, milk 185.00
Devil & Cards, full figure devil handle, BM, 5″ 175.00
Devil & Cards, water, BM, 7″ 450.00

Devil & Cards, water, new issue 200.00
Eagle, milk, mkd 260.00
Eagle, water, oldest mark 525.00
Elk, water, lg 250.00
Fishermen, boat, BM, 4″ 85.00
Forest scene, milk, pinched spout, BM, 5½″ 319.00
Goat scene, tapestry, milk 125.00
Goose Girl, water, pinch spout, gold handle, BM 225.00
Lemon, milk 135.00
Little Miss Muffet, sgnd, 4½ 75.00
Melon, milk, BM 105.00
Robin, milk, unmkd 125.00
Rose, milk 420.00
Rose Tapestry, 3 color roses, pinched spout, BM, 3½″ 165.00
Rose Tapestry, cream 200.00
Rose Tapestry, milk, corset shape, pink 165.00
Rose Tapestry, milk, lg 250.00
Sand Babies, blue, sgnd, 2½″ 95.00
Snow Babies, milk, lg 125.00
Speckled trout, milk, BM 225.00
St Bernard, water 550.00
Strawberry, stem handle, rococco leaf top, 4″ 145.00
Sunbonnet Babies, cream 140.00
Sunbonnet Babies, milk, lg 200.00
Sunbonnet Babies, washing the floor, pinched spout, 4″ . . . 165.00
Tankard, cows in pasture, 4″ 95.00
Tapestry, 3 dogs & moose, BM, 4″ 175.00
Tomato, milk, BM 110.00
Tomato, water, BM, lg 265.00
Planter, Rose Tapestry, 3 color roses, 3″ 165.00
Rose Tapestry, yellow, 2 pc 385.00
Sand Babies, gold handles 115.00
Shell, Murex, lg 150.00
Ship scene, w/insert, reticulated sides, 3¾″ 110.00
Plaque, fishing scene tapestry 250.00
Rose Tapestry, 5 color roses, 9″ 475.00
Plate, girl w/dog, 6¼″ 70.00
Girl w/dog, 8″ 80.00
Gr leaf, stem loop handle, yellow flowers, 5½″ 17.50
Jack & Jill, 6″ 75.00
Ladies in plumed hats, scalloped, 7½″ 48.00
Little Bo Peep, 6¼″ 85.00
Little Boy Blue, 6″ 85.00
Oak leaf, pearlized 95.00
Poppy, wht, pearlized, BM, 8¼″ 80.00

Rose Tapestry, 4 colors, 9¼″ 250.00

Rose Tapestry, bread **390.00**
Rose Tapestry, silver trim, 8″ **500.00**
Sand Babies, 7½″ **100.00**
Seal on sea shore, 6″ **50.00**
Snow Babies, 6½″ **65.00**
Sunbonnet Babies, 8″ **165.00**
Sunbonnet Babies, cleaning, 6¼″ **130.00**

Sunbonnet Babies washing clothes, 6″ **130.00**
Relish, Sunbonnet Babies, washing, BM, 8x4″ **250.00**
Salt & pepper, elk, BM **125.00**
    Purple grape **110.00**
    Strawberry, unmkd **45.00**
    Tomato **45.00**
Salt dip, fishing scene, BM **60.00**
    Purple grape **30.00**
    Sunbonnet Babies, unmkd **235.00**
Saucer, Arab w/horse scene **6.50**
    Jack & Beanstalk, 5¼″ **55.00**
    Sunbonnet Babies, 5½″ **125.00**
Shaving mug, w/cow scenic **275.00**
Slipper, tapestry, lady's, high heel, floral decor, BM **295.00**
Stein, elk **150.00**
String holder, rooster, wall mounted, BM **175.00**
Sugar & creamer, Corinthian, blk background, BM **75.00**
    Devil & Cards **150.00**
    Jester scene, open sugar, BM **85.00**
    Little Boy Blue, boat shaped, high handles **195.00**
    Lobster, covered sugar, sgnd **50.00**
    Oak leaf, BM **195.00**
    Pansies, purple, sgnd **250.00**
    Poppy, red, covered sugar **160.00**

Purple grapes **235.00**

Rose Tapestry, 3 color roses, covered sugar, gold handles .. **395.00**
Sunbonnet Babies, squat **250.00**
Sugar, conch shell, covered **45.00**
    Little Bo Peep, covered **90.00**
    Little Boy Blue **55.00**
    Lobster **72.50**
    Lobster, small, covered **45.00**
    Purple grape **75.00**
    Ring Around Rosie **185.00**
    Rose, covered, BM **250.00**
    Tomato **50.00**
Tea tile, Snow Babies **150.00**
    Teapot, orange, individual **175.00**
    Tomato **95.00**
Toothpick, Brittany Girl, 3 handles coming to the top **98.00**
    Cavalier scene, scuttle shape, BM, 3½″ **80.00**
    Conch shell **75.00**
    Corinthian, orange interior **50.00**
    Devil & Cards, 3″ **90.00**
    Elk **88.00**
    Hunt scene, scuttle **80.00**
    Mountain goat, 3 handled **60.00**
    Pheasant, unmkd **55.00**
    Poppy, wht **140.00**
    Rose Tapestry, basket, unmkd **225.00**
    Rose Tapestry, pink roses, ftd, w/handles **170.00**
    Snow Babies, cylinder shape on pedestal, small **150.00**
Tray, Jack & Jill, sq, 4″ **75.00**
    Sunbonnet Babies, playing card design **125.00**
Tumbler, castle scene tapestry **125.00**
Vase, castle scene tapestry, bud **125.00**
    Cavalier scene tapestry, bud, bulbous, 5″ **150.00**
    Cavaliers, red body, wht neck & shoulder, Dixon, 11½″ **60.00**
    Cow scene, roses on foot & rim, GM, 4½″ **95.00**
    Dutch boy & girl, bulbous, 9″ **110.00**
    Forest scene, 4¼″ **279.00**
    Gibson girls at top, gold rim, 4½″ **140.00**
    Girl w/doll, flow blue, unmkd, 4¾″ **125.00**
    Girl w/horse, hanging 9x4½″ **210.00**
    Goat scene tapestry, handled, 8″ **165.00**
    Jack & Beanstalk, mini handled, 3″ **100.00**
    Oak Leaf, gr glossy, 3″ across, 2¾″ tall **58.00**
    Period couple, 5¼″ **170.00**
    Rose Tapestry, 3 color roses, BM, 4″ **140.00**
    Rose Tapestry, 3 color roses, lg bottom to smaller top, 4½″ **285.00**
    Scenic tapestry, 4″ **180.00**
    Seal on sea shore, 3¾″ **95.00**
    Ship scene, 5½″ **75.00**
    Sunbonnet Babies, med **200.00**
Wall pocket, court jester, 9″ **95.00**
    Devil & Cards, unmkd **220.00**
    Grapes, blownout, leaves & vine, 9½x5½″ **220.00**
    Rose Tapestry **425.00**

Royal Bonn

    Royal Bonn is a fine-paste porcelain, ornately decorated with scenes, portraits or florals. The factory was established in the mid-1800s in Bonn, Germany; however most pieces found today are from the latter part of the century.

Bisquit jar, florals, bulbous **90.00**
Clock, iris & buds, lion head feet, 1880s, 14x10″ **650.00**
Clock, florals, gr, 5½″ **65.00**

Flowers & gold trim, blue china case, boudoir, brass works . **135.00**
Compote, scenic, sail boats on lake, 3x9½" **80.00**

Cup & saucer, Chrysanthemum, Germany **100.00**
Plate, portrait, man, blues, scalloped, hanging plate **325.00**
   Portrait, man, reticulated one side, rare **375.00**
   Urn, w/lid, scenic; obverse: florals, gold handles, finial & ft, 14¾" **275.00**
Vase, Amphora shape, allover floral decor, gold overlay, 12".. **135.00**
   Cows & farm in panel, ped, sgnd, handles, 12¼x5" dia **195.00**
   Deco floral band, turquoise, gold, bulbous base, 16" **150.00**
   Floral, bottle, gold, mkd, 13" **128.00**
   Floral decor, gold & gr bands, 5¾x6½" dia **100.00**
   Floral w/gilt edging, beige ground, gilt handles, sgnd, 10½". **115.00**
   Florals, gold, lion head handles, 1890, 14" **240.00**
   Lady's bust, sgnd, well mkd, 7x6½" dia **280.00**
   Lilac color flowers, sgnd, 8" **85.00**
   Portrait, sgnd, 12½" **295.00**
   Portrait, woman, hp, deep rose, gold, sgnd, 7½" **425.00**
   Roses, scrolled antique gold & gr trim, pastel, 20" **350.00**
   Tapestry, allover florals, trees, 12½x7" **225.00**
Wall plate, portrait, flowing blue, one side reticulated **385.00**

Royal Copenhagen

The Royal Copenhagen Manufactory was established in Denmark in about 1775 by Frantz Henrich Muller. When bankruptcy threatened in 1779, the Crown took charge, and the fine dinnerware and objects of art produced after that time carries the familiar logo, the crown over three wavy lines.

Bowl, w/mermaid, #12481, 6½x3½" **135.00**
Box, covered, gold & floral decor, mk, 1894 .... **60.00**
Cup & saucer **130.00**
Decanter, w/stopper, Rosenberg Castle, KGX, #4378 .... **50.00**
Figurines
Bear cub, w/foot in mouth, mkd: KK, Faience, #21434, 2½x3½" **35.00**
Boy, Wee Willie Winkie, w/umbrella, 6" **95.00**
Cat, grey striped, sitting, playing w/tail, #340, 7" **190.00**
   Grey w/wht chest & paws, sitting, #1759, 1803 .... **88.00**
   Sitting, w/green eyes, 5¾" **95.00**
Cockerel & hen, 1930, 10" **200.00**
Dachshund pup, chasing tail, #1407, 4½" **80.00**
   Lying on back, #1408, 3x4" **75.00**
Lhasa Apso, seated, looking backward, 6x5" **200.00**
Lovebirds, 5½" **95.00**
Mermaid on stomach, 1920 .... **150.00**
Nude, standing, 1915 .... **150.00**
Penguin, pastel colors, 3" **125.00**
Puppy, sprawling, 1 ear flipped back, #156, 7½" **280.00**
Rabbit, #1691, 1¾" **28.00**
Satyr, holding his ears as lg bird shrieks, #2113, 7x5½" **250.00**

Kneeling, holding parrot w/long tail, #752, 8x4" **250.00**
Siamese cat, #2851/3281, 7½" **165.00**

Plaque, classical scenes, pair **150.00**
   With dragon, by Krog, 1898, 12" **85.00**
Plate, dinner, Open Lace **90.00**
Platter, 14½" **250.00**
Teapot **240.00**
Vase, blue florals, 8" **45.00**
   Exotic blossom, #2687, 5" **50.00**
   Painted cactus, 4½" **55.00**
   Seascape, grass & butterfly decor, 6½" **50.00**
   Studio pottery, relief figures, sgnd Knud Kyhn, 1923, 5¾x3¾" **300.00**

Royal Copley

Royal Copley is a decorative type of pottery made by the Spaulding China Company in Sebring, Ohio, from 1939 to 1960. In addition to the Royal Copley mark, some pieces were also marked with the company's name.

Ashtray, pink bird on gr flower, 5" **4.00**
Figurine, bird, gr, blue, brown & red, 6½" **7.50**
   Blackamoor, full & kneeling figures, brown faces, holding drums, pr **38.00**
   Deer & fawn, brown **19.00**
   Indian boy standing by pot, brown, yellow & gr label **10.00**
   Oriental girls w/lg hats, pr **27.00**
   Pigtailed girl, eyes shut, pink bow in dk hair, hat **8.50**
Pitcher, pears, peaches in relief, blue, 8" **12.00**
Planter, bird on apple **8.00**
   Bird on stump, pink, yellow & blk **8.50**
   Bluebird, open center **10.00**
   Cat figural w/ball of yarn, 8x6" **18.00**
   Deer head, open center, 6½x7" **10.00**
   Girl in yellow dress w/watering can **7.50**
   Hen & rooster, orig label, 8¼" **25.00**
   In form of row of flowers, turquoise, rose & yellow, 3x7" **6.00**
   Leaping gazelles, greens, 6½x6" **8.50**
   Oriental girl w/hat, yellow pot, 8" **10.00**
   Rooster, multi color, 7½" **7.50**
Vase, horsehead, lt brown w/yellow mane, 8" **9.00**
   Raised ivy, 7" **5.00**
   Raised leaves, flat sides handles, chart & brown, 6x7½" **6.00**
   Standing Chinese girl figural, holds pot in each hand, 8" **8.50**
Wall pocket, apple **10.00**
   Chinese boy, big grey hat, rose shirt **12.00**
   Chinese girl w/big yellow hat, gr dress **12.00**
   Farm girl **7.50**
   Fruit decor **8.00**
   Indian head, lg **22.50**
   Kneeling angel, blonde hair, pink robe, label, pr **20.00**
   Rooster in relief **12.00**
   Round w/fruits, pastel, sgnd **14.00**
   Spaniel head, brown, sgnd **14.00**

Royal Crown Derby

In the latter years of the 1870s, a new firm, the Derby Crown Porcelain Company Ltd. began operations in Derby, England. Since 1890, when they were appointed Manufacturers of Porcelain to Her Majesty their fine porcelain wares have been known as Royal Crown Derby. Their earliest wares were marked with a crown over 'Derby'; often a complicated dating code indicated the year of manufacture. After 1890, the 'Royal Crown Derby, England', mark was employed; in 1921, 'Made In England' was substituted in the wording. 'Bone China' was added after 1945.

Box, ftd, 1909, 3½x3" **90.00**
Bud vase, florals on cream ground, handles end in gilt mask, 4½", pr **535.00**
Cabinet vase, florals, hp, yellow ground, 6½" **365.00**
  Trumpet shape, florals, on cream ground, hp, 8", pr **600.00**
Cake plate, Imari **200.00**
Cup & saucer, cobalt, gold, orange, peonies, gilt, 1910 . . . . . **42.00**
  Daffodils, flowers, gold, 1889 . . . . **55.00**
  Hexagon w/gold twist handle, brown decor, vines, 1891 . . . . . **70.00**
  Imari, #8540 . . . . **32.00**
  Lavender, floral sprays, sgnd, 4 cups & saucers **150.00**
  Loop handle, Imari pattern **75.00**
  Sculptured gold & wht **50.00**
Ewer, applied twist bracket handle, ovoid base, wht w/gold trim, 6½" **295.00**
Figurine, farm boy w/grapes, cabbage, 7" **785.00**
  Sealyham dog **48.00**
  'Summer', King Street Derby, 9" **275.00**
Plate, dessert, set of 6, 9" **240.00**
  Imari type, gold trim, 8½" **35.00**
  Japan pattern, 1939, 10½" **70.00**
  Mikado, blue, 10" **32.50**
Pot, covered, ftd, Imari **85.00**
Soup plate, Japan pattern, 1940, 9" dia **50.00**
Toothpick cellar, floral reserve, hp, gr ground, 3½" **235.00**
Torte stand, Imperial blank, Imari pattern #2451, 5½x9" dia . **300.00**
Trinket box, orange & blue decor, gold trim, ftd, 1909, 3", pr **175.00**
Urn, covered, center floral motif, gold, cobalt, gr, England, 9½" **675.00**
Vase, 2 handled, florals on yellow ground, 1880, 7x6" dia **235.00**
  Single hp blossom, pink ground, 10" **245.00**

Royal Dux

The Duxer Porzellan Manufactur was established by E Eichler in 1860. Located in what is now Duchcov, Czechoslovakia, the area was known as Dux, Bohemia, until WWI. Several marks have been used over the years, all variations of the acorn mark---Eichel in German meaning 'acorn'. The Art Nouveau figurines and decorative wares were imported into the United States at the turn of the century, and were marketed at moderate prices.

Bowl, girl sets on side holding flowers, oval **595.00**
Centerpiece, leaves & flowers, buds on gilded handles, 10" **60.00**
Figurine, 17th century couple, cobalt w/pastels **200.00**
  2 birds on branch, mkd, 7½" **110.00**
  Bird of Paradise, standing in marsh, 14" **90.00**
  Bird on limb, dk brown, blue-grey, 6x4" **50.00**
  Bird on stump w/pinecones, yellow w/brown, 8x7" **39.50**
  Bohemia lady w/harp on lg conch shell, 10x10¾" **495.00**
  Bohemia peasants, natural colors, pr, 11½x4" dia **595.00**
  Cockatoo on limb w/flowers, 15" **125.00**
  Cockatoo sitting on branch, 7" **46.50**
  Couple, man w/mandolin, lady w/rose, sgnd, 9x6", pr **155.00**
  Cow w/milkmaid **425.00**
  Doe & buck jumping over log, 8x12" **68.50**
  Donkey w/saddle & eye guards **295.00**
  Eagle w/head turned, full wing span, 6½x6" **60.00**
  Elephant w/trumpet up, browns w/beige, 8x11" **75.00**
  Elephant w/trunk up, beige & brown, 6½x8½" **65.00**
  Fish, dk brown & blk w/deep gr curved tail, 7½x9" **56.00**
  Fish, rearing up w/tail curled, ivory base, 8x3½" **48.00**
  German Shepherd, border collie, 8x9½" **245.00**
  German Shepherd lying w/head up, ears erect, 5x12" **55.00**
  German Shepherd sitting up, blk on tan, 8½x3½" **34.50**
  Girl, 13½" **265.00**
  Girl playing mandolin, 34" **1,500.00**
  Girl w/cow & bucket **275.00**

Hunter w/pheasant in hand, 14" **325.00**
Huntsman on horse beside 3 leaping hounds, 19x20" **600.00**
Lady w/blue dress, 10" **150.00**
Lion, walking, natural coloring, 5x9" **28.50**

Man on camel, 23½" **600.00**
Parrot sitting on perch, blue w/yellow chest **145.00**
Penguin, 6x3½" **32.00**
Polar bear, 10x15x8½" **160.00**
Polar bear walking, 8x12" **95.00**
Princess, seated, gold ruffled dress, mkd, 10x13" **220.00**
Rearing horse, lt brown, 13x7½" **165.00**
Seated nude woman, pastel coloring, 20" **400.00**
Setter, sitting, reddish brown, 6x3" **36.50**
Setter w/duck, pink triangle mk, 7x14" **120.00**
Squirrel sitting up, tail erect, brown, sgnd, 9½x9" **56.00**
Wild turkey on stump, blue chest & head, 6½x8" **56.00**
Vase, 3 lg orange poppies on gr background, 15" **125.00**
  Blown out geraniums, 2 handles, Art Nouveau design, 16" . . **165.00**
  Grapes & vine handles, 15½" **300.00**
  Oriental figures, 7½", pr **300.00**

Royal Flemish

Royal Flemish was made from the late 1880s, and was patented in 1894 by the Mt. Washington Glass Co. Transparent glass was enameled with one or several colors, and the surface divided by a network of raised lines suggesting leaded glass work. Some pieces were further decorated with enameled florals, birds or Roman coins.

Biscuit jar, embossed dragons **2,300.00**
  Roman coins, medallions, silver top & handle, 9" **2,000.00**
Cologne bottle, butterfly & daisy, 5½" **4,000.00**
Cracker jar, signed Mt Washington **1,100.00**
Ewer, chrysanthemums, heavy gold, blue & tan panels **3,800.00**
Sweetmeat, wht & yellow mums, allover gold, turtle on rim, 4" **950.00**
Vase, chrysanthemums, gold, bulbous to thin, ruffled, 13" . . **1,400.00**
  Cosmos, chrysanthemum & scrolls, waisted ovoid to thin, 13" **1,500.00**
  Jeweled, multi color enameling, 12½" **2,500.00**
  Pink w/gold floral & cupids, eagle at top, 15½" **8,000.00**
  Roman medallions, gold decor, blue, gr, pink, rust handles, 8" **1,650.00**

Royal Rudolstadt

The hard paste porcelain that has come to be known as Royal Rudolstadt

was produced in Thuringia, Germany in the early 18th century. Various names and marks have been associated with this pottery---one of the earliest was a hayfork symbol associated with Johann Frederich von Schwarzburg-Rudolstadt, one of the first founders. Variations, some that included an R, were also used.

In 1854, Earnst Bohne produced wares that were marked with an anchor and the letters EB. Wares commonly found today are those made during the late 1800s and early 20th century. These are usually marked with an RW within a shield under a crown, with the words 'Crown Rudolstadt'. Those pieces marked 'Germany' were made after 1890.

Bust, lady w/elaborate gown, deluxe **550.00**
Chocolate set, orchid & gold decor, 7-pc **290.00**
Chocolate set, pink rose garlands, 9-pc, shield & crown mk . . . **265.00**

Chocolate set, lavender astors, gold trim, pot, 4 c/s **425.00**
Compote, blue opal, cranberry trim **35.00**
Cup & saucer, w/kewpies decor **70.00**
Dish, leaf form, multi floral decor, 7x8" **30.00**
Ewer, cream floral satin, gold handle **85.00**
Ewer, gold & ivory w/large floral design, 16" **290.00**
Fruit dish, hp cherry & leaf design, pierced sides, 11" dia **35.00**
Pitcher, hp floral decor, gold handle, 2-quart **75.00**
Plate, herdsman & flock of sheep, 6" **78.00**
Plate, shaded blue & cream ground, w/daisies & violets, Prussia, 13" **90.00**
Relish, shaded blue & cream ground, w/daisies & violets, Prussia, 8x4" **24.00**
Vase, chinoiserie, resembles carved ivory **90.00**
Vase, green, w/lady & dove, 7½" **52.00**
Vase, morning glories, tapestry, 1882 . . . . **100.00**
Vase, peacock figural **45.00**

Royal Worcester

The Worcester Porcelain Company was deeded in 1751. During the first, or Dr. Wall period (so called for one of its proprietors), porcelain reflecting an Oriental influence was decorated in underglaze blue. Useful tablewares represented the largest portion of production, but figurines and decorative items were also made. Very little of the earliest wares were marked, and can only be identified by a study of forms, glazes and the porcelain body which tends to transmit a greenish cast when held to light. Late in the '50s, a crescent mark was in general use, and rare examples bare a facsimile of the Meissen crossed swords. The first period ended in 1783 and the company went through several changes in ownership during the next 80 years. The years from 1783-1792 are refered to as the Flight period. Marks were

a small crescent, a crown with 'Royal', or an impressed 'Flight'. From 1792-1807 the company was known as Flight and Barr, and used the trademark F&B or B, with or without a small cross. 1807-1813 the company was under the Barr, Flight and Barr management; this era is recognized as having produced porcelain of the highest quality of artistic decoration. Their mark was B F B.

From 1813-1840, many marks were used, but the most usual was F B B under a crown, to indicate Flight, Barr and Barr. In 1840 the firm merged with Chamberlain; and in 1852 they were succeeded by Kerr and Binns. The firm became known as Royal Worcester in 1862.

Since 1930, Royal Worcester has been considered one of the leaders in the field of limited edition plates and figurines.

Basket, cream, gold & gr decor, handled, dated 1905 . . . . **159.00**
   Gold outline, woven pattern **120.00**
   White wicker w/gold decor, 1884 . . . . **300.00**
Biscuit jar, melon ribbed, cream w/multicolor florals, w/lid, purple mk **265.00**
   Raised gold leaves, floral decor, silver plated lid & handle . . **295.00**
Bouillon, covered, pink & wht **48.00**
Bowl, basketweave, hp flowers, 8¾" dia **285.00**
   Basketweave, satin grape leaves, openwork edge, 1890s, 9" dia **350.00**
   Gilt decor, shallow, from Wall era, 1750s **250.00**
Box, covered, apples, grapes & floral hp decor, 2x2¾" dia **65.00**
Bud vase, bamboo section shape, flowers in relief, 1908 mk, 4" **80.00**
Cache pot, 3-color florals, gold rim, bird handles, 4½" **45.00**
   Dolphin handles, Chamberlain period **495.00**
Candle snuffer, monk, blk mk **40.00**
   Nun, 1936 mk, 4" **50.00**
   Plumed hat, 1901, Granger mk **95.00**
   The Cook, 1894 . . . . **85.00**
Candlestick, cherub sitting on stump, blowing horn, figural, 7¾" **365.00**
   Dated 1889, 4½" **65.00**
   Greenaway figural, 1895, 10" **600.00**
Chocolate pot, bamboo handle & finial, purple mk, 7¼" **158.00**
Cologne bottle, reticulated, wht w/gold trim, Granger, 7" **365.00**
Compote, cobalt & gold **200.00**
Creamer, floral multicolor decor on cream ground **195.00**
   Gilt decor, Chamberlain era, 3" **245.00**
Cup, demitasse, Roanoke **35.00**
Cup & saucer, floral decor, 1895 mk **100.00**
   Tea, Charlotte's Whorl, from Wall era, 1765 . . . . **435.00**
Dessert set, multicolor floral center, pink rim, 9-pc, purple mk **450.00**
Dish, free form, polychrome florals, 1891 mk, 5½" dia **60.00**
   Leaf shape, 1890 mk, 4" long **25.00**
   Old Japan Fan pattern, scalloped rim, 1760s, 7¾", pr **1,700.00**
   Ribbed, Old Japan Fan pattern, 1700s **1,300.00**
   Shell shape, floral decor, handled, 1888 mk, 4" **60.00**
Ewer, dolphin handle, lemon & coral, overall gold & tracery, 7½" **195.00**
   Floral decor, 1889, 8½" **50.00**
   Floral decor, 1891 mk, 5½" **130.00**
   Gold tracery on cream, gold applied in relief on neck, 8½" . **395.00**
   Polychrome floral decor, 1891 mk, 11" **350.00**
   Salamander handle, gold spatter, gold/silver florals, 1880 mk, 11" **495.00**
Figurine, Against the Wind, 1870s, wht glaze, 12" **495.00**
   Allegro, Midsummer Night's Dream, 1860s **950.00**
   April, girl **125.00**
   At the Meet, Doris Lindner, 7¼" **450.00**
   British Red Cross Nurse, 9" **685.00**
   Cairo Water Carrier, #1250, 1880s, 8" **475.00**
   Canary, by Doughty **110.00**
   Castinet Dancer, sgnd Hadley, 1880 . . . . **985.00**
   Child Born on Sabbath Day, Doughty **55.00**
   Chinoiserie figure **150.00**
   Countries of the World--Burma **69.00**

China **65.00**
  England **135.00**
  India **150.00**
Dandelion #3084 . . . . **150.00**
Dole Yellow Hammer #3377 . . . . **125.00**
December Child, F Doughty, 6″ **165.00**
Dog, Doris Lindner, 1938 . . . . **245.00**
Dutch Boy & Girl, #2939 & #2929, pink mk, pr . **365.00**
Fox Terrier, wht w/blk & brown spots, 1930s, 3¾″ **195.00**
Foxhound, #d, 6½″ **285.00**
Grandmother's Dress, pink or yellow **125.00**
Hedge Sparrow, #3333 . . . . **65.00**
Huntsman & Hounds, Doris Lindner, 7½″ **500.00**
Indian Brave & Squaw w/Child, Gertner, 1932, 6½″, pr **325.00**
January, boy **125.00**
Joan, Doughty **40.00**
Johnnie, #3433 . . . . **185.00**
July, Doughty **60.00**
Little Jack Horner **130.00**
March, Doughty **60.00**
Mischief, purple mk, Doughty **150.00**
Monday's Child, girl **125.00**
Mountain Bluebirds, pair **1,900.00**
Nightingale, #3337 . . . . **85.00**
Wijinsky, Doris Lindner, w/certificate & plinth **1,750.00**
Only Me, #3226 . . . . **150.00**
Palomino Stallion, Doris Lindner, w/certificate & plinth **975.00**
Parakeet, Doughty, #2663 . . . . **110.00**
Parakeet Boy, #3087 . . . . **180.00**
Polo Player, Doris Lindner, 7″ **500.00**
Robin, by Doughty **125.00**
Saturday's Child, girl, old **95.00**
Sleepy Boy, Doughty **80.00**
Sunday's Child, blue smock **85.00**
Sweet Anne, F Doughty **110.00**
Swordfish, R Van Ruyckevelt, w/certificate **200.00**
Thursday's Child, boy **115.00**
Tuesday's Child, boy, new **65.00**
Two Babies **135.00**
Water Baby **175.00**
Wednesday's Child, girl, old **95.00**
Wind, 1918, 6″ **150.00**
Yankee, impressed #C-1231, 7″ **325.00**
Flower bowl, reticulated, peach & gold, ftd, 3x5½″ **235.00**
Jar, covered, melon form, floral decor, 1889 mk, 7″ **250.00**
Jug, beige, gilded, 5¼″ **150.00**
  Raised salamander on basketweave, branch handle, 1917 mk, 6″ **225.00**
  Ruby w/gilt vine decor, 6½″ **285.00**
  Snake handle w/gilding, early mk, 5″ **400.00**
Pitcher, 3 tiers w/floral decor, 1887 mk, 9″ **180.00**
  Bamboo handle, ivory w/floral decor, gilded, purple mk, 4″ . **110.00**
  Deer antler handle, gilt decor, 10″ **110.00**
  Exotic birds, from Wall era, 8″ **400.00**
    10″ **425.00**
  Flat-back, multicolor florals on cream, gold rims, 5″ **100.00**
  Floral decor, gold reeded handle, 7½″ **300.00**
  Floral multicolor motif on cream, rococo handle, purple mk, 5″ **195.00**
  Flowers & butterfly, gr mk **140.00**
  Leaves in relief, floral decor, 1887 mk, 6¼″ . . . **150.00**
  Lion head spout, floral decor, 1880s, 6″ **160.00**
  Morning glories, gold ram's head handle, late 1800s, 9¼″ . . **225.00**
  Multicolor florals on beige, gold trim, bulbous, purple mk, 5½″ **165.00**
  Robin hp decor, sgnd, gr mk, 3¼″ **95.00**
  Shell in relief, floral motif, 1892 mk, 6¼″ **150.00**

Plate, allover floral, lt blue w/brown, border, gold, 1887, 10½″ **225.00**
  Blue rim w/raised gold floral & swag decor, set of 12, 1925, 10¼″ **350.00**
  Floral decor, free form, 1890 mk, 8″ dia **150.00**
  Magenta & blue florals, bisque satin ground, purple mk, 8″ . . **85.00**
  Multifloral on beige, 6″ **125.00**
  Ornate gold band, sgnd & dated floral center, 11″ **200.00**
  Oval, fluted rim, 1892 mk, 8½″ long **70.00**
  Pink w/enameled purple flowers, 1880s, 9″ **95.00**
  Rococo edge, floral decor, 1895 mk, 8″ dia **60.00**
  Set of 10, each w/different floral decor, scalloped, 1882 mk, 6¾″ **375.00**
  Sulgrave Manor, hp by Crease, 1929 . . . . **75.00**
Platter, 1880 mk, 13x15″ **100.00**
  Allover floral, lt blue w/brown, border, gold trim, 1887, 15″ . . **75.00**
  Allover floral, lt blue w/brown, floral border, 1887, 11½″ **40.00**
Salt, open, shell shaped **65.00**
Shell dish, beige & ivory, w/flower inside, ftd, gilt trim, 3x4½″ **170.00**
  On coral branch, wht, w/gr mk **245.00**
Soup ladle, blue ivy leaves, handle w/brown leaf, blue mk **65.00**
Spill, embossed girls w/sunflowers & cattails, matched pr, 1908, 5¼″ **495.00**
Sugar, covered, gold leaf handles, floral decor on beige, purple mk **110.00**
Sugar & creamer, floral by M Hunt, 1941, 4″ **110.00**
Tankard, floral w/gold trim on cream, 9″ **150.00**
Tea bowl & saucer, underglaze blue, from Wall era, unmkd, ca 1770 **200.00**
Tea caddy, flowers, vines & berries in gilded relief, ivorene ground, 4″ **60.00**
Teapot, flowers on tinted ground, rococo, 1894 mk, 9½″ **275.00**
  Pink & orange floral, serpent handle, gold, 1890, 5x6″ **385.00**
Vase, 3 gold serpent handles, yellow, w/leaves, gr mk **345.00**
  U-shaped, double, gilded bamboo handle & leaves, gr mk, 8x5″ **200.00**
  Bamboo, w/2 spouts, bamboo handle, 1910 mk, 8½″ **250.00**
  Bamboo shape w/bamboo section handle, gilt trim, 1885, 10″ **100.00**
  Castle & cattle hp scene, high scrolled gold handles, Granger, 8″ **300.00**
  Castle scene, 3″ **110.00**
  Cherry blossoms & multifloral decor, 1886 mk, 8″ **140.00**
  Ferns on ivory ground, gold dolphin handles, 9″ **400.00**
  Fig shape, multicolor foliage on beige, gold trim, 1900 mk, 4¼″ **195.00**
  Figural flowers, hollyhocks, cream/coral, w/handles, 8″ **360.00**
  Finches on gilded vines, squatty shape, 4½″ **100.00**
  Floral decor, 2 handles, 1891 mk, 6″ **120.00**
  Hummingbird on front, gold w/raised flowers, 1888, 13¾″ . . **485.00**
  Lotus blossoms & turtle in relief, roots form ft, 1892, 4½″ . **225.00**
  Pilgrim, yellow w/hp florals, 8¼″ **525.00**
  Reticulated ivy-shaped decor, ornate, handled, sgnd, 1880, 12″ **235.00**
  Serpent handles, foliage, gold heron & butterfly, 1880s, 8x6″ **525.00**
  Shell decor, heavy gold trim, 1888 mk, 8½x5″ dia **475.00**
Urn, figural flowers at top, beaded handles, 8¼″ **320.00**

Wall pocket, figural parakeets, bracket, 7"................. **435.00**
    Lady slipper, 1883, 8½"................................. **260.00**
    Orchid, gold, brown & beige **250.00**
    Shell shaped, wht w/brown trim, 1880s **190.00**
Waste bowl, Old Japan Fan pattern, 1760s, 6¾" dia....... **1,000.00**

Roycroft

Near the turn of the century, Elbert Hubbard established the Roycroft Printing Shop in East Aurora, N.Y. Named in honor of two 17th century printer-bookbinders, the print shop was just the beginning of a community called Roycroft, which came to be known world wide. Hubbard became a popular personality of the early 1900s, known for his talents in a variety of areas, from writing and lecturing to manufacturing. The Roycroft community became a meeting place for people of various capabilities, and included shops for the production of furniture, copper, leather items and a multitude of other wares which were marked with the Roycroft symbol, an R within a circle below a stylized cross. Hubbard lost his life on the Lucitania in 1915; production in the community continued until the Depression.

Ashtray, for pipe **30.00**
Bookends, brass w/rings **50.00**
    Copper w/leather elephant inserts...................... **95.00**
    Door & knocker design, hammered copper **38.00**
    Hammered copper, heavy, crimped edges, 3x4" **38.00**
    Owls design **60.00**
    Viking ship design **60.00**
Bowl, 8" **40.00**
    Footed, Roycroft insignia, "Buffalo Pottery", 3x9"........ **125.00**
    Plain, 10½" **45.00**
    Silverplated, ruffled, 9½" **60.00**
Calendar holder... **60.00**
Candelabra, 6 holders, 15½"............................. **65.00**
Candlesticks, copper, circle design, mkd, 6x3½", pair........ **85.00**
    Hammered brass, pair **30.00**
    Silvered, pair **85.00**
Card tray, hammered copper **65.00**
Catalog, Some Books for Sale At Our Shop, 1904 .... **35.00**
Crumb tray set, 2-pc, hammered copper, sgnd **30.00**
Desk set, 6-pc **135.00**
Diary, 1935 .... **30.00**
Doll, bean bag, 'Clownie' **65.00**
Floor lamp, hammered copper, 'Bridge' style, parrot design ... **675.00**
Inkwell, hammered brass, w/lid, 3½" dia **30.00**
    Hammered copper, hinged lid, orig insert, tapered body, mkd **58.00**

Jug, brown, 5" **23.00**
Letter opener, also is a bookmark........................ **35.00**
Mustard jar, brown, w/cover, 4½"........................ **25.00**

Napkin ring, worked silver over copper, open ended rectangle .. **35.00**
Pen tray, early... **30.00**
Pencil holder, early..................................... **60.00**
Print, hand-colored, w/verse, on Roycroft paper **50.00**
Sconce, Sheffield finish.................................. **65.00**
Tray, 8½" dia, w/6 cups **75.00**
Vase, hammered copper, mkd, 4½"...................... **35.00**
    Hammered copper, mkd, 9"........................... **140.00**
    Miniature American Beauty shape, 6" **55.00**
Wall sconce, double, w/star & moon decoration............. **85.00**

Rubina

Rubina glass was made by several firms in the late 1800s. It is a blown art glass that shades from clear to red.

Basket, twist handle **175.00**
Bowl, clear foot w/shell edge, pillar effect in glass, 4x6"....... **95.00**
Celery vase, Inverted Thumbprint, ruffled rim............... **65.00**

Cheese cover, floral enamel, faceted ball finial, 5½"........ **125.00**
Pitcher, bulbous, Thumbprint, clear handle, pontil 7"....... **135.00**
    Diamond Quilted, clear handle, 8" **150.00**
    Gold floral decor, reeded handle w/lion ft base, 6½"...... **195.00**
    Melon ribbed, tricorn scalloped rim, reed handle, 8"....... **145.00**
Rose bowl, enameled decor, 2½" **65.00**
    Royal Ivy, frosted.................................... **95.00**
Rose bowl, overshot, 8 crimp top, 3½" **95.00**
Sweetmeat, enamel decor, Moser........................ **325.00**
    In plated cart shape holder **120.00**

Rubina Verte

Rubina Verte glass was introduced in the late 1800s by Hobbs, Brocunier and Co., of Wheeling, W. Va. Its transparent colors shade from red to clear to green.

Bowl, 10" **135.00**
Bud vase, geometric, medallion, enameled, 10½" **40.00**
Celery vase, 6½" **150.00**
    Inverted Thumbprint, Hobbs #314, 6½"................. **145.00**
Compote, Honeycomb, Cambridge........................ **85.00**
Creamer, ribbing, amber handle, 5" **220.00**
Cruet, w/cut stopper, 6½" **300.00**
Pitcher, water; Coinspot, lime handle, 7½" **300.00**
    Hobnail, matching tumbler **165.00**

Inverted Thumbprint, Hobb's, Brocunier, 7".............. **210.00**
Inverted Thumbprint, sq, mouth, bulbous, 7x5½" dia **250.00**
Rosebowl, opal, crimp top, wht florals, gold scrolls, 4x4½" dia **88.00**
Sauce, sq, Hobnail **45.00**
Tumbler, 10 Row Hobnail **165.00**
Vase, corset shape, enameling, ruffled top **130.00**
    Honeycomb, 10"....................................... **125.00**
    Ruffled, pink & wht flowers, blue bow, 12x5¼" dia........ **175.00**

Ruby Glass

Ruby glass has been produced since the last century; its deep ruby color is due to the reaction of heat on the gold content of the mixture.

Candy dish, fluted edge, vertical, 'T' center handle, 7½" dia ... **18.00**
Compote, jelly, Broken Column......................... **225.00**
Decanter, World's Fair 1893, Victoria Pioneer w/orig stopper... **65.00**
Tumble-up, panel cut, New England Glass Co **275.00**
Vase, globe, pontil, 11x10" dia **85.00**
Vase, ruby w/all over enameling, pedestal, 9".............. **200.00**

Ruby Stained

Ruby flashed or stained glass was made by the applicaton of a thin layer of color over clear. It was used in the manufacture of some early pressed glassware patterns, and was often used from the Victorian era well into the 20th century for souvenir items which were often engraved on the spot with the date, location and buyers name.

Basket, handled, 'Coney Island', 3½x2½" **20.00**
Berry set, Horseshoe Medallion, 5 pc **200.00**
    Master & 6 bowls, Vincent's Valentine **275.00**
    Spearpoint Band, 7 pc **100.00**
    Thumbprint, 7 pc, round **195.00**
Bowl, berry, Spearpoint Band w/excellent gold & frost band, sm **12.00**
Box, covered w/gold trim, 4½x3½" **33.00**
    Powder, Williamsbridge, N.Y., 3" dia.................. **25.00**
Box, souvenir, gold ft, 1946, 2½", illus **35.00**
Butter, Beaded Swag, covered **95.00**
    Majestic **135.00**
    Spearpoint Band **60.00**
Cakestand, Millard, large **145.00**
Compote, Block & Fan, 7" **27.50**
    Jelly, National's Eureka............................. **110.00**
    Jelly, Thumbprint................................... **55.00**

King Crown, 9½x8½"............................. **70.00**

Thumbprint w/etching, scalloped rim, 8½" **135.00**
Creamer, Block & Lattice.............................. **55.00**
    Button Arch, souvenir, 1901......................... **22.00**
    Nail, w/etching **70.00**
    O'Hara diamond w/etching **50.00**
Cruet, Block & Lattice, orig stopper, 'Big Button'........ **125.00**
    Block & Lattice, orig stopper, tall size **105.00**
Decanter, wine; Loop & Block, orig stopper.............. **95.00**
Goblet, Fern & Berry etching, set of 6 .... **395.00**
    Roanoke **30.00**
Lady's slipper, gold trim, Shriner's Indianapolis, 1941, 4¾".... **18.00**
Match holder, Button Arches base, souvenir.............. **25.00**
Mug, Box in Box, 3" **22.00**
    Button Arches, Revere Beach, 1907, 3" **20.00**
    Hobnail, Near Cut, Coleman, Michigan, notched handle, 3" .. **20.00**
    Hobnails, Montreal, 2½" **15.00**
    Lacy Medallion, souvenir, Marlow, N.H................ **31.00**
Pepper shaker, Portland **20.00**
Pitcher & 2 tumblers, Block & Double Bar **185.00**
    Button Arches, souvenir w/names, 7¼" **30.00**
    Tankard, Truncated Cube............................ **95.00**
    Thumbprint, w/Leaf & Berry, bulbous **110.00**
    Water, Nail, etched **95.00**
    Water, Plume **125.00**
    Water, Vincent's Valentine **250.00**
Salt shaker, Heisey Punty Band, etched, 1904 .... **25.00**
    Pioneer's Victoria **45.00**
Shot glass, mug, fluted base, Revere Beach, 1906 .... **11.00**
Spooner, plain **48.00**
    Spearpoint w/frost band **50.00**
Sugar, Arched Ovals, souvenir, 1917.................... **22.00**
Syrup, Hexagon Block **135.00**
    Majestic **165.00**
    Reverse Torpedo **165.00**
    Torpedo **155.00**
Table set, Pavonia, 4 pc **255.00**
    Tacoma, 4 pc **295.00**
    Triple Triangle, 4 pc............................... **295.00**
    York Herringbone, 4 pc **210.00**
Toothpick, Button Arches, 1906 .... **20.00**
Tumbler, Button Arches at base, child's souvenir.......... **25.00**
    Chippendale, Krystol **32.00**
    Engraved, World's Fair 1893 .... **45.00**
    Hobnail w/Ruby Band **25.00**
    Late Block **25.00**
    Loop Block **28.00**
    Octagonal, cut-to-clear, Bohemian, 3" **20.00**
    Pillow Encircled etched............................. **38.00**
    Souvenir, 1906.................................... **24.00**
    Triple Triangle **35.00**

Vase, souvenir **25.00**
Water set, Block & Lattice, 7 pc, bulbous pitcher **275.00**
    Hexagonal Block, 7 pc **175.00**

Ladder w/Diamond 'Tarentum', 7 pc **385.00**
Late Block, 7 pc, bulbous pitcher **365.00**
Red Block, 7 pc **265.00**
Winina, 7 pc, floral enamel decor **325.00**
Wine, Bull's Eye, souvenir, 1908 .... **15.00**
Co-op's Royal **15.00**
Wine, footed, panel w/wheel cut floral, illus **40.00**
Witch's Pot, souvenir, metal bail **20.00**

Rugs

Hooked

Hooked rugs are treasured today for their folk art appeal. It was a craft that was introduced to this country in about 1830 and flourished its best in the New England states. The prime consideration is not age, but artistic appeal. Scenes with animals, buildings and people, patriotic designs, or whimsical themes are prefered. Condition is, of course, also a factor. Marked examples bearing the stamps of Frost & Co., Abenakee, C.R. and Ouia are highly prized.

2 dogs in forest, blk border, worn, 25x39" **35.00**
Amish, green, beige & burgandy, 22x37" **80.00**
Black dog, landscape, house w/orange roof, 21x55" **130.00**
Blue bird, raised flowers, 1875, repaired, 70x30" **700.00**
Braided border, oval, 37x54" **50.00**
Circles w/rainbow border, 1800s, 60x24" **140.00**
Dog, recumbent, cranberry, brown, green **425.00**
Dog in barrel w/playful kitten, 27x50" **175.00**
Dog on striped field, 1800s **180.00**
Fireplace scene w/spinning wheel, some wear **95.00**
Floral center on cream, green & brown border, 37x56" **45.00**
Floral sprays, stylized, red, blue, ochre on tan, 1830s, 30x37" **850.00**
Floral w/scroll design border, wool, 66x43" **130.00**
Florals in brown, green, red, minor wear, 9x12" **85.00**
Flowering vine motif, 1800s, 22½x40" **80.00**
Greens & rose, mellowed colors, 22½x24½" **40.00**
Grenfell, geese, blue w/brown & grey border, 26x40" **550.00**
Horse, 'Peater', 39x26" **800.00**
House, fence, tree & anchor, 1800s, 26x36" **365.00**
House w/trees, 3 geometric borders, 1930s, 36x32" **145.00**
Hunting scene, folk art, 1910 .... **350.00**
Indian brave, colored feathers, mended, 19x29" **175.00**
Leaping deer, 38x25" **300.00**
Leaves, colored on grey w/blk border, 24x36" **40.00**
Lion in foliage, purple border **175.00**
Moose, red striped w/2 stars over its back, 21x30" **175.00**
Overlapping stars center, star corners, 1800s, 55x40" **135.00**
Roses, red on green & tan, 1950, 53x26" **20.00**
Scene w/farmers, oxen, tree, houses **360.00**
Ship, faded colors, 28x45" **80.00**
Squares w/flowers alternate w/log cabins, 23x40" **65.00**
Stylized flowers, braided border, wool, rag & yarn, 61x30" ... **150.00**
Table rug, tree of life, 1800s, on burlap, 14x20" **165.00**
Traditional floral, black border, old, 47x23½" **30.00**

Oriental

Afghan Hatchli, rust w/meandering border, 6x4½' **600.00**
Afghan Turkoman, flat weave, allover blue diamond on red, 8x12½' **500.00**
Afshar, floral design on blue, antique, 3x4½' **300.00**
Stylized florals, rust, peach, ivory, tan, blue, 4x4½' **275.00**
Baktiari, Persia, flowers, medallion, blue, 7x5' **1,550.00**
Balouchi, geometric medallions on blue w/rust border, 7½x4' . **425.00**
Lattice on blue w/floral border, 5½x3' **275.00**
Medallions in field & border, blue, rust, 4½x3' **210.00**
Balouchistan, allover latch work pattern, rose, blue, ivory, 3x6' **250.00**
Geometrics in rust, brown and ivory, 3x5½' **325.00**

Beshir, 4 blue medallions on rust, 5x4½' **225.00**
Bidjar, blue medallion on Herati pattern red field, 8x8½' **900.00**
Florals, bird & floral border, blue w/ivory, 4x6½' **1,300.00**
Geometrics, blue, red, green, 1940, 4½x6½' **595.00**
Caucasian Kuba, geometrics, stylized birds, blue, 3½x10½' ... **300.00**
Chichi, Caucasus, boxflower rows, Kufic border, blue, 6½x4½' **4,950.00**
Chinese, floral & medallion of ivory rose & blue on navy, 3x5½' **185.00**
Daghestan, Caucasus, lattice grid, star flowers, ivory, 4x2½' . **1,425.00**
Caucasian, multi patterned, ivory, 3½x4½' **465.00**
Flame stitch, blue, pink, green, antique, 7x5½' **210.00**
Gorevan, Persia, tree of life, salmon & blue, 12x8' **1,650.00**
Hamadan, 3 geometric medallions on blue, ivory floral border, 6x3½' **250.00**
Allover stylized floral, blue field, 3½x6½' **225.00**
Camel's hair, 3x16' **900.00**
Flowers, rose field, 3½x2½' **75.00**
Medallions & spandrels, red, blue, ivory, 4x7' **220.00**
Patterned, blue w/red, 5x7' **350.00**
Persian, florals, blue & ivory, 4x7' **235.00**
Rose, blue, brown, antique, 3½x5' **160.00**
Heriz, 3 medallions, ivory borders on red, 4½x3' **150.00**
Geometric medallion, red, blue, ivory & gold, 9½x12' **1,000.00**
Persia, medallion, leaf, vines, red w/blue, 12x9½' **6,500.00**
Indo-Kashan, animals, cloud bands, ivory & rust, 8x12' **3,300.00**
Indo-Tabriz, hunting scene w/horses & animals, red, 4x6½' ... **500.00**
Isfahan, blooming tree, birds & vine, red, 3½x5' **4,000.00**
Blooming tree, flying birds, serpent, cream, 7x4½' **2,900.00**
Central medallion, vines, red, blue, ivory, 7½x4½' **6,500.00**
Paradise, animal border, branches, cream, 4½x7' **3,850.00**
Karabagh, Causasus, stripe, stylized dragons, 5x3' **2,800.00**
Rose gold and tan, 3½x4' **130.00**
Karaja, 3 medallions on rust, 3x5' **190.00**
3 medallions, rust & gold on blue, 3x4' **125.00**
Persia, 3 rows medallions, red & indigo, 11x7' **1,850.00**
Kashan, equestrian figures, cream & salmon, 4x6½' **2,400.00**
Seaweed motif, boteh medallion, red, blue, 6½x4½' ... **2,850.00**
Kazak, Caucasus, hooked diamonds, orange, 6x3½' **3,000.00**
Latchhook border, triple medallion, village decor, 3½x7' ... **225.00**
Kazvin, floral, wild rose border, red & ivory, 6x9' **3,000.00**
Kerman Laver Pictorial, antelope, pheasant, landscape, 4½x7' **3,300.00**
Kerman, fauna, foliage, animals, blue & beige, 5x7' **2,300.00**
Floral medallion, red field, 4x6½' **400.00**
Florals & medallions, wine field, 4x6' **600.00**
Millifleur field, pheasants, 6½x4½' **2,800.00**
Palmette, flower heads, claret & blue, 11½x19½' **3,000.00**
Persian, floral sprays, cream w/pastels, 9x12' **1,800.00**
Tree of life, gold, green, rose, blue on ivory, 4½x7' **525.00**
Vine palmette, leaf design, claret & blue, 26x12' **6,000.00**
Keshan, allover floral & blue medallion on rust, 10x14' **1,500.00**
Blue medallion, allover florals, 4½x7' **300.00**
Central medallion on maroon w/blue border, 7x4½" **375.00**
Floral design on red, 6x9' **950.00**
Floral on blue, 4½x7½' **450.00**
Medallion, blue on rust w/floral ornaments, 6x10' **750.00**
Yellow spandrel & blue border, 5x8' **600.00**
Khorasan, cyprus, garland, flowers, salmon & gray, 4x5½' .. **1,200.00**
Vine & trifoil border w/blue medallion on green, 10x13' .. **1,200.00**
Kildare, floral, brown, beige, blue red, by Magee Co, 11x12' .. **210.00**
Kirman, allover florals on blue, 2½x5' **475.00**
Persia, floral medallion, rose & ivory, 13x10' **8,250.00**
Persia, vases, vines, rose & blue, 8x6' **2,850.00**
Konya, prayer, red Mirhab & gold, ivory, red, blue border, 3½x5' **200.00**
Kuba, Caucasus, lattice, flowerhead stripe, rose, 6x3½' **1,850.00**
Handknotted, burnt orange w/blue, runner, 1880, 10' **1,800.00**
Kurdish, floral & geometrics on red, ivory borders, 7x4' **325.00**

Geometric ornament, ivory w/rust border, 4x5½' **550.00**

Lattice work & latch design, blue w/rust & gold, 4x7' **375.00**

Lallihan, deep red w/blue border, semi-antique, 11x18' **700.00**

Floral on red, 6 borders, 6x9½' **375.00**

Semi antique, 4½x2½' **110.00**

Lillihan mat, w/floral ornaments on gold field, 2x2½' **100.00**

Mahal, allover Herati pattern, blue, gold on rust, 8x12' **450.00**

Flower head decor, rose on blue, 6½x5' **250.00**

Mohal, sarouk type, rose, 9x12' **2,600.00**

Morroccan, rust w/allover rose medallions, handknotted, 3½x4' **265.00**

Nain, allover floral in blue & gold in ivory, 2¼x4' **500.00**

Oriental, picture of mosque scene, 1920, 30" sq **160.00**

Perpedil, Causasus, birds, indigo, orange, ivory, 6½x3½' . . . **1,850.00**

Quom, silk, Herati pattern medallion, ivory on rose, blue, 5x3½' **1,800.00**

Sarouk, allover floral on red, 9x12' **850.00**

Allover florals, central medallion, red, blue, 9x12' **2,400.00**

Allover stylized florals, rose, semi-antique, 3x4½' **975.00**

Floral border, medallion, red, blue, ivory, 4x7' **435.00**

Multi pattern, red, 9x12' **750.00**

Overall floral, 2x4' **255.00**

Sarouk Fereghan, Persian, 1900, 7x4½' **5,500.00**

Sennah, diamond medallion, semi-antique, 4½x6½' **50.00**

Medallion, ivory on blue, allover Herati decor, 5x4' **500.00**

Serab, pole medallion, natural wool, 18x3' **1,650.00**

Seraband, medallion, pineapple, terra cotta & ivory, 2x4½' . . . **225.00**

Seychour, Caucasian, 1910, mint condition, 7½x4½' **6,000.00**

Shiraz Kilim, 3 diamonds on red field, 6x4½' **400.00**

Geometric devices repeat on blue field, 5x3½' **110.00**

Zig-zag field, rust, blue & ivory, 3x4½' **150.00**

Shirred, geometric design, wool, 1875, green, gold, olive, rust . **700.00**

Shirvan, Causasus, 4 rows florals, vines, 4½x2½' **100.00**

Boteh design on red, ivory & wine border, 7½x4' **475.00**

Diamond design in red, blue, ivory, gold, brown, 3x5' **375.00**

Diamond, rust & ivory on blue, gold border, 5x9' **1,800.00**

Prayer, 4'8"x4'2" **3,000.00**

Sparta, green, rose, blue, rust & green on ivory, 5½x8' **475.00**

Overall florals on blue, red, green, blue tan border, room size **450.00**

Sultanabad, Persia, animal motif, cream, red, multi, 18x11' . **4,200.00**

Tabriz, ardebil medallion on red, ivory & blue border, 11½x17' **2,500.00**

Blossom tree, hunt design, ivory & blue, 6½x10' **1,350.00**

Floral sprays, vine, tendril border, saffron, 5x8' **2,850.00**

Flowering tree, birds, green, 7x11½' **5,000.00**

Garden design, natural wool, 8x11' **600.00**

Garden design, natural wool, 3½x5' **150.00**

Prayer, gold w/rust border w/inscription cartouches, 3x5' . . **1,400.00**

Talish, diamond, blue w/ivory border, antique, 3x6½' **825.00**

Tekke, hooked diamond border, tight weave, red, blue, wht, 3x4' **285.00**

Trans-Caucasian, patterned, antique, dark blue, 4x12' **340.00**

Turkish, brocaded flat weave, geometric on orange, 4x5½' . . . **185.00**

Turkoman, bagface, rust red field, antique, 5x2½' **150.00**

Yuruk, prayer, red, wht, brown, 4½x3½' **400.00**

Rumrill

During the early 1930s, the Red Wing Union Stoneware Company of Red Wing, Minnesota, produced pottery for George Rumrill of Little Rock, Arkansas. Rumrill not only designed the ware, but marketed it as well. In 1938 when the Shawnee Pottery Company of Zanesville, Ohio, submitted a lower bid, he awarded the contract to them, and they continued to manufacture decorative pottery for Rumrill until the early 40s. His designs can be identified by the RumRill mark or label.

Bud vase, cornucopia, w/candle holder, 4" **10.00**

Jug, tilt ball, w/ice lip, shaded gr, cream interior, 7" **20.00**

Vase, biege w/brown interior, handles, mkd 462, 7" **25.00**

Cornucopia, beige tones, 6" tall, 9½" wide top **25.00**

Double scroll handles, wht, orig label, sgnd, 8" **7.50**

Fancy handles, lg trumpet flowers around top, #491, 8" **35.00**

Lotus, blue & pink, #305, 6" **10.00**

Scroll & ring handles, grey, 7¼" **8.50**

Sea gr, swan handles, 8" **17.00**

Swan handles, 5x7" **14.00**

White w/gr interior, 500 . . . . **10.00**

Russel Wright Dinnerware

Russel Wright, one of America's foremost industrial engineers, also designed several lines of pottery dinnerware which are today becoming popular collectibles. His first line, American Modern, was manufactured by the Steubenville Pottery Company from 1939 until 1959. It was produced in a variety of solid colors, in assortments chosen to stay attune with the times.

In 1944, he designed his Iroquois line. Due in part to its thick and heavy styling, it is more easily found today than American Modern which was prone to easy damage. The earlier examples of Iroquois were heavily mottled, while later pieces were smoothly glazed. The ware was marked with Wright's signature and 'China by Iroquois'. It was marketed in fine department stores throughout the country. It also was made in a variety of lovely colors. After 1950, the line was restlyed and marked "Iroquoise China by Russel Wright".

American Modern

Ashtray **2.00**

Baker, small, grey **7.00**

Bowl, lug fruit, coral, 6¼" **4.00**

Bowl, vegetable, divided **12.00**

Bowl, vegetable, grey **8.00**

Bowl, vegetable, coral **7.00**

Casserole, covered, grey **14.00**

Celery, grey **5.00**

Coaster, chartreuse **8.00**

Creamer, seafoam **4.50**

Cup, cedar **5.00**

Cup & saucer, after dinner, coral **7.50**

Cup & saucer, blk chutney **7.50**

Cup & saucer, seafoam **5.00**

Egg cup, double, coral **10.00**

Fruit, lug, chartreuse **5.00**

Gravy boat, blk chutney **9.00**
Gravy boat, chartreuse **6.50**
Pickle dish, cedar **5.00**
Pitcher, blk chutney, water size **24.00**
Pitcher, chartreuse, water size **22.00**
Plate, 6", bean brown **2.00**
Plate, 7", chartreuse **3.50**
Plate, 8", grey **2.00**
Plate, 9¾", coral **3.50**
Plate, 10", cedar **5.00**
Plate, 13", coral **9.00**
Platter, coral **7.00**
Salt & pepper, coral **4.00**
Saucer, bean brown **2.00**
Serving dish, brown, 7x10" **5.00**
Shaker, chartreuse **3.00**
Soup, lug, grey **4.00**
Sugar, covered, coral **5.00**
Sugar & creamer, coral **8.75**
Teapot, coral **20.00**
Tray, square curled corners, chartreuse, 12" **7.00**

Iroquois
Bowl, cereal, 5", nutmeg **5.00**
Bowl, fruit, nutmeg, 5½" **5.00**
Bowl, rolled edge, pink, 8" **7.00**
Bowl, shallow, blue, 10" **7.00**
Bowl, vegetable, divided, w/lid, blue, 10¼" **18.00**
Bowl, vegetable, pink **10.00**
Coffee pot, after dinner, grey **25.00**
Covered butter, lt gr **22.50**
Cup, blue **4.00**
Cup & saucer, dk gr **5.50**
Pitcher, blue, 9" **18.50**
Plate, charcoal, 6½" **2.50**
Plate, dinner, charcoal, 10" **4.00**
Plate, dinner, yellow, 10" **2.75**
Plate, yellow, 7¼" **2.00**
Platter, blue, 14½" **12.00**
Platter, blue, round, 12¾" **10.00**
Platter, ice blue, 10" **8.00**
Salt & pepper, stacking, lt gr **7.50**
Saucer, yellow **1.50**
Soup, charcoal **7.50**
Sugar & creamer, stacked, square, charcoal **15.00**
Teapot, lt mottled gr **22.50**
Wine carafe, pink **65.00**

Iroquois Casual
Bowl, 5" berry, pink **3.00**
Bowl, 10" flared, grey **8.00**
Bowl, 8" grey **5.00**
Bowl, 8¼" pink **5.00**
Bowl, 9¾" pink **8.00**
Casserole, covered, pink **15.00**
Cup, grey **3.00**
Cup & saucer, grey **4.00**
Plate, 6¼", grey **2.00**
Plate, 7½" **3.00**
Plate, 9¾", grey **4.00**
Platter, 12½", grey **8.00**
Platter, 17½", well tree, grey **20.00**
Salt & pepper, pr **6.00**
Soup, flat, grey **4.00**
Sugar, open **4.00**
Sugar & creamer **8.00**

Russian Art

Beaker, engraved, mk: Sartov, 875 silver, 1830 . . . . **130.00**
Book, Palekh, State Museum of Palekh Art, Moscow, 1981, 320 pages **37.50**
 Palekh, Village of Artists, Moscow, 1977, 69 pages **12.00**
Box, lacquer, 3 horses, sleigh, people, sgnd, 4¾x3x½" **140.00**
 Lacquer, casket, scenic, sgnd, Fedoskino, 1952, 6x12½" . **1,150.00**
 Lacquer, hinged, sgnd, Fedoskino, 1954, 2x7" **225.00**
 Lacquered, wooden, Troika scene on lid **560.00**
 Silver w/enameling, 4" **625.00**
Candlesticks, 'Nun's lamps', brass w/etched glass shades, pr . . . **245.00**
Coffee pot, brass, double eagle mk, hinged cover **150.00**
Compote, hammered brass, ftd, oval, scrolled handles, 12x4½" . **35.00**
 Hammered copper, ftd, unmkd, 9" round, 4" high **45.00**
Console set, bowl & candlesticks, enamel on copper, Nekrasoff . **95.00**
Cup & underplate, urn shape, gr & wht on copper, Nedrossoff **165.00**
Dish, shaded enamel, peacock & birds, 3 hoofs, 4¾x3x2" . . **1,000.00**
Egg cup, w/cover, hp porcelain, man w/horses, Korniloffski . . . **175.00**
Goblet, chalice shape, engraved, mkd, Moscow, 1881, set of 6 . **285.00**
Jardiniere, brass, sgnd Imperial, mid to late 1800s, 10x8" **165.00**
Mug, silver, handle w/thumbrest, Slavic design, 3x2½" **220.00**
Salt dip, enamel, Klingert **200.00**
Salt, pair, 3-ftd, 1½x1¼" **495.00**

Sculpture, silver gilt, hollow w/fitted stopper, sgnd, 1877, 13½" **1,200.00**
Spoon, coffee, set of 6, 4¼" **1,200.00**
 Demitasse, turquoise w/wht dots, Kuzmichev, 4½" **125.00**
 Enamel, gold wash, 1889, 84 Zolotnicks **275.00**
 Salt, multicolored, round handle **125.00**
 Salt, turquoise blue, 2¾" **75.00**
 Salt, turquoise, wht dots **100.00**
 Soup, 6" **375.00**
Tea caddy, multicolor, mkd, Klingert, 1891, 4¾" **650.00**
 Tea caddy, multicolor, mkd, V Akimov, 1910, 4¾" **650.00**
 Tea caddy, silver gilt, mkd, 4¾" **125.00**
Strainer, tea, multicolored, V Akimov, 5" **750.00**
Sugar ladle, maroon ground, multicolored, 5½" **450.00**
Sugar tongs, multicolored, Kuzmichev, 3½" **450.00**
 Multicolored, V Akimov, 5" **550.00**
Sugar, w/cover, melon ribbed, silver w/gilt interior **600.00**
Tea caddy, press glass w/brass caps, oriental, 1800s, 5" **60.00**
Tea glass holder, sterling, Art Nouveau, Agafanov, 4x5½" **350.00**
Teapot, hammered brass, bulbous, hinged dome top, finial, 8" . **45.00**
 Porcelain, mkd St Petersburg, Knornilov Bros, 1800s **290.00**
Tray, brass, handmade, 6" dia **18.00**
 Hammered brass, oval, handled, mkd: Eagle, 14x7½" **35.00**
Vase, dk wood, Deco style, hand carved, 12" **65.00**
Wax carving, in shadow box, bust of man, 6½x7¼" **250.00**

Sabino

Sabino art glass was produced by Marius-Ernest Sabino in France during the 1920s and 30s. It was designed to reflect the Art Deco style of that era. In 1960, using molds he modeled by hand, Sabino once again began to produce art glass characterized by a golden opalescence. Although production continued after his death in 1971, the Sabino golden opal glass has not been duplicated.

Bird, large, feeding **57.00**
   Mini, wings up or down, ea **15.00**
   Nesting, small **23.00**
Birds on branch **1,020.00**
Birds, cluster of three **250.00**
Bowl, shell w/star, large **175.00**
Butterfly, large **183.00**
   Small, wings open or closed, ea **27.00**
Cat **23.00**
Cherub **20.00**
Chick, wings up, wings down, or drinking, ea **52.00**
Dove, small, head up or down, ea **20.00**
Dragonfly **85.00**
Elephant **21.00**
Fish, large, St Yves **64.00**
   Small **23.00**
Gazelle **29.00**
German Shepherd dog **23.00**
Hands, pair **398.00**
Isadora Duncan **910.00**
Knife rest, w/bee **21.00**
   With squirrel **21.00**
Lady & doves **290.00**
Madonna, small **32.00**
Madonna w/square or round base, 5″, ea **74.00**
Mouse **55.00**
Napkin ring, birds **21.00**
Nude silhouette statue **194.00**
Owl **67.00**
Pegingese dog, large **71.00**
Perfume bottle, 'Petalia' **67.00**

Perfume bottle, pineapple design, 5″ **150.00**
Perfume bottles, 5 dancing Art Nouveau ladies, 6¾″, pair **135.00**
Powder box, large, Bon Bonier **99.00**
Prism, 'Sabino' **54.00**
Rabbit **20.00**
Rooster, small **29.00**
Scotty dog **71.00**
Squirrel **29.00**
Storks, group **520.00**

Tray, round, w/butterfly **80.00**
   Shell, small **32.00**
   Thistle **36.00**
   Violet **36.00**
Turtle **20.00**
Vase, 'Beehive' **225.00**

   Frosted, nudes, birds **425.00**
   'LaDanse' **970.00**
   'Manta Ray' **290.00**
   'Paradise' **750.00**
   Amber, bulbous, w/relief thistle blooms **750.00**
   Amber, w/nudes & columns, molded signature, large **950.00**
   Fish, square base **124.00**
Venus De Milo, large **45.00**
Woodpecker **59.00**

Saloon Memorabilia

The period between the Civil War and the onset of the prohibition era in 1919 furnishes the most charming and collectible examples of early saloon memorabilia. Photographs of early establishments, beer steins, advertising signs and 'bar room nude' portraits are only a few of the varied items that are popular with collectors of memorabilia from the Golden Age of saloons.

Bar, teak front, upholstered armrest, metal footrail, 72x30x45″ **400.00**
Bartender's tool, silver-plated spoon, jigger cup & bottle opener, 9″ **8.00**
Beer pump, chestnut & brass, ornate **95.00**
Front bar, solid oak, raised panel, w/columns, 16 ft **1,250.00**
   Teak w/upholstered armrest, metal footrail, 72x30x45″ **400.00**
Hot Whiskey dispenser, marble base, mirrored, nickel trim, 1890s **1,200.00**
Lights, set of 5, polished brass, rewired **895.00**
Painting, oil on canvas, 3 monks drinking, sgnd, framed, 36x30″ **800.00**
   Oil on canvas, bar room nude scene, 1880, 3½x6½″ **1,250.00**
Tray, tinned sheetiron, from western frontier town, 26x19″ **55.00**
Water purifier, nickel w/glass globe, on marble base, 1896, ornate **1,000.00**

Salt Glaze

As early as the 1600s, potters used common salt to glaze their stoneware. This was accomplished by heating the salt, and introducing it into the kiln at maximum temperature. The resulting grey-white glaze was a thin, pitted surface that resembled the peel of an orange.

Candleholder, grey & blue, 3″ **18.00**
Milk jug, scenic w/gypsy tan, Jones & Walley, 1842, 9¾″ **195.00**
Minister jug, wht, Charles Heigh, 8″ **180.00**
Pitcher, acorn leaf branch style, Charles Heigh, 1848, 10″ **185.00**
   Cobalt blue floral design, Germany, 1 liter **125.00**
   Cork & edge, sleeping children in relief, English, 6″ **90.00**
   Knights in armor in high relief, English mk, 8½″ **125.00**
   Philodendron, 1857 English registry mk **90.00**
Tobacco jar, cobalt dog, cobalt knob lid, 7″ **125.00**

Salts

Before salt became refined and processed, and 'free-flowing' as we know it today, it was necessary to serve it in a 'cellar'. An innovation of the early 1800s, the master salt cellar was place by the host and passed from person to person. Smaller 'individual' salts were a part of each place setting. A small silver spoon was used to sprinkle it onto one's food.

The screw top salt shaker was invented by John Mason in 1858. In 1871, when salt became more refined, some ceramic shakers were made with pierced tops. 'Christmas' shakers, so called because of their Dec. 25, 1877 patent date, were fitted with a rotary agitator designed to break up any lumps in the salt. They were produced by the Boston and Sandwich Glass Company in various colors.

Open Salts

Acorn Band, pedestal **35.00**
Altas **7.50**
Argus, master, ftd **25.00**
Austrian, porcelain, hp roses, ball ft, set of 4, ½x2″ **35.00**
Avon, master, scalloped top, Stippled Diamond bowl **10.00**
Baccarat, sgnd, pedestal **60.00**
Basket of Flowers & Rosette, master, opal, #5 . . . . **95.00**
Basket of Flowers, milk glass **350.00**
Beaded Oval Mirror, master, ftd **15.00**
Beaded Stippled Panel, master, flat **12.50**
Boat, opal **395.00**
Boston & Sandwich, Eagle & Shield, master **225.00**
Bryce Bros, Harp pattern, round ped, Sandwich, 1840, 2x3½″ . **35.00**
Cabbage Rose, master, ftd **20.00**
Cobalt & wht, design around rim, blue enamel in bowl, 3 legs . . **95.00**
Continental, master, boat shape, ring handle, silver, 1800, 2″ . **225.00**
Cranberry **50.00**
   Flower petal shape, plated basket, w/spoon, 4x4″ **118.00**
   With vaseline applique, plated & clawfoot holder, 1½x2¾″ . . . **88.00**
Cut glass, pink & wht, overlay, silver top & bottom bands, 1¼x2″ **125.00**
Derby Hat, master, clear, 1″ **10.00**
Diamond Ornament, master, ftd **15.00**
Diamond Sunburst, master, ftd **20.00**
Duck, Art Deco, smoke crystal cut, 3″ long **55.00**
Effulgent Star **10.00**
Enameled flowers, cranberry, 1¾″ **65.00**
English, ftd, boat form, silver, 1792, 3½x5½″ **300.00**
Flowers, master, ftd, gold w/gold beading **15.00**
Giant Sawtooth, opaque wht **40.00**
Hat shaped, lavender, basket shape plated holder **88.00**
Heisey, rimmed, ftd, round, tiny diamond point, 2-pc **25.00**
Inverted Thumbprint, crystal applique, plated holder, sapphire, 2x3″ **85.00**
Japan, bowl shape, hp w/orange flower, gold rim, ½x1″ **5.00**
King's 500, cobalt blue w/excellent gold **35.00**
King's Crown **25.00**
Lenox, individual, swan, gr mk, Lenox **12.00**
Lion's heads, ftd, pewter, early 1800s, pr, 2½″ **55.00**
Loop & Dart, master, ftd **15.00**
Luck Horseshoe, master **40.00**

Mt Washington, melon rib **85.00**
   White to yellow, orange flowers, leaves, 3x1″ **90.00**
Notched Rib, round, 28 rows notched ridges, rayed bottom, 1x2″ **10.00**
Opposing Pyramids, master flat **12.50**
Paneled English Hobnail w/prisms, non-flint, 1890s, 1x1½″ **6.00**
Paneled Wheat, master, ftd **25.00**
Portland, orbed feet **12.00**
Portland Cut Log **15.00**
Portland Squirrel, individual **65.00**
Portland Tree of Life, master, ftd **75.00**
Pressed glass, Waterford type, flint, series of flutes **48.00**
Pressed Leaf, master, ftd **15.00**
Quezal, sgnd, gold, 1x2¾″ **225.00**
Ram's Heads, raised, master, hoof ft swags, gadroon border, 2x4″ **55.00**
Rib & Bead, ftd, red flash, fluted top, 2½x2¼x1¾″ **20.00**
Royal Worcester, leaf shape **20.00**
Sandwich, master, 1¾x2¾″ **85.00**
Sawtooth, master, opalescent **175.00**
   Serrated top, diamond-shape pedestal, milk glass, 2x3″ **10.00**
Scalloped lines, master, flat **12.50**
Scored Buttons, tub shape, tab handles, 2¼″ **22.00**
Shallow, cut, individual, 6 panels w/rectangle diamond points . . **15.00**
Sleigh, Stag Horn, cobalt blue **155.00**
Sprig, master, flat **55.00**
Steuben, verre de soie, copper wheel, engraved cup, silver pedestal **55.00**
Stiegel, ribbed, ogee shape, plain circular ft, 1700s, 2¼″ **175.00**
Stippled Bowl, master, ftd **12.50**
Thumbprint, 8 thumbprints, 8 point star on bottom, 1x2″ dia . . **4.00**
Tiffany, sgnd, deep gold **145.00**
Truncated Cube **5.00**
Victorian, cranberry w/gold & enamel decor, round, 1¾x3″ **65.00**
   Green, 7 petals foot **55.00**
Waterford, amber, boat shape, cut **55.00**
   High pedestal, rolled rim, 1820, 4″ **65.00**

Shakers
   mb-------mold blown
   p-------pressed patterns
AH Heisey, Punty Band, mb & p, cylinder shape w/band base, custard **68.00**
   Winged Scroll, mb & p, cylinder shape w/4 designs in relief, custard **76.00**
Apricot Band, mb, wht opaque, bark-like tree trunk, apricots at base **29.00**
Aster, mb, blue opaque, 4 sides w/raised aster, 2½″ **28.00**
Atterbury & Co, Johnny Bull, gentleman figural, mb, wht opaque **110.00**
Bakewell, Pears & Co, Little Owl, clear pressed glass w/pewter head **135.00**
Barrell, Flower Band, mb, blue opaque, fine vertical rib, 3¼″ . . **38.00**
Basket shape, rope around center, mb, red opalware, tin/celluloid top **28.00**
Biliken, mb & p, crystal w/gilt paint, impressed Billiken **63.00**
Bird, mb & p, Rubigold Carnival w/silver plated head, 2¾″ **62.00**

Bluerina w/floral enameling, pr **40.00**

Boston & Sandwich, Xmas Barrel, mold blown, vaseline, w/agitator **80.00**

Bryce Brothers, Cannon Ball, crystal w/acid-etched floral, balls at base **28.00**

Bryce, Higbee & Co, Beehive, mb & p, octagonal base, relief bees **32.00**

Buckeye, Chrysanthemum base, mb, wht ribbon opal swirl, 2½″ **48.00**

   Opal-Ribbon, short, mb, clear w/wht 'stripes' **44.00**

CF Monroe, Draped Column, above bulging base, single floral decor **54.00**

   Elephant, mb, glass, crystal w/metal head, body, 2¼″ **58.00**

   Wave Scroll, tapered w/wide base, floral decor **85.00**

Cambridge Glass Co, Star of Bethlehem, pressed, known as #2656 **32.00**

Cat, mb, pink w/metal head, 1¾″ **35.00**

Christmas, electric blue, w/agitator, Sandwich **125.00**

   Golden amber, w/pewter lid, 2½″ **55.00**

   Orig top, agitator, amethyst, sgnd, 1877 . . . . **95.00**

   With agitator, apple gr **75.00**

Consolidated Lamp & Glass, Bulging Leaf, mb, opaque---any color **33.00**

   Cone, mb, opaque---any color, cased & satin **28.00**

   Cotton Bale, mb, opaque---any color **33.00**

   Flower Assortment, mb, opaque---any color, flowers in relief . . **42.00**

   Guttate, squatty, mb, pink or wht opaque **53.00**

      Mb, pink cased glass **43.00**

   Half Cone, mb, pink or yellow cased, 2″ **67.00**

   Overlapping Shell, mb, opaque---any color **34.00**

Dithridge, bulge bottom, mb, wht opaque w/painted relief poppies **48.00**

   Corn figural, mb, custard **110.00**

   Creased Bale, mb, opaque---any color **58.00**

   Heart, mb, opaque---any color **56.00**

   Scroll & Square, mb, opaque---any color, tall square shape . . . **36.00**

   Spider Web, mb, opaque glass, squatty bulbous shape **38.00**

   Sunset, mb opaque, custard, vertical scalloped layers **40.00**

   Teardrop Bulging, mb, opaque---any color, 2 rows tear shapes **30.00**

Dog, erect ears, mb, green cased glass, sitting, metal head, 2″ . **62.00**

   Large-eared hound setting on haunches, mb, blue glass, 3¾″ . **43.00**

Domino, mb, wht opaque w/blk intaglio dots, 3″ **78.00**

Duncan & Miller, Button Arches, mb & p, souvenir, clambroth . **35.00**

Eagle Glass, Butterfly, mb & p, opalware w/butterflies in relief, 2½″ **38.00**

   Flower Blooming, mb & p, heavy opaque glass w/gilt flowers in relief **38.00**

Fostoria, Tulip Base, mb, opaque w/flower & leaves in relief . . . **32.00**

Gillinder & Son, Melon, mb, satin glass, hp floral motif, silver top **39.00**

Gunderson, Cornucopia, blown crystal, sharp ribbing & vertical panels **38.00**

Hobbs, Brockunier & Co, Acorn, mb, blk opaque **55.00**

   Pillar Sixteen, mb, blue opal, 16 vertical ribs, wht dia lattice . **60.00**

   Swirl Opalescent, mb, cranberry w/opal ribbon swirls **70.00**

Imperial, Grape Carnival, mb & p, relief grapes, Rubigold or Peacock **20.00**

   Johnny Bull, mb & p, gentleman, Rubigold or Peacock carnival **28.00**

   Mary Bull, mb & p, lady, Rubigold or Peacock **22.00**

   Sphinx, mb & p, heavy, crystal, figural Sphinx head **72.00**

Int'l Silver, bulbous w/floral cutouts, glass insert w/rayed star bottom **40.00**

Jefferson Glass Co, Circle, double, blue w/opal sheen **63.00**

   Iris With Meander, mb & p, blue w/gold decor **35.00**

   Ribbed Thumbprint, pressed, ruby-flashed, souvenir **24.00**

   Swag With Brackets, bulbous w/sq base, blue **66.00**

Lalique, intaglio, French art glass, frosted & cut, ball shape **75.00**

McKee, Colonial English, pressed brilliant crystal, 3¼″ **18.00**

   Flower Panel, hexagonal, beaded w/leaf design, mb, wht opaque **22.00**

   Intaglio Swirl, gilt colored flowers & raised vines, 3″ **32.00**

   Scrolled With Plume, mb, opaque w/multicolor decor, 3½″ . . **20.00**

Meissen, German porcelain, cylinder w/bulging ring, red & blue . **54.00**

Mt Washington, Bird Arbor, vaseline cased w/hp bird, pewter top, 4″ **115.00**

   Crown Milano, ribbed cylinder, mb, satinized opaque w/floral decor **75.00**

   Egg In Cup, hp florals, metal top w/pointed finial **105.00**

   Fig, ribbed onion shape, pointed top, hp floral decor **120.00**

   Flat End Egg, mb, wht-opaque w/hp florals **80.00**

   Flat Side Egg, mb, milk glass, satin finish, hp decor **75.00**

   Floral Dome, triangular, flat bottom, mb, wht satin, hp florals **74.00**

Lobe-5, mb, opaque wht satin, hp florals **55.00**

Lobe-6, bulbous, slim neck, 6 panels w/hp floral, mb, wht satin, 2½″ **96.00**

Loop & Daisy, salmon satin, mb, 6 looping panels w/hp daisies **76.00**

Scroll & Bulge, triangular w/3 panels, mb, wht satin, hp floral **56.00**

Squatty Lobe, variation of Tomato, hp decor, 2-pc metal top . **92.00**

Tomato, squatty melon shape, mb, wht satin, hp florals **52.00**

National Glass, Orinda, pressed, tall square shape, crystal **36.00**

   S Repeat, mb & p, blue, metal top w/pointed finial **72.00**

New England, MOP Raindrop, mb, triple cased, hp decor, pewter top **160.00**

   Rubina, bulbous, mb, acid frosted camphor to deep rose, branch **120.00**

New Martinsville, Curved Body, mb, wht opaque opal, S w/floral **30.00**

   Many Petals, ball shape w/allover raised petals, mb, wht opaque **40.00**

Northwood, Alaska Variant, bulbous, mb, blue w/hp gold floral band **74.00**

   Alaska, bulbous, mb, vaseline opal **74.00**

   Circled Scroll, bulbous, mb & p, rough pontil mk, blue or green **82.00**

   Everglades, oval, mb, purple & purple slag & clambroth **100.00**

   Jewel & Flower, bulbous, slim ringed neck, mb & p, blue opal **80.00**

Richmond & Hartley, Richmond pattern, pressed, crystal **25.00**

Riverside, Croesus, mb & p, green w/gold decor **68.00**

   Empress, tapered cylinder w/wide base, gr w/gold decor, mb & p **74.00**

Rogers-Smith, Longwy, French pottery, cylinder shape hp florals **95.00**

Sevres, bulbous, slim neck, mauve, gold, wht, hp florals, sterling trim **120.00**

Smith Brothers, Cabin In Snow, cylinder w/enamel on opal . . . **120.00**

Steuben, handcrafted crystal, trumpet shape, sterling silver top, 2¼″ **78.00**

TG Hawkes, Diamond & Star, cut crystal, 3″ **38.00**

   Diamond & Zipper, cut crystal, bulbous w/slim neck, 2½″ . . **34.00**

United States, Iowa, bulbous w/bulging panels & zippers, mb & p **42.00**

   Manhattan, tapered cylinder, mb & p, crystal **28.00**

W Virginia, Polka Dot, mb, inner layer blue, outer wht opal . . **125.00**

WL Libbey & Sons, dice figural w/hp floral decor, mb opaque . **120.00**

Samplers

    American samplers were made as early as the colonial days; English examples from the 17th century are still in existence. Changes in style and decorative motif are evident down through the years. Verses were not added until the late 17th century. By the 18th century, they were used not only for sewing experience but as an educational tool. Young ladies who often signed and dated their work embroidered numbers and characters of the alphabet, as well as fancy stitches. Fruits and flowers were added for borders, birds and animals and Adam and Eve were popular subjects. Later, houses and other buildings were included. By the 19th century, the American Eagle and the little red schoolhouse had made their appearance.

Adam & Eve, Garden of Eden w/figures, 1825, 27x25″ **1,050.00**

Adam & Eve, trees, angels, animals, verse, mounted, 1835, 17x17″ **470.00**

Adam & Eve, verse, 1811, orig frame, 15x15″ **550.00**

Alphabet, birds, old frame, English, 1780, 10x10″ **355.00**

Alphabet, building, name, old frame, English, 1822 . . . . **380.00**

Alphabet, flowers, animals, linen, sgnd, 1770, 14x12″ **125.00**

Alphabet, flowers, birds, trees, floral border, sgnd, 1825, 18″ . **385.00**

Alphabet, house, trees, birds, hearts, 1853, 19½x18″ **550.00**

Alphabet, initials, unframed, 1700s, 18x18″ **220.00**

Alphabet, name, framed, 1788, 13″ **355.00**

Alphabet, name, miniature, framed, 1802, 6x4″ **330.00**

Alphabet, numbers, birds, human figures, 10x10″ **130.00**

Alphabet, numbers, trees full of birds, sgnd, 1790, 7¾x7″ **350.00**

Alphabet, numerals, birds, deer, floral border, sgnd, 1819, 16″ **285.00**

Alphabet, numerals, inscription, 1760s **165.00**

Alphabet, numerals, verse, pine trees, florals, sgnd, 1778 . . . . . **235.00**

Alphabet, prose, florals, strawberry vines, sgnd, 1800s, 20x19″ **500.00**

Alphabet, sgnd, 1822, 4x12″ **150.00**

Alphabet, sgnd, 1871, framed, 8¾x17¼″ **230.00**

Alphabet, simple borders, sgnd, 1814, 9x12″ **165.00**

Alphabet, trees, burled frame, sgnd, 1823, 8½x8½"......... **450.00**
Alphabet, verse, birds, flowers, people, sgnd, 1773, 12x12"... **265.00**
Alphabet, verse, house, trees, people, sgnd, 1820, 16¼x17¼". **550.00**
Alphabet, verse, no name, English, 1787, 10x12".......... **180.00**
Alphanumerics, bird, pitcher motif, sgnd, 1800s, 17½x18½".. **300.00**
Alphanumerics, floral vase, bird, chair, 1800, 16x16"...... **185.00**
Alphanumerics, floral, fruit filled vases, verse, sgnd, 1813, 17½x15" **550.00**
Alphanumerics, flowering vine, sgnd, 1820, framed, 20x19"... **240.00**
Alphanumerics, fruit filled vase, floral, animals, sgnd, 1800, 8x14½" **225.00**
Alphanumerics, peafowl, houses, animals, sgnd, 1846, 21x16½" **500.00**
Alphanumerics, sgnd, 1848, framed, 11½x14½"........... **235.00**
Alphanumerics, sgnd, 1853, framed, 1800s, 16x20"........ **500.00**
Alphanumerics, vase, stag, urns, sgnd, 1800s, framed, 19x15½" **275.00**
Alphanumerics, verse, crowns, ships, sgnd, 1798, framed, 18x18" **700.00**
Alphanumerics, verse, florals, sgnd, 1800s, framed, 16½x10".. **275.00**
Animals, florals, ornithologicals, sgnd, 1831, 17x14"........ **425.00**
Birds, pots of flowers, strawberry border, verse, sgnd, 1849, 14¾" **350.00**
Birds, urns, hearts, 1826, framed, 24x27"................ **475.00**
Birds, urns, memorial, names, 1840, 16x16".............. **650.00**
Double flowers on border, hymn to benevolence, sgnd, 1828, 12½" **225.00**
Family record, sgnd, 1778-1818, framed, 23¼x22¼"....... **375.00**
Family register, floral border, stains, 1762-1844 .... **275.00**
Family register, New York, 1848, several small holes **330.00**
Family register, unfinished, unframed, small, 1821.......... **135.00**
Floral, animal, birds, houses, verse, sgnd, 1812, 20½x14½" **1,025.00**
Floral, bird devices, verse, sgnd, 1812, framed, 10½x13".... **325.00**
Floral, birds, verse, sgnd, 1830, 19½x20½"............. **300.00**
Floral, figural, animal, birds, verse, sgnd, 1838, 23½x19" **200.00**
Floral vase, prose, strawberry border, sgnd, 1828, 22x21½" .. **750.00**
Flowering vine border, verse, sgnd, 1800, 14½x18½" **350.00**
Flowers, sgnd, framed, 1822, 16"..................... **325.00**
Flowers, verse, name, old frame, 1811, 16".............. **650.00**
Geometrics, florals, animals, sgnd, 1885, frame, 15½x16".... **225.00**
Geometrics, florals, sgnd, 1829, framed, 19½x19½"........ **230.00**
House, birds, floral vase, sgnd, 1849, 23x22½"........... **475.00**
House, potted plants, trees, birds, old frame, 14".......... **275.00**
House in center, plants, birds, floral border, 1810, 10x14" ... **165.00**
Memorial verse, house, name, 1824, 14x14".............. **600.00**
Multiple decorative bands, 2 moral verses, sgnd, 1853, 17x17" **375.00**
Parrots, pots of flowers, vining borders, sgnd, 1812, 10¾x11" **400.00**
Pennsylvania, name, small holes, old frame, 1822, 16x14".... **700.00**
Somber verse, name, framed, 1850, 10x10"............... **190.00**
Stylized flowering vine border, prose, mkd, 1800s, frame, 5½x4½" **225.00**
Urn, cornucopia, vine border, verse, sgnd, 1700s, 12½x15½". **148.00**
Verses, pair, by sisters, 1833 & 1834, 16x14"............. **950.00**

Sandwich Glass

The Boston and Sandwich Glass Company was founded in 1820 by Deming Jarves in Sandwich, Mass. Their first products were simple cruets, salts, half pint jugs and lamps. They were attributed as being one of the first to perfect a method for pressing glass, a step toward the manufacture of the 'lacy' glass produced there until about 1840. Many other types of glass were made there---cut, colored, snakeskin, hobnail and opal among them.

After the Civil War, profits began to dwindle due to the keen competition of the Western factories who were situated in areas rich in natural gas and more suitable coal and sand resources. The end came with an unreconcilable dispute, and the factory closed in 1888.

Bottle, smelling salts, violin, pewter lid w/eagle, opaque blue .. **190.00**
Bowl, Industry, 6¼"................................ **170.00**
Bowl, Oak Leaf, lacy, 7½" dia **75.00**
  Peacock eye, lacy w/feather border, scrolled eye center, 7½" **158.00**
  Plume, 7½"...................................... **110.00**

Candlestick, crucifix, peacock gr, 10", pr................. **385.00**
  Hexagonal, amber, 9"............................. **365.00**
  Hexagonal, wafered, canary, 7¼"................... **185.00**
  Lacy, sq base, stepped rings, blue, 7".............. **305.00**
  Petal & loop, clambroth, wafered, 7"............... **265.00**
  Petal & loop, lt blue, 7"......................... **300.00**
Compote, Diamond Thumbprint, 7x10" dia................ **225.00**
  Flint, 8½"...................................... **90.00**
  Overshot crackle, 4½x5¾"......................... **45.00**

Cruet, cobalt, unusual color, 8"........................ **340.00**
Cup plate, Eagle #672............................... **25.00**
  Fort Pitt Eagle #676-B........................... **30.00**
  Henry Clay #565-A.............................. **25.00**
  St Louis advertising #315......................... **25.00**
Darner, lavender, blue, 5".......................... **165.00**
Dish, honey, 4".................................... **42.50**
Goblet, Arched Grape................................ **40.00**
  Ribbed Grape, flint............................. **60.00**
Lamp, whale oil, orig pewter collar, freeblown fonts, pr **130.00**
Mug, leaf design, 'Remember Me', milk glass **95.00**
Pitcher, bulbous, overshot applied reeded handle, 6½"........ **55.00**
  Bulbous, overshot w/reeded handle 10½"............ **125.00**
  Bulbous, reeded handle, clear...................... **95.00**
  Clear twist handle, wraps around neck, 8½"......... **175.00**
  Hobnail, applied handle, paneled neck, 9"........... **140.00**
  Water, rope handle, sq top, floral enameled, amber........ **495.00**
Plate, beehive, octagonal, 9"......................... **65.00**
Pomade jar, flint, amethyst bear...................... **150.00**
  With cover, basketweave, opaque blue................ **295.00**
Spill, clambroth.................................... **225.00**
Sugar & creamer, w/cover, smocking **220.00**
Sugar, Ivy, black amethyst........................... **145.00**
Toddy plate, Roman Rosette, amethyst, 5".............. **300.00**
Tumbler, tortoise shell, 3¾x2¾" dia **75.00**
Vase, icicle glass, w/clear icicles, amethyst, 12½"........ **1,000.00**
  Melon-ribs, overshot, scalloped, 6" base, 8½x4½" dia **265.00**
Whiskey taster, clear................................ **40.00**

Sarreguemines

Sarreguemines, France, is the location of Utzschneider & Co, founded

in 1770, producers of transfer printed dinnerware, figurines, and novelty ware, usually marked 'Sarreguemines'.

Dessert set, majolica, apples & leaves, sgnd, set of 10, 7″ plates **95.00**
Pitcher, Chinese scenes, yellow, brown, gr, France 6″ **25.00**
 Kate Greenaway scenes, 8″ **48.00**
 Shoemaker scenes, 8″ **135.00**
Plate, 3 rabbits, leaves in relief, verse, 8″ **28.00**
 Children's, set of 6 .... **70.00**
 Children's French caption, 5 different, each **18.50**
 Chinese scenes, yellow, brown, gr, France 7″ **8.00**
 Comical monkey, dog scene on ship, China maxim, pierced, 8″ **28.50**
 George Washington, pierced foot for hanging, sgnd, 8½″ **30.00**
 Girl, geese, sgnd Loux, 8″ **34.00**
 James Buchanan, pierced foot for hanging, sgnd, 8½″ **55.00**
 James Madison, pierced foot for hanging, sgnd, 8½″ **55.00**
 Oyster, scalloped, grey & pastel peach, 9″ **47.00**
 With copper luster bouillon, sgnd, France, 8″ plate **30.00**
Platter, sq, w/handles, Chinese scenes, yellow, gr, brown, France **40.00**
Song plate, Cadet Rouselle **25.00**
 Sur Le Pont d'Avignon **25.00**
Vase, 3 handles meet at top, grey w/red, gr, blue, gold, 15½″. **595.00**

Satin Glass

Satin glass is simply a velvety matt finish achieved through the application of an acid bath. It is a procedure used by many companies since the 19th century both here and abroad, on many types of colored and art glass.

Bowl, oval, dk rose to wht gold enameling, late 1800s **850.00**
Cracker jar, beaded drape, red **235.00**
 Bulbous, swirling ribs, plated collar, lid & bail, blue **158.00**
 Pansy decor, plated lid & bail, sgnd AJ Hall **125.00**
Cruet, bulbous, swirl ribbing, plated collar, blue **210.00**
Decanter, enamel & gold trim, clear handle, orig stopper, 14″. **165.00**
Ewer, cased, enameled birds, camphor handle, blue, 9″ **245.00**
 Fluted rim, apricot shading to wht, hp flowers, 11″ **165.00**
 Herringbone, tricorn top, gold leaves & birds decor, 11″ ... **275.00**
 Melon-ribs in aqua, gold & brown enamel, on ped 9″ **135.00**
 Melon-ribs, cased, enameled, on ped, 9″ **135.00**
 Melon-ribs, cased, w/floral enamel, 8½x4¼″ dia **100.00**
 Peach overlay, wht floral enameling, tricorn top, 10x3″ dia . **125.00**
 Pink w/florals, ruffled, frosted handle, 9½x4½″ dia **95.00**
Pitcher, lt gr background, multi-color floral decor, 8½″ **115.00**
Rose bowl, blue embossed flowers & leaves, 8 crimp top, 3¼x4″ dia **115.00**
 Ftd, pale cream, flower & bird, crimp top, 4½x4″ dia **110.00**
 Jewels, gr w/wht lining, blue florals, 4½″ **95.00**
 Pink w/enameling & gold trim, cased, 6″ **165.00**
 Red to rose coloring **140.00**
 Shell & Seaweed, pink to fuschia crimped top, 5″ **175.00**
Shell, cased, pink to camphor, enamel floral decor, 10½″ **325.00**
Sugar shaker, leaf mold, blue **145.00**
Vase, balustrade shape, cased, deep butterscotch to yellow, 9″ **160.00**
 Box pleated top, gold prunus & branches, cased, 5x3½″ ... **500.00**
 Bulbous, enameled floral decor & butterflies, cased, 7½″ ... **150.00**
 Cased wht to brown, enameled floral, 8½″ **100.00**
 Cut velvet, diamond quilted, cased, pedestalled, ruffled **225.00**
 Ftd, ruffled, peach overlay, 9x4¼″ dia **115.00**
 hp, carnations, 15½″ **140.00**
 Herringbone, quilted, lt blue w/opal sheen, 7″ **150.00**
 Melon form, fluted, peach overlay w/enameling, 10½″ **195.00**
 Pinched sides, lt blue to dk blue, yellow floral decor, 10″ .. **340.00**
 Pink to blue plums, gold foliage, Webb, 7x4¼″ dia **375.00**
 Raindrop MOP 6 sides, ruffled top, blue w/wht, 8″ **250.00**

Ruffled, camphor feet, apricot overlay w/enameled flowers, 9″ **210.00**
Stick, pinched sides, lt blue to dk blue, floral decor, 10″ ... **285.00**
Trumpet, butterscotch w/thorn overlay, pink liner, 14½″ ... **700.00**

Satsuma

Satsuma is a type of fine cream crackle-glaze pottery or earthenware made in Japan as early as the 17th century. The earliest wares, made at the original kiln in the Satsuma province, were enameled with only simple florals. Buy the late 18th century a floral brocade, or nishikide, design was favored, and similar wares were being made at other kilns under the direction of the Lord of Satsuma. In the early part of the 19th century a diaper pattern was added to the florals, and gold and silver enameling was used for accents by the latter years of the century.

During the 1850s, as the quantity of goods made for export to the Western world increased and the style of decoration began to evolve toward becoming more appealing to the Westerners, human forms such as Arhats, Kuannon, Geisha girls and Samurai warriors added.

Today the most valuable pieces are those marked Kinkozan, Shuzan, Ryuzan and Kozan. The genuine Satsuma 'mon' or mark is an X within a circle---it may appear anywhere on the ware.

Belt buckle, cobalt w/border gold decor, bejin & 2 children **55.00**
Box, decorated w/13 women, men temples **375.00**
 Genre allover decor, 1¾x4½″ dia **325.00**
Cat, left paw raised, gilt trim, 10″ **220.00**
Coffee pot, cobalt & gr, gold & enamel decor, war lords scene, 10¾″ **185.00**
 Cobalt, allover gold decor, gold panel w/scene, 1875, 10″ ... **225.00**
Cup & saucer, portrait encircled by Arhats, slip trail enameling . **15.00**
Ewer, mums w/gold edging, jewels, scroll handle, ftd, 11½ . **150.00**
Figurine, lady carrying basket w/fish, 15″ **200.00**
Ginger jar, 1000 Flowers, w/cover **475.00**
Incense burner, 100 Boys design, monkey legs, 6″ **400.00**
Jar, heart-shaped panels w/children, 4 legs, lid w/dog finial, 6½″ **105.00**

Horses & warriors, covered, 7″ **100.00**
Mums decor, lady w/dog, crab finial & handles, 1880's, 12 **450.00**
Pitcher, flowers in relief, double bamboo-shape handle, Kinkozan, 4″ **65.00**
Plate, pagoda & cherry blossoms outlined in gold, 9¾″ **75.00**
 Taisho Period, 1920s, house of S mk **35.00**
Powder box, brick w/raised slip trail enameling, scenic lid, 4¼″ dia **45.00**
Rose petal jar, bulbous, gold decor, Arhats, w/lid, 10″ **425.00**
 Figural scenes, diaper pattern lid, gold, 5x4″ dia **130.00**
Salt & pepper, figures & horses in gold, Nippon **20.00**
Sugar & creamer, raised slip trail enameling, w/scenes, 3 ftd ... **70.00**

Sugar bowl, portrait encircled by Arhats, slip trail enameling . . . **28.00**
Tea caddy, bird on prunus tree decor, brocade work on lid & handles **165.00**
   Green shaded to beige, foliage decor, w/cover & insert, 4½″ . **90.00**
Tea set, blue ground w/pastel blooming florals, 15 pc **195.00**
   Garden scenes w/heavy gold scroll work, 6 pc **145.00**
   Pot, sugar & creamer w/covers, 6 cups & saucers, 1920 . . . . **200.00**
   Prunus blossoms on blue background, 17 pc **225.00**
Teapot, floral enameling, gold trim **50.00**
Toothpick holder, sngd, 2″ **90.00**
Urn, bird in prunus tree decor, brocade work on lid & handles, 5″ **145.00**

Coral w/florals, gold handles, 3 ftd base, 15½″ **250.00**
   Footed base, griffin & tassle handles, orange w/wht peonies, 10″ **135.00**
Vase, 1000 Butterflies, 3½x2½″ **200.00**
   Art Nouveau, scenic panel on front, ca 1910, 15½″ **195.00**
   Beige w/colorful wisteria, reign mark, crest, 6″ **350.00**
   Birds & foliage, Kinkozan, sgnd, 4½″ **80.00**
   Black & gold decor, 9″ **125.00**
   Bulbous w/long neck, panels w/figures & flowers, 1850s, 6¾″ **345.00**
   Bundle form, ftd base, w/cover, 1800s, 4″ **350.00**
   Canteen shape, fine detail **350.00**
   Cobalt w/gold, figural scene, 3½″ **45.00**
   Cobalt w/large scenic panel, Geisha figural front, 1875, 12″ . **140.00**
   Cobalt, bulbous, panel scenes, 3 bejin & child, gold, 12″ . . . **155.00**
   Figural foo dogs, florals, 15½x8″ **200.00**
   Floral decor, dolphin finials, 1860s, blue imperial mk, 4″ . . . **245.00**
   Floral decor, double handled, 19″ **245.00**
   Garden scene, men & women, detailed, 4″ **395.00**
   Giesha, cherry blossoms, bulbous, 1865, 9¾″ **130.00**
   Genre, florals, heavy enamels & beading, gold trim, ftd, 11½″ **125.00**
   Heart-shaped floral reserves, animal head ears, 1850s, 5″ . . **320.00**
   Ivory w/multi-colors, genre scene, 10″ **140.00**
   Lilies, relief outlines, gold, twisted handles, Awata, 14″ **125.00**
   Matt gr, floral & gold decor, 18″ **110.00**
   Moriage decor, 1880s, 15″ **125.00**
   Multicolor florals, foo dog ears, much enameling, 15½x8″ dia **200.00**
   Nagadoni in flight, blossoms, bamboo, 24″ **2,400.00**
   Scene w/teacher & scholars, diaper pattern, heavy gold, 9½″ **175.00**
   Seated haloed Arhats, heavy gilt, 11″ **140.00**
   Spherical, overall diaper pattern, medallions w/children, 3x3″ . **40.00**
   Stick, teal to beige w/wisteria, leaves & birds, 1900, 9¾″ . . . **160.00**
   Tan, floral & gold decor, Oriental mk, 18″ **115.00**
   Tapered square w/genre scenes in reserve, floral & diaper work, 7″ **695.00**
   Theatrical scene w/costumed man & woman, late 1800s, 11″ . **95.00**

With bronze wire cover, blue Prince of Satsuma Cross mk, 8x7″ **395.00**
   Warlords pattern, gold, 1800s, 4¾″ **200.00**
   Warlords pattern, gold 1800s, 6″ **225.00**
   Wisteria & leaves, gold tracing, butterflies, w/teak stand, 2½″ **160.00**
Vases, 1000 Butterflies, 3½x2½″ dia, pr **395.00**
   Cream w/wht enamel blossoms, w/draped top, 1800s, 16″, pr **1,250.00**
   Ladies decor on front & back, cobalt & gold trim, 6½″, pr . **695.00**
   Multifloral front, gold tracing, red/gold decor, 3¾″, pr **300.00**
   Waterfall decor, 9″, pr **300.00**

Scales

In today's world of pre-measured and pre-packaged goods, it is hard to imagine the days when such products as sugar, flour, soap and candy first had to be weighed by the grocer. The variety of scales used at the turn of the century was highly diverse; at the Philadelphia Exposition in 1876, one company alone displayed over 300 different weighing devices. Among those found today, brass and iron models are the most common.

Army Medical, gr box, gold eagle imprint, 1850 . . . . **60.00**
Becker, torsion balance, w/weights, glass case, oak base **180.00**
Brass, child nude, arms up, scales on head, 6½x6½″ **40.00**
   Grain scales w/brass bucket **115.00**
   Hanging balance scales, 18″ beam, 9″ pans **150.00**
   Pharmacy scales, hanging, 7″ balance arm, 3″ pans **25.00**
   Scales, wht face, w/pan, Property of PO Department **125.00**
Buffalo Brand, country store scales, brass pan, 1880s, 29″ **135.00**
C Forschner's Improved, milk scales, hanging, brass face, 13x4¼″ **75.00**
Cast iron, scales, brass balance arm, circular base, 5 parts, 1800s **800.00**
Chatillons, cotton, lg pair w/2 weights, iron beam **27.00**
   Hanging scales, #300 . . . . **37.50**
   Hanging spring balance, w/brass face, #2, 1892 . . . . **15.50**
   Kitchen grams scales, 1941 . . . . **15.00**
Chicken, spring balance, brass face on blk iron, holding hooks . **50.00**
Columbia, Family, blk w/brass front scales, 24 pounds by ozs, 9″ **45.00**

Crescent, pat 1889, postal **15.00**
Kitchen scales, brass face **35.00**
   Penny scales, w/mirror, walnut sides & back, 6x16″ **399.00**
Computing Scale Co, meat market scales, w/orig scoop, 1904 . **150.00**
Connecticut, parcel post, 1913 . . . . **50.00**
Counter, brass **70.00**
Decetco, brass face, #100, 17½″ **45.00**
   Scale, hanging, hoop & tray, #4100, 100 pounds **100.00**
Dodge Manufacturing, micrometer scales, marble base, Yonkers, NY **175.00**
Drug Store, oak scales, marble top **85.00**
   Platform scales, walnut, brass arms & pans **125.00**
Egg scales, red, paint wear **10.00**
Empire Hardware, brass measure bars, hook, iron weights, 9½x20″ **45.00**

English, letter scales, 2 sets of weights, mahogany base, 6x10″ **245.00**
Enterprise, bulk store scales, copper scoop, ci, 20 pound, sgnd **175.00**
Fairbanks, beam scales, small **25.00**
   Counter top balance w/tin scoop, ci, #3, 8 pounds. **100.00**
   Counter top platform scales, ci, #2, 20 pounds **100.00**
   Platform scales, 500 pound **150.00**
Fairbanks Morse, beam scales, w/ceramic platform, fine **150.00**
Frary & Clark, parcel post, 1913 . . . . **50.00**
Gem, postal scales, 2 cent letter period **15.00**
Gold scales, brass, collapsible, ornate, fits in mahogany base, 15″ **175.00**
   Inside storage, ivory bar, maple box, 1870 . . . . **55.00**
   Platform, oak drawer on bottom, brass pans **95.00**
Harrison, Sovereign rocker balance **95.00**
Hatch Novelty Works, counter top store scales, ci w/double pan **64.00**
Howe Scale Co, platform scales, ci, sgnd, 1886, 23¼″ **135.00**
   Porcelain tray, 1 side, brass bar weight face **95.00**
Ideal, postal scales, zone & cost schedules shown **42.00**
Iron & brass, scales, hanging, 100 pound. **40.00**
   Scales, wall hung, 600 pound capacity. **200.00**
Jones, iron scales, brass arm, 6 weights, 2 tin pans, orig gr paint **65.00**
LF & C, #3, 25 lbs **7.50**
Landers, 50 lbs, 12″. **25.00**
   Family balance, sq, 20 pound **55.00**
Landers, Frary & Clark; parcel post, 1913 . . . . **50.00**
   Store scale, hanging, brass, iron tray **65.00**
London, brass pans, pendants, metal center post, 12x14x10″. . **95.00**
Marshall Son, hanging postal scales, clip & pendulum, mkd, Boston **70.00**
Marvel, postal scales, 3 cent, olive gr, small **23.00**
Mills Lollipop, scales, wht porcelain **565.00**
Moderne, drugstore scales, penny, Art Deco **295.00**
Morgan Bros, portable scales, wood box, London **75.00**
NYC, brass, round, serial D-5 printed on face, w/pan **95.00**
New Britain, parcel post, 1913. . . . . **50.00**
New York, hanging scales, 25 pounds **10.00**
Oakes Manufacturing, tin egg scales, painted blk **15.00**
Ohaus, triple beam scales, #1119, 20 kilos. **325.00**
PSW Co, spring balance, brass, incised eagle, 25 pounds **15.00**
Pelouze, milk scales **16.00**
Pendulum balance, w/letter-clip, small. **100.00**
Pharmacist balance, w/2-8½″ brass pans, 1890s **100.00**
Postal scales, tin, 1904. . . . . **23.00**
Royal Spring Balance, brass face, hanging, 50 pound, 12″ **18.00**
Smith, Sovereign rocker balance **85.00**
Steelyard, cast iron scales, 2 weights & hooks, small. **17.00**
   Cotton scales, iron, 3 weights, 3 hooks, lg **75.00**
   Cotton scales, (pea scales in South), iron & brass, 25 pounds . **45.00**
Stimpson, counter scales, large **135.00**
Store balance, 2 brass pans, 1870s **100.00**
The Preciso, postal scales, several schedules **60.00**
Toledo, produce scales, ci, enamel, #3655, 70 pound **150.00**
Toledo Computing, candy scales, brass pans, brass plate, 1906, 14″ **75.00**
Triner, air mail accuracy scales, enamel steel, 4 pound **60.00**
Trustee, postal scales, 3 cent letter period **12.00**
Turnstall, spring scales, brass face, 4½″. **15.00**
Unique, scales, hanging, coiled spring, 1890, 12″ **15.00**

Schafer and Vater

    Schafer and Vater operated in Volkstedt, Germany, from the last decade of the 1800s until about 1920. They produced novelties such as figural bottles, flasks, vases, etc, marked with an R within a star device.

Bottle, man's head, lg open mirrored mouth, brown, glaze **75.00**
   Merry Christmas, Santa holding tree, brown w/multirelief. . . . **25.00**

One of the Boys, man on bar stool, multicolor, 7″ **95.00**
Poison, skeleton in cloak w/tray & 3 skull jiggers, brown, 6″ **138.00**
Uncle Sam, standing profile, multicolor, 6¾″. **125.00**
Creamer, cow in dress, multicolor, 5″. **195.00**
   Fairy godmother, blue, 4″ **55.00**
   Jewels & cameo design, lavender **55.00**
   Maid w/keys, multicolor, 3½″ **55.00**
   Maid w/purse, blue, 4″ **65.00**
   Mother Goose, multicolor, 3½″. **125.00**
   Oriental w/bird, multicolor, 5″ **115.00**
Figurine, small boy w/tongue wagging, nodder **885.00**
Flask, Scotch baby in relief, drinking whiskey, porcelain, #3340 **65.00**
Lamp, miniature, lady. **125.00**
Matchholder, man w/violin, multicolor, 4″ **125.00**
Pitcher, milk maid holding jug w/key ring at side, 3½″ **110.00**
Trinket box, wht cupid on gr, in relief, pink, bisque, 2¼″ **55.00**
Vase, enameled jewels, gold rim, bronze bottom, Art Nouveau, 4″ **35.00**
Vase, pillow, cherubs in relief at top, w/jewels, lavender, bisque, 5″ **53.50**

Schneider

    The Schneider Glass Co. was founded in 1914 at Epinay-sur-seine, France. They made many types of art glass, some of which sandwiched designs between layers. Other decorative devices were applique and carved work. These were marked Charder, or Schneider.

    During the 20s, commercial art ware was produced with Deco motifs, cut by acid through two or three layers, and signed LeVerre Francais in script or with a section of inlayed filigrane. See also Le Verre Francais.

Bowl, bulbous, wht & orange, 4¼″ opening, 3¼″. **65.00**
Centerpiece, red to yellow mottled bowl, iron floral holder, sgnd **295.00**
Light shade, orange w/blue, flower bud shape, 8½″ **155.00**
Pitcher, orig paper, pink w/wht, maroon handle. **290.00**
Vase, blown out, mottled pink/orange/lavender, sgnd, 5¾″. . . **425.00**
   Full, puffy, orange & brown & wine **145.00**
   Lemon yellow, dimpled, sgnd, 6½″ **125.00**
   Orange at top, mottled grape center w/gr bottom, 10¼″. . . . **140.00**
   Pedestal, orange, brown, yellow, sgnd, France, 15½″ **275.00**
   Red w/brown tortoise shell exterior, cased on opal, 5x7″ dia **135.00**
   Sgnd, mottled, powder blue to plum at top, 8″ **295.00**
   Spatter to clear, metal collar of birds, 12″ **145.00**
   Squared oval shape, mottled pink to purple, sgnd, 13½″ . . . **295.00**

Schoolhouse Collectibles

    Schoolhouse collectibles bring to mind memories of a bygone era when the teacher rang her bell to call the youngsters to class in a one-room schoolhouse--- with both a 'hickory stick' and an apple in prominent position on her desk.

Bell, brass, burnished, ring decoration, orig bronze clapper, 11″ **80.00**
   Brass w/wood-turned handles, 6½″ **30.00**
     8½″ **45.00**
   Cast iron, complete w/frame & cradle, American Bell Foundry **1,200.00**
     Rope driven, 1870 . . . . **250.00**
Blackboard, teacher's, oak w/roll & subjects, 1903, 21x28″ **65.00**
Book, Beacon's First Reader, 1913 . . . . **4.50**
   Clark's Practical Grammar, 1864 . . . . **8.00**
   Eclectic Fourth Reader, leather, 1848 . . . . **22.00**
   McGuffey's History, 1890. . . . . **9.50**
   McGuffey's Primary History, 1884. . . . . **9.50**
   McGuffey's Reader, 1853, 3rd. **25.00**
     1866, 5th **17.50**
     1866, 6th **17.50**

1879, 3rd **10.00**
1879, 6th **15.00**
1896, 4th **10.00**
1907 . . . . **15.00**
McGuffey's Spelling, 1865 . . . . **8.50**
Olney's Practical Arithmetic, 1881 . . . . **25.00**
Ray's Practical Arithmetic, 1857 . . . . **4.50**
Sander's New Third Reader, engravings, June 7, 1867 . . . . . . **10.00**

Box, pencil, red, paper hunting scene, Made in Germany, 9″ . . . **16.50**
Box, pencil or crayon, figural wood, soldier & horse, 1930s **7.50**
Catalogue, Bradley's Kindergarten Material & School Supplies, 1911 **15.00**
Desk, pine, pegged, slant front, orig interior, 1880 . . . . **375.00**
Primitive, for 2 people **295.00**
Separate chair, ci base, Kenney Bros & Wolkins, Boston **85.00**
Table top, w/lock, Masters **275.00**
Dunce hat, 1831 . . . . **12.00**
Pencil sharpener, pistol figural, automatic **30.00**
Vertical, US Brand, 1900 . . . . **60.00**
Slate, w/wood frame, string tied, 12x9″ **16.00**
With wood frame, very old, 8½x12½″ **21.00**
Slate pencil, never used **2.00**

Scouting Collectibles

Scouting was founded in England in 1907 by a retired Major General, Lord Robert Baden-Powell. Its purpose is the same today as it was then---to help develope physically strong, mentally alert boys who were taught basic fundamentals of survival and leadership. The movement soon spread to the United States, and in 1910 a Chicago publisher, William Boyce set out to establish Scouting in America. The first World Scout Jamboree was held in 1911 in England; Baden-Powell was honored as the Chief Scout of the World. In 1926, he was awarded the Silver Buffalo Award in the United States. He was knighted in 1929 for distinguished military service, and for his scouting efforts. Baden Powell died in 1941.

Badge, any large sq 1910-20 rank or office **25.00**
Bank, Boy Scout, 1915-20 . . . . **35.00**
Book, 7th Annual Report BS of America, 144 pages, 1917 . . . . **10.00**
Archery, Boy Scout, 1929 . . . . **6.00**
Boy Scouts in the Dismal Swamp, Eaton, 1913 . . . . **8.50**
Community Boy Leadership for Executives, 1st Ed, 1921 . . . . **10.00**
Handbook, 1910 Offical BS; Seton & Powell, Doubleday **100.00**
Handbook for crew leaders, 1941 . . . . **6.00**
History of the Boy Scouts of America, Murray, 1937 . . . . **20.00**
Ninth National Conference, Boy Scout, 1951 . . . . **6.00**
Picture, National BSA Jamboree, 1950 . . . . **12.00**
Scouting for Boys, paperback, 9th Ed, Baden-Powell, 1920 . . . **20.00**
Teenage Scout Stories, Boy Scout, 1948 . . . . **6.00**
Compass, w/sundial metal case boxed, Boy Scout, 1921 . . . . . . **15.00**
First aid kit, orig contents, case, Bauer & Black, 1928 . . . . **12.00**
Game, Boy Scout, 1915-20 . . . . **35.00**
Game of Scouting for Boy Scouts, orig box, Bradley, 1920 . . . **27.50**
Handbook, scoutmaster's, hardbound, 1913-14 . . . . **20.00**
Knife, pocket, Boy Scout, Remington, 1930s **35.00**
Pocket, Boy Scout, Ulster USA, 3½″ **35.00**

Pocket, Cub Scout, Camillus NY USA, 3½″ **18.00**
Pocket, Girl Scouts of America **15.00**
Magazine, Boys Life, 1911-20 . . . . **6.00**
Match safe, Boy Scout, 1920 . . . . **10.00**
Pocket, nickled brass, round, ¾x3″ **32.00**
Medal, w/ribbon, England US Contigent, 1920 World Jamboree **200.00**
With tricolor ribbon, BSA, 1915-20 BS Eagle **45.00**
Medallion, brass, 35th Confederate Reunion **65.00**
Neckerchief, National BSA Jamboree, red, 1937 . . . . **90.00**
National BSA Jamboree, silk, 1950 . . . . **25.00**
Paperweight, pictures Cub, Boy Scout, Explorer, 3″ **15.00**
Patch, 1924 World Jamboree, small silk flag w/number **400.00**
1933 World Jamboree, silk, tan w/leaping deer **100.00**
1935 National BSA Jamboree, Washington DC **40.00**
1937 National BSA Jamboree, felt, Washington DC, 3″ **25.00**
1937 World Jamboree, cotton twill, multicolor bars **80.00**
1947 World Jamboree, w/camp names on bottom, France **50.00**
Order of Arrow, odd shaped w/# or name, 1930 . . . . **10.00**
Photo, showing woman in Girl Scout uniform, 4x5½″ **6.00**
Plate, commemorative, Baden-Powell photo, Royal Gouda, 1937 **30.00**
Print, set of 44, boxed, Norman Rockwell, 14x11″ **95.00**
Statue, Boy Scout in uniform, pledges on base **18.00**
Toy, Boy Scout, 1915-20 . . . . **35.00**
Uniform, official Boy Scout, 1910-20, w/badges **50.00**
Wall plaque, china, Baden-Powell commemorative, 1910, 7x8″ . **12.00**
Yearbook, Boy Scout, hardcover, 242 pages, 1915 . . . . **9.00**

Scrimshaw

The most desirable examples of the art of scrimshaw can be traced back to the first half of the 19th century, to the hey-day of the whaling industry. Some voyages lasted for several years; conditions on board were often dismal. Sailors filled the long hours by carving or engraving designs in whale or walrus ivory. Using the tools of their trade, they created animal figures, boxes, pie crimpers, etc., often emphasing the lines of their carvings with ink or berry stain.

Eskimos also made scrimshaw, sometimes borrowing designs from the sailors who traded with them.

American trophy of arms, flags, eagle, whale tooth, 9″ **1,300.00**
Bodkin, fist w/snake, ivory, 3½″ **110.00**
Cane, 32½″ **250.00**
Carved, female leg at end, whale ivory, 34¾″ **185.00**
Wooden shaft w/whale ivory clenched hand, 36¾″ **250.00**
Double swift, 16″ **800.00**
Double swift, 18″ **900.00**
Fin-back whale, figural, whale bone, 7″ **240.00**
Half-log, portrait of bearded sailor, MS Jack Owen, 3¼″ long . **110.00**
Jagging wheel **250.00**
With 4-tined fork **350.00**
Ladies, figural of 2, whale tooth, 1870, 4½″ **240.00**
Pie crimper, whale tooth, 6″ **325.00**
Pipe tamper, leg w/boot, bone, 2¾″ **110.00**
Ships, 2, w/3 masts, whale tooth, 6½″ long **250.00**
Walking cane, carved bone shaft, ivory knob, 1840s, 34¼″ long **375.00**
Wantage stick, wood, ivory insets, 36″ **60.00**
Whale scene, ships, whale tooth, 3½″ long **55.00**
Ships & boots, whale tooth, 6½″ long **2,750.00**
Woman, flowers, figural, ivory, 4½″ **275.00**

Seals

A seal is a device used to affix a stamp or embossment either on an official paper or on wax such as was once used on correspondence.

Board of Elections of City of NY **25.00**
Brass, deep spiral bone handle, wax **16.00**
Bronze, French, by Rubin **390.00**
Cut glass, initial S, 2½" **12.00**
Letter, brass, full bodied young man, wax **28.00**
   Brass, heavy, w/baby figure on handle **13.50**
   Sterling Nouveau style handle, blank seal **14.00**
   Wooden handle, illus **9.00**
Marlborough Savings Bank **25.00**

Wood, Oriental handcarved figurine, 2 pc **28.00**

Sebastians

   Sebastian miniatures were first produced in 1938 by Prescott W. Baston, in Marblehead, Mass. Since then, he has modeled more than 400 designs. These figurines have been sold through gift shops all over the country, primarily in the New England states. In 1976, Baston withdrew his 'Sebastians' from production. Under an agreement with the Lance Corporation of Hudson, Mass., 100 designs were selected to be produced by that company under Baston's supervision. Those remaining were discontinued. In the short time since then, the older figurines have become very collectible. A pair of very early Swedish Boy and Girl figures which originally sold in 1938, recently brought in excess of $1,000.00 at two separate auctions.

A Call From the Candy Man, Necco, Marblehead **100.00**
Abraham Lincoln, bronze, Marblehead **150.00**
   Small base, Marblehead **95.00**
   Standing **18.50**
Anne Boleyn, Marblehead **125.00**
Annie Stuyvesant, Marblehead **75.00**
Aunt Polly, blue label, #6135 . . . . **19.50**
   Old **60.00**
Baby buggy, blue label, #6303 . . . . **22.50**
Becky Thatcher, blue label, #6131 . . . . **19.50**
   Old **60.00**
Ben Franklin, blue label, #6006 . . . . **19.50**
   Marblehead **75.00**
Betsy Ross, Marblehead **50.00**
   Pewter **75.00**
Bob Cratchit, Marblehead **50.00**
Buffalo Bill & Anne Oakley **100.00**
Building days, boy & girl pr **60.00**
   Set, sgnd **75.00**
Candy store, plate, sgnd **50.00**

Charles Dickens, Marblehead, sgnd **75.00**
Children series, complete **350.00**
Clown, blue label **90.00**
Marblehead **150.00**
   Sgnd, Marblehead **165.00**
Colonial kitchen, Marblehead **50.00**
Corner Drug Store, Marblehead **60.00**
Coronado & Senora, Marblehead **150.00**
Countess Olivea, Marblehead **150.00**
Cowhand, blue label, #6508 . . . . **19.50**
Cranberry Picker, Marblehead **85.00**
Dam Van Winkle, Marblehead **75.00**
Debby Franklin, Marblehead **75.00**
Dilemma, the Cow **150.00**
Doc Berry, red **50.00**
   Sgnd **200.00**
     Blue label **150.00**
Doctor, plate, sgnd **50.00**
Donald McKay, blue label, #d **19.50**
Falstaff, Marblehead **100.00**
Falstaff & Mistress Ford **100.00**
Family Fishing **35.00**
Family Picnic **35.00**
   Sgnd **65.00**
Family Reading **40.00**
   Sgnd **45.00**
Family Sing **135.00**
   Sgnd, dated **140.00**
Fisherman, blue label, #6228 . . . . **22.50**
George Thatcher, old **60.00**
George Washington **24.00**
   Pre-Marblehead **90.00**
George Washington & Martha, Marblehead **135.00**
   Blue label, #6321 . . . . **24.50**
George Washington w/Cannon, Marblehead **50.00**
   Pewter base **95.00**
Glassblower, Marblehead **60.00**
Governor Williamsburg & Lady, Marblehead **175.00**
Grand Canyon, sgnd **75.00**
Henry VIII, Marblehead **125.00**
Herny VIII, sgnd & A Boleyn, Marblehead **200.00**
Henry Wadsworth Longfellow **200.00**
Huck Finn, blue label, #d **19.50**
In the Candy Store, sgnd **60.00**
Jefferson, blue label, #d **19.50**
Jessie Buffam, Marblehead **100.00**
Jim, Marblehead **50.00**
Joan of Arc, Marblehead **170.00**
John Adams, Pewter **95.00**
John Alden & Priscilla, Marblehead **150.00**
John Hancock, bronze, sgnd, Marblehead **200.00**
   Marblehead **150.00**
John Lafitte, Marblehead **75.00**
John Smith & Pocahontas **100.00**
Judge Thatcher, blue label, #6134 lg **9.50**
   Marblehead **50.00**
Lexington Minuteman, sgnd, Marblehead **140.00**
Lobsterman, Marblehead **50.00**
Malovolio, Marblehead **150.00**
Mark Anthony, Marblehead **150.00**
Merchants Warren National Bank **200.00**
Micawber, blue label **25.00**
Michigan Hiller, paperweight **125.00**
Motiff #1, Marblehead **50.00**

Mr & Mrs Beacon Hill, Marblehead	**240.00**
Mrs Beacon Hill, Marblehead	**130.00**
Naumkeag Indian	**200.00**
Obocell, Marblehead	**150.00**
Old Salt, blue label, #d	**19.50**
Paul Bunyan, gr label	**200.00**
Marblehead	**325.00**
Sgnd	**400.00**
Pecksniff, Marblehead	**50.00**
Pegotty, Marblehead	**50.00**
Peter Stuyvesant, Marblehead	**150.00**
Phoebe, Marblehead label	**150.00**
Pilgrims, blue label, #d	**24.50**
Marblehead	**50.00**
Pioneer Couple, blue label, #d	**24.50**
Pioneer Village, blue label, #d	**22.50**
Pocahontas, Marblehead	**125.00**
Rip Van Winkle, Marblehead	**75.00**
Robert E Lee, blue label, #d	**22.50**
Romeo, Marblehead	**95.00**
Romeo & Juliet, Marblehead	**175.00**
Sailing Days, pr	**50.00**
Sairy Gamp & Mrs Harris, Marblehead	**50.00**
Sam Houston & Margaret, Marblehead	**150.00**
Savin' Sandy, Marblehead	**120.00**
School Days, pr	**40.00**
Scrooge, Marblehead	**50.00**
Sgnd, Marblehead	**65.00**
Senora, Marblehead	**60.00**
Shaker Lady, Marblehead	**85.00**
Shaker Man, Marblehead	**125.00**
Shaker Man & Lady, Marblehead	**225.00**
Shawmut Indian	**150.00**
Shriner, Marblehead	**120.00**
Sidewalk days, pr	**125.00**
Sistine Madonna, blue	**35.00**
Skipping Rope, blue label, #d	**23.50**
Snow Days, #d, pr	**45.00**
Sgnd, pr	**55.00**
Song at Cratchet, sgnd, Marblehead	**55.00**
Speak For It, blue	**25.00**
Stearns Couple, Marblehead	**110.00**
Swan Boat, gr label, 1950	**85.00**
Swedish Boy, Marblehead	**250.00**
Switching the Freight, red	**22.00**
The Doctor, Marblehead	**60.00**
Plate	**40.00**
The Masonic Bible	**250.00**
The Piper, sgnd, Marblehead	**150.00**
The Weaver, Marblehead	**60.00**
Tom Bowline blue label, #6246	**19.50**
Marblehead	**50.00**
Town Crier, Plaque, blue	**30.00**
Plaque, red	**15.00**
Uncle Sam, Marblehead	**50.00**
Sgnd	**50.00**
Yankee Clipper Ship	**60.00**
Yankee Sea Captain	**115.00**

Sevres

Fine quality porcelains have been made in Sevres, France, since the early 1700s. Rich ground colors were decorated with hand painted portraits, scenics and florals, transfer printing or decalcomania, and are often embellish-

ed with heavy gold. These wares are the most respected of all French porcelains. Their style and design has been widely copied.

Bowl, bronze mount, floral reserve, late 1800s, 21¾" dia	**1,200.00**
Box, red & gold, hinged & ftd, 10"	**350.00**
Chamberstick, ormolu mounting, 5"	**100.00**
Condiment dish, w/3 cups, floral, gold & blue trim, 1760	**500.00**
Cup & saucer, demitasse, animals, Chateau Fontainbleu, 1846	**45.00**
Demitasse pot, w/figural scenes by Beitien, 7"	**135.00**
Dessert plate, Chateau de Fontainbleu, mkd, 1847, set of 6	**650.00**
Plate, Chateau Des Tuileries, cream, blue & gold	**265.00**
Duc de Bourgogne, blue mk, 1846, 9½" dia	**195.00**
Duchesse de Bourgogne, rose border w/3 floral medallions	**125.00**
French portrait, 10"	**135.00**
Louis XV portrait, chateau mk	**120.00**
Louis XVI portrait, cobalt blue border, gilded curliques, 10"	**260.00**
Man & woman, scenic, pink border, sgnd, pr	**300.00**
Mde Parabore, heavy gold, 9½"	**175.00**
Portrait, blue w/gold border, sgnd, 9½"	**115.00**
Portrait, green border w/gold, sgnd	**200.00**
Portrait, scalloped edge, cobalt, gilt, 10"	**130.00**
Sauce boat, attached underplate, lt blue, gold scrolls, 6½x9¾", pr	**600.00**
Serving tray, floral, gold & blue trim, 1748, 8x8"	**350.00**
Sugar & creamer, royal portrait, blue & gold floral panels, 1852	**450.00**
Tazza, blue celeste border, floral reserves w/courting scene, 1870	**300.00**
Tobacco jar, w/lid, 6"	**90.00**
Urn, blue w/hunting scenes, 1835, 15"	**375.00**
Cobalt blue w/bronze handles, 6" base, mkd, 1837, 10" pr	**950.00**
With lid, hp flowers & portrait, ormolu base, handles & rim, 11¾"	**275.00**

Sewing Items

In the early colonial days, the teaching of needlework skills were considered an important part of a young girl's education. The Victorians developed many curious yet functional sewing accessories. One of these is the sewing bird. Made of brass, wood or iron, these figural tools were designed to be clamped onto the top of the work table. Through the lever action of the tail, the beak would open and close to hold the fabric in the proper position for hand sewing. A velvet pincushion often topped them off.

The first mechanical sewing machine was invented by Thomas Paint, an Englishman, in 1790. The first American patent went to Elias Howe in 1840---but Howe took his invention to England! Not until 1846, when the Wheeler Wilson Mfg. Co. was founded, were there any truly functional home sewing machines. The first electric machine was developed by Isaac Singer in 1889.

Thimbles have long been collectible. Some were made of silver---a few in gold. Many were embossed with scrolls, engraved, and occasionally jeweled!

Hallmarked examples are especially valuable.

Book, How to Make Dresses, orig holder, Singer Sewing Co, 1924-30 **12.00**
Button; Aesop's Fables, fox & grapes, 1½″ **8.00**
  Brass, woman's head in relief, 2¼x1½″ **20.00**
  Bust of Queen Elizabeth, 1½″ **10.00**
  Celluloid, blk, round w/brass raised Gibson girl............. **3.00**
  Ceramic, Jack & Jill nursery rhyme, set of 4 .... **45.00**
  Cloisonne, pr, 1¼″ **15.00**
  German shepherd dog, encased in glass................... **3.00**
  Gold, open work, w/enameling, 1½″ **35.00**
  High wheel bicycle, ½″............................ **5.00**
  Kate Greenaway girl, 1½″ **10.00**
  Metal, bell shape, ornate **8.00**
  Ocean pearl, Occupied Japan, set of 4 on orig card, 1948 ... **10.00**
  Old, colored, American **15.00**
  On card, Deco, set of 6.......................... **4.00**
  Opal glass, pink, set of 4 .... **8.00**
  Porcelain, hp floral, 1½″ **12.00**
  St George slaying the dragon, 1″ **6.00**
  Sterling, cupid, English **10.00**
  Sterling, large heart, English **12.00**
  Sterling, mkd, set of 6, Russian, 1870, ½″............. **25.00**
  Teddy bear, ¾″ **5.00**
Buttonhole cutter, ci & brass, mechanical, sgnd, 1880, 7″ long **120.00**
  Hand forged, 1800s, 3″ **65.00**

Cabinet, pine, spool pegs, drawer, pincushion, 1900s **50.00**
Crochet hook, bone handled, tiny hook, Milwerd .12........... **3.50**
Darner, blown glass, gray w/wht loopings, 10″ **100.00**
  Double ended, blonde wood, foot-form, patented **4.00**
  Glove, embossed scrolls, ring for hanging, mkd **32.00**
  Glove, sterling **25.00**
  Stocking, end of day, 11½″ **12.00**
  Wood disc w/3″ wood handle, metal band, 1890s........... **8.00**
Darning egg, w/handle, ruby glass, 6½″ **30.00**
Drafting machine, for dress makers, made by McDowell Garment **125.00**
Embroidery machine, orig box, AC White Co, 1891 .... **40.00**
  Orig box, S & S Co, 1915 .... **40.00**
Hem gauge, ci, early, the Parisian **10.00**
  Pelouze, 1894 .... **30.00**
Loom, w/orig paint & instructions, Newcomb Loom Co, 42″ material **300.00**
Needle case, beaded roses & flower garland, 1834........... **85.00**
  Combination glove darner **50.00**

Cylindrical, carved horn, opens at 2 ends **55.00**
  Ivory **25.00**
  Sterling, embossed pigs **75.00**
  Sterling, w/handle, ornate, scrolls **28.00**
Needle threader, brass **10.00**
Pin cushion, beaded edges, rectangular fuchsia, 4 beaded stars, 3x4″ **33.00**
  Beaded Victorian velvet, scalloped, floral, 7½″ **25.00**
  Boot, beaded **45.00**
  Double scalloped shell.......................... **10.00**
  Shoe, Expo, pewter **30.00**
  Shoe, Gorham **65.00**
  Sterling, heart shaped, repousse, Reed & Barton **65.00**
  Sterling, high heeled slipper, Gorham **65.00**
  Velvet on brass log w/silver plate ped, 3x1½″........... **12.00**
Ribbon threader, heavily chased sterling, Victorian **18.00**

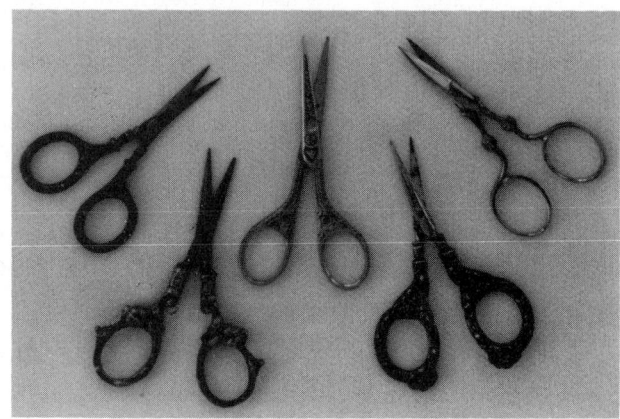

Scissors, Art Nouveau, England, silver plate, 4″............. **12.50**
  Baby faces, brass, 4″, illus **16.50**
  Daisy design on handle, 3½″, illus.................. **8.00**
  Floral, silver plate, 3″, illus **14.00**
  Gold plate, Toledo, 4″, illus **16.50**
  Fancy handles, w/star band adv **7.00**
  Gold wash, souvenir, Wendell, 4″ **35.00**
  Iron, lg handforged hallmk, very old **20.00**
  Keen Kutter, 7½″............................. **15.00**
  Ornate w/man & woman in reserve, 6½″ **12.00**
  Steel blades, 4″ brass embossed handles, 1850s **30.00**
  Tailor's hand forged, iron, 1840..................... **48.00**
  Winchester **27.50**
Sewing basket, bead & coin trim, 10½″ dia.............. **32.00**
  Grass & raffia, braided handle, 1910, 2x8½″ **30.00**
  With cover, sweet grass, 10″ dia................... **22.00**
Sewing bird, 2 red velvet cushions, Victorian **110.00**
  Brass clamp, gold washed, blue pillow............... **125.00**
  Brass embossed, clamp on, pin cushion................ **95.00**
  Brass, 1887 .... **140.00**
  Brass, double **140.00**
  Brass, small cushion below bird **120.00**
  Silver plate, dated on wing, 1853.................. **125.00**
Sewing box, dresser shape, 3-drawer, 1850s, 9½x9½x6″ **250.00**
  Velvet on tin, lace w/sixth plate tintype **135.00**
Sewing cabinet, Hepplewhite M Washington, mahogany, 29x27x13″ **450.00**
Sewing clamp, ci, open scroll work, swing arm, table screw, 4½″ **45.00**
Sewing kit, manicure set combination, silver cat decor, Germany **15.00**
  With brush, leather w/needlepoint cover, Austrian **16.00**
  With thimble **65.00**
Sewing machine, cast brass foliage, DW Clark pat 1858 ..... **245.00**
  Cast iron, hand crank, B Eldridge, Wanamaker, 1880s **65.00**
  Cast iron, hand crank, Wilcox & Gibbs, 1861, 8x11x6″ **70.00**
  Cast iron, New Remington #4...................... **70.00**

Cast iron, Singer Manufacturing Co, Spartan Great Britain . . . **35.00**
Hand crank, orig box & booklet, Improved S&E, 1897, 6½" . **75.00**
Hand crank, ornate, #60332, 1866, 7x6x4" **55.00**
Hand operated, early, MOP inlay, pawfoot, 122 yrs old **110.00**
Octagon shaped, Centennial Singer, 1851-1951 . . . . **20.00**
Portable, Remington, 1879 . . . . **125.00**
Treadle, #294, leather 12" throat **150.00**
White, hand crank, ornate w/case **45.00**
Wilcox & Gibbs, #1502, 1880s **100.00**
Sewing table, mahogany, 1820 . . . . **750.00**
Spool box, w/spool holders, drawer & pin cushion, walnut, 4½" sq **45.00**
Spool stand, embossed, ftd base, w/pin cushion, ci stand, 5½x7½" **65.00**
   Gorham **55.00**
   Sterling, plain, fancy mono **65.00**
   Walnut, 7 spools, 4" pin cushion, 4¾x6" **35.00**
Tape measure, advertising, General Electric Refrigerators, celluloid **24.00**
   Advertising, Lydia Pinkham **32.00**
   Advertising, State Bank Marietta, celluloid **12.00**
   Alarm clock figural **50.00**
   Basket of flowers, early plastic **5.00**
   Burled wood, 1840s **44.00**
   Chicken figural, brass, worm in bill turns **25.00**
   Clam figural **45.00**
   Clock figural, brass, mk Germany **9.50**
   Dog figural, stuffed, Japan **15.00**
   Dressmaker's dummy figural, plastic, 4" **15.00**
   Fishing reel treen **35.00**
   Flask figural, Indian head **55.00**
   French carriage figural, gilt, brass, red windows **75.00**
   Greek Key, sterling **50.00**
   Indian head figural, celluloid **18.00**
   Man's head figural, porcelain, fly on head pulls out tape **40.00**
   Negro figural, scarce, celluloid **100.00**
   Ostrich & small child, picture, Cawston ostrich farm **25.00**
   Owl figural, glass eyes, German round, brass & plate, 1½" . . . **22.00**
   Parrot figural, celluloid **26.00**
   Pig figural, pewter, tail turns **25.00**
   Puss & Boots, celluloid **45.00**
   Sailing ship figural **24.00**
   Scotty dog figural, w/pin cushion **40.00**
   Souvenir, World's Fair, 1904 . . . . **10.00**
   Spinning top, ivory figural **50.00**
   Sterling, embossed **65.00**
   Telephone w/pin cushion, porcelain **18.50**
   Turtle figural, movable head **48.00**
Tatting shuttle **35.00**
Thimble, aluminum, Coca Cola sewing kit, WWII **4.00**
   Bone china, Staffordshire England **9.00**
   Brass, Japan **3.00**
   Ceramic, Capo di Monte orig by KB Italy **20.00**
   Child's size **25.00**
   Cherub **100.00**
   Enamel on copper, cloisonne, gold plate **20.00**
   Genuine horn **20.00**
   Gold, 10k **85.00**
   Gold, 14k, 12 sided plain band ½", mkd, size 12 . . . . **95.00**
   Gold, 14k, Simmons **60.00**
   Gold, 14k, crochet basket, mkd, size 11 . . . . **120.00**
   Gold, 14k, decorative band & beading unmkd, size 7 . . . . . . **75.00**
   Gold, 14k, heavy, Victorian **95.00**
   Gold, 14k, ornate border **100.00**
   Gold, 14k, three churches **135.00**
   Gold, 14k, w/orig leatherette case **60.00**
   Gold, 14k, wide band of leaves, unmkd, size 7 . . . . **80.00**

Gold and sterling **70.00**
Gold plate, Old Toledo, colored band, Spain **7.00**

Hand wrought, ornate silver plate **48.00**
Iron, quilting, lg **6.00**
Lydia Pinkham **18.00**
Political, Nixon '68 . . . . **2.00**
Political, Wallace '76 . . . . **2.00**
Porcelain, Betty Boop **5.00**
Porcelain, Elvis Presley **5.00**
Porcelain, floral w/gold rim, Chinese export **6.00**
Porcelain, gold, 14k, B & G King Tut, ltd ed **27.50**
Porcelain, John Wayne **5.00**
Porcelain, Porsgrund 1st ltd Ed by AM Odegaard **20.00**
Porcelain, President & Nancy Reagan inaugural **6.00**
Porcelain, Red Cross anniversary **5.00**
Porcelain, Royal Couple wedding **6.00**
Porcelain, the space shuttle **5.00**
Silver plate, daisy design, Charles & Diana, 7/29/81 . . . . **8.00**
Silver plate, turquoise, Austria **12.50**
Sterling band **55.00**
Sterling, hand made **38.00**
Sterling decorated, Priscilla, May 1898 . . . . **25.00**
Sterling gold-washed, w/heavy raised roses **21.00**
Sterling w/14k gold wash, love birds, France **38.00**
Sterling, #7 . . . . **30.00**
Sterling, engraved border, feathers & bells, name & date **30.00**
Sterling, jewel encased top, porcelain floral band, Germany . . . **25.00**
Sterling, simple design **20.00**
Sterling, w/ornate 14k overlay bottom half **36.00**
Wht metal, My Favorite Thimble, lady w/thimble **50.00**
Thimble caddy, aluminum w/cobalt blue glass insert **12.00**
   Brass & celluloid **10.00**
   Brass & copper, donkey **16.00**
   Brass egg **30.00**
   Sterling, ornate, repousse, w/piercing **85.00**
   Sterling, w/embossments & thimble **60.00**
Thread box, silver, English, ball-shaped, birds & foliage, 1892, 3" **265.00**
Thread holder, ivory, carved, w/winders **20.00**

Shaker Items

The Shaker community was founded in America in 1776 at Niskeyuna, New York, by a small group of English 'Shaking Quakers'. The name referred to a group dance which was part of their religious rites. They were lead by Mother Ann Lee.

By 1815 their membership had grown to more than 1,000 in 18 communities as far west as Indiana and Kentucky. But in less than a decade, their numbers began to decline, until today only a handful remain.

Their furniture is prized for its originality, simplicity, workmanship and practicality. Few pieces were signed. Some were carefully finished to enhance the natural wood; a few were painted.

Although other methods were used earlier, most Shaker boxes were of oval construction with overlapping 'fingers' at the seams to prevent buckling as the wood aged. Boxes with original paint fetch double the price of an unpainted box; size and number of fingers are also considerations.

Although the Shakers were responsible for weaving a great number of

baskets, their methods are not easily distinguished from those of their outside neighbors, and it is nearly impossible without first hand knowledge to specifically attribute one to their manufacture. They were involved in various commercial efforts other than cabinetmaking---among them sheep and dairy farming, sawmills, and pipe and brick making. They were the first to raise crops specifically for seed, and to market their product commercially. They perfected a method to recycle paper, and were able to produce wrinkle free fabrics.

Advertisement, cardboard, Tannar Laxative	400.00
Basket, feather-type, mold woven, w/lid, handle	270.00
Open, palm leaf, 6-sides, 1800s, 1x6¾″ dia	35.00
Round swing handle, Enfield, Conn., mid-1800s, 13½″ dia	275.00
Round, side handles, criss cross top lacing, painted, 15½x7½″	85.00
With cover, woven, small	85.00
With handles, painted, some wear, 20″ dia	135.00
Bath tub, metal half bath	225.00
Boiler, tin, blue paint, 10x17″	135.00
Bonnet, palm	100.00
Wine velvet	100.00
Woven, child's strips of blk, machine stitched, #5 label, 9½″	55.00
Book, Kentucky Revival...Shakerism, M'Nemar, reprinted 1808	30.00
Manifesto of the Church of Christ, John Dunlavy, 1818, 6x9″	50.00
Box, Alfred, Maine	26.00
Cardboard, dried green sweet corn seed, 6½″	80.00
Round, Harvard, Mass, 1800s, 2x4″ dia	185.00
Seed, wood & tin dividers, partial front label, 4¼x11x24″	85.00
Oval, 2 shaped & chamfered finger laps, brass nails, 7¾″	115.00
Oval, 3 finger, copper tacks, old varnish finish, 3½x6x9″	350.00
Oval, 3 fingered, lid finger shorter than box finger, 2x4½″	110.00
Oval, cut out finger construction, copper tacks, varnish finish	760.00
Oval, Harvard Mass, 1¾x4½x3½″	185.00
Oval, iron nail, orig alligatored paint, sgnd, 1808, 6x11½x15½″	725.00
Oval, w/cover, 6″	75.00
Brush, horsehair, w/turned wood handle, 10¾″	22.50
With string wrapped handle, 8″	450.00
With turned wooden handle, orig red paint, 12¾″	115.00
Bucket, maple syrup, sgnd	165.00
Sap, old red & yellow paint, 'Enfield, N.H. #2'	200.00
Cheese basket, 20″	295.00
Woodpegged, cheesecloth spread over frame, 1700	350.00
Chest, cherry, 4 drawer, top bonnet drawer, cut-out ft, 42x19x43″	1,550.00
Clothespins, pair	35.00
Coffee pot, tin, 9½″	75.00
Cupboard, over 6 drawers, pine	3,900.00
Pine wall, 1-pc, cut-out ft, refinished, 68½x36x15¾″ dia	600.00
Darning egg, 2 colors of wood, Thos Fisher, Eufield, Conn., 4½″	15.00
Multiwood, very delicate handle, 6″	75.00
Dipper, tin, 15″	35.00
Drying rack, herb	150.00
Ten folding arms, center post, 4 legs	450.00
Flour bag, graham, like new condition	155.00
Food chopper	25.00
Hand mirror, oval framed, beveled glass plate, tapered handle, 1800s	40.00
Hanger, chestnut, bentwood, 24″	65.00
Clothes, wooden, w/red ribbon, 15½″	30.00
Label, butter beans & fresh tomatoes, 4½x14¾″, 2 for	45.00
Lunch box, 1835, 10x11″	150.00
Mirror rack, cherry w/5 brush pegs	900.00
Needle cushion, 5x5″	30.00
Pegboard, w/8 pegs, 55″	140.00
Pie lifter, wood handle, 2-tined	35.00
Pin cushion, split poplar trim, Alfred, Maine, 1800s, 4″ dia	75.00

Wood, sgnd: Sabbathday Lake Shaker	125.00
Rocking chair, birch, turned posts, 4 slat back, #7	165.00
Crest w/shawl bar, 3 slats, woven seat, #4, 33″	170.00
Dark brown finish, red & blk tape seat, orig label,#3	400.00
Turned finials, taped back & seat, double stretchers	185.00
Rolling pin, cherry, all 1 pc	75.00
Long clothespin handles, 19″	65.00
Sewing basket, fitted, sgnd	130.00
Sewing box, oval, pink satin lining, sgnd, 7″	125.00
Oval, w/cover & carrying handle, fitted, 3x7½″	100.00
Shaving box, 1800s	145.00
Sieve, horsehair, dk mustard, orig paint, straight lap seam, 2x5″ dia	115.00
Sunbonnet, brown & wht gingham, machine stitched, Hancock, 11″	35.00
Tray, for bean sorting	50.00
Wooden, oval, gr, 3¾x5″	150.00
Utility brush, 1800s, 10″ long	40.00
Yarn winder, hard & soft wood, sq nail construction, 26″ wheel, 32″	355.00

Shaving Mugs

In the 1870s it became a popular practice for every shaving man to have his own shaving mug. Mugs belonging to men who frequented the barber shop for their tonsorial services were often personalized with their owner's name and occupation, and kept on display on the barber's shelf. Undecorated mugs imported from Germany and France were sent to New York and Chicago and decorated to order. Because of sanitary rules and restrictions later imposed, they were eventually taken off the barbers' shelves. Today, the occupational mugs are the most valuable.

The John Hudson Moore Company produced a line of Sportsman mugs in 1953 and 54.

Applied florals, cobalt, Germany	35.00
Clambroth, wheat	35.00
Floral, hp, gold rim, soap shelf	27.50
Milk glass, Mephistopheles	20.00
Mirror on front, blue swirls, florals, Germany	65.00
Occupational, artist	250.00
Baggage car, 1910	100.00
Barbershop, w/customers	190.00
Bartender, w/2 customers	195.00
Blacksmith shoeing horse	175.00
Blacksmith w/anvil, hp, mkd A Kern BS Co Decorators, St Louis	155.00
Buggy driver w/2 horses	180.00
Butcher w/steer & tools	150.00
Cab driver w/coach & horse	180.00
Carpenter at bench	160.00

Carriage maker, w/name, D&C Co **135.00**
Conductor, floral trim, V&D Austria **100.00**
Dentist, depicts dentist at work **130.00**
Doctors name, banner on pole, Limoges **90.00**
Dry goods salesman & customer **190.00**
Farmer plowing w/2 horses **190.00**
Girl friend **135.00**
Grocery store & clerk **135.00**
High button shoe, flowers, blue & gold, name **115.00**
Horse & carriage hearse **325.00**
Horsebreeder, hp, mkd, Barbers Supply Co, Kohen Barbers . . **75.00**
Horses & carriage **300.00**
Iron puddler, man working at job, name in gold **195.00**
Locomotive, 1875 . . . . **125.00**
Milk wagon & horse **175.00**
Pharmacist, mortar & pestle **150.00**
Printer at printer case **190.00**
Railway conductor, caboose **125.00**
Roller shoe skate **275.00**
Sheep **250.00**
Steam engineer **125.00**
Pink luster, lily-of-the-valley, applied **30.00**
RS Prussia, florals **90.00**
Rose sprays, pink w/gr border, gold trim, old, mkd: Ct, lg . . . **40.00**
Scuttle, baby shoe **65.00**
    Ben Johnson **85.00**
    Bull frog **75.00**
    Chinaman **65.00**
    Elephant **80.00**
    Fish **50.00**
    Flower **25.00**
    Hen **60.00**
    Hp pink/yellow roses, brush rest handle, Germany **28.00**
    Indian **65.00**
    Negro, purple bow tie **110.00**
    Pig **40.00**
    Swan **35.00**
Show wagon omnibus, turn of the century **625.00**
Silver plated, raised floral, trimmed insert w/brush rest **40.00**
    Reed & Barton, monogram, fancy handle & feet, 1900 . . . . **60.00**
Stag, color transfer, gold trim **40.00**
Think of Me, German, raised gold letters on wht **25.00**
Toby-type, full figure, feet hold bowl, soap indentation in hat . . . **65.00**

Shawnee Pottery

The Shawnee Pottery Company operated in Zansville, Ohio, from 1937 to 1961. They produced inexpensive novelty ware---vases, flower pots and figurines---as well as a very successful line of figural cookie jars. These cookie jars and their dinnerware called the Corn Line are very popular with today's collectors.

Basket, made by Shawnee Co for Rum Rill Pottery Co, #348 . . . **27.00**
Bookends, flying geese figural, pair, #4000 . . . . **14.00**
Bowl, Tiara line console, #3504 . . . . **12.00**
Candleholder, jug, pair, mkd 1500 w/applied Rum Rill labels . . . **24.00**
    Pair, #1386 . . . . **10.00**
    Shell, pair, #1911 . . . . **10.00**
Casserole, w/cover, Kenwood Sun Dial line, blk w/wht lid . . . **18.00**
Cookie jar, basket of fruit, #84 . . . . **22.00**
    Combination bank, Smiley Pig, #60 . . . . **30.00**
    Dutch Girl, #1026 . . . . **18.00**
    Farmer Pig, w/gr kerchief **24.00**
    Hugsey Dog, wht w/blue bow around head **26.00**
    Puss'n Boots lady, red bow, wht w/yellow, hat w/red trim . . . **26.00**

Corn, butter dish w/cover, #72, Queen **30.00**
    Casserole w/lid, ovenproof, #74, 11″ **30.00**
    Coffee mug, #69, King **18.00**
    Cookie jar w/lid, #66, King **50.00**
    Creamer, #70, King **9.50**
    Individual casserole w/lid, #73 . . . . **22.50**
    Mixing bowl, #5 . . . . **12.00**
    Pitcher, #71, King, 8″ **30.00**
    Plate, #68, King **15.00**
    Plate, #89 . . . . **15.00**
    Plate, #93, King **18.00**
    Platter, ovenproof, #96 . . . . **25.00**
    Popcorn set in orig box, 6 pc, King **80.00**
    Relish tray, oblong, #79 . . . . **12.00**
    Sauce dish, #92 . . . . **18.00**
    Saucer, #91, King **5.50**
    Shakers, pair, 5½″, unmkd **18.00**
    Shakers, pair, unmkd, 3½″ **12.00**
    Sugar bowl w/lid, #78, King **15.00**
    Teapot, individual, #65, King **50.00**
    Teapot w/lid, #75, King **40.00**
    Vegetable bowl, #95, King, 6¾x9″ **25.00**
Figurine, Oriental girl mounted on a planter base, #701 . . . . . **9.00**
    Oriental, pair, #602 . . . . **12.00**
Inkwell, cat figural, #673 . . . . **10.00**
Lamps, floral hand painted, pair, pink, mkd w/paper label . . . **42.00**
    Grape encrusted, pair, wht w/gold trim, 12″ **42.00**
    Urn shaped, pair, pink **38.00**
Pitcher, cream, elephant figural, pink inside ear, wht body . . . **11.00**
    Milk, Bo Peep figural, #47, 7½″ **14.00**
    Bloodhound dog figural, #610 . . . . **7.00**
    Bow Knot, double, #519 . . . . **11.00**
    Cameo line, blue, #2505 . . . . **7.00**
    Clock figural, #530 . . . . **9.00**
    Covered wagon figural, #733 . . . . **14.00**
    Elf shoe figural, #765 . . . . **9.00**
    Kenwood line, #1608 . . . . **9.00**
    Oriental boy, #702 . . . . **9.00**
    Pekingese figural, by gr dog house, house holds plants . . . **9.00**
    Pekingese & hound figural, #61 . . . . **9.00**
    Pump figural, #716 . . . . **12.00**
    Puppy pushing buggy figural, #704 . . . . **9.00**
    Quilted round, lg, #457 . . . . **7.00**
    Ram figural, beige, #515 . . . . **10.00**
    Rocking horse figural, #526 . . . . **10.00**
    Shoe figural, #525 . . . . **10.00**
    Stylized elephant figural, blk, by brown leaf **24.00**
    Swiss boy holding duck figural, #645 . . . . **10.00**
    Touche line, ftd, #1025 . . . . **7.00**
    Touche line, #1004 . . . . **6.00**
    With attached liner, #410 . . . . **6.00**
    With attached liner, #485 . . . . **6.00**
    With attached liner, 4″ gr, #454 . . . . **6.00**

With attached tray, #495, 5" 6.00
Windmill figural, #715 .... 11.00
Wishing well, brown, #710 .... 10.50
Shakers, Farmer & Winnie, pair, 5" 14.00
Puss 'n Boots, pair 11.00
Water can, pair, wht w/blue trim, gold handle 9.00
Winnie, pair, blue collars 11.00
Teapot, Granny Ann figural, gr 24.00
Tom Tom the Pipers Son figural, #44 .... 24.00
Vase, art line, made for Rum Rill Pottery Co, #505 ... 42.00
Brown high gloss wood grain, #868 .... 9.00
Bud, made for Rum Rill, wht, bulbous base, mkd Rum Rill .. 18.00
Dolphin figural, #828 .... 12.00
Elegance line tall bud, #1402 .... 10.00
Fawn figural, gr caricature, #850 .... 11.00
Heavy gold overglaze leaf design, #805 .... 10.50
Miniature, #1135 .... 10.00
Pineapple, #839 .... 12.00
Pink w/spillover blk enamel, lg, #2146 .... 12.00
Touche line pillow, #1012 .... 6.00
Woodgrain dull finish, #879 .... 9.00
Water jug, Smiley Pig figural, 2 qt 22.00

Sheet Music

Sheet music is often collected more for the colorful lithographed covers rather than for the music itself. Transportation songs which have pictures or illustrations of trains, ships and planes; ragtime tunes which feature popular entertainers such as Al Jolson; or those with Disney characters are among the most valuable.

Adorable, 1933, Gaynor 20.00
Aladdin, 1847, Bufford, museum scene on cover 25.00
Along The Way To Waikiki, 1917, Al Jolson on cover 6.00
An Unlucky Coon, 1899, WA Cory, brown/orange cover 15.00
Animal Crackers In My Soup, 1935, Shirley Temple 20.00
Any Rags, 1902, Thos S Allan, photo of Three Mitchells 12.00
At Coontown's Picnic, 1899, Hans S Lins 15.00
At The Devil's Ball, Berlin, devils dancing on cover 14.00
Babes On Broadway, Garland cover 10.00
Barney Google 10.00
Beautiful Eyes, 1909, Whiting & De Haven, Roy Weed on cover .. 9.00
Beyond The Blue Horizon, 1930, J Buchanan & J Macdonald . 6.00
Blues Quick Step, 1836, Moores 25.00
Brownies On Parade, 1908 .... 10.00
By The Watermelon Vine Lindy Lou, 1904, TS Allen 15.00
Cain & Mable, Clark Gable on cover 13.00
Campin' On De Ole Suwanee, 1899, Lee Orean Smith 10.00
Capitol Quick Step, 1840, dedicated to the Hon Henry Clay .. 40.00
Chili Sauce Rag, 1910, HA Fischler, Negro family on cover .. 18.00
Colored Aristocracy Cake Walk, 1899, GW Bernard, blk/wht cover 25.00
Contraband, 1860, mansion w/overseer chasing black children 40.00
Fire, Fire, 1850, Tappan & Bradford, firemen & engines on cover 48.00
General Grant's March, 1862, battle scene cover 30.00
Good Ship Lollipop, Shirley Temple cover 15.00
Happy Family Polka, Sarony & Majors, family scene, sepia ... 20.00
Heigh Ho, from Snow White, Walt Disney enterprises 10.00
Hello Mary Lou, Ricky Nelson cover 10.00
Hello My Dearie, 1917, Raphael Kirchner cover 27.50
High & Mighty, John Wayne cover 15.00
How Are You Green-Backs, 1863, Bowers & Glover 40.00
How Long Will It Last, 1931, Crawford 25.00
I Got Stung, Elvis Presley cover 15.00
I Love A Piano, 1915, Irving Berlin, large size format 15.00

I Want To Hold Your Hand, Beatles 12.00
If You Want The Rainbow, 1928, Fanny Brice cover 7.00
Jealous Moon, 1918, Kerr, Zamecnik, couple sitting on moon, N.Y. 12.00
K-K-K Katy, 1913, O'Hara, published by Leo Feist, N.Y. .. 12.00
Kaiser Jubilee March, 1913, ET Paull 29.00
Know Nothing Polka, 1855, portrait of Govenor of Massachusetts 30.00
Lancers Quick Step, 1837, Moore 25.00
Lavender Blue 25.00
Lieut Clark's Quick Step, 1837, Buffard, color, portrait 50.00
Little French Mother, Rockwell cover, small 25.00
Little Annie Rooney, Mary Pickford on cover 17.00
Lone Star, 1936, S Simons, souvenir edition, cowboy & horse 18.00
Love Me Tender, Elvis Presley cover 25.00
Make Believe, 1927, Ziegfield, from Show Boat 20.00
March Of The Boy Scouts, 1912, Kocian 18.00
Marching On To Victory, 1878, temperance march 12.00
Midnight Fire Alarm, horse drawn fire engine on cover 23.00
Moon Song, 1932, picture of Kate Smith 8.00
'N Everything, 1918, Al Jolson on cover 8.00
Napoleon's Last Charge, 1910, ET Paull 12.00
New Star In Heaven Tonight, Rudolph Valentino on cover ... 14.00
One Song, from first full length Snow White feature 45.00
Ossian's Serenade, 1850, Bufford, blk/wht litho cover 25.00
Over There, 1917, Norman Rockwell cover 30.00
Over There, 1917, soldiers on stage cover 10.00
Over There, 1917, w/Nora Bayes on cover 10.00
Over Yonder Where The Lilies Grow, Rockwell cover, small .. 25.00
Pennies From Heaven, 1936, Crosby 5.00
Pershing's Crusaders March, 1918, ET Paull 10.00
Poor Old Slave, 1851, Griffin, hand-colored cover 21.00
Precious Little Thing Called Love, 1928, G Cooper & N Carroll 6.00
President Johnson's Grand March & Quick Step, 1865, Mack . 33.00
Prize Banner Quick Step, 1841, blk/wht litho, political, Whig Party 15.00
Rio Grande Quick March, 1846, Andrews, for Gen Zachery Taylor 55.00
She Reminds Me Of You, 1934, Crosby & Lombard 20.00
Silver Bell March, 1865, Blake, dedicated to Lowell Baseball Club 25.00
Silver Sleigh Bells, ET Paull, litho cover 15.00
Sit Down You're Rocking The Boat, 1913 .... 10.00
Someday My Prince Will Come, 1937, Berlin, Snow White cover 25.00
Sonny Boy, Al Jolsen on cover 16.00
Stars & Stripes Forever, 1897, John Philip Sousa Band on cover 14.00
Strenuous Life, 1901, Teddy Roosevelt cover 25.00
Take Me On A Buick Honeymoon, 1922, Black & Hickman .. 17.00
The Assassin's Vision, 1865, JW Turner, published by H Tolman 30.00
The Perfect Song, 1919, Amos 'n Andy 20.00
The Ship That Never Returned, 1865, Henry C Work 16.00
The Simple Things in Life, Shirley Temple 22.00
There's Nothing Half So Nice...Ham What Ham, 1905, Fred Fisher 35.00
They Were All Out Of Step But Jim, 1918, WWI soldiers on cover 6.50
Three Little Words, 1930, Harms, Amos n' Andy cover 16.50
Thurston March & Two-Step, 1911 .... 25.00
True Confessions, 1937, Carole Lombard on cover 6.00
Turkey In The Straw Rag, Negro cover illustration 15.00
United Nations March, ET Paull, litho cover 15.00
Waa! Hoo!, 1936, cowboy & horse on cover, picture of F Waring 7.50
Wake Up Little Susie, Everly Borthers on cover 12.00
When You Wish Upon a Star, from Pinocchio 35.00
Whippoorwill Scottish, Chandler Bros, 1836, color litho cover 26.00
Whistle While You Work, Walt Disney Enterprises 10.00
Will You Be My Teddy Bear, 1907, Anna Held cover 18.00

Shelley

Ashtray, Rose Spray 25.00

Bon-bon, florals.. **15.00**
Bowl, Rose Spray, 8½″ dia **75.00**
Butter, w/cover, Rosebud, 7¼″ dia **135.00**
Cake plate, 10″... **30.00**
    Begonia, 8x9½″ **50.00**
    Rosebud, ftd, 3x8½″................................... **85.00**
Cigarette holder, Regency, wht w/gold............. **24.00**
Coffee set, Begonia #13427, 15-pc **300.00**
Creamer, Dainty Blue, small.............................. **18.00**
Cup & saucer, aqua & wht............................... **25.00**
    Begonia w/small roses, lt gr **25.00**
    Birds inside cup, hp, #K13145 .... **42.00**
    Blue & wht daisies...................................... **25.00**
    Bouquet of flowers...................................... **25.00**
    Daffodil Time, smooth w/scallops **27.50**
    Dainty Blue **35.00**
    Demitasse, Bridal Rose #13545 .... **25.00**
        Charm.. **25.00**
        Daffodil... **25.00**
        Forget-Me-Nots w/border.................... **25.00**
        Harebell.. **25.00**
        Pansy **25.00**
        Pink & gold... **25.00**
        Rose & Red daisy............................... **25.00**
        Rose Pansy **25.00**
        Rosebud w/border **25.00**
        White & gold **25.00**
    Green & wht daisies **25.00**
    Grey & yellow flowers **25.00**
    Harebell... **28.00**
    Lily of the Valley.. **25.00**
    Light blue **25.00**
    Light blue w/blue stars **35.00**
    Light green w/roses **30.00**
    Maple Leaf **25.00**
    Mini, Campanual **55.00**
        Dainty Blue... **65.00**
        Rosebud Charm **45.00**
    Pansy **25.00**
    Peach, #15435/518 .... **40.00**
    Pink roses on lt gr **25.00**
    Pink scalloped border, #13510 .... **28.00**
    Pole Star **36.00**
    Red Roses **46.00**
    Rock garden **40.00**
    Rosebud **25.00**
    Royalty.. **25.00**
    Rust spray, Wildman **16.00**
    Summer Glory **45.00**
    Thistle **28.50**
    Vertical flutes... **25.00**
    White cup, gr leaves & gold trim **25.00**
    White outside w/gold stars **25.00**
    Wildflower **27.50**
    Woodland.. **25.00**
    Yellow inside cup & rims of saucer **25.00**
Demitasse, lt blue, pink handles, 4 c/s **180.00**
Egg cup, Rosebud.. **28.00**
Marmalade, covered **28.50**
Mustard, w/lid, rose & red daisy, 3″ **48.00**
Nappy, blue rock, fluted, 6″............................ **15.00**
Plate, 6″ **15.00**
    'Baby's plate', w/sides **70.00**
    Baby's, round, w/sides **65.00**

Blue flowers, #13777, 5½″ sq **16.00**
Children's, 5½″... **40.00**
    6½″ **45.00**
Dubarry, 8″ **15.00**
Lilac Time, 8″... **26.00**
Rose & Red daisy, 8″ **24.00**
Rosebud, 6″ **22.00**
Violets, 6″ **16.00**
Platter, Blue Rock, 12x15″.............................. **100.00**
    Dubarry, wine, 12x14″................................ **54.00**
Sauce, Lily of the Valley, 5½″......................... **20.00**
Sauce jug, w/underplate, Melody, small **30.00**
Saucer, demitasse, Bridal Rose #13545 .... **5.00**
    If the Fairies Come to Tea **10.00**
    Standard, Bridal Rose #13545 .... **7.00**
Soup, Regency, wht w/gold, 2 handles **18.00**
Sugar, Dainty Blue **18.00**
    Regency **16.00**
    White w/gold decor, #8093, 3″ **32.00**
Sugar & creamer, Apple Blossom, smooth w/scallops ... **40.00**
    Begonia w/notched edge **50.00**
    Blue Rock #13591, medium **45.00**
    Bridal Rose **45.00**
    Daffodil Time, smooth w/scallops **40.00**
    Malmesbury Abbey Crest, 1896 .... **45.00**
    Pansy, Rose, Forget-Me-Not, small, scalloped top **38.00**
    Sunrise, blk & grey border, 8 sides **65.00**
    White background w/lavender leaf design, #13639 .... **40.00**
    Wildflower **38.00**
    On Tray, dainty Dresden-type floral, pink trim ... **50.00**
        Violets **80.00**
Tea set, Rose & Red Daisy, 3-pc................... **130.00**
    Rosebud, 3-pc **145.00**
Teapot, pink, #10959/40, 3½″ **60.00**
    Rosebud **88.50**
    Wild Anemone, 5″ **48.00**
    Wildflowers, 4½″ **120.00**
Toothpick, Stock... **24.00**
Tureen, blk & yellow scenery, Deco look, sq, 8½″ ... **48.00**
    With ladle, 7″ **48.00**
Vase, birds & grape vines, MOP background, sgnd, 8½″ ... **45.00**
    10″ **55.00**
Black w/pink roses, #787/8103, 3½″................ **52.00**
    Blue dragons, #774/8315, 4½″ **180.00**
    Grape vines, sgnd, 6½″ **24.00**

Ship Model

Alaskan trawler, wood, handmade, 1900................. **100.00**
Battleship, wood, metal accessories, Naval, 39″ **70.00**
Brigantine, tight rigging, painted hull, 23″ **250.00**
Clipper ship, painted hull, figurehead, 28″ **335.00**
    Wood, fully rigged, major fittings, 1800s, 41x37″......... **600.00**
Half hull, fin keel sloop, 32″ **110.00**
Oceanliner, wood, 3 stacks, 13″ **30.00**
    Wood, painted hull, 2 stacks, 13″ **30.00**
Packet ship Living Age, wood, painted, carved, 37x39″ **400.00**
Ship in bottle, bark, lighthouse, 7″ **50.00**
    Schooner, 3½″ **40.00**
Sidewheeler, half model, shadow box, 26x33″ **335.00**
    Wood, painted hull, 19″ **65.00**
US Frigate Constitution, wood, rigged masts & major fittings, 28x36″ **700.00**
Viking ship, cased, dragon, figurehead, 11″ **75.00**
Yacht, w/sails, 20x24″ **150.00**

Silhouette

Silhouette portraits were made by positioning the subject between a bright light and a sheet of white drawing paper, the resulting shadow traced and cut out. The paper was mounted over a contrasting color and framed. The process was simplified by an invention called the Physiog-notrace, a device that allowed tracing and cutting to be done in one operation.

Experienced silhouette artists could do full length figures, scenics, ships or trains. Some of the most famous of these artists were Charles Peale Polk, Charles Willson Peale, James Elsworth and William King.

Boy, full length, sgnd, framed, 1880, 11x15¼"	**158.00**
Gentleman, profile, oval, reverse painted matt, 5x6"	**60.00**
With goatee, full length, old frame, mkd, 1838, 9½x11½"	**105.00**
Standing, litho background, birdseye frame, 11x14"	**225.00**
George Washington, blk frame, sgnd, 4x5"	**125.00**
Carved & ebonized walnut frame	**140.00**
Girls, pair, 1 w/hat, 1 w/long hair, in mahogany frame, 7"	**25.00**
Ladies & gentlemen, dancing, Victorian, 9x12"	**26.00**
Man, w/handlebar mustache & derby, orig cellophane folder, 1880	**50.00**
Man & child, blk frame, 8¾x11"	**35.00**
Man & woman, hollow cut, mkd: Daniel Hayes, Eliza Hayes, 3x3¾"	**90.00**
Martha Washington, blk frame, sgnd, 4x5"	**125.00**
Musician, w/bassoon, full length cut, old frame, 8x12"	**75.00**
Page of 9 hand cut, from August Edouart's album, 8½x11"	**125.00**
Pair, cut & mounted together, mkd: Haviland Esq, 7¾x9¾"	**75.00**
Soldier, elaborate uniform, orig blk frame, French, sgnd, 1891	**59.00**

Silver

Silver flatware is being collected today, either to replace missing pieces of heirloom sets, or in lieu of buying new patterns, by those who admire and appreciate the style and quality of the older ware. Prices vary from dealer to dealer; some pieces are harder to find and are therefore more expensive. Items such as olive spoons, cream ladles, lemon forks, etc., once thought a necessary part of a silver service, may today be slow to sell, and as a result dealers may price them low and make up the difference on items that sell more readily. Many factors enter into evaluation, popular patterns may be high due to demand, even though easily found, while scarce patterns may be passed over by collectors who find them too difficult to reassemble. In the listings that follow, HH indicates 'hollow handle'; FH, 'flat handle'.

American Classic, cocktail fork	**15.00**
Cream sauce ladle	**27.00**
FH butter spreader	**15.00**
Gravy ladle	**42.00**
HH butter spreader	**14.00**
Ice tea spoon	**25.00**
American Victorian, jelly server	**22.00**
Lemon fork	**16.00**
Master flat butter knife	**21.00**
Master HH butter knife	**19.00**
Meat fork	**42.00**
Angelique, pickle fork	**16.00**
Place fork	**25.00**
Place knife	**17.00**
Teaspoon	**17.00**
Baronial, cocktail fork	**17.00**
FH butter spreader	**17.00**
Ice tea spoon	**29.50**
Salad fork	**24.50**
Soup spoon	**24.50**
Sugar spoon	**24.50**
Tablespoon	**45.00**

Teaspoon	**20.00**
Belle Meade, place fork	**25.00**
Place knife	**17.00**
Salad fork	**21.00**
Soup spoon	**20.00**
Sugar spoon	**22.00**
Tablespoon	**42.00**
Belvedere, cocktail fork	**17.00**
FH butter spreader	**14.00**
Gravy ladle	**40.00**
Lemon fork	**15.00**
Pickle fork	**15.00**
Soup spoon	**21.00**
Sugar spoon	**21.00**
Blossom Time, jelly server	**22.00**
Master flat butter knife	**21.00**
Master HH butter knife	**19.00**
Meat fork	**42.00**
Soup spoon	**21.00**
Teaspoon	**17.00**
Brandon, berry spoon, 8¾"	**41.00**
Cream ladle, 5"	**20.00**
Fork, 7¾"	**27.00**
Gravy ladle	**28.00**
Knife, 9¾"	**17.00**
Serving spoon	**31.00**
Bridal Bouquet, ice tea spoon	**25.00**
Jelly server	**22.00**
Lemon fork	**16.00**
Meat fork	**40.00**
Pickle fork	**16.00**
Tablespoon	**42.00**
Teaspoon	**15.00**
Brocade, cream sauce ladle	**25.00**
FH butter spreader	**15.00**
Gravy ladle	**42.00**
Place fork	**26.00**
Place knife	**18.00**
Salad fork	**21.00**
Burgandy, cocktail fork	**18.50**
Cream sauce ladle	**35.00**
HH butter spreader	**16.50**
Ice tea spoon	**30.00**
Meat fork	**55.00**
Place knife	**25.00**
Buttercup, jelly server	**24.50**
Lemon fork	**18.00**
Master FH butter knife	**24.50**
Master HH butter knife	**22.00**
Sugar spoon	**25.00**
Tablespoon	**45.00**
Teaspoon	**20.00**
Camelia, HH butter spreader	**14.00**
Ice tea spoon	**25.00**
Pickle fork	**16.00**
Soup spoon	**21.00**
Sugar spoon	**21.00**
Tablespoon	**40.00**
Candlelight, cocktail fork	**17.00**
Cream sauce ladle	**27.00**
Jelly server	**24.00**
Lemon fork	**16.00**
Pickle fork	**16.00**
Salad fork	**21.00**

Soup spoon	22.00
Carpenter Hall, meat fork	55.00
Place knife	25.00
Salad fork	27.00
Soup spoon	27.50
Sugar spoon	26.50
Castle rose, ice tea spoon	25.00
Jelly server	22.00
Master FH butter knife	23.00
Master HH butter knife	20.00
Meat fork	40.00
Tablespoon	40.00
Teaspoon	18.00
Celeste, cocktail fork	17.00
Cream sauce ladle	28.00
Place fork	25.00
Salad fork	23.00
Soup spoon	23.00
Teaspoon	16.00
Chantilly, cream sauce ladle	30.00
HH butter spreader	17.00
Lemon fork	18.00
Tablespoon	45.00
Teaspoon	20.00
Chapel Bells, jelly server	20.00
Master FH butter knife	22.00
Meat fork	43.00
Place fork	25.00
Place knife	17.00
Charlemagne, ice tea spoon	30.00
Lemon fork	20.00
Pickle fork	18.00
Salad fork	25.00
Soup spoon	25.00
Sugar spoon	24.50
Teaspoon	20.00
Chased Romantique, cocktail fork	17.00
Gravy ladle	42.00
HH butter spreader	14.00
Ice tea spoon	25.00
Meat fork	42.00
Tablespoon	39.00
Chateau Rose, cream sauce ladle	27.00
FH butter spreader	17.00
Jelly server	24.00
Meat fork	43.00
Teaspoon	18.00
Chippendale, ice tea spoon	29.50
Master FH butter knife	24.50
Master HH butter knife	22.00
Meat fork	45.00
Pickle fork	19.00
Sugar spoon	24.00
Classic Rose, cocktail fork	17.00
Cream sauce ladle	30.00
HH butter spreader	18.00
Salad fork	25.00
Sugar spoon	24.50
Tablespoon	45.00
Clermont, berry spoon	50.00
Fruit knife	10.00
Ice cream fork	13.00
Ice tea spoon	13.00
Knife, 8½″	16.00
Salad fork	14.00
Teaspoon	14.00
Colfax, cocktail fork	15.00
FH butter spreader	17.00
Master HH butter knife	20.00
Salad fork	24.00
Tablespoon	41.00
Teaspoon	18.00
Country Manor, cream sauce ladle	29.00
Gravy ladle	42.00
Place fork	27.00
Place knife	18.00
Soup spoon	22.00
Courtship, gravy ladle	40.00
Ice tea spoon	26.00
Jelly server	23.00
Lemon fork	18.00
Salad fork	22.00
Sugar spoon	23.00
Craftsman, HH butter spreader	15.00
Jelly server	21.00
Lemon fork	17.00
Place knife	18.00
Tablespoon	42.00
Damask Rose, FH butter spreader	17.00
Gravy ladle	41.00
Ice tea spoon	23.00
Pickle fork	15.00
Tablespoon	41.00
Teaspoon	19.00
Debussy, ice tea spoon	32.00
Jelly server	26.50
Lemon fork	20.00
Master FH butter knife	25.00
Master HH butter knife	22.50
Teaspoon	25.00
Debutante, cocktail fork	18.50
Cream sauce ladle	35.00
Gravy ladle	55.00
Pickle fork	20.00
Place knife	25.00
Soup spoon	27.50
Tablespoon	54.00
Decor, FH butter spreader	17.50
Ice tea spoon	30.00
Master FH butter knife	25.00
Meat fork	55.00
Place fork	32.50
Place knive	25.00
Soup spoon	28.00
Della Robbia, cocktail fork	16.00
Cream sauce ladle	26.00
FH butter spreader	14.00
HH butter spreader	13.00
Jelly server	24.00
Meat fork	44.00
Diamond, master FH butter knife	22.00
Pickle fork	17.00
Place knife	18.00
Soup spoon	21.00
Teaspoon	17.00
DuBarry, cocktail fork	18.50
Gravy ladle	54.00
Jelly server	26.50

Lemon fork	20.00
Sugar spoon	26.50
Early American, cocktail fork	10.00
Dinner fork, 7¾″	29.00
Dinner knife, 9″	16.00
FH butter knife	15.00
Fork	16.00
Gravy ladle	25.00
Luncheon fork, 7″	22.00
Serving spoon	33.00
18th Century, cream sauce ladle	34.00
FH butter spreader	17.50
Master HH butter knife	22.50
Place fork	32.50
Place knife	25.00
El Grande, FH butter spreader	17.50
Ice tea spoon	29.00
Jelly server	27.00
Lemon fork	21.00
Tablespoon	54.00
El Greco, cocktail fork	18.00
HH butter spreader	16.00
Salad fork	25.00
Soup spoon	24.50
Tablespoon	45.00
Teaspoon	21.00
Eloquence, gravy ladle	56.00
Master FH butter knife	24.00
Meat fork	52.00
Place knife	24.00
Sugar spoon	27.00
Teaspoon	25.00
Enchanted Rose, buffet fork	49.00
Cocktail fork	8.00
Cream soup spoon	17.00
Fork, 7¼″	24.00
Gravy ladle	34.00
Knife, 9″	17.00
Master butter knife	18.00
Serving spoon	18.00
English Gadroon, FH butter spreader	18.00
HH butter spreader	17.00
Ice tea spoon	29.50
Jelly server	24.50
Lemon fork	18.00
Salad fork	24.50
English Provincial, cream sauce ladle	31.00
Master FH butter knife	24.50
Meat fork	45.00
Pickle fork	20.00
Soup spoon	25.50
Sugar spoon	25.50
Etruscan, cocktail fork	19.00
HH butter spreader	18.00
Ice tea spoon	29.50
Jelly server	24.50
Place fork	27.50
Place knife	20.00
Fairfax, FH butter spreader	17.00
Ice tea spoon	30.00
Lemon fork	18.00
Meat fork	44.00
Tablespoon	46.00
Teaspoon	22.00
Florentine Lace, jelly server	25.50
Master HH butter knife	22.00
Pickle fork	20.00
Salad fork	25.00
Soup spoon	25.50
Teaspoon	21.00
Florentine Northern Lights, cake knife	25.00
Dinner fork, 7¾″	38.00
Dinner knife, 9¾″	16.00
Master butter knife	21.00
Salad fork	26.00
Sugar shell	16.00
Fontaine, butter spreader	20.00
Butter server	30.00
Cocktail fork	15.00
Cream soup spoon	26.00
Fork, 7¼″	34.00
Gravy ladle	46.00
Salad fork	24.00
Salad serving set, 2 pc	140.00
Sugar shell	28.00
Tablespoon	50.00
Fontana, cocktail fork	17.00
Cream sauce ladle	28.00
Gravy ladle	44.00
Jelly server	23.00
Lemon fork	17.00
Place knife	19.00
Formality, cocktail fork	10.00
Cream soup spoon	16.00
Dinner knife, 9″	15.00
Gravy ladle	28.00
Grill fork, 7¾″	20.00
Ice tea spoon	13.00
Luncheon fork, 7″	21.00
French Provincial, HH butter spreader	16.00
Jelly server	25.00
Master FH butter knife	25.00
Master HH butter knife	22.00
Meat fork	45.00
Place fork	27.50
Teaspoon	20.00
French Renaissance, cocktail fork	18.00
FH butter spreader	19.00
Lemon fork	18.00
Salad fork	24.50
Tablespoon	45.00
Teaspoon	21.00
French Scroll, gravy ladle	43.00
HH butter spreader	15.00
Ice tea spoon	25.00
Place fork	25.00
Place knife	17.00
Salad fork	22.00
Soup spoon	22.00
George & Martha, cream sauce ladle	27.00
Gravy ladle	42.00
Master FH butter knife	21.00
Master HH butter knife	19.00
Pickle fork	16.00
Sugar spoon	22.00
Gorham, butter knife	19.00
Dessert server	25.00
Fork, 6¾″	24.00

Fork, 7½″	34.00
Knife, 10″	18.00
Salad fork	22.00
Teaspoon	16.00
Grande Baroque, HH butter spreader	16.50
Ice tea spoon	30.00
Meat fork	56.00
Place fork	32.50
Place knife	25.00
Salad fork	27.50
Tablespoon	53.00
Grand Colonial, cocktail fork	15.00
Cream sauce ladle	28.00
Ice tea spoon	25.00
Jelly server	24.00
Lemon fork	16.00
Salad fork	22.00
Grand Renaissance, FH butter spreader	17.50
Gravy ladle	54.00
HH butter spreader	16.50
Sugar spoon	26.50
Tablespoon	55.00
Teaspoon	25.00
Greenbrier, cream soup spoon	17.00
Dinner fork, 8″	28.00
Dinner knife, 9½″	15.00
FH butter knife	14.00
Ice tea spoon	15.00
Luncheon fork, 7¼″	21.00
Luncheon knife, 8¾″	15.00
Hampton Court, cocktail fork	15.00
Gravy ladle	43.00
Jelly server	23.00
Master FH butter knife	22.00
Salad fork	22.00
Teaspoon	18.00
Heiress, cake knife	25.00
Cream soup spoon	16.00
Demitasse spoon	8.00
Dinner knife, 9″	16.00
Place fork	23.00
Serving spoon	34.00
Hepplewhite, cream sauce ladle	29.00
FH butter spreader	17.00
HH butter spreader	16.00
Ice tea spoon	26.00
Place fork	26.00
Place knife	18.00
Hilton, cake knife	25.00
Demitasse spoon	8.00
Dinner knife, 9″	15.00
Serving spoon	33.00
Sugar shell	17.00
Teaspoon	15.00
Hispana, HH butter spreader	16.00
Ice tea spoon	29.00
Lemon fork	19.00
Meat fork	45.00
Place knife	21.00
Tablespoon	45.00
Hunt Club, bouillon spoon	14.00
Buffet fork, 8″	37.00
Gravy ladle	33.00
Salad fork	18.00
Serving spoon	39.00
Teaspoon	18.00
Joan of Arc, master FH butter knife	21.00
Master HH butter knife	19.00
Pickle fork	17.00
Place fork	25.00
Soup spoon	22.00
Sugar spoon	22.00
King Edward, cream sauce ladle	30.00
Ice tea spoon	29.50
Jelly server	25.50
Meat fork	45.00
Place knife	21.00
Tablespoon	45.00
King Richard, FH butter spreader	17.50
Gravy ladle	56.00
Master HH butter knife	22.50
Pickle fork	21.00
Salad fork	27.50
Sugar spoon	26.50
Lark, FH butter spreader	16.00
HH butter spreader	15.00
Lemon fork	15.00
Place knife	18.00
Soup spoon	22.00
Sugar spoon	22.00
LaScalla, gravy ladle	55.00
Jelly server	26.50
Master HH butter knife	22.50
Meat fork	54.00
Pickle fork	21.00
Teaspoon	25.00
Lasting Spring, cream soup spoon	18.00
Fork, 7¾″	30.00
Jelly server	17.00
Master butter knife	15.00
Salad fork	18.00
Serving spoon	31.00
Teaspoon	15.00
Legato, cocktail fork	15.00
Cream sauce ladle	26.00
Lemon fork	17.00
Place knife	18.00
Salad fork	22.00
Soup spoon	21.00
Tablespoon	41.00
Leonore, fork, 7″	24.00
Ice tea spoon	15.00
Knife, 9½″	17.00
Master butter knife	20.00
Serving spoon	29.00
Teaspoon	13.00
Lily of the Valley, demitasse spoon	12.00
Individual butter knife	15.00
Jelly server	15.00
Pastry fork	22.50
Pastry knife	15.00
Serving spoon	16.50
Lyric, cocktail fork	15.00
Cream sauce ladle	27.50
FH butter spreader	14.50
Master FH butter knife	19.00
Meat fork	43.50
Louis XIV, gravy ladle	43.00

HH butter spreader	16.00	Pickle fork	17.00
Jelly server	22.00	Sugar spoon	22.00
Master FH butter knife	21.00	Queen Anne, bouillon ladle	18.00
Pickle fork	15.00	Buffet fork, 8¾″	46.00
Place fork	24.00	Demitasse spoon	8.00
Pickle fork	17.00	Flat server, 6¼″	25.00
Marlborough, cream sauce ladle	31.00	Grapefruit spoon	14.00
HH butter spreader	16.50	Ice cream fork	13.00
Ice tea spoon	29.00	Mustard ladle, 5″	14.00
Lemon fork	18.00	Queen's Lace, cocktail fork	13.00
Place fork	27.50	FH butter knife	16.00
Place knife	20.00	HH jelly server	15.00
Meadow Rose, jelly server	24.50	Meat fork	40.00
Master HH butter knife	22.00	Place fork, 7¼″	25.00
Meat fork	45.00	Teaspoon	15.00
Pickle fork	19.50	Rambler Rose, cream sauce ladle	27.50
Salad fork	24.50	Gravy ladle	42.00
Sugar spoon	25.00	HH butter spreader	15.00
Medici, gravy ladle	55.50	Lemon fork	16.50
Ice tea spoon	31.00	Master FH butter knife	21.50
Master FH butter knife	25.00	Place fork	25.00
Master HH butter knife	22.50	Repousse, FH butter spreader	17.00
Meat fork	55.00	HH butter spreader	16.00
Salad fork	27.50	Ice tea spoon	29.50
Melrose, cocktail fork	18.50	Jelly server	25.00
Cream sauce ladle	36.00	Lemon fork	19.00
Gravy ladle	54.00	Soup spoon	24.00
HH butter spreader	17.00	Rhapsody, gravy ladle	43.00
Pickle fork	20.50	HH butter spreader	14.00
Tablespoon	56.00	Master HH butter knife	18.00
Milburn Rose, FH butter spreader	17.50	Meat fork	43.00
Gravy ladle	45.00	Pickle fork	16.50
Jelly server	24.50	Sugar spoon	22.00
Lemon fork	19.00	Romance of the Sea, cocktail fork	19.00
Meat fork	45.00	Gravy ladle	55.00
Tablespoon	45.00	Jelly server	26.50
Modern Victorian, ice tea spoon	24.00	Master FH butter knife	26.00
Master FH butter knife	21.00	Pickle fork	20.00
Master HH butter knife	19.00	Place knife	26.00
Meat fork	42.50	Romantique, dinner knife	15.00
Pickle fork	15.00	Individual butter knife	15.00
Soup spoon	21.50	Pastry fork	22.50
Old Colonial, cocktail fork	19.00	Pastry knife	15.00
Cream sauce ladle	35.50	Serving spoon	15.00
FH butter spreader	18.50	Tablespoon	28.50
Meat fork	55.50	Rondo, cream sauce ladle	27.50
Pickle fork	21.00	HH butter spreader	13.00
Teaspoon	25.00	Ice tea spoon	24.00
Old Master, gravy ladle	45.50	Lemon fork	15.00
HH butter spreader	16.50	Master HH butter knife	18.00
Ice tea spoon	29.50	Sugar spoon	21.50
Jelly server	24.50	Rosepoint, gravy ladle	45.50
Lemon fork	19.00	Meat fork	45.00
Tablespoon	45.50	Place fork	28.00
Orchid, cocktail fork	8.00	Place knife	20.00
Fork, 7¾″	32.00	Salad fork	24.50
Gravy ladle	32.00	Tablespoon	45.00
Knife, 9½″	17.00	Royal Danish, cocktail fork	17.00
Salad fork	19.00	HH butter spreader	16.50
Serving spoon	32.00	Ice tea spoon	29.00
Prelude, cocktail fork	14.00	Jelly server	25.00
Cream sauce ladle	27.50	Pickle fork	18.50
Master FH butter knife	21.50	Salad fork	24.00
Master HH butter knife	20.00	Savannah, FH butter spreader	16.50

Lemon fork	**17.00**
Master HH butter knife	**18.50**
Meat fork	**44.00**
Place knife	**18.00**
Soup spoon	**21.00**
Sea Rose, gravy ladle	**43.00**
HH butter spreader	**14.40**
Jelly server	**22.00**
Meat fork	**42.00**
Place knife	**17.50**
Teaspoon	**18.50**
Serenity, dinner knife, 9½″	**16.00**
Gravy ladle	**30.00**
Master butter knife	**16.00**
Salad fork	**17.00**
Serving spoon	**30.00**
Tablespoon	**18.00**
Silver Flutes, cocktail fork	**15.50**
Gravy ladle	**42.50**
HH butter spreader	**15.00**
Ice tea spoon	**25.50**
Jelly server	**22.50**
Salad fork	**21.00**
Silver Wheat, FH butter knife	**16.50**
Fork, 7½″	**29.00**
Gravy ladle	**48.00**
Jelly server	**27.50**
Pierced spoon	**55.00**
Tomato server	**54.00**
Sir Christopher, cream sauce ladle	**30.00**
FH butter spreader	**17.00**
Lemon fork	**18.50**
Master FH butter knife	**25.00**
Place fork	**28.50**
Tablespoon	**45.50**
Spanish Baroque, cocktail fork	**19.00**
Gravy ladle	**54.50**
HH butter spreader	**17.00**
Jelly server	**26.50**
Meat fork	**53.50**
Salad fork	**27.50**
Spring Glory, cocktail fork	**15.50**
FH butter spreader	**15.00**
HH butter spreader	**14.00**
Jelly server	**22.50**
Tablespoon	**40.00**
Teaspoon	**17.50**
Steiffs Rose, gravy ladle	**41.00**
Ice tea spoon	**25.50**
Master FH butter knife	**20.00**
Place fork	**26.00**
Place knife	**17.50**
Salad fork	**21.50**
Strasbourg, cocktail fork	**18.00**
FH butter spreader	**18.50**
Ice tea spoon	**28.50**
Lemon fork	**19.00**
Master HH butter knife	**22.00**
Pickle fork	**19.00**
Stravadari, cream sauce ladle	**28.00**
FH butter spreader	**16.50**
Jelly server	**21.00**
Salad fork	**20.00**
Sugar spoon	**22.00**

Teaspoon	**18.50**
Tara, cream sauce ladle	**30.00**
HH butter spreader	**17.00**
Jelly server	**24.50**
Place knife	**21.00**
Soup spoon	**25.00**
Tablespoon	**45.00**
Vivaldi, gravy ladle	**42.50**
HH butter spreader	**13.50**
Ice tea spoon	**26.00**
Lemon fork	**17.00**
Master HH butter knife	**19.50**
Meat fork	**43.00**
Wedding Bells, cocktail fork	**9.00**
FH butter spreader	**14.00**
Meat fork	**42.00**
Place fork, 7¼″	**26.00**
Serving spoon	**29.00**
Teaspoon	**14.00**
Wedgwood, master FH butter knife	**23.50**
Meat fork	**44.00**
Place fork	**45.50**
Salad fork	**24.50**
Sugar spoon	**25.00**
Teaspoon	**21.00**
Wild Rose, cream sauce ladle	**27.00**
Gravy ladle	**42.00**
Place fork	**25.00**
Salad fork	**21.00**
Sugar spoon	**21.00**
Teaspoon	**17.00**
Wildflower, cocktail fork	**15.50**
FH butter spreader	**14.50**
HH butter spreader	**13.00**
Jelly server	**22.00**
Master FH butter knife	**22.00**
Meat fork	**42.00**
William & Mary, ice tea spoon	**25.00**
Lemon fork	**16.00**
Master HH butter knife	**19.00**
Pickle fork	**16.00**
Place knife	**17.00**
Tablespoon	**40.00**

Hollowware

Until the middle of the 19th century, the silverware produced in America was custom made on order of the buyer directly from the silversmith. With the rise of industrialization, factories sprung up that manufactured silverware for retailers who often added their trademark to the ware. Silver ore was mined in abundance, and demand spurred production. Changes in style occurred at the whim of fashion. Repousse decoration (relief work) became popular about 1885, reflecting the ostentatious taste of the Victorian era. Later in the century, Greek, Etruscan and several classic styles found favor. Today, the Art Deco styles of this century are very popular with collectors.

In the listing that follows, manufacturer's name or trademark is noted first; in lieu of that information, listings are by item.

A Sanborn, napkin ring, octagonal, beaded, coin silver	**55.00**
Abraham Buteaux, coffee pot, George I London, 1725	**6,500.00**
Alvin, chocolate set, 3 pc, Art Nouveau	**550.00**
Ash tray, Peruvian, 1903 coin in center	**35.00**
Bailey & Co, tongs, 1860s, 10″	**420.00**
Bailey, Banks & Biddle, candy dish, pierced, ftd	**175.00**
Basket, fluted interior, open work handle & border, ornate, 7″	**190.00**
Pierced diamond pattern, hinged handle, Victorian, 4″	**80.00**

Bateman, salver, ornate rim, ftd, engraved crest, London, 1829, 8¼" **475.00**
Bodkin, heavy floral decor **20.00**
Bowl, open work border, sterling, 9½" dia **130.00**
   Square, sterling, heavy, 10½" wide **270.00**
   Sterling, Danish, ornate, 4 ftd, 3½x7" dia **225.00**
Box, cigarette, Thai Niello ware, on top 'to General...', 8¾" .. **325.00**
   Enameled crests, Russian, 4" **800.00**
   Gold trim, Russian, 4" **575.00**
Cake basket, repousse, London, 1770s, 10x13" dia **2,500.00**
Calderwood, sauce boat, George III, engraved coat-of-arms, 1700s **1,300.00**
   Sauce boat, ftd, Ireland, 1800s, 6x8" **1,800.00**
Caldwell, coffee service, after dinner, 3 pc, sterling **600.00**
Candlesnuffer, cone shape, long handle, sterling **48.00**
Candlesticks, etched flame design, 12" **65.00**
   Oval base & bobeches, 1793, 7½", pair **1,150.00**
Card case, scalloped, engraved bird reserve, coin silver **145.00**
Cartier, watering can, vermeil finish, 6x10" **425.00**
Cellini, bowl, rectangular, hand wrought sterling, 10x6x4" ... **185.00**
Chalice, applied grapes & leaves, gold wash interior, 14" w/lid **600.00**
Chicago Silver Co, porringer, Gustafson, 5" dia............ **140.00**
Cigar holder, ornate engraving, mkd silver 950 .... **25.00**
Cigarette case, blue gem thumbpiece, gold script, Russian, 4x3" **245.00**
Clark, snuff box, basket weave top & bottom, 1835.......... **95.00**
Coffee pot, engraved 'to Lt Gen...1951', 10½" **375.00**
   George II, scrolled spout, raised shell, ftd, 1740s **1,055.00**
Coffee/tea service, 5 pc, overall chasing, floral finials, French **2,800.00**
Coffee/tea service, Washington pattern, 5 pc, sterling **1,100.00**
Comb case, Art Nouveau, 3" **28.00**
Creamer, cow w/horns & embossed insect, 4¼x7" **590.00**
   Ovoid, flat base, floral, English, 1801, 4" **165.00**
Cup, repousse poppies, dome ped base, 1740s, 4½" dia **350.00**
Curry, chalice, scene of fire engine, repousse florals, coin silver **400.00**
Deakins & Sons, tea service, embossed, 3 pc, Sheffield, 1902 **1,800.00**
Dish, repousse florals, ftd, ornate, English, 1800s **230.00**
Dominick & Haff, bowl, 6" **34.00**
   Chop dish, oblong, shell & foliage rim, 19" **600.00**
   Dish, oblong, 12" **450.00**
   Service, 6 pc, Queen Anne **2,400.00**
   Service, after dinner, 3 pc **600.00**
Figurine, dachshund, sitting, wearing collar, sterling, 3x2" **195.00**
   Deer, 10 point buck, w/ruby eyes, standing, 5x5" **295.00**
   Knight, w/lance & sword, ivory face, vermeil work, 5½" **395.00**
   Pig, sitting, sterling, 2".............................. **90.00**
Fisher, pepper mill, made in France **40.00**
Flask, sterling, 6"..................................... **300.00**
Friedell, bowl, hand-crafted morning glory, flared ft, 3x13" dia **750.00**
   Bowl, morning glory, flared ft, 2x8 " dia **200.00**
   Platter, rim repousse & chased w/foliage, 10¾" dia........ **350.00**
Gale & Willis, creamer, engraved decor **225.00**
Gebelein, bowl, 3 curved ft, 2x6" **175.00**
Goblet, ornately decorated, Russian, 3" **80.00**
   Wine, sterling, 4½"................................. **65.00**
Gorham, ashtray, sterling, gadroon border, monogram **50.00**
   Bon-bon, shell shape, ball ft **90.00**
   Bowl, Chantilly, 10½" **280.00**
   Bowl, ftd, acanthus leaf border, 1880, 8½" **145.00**
   Bowl, oblong, acorn pattern, sterling, large **1,200.00**
   Candelabra, 3 light, Contemporary, convertible, 14", pair ... **550.00**
   Candelabra, acorn pattern, heavy, sterling, pair **1,000.00**
   Casserole, covered, oval w/pierced basket decor, sterling **600.00**
   Coffee pot, wood handle & knob, ped ft, dated 1903 ...... **215.00**
   Fruit bowl, ornate reticulated edge, sterling, 12 oz **170.00**
   Grape shears, 6½" **125.00**
   Gravy boat, w/undertray, sterling **1,000.00**

Matchbox holder, hammered, 1½x1".................... **18.00**
Mug, handled, coin silver **135.00**
Napkin ring, applied water lilies, leaves both sides **38.00**
Napkin ring, sterling, plain w/monogrammed name......... **15.00**
Pitcher, water, Athenic, daisies **1,800.00**
Plate, 9" dia **75.00**
Plate, nursery rhyme, 29 scenes at rim, 7" dia............ **110.00**
Porringer, ornate cut out handle, heavy **115.00**
Salt & pepper, hand chased, Louis XVI, monogrammed, pair **100.00**
Table set, childs, 4 pc, border w/Renaissance figures, 1890s . **350.00**
Tray, Art Nouveau, foliate shape, reticulated pansy border, 31" **3,700.00**
Tureen, Chantilly, 1900, 9x13½"...................... **1,400.00**
Vase, bulbous w/flared rim, embossed decor, 8½" **2,000.00**
Hardy & Hayes, ashtray, w/matchbox holder, ftd, hammered, sterling **98.00**
   Bread tray, embossed sloped sides, 9x12" oval............ **185.00**
Hennell, mug, medallions of Queen Victoria, London, 1883 ... **225.00**
   Tea service, pot, stand & caddy, London, 1787 .... **2,800.00**
Hester Bateman, basket, reticulated, English, 1786, 7½".... **825.00**
   Creamer, ftd, English, 1790, 6"....................... **550.00**
   Salver, George II **2,600.00**
Hodd & Son, tea set, traveling, hammered, 6 pc, 1890s, leather case **715.00**
International, tea service, Deerfield, 6 pc w/silver plated waiter **1,500.00**
Jenkens, fruit bowl, repousse, chased w/flowerheads, 1910, 9" dia **500.00**
Jensen, cheese set, 3 pc, in orig presentation box, sterling.... **135.00**
   Coffee/tea service, contemporary design, 7 pc, wood handles **16,000.00**
John Allen, creamer, ftd, 1700s, 3".................... **1,700.00**

John S Hunt, centerpiece vase, 1857, 15" **3,500.00**
Kalo, ashtray, sq w/diagonal corners, sterling, 2½" **38.00**
   Bowl, 5 section fluting, hand wrought, 6" dia............ **300.00**
   Bowl, flower form, hand wrought, 1916, 17" dia **325.00**
   Bowl, ftd, fluted, hand wrought, 9" dia **650.00**
   Tray, applied rolled edge, sterling, hand wrought, 12" dia .. **600.00**
   Tray, fluted w/curved rim, sterling, hand wrought, 6" **175.00**
Kirk & Son, bowl, molded ft, repousse, 3 scenic vignettes, 7½" dia **350.00**
   Centerpiece, boat shape, 2 handle, floral repousse, sterling.. **475.00**
   Plates, bread & butter, plain w/molded edge, set of 18 ..... **450.00**
Kirk, bookmark, embossed roses, teardrop shape, 2½"........ **55.00**
   Coaster, repousse........................ .... **40.00**
   Cocktail shaker, sterling, heavy **325.00**
   Compote, repousse floral rim, 10" dia.................. **275.00**
   Dish, coat of arms, border repousse, chased flowers, 14" dia **900.00**

Hot water kettle, w/stand & burner, floral repousse, ornate **2,300.00**

Tea service, 3 pc, etched floral, 1926 . . . . **800.00**

Teapot, foliage chasing **1,100.00**

Lebolt, goblet, hand beaten, 6″ **245.00**

Porringer w/geometric pierced handle, hand beaten, 4½″ . . . **185.00**

Loring Andrews & Co, service, 7 pc **4,000.00**

Manicure set, 6 pc w/case, 1908 hallmarked, English **89.00**

Marshall Field & Co, tray w/ sauce dish & ladle, hammered . . . **500.00**

Mirror, hand, allover floral & scroll engraving, monogram **125.00**

Mulholland, gravy boat, oval foot, wide handles, hand wrought **500.00**

Mustard pot, single handle, ornate embossing, English, 1912, hallmkd **55.00**

Napkin holder, triangular, ball ft, ornate open work, stylized bird **30.00**

Napkin ring, branch, Victorian, 3″ **135.00**

Niello, box, w/enameled farm scene, Russian, 4″ **500.00**

Novick, bowl, ftd, fluted & scalloped, hand wrought, 3½x5½″ . **385.00**

Nut dish, stem in center w/ceramic nut, sterling, 6½″ wide . . . **110.00**

Old Newburg Crafters, bread plates, hand engraved design, set of 12 **825.00**

Perfume bottle, powderhorn flask shape, ornate, 1900, 8 oz **75.00**

14k gold trim **120.00**

Perfume funnel, letters BL form handle, unmkd **24.00**

Pillbox, overall embossing, gold wash interior, ¾x1¼″ **45.00**

Poole, coffee/tea service, Georgian, 5 pc, 1930s **3,500.00**

Pratt, salt porringer, sterling, 2½″ dia **130.00**

Preisner Silver Co, tray, 8″ **65.00**

Punch bowl, sterling, 6x12″ dia **600.00**

Punch ladle, lion on bowl, woman's head handle, coin silver, 12½″ **780.00**

R & B, bowl, Francis I, 11½″ **350.00**

Randahl, bowl, fluted w/rolled edge, sterling, 6″ dia **135.00**

Candle snuffer, Liberty Bell, sterling, 7½″ **125.00**

Shell form dish, hammered, sterling, 5″ **100.00**

Redlich & Co, salt & pepper, open, w/spoons, hoof ft, glass lined **100.00**

Redlick, wine strainer, embossed rim w/head of horned god, 8½″ **110.00**

Reed & Barton, service, 5 pc & waiter tray, Grace, 1940 . . . **3,250.00**

Revere Silversmiths, candleholders, double, twist stem, 5½″, pair **175.00**

Richard Pargeter, salver, ftd, English, 1732, 7″ dia **1,100.00**

Robbins, pitcher, George III, 9¾″ **1,200.00**

Robert Breading, teapot, lid w/wood finial, handle, 1810, 6″ . . **775.00**

Robert Garrard, dinner plates, William VI, set of 6 . . . . **3,000.00**

Robert Henell, basket, George III, dbl thread border, 1792, 5¾″ **395.00**

Salts, pierced, 3 ball ft, cobalt liners, Birmingham 1922, pair . . . **48.00**

Salver, ftd, pie crust border, sterling, English, 1730, 9″ **1,000.00**

Schofield, center bowl, floral repousse, sterling, 9″ dia **700.00**

Sheffield, coffee urn, 1810, 16x30″ dia at widest point **825.00**

Shreve & Co, mug, strap band top, sterling, 3″ **285.00**

Smith, stuffing spoon, reverse tip, London, 1830s, 12″ **155.00**

Stamp holder case, Victorian, antique sterling **45.00**

Steiff, tea service, 4 pc, repousse, sterling **1,750.00**

Stone Assoc, tray, square, 11½″ **400.00**

Stove, gravy bowl w/loop handles, sterling 4¼″ **365.00**

Sugar sifter, raised scrolls & flowers, pierced blossom shape, 6½x2″ **35.00**

Tea infuser, basket weave w/roses on trellis in repousse, sterling, 2″ **115.00**

Hinged ball, pierced long handle **45.00**

Tea strainer, over-the-cup, gold wash, ornate **30.00**

Tea straws, set of 6, lotus blossom bowls, w/figural charms, MIB **95.00**

Thermometer, easel, w/figural butterflies & lilies at top, cutout base **26.00**

Thimble holder, geometric reticulated, hinged, ring, star on top **110.00**

Tiffany, condiment set, 1874 . . . . **400.00**

Tongs, scissor type, pear shape blades, embossed scrolls & flowers **85.00**

Towle, tea service, Louis XIV, 5 pc w/sterling waiter **4,700.00**

Tray, gallery, blk Bakelite base w/reticulated sides, 20x12″ oval **165.00**

Tray, tea, Mexican, 15x21″ **1,100.00**

Vase, carved animals & parrots, 7½″ **175.00**

W Ball, teapot, Greek Key band, 1830, 9½″ **1,000.00**

Wallace, bowl, Meadow Rose, 9″ **150.00**

Dressing table set, Carmel pattern, 9 pc, monogrammed **150.00**

Tray, Rose Point, 12″ **425.00**

Watson, goblet, tulip form, gold interior, 6″ **65.00**

Salt spoons, Common Wealth pattern, pair **48.00**

Tray, reticulated decorated rim, sterling, 10″ dia **140.00**

Webster, change purse, ornate border, slots for dimes & nickels **30.00**

Mug, child's, coin silver, 1840s, 2¾″ **250.00**

Teapot, sq base w/ball ft, lid w/button finial, 1900 . . . . **275.00**

Westervell, mug, overall chasing, Greek Key, dbl handle, 1845 **135.00**

Whiting, bowl, Louis XV, sterling, 10½″ **240.00**

Candy dish, ped base, w/chasing around bowl **120.00**

Pitcher, bulbous, relief shells, repousse, 1800s, 7″ **990.00**

Plate, w/ornate pierced low ft, 10″ dia **115.00**

William Cripps, teapot, bullet, George III **1,300.00**

Wilson, mug, barrel shape, coin silver, 1840s, 3″ **250.00**

Wine strainer, funnel, Sheffield **75.00**

Wood & Hughes, salts, medallion, coin silver, pair **150.00**

Sugar, w/handles, gilt interior, 1880 . . . . **285.00**

Wooley, bowl, 9½″ **300.00**

Silver Lustre Ware

Silver lustre is a type of earthenware with a metallic surface, produced in the early 1800s in Staffordshire, England. These wares were most popular prior to 1840, when the technique of electroplating was developed, and silverplated wares came into vogue.

Creamer, 4″, illus **50.00**

Ribbed on bottom half, brown inside **40.00**

Loving cup, copper lustre interior, 4½x5″ **55.00**

Sugar, covered, 4½x8″ **75.00**

Cuber, 5″, illus **75.00**

Open, ribbed on bottom half, copper inside **40.00**

Teapot, Queen Anne, 5½x9½" **165.00**
Ribbed on bottom half, flat blk handle & finial, mkd **60.00**

Silver Overlay

The silver overlay glass made during the 1800s was decorated with a cut-out pattern of sterling silver applied to the surface of the ware. Silver deposit was achieved through a chemical process involving a bath containing a solvent and dispersed silver, which was electrically attracted to a predetermined pattern on a finished glass product. Both methods of application are listed here.

Bottle, bulbous, crystal w/floral & curlicue work, 6½" **330.00**

Bowl, floral overlay, 3 toed, 3½" **35.00**
Chalice, hollow stemware, cranberry w/flowers & ferns, 8" **265.00**
Champagne, blue & clear w/engraved overlay band, 6" **28.00**
Cologne, steeple stopper, lg flowers & leaves, 2¾" base, 6¾" .. **70.00**
Decanter, gr w/lattice & floral overlay, 7½" **700.00**
    Green w/vines & flowers, Alvin, 11½" **800.00**
    Presentation, repousse stopper, emerald gr, Alvin, 1898, 11½" **795.00**
Flask, w/sterling cap, blk amethyst w/fox hunt scene, 5½" **150.00**
Perfume, clear, 3" **75.00**
    Crystal, mkd, #999/1000, 3½" **85.00**
    With stopper, dk gr, 3¾" **185.00**
Pitcher, lemonade, tilted shape, swan medallions, overall leaves, 9½" **285.00**
    Wide border of silver overlay grapes, lg **195.00**
Plate, blk amethyst w/Nouveau lily, 10-sided, 12½" **50.00**
Salt, master, amber w/floral overlay, 2" **28.00**
Sugar & creamer, clear, 4½" creamer, 5" 2-handle sugar **85.00**
Tankard, cranberry w/grapes, vines overlay, 9" **850.00**
Vase, blue irid w/floral & scroll motif, Loetz, 7" **650.00**
    Bulbous base & rim, emerald gr, 13" **645.00**
    Cranberry, mkd, 6½" **450.00**
    Green w/poppy overlay, Alvin, 8" **165.00**
    Green, 13" **675.00**
    Honey, w/irid hues of purple & pink, mkd: L Sterling **495.00**
    Pedestal, lt gr, overall design, sgnd Rockwell, 6¾" **165.00**
    Square, ftd, olive w/floral overlay, 6" **150.00**

Silver Plate

Silver plated flatware is fast becoming the focus of the attention of collectors today. In the listings that follow, prices are for pieces in like-new condition with no monogram. Worn pieces or those with monograms will be substantially less. It is generally not profitable to restore worn pieces, except those from the very valuable patterns.

Alhambra (Rogers), bouillon **8.00**
    Sugar spoon **9.00**
    Sugar tongs **20.00**
    Teaspoon **6.50**
Adoration (1847 Rogers Bros), berry spoon **15.00**
    Dinner fork **8.00**
    Gravy ladle **15.00**
    Hollow handle dinner knife **9.00**
    Salad fork **8.00**
    Teaspoon **5.00**
Arbutus (Rogers), berry spoon **22.50**
    Cream ladle **17.50**
    Dinner fork **10.00**
    Gravy ladle **17.50**
    Hollow handle dinner knife **30.00**
    Hollow handle pie server **30.00**
Berkshire (1847 Rogers Bros), berry spoon **30.00**
    Dinner fork **10.00**
    Hollow handle dinner knife **20.00**
    Jelly trowel **20.00**
    Salad fork **30.00**
    Teaspoon **8.00**
    Twisted butter knife **12.50**

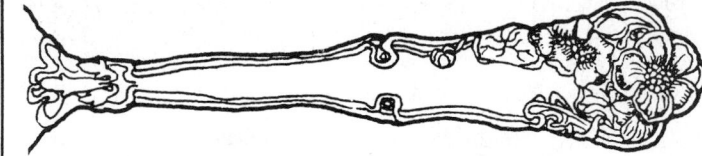

Berwick (Eagle Wm Rogers), berry spoon **35.00**
    Cold meat fork **25.00**
    Dinner fork **12.00**
    Gravy ladle **25.00**
    Hollow handle dinner knife **20.00**
    Salad fork **35.00**
    Teaspoon **8.00**
Bird of Paradise (Community), berry spoon **20.00**
    Carving set, 3 pc **50.00**
    Dinner fork **8.00**
    Hollow handle dinner knife **8.00**
    Meat fork **15.00**
    Pie server **20.00**
    Salad fork **7.00**
    Teaspoon **5.00**
Brides Bouquet (Alvin), dinner fork **20.00**
    Gravy ladle **30.00**
    Hollow handle dinner knife **25.00**
    Tablespoon **15.00**
    Teaspoon **10.00**
Caprice (Nobility Plate), berry spoon **18.00**
    Dinner fork **8.00**
    Gravy ladle **15.00**
    Hollow handle dinner knife **9.00**
    Iced teaspoon **8.00**
    Salad fork **8.00**
    Tablespoon **9.00**

Teaspoon 5.00
Carnation (+ W R Keystone), cocktail fork 12.50
   Cold meat fork........................ 25.00
   Dinner fork 10.00
   Gravy ladle........................... 25.00
   Hollow handle dinner knife.............. 30.00
   Master butter 12.50
   Oyster ladle 75.00
Charter Oak (1847 Rogers Bros), berry spoon 30.00
   Cocktail fork 20.00
   Cold meat fork........................ 25.00
   Dinner fork 10.00
   Hollow handle dinner knife.............. 25.00
   Master butter 12.50
   Salad fork 30.00
   Teaspoon 8.00

Columbia (1847 Rogers Bros), berry spoon................. 30.00
   Cold meat fork........................ 25.00
   Dinner fork 12.00
   Hollow handle dinner knife.............. 25.00
   Salad fork 35.00
   Tablespoon........................... 10.00
Coronation (Community), berry spoon 18.00
   Cold meat fork........................ 15.00
   Dinner fork 10.00
   Gravy ladle........................... 15.00
   Hollow handle dinner knife.............. 10.00
   Salad fork............................ 8.00
   Sugar spoon 6.00
   Teaspoon 6.00
Daffodil (1847 Rogers Bros), berry spoon 20.00
   Cold meat fork........................ 15.00
   Dinner fork 10.00
   Hollow handle dinner knife.............. 12.00
   Iced teaspoon......................... 12.50
   Salad fork 10.00
   Slotted serving spoon 12.50
   Teaspoon 6.00
   Tomato server 25.00
Danish Princess (Holmes & Edwards), berry spoon 20.00
   Cold meat fork........................ 15.00
   Dinner fork 9.00
   Hollow handle dinner knife............. 9.00
   Iced teaspoon......................... 10.00
   Salad fork............................ 8.00
   Teaspoon 6.00
   Tomato server 25.00

Eternally Yours (1847 Rogers Bros), berry spoon............ 20.00
   Cocktail fork 10.00
   Cold meat fork........................ 20.00
   Dinner fork 10.00
   Hollow handle dinner knife............. 10.00

Iced teaspoon......................... 10.00
Pie server........................... 20.00
Salad fork 10.00
Teaspoon 5.00
Evening Star (Community), berry spoon 20.00
   Dinner fork 10.00
   Hollow handle dinner knife.............. 10.00
   Hollow handle pie server............... 20.00
   Salad fork 8.00
   Teaspoon 5.00
   Tomato server 20.00
Exquisite 1940 (Wm Rogers & Son), cold meat fork 15.00
   Dinner fork 7.00
   Gravy ladle........................... 15.00
   Hollow handle dinner knife.............. 8.00
   Salad fork 7.00
   Teaspoon 5.00

First Love (1847 Rogers Bros), carving set, 2 pc 45.00
   Cold meat fork........................ 20.00
   Dinner fork 10.00
   Hollow handle dinner knife.............. 10.00
   Iced teaspoon......................... 10.00
   Salad fork 8.00
   Teaspoon 5.00
   Tomato server 25.00
Flair (1847 Rogers Bros), berry spoon 20.00
   Cold meat fork........................ 20.00
   Dinner fork 10.00
   Gravy ladle........................... 20.00
   Hollow handle dinner knife.............. 12.00
   Salad fork 10.00
   Teaspoon 6.00
   Tomato server 25.00
Floral (1835 R Wallace), berry spoon 35.00
   Cocktail fork 20.00
   Cold meat fork........................ 25.00
   Dinner fork 15.00
   Gravy ladle........................... 25.00
   Hollow handle dinner knife.............. 25.00
   Salad fork 30.00
   Soup ladle........................... 125.00
   Teaspoon 10.00
Grenoble (Wm A Rogers), cocktail fork 20.00
   Cold meat fork........................ 20.00
   Dinner fork 10.00
   Gravy ladle........................... 30.00
   Hollow handle dinner knife.............. 20.00
   Oyster ladle 90.00
   Salad fork 20.00
   Teaspoon 8.00

Grosvenor (Community), carving set, 2 pc, small 30.00
   Cocktail fork 8.00

Cold meat fork	15.00
Dinner fork	7.00
Gravy ladle	15.00
Hollow handle cake server	18.00
Hollow handle dinner knife	8.00
Salad fork	7.00
Teaspoon	5.00

Cold meat fork	15.00
Dinner fork	10.00
Gravy ladle	18.00
Hollow handle dinner knife	10.00
Iced teaspoon	10.00
Salad fork	10.00
Teaspoon	6.00

Heritage (1847 Rogers Bros), berry spoon 20.00

Cold meat fork	15.00
Dinner fork	10.00
Gravy ladle	15.00
Hollow handle dinner knife	10.00
Iced teaspoon	10.00
Salad fork	10.00
Teaspoon	6.00
Tomato server	20.00

Moselle (American Silver Co), berry spoon 85.00

Cold meat fork	65.00
Cream ladle	70.00
Dinner fork	20.00
Gravy ladle	70.00
Hollow handle dinner knife	35.00
Master butter	25.00
Salad fork	50.00
Sugar shell	35.00
Teaspoon	15.00

King Frederik (1847 Rogers Bros), berry spoon 20.00

Cold meat fork	20.00
Dinner fork	10.00
Gravy ladle	20.00
Hollow handle dinner knife	10.00
Salad fork	10.00
Teaspoon	6.00

LaVigne (1881 Rogers Bros), cold meat fork 20.00

Dinner fork	10.00
Gravy ladle	25.00
Hollow handle dinner knife	40.00
Master butter	12.50
Salad fork	35.00
Soup ladle	150.00
Teaspoon	8.00

Old Colony (1847 Rogers Bros), berry spoon 25.00

Cocktail fork	12.50
Cold meat fork	15.00
Dinner fork	10.00
Gravy ladle	18.00
Hollow handle dinner knife	12.00
Salad fork	10.00
Teaspoon	6.00

Orange Blossom (Wm Rogers & Son), berry spoon 25.00

Demitasse spoon	10.00
Dinner fork	10.00
Master butter	12.50
Salad fork	15.00
Sugar shell	12.50
Sugar tongs	25.00
Teaspoon	6.00
Tomato server	40.00

Milady (Community), berry spoon 18.00

Cold meat fork	15.00
Dinner fork	8.00
Gravy ladle	18.00
Hollow handle dinner knife	8.00
Pierced nut spoon	8.00
Salad fork	8.00
Teaspoon	5.00

Queen Bess 1946 (Tudor Plate), cocktail fork 10.00

Cold meat fork	12.00
Dinner fork	6.00
Gravy ladle	15.00
Hollow handle dinner knife	7.00
Iced teaspoon	10.00
Pie server	15.00
Salad fork	6.00
Teaspoon	4.00

Morning Star (Community), berry spoon 18.00

Remembrance (1847 Rogers Bros), berry spoon **20.00**
  Cold meat fork. **20.00**
  Dinner fork **10.00**
  Gravy ladle **20.00**
  Hollow handle dinner knife. **12.00**
  Iced teaspoon. **10.00**
  Salad fork **10.00**
  Teaspoon **6.00**

Silver Lace (1847 Rogers Bros), berry spoon **15.00**
  Cold meat fork. **15.00**
  Dinner fork **10.00**
  Gravy ladle **15.00**
  Hollow handle dinner knife. **10.00**
  Salad fork **10.00**
  Slotted serving spoon **12.00**
  Teaspoon **6.00**

South Seas (Community), berry spoon **18.00**
  Cold meat fork. **15.00**
  Dinner fork **10.00**
  Gravy ladle **18.00**
  Hollow handle dinner knife. **10.00**
  Iced teaspoon. **10.00**
  Salad fork **10.00**
  Teaspoon **6.00**

Spring Garden (Holmes & Edwards), cold meat fork **15.00**
  Dinner fork **8.00**
  Gravy ladle **15.00**
  Hollow handle dinner knife. **10.00**
  Pierced pie server **18.00**
  Salad fork. **8.00**
  Teaspoon **5.00**

Triumph (Deep Silver), berry spoon. **20.00**
  Cold meat fork. **18.00**
  Dinner fork **10.00**
  Gravy ladle **18.00**
  Hollow handle dinner knife. **12.00**
  Salad fork **10.00**
  Tablespoon. **10.00**
  Teaspoon **6.00**

Vintage (1847 Rogers Bros), berry spoon **35.00**
  Cocktail fork **20.00**
  Cold meat fork. **25.00**
  Cream ladle **35.00**

Dinner fork **12.00**
Gravy ladle **35.00**
Hollow handle dinner knife. **25.00**
Salad fork **35.00**
Teaspoon **8.00**
White Orchid (Community), berry spoon **18.00**
  Cold meat fork. **15.00**
  Dinner fork **10.00**
  Hollow handle dinner knife. **12.00**
  Iced teaspoon. **10.00**
  Salad fork **10.00**
  Slotted serving spoon **12.00**
  Teaspoon **6.00**

Hollowware

Barker Bros, tureen, revolving, ornate handles/ft, ivory finial, 14″ dia **275.00**
Biscuit jar, embossed collar & lid, ornate finial, trimmed twist bail **185.00**
Bowl, berry, reticulated holder w/figural ram's heads, ruby liner, 1865 **115.00**
Cocktail stirrer, wire, dated 1889 . . . . **6.00**
Coffee urn, Victorian, legs w/deer heads, dog finial, ivory trim 1868 **165.00**
Coffee/tea service, 4 sided, engraved flower & leaf, fox finials, 4 pc **280.00**
Cracker jar, etched 'Crackers' **35.00**
Gorham, candelabra, 5 branch, w/5 matching shades & holders **595.00**
Hand mirror, 'Chicago' & florals embossed, dated 1905, 4½″ . . **10.00**
Lexington, cracker jar, 'Crackers', fluted rolled rim, finial, handle **75.00**
Manning & Bowman, coffee set, 4 pc, 1925 . . . . **40.00**
Meriden, bucket, ice, hammered, heavy, ornate **25.00**
  Butter, dome top, ftd, repousse, w/insert, knife holder **40.00**
  Cocktail shaker, hammered, heavy, ornate. **65.00**
  Pitcher, tilt, engraved tigers, boy figural on spout, w/goblet, 1872 **275.00**
Middletown, spooner, pierced, medallions, ped, frosted cut liner, 1865 **65.00**
Porter Brit & Plate, basket, 4 ft w/embossed heads, on platform w/lion **50.00**
Sheffield, sugar bowl w/12 spoon hooks, bird finial on lid, 1923 **50.00**
Spoon, tea strainer **6.00**
Tufts, watch holder, girl on platform, full-figured, w/bonnet . . . **175.00**
Webster, butter dish, 1840s **25.00**
Wilcox, pitcher, engraved roses, ped base, ornate handle, 5″ . . . **25.00**
  Watch holder, semi-circle, entwined leaves decor, velvet lined **135.00**

Wm Rogers, service, 4 pc **125.00**

Sinclaire

In 1904, H.P. Sinclaire & Company was founded in Corning, N.Y. For the first 16 years of production, Sinclaire used blanks from other glassworks

for his cut and engraved designs. In 1920, he established his own glass blowing factory in Bath, N.Y. His most popular designs utilize fruits, flowers and other forms from nature. Most of Sinclaire glass is unmarked.

Bowl, rolled rim, amber, intaglio flowers in medallions, sgnd, 10½″ **40.00**
   Standard foot, cut w/diamonds under flared rim, 10″ dia ... **500.00**
   Sterling rim, 'York', 1915, 4x8¼″ **250.00**
Candlesticks, celeste blue, low mushroom style, pr **175.00**
   Spiralled hollow stems, sgnd, amber, pr **150.00**
Console set, compote & candlesticks, mkd **225.00**
Cordial, pair, faceted stem, Greek Key pattern cut into top, 3¾″ **50.00**
Decanter, teardrop mushroom stopper, sgnd **385.00**
Goblet, wine, blue band cut to clear w/florals, sgnd **125.00**
Pitcher, pedestal, #4 pattern, sgnd, 9″ **1,150.00**
Spittoon, lady's; rim engraved in leaves & acorns, sgnd, 2¾x8¼″ **450.00**
Stemware, florals, panels, swags, Fritchie rock crystal, sgnd, 4¼″ **55.00**
Tray, Georgian pattern, 13″ **195.00**
   Oval, scalloped hobstar w/fans & crosscuts, 10x7″ **150.00**
Vase, pattern #1023, 14″ **185.00**
   Pedestal, knob stem, silver threads, Adams, 24″ **995.00**
   Sgnd, Adams #2, 20″ **800.00**
   Sgnd, Stratford, 16″ **285.00**
Whipped cream set, Adelphia pattern, oval, sgnd, 2 pc **185.00**

Slag

Slag glass is a marbleized opaque glassware made by several companies from about 1870 until the turn of the century. It is usually found in purple, blue, red, orange, and green. Pink is rare and very expensive.

Bowl, purple, ftd, scalloped & serrated, beaded loops, 4½x3¾″ dia **70.00**
Butter, covered, pink w/Inverted Fan & Feather **900.00**
Butter, covered, purple, 8x9″ **180.00**
Candle, purple, Imperial, 8″ **38.00**

Celery, purple, 8½″ **125.00**
   Purple, jeweled **105.00**
Condiment set, pink, holder, pepper, mustard & open salt **110.00**
Dish, purple, rectangular w/handles, 11x6″ **80.00**
Match holder, purple **48.00**
Pitcher, water, pink w/Inverted Fan & Feather **1,200.00**
Plate, purple, closed lattice-edge, 10½″ **75.00**
Shot glass, purple, 'Just a Thimblefull', Geo Davidson, 1880, 2½″ **55.00**
Spooner, pink, Inverted Fan & Feather **295.00**
   Purple, Oval Medallion **65.00**
Sugar, covered, purple, ftd, scalloped rim, 7″ **69.00**
   Covered, purple, Scroll & Acanthus, fluted, 7″ **60.00**

Toothpick, pink, Inverted Fan & Feather **275.00**
Tumbler, water, pink, Inverted Fan & Feather, 4x2¾″ dia **395.00**
Vase, purple, crown w/lion, 3 handled, relief berries, English, 5″ **675.00**

Smith Bros. Glass

Alfred and Harry Smith founded their glassmaking firm in New Bedford, Mass., where they had been formerly associated with the Mt. Washington Glass Works, working from 1871 to 1875 to aid in establishing the decorating department there.

Smith glass is valued for its excellent enameled decoration on bisque or opal glass. Pieces were often marked with a lion in a red shield.

Bowl, cream satin w/gold, florals, beaded rim, melon rib, 9″ .. **365.00**
   Wht flower & gr leaves, gold tracing, mk rampant lion, 9″ .. **500.00**
Muffineer, melon ribbed, orig top, daisy decor, 3¼x4¼″ **275.00**
Plate, 'Santa Maria', 6½″ wide **97.00**
Sugar & creamer, covered, sgnd, blue pansy decor **185.00**
Sugar shaker, opaque wht, flower, silver top **70.00**
Syrup, squatty, w/orig plated hinged cover, enameled florals ... **165.00**
Vase, blue w/hp birds, Tauton pedestal w/bird, 11½″ **165.00**
   Opaque wht, heron decor, silver plated holder w/relief bug, 5¾″ **95.00**
   Opaque wht, pink w/heron decor, w/silver plated holder, 10¼″ **125.00**
   Orig plated stand w/hummingbird, enameled stork & foliage . **125.00**
   Pair, blue, pedestalled holders, Tauton, 11½″ **275.00**

Snow Babies

Early in the 1800s, snow babies---little figurals in white snowsuits---originated in Germany. They were made of sugar candy and were often used as decorations for Christmas trees. Later on, they were made of marzipan, a confection of crushed almonds, sugar and egg whites. Eventually, porcelain manufacturers began making them in bisque. They were popular until WWII. Some reproductions are now found on the market.

Baby, dogs pulling sled, 3x1″ **65.00**
   Falling **35.00**
   Falling over ball, 1¾″ **50.00**
   German, good coloring, 2″ **65.00**
   Holding snowball, seated, 2½″ **115.00**
   Jointed arms & legs, 3½″ **110.00**
   Jointed arms & legs, 4″ **160.00**
   Lying down, pegged, 3″ **85.00**
   On red airplane, 2″ **165.00**
   On skis, 2″ **55.00**
   On sled, red hat, German, 1½″ **50.00**
   On sled, 2 pc **125.00**
   On sled, w/open arms, Japanese, 2¾″ **55.00**
   Pulling penguins on sled **150.00**
   Pulling sled, 1¾″ **75.00**

Red hat, shoes, gloves; Germany, 1¾″ **75.00**
Reclining on side, one arm up, 2¾″ **48.00**
Sitting, 1¾″ **35.00**

Sitting w/arms out stretched, 1".......................**40.00**
Sitting w/arms outstretched, 3"......................**120.00**
Standing & waving, 1½"..............................**30.50**
With seal & ball, 2".................................**40.00**
Walking a bear, carrying object, German, 2"............**95.00**
Bisque, flange head only, 2".........................**155.00**
Boy, on skis w/poles, 2"............................**48.00**
On sled, German...................................**55.00**
Child, on skates, 2¼"..............................**37.50**
Children, dancing, 2 children, German, 1¾".........**47.50**
Sliding down roof, German.........................**200.00**
Christmas carolers, w/lantern, 3½".................**75.00**
Church, bisque, 3"................................**140.00**
Cloth body, shoulder head, bisque hands & feet, 6"........**424.00**
Eskimo, pushing twin babies in carriage, mkd, German, 2½x2½" **175.00**
German, good coloring, 2x2½".......................**75.00**
Girl, in red pushing snowball, German, 2"..............**80.00**
On sled, molded skirt, 2" long......................**115.00**
Seated, pink molded skirt, 1¼".....................**70.00**
Standing under street light w/packages & dog, German, 2"...**75.00**
Girl & boy on sled, German, 1¾"...................**25.00**
Girl & boy on sled, molded clothes, 1¾x2" long..........**120.00**
Group, 1 seated, 1 on side, 1 standing, each.........**38.00**
Baby in igloos, Santa on roof w/teddy in bag, 2½"......**165.00**
On sled, 3 babies, 2¾".............................**125.00**
Penguin, pushes sled w/children, 2"..................**75.00**
Polar bear pulling sled, German, 1¼"...............**35.00**
On his back, legs, crossed over yellow ball, 2½".........**90.00**
Standing on sled, 2"................................**95.00**
Standing, ¾".......................................**35.00**
Walking, 1½".......................................**30.00**
Walking, 2½".......................................**40.00**
With child, 2"......................................**65.00**
Santa, w/wheelbarrow, 2½".........................**65.00**
Santa on snowbear.................................**150.00**
Singers, group of 3, German, 2"....................**95.00**
Skaters, pair, boy & girl w/molded clothes, 2", each........**120.00**
Snowman, German, 1¾"..............................**40.00**
Seated w/arms & legs extended, 2¼".................**130.00**

Snuff Bottles, Boxes and Jars

The Chinese were introduced to snuff in the 17th century, and their carved and painted snuff bottles typify their exquisite taste and workmanship. These tiny bottles, seldom measuring over 2½", were made of amber, jade, ivory, and cinnabar, and often had tiny spoons attached to their stoppers. By the 18th century, some were made of porcelain, others of glass with delicate designs painted inside. Copper and brass were used only occasionally.

In the early 19th century, the use of snuff had spread to Europe and America. It was used by both the gentlemen and the ladies alike, and expensive snuff boxes and bottles were the earmark of the genteel. Some were silver or gold set with precious stones or pearls; others contained music boxes.

Bottle, amber, lg.................................**240.00**
Amber, medium..................................**160.00**
Amber, small.....................................**60.00**
Bas-relief waves & dragon pattern, rose quartz, 1¾".......**75.00**
Blanc de chine, relief molded bird on branch, 3"......**35.00**
Carved, ivory, silver, coral, turquoise...............**105.00**
Carved, reverse painted on 4 sides, 3"...............**150.00**
Chased floral pattern, silver, 2½"..................**40.00**
Chinese, blue overlay, inside painted, Peking glass.........**85.00**
Chinese, blue, reverse painting, no cover.............**70.00**

Cloisonne, turquoise, wht, blk & gold, flying cranes........**189.00**
Elder & young girl, 2¼".............................**25.00**
Famille rose porcelain, sq, spoon & stopper, 2¾".........**75.00**
Floral pattern, rose glazed, 2½"....................**25.00**
Form of a persimmon, ivory, w/spoon & stopper, 2".......**75.00**
Gold coralene top.................................**38.00**
Gourd, cloisonne, double.........................**600.00**
Hand blown, cobalt gold, lg, 1925.................**125.00**
Imari butterfly, famille noire, 2½"..................**25.00**
Imari fungus & dragon, glass stopper & spoon, 2½".......**40.00**
Ivory, carved, w/money pouch, Oriental..............**90.00**
Jade, Chinese, 1800s.............................**150.00**
Long life symbols, blue decor......................**50.00**
Monochromatic mustard, hardstone stopper & spoon, 2½"...**30.00**
Oriental man, dragon, yellow background, 3"...........**30.00**
Oriental woman, garden scene, wht background, 3".......**27.50**
Panels of flowers, cobalt blue glazed, 2½"............**25.00**
Polychrome landscape & animals, 2½"................**25.00**
Resist floral pattern, enameled, 2¼"................**25.00**
Resist prunus & bird pattern, famille jeune, 2".........**40.00**
Rose Canton, w/women, early 1800s.................**135.00**
Scholar & musician pattern, blue & wht..............**25.00**
Soapstone, carved.................................**14.00**
Temple dog & elephant, polychrome, amber top.........**125.00**
Variegated hardstone, grey to red, 2¾"..............**125.00**
Box, banded agate, top & bottom covers, oval, brass band & hinge **110.00**
Figural pocket watch, hinged lid, pewter..............**140.00**
Gold plating, round w/reverse painting on lid...........**50.00**
Stars & flowers, hinged lid, pewter, small, 1700s, 1x1½"....**75.00**
Jar, Turkish cushion, blue, gold overlay on wht china, 1½"....**20.00**
Turned wood w/pinched neck, 1800s.................**290.00**

Soapstone

Soapstone is a soft talc in rock form with a smooth, greasy-like feel, from whence comes its name. In Colonial times, it was extracted from outcroppings in large sections with hand saws, carted by oxen to mills, and fashioned into useful domestic articles such as footwarmers, cooking utensils, inkwells, etc. It was used to make heating stoves and kitchen sinks during the early 1800s. Most familiar today are the carved vases, bookends and boxes made in China during the Victorian era.

Bookends, Buddha figurals, carved, pair..............**35.00**
Dragon figurals, pair.............................**45.00**
Box, carved, cover has rose quartz elephant finial...........**68.00**
Cigarette & match holder.........................**45.00**

Figurine, Buddha, 9½"............................**300.00**
Cow, sitting, w/monkey on back, 1920s..............**35.00**
Elephant, 4"......................................**25.00**

Flowers & cactus on dk base, 1910, 12″ **100.00**
Man on horse, 7½″ **30.00**
Manchurian diplomat, full figure, w/bronze-like patina, 8″ **95.00**
Rearing horse, 6x7″ **28.00**
Set of 8, immortals, blk **300.00**
Incense burner, ornately carved, blk, 1800s **325.00**
  With 3 foo dogs **145.00**
Paint stone, 5 paint sections, carved leaves/flowers, 1900, 9″ .. **100.00**
Planter, 4x6″, 3½″ bowl, pierced leaf decor **24.00**
Snuff bottle **30.00**
Tumbler, polished, straight sided **75.00**
Vase, double, 4″ **25.00**
  Floral carvings, 4¼″ **30.00**
  Florals & leaves, 8½″ **45.00**
  Souvenir, N.Y. World's Fair **45.00**
  With 2 side vases, 1-pc, highly carved, brown shading, China, 8x8″ **85.00**

Soda Fountain Collectibles

As the neighborhood ice cream parlor becomes a thing of the past, soda fountain memorabilia, from fancy backbars to ice cream advertising, is becoming a popular field of collecting. One area of interest is the glassware used to serve the more elaborate ice cream concoctions. A sundae glass is familiar to us all, but there was also a 'mondae' glass, narrow at the bottom and flaring to a top dimension equal to one scoop! And a 'tuesdae' glass with a rim wide enough to accommodate two scoops of ice cream, side by side! At least part of their appeal is due to the mouth watering memories they revive.

Bucket, wood, 'Lemon Ice' **50.00**
Canister, girl w/cone, 'Sweetheart Sugar Cones', lg **49.00**
Chair, nickel over iron, set of 4 .... **360.00**
Cup holder, pewter, Vortex, Pat, 1915, 4½″ **8.00**
Dispenser, Cherry Julep, w/pump **450.00**
  Cherry Smash **330.00**
  Metal, hangs on wall, 'Safe-T Ice Cream Cones' **39.00**
  Straw, glass & brass, 1915, 13″ **80.00**
  Syrup, baseball shape, 'Fan Taz...Pennant Winner' **1,050.00**
Scoop, aluminum, Toledo, Oh., EZ Roll **125.00**
  Bakelite handle, model 8, Hamilton Beach **30.00**
  Brass, Gilcheist, 1930 .... **35.00**
  Brass, wood handle **25.00**
  Flat, ice cream sandwich, NP **48.00**
  Nickel over brass, cone shape, 'Delmonico', 1880s **26.00**

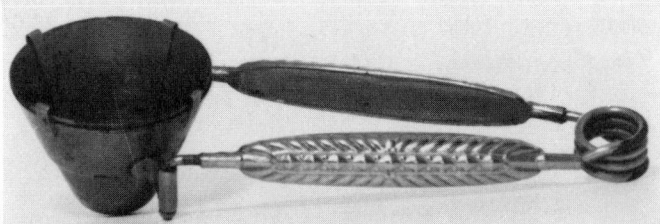

  Squeeze handle, #12 .... **25.00**
  Wood handle, cone shape, 'Quick & Easy' **45.00**
Sign, cardboard, standing, 'S&H Quality Ice Cream', 12x13″ ... **29.00**
Soda fountain back bar, arch w/stained glass, Victorian, 12′ . **6,500.00**
  Walnut, 12′ long **1,500.00**
  Wooden carved, beveled mirror, 81″x8′ **3,500.00**
Stool, bases swivel, pair, ci **20.00**

Spangle Glass

Spangle glass, also known as Vasa Murrhina, is cased art glass characterized by the metallic flecks imbedded in its top layer. It was made both abroad and in the United States during the latter years of the 19th century, and it was reproduced in the 1960s by the Fenton Art Glass Company.

Vasa Murrhina was a New England distributor who sold glassware of this type manufactured by a Dr. Flower of Sandwich, Mass. Flower had purchased the defunct Cape Cod Glassworks in 1885 and used the facilities to operate his own company. Since none of the ware was marked, it is very difficult to attribute specific examples to his manufacture.

Candlesticks, pink & gr w/mica flecks, cased, pair, 8½″ **135.00**
Chamberstick, clear applied handle & base, cased **65.00**
Ewer, blue overlay, striped, mica flaking, 8¼″ **150.00**
  Blue w/wht lining, clear thorn handle, 7½″ **120.00**
  Blue, applied handle, mica flecks, ruffled top, 8½x4½″ **135.00**
  Pink & gr w/mica flecks, cased, 10″ **145.00**
Fruit bowl, pink to cranberry, cased wht, swirl rib, 9″ **250.00**
Jar, w/lid, clear ruffled rim, mica flecks **65.00**
Rose bowl, blue to clear w/silver flecks, crimped top, 3¾″ **120.00**
  Clear petal applied feet, crimped top, 3½x3½″ dia **110.00**
  Egg shaped, yellow, gold spangled, 4″ **100.00**
  Wht lining, crimp top, mica flaking, 3½x3½″ **110.00**
  Wht lining, crimp top, silver spangled in coral pattern 3¾″ .. **95.00**
Shoe, w/clear application, cased **58.00**
Tumbler, deep oxblood w/wht spatter, mica flaked, 3¾x2¾″ dia **55.00**
Vase, blue overlay glass, wishbone feet, mica flecks, 6x3¾″ **85.00**
  Brown, blue & yellow w/mica flecks, cased, 8½″ **75.00**

Bulging panels, ruffled rim, 9½″ **165.00**
Carved, polished flowers, sgnd, 6″ **750.00**
Gold w/wht lining, crystal trim, 9″ **95.00**
Pink overlay glass w/fancy crystal rosette trim, handled, 6¾″ . **55.00**
Pink to rose, swirled pattern, mica flakes, 6½x2¾″ **65.00**
Pink w/wht lining, ruffle top, 3½″ **110.00**

Spatter Glass

Spatter glass, characterized by its multicolored 'spatters', has been made from the late 19th century to the present by American glass houses as well as those abroad. Although it was once thought to have been made entirely by workers at the 'end of the day' from bits and pieces of left-over scrap, it is now known that it was a standard line of production.

Berry, Leaf Umbrella, 5-pc set, cranberry spatter **265.00**
  Master, Leaf Umbrella, cranberry spatter **95.00**
Boot, crystal leaf & rigaree applique, 4x4½″ **65.00**

Bowl, Leaf Mold, vaseline spatter, 7¾".................. **85.00**
Box, egg shaped, ftd, hinged, florals, 3 ft, 7½x4½" **265.00**
Butter, w/cover, Leaf Umbrella, cranberry spatter **225.00**

Pitcher, Applied reed handle, browns, rust, gold, 9" **150.00**
  Reverse Swirl, spatter overlay w/blue satin **235.00**
  Ruby spatter, fluted rim, clear handle **300.00**
  Ruby w/yellow base, clear handle, fluted rim............. **320.00**
  Square mouth, dimpled sides, multicolor w/wht lining, 7½" . **225.00**
  Water, Leaf Mold, vaseline **350.00**
Rolling pin, clear w/blue & red, Victorian, 14½"............ **120.00**
Rose bowl, Leaf Mold, vaseline spatter, 4¼" **85.00**
Shade, vaseline, cranberry, wht, 5 sides, ruffled, 5½" **150.00**
Sugar & creamer, cased **35.00**
Sugar shaker, Leaf Mold, vaseline spatter................. **125.00**
  Ribbed Pillar, cranberry satin spatter.................... **95.00**
Syrup, Leaf Mold, cranberry & vaseline **265.00**
  Ribbed Pillar, cranberry satin spatter................... **125.00**
Toothpick, cranberry w/vaseline, frosted Leaf Mold, tall collar . **140.00**
Tumbler, ruby & wht **24.00**
Vase, yellow & pink, 8" **45.00**
Water set, red & wht, reeded handle, 7 pc, 7½" pitcher **240.00**

Spatterware

Spatterware is a general term referring to a type of decoration used by English potters beginning in the late 1700s. Using a brush or stick, brightly colored paint was 'dabbed' onto the soft paste earthenware items, achieving a 'spattered' effect which was often used as a border. Because much of this type of ware was made for export to the United States, some of the subjects in the central design, the schoolhouse and the eagle patterns, for instance, reflect American tastes. Yellow, green, and black spatterware is scarce and highly valued by collectors.

Bowl, dk blue & reddish brown on grey, 4¼x9" **55.00**

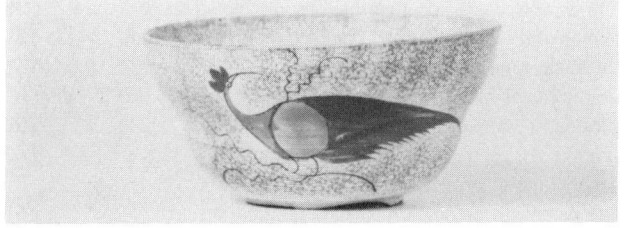

Peacock, blue spatter, 3x6¼" **200.00**

Rainbow, blue & red, 3½x6¾" dia **195.00**
Tulip in 3 colors, blue & wht spatter, 6¼" dia............ **60.00**
Yellow w/blk & red, 4½" **22.00**
Creamer, blue, high looped handle, hexagonal, 4¾"........ **235.00**
  Pink & blue spatter, octagonal, 4" **210.00**
  Red & gr spatter, 3¾"............................. **130.00**
  Red rose, gr leaves, blue, spatter handles, pearlware **250.00**
Cup, acorn design, gr leaves, brown spatter, 2½x4" dia **85.00**
  Peafowl, on bar pattern, interior peafowl gr spatter, 4" dia.. **350.00**
  Peafowl multicolored, gr, miniature, handleless **95.00**
  Rainbow, blue & ochre, 3¾".......................... **115.00**
  Rainbow, blue & red, 4" dia **95.00**
Cup & saucer, Adam's Rose, blue, cup 3" dia, saucer 4" dia.. **125.00**
  Bowknots w/dogwood, purple & red, handleless **85.00**
  Handleless **75.00**
  Holly berry design in 3 colors, blue spatter **195.00**
  Peafowl in 4 colors, red, 2½x4" cup, saucer 5¾" **295.00**
  Peafowl, red spatter border **240.00**
  Red & gr spatter, handleless......................... **65.00**
  Star pattern, red **200.00**
  Tulip in red, gr, blk, blue, lg **180.00**
Custard cup, blue spatter, handled, no lid, 3" dia **75.00**
Honey pot, tulip in red, blue, gr, blk, purple spatter, mkd B, 5½" **375.00**
Jar, w/cover, blue spatter w/gr, flaring rim, 5" **245.00**
Pitcher, design spatter, Aulk Heatherware, 6½" **65.00**
  Peacock, Adams, 13" **700.00**
Plate, blue & pink flowers, blue border, 9" **90.00**
  Blue peacock center, 8½" **300.00**
  Bowknots w/dogwood, purple & red.................... **85.00**
  Bull's eye design, blue & wht spatter, 9¾" dia **60.00**
  Early hunting stencil, stick spatter edge **115.00**
  Peafowl, blue, 8½" **300.00**
  Peafowl, multicolored, blue, Adams, 8½" **225.00**
  Peafowl, pink, Adams, 9½" **420.00**
  Persimmon pattern, blue, gr & red, 1880s, 8½" **45.00**
  Thistle w/rainbow spatter, red & gr decor **275.00**
  Tulip w/blue spatter border, Cotton & Barlow **150.00**

Platter, men on horses & trees (red transfer), 16".......... **365.00**
Saucer, blue & wht spatter, mk, 5½" dia, pr **45.00**
  Red & gr flower, cobalt blue, 1830s, 5" **65.00**
Soup plate, flower center **150.00**
  Primitive flowers w/3 colors, red & gr coarse spatter, 11½" .. **78.00**
  Star w/heavy blue spatter border, 8½" **150.00**
Sugar, thistle in red & gr, rainbow in red & blk, 4½" **65.00**
  W/cover, red, wht **200.00**
Tea set, child's wht glazed w/design spatter around the edge, 11-pc **60.00**
Teapot, peafowl, blue spatter, lg, lid rim damage only, 5½"... **400.00**

Spode-Copeland

The Spode Works were established in 1770 and continued to operate under that title until 1843. Their earliest products were typical underglaze blue printed patterns, though basalt was also made. After 1790, a translucent porcelain body was the basis for a line of fine enamel decorated dinnerware. Stone china was introduced in 1805, often in patterns reflecting an Oriental influence.

In 1833, Wm. Taylor Copeland purchased the company, continuing business in much the same tradition. During the last half of the 19th century, Copeland produced excellent parian figures and groups with such success that many other companies attempted to reproduce his work. He employed famous painters to decorate plaques, vases and tablewares, many examples of which were signed by the artist. Most of the Copeland wares are marked with one of several variations that incorporate the firm name.

Bowl, blue & wht, 7½"	35.00
Flowers & leaves, blue & wht, ironstone, Copeland 1847, 13½"	75.00
Ruffles & rings, blue, ftd, 7"	45.00
Ruffles & rings, gr, ftd, 7"	45.00
Butter, blue & wht tower scene, Copeland Spode, lg	95.00
Candlesticks, tan, paneled, scalloped base, England C/S, 3¼x4½", pr	23.00
Coffee can, gilt decor, set of 4, 1815	110.00
Coffee pot, primrose pattern, Spode	75.00
Wht classical figures, England Spode, 8½"	95.00
Cup & saucer, blue & wht, lg	45.00
Demitasse, 1850	130.00
Demitasse, dk blue scenic, Copeland	25.00
Mallard, 10" wing span, Copeland Spode	250.00

Pitcher, Chicago, depicts fire, #444, Burley, 8"	500.00
Tower, England, Copeland Spode, 20" cir, 10" tall	120.00
Velamour K220, Spode	12.50
Place setting, Country Lane, 3 pc	27.50
Planter, applied scrolls & masks in wht on blue, Copeland, 9"	375.00
Plate, brown leaf border & scene, Copeland, 10"	18.00
Impressed Copeland, 10"	18.00
Red Willoware, Copeland, 12½"	60.00
Shakespeare, blk & wht w/portrait in center, Copeland-Spode	25.00
Platter, Bridal Rose, 13"	28.00
Center scene, multicolor rim, mkd, 1882, 15½x12¼"	125.00
Towel pattern, blue, 17"	125.00
Sugar, paneled holly open blue	40.00
Toby, wht, seated, sgnd Eric Olsen NFD, Spode, 8½"	135.00
Tray, gold & floral decor, scalloped, Copeland, 2x6x10"	80.00
Tureen, covered, w/undertray, tree of India, Copeland	170.00
Vase, blue trunk, 10"	40.00

Spongeware

Spongeware is a type of factory-made earthenware that was popular during the last quarter of the 19th century. It was decorated by dabbing color onto the drying ware with a sponge, leaving a splotched design at random or in simple patterns. Sometimes a solid band of color was added. The vessel was then covered with a clear glaze and fired at a high temperature. Blue on white is the most preferred combination, but green and ivory, orange on white, or those colors in combination may also occasionally be found.

Bank, pig, brown & blue, 5¾" long	115.00
Pig, gr & wht, 5½" long	135.00
Beanpot, blue & wht, handled, wooden lid	180.00
Bottle, brown & wht, miniature, 3¾"	25.00
Set, gr on wht, relief arches, 8-10", 3 for	160.00
Bowl, blue & tan on wht, bottom impressed, 7x7" dia	25.00
Blue & wht, 2½x8½" dia	35.00
Blue & wht, crow's foot in base, 3¼x10½" dia	105.00
Blue & wht sponge spatter, salmon bands, 4¼x8" dia	50.00
Blue & wht, 13"	145.00
Blue & wht, deep, 8" dia	95.00
Blue & wht, base w/8 indentations, 1810, 3¼x10½" dia	240.00
Blue allover on orange, shallow, 2¼x7¾" dia	65.00
Blue on cream, crimped edge, 7" dia, 3½" deep	85.00
Blue over rust on tan, advertising, 4x6¼" dia	85.00
Blue, tan, wht sponge spatter, blue rim, embossed, 3½x7" dia	185.00
Bread, blue & wht, lg	210.00
Brown & gr sponge spatter, yellowware, 3x6¼" dia	20.00
Gr on cream, 8"	45.00
Gr on wht, 9"	48.00
Mixing blue & red, heavy rim, 4x7¼" dia	65.00
Mixing, blue & rust on tan, multiribbed, rolled rim, 4x7" dia	75.00
Mixing, blue & wht, 2 center bands, 5x11¼" dia	135.00
Mixing, blue & wht, 3 blue bands, tapered to bottom, 5x10¼" dia	135.00
Mixing, blue & wht, 3 center bands, cracked, 5x11"	85.00
Mixing, blue & wht, dk blue rim, fluted, 3½x9" dia	135.00
Mixing, blue & wht, round sponging, 4¾x10" dia	135.00
Mixing, blue & wht, self embossed arches design, 5½x12" dia	150.00
Mixing, blue, 15"	150.00
Mixing, dk, gr & rust, circle design, rust rim band, 4¾x10¼"	125.00
Mixing, dk gr on wht	35.00
Mixing, gr, rust lines at top & bottom, rolled rim, 4½x8" dia	65.00
Pudding, blue & wht, allover swirled design, 3½x10¼" dia	150.00
Pudding, gr over yellow clay, recessed bottom w/knob, 3½x10" dia	60.00
Red & blue on tan, embossed corn, 5"	25.00
Red & blue on tan, 10"	65.00
Rust & blue, 6"	40.00
Rust & blue, 7"	45.00
Rust & blue, 8½"	48.00
Soup, blue & wht, molded scroll rim, 9½" dia	140.00
Vegetable, blue & wht, curved edges, 8½x6½"	135.00
Yellowware w/blue, 4" dia	40.00
Yellowware w/blue, scalloped rim, minor flakes, 7½"	50.00
Yellowware w/blue, 2½x9"	50.00
Butter crock; w/lid, brown on yellow-tan, ribbed, 4½x7"	65.00
Blue & wht, wood lid, inverted U sponging, 4¾x7½" dia	90.00
Cake plate, blue & wht, 2 open handles, molded scroll rim, 10" dia	130.00
Candlestick, blue & wht, 3½"	150.00
Casserole, gr & brown on cream, 2 eared, ribbed, 4¾x8¼" dia	65.00
Salesman's sample, illus	100.00
Commode jar, grey & blue daubs	165.00
Creamer, blue & brown sponge spatter, 3"	50.00
Blue & tan on cream, rolled oats molded design, 5"	60.00
Blue & tan, embossed swirl design, 3¾"	55.00

Blue & wht, wide lip, ftd, molded scrolls, 4½" **85.00**
Gr & cream, 1800s, 5½" **80.00**
Cup, blue & wht, 2¾" **35.00**
  Blue & wht, 3" **50.00**
  Blue w/faint red threads, handleless **50.00**
Cup & saucer, blue & wht **75.00**
Cuspidor, blue & wht, 1½x5" **95.00**
Custard cup, blue & wht, 3½x4½" dia **30.00**
  Brown & blue sponge spatter, cream color ground, 4" dia ... **10.00**
  Brown on tan, 2x5½" **22.00**
  Brown sponge spatter, yellowware, 2½x4¼" dia **12.50**
  Dk gr & rust on cream, swirl embossed, tapered, 2¼x3¾" dia **40.00**
  Gr & brown on cream, ribbed, set of 6 .... **135.00**
Jar, blue & brown, cream color ground, 4¼x5½" dia **55.00**
  W/lid, blue & wht, 'butter', 4½x6½" dia **240.00**
Jardiniere, blue, wht banded, gilt, 8x10" **100.00**
Jug, blue & cream, 1 gallon **125.00**
  Dk blue on tan, 11x7" **185.00**
Match box, w/lid & striker, blue wht, applied flowers, curved, 3½" **55.00**
Mug, blue & wht, allover sponge, 3¼x3¼" **85.00**
Pan, milk, blue & wht, sponging extends over rim, 3¼x10½" dia **155.00**
Pitcher, blue & gr on cream **35.00**
  Blue & wht, 4½" **110.00**
  Blue & wht, 5½" **130.00**
  Blue & wht, 7" **145.00**

  Blue & wht, 9" **155.00**
Blue & wht, bulbous flare toward base, embossed diamonds, 9" **190.00**
Blue & wht, bulbous, molded scroll & flower rim, 6½" **130.00**
Blue & wht, cosmo, 9" **145.00**
Blue & wht, cream ground, narrow ewer shape, 6" **110.00**
Blue & wht, octagonal, 7½x5" dia **150.00**
Blue & wht, wash type, bulbous shape, 11½" **225.00**
Blue & wht, wash type, wide lip, 10½" **200.00**
Brown & gr on yellowware, 4½" **50.00**
Brown & gr on yellowware, 7¾" **70.00**
Brown & gr on yellowware, ribbed, 4½" **60.00**
Brown, yellow & gr, barrel, 8" **70.00**
Bulbous, wide lip, stripe through middle **245.00**
Dk gr & wht, 6½" **50.00**
Gr & tan on cream, advertising in blk, 4½" **90.00**
Grey & rust, applied in circles on cream ground, 7" **110.00**
Mustard, dk blue on cream, bulbous, 1880s, 6½" **85.00**
Rust on cream, fluted rim, molded flower band, 7¼" **95.00**

Wash, medium to dk gr on wht, bulbous, 10¼" **90.00**
Plate, blue & wht, 6¾" **45.00**
  Blue & wht, 8" **85.00**
  Blue & wht, 10" **100.00**
  Blue & wht, brown transfer, 9" dia **90.00**
  Blue & wht, miniature, 1870s, 4" dia **45.00**
  Gr sponge border, 9" **50.00**
  Rose & mustard, girl w/pets, Keeping School, 7" **95.00**
  Rose & mustard, girl w/pets, Now I'm Grandmother, 7" **95.00**
  Rose & mustard, girl w/pets, The Young Nurse, 7" **95.00**
Platter, blue & wht, 7½" dia **120.00**
  Blue & wht, 11¾" **125.00**
  Blue & wht, embossed foliage rim, 9¼x13½" **145.00**
  Blue & wht, oval, curved edges, molded scroll rim, 11½x7¾" **130.00**
Pot, chamber, blue & wht, 3¼x8¾" dia **150.00**
  Chamber, blue & wht, wire bail, wooden handle, 8¾x9½" dia **145.00**
  Stew, blue & wht, w/bail, 5x10" dia **130.00**
Ramekin, blue & wht, deep color, ovoid, 1½x5½x3¾" **150.00**
Salt, blue & wht **37.50**
Saucer, blue & wht, 6" dia **12.50**
Soap, blue & wht, flat, ridged **180.00**
  Blue & wht, round, covered **180.00**
Soup plate, blue & wht, 9¼" dia **40.00**
Spittoon, blue, 4x6" **140.00**
  Blue & wht, blue bands, 5½x7½" dia **75.00**
  Blue & wht, sponged circles, blue bands, 5½x7½" **75.00**
Syrup, blue & wht, advertising, 2 qt **650.00**
  Blue & wht, embossed leaves, w/bail, closed top, spout, 2 qt **650.00**
Tankard, blue & rust on tan, embossed diamonds & 3 bands, 9½" **90.00**
  Blue & wht, 7" **165.00**
  Blue & wht, 9" **190.00**
  Dk brown over yellow, 7" **125.00**

Teapot, blue & wht, 7¼" **350.00**
  Blue & wht on brown clay, 6¾" **85.00**
  Blue & wht sponge spatter, 5¼" **125.00**
Umbrella stand **575.00**
Vase, blue & wht, 4½" **40.00**
Vegetable dish, blue & wht, oblong, open, 9¼" long **40.00**
Wash set, blue & wht, bowl 13¼", sponged allover, pitcher 10" **450.00**
Waste bowl, blue & wht, 3¼x5¼" dia **30.00**

Spoons

Souvenir spoons have been popular remembrances since the 1890s; handwrought examples of the silversmiths' art are sought and appreciated for their fine craftsmanship. Commemorative, personality related, advertising, those with Indian busts, and those with floral designs are only a few of the many types of collectible spoons.

Advertising, Best Flour **14.50**
  Braniff.. **2.50**
  Campbell Kids, orig wrap **25.00**
  Formosa Oalong Tea **6.75**
  Gerber's baby spoon **5.00**
  Larkin, Globe, child, plated **24.00**
  Gold Mr Peanut.................................... **17.50**
  Kern's Founder's Month **19.50**
  Panama Pacific Expo, California Perfume Co, 1915 on reverse **17.50**
  Queensboro Bridge Bloomingdales..................... **12.50**
  Rolex-Bucherer Watches, demitasse, Tower of London in bowl **15.00**
  Towle Log Cabin **12.50**
  Walker's Grape Juice, bottle in handle, plated **38.00**
Baby, 'Bobby', straight handle **10.00**
Christmas, Dancing Indian handle w/School, Butterfield, sterling **28.00**
  Kneeling Indian, demitasse, sterling.................. **20.00**
  Michelsen 1932 .... **62.50**
  Order of the Eastern Star, sterling................... **18.00**
  Standing Indian, w/Cathedral in bowl, sterling......... **28.00**
Commemorative, Battleship Maine, plated **8.00**
  Battleship Maine, demitasse **151.00**
  Belgium King Albert, teaspoon, plated................ **15.00**
  Centennial of Lewis & Clark, 1805-1905, copper, Portland ... **45.00**
  Edward IV Coronation, sterling, orig box **100.00**
  GAR Encampment, Buffalo, 1892, demitasse............ **15.00**
  I00F, 1915, sterling, teaspoon **21.00**
  Newark, N.Y., 250th Anniversary, 1666-1916 City Hall **16.00**
Happy New Year, Father Time, pattern handle, demitasse **15.00**
  Ring Out Old, Ring In New, Cupids, sterling **120.00**
Mary Poppins, plated, 1964 .... **7.00**
Miner figural, w/pipe, pick, nugget, Mayer Bros **95.00**
Personality related, Charlie McCarthy, teaspoon, plated........ **15.00**
  Dionne Quintuplets, set, plated **125.00**
  Douglas Fairbanks, Oneida, plated **12.00**
  Earl Kitchener **4.00**
  George Washington **7.00**
  Gloria Swanson, Oneida **15.00**
  John Adams **7.00**
  Mae Murray, Oneida **15.00**
  Maire Dionne, quintuplet **25.00**

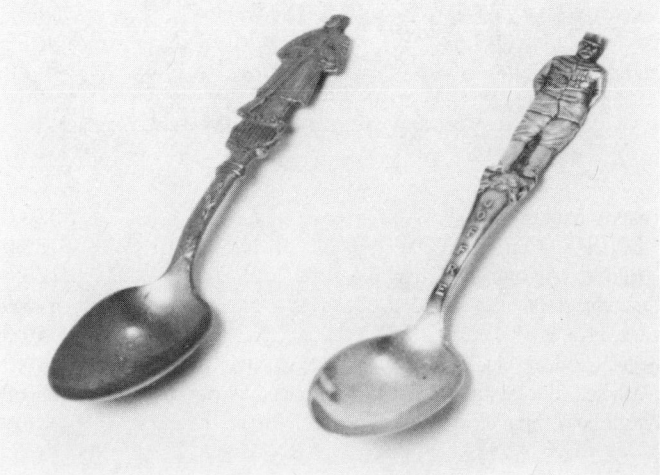

  Martin Van Buren, bronze, USA **45.00**
  Mary Baker Eddy, teaspoon, sterling **175.00**
  Norma Shearer, Oneida.............................. **15.00**
  President McKinley, teaspoon, gold wash w/flag & leaves, enameled **75.00**
  President Wm Rogers **7.00**
  Railroad, Joffre, RR conductor, plated, illus **12.00**

Ramon Navorro, Oneida **15.00**
  Rose Coghlan, Gorham actress, bowl w/gold wash, demitasse **130.00**
  Sherlock Holms, teaspoon, plated **15.00**
  Thomas Jefferson **7.00**
  Thomas Meighan, Oneida **15.00**
  Santa w/bell, fireplace scene **95.00**
Souvenir, Actors Fund Fair, sterling **295.00**
  Albuquerque, NM, Old Church of San Felipe, Indian finial, sterling **77.50**
  Alexandria, LA, Negro figural handle, demitasse, sterling..... **38.00**
  Atlantic City, early swimmers, mkd M, 1880 .... **35.00**
  Bermuda on handle, reticultated palm trees, sterling **16.50**
  Birmingham, Alabama, first house built 1871, sterling **35.00**
  Cambridge, N.Y., '93 twisted, decorated stem, demitasse ... **22.00**
  Catalina Island, Ca., full figural fish top handle, sterling **39.00**
  Chicago, plated **8.00**
  Chicago Art Institute, Indian finial, sterling **55.00**
  Chicago World's Fair............................... **20.00**
  Colorado, sterling **35.00**
  Columbia Expo, 1892, plated **8.00**
  Cumberland, B.C., twisted stem, enameled maple leaf, demitasse **20.00**
  Daytona, Fla., alligator figural **52.00**
  Denver in gold washed bowl, Indian bust handle, sterling **42.00**
  Detroit harbor, skyline handle, demitasse **50.00**
  Dionne Quintuplets, set of 5......................... **75.00**
  Elk City, sunflower handle, sterling **20.00**
  Eureka, Ca., 2 teddy bears climbing pole, sterling **70.00**
  Fish Creek, figural fish **25.00**
  Galena, Ill., Shakespear bust on handle................ **35.00**
  Galesburg, Ill., Whiting Hall, poppy handle, sterling, 5½".... **20.00**
  Galveston, Texas, in bowl, enamel water lily, teaspoon....... **25.00**
  Girl graduate **25.00**
  Gloversville w/bust of Sir Wm Johnson, demitasse, sterling ... **30.00**
  Gloversville, w/bust of Sir Wm Johnson, teaspoon, sterling ... **50.00**
  Grand Canyon of Arizona, Indian figural **120.00**
  Great Bend, Kansas, Normal College **18.00**
  Hamilton, Canada, demitasse, sterling **15.00**
  Henderson, Ky. Old Kentucky Home, cabin, woman, man, dog **45.00**
  Holland, demitasse, sterling, windmill handle, wheel turns **15.00**
  Indian Chief, full figure, Banner H Watson, teaspoon, sterling **75.00**
  Indian at well embossed, 'Saratoga', Durgin, teaspoon, sterling **75.00**
  Indian head on handle, landing of Pilgrims in bowl **25.00**
  Indian w/headdress, buffalo, teepee **34.00**
  John & Priscilla, teaspoon **45.00**
  John Harvard, Whiting sterling, orange spoon **48.00**
  Library of Congress in bowl, Capitol building handle **22.00**
  Lincoln, figure raised, 1904 .... **12.00**
  Maine state seal, brite cut engraved bowl **35.00**
  Man in the Moon, baby spoon **32.00**
  Manitou, Colorado, cutout, Pike's Peak, sterling........... **40.00**
  Michigan state seal, Shepard, teaspoon, sterling **30.00**
  Milwaukee, Wis. City Hall, Indian head in relief, florals, demitasse **50.00**
  Milwaukee, Wis., new auditorium, Indian figural on globe **68.00**
  Missouri state seal, bowl engraved, teaspoon............. **27.00**
  Montana, sterling, lg letters cover handle **39.00**
  Morman Temple, Salt Lake City, Indian finial, sterling....... **75.00**
  Mt Ranier, sterling................................. **20.00**
  New Jersey, plated **8.00**
  New Mexico, state emblem on handle, gold wash bowl, etched, 5½" **25.00**
  New Orleans, black boy eating watermelon, sterling, 5¼".... **65.00**
  Niagara Falls, Indian on handle, demitasse, sterling **30.00**
  Old man of the Mountain, teaspoon.................... **24.00**
  Ontario, tobaggan handle, demitasse, Toronto embossed bowl **20.00**
  PT Barnum autograph stem w/raised bust, sterling, pat 1881 . **45.00**
  Palm Beach, Fla., Royal Poinciana, Negro figural head, sterling **42.00**

Panama Expo, 1915, teaspoon, sterling, cutout handle **17.50**
Philadelphia, twisted feather shaped stem **30.00**
Pikes Peak, summit, gold wash in bowl, demitasse **16.00**
Port Arthur, Canada, enameled maple leaf, sterling **35.00**
Portland, Oregon, demitasse, sterling.................... **15.00**
Quebec, sterling, 5¾"..................................... **22.50**
Reading Pa., 1909, WH Luden, Anniversary 30 yrs **55.00**
Reed & Barton sterling gold wash bowl w/eagle enameled bowl **75.00**
Rhode Island, teaspoon, nautical motifs on handle **20.00**
Salem Witch, cat moon, sterling **100.00**
San Francisco, demitasse, sterling, ornate handle **12.50**
San Francisco, Palace of Fine Arts in bowl, teaspoon **20.00**
San Francisco, Pan Pac International Expo, 1915, sterling ... **40.00**
San Francisco, w/figural bear, sterling heavy **35.00**
Seattle, Washington, demitasse, sterling.................. **15.00**
South Dakota, 'Deadwood Blk Hills' **30.00**
Spokane, Washington, demitasse, sterling **15.00**
St Augustine, Fla., enameled orange & leaves, sterling **35.00**
St Augustine, Fla., figural alligator, heavy, sterling **42.00**
St Augustine, Fla., Ponce DeLeon figural, demitasse **80.00**
St Augustine, sterling enamel blossom handle, gold washed .. **35.00**
St Louis, silver plate, 1904 .... **15.00**
St Louis, sterling, lg letters cover handle................. **39.00**
St Louis, Mo., stork figural w/baby...................... **52.00**
St Paul, Minnesota, sterling **30.00**
Statue of Liberty, figural, demitasse **58.00**
Stillwater, Minn., Lake St Croix, etched bowl, sterling, 5½".. **11.00**
Summit of Pike's Peak Colorado, Indian finial, sterling **75.00**
Tacoma, Washington, demitasse, sterling................. **15.00**
The Old Elm **18.00**
Tiffany, Statue of Liberty handle, teaspoon, sterling........ **60.00**
Topeka, Kansas, sterling, ornate **22.00**
Totem pole handle, Dawson in gold washed bowl, sterling.... **28.00**
Vancouver, Canada, demitasse, sterling **15.00**
Vermont, Shepard, demitasse **32.00**
Virginia state seal handle, Jefferson Davis Mansion, Banner Watson **35.00**
Virginia, 'Jamestown 1607-1957', 3 ships, demitasse, sterling.. **15.00**
Wallace Easter, teaspoon **35.00**
Washington City, Washington Monument handle, Moore & Leading **50.00**
Waterloo, Iowa, sterling, ornate **35.00**
Watermelon bowl, black boy's head, Charles W Chrankshaw **130.00**
Watermelon enameled on bowl, Negro head handle, sterling, 5½" **25.00**
West Baden Springs Hotel, Indian bust on handle, sterling, 6¼" **75.00**
White House, Omaha in bowl, eagle on handle, teaspoon **18.00**
Wichita, Kansas, cutout, horses plow, sunflower, sterling **45.00**
Worcester, Mass., Bancroft picture front of bowl, teaspoon ... **30.00**
World's Fair, 1893, sterling, Bertha M Palmer bust, demitasse **30.00**
World's Fair, 1893, sterling, Bertha M Palmer bust, teaspoon. **50.00**
Yale in bowl, insignia on stem, demitasse **22.00**
Washington, D.C., GAR the Encampment............... **36.00**

Sports Cards

In the 1800s the American tobacco industry began using baseball cards primarily to promote sales, though the stiff cardboards also gave extra protection to their product. In this early era, sport card trading and collecting was strictly the hobby of children. The cards were discontinued, however, and it was several years before the candy and cigarette industries decided to use this promotion idea again. During the second era, which ended with the onset of WWI, sports cards were produced in gold-bordered 'T205' sets and folded styles.

After the war, 'strip cards' were produced. These were free of any advertising, and were sold strictly for the purpose of collecting. By now, adults were 'into' the hobby, but this third phase of sport card collecting and trading

was cut off at the beginning of the depression.

The fourth era began around 1933. Collecting became a much more serious hobby. One of the most important issues of these years was the Goudey Big League set. The paper shortage that resulted during WWII brought this period to an end.

The current phase began during the 1950s. Tops Gum Co. again chose the cards as a means to advertise their product, and collectors began to correspond through the aid of hobby publications. Today, those cards from before 1960 are considered the most collectible.

Baseball Cards

Aaron, Henry Louis; Bazooka, 1959 .... **250.00**
  Hires, 1958, card No 44 .... **60.00**
  Lake to Lake Dairy, 1960 .... **100.00**
  Swift's Franks, 1957, card No 13.................... **100.00**
  Topps, 1954.. **90.00**
  Topps All Star Stick Ons, 1963 .... **18.00**
  Topps Deckle Edge, 1974, card No 57 .... **25.00**
  Topps Doubleheader, 1955, card No 105 .... **60.00**
  Topps Magic Rub-offs, card No 577 .... **32.00**
  Topps Supers, 1969, card No 34.................... **100.00**
Aber, Albert Julius; Bond Bread, 1958 .... **10.00**
Abrams, Calvin Ross; Esskay Meats, 1954 .... **85.00**
Acker, Thomas James; Kahn's Weiners, 1957 .... **24.00**
  Kahn's Weiners, 1959............................. **24.00**
Adair, Kenneth Jerry; Jello, 1963, card No 61 .... **10.00**
  Post Cereal, 1963, card No 61..................... **50.00**
Adams, Charles Dwight; Mother's Cookies, 1953 .... **8.00**
Adcock, Joseph Wilbur; Topps, 1952, card No 347........ **40.00**
Agee, Tommie Lee; Kahn's Weiners, 1968 .... **5.00**
Alexander, Grover C; Topps Connie Mack All Stars, 1951 .... **300.00**
Allen, Richard Anthony; Topps, 1974, card No 39 .... **12.00**
Alou, Felipe Rojas; Topps Supers, 1969, card No 35......... **7.00**
Alou, Mateo Rojas; Topps Supers, 1969, card No 56......... **7.00**
Alston, Walter Emmons; Morrell Meats, 1960 .... **14.00**
Anderson, George Lee; Leaf Gum Co, 1960 .... **6.00**
Anson, Adrian Constantine; Goodwin & Co Champions **500.00**
Aparicio, Luis Ernesto; Topps Supers, 1969 .... **9.00**
Ashburn, Don Richie, Bazooka, 1959 .... **120.00**
Aspromonte, Robert Thomas; Post Cereal, 1963, card No 1.... **60.00**
Bando, Salvatore Leonard; Topps Baseball Greatest Moments.... **3.00**
Banks, Ernest; Bazooka, 1959 .... **180.00**
  Bowman Gum Co, 1955, card No 242 .... **30.00**
Bateman, John Alvin; Pepsi Cola, 1963 .... **300.00**
Baylor, Don Edward; Topps Supers, 1971, card No 709 .... **3.00**
Bench, Johnny Lee; Kahn's Weiners, 1968............... **18.00**
  Topps Supers, 1970, card No 660 .... **20.00**
Berra, Lawrence Peter; Drake's Cookies, 1950, card No 24 .... **80.00**
  Tip Top, 1947.................................... **50.00**
  Topps, 1955, card No 198 .... **22.00**
  Topps Current All Stars, 1951 .... **600.00**
Blasingame, Don Lee; Jello, 1963, card No 126........... **12.00**
Blasingame, Wade Allen; Kahn's Weiners, 1966............ **6.00**
Blue, Vida Rochells; Topps Supers, 1971, card No 544........ **2.50**
Boxton Red Sox, Topps, 1951 .... **100.00**
Bowa, Lawrence Robert; Topps, 1974, card No 70 .... **12.00**
Boyer, Cloyd Victor, Rodeo Meats, 1955, blue back **70.00**
Boyer, Kenton Lloyd; Bazooka, 1959 .... **140.00**
  Bazooka, 1967, card No 33 .... **140.00**
Brett, George Howard; Topps mini set, 1975, card No 228 .... **12.00**
Brock, Louis Clark; Topps, 1963, card No 472 .... **20.00**
  Topps, 1974, card No 20 .... **17.00**
Burroughs, Jeffrey Allen; Topps, 1974, card No 48 .... **10.00**
Campanella, Roy; Drake's Cookies, 1950, card No 6........ **100.00**

Stahl Meyer, 1953 . . . . **300.00**	Horner, James Robert; Topps, 1980, Super Star White **1.00**
Campaneris, Blanco Dagoberto; Topps, 1974, card No 46 . . . . . **10.00**	Howard, Elston Gene; Kahn's Weiners, 1963 . . . . **10.00**
Cardenal, Jose Domec; Topps, 1974, card No 55 . . . . **10.00**	Howard, Frank Oliver; Morrell Meats, 1961 . . . . **16.00**
Carew, Rodney Cline; Topps, 1967, card No 569 . . . . **25.00**	Hunter, James August, Bazooka, 1971 . . . . **4.00**
Topps, 1974, card No 32 . . . . **17.00**	Topps, 1974, card No 6 . . . . **17.00**
Carlton, Stephen Norman; Topps, 1974, card No 5 . . . . **14.00**	Jackson, Grant Dwight; Topps, 1966, card No 591 . . . . **1.20**
Cash, Norman Dolton; Topps Stand Ups, 1964 . . . . **16.00**	Jackson, Reginald Martinez; Topps Greatest Moments, 1971 . . . . . **7.00**
Cepeda, Orlando Manuel; Bazooka, 1959 . . . . **60.00**	Topps Mini Set, 1975, card No 300 . . . . **2.00**
Chambliss, C Christopher; Topps, 1974, card No 15 . . . . **10.00**	Topps Supers, 1969, card No 28 . . . . **26.00**
Chicago Cubs, Fatima Cigarettes Teams, 1913 . . . . **50.00**	Topps, 1969, card No 260 . . . . **4.00**
Chicago White Sox, Topps Team Cards, 1951 . . . . **60.00**	Topps, 1974, card No 61 . . . . **17.00**
Clemente, Roberto Walker; Kahn's Weiners, 1957 . . . . **80.00**	James, Charles Wesley; Topps, 1961, card No 561 . . . . **4.00**
Topps, 1968, 3-D **400.00**	Javier, Manuel Julian L; Jello, 1963, card No 159 . . . . **3.00**
Topps, 1969, card No 58 . . . . **90.00**	Jenkins, Ferguson Arthur; Kahn's Weiners, 1968 . . . . **7.00**
Clendenon, Don Alvin; Topps Stand Ups, 1964 . . . . **14.00**	Topps Supers, 1969, card No 37 . . . . **8.00**
Colvaito, Rocco Domenico; Bazooka, 1959 . . . . **180.00**	Topps, 1974, card No 59 . . . . **12.00**
Dark, Alvin Ralph; Drake's Cookies, 1950, card No 20 . . . . . . **40.00**	John, Thomas Edward; Kellogg's Cereal, 1971, card No 74 . . . **3.00**
Leaf Gum Co, 1948, card No 51 . . . . **80.00**	Nabisco Team Flakes, 1969 . . . . **6.00**
Davalillo, Victor Jose; Sugardale, 1963, card No 24 . . . . **25.00**	Topps, 1967, card No 609 . . . . **7.00**
Davis, Willie Henry; Topps, 1968, 3-D **150.00**	Johnson, Alexander; Kahn's Weiners, 1969 . . . . **5.00**
Dean, Jay Hanna; G Miller **300.00**	Topps Greatest Moments, 1971 . . . . **3.00**
Rice Stix **300.00**	Johnson, David Allen; Topps, 1971, Tattoo, card No 4 . . . . **1.50**
Dimaggio, Joseph Paul; Goudey Gum Co, 1938, card No 274 . **400.00**	Johnson, Robert Wallace; Jello, 1963, card No 96 . . . . **3.00**
Play Ball, 1940, card No 1 . . . . **200.00**	Johnstone, John William; Topps, 1968, card No 389 . . . . **1.00**
Drysdale, Donald Scott; Bazooka, 1959 . . . . **180.00**	Jones, Cleon Joseph; Kahn's Weiners, 1967 . . . . **6.00**
Donald Scott; Post Cereal, 1961, card No 160 . . . . **100.00**	Topps Supers, 1969, card No 50 . . . . **7.00**
Evans, Darrell Wayne; Topps, 1974, card No 2 . . . . **10.00**	Jones, Mack; Kahn's Weiners, 1966 . . . . **6.00**
Fairly, Ronald Ray; Kellogg's Cereal, 1974, card No 27 . . . . . **14.00**	Kahn's Weiners, 1968 . . . . **5.00**
Topps, 1968, 3-D **150.00**	Kaat, James Lee; Jello, 1963, card No 10 . . . . **12.00**
Ferguson, Joe Vance; Topps, 1974, card No 67 . . . . **10.00**	Peter's Meats, 1961, card No 7 . . . . **12.00**
Fingers, Roland Glen; Hostess, 1975, card No 52 . . . . **30.00**	Topps Greatest Moments, 1971, card No 7 . . . . **3.50**
Fischer, John Howard; Kahn's Weiners, 1967 . . . . **6.00**	Kaline, Albert William; Bazooka, 1960, card No 18 . . . . **7.00**
Fisk, Carlton Ernest; Hostess, 1975, card No 143 . . . . **40.00**	Post Cereal, 1960 . . . . **160.00**
Topps, 1974, card No 64 . . . . **14.00**	Rawling's **60.00**
Flood, Curtis Charles; Post Cereal, 1963, card No 162 . . . . . **20.00**	Topps, 1954, card No 201 . . . . **30.00**
Topps, 1968, 3-D **180.00**	Kanehl, Rodrick Edwin; Jello, 1963, card No 199 . . . . **3.00**
Foli, Timothy John; Topps, 1974, card No 19 . . . . **10.00**	Kemp, Steve; Topps, 1980, Superstars White, card No 29 . . . . . . **1.00**
Foster, George Arthur; Topps, 1971, card No 276 . . . . **1.50**	Kessinger, Donald Eulon; Kellogg's Cereal, 1971, card No 9 . . . . **3.00**
Fox, Jacob Nelson; Bazooka, 1959 . . . . **180.00**	Topps Supers, 1969, card No 18 . . . . **7.00**
Fregosi, James Louis, Topps Supers, 1969, card No 7 . . . . **8.00**	Topps, 1974, card No 52 . . . . **10.00**
Garagiola, Joseph Henry; Tip Top Bread, 1947 . . . . **16.00**	Killebrew, Harmon Clayton; Post Cereal, 1960 . . . . **120.00**
Garvey, Steve Patrick; Topps Mini Set, 1975, card No 140 . . . . **3.00**	Rawling's **60.00**
Topps, 1972, card No 686 . . . . **12.00**	Topps Supers, 1969, card No 19 . . . . **25.00**
Gibson, Robert; Jello, 1963, card No 166 . . . . **20.00**	Kingman, David Arthur; Kellog's Cereal, 1973, card No 44 . . . . **1.50**
Nabisco Team Flakes, 1969 . . . . **10.00**	Topps, 1972, card No 147 . . . . **2.00**
Topps, 1974, card No 3 . . . . **14.00**	Kluszewski, Theodore Bernard; Kahn's Weiners, 1955 . . . . . . **200.00**
Gonzalez, Pedro; Kahn's Weiners, 1966 . . . . **6.00**	Kahn's Weiners, 1958 . . . . **40.00**
Topps, 1963, card No 537 . . . . **32.00**	Koosman, Jerome Martin; Topps Supers, 1969, card No 51 . . . . **8.00**
Grich, Robert; Johnny Pro, 1973, error **3.00**	Topps, 1968, card No 177 . . . . **3.00**
Topps, 1974, card No 8 . . . . **10.00**	Topps, 1972, card No 697 . . . . **2.00**
Grote, Gerald Wayne; Topps Greatest Moments, 1971, card No 54 **3.00**	Koufax, Sanford; Bazooka, 1962 . . . . **7.00**
Guidry, Ronald Ames; Topps, 1976, card No 599 . . . . **3.00**	Bell Brand Potato Chips, 1958 . . . . **70.00**
Hansen, Ronald Lavern; Jello, 1962, card No 30 . . . . **3.00**	Morrell Meats, 1961 . . . . **24.00**
Harper, Tommy; Kahn's Weiners, 1964 . . . . **7.00**	Topps Stand Ups, 1964 . . . . **14.00**
Harrelson, Derrell McKinley; Topps Greatest Moments, 1971 . . . **3.00**	Topps, 1957, card No 302 . . . . **50.00**
Hartman, T C; Pepsi, 1963 . . . . **4.00**	Topps, 1965, card No 300 . . . . **5.00**
Hebner, Richard Joseph; Topps, 1974, card No 35 . . . . **10.00**	Kranepool, Edward Emil; Kahn's Weiners, 1967 . . . . **6.00**
Hegan, James Michael; Salem's Potato Chips **3.00**	Kubek, Anthony C, Kahn's Weiners, 1963 . . . . **10.00**
Helms, Tommy Van; Topps Supers, 1969, card No 40 . . . . . . **7.00**	Topps, 1957, card No 312 . . . . **7.00**
Henderson, Kenneth Joseph; Topps, 1971, Tattoo, card No 2 . . . **1.50**	Lee, Robert Dean; Kahn's Weiners, 1968 . . . . **5.00**
Hernandez, Keith; Topps Mini Set, 1975, card No 623 . . . . . . **1.00**	Lefebvre, James Kenneth; Bazooka, 1968, card No 2 . . . . **1.20**
Hiller, John Frederick; Topps, 1974, card No 17 . . . . **10.00**	Lemaster, Denver Clayton; Kahn's Weiners, 1965 . . . . **7.00**
Holtzman, Kenneth Dale; Milk Duds, 1971 . . . . **2.00**	Kahn's Weiners, 1966 . . . . **6.00**
Hooten, Burt Carlton, Topps, 1974, card No 18 . . . . **10.00**	Lewis, Johnny Joe; Kahn's Weiners, Atlanta, 1962 . . . . **8.00**

Lillis, Robert Perry, Pepsi, 1963 . . . . **20.00**	Mazeroski, William Stanley; Bazooka, 1959 . . . . **60.00**
Linz, Philip Francis; Topps, 1962, card No 596 . . . . **2.50**	Jello, 1962, card No 170 . . . . **12.00**
Lock, Don Wilson; Topps Stand Ups, 1964 . . . . **14.00**	Kahn's Weiners, 1959 . . . . **30.00**
Lolich, Michael Stephens; Topps Greatest Moments, 1971 . . . . . . **3.50**	Kahn's Weiners, 1961 . . . . **10.00**
Lonborg, James Reynold; Nabisco Team Flakes, 1969 . . . . **6.00**	McAuliffe, Richard John; Kahn's Weiners, 1968 . . . . **4.00**
Topps, 1968, 3-D **150.00**	McBean, Alvin O'Neal; Kahn's Weiners, 1964 . . . . **7.00**
Luzinski, Gregory Michael; Johnny Pro, 1974 . . . . **2.00**	McBride, Kenneth Faye; Bazooka, 1962 . . . . **2.50**
Topps, 1971, card No 439 . . . . **3.00**	McCarver, James Timothy; Kahn's Weiners, Atlanta, 1962 . . . . . **10.00**
Topps, 1974, card No 24 . . . . **12.00**	Topps Greatest Moments, 1971 . . . . **3.00**
Lynn, Fredric Michael; Topps Mini Set, 1975, card No 622 . . . . . **4.00**	Topps Supers, 1969, card No 61 . . . . **7.00**
Topps, 1975, card No 622 . . . . **2.00**	McCool, William John; Kahn's Weiners, 1965 . . . . **7.00**
Mahaffey, Arthur; Bazooka, 1962 . . . . **2.50**	McCovey, Willie Lee; Bazooka, 1964, card No 14 . . . . **4.00**
Jello, 1962, card No 199 . . . . **3.50**	Jello, 1962, card No 131 . . . . **10.00**
Maloney, James William; Kahn's Weiners, 1961 . . . . **8.00**	Post Cereal, 1962, card No 131 . . . . **12.00**
Kahn's Weiners, 1965 . . . . **7.00**	Topps Stand Ups, 1964 . . . . **20.00**
Kahn's Weiners, 1967 . . . . **6.00**	Topps Supers, 1969, card No 66 . . . . **20.00**
Kahn's Weiners, 1969 . . . . **5.00**	Topps, 1962, card No 544 . . . . **18.00**
Topps, 1968, 3-D **150.00**	Topps, 1974, card No 28 . . . . **14.00**
Malzone, Frank James; Jello, 1962, card No 58 . . . . **3.50**	McDowell, Samuel Edward; Kahn's Weiners, 1965 . . . . **8.00**
Mantle, Mickey Charles; Bazooka, 1951, card No 253 . . . . **350.00**	Sugardale, 1963, card No 26 . . . . **30.00**
Bazooka, 1954, card No 65 . . . . **40.00**	McLain, Dennis Dale; Topps, 1966, card No 540 . . . . **4.00**
Bazooka, 1959 . . . . **250.00**	McMahon, Donald John; Kahn's Weiners, 1965 . . . . **7.00**
Bazooka, 1963, card No 1 . . . . **100.00**	McNally, David Arthur, Topps Supers, 1969, card No 1 . . . . **8.00**
Brigg's Franks **800.00**	Melton, William; Topps, 1974, card No 68 . . . . **10.00**
Dan Dee Potato Chips, 1954 . . . . **350.00**	Menke, Dennis John; Kahn's Weiners, 1965 . . . . **7.00**
Post Cereal, 1960 . . . . **400.00**	Kahn's Weiners, 1967 . . . . **6.00**
Red Heart, 1954 . . . . **20.00**	Messersmith, John A; Milk Duds, 1971 . . . . **2.00**
Topps Supers, 1969, card No 24 . . . . **130.00**	Millian, Felix Bernardo; Topps, 1974, card No 26 . . . . **10.00**
Topps, 1952, card No 311 . . . . **1,100.00**	Mincher, Donald Ray; Peters Meats, 1961, card No 5 . . . . **12.00**
Topps, 1961, card No 578 . . . . **34.00**	Topps Supers, 1969, card No 33 . . . . **7.00**
Marichal, Juan Antonio S; Bazooka, 1966, card No 10 . . . . **4.00**	Monday, Robert James; Nabisco Team Flakes, 1969 . . . . **6.00**
Jello, 1962, card No 140 . . . . **5.00**	Topps Supers, 1969, card No 27 . . . . **8.00**
Nabisco Team Flakes, 1969 . . . . **8.00**	Moon, Wallace Wade; Hunter's, 1955 . . . . **100.00**
Post Cereal, 1963, card No 109 . . . . **14.00**	Morrell Meats, 1960 . . . . **14.00**
Topps Supers, 1969, card No 64 . . . . **10.00**	Morgan, Joseph Leonard; Kahn's Weiners, Atlanta, 1962 . . . . . . **8.00**
Topps, 1961, card No 417 . . . . **20.00**	Topps, 1971, card No 264 . . . . **5.00**
Maris, Roger Eugene; Bazooka, 1961, card No 5 . . . . **5.00**	Topps, 1972, card No 752 . . . . **3.00**
Jello, 1963, card No 16 . . . . **10.00**	Topps Greatest Moments, 1962 . . . . **8.00**
Topps, 1961, card No 576 . . . . **8.00**	Munson, Thurman Lee; Milk Duds, 1971 . . . . **4.00**
Topps, 1963, card No 120 . . . . **4.00**	Topps Greatest Moments, 1971 . . . . **8.00**
Marshall, Michael Grant; Topps Mini Set, 1975, card No 6 . . . . . **2.00**	Topps, 1971, card No 5 . . . . **3.00**
Martin, Alfred Manuel; Kahn's Weiners, 1959 . . . . **40.00**	Topps, 1974, card No 7 . . . . **17.00**
Remar, 1949 . . . . **18.00**	Murcer, Bobby Ray; Topps Greatest Moments, 1971 . . . . **3.50**
Topps, 1952, card No 175 . . . . **9.00**	Topps, 1974, card No 63 . . . . **12.00**
Martin, Joseph Clifton; Leaf Gum Co, 1962, card No 92 . . . . **3.00**	Musial, Stanley Frank; Hunter's, 1955 . . . . **250.00**
Matlack, Jonathan T; Topps, 1974, card No 44 . . . . **10.00**	Leaf Gum Co, 1948, card No 4 . . . . **30.00**
May, Carlos; Kellogg's Cereal, 1971, card No 45 . . . . **1.50**	Red Heart, 1954 . . . . **60.00**
May, David La France; Topps, 1974, card No 58 . . . . **10.00**	Royal Desserts, 1952 . . . . **50.00**
May, Lee Andrew, Kahn's Weiners, 1967 . . . . **7.00**	Topps, 1963, card No 250 . . . . **9.00**
Kahn's Weiners, 1969 . . . . **5.00**	Wheaties, 1952 . . . . **8.00**
Mayberry, John Claiborn; Topps, 1974, card No 51 . . . . **10.00**	Nelson, Roger Eugene; Topps Supers, 1969, card No 23 . . . . . . **7.00**
Maye, Arthur Lee; Jello, 1962, card No 156 . . . . **3.50**	Niekro, Joseph Franklin; topps, 1967, card No 536 . . . . **1.50**
Kahn's Weiners, 1965 . . . . **7.00**	Niekro, Philip Henry; Topps, 1964, card No 541 . . . . **2.00**
Mays, Willie Howard; Bazooka, 1959 . . . . **250.00**	Nixon, Russell Eugene; Kahn's Weiners, 1959 . . . . **17.00**
Bazooka, 1968, card No 14 . . . . **6.00**	Northrup, James Thomas; Topps Greatest Moments, 1971 . . . . . **3.00**
Bowman Gum Co, 1952, card No 218 . . . . **120.00**	Nuxhall, Joseph Henry; Kahn's Weiners, 1955 . . . . **200.00**
Brigg's Franks **750.00**	O'Dell, William Oliver; Topps Doubleheaders, 1955 . . . . **10.00**
Coca-Cola, 1952 . . . . **250.00**	O'Toole, James Jerome; Jello, 1962, card No 126 . . . . **3.50**
Robert F. Gould Inc, card No 1 . . . . **22.00**	Kahn's Weiners, 1960 . . . . **17.00**
Stahl Meyer, 1954 . . . . **700.00**	Kahn's Weiners, 1962 . . . . **8.00**
Topps Supers, 1969, card No 65 . . . . **100.00**	Kahn's Weiners, 1965 . . . . **7.00**
Topps, 1952, card No 261 . . . . **200.00**	Odom, Johnny Lee; Kellogg's Cereal, 1970 . . . . **3.50**
Topps, 1958, card No 5 . . . . **16.00**	Oliva, Antonio Pedro; Bazooka, 1965, card No 4 . . . . **4.00**
Topps, 1960, card No 564 . . . . **10.00**	Kellogg's Cereal, 1971, card No 12 . . . . **3.00**

Nabisco Team Flakes, 1969 . . . . **6.00**
Topps Supers, 1969, card No 20 . . . . **8.00**
Topps, 1974, card No 62 . . . . **12.00**
Oliver, Eugene George; Kahn's Weiners, 1965 . . . . **7.00**
Orsino, John Joseph; Topps, 1962, card No 377 . . . . **16.00**
Osteen, Claude Wilson; Jello, 1963, card No 100 . . . . **3.00**
Post Cereal, 1963, card No 100 . . . . **4.00**
Topps, 1974, card No 38 . . . . **10.00**
Otis, Amos Joseph; Kellogg's Cereal, 1971, card No 38 . . . . **3.00**
Topps, 1974, card No 1 . . . . **12.00**
Owens, James Philip; Topps Doubleheaders, 1955, card No 122 **11.00**
Pagan, Jose Antpmop; Jello, 1962, card No 132 . . . . **3.50**
Jello, 1963, card No 103 . . . . **3.00**
Pagliaroni, James Vincent; Jello, 1962, card No 63 . . . . **12.00**
Kahn's Weiners, 1967 . . . . **6.00**
Sugardale, 1963 . . . . **25.00**
Paige, Leroy Satchel, Leaf Gum Co, 1948, card No 8 . . . . **400.00**
Topps, 1953, card No 220 . . . . **20.00**
Palmer, James Alvin; Johnny Pro, 1973 . . . . **2.00**
Kellogg's Cereal, 1971, card No 60 . . . . **6.00**
Milk Duds, 1971 . . . . **3.00**
Topps, 1971, card No 570 . . . . **2.00**
Topps, 1974, card No 45 . . . . **14.00**
Pappas, Milton Steven; Jello, 1962, card No 34 . . . . **3.50**
Kahn's Weiners, 1966 . . . . **8.00**
Parker, David Gene; Topps Mini Set, 1975, card No 29 . . . . **2.00**
Topps, 1974, card No 252 . . . . **3.00**
Parker, Maurice Wesley; Topps Greatest Moments, 1971 . . . . **3.00**
Topps, 1971, Tattoo, card No 8 . . . . **1.50**
Pattin, Martin William; McDonald's, 1970, card No 6 . . . . **1.25**
Pavletich, Donald Stephen; Kahn's Weiners, 1967 . . . . **6.00**
Topps, 1962, card No 594 . . . . **2.50**
Pearson, Albert Gregory; Jello, 1962, card No 78 . . . . **3.50**
Topps Stand Ups, 1964 . . . . **14.00**
Pena, Orlando Gregory; Johnny Pro, 1973 . . . . **5.00**
Pepitone, Joseph Anthony; Topps Greatest Moments, 1971 . . . . . . **3.00**
Topps, 1962, card No 596 . . . . **2.50**
Perez, Atanasio Rigal; Kahn's Weiners, 1967 . . . . **6.00**
Kahn's Weiners, 1968 . . . . **7.00**
Kahn's Weiners, 1969 . . . . **5.00**
Topps, 1968, card No 581 . . . . **180.00**
Topps, 1974, card No 54 . . . . **12.00**
Perranoski, Ronald Peter; Bell Brand, 1962, card No 16 . . . . . . **6.00**
Perry, Gaylord Jackson; Kellogg's Cereal, 1971, card No 6 . . . . . . **6.00**
Topps, 1963, card No 169 . . . . **2.00**
Topps, 1966, card No 598 . . . . **30.00**
Topps, 1969, card No 199 . . . . **2.80**
Topps, 1970, card No 560 . . . . **2.50**
Perry, James Evan; Jello, 1962, card No 43 . . . . **3.50**
Kahn's Weiners, 1959 . . . . **17.00**
Sugardale, 1962, card No 5 . . . . **30.00**
Sugardale, 1963, card No 5 . . . . **60.00**
Petrocelli, Americo; Topps Greatest Moments, 1971 . . . . **3.00**
Topps, 1971, Tattoo, card No 11 . . . . **1.50**
Phillips, John Melvin; Kahn's Weiners, 1962 . . . . **20.00**
Sugardale, 1962, card No 14 . . . . **25.00**
Piersall, James Anthony; Bowman Gum Co, 1951, card No 306 . **8.00**
Bowman, Gum Co, 1954, card No 66 . . . . **30.00**
Piniella, Louis Victor; Topps Greatest Moments, 1971 . . . . **3.00**
Pinson, Vada Edward; Kahn's Weiners, 1959 . . . . **30.00**
Kahn's Weiners, 1961 . . . . **10.00**
Kahn's Weiners, 1965 . . . . **8.00**
Topps Stand Ups, 1964 . . . . **3.50**
Poquette, Thomas Arthur; Topps Mini Set, 1975, card No 622 . . **4.00**

Powell, John Wesley; Bazooka, 1965, card No 11 . . . . **3.00**
Topps, 1968, 3-D **180.00**
Topps, 1970, card No 38 . . . . **20.00**
Reese, Harold Henry; Bowman Gum Co, 1949, card No 36 . . . . **7.00**
Bowman Gum Co, 1950, card No 21 . . . . **8.00**
Coca-Cola, 1952 . . . . **130.00**
Topps, 1952, card No 333 . . . . **140.00**
Reichardt, Frederic Carl; Topps Supers, 1969, card No 8 . . . . . . **7.00**
Rice, James Edward; Topps Mini Set, 1975, card No 616 . . . . . . **4.00**
Topps, 1975, card No 616 . . . . **2.00**
Richardson, Robert Clinton; Jello, 1962, card No 2 . . . . **12.00**
Kahn's Weiners, 1963 . . . . **8.00**
Robinson, Brooks Calbert; Nabisco Team Flakes, 1969 . . . . **10.00**
Topps, 1957, card No 328 . . . . **50.00**
Topps, 1967, card No 600 . . . . **60.00**
Topps Supers, 1969, card No 3 . . . . **32.00**
Robinson, Frank; Kahn's Weiners, 1956 . . . . **60.00**
Topps Supers, 1969 . . . . **30.00**
Robinson, William Henry; Topps, 1968, 3-D **150.00**
Rojas, Octavio Rivas; Topps Supers, 1969, card No 55 . . . . **7.00**
Rose, Peter Edward; Bazooka, 1966, card No 38 . . . . **7.00**
Topps Supers, 1961, card No 41 . . . . **100.00**
Topps, 1974, card No 16 . . . . **25.00**
Ruth, George Herman 'Babe'; Goudey Gum Co, 1933, card No 53 **300.00**
Goudey Gum Co, 1935, card No 5A **150.00**
Sport Kings, 1933, card No 2 . . . . **100.00**
Topps Connie Mack All Stars, 1951 . . . . **700.00**
U S Caramels Famous Athletes, 1932, card No 32 . . . . **500.00**
Ryan, Lynn Nolan; Topps, 1970, card No 712 . . . . **8.00**
Topps, 1972, card No 595 . . . . **3.00**
Topps, 1974, card No 41 . . . . **14.00**
Sanguillen, Manuel DeJesus; Topps, 1974, card No 22 . . . . **10.00**
Santo, Ronald Edward; Kahn's Weiners, 1968 . . . . **5.00**
Topps Stand Ups, 1964 . . . . **16.00**
Topps Supers, 1969, card No 38 . . . . **8.00**
Topps Supers, 1971 . . . . **3.00**
Schmidt, Michael Jack; Johnny Pro, 1974 . . . . **2.00**
Kellogg's Cereal, 1975, card No 56 . . . . **1.00**
Schwall, Donald Bernard; Sugardale, 1963 . . . . **25.00**
Seaver, George Thomas; Kellogg's Cereal, 1971, card No 2 . . . . . **8.00**
Nabisco Team Flakes, 1969 . . . . **10.00**
Topps Supers, 1969, card No 52 . . . . **32.00**
Topps, 1967, card No 581 . . . . **40.00**
Topps, 1972, card No 445 . . . . **3.00**
Topps, 1974, card No 9 . . . . **20.00**
Transogram, 1970, card No 21 . . . . **2.00**
Selma, Richard Jay; Topps Supers, 1969, card No 62 . . . . **7.00**
Siebert, Wilfred Charles; Kahn's Weiners, 1966 . . . . **6.00**
Simmons, Ted Tyle; Topps, 1974, card No 10 . . . . **14.00**
Skowron, William Joseph; Jello, 1962, card No 1 . . . . **12.00**
Slaughter, Enos Bradsher; Hunter's, 1954 . . . . **130.00**
Smith, Carl Reginald; Kellogg's Cereal, 1971, card No 52 . . . . . . **3.00**
Snider, Edwin Donald; Brigg's Franks **300.00**
Stahl Meyer, 1955 . . . . **200.00**
Spahn, Warren Edward; Drake's Cookies, 1950, card No 14 . . . **80.00**
Tip Top, 1947 . . . . **60.00**
Speier, Chris Edward; Topps, 1974, card No 29 . . . . **10.00**
Stargell, Wilver Dornel; Kahn's Weiners, 1965 . . . . **8.00**
Kahn's Weiners, 1966 . . . . **20.00**
Kahn's Weiners, 1967 . . . . **16.00**
Kellogg's Cereal, 1971, card No 68 . . . . **6.00**
Topps, 1974, card No 31 . . . . **12.00**
Staub, Daniel Joseph; Nabisco Team Flakes, 1969 . . . . **6.00**
Pepsi, 1963 . . . . **10.00**

Topps, 1963, card No 544 .... **3.00**
Topps, 1968, 3-D **180.00**
Sutton, Donald Howard; Kellog's Cereal, 1971, card No 31 ..... **4.00**
Topps, 1974, card No 12 .... **12.00**
Swoboda, Ronald Alan; Topps, 1968, 3-D **150.00**
Tiant, Louis Clemente; Kahn's Weiners, 1965 .... **8.00**
Kahn's Weiners, 1969 .... **5.00**
Topps Supers, 1969, card No 13 .... **8.00**
Topps, 1974, card No 27 .... **12.00**
Torre, Joseph Paul; Kahn's Weiners, 1965 .... **9.00**
Kahn's Weiners, 1967 .... **6.00**
Topps Supers, 1969, card No 36 .... **7.00**
Uecker, Robert George; Topps, 1962, card No 594 .... **2.50**
Valentine, Robert John; Topps, 1974, card No 11 .... **10.00**
Virdon, William Charles; Hunter's, 1955 .... **110.00**
Kahn's Weiners, 1962 .... **10.00**
Walker, Harry William; Leaf Gum Co, 1948, card No 137 ..... **70.00**
Walker, Jerry Allen; Sugardale, 1963, card No 5 .... **25.00**
White, Roy Hilton; Topps Supers, 1969, card No 26 .... **7.00**
Wilhelm, James Hoyt; Topps, 1952, card No 392 .... **70.00**
Topps, 1961, card No 545 .... **6.00**
Williams, Theodore Samuel; Play Ball, 1941, card No 14 ..... **150.00**
Wills, Maurice Morning; Bell Brand, 1960, card No 20 .... **14.00**
Topps Supers, 1969, card No 49 .... **9.00**
Topps, 1967, card No 570 .... **35.00**
Winfield, David Mark; Topps, 1974, card No 456 .... **3.00**
Wood, Wilber Forrester; Topps, 1974, card No 13 .... **10.00**
Yastrzemski, Carl Michael; Post Cereal, 1963, card No 80 ..... **60.00**
Topps Stand Ups, 1964 .... **30.00**
Topps, 1974, card No 43 .... **25.00**
Zachry, Patrick Paul; Topps, 1976, card No 599 .... **1.50**
Zimmer, Donald William; Morrell Meats, 1959 .... **55.00**

Football Cards
Blanda, George; 1956, Topps **170.00**
Casares, Rick; 1957, Topps **60.00**
George, Bill; 1963, Topps **12.00**
Gifford, Frank; 1957, Topps **35.00**
Groza, Lou; 1957, Topps **35.00**
Hirsch, Elroy; 1956, Topps **170.00**
Johnson, John Henry; 1964, Topps **30.00**
Lane, Bobby; 1957, Topps **40.00**
Lilly, Bob; 1964, Topps **23.00**
Mackey, John; 1969, Topps **25.00**
Marchetti, Gino; 1963, Topps **30.00**
Meridith, Don; 1969, Topps **18.00**
Nitschke, Ray; 1969, Topps **18.00**
Olsen, Merlin; 1964 .... **22.00**
Perkins, Don; 1964, Topps **23.00**
Sayers, Gale; 1971, Topps **120.00**
Sumerall, Pat; 1957, Topps **30.00**
Taylor, Jim; 1963, Topps **30.00**
Tittle, YA; 1957, Topps **35.00**
Unitas, Johnny; 1964, Topps **60.00**
Vessels, Billy; 1957, Topps........................... **35.00**

Staffordshire

Scores of potteries sprang up in England's Staffordshire district in the early 18th century; several remain to the present time. Some of the larger companies as well as specific types of ware are listed in other sections of this book.

Figurines and groups were made in great numbers; dogs were favorite subjects. Often they were made in pairs, each a mirror image of the other.

They varied in heights of from 3″ or 4″ to the largest, measuring 16″ to 18″.

The Historical ware listed here was made throughout the district; some collectors refer to it as Staffordshire Blue ware. It was produced as early as 1820, and because much was exported to America, it was very often decorated with transfers depicting scenic veiws of well-known American landmarks. Early examples were printed in a deep cobalt. By 1830, a softer blue was favored, and within another decade, black, pink, red and green prints were used. Although sometimes careless about adding their trademark, many companies used their own border designs that were as individual as their names.

Bowl vase, gold handles, grapes in relief, 7x10″ **250.00**
Butter, w/insert, brown & wht, Garfield Pattern, LS&S Co **24.00**
Creamer, flowers in relief, verse, 6½″ **125.00**
Cup & saucer, child's, 3 nursery rhymes w/scenes, 1860s **53.00**
Dk blue, dogs, Clews **145.00**
Dk blue, girl at well, slight glaze, Clews **55.00**
Woman & child, transfer & enamel, luster resist **25.00**
Dish, pierced, on tray, Marmora, 8½x11½″................. **90.00**
With cover, figural hen on nest, gilt, 7x11″ **275.00**
Ewer, Greenaway type, boy w/duck, Stellmacher, 9½″ **110.00**
Figurine, 2 lovers sitting on grape bower, 15x9½″ **245.00**
Accordian player w/spaniel at his side, 10¾″ **110.00**
Amish couple standing on grassy mound, 8″................ **55.00**
Boy, spaniel & guitar, 13″ **140.00**
Chimney piece, boy w/ewe, 8½x6″........................ **95.00**
Chimney piece, girl on stump w/bird, 8″ **95.00**
Chimney piece, hunters w/bows, deer, clock on bottom 9½x7″ **125.00**
Chimney piece, Little Red Riding Hood, polychrome, 10″.... **90.00**
Cottage, 8½″.. **150.00**
Death of Nelson, 7½x5″................................. **130.00**
Dogs, 10¾″, pr.. **200.00**

Dog w/hare, 10x9½″.................................... **150.00**
Duck on nest.. **170.00**
Gentlemen & lady seated holding basket of flowers, 8″ **75.00**
Going to market & returning home, 9¼x8″, pr **260.00**
Group, Prince & Princess, late 1800s, 7½″ **60.00**
John Lock bust, pink toga, brown hair, gr plinth, 7″....... **180.00**
Lion, 1800s, pr...................................... **450.00**
Lion, glass eyes, tan & brown, old.................... **100.00**
Lions, reclining, glass eyes, 10x12″, pr **265.00**
Little girl spanking doll, 6″ **45.00**
Man, woman & baby, mottled brown base, pink, gr, rust & wht **95.00**
Milkmaid w/can **300.00**

Mrs Bardell **70.00**
Newspaper boy, 1800s, 13" **220.00**
Poodles, 4½", pr.. **95.00**
Queen Victoria & Prince of Wales, 1887 Jubilee, 18", pr ... **550.00**
Ram w/bacchus, 4" **150.00**
Scotchman & lady, tree behind couple, 9½" **110.00**
Seated bacchus, 7"....................................... **140.00**
Shoeshine boy, 13"....................................... **225.00**
Spaniel, tawny, glass eyes, 1870........................ **135.00**
Spaniels, rust & wht, 4", pr **165.00**
Swain in cobalt jacket, 8¼"............................... **48.00**
The Actor, handsome man in theatrical costume, 12¾" **195.00**
Uncle Tom w/Little Eva standing on his knee, 10" **250.00**
Widow, sgnd Walton, 11½"................................ **275.00**
Incense burner, thatched cottage figural, 3½".............. **85.00**
Mug, child's, blue transfer, Queen Victoria, 1838, 2¼"...... **275.00**
Child's, pink transfer, Harbor scene, 2½"................ **50.00**
Child's This Is the House That Jack Built, transfer on creamware **65.00**
Man, 1840, 5½" **20.00**
Plaque, sepia WWI scene, pierced, Grim Wades Winton, 7¼"dia **28.00**
Plate, blk & cream transfer, Botanical plants, butterfly in center, 7½" **25.00**
Blk transfer, Athens, 9"................................. **22.00**
Brown transfer, Peruvian Horsehunt, Shaw, 10"........... **38.00**
Child's, w/verse, 7"..................................... **40.00**
Corinthia Pattern, castle scene, Pink, E Challinor, 8½" **37.00**
Cow Jumped Over the Moon **55.00**
Lavender transfer, Pomerania, 10¼"..................... **26.00**
Red transfer, Palestine, Adams, 9½"..................... **40.00**
Teetotaler's, red transfer, Cold Water Army, Band of Hope, 6" **85.00**
Platter, blue & wht, oriental scenery, J Hall & Sons, 14½x11½" **11.00**
Pink, cock fighting scene, mkd, 15x11½" **125.00**
Turkey, florals, 18x15x1½" **75.00**

Urinal, nurse w/bottles, spatter decor, 12".................. **275.00**
Vase, blue & wht, portrait, landscape scene on reverse, 1870, 12" **125.00**
Figural couple on bench, tree w/bird above, 11x6" **115.00**
Mother goose, hp, 4½" **25.00**
Mottled brown ground w/butterflies, mkd Royal Staffordshire, 8" **40.00**
Vegetable, ftd w/cover, brown & wht, Garfield pattern, LS&S Co **38.00**
Watch holder, boy on 1 side, girl on other side, 11½x9¼" wide **225.00**
Whippet, orange dog reclines on gr & brown base, 1¼x3x4½" . **75.00**

Historical
Coffee pot, bird, dk blue, high dome, 11".................. **495.00**

Lafayette at Franklin's Tomb, domed, 11" **800.00**
Oriental Views, dk blue, ribbed, florals, scrolls **350.00**
Queen Anne, blue, allover floral, 11" **165.00**
Wadsworth Tower, dk blue, high dome, Enoch Wood, 11½" **1,500.00**
Creamer, horse, sleigh, dk blue, 5½"...................... **95.00**
Cup & saucer, basket of flowers, dk blue, handleless, mkd.... **110.00**
English pub view, medium dk blue, handleless **55.00**
Flute player, dk blue, Mayer............................ **85.00**
Franklin's Tomb, dk blue, scalloped rims, E&G Phillips **325.00**
Lafayette at Franklin's Tomb, blue, Woods.............. **220.00**
Sower, pink, Adams..................................... **33.00**
Virginia church, medium blue, miniature................. **150.00**
Wadsworth Tower, dk blue, shell border, Wood.......... **280.00**
Wadsworth Tower, Wood, extra lg size **325.00**
Wilkes Barre & Near Troy, lt blue, Ridgway **75.00**
Cup, Seasons, Winter, lt blue, Adams.................... **10.00**
Cup plate, Battery, dk blue, shell border, Wood, −101, 3½".. **290.00**
Battery, dk blue, trefoil border, Wood, 3" **200.00**
Blue Willow, med dk blue, Stevenson, 4¼".............. **60.00**
Casmus, dk blue, Wood, 3¾" **180.00**
Cottage in the Woods, dk blue, wood, 3¾"............. **150.00**
English View, dk blue, 3¾".............................. **50.00**
Fairmount, Brown Adams, 4"............................ **65.00**
Fort Ticonderoga, purple, Wood, 5".................... **200.00**
Hudson River View, Fairmount, pink, Clews **65.00**
Millenium, pink, 4¼".................................... **80.00**
Ship anchored, dk blue, Wood **295.00**
Valley of Shennandoah, Jefferson's Rock, blk, Wood, 4".... **100.00**
View of Newburgh, purple, Jackson, 4".................. **135.00**
Custard cup, Acorn & Oakleaf, dk blue **150.00**
Arms of the States, dk blue, Mayer **425.00**
Dessert plate, Cave Castle, blue, floral border, Enoch Wood, 8" **40.00**
Dish, Cadmus at Fort Lafayette, blue, covered, Clews, 12" long **790.00**
Girl milking cow, blue, Adams, 1830, 10" dia" **125.00**
Gravy ladle, bridge scene, blue, 8" long **80.00**
Ladle, eagle's head handle, blue **170.00**
Mug, child's, pink transfer, Harbor scene, 2½"............. **50.00**
Pitcher, American Naval Heroes, dk blue, 6".............. **650.00**
City Hall & Insane Asylum, N.Y., dk blue, Clews, 8"....... **850.00**
Erie Canal views, dk blue, small hairline, small **585.00**
Hudson, Near Fort Miller, pink, Clews, 7"............... **225.00**
Lafayette at Franklin's Tomb, dk blue, 6" **395.00**
Landing of the Pilgrims, dk blue, 3 qt **175.00**
Water Girl, dk blue, Clews, 6½"......................... **140.00**
Wilkes Barre, Vale of Wyoming, lt blue, Ridgway.......... **185.00**
Plate, Albany, City series, dk blue, 9¾"................... **275.00**
Almshouse New York, dk blue, Stevenson, 10" **625.00**
Arms of New York, deep blue, Mayer, 1840, 8½"........ **495.00**
Arms of New York, deep blue, Mayer, 10"............. **675.00**
Arms of Rhode Island, medium blue, Mayer, 8½"........ **425.00**
Arms of South Carolina, dk blue, Mayer, 5¾"........... **325.00**
Arms of the States, Fort Hamilton, N.Y., purple, 9½"...... **145.00**
Bakers Falls, blk, Clews, 9"............................. **65.00**
Baltimore & Ohio Railroad, dk blue, Wood & Sons, 10" ... **475.00**
Batalha, Portugal, dk blue, 9½"......................... **60.00**
Battery & C, pink, 7¾" **65.00**
Battery & C, purple, Jackson, 6¾"...................... **58.00**
Beauties of America, medium blue **25.00**
Beehive & Urn, dk blue, Stevenson, 10".................. **70.00**
Blue transfer, California, 1849, 9½"..................... **24.00**
Boston State House, medium blue, Enoch Wood, 6½"..... **100.00**
Capitol at Washington, dk blue, shell border, Wood, 7¾" .. **375.00**
Capitol at Washington, dk blue, vine leaf border, Stevenson, 10" **350.00**
Castle Forbes, blue, Woods, 6½"......................... **85.00**

Castle of Lavenza, dk blue, Wood, 10¼" **95.00**
Christmas Eve, dk blue, Clews, 6½" **140.00**
Church, medium blue, octagon, Ridgway, 9¾" **175.00**
City Hall, New York, blue, Ridgway, 10" **180.00**
City Hall, New York, brown, Jackson, 10¼" **70.00**
City Hall, New York, dk blue, Ridgway, 9½" **180.00**
City Hall, New York, medium blue, Ridgway, 9½" **35.00**
Commodore McDonough's Victory, deep blue, Wood, 6½" . . **165.00**
Commodore McDonough's Victory, deep blue, Wood, 7½" . . **285.00**
Constitution, dk blue, shell border, Enoch Wood & Sons, 10¼" **260.00**
Constitutional Grievances, Lovejoy, lt blue, 6" **125.00**
Coronation, blue, Clews, 10" **165.00**
Dam & Waterworks, Philadelphia, sidewheeler, dk blue, 10" **325.00**
Darmouth, dk blue, Wood, 9" **220.00**
Don Quixote & Sancho Pansa, dk blue, 6¾" **135.00**
Don Quixote & Sancho Pansa, dk blue, 9" **170.00**
Don Quixote, gr, Brameld of the Rockingham Pottery, 10" . . . **55.00**
Dr Syntax & the Bees, dk blue, Clews, 10" **165.00**
Dr Syntax Reading His Tour, dk blue, 9" **200.00**
Dr Syntax Returned From Tour, dk blue, 9" **200.00**
Dr Syntax Taking Possession of His Living, dk blue, 10" . . . **195.00**
Dr Syntax w/Dairy Maid, dk blue, 6" **160.00**
English Countryside, medium blue, 7" **15.00**
Erie Canal, dk blue, 10¼" **425.00**
Fairmount near Philadelphia, dk blue, Stubbs, 10¼" **175.00**
Fall of Montmorenci near Quebec, dk blue, Wood, shell border, 9" **255.00**
Flowers, fruit, dk blue, Stubbs & Kent, 8¾" **110.00**
Fort Conanicut, Rhode Island, purple, Jackson, 6¾" **135.00**
Franklin Flying Kite, miniature, 2½" **65.00**
    3½" **75.00**
From Wood's Italian scenery series, dk blue, 9" **65.00**
Fruit, medium blue, 10" **20.00**
Fruit & Birds, dk blue, 10" **85.00**
Fulham Church, medium dk blue, Halls, 8½" **70.00**
Gilpin's mill on the brandywine creek, dk blue, wood, 9½" . **325.00**
Hartford, Connecticut, blk, Jackson, 10" **125.00**
Hartford, Connecticut, pink, Jackson, 10" **125.00**
Hartord, Jackson, carmine, 10¼" **75.00**
Harvard College, Celtic series, lt blue, Enoch Woods, 10¼" . **125.00**
Highlands, Hudson River, dk blue, wood, 6½" **335.00**
Hindu Pagoda, dk blue, scalloped & beaded rim, Rogers, 10" **65.00**
Historical, cows, medium blue, 10" **20.00**
Historical, water works, Pennsylvania, blue, 10" **425.00**
Hoboken, dk blue, eagle border, Stubbs **250.00**
Hollywell Cottage, Cavan, Riley, medium dk blue, 10" **35.00**
Hospital Near Poissy, dk blue, Halls, 6½" **55.00**
Hospital, Boston, dk blue, Stevenson, 8¼" **250.00**
Hudson River & Junction of the Sacandaga, blk, Clews, 6¾" . **75.00**
Hudson River, Fort Edward, blk, Clews, 5¼" **55.00**
    Near Fishkill, blk, 10" **90.00**
    Near Fishkill, dk blue, 7¾" **225.00**
    Near Fishkill, sepia, Clews, 10½" **85.00**
    West Point, blk, Clews, 8" **65.00**
Hunter w/2 dogs, dk blue, Clews, 10½" **85.00**
Hunting dogs, ducks, medium dk blue, Wood, 10" **55.00**
LaGrange, Residence of Lafayette, dk blue, 10" **190.00**
Lake George, lt blue, Ridgway, 7¾" **60.00**
Landing of Gen LaFayette, Clews, 10" **175.00**
    Blue, floral border, Clews, 10" **180.00**
    Dk blue, 7¾" **190.00**
    Dk blue, 9" **195.00**
    Dk blue, Clews, 10" **285.00**
    Medium blue, 10" **200.00**
Landing of Fathers at Plymouth, 8½" **125.00**

Medium blue, Wood, 10" **150.00**
Landing of the Pilgrims, dk blue, Wood, 10" **145.00**
Llanarth Hall, Monmouthshire, dk blue, 9¾" **85.00**
MacDonnough's Victory, dk blue, Clews, 6½" **175.00**
    Dk blue, Wood, 7½" **245.00**
    Dk blue, shell border, Wood, 10¼" **325.00**
Marine Hospital, blue, shell border, Woods, 9" **240.00**
Meredith, N.H., lt blue, Ridgway, 9½" **45.00**
Millenium, purple, 7¾" **45.00**
    Red, 9" **55.00**
Mitchell & Freeman Warehouse, dk blue, Adams, 10" **210.00**
Monuments & Urns, blk, Thayer & Dean, 8¾" **65.00**
Moral Maxims, purple, Clews, 10¾" **45.00**
Narrows, Fort Hamilton, lt blue, Ridgway, 7" **45.00**
Near Sandy Hill, purple, Clews, 7¾" **55.00**
Niagara, Sheep Shearing View, dk blue, Stevenson, 10¼" . . **250.00**
Oriental scene, dk blue, 9" **40.00**
Oriental scene, medium blue, 9" **20.00**
Pains Hill, surrey, dk blue, Hall, 9¾" **75.00**
Park Theatre, dk blue, RS & W, 10" **225.00**
Pass in the Catskill Mountains, dk blue, Wood, 7½" **325.00**
Pastoral Scene, dk blue, 8½" **65.00**
Peace & Plenty, dk blue, clews, 9" **235.00**
Peach & Cherry Pattern, deep blue, Stubbs, 1820s, 6½" . . . **65.00**
Pine Orchard House, Catskills, dk blue, Wood, 10" **275.00**
Pittsfield Elm, dk blue, Clews, 6¾" **175.00**
President's House, Washington, purple, Jackson, 10" **85.00**
Quebec, dk blue, City series **245.00**
Residence of S Russel, Middletown, Conn., lt blue, Wood, 6¾" **125.00**
Sancho & the Priest & Barber, dk blue, Clews, 7½" **75.00**
Scudder's Museum, blue, Stevenson, repaired, 7½" **100.00**
Seasons, March, pink, Adams, 9½" **45.00**
Shannondale Springs, Virginia, pink, Adams, 8" **75.00**
Sheep on Lawn, States, 9" **195.00**
Shell Design, dk blue, Stubbs, 8½" **60.00**
Sheltered Peasants, dk blue, 10" **65.00**
Ship, medium blue, floral border, 9" **245.00**
Southampton, Hampshire, dk blue, irreg shell border, Wood, 7½" **250.00**
Southampton, Hampshire, dk blue, Dk blue, Wood, 7½" . . . **150.00**
States, America & Independence, dk blue, 7½" **125.00**
States, America & Independence, dk blue, Clews, 10½" **225.00**
States, dk blue, 6¾" **175.00**
States, dk blue, Clews, 8" **220.00**
States, dk blue, Clews, 9" **225.00**
The Garden Trio, dk blue, 5½" **190.00**
The Prairie Hunter, lavender, 10½" **75.00**
The Sea, Couple Dancing, pink, Adams, 8½" **35.00**
The White House, Washington, shell border, Wood, 5¾" . . . **475.00**
Transylvania University, Lexington, Ky., dk blue, Wood, 9¼" **395.00**
Trenton Falls, 3 people on rock, dk blue, Wood, 7¾" **300.00**
Union line, dk blue, irregular shell border, Wood, 10" **300.00**
Utica Tribute, Erie Canal inscription, dk blue, 7½" **375.00**
View Bakers Falls, brown transfer, Clews, 9" **30.00**
View from Ruggles House, Hudson River, lt blue, 10" **80.00**
View Near Conway, New Hampshire, deep pink, Adams, 9" . **75.00**
View of Trenton Falls, dk blue, Wood, shell border, 7½" . . . **225.00**
View on the Road to Lake George, dk blue, Stevenson, 9" . . **875.00**
Villa in Regents Park London, medium dk blue, Adams, 9" . **35.00**
Village of Little Falls, brown, Meigh, 8¼" **37.00**
Washington, pink, Enoch Wood & Sons, 7" **55.00**
Welcome Lafayette..., dk blue, embossed blue border, Clews, 10" **550.00**
William Penn's Treaty, sepia, mellowing, 9½" **32.00**
Winter View of Pittsfield, dk blue, Clews, 10" **185.00**
Woodlands Near Philadelphia, dk blue, Stubbs, 6¾" **165.00**

Platter, Advertisement for a Wife, dk blue, 15¾" **575.00**
American Marine, brown, Ashworth, 10¾" **55.00**
Boston from Dorchester Heights, brown, Meigh, 16½" **265.00**
British Views, dk blue, 18" **250.00**
Broke Hall, Suffolk, dk blue, 10¾" **265.00**
Capitol at Washington, blk, Ridgway, 19" **325.00**
Castle Garden Battery, New York, dk blue, Enoch Wood, 18½" **1,250.00**
Church St Charles-Polytechnic School, Vienna, dk blue, Hall, 19" **475.00**
Columbus, brown, Adams, 10" **95.00**
Custom House River Liffey, well & tree, dk blue, Dublin, 15x19" **700.00**
Erith on Thames, dk blue, shell border, Wood, 13" **450.00**
Harpers Ferry, West Virginia, pink, Adams, 17½" **195.00**
Highbury Cottage, London, dk blue, Adams, 9x11½" **225.00**
Hudson River, blk, Clews, 13¼" **175.00**
Landing of General Lafayette, dk blue, Clews, 17" **650.00**
Landing of General Lafayette, medium dk blue, Clews, 19".. **725.00**
Little Falls at Luzerne, blk, Clews, 17½" **295.00**
Little Falls at Luzerne, lt blue, Clews, 17¾" **275.00**
Mendenhall Ferry, dk blue, Stubbs, 16½" **750.00**
Newburgh, Hudson River, brown transfer, Clews, 15½".... **175.00**
Palace of St Cloud, France, dk blue, Hall, 17" **275.00**
Part of Regents Street, dk blue, Adams, 13½" **250.00**
Pink & wht, Parisian Chateau, Hall, 15½" **70.00**
Sheltered Peasants, dk blue, 15" **225.00**
Southwest View of La Grange, dk blue, Wood, 18½" **675.00**
St George's Chapel, dk blue, Woods, 16½" **295.00**
Teresa Pansa & the Messenger, blue, 14½" **435.00**

University Academy, West Point, Wood, 12x9½" **125.00**
View of Newburgh, purple, Jackson, 17½" **275.00**
Washington Vase, lt blue, 11x8" **32.00**
Wilkes Barre, Vale of Wyoming, lt blue, Ridgway, 8x11" ... **175.00**
Relish dish, Don Quixote, gr, Brameld of Rockingham Pottery, 11½" **95.00**
Woman in Woods w/Man Standing Nearby, dk blue, oval ... **140.00**
Sauce boat, from Foliage & Scroll Border series, dk blue..... **110.00**
Oriental, dk blue, 8" long............................. **90.00**
Sauce tureen, Gypsy, lt blue **195.00**
Saucer, Sower **13.00**
Soup plate, Baltimore & Ohio, dk blue, Wood, 10" **575.00**
Beauties of America, Octagon Church, medium blue, 10".. **155.00**
Fruit & Flowers, dk blue, Stubbs, 9¾" **75.00**
Hannibal, Battle on Elephants, lt blue, Adams, 10"......... **55.00**
Harper's Ferry, lt blue, Ridgway, 9" **80.00**
Octagon Church, Boston, dk blue, Ridgway, 10" **265.00**
Pastoral Scene w/Cows, dk blue, set of 6, 10¼" **500.00**
Peace & Plenty, dk blue, Clews, 10"..................... **175.00**

States, America & Independence, medium dk blue, Clews, 8" **175.00**
Table Rock, Niagara, dk blue, Enoch Wood, 10" **350.00**
Soup, Columbus, lavender, Adams, 10¼"................... **50.00**
Franklin Flying Kite, 3½" **75.00**
Lafayette at the Tomb of Washington, dk blue, Enoch Wood, 10" **450.00**
Millenium, lt blue, 10¼"............................... **65.00**
Peace & Plenty, dk blue, 10" **275.00**
States, Fishermen, dk blue, Clews, 10"................... **265.00**
Sugar, Floral, blue, covered **175.00**
Wadsworth Tower, Conn., dk blue, Wood **395.00**
Washington Scroll in Hand, deep blue, covered, Wood..... **450.00**
Water Girl, dk blue, open, Clews...................... **165.00**
Water Girl, dk blue, covered, Clews, flake **170.00**
Teapot, City Hall, New York, blue, Stubbs, flake **325.00**
Men Fishing Near Castle, dk blue **245.00**
Scenic, lt blue, 1840s **90.00**
Washington, Scroll in Hand, blue, ftd, 1825, 7" **525.00**
Tile, President Coolidge Home, Plymouth, Vt., wht porcelain, Adams **38.00**
Toddy plate, Landing of Lafayette, dk blue, 5½" **275.00**
Toothbrush holder, Agricultural Vase, gr, w/cover **90.00**
Tray, Franklin Flying Kite, 3x4" **90.00**
4x5½" **135.00**
Tureen, Battle of Bunker Hill, dk blue, Stevenson **4,500.00**
Beauties of America, dk blue, w/undertray, cover & ladle.. **2,500.00**
English View, dk blue, w/lid, Clews **235.00**
Franklin Flying Kite, handled, open, 2½x4½" **115.00**
Passaic Falls, N.J., dk blue, w/lid, ladle & undertray, Wood **1,550.00**
Vegetable dish, Ballston Springs, N.Y., brown, 8 sided, Meigh, 9" **125.00**
Dorney Court, dk blue, Stevenson, 9¼" **225.00**
Franklin Flying Kite, open, 3x4"........................ **135.00**
Gayhurst Buckinghamshire, dk blue, covered, ftd, Hall, 12". **325.00**
Hudson River, brown, 8¾" **150.00**
Hudson River Near Fort Miller, red, 10¾".............. **165.00**
Landing at Lafayette, sq, covered, 12¼"................ **750.00**
States, dk blue, Clews **1,600.00**
Washbowl & pitcher, Lafayette at Franklin's Tomb, blue, Woods **950.00**
Waste bowl, Landing of Lafayette, blue, floral border, 1825, 6½" **525.00**
Wadsworth Tower, dk blue, Wood, 6½"................. **275.00**

Stained Glass

There are many factors to consider in evaluating a window or panel of stained glass art. Besides the obvious factor of condition, intricacy, jeweling, beveling, and the amount of selenium (red, orange and yellow) present should all be taken into consideraton. Remember, repair work is itself an art, and can be very expensive.

Door, tulip design, wood beading effect, clear glass area, 60x23" **600.00**
Panel, armoral shield, fleur de lys, ribbons, 3 borders 36x27". **400.00**
Bug, flowers, red, amber, gr, 5x15"..................... **15.00**
Opal random ferns, drape swag borders on amber, 60x12".. **500.00**
Reaction gr & red mottled, red circles top & bottom, 36x27" **300.00**
Yellow borders, frosted center, w/oval & arcs, 48x16" **150.00**
Window, blown out, jeweled, tied, ribbon wreath medallion, 20x32" **650.00**
Cased, scenic, mountains, scrolls & geometrics 36x19" **650.00**
Clear leaded diamond cut shutters, 60x22"............... **150.00**
Golden yellow diamond pattern, 32x20" **150.00**
Jeweled banded vase, blown out red roses, 36x30" **700.00**
Opal blue, cranberry, turquoise, gothic design, 27½x23½".. **275.00**
Opal interlocking swirls w/red & gr border bands, 34x28".. **250.00**
Pennant w/anchor, 27x29".............................. **340.00**
Religious, 61x32", 1¾" thick **725.00**
Religious, set of 4, 27" wide, 6' long................. **1,500.00**
Vines & flowers, lt gr ground, purple & wht flowers **1,800.00**

Stanford

Stanford Pottery operated in Sebring, Ohio, from 1945 to 1961, when it was destroyed by fire. Decorative items and kitchenwares were produced; their Corn Line is the most popular today. Similar to Shawnee's, Stanford Corn has highly sculptured leaves and is very realistic.

Corn Line; pitcher, 7″ 25.00
  Shakers, 2¾″, pr 12.00
  Sugar & creamer, pr 12.50
  Teapot, covered, 7″ 37.00

Stangl

In 1913, the Fulper Pottery was acquired by J. Martin Stangl, who had previously been employed there as superintendant of the technical division. Under Stangl's direction, the production of dinnerware was initiated. In addition, the artwares already being made, figurines--most notably the Audubon birds modeled after the *Birds of America* series---became a large part of their output; these have become very popular with collectors in recent years. They are easily identified by the Stangl mark on the base. Stangl pottery was produced until Martin Stangl's death in 1972.

Birds

Allen Hummingbird, oval mk, #3634, 3½″ 60.00
Baltimore Oriole, sgnd 38.00
Bird of Paradise, #2040 .... 80.00
Bird of Paradise, #3408 .... 85.00
Bird of Paradise, 5½″ 60.00
Black Throated Warbler, #3814 .... 60.00
Blue Jay, w/leaf 350.00
Bluebird, #3276 .... 75.00
Bluebirds, pr, #32760 .... 135.00
Blueheaded Vireo, #3448 .... 50.00
Bob-o-link, 4″ 50.00
Brewer's Blackbird, #3591 .... 30.00
Brownheaded Nuthatch, sgnd 38.00
Cardinal, 6½″ 65.00
Cardinal, matt, #3444 .... 95.00
Carolina Wren, #33590 .... 55.00
Cerulean Warbler, #3456 .... 50.00
Chat, #3590 .... 55.00
Chestnut-backed Chickadee, #3811 .... 80.00
Chestnut-sided Warbler, #3812 .... 45.00
Chickadee, group, #3581 .... 110.00
Cockatoo, #3405 .... 50.00

Cockatoo, #3405D, pr 120.00

Cockatoo, #3584 .... 225.00
Duck, #3250B 45.00
Duck, flying, blue glaze, #3443 .... 250.00
Evening Grosbeak, 5″ 75.00
Gold Crowned Kinglet, 4″ 35.00
Gold Crowned Kinglet, group, 5½x5″ 95.00
Goldfinch, group of 4, #3635 .... 135.00
Gray Cardinal, #3596 .... 65.00
Hummingbird, #3585 .... 33.00
Hummingbird, #3634 .... 55.00
Hummingbird, double, #3599D 225.00
Indigo Bunting, #3589 .... 55.00
Kentucky Warbler, #3598 .... 45.00
Kingfisher, #3406 .... 55.00
Lovebird, #3400 .... 42.50
Lovebird, double 100.00
Nuthatch, #3593 .... 22.00
Oriole, #3402 .... 40.00
Oriole, double, #3402D 85.00
Painted Bunting, #3452 .... 65.00
Parakeets, gr, oval mk, #3582D, pr, 7″ 150.00
Parrot, w/worm, #3449 .... 150.00
Parula Warbler, #3583 .... 45.00
Pheasant, #3491 .... 175.00
Pheasant, old mk, pr 255.00
Prothonotary Warbler, #3447 .... 50.00
Red Faced Warbler, #3594, 3″ 30.00
Redstart, double, #3490D 145.00
Rivoli Hummingbird, #3627 .... 90.00
Shoeveler Duck, #3455 .... 725.00
Titmouse, #3592 .... 55.00
Wild Fowl, #4454, 9½x10″ 125.00
Wilson Warbler, #3597 .... 22.00
Wren, #3401 .... 45.00
Wren, #3401D, 6¾″ 55.00
Wren, double, #3401D 85.00
Yellow Warbler, #3447 .... 55.00

Aladdin lamp, gr, matt, 2½x5½″ 29.00
Artware, vase, blue, #1758, 12″ 12.00
  Vase, tang, #2017, 3″ 7.50
Ashtray, blue & gr, ruffled clam shell, 3½x5½x2½″ 5.00
  Figural, hp flowers 3.00
  White, #3914 .... 20.00

Basket, green, #3252 .... 45.00
Bella Rosa, server, center handle 15.00
Bittersweet, bowl, handles, small 3.00
  Salt & pepper 5.00
Blue Daisy, cup & saucer 4.00
  Dinner plate 4.50

Plate, 6″	1.00
Plate, 8″	3.50
Blueberry, butter w/cover, ¼ pound	10.00
Coffee warmer	14.00
Cup & saucer	6.00
Plate, 6″	2.00
Plate, 8″	3.50
Plate, 9″	4.00
Plate, 10″	5.00
Saucer	2.00
Tidbit server, 10″	15.00
Tray, 11¼″	7.00
Candleholder, wht Calla Lily on blue leaf, 3x4x4¼″ wide	16.00
Carafe, w/stopper, yellow & blue, hp, ribbed, wood handle, 7¾x5½″	15.00
Chickory, salt & pepper	5.00
Cigarette box, wht w/hp daisies, inked mk, 4x5″	8.00
Colonial Rose, plate, 6″	2.00
Creamer, yellow, #1388	4.00
Cup & saucer, after dinner, gr, #1388	8.00
Fruit bowl, gr, #1388, 6″	4.00
Plate, blue, 10¼″	4.50
Plate, blue, 12½″	7.00
Soup bowl w/ears, gr, 5″	6.00
Syrup, blue	6.50
Tea cup, blue	3.50
Vegetable dish, oval, blue, 9¼″	5.00
Country Garden, bowl, 5½″	3.50
Cereal bowl	4.00
Coffee pot	15.00
Coupe soup bowl	6.00
Creamer	4.00
Cup & saucer	4.00
Dinner plate	3.50
Fruit bowl	3.50
Plate, 6″	1.50
Saucer	1.00
Server, handled	6.00
Sugar & creamer, covered	3.50
Country Life, bowl, 5½″	6.00
Bowl, 8½″	6.00
Platter, oval	22.50
Sugar & creamer, covered	23.00
Vegetable plate, round, 9″	25.00
Dahlia, plate, pierced for hanging, 6″	3.50
Dish, blue, 1¼x4½x7½″	5.00
Yellow inside, rosy-tan outside, hp, 11½″	10.00
Festival, bowl, tab handle	3.00
Coffee warmer	10.00
Mug	3.50
Server, handled, 6″	3.50
Flower frog, reticulated gr over blue, 7-hole, 2½″ dia	9.00
Fruit, bean pot w/cover	25.00
Cup	6.00
Gravy tray, 9½″	3.00
Plate, 10″	5.00
Salt & pepper	10.00
Saucer	2.00
Sugar & creamer, covered	12.00
Sugar w/cover	7.50
Fruit & Flowers, cereal bowl	3.50
Plate, 6¼″	2.50
Golden Blossom, plate, 8″	5.00
Golden Grape, bowl, 10″	6.00
Cup & saucer	4.00

Dinner plate	3.50
Plate, 6″	1.00
Golden Harvest, cup	3.00
Dinner plate, 10″	12.00
Egg cup	5.00
Lug soup bowl	4.00
Kiddieware, Peter Rabbit plate	15.00
Kumquat, plate, 8″	4.00
Magnolia, coffee warmer	14.00
Plate, 8″	5.00
Orchard Song, creamer	4.00
Relish tray	6.00
Server, center handle, 10″	8.00
Pink Cosmos, cup & saucer	4.00
Dinner plate	3.50
Plate, 6″	1.00
Pink Thistle, dinner plate	3.50
Plate, 6″	1.00
Planter, figural female head, impressed Stangl USA/3418, 6½″	18.00
Prelude, sugar & creamer, covered	7.50
Rustic Garden, plate, 6″	2.00
Spun Gold, server, center handle	8.00
Star Flower, plate, 6″	2.50
Plate, 10″	5.00
Saucer	2.00
Sugar & creamer, covered	6.00
Terra Rose, blue leaf vase	6.50
Pitcher, wht w/tan, 5½″	12.00
Sunflower vase, gr & brown, 7¼″	12.50
Thistle, berry bowl	4.50
Creamer, 4″	9.50
Creamer, hp, 2½″	5.00
Cup & saucer	7.50
Dinner plate, 10″	8.50
Pie plate, 6″	3.00
Plate, 8″	5.00
Salad bowl, 12″	35.00
Salad plate, 8″	4.00
Soup bowl, flat	7.00
Sugar & creamer, covered	12.50
Tidbit server, brass center handle, 10″ dia	14.00
Vegetable dish, 11″	12.50
Tilt jug, hi-gloss yellow, ice lip, swirl relief	28.00
Town & Country, bean pot, gr	25.00
Bowl, round, gr, 8″	8.75
Butter dish, complete, gr	18.00
Cereal bowl	6.25
Chop plate, gr, 12½″	18.00
Mug, gr	6.00
Napkin rings, set of 4, honey	10.00
Pitcher, blue, 10½″	42.50
Plate, gr, 8″	6.00
Plate, gr, 10″	9.00
Platter, gr	18.00
Saucer, gr, 6″	3.00
Sugar & creamer, covered, gr	15.00
Vase, 4 overlapping leaves, wht, 11″	12.00
6 broad leaves in relief, Celedon, 4¼″	26.00
Flower panels, incised, gr & rose, 7x3¼″	28.00
Handles, reeded, scalloped, pale blue to yellow, ftd, 7″	13.00
Handles, turquoise, 7¼″	8.00
Leaf scroll, satin wht, 9x4½″	20.00
Rose, 6½″	22.00
Scalloped top, side handles, lt blue, oval, 3x3½x2½″	6.00

Shoulder handle, orange, brown, gold mottled, paper label, 3x4″ dia **12.00**
Shoulder handle, turquoise, 5½″ **7.00**
Wall pocket, turquoise **12.00**
Yellow nautilis shell, 8x5½″ **12.00**
White Dogwood, plate, pierced for hanging, 6″ **3.50**
Wig stand, blonde **165.00**
Brunette **135.00**
Wild Rose, divided vegetable dish, 10½x7″ **15.00**
Egg cup **6.00**
Plate, 10″ **6.00**
Soup bowl **3.50**
Yellow Tulip, bowl, 5¾″ **2.50**
Bowl, 9″ **5.00**
Pitcher, 4½″ **4.00**
Pitcher, 5½″ **5.00**
Plate, 6″ **1.75**
Plate, 9½″ **3.00**
Plate, 10½″ **4.50**
Salt & pepper, 2½″ **7.50**
Saucer **6.00**
Sugar w/cover **6.00**
Teapot **25.00**

Stiegel

Baron Henry Stiegel produced glassware in Pennsylvania as early as 1760, very similiar to that being made in Germany and England. Without substantiating evidence, it is impossible to positively attribute glass to his manufacture. Although other types were also produced, today the term Stiegel generally refers to any early enamel decorated glassware such as was made there---however, it is generally conceded that most glass of this type is of European manufacture.

Bar tumbler, blown 3-mold, ribbed bottom, polychrome floral border **85.00**
Bottle, amethyst, hp bird, heart & flowers, pewter stopper, 8½″ **125.00**
Clear blown ½-post, polychrome florals, pewter top, 5¾″ ... **280.00**
Flip glass, 32 ribbed panels, early, 6x4½″ **275.00**
Copper wheel engraved ornate leaves, 6x4″ **250.00**

Keeper jar, hp florals, aqua, 9½″ **1,000.00**
Mug, ribbed, enameled florals & 'Long Life', polished base, 3¾″ **75.00**
Wine, ribbed, drawn conical bowl & stem, domed circular ft, 3¾″ **75.00**

Steins

Steins have been made from pottery, pewter, glass, stoneware and porcelain, from very small up to the 2 liter size. They are decorated by etching, in-mold relief, decals, and occasionally they are hand painted. Some porcelain steins have lithophane bases. Some collectors specialize in a particular type---faience, regimental, or figural---while others limit themselves to the products of only one manufacturer. (See also Mettlach).

4F, ½ liter pot **145.00**
American Indian, blue, grey, panel w/Sioux Chief High Bear .. **125.00**
Baccuss festival decor, ivorine, 14″ **275.00**
Bismark character, in color, porcelain, ½ liter **285.00**
Blown glass, clear w/gr glass lime overlay, flower form lid **85.00**
Blue w/grey medallions, German **135.00**
Bowling scene, pewter top, German script, mkd, Victorian, ½ liter **185.00**
Ceramic, ceramic lid, German, 19″ **100.00**
Pewter & ceramic lid, Gerzit, German, 9″ **40.00**
Couple, on bench, embossed, musical, w/metal lid, German, 10½″ **75.00**

Crystal w/floral wheel cutting, pewter top, 9¾″ **200.00**
Etched leaf, floral border, ruby flashed rim, sgnd, 1883, 5½″ .. **45.00**
Figures in relief, German stoneware **105.00**
In relief, 3 color, #1266 Villeroy & Boch, ½ liter **295.00**
Floral design, German, Gesetzlich Gesghutz, .3 liter **80.00**
Four card suits, w/4 panels, hinged pewter lid **100.00**
Gaudeamus skull, character, beige w/blk trim, ½ liter, 5½″ **295.00**
Girl & boy, polychrome man & woman, lithophane base **250.00**
Grey w/incising, gr trim, pewter lid, Germany, RG451W, 6″ ... **100.00**
Hopfen U Malz Gott Erhalts, ceramic, pewter lid, 22″ **200.00**
Hunter scene, lithophane base, German, ½ liter, 9¼ **275.00**
Hand painted porcelain top, stoneware, mkd, 1864 .... **95.00**
Stoneware, grey, pewter & enamel top, Prosit, ½ liter **50.00**
Indian chief, bisque, w/lid, ½ liter **500.00**
J Reinemann **275.00**
Jager's Freund die Grune Heid, fox handle, pewter lid, 16″ ... **125.00**
Knight on horseback, ceramic, pewter lid, German, #1000, 12″. **60.00**
Landscape, painted, porcelain, pewter lid, German, 9″ **75.00**
Lowenbrau Munchen, thumbprint, pewter top **37.00**
Lumber mill, lithopane tavern scene, lion thumb rest, 10″ **150.00**
Majolica cannibal, wearing earrings & bow tie, ½ liter **225.00**
Majolica man w/pipe, tan & pink, mkd, ½ liter, 7x4″ dia **225.00**
Man & woman, embossed, musical, Auf Der Alm & Da Ist Schon **75.00**
Man smoking pipe, portrait, raised polychromed, hinged pewter lid **75.00**
Man's head, w/pipe, pottery, ½ liter **135.00**
Man, w/funnel hat, German, ½ liter **200.00**
Mettlach #1932, ½ liter **510.00**

#1940, 3 liter	1,100.00
#2090, ½ liter	550.00
Monk, w/tankard & book, music box in lid, pottery, 7″	210.00
Drinking wine, copper lid, Lenox	210.00

Monkey in hat w/book, pottery	250.00
Munich child, 7½″	209.00
#209, German, sgnd, 7½″	225.00
Munich maid, figural, ½ liter	125.00
Gesetzlich, 6″	180.00
Signed J Reineman, 1 liter	285.00
Music decor, German, 1890, 3 liter	140.00
Oriental hp face, lid hat, Germany, ½ liter	165.00
Painted scene, pewter top, Linz, 4½″	45.00
People in garden scene, ceramic, ceramic lid, Gerzit, German, 29″	350.00
Porcelain, pewter lid, German, 7½″	30.00
Regiment, German Infantry, 1910	275.00
Floral thumblift, steeple lid, 2 side scenes, porcelain, 10½″	125.00
High domed lid, draped nude on bottom, 1953, 9½″	125.00
Porcelain, ½ liter, 12½″	475.00
Seated soldier finial, griffin thumbprint, porcelain, 11″	260.00
Regimental, top figural, nude inside bottom, 1891-1893, 11″	295.00
Romatic scene, in relief, blue-gr glaze, hinged pewter lid, ½ liter	75.00
Skull, anchor mark, German, ½ liter	295.00
Tavern scene, in relief, tan background, pewter lid, sgnd, ½ liter	45.00
In relief, w/verse, hinged pewter lid, ¼ liter	75.00
Tree trunk, w/portrait, Gesetzlich	100.00
Warrior scene, ivory, deep carved, 13″	4,500.00
Wolf & grapes scene, jewel top, blue, German motto, high top, 8x6″	64.50

Steuben

The Steuben Glass Works of Corning, New York, was founded in 1903 by Frederick Carder and Thomas Hawkes. They made art glass of high quality similar to some of Tiffany's work. One of their earliest types of art glass was aurene, a metallic gold or blue. They also made verre de soie, rosaline, and silverene. In 1918, Steuben became a branch of Corning Glass Works.

Basket, rosaline w/alabaster handle	310.00
Bon-bon dish, leaf form w/leaves forming handle	160.00
Bowl, 3x10½″ wide	350.00
Calcite, pink highlights in gold interior, 2½x10″	400.00
Fluted, crystal w/blue applied threads, controlled bubbles, 9″ dia	65.00
Jade to alabaster acid cutback	680.00

Rosaline rolled rim, unsgnd, 14½″ dia	150.00
Silverene, amethyst, diamond air traps, crimped rim, 12x4″	450.00
Verre de soie, flared, engraved, irid, 7″ underplate, sgnd, 5″	185.00
Box, calcite, yellow enameled cover, copper-wheel engraved, 1½x2″	275.00
Bud vase, amethyst, sgnd, 6½″	275.00
Acid cutback, rosaline to alabaster, bulbous base, 10½″	395.00
Blue, sgnd Aurene & numbered	275.00
Candelabra, 3-candle, crystal, pr	100.00
Candlestick, baluster, pr, 10″	550.00
Calcite, twist stem	165.00
Calcite gold, engraved, 6x6″, pr	750.00
Footed, lotus leaves, 3x5″ bowl, 6x14″	850.00
French blue, Venetian style, applied prunts, #d, 8″	175.00
Green jade cup, foot & alabaster stem, sgnd, #3100, 8″	125.00
Green threading, sgnd, #379, pr, 10″	225.00
Marina blue, ribbed, double ball stem, domed ft, #2956, 12″	250.00
Ribbed blue w/clear double wafer, turned rim, sgnd, #1617, 12″	125.00
Topaz ft, gr stem & top, sgnd, 12″	260.00
Verre de soie, twisted stem, 10″	165.00
Candy dish, w/cover, rosaline w/alabaster finial	310.00
Champagne, blue bubbly, self threading, sgnd, 6″	50.00
Compote, alabaster base & stem, gr jade top flared to 8¼″ dia	147.00
Alabaster, jade, swirled, sgnd, 7″	275.00
Amber stem, Van Dyke pattern, 6x6″	110.00
French blue, teardrop stem, ruffled rim, 5x7¼″ dia	95.00
Green stem, base, Oriental striped cup, 6″	180.00
Ivory, blk base, sgnd w/fleur-de-lis, #3234, 7″ dia	375.00
Ribbed amethyst, clear stem, 3x8″	70.00
Rosaline, alabaster base, pink, 7″	610.00
Rosaline, alabaster ftd, 12″ dia	475.00
Rosaline & alabaster, 5x10″ dia	395.00
Stemmed, w/lid, deep purple, 14″	325.00
Console set, ivorene, 3-pc, lotus leaves, sgnd	795.00
Pink threads, Diamond Optic, 6″ candlesticks, 12″ bowl	400.00
Cordial, blue bubbly, self threading, sgnd, 6″	50.00
Decanter, celeste blue, ribbed body & foot, w/stopper, #3104, 9¼	225.00
Dish, circular, calcite, amber irid, 5¾″ dia	75.00
Dresser jar, alabaster footing, engraved, mkd, 2¼x2½″ dia	125.00
Alabaster footing, flowers, leaves, mkd, 3½x4½″ dia	245.00
Epergne, jade, tri-cornered, alabaster base, banner sgnd, 10¼″	595.00
Fan vase, amber ribbed top, gr ball stem & foot, sgnd, 9″	95.00
Amber w/criss-cross pattern, knobbed pedestal, sgnd, 8″	225.00
Green, 7½″	125.00
Ribbed, 4 sectioned jade body, alabaster ball foot, 8″	210.00
Ribbed, amber, 6″	90.00
Figurine, blow-fish in crystal, sgnd, 7″	395.00
Dolphin, 6″	125.00
Gazelle	275.00
Pineapple w/the internal air-twist, sgnd, 7″	395.00
Sitting fat cat w/peridox eyes, sgnd, 4x4″	210.00
Finger bowl, blue bubbly, self threading underplates, sgnd	65.00
Fruit bowl, bristol yellow, oval, engraved lion w/banner, 4½x9″ dia	225.00
Goblet, ball stem, gold ruby red, sgnd, 5¾″	65.00
Calcite stem, jade cup, 6″	80.00
Clear bowl, twisted amethyst stem, #6563	85.00
Clear w/controlled bubbles, blue threads, 9x4″	55.00
Leaf etching, pale blue, sgnd, 9½″	200.00
Ribbed bristol, swirl stem, yellow & purple, 8″	75.00
Teardrop swirl pedestal, vertical rib bowl, flared, 8″	45.00
Lamp, gr drag loop w/gold border on calcite, aurene lined, 19½″	190.00
Green jade & alabaster acid cut, pagoda scene, orig shade, 30″	850.00
Lamp base, acid cut, gr jade to alabaster, 12½x6″	890.00
Lemonade, gr parfait-form body, 3″ amber base, 6″	39.00
Pomona gr, paneled, applied threading, amber handle, 6″	65.00

Lemonade mug, swirls, gr w/alabaster handle, fleur-de-lys mkd . **105.00**
Mug, blue bubbly, self threading, handled, sgnd, 2¾″........ **45.00**
  Ivory jade, marbelized, pressed, 4″ **45.00**
Paperweight, elephant, 8″ **375.00**
Perfume, gr threaded, sgnd **140.00**
  Jade, alabaster stopper, sgnd, #1455 .... **185.00**
Pitcher, clear w/blk threading & blk faceted stopper, #7056, 10¼″ **150.00**
Plate, acid cutback, gr cut to alabaster, floral border, 7½″..... **95.00**
  Amethyst w/electric blue rim, rippled edge, sgnd, 8½″ dia .. **100.00**
  Engraved floral swan, rosaline to alabaster, 15″........... **525.00**
  Green jade, 6″.................................. **27.00**
  Green jade, raised swirl ribbed outer rim, sgnd, 8½″ dia..... **35.00**
  Rosaline, 8¾″.................................. **75.00**
Shade, calcite w/alcite etching **80.00**
  Gold aurene fishnet design over calcite, unsgnd **195.00**
  Gold aurene, gr pulled feather, diamond quilt............ **350.00**
  Green pulled feather, aurene lining, sgnd, 6¼″ **145.00**
  Reticulated **90.00**
Sherbet, blue bubbly, self threading, sgnd, 4″ **50.00**
  Green jade bowl, calcite base **145.00**
  Rosaline bowl, calcite base **155.00**
  Verre de soie, w/underplate, sgnd, set of 8 .... **495.00**
  With plate, gold aurene w/calcite **210.00**
  With underplate, clear w/bristol yellow stem, trim.......... **60.00**
Vase, acid cutback, gr jade to alabaster, pedestal foot, 9″ **375.00**
  Alabaster, double gourd, sgnd, #7447, 6″.............. **165.00**
  Blue aurene, 4″................................ **325.00**
  Blue ribbed swirl, 7″............................ **90.00**
  Blue, random bubbles, threading, 7″.................. **75.00**

Bubbles, threading, clear w/blue & topaz, 8″ **90.00**
Bubbly crystal, dome base, wide teardrop form, sgnd, 6″ ... **100.00**
Calcite w/gold aurene linings, golden peach highlights, pr, 6″ **375.00**
Clear to amethyst, pedestal, sgnd, #7090, 9″ **175.00**
Clear, grotesque pattern, 9″ **125.00**
Cornucopia, gr, ftd, 7¾″ **140.00**
Cutback jade, alabaster, Maplewood, 12″ **950.00**
Dark amethyst, flared ruffled neck, ribbed, ped, sgnd & #d, 8″ **135.00**
Diamond quilted, clear w/gr applied threads, 7″.......... **120.00**
Double acid cutback to ivorene, butterfly & coin, 7½″ ... **2,450.00**
Flared, ruffled, sgnd, 4½″ **185.00**
Folded handkerchief, clear to deep cranberry, sgnd, 9″..... **175.00**
Forest gr, 3 prong thorn, sgnd **215.00**

Gold aurene, sgnd, #2683, 8x7½″ dia **325.00**
Green jade, diagonal swirl, round base, 4-sided upper, 5½″ . **150.00**
Grotesque pattern, pedestal, clear to blue, #7089, 11″ **165.00**
Ivorene, 8½″.................................. **275.00**
Ivorene, inverted lamp shade, sgnd, 5½x5¾″ dia **180.00**
Ivory, #d, 8″.................................. **375.00**
Ivory, #d, 12″................................. **500.00**
Ivory, classic ovoid, truncated at base, top flare, 6½″ **155.00**
Ivory, donut base, flare top, vertical ribs, 5¼″ **135.00**
Ivory, Optic Rib, 7½″............................ **130.00**
Ivory, paper label, #7311, 9¼″ **400.00**
Ivory, w/gazelles, sgnd........................... **600.00**
Jade sculptured, oblong **995.00**
Jade to alabaster acid cut back, Maplewood **1,195.00**
Jade w/alabaster foot, fluted, 9″..................... **300.00**
Matzu, acid cutback, rosaline to alabaster, carved stand, 8″ **1,250.00**
Pomona gr, ball stem & foot, topaz ribbed fan top, sgnd, 8¾″ **95.00**
Poppy, #d, 5″ **1,375.00**
Rose cluthra, urn shape, big bubbles, sgnd, 10″ **775.00**
Selenium red, 8½″ diagonal swirl flare, sgnd, 7″........ **160.00**
Stylized Deco florals, blk jade acid cut back to gr, 12″ ... **1,900.00**
Topaz crystal, diagonal swirl, urn body, flared top, 7″ **95.00**
Trumpet shape, topaz diagonal swirl, pedestal, 8″ **120.00**
Trumpet vase in center, jack in the pulpit on sides, sgnd, 12″ **995.00**
Urn shape, yellow jade, 8½″...................... **1,400.00**
Verre de soie, pedestal, 5¼x3¼″...................... **60.00**
Wisteria, striped wide optic, 3 handles, #d, 10½x6¼″...... **350.00**
Wine, blue bowl, rosaline stem, Optic Rib, 8½″ **80.00**
  Blue bubbly, self threading, sgnd, 6¾″ **50.00**
  Optic Rib, green, 4½″ **25.00**
  Optic Rib, green w/clear stem, 4½″.................. **25.00**
  Ruby w/clear twist stem, 8″ **65.00**
  Selenium red w/diagonal swirl ribbed stem, sgnd, pr, 4½″.... **75.00**
  Topaz, Optic Rib, 8½″.......................... **65.00**

Stevengraph

A Stevengraph is a small picture made of woven silk, resembling an elaborate ribbon. They were created by Thomas Stevens in England in the latter half of the 1800s. They were matted and framed by Stevens, usually with his name appearing on the matt, or more commonly on the trade announcement on the back of the matt. He also produced silk bookmarks, all of which have 'Stevens' woven in silk on one of the mitered corners.

A Blessing, gr & wht on pink, no tassel, bookmark, 2x10″ **52.00**
Abraham Lincoln, memorial, w/portrait, bookmark........... **65.00**
Birthday Greetings, bookmark **45.00**
Birthday Wishes, bookmark **50.00**
Called to the Rescue, framed, sgnd, mat, 2¼x6″........... **245.00**
  Heroism at sea, framed, 10x7½″....................... **275.00**
Centennial in Philadelphia, George Washington, book mark, sgnd **85.00**
Children, 12½x8″................................. **200.00**
Declaration of Independence, framed, mat **400.00**
For Life or Death, heroism on land, framed, 10x7½″........ **350.00**
Friendship, bookmark.............................. **55.00**
Full Cry, framed, mat **275.00**
Girl, w/cap, poem & flowers, very colorful................. **55.00**
Hands Across the Sea, postcard **35.00**
Happy Christmas, bookmark, colorful bird & red roses on blk . **100.00**
Lady Godiva Procession, framed, mat **275.00**
Landing of Columbus, framed, mat **375.00**
Lusitania, postcard **175.00**
Many Happy Returns of Day, music title, silk bookmark **95.00**

Merry Christmas, verses, flags **90.00**
New Year's Wish, bookmark, rose, shamrocks, grapes on wht . **100.00**
Queen Victoria, her majesty 1837, Jubilee 1887 . . . . **250.00**
Red Riding Hood, w/'Pussy', 1888, book **145.00**
Remember Me, 1½x5" **30.00**
Richmond 1865, Lt Gen US Grant, sgnd T Stevens, Coventry . **125.00**
The Death, framed, mat **275.00**
The Good Old Days, framed, mat **340.00**
The Last Lap, 5 men on high wheel bikes in a race, sgnd, orig frame **295.00**
To My Darling, w/Mary & her lamb, verse, sgnd, bookmark **55.00**

Stevens and Williams

Stevens and Williams glass was produced at the Brierly Hill Glass Works in Stourbridge, England, for nearly a century, beginning in the 1830s. They were credited with being among the first to develop a method of manufacturing a more affordable type of cameo glass. Other lines were also made--- silver deposit, Alexandrite, and engraved rock crystal to name but a few.

Bowl, applied pears, leaves, topas w/blue ft, 6x10" **475.00**
    Floral enamel, amber ft, blue lined, 5x6" **450.00**
Cologne, floral intaglio cut overlay, pinched sides, 8x3" dia . . . **245.00**
    Gold decor, gr cut to crystal, w/stopper, 9½x3" dia **135.00**
    Green & crystal swirl striped, hallmkd collar, 9x3½" dia **165.00**
    Intaglio cut overlay, hallmkd silver collar, w/stopper, 8x3" dia **195.00**
    Ruby cut to crystal star & thumbprint, w/stopper, 8¾x2½" dia **145.00**
Pitcher, amber, w/applied aqua handle **185.00**
    Clear rushing, fluted rim, rose to amber, 7x6" **250.00**
Rose bowl, cranberry & amber striped, box pleat top, 4x4½" dia **195.00**
    Zipper pattern, crimped top, cranberry, 1886, 4½x5½" dia . **385.00**
Vase, amber & wht florals, pink to rose, scalloped rim, sgnd, 6½" **225.00**
    Applied amber leaves & wht flowers, wht, 6" **165.00**
    Applied cherries & amber leaves & rigaree, pair, 5" **275.00**
    Applied limb, leaves & acorns, scalloped top, amber rim, 10" **225.00**
    Applied plums w/stems & leaves on pink overlay, 7¼x4" dia **375.00**
    Cameo, wht blossoms & leaves on yellow satin, 7" **800.00**
    Carved wht flowers, orig label, cameo, 15" **8,500.00**
    Engraved florals w/leaves, pulled in flared top, crystal, 13½" **125.00**
    Fan, crystal w/etched florals, 3 openings, 6x3¼" **135.00**
    Green floral cameo decor, opaque background, unsgnd, 4½" **790.00**
    Jewel ware, orange & gr applied base & ft, 1866, 5" **125.00**
    Matsuy-Kn-ne, applied frosted clear glass, Rose Dubarry, #15353 **985.00**
    Pink to wht floral applique, ruffled rim, rose, 7½" **185.00**
    Squatty bowl, ruffled applied leaf, 4 crystal ball ft, 7x6½" dia **450.00**
    Vaseline opal w/applied gooseberry, 4" **200.00**

Stocks and Bonds

The interest in collecting old stocks and bonds from 1830 to about 1930

has only recently surfaced, but appears to be growing. Collectors prefer those with signatures of noted railroad and mining tycoons, as well as those with elaborate border designs, and vignettes of the early mining or railway industries. Specimen certificates, or proof copies, and certificates of large denominations are rare and valuable. Those with signatures of famous people may sell for hundreds of dollars. However, most average from $5 to $50, with the majority toward the lower side of the range.

American Drug Co South Dakota, eagle w/train, 1902 . . . . **10.00**
American Gold Mining Co Territory New Mexico, mine scene, 1902 **32.00**
Bismarck Consolidated Mines, Deadwood South Dakota, eagle, 1909 **22.00**
Boise Gold Mining Co, Washington, eagle, capitol, fort, 1890 . . **30.00**
Boston, Hartford, Erie, bond w/coupon, $1,000, 1865 . . . . **55.00**
Cayadutta Electric RR New York, ornate title banner, 1893 . . . . **22.00**
Chesapeake & Ohio RR Equip Trust, diesel loco, $1,000, 1963 . . **6.00**
Chicago & Rock Island RR Co, document certifying stocks, 1857 **150.00**
Chicago, Burlington & Northern RR, locomotive, 1887 . . . . **47.00**
Chicago, Burlington, Quincy, RR stock, vingette, cancelled, 1890 **8.00**
City of Jersy City, bond, sgnd F Boss Hague, $1,000, 1943 . . . . **18.00**
City of Philadelphia, certificate of loan, 1862 . . . . **55.00**
Cleveland, Columbus, Cincinnati & Indianapolis RR, Ohio, train, 1880 **38.00**
Colony RR, bond, 1930 . . . . **50.00**
Colorado Cen Con Mining Co, Georgetown, New York, 1888 . . . **85.00**
Confederate, 18 coupons, 8%, $50, 5/1/1861 . . . . **65.00**
    Bond, sgnd by Tyler, $1,000, 1864, 9½x7" **15.00**
    Rural scene, 7%, $1,000, 3/9/1865 . . . . **27.00**
Delaware Lack & Western, certificate, 100 shares, ABNCO **8.50**
Denver & Rio Grande RR Co Colorado, men, mine, 1886 . . . . . **47.50**
Erie RR Equip Trust, tan w/logo at top, $1,000, 1955 . . . . **3.00**
Farmer's Daughter Mining Co, Illinois, mining vignette, 1895 . . **32.00**
Illinois Central RR Co, bond, engraved, 1852, 13x15" **50.00**
Irving Trust Co, New York, 1930s **4.00**
Kaiser-Frazer Corp, auto, 1946 . . . . **12.00**
Kansas City Northwestern RR Co, bond w/coupon, $500, 1894, brown **10.00**
Kansas, Texas RR, stock certificate, good art, 1883 . . . . **6.00**
Lincoln Motor Co, Delaware, temporary certificate, 1920 . . . . . **16.00**
Merchants Union Express Co, New York, horses, wagon, 1867 **185.00**
Montana Territorial Drafts, lot of 2, 1867, 4x8" **50.00**
Nevada Utah Mines & Smelters, stock certificates, good art, 1907 **6.00**
New York & Harlem RR Co, revenue stamp, sgnd Vanderbilt, 1873 **360.00**
New York Cable Railway Co, bond w/98 coupons, red, $1,000, 1884 **18.00**
Panama Mining, stock certificate, Eagle, 1918, 10x6" **7.00**
Pennsylvania Rapid Transit, stock certificate, trolley vignette, 1914 **4.00**
Realty Syndicate, investment certificate, Ca., 6% gold, 1895 . . . **18.00**
Richmond & West Point, bond w/coupon, $1,000, 1889 . . . . **50.00**
Ringling Bros Barnum & Bailey, stock certificate, 1968 . . . . . . **120.00**
Ross Oil Co, stock certificate w/revenue stamp, 1865 . . . . **50.00**
South-Eastern Gold Mining Co, Ltd, 20 attached coupons **17.00**
Studebaker Corp, New Jersey, man shoeing horse, 1929 . . . . **80.00**
Swifterwater Mining, stock certificate, Libertyhead, 1896, 12x8" . **7.00**
The Orinoco Steam Navigation Co, stock certificate, $1,000, 1851 **175.00**
The Virginian Railway Co, orange, ABNCO, $1,000, 1945 . . . . . **11.00**
Tom Reed Gold Mines Co, Arizona, mining scene, 1919 . . . . . . **11.00**
US Internal Revenue, Special certificate, 1876-1885, 7x14¾" . . **40.00**
Union Mutual, certificate, nautical vignette, 1866-76 . . . . **75.00**
Union Traction, stock certificate, 1899 issue **4.00**
Van Noy Oil Co, Kansas City, oilfield vignette, 1918 . . . . **16.00**
Zopilote Mining Co Territory, Arizona, mining vignettes, 1908 . . **32.00**

Stockton

The Stockton Terra Cotta Company was established in 1891 in Stockton, California. In 1897, the name was changed to Stockton Art Pottery Company, and several lines of art pottery, the Rekston line among them, were

introduced. Their wares included vases, pitchers, jardinieres, umbrella stands and teapots, many of which were styled with scrolling ornate handles and graceful shapes. Some examples bear the 'Rekston' mark. The pottery closed in 1902, after a third devastating fire that destroyed their buildings.

Box, w/cover, mushrooms on brown glaze, mkd, 6″ dia **325.00**
Ewer, yellow florals on brown glaze, 10″ **250.00**
Mug, streaky brown high glaze, souvenir Iowa **55.00**
Vase, California, 9″ **125.00**
    Rekston, spider chrysanthemum decor, standard glaze, 10″ . **100.00**

Stoneware

There are three broad periods of time that collectors of American pottery can look to in evaluating and dating the stoneware and earthenware in their collections.

Among the first permanent settlers in American were English and German potters who found a great demand for their individually turned wares. The early pottery was produced from red and yellow clays scraped from the ground at surface levels. The earthenware made in these potteries was fragile and coated with lead glazes that periodically created health problems for the people who ate or drank from it.

There was little stoneware available for sale until the early 1800s because the clays used in its production were not readily available in many areas and transportation was prohibitively expensive. The opening of the Erie Canal and improved roads brought about a dramatic increase in the accessibility of stoneware clay, and many new potteries began to open in New York and New England.

Collectors have difficulty today locating earthenware and stoneware jugs produced prior to 1840, because little has survived intact. These ovoid or pear shaped jugs were designed to be used on a daily basis. When cracked or severely chipped, they were quickly discarded.

The value of handcrafted pottery is often determined by the cobalt decoration it carries. Pieces with elaborate scenes (a chicken pecking corn, a blue bird on a branch, a stag standing near a pine tree, a sailing ship, or people) may easily bring $600-$3,000 at auction.

After the Civil War, there was a need and a national demand for stoneware jugs, crocks, canning jars, churns, spittoons, and a wide variety of other pottery items. The competition among the many potteries reached the point where only the largest could survive. To cut costs, most potteries did away with all but the simplest kinds of decoration on their wares. Time-consuming brush-painted birds or flowers quickly gave way to more simply executed swirls or numbers and stenciled designs. The coming of home refrigeration and Prohibition in 1919 effectively destroyed the American stoneware industry.

Investment possibilities:

Early nineteenth century stoneware with elaborate decorations and a potter's mark is expensive and will continue to rise in price, though not as rapidly as in the past three years.

Late nineteenth century hand thrown stoneware with simple cobalt swirls or numbers is still reasonably priced and a good investment.

Mass produced stoneware (ca. 1890-1920) is available in large quantities, inexpensive, and will slowly increase in price over the decade of the 1980s.

At this point reproduction or 'fakes' are not a major concern. Much of the reproduction stoneware is dated on the bottom of the piece. The Beaumont Pottery of York, Maine, which produced 'the finest reproduction stoneware of the twentieth century' scratched the date into each piece.

Batter jug, bird w/fan tail in cobalt, handled, 4 qt **600.00**
    Brown glaze, cinderglazed top, wide spout, w/lid **75.00**
    Brown slip, w/bail handle **35.00**
    Circle decor in cobalt, tin covered spout **36.00**
    Flowers, bail handle, 1 gal **375.00**

    White glaze in & out, pouring spout **36.00**
Bottle, blue shoulder & lip, Brownell & Wheaton, 1 qt **75.00**
    Evil eye & forked tongue in cobalt, R Burge **625.00**
    R & DW Defreest in blue, 1 qt **40.00**
    Scenic, Kentucky liquor house in cobalt, wire handle, 8″ ... **200.00**
Cake crock, blue decor on crock lid, 3 gal **475.00**
    House, AO Whittemore, Havana, 3 gal **1,000.00**
Canning jar, Albany slip, raised Minnesota mk, 1 gal **1,000.00**
    Stripes in cobalt, 2 qt **75.00**
Churn, w/squiggle in cobalt, 4 gal **150.00**
    Bird decor--large, J Hart, Sherburne, 5 gal **575.00**
    Double flower in cobalt, 4 gal **195.00**
    Double tulip in cobalt, w/dasher, Cortland, 2 gal **205.00**
    Flower, branch, leaves & scrolls in cobalt; handled, w/lid, 3 gal **235.00**
    Peafowl on stump--large, J&E Norton, Bennington Vt., 6 gal **1,000.00**
    Stylized leaf decor, Wm E Warner, West Troy, 2 gal **200.00**
Cooler, flower, cobalt decor, Albany, N.Y., 2 gal **360.00**
    Grape decor in cobalt, Ft Wright & Son...Taunton, 4 gal ... **110.00**
    Slip & stylized florals in cobalt, Ottman Bros & Co, 6 gal .. **325.00**
    Stag scene, cream w/gr shading, 12¼x11″ dia **350.00**
Crock, 3 leaf decor, Haxton & Co, Fort Edward, 3 gal **120.00**
    3 simple flowers, M Woodruff, Cortland, N.Y., 5 gal **195.00**
    3 wings, Geddes, N.Y., 2 gal, 9½″ **150.00**
    Bird, Worcester Norton, 2 gal **215.00**
    Bird & flower in cobalt, S Hart, Fulton, 6 gal, 13½″ **500.00**
    Bird in bright blue, J&E Norton, Bennington, Vt., 1 gal **350.00**
    Bird in cobalt, 1 gal **250.00**
    Bird in cobalt, Caire, Pokeepsie, N.Y., 4 gal **325.00**
    Bird in cobalt, City Auction Store, 2 gal, 9″............. **125.00**
    Bird in cobalt, handled, Whites Utica, 4 gal **380.00**
    Bird on branch in cobalt, Fulper Bros, #3, 10″ **375.00**
    Bird on branch in cobalt, Norton, #3, 10″ **235.00**
    Bird on branch in cobalt, mkd, mid-1800s, 2 gal **200.00**
    Bird running, Whites Utica, 2 gal **300.00**
    Bird w/fantail in cobalt, Whites, Utica, N.Y., 4 gal **490.00**
    Bird w/song notes in cobalt, 2 gal **280.00**
    Bird w/spike tail in cobalt, Whites Utica, 3 gal **385.00**
    Bird w/stylized flower in cobalt, EP Norton...Vt., 3 gal **300.00**
    Birds on twigs in cobalt, 4 gal **490.00**
    Chicken pecking corn, Brady & Ryan, Ellenville, N.Y., 3 gal **475.00**
    Cloverleaf in cobalt, molded handles, 1½ gal **175.00**
    Cobalt decor on lid & crock, 1 gal, 4″ **375.00**
    Cobalt design, ovoid, JB Cair & Co, Pokeepsie, N.Y., 9¼″.. **300.00**
    Cobalt information, handles, Williams & Reppert, 6 gal..... **265.00**
    Deer reclining, Whites Utica, 4 gal **1,800.00**
    Double flower in cobalt, 6 gal **110.00**
    Double tulip in cobalt, handled, 2 gal **315.00**
    Fishlure in cobalt, hand thrown, 1870s, 3 gal............. **165.00**
    Floral decor in cobalt, Norton, 4 gal, 11¼″ **65.00**
    Floral decor in cobalt, Norton, 6 gal, 13″................ **140.00**
    Flower & leaf, cobalt tipped ear handles, Cowden & Wilcox, 2 gal **195.00**
    Flower & leaf in cobalt, Norton & Co, Mass., 4 gal, 11″.... **125.00**
    Flower decor in cobalt, ovoid, Wm E Warner, West Troy, 3 gal **230.00**
    Flower in cobalt, 6 gal **300.00**
    Flower in cobalt, Cowden & Wilcox, Harrisburg, Pa., 1 gal . **165.00**
    Flower in cobalt, Cowden & Wilcox...Pa., ½ gal **210.00**
    Flower in cobalt, George M Hitchcock, ½ gal **165.00**
    Flower in cobalt, ovoid, 1 gal.......................... **140.00**
    Flower in cobalt, rolled rim, Norton, 3 gal, 10½″ **85.00**
    Flowers in cobalt, EP Norton...Bennington, Vt., ½ gal **120.00**
    Flowers in cobalt, Haxston Ottman & Co...N.Y., 2 gal **110.00**
    Grape cluster, Cowden & Wilcox, Harrisburg, Pa., 2 gal ... **375.00**
    Grape cluster, orange peel surface, Ft Wright & Co, 1½ gal **100.00**
    Incised eagle w/flag, sgnd, 1860-70s, 2 gal **210.00**

Leaf decor--large & stylized, Ballard Bros, Burlington, Vt., 4 gal **145.00**
Log cabin decor in cobalt, Semour Bosworth, large **1,050.00**
Parrot in cobalt, Norton, Worcester, Mass, 4 gal **675.00**
Parrot--large, FB Norton & Co, Worcester, Mass, 3 gal **450.00**
Snake decor in cobalt, grey, handled, 2 gal **95.00**
Soldiers in cobalt, handled, WA Macquoid & Co, 3 gal **600.00**
Squiggle decor in cobalt, ½ gal **99.00**
Squiggle decor in cobalt, handled, W Roberts Binghamton, 2 gal **85.00**
Stylized deer, finch & trees in cobalt, Edmands & Co, 3 gal **2,150.00**
Tan, orange peel ground, Lyons, N.Y., 1 gal **45.00**
Tulip in cobalt, 3 gal **110.00**
Tulips & bowtie in cobalt, M Woodruff, Cortland, 4 gal **275.00**
Tulips & leaf cobalt decor, handled, 1800s, 7½" **245.00**
Woman figural decor in cobalt, 2 gal **500.00**
Wreath & flower cobalt decor, 6 gal **440.00**
Cup, urn, boat & building decor in cobalt **18.00**
Figurine, lion reclining, cobalt, Cherry Valley, N.Y. **3,600.00**
  Spaniel, Albany slip, 9" **185.00**
  Squirrel in sitting position, 1800s, 1¾" **30.00**
  Whiskey barrel on sleigh, brown & tan glaze, 4x6x6" **100.00**
Flower pot, floral cobalt decor on 2 sides, attached base **260.00**
Fruit jar, Macomb, side lid, 1899, 1 qt **15.00**
Inkwell, circular, mkd Tyler & Dillon, Albany, 2x5" **425.00**
Jar, barrel shape w/ribbing, brown, yellow, wax sealer, 6½" **88.00**
  Bowtie decor in cobalt, OL & AK Ballard, Burlington, Vt., 3 gal **120.00**
  Brown, Peoria Pottery, 9¼x9¼" dia **17.50**
  Double flower in cobalt, 2 gal **135.00**
  Double flower in cobalt, with lid, handled, Lyons, 2 gal **220.00**
  Double tulips, handled, Cortland, 2 gal **140.00**

Eagle stencil, 14½" **350.00**
Floral, Cortland, 2 gal, 10¾" **125.00**
Floral in cobalt, ovoid, OV Lewis, Greenwich, 3 gal, 12¼" ... **65.00**
Floral in cobalt, with lid, Lyons, 2 gal **185.00**
Flower, free standing handles, low, 6 qt **160.00**
Flower in cobalt, AO Whittemore, Havana, N.Y., 2 gal **195.00**
  Handled, Hart Sherburne, 2 gal **130.00**
  Lidded, Cowden & Wilcox, 1 gal **195.00**
  M Woodruff, 2 gal **165.00**
  N.Y. Stoneware, 2 gal, 9" **75.00**
  On 2 sides, 3 gal **295.00**
  Ovoid, Norton, Bennington, Vt., 4 gal **260.00**
  Ovoid, w/lid, SS Perry, Troy, 1 gal **260.00**
  Revolving, in cobalt, 1½ gal **85.00**

Stylized, in cobalt, E&LP Norton, Vt., 4 gal **240.00**
  Stylized, in cobalt, from Wiseman's China, 2 gal **150.00**
Flower & leaf in cobalt, squiggles under ears, 4 gal **330.00**
Flowers, stylized, in cobalt, 3 gal **140.00**
Flowers & leaves, revolving, in cobalt, ovoid, 4 gal **290.00**
Label in cobalt, Donagho, 8 gal, 18½ **55.00**
Leaves in cobalt on 2 sides, w/lid, 4 gal **110.00**
Man w/hat & shovel, smoking pipe, in cobalt, 2 gal **3,600.00**
Orchid in cobalt, NA White & Son, Utica, N.Y., 3 gal **250.00**
Sprigs in cobalt, ovoid, Orcutt, Humiston, Troy, 3 gal **260.00**
Streaks of cobalt, bulbous, 3½" **35.00**
Swirl in cobalt, Fenton, St Johnsburg, Vt., 1 gal **185.00**
Tulip in cobalt, ovoid, ½ gal **295.00**
Jug, 3 & double flower in cobalt, ovoid, 3 gal **140.00**
  3 & snowflake in cobalt, 3 gal **240.00**
  4 decor w/leaves, in cobalt, ovoid, S Hart, Fulton, 4 gal **165.00**
  8 vertical rods over a scroll, JM Pruden, Elizabeth, N.J., 2 gal **165.00**
  B Huber, Buffalo, N.Y., 1 gal **75.00**
  Bird, incised, in cobalt, blue wash, 1 gal **315.00**
    New York Stoneware Co, Fort Edward, N.Y., 3 gal **250.00**
    Spotted, in cobalt, J Burger Jr...N.Y., 4½ gal **780.00**
  Bird & twig in cobalt, J Norton, Bennington, Vt., 3 gal **410.00**
  Bird in cobalt, sgnd E & IP Norton, 2 gal **260.00**
  Bird in cobalt, west Troy N.Y. Pottery, 2 gal **260.00**
  Bird on branch, Charleston, 2 gal, 14½" **240.00**
  Bird on flowers in cobalt, 2 gal **280.00**
  Bird on sprig in cobalt, Haxstun & Co, Ft Edward, 1 gal ... **230.00**
  Bird on stump in cobalt, New York Stoneware Co, 2 gal ... **520.00**
  Bird on twig in cobalt, Whites Utica, 2 gal **300.00**
  Bird running, Whites Utica, 2 gal **295.00**
  Bird w/fantail in cobalt, Whites Utica, 2 gal **265.00**
  Birds in cobalt, double handled, Haxstun, Ottman, 10 gal . **1,200.00**
  Brown shiny slip, w/pour lip, E Norton & Co, Bennington, Vt. **50.00**
  Brown slip on top & bottom third, ovoid, Boston, 2 gal **225.00**
  Cream, w/ears, Porter & Frazer, W Troy, N.Y., 2 gal **285.00**
  Daisy in cobalt, unusual, Cowden & Wilcox, 2 gal **255.00**
  Deer w/fence, J&E Norton, Bennington, Vt., 4 gal **200.00**
  Devil, Brown's Pottery, 13" **25.00**
  Double flower in cobalt, Lehman & Riedinger, 2 gal **220.00**
  Double flower in cobalt, Whites Utica, 3 gal............. **140.00**
  Double thistle in cobalt, Saugerties, N.Y., 1882, 1 gal **265.00**
  Elephant face in cobalt, ½ gal **165.00**
  Fleur-de-lis incised, ovoid, C Crolius, Manhattan Wells, N.Y., 3 gal **850.00**
  Floral wreath in cobalt, PV & S Utica, N.Y., 2 gal **315.00**
  Flower in cobalt, 4 gal **120.00**
    AK Ballard, 3 gal................................. **140.00**
    H Weston, Honesdale, Pa., 2 gal **185.00**
    Handles, Somerset, 1 gal........................... **85.00**
    HN Robinson, Syracuse, N.Y., 2 gal.................. **210.00**
    Hudson, N.Y. Pottery, 2 gal **140.00**
    J & E Norton, 1 gallon **150.00**
    N Clark, Athens N.Y., 1 gal **85.00**
    Ovoid, 1 gal **85.00**
    Ovoid, Julius Norton, Bennington, 2 gal **260.00**
    Ovoid, impressed mortar & pestle, 12½"............. **400.00**
    W Hart Ogdensburgh, 3 gal **150.00**
    White's Binghamton, 2 gal **185.00**
  Flower & leaf in cobalt, White's Utica, 2 gal **150.00**
  Flower & leaves in cobalt, WJ Semour, Troy factory, 2 gal .. **145.00**
  Flower bud in cobalt, ovoid, Clark & Fox, Athens, 3 gal.... **175.00**
  Grape cluster in cobalt, mid-1800s, 2 gal **195.00**
  Grape leaves embossed, rope handle, Ohio Harvester **350.00**
  Grapes in cobalt, Wright, 1 gal **75.00**
  H in cobalt, S Hart & Son, 1 gal...................... **75.00**

Hen, rooster & flowers under 1862 & wreath in cobalt, 3 gal **3,000.00**
Herman Bernhardt, Buffalo, N.Y., 1895, in cobalt, 1 gal **75.00**
Highlights in cobalt, P Cross, Hartford, early 1800s, 15″ ... **275.00**
Incised hearts in cobalt, Charlestown, 2 gal **285.00**
Insect decor, Roberts, Binghamton, N.Y., 2 gal, 13″ **250.00**
JF Weiler, Allentown, Pa., 1 gal...................... **85.00**
Lazy S in cobalt, 1 gal **65.00**
Leaf in cobalt, Bennington, 1 gal..................... **100.00**
    Haxstun & Co, Ft Edward, N.Y., 1800s, 12″ **150.00**
    Lyons, 2 gal **140.00**
    Ovoid, 1 gal **110.00**
    Ovoid, B Nash, Unica, N.Y., 1 gal **170.00**
    Ovoid, Boynton, 2 gal **195.00**
Leaves, connected, in cobalt, ovoid, Seymour Troy, 3 gal ... **185.00**
Leaves, stylized, in cobalt, Haxstun...Ft Edward, N.Y., 3 gal . **100.00**
Leaves in cobalt, Ft Edward, New York Stoneware Co, 2 gal **120.00**
Lion, sitting position, w/fence, J&E Norton, 2 gal........ **4,500.00**
Litha Spring Water in cobalt, Londonderry, N.H., 3 gal **335.00**
Love birds w/tails crossing, J Hart, Fulton, 2 gal **550.00**
Norton & Fenton, Bennington, Vt., ovoid, 1 gal........... **85.00**
Pine tree in cobalt, 1 gal **65.00**
Profile mustached man, Haxtun, Ottman & Co, Ft Edward, 3 gal **2,500.00**
Rabbit, sgnd Julius Norton Bennington, 2 gal............ **230.00**
Rabbit & flower decor in cobalt, Norton & Fenton...Vt., 3 gal **510.00**
Robin, John Conlon & Co, 2 gal **295.00**
'Rum' in cobalt, ovoid, 4 gal **130.00**
Slip in cobalt, S Hart, Jones, 1 gal, 10¼″ **75.00**
Snowflake, blue on handle, Cowden, Harrisburg, 2 gal **150.00**
Sprig & bud in cobalt, Edmunds & Co, 2 gal............ **75.00**
Stripes in cobalt, 2 qt **85.00**
Stylized wedge, ovoid, Clark & Fox, Athens, 4 gal........ **200.00**
Thomas Furlong importer...from T Paddock..., 1 gal **90.00**
Tree design in cobalt, Norton, Bennington, Vt., 1 gal **135.00**
Tree-like decor in cobalt, Edmunds & Co, 1 gal **220.00**
With pouring spout, E&LP Norton, Bennington, Vt., 1 gal, 9¼″ **80.00**
With pouring spout, open, ears w/wire bail, N White & Co, 8¼″ **180.00**
Zigzag lines, White's Utica, 1 gal **95.00**
Milk pan, encircled w/6 flower buds, P Hermann, 1 gal **185.00**
Mug, cobalt bands **110.00**
Pitcher, Albany slip, E Norton & Co, Bennington, Vt., 1½ gal, 10½″ **45.00**
    Albany slip interior, 2 cobalt bands, applied handle, 8½″ **65.00**
     9″ **60.00**
    Band of cobalt, 1 gal **85.00**
    Bird, West Troy Pottery, 2 gal.................... **850.00**
    Bird in cobalt, 10″ **750.00**
    Bird on twig in cobalt, 2 gal **990.00**
    Brown glaze, 9″............................... **60.00**
    Cobalt decor all around, ½ gal **450.00**
    Early 1800s, 1 gal............................. **120.00**
    Flower in cobalt, 1 gal **460.00**
    Flower & teardrops incised decor, cobalt, ovoid, 1 gal...... **260.00**
    Flowers all around, RCR, Philadelphia, 2 gal **700.00**
    Leaf in cobalt, 1 gal **300.00**
    Leaf in cobalt, ½ gal **440.00**
    Leaves incised, cobalt, 1 qt **350.00**
    Tavern scene, blue-grey molded, 9½″ **120.00**
Platter, scenery in cobalt, Lombardy, Heath & Co, 1840, 12x16″ **68.00**
Pot, bluebird decor, small & incised, ovoid, 2 gal **1,000.00**
    Bluebird incised decor, I Seymour, Troy, 2 gal.......... **750.00**
    Ovoid, Paul Cushman, Albany, N.Y., 3 gal **500.00**
    Ovoid, blue mk, C Crolius, Manhattan Wells, N.Y., 4 gal ... **475.00**
Preserve jar, 3 cobalt stripes, 2 qt.................... **75.00**
Rolling pin, grey w/cobalt band, Boos Hardware, Effingham, Ill. **200.00**
Spittoon, cobalt revolving leaf, 2 gal **150.00**

Storage jar, 2 large blossoms **95.00**
Tureen, cobalt swirls decor **65.00**
Umbrella stand, tree stump form, Norton, Worcester **230.00**

Urn, fish, cobalt on wht, 1905, 18″ **650.00**
Water cooler, birds & branch decor in cobalt, flared base, 22″ **600.00**

Store

Perhaps more than any other yester-year establishement, the country store evokes more nostalgic feelings for more folks who are old enough to remember its charms---barrels for coffee, crackers, and big green pickles; candy in a jar for the grocer to weigh on shiny brass scales; beheaded chickens in the meat case outwardly devoid of nothing but feathers. Today, momentos from this segment of Americana are being collected by those who 'lived it' as well as those less fortunate.

Bolt, cabinet, oak, 144 drawers......................... **725.00**
Broom holder, round **85.00**
Butcher's drag hook, handforged, 1870 .... **40.00**

Cabinet, Clark's Spool Cotton, 4 drawers, oak............ **400.00**
    DeLavel **275.00**
    Diamond Dye, children playing....................... **450.00**
    Diamond Dye, woman washing **425.00**

Candy pan, brass, iron band under rim, 44x12″ **235.00**
  Copper, iron handles, 1880, 30″ dia, 12″ deep **200.00**
Candy scoop, brass, handle, 6″ overall **40.00**
  Tin, 6½″ overall **25.00**
Cheese cutter, iron on round wood base, counter used **100.00**
Cheese safe, counter top, pat 1892 .... **450.00**
  Mahogany, advertisement on back, 22x18″ **250.00**
  Wooden, roll top back, 3 sides glass, 22x19x22″ **395.00**
Counter, oak, 30-drawer, 144″ **2,350.00**
  Oak, seed display front, 96″ **1,000.00**
  Oak, w/cash drawer, 2 dispay areas **500.00**
Counter desk for top of country store, 29x35″ **60.00**
  Oak, orig pulls, hinged top, JP coats, 30x20x15″ **315.00**
Display cabinet, corn cob pipe, Missouri Meerschaum, pine ... **650.00**
Display tray, glass, raised sunburst pattern on bottom, 7¾x5¾″ **25.00**
Display tray shelf holder, glass, 2 pc, w/metal, 16″ **28.00**
Drugstore cabinet, 96x72″ **450.00**
Dye container, Dy-o-Las, tin, counter top, 17½x13½x8″ **250.00**
Frame, wood, w/old graining, glass top & sides, 9x20x44″ **85.00**
Grabber, long handled, picks stock off high shelves **25.00**
Grain storage bin, pine, w/roll top, 5 section **1,600.00**
Ice tongs, wood handles, lg icehouse size, latter 1800s **75.00**
Meat rack, pine, 11 handforged hooks, early, 39″ long **75.00**
Mold, milliner's bonnet, plaster of paris, 1800s **65.00**
Notion cabinet, oak counter, 35 display compartments **440.00**
Paper bags rack, wire, 10 shelves, 30″ **95.00**
Paper roll holder, wood & iron, double, illus **28.00**
Roller, wood, rolls yard goods, SD Luckett, pat 1870 .... **125.00**
Scale, fishtail, iron, flat tray, orig paint, brass arm **135.00**
  Meat, for butcher shop, Hanson, to 160 pounds........... **90.00**
Screw cabinet, cast iron, 140 drawers **310.00**
Shipping & store display, orig gr stained wood, 5 cent cigars ... **18.00**
  Wood w/paper labels, 12x8x4″ deep **45.00**
Showcase, mirror, 4 doors, 10x3x2½′ **135.00**
Showcase, plate glass, orig stock (collars), Ill. Showcase Co, 60x12″ **100.00**
  Walnut, glass door top, lg brass handle, 2 doors, 120″ ... **1,500.00**

Slicer, wood, adjustable iron blade **90.00**
Stringholder, ball hanging type, cast iron, cutouts, 6½″ dia **45.00**
  Beehive standing style, cast iron........................ **50.00**
  Cone, iron, counter bolted **30.00**
Sugar devil, iron, to loosen hardened chunks of sugar, brown .. **95.00**
Till box, solid mahogany, dovetail 4 corners drawer, 1860s, 18x9″ **195.00**
Tobacco cutters, counter type, all iron smithy made, wood handled **50.00**

Stoves

Parlor stoves range from the simple to the very ornate. Many were obviously relative to a specific style of furnishing---Rococo, Gothic, or Greek, for instance. This is due to the fact that they were first designed in wood, carved and constructed by cabinetmakers who transferred to them the decorative devices they routinely used on furniture. The wooden stove that resulted was then used as a basis for the mould.

Acme Champion, #25, wood burner, 1902, 23″ **385.00**
Acron, baseburner w/9 tiles & statue **2,200.00**
Art Grand, #12, coal heating, round, Utica, New York **310.00**
B&H, #6, 'Cool AM Handwarmer Stove, 1885', 30x16x17″ deep **285.00**
Brilliant Peoria, baseburner **1,200.00**
Charter Oak, #580, cook stove, cast iron, missing reservoir . **1,100.00**
European, solid brass & copper, shroud w/45 tiles, 62″ **1,000.00**
Excelsior, pot belly, cast iron, sm globe **90.00**
Franklin, cast iron, w/brass finials, eagle, fruit, floral, 33x40″ . **150.00**
Garett Commander, #10, ci, 3 6-panel isinglass doors, 1865... **575.00**
Home Comfort, cooking range, grey & wht enamel **685.00**
Iron Railroad, galley stove, solid copper tank, 1920 .... **350.00**

Lawson Co, Victorian, #106, 26½x14½ **140.00**
Mammouth, wood heating, cast iron, salesman's sample **225.00**
OK Marrs, wood burning, cast iron, 2′ long **205.00**
Peoria Oak, #14, wood burning round **295.00**
Pot belly, dated Jan 8, 1897 .... **250.00**
  With fancy claw foot, cast iron........................ **105.00**
Round Oak, #16, heating stove, wood or coal **320.00**
  #18, wood burning, round, chrome trim **525.00**
  Restored, 18″ **995.00**
Universal, cook stove, porcelain, gr & ivory **150.00**
Victor Peninsular, #78, parlor stove, 8 doors, 74 pc isinglass, 65″ **2,250.00**
Windsor, gas, porcelain, baby blue & wht **300.00**

Strawberry Lustre Ware

Strawberry lustre is a general term for creamware decorated with hand painted strawberries, vines and tendrils, and pink lustre trim. It was made by many manufacturers in England in the 19th century, most of whom never marked their ware.

Chop plate, 10½″ dia.................................. **85.00**
Cup & saucer **200.00**
  Handleless, lg....................................... **85.00**
  Handleless, small **75.00**
Plate, 6¾″ dia **45.00**
  7½″ dia **50.00**

9½″	65.00
10″, 1820-40	125.00
Platter, 10½x8″ dia	50.00
Relish, shell shaped, 8¾″	95.00
Sauce dish, 5″ dia	35.00
Saucer, 5¾″	20.00
Sugar, covered, S shape	175.00
Vegetable dish, covered, octagonal	350.00
Waste bowl, 4¼x6½″ dia	125.00

Stretch Glass

Stretch glass, produced from the early 1900s until after 1930, was made in an effort to emulate the fine art glass of Tiffany and Carder. The glassware was sprayed with a special finish while still hot, and a reheating process caused the coating to contract, leaving a striated, crepe-like iridescence. Northwood, Imperial, Fenton and the United States Glass Companies were the largest manufacturers of this type of glass.

Basket, green, 10″	100.00
Bowl, blue, 2x6¾″	14.00
Blue, 3x10″	27.00
Blue, collar bottom, 2½x10¼″	16.00
Blue, paneled, 9¾″	28.00
Blue, paneled, rolled-in top, 8¾x1½″	20.00
Blue, rolled edge, 6″ dia	14.00
Blue, tree-bark foot, 2¾x9½″	25.00
Blue, w/underplate, gold encrusted etching, 10″ dia	35.00
Clear, amber irid, 3½x12″	36.00
Clear, amber irid, 3 ftd, 3¾x10″	30.00
Clear, amber irid, collar bottom, 3x10″	28.00
Green, flared, 2½x9½″	25.00
Green, paneled, 3½x8¼″	25.00
Bud vase, blue, 9¾″, pr	37.00
Blue, 11¾″	22.00
Candlestick, blue, 1¾″, pr	22.00
Blue, 9¾″, pr	37.00
Blue, Fenton, 8½″, pr	50.00
Green, 3½″, pr	25.00
Green, 9¾″, pr	45.00
Green w/wht trim, 9″, pr	70.00
Candy dish, blue, w/lid, 11¼″	33.00
Green, w/lid, 9½″	25.00
Car vase, gr	25.00
Card tray, blue, ftd	28.00
Cheese & cracker, Imperial, vaseline	35.00
Cheese & cracker set, green	32.00
Cheese stand, blue	14.00
Compote, blue, 4x5½″	20.00
Blue, 15 ribs, 2½x6½″	22.00
Blue, green scalloped top, Imperial, 8½″	55.00
Blue, Imperial, 8½″	50.00
Blue, laurel lead band, 4x5½″	20.00
Blue, rolled-in top, 22 ribs, 7½x5½″ dia	18.00
Green, deep, scalloped, 5¼x6½″	24.00
Dessert set, vaseline, 8 pc, Imperial	145.00
Dish, blue, log foot, 1½x11″	25.00
Fan vase, blue, 5x6″	25.00
Green ribbed 5½x5¼″	24.00
Goblet, green w/alabaster base, 7″	40.00
Mayonnaise, vaseline, w/underplate, Imperial	25.00
Mint dish, blue, tree bark foot, 3¼x6″	25.00
Plate, blue, 8″	14.00
Blue, 12-paneled, 11″ dia	35.00

Blue irid, 8¾″	17.50
Vaseline, Imperial, 8½″	20.00
Punchbowl, blue, flared, collar bottom, 11¾x5½″	50.00
Rose bowl, green irid, ruffled top	35.00
Sandwich server, green, center handled, 10½″ dia	30.00
Serving tray, vaseline, Imperial, 13½″	45.00
Vase, blue, flared rim, vertical stripe cutting, 10x3″ dia	50.00
Clear, Imperial, 5½x4¾″	55.00
Imperial, 6x5½″	65.00

String Holders

Today, if you want to wrap and secure a package, you have a variety of products to choose from: cellophane tape, staples, etc. But in the 1800s, string was about the only available binder; thus the stringholder---either the hanging or counter type---was a common and practical item found in most homes and businesses.

Apple, chalk	25.00
Ball Shape, iron, open design, 2 part	35.00
Beehive, cast iron, orig paint fair, lg	30.00
Cast Iron, w/claw feet, ornate	55.00
French Chef	15.00
Glass dome, Plantation Parmical Co, Memphis	145.00
Gypsy kettle, cast iron ftd, advertising Jaxon Soap	130.00
Love bird, porcelain	15.00
Mammy, blk woman's head, wall, plaster, 7½″	20.00

Mammy, N S Co, 6½″	50.00
Pear, chalk	25.00
Victorian lady, china, hanging wall type	15.00
Victorian, cast iron	35.00

Sugar Shaker

Sugar shakers, or muffineers as they were also called, were used during the Victorian era to sprinkle sugar and spice onto breakfast muffins, toast, etc. They were made of art glass, in pressed patterns, and in china.

Apple Blossom, gold top, pale gr to pale blue	42.00
White opal	90.00
Aster & Leaf, gr	90.00
Austria, gold top, pale yellow w/yellow flowers, gr leaves	37.50
Bavaria, gold top, clusters of orange & purple flowers, pale gr	35.00
Beatty Honeycomb, blue opalescent	125.00

Beatty Rib, wht opal 55.00
Blown Twist, gr 65.00
   White opal 65.00
Bulbous base, wht w/lavendar 110.00
Challinor's Forget-Me-Not, pink 110.00
Chrysanthemum base, cranberry opal, glossy 150.00
Cone, blue satin 75.00
   Green cased 75.00
   Pink cased 100.00
   Yellow satin 135.00
Cranberry Optic 85.00
Crystal, cut, 7″ 45.00
Enameled decor, blue gr Flemish type glass, MW 'Fig' ... 275.00
Erier Twist, satin 175.00
Findlay Onyx, platinum or cream 250.00
Floral & bird, hp, yellow case 65.00
Forget-Me-Not, gr 125.00
Frosted Rubina, Royal Oak 170.00
Gillinder Melon, blue satinized, yellow flowers 115.00
Glossy cranberry chrysanthemum, Reverse Swirl 165.00
Guttate, pink cased 125.00
Inverted Fern, cranberry 125.00
Jeweled Heart, apple gr 95.00
Lattice, ribbed, clear opal 60.00
Leaf Mold, cranberry spatter 175.00
   Pink & wht spatter, gold flakes 135.00
   Vaseline satin spatter 150.00
Leaf Umbrella, blue cased 165.00
   Cranberry spatter 185.00
Limoges, roses, gold top, hatpin shape 35.00
Longway, blue w/yellow, gr, cream, & mauve decor in enamel, 5″ 95.00
Melligo, blue opaque 70.00

Milk glass 35.00
Mt Washington egg, blue, enameling 235.00
   Orig paper label 250.00
Netted Oak, decorated milk 65.00
Nine panel, amethyst 80.00
Optic, Hobb's, rubina 95.00
Paneled Sprig, amethyst 110.00
Pansies, egg shape, porcelain 42.00
Parian Swirl, satin cranberry spatter 95.00
Quilted Phlox, gr cased 95.00
   Pale blue case 95.00
Reverse Swirl, cranberry opal 120.00

Vaseline opal 85.00
Rib Scrolled, blue 65.00
   Green 65.00
Ribbed Pillar, cranberry spatter 85.00
   Frosted pink & wht spatter 95.00
Ridge Swirl, amber satin 75.00
Ring Neck, cranberry optic 65.00
Roses, hp, gold top, ZS & Co Bavaria 35.00
Royal Ivy, frosted rubina 150.00
Royal Oak, frosted rubina 175.00
Rubina 95.00
Spatter glass, pink, wht orig top 50.00
Star & Frost, blk, 6½″ 250.00
Swirl, blue opal 75.00
Tin, straight sides, domed top, handled, 6″ 25.00
Tiny beading, pedestal base, Meridan silver plate, 5″ 40.00
Twelve Panels, cranberry, plated domed top 72.00
Wide waisted, canary 90.00
Windows, blue opal 130.00

Summit Art Glass

Summit Art Glass Company owned by Russell and Joanne Vogelsong of Mogadore, Ohio, are producers of a line of contemporary limited edition figurines, as well as quality reproductions of antique glass toothpicks, tumblers, salt dips, etc, made from molds once used by such companies as Northwood, U.S. Glass, and Gillinder and Sons. Their glass is marked with a V in circle.

Bell, Crown Jewel 35.00
   Melanie, first bell, Pink Carnival 50.00
Butter, covered, Panelled Holly, Red Amber Slag 50.00
Covered dish, dolphin w/fish, Strawberry Tangerine Slag, 7″ ... 35.00
   Rabbit, Red Amber Slag, 5½″ 30.00
   Robin w/cherry, Strawberry Tangerine Slag, 5½″ 25.00
Melanie, Canyon Whisper 18.00
   Christmas Dream 30.00
   Lavender Rhapsody 18.00
   Lime Fantasia 20.00
   Oriental Splendor 20.00
   Oriental Surprise 20.00
   Royal Odyssey 25.00
   St Patrick's Caper 20.00
   Tom's Surprise 50.00

Sunderland Lustre

Sunderland lustre was made by various potters in the Sunderland district of England during the 18th and 19th centuries. It is characterized by a splashed-on application of the pink luster, which results in an effect sometimes referred to as the 'cloud' pattern. Some pieces are transfer printed with scenes, ships, florals or portraits.

Bowl, house pattern, 3x6″ 60.00
Chalice, pink-lavender w/excellent mottling, knob stem, 1800s, 5¼″ 175.00
Cup & saucer, cloud pattern, pink 45.00
   Cloud w/copper lustre bands 65.00
   Hand painted fruit, panels, luster bands, ftd, 1840 ...... 45.00
   Wide luster band w/leave, multi color balls 42.00
Jug, Geribaldi, rifleman, 5½″ 235.00
Lamp, red w/ivory flowers, body of lamp 10½″ 65.00
Master salt, cloud pattern 25.00
Mug, 3″ 65.00
Plaque, copper luster trim, clipper ship transfer, 7½x8½″ ... 75.00

Ships, brown transfer, Bric, Polychrome, brown rim, 8½x9½" **85.00**

Thou God Sees' Me, blk transfer w/copper luster, 7½x8½" .. **50.00**

Plate, 7¼" **24.00**

Shaker, ftd, 4" **85.00**

Teapot, pink irid cloud design, ribbed top, base, 7" **200.00**

Syracuse

Syracuse was a line of fine dinnerware which was made for nearly a century by the Onondaga Pottery Company of Syracuse, New York. Collectors of American dinnerware are focusing their attention on reassembling some of their many lovely patterns. In 1966, the firm became officially known as the Syracuse China Company in order to better identify with the name of their popular chinaware. By 1971, dinnerware geared for use in the home was discontinued, and the company turned to the manufacture of hotel, restaurant and other types of commercial tableware.

Appleblossom, cup & saucer **12.50**

Dinner plate **9.50**

Platter **20.00**

Vegetable dish **16.00**

Arcadia, ashtray **17.00**

Relish dish **14.00**

Bracelet, service for 8 .... **490.00**

Candlelight, service for 12 .... **550.00**

Canterbury, plate, china, 9½" **4.00**

Jefferson, cup **9.00**

Salad plate **8.00**

Sugar & creamer **24.00**

June Rose, coffee pot **30.00**

June Rose, creamer **10.00**

Lady Mary, service for 4, 20 pc **200.00**

Nimbus, service for 6, 40 pc **400.00**

Selma, gravy & liner **24.00**

Sharon, cake plate, handled, 10" **10.00**

Service for 8, 40 pc **400.00**

Sherwood, candle holder **30.00**

Place setting, 5 pc **50.00**

Platter **49.00**

Vegetable dish **47.00**

Sweetheart, service for 8 .... **350.00**

Smoke set, 2 trays, cigarette holder **55.00**

Tapestries

Tapestries are woven textiles that often depict elaborate pictorial designs in rich colors. The earliest examples and some of the finest were made in France in the mid-1600s. Those on the market today are scarcely anything more than cheap imitations.

Arab, street scene, framed, 56x10" **52.00**

Belgian, garden scene, 19x52" **60.00**

English bull dog, child's blocks, spelling Sigars, 1910, 18" **45.00**

Four people, 4 dogs, 2 horses, 1 deer, machine woven, 48x76" **125.00**

German, hunting scene w/horses, people, dogs, & boar, 120x60" **80.00**

Indian, street scene w/camels, merchants, palaces, old, 17½x55" **150.00**

Victorian, court scene, dog, birds, 2½x1½' **80.00**

Tea Caddies

Because tea was once regarded as a precious commodity, special boxes called caddies were used to store the tea leaves. They were made from various materials, porcelain, carved and inlaid woods, and metals ranging from painted tin or tole to engraved silver. Today all are collected.

Black lacquered w/gilt, hinged lid, scenic, 1800s, 13½x10" ... **150.00**

Brass, dovetailed, raised base, upper molded edge, dome top ... **50.00**

Iron & silver, Japanese style, fluted base, sgnd AR, 1880, 6¼" **605.00**

Mahogany, Chippendale style, marquetry fan inlay, 5x4½x5" ... **95.00**

Papier mache, pewter inserts **100.00**

Porcelain, Peking, turquoise ground, flowers & vine decor, 4½x6" **45.00**

Wood, 2 part, red & yellow apple, stemmed, 5½" **45.00**

Tea Leaf Ironstone

Tea Leaf Ironstone became popular in the 1880s, when the American middle class housewives became bored with the plain white Stone china that English potters had been exporting to this country for nearly a century. The original design has been credited to Anthony Shaw of Longport, who decorated the plain Ironstone with a hand painted copper lustre design of bands and leaves. Originally known as 'Lustre Band and Sprig', the pattern has since come to be known as Tea Leaf Lustre. It was produced with minor variations by many different firms, both in England and the United States. By the early 1900s, it had become so commonplace that it had lost much of its appeal.

Bacon rasher **45.00**

Biscuit barrel, 7x8", plated lid & collar, ribbed **265.00**

Bone dish, set of 4 .... **220.00**

Bowl, 5½" sq, Lustre Meakin **27.50**

Bowl, 6¾x9½", Meakin **45.00**

Butter, 3 pc, Meakin **70.00**

Covered, Shaw **120.00**

Butter pat, Burguess **12.50**

Meakin **8.00**

Mellor & Taylor, pr **25.00**

Cake plate, 6 sided **95.00**

Square **45.00**

Chamber pot **40.00**

Wedgwood **175.00**

Coffee pot, bulbous, handled, lid & spout, sgnd Shaw, 58 oz ... **90.00**

Creamer, 5", Shaw **150.00**

6", Burgess **100.00**

6", Shaw **165.00**

Cup & saucer, Burgess, 1860s **50.00**

Copper luster, handleless **75.00**

Handled **40.00**

Wedgwood **75.00**

Dish, 4", sq, Meakin **15.00**

4", sq, Wilkinson **15.00**

Fruit bowl, 10" dia, copper luster, pedestaled, sgnd Shaw **245.00**

Gravy boat, w/underplate, Anthony Shaw **95.00**

Wilkinson **72.50**

Pitcher, 6", Shaw **65.00**

7", Powell Bishop **68.50**

Milk, Meakin **115.00**

Plate, 8", brown rim band, Meakin, 1897 .... **22.00**

8", Clemetson **12.50**

9", Burgess **25.00**

9¾", lily-of-the-valley blank, Shaw **55.00**

10", Meakin **17.00**

10", Shaw **16.00**

Platter, 12", Meakin **32.50**

14", Mercer Taylor **65.00**

14x10", Meakin **30.00**

14¾x10½", embossed lily-of-the-valley, Shaw **55.00**

16x11½", Meakin **32.00**

17½" **75.00**

Porridge dish, A Meakin **20.00**

Salt & pepper **50.00**
Sauce, covered, Shaw **195.00**
  Square, Wedgwood **15.00**
  Wilkinson **10.00**
Shaving mug, raised berry blank, Shaw **115.00**
Soap dish, open, rectangular, Meakin **25.00**
Soup ladle, 9″ **30.00**
Spooner, flat **50.00**
Sugar, Anthony Shaw **95.00**
  Clemetson **85.00**
  Covered, Meakin **75.00**
  Powell & Bishop **60.00**

Teapot, Alfred Meakin, 8″ **125.00**
  Gold **95.00**
Toothbrush holder **55.00**
Vegetable dish, covered, Mellor-Taylor **85.00**
  Covered, oblong **65.00**
  Covered, Shaw **120.00**
  Individual **18.00**
  Ribbed sides, deep, sq, open, Wilkinson **45.00**
  Wedgwood **90.00**

Teco

Teco artware was made by the American Terra Cotta and Ceramic Company, located near Chicago, Ill. The firm was established in 1886, and until 1901, produced only brick, sewer tile and other redware.

Their early glaze was inspired by the matt green made popular by Grueby, and for nearly ten years, 'Teco green' was made---similar to Grueby, yet with a subtle silver grey cast.

The company was one of the first in the United States to perfect a true crystalline glaze. The only decorating devices used were through the modeling and glazing techniques; no hand painting was attempted. Favored motifs were naturalistic leaves and flowers.

The company broadened their lines to include garden pottery, faience tiles and panels. New matt glazes---browns, yellows, blue and rose---were added to the green in 1910. By 1922, the artware lines were discontinued; the company closed in 1920.

Teco is usually marked with a vertical impressed device comprised of a large T to the left of the remaining letters.

Bowl, rolled rim, gr matt, 6½″ dia **45.00**
Pitcher, tiger eye glaze, mkd, 4x5″ **350.00**
Vase, 4 buttress handles, gr matt, mkd, 8x5½″ **335.00**

Deco shape, gr, yellow clay highlights show, 8¾x4″ **275.00**
Matt gr, glaze, 9½″ **140.00**
Molded leaves & flowers, gr, 9″ **125.00**
Oblate, tricorn top, gr, 4½″ **50.00**
Ovoid, gr, 6″ **60.00**
Squatty bottom, thin neck, flared top, 8″ **70.00**
Wide body, thin neck, wide lip, 8″ **95.00**

Teddy Bears

The story of Teddy Roosevelt's encounter with the bear cub has been oft' recounted---with varying degrees of accuracy---so it will suffice to say that it was as a result of this incident in 1902 that the Teddy Bear got his name.

These appealing little creatures are enjoying renewed popularity with collectors today. To one who has not yet succumbed to their obvious charms, one bear seems to look very much like another. How to tell the older ones? Look for long snouts, jointed limbs, large feet and felt paws, long curving arms, and glass or shoebutton eyes. Most old bears had a humped back and were made of mohair stuffed with straw or excelsior. Cute expressions, original clothes, and, off course, good condition add to their value.

3 advertising 1920s Kellogg's stuffed bears including Goldilocks **160.00**
Bells inside ears, growler works, 1940, 16″ **225.00**
Bongo Bear, Disney, Gund manufacturer, 12″ **75.00**
Brown, 35″ **850.00**
Bully Bear, sgnd **79.50**
Celluloid, 5″ **12.00**
English, gold mohair, leather pads, lg head, glass eyes, 1925 . . **130.00**
Fabric, shoe button eyes, pre 1920s, 10½″ **90.00**
Germany mkd on foot, jointed, 2½″ **140.00**
Ideal, 75th anniversary bear, 1978 . . . . **32.50**
Jointed, brown, 1930s, 14″ **50.00**
Jointed, dk brown, glass eyes, 2½″ **165.00**
Jointed, glass eyes, 1920-30s, 16″ **225.00**
Jointed, glass eyes, gold plush, orig Worlds Fair sticker, 1940 . **185.00**
Jointed, glass eyes, straw filled, lt brown, 15″ **140.00**
Jointed, gold mohair, hump, button eyes, long arms, 1907, 10½″ **350.00**
Jointed, gold plush, glass eyes **145.00**
Jointed, gold plush, padded paws, button eyes, 2½″ **195.00**
Jointed, high button shoes, 1920s, 22″ **150.00**
Jointed, humped, straw filled, glass eyes, 19½″ **250.00**
Jointed, straw filled, 12″ **115.00**
Jointed, straw filled, hump, chubby, 30″ **425.00**
Jointed, straw filled, hump, lg **300.00**
Jointed, straw stuffing, mohair, glass eyes, WWI, 32″ **245.00**
Jointed, very old, 9″ **65.00**
Jointed, wht plush, glass eyes, 4″ **335.00**
Lambs wool, jointed, 12″ **45.00**
Lt tan, 1903, 10″ **150.00**
Merrythoughts 'Cheeky', jointed, mohair, bells in his ears, 14″ . . **58.50**
Mohair, brownish, shoe button eyes, straw filled, pre 1920s, 14″ **150.00**
Mohair, dk brown, glass eyed, straw stuffed, hump, felt pads . . **850.00**
Mohair, gold, glass eyes, 1920-30s **225.00**
Mohair, gold, jointed, straw stuffed, antique clothes, 15″ **125.00**
Mohair, gold, lg hump, canvas nose, pre 1920, 18″ **225.00**
Mohair, gold, wool coat, shoe button eyes, straw filled, 13½″ . **150.00**
Mohair, honey, shoe button eyes, wide face, 1910, 14″ **350.00**
Mohair, jointed, hump, caramel color, Hermann, 12″ **48.50**
Mohair, jointed, hump, caramel color, Hermann, 16″ **60.50**
Mohair, shoe button eyes, straw stuffed, hump, long arms, 17″ **195.00**
Mohair, yellow, straw filled, on all 4's, long nose, 14x9½″ . . . **150.00**
Musical, jointed, straw filled, 16″ **235.00**
Musical, moveable legs, by Character **65.00**

On all fours, brown mohair, felt pads, glass eyes **325.00**
On iron wheels, cinnamon, early, 12″. **400.00**
On metal wheels, w/orig gr blanket, 20″. **750.00**
Petsy, cream color, old tag. **95.00**
Pieps cloth bear, cries, 13 cm **12.00**
Plush, coffee, sitting, glass eyes, button in ear **155.00**
Plush, gold, glass eyes, chubby, 4″ **165.00**
Plush, gold, glass eyes, jointed, high shoulders, Japan label, 1930s **45.00**
Plush, gold, hump, shoe button eyes, wht muzzle, 14″ **185.00**
Plush, wht wool, velvet pads, felt eyelids, glass eyes, 1930s, 11″ **185.00**
Regal, wht curly plush, wool pads, hump, glass eyes, 21½″ . . . **200.00**
Schuco, 3″ **40.00**
Smokey, no hat. **20.00**
Standing upright, printed pads, 35″ **150.00**
Two faced, jointed, gold plush, glass eyes, 3½″. **385.00**
US Zone Germany label, jointed, 3½″ **145.00**
Wool, brown, shoe button eyes, felt pads, straw filled, 26″. . . . **250.00**

Bank, blue, bib overalls, red neckerchief, pushing flower cart, 7x7½″ **20.00**
Bear Muff **95.00**
Book, A Frightened Baby, by Burgess, 1927 . . . . **85.00**
   Fairy Tales, & Fables, soft cover, 30 pages, 1923, Goldsmith . **85.00**
   Teddies, story of 3 brown bears & the wht one **25.00**
   The Traveling Bears in the East & West, hard cover, 62 pgs, Eaton **75.00**
Cardboard bear, roller skating, moving legs & arms, 13″ **235.00**
Cookbook, teddy bears baking school, 1906. . . . . **14.00**
Dish, child's, girl feeding teddy, Salem China, 9x7″. **37.50**
Dish, pressed glass, Roosevelt Bears, Dutch children around rim, 6″ **95.00**
Game, teddy bear target game, Parker, 1906, 18x20″. **635.00**
Glass eyes, on sticks for teddies, 12″ or under. **3.00**
Muff w/teddy bear **160.00**
Paper dolls, 5 outfits, Ottmon, 1900s, 10½″ **235.00**
Perfume bottle, jointed, gold plush, glass eyes, 4¾″ **195.00**
Pin cushion, tape measure tongue, 7″ **65.00**
Pitcher, water, Teddy Roosevelt bears, Buffalo Pottery, sgnd, 1907 **595.00**
Postcard, red embroidery valentine, 1908 . . . . **15.00**
Postcard, Roosevelt bear, 1908, set of 10. . . . . **99.00**
Puppet, Max & Moritz, felt faces. **100.00**
Puzzle, paper, 1909 . . . . **25.00**
   Teddy bear camp picture, thick pieces. **14.00**

Tip tray, Roosevelt bears, 1906, 5x3″. **70.00**
Quilt, matching feather pillow, child's, 1915 . . . . **65.00**
Spoon & fork, child's figural, ABC's on back, WB/B, 4½″. . . . **100.00**
Toothpick, w/2 teddies sitting in front, porcelain, German **85.00**

Telephones

Since Alexander Graham Bell's first successful telephone communication, the phone itself has undergone a complete evolution in styles as well as efficiency. Early models, especially those wall types with ornately carved oak boxes have become of interest to collectors. Also of value are the candlestick phones from the early part of the century.

American Bell, oak, wall type, crank, refinished. **225.00**
American Phone Co, candlestick **100.00**
B&O RR, walnut, wall type, scissor extension, mkd. **300.00**
Candlestick, 1900 . . . . **50.00**
   Black, 1908 . . . . **75.00**

   Black, 1930's, 13″. **75.00**
   Glass mouthpiece, extended terminal receiver, 16″. **265.00**
   No dial type, all orig, pat 1908 . . . . **65.00**
Coin box, drug store, 1940s. **60.00**
Crank phone, 1930. . . . . **15.00**
Danish, 1912 . . . . **55.00**
   Decophone **10.00**
   Desk phone, 1912 . . . . **50.00**
   With wood trim, locking door **85.00**
Fiddle back, wall type. **250.00**
Field phone **20.00**
Graybar, wall mount, double box, w/top bells **55.00**
Kellogg, candlestick, 1901 . . . . **70.00**
   Disk phone, w/oak dovetailed ringer box **65.00**
Pay phone, old **55.00**
Schuchsardt, wall type, brass earphone, Germany, 1935 . . . . . . **140.00**
Stromberg Carlson, candlestick **95.00**
   Desk phone, w/dovetailed oak ringer bell box **75.00**
   Double box, oak, wall **290.00**
Switchboard, wood **75.00**
Wall type, oak, lg **250.00**
   Oak, short mouth piece & arm, w/batteries. **275.00**
   Oak, sm **225.00**
Western Electric, oak, bell box, cradle desk phone **60.00**
   Oak, wall type, orig gold decal, crank, 9x20½″ **225.00**
   Scissor extender, 1909 . . . . **225.00**
   Wall type, oak **225.00**

Telescopes

Old telescopes are still appreciated for the quality of the workmanship and materials that went into their production. Some of the more elaborate styles were covered in leather or ebony and the 'draws' or expansions were often brass.

Double-draw, brass, day or night, enameled barrel, 32″ **240.00**
  Enamel barrel, 18″ **110.00**
  Leather barrel, 16½″ **110.00**
  Leather cover, 30″ **135.00**
Four-draw, brass, wood barrel, case, Dolland, London, 39″ ... **440.00**
Brass, 12½″ **58.00**
  Secrtan a Paris **1,900.00**
Single draw, brass, 36″ **160.00**
  Brass, braided cover, 1890, 30″ **275.00**
  Brass, Kelvin & Wilfrid, England, 31½″ **340.00**

Teplitz

Teplitz, in Czechoslovakia, was an active art pottery center at the turn of the century. One of the many firms who operated there was the Amphora Pottery Works. Art Nouveau and Art Deco styling was favored, and much of the ware was hand decorated, with the primary emphasis on vases and figurines. Most of the wares manufactured there bear the 'Teplitz' mark, or 'Turn', a nearby city.

Bowl vase, basket of grapes in high relief, 10x7″ **225.00**
Bud vase, rooster head medallion, multi color, handled, bohemia, 5½″ **85.00**
Bust, Cleo DeMerode, wht, gold & gr w/ivy design at base, 9″ **1,500.00**
Ewer, boy w/duck, grey & gr, Stellmacher, 9″ **130.00**
Pitcher, open handle, boy & goose, brown, lg **95.00**
  Open handle, girl & goose, gr, lg **98.00**
  Squatty, girl w/horn & dog, gr **65.00**
Plated, blk transfer, near Fishkill, Hudson River, Clews, 10½″ . **85.00**
Winter view, dk blue, Pittsfield, Mass, Clews, 8½″ **175.00**
Vase, blownout figure of lady in colonial dress w/parasol, 9½″ **185.00**
  Children at play, sgnd Imperial Amphora −1321, 10½″ **379.00**
  Girls, face, jeweled headdress, long hair, sgnd, 11″ **325.00**

Green, ivory, gold w/hp florals, 11″ **50.00**
Greenaway children, 4″, pr **130.00**
Irid blue w/grape cluster, 12″ **190.00**

Lillies, nude maiden emerging from 1 lily, Amphora, 17″ ... **495.00**
Molded female head & pansies, Crown Oakware, Nouveau, 12½″ **395.00**
Reticulated, mushroom motif, 11″ **465.00**
Shell Pattern, dk blue jewels, 9″, pr **450.00**
Thistles w/gold beading, blues & gr, Art Nouveau, 6″ **65.00**

Tiffany

Louis Comfort Tiffany was born in 1848 to Charles Lewis and Harriet Young Tiffany of New York. By the time he was 18, his father's small dry goods and stationery store had grown and developed into the world reknowned Tiffany and Company.

Preferring the study of art to joining his father in the family business, Louis spent the next six years under the tutelage of noted artists. He returned to America in 1870, and until 1875 painted canvases that focused on European and North African scenes. Deciding the more lucrative approach was in the application of industrial arts and crafts, he opened a decorating studio called Louis C. Tiffany & Co., Associated Artists. He began seriously experimenting with glass, and eschewing traditionally painted-on details, he instead learned to produce glass with qualities that could suggest natural textures and effects. His experiments broadened and he soon concentrated his efforts on vases, bowls, etc., that were considered the highest achievement of the art. Peacock feathers, leaves and vines, flowers and abstracts were developed within the plane of the glass as it was blown. Opalescent and metallic lustres were combined with transparent color to produce stunning effects. Tiffany called his glass Favril, meaning hand made.

In 1900, he established Tiffany Studios, and in addition to his art glass, turned his attention full time to producing leaded glass lamp shades and household wares with metal components. He also designed a complete line of jewelry which was sold through his father's store. He became proficiently accomplished in silver work and produced such articles as hand mirrors embellished with peacock feather decor set with gems, and candlesticks with Favrile glass inserts.

Tiffany's work exemplified the Art Nouveau style of design and decoration, and through his own flamboyant personality and business acumen he perpetrated his tastes onto the American market to the extent that his name became a household word. Tiffany Studios continued to prosper until the second decade of this century, when changing tastes began to diminish his influence, and by 1920 the company had closed.

Serial numbers were assigned to much of his work, and letter prefixes indicated the year of manufacture: A-N for 1896-1900; P-Z for 1901-1905. After that the letters followed the numbers with A-N in use from 1906-1912; P-Z from 1913-1920. O marked pieces were made especially for friends or relatives; X indicated pieces not made for sale.

In the listings that follow, TS is to indicate Tiffany Studios; LCT-F, L.C. Tiffany, Favrile; and T/C is Tiffany and Company.

Ashtray, bronze, set of 3, nested, oval, TS, 1859 .... **125.00**
  Bronze, w/matchholder **60.00**
  Silvered bronze, enamel leather & nailhead decor, TS, 5″ dia **75.00**
Ashtray/matchsafe, bronze, Nautilus pattern, fish decor, sgnd, #d **325.00**
  Bronze, w/clover motif, TS **225.00**
Blotter corners, Zodiac, TS **120.00**
Blotter ends, Zodiac, long, TS **150.00**
Bon-bon, gold, ruffled, sgnd, 4½″ **250.00**
Bowl vase, amber irid millefiori blossoms, LCT-F, 7″ dia ... **1,600.00**
  Amber irid, millefiori blossoms, LCT-F, 7¼″ **1,600.00**
  Amber irid w/gr vines, bulging, w/lobed neck, LCT-F, 6″ dia **660.00**
  Blue, gentle swirl effect, LCT-F, #d, 2¾x7″ dia **895.00**
  Blue & gold irid, scalloped edges, LCT-F, #d, 2½x7″ dia ... **450.00**
  Blue irid, free-form, scalloped, sgnd & #d, 2x4″ **200.00**
  Dore bronze, rondels around edge, LCT Furnace, #d, 10″ dia **300.00**
  Gold irid, dimpled, rainbow hi-lites, intaglio leaves, LCT, 3x7″ dia **795.00**

Gr irid shading, wht feathered underside, LCT-F, #d, 12″ dia **895.00**

Pink irid w/opal stripes, stretched scalloped rim, 7″ dia **335.00**

Box, bronze, simple design, 1x5½x3½″ **140.00**

Cigar, Dore bronze, hinged, wood lined, Indian design, mkd **335.00**

Cigarette, bronze, Venetian, cedar lined, ermines on base, 5½″ dia **375.00**

Desk, Zodiac, TS.......................... **150.00**

Engraved lid & sides, gold wash interior, 3½″ dia........ **230.00**

Handkerchief, Dore bronze, Zodiac, 6x6″ **235.00**

Silver, cedar lined, T/C **280.00**

Stamp, Zodiac pattern, gr/brown patina, sgnd & #d **175.00**

Butter pat, blue, scalloped, sgnd, 3″ **185.00**

Gold irid, star-shaped dish, sgnd, 3″ dia **125.00**

Calendar holder, carmel glass, Grapevine pattern, TS, #d, 8x6¾″ **165.00**

Candelabra, bronze & glass, 4-branch, pr **2,100.00**

Candlesticks, bronze, w/bright gr Favrile cups, spread ft, TS, 17″, pr **825.00**

Candy dish, silver, leaf shape.......................... **128.00**

Clip, desk, Dore bronze, American Indian pattern **135.00**

Clock, desk, Dore bronze, Zodiac, TS **475.00**

Travel alarm, beaded front, in case, T/C **185.00**

Cocktail shaker, silver, acid-etched scene, T/C, 7½″ **605.00**

Compote, amber irid, widely flared, gilt-bronze ft, LCT Furnaces, 10″ **600.00**

Amber, Colonial pattern, 3½″ **275.00**

Gold stretch irid, rainbow colors, LCT, #d, 2¼x4½″ dia ... **300.00**

Gr pastel, intaglio Vintage pattern, sgnd, 6¼″ **650.00**

Pale gr crystal, ribbed, aqua crystal ft, sgnd & #d, 2½x4″ dia **125.00**

Pink w/irid, stretched edge, rice grain decor, LCT-F, 6x6″ dia **750.00**

Cup, gold w/applied lily-pad decor, teacup size **300.00**

Silver, baby's, ornate engraving, Dec 25, 1875, T/C........ **195.00**

Desk set, Dore bronze, cobalt jewel studded, 4-pc.......... **550.00**

Dore bronze, Zodiac, 12-pc, sgnd.................. **1,750.00**

Gilt bronze, Indian pattern, 7-pc, TS, #d **660.00**

Dish, Dore bronze, w/abstract raised border, TS, 9″ dia **85.00**

Dore bronze, floral border, 9″ dia................... **100.00**

Finger bowl, pastel yellow opal, LCT, #d **150.00**

Finger bowl & underplate, Queen's pattern, both sgnd LCT ... **475.00**

Gold Favrile, Ascot pattern, sgnd.................... **250.00**

Gold irid, intaglio Vintage pattern, LCT-F.............. **325.00**

Flower arranger, opalene, LCT-F, 2½x4″ dia base **225.00**

Flower bowl & frog, amber irid w/trailing leaves, LCT-F **780.00**

Frame, bronze, Adams pattern, sgnd & #d, 9x12″ **425.00**

Fruit bowl, LCT-F, #d, 10″ dia **300.00**

Gold, ribbed, sgnd & #d, 10″ dia **700.00**

Goblets, wine, set of 12, LCT **1,300.00**

Humidor, bronze w/gr Favrile panels, Pine Needle pattern, ovoid, 7″ **880.00**

Gr marble base, grapevine design, #30 .... **300.00**

Pine Needle pattern, w/irid glass insert, TS.............. **290.00**

Zodiac, large, TS..................................... **195.00**

Zodiac, small, TS **135.00**

Inkwell/pen tray, bronze, w/clover motif, wht liner, 9x6″ **295.00**

Jewelry, bracelet, 14k, amethyst, pearls, turquoise, diamonds **1,800.00**

Earrings, pendant, 18k, in case **1,750.00**

Ring, diamond, 18k, ¾ carat canary, in case **2,500.00**

Pendant, dragonfly.............................. **1,200.00**

Jug, silver, T/C, 1870, 5½″ **465.00**

Lamps

3 gold irid ribbed shades, metal base, sgnd, 22″ **3,500.00**

Acorn 16″ shade, on Cat's Paw adjustable base, all sgnd ... **4,450.00**

Base, bridge, gilt-bronze, harp-form support, w/5 spade ft, 4′9″ **715.00**

Bridge, heart-shaped & arched-tripod supports, gilt bronze, 4½′ **800.00**

Bronze, 6-light, 4 ftd quatrefoil, gr/brown patina, 31″ **6,600.00**

Bronze, slender paneled standard on domed ft, TS, 21″ **880.00**

Floor, bronze, simple standard, dished circular base, 3′5″ . **2,200.00**

Floor, gilt-bronze, scrolling tendrils, 4 lug ft, 5′ **3,850.00**

Bridge, acorn shade, Dore bronze base w/slender post, lily pad ft **3,200.00**

Cased pink shade w/irid waves, bronze base, TS, 4½′ **3,190.00**

Favrile glass & gilt-bronze, counter-balance, 4′7″ **715.00**

Candle, blue irid swirled base, blue/gr ruffled shade, 13″ **950.00**

Gold Favrile base w/metal insert, amber glass dome, TS .. **1,450.00**

Queen's Lace bronze base, diamond quilted shade, 24″... **1,800.00**

Candlestick, w/pulled feather design, sgnd, 13″ **995.00**

Daffodil shade, bronze base, both mkd, 20″ dia **12,000.00**

Desk, curved bronze arm holds ruffled gold irid shade, 8″ . **1,075.00**

Ochre panels, gravepine openwork, gilt-bronze base w/inset tiles **1,980.00**

Ribbed domed amber shade, bronze Zodiac base, 17x7″ dia **1,700.00**

Dragonflies & jewels on gr opal, gilt-bronze base, 33x22″ dia **41,800.00**

Dragonfly shade, reticulated bronze base, 20″ dia **21,000.00**

Floor, dogwood shade fractured ground, bronze base, 62″ .. **22,000.00**

Greek Key border shade, circular ftd gilt-bronze base, 5′3″ **15,400.00**

Geometric gr leaded 14″ shade, on 3-light base, sgnd & #d . **2,400.00**

Mottled opal gr tiles, bronze base, 22x16″ dia **3,850.00**

Hanging, brass, w/2 shades, sgnd **200.00**

Brass, w/4 shades, sgnd **300.00**

Harp base, w/gold Aurene shade, all sgnd............... **1,450.00**

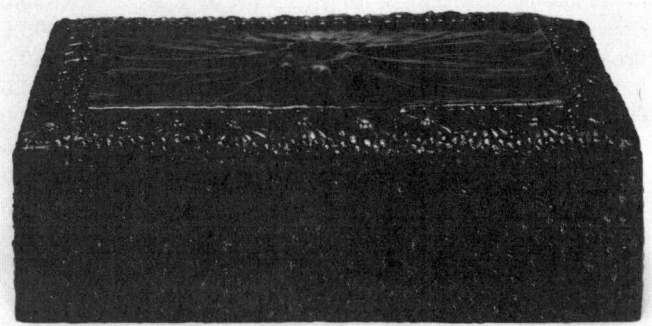

Bronze, hinged lid & cedar inner lid, lined, 9″ long **2,310.00**

Dore bronze, Zodiac pattern, sgnd, 6x6¼x2½″ **225.00**

Inkwell, bronze, Abalone pattern, sgnd & #d **215.00**

Bronze, dolphin on marble base, shell-shaped cover, 6x5″ .. **189.00**

Bronze, Pine Cone pattern, mottled gr, ball ft **359.00**

Dore bronze, Adams pattern, oval, TS **190.00**

Dore bronze, Medallion pattern, enamel background, TS ... **375.00**

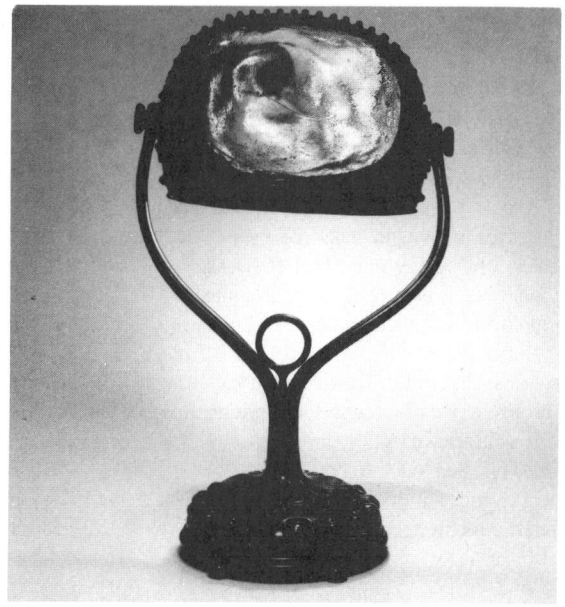

Irid turtleback tiles, Y-base w/gr glass jewels, bronze, 13″... **2,310.00**

Iris pattern 18″ shade, bronze base #318, all sgnd, 24″ **1,800.00**

Leaded shade w/gr & orange acorns, sgnd **3,400.00**

Lotus, Favrile glass & bronze, TS, 23x26″ dia........... **13,200.00**
Murano shade, gr w/pink hi-lites, bronze base, LCT & TS, 13½″ **2,586.00**
Oil, bronze base w/inset tiles, shade w/turtleback tiles **5,000.00**
Peonies decor shade, bronze 4-legged base, finial, TS, 25x18″ dia **2,200.00**
Piano, bronze leaf-molded base, 3 stems, amber irid lily shades **2,750.00**
Pomegranate shade, w/wht & pink tiles, bronze base, 21″ .. **4,675.00**
Poppies & filigree on opal gr ground, bronze base, 26x20″ dia **34,100.00**
Poppies on striated gr ground, bronze base, TS, 22x17″ dia **2,200.00**
Table, 12-light, gold Favrile lily shades, bronze etched base, 19″ **9,500.00**
   Dragonfly decor on 21″ dia shade **10,000.00**
   Geranium decor shade on turtle-back tile base, all sgnd, 17″ **13,000.00**
   Kerosene, gold Damascus stretched shade, gold base, 17″. **2,300.00**
   Pink & gold shade, bronze base, all sgnd **5,000.00**
Wild Rose shade w/mottled, peach & gr, 23x16″ dia...... **17,500.00**

Letter opener, Dore bronze, American Indian pattern **70.00**
Letter rack, Dore bronze, 3 sections, grapevine decor, 6x10″ . **365.00**
   Dore bronze, Nautical pattern, dolphins, shell center, sgnd .. **375.00**
   Zodiac pattern, TS **190.00**
Lily pad, enamel over bronze, LCT, 2½″ dia............. **475.00**
Memo pad holder, Dore bronze, Graduate pattern, TS, #d, 7x4″ **110.00**
   Zodiac pattern, TS **160.00**
Napkin holder, metal over copper, round, #1194 .... **35.00**
Nut dish, dk blue irid, ribbed & flared, sgnd, 1x3″ dia **350.00**
   Gold bowl-shape, 4 ft, sgnd, 1½x2¼″ dia............. **150.00**
Paper clip, carmel glass, Grapevine pattern, TS, #d, 3¾x2½″. **135.00**
Paperweight, bronze, bulldog, sgnd & #d **325.00**
   Carmel glass, Grapevine pattern, TS, #d, 3¾″ dia **125.00**
Parfait, blue w/rice grain, stem, sgnd, 6½″ **500.00**
Pen tray, Zodiac pattern, TS, 10″ **95.00**
Pencil, silver, floral repousse, type to hang on chain, T/C **120.00**
Pencil sharpener, sterling silver **35.00**
Pepper shaker, gold irid, silver top, LCT-F, 2¾″ **175.00**
Perfume bottle, ribbed, octagonal stopper, sgnd, 6″ **585.00**
   Silver, tiny flask shape **28.00**
   Traveling, intaglio decor, sterling connectors, 7″ **145.00**
Pitcher, gold luster, w/green leaf decor, LCT-F, 9x5½″ dia . **3,800.00**
Planter, green marble base w/grapevine design, TS, 4x11″ ... **450.00**
Plate, Dore bronze, w/Greek border, 9″ **90.00**
   Enameled bronze, LCT Furnaces, 11¼″................ **325.00**
Platter, Dore bronze, rondels around edge, LCT Furnace, #d, 12″ **210.00**
Pocket knife; blade, cork screw & bottle opener, 14k, T/C.... **100.00**
Powder box, silver, engraving on lid & sides, 4x3″ **200.00**
Punch cup, blue w/curly snails, stemmed **405.00**
   Gold w/spreading hollow stem, 3½x3¼″ dia............. **165.00**
Rocker blotter, Zodiac, TS **100.00**
Rose bowl, gold w/leaves & vine decor, LCT-F #d, 3″ **775.00**
   Gold w/leaves & vines in relief, LCT #5699A, 3″ **1,900.00**
Salt, master, wht opal & gold, LCT-F, 3½x2″ **115.00**
   Open, gold irid w/blue & silver hi-lites, pinched **150.00**
   Open, gold irid w/ruffled edge, LCT-F #1256 .... **175.00**
   Open, amber irid Favrile, crimped rims, set of 12 .... **900.00**
Sconces, brass, olive irid shade w/gold irid feathering, #d, 16″, pr **1,430.00**
   Dore bronze & Favrile w/amber irid prisms, unsgnd, 15″, pr **1,210.00**
Shot glass, gold irid, barrel w/threading around center, 1¾″ .. **135.00**
   Gold irid, pinched sides, sgnd, 1¾″ **140.00**
Tazza, amber irid, flared intaglio rim, lappet-form stem, 10″ .. **825.00**
   Decorated pink stretch border, LCT-F, 6¾″............. **375.00**
   Green w/leaf decor, stretch border, LCT-F, 6¼″ **325.00**
Teething ring, silver **35.00**
Thermometer, Dore bronze, Abalone pattern, 9″ **175.00**
Tile, blue irid, patent applied for, 4x4″ **125.00**
   Pressed glass, green, 4x4″ **55.00**
   Opal, 4x4″ **35.00**

   Red, 4x4″ **75.00**
Tobacco jar, Pine Needle pattern, w/insert, brown patina **195.00**
Toothpick holder, gold w/dimples, sgnd & #d **125.00**
Tray, brass, #d, 12″ **75.00**
   Brass, cut-out pattern, marbleized glass bottom, sgnd, 3½x9″ **195.00**
   Dore bronze, sgnd, 12″ dia **200.00**
Tumbler, gold, purple & pink, center threads, corset shape, LCT, 4″ **295.00**
Urn, Egyptian, gold Murano, reactive zipper, rainbow, 9½″ . **1,800.00**
Vase, aqua w/brown & gold marbleized areas, irid, LCT, #d, 6¼″ **2,250.00**
   Blue & green irid stripes, bronze band, 4 owls, 9″........ **1,500.00**
   Blue & purple hi-lites, pinched, lattice work, LCT-F, 4″ **950.00**
   Blue irid, ribbed, thin, 3″.......................... **310.00**
   Blue irid, ribbed round body, thin neck, flared top, 6″ **550.00**
   Blue w/millefiori decor, raised vines, TGD Co, LCT-F, 8″ . **1,750.00**
   Brown Favrile, LCT-F, 19″.......................... **3,250.00**
   Dk green over lt green opal base, silver/gold trim, irid, LCT, 7″ **2,300.00**
   Emerald green Favrile, squat, lappet shoulder band, unsgnd, 2½″ **440.00**
   Favrille, paperweight, daffodil, LCT-F, 15″ **2,100.00**
   Favrille, trumpet, mkd, 10″ **1,300.00**
   Flower form, gold irid, rainbow hi-lites, ribbed ft, sgnd, 10¼″ **1,350.00**
   Flower form, green feathers on opal, gold interior, sgnd, 11½″ **1,450.00**
   Flower form, green & wht, deep ruffles, short stem, 4½″ ... **775.00**
   Flower form, irid w/feathering, gold foot sgnd, 15″ **3,750.00**
   Flower form, gold w/blue-purple-pink inside of top, 11″ .. **2,500.00**
   Flower form, sgnd & #d, 17″ **1,500.00**
   Flower form, amber irid Favrile, waisted cup, crenated rim, 11″ **935.00**
   Garnet red, decorated, LCT-F, 3½″ **2,300.00**
   Gold, cone shape, thick round base, sgnd, 3″ **300.00**
   Gold, w/blue irid, pinched lattice top, sgnd, 4″ **1,000.00**
   Gold, w/green heart-leaves, bowl shape, sgnd, 2¾″ **675.00**
   Gold, w/wht paperweight flowers, intaglio foliage, LCT-F, 15½″ **2,250.00**
   Gold aurene, trumpet w/bronze base, LCT, 12″ **700.00**
   Gold cypriote, pinched sides, 6½″ **500.00**
   Gold irid, deep free form ribbing, sgnd & #d, 5¼″ **385.00**
   Gold irid, flared shape, fluted, sgnd, 6″ **600.00**
   Gold irid, heart shaped leaves, bowl shape w/collar, 2½″ ... **675.00**
   Gold irid, ped, flared rim, sgnd, 4″ **340.00**
   Gold irid, ribbed trumpet w/Dore bronze holder, TS, 10¾″ . **385.00**
   Gold irid, ribbed w/deep ribbed flare top, 6″ **585.00**
   Gold irid, rounded band at top, handled base, sgnd, 2″ **185.00**
   Gold irid, sgnd & #d, 3x2¾″ **330.00**
   Gold irid, sgnd, in unsgnd Dore bronze pineapple holder, 10″ **485.00**
   Gold irid, Thorn pattern, LCT #W1236, 5″ **625.00**
   Gold irid w/green & blue horizontal stripe, bowl form, LCT, 3″ **245.00**
   Gold irid w/pulled green irid flames, sgnd & d, 8″ **550.00**
   Green & gold, ribbed, #5521, 9½″ **695.00**
   Green w/feather design, flared rim, 6″ **1,450.00**
   Irid feathers, LCT #B2372, 10½″ **4,600.00**
   Opal w/gold feathers, ped ft, 8″...................... **545.00**
   Opaque green w/irid gold plumes, cobalt & gold 'eyes', 24″ **4,200.00**
   Overlay, brown cut to wht, wafer pontil, LCT-F, 8″ **2,100.00**
   Peacock blue, LCT-F, 9¾″ **525.00**
   Peacock blue millefiori, sgnd TGD Co & LCT-F **1,500.00**
   Pottery, brown crystalline drip over tan hi-gloss, 6½″ **385.00**
   Ivory w/green, molded florals, LCT #7, 8x5″ **575.00**
   Molded grape clusters, green glaze, sgnd **350.00**
   Wht bisque, tan hi-lites, molded leaves, 5″ **295.00**
   Red Favrile, spherical w/cylinder neck, LCT-F, 12″ **4,400.00**
   Rock crystal, carved florals, upper & lower handle, LCT, 7″. **825.00**
   Silver, decorated cylinder, 3 bamboo & paw supports, T/C, 6¾″ **770.00**
   Leaf engraving around top, ped ft, 8″ **235.00**
   Reticulated, w/orig cranberry liner, 1902, T/C, 8″ **395.00**
   Trumpet, T/C, 20″ **1,250.00**
   Teal blue, trumpet, w/silver casement base, LCT-F, 18″... **1,200.00**

Wht w/gold luster, green & gold feather, bronze holder, 15″ **1,025.00**

Tiffin Glass

The Tiffin Glass Company was founded in 1887, in Tiffin, Ohio, one of the many factories composing the U.S. Glass Company. Its early wares consisted of tablewares and decorative items such as lamps and globes. Among the most popular of all Tiffin wares was the black satin glass produced there during the 1940s. In 1959, U.S. Glass was sold, and in 1962, the factories were closed. The plant was re-opened in 1963, as the Tiffin Art Glass Company. They produced tableware, handblown stemware, and other decorative items.

Candlestick, blk satin, 8¼″, pr **65.00**
   Twisted, w/matching bowl, Peachblow, 8½″ **210.00**
   Vaseline satin, twist stem, bell bottom, 9½″ **35.00**
Champagne, flanders crystal, #024 . . . . **12.00**
   Persian pheasant crystal, #037 . . . . **14.00**
Cocktail, Beains Byzantine, mandrin yellow w/crystal **12.00**
   Flanders mandrin yellow w/crystal, #024 . . . . **10.00**
Compote, vaseline satin, twist stem, 7½″ **45.00**
Goblet, Beains Byzantine, mandrin yellow w/crystal **16.00**
   Cherokee Rose, beaded stem, 9 oz **22.00**
   Lafleur mandrin yellow w/crystal, #024 . . . . **18.00**
Iced tea glass, Cherokee Rose, beaded stem, 10½ oz **22.00**
Parfait, mandrin yellow & crystal, #65 . . . . **14.00**
Plate, Beains Byzantine, mandrin yellow w/crystal, 8″ **7.00**
   Flanders crystal, 8″ **6.00**
   Lafleur mandrin yellow w/crystal, 7¼″ **4.50**
Rose bowl, vaseline color **70.00**
Saucer champagne, Beains Byzantine, mandrin yellow w/crystal . **12.00**
   Champagne, Cherokee Rose, beaded stem, 5½ oz **18.50**
Sundae, Lafleur mandrin yellow w/crystal, #024, 4½″ **11.00**
Tumbler, Beains Byzantine, mandrin yellow w/crystal, ftd, 5½″ . **10.00**
Water glass, ftd, flanders mandrin yellow w/crystal, 4¾″ **10.00**

Vase, topaz, blue handles, fish, pearly, 8″ **175.00**

Tiles

Though originally strictly functional, tiles were being produced in various colors and used as architectural highlights as early as the Ancient Roman Empire. By the 18th century, Dutch tiles were decorated with polychrome landscapes and figures. During the 19th century, there were over a hun-

dred companies in England involved in the manufacture of tile; and by the Victorian era, the use of decorative tiles had reached its peak. Special souvenir editions, campaign and portrait tiles, and Art Nouveau motifs with lovely ladies and stylized examples from nature were popular. Today, these are very collectible.

Baron Limoges, pate-sur-pate, nude, 5½x6½″ **265.00**
Batchelder, castle & knight on horse, blue & gr, 6″ **65.00**
   Stylized tree decor on matt ground, hexagon, 3½″ **65.00**
Chelsea, molded female profile, high glaze, beige ground, 1881, 6x6″ **125.00**
Claycraft, Aztec design, 6x8″ **65.00**

   Cottage and bridge, 12x6″ **125.00**
   LA, mission scene on terra cotta, 6″ **40.00**
Grueby, candlestick decor, gr, wht & yellow matt glaze, 6x6″ . **200.00**
   Ship decor, gr matt glaze, 6x6″ **250.00**
Hamilton, male, female Grecian heads, brown, Mueller, 6″, pr . **200.00**
Jones-McDuffle, calendar, 1907 . . . . **55.00**
Jones-McDuffee & Stratton, calendar, J Hancock House, Boston, 1900 **45.00**
Kensington, female head w/scarf, lt brown, 1885, 6x6″ **150.00**
   Female head, gr, Mueller, 1885, 6x6″ **150.00**
Minton, historical tile, Trinity Church **50.00**
Pate-sur-pate, nude dancer **190.00**
Wedgwood, calendar, 1913-18 . . . . **55.00**
   Calendar, US Frigate, constitution, US battleship, 1911 . . . . . . **45.00**

Tinware

In the American household of the 17th and 18th centuries, tinware items could be found in abundance, from food containers to footwarmers and mirror frames. Although the first settlers brought much of their tinware with them from Europe, by 1798, sheets of tinplate were being imported from England for use by the growing number of American tinsmiths.

Tinwares were often decorated, either by piercing or painted designs, which were both freehand and stenciled. (See Toleware) By the early 1900s, many homes had replaced their old tinwares with the more attractive aluminum and graniteware.

Bathtub, w/high back, round **82.00**
Betty lamp, on stand, late, 9½″ **90.00**
Body flask, contoured, 7½x11½″ **15.00**
Box, hinged top & ends, for smoking accessories, 5x2x1″ **80.00**
   Lunch, oval, hinged door, Victorian child w/Mr Beetle, German **85.00**
Broom holder, embossed blue jays, Marcos Blue Jay, 1910 . . . . . **75.00**
Bucket, squared handle, wood grip, factory made **30.00**
Cake mold, 10x3″ **18.00**
Cake pan, tube, fluted, 8″ **10.00**
Candle holder, 5½″ **12.00**
Candle holder, saucer, w/snuffer, 4x8½″ dia **125.00**
Candle lantern, folds, mica panel, hinged compartment, mkd, 5¼″, pr **90.00**
Candle light, Christmas tree, 8 colored-glass panels, 3¼″, pr . . **100.00**
Candle maker, Pat Drummond, 1846, 8″ **435.00**

Some blue asphaltum remaininng, Pat Drummond, 1846, 8″ **395.00**
Candle mold, good handle, 12 tube, 10″ **38.00**
Dispenser, handmade, soldered, 1890, 5x3″ dia **14.00**
Document box, painted, w/key, 5x12x8″ **25.00**
Dustpan, tinner-made, star-punched center, handle **28.00**
Fly sprayer, quick loader **7.50**
Footwarmer, diamond pattern, pierced, orig wood holder **120.00**
Funnel, w/hanging loop **7.00**
Hot water bottle, w/screw cap, oval w/oval top lid, 7x10″ **15.00**
Ladyfingers pan, factory mkd **38.00**
Lamp, saucer base, acorn font, double spout, pr **220.00**
Lamp, stove shape, red glass in fire box door, mkd: Pollite Bijou, 6½″ **55.00**
Lard lamp font, blk, 4½″ **145.00**
Loaf pan, lid, 4 section, 22x13″ **25.00**
Meal funnel, maple, dovetailed 4 corners, 1860 . . . . **55.00**
Measure, handled, mug shape, 4¼x5¾″ **35.00**
Milk can, w/lid, bail, 1 gal **15.00**

Mold, bread or pudding, hinged, 9x11″ **35.00**
    Crimped edge, handle, 3½″ **14.00**
Muffin tin, shell & maple designs, early 1900s, 12½x9½″ **18.00**
Mug, shaving, handle, w/side compartment, 4½″ **68.00**
Oil can, hand made, cone shape w/hanging loop, 6″ **14.00**
Pail, lunch, integral cup, 3 part **45.00**
    Lunch, miner's, cup lid, bail, inside food tray **80.00**
    Lunch, round, wire bail, 5″ deep, 6½″ dia **18.00**
    Milk, round, late 1800s **30.00**
    Milk, slantside, brown, late 1800s **35.00**
Pan, baker's baking, tin heart, 1890s, 13x11″ **50.00**
Pastry board, w/rolling pin cradle, 22x18½″ **150.00**
Plate, portrait of woman holding lg jug, 10″ **35.00**
Stagecoach horn, Paducah, Ky. to Jackson, Tenn. route, early . **135.00**
Sugar shaker, handled, 4″ **30.00**
    Small handled, cylinder shape, plain circular foot, early 1800s, 2¼″ **27.00**
Toddy pot, rum warmer, wood disc handle, slant sides, 1840, 8″ **120.00**
Wall pocket, ornate scalloping, hand punched, 1872, 20x15½x3½″ **135.00**
Water can, At & S Fry, 1 gal **25.00**
Whale oil lamp filler, cone shaped, angled goose neck spout, 1850 **75.00**

Tobacciana

Tobacciana is the generally accepted term used to cover that field of collecting that includes smoking pipes, cigar moulds, cigarette lighters,

humidors—in short, any article having to do with the practice of using tobacco in any form.

Tobacco tin-tags, strips of metal attached to a plug of tobacco for means of brand identification, are becoming popular collectibles, expecially those featuring animals or political and patriotic themes. It is estimated that over 12,000 brands were produced.

Perhaps the most collectible variety of pipes are the Meerschums—hand carved from a clay-like medium formed by the action of the water on disintegrating sea shells on the ocean floor. Their figural bowls often portray an elaborately carved mythological character, an animal or a historical scene. Amber is often used for the stem. Other collectible pipes are corn cob (Missouri Meeschaums) and Indian peace pipes of clay or callinite.

Chosen because they introduced the white man to smoking, the cigar store Indian was a symbol used to identify tobacco stores in the 19th century. The majority of them were hand carved between 1830 and 1900, and are today recognized as some of the finest examples of early wood sculptures. When found, they command very high prices.

Ashtray, iron, eagle **21.00**
    With built in cigar cutter & match box holder, brass, Osmundo **150.00**
    Brass monkey, tail cuts, 5″ **225.00**
    Cast iron, blk woman w/basket on head, 2 pc, 5¼″ **40.00**
    Open mouth blk baby on chamber pot, metal, 6″ **20.00**
    With attached match holder, hp acorns, porcelain **90.00**
    With pipe holder, top is woman w/spread skirt, bottom bare behind **45.00**

Bottle, cigar-shape, amber glass, 5½″ **50.00**
Cigar box label, Sea Robins **3.00**
Cigar box opener, nail puller, United Cigar Stores Co **17.00**
    Nickel plate, double tapper, Beam-Dean Co **30.00**
    Nickel plate, double tapper, Coony Bayer **23.00**
    Wood handle, double tapper, Muriel Cigar **30.00**
Cigar box, dovetailed wood, advertising, 1½x14x7″ **25.00**
    Treaty Bond varieties, w/map of La. Purchase, 14x7x1½″ **27.50**
    With bottle opener, Dry Slitz, The Leading Stogie **6.00**
Cigar case, ivory, engraved silver hinges, Russian **185.00**

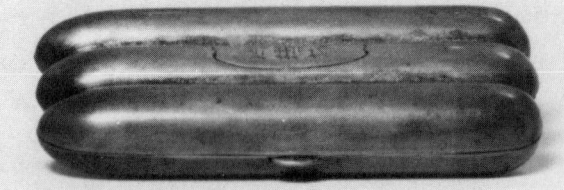

    Sterling, gilt overlay inside, for 3 cigars, 2.4 oz **60.00**
Cigar clipper, cast iron, 'Little Minister Cigars' **295.00**
    Clockwind mechanism, cast iron, Eastabrook & Eaton, 1890 **275.00**
    Scissors type, attaches to watch chain, embossed dragon **28.00**
Cigar cutter, bowing man w/top hat & tails, head turns, 8″ . . . **685.00**
    Brass cylinder, decorated, vest pocket size **18.00**
    Brass w/tortoise shell sides, loop for chain **25.00**
    Brass, styled after ships telegraph, 6″ **120.00**
    Brass, tortoise **27.50**
    Cliquot advertising, mechanical brass bottle figural **22.00**
    Counter type, mechanical, Schartz & Sons **135.00**
    Dog's head **62.00**
    Double cut, depress top, Erie Speciality Acme Cubana advertising **48.00**
    For watch chain, shape of stein **65.00**
    Horse head figural, w/flowering mane, silver colored metal, 5½″ **100.00**

Russian wolfhound head, incised '56' under neck, 6″........ **75.00**
Scissors type, brass **18.00**
Scissors type, nickelplated............................ **18.00**
Silver loop & MOP, pocket, Germany, 2½″............ **35.00**
Slide type, Moul's Liquors, New York, 1902 .... **12.00**
Store counter, picture of manufacturer, Boston Trade, 1882. **225.00**
With bulldog, Merriam's Segars **22.00**
With tray, silver, late 1800s **35.00**
Cigar holder, amber w/gold overlay bezel, orig hinged box **32.00**
Amber, 10k bezel **19.00**
Amber, gold pique, intaglio nudes, Deco **69.00**
Amber w/ornate gold overlay bezel, MIB **32.00**
Cased, carved meerschaum, 5½″ **40.00**
Celluloid, 3 pc screw type, w/leather composition box, sgnd, 3½″ **50.00**
In case, meerschaum & amber, 3″ **22.00**
Irid w/threading, unsgnd, Loetz **185.00**
Ivory, w/carved flowers & leaves **47.00**
Meerschaum & amber in fitted hinged case, 3″ **20.00**
Meerschaum, amber stem, carved full size lady, Austria **48.00**
Meerschaum, amber stem, carved horses, orig velvet case, Austria **48.00**
Meerschaum, carved jack rabbit **39.00**
Meerschaum, in case w/carved bull dog top............... **65.00**
Meerschaum, w/case & carved dog **65.00**
Cigars makers set, board w/cutter & knife, drying rack & cigar mold **140.00**
Cigar roller machine, cast iron, Winget Machine Co, 1902.... **150.00**
Cigarettes, unopened cardboard box, Zufedi, 1909............ **5.00**
Cigarette advertisements, full color, full page, lot of 37, 1920-39 **27.00**
Cigarette box, crystal w/diamond, Wedgewood style medallion, 3″ **88.00**
Hammered pewter, hinged cover, wood lined, Nekrasoff, 3¼″. **30.00**
Cigarette case, bugler, blue w/blk & yellow stripe, 3x3″ **8.50**
Floral engraved, monogram, Unger Bros, 4½x3″ **225.00**
Gold mounted brocade, carnelian ring, handle, Paris, 1935, 3¼″ **330.00**
Gold plated inside, Chagrine, English, 1900s **60.00**
Irid enamel tan & brown horses, cobalt ground, hallmkd, 3″ sq **150.00**

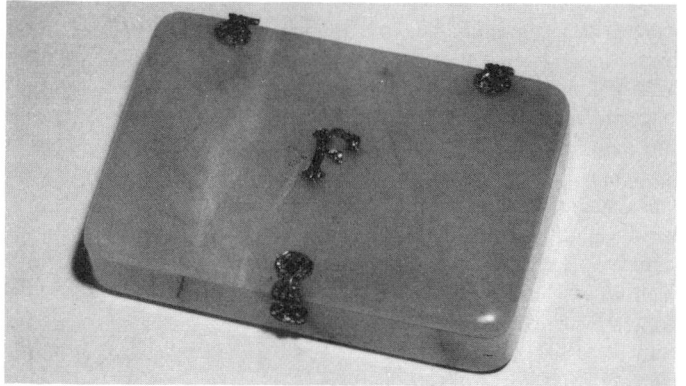

Set w/rose diamonds, rounded rectangular, gr jade, 1930 ... **880.00**
Silver, inner cover enameled w/2 nudes, sapphire thumbpiece, 4″ **605.00**
Simulated jade panels, sgnd Cartier #348, 1929, 3¼″ **2,090.00**
With compact, blk cover, rhinestone fan **35.00**
With lighter, wings emblem, blk & silver, Art Deco, Evans ... **20.00**
Cigarette cutter, bell shape, Art Nouveau, pocket model **38.00**
Blowfish wht brass, pocket model..................... **85.00**
Flat sterling, chased design, 2x5x8″ **48.00**
Ivory handle, hand model, 4½″ **45.00**
Plain sterling, bell shape, chain, pocket model **58.00**
Silver plated nickel, w/Spaniel, bird in mouth, 5¼″ **235.00**
Cigarette dispenser, carved wood, blk man's head on box...... **50.00**
Elephant figural, box, mechanical **125.00**
Tent shaped brass, copper inlay & enamel decor, 3x4″ **25.00**
Cigarette holder, Chinese, enameled wood, carved idol on stem, sgnd **25.00**
Cloisonne w/goldstone & ivory stem.................... **95.00**

Expandable, lady's, gilt w/rhinestones, Art Deco **30.00**
In case, genuine amber **28.00**
Ivory, 4¼″ **16.00**
Monk's head, bee on nose **12.00**
Retractable end, 14k, Dunhill........................ **45.00**
Cigarette paper, JG Dill's Best Tobacco **2.50**
Cigarette photo card, J Louis advertising Chesterfield cigarettes, set of 6 **6.50**
Rip Van Winkle, Piedmont, set of 8 .... **40.00**
Cigarette photo cards, Victorian women, set of 8 .... **12.50**
Cigarette roller, cast iron, elephant figural, hinged lid box on top **175.00**
Cigarette silk, 11 Indian chiefs, 2x3″.................... **9.00**
Baseball, 2x3″ **10.00**
Baseball, Thomas Leach, Pirates **30.00**
Bayou girl, Mississippi, Fatima Cigarettes, 2x3½″ **2.00**
Carlisle pendant, song, seal, 4x5½″ **3.00**
Flag girls **5.00**
Flowers **4.00**
Girl, bathing dress, parasol, May, #649, NY, 4½x6½″ **4.00**
St Barnard, #649, NY, 1¾x3½″ **1.50**
Syracuse University, sportsman, 3½x5½″ **3.00**
William McKinley, 1897-1901, 1¾x3½″ **3.00**
Zira girls, Zira cigarettes, 2½x3½″ **1.00**
Coupon catalogue, tobacco tag redempsion gifts, 48 pages **28.00**
Humidor, clear jar, w/reticulated plated panels, 1928, 6″ **40.00**
Derby silver, 3 compartments, ball feet, 1887, 10″ **120.00**

Humidor, Indian, bisque, 9½″ **150.00**
Man's head figural, smoking cigar, lid is hat, Czech **58.00**
Scenes in small medallions, flowers & animals, w/beaded border **175.00**
Skull figural, porcelain, Victoria Carlsbad, 4½x5½″ **55.00**
Lighter, bar, blk bartender shaking drink, center lighter, Ronson **350.00**
Black, red on gold, Whiz Radio, NBC, Zanesville, Ohio **26.00**
Brass, chrome plated, toylike, mkd, Buick, 1950s.......... **39.00**
Brass, looks like watch w/US soldier & baby, cigarette....... **18.00**
Coca-Cola bottle **12.00**
Counter, Midland, cigar **250.00**
Embossed cowboy w/branding iron, Rolex, advertisement **40.00**
Embossed, Smooth Sailing w/Chilton Malts, 4½″ **26.50**
Enameled, Chesterfield, cigarette **8.00**
Gas fixture, cigar store, Statue of Liberty, 40″ **475.00**
Globe-on-stand, tabletop, automatic, detailed, 5½″ **34.00**
Golden wheel w/watch **50.00**
Imari pattern 1128, Royal Crown Derby, Ronson, cigarette, 3x3½″ **95.00**
Jumpspark, Midland, cigar **265.00**
Old store countertop 'Garcia Grand', electric, cigar **43.00**

Plane figural, 4x2″ **26.00**
Plated, Reliable Pocket Lamp, 1890 .... **28.00**
Plated, oval, table model, Ronson, 2½″ **14.00**
Pull chain to light, old, Brown & Bigelow advertisement **29.00**
Shape of coin, lion rampant, Crown 1670 .... **20.00**
Ships wheel, brass, 4½″ **30.00**
Silent flame, plastic, chrome nudes, Parker of London, Art Deco, pr **55.00**
Sterling w/good engraving, Zippo **25.00**
Sterling, Adonis, flat, Ronson **10.00**
Sterling, for coffee table, cigarette **20.00**
With case, orig box, Art Deco, Ronson **32.00**
With watch, Ronson **37.50**
Match holder, w/cigar cutter, decorated metal base **48.00**
Striker ashtray, 3-hold cutter, wood & brass, Victorian **85.00**
Match safe, silver, German, Art nouveau **15.00**
Match strike, pair of tall boots, bootjack, striker next to boots .. **35.00**
Pillow cover, cigarette premium, girl w/flowers seated at window, 1905 **85.00**
Pipe, briarwood, carved gorillas, 14″ **945.00**
Briarwood, carved Indians horses, buffalo, 11″ **765.00**
Bruyere, ornate metal cover, bone stem, Czech **65.00**
China, brass, wood, hp stags, 22″ **65.00**
Cigar shaped, mkd Genuine imported Briar **17.00**
Claw foot bowl, 'O-Boy', 2½″ **20.00**
Clay, advertising w/soccer players, Western Super Mare, 8″ ... **75.00**
Clay, devil **15.00**
Clay, Indian head, mkd Germany **22.50**
Figural bowl, paper label, Gouda, early clay **70.00**
Hancarved, Bavarian painted bowl, 37½″ **60.00**
Handpainted doe & stag, complete, very old, 24″ **65.00**
Meerschaum, amber stem, dog carving, 4″ **95.00**
Meerschaum, buxom lady, w/case, 3½″ **60.00**
Meerschaum, carved eagle, metal hinged lid, bowl only **95.00**
Meerschaum, carved full figure of semi-nude, lg **225.00**
Meerschaum, claw foot, amber stem, w/case **125.00**
Meerschaum, eagle claw holding bowl, yellow stem, velvet case **125.00**
Meerschaum, in case, carved skull bowl **85.00**
Meerschaum, miniature, 2 horse carving, cherry amber stem .. **75.00**
Meerschaum, nude w/legs around pipe bowl, 6″ **365.00**
Metal lid, deer scene, wood stem, bone mouth piece, china, 40″ **65.00**
Pewter, copper lined bowl, 1700s, 4½″ **75.00**
Porcelain bowl w/woodland scene, 11″ **35.00**
Porcelain, blk forest, helmet lid, tassel, 1800s **55.00**
Porcelain, forest scene, wood & bone stem, Richard Bereks . **115.00**
Porcelain, metal fittings, applied floral decor, 2 pc, mkd, 22″ . **30.00**
Revolver shaped, old **30.00**
Wood, hand carved w/lion & deer, 6″ **60.00**
Wood stem, man apprehending boy scene on bowl, 28″ **55.00**
Pipe cleaner, w/pen knife, sterling **25.00**
Pipe holder, bronze color wht metal, dachshund, AMW 1934 .... **5.00**
Tin, advertising, 6½″ **22.00**
Tole, tin, Hanleys Peerless Ale **32.00**
Plug cutter, countertop type, cast iron, Brighton **13.00**
Lorrilard's Climax Plug **50.00**
Store counter type, Star cast iron, 1885 .... **40.00**
SW Venable & Co Tobacco **45.00**
Shipping box, Chew Kentucky Colonel, plug tobacco, wood, 8x8x6″ **20.00**
Smoking stand, embossed, iron & brass, w/attached lighter, 1930s **39.00**
Tobacco barrel label, crusader, knight, 1870s, 7x14″ **14.00**
Soldiers, 1870s, 15x15″ **18.00**
Tobacco basket, yellow, mkd Warehouse at Carthage, 39″ sq . **175.00**
Tobacco box, mahog, brass inlay, cover, Santo Domingo, 1800, 13″ **120.00**
Tobacco cutter, Arrow Cupples **30.00**
Countertop, 'Star', mkd Save The Tag **65.00**
Figural horse blade, 6½″, illus **175.00**

Pennsylvania Hardware Co, 1900 .... **38.00**
Rectangular base, 11½″, illus **65.00**
Store, Cupples Arrow & Superb **50.00**
Tobacco jar, covered, china, blk man smoking pipe, 3¾x3¼″ dia **75.00**
Man's head, mulberry red cap, blue scarf, open mouth **155.00**
Metal top, pipe finial, Handel **95.00**
Persian scene, hinged lid, mkd on bottom, #87/897 .... **325.00**
Porcelain, blk man w/earrings, 4½″ **100.00**
Smiling man w/gr Tyrolean hat, 6½″ **60.00**
Tobacco plug presses, tin w/embossed stage, mules **22.00**
Tobacco spear, handfashioned iron tip for wood stakes **25.00**
Tobacco tag, mounted & framed, 50 different, 1890s-1930s **30.00**
Tobacco tamper, brass, man figural, 1800s, 3″ **135.00**
Bronze, standing nude, round flat pedestal base, 1700s **130.00**

Toby Mugs and Jugs

The delightful drinking mug known as the Toby dates back to the 18th century, when factories in England produced them for export to the American colonies. Named for the character Toby Philpot in *The Little Brown Jug* song, the Toby was fashioned in the form of a jolly fellow, usually holding a jug of beer and a glass. Some were seated, while others were full-bodied figurals. The earlier examples were made with attention to details such as fingernails and teeth. Originally representing only a non-entity, a trend developed to portray well-known individuals such as George II, Napolean, and Ben Franklin. Among the most valued Tobies are those produced by Ralph Wood I in the late 1700s. By the mid 1830s, Tobies were being made in America.

Allerton, standing, cobalt & lustre, pr **70.00**
Bennington, 6½″ **150.00**
Clarice Cliff, jovial drinking man, lg **98.00**
Douglas Mac Arthur, Royal Winton England, 7″ **55.00**
Falstaff, Staffordshire, 1850 .... **275.00**
Father Neptune, colorful, Staffordshire-Shorter England **65.00**
George Washington, full body, squatty, polychrome, mkd, 7½″ **175.00**
Hearty Good Fellow, Staffordshire **150.00**
Herbert Hoover, Gold Medal China, political, base 5½x5¾″, 7″ **55.00**
Long John Silver, 5½″ **40.00**
Lord Nelson **140.00**
Man w/mug, woman w/hands on ears, miniature, pr, 1½″ **58.00**
Man, seated, holding jug & glass, cobalt coat, mkd, 4½x4½″ deep **55.00**
Martha Gunn, Wood, 1790 .... **700.00**
Neptune & Beefeater, 7″ **45.00**
Ralph Wood, 1770 .... **1,200.00**
Scotsman, colored, unsgnd **84.00**
Scottie, 8″ **60.00**
Scottie & Beefeater, 4½″ **30.00**
Smiling Jester, wht porcelain, unsgnd **45.00**
Toby Philpots, full body, Wood & Sons, 4½″ **75.00**
Full body, Wood & Sons, 6½″ **95.00**
Whieldon **130.00**
William Penn, coral handle, Lenox **150.00**
William Penn, mask handle, gr wreath mk, Lenox, 6½″ **145.00**
Winston Chruchill, Copeland-Spode **120.00**
Woodrow Wilson, Royal Staffordshire, 1915 .... **200.00**

Tole

The term 'toleware' originally came from a French term meaning 'sheet iron'. Today it is used to refer to paint decorated tin items. The earliest toleware was hand painted; by 1820s, much of it was decorated by means of a stencil. Among the most collectible today are those items painted by the Pennsylvania Dutch in the 1800s.

Box, flat top, yellow w/realistic red & gr floral decor, 6½x3½x2½" **165.00**
   Flower decorated, book shape, 1850, 3x3½" **150.00**
Cannister, coffee; blk, red trim, late 1800s **60.00**
   Polychrome floral, 8" **150.00**
   Tea, blk, red & yellow designs, round lid, 1800s, 5½x4" dia . **35.00**
   Tea, cone top, w/lid, 6½" **75.00**
   Tea, red, 4x2" dia **25.00**
Chest, humpback, stencil & brush work, Lynn Bell, 9½x9½x12" **70.00**
Coffee pot, gr w/gold trim, 4 glass sections, 1897, 10" **75.00**
Document box, cherries, flowers, scroll work, 7¾x4" **375.00**
   Strawberries & roses, 6x9½x7½" **575.00**

Foot tub, factory decor, 1865, 7¼x19" **125.00**
Jug, syrup, red on wht flowers, yellow accents, all orig, 4" **235.00**
Lamp, candle, adjustable shade & holder, brass shaft, saucer base, 19" **50.00**
Lunch box, painted decor, flowers, dots, fence, squiqqly lines, 8" **1,400.00**
Tea tin, orange, painted, 10" **65.00**
Teapot, gooseneck w/bird decor **1,000.00**
   Polychrome floral on blk, some wear, 10½" **900.00**
Tray, apple; orig red toleware, painted flowers **95.00**
   Bread, blk background, painted designs, japanned, 7½x12" .. **55.00**
   Bread, orig red toleware, 14x9" **55.00**
   Muffin, orig paint, stencil decor, 15" **75.00**
   Octagonal, dk brown, japanning, red & yellow design, 8¾x12¼" **200.00**
   Orig stencilling, New England origin, very old **650.00**
   Oval, bird, flowers, 20" **45.00**
   Pierced sides, open hand holes, some paint loss, 20x28" ... **150.00**
   Stencilled, Chippendale, 9x12" **170.00**

Tools

Before the Civil War, tools for the most part were handmade. Some were quite primitive to the point of crudeness, while others reflected the skill of those who took pride in their trade. Increasing demand for quality tools and the dawning of the age of industrialization resulted in tools being mass produced.

Factors important in evaluating antique tools are scarcity, usefullness and portability. Manufacturer's marks are also a consideration.

Adjustable scribe, ebony, Bushnell **65.00**
Anvil, Goodwill stoves & ranges advertisement **35.00**
Axe, broad, unmkd **20.00**
   European markings, old **85.00**
Back saw, 8" blade, Henry Diston **18.50**
Basket maker's froe & mallet, sm **55.00**
Bee smoker, wood & leather bellows **30.00**
Bit brace, brass bound, wood, W Greaver, Sheffield **110.00**
Blacksmith traveler, handmade **30.00**
Blacksmith's cone, 48" **300.00**
Blowtorch, brass, Clayton & Lambert, 9¼" **10.00**
Brace, maple, octagonal pewter ferrule, fixed spoon bit **265.00**
   Maple, ogee styling, 4 bit pads, early **675.00**
Breast drill, Goodall Pratt, 1912 .... **12.00**
Broad axe, orig paint, Barton, Rochester, NY, 1832 .... **40.00**

Buggy jack, cast iron, 26" **15.00**
Buggy wrench, cast iron, mkd **36.50**
Bullnose rabbet plane, #75 .... **18.00**
Burl maul, wht oak handle, 1700s **18.00**
Butcher saw, steel rod frame, 1" wide blade **6.00**
Cabinet clamp, iron & wood, Austin & Eddy, #1½, 1860 ..... **70.00**
Cabinet maker's burl mallet, 12x4" dia **60.00**
Cabinet maker's square, rosewood handle w/brass edge, 1869, 4½" **22.00**
Calipers, adjustable, iron, Goodall Pratt **7.00**
   Wood & brass, Stanley #136, 4" **15.00**
Carpenter's level, w/eagle, Lambert, Miliken & Stockpole **60.00**
Carpenter's mallet, burl w/hickory handle, 12½" **18.00**
Carpenter's maul, burl **55.00**
Carpenter's saw, w/iron handle **25.00**
Cement finisher, brass, embossed, wood handle, Buffum Tool Co, 8" **25.00**
Chain drill **17.00**
Cobbler's awl, thumb screw allowed varied-size points **15.00**
Crown molding plane, 6" wide **550.00**
Draftsman set, orig case, tools dated 1899, case worn **35.00**
Draw guide, Stanley #7 .... **45.00**
Draw knife, cooper's **35.00**
   With edge guard, adjustable, 12" **30.00**
   With folding handle **29.00**
   Wooden handle, Witherby #10, lg **9.00**
Drill bit set **35.00**
Fold out rule, #32½ w/caliber **20.00**
   #62 brass bound **12.00**
   Wood & brass, Stanley, 24" **15.00**
     36" **20.00**
Forge & blower, cast iron, Champion, 14x9" **165.00**
Glut, iron band, oak, very lg **12.50**
Goosewing axe **225.00**
Guage, iron, brass face, flange w/glass, lg hand, 6" **18.00**

Gauge, slitting, handfashioned, 1800s **40.00**
Hack saw, wood handle straight out, Starrett #144, 14" **7.50**
Hammer, double headed, used to nail wood cigar boxes, 4" **5.00**
Hand drill, double cogged, disc cog wheel, wood handle, 12" **8.50**
Hand pruner, cast iron, w/fancy grip handle **25.00**
Hatchet, Keen Kutter **22.00**
   Nation's Joint Smasher, 9" **35.00**
Hoof trimmers, pat 1894 .... **15.00**
Ice axe, WT Wood & Co **26.00**
Ice axe head, nickel plated **18.00**
Ice chisel, Gifford Wood **18.00**
Ice harvesting, ringed 2 prong fork bar **24.00**
Knife, bone handle, Farrier, England **18.00**
Leathercutting knife **9.00**
Leg vice, chain drive, 4" jaw **100.00**
Level, brass edges, Stanley **35.00**
   Cast iron, 3 bubbles, Jennings, 24" **45.00**
   Cast iron, 3 bubbles, Stanley, 24" **45.00**
   Cherry wood, MIB, Stanley **25.00**
   Henry Diston **25.00**
   Iron, Davis, 1883 .... **70.00**
   Stanley #0 .... **15.00**

Wood, Allas Tool, 18″ **9.00**
 Wood & brass, dovetail case, HM Pool, Easton, Mass, 30″... **50.00**
Log marker, mkd P&M **45.00**
Machinist's tool chest, walnut, sm **125.00**
Marking gauge, #91 .... **12.00**
Monkey wrench, RR, Mo. Pacific **8.00**
Panel gauge, 20″ **12.00**
Panel scribe, rosewood **35.00**
Patternmaker's scraper plane, brass, for delicate work **65.00**

Planes

Buck Bros, wood plane, coffin shape, 7½″............... **11.00**
Child Pratt Co, carpenter's plane, wooden **11.00**
Cumings, forming plane **20.00**
Gardner & Murdock, Boston, 1825-45 .... **40.00**
JP Faroe, wood plane, 16″ **15.00**
Jack plane, dovetailed helper's handles, 2″ wide **60.00**
Lamb & Brownell, plow plane w/6 irons, New Bedford, Mass. **125.00**
Lovejoy, skew rabbet plane, offset closed tote, rare **550.00**
N Spalding McLean, box plane, beech core **110.00**
Ohio Tool, plow plane, brass & iron **60.00**
Panel plane, brass, mahogany, Norris type, 15″........... **285.00**

Plow plane, cherry & brass, adjustable **95.00**
Scioto Works, #15, carpenter's plane, wooden **10.00**
 #21, wooden **18.00**
Shoulder plane, rosewood & brass, 8″ **140.00**
Spill plane, tabletop **70.00**
Stanley #2, smoothing plane **125.00**
 #5 .... **25.00**
 #6 .... **20.00**
 #20, circular plane, orig box **125.00**
 #23, wood base **23.00**
 #27, transitional plane, pre-lateral **45.00**
 #40 .... **20.00**
 #45, multi-plane **95.00**
 #55, moulding plane, orig cutters & box **190.00**
 #73, wood plane, cast iron **15.00**
 #93, cabinet plane **18.00**
 #129, transitional................................. **55.00**
 #193, fiberboard plane w/attachments & cutters **120.00**
 #605, bedrock plane **60.00**
W Brindman, carpenter's plane, wood w/curved blade, lg **12.00**

Plumb bob, all brass, miniature, ½x3″ **32.00**

Iron, 6 pound, 19″ **45.00**
Rafter square, standard knockdown...................... **40.00**
Razor blade sharpener, Twinplex....................... **15.00**
Router, carved out handle **25.00**
Rule, ivory & German silver, Stanley #40½, 3″............ **125.00**
 Wood & brass, Lufkin #171, 3″...................... **30.00**
 Wood & brass, Stanley #36, 3″...................... **30.00**
Ruler, brass, folding Boxwood, 36″..................... **35.00**
 Folding, advertising for Schuttler wagons, Bradley **11.50**
Scorp, wooden handle w/brass connectors, cleaned inside barrels **24.00**
Shears, brushmaker's, Brombacher, NY **90.00**
Shoe holder, stretcher, iron, American **5.00**
Shoe last, hand-forged iron, Z shape, 16″ **19.50**
Shoemaker hammer, sm **8.00**
Slick, Underhill Edge Tool Co **60.00**
Slitting gauge, 18″ **32.00**
 Barrel maker's, curved fence & arm, pad maple **50.00**
Spindle cutter, cast iron, Phoenix **12.00**
Spoke cutter, wheelwrights, cast iron, early **14.00**
Spur auger bit set, Russell & Jennings, #100, 1855 .... **115.00**

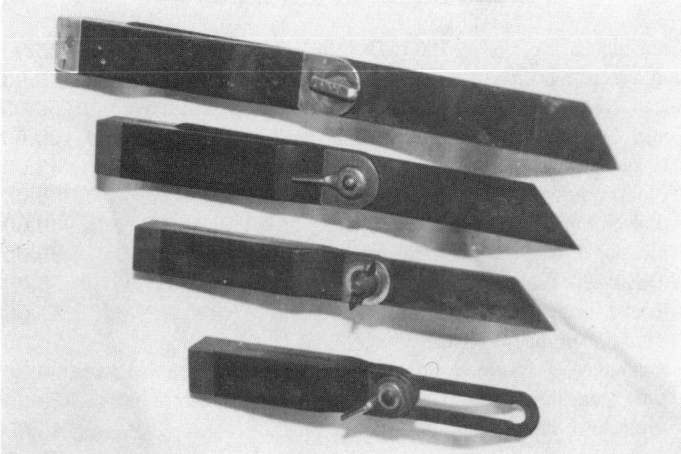

Squares, adjustable, rosewood/brass..................... **35.00**
Stapler, Acme **10.00**
Steelyard, 17″ **20.00**
Straight-edge, stainless, oak case, Taltender, 53″............ **80.00**
Tape, cloth, leather-clad case, Lufkin, 50′ **12.50**
 Metallic, leather-clad case, Lufkin, 50′ **9.50**
Tin well, miniature, handle lifts bucket, 1900s **20.00**
Transit, cast bronze, orig tripod & case, Gurley, 1880 .... **975.00**
Try square, cherry, polished iron, brass bound & inlays **30.00**
Turpentine scorp **30.00**
Ultimatum, brass, ebony, Hibernia stamp, Marples.......... **385.00**
 Brass & beech, William Marples **445.00**
 Red beech, Marples **1,300.00**
Witchet, hardwoods, brass lined throat, double blades, 1840 .. **175.00**
Wooden jointer, iron, closed tote, mkd Gardner, 27″ **28.00**
Woodworker's bench, maple, early, 32½x52x22″............ **270.00**

Toothpick Holders

Toothpick holders have been popular table accessories since the Victorian era. They were made in pressed glass patterns as well as in all types of art glass and china ware.

Baby Bootie, amber **45.00**
Baby Thumbprint, amberina **125.00**
Banded Portland, clear w/gold **25.00**
 Maiden Blush **45.00**

Basket weave, milk glass, gold trim, Bellaire	30.00
Beatty Rib, blue opal	30.00
White opal	20.00
Beveled Star, clear	25.00
Bird in Stump, amber	45.00
Bisque, dog w/bottle	20.00
Brazilian, clear	25.00
Bristol, turquoise, enamel florals & gold trim, handled, 1¾x2½"	50.00
Bundle of Cigars, clear, mkd	20.00
Bundle of Sticks, amber	27.00
Button & Daisy, V-ornament, amber, illus	35.00
Cactus, chocolate	65.00
Cane w/Scroll Band, amber flashed	50.00
Cat on Pillow, amber	45.00
Cauldron shape, gr w/3 gold feet, souvenir	10.00
Champion, gr w/gold	35.00
Green	25.00
Cherubs, electric blue, peek-a-boo	65.00
Chrysanthemum Sprig, blue custard w/gold, sgnd Northwood	235.00
Cloisonne, blue w/florals	27.50
Coal Scuttle, blue glass, wire handle	22.50
Coin Glass	75.00
Colorado, gr	35.00
Green w/mint gold, souvenir	45.00
Cordova, gr	25.00
Cut glass, egg shape on pedestal	50.00
D&M, with gold, #42	20.00
Daisy & Button amber, w/metal rim	35.00
Blue, anvil	20.00
Blue, tumbler shape	45.00
With fan brim, blue	40.00
Daisy & Button Variation, amber, metal rim & base	40.00
Daisy & Button, w/V Ornament, blue	45.00
Delaware, gr w/fair gold	65.00
Derby, figural, boy removing shoes	75.00
Diamond Spearpoint, vaseline opal	60.00
Dog w/hat, blue	50.00
Vaseline, Victorian novelty, 3¾x3¼" dia	50.00
Double Dahlia & Lens	45.00
Douglass, clear	22.00
Doulton, Dutch people scene, porcelain, handled, 1¾x2"	40.00
Doyle's 500, amber	60.00
Figural porcupine, plated, Meriden	50.00
Fish head, china	45.00
Fleur-de-lis novelty, clear	22.00
Flower & Pleat	40.00
Flute, marigold carnival	50.00
Frazier, cranberry w/enamel	45.00
Frog & Shell, amber	40.00
Frosted Hobnail, w/amber band	58.00
Garden of the Gods, stump, 1909	30.00
Gladiator w/sword, plated	55.00
Gonterman, frosted w/blue top	140.00
Harvard, ruby stained, Atlantic City, 1899	40.00
Heartband, gr w/gold, trace of souvenir	40.00
Ruby stained, souvenir	35.00
Heisey Pineapple & Fan, clear, w/gold	45.00
Heisey Ring Band, custard, unsgnd souvenir Ogunquit-by-the-Sea	30.00
Heisey Sunburst, clear, some gold	38.00
Hobnail, amber	30.00
Honeycomb, alexandrite, blue to rose to citron, 2¾x2½" dia	550.00
Horse & Cart, clear	30.00
Horseshoe & Clover, milk glass	20.00
Idyll, wht opal	135.00

Illinois, clear w/gold	30.00
Intaglio, Sunflower w/gr stained flowers	35.00
Inverted Thumbprint, lt amber, blown, ring base	35.00
Light green	50.00
Iowa, clear w/gold	25.00
Iris w/Meander, amethyst, gold	55.00
Blue opal	50.00
Clear opal	40.00
Green	25.00
Ivorina Verde, custard, gold trimmed, scalloped top, 2¼x2" dia	75.00

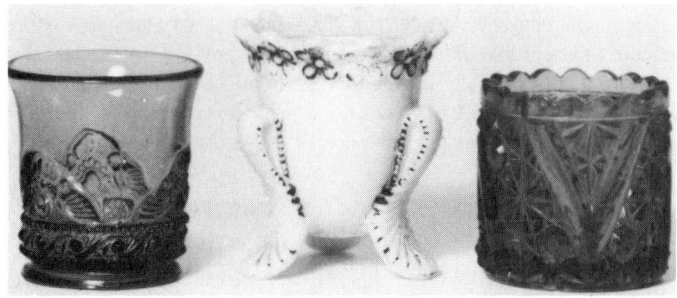

Lacy Medallion, gr w/gold, right	35.00
Ladder w/Diamonds	18.00
Leaf Mold, vaseline spatter satin	125.00
Manhattan, clear w/mint gold	35.00
McKinley head	250.00
Milk glass, baby owl, paint gone	40.00
Minnesota, clear	35.00
Monkey on Tree Stump, clear	16.00
Monkey on Tree Stump, milk glass	35.00
Mt Washington, burmese, salmon to yellow, raised florals, acid finish	250.00
New Jersey, crystal, w/gold	20.00
Palm Leaf, pink	70.00
Pansy, milk glass, 3 handled	30.00
Portieux, gr translucent, figural, Rip Van Winkle	185.00
Reverse Swirl, clear opal	40.00
Ribbed Pillar, pink & wht spatter satin	75.00
Ribbed Spiral, blue opal	85.00
Royal Co-Op, milk glass, Pontiac	18.00
Royal Ivy, rubina, frosted	65.00
Royal Oak, rubina to clear	80.00
Ruby Thumbprint	30.00
Same Old Hat, presidential campaign, 1888	48.00
Scrolled Shell, milk glass	30.00
Serrated Ribs & Panel, ruby stained	50.00
Shamrock, gr, souvenir Coney Island	30.00
Ruby stained, souvenir	30.00
Shoshone, clear	25.00
With gold	35.00
Soapstone, w/3 monkeys	25.00
Spearhead, vaseline opal	75.00
Squirrel & Stump, blue	40.00
Stork in Cattails, clear	55.00
Swirl, blue opal, tumbler shape	45.00
Take Your Pick, silverplate, 2 handles	35.00
Texas, clear w/gold	25.00
Thumbnail, clear	22.00
Tree in Meadow, Noritake gr mk, 6-sided, 2½"	60.00
Tree of Life, blue, on pedestal	35.00
Trench Mortar, amber	40.00
US Rib, gr w/gold	40.00
USA, clear	28.00
Vaseline opal, applied decor, Stourbridge, 1880	50.00
Vermont, milk glass, illus	65.00

Virginia	20.00
Wall basket, electric blue	35.00
Window, clear opal	40.00
Windows Swirl, blue opal	60.00
Wooden Pail, blue, metal bail	40.00
X-Ray, gr w/gold	60.00
York Herringbone, ruby stained w/engraving	40.00
Zipper Slash, ruby flashed, Mt Vernon	28.00

Tortoise Shell Glass

By combining several shades of glass---brown, clear and yellow---glass manufacturers of the 19th century were able to produce an art glass that closely resembled the shell of the tortoise. Some of this type of glassware was made in Germany. In America it was made by several firms, the most prominent of which was the Sandwich Glass Works.

Atomizer, 4½"	225.00
Bottle, sq shape, sloped shoulders, 6"	75.00
Straight sided w/rounded shoulders & cylindrical neck, 6¼"..	75.00
Bowl, ftd, turned down collar, amber feet, 4x8"	90.00
Console bowl, fold over rim, bubbles, polished Pontil, 12" dia ..	30.00
Plate, Sandwich, 6½" dia	165.00
Tumbler, Sandwich, 3¾x2¾"	75.00

Vase, 9½"	165.00
Urn shaped, amber & blue applied handles, 7½" pr	570.00

Toys

Toys, obviously, are fun to collect. But especially those made before WWII also represent a sound investment potential. Lithograph- printed mechanical toys, for instance, are especially popular with today's collectors, and steadily continue to increase in value year after year. Condition of any type of toy is critical---they were made for children to play with, and many that have survived to the present are in a well played-with condition, which only serves to enhance the value of those still in excellent shape. In the listings below, toys are listed by manufacturer's name when at all possible, or by type.

Battery Operated

Most mechanical battery operated toys were made from 1946 through the 1960s. It is estimated that 95% of these were made in Japan. They were distributed by such international firms as Cragston, Linemar and Rosko, although American manufacturers also marketed them, often adding their own brand name.

Animal train, MT	45.00
Barbecue Electro Toy, MIB	45.00
Blushing Willy, MIB	55.00
Brink's Armored Car, MIB	28.00
Bubble Blowing Monkey, MIB	60.00
Bubbling pup, w/flapping ears, MIB, Linemar, 1950	68.00
Busy Housekeeper, MIB	75.00
Butterfly the Flying Dog, MIB	45.00
Cable Car, tin, Japan, Alps	45.00
Champion weight lifter, MIB	55.00
Chinese Dump Truck, MIB	45.00
Clown Juggler	85.00
Cragston Crapshooter, Y Co, 9½"	65.00
Desert Patrol Jeep, MT, MIB	60.00
Dino the Dinosaur	185.00
Drinking Captain, MIB	45.00
Drumming Mickey Mouse, MIB	500.00
Ford, GT, #45	30.00
Good Time Charlie, MIB	50.00
Grandpa in Rocking Chair, San Co, 8"	100.00
Happy Santa, walking, MIB	235.00
Hungry Cat, Linemar, MIB	385.00
HY Que, hear no evil, see no evil, speak no evil, 16"	250.00
Interceptor, target game, S & E Co, 13"	95.00
Jocko, MIB	85.00
Jolly Chimp, musical	50.00
Linda Lee Laundromat, TN, MIB	45.00
Loop & Chatter Monkey, MIB	18.00
Mantini Porshe, #9	30.00
Monkey in Overalls	35.00
Moon Explorer	50.00
Papa Bear, MIB	45.00
Parrot, talks w/internal recorder	300.00
Peppy the Perky Pup, MIB	40.00
Piston Robot	55.00
Police Patrol, 3 wheel	50.00
Railroad Hand Car, KDP Co, 8"	65.00
Red Gulch Bar, K Co, 9½"	135.00
Robot 2500	18.00
Shuttling Dog Train, MIB	145.00
Shuttling Freight Train, MIB	145.00
Space Capsule	175.00
Space Explorer Ship X-7, tin	55.00
Sparky the Seal, M-T Co, 6"	90.00
Telephone Bear, MIB	125.00
Trans Continental Express, MIB	95.00
UFO-X05	35.00
VIP, the Busy Bear, S&E Co, 8"	140.00
Video Robot	48.00
Volkswagen, w/open engine, MIB, 12"	60.00

Cast Iron

Cast iron toys were made from shortly before the Civil War until the beginning of the 20th century. They are evaluated to a large extent by scarcity, complexity, design and detail.

Battleship, 14½"	200.00
Boat, Puritan	575.00
Cannon, cast iron carbide, 9"	40.00
Cop, on motorcycle, w/sidecar	40.00
Doll's stroller	65.00
Express wagon, pulled by goat, blue & wht & yellow, 8" long .	100.00
Gasoline truck, yellow, wht rubber tires, 5½"	35.00
Horse drawn surrey, w/fringed top, passenger & driver, 1906, 13½"	175.00

Marble shooter **350.00**
Motorcycle, 6″ **45.00**
Santa, w/sleigh & reindeer, 17″ **750.00**
Showboat, 11″ **500.00**
Steam engine, horse drawn **100.00**
Taxi, yellow **250.00**

Tractor & plow, 11½″ long **300.00**
Train engine, wood burning type, orig paint, 7″ **50.00**
Wheelbarrow **45.00**
Yellow kid, w/mule cart & mule, blk, orig paint **350.00**
Zeppelin, 5″ **85.00**

Companies or Country of Manufacturer

All Metals Products Co, Sambo Target Board, tin darts, 23x14″ **55.00**
Alps Co, balloon blowing monkey, 11½″ **70.00**
   Barney Bear drummer, 11″ **85.00**
   Busy Shoe Shining Bear, 10″ **85.00**
Althof Bergman, early tin milk wagon w/1 horse **800.00**
American Miniature Doll Corp, Toni w/wave solution **55.00**
Arcade, Andy Gump car, license plate, #348 . . . . **275.00**
   Avery tractor, cast iron, 5″ **225.00**
   Bus, 1940, 9″ **48.00**
   Bus, double-decker, rear stairs, #311, 8″ **325.00**
   Caterpillar w/steel tracks, diesel, 8″ **240.00**
   Chevy coupe, 8″ **365.00**
   Chester Gump horse drawn cart, 7″ **380.00**
   Chevy coupe, restored, 1924, 7″ long **375.00**
   Chevy stake truck, 9″ **650.00**
   Chevy utility coupe, 6½″ **395.00**
   Corn planter, rubber wheels **28.00**
   Dump hay rake, 7″ **70.00**
   Farm mower **27.50**
   Fire engine, 1930, 9″ **75.00**
   Ford coupe, 1934, nicked grille, 6½″ **165.00**
   Ford covered wagon, 1937, trailer only **60.00**
   Ford sedan, 1934, World's Fair taxi, 6½″ **165.00**
   Ford touring car, 5″ **145.00**
   Greyhound GMC bus, 7½″ **140.00**
   Industrial derrick **425.00**
   International truck, 11″ **125.00**
   Mack gasoline tank truck, tin tank, 13″ **695.00**
   Mack ladder truck, 3 orig ladders, repro wheels, 18″ **745.00**
   Mack truck, 5″ **60.00**
   McCormick Deering farm wagon, 2 horse **65.00**
   Model A Tudor, cast iron, orig driver, 6½″ **350.00**
   Model T Coupe, 4″ **60.00**
   Race car w/2 occupants **58.00**
   Rio coupe w/rumble seat **245.00**
   Sedan, cast iron, 1937, 8″ **95.00**
   Tractor w/cart, 8″ **50.00**
   Wrecker w/driver, 11½″ **135.00**
   Yellow Cab, 1924, 15″ **160.00**
Arnold, monkey baby riding cycle, 1940 . . . . **75.00**
   Remote control satellite, orig box **275.00**
Auburn, Cadillac, 1936 . . . . **16.50**

Milk truck, 1940, 4″ **6.00**
Truck, open bed, 1940, 4″ **8.00**
Barclay, army vehicle, 4″ **15.00**
   Radio police car, wht tires **12.50**
Bing, garage, 2 cars **400.00**
   Cruiser ship, live steam operated, 1912, 20″ **875.00**
Bliss, building blocks, ABC's & animals, paper litho, in box . . . **225.00**
   Parlor croquet set **42.50**
Buddy L, car carrier, tin cream color, 26½″ **45.00**
   Construction derrick, 24″ **75.00**
   Coupe w/orig sticker **850.00**
   Fire engine, tin hook & ladder, red, 26½″ **58.00**
   Ford pickup truck, 1921, 12″ **285.00**
   Freight carrier trailer, NM **70.00**
   Jolly Joe's popsicle wagon, 17½″ **130.00**
   Hoisting tower, orig **2,000.00**
   Pile driver **1,200.00**
   Lumber carrier w/logs, red metal, 19″ **77.50**
   Lumber truck, 1925 . . . . **165.00**
   Station wagon, wood, 18½″ **80.00**
   Steam shovel **30.00**
   Trencher, 1928 . . . . **165.00**
Buffalo Toy & Toolworks, child's bank, toy slot machine, 6x4″ . **75.00**
Carpenter, dump cart, 2 horse team **240.00**
Casige, sewing machine, boxed, made in Great Britain . . . **25.00**
   Sewing machine, painted metal, Germany, 6¾x4″ base, 6¼″ . **38.00**
Centure Engineering Co, model rocket, Astro 1, w/chute, launch pad **250.00**
Champion, ci, police motorcycle, blue, wht rubber tires, 7¼″ . . . **75.00**
   Rider & motorcycle, windup, tin, Yone, Japan, MIB, 5″ **35.00**
Chein, Aeroswing windup, MIB **185.00**
   Barnacle Bill in a barrel, 7″ **235.00**
   Chicken pulling wheelbarrow, 6x3½″ **18.00**
   Chipper Chipmunk, windup, follows a track, orig box **85.00**
   Clown barrel walker, MIB **195.00**
   Drum major, tin windup, 8½″ **50.00**
   Drummer, mechanical **75.00**
   Ferris wheel **95.00**
   Giant Ride, ferris wheel, 16″ **40.00**
   Grocery truck, windup, tin, 6″ **165.00**
   Native on alligator, windup, tin, MIB **100.00**
   Native on turtle, windup, tin, MIB **90.00**
   Player piano, w/rolls, 1950s **225.00**
   Playtime tea set, tin, 13-pc, orig box, litho **25.00**
   Popeye walker **195.00**
   Touring car, tin litho, 7″ **60.00**
Clark, auto, wood w/steel, friction, 1901 . . . . **185.00**
Coca Cola, truck, #2, 1949 . . . . **130.00**
   Truck, Buddy L, 1960 . . . . **65.00**
   Truck, Smith Miller, w/6 cases coke, 1950s **350.00**
   Truck, with bottles, 1930 . . . . **315.00**
Comic Art, Beetle Bailey character, mache figure, 7¾″ **55.00**
Converse, fire engine ladder truck, w/bell, headlight, 10″ . . . **1,300.00**
Cragston, Crap Shooter, monkey w/box **50.00**
   Helicopter, Vertol 1107 . . . . **35.00**
   Rock & Roll Monkey w/guitar **135.00**
Crescent, Mercedes Benz 2.5 litre Grand Prix **50.00**
Dent, fire snorkle wagon, 3 horse, driver **250.00**
   Ox wagon, cast iron, 2 oxen, driver, 16″ **120.00**
   Sedan, w/spare tire, stop & go light, 7½″ **700.00**
   Steam roller, cast iron, 6″ **75.00**
Doetke, Adams grader, 27″ **75.00**
   Bulldozer, 15″ **50.00**
England, tea set, Disney's Cinderella, tin **85.00**
Ertl, Rex truck mixer, w/box, 4½″ **12.00**

Tractor, International 656 . . . . **30.00**
Fernand Martin, clown, musical, 1910, costume not orig **600.00**
Fleischmann, tanker ship, windup, tin, 20″ **475.00**

France, penguin, tin, 4″ **25.00**
Gateway, sewing machine, orig box **20.00**
George Brown, dump cart, tin, 1885, 8″ **85.00**
    Peddle wagon, tin, 1880, 20″ **650.00**
German, car garage, w/auto door opener, tin, 11″ **130.00**
    Fire patrol, horsedrawn, windup, tin, 8″ **275.00**
    Minstrel, seated, hp **575.00**
    Tipp & Co, steam roller, tin, 7½x13″ **375.00**
    Scotchman figurine, papier mache windup, 10″ **155.00**
    Typewriter, 'Junior' on tin case, DRGM **150.00**
Gilbert, erector set, w/oak box, 1917, 21″ **90.00**
Girard, airmail plane, double winged **175.00**
Gropper, Buck Rogers 25th Century Chemical Laboratory, 1937 **750.00**
Gund, Fifer Pig, Disney's **75.00**
    Mad Hatter, vinylite stuffed **15.00**
Gunterman, clown, seated playing violin **750.00**
Hess, mouse, friction, orig box **100.00**
Huber, road roller, 4½″ **50.00**
Hubley, airplane, metal, wings & wheels fold **6.00**
    Borden's milk cream **450.00**
    Cement mixer, 18″ **165.00**
    Chemical truck w/ladders, 13″ **165.00**
    Coal wagon, mule, 9″ **35.00**
    Fire engine, cast iron, 8″ **130.00**
    Ice wagon, 1920, 9½″ **50.00**
    Life Saver truck, holds Life Savers, 1930 . . . . **120.00**
    Lincoln Zephyr taxicab, 7½″ **285.00**
    Lindy airplane, 10″ wing span **450.00**
    Motorcycle, cast iron, 6½″ **90.00**
    Nucar auto transport, 16½″ **265.00**
    Parcel Post Harley Davidson, side car, rider **3,500.00**
    Road roller, Huber **130.00**
    Royal Circus, 16″ **485.00**
    Telephone truck, rare, 7″ **395.00**
    Wrecker, w/rubber wheels, 1930s **50.00**
Ideal, Jiminy Cricket, orig sticker **165.00**
    Pay station wall telephone, works **25.00**
    Steve Canyon's glider bomb **35.00**
International, combine, 15″ **40.00**
Japan, automobile pulling house trailer w/table & chairs inside . . **27.50**
    Bear golfer **85.00**
    Chick, windup, boxed **35.00**
    Combat soldier, windup **18.00**
    Elephant walking, windup **125.00**
    Hungry Snake windup **75.00**

Loop plane, tin & celluloid, keywind **25.00**
Mother & baby kangaroo, windup **125.00**
Ostrich, windup **125.00**

Tropical Fish, MIB, 7½x5″ **28.00**
Kellerman, car w/driver, #144, 5″ **190.00**
Kenton, band wagon, horse w/rider, musicians **150.00**
    Buckeye ditching machine **420.00**
    Bus, cast iron, wht rubber tires, 9″ **325.00**
    Buckeye ditcher, replaced crawler chains **440.00**
    Cage truck, rare, 7″ **595.00**
    Cage truck, with bear, 9″ **550.00**
    Cement mixer **55.00**
    Coal truck, 4-pc, 18½″ **245.00**
    Contractor's wagon, blk driver, 15½″ **240.00**
    Ice truck, 7″ **165.00**
    Overland circus cage truck w/driver **225.00**
    Overland circus calliope wagon **240.00**
    Phaeton touring car, 12″ **295.00**
Keystone, steam shovel, 19″ **20.00**
Kingsbury, airplane **125.00**
    Fire truck, metal hook & ladder **55.00**
Knickerbocker, Mickey Mouse cowboy outfit, cloth, orig tag . . . **350.00**
    Minnie Mouse, w/orig tags **395.00**
Lehmann, jigger **465.00**
    Kicking mule windup **150.00**
    Sailor, climbing, metal, mechanical, MIB **70.00**
    Tut-tut windup **500.00**
    Zigzag **850.00**
Lindstrom, Little Miss sewing machine, w/motor **45.00**
    Sweeping Mammy **165.00**
Linemar, bear golfer, windup, boxed **115.00**
    Bubble Blowing Popeye **450.00**
    Buttons Pup, battery operated, boxed **200.00**
    Charlie McCarthy Crazy Car, boxed **400.00**
    Dandy Clown, windup, boxed **115.00**
    Donald & Nephews **125.00**
    Drumming Soldier **85.00**
    Engine robot, battery operated, boxed **125.00**
    Flutter Birds, battery operated, boxed **85.00**
    Girl bouncing ball, windup, boxed **85.00**
    Kangaroo, windup, boxed **85.00**
    Lady bug, windup **75.00**
    McCarthy compo bank, boxed **75.00**
    Pinky Clown, battery operated, boxed **135.00**
    Pirate, windup, boxed **125.00**
    Pluto **85.00**
    Popeye on unicycle **650.00**
    Robot tractor, battery operated, boxed **225.00**
    Santa on roof, battery operated, boxed **125.00**
    Sports car **12.50**
    Tin jumping cat squeeze toy **22.50**
    Washing Bear, battery operated, boxed **175.00**
Martin, salesman **550.00**

Marvel, Lightning Racing Cars 225.00
Marx, #3 racer, windup, tin, 5″ long 25.00
   Airmail hanger, acrobatic airplane, 19″ 250.00
   Army motorcycle, windup, tin, MIB 100.00
   Ballet dancer, w/key, windup, tin, MIB 100.00
   Bengal tiger 20.00
   Busy Bridge, windup, tin 185.00
   Busy Miners, windup, tin, MIB 70.00
   Cape Canaveral 110.00
   Cowboy rider, windup, tin, MIB 70.00
   Dapper Dan Coon Jigger, orig box 275.00
   Disney Carry-All Doll House 85.00
   Fallover Motorcycle, windup, tin, 1930s 120.00
   Fire Chief car, windup, tin, MIB 50.00
   Fire Water speed boat, windup, tin 40.00
   G-Man Pursuit Car, works 195.00
   Gepetto, twistable 35.00
   Hee Haw Balky Mule 150.00
   Hop-A-Long Cassidy, on rocking horse, tin 140.00
   Jumping Jeep 85.00
   Merrymakers 465.00
   Military airplane, windup, tin, MIB 85.00
   Mother Goose, windup 225.00
   Motorcycle, w/delivery attachment, windup, tin, 9½″ 115.00
   Mystic Motorcycle, windup, tin, orig box, 4½″ 35.00
   National Defense, target shooting game w/matching gun, tin . . 40.00
   Police siren motorcycle, windup, tin, MIB 100.00
   Roadster convertible, windup, w/Mickey, Minnie, Donald & Huey 485.00
   Running Scottie, windup, tin, MIB 40.00
   Sky Bird Flyer, windup, tin, MIB 175.00
   Speedboy Delivery, windup, tin, MIB 95.00
   Streamline Speedway, windup, tin, MIB 100.00
   Toto Acrobat, windup, tin 165.00
   Tower airplane, 2 planes around tower, windup, tin, MIB 90.00
   Toytown Milk Wagon, orig box 85.00
   Tricky Taxi, red, blk & wht, windup, tin 20.00
   Tumbling Monkey, windup, tin, MIB 60.00
   Turnover Tank, windup, tin, MIB 30.00
   Union Station Train set, windup, MIB 95.00
   USA Army truck, windup, tin 65.00
   War ship, windup, tin, MIB 50.00
   Yellow Cab, windup, tin, MIB 65.00
Matchbox, 1926 Bugatti #6 . . . . 45.00
   1928 Mercedes #10 . . . . 45.00
Mattel, music box carousel, w/Indians & cowboys, 9x9½″ dia . . . 40.00
Muller & Kadeder, clockwork carousel w/6 bisque headed dolls 8,500.00
Nifty, truck, tin, 9½″ long 475.00
Nonpareil, ambulance 30.00
Orkin, motor boat w/key, 29″ 500.00
Penny Toy, squirrel in cage 110.00
Realistic, Baseball Game, w/tin players 65.00
Renwal, Duesenberg model car, 1934, mint in plastic case 25.00
   High chair 10.00
Schuco, drummer 65.00
   Frog, windup, boxed 45.00
Singer, sewing machine, boxed, made in Germany 35.00
Smitty, box truck, trailer, 6 wheeler 20.00
   Semi, 6 wheel tractor, PIE, 29″ 125.00
Strauss, Alabama Coon Jigger, 1910, 10″ 185.00
   Dizzie Lizzie 70.00
   Jenny the Balky Mule 225.00
   Leaping Lena, car splits & bucks, windup, tin 275.00
   Speed boat, the Ferdinand, windup, tin 50.00
   Trik-Auto, windup, tin 25.00

Wildfire 195.00
Structo, camper w/cloth top, 12″ 10.00
   Delivery storage truck 7.50
   Delivery truck, tin, electric lights 125.00
   Earthmover 30.00
   Utility truck, 21″ 40.00
Sun Rubber, tank 8.50
T-N Co, milk drinking kitty, 10″ 65.00
Technofix, Coney Island ride, windup, MIB 85.00
   Fire engine, extension ladder, 8″ 65.00
   Motorcycle racer, 7″ 65.00
   Motorcycle, windup, tin, US Zone Germany, MIB 125.00
Tommy Toy, beer truck, w/wooden barrels, 1930s 16.50
Tonka, Carnation milk truck, 1950, 12″ 50.00
   Dump truck, 11½″ 50.00
Tootsietoy, antiaircraft gun truck, wht tires 12.50
   Armored car, 4″ 25.00
   Buick roadster, 1926 . . . . 28.00
   Bulldozer, rubber treads, movable plow, 1950 . . . . 15.00
   Chevrolet roadster, 1926 . . . . 25.00
   Convertible, 6 wheel, Graham, 1932 . . . . 35.00
   Farm tractor 25.00
   Jeep, late 1940s 25.00
   Kayo 125.00
   Motors Rol-Ezy set, #5419 . . . . 165.00
   Pick-up truck, plastic tires 9.00
   Plane, Curtis P-40, 1941 . . . . 45.00
   Plance, US Navy 6.00
   Uncle Walt 125.00
   Kiddy Cyclist tin windup, MIB 100.00
   Lincoln Tunnel, tin windup, 3½x24″ 225.00
   Sedan, in garage, 1930 . . . . 50.00
   Town car, 5 wheel, Graham, 1932 . . . . 55.00
   US Mail Airmail Service 20.00

Unique, Dog Patch Band, 1945 . . . . 375.00
   Gertie the Galloping Goose 40.00
   Jazzbo Jim the dancer, 1921 . . . . 145.00
United Electrical Mfg, electric plane, 2 planes on pylon, 20″ . . 850.00
Walt Disney Production, Donald Duck spongy rubber figurine, 11″ 20.00
   Pluto, windup, hard plastic, 5½x5½″ 18.50
   TV Storyteller 125.00
Wilkins, fire truck, clockwork, 1880 . . . . 400.00

Wolverine, Bizzy Andy trip hammer, orig box 65.00
   Diving submarine, windup, tin, MIB 75.00
   Drummer boy, 14" 85.00
   Magic Auto Race, MIB 100.00
   Shooting gallery, 18x11" 60.00
   Spot Shot Skill Game 30.00
Wyandotte, construction co excavator 55.00
   Convertible w/movable top, steel 40.00
   Coupe, 6" 25.00
   Man on flying trapeze, MIB 125.00
   Red Ranger Ride 'em Cowboy, 1930 . . . . 30.00
   Steam shovel, wood wheels, rotating cab 28.00
   Truck, high bed, 6½" 28.00
Jiff, bus, MA Nerster, 6½" 30.00
   Zilotone, w/3 records, windup, tin 325.00
Zylmex, tanks 4.00

Farm Toys
190Xt, tractor 75.00
Allis Chalmer, tractor, 7030 . . . . 60.00
   Tractor, 8550 . . . . 75.00
   Tractor, D-17 . . . . 200.00
   Tractor, WD, plastic 230.00
Avery, tractor 180.00
Case, disc, 4 gang, Ertl 10.00
   Farm wagon, Ertl 6.00
   Paddle tractor, no paint 80.00
   Plow, 4 bottom, Ertl 5.00
   Tractor, 1030 . . . . 70.00
   Tractor, 1070 . . . . 80.00
Cockshutt, tractor, 1850 . . . . 150.00
Ford, tandem disc w/folding roller gangs, Ertl 5.00
   Tractor, 8N-1939, 1959s, Auburn 8.00
   Tractor, commander 6000, 1963, Hubley 50.00
   Wagon, Ertl 10.00
Fordson, tractor, Dexta, Crescent Toys 65.00
Gleaner, combine, 1-32 . . . . 50.00
International Harvester, combine, 815 . . . . 70.00
   Combine, pull type w/belt conveyer, 1950s 50.00
   Drill seeder, steel, Tru-Scale 25.00
   Forage harvester, steel, Tru-Scale 45.00
   Four wheel wagon, steel, Tru-Scale 20.00
   Paddle tractor 95.00
   Slip scoop, Slick 15.00
   Tractor, 1206 . . . . 75.00
   Tractor, 2x2" 100.00
   Tractor, 96 . . . . 30.00
   Tractor 110.00
   Paddle tractor 95.00
John Deere, combine w/belt conveyer, steel, Tru-Scale 45.00
   Manure spreader hi-side, steel, Ertl 30.00
   Mounted picker, 227 . . . . 27.50
   Plow, trailer, steel, Ertl/Eska 50.00
   Tractor, 730 . . . . 190.00
   Tractor, 7520 . . . . 87.50
   Tractor, D 550.00
   Two-row corn picker, steel, Ertl 50.00
Massey-Ferguson, tractor, 1150 . . . . 72.50
Massey-Harris, tractor, 44 . . . . 250.00
Minneapolis-Moline, tractor, LPG-1967, Ertl 60.00
   Tractor, Z-1937, Acor 35.00
New Holland, baler, zinc alloy die cast, Ertl 25.00
   Combine, zinc alloy die cast, Ertl 75.00
   Windrower, zinc alloy die cast, Ertl 50.00
New Idea, spreader 26.00

Oliver, baler 40.00
   Disc, aluminum & steel, Slik 20.00
   Tractor w/mounted picker, 77 . . . . 205.00
   Tractor, 1800-1963, zinc alloy die cast, Ertl 500.00
   Tractor, 1800 . . . . 195.00
   Tractor, 70-1936, 1940s, zinc alloy die cast, Slik 35.00
   Tractor, 880 . . . . 200.00
   Two-row corn picker, steel, Slik 80.00

Guns & Bombs
    Though toy guns were patented as early as the 1850s, the cap pistol was not invented until 1870, when paper caps that were primarily developed to detonate muzzle loaders became available. Some of the earlier models were very ornate, and were occasionally decorated with figural heads. Most are marked with the name of their manufacturer--Ace, Daisy, Bulldog, Victor and Excelsion are most common.

Ace, cast iron cap gun, 1930s, 5" 12.00
Aim to Save, 1909 . . . . 100.00
Banner, cast iron mechanical blank shooter 35.00
Big Bill, cast iron cap gun, USA Kilgore, 1935 . . . . 8.50
Big Chief, cast iron cap gun, mkd K/star, Kilgore, 1935 . . . . . . 12.00
Bomb, A Lincoln 275.00
   Admiral Dewey 110.00
   Chinaman 80.00
   Dog's head 85.00
   George Washington 125.00
Boy's delight, cast iron cap gun, pat June 1891 . . . . 60.00
Buffalo Bill, cast iron cap gun, Kenton, pat Sept 23, 13½" 35.00
Cap cane, American Repeater, model 9 . . . . 35.00
   National, 1909 . . . . 35.00
Cap pistol, animated, w/locomotive 135.00
   Captain Kilgore, w/orig box 28.00
Cavalier, cast iron cap automatic Kilgore, 1935, 4½" 17.00
Cowboy, cast iron cap gun, Stevens, USA, 1930 . . . . 35.00
Daisy Cinematic picture pistol, 1940s 40.00
Daisy Pal, cast iron cap gun 12.00
Dick, cast iron cap gun, Hubley, 1930, 6" 12.00
Dude, cast iron cap gun, plastic grips, Kenton, 1941 . . . . 14.00
Federal, cast iron cap gun, Kilgore, 1920, pat Dec 14, USA . . . 18.00
Frontier, cast iron cap gun, dog's head, Ives, pat, 1890 . . . . . 120.00
Hi-ho, cast iron cap gun, Kilgore, 1940, 6½" 17.50
King, cast iron cap gun, pat 1879 . . . . 18.00
Lightning express, animated cap pistol 100.00
Lock w/key shape, cap gun, animated action, Hubley, 4½"x1¼x3¼" 72.50
Long Boy, cast iron cap gun, Kilgore, USA, 1922, 11" 25.00
National, cast iron cap gun, USA 65.00
Old Ironsides, cast iron cap gun, 11" 45.00
Presto, cast iron cap gun, Kilgore, 1940, 5" 15.00
Scout, cast iron cap gun, Stevens, USA, 1935, 7" 15.00
Sparkling Space Gun, Marx 12.00
The Sheriff, cast iron cap gun, Stevens, 1940, 8" 13.00
Trooper Safety, cast iron cap gun, Kilgore, 1925, 10" 20.00
UNXLD, steel cap automatic nickel plate, 6½" 10.00
Westo, cast iron cap gun, Kenton, 1936, 7" 12.00
Yellow Kid, cap bomb 50.00

Pedal Toys
Bicycle, sidewalk, w/sidecar 2,500.00
Bi-plane, 54" 500.00
Cannonball Express, 37" 235.00
Car, Winner, 1906 . . . . 300.00
Fire truck, Mack 332.00
Hudson, w/lights, orig paint, 1937 . . . . 550.00
Packard, wire wheels 650.00
Tractor, John Deere, 1947 . . . . 90.00
   John Deere, cast iron, Arcade 325.00

Minneapolis Moline 400 . . . . **60.00**
Velo King, tricycle, 1916 w/orig label **600.00**

Primitives

Carousel, tin, windup, 3 pr mounted horses, 1880s, 12x20″ . **1,650.00**
Children's building blocks, set of 16, 2½″ sq, 1830 . . . . **45.00**
Circus clown clapper, wood, cloth, metal, mkd, 1800s **275.00**
Hobby horse, wood, fence style brace, Victorian, 49″ **850.00**
Noah's Ark, 13x24″ long **2,500.00**
Rattle w/whistle, tin, 90-100 yrs old **45.00**
Rocking horse, orig paint & leather saddle, 1880s **330.00**
Sled, child's, wood, red, 1920s, 10½x27″ **65.00**
Symnetroscope, tin & wood, orig paint, pat 1899 . . . . **75.00**
Tin pail, hand stippled, raised flowers, 1888, 5½″ **37.50**
Wooden horse pulling 2 wheel cart, litho covered, 5½x13½″ long **165.00**

Schoenhut

From 1872-1933, Schoenhut produced toys, dolls, games and puzzles. Their circus toys were made as early as 1903 and are the most highly prized examples of their work. They also made a similar series of farm pieces, as well as several comic characters. Though they were never marked, Schoenhut figures are easily recognized by their jointed wood bodies, strung together with elastic cords. Early examples were made with glass eyes, rather than painted eyes, and are more valuable.

Acrobat, bisque head **250.00**
Ball, circus **20.00**
Bareback Rider, Bisque head, blonde molded hair, orig clothes **675.00**
Barney Google, all orig, regular size **275.00**
Barrel **15.00**
Build-a-Village, 5 buildings, orig box **85.00**
Burro, glass eyes **230.00**
Camel, 2 humps **165.00**
    Circus, 1 hump **150.00**
    Glass eyes **350.00**
Cat, felix, 7½″ **200.00**
Chair **14.00**
Chimpanzee **250.00**
Circus horse, w/saddle, 11″ **85.00**
Clown, hobo, 8″ **100.00**
    Mechanical, compo head & hands, blue glass eyes, 16″ **350.00**
    Orig outfit, regular size **75.00**
Donkey, circus **60.00**
    Painted eyes, small **85.00**
Elephant, circus, reduced size **85.00**
    Painted eyes, regular size **150.00**
Farmer's wife, orig clothes, w/milk pail **350.00**
Felix the Cat, 4″ **185.00**
Giraffe, painted eyes, regular size **225.00**
Hippo, glass eyes **230.00**
Horse, brown, regular size **110.00**
    Dapple grey, regular size **115.00**
Humpty Dumpty Circus, animals, clowns, props, 20 pc, 1911 . . **750.00**
    Tent, side show panels, 31 pc **4,000.00**
Indoor golf game, complete **1,450.00**
Ladder, lg **14.00**
    Small **12.00**
Lamb, glass eyes, regular size **300.00**
Mary, orig clothes & straw hat **325.00**
Naval War Toy Game, orig box **285.00**
Ostrich, circus **275.00**
Piano, 5-key, upright, mahogany, 6½″ long, 5″ deep, 5¾″ high **75.00**
    6-key **45.00**
    10x13″ ex **130.00**
    14 key, toy, 1900 . . . . **87.00**
    Child's, solid cherry wood, mkd **65.00**
Pluto, no blanket, regular size **175.00**

Poodle, circus, 8″ **125.00**
    Regular size **175.00**
Ringmaster, bisque, 8″ **375.00**
Roly Poly, clown, 6″ **175.00**
    Dutch Boy, 4″ **145.00**
Seal, Robbie, 1940s **100.00**
Submarine & Dreadnought, in box, 1915 . . . . **95.00**
Tent, lg **1,100.00**
Tiger, regular size **125.00**
Train station, w/label, all orig **225.00**
Trinity chimes **110.00**
Tub, wooden **15.00**
Zylophone, w/Victorian children decor **25.00**

Steiff

Margaret Steiff began making her felt stuffed toys in 1800, in Germany. The animals she made were tagged with an elephant in a circle. Her first teddy bear, made in 1903, became such a popular seller that she changed her tag to a bear. Felt stuffing was replaced with excelsior and wool, and when it became available, foam was used. In addition to the tag, look for the 'Steiff' ribbon, and the botton inside the ear.

Aligator, Gaty, tagged **45.00**
Bassett Hound, orig blue collar, squeaker works, head jointed, 7″ **65.00**
Beagle, puppy, red collar, sitting, has button, late 1960s, 4½″ . . **35.00**
Beaver, mohair **45.00**
Bird, mohair **45.00**
Boxer, sitting, mohair **45.00**
    Standing, mohair **45.00**
Camel, velvet legs, face, 6″ **50.00**
Cocker, hand puppet **40.00**
Crocodile, hand puppet **27.00**
Dachshund, Hexie, mohair **45.00**
Deer, mohair **45.00**
Dog, hand puppet **20.00**
Donkey, Grissy, tagged **45.00**
Duck, mohair **45.00**
Elephant, metal ear tag & paper tag **85.00**
Fox, metal ear tag & paper tag **85.00**
    Terrier, hand puppet **40.00**
Foxy Dog, orig, #1310.0 . . . . **275.00**
Froggy, tagged, 5″ **50.00**
German shepherd, red collar, no tag, 7″ **100.00**
Giraffe, mohair, 1948, 8₉ **1,300.00**
    Mohair, tagged **50.00**
Goat, standing, felt horns, 6½″ **50.00**
Halloween Cat, pink bow, 13″ **70.00**
Hedgehogs, boy & girl, pr **185.00**
Hippo, Nosy, tagged, 5″ **50.00**
Hog, tagged, 11″ **65.00**
Horse, cream w/lt brown markings, open mouth, 1950s, 8″ . . . **50.00**
Husky, wht w/squeaker, no tag, 9″ **125.00**
Kangaroo, tagged, 5½″ **85.00**
Kitten, wht mohair w/brown swirls, sitting, gr eyes, late 1940s, 4″ **40.00**
Lamb, sleeping, mohair, 10″ **40.00**
Leopard, luminous glass eyes, lying down, 1960s, 13″ **135.00**
    Reclining, 36″ **280.00**
Lion, w/button, 10″ **50.00**
    Sitting, 9x14″ **100.00**
    Sitting, mohair **45.00**
    Standing, 7x7″ **68.00**
Llama, standing, wht, spotted, tagged, 11″ **95.00**
    Tagged, 6½″ **80.00**
Lucki, tagged, 8″ **65.00**
Lamb, sleeping, mohair, 10″ **40.00**
Leopard, luminous glass eyes, lying down, 1960s, 13″ **135.00**

Reclining, 36″ **280.00**
Lion, w/button, 10″ **50.00**
  Sitting, 9x14″ **100.00**
  Sitting, mohair **45.00**
  Standing, 7x7″ **68.00**
Llama, standing, wht, spotted, tagged, 11″ . **95.00**
  Tagged, 6½″ **80.00**
Lucki, tagged, 8″ **65.00**
Monkey, fully jointed, 17″ **160.00**
  Jocko, 15″ **45.00**
  Jocko, has tags & buttons, fully jointed, late 1940s, 6″ **65.00**
  Jocko, fully jointed, 1960s, 13½″ **125.00**
  Jocko, sitting, jointed, tagged, 9″ **60.00**
Mopsy Dog, sitting, jointed head, 9″ **78.00**
Parrot, mohair, 5″ **40.00**
Peacock, full tail spread, 91″ across **750.00**
  Tail down, 8′ long **750.00**
Pekingese, standing, jointed, long mohair, 5″ **40.00**
Peky, dog, swivel neck, tagged, 6″ **50.00**
Penguin, baby, blk velvet wings, wht stripe on center of head, 1950s **40.00**
  Mohair, tagged, 3½″ **20.00**
  Mohair, tagged, 8″ **48.00**
Polar bear, wht, on all fours, head jointed, 1950s, 6″ **60.00**
Pony, cream w/lt brown, red saddle & bridle, mid 1950s, 5″ . . . **45.00**
  On wheels, 24x29″ **265.00**
Poodle, lying down, mohair, no tags, 16″ . . . **50.00**
  Miniature, blk, tagged, 1950s, 12″ **100.00**
  Snobby, grey, jointed legs, mohair, tagged, 1950s, 6″ . . . **40.00**
  White, fully jointed, straw filled **50.00**
Pucki, tagged & button, 7″ **65.00**
Rabbit, hand puppet **27.00**
  Jumping, mohair, wood wheels, 1900s, 5½x10½″ . . . **230.00**
  Manni, brown w/wht, blk tipped ears, begging, 1950s, 5″ . . . **55.00**
  Pummy, lt brown w/wht, crouching, mohair, 1960s, 8″ . . . **55.00**
  Running, 7″ **70.00**
  Running, 8″ **80.00**
  Sitting, mohair, jointed front legs, 17″ . . **185.00**
  Standing, 10″ **35.00**
Reindeer, standing, mohair, tagged, felt antlers, 5½″ **70.00**
  Tagged, 14″ tall, 12″ long **100.00**
Rhino, standing, 4x7″ **50.00**
Rooster, multi color, tagged, 8″ **65.00**
Samoyede, mohair **45.00**
Seal, 5″ **48.00**
Seal, Robby, 7″ **68.00**
Snucki, 5½″ **70.00**
Spaniel, blk & wht, standing, 4″ **35.00**
  Jointed head, no tag, 6½″ **60.00**
Squirrel, tagged, 5½″ **45.00**
St Bernard, sitting, jointed head, button in ear, 1950s, 7″ **60.00**
Tabby cat, Lizzy, 10″ **68.00**
Tabby, hand puppet **27.00**
Teddy bear, jointed old tags, lt brown, 7½″ . **100.00**
Terrier, felt ears, mid 1950s, 4″ **20.00**
  Fox; mohair, tagged, 6½″ **50.00**
  Fox; standing, 1950s, 7″ **60.00**
  Fox; wirehaired, mohair, head turns, 17″ . **120.00**
  Red collar, grey w/tags, 9″ **115.00**
Tiger, hand puppet **27.00**
  Lying down, 10″ **60.00**
  Standing, 3½″ **40.00**
  Yellow-gr glass eyes, lying, 1960s, 14″ . . **80.00**
Wittie Owl, tagged, 10″ **68.00**
Zebra, button in ear, 7″ **70.00**

Mohair, tagged, 9″ **65.00**
Tagged, 5½″ **60.00**

Toy Soldiers

    Toy soldiers were popular playthings with children in the 19th century. They were made by many European manufacturers in various sizes, until 1848, when a standard size of approximately 1⅓″ was established. The most collectible of all toy soldiers were made in England by Britains Ltd. from 1893-1966. In America, some of the important manufacturers were Barclay, Manoil, Grey and All-Nu.

Auburn, cavalry officer, mounted **32.00**
  Sound detector **16.50**
  Stretcher-bearer **3.50**
Barclay, soldier, walking dog, tin helmet, after 1934 . . . . **20.00**
  Ambulance, #50, 3½″ **8.00**
  Beer truck, w/barrels, #377 . . . . **16.50**
  Cannon car, w/gun & gunner, 4″ **7.50**
  Chrysler Airflow, 1936, 4″ **7.00**
  Cowboy w/pistol, after 1934 . . . . **7.50**
  Doctor w/stethoscope, after 1934 . . . . . . **12.00**
  Drummer, tin helmet, long stride **10.00**
  Flagbearer, tin helmet, long stride **14.00**
  Indian on rearing horse, 1920 . . . . **7.50**
  Japanese, charging w/rifle, 1937 . . . . . . **30.00**
  Kneeling w/pigeons, tin helmet, 1934 . . . **11.00**
  Kneeling, firing, after WWII **16.50**
  Machine-gunner, kneeling, long stride . . . **10.00**
  Marching, shoulder arms, short stride . . . **9.00**
  Marching, w/pack, tin helmet, after 1934 . **6.50**
  Motorcyclist, after 1934 . . . . **12.00**
  Naval officer, cap w/tin top, short stride . . **14.00**
  Nurse, kneeling, after 1934 . . . . **14.00**
  Officer on rearing horse, arm moves sword . **12.00**
  Officer w/gas mask, cast helmet **18.00**
  Railroad porter, blk **7.50**
  Sitting w/rifle, tin helmet, after 1934 . . . **11.00**
  Soldier on horse, steel helmet, 1930s, 2″ . **5.50**
  Standing, firing, after WWII **11.00**
  Two soldiers on raft, cast helmets **35.00**
  US Army truck, rubber tires **12.00**
  Wounded on crutches, after 1934 . . . . . . **9.00**
Britains, 2nd life guards, #43, orig box **350.00**
  Arabs, #9291, 4 pc, MIB **100.00**
  Arabs, #9391, 12 pc, MIB **200.00**
  Band of Royal Horse Guards, #103, 12 pc, 1900 . . . . **2,200.00**
  Band of Salvation Army, #10, 24 pc **900.00**
  Belgian Chasseurs, 33P, set in box **50.00**
  Camel figure, from set #131, 1910, 3″ . . **560.00**
  Camel corps, #9265, 5 pc, MIB **100.00**
  Cameron highlanders, #9334, 14 pc, MIB . **200.00**
  Canada RCMP, #9256, 4 pc, MIB **100.00**
  Confederate Cavalry, #9286, 4 pc, MIB . . **100.00**
  Confederate Cavalry, #9386, 11 pc, MIB . **200.00**
  Coronation display, #1477, in box, 1937 . **1,500.00**
  Coronation set w/king & queen, 8 horses . **400.00**
  Cossacks, #9273, 4 pc, MIB **100.00**
  Cowboys, #9188, 6 pc, MIB **100.00**
  Eastern people, #1313, 11 pc **1,900.00**
  Egyptian Infantry, 117, boxed **135.00**
  Elephant ride, #252, orig box **280.00**
  Fourth Bombay Grenadiers, 68, set in box . **165.00**
  Fox hunt, #9655, 16 pc, MIB **200.00**
  France Cuirassiers, #9266, 4 pc, MIB . . . **100.00**
  Full cry, #9656, 16 pc, MIB **200.00**
  Fusiliers, #9345, 11 pc, MIB **200.00**

George VI, coronation coach, 1470, MIB **100.00**
Grenadier Guards, #9321, 15 pc, MIB. **200.00**
Indian lancers, #9262, 4 pc, MIB. **100.00**
Indian skinners, #9261, 4 pc, MIB **100.00**
Indians & cowboys, #9390, 10 pc, MIB **200.00**
Indians, #9189, 6 pc, MIB **100.00**
Indians, #9389, 10 pc, MIB **200.00**
Knights, #9192, 4 pc, MIB **100.00**
Knights, #9392, 9 pc, MIB **200.00**
Knights, #9398, 11 pc, MIB **200.00**
Life guards, #9205, 4 pc, MIB **100.00**
Mexico's Pride, #186, orig box **950.00**
Pilots of the German Luftwaffe, 1895, MIB **300.00**
Red army guards in overcoats, #1027, boxed **115.00**
Royal Corps of Signals, 1791, set in box **165.00**
Royal Welsh fusiliers, 23rd foot, #74, orig box, 1920s. **200.00**
Scots guards, #9306, 12 pc, MIB. **200.00**
Signal, corps, #9153, MIB **100.00**
South African Mounted Infantry, set #38, 5 pc **700.00**
The 'Village Idiot', set #587 . . . . **340.00**
The Evzones, scarlet, orig box, #196 . . . . **200.00**
The Royal Army Medical Corps, 145, boxed. **265.00**
Two-seater coupe w/wht wheels, orig box. **1,100.00**
Union cavalry, #9287, 4 pc, MIB **100.00**
Union cavalry, #9387, 11 pc, MIB **200.00**
Union Infantry, #9187, 6 pc, MIB **100.00**
US Infantry Squad, 264, set, MIB **65.00**
US Marines, 228, set in box **90.00**
US Cavalry, #9380, 11 pc, MIB **200.00**
USA Sailors, #9187, MIB **100.00**
Venezuelan military school, set #2100, 20 pc **600.00**
Welch guards, #9127, MIB **100.00**
Worcestershire regiment, set #18, 10 pc **360.00**
Zulu warriors, 9190, 7 pc, MIB **100.00**

Britians Ltd, Royal Scots Greys, End Dragoon 6B, set in box . . **70.00**

Grey Iron, cadet, 2, early **7.00**
Girl in riding suit, American family. **6.00**
Hold-up man, 12/1. . . . . **6.00**
Nurse & wounded soldier, D26. . . . . **40.00**
Old colored man, sitting, American family **5.00**
Pirate w/sword, 16/5 . . . . **6.00**
US Doughboy grenade thrower, 6/4 . . . . **12.50**
US Doughboy w/bayonet, 4/6 . . . . **12.00**
Woman in bathing suit, American family **6.00**

Heyde, French Cavalry & artillery display, 42 pc **700.00**
Spanish American War display, 24 pc **850.00**

Manoil, bicycle dispatch rider, 50 . . . . **14.00**
Farmer sowing grain, Happy Farm series **6.00**
Indian, w/knives, both feet on base, 22 . . . . **6.00**
Parade, hollow base, 8 . . . . **13.00**
Radio operator, standing, 88 . . . . **23.00**
Sailor, hollow vase, 14 . . . . **40.00**
Scarecrow w/top hat, Happy Farm series **11.00**
Sniper, folding rifle, 26 . . . . **33.00**
Soldier w/camera, 61 . . . . **16.50**
Soldier w/gun, charging, 37 . . . . **13.00**
Ten metal figures, 17 cutouts, Happy Farm set **100.00**
Water wagon, #72 . . . . **10.00**

McLoughlin Bros, soldiers, cardboard/wood, 1900, 50 pc **200.00**

Playwood Plastics, matching gun team, 2 men **4.00**
Seated at matching gun. **4.00**

Tommy toy, Little Miss Muffet, 1936. . . . . **16.50**
Old Mother Hubbard, 1936 . . . . **20.00**

Trains

Electric trains were produced as early as the late 19th century. Names to look for are Lionel, Ives, and American Flyer.

American Flyer, #21160, Reading lines, S-guage, 4-4-2, w/tender **30.00**
#3110, 0-4-4, headlight in cab, O-gauge **120.00**
#4635 Shasta, S-guage, red w/brass trim **425.00**
#4644 Af Shasta, S-guage, red & grey **375.00**
#9900, Burlington Zephyr windup, O-guage, litho **245.00**
Baggage #1200, O-guage, litho, 4 wheel **30.00**
Box car #24039, Rio Grande Cookie, S-guage **50.00**
Box car #4642, S-guage, red & blk **280.00**
Caboose #930, S-guage, brown **7.00**
Caboose #24603, S-guage **11.00**
Caboose #24631, S-guage, radio, yellow & red **23.00**
Caboose #24636, S-guage **5.00**
Cattle car #629, S-guage, maroon **17.00**
Circus Pullman #649, S-guage **80.00**
Container car #24575, Borden, S-guage **30.00**
Covered hopper #924, S-guage. **10.00**
Crane #906, S-guage **30.00**
Franklin car #30, western type, S-guage **35.00**
Gondola #804, S-guage **18.00**
Industrial hoist #24569, S-guage, brown **25.00**
Log unloading car #914, S-guage **28.00**
Lumber car #42597, CNW, S-guage, Bakelite base **30.00**
Railway Express car #718, S-guage, w/button & trip **40.00**
Railway post office car, Nationwide lines, O-guage **35.00**
Rocket launcher, w/metal base car, S-guage **18.00**
Searchlight car #634, S-guage **13.00**
Steam loco #283, 4-6-2, S-guage **45.00**
Steam loco #302, Reading lines, S-guage, metal body **35.00**
Steam loco #322, 4-6-4, smoke unit tender. **90.00**
Bassett-Lowke, live steam 2-6-0 LMS Magul, 6 wheel tender, track **1,500.00**
Bing, #3105, 0-4-0, O-guage w/tender, 14½" **170.00**
Freight station, cast chimney, litho, 12x6" **120.00**
Passenger coach, #1 guage. **130.00**
Street car, yellow & brown & orange litho, track, box, 8½". **950.00**
Windup & tender, #1 guage, 0-4-0 . . . . **575.00**
Carette, street car, O-guage, eleric, track, orig box **1,100.00**
Tender, #1 guage, live steam 0-4-0, 4 wheel **1,500.00**
Carlisle & Finch, mining loco, 0-4-0, piece of display track . . . **860.00**
Windup loco, 0-4-2, O-guage, no tender **200.00**
Engine & Tender, S-guage scale 4-6-0, all brass. **3,000.00**
Fleischmann, goods van, Hi O-guage, brakeman's cabin, 7" . . **40.00**
Ore car, 7" **45.00**
Ives, #3241R, S-guage, dk gr. **330.00**
Block Semaphore #330, #2 guage, orig box **105.00**
Buffet car #130, O-guage, green roof, yellow & pink litho **70.00**
Engine #3236, S-guage, cast frame, orange. **240.00**
Gondola #128, O-guage, dk gr & grey **30.00**
Gondola, cast iron w/old repaint, 6" **100.00**
Locomotive, early cast floor, 4-4-0, old repaint, 10" **240.00**
Station #144, w/ticket office, litho **110.00**
Kingsbury, engine & tender, early tin friction, red & gold, 17" **130.00**
Lionel, #1004 Baby Ruth, orange & blue **12.00**
#1103 Peter Rabbit Chick Mobil, O-guage, orig box. **1,250.00**
#254, O-guage, olive & orange stripe, vents **220.00**
#6025 Gulf Black Chemical car **15.00**
#7806, 1976 Christmas Greetings car, MIB. **200.00**
Box car #2458, semi scale, all metal **44.00**
Box car #655, yellow & maroon **35.00**
Builder motor #2, S-guage **260.00**
Caboose #1682, red & yellow & blk litho **12.00**
Caboose #6257, red, Lionel lettering **7.00**

Caboose #657 . . . . **25.00**
Caboose #817, red w/nickel trim, orig box **85.00**
Cattle car #813, orange w/brass trim **85.00**
Crane #810, blk & orange & maroon & peacock booms **95.00**
Diesel loco #1055, Texas Special **40.00**
Diesel loco #2041, Rock Island Twin A, blk & red **125.00**
Diesel loco #211, Texas Special, Twin A, orig box **70.00**
Diesel loco #2245, Texas Special B Unit, MIB **190.00**
Diesel loco #225, C&O **50.00**
Diesel loco #231, Rock Island, red & blk, MIB **85.00**
Diesel loco #2348, Minnesota & St Louis **310.00**
Diesel loco #2365, C&O **160.00**
Diesel loco #2383, Western Pacific Dummy A, orig box **170.00**
Diesel loco #250E, orange & terracotta frame, E on door . . . **430.00**
Diesel loco #252, lt olive **110.00**
Diesel loco #623 . . . . **90.00**
Diesel loco #624, C&O **100.00**
Diesel loco #628, NP 44 ton switcher **95.00**
Diesel loco #634, AT & SF switcher **65.00**
Diesel loco #635, UP switcher, yellow & red **155.00**
Engine, #8, S-guage, red **170.00**
Gondola #1717, lg O-guage, 8 wheel, orig box **40.00**
Gondola #652, nickel trim **35.00**
Hopper #653, pea gr w/brass **35.00**
Milk car #3472 . . . . **20.00**
Milk car #3662, Long O Guage, wht w/brown **30.00**
Searchlight car #820, burnt orange & blk **80.00**
Steam loco #1060, 2-4-2 w/tender **30.00**
Steam loco #1656, w/bell ringing tender, orig loco box **320.00**
Steam loco #1688, w/#2689 WX tender, gunmetal, orig box . **210.00**
Steam loco #2018, 2-6-4 e/#2466 WX tender **60.00**
Steam loco #2026, 2-6-4 w/whistle tender **60.00**
Steam loco #671, 6-8-6 w/#2671 W tender, 12 wheel **315.00**
Steam loco #726, 2-8-4 w/#2426 W tender, orig box **670.00**
Steam loco #726, 2-8-4 w/#2426 W tender **420.00**
Steam loco #726, early type w/#2224 tender **370.00**
Steam loco #8040, w/plastic tender **18.00**
Tank car #1680, latch couplers, Sunoco **13.00**
Marklin, crane car, 8" **85.00**
Gondola #17610, sand type, gr, 6½" **50.00**
Goods Van #17910, w/brake cabin **75.00**
Goods Van, O-guage **100.00**
Lumber car, #17720, w/brake house **70.00**
Lumber car, #17720 . . . . **50.00**
Passenger coach #17250, w/opening doors **60.00**
Windups
Bear Cub, pours & drinks milk, in box **30.00**
Billiards Player, 1910 . . . . **500.00**
Blacksmith Bear, MIB **65.00**
Boxing Bunny, MIB **45.00**
Bucking Bronco, 1920, 8" **275.00**
Bunny Drummer, MIB **45.00**
Camel, 1900 . . . . **200.00**
Carousel, tin & celluloid, w/bunny on cart, MIB, Japan **30.00**
Tin & celluloid, w/chicks, Japan **35.00**
Clown playing violin **25.00**
Crazy Clown, Japan **45.00**
Dairy Wagon, Toylands, 10x4½" **165.00**
Disneyland Ferris Wheel **200.00**
Donald the Drummer, Marx **70.00**
Egg Head, MIB **65.00**
Elephant on tricycle, Germany, 8" **90.00**
Fox magician **65.00**
French fur juggling monkey **195.00**

German tank, w/sparker, 3" **30.00**
Girl bouncing ball, cloth plaid skirt, 5½" **15.00**
Golden Arrow Racer, Kingsbury, 20" **260.00**
Jazz Bo Jim, orig box **325.00**
Jumping Clown **125.00**
Knitting Cat, MIB **45.00**
Limping Lizzard, Marx **90.00**
Monkey Acrobat, MIB **45.00**
Nutty Mad Indian, Marx **45.00**
Pixie phone, litho, US zone **85.00**
Planet robot, MIB **60.00**
Pluto, drum major, MIB **190.00**
Pool Players, 2 players, 14½" **100.00**
Rabbit, plush **30.00**
Wood & felt, Japan **20.00**
Roller Skating Bear, TPS **225.00**
Sightseeing bus, W Germany, 2" **8.00**
Singing bird, TN **45.00**
Singing canary, W Germany **90.00**
Sparky Bird, MIB **145.00**
Sparky, robot, MIB **70.00**
Toonerville Trolley, tin **450.00**
Trapeze Artist, Japan **124.00**
Trumpet player, tin & vinyl **45.00**
Turkey, Germany **125.00**
Uncle Wiggily, He Goes a Ridin', 1935 . . . . **125.00**
Woodpecker on tree stump, fabric & composition **45.00**

Trade Signs

Trade signs were popular during the 1800s. They were usually made in an easily recognizable shape that one could mentally associate with the particular type of business it was to represent, and were especially appropriate in the days when many customers could not read.

Apothecary trade, early wooden, 'Pills Bitters Ointments Lotions' **135.00**
Armitage Tailor, hanging tin, wood, early **70.00**
Atlas Assurance Co, porcelain, Atlas holding world **165.00**
Barber Shop, lg razor **85.00**
Blacksmith trade, sheet iron, running horse, 1860, 17x30" . . . **350.00**
Buffalo Steamboat, picture of steamboat, insert shows buffalo w/boat **495.00**
Dentist, wood, painted, Dr C Leefmans **27.50**
Elk Hartford Insurance, reverse painting on glass, framed **85.00**
Great American Indemnity Co, brass, NY **85.00**
Haberdasher, top hat, glove, early 1900s **700.00**
Ice cream, sundae, 10 cents, 62x25" **155.00**
Iron butcher's trade, old meat saw w/bull on top, 36x14½" . . . **475.00**
Jewelry, diamonds, gifts, repairing, tin, 1910, 10x29" **24.00**
Tin, woman w/lg diamond ring, 36x12" **95.00**
Jeweler & Optician, tin, lg pocket watch, 12x36" **90.00**
Jewelry store trade, cast iron, have face, needs repaint **265.00**
National Union Fire Insurance, reverse on glass, 31½x19½" . . **350.00**
Norwich Fire Insurance, reverse glass, woman holding scales & sword **550.00**
Optical Department, pointing hand **85.00**
Optician, tin, lg eye glasses, 36x12" **125.00**
Optometrist, reverse glass, eye at top, wire rim glasses **165.00**
Pearce's Sporting Goods, tin, fish shape **145.00**
Pocket watch trade, metal, lg **225.00**
Saw trade, cast iron & steel, advertising Henry Disston Saws . . **375.00**
Steel saw, lg, Henry Disston & Sons **475.00**
Tin, man in overcoat, umbrella & bowler, 12x49" **95.00**
Usher's Whiskey, reverse on glass, 26x15½" **285.00**

Tramp Art

Today considered a type of American folk art, tramp art was made from the late 1800s until after the turn of the century. Often produced by 'tramps' and 'hobos' from wooden materials which could be scavenged---crates and cigar boxes for instance---articles such as jewelry boxes and picture frames were usually decorated by chip-carving and stained.

Box, ornate brass, ftd **75.00**
  Shell decor **155.00**
  Dovetailed, 2 layer carved details **44.00**
  Dovetailed, octagonal, hinged lid, 1930s, 4½x9½" **28.00**
  Drawer **75.00**
Cupboard, 2 glass doors over 2 doors & drawer, 1886, 60x45x14" **575.00**
Doll's dresser, w/mirror **145.00**

Frame, 17x15" **80.00**
  Gold paint, heart & leaf design, 1900, 23x16" **70.00**
  Walnut, orig paint, crown of thorns style, 34x19" **125.00**
  With carved easel, elaborate, 8x12" **95.00**
Match holder, double, vine & leaves, strike in center **20.00**
Picture, oval, leaves & berries frame, squirrel litho, 9x11" **35.00**
Picture easel, table top, bentwood **12.00**
Plant stand **185.00**
Sewing stand **80.00**
Wall pocket, triangular back w/rosettes, painted details, 11" . . **105.00**
  With shelf **65.00**

Traps

Any System, Los Angeles, CA. Pro, 1925, 1½x5" **32.00**
Bear, handwrought iron, late 1800s 180.00
  Kodiak, #6 . . . . **260.00**
  Newhouse, #15 . . . . **375.00**
Big triumph, double spring, −4, w/5' drag chain, 19" long **12.00**
Bird, spring operated, jams in tree, wood & iron, 1700s, 8" . . **165.00**
Calpro ant extermination gr crockery, 1925 . . . . **20.00**
Double jaw, True Value #1, old **9.00**
Fly, balloon, National Manufacturing Co, pat 1875, 7" **70.00**
  Wire screen, cone shaped, removable base, 10" **45.00**
Mouse, Peerless, wood & tin, 10½" **40.00**
  Tinware, old, runway trap, 4½" **14.00**

Wire cage, 1850, 4x9" **21.00**
Rat, sheet iron, old, 6" **7.50**
Single spring, Onida, #0, set of 3 . . . . **5.00**
Wolf, handwrought iron, late 1800s **90.00**
  Newhouse, #4½ **60.00**

Trivets

Although a decorative item today, the original purpose of the trivet was much more practical. They were used to protect tabletops from hot serving dishes; and irons, heated on the kitchen range, were placed on trivets during the pressing proccess to protect work surfaces. The first patent date was 1869, and many of the earliest trivets bore portraits of famous people or patriotic designs. Florals, birds, animals and fruit were also used.

Brass hearth, pierced round shaped top, turned legs, 1800s **80.00**
  Pierced sq shaped top, turned legs, early 1800s **125.00**
Christmas tree, w/fox on shield shape, 1800s, 7½x4" **45.00**
Clawfoot, lightly impressed design **15.00**
Colebrookdale Iron Co, Pottstown, Pa., #2 . . . . **50.00**
Heart shape, iron, w/feet **125.00**
Hearts, cutout, chairback, for keeping tea warm **65.00**
Horseshoe shape, Good Luck to All Who Use This Stand, iron . **30.00**
Lacy cast iron, stovepipe or trivet, sq, stars & circles pattern, 1860 **75.00**
Mrs Potts Co, Philadelphia, Pa., ftd, for sadirons **14.00**
Musical lyre, brass & iron, handles & feet, 4x7½" **35.00**
Open crown, cast iron, ftd, Maltese cross **18.00**
Triangle, wrought iron, 18" sides **45.00**
Universal Tool, cast iron pot, kettle & lid lifter, 1881 . . . . **45.00**

Wire loop sides, 3 feet, 12" **75.00**
Wrought iron, riveted w/turned & carved wooden handle, 10½x4½" **55.00**

Trolls

The modern day version of the Troll was designed in 1952 by Helena and Martti Kuuskoski, of Tampere, Finland. Those made by DAM and those marked with a horseshoe are among the most valuable, since both are made from the original Kuuskoski design. Many copies have been produced, the best of which are the Wishniks, made by the Uneeda Doll Co. These were first marketed in 1979 and are currently available.

Troll animals are scarce, and valued in the $10 to $45 range

Baby boy, bisque, lavender hair, sucks red sucker, no shirt, 5½". **8.00**
Bank, boy, dam, orange hair, short cape w/felt pants, 7" **15.00**
  Caveman, plastic inset eyes, pasted fur, mkd, 8½" **13.00**
  Dam, Santa, wht hair & beard, Santa suit, 7" **17.50**
  White hair, w/jumper, 7¼" **12.00**
Batman, red suit, yellow belt, blk cape, blk felt mask **8.00**
Bear **20.00**
Bowler, lt blue hair, glued-on felt pants, blk bowling ball, Japan, 4½" **10.00**
Boy, dam, felt shirt & short pants, 11" **45.00**
Boy, modern troll look, short hair, playing guitar, Art #708, 6½" **25.00**

Bride, Wishnik, pasted mohair hair, 5½″ **8.00**
Caveman **10.00**
Cheerleader, molded clothes body, rubbery hard vinyl, wht gloves, 3″ **9.00**
 Wishnik, felt outfit, 5½″ **8.00**
Clown, painted eyes & nose, round ears, glued fun fur hair, 8½″ **14.00**
Cowboy **10.00**
Cowgirl **10.00**
Dam, 12″ **45.00**
 Caveman, orig tag **55.00**
Doctor, Wishnik, wht & brown long hair, orig package, 3″ **7.00**
Donkey, dam, sitting position, mohair hair, plastic eyes, 3″ **15.00**
Fox **15.00**
Frankenstein, blue vinyl body & head, painted head, 3½″ **13.00**
Giraffe, troll-like, mohair hair **50.00**
Girl, dam, pink felt skirt w/straps, jointed head, 11″ **45.00**
 Hard vinyl painted body, 1 eye closed, gray hair, Art #125, 6″ **18.00**
Gorilla **15.00**
Graduate girl, dam, wht felt graduate outfit, w/diploma, 11″ **55.00**
Groom, Wishnik, pasted mohair hair, 5½″ **8.00**
Hand puppet, terry troll, Knickerbocker, mkd **11.00**
Horned, flesh colored, blue fur on bottom & head, tufted tail, 4″ **8.00**
House **25.00**
Hula girl, Wishnik, skirt rooted into waist, pasted mohair hair, 5½″ **20.00**
Leprechaun, cloth stuffed, mohair hair, inset plastic eyes, 11″ . . **35.00**
Man, bald head, salt & pepper hair on sides, gr overalls, Art #111, 9″ **45.00**
Mother, bisque, one tooth, lg nose, 5½″ **8.00**
Native-like, troll body w/native head, rooted nylon hair, 7″ **8.00**
Old jockey, red shirt, gr pants, plastic eyes, Art #209, 21½″ . . **128.00**
Orange hair, purple velvet clothes, 3″ **8.00**
Pixie face, troll body, lavender painted hair, painted features, 7″ . **7.00**
Playboy bunny, blk felt, wht pom-pom tail, aqua mohair hair, #25, 6″ **20.00**
Pom-pom head, charm, plastic, thread pom-pom for hair **3.00**
Puff head, flesh colored, painted eyes, yellow yarn puff hair, 2″ . **10.00**
Russian Viking, one tooth, amber eyes, gray hair, felt outfit, 7″ . **25.00**
Sailor, dam, wht cloth outfit, wht hair fading to dk, 11″ **60.00**
Smokey Mountain troll, girl, orange braids, holds lg pine cone, 20″ **28.00**
Sock-it-to-me, Wishnik, pink hair, no clothes **18.00**
Tailed troll, dam, fur tuft tail, wide low body, pasted hair, 7″ . . . **16.00**
Troll family, wall plaques, molded metal, set of 5 persons **38.00**
True troll, sit down, hair on head & body, hands & feet stick out, 3½″ **10.00**
True troll, Tiny Tim, sit down, checkered shirt, tie, long hair, 3″ **10.00**

Two-headed, gr trousers w/buttons, w/stick in 1 hand, Art #101, 12″ **80.00**
 Wishnik, vinyl body, extra wide head w/2 faces, 3″ **15.00**
Vampire, rubbery, pointed ears, painted face, plastic eyes, 3″ . . . **6.00**
Viking, wooden, wood shield & hammer-like weapon, 3½″ **4.00**
Woman, salt & pepper gray hair, pot bellied, fur skirt, Art #121, 8½″ **28.00**

Trunks

In the days of steam boat voyages, stage coach journeys, and railroad travel, trunks were used to transport clothing and personal belongings. Some, called 'dome top' or 'turtle backs' were rounded on top to better accomodate mi-lady's finery. Today, some of the more interesting examples are used in various ways in home decorating. For instance, a flat topped trunk may become a coffee table, while a smaller dome top style may be 'home' for antique dolls or a teddy bear collection.

Camel back, child's **25.00**
 With tray, portrait inside lid, Germany, 1825, 4x2½″ **210.00**
Dome top, potato stamp decor, yellow & blk on red, 22x12x12″ **375.00**
 With fitted, padded & lined inside, refinished outside **295.00**
 Wood, polychrome decor on blk, 28x11x14″ **550.00**
Flat top, butternut & pine, w/orig wrought iron trim, 1870 . . . **100.00**
 With tray, padded & lined inside **185.00**
Norwegian rosemaled, 1852 . . . . **550.00**

Salesman's, cowhide, cedar-lined lid, cloth lined, 1866, restored **300.00**
Stagecoach trunk, Jenny Lind, brassbound, leather, 1850 . . . . . **450.00**
 Tooled decor, leather, 104 brass buttons, 1868 . . . . **225.00**
Swell top, wrought iron handles, dovetail construction, mkd, 1820 **70.00**
The Long Island Express, bentwood side handles, 24x11x10″ . . **95.00**
Travel trunk, pine, ironbound **125.00**

Tuthill

Bowl, flat, 3 feet, vintage **735.00**
Compote, Rosaceae Pattern, sgnd, octagonal, 8x6″ **650.00**
Ice cream tray, 14x7″ **400.00**
Nappy, handled, Phlox Pattern, intersecting bands of hobstars, 7″ **225.00**
 Scalloped w/hobs & crosshatching, sgnd, 7″ dia **125.00**
Pickle dish, Rosaceae Pattern, sgnd, 4½x7″ **325.00**
Plate, Floral Pattern, cut class, sgnd, 10″ **395.00**
Tankard, deep cutting, blackberry, 12½″ **350.00**
Tray, sgnd, 1900s, 13½″ **525.00**
Water set, Cut Rose Pattern, sgnd, 7 pc **850.00**

Typewriters

The first commercially produced standard office typewriters were made in 1873 by Remington, although some experimental models were used as early as 1850. They attracted little serious interest as a business asset until the early 20th century. In 1905, the original keyboard was accepted as standard. The electric typewriter was patented in 1871, but it was not until 1902 that it was commercially manufactured. The first of this type was made in

the United States by Blickensderfer Electric; these are very rare today.

American Visible	100.00
Bennett, portable w/case, small, last pat 1908, 10¾x4¾x2½"	35.00
Blickersderfer, wood case	75.00
Blickersderfer Electric	500.00
Boston	200.00
Brooks	200.00
Cash	125.00
Corona, orig case, roller folds over keys, 1917, 9x10x6"	40.00
Crandall, new model	200.00
Crown	150.00
Densmore	75.00
Ford	150.00
Fox, metal case, early 1900s	80.00
German, junior model –3, metal	60.00
Hammond, in case, folding model –26	70.00
Portable, 3-row keyboard, 1907	120.00
Wooden case, pat 1880	250.00
Hammond Multiplex, wood case	75.00
Harris, visible #4	12.00
Horton	500.00
Keystone	75.00
Lasar	125.00
McCool	100.00
Munson	100.00
O'Dell #4, Chicago, 1885	75.00
Oliver #3, visible	30.00
#5, metal cover	48.00
#5, oak cover, ivory color keys	100.00
#5, standard visible	32.50
#9, old	59.00
Peoples	150.00
Rem-Sho	125.00
Remington –2, w/wood roller, 1890	50.00
Saturn	300.00
Schmidt Premier, 1892	95.00
Shole & Glidden	250.00
Smith Premier –1	65.00
Underwood, standard portable in case, 1921	45.00
World	100.00

UHL Pottery

Founded in Evansville, Ind., in 1854 by German immigrants, the ULH Pottery was moved to Huntington, Ind., in 1908 because of the more suitable clay available there. Their products were stoneware— Acorn Ware jugs, crocks and bowls, which were marked with the acorn logo and UHL Pottery; and pitchers, mugs and vases in simple shapes and solid glazes marked with a circular ink stamp containing the name of the pottery and 'Huntington, Indiana'. The pottery closed in the mid-40s.

Churn, 2 handled, 2 gal	45.00
Jug, miniature, brown & cream, blue lettering, advertising	50.00
Pitcher, grape cluster on trellis, set of four blue & wht interior	550.00
Head of Lincoln, deep blue, 4¾"	135.00
Head of Lincoln, deep blue, 6"	225.00
Head of Lincoln, deep blue, 7"	235.00
Head of Lincoln, deep blue, 8"	250.00
Head of Lincoln, deep blue, 10"	400.00
Redware masked spout, mkd UHL-USA, 8"	85.00

Universal

Universal Potteries Incorporated operated in Cambridge, Ohio, from 1934 to 1956. Many lines of dinnerware and kitchen items were produced, in both earthenware and semi-porcelain. In 1956, the emphasis was shifted to the manufacture of floor and wall tiles, and the name was changed to the Oxford Tile Company, Division of Universal Potteries. The plant was closed in 1976.

Cake plate, yellow	5.00
Chop plate, 13"	5.50
Cream soup, w/tab handle, 7"	3.00
Cup, gr	3.50
Dinner plate, blue, 9"	4.00
Plate, round, tab handle, 10"	3.50
Water jug, cream glaze, tilted, floral decal, Universal, Cambridge	28.00

Val St. Lambert

Since its inception in Belgium at the turn of the 19th century, the Val St. Lambert Cristalleries has been involved in the production of high quality glass, specializing in cameo.

Ashtray, heavy crystal, blue overlay cut to clear	75.00
Candlestick, frosted Virgin Mary, 3 cherubs at ftd base, sgnd, 12"	120.00
Decanter, w/stopper, cameo, purple floral, frosted ground, sgnd, 9½"	670.00
Horn of plenty, double, 6 sided base, sgnd	75.00
Rose bowl, w/bats, castles & moon, gray & blk cameo, 6"	850.00
Vase, cameo, bronze overlay foliage, cobalt glass floral, sgnd, 12"	565.00
Swirled ribs from base to wide flared top, red/pink/clear, 6¼"	250.00

Valentines

Pagan ritual once held that on Valentine's Day the birds of the air elected to choose their mates; and as this premise was eagerly adopted by the homo sapien speci, romantic poems became a familiar expression of one's intentions. By the mid-1800s, comical hand colored lithographic and wood block prints were mass produced both here and abroad. At the turn of the century, the more romantic, often mechanical German imports forced many American companies out of business. Today's collectors often specialize: comic, postcards, mechanical, Victorian, Kewpies, Greenaway characters, or those signed by a specific artist are among many well established categories.

3D, early, 2 for	10.00
Black boy, w/watermelon, hand made, painted, 1900s, 5½x7"	35.00
Booklet, embossed, lace-effect, 4 pages, 1870s, 5x7"	18.00
Boy, running, Germany	7.50
Cat & mouse, Germany, 1933	15.00
Charles Magnus, litho mechanicals, New York, 1850-70	30.00
Clapsaddle	15.00
Clapsaddle, International Art Co, heart, 1900s, 6x7"	25.00
Die cut, children playing	4.00
Little girl, floral border, 1905, 6x7"	3.00
EA Howland, Massachusetts, 1840-50	25.00
Esther Howland, w/colored wafers, 1850s, 2½x4"	30.00
Expanding tissue, Beistle, 1925, lg	7.50
Fold out, boy & girl w/umbrella, 2 pc, 1920, 6x9"	16.00
Boy & girl w/wheelbarrow, die cut, 1920, 3x4"	8.00
Children, roses, die cut	24.00
Cupids & roses, die cut"	18.00
Germany, 1905	8.00
Girl w/wheelbarrow, other children, 4 pc, 1928	22.00
Merry-go-round, cupids, 7½"	7.00
Mother, children, die cut, illus	28.00
Victorian, small	5.00
George C Whitney, Massachusetts, layered, 1870s, 6x4½"	15.00
Heart, turn catch, out pops cupid's arrow & inner heart, 2"	10.00

Jiggs, 1930s **10.00**
Kewpie, violets **17.50**
Lacy, 2 fold lacy, open up, child riding dragonflies **25.00**
Mechanical, boy playing tub drum w/wrench, German litho **12.00**
   Cat w/camera, Saxony, 1925, 5x6" **24.00**
   Girl on balcony, 1920s, 7x8½" **15.00**
   Lad w/camera, lens shows kittens & heart, 1930s, 5x7½" **15.00**
   Perry at North Pole, Nister **50.00**
   Revolving cats, verses, Bavaria, 7½" **17.00**
Mickey Mouse, 1939 . . . . **25.00**
Nister, owl fan **18.00**
Penny Dreadfuls, Hallmark, 1900, 11x14" **5.00**
Postcard, 1 cent **5.00**
Prang, 1878, 2x3½" **20.00**
   Fan, late 1800s **24.00**
Pull out, lg **5.00**
   Small **3.00**
Punch-out book, unused, 14 pages, 1940 . . . . **12.00**
Snow White, pull-tab, 1938 . . . . **7.50**
TW Strong, embossed w/mirrors & lace, 1840s, 8x10" **65.00**
Teddy bear, red embroidery, valentine postcard, 1908 . . . . **15.00**
   Squeaker, moveable head, 8½" **52.00**
Token of love, Germany **15.00**
Tuck, Campbell Kid, girl w/teddy, easel **20.00**
   Figural **25.00**
   Fringed, colorful **5.00**
Victorian, lacy, pops out, doves, little girl, fancy car, 4x7" **12.00**

Vallerysthal

Fine glasswares have been made in Vallerysthal, France since the middle of the 19th century.

Box, w/cover, frosted English Setter, clean base, mkd **85.00**
Candlesticks, female figures, 10½", pr **145.00**
   Joseph & Mary figurals, sgnd, pr **200.00**
Compote, sq topped, allover lacy decor, blue milk glass, 6¼x6¼" **140.00**
Vase, Diamond Quilt, gr crystal w/multi color enamel thistle, sgnd, 8" **275.00**

Van Briggle

The Van Briggle Pottery of Colorado Springs, Colorado, was established in 1901 by Artus Van Briggle, whose early career had been shaped by such notables as Karl Langenbeck and Maria Nichols Storer. His quest for several years had been to perfect a completely flat matt glaze, and upon accomplishing his goal, he opened his pottery. His wife Anne worked with him, and they, along with George Young, were responsible for the modeling of the wares. Their work typified the flow and form of the Art Nouveau movement, and the shapes they designed played as important a part in their success as their glazes. Some of their most famous pieces were Despondency, Lorelei and Toast Cup.

Increasing demand for their work soon made it necessary to add to their quarters as well as their staff. Although much of the ware was eventually made from molds, each piece was carefully trimmed and refined before the glaze was sprayed on. Their most popular colors were rose, blue, green, and grey.

Van Briggle died in 1904, but the work was continued by his wife. New facilities were built and by 1908, in addition to their artware, tiles, garden ware, and commerical lines were added.

By the '20s, the emphasis had shifted from art pottery to novelties and commercial wares. As late as 1970, reproductions of some of the early designs continued to be made.

Until about 1920, most pieces were marked with the date and shape number. Before Van Briggle's death, Roman numerals identified the artist: I for Anne, II for Harry Bangs, and III for Van Briggle. The AA mark was the earliest mark; Colorado Springs, Colorado was used after 1920; and USA was added from 1922 to 1930.

Ashtray, ming blue, CS, 1½x7" **15.00**
   Persian rose, triangular, CS, 1x7x4" **20.00**
   Trapezoid, turquoise, 6¾x4" wide **20.00**
Bookends, owl, dk brown & gr, #645, 1920 . . . . **60.00**
   Owl, gray-blue, 1920 . . . . **100.00**
   Owl, gray-gr shading to cobalt **60.00**
   Puppies, ming blue, 5x4½" **70.00**
Bowl, #903, 1915, 2" **110.00**
   3-hole flower frog, turquoise, dragonflies, #903, 8½" **70.00**
   Acorn & oak leaf rim, #111 CS, 6" **35.00**
   Bubbly powder blue glaze, #330 . . . . **50.00**
   Dragonfly decor, ming blue, muddy clay, #903D, 2½x8¼" . . . **75.00**
   Hand thrown, crimped edges, twisted handles, 3x8" **30.00**
   Leaves decor, gr matt over brown, before 1930, 4x7½" **40.00**
   Leaves, rose, 2½x3¼" **23.00**
   Leaves, turquoise, 3x2" **17.00**
   Molded dragonflies, brown matt w/gr, 1914" **100.00**
   Persian rose, #903, 1915, 2x8" **110.00**
   Persian rose, geometric, Van B 20 (1920), 3½x6" **80.00**
   Persian rose, muddy clay, 5x8" **65.00**
   With flower frog, dragon fly, frog, blue, USA #903D **95.00**
   With frog, oblong, floral, frog has stylized tulips, #777, 8¼" . **45.00**
   Yucca leaves, turquoise, 4½x5½" **33.00**
Bud vase, mountain craig brown, CS, 8" **28.00**
Candlestick, plain, 7 sided, 10¼x5½" at base **40.00**
Conch, ming turquoise, 42 CS, 9" **30.00**
Creamer, turquoise, hexagonal, 2" **110.00**
Cup, 6 incised panel lines, turquoise, 3½" dia **33.00**
   Matt pink, #708, 5" **500.00**
Donkey, turquoise, 3¾x4" long **35.00**
Elephant, Persian rose, triangle ears, AA, 4x7½" **75.00**
   Trunk raised, turquoise, 4x3" **35.00**
Ewer, gr drip glaze, 50 Anna Van Colo Springs, 6" **18.00**
Lamp, Damsel from Damascus, w/orig shade **265.00**
   With butterflies, ming blue, orig shade, CS, 11½" base **160.00**
Owl on stump, high glaze brown, sgnd Anna, 9½" **300.00**
Paperweight, figural rabbit, gr to brown, 3" **60.00**
Pitcher, Persian rose, 1918, 5" **45.00**
   Persian rose, Colo Springs Original, 4" **25.00**
Planter, shell form, ming blue, CS, 3½x9" **25.00**
Vase, '840' blue, 1906, 4½" **150.00**

3-faced Indian, mulberry, Colo Springs mk, 11" **160.00**

5 dicotyledons, 2″ mouth, 3x2″ **33.00**
6 leaves around rim, turquoise, 4¼x3¾″ **45.00**
Bird of paradise, turquoise, 8¼″ **23.00**
Blue, #649, 1917, 10¾″. **210.00**
Butterflies, rose, 4x4″. **35.00**
Crocus & roots, turquoise, 5″ **40.00**
Despondency, 16″. **425.00**
Embossed floral design, 2 handled, #422, 1907, 3½x4½″ . . **195.00**
Extruded long stems w/leaf at top, flared, 1906, 6¾″ **145.00**
Floral decor, ming blue, 1917, 11″. **210.00**
Heart shaped leaves, rose, 5¼″ **33.00**
Incised band of leaves, wht matt, mkd, 17″ **300.00**
Indian heads, brown matt, 1930, 11″ **125.00**
Leaf decor, ming blue, #840 (1908-1911), 4½″ **150.00**
Leaves & flowers, #645, 4x3¼″ dia **45.00**
Leaves & violets, brown, 4¼″ **33.00**
Leaves & violets, rose, 4″. **30.00**
Leaves & violets, turquoise, 4¼″ **23.00**
Maroonish, 1917, 7½″ **85.00**
Ming blue, muddy clay, 8″ **85.00**
Moth decor, gr & purple, 1915, 6″ **165.00**
Persian rose, flowers & leaves, #503, 9½x4½″. **70.00**
Persian rose, leaf decor, 1919, 7″ **125.00**
Persian rose, leaf decor, 1917, 4″ **140.00**
Persian rose, rectangular w/notched lip, CS, 3½x4″. **22.00**
Persian rose, USA, 7½″ **45.00**
Rose, #847, 1917, 4″ **140.00**
Rose, 1918, 2¼″ **85.00**
Rose, long leaves, 8x2¼″ **40.00**
Squatty, blue, 1905, 3″. **185.00**
Thick texture, pea gr matt, 1905, 4″. **325.00**
With handles, leaves at base, olive matt, #232, 1904, 9½″. . **600.00**
With handles, leaves, matt blue w/gr & purple, 1910, 13″. . . **110.00**
With handles, ming blue, CS, #774, 13½″ **65.00**
Water set, blk gloss glaze, 9 pc. **95.00**

Vance Avon

Although pottery had been made at Tiltonville, Ohio, since about 1880, the ware manufactured there was of little significance until after the turn of the century, when the Vance Faience Co. was organized for the purpose of producing quality art ware. By 1902, the name had been changed to the Avon Faience Co, and late in the same year they and three other West Virginia potteries incorporated to form the Wheeling Potteries Co. The Avon branch operated in Tiltonville until 1905, when production was moved to Wheeling. Art pottery was discontinued.

From the beginning, only skilled craftsmen and trained engineers were hired. Wm. P. Jervis and Frederick Hurten Rhead were among the notable artists responsible for designing some of the early art ware. Some of the ware was slip decorated under glaze, while other pieces were molded with high relief designs. Examples with squeeze bag decoration by Rhead are obviously forerunners of the Jap Birdmal line he later developed for Weller. Ware was marked Vance F. Co; Avon F. Co, Tiltonville; or Avon W. Pts. Co.

Jug, high glaze mahogany, Art Nouveau shape, mkd 'F', 5½x6¼″ **95.00**
Vase, floral, squeeze bag, mkd, 4½″ **400.00**
Gr scrolls, blk, impressed Vance F Co, 4x5½″. **250.00**
Mermaids in relief, bulbous, 3 color, Art Nouveau, 12x10″. . **400.00**
Orange w/incised gr trees, brown trunks, 11″. **325.00**
Orange w/incised gr trees, brown trunks, Rhead, 7x4″ **250.00**

Vaseline

Vaseline, a greenish yellow type of glass whose color was achieved by adding uranium oxide to the batch, was made in large quantities during the Victorian era. It was used for pressed glass tablewares, vases and souvenir items.

Bowl, frosted, garlands of roses, 10″. **95.00**
Creamer, Wooden Pail **50.00**
Dresser box, hinged top, gold & enamel decor **110.00**
Mug, Dewey **60.00**
    Three Panel **40.00**
Pitcher, Button & Mitre, 8½″ **130.00**
Slipper, Daisy & Button **68.00**
Sugar, w/cover, Dewey, table size **80.00**
    With cover, Wooden Pail **85.00**
Vase, ground pontil, ruffled top, 14″. **65.00**
    Ruffled rim, panels, knob & wafer stem, 12″ **675.00**
    Scalloped rim, ftd, loop pattern, 10½″ **185.00**
    Stemmed, paneled, ruffled top, 9½″ **165.00**
    Thousand Eye, 9″. **70.00**

Venetian Glass

Venetian glass is a thin, fragile glass, usually colored, with an iridescence similar to that of Carnival glass. It was produced on the island of Murano, near Venice, from the 13th century to the early 1900s.

Candlestick, lady holding 2 candles, blue, 10½″ **115.00**
Champagne, cranberry bowl & base, gold flecked clear dolphin stem **40.00**
Compote, gr base, scalloped top, dolphin stem, gold dust, 8″ . **110.00**
Cornucopia, dk red w/clear dolphins, gold flakes at base, 11½″ **145.00**
    Dark red, clear grapes at base, lightly ribbed, pr **225.00**
Goblet, gilt scrolls, lg wht enamel portrait of Moses, 6¾″ **300.00**
Liqueur decanter, cranberry & lace, rough pontil, 13″ **125.00**
Vase, pink swirl, dk pink ruffled collar, pink rimmed foot **95.00**
Wine, pink frosted w/clear fluted wings, latticinio stem, 11″. . . **340.00**

Verlys

Verlys art glass, made by the French Holophane Company of Verlys, France, after 1931, was made in crystal with acid finished relief work in the Art Deco style. Colored and opalescent glass were also used.

In 1935, an American branch opened in Newark, Ohio. The wares they produced were very similar, but less expensive.

Both producers signed their wares 'Verlys'---the American branch by etching, the French with a molded signature.

Ashtray, swallows, directoire blue, sgnd **125.00**
    Swallows, clear, sgnd, 4½x3½″ **65.00**
Bowl, birds & fish, script sgnd, 14″ **175.00**
    Blueish opal fish, tails form lug handles, sgnd, 19½″ **349.00**
    Electric blue, molded flaring fronds on underside, sgnd, 11¾″ dia **125.00**
    Electric blue, partially frosted, molded sgnd, 3x11¼″ dia . . . **165.00**
    Frosted rose, molded sgnd, 2½x5″ **50.00**
    Frosted water lily, sgnd, 13¾″ **155.00**
    Orchid, crystal, etched, 14″ **142.00**
    Poppy, script sgnd, 13½″ **125.00**
    Shallow, opal birds & honeybees decor, 11½″ **250.00**
    Thistle, etched crystal, unsgnd, 2½x8½″ dia **55.00**
    Water lily, frosted, sgnd, 13¾″ **195.00**
Box, topaz butterfly, 6½″ **300.00**
Candle holders, water lily, pr. **117.00**
Dish, frosted figural duck, molded sgnd **85.00**
Vase, acid w/clear berries, rice pattern, 7″. **110.00**
    Frosted half-moon w/lovebirds, sgnd, 4½x6¼″ **90.00**
    Frosted lovebirds, fan shape. **110.00**
    Frosted wheat panels, American, 9½″ **140.00**

Gem, polished circles, rice pattern, frosted, sgnd, 7″ **135.00**
Gems pattern, script sgnd in 2 places **125.00**
Half-moon, lovebirds, sgnd, 4½x6″ **100.00**
High relief decor, opal, 6x6½″ **175.00**
Lance, crystal frosted, sgnd **150.00**
Mandarin, sgnd **289.00**
Spring & autumn scenes, sgnd, dated **275.00**
Summer & winter scenes, sgnd Carl Schmitz, dated, 8″ **250.00**
Thistle, opal & clear, 9½″ **195.00**

Vernon Kilns

Vernon Potteries Ltd. was established by Fay G. Bennison in Vernon, California in 1931. The name was later changed to Vernon Kilns, and until it closed in 1958, dinnerware and figurines were their primary products. Among its wares most sought by collectors today are items designed by such famous artists as Rockwell Kent and Walt Disney.

Autumn Leaf, fruit dish, 1932, 5½″ **6.00**
Bennison, bowl, gray, 3x12″ **24.00**
Bird Pottery, cup & saucer, beige **12.00**
  Plate, beige, 9½″ **5.50**
Blossom Time, candy dish, 5 petals, 10″ **25.00**
Brown-Eyed Susan, casserole, w/cover **40.00**
  Plate, 10½″ **4.00**
  Plate, 12″ **12.00**
Bulb bowl #101, Poxon, blend of color, high glaze, 10″ dia. . . . **75.00**
Bust, lady, Art Deco, Jan Bennison design, 1835, 12″ **175.00**
Cactus, dinner plate, 1932, 9½″ **6.00**
Casual California, carafe, turquoise **12.00**
  Dinner plate, Turnbull design, T-630 . . . . **20.00**
  Plate, yellow, 6″ **2.50**
  Saucer **1.50**
Chintz, plate, 7″ **4.00**
Coral Reef, salt & pepper **25.00**
Coronado, plate, orange, 9½″ **3.50**
Cup & saucer, Santa Claus **20.00**
Disney, bowl, decorated mushroom, Fantasia #120 . . . . **175.00**
  Bowl, mushroom, pink, 1940, 7x12″ **70.00**
  Bowl, satyr, Fantasia #124, 1940 . . . . **140.00**
  Dumbo, 1941 . . . . **55.00**
  Ostrich, Fantasia, 1940 . . . . **190.00**
  Plate, Nutcracker pattern, 10½″ **40.00**
  Sprite, Fantasia, 1940 . . . . **75.00**
  Timothy Mouse, 1941 . . . . **55.00**

Vase, Art Deco Nude, Disney copyright, 10″ **45.00**
Dolores, pitcher, 5″ **15.00**

Early California, creamer, w/cover, dk brown **7.00**
  Demitasse pot, orange **55.00**
  Platter, 12″ **8.00**
  Salt & pepper, blue **6.50**
  Vegetable dish, oval, blue, 7x9½″ **6.00**
Early days, cup & saucer, scalloped, pink **10.00**
Figurine, Gary Cooper, 16½″ **400.00**
  Dorothy Lamour, 10″ **275.00**
  Godey Lady, ivory, by Hamilton Sisters, 10″ **75.00**
Gingham, coupe soup **5.00**
  Creamer **7.00**
  Cup & saucer **7.50**
  Dinner plate **5.00**
  Gravy **6.00**
  Pitcher, water, 3 qt **16.50**
  Plate, 6″ **2.50**
  Plate, 9½″ **4.50**
  Plate, 10½″ **6.00**
  Platter, 12″ **12.00**
  Saucer **1.00**
  Soup, flat **5.00**
  Sugar, w/cover **8.00**
  Tumbler **9.50**
  Vegetable dish, 9″ **8.50**
Hawaiian Flowers, coffee pot, 8″ **39.00**
  Creamer, maroon, Aloha **8.00**
  Cup & saucer, maroon, Aloha **12.00**
  Plate, maroon, Aloha, 9½″ **8.00**
  Teapot, pink, Aloha **35.00**
Heyday, creamer **4.00**
  Cup **4.50**
  Gravy boat **6.00**
  Plate, 6″ **2.50**
  Plate, 7½″ **3.00**
  Plate, 10½″ **4.50**
  Salt & pepper **6.50**
  Saucer **2.00**
  Sugar, w/cover **5.00**
Homespun, chop plate, round **17.50**
  Creamer **6.00**
  Cup & saucer **7.50**
  Cup **6.00**
  Dinner plate **5.00**
  Drip bowl, 5″ dia **5.00**
  Egg cup, double **7.00**
  Fruit dish **3.50**
  Plate, 6″ **2.50**
  Platter, 12″ **10.00**
  Salt & pepper **6.50**
  Sugar w/cover **8.50**
  Vegetable dish, 9″ **6.50**
Indiana, ashtray, maroon **8.00**
Ingraham, cup & saucer **8.50**
  Plate, 7½″ **3.50**
  Plate, 9¾″ **6.00**
Joy, platter, 12½″ **15.00**
Lei Lani, chip & dip, 14″ **45.00**
  Dinner plate, Don Blanding design, 10½″ **25.00**
  Plate, 9½″ **30.00**
Mayflower, creamer, 4″ **8.00**
McArthur, plate **15.00**
Mexicana, platter, 1932, 11½″ **14.00**
Milkweed Dance, bowl, blue, Walt Disney, 1942, 8½″ **42.00**
Mississippi, ashtray, blue & wht, 5½″ **13.00**

Modern California, creamer, blue 7.00
   Cup, gr 6.50
   Cup & saucer 9.50
   Dinner plate, 9½″ 4.50
   Egg cup, pistachio 6.00
   Fruit dish, 5½″ 4.00
   Plate, gr, 12″ 8.00
   Platter, oval, 14″ 17.50
   Salad plate 3.00
   Salt & pepper, 3″ 9.00
   Saucer, pink 2.00
   Vegetable bowl, lavendar, 9″ dia 10.00
Mug, child's, Vernon China Poxon; baby in cradle decor 14.00
Native California, bowl, cereal, yellow 3.00
   Dinner plate, blue 3.00
   Platter, turquoise, 14″ 10.00
Organdie, bowl, 5¾″ 4.50
   Bowl, 7½″ 6.00
   Bowl, 8¾″ 15.00
   Bowl, divided, 11½″ 8.00
   Bowl, rimmed, 9″ 8.00
   Butter, w/cover 12.00
   Butter pat 7.00
   Casserole, covered 25.00
   Chop plate, 12″ 8.50
   Creamer 5.00
   Cup & saucer 7.50
   Egg cup 7.00
   Flat soup 5.00
   Gravy 6.00
   Plate, 6¼″ 2.00
   Plate, 7½″ 3.00
   Plate, 9¾″ 6.00
   Plate, 12″ 10.00
   Platter, 12½″ 12.50
   Salt & pepper 8.00
   Sugar, w/cover 6.00
   Tumbler, 5½″ 8.00
   Vegetable dish, divided 20.00
   Vegetable dish, round, 8″ 7.00
Plate, Bits of the Old South, 8½″ 30.00
   Cocktail Hour, 8½″ 18.00
   Commemorative, Big Spring Centenial, 10½″ 17.50
   General MacArthur, 1st edition, 10½″ 18.00
   Honolulu, hand-tinted, 10½″ 22.00
   Los Angeles, 10½″ 17.50
   Moby Dick, blue, by Rockwell Kent, 10½″ 40.00
   Notre Dame, hand-tinted, 10½″ 26.00
   Plane, 10½″ 40.00
   Poxon, hp peacock, 9½″ 30.00
   Presidential Gallery #1, 12½″ 30.00
   Salamina, by Rockwell Kent, 10½″ 70.00
   Train, 10½″ 40.00
   Vernon China Poxon, game decal, sgnd RK Becker 55.00
Roffio, plate, 7½″ 2.50
   Platter 8.00
   Salt & pepper 6.00
   Vegetable dish, 7″ 5.00
   Vegetable dish, 8½″ 6.00
States, plate; Arizona, blue 15.00
   Arkansas, Hot Springs, blue 15.00
   California, blue, leaf edge 14.00
   California, San Francisco, Fisherman's Wharf 14.00
   Colorado, blue 15.00

Connecticut, blue 14.00
Florida, maroon, leaf edge 14.00
Georgia, Capitol Building, blue 14.00
Indiana, song, blue 25.00
Iowa, song 14.00
Kentucky, Blue Grass State 14.00
Lousiana 14.00
Maine 14.00
Maryland, My Maryland, blue 14.00
Michigan, Detroit 14.00
Missouri, maroon 15.00
Nevada, Reno, maroon 14.00
New Mexico, Carlsbad Caverns 14.00
Ohio, maroon 15.00
Oregon, 10½″ 17.50
Pennsylvania, Philadelphia 14.00
South Dakota, Mt Rushmore 14.00
Tennessee, Volunteer State 14.00
Texas, multi color 25.00
Utah, multi color 25.00
Vermont, blue 14.00
Wisconsin, blue 14.00
Tam O'Shanter, bowl, mixing, 7″ 10.00
   Cup & saucer 8.50
   Teapot 20.00
Tickled Pink, salad plate, Vernonware, 7½″ 4.50
Tweed, carafe 20.00
Ultra-California, creamer, pink 4.50
   Plate, pink, 9½″ 3.50
   Plate, pink, 14″ 9.00
   Platter, gr 8.50
   Sugar & creamer, lt gr 10.00
Vase, El Camino Real, hexagonal, bisque finish, 10″ 115.00
   Milady, May & Vieve Hamilton design, 7½″ 30.00
Vernonware, pitcher, lt blue 8.00
Will Rogers, plate, leaf edge, maroon 24.00
Winchester 73, cup & saucer, Davidson 22.50
   Plate, Davidson, 6″ 7.50
   Plate, Davidson, 7½″ 9.00
   Plate, dinner, Davidson, 10½″ 26.00

Verre de Soie

Literally meaning glass of silk, this type of glass is named for its lovely, almost pearl like lustre.

Bisquit barrel, lime w/gr & amethyst threads, cover, bail 240.00
Bowl, copper wheel decorated, sgnd by Hawkes, 5x7″ 250.00
   Etched floral loops, unsgnd, 3½x10″ dia 155.00
   Irid, #2941, 4x14″ dia 90.00
   Low, gr threading, sgnd F Carder 75.00
Bud vase, ftd, wht to yellow, quilted pattern, 7x4″ dia 155.00
Centerpiece, edged w/applied rosaline, center melon ribbed, 2½x19″ 265.00
Finger bowl, w/underplate 6″ dia, bowl 2½x4¾″ dia 100.00
Nut dish, blue rim, applied prunts, Steuben, 3″ dia 38.00
Perfume, dk blue, flame stopper, Steuben 165.00
Sherbet, w/underplate, mkd MS 50.00
Sugar bowl, cobalt handles, Steuben, lg 47.00
Vase, applied gr leaves, impressed dimples, 5½″ 120.00
   Bulbous w/tapered neck, pink satin, 4½″ 100.00
   Hawkes cutting, 7″ 140.00
   Wheel engraved, sgnd Hawkes, Steuben, 10″ 335.00

Villeroy and Boch

The firm of Villeroy and Boch, located in Mettlach, Germany, was brought about by the merger of three German factories in 1841---the Wallerfangen factory, founded by Nicholas Villeroy in 1787; the Mettlach factory, founded by Jean Francis Boch in 1809; and his father's factory in Septfontaines, established in 1767. Villeroy and Boch produced many varieties of wares, including earthenware with printed underglaze designs, and the famous Mettlach steins. The company made use of a variety of marks, including the castle mark with the name 'Mettlach'. See also Mettlach.

Beaker, #2968	**48.00**
Bread & butter, Dresden Amalienburg	**3.00**
Box, rust & yellow hp florals, 3½x4″	**60.00**
Cake plate, Dresden, 12″	**50.00**
Cup & saucer, demitasse, Dresden Amalienburg	**10.00**
Tea, Dresden Amalienburg	**12.50**

Dinnerware, cup & saucer, blue & wht	**14.00**
Sauce dish, illus	**7.50**
Dish, illus	**14.00**
Plate, 8, illus″	**9.00**
Pitcher, blue w/wht design, Dresden Saxony Concord	**30.00**
Plaque, WWI battleship scene, 12″	**200.00**
Boat scene, blue & wht, #2305, 10¼″	**90.00**
Dresden Altsladt, 12″	**150.00**
Heidelberg Schlohs, 12″	**150.00**
Plate, hanging, pronghorn sheep, delft type, 12″	**75.00**
Majolica, gr & turquoise w/elves decor, 7¾″	**18.00**
Platter; Dresden Amalienburg, 12″	**14.50**
14″	**35.00**
Salad, Dresden Amalienburg	**5.00**
Serving dish, covered w/handles, Dresden Amalienburg, 12″	**45.00**
Serving tray, in silver holder w/handles, Dresden Amalienburg	**45.00**
Soup bowl, Dresden Amalienburg	**7.00**
Soup tureen, covered & handled, individual, Dresden Amalienburg	**10.00**
With lid & underplate, Dresden Amalienburg	**75.00**
Tile, blk rag doll sits w/sunbonnet babies doll, 6″	**98.00**
Trivet, Dresden Amalienburg	**3.00**
Tumbler, girl w/pitcher, peacock on tray, ¼ liter	**60.00**
Vase, handles, applied leaves & vines, silver lustre, 8″	**75.00**
Pierced top, raised wht florals, silver lustre leaves, 8″, pr	**295.00**
Yellow ground w/wht design in relief	**75.00**

Volkmar

Charles Volkmar established a workshop in Tremont, New York, in 1882. He produced art ware decorated under the glaze in the manner of the early barbotine work done at the Haviland factory in Limoges, France. He relocated in 1888 in Menlo Park, New Jersey, and together with J.T. Smith establish-

ed the Menlo Park Ceramic Co. for the production of art tile; the partnership was dissolved in 1893.

From 1895 until 1902 Volkmar located in Corona, New York, first under the name Volkmar Ceramic Company, later as Volkmar and Cory, and for the final six years as Crown Point. During this period he made art tile, blue underglaze Delft type wares, and colorful polychromed vases, etc. The Volkmar Kilns were established in 1903 in Metuchen, N.J. by Volkmar and his son.

Wares were marked with various devices consisting of the Volkmar name, initials, or 'Crown Point Ware'.

Bowl, rubbery textured, gr, 3″	**165.00**
Pitcher, matt gr	**100.00**
Vase, handles, ovoid w/sq neck, gr	**225.00**

Wade

George Wade and Son, Ltd., of England, makes inexpensive ceramic character figures and giftware that is becoming popular with collectors. Several lines have been produced: Little Creatures; Nursery Favorites and mini-Nursery Rhyme Characters; and a new series called Whimsey-On-Why, a typical English village in miniature.

Little Creatures

Angel Fish	**2.00**
Brown Turtle	**8.00**
Butterfly	**8.00**
Crocodile	**6.00**
Fawn	**2.00**
Green Fish	**8.00**
Green Frog	**8.00**
Hedgehog	**2.00**
Kangaroo	**2.00**
Pig	**2.00**
Poodle	**8.00**
Sea Lion	**8.00**
Walrus	**2.00**
Zebra	**2.00**

Nursery Favorites

Goosey Gander	**7.50**
Jack Horner	**7.50**
King Cole	**7.50**
Miss Muffet	**7.50**
Polly & Kettle	**7.50**
Queen of Hearts	**7.50**
Tom Piper	**7.50**
Tommy Tucker	**7.50**

Nursery Rhyme & Fairy Tale Figurines

Cat & Fiddle, tan cat standing on hind legs playing fiddle, 1¾″	**4.50**
Gingerbread Man, br cookie man standing on gr & brown base, 1¾″	**4.50**
Jack, boy sprawled backward on his behind, 1¼″	**4.50**
Jill, girl fallen to knees leaning back on her left elbow, 1¼″	**4.50**
Little Bo Peep, girl holding a hooked staff, tan figure, blue apron, 1¾″	**4.50**
Miss Muffet, young lady sitting on a hassock holding a dish, 1½″	**4.50**
Mother Goose, woman dressed in long tan dress, goose beside her, 1¾″	**4.50**
Puss in Boots, tan cat w/gray boots, 1¾″	**4.50**
Red Riding Hood, girl holding basket, tan dress, red cape, 1¾″	**4.50**
Woman & Shoe, shoe-shaped house, woman in tan & brown, 1½″	**4.50**

Walley

The Walley Pottery operated in West Sterling, Massachusetts, from 1898-1919. Some pieces were marked 'WJW'.

Bowl, inverted lip, matt browns, gr highlights, drip glaze, 3½x6″ **300.00**
   Low, brown to gr, drip glaze **225.00**
Bud vase, gr w/oxblood, 5″ **85.00**
Vase, gr, high glaze, carved, 7¼″ **400.00**

Wannopee

The Wannopee Pottery, established in 1892, developed from the reorganization of the financially insecure New Milford Pottery Co. of New Milford, Conn. They produced a line of mottled glaze pottery called 'Dutchess', and a similar line in porcelain. Both were marked with the impressed sunburst W, with 'Porcelain' added to indicated that particular body type.

In 1895, semi-porcelain pitchers in three sizes were decorated with relief medallion cameos of Beethoven, Mozart and Napoleon. Lettuce-leaf ware was first produced in 1901, and used actual leaves in the modeling. Scarabronze, made in 1895, was their finest artware. It featured simple Egyptain shapes with a coppery glaze. It was marked with a scarab, either impressed or applied.

Production ceased in 1903.

Chamberstick, bowl form w/handle, olive, blue flame, 4x4″ **60.00**
   Green twisted, 9″ **110.00**
Ewer, blown, tan flambe glaze, 4″ **50.00**
Oil lamp, shade, orig font, 3 feet, brown glaze, #79, 20½″ . . . **200.00**
Pitcher, high glaze, mkd, 4½″ **50.00**

Planter, mottled brown & gold, signed, 4x8″ **150.00**
Vase, brown cream, gr, 10x7½x2½″ **75.00**
   Fluted lip, hand thrown, impressed, brown & blue, 10″ **130.00**
   Panel neck, ruffled rim, mottled metallic brown, 10″ **75.00**

Warwick

The Warwick China Company operated in Wheeling, West Virginia from 1887 until 1936. They produced both handpainted and decaled plates, vases, tea and coffee pots, pitchers, bowls and jardiniers featuring lovely florals or portraits of beautiful ladies done in luscious colors. Backgrounds were usually blendings of brown and beige, but ivory was also used.

Various marks were employed, all of which incorporate the Warwick name.

Biscuit jar, pale violets, hp, cream matt finish, melon shape **95.00**
Bowl, flow blue, gold trim, 9″ **50.00**
   Pinecones, brown, gold, w/underplate 11½″, 3x9″ **65.00**
Butter crock, w/lid **250.00**
Chocolate pot, wht w/cherry decor, 8″ **85.00**
Ewer, rose decor, 7″ **65.00**
Mug, monk & jolly top-hatted man drinking, 1887, BPOE **45.00**
   Poppies **15.00**
   Red cardinal, standard brown glaze, IOGA **45.00**
Pillow vase, portrait on brown, 9″ **120.00**

Pitcher, cider, fisherman w/pipe portrait, pinched spout, IOGA **135.00**
   Floral & strawberry on cream ground, melon ribbed, mkd . . . **115.00**
   Monk, brown, 7½″ **95.00**
   Poppies **65.00**
Plate, elk, 10½ **75.00**
   Indian chief, 9½″ **110.00**
Relish, pansy, flow blue, 11½″ **95.00**
Shaving mug, Indian portrait **120.00**
Tankard, Indian Chief, brown tones, 11″ **375.00**
Trumpet vase, acorn & oak leaf decor, tan & brown, scalloped, 15″ **95.00**
   Floral decor, brown, 15″ **110.00**
   Poppy decor, 12″ **35.00**
Vase, brown, floral, bulbous, 7″ **50.00**
   Brunette in feathered stole portrait, pink **225.00**
   Floral decor, yellows & browns, bulbous, 4″ **55.00**
   Horn of plenty, 9″ **45.00**
   Lady portrait, twig handle, 11¾″ **135.00**
   Pink & red flowers on vine, double twig handle, IOGA, 12″ . . **65.00**
   Poinsettia decor, red ground, handled, 10″ **70.00**
   Poppy decor, brown glaze, pillow shape, 8″ **50.00**
   Portrait, red overglaze, twig handles, IOGA, 10½″ **165.00**

   Portrait, bisque ground, brown & tan, sgnd MI **165.00**
   Stick, orange poppies, 12″ **75.00**
   Wild rose, blue, 8½″ **110.00**
   Young girl portrait, IOGA **110.00**
Wash set, pink, gr & gold, scalloped, pitcher 12″, bowl 16″ . . **365.00**

Wash Sets

Before the days of running water, bedrooms were standardly equipped with a wash bowl and pitcher as a matter of neccessity. A 'toilet set' was comprised of the pitcher and bowl, toothbrush holder, covered commode, soap dish, shaving dish and mug. Through everyday usage, the smaller items were often broken, and today it is unusual to find a complete set.

Porcelain sets decorated with florals, fruits, or scenics were produced abroad by Limoges in France; and some were imported from Germany and England. During the last quarter of the 1800s and until after the turn of the century, American-made toilet sets were manufactured in abundance. Tin and graniteware sets were also used.

Art Deco, Limbach China, red & yellow sprays of roses, 14-pc. **295.00**
   White porcelain w/stylized roses, bowl 12″ dia, pitcher 11″ . **165.00**
Buffalo Pottery, Cairo pattern, 9-pc wash set **350.00**

F & Sons Burslem, blue, white, gold trim	**500.00**
Flow blue, poppies, w/soap dish	**395.00**
JG Meakin, Hanley England, wht ironstone	**150.00**
Keeling & Co, Ly Sol Ware, cobalt & gold, floral band	**175.00**
Mason's, ironstone, blue & rust; w/gold scale dragon handle	**395.00**
Meakin & Co, Hanley, England, ironstone, gr & pink shading	**65.00**
Smith Phillips, wht w/bluebells, 6-pc	**185.00**
Sponge spatter, blue & wht, bowl 14¾" dia, pitcher 11½"	**360.00**
Spongeware, blue & wht w/bands	**325.00**
Staffordshire china, blue spatterware, chamber set, 10-pc	**800.00**
Thomas Demmock & Co, Staffordshire, Koolin Ware, oriental motif	**250.00**
Wood's, Tivoli, Staffordshire blue & wht, chamber set	**125.00**
Yale, ironstone, wht & gold, 7-pc	**275.00**

Watches

First made in the 1500s in Germany, early watches were actually small clocks, suspended from the wrist or belt. By 1700, they had become the approximate shape and size we find today. The first watches produced in America were made in 1810. The well known Waltham Watch Company was established in 1850, and their inexpensive 'Waterbury' models were produced by the thousands.

Gold watches became a status symbol in the late 1800s, and were worn by both men and women on chains with fobs or jeweled slides. Ladies sometimes fastened them to their clothing with pins often set with jewels. The chatelaine watch was worn at the waist, only one of several items such as scissors, coin purses or needlecases, each attached to small chains. During this period, movements and cases were often bought separately, so inexpensive cases may sometimes be found containing well-jeweled movements, or the contrary may be true.

Most turn of the century watch cases were gold filled and are plentiful today. Open face and hunting case watches of the 1890s were solid gold or gold-filled and were often elaborately designed with several colors of gold. 18k cases are rare, and 22k cases are very valuable! Sterling cases, though interest in them is on the increase, are not in great demand.

Key:

Double sunk dial---------d/s	Railroad----------------r/r
Hunter case--------------h/c	Size----------------------s
Jewel--------------------j	Yellow gold filled-----y/g/f
Open face----------------o/f	

AWW Co, 16s 7j, J Boss, h/c, engraved	**165.00**
18s 7j, key wind & set, coin silver, o/f	**125.00**
18s 7j, o/f	**65.00**
Adam & Eve, Garden of Eden animated, erotic movement	**135.00**

Alpine, keywind, cylinder escapement, Paris, o/f	**225.00**
Appleton Tracy, 18s 17j, key wind & set, sterling o/f	**135.00**
Audemars Piguet & Co, 19j, platinum, o/f, 1925	**880.00**
Automatic Watch Co, sterling, digital, 1885	**275.00**
Burlington, 21j, 14K gold strata case, adjusted to temperature	**95.00**
21j 16s, o/f	**65.00**
Burlington Special, 19j	**145.00**
C H Meylan, 15j, platinum, diamond, enamel, diamond/onyx chain	**2,530.00**
Cartier, 19j, champleve bezel, wht gold & pearl chain pencil	**3,300.00**
Cervine, gold filled case, 1915, o/f	**35.00**
Cloisonne, lady's, blue on silver w/tiny gold birds	**475.00**
Columbus, 18s, silver, o/f	**275.00**
Railway King, 18s, y/g/f case	**200.00**
Connecticut Watch Co, Liberty, pin lever, wind & set from back	**70.00**
Deco, lady's, diamonds & 14K wht gold	**300.00**
Dudley, 19j, 14K gold, Masonic, glass front & back	**2,150.00**
Dueber, 21j 18s, 5 position, full plate, gold filled o/f	**145.00**
E Guberlin, 16j, gold & champleve, w/knife & 14K chain, 1920s	**1,100.00**
Elgin, 0s, 7j, lady's lapel, initials, sterling h/c	**95.00**
0s, 14K, 15k, h/c, initial engraving	**175.00**
3/0s, 14K gold, vine & leaf pattern, h/c	**385.00**
6s, lever set, 14K gold, h/c	**225.00**
6s 7j, Deuber, lever, gold filled, ornate, h/c	**240.00**
6s 7j, h/c	**185.00**
6s 15j, #20069025, 14K gold, h/c	**600.00**
8s, #1141341, 14K gold, lever set, h/c	**465.00**
8s 15j, engraved h/c	**175.00**
12s 7j, gold filled, o/f	**48.00**
12s 7j, gold hands, h/c	**145.00**
12s 7j, J Boss, 25 yr, h/c	**180.00**
12s 17j, 25 yr, h/c	**165.00**

14k multicolor gold, h/c, porcelain dial	**2,000.00**
15j, base metal, o/f case	**60.00**
15j, BW Raymond, gold filled, o/f	**80.00**
15j, lady's 20 yr case, engraved h/c	**110.00**
16s, y/g/f h/c	**100.00**
16s 7j, initialed, engraved, J Boss h/c	**190.00**
16s 17j, gold filled h/c	**125.00**
16s 17j, multicolor dial, gold filled h/c	**150.00**
16s 19j, BW Raymond, o/f	**65.00**
16s 21j, BW Raymond, r/r	**165.00**

16s 21j, Father Time, y/g/f, o/f **135.00**
17j, nickel case, o/f **58.00**
17s 17j, Convertible, lever set, gold filled h/c **300.00**
18s 14K gold, h/c **700.00**
18s 7j, coin silver, key wind, o/f **90.00**
18s 7j, key wind & set, sterling o/f **90.00**
18s 7j, silveroid case **48.00**
18s 17j, full plate, lever, gold filled h/c **165.00**
18s 17j, GM Wheeler, coin silver case, o/f **155.00**
21j 571, BW Raymond, J Boss, 10K gold filled case **95.00**
22j 16s, New British Admiralty BW Raymond, in box **250.00**
70s 7j, Ryerson, #27637, 1868, silver h/c **365.00**
Four dial, calendar pocket watch **250.00**
French, 00s, 18k, hand engraved florals w/rose cut diamonds . **300.00**
Geneva, keywind, porcelain dial, coin silver h/c **50.00**
Gruen Verithin, 10s, 14K gold **350.00**
Guinand, 16s 7j, split second timer, o/f **80.00**
Haas Neveux, 29j, 18k, Minute Repeater, in silk & leather case **7,500.00**
Ham 992, 16s 21j, Montgomery dial, gold filled, o/f **170.00**
Ham Navigator, 16s 22j, 24 hour dial, second hand, o/f **160.00**
Hamilton, 10s 23j, 923 orig y/g/f, o/f **130.00**
10s 23j, 945, orig y/g/f, o/f **130.00**
12s 23j, 920, orig y/g/f, o/f **125.00**
12s 23j, 922, orig y/g/f, o/f **130.00**
16s 17j, 968, gold jewel settings, Boss, o/f **400.00**
16s 17j, 987, gold filled o/f, r/r type dial **95.00**
16s 17j, #899871, lever set, gold filled, o/f **85.00**
16s 19j, 996, gold filled, o/f **190.00**
16s 21j, 990, orig y/g/f **160.00**
16s 21j, 992B, orig yellow r/r **145.00**
17j, 912, 14K gold filled case, o/f double back **85.00**
17j, 924, 25 yr gold filled case, o/f **90.00**
17j, lever set, base metal case, o/f **48.00**
18s 16j, 930 . . . . **150.00**
18s 17j, full plate, lever, damasceening, o/f **135.00**
18s 21j, 940, gold filled, damasceened, Extra, o/f **365.00**
18s 21j, #212872, full plate, damasceened, o/f **145.00**
18s 23j, 946, y/g/f, o/f **400.00**
#21, chronometer, in orig box **1,650.00**
#22, chronometer **590.00**
21j, 10K gold, Ball, glass front **380.00**
21j, 992 . . . . **95.00**
21j, 992, montgomery dial, r/r, orig case **95.00**
21j, 992, o/f **170.00**
914-14K, orig **195.00**
950 orig **335.00**
Hampden, 3/0 14 K gold, lady's, engraved h/c **275.00**

10k gold, double plated, 1895 . . . . **240.00**

16s 7j, lever set **160.00**
16s 23j, decorated dial, h/c **485.00**
18s 7j, key wind & set, silvern, o/f **120.00**
18s 7j, key wind & set, Springfield, Ma., o/f **120.00**
18s 23j, New Railroad, silveroid o/f **160.00**
21j, lever set, 20 yr gold plated case, o/f **200.00**
23j **195.00**
Howard, 12s, #1000736, 14K, script engraving **300.00**
12s 17j, gold filled, o/f **95.00**
12s 23j, orig Howard case **200.00**
12s 23j, orig case **200.00**
14s 17j, gold filled, engraved, o/f **140.00**
16s 23j, series O, orig yellow gold case **475.00**
17j, 14K gold case, adjusted 3 positions, orig box **350.00**
19j **200.00**
21j **200.00**
Illinois, 12s 21j, h/c **200.00**
12s 23j, GR410, y/g/f, o/f **175.00**
15j, Monarch, key & stem wind transition, 1884 . . . . **160.00**
16s, Benedict Bros, 18K gold **320.00**
16s 17j, Bridge model, 25 yr, h/c **185.00**
16s 19j, Sangamo Special, orig y/g/f case **550.00**
16s 21j, A Lincoln, lever set, o/f **175.00**
16s 21j, Bunn special, gold filled case **340.00**
16s 23j, BW Raymond Up & Down, y/g/f & r/r case **440.00**
16s 23j, Sangamo, y/g/f o/f **290.00**
16s 23j, Sangamo Special, y/g/f o/f **325.00**
18s, Independent Watch Co, Fredonia N.Y., stem wind, silver o/f **250.00**
18s, KW Currier #5914 . . . . **175.00**
18s, KW Nickel, 'Benicia' **100.00**
18s, sgnd President, key wind, silver o/f **175.00**
18s 7j, lever, h/c **185.00**
18s 17j, Bunn, orig script dial, y/g/f o/f **150.00**
18s 17j, key wind & set, silvern o/f **135.00**
18s 17j, Miller, silveroid case, cup type o/f **120.00**
23j, Bunn, 60 hour **550.00**
23j ruby, Bunn Special, o/f **680.00**
Ingraham, 10/0 in 16s case, pin lever **28.00**
Keystone, 18s 7j, gold filled h/c **185.00**
Lindbergh, New York to Paris, w/fob, hand engraved **250.00**
Longines, 00s, 14K, o/f, porcelain dial w/blue enamel, engraved **220.00**
16s, 8 day, up/down indicator, gold filled, o/f **550.00**
Luth Feres, Tocle, 8s, silver o/f, fuses **160.00**
Manistee Watch Co, 16s 17j, silver h/c, rare **275.00**
Marion, 18s, KWE Rollo, butterfly cutout **275.00**
Masonic, w/masonic dial, y/g/f o/f **100.00**
Musical, disc movement, gold case **4,000.00**
New England Watch Co, Duplex, skeletonized model **240.00**
Skeleton watch **385.00**
New Haven Clock Co, 2s, Tip Top, pin lever **35.00**
6s, pin lever, o/f **40.00**
18s 15j, #778013, keywind & set, o/f **475.00**
Omega, 12s 14K gold, thin opera case **300.00**
Patek Philippe, 12s, 18K orig case **775.00**
18j, platinum & diamond o/f, #193792 . . . . **1,320.00**
Pennsylvania Special, 17j, 14K gold h/c **950.00**
Plan watch, 18s 17j, full plate, engraved h/c **185.00**
Rockford, 16-7 . . . . **69.50**
18s 11j, #16255, key wind & set, silver h/c, rare **575.00**
18s, #9416, key wind, silver o/f **260.00**
Key wind, silver chain, #968, 6 oz silver h/c **950.00**
SI Tobias & Co, 16s, 17j, o/f, English Fusee, w/monastery **500.00**
Seth Thomas, 6s 7j, lever, h/c **175.00**
South Bend, 16s 9j, #209, 20 yr case, o/f **85.00**

16s 15j, y/g/f case, multicolor dial 85.00
18s 17j, y/g/f case 85.00
Stop watch, Dan Patch.................................. 550.00
Studebaker, 12, 21j, y/g/f case........................ 150.00
Swiss, 6s, 18K gold, key wind, h/c 225.00
  6s 7j, 14K gold, lever set, h/c 285.00
  12s, 18K gold, key wind, h/c 500.00
  12s, 18K gold, key wind, engraved gold dial, floral case, o/f . 400.00
  12s, 18K, h/c, machine turned w/blk enameling 490.00
  14s, 18K gold, very decorative hands, o/f 450.00
Swiss Calender Watch, 16s, moon phases, silver, o/f 375.00
Touchon & Co, 19j, platinum o/f, platinum chain, #44362 .... 770.00
  For Tiffany, 19j, gold, platinum w/champleve, o/f 550.00
Trenton, 6s 7j, gold filled h/c 100.00
US Marion AH Wallis, key wind 485.00
US Watch Co, 18s, #34747, Asa Fuller, Marion N.J., 5 oz, silver h/c 350.00
United States Watch Co, 15j, Edwin Rollo, #624Z, silver h/c .. 500.00
  18s 17j, engraved plates, gold filled h/c................ 200.00
Waltham, 0s, 14K, bullet & floral engraving, h/c 290.00
  0s, 14K, engraved half moons w/diamonds 250.00
  0s, 14K gold hands, h/c 300.00
  0s, 14K, vine & leaf pattern w/diamond star cut, h/c 240.00
  3/0s, 14K, h/c, wear on engraving 250.00
  3/0s 15j, 14K gold, bullet case w/village scene, h/c 250.00
  3/0s 15j, 14K gold, initials, o/f....................... 130.00
  6s, #312348, 14K gold, lever set, h/c 335.00
  6s, #3130177, 14K gold, h/c 285.00
  6s, #8584967, 14K gold, multicolor case, h/c 590.00
  6s, 14K, lever set, floral & village scene engraved 375.00
  6s 7j, Deuber gold filled h/c, engraved 240.00
  6s 17j, lady's, gold filled h/c......................... 125.00
  10 Ligne Maximus, gold filled, o/f 120.00
  10s, 21j, Col A Maximus 190.00
  12s 17j, 14K gold, lg numerals & hands, o/f 325.00
  12s 17j, Colonial series, see through case 72.00
  14K gold, #6011885, h/c 350.00
  16s 7j, Traveler, 20 yr o/f........................... 80.00
  16s 19j, Riverside 55.00
  16s 21j, Cresent, r/r dial, o/f 165.00
  16s 21j, Maximus, 900 made, y/g/f, h/c 525.00
  16s 21j, Model 88 Maximus, 200 made, y/g/f, o/f 525.00
  16s 23j, Vanguard, orig case 120.00
  17s 23j, Vanguard, y/g/f & r/r case 135.00
  18s 7j, sterling, lever set, engraved h/c 185.00
  18s 11j, Wm Ellery, lever, sterling h/c................. 185.00
  18s 15j, #5510, key wind, 1st run Appleton Tracy........ 600.00
  18s 15j, coin case Appleton Tracy 95.00
  18s 17j, PS Bartlett, Fogg's Pat, silveroid o/f 135.00
  18s 19j, Vanguard, o/f 140.00
  18s 23j, Vanguard, d/s, y/g/f, r/r case 140.00
  19j, 14K gold, rosewood cased, h/c 675.00
  19j, Riverside, o/f 185.00
  21j, 845, r/r, orig case 95.00
  23j, Vanguard, gold filled, o/f....................... 400.00
Wristwatch, Audemars Piguet, platinum & diamonds, 1925 ... 440.00
  Baum & Mercier, ladies, 14K gold w/leather strap 350.00
  Omega, ladies, 18K gold attached band 650.00
  Rolex, oyster perpetual date, 14K gold Jubilee band 995.00
  Navigators WWII 50.00

Watch Fobs

Watch fobs have been popular since the last quarter of the 19th century. They were often made by retail companies to advertise their products.

Souvenir, commemorative, and political fobs were also produced---all are popular collectibles today.

Abrahamson Fur Co 50.00
Adam's Road Machinery, mowing hillside, advertising 46.00
Adamant Suit, Rosenthal Bros, NY, boy in knickers sitting in box 30.00
Allies European War, 1914 .... 35.00
Allis-Chalmers, 140,000 pounds, aqua & yellow, silver wash 11.00
Amber glass, w/profile of classical goddess 8.00
American Legion, Milwaukee 1941 .... 18.50
American Old Time Insurance, Indian head 20.00
Angelica Jacket, porcelain baker 40.00
Art Nouveau, yellow gold, round, scroll work, opens as locket, 1912 145.00
Atkins Hand Saw, figural, ribbon type 65.00
Avery, bulldog 85.00
  Kerosene tractor 75.00
BPOE, #49, 1919, Albany N.Y., red enamel star, bronze 15.00
BSA, red sunburst on chrome 7.00
Baseball 15.00
Basketball, brown color on metal 6.00
Beaded, blk & gold beads 15.00
Beck Sweet Feed, Edgar Morgan, Memphis Tenn., donkey, celluloid 45.00
Boy Scout 50.00
Brass, w/amethyst stone, ornate brass slide set............ 10.25
Brockway Trucks, husky on snow, wht & red enamel on chrome 15.00
Bronze, arrow w/horse's head & horseshoe, 1½"............ 7.00
Brotherhood of RR Trainmen 10.00
Buffalo Bill, Pawnee Bill, gold plated 45.00
Buffalo Springfield Steam Roller Co, bronze, orig strap, 1920 .. 65.00
Buick, w/blue ground 35.00
Buick Motors Cars, valve in head, advertising............. 60.00
Case, cross mount 85.00
  Eagle, oval 50.00
  Plow works 65.00
Cat DC21 .... 25.00
Caterpillar, Perkins Machinery Co, South Hadly, Mass., pewter . 14.00
Century of Progress, 1934 .... 30.00
Chicago Exposition 1933, Research Industry 1833-1933, Deco.. 13.00
Columbus Suit, Boston 22.00
Commonwealth of Kentucky, United We Stand, Divided We Fall 35.00
Cox-Roosevelt, presidential campaign, jugate type 62.00
Cyrus Hall McCormick, 2 men, horse & reaper, 1831-1931 .... 50.00
Dartmare Pixie, brass 15.00
Denver US Aeronautical Light, arrowhead shape, 1929, pewter . 15.00
Des Moines Silo, celluloid 25.00
Diamond Reo Trucks, world's most experienced, pewter 11.00
E Atkins Co, Silver Steel Saws, mesh type w/figural hand saw .. 65.00
E-Z Ola, brass, w/fancy emblem 12.50
Eagle, figural, Independence Day 1918 .... 25.00
Egyptian, bronze strap type, 4 linked sections of relief figural, sgnd 95.00
  Old strap type, Egyptian scenes, w/H Carter coin, sgnd 50.00
English, rose gold, 9K, cutout work, hand tooling, crest design . 95.00
Estey, Merchants/Bankers Schools N.Y., scalloped, blue & wht.. 20.00
Eucha, w/watch 25.00
Euclid, earthmoving truck, BUC Hawler, bronze 10.00
Fireman's hat, 3-D, gold plated, leather strap 23.00
Fisher, body 35.00
Football, brown on metal 6.00
Fordson, tractor 100.00
Frost King, gas engine advertising...................... 75.00
Gesanguerein Concordia, Altoona Penn., 1916, gold washed ... 30.00
Gibson girl, leather back, old & unusual 22.50
Gold, 10k, lions head in high relief, gr jewels in lions mouth .. 125.00
Gold, w/amber jewels, attached to 15 connecting bars, ornate .. 25.00

Green River Whiskey **30.00**
Gypsy Tour, 1917 .... **65.00**
H Miller Manufacturing Co **90.00**
Hamlight, lantern **85.00**
Harley Davidson **65.00**
Heinz 57 .... **22.50**
Herschel Oil, figural sickle blade, tempered **35.00**
Hoffman Barber Supplies **25.00**
Hub Furniture, porcelain wagon wheel hub **75.00**
IATSE, Louisville Kentucky, June 1940, gold plated brass **15.00**
  28th Convention, June 21-18, 1926, gold washed **23.00**
IHC, tractor **35.00**
Indian chief head **30.00**
Indian Motorcycles, figural arrowhead **55.00**
International Harvester, 2 worlds **60.00**
  Bucking bronco **35.00**
  New Orleans, advertising **22.00**
International Watch Fob Association, cutout Case tractor **22.50**
Iowa State Seal **35.00**
JD Adams Co, man on grader & 1 man pushing wheelbarrow .. **55.00**
John Deere, MOP **75.00**
  Round front, deer head & initial D, pewter **12.00**
Kansas Pacific RR, steer's head star, 1874, advertising **30.00**
Kelly Springfield Tires, tire, women **95.00**
Kit Carson, Denver, Colorado **30.00**
Labor Day, Des Moines, Sept 1, 1913 .... **32.00**
Lady's head, embossed as Liberty, 13 stars around edge **30.00**
Laflin, Rand Rifle Powder, orange, cannon, ornate, advertising . **40.00**
Larkin Nationwide Contest Winner 1916, USA shape, gold wash **30.00**
Lee Broom **35.00**
Leisey Brewing Co, advertising **75.00**
Leroi Neumatic Air Tools, pewter **12.00**
Lincoln, w/eagle & shield, E Pluribus Virum, old pewter **20.00**
Lion Brand Fertilizer, embossed lion **45.00**
Lone Star Cement, porcelain **25.00**
Luther League, 36th annual convention, 1929, pewter **14.00**
Lyre, in relief, Art Nouveau, dk metal **10.00**
Mack, bulldog, performance counts, bronze **11.00**
  Truck & trailor center, West Virginia, colors on chrome **15.00**
  Truck shape, Mack off highway trucks, brass **11.00**
Magobar **50.00**
Man of War **35.00**
Masonic, 1913 .... **25.00**
  Sq & compass, MOP buckle, alligator strap **125.00**
Massachusetts State Seal, silver plated **15.00**
Meadow Gold Butter, celluloid insert **40.00**
Metal Workers Convention, Montreal **25.00**
Mexican Border Service, 1916 .... **17.50**
Miami, 1934, bronze **15.00**
Michelin Earth Mover Tires, Michelin Tire Corporation, pewter . **12.00**
Milwaukee Wisconsin, the Badger State, Aug 2-7, 1953, bronze. **10.00**
Minnehaha Falls **22.00**
Missouri State Seal **18.00**
Monarch Ranges **65.00**
NY Buffaloes **15.00**
NYS Federation of Labor, organized 1864, gold plastic **10.00**
NYS Firemen's Association, gold washed **17.00**
Nantucket Encampment **20.00**
New Jersey State Seal, silver on brass **11.00**
New York City Seal, silver on brass **10.00**
North American Gasoline Conference 1907, Oklahoma seal **35.00**
Northern Rock Island, plow **85.00**
Noursman, w/club, embossed **38.00**
Old Senate House, Kingston N.Y., bronze **10.00**

Old Style Lager, figural, tricolor porcelain **35.00**
Oliver Oc 9 Crawler **55.00**
Oliver Typewriter, embossed **35.00**
Our Choice, Bryon Kern **20.00**
  Tabt & Sherman, pewter **20.00**
Our Freedom Must Live, 1960, copper **7.00**
Owl Brand Coffee **35.00**
Pathfinder Compass, embossed Indian chief **45.00**
Penn State Elk's Revision, Eastan 1927, bronze **15.00**
Playboy Bunny, MMcDean England, wht, blk & chrome **6.00**
Polar Bear Flour, figural bear **35.00**
Polarine Motor Oils, embossed bear **35.00**
Polly Parrot Shoes, color cello **45.00**
Remington, 100th anniversary, 1916, brass **125.00**
  National letter writing contest, 1913 .... **125.00**
Reo **40.00**
Roosevelt, Fairbanks **28.00**
Roosevelt Dam **20.00**
SS Catalina Casino **25.00**
Sal Vet **45.00**
Salvation Army, blue enamel shield on brass **10.00**
San Francisco Liberty Bell **35.00**
San Francisco Railway, w/cable car figure **7.50**
Satisfaction Coffee **50.00**
Shield w/Navy, anchor **26.00**
Silk Association of America, A Filo Corona 1872, colors on gold plate **20.00**
Simmons Keen Kutter **65.00**
Souvenir Buffalo Bill, circus, early 1900s, gold on brass **17.50**
Square w/rounded edges, center diamond, hair plaited on sides **150.00**
St Louis Expo, 1904, Palace of Liberal Arts **36.00**
Standard Varnish Works **22.50**
Starett Tools **25.00**
Statue of Liberty, silver wash on brass **12.00**
Sterling Shield, warships & airplane **20.00**
Teddy Roosevelt, ribbon fob **240.00**
Trojan, 4 wheeler **12.00**
UMW Tri Districts Shemokin, 1922, gold plated brass **20.00**
US Military Acadamy, dedicated Oct 1908, gold washed bronze . **30.00**
US Steel, EH Gary **37.50**
US Tires **17.50**
University of Iowa, 1915 .... **52.00**
VFW, US for freedom 1917, 1918, 1945, bronze **11.00**
Victorian, gold filled, 2 hanging from watch clasp **35.00**
WS Tyler Co, Cleveland, Ohio, figural fence **40.00**
William Jennings Bryan **140.00**
William Taft **35.00**
Wisconsin State Seal **18.00**
Woodsman of the World, gold, w/braided human hair chain **75.00**
York Congress Session, 1927, anniversary **30.00**

Waterford

The Waterford Glass Company operated in Ireland from the late 1700s until 1851 when the factory was closed. One hundred years later, in 1951, another Waterford glass works was instituted that produced glass similar to the 18th century wares---crystal glass, usually with cut decoration. Today, Waterford is a generic term referring to the type of glass first produced there.

Claret jar, w/stopper, diamond & paneled facet, scalloped base, 7½" **90.00**
Decanter w/stopper, paneled/ribbed/Coin Spot, flare neck 1780, 11" **200.00**
Heart pendant, w/heavy sterling chain, cut glass, 20" **30.00**
Salt, master, high pedestal, rolled rim, crystal, 4" **65.00**
Urn, ftd, oval flutes & bull's eyes, tall finial, 14" **285.00**

Watts

During the '50s and '60s, Watts Pottery Company of Zanesville, Ohio, produced a line that is becoming popular with collectors of American kitchenware. Their ovenware line is decorated with bold brush strokes of color on a buff glazed background. A variety of patterns may be found, the most familiar are the apple, star flower, rooster, tulip and grape. Much of the ware was made for advertising premiums and is often found stamped with the name of a retail company.

Bowl, advertising Cascade Oil, 6½″ **7.50**
  Black w/pink & blue florals, 11″ **12.00**
  Cereal, red flower, 6″ **6.50**
  Flat, red apple, 5¾″ **5.00**
  Mixing, apple **6.00**
    Blue, pink stripe, mkd Tangeman Grocery, 6″ **15.00**
    Cherry, 6½″ **6.50**
    White, blue stripe, set of 3, 5¼″, 6¼″, 7″ **15.00**
  Red flower, 5″ **4.50**
Cookie jar, apple, bean pot shape, covered **25.00**
Creamer, w/red floral **11.00**
Mug, poinsettia, 4¾″ **6.50**
Pie pan, apple, advertisement **16.00**
Pitcher, red apple, 4″ **5.00**
  6″ **9.50**
  7″ **12.00**
  With 4 mugs, mkd **50.00**
  Starflower, 8″ **15.00**
Soup bowl, red apple, 5½″ **4.00**

Wave Crest

Wave Crest is the trademark used on a line of creamy opaque glassware manufactured by the C.F. Monroe Company of New York, who operated there from 1892 until 1916. Vases, boxes, tablewares and humidors in swirled and blown out shapes were either hand painted or transfer printed with florals, scenics or portraits. Many pieces were enhanced with ornately scrolled ormolu handles, feet or rim decor. Several marks were used: the black mark, Trade Mark Wave Crest; the Red Banner mark; and the paper label, Wave Crest Ware, Patented Oct 4, 1892.

Basket, blue w/floral enameling, puffy egg crate, 6½″ **435.00**
Biscuit jar, brown & yellow roses, pewter top, 8″ **195.00**
  Florals, Helmschmeid swirl, plated lid, sgnd, 7½″ **385.00**
  Flowers, sq, puffy, numbered **375.00**
Bon-bon, lavender & blue florals, hp, w/handles, sgnd, 3¾″ dia **115.00**
Box, baroque shell, floral, 7″ round **400.00**
  Cigars, puffy, hinged cover, sgnd, 7″ **950.00**
  Cigars, swirl & floral enamel, 'cigars' in gold, sgnd, 6″ **449.00**
  Clovers, hp, embossed, blk mark, 6x5″ **445.00**
Box, Daisies, 3½x7″ **650.00**
  Deck of cards, blownout, sgnd **235.00**
  Double portrait of courting couple, embossed, blk mark, 5½″ dia **665.00**
  Enamel flowers, blue, 4x3″ **185.00**
  Enameled wht spray on wht ormolu rim, hinged cover, 2½x3″ dia **200.00**
  Fall decor, robin egg blue, embossed, blk mark, 7″ **625.00**
  Floral enamel, gold decor, swirls, label, hinged, 4x7″ **650.00**
  Florals, blue, embossed rococo, ftd, hinged lid, 3½″ dia **300.00**
  Florals, embossed, hinged cover, 5″ dia **400.00**
  Florals, hp, brass ormolu, base ftd, 4″ dia **285.00**
  Glossy w/florals, Helmschmeid swirl, 5″ **365.00**
  Handkerchief, ribbon scenic, brass base, ftd, 6½x7″ dia **960.00**
  Hinged, orig lining, sgnd, colorful, 5½ ″ **325.00**
  Hp scene w/woman, child & chicken, sgnd, 3½″ dia **250.00**

Jewel, 2 cherubs gardening, pale gr ground, 5½″ dia **525.00**
Jewel, floral decor on wht, plated rim, Helmschmeid swirl, 6″ dia **275.00**
Jeweled, ftd, hinged cover, 5x5″ **600.00**
Pink florals encircle cupid, blue, covered, 3½″ **750.00**
Pink florals, hp, silver ormolu rim, octagonal, sgnd, 6″ **485.00**
Pink, blue & wht flowers, pink & blue, hinged, sgnd, 4x7″ dia **450.00**
Powder, hp blue flowers, Helmschmeid swirl, mkd **150.00**
Scrolls & enamel decor, pink, hinged cover, 4½x5″ dia **375.00**
Scrolls & floral decor, aqua, hinged, oval, 3½x5¼″ **325.00**
Scrolls, pink & wht ground, hinged cover, 7″ dia **395.00**
Shell mold, blue florals, pink, 3″ **300.00**
Sprays of flowers, ftd ormolu w/lion head & paws, 5½x7″ . . . **775.00**
Swirl w/florals, pink lining, hinged cover, unmkd, 2½x3″ . . . **165.00**
Swirl, unmkd, 4½″ **200.00**
Zinnia lid in pink, blownout, hp decor, sgnd, 4½″ **595.00**
Carafe, satin finish, paneled, pewter neck **300.00**
Cigar set, pink apple blossoms, ormolu beading, ftd, 3 pc **425.00**
Dish, scroll mold w/florals, ormolu collar, blownout, 3½″ dia . . **100.00**
  Swirl, pink banner, squarish w/round brass rim, open, 3″ . . **85.00**
Dresser bowl, lavender, 4″ **165.00**
Dresser box, mill scene, gr gound, orig liner, sgnd, 3x4″ **295.00**
Dresser jar, yellow floral, pink, sgnd, w/lid, 4x4″ **250.00**
Fernery, floral, yellow, 8″ **180.00**
  Flowers & vine, puffy, insert, unsgnd, lg **250.00**
Ferner, ringed brass liner, sgnd, 7″ **35.00**
Jewel box, 2 cherubs gardening, pale gr ground, 4½″ dia **525.00**
  Floral decor on wht, plated rim, Helmschmeid swirl, 6″ dia . **275.00**
Jewel stand, blue florals, hp, w/handle on pedestal, 3¼x3¼″ . . **125.00**
Jewel tray, ormolu ftd w/lion heads, sgnd, 7″ dia **285.00**
Match holder, embossed, ormolu feet, 2″ **350.00**
Napkin ring, hp blue forget-me-not, wht satin ground, mkd, 1896 **125.00**
Oil lamp, morning glory reserves w/scenics **325.00**
Photo receiver **365.00**
Pin dish, sunflower mold, floral, ormolu handles, 3½″ **120.00**
Pin holder, blk mk, open 2 handles **75.00**
Pin tray, pink flowers, deep blue, sgnd, open, 4½″ **145.00**

Pitcher, floral enamel, silver handle, 3½″ **200.00**
Salt & pepper, daisy petal pattern, pr **105.00**
  Emb swirls, sq **120.00**
  Floral decor, Helmschmeid swirl **75.00**
  Forget-me-nots, tall **65.00**
  Puffy floral **95.00**
Salt, pink w/hp, Helmschmeid **125.00**
Sugar & creamer, floral decor, swirl, blue to ivory, Helmschmeid **425.00**
  Mushrooms, floral, swirl, plated cover **325.00**
  Pink apple blossoms, Helmschmeid **650.00**
Syrup, floral decor w/pink beading separating panels, twisted . . **175.00**
Vase, beading, pink & wht, ormolu, unsgnd, pr **350.00**

Chrysanthemums on ormolu mountings, gold handles & ft, 13½″ **895.00**
Florals in russet cartouche, hp, ormolu handles & feet, 12″ . **875.00**
Gr beaded florals, applied wht baroque shells, olive gr ground, 14″ **595.00**
Maiden & cherubs, hp, brass ormolu handles & feet, 17½″ **1,375.00**

Wax

The craft of wax modeling flourished after a very successful showing in 1851 at the Great London Exhibition, and continued to be of interest throughout the century. Many painstaking hours were put into each article. Instruction in the craft was published in the book *Handbook of Modelling Wax*. Upon completion, the project was often framed in glass for protection.

Angel, 4″ **40.00**
Banana vendor, blk man w/bulging eyes, 5½″ **425.00**
Bust of Napoleon, in orig shadow box frame **195.00**
Bust portrait, in shadow box frame, 5x6″ **155.00**
Chicken vender, blk woman **400.00**
Plaque, Whist at Wardles, Mr Pickwick, shadow box frame . . . **105.00**

Weapons

Among the varied areas of specialization within the broad category of weapons, guns are by far the most popular. Muskets are among the earliest firearms; they were large-bore shoulder arms, usually firing black powder, with separate loading of powder and shot. Some ignited the charge by flintlock or caplock, while later types used a firing pin with a metallic cartridge. Side arms, referred to as such because they were worn at the side, include pistols and revolvers. Pistols range from early single-shot and multiple barrels to modern types with cartridges held in the handle. Revolvers were supplied with a cylinder that turned to feed a fresh round in front of the barrel breech. Other firearms include shotguns, which fired round or conical bullets and had a smooth inner barrel surface, and rifles, so named because the interior of the barrel contained spiral grooves (rifling) which increased accuracy.

In the listing below, f/l is flintlock; f/s is full stock; cal is caliber.

Bayonet w/scabbard, Swedish, 1896 . . . . **24.00**
Cannon, 1600s, 7′ **695.00**
Dagger, curved w/ivory handle, engraved sheath, 8½″ **25.00**
  Silver, ornate engraving, w/sheath & velvet lined case **125.00**
Guns
Boot pistol, engraved steel frame, walnut stock, mid-1800s **100.00**
  Percussion, screw-off barrel, 1848, LEG proof **200.00**
Carbine, 1873 Springfield **325.00**
Colt, 1860 Army **415.00**
Derringer, Colt #3, serial #1549 . . . . **250.00**
  Colt 41 cal, rim fire, brass frame, 1800s **350.00**
  Remington, 4 barrel, 32 cal, pat Oct 1861 . . . . **265.00**
Long rifle, Ky., curly maple f/s, f/l, silver/brass inlays, carved, 58″ **900.00**
  Kentucky, carved f/s, brass mounts, late 1700s, G Kopp **500.00**
  Kentucky, f/s, percussion lock plate, brass inlay, Tyron Philad **550.00**
  Kentucky, walnut f/s, percussion lock, octagon barrel, 61″ . . **650.00**
Luger, 1917 German, 9″ barrel stock/rifle, case mkd KBAG 1916 **7,500.00**
  1940 S42, NRA **650.00**
Musket, American f/l, walnut stock w/US Eagle Springfield mk, 1810 **375.00**
  Colt, Civil War, 58 cal percussion **500.00**
  Full walnut stock w/brass furniture, Brown Bess, late 1700s . **475.00**
  Full walnut stock, 69 cal, US contract 1798, Conn. mk **300.00**
  Harper's Ferry, early percussion conversion, 69 cal, 1829 . . . **650.00**
  Springfield 1795, type III, 69 cal, 57″, 1816 . . . . **950.00**
  Springfield 1863, 58 cal, contract model, all orig **475.00**
  Springfield Civil War 1864, 58 cal **375.00**
Muzzle-loader, child's size, maple w/brass inlay **700.00**
Pistol, dueling, Paris, 1830s, 38 cal, hexagonal barrel, 11″ . . **1,200.00**
  F/l, ornate silver & gold inlay, walnut, 1830s **580.00**

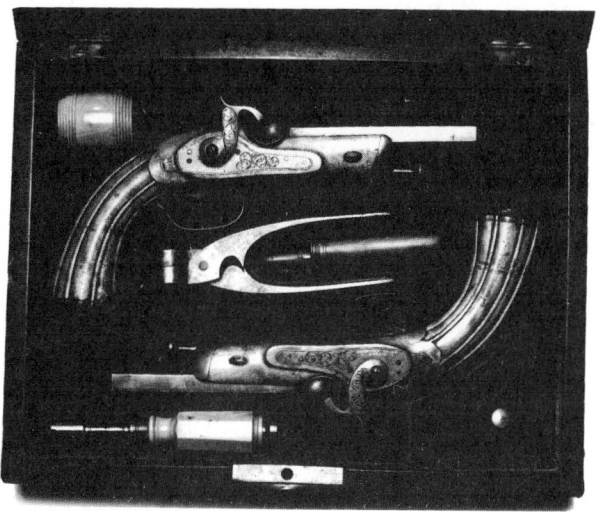

French, 60 cal, 1850s, in box w/accessories **1,000.00**
Hero S S, brass frame **150.00**
Hopkins & Allen 'Dictator', mounted in display frame, 1860s . **70.00**
Kentucky-type, carved, engraved, small, 1780s **565.00**
Pirate's dbl-barrel, early percussion **325.00**
Remington M1871 rolling block, civilian model **500.00**
Remington vest pocket 22 cal w/walnut stocks, 1860s **175.00**
Ryan & Watson, brass cannon-barrel, Revolutionary War officer's **550.00**
Smith & Wesson, 22 cal, tip-up, 1890s **125.00**
Pocket gun, Stevens, 1878, 22 cal tip-up **160.00**
  Forehand & Wadsworth 1861, sidehammer 22 cal **170.00**
  Marlin 1878, 32 cal **155.00**
  Smith & Wesson, 1877, 32 cal **155.00**
  Stevens 1878, 22 cal tip-up **160.00**
Revolver, Army Colt 44, 1860 . . . . **275.00**
  Colt 1855 root side 2 hammer, 28 cal percussion **2,255.00**
  Colt 1877 Lightning, storekeeper's model, 32 cal, 3½″ barrel **290.00**
  Colt 31 cal, 1849 . . . . **235.00**
  Marlin 32 cal, nickel over brass frame, gutta percha grips, 1800s **110.00**
  Remington, cap & ball, DA new model, pat 1858, w/holster . **525.00**
  Smith & Wesson, #2 Civil War Army, 32 rf cal, 6″ barrel . . **325.00**
  Smith & Wesson, 22, 1st US, pat 1855, #1, 2nd issue **250.00**
  Smith & Wesson, model #2, 2nd issue, 1885, 38 cal, 3½″ barrel **275.00**
Rifle, Ballard Pacific, 38-50 . . . . **260.00**
  Harper's Ferry, dated 1852, walnut stock **350.00**
  Kentucky Perc, 42 cal, octagonal bbl, tiger maple stock **925.00**
  Kentucky f/l, 40″ barrel, full maple stock, brass **600.00**
  Kentucky, curly maple, sgnd, 1865, 58″ **600.00**
  Kentucky, f/s, tiger maple, barrel mkd 'In Riling' **425.00**
  Kentucky, half-stock, 14½″ powder horn, 51″ **450.00**
  Marlin Ballard Lever Action, 22 cal, octagon barrel **300.00**
  Mauser 1891, w/bayonet & scabbard, M **250.00**
  Percussion breech loading, 1830s **325.00**
  Springfield, model 1884, 4570 cal **175.00**
  Stevens Ideal Model 45, 22 cal, dbl triggers, 44½ action . . . **370.00**
  Winchester 1873, 44 cal **1,500.00**
  Winchester 1906, 22 cal **250.00**
  Winchester 22 cal, 1890 pump **200.00**
  Winchester Hornet, 22 cal, single shot **245.00**
  Winchester model 1886, 40-82 cal **1,200.00**
Shotgun, dbl muzzle-loading, stock w/carved glass-eyed Indian . **350.00**
  Dbl-barrel, carved walnut stock, Remington Arms Co **260.00**
  German Drilling, 3-barrel **450.00**
  John Conover, dbl-barrel, 12-gauge **150.00**
  Parker, 12 gauge, dbl-barrel hammers **800.00**
  Springfield 1881 Forager, trapdoor, all original **800.00**

Wells Fargo, dbl-barrel **750.00**
Winchester Model 12, 16 gauge **350.00**
Winchester 12 gauge trap, Monte Carlo stock **480.00**
Saber, w/scabbard, Civil War Cavalry, US mkd **170.00**

Sword

Bone & brass handle, 19″ curved blade w/scabbard, Persian . . . **20.00**
Brass hilt, 27″ slightly curved blade mkd Toledo 1840 . . . . **35.00**
Indian Talwar, gold inlay, 1750s **300.00**
KKK, complete & mkd, 1870s **350.00**
Russian Cavalry, brass handle & furniture on scabbard, 1905 . . **125.00**
Samari, 1930, all original **275.00**
Silver mountings on wood scabbard and wood hilt, ornate **100.00**

Weathervane

The earliest weathervanes were of handmade wrought iron and were generally simple angular silhouettes with a small hole suggesting an eye. Later, copper, zinc and polychromed wood with features in relief were fashioned into more realistic forms. Ships, horses, fish, Indians, cocks, and angels were popular motifs.

In the 19th century, silhouettes were often made from sheet metal. Wooden figures became highly carved and were painted in vivid colors. E.G. Washburne and Co, in New York, was one of the most prominent manufacturers of weathervanes during the last half of the century.

Today, these early weathervanes are valuable examples of early American folk art.

Arrow, copper & iron, 1900, 30″ long **225.00**
Butterfly, sheet metal, late 1800s **1,100.00**
Car, w/driver, open, tin, iron arrow **150.00**
Cow, copper spear, painted iron, directional, lightning rod **225.00**
Lightning rod & ball, old, 7x9″ **165.00**
Sheet iron w/old paint, 1900, 18x32″ **265.00**
Tin on tin cone, red ball, w/lightning rod **170.00**
Deer, full body jumping, iron head & horns, copper body, 24x28″ **750.00**
Ear of corn, zinc, wht milk glass ball, 1890 . . . . **350.00**
Horse, lightning rod & ball, old, 9″ **165.00**
Running, carved, polychromed, wooden, 38″ **1,100.00**
Running, copper, 1800s, 32″ **400.00**
Running, sheet metal, yellow paint, 19x38″ **300.00**
Sheet iron, orig lacy iron arrow directional, 10½x24″ **145.00**
Sheet tin, old yellow paint, 37x16″ **275.00**
Pig, full bodied, copper **175.00**
Tin & cast iron, arrow, early 1900s, 5½x19″ **100.00**
Zinc & cast iron, directional, w/lighting rod, 8″ **125.00**
Ram, tin, copper rod, red ball, 14x12″ **125.00**
Rooster, sheet iron, hand made **1,400.00**
Stylized, cutout sheet metal **130.00**
Wooden, blk & red paint, 15x14″ **330.00**
Sunflower, copper, 1880 . . . . **550.00**
Whale, copper **625.00**

Weaving

Early Americans used a variety of tools and a great amount of time to produce the material from which their clothing was made. Soaked and dried flax was broken on a flax brake to remove waste material. It was then tapped and stroked with a scutching knife. Hackles further removed waste and separated the short fibers from the longer ones. Unspun fibers were placed on the distaff of the spinning wheel for processing into yarn. The yarn was then wound around a reel for measuring. Three tools used for this purpose were the niddy-noddy, the reel yarn winder, and the click reel. After it was washed and dyed, the yarn was transferred to a barrel-cage or squirrel-cage swift and fed onto a bobbin winder.

Today, flax wheels are more plentiful than the large wool wheels, since

they were small and could be more easily stored and preserved. The distaff, an often discarded or misplaced part of the wheel, is very scarce. French spinners from the Quebec area painted their wheels. Many have been stripped and refinished by those unaware of this fact. Wheels may be very simple or have a great amount of detail, depending upon the owner's ethnic background and the makers skill.

Distaff, handfashioned wood, 4 flax, wool or tow in spinning, 1700s **100.00**
Flax breaker, thin cup 1-pc wood handle & breaking edge **60.00**
Flax hackle, rose top, sharp nails driven in from reverse side . **165.00**
Flax wheel, orig treadle, bobbin & rotating wheel, Windsor, 1700s **200.00**
Niddy-noddy, hickory, turned, mortised, pinned joints, 19″ **80.00**

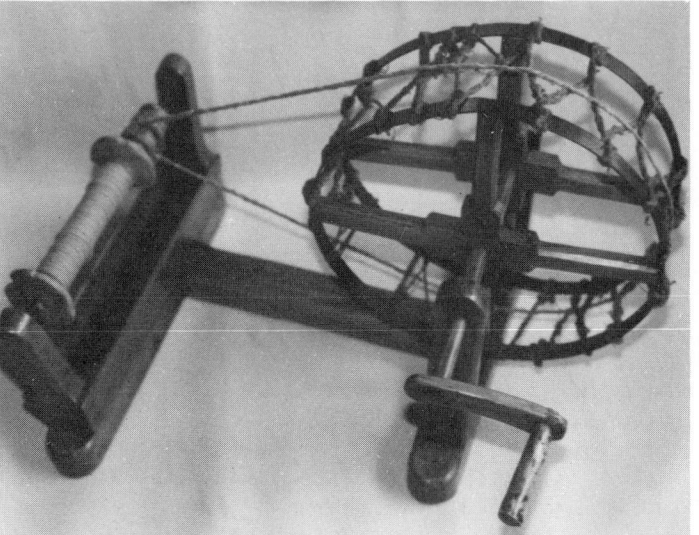

Quill (bobbin) winder, handturned wheel, 18th century **225.00**
Spinning wheel, complete, German, 1850 . . . . **150.00**
Wilder, Keene, NH **245.00**
Wood w/some manufactured cast iron parts, 30″ wheel **195.00**
Wooden, early primitive, lg **300.00**
Tape loom, domed top, cutout sides, round bottom edges, 21½x8″ **125.00**
Poplar, dovetailed, crests, reel w/ratchet, 20½x17½x7¾″ . . . **310.00**
Weaver's stool, lathe turned maple, iron stretchers, 1800s **85.00**
Wool carders, handled wood paddles, tiny wire teeth, pair **25.00**
Yarn swift, folding wood strips **129.00**
Yarn winder, handmade 2-pc, lg wheel & stand w/counting device **175.00**
Turned legs, rectangular chamfered base, 1700s **70.00**
Walnut, adjustable 4-arm table top, clamps on table **45.00**

Webb

Thomas Webb and Sons have been making fine art glass in Stourbridge, England, since 1837. Besides their fine cameo glass, they have also made enameled ware, and pieces heavily decorated with applied glass ornaments. The butterfly is a motif that has been so often featured that it often helps to identify Webb's work.

Bowl, cameo, salmon overlay, pearlized wht underside, butterfly, 10″ **600.00**
Ivory, amber feet, pink lining, floral enamel, 5x7½″ **700.00**
Satin, brown, ftd, 6 crimp top, 3 reeded gold feet, 4x5¾″ dia **650.00**
Cruet, tall stopper, twisted handle, blue w/clear amber base, 10½″ **325.00**
Ewer, satin, yellow w/applied handle **145.00**
Finger bowl, cameo, underplate, 3 color, flowers & butterfly, sgnd **3,250.00**
Jar, cameo, plated cover & handle, red ground w/wht morning glory **875.00**
Loving cup, bronze, glass pedestal, 2 scroll handles, unsgnd, 5½″ **75.00**
Perfume bottle, cameo, blue satin sphere, silver cap, 3½″ **875.00**
Cameo, citron, flowers, sgnd, 5½″ **1,250.00**
Cameo, lay down, wht flowers on blue, 4″ **645.00**

Cameo, sterling top, sgnd, 4½″ **1,450.00**
Pitcher, aqua, bird & floral decor in yellows & pinks **275.00**
Plaque, cameo, William E Gladstone, sgnd, 2½″ **2,500.00**
Rose bowl, satin, blue blossoms, box pleated top, 3¾x2½″ dia **375.00**
   Satin, brown w/gold prunus blossoms, butterfly, 2¼x2¼″ . . . **395.00**
Scent bottle, satin, gold prunus, brown, reclining, 4x1½″ **395.00**
Urn, ftd w/handles, bronze, 5½″ **80.00**
   Satin, pink rim & handles, acorn finial, brass top, 8″ **195.00**
Vase, bronze with blue/grey lining, 12″ **135.00**
   Bronze w/gold trim, 2 gold butterflies, unsgnd, 6½″ **400.00**
   Bronze, teal body, 4 depressions, sgnd, 4½″ **60.00**
   Cameo, blue floral decor, 2 handles, sgnd twice, 11″ **11,500.00**
   Cameo, blue frosted w/wht opaque florals, 10¾x3½″ **2,450.00**
   Cameo, blue, w/butterfly & wht flowers on pink, 5″ **900.00**
   Cameo, citron floral & butterfly decor, sgnd, English, 8″ . . **1,350.00**
   Cameo, ivory w/ruffled top, sgnd, 4″ **550.00**
   Cameo, raisin colored, 2 handles, 9″ **10,500.00**
   Cameo, red to pink, gold bee, florals, 8½″ **365.00**
   Cameo, red w/wht ferns, butterfly, 8″ **850.00**
   Cameo, white deep cut roses over blue, sgnd, 9x6″ **3,500.00**
   Corset shape, calcite w/orange luster, 8½″ **125.00**
   Fishscale, bulbous, narrows at bottom & top, mkd, pink **450.00**
   Intaglio, enameled, swamp w/tortoise & bird, 9¾″ **2,090.00**
   Lace design, glossy cerise, wht cased, 10¼x7″ **320.00**
   Lime, wht, 4½″ **600.00**

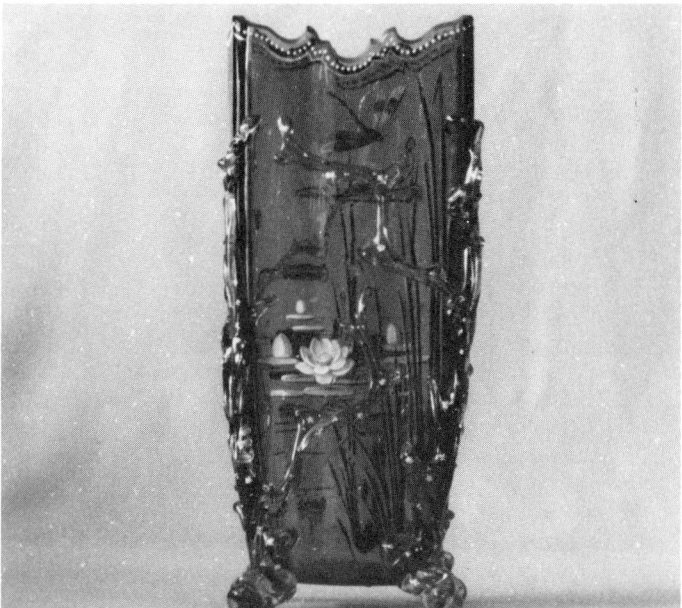

Pink w/blue applied branches & ft, 12½″ **375.00**
Queensware Burmese, 6 point top, sgnd **435.00**
Rainbow swirl, pink, yellow, blue w/wht lining, 6½″ **875.00**
Satin, Burmese, berry prunt, brass tripod holder, 3¾″ **525.00**
Satin, gold prunus decor, shaded yellow, 4¼x3¼″ dia **265.00**
With handles, 5-petaled flower, leaves, sgnd, 5″ **825.00**
Woodall Cameo, Paris Expo 1880, bottom mkd, 7½″ **6,500.00**

Wedgwood

Josiah Wedgwood established his pottery in Burslem, England, in 1759. He produced only utilitarian molded earthenwares until 1770, when new facilities were opened at Etruria. It was there he introduced his famous basalt and jasper ware.

Jasperware, an unglazed fine stoneware decorated with classic figures in white relief, was usually produced in blues, but it was also made in ground colors of green, lilac, yellow, black or white. Occasionally, 3 or more colors were used in combination. It has been in continuous production to the present day, and is the most easily recognized of all the Wedgwood lines.

Though his Jasperware was highly acclaimed, on a more practical basis his creamware was his greatest success. Due to the ease with which it could be potted, and because its lighter weight significantly reduced transportation expenses, Wedgwood was able to offer 'china' ware at affordable prices. Queen Charlotte was so pleased with the ware that she allowed it to be called 'Queen's Ware'. Most creamware was marked simply 'Wedgwood'. (Wedgwood & Co. and Wedgewood are marks of other potters).

From 1769 to 1780, Wedgwood was in partnership with Thomas Bently; art wares of the highest quality bear the mark indicating this partnership.

Moonlight lustre, an all-over splashed-on effect of pink intermingling with grey, brown or yellow, was made from 1805 to 1815. Porcelain was made, though not to any great extent, from 1812 to 1822. Both of these types of wares were marked 'Wedgwood'.

Stone china and Pearl ware were made from about 1820 to 1875. Exampes of either may be found with a mark to indicate their body type.

During the late 1800s, Wedgwood produced some fine Parian and Majolica. Creamware, hand painted by Emile Lessore, was sold from about 1860 to 1875.

Nearly all of Wedgwood's wares are clearly marked. 'Wedgwood' was used before 1891, after which time 'England' was added. Most examples marked 'Made In England' were made after 1910. 'Wedgwood' in sans serif type was used after 1929. A detailed study of all marks is recommended for accurate dating.

WW--------Wedgwood
WWE--------Wedgwood England

Ale jug, Cambridge, redware, inlaid decor wht & yellow, mkd, 1868 **150.00**
Ashtray, Jasper, dk blue, Pegasus, 3½″ **27.50**
Basket, w/underplate, creamware, brown twig decor, 1830 . . . . **435.00**
Beaker, Jasper, blue & wht, 4″ **200.00**
Biscuit barrel, acorn & leaf on lid, acorn finial, 8½″ **350.00**
   Jasper, blk & wht classical figures **390.00**
   Jasper, blue & wht, classic figures, WW **265.00**
   Jasper, gr, cupid, female figures, plated cover, bail handle, 1874 **195.00**
   Jasper, lilac & wht **475.00**
Biscuit jar, Franklin, Washington, Lafayette, 7½″ **350.00**
   Jasper, 3 colors, blk & gold bands, WW, 7x5″ **750.00**
   Jasper, blue & wht silver top & handle **125.00**
Bottle, green, blue, lilac & wht, 1860s **2,800.00**
Bowl, basalt, Dancing Hours, WW, 8″ **600.00**
   Basalt, Lady Templetown, 1790, 7″ dia **1,275.00**
   Butterfly lustre, blue & gold w/in, flame w/out, 6½x3″ **350.00**
   Chinese red w/blue & wht, octagon, 12″ **450.00**
   Daventry lustre, ruby, sgnd & #d, 9″ **1,350.00**
   Dragon lustre, 4¼″ **90.00**
   Dragon lustre, #Z9829, 6½″ **395.00**
   Dragon lustre, blue w/out, pearl green w/in, 9″ **750.00**
   Fairyland lustre, butterflies w/in & w/out, #Z430/F, 2x4″ . . . **250.00**
   Fairyland lustre, butterfly at bottom, yellow/orange, 2x4″ . . . **275.00**
   Fairyland lustre, garden of paradise, fruit, 2x11″ **1,850.00**
   Fairyland lustre, hummingbird decor, 2½x4½″ **275.00**
   Fairyland lustre, marston, elves, sunset, bat, insects, bird, 2x4″ dia **850.00**
   Hummingbird lustre, #Z5294, 9½″ **595.00**
   Jasper, blue & wht, classic figures, 2½x4″ **70.00**
   Jasper, blue & white, WW, 5x11″ **395.00**
   MOP and Oriental decor w/in, orange & gold w/out, octagonal **500.00**
Box, dragon lustre, blue, round w/lid, 6″ **650.00**
   Heart shape, w/cover, crimson **525.00**
   Hummingbird lustre, widow finial, 5½″ dia **695.00**
   Jasper, blk & wht, heart shape, w/lid MIE **50.00**
   Queen Elizabeth, on royal blue, 1953 . . . . **85.00**

Bud vase, hummingbird lustre, blue, 5¼" **195.00**
  Jasper, yellow & black, mkd WW, 7" **625.00**
Bust, basalt, Burns, mk WW, 14½" **650.00**
  Basalt, Lord Byron, 1850s, 8½" **875.00**
  Basalt, Rousseau, fur cap & collared coat, WW, 6x4" **425.00**
  Parian, Milton, by EW Wyon, mk WW, 1850s, 14½" **850.00**
Cake Plate, pearlware, incised, scenic w/fruit border **125.00**
Candlesticks, classical decor, lg, pr **485.00**
  Terra cotta, w/blk relief, pr **85.00**
Chess pieces, Jasper, wht, each **275.00**
Chocolate pot, Queen's ware, green leaf decor, 1840, 4" **110.00**
Coffee pot, basalt, turned body, acanthus handle & spout, 10¾" **475.00**
  Caneware, glazed, 9" **250.00**
Condiment set, Jasper, 3 colors, bamboo lattice decor, WW .. **425.00**
Creamer, 1925-30, 1¾x3½" **150.00**
Cress basket, w/stand, creamware, woven lattice work, oval, gilt, 8x9" **235.00**
Cup, brown w/sailing sloops, 2" **22.00**
  Creamware, wine tasters, 1785, 3½" dia **450.00**
  Fairyland lustre, melba, MOP, elves, kewpies, ftd, 3x4¼" dia **1,000.00**
Cup & plate, Lady Templetown, 1790 .... **1,390.00**
Cup & saucer, basalt **50.00**
  Basalt, husk & berry decor, turned body............. **165.00**
  Demitasse, basalt, mk WW **225.00**
  Demitasse, creamware, intertwined ribbon handle, 1790...... **95.00**
  Demitasse, lustreware, silver around cup **395.00**
  Jasper, blue & wht, birds, made for bird feed shop **395.00**
  Jasper, blue & wht, MIE.......................... **125.00**
  Pearlware, miniature, 'blue willow', 1½x2½" **125.00**
  Terra cotta, wht relief **85.00**
Dish, creamware, E Lessore, 'The Trio', scalloped, 9½x7¼x1½" **1,000.00**
  Creamware, oval, basket design, 7x9" **45.00**
  Creamware, pierced border, oval, impressed, 1830 .... **95.00**
  Queen's ware, E Lessore, children scenic, oval, 3¼x5" **375.00**
Egg cup, glazed drab, gold trim **125.00**
Ewer, basalt, 15½" **350.00**
  Basalt, gilded, 1860s, 15" **1,850.00**
Figurine, basalt, Cupid & Psyche, 1850, 8½" **1,750.00**
  Monkey & baby, cream glaze, J Skeaping, 7¾x7¼x3" **595.00**
Flower frog, basalt, figural egret, WWE, 7½" **650.00**
Games dish, Caneware, w/insert, early, 10" long **425.00**
Ginger jar, fairyland luster, rainbow, 9" **2,200.00**
Jardiniere, basalt, mythological figure, lion head decor, 7¼x7¾" **395.00**
  Basalt, lion heads, grapes, figures, 5" **175.00**
  Jasper, 3 colors, blk figures on yellow, 7x7" **440.00**
  Majolica, scroll & leaf decor, 4 colors, 4 ram heads, 7x7¼". **225.00**
  Jasper, blk & wht, mythological, 4½x5" **450.00**
Jug, creamware, glazed interior, 1920s, 3¾x3½" **135.00**
  Jasper, blue & wht, ladies & cherubs, WW, 5x4½" **125.00**
  Jasper, blue & wht, ladies, mk WW, 7x5" **135.00**
  Jasper, blue & wht, miniature **85.00**
  Josiah Wedgwood Bicentenary, brown/cream, acorn rim **195.00**
  Milk, Jasper w/hinged pewter lid, grape border, 8" **265.00**
Match holder, w/strike & cover, embossed figured on blue **165.00**
Mug, crimson, WWE, 5½" **650.00**
Pin tray, 1920s, 6x2" **135.00**
Pitcher, Franklin & Washington medallions, vintage rim, 8½". **500.00**
  Basalt, basketweave sides, 4x4" **115.00**
  Commemorative, by WW & Sons for Messrs, 5"........... **60.00**
  Copper lustre, fallow deer, 3½" **25.00**
  Jasper, blue, classic figures, WWE, 8" **115.00**
  Jasper, blue, Greek key & classic figures, 5½" **115.00**
  Jasper, green, classical figures, 4" **210.00**
  Jasper, green, classical figures, 8" **495.00**
  Pearlware, blue & wht, miniature **75.00**

Silver resist, hound handle, 4"........................ **35.00**
Silver resist, hunting scene, hound handle, 6½" **110.00**
Place setting, Columbia, 5 pc........................ **80.00**
  Petersham, 5 pc................................ **45.00**
  Swallow, 5 pc.................................. **50.00**
Plant pot holder, majolica, figural child, blue & cream, 15"... **450.00**
Plaque, basalt, cupid w/pipes, Rosso Antico, 5x3" **425.00**
  Basalt, oval, 'Erato, Muse of Erotic Poetry', framed, 6x4¾". **350.00**
  Basalt, oval, Marriage of Baccus & Ariadne, framed, 8¼x6¼" **450.00**
  Basalt, oval, Venus & Cupid, framed, 6x4¾" **350.00**
  Classic figure, ormolu frame, 9"................... **450.00**
  Jasper, 3 colors, w/orig frame **800.00**
  Jasper, blk & wht, undraped bacchanalian boys, 4¾x9¾". **1,000.00**
  Jasper, lt blue & wht, Napoleon, framed, 1820, 8½" **590.00**
  JFK, framed, blk **20.00**
Plaques, Elizabeth II & Philip, jasper ovals, creamware frames, pr **350.00**
Plate, creamware, heraldic, 1700s, 9".................. **150.00**
  Creamware, Kruger Nat'l Park, litho scenes, animals, 10½", pr **95.00**
  Creamware, nude w/child, WW only, hp, artist sgnd, 9½" .. **135.00**
  Creamware, Red Riding Hood & Wolf, 1800, 10" **225.00**
  Creamware, ribbon edge, some gilt, 1790, 9½" **95.00**
  Denison Univ Centennial, 1931, pk & wht, 5 for **75.00**
  Dessert, green w/relief grapes, basket.............. **36.00**
  Eturia, harbor scene, pink & red ship, 6" **25.00**
  Eturia, harbor scene, pink & red ship, 8" **40.00**
  Ferrare pattern, canal scene, floral border, blue /wht **28.00**
  Garden Club of America, set of 10 .... **125.00**
  Historical, Library of Congress, bk blue, 9" **28.00**
  Historical, Mayflower, Plymouth Harbor, dk blue, 9" **28.00**
  Historical, Mount Vernon, dk blue, 9"................ **24.00**
  Historical, the Capitol, dk blue, 9".................. **24.00**
  Jasper, Collector's Society, 1969-79 .... **750.00**
  Jasper, Ivanhoe, Rebecca Gives Purse to Gurth **40.00**
  Jasper, Rebecca Repelling the Templar Scene, blue, 10"..... **55.00**
  Kate Greenaway type, August, polychrome, 10" **150.00**
  Kate Greenaway type, February, 10" **150.00**
  Kate Greenaway type, May, 10" **150.00**
  Majolica, 1800s, 8½" **65.00**

Majolica, straw bonnet, 13x11" **125.00**
Platter, Newport, scalloped, 14" **22.00**
Potpourri, moonlight lustre, covered, 1810 .... **1,000.00**

Pearlware, flowers, butterflies, loop handle, 16½x12" **2,250.00**
Salt & pepper, Jasper, blue & wht, cupids, 4x2½", pr **110.00**
Scurier, terra cotta edge, blk Capri decor, covered, 6½" **325.00**
Serving piece, leaf shape, green, 10" to tip of handle **90.00**
Sherbet, Fairyland lustre, cranes & dog, blue & green, 3x4" .. **525.00**
Spill, Caneware, crescent shape, blue applied floral, WW, 3¾" **215.00**
Stick vase, creamware, Worcester decor, gr/rust, gold leaves, 5¼", pr **325.00**
Sugar, basalt **125.00**
    Caneware, w/lid, 6" **250.00**
    Covered, 1925, 4x4½" **135.00**
Sugar & creamer, Jasper, blk & wht **230.00**
Sugar box, basalt, widow finial, w/lid, 1810 . . . . **425.00**
Syrup, Jasper, blue & wht **125.00**
Tablet, Jasper, Bringing Home the Game & Music, 2½x7½" .. **100.00**
Tea set, Jasper, blue & wht, WW only, 3 pc **275.00**
    Stoneware coated w/copper, electroplated w/platinum, 3-pc **1,000.00**
Teapot, 1925, 5½" **195.00**
    Basalt **125.00**

Basalt, floral relief, 10½" **750.00**
Basalt, widow finial on cover, 4¾x7¼" **250.00**
Drabware & lavender, 1800s, 7" **250.00**
Dragon handle & spout, 1864, imp WW **250.00**
Jasper, dk blue/wht WWE, lg **145.00**
Queen's Ware, #223, band of leaves & grapes, lg **90.00**
Queen's Ware, commemoration, Coronation Edward, VII **75.00**
Rust & wht, urn mk, pre 1891 . . . . **100.00**
Tile, calendar, State House, Boston, 1895 . . . . **60.00**
    Calendar, Washington Elm, 1809 . . . . **65.00**
Toby jug, Elihu Yale **145.00**
Urn, Jasper, blk & wht, w/lid, on pedestal, bolted base, lid, 10" **695.00**
    Jasper, lt blue, Dancing Hour, w/lid, 1800s, 9", pr **1,350.00**
    Jasper, terra cotta w/black relief **900.00**
    Queen's Ware, cream w/applied blue decor, lid, Eng, 7" **125.00**
    Queen's Ware, cream w/applied blue decor, w/lid, Eng, 12" . **175.00**
Vase, dragon lustre, w/lid, blue, 12" **485.00**
    Fairyland lustre, gold dragon on blue, 8" **300.00**
    Jasper, blue & wht, bottle shape, WW, 1867, 7" **135.00**
    Jasper, blue & wht, classical figures, WWE, 8x5" **350.00**
    Jasper, blue & wht, mk WW, 8¾", pr **795.00**
    Jasper, Portland, blk & wht, 5" **285.00**
    Jasper, Portland, blue & wht, WWE, 7" **375.00**
    Urn shape, bone china, twisted handles, florals, 1880, 5½" . **195.00**
Waste bowl, glazed interior, 1925, 2¼x4½" **150.00**
Wine cask marker, parian **85.00**

Weller

The Weller Pottery Company was established in Zanesville, Ohio, in 1882, the outgrowth of a small one-kiln log cabin works Sam Weller had operated in Fultonham. Through an association with Wm. Long, he entered the art pottery field in 1895, producing the Lonhuda ware Long had perfected in Steubenville, six years earlier. His famous Louwelsa line was merely a continuation of Lonhuda, and was made in at least 500 different shapes until 1924.

Many fine lines of artware followed under the direction of Charles Babcock Upjohn, art director from 1895 to 1904: Dickens Ware (1st line), underglaze slip decorations on dark backgrounds; Turada, featuring applied ivory bands of delicate openwork on solid dark brown backgrounds; and Aurelian, similar to Louwelsa, but with a brushed-on rather than blended ground.

One of their most famous lines was 2nd Line Dickens, introduced in 1900. Backgrounds, characteristically caramel shading to turquoise matt, were decorated by sgraffito with animals, golfers, monks, Indians, and scenes from Dickens novels. The work is often artist signed.

Sicardo, 1903, was a metallic lustre line in tones of flame, rose, blue, green or purple, with flowing art Nouveau patterns developed within the glaze itself.

Frederick Hurten Rhead, who worked for Weller in 1903-04 created the prestigious Jap Birdmal line, decorated with geisha girls, landscapes, storks, etc., accomplished through application of heavy slip forced through the tiny nozzle of a squeeze bag. Other lines to his credit are L'Art Nouveau, produced both in high gloss brown and matt pastels, and 3rd Line Dickens, often decorated with Cruikshank's illustrations in relief.

Other early artware lines were Eocean, Floretta, Hunter, Perfecto, Dresden, Etched Matt and Etna.

In 1920, John Lessel was hired as Art Director, and under his supervision several new lines were created. LaSa, LaMar, Marengo and Besline attest to his expertise with metallic lustres.

The last of the artware lines and one of the most sought after by collectors today is Hudson, first made during the early 1920s. Hudson, a semi-matt glazed ware, was beautifully artist decorated on shaded backgrounds with florals, animals, birds and scenics. Notable artists often signed their work, among them Hester Pillsbury, Dorothy England Laughead, Ruth Axline, Claude Leffler, Sarah Reid McLaughlin, E.L. Pickens, and Mae Timberlake.

During the '30s, Weller produced a line of gardenware and naturalistic life sized figures of dogs, cats, swans, geese and playful gnomes.

The depression brought a slow steady decline in sales, and by 1948, the pottery was closed

Ardsley, candleholders, 3", pr **50.00**
    Candleholders, lotus shape, 3", pr **70.00**
    Console set, cattail bowl, fish frog **220.00**
    Console set, freeform bowl, lily frog **135.00**
    Corner vase, iris, 7" **90.00**
    Double vase, 9½" **60.00**
    Double wall pocket, 11½" **85.00**
    Fan vase, cattails, 8" **55.00**
    Vase, 10½" **85.00**
    Trumpet shape, 11½ **55.00**
    Vase, tulip & leaf, freeform, 7" **55.00**
    Wall pocket, double pocket w/cattails, 12" **50.00**
Atlas, bowl, #C-3, 4" **45.00**
    Candleholders, #C-12, pr **45.00**
    Dish w/cover, star shape, #C-2" **80.00**
    Star dish, #C-2 . . . . **45.00**
    Vase, 10½" **65.00**
    Vase, 13" **85.00**
Aurelian, jard & ped, iris, twisted mold, 38" **1,200.00**

Tankard, corn, 12½″	600.00
Tankard, grapes, sgnd E Roberts, 16½″	500.00
Vase, daffodils, sgnd TJW, 16″	800.00
Baldin, vase, apple branch, 9½″	140.00
Vase, blue w/apple branch, 11″	190.00
Vase, yellow apple branch, bulbous bottom, 9½″	250.00
Barcelona, oil jar w/handles, 25½″	750.00
Pitcher, 8″	140.00
Vase, bulbous, scalloped narrow rim, handles, 8″	120.00
Vase, cylinder, 7″	85.00
Besline, candlestick, 10½″	150.00
Vase, full shoulder curving to narrowed base, 12″	550.00
Vase, high shoulder, straight sides, 11″	550.00
Blo' Red, vase, 7″	70.00
Vase, 9½″	135.00
Vase, tassel handles, 3½″	50.00
Blossom, basket, 6″	25.00
Cornucopia, 6″	25.00
Double cornucopia, 6½″	30.00
Double vase, 12½″	90.00
Vase, 6″	20.00
Window box	40.00
Bouquet, console bowl, #B-12, 5x12½″	35.00
Pitcher, #B-18, 9½″	60.00
Urn vase, #B-6, 5″	30.00
Vase, #B-5, 5½″	25.00
Vase, cylinder top half, bulbous bottom, 15″	60.00
Blue & Decorated, 6 panel body w/florals, 9½″	165.00
Floral rim band, cylinder, 8½″	100.00
Shoulder band w/florals, 7½″	110.00
Blue Drapery, bowl, 3x5½″	35.00
Candlestick or lamp base, 9½″	35.00
Planter, 4″	30.00
Vase, 4″	25.00
Vase, 6″	30.00
Wall pocket, 9″	60.00
Blue Ware, comport, floral & fruit garlands, 5½″	125.00
Jardiniere, classic figure, 6½″	100.00
Jardiniere, classic figure, 10″	100.00
Jardiniere, w/2 angels, 8½″	200.00
Jardiniere, w/4 angels, 9″	200.00
Lamp base, shoulder band, 9″	100.00
Vase, classic figure, 8½″	110.00
Vase, classic figure, wht fluted base, 13″	150.00
Vase, floral & scroll panels, 10″	350.00
Vase, classic figure w/lyre, 8½″	110.00
Bonito, candleholder, bowl w/2 sm loop handles, 3½″	50.00
Candleholders, 1½″, pr	65.00
Vase, C scroll handles, 5″	60.00
Vase, U shape, tab handles, 4″	40.00
Vase, U shape on disk ft, sgnd HP, 6″	75.00
Vase, bulbous, tab handles, 10½″	250.00
Vase, ornate handles, sgnd NW, 7″	80.00
Vase, trumpet flare, 5″	45.00
Brighton, 2 canaries, 4″	10.00
2 parrots on curving perch, 9″	220.00
2 penguins, 5″	135.00
Bluebird on stump, 6″	100.00
Bluebird, wings spread on stump w/fruit, 7½″	210.00
Bluebird, wings spread, tail upward, 5″	100.00
Crow, 6½″	400.00
Flamingo w/foliage, 6″	100.00
Hanging parrot w/spread wings, 15″	350.00
Kingfisher, 6½″	100.00

Kingfisher on perch, 9″	100.00
Parrot on curving perch, 12½″	265.00
Parrot on curving perch, 13½	320.00
Parrot on perch, 7½″	210.00
Wall pocket, black bird figural on 3-prong branch, 15″	250.00
Wall pocket, woodpecker figural on 2-prong branch, 12″	150.00
Woodpecker, on branch pile, 6½″	110.00
Bumble bee, 2¼″	50.00
Burntwood, plaque, bird in tree, 12″	150.00
Plate, 1910, Odd Fellows, 7″	60.00
Stylized florals, black rim band, 7″	85.00
Vase, birds & florals, 8½″	135.00
Vase, chickens & roosters, 9″	150.00
Vase, Egyptian chariot motif, 7″	85.00
Vase, grapes & vines, 6½″	80.00
Vase, stylized florals, black rim band, 7″	85.00
Vase, stylized florals, full body, 8″	130.00
Vase, stylized florals & leaves, 5″	40.00
Butterfly, 2″	40.00
3″	55.00
Cactus, boy w/bag, 5″	85.00
Camel, 4″	75.00
Cat, 5½″	75.00
Duck, 4½″	85.00
Elephant, 4″	110.00
Frog, 4″	85.00
Pan w/lily, 5″	75.00
Snail, 3½″	85.00
Cameo, basket, 7½″	30.00
Footed bowl, 4″	25.00
Hanging basket, 5″	60.00
Vase, square, 8½″	25.00
Vase, w/handles, 5″	25.00
Window box	30.00
Cameo Jewell, jardiniere & ped, 34″	800.00
Umbrella stand, 22″	450.00
Umbrella stand, jewels, no medallion, 20½″	275.00

Cat, white, 15″	1,600.00
Chanticleer Rooster, 7″	135.00
Chase, fan vase, 8½″	200.00
Vase, ovoid w/short neck section, 6½″	175.00
Vase, wide rim, convex sides, disk ft	160.00
Chengtu, bowl vase, 3½″	55.00
Jar, flat cover, 8″	135.00
Jar, lid w/knob, 12″	160.00
Jardiniere, 5½″	75.00
Vase, 4 shaped panels, 8″	70.00
Vase, elongated ovoid, 7½″	60.00
Vase, slender neck, full body, 11½″	85.00

Clarmont, candleholder, 8″ **75.00**
   Candleholder, 10″ **100.00**
   Vase, waisted, double handles, 8″ **160.00**
Classic, bowl w/9″ goose boy, 14½″ **180.00**
   Fan vase, 5″ **55.00**
   Plate, 11½″ **45.00**
   Vase, 6½″ **50.00**
   Wall pocket, 6″ **65.00**
   Wall pocket, 6x8½″ **80.00**
   Window box, 4″ **70.00**
Claywood, mug, stylized florals, 5″ **75.00**
   Candleholder, 5″ **35.00**
   Spittoon, 4½″ **100.00**
   Vase, floral panels, square, 8½″ **50.00**
   Vase, floral shoulder band, bowl shape, 3½″ **35.00**
   Vase, spider web, 5½″ **45.00**
   Vase, stylized florals, 5″ **40.00**
   Vase, stylized star flowers, 5½″ **40.00**
Cloudburst, bowl, 4x9″ **100.00**
   Vase, 4½″ **80.00**
   Vase, full bodied, 10½″ **250.00**
   Wall pocket, 5½″ **35.00**
Coppertone, ashtray w/frog, 6½″ **90.00**
   Basket, floral relief, 8½″ **70.00**
   Candleholder, waterlily w/turtle figural, 3″ **110.00**
   Frog figural, 4″ **85.00**
   Pitcher, fish handle, 7½″ **50.00**
   Vase, 6½″ **20.00**
   Vase, bulbous w/large handles, 7″ **55.00**
   Vase, frog handles, bulbous, 8″ **180.00**
   Vase, Pumila motif, 6½″ **35.00**
Copra, basket, florals, 11″ **225.00**
   Jardiniere, tulips, ring handles, 8″ **130.00**
   Vase, hollyhocks, ring handles, 10″ **180.00**
Cornish, bowl, 4″ **35.00**
   Bowl, 7½″ dia **25.00**
   Jardiniere, 7″ **80.00**
   Vase, ovoid w/tab handles, 7″ **30.00**
Creamware, mug, floral, hand decorated, 5″ **125.00**
   Mug, grape decal **75.00**
   Teapot, lilac decal, 5″ **125.00**
   Vase, grapes & leaves, blue on ivory, 11½″ **275.00**
Cretone, vase, blk w/wht figures, 7″ **350.00**
   Vase, cream w/brown figures, 8″ **275.00**
   Vase, yellow w/brown figures, unusual color, 3½″ **350.00**
Darsie, bowl vase, 5½″ **35.00**
   Flower pot, 5½″ **30.00**
   Vase, 5½″ **25.00**
   Vase, bulbous, 9½″ **65.00**
   Vase, cylinder, 7½″ **30.00**
Delsa, basket, 7″ **35.00**
   Pitcher, #10, 7″ **30.00**
   Vase, 6″ **20.00**
   Vase, ped ft, handles, 6″ **30.00**
Delta, vase, irises, blue on blue, sgnd Pillsbury, 10″ **300.00**
Dickens, 1st Line, jardiniere, morning glories, 8½″ **225.00**
   lst Line, jug, ear of corn on lt brown, 6½″ **325.00**
   lst Line, lamp, cherries, 3 toed, loop handles, 11″ . . **1,100.00**
   lst Line, mug, border of medallions in relief, 6″ **250.00**
   lst Line, mug, florals, 7″ **375.00**
   lst Line, mug, leaves & berries, 4½″ **235.00**
   lst Line, mug, portrait of the Admiral, sgnd MM, 4½″ **900.00**
   lst Line, pillow vase, portrait of woman on shaded ground, 7″ **2,200.00**
   2nd Line, Captain humidor, 7″ **600.00**

2nd Line, Chinaman humidor, 6″ **850.00**
2nd Line, Irishman humidor, 6½″ **600.00**
2nd Line, jug, Mt Vernon Bridge, sgnd UJ, 5½″ **450.00**
2nd Line, mug, nudes, shield w/'Prost', hi gloss, 5½″ **700.00**
2nd Line, skull humidor, 5½″ **1,175.00**
2nd Line, tankard, Chief Blackbear, AD & A Dautherty, 12″ **2,000.00**
2nd Line, Turk humidor, 7″ **675.00**
2nd Line, vase, Bald Eagle, ovoid, sgnd Anna Dautherty, 10″ **1,400.00**
2nd Line, vase, Black Bear, sgnd Anna Dautherty, 10″ . . . **1,400.00**
2nd Line, vase, boy w/trees, slightly concave, sgnd RGT, 12½″ **1,200.00**
2nd Line, vase, cavalier, blue on blue gloss, sgnd, JH, 13½″ **900.00**
2nd Line, vase, Chief Hollowhorn Bear, A Dautherty, 13½″ **2,000.00**
2nd Line, vase, cupids, 4 sides extend to feet, 11½″ **600.00**
2nd Line, vase, Dombey & Son, sgnd W Gibson, 10½″ **700.00**
2nd Line, vase, Don Quixote & Sancho, EL Pickens, 16″ . **1,750.00**
2nd Line, vase, fishermen by stream, 15½″ **1,500.00**
2nd Line, vase, hunting dog, sgnd EL Pickens, 9″ **1,300.00**
2nd Line, vase, knight on horse w/trees, slender, Upjohn, 14″ **1,350.00**

2nd Line, vase, mont, 10″ **1,000.00**
2nd Line, vase, mountain man w/rifle, sgnd Dunlavy, 16″ . **1,200.00**
2nd Line, vase, nymph in wht gown, sgnd Dusenbury, 12″ . . **675.00**
2nd Line, vase, rabbit, water lily pads, cylinder, 17″ **1,200.00**
2nd Line, vase, shepherd & sheep, 15″ **1,500.00**
2nd Line, vase, The Inns Scene, 3 men at table, 13″ **975.00**
3rd Line, carafe w/cup, David Copperfield, sgnd R, 14½″ . . . **900.00**
3rd Line, circle vase w/sq neck, Dombey & Son, sgnd P, 7½″ **650.00**
3rd Line, creamer, Charles Dickens on disk, 4″ **350.00**
3rd Line, inkwell, Income 20#, expenditure 19-6, sgnd R, 2½″ **500.00**
3rd Line, mug, 2 handles, man, waist up w/pipe, 4″ **500.00**
3rd Line, mug, Master Bellin, 5″ **375.00**
3rd Line, tankard, Squeers, sgnd, 12½″ **600.00**
3rd Line, vase, 2 handles, woman in bonnet, 6″ **325.00**
3rd Line, vase, 'Bailey' on base, rim handles, 9½″ **450.00**
3rd Line, vase, Carker Combey & Son, flat flare rim, 13″ . . **650.00**
3rd Line, vase, King, 11″ **450.00**
3rd Line, vase, Mr Weller Sr, wide flare w/rim handles, 8″ . . **750.00**
3rd Line, vase, Wilker Mcawber, David Copperfield, LS, 10½″ **600.00**
Dragonfly, 3¼″ **65.00**
Dupont, Jardiniere, 7½″ **125.00**
   Planter, square reticulated rim **60.00**
   Vase, large cylinder, 10″ **125.00**
Eocean, umbrella stand, nastursium, 22½″ **600.00**
   Vase, apple blossoms, grey/ivory, sgnd LJB, 13″ **450.00**
   Vase, cherries, cylinder, w/6 rim handles, 16″ **450.00**

Vase, florals, cream on ivory, sgnd M Rauchfuss, 12½″ **350.00**
Vase, owl in tree, moon behind, greys, sgnd EB, 10½″... **1,200.00**
Vase, spider mums, 6 rim to shoulder handles, sgnd EP, 20½″ **300.00**
Vase, thistle blooms, grey & ivory w/purple, panels, 7½″ ... **300.00**
Vase, wild roses, greys/ivory sgnd LJB, 11½″............ **300.00**
Vase, wild roses, rose & mauve, sgnd AH, 13½″......... **400.00**
Eocean-Late Line, bud vase, florals, 5″.................... **75.00**
  Bud vase, florals, 6½″............................. **80.00**
  Vase, florals & berries, sgnd MT, 10½″............. **175.00**
  Vase, poppies, 8½″................................ **150.00**
  Vase, poppies, 13″................................ **450.00**
Ethel, fan vase, no cameo, 6″ **55.00**
  Vase, 9½″ **175.00**
  Vase, 11½″ **200.00**
Etna, mug, cherries, 5½″ **125.00**
  Pitcher, clover blossom, 6½″...................... **140.00**
  Vase, Beethoven medallion, 12″................... **350.00**
  Vase, floral, 6″ **50.00**
  Vase, florals, heavy handles, 11″ **190.00**
  Vase, grapes, tendrils, angle shoulder, grey/rose, 15″...... **235.00**
  Vase, pansies blown out, grey/rose, 6½″........... **100.00**
  Vase, Pope medallion, pearls, jewels, 10″ **220.00**
  Vase, rose, blown out, ear handles on ovoid, 9″ **185.00**
  Vase, wild roses, grey/rose, 5½″ **60.00**
Flask, All's Well, 4″ **135.00**
  BPOE, w/elk, 4½″ **85.00**
  Dust Remover, 6″ **135.00**
  F O E, 5½″ **85.00**
  Never Dry, 6″ **135.00**
  Old Kentucky, 5″ **135.00**
  P A P, Loyal Order of Moose, 4½″................. **85.00**
  Suffer-E-Get, 6″................................. **135.00**
  Take a Plunge, 6″ **135.00**
Flemish, comport w/cover, rose finial & base decor, 8½″..... **150.00**
  Inkwell, 2 blue birds under arching branches, 4½x7″ **425.00**
  Jard & ped, stylized florals, incised lines, 26½″.......... **420.00**
  Jardiniere, geranium leaves, 7½″ **85.00**
  Jardiniere, peonies in panels, 7½″ **110.00**
  Tub, basketweave w/florals, 4½″ **50.00**
  Umbrella stand, stylized trees, apples, 22″ **650.00**
  Vase, leaves & berries at base, flared shape, 6½″ **135.00**
Fleron, batter pitcher, 11½″ **130.00**
  Bowl, folded scalloped rim, 3x5½″ **45.00**
  Vase, handles, 19½″............................. **150.00**
  Vase, waisted, pinched rim, 8½″ **65.00**
Floral, double vase, 5½″ **20.00**
  Vase, #F-2 .... **20.00**
  Vase, 6½″ **30.00**
Florala, candleholder, 11″ **35.00**
  Console bowl, 11″ **35.00**
  Double bud vase, 5″ **65.00**
  Wall pocket, 10″ **55.00**
  Vase, berries, blown out, broad shoulder, 13½″........... **265.00**
  Vase, cherries in relief, green ground, 12″........... **330.00**
  Vase, floral rim, bulbous base, grey, rose, 13½″ **160.00**
  Vase, floral, grey/ivory w/rose, 5½″............... **60.00**
  Vase, florals, grey/ivory/pink, convex sides, 19″ **350.00**
Floretta, ewer, floral, grey/ivory, w/rose, 6″ **80.00**
  Tankard, grapes in relief, brown glaze, 10½″........... **135.00**
  Vase, berries, blown out, broad shoulder, 13½″........... **265.00**
  Vase, cherries in relief, green ground, 12″........... **330.00**
  Vase, floral rim, bulbous base, grey, rose, 13½″ **160.00**
  Vase, floral, grey/ivory w/rose, 5½″............... **60.00**
  Vase, florals, grey/ivory/pink, convex sides, 19″ **350.00**

Vase, grapes in relief at shoulder, concave sides, brown, 17″ **165.00**
Vase, grapes in relief, brown glaze, 7½″................. **85.00**
Vase, grapes, blown out shape, grey/ivory w/purple, 5½″.... **100.00**
Vase, ornate handles, brown glaze, 7½″................. **125.00**
Vase, poppy at rim, rose, grey & ivory, 11½″............. **185.00**
Florenzo, basket, 5½ **55.00**
  Double bud vase, 5½″ **40.00**
  Planter, square, 3½″............................. **35.00**
  Vase, 7″ **55.00**
  Vase w/frog cover″ **100.00**
  Window box″ **35.00**
Forest, basket, slender V shape, 8½″..................... **110.00**
  Bowl, #3, 2½″ **35.00**
  Hanging basket, 8″ **130.00**
  Jard & ped, 26″ **475.00**
  Jardiniere, 4½″ **95.00**
  Jardiniere, 7″ **100.00**
  Jardiniere, 8½″ **200.00**
  Pitcher, hi gloss, 5″ **130.00**
  Teapot, hi gloss, 4½″............................ **185.00**
  Tub planter, #3, 3½″ **60.00**
  Tub planter, w/handles, 6″ **65.00**
  Vase, concave sides, 8″.......................... **70.00**
  Vase, concave sides, 12″......................... **120.00**
  Vase, concave sides, 13½″........................ **130.00**
  Vase, cylinder, 8″ **65.00**
  Window box, 5¼x14¼″ **200.00**
Fruitone, bud vase, 11½″ **85.00**
  Vase, handles, 4½″ **50.00**
  Vase, ovoid, 6″ **85.00**
  Vase, paneled, 8″ **150.00**
  Wall pocket, 5½″ **80.00**
Garden ornament, banjo frog, 13½″...................... **400.00**
  Fisher boy, 21″ **600.00**
  Gnome, 14″ **400.00**
  Pan w/fife, 16½″ **600.00**
Glendale, double bud vase, bluebird, 7″.................. **125.00**
  Plate w/frog, seagulls & nest w/eggs, 15½″......... **225.00**
  Vase, 2 parrots on branch, 8½″ **300.00**
  Vase, bird among flowers, butterflies, foliage, 12″ **325.00**
  Vase, bird, nest, stream & mountains, 12″......... **350.00**
  Vase, bluebird w/nest, slender shape, 10″......... **195.00**
  Vase, brown bird among trees, 5″ **125.00**
  Vase, brown bird, 6″............................ **180.00**
  Vase, brown birds & nest w/eggs, bulbous, 9″ **350.00**
  Vase, flying brown bird, 6½″ **200.00**
  Wall pocket, 2 yellow birds, triangle over ½ circle, 7½″.... **100.00**
  Wall pocket, bluebird w/chicks in nest, cornucopia, 12½″ .. **100.00**
Gloria, double vase, 4½″ **25.00**
  Pitcher, 9″..................................... **40.00**
  Vase, 12½″ **85.00**
  Vase, w/handles, 5½″ **20.00**
Glouster Woman, 11½″ **260.00**
Goldenglow, bowl, 3½x16″ **60.00**
  Bud vase, 3 ft, 8½″ **35.00**
  Jar on ft w/cover, 8″ **90.00**
  Triple candleholder, 3½″ **40.00**
  Triple candleholder, 7½″ **50.00**
  Vase, 2 handles, 1 low, 1 high, 6″................ **45.00**
  Wall pocket, 11″................................ **55.00**
Graystone Garden Ware, birdbath, Regal, 21½″ **165.00**
  Jardiniere & ped, 28″........................... **175.00**
Greenbriar, ewer, double handle, 11½″ **165.00**
  Pitcher, 10″.................................... **160.00**

Vase, 6″ **55.00**
Vase, full bodied, 6½″ **85.00**
Vase, wing handles, 7½″ **110.00**
Greora, strawberry jar vase, 8½″ **115.00**
Strawberry pot, 5″ **70.00**
Vase, cylinder, 11½″ **130.00**
Vase, pointed handles, full body, 9″ **90.00**
Vase, triangular w/3 ft, 4½″ **50.00**
Hobart, bowl, 3x9½″ **45.00**
Bowl, w/nudes flower frog, 12″ dia **165.00**
Candleholder, nude, 6″ **110.00**
Girl w/flowers, 8½″ **65.00**
Nude, double bud vase, 10″ **120.00**
Nude, ivory glaze, flower frog, 8½″ **70.00**
Hudson, iris, wht on blues, cylinder, sgnd Axline, 8½″ **200.00**
Vase, 3 egrets fly over lake, sgnd Pillsbury, 9″ **1.100.00**
Vase, clover leaves & blossoms, on blue, sgnd LBM, 7″ **180.00**
Vase, hollyhocks, pink, wht, blue, 12″ **350.00**
Vase, lilacs, sgnd McLaughlin, 12″ **350.00**
Vase, man on horse, mountains, sgnd Timberlake, 9″ **1,300.00**
Vase, owl, trees in moonlight, sgnd Pillsbury, 9″ **1,100.00**
Vase, parrots, florals, foliage, sgnd Timberlake, 8″ **1,250.00**
Vase, pine trees & cabin, snow covered, sgnd Pillsbury, 9½″ **1,300.00**
Vase, plums & berries, bulbous w/handles, sgnd Pillsbury, 13½″ **550.00**
Vase, snowcapped mountain, blk trees, full body, Pillsbury, 12″ **1,600.00**
Vase, tiger among foliage, 8″ **1,100.00**
Vase, yellow irises, leaves on blue-tan, sgnd Pillsbury, 15″ . . **450.00**
Wall pocket, wht w/thorny branches & blossoms, 8″ **150.00**
Hudson-Light, vase, lily of the valley, 4½″ **80.00**
Hudson-Perfecto, bowl vase, morning glories, 5½″ **165.00**
Vase, floral stocks, lavenders, sgnd DE, 6½″ **135.00**
Vase, irises, lavenders, 9″ **140.00**
Vase, irises, purple on mauve, full body, Leffler, 13½″ **550.00**
Vase, jonquils, blue, green & ivory, sgnd DE, 4½″ **175.00**
Vase, pine cones, very bulbous, sgnd Leffler, 10″ **450.00**
Vase, spider mums, bulbous, sgnd Leffler, 9½″ **360.00**
Vase, tiger lilies, mauve values, lt green, Leffler, 13½″ **450.00**
Hunter, pillow vase, duck by water, 4¾″ **550.00**
Vase, birds, wings spread, sgnd UJ, 7½″ **550.00**
Vase, elk, rim to shoulder handles, 6½″ **600.00**
Ivoris, console bowl, w/frog, dogwood in relief, 3½x10″ **65.00**
Ginger jar w/lid, intaglio design, 8½″ **75.00**
Jar w/cover, wild rose in relief, 5″ **50.00**
Powder box w/cover, pointed finial, 4″ **50.00**
Vase, ornate handles, 6″ **30.00**
Ivory, jard & ped, florals in panels, 27½″ **400.00**
Jardiniere, squirrel in tree, 6½″ **55.00**
Letter pocket, eagle, 9″ **165.00**
Planter, couple by fence w/gate, 5″ **60.00**
Planter, dragonfly in relief, 4″ **50.00**
Vase, female forms in panels, 12″ **125.00**
Vase, oak leaves, cylinder, 10″ **50.00**
Wall pocket, ram, 10½″ **225.00**
Wall pocket, stag head, 9″ **225.00**
Window box, 6x15½″ **60.00**
Jap Birdimal, mug, geisha girl, 5″ **1,000.00**
Oil pitcher, sgnd HMR, 10½″ **900.00**
Vase, geisha girl, 4″ **650.00**
Vase, geisha girl, sgnd VMH, buldging base, cylinder top, 13″ **1,600.00**
Vase, scenic w/trees, squeeze bag, blue on grey, 14″ **575.00**
Vase, stork, slight concave cylinder, 7″ **300.00**
Vase, storks, squat w/pinched sides, 4″ **350.00**
Jewell, jardiniere, jewels at shoulder, 7½″ **125.00**
Mug, cameo in vine vignette, jewell base band, 6½ **250.00**

Vase, 4 vertical shoulder posts & neck band, 9½″ **160.00**
Vase, stylized trees, 9″ **150.00**
Vase, stylized trees w/jewells, 10½″ **190.00**
Juneau, bud vase, 6″ **40.00**
Vase, 6½″ **65.00**
Vase, w/handles, mid angle, 8″ **85.00**
Kenova, bowl vase, floral, 5½″ **110.00**
Vase, morning glories, 6½″ **75.00**

Vase, rose, 8″ **140.00**
Klyro, basket, 7″ **75.00**
Bud vase, 8½″ **45.00**
Candleholder, 9½″ **50.00**
Circle vase, 8″ **85.00**
Fan vase, 6″ **50.00**
Planter, square, 3½″ **50.00**
Planter, square, 4″ **60.00**
Wall pocket, 7½″ **60.00**
Wall pocket, circle shape, 6″ **25.00**
Knifewood, tobacco box, foxes, 3½″ **125.00**
Tobacco jar, hunting dog, trees, 7″ **375.00**
Vase, peacock, 9″ **150.00**
Vase, squirrel, oak leaves, 11″ **200.00**
Wall pocket, daisies on textured ground, 8″ **125.00**
L'Art Nouveau, bank, corn figural, 8″ **140.00**

Bowl, 3″ **175.00**
Mug, florals & scrolls, 5″ **185.00**
Pitcher, flower spout, 12½″ **265.00**
Tankard, scrolls & floral rim, 14½″ **285.00**
Vase, florals, base buldge, cylinder neck, 8″ **85.00**
Vase, poppy at rim, wide shoulder, 13½″ **175.00**
Vase, square w/floral rim, 12″ **140.00**
Wall pocket, 6½″ **125.00**
LaMar, lamp, full bottom half, slender neck, 16″ **375.00**
Vase, flare rim, short neck, full body, 11½″ **295.00**

Vase, full at shoulder, tapers, 6″ **100.00**
Vase, lake scenic w/trees, teardrop body, cylinder neck, 14½″ **450.00**
Vase, rimless, low shoulder angle, 8½″ **160.00**
Vase, slender, 7½″ **135.00**
LaSa, bowl vase, cross & tiny wht florals, 3½″ **150.00**
   Bud vase, slender 4-panel flare, 6½″ **165.00**
   Vase, palm trees, heavy body w/high shoulder, flare rim, 13½″ **500.00**
   Vase, spider mum in wht, 6″ **160.00**
   Vase, trees, 6½″ **175.00**
   Vase, trees, ovoid body w/flare rim, 8″ **225.00**
Lavonia, Hobart girl, 7½″ **70.00**
   Vase, slender bottom w/3 vertical handles, 9″ **65.00**
   Vase, thistles, 10″ **85.00**
Lebanon, vase, 2 handled jug, oxen, men, 9″ **325.00**
   Vase, flared w/3 supports at rim, men on camels, 9″ . . . **275.00**
Lido, candleholder, double, 2½″ **45.00**
   Console bowl, 3½x12″ **35.00**
   Fan vase, 7½″ **25.00**
   Pitcher, 10½″ **50.00**
   Planter, 2x9″ **25.00**
   Vase, 4″ **25.00**
   Vase, 7″ **30.00**
   Vase w/handles, 10½″ **75.00**
Lorbeek, bowl w/frog, 5″ **80.00**
   Candleholders, 2½″, pr″ **45.00**
   Console set, bowl w/frog, 3x14″ **140.00**
   Fan vase, 7″ **65.00**
   Wall pocket, 8½″ **65.00**
Lorber, jardiniere, satyrs, vineyard, 10″ **150.00**
   Vase, elongated ovoid w/neck band, satyr, vineyard, 13″ **350.00**
Loru, bowl, 4″ **25.00**
   Cornucopia, 4″ **20.00**
   Vase, 8″ **40.00**
   Vase, 10″ **60.00**
Louella, basket, 6½″ **100.00**
   Bowl, 3x5″ **35.00**
   Hair receiver, 3″ **55.00**
   Vase, ring handles, 8″ **130.00**
Lustre, basket, draped effect, 6½″ **60.00**
   Candlestick, 8″ **50.00**
   Comport, 3 vertical bars surround ped, 7″ **55.00**
   Vase, straight sides, 8½″ **65.00**
   Wall pocket, 5½″ **25.00**
   Wall pocket, 7½″ **50.00**
Luxor, bud vase, 7½″ **30.00**
   Vase, concave sides, 9″ **45.00**
   Vase, concave sides, 10½″ **55.00**
Louwelsa, clock, florals, 10½x10½″ **600.00**
   Ewer, full blown rose, trilobe rim, 10″ **200.00**
   Ewer, leaves, slender neck, sgnd JB, 6½″ **170.00**
   Ewer, wild flowers, shoulder handle, 7″ **165.00**
   Humidor, leaves & berries, wood lid, sgnd CA, 5½″ **380.00**
   Jard & ped, thistles, ruffled, sgnd, 33″ **800.00**
   Jug, cherries, top handle, sgnd D, 6½″ **160.00**
   Mug, leaves & berries, sgnd EA, 6″ **275.00**
   Mug, leaves and berries, 4½″ **140.00**
   Pillow vase, floral, sgnd, M, 4″ **145.00**
   Pitcher vase, florals, squat shape, sgnd AC, 3″ **140.00**
   Pitcher, florals, integral circle handle, 3 toed, sgnd MT, 5″ . **175.00**
   Tankard, monk portrait, LJ Burgess, 12½″ **1,800.00**
   Umbrella stand, foliage, 21″ **500.00**
   Vase, daffodil, broad shoulder, sgnd LB, 7″ **165.00**
   Vase, daffodils, full shoulder, waisted, sgnd VA, 6½″ . . . **165.00**
   Vase, florals, 3 toes & integral handles, sgnd MH, 5″ . . . **170.00**

Vase, grapes in 2 colors, sgnd Lybarger, ovoid, 17″ **700.00**
Vase, grapes, trumpet neck, CJ Dibowsky, 25″ **1,150.00**
Vase, Indian in full headdress, sgnd Burgess, 11½″ **2,500.00**
Vase, pansies, flattened spheres, lg bottom, sm neck, 3½″ . **140.00**
Vase, pansies, high shoulder, 5″ **115.00**
Vase, poppies, integral shoulder handles, Haubrich, 23½″ . . **675.00**
Vase, wild rose, globular w/sm neck, sgnd EA, 5½″ **160.00**
Vase, young Spotted Eagle, sgnd M Rauchfuss, 14″ **2,000.00**
Louwelsa-Blue; florals, cylinder, 10″ **400.00**
   Florals, cylinder, 10½″ **500.00**
   Florals, slender shape, 6½″ **325.00**
   Jug vase, pansies, squat sphere, 3″ **350.00**
   Mug, leaves, 5½″ **600.00**
Malvern, bud vase, 8½″ **40.00**
   Circle vase, 8″ **55.00**
   Jard & ped, 29½″ **420.00**
   Pillow vase, 6½″ **50.00**
   Pillow vase, 8½″ **70.00**
   Vase, 5½″ **25.00**
   Vase, 9″ **60.00**
   Wall pocket, 11″ **65.00**
Mammy Line, cookie jar, 11″ **175.00**
   Creamer, 3½″ **125.00**
   Sugar w/cover, 3½″ **125.00**
   Syrup pitcher, 6″ **150.00**
   Teapot, 8″ **175.00**
Marbleized, comport, 8″ **150.00**
   Vase, flares to low buldge, 4½″ **100.00**
   Vase, trumpet, 7½″ **120.00**
Marengo, vase, 6 panel ovoid, 8″ **185.00**
   Wall pocket, 8½″ **100.00**
Marvo, bowl vase, 5″ **40.00**
   Bud vase, 9″ **30.00**
   Double bud, 5″ **30.00**
   Double bud w/bars, 4½″ **55.00**
   Hanging basket, 5″ **75.00**
   Pitcher, 8″ **115.00**
   Vase, cylinder, 8½″ **30.00**
   Vase, cylinder, 10″ **35.00**
   Vase, oak leaf, 9″ **30.00**
   Vase, trumpet shape, 11½″ **75.00**
   Wall pocket, 8½″ **40.00**
Matt Floretta, tankard, apples & leaves, sgnd, CD, 13½″ . . . **450.00**
   Tankard, pears, 10½″ **280.00**
Melrose, basket, grapes, 10″ **180.00**
   Console bowl, roses, 5½x8½″ **100.00**
   Vase, berries, handles, swirled modeling, 8½″ **100.00**
   Vase, rose, handles, dimples, 5″ **75.00**
Mi-Flo, bowl, 4″ **30.00**
   Vase, 7″ **45.00**
   Vase, pointed handles, 9½″ **80.00**
Mirror Black, bowl, 11″ **50.00**
   Double bud vase, open vine work, 9″ **55.00**
   Strawberry jar, 6½″ **65.00**
   Vase, concave sides, top to base handles, 8″ **60.00**
   Vase, trumpet shape, 5½″ **25.00**
   Vase, wide shoulder, 12″ **125.00**
   Wall pocket, 8″ **55.00**
Modeled Etched Matt, vase, floral, wide top over cylinder, 10″ **185.00**
   Vase, fruit & branches, concave sides, 10½″ **225.00**
   Vase, grapes, leaves & vines, 14″ **325.00**
   Vase, rose, ovoid w/short cylinder neck, 6½″ **165.00**
   Vase, rose, square shape, 10″ **200.00**
Muskota, 2 geese flower frog, 6″ **160.00**

2 hunting dogs, 7½″ **300.00**
Bowl w/spread wing geese, 4½″ **110.00**
Elephant figural, 7½x12½″ **575.00**
Fence, 5″ **140.00**
Fish & stump, 5″ **80.00**
Fishing boy on driftwood, 6½″ **100.00**
Foxy Grandpa incense burner, 4″ **140.00**
Gate w/pots & cat, 7″ **400.00**
Girl, hand to hair, 4″ **70.00**
Girl on stump at fork of tree, 8½″ **135.00**
Girl w/flowers & hat, 9″ **150.00**
Girl w/hoop skirt powder box, 7″ **150.00**
Nude on rock flower frog, 8″ **130.00**
Neiska, bowl, 3 toed, 4″ **30.00**
Vase, 6″ **20.00**
Vase, ornate handles, 6″ **30.00**
Noval, bowl, 3½x8″ **55.00**
Bowl, 3½x9½″ **65.00**
Candleholder, 9½″ **120.00**
Comport, 5½″ **60.00**
Vase, 6″ **55.00**
Novelty, 3 pig ashtray, 4″ **70.00**
Dog w/bone ashtray, 4½″ **75.00**
Frog & lotus, 4″ **45.00**
Jar, Man, 6″ **75.00**
Monkey on peanut, 5x8″ **45.00**
Pot, Woman, 2½″ **45.00**
Sitting dog ashtray, 5″ **60.00**
Wall pocket, face, 10″ **85.00**
Wall pocket, pitcher, 7½″ **60.00**
Wall pocket, teapot, 9″ **65.00**
Oak Leaf, basket, 7½″ **35.00**
Basket, 9½″ **40.00**
Pitcher, 8½″ **40.00**
Pitcher, 14″ **100.00**
Wall pocket, 8½″ **40.00**
Window box, 6″ high **35.00**
Ollas water bottle, w/underplate **75.00**
Panella, basket, 7″ **35.00**
Bowl, footed, 3½″ **25.00**
Jar w/cover, footed, 6½″ **45.00**
Vase, w/handles, 6½″ **25.00**
Wall pocket, 8″ **45.00**
Paragon, vase, ball shape, 6½″ **80.00**
Vase, ovoid, maroon, 7½″ **90.00**
Vase, wide rim, slightly convex sides, 7½″ **85.00**
Parian, vase, 8½″ **65.00**
Vase, 13″ **100.00**
Wall pocket, 10″ **80.00**
Pastel, circle vase, 6″ **45.00**
Pitcher, 10″ **50.00**
Planter, #P3, 4x7″ **35.00**
Planter, 4x8″ **30.00**
Planter, heart shape, 6″ **40.00**
Vase, #P-14, 6½″ **20.00**
Patra, basket, 5½″ **75.00**
Bowl, 3 ft, shape, #13 .... **45.00**
Vase, 5″ **55.00**
Vase, 2 handles, shape #6, 4½″ **40.00**
Vase, shape #15, 8″ **55.00**
Patricia, bowl, 6 geese, long necks, 8″ **215.00**
Bowl, spread wing duck figurals, 7″ **165.00**
Pelican planter, 5″ **90.00**
Swan planter, 5″ **40.00**

Vase, duck head handles, 4″ **30.00**
Vase, swan neck handles, 8½″ **90.00**
Pearl, basket, small, 6½″ **130.00**
Bowl, 3x6″ **50.00**
Bud vase, 5″ **40.00**
Candleholders, 8½″ pr **115.00**
Console bowl, 3x10″ **65.00**
Vase, 6″ **75.00**
Vase, 9″ **200.00**
Wall pocket, 8″ **75.00**
Wall pocket, 8½″ **85.00**
Perfecto (Matt Louwelsa), ewer, berries & thorns, sgnd HP, 17″ **725.00**
Ewer, dandelion puff, 12″ **470.00**
Ewer, ears of corn, sgnd A Haubrich, 12″ **725.00**
Vase, roses & leaves, pink/grey, cylinder, 14″ **450.00**
Wall pocket, florals on blue-gray, sgnd, HP, 7″ **165.00**
Pesca, Old Man w/Fish, 12½″ **235.00**
Pierre, cookie jar, 10″ **65.00**
Creamer **15.00**
Pitcher, 5″ **30.00**
Pitcher, 7½″ **45.00**
Sugar **15.00**
Teapot, 8½″ **60.00**
Pumila, bowl w/underplate, 4″ **35.00**
Bowl, 3½″ **25.00**
Console plate, 3x12″ **50.00**
Vase, flare rim, 9½″ **55.00**
Wall pocket, 7″ **60.00**
Raceme, vase, ball shape, 9″ **250.00**
Ragenda, urn, high angle shoulder, pink, 6½″ **40.00**
Vase, cylinder w/side drape, maroon, 12″ **65.00**
Vase, sphere, blue, 9″ **60.00**
Raydance, vase, 7½″ **35.00**
Vase, 8″ **35.00**
Vase, 9″ **60.00**
Regal, console bowl, 2½x11″ **30.00**
Hanging basket, 5½″ **75.00**
Pitcher, teardrop panel, 11″ **45.00**
Vase, teardrop panel, handles, 9″ **35.00**
Vase, tri-level side panels, 9″ **40.00**
Roba, pitcher, 6″ **45.00**
Pitcher, 11″ **70.00**
Planter, 4x6″ **30.00**
Vase, w/handles, 13″ **90.00**
Wall pocket, 10″ **50.00**
Rochelle, vase, apple blossoms, pink & wht on brown, 6″ **200.00**
Vase, roses, yellow on shaded brown matt, 13″ **325.00**
Roma, bowl, roses, handles, 3″ **35.00**
Candleholder, band of roses, bobeche over sm handles, 10½″ **35.00**
Console w/liner, grapes & vines, 6½x18″ **150.00**
Door stop, basket of flowers **95.00**
Letter pocket, florals on wht, 4½x7½″ **125.00**
Planter, log shape w/floral swags, 3x10½″ **45.00**
Pot, reticulated rim, 3½″ **25.00**
Vase, floral swags, 9″ **35.00**
Vase, reticulated rim, wreath decor, cylinder, 6½″ .. **25.00**
Vase, roses, rim handles, 6″ **30.00**
Wall pocket, basket w/flowers, Dupont motif, 10″ **50.00**
Wall pocket, cornucopia w/bow & florals, 8½″ **45.00**
Wall pocket, floral swag, reticulated rim, 6″ **30.00**
Wall pocket, fluting & 3 roses on tapering shape, 7″ ... **40.00**
Rosemont, jard & ped, black gloss w/wht florals, 25½″ ... **465.00**
Jardiniere, 4 daisy clusters, blk gloss, 7″ **160.00**
Jardiniere, apple branch on blk & wht blocks, 5″ **85.00**

Jardiniere, bluebird, flowering branch, 6½″ 160.00
Jardiniere, crowned heads, fruit clusters, blk gloss, 4½″ 125.00

Vase, bluebird, flowering branch, 10″ 300.00
Vase, bluebird, leaves, 10½″ 300.00
Rudlor, console bowl, 4½x17½″ 50.00
   Vase, 6″ 25.00
   Vase, 9″ 45.00
Sabrinian, baskets, 7″ 125.00
   Candleholder, fish standard, 6½″ 55.00
   Pitcher, 10½″ 165.00
   Planter, 4½″ 70.00
   Vase, shell body, seahorse head handles, 12″ 265.00
   Vase, twisted w/seahorses, 9½″ 140.00
   Wall pocket, 8½″ 55.00
   Window box, 3½x9″ 90.00
Scandia, bowl, 3x6″ 60.00
   Vase, 9″ 70.00
   Vase, cylinder, 6″ 40.00
Senic, pillow vase, #S-11, 7½″ 40.00
   Planter, #S-17, 5½″ 55.00
   Vase, #S-4, 5½″ 35.00
   Vase, #S-9, 8″ 50.00
   Vase, #S-14, 10″ 55.00
Sicardo, mug, 3½″ 470.00
   Pillow vase, scalloped w/handles, 6x10″ 500.00
   Vase, elongated ovoid, 9″ 325.00
   Vase, flaring to side base, 4½″ 265.00
   Vase, low body angle, 5″ 265.00
   Vase, low body buldge, long cylinder neck w/flared rim, 15½″ 450.00
   Vase, pear shape w/curving half handles, 6″ 550.00
   Vase, sharp shoulder angle tapers to base, 6″ 400.00
   Vase, sharp twist, 5″ 265.00
   Vase, stylized florals, 4½″ 295.00
Silva, the Dancer, 8″ 135.00
Silvertone, basket, 13″ 185.00
   Candleholders, 3″, pr 60.00
   Double bud vase, 6″ 60.00
   Vase, bulbous, fluted w/handles, 8½″ 125.00
   Vase, curved handles close to body, 11½″ 135.00
   Vase, cylinder neck w/straight handles, round bottom, 10″ . . 180.00
   Vase, w/handles, slender, 9″ 140.00
Softone, candleholder, 2½″ 25.00
   Double bud vase, 9″ 30.00
   Hanging basket, 10″ 55.00

Pitcher, 9½″ 35.00
Planter, 4x8″ 35.00
Vase, 11″ 45.00
Souevo, bowl, brick, ivory band w/'swastika' decor, 2½x6″ 85.00
   Pot, brick, narrow rim, ivory band on wide flared body, 6½x8″ 150.00
   Tobacco jar, brick w/incised Greek Key motif, 6″ 225.00
   Wall pocket, brick, ivory top section w/C motif in blk, 9½″ . . 55.00
Squirrel, lawn ornament, 12″ 600.00
   On bowl, 5½x7″ 60.00
Stellar, vase, black w/wht stars, 5″ 120.00
   Vase, wht w/blue stars, 6″ 110.00
Sydonia, candleholder, double, 7″ 50.00
   Cornucopia, 8½″ 65.00
   Double vase, 7½″ 60.00
   Fan vase, 9½″ 90.00
   Planter, 4″ 35.00
   Triple bud vase, 8½″ 70.00
Tivoli, vase, wht, flared cylinder, 8½″ 90.00
   Vase, wht, funnel shape, 6″ 60.00
   Vase, wht, width at shoulder, 9½″ 100.00
Turada, lamp base, 4 toed, 8″ 800.00
   Mug, 6″ 265.00
   Tobacco jar, 8½″ 300.00
   Umbrella stand, 21″ 750.00
Turkis, vase, 5″ 40.00
   Vase, fluted rim, 8″ 80.00
   Vase, full bodies, large handles, 14″ 135.00
   Vase, square cylinder body w/wing handles, 7″ 80.00
Tutone, console bowl, triangular 110.00
   Vase, 11″ 90.00
   Vase, 3 tab ft, ball body, 4″ 30.00
   Vase, 4 tab ft, elongated ovoid, 6½″ 45.00
   Vase, cylinder, 12½″ 85.00
   Vase, w/candleholder, 7″ 50.00
   Wall pocket, 10½″ 60.00
Utility Ware, bean pot w/lid, 5½″ 30.00
   Casserole in metal frame, 5x7½″ 50.00
   Cup, 2″ 15.00
   Mug, 4″ 30.00
   Mustard pot w/metal holder, 2½″ 30.00
   Pitcher, 6″ 45.00
   Teapot, 4″ 35.00
   Tumbler, 4″ 12.00
Velva, console bowl, 3½x12½″ 65.00
   Vase, bulbous body, short wide neck, 9″ 55.00
   Vase, ovoid, 6″ 40.00
   Vase, slim convex shape, 9½″ 65.00
Velvetone, batter jug, 10″ 135.00
   Pitcher, 10″ 125.00
   Vase, fluted rim, milk can handles, 9½″ 100.00
Voile, fan vase, 7″ 45.00
   Fan vase, 8″ 75.00
   Jardiniere, 6″ 85.00
Warwick, basket, 9″ 135.00
   Circle vase, 7″ 65.00
   Console bowl, 10½″ 100.00
   Double bud vase, 8½″ 55.00
   Double vase, 4½″ 45.00
   Planter, 1 handle, 3 ft, 3½″ 60.00
   Planter w/frog cover, 5″ 70.00
   Vase, cylinder, 9½″ 55.00
Weller Faience, poppy, orange on brown, handles at mid section, 8″ 550.00
   Vase, abstract, yellow & blue on black, 13″ 400.00
White & Decorated, bowl vase, florals at rim, 4″ 100.00

Vase, florals, 6 panels, 9½″ **160.00**
Vase, florals over wide band, trumpet shape, 10½″ **165.00**
Wild Rose, basket, 5½″ **25.00**
  Double vase, 6″ **25.00**
  Triple candleholder, 6″ **50.00**
  Vase, 6½″ **25.00**
  Vase, flaring, 4 toed, 7½″ **30.00**
Woodcraft, apple branch on bark ground, 13″ **110.00**
  Basket, acorn design, 9½″ **160.00**
  Bowl, reticulated, twigs, 3½″ **50.00**
  Bud vase, by water lily, on pad, 7″ **75.00**
  Hanging basket, long funnel shape, fruit, 6″ **60.00**
  Jardiniere, woodpecker & squirrel figurals, oak leaves, 9½″ . **250.00**
  Jardiniere, woodpecker figural on side of stump, 5½″ **165.00**
  Jardiniere, woodpecker on stump w/daffodils, 5″ **225.00**
  Lamp, owl between 2 bulbs, entwined branches, 13½″ **275.00**
  Lamp, owls on tree, 12½″ **250.00**
  Mug, foxes in den, 6″ **165.00**
  Planter, foxes in den, 5½″ **30.00**
  Tankard, foxes in den, 12½″ **500.00**
  Vase, owl & fruit on tree, open front, 16″ **375.00**
  Vase, plums on branch, 12″ **150.00**
  Wall pocket, 2 bird figurals w/nest, branches & florals, 14½x12½″ **300.00**
  Wall pocket, owl in den, 10″ **100.00**
  Wall pocket, purple plums on 4-forked branch, figural, 9″ ... **75.00**
Woodrose, bowl, 2½x8½″ **45.00**
  Jardiniere, 3½″ **35.00**
  Jardiniere, 7″ **115.00**
  Vase, 4″ **35.00**
  Vase, cylinder, 7″ **40.00**
  Wall pocket, 5½″ **65.00**
Zona, baby plate, rolled edge, 7½″ **30.00**
  Bowl, apple branches, 5½″ **15.00**
  Bowl, apple branches, 9½″ **25.00**
  Juvenile Line, bowl, w/rabbit & bird, 5½″ **30.00**
  Juvenile Line, milk pitcher, 3½″ **50.00**
  Pickle dish, twig center handle, 11″ **65.00**
  Pitcher, apple branches, 6″ **70.00**
  Pitcher, apple branches in sq reserves, 7″ **110.00**
  Pitcher, kingfisher in sq reserves, natural colors, 8″ **135.00**
  Pitcher, kingfisher in sq reserves, rose glaze, 8″ **135.00**
  Pitcher, zinnias, rose on ivory, 7½″ **135.00**
  Plate, apple branches, 7½″ **20.00**
  Plate, apple branches, 10″ **25.00**
  Plate, apple branches, closed handles, 9½″ **25.00**
  Platter, apple & grape clusters, 12″ **30.00**
  Tea set, apple branches, 3 pc″ **165.00**
  Tea set, floral branches, 3 pc″ **220.00**
  Umbrella stand, girls w/floral garlands, 20½″ **450.00**
  Vase, apple branches, twig handles, 9″ **70.00**
  Wall pocket, iris & leaves, 8″ **30.00**

Western Americana

Relics from the era of the Western Frontier to the age of the cowboys hold a fascination for many. Leather items, such as holsters, saddles and chaps, are often elaborately hand tooled and sometimes bear the mark of their makers. 'California' spurs were ornate, sometimes inlaid with silver work, and are considered very desirable among today's collectors. So are those stamped McChestney, Kelly, G.A. Bischoff and Co., and J.O. Bass.

Sheriff's badges, old photographs, Express memorabilia and barbed wire--in short, anything from the Old West is being collected!

Anvil, blacksmith's, old, 8¾x24½x9″ **160.00**

Barbed wire, Allis, Buckthorn, pat 1881, 18″ .... **.60**
  Baker, Champion, pat 1881, 18″ .... **.30**
  Beers, Flopover, pat 1880, 18″ .... **.60**
  Brinkerhoff, Lance Ribbon, pat 1881, 18″ .... **.60**
  Burrows, Star, pat 1877, 18″ **110.00**
  Case, Washer Barb, pat 1882, 18″ **49.00**
  Cook, Fin, pat 1882, 18 ″ **80.00**
  Crandal, Zigzag, pat 1881, 18″ .... **.90**
  Crowell, Saddle Barb, pat 1879, 18″ **1.75**
  Decker, Parallel, pat 1882, 18″ **5.50**
  Dodge, Star, pat 1881, 18″ **440.00**
  Ellwood, Spread, pat 1874, 18″ .... **.60**
  Glidden, Common, pat 1874, 18″ .... **.30**
  Gunderson, Snake, pat 1883, 18″ **1.75**
  Haish, 'S' Barb, pat 1874, 18″ .... **.60**
  Halner, Greenbriar, pat 1878, 18″ **2.50**
  Harsha, Nail & Arrow Barb, pat 1876, 18″ **110.00**
  Hill, Caged Barb, pat 1881, 18″ **440.00**
  J W Griswold, Chain Link Wire, pat 1819, 18″ **2.50**
  Kelly, Diamond Barb, pat 1868, 18″ .... **.30**
  Kennedy, 3 Point Barb, pat 1874, 18″ **2.25**
  Knickerbocker, wrapped 'Y' barb, pat 1876, 18″ **11.00**
  Lenox, Knox Line, pat 1883, 18″ **2.25**
  Merrill, Twirl, pat 1874, 18″ .... **.60**
  Miles, Staple Barb, pat 1883, 18″ **1.20**
  Munson, Double Z, pat 1879, 18″ **220.00**
  Nadelhoffer, 'N' barb, pat 1883″ .... **.90**
  Pond, Traingle, pat 1883, 18″ **190.00**
  Reynolds, Necktie, pat 1877, 18″ **1.25**
  Ross, Vicious 4 Point, pat 1879, 18″ .... **.30**
  Stover, Clip, pat 1875, 18″ **7.75**
  Upham, Snail, pat 1881, 18″ **1.25**
  Westgarth, Webbed Arrowplate, pat 1881, 18″ **35.00**
  Wormley, 'Y' barb on 3 lines, pat 1875, 18″ **5.50**
Bit, gal leg w/studded head stall, mkd Byermann's **195.00**
  Silver, mounted on bridle, 1930s **200.00**
Box, wooden, old, Adams Express Company, 12x23x11½″ ... **120.00**
Branding iron, initials, late 1800s, 4x4x18″ **40.00**
  JC Marble & Co **40.00**
Bridle rosettes, silver, pr **15.00**
Buggy neck yoke **16.00**
Chaps, angora **175.00**
Chaps, brown w/gr leather trim, studs in waist & down sides, 33″ long **50.00**
  Heavy leather w/10 silver medallions & 2 pockets **95.00**
Collar & mirror, w/hames **45.00**
Cuffs, tooled, mkd Clark **90.00**
Curry comb, cast iron, wood handle, tail comb, Fitch pattern **7.50**
Hames, iron, w/brass knobs, pr **15.00**
Hames, wooden **25.00**
Harness, single, breast collar type w/shaft thimbles & matching bridle **40.00**
Hat band, horsehair **29.00**
Hitching post, iron tree trunk, rare **150.00**
  With ring, cast iron, horse head **150.00**
Hoof trimmer, perforated iron handle, pat 1903 .... **9.50**
Horse bit, old **12.00**
Horse bridle rosettes, brass, oval shaped, pr **8.00**
Oil on canvas, Autumn Moon by Bill Remar, framed, 24x12″ ... **85.00**
  Pale Moon by Bill Remar, framed, 14x11″ **65.00**
  Santa Fe Ranch Home by Arthur Haddock, 12x16¼″ **800.00**
  Solitude by Bill Remar, 17½x25½″ **225.00**
Pallet knife oil, Grand Tetons, landscape by Bill Freeman, 18x24″ **250.00**
Pen & ink, Monument Valley Ariz., Aug 1922, by M Dixon, 4x5½″ **650.00**
  Onion Valley, Nevada, July, 1929, by Maynard Dixon **850.00**
Pencil drawing, Brittany Boats by Edgar Alwin Payne, 12x12″. **300.00**

Photograph, of CH Russell, at easel, matted & framed, 1918, 14x11″ **55.00**
Pistol, colt open top, 22 caliber, brass frame, 1873 . . . . **130.00**
   Muff, folding trigger, multi-shot, 32 caliber, Victorian **90.00**
Print, 4 prehistoric natives attack a mammoth, by Bob Edgar, 8x10″ **25.00**
Rifle scabbard, fits Winchester lever action, Denver mkd **75.00**
Saddle, Fremont, early 1900s **65.00**
   Mueller roping, w/matching bridle & breast collar **250.00**
   Orig rodeo contest #1, early 1900s **125.00**
Saddle bag, hand tooled, small **195.00**
Sign, metal, old, Wells Fargo & Co, 12x12″ **80.00**
   Porcelain over steel, Wells Fargo Pony Express Overland Mail **69.50**
Spur, w/lg spiked rowel, handforged **12.00**
   George Parker & Sons, Never Rust Silver, pr **30.00**
   Old, pr **25.00**
   Polished aluminum, w/straps, pr **28.50**
   Presentation, World's Champion Rodeo 1958, Pillsbury Best Feeds **37.50**
   Silver overlay, Crockett, early mkd **190.00**
Stagecoach time table, California & Oregon, 1881 Overland, 15″ **450.00**
Stirrup, side saddle **5.50**
Stirrups, all different, set of 12 . . . . **115.00**
Strongbox, Wells Fargo, sgnd **2,800.00**
Wagon hubs, wooden **10.00**
Wagon jack, Conestoga, iron **120.00**
   Wooden, stenciled Miller's Jack **35.00**
Wagon spring seat **95.00**
Wagon wheel, wooden **55.00**
Wagon whip holder, cast iron, 7½″, 1850s **15.00**
Wheel, iron **15.00**
Wrist cuffs, tooled leather **60.00**

Wheatley

    In 1880, after a brief association with the Coultry Works, Thomas J. Wheatley opened his own studio in Cincinnati, Ohio, claiming to have been the first to discover the secret of underglaze slip decoration on an unbaked clay vessel. He applied for and was granted a patent toward that end. Demand for his ware increased to the place that several artists were hired to decorate the ware. The company incorporated in 1880 as the Cincinnati Art Pottery, but until 1882, it continued to operate under Wheatley's name. Ware from this period is marked T.J. Wheatley, or T.G.W. and Co., and it may be dated.

Mug, gr matt, pretzel handle, 7¼″ **110.00**
Vase, 6¾″ **300.00**

Circle, w/daisy, 8″ **700.00**

Daisy spray, gray ground, flattened oblong shape, sgnd, 9½x7¼″ **400.00**
With flowers, 1880s, 6½″ **490.00**

Whites Utica

Butter, wood lid, cobalt, daisies & leaves, no bail, 1 qt, 5x5¼″ dia **80.00**
Honey jar, wood lid, embossed surface, grape & leaf spray **65.00**
Humidor, cigars, snake lid **200.00**
Jar, flared, w/lid, self embossed diamond surface, 'cigars', 7½″ **200.00**
Mug, rounded, buffalo, 3 drinking men, gold imprint, 4½x3¼″ dia **125.00**
Pitcher, embossed bark surface, daisies allover, 6¾x3½″ dia . **127.50**
Tankard, drinking monk, embossed diamond surface, leaves, 10″ **135.00**
Tobacco jar, bulbous, pointer dog molded in relief, label, 7x6″ **124.00**
   Bulbous, wood lid, horse head & beaded ring, 4½x4½″ dia . . **90.00**

Wicker

    Wicker is the basket-like material used in many types of furniture and accessories; it may be made from bamboo cane, rattan, reed or artificial fibers. It is airy and light weight, and very popular in hot regions.

    Imported from the Orient in the 18th century, it was first manufactured in the United States in about 1850. The elaborate, closely woven Victorian designs belong to the mid-to-late 1800s, and the simple styles with coarse reedings usually indicate a post-1900 production. Art Deco styles followed in the '20s and '30s.

    The most important consideraton in buying wicker is condition---it can be restored, but only by a professional. Age is an important factor, but be aware that 'Victorian-look' furniture is being manufactured today. A clue to age is in the type of weave. Light-weight, closely woven material indicates a pre-1900 production date.

Basinet, loose weave, braid trim, no hood, bottom rack **80.00**
Basket, circular, tight weave waste basket **15.00**
   Large oval, loose weave, laundry type, w/handles **20.00**
   Large, medium weave hamper-like, w/handles **30.00**
   Rectangular, loose weave waste w/handles **20.00**
   Small rectangular picnic-like w/handles, decorated sides **15.00**
Carriage, baby, w/adjustable hood, side window & design **120.00**
   With adjustable hood, tight weave **110.00**
   With adjustable hood, sideview window **120.00**
Cart, tea, tight weave, bottom shelf front wheels, top tray **260.00**
Chair, cane, w/braided trim, square cushioned seat **125.00**
   Child's, rocker, rounded back & seat, tight braid trim **200.00**
   Child's, rocker, Victorian, high back **200.00**
   High back, Victorian, ornate scrolled design **175.00**
   High cushioned back & seat, short peg legs **150.00**
   High floral cushioned back & seat, low seat, short legs **110.00**
   High oval back, w/curved arm rests, square cushion seat **145.00**
   Patio, low fanback, round seat, ornate scrolled design **235.00**
   Rocker, cane 5-sided braid trim, cushion seat **175.00**
   Rocker, cushioned, round back, tight weave, arm rest **170.00**
   Rocker, floral cushioned, w/tight braid weave trim **125.00**
   Rocker, loose weave, square back w/high arm rest **240.00**
   Rocker, low back w/loose weave, cushioned seat & back **120.00**
   Rocker, square back & seat w/loose weave & arm rest **110.00**
   Rocker, tight weave curved back & sides, cushion seat **150.00**
   Rocker, tight weave high back w/design, square cushion seat **150.00**
   Rocker, tight weave pointed back, square cushioned seat . . . **150.00**
   Rocker, tight weave, low sides & seat, design on back **300.00**
   Rocker, tight weave, wide arm rests, square cushioned seat . **200.00**
   Rocker, Victorian, w/low small arm rest **240.00**
   Rocker, w/cane, curved back & sides, square cushion **120.00**
   Round back chair, square seat, straight legs **115.00**
   Round back, cane w/weave for trim, cushioned seat **150.00**

Round back, curved arm rests & loose weave square seat ... **185.00**
Round cushioned back & seat, tight weave trim **150.00**
Square back, loose weave, w/arm rest **175.00**
Tight weave, half open round back, cushioned seat **150.00**
Tight weave, round back, loose square cushion **150.00**
Tight weave, short legs, round back, cushioned seat **200.00**
Tight weave, w/diamond design, square cushioned seat **270.00**
Wing back, loose weave with side arm rests **175.00**
Davenport, braided look, rounded back, rounded arms cushion seat **400.00**
Cane, square back, 6 individual cushions **185.00**
Cane w/rounded back & cushion seat **250.00**
Curved back, loose weave, wide tight weave trim, cushion seat **230.00**
Curved back, loose weave, cushioned seat **430.00**
Curved, cane, unusual diamond design, cushion seat **280.00**
Floral, cushioned, curved back & seats, loose woven **240.00**
Half tight & half loose weave back, cushion seat **230.00**
Large, cushioned back & seat w/upholstry on bottom **280.00**
Light & dark wicker, tight weave, round back **320.00**
Tight weave, curved back, w/3 floral cushions........... **210.00**
Tight weave, low center back, lg wings, 3 cushions **440.00**
Tight weave, round back w/diamond design, cushioned seat . **275.00**
Tight weave, wing back, striped cushion seat **280.00**
Desk w/chair, tight weave, drawers, curved top, high back **380.00**
Tighter weave, flat top, high back chair **330.00**
Footstool, cane legs w/floral cushion, rectangular........... **55.00**
Cane base w/cushion on top, square **45.00**
High chair, loose weave, braid trim high back **155.00**
Victorian, w/high back & scroll design................. **155.00**

Lamp, 16"... **100.00**
Desk, tight & loose weave, over kerosene lamp **75.00**
Floor, tight weave pole & shade, open top shade......... **125.00**
Floor, tight weave pole w/loose weave shade, dome-shape w/fringe **110.00**
Table, round dome shade w/fringe, tight weave base **40.00**
Table, umbrella-like shade, loose weave, square base **110.00**
Lounge, back & arm rest, cushioned, tight weave **390.00**
Back, rail on one side & curved around foot, cushion **500.00**
Lounges, flat, tight weave, flat cushion **210.00**
Settee, loose weave, ½ cushioned back & cushioned seat.... **280.00**
Tight weave, curved back, w/partial loose weave back **190.00**
Tight weave, ½ cushioned back, cushioned seat.......... **255.00**
Stand, fern, loose weave, rectangle, w/arch & birdcage **280.00**
Fern, tight weave, bowl shape w/rim on footed pole **75.00**
Fern, tight braided weave, rectangular, 4 straight legs **100.00**

Fern, tight weave, oval shape, curved legs............... **180.00**
Fern, tight weave, rectangular, diamond braid design....... **110.00**
Stroller, baby, adjustable hood, side diamond design........ **110.00**
Baby, adjustable hood w/window, side design **100.00**
Baby, plain w/loose weave & no hood **90.00**
Swing, curved back, tight weave seat & trim round back **250.00**
Loose weave back, tight weave seat & trim, square back.... **225.00**
Square back, cushioned back & seat, tight & loose weave... **280.00**
Table, rectangle, light color, oak top w/bottom shelf **95.00**
Oak top, wicker sides & legs **100.00**
Table, corner; 2 shelves, tight weave, square shape......... **150.00**
Table, end; round, tight weave, stool-like **110.00**
Round, with 2 shelves, tight weave **180.00**
Table, library; oak top, lower shelf, tight weave **150.00**
Oak top, tight weave sides & legs, decorative end panels ... **245.00**
Table, magazine; 2 shelves, flat top, tight weave, rectangular .. **115.00**
Table, round; lg, tight weave, diamond design in square woven base **325.00**

Willets

The Willets Manufacturing Company of Trenton, New Jersey, produced a type of beleek porcelain during the late 1880s and 1890s. Examples were often marked with a coiled snake that formed a 'W', with 'Willets' below, and 'Belleek' above.

Bowl, blk band, leaves & blackberries, lizard handles, 4½x10½" **195.00**
Bowl, fluted, bouillon, cobalt, gilt trim **325.00**
Gold handles, gold floral trim, 6" dia **145.00**
Rose bowl type, hp, sgnd, 1912, 4¾x8" dia **70.00**
Butter tub, ivory **30.00**
Charger, hand sponged rim, Arno, 16"................... **28.00**
Claret pitcher, dragon handle, bearded face spout, red mk, 11½" **360.00**
Cup & saucer, chocolate, facet decor, wht & gold **85.00**
Demitasse cup & saucer, embossed gold & floral trim **65.00**
Dish, heart shape, fluted edge, flowers **65.00**
Hatpin holder, hp floral, 5"............................ **125.00**
Mug, gold & dk gr, sgnd, 1906, 5½" **185.00**
Hp blackberries, shaded blue ground **70.00**
With currants.. **68.00**
Pitcher, tankard, blue/gr on cream, gold & blue handle, sgnd, 7" **149.00**
Punch cup, gr & sterling shamrock overlay, rare **125.00**
Salt dip, ruffled rim, applied beading & gold **16.00**
Swan, iridescent luster, small.......................... **22.00**
Lavender & gilt trim, small............................ **24.00**
Tankard, floral relief, hp raspberries, 14"................. **365.00**
Vase, apple blossom decor, rose & blue ground, brown mk, 8" **175.00**
Blue w/bluebirds, foliage, artist sgnd, 12"................ **400.00**
Hp floral, 1909, 11½" **229.00**
Lavender ground w/small red roses, 14" **250.00**
Pink poppy, birds, foliage on shaded ground, 10x3" **120.00**
Violet decor, 9".................................... **220.00**

Willow Ware

Willow Ware, inspired no doubt by the numerous patterns of the blue and white Nanking imports, has been popular since the late 18th century, and has been made in as many variations as there were manufacturers. English transfer wares by such notable firms as Allerton and Ridgway are the most sought after and the most expensive. Japanese potters have been producing Willow patterned dinnerware since the late 1800s and American manufacturers followed suit. Although blue is the color most commonly used, mauve, black and even multicolor Willow Ware may be found. Complimentary glassware, tinware and linens have also been made.

Bowl, Booth, #453, 1906, 9″	**22.50**
Buffalo, 1911, 5″	**15.00**
Burleigh, 9″	**22.00**
Oval, 10″	**27.50**
With domed cover, sq, 9″	**90.00**
With flat lid, round	**65.00**
With handles, scalloped	**55.00**
Carr, 5¼″	**6.50**
Copeland, shallow, 9″ dia	**30.00**
HA & Co, England, oval, 2x8½″	**25.00**
Homer Laughlin, 5¼″	**4.00**
6¼″	**4.50**
9½″	**12.00**
Japan, blk mk, 5¾	**4.50**
Blue mk, 5¼″	**4.00**
Wide flange rim, 6½″	**4.50**
Minton, flow blue, 8″ dia	**70.00**
Ridgway, 7½″	**20.00**
8½″	**22.00**
Royal, 9″	**8.50**
Unmkd, 5¼″	**2.00**
Ventonware, 4¾″	**5.00**
8½″	**15.00**
Wedgwood, 8″	**25.00**
Wedgwood & Co, 8½x11″	**40.00**
Butter, w/cover; Allerton	**150.00**
Ridgway mkd	**50.00**
Butter pat, Allerton	**16.50**
Cake plate, Homer Laughlin, 6¼″	**2.50**
Japan, 6″	**2.50**
Canister, Morylaneo Japan, 4″ sq lid, 7½″	**12.50**
Casserole, w/cover, Royal Venton, Steventon & Sons, 2½x10″	**35.00**
Cereal, Burleigh	**10.00**
Chamber pot, Dulton, 1895	**165.00**
Cheese keeper, Burleigh	**60.00**
Child's set, 21 pcs, made in Japan	**100.00**
Chop plate, Royal, gr mk, 10½″	**12.00**
Coffee pot, Burleigh, 8 cup	**60.00**
Creamer, Burleigh	**25.00**
Homer Laughlin	**6.50**
Japan, blk mk	**7.50**
Swinnerton	**10.00**
Cup & saucer, Allerton, a-wreath mk, 4″ cup	**18.00**
Scalloped	**22.00**
Buffalo, 1905	**27.50**
Burleigh	**18.00**
Homer Laughlin	**6.00**
Japan	**5.50**
Blk mk	**7.50**
Child's	**5.50**
Low, unmkd	**3.50**
Meakin, England	**8.50**
Occupied Japan	**15.00**
Ridgway, bouillon	**22.50**
Breakfast	**16.50**
Wedgwood, unicorn mk, lg	**16.50**
Wood's	**10.00**
Cup, Japan, child's, blue mk	**3.50**
Made in England	**6.00**
Myott & Son	**8.50**
Occupied Japan, blue mk	**8.00**
Ridgway	**14.00**
Demitasse cup, Buffalo, 1916	**18.00**
Ridgway	**13.50**
Demitasse cup & saucer, Burleigh	**15.00**
Ridgway	**22.50**
Egg cup, Burleigh, double, 4″	**16.00**
Ginger jar	**35.00**
Gravy boat, 7″	**35.00**
Allerton	**39.00**
Ridgway	**35.00**
Royal Venton, John Steventon & Son	**25.00**
Side handle, 'Gravy Lean'	**12.00**
Gravy boat, w/stand; Burleigh	**50.00**
Japan, 4½x3½″	**12.00**
Grill plate, Occupied Japan, Motijama, 10″	**7.00**
Hot water dish, pattern on outside, very rare	**100.00**
Marmalade, Japan	**39.50**
Mug, Japan	**6.00**
Stacking, unmkd	**4.50**
Pepper jar, w/cover, Morylaneo Japan, 2½″ sq, 4″	**5.00**
Pitcher, 6 sided w/lg neck, pewter lid, GH & C Co, 1900, 7x5″ dia	**65.00**
Buffalo Pottery, gold trim, 1907, 5″	**65.00**
Mason's Ironstone, octagonal w/serpent handle, 5″	**90.00**
Plate, AB Jones Grafton, 6″	**4.00**
Adams, Staffordshire, 7½″	**8.50**
Allerton, a-wreath mk, 6″	**8.50**
A-wreath mk, 7″	**10.00**
A-wreath mk, 9″	**16.50**
Scalloped, 9″	**15.00**
Scalloped, old mk, 7″	**10.00**
B&L, 1888, 10½″	**15.00**
Booth, #453, 1906, 8″	**14.00**
Buffalo, 1909, 6″	**12.00**
1909, 9″	**20.00**
1911, 8½″	**18.00**
Scalloped, 1905, 8″	**22.00**
Scalloped, 1907, 8″	**20.00**
Burleigh, 10½″	**18.00**
Bread & butter	**8.00**
Salad, 8″	**11.00**
Copeland, 1882, 7½″	**12.00**
1882, 9″	**16.00**
1882, 10″	**18.00**
Scalloped, 9″	**16.00**
Dudson, Wilcox & Tell, 6¼″	**4.50**
8″	**7.50**
10″	**12.00**
Homer Laughlin, 6¼″	**1.50**
7¼″	**4.00**
9¼	**6.50**
Ideal, 10¼″	**7.00**
11¼″	**12.00**
Japan, 7½″	**4.50**
9″	**6.00**
Blk mk, 6″	**2.00**
Blk mk, 9¼″	**6.00**
Blue mk, 6″	**2.50**
Child's, 3¾″	**2.50**
Johnson Bros, sandwich, 8″ sq	**55.00**
Maastrich, Holland, 9″	**17.50**
Soup, 9½″	**15.00**
Meakin, England, 9¾″	**8.50**
Occupied Japan, 9¼″	**7.50**
Olde Alton, 9″	**12.00**
Paden City, 7½″	**6.00**
9″	**8.50**
Ridgway, 9″	**12.00**

10″	**14.00**
Roya USA, 9¼″.................................	**4.00**
Handled, 10½″	**5.00**
Royal, gr mk, 9″	**6.00**
Royal Venton, John Steventon & Son, 10″..............	**12.00**
Shaw, 8″	**19.00**
9″	**22.00**
Staffordshire, 9″	**22.00**
Stone china, 9″	**22.00**
Swinnerton, 6½″	**4.50**
Unmkd, 6″	**1.00**
7¼″.....................................	**2.00**
9¾″.....................................	**4.50**
Ventonware, 9″	**9.00**
Wedgwood, 9″	**12.00**
Wedgwood Stoneware, scalloped, 10″	**18.00**
Wood's, 9″	**8.00**
10″	**12.00**
Yorktown, cockle, 3″	**24.00**
Platter, Adderlay, 11x14″.......................	**40.00**
Allerton, a-wreath mk, 9x11″	**30.00**
B&S, stoneware, impressed mk, 12½x10″	**150.00**

Buffalo, 1909, 14x11″................................	**55.00**
Burleigh, 12″	**30.00**
14″	**40.00**
16″	**65.00**
Copeland, 1882, 7x9″.........................	**40.00**
1882, 8x11″..............................	**50.00**
1883, 13x17″.............................	**80.00**
1883, 15x20″.............................	**110.00**
Crown mark, 14x18″..........................	**75.00**
EBJEL, 9x12½″...............................	**32.00**
ER & Jel, 13¼″	**45.00**
Homer Laughlin, 9x12″	**12.00**
11x13″	**22.50**
Japan, 12½″	**10.00**
Blk mk, 12¾″	**15.00**
Paden City, oval, impressed mk, 11¾″..........	**15.00**
Ridgway, 9x12″..............................	**27.50**
Staffordshire, 1800s, 12x15″	**65.00**
Unmarked, 8½x11″............................	**22.00**
Unmarked, Early, 15x19″......................	**70.00**
Well & tree, 15x18″	**165.00**
Salt box, Morylaneo Japan, hanging, wooden lid	**15.00**
Sauce dish, Allerton, a-wreath mk, 5½″	**8.50**

Burleigh	**8.00**
Homer Laughlin, 5″	**2.50**
Japan, 5¼″	**3.00**
Saucer, Allerton, 6″	**2.50**
Buffalo, 1908, 6″	**7.00**
Child's, 3¾″.................................	**4.00**
Dudson, Wilcox & Tell	**1.50**
Homer Laughlin	**1.00**
Japan, blk mk	**1.00**
Meakin, England	**1.50**
Paden City, impressed mk	**2.00**
Roya USA	**1.00**
Unmkd	**1.00**
Soup, Allerton, a-wreath mk, 7½″...............	**12.00**
Flat	**29.50**
Scalloped, 7″	**23.00**
Scalloped, 9″	**32.00**
Burleigh, rimmed	**14.00**
Dudson, Wilcox & Tell, 8″	**8.50**
Homer Laughlin, 8″	**6.00**
Japan, rimmed, blue mk, 7½″..................	**7.50**
Occupied Japan, flat	**15.00**
Podmore Walker, 1860s, 9″....................	**17.00**
Ridgway, 7″	**12.00**
Roya USA, rimmed, 8¼″.......................	**4.50**
Unmkd, 8½″	**4.50**
Spooner, Ridgway	**20.00**
Sugar, Allerton, England	**45.00**
Sugar, w/cover	**6.00**
Buffalo, 1907	**30.00**
Burleigh	**35.00**
Japan, blk mk	**8.50**
Ridgway	**22.50**
Sugar & creamer, Allerton, w/cover	**42.00**
Royal	**8.50**
Tea bowl, scalloped rim, unusal designs, 1810	**25.00**
Tea cup & saucer, Allerton, a-wreath mk	**22.00**
Tea jar, Rington, rare	**145.00**
Teapot, Burleigh, 6 cup	**55.00**
Dulton, late 1800s...........................	**80.00**
Japan, lg...................................	**60.00**
Rington, 4 cornered, limited tea merchants, 7″	**75.00**
Tumbler, juice, set of 4, 3½″....................	**25.00**
Set of 5, 3¾″...............................	**35.00**
Set of 6, 5″.................................	**45.00**
Tureen, Burleigh, lg	**200.00**
Vegetable bowl, Allerton, 9″	**30.00**
Copeland, w/cover & handles, 1882, 7x10″..............	**80.00**
Homer Laughlin, round, 8¾″...................	**12.00**
Japan, child's, w/lid, blue mk, 4¼″	**4.50**
Oval, 10½″	**8.00**
With cover, round	**28.00**

Winchester

The Winchester Repeating Arms Co. lost their important government contract after WWI, and of necessity turned to the manufacture of sporting goods, hardware items, tools, etc., to augment their gun production. Between 1920 and 1931, over 7,500 different items, each marked Winchester Trademark USA, were offered for sale by thousands of Winchester Hardware stores throughout the country. After 1931, the firm became Winchester-Western.

Advertisement, framed, blacks, skunk, log, 1908, 31x23″	**385.00**

Color flyer, Nublack & New Rival shotgun shells, 1915, 3x3″ . **10.00**
Advertising envelope, 2 men, 1 w/rifle, 1 w/pistol, W brand motto **18.00**
  Winchester rifles **25.00**
Auger bit **7.00**
Axe, hunters **50.00**
BB's, in orig package **5.00**
Banner, oilcloth, shooting gallery, 57x60″ **250.00**
  Silk type **35.00**
Barber shears, 7½″ **45.00**
Battery, dry cell, #6 . . . . **20.00**
Bit **12.50**
Block plane **25.00**
Bushel scale, brass, no bucket **75.00**
Calendar, bear coming around rock, 1926 . . . . **200.00**
Can opener **39.00**
Carbine, Indian decorated, MI873 . . . . **895.00**
Catalog, 1902 . . . . **125.00**
  1922, pocket, guns & amo, 30 pages **6.00**
  1932 . . . . **23.00**
Chisel, wood **25.00**
Counter top mat, padded, w/horse & rider, 47x54″ **17.50**
Display cabinet, razor blade, Winchester-Simmons **75.00**
Drill bit extension **65.00**
  #1209 . . . . **21.00**
Flashlight, 2 cell, pat 1926 . . . . **15.00**
  3 cell, pat 1925 . . . . **22.50**
  6 cell, brass **28.00**
  Copper, mkd **25.00**
Flat file **30.00**
Flyrod, telescoping, #5090, 8½″ **95.00**
Food chopper, W11 . . . . **45.00**
  W32 . . . . **50.00**
Food grinder, extra blades **40.00**
Hammer, ball peen **30.00**
Hammer, claw, 10 oz **110.00**
Hand saw, #10 . . . . **25.00**
  18″ **47.50**
Hand trap thrower, 1919 . . . . **55.00**
Hatchet, claw pattern **50.00**
  Head only, household half pattern **40.00**
Ice pick **8.00**
Ice skates **30.00**
Knife, Barlow, 2 blade, #2701 . . . . **85.00**
  Pruning, #1610 . . . . **155.00**
  Steel **35.00**
Level, 12″ **50.00**
Loading tool, 38-55, Winchester Rep Arms Co, Feb 18, 1894, mkd **28.50**
Meat cleaver **75.00**
Meat fork **30.00**
Padlock **45.00**
Paperweight, glass **60.00**
Pinback, Winchester Rifle, 1900 . . . . **36.00**
Pliers, short nose, side cutting chain, #2139, 10″ **50.00**
Pocket watch **200.00**
Poster, hunter & pheasant, 1955, 28x42″ **17.50**
  Ram & hunter, 1904, 15x26″ **250.00**
Potato fork **45.00**
Razor, w/razor strap **110.00**
Rod & reel **150.00**
Roller skates **30.00**
Ruler, folding, boxwood **45.00**
S wrench **32.50**
Saw, old **25.00**
Screwdriver, #7122 . . . . **23.00**

#7126, 8″ **47.50**
Brass bolster, 7″ **15.00**
Cabinet, #7113, 4″ **30.00**
July special **35.00**
Mechanical 4″ **20.00**
Mechanical 6″ **25.00**
Regular 3″ **35.00**
Sharpening steel #1768 . . . . **40.00**
Shotshells, window, brass, 12 for **40.00**
  Window, Nublack, 12 for **30.00**
  Window, Rival, 12 for **30.00**
Sign, enamel, Gun Advisory Center **65.00**
Spatula **45.00**
Stillson, 6″ **15.00**
Store box, holds 10 rifles, wooden dovetailed **160.00**
Straight razor, box w/orig instructions **60.00**
Sunglasses **15.00**
Whistle **70.00**
Wrench, open end **23.00**
  Pipe, 10″ **40.00**
Yardstick **145.00**

Windmill Weights

Chicken, ci, blk paint, 51 lbs, 19x19″ **650.00**
Dempster horse, ci, blk, 13 lbs, 16½x17″ **350.00**
Eclipse moon, ci, 22 lbs, 10″ wide **155.00**
Elgin rooster, ci, folksy design, 45 lbs, 16x17x4″ **400.00**
  Ci, partial base, 23 lbs, 12x17″ **500.00**
Fairbury bull, ci, blk, 38 lbs, 18x24½″ **650.00**
Hummer rooster, ci, wht & red, 8 lbs, 9x10″ **350.00**

Witch Balls

  During the 1800s, these blown glass balls, sometimes filled with holy water, were either hung in a window or placed in a prominent place in the home to protect it from danger and evil.

Amber glass **65.00**
Amber, rough pontil, 4½″ **110.00**
Glass w/loop designs, in stand, 6″ **300.00**

Opal glass w/pastel speckles **75.00**
Pigeon blood, blown glass, 3¼″ dia **30.00**
Sapphire blue, bottle stopper, blown glass, 3″ dia **35.00**

Wood Carvings

Wood sculptures represent an important section of American folk art. Wood carvings were made not only by skilled woodworkers, such as cabinetmakers, carpenters, etc., but by amateur 'whittlers' as well. They take the form of circus-wagon figures, carousel animals, decoys, busts, figurines, and cigar store Indians. Oriental artists show themselves to have been as proficient with the medium of wood as they were with ivory or hardstones.

Arhat of Sennin, w/lion, inlaid horn, ivory, China, 10x16″ **550.00**
Boxer, pine, 11″ **350.00**
Cigar store Indian, 13½″ **55.00**
    Princess, life size, orig paint **1,200.00**
Dog, seated, early 1900s, 9x8x3½″ **185.00**
Eagle, pilot house, stained finish, 1800s, 30x15x30″ **1,500.00**
Head, polychromed, 7″ **500.00**
Horned Owl, cypress root, late 1800s, 1¼x4″ **65.00**
Horse, primitive, gray, blk & wht, 1900s, 8½x6x1¾″ **110.00**
Indian chief, primitive, gold, red, blk & yellow paint, 8″ **80.00**
Man, Oriental w/foo dog, ivory eyes, teeth, teakwood, 12″ **125.00**
Muskrat, old blk paint, early 1900s, 20″ **220.00**
Ornament w/elephants, teakwood, Ceylon, India, 1921 .... **100.00**
Owl, orig wht paint, gr eyes, 1920s, 15x6½x6″ **255.00**
Penguin, orig paint, 1850s, 4″ **70.00**
Pine board, oak branch w/leaves & acorns, 20x10½″ **35.00**
Portrait, man, walnut, punched background, 1930, 8½x7″ **32.00**
Spaniel, seated, blk, wht, gr & red paint, early 1900s, 3″ **25.00**
Turtle, primitive, 1800s **145.00**
Water buffalo, teakwood, weighs 300 pounds **950.00**

Woodenware

Woodenware, or treenware as it is sometimes called, generally refers to those wooden items used in the preparation of food, such as spoons, bowls, food molds, etc. Common during the 18th and 19th centuries, these wares were designed from a strictly functional veiwpoint, and were used on a day-to-day basis. With the advent of the Industrial Revolution, bringing new materials and products, many of the old wooden wares were simply discarded. Today, original hand-crafted American woodenwares are extremely difficult to find.

Apple drying rack, slats-framed 3 sides, 4 removable legs, 1880 . **98.00**
Applebutter paddle, 18 holes, paddle stirrer, 20x5½″, 60″ long. **40.00**
    Bored holes, 12½x2″ handle, 29½″ **48.00**
Barrel, for nutmeg storage, mustard paint, 4x2″ dia **25.00**
Bowl, burl, 1800s, 5x13″ dia............................ **650.00**

Burl, 16½″ **500.00**
Burl, 21″ dia... **850.00**

Burl, 2½x7″ dia **350.00**
Burl, handmade, handled, 3x6″ dia **250.00**
For cheese mixing, hand carved sycamore, 1830 .... **225.00**
Handmade, 11″ **60.00**
Maple, oval, 25½″..................................... **85.00**
Rectangular w/flat bottom, old red paint, 25″ **350.00**
Box, quartered oak, inset hinges, 1880s, 29x15½x7½″ deep .. **350.00**
Box, dovetailed, hinged inset cover, 6x12x9½″ deep.......... **12.00**
    Egg, metal banding, iron lock, covered, spring clasp, 9¾x13x15½″ **12.00**
    Egg, old red paint, 12x12x6″........................... **30.00**
    Open, pumpkin color, grained, dovetailed, 10½x14½x6¾″ ... **12.00**
    Pantry, covered, painted gr, 5½″ **12.00**
    Pine, domed, red w/traces of blk grain paint, 16x9x8″ **200.00**
    Pine, holds utensils, orig red stain, cutout handle **68.00**
    Poplar, hinged lid, traces blue paint, 36¼x16x17″ deep ... **185.00**
Bread peel, poplar, long handle, mid 1800s, 54″............. **75.00**
Breadboard, pine, hanging eye cut in 1 pc wood, 12x10″ **75.00**
    Pine, lollipop handle, 21¾″ long, 14″ dia **90.00**
Bucket, mincemeat, lid, 10″ top dia, 13″ base dia, 11″ **75.00**
    Sugar, floor standing, red, old **225.00**
    Sugar, stave constructed, orig paint, 14½″ **115.00**
    Sugar, wrapped loops, lid, flat handle, 1890, 7x5″ dia...... **150.00**
    Water, 1 pc wood, self side handles, rope bail **95.00**
    Water, oak, iron bands, for usage on waterbench.......... **95.00**
Butcher's block, sycamore, Amish 'shonk' carved in side **650.00**
Butter churn, lg Maine wooden, 1866..................... **285.00**
Butter roller, hand carved birch, in wooden pinned yoke **150.00**
Butter worker, tiger maple, good signs of age & use **95.00**
Butter worker table, maple, butter roller & wood handle, 33x43x17″ **250.00**
    With deep well & hexagon roller, 1800s **300.00**
Candle drying rack, pine, 2 X-ed arms mortised at center of post **130.00**
Canteen, oak, handmade................................ **65.00**
Cheese drainer, Windsor style, arrow shaped slats, 19½″..... **450.00**
Cheese ladder, wild cherry **85.00**
Churn, barrel stave construction forms single handle, 18″ **340.00**

Hand made, willow wrapped, 34″....................... **195.00**
Cookie mold, musketeer on a saddle strapped to a chicken, lg.. **95.00**
Cookie roller, handcut from 1 pc birdseye maple............. **30.00**
Cracker pricker & biscuit stamp, oval w/turned handle, 1½x2½″ **165.00**
Dipper, honey; maple, wide ridges on one end, 13″ long, 8″ dia **40.00**
    Honey; turned maple, double ring turning, 1830, 7″ long **20.00**
Dough bowl, 4¼x17½x9½″ **165.00**

Hand carved maple, 26x13½" **225.00**
Walnut burl, 1700s, 16½" dia, 6" deep **450.00**
Dough box, cherry, 4 leg frame, l pc lid, self handles, 1860, 30x14" **275.00**
Dough tray, chestnut, 1 pc w/handles, 25x14x5½" deep **200.00**
Hard carved pine, 1840, 24" **45.00**
Dough trough, cherry, no lid, slanted sides, 1830, 26x12½" . . **225.00**
Pine, on 4 leg frame, self handles, 1860, 28x13½x10" deep **250.00**
Food stomper, handcarved poplar **19.00**
Ironing board, folding, poplar, stepstool when folded, 14" widest part **55.00**
Ladle, hand carved, bowl, 3½" dia, 9" long, 2" deep **55.00**
Handcarved maple, 1 pc wood, 1860, 12½" **40.00**
Treen, hand carved, off center handle, 4" dia bowl, 14" long . **65.00**

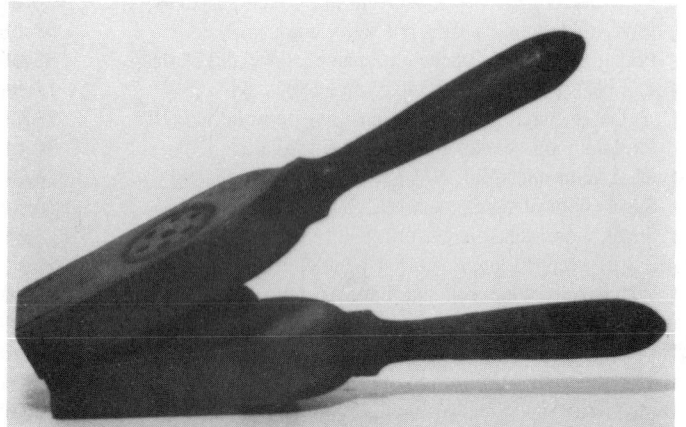

Lemon squeezer **50.00**
10" long **60.00**
Mash agitator, handfashioned wood, 8" handle **85.00**
Masher, hickory, pestle on one end, bulbous center turning, 12" long **30.00**
Meatblock, maple, Pennsylvania Amish, 13x11¾x8½" **215.00**
Mortar, burl, excellent figure, 6" **135.00**
Mortar & pestle, hickory, maple pestle, 1700s **85.00**

Lignum vitae, 5½", 8" **145.00**
Maple, hickory pestle, iron band, 1600s **450.00**
Tiger maple, honey maple pestle, 1700s **225.00**
Walnut, maple pestle, lg **95.00**
Noggin, maple, 1800s, 8¼" **160.00**
Noodle roller, maple, corrugations good condition, 1850, 20" long **58.00**
Noodle rolling pin **10.00**

Paddles, butter, handcut variations in maple & hickory, 10" . . . **35.00**
Peel, pie, ball-end, 23" handle, 5" wide flat blade, 1840-50 . . . . **75.00**
Plate, burl, wide rim, shallow, 9" **165.00**
Potato masher, maple **17.00**
Rolling pin, birdseye maple, 1 pc carved wood, 1800s **45.00**
Old **20.00**
Springerli, 16 carved designs, red handles, Germany **25.00**
Springerli, 20 carved designs, 1800s, 14½" long **100.00**
Tiger maple, 2 handles **65.00**
Saltbox, pine, lid, handcarved, 1700s, 2x3¼" dia **90.00**
Slawcutter, dovetailed, 34½x12½" **20.00**
Soap mold, 2 pc pine, handle on liftout part, 6x3x3" deep **29.00**
Soft-soap scoop, hand carved, rectangular, 1 pc wood, 1½x6¼" **75.00**
Spatula, cherry, heart carved center, 1700s **75.00**
Spoon, hanging, maple, shovel shape, carved hook, 14" **60.00**
Spoonholder, handcarved walnut wall hanger, early, 36"long . . **145.00**
Springerli board, 6 hand carved patterns, 3½x6½" **70.00**
Sugar, raised bands, pail shaped, round lid, 1 pc wood, 5x6" . . **85.00**
Trencher, hard carved, small **55.00**
Tub, cedar, iron banded staves, 14x25" dia **125.00**
Oak, iron banded staves, 14x10" dia **80.00**
Vinegar pump, w/spigot **52.00**
Washboard, handcarved wood, small rolls **75.00**
Washstick, blk walnut, handcut corrugations & end handle, 29x4" **185.00**
Dolly Peg, to hand agitate garments in tub **125.00**
Handcarved maple, 31" long **20.00**
Handcarved, 2 prong, 25" long **32.00**
Handcut hickory, lye soap stained, 34" long **45.00**
Pose stick, hickory, to turn agitate clothes in tub, 1800s **50.00**
With caged ball, whimsey handle, handcarved, 33" long **125.00**

Wood, Enoch and Sons

Enoch Wood began his own business in Burslem, England, about 1784. By 1790, he was in partnership with James Caldwell, and until 1818 he was best known for his busts and plaques.

From 1818 to 1846, the firm was known as Enoch Wood and Sons. They produced the underglaze blue transfer dinnerware patterns, many of which were specifically designed for export to America.

Cup & saucer, purple transfer, eagle on rock, Wood **150.00**
Plate, pink transfer, Washington, Enoch Wood & Sons, 7" **50.00**
Red turkey transfer, polychrome border, Wood, 7" **250.00**
Teapot, blk flowers & eagles, griffin spout, Enoch Wood, 1792-1818 **180.00**
Toby, seated man w/pipe, tri-corner hat, 5½" **140.00**
Vegetable dish, Buddha pattern, blue & wht, covered, Wood & Sons **85.00**

World's Fairs and Expos

Since 1851 and the Crystal Palace exhibit in London, World's Fairs and Expositions have taken place at a steady pace, except during wartime. These events have been the source of tens of thousands of souvenirs, and collectors today find the possibility of locating representative examples an exciting challenge.

1876 Centennial, Philadelphia
Hatchet, ci, open work bust of George Washington **45.00**
Scarf, silk, Machinery Hall **40.00**
Slipper, ladies, wht satin glass **35.00**
Vase, frosted glass, hand w/torch, 6" **30.00**
1893 Columbian, Chicago
Art portfolio, 2 parts, 22 litho color plates **50.00**
Bell, 5" **6.00**
Book, World's Columbian Expo & Guide to Chicago & St Louis **35.00**

Bowl, ironstone w/brown transfer, 8½″ **40.00**
Butter crock **300.00**
Clock case, figural, tool, Keystone Co **4.50**
Foldout, glossy views of buildings, advertising back **22.00**
Handkerchief, silk, gold, machinery building **45.00**
    With fisheries building **28.00**
Inkwell, globe w/view of fair, opens **120.00**
Mug, stoneware, incised, florals all in cobalt blue **65.00**
Pitcher, Doulton-Lambeth, 7½″ **300.00**
Playing cards, landing of Columbus **85.00**
Spoon, demitasse **10.00**
Towel, fringed, George Washington portrait in center, 38″ long . **55.00**
Vase, opaline glass, government building **50.00**
Watch fob, pendants & medal **35.00**

1895 Atlantic City Expo
Decanter, w/stopper, clear, 6 cups, etched **125.00**
Napkin ring, shell **28.00**

1898 Omaha
Cup, child's **19.00**

1901 Pan American
Clock, shape of frying pan **59.00**
Frame, round, jeweled, advertisement of fair, 2½″ **25.00**
Glass, Manufacturing & Liberal Arts Buildings, 3½″ **25.00**
Locket, brass w/embossed buffalo **40.00**
Mirror **18.00**
Paperweight, rectangular, glass, etched monogram **24.00**
Spoon, McKinley & Temple of Music, sterling **22.50**

1904 St Louis, Mo.
Book, souvenir book, day & night scenes **25.00**
Card, aluminum, set of 10, erotica, 3½x2x¼″ **65.00**
Match safe, Palace of Electricity **45.00**
Medallion, half dollar size **18.50**
Money clip, brass, Coca-Cola, Tiffany Studios **50.00**
Mule, Shoe Me **35.00**
Napkin rings, aluminum, pr **25.00**
Paperweight, Cascade Gardens under dome, surrounded by horseshoe **45.00**
Picture, Jefferson, Napolean & exhibit building **55.00**
Pincushion, shoe, silver plate, 6″ **24.00**
Pitcher, crockery, US Government building, 2½″ **35.00**
Plate, china, colored transfer, Palace of Electricity, blue trim, lg **22.00**
    Liberal Arts, 7″ **15.00**
    Palace of Manufacturers **30.00**
Spoon **16.00**
Sugar bowl, Palace of Varied Industries, 2½″ **45.00**
Tumbler, milk glass **25.00**
Vase, china, Missouri State building, 3½″ **45.00**
    Metal, wht, Cascade Gardens, 3″ **35.00**
    Metal, wht, Palace of Liberal Arts, 3½″ **45.00**

1909 Alaska Yukon Pacific
Plate, views of fair **40.00**

1915 Panama Pacific
Album, color photos **45.00**

1933 Chicago Worlds Fair
Bank, carved, scenic Dutch shoe **20.00**
    Tin **28.00**
Book, hardcover, Chicago's World's Fair **15.00**
Bracelet, brass **14.00**
Cigarette case, sterling **60.00**
Cream & sugar, 4½″ **150.00**
Crumb set, metal **85.00**
Game, pinball, 11x17″ **65.00**
Handkerchief, Japanese silk **20.00**
License plate holder, brass, emblem Century of Progress **22.00**
Map, Conoco Map of Fair & Chicago **4.00**

Menu, Swedish produce exhibit **2.00**
Pencil, lady's mechanical **10.00**
Picture, official **13.00**
Plate, federal building, Picard **20.00**
Playing cards **25.00**
Postcard, Baltimore & Ohio Railroad, set of 12, colored **75.00**
Stubs, observatory tickets, 3 . . . . **2.00**
Tea strainer, underplate, kettle shape **12.50**
Ticket, admission, color **2.00**

1933 San Diego Expo
Bracelet **6.00**

1939 New York World's Fair
Book, flip, Bromo Seltzer ad **6.00**
Bottle, milk glass, 9¼″ **15.00**
Compact, powder & rouge, Trylon & Perisphere, felt case **20.00**
Kan-o-seat, wooden, cane & slide out seat forms chair, 35″ long **32.00**
Letter case, brass, ivory enameled, 3½x5½″ **52.00**
Newspaper, New York Times special, 73 pages **35.00**
Plate, blue, ironstone **25.00**
Poster, railroads on parade, yellow & blue type headlines, 40x26″ **500.00**
Poster stamps, sheet of 54 . . . . **12.00**
Salt & pepper, Lenox **68.00**
Scarf **9.00**
Vase, salmon color, wht raised Trylon & Perisphere, 5¼″ **125.00**

1939 San Francisco
Knife, pink depression glass fruit, orig red carton **26.50**
Plate, multicolored, 10″ **17.50**
Viewer, w/6 movie views **15.00**

1964 New York
Ashtray, covered, brass, 4½″ dia **7.00**
Playing cards **18.00**

Wrought Iron

Until the middle of the 19th century, almost all the iron hand forged in America was made in a material called wrought iron. When wrought iron rusts, it appears grainy, while the mild steel that was used later shows no grain, but pits to an orange peel surface. This is an important aid in determining the age of an ironwork piece.

Candle snuffer, scissor type, 1700s **75.00**
Ladle, 17½″, 5½″ dia **35.00**
Sea horses, figural, 1920s, pr, 9″ **100.00**
Toaster, 2 slices, on frame w/3 legs, handle, 16½″ long **130.00**
Trivet, heart on 3 feet, 2x5½″ **60.00**
    Serpentine, 3 flat feet, compact design, 1700s, 2½″ high . . . **150.00**

Yellowware

Yellowware is an inexpensive, plain type of earthenware, so called because of the color of the clay used in its manufacture. Pieces may vary from buff to yellow to nearly brown; the glaze itself is clear. Some yellowware was decorated with blue, white, brown or black bands, but it was seldom relief molded.

Yellowware was made to a large extent in East Liverpool, Ohio, but other Ohio potteries, as well as some in Pennsylvania and Vermont also produced it. English yellowware has a harder body composition. Because it was not often marked, it is almost impossible to identify the manufacturer.

There is a growing interest in this type of pottery, and consequently, prices are continually increasing.

Bedpan **15.00**
Bowl, 3 brown bands, 8¾″ **15.00**
    13″ **30.00**

14″, Roseville, Ohio **35.00**
Crown bottom, blue & brown bands, embossed pattern, set of 4 **65.00**
Mixing, set of 5, girl w/sprinkling can in garden, 6-10″ **95.00**
Rolled rim, 2 wht & 2 narrow brown bands, 7¼″ **10.00**
   9¼″ **18.00**
   12″ **25.00**
With pouring spout **35.00**
Wht & dripped mocha band, 8″ dia **27.50**
Butter, w/cover, 2 wht & 2 brown rings, 4½x5½″ dia **45.00**
With cover, heavy wht & 2 narrow wht bands, 'Butter', 5x6½″ dia **50.00**
Chamber pot, wht stripes, miniature, 2¾″ **25.00**
Cuspidor, embossed, molded scroll design, 8 sided, Victorian, 1800s **45.00**
Custard, 3 blue bands, set of 6 . . . . **60.00**
Match box, molded shell on sides & lid, mid 1800s, 4½x3½″ . . **70.00**
Milk bowl, 2 thin wht stripes **45.00**
Milk pan, 3¾x13″ dia **35.00**
Pie plate **32.00**

Pitcher, advertising, wht band, 8″ **65.00**
  pancake, raised blue flower spray, bulbous, 7x6″ dia **35.00**
  Pancake, raised decor, self embossed barrel staves, 4½x4″ dia **25.00**
  Rim, mask spout silver resist, scenic transfer, 6″ **255.00**
  Rose, basketweave **60.00**
Pudding mold, corn pattern, 8x5½″ **35.00**
Rolling pin **100.00**
Soap dish, 2x6x3¾″ **65.00**
Spittoon, embossed scrolls, Victorian **45.00**
Watering can, girl, garden; repeat design, 9″ **28.00**

Zanesville Art Pottery Co.

Prior to 1900, this company was known as The Zanesville Roofing Tile Company; then it was reorganized, and production shifted to the manufacture of art pottery. Their most familiar line, La Mora, was made in both the standard brown glaze as well as in a matt version very similar to Owens Matt Utopia.

The plant was sold to The Weller Pottery Company in 1920.

Pitcher, milk, brown glaze, LaMora, mkd, 6″ **115.00**
Vase, LaMora, sgnd LS, 6″ **135.00**

Zsolnay

Zsolnay pottery has been made in Hungary since the mid-1800s. Early wares were highly ornamental--some in high relief Art Nouveau motifs, others depending on surface decoration for their appeal. Today, the firm produces

figurines with an iridescent glaze which are becoming very collectible.

Basket, 4 sided, ftd, stationary handle, 9¼″ **165.00**
  4 sided, ftd, stationary handle, reticulated, flared, 8½″ **195.00**
Bear, irid gr **100.00**
Bird, gr irid, sgnd, Made in Hungary, 6″ **85.00**
Bison **110.00**
Bowl, burgundy & gold, ftd, old, underglaze tower mk, 7″ **127.00**
  Heart shaped, full mk **360.00**
  Reticulated decor, turned up, oval **450.00**
  Reticulated top, enameling, small **68.00**
  Shell shape, scroll handle, reticulated, flowers, 9¾x8″ **350.00**
Bud vase, enamel decor, 3″ **65.00**
Castle, castle mk **105.00**
Deer **22.00**
Ewer, flowers, gold beading, 7¼″ **265.00**
  Olive gr w/multi color florals, pink griffin handle, 9½″ **350.00**

Reticulated leaf mounts, scrolls & beading, castle mk, 12″ . . **300.00**
Nude, bending backwards, Deco, 10″ **170.00**
Owl, 2½″ **75.00**
Pillow vase, reticulated collar **130.00**
Pitcher, Persian, reticulated reserves, florals, gold, 8″ **400.00**
  Standing & stooping women, Deco type, 6″ **185.00**
Planter, 4 reticulated panels, 4 color floral design **125.00**
Plaque, gold foil ground w/portrait, old mk underglaze, 10″ . . **250.00**
Rose bowl, melon shape, glazed, sgnd, 5″ **145.00**
Tumbler, castle mk **155.00**
  Lustre w/nudes in relief, vineyard, 6½″ **80.00**
Vase, blue irid, bulbous, scallop top, flame mk, 6″ **95.00**
  Cream, 5 loop, jeweled handles, 8½″ **245.00**
  Double wall base, reticulated, cobalt, beige, gold, steeple mk **389.00**
  Double wall, reticulated melon shape base, 3 color, 10″, pr . **575.00**
  Double walled allover reticulation, 3 color, 6½″ **389.00**
  Electric blue ground, gold traced, sgnd w/cathedral mk, TJM, 13″ **295.00**
  Full reticulated, cobalt & gold, 6½″ **375.00**
  Irid gold w/ladies in relief, 8″ **295.00**
  Irid, gold sunburst on wine ground, house mk, 3¾x3¾″ . . **350.00**
  Pink & yellow roses, gold trim, 3 handled, 12″ **275.00**
  Reticulated, closed top, open applied loops, lt blue, 14½″ . . **570.00**
  Tree form base, flared, mustard w/magenta metallic rose **185.00**

Arizona

Tere Hagan,
P.O. Box 26004, Tempe, 85282
Author Collector Books on silver plated flatware

California

Bob Jackson
2909 E. Hatch Road, Modesto, 95351
Bear Country, Inc.; Buy & sell American art pottery

Cindy Chapman
18661 Pasadero Drive, Tarzana, 91356
Dealer in Peters & Reed, Zaneware

Dorene Paoluccio
3530 Kiernan, Modesto, 95366
Samplers, dolls, toys, quilts, coverlets & early portraits

J. Douglas Scott, Inc.
P.O. Box 3620, San Diego, 92103, 714-298-3056
Pottery of all types, send SASE for list

Jeo Jeozane Antiques & Collector Items
715 Avalon Court, San Diego, 92109
Specializing in old hatpins and holders

Jerry Harrington
925 L St., Suite #890, Sacramento, 95810
American art pottery, books and tiles

John & Anne DeMelio
1505 Old Fashioned Way, Anaheim, 92804
Buy, sell and trade American pottery

Maxine Nelson
Box 1686, Huntington Beach, 92647
Author, Collector Books on Vernon Kiln pottery

Mike Brooks
3529 Lincoln Avenue, Oakland, 94602
Buy or trade early typewriters

Rick & Mercy Medina
1414 Marine Avenue, Wilmington, 90744
The Fan Man, ceiling fan repairs, replacements; buy & sell

Connecticut

Fred Morth
282 Maubuc Ave, E. Hartford, 06118
Specializing in aviation collectibles

Florida

C.L. Watford
8751 S.W. 85 St., Miami, 33137, 305-595-8751
Want to buy HLC Va. Rose, pg 143 Hux book, unusual pieces

Hensel's Antiques and Clock Shoppe
2707 MacDill Ave., Tampa, 33609
Buy & sell, clock, watch and jewelry repair

Kathryn McNerney
Northwoods Apt II, #221, 4051 Olive Rd., Pensacola, 32504
Author Collector Books on blue & white, primitives, tools

Sherrie & Barry Hershone
952 Versailles Circle, Maitland, 32751
The Antique Emporium, American art pottery

Steve Smith
5601 S.W. 76th St., Miami, 33843
Civil War memorabilia, paper only

Suzan Schroeder
3301 Ramblewood, Dr. N., Sarasota, 33577
Send dbl stamped LSASE for 8 pg Barbie list, revised monthly

The Glass Menagerie Warehouse, Inc.
40½ W. Colonial Dr., Orlando, 32801
Specializing in Imperial porcelain

The Silver Queen
778 N. Ind. Rocks Rd., Belleair Bluffs, 33540, 813-581-6827
Silver, pattern matching service

Georgia

Mike & Diane Cole
Box 174, Martin, 30557
American art pottery, Rookwood, Owens, Lonhuda

Illinois

Don Raycraft, R.R. 8, Normal, 61761
Specializing in stoneware & baskets
Author Collector Books on stoneware & baskets

Doris & Burdell Hall
210 W. Sassafras Drive, Morton, 61550
B&B Antiques, authors of book on Morton pottery

Larry & Jane Lafary
2316 N. Knoxville Ave., Peoria, 61640, 309-686-0100
Larry's Antiques, American art pottery, general line

Louise & Jim Kelsey
112 Brahms Court, Glendale Hts., 60137
Barrington Antique Market, Kelsey Rd, art pottery

Rev. Leslie Wolfe
Box 66, Villa Grove, 61956, 217-832-8073
Angel's Roost Antiques, Royal Copley, Fiesta, Abingdon

Yesterday's Paper, Inc., Box 294, Naperville, 60566
Stocks, bonds, paper Americana
WWII aviation, especially magazines

Indiana

Bill Edwards
423 N. Main, Rushville, 46173
Author Collector Books on carnival glass

Dean J. Armstead
1105 32nd St., South Bend, 46615
Specializes in Fulper pottery

Florence Adams
R.R.3, Covington, 47932
Specializes in teapots

Howard Kendall
Rt. #6, Box 88, Greencastle, 46135, 317-653-6370
Antique firearm restoration & custom built long rifles

Jim Trice
268 Meadow Lark Lane, Bremen, 46506
Author Collector Books on butter molds

Judy & Dick Frey
716 4th St., Covington, 47932
Specializes in cloisonne, baskets, art pottery

Marvin & Jeanette Stofft
Marnette Antiques, 812-547-5707
Ohio art pottery, cut glass, R.S. Prussia, buy & sell

Ronald R. Plew, Sr.
9648 W. Morris St., Indianapolis, 46231, 317-839-5908
Indy 500 Museum, buy, sell or trade Indy memorabilia

Susan Miller
1103 Waynetown Rd., Crawfordsville, 47933
Tea Leaf, Autumn Leaf, author of book on Trolls

Virgil Scowden
303 Lincoln, Williamsport, 47993, 317-762-3408
Antiques Museum, general line, tours

Iowa

Bill Bilsland
1808 C. St. S.W., Cedar Rapids, 52420
Specializes in Old Sleepy Eye

Broken Kettle Book Service
RR 1, Akron, 51001
Catalogues & manuals, out of print books

G.G. Larson
RR #2, Fort Dodge, 50501
Specializes in American art pottery

Gabe's Antiques
232 S. Summit B-3, Iowa City, 52240
Specializes in American art pottery

Gary Huxford, 503 W. Pine, Marengo, 52301
Want to buy marbles: ornamental china,
lutz, sulphides, end-of-day, clambroth

Hal & Bea Moore
RR 3 Box 186, Washington, 52353
Halbea Antiques, American pottery

Harold & Ruth Nichols
632 Agg Ave., Ames, 50010
Buy & sell American art pottery

Main St. Antiques & Art
110 W. Main, Box 340, West Branch, 52358, 319-643-2065
Folk art, country Americana, the unusual

Kansas

Harriet Richardson
701 15th St., Box 768, Hoxie, 67740
Buying pie birds & other pie venting devices

Joleen A. Robison
502 Lindley Dr., Lawrence, 66044
Author Collector Books advertising dolls

Kentucky

Gene Florence
Box 7186H, Lexington, 40522
Author Collector Books on Depression, Occupied Japan

Roy M. Willis
Box 428, Lebanon Junction, 40150, 502-833-4427
Whiskey decanters, especially Ski Country, Wild Turkey

Wes Johnson, Cracker Jack Collector
1725 Dixie Highway, Louisville, 40210
Wants tin, cast metal, plastic toy prizes, advertising

Louisiana

Sanchez Antiques & Auction Galleries
4730 Magazine St., New Orleans, 70115
Specializing in prints

Maine

Manuel & Barbara Rimer
115 Vermont St., W. Roxbury, 02132
Buy & sell Saturday Evening Girls pottery

Orphan Annie's, Art Nouveau, Art Deco clothing
96 Court St., Auburn, 04210
Accessories, clothing 1890-1950s, unusual lamps, collectibles

Maryland

Bob Banks
18901 Gold Mine Court, Brookeville, 20833
Wants old & unusual flags

Harry Goldman
3516 Milford Mill Road, Baltimore, 21207
Specializing in automobilia

Richard Fulper, Jr.
8006 Carey Branch Dr., Oxon Hill, 20022
Specializing in Fulper pottery

Massachusetts

Gloria C. Kluever, Blue Plate Antiques
P.O. Box 124, Sherborn, 01770
Flow blue matching serivce, send SASE for reply

Peter Schriber
Box 199, Hadley, 01035, 413-527-5656
Buy, sell, appraise early American stoneware

Michigan

Mike & Connie Nickel
Box 2374, Grand Rapids, 49501
Specializing in American art pottery

Leo's Jewelry & Gifts
34900 Michigan Ave., Wayne, 48184
Hummels, Royal Doulton, Lladro, Rockwell, etc.

Richard Keiler
855 Emerald N.E., Grand Rapids, 49503
American art pottery, Gonder, Peters & Reed

Minnesota

Cork Marcheschi, Art Deco pottery
2418 Stevens Ave. So., Minneapolis, 55404
Longwy, Keith Murray, Boch, Carlton, Cowan, Futura

Stanley Baker
2525 Pahl Ave., N.E., Minneapolis, 55418
Author Collector Books on railroadiana

Missouri

Back Issue Magazines
Box 26012, Kansas City, 64196
Magazine replacement service

Brenda Roberts
Rt. 2, Marshall, 65340
General line, author Collector Books on Hull Pottery

Dick & Juanita Bosworth, Kansas City Trade Winds
7307 N.W. 75th St., 64152
Roseville, Weller, Rookwood, Niloak, etc.

Glen Enloe
1053 E. 8th St., 46053
Buy & sell bottle openers, cigar box openers

Helen Brink
2210 N. Pursell Rd., Gladsone, 64118
Depression era china, glass

Morton Werner
20 Ridgemoor, Clayton, 63105
Specializes in fire marks, insurance signs

Pat Smith
Independence, 816-461-3900
Author Collector Books doll book series

Whetstone Antiques, Box 57, Williamsburg, 63388
Glass, china, silver, primitives, furniture
American dinnerware, pottery

Nebraska

Lloyd Hedman
5033 Spencer, Omaha, 68104
Advertising letter openers & old turtles, any type

Margaret James
311 N. 56th St., Lincoln, 68504
Author Collector Books on black glass

New Hampshire

Dave Bowers
Box 1224-CN, Wolfeboro, 03894
Buy & sell prints, postcards, music related items

New Jersey

Cybis, 65 Norman Ave., Trenton, N.J., 06818
Producers of Cybis Porcelains

Herman & Florence Lotstein
7220 Browning Rd., Pennsauken, 08110
Railroadiana, trains, books, china & silver, buy & sell

M. Grimley
P.O. Box 244, Oakland, 07436
Buying fire department memorabilia

Those Were The Days, Memorabilia, Box 186, Fairview, 07022
Buy & sell baseball cards, presidential campaign buttons
U.S. coins, autographs, send $1 for list

New York

A. Wunsch, 4297 Ludwig Lane, Bethpage, 11714
Wanted: Owens art lines, Weller art lines, Peters & Reed
Zaneware, McCoy, Olympia, Kenton Hills, Lonhuda

Bonnie Breslauer
2580 Ocean Parkway, Brooklyn, 11235
Frankart, Art Deco, American art pottery

Ed & Cassie Gisel
50 Surfside Pkwy., Cheektowaga, 14225
American art pottery: buy, sell & trade

Fenner's Antiques, 2611 Ave. S, Brooklyn, 11229
SASE for info about lists re: jewelry, glass
European china, books, porcelain, pottery

Gene Christian, 3849 Bailey Ave., Bronx, 10463
Wanted: Foreign Legion; U.S., French, British Forces
Yangtse Gunboats, Military Kukris, Chinese Forces pre 1949

Glentiques, Ltd.
P.O. Box 337, Glenford, 12433
Steins & Mettlach plaques

Joan Van Patten
3 Colina Lane, Clifton Park, 12065
Author Collector Books on Nippon

Paul P. Luchsinger, Alpine Antiques
9 Split Rd., Pittsford, 14534, 716-381-3950
Buy & sell corkscrews & other wine related items

The China Match
9 Elmford Road, Rochester, 14606
Specializing in Syracuse China

Whispering Pines Antiques
9853 Caughdenoy Rd., Brewerton, 13029
Buy & sell, canning jars

North Carolina

Bert Spilker
2556 Booker Creek Rd., Chapel Hill, 27514
Buying ornate keys & locks before 1800

Ohio

Bernice & W.E. Lyon
Columbus, 43220
Specializing in art tiles

Betty Blair, Golden Apple Antiques
403 Chilicothe, Jackson, 45640
General line, pottery, furniture, silver

Betty Ward, Betty's Antiques
7525 E. Pike, Norwich, 614-872-3045
Located in Stage Coach Mall, general line

Bunny Walker, Box 502, Bucyrus, 44820, 419-562-8355
Write for lists re: Teddy bears
Toys, dolls, pie birds, reamers & pottery

Debbie & Bill Rees, Zanes Trace Antiques
3630 E. Pike, Zansville, 43701
Buy & sell Rv & Weller; want Rv wallpockets & Juvenile

Don & JoAnne Calkins, Calkins Antiques Company
1068 Sylvan Ave., Lakewood, 44107
Art pottery, especially Cowan, Clewell & Rookwood

Don Treadway, American Art Pottery
P.O. Box 8924, Cincinnati, 45208
Buy & sell Newcomb, Grueby, Pewbic, Overbeck

Federation Antique Furnishings, 2700 Observatory, Cincinnati
Chinese export porcelain, early English porcelain
American furniture, folk art, early quilts

Jim Sneed, Pottery Shack
108 N. Cooper Ave., Cincinnati/Lockland, 45215
Specializing in American pottery

Lewis & Alice Bettinger
Canton, 44780, 216-454-4863
Specializing in American art pottery

Mary Joung
1040 Greenridge Dr., Kettering, 45429
Author Collector Books on paper dolls

Maxine Ferguson, Wayside Antiques
2290 E. Pike, Zanesille, 43701
General line, furniture, dolls, pottery, glass

Nancy Darrow
50 Orchard Rd., Akron, 44313
American art pottery, specializing in Clewell

Paul Miller; Jabe Tarter, Akron, 44302, 216-376-1337
Specializing in Degenhart, Ltd. edition glassware
Degenhart price guide, $5 from authors

Sam & Faydell Schott
806 Warner Rd., Akron, 44300
Specializing in art pottery

Stagecoach Antique Mall
Rt. 40, ½-mile west of I-70, Norwich Exit 16
7527 East Pike, Norwich, 43767

Oklahoma

Phyllis & Tom Bess
14535 E. 13th St., Tulsa, 74108
Authors of Frankoma Treasures; buy, sell & trade Frankoma

Pennsylvania

Ann Lloyd
4302 June Meadow Drive, Doylestown, 18901
Dolls & miniatures

Charles Reuter
P.O. Box 71, Mount Joy, 17552
Buy & sell cigarette silks, cards, antique watches

DLK Antiques, 2778 Richland St., Johnston, 15904
Buy & sell: Animated clocks, pre-1890 sewing machines
Occupied Japan, space toys, pre-prohibition items

Jim Bragg
1216 Nimick Avenue, Monaco, 15061
Buy & sell marbles

Joseph A. Weber, 604 Centre St., Ashland, 17921
717-875-4787 or 717-875-4401
Jukeboxes & typewriters

Rhode Island

Music Man, 87 Tillinghast Ave., W. Warwick, 02893
Wanted: old banjos, guitars, mandolins, concertinas, flutes
Harps, violins, violas, cellos, basses, etc., in good shape

South Carolina

David Powell
1125 Courtland Ave, Florence, 29501
Buys N.C. pottery, i.e.: Jugtown, Ben Owens, Rainbow

Tennessee

E.S. Stone
P.O. Box 12574, Memphis, 38112
Photographica; wanted: collectible old cameras

Texas

L.R. Docks
P.O. Box 32932, San Antonio, 78216
Specializing in records

R.J. Sayers, P.O. Box 246, Andrews, 79714
Boy scouting memborabilia, want patches, medals, souvenirs
From 1920, '24, '33, '37 & '47 World Jamborees

Virginia

H.W. O'Kennon
2204 Haviland Dr., Richmond, 23229
Want to buy comic books 1935-65, send list for offer

Wisconsin

Continental Hobby House
P.O. Box 193, 1616 N. 3rd St., Sheyboygan, 53081
Meissen, KPM porcelain, gambling devices, slot machines

Bob & Delores Cowan
218 Lawrence Court, Appleton, 54911
Specializing in Cowan pottery

Finch's Nest, 21400 Red Fox Dr.
P.O. Box 126, Brookfield, 53005
Dealer in Ferrandiz

Steve Lange
Box 33, Waldo, 53093
Automobilia, old radios & wireless items pre-1930

Clubs, Newsletters and Catalogues

A&M Sales, 197 Melville Rd., Huntington Sta., N.Y., 11746
Order Collectors Guide to RR Dining Car Flatware
Dominy & Morgenfruh, $4.50 pp

Alingh Dimensional Images, Inc.
2705 70th, Des Moines, Iowa, 50322
Send SASE for information on comic strip legends catalogue

American Art Pottery Newsletter
P.O. Box 714, Silver Spring, Md., 20901
Newsletter serving American Art Pottery Assoc.

American Historical Publication
231 Rock Ridge Rd., Millersville, Md., 21108
Order book re: Harrison Fisher, $15; Robert Robinson, $13

Barbed Wire Associaton of New Mexico
Don Sowle, 2816 Camino Principe, Santa Fe, 875501

Benjamin Moulton, B&B Collectibles
R.R. 21, Box 103, Terre Haute, Ind., 47802
Send SASE for informaton re: Hall China Newsletter

California Spectrum
11057 Ocean Dr., Culver City, Ca., 90230
Complete Collectors Guide to Bauer Pottery

Depression Glass Daze
12135 N. State St., Otisville Mi., 48463

Dixie Flyer Railroad Memorabilia Newsletter
Seth H. Bramson, 8035 Cecil St., Miami Beach, Fla., 33141
Send $1 & SASE for sample

Don Bull, 64 October Lane, Trumbull, Conn., 06661
Buy & sell corkscrews w/beer & brewery advertising
SASE for ordering information re: Book on Corkscrews

East Coast Casino Antiques
98 Main St., Fishkill, N.Y., 12524
$4 for 80 pg catalogue re: gambling paraphernalia

Elephant Collectors Newsletter
Richard Massiglia, Box CY-7, Boston, Mass., 02215

Fenton Art Glass Collectors of America
P.O. Box 2441, Appleton, Wisc., 54913

Fiesta Collectors Association
Dan Anderson
P.O. Box 100582, Nashville, Tenn., 37210

Geisha Girl Porcelain, Newsletter
P.O. Box 925, Orange, N.J., 07051

International Club for Collectors of Hatpins & Holders
Lillian Baker, founder
15237 Chanera Avenue, Gardena, Ca., 90249

J. & C. Antiques, Box 210, Lehigh, Ks., 67073
Dealers in Sabino glass
Send $2.50 for photos and price list

Melton's Antiques
P.O. Box 1311, Indian River Rd., Chesapeake, Va., 23325
SASE for information re: Dolls newsletter

National Reamer Collectors Association
Dee Long
112 S. Center, Lacon, Ill., 61540

Occupied Japan Collectors Club, Robert Gee, founder
18309 Faysmith Ave., Torrance, Ca., 90504
Buy, sell, aid with info re: items marked MIOJ

Rick & Barb Botts
2545 S.E. 60th Court, Des Moines, Iowa, 50317
Monthly newsletter serving the jukebox collector

Roberta B. Etter, P.O. Box 22, Oradell, New Jersey, 07649
$3 for sample: Photographic Catalogue, 32 pgs, illus
Quarterly, daguerreotypes, cameras, stereo views, etc.

Sally Carver
179 S. St., Chestnut Hill, Maine, 02167
SASE for informaton re: postcard auctions

The Glaze, Pottery Collectors Newsletter
535 E. Norman, Springfield, Mo., 65807

Timothy J. Huges, 2410 N. Hills Dr., Williamsport, Pa., 17701
Newspapers & magazines before 1870
SASE for information re: fine catalogues

We wish to thank the following auction houses for allowing us to reproduce protographs from their fine catalogues:

Adam A. Weschler & Son
905-9 E Street Northwest
Washington, D.C., 20004

C. E. Guarino
Box 49
Denmark, ME, 04022

C. G. Sloan & Company, Inc.
715 13th Street, N.W.
Washington, D.C., 20005

Christie's East
219 East 67th Street
New York, N.Y., 10021

Continental Auctions, Div. Continental Hobby House
Heinz A. Mueller
P.O. Box 193, Sheyboygan, Wisc., 53081

Early American Toys
Lloyd W. & Ruth K. Ralston
447 Stratfield Rd., Fairfield, Conn., 06432

Garths Auctions Inc.
2629 Stratford Road, Box 315
Delaware, Ohio, 43015

Jack Sellner
P.O. Box 1113
Scottsdale, AZ, 85252

Milwaukee Auction Galleries, Ltd.
4747 W. Bradley Rd.
Milwaukee, Wisc, 53223

Sotheby's
1334 York Ave.
New York, N.Y., 10021

Books On Antiques & Collectibles

Published By COLLECTOR BOOKS
(All are well illustrated and contain current values.)

Most of the following books are available at local book sellers or antique dealers, and on loan from your public library. If you are unable to locate certain titles in your area you may order by mail from COLLECTOR BOOKS, P.O. Box 3009, Paducah, KY 42001. Add $1.00 for postage and handling for the first book ordered and $.65 for each additional book. Include item number, title, and price when ordering. Allow 14 to 21 days for delivery.

Item #	Title & Author	Price
	Books On Glass	
1321	Collector's Encyclopedia of Depression Glass, Fifth Edition, Florence	$17.95
1372	Depression Glass Pocket Guide, Revised 3rd Edition, Florence	9.95
1364	The Collector's Encyclopedia of Akro Agate, Florence	9.95
1005	The Standard Cut Glass Value Guide, Evers	8.95
1006	Cambridge Glass I, 1930-34	14.95
1007	Cambridge II, 1949-1953	14.95
1368	Standard Encyclopedia of Carnival Glass, w/3rd Edition of Std. Carnival Price Guide, Edwards	24.95
1391	Millersburg Crystal Glassware, Edwards	5.95
1365	World of Salt Shakers, Lechner	9.95
1218	Early 20th Century Lighting Fixtures	11.95
1307	Black Glass, James	5.95
1396	Elegant Glassware of the Depression Era, Florence	17.95
1379	Collector's Encyclopedia of Glass Candlesticks, Archer	19.95
1380	Collector's Encyclopedia of Pattern Glass, McCain	12.95
	Books On Pottery	
1311	Collector's Encyclopedia of R.S. Prussia, Gaston	24.95
1033	The Collector's Encyclopedia of Weller Pottery, Huxford	24.95
1034	Encyclopedia of Roseville Pottery, Huxford	19.95
1035	Encyclopedia of Roseville Pottery, 2nd Series, Huxford	19.95
1039	The Collector's Encyclopedia of Nippon Porcelain, Joan Van Patten	19.95
1350	The Collector's Encyclopedia of Nippon Porcelain, Second Series, Joan Van Patten	19.95
1358	McCoy Pottery Encyclopedia, Huxford	19.95
1041	Brush-McCoy Pottery Encyclopedia, Huxford	17.95
1037	Collector's Encyclopedia of Occupied Japan, 1st Series, Florence	12.95
1038	Collector's Encyclopedia of Occupied Japan, 2nd Series, Florence	12.95
1045	Red Wing Pottery, Simon	8.95
1210	Collector's Encyclopedia of Limoges Porcelain, Gaston	19.95
1284	The Collector's Encyclopedia of Fiesta, Fourth Edition, Huxford	9.95
1312	Collectible Blue & White Stoneware, McNerney	9.95
1343	Franciscan Ware, Enge	9.95
1344	Shawnee Pottery, Simon	8.95
1346	Decorated Country Stoneware, Raycraft	5.95
1377	Collector's Encyclopedia of American Dinnerware, Cunningham	24.95
	Books On Dolls	
1066	The Collector's Encyclopedia of Half-Dolls, Marion & Werner	29.95
1067	Madame Alexander Dolls, Smith	19.95
1068	Madame Alexander Dolls, 2nd Series, Smith	19.95
1069	Price Guide only for above Madame Alexander Books	3.95
1357	Madame Alexander Ladies of Fashion, Uhl	19.95
1073	Shirley Temple Dolls & Collectibles, Smith	17.95
1074	Shirley Temple Dolls & Collectibles II, Smith	17.95
1076	Antique Collector's Dolls I, Smith	1795
1077	Antique Collector's Dolls II, Smith	17.95

Item #	Title & Author	Price
1079	Modern Collector's Dolls I, Smith	17.95
1080	Modern Collector's Dolls, 2nd Series, Smith	17.95
1081	Modern Collector's Dolls, 3rd Series, Smith	17.95
1082	Modern Collector's Dolls, 4th Series, Smith	17.95
1375	Effanbee Dolls, Smith	19.95
1214	German Dolls, Smith	9.95
1319	Armand Marseille Dolls, 2nd Series, Smith	9.95
1286	French Dolls, Second Series, Smith	9.95
1089	Patricia Smith's Doll Values Antique to Modern	8.95
1090	Pat Smith's Doll Values Antique to Modern, Series II	8.95
1093	Kestner and Simon & Halbig Dolls, Smith	7.95
1105	Advertising Dolls, Robison	9.95
1106	Collector's Guide to Paper Dolls, Young	9.95
1209	China & Parian Dolls, Smith	9.95
1310	The Troll Book, Miller	5.95
1347	Barbie Dolls, Manos	5.95

Books On Primtives & Furniture

1212	The Marketplace Guide to Oak Furniture Styles & Values, Blundell	17.95
1283	Marketplace Guide to Victorian Furniture, Blundell	17.95
1279	Victorian Furniture, Our American Heritage, McNerney	8.95
1118	Antique Oak Furniture, Hill	7.95
1123	Primitives & Folk Art, Our Handmade Heritage, Thuro	17.95
1124	Primitives, Our American Heritage, McNerney	8.95

Other Collectibles

1125	1000 Fruit Jars, 4th Edition	4.95
1126	Red Book of Fruit Jar III, Creswick	11.95
1128	Bottle Pricing Guide, 3rd Edition, Cleveland	7.95
1342	American Beer Can Encyclopedia, 1982-1983 Edition, Toepfer	7.95
1154	Antique Tools, Our American Heritage, McNerney	8.95
5088	World War II German Military Collectibles, McCarthy	6.95
1392	Modern Guns, Revised 4th Edition, Quertermous	11.95
1285	Wanted to Buy	7.95
1287	Railroad Collectibles, Baker	8.95
1277	Silverplated Flatware, Hagan	14.95
1172	Standard Antique Clock Guide, Wescott	11.95
1181	100 Years of Collectible Jewelry, Baker	8.95
1308	The Basket Book, Raycraft	5.95
1309	Metal Molds, Bunn	5.95
1383	Sea Shells, Glassmire	5.95
1384	Coffee Mills, Friend	5.95
1385	Police Relics, Virgines	5.95
1374	Antique Purses, Holiner	9.95
1377	Elvis Collectibles, Cramor	12.95
1211	Flea Market Trader, Revised 4th Edition, Quertermous	7.95

COLLECTOR BOOKS
P.O. Box 3009
Paducah, Kentucky 42001